THE ENCYCLOPAEDIA OF ISLAM

THE ENCYCLOPAEDIA OF ISLAM

NEW EDITION

PREPARED BY A NUMBER OF
LEADING ORIENTALISTS

EDITED BY

P. J. BEARMAN, TH. BIANQUIS, C. E. BOSWORTH,
E. VAN DONZEL AND W. P. HEINRICHS
ASSISTED BY C. OTT

UNDER THE PATRONAGE OF
THE INTERNATIONAL UNION OF ACADEMIES

VOLUME XII

SUPPLEMENT

LEIDEN
BRILL
2004

The preparation of this volume of the Encyclopaedia of Islam was made possible in part through grants from the Research Tools Program of the National Endowment for the Humanities, an independent Federal Agency of the United States Government; the British Academy; the Oriental Institute, Leiden; Académie des Inscriptions et Belles-Lettres; and the Royal Netherlands Academy of Sciences.

The articles in this volume were published in double fascicules, the dates of publication being:

1980: Fascs. 1-2, pp. 1-128
1981: Fascs. 3-4, pp. 129-256
1982: Fascs. 5-6, pp. 257-423
2003: Fascs. 7-8, pp. 425-572
2004: Fascs. 9-10, pp. 573-716
2004: Fascs. 11-12, pp. 717-844

ISBN 90 04 13974 5

PRINTED IN THE NETHERLANDS

AUTHORS OF ARTICLES IN THIS VOLUME

For the benefit of readers who may wish to follow up an individual contributor's articles, the Editors have listed after each contributor's name the pages on which his or her signature appears. Academic affiliations are given (for a retired scholar, the place of his/her last known academic appointment, when known).

In this list, names in square brackets are those of authors of articles reprinted or revised from the first edition of this *Encyclopaedia* or from the *Shorter Encyclopaedia of Islam*. An asterisk after the name of the author in the text denotes an article reprinted from the first edition which has been brought up to date by the Editorial Committee; where an article has been revised by a second author his or her name appears within square brackets after the name of the original author. The large number of deaths among the contributors of this Supplement volume reflects the fact that the first three double fascicules were published in the early 1980s, 20-odd years before the last three fascicules. Every effort was made to ascertain whether a contributor to the Supplement volume had died, or moved, in the time it took to complete and publish this Supplement, but it is very possible that some contributors not noted as having passed away, are no longer living, and that an affiliation may be passé.

A. Abdel Nour, Paris. 49
the late J. Abdel-Nour, Beirut. 162
K. Abu Deeb, University of London. 278
M. Achena, Paris. 15, 305
Virginia H. Aksan, McMaster University, Hamilton, Ontario. 714
H. Algar, University of California, Berkeley. 24, 52, 96, 135
the late M. Athar Ali, Aligarh Muslim University. 3, 55, 57, 63, 177, 313, 331, 361, 379, 411, 420
R.M.A. Allen, University of Pennsylvania, Philadelphia. 58, 548, 637
the late Joan Allgrove, University of Manchester. 148
Mohammad Ali Amir-Moezzi, Ecole Pratique des Hautes Etudes, Paris. 754
R. Amitai, Hebrew University, Jerusalem. 722
P.A. Andrews, University of Cologne. 839
W.G. Andrews, University of Washington, Seattle. 832
Ghaus Ansari, University of Vienna. 636
A. Arazi, Hebrew University, Jerusalem. 352
S.A. Arjomand, State University of New York, Stony Brook. 531
J.-L. Arnaud, Centre National de la Recherche Scientifique (IRMC), Tunis. 623
Ali S. Asani, Harvard University. 483
T. Atabaki, University of Utrecht. 621
Françoise Aubin, Centre National de la Recherche Scientifique, Paris, 527
Hatice Aynur, Yildiz Technical University, Istanbul. 774, 835
J.-L. Bacqué-Grammont, Centre National de la Recherche Scientifique, Paris. 59
Eva Baer, Hebrew University, Jerusalem. 204, 407
the late G. Baer, Hebrew University, Jerusalem. 179, 322, 370, 379, 410, 421
M.A. al-Bakhit, Āl al-Bayt University, Mafraq, Jordan. 556
T. Bauer, University of Munster. 722
the late A.F.L. Beeston, University of Oxford. 337
M.A.J. Beg, Cambridge. 59, 172, 241, 268, 304, 323, 342, 350, 463, 660, 759
Doris Behrens-Abouseif, University of London. 588
J.A. Bellamy, University of Michigan, Ann Arbor. 179
J.E. Bencheikh, University of Paris. 25, 26
M. Bergé, Bordeaux. 27
Lidia Bettini, University of Florence. 667
Th. Bianquis, University of Lyons. 503, 599, 687, 812
[W. Björkman, Uppsala]. 508
J.R. Blackburn, University of Toronto. 31
Sheila S. Blair, Boston College. 458
J. Blašković, Prague. 171
F.C. de Blois, Royal Asiatic Society, London. 600, 631
J.M. Bloom, Boston College. 458
M. Boivin, Ecole des Hautes Etudes en Sciences Sociales, Paris. 681
S.A. Bonebakker, Zeist. 362, 695
C.E. Bosworth, University of Manchester. 10, 83, 103, 115, 116, 119, 125, 127, 129, 149, 154, 173, 176, 195, 222, 235, 238, 246, 270, 279, 280, 285, 302, 305, 309, 326, 327, 329, 332, 367, 368, 376, 378, 382, 384, 387, 395, 398, 411, 458, 459, 460, 462, 502, 507, 509, 527, 529, 542, 543, 547, 550, 556, 602, 618, 632, 636, 637, 662, 682, 683, 684, 686, 695, 696, 699, 703, 710, 713, 736, 817
Ch. Bouyahya, Tunis. 12
G. Böwering, Yale University. 313
the late J.A. Boyle, University of Manchester. 203
V.I. Braginsky, University of London. 729
Yu. Bregel, Indiana University, Bloomington. 46, 98, 169, 228, 281, 340, 420
J.T.P. de Bruijn, University of Leiden. 22, 63, 83, 236, 334, 416, 831
P. Buresi, University of Paris. 822, 844
the late Cl. Cahen, University of Paris. 4
J. Calmard, Centre National de la Recherche Scientifique, Paris. 104
the late M. Canard, University of Algiers. 37
A. Carmona, University of Murcia. 679
Lucy Carroll, Decatur, Georgia. 566
J. Carswell, University of Chicago. 277
M.G. Carter, University of Oslo. 546
P. Chalmeta, University of Madrid. 82
E. Chaumont, Centre National de la Recherche Scientifique, Aix-en-Provence. 769
P. Chelkowski, New York University. 461
Youssef M. Choueiri, University of Exeter. 606, 712
A. Christelow, Idaho State University. 559, 569
Mirena Christoff, Brown University. 790
Nathalie Clayer, Centre National de la Recherche Scientifique, Paris. 462
the late J.W. Clinton, Princeton University. 84
Anna Contadini, University of London. 591
M. Cook, Princeton University. 646
M. Côte, University of Aix-en-Provence. 699
V. Crapanzano, City University of New York. 53, 351

Stephanie Cronin, University of London. 675
Yolande Crowe, Geneva. 810
F. Daftary, Institute of Ismaili Studies, London. 528, 633, 635, 713
R.E. Darley-Doran, Winchester. 594
G. Dávid, Eötvos Loránd University, Budapest. 542
Anne-Marie Delcambre, Paris. 207
Bettina Dennerlein, Centre for Modern Oriental Studies, Berlin. 560
F.M. Denny, University of Colorado, Boulder. 642
the late G. Deverdun, Paris. 29, 48, 103, 114, 132, 336, 378, 422
A. Dietrich, University of Göttingen. 43, 52, 78, 87, 115, 129, 131, 156, 157, 198, 250, 264, 277, 310, 314, 350, 371, 376, 380, 383, 397, 410
the late M.W. Dols, California State University, Hayward. 274
E. van Donzel, University of Leiden. 541, 697, 701
Nelly van Doorn-Harder, Valparaiso University, Valparaiso, Indiana. 682
S.A. Dudoignon, Centre National de la Recherche Scientifique, Strasbourg. 766
the late Ch.-E. Dufourcq, University of Paris. 308
R.Y. Ebied, University of Sydney. 36, 38, 40, 55, 136, 162, 267, 354, 371, 383, 410, 466
Anne-Marie Eddé, Centre National de la Recherche Scientifique, Paris. 511, 518, 545
A.S. Ehrenkreutz, University of Michigan, Ann Arbor. 121
R. Eisener, Humboldt University, Berlin. 468
Taïeb El Achèche, University of Tunis. 643
Mohamed El Mansour, University Mohammed V, Rabat. 634
the late N. Elisséeff, University of Lyons. 117
the late L.P. Elwell-Sutton, University of Edinburgh. 41, 73, 84, 92, 170
W. Ende, University of Freiburg. 640, 642
G. Endress, University of Bochum. 606
Sibel Erol, New York University. 538
J. van Ess, University of Tübingen. 14, 15, 90, 227, 358, 365, 392, 510, 546, 633
T. Fahd, University of Strasbourg. 771
Suraiya Faroqhi, University of Munich. 477, 480, 716
Ahmed Farouk, Ecole Pratique des Hautes Etudes, Paris. 807
G. Féhérvari, University of London. 327
M.Ch. Ferjani, University of Lyons. 482
I. Ferrando, University of Cadiz. 501, 545
R. Firestone, Hebrew Union College, Los Angeles. 703
the late H. Fleisch, Saint-Joseph University, Beirut. 290
W. Floor, Bethesda, Maryland. 731
Ch.H. de Fouchécour, University of Paris. 620
Ersilia Francesca, University L'Orientale, Naples. 786
R.M. Frank, Catholic University of America, Washington, D.C. 32, 348
Y. Friedmann, Hebrew University, Jerusalem. 163
M. Gaborieau, Centre National de la Recherche Scientifique, Paris. 768
the late F. Gabrieli, University of Rome. 31
M. Gammer, Tel Aviv University. 486
H. Gaube, University of Tübingen. 157, 229, 514, 515
G.J.H. van Gelder, University of Oxford. 635, 640, 668
E. Geoffroy, University of Strasbourg. 724
Ahmad al-Ghumari, Ministry of Culture, Sanaa. 723
Erika Glassen, University of Freiburg-im-Breisgau. 383
R. Gleave, University of Bristol. 517, 535, 570
the late L. Gölvin, University of Aix-Marseilles. 145
L.P. Goodson, U.S. Army War College. 787
P. Gorokhoff, Paris. 249
W.J. Griswold, Colorado State University, Fort Collins. 239
A.H. de Groot, University of Leiden. 282, 511
P. Guichard, University of Lyons. 763, 766
A. Guimbretière, Paris. 107
A.J. Gully, University of Exeter. 725
the late U. Haarmann, Free University, Berlin. 408
the late M. Hadj-Sadok, Paris. 405
the late Abdul-Hadi Hairi, Mashhad. 54, 55, 71, 72, 77, 111, 158, 292, 343, 366
W. Hale, University of London. 681
H. Halm, University of Tübingen. 207, 237
S.K. Hamarneh, Smithsonian Institution, Washington, D.C. 391
A.C.M. Hamer, Tehran. 50
A. Hamori, Princeton University. 555
Shah Mahmoud Hanifi, James Madison University, Harrisonburg, Virginia. 508, 763
M. Şükrü Hanioğlu, Princeton University. 678
Mohibbul Hasan, Aligarh. 114, 132, 156, 167, 325, 328, 329, 333, 354, 366, 423
Mushirul Hasan, Jawaharlal Nehru University. 481
Sohail H. Hashmi, Mount Holyoke College, South Hadley, Massachusetts. 794
the late J.A. Haywood, Lewes, Sussex. 47, 75, 102, 107, 359
G. Hazai, University of Budapest. 814
W.P. Heinrichs, Harvard University. 518, 658, 669, 710, 830, 831
Metin Heper, Bilkent University. 470
C.J. Heywood, University of London. 316
the late D.R. Hill, Great Bookham, Surrey. 267, 374
A. Hofheinz, Centre for Modern Oriental Studies, Berlin. 556
C. Holes, University of Oxford. 843
P.M. Holt, Oxford. 20, 524, 594, 608, 613, 810
W. Holzwarth, University of Halle. 820
M.B. Hooker, Australian National University, Canberra. 569
Virginia Matheson Hooker, Australian National University. 598
D. Hopwood, University of Oxford. 9, 70
B. Hourcade, Centre National de la Recherche Scientifique, Paris. 604
the late I. Hrbek, Prague. 171
R.S. Humphreys, University of California, Santa Barbara. 206
A.O. İcimsoy, Marmara University. 616
A. Gül İrepoğlu, University of Istanbul. 548
the late Fahir İz, Boğaziçi University. 42, 47, 50, 55, 61, 63, 64, 82, 91, 96, 99, 129, 150, 168, 170, 280, 282, 283, 284, 308, 324, 329, 349, 359
Mawil Y. Izzi Dien, University of Wales, Lampeter. 767
P. Jackson, University of Keele. 117, 240, 242, 336, 421
J. Jankowski, University of Colorado, Boulder. 625, 627
Marilyn Jenkins, Metropolitan Museum of Art, New York. 262
Éva M. Jeremiás, Eötvos Loránd University, Budapest. 448
Penelope C. Johnstone, University of Oxford. 60

the late T.M. JOHNSTONE, Oxford. 340
F. DE JONG, University of Utrecht. 18, 41, 44, 94, 121, 123, 133, 209, 244, 263, 279, 371, 408, 411
G.H.A. JUYNBOLL, Leiden. 393
M. KABLY, Rabat University. 805
MEHMET KALPAKLI, Bilkent University, Ankara. 832
N.J.G. KAPTEIN, University of Leiden. 614
A. KARAHAN, Istanbul. 83
M. KEENE, Metropolitan Museum of Art, New York. 262
BARBARA KELLNER-HEINKELE, Free University, Berlin. 707, 838
J.B. KELLY, London. 42, 332, 419
C.S. KESSLER, University of New South Wales, Sydney. 520
R.G. KHOURY, University of Heidelberg. 88
M. KIEL, University of Utrecht. 331
M.J. KISTER, Hebrew University, Jerusalem. 232
the late J. KNAPPERT, University of London. 352, 643
A. KNYSH, University of Michigan, Ann Arbor. 501
E. KOHLBERG, Hebrew University, Jerusalem. 723
G.L. KOSTER, University of Indonesia. 729
A.K.S. LAMBTON, Kirknewton, Northumberland. 336
W. and FIDELITY LANCASTER, Orkney. 466
J.M. LANDAU, Hebrew University, Jerusalem. 40, 297, 382
D. LANGE, University of Bayreuth. 569
J.D. LATHAM, University of Manchester. 46, 113, 125, 126, 153, 377, 389, 398, 399
G. LAZARD, University of Paris. 35
M. LECKER, Hebrew University, Jerusalem. 662, 695
G. LEISER, Vacaville, California. 578
T. LEISTEN, Princeton University. 571
D.D. LESLIE, Australian National University, Canberra. 748
P. LETTINCK, International Institute of Islamic Thought and Civilization, Kuala Lumpur. 770
[G. LEVI DELLA VIDA, Rome]. 702
the late N. LEVTZION, Hebrew University, Jerusalem. 167
L. LEWISOHN, University of London. 785
P. LORY, Ecole Pratique des Hautes Etudes, Paris. 556, 613, 823
J. MCCARTHY, University of Louisville. 221
[D.B. MACDONALD, Hartford, Connecticut]. 154, 323
the late D.N. MACKENZIE, University of Göttingen. 158, 425
W. MADELUNG, University of Oxford. 19, 22, 26, 49, 57, 130, 233, 236, 335, 343, 357, 363, 380, 393, 401, 402, 557, 756, 841
the late G. MAKDISI, University of Pennsylvania, Philadelphia. 30, 194, 195
IFTIKHAR H. MALIK, Bath Spa University College. 679
the late P. MARTHELOT, Ecole Pratique des Hautes Etudes, Paris. 423
U. MARZOLPH, Enzyklopädie des Märchens, Göttingen. 817
R. MATTHEE, University of Delaware. 612, 717
ASTRID MEIER, University of Zurich. 828
[TH. MENZEL]. 763
EBRAHIM MOOSA, Duke University, Durham, North Caroliina. 754
H. MOTZKI, University of Nijmegen. 698
R. MURPHEY, University of Birmingham. 767, 837
F.C. MÜTH, University of Mainz. 525
SEYYED HOSSEIN NASR, George Washington University, Washington, D.C. 309
I.R. NETTON, University of Leeds. 795
E. NEUBAUER, University of Frankfurt. 64, 116, 128, 183, 284, 409, 547
D. NICOLLE, University of Nottingham. 746
the late K.A. NIZAMI, Aligarh Muslim University. 475, 573, 578
MAHMOUD OMIDSALAR, California State University, Los Angeles. 781
NICOLE A.N.M VAN OS, University of Leiden. 640
CLAUDIA OTT, University of Erlangen. 668
AYLIN ÖZMAN, Hacettepe University, Ankara. 468, 812
J. PAUL, University of Halle. 524, 538
the late CH. PELLAT, University of Paris. 17, 18, 20, 23, 24, 26, 27, 31, 32, 33, 35, 39, 56, 80, 92, 113, 118, 122, 124, 128, 157, 191, 223, 224, 225, 234, 247, 264, 266, 284, 303, 312, 355, 381, 386, 388, 390, 394, 476
C.R. PENNELL, University of Melbourne. 634
B. PÉRI, Eötvös Loránd University, Budapest. 815
R. PETERS, University of Amsterdam. 368, 644
J.E. PETERSON, Tucson, Arizona. 819
CH. PICARD, University of Paris. 514
ELIZABETH PICARD, Centre National de la Recherche Scientifique, Aix-en-Provence. 673
the late G.F. PIJPER, Amsterdam. 368
X. DE PLANHOL, University of Paris. 328
I. POONAWALA, University of California, Los Angeles. 61, 62, 70, 358, 407
A. POPOVIC, Centre National de la Recherche Scientifique, Paris. 188, 752
the late L. POUZET, Saint-Joseph University, Beirut. 773
B. RADTKE, University of Utrecht. 748
F.J. RAGEP, University of Oklahoma, Norman. 502
MUNIBUR RAHMAN, Oakland University, Rochester, Michigan. 505, 512
J. RAMÍREZ, University of Cordova. 724
S.A. AL-RASHID, King Saud University, Riyadh. 199
W. RAVEN, University of Frankfurt. 756
A. RAYMOND, University of Aix-en-Provence. 554
M. REKAYA, University of Paris. 299
the late G. RENTZ, Washington. 50, 235
M.E.J. RICHARDSON, University of Manchester. 102
A. RIPPIN, University of Victoria, British Columbia. 842
D. RIVET, University of Paris. 730
the late S.A.A. RIZVI, Australian National University, Canberra. 126
the late U. RIZZITANO, University of Palermo. 64
CH. ROBIN, Centre National de la Recherche Scientifique, Aix-en-Provence. 506, 723, 821, 832, 834
F.C.R. ROBINSON, University of London. 5, 74, 248, 294, 361, 526
J.M. ROGERS, London. 681
L. ROGLER, Centre for Modern Oriental Studies, Berlin. 560
W. ROLLMAN, Wellesley College, Wellesley, Massachusetts. 840
the late F. ROSENTHAL, Yale University. 91, 463
S. ROSENTHAL, University of Hartford, Connecticut. 168
E.K. ROWSON, New York University. 73
U. RUBIN, Tel Aviv University. 574, 661
U. RUDOLPH, University of Zurich. 528, 815
J. SADAN, Tel Aviv University. 100, 601
ABDULLAH SAEED, University of Melbourne. 692, 711
ABDEL HAMID SALEH, Geneva. 389, 390

Kamal S. Salibi, Royal Institute for Inter-Faith Studies, Amman. 39, 269, 603
A.I. Salim, Nairobi. 248
A. Samb, Dakar. 183
Jasna Samic, Belgrade. 507
F. Sanagustin, University of Lyons. 550, 628, 641
R. Santucci, Institut National des Langues et Civilisations Orientales, Paris. 241
A. Savvides, Aegean University, Rhodes. 544, 617, 837
R. Schick, Henry Martyn Institute, Hyderabad. 514
A. Schippers, University of Amsterdam. 670
G. Schoeler, University of Basel. 540
O. Schumann, University of Hamburg. 151, 152, 203, 510, 608, 762, 838
R. Sellheim, University of Frankfurt. 632
C. Shackle, University of London. 684
Irfan Shahid, Georgetown University, Washiington, D.C. 230
Miri Shefer, Tel Aviv University. 811
P. Shinar, Hebrew University, Jerusalem. 387, 402, 423
A. Shivtiel, University of Leeds. 779
S. von Sicard, Selly Oak Colleges, Birmingham. 577, 630
A. Sidarus, University of Evora. 396
Iqtidar H. Siddiqui, Aligarh Muslim University. 2, 11, 67, 74, 106, 122, 203, 312, 353, 360, 409, 686
N. Sims-Williams, University of London. 426
G.R. Smith, University of Manchester. 339, 388, 420, 516, 543
F. Sobieroj, University of Jena. 772
Priscilla Soucek, New York University. 453
M. Souịssi, University of Tunis. 414
F. Spuhler, Museum of Islamic Art, Berlin. 144
F.H. Stewart, Hebrew University, Jerusalem. 536
W. Stoetzer, University of Leiden. 483
J. Strauss, University of Strasbourg. 734
[M. Streck. Jena]. 605
G. Strohmaier, German Academy of Sciences, Berlin. 270
Abdus Subhan, Asiatic Society, Calcutta. 124, 206, 246, 325
Jacqueline Sublet, Centre National de la Recherche Scientifique, Paris. 289, 296, 322, 393
Yasser Tabbaa, Oberlin College. 696
M. Talbi, University of Tunis. 173
J.K. Teubner, Brussels. 3, 105
H.G.B. Teule, University of Nijmegen. 809
W.M. Thackston, Harvard University. 816
Ahmed Toufiq, Ministry of Habous and Islamic Affairs, Rabat. 810
G. Troupeau, Institut National de Langues et Civilisations Orientales, Paris. 16, 38
Tomohiko Uyama, Hokkaido University, Sapporo. 520
M. Valor, University of Seville. 724
J.-P. Van Staëvel, University of Paris. 513
the late P.J. Vatikiotis, University of London. 302
G. Veinstein, Collège de France, Paris. 505
J. Vernet, University of Barcelona. 544
Chantal de La Véronne, Centre National de la Recherche Scientifique, Paris. 807
Maria J. Viguera, University Complutense of Madrid. 92
the late F. Viré, Centre National de la Recherche Scientifique, Paris. 20, 87, 176, 244, 289, 296, 322, 393
G.J.J. de Vries, University of Utrecht. 61, 135
the late Jeanette Wakin, Columbia University. 198, 690
W. Montgomery Watt, University of Edinburgh. 131
L. Wiederhold, University of Halle. 727
S. Wild, University of Bonn. 250
J.C. Wilkinson, University of Oxford. 356
the late R. Bayly Winder, New York University. 4, 306
M. Winter, Tel Aviv University. 799
J.J. Witkam, University of Leiden. 45, 381, 469
Christine Woodhead, University of Durham. 616
O. Wright, University of London. 511
M. Yalaoui, University of Tunis. 63, 306
M.E. Yapp, University of London. 66
S. Yerasimos, University of Paris. 475
the late M.J.L. Young, University of Leeds. 55, 136, 162, 199, 267, 354, 371, 383, 410, 466
Th. Zarcone, Centre National de la Recherche Scientifique, Paris. 522
A.H. Zarrinkoob, Tehran. 44, 208, 240, 406
M. Zekri, University of Evora. 556
F.J. Ziadeh, University of Washington, Seattle. 526
A. Zysow, Harvard University. 533, 690, 706

ABBREVIATED TITLES OF SOME OF THE MOST OFTEN QUOTED WORKS

Abu 'l-Fidā', *Taḳwīm* = *Taḳwīm al-buldān*, ed. J.-T. Reinaud and M. de Slane, Paris 1840

Abu 'l-Fidā', *Taḳwīm*, tr. = *Géographie d'Aboulféda, traduite de l'arabe en français*, vols. i, ii/1 by M. Reinaud, Paris 1848; vol. ii/2 by St. Guyard, 1883

Aghānī[1] or [2] or [3] = Abu 'l-Faradj al-Iṣfahānī, *al-Aghānī*; [1]Būlāḳ 1285; [2]Cairo 1323; [3]Cairo 1345-

Aghānī, Tables = *Tables alphabétiques du Kitāb al-Aghānī*, rédigées par I. Guidi, Leiden 1900

Aghānī, Brünnow = *The XXIst vol. of the Kitāb al-Aghānī*, ed. R.E. Brünnow, Leiden 1883

ALA = *Arabic Literature of Africa*, ed. R.S. O'Fahey and J.O. Hunwick, Leiden 1993-

'Alī Djewād = *Memālik-i 'Othmāniyyenīn ta'rīkh we djughrāfiyā lughāti*, Istanbul 1313-17/1895-9

'Alī Mubārak, *Khiṭaṭ* = *al-Khiṭaṭ al-tawfīḳiyya al-djadīda li-Miṣr al-Ḳāhira wa-mudunihā wa-bilādihā 'l-ḳadīma wa 'l-shahīra*, 20 vols., Būlāḳ 1304-6

Anbārī, *Nuzha* = *Nuzhat al-alibbā' fī ṭabaḳāt al-udabā'*, [1]Cairo 1294; [2]Stockholm, etc. 1963

'Awfī, *Lubāb* = *Lubāb al-albāb*, ed. E.G. Browne, London-Leiden 1903-6

Babinger, *GOW* = F. Babinger, *Die Geschichtsschreiber der Osmanen und ihre Werke*, 1st ed., Leiden 1927

Baghdādī, *Farḳ* = *al-Farḳ bayn al-firaḳ*, ed. Muḥammad Badr, Cairo 1328/1910

Balādhurī, *Futūḥ* = *Futūḥ al-buldān*, ed. M.J. de Goeje, Leiden 1866

Balādhurī, *Ansāb* = *Ansāb al-ashrāf*, i, ed. M. Ḥamīd Allāh, Cairo 1960; iii, ed. 'Abd al-'Azīz al-Dūrī, Beirut 1978; iv A, ed. Iḥsān 'Abbās, Beirut 1979; iv B and v, ed. M. Schlössinger and S.D.F. Goitein, Jerusalem 1936-9

Barkan, *Kanunlar* = Ömer Lûtfi Barkan, *XV ve XVI inci asırlarda Osmanlı Imparatorluğunda ziraî ekonominin hukukî ve malî esasları*, I. *Kanunlar*, Istanbul 1943

Barthold, *Four studies* = V.V. Barthold, *Four studies on the history of Central Asia*, tr. V. and T. Minorsky, 3 vols., Leiden 1956-63

Barthold, *Turkestan* = W. Barthold, *Turkestan down to the Mongol invasion*, London 1928 (GMS, N.S. V)

Barthold, *Turkestan*[2] = *ibid.*, revised edition, London 1958

Barthold, *Turkestan*[3] = *ibid.*, revised and enlarged ed., London 1968

Blachère, *HLA* = R. Blachère, *Histoire de la littérature arabe*, 3 vols., Paris 1952-64

de Blois, *Persian literature* = F. de Blois, *Persian literature, a bio-bibliographical survey, begun by the late C.A. Storey*, vol. v, London 1992-

Brockelmann, I, II = C. Brockelmann, *Geschichte der arabischen Literatur (GAL)*, zweite den Supplementbänden angepasste Auflage, Leiden 1943-9

Brockelmann, S I, II, III = *GAL*, Erster (zweiter, dritter) Supplementband, Leiden 1937-42

Browne, *LHP* = E.G. Browne, *A literary history of Persia*, 4 vols., London and Cambridge 1902-24

Browne, ii = E.G. Browne, *A literary history of Persia, from Firdawsi to Sa'di*, London 1908

Browne, iii = E.G. Browne, *A history of Persian literature under Tartar Dominion*, Cambridge 1920

Browne, iv = E.G. Browne, *A history of Persian literature in modern times*, Cambridge 1924

Caetani, *Annali* = L. Caetani, *Annali dell'Islam*, Milan 1905-26

Camb. hist. Iran = *The Cambridge history of Iran*, 7 vols., Cambridge 1968-91

Camb. hist. Ar. lit. = *The Cambridge history of Arabic literature*, ed. A.F.L. Beeston *et alii*, 4 vols., Cambridge 1983-92

Chauvin, *Bibliographie* = V. Chauvin, *Bibliographie des ouvrages arabes ou relatifs aux Arabes*, Liége 1892-1922

Clauson, *Etymological dictionary* = Sir Gerard Clauson, *An etymological dictionary of pre-thirteenth century Turkish*, Oxford 1972

Creswell, *Bibliography* = K.A.C. Creswell, *A bibliography of the architecture, arts and crafts of Islam to 1st Jan. 1960*, Cairo 1961

Ḍabbī = *Bughyat al-multamis fī ta'rīkh ridjāl ahl al-Andalus*, ed. F. Codera and J. Ribera, Madrid 1885 (BAH III)

Damīrī = *Ḥayāt al-ḥayawān* (quoted according to titles of articles)

Dawlatshāh = *Tadhkirat al-shu'arā'*, ed. E.G. Browne, London-Leiden 1901

Dhahabī, *Ḥuffāẓ* = *Tadhkirat al-ḥuffāẓ*, 4 vols., Hyderabad 1315 H.

Dictionnaire arabe-français-anglais = *Dictionnaire arabe-français-anglais* (*langue classique et moderne*), Paris 1963-

Djuwaynī = *Ta'rīkh-i Djihān-gushā*, ed. Muḥammad Ḳazwīnī, Leiden 1906-37 (GMS XVI)

Djuwaynī-Boyle = *The history of the World conqueror*, by 'Aṭā-Malik Djuwaynī, tr. J.A. Boyle, 2 vols., Manchester 1958

Doerfer, *Elemente* = G. Doerfer, *Türkische und mongolische Elemente im Neupersischen*, Wiesbaden 1963-

Dozy, *Notices* = R. Dozy, *Notices sur quelques manuscrits arabes*, Leiden 1847-51

Dozy, *Recherches*[3] = R. Dozy, *Recherches sur l'histoire et la littérature de l'Espagne pendant le moyen-âge*, [3]Paris-Leiden 1881

Dozy, *Suppl.* = R. Dozy, *Supplément aux dictionnaires arabes*, Leiden 1881 (repr. Leiden-Paris 1927)

EMA[1] = K.A.C. Creswell, *Early Muslim architecture*, 2 vols., Oxford 1932-40

EMA[2] = K.A.C. Creswell, *Early Muslim architecture*, [2]London 1969-

Fagnan, *Extraits* = E. Fagnan, *Extraits inédits relatifs au Maghreb*, Alger 1924

Farhang = Razmārā and Nawtāsh, *Farhang-i djughrāfiyā-yi Īrān*, Tehran 1949-53

Firishta = Muḥammad Ḳāsim Firishta, *Gulshan-i Ibrāhīmī*, lith. Bombay 1832

Gesch. des Qor. = Th. Nöldeke, *Geschichte des Qorāns*, new edition by F. Schwally, G. Bergsträsser and O. Pretzl, 3 vols., Leipzig 1909-38

Gibb, *HOP* = E.J.W. Gibb, *A history of Ottoman poetry*, 7 vols., London 1900-9

Gibb-Bowen = H.A.R. Gibb and Harold Bowen, *Islamic society and the West*, London 1950-7

Goldziher, *Muh. St.* = I. Goldziher, *Muhammedanische Studien*, 2 vols., Halle 1888-90

Goldziher, *Vorlesungen* = I. Goldziher, *Vorlesungen über den Islam*, Heidelberg 1910

Goldziher, *Vorlesungen*[2] = 2nd ed., Heidelberg 1925

Goldziher, *Dogme* = *Le dogme et la loi de l'Islam*, tr. F. Arin, Paris 1920

Gövsa, *Türk meşhurları* = İbrahim Alâettin Gövsa, *Türk meşhurları ansiklopedisi*, Istanbul 1946

Ḥādjdjī Khalīfa, *Djihān-nümā* = Istanbul 1145/1732
Ḥādjdjī Khalīfa = *Kashf al-ẓunūn*, ed. Ş. Yaltkaya and Kilisli Rifat Bilge, Istanbul 1941-3
Ḥādjdjī Khalīfa, ed. Flügel = *K. al-ẓ.*, Leipzig 1835-58
Ḥamd Allāh Mustawfī, *Nuzha* = *Nuzhat al-ḳulūb*, ed. G. Le Strange, Leiden 1913-19 (GMS XXIII)
Hamdānī = *Ṣifat Djazīrat al-ʿArab*, ed. D.H. Müller, Leiden 1884-91
Hammer-Purgstall, *GOR* = J. von Hammer(-Purgstall), *Geschichte des Osmanischen Reiches*, Pest 1828-35
Hammer-Purgstall, *GOR²* = *ibid.*, 2nd ed., Pest 1840
Hammer-Purgstall, *Histoire* = *ibid.*, tr. J.J. Hellert, 18 vols., Bellizard [etc.], Paris [etc.], 1835-43
Hammer-Purgstall, *Staatsverfassung* = J. von Hammer, *Des Osmanischen Reichs Staatsverfassung und Staatsverwaltung*, 2 vols., Vienna 1815 (repr. 1963)
Houtsma, *Recueil* = M. Th. Houtsma, *Recueil des textes relatifs à l'histoire des Seldjoucides*, Leiden 1886-1902
Ḥudūd al-ʿālam¹ = *Ḥudūd al-ʿālam. The regions of the world*, tr. V. Minorsky, London 1937 (GMS, N.S. XI)
Ḥudūd al-ʿālam² = *ibid.*, 2nd revised and enlarged ed., London 1970
Ibn al-Abbār = *K. Takmilat al-Ṣila*, ed. F. Codera, Madrid 1887-9 (BHA V-VI)
Ibn al-Athīr, ed. Tornberg = Ibn al-Athīr, *al-Kāmil fi 'l-tawārīkh*, ed. C.J. Tornberg, 12 vols., Leiden 1851-76
Ibn al-Athīr, ed. Beirut = *ibid.*, 13 vols., Beirut 1385-7/1965-7
Ibn al-Athīr, trad. Fagnan = *Annales du Maghreb et de l'Espagne*, tr. E. Fagnan, Algiers 1901
Ibn Bashkuwāl = *K. al-Ṣila fi akhbār a'immat al-Andalus*, ed. F. Codera, Madrid 1883 (BHA II)
Ibn Baṭṭūṭa = *Voyages d'Ibn Batouta*, Ar. text, ed. with Fr. tr. by C. Defrémery and B.R. Sanguinetti, 4 vols., Paris 1853-8
Ibn Baṭṭūṭa, tr. Gibb = *The travels of Ibn Baṭṭūṭa*, Eng. tr. H.A.R. Gibb, 3 vols., Cambridge 1958-71
Ibn al-Faḳīh = *Mukhtaṣar K. al-Buldān*, ed. M.J. de Goeje, Leiden 1886 (BGA V)
Ibn Ḥawḳal = *K. Ṣūrat al-arḍ*, ed. J.H. Kramers, Leiden 1938-9 (BGA II, 2nd edition)
Ibn Ḥawḳal-Kramers-Wiet = Ibn Hauqal, *Configuration de la terre*, tr. J.H. Kramers and G. Wiet, 2 vols., Beirut 1964
Ibn Hishām = *Sira*, ed. F. Wüstenfeld, Göttingen 1859-60
Ibn ʿIdhārī = *K. al-Bayān al-mughrib*, ed. G.S. Colin and E. Lévi-Provençal, Leiden 1948-51; vol. iii, ed. E. Lévi-Provençal, Paris 1930
Ibn al-ʿImād, *Shadharāt* = *Shadharāt al-dhahab fi akhbār man dhahab*, Cairo 1350-1 (quoted according to years of obituaries)
Ibn Isḥāḳ, tr. Guillaume = *The life of Muḥammad, a translation of Isḥāq's (sic)* Sīrat Rasūl Allāh, tr. A. Guillaume, Oxford 1955
Ibn Khaldūn, *ʿIbar* = *K. al-ʿIbar wa-dīwān al-mubtada' wa 'l-khabar, etc.*, Būlāḳ 1284
Ibn Khaldūn, *Muḳaddima* = *Prolégomènes d'Ebn Khaldoun*, ed. E. Quatremère, Paris 1858-68 (*Notices et Extraits* XVI-XVIII)
Ibn Khaldūn-Rosenthal = *The Muqaddimah*, trans. from the Arabic by Franz Rosenthal, 3 vols., London 1958
Ibn Khaldūn-de Slane = *Les prolégomènes d'Ibn Khaldoun*, traduits en français et commentés par M. de Slane, Paris 1863-8 (repr. 1934-8)
Ibn Khallikān = *Wafayāt al-aʿyān wa-anbā' abnā' al-zamān*, ed. F. Wüstenfeld, Göttingen 1835-50 (quoted after the numbers of biographies)
Ibn Khallikān, ed. ʿAbbās = *ibid.*, ed. Iḥsān ʿAbbās, 8 vols., Beirut 1968-72
Ibn Khallikān, Būlāḳ = *ibid.*, ed. Būlāḳ 1275
Ibn Khallikān-de Slane = *Kitāb Wafayāt al-aʿyān*, tr. Baron MacGuckin de Slane, 4 vols., Paris 1842-71
Ibn Khurradādhbih = *al-Masālik wa 'l-mamālik*, ed. M.J. de Goeje, Leiden 1889 (BGA VI)
Ibn Ḳutayba, *al-Shiʿr* = Ibn Ḳutayba, *Kitāb al-Shiʿr wa 'l-shuʿarā'*, ed. M.J. de Goeje, Leiden 1900
Ibn al-Nadīm, *Fihrist* = Ibn al-Nadīm, *K. al-Fihrist*, ed. G. Flügel, 2 vols., Leipzig 1871-2
Ibn al-Nadīm, tr. Dodge = *The Fihrist of al-Nadīm*, tr. B. Dodge, 2 vols., New York and London 1970
Ibn Rusta = *al-Aʿlāḳ al-nafīsa*, ed. M.J. de Goeje, Leiden 1892 (BGA VII)
Ibn Rusta-Wiet = *Les Atours précieux*, Fr. tr. G. Wiet, Cairo 1955
Ibn Saʿd = *al-Ṭabaḳāt al-kubrā*, ed. H. Sachau *et al.*, Leiden 1905-40
Ibn Taghrībirdī = *al-Nudjūm al-zāhira fī mulūk Miṣr wa 'l-Ḳāhira*, ed. W. Popper, Berkeley-Leiden 1908-36
Ibn Taghrībirdī, Cairo = *ibid.*, ed. Cairo 1348ff.
Idrīsī, *Maghrib* = *Description de l'Afrique et de l'Espagne*, ed. R. Dozy and M.J. de Goeje, Leiden 1866
Idrīsī-Jaubert = *Géographie d'Édrisi*, Fr. tr. P. Amédée Jaubert, 2 vols., Paris 1836-40
Iṣṭakhrī = *al-Masālik wa 'l-mamālik*, ed. M.J. de Goeje, Leiden 1870 (BGA I) (and reprint 1927)
Justi, *Namenbuch* = F. Justi, *Iranisches Namenbuch*, Marburg 1895
Juynboll, *Handbuch* = Th.W. Juynboll, *Handbuch des islāmischen Gesetzes*, Leiden 1910
Kaḥḥāla, *Nisā'* = ʿUmar Riḍā Kaḥḥāla, *Aʿlām al-nisā' fī ʿālamay al-ʿArab wa 'l-Islām*, 5 vols., Damascus 1379/1959
Khʷāndamīr = *Ḥabīb al-siyar*, Tehran 1271
Kutubī, *Fawāt*, ed. Būlāḳ = Ibn Shākir al-Kutubī, *Fawāt al-wafayāt*, 2 vols., Būlāḳ 1299/1882
Kutubī, *Fawāt*, ed. ʿAbbās = *ibid.*, ed. Iḥsān ʿAbbās, 5 vols., Beirut 1973-4
LA = *Lisān al-ʿArab* (quoted according to the root)
Lambton, *Landlord and peasant* = A.K.S. Lambton, *Landlord and peasant in Persia: a study of land tenure and revenue administration*, London 1953
Lane = E.W. Lane, *An Arabic-English lexicon*, London 1863-93 (reprint New York 1955-6)
Lane-Poole, *Cat.* = S. Lane-Poole, *Catalogue of oriental coins in the British Museum*, London 1877-90
Lavoix, *Cat.* = H. Lavoix, *Catalogue des monnaies musulmanes de la Bibliothèque Nationale*, Paris 1887-96
Le Strange = G. Le Strange, *The lands of the Eastern caliphate*, ²Cambridge 1930
Le Strange, *Baghdad* = G. Le Strange, *Baghdad during the Abbasid caliphate*, Oxford 1924
Le Strange, *Palestine* = G. Le Strange, *Palestine under the Moslems*, London 1890
Lévi-Provençal, *Hist. Esp. Mus.* = E. Lévi-Provençal, *Histoire de l'Espagne musulmane*, new ed., 3 vols., Leiden-Paris 1950-53
Lévi-Provençal, *Chorfa* = E. Lévi-Provençal, *Les historiens des Chorfa*, Paris 1922
MAE = K.A.C. Creswell, *The Muslim architecture of Egypt*, 2 vols., Oxford 1952-9
Maḳḳarī, *Analectes* = *Nafḥ al-ṭīb fī ghuṣn al-Andalus al-raṭīb (Analectes sur l'histoire et la littérature des Arabes de l'Espagne)*, Leiden 1855-61
Maḳḳarī, Būlāḳ = *ibid.*, ed. Būlāḳ 1279/1862
Marquart, *Ērānšahr* = J. Marquart, *Ērānšahr nach der Geographie des Ps. Moses Xorenacʿi*, Berlin 1901
Marquart, *Streifzüge* = J. Marquart, *Osteuropäische und ostasiatische Streifzüge: ethnologische und historisch-*

topographische Studien zur Geschichte des 9. und 10. Jahrhunderts (c. 840-940), Leipzig 1903
Maspero-Wiet, *Matériaux* = J. Maspero et G. Wiet, *Matériaux pour servir à la géographie de l'Egypte*, Cairo 1914 (MIFAO XXXVI)
Masʿūdī, *Murūdj* = *Murūdj al-dhahab*, ed. C. Barbier de Meynard and Pavet de Courteille, 9 vols., Paris 1861-77; ed. and tr. Ch. Pellat, *Les prairies d'or*, 7 vols. text and 4 vols. translation, Paris-Beirut 1962-89 (cited according to paragraph)
Masʿūdī, *Tanbīh* = *K. al-Tanbīh wa 'l-ishrāf*, ed. M.J. de Goeje, Leiden 1894 (BGA VIII)
Mayer, *Architects* = L.A. Mayer, *Islamic architects and their works*, Geneva 1956
Mayer, *Astrolabists* = L.A. Mayer, *Islamic astrolabists and their works*, Geneva 1958
Mayer, *Metalworkers* = L.A. Mayer, *Islamic metalworkers and their works*, Geneva 1959
Mayer, *Woodcarvers* = L.A. Mayer, *Islamic woodcarvers and their works*, Geneva 1958
Mez, *Renaissance* = A. Mez, *Die Renaissance des Islams*, Heidelberg 1922
Mez, *Renaissance*, Eng. tr. = *The renaissance of Islam*, Eng. tr. Salahuddin Khuda Bukhsh and D.S. Margoliouth, London 1937
Mez, *Renaissance*, Sp. tr. = *El renacimiento del Islam*, Sp. tr. S. Vila, Madrid-Granada 1936
Miquel, *Géographie humaine* = A. Miquel, *La géographie humaine du monde musulman jusqu'au milieu du 11e siècle*, 4 vols., Paris-The Hague 1973-88
Mīrkhwānd = *Rawḍat al-ṣafā*, Bombay 1266/1849
Miskawayh, in *Eclipse of the ʿAbbasid caliphate* = Miskawayh, *Tadjārib al-umam*, in *The eclipse of the ʿAbbasid caliphate*, ed. and tr. H.F. Amedroz and D.S. Margoliouth, 7 vols., Oxford 1920-21
Muḳaddasī = *Aḥsan al-taḳāsīm fī maʿrifat al-aḳālīm*, ed. M.J. de Goeje, Leiden 1877 (BGA III)
Munadjdjim Bashī = *Ṣaḥāʾif al-akhbār*, Istanbul 1285
Nallino, *Scritti* = C.A. Nallino, *Raccolta di scritti editi e inediti*, Rome 1939-48
ʿOthmānlî müʾellifleri = Bursalî Meḥmed Ṭāhir, *ʿOthmānlî müʾellifleri*, Istanbul 1333
Pakalın = Mehmet Zeki Pakalın, *Osmanlı tarih deyimleri ve terimleri sözlüğü*, 3 vols., Istanbul 1946ff.
Pauly-Wissowa = *Realenzyklopaedie des klassischen Altertums*
Pearson = J.D. Pearson, *Index Islamicus*, Cambridge 1958; S I = *Supplement, 1956-60*
Pons Boigues = *Ensayo bio-bibliográfico sobre los historiadores y geógrafos arábigo-españoles*, Madrid 1898
PTF = *Fundamenta philologiae turcica*, ed. J. Deny *et alii*, 2 vols., Wiesbaden 1959-64
Rypka, *Hist. of Iranian literature* = J. Rypka *et alii*, *History of Iranian literature*, Dordrecht 1968
Ṣafadī = *al-Wāfī bi 'l-wafayāt. Das biographische Lexikon des Ṣalāḥaddīn Ḫalīl ibn Aibak aṣ-Ṣafadī*, ed. H. Ritter, S. Dedering *et alii*, 22 vols., Wiesbaden-Beirut-Damascus 1962-
Samʿānī, *Ansāb*, fasc. = *K. al-Ansāb*, facsimile edition by D.S. Margoliouth, Leiden 1912 (GMS, XX)
Samʿānī, ed. Ḥaydarābād = *ibid.*, ed. M. ʿAbd al-Muʿīd Khān *et alii*, 13 vols., Ḥaydarābād 1382-1402/1962-82
Santillana, *Istituzioni* = D. Santillana, *Istituzioni di diritto musulmano malichita*, Roma 1926-38
Sarkīs = Yūsuf I. Sarkīs, *Muʿdjam al-maṭbūʿāt al-ʿarabiyya*, Cairo 1346/1928
Schwarz, *Iran* = P. Schwarz, *Iran im Mittelalter nach den arabischen Geographen*, Leipzig 1896-1921
Sezgin, *GAS* = F. Sezgin, *Geschichte des arabischen Schrifttums*, 9 vols., Leiden 1967-84
Shahrastānī = *al-Milal wa 'l-niḥal*, ed. W. Cureton, London 1846
Sidjill-i ʿOthmānī = Meḥmed Thüreyyā, *Sidjill-i ʿOthmānī*, Istanbul 1308-16
Snouck Hurgronje, *Verspr. Geschr.* = C. Snouck Hurgronje, *Verspreide Geschriften*, Leiden 1923-7
Sources inédites = Comte Henry de Castries, *Les sources inédites de l'histoire du Maroc*, première série, Paris [etc.] 1905-, deuxième série, Paris 1922
Spuler, *Horde*¹ = B. Spuler, *Die Goldene Horde, die Mongolen in Russland*, 1st ed., Leipzig 1943
Spuler, *Horde*² = *ibid.*, 2nd ed., Wiesbaden 1965
Spuler, *Iran* = B. Spuler, *Iran in früh-islamischer Zeit*, Wiesbaden 1952
Spuler, *Mongolen*¹ = B. Spuler, *Die Mongolen in Iran*, 1st ed., Leipzig 1939
Spuler, *Mongolen*² = *ibid.*, 2nd ed., Berlin 1955
Spuler, *Mongolen*³ = *ibid.*, 3rd ed., Berlin 1958
Storey = C.A. Storey, *Persian literature: a biobibliographical survey*, London 1927-
Survey of Persian art = ed. by A.U. Pope, Oxford 1938
Suter = H. Suter, *Die Mathematiker und Astronomen der Araber und ihre Werke*, Leipzig 1900
Suyūṭī, *Bughya* = *Bughyat al-wuʿāt*, Cairo 1326
TA = Muḥammad Murtaḍā b. Muḥammad al-Zabīdī, *Tādj al-ʿarūs* (quoted according to the root)
Ṭabarī = *Taʾrīkh al-rusul wa 'l-mulūk*, ed. M.J. de Goeje *et al.*, Leiden 1879-1901
Taeschner, *Wegenetz* = F. Taeschner, *Das anatolische Wegenetz nach osmanischen Quellen*, 2 vols., Leipzig 1924-6
Taʾrīkh Baghdād = al-Khaṭīb al-Baghdādī, *Taʾrīkh Baghdād*, 14 vols., Cairo 1349/1931
Taʾrīkh Dimashḳ = Ibn ʿAsākir, *Taʾrīkh Dimashḳ*, 7 vols., Damascus 1329-51/1911-31
Taʾrīkh-i Guzīda = Ḥamd Allāh Mustawfī al-Ḳazwīnī, *Taʾrīkh-i guzīda*, ed. in facsimile E.G. Browne, Leiden-London 1910
TAVO = *Tübinger Atlas des Vorderen Orients*, Wiesbaden 1977-93
Thaʿālibī, *Yatīma*, ed. Damascus = *Yatīmat al-dahr fī maḥāsin ahl al-ʿaṣr*, 4 vols., Damascus 1304/1886-7
Thaʿālibī, *Yatīma*, ed. Cairo = *ibid.*, ed. Muḥammad Muḥyī al-Dīn ʿAbd al-Ḥamīd, 4 vols., Cairo 1375-7/1956-8
Tomaschek = W. Tomaschek, *Zur historischen Topographie von Kleinasien im Mittelalter*, Vienna 1891
Weil, *Chalifen* = G. Weil, *Geschichte der Chalifen*, Mannheim-Stuttgart 1846-82
Wensinck, *Handbook* = A.J. Wensinck, *A handbook of early Muḥammadan Tradition*, Leiden 1927
Wensinck, *Concordances* = A.J. Wensinck *et alii*, *Concordances et indices de la tradition musulmane*, 7 vols., Leiden 1936-79
WKAS = *Wörterbuch der klassischen arabischen Sprache*, Wiesbaden 1957-
Yaʿḳūbī = *Taʾrīkh*, ed. M.Th. Houtsma, Leiden 1883
Yaʿḳūbī, *Buldān* = ed. M.J. de Goeje, Leiden 1892 (BGA VII)
Yaʿḳūbī-Wiet = *Yaʿḳūbī. Les pays*, Fr. tr. G. Wiet, Cairo 1937
Yāḳūt, ed. Wüstenfeld = *Muʿdjam al-buldān*, ed. F. Wüstenfeld, 5 vols., Leipzig 1866-8
Yāḳūt, ed. Beirut = *ibid.*, 5 vols., Beirut 1374-6/1955-7
Yāḳūt, *Udabāʾ* = *Irshād al-arīb ilā maʿrifat al-adīb*, ed. D.S. Margoliouth, Leiden 1907-31 (GMS)
Zambaur = E. de Zambaur, *Manuel de généalogie et de*

chronologie pour l'histoire de l'Islam, Hanover 1927 (repr. Bad Pyrmont 1955)

Zinkeisen = J. Zinkeisen, *Geschichte des osmanische Reiches in Europa*, Gotha 1840-83

Ziriklī, *Aʿlām* = K̲h̲ayr al-Dīn al-Ziriklī, *al-Aʿlām, ḳāmūs tarād̲j̲im li-as̲h̲har al-rid̲j̲āl wa 'l-nisā' al-ʿArab wa 'l-mustaʿribīn wa 'l-mustas̲h̲riḳīn*, 10 vols., Damascus 1373-8/1954-9

Zubayrī, *Naṣab* = Muṣʿab al-Zubayrī, *Nasab Ḳurays̲h̲*, ed. E. Lévi-Provençal, Cairo 1953

ABBREVIATIONS FOR PERIODICALS ETC.

AARP = *Art and Archaeology Research Papers.*
AAS = *Asian and African Studies.*
Abh. A. W. Gött = *Abhandlungen der Gesellschaft der Wissenschaften zu Göttingen.*
Abh. K. M. = *Abhandlungen für die Kunde des Morgenländes.*
Abh Pr. Ak. W. = *Abhandlungen der preussischen Akademie der Wissenschaften.*
Afr. Fr. = *Bulletin du Comité de l'Afrique française.*
AI = *Annales Islamologiques.*
AIEO Alger = *Annales de l'Institut d'Études Orientales de l'Université d'Alger* (N.S. from 1964).
AIUON = *Annali dell'Istituto Universitario Orientale di Napoli.*
Anz. Wien = *Anzeiger der [kaiserlichen] Akademie der Wissenschaften, Wien. Philosophisch-historische Klasse.*
AO = *Acta Orientalia.*
AO Hung. = *Acta Orientalia* (*Academiae Scientiarum Hungaricae*).
APAW = *Abhandlungen der preussischen Akademie der Wissenschaften.*
ArO = *Archiv Orientální.*
ARW = *Archiv für Religionswissenschaft.*
ASAE = *Annales du Service des antiquités de l'Égypte.*
ASI = *Archaeological Survey of India.*
ASI, NIS = *ibid.*, New Imperial Series.
ASI, AR = *ibid.*, Annual Reports.
AÜDTCFD = *Ankara Üniversitesi Dil ve Tarih-Coğrafya Fakültesi Dergisi.*
BAH = *Bibliotheca Arabico-Hispana.*
BASOR = *Bulletin of the American Schools of Oriental Research.*
BEA = *Bulletin des Études Arabes, Alger.*
Belleten = *Belleten* (of *Türk Tarih Kurumu*).
BÉt. Or. = *Bulletin d'Études Orientales de l'Institut Français de Damas.*
BFac. Ar. = *Bulletin of the Faculty of Arts of the Egyptian University.*
BGA = *Bibliotheca geographorum arabicorum.*
BIE = *Bulletin de l'Institut d'Égypte.*
BIFAO = *Bulletin de l'Institut Français d'Archéologie Orientale du Caire.*
BiOr = *Bibliotheca Orientalis.*
BJRUL = *Bulletin of the John Rylands University Library, Manchester.*
BRAH = *Boletín de la Real Academia de la Historia de España.*
BSE = *Bol'shaya Sovetskaya Éntsiklopediya* (Large Soviet Encyclopaedia) 1st ed.
BSE[2] = *ibid.*, 2nd ed.
BSL[P] = *Bulletin de la Société de Linguistique de Paris.*
BSMES or *BRISMES* = *British Society for Middle Eastern Studies Bulletin*, continued as *British Journal of Middle Eastern Studies.*
BSO[A]S = *Bulletin of the School of Oriental [and African] Studies.*
BTLV = *Bijdragen tot de Taal-, Land- en Volkenkunde [van Nederlandsch Indië].*
BZ = *Byzantinische Zeitschrift.*
CAJ = *Central Asiatic Journal.*
CHIr = *Cambridge History of Iran.*
COC = *Cahiers de l'Orient contemporain.*
CSCO = *Corpus Scriptorum Christianorum Orientalium.*
CT = *Cahiers de Tunisie.*
EI[1] = *Encyclopaedia of Islam*, 1st edn.
EIM = *Epigraphia Indo-Moslemica.*
EIr = *Encyclopaedia Iranica.*
ERE = *Encyclopaedia of Religions and Ethics.*
EW = *East and West.*
GaP = *Grundriss der arabischen Philologie.*
GGA = *Göttingische Gelehrte Anzeigen.*
GIPh = *Grundriss der iranischen Philologie.*
GJ = *Géographical Journal.*
GMS = *Gibb Memorial Series.*
Gr. I. Ph. = *Grundriss der Iranischen Philologie.*
Hdb d. Or = *Handbuch der Orientalistik.*
HUCA = *Hebrew Union College Annual.*
IA = *Islâm Ansiklopedisi.*
IBLA = *Revue de l'Institut des Belles Lettres Arabes*, Tunis.
IC = *Islamic Culture.*
IFD = *Ilahiyat Fakültesi Dergisi.*
IHQ = *Indian Historical Quarterly.*
IJMES = *International Journal of Middle Eastern Studies.*
ILS = *Islamic Law and Society.*
IOS = *Israel Oriental Studies.*
IQ = *The Islamic Quarterly.*
Iran JBIPS = *Iran, Journal of the British Institute of Persian Studies.*
Isl. = *Der Islam.*
JA = *Journal Asiatique.*
JAfr S. = *Journal of the African Society.*
JAL = *Journal of Arabic Literature.*
JAnthr. I = *Journal of the Anthropological Institute.*
JAOS = *Journal of the American Oriental Society.*
JARCE = *Journal of the American Research Center in Egypt.*
JASB = *Journal of the Asiatic Society of Bengal.*
JBBRAS = *Journal of the Bombay Branch of the Royal Asiatic Society.*
JE = *Jewish Encyclopaedia.*
JESHO = *Journal of the Economic and Social History of the Orient.*
JIMMA = *Journal of the Institute of Muslim Minority Affairs.*
JIS = *Journal of Islamic Studies.*
J[R] Num. S. = *Journal of the [Royal] Numismatic Society.*
JNES = *Journal of Near Eastern Studies.*
JPak. HS = *Journal of the Pakistan Historical Society.*
JPHS = *Journal of the Punjab Historical Society.*
JPOS = *Journal of the Palestine Oriental Society.*
JQR = *Jewish Quarterly Review.*
JRAS = *Journal of the Royal Asiatic Society.*
J[R]ASB = *Journal and Proceedings of the [Royal] Asiatic Society of Bengal.*
JRGeog. S. = *Journal of the Royal Geographical Society.*
JSAI = *Jerusalem Studies in Arabic and Islam.*
JSFO = *Journal de la Société Finno-ougrienne.*
JSS = *Journal of Semitic Studies.*
JTS = *Journal of Theological Studies.*
KCA = *Körösi Csoma Archivum.*
KS = *Keleti Szemle* (Oriental Review).
KSIE = *Kratkie Soobshčeniya Instituta Étnografiy* (Short communications of the Institute of Ethnography).
LE = *Literaturnaya Éntsiklopediya* (Literary Encyclopaedia).
MDOG = *Mitteilungen der Deutschen Orient-Gesellschaft.*
MDPV = *Mitteilungen und Nachrichten des Deutschen Palästina-Vereins.*
MEA = *Middle Eastern Affairs.*
MEJ = *Middle East Journal.*
Méms. DAFA = *Mémoires de la Délégation Française en Afghanistan.*
MES = *Middie East Studies.*
MFOB = *Mélanges de la Faculté Orientale de l'Université St. Joseph de Beyrouth.*

MGMN = *Mitteilungen zur Geschichte der Medizin und Naturwissenschaften.*
MGWJ = *Monatsschrift für die Geschichte und Wissenschaft des Judentums.*
MIDEO = *Mélanges de l'Institut Dominicain d'Études Orientales du Caire.*
MIE = *Mémoires de l'Institut d'Égypte.*
MIFAO = *Mémoires publiés par les membres de l'Institut Français d'Archéologie Orientale du Caire.*
MMAF = *Mémoires de la Mission Archéologique Française au Caire.*
MME = *Manuscripts of the Middle East.*
MMIA = *Madjallat al-Madjma' al-'Ilmī al-'Arabī,* Damascus.
MO = *Le Monde oriental.*
MOG = *Mitteilungen zur osmanischen Geschichte.*
MSE = *Malaya Sovetskaya Éntsiklopediya* (Small Soviet Encyclopaedia).
MSFO = *Mémoires de la Société Finno-ougrienne.*
MSL[P] = *Mémoires de la Société Linguistique de Paris.*
MSOS Afr. = *Mitteilungen des Seminars für Orientalische Sprachen, Afrikanische Studien.*
MSOS As. = *Mitteilungen des Seminars für Orientalische Sprachen, Westasiatische Studien.*
MTM = *Millī Tetebbü'ler Medjmū'asï.*
MUSJ = *Mélanges de la Faculté orientale de l'Université St.-Joseph.*
MW = *The Muslim World.*
NC = *Numismatic Chronicle.*
Nak. W. Gött = *Nachrichten von der Gesellschaft der Wissenschaften zu Göttingen.*
NZ = *Numismatische Zeitschrift.*
OC = *Oriens Christianus.*
OLZ = *Orientalistische Literaturzeitung.*
OM = *Oriente Moderno.*
PEFQS = *Palestine Exploration Fund. Quarterly Statement.*
Pet. Mitt. = *Petermanns Mitteilungen.*
PO = *Patrologia Orientalis.*
PPUAES = *Publications of the Princeton University Archaeological Expedition to Syria.*
PTF = *Philologiae Turcicae Fundamenta,* Wiesbaden 1959-.
QDAP = *Quarterly Statement of the Department of Antiquities of Palestine.*
QSA = *Quaderni de Studi Arabi.*
RAAD = *Revue de l'Académie Arabe de Damas.*
RAfr. = *Revue Africaine.*
RCAL = *Rendiconti de l'Academia dei Lincei.*
RCEA = *Répertoire chronologique d'Épigraphie arabe.*
REJ = *Revue des Études Juives.*
Rend. Lin. = *Rendiconti della Reale Accademia dei Lincei, Classe di scienze morali, storiche e filologiche.*
REI = *Revue des Études Islamiques.*
RHR = *Revue de l'Histoire des Religions.*
RIMA = *Revue de l'Institut des Manuscrits Arabes.*
RMM = *Revue du Monde Musulman.*
RMMM = *Revue des Mondes musulmans et de la Mediterranée.*
RN = *Revue Numismatique.*
RO = *Rocznik Orientalistyczny.*
ROC = *Revue de l'Orient Chrétien.*
ROL = *Revue de l'Orient Latin.*
ROMM = *Revue de l'Occident musulman et de la Mediterranée.*
RSO = *Rivista degli studi orientali.*
RT = *Revue Tunisienne.*
SB. Ak. Heid. = *Sitzungsberichte der Heidelberger Akademie der Wissenschaften.*
SB. Ak. Wien = *Sitzungsberichte der Akademie der Wissenschaften zu Wien.*
SBBayer. Ak. = *Sitzungsberichte der Bayerischen Akademie der Wissenschaften.*
SBPMS Erlg. = *Sitzungsberichte der Physikalisch-medizinischen Sozietät in Erlangen.*
SBPr. Ak. W. = *Sitzungsberichte der Preussischen Akademie der Wissenschaften zu Berlin.*
SE = *Sovetskaya Étnografiya* (Soviet Ethnography).
SO = *Sovetskoe Vostokovedenie* (Soviet Orientalism).
Stud. Ir. = *Studia Iranica.*
Stud. Isl. = *Studia Islamica.*
S.Ya. = *Sovetskoe Yazïkoznanie* (Soviet Linguistics).
TBG = *Tijdschrift van het Bataviaasch Genootschap van Kunsten en Wetenschappen.*
TD = *Tarih Dergisi.*
THITM = *Türk Hukuk ve İktisat Tarihi Mecmuasi.*
TIE = *Trudï instituta Étnografiy* (Works of the Institute of Ethnography).
TM = *Turkiyat Mecmuası.*
TOEM/TTEM = *Ta'rīkh-i 'Othmānī* (*Türk Ta'rīkhi*) *Endjümeni medjmū'asï.*
UAJb = *Ural-altäische Jahrbücher.*
Verh. Ak. Amst. = *Verhandelingen der Koninklijke Akademie van Wetenschappen te Amsterdam.*
Versl. Med. Ak. Amst. = *Verslagen en Mededeelingen der Koninklijke Akademie van Wetenschappen te Amsterdam.*
VI = *Voprosï Istoriy* (Historical Problems).
WI = *Die Welt des Islams.*
WI, n.s. = *ibid.,* new series.
Wiss. Veröff. DOG = *Wissenschaftliche Veröffentlichungen der Deutschen Orient-Gesellschaft.*
WO = *Welt des Orients.*
WZKM = *Wiener Zeitschrift für die Kunde des Morgenländes.*
ZA = *Zeitschrift für Assyriologie.*
ZAL = *Zeitschrift für Arabische Linguistik.*
ZATW = *Zeitschrift für die alttestamentliche Wissenschaft.*
ZDMG = *Zeitschrift der Deutschen Morgenländischen Gesellschaft.*
ZDPV = *Zeitschrift des Deutschen Palästinavereins.*
ZfN = *Zeitschrift für Numismatik.*
ZGAIW = *Zeitschrift für Geschichte der Arabisch-Islamischen Wissenschaften.*
ZGErdk. Birl. = *Zeitschrift der Gesellschaft für Erdkunde in Berlin.*
ZS = *Zeitschrift für Semitistik.*

LIST OF TRANSLITERATIONS

SYSTEM OF TRANSLITERATION OF ARABIC CHARACTERS:

Consonants

ء	’ (except when initial)	ز	z	ق	ḳ
ب	b	س	s	ك	k
ت	t	ش	sh	ل	l
ث	th	ص	ṣ	م	m
ج	dj	ض	ḍ	ن	n
ح	ḥ	ط	ṭ	ه	h
خ	kh	ظ	ẓ	و	w
د	d	ع	‘	ي	y
ذ	dh	غ	gh		
ر	r	ف	f		

Long Vowels

أى	ā
و	ū
ي	ī

Short Vowels

ـَ	a
ـُ	u
ـِ	i

Diphthongs

ـَو	aw
ـَي	ay
ـِيّـ	iyy (final form ī)
ـُوّ	uww (final form ū)

ة a; at (construct state)

ال (article), al- and ’l- (even before the antero-palatals)

PERSIAN, TURKISH AND URDU ADDITIONS TO THE ARABIC ALPHABET:

پ	p	ژ	zh	ٹ	ṫ	ڑ	ŕ
چ	č	ك or F	g (sometimes ñ in Turkish)	ڈ	d́	ں	ṇ

Additional vowels:

a) Turkish: e, i, o, ö, ü. Diacritical signs proper to Arabic are, in principle, not used in words of Turkish etymology.
b) Urdu: ē, ō.

For modern Turkish, the official orthography adopted by the Turkish Republic in 1928 is used. The following letters may be noted:

c = dj	ğ = gh	j = zh	k = k and ḳ	t = t and ṭ
ç = č	h = h, ḥ and kh	ş = sh	s = s, ṣ and th	z = z, ẓ, ḍ and dh

SYSTEM OF TRANSLITERATION OF THE RUSSIAN ALPHABET:

а	a	е	e	к	k	п	p	ф	f	щ	shč	ю	yu
б	b	ж	ž	л	l	р	r	х	kh	ы	i̊	я	ya
в	v	П	z	м	m	с	s	ц	ts	ь	’	ѣ	ě
г	g	и	i	н	n	т	t	ч	č	ъ	‘		
д	d	й	y	о	o	у	u	ш	sh	э	é		

ADDENDA AND CORRIGENDA

VOLUME I
P. 702ᵃ,   **ASHRAF ʿALĪ**, *add to Bibl.*: Barbara Daly Metcalf, *Perfecting women: Maulana Ashraf ʿAli Thanawi's Bihishti Zewar, a partial translation with commentary*, Berkeley 1990.

VOLUME IV
P. 1091ᵇ,   **KHĀSĪ**, l. 38, *for* Ustād͟h D͟jawhar [*q.v.*] *read* Ustād͟h D͟jawd͟har [*q.v.*]

VOLUME VII
P. 560,   **MUNAD͟JD͟JIM**, Banū 'l-, note 7 to genealogical tree, *for* *Taʾrīk͟h Bag͟hdād*, iv, 318, nr. 2122, *read* *Taʾrīk͟h Bag͟hdād*, v, 215, nr. 2688

VOLUME IX
P. 353ᵃ,   **SHARḲĀWA**, *add to Bibl.*: D.F. Eickelman, *Moroccan Islam: tradition and society in a pilgrimage center*, Austin 1976.

VOLUME X
P. 89ᵇ,   al-**TAFTĀZĀNĪ**, ll. 14-15 from bottom of article, *for* and a polemical refutation of Ibn al-ʿArabī's *Fuṣūṣ al-Ḥikam, read* The refutation of the doctrine of Ibn al-ʿArabī often ascribed to al-Taftāzānī was written by his pupil ʿAlāʾ al-Dīn Muḥammad al-Buk͟hārī (d. 841/1430). See Bakrī ʿAlāʾ al-Dīn, *ʿAbd al-G͟hanī al-Nābulusī: al-Wud͟jūd al-ḥaḳḳ*, Damascus 1995, 15-30.

P. 664ᵇ,   al-**ṬŪR**, *add to Bibl. on the Arabic mss. of St. Catherine's*: Y.E. Meimaris, *Katalogos ton neon arabikon kheirographon tes hieras mones Hagias Aikaterines tou Orous Sina*, Athens 1985.

P. 868ᵃ,   ʿ**UNAYZA**, *add to Bibl.*: Soraya Altorki and D.P. Cole, *Arabian oasis city: the transformation of ʿUnayzah*, Austin 1989.

VOLUME XI
P. 1ᵇ,   **VID͟JAYANAGARA**, l. 5 from bottom of first paragraph, *for* Konkar [*q.v.* in Suppl.] *read* Konkan [*q.v.* in Suppl.]

P. 126ᵇ,   **WĀLIBA** b. al-**ḤUBĀB**, l. 3, *for* 2nd/9th century *read* 2nd/8th century.

P. 169ᵇ,   **WĀSIṬ**, *add after l. 37*: During the struggle for ʿIrāḳ under al-Maʾmūn, there were, however, small issues of silver from Wāsiṭ in the years 200 and 203, and occasional issues in copper in 147, 167, 177 and 187 or 9.

P. 174ᵃ,   **WASM**, *add to Bibl.*: A second general study is E. Littmann, *Zur Entzifferung der thamudenischen Inschriften*, Berlin 1904, 78-104, which argues that most of the brands originate from the South Semitic alphabet in its North Arabian form.

P. 177ᵇ,   **WATHANIYYA**, *add to Bibl.*: G.R. Hawting, *The idea of idolatry and the emergence of Islam. From polemic to history*, Cambridge 1999.

P. 227ᵇ,   al-**YADĀLĪ**, l. 14 from bottom, *for* (19 lines) *read* (19 folios)

opp P. 264,   **YĀḲŪT** al-**RŪMĪ**, map, *for* Oxus (Sayḥūn) *read* Oxus (D͟jayḥūn), *and resitutate Cairo on the right-side of the Nile*

P. 292ᵃ,   **YARMŪK**, *add to Bibl.*: W.E. Kaegi, *Heraclius, Emperor of Byzantium*, Cambridge 2003, 237-44.

P. 345-6,   al-**YŪNĪNĪ**, *add the following table*:

Genealogical tree of the family of Mūsā al-Yūnīnī, author of *Dhayl Mirʾāt al-zamān*

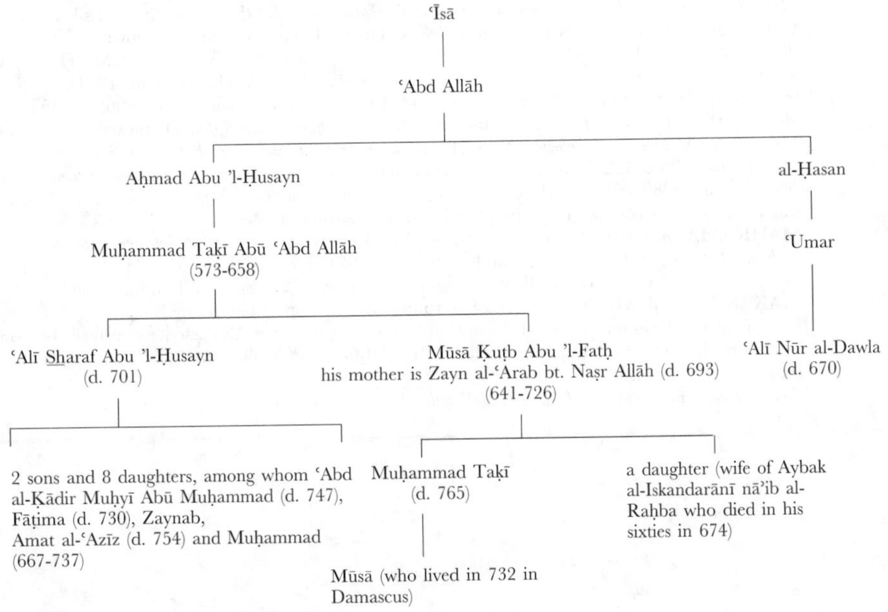

P. 361b, **YŪSUF** AND **ZULAYKHĀ**, *add to Bibl.1.(c)*: ed. Aʿlā-Khān Afṣaḥzād and Ḥusayn Aḥmad Tarbiyat, in *Mathnawī-yi Haft awrang*, ii, Tehran 1378 *sh.*/1999, 19-209.

P. 364a, **ẒĀʾ**, ll. 23-25, *read* a voiceless /ṭ/ for /ḏ/ is attested in some Northern Yemeni dialects . . ., and a voiceless /ṭ/ for /ḏ/ occurs in North African sedentary dialects
l. 42, *read* Uzbekistan-Arabic) with /ḏ/ > /y/,

P. 371b, **ZABĪD**, *add to Bibl.*: Barbara E. Croken, *Zabîd under the Rasulids of Yemen, 626-858 AH/1229-1454 AD*, unpubl. Ph.D. diss. Harvard University 1990; *Zabīd. Patrimoine mondiale*, in *Saba, revue trimestrielle*, v-vi (1999); ʿAbd al-Raḥmān b. ʿAbd Allāh al-Ḥaḍramī, *Zabīd. Masādjiduhā wa-madārisuhā al-ʿilmiyya fi ʾl-taʾrīkh*, Damascus 2000.

P. 404b, **ZĀʾIRDJA**, *add before final paragraph*: As for the history of numbers, in his description of the *zāʾirdja* Ibn Khaldūn called attention to the use of Arabic characters (*abdjād* [*q.v.*]) and *zimām*, or administrative, numerals, as well as *ghubār*, denoting the nine figures of Indian origin. With regard to the *zimām* numerals, this statement allows G.S. Colin to date the entry of the system of Greek numerals into Morocco and to declare that the *zimām* had spread in hermetic circles at the same time. But given their administrative, commercial or diplomatic use, recourse to them did not signify that they required the use of a code-breaker (*De l'origine grecque des 'chiffres de Fès' et de nos 'chiffres arabes'*, in *JA*, ccxxii [1933], 193-215). R. Lemay points out, from two astrological manuscripts, B.N. ar. 2582 (attributed to Abū Maʿshar), a MS from the 18th century (?), fol. 2r, and B.N. ar. 2584, fol. 2r, the list of correspondences between *abdjād* numerals and *zimām* (*Arabic numerals*, in *Dictionary of the Middle Ages*, ed. J.R. Strayer, i, New York 1982, 386ff.).

P. 548a, AL-**ZUBAYDĪ**, l. 4, *for* great-great-great-grandfather *read* great-great-great-great-grandfather

P. 548b, l. 30, *for* He died there on 1 Djumādā II *read* He died there on 1 Djumādā II 379

SUPPLEMENT

P. 20b, **ABU ʾL-BAYḌĀʾ** AL-**RIYĀḤĪ**, *add after the last sentence of the text*: He was also the *rāwī* of Abū Nuwās, and the latter has devoted a *marthiya* to him (*Dīwān*, ed. Ghazālī, Cairo 1953, 572-4; cf. E. Wagner, *Abū Nuwās*, Wiesbaden 1965, 356).

P. 28b, **ABŪ MĀḌĪ**, *add to Bibl.*: G.D. Salīm, *Ī. Abū Māḍī (1889-1957): dirāsāt ʿanhu wa-ashʿāruh al-madjhūla*, Cairo 1980.

P. 58a, AL-ʿ**AḲḲĀD**, l. 6, *for* Ḥāfiẓ Ibrāhīm *read* Shukrī

P. 103a, **AʿYĀṢ**, *add to Bibl.*: M.J. Kister, *"Call yourselves by graceful names . . ."*, in *Lectures in memory of Professor Martin B. Plessner*, Jerusalem 1976, 16, 25.

P. 163b, **ČAČ-NĀMA**, *add to Bibl.*: I. Habib, *A study of Ḥajjāj b. Yūsuf's outlook and policies in the light of the Chachnāma*, in *Bull. of the Inst. of Islamic Studies*, Aligarh, vi-vii (1962-3), 34-48.

P. 167a, **ČAD**, *add at the end of the article*: These negotiations finally resulted in the formation of a Transitional Government of National Union (GUNT), which did not, however, bring the internal dissensions to an end. The civil war started up again in 1980, and M. Goukouni Oueddaï secured victory over his opponents, thanks to the help of Libyan forces; he has even announced a plan for a union between Chad and Libya, but the FAN (Armed Forces of the North) continue the struggle in the eastern part of the country, simultaneously against the Libyans and the government troops (March 1981).

P. 241b, AL-**DJĀMIʿA** AL-ʿ**ARABIYYA**, *add at the end of the article*: In consequence of the treaty between Egypt and Israel and the Camp David negotiations, the seat of the Arab League has been moved to Tunis, and Shādhlī Ḳlēbī was elected Secretary General (27 June 1979).

P. 408a, AL-**IDRĪSĪ,** *add at the end of the article*: The oldest manuscripts (Princeton of 754/1353, Taymūriyya of 877/1473 and Manchester of 887/1482) and Ibn Abī Ḥadjala (*Sukkardān* [together with al-ʿĀmilī's *al-Mikhlāt*], 2Beirut 1399/1979, 460) give the title *Anwār ʿulwiyy al-adjrām*. In the *Anwār* al-Idrīsī mentions other books he wrote: *K. al-Adwār wa ʾl-fatarāt*, *K. al-Djawhara al-yatīma fī akhbār Miṣr al-ḳadīma* and *K. Maṭlaʿ al-ṭāliʿ al-saʿīd fī akhbār al-Ṣaʿīd*; the latter title possibly served al-Udfuwī as a model for his prosopography of Upper Egyptian men of renown.
Add to Bibl.: al-Udfuwī, *al-Ṭāliʿ al-saʿīd al-djāmiʿ asmāʾ nudjabāʾ al-Ṣaʿīd*, ed. S.M. Ḥasan, Cairo 1966, 179-81, 534-6; Ibn Ḥadjar al-ʿAskalānī, *Lisān al-mīzān*, Ḥaydarābād 1331, v, 262, no. 902; al-Suyūṭī, *Ḥusn al-muḥāḍara*, ed. M. Abu ʾl-Faḍl Ibrāhīm, Cairo 1387/1968, i, 554; Ziriklī, *al-Aʿlām*, 2Beirut 1399/1979, vi, 208b-c; Kaḥḥāla, *Muʿdjam al-muʾallifīn*, Damascus 1379/1960, ix, 174a-b; A. Mingana, *Catalogue of the Arabic manuscripts in the John Rylands Library in Manchester*, Manchester 1934, 422-5, no. 262; U. Haarmann, *Regional sentiment in medieval Islamic Egypt*, in *BSOAS*, xliii (1980), 55-66; M. Cook, *Pharaonic history in medieval Egypt*, in *SI*, lvii (1983); a critical edition of *Anwār* has been prepared by U. Haarmann (Beirut 1991).

P. 566b, **MAḤKAMA**, *add to Bibl.*: See the writings by D. Pearl, in particular *Interpersonal conflict of laws in India, Pakistan, and Bangladesh*, London-Bombay 1981; idem and W. Menski, *Muslim family law*, London 1998 (rev. ed. of D. Pearl, *A textbook on Muslim personal law*, London 21987).

P. 570a, **MAḲĀṢID** AL-**SHARĪʿA**, l. 3, *for* of a ruling *read* of a possible ruling
1st line of third paragraph, read *Istiṣlāḥ* and *istiḥsān* [*q.vv.*] were discussed extensively by Mālikīs.
l. 2 from bottom, *for* Muḥammad Ṭāhir b. ʿĀshūr, *read* Muḥammad al-Ṭāhir b. ʿĀshūr; *and change same in Bibliography*.
Add to Bibl.: Ṭūfī, *Sharḥ Mukhtaṣar al-Rawḍa*, Beirut 1987-89.

A

AL-ʿ**ABBĀS** B. **AḤMAD** B. **ṬŪLŪN**, eldest son f Aḥmad b. Ṭūlūn [*q.v.*]. When the latter set off or the conquest of Syria, he entrusted the govern-ent of Egypt to al-ʿAbbās, his designated heir, but l-ʿAbbās was very soon persuaded to take advantage f his father's absence to supplant him. Warned by he vizier al-Wāsiṭī, Ibn Ṭūlūn got ready to return to gypt, and his son, after having emptied the treasury nd got together considerable sums of money, went ff with his partisans to Alexandria, and then to Barḳa. As soon as he got back, on 4 Ramaḍān 265/30 April 879, Ibn Ṭūlūn tried to bring him back to reason, nd, promising him pardon, sent to him a letter, whose text has been preserved by al-Ḳalḳashandī (*Ṣubḥ*, vii, 5-10; reproduced also by Ṣafwat, *Djamharat rasāʾil al-ʿArab*, iv, 366-73); but the rebel remained deaf to all these approaches and decided to invade Ifrīḳiya at the head of a force of 800 cavalry and 10,000 black infantry, swollen along the way by some local contingents.

Al-ʿAbbās then claimed that the caliph al-Muʿtamid had named him as governor of Ifrīḳiya and demanded of the Aghlabid Ibrāhīm II that he should yield place to him. The latter responded by sending against him a force of cavalry, which met up with him at Labda but did not venture an engagement. Al-ʿAbbās now sacked Labda, even though the governor there had decided to yield to him, and then went on to lay siege to Tripoli. The Ibāḍī leader Ilyās b. Manṣūr al-Nafūsī organised resistance, and with the help of reinforcements sent by Ibrāhīm II, succeeded in putting the rebel army to flight (middle of 267/ winter 880-1). Al-ʿAbbās was compelled to return to Egypt, but was captured in the course of a battle outside the city of Alexandria with an army sent by Ibn Ṭūlūn. He was brought to Fusṭāṭ, led round on a mule (Yāḳūt, *Udabāʾ*, vii, 183), condemned to execute personally the poet Djaʿfar b. Muḥammad b. Aḥmad b. Ḥudhār and others of his retinue considered to be responsible for his revolt, and finally flogged and thrown into prison. He probably did not remain there long, but his attitude nevertheless removed him from all possibility of succession to the throne of Egypt. On Ibn Ṭūlūn's death (Dhu 'l-Ḳaʿda 270/May 884), it was his son Khumārawayh [*q.v.*] who followed him, and al-ʿAbbās's protests were extinguished in blood.

Bibliography: The events are recounted in great detail by Balawī, *Sīrat Aḥmad b. Ṭūlūn*, ed. M. Kurd ʿAlī, Damascus 1358, 252-5, and Kindī, *Wulāt Miṣr*, Beirut 1959, 246-50; these basic sources and the data of other historians have been utilised by M. Talbi, *Emirat aghlabide*, 347-52.

(ED.)

ʿ**ABBĀS SARWĀNĪ**, historian of the Mughal period in India.

Little is known about him personally, but he was a member of a Sarwānī Afghān family which had settled in Banūr town (in the *sarkār* of Sirhind). His ancestor got 2,000 *bīghās* of land as a maintenance grant during the reign of Bahlūl Lōdī. It was resumed by Bābur in 932/1526, and Shaykh Bāyazīd Sarwānī, the grandfather of ʿAbbās, had to leave for Rōh for this reason. Shēr Shāh Sūr restored it to Shaykh Bāyazīd when the latter returned after the expulsion of the Mughals in 947/1540. Islām Shāh Sūr also renewed it to Shaykh ʿAlī, the father of ʿAbbās. In 987/1579, it was again resumed by the state. ʿAbbās then entered the service of Sayyid Ḥamīd, a scholarly officer of Akbar. In 990/1582 he compiled at the instance of Akbar his famous *Tuḥfa-yi Akbar Shāhī*, generally known as the *Taʾrīkh-i Shēr Shāhī*. It is however, a biography of Shēr Shāh Sūr and not history in the true sense.

The *Tuḥfa-yi Akbar Shāhī* was compiled when the short-lived Sūr dynasty had already passed into the limbo of history; and there was no hope left for the revival of Afghān power. Now an Afghān writer could get satisfaction only in magnifying the Afghān rule, so that ʿAbbās was in his work inevitably nostalgic about the past of the Afghāns. In fact, he compiled his work with preconceived notions, practising the economy of truth when the facts were disparaging. Moreover, he is not a first-hand source. All, or almost all, his narratives relating to the life and career of Shēr Shāh are based on the information supplied by the Sarwānī nobles who had served under the Lōdīs and the Sūrs and with whom he was connected by his own marriages. As descendants of Khān-i Aʿẓam ʿUmar Khān Sarwānī, the premier noble of the Lōdī Sultans, they were not expected to enquire about Shēr Shāh's background, who had himself, and his father before him, been their servants before his rise to sovereignty. For this reason, information gathered by ʿAbbās about Shēr Shāh's early career from his Sarwānī relations contains important gaps, some of which are filled by Mushtāḳī's rambling account, available in the *Wāḳiʿāt-i Mushtāḳī*. Despite its defects, the *Tuḥfa-yi Akbar Shāhī* is regarded as the major source for Shēr Shāh's reign. It furnishes fairly detailed data about the early life of Shēr Shāh and provides clues to important facts about his statesmanship. Later works, such as the *Taʾrīkh-i Khān-i Djahānī* of Niʿmat Allāh Harawī, *Taʾrīkh-i Shāhī* of Aḥmad Yādgār and *Taʾrīkh-i Dāwūdī* of ʿAbd Allāh, all compiled during the reign of the Emperor Djahāngīr, contain very little additional information with regard to Shēr Shāh.

Bibliography: ʿAbbās Sarwānī, *Tuḥfa-yi Akbar Shāhī*, ed. Imām al-Dīn, Dacca 1964; Sir H. M. Elliot and J. Dowson, *The history of India as told by its own historians*, iv, 301-433; Storey, i, 513-5; I. H. Siddiqui, *History of Shēr Shāh Sūr*, Aligarh 1971; S. A. A. Rizvi, *Religious and intellectual history of the Muslims in Akbar's reign*, New Delhi 1975, 234-8. (I. H. SIDDIQUI)

ABBREVIATIONS, sigla and conventional signs are nowadays called in Arabic *mukhtaṣarāt* "abridgements" or *rumūz* "symbols", but there does not seem to have been any specific term for them in the classical period, even though from the very beginnings of Islam copyists, scribes and specialists in all sorts of disciplines were led to use them. This is why it has been thought suitable to bring together here a list of the main abbreviations found in the mediaeval texts, together with some examples of those taken up by our contemporaries.

One should first of all recall that a certain number of the surās of the Ḳurʾān begin by groups of letters (the *fawātiḥ* or *ḥurūf muḳaṭṭaʿa/āt*), which remain curiously inexplicable despite the many interpretations thought up by inventive minds; the reader will find a table of them in the article AL-ḲURʾĀN, where the signs indicating pronunciation to be found in various editions of the Holy Book are also considered.

It should also be noted that if the verb *sammā*, means notably "to pronounce the formula *bi-smi llāh al-raḥmān al-raḥīm*," the formula itself is called the *basmala* [*q.v.*], whose form is obvious; cf. also the *ḥamdala*, the formula *al-ḥamdu li-llāh* "praise be to God", etc.

It is precisely these pious or optative formulae which, because of their frequency, led copyists and scribes to adopt various abbreviations, of which the most frequent are: *tʿ* = *taʿālā* "may He be exalted"; *ṣ* = *ṣallā llāh ʿalayh*, and *ṣlʿm* = *ṣallā llāh ʿalayhi wa-sallam* "may God confer His blessings [on the Prophet] and grant him peace"; *ʿm* = *ʿalayhi al-salām* "peace be upon him [sc. upon a prophet]"; *rḥ* = *raḥimahu llāh* "may God have mercy on him"; and *rḍh* = *raḍiya llāh ʿanhu* "may God be pleased with him" after the name of a deceased person.

For their part, copyists used conventional signs, amongst which one may mention: *ṣ* = *ṣawābuhu* "the correct reading, to be read ..."; *b* = *baʿda* "after" or *kh* = *muʾakhkhar* "placed after" and *ḳ* = *ḳabla* "before" to show that two words should be transposed (or also *m* = *muʾakhkhar* and *m* = *muḳaddam* for the same inversion); *ṣḥ* = *muṣaḥḥaḥ* "corrected, verified, the correct reading"; *kh* = *khaṭaʾ* "error" or *nuskha ukhrā* "another manuscript = variant"; *m* = *mudradj* "a word straddling two hemistiches of a verse"; *alkh* = *ilā akhirihi* "etc."; *h* or *ah*=*intahā* "end of quotation".

In technical works on grammar, theology, law, etc., the following may occur: *dj* = *djamʿ* "plural"; *djdj* = *djamʿ al-djamʿ* "double plural"; *m* = *muʾannath* "feminine", but also *matn* "text of the *ḥadīth*, etc."; *sh*=*sharḥ* "commentary" and *shāriḥ* "commentator"; *thnā* or *nā* = *ḥaddathanā* "there related to us"; *anā* = *anbaʾanā* or *akhbaranā* "[he] related to us (especially of a historical or other tradition"; *m* or *alm* = *(al)-maʿrūf* or *(al)-mashhūr* "(the) well-known, (the) famed"; *alẓ* = *al-ẓāhir* "the obvious, literal sense"; *wẓ* = *wa-ẓāhiruhu* "and its literal sense"; *ḥ* = *taḥwīl* "change in the *isnād*"; *ṣ* = *muṣannaf* "*ḥadīth* work" or *muṣannif* "author (of the work)"; *alm* = *al-muṣannif* "the author"; *yḳ* = *yuḳāl* "it is said"; *aṣ* = *aṣlan* "by no means, absolutely"; *ayḍ* = *ayḍan* "also, equally"; *s* = *suʾāl* "question"; *dj* = *djawāb* "reply"; *n* = *bayānuhu* "its explanation"; *ḥ* = *ḥaḳīḳa* "realit[y] "in truth"; *b* = *bāṭil* "false"; *(al)mḥ* = *(al)-mu*[...] "what is absurd, improbable"; *mm* = *mamnūʿ* "i[m]possible, absurd"; *(f)lā nm* = *(fa)-lā nusallim* "we [do] not admit, recognise"; *ḥ, fḥ* = *(fa)-ḥīnaʾidhin* "a[nd] then, consequently"; *lā mḥh* = *la maḥālata* "witho[ut] any doubt"; *kk* = *kadhālika* "thus"; *almṭ* = *al-maṭ*[...] "the desired aim" or *al-muṭlaḳ* "the absolute".

Also found are: *s* = *sāʿa* "hour", *d* = *daḳ*[...] "minute", and the names of the months: *m* = *M*[u]*ḥarram*, *ṣ* = *Ṣafar*, *rā* = *Rabīʿ* I, *r* = *Rabīʿ* II, *djā* = *Djumādā* I, *dj* = *Djumādā* II, *b* = *Radjab*, *sh* = *Shaʿbān*, *l* = *Shawwāl*, *n* = *Ramaḍān*, *dhā* = *Dhu Ḳaʿda* and *dh* = *Dhu 'l-Ḥidjdja*.

It will be noted that these abbreviations are oft[en] formed by the first letter of the word; another lett[er] may sometimes be chosen, without always there bei[ng] a care to avoid confusion, so that it may well happ[en] that the groups of letters have an ambivalence, whi[ch] is not, however, very confusing.

At the present time, the proliferation of sigla, a[nd] the perennial desire to save time have multiplied t[he] use of abbreviations, especially in the press and [in] commercial and financial documents, but also [in] scholarly works with an apparatus criticus, whe[re] one may find e.g. *dj* = *djuzʾ* "volume", *ṣ* = *ṣaf*[*ḥa*] "page", *s* = *saṭr* "line", *w* = *waraḳa* "leaf, folio" *a* and *b* or *w* and *ẓ* = *wadjh* and *ẓahr* "recto an[d] verso", *m* = *masīḥī/iyya* "A.D.", *h* = *hidjrī/iy*[*ya*] "A.H.", *m* = *malzama* "signature", *khṭ* = *makhṭ*[*ūṭ*] "manuscript", *ṭ* = *ṭabʿa* "printed edition", etc.

An international abbreviation has yielded, as els[e]where, a genuine noun: *al-Yūna/iskū* "UNESCO" Expressions denoting Unions or Federations are re[-]placed by initials: *dj.ʿ.m* = *al-djumhūriyya al-ʿara*[*]biyya al-muttaḥida* "the United Arab Republic" *a.ʿ.m* = *al-imārāt al-ʿarabiyya al-muttaḥida* "th[e] United Arabic Emirates", etc. Money and currencie[s] weights and measures are not outside this genera[l] tendency: *l.l.* = *līra lubnāniyya* "Lebanese pound" *d* = *dīnār* (and also *daktūr* "doctor"); *dj. m.* = *dju*[*]nayh miṣrī* "Egyptian pound"; *m* = millieme or *mit*[*r*] "metre"; *km* = *kīlūmitr* "km"; *s.m./ṣ.m.* = *s/ṣanti*[*]mitr* "cm"; *f* = *faddān* "feddan", etc. Addresses ofte[n] have *ṣ.b.* = *ṣundūḳ al-barīd* "postal box", and com[-]mercial letter headings *sh.m.m* or *sh.a.l* = *sharik*[*a*] *maḥdūdat al-masʾūliyya* "Ltd. Co.".

The list of abbreviations could be considerably pro[-]longed, but our list will be limited to those give[n] above; one should however add that magazines an[d] periodicals often use these to such an extent tha[t] only the initiates can unravel them. G. Oman (se[e] *Bibl.*) has mentioned, as characteristic: *m.m.* = "Marilyn Monroe", and *b.b.* = "Brigitte Bardot"!

Bibliography: W. Wright, *Arabic grammar*, i, 25-6; M. Ben Cheneb, *Liste des abréviations employées par les auteurs arabes*, in *RAfr.* 302-3 (1920-1), 134-8; G. Oman, *Abbreviature e sigle nell' arabo moderno*, in *OM* (1961), 800-2. (ED.)

ʿABD ALLĀH B. **ABĪ BAKR** AL-**MIYĀNADJĪ**, called ʿAYN AL-ḲUḌĀT AL-HAMADHĀNĪ, Shāfiʿī jurist and Ṣūfī martyr, born at Hamadhān in 492/1098. Born of a line of scholars, he studied Arabic grammar, theology, philosophy and law, and he is said to have, as an already precocious scholar, started his first book at the age of 14. Also, at the approach of puberty, he became a convert to Ṣūfism. In 517/1123, at the age of 25, he seems to have met Aḥmad al-Ghazālī, brother of the great theologian Muḥammad al-Ghazālī, who is said to have initiated him into Ṣūfī meditation and dancing, thus completing his spiritual conversion. Other masters of his e Muḥammad b. Ḥammūya and a certain Baraka. Iis spiritual reputation soon gained him many ;iples, and he spent all his time in oral and written ching, sometimes going beyond the limits of his ysical strength for this and having then to retire two or three months for recuperation. His activi- soon provoked the hostility of the orthodox ologians. Provoked by his teachings on the nature sainthood and prophethood and on submission to Ṣūfī *shaykh*, and objecting to his usage of Ṣūfī minology which gave the impression that he him- laid claim to prophetic powers, they brought an :usation of heresy against him before the Saldjūk ier in ʿIrāḳ, who imprisoned him in Baghdād. It s there that he wrote his apologia, the *Shakwā gharīb*. Some months later he was set free and urned to Hamadhān, but shortly afterwards, at time of the Saldjūḳ sultan Maḥmūd's arrival igned 511-25/1118-31), he was executed in a bar- rous manner during the night of 6-7 Djumādā II 6/6-7 May 1131 at the age of 33. His premature ath seems to have prevented al-Hamadhānī from unding a Ṣūfī monastery, setting up a Ṣūfī group and signating a successor; nevertheless, his numerous orks, written in a fine style, have always found an dience.

His published works include his *Shakwā 'l-gharīb n al-awṭān ilā buldān al-ʿulamāʾ*, an apologia in rabic (ed. and Fr. tr. Mohammed ben Abd-el-Jalil, *JA* (1930), 1-76, 193-297; ed. ʿAfīf ʿUsayrān, *ʾuṣannafāt-i ʿAyn al-Ḳuḍāt-i Hamadhānī*, Tehran 341/1962; Eng. tr. A. J. Arberry, *A Sufi martyr, e apologia of ʿAin al-Quḍāt al-Hamadhānī*, London 969); *Risāla-yi Lawāʾiḥ*, on mystic love, in Persian, l. Raḥīm Farmanish, Tehran 1337/1958; *Zubdat al- ḳāʾiḳ*, in Arabic, ed. ʿUsayrān, in *op. cit.*; *Tam- īdāt* or *Zubdat al-ḥaḳāʾiḳ fi kashf al-daḳāʾiḳ*, in ersian, ed. ʿUsayrān, in *op. cit.*, twice tr. into urkish; *Nāmahā* or *Maktūbāt*, *Makātīb*, letters, in ersian, ed. ʿAlīnaḳī Munzawī and ʿUsayrān, 2 vols., eirut and Tehran 1390/1971; *Risāla-yi yazdānshi- ākht*, ed. Bahman Karīmī, Tehran 1327/1948; and *ḥwāl u āthār*, ed. Farmanish, Tehran 1338/1959.

Bibliography: Sandilāhī, *Makhzan al-gharāʾib*, Bodl. Pers. ms. 395, 1523; Brockelmann, I, 490, S I, 674-5; F. Meier, *Stambuler Handschriften dreier persischer Mystiker*, in *Isl.*, xxiv (1937), 1-9.

(J. K. Teubner)

ʿABD ALLĀH SULṬĀNPŪRĪ, called Makhdūm al-Mulk, son of Shaykh Shams al-Dīn of Sulṭānpūr Pandjāb), a leading Indian theologian of the oth/16th century. He studied under Mawlānā ʿAbd al-Ḳādir of Sirhind, and acquired renown as a scholar and for his command over Muslim jurisprudence, the- ology and history. He was held in high esteem by Humāyūn [*q.v.*], and Shēr Shāh (947-52/1540-5) gave him the title of *Ṣadr al-Islām*; under Islām Shāh (952-61/1545-54) he was the principal adviser of the king in religious affairs. Upon his return in 962/1555, Humāyūn again conferred on him the title of *Shaykh al-Islām*, and under the next king Akbar [*q.v.*], he received the title of *Makhdūm al-Mulk*. In 987/1579 he went to the Ḥidjāz and was received with much respect by the *Muftī* of Mecca. Makhdum al-Mulk, however, returned to India without performing the Pilgrimage, and is said to have issued a *fatwā* to the effect that the *Ḥadjdj* was not obligatory on the people of India because the journey by sea could not be undertaken without the European passports bearing the pictures of Mary and Jesus and because the land route lay through Shīʿī Persia.

Makhdūm al-Mulk was one of the signatories of the *Maḥḍar* of 987/1579 giving a high religious position to Akbar, but subsequently disowned it; he was in fact a very orthodox Sunnī and drew much criticism from Abu 'l-Faḍl. He died in 990/1582 in disgrace.

Bibliography: Abu 'l-Faḍl, *Akbar-nāma*, Bibl. Ind., Calcutta 1873-87; ʿAbd al-Ḳādir Badāʾūnī, *Muntakhab al-tawārīkh*, Bibl. Ind., Calcutta 1864-9; Shāh Nawāz Khān, *Maʾāthir al-umarāʾ*, iii, Bibl. Ind., Calcutta 1888-91; Aziz Ahmad, *Studies in Islamic culture in the Indian environment*, Oxford 1964, 29-30, 168-9; S. A. A. Rizvi, *Religious and intellectual history of the Muslims in Akbar's reign*, New Delhi 1975, 71-2 and index.

(M. Athar Ali)

ʿABD al-ʿAZĪZ b. ʿAbd al-Raḥmān b. Fayṣal Āl Suʿūd (*ca.* 1291-1373/*ca.* 1880-1953), founder king (regn. 1319-73/1902-53) of the Kingdom of Suʿūdi Arabia. His mother was Sāra b. Aḥmad al-Sudayri. At four, ʿAbd al-ʿAzīz was entrusted to a tutor and became a *ḥāfiẓ* at eleven. Simultaneously (1309/1891), at al-Mulayda the Āl Rashīd of Ḥāʾil [*q.v.*] defeated and expelled the Suʿūds from Nadjd, so that ʿAbd al-ʿAzīz grew up subsequently in al-Kuwayt, his father's exiled home.

In 1319/1902, the young hot blood retook al-Riyāḍ, expelled the Rashīdi governor, and proclaimed the restored Suʿūdi rule. Central Nadjd soon re-pledged loyalty to the Suʿūds, and al-Ḳaṣīm [*q.v.*] was gradually brought in. By 1330/1912, ʿAbd al-ʿAzīz had restored Suʿūdi rule throughout Nadjd.

In 1912, ʿAbd al-ʿAzīz inaugurated his most imaginative policy, that of settling Bedouin in Wahhābism-centred agricultural colonies whose members were known as al-Ikhwān ("the brothers") [*q.v.*]. This movement simultaneously furthered Wahhābism, provided a new military force, reduced tribalism, and increased agricultural production; it brought with it profound social change, and the movement at its height counted some 150 colonies, one with 10,000 people. Ikhwānīs played a leading role in subsequent conquests, but ultimately revolted, charging the king with religious laxity, so that the founder of the Ikhwān himself suppressed them (1348/1930).

On the eve of World War I, ʿAbd al-ʿAzīz expelled the Ottomans from eastern Arabia thus acquiring access to the sea. For ʿAbd al-ʿAzīz., this war constituted a period of watchful waiting, but with the war's end, he resumed expansion. Djabal Shammar [*q.v.*] was occupied in 1340/1921 and its dependencies the next year. In 1337/1919 ʿAbd al-ʿAzīz won an important border fight with the Hāshimīs, and in 1338/1920 annexed upland ʿAsīr [*q.v.*]. The end of his festering quarrel with the Hāshimīs began when the Hāshimī king, al-Ḥusayn, somewhat vaingloriously assumed the caliphate (1342/1924). The Ikhwān, affronted, entered al-Ṭāʾif, and Mecca opened its gates, despite the Hāshimīs' descent from the Prophet and long tenure in al-Ḥidjāz. By 1344/1926, ʿAbd al-ʿAzīz was proclaimed king of al-Ḥidjāz. His realm, now quite independent, stretched solidly across the peninsula in the first such broad unification in Arabia for many centuries. In addition, responsibility for the holy places, well discharged, converted ʿAbd al-ʿAzīz from the leader of a minor sectarian polity into a central figure in Muslim and international eyes. His one remaining external dispute, with al-Yaman, was settled by a military victory followed by a treaty (1352/1934). In the same year, he unified his government as the Kingdom of Suʿūdi Arabia. ʿAbd al-ʿAzīz treated defeated enemies magnanimously and, especially in al-Yaman, wisely restrained himself. Much of this period was also spent negotiating with Britain; demarcated borders gradually emerged. During World War II, he maintained formal neutrality, but tilted toward the Allies, subsequently joining the United Nations and the Arab League.

Internally, this commanding monarch ruled traditionally but with his own extra wisdom and strength. He oversaw the successful implantation of the high-technology, American-run petroleum industry into an ultra-traditional society, from a first commercial find in 1356/1937 to the point when, at his death, production approached 1 million barrels/day and gave an annual revenue of $ 200 million. Oil revenues financed dramatic developments: water supplies, airports, telephones and radios, roads, electricity, deep water ports, a railroad, hospitals, and schools. ʿAbd al-ʿAzīz had a "marked tendency to uxoriousness". A study of 1952 indicates that he had 35 living sons. The number of his wives, many married ephemerally, was a legendary 300; in addition, he had concubines and slave women. Yet to some wives, he was faithful and always within the letter of Ḳurʾānic law.

All in all, ʿAbd al-ʿAzīz laid the bases for the modernisation of his country and was one of the greatest leaders to arise in the Arabian peninsula.

Bibliography: Amīn al-Rayḥāni, *Taʾrīkh Nadjd wa-mulḥakātih*, Beirut 1928; A. Rihani, *Ibn Saʾoud of Arabia: his people and his land*, London 1928; Fuʾād Ḥamza, *al-Bilād al-ʿArabiyya al-Suʿūdiyya*, Mecca 1936; Ḥāfiẓ Wahba, *Djazīrat al-ʿArab fi ʾl-ḳarn al-ʿishrīn*², Cairo 1946; Dj. ʿAbduh, *Insān al-Djazīra: ʿarḍ djadīd li-sīrat al-Malık ʿAbd al-ʿAzīz Āl Suʿūd*, Cairo 1954; H. St. J. B. Philby, *Saʿudi Arabia*, London 1955; Ṣalāḥ al-Dīn al-Mukhtār, *Taʾrīkh al-Mamlaka al-ʿArabiyya al-Suʿūdiyya*, Beirut 1957; Ḥāfiẓ Wahba, *Khamsūn ʿām fī Djazīrat al-ʿArab*, Cairo 1960; Suʿūd b. Hadhlūl, *Taʾrīkh Mulūk Āl Suʿūd*, al-Riyāḍ 1961; D. Howarth, *The Desert King: a life of Ibn Saud*, London 1964; Amīn Saʿīd, *Taʾrīkh al-Dawla al-Suʿūdiyya*, Beirut 1964; G. Troeller, *The birth of Saudi Arabia: Britain and the rise of the house of Saʿud*, London 1976.

(R. BAYLY WINDER)

ʿABD AL-ʿAZĪZ B. YŪSUF (Abu ʾl-Ḳāsim al-Ḥakkār?), the private secretary and trusted adviser of the Būyid *amīr* ʿAḍud al-Dawla [*q.v.*] from the very beginning to the end of his reign, and then three times alternatively the vizier and in disgrace in regard to his sons Ṣamṣām al-Dawla and Bahāʾ al-Dawla [*q.v.* below]. He is the author of a collection of official correspondence (*inshāʾ*), largely preserved in ms. Petermann 406 (Ahlwardt 8625), which is however limited to the period of ʿAḍud al-Dawla's reign (some fragments lacking here are cited in al-Thaʿālibī, *Yatīma*, ii, 89-90) and which, without securing him a place equal to his contemporaries Abū Isḥāḳ al-Ṣābiʾ and Ibn ʿAbbād, merits the historian's consideration, above all for the narrative of events of the reign.

Bibliography: Abū Shudjāʿ al-Rūdhrāwarī, continuation of the Miskawayh's *Tadjārib al-umam*, ed. and tr. Amedroz and Margoliouth in *The eclipse of the ʿAbbasid caliphate*, iii and vi (see index, vii, 2); Thaʿālibī, *Yatīma, loc. cit.*; Cl. Cahen, *Une correspondance buyide inédite*, in *Studi orientalistici ... Levi della Vida*, i, 85-96; J. Chr. Bürgel, *Die Hofkorrespondenz ʿAḍud al-Daulas ...*, Wiesbaden 1965; H. Busse, *Chalif und Grosskönig, die Buyiden im Iraq (945-1055)*, Beirut 1969, esp. 240 ff.

(CL. CAHEN)

ʿABD AL-BĀRĪ, ḲIYĀM AL-DĪN MUḤAMMAD, ea 14th/20th century *ʿālim* and *pīr* of the Farangī M ḥalī family [*q.v.* below]. Born in Lucknow in 12 1878, he was descended on his father's side fron distinguished line of *pīr*s and on his mother's s from Malik al-ʿUlamāʾ Mullā Ḥaydar (d. 1256/1840- who had established the Hyderabad (Deccan) bran of the Farangī Maḥall family. ʿAbd al-Bārī w brought up in Lucknow, where he studied under ma teachers, notably his uncle ʿAbd al-Bāḳī and ʿA al-Ḳuḍāt, the prominent pupil of ʿAbd al-Ḥayy [*q.v* He travelled to the Ḥidjāz three times, in 1309/189 2, 1321/1903-4 and 1330/1911-2, and also visited oth parts of the Ottoman Empire. In Medina, where came to know Sharīf Ḥusayn of Mecca, he bo studied *ḥadīth* under Sayyid ʿAlī Witrī and taugh

With Abu ʾl-Kalām Āzād, ʿAbd al-Bārī was t first Indo-Muslim scholar to play a major role modern Indian politics. He came to the fore as Mu lims of the subcontinent became agitated over even in the Ottoman Empire just before World War On In 1913, after returning from Mecca, with Mush Ḥusayn Ḳidwāī, he founded the Andjuman-i Khu dām-i Kaʿba [*q.v.* below]. After the War he played leading part in launching the Indian *Khilāfat* mov ment: leading in 1918 the first *ʿulamāʾ* to attend th All-India Muslim League sessions, developing a alliance with Mahatma Gandhi, helping to organis the Central Khilāfat Committee in 1919, and through out driving the agitation more extreme till in 192 the Khilāfat movement adopted a policy of non-co operation with the British government and, under it influence, so did the Indian National Congress. I these years ʿAbd al-Bārī's influence was at its zenith a fact marked, at least among Indian *ʿulamāʾ*, by hi election as the first president in 1919 of the *Djamʿiyyat-i ʿulamāʾ-i Hind*, which he had played a majo part in establishing. But gradually in 1921 and 192 he began to draw apart from the politicians as they refused to accept his view that force should be used to defend the *Khilāfat*. By 1923 the resurgence of communalism had driven him to defend Islam in India at the cost of Hindu-Muslim unity. Moreover, he continued to fight for the *Khilāfat*, although the issue had ceased to interest politicians. From 1925 he led the tremendous protest in India against Ibn Saʿūd, and died on 4 Radjab 1344/19 January 1926 while in the midst of his campaign.

ʿAbd al-Bārī knew that Muslims had to face the problems posed by the modernisation of their society. He was willing to support Muslims who sought western learning, sending boys to Aligarh College and making a donation to the Muslim University movement. In an endeavour designed to equip the children of *ʿulamāʾ* and *pīr*s for modern life along traditional lines, he established the Madrasa-yi ʿĀliya Niẓāmiyya at Farangī Maḥall in 1905. This offered an improved form of the Dars-i Niẓāmiyya, making "modern" subjects such as algebra and geography compulsory and offering practical subjects such as English to higher classes. ʿAbd al-Bārī was no less concerned about the future of mysticism. He felt that the ignorance of those who were mystics, as well as that of those who were not, was damaging the reputation of *taṣawwuf*. He was particularly concerned that mystics should adhere strictly to the *Sharīʿa*. It was on this account that around 1914 he revived a plan, first mooted by his father and others in 1896, to establish a *madrasa* to teach Islamic mysticism systematically. The plan was adopted as the aim of the *Bazm-i Ṣūfiyya-yi Hind*, an organisation which, with the support of many leading Indian mystics, was founded

ing the *ʿUrs* of Muʿīn al-Dīn Čis͟htī at Ad͟jmīr in 6.

Abd al-Bārī was one of the great teachers of his e, having at least 300 pupils. He wrote 111 books l pamphlets displaying wide learning in Persian as ll as Arabic; as was customary in the Farangī hall family, Ḥanafī jurisprudence was his most portant field. Initiated into the Ḳādirī-Razzāḳī l Čis͟htī-Niẓāmī *silsilas*, he was an influential *pīr*, mbering several leading politicians, including Mu- nmad and S͟hawḳat ʿAlī [*q.v.*], amongst his *murīds*. independent-minded but emotional man, ʿAbd Bārī was guided by the need to defend and engthen Islam. He achieved fame and success, in rt because of what he did but also in part because who he was: the dominant member in his genera- n of the widespread and talented Farangī Maḥall nily. In recent years he has been this family's most stinguished product.

Bibliography: There is a biography of ʿAbd al-Bārī, Mawlawī ʿInāyat Allāh, *Risāla-yi ḥasrat al-āfāk ba wafāt mad͟jmūʿat al-ak͟hlāḳ*, Lucknow n. d.; see also Mawlawī ʿInāyat Allāh, *Tad͟hkira-yi ʿulamāʾ-i Farangī Maḥall*, Lucknow 1928. For ʿAbd al-Bārī's views on mysticism, see Nūr al-Ḥasan Ad͟jmīrī, *K͟hādimāna guzāris͟h*, Lucknow 1923 and ʿAbd al-Bārī, *ʿUrs Ḥaḍrat Bānsa*, Lucknow n. d., and for his views on education, see Alṭāf al-Raḥmān Ḳidwāī, *Ḳiyām-i niẓām-i taʿlīm*, Lucknow 1924. His political career is covered by Francis Robinson, *Separatism among Indian Muslims: the politics of the United Provinces' Muslims 1860-1923*, Cambridge 1974, chs. vii-ix, and Afzal Iqbal, *The life and times of Mohamed Ali*, Lahore 1974, 336-40.

(F. C. R. Robinson)

ʿABD al-LAṬĪF ČELEBI [see Laṭīfī].

ʿABD al-NĀṢIR, D͟jamāl, Egyptian comman- er and statesman. His father, ʿAbd al-Nāṣir Iusayn, came from the village of Banī Murr near syūṭ in Upper Egypt. He was a clerk in the post ffice and in 1915 moved to Alexandria. In 1917 he narried the daughter of an Alexandrian coal mer- hant and on January 15th 1918, his first son, D͟jamāl, vas born. The father was transferred several times luring his son's early childhood and it was in Asyūṭ hat D͟jamāl began his primary education. At the ge of seven he was sent to Cairo to live with his ncle and to study there instead of moving around with his father. He also spent some time in the family village of Banī Murr when he was able to observe the ife of the Egyptian peasant—its poverty and its daily toil, its dignity and solidarity. The village was a microcosm of Egyptian rural society. ʿAbd al-Nāṣir's family belonged to the middle layer of small ptoprietors and tenants, a class largely dominated by others yet from which there was some outward movement into the towns and cities through education and government employment. This class gave ʿAbd al-Nāṣir his roots in the Egyptian countryside and also his escape into another world.

In Cairo he went to al-Naḥḥāsīn school in K͟hān al-K͟halīlī where he was able to experience at first hand the life of the bustling crowded quarters of Cairo, that other aspect of the poverty of Egypt. During this period he was greatly affected by the death of his mother and by his father's early remarriage. This experience turned him against his father and strengthened his independence and perhaps also his introspection. He was noted from then on for his seriousness and thoughtfulness.

After an interval with his family in Alexandria ʿAbd al-Nāṣir moved to Cairo where he spent five decisive years, 1933-8. He went to al-Nahḍa school and began to mix study with militant activity, protesting both against the British presence and the policies of the Egyptian politicians. He was exposed to the political currents of the time, of the *Wafd*, the National Party (*al-Ḥizb al-Waṭanī*) and especially *Miṣr al-Fatāt*, the Fascist-type movement found by Aḥmad Ḥusayn. He felt deeply and personally the problems of Egypt and began to assume them inwardly himself, unconsciously following the example of those future leaders who take upon themselves the burdens of their people, and also searching for a future pattern for his own life. He admired the *Wafd* centred around its leader, Muṣṭafā Naḥḥās; he occasionally marched with *Miṣr al-Fatāt*. He wrote at the time: "[The Egyptian] only needs a leader who will lead him to battle".

In November 1935, when the British opposed the re-establishment of the Egyptian constitution, ʿAbd al-Nāṣir marched with students on to the streets of Cairo and was wounded by a bullet fired by British troops. He was identified as an agitator and asked to leave his school. After a few months in 1936 as a law student in Cairo University, his sense of disillusion with the politicians who had "surrendered" to the British by signing the 1936 Treaty and with what he saw as the indifference of his fellow-students, led him to seek to join the army, in his opinion the best means available for effecting change. He had passed through his early personal crisis and took to the army as a positive means of action.

In 1936 the Egyptian army had lifted its restrictions on the middle and lower classes entering the officer corps. ʿAbd al-Nāṣir was a member of the second entry of such men, an officer cadet in 1937 at the age of nineteen in the ʿAbbāsiyya Military Academy. He was attracted to military life with its discipline and study, and was quickly promoted. Of his future companions in the revolution, he met ʿAbd al-Ḥakīm ʿĀmir in the academy and Zakariyyā Muḥyī al-Dīn and Anwar al-Sādāt in his first posting to upper Egypt. It is difficult to maintain that their plotting began at once but, being of similar age and background, they were united in their disrespect and even contempt for their senior officers, and this attitude was confirmed when he again met ʿĀmir during their assignment to the Sudan.

The German successes in Libya and Egypt in 1940-1 led some Egyptian officers to see in the Axis their deliverers from British occupation. ʿAbd al-Nāṣir stayed aloof from making approaches to the Germans, but his anger was aroused in February 1942 when Sir Miles Lampson, the British High Commissioner, with the support of British tanks imposed on King Fārūḳ a *Wafd* cabinet under Naḥḥās. ʿAbd al-Nāṣir was ashamed that the army had taken no counteraction, but he at least felt that some officers had been shaken out of their apathy. In 1943 he was appointed an instructor at the Military Academy, and during his time there was able to make contact with a number of younger Egyptians who were also like him fired by the aim of liberating their country.

The period 1945-52 bears, with hindsight, the signs of the end of an era. Several factors combined to ensure that change eventually became inevitable. King Fārūḳ's political erraticness and scandalous private life debarred him as a serious political leader. The *Wafd* had lost most of its credibility, and the more extreme movements were left to clamour for a central role. The Arab disaster in Palestine had a profound effect on the minds of young Egyptian army officers, and the British reluctance to evacuate troops first from the towns and then from the Suez Canal Zone confirmed their suspicions about the survival of British imperialist aims. The period was one of ferment and tension, so that even a personality less politically sensitive than ʿAbd al-Nāṣir could not have remained unaffected, and he was in a sense torn during this period between his position as staff officer and his interests in "revolutionary" movements. He was introduced to Marxism by K͟hālid Muḥyī al-Dīn, a fellow officer and cousin of Zakariyyā, to the *Ik͟hwān al-Muslimūn* by al-Sādāt, and to the left wing of the *Wafd* by Aḥmad Abu 'l-Fatḥ and others. At this time a group of officers began to meet regularly, comprising the above together with ʿĀmir, T͟harwat ʿUkās͟ha and one or two others. These so-called *Dubbāṭ al-Aḥrār* ("Free Officers") did not yet coalesce as a movement, having no common ideology but a determination to transform Egypt; but the figure of D̲jamāl ʿAbd al-Nāṣir emerged here as a leader.

It was events outside Egypt which decisively placed the Free Officers on course outwards revolution. In May 1948 the Egyptian army advanced into Palestine in an attempt to destroy the new state of Israel. ʿAbd al-Nāṣir was commanding officer of a unit, and was immediately dismayed by the inefficiency and lack of preparedness of the Egyptians who were fighting against greatly inferior numbers; in the fighting he was himself wounded in the chest. After the second United Nations armistice (during which the Haganah improved its positions), the battle for the Negev began in October. ʿAbd al-Nāṣir and his unit were trapped at Fallūd̲ja, but together with several other Free Officers they held out against the Israeli forces and were eventually able to counter-attack. In retrospect, ʿAbd al-Nāṣir saw this episode as a symbol of their determination to pursue the real fight against all those forces which opposed Egypt. He had fought the Israelis and had even admired them in their successful bid to oust the British from Palestine (during one armistice he had had an opportunity to talk to an Israeli officer), and had himself become more widely known. One general also made his name for heroism in the Palestine war, Muḥammad Nad̲jīb (Neguib).

The army returned home bitter in defeat and determined to begin the "real" struggle. The Free Officers began to issue propaganda denouncing the King, the régime and the army, to infiltrate the government, and to co-operate with other organisations. In October 1951 the Egyptian government abrogated the 1936 Treaty, and this action signalled the beginning of guerilla activity against the British troops remaining in the Canal Zone. The Free Officers played a certain part, issuing arms and training commandos, but it was largely students and members of the *Ik͟hwān* who bore the brunt of the fighting; ʿAbd al-Nāṣir himself was biding his time conserving his energies.

Tension was also rising in Cairo. A particularly severe British retaliatory attack on the Ismāʿīliyya barracks in January 1952 led to Black Saturday, January 26th, when much foreign and Egyptian property in Cairo was burned and several lives lost. Students, *Ik͟hwān* and the mob rampaged in a fury of revenge, and the army and police intervened only late in the day. It is still not clear who instigated the riots and how large a part, if any, the Free Officers played; but the events had at least demonstrated the desperate fury of the country and the lack of any solution offered by the régime.

Fārūḳ and his entourage continued their improvident course, seemingly careless of the country's pli[g
The Free Officers decided that a coup could no lon
be postponed and began to make their final plans
July. The government had moved for the summer
Alexandria, and two army units favourable to
Free Officers were about to move to Cairo. On 2
July it became known that Fārūḳ was to appoin
new government, one of whose first actions would
to arrest some of the Officers. The latter advan
their plans; by the morning of 23rd July the key ar
and communications posts had been taken, w
hardly a shot fired and only two lives lost. Althou
ʿAbd al-Nāṣir had been the leader, General Muḥa
mad Nad̲jīb, the older and better-known man, b
came the new Commander-in-Chief, while argume
raged over the future form of government—shou
there be co-operation with civilian politicians, a
what was to be the fate of Fārūḳ?

ʿAlī Māhir, an ex-premier, headed the new gover
ment. ʿAbd al-Nāṣir stood out for the exile, rath
than the execution, of Fārūḳ, and the ex-king sail
from Alexandria on 26th July. Nad̲jīb supervised t
abdication while ʿAbd al-Nāṣir remained in Cai

Muḥammad Ḥasanayn Haykal has divided t
political life of ʿAbd al-Nāṣir (known in Egypt
"The Lion") into three parts: 1952-6, the Lion fre
1956-67 the Lion chained; 1967-70 the Lion wounde
By this division, Haykal saw him free until the Su
invasion to concentrate on Egyptian affairs; aft
1956 he became chained to Arab and world affai
and a prisoner of his own success and personalit
after the Arab-Israeli war of 1967 he was gradual
weighed down by the burdens of office. These div
sions may be qualified and modified, however. Durin
the whole of his political life he was attempting bot
to legitimise his rule and to give Egypt a lastin
political and social system. Until 1956 he was largel
concerned with Egyptian internal affairs, but Sue
thrust him on to the world stage, and while chainin
him, in Haykal's phrase, he was at the peak of h
popularity and success, at least until the dissolutio
of the Syrian-Egyptian union in 1961. The perio
1961-7 saw him more closely chained and less success
ful, until the disaster of 1967, by which he was mor
tally wounded.

The Free Officers had no definite political pro
gramme before or at the beginning of their régime
No one ideology motivated the seizure of power; they
had rather vague ideas about national independence
modernisation, democratisation, social justice and
equality. The first years of power entailed a more
precise defining of these ideas and forced ʿAbd al-Nāṣir to determine his role in the new system. He was
the centre of the new ruling body, the Revolution
Command Council (R.C.C.) (*Mad̲jlis Ḳiyādat al-T͟hawra*), although Nad̲jīb was its president, replacing
ʿAlī Māhir in September 1952, and ʿAbd al-Nāṣir not
yet publicly acknowledged.

The régime's first declared objective had been the expulsion of the British, and negotiations began immediately over the evacuation of the Canal Zone. Secondly, the direction of domestic policy was established by the agrarian reform law of September 1952 by which no one was allowed to hold more than 200 feddans of land. Thirdly, the régime set about eliminating opposition, i.e. the *Wafd* and especially the *Ik͟hwān*, who reacted by trying to foment opposition in the army, police and universities. In the early months of 1954 the *Ik͟hwān* waged what ʿAbd al-Nāṣir termed a *d̲jihād* against the régime, in an attempt to seize power themselves.

Within the Revolution Command Council, dis-sions arose between General Nadjīb, now President the Egyptian Republic, and the younger officers. e older man had gained considerable popularity, t was opposed by his colleagues, who accused him re-establishing relations with the old politicians d wanting to send the army back to its barracks. ere were demonstrations in his favour, and the aos of pre-revolutionary days seemed about to re- n. This was unthinkable to ʿAbd al-Nāṣir with his eply authoritarian character, and he and like- nded colleagues isolated Nadjīb by the end of arch 1954; he remained as titular president of the public, while ʿAbd al-Nāṣir became president of the C.C. with *de facto* power.

In July 1954, ʿAbd al-Nāṣir signed a treaty with e British under which the Canal base would be evac- ted within twenty months with the provision that could be "re-activated" by the British in the event an attack by an outside power on an Arab country on Turkey. To many Egyptians, this was a capit- ation to the West and was strongly opposed by e *Ikhwān*. On 24 October 1954 ʿAbd al-Nāṣir was ldressing a crowd in Alexandria justifying the treaty hen a member of the *Ikhwān* attempted to assassi- ate him. Haykal described this as a turning point in bd al-Nāṣir's career. Having already gained control the army and state, his survival might also be seen as onfirmation of that control, for charismatic leaders an only gain in prestige from "miraculously" surviving ssassination attempts. ʿAbd al-Nāṣir now dominated ne Revolution Command Council, the cabinet, the ree Officers and through them the Liberation Rally, is first attempt to organise political support. The *ukhābarāt* (secret police) were his means of super- ising the two latter bodies, and the basis of the égime was the army, whose members penetrated nost aspects of civil life.

1955 was the year in which ʿAbd al-Nāṣir won his personal battle, and found the role he had written bout in his *Falsafat al-thawra* "Philosophy of the evolution": "In this region in which we live there s a role wandering aimlessly about seeking an actor to play it". In his writing he had criticised the masses for not enthusiastically following him after the coup. Now he was presented with a cause in which to lead them. The British had established the Baghdād Pact with Nūrī al-Saʿīd of ʿIrāḳ as the lynch-pin. ʿAbd al-Nāṣir, aware that he was compromised over the Suez base agreement, saw the Pact as an attempt by Britain, and especially by Eden, to maintain domination in the Middle East, and even to shift the centre of power away from Egypt to ʿIrāḳ, hence he determined to oppose it. In February 1955 he was visited by the proponents of non-alignment, Tito and Nehru, and was greatly influenced by them, especially by the Yugoslav. At the same time an Israeli attack on Gaza convinced him that the Americans were attempting to exploit his vulnerability. He now began to seek arms, first unsuccessfully from the West, and then from the Communist bloc.

His participation in April in the Bandung Conference of Non-aligned Nations made a deep impression on him, for he was hailed as a leader in the anti-colonialist fight and welcomed by an enthusiastic crowd on his return to Cairo. Seven months later he announced an arms contract with Czechoslovakia, though he was loath to sever contacts with the West, and in November he opened negotiations with Britain and America for a loan to finance the construction of the Aswān High Dam. In January 1956 a loan by the West was announced with conditions, notably that Egypt's budget had to be supervised by the lenders. ʿAbd al-Nāṣir hesitated for a time, having alienated France by his support of the Front de Libération Nationale in Algeria and Britain by his approval of King Ḥusayn's dismissal of General Glubb in Jordan; and finally in July the offer of the loan was withdrawn because, according to the U.S. Department of State, of doubts about Egypt's "ability to devote adequate resources to assure the project's success".

Such a rebuff was a severe blow to a man of ʿAbd al-Nāṣir's temperament and he reacted angrily. Under a new constitution he had been elected President, with both the powers of head of state and of government, in June with 99.9 per cent of the votes. He announced the nationalisation of the Suez Canal, against which the British Prime Minister, Anthony Eden, reacted by denouncing the takeover as illegal; he also saw ʿAbd al-Nāṣir as a dictator threatening British security who had to be removed. To the Egyptians, however, the Canal was the symbol of imperialism and ʿAbd al-Nāṣir was the man who had defied the Old World and who had asserted the rights of the newly-independent. His popularity in Egypt was enormous and he was convinced that he could withstand Western attempts to make him retract.

Britain, France and Israel combined to attack Egypt, each for their own reasons, but united in fear and hatred of ʿAbd al-Nāṣir, after attempts to organise forms of international supervision of the Canal had failed. On October 29th Israeli troops crossed into Sinai and the following day were reported to be within 20 miles of the Canal. The British and French ultimatum ordering both Egypt and Israel to withdraw to ten miles on either side of the Canal, was rejected by ʿAbd al-Nāṣir, and two days later British planes raided Cairo. On November 5th British and French troops landed in Port Said. ʿAbd al-Nāṣir convinced his followers of Egypt's ability to resist, but he was in fact facing defeat, and was only saved by American and Soviet pressure on his attackers. All foreign troops were compelled to leave Egyptian territory, and he emerged as victor in defeat, more popular and powerful than before, and a world figure.

His very success bore within itself the seeds of danger. He had confronted Israel and the West, not only on behalf of Egypt but also of other parts of the Arab world. He was being drawn into the politics of Arabism, with its twin goals of unity and the destruction of Israel, reaction and colonialism. Egypt, the strongest Arab state with its powerful leader, was the natural centre of the Arab world. ʿAbd al-Nāṣir had already shown his support for the Algerian national movement and thereby alienated France. The Voice of the Arabs radio broadcast continual anti-Western propaganda from Cairo. ʿAbd al-Nāṣir had rejected President Eisenhower's offer of American military support. At the same time Syria, the other centre of Arabism seemed to be slipping into a chaotic situation. Several factions, Baʿthists, Communists and rival nationalist groups, were competing for power. In January 1958 Syrian spokesmen informed ʿAbd al-Nāṣir that only union with Egypt could save their country. He was not immediately convinced, despite his professed belief in Arab unity, and made strong conditions for the Syrians which they nevertheless readily accepted. At the end of January the United Arab Republic came into existence with ʿAbd al-Nāṣir as president, welcomed with relief by the Syrians but not, it seemed, with any great enthusiasm by the Egyptian leader himself, nor by the Egyptian people, some of whom regretted the disappearance of the name of Egypt.

However, he received a great popular welcome in

Syria and appeared determined to make the union a success, if only by imposing his own will on the Syrians. Such an attitude was bound to cause resentment, and socialist measures, the dismissal of army officers, purges of politicians and the arrogant behaviour of ʿAbd al-Nāṣir's man in Syria, ʿAbd al-Ḥamīd Sarrādj, all contributed to increase feelings of bitterness. By early 1961 the union was falling apart and in September a group of Syrian officers unilaterally took Syria out of the U.A.R.

ʿAbd al-Nāṣir was stunned, but, after a momentary determination to oppose the split by force, reluctantly withdrew Egyptian troops from Syria. To salvage his self-esteem and perhaps to keep the door open for further unions, he retained the title of U.A.R. for Egypt. His political life was complicated by another factor. The ʿIrāḳīs had overthrown the monarchy in July 1958, had proclaimed their revolution and were disputing with him the leadership of the Arab world. Rivalry was intense, especially as ʿIrāḳ claimed Soviet support and had refused to join the U.A.R. He had been dragged deep into inter-Arab disputes and saw his energies diverted into unprofitable avenues.

After the break-up of the U.A.R., ʿAbd al-Nāṣir felt isolated and to some extent withdrew into Egyptian affairs. In a speech of October 1961 he made some surprising admissions; "We fell victim to a dangerous illusion, to which we were led by an increasing confidence in ourselves and in others". He had neglected the economic development and the political organisation of Egypt. He would summon a congress of popular forces which would chart a more socialist and democratic course. In Egypt he had become in all senses the *raʾīs*, enjoying absolute power and now being corrupted by that power. He was the father-figure, protected by the *mukhābarāt*, imprisoning and torturing Communists, with an all-powerful police, and with judicial corruption. His entourage both protected and isolated him. He owed his popularity to the masses, yet he distrusted them, and none of his plans to involve the people more directly in government had very great success. He moved cautiously and pragmatically, approaching a socialist solution slowly. Despite his reliance on Russia, he had persecuted Egyptian Marxists and had no intention of imposing a totally communist programme on the country.

During the fifties there had been some nationalisation, but it was not until July 1961 that ʿAbd al-Nāṣir announced more radical measures. He introduced "Arab socialism" into Egypt—land ownership was reduced to a maximum of 100 feddans; banks and many other companies were nationalised; property was sequestrated; and the economy was to be totally planned. Smaller businesses were left in private hands. ʿAbd al-Nāṣir was clearly reluctant, however, to follow too closely the Soviet pattern. His socialism was to be built on "national friendship" rather than class warfare and there was to be no enforced collectivisation of the peasantry. The Congress of Popular Forces was convened in May 1962 to discuss and approve a National Charter which embodied the ideology of the régime. A new single party, the Arab Socialist Union, was founded to succeed the National Union which had already taken the place of the earlier Liberation Rally.

The A.S.U. was ʿAbd al-Nāṣir's attempt to involve the people, in a strictly supervised way, in the government of Egypt. That it largely failed was partly due to the scarcity of enthusiastic and well-trained cadres. Traditional centres of power still held sway in many of the Egyptian villages and no great enthusiasm w shown for the A.S.U. In an attempt to strengthen Union, ʿAbd al-Nāṣir even released impriso Marxists, some of whom in 1964 agreed to work wi in the organisation.

ʿAbd al-Nāṣir's economic policies were obviou influenced by his relationship with the Soviet Un and Yugoslavia. He rejected Communism and v categorised by Soviet ideologists as a bourge nationalist, yet he was dependent on Russia for a and Krushchev considered him an ally in the Mid East. Apart from arms, Russia had in 1960 agreed finance the construction of Aswān Dam, which b came both the symbol of Russo-Egyptian co-ope tion and of Egypt's rebirth. The dam was built transform Egypt's economy and agriculture. It h not succeeded in all the ways intended, and in mo ways than one it is ʿAbd al-Nāṣir's monument.

Despite his intention to concentrate on intern affairs, ʿAbd al-Nāṣir's reputation and Egypt's p sition in the Arab world obliged him to continue play a leading role. The most serious interventio was in the Yemen where in the autumn of 1962 a uprising had driven out the Imām. A republic was pr claimed which was immediately threatened by Sau backed royalist forces. ʿAbd al-Nāṣir sent an Egy tian army to support the revolution, an action he lat regretted, for it was trapped for five years with continuing drain of men and equipment, diverte away from a confrontation with Israel, the insolub problem of his lifetime.

The Israelis had withdrawn from the Suez Cana after 1956, and United Nations troops had moved i between Israel and Egypt. The Arabs had mad various plans for and propaganda about the destruc tion of Israel, but ʿAbd al-Nāṣir seemed determine not to let Egypt be engaged in war before the arm was ready, or until Arab unity was achieved. How ever, he joined a pact with Syria in 1966 which trap ped him into confrontation. Both Syria and Jorda clashed with Israel and he found himself shoulderin their burdens and being ineluctably drawn into a conflict. He was now heard to talk of destroying Israel and of the impossibility of co-existence. ʿAbd al-Ḥakīm ʿĀmir and others convinced him that th army was strong and prepared, though after the war ʿAbd al-Nāṣir claimed that he had not wanted to fight.

According to his version of the events leading to the war, in May he asked U Thant to withdraw the U.N. Emergency Force from the Israeli-Egyptian frontier, thus allowing the Egyptian army to face Israeli troops directly. The Russians had informed him that the Israelis were preparing to attack Syria, and by his moves in Sinai he intended to deter them; this information seems to have been either incorrect or at least exaggerated. ʿAbd al-Nāṣir claimed that the U.N. responded by insisting on withdrawing their troops both from the frontier and from Sharm al-Shaykh. The U.N. version is that Egyptian troops appeared at Sharm al-Shaykh and forced the U.N. to withdraw. Whichever version is correct, Egyptian troops were soon at the entrance to the Gulf of ʿAḳaba and blockading the Straits of Tirān to Israeli shipping, and it was clear that Israel could not leave such a challenge unanswered. According to eyewitnesses in Cairo ʿAbd al-Nāṣir appeared at the time to be borne down by the inexorable, and he spoke of a moment of decision: either Israel must accept new discussions on the Palestine problem or war was inevitable.

ʿĀmir and Shams Badrān, the Egyptian War Minister, urged him in vain to strike first. Israel settled e matter by a pre-emptive attack on June 5th which stroyed the Egyptian air force on the ground. By ne 9th Egypt accepted a cease-fire, with Israeli ops once again on the Suez Canal. ʿAbd al-Nāṣir d led his country to a catastrophic defeat. He had excuses. On television on June 9th he admitted his ilures and announced his resignation. The reaction as immediate. All Egypt, it seemed, begged him to ay. Egypt and ʿAbd al-Nāṣir had together been deated, and Egypt without him was unthinkable; the entification between leader and people appeared tal. His resignation was rejected and the following ay he resumed office.

His prestige was, however, diminished, a fifth of is country occupied, the Canal closed; he was conronted by a powerful enemy, and his armed forces ere shattered. In the short period left of his life here was little he could do to restore the situation, et as leader he was forced to try. Even the army as not prepared totally to support him. ʿĀmir was lamed for the defeat, arrested and allowed (or forced) o commit suicide, Badrān was imprisoned for life. Members of the secret police were arrested. In February 1968 the Air Force commanders were senenced to imprisonment. Even so, the Egyptian people were not satisfied with ʿAbd al-Nāṣir's actions, and there was criticism of him, of the system and of the leniency of the sentences on the Air Force officers.

He responded by increasing the sentences and by urging the Arab Socialist Union to play a more creative and active role. This did not satisfy the people, and in late 1968 there were demonstrations in favour of more political freedom and even demands for his resignation. He had been called back by the people yet was unable to fulfil their expectations.

On the international scene, he was able to offer little that was constructive. At the Khartoum Arab summit in September 1967 he endorsed the Arab refusal to recognise or to negotiate with Israel, although he also seemed to accept the U.N. resolution 242 which entailed recognition of the sovereignty of all states in the Middle East. Soviet support in rebuilding his army at least gave him a position from which he could face Israel on a more equal footing. It led him to launch the war of attrition in 1969-70 during which the Israeli air force on several occasions attacked Egyptian territory. ʿAbd al-Nāṣir personally and on behalf of the Arabs could not bring himself to the point of negotiating a peace treaty with Israel, despite Soviet and American pressure. He made several moves which seemed to be leading towards negotiation, but he remained fettered by his position in the Arab world.

On 24 September 1970 King Ḥusayn of Jordan and Yāsir ʿArafat of the Palestine Liberation Organisation met in Cairo under ʿAbd al-Nāṣir's aegis to try to achieve reconciliation after Ḥusayn's suppression of the attempted Palestinian take-over in Jordan, and this was his last achievement. On September 28th he died of a heart attack, having suffered from diabetes for ten years and later from arteriosclerosis of his right leg. Despite a previous heart attack in September 1969 he had continued to work until the very end. His funeral in Cairo was marked with astonishing scenes of grief, devotion and disbelief amongst the thousands who surrounded his coffin. It was as though in a very real sense part of the soul of Egypt had died with him.

It is also possible that the mass hysteria of that day contained within itself a grain of relief. ʿAbd al-Nāṣir had dominated Egyptian life for some fifteen years and perhaps by 1970 Nasserism had run its course. He had guided Egypt through a period of intense change and political adjustment. He had seen the end of French and British imperialism and had felt his way towards a new relationship both with the United States and the Soviet Union. He had led Egypt into a relationship with an Arab world newly-conscious of its power and independence. He had had to face the problem of confronting Israel on behalf of that Arab world. As Haykal wrote, these historical conditions formed his destiny and laid on him a burden too great for any one man to bear, or in the words of another commentator, "being unable to solve Egypt's problems, [he] chose to incarnate them".

ʿAbd al-Nāṣir was thoroughly Egyptian, a Ṣaʿīdī who gave back to Egypt a sense of dignity. He remained a man of simple tastes and hard work who continued to live modestly in Cairo. His close friends were almost all political allies and he created with them an atmosphere of intrigue and conspiracy in government. He ruled Egypt through this élite, together with a network of interlocking security systems. He was cunning, mistrustful and a conspirator. He even distrusted the army, which he supervised with the *mukhābarāt*. He was a naturally passionate man, not averse to the use of violence and torture to subdue his opponents. He did not know how to create lasting institutions nor how to gather around him a strong governmental team.

He clearly inspired devotion both among his colleagues and among the masses in Egypt and elsewhere. His figure dominated Arab politics and gave rise to the formation of Nasserist parties in other countries. He was the symbol for many of Arab resistance to foreign influence and to internal reaction. He was the leader who, in Weber's terms, was able to lead the break-through in Egypt's history.

Bibliography: Much has been written about ʿAbd al-Nāṣir and Egypt under his régime. A survey of English and French studies written before 1967 can be found in D. Hopwood, *Some Western views of the Egyptian revolution*, in P. J. Vatikiotis, ed., *Egypt since the revolution*, London 1968. The most important works specifically on Djamāl ʿAbd al-Nāṣir appearing since that date are: J. Lacouture, *Nasser*, Paris 1971 (and Engl. tr., London 1973); R. Stephens, *Nasser*, London 1971; R. H. Dekmejian, *Egypt under Nasir*; *a study in political dynamics*, Albany, N.Y. 1972; A. Nutting, *Nasser*, London 1972; *Egypt and Nasser*. 3 vols. (Facts on File) New York 1973; M. H. Heikal, *The Cairo documents*. London 1973. Many works in Arabic have been published, especially since his death, both laudatory and critical, and these are too numerous to list here. One of the most revealing is by Haykal, *ʿAbd al-Nāṣir wa ʾl-ʿālam*, Beirut 1972. Essential is ʿAbd al-Nāṣir's own *Falsafat al-thawra*, Cairo 1956 (English tr., Washington D.C. 1956). Also of use are memoirs by his colleagues, Anwar al-Sādāt, *Revolt on the Nile*, New York 1957, and Mohammed Neguib, *Egypt's destiny*, London 1955. Many of his speeches were also published.

(D. Hopwood)

ʿABD AL-RAḤMĀN B. **ḤASSĀN** B. THĀBIT AL-ANṢĀRĪ, poet of Medina and Damascus in the early Islamic period and son of the more famous eulogist of the Prophet, Ḥassān b. Thābit [*q.v.*]. He seems to have been born in *ca.* 6/627-8 or 7/628, and apart from visits to the Umayyad capital, to have spent most of his life in Medina. He died there, according to Ibn Ḥadjar, *Tahdhīb*, vi, 162-3, in *ca.* 104/722-3 at the age of 98 lunar years, long-lived like his father.

His father had latterly become a stróng advocate of vengeance for ʿU<u>th</u>mān and a supporter of Muʿāwiya's cause, and ʿAbd al-Raḥmān likewise became embroiled in the controversies of the day, including with the poet and supporter of the ʿAlids, Ḳays b. ʿAmr al-Nad<u>j</u>ā<u>sh</u>ī [q.v.]. ʿAbd al-Raḥmān himself apparently was of a distinctly provocative and irascible nature, much given to satirising his contemporaries, and he also clashed with the Umayyad poet-prince ʿAbd al-Raḥmān b. al-Ḥakam, brother of the future caliph Marwān (see A<u>gh</u>ānī¹, xiii, 150-4, xiv, 123 f. = ed. Beirut, xiii, 279-86, xiv, 284 ff.), and then with the heir to the throne Yazīd b. Muʿāwiya over an alleged slight to the latter's sister in the nasīb of one of ʿAbd al-Raḥmān's poems (see Lammens, Études sur le règne du calife omaiyade Moʿâwia Iᵉʳ, in MFOB, ii (1907), 149-51); the moderation of Muʿāwiya protected him from retaliation, although the incident may possibly have sharpened the satires of Yazīd's protégé al-A<u>kh</u>ṭal [q.v.] against the Anṣar in general. ʿAbd al-Raḥmān was also a companion of his younger Anṣārī contemporary, the poet ʿAbd Allāh b. Muḥammad al-Aḥwaṣ [q.v.]. Only fragments of his verses have survived; these are significant, however, as showing a transitional stage to the poetry of the Ḥid<u>j</u>āzī school of al-Aḥwaṣ and then of ʿUmar b. Abī Rabīʿa [q.v.], though he was clearly inferior in poetic talent to his father.

ʿAbd al-Raḥmān's son Saʿīd was also a poet of this Ḥid<u>j</u>āzī lyrical tradition, to judge by the few citations of his work in the A<u>gh</u>ānī and other sources. He spent some of his career in the Ḥid<u>j</u>āz and some in Syria at the court of Yazīd b. ʿAbd al-Malik and then in the latter's son al-Walīd's circle during Hi<u>sh</u>ām's caliphate; the date of his death is unknown. See R. Blachère, Hist. de la litt. arabe, iii, 625, and Sezgin, GAS, ii, 423.

Bibliography: There is no specific biography of ʿAbd al-Raḥmān in the A<u>gh</u>ānī, but see the Tables alphabètiques for references there to him. The scattered references of the ṭabaḳāt literature, etc., are given in Blachère, op. cit., ii, 316-17, and Sezgin, ii, 422-3, see also Brockelmann, S I, 68, and Ziriklī, Aʿlām, iv, 74. Of secondary literature, see in addition to the above, F. Schultess, Über dem Dichter al Naǧāšī und einige Zeitgenossen, in ZDMG, liv (1900), 421-74 (material from al-Zubayr b. Bakkār's Muwaffaḳiyyāt); Lammens, loc. cit.; and W. ʿArafat, Dīwān of Ḥassān ibn Thābit, London 1971, i, Introd., 6-7. The surviving verses and fragments of ʿAbd al-Raḥmān's poetic work have recently been gathered together by S. Makkī al-Ānī, <u>Sh</u>iʿr ʿAbd al-Raḥmān b. Ḥassān al-Anṣārī, Baghdad 1971.   (C. E. Bosworth)

ʿABD AL-RAZZĀḲ AL-LĀHID<u>J</u>Ī [see LĀHID<u>J</u>Ī].

ʿABD AL-SALĀM B. MUḤAMMAD B. AḤMAD AL-ḤASANĪ AL-ʿALAMĪ AL-FĀSĪ, Moroccan astronomer and physician of the 19th century who lived in Fās, dying there in 1313/1895. Like some others of his fellow-countrymen, he tried to improve the instruments used for calculating the hours of the prayers (tawḳīt [q.v.]), and he describes one of these invented by himself in his Ir<u>sh</u>ād al-<u>kh</u>ill li-taḥḳīḳ al-sāʿa bi-rubʿ al-<u>sh</u>uʿāʿ wa 'l-ẓill. Besides some commentaries (in particular, on al-Wazzānī, called Abdaʿ al-yawāḳīt ʿalā taḥrīr al-mawāḳīt, Fās 1326/1908), he wrote a Dustūr abdaʿ al-yawāḳīt ʿalā taḥrīr al-mawāḳīt (ms. Rabat K 980), which aimed at being a general manual based in part on translations of western scientific works, which he had got to know about in Cairo, where he had gone to study medicine; on his return, he also wrote a commentary on the Ta<u>dh</u>kira

of al-Anṭākī [q.v.], called Ḍiyāʾ al-nibrās fī ḥall mu[~] dāt al-Anṭākī bi-lu<u>gh</u>at ahl Fās (ed. Fās 1318/19[~] 2nd edn., N.D.; with his treatise on haemorrhoids the margins) and composed a reclassification of material in this same work in al-Tabṣira fī suhū al-intifāʿ bi-mud<u>j</u>arrabāt al-Ta<u>dh</u>kira. He furtḥ wrote an ur<u>dj</u>ūza on surgery, but left unfinished dictionary of technical terms found in medical wo[~] translated into Arabic. This author accordingly mai the transition between traditional medicine and t modern medicine, of which he had been able to a quire some idea during his stay in Cairo.

Bibliography: Ibn ʿAbd Allāh, al-Ṭibb wa aṭibbāʾ bi 'l-Ma<u>gh</u>rib, Rabat 1380/1960, 86-9; Lakhdar, La vie littéraire au Maroc, Rabat 197 361-4 and bibl. given there.   (ED.)

ʿABD AL-WAHHĀB BUKHĀRĪ, <u>Sh</u>AYKH, Sū saint of Muslim India.

He was the son of Muḥammad al-Ḥusaynī a Bu<u>kh</u>ārī, the descendant of Sayyid D<u>j</u>alāl al-D Bu<u>kh</u>ārī, who had come to Multān from Central As and then settled down in Uččh at the instance of h pīr, <u>Sh</u>ay<u>kh</u> Bahāʾ al-Dīn Zakariyyāʾ Suhrawardī Multān. His descendants became distinguished Su[~] rawardī saints during the latter half of the 8th/14t century owing to the eminence of Ma<u>kh</u>dūm D<u>j</u>ahān yān. ʿAbd al-Wahhāb received his early religiou instruction in Uchha and then went to Multān fo higher education. He is reported to have studied th religious sciences under <u>Sh</u>ay<u>kh</u> Aḥmad <u>Kh</u>aṭṭū i Aḥmadābād (in Gud<u>j</u>arāt). At an early age, he wen to Arabia on pilgrimage and whilst there benefite from local scholars. On his return to India he settle down in Dihlī, as most of the Suhrawardī saints c Uččh and Multān had moved there. He there becam the murīd of <u>Sh</u>ay<u>kh</u> ʿAbd Allāh Suhrawardī, the so of <u>Sh</u>ay<u>kh</u> Yūsuf Multānī and son-in-law of Sulta Bahlūl Lōdī. He also became an associate of Sultan Sikandar Lōdī. After some time, he left on the pil grimage to Arabia for a second time. This time he went from Gud<u>j</u>arāt by ship, having on his previous trip travelled by land.

On his return to Āgra, in the beginning of the 10th/16th century. The Sultan accorded him a grand reception. In the year, 915/1509, he was sent to the Central Indian fort of Narwar (in modern Madhya Pradesh) which had been just been conquered and renamed by the Sultan Ḥiṣār-i Muḥammad, so that he could serve the religious cause there. Acting as <u>Sh</u>ay<u>kh</u> al-Islām, he supervised the construction of mosques and madrasas, and some mosque inscriptions contain his praise. In the same year, ʿAbd al-Wahhāb Bu<u>kh</u>ārī completed his commentary on the Ḳurʾān, in which the meaning of every verse was explained from a Ṣūfī point of view. The work is not extant, and only a few extracts, quoted by <u>Sh</u>ay<u>kh</u> ʿAbd al-Ḥaḳḳ in his A<u>kh</u>bār-al-a<u>kh</u>yār, are known.

ʿAbd al-Wahhāb Bu<u>kh</u>ārī's association with the Sultan enhanced his influence and prestige in the ruling class, and as a result, a number of scholars and Ṣūfīs got stipends and land-grants from the state for their maintenance on his recommendation. But his relations with Sultan Sikandar Lōdī became strained towards the close of the latter's reign. It is said that on his arrival in Āgra from Narwar, the <u>Sh</u>ay<u>kh</u> advised the Sultan to grow a beard as it was not proper for a Muslim monarch to shave his beard. The sultan tried to avoid discussion over the matter by giving evasive replies. Against the royal wishes, the <u>Sh</u>ay<u>kh</u> insisted on eliciting a promise from the sultan. However, the sultan got annoyed and became quiet. On the departure of the <u>Sh</u>ay<u>kh</u>, he expressed his resentnt, remarking that he had become presumptuous er royal favour to him and that he did not know at it was because of this that people kissed his feet. hen the Shaykh came to know of the sultan's re- ark through a courtier, he left Āgra in disgust and en spent the rest of his life in seclusion in Dihlī. e died in 931/1525 and was buried in Dihlī near the mb of his *pīr*, Shaykh ʿAbd Allāh.

Bibliography: Shaykh Rizḳ Allāh Mushtāḳī, *Wāḳiʿāt-i Mushtāḳī*, Ms. British Museum Add. 11,633; Shaykh ʿAbd al-Ḥaḳḳ Muḥaddith, *Akhbār al-akhyār*, Dihlī 1914; ʿAbd Allāh, *Taʾrīkh-i Dāwūdī*, ed. Shaykh ʿAbd al-Rashīd, Aligarh 1954; Aḥmad Yādgār, *Taʾrīkh-i Shāhī*, ed. M. Hidāyat Ḥusayn, Calcutta 1939; Aḥmad Khān, *Shadjara-yi-Suhraward*, Ms. Riza Library, Rampur; *Epigraphia Indica*, Arabic and Persian Supplement 1965, ed. Z. A. Desai, Calcutta 1966.

(I. H. Siddiqui)

ʿABD AL-WAHHĀB, Ḥasan Ḥusnī b. Ṣāliḥ b. Abd al-Wahhāb b. Yūsuf al-Ṣumādiḥī al-Tudjībī, orn in Tunis 21 July 1884 and died at Salammbo in he suburbs of Tunis November 1968, was a polygraph and scholar born into a family of dignitaries and high officials of the Tunisian state. His eponymous grandfather, ʿAbd al-Wahhāb b. Yūsuf, served in positions of administration and protocol in the entourage of the Beys while his father, Yūsuf b. ʿAbd al-Wahhāb, a senior official and interpreter with various Tunisian delegations in Europe, occupied a number of administrative posts under the French Protectorate, including that of *ʿāmil*, governor, of Gabès and of Mahdia; passionately interested in history, he wrote a history of Morocco that has never been published.

In 1904, on the death of his father, Ḥasan Ḥusnī ʿAbd al-Wahhāb was obliged to interrupt his short-lived higher studies in Paris where he was following a course in Political Science, for an administrative career in Tunis which was to last from 1905 to 1920.

Governor or *ʿāmil* successively of Djabanyāna in 1925, Mahdia in 1928 and Nabeul in 1935, he exerted himself particularly in the extension of education and the diffusion of culture in these regions through the establishment of primary schools in the Caïdate of Djabanyāna, through weekly lectures on the history of Tunis which he himself gave in Mahdia, and through the provision of books for the libraries of this town and of Nabeul.

Returning to the central administration in Tunis, in 1939 he was given responsibility, having been pensioned off, for the supervision of the *Habous* (properties held in mortmain). From May 1943 to July 1947, he was minister of the Pen (Chancellery and Internal Affairs) of the last Bey of Tunis Lamine or al-Amīn I.

Following the independence of Tunisia, he directed, from 1957 to 1962, the Institute of Archaeology and Arts where he introduced young Tunisians to archaeological pursuits, founded five museums in different parts of the country, of which four were museums of Arab-Islamic art to which he donated the whole of his private collection, and at the same time stimulated artistic and archaeological activity by the publication of articles and the writing of prefaces to books which he encouraged and assisted scholars to write.

His vocation as historian of Tunisia, put into effect from 1905 onward by the courses in the history of Tunisia which he gave at the *Khaldūniyya* [*q.v.*] and in the history of Islam which he conducted at the École Supérieure de Langue et Littérature Arabes from 1913 to 1924, was assisted by his transfer in 1920 to the General Archives of Tunisia, where he inaugurated a card-index system, then to the Supervision of *Habous*, and also by his work as governor in various parts of Tunisia, which enable him to gain a better acquaintance with the country, its recent history, its hitherto ignored cultural patrimony, its peoples, their ethnology and dialects. In 1933, he gave a series of lectures at the Institut des Études Islamiques at the University of Paris.

A member from its foundation in 1932 of the Arabic Language Academy of Cairo, in which he in effect represented the three countries of the Maghrib, he took an active part in the work of the various commissions, distinguishing himself by "an open-minded approach striving to conciliate modern needs with the norms of Muslim civilisation". He was also a member of the Academy of Damascus from its creation, of the Academy of Baghdad, a corresponding member of the French Académie des Inscriptions et Belles Lettres from 1939, of the Egyptian Institute, and of the Madrid Academy of History, and of the executive committee of the *EI*.

As official delegate of the Tunisian government, he participated, from 1905, in the work of the majority of the International Congresses of Orientalists as well as in a number of seminars, which enabled him to forge fruitful and lasting relationships with numerous orientalists and oriental scholars.

While the title of Doctor *honoris causa* of the Academy of Cairo in 1950, and of the Academy of Algiers —then French—in 1960, confirmed the scholar's prestige, the Prize of the President of the Tunisian Republic crowned, on the very eve of the death of H. H. ʿAbd al-Wahhāb (7 November 1968), the achievements of a long and hard-working life.

His works comprise:

(a). In Arabic: *al-Muntakhab al-madrasī min al-adab al-tūnisī*, Tunis 1908, re-published in Cairo in 1944 and again in Tunis in 1968 in a new version under the title *al-Mudjmal*; *Bisāṭ al-ʿaḳīḳ fī ḥaḍārat al-Ḳayrawān wa shāʿirihā Ibn Rashīḳ*, Tunis 1912; *Khulāṣat taʾrīkh Tūnis*, a summary of the history of Tunisia, published three times between 1918 and 1953 and brought up to date with each edition; *al-Irshād ilā ḳawāʿid al-iḳtiṣād*, Tunis 1919; *Shahīrāt al-tūnisiyyāt*, Tunis 1934, 2nd ed. 1966; *al-Tārī*, in *al-Madjalla al-Zaytūniyya*, Tunis, May 1940; *Nissīm Ibn Yaʿḳūb*, in *al-Nadwa*, Tunis, January 1953; *al-ʿInāya bi 'l-kutub wa-djamʿihā fī Ifrīḳiyā al-tūnisiyya*, in *RIMA*, i, (1955), 72-90; *al-Imām al-Māzarī*, Tunis 1955; *Waraḳāt ʿan al-ḥaḍāra al-ʿarabiyya bi-Ifrīḳiya al-tūnisiyya*, Tunis 1965-72 (3 vols.); *al-ʿArab wa 'l-ʿumrān bi-Ifrīḳiya*, in *al-Fikr* (Dec. 1968), 28-31.

(b). In French: *La domination musulmane en Sicile*, Tunis 1905; *Coup d'oeil général sur les apports ethniques étrangers en Tunisie*, Tunis 1917; *Le développement de la musique arabe en Orient, au Maghreb et en Espagne*, Tunis 1918; *Un témoin de la conquête arabe de l'Espagne*, Tunis 1932; *Deux dinars normands frappés à Mahdia*, in *RT* (1930), 215-18; *Un tournant de l'histoire aghlabide, l'insurrection de Manṣūr Ṭunbudhī, seigneur de la Muḥammadiyya*, in *ibid.* (1937), 343-52; *Du nom arabe de la Byzacène*, in *ibid.* (1939), 199-201; *Villes arabes disparues*, in *Mélanges W. Marçais*, Paris 1950, 1-15; *Le régime foncier en Sicile au Moyen-Age* (*IXe et Xe s.*), ed. and tr. of the *K. al-Amwāl* of al-Dāwūdī (in collaboration with F. Dachraoui), in *Études d'Orientalisme dédiées à la mémoire d'E. Lévi-Provençal*, Paris 1962, ii, 401-44.

(c). Editions of texts: *Aʿmāl al-aʿlām of Ibn al-Khaṭīb* (section relative to Ifrīḳiya and to Sicily), in *Centenario della nascita di M. Amari*, Palermo 1910, ii, 423-94; *Rasāʾil al-intiḳād* of Ibn S̲h̲araf, Damascus 1912; *Malḳā al-sabīl* of al-Maʿarrī, Damascus 1912; *Waṣf Ifrīḳiya wa-'l-Andalus* of Ibn Faḍl Allāh al-ʿUmarī, Tunis 1920; *Kitāb Yafʿūl* of al-S̲ā̲g̲h̲ānī, Tunis 1924; *al-Tabaṣṣur bi 'l-tidjāra* of al-Dj̲āḥiẓ, Damascus 1933, Cairo 1935 and Beirut 1966; *Adab al-muʿallimīn* of Muḥammad b. Saḥnūn, Tunis 1934; *al-Dj̲umāna fī izālat al-raṭāna*, anon., Cairo 1953; *Riḥla* of al-Tidj̲ānī, Tunis 1958.

His works also include a number of articles in Arabic and in French, some of them still unpublished, the others appearing in the *Encyclopaedia of Islām* and in periodicals of Tunisia, Europe and the Orient (see *al-Fikr* [Dec. 1968], 96, with a list of his articles published by this journal, some of which, as well as some of the titles mentioned above, have been reproduced in *Waraḳāt*, either because they are in a suitable context there or because their original edition has been exhausted).

Manuals or monographs, these works are for the most part dedicated to Arab history and civilisation in Tunisia in a perspective which embraces literature and also linguistic and religious studies, without however neglecting the "exact sciences" and the arts. They prefigure the author's greatest work, the fruit of sixty years of patient research, his *Kitāb al-ʿUmr*, the "work of his life", a posthumous work in several still unpublished volumes, a collection of biographical notes on some thousand scholars and men of letters who lived and worked in Tunisia since the Arab conquest, which he seems already to have foreshadowed in 1953 under the title *Taʾrīk̲h̲ Tūnis al-kabīr* "Great history of Tunisia" (Preface to the 3rd ed. of *K̲h̲ulāṣat taʾrīk̲h̲ Tūnis*), and publication of which he had entrusted to a Tunisian scholar M. el Aroussi el Metoui (see especially *al-Fikr* [Dec. 1968], 86).

His only known experiment in the fictional genre, a short story, *Dernière veillée à Grenade*, written in French (in *La Renaissance nord-africaine*, Tunis no. 3, March 1905) and translated into Arabic (by Hamadi Sahli in *Ḳiṣaṣ*, Tunis, no. 17, Oct. 1970), prefigures the concern motivating him, in all his studies, for the revival of Arab-Muslim civilisation; in addition, he reveals gifts as a writer whose style and poetic imagination have already been noted (see Ch. Bouyahia, review of *Waraḳāt*, ii, in *Ḥawliyyāt al-Dj̲āmiʿa al-Tūnisiyya*, iv [1967], 166-70).

Through the abundant wealth of his scientific contribution, which goes beyond the Tunisian domain into the broader spheres of Arab-Muslim culture, through the clarity of expression, the tautness and elegance of style, the work of Ḥ. Ḥ. ʿAbd al-Wahhāb, so varied in its unity, has already inspired and guided generations of scholars. Moreover, the influence of the scholar and the master, whose *madjlis*, the last of its kind perhaps in Tunisia, was a veritable school, continues to be felt today, thanks to his collection of manuscripts, some thousand volumes strong, which he presented to the National Library of Tunis, where they constitute the bequest that bears his name (see catalogue published in *Ḥawliyyāt al-Dj̲āmiʿa al-Tūnisiyya*, vii [1970], 133-272 and the announcement of the gift in his speech accepting the Prize of the President of the Republic of Tunisia, in *al-Fikr* [Dec. 1968], 85-7).

Bibliography: (in addition to references given in the article): For Ḥ. Ḥ. ʿAbd al-Wahhāb's life: the sole source is his *Autobiography*, which appeared mainly in the Tunis daily *al-ʿAmal* for 8 Nov. 1968; *al-Fikr*, Dec. 1968, 87-95; *Ḥawliyyāt al-Dj̲āmiʿa al-Tūnisiyya*, vi (1969), 35-55; *Wara-*

ḳāt, iii, 1972, 11-29; largely used by Muḥamm Mahdī ʿAllām, *al-Madj̲maʿiyyūn*, Cairo 1966, 66 and by Hilāl Nādj̲ī, *Ḥasan Ḥusnī ʿAbd al-Wahhā* in *al-Adīb*, Beirut, April 1967; and resumed in *Fikr* (Nov. 1968), 6-7. For his works: Ch. Bouy hia, reviews of the 3 vols. of *Waraḳāt*, in *Ḥawliy* . . ., iii (1966), 215-27; iv (1967), 161-70; xi (197 275-94; idem, *Ḥasan Ḥusnī ʿAbd al-Wahhāb Ḥawliyyāt* . . ., vi (1969), 7-9; M. Chemli, revie of *S̲h̲ahīrāt al-tūnisiyyāt*, in *Ḥawliyyāt* . . ., (1966), 287-92; R. Hamzaoui, *Masālik al-lug̲h̲a m k̲h̲ilāl ḥayāt Ḥ. Ḥ. ʿAbd al-Wahhāb wa aʿmālih l Madj̲maʿ al-lug̲h̲a al-ʿarabiyya*, in *Ḥawliyyāt* . . iv (1969), 11-33; idem, *l'Académie de langue ara du Caire, histoire et œuvre*, Tunis 1975, 97-9, a index; see also Sarkīs, *Muʿdj̲am al-maṭbūʿāt*, Cai 1928, 758-9; Muḥammad Maṣmūlī, Ḥ. Ḥ. ʿAbd a Wahhāb hal māt? in *al-Fikr*, (Dec. 1968), 38-4 Ch. Klibi, in *ibid.*, 76-82; A. Demeerseman, *I memoriam*, in *IBLA*, 1968, No. 2, pp. i-iv.

(Ch. Bouyahia)

ABDELKADER [see ʿABD AL-ḲĀDIR].
ABDICATION [see TANĀZUL].
ABJURATION [see MURTADD].
ABKARIUS [see ISKANDAR AG̲H̲A].
ABROGATION [see NĀSIK̲H̲ WA-MANSŪK̲H̲].
ABSOLUTION [see KAFFĀRA].
ABSTINENCE [see TABATTUL].
ABŪ 'L-ʿABBĀS AḤMAD B. ʿABD ALLĀH [se ABŪ MAḤALLĪ].

ABŪ 'L-ʿABBĀS AL-AʿMĀ [see AL-AʿMĀ AL TUṬĪLĪ].

ABŪ ʿABD ALLĀH AL-BAṢRĪ, AL-ḤUSAYN B ʿALĪ B. IBRĀHĪM AL-KĀG̲H̲ADĪ, called (AL-)Dj̲UʿAL "Dungbeetle", influential Muʿtazilī theologian and Ḥanafī jurist, died 2 Dhu 'l-Ḥidj̲dj̲a 369/19 June 980 in Bag̲h̲dād. He was born in Baṣra, at an uncertain date (293/905-6 according to *Taʾrīk̲h̲ Bag̲h̲dād*, viii, 73, ll. 20 ff., following ʿAlī b. al-Muḥassin al-Tanūk̲h̲ī and Hilāl al-Ṣābiʾ; 308/920-1 according to the *Fihrist*, ed. Flügel, 174, pu.; 289/902 according to Ṣafadī, cf. Kaḥḥāla, *Muʿdj̲am al-muʾallifīn*, iv, 27, n. 1). The nickname Dj̲uʿal is not used in Muʿtazilī or Ḥanafī sources.

He left Baṣra at an early age, possibly forced by the constant danger presented by the Ḳarmathians [see ḲARMAṬĪ] since 311/923. He entertained contacts with the representatives of the Baṣran school of the Muʿtazila who lived now in ʿAskar Mukram in K̲h̲ūzistān, with Abū Hās̲h̲im (died 321/933) and especially with Abū Hās̲h̲im's disciple Ibn K̲h̲allād [q.v.]. But he lived mainly in Bag̲h̲dād, where he studied Ḥanafī law with Abu 'l-Ḥasan al-Kark̲h̲ī (died 340/952; cf. *GAS*, I, 444). With respect to his theological views, he was isolated there; during the late years of al-K̲h̲ayyāṭ (died *ca.* 300/913 [q.v.]) the Muʿtazila had lost much of its prestige, perhaps due to the scandal caused by the books of Ibn al-Rāwandī [q.v.], and the wing of the school which still maintained some influence in the capital, namely Ibn al-Ik̲h̲s̲h̲īd (270-326/883-938 [q.v.]) with his disciples, strongly opposed Abū Hās̲h̲im's ideas. Abū ʿAbd Allāh therefore suffered serious deprivation during his studies (cf. the stories in Ḳāḍī ʿAbd al-Dj̲abbār, *Faḍl al-iʿtizāl*, ed. Fuʾād Sayyid, 325, pu. ff.; also in Ibn al-Murtaḍā, *Ṭabaḳāt al-Muʿtazila*, 105, ll. 15 ff.). His teacher Abu 'l-Ḥasan al-Kark̲h̲ī entertained relations with the Ḥamdānid Sayf al-Dawla (333-56/944-67) who rivalled with the Būyids in the game for political power in ʿIrāḳ (cf. *Faḍl al-iʿtizāl*, 326, ll. 17 f.); when he suffered from a stroke in 340/952, his disciples, among them Abū ʿAbd Allāh, apached the prince for financial support (cf. *Taʾrīkh* *ḡhdād*, x, 355, ll. 4 ff.). This may have initiated ɩt least strengthened those moderate Shīʿī leanings which Abū ʿAbd Allāh became well-known after- :ds. He used them, however, in order to win the our of Būyid and Zaydī circles which had become isive after Muʿizz al-Dawla had succeeded in tak- over Baghdād in 334/945. He found support with ʿizz al-Dawla's *wazīr* al-Ḥasan b. Muḥammad al- hallabī (339-52/950-63; cf. Hamdānī, *Takmilat* *ʾrīkh al-Ṭabarī*, ed. Kanʿān, 186, ll. 13 ff., and ū Ḥayyān al-Tawḥīdī, *al-Imtāʿ wa 'l-muʾānasa*, iii, 3, l. 10), who liked to surround himself with jurists . Thaʿālibī, *Yatīmat al-dahr*, ed. ʿAbd al-Ḥamīd, ii, 5, ult. ff.). Muʿizz al-Dawla himself did penitence his presence during his last disease, in 356/967 (cf. ımdānī, 192, apu. ff.). He gave private lessons in *'ām* to the Zaydī pretender Abū ʿAbd Allāh Mu- ımmad b. al-Ḥasan (304-59/916-70) whom he man- ed to persuade, at the instigation of Muʿizz al- ıwla, to become *naḳīb al-ashrāf* in 349/960 (cf. al- ākim al-Djushamī, *Sharḥ al-ʿuyūn*, ed. Fuʾād Say- l, Tunis 1974, 372, ll. 16 ff.; Hamdānī, 188, l. 16; n ʿInaba, *ʿUmdat al-ṭālib*, Nadjaf 1380/1961, 84, t. ff.). When his disciple proclaimed himself *imām* Gīlān under the title al-Mahdī li-dīn Allāh in 353/ 4, Abū ʿAbd Allāh saw himself exposed to perse- ıtion by the mob of al-Karkh who had been insti- .ted against him by a member of the ʿAlid aris- cracy, but his great prestige even among those who d not share his political leanings, saved him from ıe banishment planned by the government (cf. al- āṭik bi 'l-ḥaḳḳ, *al-Ifāda fī taʾrīkh al-aʾimma al-sāda*, s. Leiden Or. 8404, fol. 63b, ll. 5 ff.; shorter version so in al-Ḥākim al-Djushamī, 372, apu. ff.). Later ı he counted among his pupils Aḥmad b. al-Ḥusayn -Muʾayyad billāh (333-411/944-1020) and his brother bū Ṭālib al-Nāṭiḳ bi 'l-ḥaḳḳ (340-424/951-1033) who, lthough originating from an Imāmī family, took up ıe Zaydī claims in the Caspian region (cf. Madelung, *)er Imam al-Qāsim ibn Ibrāhīm*, Berlin 1965, 177 ff.).

Of greatest importance for his school and for the ictory of Abū Hāshim's ideas was his friendship ʼith the Ṣāḥib Ibn ʿAbbād, whom he may have met ʼhen he came to Baghdād in 347/958 with Muʾayyid l-Dawla, and whom he hailed as the "support of eligion" (*ʿimād al-dīn*) or even as the expected Iahdī, although in the latter case only in a meta- horical sense. This must be dated to the year 366/ 76 or somewhat later, when the Ṣāḥib had been ominated *wazīr* by Muʾayyid al-Dawla in Rayy. He ɾdered Abū ʿAbd Allāh's epistle to be reproduced n golden letters and sent it among other gifts to Ḳābūs b. Wushmgīr [*q.v.*] who took over power in Ṭabaristān and Gurgān in the same year (cf. Tawḥīdī, *Akhlāḳ al-wazīrayn*, ed. Ṭandjī, 202, ll. 3 ff. and 208, l. 6 ff.). He addressed Abū ʿAbd Allāh with the title *al-shaykh al-murshid* and agreed, in 367/978, on his recommendation to take over into his service his most promising disciple, ʿAbd al-Djabbār b. Aḥmad [*q.v.*], the later *ḳāḍī al-ḳuḍāt* of Rayy. Abū ʿAbd Allāh, at the peak of his influence, seems to have been in ill health; Abū Ḥayyān al-Tawḥīdī remembered having seen him in 360/971, on the occasion of a reception for scholars given by ʿIzz al-Dawla, when the guests were conducted to him and when he was too weak to answer an attack launched at him by his colleague ʿAlī b. ʿĪsā al-Rummānī, who represented the school of Ibn al-Ikhshīd (cf. *Akhlāḳ al-wazīrayn*, 202, ll. 11 ff.). He was buried in the *turba* of his teacher al-Karkhī; the mourning prayer had been said by the Muʿtazilī grammarian Abū ʿAlī al-Fārisī (286-377/900-87) who was in his eighties himself (cf. *Taʾrīkh Baghdād*, viii, 73, l. 19 and 74, l. 2).

Abū Ḥayyān did not like him, just as he disliked everybody connected with the Ṣāḥib Ibn ʿAbbād. In his *Imtāʿ* (i, 140, ll. 3 ff.) he gives a sharpsighted characterisation of Abū ʿAbd Allāh's personality: imaginative, but bad in rhetorics and awkward in discussion; avid of wealth and prestige, but strongly committed to his "people"; skilfully using his political influence—a typical social climber. Several times he stresses the fact that Abu 'l-Ḳāsim ʿAlī b. Muḥammad b. ʿAllāh al-Wāsiṭī, who seems to have been Abū ʿAbd Allāh's closest assistant for some time (cf. *Faḍl al-iʿtizāl*, 329, l. 9), left him out of personal disgust (cf. *Imtāʿ*, i, 140, ll. 10 ff., and ii, 175, ll. 10 ff.; *Akhlāḳ*, 213, ll. 5 ff.). He also mentions a number of other disciples (*Akhlāḳ*, 202, ll. 7 ff.), most of them young people from Khurāsān (*ibid.*, 210, ll. 12 f.), whom he calls a "bunch of unbelievers" and whose names were, as a matter of fact, usually not taken over into the Muʿtazilī *ṭabaḳāt*-literature. This bad reputation is perhaps to be explained by a certain trend towards scepticism (*takāfuʾ al-adilla*) for which at least one of them, Abū Isḥāḳ Ibrāhīm b. ʿAlī al-Naṣībī, was well known (cf., e.g., Tawḥīdī, *Muḳābasāt*, ed. Muḥ. Tawfīḳ Ḥusayn, Baghdād 1970, 159 f.), and which Abū Ḥayyān tries to impute to Abū ʿAbd Allāh, too (cf. *Akhlāḳ*, 212, ll. 5 ff., with reference to a conversation between Abū ʿAbd Allāh and Abū Sulaymān al-Manṭiḳī).

Abū ʿAbd Allāh's ideas have to be reconstructed mainly from the numerous quotations found in the works of Ḳāḍī ʿAbd al-Djabbār. The Ḳāḍī recognises his indebtness himself (cf. *Mughnī*, xx², 257, ll. 4 ff.), although frequently he did not share his teacher's opinions. He dictated some of his books in the presence of Abū ʿAbd Allāh, obviously when he lived in his house in Baghdād (cf. al-Ḥākim al-Djushamī, *Sharḥ al-ʿuyūn*, 366, ll. 5 f.); when he began his *Mughnī*, Abū ʿAbd Allāh was still alive (cf. xx², 258, ll. 8 ff.). A full evaluation of Abū ʿAbd Allāh's originality is, however, not yet possible. We get quite a lot of information about his pro-Shīʿī (Zaydī) arguments which he proferred in his *K. al-Tafḍīl* (for the title. cf. Ibn al-Murtaḍā, *Ṭabaḳāt al-Muʿtazila*, 107, l. 5). He based himself mainly on Shīʿī traditions, the trustworthiness of which he tried to prove with rational speculations about their historicity. Moreover, he practiced what was called *muwāzanat al-aʿmāl*, i.e. he weighed the virtues of ʿAlī and Abū Bakr against each other. In this he seems to have taken up the arguments of al-Iskāfī (died 240/854 [*q.v.*]), and he had to criticise Abū ʿAlī al-Djubbāʾī; he obviously avoided, however, open disagreement with Abū Hāshim (cf. *Mughnī*, xx¹, 216, ll. 7 ff.; 223, ll. 6 f.; 241, ll. 17 ff.; xx², 120, ll. 13 ff.; 122, ll. 3 ff.; 124, ll. 7 ff.; 125, ll. 4 ff.; 131, ll. 3 ff.; 132, ll. 19 ff.; 140, ll. 3 ff.). He never made any concessions to *rafḍ*; he drew Muʿizz al-Dawla's attention to the fact that ʿUmar had accepted Islam very early and that ʿAlī had given his daughter Umm Kulthūm in marriage to him (cf. Hamdānī, *Takmila*, 192, ult. ff.).

He showed great interest in epistemology, probably because of the fact that Abu 'l-Ḥasan ʿAlī b. Kaʿb al-Anṣārī, a member of the rival school of Ibn al-Ikhshīd, still defended the ideas of al-Djāḥiẓ in his circle, among them certainly al-Djāḥiẓ's famous apriorism (cf. Tawḥīdī, *Akhlāḳ*, 203; for al-Djāḥiẓ, van Ess, in *Isl.*, xlii (1966), 169 ff. and Vajda in *SI*, xxiv (1966) 19 ff.). He transmitted Djubbāʾī's *K. Naḳḍ al-maʿrifa*, a critique of Djāḥiẓ's *K. al-Maʿrifa*, and added remarks to it, obviously in his own *K. al-Maʿrifa* (cf. *Fihrist*, ed. Flügel, 175, ll. 4 f.), which were taken over by the Ḳāḍī ʿAbd al-Djabbār in his *Taʿlīḳ Naḳḍ al-maʿrifa* (cf. Ḥākim al-Djushamī, 367, ll. 10 f.). The book is quoted in *Mughnī*, xii, 131, ll. 19 ff.; the other numerous references (cf. *Mughnī*, xii, 9, ll. 7 ff.; 11, ll. 16 ff.; 12, ll 11. ff.; 28, ll. 9 ff.; 33, ll. 5 ff.; 46, ll. 5 ff.; 75, ll. 13 ff.; 81, ll. 5 ff.; 102, ll. 8 ff.; 118, ll. 6 ff.; 133, ll. 13 ff.; 187, ll. 18 ff.; 372, ll. 15 ff.; 442, ll. 12 ff.; 446, ll. 10 ff.; 513, ll. 15 ff.; 521, ll. 6 ff.; 532, ll. 5 ff.) may equally well go back to his *K. al-ʿUlūm* which is explicitly mentioned in *Mughnī*, xii, 235, l. 16.

In juridical hermeneutics, he departed from Abu 'l-Ḥasan al-Karkhī's ideas. But he seems to have surpassed his teacher in many respects. Some of his views are quoted with the additional remark that he had them *ʿan Abi 'l-Ḥasan*; frequently, however, his name is mentioned alone. He impressed later generations with the precision of some of his definitions, but also with subtle speculations on *ʿāmm* and *khāṣṣ*, on *idjmāʿ*, on the *ratio legis* (*ʿilla*) in *ḳiyās*, on *akhbār*, on *naskh* (which, in contrast to many of his contemporaries, he also allowed concerning *ḥadīth*), etc. Numerous, although scattered, material is found in *Mughnī*, xvii, in Abu 'l-Ḥusayn al-Baṣrī's [*q.v.*] *Muʿtamad fī uṣūl al-fiḳh* (cf. the index), and in an as yet unidentified work on *uṣūl al-fiḳh* preserved in the Vatican library (Ms. Vat. arab. 1100; cf. Levi Della Vida, *Elenco dei manoscritti*, 145 f., and Madelung, *Qāsim ibn Ibrāhīm*, 179 f.). Abū ʿAbd Allāh's own works in this domain, among them a *K. al-Uṣūl* and a *K. Naḳḍ al-futyā* (cf. *Faḍl al-iʿtizāl*, 326, l. 20), seem to be lost. In the "ethical" chapters of *uṣūl al-fiḳh*, he circumscribed, like Ḳāḍī ʿAbd al-Djabbār, the good only in a privative way (cf. ʿAbd al-Djabbār, *al-Muḥīṭ*, ed. ʿAzmī, 239, ll. 13 ff.); the affirmative definition was apparently reserved for evil, which recieved the greater share of attention. Evil is never chosen by man for the sake of itself, but only when he sees a need for it (cf. G. Hourani, *Islamic rationalism*, Oxford 1972, 95). Whereas Djubbāʾī and Abū Hāshim believed that the state of mind of an agent determines the quality of evil (evil becoming neutral when performed during sleep or in the state of unconsciousness), Abū ʿAbd Allāh upheld a more differentiated position (cf. *ibid.*, 41 f.). His ideas on *furūʿ* were formulated in his commentary on Karkhī's *Mukhtaṣar*, but also in some monographs where he treated the lawfulness of drinking *nabīdh* or of performing one's prayer in Persian (two typical Ḥanafī tenets) and the *mutʿa* marriage (which he deemed unlawful, in accordance with Zaydi *fiḳh* and in disagreement with Imāmī opinion; cf. *Fihrist*, 208, pu. f.).

In theology proper, he followed the line of the Baṣran school. Only a few personal traits can be recognised with sufficient certainty. In at least three treatises he attacked the doctrine of the eternity of the world, two of them focussing their polemics on special persons, Ibn al-Rāwandī and al-Rāzī (cf. *Fihrist*, 175, ll. 3 f.; 174, ult. f.; 175, l. 2). When he explained creation as an act of thinking (*fikr*) in order to avoid all material connotations, he seems to have taken philosophical critique into consideration (cf. Ḳāḍī ʿAbd al-Djabbār, *Sharḥ al-uṣūl al-khamsa* 548, ll. 11 ff.; *Muḥīṭ*, 332, ll. 15 f.). He attacked al-Rāzī also for his book against Abu 'l-Ḳāsim al-Balkhī, probably about divine knowledge (cf. *Fihrist*, 175, ll. 1 f., and *Abi Bakr Rhagensis opera philosophica*, ed. P. Kraus, 167 f.). He did not accept the idea of *luṭf*; we never know whether an event which we interpret as a special "grace" (*luṭf*) somebody is not the ruin of somebody else (*Mughnī*, xiii, 67, ll. 15 ff.; also 155, ll. 4 ff.; viously both quotations from his *K. al-Aṣlaḥ*, gether with xiv, 62, ll. 12 f.). He refuted Ashʿa *K. al-Mūdjiz* (cf. al-Nāṭik bi 'l-ḥaḳḳ, *Ifāda*, fol. 6 ll. 5 ff. and Ḳāḍī ʿAbd al-Djabbār, *al-Muḥīṭ*, 3 l. 4; also al-Ḥākim al-Djushamī, 372, ll. 1 f., wh *naḳḍ* is to be read instead of *baʿḍ*; R. McCarthy, *T theology of al-Ashʿarī*, Beirut 1953, 167, 211 f., 22 Altogether, more than 20 titles of books can be trace

Bibliography: 1. Primary sources. Ḳā ʿAbd al-Djabbār, *Faḍl al-iʿtizāl*, 325 ff.; ide *Tathbīt dalāʾil al-nubuwwa*, ed. ʿAbd al-Kar ʿUthmān, 627, ll. 10 ff.; Abū Rashīd in A. Bira *Die atomistische Substanzenlehre aus dem Buch d Streitfragen zwischen Basrensern und Bagdadense* Berlin 1902, 27 and 73, n. 2; Ibn al-Murtaḍ *Ṭabaḳāt al-Muʿtazila* 105 f.; *Taʾrīkh Baghdād*, vi 73 f. no. 4153 (on which depend Ibn al-Djaw *Muntaẓam*, viii, 101, no. 131 and Ibn Ḥadjar, *Lisā al-mīzān*, ll, 303, ll. 6 ff.); Hamdānī, *Takmil Taʾrīkh al-Ṭabarī*, Index s.v. al-Baṣrī; Shīrā *Ṭabaḳāt al-fuḳahāʾ*, ed. ʿAbbās, Beirut 1970, 14 pu. f. (on which depends Ibn al-ʿImād, *Shadhar al-dhahab*, iii, 68, ll. 4 f.); Ibn Abi 'l-Wafāʾ, *a Djawāhir al-muḍīʾa*, ii, 260, no. 140 (erroneous under Abu 'l-ʿAlāʾ); Ibn al-Nadīm, *Fihrist*, e Flügel, 174, ll. 21 ff. (among the theologians), an 208, ll. 26 ff. (among the jurists); Abū Ḥayyā al-Tawḥīdī, *Akhlāḳ al-wazīrayn*, ed. Ṭandjī, Da mascus 1965, 200 ff.; idem, *al-Imtāʿ wa 'l-muʾānasa* i, 140, ii, 175, iii, 213; Ibn Taghrībirdī, *al-Nudjūm al-zāhira*, Cairo 1348 ff., iv, 135, ll. 13 ff.; Dha habī, *Siyar aʿlām al-nubalāʾ* (ms.); Ṣafadī, *al-Wāf bi 'l-wafayāt* (ms.); Ziriklī, *al-Aʿlām*, ii, 266; Kaḥ ḥāla, *Muʿdjam al-muʾallifīn*, iv, 27 (and iv, 19 with wrong name and date of death). 2. Studies M. Horten, *Die philosophischen Systeme der speku lativen Theologen im Islam*, Bonn 1918, 443 f.; W Madelung, *Der Imām al-Qāsim ibn Ibrāhīm*, Berlin 1965, index s.v.; Iḥsān ʿAbbās, in *al-Abḥāth*, xi (1966), 189 ff.; H. Busse, *Chalif und Grosskönig*, Beirut 1969, 439 ff.; G. Hourani, *Islamic rationalism*, Oxford 1972, index s.v.; J. Peters, *God's created speech*, Leiden 1976, index s.v.

(J. VAN ESS)

ABU 'L-ʿALĀʾ AL-RABAʿĪ [see ṢĀʿID AL-BAGHDĀDĪ].

ABŪ ʿALĪ AL-FAḌL B. MUḤAMMAD AL-MURSHID AL-FĀRMADĪ, one of the greatest Ṣūfī masters of the 5th/11th century, born in 402/1011-12 at Fārmad, a small town in the vicinity of Ṭūs in Khurāsān, and the contemporary of the caliph al-Ḳādir and the Saldjūḳ princes Ṭoghrïl, Alp Arslan and Malik Shāh. He was highly respected by various political and religious dignitaries, including by the celebrated minister of the Saldjūḳs, Niẓām al-Mulk, who sought his advice and his spiritual favour. He was also respected as an eloquent preacher, and appreciated for his breadth of knowledge and the beauty of his oratorical language. He approached Ṣūfism after profound studies in the religious sciences, and can therefore be classified as one of the scholarly mystics. When he came to Nīshāpūr, he became one of Abu 'l-Ḳāsim Ḳushayrī's circle of students, and it seems to have been the latter who turned him towards preaching and who stimulated him to study profoundly the religious sciences. In his Ṣūfī training, he was directed spiritually by two great masters, Abu 'l-Ḳāsim Djurdjānī and Abu 'l-Ḥasan Kharaḳānī [*q.v.*]. The author of the *Asrār al-tawḥīd* relates in an

ꜛdotal form the circumstances of al-Fārmadī's adꜛon to Ṣūfism under Ḳushayrī's direction first of and then under that of Djurdjānī, who encouraged to preach from the pulpit and later gave him the d of his daughter in marriage. None of al-Fārꜛdī's works remain, apart from a few brief poems Arabic and a few sentences displaying his philosꜛy and thought. However, his influence on culꜛal life and mysticism can be gauged from the fact t the *Imām* al-Ghazālī [*q.v.*] was one of his pupils cites traditions on his authority. He was accordꜛly considered as the greatest Ṣūfī luminary of his , who lustre is seen in the fame of his great disciple. Fārmadī died in his native town in 477/1080.

Bibliography: Muḥammad b. al-Munawwar, *Asrār al-tawḥīd*, ed. Dhabīḥ Allāh Ṣafā', Tehran 1332/1953, 128-31, 196-7, 199-200, tr. M. Achena, *Les étapes mystiques du shaykh Abu Saʿid*, Paris 1974, 136-8, 186, 189; Djāmī, *Nafaḥāt al-uns*, 368; Maʿṣūm ʿAlī Shāh, *Ṭarā'iḳ al-ḥaḳā'iḳ*, 1339/1921, ii, 308, 322, 350, 352-5; *Nāma-yi dānishwarān*, Tehran 1959, vii, 306. (M. ACHENA)

ABŪ ʿALĪ AL-FĀRISĪ [see AL-FĀRISĪ].

ABŪ ʿALĪ AL-YŪSĪ [see AL-YŪSĪ].

ABU 'L-ʿAMAYTHAL, ʿABD ALLĀH B. KHULAYD SAʿD (d. 240/854), a minor poet who claimed to a *mawlā* of the Banū Hāshim and who was origiꜛlly from Rayy. He was in Khurāsān in the service Ṭāhir b. al-Ḥusayn [*q.v.*] as a secretary and as ꜛtor to Ṭāhir's son ʿAbd Allāh, whose children he ꜛrther tutored and whose secretary and also libraꜛan he was. In particular, he had the duty of judging ꜛe value of the poems addressed to his master, and was in this capacity that he came to reject a poem y Abū Tammām, who protested violently. He was, ꜛdeed, very much attached to the classical ways, ꜛd it was doubtless for this reason that al-Ma'mūn ꜛ appreciated his poetic work, finding it superior ꜛ that of Djarīr. Bedouin in tradition and classical ꜛ mould, this poetry was largely made up of eulogies f the two Ṭāhirids, though nothing has survived of is poems addressed to Ṭāhir. His *dīwān* amounted to ꜛoo leaves, according to the *Fihrist*, 234, and also ꜛontained eulogies of the sons of Sahl, al-Ḥasan and ꜛl-Faḍl.

Abu 'l-ʿAmaythal ranks equally as a philologist, ꜛo whom various works of a technical character are ꜛttributed, sc. the *K. al-Tashābuh* (*al-Tashābīh?*), *K. ꜛl-Abyāt al-sā'ira* and *K. Maʿānī 'l-shiʿr*; F. Krenꜛkow published in 1925 his *K. al-Ma'thūr fī-mā 'ttafaḳa ꜛafẓuhu wa-khtalafa maʿnāhu*.

Bibliography: Djāḥiẓ, *Bayān*, i, 280; idem, *Ḥayawān*, i, 155, vi, 316 where, unless the text is corrupt, he is curiously described as a *rādjiz*; Ibn Ṭayfūr, *K. Baghdād*, Cairo 1368/1949, 164; Ibn Ḳutayba, *ʿUyūn*, i, 85; Ibn al-Muʿtazz, *Ṭabaḳāt*, 135-6; *Fihrist*, 72-3, 234; Ḳālī, *Amālī*, i, 98; Bakrī, *Simṭ al-la'ālī*, 308 and index; Āmidī, *Muwāzana*, Cairo 1961-5, i, 20-1; Marzubānī, *Muwashshaḥ*, 14; Ibn Khallikān, *Wafayāt*, No. 344, tr. de Slane, ii, 55-7; al-Rāghib al-Iṣfahānī, *Muḥāḍarāt*, i, 102; Ibn ʿAbd Rabbihi, *ʿIḳd*, i, 59; Yāḳūt, *Buldān*, iii, 832, iv, 796; Ibshīhī, *Mustaṭraf*, i, 84; Yāfiʿī, *Mir'āt al-djanān*, ii, 130-1; Nuwayrī, *Nihāya*, vi, 85; Ibn Abī Ṭāhir Ṭayfūr, *K. Baghdād*, Cairo 1368/1949, 164; Brockelmann, S I, 195; C. E. Bosworth, *The Ṭāhirids and Arabic culture*, in *JSS*, xiv (1969), 58; J. E. Bencheikh, *Les voies d'une création*, Sorbonne thesis 1971, unpubl., 108 and index. (ED.)

ABŪ ʿAMMĀR ʿABD AL-KĀFĪ B. ABĪ YAʿḲŪB B. ISMĀʿĪL AL-T(A)NĀW(A)TĪ, Ibāḍī theologian who lived in the middle of the 6th/13th century. He studied in the oasis of Wargla/Wardjlān (in modern Algeria) with Abū Zakariyyā' Yaḥyā b. Abī Bakr, the famous Ibāḍī historian (cf. *EI*², I, 167), and also in Tunis, with what must have been Sunnī authorities there. He was a tribesman, and as such he does not entirely fit the model of the bourgeois scholar; he is reported to have come with his herds to the Mzāb and to have proselytised among the tribes of that region, one which was to become a stronghold of Ibāḍī faith later on.

His main work is the *K. al-Mūdjiz* (*Mūdjaz?*) *fī taḥṣīl al-su'āl wa-takhlīṣ al-ḍalāl* (or *wa-talkhīṣ al-maḳāl*), a rather voluminous manual of Ibāḍī theology and polemics against contrary opinions (for its contents cf. *ZDMG*, cxxvi (1976), 56 f.; for manuscripts, cf. *ibid.*, 56; Kubiak, in *RIMA*, (1959), 21, no. 26; Schacht, in *Revue Africaine*, c (1956), 391, no. 80; also in the libraries of Maḥfūẓ ʿAlī al-Bārūnī, Djerba, and Ayyūb Muḥammad, Djannāwan, Djādjū; ʿAmmār Ṭālibī, Univ. of Algiers, is preparing an edition). In addition, he wrote a commentary to the anonymous *K. al-Djahālāt*, a brief collection of questions and answers used by Ibāḍī missionaries for theological discussion (cf. *ZDMG*, cxxvi (1976), 43 ff.). His *K. al-Istiṭāʿa* seems to be lost. In *fiḳh* he dealt with the law of inheritance; his *K. al-Farā'iḍ* exists in a printed edition (cf. Schacht in *Rev. Afr.*, c (1956), 387, no. 52). Among his historical works are a *K. al-Siyar* (for mss., cf. Schacht, *op. cit.*, 141, and Lewicki, in *RO*, xi (1935), 165 n. 7: preserved?) and a *Mukhtaṣar ṭabaḳāt al-mashāyikh* (cf. Ennami, in *JSS*, xv (1971), 86, no. 17-1, and note by van Ess in *ZDMG*, cxxvi (1976), 57). An epistle concerning the problem of *al-waʿd wa 'l-waʿīd* addressed to him by a certain ʿAbd al-Wahhāb b. Muḥammad b. Ghālib b. Numayr al-Anṣārī was incorporated by his contemporary Abū Yaʿḳūb Yūsuf b. Ibrāhīm al-Wardjlānī (died 570/1174; cf. *GAL*, S I, 692) into his *K. ad-Dalīl li-ahl al-ʿuḳūl* (cf. lith. Cairo 1306, 54-72).

Bibliography: (apart from the references mentioned in the article): Shammākhī, *Siyar* (lith. Cairo 1301/1883), 441 ff.; A. de C. Motylinski, in *Bull. Corr. Afr.*, iii (1885), 27, no. 68; T. Lewicki, in *REI*, viii (1934), 278, in *Fol. Or.*, iii (1961), 33 ff., and in *Cahiers d'histoire mondiale*, xiii (1971), 86; A. Kh. Ennami, *Studies in Ibāḍism* (Diss. Cambridge 1971, unpublished), 292 ff. (J. VAN ESS)

ABŪ ʿAMR AL-SHAYBĀNĪ, ISḤĀḲ B. MIRĀR, one of the most important philologists of the Kūfan school in the 2nd/8th century, and the contemporary of the two great figures of the rival Baṣran school, Abū ʿUbayda and al-Aṣmaʿī [*q.vv.*]. He was born in *ca.* 100/719 at Ramādat al-Kūfa, and derived his *nisba* from the Banū Shaybān because he was their neighbour and client and because he also acted as tutor to the sons of certain members of the tribe. After having studied under the masters of the Kūfan school, such as al-Mufaḍḍal al-Ḍabbī, he went out into the desert, where he lived for a considerable time amongst the Bedouins, collecting tribal poetry. Then he settled in Baghdād, where he taught until his death at an advanced age, since he died in *ca.* 210/825, by then more than a centenarian, leaving behind him sons and grandsons who transmitted his works. Amongst his pupils were the main Kūfan grammarians, sc. Thaʿlab, Ibn al-Sikkīt and Ibn Sallām [*q.vv.*].

Al-Shaybānī was famed above all as a transmitter (*rāwiya*) of old poetry. Thaʿlab records that he left for the desert armed with two inkholders and did not return until the ink had been exhausted. According to his son ʿAmr, he collected the poetry of over 80 tribes, which he wrote out and arranged with his own hands in separate collections and then placed in the mosque of Kūfa. The collections have not come down to us, but they were abundantly used by later anthologists.

However, al-Shaybānī was equally known as a lexicographer especially interested in rare words (*nawādir*) and in dialect words and phrases (*lughāt*). Only one of the many works in this sphere attributed to him by the biographers has survived, the *K. al-Djīm*, so-called because it was unfinished and did not go beyond the fourth letter of the alphabet, although the sources term it equally the *K. al-Nawādir*, *K. al-Ḥurūf* and *K. al-Lughāt*. According to F. Krenkow, who proposed to edit it after the unique manuscript preserved in the Escurial, this work is a dictionary of words peculiar to the speech of the many tribes from whom al-Shaybānī collected poetry. It is of great lexical richness, and is all the more important for the knowledge of the old dialects, since Krenkow found from a detailed perusal of the *Lisān al-ʿArab* that later lexicographers did not use al-Shaybānī's work.

Finally, he is also said to have been a traditionist worthy of being relied upon, transmitting a large number of authentic *ḥadīth*s; his most celebrated pupil here was the *imām* Aḥmad b. Ḥanbal, whose son ʿAbd Allāh transmitted al-Shaybānī's work called the *K. Gharīb al-ḥadīth*.

The post-Ibn al-Nadīm biographers attribute to Abū ʿAmr al-Shaybānī several works which, according to the *Fihrist*, belong really to his son ʿAmr.

Bibliography: Brockelmann, I, 116, S I, 179; *EI*[1], art. *al-Shaibānī* (Krenkow); Kaḥḥāla, *Muʾallifīn*, ii, 238. (G. Troupeau)

ABU 'l-ʿANBAS al-ṢAYMARĪ, Muḥammad b. Isḥāḳ b. Ibrāhīm b. Abi 'l-Mughīra b. Māhān (213-75/828-88), a famous humorist of the ʿAbbāsid court, who was also a *faḳīh*, astrologer, oneiromancer, poet and man of letters, and who wrote some forty works, both serious and jesting, even burlesque and obscene. Of Kūfan origin, he was first of all *ḳāḍī* in the district from which he derived his *nisba*, Ṣaymara, near Baṣra, at the mouth of the Nahr Maʿḳil, but his vivid penchant for coarse humour very early earned him a reputation as a buffoon sufficient for him to be admitted to the court circle of al-Mutawakkil (232-47/847-61), whose courtier he now became. It is likely that he remained at court under his successors, and he is known to have enjoyed the favour of al-Muʿtamid (256-79/870-92). He died in the capital, but was buried at Kūfa.

Abu 'l-ʿAnbas was quite an original character, and one is tempted to speak of his personality as being a split one, even though we are lacking in knowledge about the chronology and actual content of his works. It is well known that, from earliest Islamic times, the profession of buffoon paradoxically developed in Arabia (see F. Rosenthal, *Humour in early Islam*, Leiden 1956), but the fame of the humorists of the period was built essentially on their skill in making up amusing stories or in indulging in clowning to distract their masters, without really taking part in literary activity (it is insulting to number amongst them, as certain critics have gone so far as to do, a Djāḥiẓ, whose humour was of a quite different quality). Now, if our interpretation of the titles of Abu 'l-ʿAnbas's works, listed in the *Fihrist* (151, 278; ed. Cairo, 216, 388) and Yāḳūt's *Muʿdjam al-udabāʾ* (xviii, 8-14 = *Irshād al-arīb*, vi, 401-6) is correct, he may be considered on one hand, if not the creator, at least a prominent representative of a type of literature which was to culminate in the *maḳā*[...] and then in a burlesque or obscene type of *a*[...] and on the other hand, as an astrologer, a *mutaka*[...] and perhaps even a serious depictor of society.

At the court, he acted as royal jester, and [...] occasion, he would be charged with expressing, i[...] facetious, impertinent and personal manner, the c[...] iph's own feelings or opinions (see especially [...] oft-quoted episode concerning his reply to al-Buḥt[...] when the latter had been rather offensive: al-Ṣ[...] *Ashʿār awlād al-khulafāʾ*, ed. J. Heyworth-Dun[...] London 1936, 325; al-Masʿūdī, *Murūdj*, vii, 202-4 § 2885-8; *Aghānī*[1], xviii, 173 = ed. Beirut, xxi, 5[...] al-Ḥuṣrī, *Djamʿ al-djawāhir*, 15-16; Yāḳūt, *Udab*[...] xviii, 12-14; etc.). Like his predecessors, he co[...] also make up amusing stories, since we read that th[...] were gathered together, with his poetry, in an in[...] pendent volume, passages from which may be fou[...] in authors like Ibn ʿAbd Rabbihi (*ʿIḳd*, Cairo 19[...] iv, 148) and even Ibn al-Djawzī (*Akhbār al-ḥamḳā* [...] *'l-mughaffalīn*, Damascus 1345, 85, 111, 141, 14[...] and which attests the influence exercised by the i[...] imitable Djāḥiẓian *adab* on the most serious of a[...] thors. In this respect, Abu 'l-ʿAnbas probably differ[...] very little from other "humorous figures" who, as v[...] know from the *Fihrist*, left behind collections [...] stories; but he is distinguished from them by a seri[...] of works whose titles lead one to think that they we[...] burlesque or scabrous. The *K. Faḍl al-sullam ʿalā* [...] *daradj* "Superiority of the ladder over the staircase" for example, must have been purely humorous, b[...] the *K. Nawādir al-ḳawwād(a)* "Remarkable stori[...] about pimps", to mention only this one work, mus[...] certainly have descended to pornography. After al[...] there emerges from a conversation between Abu '[...] ʿAnbas and his crony Abu 'l-ʿIbar (al-Ṣūlī, *loc. cit.* *Aghānī*, ed. Beirut, xxiii, 77-8) that if he had aban[...] doned scholarship (*ʿilm*) for *sukhf* and *raḳāʿa* i.e. ob[...] scenity and burlesque, it was because these last wer[...] much more profitable and lucrative. In the course o[...] this dialogue, which took place in al-Mutawakkil'[...] caliphate, Abu 'l-ʿAnbas declares that he has writte[...] over 30 works on *sukhf* and *raḳāʿa*; does this mea[...] that the lists which we possess are very incomplete that the works which appear to be serious in conten[...] are not serious at all, or that after al-Mutawakkil's death, this writer came back again to topics less frivolous than certain titles would suggest?

Some of these titles recall works of al-Djāḥiẓ, to the extent that C. E. Bosworth (see *Bibl.*) has wondered whether Abu 'l-ʿAnbas might have plagiarised the former writer's work; the possibility of an influence here must be seriously considered, since one finds in the list a *K. al-Ikhwān wa 'l-aṣdiḳāʾ* and a *K. Masāwī 'l-ʿawāmm wa-akhbār al-sifla wa 'l-aghtām* and even a *K. al-Thuḳalāʾ* "Book of Bores"; in order to know the truth here, it would be necessary to know what lay behind these titles.

The poetry of al-Ṣaymarī has been referred to above; to judge by those poems available for reading, they were not all licentious and scatological, since they include the well-known line "How many sick persons have survived the physician and visitors, when all hope of cure had been given up".

The lists bring out the existence of at least one work which seems to be of a theological nature, the *K. Taʾkhīr al-maʿrifa*, which is alone cited—and doubtless deliberately—by Yāḳūt in his *Muʿdjam al-buldān* (s.v. Ṣaymara), whilst the same author enumerates some 40 titles in his *Irshād al-arīb*. In fact, Abu 'l-ʿAnbas, called by Abu 'l-ʿIbar a *mutakallim*, must apparently have been a Muʿtazilī, and because

.is he was dignified by being cited by Ibn Batta
.aoust, *La profession de foi d'Ibn Batta*, Damascus
, 170) amongst "the people of infidelity and
:", who for him mean the Muʿtazila. On another
, one finds other titles which give the impres-
that Abu 'l-ʿAnbas was equally interested in
entific" topics. If his *K. al-Radd ʿalā 'l-mutaṭa-
ᵢn*, directed against charlatans and homeopathic
sicians, strictly speaking belongs to the depicting
ociety, his *K. al-Radd ʿalā Abī Mikhāʾīl al-Ṣay-
ni* (?) *fi 'l-kimiyāʾ* may not be a general refuta-
of alchemy, and his *K. al-Djawāris̲h̲ wa 'l-dar-
ūt* might lead one to take him for a pharmacol-
t. The *K. Tafsīr al-ruʾyā* is quite explicable, since
rocriticism can be connected with astrology,
ch gave Abu 'l-ʿAnbas a lasting fame. In fact, if
above-mentioned works suffered from the reaction
ietistic circles against *sukh̲f* and *hazl* in general,
ling the *warrāḳūn* to cease at an early date copy-
them, Ṣaymarī's name still appears in manuscript
logues, even though the titles given there hardly
respond at all to the following ones, figuring in the
y lists: *K. al-Mawālīd*, *K. Aḥkām al-nudjūm*, *K.
Mudkhal ilā s̲h̲ināʿat al-nudjūm* and *K. al-Radd ʿalā
unadjdjimīn*. In fact, a *K. Aṣl al-uṣūl* attributed
ᵢim is preserved in both the B.N. of Paris (6608)
l the B.M. of London (Suppl. Rieu, 775; cf.
ockelmann, S I, 396), but Ibn al-Nadīm asserts
t he appropriated the *K. al-Uṣūl* of Abū Maʿs̲h̲ar,
l al-Ḳifṭī (*T. al-Ḥukamāʾ*, ed. Lippert, Leipzig
·3, 410) accuses him of plundering other people's
tings and putting them forward as his own compo-
ons. There are several extant manuscripts of an-
ᵢer work, the *K. fi 'l-Ḥisāb al-nudjūmī*, but the *K.
ᵢkām al-nudjūm* mentioned in the early lists and by
ockelmann is merely the opening of the *Ḥisāb
ᵢjūmī*, whose copy preserved in the Vatican is
ᵢeresting, since it is dated 30 Rabīʿ I 1221/17 June
06 and testifies to the continuing successfulness of
s manual of astrology, and at the same time to the
pect accorded to the author, al-Ṣaymarī, depicted
a most learned philosopher who left a masterpiece
posterity. G. Levi della Vida (*Elenco di mano-
itti arabo islamici della Biblioteca Vaticana*, Vatican
ᵢy 1935, Nos. 955/8 and 957) is not far wrong in
ᵢinking that we have here another redaction of the
Aṣl al-uṣūl, hence in the end, of a recasting of
ᵢū Maʿs̲h̲ar's work. Consequently, it seems that
ᵢere is nothing left of Abu 'l-ʿAnbas's genuine work,
ᵢich therefore enjoys in the "scientific" sphere a
ᵢurious reputation. Even so, he must have enjoyed
ᵢertain importance, since Ibn Baṭṭa felt the need to
ᵢiticise him. Also, as well as the *adab* writers who
ᵢote anecdotes of his, one famous author, Badīʿ al-
ᵢmān, thought to make him a kind of romantic per-
ᵢnality by reserving for him the *maḳāma* of Ṣaymara,
which Abu 'l-ʿAnbas is both narrator and hero.
. this, he tells how, after having been rich and
ᵢspitable, he had been abandoned by his friends,
ᵢd been transformed into a vagabond in the style of
ᵢe age and hence able to acquire a knowledge of the
ᵢivolous poetry of the elegant circles and of the *sukh̲f*
ᵢ the professional entertainers sufficient for him to
ᵢcover his old position in Bag̲h̲dād and then take his
ᵢvenge on his faithless former friends.

Bibliography: In addition to the sources cited
in the article, see K̲h̲aṭīb Bag̲h̲dādī, *Taʾrīkh̲*, i, 238;
Akhbār al-Buḥturī, index; Ḳifṭī, *al-Muḥammadūn
min al-s̲h̲uʿarāʾ*, Beirut 1390/1970, No. 101; Ibn al-
Djarrāḥ, *Waraḳa*, 5; Marzubānī, *Muʿdjam*, 393;
idem, *Muwas̲h̲s̲h̲aḥ*, 285; Ibn al-Djawzī, *Muntaẓam*,
vi, 99; Ibn Tag̲h̲rībirdī, *Nudjūm*, iii, 74; Suter,

Mathematiker, Leipzig 1900, 30; Kaḥḥāla, ix, 38;
Ziriklī, vi, 202; F. Bustānī, *DM*, iv, 486-7; M. F.
G̲h̲azi, in *Arabica*, iv (1957), 168; Ch. Pellat, *Un
curieux amuseur bagdādien: Abu 'l-ʿAnbas as-Ṣay-
marī*, in *Studia or. in mem. C. Brockelmann*, Halle
1968, 133-7; C. E. Bosworth, *The mediaeval Islamic
underworld*, Leiden 1976, i, 30-2; Muḥammad Bāḳir
ʿAlwān, *Abu 'l-ʿAnbas Muḥammad b. Isḥāḳ al-Ṣaymarī*, in *al-Abḥāth*, xxvi (1973-7), Arabic section,
35-50.　(Ch. Pellat)

ABŪ 'L-ASAD AL-ḤIMMĀNĪ, Nubāta b. ʿAbd
Allāh, minor poet of the ʿAbbāsid period,
originally from Dīnawar. His talent was only moderate, and it was ʿAllawayh/ʿAllūya who rescued him
from oblivion, since this singer, the poet's friend,
introduced him to the great men of the age and,
above all, set some of his verses to music, so that
they enjoyed a great success. His career seems to
have been quite a lengthy one. He is found, first
of all, satirising as early as 153/770 two of al-Manṣūr's
mawālī, Ṣāʿid and Maṭar (al-Djahs̲h̲iyārī, *Wuzarāʾ*,
124), and then frequenting Abū Dulaf al-ʿIdjlī [see
AL-ḲĀSIM B. ʿĪSĀ], at whose court he was however
eclipsed, it is said, by ʿAlī b. Djabala [see AL-ʿAKAW-
WAK]. After having previously sung the praises of the
ruler of al-Karadj [q.v.], he launched at him a somewhat coarse diatribe and then turned to the former
secretary of al-Mahdī, al-Fayḍ b. Abī Ṣāliḥ (on whom
see Sourdel, *Vizirat*, index), whose praises he now
sang (al-Djahs̲h̲iyārī, 164; Ibn al-Ṭiḳṭaḳā, *Fakhrī*, ed.
Derenbourg, 256, calls the poet Abu 'l-Aswad). But
the chronology of these events is uncertain, and it is
even probable that, contrary to what the *Ag̲h̲ānī*
asserts, his relations with al-Fayḍ (who died in 173/
789-90) were anterior to his stay with Abū Dulaf.
Amongst those whose patronage he sought, one even
finds Aḥmad b. Abī Duʾād [q.v.], who gave him a
modest gift and begged him to cease importuning
him. It is, on the other hand, dubious that he was
able to make a claim upon ʿAlī b. Yaḥyā al-Munadjdjim (d. 275/888-9) and to address to him a lengthy
anti-S̲h̲uʿūbī satire; but the intermediary whom he
thanks for having secured for him satisfaction could
well have been Ḥamdūn b. Ismāʿīl [see IBN ḤAMDŪN].

To judge by the few extant fragments of his verse,
Abu 'l-Asad had no compunction about composing
scabrous epigrams in order to get his revenge on people
for the neglect which he sometimes received where
he had expected a reward. But he was also able to
express very delicate feelings, as in his elegy on
Ibrāhīm al-Mawṣilī (d. 188/804 [q.v.]), whose outspokenness was nevertheless criticised.

Bibliography: In addition to references given
in the article, see *Ag̲h̲ānī*, xiv, 124-35; Bustānī,
DM, iv, 171.　(Ed.)

ABŪ ʿĀṢIM AL-NABĪL, AL-Ḍaḥḥāk b. Makhlad
b. Muslim b. al-Ḍaḥḥāk al-S̲h̲aybānī al-Baṣrī,
traditionist, born at Mecca in 122/740 but established subsequently at Baṣra, where he transmitted
from a host of scholars (notably al-Asmaʿī) a large
quantity of *ḥadīth*s gathered by himself, and especially from several *tābiʿī*s or Successors. He was considered as trustworthy, and some of his *ḥadīth*s were
included in the great collections; his biographers assert that he never fabricated a single one, although
he is said to have declared that pious men never lie
so much as in regard to traditions from the Prophet
(Goldziher, *Muh. Stud.*, ii, 47, Eng. tr. 55). It is said
that he was never seen with a book in his hand and
that we was knowledgeable about *fiḳh*. Despite such
details as these, little is known of his life. Physically,
he was remarkable for the size of his nose, and this

particularity is one of the explanations given for his name of al-Nabīl. It is also recorded that he owed this name to his habit of wearing fine clothes, or because he freed his own slave in order to release S̲h̲uʿba [*q.v.*] from his oath not to transmit *ḥadīt̲h̲*s for a month. A final explanation seems the most plausible; some elephants passed through Baṣra, and all the population rushed out to see the spectacle, whilst he however stayed with his master Ibn D̲j̲urayd̲j̲ [*q.v.* in Suppl.], who gave him the title of "noble". He probably died on 14 D̲h̲u 'l-Ḥid̲j̲d̲j̲a 212/5 March 828 at Baṣra.

Bibliography: D̲j̲āḥiẓ, *Bayān*, ii, 38; Ibn Saʿd, *Ṭabaḳāt*, vii, 295; *Fihrist*, ed. Cairo, 163; Ibn Ḥad̲j̲ar, *Tahd̲h̲īb*, iv, 450-3; Ibn al-ʿImād, *S̲h̲ad̲h̲arāt*, ii, 28; Bustānī, *DM*, iv, 416. (Ch. Pellat)

ABU 'L-ʿAZĀʾIM, Muḥammad Māḍī, an Egyptian and a political activist, was born in the town of Ras̲h̲īd on 27 Rad̲j̲ab 1286/2 November 1869 and grew up in the village of Maḥallat Abū ʿAlī near Dasūḳ in the present-day G̲h̲arbiyya province. He studied at al-Azhar [*q.v.*] and at Dār al-ʿUlūm [*q.v.*]. He graduated in 1308/1890-1 and spent the subsequent twenty-five years as a teacher at various provincial government schools in Egypt and the Sudan as well as at Gordon College in Khartoum. At the latter establishment he taught Islamic Law from 1905 until August 1915, when he was forcibly repatriated to Egypt—following his refusal to declare himself in support of British administrative reforms in the Sudan, and his public opposition to these—where his freedom of movement was restricted to al-Minyā province. About a year later, in 1916, he was allowed to take up residence in Cairo, where he devoted himself to the propagation of his own conception of the S̲h̲ād̲h̲iliyya [*q.v.*] order, into which he had been initiated by Ḥasanayn al-Ḥiṣāfī [*q.v.*]. He had been actively proselytising on behalf of his *ṭarīḳa* [*q.v.*], which became known as al-ʿAzamiyya al-S̲h̲ād̲h̲iliyya, already since the beginning of his teaching career, and had obtained a substantial following for himself in Egypt as well as in the Sudan. Al-ʿAzamiyya distinguished itself by the stress it placed upon inner-worldly asceticism in conjunction with active social commitment in conformance with the precepts of the Law, as opposed to the retraitist other-wordly asceticism and its underlying relatively negative appreciation of life in this world, as found implicitly or explicitly in the teachings of many *ṭarīḳa*s. After 1916, however, when settled in Cairo, Muḥammad Māḍī ceased to look upon himself as merely head of a *ṭarīḳa*, but assumed the more comprehensive role of religious reformer (*mud̲j̲addid*) instead, and consequently presented his *ṭarīḳa* as his conception of a revitalised Islam, which he elaborated over the following years in a variety of books and articles, notably in the periodicals *al-Saʿāda al-Abadiyya* (a bi-monthly published by one of Muḥammad Māḍī's disciples, ʿAlī ʿAbd al-Raḥmān al-Ḥusaynī, from 1914 until 1923) and *al-Madīna al-Munawwara* (a weekly published from 1925 until 1927, and after 1927 until 1929, when it was merged with *al-Fātiḥ*, a periodical of the Aḥrār al-Dustūriyyīn, edited by Muḥammad Maḥmūd, as *al-Fātiḥ wa 'l-Madīna al-Munawwara*). The majority of these books as well as the periodicals were printed by the Maṭbaʿa al-Madīna al-Munawwara, a press established by Muḥammad Māḍī in early 1919. In his aversion to the British presence in Egypt, he committed himself to the case of the nationalists during the revolution of 1919, when he was twice arrested. On 20 March 1924, less than three weeks after the abolition of the caliphate in Turkey [see K̲h̲alīfa], he organ a meeting in Cairo, which was attended by sch and religious dignitaries from all over the Isl world, in order to discuss the implications of event. This meeting ended in the foundation of so-called D̲j̲amāʿat al-K̲h̲ilāfa al-Islāmiyya bi-W al-Nīl under his presidency. Because of its histo consequences, the foundation of this organisa must be considered as Abu 'l-ʿAzāʾim's most not achievement. It allowed him to mobilise an effec world-wide opposition against King Aḥmad Fuʾ candidacy for the caliphate—to which he objec for religious and political reasons (cf. Aḥmad S̲h̲a *Ḥawliyyāt Miṣr al-siyāsiyya*, Cairo 1929, iii, 105 —and thus determined the outcome of the Caliph Conference held in Cairo in May 1926 and brou activity in support of Aḥmad Fuʾād's candidacy an end. Muḥammad Māḍī died on 28 Rad̲j̲ab 13 4 October 1937 and was buried in his *zāwiya* [*q* in Cairo near the mosque of al-Sulṭān al-Ḥanafī. H his shrine as well as the shrine of his son Aḥm (d. 1970), who succeeded him as head of the *ṭarī* may be visited in a newly-built mosque (opened January 1962), which houses the headquarters of ʿAzamiyya *ṭarīḳa*.

Bibliography: The most extensive biograp is ʿAbd al-Munʿim Muḥammad S̲h̲aḳraf, *al-Im Muḥammad Māḍī Abu 'l-ʿAzāʾim, ḥayātuhu, d hāduhu, āt̲h̲āruhu*, Cairo 1972. It contains the te of various relevant documents, evaluates l poetry, clarifies his position with respect to t idea of *al-insān al-kāmil* [*q.v.*], sets forth his co ception of *tawḥīd* (based upon an unpublish treatise), and lists and summarises his works. these must be added *Min d̲j̲awāmiʿ al-kalim*, Ca 1962; *al-Wad̲j̲dāniyyāt* (ed. ʿAbd Allāh Māḍī A 'l-ʿAzāʾim), Cairo n.d.; *Dīwān* (ed. Muḥammad Bas̲h̲īr Māḍī Abu 'l-ʿAzāʾim), Cairo n.d. (mimec *al-Ṭarīḳa al-ʿAzamiyya* (ed. Maḥmūd Māḍī A 'l-ʿAzāʾim), Cairo 1328/1910, (important for h affiliations with various *ṭarīḳa*s); and *al-S̲h̲ifāʾ m maraḍ al-tafriḳa*, Cairo n.d., which caused t temporary imprisonment of Muḥammad Māḍī wh it was interpreted as a concealed attack upon Ki Aḥmad Fuʾād (cf. *al-Wad̲j̲dāniyyāt*, 8). The treati *Wasāʾil iẓhār al-ḥaḳḳ*, Cairo n.d., should be e cluded from S̲h̲aḳraf's enumeration. It was writte by Muḥammad's brother, the journalist Aḥma Māḍī (d. 1893), who had founded the newspap *al-Muʾayyad* together with ʿAlī Yūsuf [*q.v.*]. Th treatise was published for the first time in Cai in 1914, by Aḥmad's brother Maḥmud. The autho ship was falsely assigned to Muḥammad Abu ' ʿAzāʾim by his son and successor Aḥmad in th subsequent editions published under his auspice For additional biographical materials, see Muḥam mad ʿAbd al-Munʿim K̲h̲afād̲j̲ī, *al-Turāt̲h̲ al-rūḥ li 'l-taṣawwuf al-islāmī fī Miṣr*, Cairo n.d., 17 For details about the history of the al-ʿAzamiyy *ṭarīḳa* and further references, see also F. de Jong *Two anonymous manuscripts relative to the Ṣūf orders in Egypt*, in *Bibliotheca Orientalis*, xxx (1975), 186-90. For the ʿAzamiyya in the Sudan see J. S. Trimingham, *Islam in the Sudan*, Londo 1949, 239 f. On his *mawlid*, see J. W. McPherson *The moulids of Egypt*, Cairo 1940, 140 ff. A smal collection of letters written by Muḥammad Māḍ and transcripts thereof, which are in the possessio of the ʿAzamī family, is preserved on microfilm a Leiden University Library. (F. de Jong)

ABŪ BAKR IBN ʿABD AL-ṢAMAD [see ʿAbd al-Ṣamad].

BŪ BAKR IBN AL-**ʿARABĪ** [see IBN AL-ʿARABĪ].

BŪ BAKR AL-**AṢAMM** [see AL-AṢAMM in pl.].

BŪ BAKR AL-**KHARĀʾIṬĪ** [see AL-KHARĀ-.

BŪ BAKR AL-**ZUBAYDĪ** [see AL-ZUBAYDĪ].

BU 'L-BARAKĀT AL-ʿALAWĪ AL-ZAYDĪ, ʿUMAR BRĀHĪM B. MUḤAMMAD, Kūfan grammarian, isprudent, Ḳurʾān scholar and tradition- He was born in Kūfa in 442/1050-1, heard *ḥadīth* is home town and Baghdād, and stayed for some e, together with his father, in Damascus, Aleppo Ṭarābulus. In Aleppo he read in 455/1063 the *l-Īḍāḥ* of Abū ʿAlī al-Fārisī which he later trans-ted in Kūfa. There he finished on 5 Ramaḍān 464/ May 1072 the reading of the *K. al-Djāmiʿ al-kāfī*, extensive collection of Kūfan Zaydī *fiḳh* doctrine the Sayyid Abū ʿAbd Allāh Muḥammad b. ʿAli Alawī. He read it with the Sayyid ʿAbd al-Djabbār l-Ḥusayn b. Muʿayya, who had heard it from the hor, though he also transmitted directly from Abū d Allāh al-ʿAlawī with an *idjāza*. He taught and the prayer in the mosque of Abū Isḥāḳ al-Sabīʿī. his works on grammar, a commentary on the *K. Lumaʿ* of Ibn Djinnī is extant in manuscript (see ockelmann, S I, 192). A descendant of Zayd b. ʿAlī, u 'l-Barakāt personally adhered to Zaydī Shīʿī iefs, though he generally concealed them from his nnī students and gave legal *fatwā*s according to nafī doctrine. Only to Shīʿīs did he transmit par-an Shīʿī *ḥadīth*s and rendered *fatwā*s according to ydī law. In agreement with the Zaydī creed in his ne, he upheld the doctrine of human free will and createdness of the Ḳurʾān. He died on 7 Shaʿbān 9/2 February 1145 in Kūfa.

Bibliography: Samʿānī, f. 283b; Ibn al-Anbārī, *Nuzhat al-alibbāʾ*, ed Muḥ. Abu 'l-Faḍl Ibrāhīm, Cairo 1967, 399 f.; Ibn al-Djawzī, *al-Muntaẓam*, Ḥaydarābād 1357-59/1938-41, x, 114; Yāḳūt, *Udabāʾ*, xi, 12-14; Ibn al-Ḳifṭī, *Inbāh al-ruwāt*, ed. Muḥ. Abu 'l-Faḍl Ibrāhīm, Cairo 1950-73, ii, 324-7; al-Dhahabī, *Mīzān al-iʿtidāl*, ed. A. M. al-Bidjāwī, Cairo 1382/1963, iii, 181; Ibn ʿInaba, *ʿUmdat al-ṭālib*, ed. Muḥ. Ḥasan Āl al-Ṭāliḳānī, Nadjaf 1380/ 1961, 263; Ibn Ḥadjar, *Lisān al-mīzān*, Ḥaydarābād 1331/1913, iv, 280-2; Ṣārim al-Dīn Ibrāhīm b. al-Ḳāsim, *Ṭabaḳāt al-Zaydiyya*, ms. photocopy no. 290 Cairo, Dār al-Kutub, 314.

(W. MADELUNG)

ABŪ BARĀḲISH (A.) a name, no longer in use, ven, according to localities, to two birds whose illiant plumage is characterised by iridescent colours shows a colour-scheme varying in the course of e seasons. The quadriliteral root *B-R-Ḳ-Sh*, prob-ly derived from the triliteral *R-B-Ḳ*, has, like *Ḳ-Sh*, the sense of "to be variegated, mottled" d the substantive *birḳish* indicates the result, synon-nous with *talawwun*. The plural *barāḳish* has a perlative quality in expressions such as *bilād barā-ish* "a land decked with flowers" and it is used as a rename; it was the name of the wife of Luḳmān .v.], and of a bitch that became proverbial for her ility to foresee and to foretell with her barking e return to camp of the horsemen of her tribe. s for the plural of the composite noun *abū barāḳish*, would theoretically be *ābāʾ barāḳish*, but this form not found in literature.

) According to the uniform definition provided by rab lexicographers, the true *abū barāḳish* corre-ponds to this description: "a small bird of the bushes ith a greyish head, a scarlet breast and dark lower arts. Just like the porcupine, when excited it ruffles up all its plumage, showing a whole range of glittering colours". (al-Damīrī, *Ḥayāt al-ḥayawān*, i, 162, and root *B-R-Ḳ-Sh* in the Arabic dictionaries.) Though restrained and concise, this ornithological information is sufficient to identify the *abū barāḳish* as a ploceid, the male in the nuptial plumage of the weaver-bird (*tanawwuṭ nassādj*) the flame-coloured Franciscan or Grenadier, the English Durra-bird (*Euplectes oryx franciscana*), a resident both of the Sudan and of the southern coasts of the Red Sea. In fact, this industrious and gregarious bird, smaller in size than the house sparrow and with plumage that is generally brownish and rather dull, abruptly changes its livery in the mating season and its feathers become soft, velvety, long and finely shaped; the colours are striking: the breast, the back, the upper and lower caudal feathers covering the short tail (whence the expression found in some authors *thaḳīl al-ʿadjz*) are of the purest pink, while the crown of the head and the stomach have a sheen of glistening black. Nubia is the favourite territory of this bird, which was one of the first to be exported and which very soon came to be known to the Arabs. In the period of mating, the male courts three or four females, making a show of bringing them grains of millet, and throughout the period of nestbuilding he constantly asserts his proprietory rights by fluttering and hovering beneath each nest and ruffling all his feathers which sparkle in the light, accompanying his performance with a loud rustling of wings (*ḥafīf*). After the hatching of the young, the actor abandons his deceptive guise and returns to the gregarious life in large flocks whose greed causes sometimes considerable havoc in the cereal crops. The spectacular variations in colour of the plumage of the Grenadier weaver-bird provided for a poet of the Banū Asad an image whereby to stigmatise the inconstant nature of his enemies, and his proverbial lines (written in *kāmil metre*) *ka-abī barāḳisha kulla law | nin lawnu-hu yatakhayyalu* "like *abū barāḳish*, whose colour resembles all colours", have determined the way in which the bird is remembered (see Ibn Ḳutayba, *Adab al-kātib*, Cairo 1355/1936, 204; al-Damīrī, *loc. cit.*; *LA*),

(2) For al-Ḳazwīnī (*ʿAdjāʾib al-makhlūḳāt*, in the margins of al-Damīrī, ii, 252) and for him alone, the *abū barāḳish* is a wader with a pleasant-sounding cry, with red beak and feet, of a size close to that of the stork and with plumage fluctuating in colour, in reds, greens, yellows and blues. The livery of this attractive wading-bird apparently provided Byzantine weavers with the inspiration for the creation of the precious dove-coloured shot silk called *abū ḳalamūn* [*q.v.*], a name which conversely was applied to the bird. Now, the only wader of the Mediterranean and oriental regions perfectly fitting this description is the Porphyrion or Blue Taleva/Purple Gallinule (*Porphyrio porphyrio*), better known however under the grandiose name of "Sultan-fowl". This marshland bird, half-a-metre in height, has feet and beak of a fine coral red and on its forehead a knob of the same colour; its rich blue plumage varies from indigo to turquoise with flashing tints of green, purple and bronze. When alarmed, the Sultan-fowl emits a brief, trumpet-like sound. Its Spanish name is "calamon", a vestige of the Arabic *ḳalamūn*, while Egypt has retained its ancient Greek name πορφυρίων arabised as *furfūr/furfur*, pl. *farāfīr*; Syria and ʿIrāḳ call it *burhān* and *suḥnūn*. All these countries and Persia are also familiar with the "green-backed" sub-species (*Porphyrio aegypticus* or *madagascarensis*), very closely related to the main species and bearing the

names *dīk sulṭānī* "sultan-cock", *dīk al-mā'* "water-cock" and *farkha sulṭāniyya* "sultan-pullet". The Sultan-fowl, easily domesticated, was highly thought of among the Persians, the Greeks and the Romans; it was bred in temples and placed under the protection of the gods. In Egypt, it is not unusual to see it in rural areas co-existing peaceably with domestic poultry. Because of the splendour of its plumage, the Persians awarded it the title *shāhmurgh* "king-bird", arabised in the forms *shāhmurk*, *shāhmurkī*, *shāmūrk*, *shamurk*, *shāhmurdj*, *shahmurdj*. In legends and stories of Persian origin, while the lion is the king of the animals, it is the Sultan-fowl that sits on the throne of the feathered race, and the peacock is only the vizier (see *Rasā'il Ikhwān al-Ṣafā'*, Beirut 1957, ii, 248 ff). Al-Djāḥiẓ several times cites the Sultan-fowl (*Ḥayawān*, passim) as feeding on flies and small reptiles, which is accurate, the diet of this wader being both vegetable and carnivorous; having killed its prey with a violent blow of the beak, it holds it with one foot and tears it with the other, carrying off the morsels of flesh in its beak.

Thus the *abū barāḳish* of the poet of Asad was a weaver-bird, while al-Ḳazwīnī saw it as the Sultan-fowl, worshipped in antiquity, and one is inclined to believe that it was on his own authority that this naturalist, perhaps not knowing the Grenadier weaver-bird, identified the *abū barāḳish* with the *abū ḳalamūn/shāhmurk*; but his decision was regarded as law by his successors, and it should be recognised as such.

(3) In the Ḥidjāz, through a confusion on the part of the children of the nomads, attested by the philologist al-Azharī, *abū barāḳish* was used in place of *birḳish* to denote the chaffinch (*Fringilla coelebs*), a finch well-known in all the Arabic-speaking countries and also called *shurshur* (in the Maghrib, *shershir*, *berḳesh*, *zāneb*); this was simply an error ascribable to childish ignorance.

Finally, we may ignore the totally unfounded identification of the *abū barāḳish* with the bullfinch (*Pyrrhula pyrrhula*) suggested by the encyclopedia *al-Mawsū'a fī 'ulūm al-ṭabī'a* (Beirut 1965, i, no. 154), this western bird being practically unknown in the Near East, in Arabia, in Egypt and the Maghrib.

Bibliography: In addition to references given in the text, there are mentions of the *abū barāḳish* in al-Ḳalḳashandī, *Ṣubḥ*, ii, 76; Kushadjim, *Maṣāyid* . . , Baghdād 1954, wholly imprecise. Ornithology: A. Ma'lūf, *Mu'djam al-ḥayawān*, Cairo 1932, 111, 197; B. Al-Lūs (Allouse), *al-Ṭuyūr al-'irāḳiyya*, ii, Baghdād 1961, 29-30; A. E. Brehm, (*L'homme et les animaux*) *Les oiseaux*, Fr. edn. revised by Z. Gerbe, Paris 1878 ii, 701-3; F. O. Cave and J. D. Macdonald, *Birds of the Sudan*, London 1955, 374; R. D. Etchécopar and F. Hue, *Les oiseaux du nord de l'Afrique*, Paris 1964, 191-5 and 600 (index of Arabic names by F. Viré); idem, *Les oiseaux du Moyen-Orient*, Paris 1970; R. N. Meinertzhagen, *Birds of Egypt*, London 1930; L. Delapchier, *Les oiseaux du monde* (Atlas), Paris 1959, i, 125, ii, 130. (F. Viré)

ABU 'L-BAYḌĀ' AL-RIYĀḤĪ, As'ad b. 'Iṣma, one of the most famous informants of the Baṣran philologists in the 2nd/8th century, notably, of al-Aṣma'ī [*q.v.*]. This Bedouin teacher, settled in southern 'Irāḳ, may have received his curious *kunya* (*bayḍā'* = "desert") from the admirers forming a circle around him. He also wrote poetry, transmitted by another teacher, a certain Abū 'Adnān, who is allegedly the author of several works (in particular, of a *K. al-Naḥwiyyīn* and a *K. Gharīb al-ḥadīth*, *Fihrist*, 68), and whom al-Djāḥiẓ praised greatly his erudition and his fine language (*Bayān*, 1, 2 Abu 'l-Bayḍā' also had as his *rāwiya* his son-in 'Amr b. Kirkira [*q.v.*], but his poetic work is aln wholly lost.

Bibliography: Djāḥiẓ, *Bayān*, i, 66, *Fihrist*, 66; Ibn Ḳutayba, *'Uyūn*, i, 71; Marzub *Muwashshaḥ*, 118, 183; Suyūṭī, *Muzhir*, ii, Yāḳūt, *Udabā'*, vi, 89-90; Bustānī, *DM*, iv, (Ch. Pella

ABŪ ḌABĪ [see abū ẓabī].

ABŪ DĀWŪDIDS [see bānīdjūrids].

ABU 'L-DHAHAB, *kunya* of Muḥammad B a grandee of Ottoman Egypt. Acquired a *mamlūk* by *Bulūṭ ḳapān* 'Alī Bey [*q.v.*] (the d 1175, given in Djabartī, *'Adjā'ib*, i, 417, is obvio incorrect), he became the chief officer in his mast household as *khāzindār* in 1174/1760. When in 11 1764-5 he was raised to the beylicate, he obtai his *kunya* by distributing a largesse of gold. In 11 1770 he commanded the expeditionary force sent 'Alī Bey to install a Hāshimite protégé in Mecca. commander of the force sent by 'Alī Bey in 1185/1 to co-operate with Ẓāhir al-'Umar against 'Uthm Pasha al-Ṣādiḳ, governor of Damascus, he captu the city, but, when the citadel was on the point surrender, withdrew with all his troops to Egy This curious development has been ascribed (e.g. Volney) to the secret negotiations of 'Uthmān Pasl the *iltizām* of Gaza and al-Ramla, which Abu Dhahab received in this same year (Cohen, *Palesti* 49) may have been his reward. As master of an ceptionally large household of *mamlūk*s and bla slaves (*'abīd*), and as the head of a faction, he s ceeded in 1186/1772 in ousting 'Alī Bey, who soug refuge with Ẓāhir al-'Umar. Lured into returning Egypt with a small force, 'Alī Bey was defeated al-Ṣāliḥiyya, and died a few days later (Ṣafar 11 May 1773). Abu 'l-Dhahab was now the effecti ruler of Egypt, where he established peace and curity, so that internal trade revived. Unlike 'Alī Be he followed a policy of ostentatious loyalty to t sultan, and was gratified by investiture as *amīr Mi* i.e. *shaykh al-balad* (Rabī' I 1187/June 1773). He w nevertheless as determined as his former master control Syria, where he represented himself as t defender of the sultanate against the rebel, Ẓāhir 'Umar. The *sandjaḳ* of Gaza and al-Ramla was co ferred on him in 1187/1773 (Cohen, *Palestine*, 14 The fact that he obtained the appointment as vicer of Egypt of a fugitive Palestinian notable, Muṣṭa Pasha Ṭūḳān al-Nābulusī (not a member of the 'Aẓ family, as stated in Djabartī, *'Adjā'ib*, i, 418; Cohen, *Palestine*, 56, n. 97), may also be linked wi his Syrian aims. Early in 1189/March 1175, he led h army into Palestine to overthrow Ẓāhir. Jaffa w captured, and a massacre ensued. Ẓāhir fled fro Acre, his capital, which was about to fall, when Ab 'l-Dhahab died suddenly of fever. His troops returne forthwith to Cairo.

Bibliography: 'Abd al-Raḥmān b. Ḥasan a Djabartī, *'Adjā'ib al-āthār* (Būlāḳ edn.), i, anna for the years indicated and obituary of Abu ' Dhahab on pp. 417-20; Volney, *Voyage en Égypt et en Syrie* (ed. Jean Gaulmier), Paris and Th Hague 1959, especially pp. 78-94 (dates on pp. 91- inaccurate); Amnon Cohen, *Palestine in the 18t century*, Jerusalem 1973. (P. M. Holt)

ABŪ DJA'FAR AL-ANDALUSĪ [see al-ru'aynī

ABŪ DJA'FAR AL-RU'ĀSĪ [see al-ru'āsī].

ABŪ DJA'FAR AL-ṬŪSĪ [see al-ṭūsī].

ABU 'L-DJĀRŪD [see al-djārūdiyya].

BŪ DULAF AL-ʿ**IDJLĪ** [see AL-ĶĀSIM B. ʿĪSĀ].

BU 'L-FAḌĀʾIL [see ḤAMDĀNIDS].

BU 'L-FARADJ B. **MASʿŪD RŪNĪ**, Persian t of the Ghaznawid period, was born and d at Lahore, according to ʿAwfī, the earliest and t trustworthy authority for his life. The *nisba* ī has been related by Indian writers of the 16th 17th centuries to a place by the name of Rūn he vicinity of Lahore (cf. e.g. Badāʾūnī, *Mun-ab al-tawārīkh*, i, Calcutta 1864, 37; *Farhang-i hāngīrī* and *Burhān-i ķāṭiʿ*, s.v.). But already Ba-nī had to admit that this place could not be found where in that area. Others (e.g. Luṭf-ʿAlī Beg ar, *Ātashkada*, lith. Bombay 1299/1882, 122) have gested an origin from Rūna, a village in the ht-i Khāwarān near Nīshāpūr. This would mean Abu 'l-Faradj was descended from Khūrāsānian lers in the Pandjāb who must have come there r the conquest of the region by the Ghaznawids he early 5th/11th century. The mentioning of a ān origin that can be met with in some other rces probably goes back to a confusion with an-er Ghaznawid poet, Abu 'l-Faradj Sidjzī.

he date of his birth is not known. Chronological cations that can be derived from his work make ikely that he started his career as a poet of the rt of Lahore some time before Sayf al-Dīn Maḥ-d was installed there by his father Sulṭān Ibrā- as a viceroy (*wālī*, or *mālik*) of Ghaznawid Hin-tān in 469/1076-7. Abu 'l-Faradj appears to have ained his position at the court of Lahore also ler the successor of Sayf al-Dīn the later Sulṭān sʿūd III, who was in residence there from 480-92/ 7-99 (cf. on events in India under these two vice-s, C. E. Bosworth, *The later Ghaznavids, splendour l decay: the dynasty in Afghanistan and northern lia 1040-1186*, Edinburgh 1977, 65-8). As he ad-sses the latter in most of the poems he wrote for n by the title of *malik*, it may be concluded that y belong to this period. The last poem by Abu 'l-radj that can be dated with certainty is an ode he ote at the occasion of the accession to the throne Lahore of Masʿūd's son Shērzād after his father had come Sulṭān of Ghazna.

The relationship between the poet and the central aznawid court is not quite clear. He wrote several ems for Sulṭān Ibrāhīm and, according to ʿAwfī, ced a *ķaṣīda* addressed to the sultan at the be-ning of his *Dīwān*. There are also poems preserved ich bear dedications to prominent officials of the ntral government, like the *ʿāriḍ-i lashkar* Manṣūr Saʿīd Maymandī who patronised other poets of s period as well. But apart from that, there are no dications of a stay of Abu 'l-Faradj at Ghazna for y long period of time. As Lahore was a base incursions into Hindu territory, in which the ltan and his retinue also participated from time time, most of these poems may very well have en written while the patrons from Ghazna were aying at that city temporarily on their way to a mpaign

It seems, therefore, likely that the scene of Abu Faradj's career was mainly, if not entirely, the urt of Lahore, where the young princes showed a eater interest in poetry than the Sultan himself, ho has been depicted by historians as a stern and ous man. The only contemporary poet who as far as e know now was in personal contact with Abu 'l-aradj was Masʿūd-i Saʿd-i Salmān [*q.v.*], another anian born in the Pandjāb. But the former is to be stinguished from the Abu 'l-Faradj whom Masʿūd eld responsible for his banishment from the court. (cf. *Dīwān-i Masʿūd-i Salmān*, ed. Rashīd Yāsimī, Tehran 1319/1940, Introduction).

The modern Iranian scholar Djalāl al-Dīn Humāʾī has connected one of the poet's *ķaṣīda*s with the conquest of Ķannawdj by Sulṭān Masʿūd III which he dates between 500 and 508 A.H. This would provide an approximate dating for the death of Abu 'l-Faradj (cf. *Dīwān-i ʿUthmān-i Mukhtārī*, ed. Humāʾī, Tehran 1341/1962, 654 ff. and *passim*, and Bosworth, *op. cit.*, 85).

The work of Abu 'l-Faradj, as we know it now, consists mostly of *ķaṣīda*s, and further of some quatrains and *muķaṭṭaʿāt*, as well as a few *ghazal*s of a pre-classical type. The *ķaṣīda*s are comparatively short poems in which the emphasis is laid on the panegyric. In many cases, the conventional *nasīb* has been left out altogether. The poet developed the style of the panegyrical address of the Sāmānid and early Ghaznawid poets into various new directions. The texture of his verse became more knitted through the use of uncommon compounds, original metaphors and hyperboles, and through a greater density in the handling of rhetorical artifices. He also introduced references to elements of religious lore or of the sciences into his poetry with an unprecedented frequency. Through all these features, the work of Abu 'l-Faradj heralds the great change in poetical style which took place in the course of the 6th/12th century and is commonly designated as the development from the Khūrāsānian into the ʿIrāķī style (for brief analyses of the main characteristics of Abu 'l-Faradj's poetry, see the works by Ṣafā, Maḥdjūb and Dāmghānī mentioned in the bibliography).

The stylistic originality of Abu 'l-Faradj was already recognised by his contemporaries and the immediately-following generations of poets. A remarkable instance of his influence is on Anwarī, one of the great masters of the Persian *ķaṣīda*, who did not conceal his indebtedness to this predecessor. The traces of this influence can be noticed in many ways, varying from direct quotations to a more general similarity of ideas, motifs and forms of expressions (cf. *Dīwān-i Anwarī*, ed. by M. T. Mudarris-i Raḍawī, i, Tehran 1347/1968, 104-8).

The wide range of Abu 'l-Faradj's influence is further attested by the many quotations from his poems in the *Kalīla wa-Dimna* adaptation by Naṣr Allāh Munshī, written about 540/1145-6, and by the frequent use of his verses as *shawāhid* by Shams-i Ķays in his textbook on the theory of poetry. In more recent times, a renewed interest in his work emerged after the "return" (*bāzgasht*) to the earlier styles of Persian poetry which occurred in Iran during the late 12th/18th century (cf. Riḍā-Ķulī Khān Hidāyat, *Madjmaʿ al-fuṣaḥāʾ*, *muķaddama*). The perpetual war waged with the non-Muslim neighbours of Ghaznawid Hindūstān is often reflected in his poems. But the identification of events and placenames is still hampered by the philological unsufficiencies of the text of the *Dīwān* as it is accessible at this moment.

It cannot be doubted that the collections of Abu 'l-Faradj's poems differed already at an early date as far as their contents and arrangement are concerned. Even Anwarī could only find a selection (*intikhāb*) from which to make his own copy. The poem opening the *Dīwān*, according to ʿAwfī (= ed. Dāmghānī no. 53), is not the same as that which opens the collections contained in the oldest manuscripts known so far. The first printed text was an addition in the margin to a lithograph of the *Dīwān* of ʿUnṣurī (ed. by Āķā Muḥammad Ardakānī, Bombay 1320). A critical edition was published by K. I. Čaykin as an annex (ḍamīma) to *Armaghān*, vi (Tehran 1304/1925) with a biography and annotations to the text by Muḥammad ʿAlī Nāṣiḥ. The recent edition by Maḥmūd Mahdawī Dāmghānī reproduces the text of its predecessor, adding variant readings from two ancient manuscripts, viz. a copy in the Chester Beatty Library (cf. *A catalogue of the Persian manuscripts and miniatures*, Dublin 1959, 4, no. 103) and a copy in the British Museum (cf. Ch. Rieu, *Supplement to the catalogue of the Persian manuscripts*, London 1895, 141, no. 211). Many manuscripts of the *Dīwān*, or of smaller collections of poems, still await to be examined (see e.g. A. Munzawī, *Fihrist-i nus̲h̲ahā-yi k̲h̲aṭṭī-yi fārsī*, iii, Tehran 1350/1971, 2214-6, nos. 21375-417; Aḥmed Ateş, *İstanbul kütüphanelerinde Farsça manzum eserler*, i, Istanbul 1968, 212).

Bibliography: In addition to the works mentioned in the article, Niẓāmī ʿArūḍī, *Čahār maḳāla*, Tehran 1955-7, *matn* 44, cf. *taʿlīḳāt* 115 ff., 194, 226; Abu 'l-Maʿālī Naṣr Allāh Muns̲h̲ī, *Tard̲j̲ama-yi Kalīla wa-Dimna*, Tehran 1343/1954; ʿAwfī, *Lubāb*, ed. Browne, ii, 241-5; ed. Nafīsī,Tehran 1335/1956, 419-23, cf. *taʿlīḳāt* 714 ff.; S̲h̲ams al-Dīn Muḥammad b. Ḳays al-Rāzī, *al-Muʿd̲j̲am fī maʿāyīr as̲h̲ʿār al-ʿad̲j̲am*, Tehran 1338/1959; Amīn Aḥmad Rāzī, *Haft iḳlīm*, Tehran 1340/1961, i, 339-44; Luṭf-ʿAlī Beg Ād̲h̲ar, *Ātas̲h̲kada*, lith. Bombay 1299 A.H., 136-9; Riḍā-Ḳulī K̲h̲ān Hidāyat, *Mad̲j̲maʿ al-fuṣaḥāʾ*, lith. ed. Tehran 1295 A.H., i, 70-8; Ch. Rieu, *Catalogue of the Persian manuscripts in the British Museum*, ii, 547-8; Dihk̲h̲udā, *Lug̲h̲at-nāma*, s.v.; D̲h̲. Ṣafā, *Taʾrīk̲h̲-i adabiyyāt dar Īrān*, ii, Tehran 1339/1960, 470-6 and *passim*; Ḥusayn Nāyil, *Abu 'l-Farad̲j̲ Rūnī*, in *Āryānā* (Kabul) xxii/1-2 (1342/1963), 19-24; M. D̲j̲. Mahd̲j̲ūb, *Sabk-i K̲h̲urāsānī dar s̲h̲iʿr-i fārsī*, Tehran 1345/1966, 575-81 and *passim*; Maḥmūd Mahdawī Dāmghānī,*muḳaddama* and *taʿlīḳāt* to *Dīwān-i Abu 'l-Farad̲j̲ Rūnī*, Mas̲h̲had 1348/1969.   (J. T. P. DE BRUIJN)

ABU 'L-FARAD̲J̲ IBN AL-ṬAYYIB [see IBN AL-ṬAYYĪB].

ABU 'L-FATḤ AL-BALAṬĪ [see AL-BALAṬĪ in Suppl.].

ABU 'L-FATḤ AL-BUSTĪ [see AL-BUSTĪ].

ABU 'L-FATḤ AL-DAYLAMĪ AL-ḤUSAYN B. NĀṢIR B. AL-ḤUSAYN, AL-NĀṢIR LI-DĪN ALLĀH, Zaydī Imām. There are some variants in the sources in regard to his own, his father's and his grandfather's personal names. He belonged to a Ḥasanid family which had been prominent in Abhar for some generations. Nothing is known about his life before he came to the Yaman after 429/1038 claiming the Zaydī imāmate. He gained some tribal support in northern Yaman and established himself in the Ẓāhir Hamdān region where he built the fortress and town of Ẓafār [q.v.] near Dhū Bīn. In 437/1045-6 he entered and pillaged Ṣaʿda, the stronghold of the descendants of al-Hādī ila 'l-Ḥaḳḳ [q.v.], and committed a slaughter among the Banū K̲h̲awlān living in the area. Still in S̲h̲awwāl 437/April-May 1046 he occupied Ṣanʿāʾ. In the following year he gained briefly the allegiance of D̲j̲aʿfar b. al-Ḳāsim al-ʿIyānī, leader of a Zaydī faction which expected the return of his brother, the *Imām* al-Ḥusayn al-Mahdī [q.v.], as the Mahdī. D̲j̲aʿfar soon revolted against him, together with the Sulṭān Yaḥyā b. Abī Hās̲h̲id b. al-Ḍaḥḥāk, chief of the Hamdān, and expelled his representatives from Ṣanʿāʾ. Thereafter the Imām and D̲j̲aʿfar fought each other with changing fortunes for the possession of the fortresses of At̲h̲āfit and ʿAd̲j̲īb. The situation of Abu 'l-Fatḥ deteriorated further after ʿAlī b. Muḥammad al-Ṣulayḥī occupied the D̲j̲abal Masār in 439/1047 and

quickly expanded his power over large areas of Yaman. The *Imām* was soon deserted by most of followers and was forced to move from town to to In Rabīʿ I 444/July 1052 al-Ṣulayḥī defeated killed Abū Hās̲h̲id b. Yaḥyā b. Abī Hās̲h̲id and possession of Ṣanʿāʾ. Abu 'l-Fatḥ now correspon with Nad̲j̲āḥ, the lord of the Tihāma, inciting against al-Ṣulayḥī. When he invaded the Balad later in the year 444/1052-3, he was defeated killed by al-Ṣulayḥī, together with some seventy porters, at Nad̲j̲d al-D̲j̲āḥ and was buried in Radm His descendants were later known in the Yamar the Banu 'l-Daylamī.

His Ḳurʾān commentary *al-Burhān* is extant manuscript (*Fihrist kutub al-k̲h̲izāna al-Mutawa. liyya*, Ṣanʿāʾ n.d., 12; *Dār al-kutub: Ḳāʾimat mak̲h̲ṭūṭāt al-ʿarabiyya al-muṣawwara bi 'l-mīkrūf min al-D̲j̲umhūriyya al-ʿArabiyya al-Yamaniy Cairo 1967, 6). A refutation of the Muṭarrifiyya [ṣ sect is also ascribed to him.

Bibliography: Ḥumayd al-Muḥallī, *al-Ḥadd al-wardiyya*, ii, ms. Vienna, Glaser 116, ff. 11 113b; Yaḥyā b. al-Ḥusayn, *G̲h̲āyat al-amānī ak̲h̲bār al-ḳuṭr al-Yamānī*, ed. S. ʿAbd al-Fat ʿĀs̲h̲ūr and M. Muṣṭafā Ziyāda, Cairo 1388/1968 246 f., 250; al-ʿArs̲h̲ī, *Bulūg̲h̲ al-marām*, ed. Anas Mārī al-Karmalī, Cairo 1939, 36 f.; H. C. K Yaman, London 1892, 229 f.; Ḥ. F. al-Hamdā *al-Ṣulayḥiyyūn*, Cairo [1955], 82; W. Madelun *Der Imam al-Ḳāsim ibn Ibrāhīm*, Berlin 1965, 2 (W. MADELUNG)

ABU 'L-FATḤ AL-ISKANDARĪ [see AL-HAM DHĀNĪ].

ABŪ ḤAFṢ AL-S̲H̲IṬRANDJĪ [see AL-S̲H̲IṬRA DJĪ].

ABU 'L-ḤASAN AL-AḤMAR, the usual name a philologist of Baṣra called ʿAlī b. al-Ḥasan/a Mubārak, who was taught by al-Kisāʾī [q.v.], who eager pupil he was; after his master, he became tut to the future caliphs al-Amīn and al-Maʾmūn. T biographical sources record that al-Aḥmar w. originally a member of al-Ras̲h̲īd's guard, so tha being very attracted to the study of philology, b was unable to attend al-Kisāʾī's teaching session except when he was not on duty in the palace. Whe the master came to give lessons to the young prince al-Aḥmar rushed towards him, both when he went and when he came out took his stirrup and escorte him, whilst firing questions on grammar at hin When al-Kisāʾī was afflicted by leprosy and unabl to teach the princes any longer, he was afraid les one of the great grammarians of the period, Sība wayh or al-Ak̲h̲fas̲h̲ [q.vv.] might take his place; s he recommended as his own successor al-Aḥmar, wh was in the end confirmed in the post. The biographica sources mention in this connection the custom where by, after the first lesson, the new tutor received a the furnishings of the room in which he had beer teaching; al-Aḥmar, whose house was too small t take this, saw himself offered now both a house anc two slaves, one of each sex. Each day, he went along to learn that morning's lesson from al-Kisāʾī, whc every month came to question his pupils in al-Ras̲h̲īd's presence. In this way, al-Aḥmar acquired a vast amount of knowledge. He is said to have known 40,000 s̲h̲awāhid verses and complete ḳaṣīdas, but he had no pupils and did not transmit al-Kisāʾī's knowledge orally. This latter rôle devolved on his rival al-Farrāʾ [q.v.], but he was the author of two works, the *K. al-Taṣrīf* and the *K. Tafannun al-bulag̲h̲āʾ*. He died on the Pilgrimage road in 194/810.

Bibliography: *Fihrist*, 98; K̲h̲aṭīb Bag̲h̲dādī,

. *Baghdād*, xii, 104-5; Abu 'l-Ṭayyib al-Lughawī, *arātib al-naḥwiyyīn*, Cairo 1955, 89-90; Zubaydī, *abaḳāt*, 147, Ḳifṭī, *Inbāh*, Cairo 1369-74/1950-5, 313-17; Anbārī, *Nuzha*, 59; Masʿūdī, *Murūdj*, , 321-2 = § 2523; Yāḳūt, *Udabāʾ*, xii, 5-12; uyūṭī, *Bughya*, 334; M. al-Makhzūmī, *Madrasat -Kūfa*, Baghdād 1374/1955, 102; Bustānī, *DM*, , 250-1; Ziriklī, *Aʿlām*, v, 79. (CH. PELLAT)

BU 'L-ḤASAN AL-ANṢĀRĪ, ʿALĪ B. MŪSĀ B. B. ARFAʿ (Rāfiʿ) RĀSUH AL-ANDALUSĪ AL-YYĀNĪ (515-93/1121-97), a preacher of Fez, member of a family of whom one person (Ibn ʿ Rāsuh) is mentioned in the 5th/11th century Toledo as a composer of *muwashshaḥāt* (Ibn al-ṭīb has preserved ten examples in his *Djaysh al-shīḥ*, Nos. 49-58; cf. S. M. Stern, *Les chansons arabes*, Palermo 1953, 43-4; E. García Gómez, *rica de la moaxaja y métrica española*, in *al-And.*, ix (1974), 25). ʿAlī b. Mūsā's fame rests on a m in 1,414 verses (rhyme -*ṭā*, metre *ṭawīl*) on the ject of alchemy and variously called *Dīwān shu-r al-dhahab fi 'l-ṣināʿa al-sharīfa/fī fann al-salāmat*, *Dīwān al-shudhūr wa-taḥḳīḳ al-umūr*. This poem's at vogue, whose author gained the name "Poet of alchemists and alchemist of the poets", is shown the great number of mss. and commentaries ex-t, and it was said that if he could not teach the king of gold, he could at least teach *adab*. Further-re, this poet-alchemist left other writings, of a gious nature, *al-Ṭibb al-rūḥānī bi 'l-Ḳurʾān al-mānī* (ms. BN. 2643) and *Djihāt fī ʿilm al-tawdjīhāt* s. B.N. 3253).

Bibliography: Maḳḳarī, ii, 410; Kutubī, *Fawāt*, No. 319, ed. Iḥsān ʿAbbās, ii, 181-4; Bustānī, *DM*, v, 252; Brockelmann, I, 496, S I, 908, 2nd edn. I, 54. (ED.)

ABU 'L-ḤASAN AL-BATTĪ, AḤMAD B. ʿALĪ, et and littérateur, originally from al-Batt in āḳ (Yāḳūt, i, 488), who was a member of the staff al-Ḳādir's chancery (reigned 381-422/992-1031). en the future caliph had in 381/991 to flee from Ṭāʾiʿ, al-Battī had already been in his service, ce it was with him that al-Ḳādir sought refuge. nce as soon as he succeeded to the caliphate, he pointed al-Battī to his *dīwān*, where he was in arge of the postal service and of intelligence. A ʿtazilī in theology and a Ḥanafī in *fiḳh*, he had eviously specialised in study of the Ḳurʾān and *dīth*, but with his new duties, he soon became for colleagues the archetypal *adīb* with a vast know-lge of literature, a fine hand for calligraphy, and a tain talent for letter-writing and versifying which ade him well-renowned. Since he was extremely tty, had a fierce humour and quick repartee, pos-ssed a great store of anecdotes which he could retail a sparkling fashion and had a good knowledge music and singing, he shone with special bright-ss in the circles of the Būyids. He was intimately ked with al-Sharīf al-Raḍī [*q.v.*] who, on his death, Shaʿbān 405/Jan.-Febr. 1015, dedicated to him his st composition; al-Sharīf al-Murtaḍā [*q.v.*] likewise rote an elegy on him. His own poetry was com-ratively mediocre, and it was really as a *rāwī* that excelled. However, three works are credited to m, a *K. al-Ḳādirī*, a *K. al-ʿAmīdī* and a *K. al-akhrī*, whose contents are unknown but which must ve been biographical in nature.

Bibliography: Tawḥīdī, *Imtāʿ*, iii, 100; Tanū-khī, *Nishwār*, Cairo 1392/1972, iv, 256, v, 224, 225, vii, 24; Khaṭīb Baghdādī, *T. Baghdād*, iv, 320, xiv, 328; Sibṭ Ibn al-Djawzī, *Muntaẓam*, vii, 263; Ṣafadī, *Wāfī*, vii, 231-4; Ibn al-Athīr, ix, 175; Yāḳūt, *Udabāʾ*, iii, 254-70 (details here also on the dress of the *kuttāb*); Bustānī, *DM*, iv, 253; Ziriklī, *Aʿlām*, i, 165; Kaḥḥāla, *Muʾallifīn*, i, 319. (ED.)

ABU 'L-ḤASAN DJILWA, MĪRZĀ, Persian philosopher, poet and recluse. He was born in 1238/1823 in Aḥmadābād, Gudjarāt, where his father, Mīrzā Sayyid Muḥammad, member of a *sayyid* family from Ardistān, was engaged in trade. After a brief period in Bombay, Djilwa was brought to Iṣfahān by his father at the age of seven and began his education. When his father died seven years later, he decided to devote himself to learning, conscious of the scholarly and literary traditions of his family: Mīrzā Rafīʿ al-Dīn Nāʾīnī (d. 1082/1671), a celebrated theologian and jurist, was among his ancestors; the poet Midjmar (d. 1225/1810) had been his paternal uncle; and even his father had composed poetry under the pen-name of Maẓhar. Djilwa took up residence at the Kāsagarān *madrasa* and soon developed a predilection for the rational sciences, in particular, for metaphysics. It was also at this time that he began the composition of poetry under the pen-name of Djilwa, which became the appellation by which he was generally known. In his autobiographical sketch, Djilwa does not mention the name of any of his teachers in Iṣfahān, remarking only that he soon tired of attending their lectures and therefore began to study independently and himself to offer instruction (le Comte Arthur de Gobineau, in his *Les religions et les philosophies dans l'Asie Centrale*, new ed., Paris 1928, 85, mentions a certain Mullā Abu 'l-Ḥasan Ardistāni whose teachers were Muḥammad Ḥasan Gīlānī and Mīrzā Muḥammad Ḥasan Nūrī; it is possible that this Abu 'l-Ḥasan is identical with Djilwa). In 1274/1857 he came to Tehran and took up residence in the Dār al-Shifāʾ *madrasa*; the two narrow rooms allotted him there were to be his home for the remaining forty years of his life. He lived the life of a recluse, and although he had a number of aristocratic admirers and friends, such as Mīrzā Maḥmūd Khān Māzandarānī Mushīr al-Wizāra, who pressed invitations upon him, he scarcely ever left the *madrasa*. Surprisingly, however, despite his deep roots in traditional philosophy, Djilwa is recorded to have been a member of Mīrzā Malkum Khān's pseudo-masonic organisation, the *farāmūshkhāna*, and to have attended its meetings in the house of Djalāl al-Dīn Mīrzā (H. Algar, *Mirza Malkum Khan: a study in the history of Iranian modernism*, Berkeley and Los Angeles 1973, 49-50). The only journey outside Tehran that he undertook was a brief one to Gīlān and Ādharbāydjān. He received at the *madrasa*, with some disdain, visits by Nāṣir al-Dīn Shāh and the British orientalist, E. G. Browne (Browne, *A year amongst the Persians*, Cambridge 1927, 162). Among his principal pupils were the Niʿmatullāhī Ṣūfī, Maʿṣūm ʿAlī Shāh (d. 1324/1926) (see his *Ṭarāʾiḳ al-ḥaḳāʾiḳ*, ed. Muḥammad Djaʿfar Maḥdjūb, Tehran 1339/1960, iii, 507), Sayyid Hāshim Ushkūrī (d. 1332/1914) (see Muḥammad Ḥirz al-Dīn, *Maʿārif al-ridjāl fī tarādjim al-ʿulamāʾ wa 'l-udabāʾ*, Nadjaf 1384/1964, iii, 271), and Sayyid Ḥusayn Bādkūbaʾi (see preface by S. H. Naṣr to his translation of Muḥammad Ḥusayn Ṭabāṭabāʾī's *Shiʿite Islam*, Albany, N.Y. 1955, 22). Djilwa died in 1314/1897 and was buried in Rayy near the tomb of Ibn Bābūya. Later, an impressive structure was built over his grave by Mīrzā Aḥmad Khān Naṣīr al-Dawla and Sulṭān Ḥasan Mīrzā Nayyir al-Dawla. Djilwa was described by Maʿṣūm ʿAlī Shāh as the "renewer of peripatetic philosophy in the fourteenth (Hidjrī) century", as opposed to his friend and contemporary,

Āķā ʿAlī Ḥakīm-Ilāhī, who followed the school of illuminationism (*ishrāķ*) (*Ṭarā'iķ al-ḥaķā'iķ, loc. cit.*). But despite his great fame, he never composed original works, regarding independent writing on philosophy as "difficult or even impossible" after the achievements of his predecessors (autobiographical sketch quoted by Muḥsin al-Amīn in *Aʿyān al-Shīʿa*, Beirut 1380/1960, vi, 216), and he preferred instead to write commentaries and glosses on the work of Avicenna and Mullā Ṣadrā. Two of these have been printed in the margin of Ṣadrā's *Sharḥ al-Hidāyat al-Athīriyya*, Tehran 1313/1895. His *Dīwān* is also said to have been published.

Bibliography: in addition to the works mentioned in the text, see ʿAbbās b. Muḥammad Riḍā Ķummī, *Hadiyat al-aḥbāb*, Nadjaf 1349/1930, 11; Mīrzā Muḥammad ʿAlī Mudarris, *Rayḥānat al-adab*, Tabrīz n.d., i, 419-20; Muḥsin al-Amīn, *Aʿyān al-Shīʿa*, Beirut 1380/1960, vi, 214-16 (including, in Arabic translation, the autobiographical account of Djilwa first printed in *Nāma-yi dānishwarān-i nāṣirī*); Mahdī Bāmdād, *Sharḥ-i ḥāl-i ridjāl-i Īrān dar ķarnhā-yi 12 va 13 va 14-i Hidjrī*, Tehran 1347/1968. (H. ALGAR)

ABU 'L-ḤASAN AL-MAGHRIBĪ, MUḤAMMAD B. AḤMAD B. MUḤAMMAD, poet and littérateur of the 4th/10th century whose origin is unknown. He seems to have undergone many vicissitudes, since he appears in the service of Sayf al-Dawla, of al-Ṣāḥib Ibn ʿAbbād and of the ruler of Khurāsān, where he met Abu 'l-Faradj al-Iṣfahānī, and he also resided in Egypt, in the Djabal, and in Transoxania, at Shāsh. The surviving verses of this great traveller are occasional pieces without any great originality, but he seems also to have been the author of several epistles and books, in particular, of a *Tuḥfat al-kuttāb fi 'l-rasā'il* and a *Tadhkirat/Mudhākarat al-nadīm*, in which there were no doubt pieces of advice on style and valuable data on the literary circles of the age. He is also famed from the fact that he was probably the transmitter of al-Mutanabbī's work in the lands of the east, since Yāķūt says of him that he was the *rāwiya* of the celebrated poet, encountered at Baghdād. However, if he made an apologia for the poet in his *K. al-Intiṣār al-munabbī ʿan faḍā'il al-Mutanabbī*, followed by a *Baķiyyat al-Intiṣār al-mukthir li 'l-ikhtiṣār*, he was equally the author—for reasons unknown to us—of a *K. al-Nabīh/Tanbīh al-munabbī ʿan radhā'il al-Mutanabbī*, which must be the oldest criticism of the poet's work.

Bibliography: Thaʿālibī, *Yatīma*, iv, 81; Yāķūt, *Udabā'*, xvii, 127-32; R. Blachère, *Abou ṭ-Ṭayyib al-Motanabbî*, Paris 1935, 227, 273-4; Bustānī, *DM*, iv, 264. (ED.)

ABU 'L-ḤASAN AL-RABAʿĪ [see AL-RABAʿĪ].

ABU 'L-ḤASAN AL-RUMMĀNĪ [see AL-RUMMĀNĪ].

ABŪ ḤAYYĀ AL-NUMAYRĪ, the usual name for AL-HAYTHAM B. AL-RABĪʿ B. ZURĀRA, a minor poet of Baṣra of the 2nd/8th century. The date of his death is given variously in the biographical sources, with dates ranging from 143/760 to 210/825, and the only point of reference which we have is the fact that he was considered as the *rāwiya* of al-Farazdaķ (d. 110/728). Of Bedouin origin, Abū Ḥayyā must have lived for quite a long time in the desert, to judge by the verses which al-Djāḥiẓ cites in his *K. al-Ḥayawān*, and which other, subsequent authors cite, apparently considering him as an authority. This is not, however, the image that one gains of this personage by reading the notices of him in the biographical sources, since he became legendary for his cowardice (stories of his sword, pompously c *Luʿāb al-maniyya*, of a dog which frightened hi death, etc.), his tendency to romance and to b about outstanding deeds of valour (in particula claimed to be able to converse with the *djinn*), his weakness of mind (*lūtha*), which led to his b sometimes grouped amongst those possessed (espe ly as he was allegedly epileptic); more indulge al-Djāḥiẓ merely classes him amongst the fo persons, *nawkā*, and forebears to reproduce anecd in which he is the hero and which could very we invented tales.

The biographers state and repeat that Abū Ḥa wrote eulogies to the last Umayyads and the ʿAbbāsids, but it very much seems, unless one is taken, that none of his panegyrics have been served. They further state that he wrote *urdjūza* well as *ķaṣīdas*, but the great majority of his viving verses are not in *radjaz* at all. Accordin the *Fihrist*, 231, his *dīwān* took up 50 leaves, one must accept that this work was not lackin quality, since isolated verses and fragments appreciated by the critics. Although accusing of some defects, notably a characteristic ingenu ness (al-ʿAskarī, *Ṣināʿatayn*, 165; al-Marzub *Muwashshaḥ*, 227-8), they remark that his style free from affectation and padding, though someti difficult; Abū ʿAmr Ibn al-ʿAlā' even judged Ḥayyā to be superior to his fellow-tribesman al-[*q.v.*]. As a rule, the pieces of poetry which have b preserved have a descriptive, bacchic, satirical elegiac character; according to Ibn al-Mu'tazz, verses inspired by his wife, who died when still you were often quoted.

Bibliography: (in addition to references in article): Djāḥiẓ, *Bayān*, i, 385, ii, 225, 229-30; id *Ḥayawān*, index; Ibn Ķutayba, *Shiʿr*, 749-50; i *ʿUyūn*, index, idem, *Maʿārif*, 87; Abū Tamm *Ḥamāsa*, ii, 105, 133; Buḥturī, *Ḥamāsa*, 287; al-Muʿtazz, *Ṭabaķāt*, 61-3; Ķālī, *Amālī*, i, 69, 185; Bakrī, *Simṭ al-la'ālī*, i, 97, 244; Mubar *Kāmil*, index; *Aghānī*, ed. Beirut, xvi, 235-9; *Mukhtār min shiʿr Bashshār*, ed. 1353, 38, 39, 2 Ibn ʿAbd Rabbih, *ʿIķd*, index; Marzubānī, *M djam*, 193; Ḥuṣrī, *Zahr al-ādāb*, 14-5, 198, 218-idem, *Djamʿ al-djawāhir*, 217-9, 292, 22-3, 2 477-8; Ibn Ḥadjar, *Iṣāba*, iv, No. 327; Ām *Mu'talif*, 103; Ibn al-Djawzī, *Akhbār al-ḥamķā 'l-mughaffalīn*, Baghdād 1966, 226; Yāķūt, *Buld* iii, 35; Baghdādī, *Khizāna*, ed. Būlāķ, iii, 154, 283-5; Ibshīhī, *Mustaṭraf*, i, 305; ʿAskarī, *Ṣinā tayn*, 165, 208; idem, *Dīwān al-maʿānī*, ed. 19 ii, 127; Suyūṭī, *Muzhir*, index; R. Basset, *Mill un contes*, i, 536; Pellat, *Milieu*, 160; Bustānī, *D* iv, 281-2; Ziriklī, *Aʿlām*, ix, 114; Wahhābī, i, 1 70. (CH. PELLAT)

ABŪ HIFFĀN, ʿABD ALLĀH B. AḤMAD B. ḤA AL-MIHZAMĪ, collector of poetical *akhbār*, *rā* and poet in Arabic, (died between 255/869 a 257/871. Virtually nothing is known of his life, exce that he came from a Baṣran family stemming fr the B. Mihzam of ʿAbd al-Ķays, and that he glori in his Arab origin. He led a fairly poor and constrict life, to the point that he had to sell his clothing procure food, and he complains of this frequently his verses.

His reputation arises primarily from his role as transmitter of poetical *akhbār*, and he has a place the *isnāds* or chains of supporting transmitters several important works, such as the *K. al-Aghā* the *Muwashshaḥ* of al-Marzubānī and the works al-Ṣūlī and Ibn al-Djarrāḥ. He knew the circles poets very well, and previous to his own activity, ous of his paternal and maternal uncles had ialised in the collection and transmission of liter- anecdotes. He was in contact with Abū Nuwās, se protégé and *rāwī* he was, and through this nection he developed, and came in his own right follow the activities of the great contemporary ts, and especially, of the libertine poets. As well his own master Abū Nuwās, he frequented the npany of al-Ḥusayn b. al-Ḍaḥḥāk, al-Buḥturī, al- uraymī, and also al-Djāḥiẓ, Thaʿlab, al-Mubarrad,

Ie himself put together a work called the *Akhbar Nuwās*, which has come down to us, and a *K. āʿat al-shuʿarā*ʾ and a *K. Akhbār al-shuʿarā*ʾ, of ich no trace has survived but were certainly used the 3rd and 4th centuries by several writers of *adab* rks.

Abū Hiffān was also a poet, but only a few dozen his verses have been preserved, sc. fragments of ogies addressed to ʿAlī b. Yaḥyā al-Munadjdjim d ʿUbayd Allāh b. Yaḥyā b. Khāḳān; of satires ad- essed to Aḥmad b. Abī Duʾād and al-Buḥturī; epi- ammatic exchanges, not always in the best of taste, th Abū ʿAlī al-Baṣīr, Saʿīd b. Ḥumayd, Abu 'l- ynāʾ and Yaʿḳūb al-Tammār, all these being his mpanions in nocturnal sessions; and a few love rses. It is surprising that nothing has come down us from his wine poetry, which Ibn al-Muʿtazz says joyed a wide currency. Altogether, Abū Hiffān was minor poet who has contributed, through his anec- tes, to our knowledge of the history and sociology poetry in the 2nd/8th and 3rd/9th centuries.

Bibliography: ʿA. Aḥmad Farrādj has edited the *Akhbār Abī Nuwās*, Cairo 1373/1953 (an edition with numerous verses in the text censored) with a bibliographical note, to be completed by Bencheikh, *Les voies d'une création*, typescript thesis, the Sorbonne 1971, i, 116-7, and idem, *Les sècrétaires poètes et animateurs de cénacles aux IIe et IIIe siècles de l'hégire*, in *JA* (1975), 265-315.

(J. E. BENCHEIKH)

ABU 'L-ḤUSAYN AL-BAṢRĪ, MUḤAMMAD B. ʿALĪ B. AL-ṬAYYIB B. AL-ḤUSAYN, Muʿtazili theologian. Little is known about his education nd early career. He originated from Baṣra where he eard *ḥadīth*. As he studied *kalām* and *uṣūl al-fiḳh* ith Ḳāḍī ʿAbd al-Djabbār [*q.v.*], he must have isited Rayy for some time. With the Christian Abū ʿAlī b. al-Samḥ, a student of Yaḥyā b. ʿAdī, he tudied philosophy and sciences, presumably in Baghdād. This is attested by a manuscript containing his redaction of the notes of Ibn al-Samḥ on the *Physics* of Aristotle. He may have also studied nd practised medicine for some time if he is, as as been suggested, identical with the Abu 'l-Ḥusayn l-Baṣrī mentioned by Ibn Abī Uṣaybiʿa as a physiian contemporary with Abu 'l-Faradj b. al-Ṭayyib. Al-Dhahabī refers to him as *al-ḳāḍī*, but there is no other evidence that he ever held an official position. During the later part of his life he taught and wrote n Baghdād. As his two *uṣūl al-fiḳh* works, the *Sharḥ al-ʿUmad* and the *K. al-Muʿtamad*, were composed still before the death of his teacher ʿAbd al-Djabbār in 415/1024-5, he must have begun his teaching career in Baghdād before that date. He died in Baghdād on 5 Rabīʿ II 436/30 October 1044. The fact that the Ḥanafī *ḳāḍī* Abū ʿAbd Allāh al-Ṣaymarī led the funeral prayer for him indicates that he belonged to the Ḥanafī *madhhab*, not to the Shāfiʿī as suggested by some sources.

Of his works on the *uṣūl al-fiḳh*, his commentary (*sharḥ*) on ʿAbd al-Djabbār's *K. al-ʿUmad* appears to be lost. His *K. al-Muʿtamad*, written later, has been edited together with his *Ziyādāt al-muʿtamad* and *K. al-Ḳiyās al-sharʿī* (ed. M. Hamidullah, Damascus 1965). This work became popular also among non-Muʿtazilī scholars and, according to Ibn Khallikān, formed the basis of Fakhr al-Dīn al-Rāzī's *K. al-Maḥṣūl*. None of his *kalām* works appears to be extant. The largest one, *K. Taṣaffuḥ al-adilla*, remained unfinished, as he had only reached the chapter on the *visio beatifica* before he died. On the *K. Ghurar al-adilla*, Ibn Abi 'l-Ḥadīd [*q.v.*] wrote a commentary. A short fragment on the question of the imāmate extant in manuscript (Vienna, Glaser 114) is probably an extract from his *K. Sharḥ al-Uṣūl al-khamsa*. His theological doctrine can, however, be recovered from later references and especially from the extant parts of the *K. al-Muʿtamad fī uṣūl al-dīn* (ms. Ṣanʿāʾ) of his student Maḥmud al-Malāḥimī, who quotes the *K. Taṣaffuḥ al-adilla* extensively. Also lost are his refutations of two works of the Imāmī Sharīf al-Murtaḍā, his contemporary in Baghdād: the *K. al-Shāfī* on the imāmate and the *K. al-Muḳniʿ* on the doctrine of the concealment (*ghayba*) of the Twelfth *Imām*.

In his doctrine, Abu 'l-Ḥusayn al-Baṣrī was deeply influenced by the concepts of the philosophers and diverged from the Bahāshima, the school of Abū Hāshim al-Djubbāʾī represented by his teacher ʿAbd al-Djabbār. He was therefore shunned by the Bahāshima, who accused him of refuting his Muʿtazilī *shaykhs* in an unfair and injurious manner. This charge is repeated by al-Shahrastānī, who maintains that he was really a philosopher in his views (*falsafī al-madhhab*) but the Muʿtazilī *mutakallimūn* were not aware of this fact. Ibn al-Ḳifṭī, too, suggests that he concealed his philosophical views under the forms of expression of the *kalām* theologians in order to guard himself from his contemporaries. Notable points on which he differed from the Bahāshima were his rejection of their theory of modes (*aḥwāl*) [*q.v.*] and their thesis that the non-existent (*maʿdūm*) is a thing, his indecision about their theory of atomism, his admission of the miracles of saints (*karāmāt*), and his reduction of the divine attributes of will, hearing and seeing to that of knowledge. Evidently also under the influence of the doctrine of the philosophers, he affirmed that the acts of man occur necessarily in accordance with their motive (*dāʿī*) thus, as Fakhr al-Dīn al-Rāzī pointed out, in effect undermining the Muʿtazilī doctrine of human free will.

Abu 'l-Ḥusayn's school was continued by his students, the Khwārazmian Maḥmūd b. Muḥammad al-Malāḥimī and Abū ʿAlī Muḥammad b. Aḥmad b. al-Walīd al-Karkhī (d. 478/1086) who, like his teacher, also studied logic and philosophy and taught in Baghdād. According to Ibn al-Murtaḍā, Fakhr al-Dīn al-Rāzī adopted many of his views on the "subtleties" (*laṭīf*) of *kalām*, i.e. matters not touching fundamental dogma. His theological doctrine progressively exerted a strong influence among the Imāmiyya and, to a lesser extent, among the Zaydiyya.

Bibliography: *Taʾrīkh Baghdād*, iii, 100; al-Ḥākim al-Djushamī, *Sharḥ al-ʿUyūn*, in *Faḍāʾil al-iʿtizāl*, ed. Fuʾād Sayyid, Tunis 1393/1974, 387; Shahrastānī, 19, 32, 57, 59; idem, *Nihāyat al-aḳdām*, ed. A. Guillaume, Oxford 1931, 151, 175, 177, 221, 257; Fakhr al-Dīn al-Rāzī, *Iʿtiḳād firaḳ al-muslimīn wa 'l-mushrikīn*, ed. Muṣṭafā ʿAbd al-Rāziḳ, Cairo 1356/1938, 45; Ibn al-Ḳifṭī, *Taʾrīkh al-ḥukamāʾ*, ed. J. Lippert, Leipzig 1903, 293 f.;

Ibn Khallikān, *Wafāyāt*, ed. Iḥsān ʿAbbās, Beirut 1968-72, iv, 271 f.; al-Dhahabī, *Mīzān al-iʿtidāl*, ed. ʿAlī Muḥ. al-Bidjāwī, Cairo 1963, iii, 654 f.; idem, al-ʿIbar, iii, ed. Fuʾād Sayyid, Kuwait 1961, 187; al-Īdjī, *al-Mawāḳif*, ed. Th. Soerensen, Leipzig 1848, 106-12; al-Ṣafadī, *al-Wāfī*, iv, ed. S. Dedering, Damascus 1959, 125; Ibn Abi 'l-Wafāʾ, *al-Djawāhir al-muḍīʾa*, Ḥaydarābād 1332, ii, 93 f.; Ibn al-Murtaḍā, *Ṭabaḳāt al-muʿtazila*, ed. S. Diwald-Wilzer, Wiesbaden 1961, 118 f.; A. S. Tritton, *Muslim theology*, London 1947, 193-5; S. M. Stern, *Ibn al-Samḥ*, in *JRAS* (1956), 33-41; M. Hamidullah, introd. to edition of *K. al-Muʿtamad*; *GAS*, I, 627. The section on consensus in the *K. al-Muʿtamad* has been translated and analysed by M. Bernand, *L'accord unanime de la communauté . . . d'après Abū 'l-Ḥusayn al-Baṣrī*, Paris 1970.

(W. MADELUNG)

ABŪ ḤUZĀBA, AL-WALĪD B. ḤUNAYFA (b. Nahīk in Ṭabarī, ii, 393) AL-TAMĪMĪ, a minor poet of the 1st/7th century. He was a Bedouin who settled at Baṣra and was a panegyrist, at the time of Ziyād b. Abīhi (45-53/665-72) or shortly after, of ʿAbd Allāh b. Khālid b. Asīd, governor of Fārs. His family urged him strongly to join the circle of Yazīd b. Muʿāwiya, before the latter's assumption of the caliphate (60/680); he finally decided to try his luck, but was not received by the prince, and he returned to Baṣra and joined up with the army. He was sent to Sīstān (Sidjistān), and from 60/680-1, under the orders of Salm b. Ziyād, he sang the praises of the governor Ṭalḥa al-Ṭalaḥāt [*q.v.*]; he recited a funeral elegy on the latter which contained critical aspersions on Ṭalḥa's successor, ʿAbd Allāh b. ʿAlī al-ʿAbshamī, who had shown himself less generous to the poet. He also had occasion in Sidjistān to mourn the death of a certain Nāshira al-Yarbūʿī killed at the time of Ibn al-Zubayr, in an elegy set to music by Ibn Djāmiʿ [*q.v.*]. Finally, he returned to Baṣra and then, after various adventures, rallied to the cause of Ibn al-Ashʿath [*q.v.*] and was possibly killed at the same time as him (85/704).

Abu Ḥuzāba had the reputation of turning nasty when his hopes of reward were disappointed. He has left behind a certain number of *radjaz* poems, as well as *ḳaṣīda*s which have kept his name from falling into oblivion.

Bibliography: Djāḥiẓ, *Ḥayawān*, i, 255, iii, 381-2; idem, *Bayān*, iii, 329; Ibn al-Kalbī-Caskel, Tab. 72 and ii, 586; Muṣʿab al-Zubayrī, *Nasab Ḳuraysh*, 188; Balādhurī, *Ansāb*, ivb, 153; *Aghānī*, ed. Beirut, xxii, 271-82; Āmidī, *Muʾtalif*, 64; Dhahabī, *Mushtabih*, 160; Bustānī, *DM*, iv, 247.

(CH. PELLAT)

ABU 'L-ʿIBAR, ABU 'L-ʿABBĀS MUḤAMMAD B. AḤMAD B. ʿABD ALLĀH AL-HĀSHIMĪ, burlesque poet and member of the ruling family, who was born in *ca.* 175/791-2 in the reign of al-Rashīd and who died in 252/866, probably assassinated by an ʿAlid partisan. He is known by the name of Abu 'l-ʿIbar, a sobriquet which he made up himself, adding a letter each year, and in the end making it unpronounceable. He was carefully educated, had an acute literary sense and was a fine connoisseur of poetry. The severe al-Maʾmūn did not appreciate him, and even imprisoned him, but he welcomed the accession of al-Mutawakkil, giving himself up to all sorts of amusing deeds.

Since he felt his way blocked by the great poets of his time, and in particular, by Abū Tammām and al-Buḥturī, he found it more profitable to devote himself to *ḥumḳ* and *sukhf*, thereby illustrating a tradition which was to continue with e.g. Ibn al-Ḥadjdjādj and Ibn al-Habbāriyya [*q.vv.*]. Abu 'l-ʿI did not allow his membership of the caliphal fa to constrict him, and cultivated a real burlesque in his own life and writings, in which he displa acrobatics. In reality, under the form of burles satire is often hidden, and under the form of foonery, an element of suffering. Whether he inv new words, writes phrases devoid of sense, wit parodies a scholar, or fishes with a line in the p of the caliphal palace, he goes quite contrary to accepted cultural norms, defies the usual patte confronts an atmosphere of seriousness with droll and in short, gives himself up to grotesque piece clowning which might have opened up a way for original and new strain in Arabic literature. But this, Arabo-Islamic culture would have had to acc new values alien to its own ones. The terms of *ḥu* and *sukhf* show clearly the lack of esteem for th tentative efforts, which never had any really frui consequences [cf. ABU 'L-ʿANBAS above].

Bibliography: *Aghānī*, xxiii, 76-86; Ṣūlī, *A bār al-Buḥturi*, 170-1; idem, *Awrāḳ*, ii, 323- Kutubī, *Fawāt al-wafayāt*, ii, 354-6, No. 3 *Fihrist*, 223-4; Yāḳūt, *Udabāʾ*, xvii, 122-7; Muḥa mad b. Dāwūd al-Djarrāḥ, *Waraḳa*, 120-1; cf. J. Bencheikh, *Le cénacle d'al-Mutawakkil, contribut à l'étude des instances de légitimation littéraire*, *Mélanges Henri Laoust* = *BEO*, xxix [1977].

(J. E. BENCHEIKH)

ABŪ ʿIMRĀN AL-FĀSĪ, MŪSĀ B. ʿĪSĀ B. A ḤĀDJDJ/ḤADJDJĀDJ (?), Mālikī *faḳīh*, probab born between 365/975 and 368/978 at Fās into Berber family whose *nisba* is impossible to reco struct. No doubt to complete his studies, but perha also because of other reasons hard to discern, he we to settle in al-Ḳayrawān, where his master was particular al-Ḳābisī (d. 403/1012 [*q.v.*]). He is know to have stayed in Cordova with Ibn ʿAbd al-Ba [*q.v.*] and to have profited by the chance to follo the lectures of various scholars there, which his bio raphers list, without however giving the date this journey. Soon after the end of the century, went to the East, possibly spending some years Mecca, since he made the Pilgrimage several time and deriving further instruction from the *fuḳahāʾ* the Holy City. In 399/1008-9 he was in Baghdā benefiting from the teaching of al-Bāḳillānī (d. 40 1013 [*q.v.*]), a Mālikī like himself but an Ashʿarī *kalām*, and it was in the ʿIrāḳī capital that he ha the revelation of a theological doctrine in whose su sequent diffusion in the West he was to take pa (see H. R. Idris, *Essai sur la diffusion de l'ašʿarism en Ifrîqiya*, in *Cahiers de Tunisie*, ii (1953), 134-5 He returned to Mecca from Baghdād, and then in *ca* 402/1011 returned via Egypt to al-Ḳayrawān, whic he never seems then to have left apart from a las journey to the East in *ca.* 425/1033-4 or 426/1034-5 He died on 13 Ramaḍān 430/8 June 1039 in hi adopted home; al-Muʿizz b. Bādīs [*q.v.*] was presen at his funeral, together with a great crowd, and hi tomb has henceforth been venerated as equal to tha of a saint. His descendants still live in al-Ḳayrawān

His biographers stress the breadth and diversity of his education, and mention in detail the numerou teachers whose courses he followed, both at al-Ḳayra wān and during his travels; and they make him in some way the heir of Mālikī teaching at the opening of the 4th/10th century. Nor do they omit to list al the pupils who thronged his courses, and they give the impression that he exercised a deep influence on intellectual activity in the juridical-religious domain. He was at the outset a specialist on the seven readings he Ḳurʾān, and then after his return from the t, turned to *ḥadīth* and *fiḳh* and, to some extent, *im*. He attracted a host of disciples not only from ḳiya, but even from Spain, Sicily and Morocco, several of these later made a name for themes. Furthermore, he kept up a correspondence h scholars in distant places, who consulted him points of doctrine, and he even gave *idjāza*s at a tance. It would be tedious to enumerate here all pupils of his mentioned by biographers but one uld mention that they included Ibn Sharaf [*q.v.*], a person homonymous with the name of the hor of the *ʿUmda*, ʿAbd Allāh Ibn Rashīḳ (d. 419/ 8), who was also a poet, and dedicated to him the ater part of his verse (see Ch. Bouyahia, *La vie éraire en Ifriqiya sous les Zirides*, Tunis 1972, 67,).

Two other pupils of Abū ʿImrān's ought to be menned also because they were associated with import historical events. At a date which, with Ibn ī Zarʿ (*Ḳirṭās*, 122-3) can be fixed at 427/1035-6 ilst Ibn Khaldūn, *Berbères*, ii, 67, places the events 440/1048-9, Ibn ʿIdhārī, *Bayān*, iii, 242, in 444/ 52-3 and Ibn al-Athīr, ix, 258-9, in 447/1056, which unlikely), the Lamtūna chief Yaḥyā b. Ibrāhīm ssed through al-Ḳayrawān whilst returning from Pilgrimage, attended Abū ʿImrān's courses and, lising the depth of his compatriots' ignorance, ked the great scholar to designate one of his folvers to go and teach them. Abū ʿImrān then recmended to him one of his former pupils called gʷag (Wadjdjādj in Arabic transcription), who had urned to his own land, and this latter scholar in rn designated ʿAbd Allāh b. Yāsīn (see al-Bakrī, *scription de l'Afrique septentrionale*, new edn. Paris 65, 165-6/311-12; *al-Ḥulal al-mawshiyya*[1], 9; A. Bel, *religion musulmane en Berbérie*, Paris 1938, 215; Marçais, *La Berbérie musulmane et l'Orient au oyen âge*, Paris 1946, 238; H. Terrasse, *Histoire du aroc*, Casablanca 1949, i, 214; J. Bosch Vilá, *Los morávides*, Tetuan 1956, 49; and see AL-MURĀṬŪN). Now the anonymous author of the *Mafākhir Barbar* (ed. E. Lévi-Provençal, *Fragments historiques sur les Berbères au moyen âge*, Rabat 1934, 69) ates that these two men impelled the Almoravids to pand out of the Sahara on the order (*bi-amr*) of ū ʿImrān.

One would like to have exact details about this, it if the assertion is true, it shows the influence of e Ḳayrawānī *faḳīh*, which was, at all events, a ofound one. His pupils transmitted his oral teachgs and doubtless also his works (cf. Ibn Khayr, *ahrasa*, i, 440), which do not however seem to have en very numerous. Some of his *fatwā*s have been eserved, in particular by al-Wansharīsī in his *Miʿyār* ut one should be careful, since the name "Abū mrān al-Fāsī" was fairly widespread; see e.g. ockelmann, S II, 961; a *K. al-Dalāʾil wa 'l-aḍdād* mentioned in the *Miʿyār*, x, 105, and a manuscript *al-Iḥkām li-masāʾil al-aḥkām al-mustakhradja min itāb al-Dalāʾil wa 'l-aḍdād li-Abī ʿImrān al-Fāsī* has so been catalogued (1342-D. 1444) at Rabat). His *. al-Taʿālīḳ ʿalā 'l-Mudawwana* is one of the Ḳāḍī yāḍ's sources (*Madārik*, i, 56), who cites him freiently. He is moreover said to have made a selection *ḥadīth*s which was especially important and covered hundred leaves, and a *Fahrasa* is attributed to him; nally, a manuscript of his *Naẓāʾir* is mentioned as xisting at Algiers (Brockelmann, S I, 660-1). Some erses are also attributed to him.

Bibliography: In addition to sources already cited, see: Western biographical sources: ʿIyāḍ, *Tartīb al-Madārik*, ed. A Bakīr, Beirut n.d., iv, 702-6 and index; Ibn Nādjī, *Maʿālim al-īmān*, Tunis 1320, iii, 199-205; Ibn Farḥūn, *Dībādj*, Cairo 1329, 344-5; Tādlī, *al-Tashawwuf ilā ridjāl al-taṣawwuf*, ed. A. Faure, Rabat 1958, 64-6; al-Wazīr al-Sarrādj, *al-Ḥulal al-sundusiyya*, ed. al-Hīla, Tunis, ix, 272-3; Ḥumaydī, *Djadhwa*, Cairo 1952, No. 791; Ibn Bashkuwāl, *Ṣila*, No. 1223; Ḍabbī, *Bughya*, Madrid 1884, No. 1332; Ibn al-Abbār, *Takmila*, No. 679 — Oriental biographical sources: Ibn al-Djazarī, *Ḳurrāʾ*, No. 3691; Dhahabī, *Ḥuffāẓ*, iii, 284-6; Yāḳūt, *Buldān*, iii, 807; Ibn Taghrībirdī, *Nudjūm*, v, 30 (on p. 77, he makes Abū ʿImrān die in 458); Ibn al-ʿImād, *Shadharāt*, iii, 247-8; F. Bustānī, *DM*, iv, 483; Ziriklī, *Aʿlām*, viii, 278. — Studies: H. R. Idris, *Zīrides*, index; idem, *Deux maîtres de l'école juridique kairouanaise . . .*, in *AIEO Alger*, xiii (1955), 42-60 (detailed study, with rich bibliography). (CH. PELLAT)

ABŪ ISḤĀḲ AL-FĀRISĪ, IBRĀHĪM B. ʿALĪ (d. after 377/987), celebrated grammarian and also lexicographer of the golden age of grammatical studies in Baghdād during the 4th/10th century, and equally a poet. As a pupil of Abū ʿAlī al-Fārisī (d. 377/987 [*q.v.*]) and of al-Rummānī (d. 384/994 [*q.v.*]), he belonged to the second generation of grammarians of this century, and more especially, to the first group "moulded by the pupils of al-Mubarrad", and he assured "the triumph of the method of Baṣra in Baghdād" (G. Troupeau). He wrote several works, in particular, on prosody, and like his master Abū ʿAlī al-Fārisī somewhat earlier, criticised the work of the poet al-Mutanabbī.

Bibliography: Yāḳūt, *Udabāʾ*, i, 204-5; Suyūṭī, *Bughya*, 184; G. Troupeau, *La grammaire à Baġdād*, in *Arabica*, ix (1962), 399; R. Blachère, *Abou ṭayyib al-Motanabbî*, Paris 1935, 242. (M. BERGÉ)

ABU 'L-ḲĀSIM AL-FAZARĪ [see AL-FAZARĪ].

ABU 'L-ḲĀSIM AL-MADJRĪṬĪ [see AL-MADJRĪṬĪ].

ABU 'L-ḲĀSIM AL-WĀSĀNĪ [see AL-WĀSĀNĪ].

ABŪ KHALĪFA AL-DJUMAḤĪ [see AL-FAḌL B. AL-ḤUBĀB in Suppl.].

ABŪ MĀḌĪ, ILIYYĀ (1889-1957), poet and journalist of Lebanese origin, who spent his childhood in the village of al-Muḥaydiṯha near Bikfayā, his birthplace, but left his native land at the age of 11 to help his maternal uncle with his business in Alexandria. During his stay of some dozen years in Egypt, he was able to find time to acquire an advanced literary education, to learn a lot of classical and modern poetry and to frequent the circles of intellectuals who were in varying degrees engaged in political activities which roused the authorities' suspicions. Like so many of his compatriots, he began early to write poetry, which gave him an initial fame, and he was even able in 1911 to publish at Alexandria a first collection called *Tadhkār al-māḍī, Dīwān Īliyyā Ḍāhir Abū Māḍī*, which the critics were unanimous in considering of no great literary value. In this same year of 1911, he decided to leave for the United States and rejoin his brother, who was a merchant like his uncle. He then spent several years in Cincinnati, where he continued to write verse, and then abandoned trade for poetry and journalism, and went in 1916 to New York. There he published on arrival, under the title of *Dīwān Īliyyā Abū Māḍī*, a second edition of his first collection, but now augmented by some poems on social questions and inspired by Arabism and nationalism, which he had avoided inserting in the *Tadhkār al-māḍī*. Both these editions are very rare today, but they add nothing to the poet's fame and have only an historical interest.

In New York, Abū Māḍī threw himself into journalism and took charge of editing *al-Madjalla al-ʿarabiyya* and then *al-Fatāt*. It is at this point that he became connected with the great names of *mahdjar* literature who were to found *al-Rābiṭa al-ḳalamiyya*; it was also there that he married the daughter of Nadjīb Diyāb, director of the *Mirʾāt al-Gharb*, of which he became chief editor 1918-29, i.e. until the time when he founded the monthly *al-Samīr*, which he transformed into a daily in 1936 and directed till his death on 23 November 1957.

Abū Māḍī's talent began to take shape in New York, with his poetic work partly spread by the periodicals to which he contributed and brought together in a new *dīwān*, *al-Djadāwil* (New York 1927; reprinted at Nadjaf three times between 1937 and 1949); with his fame thus assured, his poetic talent became more widely known in his last collection published during his lifetime, *al-Khamāʾil* (New York 1940; 2nd edn. Beirut 1948, with additions). Some further poems were collected together in 1960, after his death, as *Tibr wa-turāb*.

Within the limits of this brief article, it is not possible to go into the details of Abū Māḍī's poetic achievement, but the most striking feature for the reader is what might be called the philosophical tone of many of the poems, a succinct philosophy conveyed as a scepticism which is stressed many times. In this respect, the famous quatrains which appear in the *Djadāwil* and which have been thought worthy of separate publication under the title of *al-Ṭalāsim*, are characteristic; musing on the origins of man, the poet replies to the questions put in each strophe by a *lastu adrī* "I do not know" (which has inspired the *shaykh* Muḥammad Djawād al-Djazāʾirī to compose a reply: in his *Ḥall al-Ṭalāsim* [Beirut 1946], each strophe ends, somewhat presumptuously, with an *anā adrī* "I myself know"). His social, political and nationalist themes, already animating his first *dīwān*, became more refined and precise, and the poet was moved to act as a moralist in a well-known piece, *al-Ṭīn*, which condemns human pride, commends humility and advocates equality (see a commentary in Dj. Rikābī *et alii*, *al-Wāfī fi 'l-adab al-ʿarabī al-ḥadīth*, Damascus 1963, 180-4; Fr. tr. in *Anthol. de la littérature arabe contemporaine*, iii, *La poésie*, by L. Norin and E. Tarabay, Paris 1967, 83-4). But the poet, in spite of his disquiet and his philosophical doubt, nevertheless had an optimistic and lively character which made him love life just as it is and made him proclaim his faith in the lasting value of art and literature. In his *Khamāʾil*, he chanted the praises of Lebanon, which at bottom he knew very poorly, and expressed his nostalgia for his native country, which he did not see again till 1948.

In regard to poetic technique, one might have expected Abū Māḍī to utilise free verse (*al-shiʿr al-ḥurr*), but in fact he remained faithful to classical metres, which he only abandoned in order to adopt a strophic pattern or, in his narrative poem of 79 verses *al-Shāʿir wa 'l-sulṭān al-djāʾir* (1933), to be able to employ several metres and sometimes alter the rhyme.

Abū Māḍī's successful poetical work, with its immediate accessibility to the reader, has tended to obscure his work as a journalist and the quality of his prose. It would undoubtedly be an exaggeration to maintain that all his contributions to the numerous *mahdjar* periodicals, on which he collaborated, are poems in prose. However, the poet's personality comes through constantly in his editiorals and in his articles, admittedly those on literary topics, but in those on political, economic and social questi which he treats in an eminently poetic fashion, playing his reflective attitude and allowing the s preoccupations as those of his verses to ap through.

Bibliography: Abū Māḍī has already made the subject of some studies, amongst w are Fatḥī Ṣafwat Nadjda, *Īliyyā Abū Māḍī w ḥaraka al-adabiyya fi 'l-mahdjar*, Baghdad 1 Zuhayr Mīrzā, *Ī. Abū Māḍī, shāʿir al-mahdjar akbar*, Damascus 1954; ʿAbd al-Laṭīf Sharār *Abū Māḍī*, Beirut 1961. Works on the litera of the *mahdjar* naturally include material on Māḍī's work; on his prose, see in particular, ʿ al-Karīm al-Ashtar, *al-Nathr al-mahdjarī*, Be 1964, index; idem, *Funūn al-nathr al-mahdj* Beirut 1965, index. Amongst the numerous arti devoted to him, see Ilyās Abū Shabaka, *Ī. Māḍī*, in *al-Muḳtaṭaf*, October 1932; Dj. ʿAbd Nūr, *Ī. Abū Māḍī*, in *al-Ādāb*, 1953; idem, in *D rat al-maʿārif*, v, 101-4 (with bibliography); G. Selim, *The poetic vocabulary of Īlîyâ Abû M (1889?-1957): a computational study of 47, 766 tent words*, Ph. D. thesis, Georgetown Univ. 1 (unpublished); R. C. Ostle, *Ī. Abū Māḍī and Ar poetry in the inter-war period*, in idem (ed.), *Stu in modern Arabic literature*, Warminster 1975, 45; Salma Khadra Yayyusi, *Trends and movem in modern Arabic poetry*, Leiden 1977, i, 123-35.

(Ed.

ABŪ MAḤALLĪ (al-Maḥallī on coins) al-Fil al-Sidjilmāssī, the name by which Abu 'l-ʿAb Aḥmad b. ʿAbd Allāh is known, one of the ch pretenders who took part in the ruin of Moro during the agony of the Saʿdid [*q.v.*] dynasty whose brief spell of success has a useful illustra value.

We know by his autobiography, which forms beginning of his still-unpublished book, the *K Iṣlīt al-khirrīt fi 'l-ḳaṭʿ bi-ʿulūm al-ʿifrīt*, but wh al-Ifrānī gives in his *Nuzha*, that he was born Sidjilmāssa in 967/1559-60 into a family of juri which were said to be descended from the Proph uncle. His father was a *ḳāḍī*, and in the first insta took charge of his son's education, and then s him to complete his studies at Fās, where the you man spent several years. After the accession Aḥmad al-Manṣūr and the end of the troubles wh had racked northern Morocco, he went to visit tomb of the Berber saint Abū Yaʿazza [*q.v.*]; th despite the great distrust he had felt for mystics, became a convert to Ṣūfism and attached himself the *shaykh* Muḥammad b. Mubārik al-Zaʿīrī and li for eight years close to him. His master then s him to Sidjilmāssa "in order to bring blessing on inhabitants". In 1002/1594 Abū Maḥallī made Pilgrimage to Mecca. On his return, he visited eastern provinces of Morocco and finally settled w his family in the Sāwra valley, and in some place known to us now, devoted himself to God.

It was at this point that this first-rate jurist, n deeply affected by mysticism, proclaimed that had received divine inspiration and gave himself to be the *mahdī*. Al-Yūsī says that he was no lon content to put together, in an elegant style, le works or mediocre poetry, but began to deal w subjects which showed that he had reached the po of possessing divine grace (*dhawḳ*) up to a cert degree. He probably also had within in him son thing of the thaumaturge, like so many other clai ants to such powers. When in 1019/1610 he lear the sultan Muḥammad al-Shaykh II had handed the town of Larache (al-ʿArāʾish [*q.v.*]) to the ıiards, he shared in the popular indignation, fan- the general wave of xenophobia and skilfully sed the occasion to launch an appeal for the holy and to proclaim the downfall of the Saʿdids. ı a few hundred followers inflamed by his words promises, he managed to seize Sidjilmāssa from egal governor and set up there the reign of jus- His prestige grew so great that he was recog- l as far away as Timbuctu and received delega- s from distant tribes and even from the town of ıcen. He further began negotiations with the ya of Dilāʾ [*q.v.* below].

awlāy Zaydān, Muḥammad al-Shaykh II's her, who was ruling over Marrakesh and its on, took fright and organised a powerful army e valley of the Wādī Draʿ. Abū Maḥallī marched hem immediately, and his opponents, convinced he was supernaturally aided, laid down their s and were crushed.

he pretender, benefitting from the sound advice renegade commander, did not hesitate to march Marrakesh at the head of his rough and savage ıran followers, whose numbers increased daily. lāy Zaydān offered no resistance and retreated afi. On 20 May 1612 Abū Maḥallī occupied the l *ḳaṣaba* and adopted all the insignia of royalty; since supplies of gold continued to arrive in rakesh, he had minted in his own name fine-quali- old coins. Nevertheless, although he disapproved oreign occupation of Moroccan territory, he had sense to allow Christian merchants to continue r commercial activities. It is thanks to these last we have first-hand information about the claim- and the immense prestige which he enjoyed ngst the troops and the peoples whom he had ıght under his control.

awlāy Zaydān had prudently to leave Safi for the where he got into contact with another religious er, Yaḥyā b. ʿAbd Allāh b. Saʿīd al-Ḥāḥī, who yed great fame and who promised to expel Abū allī from Marrakesh. He gathered together erous bodies of troops and soon appeared with n near the southern capital. Abū Maḥallī came to do battle at the head of his faithful Saharan ps, but at the beginning of the engagement was d by a shot. His army believed that the divine our had abandoned it and was unable to resist the ck. On 30 November 1613 Yaḥyā occupied the and had his rival's head hung above the gateway he *ḳaṣaba*.

he tragic spiritual and mental process which led ious scholar to seek after temporal power and ı to give himself out as a Messiah, finally ending ike a sorcerer's apprentice, remained in the Moroc- mind as such a baleful example that the chroni- s only mention it whilst at the same time praying the divine pardon to Abū Maḥallī.

Bibliography: M. El Oufrānī (al-Ifrānī), *Nuzhet lhādi, histoire de la dynastie sa'adienne au Maroc 1511-1670*). Ar. text and Fr. tr. O. Houdas, Paris 888-9, index; Ḥ. al-Yūsī, *Kitāb al-Muḥāḍarāt*, lith. ās 1317/1899, 90-1; H. de Castries, *Sources in- lites de l'histoire du Maroc*, 1ère série, *Saadiens 1530-1600*), *Pays Bas*, ii, Paris 1907 (index); P. de énival, *ibid.*, 1ère série, *Saadiens (1530-1600) ngleterre*, ii, Paris 1925; G. S. Colin, *Chronique noyme de la dynastie saadienne*, Collection de extes arabes publ. par l'I. N. F. M., Paris 1934; partial fr. tr., based on a defective text, was ublished in 1924, at Algiers, by E. Fagnan, *Extraits inédits sur le Maghreb*, v, 442-4; J. D. Brèthes, *Contribution à l'histoire du Maroc par les recherches numismatiques*, Casablanca [1939], 211 and pl. xxviii; A. al-Nāṣirī, *Kitāb al-Istiḳṣā*, vi, *al-Dawla al-Saʿdiyya*, new annotated edn., Casablanca 1955; R. Le Tourneau, *Abū Maḥallī, rebelle à la dynastie saʿdienne* (1611-1613), in *Studi orientalistici in onore di G. Levi Della Vida*, ii, Rome 1956; J. Berque, *Al-Yousī, problèmes de la culture marocaine au XVIe siècle*, Paris 1958, 62-4; R. Le Tourneau, *La décadence saʿdienne et l'anarchie marocaine au XVIIe siècle*, in *Annales de la Faculté des Lettres d'Aix*, xxxii (1960), 187-225. (G. Deverdun)

ABŪ MANṢŪR B. YŪSUF, in full ʿAbd al-Malik b. Muḥammad b. Yūsuf, wealthy Ḥanbalī merchant, the most important patron of the Ḥanbalī movement and a staunch supporter of the ʿAbbāsid caliphate in the 5th/11th century. Abū Manṣūr b. Yūsuf was for Baghdād and the caliph what Niẓām al-Mulk was for Khurāsān and the sultan. Both distinguished themselves from among their contemporaries by their political and administrative genius, as well as by their wealth and power, Abū Manṣūr accumulating his wealth through commerce, and Niẓām al-Mulk through power which he exercised in the name of the sultan.

In 453/1061, Abū Manṣūr saw to the destitution of the caliphal vizier Abū Turāb al-Athīrī whom he had replaced by Ibn Dārust. In 447/1055 it was Abū Manṣūr who had influenced the caliph to appoint Abū ʿAbd Allāh al-Dāmaghānī, a Ḥanafī, as *ḳāḍī 'l-ḳuḍāt* in order to placate the Ḥanafī Saldjūḳ conquerors. Three years later, Abū Manṣūr, who had been on friendly terms with the Saldjūḳs, was thrown into prison by Basāsīrī on the latter's return to Baghdād during the absence of his archenemy the Saldjūḳ Ṭoghrīl Beg. It was only after paying great sums of money that Abū Manṣūr regained his freedom, but he did not feel entirely safe until Ṭoghrīl Beg had returned to Baghdād, wresting it from the hands of Basāsīrī, stripping the latter of all the wealth he had accumulated, and killing him. In the affair of the marriage of Ṭoghrīl Beg with the caliph's daughter, a marriage which scandalised the caliph, Abū Manṣūr, along with Abū ʿAbd Allāh al-Dāmaghānī, played the role of mediator between caliph and sultan.

Abū Manṣūr b. Yūsuf was known for his good works and for the favours which he bestowed upon his contemporaries. Among his works was the reconstruction of the ʿAḍudī Hospital, al-[Bi]Māristān al-ʿAḍudī, which he also endowed with *awḳāf* properties in order to provide for its needs in perpetuity. Among those who benefitted from his largesse were the Ḥanbalī *ʿulamāʾ* and ascetics who enjoyed a great following among the masses, the preachers, the leading Hāshimīs and their followers, the Saldjūḳs' functionaries, including *shiḥna*s and the *ʿamīd*s, as well as the Bedouin and Turkish *amīr*s.

This wide influence enjoyed by Abū Manṣūr did not please Niẓām al-Mulk, and the rivalry between these two influential men can be seen in some of the events of the period. The founding of the Niẓāmiyya *madrasa* in Baghdād (inaugurated in 459/1067) is an instance in point. Abū Isḥāḳ al-Shīrāzī, for whom the *madrasa* was founded, having refused to assume the chair of law for religious reasons (the *maghṣūb*, or misappropriated character of the materials), was replaced by another Shāfiʿī, Ibn al-Ṣabbāgh, chosen by Abū Manṣūr, with the concurrence of the caliph. The founding of the *madrasa* by Niẓām al-Mulk appears to have been considered by Abū Yuṣūf as interference in the latter's sphere of interest.

The rivalry between these two powerful and influential men also expressed itself quite clearly in the ideological sphere. While Abū Manṣūr was the great support and consolation of the traditionalist *ʿulamāʾ* in Baghdād, men belonging essentially to the Ḥanbalī movement, Niẓām al-Mulk supported the rival Ashʿarī movement. And whereas Niẓām al-Mulk lent his support and bestowed his patronage upon men of the rationalist Muʿtazilī movement, Abū Manṣūr had reduced the Muʿtazilīs to silence in Baghdād. It was because of him that the great Muʿtazilī professor of the period in Baghdād, Abū ʿAlī b. al-Walīd, could not publicly profess his teachings in that city. The riot which occurred in Baghdād in 460, led by the traditionalists against Ibn al-Walīd, was caused by the latter's reappearance in public to teach Muʿtazilism; Abū Manṣūr had disappeared from the scene at the beginning of that year. There is some evidence indicating that Abū Manṣūr's death was not a natural one, and that he had paid with his life for interfering with Niẓām al-Mulk's plans. For instance, the contemporary Ibn al-Bannāʾ, writing in his *Diary* about five months after the death of Abū Manṣūr, mentions a dream in which he saw Abū Manṣūr walking barefoot and, upon asking him the cause, replied saying that that "was the way to walk for those who complain of wrongdoing" (*hādhā ... mashy al-mutaẓallimīn*). Elsewhere in the *Diary* (ii, 26, 47), the following invocation is made: "May God have mercy on the *blood* of [Abū Manṣūr] Ibn Yūsuf". The word *blood*, in this context, implies *bloodshed*, blood calling for revenge, or for justice. It is perhaps significant that the title *al-Shaykh al-Adjall* "the most eminent *Shaykh*", applied only to Abū Manṣūr during his lifetime, is found later applied not only to his two sons-in-law, Ibn Djarada and Ibn Riḍwān, but also to Niẓām al-Mulk (E. Combe *et al.*, *Répertoire*, vii, Nos. 2734, 2736, 2737).

The two sons-in-law of Abū Manṣūr, though they inherited from their father-in-law his title, presented no threat to Niẓām al-Mulk. Ibn Riḍwān succeeded to Abū Manṣūr's position of influence with the caliph; but far from following in the footsteps of his father-in-law in opposing Niẓām al-Mulk, he became reconciled with him by effecting a marriage between his daughter and Niẓām al-Mulk's son. On the other hand, Ibn Djarada seems to have inherited the place of honour enjoyed by his father-in-law with the traditionalists, for whom he founded mosque-colleges (*masdjid*) in Baghdād.

Bibliography: G. Makdisi, *Ibn ʿAqīl et la résurgence de l'Islam traditionaliste au XIe siècle* (*Ve siècle de l'hégire*), Damascus 1963, 274 and n. 3 (bibliography cited); idem, *Muslim institutions of learning in eleventh-century Baghdad*, in *BSOAS*, xxiv (1961), 30, 35-7; idem, *Nouveaux détails sur l'affaire d'Ibn ʿAqīl*, in *Mélanges Louis Massignon*, Damascus 1967, iii, 91-126, *et passim*; idem, *Autograph diary of an eleventh-century historian of Baghdad*, in *BSOAS*, xviii-xix (1956-7), xix, 285, 296-7 *et passim*. (G. Makdisi)

ABŪ MISMĀR, al-Sharīf Ḥammūd b. Muḥammad b. Aḥmad al-Ḥasanī, an important *sharīf* of Abū ʿArīsh who in the early years of the 19th century defended his independent state, based on the coastal plain of ʿAsīr [*q.v.*] (Tihāmat ʿAsīr) and embracing most of the Tihāma region of Yemen, against the encroachments of the Wahhābī Āl Saʿūd of Nadjd, the Zaydī *imām*s of Ṣanʿāʾ and the Ottomans under Muḥammad ʿAlī. Born in or before 1170/1756-7, he was descended from the Āl Khayrāt *sharīf*s who emigrated from Mecca to the al-Mikhlāf al-Sulaymānī district of lowland ʿAsīr early in the 11th/17th century. death occurred in 1233, probably during Rama July 1818 but possibly several months earlier.

While serving as the Zaydī *imām*'s governo Abū ʿArīsh in the mid-18th century, Sharīf Aḥ Ḥammūd's grandfather, declared his family's i pendence, although the *imām*'s suzerainty was ognised. Ḥammūd assumed power in about 1215/1 1, and shortly afterwards had to expel a troubles Wahhābī agent of ʿAbd al-ʿAzīz (d. 1218/1803), chief of the Āl Saʿūd. But when in 1217/1802-3 ʿArīsh was captured by Abū Nukṭa (d. 1224/18 the Wahhābī *amīr* of upland ʿAsīr, Ḥammūd decl allegiance to ʿAbd al-ʿAzīz. He undertook to certain taxes to the Wahhābī chief and send a to al-Dirʿiyya as hostage, in return for which he appointed ʿAbd al-ʿAzīz's governor of lowland ʿ Aided by Wahhābī reinforcements, Ḥammūd su quently captured from the old Zaydī *imām*, Manṣūr bi'llāh ʿAlī (1189-1224/1775-1809), and ad to his own lands, the bulk of the Tihāma regio Yemen, including such centres as al-Luḥayya, Ḥudayda, Bayt al-Fakīh, Zabīd and al-Ḥays, not Mocha.

Ḥammūd's allegiance to the Wahhābīs was nominal; and early in 1224/1809 he conspired Aḥmad, the heir apparent to Imām al-Manṣūr to replace Wahhābī suzerainty with that of Zaydī *imām*, on condition that he himself was allo to retain the Tihāma lands already under his con Although his forces were twice defeated by thos Abū Nukṭa later that year, and despite occasi Wahhābī forays into the northern Tihāma therea Sharīf Ḥammūd was able, with the aid of his compe vizier, Sharīf al-Ḥasan b. Khālid al-Ḥāzimī, to control of both his ancestral lands and the exten Tihāma territories acquired with Wahhābī help. flirted alternately with the *imām* in Ṣanʿāʾ and Wahhābī chief in al-Dirʿiyya just enough to fores a serious military intervention by either.

Initially disposed to cooperating with Muḥamm ʿAlī against the Wahhābīs (1229/1814), Ḥammūd c ed towards him, owing to a series of Wahhābī victo over the Ottomans and his fear of the Egypt viceroy's designs upon his lands. In 1233/1818, a few days before his death, Ḥammūd's forces ne annihilated an Egyptian army. His son Aḥmad r after him for about a year before submitting Muḥammad ʿAlī's commander in the south and be sent to Egypt where shortly he died. Altho Ḥammūd's lands were restored by the Ottoman tan to the *imām*, the governorship of lowland ʿ was awarded to a nephew of Ḥammūd.

Bibliography: The basic source for the lif Sharīf Ḥammūd Abū Mismār is his unpublished ography, *Nafḥ al-ʿūd*, by ʿAbd al-Raḥmān al-B kalī (a ms. of which is in the al-ʿAḳīlī private col tion at Djāzān). This treats of the *sharīf*'s life 1225/1810-11, the remaining years being cove by al-Ḥasan b. Aḥmad ʿĀkish in a *dhayl* entit *Nuzhat al-ẓarīf*. Other mss. in which Sharīf Ḥamm figures, sometimes prominently, are Luṭf A Djiḥāf, *Durar nuḥūr al-ḥūr*; ʿĀkish, *al-Dībādj khusrawānī*; al-Ḥasan b. ʿAbd al-Raḥmān al-K kabānī, *al-Mawāhib al-saniyya*; and Badr al- Muḥammad al-Kibsī, *al-Laṭāʾif al-saniyya*. Of th works, *Nafḥ al-ʿūd*, its *dhayl* and al-*Dībādj* w consulted by Muḥammad b. Aḥmad ʿĪsā al-ʿA in Part 1 of his *Min taʾrīkh al-Mikhlāf al-Sul mānī*, Riyadh 1958.

Other works providing useful information ab Sharīf Ḥammūd's life are al-Shawkānī, *al-Badr* *li*ᶜ, Cairo 1348/1929-30, i, 240 f.; Shānīzāde, *a*ᵓ*rīkh*, Istanbul 1290-1/1873-4, iii, 30 ff.; Ibn ishr, ᶜ*Unwān al-madjd*, Riyadh 1967, 132-210, *ıssim*; Zabāra, *Nayl al-waṭar*, Cairo 1348/1929-30, *passim*; C. Niebuhr, *Description de l'Arabie*, Paris 779, ii, 107; Henry Salt, *A voyage to Abyssinia*, ondon 1814, 123 ff.; J. L. Burckhardt, *Notes on e Bedouins*, London 1831, ii, *passim*; R. L. Play-ıir, *A history of Arabia Felix*, Bombay 1859, 119-4. (J. R. BLACKBURN)

BU 'L-MUṬAHHAR AL-AZDĪ, an Arab ter who lived in the 5th/11th century, but since nown biographical source mentions him, his dates the milieu within which he lived can only be rred from his sole surviving work, the *Ḥikāyat 'l-Ḳāsim* (one should however add the informa- of al-Bākharzī (d. 467/1075), who says that he w in Iṣfahān a writer called Abū Muṭahhar, very ly our author). He must have lived between Bagh- and Iṣfahān, as emerges from a *munāẓara* be-en the two cities given in the *Ḥikāya*, before the djūḳ assumption of power in ᶜIrāḳ, which he never ntions. Concerning the rest of his work, he himself ntions an *Ḥikāya badawiyya*, now lost, and al-kharzī a *Ṭirāz al-dhahab* ᶜ*alā wishāḥ al-adab* (as-ning that the same person is involved).

The *Ḥikāyat Abi 'l-Ḳāsim al-Baghdādī* (ms. Brit. s. Add. 19,313; ed. A. Mez, Heidelberg 1902) has nained till now a unique work in classical Arabic rature, a conscious variation of the highly-preciated *maḳāma* genre [*q.v.*] which al-Hamadhānī d just launched and which al-Ḥarīrī (who lived t one or two generations after our author) was bring to perfection. The novelty of the *Ḥikāya* of u 'l-Muṭahhar in relationship to the *maḳāma* of above two authors is the displacement of the tre of interest from the purely linguistic and for-l aspect to the representation of a character and environment in a genuine *mimesis* of reality (in s case, the bourgeois environment of Baghdād, h its bons viveurs and drinkers, amongst whom u 'l-Ḳāsim displays his bravura style and his va-bond's effrontery). This bravura style is also a guistic one, and Abu 'l-Muṭahhar attaches himself this means to the *maḳāmāt* writers; but whilst the ter remain merely that, and their heroes al-Is-ndarī and al-Sarūdjī offer us nothing more than omewhat monotonous and stereotyped cliché figure a rogue, al-Azdī's Abu 'l-Ḳāsim is wholly alive, d to be compared more with the characters in tronius's *Satyricon* and the "pícaros" of Spanish rrative literature. The text of the *Ḥikāya* raises lot of philological problems for the language and metimes the jargon used in it, but its literary im-rtance is far from being limited to pure philology; e work of this 5th/11th century ᶜIrāḳī writer, him-lf almost unknown, remained an isolated effort of time, but heralding fields of interest and artistic rrents of the future.

Bibliography: Mez, in the introd. to his edition; the arts. *Ḥikāya* in *EI*[1] and *EI*[2] by Macdonald and Pellat respectively; F. Gabrieli, in *RSO*, xx (1942), 33-45. (F. GABRIELI)

ABŪ NUKHAYLA AL-ḤIMMĀNĪ AL-RĀDJIZ, a ɔet of Baṣra who owed his name to the fact that s mother gave birth to him by a palm tree (*nakhla*). e was given the *kunya*s of Abu 'l-Djunayd and Abu ᶜIrmās and the name of Yaᶜmar (or Ḥazn, or Ḥabīb Ḥazn) b. Zāᵓida b. Laḳīṭ, but it is possible that he rged a fictitious genealogy to attach himself to the ıᶜd b. Zayd Manāt of Tamīm; in fact, al-Farazdaḳ, gry at being released from jail at his intervention, calls him a *daᶜī*, and Ibn al-Kalbī does not cite him in his *Djamhara*. It is said that he was ejected by his father, on account of his ingratitude, and spent some time in the desert, where he improved his knowledge of the Arabic of the Bedouins and gained a certain fame. He then went to Syria and succeeded in attaching himself to Maslama b. ᶜAbd al-Malik [*q.v.*], despite a personal inhibition which led him at first to attribute to himself an *urdjūza* of Ruᵓba [*q.v.*], and then afterwards addressed eulogies to Hishām b. ᶜAbd al-Malik and his successors, who showed their favour to him and gave him the largesse of which he was avidly hungry. He nevertheless had no scruples in going and presenting himself to Abu 'l-ᶜAbbās al-Saffāḥ and in reciting to him an *urdjūza* in *dāl* which he had previously dedicated to Hishām. His panegyrics of the first ᶜAbbāsids, filled with attacks on his former patrons, gained him the title of "poet of the Banū Hāshim", but his greed led in the end to his downfall. He wrote, and caused to be widely spread, a poem in which he urged al-Manṣūr to proclaim his own son Muḥammad (al-Mahdī) as heir-presumptive instead of ᶜĪsā b. Mūsā, whom al-Saffāḥ had designated heir. The caliph generously rewarded him and followed his advice, but he instructed him to flee to Khurāsān. However, one of ᶜĪsā's agents pursued him, slaughtered him, stripped the skin from his face and threw his corpse to the vultures. This took place at some time shortly after 136/754.

Abū Nukhayla wrote some *ḳaṣīda*s, but above all favoured *radjaz*; he was involved in poetic contests with another famous *rādjiz*, al-ᶜAdjdjādj [*q.v.*] and left behind a body of work considered good enough to be formed into a *dīwān*. This poetry is not always easy to understand, because of the Bedouinisms which abound in it, but it has a verve which is sometimes fairly coarse and a humour which disarmed his opponents and made his audience laugh, these last being more or less inclined accordingly to open their purse-strings. This was, indeed, the poet's sole object, and he seems to have been an inveterate demander of money. Cutting epigrams are to be found side-by-side with poems on hunting themes, elaborate panegyrics and unexpected elegies, since, despite an innate sense of ingratitude, the poet knew occasionally how to display his thanks, and especially after the death of al-Muhādjir b. ᶜAbd Allāh al-Kilābī, who had been a kindred spirit. The critics, and especially Ibn al-Muᶜtazz, considered him to have been a born poet, and much appreciated his work, which was widely-distributed in the 3rd/9th century.

Bibliography: Djāḥiẓ, *Ḥayawān*, ii, 100 and index; idem, *Bayān*, iii, 225, 336; Ibn Ḳutayba, *Shiᶜr*, 583-4; Ibn al-Muᶜtazz, *Ṭabaḳāt*, 21-3; Ibn Durayd, *Ishtiḳāḳ*, 154; idem, Djamhara, iii, 504; Ṭabarī, iii, 346-50; Masᶜūdī, *Murūdj*, vi, 118-20 = § 2332; *Aghānī*, ed. Beirut, xx, 360-92; Ṣūlī, *Awlād al-khulafā*ᵓ, 310-14; Ḥuṣrī, *Zahr al-ādāb*, 925; Baghdādī, *Khizāna*, ed. Būlāḳ, i, 78-80 = ed. Cairo, i, 153-7; Ibn ᶜAsākir, *Ta*ᵓ*rīkh Dimashḳ*, ii, 318-22; Ghars al-Niᶜma, *Hafawāt*, index; Marzubānī, *Muwashshah*, 219-20; Ibn al-Shadjarī, *Ḥamāsa*, 117; Āmidī, *Mu*ᵓ*talif*, 193-4; Ibn al-ᶜImād, *Shadharāt*, i, 195; Nallino, *Littérature*, 159-60; Pellat, *Milieu*, 159-60; O. Rescher, *Abriss*, i, 223; A. H. Harley, *Abu Nukhaylah, a postclassical Arab poet*, in *JRAS Bengal*, 3rd series, iii (1937), 55-70; Bustānī, *DM*, v, 145-7; Ziriklī, *Aᶜlām*, viii, 331. (CH. PELLAT)

ABŪ RAKWA [see AL-WALĪD B. HISHĀM].

ABŪ RASHĪD AL-NĪSĀBŪRĪ, SAᶜĪD B. MUḤAMMAD, a theologian of the Muᶜtazilī tradition of Baṣra and disciple of ᶜAbd al-Djabbār al-Hamadhānī [*q.v.*]. Originally a follower of the Muʿtazilī school of Baghdād, Abū Rashīd frequented the lectures of ʿAbd al-Djabbār, whose doctrine he came to follow in its entirety, surrendering his former adherence to the teaching of al-Kaʿbī and the Baghdādīs. Subsequently, having given up his circle (*ḥalḳa*) at Nīsābūr, he took up permanent residence at Rayy where, after the death of ʿAbd al-Djabbār in 415/1025, he became the acknowledged leader of the Baṣran Muʿtazila. The date of his death is unknown. Abū Rashīd's teaching insofar as it is revealed in the presently available sources, is essentially undistinguishable from that of ʿAbd al-Djabbār. His works include (1) *K. al-masāʾil fi 'l-khilāf bayn al-Baṣriyyīn wa 'l-Baghdadiyyīn* (Berlin 5125 = Glaser 12), the first part of which was published with a translation by A. Biram, *Die atomistische Substanzlehre aus dem Buch der Streitfragen*, Berlin 1902; a paraphrase of much of the work is found in M. Horten, *Die Philosophie des Abu Raschid*, Bonn 1910. This work (entitled in several of the section headings *al-Masāʾil fi 'l-khilāf bayn shaykhinā Abī Hāshim wa 'l-Baghdādiyyīn*) contains rather fulsome expositions of a number of the Baṣrans' philosophical theses, set forth against unelaborated theses of al-Kaʿbī, and grouped under fourteen major topics; and (2) *Ziyādāt al-Sharḥ* (cited in *K. al-Masāʾil*, fol. 112v°), of which a lengthy portion of the first part is published by M. Abū Rīda under the title *Fi 'l-tawḥīd*, Cairo 1969 and a large part of a later section, though in a different rescension, is found in British Museum ms. Or. 8613. The *Sharḥ* in question is a work of Ibn Khallād, a disciple of Abū Hāshim [*q.v.*], that appears to have been completed by ʿAbd al-Djabbār. Other works, not currently known to have survived, are (3) *Dīwān al-uṣūl*, a lengthy work written for *taʿlīḳ* at the direction of ʿAbd al-Djabbār, divided into two sections, the first philosophical and the second theological, viz. (a) *al-Djawāhir wa 'l-aʿrāḍ* and (b) *al-Tawḥīd wa 'l-ʿadl*; (4) *al-Tadhkira*; (5) *K. al-Djuzʾ*; (6) *K. al-Shahwa*; (7) *Masāʾil al-khilāf baynanā wa-bayn al-Mushabbiha wa 'l-Mudjbira wa 'l-Khawāridj wa 'l-Murdjiʾa*; and (8) *Naḳḍ ʿalā aṣḥāb al-ṭabāʾiʿ*.

Bibliography: Besides the works cited in the text, see Ibn al-Murtaḍā, *Ṭabaḳāt al-Muʿtazila*, ed. S. Diwald-Wilzer, Wiesbaden 1969, 116; R. Martin, *A Muʿtazilite treatise on prophethood*, diss. New York University 1976 unpublished; R. Frank, *Beings and their attributes*, Albany 1977, index; and also Brockelmann, S I, 244 and Sezgin, *GAS*, ii, 626 f. (R. M. Frank)

ABŪ RIYĀSH AL-ḲAYSĪ, Aḥmad b. Ibrāhīm al-Shaybānī, *rāwī*, philologist and poet, originally from Yamāma, who settled at Baṣra and was famous at the beginning of the 4th/10th century for his exceptional knowledge of the Arabic language, genealogies and ancient poetry. He was a former soldier who had become a civil servant, and had the job of levying dues on the ships coming to ʿAbbādān. He was totally lacking in education and in tidiness, but his knowledge led to his faults being excused and overlooked. He had a powerful voice, and he spoke in the Bedouin fashion, expressing the *iʿrāb*, at a time when this was normally neglected in the spoken language. He was said to pose as a Zaydī. He died in 339/950 (but in 349/960, according to al-Suyūṭī, who moreover calls him Ibrāhīm b. Aḥmad).

His clashes with Ibn Lankak (d. 360/970 [*q.v.*]), who found in his lack of cleanliness a vein of attack easy to exploit, would have been enough to save him from oblivion, but Yāḳūt, *Udabāʾ*, xix, 6, goes as far as to assert that Ibn Lankak was eclipsed by al-Mutanabbī (d. 345/965) and by Abū Riyāsh, who l at this time were outstanding. If such an asser is valid for the first-named poet, it hardly se justified in regard to the second, since if Abū Riy had been poet of remarkable quality, it is likely posterity would have preserved his work more c fully; whereas only a limited number of his ve are extant, notably, apart from his replies to Lankak, a piece in praise of al-Muhallabī [*q.v.*], wh nevertheless drew down on himself the poet's c cising Abū Riyāsh; he himself owed part at leas his fame to al-Tanūkhī (d. 384/994 [*q.v.*]), who been his pupil, and to Abu 'l-ʿAlāʾ al-Maʿarrī 449/1058 [*q.v.*]). Abū Riyāsh is said not to have preciated Abu Tammām's work, but neverthe wrote a commentary on the latter's *Ḥamāsa*, wh was criticised by al-Ḳifṭī but used especially by Baghdādī (who does not, however, cite it in the of sources of his *Khizāna*, ed. Cairo, i, 33), and thought it opportune to put together in his turn anthology called *al-Ḥamāsa al-Riyāshiyya* (in the a ḤAMĀSA, the reading *Abū Dimās* taken from *Fihrist*, ed. Cairo, 120, should be corrected to A Riyāsh). This anthology must have enjoyed a cert fame, since al-Maʿarrī did not esteem his reputat damaged by completing a commentary on it, wh title only is known, *al-Riyāsh al-muṣṭaniʿī* (Yāḳ *Udabāʾ*, iii, 157, in the biography of Abu 'l-ʿAlāʾ; M. Saleh, in *BEO*, xxiii (1970), 278).

Bibliography: Thaʿālibī, *Yatīma*, ii, 120 Ḳifṭī, *Inbāh*, ed. Cairo 1950, 25-6; Tanūkhī, *Ni wār*, ed. Cairo 1392/1972, ii, 158; Yāḳūt, *Udab* ii, 123-31; Ṣafadī, *Wāfī*, vi, 205, No. 2669; Suyū *Bughya*, 178; Fück, *ʿArabīya*, Fr. tr., 178; Bustā *DM*, iv, 314. (Ch. Pellat)

ABŪ SAʿD AL-MAKHZŪMĪ, the name curren given to ʿĪsā b. Khālid b. al-Walīd, minor po of Baghdād whose fame stems from his clashes wi Diʿbil [*q.v.*]. The long dispute between the two po was clearly a manifestation of the latent confl between the partisans of Yemen and those of Niz and it was probably provoked by the famous *ḳaṣī* of Diʿbil in praise of the South Arabs (ʿAbd al-Kar al-Ashtar, *Shiʿr Diʿbil*, Damascus 1964, No. 212), which Abū Saʿd replied by a poem in *-rāʾ* whi achieved some fame in its time. After this incider the Banū Makhzūm might well have closed their do to Diʿbil, but the fear which he inspired in them l them at that point to deny to their defender ar connection with their clan, and on the advice of a Maʾmūn, they issued a formal declaration to th effect (*Aghānī*, ed. Beirut, xx, 127, 130). Abū Saʿ who claimed to be descended from al-Ḥārith Hishām, then had inscribed on his ring *al-ʿAbd al-ʿAbd*; and al-Djāḥiẓ himself calls him *daʿī Ba Makhzūm* (*Bayān*, iii, 250-1; *Ḥayawān*, i, 265). Tl *Aghānī*, which has no special notice on Abū Saʿ gives in its section on Diʿbil (xx, 121 ff.) some detai on the two poets' attitudes and on the measures use by the latter expressly to humiliate his opponen Having, in an epigram, dubbed Abū Saʿd as Ḳawṣa (a metonymy denoting a woman, but Ibn Ḳawṣa means pariah), Diʿbil hired children to chant it round the streets (*Shiʿr Diʿbil*, No. 119; *Aghānī*, x 123, 131; Ibn al-Muʿtazz, *Ṭabaḳāt*, 140), which e raged Abū Saʿd. For his own part, he took care incite al-Maʾmūn (*Aghānī*, ii, 130) against the po of the South Arabs who had abused him in one c his poems, and even asked him for authorisation bring Diʿbil's head to the caliph (*Aghānī*, xx, 93, 13 132); but the caliph refused this request, and advise him to limit himself to replying to the attacks. Diʿb

:edly even tried to murder his enemy (*Aghānī*, :27); and if the report in *Aghānī*, xx, 125-7, of an ırent reconciliation is authentic, it must indicate Saʿd's duplicity. Various pieces aimed against have been gathered in *Shiʿr Diʿbil*, Nos. 68, 81, 119, 223, 235; see also p. 293).

bū Saʿd was also exposed to attacks from Diʿbil's ;in, the son of Abu 'l-Shīṣ (*Aghānī*, xx, 130-1; *Diʿbil*, 349), but he on his part made al-Ashʿath)jaʿfar al-Khuzāʿī his target, and the latter had Saʿd flogged with a hundred lashes (Ibn al-tazz, *Ṭabaḳāt*, 139-40). In the end he left Baghdād eek shelter at Rayy, where he died in the caliphate l-Wāthiḳ *ca.* 230/845 (*ibid.*).

t is interesting to note that not only did Abū l take the trouble to introduce one of his own ;es into a poem by Diʿbil (*Aghānī*, xx, 124), but that a certain number of pieces are attributed one or the other poet at the same time (*Shiʿr bil*, 289, 313, 322, 338). As well as the epigrams ed at his enemies, Abū Saʿd addressed praises to la'mūn and wrote several pieces glorifying Nizār; *Aghānī*, xx, 128, even speaks of a *daftar al-āriyyāt*. Diʿbil's fame, since his works were spread and wide, threw Abū Saʿd's work into the shade, ough this last is by no means of inferior quality. believe al-Marzubānī, *Muwashshaḥ*, 329, Abū ımām would have given half of his own work a hemistich by Abū Saʿd which he particularly reciated. Abū Saʿd, who constituted himself as ender of the North Arabs and by that fact also defender of Sunnism against the Shīʿī Diʿbil, at ime of ethnic and religious conflicts, deserves to no longer ignored by historians of Arabic litera-e; it happens fortunately that Razzūḳ Faradj zzūḳ has just endeavoured to put together his vān (Baghdād, 1971).

Bibliography: ʿAbd al-Karīm al-Ashtar, *Shiʿr Diʿbil*, index; idem, *Diʿbil b. ʿAlī al-Khuzāʿī*, 2nd dn. Damascus 1967, 145 ff. and index; Ibn Ḳu-ayba, *ʿUyūn al-akhbār*, i, 190; Djāḥiẓ, *Bayān*, iii, 250; idem, *Ḥayawān*, i, 262, 265; Marzubānī, *Muwashshaḥ*, 329, 347; idem, *Muʿdjam*, 98, 260; Nuwayrī, *Nihāya*, ii, 91; Ḥuṣrī, *Zahr al-ādāb*, 320; Ibn al-Muʿtazz, *Ṭabaḳāt*, 126, 139-41; Bustānī, *DM*, v, 339-40; Ziriklī, *Aʿlām*, v, 286; introd. to his *Dīwān*. (Ed.)

ABŪ SAʿĪD AL-KHAṬṬĀBĪ [see AL-KHAṬṬĀBĪ].

ABŪ SAʿĪD AL-SĪRĀFĪ [see AL-SĪRĀFĪ].

ABŪ SAYYĀRA, ʿUMAYLA B. AL-AʿZAL B. KHĀLID -ʿADAWANĪ, a personage of the end of the āhiliyya, said to have been the first to fix the *a* or pecuniary composition for murder at 100 nels and the last to lead the pilgrims, either at departure for ʿArafāt (*ifāḍa*) or from al-Muzdalifa Minā (*idjāza*), since the sources disagree on this int, and the more careful authors merely use the pression *dafaʿa bi 'l-nās*. This man, who probably ed his *kunya* to this function of his, a privilege of Ḳaysī tribe of ʿAdwān (see Ibn al-Kalbī-Caskel, b. 92 and ii, 142), became proverbial because he is d to have exercised this office, always mounted the same black ass (which was, however, according al-Aṣmaʿī and others, a she-ass, sometimes further scribed as one-eyed), for 40 years. As al-Djāḥiẓ usingly points out (*Ḥayawān*, i, 139), no-one can ubt the longevity of this animal which, amongst asses, lived the longest time; it gave rise to a overb *aṣaḥḥ min ʿayr Abī Sayyāra* "more sturdy an Abū Sayyāra's ass" (al-Maydānī, *Amthāl*, i, 422- Abū ʿUbayd al-Bakrī, *Faṣl al-maḳāl fī sharḥ K. al-mthāl*, Beirut 1391/1971, 500-1); al-Djāḥiẓ provides a variant (*Ḥayawān*, ii, 257), *aṣbar min* ... "having greater endurance than ...".

Abū Sayyāra is compared, because of his humility, with ʿUzayr [*q.v.*] and with Christ, and his ass is cited by prominent people who preferred this humble form of mount.

Bibliography: In addition to the references in the article, see Djāḥiẓ, *Ḥayawān*, vii, 215; idem, *Bayān*, i, 307-8; idem, *Bukhalā'*, 187; Ibn Hishām, *Sīra*, i, 122; Ṭabarī, i, 1134; Azraḳī, *Makka*, 120-1; Ibn Durayd, *Ishtiḳāḳ*, 164; Masʿūdī, *Murūdj*, iii, 116 = § 964; Thaʿālibī, *Thimār al-ḳulūb*, 295; *Naḳā'iḍ*, ed. Bevan, 450; *DM*, iv, 373. (Ch. Pellat)

ABŪ SHABAKA, ILYĀS (usual orthography, Elias Abou Chabakeh), Maronite poet, journalist and translator (1903-47). He was born in Providence, R.I., whilst his parents were travelling in the United States, but he spent all his life in Lebanon, dividing his time between his home in the village of Zūḳ Mīkhā'īl (in Kisrawān), from which his family came, and the cafés and editorial offices of Beirut, to which he went each day.

His father held some estates in the region of Khartoum, but in 1914, when he went there, was murdered by bandits. Hence the young orphan had soon to interrupt his studies, especially as the French school at ʿAynṭūra, where he had been enrolled, was closed by the authorities during the First World War. He then resumed his studies, but never finished them, preferring to complete his education by plunging into reading the Bible and the French Romantics, which early inspired his first literary efforts. He was compelled to earn a living, hence taught for a while, but also contributed to several Lebanese newspapers, did translations, at the request of publishers, of a series of novels and dramas by French authors as varied as Lamartine, Henry Bordeaux, Voltaire, Edmond Rostand, Molière, the Abbé Prevost, Bernardin Saint-Pierre or Choukri Ghanem, and was even employed as a translator in the press and radio services of the French High Commission during the Second World War. He died of leukaemia on 27 January 1947.

The greater part of Abū Shabaka's original work is made up of seven collections of poems. The first, *al-Ḳithāra* (1926) contains juvenilia which attest at the same time his great inexperience and a distinct poetic talent. This latter is clearly affirmed in *Afāʿī 'l-Firdaws* (1938), in which the poet has gathered together thirteen pieces written between 1928 and 1938. The basic source of his inspiration is love, its transports, its joys and its sufferings, and there can be clearly seen the influence of the French Romantics in this collection, which the native critics regard as one of the master-pieces of Lebanese poetry. Romantic feelings of nature inspire the next *dīwān*, *al-Alḥān*, a real hymn to nature as well as being at the same time a poetic description of the life of the Lebanese peasants. The poet reverts to the theme of love with *Nidā' al-ḳalb* (1944) and *Ilā 'l-abad* (1945). In this very same year, 1945, there appeared *Ghalwā'*, whose title is an anagram of the name Olga, the woman whom he had at last married after ten years of betrothal and who had naturally been his principal muse. Finally, in 1958 Abū Shabaka's friends put together in *Min Ṣaʿīd al-āliha* a number of pieces of occasional verse already published in periodicals.

Abū Shabaka had a deeply religious mind, a tormented soul, and was a enthusiastic reader of the Romantics. He was undoubtedly one of the main representatives of a school which has, in Lebanon, followed, with a certain amount of side-stepping, a tendency long dormant in the West. This romantic movement is now outmoded in the East itself, but Abū Shabaka's work continues to attract young readers who appreciate pure poetry and have little taste for the politico-social preoccupations of engaged poets, who tend moreover to break loose from classical metres. Abū Shabaka generally respects these last, although he may at times adopt a strophic form or vary the rhymes and metres, as in *Ghalwāʾ*.

As well as his translations and a great number of articles which he left behind, Abū Shabaka wrote, as one might have expected, a *Lāmartīn* (1935) and a study of comparative literature, *Rawābiṭ al-fikr wa 'l-rūḥ bayn al-ʿArab wa 'l-Ifrandj* (1943). Lastly, a series of portraits of literary and political personalities, which appeared in *al-Maʿriḍ*, have been gathered together in one volume, *al-Rusūm* (1931).

Bibliography: The main studies are a collection of articles about the poet and dedicated to his memory by the most prominent names in contemporary Lebanese literature, *Ilyās Abū Shabaka*, Beirut 1948; Razzūḳ Faradj Razzūḳ, *Ilyās Abū Shabaka wa-shiʿruhu*, Beirut 1956; and Īliyyā al-Ḥāwī, *Ilyās Abū Shabaka, shāʿir al-djaḥīm wa 'l-naʿīm*, Beirut n.d. See also *Anthologie de la littérature arabe contemporaine*, iii, *La Poésie*, by L. Norin and E. Tarabay, Paris 1967, 96-8; A. Miquel, *Réflexions sur la structure poétique à propos d'Eliās Abū Šabaka*, in *BEO*, xxv (1972), 265-74; Salma Khadra Jayyusi, *Trends and movements in modern Arabic poetry*, Leiden 1977, ii, 424-52. Bustānī, *DM*, iv, 367-8 (art. by F. Bustānī, with bibl.). A thesis is now in the course of preparation at the Sorbonne on poetic image in the work of Abū Shabaka. (Ed.)

ABŪ SHĀDĪ, Aḥmad Zakī (1892-1955), Egyptian physician, journalist, writer and poet, a man of an astonishing variety of diverse activities.

Born in Cairo on 9 February 1892, he had his primary and secondary education in his natal city, and then in 1912 went to study medicine in London, where he specialised in microbiology; at the same time, he became especially interested in apiculture and acquired quite an extensive knowledge of Anglo-Saxon culture and life which was to exert a deep influence on his literary production. On returning to Egypt in 1922, he was appointed to do research in microbiology, but also became at the same time busy with many other fields, and soon became secretary of several associations of beekeepers, agricultural industrialists, poultry rearers, etc. Furthermore, he quickly took over at the same time the secretaryship of the *Apollo* group inspired by Aḥmad Shawḳī and Khalīl Muṭrān. It was he who created and directed the journal *Apollo* from 1932 to 1934, at a time when he had just founded three other journals of a totally different nature: *Mamlakat al-naḥl* (1930), *al-Dadjādj* (1932) and *al-Ṣināʿāt al-zirāʿiyya* (1932). All these responsibilities in no way kept Abū Shādī from giving talks and lectures, from writing articles on all the subjects which interested him, and above all, from throwing himself into a literary activity which gives the impression of a remarkable breadth. A man like himself, rather too restless, inevitably provoked jealousies and enmities in those circles which were not ready to accept his ideas, especially those on modern poetry. It was perhaps the reactions to his innovations which made him in 1946 decide to emigrate to the United States. He worked on the transmissions of The Voice of America from New York and then Washington, where he died on 12 April 1955.

It is extremely difficult, in this brief notice evaluate his role in the evolution of contempo Arabic poetry and to enumerate and classify his positions of his ideas and the totality of his lite work. The latter is largely composed of poetry theatrical works, and is characterised at base by inspiration which is primarily Egyptian, both Ph onic and Arab. He embarked on almost every po genre, at times giving himself up to romanticism at times to symbolism, and even went so far as found in 1936 an ephemeral journal called *Adabī* " literary work". With regard to form, Abū Shādī u the framework of the *muwashshaḥ* [*q.v.*] and o strophic structures, but he was above all the ponent of blank verse (*al-shiʿr al-mursal*) and of verse (*al-shiʿr al-ḥurr*), under the simultaneous fluence of Anglo-Saxon poetry and of that of *mahdjar*, and he tried to launch a literary movem in this sense.

In various commentaries which accompanied collections, as also in his articles explaining his id and his work of criticism *Masraḥ al-adab* (Cairo 19 8), he insisted on the primordial importance in poe of metre; he freed himself from the fetters of rhy but respected up to a certain point classical met at the same time mixing different metres in one a the same poem (on this question and on Abū Shā influence, see S. Moreh, *Free verse* (al-shiʿr al-ḥ *in modern Arabic literature: Abū Shādī and his sch 1926-46*, in *BSOAS*, xxx/1 (1968), 28-51).

If he had enemies, he also made friends and mirers who busied themselves in collecting toget his poetry into more or less coherent collectio Hence there appeared in this way *Miṣriyyāt* (192 *al-Shafaḳ al-bākī* (1926); *Amīn wa-ranīn aw ṣu min shiʿr al-shabāb* (1925), on the initiative of Ḥ. al-Djaddāwī; *Shiʿr al-widjdān* (1925), on the initiat of Muḥ. Ṣubḥī; and *al-Muntakhab min shiʿr Abī Sh* (1926) by ʿAbd al-Ḥamid Fuʾād.

As for the *dīwān*s published by Abū Shādī hims the main ones of these are *Waṭan al-Farāʿina* (192 *Ashiʿʿa wa-ẓilāl* (1931); *al-Shuʿla* (1933); *Aṭyāf rabīʿ* (1933, with an introduction by Khalīl Muṭ and others); *Aghānī Abū Shādī* (1933); *Andāʾ al-fa* (1934: poems of his youth); *al-Yanbūʿ* (1934); *Fa al-ʿubāb* (1935); *al-Kāʾin al-thānī* (1935); *ʿAwdat rāʿī* (Alexandria 1942); and *Min al-samāʾ* (New Yo 1949). There must also be still further unpublish collections of poems written in America.

As well as his *dīwān*s, Abū Shādī left behind so fifteen novels and theatrical pieces whose Pharao and Arab inspiration is comparable with that of poetry and in which the use of blank verse is n uncommon: *Zaynab, nafaḥāt min shiʿr al-ghi* (1924); *Mafkharat Rashīd* (1925); *ʿAbduh Bek* (192 *al-Āliha* (1927, a symbolist opera); *Iḥsān* (1927, Egyptian drama); *Ardashīr* (1927, an opera); *Akhn ton* (1927, an opera); *Néfertiti*; *Maʿshūkāt Ibn Ṭūlū* and *al-Zibbāʾ malikat Tadmur* (1927); *Bint al-Ṣaḥ* (1927, an opera); *Iḥtiḍār Imriʾ al-Ḳays*; *Ibn Zayd fī sidjnihi*; *Bayrūn wa-Tīrīz*; and *Mahā* (a love stor

It is not possible here to speak at length abo Abū Shādī's scientific works, but one should menti that he was at the same time the theoretician free verse and the promoter of apiculture in Egyp notably with his *Tarbiyat al-naḥl* (1930). Not fo getting that he was a physician, he also wrote *Ṭabīb wa 'l-maʿmal* (1928); and not forgetting eith that he was a Muslim, he explained why he was a b liever in his *Limā anā muʾmin* (1937) and publish in the year he died *al-Islām al-ḥayy*, all of whi had not prevented him from praising freemasonry

Rūḥ al-māsūniyya (1926). Finally, one should .tion his verse translation of the quatrains of ıar Khayyām and Ḥāfiẓ (1931), as well as the one ›hakespeare's *The Tempest*.

his brief survey can only give a partial idea of exceptional personality, one who was discussed criticised, but also admired, and who merits :icular interest.

Bibliography: In addition to S. Moreh's ar-cle, the main monographs on him are Muḥammad Abd al-Ghafūr, *Abū Shādī fi 'l-mīzān*, Cairo 1933; . A. Edhem, *Abushady, the poet. A critical study ith specimens of his poetry*, Leipzig 1936; and ıuḥammad ʿAbd al-Fattāḥ Ibrāhīm, *Aḥmad Zakī bū Shādī, al-insān al-muntidj*, Cairo 1955. See also ›ustānī, *DM*, iv, 373-4 (with bibliography); and '. K. Kotsarev, *Pisateli Egipta*, Moscow 1975, 31-4 with bibl.), and index; Salma Khadra Jayyusi, *'rends and movements in modern Arabic poetry*, ,eiden 1977, ii, 370-84. (Ed.)

ABŪ SHAKŪR BALKHĪ, born possibly in 300/-13, one of the most important Persian :ts of the Sāmānid period. ʿAwfī's *Lubāb al-albāb* :ibutes to him a *mathnawī* in the *mutaḳārib* metre ed the *Āfarīn-nāma*, completed in 336/947-8 and bably dedicated to the *amīr* Nūḥ b. Naṣr (331-43/-54). Nothing is known about his life, but allusions ıis verses suggest that he was a professional poet l had known setbacks in life. The only surviving ts of his work are short fragments and isolated ses quoted in dictionaries, anthologies and a few er works. These comprise some 60 lyrical distichs l some fragments of *mathnawīs* in various metres, t above all, about 140 *mutaḳārib* distichs which st belong to the *Āfarīn-nāma*, to which one should haps add almost 175 distichs cited anonymously the *Tuḥfat al-mulūk* of ʿAlī b. Abī Ḥafṣ Iṣfahānī h/13th century), which seem to be extracts from same work. This last was apparently a collection anecdotes illustrating moral sentiments; maxims l moral sayings are prominent in the extant verses Abū Shakūr, who was certainly the chief heir ıongst the Persian poets of the 4th/10th century the wisdom literature of pre-Islamic Iran. He must ve enjoyed a great renown in his time; Manūčihrī ntions him as one of the ancient masters, along th Rūdakī and Shahīd Balkhī.

Bibliography: There is an edition of the frag-ments with a French translation, together with a notice on the poet and a bibliography, in G. Lazard, *Les premiers poètes persans*, Tehran-Paris 1964, i, 94-126, ii, 78-127; see also J. Rypka, *History of Iranian literature*, Dordrecht 1968, index.

(G. Lazard)

ABŪ SHURĀʿA, Aḥmad b. Muḥammad b. ḳurāʿa al-Ḳaysī al-Bakrī, minor poet of Baṣra ıo, during the course of the 3rd/9th century, took rt in the social and intellectual life of his native wn, and hardly left it, it seems, except to make e Pilgrimage or to visit places very close at hand. ır the rest, his life is poorly documented. It seems likely that he was able, as Ibn al-Muʿtazz asserts *'abaḳāt*, 177-8), to praise al-Mahdī (158-69/775-85) ıring the latter's lifetime, to have reached an ad-nced age in al-Maʾmūn's time and to die in the liphate of al-Mutawakkil (232-47/847-61). In the :st place, the *Aghānī* speaks of his relations with rāhīm b. al-Mudabbir (d. 279/892-3 [see ibn al-udabbir]) at Baṣra, where the latter, according to s own words, acted as governor (it is not impossible ıat he was governor there before 252/866, but he is ıly mentioned as tax-collector in Ahwāz in *ca.* 250/864). One item of information concerning Abū Shurāʿa's meeting with Diʿbil (d. 246/860 [*q.v.*]) in Ahwāz is of no help. Moreover, al-Djāḥiẓ, so far as is known, cites him only once (*Rasāʾil*, ed. Hārūn, ii, 314), re-peating an epigrammatic verse aimed at al-Sidrī (cf. *Aghānī*, xxii, 435), whilst Abū Shurāʿa's name would certainly figure more often if he had been older. Moreover, several other authors cite five fairly me-diocre verses of his (see Pellat, *Milieu*, 166) which he is said to have composed on al-Djāḥiẓ's death (255/868). Finally, his son Abu 'l-Fayyāḍ Sawwār, who was also a poet, went to Baghdād after 300/913, and it was he who indirectly furnished Abu 'l-Faradj with most of the information about his father. All these pieces of information lead one to think that Abū Shurāʿa died after 255 at a considerable age.

Although he was reputed to have written epistles and to have delivered eloquent discourses, he was mainly known as a versifier, and Abū Bakr al-Ṣūlī even deigned to gather his works into a *dīwān* (*Fihrist*, 216). According to the *Aghānī*, his poetry was in the Bedouin tradition and fairly obscure, but the part of it now extant does not allow of a categorical judgement. As well as verses inspired by his ruinous generosity, he wrote mainly some fairly coarse epi-grams, an attractive poem on Ibn al-Mudabbir's departure and some occasional verses which reflect the idle way of life led in Baṣra at this time by the poets, always lying in wait for some reward or ready to heap ridicule on some patron who had disappointed them.

Bibliography: In addition to the references given above, see *Aghānī*, ed. Beirut, xxii, 178-9, 429-50; Marzubānī, *Muwashshaḥ*, 219; idem, *Muʿdjam*, 431 ff.; Khaṭīb Baghdādī, *Taʾrīkh*, xii, 219-20; Mubarrad, *Kāmil*, 306; Sandūbī, *Adab al-Djāḥiẓ*, 195; Bustānī, *DM*, iv, 383-4. (Ch. Pellat)

ABŪ SINBIL, an ancient village on the western side of the Nile between the first and second cataracts, in lat. 22° 22 north and long 31° 40 east. It lies *ca.* 175 miles south of Aswān. The French discoverers of the two huge rock-hewn temples built by Ramses II (1304-1237 B.C.) referred to it as Ipsamboul at the beginning of the 19th century. The name Abū Sinbil is a popular arabicisation ("father of an ear of corn") of the local Nubian designation, which is also known by many other variants in the spelling, e.g. Abū Simbil/Sinbūl/Sunbul/Sunbūl.

Abū Sinbil later became known as Farīḳ in the Official Government Register, being one of the vil-lages within the financial jurisdiction of the Ibrīm (Piromi, *ca.* 35 miles north of Abū Sinbil) district until 1272/1855 when it became a separate adminis-trative unit. In 1917 the name Farīḳ was dropped, and the village was given its former name, Abū Sin-bil. Its irrigated land extends over several hundreds of acres.

Abū Sinbil became famous as the site of two rock temples which gave it its special artistic and religious significance. The temples, which represent some of the most spectacular examples of ancient Egyptian architecture, were unknown to the outside world un-til the discovery of the Smaller Temple by J. L. Burckhardt in 1813, and its opening by the Italian engineer Giovanni Belzoni in 1817.

The Great Temple of Abū Sinbil is carved in the rock and stands 33 m. high and 38 m. wide. The façade shows four colossal seated figures of Ramses II, two on either side of the entrance to the temple, each measuring 20 m. high. Ramses II dedicated this temple to the sun gods Amon Rē of Thebes and Rē-Horakhti of Heliopolis.

Less than 50 yards away was constructed the Smaller (northern) Temple, which was dedicated to Queen Nefertari, wife of Ramses II, in homage to the goddess Hathor. Its façade is decorated with six 35-foot statues of the Pharaoh and his wife.

The Abū Sinbil cliff had been buried by large sand drifts, which covered the Great Temple until its rediscovery by Burckhardt. But the Smaller Temple, which had not been buried, served the inhabitants of the nearby village Bilyānī (*ca.* 5 miles from Abū Sinbil) as a refuge from marauding Bedouin tribes from Nubia. Only modern Arab authors give particulars about the Abū Sinbil temples, based on French sources, and reports of the French archeological expedition which undertook the excavations at Abū Sinbil in the 19th century.

The original site was submerged by the Nile in 1966 as a result of the building of the Aswān High Dam. The two temples were salvaged from the rising waters of the Nile by sawing them into sections and re-erecting them on top of the rock face from which they were originally hewn.

Bibliography: ʿAlī Pa<u>sh</u>a Mubārak, *al-<u>Kh</u>iṭaṭ al-tawfīḳiyya al-<u>dj</u>adīda*, Būlāḳ 1305, viii, 14-15; G. Rawlinson, *A history of Ancient Egypt*, London 1881, ii, 318-20; E. A. Wallis Budge, *Cook's Handbook for Egypt and the Sudan*[3], London 1911, 259-66; A. E. P. Weigall, *A guide to the Antiquities of Upper Egypt*, London 1913, 565-76; P. Bovier-Lapierre *et alii*, *Précis de l'histoire d'Égypte*, Paris 1932, i, 160-1; S. Mayes, *The Great Belzoni*, London 1959, 132 ff.; Muḥammad Ramzī, *al-Ḳāmūs al-<u>dj</u>ug<u>h</u>rāfī li 'l-bilād al-Miṣriyya*, Cairo 1963, ii/4, 230-1; W. MacQuitty, *Abu Simbel*, London 1965, *passim*; G. Gerster, *Saving the ancient temples at Abu Simbel*, in *National Geographic Magazine*, cxxix/5 (1966), 694-742. (R. Y. Ebied)

ABŪ TA<u>GH</u>LIB Faḍl Allāh al-<u>Gh</u>aḍanfar al-Ḥamdānī, ʿUddat al-Dawla, Ḥamdānid *amīr* of Mosul [see ḥamdānids] and son of the *amīr* al-Ḥasan Nāṣir al-Dawla and a Kurdish mother, Fāṭima, born 328/940. He seems to have had a certain authority over his younger brothers, and when their father grew old, Abū Tag<u>h</u>lib seems to have obtained tacitly from them, except for Abu 'l-Muẓaffar Ḥamdān, who was born of another mother, authority to depose their father and imprison him in the stronghold of Ardumu<u>sh</u>t in the <u>D</u>jabal <u>D</u>jūdī to the north-east of Mosul. This operation was carried out with the complicity of Fāṭima in <u>D</u>jumādā I 356/beginning of May 967, and Nāṣir al-Dawla died there on 12 Rabīʿ I 358/3 February 969. As this act of deposition had been carried out without Ḥamdān's agreement, and Ḥamdān controlled the towns of Niṣībīn, Māridīn and Raḥba, with the addition of Rakka, seized on the death of the Ḥamdānid of Aleppo Sayf al-Dawla, Abū Tag<u>h</u>lib secured support from the Būyid *amīr al-umarā'* in Bag<u>h</u>dād and master of the caliphate Ba<u>kh</u>tiyār, and attacked Ḥamdān, forcing him to surrender Raḳḳa and evacuate Raḥba.

Abū Tag<u>h</u>lib continued the war against Ḥamdān, but the latter now obtained Ba<u>kh</u>tiyār's support and re-entered Raḥba, whilst certain of Abū Tag<u>h</u>lib's other brothers now turned on him and took Ḥamdān's side. But a new offensive by him forced Ḥamdān to flee for refuge with the Būyid in Bag<u>h</u>dād. He now was able to consolidate his power in Mosul, seizing his brother's possessions and endeavouring to unite under his authority the territories of the Ḥamdānid amīrate of Aleppo held by his cousin, Sayf al-Dawla's son, and obtaining from the caliph al-Muṭīʿ lillāh an investiture patent for the united amīrates of Mosul and Aleppo. He extended his authority over Di Bakr and Mayyāfāriḳīn, where he left Sayf al-Daw mother and his sister <u>D</u>jamīla with a certain amc of authority, then seized Ḥarrān and Diyār Mu (359-60/969-70). Recalling that his father Nāṣir Dawla had been *amīr al-umarā'* in Bag<u>h</u>dād, whe he had been dislodged in 334/945 by the Būyid Mu al-Dawla, Ba<u>kh</u>tiyār's predecessor, Abū Tag<u>h</u>lib dreamed of recovering this rôle in Bag<u>h</u>dād and coming the real master of the caliphate. For his p Ba<u>kh</u>tiyār, with whom Ḥamdān was now living, urged by the latter into warfare with Abū Tagh

However, Ba<u>kh</u>tiyār preferred to make an ent with Abū Tag<u>h</u>lib and to conclude an agreement v him confirming this last in his possessions, incluc Diyār Muḍar and Diyār Bakr, and this was se by Abū Tag<u>h</u>lib's marriage with one of Ba<u>kh</u>tiy daughters. It is probable that one of the reasons hind this agreement was the threat to both par from Fāṭimid ambitions. Hence both of them g help to the Fāṭimids' enemy, the Ḳarmaṭī c Ḥasan al-Aʿṣam, who received subsidies from th and was accordingly with their help briefly able seize Damascus. Nevertheless, in the end Ba<u>kh</u>ti yielded to Ḥamdān's solicitations. In 363/973 marched against Mosul and took up a position Dayr al-Aʿlā to the north of the town. Abū Tag evacuated the town and made a diversion southwa as far as the gates of Bag<u>h</u>dād, provoking m exitement there. He then retired towards Mosul, Ba<u>kh</u>tiyār, though numerically stronger, entered i negotiations with Abū Tag<u>h</u>lib, who obtained an vantageous agreement. On returning to Bag<u>h</u>dād, considering Abū Tag<u>h</u>lib's position as over-adv tageous, he launched another expedition aga Mosul. Again, negotiations were begun; Abū Tag agreed to pay tribute to the Būyid, and recei from the caliph the *laḳab* of ʿUddat al-Dawla "S port of the dynasty" in 974. His relations with Ba tiyār remained friendly, and he gave support to latter when the Būyid had to face a rebellion of Turkish mercenary troops in Bag<u>h</u>dād itself.

The rebellion of the Turkish troops had led Ba tiyār to appeal also to the head of the family, Ru al-Dawla, who authorised ʿAḍud al-Dawla, ruler Fārs, to march on Bag<u>h</u>dād, thus favouring the a bitions of the latter, who dreamed of securing ʿIr Abū Tag<u>h</u>lib, pressed by the Turks who had ov thrown Ba<u>kh</u>tiyār, had left Bag<u>h</u>dād. ʿAḍud Dawla expelled the Turks, but now received the to submission of Ba<u>kh</u>tiyār, whom he forced to abdica and also made an agreement with Abū Tag<u>h</u>lib, up whom depended the supply of provisions for the ci the treaty previously made between Abū Tag<u>h</u>lib a Ba<u>kh</u>tiyār was renewed and the Ḥamdānid excu fromt he payment of tribute. However, Rukn Dawla showed his opposition to ʿAḍud al-Daw treatment of Ba<u>kh</u>tiyār and recalled ʿAḍud al-Daw Ba<u>kh</u>tiyār accordingly resumed power in Bag<u>h</u>d But when Rukn al-Dawla died in 366/977, ʿAḍud Dawla, who had never renounced his ambitions ʿIrāḳ, returned to Bag<u>h</u>dād in November 977.

Abū Tag<u>h</u>lib's position now appeared firm. I Ḥamdān, who had always remained in Ba<u>kh</u>tiyā entourage, persuaded the latter to attack Mosul, a Ba<u>kh</u>tiyār advanced as far as Takrīt. Abū Tagh acted skilfully. He promised to aid Ba<u>kh</u>tiyār in covering Bag<u>h</u>dād and getting free of ʿAḍud al-Daw provided he would surrender to him Ḥamdān, a he marched on Bag<u>h</u>dād in concert with Ba<u>kh</u>tiy But ʿAḍud al-Dawla defeated them near Sāmarrā a captured Ba<u>kh</u>tiyār, whilst Abū Tag<u>h</u>lib fled. ʿA

)awla entered Mosul itself in June 978 and re- ɪd to negotiate in any way with Abū Taghlib. The er fled to Niṣībīn and thence to Mayyāfāriḳīn, sued by the Būyid troops. Deciding not to go 3itlis, where his sister Djamīla had taken refuge, ntered the Kurdish mountain region of the Tigris uent of the Khābūr al-Ḥasaniyya, perhaps with hope of shutting himself up in the Ḥamdānid nghold of Ardumusht. But in the end he decided nake for the region of the Tigris sources and the ıt loop of the Euphrates, where was the Byzantine ɜl Sklēros, with whom he had been in contact and whom he had promised help against the imperial ɔps. He was pursued by ʿAḍud al-Dawla's forces, had an engagement with them at the beginning 368/August 978 in the mountain region near Ḥiṣn ād (Kharpūt), territory held by Sklēros. He was ɔrious in this, and stayed for some time at Ḥiṣn ād. He hoped for a victory by Sklēros over the erial army and help from the latter to reconquer sul, but Sklēros was subsequently beaten. Abū ghlib arrived at Āmid in Diyār Bakr, having learnt t Mayyāfāriḳīn, held by his supporters, had been tured by the Būyids; he now fled with Djamīla Raḳḳa, abandoning Diyār Bakr and Diyār Rabīʿa ʿAḍud al-Dawla.

'he Būyid *amīr* rejected attempts by Abū Taghlib negotiate with him, and he was unable to count any help from his cousin Abu 'l-Maʿālī Saʿd al- wla in Aleppo, who had just recognised the su- ainty of ʿAḍud al-Dawla. He now further aban- ɪed Diyār Muḍar, which had till then remained ler his control, and decided to make for Fāṭimid itory and go to Damascus, not daring however, to to Egypt itself. Abandoned by various of his thers, exposed to the hostility of both the Fāṭimid ɔps and those of the rebel master of Damascus, ssām, he attempted, with the support of one of the ıb tribes of Syria, the ʿUḳayl, to capture Ramla in lestine from the Ṭayyī Mufarridj b. Daghfal b. Djarrāḥ. But he clashed with Fāṭimid troops, and Ṣafar 369/end of August 979 he and his allies were eated and he was handed over to Mufarridj, who, tead of delivering him to the Fāṭimid commander, ed him with his own hand. It seems that Abū ghlib was killed at the instigation of ʿAḍud al- wla, whom Mufarridj had recognised as suzerain 371 (see Madelung, in *JNES*, lxxvi (1967), 22, 29).

Such was the end, at the age of 40, of the last mdānid of Mosul, of Nāṣir al-Dawla's son, and of Ḥamdānid amīrate of Mosul, where new powers re now installed but where memories of the Ḥam- ıids long remained in the minds of the local popu- ion.

Bibliography: See for this, M. Canard, *Histoire le la dynastie des H'amdânides de Djazira et de Syrie*, i, Algiers 1950, where the vicissitudes of Abū Taghlib's career are set forth in ch. vi, 541-72.

(M. CANARD)

ABU 'L-ṬAMAḤĀN AL-ḲAYNĪ, ḤANZALA B. AL-ARḲĪ, *Mukhaḍram* Arab poet, considered to one of those endowed with an unduly long life -Sidjistānī, *K. al-Muʿammarīn*, ed. Goldziher, in *h. zur arab. Philologie*, ii, 62, asserts that he lived ɔ years). During the *Djahiliyya* he led the life of a gand or *ṣuʿlūk* [*q.v.*] and of a libertine (especially, Mecca, in the company of al-Zubayr b. ʿAbd al- ṭṭalib), and he does not seem to have altered his ys in any measure after his conversion to Islam. is said to have been killed at Adjnādayn [*q.v.*] in /634, but F. Bustānī (*DM*, iv, 408-9) believes that he died *ca.* 30/651, whilst the *Aghānī* asserts that he spent his last years among the Banū Shamkh of Fazāra, with whom he had sought refuge from the efforts of the authorities to arrest him for a crime committed by him. This source (ed. Beirut, xiii, 3-13) also recounts adventures of his whose authenticity raises serious doubts. It tells how Abu 'l-Ṭamaḥān managed to set free Ḳaysaba b. Kulthūm (on whom see Ibn al-Kalbī-Caskel, Tab. 240 and ii, 464), who had been captured during the course of the pilgrim-age; and it dilates on his own capture during a battle between two groups of the Ṭayyiʾ (Badjīla and al-Ghawth) and his ransoming by Budjayr b. Aws al-Ṭāʾī, who set him free and received eulogies in verse.

It is difficult to get an idea of Abu 'l-Ṭamaḥān's poetic work, since although this was collected together into a *Dīwān* by al-Sukkarī (*Fihrist*, 224), only fragments of this have been preserved, and this only thanks to their fame, which led to several of them being set to music. The authenticity of the most-oft cited verse (metre *ṭawīl*, rhyme *thaḳībuh*) should nevertheless be regarded with caution; it appears in Djāḥiẓ (*Ḥayawān*, iii, 93) in a fragment attributed to Laḳīṭ b. Zurāra and given immediately after that of Abu 'l-Ṭamaḥān, of which it forms part in the other sources; Ibn Ḳutayba (*ʿUyūn*, iv, 24; *Shiʿr*, 692) expressly attributes it to Laḳīṭ.

Finally, the existence of at least three poets bearing this same *kunya* (see al-Āmidī, *Muʾtalif*, 149-50) should demonstrate the need for the greatest prudence.

Bibliography: In addition to references given in the text, see Djāḥiẓ, *Bayān*, i, 187, iii, 235, 237; idem, *Ḥayawān*, iv, 473; Ibn Ḳutayba, *Shiʿr*, 348-9; Buḥturī, *Ḥamāsa*, 294; Abū Tammām, *Ḥamāsa*, ii, 77-8, 258; Ibn al-Kalbī-Caskel, ii, 298; Mubarrad, *Kāmil*, 46-7, 100, 436; Ibn Durayd, *Ishtiḳāḳ*, 317; *Naḳāʾiḍ*, ed. Bevan, 670; Kushādjim, *Maṣāyid*, Baghdād 1954, 207, 209; ʿAskarī, *Ṣināʿatayn*, 360; Marzubānī, *Muwashshaḥ*, 75, 78, 244; idem, *Muʿdjam*, 149-50; Baghdādī, *Khizāna*, ed. Būlāḳ, iii, 426; Ibn Hadjar, *Iṣāba*, No. 2011; Yāḳūt, *Buldān*, ii, 154; Murtaḍā, *Amālī*, ed. 1907, i, 185; Wahhābī, *Marādjiʿ*, i, 193-4; Ziriklī, ii, 322-3; Blachère, *HLA*, 318.

(ED.)

ABU 'L-ṬAYYIB AL-LUGHAWĪ, ʿABD AL-WĀḤID B. ʿALĪ AL-ḤALABĪ, grammarian of the 4th/10th century, interested above all in lexicography (*ʿilm al-lugha*), whence his surname. He came originally from ʿAskar Mukram in Khūzistān, but left his natal town for Baghdād, where he studied under Abū ʿAmr al-Zāhid and Abū Bakr al-Ṣūlī. Then he moved to Aleppo, whose ruler, Sayf al-Dawla, was attracting scholars from all disciplines. It was thus in Aleppo that Abu 'l-Ṭayyib found himself competing with the grammarian Ibn Khālawayh [*q.v.*], who had followed the same masters at Baghdād as himself and who had become tutor to Sayf al-Dawla's son. Abu 'l-Ṭayyib was killed in the massacre by the Byzantines when Aleppo was captured in 351/962. His most famous pupil was Ibn al-Ḳāriḥ, to whom Abu 'l-ʿAlāʾ al-Maʿarrī presented his *Risālat al-Ghufrān*, giving there information on Abu 'l-Ṭayyib's works, many of which, he stated, perished in the sack of Aleppo. His extant works include the following: *K. Marātib al-naḥwiyyīn*, ed. M. Abu 'l-Faḍl Ibrāhīm, Cairo 1955; *K. Shadjar al-durr*, ed. M. ʿAbd al-Djawād, Cairo 1957; *K. al-Ibdāl* and *K. al-Muthannā*, ed. Tanūkhī, Damascus 1960, *K. al-Itbāʿ*, ed. Tanūkhī, Damascus 1961; and *K. al-Aḍdād*, still unpublished. In regard to the *K. al-Furūḳ*, cited by al-Suyūṭī in his *Muzhir*, i, 447, this seems to have been lost.

Bibliography: Brockelmann, S I, 190; Kaḥḥāla, *Muʿdjam*, vi, 210; ʿIzz al-Dīn al-Tanūkhī, in *MMIA*, xxix, 175-83. (G. TROUPEAU)

ABŪ USĀMA AL-HARAWĪ, DJUNĀDA B. MUḤAMMAD, grammarian and lexicographer of the 4th/10th century, a native of Harāt in Khurāsān. He was the pupil of Abū Manṣūr al-Azharī and Abū Aḥmad al-ʿAskarī, whose works he transmitted. After residing at Shīrāz, where he frequented the circle of the vizier the Ṣāḥib Ibn ʿAbbād [*q.v.*], he went off to Cairo. There he taught in the Nilometer mosque (*Djāmiʿ al-Miḳyās*) and, in company with the traditionist ʿAbd al-Ghanī b. Saʿīd al-Miṣrī and the grammarian ʿAlī b. Sulaymān al-Anṭākī, he held lectures at the House of Knowledge (*Dār al-ʿIlm*). He was subsequently accused of preventing the rising of the Nile by casting spells on it, condemned to death by the caliph al-Ḥākim and executed in 399/1009. His biographers only provide the name of one of his pupils, that of Abū Sahl al-Harawī, and they attribute no works to him; however, a commentary by him, on the *Muʿallaḳa* of Imruʾ al-Ḳays, has come down to us.

Bibliography: Brockelmann, S I, 36; Sezgin, *GAS*, ii, 52; Yāḳūt, *Irshād*, ii, 426; Ibn Khallikān, *Wafayāt*, i, 372, tr. de Slane, i, 337; Suyūṭī, *Bughya*, 213. (G. TROUPEAU)

ABU 'L-WALĪD AL-BĀDJĪ [see AL-BĀDJĪ].

ABU 'L-YUMN AL-ʿULAYMĪ [see MUDJĪR AL-DĪN].

ABŪ ZAʿBAL, an ancient village in Lower Egypt *ca.* 15 miles north of Cairo. Its original name was al-Ḳuṣayr, under which designation it is mentioned by Ibn Mammātī (d. 606/1209) in his *Kitāb Ḳawānīn al-dawāwīn*. It became known as Abū Zaʿbal from the end of the Mamlūk period, the first record of this name being found in a deed of *waḳf* granted by Khāyir Bey al-Djarkasī, Ottoman governor of Egypt 923-8/1517-21, dated 10th Radjab 926. It had a population of approximately 2,000 people towards the end of the 19th century.

In 1827 Muḥammad ʿAlī founded a School of Medicine in Abū Zaʿbal, which was chosen because of its convenient location near the barracks of his army. The School was attached to the largest military hospital in Egypt, which had been built in Abū Zaʿbal in 1825. Muḥammad ʿAlī appointed the Frenchman Clot Bey (then Physician and Surgeon-in-Chief of the Egyptian army) as its first director. In order to overcome the difficulty posed by the language barrier between the students and the French and Italian professors, Clot Bey appointed a team of interpreters who were also entrusted with the translation into Arabic of the necessary medical textbooks. The first of these translations, *al-Ḳawl al-ṣarīḥ fī ʿilm al-tashrīḥ*, was printed at the press of the Medical School of Abū Zaʿbal (also founded by Muḥammad ʿAlī) in 1248/1832 (the first book to be printed in Abū Zaʿbal).

To the Abū Zaʿbal School of Medicine were later added the School of Pharmacy (1830), the School of Veterinary Medicine (1831) and the School of Obstetrics (1832). The Medical School was transferred in 1837 to its present site at Ḳaṣr al-ʿAynī (Cairo), a palace built in 870/1466 by Aḥmad b. al-ʿAynī, grandson of the Sultan Khushḳadam.

The area around Abū Zaʿbal was the scene of considerable military activity during the Napoleonic occupation, Abū Zaʿbal itself being twice attacked by the French troops. When Napoleon's troops demanded an impost for the upkeep of the military from the people of Abū Zaʿbal on the 23 Ṣafar 1213/7 August 1798, they refused to give it, and a result the French sacked the village and set it fire. Five months later the French attacked A Zaʿbal again and seized all the cattle and the bea of burden (on 30 Radjab 1213/11 January 1799). Djabartī also records that Abū Zaʿbal was loo on 6 Djumādā I 1207/23 December 1792 by Mu Bey and his Mamlūk soldiers, who killed about 25 the villagers, and arrested and imprisoned the *shay* of Abū Zaʿbal.

Today Abū Zaʿbal is well-known for the la prison situated there.

Bibliography: ʿAbd al-Raḥmān al-Djaba *ʿAdjāʾib al-āthār fi 'l-tarādjim wa 'l-akhbār*, Bū 1297/1880, ii, 239-40, iii, 13, 14, 38; Muḥamm Amīn al-Khāndjī, *Mundjam al-ʿumrān fī 'l-mus drak ʿalā muʿdjam al-buldān* [of Yāḳūt al-Rūr Cairo 1325/1907, i, 109; Aḥmad ʿIzzat ʿAbd Karīm, *Taʾrīkh al-Taʿlīm fī ʿaṣr Muḥammad ʿ* Cairo 1938, 251-316; Naguib Mahfouz Pasha, *history of medical education in Egypt*, London 19 14-16; Djamāl al-Dīn al-Shayyāl, *Taʾrīkh al-T djama wa 'l-ḥaraka al-thaḳāfiyya fī ʿaṣr Muḥa mad ʿAlī*, Cairo 1951, *passim*; Abu 'l-Futūḥ R wān, *Taʾrīkh Maṭbaʿat Būlāḳ*, Cairo 1953, 354 Muḥammad Ramzī, *al-Ḳāmūs al-djughrāfī li'l-bi al-Miṣriyya*, ii/1, Cairo 1954-5. 31. (R. Y. EBIED)

ABŪ ZAKARIYYĀʾ AL-FARRĀʾ [see AL-FARRĀ

ABŪ ZAYD AL-ḲURASHĪ, MUḤAMMAD B. A 'L-KHAṬṬĀB, *adīb* of the end of the 3rd/9th or the beginning of the 4th/10th century, and kno only as the author of the *Djamharat ashʿār al-ʿArab* (ed. Būlāḳ 1308/1890). No personal deta about the author can be derived from this collecti and the only relevant data are two *isnād*s, one (p. going back to al-Haytham b. ʿAdī (d. *ca.* 206/8 [*q.v.*]) through two intermediaries, and the other 14) going back to Ibn al-Aʿrābī (d. 231/846 [*q.v.* through one intermediary; these *isnād*s would th allow us to date the *Djamhara* approximately to t end of the 3rd century. The mention (p. 165) of t *Ṣaḥāḥ* of al-Djawharī (d. *ca.* 398/1107-8 [*q.v.*]) is pro ably a reader's note incorporated in the text by copyist. Another problem is raised by the referen to a certain Mufaḍḍal, falsely identified (p. 1) wi al-Mufaḍḍal al-Ḍabbī (d. *ca.* 170/786 [*q.v.*]), for th cannot be a case here of the author of the *Mufa ḍaliyyāt*; Brockelmann surmised that Abū Zayd Ḳurashī and al-Mufaḍḍal might be two pseudony referring to Abū Zayd al-Anṣārī (d. 215/831 [*q.v* and to the Kūfan anthologist, but this hypothe hardly seems tenable. A. J. Arberry, for his pa (*The seven odes*, London 1957, 23) prudently sugges but without insisting upon this, an identification Abū Zayd with ʿUmar b. Shabba (d. 262/875-6 [*q.v.*

After an introduction containing observations the value of poetry for the philological point of vi and on Muḥammad's interest in it, a comparis between the language of the Ḳurʾān and that of t poets, a judgment on the merits of these last a some fragments attributed to Adam, Satan, t angels, the djinn, etc., the *Djamhara* comprises *ḳaṣīda*s written by 49 poets of the *Djāhiliyya* a the beginnings of Islam. These poems are divid into 7 groups, each of which should comprise 7 poe but ʿAntara, mentioned in the introduction as o of the 7 of the second group, figures in the end (the printed edn., though not in all the mss.) among the authors of the *muʿallaḳāt*, so that this particul group comprises 8 poems and the following one only. Abū Zayd chose the following terminolog *muʿallaḳāt*, *mudjamharāt*, *muntaḳayāt*, *mudhahhab* *ḥbahāt, marāt͟hī, mas͟hūbāt* and *mulḥamāt*. He certly is lacking in any critical spirit, but his *Djam-*, which possesses no outstanding originality, rs some interesting variants and also the advan- of grouping together for the first time the *allaḳāt* [*q.v.*] and of reflecting the public's taste time when the *ruwāt* had gathered together a siderable number of poetic productions and it had ome convenient to select and to classify those ch would ultimately constitute the Arabic humans and, on the whole, the classical ideal.

Bibliography: Ibn Ras͟hīḳ, *ʿUmda*, index; ag͟hdādī, *K͟hizāna*, ed. Cairo i, 33; F. Hommel, in *ctes du VIe Congrès Intern. des Orientalistes*, 387-08; Nöldeke, in *ZDMG*, xlix, 290-3; M. Nallino, *RSO*, xiii/4 (1932), 334-41; Brockelmann, S I, 8-9; Blachère, *HLA*, index; A. Trabulsi, *La critique poetique des Arabes*, Damascus 1955, 28-30; *M*, iv, 331. (CH. PELLAT)

BŪ ZAYD AL-SĪRĀFĪ [see AK͟HBĀR AL-ṢĪN WA-IND in Suppl.].

BŪ ZURʿA, the *kunya* by which the S͟hāfiʿī olar and jurist ʿAḤMAD B. ʿABD AL-RAḤĪM, ed IBN AL-ʿIRĀḲĪ, was best known. Abu Zurʿa, son of a prominent S͟hāfiʿī jurist of Kurdish origin, born in Cairo on 3 Dhu 'l-Ḥijja 762/14 October 1. His mother was the daughter of a Mamlūk cer. For a time his father was the *ḳāḍī* of Medina. ī Zurʿa studied in Cairc, Damascus, Mecca and lina, and completed his education at an early age. began his career as a *mudarris*, teaching *ḥadīt͟h* jurisprudence in various *madrasas* in Cairo. pointed deputy S͟hāfiʿī *ḳāḍī* of Cairo, probably in /1390, he held this and other judicial positions side the capital for twenty years, before he reed to resume his original function as *mudarris*. 822/1419, he was summoned by Sultan Ṭaṭar to ıme the position of S͟hāfiʿī grand *ḳāḍī* of Cairo— foremost judicial office in the Mamlūk empire. strict and honest manner in which he discharged functions as chief magistrate won him the eny of powerful Mamlūk *amīrs*, who pressured ar's successor, Barsbāy, into dismissing him from office in 825/1421, after a tenure of barely four- months. Abū Zurʿa died on 27 Shaʿbān 826/ ugust 1423, a few months after his dismissal.

At a time when corruption in the judiciary was npant, and when prominent jurists were spending ge fortunes to secure high judicial appointments, ū Zurʿa stands out as a jurist and *ḳāḍī* of unusual egrity. A scholar of great prominence, he was also owned for his personal modesty; upon his appointnt as grand *ḳāḍī*, he proceeded to exercise his ctions in his ordinary clothes, and considerable orts had to be exerted before he was persuaded don the customary ornamental robes for the digy of the office. His contemporaries were unaniıus in the praise of his character, learning and nmand of the Arabic language. He left a number works on *ḥadīt͟h* and jurisprudence, which were stly commentaries on earlier works; he also wrote other subjects and left a compilation of obituaries the years 762-93 A.H. (now lost), an anthology of ecdotes about hypocrites (*Akhbār al-mudallisīn*), commentary on an *urd͟jūza* (versified tract) on ebra, and some scattered verse.

Bibliography: Sak͟hāwī, *al-Ḍawʾ al-lāmiʿ*, i, 336-44; Ibn Tag͟hrībirdi, *Nud͟jūm*, vi, 514, 516, 563, 578; Suyūṭī, *Ḥusn al-muḥāḍara fī ak͟hbār Miṣr wa 'l-Ḳāhira*, Cairo 1321, ii, 116; Brockelmann, II, 66-7; ʿUmar Riḍā Kaḥḥāla, *Muʿd͟jam al-muʾallifīn*, , 270-1. (K. S. SALIBI)

ABYAḌ, GEORGES (b. Beirut, 5 May 1880; d. Cairo, 21 May 1959), a Syrian Christian who became a prominent protagonist of the modern Egyptian theatre. After acting in school-plays, Abyaḍ attempted a career as a clerk; unhappy with this work, he moved in 1898-9 to Egypt, then the centre of the young theatre in Arabic. In Alexandria and Cairo, he attended theatrical performances, both local and foreign, then, with a group of Egyptian amateurs, repeatedly tried his own hand, with some success. The turning point in his career came when the Khedive ʿAbbās II Ḥilmī awarded him a stipend to study acting in France, where Abyaḍ stayed from 1904 to 1910. Sylvain, Director of the *Conservatoire* in Paris, became his teacher, mentor and model; but he was also impressed and inspired by such leading actresses as Sarah Bernhard. Upon his return to Egypt, Abyaḍ commissioned the translation of several plays into literary Arabic, without colloquialisms or slang, and assembled a troupe in Cairo to perform these and other works. In 1912, with packed halls, his troupe was virtually the first to perform plays in Arabic without music—for Abyaḍ introduced music, vocal or instrumental, only when it was organic to the play. The troupe was organised and re-organised, and it played in Cairo as well as on repeated tours in Egypt and other Arab lands. Although Abyaḍ sometimes had to act in vernacular comedies and dramas (to please and attract the public), his forte remained the tragedy in literary Arabic. From 1927, he acted occasionally in broadcast plays, and, in 1930, started to teach acting and diction at the newly-established Institute of Dramatic Arts and at various universities and schools. In 1931-2 he acted in the first Arabic talking film, a musical entitled *The Song of the heart*. Abyaḍ retired from the State National Theatre in 1942, but he continued to lecture, direct plays, and occasionally act in Egyptian films. He was the first President of the Actors' Union, which was established in 1943. Until his death, he was active in the intellectual circles of Cairo and Alexandria. Abyaḍ's main merits were that, almost single-handed, he created a classical non-musical Egyptian theatre in literary Arabic, modelled on the modern French theatre; he encouraged the production of translated and original plays; and he increased the respectability of acting as a profession, socially and financially (paying his actors a regular and adequate salary).

Bibliography: *al-Hilāl*, xx (1 Apr. 1912), 436-8; xxi (1 Nov. 1912), 125-6; xxxiii (1 June 1925), 906-9; Muḥammad Taymūr, *Muʾallafāt*, ii, Cairo 1922, 131-49, 161-2, 213 ff., 232-3, 236 ff., 241-58, 276-7, 285-6, 290 ff., 303-4; N. Barbour, *The Arabic theatre in Egypt*, in *BSOAS*, viii (1935-6), 178-81; Fāṭima al-Yūsuf, *D͟hikrayāt*, Cairo 1953, 27-31, 36-7; Muḥammad Yūsuf Nad͟jm, *al-Masraḥiyya fi 'l-adab al-ʿArabī al-ḥadīt͟h*, Beirut 1956, 152-67, 245, 256, 415, 446, 449-50; J. M. Landau, *Studies in the Arabic theater and cinema*, Philadelphia 1958, 75-87, 93, 100, 113, 166, 189 (Arabic tr. by Aḥmad al-Mag͟hāzī, Cairo 1972); Muḥammad Mandūr, *al-Masraḥ*², Cairo 1963, 40-2; Tawfīḳ al-Ḥakīm, *Sid͟jn al-ʿumr*, Cairo n.d. [1964], 140-3 (Italian tr. by G. Belfiore, *La prigione della vita*, Rome 1976, 87-9); Muḥammad Kamāl al-Dīn, *Ruwwād al-masraḥ al-miṣrī*, Cairo 1970, 81-2, 85, 89-91, 106; Suʿād Abyaḍ, *D͟jūrd͟j Abyaḍ: al-masraḥ al-miṣrī fī miʾat ʿām*, Cairo 1970; Fāṭima Rus͟hdī, *Kifāḥī fi 'l-masraḥ wa 'l-sinimā*, Cairo 1971, 28-30; Maḥmūd Taymūr, *Ṭalāʾiʿ al-masraḥ al-ʿarabī*, Cairo n.d., 43-7, 52-3; Aḥmad S͟hams al-Dīn al-Ḥad͟jd͟jād͟jī, *al-ʿArab wa fann al-masraḥ*, Cairo 1975, 85-7; T. A. Putintsiyeva, *Tisyača i odin god Arabskogo teyatra*, Moscow 1977, 164-8, 171, 177, 200, 209, 228, 262.

(J. M. LANDAU)

AL-**ABYĀRĪ**, SH̲AYK̲H̲ ʿABD AL-HĀDĪ NAD̲J̲Ā B. RID̲WĀN B. NAD̲J̲Ā B. MUḤAMMAD, a leading Egyptian author and grammarian who was born in 1236/1821 in Abyār in the Gh̲arbiyya province of Lower Egypt. He was brought up in Abyār where he received his early education from his father and in one of the *kuttāb*s of the town. He studied at al-Azhar and later became a teacher there. Ismāʿīl Pas̲h̲a entrusted him with the instruction of his children, and Tawfīḳ Pas̲h̲a appointed him *imām* and *muftī* of his entourage, a post which he held until his death on 18 Dh̲u 'l-Ḳaʿda 1305/28 July 1888. He belonged to the Shāfiʿī *madh̲h̲ab*.

Al-Abyārī is credited with the authorship of more than 40 books on various subjects, including grammar, Islamic mysticism, *fiḳh* and *ḥadīth*. He corresponded with a number of leading scholars, including Ibrāhīm al-Aḥdab and Nāṣif al-Yāzid̲j̲ī. The collection of his correspondence with Ibrāhīm al-Aḥdab in Beirut and with others on literary and linguistic topics, *al-Wasāʾil al-adabiyya fi 'l-rasāʾil al-aḥdabiyya*, was published in Cairo in 1301/1883. A dispute on certain linguistic matters between Aḥmad Fāris al-S̲h̲idyāḳ and Sulaymān al-Ḥarīrī al-Tūnisī led to an adjudication of the questions at issue by al-Abyārī, which judgement appeared in print in Cairo in 1279/1862 under the title *al-Nad̲jm al-th̲āḳib*. A number of his works remain unpublished.

Bibliography: ʿAlī Pas̲h̲a Mubārak, *al-K̲h̲iṭaṭ al-tawfīḳiyya al-d̲jadīda*, viii, Būlāḳ 1305/1888, 29; E. Zakh̲kh̲ūra, *Mirʾāt al-ʿaṣr fī taʾrīkh̲ wa-rusūm akābir al-rid̲jāl bi-Miṣr*, i, Cairo 1897, 239-40; Ḥasan al-Sandūbī, *Aʿyān al-bayān*, Cairo 1914, 222-31; D̲j̲ūrd̲j̲ī Zaydān, *Tarād̲jim mas̲h̲āhir al-s̲h̲arḳ fi 'l-ḳarn al-tāsiʿ ʿas̲h̲ar*, ii, Cairo 1903, 144-5; Sarkīs, *Muʿd̲jam al-maṭbūʿāt al-ʿarabiyya wa 'l-muʿarraba*, Cairo 1928, 358-61; al-Ziriklī, *al-Aʿlām*, iv, 322-3; Zakī Muḥammad Mud̲jāhid, *al-Aʿlām al-s̲h̲arḳiyya fi 'l-miʾa al-rābiʿa ʿashra al-hid̲jriyya*, ii, Cairo 1950, 138-9; Kaḥḥāla, *Muʿd̲jam al-muʾallifīn*, vi, 203-4.

(R. Y. EBIED)

ACCESSION TO THE THRONE [see BAYʿA, K̲H̲ILĀFA].

ACCIDENT [see ʿARAḌ].

ACQUISITION [see KASB].

ACRIDOIDS [see D̲J̲ARĀD].

ACROBAT [see D̲J̲ĀNBĀZ].

ACT, ACTION [see ʿAMAL, FIʿL].

ADAGE [see MATHAL].

ĀDARRĀḲ, the name of a family of Berber "physicians", whose ancestor, Abū ʿAbd Allāh Muḥammad (d. 1070/1658-60) left the Sūs and settled at Fās; he must have used completely empirical methods, but nevertheless obtained significant results. Ibn S̲h̲akrūn [*q.v.* in Suppl.] was the pupil of a certain Aḥmad b. Muḥammad Ādarrāḳ, who was probably the son of the above-mentioned person, but the best-known member of the family was this Aḥmad's son, ABU MUḤAMMAD ʿABD AL-WAHHĀB B. AḤMAD (b. *ca.* 1077/1666, d. 28 Ṣafar 1159/22 March 1746), who was attached to Mawlāy Ismāʿīl (1082-1139/1672-1727). ʿAbd al-Wahhāb had also received a traditional education and had a certain talent as a versifier. In actuality, apart from a few poems of an ethico-philosophic nature, a *ḳaṣīda* in praise of the saints buried at Meknès (*Manẓūma fī madḥ ṣāliḥī Miknāsat al-zaytūn*), his biographers mainly mention some pieces having a certain connection with medecine: these comprise first of all a commentary on

the *Nuzha* of al-Anṭākī and two *urd̲jūza*s, one c plementing that of Ibn Sīnā, the other on the su of smallpox (these works apparently lost); the *ḳaṣīda* of 31 verses on the fine qualities of (*naʿnaʿ*), which exists in ms. (Rabat D 158 an 1131; partial tr. in Renaud, *Médecine*, 104-5; L dar, 189); and finally, an *urd̲jūza* of 179 verse syphilis (*ḥabb al-Ifrand̲j*), based largely on al-Anṭ *Nuzha* and on the *risāla* of Ibn S̲h̲akrūn on sars rilla (*fi 'l-ʿus̲h̲ba al-hindiyya*), text published an by Renaud and Colin, *Mal franc*, Arabic text 25 tr. 81-94.

Another Ādarrāḳ called Aḥmad is also cited physician to Sīdī Muḥammad b. ʿAbd Allāh (1 1204/1757-90).

Bibliography: Ibn Zaydān, *Itḥāf aʿlām al-* Rabat 1347-52/1929-33, v, 400-7; Ḳādirī, N *al-math̲ānī*, lith. Fās 1310, i, 226, ii, 251; Katt *Salwat al-anfās*, lith. Fās 1316/1898, ii, 34; Al sūs, *al-D̲jays̲h̲ al-ʿaramram*, lith. Fās 1336/1 94 ff.; Lévi-Provençal, *Chorfa*, 310-11; H. P Renaud, *Médecine et médecins marocains*, in A l *Alger*, iii (1937), 99-106; idem and G. S. Cc *Documents marocains pour servir à l'histoire "mal franc"*, Paris 1935, 31-5; M. Lakhdar, *La littéraire au Maroc*, Rabat 1971, 187-90 and l cited there. (ED

AL-**ʿADAWĪ**, MUḤAMMAD ḤASANAYN MAK̲H̲I Azharī scholar and administrator, one-t s̲h̲ayk̲h̲ of the Aḥmadī mosque in Ṭanṭā, born 5 Ramaḍān 1277/18 March 1861 in the village of F ʿAdī, near Manfalūṭ in the Upper Egyptian prov of Asyūṭ.

After the completion of his studies at al-Azhar [c in 1305/1887-8, when he was granted the degree ʿālim [see ʿULAMĀʾ], and a short period of teach at that institution, he was appointed Director of Azhar Library which was established and organi at his initiative. His commitment to the cause reform in al-Azhar gave his further career its cont and significance when, in the various high administ tive offices he held within this institution—the m notable of which were the offices of *mudīr al-Az* and of the Religious Institutes attached to it, *mu tis̲h̲ al-awwal* and *wakīl al-Azhar*— as well as in period in which he held the office of s̲h̲ayk̲h̲ of Aḥmadī mosque in Ṭanṭā, he was able to give spiration and direction to the reformist efforts Aḥmad S̲h̲afīḳ, *Mud̲h̲akkirātī fī niṣf ḳarn*, Cairo 19 ii/2, 137 f., 140, 182, 233). He continued to do so af his resignation from all his administrative functi following a dispute with the Egyptian Sultan Ḥusa Kāmil in 1915 (see ʿAbd al-Mutaʿāl al-Saʿīdī, *Taʾr al-iṣlāḥ fi 'l-Azhar wa-ṣafaḥāt min al-d̲jihād fi 'l-iṣl* Cairo n.d., 142 ff.).

From the latter year onwards, he committed hi self mainly to private teaching and to the writing a variety of books and tracts, of which some fo were published, largely pertaining to legal issues a to *taṣawwuf* [*q.v.*]. He was an active member of t S̲h̲arḳāwiyya branch of the K̲h̲alwatiyya [*q.v.*] a among the principal disciples of its founder Aḥm b. S̲h̲arḳāwī al-K̲h̲alifī (1834-98). He died in Muḥ ram 1355/April 1936.

Bibliography: In addition to the references the article, see the biographies by Ilyās Zakh̲kh̲ū *Mirʾāt al-ʿaṣr fī taʾrīkh̲ wa-rusūm akābir rid̲ Miṣr*, Cairo 1897, ii, 455; K̲h̲ayr al-Dīn al-Ziriklī, *Aʿlām*, Cairo 1954-9, vi, 326; Muḥammad ʿAbd al-Ḥid̲jād̲jī, *Min aʿlām al-Saʿīd fi 'l-ḳarn al-rā ʿas̲h̲r al-hid̲jrī*, Cairo 1969, 93-112, and Za Muḥammad Mud̲jāhid, *al-Aʿlām al-s̲h̲arḳiyya fi* i'a al-rābiʿa ʿashra al-hidjriyya, Cairo 1950, ii, 50, where additional references may be found as ell as an enumeration of al-ʿAdawī's writings. A milar list may be found appended to several of -ʿAdawī's publications. To these must be added -Taḳrīr al-awwal li-mashyakhat al-Djāmiʿ al-ḥmadī ʿan sana 1316 dirāsiyya, Cairo 1327/1909, hich was drawn up by him at the time when he as shaykh of the Aḥmadī mosque in Ṭanṭā. For a ummary of the reforms and improvements im-lemented by him at the Aḥmadī mosque, when e was in charge of that institution, see Dhikrā shrīf Samū al-Djanāb al-ʿAlāʾ al-Khudaywī al-Iuʿaẓẓam ʿAbbās Ḥilmi al-Thānī li 'l-Djāmiʿ wa Maʿhad al-Aḥmadī, sana 1332, Cairo 1332/1913-4, 9 f. (F. DE JONG)

ʿADĪ B. **ARṬĀT** AL-FAZARĪ, ABŪ WĀTHLA, offi-l in the service of the Umayyads who erned ʿIrāḳ from Baṣra between 99/718 and 101/ . He was appointed to this office by ʿUmar b. d al-ʿAzīz in place of Yazīd b. al-Muhallab, and ived the order to arrest all the sons of al-Muhal-. He managed to get hold of al-Mufaḍḍal, Ḥabīb, rwān and Yazīd, but the latter escaped and re-ned to the attack. ʿAdī then raised the troops of ra and had a trench dug round the town to pre-t the rebels from breaking in, but these measures l no effect. In the event, Yazīd managed to get session of Baṣra without much difficulty, and ered the arrest of ʿAdī, who was killed at Wāsiṭ 102/820-1 by Muʿāwiya b. Yazīd. There is, first all, attributed to this governor's name a canal avated at Baṣra in order to bring a satisfactory ply of drinking water, the *Nahr ʿAdī*, and second-an epidemic which broke out in 100/719, the *ṭāʿūn dī*.

Bibliography: Djarīr, *Dīwān*, 241; *Naḳāʾiḍ*, ndex; Djāḥiẓ, *Bayān*, index; Ibn Ḳutayba, *Maʿ-ārif*, index; *Ṭabarī*, index; Balādhurī, *Futūḥ*, 77, 349, 359, 369-70; Ibn al-Kalbī-Caskel, Tab. 130 and i, 138; Yaʿḳūbī, *Hist.*, ii, 362, 370, 373; idem, *Buldān*, tr. Wiet, 94, 124; Mubarrad, *Kāmil*, index; Masʿūdī, *Murūdj*, v, 453-4, 457 = § 2206, 2209; dem, *Tanbīh*, index; Khaṭīb Baghdādī, *Taʾrīkh*, xii, 306; Ibn al-Athīr, v, 31, 42, 53, 64; Yāḳūt, i, 643, iv, 841; Ibn Abi 'l-Ḥadīd, *Sharḥ*, i, 303; Cae-tani, *Chronographia*, 1205, 1239, 1244, 1248, 1260; Ṣ. al-ʿAlī, in *Sumer*, vii (1952), 78; Pellat, *Milieu*, ndex; Ziriklī, vi, 8. (ED.)

ADĪB PĪSHĀWARĪ, SAYYID AḤMAD, Persian et, was born *ca.* 1844 in the district of Pīshāwar eshawar) in north-west India to a clan of nomadic *yyids* who traced their spiritual lineage back to ihāb al-Dīn Suhrawardī. While he was still a boy, s father and most of his male relatives were killed fighting against the British government. He him-lf escaped to Kābul, and after spending several ars in Ghaznīn, Harāt and Turbat-i Shaykh Djam, ttled in Mashhad, where he studied under a number distinguished divines. For two years he was in bzawār at the feet of the famous Mullā Hādī Sab-wārī. During his stay in Mashhad he became known *Adīb-i Hindī*, "the Indian scholar". In 1884 he oved to Tehran, where he spent the rest of his life, d was honoured by Nāṣir al-Dīn Shāh. He died in 30. His writings include a *dīwān* of 4,200 Persian d 370 Arabic verses, a *mathnawī* poem in the *muta-rib* metre, the *Ḳayṣar-nāma*, dedicated to the erman Kaiser and describing the events of the 1914- war, two philosophica essays, a commentary on e *Taʾrīkh-i Bayhaḳī*, and an incomplete Persian anslation of Avicenna's *Kitāb al-Ishārāt*.

Although his mother-tongue was Pashto, Adīb Pīshāwarī was regarded as a master of the Persian language, his wide reading and powerful memory en-abling him to clothe his ideas in a high literary style. Nevertheless, although he took no active part in public affairs and lived an unwordly life, his poems show that he was well-acquainted with world events; he commented freely on such matters as the Russo-Japanese War, India's fight for freedom, pan-Islam, and the Great War. His early tragic experience had given him a lasting hatred of British imperialism, from which no doubt his support for the Kaiser in part stemmed. At heart he was a fervent nationalist and patriot. At the same time he placed no reliance on patrons, and was never known to have composed a panegyric. He may be regarded as the first of the new generation of poets who abandoned the classical themes and wrote about subjects closer to the lives of ordinary people.

Bibliography: Adīb's *Dīwān* was edited by ʿAlī ʿAbd al-Rasūlī, Tehran 1933. His edition of the *Taʾrīkh-i Bayhaḳī* was published in Tehran in 1889, and the commentary was incorporated with corrections in Saʿīd Nafīsī's edition, 3 vols., Tehran 1940-53. The *Ḳayṣar-nāma* has never been pub-lished. Biographical information in: M. Ishaque, *Sukhanwarān-i Īrān dar ʿaṣr-i ḥāḍir*, i, Calcutta 1933, 1-8; Rashīd Yāsimī, *Adabiyyāt-i muʿāṣir*, Tehran 1937, 10-3; M. Ishaque, *Modern Persian poetry*, Calcutta 1843, *passim*; Sayyid Muḥammad Bāḳir Burḳaʿī, *Sukhanwarān-i nāmī-yi muʿāṣir*, i, Tehran 1950, 1-2; J. Rypka, *Iranische Literatur-geschichte*, Leipzig 1959, 356-7; ibid., *History of Iranian literature*, Dordrecht 1968, 374-5; Bozorg Alavi, *Geschichte und Entwicklung der modernen persischen Literatur*, Berlin 1964, 34-5. (L. P. ELWELL-SUTTON)

ADİVAR, ʿABD AL-ḤAḲḲ ʿADNĀN, modern Turkish ABDÜLHAK ADNAN ADIVAR, Turkish author, scholar and politician (1882-1955). He was born in Gelibolu (Gallipoli), while his father Aḥmed Bahāʾī, who came from a prominent *ʿulamāʾ* family of Istanbul, was *ḳāḍī* there. He studied medi-cine at the University of Istanbul and while a stu-dent, contributed to various newspapers and was in trouble with the Ḥamīdian police. Upon graduation he fled to Europe, spent a year in Paris and Zürich and settled in Berlin where he became an assistant in the Faculty of Medicine. After the restoration of the Constitution in July 1908, he returned to Turkey, taught at the University of Istanbul and was Dean of the Faculty of Medicine (1909-11). As a prominent member of the powerful Committee of Union and Progress (CUP), he contributed substantially to re-organising the Red Crescent and the Department of Health. In 1917 he married, by proxy, the prominent writer Khālide Edīb [*q.v.*]. Elected a deputy in the post-Armistice Ottoman Parliament, Dr. ʿAdnān (as he was known until 1940 when he took the family name Adıvar) left Istanbul secretly with his wife in order to avoid certain arrest and deportation by the British, and joined the Nationalist government in Ankara (April 1920), where he served as Minister of Health and of the Interior and as Deputy Speaker of Parliament. Later he joined dissident generals and former members of the CUP, with whom he founded the Progressive Republican Party (*Teraḳḳīperver Djumhūriyyet Fırḳası* [*q.v.*]), which represented the main opposition to Muṣṭafā Kemāl Pasha (1924). In the summer of 1926, a Unionist conspiracy to assas-sinate Muṣṭafā Kemāl was discovered and several people were arrested. Dr. ʿAdnān was tried in his absence as he had been in Europe for some months. Although he was acquitted, he and his wife did not return to Turkey until 1939. They lived in England and later in France where he worked as lecturer at the École de Langues Orientales Vivantes in Paris, together with Jean Deny (1929-39).

When Ḥasan ʿĀlī Yüdjel (Yücel), the reforming Minister of Education (1938-46) decided that a Turkish edition of the *Encyclopaedia of Islām* should be published, he appointed Adnan Adıvar its chief editor (1940); the latter organised the secretariat of the *İslâm Ansiklopedisi* and successfully launched and directed it as an independent deputy (1950-4). He died in Istanbul on 1 July 1955.

Adnan Adıvar's main work is his book on the history of science in Turkey, prepared during his exile in France: *La science chez les Turcs ottomans* (Paris 1939), which he revised and enlarged in the second edition in Turkish, *Osmanlı Türklerinde ilim* (Istanbul 1943), where for the first time all the extensive data on the subject are put systematically together. Apart from an essay on Faust (*Faust, tahlil tecrübesi*, Istanbul 1939) and a study of the conflict of religion and science in history; *Tarih boyunca ilim ve din* (2 vols., Istanbul 1944), his remaining work consists of essays and articles on problems of general culture, history, science and politics which he published in daily papers; some of these have been put together in *Bilgi Cumhuriyeti haberleri* (1945), *Dur, düşün* (1950) and *Hakikat peşindeki emeklemeler* (1954).

Bibliography: *Yeni ufuklar*, special number, August 1955; Halide Edib Adivar, *Doktor Abdülhak Adnan Adıvar*, Istanbul 1956; Tahir Alangu, *100 ünlü Türk büyüğü*, ii, Istanbul 1974, 1259-65.

(Fahir İz)

ʿADJMĀN, the smallest of the seven shaykhdoms of Trucial ʿUmān, which now comprise the United Arab Emirates (*al-Imārāt al-ʿArabīyya al-Muttaḥida* [*q.v.* below]). The shaykhdom proper measures about 100 square miles in extent, and there are two small enclaves, Masfūt and Manāma, in the interior. The total population is around 5,000. The leading tribal elements are the Ḳarātisa, Hamīrat and Āl Bū Dhanayn sections of the Āl Bū Khuraybān branch of the Naʿīm (or Nuʿaym), which is also to be found in the Buraymī Oasis and its vicinity. The ruling *shaykh*, from the Ḳarātisa section, is Rashīd b. Ḥumayd, who succeeded in 1347/1928-9.

Throughout the 13th/19th century ʿAdjman was little more than a client state of the neighbouring Ḳasīmī shaykhdom of Shārdja (al-Shārika [*q.v.*]). It subscribed independently, however, to the various engagements concluded between the Trucial Shaykhs and the British government during the century, from the General Treaty of Peace in 1235/1820 to the "Exclusive" Agreements of 1309/1892. Early in the century, as a consequence of Saʿūdi penetration of the area, the Āl Bū Khuraybān of ʿAdjmān, like most of their fellow Naʿīm, were converted to the Wahhābī pratice of Islam.

ʿAdjman's economy until recent years depended wholly upon fishing and subsistence agriculture. It is now sustained primarily by grants from the wealthier members of the UAE, notably Abū Dhabī (Ẓabī), and by concessionary payments from the Occidental Oil Company for exploratory rights in ʿAdjman territory and waters. (J. B. Kelly)

ADMIRAL [see ḳapudan].

ADVENTURER [see ḳazaḳ].

AFĀWĪH (pl. of *afwāh*, sing. *fūh*) are spices, aromatic substances, which are added to food and beverages in order to increase pleasant flavour and promote digestion. In general they are vege products which are active through their conten volatile oils or pungent substances. The classific according to the individual constituents of p (fruits and seeds, blossoms and buds, peel, roots, in use at present, does not seem to have bee practice realised anywhere. It is possible that Ḥanīfa al-Dīnawarī (end 3rd/9th century) has th mind when he says that *al-afwāh* fall under va classes and types (*aṣnāf wa-anwāʿ*), and then qu a verse each of Dhu 'l-Rumma and of Djamīl ʿUdhrī], according to which there is a distin between *afwāh al-nawr* and *afwāh al-buḳūl* (*Kitā Nabāt. The book of plants*, part of the monog section, ed. B. Lewin, Wiesbaden 1974, 200 f., 757). An unsystematic list of food spices, an which are included the most common like salt (*m* is to be found in Ibn Ḳutayba, *ʿUyūn al-akhbar* Cairo 1348/1930, 296-9, under the heading *ma al-ṭaʿām*, where *maṣāliḥ* must have the plain mea of "spices, food-flavourings". In Arabic the mea of *afāwīh* is not sharply marked off from *ʿiṭr* "scents", and *ʿaḳḳār* (plur. *ʿaḳāḳīr*, *ʿuḳḳār*), "dr [see ʿaṭṭār]. The lexicographers call *al-afwāh* w is added to scents, and *al-tawābil* what is adde food (see Lane, s.v. *fūh*).

Specific monographs on *al-afāwīh* do not seen be known. These substances are treated in their propriate places in works on botany, pharmacog tics, medicine, knowledge of commodities, ency paedias and other writings. A list which is, t certain extent, representative for the 4th/10th tury, is to be found in al-Masʿūdī, *Murūdj*, i, containing 25 main kinds of spices: 1. *sunbul* sp nard, 2. *ḳaranful* clove, 3. *ṣandal* sandalwood *djawzbuwwā* nutmeg, 5. *ward* rose, 6. *salīkha* ca 7. *zarnab* (meaning doubtful, cf. Meyerhof's edi of Maimonides, *Sharḥ asmāʾ al-ʿuḳḳār*, no. 137) *ḳirfa*, cinnamon, 9. *ḳarnuwa* (a kind of sonchus? Ibn al-Bayṭār, *al-Djāmiʿ*, Būlāḳ, iv, 17, tr. Lec no. 1775), 10. *ḳāḳulla* cardamom, 11. *kubāba* cu 12. *hālbuwwā* small cardamom, 13. *manshim* ca balsam, 14. *fāghira* xanthoxylum, 15. *maḥlab* mor 15. *wars* Flemmingia rhodocarpa, 17. *ḳusṭ* costus, *aẓfār* (*al-ṭīb*), Strombus lentiginosus, 19. *birank* belia Ribes, 20. *ḍarw* lentisk gum, 21. *lādhan* la num, 22. *mayʿa* aromatic gum of the storax tree, *ḳanbīl* Mallotus philippinensis, 24. *ḳaṣab al-dha* calamus, 25. *zabāda* civet.—Notable is the fact t one of the oldest and most utilised spices, pep (*fulful*), with its *ca.* 700 different kinds, does appear in this inventory.

In the section on knowledge of commodities in handbook on mercantile science, Shaykh Abu 'l-F Djaʿfar al-Dimashḳī (probably 6th/12th century) e merates, under the term *saḳaṭ* (plur. *asḳāṭ*, stri speaking "refuse"), a list of spices which is q different from that of al-Masʿūdī (*Kitāb al-Ishāra maḥāsin al-tidjāra ilkh.*, Cairo 1318/1900, 21-4): un the "small spices" (*al-saḳaṭ al-ṣaghīr*) he menti only the rhubarb (*rāwand*) and leaves the others as being less important, but under the "great spic (*al-saḳaṭ al-kabīr*) he reckons: 1. *nīl* indigo, 2. *baḳ* sapanwood, 3. *fulful* pepper, 4. *lubān* frankince 5. *maṣṭakā* gum mastic, 6. *dārṣīnī al-ṭaʿām* fo cinnamon, 7. *āl* yellow ginger, 8. *zandjabīl* gin 9. *zurunbād* redowary-root, 10. *khūlandjān* galing 11. *ḳusṭ* costus, 12. *lādhan* ladanum, 13. *ihlīlad* kinds of myrobalan (see concerning this list, E.Wie mann, *Aufsätze zur arabischen Wissenschaftsgeschic* ed. W. Fischer, Hildesheim 1970, ii, 11-5; H. Rit in *Isl.* vii [1917], 17 f.).

ttered or unsystematically-arranged material .e knowledge of spices is to be found, as can be ted, in the encyclopaedias of the Arabic and ın literature. Preliminary statements already .r in al-Khwārazmī's *Mafātīḥ al-ʿulūm* (ed. van n, Leiden 1895) under medicaments (169-80), ample material is given by Nuwayrī, *Nihāyat* b, the entire twelfth volume of which (Cairo 1937) is devoted to this subject; scents (*ṭīb*), mery (*bakhūrāt*), many kinds of Galia moscata *ālī*), perfumes made of aloe with various ad- ıres (*nudūd*), distillates (*mustaḳṭarāt*), oils (*ad-* and certain perfumes (*naḍūḥāt*). Among these :s we find also descriptions of some of the spices ly mentioned, such as sandalwood (39-42), nard (43 f.), cloves (45-8), costus (49-51), etc. ıis is mixed up with detailed statements about materials which can be counted among spices with reservations or in no way at all. As in ıeval Europe, ground spices were often adulter- especially in times of distress. Here we only the original work of Djawbarī (*ca.* 615/1218), *al-Mukhtār fī kashf al-asrār wa-hatk al-astār*, ı allegedly informs traders about deceitful de- in commerce and trade; it was printed several in the Orient and urgently deserves a critical ın (now in preparation by S. Wild). The section lulterations of spices and perfumes was trans- into German by E. Wiedemann (*op. cit.*, i, 1970, 2).

ıce there is hardly any spice which was not at ame time used as medicament, it is no wonder the most comprehensive material on spices is to und in the pharmacopoeias. These are essentially l on the *Materia medica* (ὕλη ἰατρική) of Dio- les [see DIYUSḲŪRIDĪS]. This work, translated into ic at an early period, lived on in the Islamic world er-new compilations, expanded by a great num- f drugs which the Arabs had come to know in ourse of their conquests. The material is to be l on the one hand in pharmacognostic and maceutical monographs, the development of h came to a certain conclusion with Ibn al- ār's great compilation, and on the other hand ıe pharmaceutical sections of compendia on :al medicine [see ṬIBB]. It should, however, be mbered that in these works spices are entered described as medicines in the first place, not as iments.

gether with cambric textiles, spices were con- ed as the most fashionable luxury; both prod- are often mentioned together as the most lucra- ones (Mez, *Renaissance*, 452 ff.). In Egypt, where long time corn had offered the best chances for stment, spices and drugs took its place after the ades. In the later Middle Ages, the spice trade, the pepper trade in particular, was mainly in the ıs of Egyptians and Venetians. A good survey on spice trade under the Ayyūbids and Mamlūks is found in G. Wiet, *Les marchands d'épices sous les ns mamlouks*, in *Cahiers d'histoire égyptienne*, vii (1955), 81-147, with a rich bibliography. 'ever, the author does not deal with particular s, but with their general trade. Under the pro- on of the sultans this trade was carried out by rtant bodies of merchants, who forwarded the s from India and South-East Asia to Europe by of Egypt through the Red Sea or by way of ı through the Persian Gulf. About these trading panies and their monopoly we have some detailed :mation, especially about the wealthy Kārimī , who controlled the spice trade between the Yemen and Egypt. The "spice-wars" with the European ports in the Mediterranean, started by the Ayyūbids and continued by the Mamlūks and the Ottoman Turks, were waged on both sides with great ruthlessness. Internal policy was carried out, just as rigorously, especially by the Mamlūks: in 832/1429 Barsbāy founded a state monopoly of pepper and three years later he forced the wholesale merchants to buy from him for 80 *dīnār*s a *ḥiml* the pepper which they had sold to him earlier for 50 *dīnārs*. Even so, Ḳānṣawh al-Ghawrī not only maintained this monopoly system, but imposed additional heavy taxes on the merchants. Hopes of cutting out Egyptian middlemen were the decisive inducement for the Spanish and the Portuguese to search for a direct sea-route to India; but after the conquest of the Moluccas in 1607, the Dutch snatched the monopoly of the spice trade away from the Portuguese.

Bibliography: W. Heyd, *Histoire du commerce du Levant au Moyen-Âge*, ii, Leipzig 1886 (new impr. Amsterdam 1959), 563-676; S. Y. Labib, *Handelsgeschichte Ägyptens im Spätmittelalter (1171-1517)*, Wiesbaden 1965 (solid investigation with valuable evidence, see index); L. Kroeber, *Zur Geschichte, Herkunft und Physiologie der Würz- und Duftstoffe*, Munich 1949, *passim*; F. A. Flückiger, *Pharmakognosie des Pflanzenreiches*[3], Berlin 1891, index; H. A. Hoppe, *Drogenkunde*[7], Hamburg 1958; *The legacy of Islam*[2], 217, 227, 234 with Bibl. at 243. Of the pharmacognostic and medical works, the following selection may be mentioned: Ibn Sīnā, *al-Ḳānūn fi 'l-ṭibb*, i, Būlāḳ 1294, 243-470; Bīrūnī, *K. al-Ṣaydala*, ed. and tr. Ḥakīm Muḥ. Saʿīd, Karachi 1973; Maimonides, *Sharḥ asmāʾ al-ʿuḳḳār. Un glossaire de matière médicale*, éd. M. Meyerhof, Cairo 1940, index; Ibn al-Bayṭār, *al-Djāmiʿ li-mufradāt al-adwiya wa 'l-aghdhiya*, i-iv, Būlāḳ 1291, partial tr. L. Leclerc in *Notices et extraits des manuscrits de la Bibliothèque Nationale*, xxiii, Paris 1877; xxv, 1881; xxvi, 1883.

(A. DIETRICH)

AFḌAL AL-DĪN TURKA, more frequently referred to as Khwādja Afḍal-i Ṣadr, was a famous theologian in the reign of the Tīmūrid Shāhrukh Mīrzā [*q.v.*], and a member of an originally turcophone family of Iṣfahān, whence the appelation Turka. In 845/1441, when Shāhrukh appointed his own grandson, Muḥammad b. Bāysonḳor as governor of a part of ʿIrāḳ-i ʿAdjamī (al-Djibāl), Afḍal al-Dīn Turka was among the learned courtiers of this young prince. But later when, in consequence of Muḥammad's revolt, Shāhrukh came to Iṣfahān, Afḍal al-Dīn together with a number of other leading figures, were arrested as Muḥammad's accomplices and put to death by the order of Shāhrukh with no further inquiry (Ramaḍān 850/November 1446). Afḍal al-Dīn is responsible for a partial translation of Shahrastānī's *Kitāb al-Milal wa 'l-niḥal*, in which contrary to the original author, he did not confine himself to expose only the heretical doctrines, but endeavoured also to refute these heresies. This translation was originally made in 843/1439 for Mīrzā Shāhrukh, but later when Muḥammad b. Bāysonḳor came to ʿIrāḳ-i ʿAdjamī, a new version of the book was dedicated to him. Among other famous dignitaries of the Turka family we know of another Afḍal al-Dīn Turka (d. 991/1583), a grandson of our Khwādja Afḍal al-Dīn, and also a famous theologian of the Ṣafawid period who held for a time the office of *ḳāḍī* and *mudarris*, at Ḳazwīn, under the Ṣafawid Shāh Ṭahmāsp I.

Bibliography: Dawlatshāh, *Tadhkirat al-shuʿarāʾ*, ed. Browne, 339; Aḥmad b. Ḥusayn al-

Kātib, *Taʾrīkh-i djadīd-i Yazd*, ed. I. Afshār, Tehran 1966, 241-2; Abū Bakr-i Tihrānī, *Kitāb-i Diyārbakriyya*, ed. Necati Lugal and Faruk Sümer, Ankara 1962, 285-8; ʿAbd al-Razzāḳ Samarḳandī, *Maṭlaʿ-i saʿdayn*, ii, 1946, 862-3; Ḥasan-i Rūmlū, *Aḥsan al-tawārīkh*, Tehran 1970, 260; Mudarris-i Khiyābānī, *Rayḥānat al-adab*, Tehran 1326/1947, i, 412-3; Djalālī-yi Nāʾīnī, ed., *Tardjuma-yi al-Milal wa 'l-niḥal*, Tehran 1335/1956, 34-57 cf. Iskandar Beg Munshī, *ʿĀlamārā-yi ʿAbbāsī*, index.

(A. H. Zarrinkoob)

AL-ʿAFĪFĪ, ʿAbd al-Wahhāb b. ʿAbd al-Salām b. Aḥmad b. Ḥidjāzī, an Egyptian mystic belonging to the Shādhiliyya [*q.v.*] order, after whom one of its branches is named al-ʿAfīfiyya. He was born in Minyat ʿAfīf in the present-day Minūfiyya province in the last quarter of the 17th century. After a period of study at al-Azhar under a number of notable scholars like the Mālikī *muftī* Sālim b. Aḥmad al-Nafrāwī, and Aḥmad b. Muṣṭafā al-Sikandarānī al-Ṣabbāgh, he taught the *Ṣaḥīḥ* of Muslim at the *madrasa al-ashrafiyya* and confined himself to an ascetic way of life based upon the precepts of the Shādhiliyya order. He had been initiated into this *ṭarīḳa* [*q.v.*] by the son of the founder of the Moroccan Ṭayyibiyya [*q.v.*], the Wazzānī *sharīf*, Mawlā Aḥmad al-Tihāmī al-Tawwātī (d. 1715), from whom he had also received the *khilāfa* [*q.v.*]. In addition he held an *idjāzat khilāfa* of the Khalwatiyya order issued to him by Muṣṭafā Kamāl al-Dīn al-Bakrī [*q.v.*].

His contacts with the Mamlūk *amīr*s who used to come and visit him in his house in Ḳaṣr al-Shawḳ and the generous way in which he gave away to his *murīdūn* most of what was presented to him as pious donations caused his circle of adepts to increase and to spread into the rural areas.

When he died on 12 Ṣafar 1172/15 October 1758, he was buried close to the mosque of Ḳāyit Bāy in a grave which was swept away by a torrent in the year 1178/1764-5. After this event his body was reinterred at a much higher site in the same area where a domed shrine was constructed over his tomb, together with a number of adjacent buildings at the expense of Muḥammad Katkhudā Abāẓa, a Mamlūk *amīr* and onetime *katkhudā* [*q.v.*] of Muḥammad Bey Abu 'l-Dhahab [*q.v.*]. As reported by ʿAbd al-Raḥmān al-Djabartī, *ʿAdjāʾib al-āthār*, Būlāḳ 1297, i, 220 f., and iv, 163, the yearly *mawlid*, about which he makes highly derogatory remarks, was not celebrated until after this event. At the end of the 19th century it had become one of the larger popular *mawlid*s in Cairo (cf. J. W. McPherson, *The moulids of Egypt*, Cairo 1941, 50, 174; Murray's *Handbook of Egypt 1888*, 209), and lasted for eight days (cf. ʿAlī Mubārak, *Khiṭaṭ*, v, 50 f., xvi, 73). According to McPherson, 174, the *mawlid* was not celebrated any more by 1940, but in the fifties celebrations were held again (cf. *Madjallat al-Islām wa 'l-Taṣawwuf*, i (Cairo 1958), no. 6, 82).

Al-ʿAfīfī has left no writings of his own, but his teachings have been summarised by one of his disciples ʿAbd al-Raḥmān b. Sulaymān al-Ghuraynī, in *Risālāt al-Silsila*, and they mirror Shādhilī teaching as formulated by Aḥmad Zarrūḳ. The latter's *waẓīfa* [*q.v.*], known as *Safīnat al-Nadjāʾ* [*li-man ila 'llāh iltadjaʾ*] was incorporated into the *ṭarīḳa*'s liturgy and was adopted as part of the daily office prescribed for the *ṭarīḳa*'s members, to whom two of al-Zarrūḳ's treatises, *Risālat al-Uṣūl* and *Risālat al-Ummahāt* became standard reading at a later period, towards the end of the 19th century.

Followers of the ʿAfīfiyya order have been criticised on various grounds for wearing yellow headge imitation of al-Zubayr b. ʿAwwām [*q.v.*], who cording to one tradition, wore a yellow turban o day of the battle of Badr. In defence of headge this colour, a small treatise was published by order, written by Ibrāhīm al-Sadjīnī under the *al-Aman al-akbar fī ʿayn man ankara libs al-ʿ*

Two branches of the al-ʿAfīfiyya *ṭarīḳa* were a in Egypt in 1958 (cf. Muḥammad Maḥmūd ʿA *al-Taṣawwuf al-islāmī, risālatuhu wa-mabādi māḍiyuhu wa-ḥāḍiruhu*, Cairo 1958, 72, 74).

Bibliography: The biographies by ʿAlī M rak, *Khiṭaṭ*, xvi, 72 f.; al-Ḥasan b. Muḥamma Kūhin, *Ṭabaḳāt al-Shādhiliyya al-kubrā*, 1347/1928-9, 157 f.; and Muḥammad al-B. Ẓāfir, *al-Yawāḳīt al-thamina fī aʿyān ʿālim Madīna*, Cairo 1324-5/1906-7, are essentially produced from ʿAbd al-Raḥmān al-Djab *ʿAdjāʾib al-āthār*, i, 220 f. A short biography be found in Muḥammad Khalīl al-Murādī, *Si durar fī aʿyān al-ḳarn al-thānī ʿashar*, Ista Būlāḳ 1291-1301/1874-83, iii, 143 f., which utilised by Yūsuf b. Ismāʿīl al-Nabahānī, *Dj karāmāt al-awliyāʾ*, Cairo 1329/1911, ii, 139 the construction of the mosque of al-ʿAfīfī in second half of the 19th century, see ʿAlī Mub *Khiṭaṭ*, v, 51. Information about descendan al-ʿAfīfī and *ʿulamāʾ* buried in the precincts o mosque may be found in Abu 'l-Ḥasan Nū Dīn ʿAlī b. Aḥmad al-Sakhāwī, *Tuḥfat al-a wa-bughyat al-ṭullāb fi 'l-khiṭaṭ wa 'l-mazārā 'l-taradjim wa 'l-biḳāʿ al-mubārakāt*, Cairo 1937 The treatises by Aḥmad al-Zarrūḳ, ʿAbd al- mān al-Ghuraynī and Ibrāhīm al-Sadjīnī, refe to in this article were published by ʿAfīfī al-W ḳād in a collection under the title *Hidāyat al- ilā madjmūʿ al-rasāʾil*, Cairo 1316. The order's c of transmission of the *waẓīfa* and the *sanad* [which are given in the treatise by ʿAbd al-Raḥ al-Ghuraynī referred to in this article, figure in ʿAbd al-Ḳādir Zakī, *al-Nafḥa al-ʿaliya fī a al-Shādhiliyya*, Cairo 1321, 220 f. (photomecha reprint: Ṭarābulus (Libya) 1971).

A manual of religious instruction and mys practice intended for the members of the ʿAfīf order was written by one of its *khalīfa*s, Sa ʿAbd al-Nabī Muḥammad Khaḍir, *al-Irshādā dīniyya*, al-Minyā n.d. [1970]. Prayer manual al-ʿAfīfiyya are Fuʾād Ramaḍān, *Madjmūʿat al* Cairo n.d.; and Aḥmad Ḥasan (ed.), *Madjm awrād wa-aḥzāb li 'l-sāda al-Shādhiliyya*, C 1351/1932-3.

(F. de Jon

AFLĪMŪN, Fulaymūn, Iflīmūn, the Gr rhetorician and sophist Antonius Polemon 88-144 A.D.) of Laodicea (near modern Deñizli [in western Turkey). He lived most of his life Smyrna, and was the author of a book on phys nomy, which has been preserved, apart from single Greek quotation, in an Arabic translation o The translator is not known. Polemon's book *Aflīmūn fi 'l-firāsa*) presents the characteriolog physiognomy, in contrast to the branch of physio my which aims at medical morphoscopy [see firā It was believed that characteriological physiogno provided an insight into someone's character means of a skilful interpretation of his physical pearance (*al-istidlāl bi 'l-khulḳ al-ẓāhir ʿalā 'l-k al-bāṭin*). Polemon's book is divided into 70 chapt Ch. 1 treats the characteristics of the human and ch. 2 the characteristics of animals from wh by analogy, conclusions can be drawn about hu nature; these constitute about half of the book. T v chs. 3-30 on the different parts of the body, 31-5 on the different nations of the world, chs. on the colour of the parts of the body, chs. on the growth of hair on the parts of the body, 49-50 on the movements of the body, chs. 51-66 veral outspoken character types, and chs. 67-70 everal other topics connected with foretelling one's destiny. The book appears to be authentic, n be seen from the many Greek examples; thus ion is made of Oedipus (ed. Hoffmann, 111, 7), ne (*ibid.* 119, 14), Lydia and Phrygia (*ibid.* 139, Egypt, Macedonia, Phoenicia, Cilicia and Scythia 237, 14-239, 2). The eyes of the Roman Em-r, Hadrian of whom Polemon was a favourite, escribed (*ibid.* 149, 4). Polemon's opponent, Fa-us, is only too well recognisable in the anon-us and malicious description on p. 161,8 ff. sion to the attempt on the Emperor's life is made 141,1 ff.

lemon does not give a theoretical introduction is method. He used materials from the *Physio-icon* of Ps. Aristotle and gave his book a lively by including anecdotes about contemporaries avoiding a monotonously scientific treatment of ubject (Stegemann, 1345-7). Polemon's name is tioned by al-Djāḥiẓ (d. 255/868 [*q.v.*]) in his *awān*, ed. ʿA. M. Hārūn, Cairo 1938, iii, 146, 75, 284), with extensive quotations on the phys-omy of the dove (*firāsat al-ḥamām*), none of h however can be found in the Arabic physiogno-n as it exists now. Ibn al-Nadīm (d. 377/987) mentions Polemon's book and, without naming uthor, a *Firāsat al-ḥamām* (*Fihrist*, ed. Flügel, . Mention of Polemon is also made by Ibn Ḥazm /1022 [*q.v.*]) in his *Ṭawḳ al-ḥamāma* (ed. D. K. of, Leiden 1914, 30). The quotation by Ibn Ḥazm ly a faint echo of Polemon, ed. Hoffmann, 169, An anecdote about Polemon and Hippocrates (a e anachronism) in Ps. Aristotole, *Sirr al-asrār* ed. Foerster, ii, 187-90) found its way into Ibn iftī (d. 646/1248 [*q.v.*]), *Taʾrīkh al-Ḥukamāʾ*, ed. ert, Leipzig 1903, 91 l. 12-92 l. 2 and into Ibn Uṣaybiʿa (d. 668/1270 [*q.v.*]), *ʿUyūn al-anbāʾ*, ed. ler, Königsberg 1884, i, 27-8.

olemon's book was widely used and epitomised. Arabicised short version is the edition of M. R. abbākh, Aleppo 1929. The characteristics of the ral nations of the Hellenistic world (ed. Hoffman, 9, ed. al-Ṭabbākh, 46) are applied to peoples of Islamic world. Another short version is MS ha 85 (3) (see bibliography), which lacks the ific Greek characteristics but is less adapted to mic taste than the Aleppo version. An evaluation he texts written under the name of Polemon has been undertaken so far. Polemon's book was bably a primary source of al-Dimashḳī (d. 727/ 7 [*q.v.*]), *K. al-Siyāsa fī ʿilm al-firāsa* (cf. Brockel-n, S II, 161) and Ibn al-Akfānī (d. 749/1348]), *Asās al-riyāsa fī ʿilm al-firāsa* (MS Paris, BN, b. 2762). *Firāsa* was, and still is, a popular science its uses both in court life, human relationships the slave trade. The exact impact, directly or rectly, of Polemon's work on the numerous tracts physiognomy of later times, cannot now easily be erned.

Bibliography: On Polemon in general see the rt. *Polemon* (by W. Stegemann) in Pauly-Wissowa, xi/2, cols. 1320-57, and F. Sezgin, *GAS*, iii, 352-3. n Polemon's position in the Arabic *firāsa* tradi-ion, see T. Fahd, *La divination arabe*, Strasbourg 966, 384-6, and Y. Mourad, *La physiognomie rabe* ..., Paris 1939, 44-6, with the literature cited there. Polemon's book was edited by G. Hoffmann, in R. Foerster, *Scriptores physiognomonici Graeci et Latini*, Leipzig 1893, i, 93-294 (= MS Leiden Or. 198 (1)). The only Greek quotation of Polemon preserved is given in *ibid*, i, p. LXXVI. A Ps-Polemonic treatise is mentioned in *ibid*; ii, 147-60 (= MS Gotha Arab. 85 (3)). Other MSS. of treatises going under the name of Polemon are mentioned by Fahd, *op. cit.* 384-6; Ullmann, *Medizin*, 96; Foerster, *Script. phys.*, i, p. LXXXVII (identical with Ḥādjdjī Khalīfa, ed. Flügel, vii, 297, and (?) with MS Nuruosmaniye, *Defter*, no. 2388); and M. R. al-Ṭabbākh in his edn., introd. p. 2. The Greek physiognomicon ascribed to Polemon in *Aeliani variae Historiae Libri XIIII*, Rome 1545, ff. 79-91 is not authentic, as has been demonstrated by R. Foerster, in *De Polemonis Physiognomonicis dissertatio*, Kiel 1886, 10 ff. (J. J. WITKAM)

ĀFRĀG (AL-MANṢŪRA), an 8th/14th century Marīnid royal camp-town (whence its name), commanding Ceuta from the heights west of the peninsula on which this old Moroccan (now Spanish) seaport is situated. Its site lies in an area of modern suburban development: in the north-east the line of its west wall stops short of the Ceuta-Punta Blanca coast road (Carretera de la Playa Benitez), and, from south-west to north-east, the trapezoid site is bisected lengthways by the Carretera de Torrones. More than half a kilometer of the west wall, including the remains of one of its three original gates, Bāb Fās, and its towers has survived. Construction techniques suggest Andalusian influence.

Āfrāg owed its existence to that of Ceuta, which, from around 1250, had acquired growing economic and strategic importance and become the great *entrepôt* of the western Mediterranean, boasting an economy thriving on commerce and privateering. Militarily, it was ideally suited to assist Islam in its struggle to maintain its increasingly precarious foothold in Spain: it had ships, harbours and a seafaring population equipped for war by land and sea; in good weather its ships could rapidly cross to Algeciras; its fortifications were formidable and, on its landward side, impregnable. However, because it could easily withstand assault and siege from the mainland, it had long enjoyed a profitable measure of independence and, at times under the ʿAzafids [*q.v.*], escaped Marīnid control altogether. Accordingly, when in 728/1327-8 the total collapse of ʿAzafid authority was followed by internal dissension, the Marīnid sultan Abū Saʿīd decided to assert his authority there once and for all. Among measures to achieve this end were decisions to demolish Ceuta's Outer Suburb (*al-rabaḍ al-barrānī*) wall, the most formidable barrier to access from the west, and to impart solidity and permanence to what had doubtless been the site of many an earlier siege camp. Like a similar foundation built by a dynastic predecessor outside Tlemcen, it was given the name al-Manṣūra. Abū Saʿīd is credited with the construction of a palace there with adjacent mosque as well as other buildings. Most of the wall and fortifications, however, seem to have been the work of Abu 'l-Ḥasan (931-52/1331-51). In the 9th/15th century Āfrāg was regarded as a suburb of Ceuta. Much of the place was still standing in the 18th century.

Bibliography: B. Pavón Maldonado, *Arte hispanomusulmán en Ceuta y Tetuán*, in *Cuadernos de la Alhambra*, vi (1970), 72-6; J. D. Latham, *The strategic position and defence of Ceuta in the later Muslim Period*, in *Orientalia Hispanica*, ed. J. M. Barral, i/1, Leiden 1974, 454 and *passim* (also in *Islamic Quarterly*, xv (1971), 195-7 and *passim*); al-Anṣārī, *Ikhtiṣār al-akhbār*, ed. E. Lévi-Provençal with title *Description musulmane au xve siècle*, in *Hespéris*, xii (1931), 145-76, ed. Ibn Tāwīt in *Tetuán* (1959), ed. A. Ben Mansour, Rabat 1969, *passim*; Spanish tr. by J. Vallvé Bermejo, in *Al-Andalus*, xxvii (1962), 398-442). (J. D. LATHAM)

ĀGAHĪ, poetical name of MUḤAMMAD RIḌĀ MĪRĀB B. ER NIYĀZ BEK, Khīwan historian, poet and translator, born 10 Dhu 'l-Ḳaʿda 1224/17 December 1809 in the township Ḳiyāt, near Khīwa, in Khwārazm.

He belonged to Uzbek tribe of Yüz and to an aristocratic family, whose members were hereditary *mīrāb*s (in the Khānate of Khīwa there were four high officials with the title *mīrāb*, members of the khān's council consisting of 34 *ʿamaldār*s). His uncle was Shīr Muḥammad Mīrāb with the poetical name Muʾnis [*q.v.*], a poet, translator and historian. Āgahī studied in a *madrasa* and especially under his uncle, whom he repeatedly calls his *ustād*. After the death of Muʾnis in 1244/1829, he received the title and the post of his uncle (Āgahī, *Riyāḍ al-dawla*, MS. of the Leningrad Branch of the Institute of Oriental Studies of the Academy of Sciences of the USSR, E-6, f. 334a). As a *mīrāb* he supervised the irrigation system in the country (a special interest in irrigation is noticeable in his historical works), but also, as other high officials, he usually accompanied the khāns of Khīwa in their military campaigns. In 1255/1839 he was ordered by Allāh-Ḳulī Khān to complete the history of the Khānate of Khīwa *Firdaws al-iḳbāl* written by Muʾnis, which had remained unfinished after his death (see *Firdaws al-iḳbāl*, MS. of the Leningrad Branch of the Institute of Oriental Studies, C-571, f. 445a-b). Having completed this work, carrying it to the death of Muḥammad Raḥīm Khān, 1240/1825, Āgahī proceeded with separate histories of Allāh-Ḳulī Khān and his successors, thus becoming a kind of official historiographer of the Khānate of Khīwa (formally such a post did not exist in the khānate). In 1268/1851 he resigned from the post of *mīrāb* because of an illness (see his *Djāmiʿ al-wāḳiʿāt-i sulṭānī*, MS. of the Leningrad Branch of the Institute of Oriental Studies, E-6, f. 488a-b) and dedicated all his time to literary work until his death in 1291/1874, shortly after the Russian conquest of Khīwa (see Muḥammad Yūsuf Bek Bayānī, *Shadjara-yi Khwārazmshāhī*, MS. of the Institute of Oriental Studies in Tāshkent No. 9596, f. 4b).

His literary production in Čaghatāy was very considerable. Besides the continuation of the *Firdaws al-iḳbāl* of Muʾnis he wrote five other historical works, continuing one after the other till 1289/1872: (1) *Riyāḍ al-dawla*, history of Allāh-Ḳulī Khān (1240-58/1825-42) and the first two years of the reign of Raḥīm-Ḳulī Khān (1258-9/1843-4); (2) *Zubdat al-tawārīkh*, history of Raḥīm-Ḳulī Khān (1258-62/1843-6): (3) *Djāmiʿ al-wāḳiʿāt-i sulṭānī*, history of Muḥammad Amīn Khān (1262-71/1846-55), ʿAbd Allāh Khān (1271/1855) and Ḳutlugh Murād Khān (1271-2/1855-6); (4) *Gulshan-i dawlat*, history of Sayyid Muḥammad Khān (1272-81/1856-64); and (5) *Shāhid-i iḳbāl*, history of the first eight years of the reign of Sayyid Muḥammad Raḥīm Khān II (1281-9/1864-72). Except for the *Firdaws al-iḳbāl* and the greater part of the *Riyāḍ al-dawla*, all of them are contemporary chronicles arranged in annalistic form, with their main subdivisions being the years of reign of respective khāns. Āgahī's accounts are based on his own observations as well as reports of other eyewitnesses, and, in some cases, on official documents. These chronicles are the most outstanding work of Central Asian historiography "in regard to th nuteness of account and the quantity of facts" they comprise (Barthold). His Turkī *dīwān* en *Taʿwīdh al-ʿāshiḳīn* includes mainly *ghazal*s, bu *ḳaṣīdas*, *mathnawīs*, *mukhammasāt*, etc.; he wrot some poems (mostly *ghazals*) in Persian.

Āgahī was also a prolific translator. At the b ning of his literary career he continued the t lation into Čaghatāy on the *Rawḍat al-ṣafā* Mīrkhwānd [*q.v.*] begun by Muʾnis (Āgahī trans the second half of vol. ii, vol. iii and, allegedly, vii), and later translated a number of other Pe works: *Taʾrīkh-i djahān-gushā-yi Nādirī* by Mu mad Mahdī Khān; *Durra-i Nādirī* by the same au the 3rd vol. of *Rawḍat al-ṣafā-yi Nāṣirī* by Riḍā Khān; the *Gulistān* by Saʿdī; *Yūsuf wa-Zulaykh* Djāmī; *Haft paykar* by Niẓāmī (a prose translat *Shāh wa-gadā* by Hilālī; *Zubdat al-ḥikāyāt* by Mu mad Wārith; the *Ḳābūs-nāma*; the *Akhlāḳ-i Mu* by Ḥusayn Kāshifī; and the *Miftāḥ al-ṭālibī* Maḥmūd Ghizhduwānī (cf. Storey, i/2, 973) (exist MSS. of all above-mentioned translations Bibliography). In the preface to his *dīwān* he tions also several other translations made by manuscripts of which, however, have still not been discovered: a *Ẓafar-nāma* [apparently by Sh al-Dīn Yazdī]; *Salamān wa-Absāl* by Djāmī; *Bahāristān* by Djāmī; [the memoirs of] Wāṣif Storey-Bregel, 1123-6); *Tadhkira-yi Muḳīm-Kh* *Ṭabaḳāt-i Akbar-Shāhī*; the *Hasht bihisht* by Khusraw; and also a *sharḥ* to the *Dalāʾil al-kh* from Ottoman Turkish.

Bibliography: V. V. Bartol'd, *Istoriya kul noy zhizni Turkestana* (1927), in *Sočineniya*, 285-6; P. P. Ivanov, in *Materiali po istorii turk i Turkmenii*, ii, Moscow-Leningrad 1938, 23-7 Munirov, *Āgahī* [in Uzbek], Tāshkent 1959; i Munis, *Āgahī wa Bayānīning tarikhi atharla* Uzbek], Tāshkent 1961; R. Madjidi, *Āgahī lir* [in Uzbek], Tāshkent 1963; J. Eckmann, in *P logiae turcicae fundamenta*, ii, 389-90; H. F. man, *Turkish literature*, section iii, Utrecht 1 i/2, 48-52 (with additional references). On the of his original historical works see, besides above-mentioned sources, L. V. Dmitriyev alii, *Opisaniye tyurkskikh rukopisey Inst narodov Azii*, i, Moscow 1965, 106-18 (Nos. 97 100-2, 105-7, 110); *Sobraniye vostočnikh rukop Akademii nauk Uzbekskoy SSR*, Tāshkent, i, vii, 33-7. The MS. in the Istanbul Unive Library TY 82 (the only one known outside Soviet Union) contains *Firdaws al-iḳbāl*, *Riyā dawla* and *Zubdat al-tawārīkh*. Russian translat of extracts from historical works: V. V. Bar (1910), in *Sočineniya*, ii/2, 400-13 (epitomised tr lation from *Shāhid-i iḳbāl*); *Materiali po is karakalpakov*, Moscow-Leningrad 1935, 12 *Materiali po istorii turkmen i Turkmenii*, ii, Mos Leningrad 1938, 384-638. MSS. of the *dīwān*: *Sobraniye vostočnikh rukopisey Akademii n Uzbekskoy SSR*, vii, 128-9; separate poems: *ibid.*, ii, 358, v, 125, vii, index. The *Dīwān* published lithographically in Khīwa in 1300/ and 1323/1905 and in modern Cyrillic transcrip in 1960 in Tāshkent (partial edition only). On MSS. of his translations of Persian historical w see Storey-Bregel, 374, 375, 479, 910, 913; *So niye vostočnikh rukopisey Akademii nauk Uzbeks SSR*, iii, 111, v, 107, vii, 48, 68-9, 217-8.

(YU. BREGE

ĀGHĀ ḤASHAR KASHMĪRĪ (1879-1935),

-known Urdu dramatist. His actual name Āghā Muḥammad Shāh and Ḥashar his *takhalluṣ*, his *nisba* alludes to the country of origin of his r. The latter came from Kashmīr, and settled in res as a merchant. Here Āghā Ḥashar was born educated, until in 1897 he ran away from home made for Bombay. He feared his father's wrath is misuse of money entrusted to him; and his tite for the new Urdu drama form, which was ishing in Bombay, had been whetted by the visit theatrical company to Benares. He worked as wright for various companies in Bombay, and equently in several provincial capitals such as erabad and Madras, writing over thirty plays. y of them were extremely successful, and earned a fine reputation, and also considerable wealth, h, however, he quickly dissipated. He later ed in films. He died and was buried in Lahore. hen he entered the field, the main lines of the dramatic form were already established. Āghā ar, by his technical brilliance and command of age raised it to its highest point. The form was ly challenged until after the 1939-45 War. mon elements in the form were: the use of poetry rhymed prose, often rhetorical to the point of bast, prose being reserved for comedy or social a; the development of subsidiary plots along-the main one, as in Shakespeare; and historical eroic themes, based on either Islamic and Indian es or Shakespeare and other English dramatists, se plays were freely adapted, with changes in tions and names of characters. Social themes also employed. Violence and death were common tage, as in *Sohrāb-o-Rustum* (1929, publ. Lahore): yet adaptations of Shakespeare's tragedies it be given happy endings—thus *Safed Khwun* 7, publ. Lahore 1954), based on *King Lear*.

Bibliography: For accounts of earlier Urdu ama, see Muhammad Sadiq, *History of Urdu erature*, London 1964, 393-9; Ram Babu Sak-na, *History of Urdu literature*, Allahabad 1927, 6-67; J. A. Haywood, *Urdu drama—origins and rly development*, in *Iran and Islam—in memory of ladimir Minorsky*, ed. C. E. Bosworth, Edinburgh 71, 293-302. Accounts of Āghā Ḥashar and his amatic art are to be found in Wakkār ʿAẓīm, *ghā Ḥashar awr un ke drāme*, Lahore 1956; and em, *Urdū drāma—taʾrīkh-o-tanḳīd*, Lahore 1957. or the texts of the plays, those published by Urdu arkaz, Lahore, are recommended. Other and ear-r editions are based on information supplied by tors; many were published in the author's life-me without his authority. They differ substan-ally from Āghā Ḥashar's manuscripts, many of hich are in the Nawāb of Rampūr's library. Of e Urdu Markaz series, apart from the two men-oned in the text, the following may be noted: *ayd-i-haws* based on Shakespeare's *King John* 954); *Asīr-i-ḥirṣ*, based on Sheridan's *Pizarro* 954); *Khwubṣūrat balā* (1954); and *Pahla piyār Balwā mangal* (1955). (J. A. Haywood)

GHAOGHLU, Aḥmed (originally Aḥmed Agha-, later Aghaoghlu Aḥmed and after 1934 Ahmet oğlu), Turkish writer and journalist (1869-). Born in Shusha, a town in the Ḳarabāgh [*q.v.*] on of Ādharbāydjān, he was educated in his home and Tiflis (Tbilisi) and later studied political nce in Paris. In 1894 he returned home, where collaborated with progressive and nationalist in-ectuals like Ḥusayn-Zāde ʿAlī, Ismāʿīl Gaspīralī sprinski) [*q.v.*] and ʿAlī Merdān Topčïbashï and tributed to various papers. After the restoration of the Constitution in Turkey in 1908, he went to Istanbul, joined the Committee of Union and Progress (CUP) and became a leader writer of the French daily *Jeune turc*. Together with Ḍiyā Gökalp, Yūsuf Akčura and Meḥmed Emīn (Yurdakul) he became one of the promoters of the Turkism movement (*Türkčülük*) which developed, with the foundation in June 1911 of the nationalist association Turkish Hearth (*Türk Odjaghï*) and its organ *Türk yurdu*, into an influential current in Turkish intellectual life after 1912. In 1913 Aghaoghlu was appointed professor of Turkish history in Istanbul University and continued his contributions to various papers. Elected deputy to Parliament and a member of the executive board (*Merkez-i ʿUmūmī*) of the CUP, in 1917 he accompanied the Turkish expeditionary force to the Caucasus as a political officer. On his return to Istanbul he was arrested by the British and exiled to Malta with other leading CUP members. Freed from Malta in July 1921, he joined the Nationalists in Ankara and was appointed director general of the Press. Elected to the Grand National Assembly, he contributed at the same time to the semi-official daily *Ḥākimiyyet-i milliyye* and taught at the newly-established Faculty of Law in Ankara. He was one of the founders of the short-lived Liberal Party (*Serbest Fırka*) of August 1930 and following its abolition in November of the same year, retired from political life, teaching in the Istanbul Faculty of Law until his retirement in 1933. He died in Istanbul on 19 May 1939.

Essentially a journalist and politician, Aghaoghlu is the author of the following major works: (1) *Üč medeniyyet* ("Three civilisations") Istanbul 1927, 2nd ed. in Roman script *Üç medeniyet*, Istanbul 1972; (2) *Serbest insanlar ülkesinde* ("In the land of free people"), Istanbul 1930; (3) *Devlet ve fert* ("State and individual"); and posthumously, (4) *Serbest Fırka hatıraları* ("Reminiscences of the Liberal Party"). Istanbul 1949. Aghaoghlu's innumerable articles published in various dailies have not been published in book form.

Bibliography: Samet Ağaoğlu (his son), *Babamdan hatıralar*, Istanbul 1940 (contains the author's reminiscences of his father, Aghaoghlu's own incomplete memoirs and impressions of a number of writers on A. A.); *idem*, *Babamın arkadaşları*[2] ("My father's friends"), Istanbul 1969. (Fahir İz)

AGRICULTURE [see filāḥa].

AGUEDAL [see āgdāl].

AḤĀBĪSH [see ḥabash, ḥabasha].

al-**AḤDAB** [see ibrāhīm al-aḥdab].

AḤMAD al-HĪBA, a religious leader of southern Morocco, and ephemeral pretender to the Sharīfian throne, known above all as al-Hība. He was born in Ramaḍān 1293 or 1294/September-October 1876 or 1877, the fourth son of the famous Shaykh Māʾ al-ʿAynayn [*q.v.*]. He was brought up and educated in his father's bosom, and his natural talents and temperament gave his teachers high literary hopes of him.

When his father died at Tiznīt in Shawwāl 1328/November 1910, he succeeded him at the head of the *murīdūn* of the order and was then at the peak of his responsibilities. However, when there was announced the signing of the Protectorate Treaty between France and sultan Mawlāy al-Ḥāfiẓ [*q.v.*], followed by the rumour of the latter's death and of the murder of the *ʿulamāʾ* of Fās by the French, he proclaimed himself sultan, organised his own *makhzan* [*q.v.*] and launched throughout the Sūs, and then through all Morocco, appeals for resistance. Soon the tribes of the South (except for the ports) rallied to him, and before official letters announcing the accession of Mawlāy Yusūf [*q.v.*] could arrive, he appointed fresh officials with high responsibilities in the regions which had recognised him. He then used the way via Tīzī n'Maʿshū and followed the road to Marrakesh in an imperial procession. When he arrived before the southern capital, he met with hostility from the high political leaders, but was received with joy by the people of the Ḥawẓ [*q.v.*]. The new sultan entered Marrakesh on Sunday, 5 Ramaḍān 1330/18 August 1912, occupied the *ḳaṣaba* and installed himself in the palace of the ʿAlawīs. He had to face grave troubles immediately. Profiting by the great unrest which had seized people's hearts and minds, the *ʿasākir* troops, the floating population of the city and the hungry hordes which had followed the new *amīr* from Taroudannt, launched themselves into sacking the shops and imposing all sorts of exactions on the populace.

Al-Hība had secured the handing-over to himself of the few French residents, including the vice-consul of France, who had attempted to flee the city. In an endeavour to save their lives, Gen. Lyautey's troops got the order to go by forced marches to Marrakesh. Aḥmad al-Hība sent out to confront them about 5,000 men, who were crushed on 6 September at Sīdī Bū ʿUthmān by Col. Mangin's column, in every way better-armed and better-led than the pretender's force. In front of the rapid French advance, al-Hība and his remaining supporters, the "blue men" quickly evacuated the city which they had occupied three weeks previously and fled into the Atlas, pursued by all those who has suffered from their extortions and insolent behaviour. Col. Mangin entered Marrakesh on 7 September 1912, with an enthusiastic welcome from the Jewish community; the majority of the Muslim population sullen and silent. Sultan Mawlā Yūsuf was then proclaimed, in an atmosphere of general relief, by the great religious and political leaders of the city and of the surrounding region, wearied by the disorders and insecurity.

Al-Hība withdrew first of all to base, whence he "reigned" over the Sūs over nearly eight months, after having refused nomination as the sultan's *khalīfa* over all the south of Morocco. He was then expelled from his capital by the Sharīfian *maḥallas* [*q.v.*] sent against him from Marrakesh, and finally, continually defeated but always remaining proud, he died at Tiznīt in dignity on 18 or 24 Ramaḍān 1337/17 or 23 June 1919.

Bibliography: Ladreyt de Lacharrière, *Grandeur et decadence de Mohammad al-Hiba*, in *Bulletin de la Société de Géographie d'Alger et de l'Afrique du Nord* (1912), No. 65; ʿAbbās b. Ibrāhīm al-Marrākushī, *al-Iʿlām bi-man ḥalla Marrākush*, i, Fās 1355/1936, 289-303; Gen. Lyautey, *Rapport général sur la situation du Protectorat du Maroc du 31 Juillet 1914*, Rabat N.D., 13-15; F. Weisgerber, *Au seuil du Maroc moderne*, Rabat 1947, chs. xxii-xxiv; G. Deverdun, *Marrakech, des origines à 1912*, Rabat 1959, i, 548-9; M. M. al-Sūsī, *al-Maʿsūl*, Rabat 1380/1960, iv, 101-246 (very full and lively account of the pretender and his adventures).

(G. DEVERDUN)

AḤMAD B. **ʿĪSĀ** B. ZAYD B. ʿALĪ B. AL-ḤUSAYN B. ʿALĪ B. ABI ṬĀLIB, ABŪ ʿABD ALLĀH, Zaydī leader and scholar, was born on 2 Muḥarram 157/22 November 773 in Kūfa. His father ʿĪsā b. Zayd, who was supported by many Zaydīs as their candidate for the imāmate, had gone into hiding in the houses of the Kūfan Zaydī traditionist al-Ḥasan b. Ṣāliḥ b. Ḥayy [*q.v.*] after the failure of the revolt of Ibrāhīm b. ʿAbd Allāh [*q.v.*] in 145/762-3. Afte death of his father in 166/783 and of al-Ḥasa 167/783-4, Aḥmad and his brother Zayd were bro to the caliph al-Mahdī, who took charge of thei bringing. He permitted them to reside in Me where Zayd died. Aḥmad remained there unt was denounced to the caliph Hārūn al-Rashī being alleged that the Zaydīs were gathering ar him. On the order of the caliph, he and another ʿ al-Ḳasīm b. ʿAlī b. ʿUmar, were brought to Bag and put under the custody of al-Faḍl b. al-R They escaped, however, and Aḥmad b. ʿĪsā, accor to al-Ṣafadī, led a revolt in ʿAbbādān in 185 but soon fled and went into hiding in Baṣra. date for Aḥmad's escape and concealment wou gree well with the report of al-Ṭabarī (iii, 651) Thumāma b. Ashras was imprisoned by Hārūn in 802 "because he had been lying in the matter of mad b. ʿĪsā" and the report of al-Djahshiyārī *wuzaraʾ*, ed. Muṣṭafā al-Saḳḳāʾ, Cairo 1357/1938, that the Barmakid Yaḥyā b. Khālid, when he into disgrace in the same year, was accused of ha sent 70,000 *dīnār*s to Aḥmad in Baṣra. Al-Yaʿḳ account (*Taʾrīkh*, 512) that Aḥmad was seized imprisoned in al-Rāfiḳa in 188-804 appears mista and the date may refer merely to the capture execution of Ḥādir, the servant and assistant of mad, reported in the same account. According to report, Aḥmad was discovered in Kūfa in the tim the caliph al-Mutawakkil, but left free becaus was afflicted with cataracts. He died, after ha become blind, in Baṣra on 23 Ramaḍan 247/1 De ber 861.

Like his father, Aḥmad was considered by m Kūfan Zaydīs as the most suitable candidate for imāmate, though he refused, after his initial fai to become involved in any revolutionary acti He was also accepted by his followers as an aut tative teacher in religious matters. His doctrine collected by some Zaydī transmitters who had ac to him, in particular by the foremost Kūfan Z scholar of the 3rd/9th century, Muḥammad b. Ma al-Murādī (d. *ca.* 290/903), whose *K. Amālī Aḥm ʿĪsā* (with additions from the transmission of o Zaydī authorities) is extant in manuscript. His doctrine was based primarily on the traditions tr mitted by Abū Khālid al-Wāsiṭī from Zayd b. [*q.v.*] and by Abu 'l-Djārūd from Muḥammad al-Bā though he occasionally also relied on other tradit or taught on his own authority. He thus represe a more strictly Zaydī (Djārūdī) outlook, conside only the *ḥadīth* of the *Ahl al-Bayt* as authorita in contrast to his father who, in accordance with view of the Batriyya [*q.v.*], accepted the *ḥadīth* tr mitted by the Muslim community at large. C cerning the imāmate, however, he stood close to Batriyya, apparently admitting the legitimacy of caliphate of Abū Bakr and ʿUmar. In theology upheld the majority views of the early Kūfan Za yya. He supported predestination and the creatio the acts of men by God versus human free will, the Muslim sinner to be an "unbeliever by ing tude" (*kāfir niʿma*) though not a polytheist (*mush* and refused to take a definite position concer the question of the createdness of the Ḳurʾān. the first of these doctrines he sharply differed f his contemporary al-Ḳāsim b. Ibrāhīm [*q.v.*], wh positions were closer to Muʿtazilī views.

His religious doctrine became one of the *madhhab*s to which the Kūfan Zaydīs adhered in 4th/11th century. Some Zaydīs are said to have stricted the imāmate to his descendants. His po

y among the Sh̲īʿa is also reflected by the fact
the leader of the Zand̲j̲ rebellion [see ʿALĪ B.
AMMAD AL-ZAND̲J̲Ī] for some time claimed to be
randson.

Bibliography: Abu 'l-Farad̲j̲ al-Iṣfahānī, *Ma-
til al-Ṭālibiyyīn*, ed. Aḥmad Ṣaḳr, Cairo 1368/
49, 420-5, 619-27; al-Tanūkh̲ī, *al-Farad̲j̲ baʿd al-
idda*, Cairo 1357/1938, i, 120 f.; Abū Nuʿaym al-
ʿahānī, *D̲h̲ikr akh̲bār Iṣfahān*, ed. S. Dedering,
iden 1931, i, 80 (the account seems to rest at
ist partially on a confusion with another ʿAlid);
Ṣafadī, *al-Wāfī*, vii, ed. Iḥsān ʿAbbās, Wiesbaden
69, 271 f.; Ibn ʿInaba, *ʿUmdat al-ṭālib*, ed. Muḥ.
asan Āl al-Ṭāliḳānī, al-Nad̲j̲af 1380/1961, 288-90;
. Madelung, *Der Imam al-Ḳāsim ibn Ibrāhīm*,
erlin 1965, 80-3 and index s.v. Aḥmad b. ʿĪsā b.
aid.   (W. MADELUNG)

ḤMAD B. MUḤAMMAD or MAḤMŪD, called
N AL-FUḲARĀʾ, Transoxanian author of an
ortant work on the religious leaders and saints of
hārā, the *Kitāb-i Mullāzāda* or *Kitāb-i Mazārāt-i
hārā*, in which the cemeteries of the city and
r occupants are described. Since the last date
tioned in the book is 814/1411-12, the author
t have lived in the reigns of Tīmūr and Sh̲āh-
h [see TĪMŪRIDS]. From the number of extant
uscripts, the work was obviously popular in Cen-
Asia. Extracts from it were first given by Bar-
d, *Turkestan v epokhu Mongolskago nashestviya*, i,
sty, 166-72, and a lithograph appeared at New
hārā in 1322/1904. Of secondary sources, see
hold, *Turkestan*, Eng. tr.³, 58; Storey, i, 953;
Pritsak, *Āl-i Burhān*, in *Isl.*, xxx (1952), 95-6
critical text of the *K.-i Mullāzāda* mentioned here
eing in preparation as a Göttingen thesis never in
materialised).

Bibliography: Given in the article.   (ED.)

ḤMAD B. MUḤAMMAD AL-BARḲĪ [see AL-
Ḳ̲Ī, in Suppl.].

ḤMAD PASH̲A KŪČŪK ("the small"), d.
5/1636, Ottoman military commander who
k a prominent part in the revival of the Ottoman
ire under Murād IV (1033-49/1623-40). Of Al-
ian origin, he began as a soldier and became com-
adant of the Türkmen troops. He became governor
Jamascus for the first time in 1038/1629, but was
recalled by the Porte to become governor of
ahya. The sultan then charged him with suppres-
the revolt of Ilyās Pasha, who was ravaging
tolia, and he rapidly achieved success here and
ught the rebel back a prisoner to Istanbul (1042/
2). He then became governor of Damascus again,
the charge of pacifying the Druze country, and
lst passing through the region of Aleppo sup-
ssed the endemic state of revolt of the nomads
he mountainous zone to the north-west of the
.

ḥmad Pasha easily managed to master the revolt
akhr al-Dīn II [q.v.], whom he took captive (1043/
3-4). As a reward for his many services, Murād
appointed him to the vizierate with three *tugh̲*s
bestowed upon him, by a *firmān* of 1046/1636,
whole of Fakh̲r al-Dīn's wealth, which included
nerous buildings in Ṣayda, one of which was the
n for rice in the quarter near the port in the north-
tern sector of the town (and not the kh̲ān of the
nch, as often stated, including by P. Schwarz in
art. SIDON). Aḥmad Pasha used these revenues
a *wakf* in favour of the Holy Cities in Arabia and
kiyye which he had built in the southern part of
mascus, outside the Bāb Allāh on the pilgrimage
te; this is accordingly one of the rare monuments

built in Damascus in the first half of the 17th century
(it is known today as the mosque of al-ʿAssālī).

The pacification of Lebanon was hardly finished
when he joined the forces campaigning against Persia
as commander of the Ottoman vanguard, and he distinguished himself above all at the time of the great
battle of Tabrīz. In the following year, Murād IV
entrusted to him the defence of al-Mawṣil, where he
found a glorious death in battle against the Persian
troops (20 Rabīʿ II 1046/21 September 1636). He was
buried in his *tekiyye* in Damascus.

It seems that during his Lebanese expedition,
Aḥmad Pasha showed his usual severity, so much so
that remembrance of "the year of Küčük" remained
stamped on the popular memory in Mount Lebanon.
Indeed, the Porte did not hesitate on future occasions
(notably in 1214/1799) to remind the Druzes of this
harshness. The terrible legacy of fear left behind in
the local consciousness is probably the origin of the
Lebanese legend of "Küčük". Aḥmad Pasha is represented as a polished traitor who engineered the
ruin of his benefactor and then seized his possessions.
The legend relates in effect that Aḥmad Pasha was
an orphan brought up by Fakh̲r al-Dīn II, who appointed him tax-collector for southern Lebanon, but
since he committed various financial defalcations, he
had to leave his service and then sought Fakh̲r al-
Dīn's ruin by accusing him at the Porte of wanting
to make himself independent, for which he was rewarded by the wealth of the Maʿns.

Bibliography: There is a long, fairly confused
biography in Muḥibbī, *Kh̲ulāṣat al-ath̲ar*, Cairo
1862, i, 385-8, who, together with Sāmī Bey (*Ḳāmūs
al-aʿlām*, Istanbul 1888, i, 797), emphasises his
courage and fidelity to Murād IV. Extracts from
the text of the *wakfiyya* of Aḥmad Pasha are in the
Ẓāhiriyya at Damascus, No. 8518 (history), containing in particular the description of Fakh̲r al-
Dīn's possessions; see A. Abdel Nour, *Étude sur
deux actes de waqfs du XVIᵉ et du XVIIᵉ siècles des
wilayets de Damas et de Sayda*, Sorbonne thesis
1976. For a detailed account of Aḥmad Pasha's
death, see Naʿīmā, *Taʾrīkh̲*, Istanbul 1866, iii, 291-
2. On his official career, see Von Hammer, *Histoire*,
Paris 1838, ix, 275-6. On the "year of Küčük", see
Chebli, *Fakh̲r al-Dīn II Maʿn*, Beirut 1936, 186 ff.
One of the oldest versions of the Lebanese legend
of Küčük is to be found in ʿĪsā al-Maʿlūf, *Taʾrīkh̲
al-amīr Fakh̲r al-Dīn al-Maʿnī al-th̲ānī²*, Beirut
1966, 202-10.   (A. ABDEL NOUR)

AḤMAD-I RŪMĪ, Persian Ṣūfī and author,
who lived and worked in India in the first half of the
8th/14th century. Little is known of his life except
that he travelled from kh̲ānaḳāh [q.v.] to kh̲anaḳāh,
preaching and composing his moralistic treatises for
the residents of these convents. He has been incorrectly identified as Aḥmad b. Muḥammad
Rūmī al-Ḥanafī (Ḥād̲j̲d̲j̲ī Kh̲alīfa, iv, 582) and by Massignon as Sulṭān-i Walad's grandson, Aḥmad Pasha.

Aḥmad's most popular work, the *Daḳāʾiḳ al-ḥaḳā-
ʾiḳ*, is divided in 80 chapters, each opening with an
āya or *ḥadīth̲*, which serves as a starting point for the
discussion of some aspect of Ṣūfī doctrine. Mawlānā
D̲j̲alāl al-Dīn Rūmī [q.v.] is quoted frequently, and
each chapter is concluded by a short *math̲nawī* in
imitation of Mawlānā. Like his later, similar composition, *Umm al-Kitāb* (727/1327) it is a first instance of a class of works expounding Mawlānā's
teachings, without however constituting an actual
attempt at a commentary of the *Math̲nawī* (as Furū-
zanfar would have it in his *Sh̲arḥ-i Math̲nawī*, i,
Tehran 1346, 10).

cyclopaedia of Islam, Suppl.

4

The instruction of the convent's residents takes a more practical turn in *al-Daḳāʾiḳ fi ʾl-ṭarīḳ*, a lengthy *mathnawī* in 12 chapters on the relation between *murshid* and *murīd*. Although Aḥmad describes himself as a "follower of Mawlānā", from his exposition of Ṣūfī praxis he does not appear as a Mawlawī in the strict sense of the word. Rather, Aḥmad's works indicate that Ṣūfī life in the 8th/14th century did not have to be organised along the formal lines of the later great orders.

One instance of lyrical poetry (a *ghazal*) occurs in a *Mathnawī* manuscript in Edinburgh (Hukk, Ethé, Robertson, *Descriptive catalogue*, no. 281).

Bibliography: A. C. M. Hamer, *An unknown Mawlawī-poet: Aḥmad-i Rūmī*, in *Studia Iranica*, iii (1974), 229-49. (A. C. M. Hamer)

AḤMADĪ, a town about 30 years old some 20 km. south of Kuwayt City. During the early days of exploration for oil in Kuwayt, the Kuwait Oil Company (KOC), then owned in equal shares by the Anglo-Iranian Oil Company (later renamed British Petroleum) and by the Gulf Oil Corporation of the United States, established its base camp at Magwa (al-Maḳwa) not far north-west of the ridge known as Dhahr (al-Ẓahr), which with an elevation of *ca.* 120 m. is one of the few fairly high places in the state. In 1356/1938 KOC discovered oil south of the ridge at Burgan (Burḳān), destined to become one of the largest oil fields in the world. The involvement of Britain and later the United States in the Second World War delayed the first export of oil until 1365/1946. KOC gradually moved its field headquarters to the desert area of the ridge, which was renamed Aḥmadī (in Arabic al-Aḥmadī) in honour of Shaykh Aḥmad Āl Djābir Āl Ṣabāh, then the Ruler of Kuwayt. Oil from Burgan and other fields, including one called Aḥmadī, is brought to a tank farm on the ridge, whence it flows by gravity to the nearby coast for shipment from the terminal of Mīnāʾ al-Aḥmadī. The company built at Aḥmadī a planned community with many amenities designed especially for the comfort and pleasure of the expatriate staff (British, Americans, etc.). With the passage of time, Kuwaytīs in increasing numbers received the training necessary to qualify them for higher positions in the company. The government also inaugurated and expanded in stages its participation in the ownership of KOC, culminating in a complete takeover in 1394/1975, with the original owners being retained to lend a hand in the operations. The town and the indigenous parts of the state have thus moved towards full integration.

Aḥmadī town is also the seat of the Aḥmadī Governorate (*muḥāfaẓa*). As Kuwayt endeavours to diversify its economy in order to escape undue dependence on the export of oil and natural gas, emphasis is placed on industrialisation. The largest industrial area in the state is now Shuaiba (al-Shuʿayba) on the coast of the Governorate south of Mīnāʾ al-Aḥmadī, with huge plants for generating electricity, distilling sea water, and manufacturing petrochemicals.

Bibliography: In addition to the general bibliography for KUWAYT, see *al-ʿArabī*, Kuwayt, Shawwal 1395 and Rabīʿ II 1396; *Madjallat Dirāsāt al-Khalīdj*, Kuwayt, Radjab 1396; *The Kuwaiti Digest*, Kuwayt, Jan.-Sept. 1976. (G. Rentz)

AL-**AḤMAR** [see ABU ʾL-ḤASAN AL-AḤMAR, in Suppl.].

AḤMED, FAḲĪH, or AḤMED FAḲĪH, early Anatolian Turkish poet whose identity and date are controversial. He is accepted to be the author of the *Čarkh-nāme*, a poem of about eighty couple *ḳaṣīda* form, which is found in the *Madjma naẓāʾir*, compiled in the early 16th centur Ḥādjdjī Kemāl of Egirdir. It was first publishe M. Fuʾād Köprülü as a specimen of early century Turkish verse (*Anatolische Dichter i Seldschükenzeit, ii, Aḥmed Faḳīh*, in *KCsA*, ii (1 20-38). Mecdut Mansuroğlu, who edited the wo transcription, modified the text of the 16th cer manuscript, adapting it to the linguistic ch teristics of the 13th century. Recent researc T. Gandjei (*Notes on the attribution and date o "Čarḫnāma"*, in *Studi preottomani e ottomani, del Convegno di Napoli*, Naples 1976, 101-4) s that there has been a confusion among se Faḳīh Aḥmeds and Aḥmed Faḳīhs mentioned i sources and that the *Čarkh-nāme* attributed to o these cannot linguistically be dated earlier thar late 14th century. The *Čarkh-nāme*, which is wr in the literary language of early Anatolian ((man) Turkish, repeats some of the *leitmoti dīwān* poetry: life is short, all the signs indicate the end is near; none, even prophets and kings escape death; consider the day of Judgement repent; etc. (For a paraphrase in modern Tu and evaluation of the poem, see Fahir İz, *türk edebiyatinda nazım*, ii, Istanbul 1967, Intro tion).

Bibliography: A. Bombaci, *Storia letteratura turca*, Milan 1969, 270. (Fahir İ

AḤRĀR, KHWĀDJA ʿUBAYD ALLĀH B. MAḤ NAṢĪR AL-DĪN (806-95/1404-90), a *shaykh* of Naḳshbandī order under whose auspice became firmly rooted in Central Asia and spread to other regions of the Islamic world; furtherm the effective ruler of much of Transoxania for decades. He was born in Ramaḍān 806/March in the village of Bāghistān near Tashkent in family already renowned for its religious and scho interests. It was his maternal uncle, Ibrāhīm Sh who first assumed the task of educating him and sent him to pursue his studies in Samarḳand. Bec of illness and lack of inclination on his part, A soon abandoned his studies in Samarḳand, according to his own admission never mast "more than two pages of Arabic grammar". Thro out his life, indeed, he manifested a certain dis for formal religious learning, assigning more portance to the enactment of the *Sharīʿa* and practise of Ṣūfism. At the age of 24, Aḥrār wen Herat, and it was evidently there that his ac interest in Ṣūfism was awakened. He associ with numerous *shaykhs* of the city without, howe offering his formal allegiance to any of them. master to whom he gave his devotion was ins Yaʿḳūb Čarkhī (d. 851/1447), one of the princ successors of Bahāʾ al-Dīn Naḳshband, eponym founder of the Naḳshbandī order, who had Bukhārā after the death of his master to settle in Badakhshān and then in the remote provinc Čaghāniyān. Aḥrār had already had some dealing Samarḳand with another Naḳshbandī *sha Khwādja* Ḥasan ʿAṭṭār, son-in-law of Bahāʾ al- Naḳshband, but ʿAṭṭār had seen little sign in hi spiritual talent, and advised him instead to le the martial arts. Returning from Čaghāniyān Tashkent in about 835/1431, Aḥrār establis himself as chief Ṣūfī *shaykh* of the city.

Aḥrār's rise to political prominence came in 8 1451, when he extended to the Tīmūrid prince A Saʿīd assistance that proved decisive in enab him to capture the Tīmūrid capital of Samarḳa rding to the account found in the biographies of r, Abū Saʿīd, defeated in battle by a rival e, ʿAbd Allāh Mīrzā, fled northward to Tash- , and in the course of his flight dreamed of the rated saint, Aḥmad Yasawī [*q.v.*]. Yasawī duced him to a luminous figure who would im in his struggle. Describing the figure he had med of to the people of Tashkent, Abū Saʿīd told that it was none other than Khwādja yd Allāh Aḥrār. Aḥrār was at the time absent Tashkent, and it was at the small town of ent (Fārkat) outside the city that Abū Saʿīd to meet him. Aḥrār consented to aid him, on ition that he use his rule to enforce the *Sharīʿa* to alleviate the lot of the people. In the ensuing le, ʿAbd Allāh Mīrzā was defeated, and Abū d entered Samarḳand, soon to be followed by ār. Abū Saʿīd's battle against ʿAbd Allāh Mīrzā been won, in reality, by his Uzbek auxiliaries, manded by Abu 'l-Khayr Khān; it is said that had intervened at the request of Aḥrār, but is uncertain. In any event, Abū Saʿīd felt him- to be in the debt of Aḥrār and even, according the chronicler ʿAbd al-Razzāḳ Samarḳandī, garded himself as being under his orders". ār's domination of Samarḳand became complete 61/1457 when Abū Saʿīd transferred his capital Herat. It survived the death of that prince in '1469, this death occurring in the course of a strous campaign undertaken with Aḥrār's ice; Abū Saʿīd's son, Sulṭān Aḥmad, proved even e devoted to Aḥrār than his father had been. here are a number of episodes, apart from the quest of Samarḳand in 855/1451, that may be tioned as particularly illustrative of Aḥrār's tical influence; his organisation of the defence of narḳand against an army from Khurāsān in /1454; his success in 865/1460 in persuading Abū īd to abolish the *tamgha* in Bukhārā and Samar- d, and to promise the abolition of it and all er non-*sharʿī* imposts throughout his realm; his liation between Abū Saʿīd and a rebellious prince, hammad Djūkī, at Shāhrukhiyya in the years /1461 and 867/1463; and his arbitration of three flicting claims for the possession of Tashkent in /1485.

Aḥrār expounded the reasons for his political ac- ity in a number of explicit utterances, which ke it clear that he sought ascendancy over rulers order to secure justice and the implementation the *Sharīʿa*. He is thus reported as saying: "there st stand between the people and their ruling ds one capable of checking violence and oppres- n. The people are helpless, and have no recourse inst the great. Hence it is necessary to convince gs not to transgress against God's law or to tor- nt the people" (Mīr ʿAbd al-Awwal Nishāpūrī, *smūʿāt*, ms. Institut Vostokovedeniya, Uzbek ademy of Sciences, Tashkent 3735, f. 131b). s sense of political mission is also apparent from following utterance: "if we acted only as *shaykh* this age, no other *shaykh* would find a *murīd*. t another task has been assigned to us, to protect Muslims from the evil of oppressors, and for the e of this we must traffic with kings and conquer ir souls, thus achieving the purpose of the Mus- s" (Fakhr al-Dīn ʿAlī Ṣafī, *Rashaḥāt ʿayn al- yāt*, Tashkent 1329/1911, 315).

In fulfilling this role, Aḥrār was aided by the adual accumulation of a vast amount of wealth, ich permitted him to bestow patronage and arity as well as to exercise political influence. He may, indeed, have been the largest landowner in Transoxania of his time. Documents survive indi- cating that he owned 30 orchards, 64 villages with their surrounding lands and irrigation canals, and scores of commercial establishments and artisan workshops in different cities (O. D. Čekhovič, *Samarkandskie dokumenti XV-XVI vv.*, Moscow 1974). Some of this property, worked partly by slaves of Indian origin, was used for the upkeep of Naḳshbandī *khānaḳāh*s, but it is evident that in many cases the purchase of land by Khwādja Aḥrār was purely nominal; the property remained in the effective ownership of the sellers, who benefited from the security and prestige bestowed by the name of Aḥrār.

In addition to thus establishing, in his own person, Naḳshbandī supremacy in Transoxania, Aḥrār ex- tended the influence of the order to other regions. One of his principal followers, Muḥammad Ḳāḍī, trav- elled to the Mughal rulers of Farghāna and obtained their adhesion to the Naḳshbandī order, thus laying the foundation for several centuries of both spirit- ual and temporal rule by Naḳshbandī *khwādjas* in Eastern Turkestan (see Muḥammad Ḥaydar Dughlāt, *Taʾrīkh-i Rashīdī*, ms. British Museum or. 157, f. 67b). Others undertook to travel to the presence of Aḥrār in Samarḳand; by way of example we can mention Mawlānā ʿAlī Kurdī of Ḳazwīn and Shaykh ʿAyān Kāzarūnī, who introduced the Naḳshbandiyya to western and southern Iran before it was swept away by the Ṣafavids (Muḥammad b. Husayn b. ʿAbd Allāh Ḳazwīnī, *Silsil-nāma-yi Khwādjagān-i Naḳshband*, ms. Istanbul, Laleli 1381, f. 13a. Ff. 10a-14a of this work contain a complete list of the *murīd*s of Aḥrār). Possibly most significant was the transmission of the Naḳshbandī order to Turkey by another *murīd* of Aḥrār, Mollā ʿAbd Allāh Ilāhī, since whose time the Naḳshbandī order has main- tained an uninterrupted presence among the Turks (see Kasim Kufralı, *Molla İlahi ve kendisinden sonraki Nakşbendiye mühiti*, in *Türk Dili ve Edebiyatı Dergisi*, iii [October 1948], 129-51).

Aḥrār died in Rabīʿ al-Awwal 895/February 1490, and a decade later Tīmūrid rule in Transoxania came to an end. Muḥammad Shaybānī, the Uzbek con- queror of Transoxania, showed himself hostile to the sons of Aḥrār, confiscating much of the property they had inherited from their father, and putting to death Khwādja Muḥammad Yaḥyā, his second and favourite son. However, Muḥammad Shaybānī's nephew, ʿUbayd Allāh Khān, restored the major part of their lands and took pride in the coincidence of his name with that of the great Aḥrār. In general, the posthumous repute and influence of the *khwādja* were great, and the various branches of the Naḳsh- bandī order that descended from him played a major role in the history of Central Asia down to the Russian conquest.

Bibliography: Materials on the life of Aḥrār are unusually copious. A complete bibliography is given in Hamid Algar, *The origins of the Naqsh- bandi order*, ii (forthcoming), which contains a full discussion of the career of Aḥrār. Here the following primary sources—all of them in Persian—will be mentioned: Mīr ʿAbd al-Awwal Nishāpūrī, *Masmūʿāt*, ms. Institut Vostokovedeniya, Uzbek Academy of Sciences, Tashkent 3735; Fakhr al-Dīn ʿAlī Ṣafī, *Rashaḥāt ʿayn al-hayāt*, Tashkent 1329/1911 (numerous other editions also exist, as well as Arabic and Turkish translations); Mu- ḥammad Ḳāḍī, *Silsilat al-ʿārifīn wa-tadhkirat al-ṣiddīḳīn*, ms. Istanbul, Haci Mahmut Efendi

2830; and Mawlānā <u>Sh</u>ay<u>kh</u>, *Manāḳib-i <u>Kh</u>ʷād̲j̲a Aḥrār*, ms. Institut Vostokovedeniya, Uzbek Academy of Sciences, Ta<u>sh</u>kent 9730. There is mention of Aḥrār in most of the Tīmūrid chronicles, and a long encomium of him in ʿAbd al-Raḥmān D̲j̲āmī's *Nafaḥāt al-uns* (pp. 406-13 of the edition published in Tehran in 1336/1957 by Mahdī Tawḥīdīpūr). Most later manuals of Naḳ<u>sh</u>bandī biography also contain accounts of Aḥrār, generally based on the *Ra<u>sh</u>aḥāt*; see, for example, Muḥammad Amīn al-Kurdī, *al-Mawāhib al-sarmadiyya fī manāḳib al-Naḳ<u>sh</u>bandiyya*, Cairo 1329/1911, 155-72. Averse to formal learning, Aḥrār did not leave many writings; there survive from him, however, a commentary on a quatrain of obscure meaning attributed to Abū Saʿīd b. Abī 'l-<u>Kh</u>ayr, *Sharḥ-i hawrāʾiyya* (published by V. A. Zhukovskii as an appendix to his edition of Muḥammad b. al-Munawwar's *Asrār al-tawḥīd*, St. Petersburg 1899, 489-93), and two treatises, entitled *Risāla-yi wālidiyya* and *Faḳarāt* (numerous mss. of both are to be found in European, Turkish and Soviet collections; the former has been translated into both Ottoman and Čaghatāy Turkish). Some of his correspondence has also been preserved in Soviet collections, partly in autograph; see, for example, ms. Institut Vostokovedeniya, Tajik Academy of Sciences, Dushanbe 548. The branches of the Naḳ<u>sh</u>bandiyya descending from <u>Kh</u>ʷād̲j̲a Aḥrār are enumerated in Kamāl al-Dīn al-Ḥarīrī, *Tibyān wasāʾil al-ḥaḳāʾiḳ*, ms. Istanbul, Ibrahim Efendi ff. 34a-41b. Scholarly writing on Aḥrār has been done up to the present almost entirely in Russian: mention may be made of the pages devoted to Aḥrār in V. V. Bartold's *Ulug Beg i ego vremya*, reprinted in *Sočineniya*, Moscow 1964, ii (2), 121-4, 205-17, Eng. tr. V. and T. Minorsky, in *Four studies on the history of Central Asia*, ii, Leiden 1958, 117-18, 166-77, and a number of more recent studies concentrating on the socio-economic aspects of Aḥrār's activity: R. N. Nabiev, *Iz istorii politiko-ekonomičeskoi zhizni Maverannakhra XV v.* (*zametki o <u>Kh</u>odzha-Akhrare*), in *Velikii Uzbekskii Poet—Sbornik Statei*, Ta<u>sh</u>kent 1948, 25-49; Z. A. Kutbaev, *K istorii vakufnykh vladenii <u>Kh</u>odzha Akhrara i ego potomkov*, doctoral thesis, Ta<u>sh</u>kent University 1970; and O. D. Čekovič, *Samarkandskie Dokumenty XV-XVI vv.*, Moscow 1974.

(HAMID ALGAR)

AHRUN (AHRŪN) B. Aʿyan AL-Ḳass, "the priest", presbyter and physician, who lived in Alexandria probably in the 7th century and belonged, with Paulus of Aigina, to the last great medical scholars produced by the Alexandrian School. A satirical verse of al-Ḥakam b. ʿAbdal [*q.v.*], in which a tax official of ʿAbd al-Malik b. Bi<u>sh</u>r b. Marwān, governor of Baṣra, is advised to have the offensive smell of his breath and nose cured by Ahrun before presenting himself to the *amīr* (D̲j̲āḥiẓ, *Ḥayawān*, i, Cairo 1949-50, 247, 14 = 249, 8 = 250, 2; Ibn Ḳutayba, *ʿUyūn*, Cairo 1930, iv, 62; *Aghānī*, Cairo 1928, ii, 424), possibly offers a *terminus post quem* for the period in which Ahrun lived. ʿAbd al-Malik b. Bi<u>sh</u>r was governor under Yazīd II in 102/720-1 (Ṭabarī, ii, 1433, 1436).

Ahrun (probably = Ἄρρων) allegedly composed a medical compendium (Πανδεκτης, Σύνταγμα?) consisting of 30 books, which was translated into Syriac by a certain Gōsiōs (*The Chronography of Gregory Abu 'l-Faraj ... Bar Hebraeus*, tr. Budge, Oxford 1932, 57; see also M. Meyerhof in *Isl.*, vi

(1916), 220 f.). Māsard̲j̲uwayh is said to have t lated the work afterwards into Arabic unde title *al-Kunnā<u>sh</u>* and to have added two more b The information on this procedure is, how defective and inconsistent (see *Fihrist*, 297; D̲j̲uld̲j̲ul, *Ṭabaḳāt*, ed. F. Sayyid, 61; Ḳifṭī, *Ḥuk* ed. Lippert, 80; Ibn Abī Uṣaybiʿa, *ʿUyūn al-anb* 109; Ṣāʿid, *Ṭabaḳāt*, ed. Cheikho, 88; Barhebr *Duwal*, ed. Ṣālḥānī, 157). The data are the uncertain because it is not known when M d̲j̲uwayh was living. According to Ibn D̲j̲u he is said to have translated Ahrun's work unde caliphs Marwān (64-5/684-5) or ʿUmar b. ʿAb ʿAzīz b. Marwān (99-101/717-20); accordin others he belongs to the 2nd/8th or 3rd/9th tury.

In any case, the *Kunnā<u>sh</u>* must have been h appreciated (*Kunnā<u>sh</u> fāḍil afḍal al-kanānī<u>sh</u> ḳadīma*, Ḳifṭī, *Ḥukamāʾ*, 324), although it very badly arranged and difficult to consult for specialists, according to the judgement of Sahl Bi<u>sh</u>r b. Yaʿḳūb al-Sid̲j̲zī (4th/10th cent For example, the twenty kinds of headaches (ṣ are said to have been brought together in one p while their causes, symptoms and treatments discussed separately in various places. The sub matter could thus only be mastered by len readings (see Dietrich, *Medicinalia arabica*, tingen 1966, Arabic text, 6 ff.). Al-Mad̲j̲ūsī (*K al-Malakī*, i, Būlāḳ 1294, 4 f.) remarks that the v is bad and without value, especially for those had not read Ḥunayn b. Isḥāḳ's translation—w thus also did exist.

The *Kunnā<u>sh</u>* has not been preserved in comp manuscript, but it has survived in many quotati especially in al-Rāzī's *Ḥāwī*. They have b brought together by Ullmann, *Die Medizin Islam*, 88 f., and by Sezgin, *GAS*, iii, 167 f. T can certainly be enlarged through systematic resea see e.g. Maimonides, *Sharḥ asmāʾ al-ʿuḳḳār*, Meyerhof, Cairo 1940, no. 247; Ibn al-<u>Kh</u>a *Kitāb ʿamal man ṭabb li-man ḥabb*, ed. Maria Vazquez de Benito, Salamanca 1972, 89, 132, 140. A judgment on the work will only be permi after all the quotations attainable have been c piled systematically with the greatest poss completeness. Rāzī more than once quotes abstract from the *Kunnā<u>sh</u>* under the title *Fāʾiḳ*. It could not be verified whether the *Adwiya al-ḳātila*, mentioned by S. Munad̲j̲d̲j̲id *RIMA*, v (1959), 278, is indeed a work of Ahrun, Munad̲j̲d̲j̲id considers the attribution as doubt

Bibliography: given in the article. further, Ullmann and Sezgin, and for the o literature, L. Leclerc, *Histoire de la méde arabe*, i, 1876, 77-81. (A. DIETRICH)

ʿĀʾISHA ḲANDĪSHA, a female spirit, div sely referred to as a *d̲j̲inniyya* (a female *d̲j̲i* [*q.v.*]), an *ʿafrīta* [see IFRĪT] or a *ghūla* [see GHŪL], the peoples of northern Morocco. Westerma classifies her as one of the "individual spirits" wh characteristics are more explicitly elaborated th those of the run-of-the-mill *d̲j̲inn*. Although ther some difference of belief in her attributes, ʿĀʾi<u>s</u> Ḳandī<u>sh</u>a is said generally to appear as either wondrous beauty or an old, wrinkled hag wit elongated nipples, pendulous breasts, and lc finger nails. In both manifestations she has a hoc foot of a camel, a goat, or an ass. She it thought to jealous, arbitrary, whimsical, and quick-tempere ever-ready to strangle or strike those who ha offended her. Her victims, at least in the area arou ās, must undergo the rituals of the Ḥamādis͟ha n Suppl.], her special devotees, to be rid of the toms of her attack: paralysis, sudden deafness, ness, or mutism. In her beautiful manifestation an insatiable temptress. Once a man has suc-ed to her—he is said to be married to her—he is r absolute power and must follow her every nand. His only redress is to plunge a steel knife he earth before giving into her.

ʾis͟ha Ḳandīs͟ha is said to be married to a far laborated *d̲j̲innī*, Ḥammu Ḳiyu, and to live in earth or under a river. Along the Moroccan al she is thought to live in the sea. The Ḥa-s͟ha claim that her favourite home is a grotto r a giant fig tree, near the sanctuary of Sīdī . Ḥamdus͟h, one of the saints whom they vener-on the D̲j̲ebel Zarhūn. This grotto is visited by ha Ḳandīs͟ha's followers, especially by women are anxious for children or for relief from trual cramps and other gynaecological com-ts. Such women smear henna on their ailing and make a promise (*ʿār* [*q.v.* in Suppl.]) to fice a chicken or goat if they are relieved of complaint. During the *musem*, or annual image [see MAWSIM], to Sīdī ʿAlī's sanctuary, grotto is the scene of wild, trancelike dances in h some of ʿĀʾis͟ha Ḳandīs͟ha's female followers el in the mud in imitation of pigs. ʿĀʾis͟ha dīs͟ha is said to like henna and to fear iron and . Her favourite colours are red and black. She a preference for black benzoin and certain Ḥamā-a melodies.

ʾis͟ha Ḳandīs͟ha is often indigenously confused similar female spirits. She is, of course, iden-ble with other female spirits in North Africa and Middle East. Westermarck has related her ship to that of Astarte. The Ḥamādis͟ha claim she was brought north from the Sudan by one neir saints, Sīdī Aḥmad Dg͟hug͟hī.

Bibliography: E. A. Westermarck, *Ritual d belief in Morocco*, London 1926; V. Crapan-no, *The Ḥamadsha: a study in Moroccan eth-psychiatry*, Berkeley 1973; idem, *Mohammed d Dawia*, in V. Crapanzano and V. Garrison ds.), *Case studies in spirit possession*, New York 977. (V. CRAPANZANO)

ḲĀ K̲H̲ĀN KIRMĀNĪ, MIRZA ʿABD AL-ḤUSAYN, known as Bardsīrī (*ca.* 1270-1314/1853-96), a dernist thinker of 19th century Iran. He be-ged to a well-to-do family of Kirmān. He studied sian and Arabic literature, Islamic history, *fiḳh*, *l*, *ḥadīt̲h̲*, mathematics, logic, natural philosophy, mediaeval medicine under several teachers such Mullā D̲j̲aʿfar, Ḥād̲j̲d̲j̲ī Āḳā Ṣādiḳ, and Sayyid wād Karbalāʾī. He also learned some English, nch, Turkish and Old and Middle Persian. In 8/1880 he assumed a position in the Kirmān venue Office. After approximately three years, vever, he suddenly abandoned his job and secretly Kirmān for Iṣfahān because he was not willing o-operate with the Nāṣir al-Dawla, the oppressive ernor at that time of Kirmān. Thereafter he began work for the governor of Iṣfahān, Ẓill al-Sulṭān, at the same time he continued to study French der the Jesuits. Because of the trouble that the ṣir al-Dawla created for him, he, together with his se friend, S̲h̲ayk̲h̲ Aḥmad Rūḥī, went to Tehran 1303/1885, but he could not stay there for the ne reason. He and Rūḥī therefore, after spending few months in Mas̲h̲had, proceeded to Istanbul vards the end of 1303/1886. Soon afterwards, they th went to Cyprus and each married a daughter of the then Bābī leader, Mīrzā Yaḥyā Nūrī, known as Ṣubḥ-i Azal.

While in Istanbul, Āḳā K̲h̲ān was living in poor circumstances; his mother and his brother had de-prived him of the wealth to which he was due by inheritance. He had therefore to live on a modest income earned through teaching, as well through contributing to the Persian newspapers, such as the *Ak̲h̲tar* of Istanbul and Malkam K̲h̲ān's *Ḳānūn* published in London. He was one of the outspoken opponents of the 1890 Persian Tobacco Concession and other concessions granted by the S̲h̲āh, and his sharp criticism of Nāṣir al-Dīn made the latter so angry that "... while kicking the ground and chewing his lips, the S̲h̲āh said: 'Anyone who establishes correspondence with Āḳā K̲h̲ān, I will demolish his house over his head' " (Yaḥyā Dawlatābādī, *Taʾrīk̲h̲-i muʿāṣir yā ḥayāt-i Yaḥyā*, i, Tehran 1957, 125).

In addition to his press campaign, Āḳā K̲h̲ān joined the Pan-Islamic group headed by another bitter critic of the S̲h̲āh, Sayyid D̲j̲amāl al-Dīn Asadābādī "Af-g̲h̲ānī", and he also corresponded with the Persian *ʿulamāʾ* of ʿIrāḳ. Because of these anti-S̲h̲āh activi-ties, the Iranian government urged the Turkish autho-rities to extradite Āḳā K̲h̲ān and his close associates to Iran. This development coincided with the 1893-4 Armenian unrest in Turkey, and Āḳā K̲h̲ān was ac-cused of cooperation with the rebels. An arrangement was therefore made that Turkey should exchange Āḳā K̲h̲ān and his friends for the rebellious Arme-nians who had fled to Iran. In the meantime (1314/1896), Nāṣir al-Dīn S̲h̲āh was assassinated by a dis-ciple of Afg̲h̲ānī, Mīrzā Riḍā Kirmānī; this incident expedited the process of Āḳā K̲h̲ān's extradition. Finally, in Ṣafar 1314/July 1896 Āḳā K̲h̲ān, together with two friends, Rūḥī and Ḥasan K̲h̲ān K̲h̲abīr al-Mulk, were beheaded in Tabrīz while Muḥammad ʿAlī Mīrzā, the later S̲h̲āh, was watching the scene.

Āḳā K̲h̲ān has been recognised as a distinguished forerunner of modernist thinking in Iran, of greater intellectual calibre than other contemporaries such as Malkam K̲h̲ān, Āk̲h̲ūnd-Zāda, and Mustas̲h̲ār al-Dawla Tabrīzī; for one thing, his linguistic ability provided him with a broader access to European sources on social, political, and philosophical thought. Despite his Pan-Islamic activity, he was anti-religious and quite hostile to many traditional practices.

As a modern school of thought, Bābīsm attracted Āḳā K̲h̲ān and for a while he became one of its ad-herents. Later, however, he turned against Bābīsm, and considered all religious sects to be useless (Firī-dūn Ādamiyyat, *Andīs̲h̲ahā-yi Mīrzā Āḳā K̲h̲ān Kir-mānī*, Tehran 1967, 66). In his thinking, he was in-fluenced by European thinkers such as Voltaire, Spencer, Rousseau, Montesquieu, and Guizot.

Āḳā K̲h̲ān's works, many of them unpublished and incomplete, include detailed accounts of materialism, anarchism, nihilism, nationalism, and the philosophy of religion. He had modernist interpretations of his-tory and suggested a new methodology for Persian historiography; in regard to the arts, and particularly literature, he believed that they should be responsible to and representative of society. In his treatment of society, he proclaimed that "Wealth consists essen-tially of (1) material objects such as metals and mines, and (2) the labourers' wages. The true criterion for wealth is physical as well as intellectual labour alone ... not silver and gold, which are the means of ex-change alone" (*ibid.*, 237-8).

Bibliography: Āḳā K̲h̲ān Kirmānī, *Has̲h̲t bihis̲h̲t*, Tehran 1960; idem, *Haftād u du millat*, Berlin 1924; idem, *Nāma-yi ʿibrat*, in *Rastāk̲h̲īz*, i

(1924), 406-12; idem, *Āʾīna-yi sikandarī* (*Tārīkh-i Īrān*), Tehran 1906; Abdul-Hadi Hairi, *European and Asian influences on the Persian Revolution of 1906*, in *Asian Affairs*, N.S. vi (June 1975), 155-64; idem, *The idea of constitutionalism in Persian literature prior to the 1906 Revolution*, in *Akten des VII. Kongresses für Arabistik und Islamwissenschaft, Göttingen, 15. bis 22. August 1974*, Göttingen 1976, 189-207; Firīdūn Ādamiyyat, *Īdeuluzhī-yi nahḍat-i mashrūṭiyyat*, i, Tehran 1976; idem, *Fikr-i dimukrāsīyi idjtimāʿī dar nahḍat-i mashrūṭiyyat-i Īrān*, Tehran 1975; idem, *Sih maktūb-i Mīrzā Fatḥ ʿAlī, sih maktūb va ṣad khaṭāba-yi Mīrzā Āḳā Khān*, in *Yaghmā*, xix (1966), 362-7, 425-8; idem, *Andīshahā-yi Mīrzā Fatḥ ʿAlī Ākhūnd-Zāda*, Tehran 1970; M. Muʿīn, *Farhang-i fārsī*, v, Tehran 1966, under "Āḳā Khān"; Muḥammad Taḳī Malik al-Shuʿarāʾ Bahār, *Sabk-shināsī*, iii, Tehran 1958; Aḥmad Kasrawī, *Taʾrīkh-i mashrūṭa-yi Iran*, Tehran 1965; Mahdī Malik-Zāda, *Taʾrīkh-i inḳilāb-i mashrūṭiyyat-i Īrān*, i, Tehran 1949; Nāẓim al-Islām Kirmānī, *Tāʾrīkh-i Bīdāri-yi Īrāniyān*, i/1-3, and *Muḳaddima*, Tehran 1967; Nikki R. Keddie, *The origins of the religious-radical alliance in Iran*, in *Past & Present: A Journal of Historical Studies*, xxxiv (1966), 70-80; idem, *Religion and irreligion in early Iranian nationalism*, in *Comparative Studies in Society and History*, iv/4 (1962), 265-95; idem, *Religion and rebellion in Iran: the Tobacco Protest of 1891-1892*, London 1966; E. G. Browne, *Press and poetry of modern Persia*, Cambridge 1914; idem, *The Persian Revolution of 1905-1909*, Cambridge 1910; idem, *Materials for the study of the Bābī religion*, Cambridge 1918; Naṣr Allāh Fatḥī, *Taʾrīkh-i shānzhmān-i Īrān, kitābī ki muntasab bi Mīrzā Āḳā Khān Kirmānī ast . . .*, in *Nigīn*, ii/9 (1967), 33-7; Ismāʿīl Rāʾīn, *Andjumanhā-yi sirrī dar inḳilāb-i mashrūṭiyyat-i Īrān*, Tehran 1966; Khānbābā Mushār, *Muʾallifīn-i kutub-i čāpī-yi fārsī va Arabī*, iii, Tehran 1962, nos. 754-6; Hamid Algar, *Mīrzā Malkum Khān: a biographical study of Iranian modernism*, Berkeley 1973; Bāstānī Pārīzī, *Talāsh-i maʿāsh*, Tehran 1968; Khān Malik Sāsānī, *Siyāsatgarān-i dawra-yi Ḳādjār*, i, Tehran 1959; ʿAlī Amīn al-Dawla, *Khāṭirāt-i siyāsī*, Tehran 1962; Muhammad Ḳazwīnī, *Wafayāt-i muʿāṣirīn*, in *Yādgār*, iii/10 (1947), 12-25; Saʿīd Nafīsī, *Duktur ʿAlī Akbar Khān Nafīsī Nāẓim al-Aṭibbā*, in *Yādgār*, 11/4 (1946), 52-60; J. Morier, *Sarguzasht-i Hādjdjī Bābā-yi Iṣfahānī*, tr. Mīrzā Ḥabīb Iṣfahānī, Calcutta 1924; Mangol Bayat Philipp, *The concepts of religion and government in the thought of Mīrzā Āqā Khān Kirmānī, a nineteenth-century Persian revolutionary*, in *IJMES*, v (1974), 381-400; Muḥammad Gulbun, *Mādjarā-yi ḳatl-i Mīrzā Āḳā Khān Kirmānī, Shaykh Aḥmad Rūḥī, va Mīrzā Ḥasan Khān Khābīr al-Mulk*, in *Yaghmā*, xxiv/4 (1971). See also Āzādī in Suppl.

(Abdul-Hadi Hairi)

ĀḲĀ NADJAFĪ, Ḥādjdjī Shaykh Muḥammad Taḳī Iṣfahānī (1845-1931), member of a very powerfully-established clerical family of Iṣfahān and himself an influential and wealthy religious authority in that city. Contrary to some of his clerical contemporaries, such as Mīrzā Ḥasan Shīrāzī and Muḥammad Kāẓim Khurāsānī [*q.v.*], Āḳā Nadjafī was not known as being devoted to the welfare and prosperity of the Muslims in general and the Iranians in particular. Rather, he has often been referred to as a grain hoarder, a venal, power-hungry religious leader, a usurper of other people's property, and an unjust judge. After his primary education under his father, who was also a powerful cleric, he we[nt to] Nadjaf and studied *fiḳh* and *uṣūl* under Shīrāz[ī and] others. After his father's death in 1883, Āḳā N[adjafī] was widely recognised as a religious leader in Iṣfa[hān;] he led the prayers in congregation in the Shāh mo[sque] and performed judicial duties at home. Despit[e a] governmental injunction, he went as far as to ex[ecute] the judgements which he himself passed on civi[l and] criminal cases. Many books on prayers, ethics, and other Islamic subjects have been ascribed t[o him] and were published at his own expense, but [it is] believed that they were not in reality writte[n by] himself (Mahdī Bāmdād, *Sharḥ-i ḥāl-i ridjāl-i* . iii, Tehran 1968, 327). Since he was a wealthy [land]owner, he naturally had much in common wit[h the] feudal governor of Iṣfahān, Ẓill al-Sulṭān; they [often] worked together, although at times this co-oper[ation] was replaced by hostility, conspiracy, and stru[ggle.] Āḳā Nadjafī has been held responsible for [two] major disorders in Iṣfahān and Yazd, in which [many] people were murdered, on the accusations of Bā[bism] and irreligiosity: once in 1890 and another tim[e in] 1902, both of which resulted in Āḳā Nadjafī's ba[nish]ment to Tehran. He, along with many other pe[ople,] protested against the Tobacco Concession of [1890] being given to a British company; he also favo[ured] the Persian Constitutional Revolution of 1906[. In] both cases Āḳā Nadjafī appears less as a genuine l[over] of freedom than as an opportunist who hoped t[o in]crease his prestige, wealth, and influence in the [wake] of those national movements. To preserve his p[ower] and wealth, Āḳā Nadjafī declared as unbelievers, [and] even at times had murdered, those who opposed [him] or who were critical of him (Mahdī Malik-Z[āda,] *Taʾrīkh-i inḳilāb-i mashrūṭiyyat-i Īrān*, i, Te[hran] 1949, 166). Moreover, by 1911, Āḳā Nadjafī and [his] sons had made a volte-face and wished "to place t[heir] extensive landed property under foreign protecti[on"] (Cd. 5656. *Persia*, No. 1 (1911), G. Barclay, t[o] Grey, Feb. 25, 1911, London 1911, CIII, p. 30).

Bibliography: Abdul-Hadi Hairi, *Shīʿism [and] constitutionalism in Iran: a study of the role pla[yed] by the Persian residents of Iraq in Iranian poli[tics]*, Leiden 1977; idem, *Why did the ʿUlamā partici[pate] in the Persian revolution of 1905-1909?*, in *WI*, (1976), 127-54; Ḥasan Djābirī Anṣārī, *Taʾrī[kh-i] Iṣfahān va Ray va hama-yi djahān*, Tehran 19[..]; Āghā Buzurg Ṭihrānī, *Ṭabaḳāt aʿlām al-Shīʿa*, Nadjaf 1954; Yaḥyā Dawlatābādī, *Taʾrīkh-i m[uʿā]ṣir yā ḥayāt-i Yaḥyā*, i, Tehran 1957; Aḥmad K[as]rawī, *Taʾrīkh-i mashrūṭa-yi Īrān*, Tehran 19[..;] idem, *Taʾrīkh-i hidjdahsāla-yi Ādharbāyd[jān]*, Tehran 1961; Nūr Allāh Dānishwar ʿAlawī, *[Taʾ]rīkh-i mashrūṭa-yi Īrān va djunbish-i waṭanp[arā]stān-i Iṣfahān va Bakhtiyārī*, Tehran 1956; Nā[ẓim] al-Islām Kirmānī, *Taʾrīkh-i bīdārī-yi Īrāniyān*, [in]trod., i-ii, Tehran 1967, 1970; Muḥammad Ḥa[san] Khān Iʿtimād al-Salṭana, *Rūznāma-yi khāṭi[rāt]*, Tehran 1971; ʿAbd al-Ṣamad Khalʿatbarī, *Sha[rḥ-i] mukhtaṣar-i zindigānī-yi sipahsālār-i Aʿẓam [Mu]ḥammad Walī Khān Tunukābunī*, Tehran 19[..;] Aḥmad Tafrishī Ḥusaynī, *Rūznāma-yi akhb[ār-i] mashrūṭiyyat va inḳilāb-i Īrān*, Tehran 1972; an[on]ymous, *Ruʾyā-yi ṣādiḳa*, n.d., n.p.; G. R. Ga[rth]waite, *The Bakhtiyārī Khāns, the government of I[ran] and the British, 1846-1915*, in *IJMES*, iii (19[..]), 24-44; ʿAbbās Mīrzā Mulkārā, *Sharḥ-i ḥāl*, Teh[ran] 1946; ʿAbd Allāh Mustawfī, *Sharḥ-i zindigānī-[yi] man*, i, Tehran n.d.; Muḥammad ʿAlī Sayy[āḥ,] *Khāṭirāt-i Ḥādjdjī Sayyāḥ yā dawra-yi khawf [va] waḥshat*, Tehran 1967; Mahdīḳulī Hidāyat, *Khāṭ[irāt] va khaṭarāt*, Tehran 1965; Masʿūd Mīrzā Ẓill ṭān, *Ta'rīkh-i sarguzasht-i Mas'ūdī*, Tehran ›7; Muḥammad Ḥirz al-Dīn, *Ma'ārif al-ridjāl*, Nadjaf 1964; 'Alī Wā'iẓ Khiyābānī, *Kitāb-i ›amā-'i mu'āṣirīn*, Tehran 1946; Muḥammad ›ī Mudarris, *Rayḥanat al-adab*, i, iii, 1967; ›usayn Sa'ādat Nūrī, *Ẓill al-Sulṭān*, Tehran 1968; ›mid Algar, *Religion and state in Iran 1785-1906: role of the Ulama in the Qajar period*, Berkeley ›69; E. G. Browne, *The Persian revolution of ›05-1909*, Cambridge 1910; Firuz Kazemzadeh, *›ssia and Britain in Persia*, 1864-1914, New ›aven 1968; Nikki R. Keddie, *Religion and ›ellion in Iran: the tobacco protest of 1891-1892*, ›ndon 1966; A. K. S. Lambton, *Persian political ›cieties 1906-11*, in *St. Antony's Papers*, No. 16, ›ndon 1963, 41-89. (ABDUL-HADI HAIRI)

›KAGÜNDÜZ, Turkish writer and novelist ›6-1958) whose original name was Ḥusayn 'Awnī. ›is writings he used the pen-name Enīs 'Awnī ›h he later changed to Akagündüz. The son of an ›y major, he was born in a village of Alasonia, Salonica, and was educated at the Kuleli ›tary high school and the War College (*Mektebi ›iyye*), which he left because of ill health, being to Paris for treatment where, for three years, ›attended the courses of the Academy of Fine › and the Faculty of Law. Back in Salonica, he ›nteered for the Action Army (*Ḥareket ordusu*) ›h was sent to quell the mutiny of 13 April 1909 *Mart waḳ'asi*) in Istanbul. He was active as a ›nalist until 1919, when, because of his enthu›tic support of the Nationalists in Anatolia, he arrested by the British and deported to Malta. ›d by the Nationalist government, he settled in ›ara where he combined the functions of a Member ›arliament with his career as a writer. He died in ›ara on 7 November 1958.

›kagündüz started his career in Salonica in close ›tionship with his friend 'Ömer Seyf el-Dīn, as ›et, short story writer and playwright. But he is ›narily known as a novelist. Apart from his collec› of verse *Bozghun* ("Débâcle", 1913) and his plays *›hterem ḳātil* ("Respectable assassin", 1914) and *›i yıldırım* ("Blue thunderbolt", 1934), he is the ›hor of several volumes of short stories and more ›n sixty novels, the most famous of which are *›men yıldızı*, ("The star of Dikmen", 1928); *Iki ›gü arasında* ("Between two bayonets", 1929); *›y ana* ("The step-mother", 1933) and *Yayla* › ("The girl of the plateau", 1940). Akagündüz's ›ophisticated novels and short stories, written in unpolished style with no claim to literary value, ›ch were immensely popular in the 20s and early , treat, with a certain element of realism, mainly sentimental or tragic themes among ordinary ›ple.

Bibliography: *Yeni yayınlar*, February 1960 ›complete list of works; Behçet Necatiğil, *Edebiya›mızda isimler sözlüğü*[8], Istanbul 1975.

(FAHİR İZ)

›AḲĀR (A.), a legal term denoting "immovable ›perty", such as houses, shops and land, as ›osed to *māl manḳūl* ("movable property"). As ›h, *'aḳār* is identical with "realty" or "real proper›". All property which is *'aḳār* is non-fungible *›mī*), but the two terms are not co-extensive, since ›mals, furniture, etc. are *ḳīmī*, although they do ›t constitute *'aḳār*.

The owner of *'aḳār* is deemed also to be the owner anything on it, over it or under it, to any height depth, so that ownership of land includes owner›p of minerals beneath it and buildings and plants on it. Like personalty, realty may be held in joint ownership in Islamic law, without the shares being allocated (*mushā'*). As regards ownership of the foreshore and new land formed by natural processes, this is vested in the state in modern Islamic countries.

Bibliography: Muṣṭafā Aḥmad al-Zarḳā', *al-Fiḳh al-islāmī fī thawbih al-djadīd*, Damascus 1968, and bibliography there cited; for examples of how items of *'aḳār* are described and defined in legal documents, see R. Y. Ebied and M. J. L. Young, *Some Arabic legal documents of the Ottoman period*, Leiden 1976.

(R. Y. EBIED and M. J. L. YOUNG)

AKBAR B. AWRANGZĪB, Mughal prince. His mother dying when he was an infant, he was very affectionately brought up by Awrangzīb [*q.v.*]. In 1090/1679 he was deputed to lead an army against the Rathors, and after initially taking a vigorous part in the operations, he was won over to their side by the rebels. His own reasons for his defection are given in a letter to Awrangzīb in 1092/1681, where he criticises his father's hostility to the Rādjputs. However, his attempt at a surprise attack on his father at Adjmēr failed, and he had to flee, first to Shambhadji, the Marāṭhā ruler (1680-9), and then to Persia; where he died in 1116/1704; until his death, Awrangzīb continued to feel some anxiety of a threat from Persia.

A large number of letters written on behalf of Akbar are preserved in the well-known collection of Awrangzīb's letters, the *Ādāb-i 'ālamgīrī* (see *Bibl.*).

Bibliography: Muḥammad Hāshim Khāfī Khān, *Muntakhab al-lubāb*, ii, Bibl. Ind., Calcutta 1860-74; *'Arḍ-dāsht* of Shāhzāda Muḥammad Akbar to the Emperor Awrangzīb, Royal Asiatic Society London, MS. No. 173; *Ādāb-i 'ālamgīrī*, numerous mss.; see V. J. A. Flynn, *Ādāb-i 'ālamgīrī, an English translation ...*, Australian National Univ., Canberra Ph. D. thesis 1974, unpublished. (M. ATHAR ALI)

AKHBĀR AL-ṢĪN WA 'L-HIND, the title by which are now designated two narratives concerning China and India which have, for various reasons, attracted the attention of Arabists.

Ms. 2281 of the B. N. contains amongst other things: I. fols. 2a-23b, an untitled and anonymous text which constitutes the basis of the work; and II. fols. 24a-56a, a sequel to the preceding, of which the author is named as Abū Zayd al-Sīrāfī.

In 1718, the Abbé Renaudot published in Paris, under the title *Anciennes relations des Indes et de la Chine, de deux voyageurs mahométans qui y allèrent dans le neuvième siècle, traduites d'arabe, avec des remarques sur les principaux endroits de ces relations*, a version of I and II, which was in its turn translated into English and Italian; since he had supplied no precise information regarding the origin of the text, Renaudot was accused of committing a hoax, but the original (the actual ms. 2281, to which was added, as no. 2282, the copy made by the translator himself) was subsequently found in the Bibliothèque Royale and printed through the good offices of Langlès; it was, however, M. Reinaud who put it into circulation 34 years later, accompanied by a new annotated translation and an introduction, under the title *Relations des voyages faits par les Arabes et les Persans dans l'Inde et Chine dans le IX*[e] *siècle de l'ère chrétienne* (Paris 1845, 2 vols.). In 1922 G. Ferrand produced a new translation, *Voyage du marchand arabe Sulaymân en Inde et en Chine, rédigé en 851, suivi de remarques par Abû*

Zayd Hasan (*vers 916*), as vol. vii of the *Classiques de l'Orient*. Finally, in 1948, J. Sauvaget published in Paris the text, a translation of and a lavish commentary on no. I, as Aḫbār aṣ-Ṣīn wa 'l-Hind, *Relation de la Chine et de l'Inde rédigée en 851*.

Independently of the reactions provoked by Renaudot's version (see Sauvaget, p. xvi), the anonymity of the first of these narratives has given rise to discussions and hypotheses. Quatremère (in *JA* (1839), 22-5), thought rather unwisely to attribute it to al-Masʿūdī [*q.v.*]; Reinaud, on the basis of the name of Sulaymān al-Tādjir which is quoted in the text (§ 12 of the Sauvaget edition), thought that this last was the author; G. Ferrand, adopting this point of view, entitled his work *Voyage du marchand arabe Sulaymān*, and V. Minorsky (*Ḥudūd al-ʿālam*, index) is seen to follow him deliberately in speaking only of "Sulaymān the Merchant". It is true that these authors can claim support from an important authority, since Ibn al-Faḳīh refers (*Buldān*, 11; tr. H. Massé, 14) to Sulaymān al-Tādjir in a context other than the narrative in which his name appeared. However, H. Yule (*Cathay and the way thither*, London 1866, pp. cii-ciii) and after him P. Pelliot (in *T'oung-Pao*, xxi (1922), 401-2, xxii (1923), 116) have drawn attention to the fact that this Sulaymān was apparently only an informant, among others who remained anonymous.

As for the general title, it may be deduced from a remark figuring at the beginning of the "sequel" written by Abū Zayd, who says that his own contribution is *al-kitāb al-thānī min akhbār al-Ṣīn wa 'l-Hind*; even if these words are more a general indication of the contents of the work, later authors have considered them as a title, notably al-Bīrūnī who, in his *Nubadh fī akhbār al-Ṣīn* (ed. Krenkow, in *MMIA*, xiii (1935), 388), claims to borrow a fact from the *Kitāb Akhbār al-Ṣīn*, and there is no reason not to adopt this solution.

The anonymous narrative is called *al-Kitāb al-awwal* by Abū Zayd, who gives the precise date of 237/851. On the other hand, that of the *kitāb al-thānī* is not so precisely known; but we possess some information on the author of this "sequel", thanks to al-Masʿūdī, who incidentally commits an error in calling him, probably inadvertently, Abū Zayd Muḥammad b. Yazīd al-Sīrāfī, although he himself says that his surname is al-Ḥasan. The author of the *Murūdj* declares (i, 321 = § 351) that he met Abū Zayd at Baṣra, where he was resident in 303/915-16, and that he received information from him; in reality, Abū Zayd must have supplied him with the text of the two narratives which were put to extensive use in the *Murūdj*, often distorted by al-Masʿūdī's zeal for elegance.

Texts I and II are quite dissimilar; both are clearly recollections of journeys in exotic lands, but if the first is characterised by the quality of the observations of the author or of the merchants who gave him the information and probably constitutes the most ancient account of China, the second, later by about 70 years, seems less reliable. While the first narrative, without pretension of any sort, is in general exact and spontaneous, that of Abū Zayd, which had itself been moreover commissioned, is more laboured, gives much space to sailors' stories and to marvels, and betrays the tendency, resisted however by al-Djāḥiẓ, to introduce fables into this form of *adab*.

Other authors than al-Masʿūdī have exploited, directly or indirectly, admitting it or not, the *Akhbār al-Ṣīn wa 'l-Hind* (see Sauvaget, pp. xxiii-xxix), and it is astonishing that only one ms. of i survived. It is, however, not impossible that ı of it were detached and passed into the oral dor which would explain why at a fairly early date texts ceased to be copied, although these texts originally intended for a literate public.

Bibliography: Pre-1948 references appea Sauvaget's work. See further, I. Kračkovs *Arabskaya geografičeskaya literatura*, Mos Leningrad 1957, 141-2; A. Miquel, *La géogra humaine du monde musulman*², Paris 1973, 11 and index.

(CH. PELLA

AKHBĀRIYYA, in Ithnā ʿAsharī Shīʿism, m those who rely primarily on the traditi *akhbār*, of the *Imāms* as a source of religious kı ledge, in contrast to the Uṣūliyya [*q.v.*], who adr larger share of speculative reason in the princi (*uṣūl*) of theology and religious law. Oppo traditionalist and rationalist currents were appa in the Ithnā ʿAsharī Shīʿa from its beginnings in 2nd/8th century. In the Buwayhid age, the t leading scholars, al-Mufīd (d. 413/1022), al-Murt (d. 436/1044) and the Shaykh al-Ṭūsī (d. 460/1c in confrontation with the traditionalist schoo Ḳumm, put the rationalist Uṣūlī doctrine on a basis by adopting Muʿtazilī theological princi and elaborating a distinctive Ithnā ʿAsharī metho ogy of jurisprudence (*uṣūl al-fiḳh*). Akhbāriyya Uṣūliyya are first mentioned as antagonistic fact by ʿAbd al-Djalīl al-Ḳazwīnī, an Ithnā ʿAs scholar of Rayy writing *ca.* 565/1170, who cha terises the former as narrowly traditionalist literalist, the latter as basing the fundamentals religion on reason and rational investigation.

Akhbārī opposition to the predominant U trend remained latent during the following centur until Mullā Muḥammad Amīn b. Muḥamn Sharīf al-Astarābādī (d. 1033/1624), encoura by his teacher Mīrzā Muḥammad b. ʿAlī al-Ast bādī (d. 1028/1619), articulated the Akhbārī posit in his *K. al-Fawāʾid al-madaniyya* and thus beca the founder of the later Akhbārī school. He propo to restore the early Akhbārī doctrine which remained undisputed until the time of al-Kula (d. 328/929) and vigorously criticised the innovati of the three famous scholars of the Buwayhid and, even more so, of the ʿAllāma al-Ḥillī (d. 7 1325), the Shahīd al-Awwal Muḥammad b. Ma al-ʿĀmilī (d. 786/1384) and the Shahīd al-Th Zayn al-Dīn al-ʿĀmilī (d. 966/1558) in the *u al-fiḳh* and theology. The basic theses which affirmed against the Uṣūlī position included doctrine that the *akhbār* of the *Imāms* take prec ence over the apparent meaning of the Ḳurʾān, *ḥadīth* of the Prophet and reason, since the *Imā* are their divinely appointed interpreters. apparent meaning of the *akhbār* which were accep as sound (*ṣaḥīḥ*) by the early Ithnā ʿAsharī cc munity provide "customary certainty" (*ya. ʿādī*), not merely probability (*ẓann*) as the Uṣ *mudjtahids* maintained. All *akhbār* contained in four canonical collections of the Ithnā ʿAshariy belong to the category of *ṣaḥīḥ*. The categoı besided *ṣaḥīḥ* and *ḍaʿīf*, weak, which the ʿAllā al-Ḥillī, in imitation of Sunnī practice, introduc with regard to the reliability of the transmitte are irrelevant. Also, consensus (*idjmāʿ*), which been handled too laxly by the *mudjtahids*, is va only if the inclusion of the *Imām* is absolutely cert and thus does not provide a source of the law separ from the *akhbār*. *Idjtihād*, leading to mere *ẓa* and *taḳlīd*, i.e. following the opinions of a *mudjtah* orbidden. Every believer must rather follow the ār of the *Imāms*, for whose proper understanding ore than a knowledge of Arabic and the specific inology of the *Imāms* is needed. If an apparent ict between two traditions cannot be resolved he methods prescribed by the *Imāms*, *tawakkuf*, ention from a decision, is obligatory.

ie Akhbārī school flourished during the following centuries. Muḥammad Amīn al-Astarābādī's hing was expressly endorsed by the elder al-jlisī, Muḥammad Taḳī (d. 1070/1660), and ›ted by Mullā Muḥsin Fayḍ al-Kāshānī (d. *ca.* ›/1680), both inclining to Ṣūfism and philosophy. influential champion of Akhbārī doctrine was urr al-ʿĀmilī [*q.v.*] (d. 1104/1693), author of a collection of *akhbār* of the *Imāms*, *Tafṣīl* ›'il al-shīʿa ilā aḥkām al-sharīʿa*, who strictly ered to, and refined, Akhbārī methodology, aining, however, from any polemics against the ›jtahids*. His contemporary ʿAbd ʿAlī b. Djumʿa Arūsī al-Ḥuwayzī, author of the Ḳurʾān com-tary *Nūr al-thiḳalayn*, also staunchly supported bārī views. Al-Astarābādī's verbal attacks the Uṣūlī *mudjtahids* were resumed by ʿAbd h b. Ḥādjdj Ṣāliḥ al-Samāhīdjī al-Baḥrānī 1135/1723), who in his *Munyat al-mumārisīn fī* *vibat suʾālāt al-shaykh Yāsīn* expounded some y points of conflict between the Akhbārīs and *mudjtahids*, and by the *Muḥaddith* ʿAbd ʿAlī b. nad al-Dirāzī al-Baḥrānī (d. 1177/1763-4) in his *ā' maʿālim al-shīʿa*. Among the more moderate porters of Akhbārī positions were ʿAbd Allāh al-Ḥādjdj Muḥammad al-Tūnī al-Bushrawī 1071/1666), author of *al-Wāfiya fī uṣūl al-fiḳh*, Sayyid Niʿmat Allāh al-Djazāʾirī al-Shushtarī 1112/1700), and Yūsuf b. Aḥmad al-Baḥrānī (d. 6/1773), brother of the previously mentioned d ʿAlī b. Aḥmad and author of the *Luʾluʾat al-rayn* and of the extensive and popular *fiḳh* work *Ḥadāʾiḳ al-nāḍira*. The latter originally upheld e Akhbārī doctrine, but later he espoused an ermediate position between the two factions and med al-Astarābādī for having opened the door of idering the *mudjtahids* and splitting the ranks of Shīʿa.

n the second half of the 12th/18th century, ūlī doctrine was forcefully restated by Muḥam-d Bāḳir al-Bihbihānī (d. 1208/1793-4) in his *al-tihād wa 'l-akhbār* and other works. He went so as to denounce the Akhbārīs as infidels and was le to break their dominant position in Karbalāʾ. e last prominent representative of the Akhbāriyya, *Muḥaddith* Muḥammad b. ʿAbd al-Nabī an-sābūrī al-Akhbārī, author of a *K. Munyat al-rtād fī nufāt al-idjtihād*, countered with polemical uperation and cursing of the *mudjtahids*. He gained favour of the Ḳādjār Shāh Fatḥ ʿAlī Shāh for ne time, but, having been denounced by the aykh Djaʿfar Kāshif al-Ghiṭāʾ [*q.v.*], was eventual-exiled to ʿIrāḳ and, in 1233/1818, was killed by a ›b in al-Kāẓimayn. Thereafter the Akhbāriyya pidly declined. The only Akhbārī community own to have survived to the present is in the gion of Khurramshahr and Ābādān.

Bibliography: ʿAbd al-Djalīl al-Ḳazwīnī al-Rāzī, *K. al-Naḳḍ*, ed. Djalāl al-Dīn Urmawī, maʿrūf bi-Muḥaddith, Tehran 1331/1952, 2, 256, 291, 301, 304, 492; Muḥammad Amīn al-Astarā-bādī, *al-Fawāʾid al-madaniyya*, Tehran 1321/1904; Muḥammad al-Dizfūlī, *Fārūḳ al-ḥaḳḳ*, printed together with Djaʿfar Kāshif al-Ghiṭāʾ, *al-Ḥaḳḳ al-mubīn*, Tehran 1319/1901; al-Khwānsārī, *Rawḍāt al-djannāt*, ed. A. Ismāʿīliyān, Ḳumm 1390-2/1970-2, i, 120-39; G. Scarcia, *Intorno alle controversie tra Aḫbārī e Uṣūlī presso gli Imāmiti di Persia*, in *RSO*, xxxiii (1958), 211-50; A. Falaturi, *Die Zwölfer-Schia aus der Sicht eines Schiiten: Probleme ihrer Untersuchung*, in *Festschrift Werner Caskel*, ed. E. Gräf, Leiden 1968, 80-95.

(W. MADELUNG)

ʿĀḲIL KHĀN RĀZĪ, MĪR MUḤAMMAD ʿASKARĪ, Mughal official and commander. He came from a family of the Sayyids of Khwāf [*q.v.*] in Khurāsān, but was born in India. He was in the service of Prince Awrangzīb from the very beginning. When Awrangzīb left the Deccan to contest the throne in 1068/1658, ʿĀḳil Khān was left in charge of the city of Dawlatābād. Subsequently, he was promoted to the rank of 1,500/1,000 and was made *fawdjdār* [*q.v.*] of the Dōāb. In 1092/1681 he was appointed as *ṣūbadār* of Dihli, and he held this post till his death in 1108/1696-7, having been promoted to the rank of 4,000/1,000.

A work called the *Wāḳiʿāt-i ʿālamgīrī or Ẓafar-nāma-yi ʿālamgīri* is ascribed to him. This contains a very interesting, but on occasions a highly-coloured, account of the war of succession and the opening years of Awrangzīb's reign. It does not always present a very flattering picture of Awrangzīb, and contains much information not found in the official history, the *ʿĀlamgīr-nāma*. ʿĀḳil Khān was devoted to literary pursuits and was interested in poetry, leaving behind a *Dīwān* and a number of *mathnawī* poems.

Bibliography: ʿĀḳil Khān Rāzī, *Wāḳiʿāt-i ʿālamgīrī*, ed. Ẓafar Ḥasan, Aligarh 1945 (see Storey, i, 584-5); Muḥammad Kāẓim, *ʿĀlamgīr-nāma*, Bibl. Ind., Calcutta 1865-73; Sāḳī Mustaʿid Khān, *Maʾāthir-i ʿālamgīrī*, Bibl. Ind., Calcutta 1871; Shāh Nawāz Khān, *Maʾāthir al-umarāʾ*, ii, Bibl. Ind., Calcutta 1888; M. Athar Ali, *The Mughal nobility under Aurangzeb*, Bombay 1966.

(M. ATHAR ALI)

AL-**ʿAKKĀD**, ʿABBĀS MAḤMŪD, one of the most influential figures in the development of Egyptian culture in the first half of the 20th century, littérateur, journalist, educator, polemicist and critic. Born in Aswān in 1889, he did not complete his secondary education but moved to Cairo at the age of fourteen. While taking a series of minor posts in the civil service, he began to make up for his lack of formal education by reading widely. He was particularly interested in literature, philosophy and the natural sciences, and among his greatest contributions was to pass on to a younger generation of Egyptians a synthesis of his views on these and other subjects. His writings on aesthetics and poetic theory show a strong influence of English writers such as Hazlitt, Coleridge, Macaulay, Mill and Darwin, and he was also acquainted with the ideas of Lessing, Schopenhauer and Nietzsche among the German philosophers. It was early in the 1910s that al-ʿAkkād met Ibrāhīm al-Māzinī, and the two men formed a firm friendship based both on a love of poetry (especially that of the English Romantics found in such works as Palgrave's *The Golden Treasury*) and on a distaste for the conventions of the neo-classical school of Egyptian poets personified by Aḥmad Shawḳī and Ḥāfiẓ Ibrāhīm. Al-ʿAkkād wrote the Introduction to al-Māzinī's first collection of poetry (1913) and published two collections of his own during this decade, *Yaḳẓat al-ṣabāḥ* (1916) and *Wahadj al-ẓahīra* (1917). The same views on poetry were also shared by a third writer, ʿAbd al-Raḥmān

S͟hukrī, the best poet of the group. These three are often referred to as the "Dīwān School", but that is somewhat of a misnomer in that al-ʿAḳḳād and al-Māzinī alone were the authors of *al-Dīwān*, a blistering piece of criticism in which al-Māzinī accused Ḥāfiẓ Ibrāhīm of madness and confusion while al-ʿAḳḳād attacked S͟hawḳī's occasional poetry in the most caustic of terms. The three men seemed to have shared a common view of the nature and rôle of poetry, but it was al-ʿAḳḳād who provided much of the critical impetus for which the group is primarily remembered.

At the conclusion of the First World War, al-ʿAḳḳād became closely associated with Saʿd Zag͟hlūl, the leader of the Wafd, and began to write articles for the party's newspaper, *al-Balāg͟h*. Many of these articles on literature, aesthetics, religion and history were later collected into book form under such titles as *Murād͟jaʿāt fi 'l-ādāb wa 'l-funūn* and *Muṭālaʿāt fi 'l-kutub wa 'l-ḥayāt*. During the regime of Ismāʿīl Ṣidḳī in the early 1930s when the constitution was revoked, al-ʿAḳḳād's fervent convictions led him to undertake the considerable risk of publishing a work criticising the ruling authorities, *al-Ḥukm al-muṭlaḳ fi 'l-ḳarn al-ʿis͟hrīn*, for which he was imprisoned for nine months. This decade also saw the appearance of three more volumes of his poetry (*Waḥy al-arbaʿīn*, *Hadiyyat al-karawān*, and *ʿĀbir sabīl*), the novel, *Sāra*, and a series of biographies on famous figures from the early history of Islam. These latter works seem to form part of a trend in the 1930s whereby Egyptian intellectuals (including Ṭāhā Ḥusayn and Muḥammad Ḥusayn Haykal) turned their attentions to religious biographical themes.

In 1938, al-ʿAḳḳād abandoned the Wafd Party and joined the breakaway Saʿdist group led by Aḥmad Māhir and al-Nuḳrās͟hī. However, the self-reliance and outspokenness which had served his purpose as a younger man seem to have turned progressively to scepticism, arrogance and extreme conservatism. He left the Saʿdist group and became essentially a one-man party. In the literary sphere, he not only vigorously opposed the new free verse poetry which began to emerge following the Second World War, but also changed his mind about the possibilities of blank verse in Arabic, something which he had encouraged S͟hukrī to experiment with in the earlier part of their careers. He joined a number of other conservative critics in opposing "committed" literature; in fact, as David Semah notes (*Four Egyptian literary critics*, Leiden 1974, 25) he seemed unwilling to accept any kind of criticism of his own views or to tolerate the idea that some of his earlier theories had been superseded.

Al-ʿAḳḳād's contributions to creative literature tend to be of interest more for historical reasons than for their intrinsic literary merit. He composed a large number of personal poems as well as some occasional ones, and translated a number of works from English (see Mustafa Badawi, *A critical introduction to modern Arabic poetry*, Cambridge 1975, 109 ff.). In his novel, *Sāra*, the psychological insights into the relationship of the two lovers may have been on a new level of sophistication when compared with previous works in this genre, but the element of doubt and questioning which pervades the work (six of the chapters have questions as their title) reduces it to an almost abstract analytical plane. Several commentators have also pointed out that the attitude to women found in this work is more than a little autobiographical (Aḥmad Haykal, *al-Adab al-ḳaṣaṣī wa 'l-masraḥī*, Cairo 1971, 164; Hilary Kilpatrick, *The modern Egyptian n*[...] London 1974, 32; ʿAbd al-Ḥayy Diyāb, *al-Mar*[...] *ḥayāt al-ʿAḳḳād*, Cairo 1969, 100 ff.).

The views of al-ʿAḳḳād on aesthetics and po[...] theory propounded so forcibly in many of his w[...] are also clearly visible in his writings on other po[...] both ancient and modern. While he wrote nume[...] articles on ancient poets during the 1920s (suc[...] on Imru 'l-Ḳays, Abū Nuwās, Bas͟hs͟hār b. B[...] and al-Mutanabbī), it is his study of Ibn al-R[...] published in book form in 1931, *Ibn al-Rūmī, ḥa*[...] *tuhu min s͟hiʿrihi*, which is widely regarded as [...] best literary study and especially as the one w[...] permits al-ʿAḳḳād to use his own theories on psyc[...] ogy, race and poetics in an analysis of this somew[...] neglected poet. Al-ʿAḳḳād's introduction of s[...] objective criteria, often based on non-liter[...] information, into the analysis of literature led [...] new insights into the Arabic poetic tradition [...] ancient times. However, it also tended to place m[...] emphasis on the writer than the work of literat[...] and it was left to the next generation (and especi[...] Muḥammad Mandūr) to restore importance to [...] work itself in literary analysis, while fusing into [...] critical process the best elements of the theo[...] which al-ʿAḳḳād had developed.

In 1960, he was awarded the State Appreciat[...] Prize for his contribution to Egyptian literat[...] S͟hawḳī Ḍayf's work, *Maʿa 'l-ʿAḳḳād* (Iḳraʾ Se[...] no. 259, Cairo 1964) shows a picture of the a[...] bachelor browsing in the natural science section[...] his library (opp. p. 65). He died in 1964.

Bibliography: (in addition to those wo[...] already cited in the text of the article): S͟ha[...] Ḍayf, *al-Adab al-ʿarabī al-muʿāṣir fī Miṣr*, Ca[...] 1961, 136; ʿAbd al-Ḥayy Diyāb, *ʿAbbās al-ʿAḳḳ*[...] *nāḳidan*, Cairo 1965; Mounah Khouri, *Poe*[...] *and the making of modern Egypt*, Leiden 19[...] passim; S. Moreh, *Modern Arabic poetry 1800-19*[...] Leiden 1976, passim; Nadav Safran, *Egypt*[...] *search of political identity*, Cambridge, Mass. 19[...] A. M. K. Zubaydī, *Al-ʿAḳḳād's critical theor*[...] *with special reference to his relationship with* [...] *Dīwān school and to the influence of Europe*[...] *writers upon him*, University of Edinburgh Ph. [...] thesis, 1966, unpublished; idem; *The Dīw*[...] *School*, in *JAL*, i (1970), 36; Salma Kha[...] Jayyusi, *Trends and movements in modern Ara*[...] *poetry*, Leiden 1977, i, 153-4, 163-75.

(R. Allen)

AKKĀR (A.), pl. *akara* (abstract *ikāra*), litera[...] "tiller, cultivator of the ground", a word of Aram[...] origin (see Fraenkel, *Die aramäischen Fremdwör*[...] *im Arabischen*, 128-9), borrowed into Arabic, a[...] parently in the post-Islamic period (it does n[...] appear in the Ḳurʾān), and applied to the pea[...] antry of Aramaean stock in Syria and ʿIrā[...] accordingly, the term had in Arabic eyes, like t[...] name *Nabaṭ*, a pejorative sense (see *LA*[1], v, 85-[...] Some of these peasants were sharecroppers w[...] cultivated lands of wealthy landlords for one-six[...] or one-seventh share of the produce and on *muḳāsa*[...] [*q.v.*] terms of contract (cf. Abū Yūsuf, *al-K͟harā*[...] Būlāḳ 1884, 52; Ibn Ḥawḳal, *Ṣūrat al-arḍ*, e[...] Kramers, 218). Following the Arab conquest of t[...] Fertile Crescent, the *akara* paid the lowest amount [...] poll-tax (*d͟jizya*) at the rate of 12 *dirhams* per he[...] per annum (Balādhurī, *Futūḥ*, 271).

Social and economic conditions deteriorated f[...] the *akara* during the ʿAbbāsid period. One finds the[...] as itinerant farm labourers moving from village [...] village in search of work and working on esta[...]

and for the highest bidder among landlords ..ī, *Wuzarāʾ*, ed. Amedroz, 259). They also worked ..ands owned by Christian monasteries (Shābushtī, ..*iyārāt*, 214-15). In a typical story we read of a ..ain *akkār* who was employed by a rich man of ..ra as a domestic servant, possibly out of farming ..on. His work included husking rice, grinding it .. mill turned by an ox, and making bread for his ..ter (Djāḥiẓ, *Bukhalāʾ*, Cairo 1963, 129). Djāḥiẓ evidently recorded in the story of the *akkār* and employer the tale of the toiling labourers and hard task-master of this epoch. Djāḥiẓ also men..s a certain *mashāyikh al-akara* (elder of the ..*a*), which may be indicative of some form of ..nised social grouping of the *akara* headed by a ..red Shaykh (cf. *Ḥayawān*, v, 32). The rural ..ulation of the Sawād of ʿIrāḳ, at least, seems to ..e continued to be Aramaic-speaking into the ..9th century and perhaps until later; cf. the ..cdote of al-Muʿtaṣim and the old *Nabaṭī* peasant ..the Sawād in Masʿūdī, *Murūdj*, vii, 113-4 = § ..6.

Bibliography: In addition to references given ..n the article, see also Tanukhi, *al-Faradj baʿd ..l-shidda*, Cairo 1903, i, 125-6; Thaʿālibī, *Thimār ..l-ḳulūb*, Cairo 1908, 195; al-Ṣābī, *The historical ..emains of Hilāl al-Ṣābī*, Leiden 1904, 91, 216, 254, ..l-Nawbakhtī, *Firāḳ al-Shīʿa*, Istanbul 1931, 61; ..ane, *Lexicon*, i, 70-1; M. A. J. Beg, *Agricultural ..nd irrigational labourers in the social and economic ..ife of ʿIraq during the Umayyad and ʿAbbasid ..aliphates*, in *IC* (January 1973), 15-22.

(M. A. J. Beg)

..L-**AḲSARĀYĪ**, Karīm al-Dīn Maḥmūd b. Mu..mmad, historian of Anatolia under the Sal..ḳs and Il-Khānids. The date of his birth is ..known, but it seems that he died at an advanced .. in the 720/1320s. As an official in the Il-Khānid ..vice, he was attached to the retinue of Mudjīr ..Dīn Amīr Shāh (the representative of the Mongol ..al department in Saldjūḳ Anatolia, and then ..*ib* from 1281 to 1291) until the latter's death .. 1302. Ghāzān Khān then appointed him *nāẓir* intendant of the *awḳāf* in the Saldjūḳ territories, ..d an uncertain date he acted as military comman..nt (*kutwāl* [see kōtwāl]) of Aḳsarāy, his natal ..vn. He enjoyed a privileged view of the events of .. time, and in 723/1323 put together in Persian .. chronicle the *Musāmarat al-akhbār wa-musāyarat ..akhyār* which is, together with Ibn Bībī's work, ..e of the essential sources for Anatolian history in ..e period of Mongol domination. This period forms ..e subject of the fourth and last chapter of the work, ..e most important one, since it takes up three..arters of the book and covers some 75 years ..ntemporary with al-Aḳsarāyī himself. The chronicle .. known only in two manuscripts (Ayasofya 3143, ..pied in 734/1334, and Yenicami 827, copied in ..5/1345, both now in the Süleymaniye Library in ..tanbul), and was hardly used by subsequent ..storians, with the exceptions of Ḳāḍī Aḥmad of ..gde (14th century) and the Ottoman compiler ..ünedjdjim Bashī (d. 1702), until it was rediscovered .. Turkish historians at the end of the 19th century. .. his preface to his critical and annotated edition .. the text, Osman Turan conveys all the information ..nown about the author, and gives an account of ..evious studies on the latter and his book.

Bibliography: *Müsâmeret ü-ahbâr. Mogollar zamanında Türkiye Selcukları tarihi*, Mukaddime ve haşiyelerle tashih ve neşreden Dr. Osman Turan, Ankara 1944; Fikret Işıltan, *Die Seltschuken Geschichte des Akserayî*, Leipzig 1943 (summary translation in German of the fourth chapter of the history).

(J.-L. Bacqué-Grammont)

AḲŪNĪṬUN (Greek ἀκονιτον) appears frequently in Arabic medical writings as a particularly deadly poison originating from a plant root; it can denote a substance either (A) from the Mediterranean region, or (B) from India. Synonyms for (A) include *khāniḳ al-nimr*, *khāniḳ al-dhiʾb*, *ḳātil al-nimr* and *bīsh*. This last, however, is the name generally accepted for (B). Aḳūnīṭun thus well exemplifies a constant problem of Arabic botanical literature: identification today of the actual plant referred to and of its Greek equivalent.

(A) Mediterranean region: ἀκονιτον as a poison in Greek writings: remedies are given by Nicander in his *Alexipharmaca* (95, lines 11-73). Theophrastos describes two types, (a) ἀκονιτον with a prawn-shaped root; (b) θηλυφονον or σκορπιον able to cure scorpion bite (*HP*, 9.16.4 and 9.18.2). Cf. Paulus of Aegina (Eng. tr. F. Adams, London 1844-8, III.28). Dioscorides similarly lists two types, in the reverse order, described in much the same terms: (i) = (b) above, with synonyms παρδαλιαγχης, καμμαρον, θηλυφονον, κυνοκτονον, μυοκτονον (IV.77); (ii) = (a) above, synonym λυκοκτονον (IV.78). When Dioscorides was translated into Arabic, the possibility of regional variation in species was not always considered; some Greek names were transliterated, but in time most were given standard equivalents in Arabic. In the Julia Anicia MS, 6th century, marginal notes in Arabic explain ἀκονιτον (i) as *aḳūnīṭun* and *khānik al-nimr*; (ii) as *khāniḳ al-dhiʾb* (f. 66b).

The Arabic version of these sections (Bodleian MS Hyde 34) gives as synonyms for (i) *nabbāl* and *khāniḳ al-nimr* (f. 123a, marginal note). *Nabbāl* occurs also in the *Tafsīr* to Dioscorides by Ibn Djuldjul (Madrid, Biblioteca Nacional MS 4981, f. 7a); in Ibn Djuldjul's *Supplement* to Dioscorides (MS Hyde 34, f. 198b) *nabbāl* is mentioned as a poisonous plant whose antidote is *bustān abrūz* (*Amaranthus tricolor* L.). Cf. F. J. Simonet, *Glosario de voces ibéricas y latinas usadas entre los mozárabes*, Madrid 1888, 395.

(B) India: *Bīsh*, although sometimes considered a synonym for *aḳūnīṭun*, refers to a far more poisonous plant (probably *Aconitum ferox* Wall) and is described as the most deadly of plant poisons by such writers as Thābit b. Ḳurra (*Dhakhīra*, ch. xxv, 143 (298)), Djābir b. Ḥayyān (*Gifte*, 56 = f. 46a-b, 104 = f. 95b, 185 = f. 179a), Ibn Waḥshiyya (*Poisons*, 84-5, 108), Ibn Sīnā (*Ḳānūn*, I, 276, III, 223), al-Bīrūnī (*Ṣaydana*, Arabic 81, Eng. 53). Most agree that there is little if any hope of recovery, even if the Great *Tiryāḳ* is administered. Ibn Sīnā distinguishes clearly between *bīsh* and the plant known as *khāniḳ al-dhiʾb* etc., the latter being described separately (I, 424, 460).

(C) Possible identifications: Although (A) *Aḳūnīṭun* is often equated with an *Aconitum* sp. (e.g. Ghalib I.86, Nos. 1752-7, Issa 5.1, cf. W. Schmucker, *Die pflanzliche und mineralische Materia Medica im Firdaus al-Ḥikma des Ṭabari*, Bonn 1969, 126, No. 157, where *bīsh* = ἀκονιτον), a modern botanist thinks it likely that the ἀκονιτον of Dioscorides was (i) a *Doronicum* sp., (ii) a *Delphinium* sp., possibly *D. staphisagria* or *D. elatum*. In the case of (B) *bīsh*, this did not have to be identified in the growing state, but was known to the Arabs as a deadly poison from India (Issa 4.19).

Bibliography: Dioscorides, *De materia medica*, ed. D. G. Kühn, Leipzig 1829; Dioscorides, *Codex*

Aniciae Iulianae picturis illustratus, nunc Vindobonensis Med. Gr. 1, Leiden 1906 (phototype edn.); *La Materia Médica de Dioscórides*, ii, ed. C. E. Dubler and E. Terés, Tetuan 1952; Bodleian MS Hyde 34; Theophrastus, *History of Plants*, ed. and tr. A. Hort, Loeb edn. London 1916; Nicander, *Alexipharmaca*, ed. A. S. F. Gow and A. F. Scholfield, Cambridge 1953; ʿAbd Allāh b. Aḥmad b. al-Bayṭār, *al-Djāmiʿ li-mufradāt al-adwiya wa 'l-aghdhiya*, Cairo 1874; Thābit b. Ḳurra, *K. al-Dhakhīra fī ʿilm al-ṭibb*, ed. G. Sobhy, Cairo 1928; Rabban al-Ṭabarī, *Firdaws al-ḥikma*, ed. M. Z. Siddiqi, Berlin 1928; *The abridged version of "The Book of Simple Drugs" of Ahmad ibn Muhammad al-Ghâfiqî...*, ed. M. Meyerhof and G. Sobhy, Cairo 1932-40; Maimonides, *Sharḥ asmāʾ al-ʿuḳḳār*, ed. M. Meyerhof, Cairo 1940; *Das Buch der Gifte des Ǧābir Ibn Ḥayyān*, tr. A. Siggel, Wiesbaden 1958 (with facsimile text); Ibn Sīnā, *al-Ḳānūn fi 'l-ṭibb*, 3 vols., repr. Baghdād n.d. [= 1970?]; Ibn Waḥshiyya (translation): M. Levey, *Medieval Arabic toxicology: the Book on Poisons of Ibn Waḥshīya and its relation to early Indian and Greek texts*, Philadelphia 1966; al-Bīrūnī, *K. al-Ṣaydana fi 'l-ṭibb*, ed. and tr. H. M. Said, Karachi 1973; M. Levey, *Early Arabic pharmacology*, Leiden 1973; M. Meyerhof, *The article on aconite from al-Beruni's kitab as-Saydana*, in *IC*, xix/4 (1945); P. Johnstone, *Aconite and its antidote in Arabic writings*, in *Journal for the History of Arabic Science*, i/1 (1977); A. Issa, *Dictionnaire des noms des plantes en latin, français, anglais et arabe*, Cairo 1930; A. Siggel, *Arabisch-Deutsches Wörterbuch der Stoffe aus den drei Naturreichen*, Berlin 1950; E. Ghalib, *Dictionnaire des sciences de la nature*, Beirut 1965. (P. Johnstone)

ĀL-I AḤMAD, Sayyid Djalāl, Iranian prose writer and ideologist (1923-69). His œuvre may be tentatively classified as comprising literary fiction on the one hand (*ḳiṣṣa, dāstān*), and essays and reports on the other hand (*maḳāla, guzārish*). This classification, however, only follows the author's own designation. Āl-i Aḥmad lacks the technical concern and sophistication of a contemporary like Ṣādiḳ Čūbak, and in terms of formal structure, this tends to blur the dividing lines, not merely between the "novel" (*ḳiṣṣa*) and the "short story" (*dāstān*), but also between the *dāstān*, often approaching the "narrative essay", and the *maḳāla*. Among biographical data, three factors stand out for their crucial influence on Āl-i Aḥmad's career as a writer: his birth in a Tehrani family of lower Shīʿī dignitaries; his occupation as a professional schoolteacher; and his vivid interest and, for a brief period, active participation in national politics.

The religious element is reflected in the early collections of short stories *Dīd wa bāzdīd* (1945), *Sih-tār* (1948) and *Zan-i ziyādī* (1952). Written after the "flight" from his traditional family background and adherence to the leftist ideologies of post-war political parties, they offer an ironic picture of the religious milieu of lower and middle class Tehran. A similar, if more outspoken aloofness pervades his *ḥadjdj*-diary of 1966, *Khassī dar mīḳāt*. While preserving a personal piety throughout his life, Āl-i Aḥmad is the critical observer, rather than the raptured participant. A tone of irony is seldom absent; yet it is generally mild and benevolent, occasionally even slightly nostalgic.

His life-long experiences as a schoolteacher prompted an interest in educational and, more broadly, cultural issues, as expressed in some of his
most vitriolic articles (notably in *Sih maḳāla-i d*
(1959)). Moreover, they inspired the "nov
Mudīr-i madrasa (1958) and *Nafrīn-i zamīn* (19
The former especially, which relates the aliena
of a provincial school-principal, is counted among
most successful literary achievements. If indel
to an earlier prose-experiment in French literat
i.e. *Voyage au bout de la nuit* by Louis-Ferdin
Céline (1932), *Mudīr-i madrasa* convincingly es
lished Āl-i Aḥmad's reputation as an innovato
Persian literary style. Its highly economic use
words, abundant colloquialisms and vivid, stacc
rhythm has been described in a laudatory fashion
inshāʾ-i kārīkātūrī by Djamālzāda (cf. bibliograp

Some similarity exists between the developmen
Āl-i Aḥmad's religious attitudes and his polit
ones. After an intensive exposure to the ortho
milieu in the early stages (as son of a Shīʿī *rūḥānī*
a devoted and prominent member of political parti
he proved in both instances incapable of conform
to collective, organised loyalty. His membershi
the recently established communist *Tūda* pa
lasted from 1944 until early 1948 only; his subsequ
adherence to the "anti-Stalinist" faction of Kh
Malikī ended in early 1953, following bitter exp
ences with personal rivalries within this "Third For
movement. He left the forum of organised polit
never to return. Among the literary documents
this political career, the short stories collected
Az randjī-kih mībarīm (1947) belong to the *T*
period. First printed at the party-press *Shuʿlau*
it constitutes an effort to create "socialist-reali
literature. With its very explicit commitment,
some ways reminiscent of Buzurg ʿAlawī's work
lacks the ironic, observing distance common
Āl-i Aḥmad's remaining œuvre, and was afterwa
considered a failure by the author himself. *Za*
ziyādī was written after the breakaway from
Tūda, and contains the story *Khudādād-khān*,
sarcastic description of the ambitions, hypocrisy a
luxuries of a leading party executive. The ideologi
importance of this collection further lies in the int
duction which the author added to the second edit
(1963), *Risāla-i Pawlūs bi-kātibān*. A "testame
according to the writer, it calls for literary hone
and commitment. In a less biblical fashion, t
theme dominates many of his other essays: t
conviction that "in our land, writing literature mea
waging a battle for justice", and that "the pen h
become a weapon". Since the ending of the Mossade
experiment in August 1953 and Āl-i Aḥmad's d
parture from party-politics, he saw this battle
justice as a cultural, rather than political one.
primary target is not the external force of oppressi
but the spirit of submissiveness which had turn
his countrymen into voluntary, even zealous se
vants. This phenomenon was diagnosed as *gha*
zadagī ("western-struckness" sc. blind worship a
imitation of western civilisation), and its causes a
symptoms are described at length in the essay of t
same name (1962), which, in spite of its prom
confiscation by the authorities, remained Ā
Aḥmad's most widely read and most hotly debat
work. In search of a cure, he calls for an "inn
revolt" (*ḳiyām-i durūnī*): a return to the classic
virtues of unconditional devotion and self-sacrifi
This *shahādat* forms the central theme of *Nūn*
'l-ḳalam (1961), an allegory tale explaining t
failure of contemporary leftist movements.

Finally, mention should be made of the region
monographs which the author composed during h
numerous travels throughout the country, trying

pture the "majesty" (ʿ*iẓmat*) and "authenticity" *at*) which he could no longer find in the capital. *īzān* (1954), *Tātnis̲h̲īn-hā-i Balūk-i Zahrā* (1958) *D̲j̲azīra-i K̲h̲ārg* (1960) have appeared as separate mes; comparable studies of K̲h̲ūzistān, Yazd and outskirts of the Kawīr have been included in his cted essays.

Bibliography: 1. Works by Āl-i Aḥmad, addition to those mentioned in the text: *rguzas̲h̲t-i kandū-hā* (1333 *sh.*) is a symbolic *ṣṣa* dealing with the abortive oil-nationalisation 51-3. Not included in the four collections menoned above are the short stories *D̲j̲as̲h̲n-i farzanda*, *K̲h̲ʷāhar wa ʿankabūt*, *K̲h̲ūnāba-i anār*, *awhar-i Amrīkāʾī* and *Guldastahā wa falak*. The rst one is available through M. A. Sipānlū's thology *Bāz-āfarīnī-yi wāḳiʿiyyat* (Tehran 1352 .[3]). The other ones have been collected in the sthumously-edited and only narrowly distributed *and̲j̲ dāstān* (1350 *sh.*), which also contains a ort autobiographical sketch dated Day 1347 *sh.*: *at̲h̲alan s̲h̲arḥ-i aḥwālāt*. The majority of Āl-i ḥmad's numerous essays and travel reports were rst published in periodicals and afterwards reinted in the collections *Haft maḳāla* (1334 *sh.*), *ih maḳāla-i dīgar* (1337 *sh.*), *Arzyābī-yi s̲h̲itābzāda* 344 *sh.*) and *Kārnāma-i sih-sāla* (1348 *sh.*). These ollections, however, are far from exhaustive, and substantial number of articles remains scattered ver the various magazins, for the later period otably *Andīs̲h̲a wa hunar*, *Āris̲h̲* and *D̲j̲ahān-i aw*. Certain other writings were completed by e author before his death, but have not yet been eemed suitable for publication. These include a ovel (*Nasl-i d̲j̲adīd*) and diaries of his travels to urope, the United States and the Soviet Union. f the latter, two fragments have appeared in *unar wa sīnimā*, Nos. 1 (18 *Ād̲h̲ar* 1345) and (25 *Ād̲h̲ar* 1345). Translations prepared by l-i Aḥmad were almost without exception done om or via French; well-known among these are is rendering of works by André Gide, Albert amus, Eugene Ionesco and Dostoievski. Transtions made from Āl-i Aḥmad's writings include *he old man was our eyes*, a monography on the oet Nīmā Yūs̲h̲īd̲j̲, in *The Literary Review*, utherford N.J., xviii (1974), 115-28, *The pilgrimge*, in *Life and letters*, lxiii (1949), 202-9, *Someone se's child*, in *Iranian Studies*, i (1968), 161-9, nd *The school principal*, by J. K. Newton and . C. Hillmann, Minneapolis and Chicago 1974; ne preface to this volume also contains an English ranslation of the story *Guldān-i čīnī*.

2. Studies. See the cursory remarks in H. amshad, *Modern Persian prose literature*, Cambridge 1966, 125-6; B. Alavi, *Geschichte und ntwicklung der modernen persischen Literatur*, erlin 1964, 221-2; Miloš Borecký, in *MEJ*, vii 953), 238-9; and M. Zavarzadeh, in *MW*, lviii 968), 311-12. Opinions of Iranian critics may be ound in the special Āl-i Aḥmad issue of the eriodical *Andīs̲h̲a wa hunar*, v (1343 *sh.*), 344-489, ncluding also a lengthy interview with the author. or more specific discussions, cf. D̲j̲amālzāda's eview of *Mudīr-i madrasa* in *Rahnamā-yi Kitāb*, i 1337 *sh.*), 166-78; Riḍā Barāhinī, *Ḳiṣṣa-niwīsī*, ehran 1348 *sh.*[2], 416 ff.; G. L. Tikku, in *idem* ed.), *Islam and its cultural divergence*, Urbana, hicago and London 1971, 165-79; and G. R. Sabri-abrizi, in *Correspondance d'Orient* 11, Brussels 970, 411-18.

(G. J. J. de Vries)

ʿALĀʾ al-DĪN K̲H̲ALD̲J̲Ī [see K̲h̲ald̲j̲īs].

al-ʿALAMĪ, ʿABD al-ḲĀDIR [see Ḳaddūr al-ʿAlamī].

ALANGU, Tahir, Turkish author and literary critic (1916-73). The son of a naval officer, he was born in Istanbul and graduated from the Department of Turkish Studies of Istanbul University (1943). He taught Turkish literature in various high schools until 1956, when he was appointed to Galatasaray Lycée in Istanbul where he taught until his death on 19 June 1973. During the last few years of his life he was also a part-time lecturer at Boğaziçi University in Istanbul.

Two leading themes of his many books and large number of articles are firstly, Turkish folk-lore, and secondly, the modern Turkish novel and short story. As a literary critic and research worker, his judgments are based on sound scholarly research and are (with rare exceptions when his close friends are involved) balanced, responsible and fair. Alangu is the author of the following major works: *Cumhuriyetten sonra hikâye ve roman*, 2 vols, Istanbul 1959 and 1965, a comprehensive study on Turkish short story writers and novelists of the 1920-50 period, with copious examples of their works; *Ömer Seyfettin*, Istanbul, 1968, a monograph in the form of biographical novel of this pioneer of the modern Turkish short story; and his posthumous *100 ünlü Türk eseri*, 2 vols, Istanbul 1974, an anthology from 100 famous works from Turkish literature, with introduction and comments. The second volume of this work covering the last hundred years (1870-1970) is particularly valuable as it is based mainly on his own research. Unfortunately, many of his articles published in various journals and reviews have not yet been collected into book form. Alangu translated (from the German) several authors, and particularly from the Israeli author Samuel Agnon.

Bibliography: Mehmet Seyda, *Edebiyat dostları*, Istanbul, 1970; Behçet Necatiğil, *Edebiyatımızda isimler sözlüğü*[8], 1975, s.v. (Fahir İz)

ʿALĪ b. ḤANẒALA b. ABĪ SĀLIM al-Maḥfūzī al-Wādiʿī al-Hamdānī, succeeded ʿAlī b. Muḥammad b. al-Walīd [*q.v.*] as the sixth *dāʿī muṭlaḳ* of the Mustaʿlī-Ṭayyibī Ismāʿīlīs in Yaman in 612/1215. As the country was passing through a critical period of internal strife after its occupation by the Ayyūbids, the *dāʿī* pursued a policy of non-interference in politics. He maintained good relations both with the Ayyūbid rulers of Ṣanʿāʾ and the Yāmid sulṭāns of Banū Ḥātim in D̲h̲amarmar which enabled him to carry out his activities without much difficulties. He died on 12 or 22 Rabīʿ I 626/8 or 18 February 1229.

Both his compositions, *Simṭ al-ḥaḳāʾiḳ* and *Risālat Diyāʾ al-ḥulūm wa-miṣbāḥ al-ʿulūm*, concerning *al-mabdaʾ wa 'l-maʿād*, are considered important works on *ḥaḳāʾiḳ* [*q.v.*]. The former, edited by ʿAbbās al-ʿAzzāwī (Damascus 1953), is a *rad̲j̲az* poem, whereas the latter is an elaborate treatment of the subject and exists in manuscript.

Bibliography: The main biographical source, Idrīs b. al-Ḥasan, *Nuzhat al-afkār*, still in manuscript, is studied by Ḥ. F. al-Ḥamdānī, *al-Ṣulayḥiyyūn*, Cairo 1955, 291-7; Ḥasan b. Nūḥ al-Bharūčī, *Kitāb al-Azhār*, i, ed. ʿĀdil al-ʿAwwā, in *Muntak̲h̲abāt Ismāʿīliyya*, Damascus 1958, 195, 247; Ismāʿīl b. ʿAbd al-Rasūl al-Mad̲j̲dūʿ, *Fihrist*, ed. ʿAlī Naḳī Munzawī, Tehran 1966, 196-7, 269-70. For a detailed account, see Ismail Poonawala, *Biobibliography of Ismāʿīlī literature*, Malibu, Cal. 1977. (I. Poonawala)

ʿALĪ B. MUḤAMMAD B. DJAʿFAR B. IBRĀHĪM
B. AL-WALĪD AL-ANF AL-ḲURASHĪ, the mentor of
ʿAlī b. Ḥātim al-Ḥāmidī [q.v.], whom he succeeded
as the fifth dāʿī muṭlaḳ of the Mustaʿlī-Ṭayyibī
Ismāʿīlīs in Yaman in 605/1209, came from a prominent al-Walīd family of Ḳurays̲h̲. His great-grandfather Ibrāhīm b. Abī Salama was a leading chieftain
of the founder of the Ṣulayḥid dynasty ʿAlī b.
Muḥammad al-Ṣulayḥī, and he was sent by the
latter on an official mission to Cairo. He studied
first under his uncle ʿAlī b. al-Ḥusayn and then
under Muḥammad b. Ṭāhir al-Ḥārithī. After al-
Ḥārithī's death, Ḥātim b. Ibrāhīm al-Ḥāmidī [q.v.]
appointed ʿAlī b. Muḥammad as his deputy in
Ṣanʿāʾ. He lived in Ṣanʿāʾ and died there on 27
Shaʿbān 612/21 December 1215 at the age of ninety.
He headed a distinguished family of dāʿīs: for
approximately three centuries the headship of the
daʿwa was held by his descendants.

He was a prolific author and his works are held
in high esteem by the community. The following
works are extant. On ḥaḳāʾiḳ: 1. Tād̲j̲ al-ʿaḳāʾid,
ed. ʿĀrif Tāmir, Beirut 1967, English tr. (in summary form) W. Ivanow, Creed of the Fatimids,
Bombay 1936. 2. Kitāb al-D̲h̲ak̲h̲īra, ed. Muḥammad
al-Aʿẓamī, Beirut 1971. 3. Risālat D̲j̲īlāʾ al-ʿuḳūl,
ed. ʿĀdil al-ʿAwwā in Muntak̲h̲abāt Ismāʿīliyya,
Damascus 1958, 89-153. 4. Risālat al-Īḍāḥ wa 'l-
tabyīn, ed. R. Strothmann, in Arbaʿa kutub Ismāʿīliyya, Göttingen 1943, 138-58. 5. Risāla fī maʿnā
al-ism al-aʿẓam, ed. Strothmann in ibid., 171-7.
6. Ḍiyāʾ al-albāb. 7. Lubb al-maʿārif. 8. Lubāb al-
fawāʾid. 9. Risālat mulḥiḳat al-ad̲h̲hān. 10. al-Risāla
al-mufīda, a commentary on the ḳaṣīdat al-nafs
ascribed to Ibn Sīnāʾ. Refutations: 11. Dāmig̲h̲
al-bāṭil, refutation of al-G̲h̲azālī's al-Mustaẓhirī.
12. Muk̲h̲taṣar al-ʿuṣūl, refutation of Sunnīs, Muʿtazilīs, Zaydīs and Falāsifa who deny God all attributes.
13. Risālat tuḥfat al-murtadd, ed. Strothmann in
Arbaʿa kutub Ismāʿīliyya, 159-70, a refutation of
the Ḥāfiẓī-Mad̲j̲īdī daʿwa. Miscellaneous: 14.
Mad̲j̲ālis al-nuṣḥ wa 'l-bayān. 15. Dīwān, eulogies
of the Imāms and his teachers, elegies, and valuable
historical information about contemporary events
in Yaman.

ḤUSAYN B. ʿALĪ, son of the preceeding, He
succeeded Aḥmad b. al-Mubārak b. al-Walīd as the
eighth dāʿī muṭlaḳ. He lived in Ṣanʿāʾ and died there
on 22 Ṣafar 667/31 October 1268. His writings deal
mainly with ḥaḳāʾiḳ. The following works have
survived. 1. Risālat al-Īḍāḥ wa 'l-bayān. The section
about the fall of Adam has been edited by B. Lewis
in An Ismāʿīlī interpretation of the fall of Adam, in
BSOS, ix (1938), 691-704. 2. al-Risāla al-waḥīda
fī tathbīt arkān al-ʿaḳīda. 3. ʿAḳīdat al-muwaḥḥidīn.
4. Risālat al-īḍāḥ wa-'l-tabṣīr fī faḍl yawm al-G̲h̲adīr.
5. Risāla Māḥiyyat al-zūr. 6. al-Mabdaʾ wa 'l-maʿād,
ed. and tr. H. Corbin, in Trilogie Ismaëlienne, Tehran
1961, 99-130 (Arabic pagination), 129-200.

ʿALĪ B. ḤUSAYN, son of the preceeding. He
succeeded his father as the ninth dāʿī muṭlaḳ. He
lived in Ṣanʿāʾ and then moved to ʿArūs, but following the Hamdānid repossession of Ṣanʿāʾ, he
returned and died there on 13 D̲h̲u 'l-Ḳaʿda 682/
2 February 1284. His al-Risāla al-kāmila is extant.

Bibliography: Ḥātim al-Ḥāmidī, Tuḥfat al-
ḳulūb, in manuscript, (edition being prepared by
Abbas Hamdani); Idrīs b. al-Ḥasan, Nuzhat al-
afkār, manuscript used by Ḥ. F. al-Ḥamdānī, al-
Ṣulayḥiyyūn, Cairo 1955, 284-91; Ḥasan b. Nūḥ
al-Bharūči, Kitāb al-Azhār, i. ed. ʿĀdil al-ʿAwwā
in Munta·abāt Ismāʿīliyya, Damascus 1958, 191,

193-4, 198, 247-8; Ismāʿīl b. ʿAbd al-Rasū
Mad̲j̲dūʿ, Fihrist, ed. ʿAlī Naḳī Munzawī, Te
1966, 41-2, 80, 93-5, 123-7, 131, 140, 151,
200-1, 229-37, 244-6, 257, 278. For a full descri
of works and sources, see Ismail Poonawala,
bibliography of Ismāʿīlī literature, Malibu, Cal.
(I. POONAWA)

ʿALĪ B. MUḤAMMAD AL-TŪNISĪ AL-IY
pro-S̲h̲īʿī poet of Ifrīḳiya, who was, acco
to Ibn Ras̲h̲īḳ (Ḳurāḍa, 102), in the service o
Fāṭimid caliphs al-Ḳāʾim, al-Manṣūr and abov
al-Muʿizz, whom he joined in his new capit
Egypt, despite his great age and the hazards o
journey. It was probably in Cairo that he die
the same year as his protector, 365/976, accordir
Ḥ. Ḥ. ʿAbd al-Wahhāb (Taʾrīk̲h̲, 96), but later
this, according to Ch. Bouyahia (Vie littéraire,
these two authors place his birth in Tunis, appar
in order to explain his ethnic of al-Tūnisī, whic
the 4th/10th century, and even later, referred m
to a small place adjacent to the ruins of Carthag
Ḳāḍī Nuʿmān, K. al-Mad̲j̲ālis wa 'l-musāyarāt
Yalaoui-Feki-Chabbouh, Tunis, 1978, 203, 332-3,
al-Bakrī, ed. de Slane, 37). This nisba has ca
him to be often confused with a later homo
ʿAlī b. Yūsuf al-Tūnisī, also the eulogist of a
Manṣūr and an al-Muʿizz, but this time, Zīrids
Bouyahia, loc. cit.). On the other hand, the e
al-Iyādī leads one to postulate an Arab origin,
Iyād being a component of a section of the Banū
the Ath̲bād̲j̲, who had established themselves in
region of Msila (see P. Massiéra, Msila du X
XVe siècles, in Bull. de la Soc. hist. et archéo.
Sétif, ii [1941], repr. in CT, No. 85-6).

The poet's fame reached the Spanish shores i
own lifetime; an anecdote of the same Ibn Ra
(ʿUmda, i, 111) shows us the Andalusian Ibn H
[q.v.] on his arrival in al-Ḳayrawān involve
hostilities with the poets already established t
but making specific mention only of al-Iyādī. H
ever, despite the high esteem in which later cr
held him, such as Ibn S̲h̲araf (Questions de cri
littéraire, ed. Ch. Pellat, Algiers 1953, 9), no p
of his has come down to us in complete form; is
attributable to later Sunnī ostracism of the
after the sudden change to the Zīrid régime,
change in literary tastes? Whatever the reason
be, out of the 105 verses which the present w
has been able to gather together (Ḥawliyyāt, 1
97), only two fragments are S̲h̲īʿī in inspiration. T
however are preserved by pro-Fāṭimid authors, t
being firstly a rather poignant and moving rela
of the end of Abū Yazīd, "the man on the donk
(Sīrat Ustād̲h̲ D̲h̲awd̲h̲ar, Cairo, 48, tr. M. Can
69) and secondly a eulogy in honour of al-Ma
(Dawādārī, Kanz al-durar, vi, 117). The remai
is made up of well-turned, descriptive fragme
which abound richly in images, hence admired
gathered together for this reason by the antholog
thus out of these last, al-Ḥuṣrī (Zahr, 189, 314, 1
reproduces a description of the Fāṭimid fleet, a
with the fearsome Greek Fire, a picture of a gallo
horse and a tableau of the splendours of the I
Palace, Dār al-Baḥr, at Manṣūriyya.

In sum, al-Iyadi seems to have been a great p
quite apart from his Fāṭimid allegiance, but
knowledge of his poetry—apart from his tale
remains till now only fragmentary.

Bibliography: Ibn Ras̲h̲īḳ, Ḳurāḍat al-d̲h̲a
ed. Bouyahia, Tunis 1972; Ḥ. Ḥ. ʿAbd al-Wah
Mud̲j̲mal taʾrīk̲h̲ al-adab al-tūnisī, Tunis 1968,
Ch. Bouyahia, La vie littéraire en Ifriqiya sou

rides, Tunis 1972; M. Yalaoui, *Poètes ifriqiyiens ntemporains des Fatimides*, in *Ḥawliyyāt al-ʾāmiʿa al-Tūnisiyya* (Annales de l'Université de nis), 1973. (M. YALAOUI)

LĪ EMĪRĪ (1858-1924), Turkish bibliophile scholar. He was born in Diyārbekr, the son Iehmed Sherīf, a wealthy merchant from a ly prominent family. He learnt Arabic, Persian the Islamic sciences from his great-uncle and ate tutors. At the age of 18 he published in the paper *Diyārbekr* a *djülūsiyye*, a poem com-orating the enthronement of Murād V which e his name widely known in educated circles. n ʿĀbidīn Pasha (the *Mathnāwī* commentator) e in 1879 to Diyārbekr as president of the com-ee of reform for the eastern provinces, he ap-ted ʿAlī Emīrī as secretary, and later took him alonika when he became the governor of that ince. Thus there began his career as a civil ant which was to last for three decades. He served iverse parts of the Empire until he retired in . He died in Istanbul on 20 January 1924.

life-long passionate collector of rare books, he d many important manuscripts from destruction the unique copy of Kāshgharī's *Diwān lughāt rk*), and made copies of the rare books which ould not purchase. He conveyed his invaluable ction to the Shaykh al-Islām Fayḍ Allāh Efendi ary at Fātiḥ in Istanbul (1916), then re-named Millet Library, of which he remained Director his death. ʿAlī Emīrī wrote *dīwān* poetry with t ease and facility (but with not much talent), his enormous output of several volumes is among personal papers in the Millet Library. Except he biographies of poets of his native Diyārbekr *lhkire-yi shuʿarāʾ-yi ʿĀmid*, Istanbul 1325 *rūmī*/), very little of his research work on the Otto-poets (with special emphasis on sultan and ce poets), has been published (and that mainly is journal *ʿOthmānlî taʾrīkh we edebiyyat medjmū-*, founded in 1920, 31 issues). ʿAlī Emīrī followed, ethod and approach, the tradition of the classical *kire* [*q.v.*] writers. The bulk of his manuscript s is in the Millet Library. His study on the East-provinces, *ʿOthmānlî wilāyat-i sharkiyyesi*, nbul 1334 *rūmī*/1918, was of great use and was reciated by the Nationalists in Ankara; Muṣṭafā nāl Pasha (Atatürk) personally gave financial to him in his old age. The list of ʿAlī Emīrī's er publications are given in Aḥmed Refīḳ and ülemin M.K. Inal (see Bibl. below).

Bibliography: Aḥmed Refīḳ, *A.E.* in *TTEM*, o. 78 (1924); Ibnülemin M.K. Inal, *Son asır türk irleri*, i, Istanbul 1930, 298-314; Muzaffer Esen, *stanbul ansiklopedisi*, ii, Istanbul 1959, s.v. (FAHİR İZ)

LĪ MARDĀN KHĀN, AMĪR AL-UMARĀʾ, a itary commander of Kurdish origin, was one he prominent nobles of Shāh ʿAbbās of Persia. ing the reign of Shāh Ṣafī (1038-52/1629-42) he ne under a cloud. He thereupon went over to the ghal Emperor Shāh Djahān (1037-68/1628-58) handed over the fort of Ḳandahār [*q.v.*] to the ghals. He was given the rank of 5,000/5,000 by new master in 1048/1638 and was appointed ernor of Kashmīr. In 1050/1640 he was promoted 7,000/7,000 and was appointed governor of the djāb. In 1641 he was appointed governor of bul in addition to the Pandjab.

Ali Mardān Khān was connected with the con-ıction of a major canal running from Ravi to iore, and laid out the famous Shalamār garden at Lahore. He died in 1067/1657 and was buried in his mother's tomb at Lahore.

Bibliography: ʿAbd al-Ḥamīd Lāhorī, *Bādshāh-nāma*, ii, Bibl. Ind., Calcutta 1868; continuation by Muḥammad Wārith, *Bādshāh-nāma*, I. O. MS., Ethé 329 (see Storey, i, 574-7); Shāh Nawāz Khān, *Maʾāthir al-umarāʾ*, ii, Bibl. Ind., Calcutta 1888-91; H. I. S. Kanwar, *ʿAli Mardan Khan*, in *IC*, xlvii (1973), 105-19. (M. ATHAR ALI)

ʿALLĀL AL-FĀSĪ, MUḤAMMAD, Moroccan statesman and writer (1907-74). Born at Fās, he was educated at the university of al-Ḳarawiyyīn [*q.v.*]. From the age of 18 onwards, he took part in the diffusion throughout Morocco of the progressive movement of the Salafiyya [*q.v.*], and his militant attitude in favour of local nationalist aspirations, as well as his oratorical powers, soon led the government to confine him to a house, under guard, at Tāza. He was freed in 1931 and returned to Fās, where he began to lecture at the Ḳarawiyyīn; these lectures were however boycotted by certain religious leaders who feared that his unrestrained political attitudes might well cause difficulties for the Moroccan authorities in their relations with the French Protectorate. Al-Fāsī then took part in the delegation of the most influential nationalist leaders to the sultan of Morocco in 1934, when the document called *Maṭālib al-shaʿb al-maghribī* ("Demands for reform of the Moroccan people"), the first catechism of the nationalist movement, consisting of a complete programme for the reform and renovation of the land, especially in the politico-social sphere, was presented to the sovereign. The tergiversations and delays of the speakers engaged in this exasperated the more ardent of patriots, and led the *Kutlat al-ʿamal al-waṭanī al-maghribiyya* ("Moroccan bloc for national action") which had until 1934 worked in the background, to intensify its activities. Disorders broke out in 1936 in Fās, Salé and Casablanca, and the leaders of the bloc, including ʿAllāl al-Fāsī, were arrested. After their freeing almost immediately, the bloc decided to disband itself, and two parties were then formed, *al-Ḥaraka al-ḳawmiyya* and *al-Ḥizb al-waṭanī li-taḥḳīḳ al-maṭālib*, which merged in 1943 to form the single party of the *Istiḳlāl*, led from 1946 onwards by al-Fāsī. In the following year he fled to Cairo, where he organised the resistance movements against the French and Spanish Protectorates from a centre in the *Maktab al-Maghrib al-ʿarabī* founded in the Egyptian capital. He returned to Morocco in 1956, the year when his country gained its independence, and was nominated Professor of Islamic Law at Rabat and Fās and then Minister of State entrusted with Islamic affairs and a Deputy.

ʿAllāl al-Fāsī's work as a publicist, as well as a politician, continued to be most intense. At the beginning of 1957 he founded the newspaper *Le Sahara marocain* in order to promote the inclusion of Mauretania in Morocco, and in 1962, the monthly review *al-Bayyina*, which was at the same time Pan-Arab and Pan-Islamic and also concerned with culture and social progress. In all his work, the writer dealt with topics and problems of the Maghrib's history and politics, above all in regard to the modern and contemporary periods, with the exception of his *Maḳāṣid al-sharīʿa al-islāmiyya wa-makārimuhā* (Casablanca, n.d.), in which the author gathered together his lectures on law at the Faculty. Two books are devoted to an historico-juridical analysis of the French and Spanish Protectorates over Morocco: *al-Ḥimāya fī Marrākush min al-widjha al-taʾrīkhiyya wa 'l-ḳānūniyya* and *Ḥimāyat Isbāniyā fī Marrākush min al-widjha al-taʾrīkhiyya wa 'l-ḳānūniyya* (publ. in Cairo 1947). His *al-Maghrib al-ʿarabī min al-ḥarb al-ʿālamiyya al-ūlā ilā 'l-yawm* (Cairo 1955), on the other hand, belongs to the usual class of historical compilations. His essay on *al-Ḥaraka al-istiḳlāliyya fi 'l-Maghrib al-ʿarabī* (Cairo 1948, 2nd ed. 1956) may be considered as an unpretentious contribution to our knowledge of Maghribī nationalism, especially in Morocco; there exist of these an English translation (New York 1954, repr. 1970) and a Spanish one. Other works comprise collections of lectures given in various capitals of the Arab world (as in *Ḥadīth al-Maghrib fi 'l-Mashriḳ*, Cairo 1956) and radio talks (as in *Nidāʾ al-Ḳāhira*, Rabat 1959)—these last revealing the passionate character of the writer's political beliefs. *Al-Naḳd al-dhātī* (Cairo 1952), of which there even exists a Chinese translation, is a self-criticism of the Arab world (particularly in regard to Morocco), in which the author analyses with a careful dialectic the recent past, and above all the present, in order to discern exactly the most effective way for Arabism to face up to the exigencies of modern life and to become part of European civilisation without at the same time renouncing its own particular genius and identity. In this, ʿAllāl al-Fāsī places himself in the forefront of the ideology of Islamic fundamentalism with its roots in Muḥammad ʿAbduh's *q.v.*] thought, but at times he goes beyond this basic model when it is a question of penetrating more clearly to the heart of western thought.

Bibliography: There is information on ʿAllāl al-Fāsī in all the numerous works (mainly in French) on Morocco. There is a good source of documentation on his political activity in *Oriente Moderno*, esp. xvii (1937), 595, xix (1939), 429-30, and xxxii (1952), 1-31 *passim*. See also Anouar Abdel-Malek, *Anthologie de la littérature arabe contemporaine*. ii. *Les essais*, Paris 1965, 190-6; and A. Laroui, *L'idéologie arabe contemporaine*, Paris 1967, passim. (U. Rizzitano)

ʿALLAWAYH AL-AʿSAR, Abu 'l-Ḥasan ʿAlī b. ʿAbd Allāh b. Sayf, court musician in early ʿAbbāsid times, died in or shortly after 235/850. He was of Soghdian origin, *mawlā* (*al-ʿitḳ*) of the Umayyads and *mawlā* (*al-khidma*) of the ʿAbbāsids. Ibrāhīm and Isḥāḳ al-Mawṣilī taught him the "classical" *ḥidjāzī* music, but he prefered the "romantic" style of Ibrāhīm b. al-Mahdī and introduced "Persian melodies" (*nagham fārisiyya*) into Arab music. As a court musician, he started in the third class (*ṭabaḳa*) under Hārūn al-Rashīd and continued to serve the caliphs up to al-Mutawakkil, but suffered from the rivalry of his more brilliant colleague Mukhāriḳ. ʿAllawayh is described as being a master musician (*mughannī ḥādhiḳ*), an excellent lutenist (*ḍārib mutaḳaddim*)—being left-handed he used an instrument stringed in reverse order—and a skilful composer (*ṣāniʿ mutafannin*). Abu 'l-Faradj al-Iṣbahānī recorded 80 of his songs, using sources like ʿAllawayh's own *Kitāb* (or *Djāmiʿ*) *al-Aghānī* and the songbooks of ʿAmr b. Bāna, Ibn al-Makkī, Ḥabash and al-Hishāmī.

Bibliography: *Aghānī*³, xi, 333-60 (main source, see also indices); Ibn Ṭayfūr, *Kitāb Baghdād*, Cairo 1949 (see indices); Ibn ʿAbd Rabbih, *ʿIḳd*, vi, Cairo 1949, 31, 33, 37; Djāḥiẓ, *Bayān*, i, 132; Ṣūlī, *Awrāḳ* (*Ashʿār awlād al-khulafāʾ*), 30; Nuwayrī, *Nihāya*, v, 9-13; O. Rescher, *Abriss der arabischen Literaturgeschichte*, ii, Stuttgart 1933, 81-3; H. G. Farmer, *History of Arabian music*, 123; Kh. Mardam, *Djam al-mughannīn*, Damascus 1964, 163-4. (E. Neubau

ALUS, Sermed Mukhtār, modern Tu Sermet Muhtar Alus, Turkish writer (1952). He was born in Istanbul, the son of A Mukhtār Pasha, the founder of the Military Mu and a teacher at the War College. Educated m privately at Galatasaray Lycée, he studied graduating in 1910. As a student, he founded two friends, the humorous paper *El-Üfürük* (and contributed essays and cartoons to an humorous paper *Davul* (1908-9). His early in in philosophy and social studies did not last and he turned to the theatre. Between 1918 1930, apart from a number of short stories v he contributed to various papers, he concent exclusively on the theatre, writing and ada from the French many plays, some of which performed in the Istanbul Municipal theatre *al-Bedāyiʿ*). Some of his plays were serialise satirical weeklies (*Akbaba* and *Amcabey*). The 1931 was a turning point in his literary career began to publish in the newspaper *Akşam* ske of everyday life in Istanbul at the turn of the tury, *Otuz sene evvel Istanbul* ("Istanbul thirty ago") which were followed by stories, essays, biographical sketches, novels, etc. serialised in same paper and in the dailies *Son posta*, *Cumhu Vatan*, *Vakit*, etc. and in the periodicals *Yed Hafta*, *Yeni mecmua*, etc., all describing life in sions, villas, *yalıs* (sea-side villas), famous res or in the humble homes of Istanbul during the decade of Ḥamīdian era.

An extremely prolific writer, he produced tinuously until his death in Istanbul on 18 May 1 Unfortunately the great bulk of his output (art essays, short stories, novels, memoirs) always companied by his own designs and sketches, rem scattered in many dailies and periodicals. Four o novels have been published in book form: *Kıv Paşa* (1933), *Pembe maşlahlı hanım* (1933), *zengininin gelini* (1934), *Eski Çapkın anlatıyor* (1 The plots in these novels, as in all Alus's writ are loose and unimportant, and are only a pre for describing and reporting the conversations o pet characters, who are Ḥamīdian pashas, beauties or toughs, snobs and simple people. is the last representative of the popular entert ment narrative school inaugurated by Aḥmed Mi and continued by Ḥusayn Raḥmī, Aḥmed Rāsim O. Dj. Ḳaygīlī [*q.vv.*]; perhaps he is more akin the latter in that he is more entertaining and plistic without high claims to any moral or p sophic conclusions. In spite of his often unpolis even sloppy, style and his weakness for the farc his work has a great documentary value for spoken language, way of life, customs and folk of the period.

Bibliography: Reşat Ekrem Koçu, in *İsta ansiklopedisi*, Istanbul, 1958-69, s.v. (the m source for all subsequent studies); Metin A *Meşrutiyet döneminde Türk tiyatrosu*, Ank 1971, 112. (Fahir İ

ʿAMʿAḲ, Shihāb al-Dīn Bukhārī, one of leading Persian poets at the court of the I Khāns (Ḳara-Khānids) [*q.v.*] of Transoxania. I sources ascribe to him the *kunya* Abu 'l-Na (e.g. Taḳī al-Dīn Kāshānī). It is not certain whe ʿAmʿaḳ is a personal name or a *laḳab* used as a p name. It cannot be connected with any exis Arabic, Persian or Turkish word. Dh. Ṣafā

ested a corruption of an original ʿaḳʿaḳ ("mag-
which occurs as the name of the poet in a
uscript of the *Dīwān* of Sūzanī. S. Nafīsī con-
red a possible Soghdian origin. The forms
iḳ and ʿAmīḳī, which can be found in some
uscripts of the *Bahāristān* of Djāmī, are certainly
e rejected.

mʿaḳ was born in Buk̲h̲ārā, probably before
middle of the 5th/11th century. If any of the
s given for his death by later biographers viz.
(e.g. Dawlats̲h̲āh and Riḍā-Ḳulī Khān Hidāyat),
(Taḳī al-Dīn Kās̲h̲ānī) or 551 (Ṣādiḳ b. Ṣāliḥ
ānī in *S̲h̲āhid-i Ṣādiḳ*) is correct, he would
lived to become a centenarian.

ie earliest datable poems that are attributed to
ʿaḳ are ḳaṣīdas written for the Ilek-K̲h̲ān Naṣr
brāhīm (460-72/1068-80). The poet must have
d at least till 524/1129-30, according to the
dote that he was ordered to write an elegy for
n Sand̲j̲ar's daughter Māh-i Mulk K̲h̲ātūn, whose
h occurred in that year (Dawlats̲h̲āh, on the
ority of ʿAmʿaḳ's contemporary Khātūnī), or
later if the prince Maḥmūd named in a frag-
tary poem is identical with the Ilek-K̲h̲ān who
put on the throne of Samarḳand by Sand̲j̲ar in
132.

ready during the short reign of K̲h̲iḍr b. Ibrāhīm
-3/1080-1), ʿAmʿaḳ appears to have reached a
inating position at the court of Samarḳand. The
about his rivalry with Ras̲h̲īdī, told in the
r maḳāla, pictures him as an *amīr al-s̲h̲uʿarāʾ*. In
ater years he is said to have lived a secluded
communicating with his patrons through a son
he name of Ḥamīdī or Ḥamīd al-Dīn. ʿAmʿaḳ
wrote a poem for the Sald̲j̲ūḳ ruler Alp Arslān.

though the greater part of ʿAmʿaḳ's poetry
is to have been lost, a small number of his ḳaṣīdas
been preserved in anthologies or in mad̲j̲mūʿa
uscripts. There are also some quatrains attributed
is name. A mat̲h̲nawī-poem on the theme of
if and Zulayk̲h̲ā, which is said to have been
en in such a way that it could be scanned ac-
ing to two different metres, has, however, left
ace.

spite of this early loss of the *dīwān*, estimated
,000 bayts (*Haft iḳlīm*), ʿAmʿaḳ appears to have
a remarkable influence on the poetry of his
emporaries as well as on that of the following
ration. No one less than Anwarī styled him
aster of poetry" (*ustād-i suk̲h̲an*), and designed
of his poems on a model provided by ʿAmʿaḳ
Dīwān-i Anwarī, i, Tehran 1347², 205, 274).
reputation was based, first of all, on the clever
ʿAmʿaḳ made of rhetorical artifices which were
a novelty in his time. A fragment of one of his
das, in which the words mūr ("ant") and mūy
ir") have been used in every line, is often quoted
n example of this. ʿAmʿaḳ was also renowned
writer of elegies, but nothing more than the
lines he wrote at the request of Sand̲j̲ar has been
erved.

iother notable feature of ʿAmʿaḳ's poetry is
ise of long and elaborate prologues to his odes.
most extreme example of this, a prologue of
bayts, contains the conceit of a spiritual journey
imaginary world on the back of the donkey of
combined with satirical hints to the poet's rivals
ān, ed. Nafīsī, 141 ff.). ʿAmʿaḳ had a distinct
for fantastic images; in one of his many des-
ions of nocturnal scenes, the night is represented
preacher who from his pulpit extols the virtues
ie poet's native town Buk̲h̲ārā (*op. cit.*, 176 ff.).

According to Dh. Ṣafā, the "fantastic simile"
(*tas̲h̲bīh-i k̲h̲iyālī*) is also a major characteristic of
the imagery ʿAmʿaḳ applied to the individual lines
of his poems.

Bibliography: The *Dīwān* of ʿAmʿaḳ published at Tabrīz, 1307 *sh.* (624 *bayt*s) is unreliable,
as it contains several poems that actually belong
to other poets. S. Nafīsī has assembled a collection
of 806 *bayt*s from various sources in *Dīwān-i
ʿAmʿaḳ-i Buk̲h̲ārī*, Tehran 1339/1960. This volume
lacks, however, precise references on the provenance
of each item. The ḳaṣīdas written for the Ilek-
K̲h̲āns have also been inserted into the taʿlīḳāt to
Nafīsī's edition of *Taʾrīk̲h̲-i Bayhaḳī*, Tehran 1332/
1953, iii, 1301-23.

The most important sources containing
fragments of his poetry are: ʿAwfī, *Lubāb*,
ed. Browne, 181-9, ed. Nafīsī, 378-84, cf. *taʿlīḳāt*,
686-94; Ras̲h̲īd-i Waṭwāṭ, *Ḥadāʾiḳ al-siḥr*, Tehran
1308/1929, 44-5; S̲h̲ams al-Dīn Muḥammad b.
Ḳays al-Rāzī, *al-Muʿd̲j̲am fī maʿāyīr as̲h̲ʿār al-
ʿad̲j̲am*, Tehran 1338/1959, 351, 381; Djād̲j̲armī,
Muʾnis al-aḥrār fī daḳāʾiḳ al-as̲h̲ʿār, ii, Tehran
1350/1971, 499; Dawlats̲h̲āh, 64-5; Djāmī, *Bahāristān*, Dushambe 1972, 107; Amīn Aḥmad Rāzī,
Haft iḳlīm, Tehran 1340/1961, iii, 409-20; Ḳāsimī,
Sullam al-samawāt, Tehran 1340/1961, 53, cf.
ḥawās̲h̲ī, 303-4; Luṭf-ʿAlī Beg Ād̲h̲ar, *Ātas̲h̲kada*,
lith. Bombay 1299 A.H., 337-42; Riḍā-Ḳulī Khān
Hidāyat, *Mad̲j̲maʿ al-fuṣaḥāʾ*, lith. Tehran 1295
A.H., i, 345-50, ed. Tehran 1336/1967, ii, 879-88.

For manuscripts of mad̲j̲mūʿa's containing
poems by ʿAmʿaḳ, see E. Blochet, *Catalogue des
manuscrits persans de la Bibliothèque Nationale*,
Paris 1912, ii, 48 ff.; Ch. Rieu, *Catalogue of Persian
manuscripts in the British Museum*, London 1881,
ii, 869, *Supplement*, 105; A. J. Arberry, in *JRAS*
(1939), 379; A. Munzawī, *Fihrist-i nusk̲h̲ahā-yi
k̲h̲aṭṭi-yi fārsī*, iii, Tehran 1350/1971, 2551, nos.
24876-9.

Bibliographical references to ʿAmʿaḳ are
to be found in Niẓāmī Arūḍī, *Čahār maḳāla*, Tehran
1955-7, *matn* 44, 73, 74, cf. *taʿlīḳāt* 138 ff., 232 f.
and 615, as well as in the tad̲h̲kira works mentioned
above. See further Browne, ii, 298, 303, 335 f.;
Dh. Ṣafā, ʿAmʿaḳ-i Buk̲h̲arāʾī, in *Mihr* iii (1314-15
A.S.H.), 177-81, 289-95, 405-11; idem, *Taʾrīk̲h̲-i
adabiyyāt dar Īrān*, ii, Tehran 1339/1960³, 535-47;
E. E. Bertel's, *Istoriya persidsko-tadžikskoy litera-
turī*, Moscow 1960, 461-6 and *passim*; S. Nafīsī,
muḳaddama to his edition of the *Dīwān*, 3-127
and 206 ff.; Yu. N. Marr and K. I. Čaykin, *Pis'ma
o persidskoy literature*, Tiflis 1976, 119-25.

(J. T. P. de Bruijn)

AMĀN ALLĀH, Amīr of Afg̲h̲ānistan and the
successor and third son of Ḥabīb Allāh [*q.v.*] by his
chief wife, ʿUlyā Ḥaḍrat (d. 1965). He was born on
2 June 1892 in Pag̲h̲mān and educated at the Military
Academy. Intelligent, energetic and hardworking,
he was attracted to the nationalist and Islamic
modernist ideas of Maḥmūd Ṭarzī (1866-1935), the
editor of *Sirād̲j̲ al-ak̲h̲bār*, and in 1914 married
Ṭarzī's daughter, Soraya (T̲h̲urayyā) (d. 21 April
1968). At the time of his father's murder on 20 February 1919, Amān Allāh, as Governor of Kābul, controlled the capital with its garrison, arsenal and
treasury. Supported by the army, the younger
nationalists and the Bārakzay faction, he resisted
the claims of his uncle, Naṣr Allāh, and his eldest
brother, ʿInāyat Allāh, and was recognised as *amīr*
on 28 February.

Amān Allāh promptly asserted Afg̲h̲ānistan's independence from British control of her foreign relations. Possibly hoping to promote his goal by the threat of war, he despatched forces to the Indian frontier, but hostilities commenced on 3 May and endured until an armistice at the beginning of June (the Third Afghan War). By the Treaty of Rāwalpindi (8 August 1919) Britain recognised, by implication, Afghānistān's independence, although the Durand Line remained the frontier. After further negotiations at Mussoorie (April-July 1920) and in Kābul, a treaty of good neighbourliness was signed by Britain and Afghānistān on 22 November 1921. In the meantime Amān Allāh had obtained international recognition through treaties with the USSR (28 February 1921) and Turkey (1 March 1921). Relations were also established with Italy, France and Iran. In the early years of his reign Amān Allāh espoused a Pan-Islamic policy involving support for Indian Muslims, friendship with Turkey and Iran and the creation of a Central Asian federation under Afghān leadership including Bukhārā and Khīwa, but the reassertion of Soviet control over Turkistān put an end to this project.

Amān Allāh's internal policy was one of rapid modernisation. His reforms came in two main bursts. In the period 1921-4 he reformed the structure of Afghān government, introducing the first budget (1922), constitution (1923), and administrative code (1923). He introduced legal reforms including a family code (1921) and a penal code (1924-5). The legal reforms were partly the work of ex-Ottoman advisors and influenced by Islamic modernism, being derived largely from the *Sharīʿa* but replacing *ʿulamāʾ* control by that of the state. Education was central to his reforms and he established new secondary schools and sent Afghān students abroad. His support of female education gave rise to bitter criticism from traditional groups. Amān Allāh made some effort to promote economic development by fostering communications (aircraft, radio and telegraph introduced, and railway surveys begun), reforming the currency (the rupee replaced by the *afghānī*), reorganising the customs, and helping light industry. The principal economic success of his reign, however, owed nothing to his efforts; this was the development of the *Karakūl* and carpet industries following Uzbek immigration into the northern provinces. There was also some agricultural development. Amān Allāh's reforms were financed largely from domestic resources and lack of money imposed constraints which were especially marked in his military reforms. With the aid of foreign instructors (mainly Turks) Amān Allāh sought to develop a non-tribal national militia based on conscription for short periods, and at the same time to reduce military spending. The result was strong tribal opposition to conscription, and a disaffected, discontented and inefficient army. Hostility to centralisation, conscription and certain social reforms lay behind the Khōst [*q.v.*] rebellion in 1924, which was suppressed only after a protracted struggle. For a time Amān Allāh was obliged to abate his reforming zeal.

In December 1927 Amān Allāh departed for a tour of Europe, returning to Kabul on 1 July 1928. His object, he explained, was to discover the secrets of progress; his conclusion was that these were the discarding of outworn ideas and customs. He summoned a national assembly (*Loe Djirga*) (28 August-5 September) and dressed the delegates in European clothes to hear his new ideas. At the last moment he was persuaded to omit his most far-reaching proposals, but his announced changes in the constitution, new social reforms, and increased t
were sufficiently disturbing to his hearers.
abashed, Amān Allāh repeated his proposals
further series of five three-hour speeches deliv
between 30 September and 4 October to an inv
audience, which was treated to the spectacl
Queen Soraya dramatically unveiling herself.

Enraged by the social reforms, by their diminu
of their own authority, and by new proposals
Amān Allāh to examine them in their profici
to teach and to expel those trained at Deoband
ʿulamāʾ, under the leadership of the Hazrat fa
of Shor Bazaar, denounced Amān Allāh as an inf
The Āmir arrested the leaders, but in Nover
found himself confronted by two tribal ris
supported by *ʿulamāʾ*, one in the vicinity of Dja
bād, involving the Shinwārīs and other tr
and the second in the Kūhistān, led by a Tā
bandit known as Bačča-yi Saķaw. His inadeq
forces divided, Amān Allāh was unable to resist
attack on Kābul from the Kūhistān, and his bel
withdrawal of nearly all his reforms did not pa
the rebels. On 14 January 1929 Amān Allāh abdic
in favour of ʿInāyat Allāh and fled to Ķanda
ʿInāyat Allāh also abdicated on 18 January and
Bačča became ruler of Kābul with the title of H
Allāh II. At Ķandahār Amān Allāh rescinded
abdication on 24 January and sought help
Britain (which remained neutral), from the U
(which briefly sent troops to northern Afghānis
and from Afghān tribes. Although Amān Allāh
ceived help from the Hazāras and some other tr
he failed to command the support of the Dur
and the majority of the Ghalzays, and was fo
to turn back his advance on Kābul at Ghazna.
23 May he left Afghānistān for India and on 22
sailed from Bombay to exile in Rome. He die
Switzerland on 26 April 1960 and was brought h
and buried at Djalālābād.

Bibliography: The older biographies of A
Allāh such as those by R. Wild, London 1932
Ikbal Ali Shah, London 1933 have little v
by comparison with modern studies based
the British archives. See Rhea Talley Stev
Fire in Afghanistan 1914-1929, New York 1
L. B. Poullada, *Reform and rebellion in Afgha
tan, 1919-1929*, Ithaca 1973; L. W. Ada
Afghanistan 1900-1923, Berkeley and Los Ang
1967, and idem, *Afghanistan's foreign affair
the mid-twentieth century*, Tucson 1974; V.
gorian, *The emergence of modern Afghanis*
Stanford 1969. All these latter works con
valuable further bibliographies. (M. E. YAP

AMĪD TŪLAKĪ SŪNĀMĪ, KHWADJA ʿA
AL-DĪN FAKHR AL-MULK, poet of Muslim In
He was born in Sūnām, an important town (no
the district of Patiala in the Indian part of
Pandjāb) that had emerged as a centre of cul
and learning in the 7th/13th century. ʿAmīd ca
himself Tūlakī along with Sūnāmī because his fa
was said to have migrated from Tūlak in Khur
to India. In the art of poetry, he was the dis
of a famous master, Shihāb Mahmrā. He starte
career as a poet in Multān, which had become
capital of a short-lived kingdom under Malik
al-Dīn Khān-i Ayāz and his son, Tādj al-Dīn
Bakr (who died in 638/1241). Two of his *kaṣ*
preserved in mediaeval anthologies are in prais
Sultan Tādj al-Dīn. On the death of patron
moved from Multān to Dihlī, and during the r
of Sultan Balban he was appointed *mustawfī* of
district of Multān and Uččh, placed under the ch

rince Muḥammad, who was later known as
ı-i Shahīd.
mīd's *dīwān* is not extant, but the poems
ained in mediaeval anthologies and other literary
s give us an idea of his greatness and excellence
e art of poetry, showing that he was one of the
nguished poets of the Dihlī Sultanate during
th/13th century, contributing to the growth of
-Persian literature. It emerges from his poems
he was interested in the philosophy of *Ishrāḳ*
uminative wisdom as propounded and advocated
haykh Shihāb al-Dīn Suhrawardī (d. 587/1191).
ke most of his contemporaries, ʿAmīd was basi-
a poet of the *ḳaṣīda*, and his known poems
ly comprise panegyrics on rulers, princes and
emen. Among his poems, there are also one
jīʿ-band, two *ghazal*s and one *hazl* (humorous
ı); their characteristic features are simplicity,
taneity, freshness of thought and beauty of
on. His *ḥabsiyyāt* (poems written in prison and
cting the prisoner's life [see ḤABSIYYA below])
light on the actual conditions in mediaeval
It should also be stressed that his *ghazals*,
those of Shaykh Djamal of Hānsī, paved the
for the *ghazal*'s subsequent popularity as an
pendent branch of poetry.

Bibliography: ʿAbd al-Ḳādir Badāʾūnī, *Mun-khab al-tawārīkh*, i, Bibl. Ind. edn., Calcutta 69; Aḥmad Kulātī Iṣfahānī, *Muʾnis al-aḥrār*, S. Ḥabīb Gandj Collection, Mawlānā Āzād brary, Aligarh; Taḳī Kashī, *Khūlāṣat al-ashʿār*, S. Khudā Bakhsh Library, Patna; Ḥusayn ndjū, *Farhang-i Djahāngīrī*, Newal Kishore edn.; bal Husain, *The early Persian poets of India*, atna 1937; Nāẓir Aḥmad, *ʿAmīd Tūlakī Sūnāmī*, *Fikr-o-Naẓr* (*Urdu Quarterly*), (October 1964), ligarh Muslim University, Aligarh.

(I. H. SIDDIQUI)

MĪN AL-ḤUSAYNĪ, *muftī* and Palestinian ler. He was born in Jerusalem in 1893, the son ʾāhir al-Ḥusaynī. The Ḥusaynīs were a leading ily in Jerusalem who claimed Sharīfī lineage ough this was disputed by others, as on two sions the line had passed through female members he family. They had often held the office of *tī* in the past, and three had been *muftī* in the od immediately before 1821: Muṣṭafā, Amīn's dfather; Ṭāhir, his father; and Kāmil, his elder her by another mother. The holding of this e enhanced the standing of the family, other nbers of which had held other high positions, uding that of Mayor of Jerusalem and of deputy he Ottoman parliament. Thus Amīn came from mily used to the prestige and authority of high e and also to rivalry on the part of the other ing families in Jerusalem. Moreover, the concept erusalem as the third holiest city in Islam and of erving it as such must have been at the very tre of their thoughts. The office of *muftī* gave the aynīs a special role in this act of preservation.

mīn al-Ḥusaynī had a varied education. He first nded a local Muslim school and then the Ottoman e school in Jerusalem. It seems that he also nded for a year the school of the Alliance Is-ite Universelle where he studied French. In 1912 went to Cairo and entered al-Azhar, but stayed than a year and left without graduating and hout the title of *ʿālim*. He immediately went to ke the *ḥadjdj*, from which he returned to Jerusa-. His religious education was incomplete and not qualify him for the office of *muftī*. Further cation was received in the Ottoman army in which he served during the First World War. He undertook his basic training in the School of Officials, the *Mülkiyye*, in Istanbul and at the Military Academy. His war years were spent chiefly in an office in Izmīr. By virtue of this training he was permitted to wear the *tarbūsh*, the symbol of an Ottoman official but not of a religious dignitary.

On the conclusion of the war, Amīn returned to Jerusalem which was to be the base of his activities for the next nineteen years. He worked as teacher, translator and civil servant, but he soon turned to journalism and direct political activity. He was an intensely political man, possessed of great energy and organising ability and from the first inspired by two deeply-held ideas, Arab nationalism and a hatred of the Zionist attempt to change the character of Palestine. For him, Palestine was an Islamic Arab country belonging to the wider Arab world and he believed that any alteration of its basic Arab character would isolate it and its inhabitants from their Arab neighbours. He was convinced that the Palestinians had the right to determine the future form of government of their country, a right possessed by neither the British government nor the Zionist organisation. He also believed that European Jews settling in Palestine would spread customs and usages alien to the more traditional Islamic way of life. If change was to come in Palestine, it should be organic and internal and not imposed from outside. He devoted the rest of his life to a vain attempt to stem this tide of change.

Opposition to Zionism amongst the Arabs of Syria and Palestine grew in intensity once Jerusalem and Damascus had fallen to the Allied forces. The opposition was led by a group of young Palestinians, foremost amongst whom were Amīn al-Ḥusaynī and ʿĀrif al-ʿĀrif. Verbal opposition in speeches and newspapers led to street demonstrations in September 1919. Editorials and sermons called for the shedding of Jewish blood if protests went unheeded. Amīn began to organise small groups of *fidāʾiyyūn* whose task was to strike against the Jews and the British. When in March 1920 the Syrian National Congress voted for Syrian independence, Palestine Arabs took to the streets in the belief that their country was included in the new state. ʿĀrif's newspaper *Sūriyya al-Djanūbiyya* published the headline: "Arabs arise! The end of the foreigners is near. Jews will be drowned in their own blood". Because of the Amīr Fayṣal's lack of strong leadership, the Palestinians tended to separate from his state and follow their own path. In April, the Arabs of Jerusalem in the prevailing tense atmosphere exploded from a demonstration into an assault on the Jewish population.

Amīn, who was leading the demonstration, was reported to have tried to restrain the rioters, but two days of trouble left five Jews dead and 211 wounded and four Arabs dead and 21 wounded. During the disturbances, Vladimir Jabotinsky's Jewish Self-Defence Group attempted to assassinate Amīn and ʿĀrif, whose *fidāʾiyyūn* tried to retaliate. British intelligence forestalled these attempts and the two had to flee to Transjordan after having been accused of provoking the riots. This was the first of a series of charges laid against Amīn during his lifetime. His precise role in the provocation can never be ascertained, but it is certain that he approved of all actions taken to discomfort the Jewish population and that he was not averse to the shedding of blood. The concepts of *djihād* and of the *fidāʾī* were in Islamic history associated with the possibility of death in the pursuit of a goal. All Muslims could be summoned to a *djihād* in defence of Islam against a perceived threat, while the *fidāʾī* was always prepared to die himself while assassinating an opponent.

The first British High Commissioner in Palestine, Herbert Samuel, pardoned Amīn in August 1920 and he returned to Jerusalem. Samuel had issued the pardon in order to try to calm Arab feeling and to attempt to enlist Arab support for his policies. In March 1921 the *muftī* of Jerusalem, Kāmil al-Ḥusaynī, died. The British authorities had assumed the mantle of the Ottoman government and consequently the responsibility for religious appointments. In an election, local *ʿulamāʾ* had to select three candidates for the office of *muftī*, one of whom would be approved by the government. The al-Ḥusaynī family campaigned for their nominee, *Ḥādjdj* Amīn, but he was not one of the three selected in April. It appeared however that he had some popular support in the country and the government was loathe to go against the wishes of the people. Samuel eventually decided that Amīn was his man and in May he was appointed Grand Mufti (*al-muftī al-akbar*), a title given by the British to enhance the status of the office.

Amīn's appointment as head of the Muslim community in Palestine did not settle the problem of the Muslim religious organisation of the country. In Ottoman times, the *sharīʿa* courts had come under the general jurisdiction of the *Shaykh al-Islām* and the *waḳf*s had been administered by the Ministry of *Awḳāf*. The British assumed responsibility for these, but the Muslims soon demanded that they be allowed to run their own religious affairs. The government concurred and the Supreme Muslim *Sharīʿa* Council (*al-Madjlis al-Sharʿī al-Islāmī al-Aʿlā*) was elected by leading Muslims. *Ḥādjdj* Amīn was chosen as *Raʾīs al-ʿUlamāʾ* and President of the Council, as he later maintained, for life. He had thus, as a young man, consolidated his position as leader of the Palestinian Arabs both in their religious and their secular affairs. In March 1921 he wrote a Memorandum to the British Colonial Secretary, Winston Churchill, in which he outlined Palestinian resistance to Zionism and the ideas which were the foundation of his future policy—the complete prohibition of Jewish immigration, the abolition of the Jewish National Home and the establishment of an Arab government of Palestine.

The period 1921-9 was used by the Muftī to build up his following. As President of the Supreme Muslim Council, he controlled the *waḳf* revenues, which were not used exclusively for charitable purposes. Preachers were paid to disseminate political propaganda and those who did not support his policies were dismissed. Financial assistance was given to Arab schools to instruct their pupils in the Arab nationalist spirit. Demonstrations and boycotts were encouraged. Money was also used to enhance the status of Jerusalem and its mosques in the Islamic world. To Amīn, the area of the *Ḥarām* was the very centre and symbol of his aspirations to preserve Jerusalem and Palestine as Arab and Islamic. In 1928 a screen was set up by the Western Wall of the sanctuary to separate male and female Jewish worshippers. This move was taken as a reason for protest and seen by Muslims as a Jewish encroachment on the *Ḥarām*. The Muftī felt the threat deeply, and encouraged propaganda to the effect that the Jews were planning to take over the Muslim holy places. A year later feelings between the two communities became so exacerbated that the Arabs attacked and committed atrocities amongst the Jews. 133 were killed b Arabs and 116 Arabs killed by police action. subsequent British government report did not a the Muftī directly of provoking the attacks, blamed him for not doing enough to forestall and for having played upon public feeling. agitation had been conducted in the name religion of which, in Palestine, he was head. British still saw him as a force for modera whereas it is clear that he was committed t uncompromisingly anti-Zionist policy and tha would do everything in his power to frustrate establishment of a Jewish National Home.

In 1931 he convened a Pan-Islamic Conferen Jerusalem which he attempted to use as a plat to further his anti-Zionist policy, although position was challenged by other Palestinian lea He later travelled to other Muslim countries to political support and to raise funds. In 193 helped to found the Palestine Arab Party, a Ḥus organisation under the presidency of Djamāl, Muftī's cousin. The Party's policy was that of himself, and it attempted to prohibit the fu sale of Arab land to Jewish settlers.

The year 1936 was a time of rising tensio Palestine, culminating in the Arab revolt. Th crease in Jewish immigration caused by the ri Nazism led the Arabs to fear the future take of their country by the Zionists. In April an Higher Committee of Christians and Muslims formed under the leadership of Amīn. It immedi supported a general strike, to be called off v the British government suspended Jewish immi tion. Murderous attacks on Jews began to occur, the brunt of the Arab effort was quickly tu against the British and those Arabs considered loyal. The strike and the unrest continued October. The British Commission appointed investigate the disturbances apportioned a l share of the blame for them to the Muftī. The Higher Committee under his chairmanship clearly instigated illegal acts and had not demned sabotage and terrorism. The Muftī seen and encouraged the revolt as a moven of the people, largely peasants, who had riser defend their country and their rights.

The British still clung to their hope of u Amīn as a moderating influence, but after assassination of a government officer in Septen 1937, stricter regulations were introduced. Arab Higher Committee was declared illegal Amīn was removed from his post as presiden the Supreme Muslim Council. Six members of former were arrested and deported (although Dja al-Ḥusaynī escaped) and the Muftī, fearing ar himself, fled to Lebanon. From there he fough propaganda war against the British, while his lowers contributed to the continuing unrest Palestine or set about eliminating members of r clans. He was not allowed to attend the Lon Conference on the future of Palestine in Febru 1939, although a four-man delegation of member the disbanded Higher Committee was present.

In October 1939 the Muftī made another m this time to ʿIrāḳ. As German successes multip in the Second World War, he began to make proaches to the Nazis in the hope that at the en the war he would be on the winning side. He s his private secretary to Berlin in September 1 to ask for German commitments to the Arab recognition of the complete independence of Arab countries, the abrogation of the manda he right of the Arabs to solve the Jewish question ılestine "in the national and racial interest on German-Italian model". These latter words the Nazi Secretary of State's report of his ersation with Amīn's secretary, and it is not exactly what the Muftī knew in Baghdād in ember 1940 of the "model" on which the Nazis solving the Jewish problem and how he would y it in Palestine. However, his letter was noted erlin and he was able to build on it later. His German feelings led to him to support Rashīd al-Gaylānī, the anti-British ʿIrāḳī politician had become Prime Minister in March 1940. both sought promises of material support the Axis, and in April 1941 al-Gaylānī and his orters carried out a shortlived pro-German . Promised German support was too little and ate, and a small British force was able to unseat Amīn had issued a *fatwā* urging all Muslims ipport the coup and to fight the British, and ı it failed he had once again to flee, via Iran aly.

e was warmly welcomed by Mussolini who hoped se him for his own purposes. The Muftī was interested in negotiating with the senior partner e Axis in Berlin, and he arrived there in November 1941. Al-Gaylānī arrived later the same th and the two disputed for the position of esman for the Arab cause. Amīn claimed that vas the leader of the Arab national movement. was the first to be received on November 20th Hitler to whom he repeated his request for the al recognition by Germany of the independence e Arab countries. The Führer was non-committal. ertheless the Muftī assured him of the friendship co-operation of the Arabs.

he period that the Muftī spent in Nazi Germany, ember 1941 to May 1945 is the most controversial is life. He had fled to Germany to escape the ish and because he believed that the Axis would the war. As a strict Muslim he could have had e sympathy with National Socialism as such, his chief aim in life of ridding Palestine of the s coincided hideously with the Nazi final solution the Jewish "problem". He therefore used all ilable anti-British and anti-Jewish sources in the e hope that he would be recognised by the Axis he ruler of an independent Arab state. He never ained written pledges from the Germans (although Italians were more forthcoming), and he was l to the limit by Nazi propaganda. The Germans vided staff and finance for *Das Arabische Büro* ı which the *Grossmufti* was able to send propada, both printed and broadcast, to the Middle t. He issued calls to the Arabs to rise against the tish and the Jews and to destroy them both. ıly when Britain and her Allies are destroyed will Jewish questions, our greatest danger be definitely lved" (broadcast of 11th November 1942). He helped to organise fifth columns in the Middle t and to establish Muslim and Arab units to ıt in the German armies.

he greatest suspicions surround his attitude to, knowledge of, and his possible encouragement of Nazi extermination policy. Calls to Palestinians ise and kill the Jewish settlers had been frequent ce the Balfour Declaration; they had been the dlines of newspapers and the slogans of demonıtions, but they became much more sinister when claimed in Nazi Germany. The evidence produced condemn him is difficult to substantiate. He is d to have been befriended by Eichmann, one of the chief executives of Hitler's policy. During his trial in Jerusalem in 1961, Eichmann denied having known the Muftī well, having met him only once during an official reception. The evidence for the friendship came from Dieter Wisliceny, one of Eichmann's aides, who months before the Nuremberg trials had begun to prepare an alibii for himself at the expense of Eichmann. Wisliceny went much further and accused the Muftī of being an "initiator" of the extermination policy. Other evidence of the Muftī's alleged role came from Rudolf Kastner (a Jewish leader in Hungary), who reported that Wisliceny had told him that "*According to my opinion*, the Grand Mufti . . . played a role in the decision . . . to exterminate the European Jews . . . *I heard say* that, accompanied by Eichmann, he has visited incognito the gas chamber at Auschwitz". These reports coming only from Wisliceny must be questioned until substantiated from other sources.

It *has* been established that Amīn actively tried to prevent the emigration of Jews to Palestine from Nazi-occupied countries. With his aims in mind it is understandable that he would try to prevent an expansion of the Jewish population in Palestine. By his protests he might have influenced German actions, although Hitler had long ago formulated a policy of extermination which could not be contradicted. Eichmann had once offered the lives of a million Hungarian Jews for 10,000 trucks, but Hitler had insisted on extermination. All the Jews in Hungary had been condemned to death, and the voice of the Muftī was insignificant.

A further piece of evidence which has been adduced to condemn him is a broadcast he made in September 1944 in which he referred to the eleven million Jews of the world, when it is said that before the Second World War it was well known that the world Jewish population was seventeen million. Thus, it is alleged, the Muftī knew that precisely six million Jews had been murdered. In September 1944 the holocaust had not been completed, as Eichmann continued his activities at least into October 1944. Moreover, Eichmann is said to have spoken of 5 million victims. The Muftī's figure does not prove that he, alone with the top Nazi leaders, knew the full horror, but neither does it disprove that he knew at least in general terms of German atrocities. At a press conference in 1961 he denied that he knew Eichmann and that he had visited the camps. By his presence in Germany, by his propaganda and other activities, by his protests against Jewish emigration, he gave moral authority to Nazi policy. He was, however, never brought to trial as a war criminal, for the technical reason that he was not, from the British point of view, an enemy national. Amīn had chosen the wrong side in the war but as a Palestinian Arab nationalist he had had little choice. If the Nazis won they would adopt an anti-Jewish policy in Palestine, if the British, then they would continue to support the establishment of a Jewish National Home.

When the outcome of the war was clear he escaped again, first to Paris, 1945-6, and then back to the Middle East, to Egypt. During the war Palestinian politics had been rather muted, but in 1944 the Ḥusaynīs had decided to re-establish the Palestine Arab Party and soon called for the return to the exiled Ḥusaynī politicians. Amīh began to try to regain his former position and influence. He had become the symbol of Arab opposition to Zionism, and the Arab League, in an effort to end political quarrels amongst the Palestinians, ordered the dissolution of the Arab Higher Committee and the Higher Front (the anti-Ḥusaynī body) and the formation of the Arab Higher Executive with the Muftī as its chairman. He was not allowed by the British to return to Palestine and had to direct the resistance from outside. He continued to follow an uncompromising line, boycotting the United Nations Special Committee on Palestine, refusing to contemplate any partition plans, and urging total opposition to the Zionists. As violence on both sides increased, the Higher Executive at the end of 1947 began to organise and direct military resistance. An Arab Liberation Army, owing partial allegiance to the Muftī, was created which later attempted to co-operate with other Arab armies.

Inter-Arab rivalry hindered co-operation, and after the proclamation of the State of Israel a split grew over Transjordan's ambitions in the West Bank of the Jordan. Egypt supported the Muftī and allowed him to settle in Gaza, where he announced in September 1948 the formation of a Palestine government. A self-constituted Assembly elected him its president and several Arab governments recognised the Gaza régime. However, the rump of Palestine was under Transjordanian control and its final annexation in April 1950 was not opposed by the Arab League. Henceforward the Muftī lost any real base of power and spent the rest of his life vainly trying to rally support for an effort to destroy Israel. Amīr ʿAbd Allāh of Transjordan appointed his own *muftī* and president of the Muslim Supreme Council.

In July 1951 ʿAbd Allāh was assassinated and Amīn was thought to be implicated although this was never conclusively proved. In 1951 he chaired a World Muslim Conference which he used as a platform to publicise his policy. He attended the Bandung Afro-Asian Conference in a minor capacity, having to accept the predominance of President ʿAbd al-Nāṣir [*q.v.* in Suppl.]. In fact, the latter's lack of regard for him caused him to move to Beirut in 1959. He had more freedom of action in Lebanon, but no more authority. He tried various alliances, with President Ḳāsim of ʿIrāḳ, with the Saʿūdīs, with Jordan, all to no avail. In the shifting sands of inter-Arab politics, Amīn was now of little account. He moved about, to Damascus, to al-Riyāḍ and back to Beirut. In the Palestine movement, first Aḥmad Shuḳayrī and then the Palestine Liberation Organisation took over precedence.

Al-*Ḥādjdj* Amīn died in Beirut on July 4th 1974. To the end, he proclaimed his unwavering belief that *his* country had been illegally given away by foreigners to other foreigners, both of whom had scant regard for its Arab and Islamic character. He spent his adult life trying to prevent a change in the character of Palestine. Through his intransigence, his desire to dominate his rivals and his inability to distinguish between his personal aspirations and his political goals, he ended by losing everything for himself and almost everything for the Palestinian Arabs.

Bibliography: Two works deal specifically with the Muftī, M. Pearlman, *Mufti of Jerusalem*, London 1947, written in an attempt to have him tried as a war criminal, and J. B. Schechtman, *The Mufti and the Fuehrer*, New York and London 1965, a fairer work but one taking too much for granted from Pearlman. Otherwise, references have to be sought in the many histories of the Palestine problem, and in works dealing with German relations with the Middle East and with Nazi policy towards the Jews. (D. Hopwood)

AMĪNDJĪ B. DJALĀL B. ḤASAN, an em Mustaʿlī-Ṭayyibī Ismāʿīlī jurist of India, the son of the twenty-fifth *dāʿī muṭlaḳ*. He liv Aḥmadābād in Gudjarāt and died there o Shawwāl 1010/6 April 1602. His works deal m with jurisprudence and are considered a authority on legal matters after the works c Ḳāḍī al-Nuʿmān [*q.v.*]. The following works been preserved: 1. *Masāʾil Amīndjī b. Djalā* the form of questions, answers, and anecdotes be on legal issues, hence also known as *Kitāb al-*. *wa 'l-djawāb*. The book contains many prob that are typically Indian, and although the bo in Arabic, the author uses many local Gujarati w and expressions. 2. *Kitāb al-Ḥawāshī*, consistir problems in the form of questions and ans relating to the text of al-Ḳāḍī al-Nuʿmān's *Da al-Islām* and *Mukhtaṣar al-āthār*. The problems cussed in the book throw some light on the s history of the Ismāʿīlī Bohra community. 3. *I al-mawārīth*, concerning inheritance. 4. *Sharḥ muntakhaba al-manẓūma*, a commentary on al-. al-Nuʿmān's *al-Urdjūza al-muntakhaba* on j prudence. 5. *Sharḥ Asās al-taʾwīl wa-taʾwīl al-daʿ* a commentary on al-Ḳāḍī al-Nuʿmān's *Asās taʾwīl* and *Taʾwīl al-daʿāʾim*.

Bibliography: Ismāʿīl b. ʿAbd al-Rasū Madjdūʿ, *Fihrist*, ed. ʿAlī Naḳī Munzawī, Te 1966, 37-8; Ḳuṭb al-Dīn Burhānpūrī, *Mun al-akhbār*, manuscript; Muḥammad ʿAlī b. M Djīwābhāʾī, *Mawsim-i bahār*, Bombay 130 1883-94, iii, 206, 252; Asaf A. A. Fyzee, *Com dium of Fatimid law*, Simla 1969 (both the w of Amīndjī b. Djalāl, Nos. 1 and 2 are use sources); Ismail Poonawala, *Biobibliograph Ismāʿīlī literature*, Malibu, Cal. 1977.

(I. Poonawal

AMĪR KABĪR, Mīrzā Muḥammad Taḳī K (*ca.* 1222-68/1807-52), the most prominent reforn statesman of 19th century Iran. He was a so Karbalāʾī Ḳurbān, the chief cook of the Ḳā ministers ʿĪsā and Abu 'l-Ḳāsim Ḳāʾimmaḳ through whom he found his way to the Ḳādjār r court. After receiving the necessary educatio Arabic and Persian studies, he began his secret position in the court and rapidly achieved in cession the important titles of "Mīrzā", "Kh "Wazīr-i Niẓām", "Amīr-i Niẓām", and finally highest of all, "Amīr-i Kabīr Atābak-i Aʿẓam". also married Nāṣir al-Dīn Shāh's sister, ʿIzzat Dawla.

The Amīr Kabīr served the Persian governm in different capacities such as the State Accoun of Ādharbāydjān in *ca.* 1240-5/1829-34 and Minister of the Army in 1253/1837. Before b appointed as Grand Vizier in 1264/1848, the A Kabīr took part in three diplomatic missions. 1244/1828 he went to St. Petersburg with Khus Mīrzā in order to settle the problems caused by murder of Griboyedov, the Russian special en to Iran. The second diplomatic mission was accompanying, in 1253/1837, the then Crown Pri Nāṣir al-Dīn Mīrzā, to Erivan for a meeting v the Russian Emperor. The Amīr was also appoin as the head of the Iranian mission to the "Erzur Conference", which was held in Erzurum in 1259 1843-6 to deal with Ottoman-Persian territorial border disputes.

During these missions to Russia and Turkey, Amīr studied closely the processes of modernisat in those countries. In his term of office as a Gr Vizier, therefore, he made strenuous efforts to uce certain modernising measures into his own ıtry. He took steps, for instance, towards the larisation of Iranian legal systems, the separation eligion and state, toleration towards religious orities, publication of newspapers, abolition of monial titles, foundation of modern factories and ols, and so on. He did not, however, pay much ntion to the limitation of the monarchic absolute er by establishing a law-making body in Iran; his problem, he had reportedly said, "I had the ıtion of [establishing] constitutionalism (*kon-siyun*), but my big obstacles were the Russians" īdūn Ādamiyyat, *Maḳālāt-i taʾrīkhī*, Tehran 1973,).

ı the course of his service as a Grand Vizier, the ır created many domestic and foreign enemies himself because, on the one hand, he limited ery, injustice, and abuses of power committed government officials and high dignitaries at court, ıding the Shāh's mother, Mahd ʿUlyā, and on other hand he opposed the Anglo-Russian inter-tions in Iranian affairs. This hostility at court, ther with the Anglo-Russian intervention, finally ıght about the Amīr's execution in Kāshān some months after his dismissal from the Grand erate, and the succession to that position of Nūrī, a protégé of the British.

Bibliography: Akbar Hāshimī Rafsandjānī, *mīr Kabīr yā ḳahramān-i mubāraza bā istiʿmār*, 'ehran 1967; ʿAbbās Iḳbāl, *Mīrzā Taḳī Khān mīr Kabīr*, Tehran 1961; Ḥusayn Makkī, *Zin-igānī-yi Mīrzā Taḳī Khān-i Amīr Kabīr*, Tehran 958; Firīdūn Ādamiyyat, *Amīr Kabīr va Īrān*, 'ehran 1969; J. H. Lorentz, *Iran's great reformer f the nineteenth century: an analysis of Amir Kabir's reforms*, in *Iranian Studies*, iv (1971), 5-103; Yaḥyā Dawlatābādī, *Kunfirāns rādjiʿ bi mīr Kabīr*, Tehran 1930; Ḳudrat Allāh Rūshanī aʿfaranlū, ed., *Amīr Kabīr va Dār al-Funūn*, 'ehran 1975 (a collection of speeches delivered y several Iranian scholars). See also the general istories of 19th century Persia.

(Abdul-Hadi Hairi)

AMĪR NIẒĀM, Ḥasan ʿAlī Khān Garrūsī 36-1317/1820-99) was born into a distinguished rdish family of the Garrūs district in western n. His ancestors and relatives held important itions at the courts of the Tīmūrīds, the Ṣafawīds, Afshārīds, the Zandīs, and finally the Ḳādjārs. er studying Persian, Arabic, history. and callig-hy, he began his government service at the age seventeen and, as a commander of the Garrūs iment, he helped Muḥammad Shāh Ḳādjār's ıy to lay siege to the city of Harāt in 1253/1837. er that, the Amīr Niẓām (a title which he received n Nāṣir al-Dīn Shāh in 1302/1884) continued his ninistrative, political, military, and diplomatic ies with little interruption for approximately years. His military missions include his victorious ticipation in the 1265/1848 expedition to Mashhad, that of 1273/1856 to Harāt. He was also one of se military commanders who ended the Bābī vement in Zandjān in 1267/1850 and that of the kshbandī Ṣūfīs led by Shaykh ʿUbayd Allāh in rdistān in 1297/1879; the former success gained Amīr Niẓām the title of "aide-de-camp" to Nāṣir Dīn Shāh, and the latter the governorship of five stern regions in Iran.

ın the sphere of civil offices the Amīr Niẓām served, ong other things, as Director of the Office of yal Effects and Treasuries (1273-5/1856-8), as a mber of the Grand Consultative Assembly (1283-8/1866-71), as Minister of Public Works (1289-99/1872-81), and as Governor of Kurdistān, Kirmān-Balūčistān, and other provinces at various times.

As Nāṣir al-Dīn Shāh's special political envoy, the Amīr Niẓām went to Europe and met the heads of state in London, Paris, Berlin, Brussels, and a few other European capitals in 1275/1858. It was on this trip that he was accompanied by 42 students seeking further education in Europe. Later, from 1276/1859 to 1283/1866, he was appointed Minister Plenipoten-tiary in Paris.

The Amīr Niẓām is known to have refused to co-operate with the Shāh in putting into effect the Tobacco Régie Concession of 1890 which had caused wide-spread unrest in Ādharbāydjān. For this reason, he resigned from his position as vizier to the Shāh's heir-apparent in that province (Muḥammad Ḥasan Khān Iʿtimād al-Salṭana, *Rūz-nāma-yi khāṭirāt*, Tehran 1971, 765-70 and *passim*). Curzon held that "the Amīr-i Niẓām was reputed to be a strong Russophile" (*Persia and the Persian question*, i, repr. London 1966, 415, 431). Besides, the Iʿtimād al-Salṭana reported that the Russians were insisting in sending the Amīr Niẓām back to his previous position in Ādharbāydjān (*Rūz-nāma*, 773). We also know that the Amīr Niẓām was popular with the Russians to the extent that he received the insignia of the order of the "White Eagle" from the Russian Emperor (Amīr Niẓām, *Munshaʾāt*, Tehran 1908, 14). It would accordingly probably be safe to assume that, in his opposition to the Tobacco Concession, the Amīr Niẓām was not inspired by a desire to protect national interests, but was, rather, protecting the interests of the Russians, the latter power being a firm opponent to the Concession.

The Amīr Niẓām had continued contacts with the West through his diplomatic missions abroad. He was one of the distinguished companions of Nāṣir al-Dīn Shāh during the latter's trip of 1290/1873 to Europe (Nāṣir al-Dīn Shāh, *Safar-nāma*, Tehran 1964, 12), a trip in which "Our principal goal", said the Shāh, "... is to learn about the basis of reform, development, and the means of interests and progress. We would like to see in person, and choose those things which are instrumental for the welfare and progress of the people in other countries" (Abdul-Hadi Hairi, *Shīʿism and constitutionalism in Iran: a study of the role played by the Persian residents of Iraq in Iranian politics*, Leiden 1977, 15). In addition, the Amīr Niẓām was closely associated with intel-lectuals such as Malkam Khān and Yūsuf Khān Mustashār al-Dawla Tabrīzī, two men who were widely known as apostles of modernist ideas (idem, *The idea of constitutionalism in Persian literature prior to the 1906 Revolution*, in *Akten des vii. Kongresses für Arabistik und Islamwissenschaft, Göttingen, 15. bis 22. August* 1974, Göttingen 1976, 189-207). He even reportedly signed an oath, together with a number of Persian modernist thinkers, to work to-wards "the progress of our beloved people and country" (Firīdūn Ādamīyyat, *Andīsha-yi taraḳḳī va ḥukūmat-i ḳānūn: ʿaṣr-i Sipahsālār*, Tehran 1972, 249 ff.).

Despite all these facts, however, the Amīr Niẓām seems in practice to have followed very much the traditional ways characteristic of despotic régimes. Thus it is reported that he used to burn in furnaces bakers who were believed to have overcharged their customers, and mutilated Kurds when he was sent to suppress their uprisings. At one time, his hostility towards modernisation went so far as to have ʿAlī Ḳulī Ṣafarov bastinadoed and his Tabrīz newspaper

Iḥtiyādj banned in 1316/1898 because Ṣafarov had advocated the idea of industrialisation in Iran (Mahdī Bāmdād, *Sharḥ-i ḥāl-i ridjāl-i Īrān*, i, Tehran 1968, 367, under "Ḥasan ʿAlī").

The Amīr Niẓām's reputation as a learned man, a stylistically distinguished prose writer, an excellent calligrapher, and a tough bureaucrat made him so highly respected in the royal court that at one time, in 1316/1898, even Muẓaffar al-Dīn Shāh preferred to side with the Amīr Niẓām in the latter's conflicts with the royal heir-apparent, Muḥammad ʿAlī Mīrzā (Mahdī Ḳulī Hidāyat, *Khāṭirāt va khaṭarāt*, Tehran 1965, 98-9). Among foreign observers, Curzon called him "a man of very strong will and determination" (*Persia*, i, 431). Dr. J. B. Feuvrier admired him as a "vieillard d'une intelligence supérieur, d'une grande expérience et d'une sagesse consommée" (*Trois ans à la cour de Perse*, Paris, n.d., 86).

The Amīr Niẓām wrote a book called *Pand-nāma-yi Yaḥyawiyya*; it consists of counsels given to a child of his, and has been published several times since 1315/1897 in Tehran and Tabrīz. This short book is also included in a collection of his epistolary prose called *Munshaʾāt*, already cited. This comprises letters written by the Amīr Niẓām to many Iranian political and religious figures, and provides much interesting and useful information about 19th century Iran. Some of his epistolary works can also be found in ʿAbbās Iḳbāl, *Amīr Niẓām Garrūsī*, in *Yādgār*, iii/6-7 (1947), 8-33, and in some other references given in the Bibliography below.

Bibliography: Amīr Niẓām Garrūsī, *Matn-i yak maktūb muwarrakh-i 1311*, in *Hunar va mardum*, N.S., nos. 41-2 (1967); idem, *Yak nāma*, in *Nashr-iyya-yi farhang-i Khurāsān*, iv/4 (1960), 30-1; Firīdūn Ādamiyyat, *Amīr Kabīr va Īrān*, Tehran 1969; Karīm Kishāwarz, *Hazār sāl nathr-i pārsī*, v, Tehran 1967; Sayyid Nasr Allāh Taḳawī, *Andarz-nāma-yi Amīr Niẓām Garrūsī*, Tehran 1935; Muḥammad Ḥasan Khān Iʿtimād al-Salṭana, *al-Maʾāthir wa 'l-āthār*, Tehran 1888; idem, *Mirʾāt al-buldān-i Nāṣirī*, ii, Tehran 1877; Dūst ʿAlī Muʿayyir al-Mamālik, *Ridjāl-i ʿaṣr-i Nāṣirī*, in *Yaghmā*, viii (1955), 369-73; Khānbābā Mushār, *Muʾallifīn-i kutub-i čāpī-yi fārsī va Arabī*, ii, Tehran 1961, nos. 679-81; Ghulām Ḥusayn Muṣāḥib, ed., *Dāʾira al-maʿārif-i fārsī*, i, Tehran 1966, 253, under "Amīr Niẓām"; Ḥusayn Maḥbūbī Ardakānī, *Taʾrīkh-i muʾassasāt-i tamaddunī-yi djadīd dar Īrān*, Tehran 1975; Aḥmad Kasrawī, *Taʾrīkh-i mashrūṭa-yi Īrān*, Tehran 1965; Muḥammad Muʿīn, *Farhang-i fārsī*, vi, Tehran 1973, under "Garrūsī"; ʿAlī Amīn al-Dawla, *Dastkhaṭṭī az Amīr Niẓām*, in *Waḥīd*, ii, no. 11 (1965), 70-1; idem, *Khāṭirāt-i siyāsī*, Tehran 1962; Bāstānī Pārīzī, *Talāsh-i āzādī*, Tehran 1968; E. G. Browne, *The Persian revolution of 1905-1909*, Cambridge 1910; Saʿīd Nafīsī, *Ḥasan ʿAlī Khān Amīr Niẓām*, in *Waḥīd*, iii, no. 2 (1965), 101-12; Aḥmad Suhaylī Khwānsārī, *Sifārat-i Amīr Niẓām va iʿzām-i dānishdjūyān-i Īrānī bi Urūpā barāy-i awwalīn bār*, in *Waḥīd*, i, no. 4 (1964), 18-20; Manṣūr Taḳī-Zāda Tabrīzī, *Buzurgān-i ḥusn-i khaṭṭ wa khushniwisān: Amīr Niẓām*, in *Waḥīd*, no. 197 (1976), 511-3, 515; Fereshteh M. Nouraie, *Taḥḳīḳ dar afkār-i Mīrzā Malkam Khān Nāẓim al-Dawla*, Tehran 1973; Ābbās Mīrzā Mulkārā, *Sharh-i ḥāl*, Tehran 1946; Nāẓim al-Islām Kirmānī, *Taʾrīkh-i bīdāri-yi Īrāniyān: muḳaddima*, Tehran 1967; ʿAlī Afshār, *Shūrish-i Shaykh ʿUbayd Allāh*, included in Mīrzā Rashīd Adīb al-Shuʿarāʾ, *Taʾrīkh-i Afshār*, Tehran 1967; Mahdī Khān Mumtaḥin al-Dawla Shaḳāḳī, *Khāṭirāt*, Te 1974.

(ABDUL-HADI HAIR

AL-ʿĀMIRĪ, ABU 'L-ḤASAN MUḤAMMAD B. YŪ philosopher who lived mainly in Persia, born e in the 4th/10th century in Khurāsān, where he stu with the well-known geographer and philoso Abū Zayd al-Balkhī [see AL-BALKHĪ]. From a 355/966 he spent some years in Rayy, enjoying patronage there of the Būyid vizier Abu 'l-Fa al-ʿAmīd, and of his son and successor Abu 'l-I [see IBN AL-ʿAMĪD]. Al-ʿĀmirī also visited Bagh at least twice, in 360/970-1 and again in 364/97 There he met many of the leading intellectua the day, but according to al-Tawḥīdī he was coldly received, being regarded as an unc provincial. By 370/980 he had returned to Khurā where he dedicated a treatise to the Sāmānid v Abu 'l-Husayn al-ʿUtbī (d. *ca.* 372/982), and c posed another in Bukhārā in 375/985-6. Al-ʿĀ died in Nīshāpūr on 27 Shawwāl 381/6 Jan 992.

In his *K. al-Amad ʿala 'l-abad* (MS Istanbul Se 179, edition by E. K. Rowson forthcoming), wri only six years before his death, al-ʿĀmirī gives a of his works, comprising seventeen titles, of w four are known to be extant: *K. al-Ibṣār wa 'l-mu* (MS. Cairo, Taymūriyya *ḥikma* 98) on optics; works on predestination, *Inḳādh al-bashar min djabr wa 'l-ḳadar* and *al-Taḳrīr li-awdjuh al-ta* (together in MS Princeton 2163 (393B)); an philosophical defense of Islam entitled *K. al-Iʿ bi-manāḳib al-Islām* (ed. A. Ghurāb, Cairo 19 Omitted from the list are his Aristotelian comme ries, three of which (on the *Categories*, *Poste Analytics*, and *De Anima*) he cites elsewhere. missing from the list is the *Fuṣūl fi 'l-maʿālim ilāhiyya* (MS Istanbul Esat Ef. 1933), a metaphys work which paraphrases large sections of the fam *K. al-Khayr al-maḥḍ* (known in Latin as the *L de causis*). Another work possibly to be attribu to al-ʿĀmirī is the doxographical *K. al-Saʿāda 'l-isʿād* (facs. ed. M. Minovi, Wiesbaden 1957-8).

Al-ʿĀmirī's philosophy is a rather conventic amalgam of Neoplatonism and Aristotelianism, type familiar from works by such figures as contemporary Miskawayh [*q.v.*], but his partic concern seems to have been to justify the pur of philosophy to the religious establishment. In *Iʿlām* he attempts to show the *ʿulamāʾ* how losophy and Islam can be seen as complement rather than contradictory, illustrating his point using philosophical methods in a programm demonstration of the superiority of Islam to ot religions. The *Amad* similarly combines philosoph and dogmatic evidence in a discussion of the after as well as giving the *ʿulamāʾ* an elementary (highly apologetic) introduction to the Greek losophers. This conciliatory attitude towards Is represents a conscious continuation of the tradit initiated by al-Kindī [*q.v.*], the master of al-ʿĀmi master al-Balkhī.

Al-ʿĀmirī's only pupil of note was Ibn Hi [*q.v.*], and his influence on later figures seems have been minimal. The massive impact of Sīnā, who began writing shortly after al-ʿĀmi death, all but obliterated his memory.

Bibliography: Abū Ḥayyān al-Tawḥ *Akhlāḳ al-wazīrayn*, ed. M. al-Ṭandjī, Damas 1965, 355 f.; 410 ff., 446 f.; idem, *al-Muḳaba* ed. H. al-Sandūbī, Cairo 1929, index; idem, *Imtāʿ wa 'l-muʾānasa*, ed. A. Amīn and A. al-Za Beirut 1953, indices; Abu Sulaymān al-Sidjistā *wān al-ḥikma*, ed. ʿA. Badawī, Tehran 1974, ff., 307 ff.; Ibn Sīnā, *al-Nadjāt*, Cairo 1357/1938, ɪ; Yāḳūt, *Udabāʾ*, i, 411 f.; al-Kutubī, *Fawāt wafayāt*, ed. M. ʿAbd al-Ḥamīd, Cairo 1951, 95; full bibl. in M. Minovi, *Az khazāʾin-i kiyya*, in *Revue de la faculté des lettres de l'Université de Tehran*, iv/3 (1957), 60-87; Brockelmann, I, 744, 958, 961; F. Rosenthal, *State and religion ording to Abu 'l-Ḥasan al-ʿĀmirī*, in *IQ*, iii)56), 42-52; M. Arkoun, *Logocentrisme et vérité igieuse dans la pensée islamique d'après al-Iʿlām manāḳib al-Islām d'al-ʿĀmirī*, in *Stud. Isl.*, xv (1972), 5-52; M. Allard, *Un philosophe ologien: Muḥammad b. Yūsuf al-ʿĀmirī*, in *HR*, clxxxvii (1975), 57-69. (E. K. Rowson)

MĪRĪ, Mīrzā Muḥammad Ṣādiḳ Adīb al-ālik, Persian poet and journalist, was . at Kāzarān near Sulṭānābād (mod. Arāk) in . On his father's side he was directly descended Mīrzā Abu 'l-Ḳāsim Ḳāʾimmaḳām Farāhānī, esman and writer of the early 19th century, e his mother was a member of the same family. r his father's death in 1874 the family was in us financial difficulties, until in 1890 Mīrzā ḳ took service with Amīr-i Niẓām Garrūsī, n he accompanied to Tabrīz, Kirmānshāh and an. During this period he acquired the titles *r al-Shuʿarāʾ* (whence his *takhalluṣ* Amīrī) and *Adīb al-Mamālik*. In 1894 he was in charge he Government Translation Bureau in Tehran. years later he returned to Tabrīz, and after ng theological qualifications became Vice-cipal of the Luḳmāniyya College of science medicine. For a time he published *Adab*, a ary and scientific journal, and in 1900 travelled way of the Caucasus and Khīwa to Mashhad, in 1903 to Tehran, in both of which cities he med publication of his journal. 1904 saw him Baku, where he edited a Persian supplement to Turkish periodical *Irshād*. After the Constitutional Revolution of 1906 he became editor of *djlis*, the record of the National Assembly debates, later of the official periodicals *Rūznāma-yi vlatī-yi Īrān* and *Āftāb*; in between he started own journal, *ʿIrāḳ-i ʿAjam*. In 1911 he entered judicial service and held posts in Simnān, udjbulāgh, Sulṭānābād and Yazd. He died in ran in 1917.

mīrī had a wide range of interests from geoghy, mathematics and lexicography to history, rature and astrology. He was well-versed in sian and Arabic, in both of which he composed ms, and was familiar with a number of other guages. However, he was no ivory tower poet; poems, following the new trend to re-unite rature and daily life, reflect the turbulent politics his time, in which he was generally on the side the Constitutionalists. His later writings are rked by social satire and revolutionary fervour.

Bibliography: Amīrī's *Dīwān-i kāmil* was dited by Waḥīd Dastgirdī, Tehran 1933. Biographical information in: E. G. Browne, *Literary istory of Persia 1500-1924*, Cambridge 1924, epr. 1930, 346-9; M. Ishaque, *Sukhanwarān-i rān dar ʿaṣr-i ḥāḍir*, ii, Calcutta 1937, 48-63; Rashīd Yāsimī, *Adabiyyāt-i muʿāṣir*, Tehran 1937, 20-2; M. Ishaque, *Modern Persian poetry*, Calcutta 1943, *passim*; Muḥammad Ṣadr Hāshimī, *Taʾrīkh-i ljarāʾid wa madjallāt-i Īrān*, i, Tehran 1948, 80-98; J. Rypka, *Iranische Literaturgeschichte*, Leipzig 1959, 336-7; ibid., *History of Iranian literature*, Dordrecht 1968, 375-6; Bozorg Alavi, *Geschichte und Entwicklung der modernen persischen Literatur*, Berlin 1964, 35-6. (L. P. Elwell-Sutton)

ʿAMR b. KIRKIRA, Abū Mālik al-Aʿrābī, *mawlā* of the Banū Saʿd, had learnt the *ʿarabiyya* in the desert and had settled at Baṣra. Since his mother had married Abu 'l-Baydāʾ [*q.v.*], he acted as *rāwiya* to this last, but he owed his fame to his incomparable knowledge of the Arabic language, since, according to an oft-mentioned tradition, he knew it in its entirety, whereas al-Aṣmaʿī had only one-third of it, Abū ʿUbayda (or al-Khalīl b. Aḥmad) half of it and Abū Zayd al-Anṣārī (or Muʾarridj) two-thirds of it. His speciality was rare words. Abū Mālik was allegedly the author of at least two works, a *K. Khalḳ al-insān* and a *K. al-Khayl*. Al-Djāḥiẓ was one of his auditing students.

Bibliography: Djāḥiẓ, *Bayān*, iv, 23; idem, *Ḥayawān*, iii, 525-6; *Fihrist*, 66; Suyūṭī, *Muzhir*, ii, 249-50; idem, *Bughya*, 367; Zubaydī, *Ṭabaḳāt*, 139; Anbārī, *Nuzha*, 82; Yāḳūt, *Udabāʾ*, xvi, 131-2. (Ed.)

AMRŌHĀ, a district and town of mediaeval northern India, now a town. It arose as a metropolitan centre after the accession of Sultan Ghiyāth al-Dīn Balban to the throne of Dihlī in 664/1266. Since the Rādjpūt Rādjā of Kētehr or Katahr [*q.v.*] (modern Bareilly district in the U.P.) rose in rebellion and carried his depredations as far as the *iḳṭāʿ* of Badāʾūn, Balban attacked him in his own region, and having cleared the vast district, carved out the *iḳṭāʿ* of Amrōhā that comprised the area of the modern districts of Bareilly, Murādābād, Rāmpūr and Bidjnore in Western Uttar Pradesh. For the consolidation of his authority, he brought the *iḳṭāʿ* under direct, *khāliṣa* administration and appointed efficient officers. As a result of this, the town of Amrōhā soon developed considerably with public buildings, a fort, mosques, *madrasa*s and Ṣūfī *khānḳāh*s; Among all these, only the mosque constructed by an officer of Sultan Muʿizz al-Dīn Kayḳubād in 686/1287 is intact.

In the 8th/14th century Amrōhā became a centre of Muslim culture, and was held by a high noble of the sultanate. For instance, the Prince Khiḍr Khān, the eldest son of Sultan ʿAlāʾ al-Dīn Khaldjī, was appointed its governor towards the close of his father's reign. In the time of Muḥammad b. Tughluḳ, (725-52/1325-51), Ibn Baṭṭūṭa found Amrōhā a beautiful city, placed under the joint responsibility of a number of important nobles. ʿAzīz Khammār, the governor, was in charge of its revenue affairs, while Shams al-Dīn Badakhshānī acted there as the army commandant. Besides, there was a *ḳāḍī*, Sayyid Amīr ʿAlī, to administer justice; a *shaykh al-Islām*, charged with the duty of looking after the religious affairs and providing maintenance land for the scholars, saints and other deserving persons; and 4,000 royal slaves stationed there under Malik-Shāh for military service. The Ḥaydarī *ḳalandar* dervishes also settled down there in quite large numbers.

During the reign of Sultan Fīrūz Shāh, Amrōhā lost its importance as a provincial capital, for administrative headquarters were shifted from here to Sambhal because of the contumacious activities of the Katehriya Radjpūt *zamīndārs*. However, Amrōhā continued as a centre of culture and learning, with many saints and scholars. Shaykh Čāʾildā, a descendant of Shaykh Farīd al-Dīn Gandj-i Shakar of Adjodhān, was a respectable Ṣūfī saint in Amrōhā during the reign of Sultan Sikandar Lōdī. The Masnad-i ʿĀlī Maḥmūd Khān Lōdī, the governor of the territory of Sambhal, gave Shaykh Čāʾildā two villages in maintenance grant in the *pargana* of Nindru (now in the district of Bid̲j̲nore).

During the Mug̲h̲al period, Amrōhā also produced famous Ṣūfīs and scholars, such as S̲h̲ayk̲h̲ Ibban Čis̲h̲tī during the reign of Akbar. Mīr Sayyid Muḥammad, the famous Mīr ʿAdl (Chief justice) and Mawlānā Allāhdād (d. 990/1582), a leading scholar, also belonged to Amrōhā. Maṣḥafī Amrōhāʾī, the famous Urdu poet of the 18th and 19th centuries, was also born and educated there. Wiḳār al-Mūlk, an associate of Sir Sayyid Aḥmad K̲h̲ān and one of the founder members of the Aligarh Movement, also hailed from Amrōhā. It is now a *taḥṣīl* headquarters in the district of Murādābād in Uttar Pradesh.

Bibliography: Abu 'l-Faḍl, *Āʾīn-i Akbarī*, Eng. tr. Jarrett, Bibl. Ind. Calcutta 1927; ʿAbd al-Ḳādir Badāʾūnī, *Muntak̲h̲ab al-tawārīk̲h̲*, iii, Bibl. Ind., Calcutta 1868; Ḍiyāʾ al-Dīn Baranī, *Taʾrīk̲h̲-i Fīrūz S̲h̲āhī*, ed. Sir Syed Ahmad Khan, Bibl. Ind., Calcutta 1862; Ibn Baṭṭūṭa, *Riḥla*, iii, 436-40, Eng. tr. Gibb, iii, 762-4; ʿIṣāmī, *Futūḥ al-salāṭīn*, ed. Usha, Madras 1948; S̲h̲ayk̲h̲ ʿAbd al-Ḥaḳḳ Muḥaddit̲h̲, *Ak̲h̲bār al-ak̲h̲yār* Dihlī 1914; S̲h̲ams Sirād̲j̲ ʿAfīf, *Taʾrīk̲h̲-i Fīrūz S̲h̲āhī*, Bibl. Ind., Calcutta 1890. (I. H. SIDDIQUI)

AL-**ĀMULĪ** [see ḤAYDAR-I ĀMULĪ, in Suppl.].

AND̲J̲UMAN-I K̲H̲UDDĀM-I KAʿBA, a religious society founded by Indian Muslims in their period of great pan-Islamic fervour just before World War One. The And̲j̲uman was started by Mawlānā ʿAbd al-Bārī [*q.v.* above] and Mus̲h̲īr Ḥusayn Ḳidwāī [*q.v.*] of Lucknow who hoped to be able to defend Mecca and Medina by raising ten million rupees to build dreadnoughts and airships and to maintain armed forces. Such an ambitious programme proved impracticable, and the final constitution of the organisation published early in 1332/1914 declared that to defend the Holy Places it would: "(a) preach the aims and objects of the And̲j̲uman to Muslims generally; invite them to join it; and induce them to render sincere service to the holy places; (b) spread Islamic ethics in the neighbourhood of the holy places; invite the attention of the inhabitants of those places to a knowledge of the religion; promote intercourse and unity among them; and persuade them to the allegiance and assistance of the guardian of the holy places; (c) promote relations between Muslims and the holy places and extend and facilitate means of communication with the holy places".

The leaders of the And̲j̲uman came in large part from young western-educated Muslims of pan-Islamic predilections, for instance, Muḥammad and S̲h̲awḳat ʿAlī [*qq.v.*], Dr. M. A. Anṣārī and Mus̲h̲īr Ḥusayn Ḳidwāī, and *ʿulamaʾ* who were in some way connected with the Farangī Maḥall family [*q.v.* below] of Lucknow, for instance, ʿAbd al-Bārī, S̲h̲āh Aḥmad As̲h̲raf of Kačawča and ʿAbd al-Mad̲j̲īd Ḳādirī of Badāʾūn. The *ʿulamāʾ* of Deoband, landlords, and men closely associated with government, were conspicuous by their absence. Nevertheless, many, including women, joined the And̲j̲uman. By S̲h̲awwāl 1332/September 1914 the And̲j̲uman had over 17,000 members, a central organisation in Dihlī and branches throughout India: moreover, it had grown faster and spread more widely than any other Indo-Muslim organisation.

The achievements of the And̲j̲uman, however, were limited. One problem was that the Government of India, suspicious of the alliance between young western-educated politicians and *ʿulamāʾ*, refused to support it. The And̲j̲uman's work was restricted to the *Ḥad̲j̲d̲j̲*, and here S̲h̲awḳat ʿAlī strove to im[prove] the conditions of Indian pilgrims and attempt[ed to] break the European monopoly of the pilgrim [traffic] by setting up, with Turkish aid, a wholly M[uslim] shipping company. But the outbreak of World [War] One and the closing of the *Ḥad̲j̲d̲j̲* route put a[n end] even to this work, and the organisation, witho[ut] obvious function, fell apart amidst squabbles bet[ween] the *ʿulamāʾ* and the young politicians. In 1334, ʿAbd al-Bārī moved its central office to Luc[know] and the organisation was last talked of in 1336, when he tried to restart it as a vehicle for a cam[paign] to release Muslims who had been interned d[uring] the War.

The importance of the And̲j̲uman lies mo[re in] what it portended than in what it achieve[d. In] working to protect the Holy Places, the leading Islamic politicians of the day, S̲h̲awḳat and Mu[ḥam]mad ʿAlī, met ʿAbd al-Bārī and became *murī[d]* [of] this very important *pīr*. More generally, y[oung] western-educated politicians came to appreciat[e the] widespread influence in Indo-Muslim societ[y of] *ʿulamāʾ* like those of the Farangī Maḥall fa[mily]. These same people were to come together a[gain] after World War One to organise a much gr[eater] effort for a pan-Islamic cause, the *K̲h̲ilāfat* m[ove]ment [*q.v.*].

Bibliography: Mawlawī ʿInāyat Allāh, *Ris[āla]* *ḥasrat al-āfāḳ ba wafāt mad̲j̲mūʿat al-ak[...]* Lucknow n.d. 16-17; Francis Robinson, *Separa[tism]* *among Indian Muslims: the politics of the U[nited]* *Provinces' Muslims 1860-1923*, Cambridge [...] 208-12, 214-15, 279, 281, 287.

(F. C. R. ROBINSO[N])

ANĪS, MĪR BĀBAR ʿALĪ (1217-91/1802[...]) Urdu poet, was born in Fayḍābād (Fyzabad) [...] into a family which had produced five generat[ions] of poets. Some of these, including his father K̲h̲[...] wrote the characteristically Indian type of *mart̲[h̲iya]* which thrived at public recitals in Lucknow, ca[pital] of the S̲h̲īʿī Nawābs of Oudh. This type, which [...] have originated in the Deccan, was devoted to [the] martyrdom of al-Ḥusayn b. ʿAlī at Karbalāʾ (61/6[80]). Anīs moved to Lucknow as a young man, and dev[oted] his life to writing poetry, especially *marāt̲h̲ī*. [He] became the leading exponent of this form; thous[ands] attended his readings in Lucknow, and in o[ther] Indian cities which he occasionally visited late[r in] life. Some critics thought his contemporary and r[ival] Dabīr superior, but this view is now discounted. [By] the time Anīs began writing, the main lines of [the] Indian *mart̲h̲iya* had already been foreshadowe[d but] not fully established; and he used it to the [...] Formerly in quatrains, it was now almost alway[s in] *musaddas* form. Starting as a short emotional [and] devotional lament, it was lengthened to ove[r a] hundred verses of varied content. Alongside [the] incidents involving al-Ḥusayn and his followers [at] Karabalāʾ, Anīs includes description of nature, s[uch] as landscape, the desert, and storms; chara[cter] sketches of the protagonists; the horse, the sw[ord,] warlike accountrements; and a philosophising w[hich] gave universality to a superficially restricted the[me]. The language employs all the devices of rhet[oric] (*balāg̲h̲a*), yet there is an inherent simplicity [and] sincerity which contrasted strongly with the U[rdu] *g̲h̲azal* [see GHAZAL, iv] then in vogue. It consequen[tly] won the approval of forward-looking critics [and] poets such as Ḥālī and Āzād, and occupies an [im]portant place in Urdu literary history. It says m[uch] for Anīs's artistry that he managed to sustain inte[rest] in an output estimated at 250,000 verses; but i[...]

ily surprising that the form ceased to be widely ivated after the end of the 19th century.

Bibliography: Critical accounts of Anīs and s *marāthī* may be found in Muhammad Sadiq, *istory of Urdu literature*, London 1964, 155-63; bu 'l-Layth Ṣiddīḳī, *Lakhnāū kā dabistān-i shāʿirī*, ahore 1955, which also contains examples from :evious and subsequent *marthiya* poets. Ram abu Saksena's *History of Urdu literature*, Allaabad 1927, in a general chapter on "Elegy and egy writers" (123 ff.), contains a genealogical .ble of Anīs's family (p. 136), showing the poets . the family before and after him.

Among critical studies of Anīs are Amīr Aḥmad, *ādgār-i Anīs*, Lucknow 1924, and Djaʿfar ʿAlī hān, *Anīs kī marthiya nigārī*, Lucknow 1951. ıiblī Nuʿmānī's *Muwāzana-yi-Anīs-o-Dabīr* is still ıe standard comparison of the two poets, though ɜavily weighted in Anīs's favour. There are ımerous editions of Anīs's poetry, none complete. ne of the fullest is *Marāthī Anīs*, ed. Nāʾib usayn Naḳwī Amrotā, 4 vols., Karachi 1959. he three-volume edition of Nawāb Ḥaydar Djang, adāūn 1935, is less full, but has an introduction y Niẓām al-Dīn Ḥusayn Niẓāmī Badāūnī.

(J. A. Haywood)

NṢĀRĪ, Shaykh Murtaḍā, despite his being er unknown in the West, is considered to have a Shīʿī *mudjtahid* whose widely-recognised ;ious leadership in the Shīʿī world has not yet ı surpassed. He was born into a noted but finan-.y poor clerical family of Dizfūl, in the south of ı, in 1214/1799; his lineage went back to Djābir Abd Allāh Anṣārī (d. 78/697), a Companion of Prophet. After learning the recitation of the ·ʾān and related primary subjects, Anṣārī studied er his uncle Shaykh Ḥusayn Anṣārī until 1232/ 5 when he, accompanying his father, Muḥammad in, went to visit the shrine cities of ʿIrāḳ. While Karbalāʾ, he attended the teaching circle of the Shīʿī leader, Sayyid Muḥammad Mudjāhid (d. 2/1826), who found Anṣārī a man of extraordinary us and urged Anṣārī's father to let his son remain Karbalāʾ. Anṣārī then studied under Mudjāhid il *ca.* 1236/1820, when Anṣārī, together with dreds of other Iranian people, fled from Karbalāʾ to the pressures imposed by the Ottoman gover-at Baghdād, Dāwūd Pasha, after the growth of Perso-Ottoman hostility at that time (S. H. Long-, *Four centuries of modern Iraq*, Oxford 1925, -9; Sir Percy Sykes, *A history of Persia*, ii, repr. .don 1963, 316 ff.). Anṣārī then returned to fūl.

ı *ca.* 1237/1821, Anṣārī again went to Karbalāʾ attended the circle of the famous *mudjtahid* lā Muḥammad Sharīf al-ʿUlamāʾ (d. 1245/1829). *ca.* 1238/1829 he proceeded to Nadjaf and con-ıed his studies under Shaykh Mūsā Kāshif al-ṭāʾ (d. 1241/1825), and after a year or so he again rned to his home town, Dizfūl. Heading for hhad in 1240/1824 with the intention of attending circles for religious learning in different Iranian ɜs, Anṣārī joined the teaching circle of Shaykh d Allāh Burūdjirdī (d. *ca.* 1271/1854) in Burūdjird ɔd al-ʿAzīz Ṣāḥib al-Djawāhir, *Dāʾira al-maʿārif slāmiyya: Īrān va hama-yi maʿārif-i Shīʿa-yi imiyya-yi Ithnāʿashariyya*, ii, n.d., 155, under ad Allāh") and that of Sayyid Muḥammad Bāḳir ftī (d. 1270/1853) in Iṣfahān (Anṣārī's biography :ten by Muḥammad Riḍā al-Raḍawī al-Khwānsārī , in Anṣārī, *Kitāb al-Matādjir* (*al-Makāsib*), ran 1908, 1), each for no more than a month. When Anṣārī met Mullā Aḥmad Narāḳī (d. 1245/1829) in Kāshān, he decided to remain there because he found Narāḳī's circle most congenial for learning. Narāḳī also found Anṣārī exceptionally knowledgeable, saying that within his experience he had never met any established *mudjtahid* as learned as Anṣārī, who was then *ca.* thirty years of age (Murtaḍā al-Anṣārī, *Zindigānī va shakhṣiyyat-i Shaykh-i Anṣārī ḳuddisa sirruh*, Aḥwāz (*sic*) 1960, 69).

In 1244/1828, Anṣārī left Kāshān for Mashhad, and after a few months living there he went to Tehran. In 1246/1830, he returned to Dizfūl, where he was widely recognised as a religious authority, despite the presence of other important *ʿulamāʾ* in that town. It is said that Anṣārī suddenly left Dizfūl secretly after sometime because he, as a religious-legal judge, was put under pressure to bring in a one-sided verdict in a legal case. He then arrived in Nadjaf in *ca.* 1249/1833 and joined the teaching circle of Shaykh ʿAlī Kāshif al-Ghiṭāʾ (d. 1254/1838) and, according to some sources, that of Shaykh Muḥammad Ḥasan Ṣāḥib al-Djawāhir (d. 1266/1849), but each for only a few months, and soon organised his own teaching circle independently.

Anṣārī's life as a distinguished religious scholar entered a new phase in 1266/1849 after he had received an overwhelming recognition from all the Shīʿī communities which formed a population then estimated at 40 million across the Muslim world, so that the institution of *mardjaʿ-i taḳlīd* [*q.v.*] reached its highest point. "The Twelver Shīʿī population of Iran," wrote one of Anṣārī's contemporaries, Muḥammad Ḥasan Iʿtimād al-Salṭana, "and the numerous Shīʿī groups who live in India, in Russia, in some of the Ottoman provinces, and in several other cities of Afghānistān, Turkistān, and elsewhere used to send to Anṣārī their endowment funds, alms taxes, one-fifth of their annual savings . . . and other similar payments, which amounted to 200,000 *tūmān*s [*ca.* $ 30,000.00] annually" (*al-Maʾāthir wa 'l-āthār*, Tehran 1888, 136-7).

Despite his vast income and his overwhelming leadership, Anṣārī, according to a number of eyewitness accounts, nevertheless denied his family a comfortable life and himself lived an ascetic life, as was evident from his appearance (cf. *inter alia*, Muḥammad Ḥirz al-Dīn, *Maʿārif al-ridjāl*, ii, Nadjaf 1964, 399-404). Instead, he gave the money to the poor and needy, to the students of religious schools, and at times to those Muslims who, on their way to visit the shrine of Imām Riḍā in Mashhad, were taken captive by the Turkomans. When Anṣārī died in 1281/1864 his wealth and belongings were worth only seventeen *tūmān*s (less than three dollars), for an equal amount of which he was in debt. One of his followers therefore took charge of the funeral expenses.

Anṣārī's piety, and above all his scholarly qualifications, deserved of course such recognition, but other factors also were certainly instrumental in establishing his leadership: the then great *mardjaʿ-i taḳlīd*, Ṣāḥib al-Djawāhir, shortly before his death declared Anṣārī to be the legitimate sole *mardjaʿ-i taḳlīd* of the Shīʿa. This endorsement was compounded with the earlier death of other distinguished religious authorities such as Shaykh Muḥammad Ḥusayn Ṣāḥib al-Fuṣūl (d. 1261/1845). In addition, this development was preceded by the gradual decline of Iṣfahān as religious centre, a process which had begun its course since the fall of the Ṣafawīd dynasty and was accelerated by the death of such religious authorities of Iṣfahān as Shaftī and Ibrāhīm

Karbāsī (d. 1262/1845). Consequently, Nadjaf began then to enjoy an unprecedented attention from the Shīʿa of Iran, and most of this attention was certainly focused on the person of Anṣārī.

Anṣārī not only established a new era in the history of the Shīʿī leadership but was also an important figure in the field of Shīʿī jurisprudence, being credited with introducing a new methodology in the field of *uṣūl*. His interpretation, for instance, of the "principle of no harm" (*ḳāʿida lā ḍarar*), which had long engaged the Shīʿī *ʿulamāʾ*, opened up a more settled way for practising *idjtihād* in general and for dealing with the problem of private ownership in particular. Anṣārī's system in jurisprudence laid great importance on the *mardjaʿ-i taḳlīd*'s being the most learned man of his time; he said that *ʿaḳl* (reason) and *ʿurf* (social conventions and common practices) are to be taken as criteria and bases for introducing new laws. His name is also mentioned as an authority with original views on such *uṣūl* subjects as the principles of *istiṣḥāb*, *barāʾa*, and *ẓann*, each of which were the subject of an independent study done by Anṣārī (for a concise definition of the above terms, cf. Djaʿfar Sadjdjādī, *Farhang-i ʿulūm-i naḳlī va adabī*, Tehran 1965, 51-3, 136, 359).

Anṣārī's school of thought has been clearly dominant in the Shīʿī clerical circles since the middle of the 19th century, and his views have been discussed and adopted by most of the Shīʿī *ʿulamāʾ*. A descendant of Anṣārī's brother has listed the names of 144 *mudjtahid*s who have written commentaries on Anṣārī's various books (Anṣārī, *Zindigānī*, 354-87). Anṣārī's influence on the later *ʿulamāʾ* can also be found in the bio-bibliographical dictionaries compiled on the Shīʿī authorities (cf. *Bibl.*). The influence of Anṣārī's ideas is further seen in the laws made for various Shīʿī communities, because many of those who were involved in the process of law-making were either Anṣārī's disciples or were indirectly under the influence of his thought. The Persian civil law which was substantially based on the Shīʿī jurisprudence may be mentioned as an example; and the man who "translated into Russian the Islamic law according to which the Muslims of Caucasus were being tried in the legal courts" was Mīrzā Kāẓim Bey, a disciple of Anṣārī (Mahdī Khān Mumtaḥin al-Dawla Shakākī, *Khāṭirāt*, Tehran 1974, 110).

Anṣārī's circle of teaching was attended by numerous pupils, many of whom became great *mardjaʿ-i taḳlīd*s of their times, e.g. Ḥusayn Kūhkamarī (d. 1291/1874), Muḥammad Īrwānī (d. 1306/1888), Ḥabīb Allāh Rashtī (d. 1312/1894), Muḥammad Ḥasan Shīrāzī (d. 1312/1894), and Muḥammad Kāẓim Khurāsānī (d. 1329/1911). There are also reports that Sayyid Djamāl al-Dīn Asadābādī "Afghānī" was also a pupil of Anṣārī (Aṣghar Mahdawī and Īradj Afshār, *Madjmūʿa-yi asnād va madārik-i čāpnashuda dar bāra-yi Sayyid Djamāl al-Dīn mashhūr bi Afghānī*, Tehran 1963, 20) and that Afghānī studied in Anṣārī's circle for four years prior to Afghānī's departure from Nadjaf in 1270/1854 (Mīrzā Luṭf Allāh Khān Asadābādī, *Sharḥ-i ḥāl va āthār-i Sayyid Djamāl al-Dīn Asadābādī maʿrūf bi Afghānī*, Berlin 1926, 21-2; but these accounts are controversial. It cannot be accepted that Anṣārī, despite his great caution in issuing a certificate of *idjtihād*, gave one to Afghānī, then only sixteen years of age (Khān Malik Sāsānī, *Siyāsat-garān-i dawra-yi Ḳādjār*, i, Tehran 1959, 186, nor has Luṭf Allāh Khān been correctly quoted by Nikki R. Keddie that "Shaikh Murtazā gave Jamāl ad-Dīn an *ijāzeh* (certificate of advanced knowledge)" (*Sayyid Jamāl ad-Dīn "al-Afghānī": a political biography*, Berkeley and Los Angeles 1972, 15 rather, Luṭf Allāh reported that Anṣārī ga certain certificate to Afghānī's father (Asadā *op. cit.*, 15, 21 and the Arabic translation of As bādī's book by ʿAbd al-Naʿīm Muḥammad Ḥasan Beirut 1973, 64; see also Abdul-Hadi Hairi, *An ahā-yi Sayyid Djamāl al-Dīn Asadābādī dar mūn-i inḥiṭāṭ-i musalmānān va inḳilāb-i mashrūṭi i Īrān*, in *Vaḥīd*, nos. 225-9 [1978], 47-52, 5 etc.).

Despite his being a one-eyed man, Anṣārī was c productive in writing. According to a report wrote over thirty books (Anṣārī, *Zindigānī*, 13 twenty-four of which are listed as Anṣārī's publi works in Khānbābā Mushār, *Muʾallifīn-i ku čāpī-yi fārsī va Arabī*, vi, Tehran 1965, nos. 126 many of these books have been published se times in India, ʿIrāḳ, and Īrān since 1267/1850. of his works are especially frequently consulted have been considered by the Shīʿī *ʿulamāʾ* to b exceptional importance: *Farāʾiḍ al-uṣūl* (*al-Ras* on *uṣūl* and *al-Makāsib* on *fiḳh*, which were published in Tehran in 1268/1851 and 1280/ respectively. Both these have constantly been as text books in all Shīʿī circles.

One of the financial foundations with which m of the Shīʿī *ʿulamāʾ* of ʿIrāḳ were knowingl unknowingly connected was the so-called "O Bequest". It was, in the words of the British Mini of Tehran, a "powerful lever which helped to pro good relations between the Persian ecclesiastics myself and . . . afforded opportunities for influen the leading Persian Ulema" (Sir Arthur Hardi *A diplomatist in the East*, London 1928, 323-4). British authorities, however, did not succee influencing Anṣārī through the Oudh Beq (Sayyid Muḥsin Amīn, *Aʿyān al-Shīʿa*, xl, Be 1960, 43-6). He received money only for a short pe of time, and then rejected further sums (Maḥ Maḥmūd, *Taʾrīkh-i rawābiṭ-i siyāsī-yi Īrān Ingilīs*, vi, Tehran 1953, 1743).

In the arena of politics and public affairs, An was quite inactive. He refused to make use of influence in the interest of his followers. Persia otherwise, in their political and other strug Theoretically, however, he believed that the *ʿula* are not only the custodians of religions, but are unquestionably responsible for judicial and polit affairs also (Hairi, *Shiʿism and constitutionalism Iran: a study of the role played by the Persian resid of Iraq in Iranian politics*, Leiden 1977, 60). Anṣā lack of interest in social and political issues been criticised by contemporary modernist think Fatḥ ʿAlī Ākhūnd-Zāda, for instance, said: "God not given Anṣārī enough insight to understand Īrān is in the state of collapse and why the Irani are suffering abasement" (*Alifbā-yi djadīd maktūbāt*, Baku 1963, 121), and Aḳā Khān Kirm [*q.v.* above] believed that Anṣārī contributed to people's ignorance and perplexity (Firīdūn Ād iyyat, *Andīshahā-yi Mīrzā Āḳā Khān Kirm* Tehran 1967, 66).

On the other hand, his aloofness from poli was warmly welcomed by the political authorit who seem to have taken it as a sign of his asceticí Thus we come across the reports that the gove of ʿIrāḳ referred to him as the Greatest Fārūḳ one who distinguishes truth from falsehood) that the British Ambassador allegedly said: "An is either Jesus himself or his special deputy on ear (Ḥasan Khān Shaykh Djābirī Anṣārī, *Taʾrī Iṣfahān va Ray va hama-yi djahān*, Tehran 19 e the front cover). The cult formed around him ome people to say that Anṣārī had met with the fth *Imām*.

ṣārī has also been praised in Bābī literature as a man renowned for his tolerance, his wisdom, nderstanding justice, his piety and nobility of acter"; the leader of the Bahā'īs, Mīrzā Ḥusayn Nūrī known as Bahā' Allāh [*q.v.*], included rī among "those doctors who have indeed drunk ie cup of renunciation"; ʿAbbās Efendī (ʿAbd ahā') also referred to Anṣārī as "the illustrious erudite doctor, the noble and celebrated scholar, seal of seekers after truth" (Shoghi Effendi, *God es by*, Wilmette, Illinois 1944, 143). Anṣārī is praised because he did not share the condem- on by other Shīʿī *ʿulamā'* of the Bābī faith and ls. He did not attend the meeting convened he Shīʿī *ʿulamā'* in Kāẓimayn in *ca.* 1863 for mining on the banishment of Bahā' Allāh and adherents from ʿIrāḳ (Muḥammad Khān Zaʿīm awla, *Miftāḥ Bāb al-abwāb*, Cairo 1903, 347). ording to Bābī sources, he did attend the meeting, as soon as he was informed of the *ʿulamā'*'s al design, he left, declaring that he was not ainted with the new faith and that he had not essed in the Bābīs' demeanour anything at ance with Islam (E. G. Browne, ed. and tr., *aveller's narrative written to illustrate the episode e Bāb*, ii, Cambridge, 1891, 86-7).

lthough Bābism appeared at the outset as a ious sect within Shīʿism, it did eventually assume riety of political aspects, aspects which Anṣārī very reluctant to deal with. It seems, therefore, Anṣārī's lack of publicly-expressed opinions here substantially a result of his lack of interest in cautious attitude towards issues of political and ic significance.

nṣārī, however, remote from politics, did train iples who made use of the highly influential tion he had earned for the Shīʿī *ʿulamā'* of ʿIrāḳ their taking part in contemporary social and tical movements; thus Mīrzā Ḥasan Shīrāzī ed a *fatwā* against the Tobacco Concession (cf. *alia*, Firuz Kazemzadeh, *Russia and Britain in sia, 1864-1914*, New Haven 1968, 241 ff.), and rāsānī [*q.v.*] actively supported the 1906-11 sian Revolution and helped to depose the then sian monarch (Abdul-Hadi Hairi, *Why did the mā participate in the Persian Constitutional olution of 1905-1909?*, in *WI*, xvii (1976), 127-54).

Bibliography: In addition to the sources men- oned in the text, see Muḥammad ʿAlī Mudarris, *ayḥānat al-adab*, i, Tabriz 1967; ʿAbbās Ḳummī, *adiyyat al-aḥbāb*, Nadjaf 1929; idem, *Fawā'id -raḍawiyya fī aḥwāl ʿulamā' al-madhhab al- aʿfariyya*, Tehran 1947; idem, *al-Kunā wa -alḳāb*, 3 vols., Nadjaf 1956; ʿAlī Maḥfūẓ, *Sirr aḳā' al-Nadjaf wa-khulūd al-ʿulamā'*, in *Madjallat l-Nadjaf*, no. 10 (1957), 6 ff.; Hamid Algar, *eligion and state in Iran 1785-1905*, Berkeley and os Angeles 1969; Muḥammad Bāḳir Khwānsārī, *awḍāt al-djannāt*, Tehran 1889; Mīrzā Ḥusayn ūrī, *Mustadrak al-wasā'il*, iii, Tehran 1949; Alī al-Wardī, *Lamaḥāt idjtimāʿiyya min ta'rīkh l-ʿIrāḳ al-ḥadīth*, i-iv, Baghdād 1969-74; Ghulām Iusayn Muṣāḥib, ed. *Dā'ira al-maʿārif-i fārsī*, i, 'ehran 1966; ʿAbd al-Ḥusayn Amīnī, *Shuhadā' l-faḍīla*, Nadjaf 1936; Muḥsin al-Mu'min, *al- Vadjaf al-ashraf: ʿUlamā' al-dīn al-aʿlām wa-bayān anhum*, in *Madjallat al-Rābiṭa al-Arabiyya*, no. 193 1938), 28 ff.; Murtaḍā Mudarrisī, *Ta'rīkh-i awābiṭ-i Īrān va ʿIrāḳ*, Tehran 1972; Muḥam- mad Tunukābunī, *Ḳiṣaṣ al-ʿulamā'*, Tehran 1886; Ḥabīb Allāh Sharīf Kāshānī, *Lubb al-albāb fī alḳāb al-aṭyāb*, Tehran 1958; Shaykh Djaʿfar Maḥbūba, *Māḍī al-Nadjaf wa-ḥāḍiruhā*, i, Nadjaf 1958; Muḥammad Ḥusayn Nāṣir al-Shariʿa, *Ta'rīkh-i Ḳum*, Ḳum 1971; Muḥammad ʿAlī Tamīmī, *Mashhad al-Imām*, ii, Nadjaf 1954; Āghā Buzurg Ṭihrānī, *Muṣaffā al-maḳāl fī muṣan- nifī ʿilm al-ridjāl*, Tehran 1959; idem, *al-Dharīʿa ilā taṣānīf al-Shīʿa*, i-xx, 1936-74; idem, *Ṭabaḳāt aʿlām al-Shīʿa*, i-ii, Nadjaf 1954-62; Muḥammad Mahdī al-Aṣfā, *Murūr ḳarnin ʿalā wafāt al-Shaykh al-Anṣārī*, in *Madjallat al-Nadjaf*, iv, no. 8 (1961), 29 ff.; Muḥammad Hāshim Khurāsānī, *Muntakhab al-tawārīkh*, Tehran n.d.; Mullā ʿAlī Wāʿiẓ Khīyā- bānī, *Kitāb-i ʿulamā'-i muʿāṣirīn*, Tabrīz 1946; Naṣr Allāh Turāb Dizfūlī, *Lamaʿāt al-bayān*, n.p., n.d.; Ḥabīb Allāh Rashtī, *Badā'i al-afkār*, Tehran ?, 1895; ʿAlī Akbar Nihāwandī, *Akhlāḳ-i rabīʿī: bunyān-i rafīʿ*, Tehran 1926; Yaḥyā Dawlatābādī, *Ta'rīkh-i muʿāṣir yā ḥayāt-i Yaḥyā*, i, Tehran 1957; Muḥammad Mahdī al-Kāẓimī, *Aḥsan al- wadīʿā*, i-ii, Nadjaf 1968; Homa Pakdaman, *Djamal-Ed-Din Asad Abadi dit Afghani*, Paris 1969; ʿAbbās ʿAlī Kaywān Ḳazwīnī, *Kaywān- nāma*, Tehran 1929; Muḥammad Ṭāhā Nadjafī, *Itḳān al-maḳāl fī aḥwāl al-ridjāl*, Nadjaf 1921; ʿAbd Allāh Mamaḳānī, *Tanḳīh al-maḳāl fī aḥwāl al-ridjāl*, Nadjaf 1933; Djaʿfar Khalīlī, *Mawsūʿa al-ʿAtabāt al-muḳaddasa*, 4 vols., Baghdād 1965-6; ʿAbd al-Raḥīm Muḥammad ʿAlī, *al-Muṣliḥ al- mudjāhid al-Shaykh Muḥammad Kāẓim al-Khurā- sānī*, Nadjaf 1972; Nādjī Wadāʿa, *Lamaḥāt min ta'rīkh al-Nadjaf*, i, Nadjaf 1973; Muḥammad Muʿīn, *Farhang-i aʿlām*, v, Tehran 1966, under "Anṣārī"; Murtaḍā Āl Yāsīn, *Uslūb al-dirāsa al-dīniyya fī madrasa al-Nadjaf*, in *Madjallat al-Nadjaf*, i, no. 3 (1956), 2 ff.; ʿAbd Allāh al- Mudarris al-Ṣādiḳī al-Iṣfahānī, *Lu'lu' al-ṣadaf fī ta'rīkh al-Nadjaf*, Iṣfahān 1959; ʿAbbās Iḳbāl, *Ḥudjdjat al-Islam Ḥādjdj Sayyid Muḥammad Bāḳir Shaftī*, in *Yādgār*, v, no. 10 (1949), 28-43; Mīrzā Ḥusayn Hamadānī, *Ta'rīkh-i djadīd*, ed. E. G. Browne, Cambridge 1893; Ismāʿīl Rā'īn, *Ḥuḳūḳ bigīrān-i Ingilīs dar Iran*, Tehran 1969; Khān Malik Sāsānī, *Dast-i pinhān-i siyāsat-i Ingilīs dar Īrān*, Tehran 1950; Muḥammad ʿAlī Muḥammad Riḍā Ṭabasī, *Dhikrā Shaykhinā al- Anṣārī baʿd ḳarnin*, Nadjaf 1961 (?); art. *Anṣārī, Shaykh Murtaḍā*, in *Lughat-nama-yi Dihkhudā*, no. 86, 1963, 408; Ḍiyā' al-Dīn al-Dakhīlī, *Ta'rīkh al-ḥayāt al-ʿilmiyya fī djāmiʿ al-Nadjaf al-ashraf*, in *Madjallat al-risāla*, vi (1938), 1509-11, 1555-8.

(ABDUL-HADI HAIRI)

ANTHROPOID [see ḳird].

ANZARŪT, greek σαρκοκολλα, is a gum-resin from a thorn-bush which cannot be identified with certainty; known from antiquity, it is used for medical purposes. Synonyms are: *anzarūṭ*, *ʿanzarūt*, *kuḥl fārisī*, *kuḥl kirmānī*; in Persian: *anzarūt* or *andjarūt*, *tashm* (< *čashm*), *kandjubā*, *kandjudha*, *kandjudak*, *bāzahr-i čashm* (so instead of *zahr djashm*, Anṭākī, *Tadhkira*, see *Bibl.* below). Much has been written on this drug. Formerly, the species Penaea, belonging to the Thymelaeaceae, was generally con- sidered to be the original plant, namely either *Penaea mucronata* L., or *P. Sarcocolla* L. or *P. squamosa* L. But in 1879 W. Dymock was able to prove that at least the Persian Sarcocolla is the product of what he called *Astragalus Sarcocolla* Dym. (Leguminosae). Widely known in antiquity, the drug has practically disappeared from the

European store of medicines, but, according to
Meyerhof, it is still well-known in the Orient, especially in the drugmarket in Cairo.

According to Dioscorides, the yellowish bitter resin
was above all useful for causing new flesh wounds
(σάρξ "flesh"; κόλλα "glue") scar over. Already al-
Kindī used it as component of a good number of
recipes (*Aḳrābāḏhīn*, see *Bibl.* below), among others
for leprosy. The most detailed description is given
by Ibn al-Bayṭār on the basis of Greek and Arabic
sources as well as his own observations. The resin
consumes the festering flesh of putrescent abscesses,
assists the ripening of tumours, carries away mucus
and yellow gall, and is a remedy for inflammations
of the eye, for agglutinating eyelids and for excessive
secretion of the eye. Taken internally, the resin is a
strong purgative, but causes also the hair to fall
out. The best Sarcocolla consists of crushed, white
seeds, mixed with walnut oil. Measured out in different ways, it can be mingled with other drugs
(sagapenum, myrobalanum, aloes, bdellium, etc.).
When taken neat, the resin can be lethal; therefore,
the dose should not be more than $2^1/_4$ *dirham*s. Ibn
al-Bayṭār, however, maintains that he saw in Egypt
women partaking, immediately after a bath, of up
to 4 ounces of *anzarūt*, together with the pulp of
the yellow melon, hoping to increase thus their
corpulence.

Bibliography: Dioscurides, *Materia medica*, ed.
M. Wellmann, ii, Berlin 1906, 102 (= lib. iii, 85);
La 'Materia médica' de Dioscorides, ii (Arab. tr. of
Iṣṭafan b. Basīl) ed. C. E. Dubler and E. Terés,
Tetuán 1952, 280 f.; *The medical formulary or
Aqrābāḏhīn of al-Kindī*, tr. M. Levey, Madison,
etc. 1966, 236 (no. 25); Bīrūnī, *K. al-Ṣaydala*, ed.
Muḥ. Saʿīd, Karachi 1973, Arabic, 70 f., Eng.,
45 f.; Ghāfiḳī, *al-Djāmiʿ fi 'l-adwiya al-mufrada*,
Ms. Rabat, Bibl. Gén. ḳ. 155 I, fols. 26b-27a; *The
abridged version of 'The Book of simple drugs' of
... al-Ghâfiḳî by ... Barhebraeus*, ed. and tr.
M. Meyerhof and G. P. Sobhy, Cairo 1932, no. 37;
Suwaydī, *K. al-Simāt fi asmāʾ al-nabāt*, Ms. Paris
ar. 3004, fol. 15b, 137b; Ibn Biklārish, *K. al-
Mustaʿīnī*, Ms. Naples Bibl. Naz. III, F. 65, fol.
14b; Ibn al-Djazzār, *al-Iʿtimād*, Ms. Ayasofya 3564,
fol. 13b; Zahrāwī, *Taṣrīf*, Ms. Beşir Aǧa 502,
fol. 500a, 7; Maimonides, *Sharḥ asmāʾ al-ʿuḳḳār.
Un glossaire de matière médicale* ... ed. M. Meyerhof, no. 4; Ibn al-Bayṭār, *al-Djāmiʿ*, Būlāḳ 1291,
i, 63 f., tr. L. Leclerc, *Notices et extraits* ... xxiii/1,
Paris 1877, no. 171; Ghassānī, *al-Muʿtamad fi
'l-adwiya al-mufrada* ed. M. al-Saḳḳāʾ, Beirut
1395/1975, 10; *Die pharmakologischen Grundsätze
des Abu Mansur* ... Harawi, tr. A. Achundow,
Halle 1893, no. 34; *Tuḥfat al-aḥbāb*, ed. H. P. J.
Renaud and G. S. Colin, Paris 1934, no. 35; Rāzī,
al-Ḥāwī, xx, Ḥaydarābād 1387/1967, no. 44; Ibn
Sīnā, *Ḳānūn*, i, Būlāḳ, 248; Ibn Hubal, *al-
Mukhtārāt fi 'l-ṭibb*, Ḥaydarābād 1362, ii, 23 f.;
Dāwūd al-Anṭākī, *Tadhkirat ūli 'l-albāb*, Cairo
1371/1952, i, 60; Nuwayrī, *Nihāyat al-arab*, xi,
Cairo 1935, 315; *El Libro Agregà de Serapiom*, ed.
G. Ineichen, ii, Venice 1966, 196; H. G. Kircher,
*Die "einfachen Heilmittel" aus dem "Handbuch
der Chirurgie" des Ibn al-Quff*, Bonn 1967, no. 1;
W. Schmucker, *Die pflanzliche und mineralische
Materia medica im Firdaus al-ḥikma des ʿAlī ibn
Sahl Rabban aṭ-Ṭabarī*, Bonn 1969, no. 79.

(A. DIETRICH)

APE [see ḲIRD].

ʿĀR (A.), "shame, opprobrium, dishonour",
has undergone in North Africa a semantic evolution
analogous to that of the root *ḏh.m.m.* of clas
Arabic, arriving at a sense close to that of *ḏhī*
[*q.v.*], that is to say, of "protection", with nua
which should be taken into account. A formula
as *ʿārī ʿalayk/ʿalīk*, "my shame upon you", con
visibly a threat against the person to whom
addressed and means in effect "the shame sha
yours if you do not grant my request" (cf. W. Mar
Textes arabes de Takroûna, Paris 1925, 200, 2
where the challenge is addressed to a deceased ṣ
and the appeal is for rain). When applied to a li
person the formula presupposes a transfer of
sponsibility accompanied by a mystical sanc
the divine malediction which will not fail to a
the man whose refusal is unjustified. To this s
of *ʿār*, current even in Tunisia, there is adde
Morocco (where the term was adopted by Be
in the form *aʿar*, *lʿar*), a new sense which appea
expressions of the type: *anā f-ʿarǝk* "I am in
ʿār—under your protection" (cf. W. Marçais, *T
arabes de Tanger*, Paris 1911, 396). The sens
"conditional malediction" (E. Westermarck,
*vivances païennes dans la civilisation mahomé
Paris 1935, 87) continues to underly it, and i
"mystical responsibility" (G. Marcy, *Le droit
tumier zemmoûr*, Algiers-Paris 1949, index, s.v. a
we pass into the material world when *ʿār* come
designate the indemnity due in cases of breac
honour.

In fact the "throwing" (Arabic verb: *rma*, Ber
gǝr) of the *ʿār* is effected by means of practice
ready in part attested in the pre-Islamic period,
example touching the pole or the cords of a t
taking a child in one's arms, etc. (see Wellhau
Reste, 223 ff.), which permitted a solitary perso
a fugitive to obtain the status of *dakhīl* or of
and in consequence the protection of an individ
a clan or a tribe (cf. B. Farès, *L'honneur chez
Arabes avant l'Islam*, Paris 1932, 88-9). J. Che
(*Le droit dans la société bédouine*, Paris 1932, 222
has called attention to three terms in current
of which the connotations are close:

(1) *dakhīl* "an oppressed or hunted man who s
the aid of his own tribe", according to a ritual c
prising especially a gesture of humility; this prac
introduced by the formula *anā dākhil ʿalayk*, c
stitutes the *dakhala* and implies, on the part of
beneficiary, a recompense for the services rend
by the protector, henceforward responsible for
conduct of the affair in which his intervention
been sollicited. A much attenuated vestige of
type of requisition survives in the Oriental express
dakhīlak, which means nothing more than "I
you";

(2) *ṭanīb* "a man who, to safeguard his rights
escape from justice or to save his life, leaves
clan of his birth, alone or with his family and g
to establish himself in a different tribe which prom
to assist him". This term is to be linked with *ṭu
"tent-cord" [see KHAYMA], the suppliant being oblig
originally, to touch at least a cord of the t
of the one to whom he appeals; while in Moro
this gesture is still a part of the ritual, it has b
forgotten in the Orient, where the *ṭanīb* pronou
the same formula as the *dakhīl*, but enjoys a wi
protection and owes no indemnity; and

(3) *ḳaṣīr*, also a refugee, but entitled to make
of his prestige among his former group with wh
he has not severed all relations.

In all the cases cited above, the Bedouin who
granted his protection cannot again withdraw
and if he falls short of his obligations, tacit or

he will be forever marked by dishonour. Thus
turn to the primitive sense of the word *ʿār*,
is not however used in the Orient in the same
as in Morocco. J. Chelhod (*op. laud.*, iii), who
lrawn attention to the use of this word to
ıate a spouse (*ʿārī* = my wife), links it to
"nudity, modesty, etc.", but the two words
ɔt belong to the same root and, what is more
'honour" is also used in the same sense (for
l, see A. Jaussen, *Coutumes des Arabes au pays
oab*[2], Paris 1948, 45, n. 3). In this case, *ʿār*
l seem rather to imply the idea that dishonour
l affect the husband who did not protect his
one dare not go so far as to attribute to this
the sense of "protection", but there is found
a notion firmly rooted in the Arab mentality,
otion of honour upon which B. Farès has founded
ntire thesis.

e Moroccan *ʿār* thus implies a transfer of
nsibility and of obligation, for the supplicatee,
cord his protection to the suppliant, in default
hich dishonour falls on the former, who is
ed to give satisfaction to the latter. This transfer
operate in a number of ways, with variable
quences. The most simple consists in saying
ılīk "the *ʿār* on you" and making a material
ct with the person to whom the appeal is
, for example touching the edge of his turban,
ying one's hand upon him or his mount. More
ıs is the case of a man guilty of a crime or a
eed and pursued by his enemies: the pursuit
cease as soon as the suppliant has touched the
or the pole of the tent of the supplicatee or has
trated his home: the result is still more spec-
ar when the latter is an interested party of the
iant's victim. However, in such serious cases a
efficacious means consists in slaughtering an
al (Arabic *dbīḥa*, Berber *tam ghrust*) without
ouncing the *basmala*, so as to preclude the eating
s flesh, on the threshold of the house or at the
ınce of the tent of the member of the alien
to whom appeal has been made. The latter is
ed to grant the request presented in this manner
the instant that he sets foot in the pool of
l or simply perceives it; here the efficacy of the
edure is due to the blood [see DAM, in the Supple-
], which possesses magic power. Finally, to
al for the aid of another tribe, to address a
est to the authorities or to give force to a sub-
on to central government, recourse would made
ıe *tʿargība* which consisted in hamstringing a
, a camel or a bull and placing it in the posture
suppliant.

her procedures are still employed (see E.
ermarck, *op. laud.*, 87-107) which may be
ed over without comment except to recall that
persons sollicited are not permitted to refuse
that they are bound, whatever their inner
ıation, to protect the suppliant, and whatever
circumstances, to provide him with hospitality:
vate house, and in more serious cases where the
as been imposed on the tribe, a mosque, or the
of a saint enjoying a right of asylum rarely
ted.

ere was quoted at the beginning of this article
xample of *ʿār* exercised with regard to a Tunisian
. The Moroccans also use it towards their saints
below), to whom they offer sacrifices to obtain
intercession; they also employ other procedures
ps of stones, votary offerings, etc.) which doubt-
rely more on sympathetic magic than on *ʿār* in
true sense of the word. In the same way, they
assure themselves of the neutrality of *dj*inns by
immolations which could be interpreted as offerings
and therefore unrelated to *ʿār*.

The latter is imposed, so it is understood, to obtain all sorts of things, from the most banal to the most important; to obtain pardon for an offence, to assure oneself of an intervention, to protect oneself from an enemy, to bring about a change of mind on the part of a father who has refused to give his daughter in marriage to a suitor, to oblige the parents of a murdered man to accept the *diya* and not to insist on vengeance on the guilty party; a douar can even impose it on another whose co-operation it is seeking, for example in the harvest.

Women can also have recourse to the *ʿār*, under the same conditions as men or using procedures of their own. In certain Berber tribes of Morocco, a woman who wishes to leave her husband may take refuge in an alien tent or house, kiss a beam or handle the mechanism of a mill: from that moment, the owner of the property must marry her and compensate the abandoned husband, or ... take flight. A fugitive who has succeeded in sucking a woman's nipple obtains her protection and that of her husband, and cases are known of adoption by suckling (see G. Marcy, in *RAfr.*, lxxix (1936), 957-73) or even by simulated suckling [see for instance AL-KĀHINA].

As regards adoption, which does not exist in Islamic law, a particular aspect of *ʿār* in certain Berber tribes is an institution concerning an individual called, with nuances, *amazzal, amzyad, amḥaz, amḥars, awrith*, etc. It occurs in the case of a stranger to the group who, usually after committing some offence in his own clan (also sometimes one refused by a father whose daughter he has asked for in marriage), has imposed the *ʿār* and obtained the protection of another group which he makes henceforward the beneficiary of his work. He becomes *amazzal* when his protector has given to him in marriage his own daughter or another woman over whom he holds the right of *djabr* [*q.v.* in Suppl.]; the marriage-price must be paid in work over a prescribed period. If the head of the family so decides, the *amazzal* may be adopted and may enjoy all the rights of a legitimate son, even though he is the daughter's husband. In certain parlances, a distinction is drawn between the *amḥars*, a term designating the stranger adopted by a man, and the *amazzal* in the true sense of the word; in this last case, a widow who is the head of a family may adopt a stranger whom she makes her concubine and whom she has the right to reject or to marry legally when the pre-arranged marriage-price has been paid in full. This institution gives rise to judicial arrangements, the details of which cannot be discussed here (see G. Marcy, *Zemmour*, index; G. Surdon, *Institutions et coutumes des Berbères du Maghreb*, Tangier-Fez 1938, 244-50).

In spite of the absence, in Berber speech, of an original term to designate *ʿār*, it is quite certain that this custom presents a number of autochtonous features which justify a treatment distinct from that of the ancient *djiwār* and its aspects which define within strict limits the protection accorded by oriental Bedouin to strangers to their tribe. However, orthodox opinion is particularly worried by the practice of throwing one's cloak or turban on the tomb of a saint, or furthermore, of slaughtering an animal there as a form of *ʿār*, and the *fuḳahāʾ* make the comment that the deceased would not be able alone to fulfil the request. They object in other ways besides to the use of the word *ʿār*, and only permit these rites when their object is to obtain the *baraka* of the saint or when an animal is sacrificed for the distribution of its meat to the guardians of the sanctuary (see al-Kattānī, *Salwat al-anfās*, i, 54-6).

Bibliography: In addition to references given in the article, see G. Kampffmeyer, *Texte aus Fes*, Berlin 1909 (text V); E. Westermarck, *Ritual and belief in Morocco*, London 1928; idem, *L'ʿâr, the transference of conditional curses in Morocco*, in *Anthropological essays presented to E. B. Tylor*, Oxford 1907, 361-74; A. Jaussen, *Coutumes des Arabes au pays de Moab*², Paris 1948, 187-220.

(CH. PELLAT)

ARAGHŪN, Arabic name corresponding to the Spanish Aragon. In fact, this word has both a geographical and a political sense. As a geographical term, it refers to a river, dominated by the fortress of Shantamariyya, the first of the defensive system of Navarre (al-Ḥimyarī, *Rawḍ*, no. 105). This water-course rises on the southern slope of the Pyrenees, near Canfranc; after passing the town of Jaca, the Sierra de la Peña diverts it towards the west, watering Berdun, Tiermas, Sangüesa, Rocaforte, Aibar, Caparroso and Villafranca before joining the Arga and flowing into the Ebro in Navarre.

This *Wādī Araghūn* would seem to constitute the natural path of incursion into the Christian kingdom of Navarre. Having followed the river as far as Sangüesa, the Muslim forces followed the course of its tributary the Irati, in the direction of Pamplona. This is to be inferred from *Bayān*, ii, 148, "Muḥammad b. ʿAbd al-Malik al-Ṭawīl marched in 298/911 towards Aragon with the object of capturing Pamplona and linking up there with ʿAbd Allāh b. Muḥammad b. Lubb." This is precisely the route used in the famous campaign of ʿAbd al-Raḥmān III in 312/924. The forces of the caliph, coming from Tudela, attacked the stronghold of Ḳarḳastal/Carcastillo on the river Aragon, Marḳwīz/Marcuella, Sangüesa, Rocaforte and Aibar, Lumbier and Pamplona (*Muḳtabis*, v, 123; *Bayān*, ii, 186; A. Cañada, *La Campaña musulmana de Pamplona. Año 924*, Pamplona 1976). In 325/937 we find the same juxtaposition of details when the general Aḥmad b. Muḥammad b. Ilyās was sent, with 1,500 horsemen, on a reconnaissance expedition, *ilā basīṭ Banbalūna wa-wādī Araghūn* (*Muḳtabis*, v, 271).

For Rāzī it was also a mountain range (*Crónica moro...*, ed. Catalan, Madrid 1975, 48-9) "E en su termino (de Huesca) ha... otro (castillo) que ha nonbre Tolia, yaze cerca de la sierra de Aragon. E Aragon es muy nombrada sierra entre las Españas. E en ella yazen dos castillos muy buenos, el uno ha nonbre Sen e el otro Ben; e yazen en dos peñas que son encima de la sierra de Aragon, e corre por entre ellos un rrio de Flumen... E de las sierras... e logares nombrados en fortaleza, son en aquella tierra que se ayunta con monte Aragon que ha nonbre Monte Negro, e non lo podra pasar ome a cavallo, que ande bien, en menos de tres dias." Al-ʿUdhrī (*Masālik...*, 56) states that the town and district of Huesca "lies in the vicinity of the *Djabal Araghūn*, renowned among the Christians."

If it is accepted that this valley was the route employed by the various Muslim expeditions, not only towards the Christian centre of Jaca but also, and especially, towards Navarre, it must be assumed that it was organised as a "frontier" for the defence of Pamplona. This defensive function would create a centre for resistance and for counter-attacks. The "reconquest" of the valley of the Ebro would been an enterprise of Aragon rather than Na just as Castille had absorbed the old kingdo Leon. The Christian advance at the expense Andalus would henceforward be the product of two "frontier" forces, *Kashtāla* [*q.v.*] and Ara

In fact, these two kingdoms were to share bet themselves their future conquests. This gave ri various formal treaties: Tudellen (1151), Ca (1179) and Almizra (1244) (Roque Chabas, *Di de la conquista de España nueva entre Arag Castilla*, in *Congreso Hist. Aragón*, Barcelona 1 in which were fixed the respective zones of the expansion of Aragon and Castille. The fo having achieved by 1238 its own particular "r quest", turned its attention to the sea. It was that there took shape the broad outlines of its p towards Africa (Ch. E. Dufourcq, *L'Espagne cat et le Maghrib aux XIII et XIV siècles*. Paris 1 the Mediterranean (Corsica, Sardinia, Sicily, an kingdom of Naples—in competition with the Ang dynasty), annexation of part of the Byzantine en (the duchies of Athens and of Neopatria), of island of Cyprus, and commercial relations Mamlūk Egypt (A. Masia de Ros, *La Coron Aragón y los estados del Norte de Africa*, Barce 1951; A. Lopez de Meneses, *Los consulados cata de Alejandria y Damasco en el reinado de Pedro I Ceremonioso*, Saragossa 1956; F. Giunta, *Arag e Catalani nel Mediterraneo*, Palermo 1959; Nicolau d'Olwer, *L'expansio de Catalunya Mediterrania Oriental*, Barcelona 1926). After union of the kingdoms of Aragon and Castill 1474, Spain inherited this interventionist lin the Mediterranean: attempts at invasion of Al in 1519 and 1541 (directed against the piracy of Barbarossa brothers [see ʿARŪDJ and KHAYR AL BARBAROSSA]), conquest of the island of Dj (1520), the capture of La Golletta at Tunis (1 (E. G. Ontiveros, *La politica norteafricana de Carl* Madrid 1950) and the battle of Lepanto AYNABAKHTI] in 1571.

But Araghūn above all has a political sense. cording to al-Ḥimyarī (*Rawḍ*, no. 8), "it is the n of the territory of Gharsiya b. Shandjuh, compri cantons (*bilād*), staging posts (*manāzil*) and distr (*aʿmāl*)". According to Maḳḳarī (*Nafḥ*, ed. Beiru 137), "The fifth region passed through Toledo Saragossa and their environs, towards the terri of Aragon, to the south of which lies Barcelor As a political concept, its borders were consta changing. Just as al-Andalus did not cease to c tract in the course of the centuries, *Araghūn* stantly expanded. So its history is founded on recession of the Muslim *thaghr al-aʿlā* [*q.v.*], sc the Upper March. Its growth took place at expense of the neighbouring Hispano-Arab sta the Banū Ḳasī, Tudjībids, Banu 'l-Ṭawīl, B Hūd, Banū Razīn, Almoravids, Banū Ghāniya Banū Mardanīsh [*q.vv.*], following a continuous vance during the 11th-13th centuries. The princ landmarks of this "reconquest" are the taking Graus (1083), Monzón (1089), Alquézar (10 Almenara (1093), Huesca (1096), Barbastro (11 Balaguer (1105), Ejea and Tauste (1106), Tama (1107), Morella and Belchite (1117), Saragossa (11 Tarazona and Tudela (1119), Calatayud and Dar (1120), Alcañiz (1124), Tortosa (1148), Lérida, Fr and Mequinenza (1149), Teruel (*ca.* 1157), Valdero (1169), Caspe (1171), Majorca (1229), Morella (12 Burriana (1233), Peñiscola (1234), Ibiza (12 Valencia (1238) and Minorca (1287). The expans astile was fundamentally local, while that of on took place in a wider context. Alfonso I was sense a crusader. The author of the *Ḥulal ḥiyya* (76) tells us that for his epic raid in 6 against the Levante and Andalusia—which ght back numerous Mozarabs [*q.v.*]—"He chose, bled and equipped 4,000 horsemen of Aragon, n they selected with their squires. They agreed wore by the Gospel that not one of them would t his companion". First of all, a psychological sive took place (articles by D. M. Dunlop, tler and A. Turki, in *Al-Andalus*, 1952, 1963 1966; Chalmeta in *RUM*, xx, 1972), followed e Council of Toulouse in 1118 which proclaimed xpedition against Muslim Spain. There was also cipation by numerous French troops, creating ater "mass movement" and a change of tactics. nical innovations (catapults and mobile siege- rs built by an expert, a veteran of the sieges of , Antioch, and especially Jerusalem, Gaston de n) made possible the capture of strongholds rto impregnable. The great campaigns of James I Conqueror (the Balearic islands in 1229 and ncia in 1238) were also to be considered as a de (R. I. Burns, *The Crusader kingdom of ncia*, Cambridge, Mass. 1967). The royal house ragon was systematically more tolerant than le towards the conquered Muslims. The treaties pitulation seem all to have been inspired by eed to retain labourers and peasants (hence this a policy different from "repopulation"). The example was to be that of the conquest of ncia by the Cid in 1094. Those, subsequently, aragossa, Tudela and Tortosa, as well as the ones signed by James I, also correspond to scheme (R. M. Menendez Pidal, *La España del* Madrid 1956, 483-93; R. I. Burns, *Islam under rusaders*, Princeton 1973, 118-38, 173-83). These mstances explain the importance of the Mudéjars and Macho Ortega, *Condición social de los ejares aragoneses* (s. *XV*) in *Mem. Fac. Fa. goza*, i (1923), 137-319, and L. Piles, *La situación l de los moros de realengo en la Valencia del V*, Madrid 1949), and later of the Moriscoes and T. Halperin Donghi, *Un conflicto nacional: scos y cristianos viejos en Valencia*, in *CHE*, -xxiv (1955), 5-115; xxv-xxvi (1957), 83-250; , *Recouvrements de civilisation: les morisques du ume de Valence au XVI s.*, in *Annales*, xi (1956), 32; J. Reglá, *Estudios sobre los moriscos*, Valencia ; M. S. Carrasco Urgoiti, *El problema morisco Aragón al comienzo del reinado de Felipe II*, ncia 1969) in these regions where they were st always vassals of local lords and bore the e of "exarico"/*sharīk* (E. Hinojosa, *Mezquinos y icos. . .*, in *Obras*, Madrid 1948, 245-56). It is permanence of this *modus vivendi* which explains fact that the vast majority of aljamiada [*q.v.*] ature comes from this region.

r the Arab historians, *Araghūn* means not only gion but also all the territories of the political y embodied in the Kingdom of Aragon. In this ext are included Catalonia, the Balearic Islands Valencia. Al-Marrakūshī (*Muʿḏjib*, 50-1, 235, defines its extent in 621/1224 thus: "The Banū possessed the towns of this region (al-Andalus), osa and its environs, Saragossa and its environs, a, Lérida and Calatayud. They are now in the ls of the "Franks", belonging to the prince of elona, and constitute the country known as ghūn. The latter has the borders of the kingdom Barcelona, to the French frontier. Neighbouring the Banū Hūd, there used to be Abū Marwān ʿAbd al-Malik b. ʿAbd al-ʿAzīz. . . who possessed Valencia and its surrounding territory. The Frontier was under the control of Abū Marwān b. Razīn, whose rule extended as far as the frontiers of Toledo. The four parts of Spain are ruled by four kings: one is constituted by the afore-mentioned Aragon and lies to the south-east. . . The first town, at the south-east border on the Mediterranean coast, is Barcelona, followed by Taragona, then Tortosa. In this region, the non-coastal cities are Saragossa, Lérida, Fraga, and Calatayud all under the rule of the king of Barcelona. It is the region called *Araghūn*". For Ḥimyarī (*Rawḍ*, no. 182), "Majorca lies one day's sail from Barcelona, *min bilād Araghūn*", and in 636/1238 "the Rūm entered into possession of Valencia, demanding capitulation and James/ *Ḏjākmuh malik Araghūn* took control of it". Finally, we find the equation *Araghūn* = the territories of the Kingdom of Aragon clearly expressed in the 14th century. Ibn Khaldūn (*ʿIbar*, ed. Beirut, iv, 395) declares: "As for the king of Barcelona, in the Levante of al-Andalus, his territories are extensive and his kingdom is great. The latter includes Barcelona, Aragon, Jativa, Saragossa, Valencia, Dénia, Majorca, and Minorca." Speaking of the taking of Valencia by James I, he describes him as *malik* or *ṭāghiyat Araghūn*.

The origin of the future Navarre-Aragon heartland apparently dates back to the period of the Muslim invasions. It seems in fact that the Arabs only penetrated fairly superficially into the region of the Pyrenees (F. Codera, *La dominación arabiga en la Frontera Superior*, Madrid 1879; idem, *Limites probables de la conquista arabe en la cordillera pirenaica*, in *BRAH* (1906); J. Millas Vallicrosa, *La conquista musulmana de la region pirenaica*, in *Pirineos* (1946), ii, 53-67). Thus "the regions lying beyond the sierras of Santo Domingo and Guara, of Alquézar in Sobrarbe, Roda in Ribagorza, Agar in Pallars, like the highlands of Urgel, Bergada, Ripolles and Besalu in Catalonia" were not occupied.

Although the texts lack precision, they agree in asserting that Mūsā b. Nuṣayr [*q.v.*] conquered Saragossa in 96/714. He marched for twenty days and captured a sea-port town, probably Taragona, if we are to believe the *Cronica del moro Rasis* (41-2), which attributes this deed to "Tarife, el fijo de Nazayr". Pamplona capitulated before 100/718, during the emirate of al-Ḥurr, and the *tābiʿis* ʿAlī b. Rabāḥ al-Lakhmī and Ḥanash b. ʿAbd Allāh al-Ṣanʿānī (Ibn al-Faraḍī, no. 913) countersigned it. This was hardly a durable submission, since "ʿUḳba conquered Narbonne. . . . Pamplona, where he established Muslims" (*Bayān*, ii, 29) and the *amīr* Yūsuf hurried thither with clearly insufficient forces, "Sulaymān b. Shihāb and al-Ḥusayn b. Dadjn against the Vascons of Pamplona" (*Akhbār madjmūʿa*, 75). After seven years of siege, Huesca surrendered (al-ʿUḏhrī, 56-7) on conditions similar to those of Tudmīr [*q.v.*], under the governorship of al-Ḥurr or of al-Samḥ: "When the Muslims penetrated into Spain, the inhabitants of the mountain fortresses of Lérida and the High Aragon made a pact with them, and paid them tribute, without any argument" (*Crónica Rasis*, 42-3).

In 132/750, the situation of the valley of the Ebro began to pose serious problems when Yūsuf al-Fihrī sent there, as *wālī*, his adviser and *alter ego* al-Ṣumayl. In 136/753, there broke out the rebellion of ʿĀmir and the Banū Zuhra b. Kilāb, who, at the head of a coalition of Yemenīs and Berbers besieged him in

Saragossa. The Ḳaysīs relieved al-Ṣumayl while ʿAbd al-Raḥmān I attempted a crossing to Spain. (*Akhbār*, 62-79). Later the *amīr* sent there his trusted lieutenant, the *mawlā* Badr. The Yemenīs Sulaymān b. Yaḳẓān al-Kalbī and al-Ḥusayn b. Yaḥyā al-Anṣārī, by promising Saragossa to Charlemagne, encouraged him to undertake his ill-fated expedition of 778. This Upper March was always an extremely volatile zone and politically very unstable. We find there the Tudjībid Banū Salama in the region of Huesca, ousted by the "reign" of Bahlūl b. Marzūḳ. The loyal ʿAmrūs b. Yūsuf re-established authority there in the name of al-Ḥakam I, but the representative of the *muwallad* family of the Banū Ḳasī, Mūsā b. Mūsā [*q.v.*], rebelled in 842 at Tudela, took possession of Saragossa and Huesca and declared himself the "third king of Spain". To curb him, the *amīr* Muḥammed installed at Calatayud and Daroca the Tudjībid Banū Muhādjir who, having succeeded, transformed themselves into autonomous "lords" of the March of a more-than-changeable loyalty. In the north, we find in the 10th century the Banū Shabrīṭ b. al-Ṭawīl at Huesca. All these peoples did not hesitate to play the Franks, the Arabs, the *muwallads* and the Navarro-Aragonese (with whom they had family ties) off against their rivals, Muslim as well as Christian. Such was also the policy of the Banū Hūd, who employed the Cid and were able for a long time to balance the ambitions of the Almoravids, the Aragonese, the Catalans, the Navarrese and the Castillians. In fact, it seems that, in about 228/843 there was legal recognition of the North-Pyrenean enclaves by the emirate of Cordova. Thanks to an annual tribute of 700 *dīnārs* and the status of vassalage, there was *iḳrār* [*q.v.*] of the territories of Iñigo and of Sancho (al-ʿUdhrī, 30).

Bibliography: In addition to sources mentioned in the article, see J. Alemany, *La geografía de la Peninsula ibérica en los autores árabes*, Granada 1921; C. Dubler, *Las laderas del Pirineo según al-Idrīsī*, in *Andalus*, xviii (1953), 337-73; F. Ḥernandez, *El Monte y la provincia del Puerto*, in *ibid.* xvii, (1952) 319-68; H. Monès, *Taʾrīkh al-djughrāfiya... fi 'l-Andalus*, Madrid 1967; Afif Turk, *El reino de Zaragoza en el s. XI*, Madrid 1975; J. Bosch, *Historia de Albarracin musulmán*, Teruel 1959; J. Font y Rius, *La reconquista de Lérida*, Lérida 1949; A. Huici Miranda, *Historia de Valencia musulmana*, Valencia 1969; J. Lacarra, *Historia del reino de Navarra*, Pamplona 1972; idem, *La conquista de Zaragoza por Alfonso I*, in *Andalus*, xii, (1947), 65-96; idem, *La reconquista y repoblación del valle del Ebro*, in *Est. E. M. C. Aragón*, ii (1946), 39-83; idem, *La repoblación de Zaragoza por Alfonso el Batallador*, in *Est. Ha. Social, Esp.* Madrid 1949, 205-23; idem, *Origenes del condado de Aragón*, Saragossa 1945; E. Lévi-Provençal, *Hist. Esp. mus.*, index; J. Millas, *El texts d'historiadors musulmans referentes a la Catalunya carolingia*, in *Quadernos d'Estudi*, xiv (1922); M. Pallares Gil, *La frontera sarracena en tiempo de Berenguer IV*, in *Bol. Ha. Geo. Bajo Aragón*, iv (1907). (P. CHALMETA)

ARAT, REŠHĪD RAḤMETĪ, up to 1934 G. R. RACHMATI, modern Turkish REŞİD RAHMETİ ARAT, Turkish scholar and philologist (1900-64). Born at Eski Üdjüm, to the south-west of Kazan, he was the son of ʿAbd al-Reshīd ʿIṣmet Allāh, of a family of *mudarrisūn* who emigrated from Kazan and set up a "hereditary" *madrasa* there. He attended various schools in his home town, and later in Ḳizīlyar (Petropavlovsk) and in Harbin in Manchuria where he finished high school (1921). He joined cu associations of the Kazan Tatars in Harbin contributed to various papers. In December 19 left for Germany and he enrolled in Berlin Unive where he was trained in Turkish philology by Bang. He obtained his Ph. D. in 1927 with a on *Die Hilfsverben und Verbaladverbien im Altai* which was published in *Ural-altäische Jahrb* viii/1-4 (1927), 1-66. He then joined the tea staff of the Department of Oriental languages a University. In the same year he married Dr. R also from the Kazan area, whom he had m Harbin. In 1928 he was made a research assista the Prussian Academy. In 1933, following the versity reform in Turkey, he was offered the of Turkish philology in the University of Ist where he taught until his death. He was the di of the Institute of Turcology (1940-50) founde Fuʾād Köprülü in 1924 and a visiting profess the SOAS London (1949-51). He died in Istanb 29 November 1964. R. R. Arat, who contri greatly in introducing the historic and compa approach to studies of Turkish language and dia was a scholar who preferred to limit his efforts given area and to deepen it rather then spread many problems and cognate fields. He rem strictly interested in linguistic and philological lems and text criticism. He is the author of th lowing major works: *Zur Heilkunde der Uig* 2 vols, Berlin 1930-2; *Die Legende von Oghuz Q* (with W. Bang), Berlin 1932; *Türkische Turfan* vii, Berlin 1936; *Un yarlık de Mehmed II, le quérant*, in *Annali RISON*, xx (1940); Bābur, *V* 2 vols, Ankara, 1943-6; *Ḳutadgu Bilig* (critica tion), Istanbul 1947; *ʿAtebetü 'l-ḥaḳāyiḳ* (critica tion and modern Turkish paraphrase), Istanbul *Yusuf Has Hacib, Kutadgu bilig* (Modern Tu paraphrase), Ankara, 1959; *Türk şivelerinin ta* fn *TM*, x (1953), 59-139 (a summary of form tempts to classify Turkish dialects, together w new proposal; under the influence of his own di Arat insisted on using the term *şive* (accent) in of *lehçe* (dialect) of standard Turkish); *Eski türk* (Pre-Islamic and early Islamic Turkish verse, modern Turkish paraphrase and notes), posthu Ankara 1965.

Bibliography: *Reşit Rahmeti Arat icin—A* morial volume published by Türk Kültü Araştırma Enstitüsü, Ankara 1966, pp. x, (the principal source for biographical and b graphical data on Arat up to the date of lication). (FAHİR

ARBAʿŪN ḤADĪTHAN, a genre of lite and religious works centred round 40 *ḥadīt* the Prophet.

This type of work has arisen, from one aspect, the *ḥadīth* which says "The member of my munity who learns 40 *ḥadīths* connected wit prescriptions of the faith will be raised to li God among the authorities on the law and scholars", and from another aspect, from ce secondary factors: the desire to be covered b Prophet's grace, the hope of escaping the to of hell-fire, the intention of enabling oneself t the great ones, etc.

Works in this category of *arbaʿūn ḥadīthan* be written in prose, verse or in the two comb The contents may also differ; some writers compilers are content to gather together the *ḥa* others add to them explanations, whilst yet o adorn and complete these texts by means of acco *āyāt* and homilectic material. The elements of is general category are selected according to ing principles: *aḥādīth̲ ḳudsiyya*, of divine ·ation [see ḤADĪTH ḲUDSĪ]; *k̲h̲uṭba*s of the het; *ḥadīth̲*s chosen from amongst those texts for learning by heart; etc. *Arbaʿūn* collections lso found centred on a particular subject: the ties of the Ḳurʾān, the essential principles of , the Prophet and his Companions (or even his en and grandchildren), sects and mysticism, ledge and the scholar, politics and law, the war, social and moral life, etc.

e genre is called *čihil ḥadīth̲* by the Persians and *hadīth̲* by the Turks. It developed first of all in ic and developed extensively. Amongst the t collections are those of Abū Bakr al-Ād̲j̲urrī 30/942) and of Ibn Wadʿān (d. 494/1101). But most celebrated is that put together by Muḥyī Abū Zakariyyāʾ Yaḥyā al-Nawawī (631-76/ 77), the object of numerous commentaries in ic and translations into other Islamic languages. first *čihil ḥadīth̲* collections in Persian which come down to us were written in the 6th-7th/ 13th centuries, sc. the *Ṭabīb al-ḳulūb* of Muḥam- b. Muḥammad b. ʿAlī al-Farawī and *al-Arbaʿūn hāʾī* of ʿImād al-Dīn Ḥasan b. ʿAlī. However, most famous and most widely-disseminated col- n is that composed in quatrains, the *Tard̲j̲uma- baʿīn ḥadīth̲* of ʿAbd al-Raḥmān D̲j̲āmī (817-98/ 92). The works of Nawawī and D̲j̲āmī were lated into Turkish and published on many ions.

should further be noted that the Turks not only ciated highly the genre in question, but also osed didactic works full of teaching points. The t one of these in Turkish known to us is the *i al-farādīs* of Maḥmūd b. ʿAlī (8th/14th cen- , followed in the next one by Kemāl Ummī slation after 815/1412) and also ʿAlī S̲h̲īr Newāʾī 906/1441-1501), and then in the 10th/16th cen- by Fuḍūlī (?885-963/?1480-1556), Uṣūlī (d. 568), Newʿī (942-1007/1535-99), ʿĀs̲h̲ıḳ Čelebi iʿa (translation 979/1571) and Muṣṭafā ʿĀlī slation 1005/1597). This work of translation urther pursued with enthusiasm in succeeding ries, the most important works being those of ned K̲h̲āḳānī (1011/1603), Ismāʿīl Rusūk̲h̲ī (d. 1631), Yūsuf Nabī (1052-1124/1642-1712), ʿOth- zāde Tāʾib (1120/1708), Münīf (1145/1733), r Ḍiyāʾ al-Dīn (publ. 1326/1908) and Aḥmed n (publ. 1343/1925).

Bibliography: Abdülkadir Karahan, *Islâm- rk edebiyatında kırk hadîs*, Istanbul 1954; idem, *mîʾin Erbaînʾi ve türkçe tercümeleri*, Istanbul 52; idem, *Türk edebiyatında arapçadan nakledil- kırk hadîs tercüme ve şerhleri*, Istanbul 1954; m, *Aperçu général sur les quarante ḥadīth̲s dans littérature islamique*, in *SI*, iv (1955), 39-55.

(ABDÜLKADIR KARAHAN)

GHIYĀN, the name found in mediaeval times district of northern K̲h̲urāsān. It lay to outh of Kūčān/K̲h̲abūs̲h̲ān [*q.v.*], straddling the region of the modern Kūh-i S̲h̲āh D̲j̲ahān and Kūh-i Binālūd, around the sources of the Kas̲h̲af- It is not to be identified with the district of jarm [*q.v.* in Suppl.] lying further to the west, s done by Le Strange, *The lands of the Eastern hate*, 392, an error perpetuated by B. Spooner s *Arghiyān. The area of Jājarm in western āsān*, in *Iran, Jnal. of the British Institute of an Studies*, iii, (1965), 97-107). The name of iyān's *chef-lieu*, Rāwnīr, appears in the *Ḥudūd am*, tr. Minorsky, 103, as Rāwīnī (restored by Aubin as Rāwnīr, see Bibl.); the correct form Rāw(a)- nīr is further given in Yāḳūt, *Buldān*, ed. Beirut, i, 153, as the *ḳaṣaba* of this district of 71 villages, and by Samʿānī, *Ansāb*, ed. Hyderabad, i, 167-70, who visited the district personally and who has a long list of the *ʿulamāʾ* of Arg̲h̲iyān.

In Tīmūrid times, we find the administrative coupling D̲j̲ahān u Arg̲h̲iyān, and then in the Ṣafawid period, D̲j̲ahān-i Arg̲h̲iyān is linked with the district of Kalīdar (thus as a single *tiyuldār* under S̲h̲āh Ṣafī in 1046/1636). By modern times, however, the name of Arg̲h̲iyān dropped out of usage.

Bibliography: In addition to the sources mentioned in the article, see the penetrating dis- cussion of J. Aubin in *Réseau pastoral et réseau caravanier. Les grand' routes du Khurassan à l'époque mongole*, in *Le monde iranien et l'Islam*, i (Geneva-Paris 1971), 109 ff. (C. E. BOSWORTH)

ʿĀRIF ČELEBĪ, dervish mystic, grandson of Mawlānā D̲j̲alāl al-Dīn Rūmī and the third *k̲h̲alīfa* of the Mawlawiyya order, was born at Konya on 8 D̲h̲u 'l-Ḳaʿda 670/7 June 1272 as a son to Sulṭān Walad and Fāṭima K̲h̲ātūn, the daughter of the goldsmith Ṣalāḥ al-Dīn. His actual name was D̲j̲alāl al-Dīn Farīdūn. Mawlānā, who named him thus after his two grandfathers, gave him also the by-name Amīr ʿĀrif, from which the commonly-used Turkish form Ulu ʿĀrif has been derived.

An extensive biography with many hagiographic traits is contained in the eighth chapter of the *Manāḳib a'-ʿārifīn* by Aflākī [*q.v.*]. Being one of ʿĀrif's pupils, Aflākī was an eyewitness to a great part of his life and accompanied him on a number of his travels. ʿĀrif frequently wandered through Anatolia, but he made journeys to ʿIrāḳ and Persia as well. On one occasion, Sulṭān Walad sent him to the court of the Īl-K̲h̲ān at Sulṭāniyya to remonstrate against the pro-S̲h̲īʿa policy adopted by Öld̲j̲eytü. In 712/1312, ʿĀrif succeeded his father as the head of the Mawlawiyya. His death occurred at Konya on 23 D̲h̲u 'l-Ḥid̲j̲d̲j̲a 719/5 November 1320. His tomb is still extant in the Mawlawī *türbe*.

The anecdotes related by Aflākī depict ʿĀrif as a colourful personality. Through his conduct, he ex- pressed the antinomian tendencies inherent in the Mawlawī tradition from its origin. He acted like a *rind* dervish and indulged in long and exhaustive *samāʿ* sessions which often gave rise to scandal.

Unlike his ancestors, ʿĀrif was neither prominent as a scholar nor as a writer. The only works known to us are collections of his *g̲h̲azal*s and his quatrains which were all written in Persian. The rareness of these poems both in separate manuscripts and in collections of Mawlawī poetry suggests that they were not very highly appreciated in the literary tradition of the order. A manuscript in the Leiden University Library contains a collection of ʿĀrif's *g̲h̲azal*s and *rubāʿī*s under the heading *al-Asrār al-ʿĀrifiyya* (Or. 1676 B/8, ff. 89a-130a).

Bibliography: Aflākī, *Manāḳib al-ʿārifīn*, ed. Tahsin Yazıcı, Ankara 1961, ii, 825-974; H. Ritter, *Philologika XI*, in *Isl.*, xxvi (1942), 127; Feridun Nafiz Uzluk, *Ulu Ârif Çelebinin rubaileri*, Istanbul 1949; Abdülbaki Gölpinarli, *Mevlanâʾdân sonra Mevlevilik*, Istanbul 1953, 65-95; idem, *Mevlânâ Müzesi yazmalar kataloğu*, Ankara 1971-2, ii, 211; iii, 21 f. (J. T. P. DE BRUIJN)

ʿĀRIF, MĪRZĀ ABU 'L-ḲĀSIM, Persian revo- lutionary poet and satirist, was born in Ḳazwīn *ca.* 1880, and after studying Persian, Arabic, callig- raphy and music, became a *rawḍak̲h̲ʷān*, an occu- pation that he abandoned after his father's death

At 17 he married a young girl against her parents' wishes, and two years later was obliged to divorce her; he never married again. Leaving for Tehran, he took service at the court of Muẓaffar al-Dīn Shāh, where his singing attracted the attention of the sovereign and leading courtiers. Court life, however, did not appeal to him, and he returned to Ḳazwīn, where he remained until the 1906 Constitutional Revolution, of which he was one of the leading spirits. His outspoken and reckless verses, usually sung at public concerts, made him many enemies, including even his former friend the poet Īradj Mīrzā. In 1915 he joined the *muhādjarat* to Kirmānshāh, whence he went to Istanbul, returning to Persia in 1919. During the next few years he gave his support successively to Col. Muḥammad Taḳī Khān, the dissident gendarmerie officer in Khurāsān, Sayyid Ḍiyāʾ, and Riḍā Khān. In 1924 he campaigned in favour of the establishment of a republic, but after the accession of Riḍā Khān to the throne he was unable to continue his public concerts, and retired on a small government pension to Hamadān, where he died in poverty in 1934. His *Dīwān* was published in Berlin in 1924 together with an autobiography on the lines of Rousseau's *Confessions*.

ʿĀrif was a man of dervish-like disposition, and had no use for material wealth or respect for authority and position. His poetry is full of social satire, attacks on corruption, and nostalgia for Persia's great past, all couched in popular language free from classical artificialities.

Bibliography: After the edition of ʿĀrif's *Dīwān* published by Riḍā-zāda Shafaḳ, in Berlin 1924, further writings appeared in M. R. Hazār, *ʿĀrif-nāma-yi Hazār*, Shīrāz 1935, and Sayyid Hādī Ḥāʾirī Kūrūsh, *Djild-i duwwum-i dīwān-i ʿĀrif*, Tehran 1942. Biographical information is to be found in E. G. Browne, *Press and poetry of modern Persia*, Cambridge 1914, 250-2; M. Ishaque, *Sukhanwarān-i Īrān dar ʿaṣr-i ḥāḍir*, i, Calcutta 1933, 191-218; Rashīd Yāsimī, *Adabiyyāt-i muʿāṣir*, Tehran 1937, 69-70; M. Ishaque, *Modern Persian poetry*, Calcutta 1943, *passim*; Sayyid Muḥammad Bāḳir Burḳaʿī, *Sukhanwarān-i nāmī-yi muʿāṣir*, i, Tehran 1950, 159-61; J. Rypka, *Iranische Literaturgeschichte*, Leipzig 1959, 352-3; ibid., *History of Iranian literature*, Dordrecht 1968, 372-3; Bozorg Alavi, *Geschichte und Entwicklung der modernen persischen Literatur*, Berlin 1964, 36-44. (L. P. Elwell-Sutton)

ʿĀRIFĪ, Mawlānā Maḥmūd, Persian poet. Virtually nothing is known of the life of ʿĀrifī except the approximate dates of his birth and death (791-853/1389-1449), and that he belonged to the circle of poets that flourished at the court of Shāh Rukh [*q.v.*] in the first half of the 9th/15th century.

The best-known of his works is a brief *mathnawī* of some 500 *bayt*s entitled *Gūy u čūgān* or *Ḥālnāma*, which he composed in just two weeks during his fiftieth year to honour a prince Muḥammad, assumed to be Muḥammad b. Bāysonḳor (Browne, *LHP*, iii, 496). The subject of the poem is a mystical romance between a dervish and a prince whom he first sees playing polo. The game of polo provides the predominant imagery. R. S. Greenshields published an edition of this work, of which there are many good manuscripts, in 1931, and a translation of it under the title *The Ball and polo stick or Book of ecstasy*, in 1932 (both at London).

According to Dawlat-Shāh, ʿĀrifī was the author of numerous panegyrics of the kings and princes of his day, and of *ghazal*s and *ḳiṭʿas* as well. The same source says that in addition he composed ten l[...] in verse addressed to Khʷādja Pīr Aḥmad b. [...] and a versified work on Ḥanafī *fiḳh* called *M*[...] *budd madhhab Imām Aʿẓam*. None of these [...] has yet been published.

Although the authors of contemporary *tadh*[...] credit him with an elegant style and conside[...] popularity, in the modern period his works [...] received only cursory mention.

Bibliography: ʿAlīshīr Nawāʾī, *Madjāli*[...] *nafāʾis, madjlis-i awwal*; Dawlat-Shāh, *Tadh*[...] ed. Browne, 439-40; Browne, *LHP*, iii, 490, 4[...] E. Yār-Shāṭir, *Shiʿr-i fārsī dar ʿahd-i Shāh*[...] Tehran 1334/1956, 101-2, 176-8, 216-7. (J. W. Clint[...]

ARĪN [see ḳubbat al-arḍ].

ARNAB (A.), pl. *arānib*, in poetry, *al*-[...] Grammatically this noun is feminine and de[...] the hare, with the general meaning of a le[...] either as a collective noun, or specifically the doe [...] (see Ch. Pellat, *Sur quelques noms d'animau*[...] *arabe classique*, in *GLECS*, viii, 95-9). In al[...] Arabic dialects the term maintains this mea[...] but in Maghribī two plural forms are found, *ra*[...] and *arnānib*. Today its archaic synonym *ḳuwāʿ* [...] *ḳuwāʿa*) seems to have been forgotten. Arabic [...]cographers relate *arnab* to a root *r-n-b* (see [...] according to the rules of triliteralism, but its [...]mology should perhaps be sought in Sumeria[...] Akkadian, from which a number of animal and [...] names in Arabic are derived (like *dhiʾb*, *gh*[...] *iwazz*, *kurkī* etc.). Semantic equivalents to *arna*[...] *khargūsh* in Persian, *tavsan* in Turkish, *awtu*[...] *iwtal*, fem. *tawtult*, pl. *tiwtalin*) in Berber o[...] Maghrib, *emerwel* (pl. *imerwelen*, fem. *teme*[...] pl. *timerwelīn*) from the verb *erwel*, "to flee" [...] Tamahaḳ, while *abekni* (pl. *ibekniten*, fem. *tab*[...] pl. *tibeknītīn*) is little used.

Among the order of lagomorphs and the fam[...] leporids, the genus *lepus* is represented in Is[...] lands predominantly by the *lepus capensis* or [...] hare. Its breeding ground stretches from Africa ([...] of Good Hope) to China (Shantung, bordering o[...] Yellow Sea of Asia). In the Mediterranean zone [...] found with the plains species, *l. granatensis* (S[...] *l. schlumbergeri* and *l. sherif* (Morocco), *l. me*[...] *raneus* and *l. kabylicus* (Algeria) *l. tunetae* (Tu[...] and *l. rotschildi* (Egypt); in western Morocc[...] smaller *l. atlanticus* is also found. In the hill[...] found *l. marocanus* and *l. pediaeus* (Morocco)[...] *l. sefranus* (Algeria). The characteristically d[...] hare, *l. arabicus*, is found on the borders o[...] Sahara, together with *l. pallidior*, *l. harterti* [...] *l. barcaeus*, from Morocco to the Sinai peninsu[...] systematic study of the hares of the Arabian P[...]sula has yet to be made. The species *l. europa*[...] represented in the Near East in several iso[...] places as well as *l. syriacus* (Lebanon) and *l. j*[...] (Palestine).

Literary authorities differ about the gender c[...] noun *arnab*; some see it as masculine with a[...]sociated feminine *arnaba* (see *al-Ifṣāḥ fī fiḳh al-l*[...] Cairo 1929, 391), but country people, both sede[...] and nomadic, knew from very early times h[...] distinguish the sex and age of hares by a sp[...] terminology which is unambiguous. The mal[...] buck, was called *khuzaz* (pl. *khizzān*, *akhizz*[...] *ḥawshab* or *ḳuffa* (Maghribī *ʿakrūsh*). The fema[...] doe, was named *ʿikrisha* (Saʿūdī, *ʿidana*); [...] suckling she was called *djaḥmarish*. The levre[...] called *khirniḳ* (pl. *kharāniḳ*) or the *khawtaʿ*, an[...] weanling *suḥla* (Maghribī *kharbūsh*, *ḥarbūsh*; Tam[...]

ḏewel, pl. iberḏewēlen, fem. teberḏewelt, pl. tiber-ʾlīn). From an ethnological point of view, these ıtry folk knew the habits of the hare in detail its simple form or lair (*makā* / *makʾ* / *makw*, pl. *ʾ*, *khitl*, Maghribī, *margad*) did not escape the of the herdsmen; it was found facing the pre-ng wind behind a tuft of grass. Regions where s were plentiful were named *muʾarniba*/*murniba* *akhazza* or *mukharnika*, according to whether ts or young hares were predominant. Most of Bedouin observations about the leporids have recorded by the naturalists al-Ḳazwīnī (*ʿAdjāʾib akhlūḳāt*, ii, 215-17, margin), al-Damīrī (*Ḥayāt ıyawān al-kubrā*, Cairo 1356/1937, i, 20-3) and cially al-Djāḥiẓ (*Ḥayawān*, vi and *passim*). From e records scholars can learn that the hare has inside its cheeks, that it dozes with its eyes wide , and that it is always on the alert and flees at slightest danger, which has gained it a universal tation as a coward. The doe, like a bitch or ass, menstruates from time to time and because ıis impurity in the family of leporids, the species not mounted by the djinn. The passion of the linked with the phenomenon of superfoetation ertilising the doe led to a popular belief in the changing sex annually. In antiquity, it was also sidered to be a case of hermaphroditism.

he enormous length of the hare's back legs in parison with its front legs allows it to run ex-ıely swiftly, and this is its chief means of defence. an thwart the best saluki tracker set on its s, especially on hard and hilly ground where it make turns and back-casts (*murāwagha*) fre-ntly, whence the saying "to swerve more than a ", and the nicknames the hunters give it em-sise its speed, like *darrāma*, *dāmika hudhama*, *aṭṭiʿat al-suḥūr* and *al-niyāṭ*. When a hare is orised at its form, the leap (*nafdja*) it makes is nstantaneous and impetuous that it has become llustration of the brevity of life on earth compared h the life beyond, as in the expression in *ḥadīth* *ı mā al-dunyā fi ʾl-ākhira illā ka-nafdjati arnab* mpared with the world hereafter, this present ld is like a hare's leap" (*Ḥayawān*, vi, 352-3). ause of the many ruses they devise to avoid the nds, hares and foxes are considered the most icult of animals to catch. When hard pressed on e ground, one of the commonest tricks is the *bīr* (*Ḥayawān*, vi, 357), which is an instinctive mpt to blur the tracks by placing the body ght on the back foot only. The back of the foot a pad which is covered with hair and thus vents the toes and claws from marking the und.

The hare is certainly one of the most highly-zed game animals in Muslim countries, as else-ere. To catch it, man has employed all kinds of enuity; he has caught it with nets (*ḥibāla*, pl. *āyil*), snares (*sharak*, pl. *ashrāk*) and traps (*mighwāt*, *maghāwī*; *mughawwāt*, pl. *mughawwayāt*; *ḥukna*, *ḥukan*), and he has hunted (*ṭarada*) with the help trained beasts (*ḍawārī*) like the gazehound (*salūḳī* *ūḳī*, pl. *-iyya*), which always hunts by sight, and nters or other hounds (*zaghārī*, pl. *-iyya*, Maghribī *ūs*, pl. *ṭawāris*) which hunt by scent. The Persian x (*ʿanāḳ al-arḍ*) and trained birds of prey (*dja-wiḥ*) are also used. He has used various weapons attack the hare like the thrown cudgel (*hirāwa*, *rīṭa*/*zarwāṭa*), which the young shepherds of the ins of the Maghrib can wield so skilfully, as well the sling (*mikhdhafa*, *miḳlāʿ*), the bow, then the ss-bow and eventually firearms. As well as man, the hare is surrounded by a number of natural enemies, carnivores and rapacious predators; it is especially threatened by the tawny eagle (*aquila rapax*) which is appropriately called *ʿuḳāb al-arnab* or *ṣaḳr al-arnab*. Hare flesh has no fat or tendons, owing to the alimentary eclecticism of the animal. It is instinctively attracted to certain aromatic and sweet plants, and the Bedouin expression *arnab al-khulla*, "the hare of the sweet plants" summarises the appreciation of the gourmet and the glutton (*Ḥayawān*, iv, 134). The gastronomic authority Abu ʾl-Wadjīh al-ʿUklī, a man of the desert and one of the informants of al-Djāḥiẓ, gave pride of place to the hare in the metaphor "If the uromastix-lizard (*ḍabb* [*q.v.*]) had been a chicken, the hare would be a francolin (*durrādj*)" (*Ḥayawān*, vi, 353). Oriental cookery books esteem hare highly in their chapters on meats (see M. Rodinson, *Recherches sur les documents arabes relatifs à la cuisine*, in *REI* [1949], 107). To serve jugged hare (*arnabī*) or roast saddle of hare (*ʿadjz mashwī*) to a guest was a mark of honour, especially if one kept the kidneys for him; these were regarded as the finest morsel, as can be seen from the pituresque maxim *aṭʿim akhā-ka min kulyat al-arnab* "feed your brother with hare's kidneys", which meant using the tenderest words to console a friend in difficulty.

Al-Djāḥiẓ draws attention to the double benefit which the hare provides. Apart from its highly desirable flesh, its fine warm pelt also has a commercial value in the fur trade [see FARW] and the textile industry. An anonymous satirical line of verse (*Ḥayawān*, vi, 360) alludes to the trade in these terms: "When gentle folk move (among them), it is to see them touching hare skins with their hands wide open". The sentence expresses the scorn which has always attached to rabbit skin dealers. Rabbit skin is not distinguished from hare skin in the making of fabrics called *muʾarnab*/*murnab* and certain felts. The fur is also used to line gloves and slippers and to trim winter bonnets. It is not inconceivable that they were also used as counterfeit furs, which would normally be more highly priced, but the secrets of dyeing and other treatments were known only to the tricksters. The colour of the fur can vary from light brown almost to blonde according to the hare's habitat, and certain beige materials are called *marnabānī* "hare coloured"; conversely, in popular French the hare is known as "capuchin" because of the brown habit worn by the monks of that order. The hare's tail is black on top and immaculately white underneath; it is conspicuous even from a distance because the tuft is always erect. The Saharans have a name *(a)bū nawwāra*, "the one with the flower" which is used for the hare as well as for the fox.

As Islam expanded westwards to Spain and north-eastwards to the Indus, Arabs were introduced to a second leporid, the rabbit (*Oryctolagus cuniculus*), both wild and domestic. Since there was no specific term for rabbit in the *ʿarabiyya*, *arnab* was used. At first they regarded the wild rabbit simply as a small hare, and it was sometimes called "levret" (*khirnik*). The duality of the term *arnab* in the East to cover hare and rabbit is a source of constant confusion, but one of the first to find difficulty with it was Ibn al-Muḳaffaʿ. When he was translating the fables of Bidpay from Pahlavi, he encountered the typically Indian episode of the elephants who were looking for water and trampled over a rabbit warren (*arḍ li ʾl-arānib*), crushing the inhabitants in their burrows (*djuḥr*, pl. *adjhār*, *adjḥira*, *djaḥara*), but the clever rabbit Fayrūz (= Felix) became their spokesman and drove away the elephants by a trick (see *Kalīla wa-Dimna*, Cairo 1931, 207-9). This story could not possibly be concerned with hares, for they do not live in colonies and they do not tunnel underground. Once the domestic rabbit was being bred on a large scale, it became necessary to add epithets to *arnab* to make the word more specific; *arnab barriyya* or *waḥshiyya* was used for the hare, and *arnab ahliyya* or *dādjina* or *baladiyya* for the domestic rabbit, but the wild rabbit hardly had any specific name. In the Muslim West the same confusion did not arise, because in Spain as well as in the Maghrib the wild and domestic rabbit kept its original Latin name *cuniculus* in Arabised form (compare Fr. *connil* or *connin*, Provençal *counièu*, Sp. *conèjo*, Port. *coêlbo*, It. *coniglio*, Eng. *cony*, Ger. *Kaninchen*, Swed. *kouin*). The Hispano-Arabic names *kunilya/ ḳunilya, ḳullīn, ḳulayn* are still found in the Maghrib as *ḳanīn/ganīn* (sing. *-a*, pl. *-āt* and *ḳnāyen/gnāyen*), *ḳalīn* (pl. *ḳlāyen*), *ḳūnīn/gūnīn*, *ganūn* and Kabyle *agunin* (pl. *iguninen*). Besides *arnab*, Hispanic languages use *labbay* (pl. *-āt*), ultimately derived from Ibero-Roman *lapparo* (from *leporis*, Sp. *liebre*, Catalan *llèbre*, Prov. *lèbre*, Fr. *lièvre/lapereau/lapin*). As for Tunisia, Ibn Saʿīd (in al-Maḳḳarī, *Analectes*, i, 122) notes that the practice of raising rabbits for fur was introduced there from Spain in the 7th/13th century; the wild rabbit is to be found only on some coastal islets, but it is common in Algeria (*cuniculus algirus*) and in northern Morocco.

According to Ḳurʾānic law, the flesh of a hare which has had its throat cut ritually may be consumed; the doctors of law agree unanimously about this, for the hare is a product of hunting and the animal is herbivorous and not carnivorous. It is true that some *ḥadīth*s suggest that the Prophet Muḥammad abstained from eating hare, but no-one accepts this as a formal prohibition [but see ḤAYAWAN concerning the Rāfiḍīs]. This permission extended *ipso facto* also to the rabbit when the animal was introduced to Muslims. In al-Andalus, the rabbit was highly prized and the only restriction imposed on it was that it should not be sold around the Great Mosque. Instead, a place was chosen by the *muḥtasib* and there they had to be offered for sale properly slaughtered and skinned so that the meat could be seen to be fresh (see Ibn ʿAbdūn-Lévi-Provençal, *Séville musulmane au début du XIIe siècle*, Paris 1947, 95-6).

In pre-Islamic times the Arabs attached great power to the hare's foot as a talisman (*kaʿb al-arnab*). It was considered to be a protection against all evil spells, and mothers would affix one of their children to preserve them from the evil eye [see ʿAYN]. Every man who went into a strange village would equip himself with one to protect him from evil spells, which were always to be feared in unknown territory.

In Greek medicine a number of specific virtues were accorded to particular organs of the hare. The flesh was thought to have laxative and aphrodisiac properties. Later Arab medicine confirmed the views of Hippocrates and Galen on this subject, but added some new empirical prescriptions. Perhaps the most important parts were the brain and the gastric juices (*infaḥa*); the brain was the best remedy for trembling and senility, and it could be applied to an infant's gums to suppress the pain in teething, but if it was mixed with camphor and drunk it was thought to be an infallible love philtre. The gastric juices and stomach tissue were mixed into a potion with a vinegar base and used as an antidote fc kinds of poison. It is interesting that modern sci whether by chance or not, knows no proven rer which has any real chance of fighting the pois the phalloïdine (death's cap) fungus other thar absorption of a mixture of minced brains and s achs of leporids. Perhaps after all, Arab emp medicine was not just pure fancy. Dried and dered hare's blood had recognised healing qua for sores and wounds and helped to extract fo bodies like splinters and thorns; it was also use treat arrow wounds. In surgery, leporid hair used instead of cotton wool as an absorbent tan and as a cap for ruptured veins and arteries.

Since Sāsānid times in Iran, hares and ral have held a position of not negligible importan the field of Muslim art. They figure either decorative motif incorporated into a hunting s or are themselves the main theme of inspira Besides the mass of Persian miniatures, prob the most typical representations of leporids ar illustrations of the incident mentioned above, w the wily Fayrūz harangues the king of the elepha it is found in Syrian manuscripts of the 8th/ century of *Kalīla wa-Dimna* (Paris B.N., ms. 3467, fol. 70, and Oxford Bodl. Libr., Pococke fol. 99). Iranian ceramics, which also inspired t of Fāṭimid Egypt, frequently incorporate the n of "the hare". There is a glazed ewer from Gu (6th/12th century, Paris Mus. Arts Déc.) whic decorated on its bulged-out sides with a friez hares chasing each other in an endless circle. Ano example is the remarkable glazed Fāṭimid cu the 5th/11th century (Paris Louvre, coll. F. Sa with its white base decorated with a beautiful strolling among the flora, symbolised by the sty Kūfic inscription on its margin. Persian silks carpets from every period, but especially from of the Ṣafawid dynasty (10th/16th century), as their inborn taste for nature. Animals are portra as living in an earthly paradise, with hares gazelles gambolling among their carnivorous ener and there are hunting scenes commemorating fam slaughters by battues, of which the Chosroes wer fond. All these interpretations have been caref represented in bronze, copper and ivory, and also hares and gazelles have their proper place. Fāṭimid goldsmiths in Egypt, following their Per predecessors, were skilled in portraying animals birds in metal, even on commonplace objects, a shown by the famous "hare on the alert" brc aquamanile. This is the proud possession of Museum of Brussels (coll. Stoclet), and natural are amazed at its realism. The same Persian ani themes are found on carved ivory caskets (py from Egypt through Sicily to Muslim Spain, anc Mesopotamia they are even found on the stone lintels and door cases in Artuḳid art (6th/1 century).

In zoology, the name *arnab baḥrī*, transla from the Latin *lepus marinus*, "sea hare", has b given to *aplysia depilans*, a nudibranch mollusc of order *op isthobranchia*. It is found widely in the s and ancient man treated it with a profound disg as much for its hideous appearance (it looks lik slug with a hare's head) as for the nauseating vi secretion which it emits in self-defence and wh was thought to be a deadly poison (see al-Dam *op. cit.*, i, 23).

Finally, in astronomy *al-arnab* "Alarnab" is Hare constellation found beneath the left foot Orion, the legendary hunter. The first star of stellation is called "Arneb" (α *Leporis*, mag. 2.7; A. Benhamouda, *Les noms arabes des étoiles*, in :O Algers [1951], 179-80).

Bibliography: Besides the works already ted, see al-Kushādjim, *Kitāb al-Maṣāyid wa -maṭārid*, ed. A. Talas, Baghdad 1954, 146-8; -Ḳalḳashandī, *Ṣubḥ*, ii, 46; Amīn al-Maʿlūf, *Iuʿdjam al-ḥayawān*, Cairo 1932, 150; Ibn Sīduh, *-Mukhaṣṣaṣ*, viii, 76-9; G. Benoist, *Lièvres et vrauts*, Paris 1946; L. Blancou, *Géographie cynégétique du monde* (coll. Que sais-je?), Paris 1958; .. Hanoteau and A. Letourneux, *La Kabylie et les outumes kabyles*, i, Paris 1893; D. L. Harrison, *he mammals of Arabia*, London 1972, iii, 385-95; . Lavauden, *La chasse et la faune cynégétique en unisie*, Tunis 1920, 12-13; idem, *Les vertébrés du ahara*, Tunis 1926, 45-6; H. Lhote, *La chasse hez les Touaregs*, Paris 1951, 134; G. Migeon, *Ianuel d'art musulman* (Arts plastiques et industriels), Paris 1927; G. Mountfort, *Portrait of a esert*, London 1965, and French tr. *La vie d'un ésert*, Paris 1966, 112. (F. Viré)

RMOUR [see SILĀḤ].

RT [see FANN].

S, Arabic for the myrtle, *Myrtus communis* (Myrtaceae), the well-known fragrant, evergreen ub, growing to over a man's height. The term, ived from Akkadian *āsu* came into Arabic through maic *āsā*; the Greek term μυρσίνη (μύρτος) exists as *marsīnī* (and variants). Much material has n collected by I. Löw (*Die Flora der Juden*, ii, -74), among which are many, more or less locally-ined synonyms. Occasionally, myrtle is menied in the *ḥadīth* (Dārimī, see Wensinck, *Conlance*, i, 132b), by the Arab botanists and in the ses quoted by them (Dīnawarī, *K. al-Nabāt*, ed. Lewin, Uppsala-Wiesbaden 1953, 25 f.; Aṣmaʿī, *al-Nabāt*, ed. al-Ghunaym, Cairo 1392/1972, 32), the plant was mainly used as medicine. Like scorides, the Arabs knew the black garden-myrtle *ās al-bustānī al-aswad*) and the white field-myrtle *ās al-barrī al-abyaḍ*), the leaves, blossoms and ries of which occasioned positive therapeutic ılts. The scent of the myrtle mitigates headaches invigorates the heart. The extract is suitable hipbaths which cure ulcers of the fundament and rus; as a beverage it calms down the spitting of od and cures coughs and diarrhoea. Dried and verished leaves of the myrtle remove putrescent ls and facilitate the growing of new flesh. Rāzī, erwise critical and not given to superstition, curily enough declares in his *Kitāb al-Khawāṣṣ* eserved in Latin; of the Arabic text, only quoions are known) that a man, suffering from a in the inguinal region, may find mitigation by ting the stalk of a myrtle around his finger by y of a ring. The manifold symbolical meaning ributed to the myrtle on festive occasions by the aelites, Greeks and Romans seems to have reined unknown to Islam; according to an Arab end, it was brought from Paradise by Adam (Löw, *cit.*, 269).

Bibliography: (besides the works quoted in he article): Dioscorides, *Materia medica*, ed. M. Wellmann, i, Berlin 1907, 105 f. (= lib. i, 112); *La 'Materia médica' de Dioscorides*, ii (Arabic tr. Iṣṭafan b. Basīl), ed. Dubler and Terés, Tetuán 1952, 109 f.; Bīrūnī, *Ṣaydala*, ed. H. M. Saʿīd, Karachi 1973, Arabic, 33 f., Eng. 22 f.; Ghāfiḳī, *Djāmiʿ*, Ms. Rabat, Bibl. Gén. ḳ. 155 I, fols. 9a-10b; *The abridged version of "The Book of the simple drugs" of ... al-Ghâfiqî by ... Barhebraeus*, ed. Meyerhof and Sobhy, Cairo 1932, no. 37; Suwaydī, *Simāt*, Ms. Paris ar. 3004, fols. 17b-18a, 174b-175a; Ibn Biklārish, *Mustaʿīnī*, Ms. Naples, Bibl. Naz. iii, F. 65, fol. 14 f.; Ibn al-Djazzār, *Iʿtimād*, Ms. Ayasofya 3564, fols. 14a-15a; Maimonides, *Sharḥ asmāʾ al-ʿuḳḳār*, ed. Meyerhof, no. 10; Ibn al-Bayṭār, *Djāmiʿ*, Būlāḳ 1291, i, 27-30, tr. Leclerc, nos. 69, 70; *Die pharmakologischen Grundsätze des Abu Mansur ... Harawi*, tr. A. Achundow, Halle 1893, no. 10; Rāzī, *Ḥāwī*, xx, Haydarābād 1387, no. 23; Ibn Sīnā, *Ḳānūn*, i, Būlāḳ, 245 f.; Ibn Hubal, *Mukhtārāt*, Ḥaydarābād 1362, ii, 17 f.; Nuwayrī, *Nihāyat al-arab*, xi, Cairo 1935, 239-42 (important); H. G. Kircher, *Die "einfachen Heilmittel" aus dem "Handbuch der Chirurgie" des Ibn al-Quff*, Bonn 1967, no. 16; W. Schmucker, *Die pflanzliche und mineralische Materia medica im Firdaus al-ḥikma des ʿAlī ibn Sahl Rabban aṭ-Ṭabarī*, Bonn 1969, no. 19. (A. Dietrich)

AL-**ASAD** [see MINṬAḲAT AL-BURŪDJ].

ASAD B. **MŪSĀ** B. **IBRĀHĪM** B. ʿABD AL-MALIK B. MARWĀN B. AL-ḤAKAM AL-UMAWĪ, Arab traditionist and author of ascetic writings. He was born in Egypt in 132/750 (according to others in Baṣra (Ibn Ḥadjar, *Tahdhīb*, i, 260), and died in Egypt in 212/827. He made his reputation as a *ḥāfiẓ*, *rāwī* or *akhbārī*, had disciples and was nicknamed Asas al-Sunna. He exchanged *ḥadīths* with the majority of the Egyptians who are known to us from this period, in particular with ʿAbd Allāh b. Lahīʿa (97-174/715-90) and al-Layth b. Saʿd (94-175/713-91), a great master and one of the richest men in Egypt, into whose house he entered in disguise, following his flight from the persecution of the Umayyad family to which he himself belonged (Abū Nuʿaym, *Ḥilya*, vii, 321 ff.), but also with ʿAbd Allāh b. al-Mubārak (118-81/736-97), an author of ascetic writings who, among his numerous masters, exercised the most profound influence on him, although the texts that are available to us show very few signs of this influence *expressis verbis*. Opinion is divided among Arab-Islamic writers as to the value of Asad's activity as a traditionalist; while al-Bukhārī calls attention to the reputation of his *ḥadīth*, al-Nasāʾī refutes this statement to some extent in declaring that he is "worthy of belief, but he would have done better not to write" (Dhahabī, *Ḥuffāẓ*; Ibn Ḥadjar, *Tahdhīb*). Since then, the tendency has been to attack him vociferously, pointing out the exaggerated side of his traditions, as is indicated by Ibn Khaldūn's resumé on this subject (*Muḳadimma*, 564-6). This distrust, like that shown towards the work of Ibn Isḥāḳ and many authors of the early period of Islam, is explained, not so much by the fact that some of his traditions go beyond the serious framework accepted by Muslim theological good sense, as by the fact that Ibn Mūsā was under no obligation to masters recognised as such by the major schools of *ḥadīth*. On this basis, the author's fate was no better than that of his master Ibn Lahīʿa, whose material has been taken into consideration and propagated by other means, and especially under other names (see R. G. Khoury, *Asad*, 28).

Asad is known primarily as transmitter of the *Kitāb al-Tīdjān* of Ibn Hishām, more particularly of the part that is associated with Ibn Munabbih (Abbott, *Studies*, i, 12; R. G. Khoury, *Wahb b. Munabbih*, 286 ff., esp. 292). Asad's interest in the Yemenī heritage is no doubt explained by the influence of the policies of Muʿāwiya on all his descendants, but also by the author's wish to borrow material for his own writings from a *ḳāṣṣ* as famous as Wahb. As a transmitter, he is also encountered in a number of historical and ascetic books, like the *Futūḥ Miṣr* of Ibn ʿAbd al-Ḥakam (see *Bibl.*), where there is a large number of traditions linked with his name; these are, like the majority of those attributed to his Egyptian masters, of an ascetic and pious nature. Other works are further attributed to him: *Musnad Asad b. Mūsā* (Ibn Khayr, *Fihrist*, 141-2; Ibn al-Faraḍī); the four versions mentioned by the *isnād*s of Ibn Khayr were the work of one Naṣr b. Marzūḳ. Not one of them seems to have appeared in book form. Then there is a treatise entitled *Risālat Asad b. Mūsā ilā Asad b. al-Furāt* [142-213/759-828] *fī luzūm al-sunna wa 'l-taḥdhīr min al-bidaʿ* (Ibn Khayr, 299) (see R. Sayid, who seems to have discovered a manuscript of it). Ibn Khayr (270) also mentions *Faḍāʾil al-tābiʿīn*, a book that he attributes to Saʿīd, son of Asad, which Ibn Hadjar had seen in two volumes and which apparently contained, according to the last-named, a great deal of information afforded by the father (Asad) and his circle (Ibn Ḥadjar, *ibid.*). Finally, there is the *Kitāb al-Zuhd wa 'l-ʿibāda wa 'l-waraʿ* (Ibn Khayr, 270; Ḥādjdjī Khalīfa, v, 91); this book seems to have been the author's most important work, and according to Ibn Khayr comprised several books (*kutub*) corresponding to the three parts of the title which he supplies. Unfortunately, only two copies of the *Kitāb al-Zuhd* are available to us, one of them preserved in Berlin (Sprenger, 495) the other in Damascus (Ẓahiriyya, madj. 100/1). The first was edited by Leszynsky who, in the guise of an introduction, devoted a study to the traditions of the book and compared them with their parallels in Judaism and Christianity, but was not at all concerned with the author himself. The author of the present article has re-edited this copy, also taking account of the second, and adding to it all the "certificates of reading" in both of them, with a study of Asad (see *Bibl.*). It will be appreciated that the word *kitāb* is used here in the most flexible sense, seeing that one of the two copies begins with the word *bāb*, which tends to give to all the *kutub* cited by Ibn Khayr on this subject the dimensions of a single work. This book perhaps best illustrates the influence of the author and his importance in the sphere of ascetic and pious literature in general from the formative period of Islam, for it is the second work of its kind, after the *Kitāb al-Zuhd wa 'l-raḳāʾiḳ* of ʿAbd Allāh b. al-Mubārak, which provided a model for it, both in content and in title, although Asad does not acknowledge this. It is made up of a collection of traditions with eschatological questions, while the other lost portions, corresponding to the *Kutub al-ʿIbāda wa 'l-waraʿ* mentioned by the bibliographer must have contained the remainder of the themes encountered in the work of Ibn al-Mubārak; piety, ascetic meditation, etc. (see Khoury, *Asad*, 39 ff.; Abbott, *Studies*, ii, 237 ff.).

Bibliography: Abū Nuʿaym, *Ḥilya*, vii, 321 ff.; Dhahabī, *Mīzān*, i, 207; idem, *Ḥuffāẓ*, 1375/1955, i, 402; Ḥādjdjī Khalīfa, v, 91; Ibn ʿAbd al-Ḥakam, *Futūḥ Miṣr*, ed. Torrey, index; Ibn Abī Ḥātim, *Djarḥ*, i, 338; Ibn al-Faraḍī, no. 484; Ibn Ḥadjar, *Tahdhīb*, i, 260; Ibn Khaldūn, *Muḳaddima*, Beirut 1961, 564-5, tr. Rosenthal, ii, 170-1; Ibn Khayr al-Ishbīlī, *Fihrist*, 141-2, 270, 299; Ibn Hishām, K. *al-Tīdjān*, 2 ff.; Ibn al-Mubārak, K. *al-Zuhd wa 'l-raḳāʾiḳ*, ed. Aʿẓamī, 1966; ʿUmar al-K *Faḍāʾil Miṣr*, Cairo 1971, index; N. Abl *Studies*, i, Chicago 1957, index, ii, 1967, 23 where Asad is suggested as the possible authc a two-page collection of traditions on papy F. Krenkow, *The two oldest books on Arabic folk* in *IC*, ii (1928), 55 ff.; R. G. Khoury, *Import et authenticité des texts de Ḥilyat al-awliyāʾ*, i (1977), 94-6; idem, *Wahb b. Munabbih*, Wiesb 1972, 286 ff.; Brockelmann, S I, 257, 351; Se *GAS*, i, 354-5. The main studies on Asad's w are: R. Leszynsky, *Mohammedanische Traditi über das jüngste Gericht. Eine vergleichende St zur jüdisch-christlichen und mohammedanis Eschatologie*, Kirchhain 1909 (contains an ed the *K. al-Zuhd*, based on the Berlin ms., wi study); R. G. Khoury, *Asad b. Mūsā*, *Kitāb Zuhd*, new ed., with a study, Wiesbaden 1 R. Sayid is preparing in Beirut an ed. of As *Risāla*. (R. G. Khour

al-**AṢAMM**, Abū Bakr ʿAbd al-Raḥmān Kaysān, died 200/816 or 201/817, early th ogian and *mufassir*, commonly counted am the Muʿtazilīs, although always treated as an sider by the Muʿtazilī *ṭabaḳāt*. In his youth he ser together with other *mutakallimūn* like Muʿamr Ḥafṣ al-Fard and Abū Shamir al-Ḥanafī, as *adl* (*ghulām*) to Maʿmar Abu 'l-Ashʿath, a Baṣran sician with certain "philosophical" leanings *Fihrist*, ed. Flügel, 100, ll. 28 ff.). In the later c of Ḍirār b. ʿAmr [*q.v.*], i.e. in the last quarter of 2nd century A.H., he created in Baṣra a circle of own. Abu 'l-Hudhayl did not like him; he ca him, with a Persian expression, *kharbān*, the "donl driver", obviously alluding to his low origin Malaṭī, *Tanbīh*, ed. Dedering, 31, ll. 12 ff.). But 'l-Hudhayl became influential only when he been called to Baghdād by al-Maʾmūn after 204/ at a rather advanced age; in Baṣra al-Aṣamm se to have enjoyed the higher prestige (cf. Ḳāḍī ʿ al-Djabbār, *Faḍl al-iʿtizāl*, ed. Fuʾād Sayyid, ll. -5 and pu. f.). This may be due to his even relations with the Ibāḍiyya who had, at that ti not yet entirely left the town (Abū Ḥayyān Tawḥīdī introduces him as *ṣāḥib al-Ibāḍiyya* in *Baṣāʾir*, ed. Kaylānī, ii, 825, ult. f.). But it may be attributed to the fact that he was a prolific wri Ibn al-Nadīm mentions 26 books, none of whic unfortunately preserved (cf. *Fihrist*, ed. Fück, *Shafīʿ comm. volume*, 68, ll. 5 ff.). All of them trea of theological and juridical subjects. But he se also to have been a poet (if the ʿAbd al-Raḥmān Kaysān mentioned by Djāḥiẓ, *Ḥayawān*, iv, ll. 6 ff. is identical with him; cf. Goldziher, *Isl.* (1916), 174, n. 2). At least he was known to eloquent; al-Djubbāʾī still acknowledged him as s (cf. *Faḍl al-iʿtizāl*, 267, l. -6 and 268, l. 3; also aphorism mentioned in Djāḥiẓ, *Bayān*, i, 80, ll. 1 With the authority of an expert, he passed a sev judgment on Ibn al-Muḳaffaʿ (cf. Djāḥiẓ, *Dha akhlāḳ al-kuttāb*, in *Rasāʾil*, ed. ʿAbd al-Sa Muḥammad Hārūn, ii, 195, ll. 7 ff.).

His solidarity with certain Muʿtazilī ideas is tested by his repeated polemics against the destinarians (al-Mudjbira; cf. titles nos. 5 and in the *Fihrist*, also no. 11) and by his reflecti about tawḥīd (cf. title no. 3). But he did not acc the tenet of *al-manzila bayn al-manzilatayn* Ashʿarī, *Maḳālāt al-Islāmiyyīn*, 269, ult. ff.); he lieved that the *fāsiḳ* remains a believer because his monotheistic creed and because of the g deeds he has performed (ibid., 270, ll. 9 ff.).

will nevertheless be condemned to eternal shment; for this al-Aṣamm did not base himself, his Muʿtazilī colleagues, on Ḳurʾānic evidence :h refers to unbelievers), but on the unanimous ment of the community (ibid., 278, ll. 3 ff.; Ibn n, *Fiṣal*, iv, 45, ll. 10 ff. seems to be a wrong ralisation). His ideas on the principle of *al-amr -maʿrūf wa 'l-nahy ʿan al-munkar* (cf. *Fihrist*, no. 9) equally did not entirely correspond to e of other Muʿtazilīs (cf. As͟hʿarī, 278, ll. 7 ff.); ased himself on a peculiar exegesis of sūra III, (cf. Ibn Ḥazm, *Fiṣal*, iv, 171, ll. 10 ff.). He wrote t the createdness of the Ḳurʾān at a moment 1 other Muʿtazilīs did not yet touch the problem title no. 2); a fierce opponent of this doctrine, d b. Hārūn (died 205 or 206/820-822), saw him as in line with Bis͟hr al-Marīsī, who was younger he and whom he may have influenced (cf. hārī, *K͟halḳ al-afʿāl*, in Nas͟hs͟hār-Ṭālibī, *ʿAḳāʾid laf*, 129, ll. 16 ff.). It was perhaps for this reason T͟humāma b. As͟hras recommended him to al-mūn when the caliph was still in Marw (cf. *ist*, ed. Fück, 67, ll. -4 ff.). He clashed with ıām b. al-Ḥakam, certainly because of his ngly anti-S͟hīʿī feelings (cf. *Faḍl al-iʿtizāl*, 267, f. and title no. 13), but also because of His͟hām's thropomorphism" (cf. title no. 10), and he at-:ed the *zanādiḳa* and the Dahriyya, probably in espondence with the policy pursued by al-Mahdī -69/775-85) and his successors (cf. titles no. 24 15).

he theological doctrine most strongly connected Aṣamm's name was his denial of the accidents *āḍ*), which put him in opposition to Ḍirār b. r [*q.v.*] and may have brought him into a certain nection with His͟hām b. al-Ḥakam [*q.v.*; cf. vḥīdī, *Baṣāʾir*, ii, 825, ult. ff.]. He seems to have :eeded from a sensualistic basis: only bodies are ble; qualities appearing on them cannot subsist themselves and can therefore not be ascribed a ırate existence (*ibid.*, also As͟hʿarī, *Maḳālāt*, 335, 2 ff.). In comparison with Ḍirār's ideas, this was ıaps not so much a difference in substance but xplanation and in the conceptual apparatus. Like ār, he was led to deny a separate existence of the l (cf. As͟hʿarī, *Maḳālāt*, 335, ll. 12 ff., and 331, ff.; Ibn Ḥazm, *Fiṣal*, iv, 70, l. 4 and 74, ll. 4 f.); him he seems to have rejected the idea of *kumūn* .; cf. As͟hʿarī, 328, ll. 14 f.). In any case, he was an atomist; this is why he was attacked for his trine by Abu 'l-Hud͟hayl, who tried to show that dical obligations are normally not concerned with n as a whole, but with one of his accidents (e.g. prosternation in prayer, or his being flogged in e of adultery; cf. *Faḍl al-iʿtizāl*, 262, apu. ff.). hām al-Fuwaṭī, a disciple of Abu 'l-Hud͟hayl, ms to have been mainly shocked by the ensuing ial of movement (which, understood in a very ad sense, was considered as the only accident by Naẓẓām; cf. the title of Fuwaṭī's book in *Fihrist*, Fück, 69, l. 1). Many opponents and, influenced their polemics, the later heresiographers, tended understand Aṣamm's denial of the accidental racter of qualities as a denial of qualities as such As͟hʿarī, 343, ll. 12 ff.; Bag͟hdādī, *Farḳ*, 96, 3 f./116, ll. 3 f.; *idem*, *Uṣūl al-dīn* 7, ll. 14 ff. etc.). consequently also regarded the Ḳurʾān as a ly, and may have derived its createdness from s; God is the only essence which is not a body. der this aspect, the doctrine seems to have been :en over by D͟jaʿfar b. Mubas͟hs͟hir (*q.v.*; cf. hʿarī, 583, ll. 4 ff.).

In addition to these ideas, al-Aṣamm is frequently mentioned for his unusual views concerning political theory. Government (*imāma*) was according to him not an obligatory attribute of human society; the ideal community is the community of the righteous which can do without a ruler (cf. Bag͟hdādī, *Uṣūl al-dīn*, 272, l. 10 and 271, ll. 14 f.; many later sources like Māwardī, *al-Aḥkām al-sulṭāniyya*, ed. Enger, 3, l. 7; G͟hazzālī, *Faḍāʾiḥ al-Bāṭiniyya*, ed. Badawī, 170, ll. -5 ff.; Rāzī, *al-Muḥaṣṣal*, 176, ll. 9 f. etc.). Government is therefore not prescribed by reason nor by revelation, but is a mere practical measure against human iniquity. Theoretically speaking, universal knowledge of the Ḳurʾān should be sufficient in order to keep a society in order (cf. Pazdawī, *Uṣūl al-dīn*, ed. Linss, 186, ll. 11 ff.); but the reality being imperfect, the Muslims always decided to choose somebody as their *imām*. This can only be done by consensus (cf. As͟hʿarī, 460, ll. 6 f.; Bag͟hdādī, *Farḳ*, 150, ll. 4 f. / 164, ll. 1 ff.; etc.), and once somebody has been agreed upon, the election is irreversible, even if a more appropriate (*afḍal*) candidate presents himself afterwards (cf. al-Nās͟hiʾ al-akbar, *Uṣūl al-niḥal*, ed. van Ess, § 99). Armed resistance against a ruler is only allowed if this person has seized power in an unjust way and if the leader of the rebellion has been agreed upon by consensus (cf. As͟hʿarī, 451, ll. 12 f.).

Applied to the historical reality of the past, this meant that al-Aṣamm accepted Abū Bakr and ʿUmar as the most appropriate candidates in the moment of their election. After ʿUmar's death, the *afḍal* was ʿAbd al-Raḥmān b. ʿAwf, who demonstrated his virtue by renouncing the caliphate for himself; ʿUt͟hmān was only second in rank after him (cf. Nās͟hiʾ, *Uṣūl al-niḥal*, § 100). In contrast to him, ʿAlī was not elected by a *s͟hūrā*, i.e. by consensus; his government was therefore unrighteous (ibid., § 101). This does not mean that all his measurements were unlawful *per se*; in the case of his war against Ṭalḥa and Zubayr and of his establishing the arbitration at Ṣiffīn, an impartial assessment would have to proceed from his intentions and those of his opponents, whether he acted out of mere despotism or in order to put things right again. But as these intentions are no longer known, we have to suspend judgment. It is clear, however, that Ṭalḥa and Zubayr had a certain superiority over ʿAlī (perhaps because they sought revenge for ʿUt͟hmān) and that Abū Mūsā al-As͟hʿarī was right when he deposed ʿAlī in order to give his community a single ruler (cf. al-Mufīd, *K. al-D͟jamal*, Nad͟jaf 1382/1963, 26, ll. 16 ff., tr. M. Rouhani, *La victoire de Bassora*, Paris 1974, 17, and, shorter, As͟hʿarī, 457, ll. 13 ff.; ibid., 453, ll. 13 ff.). Muʿāwiya was right in his resistance against ʿAlī, because he had been legally appointed governor of Syria by ʿUmar and confirmed in his office by ʿUt͟hmān; he would have only been obliged to hand over Syria to a ruler who had been elected by consensus (cf. Nās͟hiʾ, § 102).

Thus far Aṣamm's theory could be learnt from his books, mainly his *K. al-Imāma* (cf. *Fihrist*, title no. 7) which, for understandable reasons, encountered opposition especially from the S͟hīʿīs and from theologians sympathetic to them: from Bis͟hr b. al-Muʿtamir (cf. *Fihrist*, ed. Flügel, 162, l. 21), probably from the early S͟hīʿī Faḍl b. S͟hād͟hān (died 260/874; cf. Ṭūsī, *Fihrist*, 150, ll. 10 f.) and even much later from the *s͟haykh* al-Mufīd (died 413/1022), who also seems to quote from the original in his *K. al-D͟jamal*, 26, ll. 16 ff. Al-Nās͟hiʾ also preserves, however, an oral tradition from Aṣamm's closest adherents saying that there may be several rulers at once in the Muslim community, provided that they are legally elected and co-ordinate their efforts in righteousness. He based this theory on the fact that the Prophet appointed governors for different regions and that, after his death, his prerogative had been transferred to the population of these regions, who may decide according to their consensus. For his own time, al-Aṣamm deemed this even to be the better solution: a condominium, with its smaller political entities, would allow closer contact between the people and the ruler (cf. §§ 103 f.). As to the origin of these ideas, Goldziher suggested the influence of the Pseudo-Aristotelian Περὶ βασιλείας which may have been translated thus early (cf. *Isl.*, vi (1916), 176 f. and Cheikho's edition of the text in *Machriq*, x (1907), 311 ff.; for an analysis of the text itself S. M. Stern, *Aristotle on the World State*, Oxford 1968, passim, M. Grignaschi in *BEO*, xix (1965-6), 14 and M. Manzalaoui in *Oriens*, xxiii-xxiv (1974), 202). But it seems easier to assume that they were stimulated by discussions in Ibāḍī circles in Baṣra (cf. *EI*[2], III, 658a, and Bosworth, *Sīstān under the Arabs*, 88).

Aṣamm's high appreciation of the consensus led him to the theory that the *ʿulamāʾ*, if they are sufficient in number not to agree on a lie, are able to issue laws (cf. As͟hʿarī 467, l. 6 f.). For their *id͟jtihād* is not a matter of mere probability; every true judgment is based upon an irrefutable proof. Among *mud͟jtahidūn* of different opinions, therefore, only one is right (cf. Abu 'l-Ḥusayn al-Baṣrī, *al-Muʿtamad*, ed. Hamidullah, 949, ll. 10 ff.). In principle, there is no difference between juridical and dogmatical verities in this respect (cf. Ḳāḍī ʿAbd al-D͟jabbār, *al-Mug͟hnī*, xvii, 369, ll. 17 ff.); but we may distinguish between errors which lead to unbelief (about God and prophecy), other ones which lead only to sinfulness (*fisḳ*; about the *ruʾya* or about *k͟halḳ al-Ḳurʾān*, e.g.) and those which result in the mere imputation of a fault (*taʾt͟hīm*) as in juridical questions (cf. G͟hazālī, *Mustaṣfā*, ii, 107, ll. -6 ff.; S͟hīrāzī, *Lumaʿ*, Cairo, Ṣubayḥ, n.d., 76, ll. 17 ff.; Māwardī, *Adab al-ḳāḍī*, Bag͟hdād 1391/1971, i, 532 no. 1234; Āmidī, *Iḥkām*, iv, 244, ll. 7 ff.). Because of this rational criterion, even a sinful *ḳāḍī* may pass righteous judgments (cf. Māwardī, ibid., i, 634, no. 1579). On the other hand, the *āḥād*, isolated traditions (which, at that time, must have comprised the majority of *ḥadīt͟h* in the view of the Muʿtazila), cannot claim any value as criteria (ibid., i, 376, no. 787). In these ideas, which seem to have been characteristic for Baṣra (cf. Masʿūdī, *Tanbīh*, 356, ll. 10 ff.), al-Aṣamm was followed by Bis͟hr al-Marīsī [*q.v.*] and Abū Isḥāḳ Ibrāhīm b. Ismāʿīl Ibn ʿUlayya, who had been his *adlatus* s*g͟hulām*) and who founded a quite influential juridical school in Egypt (he died, like al-Marīsī, in 218/832, cf. *Taʾrīk͟h Bag͟hdād*, vi, 20 ff. no. 3054, etc.; there were adherents of his in Rāmhurmuz even in the 4th/10th century, cf. *Faḍl al-iʿtizāl*, 316, l. 3).

A rational trend appears also to have permeated al-Aṣamm's *Tafsīr*. He defines the *muḥkamāt* as those verses, the veracity of which cannot be denied by any opponent as, e.g., all statements about the past; the *mutas͟hābihāt* are verses which tell something about the future and which reveal their truth only after reflection as, e.g., statements about the Last Judgment (cf. As͟hʿarī, 223, ll. 3 ff.; Bag͟hdādī, *Uṣūl al-dīn*, 222, ll. 4 ff.; Rāzī, *Mafātīḥ al-g͟hayb*, Cairo n.d., vii, 182, ll. -5 ff.). There are thus no verses which remain permanently obscure to human reason. Al-Aṣamm seems to have concentrate the meaning of entire passages (*maʿnā*); he di deal with philological problems. The verse conta the problematic word *abb* (sūra LXXX, 31) is co by him among the *muḥkamāt*. Naẓẓām criticise arbitrariness and did not distinguish him from Muʿtazilī commentators like Kalbī or Muḳāt Sulaymān (cf. D͟jāḥiẓ, *Ḥayawān*, i, 343, ll. translated by Goldziher, *Richtungen der Kora legung*, 111 f.). But he was quoted exclusivel D͟jubbāʾī in his lost *Tafsīr* (although perhaps for one passage; cf. *Faḍl al-iʿtizāl*, 268, ll. 1 f.) later on by Māturīdī in his *Taʾwīlāt ahl al-s* (cf. i, 59, ll. 4 ff.; 95, ll. 8 f.; 103, ll. 1 ff.), by Aḥ b. Muḥammad al-T͟haʿlabī al-Nīs͟hābūrī (died 1035) in his *Kas͟hf wa 'l-bayān* (cf. *GAS*, i, 615 Ḥākim al-D͟jus͟hamī (died 494/1101) in his volumi *Tafsīr*, and by Fak͟hr al-Dīn al-Rāzī in his *Ma al-g͟hayb* (cf. iii, 230, ult. ff.; ix, 160, ll. 13 ff. D͟jāḥiẓ uses the work sometimes (cf. *Ḥayawān* 73, ll. -4 ff.; also 205, ll. 6 ff.?), and Ṭabarī have known it, although he does not mentio Aṣamm by name. But it was interesting main theologically-minded commentators and acces obviously only in the East. Whether the ms. Ali 53/8 really contains the text (cf. *GAL*, S II, no. 7) has still to be checked.

This Baṣran Muʿtazilī should not be confou with another Muʿtazilī by the name of Abū al-Aṣamm who lived in Egypt and who initi the *miḥna* there at the instigation of Ibn Abī Du He was called Naṣr b. Abī Layt͟h and was at one generation younger than ʿAbd al-Raḥmā Kaysān (cf. Ḳāḍī ʿIyāḍ, *Tartīb al-madārik*, B 1387/1967, i, 516, ll. -5 ff.; 527, ll. 6 ff.; 564, p etc.; cf. the index).

Bibliography: Given in the article, but also amongst sources: As͟hʿarī, *Maḳālāt*, l. 2; 456, ll. 9 ff.; 458, ll. 3 ff.; 564, ll. 3 f.; N bak͟htī, *Firaḳ al-S͟hīʿa*, 14, ll. 1 ff. = Ḳun *Maḳālāt*, 14, ll. 3 f.; Ibn Baṭṭa, *Ibāna*, ed. Lac 91, ll. 15 f. and 92, l. 16; al-S͟harīf al-Murtaḍā *Fuṣūl al-muk͟htāra*[2], i, 63, ll. 10 ff.:[3] 68, 4 ff.; ʿAbd al-D͟jabbār, *al-Mug͟hnī*, xx[2], 61, ll. Bag͟hdādī, *al-Farḳ bayn al-firaḳ*, 95, l. 7; id *Uṣūl al-dīn*, 7, ll. 14 ff. and 36, ult. ff.; Abū Y *al-Muʿtamad fī uṣūl al-dīn*, ed. Haddad, 37, and 222, ll. 3 ff.; D͟juwaynī, *al-S͟hāmil*, i, 168, Pazdawī, *Uṣūl al-dīn*, ed. Linss, 11. pu. f.; S͟h rastānī, *Milal*, 19, ll. 3 ff.; 51, ll. 5 ff.; 53, ll. Ibn al-Murtaḍā, *Ṭabaḳāt al-Muʿtazila*, ed. Diw Wilzer, 56, ll. 17 ff.; Ibn Ḥad͟jar, *Lisān al-mī* iii, 427, ll. 2 ff.; Dāwūdī, *Ṭabaḳāt al-mufassirīn*, ʿAlī Muḥammad ʿUmar, Cairo 1392/1972, i, no. 258. Studies: M. Horten, *Die philosophis Systeme der spekulativen Theologen im Islam*, B 1912, 298 f.; A. S. Tritton, *Muslim theol* London 1947, 126 f.; A. N. Nader, *Le sys philosophique des Muʿtazila*, Beirut 1956, in s.v. Abū Bakr al-Aṣam (*sic*); H. Brentjes, *Imamatslehren im Islam*, Berlin 1964, 43, W. Madelung, *Der Imam al-Qāsim ibn Ibrāh* Berlin 1965, 42 f.; E. Gräf, in *Bustān*, x/2-3 (19 44; H. Laoust, *La politique de Ġazālī*, Paris 1 231; H. Daiber, *Das theologisch-philosophi System des Muʿammar ibn ʿAbbād al-Sulamī*, Be 1975, Index s.v. (JOSEF VAN ES

ASĀṬĪR AL-AWWALĪN "stories of ancients," a phrase occurring nine times in Ḳurʾān (VI, 25/25, VIII, 31/31, XVI, 24/26, XX 83/85, XXV, 5/6, XXVII, 68/70, XLVI, 17 LXVIII, 15/15, and LXXXIII, 13/13; see also ɔ8ob, s.v. KHALḲ) and there "put exclusively in mouth of unbelievers. . . expressing themselves ıst the Ḳur'ānic revelation or, more specifically, ıst the doctrine of the Resurrection, by referring he *asāṭīr* of the former (generations) when .ar, and in their opinion silly, things could .dy be found without being accepted" (R. Paret, *Koran, Kommentar*, Stuttgart 1971, 137). The nentators (e.g. al-Ṭabarī, to VIII, 31) connected se at one point with the opponent of the Prophet, aḍr b. al-Ḥārith. Travelling as a merchant to or al-Ḥīra, he saw Christians praying and read- :he Gospels and, upon returning to Mecca, com- d their activities to the Prophet's allegedly ar worshipping. More interestingly, another ver- (Ibn Hishām, 191 f.) says that al-Naḍr compared Prophet's story-telling unfavourably with "the es of the Persian kings and the stories of Rustum Isfandiyār" he had learned in al-Ḥīra.

e fact that, with the exception of XXV, 5/6, all rrences are at the ends of verses suggests a set ession that had been long in use. The appearance *āṭīr* in a verse by the *mukhaḍram* poet ʿAbd Allāh .-Ziʿbarā, although attribution and date are un- ain, seems to support the assumption of its ency in Mecca in pre-Islamic times (cf. J. Horo- *Koranische Untersuchungen*, Berlin-Leipzig 1926, A. Jeffery, *The foreign vocabulary of the Qur'ān*, ɔda 1938, 56 f.; P. Minganti, in *RSO*, xxxviii, 3), 326 f., 351). With its general meaning hardly ɔubt, most of the discussion has concerned the ımatical form and, more generally, the derivation e word. It was declared a *plurale tantum*, or else ely hypothetical singular forms were recon- :ted (Lane, 1358b). Its widely accepted derivation *s-ṭ-r* led to meanings such as "writings, written ɔunts, stories)." It was glossed "lying stories," *sādjīʿ* "rhymed prose pieces," or, frequently, *hāt* "obscure and confused statements." It was ained as reflecting *s-ṭ-r ʿalā* in the sense of "mak- up embellished stories for" (Ibn al-Athīr, *al- iya*, s. rad.). Later Muslims (as, strangely, also odern scholar, D. Künstlinger, in *OLZ*, xxxix 6), 482), imbued with respect for the cultural evements of the "ancients," would ask themselves the phrase should have been used in a negative when "the ancients wrote things containing vledge and wisdom which it was not blame- hy to state", and give the answer that use of as meant to criticise the Ḳur'ān as unrevealed s difficult and obscure (Ibn al-Djawzī, *Zād al- r*, Damascus 1384-8, iii, 20, to VI, 25).

ientalists, beginning, it seems, with Golius, have ested a derivation from Greek *historia*; see, the references in T. Nöldeke and F. Schwally, *hichte des Qorāns*, i, 16; Horovitz; Jeffery; Köbert, in *Orientalia, N.S.*, xiv (1945), 274-6; osenthal, *A History of Muslim historiography*², en 1968, 28 f.; Paret, *op. cit.*). This is philologi- possible and would make good sense. However, ıer this etymology nor another connecting the l with Syriac *sh-ṭ-r* "stupidities" (Künstlinger) ɔe supported by proof, nor is there any compelling ence for a South Arabian origin. For the time g, its connection with Arabic *s-ṭ-r* "to write" sibly supported also by Ḳur'ān, XXV, 5/6) ars to have the best claim to being correct.

Bibliography: given in the article.

(F. ROSENTHAL)

SHĪK WEYSEL, modern Turkish ÂŞIK VEYSEL 4-1973), Turkish folk poet and the last great esentative of the tradition of *Sāz shāʿirleri* [see ḲARADJAOGHLAN]. He was born in Sivrialan, a village near Sharḳīshla of Sivas province, the son of a farmer, Ḳara Aḥmed, whose family name of Shātīr-oghlu Weysel rarely used. Loss of sight in both his eyes at the age of seven followed smallpox. At ten he began to chant poetry accompanied by his instrument the *sāz* [*q.v.*]. An *ʿāshiḳ* of his own village and other wandering folk poets whom he came across and who discovered his talent, taught him poetry and music and encouraged him to continue. In 1931, in a traditional gathering of folk poets at Sivas, he was hailed as a prominent *ʿāshiḳ*. In 1933 he joined, as a volunteer, the 10th Anniversary celebrations of the Turkish Republic in Ankara, to which he went wandering on foot during several months, accompanied by a friend. He went all over Anatolia reciting his poems and playing his *sāz*. He performed many times on Ankara and Istanbul radios. For a short while (1942-4) he taught folk songs in the Village Institutes [see KÖY ENSTITULERI]. He died in his village on 21 March 1973. ʿĀshīḳ Weysel was married and had six children. Differing from many contemporary folk poets who joined the "social protest" literature of most modern writers, ʿĀshīḳ Weysel preferred to follow the classical tradition of folk poetry in the line of Ḳaradjaoghlan, Emrāh, Rukhṣatī and others, and he sang of love, friendship, nostalgia, separation, life's mutability and death. He is the author of *Deyişler* (1944) and *Sazımdan sesler* (1950). His collected works have been edited by Ümit Yaşar Oğuzcan as *Dostlar beni hatırlasın* (1970).

Bibliography: Ü. Y. Oğuzcan, *Aşık Veysel, hayatı ve şiirleri* Istanbul 1963; S. K. Karaalioğlu, *Resimli Türk edebiyatçıları sözlüğü*, Istanbul 1974, s.v.

(FAHİR İZ)

ASHRAF AL-DĪN GĪLĀNĪ, Persian journalist and poet, was born in Rasht in 1871. He completed his early studies in Ḳazwīn, and from 1883 to 1888 was a theological student in Nadjaf. Returning to Rasht, he earned his living as a letter-writer until the Revolution of 1906, when he began the publication of *Nasīm-i Shimāl* (a name that he also sometimes used as his *takhallūṣ*). This weekly journal was suppressed after the counter-revolution of Muḥammad ʿAlī Shāh in 1908, but the following years Ashraf accompanied the Constitutionalist forces on their successful occupation of Tehran, where he resumed publication of his journal. Although he admired Riḍā Khān, he abandoned public life after the latter's accession to the throne in 1925, and devoted himself to literary pursuits. Apart from his poems, which mostly first appeared in *Nasīm-i Shimāl*, he wrote a novel in verse and prose and works on history and philosophy. He died in poverty and ill-health in 1934.

Though Ashraf's poetic talent was not up to the level of some of his contemporaries, he was an influential innovator in the use of colloquial vocabulary and style. He was an ardent supporter of constitutionalism and social reform, including the emancipation of women, and a fervent patriot who often cited the example of Persia's great past. *Nasīm-i Shimāl* was regarded as one of the best literary journals of its day.

Bibliography: Ashraf's poems were collected in *Bāgh-i Bihisht*, Tehran 1919, and *Djild-i duwwum-i Nasīm-i Shimāl*, Bombay 1927. Biographical details in: E. G. Browne, *Press and poetry of modern Persia*, Cambridge 1914, 182-200; M. Ishaque, *Sukhanwarān-i Īrān dar ʿaṣr-i ḥāḍir*, i, Calcutta 1933, 146-70; ibid., *Modern Persian poetry*, Calcutta 1943, passim; Sayyid Muḥammad Bāḳir

Burḳaʿī, *Sukhanwarān-i nāmī-yi muʿāṣir*, ii, Tehran 1951, 250-5; Muḥammad Ṣadr Hāshimī, *Tāʾrīkh-i djarāʾid wa madjallāt-i Īrān*, iv, Tehran 1953, 295-9; Bozorg Alavi, *Geschichte und Entwicklung der modernen persischen Literatur*, Berlin 1964, 51-5. (L. P. Elwell-Sutton)

ASHTURKA, Asturka, the Spanish town of Astorga, the Asturica Augusta of the Roman period, capital of the Conventus Asturum, already by then a focal point for communications (J. M. Roldán, *Iter ab Emerita Asturicam. El camino de la Plata*, Salamanca 1971), and later a halting-point on the "route of the herds" (R. Aiken, *Rutas de trashumancia en la Meseta castellana*, in *Estudios geográficos*, xxvi (1947), 192-3) and on the "road to St. James" (C. E. Dubler, *Los caminos a Compostela en la obra de Idrisi*, in *And.*, xiv (1949), 114; N. Benavides Moro, *Otro camino a Santiago por tierra leonesa*, in *Tierras de León*, v (1964). Al-ʿUdhrī compares it with Saragossa (F. de la Granja, *La Marca Superior en la obra de al-ʿUdrī*, in *Estudios Edad Media Corona Aragón* (1967), 456). Astorga was another *urbs magnifica*, although Theodoric destroyed it in 456 (A. Quintana, *Astorga en en tempo de los suevos*, in *Archivos Leoneses* (1966). Al-Idrīsī says that Astorga was "a small town, surrounded by a green countryside" (E. Saavedra, *La geografía de España del Edrisi*, Madrid 1881, 67, 80; Ḥ. Muʾnis, *Taʾrīkh al-djughrāfiya wa 'l-djughrāfiyyīn fi 'l-Andalus*, Madrid 1967, 265).

Astorga was captured by Ṭāriḳ b. Ziyād in 95/714. In 718 there was formed to the north of it the kingdom of the Asturias, which nevertheless did not include all the territory of the Conventus Asturum (G. Fabre, *Le tissu urban dans le N.O. de la péninsule ibérique*, in *Latomus* (1970), 337). The region was settled by Berbers, who rose against the Arabs in 123/740-1 (*Akhbār madjmūʿa*, 38, tr. 48). The Christian advance which overcame the Muslims and expelled them from the whole of Djalīḳiya (133/750-1) compelled them "to cross the mountains towards Asturḳa" (*ibid.*, 62, tr. 66). It seems definite that in this region, the Berber element has left behind an enduring ethnic imprint (= Maragatos (?); P. Guichard, *Al-Andalus. Estructura antropológica de una sociedad islámica en Occidente*, Barcelona 1976, 143 n. 5, 146). Alfonso I reconquered Astorga in 753-4, but it was not repopulated till *ca.* 854 (C. Sanchez Albornoz, *Despoblación y repoblación del valle del Duero*, Buenos Aires 1966, 261-2; *idem*, *Repoblación del reino asturleonés. Proceso, dinámica y proyecciones*, in *CHE*, liii-liv (1971), 236-49) or in 860 (J. M. Lacarra, *Panorama de la historia urbana en la peninsula desde los siglos V al X*, in *Settimane. . . Spoleto*, 1958, 352). In 179/795 the town was attacked by Hishām I's general ʿAbd al-Karīm b. Mughīth (A. Fliche, *Alphonse II le Chaste et les origines de la reconquête chrétienne*, and A. de la Torre, *Las etapas de la reconquista hasta Alfonso II*, in *Estudios sobre la Monarquía asturiana*, Oviedo 1971, 115-31, 133-74). In 267/878, al-Mundhir launched an expedition against Astorga. We possess documents dating from that year proving the presence there of Mozarabes (M. Gómez Moreno, *Iglesias mozárabes*, Madrid 1919, 107-11), who played a key role in the repopulating of the town (L. C. Kofman and M. I. Carzolio, *Acerca de la demografía astur-leonesa y castellana en la Alta Edad Media*, in *CHE*, xlvii-xlviii (1968), 136-70). Under Alfonso III, Astorga, by now properly organised, was part of a defensive line with Coimbra, Leon and Amaya (Sanchez Albornoz, *Las campañas del 882 y del 883 que Alfonso III esperó en León*, in *León y su historia*, i (1969), 169-82). The bish[…] was re-established there (A. Quintana Prieto[…] *obispado de Astorga en los siglos IX y X*, As[…] 1968), and its bishops played an important ro[…] political life (L. Goñi Gaztambide, *Historia* […] *Bula de la Cruzada en España*, Vitoria 1958, […] 155, 184, 203, 386, 521, 681, 683; H. Salv[…] Martínez, *El "Poema de Almería" y la épica romá*[…] Madrid 1975, 48-9, 399). It was attacked b[…] Manṣūr Ibn Abī ʿĀmir [*q.v.*] in 385/995. It fell int[…] cay at the beginning of the 14th century. In the […] century the "marquisate of Astorga" was fo[…] there (A. Seijas Vazquez, *Chantada y el señor*[…] *los Marqueses de Astorga*, Chantada 1966).

Bibliography: Sources: Lévi-Provençal, *H*[…] i, ii, indices; Sanchez Albornoz, *Origenes d*[…] *Nación española: Estudios críticos sobre la His*[…] *del Reino de Asturias*, Oviedo 1972; M. Diaz y I[…] *La historiografía hispana desde la invasion d*[…] *hasta el año 1000*, in *Settimane . . . Spoleto*, 1[…] 313-43. There exists an outstanding monograp[…] M. Rodríguez Díaz, *Historia de la muy noble,* […] *y benemérita ciudad de Astorga*, Astorga 1909. (M. J. Viguer[…]

ASMĀʾ Bint ʿUmays b. Maʿd al-Khathʿami[…] a contemporary of the Prophet (d. 39/659[…] Her mother, Hind bint ʿAwf b. Zubayr, calle[…] ʿAdjūz al-Djurashiyya, was famous through […] illustriousness of her sons-in-law, amongst w[…] were included the Prophet, al-ʿAbbās b. ʿAbd[…] Muṭṭalib and Ḥamza b. ʿAbd al-Muṭṭalib […] Ḥabīb, *Muḥabbar*, 91, 109), as well as of Asm[…] husbands. In fact, the latter probably marrie[…] the first place Rabīʿa b. Riyāḥ al-Hilālī, by w[…] she had three sons, Mālik, ʿAbd Allāh and […] Hubayra; but all the sources agree that she […] successively the wife of (1) Djaʿfar b. Abī Ṭālib, […] whom she had three further sons, ʿAbd Allāh, ʿ[…] and Muḥammad, with whom she emigrated […] Abyssinia, where she saw for the first time b[…] introducing them subsequently into usage in Ara[…] the continuance of Djaʿfar's line was assumed […] Muḥammad; (2) Abū Bakr, by whom she […] Muḥammad; and (3) ʿAlī b. Abī Ṭālib, by whom […] further had Yaḥyā. Despite all these marriages, […] was not considered to be one of the famous *muta*[…] *widjāt*, and the number of sons which she bro[…] into the world does not seem to have attra[…] particular attention.

On the other hand, she is considered to be […] authoress of a *Kitāb* which Yaʿḳūbī cites (*Histo*[…] ii, 114, 128) and which must have contained *ḥa*[…] of the Prophet; that Asmāʾ should have made s[…] a compilation, which would circulate in Shīʿī cir[…] is a priori suspect, even though ʿAlī's main w[…] Fāṭima, would have been able to hand on to As[…] the doings and happenings concerning her fat[…] Furthermore, the Sunnīs seem to have accepted […] with reservations *ḥadīths* transmitted by this wo[…] (cf. I. Goldziher, *Muh. Studien*, ii, 9, Fr. tr. […] Bercher, Paris 1952, 10-11, Eng. tr. Barber […] Stern, London 1967-71, ii, 22).

Bibliography: Ibn al-Kalbī-Caskel, *Djamh*[…] Tab. 226 and ii, 198; Zubayrī, *Nasab Ḳuraysh*, […] 277; Ibn ʿAbd al-Barr, *Istīʿāb*, iv, 234-6; Ibn S[…] *Ṭabaḳāt*, viii, 205-9; Ibn Ḳutayba, *Maʿārif*, ind[…] Masʿūdī, *Murūdj*, iv, 181-2, v, 148 = §§ 1515-[…] 1908; Balādhurī, *Futūḥ*, 451-5; Nawawī, *Tah*[…] *al-asmāʾ*, 825; Maḳdisī, *al-Badʾ wa 'l-taʾrīkh*, […] 137; Ibn Ḥadjar, *Iṣāba*, iv, No. 51; Caet[…] *Annali*, x, 231-5.

(Ch. Pellat[…]

-ASMAR, ᶜABD AL-SALĀM B. SALĪM AL-
RŪRĪ, 16th century revivalist of the ᶜArūs-
order, was born on 12 Rabīᶜ I 380/16 July
in the coastal oasis of Zlīṭen (Zalīṭan, Zlīṭan;
lete forms, Zalīṭan, Yazlīṭan, Yazlīṭīn, Izlīṭan)
Tripolitania. He belonged to the Faytūriyya
ꞏātir) tribe, whence his laḳab, while the nickname
smar was given to him by his mother who had
ordered to do so in a dream. He received his
ꞏ mystical training from ᶜAbd al-Wāḥid alālī, a k̲h̲alīfa [q.v.] of the ᶜArūsiyya order, who
ated him into this ṭarīḳa [q.v.] and to whose
e of disciples he belonged for seven years. Ac-
ᵢng to the canonised history of the order, he
ᵢved additional instruction from eighty other
k̲h̲s before he started to manifest himself as the
ꞏalist of al-ᶜArūsiyya, whose coming had been
ᵢicted by the founder of this ṭarīḳa Aḥmad b.
ᵢs (d. 868/1463). His proselytising efforts ined him in tribal rivalries and led to accusations
orcery and heresy being brought against him.
various occasions he was expelled from villages
from tribal territories, where he must have
ᵢsed the hostility of the population because of
ᵢenunciations of the prevailing marriage customs
WK, 113; see Bibliography), mourning rites
WK, 117), and of the relatively free social inter-
ꞏgling of the sexes in tribal society (see e.g. WK,
ꞏ. He was expelled from the town of Tripoli,
ꞏe he had settled in the early 16th century, and
ꞏe he had become an increasingly popular religious
ꞏer, by the local ruler, who may well have con-
red ᶜAbd al-Salām's proselytising activities as
ꞏt of a Ḥafṣid [q.v.] plot aimed at his overthrow
the re-establishment of the dynasty's power in
ꞏarea. The actual revival of the ṭarīḳa did not
ꞏt until after he again took up residence in Zlīṭen,
ꞏre he established a zāwiya [q.v.] in the territory
ꞏne of the local tribes, the Barāhima, who had
ꞏe to accept his claims to sainthood. Here he died
Ramaḍān 981/January 1574.
ᵃbd al-Salām al-Asmar gave a new direction to
original ᶜArūsiyya of which he amended the ritual
ꞏ to which he added his own body of teachings.
ꞏobliged his adherents to wear white clothes (WK,
ꞏff.), forbade smoking (WK, 70), and introduced
playing of the bandīr (duff) during the ḥaḍra
ꞏ], claiming that he had received an authorisation
ꞏthis effect from heaven (al-Mulayd̲j̲ī, 257 ff.; see
ꞏiography). In addition, he prohibited self-mutila-
ꞏ during the ḥaḍra (WK, 201) and stressed the
ꞏortance of attending these occasions by pro-
ꞏming that attendance was half the wird [q.v.] and
ꞏt absence consequently meant abandoning the
ꞏd (WK, 170; Rawḍat, 307), which had come to
ꞏsist of a number of awrād composed by ᶜAbd al-
ꞏām himself, in addition to the original ᶜArūsī wird
Mulayd̲j̲ī, 393 ff.). He claimed that the ᶜArūsiyya
ꞏe the original S̲h̲ād̲h̲iliyya [q.v.], which was the
ꞏḳa practised by the most intimate companions
the Prophet (Rawḍat, 104), and that its out-
ꞏnding nature was testified to by the fact that in a
ꞏaculous act, the angels had written the names of
s̲h̲ayk̲h̲s mentioned in the silsila [q.v.] on the lawḥ
ꞏaḥfūẓ [q.v.] (WK, 267). Moreover, he taught that
ꞏbody who knew his speech by heart, i.e. who
morised everything which had been written down
ꞏe himself was an analphabetic—of that which
had ever said (which was partly codified in ḳaṣīdas
ꞏ.] sung during the ḥaḍra and on other ceremonial
ꞏasions) would be protected by God in this world
ꞏ in the next (WK, 217), and that his adherents

would be assisted by him, wherever they were, by
means of his miraculous omnipresence (WK, 262;
this belief is also expressed in the introductory lines
to every ḳaṣīda composed by him, viz. al-asmar fī
kullⁱⁿ dīwān, kursīhi fī 'l-wasaṭ al-ᶜalī. . .). Members
of the order were moreover required to direct their
lives in accordance with a number of ethical precepts
and admonitions elaborated by ᶜAbd al-Salām in a
set of rules known as al-Waṣiyya al-kubrā, which is
very similar to the Ṣūfī tracts on ādāb [q.v.] of earlier
eras. To abandon the ṭarīḳa was considered as equal
to apostasy and would, as was taught, not be considered as such only by those belonging to the
order, but by God himself (WK, 260). ᶜAbd al-Salām
exhorted his adherents to adopt al-Sanūsī's ᶜaḳīda
in matters of tawḥīd (WK, 3), but urged them at
the same time to pay tribute to Ibn al-ᶜArabī as the
greatest walī [q.v.] of all times—except for the
Prophets and the companions of the Prophet Muḥammad—and stressed him as the pillar of the ṭarīḳa
(WK, 245).

The period in which ᶜAbd al-Salām lived, largely
coincided with the turbulent era in which the
Ḥafṣids, the Spaniards, local tribal chiefs, the
Knights of Saint John and the Ottomans, had all
become involved in the struggle for control of
Tripolitania. This caused conditions of life to become
increasingly unsettled, and must have made it possible for an exclusivist mystical salvationist movement, like the one into which the original ᶜArūsiyya
had been elaborated by ᶜAbd al-Salām, to flourish
and spread the way it did.

Throughout the collections of sayings and texts
attributed to ᶜAbd al-Salām al-Asmar, the ṭarīḳa is
referred to as al-ᶜArūsiyya. It does not seem to
have been referred to as al-Salāmiyya until in the
19th century in Tunisia (cf. Muḥammad Muḥammad
Mas̲h̲īna, al-Anwār al-ḳudsiyya fī 'l-kas̲h̲f ᶜan ḥaḳīḳa
al-ṭarīḳa al-Salāmiyya al-S̲h̲ād̲h̲iliyya, Cairo 1365,
9), where the order had obtained a substantial membership, in particular in the southern parts (cf.
Mustafa Kraïem, La Tunésie pré-coloniale, Tunis
1973, ii, 129).

Nowadays, the names ᶜArūsiyya and Salāmiyya
are used more or less synonymously throughout
North Africa, except for Egypt where the names
refer to two distinct branches, which emerged there
in the 19th century. Active lodges of the ṭarīḳa of
ᶜAbd al-Salām may be found in Tunisia (see al-Ṣādiḳ
al-Rizḳī, al-Ag̲h̲ānī al-Tūnisiyya, Tunis 1967, 129 ff.),
in Egypt, where it has a wide-spread membership
(see Ibrāhīm Muḥammad al-Faḥḥām, Ibn ᶜArūs wa
'l-ṭarīḳa al-ᶜArūsiyya, in al-Funūn al-s̲h̲aᶜbiyya, iv
(Cairo 1970), no. 15, 71), and in Libya (see D̲j̲amīl
Hilāl, Dirāsāt fī 'l-wāḳiᶜ al-Lībī, Tripoli 1969, 141 f.;
ᶜAbd al-D̲j̲alīl al-Ṭāhir, al-Mud̲j̲tamaᶜ al-Lībī, dirāsāt
id̲j̲timāᶜiyya wa-ant̲h̲rūbūlūd̲j̲iyya, Ṣayḍā/Beirut
1969, 325ff.; and al-Muslim, xx (Cairo 1969), no.i, 23).
The shrine of ᶜAbd al-Salām at Zlīṭen has significance, as a centre of pilgrimage; religious education
is provided at the establishment attached to it
known as al-maᶜhad al-asmarī (cf. Mulayd̲j̲ī, 23).

Bibliography: al-Waṣiyya al-kubrā (abbreviated in the article as WK, with reference to the para-
graphs in which it is sub-divided), also known as
Naṣīḥat al-murīdīn li 'l-d̲j̲amāᶜa al-muntasibīn li
'l-ᶜArūsī, was published in Cairo n.d., in Tripoli
(cf. O. Depont and X. Coppolani, Les confréries
religieuses musulmanes, Algiers 1897, 339-49, 351),
and in Isḥāḳ Ibrāhīm al-Mulayd̲j̲ī, Fī hāmis̲h̲
ḥayāt Sīdī ᶜAbd al-Salām al-Asmar, Tripoli 1969,
422-529. This book contains also ᶜAbd al-Salām's

Waṣiyya al-ṣughra (which is essentially a summary of *the Waṣiyya al-kubrā*), the texts of various prayers (*aḥzāb*) composed by him (402-19), a collection of his admonitions as well as a list of works (largely unpublished) containing data about al-Asmar's life (247 ff.). The biography presented in it is based upon oral information collected by the author (cf. 93) and upon materials contained in Muḥammad b. Muḥammad b. Makhlūf al-Munastirlī, *Tanḳīh rawḍat al-azhār wa-munyat al-sādāt al-abrār fī manāḳib Ṣīdī ʿAbd al-Salām al-Asmar*, Tunis 1325/1907-8. This work, also known under the title *Mawāhib al-raḥīm fī manāḳib Mawlānā al-Shaykh Sīdī ʿAbd al-Salām Ibn Salīm* (cf. *Tanḳīh*, 4), is an abridgement of the unpublished *Rawḍat al-azhār wa-munyat al-sādāt al-abrār fī manāḳib Ṣāḥib al-Ṭār*, by Karīm al-Dīn al-Barmūnī, a disciple of ʿAbd al-Salām al-Asmar. A sample of al-Asmar's poetry, reflecting his ideas, may also be found in al-Rizḳī's book referred to in the article and in ʿAbd al-Salām al-Asmar, *Safīnat al-buḥūr*, Cairo 1969. For a defence of playing the *bandīr* (*duff*) in this *ṭarīḳa*, see Muḥammad Muḥammad Mashīna, *Risālat al-ḳawl al-maʿrūf fī aḥkām al-ḍarb bi 'l-dufūf*, contained in Mashīna's *al-Anwār al-ḳudsiyya* (see the article). For details about the history of al-Salāmiyya and al-ʿArūsiyya in Egypt and further references, see F. De Jong, *Ṭuruq and ṭuruq-linked institutions in 19th century Egypt, passim*, Leiden 1978. In addition to these references and the references in the article, see the biographies by Ṭāhā Muḥammad Mashīna al-Tādjūrī, *al-Ṭarīḳa al-Salāmiyya al-Shādhiliyya*, in *Madjallat al-Islām wa 'l-Taṣawwuf* (1959), no. 10, 79-81; Sālim b. Hamūda, *al-Shaykh ʿAbd al-Salām al-Asmar*, in *al-Muslim* xiii (Cairo 1962), no. 8, 16-20; Muḥammad al-Bashīr Ẓāfir, *al-Yawāḳīt al-thamīna fī aʿyān madhhab ʿālim al-Madīna*, Cairo 1324-5/1906-7, 200 f.; Muḥammad ʿAbd al-Ḥayy al-Kattānī, *Fihris al-fahāris*, Cairo 1346/1927-8, i, 147. (F. DE JONG)

ASSASSINS [see ḤASHĪSHIYYA].

ASSOCIATION [see ANDJUMĀN, DJAMʿIYYA].

ASYLUM [see BAST, BĪMĀRISTĀN].

ʿATABĀT (A. "thresholds"), more fully, *ʿatabāt-i ʿāliya* or *ʿatabāt-i muḳaddasa* ("the lofty or sacred thresholds"), the Shīʿī shrine cities of ʿIrāḳ—Nadjaf, Karbalāʾ, Kāẓimayn and Sāmarrā [*q.vv.*]—comprising the tombs of six of the *Imāms* as well as a number of secondary shrines and places of visitation.

Nadjaf, 10 km. to the west of Kūfa, is the alleged site of burial of ʿAlī b. Abī Ṭālib (d. 41/661) (another shrine dedicated to ʿAlī is that at Mazār-i Sharīf in Northern Afghanistan; see Khwadja Sayf al-Din Khudjandī, *Karwān-i Balkh*, Mazār-i Sharīf, n.d., 18 ff.). His tomb is said to have been kept secret throughout the Umayyad period, and was marked with a dome for the first time in the late 3rd/9th century by Abu 'l-Haydjāʾ, the Ḥamdānid ruler of Mosul; this early structure was repaired and expanded by ʿAḍud al-Dawla the Buwayhid in 369/979-80 (Ibn al-Athīr, viii, 518). Karbalāʾ, 100 km. to the south-west of Baghdād, the site of the martyrdom and burial in 61/680 of Ḥusayn b. ʿAlī, became very early a centre of Shīʿī pilgrimage; according to Shīʿī tradition, the first pilgrim was Djābir b. ʿAbd Allāh, who visited the site forty days after the death of Ḥusayn. Endowments were settled on the shrine (known as Mashhad al-Ḥāʾir, "shrine of the garden pool") by Umm Mūsā, mother of the ʿAbbāsid caliph al-Mahdī (Ṭabarī, iii, 752), but it was temporarily destroyed in 236/850 by an ʿAbbāsid less favourable to the Shīʿa, Mutawakkil: he caused the site to be flooded (Ṭa iii, 1407). By the time that Ibn Ḥawḳal vis Karbalāʾ in 366/977, the shrine had evidently restored (ed. J. H. Kramers, i, 166), and it expanded, like that at Nadjaf, by ʿAḍud al-D in the late 4th/10th century (Ibn al-Athīr, *loc. cit*

From the Buwayhid period onward, Nadjaf Karbalāʾ, the two most important of the *ʿat* have in fact had a common destiny, each recei patronage and pilgrimage from the successive querors and rulers of ʿIrāḳ. Thus Malik Shāh Saldjūḳ visited both Nadjaf and Karbalāʾ in 1086-7 and bestowed gifts on the shrines (Ibn Athīr, x, 103). Spared by the Mongol invaders, two shrines prospered under Il Khānid rule. ʿ al-Dīn Djuwaynī Ṣāḥib al-Dīwān had a hos erected at Nadjaf in 666/1267 to accomodate grims, and also began the construction of a c linking the city with the Euphrates (ʿAbbās ʿAzzāwī, *Taʾrīkh al-ʿIrāḳ bayn iḥtilālayn*, Bagh 1354/1935, i, 263, 310). In 703/1303, Ghāzān K visited both shrines: in Nadjaf he built a lodging the *sayyid*s resident there (*dār al-siyāda*), toge with a further hostel for pilgrims, as well as impro the canal constructed by Djuwaynī, and he besto similar favours on Karbalāʾ (Rashīd al-Dīn Allāh, *Taʾrīkh-i mubārak-i Ghāzānī*, ed. K. J London 1940, 191, 203, 208). After his captur Baghdād in 803/1400, Tīmūr made a pilgrimag Nadjaf and Karbalāʾ and presented gifts to shrines (al-ʿAzzāwī, *op. cit.*, ii, 240).

In the 10th/16th century, ʿIrāḳ became an ob of dispute between the Ṣafawids and the Ottom and both sides endowed and patronised the shr of Nadjaf and Karbalāʾ during their periods control. Shāh Ismāʿīl the Ṣafawid visited and stowed gifts on the two shrines in 914/1508, as as restoring the canal at Nadjaf dug in Il Khā times (al-ʿAzzāwī, *op. cit.*, iii, 316, 341). Su Sulaymān Ḳānūnī made a similar pilgrimage Nadjaf and Karbalāʾ after his conquest of ʿIrā 941/1534, and had a new irrigation canal dug Karbalāʾ, called *al-nahr al-sulaymānī* after (al-ʿAzzāwī, *op. cit.*, iv, 29, 36-7). Shāh ʿAbbā restored ʿIrāḳ and the *ʿatabāt* to Ṣafawid con in 1032/1623; this new occupation, terminated Murād IV in 1048/1638, led to a further enrich and expansion of the shrines at both Nadjaf Karbalāʾ. Again in the years 1156-9/1743-6, part ʿIrāḳ, including Nadjaf and Karbalāʾ, were tem rarily removed from Ottoman sovereignty, this t by Nādir Shāh; he is variously reported to have the main dome at Karbalāʾ gilded, and to h plundered the treasury at the shrine. This was last time that Ottoman rule of ʿIrāḳ was threate from Iran, but throughout the 13th/19th cent royal Iranian patronage of both Nadjaf and Karb continued, and it is this that accounts for the lar Iranian appearance of the shrines in the present Āghā Muḥammad Khān, the first Ḳādjār mona had the dome at Karbalāʾ regilded, and endo the tomb at Nadjaf with a golden grill (H. Al *Religion and state in Iran, 1785-1906*; *the role of Ulama in the Qajar period*, Berkeley and Los Ang 1969, 42). Following his example, Fatḥ ʿAlī S had the minarets at Karbalāʾ gilded, as well reconstructing the dome out of gold bricks; Muḥ mad Shāh provided for the repair of the dam inflicted on Karbalāʾ by the Wahhābīs during t incursion of 1216/1801; and Nāṣir al-Dīn Shāh him visited the *ʿatabāt* in 1287/1870 and commissio ous work in Nadjaf, Karbalāʾ and Kāẓimayn ar, *op. cit.*, 48, 104, 167). Gifts and endowments also sent to the *ᶜatabāt* by the rulers of various principalities in India, especially Oudh (J. N. ister, *The Shīᶜa of India*, London 1953, 107, 112, 3).

āẓimayn (also known as Kāẓimiyya), the third e *ᶜatabāt*, formerly a separate city on the right of the Tigris but now virtually a suburb of dād, is the site of the tombs of the seventh and h *Imāms*, Mūsā al-Kāẓim (d. 186/802) and ammad al-Taḳī (or al-Djawād) (d. 219/834). It pies a geographically central place among the āt, being situated between Sāmarrā to the h and Nadjaf and Karbalāʾ to the south, and always received a steady flow of pilgrims. Unlike iaf and Karbalāʾ, it did not escape the Mongol sion unscathed, and was extensively damaged fire during conquest of Baghdād in 656/1258. t of the existing structures in Kāẓimayn date the time of Shāh Ismāᶜīl, who was particularly sh with his patronage in Kāẓimayn because of claim to descent from the seventh *Imām*. The k begun under his auspices was completed by an Sulaymān in 941/1534 and restored and ex-ded by several Ḳādjār monarchs in the 19th ury. The major courtyard (*ṣaḥn*) at Kāẓimayn built in 1298/1880 by Farhād Mīrzā, a Ḳādjār ce. Also buried in Kāẓimayn are two early Shīᶜī lars, Sharīf al-Raḍī (d. 406/1015) and Sharīf urtaḍā (d. 436/1044); two sons of Mūsā al-Kāẓim, āᶜīl and Ibrāhīm; Ṭāhir b. Zayn al-ᶜĀbidīn, a of the fourth *Imām*; Khadīdja bint al-Ḥasan; Fāṭima bint al-Ḥusayn (L. Massignon, *Les saints ulmans enterrés à Bagdad*, in *Opera minora*, ed. Moubarac, Beirut, iii, 100-1).

āmarrā, the fourth of the *ᶜatabāt*, contains the bs of the tenth and eleventh *Imāms*, ᶜAlī al-Naḳī 254/868) and Ḥasan al-ᶜAskarī (d. 260/873), as as the cistern (*sardāb*) where the twelfth *Imām*, ammad al-Mahdī, entered the state of occultation *yba*) in 260/873 and where too he is destined to pear at the beginning of his renewed manifesta- at the end of time.

he *ᶜatabāt* play a role of great importance in the of Shīᶜī Islam, functioning almost as a secondary *a*. They are above all places of pilgrimage (*ziyārat*), ted by countless Shīᶜīs from Iran, the Indian sub-tinent and elsewhere. Pilgrimage to the *ᶜatabāt* sists primarily of circumambulating the sacred bs while reading a series of traditional prayers *āratnāma*) and fervently caressing the golden s enclosing the tombs; one may also seek the rcession of the *Imāms* or make to them a vow *dhr*). Karbalāʾ, which contains the tombs not of Ḥusayn but also of his half-brother, ᶜAbbās, his son, ᶜAlī Akbar, is in particular much fre-nted by pilgrims, who after their return home prefix the title "Karbalāʾī" to their names. The of Karbalāʾ, having been moistened with the od of Ḥusayn, is deemed to possess special proper-; from it is generally fashioned the clay disc *hr*) on which the Shīᶜa place their foreheads when strating in prayer. When diluted in water, the also yields a beverage (*āb-i turbat*) thought to e theurgical and curative properties; the sick, dying, and women in labour are caused to imbibe and it is lightly sprinkled over the face and lips he dead (H. Massé, *Croyances et coutumes persanes*, is 1938, i, 38, 96; B. A. Donaldson, *The wild rue*, don 1938, 205). The dust accumulating on the l around the tomb of Ḥusayn is also highly re-garded; it is carefully collected for its curative properties (Donaldson, *op. cit.*, 67), and is sometimes used in India as a lining for tombs (Hollister, *op. cit.*, 155). Burial at the *ᶜatabāt* is considered highly desirable, again with a marked preference being shown for Karbalāʾ; corpses are often transported for burial from Iran and India to the *ᶜatabāt*, where vast cemeteries have sprung up, particularly at Nadjaf and Karbalāʾ. Traditionally numerous pious Shīᶜīs have also gone to spend their last years in the *ᶜatabāt* as "neighbours" (*mudjāwirūn*) to the *Imāms*.

The *ᶜatabāt* have also occupied an important place in the intellectual and theological life of Shīᶜīsm, the *madrasas* situated there drawing scholars and students from every region of Shīᶜī population; Nadjaf, frequently entitled Dār al-ᶜIlm, is the chief centre of learning today in the Shīᶜī world. In the 12th/18th century, after the Afghān sack of Iṣfahān, many Iranian Shīᶜī scholars took refuge in the *ᶜatabāt*, and it was there—above all in Karbalāʾ—in the last quarter of the century that the long-standing contro-versy between the Akhbārī and Uṣūlī schools of *fiḳh* was settled in favour of the latter. Although centres of religious learning revived in Iran in the Ḳādjār period, the *ᶜatabāt* continued to exert their attraction, and most leading scholars either resided and taught there, or studied for a time before returning to Iran. When in the late 19th and early 20th centuries an important segment of the Iranian *ᶜulamāʾ* clashed with the Ḳādjār monarchy and supported the con-stitutional movement, the *ᶜatabāt*—particularly Nadjaf—came to function as an important base of clerical operations beyond the reach of the Iranian state. The role of three great constitutionalist *mudjtahids* resident in Nadjaf—ᶜAbd Allāh Māzan-darānī, Muḥammad Kāẓim Khurāsānī and Mīrzā Ḥusayn Khalīlī Ṭihrānī—deserves particular mention (see Abdul-Hadi Haʾiri, *Shīᶜsm and constitutionalism in Iran: a study of the role played by the clerical resi-dents of Iraq in Iranian politics*, Leiden 1977). *Mutatis mutandis*, Nadjaf has fulfilled a similar function in recent years, following the exile there in 1963 of Āyat Allāh Khumaynī. The Shīᶜī *ᶜulamāʾ* resident in the *ᶜatabāt* have also exerted influence on the 20th century history of ᶜIrāḳ; they played, for ex-ample, a directive role in attempts to thwart the imposition of a British mandate on the country (ᶜAbd Allāh Fahd al-Nafīsī, *Dawr al-Shīᶜa fī taṭawwur al-ᶜIrāḳ al-siyāsī al-ḥadīth*, Beirut 1973, 80 ff.).

Finally, mention may be made of the fact that the *ᶜatabāt* are of interest not only to the Ithnā ᶜAsharī Shīᶜa, but also to the adherents of various branches of Ismāᶜīlism; although they hardly ever make the *ḥadjdj*, they frequently perform pilgrimage to Nadjaf and Karbalāʾ (Hollister, *op. cit.*, 289, 391) and it is probable that a number of Nizārī *Imāms* of the post-Mongol period are buried in Nadjaf (W. Ivanow, *Tombs of some Persian Ismāᶜīlī Imams*, in *JBBRAS*, xiv (1938), 49-52). The Bektashīs, who in many ways may be considered a crypto-Shīᶜī sect, also used to maintain *tekkes* in Nadjaf, Karbalāʾ and Kāẓimayn (al-ᶜAzzāwī, *op. cit.*, iv, 152-3; Murat Sertoğlu, *Bektaşılık*, Istanbul 1969, 319).

Bibliography: in addition to references cited in the text: A. Nöldeke, *Das Heiligtum al-Husains zu Kerbela*, Berlin 1909; E. Herzfeld, *Archäologische Reise im Euphrat- und Tigrisgebiet*, Berlin 1919, ii, 102 ff., 145 ff.; Le Strange, *Lands of the Eastern Caliphate*, 56, 76-9; D. M. Donaldson, *The Shīᶜite religion*, London 1933 (numerous references); ᶜImād al-Dīn Ḥusaynī Iṣfahānī, *Taʾrīkh-i*

Dj̲ug̲h̲rāfiyāʾi-yi Karbalā-yi Muʿallā, Tehran 1326/1947; Dj̲aʿfar al-S̲h̲ayk̲h̲ Bāḳir Āl-Maḥbūba, Māḍī al-Nadj̲af wa-Ḥāḍiruhā, Nadj̲af 1955-7, 3 vols.; ʿAbd al-Dj̲awād al-Kilīddār Āl-Ṭaʿma, Taʾrīk̲h̲ al-Karbalāʾ wa-ḥāʾir al-Ḥusayn ʿalayhi ʾl-salām, Nadj̲af 1387/1967; Dj̲aʿfar al-K̲h̲alīlī, Mawsūʿat al-ʿatabāt, Bag̲h̲dād 1382-92/1969-72, vol. i, Karbalāʾ, vols. ii and iii, Nadj̲af, vol. iv, Sāmarrā.

(H. Algar)

ATAČ, Nūr Allāh, modern Turkish Nurullah Ataç (1898-1957), prominent Turkish essayist and literary critic, the guiding spirit of the Turkish contemporary linguistic and literary renewal for two decades (1935-55). Born in Istanbul, the son of Meḥmed ʿAṭāʾ, civil servant and writer (1856-1919), better known as the translator of J. von Hammer's *GOR* (from the French version), Atač signed his writings as Nūr Allāh ʿAṭāʾ until the introduction of family names in 1934, when he changed ʿAṭāʾ into Atač and later dropped Nūr Allāh altogether. Of his various pen-names, the most frequently used one was Kavafoğlu. Atač's education was irregular. He attended various schools (including Galatasaray for four years and then the Faculty of Letters), without finishing either. Although he spent some time in Switzerland during the First World War, his thorough knowledge of the French language and literature was, like all his accomplishments, mainly self-acquired. Atač made his living as a teacher, translator and constant contributor to a great number of newspapers and periodicals. He taught French literature and French in various schools of Istanbul, Ankara and the provinces, and served as a translator in government departments including the office of the President of the Republic. He died in Ankara on 17 May 1957.

Atač started his literary career in 1921 with poems, critical reviews and theatrical criticism in the famous fortnightly *Dergāh*, to which all the leading writers of the time and many young talents were contributors. At this period he was particularly interested in the theatre and wrote theatre reviews mainly in the daily *Aks̲h̲am* (see Metin And, *Ataç tiyatroda*, Istanbul 1973). Later he concentrated on literary criticism, and closely following the day-to-day developments of the literary scene, wrote articles of criticism untiringly in more than sixty newspapers and periodicals, particularly in *Aks̲h̲am, Akşam, Ḥākimiyyet-i milliyye, Milliyet, Varlık, Yeni adam, Tan, Son posta, Haber, Tercüme, Ülkü, Türk dili, Cumhuriyet, Pazar postası, Dünya*, and most frequently of all, *Ulus* (see Konur Ertop, *Ataç bibliyoğrafyası*, in *Ataç*, ed. *Türk Dil Kurumu*, Ankara 1962). Atač developed the essay, a much-neglected field in Turkish literature, into an independent *genre* of which he became a recognised master, and had many followers. He wrote thousands of essays on literature, classical and modern, on cultural change and problems of culture in general, on individual writers, etc. with a very personal, natural, concise and unadorned style. In the early 1940s he espoused the language reform movement and gave it great support and impetus, increasing its prestige in literary circles. It is no exaggeration to say that he became the greatest master of the nascent contemporary Turkish prose, and his style was taken as the model by many young writers. This prose was to supersede that of the pre-1930 masters like R. K̲h̲. Karay, Res̲h̲ād Nūrī Güntekin [*q.vv.*] and others. Although Atač's authority as a literary critic is controversial because he chose a subjective and impressionistic approach to criticism according to his own temperament and per[...] taste, it is unanimously accepted that it is his [...] flair as a critic which discovered and launched [...] young talents on to the literary scene (e.g. C[...] Veli Kanık, F. H. Dağlarca, etc.). Restless, i[...]tient, aggressive by temperament and equipped [...] a piercing mind and armed with "methodical do[...] Atač waged an unrelenting war against fanati[...] intolerance, sentimentality, "poetical" artifici[...] clichés and ready-made thoughts and form[...] He was a conscious extremist in language reform[...] believed that only the "self-sacrifice" of som[...] tremists would nullify the harm caused by [...] ultra-conservatives. Atač studied 15th century [...] works, particularly Merdj̲ümek Aḥmed's mas[...] translation of Kay Kāʾūs's *Ḳābūs-nāma* [see [...] kāʾūs b. iskandar] and used them as the mod[...] a new style. He experimented successfully wi[...] new syntax which included inversion (*devrik tü*[...] which naturally exists in spoken Turkish and w[...] was frequently used in early Turkish writings b[...] the syntax of the written Turkish was "fro[...] Atač coined a number of neologisms, some of w[...] survived and were incorporated into the lang[...] (for a list of Atač's neologisms, see *Ataçın sözcü*[...] ed. Türk Dil Kurumu, Ankara 1963). Atač [...] several thousand essays and articles, some of w[...] (mostly his post-1940 writings) have been publ[...] in book form in 10 volumes: *Günlerin getirdiği* (1[...] *Karalama defteri* (1952), *Sözden söze* (1952) *Ar*[...] (1954), *Diyelim* (1954), *Söz arasında* (1957), *Oku*[...] *mektuplar* (1958), *Günce* (1960), *Prospero ile Ca*[...] (1961), *Söyleşiler*, 2 vols. (1964) Atač's diaries c[...]ing the years 1953-7 have been published in [...] volumes as *Günce*, Ankara 1972.

Atač also made perfect examples of literary t[...]lation in Turkish. He translated more tha[...] literary works from ancient Greek, Latin and Ru[...] authors (via French), and in particular, directly [...] French, the most famous of which being his t[...]lation of Stendhal's *Le rouge et le noir* rendere[...] *Kırmızi ve siyah* (1941), second edition as *Kı*[...] *kara* (1946).

Bibliography: Tahir Alangu, *Ataçʾa s*[...] Ankara 1959; Konur Ertop, Introduction t[...] complete works published by *Varlık*: *Gün*[...] *getirdiği-karalama defteri*, Istanbul 1967, [...] Asım Bezirci, *Nurullah Ataç, eleştiri anlayı*[...] *yazıları*, Istanbul 1968; Mehmed Salihoğlu, *A*[...] *gelen*; Türk Dil Kurumu (ed.), *Ölümünün 10*[...] *dönümünde Ataçʾı anış*, Ankara 1968.

(Fahir [...])

ATALİḲ, Turkic title which existed in Ce[...] Asia in the post-Mongol period, with the same ori[...] meaning as the title *atabeg* [see atabak].

In the *ulus* of Dj̲uči (the Golden Horde) an[...] immediate successors, as in the k̲h̲ānates of Ḳ[...] and Ḳïrïm and the *ulus* of S̲h̲iban (Aḳ Orda), as [...] as in the Čag̲h̲atāyid state in Mog̲h̲olistān, the *a*[...] was, in the first place, a guardian and tutor [...] young prince and, in this capacity, an actual gov[...] of his appanage. The sovereign himself (k̲h̲ā[...] sulṭān) also had an *atalïḳ* who was his close couns[...] and confidant, often playing the role of the [...] minister. The *atalïḳ*s were nominated from a[...] the Turkic tribal nobility, the senior begs (*a*[...] It seems that, according to Turkic nomadic cus[...] a ruler should always have an *atalïḳ*; it was a [...] of control over his conduct exercised by the [...] aristocracy. Tīmūrid and S̲h̲aybānid sources [...] also use, instead of the term *atalïḳ* and in the [...] meaning, the term *atakä*, or *ätäkä* (most prob[...]

ntracted form from *ata-äkä*, or *atabeg-äkä*, *atalïk*-where *äkä* is "the elder brother", which was a usual form of polite address in Eastern Turkic, ed to proper names and titles). The post of *atakä* *lïḳ*) was entrusted often to a *kökältās̲h̲* "foster-her" (also *ämildās̲h̲*); these persons were brought together with the princes of the ruling dynasty, ch created a special relationship (*kökältās̲h̲ī*) veen the two sides (see *Tawārīk̲h̲-i guzīda-i* *at-nāma*, ed. by A. M. Akramov, Tashkent 1967, mile 270, lines 4250-4, and 272; Russian tr. the *S̲h̲aybānī-nāma* by Binā'ī, in *Materialï po ii kazak̲h̲skik̲h̲ k̲h̲anstv XV-XVIII vekov*, Alma-1969, 98, 100; V. V. Vel'yaminov-Zernov, *edovaniye o Kasimovskik̲h̲ tsaryak̲h̲ i tsarevičak̲h̲*, 2, St. Petersburg 1864, 438; V. V. Bartol'd, *neniya*, ii/2, 212; G. Doerfer, *Türkische und golische Elemente in Neupersischen*, ii, 9 (No. 419), (No. 343), iv, 402-3, with further references).

n the Uzbek k̲h̲ānates of Central Asia, the ning of the title *atalïḳ* was gradually transformed. Buk̲h̲ārā, till the beginning of the 18th century, e great *atalïḳ*" (*atalïḳ-i buzurg*) was the senior r and the first minister (hence his epithets *dat al-umarā'* and *wizārat-panāh*). In the As̲h̲tar-nid period, he often appears in historical sources ether with the *dīwān-begi* [*q.v.* below], who was second figure in the government. He could be the same time governor of a province; *atalïḳ* angtus̲h̲ Biy, who was *ḥākim* of Samarḳand in first half of the 17th century and became famous his building activity, was a semi-independent r. There was also, besides him, an *atalïḳ* of the n's heir residing in Balk̲h̲ with the same func-s in his respective region. In the reign of ʿUbayd āh K̲h̲ān (1114-23/1702-11), the *ḳosh-begi* [*q.v.*] ame the head of the civil administration in k̲h̲ārā, he being an official of mean origin—bably as an attempt of the k̲h̲ān at cutting down influence of the Uzbek aristocracy. But the ortance of the *atalïḳ* did not diminish; already lier, at the end of the 17th century, the *atalïḳ* in k̲h̲ became independent ruler of this province, in the middle of the 18th century Muḥammad ḥīm Atalïḳ of the Mangït [*q.v.*] tribe founded a v ruling dynasty in Buk̲h̲ārā, having killed the last in of the As̲h̲tark̲h̲ānids. Muḥammad Raḥīm was claimed k̲h̲ān in 1170/1756; his uncle and suc-sor Dāniyāl Biy (1172-99/1758-85) preferred to main *atalïḳ*, enthroning puppet k̲h̲āns of Čingizid gin, but his son S̲h̲āh Murād eliminated these āns and proclaimed himself *amīr*, which later nained in Buk̲h̲ārā the title of the Mangït rulers excellence. In the administrative manual *djmaʿ al-arḳām* compiled under S̲h̲āh Murād 1212/1798, the post of *atalïḳ* is defined as that senior *amīr*, who was charged specifically with ersight of the irrigation of the Zarafs̲h̲ān valley m Samarḳand to Ḳarakul, and, at the same e, was the *mīrāb* of the main city canal of Buk̲h̲ārā, d-i S̲h̲ahr, as well as *dārūg̲h̲a* [*q.v.*] of the *rabaḍ* Buk̲h̲ārā (see facsimile in *Pis'menniye pamyatniki stoka 1968*, Moscow 1970, 50-1; cf. A. A. Semenov, *Sovetskoye vostokovedeniye*, v [1948], 144-7). But eady in the first half of the 19th century, the *lïḳ* became a purely honorary rank (the highest the hierarchy of 15 ranks in Buk̲h̲ārā) given very ely. In 1820 a semi-independent governor of ṣār, father-in-law of the *amīr*, had this rank (see Meyendorff, *Voyage d'Orenburg à Boukhara, fait 1820*, Paris 1826, 259; cf. V. L. Vyatkin, in *estiya Sredneaziatskogo otdela Russkogo geografi-českogo obs̲h̲čestva*, xviii [1928], 20); in 1840 the *atalïḳ* was also a father-in-law of the *amīr*, a ruler of S̲h̲ahrisabz (see N. K̲h̲anïkov, *Opisaniye Buk̲h̲ars-kogo k̲h̲anstva*, St. Petersburg 1843, 185). Under the last two *amīr*s, only the governor of Ḥiṣār (who had also the title *ḳos̲h̲-begi*) was given the rank of *atalïḳ*.

In the K̲h̲ānate of K̲h̲īwa, *atalïḳ* was originally also a guardian and counsellor of the k̲h̲ān and of princes (sulṭāns) who ruled in their appanages. Abu 'l-G̲h̲āzī [*q.v.*] in his *S̲h̲adjara-yi Turk* (ed. Desmaisons, text, 252, tr. 269) says about an *atalïḳ* (in the middle of the 16th century) that he was "the mouth, tongue and will" (*ag̲h̲ïzï, tili wa ik̲h̲tiyārï*) of his sulṭān. Russian sources of the 17th century compare the *atalïḳ*s in K̲h̲īwa with the Russian boyars (see *Materialï po istorii Uzbekskoy, Tadžikskoy i Turk-menskoy SSR*, Moscow-Leningrad 1931, 266). According to Mu'nis [*q.v.*] (*Firdaws al-iḳbāl*, MS. of the Leningrad Branch of the Institute of Oriental Studies, C-571, f. 65b), Abu 'l-G̲h̲āzī K̲h̲ān, reorganising the administration of the k̲h̲ānate, established posts of four *atalïḳ*s, who were members of the k̲h̲ān's council of 34 *ʿamaldār*s. Later they were called "the great *atalïḳ*" (*ulug̲h̲ atalïḳ*, cf. *ibid.*, ff. 112a, 118b); they represented four tribal groups (*tupä*) into which all K̲h̲ʷārizmian Uzbeks were divided: Uyg̲h̲ur and Nayman, Ḳungrat and Ḳiyat, Mangït and Nukuz, Ḳanglï and Ḳïpčaḳ. One of the "great *atalïḳ*s" was the *atalïḳ* of the k̲h̲ān (see *ibid.*, ff. 69b, 101b). In the first half of the 18th century, the *atalïḳ* of the k̲h̲ān was a most powerful figure in K̲h̲īwa, but from the 1740s onwards he was pushed somewhat into the background by another dignitary, the *ïnaḳ* [*q.v.* below]. It is not clear whether in the time of Abu 'l-G̲h̲āzī there existed only the four *atalïḳ*s mentioned by Mu'nis; but in the middle of the 18th century there was quite a number of them. In 1740 a letter to the inhabitants of K̲h̲īwa sent by the K̲h̲īwan dignitaries from the camp of Nādir S̲h̲āh was signed by eleven *atalïḳ*s (see *Geografičeskiye izvestiya*, 1850, 546-7). Apparently, already at that time, as in the 19th century, the title *atalïḳ* was given also to the chiefs of the Uzbek tribes; such an *atalïḳ* was senior *biy* in his tribe, and his title was usually hereditary, though it had to be confirmed by the k̲h̲ān. In the 19th century this title was granted also, as a purely honorary distinction, to some Turkmen tribal chiefs (see Yu. Bregel', in *Problemï vostoko-vedeniya*, 1960, No. 1, 171; cf. idem, *K̲h̲orezmskiye turkmenï v XIX veke*, Moscow 1961, 129). In 1859 this title was introduced also for the chiefs of the Karakalpak tribes (see Yu. Bregel', *Dokumentï ark̲h̲iva k̲h̲ivinskik̲h̲ k̲h̲anov po istorii i étnografii karakalpakov*, Moscow 1967, 58). The number of the "great *atalïḳ*s" increased before 1873 from four to eight (see A. L. Kuhn's papers in the Archives of the Leningrad Branch of the Institute of Oriental Studies, file 1/13, 105-6). As distinct from the other tribal chiefs, they were considered among the *umarā-yi ʿaẓām*. The *atalïḳ* of the k̲h̲ān, who in the 19th century always belonged to the k̲h̲ān's tribe, the Ḳungrat [*q.v.*] and was mostly a relative of the k̲h̲ān, was considered as the senior *amīr* in the k̲h̲ānate; in the first half of the 19th century he still exercised some influence as the k̲h̲ān's counsellor, but later this post lost its importance.

Less is known about the role of *atalïḳ*s in the K̲h̲ānate of K̲h̲oḳand [*q.v.*]. The ruler of Farg̲h̲āna and the founder of the Ming dynasty of this k̲h̲ānate, S̲h̲āhruk̲h̲ Biy (early 18th century) received the title *atalïḳ* from the k̲h̲ān of Buk̲h̲ārā (see V. P. Nalivkin, *Histoire du khanat de Khokand*, Paris 1889,

68). In the 19th century, governors of large provinces (such as Tāshkent and Khudjand) also sometimes had this title; they could be not only Uzbeks: Ḳanāʿat Shāh Atalīḳ, the governor of Tāshkent in 1850s and early 1860s, was a Tādjīk. Apparently, the *atalīḳ* in the Khānate of Khoḳand, as well as in Bukhārā of the same period, was considered rather an honorary rank than an official post.

In Eastern Turkestan under the Čaghatāyids in the 16th and 17th centuries, the title *atalīḳ* preserved its original meaning. The governors of provinces (princes of the ruling house), the khān's heir and the khān himself had their *atalīḳ*s, who were always senior Turkic *bek*s. The *atalīḳ* of the khān was at the same time the governor (*ḥākim*) of Yārkand, and that of the heir the governor of Aḳsu or Khotan (see Shāh Maḥmūd Čurās, *Taʾrīkh*, ed. by O. F. Akimushkin, Moscow 1976, text 30, 52, 64 et *passim*). The ruler of the last independent Muslim state in Eastern Turkestan, Yaʿḳūb Bek [*q.v.*], styled himself Atalīḳ Ghāzī; apparently he received the title of *atalīḳ* on being sent from Khoḳand to Kāshghar as a counsellor and guardian of Buzurg Khʷādja.

Bibliography: in addition to the works mentioned in the text, see V. V. Bartol'd, *Sočineniya*, ii/2, 390, 394; A. A. Semenov, in *Materialī po istorii tadžikov i uzbekov Sredney Azii*, ii, Stalinabad 1954, 61; H. Howorth, *The history of the Mongols*, ii, 869-70; G. Doerfer, *Türkische und mongolische Elemente in Neupersischen*, ii, 69-71 (No. 490); M. F. Köprülü, *İA*, art. *Ata*, at the end.

(Yu. Bregel)

ATAY, Fāliḥ Rīfḳī, Turkish writer, journalist and politician (1894-1971). He was born in Istanbul, the son of Khalīl Ḥilmī, an uncompromising traditionalist and *imām* of a mosque at Djibāli on the Golden Horn. He was educated at Merdjān high school, where his teacher, the poet Djelāl Sāhir, encouraged him to publish his early poems, and at the Faculty of Letters. His elder brother, a progressive officer, provided him with all the advanced literature from Nāmīḳ Kemāl to Tewfīḳ Fikret [*q.vv.*]. Fāliḥ Rīfḳī began his career as a journalist in 1912 in Ḥusayn Djāhid's [*q.v.*] *Ṭanīn*, the organ of the Committee of Union and Progress (CUP), where he wrote once a week his *Istanbul mektūblarī* ("Istanbul Letters)." These and his later articles in the same paper during the Balkan War were full of emotional, patriotic and anti-reactionary spirit. After serving briefly in the chancery of the Sublime Porte, he was appointed to the Private Secretariat of Ṭalʿat Pasha [*q.v.*], then Minister of the Interior, whom he accompanied on his trip to Bucharest, whence he sent his first travel notes, a *genre* in which he would later excel. He was at the same time contributing to various periodicals, particularly *Shehbāl*. At the outbreak of the First World War he was called up as a reserve officer and accompanied Djemāl Pasha [*q.v.*], the Commander of the Fourth Army in Syria, as his adjutant and private secretary. When Djemāl Pasha returned to Istanbul as Minister of the Navy, he appointed him deputy-director of his secretariat which he combined with instructor at the naval N.C.O.s' school. When at the end of the War the CUP leaders fled the country, Fāliḥ Rīfḳī founded, with three of his friends, the daily *Akshām*, becoming known as a staunch defender of the Nationalist movement in Anatolia (1918-22) versus the journalists who backed the collaborationist Istanbul government. In the autumn of 1922 he left for Izmir, which had just been liberated on 9 September, to meet Muṣṭafā Kemāl Pasha, who had invited him toge with other prominent journalists. Muṣṭafā Ke told them that "the real battle is beginning n and urged them to enter political life. Elected de for Bolu in 1923, Fāliḥ Rīfḳī became the le writer of the daily semi-official *Ḥākimiyyet-i mi* (later re-named *Ulus*) founded by Muṣṭafā Ke He remained in Parliament for 27 years until defeat of the Republican People's Party in general elections of 14 May 1950, when he mo to Istanbul and wrote a weekly column in *Cumhu* until he founded his own daily *Dünya*, which published until his death in Istanbul on 20 M 1971.

Essentially a journalist and always conce with the "topical", Atay had literary talents beyond those of a routine journalist. He exce in the essay, sketches, travel notes and auto graphical writing. An anti-traditionalist and a d cated Kemalist, he devoted all his writing caree defend and support the reforms achieved by Republican régime. He fought relentlessly and compromisingly for the survival of a modern, gressive and secular Turkey. No matter what wrote about, the lesson which he drew remained same: No going back.

A great master of modern Turkish prose, he u like R. Kh. Karay and ʿÖmer Seyf el-Dīn [*q.vv.*] spoken Turkish of ordinary people and wrote i concise, but vivid, colourful and very personal st carefully avoiding all artificialities of the ea generations of writers. Except for certain dou towards the end of his life, Atay was a great s porter of the language reform movement, revi by government support in the 1930s, and his hand of the reformed language became the model young writers until the appearance of Nūr A Atač [*q.v.* above], the linguistic and literary "gu of the generations between the 1940s and late It is perhaps because of this fascinating style t his readers are seldom worried about the lack depth in some of his writings, which brillia observe, describe and report, but do this with much sophistication. Atay is the author of m than thirty works, but the great bulk of his ess and articles published in newspapers and periodic have not yet been published in book form. major works are: (1) *Atesh we günesh* (1918) a *Zeytindaği* (1932), the two published in one volu as *Zeytindaği* (1970), impressions of the First Wo War in Palestine and Syria which are powe sketches of the end of the Ottoman Empire; *Den ṣırı* (1931), *Yeni Rusya* (1931), *Taymis kıyıl* (1934), *Tuna kıyıları* (1934), *Hind* (1944) are e cative travel notes on respectively Brazil, Sov Russia, England, the Balkans and India; *Geze gördüklerim* (1970), selections from travel not *Çankaya* (in two vols., 1961, revised one volu edition, 1969) is the most important and comp hensive of Atay's many books on Atatürk and achievements. It has powerful sketches of Atat and interesting character-studies of the many peo of his time. The second edition has been substantia altered in places and anti-İnönü passages have be borrowed from Y. K. Karaosmanoğlu's politi memoirs (*Politikada 45 yıl*, 1968) and introdu here to discredit the former Commander of t Western Front during the War of Liberation, bo writers having broken with İsmet İnönü, for politi reasons, towards the end of their lives; *Başve inkılapçı* (1954), a monograph on ʿAlī Suʿāvī (18 78), the controversial writer and revolutionary.

Bibliography: Baki Süha Ediboğlu, *Falih ıfkı Atay konuşuyor*, Istanbul 1945; B. Necatiğil, *debiyatımızda isimler sözlüğü*, Istanbul 1975, s.v.; ahir Alangu, *100 ünlü Türk eseri*, ii, Istanbul 974, 1124-31. (Fahir İz)

THĀTH (A.), furniture. The Arabic language s terms adequate to express the concept of iture. Taking into account the mutual over-ing of the notions of "furniture", "table-ware", pets", "household objects" and "utensils", bic frequently has recourse to approximative ıs and to broader categories (combinations of expressions, for example (*farsh* = carpets, bed- and furniture; *āla* = crockery and household ects; *farsh* and *āla* may be used in combination; = utensils etc.; *athāth* = literally, belongings, ous household objects and (especially in modern bic) furniture; *farsh* and *athāth* may be used in bination; *matāʿ* = personal property, domestic ıs, etc.).

n the mediaeval Muslim home, life was conducted tively close to the ground. Meals were served the diners in a kind of "serving-dish" with or out legs (the receptacle being separable from its port or not, as the case might be) which was laid a carpet on the floor. The diners did not have ividual plates but served themselves directly n the dish placed on a low table (*khuwān, māʾida, sak, fāthūr, mudawwara, muḥawwal, muʿtaṣamāt, āṭ*, the majority of these terms indicating a very ll round table; some, like *simāṭ*, a low oblong le) each of them sitting on a "seat" adapted to appropriate height (a cushion [*wisāda, mirfaḳa, ʾa, miswara, numruḳ*, and even *mikhadda* which originally a pillow], a pair of cushions super-osed, a cushion folded in two, the carpet itself,). The table was removed from the room as soon the meal was completed.

t is understandable that such scenes should have led western travellers and even some orientalists o described the interior of the Muslim household being "empty", "uninhabitable", etc., without sidering that the dimensions of furniture are quently adapted to the way of life, to the manner sitting, and to taste. However it would be incor-t to suppose that all mediaeval Arabic furniture s low. Carpenters and other craftsmen constructed stles and benches of a fair height for various poses outside the private house; they also made irs with legs of wood or metal [see KURSĪ] and one-like seats (*sarīr, takht*), but such seating angements were not used at meal-times. A high ol was somewhat exceptional in the Middle Ages l it focussed attention on the person seated there prince, the head of the family, sometimes an linary individual) in relation to the others present. The hierarchy of heights in sitting (on a throne, a high stool, on two superimposed cushions, on e cushion folded in two, on a single ordinary cush-, on the carpet itself, on the ground, this last sition indicating humiliation, humility or mourn-) only reflects the categories and class-distinctions etiquette. Another aspect of the stratification of sses is reflected in the range of materials and alities: beds with legs, a sign of luxury, beds with-t frames, and lower down the scale the *martaba*, good-quality mattress stuffed with down, simple ttresses laid on the ground and serving as a bed night, simple mattresses, mats and carpets for eping on, piles of rags and scraps of clothing for e same purpose (only the poorest slept on the ound); cushions and pillows stuffed and covered with choice materials, silk for example, and at the other end of the scale, rags or simply a stone serving as pillow for a poor man.

The very high "western style" thrones such as those appearing in Umayyad iconography, seem to have been copied from Byzantine models and do not reflect true conditions in the court (see V. Strika, in *AIUON* xiv/2 (1964), 729-59); but cf. O. Grabar, in *Studies in memory of Gaston Wiet*, Jerusalem 1977, especially 53-6, who puts into perspective the remarkable development of etiquette already taking place in the Umayyad court). According to mediaeval texts, another kind of throne, a long sofa for reclining, was quite widely known in the courts of the Umayyads, of the ʿAbbāsids and of local princes (such as the Ikhshīdids). The sovereign could invite a friend to sit beside him, on the same *sarīr* (hence quite a long seat); he could alternatively recline on it. The overlapping of the concepts mattress-seat-throne-bed (for example, from the Persian; *takht* can mean any of the following: board, seat, throne, sofa, bed, calculating tablet, chest or box) did not prevent the evolution of ceremonial and the differentiation of functions (a seat or a throne for public or solemn audience, or for private audience, feasts etc.) from establishing or re-establishing in usage thrones and narrow seats (of Persian manufacture, for example) and long and more elaborate thrones. Towards the end of the 3rd/9th and the beginning of the 4th/10th centuries, the use of the bed with frame (for reclining and sleeping) became fashionable in high society and among the bourgeoisie. The belief of certain orientalists that the bed did not exist in the mediaeval Muslim world is only partially correct: unsprung mattresses were more common (even in documents from the Cairo Geniza, many mattresses are to be found serving as relatively inexpensive beds; among the dowries of young brides there is mention of a very small number of beds with frames, extremely expensive, and between these two categories is the *martaba*, which would correspond in function with the divan-bed of the present day).

To return to the subject of tables: *māʾida, khuwān* and *sufra* are synonymous: they refer to the small eastern "table", the first two to a solid "table" (the attempts on the part of mediaeval philologists to differentiate between them were quite arbitrary) while the third (and sometimes also *naṭʿ*, as well as *māʾida*, exclusively in the context of the Ḳurʾān and its commentaries and in certain passages in the literature of *ḥadīth*) was applied to a skin stretched out on the ground and serving, not only among the early Bedouins, but also in circles of sedentary Arabic civilisation, various functions in the home and in the country (in dialect, *sufra* is an ordinary table and *sufradji* is a waiter in a restaurant or a cafe). This is one of the characteristic cases which raises the question whether the continuity of sedentary habits (from the Persians, Byzantines, from the ancient Syrian and Egyptian stocks, etc.) was an exclusive characteristic of daily life in the mediaeval Muslim world, in the sense that it is reflected in the use of furniture, and if there was not here a minimal contribution on the part of the Bedouin element, betrayed in the spread of ancestral customs through the disappearance of the high furniture of the Byzantine metropolis in favour of the low furniture which existed in Iranian civilisation and in certain local Aramaeo-Syrian and ʿIrāḳi centres, as is revealed by the mediaeval lexicographers and commentators (*ṭustkhuwān* and *fāthūr*, for example). Nevertheless, specimens of wooden furniture from the Middle Ages are available to us and we have ceramic objects designed to imitate them (supports sometimes containing cavities to accommodate jugs, resembling the supports-plus-shelves attested by the texts; some of these still exist today: *mirfaʿ* or *kursī*-plus-*ṣīniyya*, in various Muslim lands lying far apart from one another); iconography also shows a certain standardisation, in spite of regional styles, of way of life and of taste throughout the whole of the Muslim world (household objects, such as tables, being exported from one country to another).

The mediaeval Muslims made use of a whole range of chests, cases and boxes (*ṣundūḳ*, *takht*, *ḳamṭara*, *muḳaddima*, *safaṭ*), as well as recesses and racks (*rufūf*), but they had no cupboards as such.

The Mongols introduced the use of a higher type of square table, but the essential nature of the "oriental style" way of life has been preserved up to the very threshold of the modern age (Turkish and Persian miniatures attest this, *grosso modo*). Even in the 19th and early 20th centuries, travellers, writers and orientalists (E. Lane for Egypt, Lortet for Syria, E. Jaussen for Palestine, for example) were still describing such a way of life; some elements (such as beds with frames) introduced from abroad, or under foreign influence, were still called *frandjī* in certain semi-urban centres, at the beginning of the present century. The modern age has made fashionable the use of European style furniture and the original form of the "oriental" way of life, with its abundant taste and comfort, has tended to disappear.

Bibliography: J. Sadan, *Le mobilier au Proche-Orient médiéval*, Leiden 1976 (esp. the bibliographical index, 155-69). (J. SADAN)

ATHŪR, modern ḲALʿAT SHARḲĀT, a large ancient mound on the west bank of the River Tigris in the *vilāyet* of Mawṣil, about 250 km. north of Baghdād and about 100 km. south of Mawṣil, in 35° 30′ N and 45° 15′ E. It is strategically placed on a spur of the Djabal Ḥamrīn and is identified with Ashur, one of the capital cities of ancient Assyria. In the middle of the 3rd millennium, it was occupied by migratory tribes coming either from the west or the south, and was venerated as the religious and sometime political centre of Assyria until it was captured by the Babylonians in 614 B.C. This battle devastated the city and it was not reoccupied as a city again. Ashur is the name not only of the place but also of the local deity, and it occurs in Akkadian, Aramaic and Greek sources. The site was known by the Turks under the name Ṭopraḳ Ḳalʿe, "Earth Citadel". The meaning of the element *sharḳāt* in the Arabic name is not known, but it is probably to be explained as an independent proper name. It is not mentioned by Arab geographers; the earliest reference to it is in the 18th century, and it is the name used by later Western travellers.

The site was described by C. J. Rich, who visited it in March 1821, and it was subsequently investigated by J. Ross (1836), W. Ainsworth with E. L. Mitford, A. H. Layard and H. Rassam (1840), and again by Layard and Rassam (1847) on behalf of the British Museum, when an important statue of Shalmaneser III (858-825 B.C.) was found. In 1849, after excavations by J. Talbot, J. Oppert, F. Hincks and H. C. Rawlinson, an inscribed historical prism recording the history of the reign of Tiglath Pilesar III (744-727 B.C.) was found, and two duplicate copies of this inscription were discovered by Rassam in 1853 in further British Museum excavations under the general supervision of Rawlinson. Several inscrip-tions from the reign of Adad Nirari III (810-783 I were discovered by G. Smith in 1873. The r rigorous excavation of the site was conducted bet 1903-13 by the Deutsche Orient Gesellschaft, by R. Koldewy and then by W. Andrae and ot which followed the presentation of the site to K Wilhelm II by Sultan ʿAbd al-Ḥamīd II.

To the north and east the site is naturally prote by the river and the escarpment, and the necessary fortifications were buttressed w Sennacherib (704-681 B.C.) records the buil of a semicircular sallyport tower of rustic masonry which is probably the earliest of its k To the south and west it was more heavily forti After an early period of dependence upon the s during the Third Dynasty of Ur (2112-2004 B it begins a separate history. Evidence about lif Ashur for the earliest period comes from the d ments of an Assyrian group of traders workin Anatolia at the ancient city of Kanesh, mo Kültepe, in Turkey, but the earliest palace is tha Shamshi Adad I (1813-1781 B.C.), and spac private houses with family vaults beneath the fl have been found in the north-western area. Muc the history of this period has to be reconstructed f an archive of the letters of Shamshi Adad which discovered at Mari (modern Tell Ḥarīrī) in eas Syria. He controlled Ashur after it had been sub to Naram Sin of Eshunna (modern Tell Asm Although he did not use Ashur as his capital preferring Shubat Enlil (modern Chagar Bazar) did build there a temple to Enlil, the local go Nippur (modern Niffar), and the one who tr tionally named the king and entrusted to him symbols of royal power.

During the period of Cassite domination in M potamia, Puzur Ashur III (*ca.* 1490 B.C.), ma treaty with Burnaburiash I of Babylon, and Ashur he records rebuilding part of the Ishtar te and a section of the southern city wall. Buil operations of this kind are often recorded on cones which were inserted between the course the new brickwork. Ashur Nadin Akhe II (1402-1 B.C.) secured Egyptian support for his country teceived gifts of gold from the Pharaoh.

Official lists of the Assyrian kings have been fo and these are an essential source for establishin framework of the classical history of the site. T often contain more than fifty names and record length of each reign. Other lists record the name the temples there, but only a few of the 34 mentio have actually been identified. The architect features of these early buildings are similar to t of Old Babylonian buildings, but the lengthenin the sanctuary on its main axis and the positio of an altar in a deep recess are distinctively Assy features.

The traditional founder of the Assyrian em was Ashur Uballiṭ (1365-1330). At the beginnin his reign he was subject to Tushratta of Mita but in 1350, with the help of Supplilulíumas, Hittite king, he was able to attack and annexe Mitanni areas in northeast Mesopotamia. As Uballiṭ called himself *šarru rabu*, the great k equal in status to the Pharaoh, and was a se threat to the Babylonians. Two of his letters Akhnaten have been preserved in the famous arch from Tell al-Amarna, Egypt (see Knudtzon (19 nos. 15-16). He called his country *mat Aššur*, Land of Ashur, while the older name of Suba was used by the Babylonians, possibly in a de catory sense. Even so, Assyrian royal inscripti

composed in the Babylonian dialect of Akkadian
use, presumably, such language had a tradi-
al air of refinement. His son Enlil Nirari (1329-
B.C.) fought against Babylon, and Arik Din Ili
9-1308 B.C.) harassed the Akhlamu, the Semitic
s to the west. Adad Nirari I (1307-1275 B.C.),
is battles with the Cassites and the Mitanni, was
tually able to unite Mesopotamia into an empire,
the territory he gained was later eroded because
he rise of the Hittites and the unsatisfactory
nces against the tribes to the east.
almaneser I (1274-1245 B.C.) records building
w royal city in the north at Kalkhu (modern
Nimrūd) and his son Tukulti Ninurta I (1244-
B.C.), also built a new residence but much
er, just to the north-east, which he named
Tukulti Ninurta, "the Quay of Tukulti Ninurta"
dern Tulūl ʿAḳr). He records having captured
duk god of Babylon, and a figure of primary
ortance in Babylonian mythology who was later
e assimilated into Assyrian versions of religious
s. Despite these alternative capitals, Ashur was
used as a political centre from time to time, yet
radually became primarily a religious centre.
the 10th century B.C. it was overshadowed by
khu and Nineveh, and the later kings chose these
hern sites as capitals from which to administer
r empire.
he city was attacked and devastated by the
ylonian ruler Nabopolassar (625-605 B.C.) in
B.C. two years before he destroyed Nineveh
brought the Assyrian empire to an end. After-
ds, there is only scanty documentation from
h to reconstruct the history of this important
Under the Babylonians, it was probably only
sely inhabited, for Cyrus the Great, when he
quered Babylon in 539 B.C., claims: "To the
ed cities on the other side of the Tigris as far as
ur ....., the sanctuaries of which have been
s for a long time, I returned the images which
to live therin and established for them perma-
sanctuaries" (from the *Cyrus Cylinder*, the basic
orical source for the Persian conquest of Babylon).
name occurs again in the Old Persian text of the
stun Inscription but the only other inscriptional
ence comes from Aramaic documents from the
these used to be dated to the Parthian period,
taken as evidence that the names of the old
rian gods survived in the community until the
century A.D., but they are now said to come
the 7th century B.C. As a geographical name
ırā may refer simply to the town but in Greek
ces it is clear that 'Ατουρία refers to the whole
hern area. The site seems definitely to have
ined in importance under the Sāsānids, and
r in Syriac indicates simply a parish which
inued until the late Middle Ages.
he Arab geographers refer to Athūr (sometimes
ten Aḳūr); it is, however, defined by them not
modern Ḳalʿat Sharḳāt but as an earlier name for
ṣil, and also as the name of the province which
later called al-Djazīra [*q.v.*]. The ruin associated
the name is described as near to al-Salāmiyya,
n. N.W. of Nimrūd. They also make the obser-
on that al-Djazīra, which practically coincides
rea with Assyria, is a name derived from Athūr.
ough it is clear that a ruin was still known at
site, the name Athūr has been transferred er-
eously to the ruin near al-Salāmiyya; this trans-
tion was influenced by the fact that there were
famous capitals of Assyria in the north and is
ilar to the case of Baghdad, which travellers of the Middle Ages until Pietro della Valle (1616-17) considered to be the site of ancient Babylon. According to Layard (1853), 165, the hill in the corner of the ruins of Nimrūd was still called "Tell Athūr".

It is surprising that there appears to be no mention of the name Sharḳāt before the narratives of European travellers. Rich (1821) mentions it, and it is described more fully by Layard (1849), 3, who says "We entered Mosul on 10th April 1846. During a short stay in that town we visited the great ruins which have been generally believed to be the remains of Nineveh. We rode also into the desert and explored the mound of Kalah Shergat, a vast ruin on the Tigris about fifty miles below its junction with the Zab". He did not identify it with Ashur; all he could say was, "A few fragments of pottery and inscribed bricks discovered after a careful search amongst the rubbish which had accumulated around the base of the great mound, served to prove that it owed its construction to the people who had founded the city of which Nimrod is the remains" (*loc. cit.*). But later, during the river trip from Mawṣil to Baghdād, he was told of a connection in folklore between the two names, based on the ancient dam in the river: "The Arab explained the connection between the dam and the city built by Athur, the lieutenant of Nimrod, the vast ruins of which were then before us, and its purpose as a causeway for the mighty hunter to cross to the opposite palace now represented by the mound of Hammam Ali." (*op. cit.*, 6). These traditions may still survive in local villages.

Today the site is situated on the edge of the rainfall zone, so that agriculture relies on artificial irrigation. Local inhabitants often rely on employment outside the village to supplement their income, and some of the men and boys have become particularly skilful assistants for archaeological excavations. Most of the settled population belong to the Djubūr tribe; although the *shaykh* of this branch lives at Kayyārā further up the valley, there is a mansion at Sharḳāt, 8 km. north of the site, belonging to Shaykh Adjil al-Yawir of the Shammar. The population density of the area is 4.8 per sq. km., which reflects its relative poverty. Sharḳāt is the headquarters of a *nāḥiya*, the smallest administrative unit in ʿIrāḳ.

Bibliography: For a general topographical description of the area, see Admiralty, Intelligence Division, *Geographical Handbook: Iraq and the Persian Gulf*, London 1944; R. Dussaud, *Topographie historique de la Syrie antique et médiévale*, Paris 1927 and G. Tchalenko, *Villages antiques de la Syrie du Nord*, Paris 1953. The site itself is fully described by E. Unger, in E. Ebeling and B. Meissner, *Reallexicon der Assyriologie*, Leipzig 1928, 170-96, but for an accurate historical assessment, more modern works should be consulted. See in general, I. E. S. Edwards *et alii* (eds.), *Cambridge Ancient History*, Cambridge 1973, Part ii, Ch. 1 (by J. R. Kupper), Ch. 2 (by M. S. Drower) and Ch. 5 (by C. J. Gadd), and more specifically D. Oates, *Studies in the ancient history of Northern Iraq*, London 1968.

The official reports of the excavations are given by W. Andrae, with others as indicated, in the following volumes of *Mitteilungen der Deutschen Orient Gesellschaft*, xx (1903, R. Koldewy); xxi, xxii, xxv (1904); xxvi-xxix (1905); xxxi-xxxiii (1906); xxxiii, xxxvi, xxxvii (with J. Jordan) (1908); xl, xlii (1909, with J. Jordan); xliii-xliv (1910); xlv, xlvii (1911); xlviii-xlix (1912, with J. Jordan); li (1913, with P. Maresch); liv (1914, with H. Luhrs and H. Lucke); lxi (1921); lxiii (1924); lxxi (1932, H. J. Lenzen); lxxii (1935) and lxxvi (1938). A series of monographs by Andrae and others have been published in the following volumes of *Wissenschaftliche Veröffentlichungen der Deutschen Orientgesellschaft*: x (1909); xxiii (1913); xxiv (1913); xxxix (1922); lvii (with H. J. Lenzen, 1933); lviii (1935); xlvi (1924); liii (1931).

In the same series, editions of the cuneiform texts discovered at the site have been published as follows: xvi (1911) and xxxvii (1922) by L. Messerschmidt and O. Schroeder; xxviii and xxiv (1915-23) by E. Ebeling; xxxv (1920) by Schroeder; lxiv (1954) and lxvi (1955) by C. Preusser; lxv (1954) and lxvii (1955) by A. Haller; lxii (1956) by F. Wetzel and others. The Aramaic ostraca and tablets were published originally by M. M. Lidzbarsky, also in the same series, xxxviii (1921), but the more recent edition by H. Donner and W. Rollig, *Kanaanäische und aramäische Inschriften*, 2nd ed., Wiesbaden 1969, Texts 233 and 234-6, should now be used.

The Arab geographers referring to the site are as follows: Ibn Rustih, 104, tr. Wiet, 115, equating Athūr with Mawṣil; and Yāḳūt, i, 119, 16; 340, 5; 118, 18. For Djazīrat Aḳūr, see *ibid.*, ii, 72, 13; 231, 9, which coincides with the Iḳlīm Athūr/Aḳūr, "the region of Ashur", mentioned only by al-Muḳaddasī, 20, 3 (see also 27, 10, and 28, 7). For [Djazīrat] Aḳūr as an older name for the Djazīra, see also Le Strange, *The lands of the Eastern Caliphate*, 86.

For the records of early travellers, see C. J. Rich, *Narrative of a residence in Koordistan*, London 1836, ii, 137 ff.; J. Ross, in *JRGS*, ix (1839), 451-3; W. Ainsworth with A. H. Layard and E. L. Mitford, in *JRGS*, xi (1842), 4-8; Layard, *Nineveh and its remains*, London 1849, ii, 45-63, 245, 581; idem, *Discoveries in the ruins of Nineveh and Babylon*, London 1853; V. Place, *Ninive et l'Assyrie*, Paris 1867-70; H. Rassam, *Asshur and the land of Nimrod*, New York 1897.

(M. E. J. Richardson)

ĀTISH, Khwādja Ḥaydar ʿAlī (d. 1263/1847), Urdu poet, was born in Faizabad (Fayḍābād [*q.v.*]) probably around 1191/1778, according to A. L. Ṣiddīḳī (see *Bibl.*, below). His ancestors are said to have originated in Baghdād, whence they came to Dihlī. His father moved from there to Fayḍābād and died during the poet's youth. As a result, Ātish's formal education was curtailed, though he supplemented it by avid reading. In early manhood, he led the life of a fop and a roué, and carried a sword. But his aptitude for poetry was noticed, and he was taken to Lucknow. There he was trained by the poet Shaykh Ghulām Hamadānī Muṣḥafī, and was soon recognised as a leading *ghazal* poet, along with his chief rival, Shaykh Imām Bakhsh Nāsikh. Such poetical rivalries were a familiar feature of Lucknow cultural and social life, but—as we see in the case of Ātish—they did not always involve personal animosity. Indeed, he ceased to write poetry after the death of his rival.

Modern critics regard Ātish as the greater poet of the two. Urdu *ghazal*, as he found it, tended to be rich in vocabulary and ornate in style, with similes, metaphors, and other rhetorical devices which were at times far-fetched and exaggerated. Ideas were largely stereotyped, with much concentration on the physical features of the beloved such as tresses (*zulf*) and face (*rukhsār*) as in Persian models. Ātish seems to have been an independent-minded eccentric in his private life, and this is reflected in his pc to some extent. He would not write poetry patronage, though he accepted a small pension the King of Oudh (Awadh [*q.v.*]). He spurned we living like a dervish in a broken-down house. He humble to the poor but haughty to the wealthy his verse, he was not a great innovator, but ne was he a slavish imitator of time-honoured poe techniques. Thus while he did not radically ch the form and style of *ghazal*, he frequently ap less artificial than his predecessors and conte raries, writing in a more natural language near everyday speech as used by the educated of Luck perhaps his lack of formal education encouraged tendency. He was criticised for using non-lite turns of phrase, and mis-spelling Arabic words– latter perhaps deliberately, in the interests of of prosody, or to reflect actual pronunciation of words in Urdu. In short, we at times sense spontai and even sincerity in his verse, and his lite language became accepted as a model. His poe output of over 8,000 verses is practically ent composed of *ghazals*.

Bibliography: Ātish's poetry was publi originally in two *dīwāns*—the first in 184 Lucknow under the poet's supervision; the sec which contains many of his best poems, published in the same city after his death by pupil, Mīr Dūst ʿAlī Khalīl in 1268/1851. M editions of his collected poetry have since published, for example the *Kulliyyāt* in Cawn 1871 and 1884. There is a useful introductio Ẓāhir Aḥmad Ṣiddīḳī in *Kulliyyāt-i Ātish*, habad 1972. Short critical accounts of the pc will be found in Muḥammad Ḥusayn Āzād, *ḥayāt*, 379-93 in the Lahore edition of 1950; 'l-Layth Ṣiddīḳī, *Lakhnāu kā dabistān-i-shā* Lahore 1955, 525-41; Muḥammad Sadiq, *His of Urdu literature*, London 1964, 138; and Babu Saksena, *History of Urdu literature*, habad 1927, 111-13. Further information ma found in Shaykh Ghulām Hamadānī Muṣ *Riyāḍ al-fuṣaḥā*ʾ, Dihlī 1934, 4-9; Karīm al and Fallon, *Tadhkira-i-shuʿarāʾ-i-Hind*, Dihlī 1 354; Ṣafīr Balgrāmī, *Djalwa-i-khiḍir*, 2 vols., Bihar 1882, ii, 106 f.; Khwādja ʿAbd al-R ʿIshrat Lakhnawī, *Āb-i baḳā*ʾ, Lucknow 1 11-19, 170-7; *Memoirs of Delhi and Faiza* English tr. of Fayḍ Bakhsh, *Taʾrīkh-i-faraḥ bak* Allahabad 1889, 266-302; and Iʿdjāz Ḥus *Kalām-i-Ātish*, Allahabad 1955. For a gen picture of Lucknow cultural life in the first of the 19th century, see Abdul Halim Sharar E. S. Harcourt and Fakhir Husain, *Lucknow: last phase of an oriental culture*, London 1975.

For further bibliographical material, see K al-Raḥmān Aʿẓamī and Murtaḍā Ḥusayn F art. *Ātish*, in *Urdu Encyclopaedia of Islam*, La 1962 ff., i, 10-14. (J. A. Haywoo

ATLANTIC [see al-baḥr al-muḥīṭ].

AVARICE [see bukhl].

AVRAM CAMONDO [see camondo].

AWRABA, a Berber tribe of Morocco. Khaldūn, *ʿIbar*, Fr. tr. de Slane, i, 286, provides the information which we have on the early his of this tribe, which formed part of the seden Barānis [*q.v.*]. Certain of these appear to have Christians. At the time of the Muslim conq they held the premier place among the North Afr Berber tribes because of their forcefulness and bravery of their warriors. Ibn Khaldūn also g us the names of the tribe's main branches and th e most outstanding chiefs whom they had before Arabs' arrival. The celebrated Kusayla [*q.v.*], was probably a Christian, is said to have been *amīr*, as of all the Barānis. He rebelled, and defeated and killed in 62/682, and it was after death that the Awraba (or Awriba?) no longer cted the resistance against the invaders.

e tribe makes its real appearance in the history Iorocco by making Shīʿī doctrines triumphant e, even though these were contrary to the ridjī ones embraced by the Berbers in the eding century. It was indeed under the protection e Awraba chief, Abū Laylā Isḥāḳ b. Muḥammad Abd al-Ḥamīd, that the ʿAlid fugitive Idrīs I] established himself in 172/788 at Walīla, the ent Roman town (the present Volubilis), situated he little mountain massif of Zarhūn, north of nès.

hese mountain folk called themselves descendants e Awraba of the Aurès, driven out of the central hrib after Kusayla's death, as also were those ents of the Awraba to be found in the regions he Zāb [*q.v.*] and the Ouarsenis [*q.v.*].

ike several of the northern Moroccan tribes, the aba professed Muʿtazilī doctrines; they were rdingly favourable to the ʿAlids and regarded nomination of an *imām* as a necessary obligation the community. This is why Abū Laylā could out difficulty have himself proclaimed sovereign *m* of his own tribe and of the neighbouring tribes amaḍān 172/5 February 789) a few months after s's arrival in the Zarhūn. The Awraba then successfully took part in Idrīs I's work of Islamisation. s II showed his gratitude badly towards his er's benefactor, since he had him executed years later, on the accusation of having relations the Aghlabid ruler of al-Ḳayrawān, who recognised the authority of the hated ʿAbbāsids, but this on was doubtless also from reasons of local tics.

t Idrīs II's death (213/828) and after the disous division of Morocco between his sons, troubles ke out within the principalities thereby established. The Awraba and the Berber coalition put end to them (221/836) by giving allegiance to the e-years old ʿAlī b. Muḥammad, ruler of Fās, ring tutelage over the kingdom till the young *m*'s majority. ʿAli died after a peaceful reign 13 years. New disputes now divided Morocco ween rival factions, and finally, in 251/866, the raba recognised ʿAlī's cousin, ʿAlī b. ʿUmar.

wraba were still in contact with the principality Nukūr [*q.v.*], and in mediaeval times, they were be found in Algeria, at Niḳaws (N'gaous) and in region of Bône. They never disappeared comtely, and re-appear in the historical texts, e.g. ler the Almohads; at first (559/1164) they espoused cause of a rebel and were opposed to the Almos, but then in 580/1184 rallied to them in order go and fight in Spain. They appear further under Marīnids, being specially mentioned in the texts cerning the meetings for the holy war in aldalus, and one of them commanded the renowned lunteers for the faith". In 707/1308, some Awraba efs involved in the revolt of a pretender, were cuted on the orders of the sultan Abū Thābit, their bodies exposed in crucifixion on the enling walls of Marrakesh.

At the present time, some of their former tribes e Ladjāya, Mazyata and Raghiwa) are established the banks of the Wādī Wargha, to the north of Zarhūn.

Bibliography: al-Nāṣirī, *K. al-Istiḳṣā*, index; ʿAbd Allāh Gannūn, *al-Umarāʾ Idrīs*, in *Mashāhir ridjāl al-Maghrib*, No. 33; and see arts. BARĀNIS, BERBERS, IDRĪS I and II, IDRĪSIDS, KUSAYLA, WALĪLA. (G. DEVERDUN)

AʿYĀṢ, a component group of the Meccan clan of Umayya or ʿAbd Shams, the term being a plural of the founder's name, a son of Umayya b. ʿAbd Shams b. ʿAbd Manāf b. Ḳuṣayy called al-ʿĪṣ or Abu 'l-ʿĪṣ or al-ʿĀṣ(ī) or Abu 'l-ʿĀṣ(ī) or ʿUwayṣ, these being given in the genealogical works as separate individuals, but doubtless in fact one person (on the two orthographies al-ʿĀṣ and al-ʿĀṣī, the former explicable as an apocopated Ḥidjāzī form, see K. Vollers, *Volkssprache und Schriftsprache im alten Arabien*, Strassburg 1906, 139-40). The group formed a branch of the clan parallel to that of Ḥarb b. Umayya, from whom descended Abū Sufyān, Muʿāwiya [*q.vv.*] and the Sufyānids. Amongst the sons of al-ʿĀs, etc., were ʿAffān, father of the caliph ʿUthmān [*q.v.*]; al-Ḥakam, father of the caliph Marwān I [*q.v.*] and progenitor of the subsequent Marwānids; Saʿīd [*q.v.*], governor of Kūfa under ʿUthmān and of Medina under Muʿāwiya b. Abī Sufyān; and al-Mughīra, whose son Muʿāwiya was the mutilator of the Prophet's uncle Ḥamza b. ʿAbd al-Muṭṭalib and the father of ʿAbd al-Malik b. Marwān's mother ʿĀʾisha.

Because of the strenuous hostility shown to the Prophet by al-ʿĀṣ (he was killed, a pagan, at Badr) and his son Muʿāwiya, and because of al-Ḥakam's ambiguous role in the first years of Islam (as the "accursed one" banished by the Prophet), the family was often regarded by later Islamic sources with especial rancour; Saʿīd b. al-ʿĀṣ, however, found some contemporary favour with the Hāshimī clan and the supporters of ʿAlī, see Lammens, *Moʿâwia Ier*, in *MFOB*, i (1906), 27-8.

Bibliography: see Ibn al-Kalbī-Caskel, *Ğamharat an-nasab*, i, *Tab.* 8, 9, ii, *Register*, 202; Zubayrī, *Nasab Ḳuraysh*, ed. Lévi-Provençal, 98-9; Ibn Durayd, *Ishtiḳāḳ*, ed. Wüstenfeld, 45 ff., 103, ed. Cairo 1378/1958, 73 ff., 166. See also UMAYYA B. ʿABD SHAMS. (C. E. BOSWORTH)

ĀYATULLĀH (ĀYAT ALLĀH, current orthography Ayatollah), a title with an hierarchical significance used by the Imāmī, Twelver Shīʿīs, and meaning literally "Miraculous sign (*āya* [*q.v.*]) of God". In order to understand its sense and its implications, one has to consider the recent evolution of certain institutions worked out by the Imāmī *ʿulamāʾ*.

Since the dominating attitude of Imāmism has been dictated by the doctrine that all political power —even if exercised by a Shīʿī—is illegitimate during the occultation of the Hidden Imām, it has only been comparatively late, from the Ṣafawid period (907-1135/1501-1722) onwards, that political theories have taken shape and an hierarchy within the top ranks of the *mudjtahid*s [*q.v.*] has been formed. After their long disputes against the Akhbārīs [see AKHBĀRIYYA in Suppl.] and Ṣūfīs, the Uṣūlīs [*q.v.*] in the course of the 19th century elaborated the theory according to which at every given moment there could only be one unique *mardjaʿ-i taḳlīd* [*q.v.*] "source of imitation" (see Algar [1969], 5-11, 34-6, 162-5, etc.; Binder, 124 ff.). This title of *mardjaʿ-i taḳlīd* [*q.v.*] was subsequently applied retrospectively to numerous *mudjtahid*s (for lists of the *nāʾib-i ʿāmm*s of the Hidden Imām going back to Muḥammad Kulaynī, d. 329/940, see Bagley [1972], 31; Fisher, 34-5; Hairi, 62-3). During the 1960s, several discussions took place concerning the manner of selection and the functions of the *mardjaʿ-i taḳlīd*, at the very time when the Āyatullāh Burūdjirdī (d. 1961), recognised as the sole *mardjaʿ-i taḳlīd* by the mass of Imāmī Shīʿīs, disappeared (Algar [1972], 242; for some reserves about this recognition, see Binder, 132). Drawn up by religious leaders and laymen, a collective work called *Baḥthī dar bāra-yi mardjaʿiyyat va rūḥāniyyat*, dealing in particular with Imāmī institutions and on links with the political authority, appeared at Teheran in December 1962 (a brief analysis by Lambton, 121-35). After the disappearance of Burūdjirdī —whose attitude to politics had been one of quietism —the institution of the *mardjaʿiyyat* seems to have spread out widely (in 1976, there were six *mardjaʿ-i taḳlīd*s of first rank, including the Āyatullāh Khumaynī; Fisher, 32). However, from 1963 onwards, a certain consensus seems to have grown up around the Āyatullāh Khumaynī, the main religious opponent of the Pahlavī régime (Algar [1972], 243); but it also seems that the consensus over the *mardjaʿiyyat-i kull* of the Āyatullāh Muḥsin Ḥakīm Ṭabāṭabāʾī of Nadjaf (d. 1970) was at least partially realised in *ca.* 1966 (Bagley [1970], 78, n. 7; this *āyatullāh* enjoyed the favour of the Shah; see Algar [1972], 242-3).

From the time of the protest against the Tobacco Concession (1891-2), the *mardjaʿ-i taḳlīd*—who at that period resided in the holy places of ʿIrāḳ, the ʿAtabāt [*q.v.* in Suppl.]—often took the lead in the fight of opposition to Ḳādjār autocracy and to foreign domination. This association of the *mudjtahid*s with political opposition seems to have been clearer with the grant of the title *āyatullāh.* In practice, this *laḳab* seems first of all to have designated the two great leaders of the constitutional revolution, the *sayyid*s ʿAbd Allāh Bihbahānī and Muḥammad Ṭabāṭabāʾī (*Lughat-nāma-yi Dihkhudā*, s.v. *Āyatullāh*). It has since been applied to numerous great *mudjtahid*s (sometimes retrospectively), independently, it appears, of their political attitudes. It tends to replace in current usage (but not in the actual hierarchy) certain titles such as that of *ḥudjdjat al-Islam* which nowadays can mean any and every *ākhund* (this latter term tending, despite its pejorative character, to supplant that of *mullā*).

As with that of *mardjaʿ-i taḳlīd*, attribution of the title is above all a question of opinion. In effect, above the title of *mudjtahid* the level of respect accorded and the religious chief's charisma depend on the consensus of the mass of faithful. The *āyatullāh* is placed at the top of the hierarchy, amongst the élite of the great *mudjtahid*s. At the summit of all is to be found the *āyatullāh al-ʿuẓmā* (the "greatest miraculous sign of God"), the supreme *mardjaʿ-i taḳlīd* or *mudjtahid*. This rank seems to have been first of all accorded to Burūdjirdī (Binder, 132). There seems also to be at Ḳum a limited sort of college which makes decisions about the title (*ibid.*, 134). This clearly reinforces the position of Ḳum, which has become the "symbolic capital" of Iran since the Āyatullāh Khumaynī's return (the title *Imām* sometimes applied to him seems to be taken from ʿIrāḳī usage).

Although they are sometimes of modest origin, the great majority of *āyatullāh*s are now *sayyid*s (whereas the great *ʿulamāʾ* of the past were not always from this class). Marriages and alliances traditionally reinforce the strength of religious leadership (see Fischer, genealogical tables, 33-4). Whether he be *mardjaʿ-i taḳlīd* or not, the *āyatullāh* excercises a double role of manager within his sphere of activity. On the administrative level, he controls the levying of various religious taxes, the direction of pious and property in mortmain (*waḳf* [*q.v.*], controlle the state under the Pahlavī régime), the distribu of various grants and alms, the administratio centres of learning, etc.; on the intellectual spiritual level, he is responsible for education. influence on the social level is limited by his fait followers: the students and those who bring t financial support to him (Fisher, 41).

The role and influence of the Iranian *āyatul* are now very diverse. Their prerogatives have creased through the progressive installation of Islamic Republic since the events of winter 197 But, despite the abolition of the monarchy, they inevitably subject to all the hazards of polit power and to the pressures of antagonistic fo (secularism, communism, the growth of nationalis religious particularisms, etc.). There is at least *āyatullāh* in each province and several in each n centre of religious teaching (*ḥawḍa-yi ʿilmī*). T there are 14 traditional *madrasa*s at Ḳum directe *āyatullāh*s, of whom some have attained the ran *mardjaʿ-i taḳlīd* (Fisher, table, 23).

Bibliography: (for works in Persian, diffi to find outside Iran, see the bibliographies citec Algar, Bagley, Fisher and Hairi); A. K. S. La ton, *A reconsideration of the position of the ma al-taqlīd and the religious institution*, in *St. Isl.*, (1964), 115-35; L. Binder, *The proofs of Islam: gion and politics in Iran*, in *Arabic and Islamic dies in honor of Hamilton A. R. Gibb*, ed. G. M disi, Leiden 1965, 118-40; H. Algar, *Religion state in Iran 1785-1906*, Berkeley-Los Angeles 19 idem, *The oppositional role of the Ulama twentieth-century Iran*, in *Scholars, saints and Su* ed. N. R. Keddie, Berkeley-Los Angeles 1972, 55 (see also N. R. Keddie, *The roots of the Ulan power in modern Iran*, in *ibid.*, 211-29, first p lished in *St. Isl.*, xxix [1969], 31-53); F. R. Bagley, *Religion and the state in modern Iran* in *Actes du Ve Congrès international d'arabisc et islamisants*, Brussels 1970, 75-88, *II*, in *I ceedings of the VIth Congress of Arabic and Isla Studies*, Visby-Stockholm 1972, ed. F. Rundg Uppsala 1975, 31-44; M. J. Fisher, *The Qum rep an anthropological account of contemporary Shii* draft (typewritten report), July 1976; Abdul-H Hairi, *Shiʿism and constitutionalism in Iran*, Lei 1977.

(J. CALMARD)

ʿAYN AL-ĶUḌĀT AL-HAMADHĀNĪ, ʿA ALLĀH B. ABĪ BAKR AL-MIYĀNADJĪ, Shāfiʿī jur and Ṣūfī martyr, born at Hamadhān in 492/10 Born of a line of scholars, he studied Arabic gramm theology, philosophy and law, and as an alre precocious scholar, began writing his books at age of 14. Also, at the approach of puberty, he came a convert to Ṣūfism. In 517/1123, at the of 25, he seems to have met Aḥmad al-Ghaz brother of the great theologian Muḥammad Ghazālī, who initiated him into Ṣūfī meditation dancing, thus completing his spiritual conversi Other masters of his were Muḥammad b. Ḥammi and a certain Baraka.

His spiritual reputation soon gained him m disciples, and he spent all his time in oral written teaching, sometimes going beyond the lin of his physical strength for this and having t to retire for two or three months for recuperati His activities soon provoked the hostility of orthodox theologians. Provoked by his teachings the nature of sainthood and prophethood and submission to the Ṣūfī *shaykh*, and objecting to e of Ṣūfī terminology which gave the impression he himself laid claim to prophetic powers, they ght an accusation of heresy against him before Saldjūḳ vizier in ʿIrāḳ, who imprisoned him in ıdād. It was there that he wrote his apologia, *Shakwā 'l-gharīb*. Some months later he was set and returned to Hamadhān, but shortly afterls, at the time of the Saldjūḳ sultan Maḥmūd's ·al (reigned 511-25/1118-31), he was executed in :barous manner during the night of 6-7 Djumādā 26/6-7 May 1131 at the age of 33. His premature h seems to have prevented Hamadhānī from ding a Ṣūfī monastery, setting up a Ṣūfī group designating a successor; nevertheless, his numerworks, written in a fine style, have always found ıudience.

is published works include his *Shakwā 'l-gharīb al-awṭān ilā ʿulamāʾ al-buldān*, an apologia in ›ic (ed. and Fr. tr. Mohammed ben Abd-el-Jalil, *JA* (1930), 1-76, 193-297; ed. ʿAfīf ʿUsayrān, *annafāt-i ʿAyn al-Ḳuḍāt al-Hamadhānī*, Tehran :/1962; Eng. tr. A. J. Arberry, *A Sufi martyr, apologia of ʿAin al-Quḍāt al-Hamadhānī*, London); *Risāla-yi Lawāʾiḥ*, on mystic love, in Persian, Raḥīm Farmanish, Tehran 1337/1958; *Zubdat aḳāʾiḳ*, in Arabic, ed. ʿUsayrān, in *op. cit.*; *ahīdāt* or *Zubdat al-ḥaḳāʾiḳ fī kashf al-daḳāʾiḳ*, in sian, ed. ʿUsayrān, in *op. cit.*, twice tr. into kish; *Nāmahā* or *Maktūbāt, Makātib*, letters, in sian, ed. ʿAlīnaḳī Munzawī and ʿUsayrān, 2 vols., ut and Tehran 1390/1971; *Risāla-yi yazdānshi-ht*, ed. Bahman Karīmī, Tehran 1327/1948; and *vāl u āthār*, ed. Farmanish, Tehran 1338/1959.

Bibliography: Sandilāhī, *Makhzan al-gharāʾib*, ›odl. Pers. ms. 395, 1523; Brockelmann, I, 490, I, 674-5; F. Meier, *Stambuler Handschriften dreier ersischer Mystiker*, in *Isl.*, xxiv (1937), 1-9.

(J. K. TEUBNER)

ʿAYN AL-MULK MULTĀNĪ, official and miliy commander under the Dihlī sultans of India. His actual name and early career are not known. temporary writers mention him by his honorific , ʿAyn al-Mulk, with the *nisba* Multānī because hailed from Multān; the 9th/15th century chron- Yaḥyā Sirhindī calls him ʿAyn al-Mulk-i Shihāb ifying that his father's name was Shihāb. How-, ʿAyn al-Mulk Multānī started his career in the n of Sultan ʿAlāʾ al-Dīn Khaldjī (695-715/1296-6), and soon attained to an important position he official hierarchy, showing excellence in both manship and military generalship. Amīr Khusraw wers praises on him in his works, depicting him ı learned statesman in peace time and a veteran eral on the battlefield. Ḍiyāʾ al-Dīn Baranī aks of him as one who was wise in counsel, widely velled, ripe in experience and much distinguished his sagacity and successful tackling of complicated blems.

His first important assignment was his posting in wā as the *muḳṭaʿ* or governor of Dhār and idjayn in 704/1305. In Mālwā, he not only condated the sultan's rule, but also subdued the alcitrant *zamīndārs* of Central India. In 716/1316, held the territory of Deogīrī (in modern Mahahtra), when he was recalled to Dihlī by Malik ʾib just after Sultan ʿAlāʾ al-Dīn had died. En te he received another order from Dihlī directing to proceed to Gudjarāt, where rebels had caped the province. In compliance to Malik Nāʾib's er, ʿAyn al-Mulk turned aside, but had to halt Čitōr as many fellow-nobles in the royal army ısed to march after Malik Nāʾib had been killed and the policy of the new ruler, Sultan Ḳuṭb al-Dīn Mubārak Shāh, was not known. After a few days, the new Sultan sent him and other nobles *farmāns* ordering them all to go to Gudjarāt and establish peace and order there.

On arrival, ʿAyn al-Mulk tried to solve the problem diplomatically. He wrote to the leaders of the rebellion that the murder of their leader Alp Khān had already been avenged, as the culprit (Malik Nāʾib) was now dead, and for this reason they should not persist in rebellion. He also warned them of the serious consequences if they did not submit to the central authority. In response to his letter, many rebels joined his camp. Only Ḥaydar and Zīrak fought against the royal army and they were easily routed. Having settled the affairs of Gudjarāt, he then returned to Dihlī.

In 718/1318, he was sent to Deogīrī when Malik Yak Lakhī, the local *muḳṭaʿ*, rose in rebellion. This time he was appointed as *wazīr*, with Malik Tādj al-Dīn, son of Khʷādja ʿAṭāʾ as *Mushrif* and Mudjīr al-Dīn Aburdja as military commandant. In 720/1320, he was present in Dihlī when Sultan Ḳuṭb al-Dīn Mubārak Shāh was killed by the allies of Khusraw Khān. Though ʿAyn al-Mulk was not in alliance with Khusraw Khān, the latter honoured him with the title of ʿAlam Khān in order to win him over to his side. Soon afterwards, Ghāzī Malik, the *muḳṭaʿ* of Depālpur, organised a movement against Khusraw Khān aiming at revenge for the murder of Ḳutb al-Dīn Mubārak Shāh, persuading all the important nobles, including ʿAyn al-Mulk, to help him against the regicide. ʿAyn al-Mulk, afraid of Khusraw Khān's agents, showed Malik Ghāzī's letter to the usurper, and thus assured him of his own loyalty. Ghāzī Malik, anxious to win him over, again wrote a letter to him. This time ʿAyn al-Mulk expressed his sympathy with Ghāzī Malik's undertaking and promised not to participate in the battle against any party because he was in Dihlī, surrounded by the allies of Khusraw, and could not take up arms against him. On achieving the throne, Ghāzī Malik, who assumed the title of Sultan Ghiyāth al-Dīn, and apparently retained ʿAyn al-Mulk Multānī in his service.

According to ʿIṣāmī, ʿAyn al-Mulk joined Ulugh Khān (later Sultan Muḥammad b. Tughluḳ) on the Warangal expedition of 722/1322. Since the siege of Warangal became prolonged and Ulugh Khān insisted on capturing the citadel, the officers got tired and many of them mutinied, although ʿAyn al-Mulk remained loyal. This was the last expedition that he had joined, for we do not hear of him afterwards.

Certain mediaeval as well as modern scholars have confused ʿAyn al-Mulk Multānī with ʿAyn al-Mulk Māhrū, who is the author of the famous work, *Inshāʾ-i Māhrū*. Māhrū was a noble of Muḥammad b. Tughluḳ's and Fīrūz Shāh's entourage. ʿIṣāmī distinguishes ʿAyn al-Mulk Multānī from Māhrū by calling the latter ʿAyn al-Dīn. Ḍiyāʾ al-Dīn Baranī differentiates between them by making different statements about their qualities, stating that ʿAyn al-Mulk Multānī could not only wield the sword successfully but was also adept in diplomacy and penmanship, while Māhrū had no experience of military generalship, since he belonged to the class of scribes and clerks. Shams al-Dīn Sirādj ʿAfīf presents Māhrū as the creature of Muḥammad b. Tughluḳ. Further, most of the letters and documents contained in the *Inshāʾ-i Māhrū* were drafted in Fīrūz Shāh's reign, and only a few belong to the time of Muḥammad b. Tughluḳ; there is no letter written by Māhrū during the reigns of the latter's predecessors. In short, ʿAyn al-Mulk Multānī and ʿAyn al-Mulk Māhrū were two different persons belonging to different generations.

Bibliography: Shams al-Dīn Sirādj ʿAfīf, *Taʾrīkh-i Fīrūz Shāhī*, Bibl. Ind. Calcutta 1890; Amīr Khusraw, *Dewal Rānī Khiḍr Khān*, Aligarh 1917, idem, *Tughluḳ-nāma*, Hyderabad, Deccan 1933; Ḍiyāʾ al-Dīn Baranī, *Taʾrīkh-i Fīrūz Shāhī*, Bibl. Ind., Calcutta 1862; Ibn Baṭṭūṭa, *Riḥla*, iii, 341-54, tr. Gibb, iii, 720-6; ʿIsāmī, *Futūḥ al-salāṭīn*, ed. Usha, Madras 1948; Muḥammad Bihāmad-Khānī, *Taʾrīkh-i Muḥammadī*, MS. British Museum, Or. 137; Yaḥyā Sirhindī, *Taʾrīkh-i Mubārak-Shāhī*, Bibl. Ind., Calcutta 1931; ʿAyn al-Mulk Māhrū, *Inshāʾ-i Māhrū*, ed. Shaykh ʿAbd al-Rashīd, Lahore 1965. (I. H. Siddiqui)

AYTĀKH AL-TURKĪ (d. 235/849), a Khazar military slave or *ghulām* [*q.v.*] who had been bought in 199/815 by the future caliph al-Muʿtaṣim, and who played an important role in the reigns of his master, of al-Wāthiḳ and of al-Mutawakkil. At the opening of al-Wāthiḳ's caliphate, he was, with Ashnās, the "mainstay of the caliphate". After being commander of the guard in Sāmarrā, in 233/847 he was made governor of Egypt, but delegated his powers there to Harthama b. Naṣr (Ibn Taghrībardī, *Nudjūm*, ii, 265; al-Maḳrīzī, *Khiṭaṭ*, ed. Wiet, v, 136). It was he who, in this same year, seized and put to torture the vizier Ibn al-Zayyāt. At this time, he was combining the functions of *ḥādjib*, commander of the caliphal guard, intendant of the palace and director of the postal and intelligence system; but he laid these duties down in 234/848 in order to go on the Pilgrimage. When he returned, he was arrested by Isḥāḳ b. Ibrāhīm b. Muṣʿab, and he died of thirst in prison the following year. It is said that al-Mutawakkil confiscated from his house a million *dīnārs*.

Bibliography: Ṭabarī, index; Yaʿḳūbī, *Historiae*, ii, 586; idem, *Buldān*, 256, tr. Wiet, 45; Masʿūdī, *Murūdj*, index, Ghars al-Niʿma, *Hafawāt*, 80, 362-5; Ibn al-ʿImād, *Shadharāt*, ii, 80 (under year 234); Ibn al-Athīr, vii, 29; Tanūkhī, *Nishwār*, index; Sourdel, *Le vizirat ʿabbāside*, index. (Ed.)

ĀZĀD, Abu 'l-Kalām, reviver of Muslim thought in India and influential politician of the first half of the 20th century. Born in Mecca in 1888, he received in Calcutta, where his family settled in 1898, an austere and rigorously orthodox education. With great precocity he made his début in the literary world at the age of fourteen with an article published in the Urdu language magazine *Makhzan*. At the age of sixteen he made the acquaintance of the remarkable poet Alṭāf Ḥusayn Ḥālī [*q.v.*], on whom he made a strong impression, and shortly after he met Mawlānī Shiblī Nuʿmānī who immediately recognised his exceptional qualities and took him to Lucknow to teach him journalism, entrusting to him the editing of his journal *al-Nadwa*.

In July 1912 Abu 'l-Kalām Āzād published the first issue of his journal *al-Hilāl*, which very quickly earned him a vast audience, thanks to the original composition of the publication, to its articles dealing with subjects of the most burning relevance, and to the fiery and poetic style of the author. This enterprise was suspended by the British government at the start of the 1914-18 war, and Abu 'l-Kalām Āzād then launched, in 1915, another periodical, *al-Balāgh*, which had only a short existence since the writer was expelled from Bengal in 1916. The texts published in *al-Hilāl* and *al-Balāgh* have been collected in two volumes bearing the title *Maḳālāt-i-Āzād*.

Abu 'l-Kalām Āzād continued and extended work begun by Shiblī with the object of encoura the *ʿulamāʾ* to participate in the most modern d opments of civilisation. As a theologian experie in the disciplines of the most traditional reli thought, he provoked the *ʿulamāʾ* into an increasi sharp awareness of social and political probl In 1920 he rejoined the ranks of the Indian Con Party and participated more or less overtly in *Djamʿiyyat al-ʿulamāʾ-i-Hind* [see djamʿiyya. I and Pakistan], an Indian association of Mu theologians which showed itself always sympat to a political scheme of nationalistic tendency, the object of driving the British colonial power Indian territory. An ardent opponent of Sir Sa Aḥmad Khān (1817-1898 [*q.v.*]) and of the mover which the latter launched in founding the unive of ʿAlīgaṛh, Abu 'l-Kalām Āzād revived the Islamic proposals of the great reformist Dj al-Dīn al-Afghānī and exhorted the Muslims of I not to remain passive observers of the uphea which were transforming the world, but to asso themselves with the struggle whose primary ob was to free them from the foreign yoke, so they could subsequently participate actively in complex and fruitful changes which, in the mo era, contribute to the prosperous life of free nat But was there not in this attitude a contradic between pan-Islamism, ideally asserted, and natic ism as constantly practised in a context wher the event, India, once independent, could no other than a nation dominated by the H community?

In the more strictly theological sphere, 'l-Kalām Āzād expressed his opposition to Sir Sa in numerous articles in *al-Hilāl* and especiall the introduction to his celebrated work *Tardju al-Ḳurʾān*, a project which he had conceived w he established himself at Rānčī after his expul from Bengal in 1916, but of which the first part not published until 1931. According to Abu 'l-K Āzād, the Ḳurʾān must be disencumbered of artificial interpretations founded on a philoso and a terminology more or less borrowed from Greeks; it is necessary also to resist the tempta of wishing to consider the Holy Book only from point of view of its conformity with newly-discov scientific laws. If we wish to restore to the Ḳu its original atmosphere, the exercise of *idjtihād* r become a vital experience, in the course of w each article of faith will be confronted by the abra forces of scepticism so that the individual emerge from the process more positive in his b and more enthusiastic in his actions.

When in 1947 the Indian sub-continent divided to permit the creation of Pakistan, 'l-Kalām Āzād chose to stay in India, and he bec minister of National Education in the Central Gov ment, a post which he held until his death in 195

Attention should also be drawn to two other portant works by this author, who contributed m to the development of the Urdu language: *Tadh* (published in 1920), a selection of autobiograp memories, and especially *Ghubār-i Khāṭir*, which the form of a collection of letters addressed friend by Abu 'l-Kalām Āzād during his impri ment in the fort of Aḥmadnagar between 9 Au 1942 and 15 June 1945. Finally, the work which author wrote in English, *India wins freedom* (Calc 1959) constitutes a valuable document for historian.

Bibliography: Badr al-Ḥasan, *Maḍāmīn-i-*

·Kalām Āzād, Delhi 1944; A. H. Alberuni, *Makers Pakistan and modern Muslim India*, Lahore)50; S. M. Ikram, *Mawdj-i Kawthar*, Lahore)54; Abu 'l-Kalām Āzād, *Speeches of Maulānā zād*, Government of India 1956; *Nawā-i-Āzādī*, ombay 1957; W. Cantwell Smith, *Islam in modern istory*, Princeton 1957; *Abu 'l-Kalām Āzād, a emorial volume*, New York 1959; Khalid bin ayeed, *Pakistan: the formative phase*, Karachi)60; A. Guimbretière, *Le réformisme musulman Inde*, in *Orient*, nos. 16, 18 (Paris 1961); Ziya -Hasan Faruqi, *The Deoband school and the emand for Pakistan*, London 1963; Abū Saʿīd azmī, *Abu 'l-Kalām Āzād*, Lahore N.D.; Aziz hmad, *Islamic modernism in India and Pakistan 857-1964*, London 1967, 175-85; P. Hardy, *Partners in freedom—and true Muslims, the political ought of some Muslim scholars in British India 912-1947*, Lund 1971. (A. GUIMBRETIÈRE)

ZĀD, MUḤAMMAD ḤUSAYN (1830-1910), Urdu ter, was a leading exponent of "new" Urdu se, and a pioneer of the reaction against the sian tradition in Urdu poetry, with its emphasis *ghazal* and its preoccupation with ornate, stylised guage.

orn in Dihlī, he was the son of one of the first ling journalists of north India. He was educated Delhi College, and acquired a mastery of both bic and Persian. By 1854, he was editor of his ıer's newspaper, the *Dihlī Urdū Akhbār*. A love poetry was fostered in him by the poet Dhawḳ 39-1854), who was a friend of his father's. However, the Indian Mutiny of 1857 and its aftermath pletely changed his life, and its effect probably er left him. His father was executed for treason the British authorities, and he himself fled and ame a wanderer. In 1864 he arrived in Lahore, ere he was to reside for the remainder of his life. obtained a minor post in the Panjab Ministry of olic Instruction. He twice visited Persia, and in 5 he accompanied an Indian Government secret sion to Bukhārā, aimed at investigating Russian etration of that region.

n his early years in Lahore, he quickly won the fidence of local British dignatories, including onel Holroyd, Director of Public Instruction. wrote several educational works, including a sian course in two books, and, in Urdu, Volume ii *Ḳiṣaṣ-i-Hind*, a three-volume series of Indian torical stories. Though designed for students, the ter book won the admiration of more mature ders, for its vivid style. In 1865 Dr. G. W. Leitner, ncipal of Government College, founded the *djumān-i Pandjāb*, a literary society, and Āzād s appointed secretary in 1867. One project of the iety was to encourage the reform of Urdu poetry, l Āzād threw himself whole-heartedly into this. r nearly a year, monthly *mushāʿaras* (poetical tests) were held, a set theme being specified in vance for each meeting. These themes, which luded "the rainy season", "winter" and "patriot-", were chosen to discourage the use of antique tical diction. Āzād opened the series with a lecture the nature of poetic art, and wrote poems for the etings. Nevertheless, even allowing for criticism sed on prejudice or personal animosity, Āzād's etry hardly enhanced his reputation; and it was t he, but Alṭāf Ḥusayn Ḥālī, [*q.v.*] who also took rt in the *mushāʿaras*, who came to be recognised the pioneer of the "new" poetry, both for his se and his critical writings. Nevertheless, a reraisement of Āzād's verse is overdue. It is uneven in quality; but there is strength and drive behind a poem like *Ūlū 'l-ʿazmī* (Resolution).

Āzād wrote some important prose works, which were better received than his verse, and indeed ultimately gained him recognition as a great—some would say the greatest—master of Urdu prose. Yet he was destined never to be free from some hostile, even carping, criticism. *Nayrang-i khayāl* (1880) is a collection of thirteen allegorical essays, translated—with minor changes and interpolations—from the English of Samuel Johnson, Addison and their contemporaries. *Sukhandān-i-Fārs*, based on his lectures on Persian language and literature, dates from 1872, but was not published until 1907. However, his fame rests chiefly on his long critical account of Urdu poetry, *Āb-i-ḥayāt* (1881). His last major work, *Darbār-i-akbarī* (1898), is a dazzling account of the court of the Mughal emperor Akbar [*q.v.*], but, despite its rich style, it is often described as a failure. Āzād's prose is imaginative and colourful, far removed from the straightforward style of Sir Sayyid Aḥmad Khān and Ḥālī. Muhammad Sadiq (*History of Urdu literature*, 300) says that it "recalls old patterns in its syntactical peculiarities and word-arrangement", and adds, perhaps with a little exaggeration, that its syntax seems Persian. Āzād was not directly involved in the ʿAlīgaṙh Movement, but was highly respected by its leaders. Ḥālī wrote complimentary reviews of *Nayrang-i-khayāl* and *Āb-i-ḥayāt*.

The last twenty years of Āzād's life were marred by periods of mental illness bordering on insanity. Personal tragedies, and overwork—including his edition of Dhawḳ's *Dīwān*—have been blamed for this. He died in Lahore in 1910.

Bibliography: In addition to information given above, some of the many reprints of Āzād's works may be mentioned; thus for *Āb-i-ḥayāt*, Lahore 1950, Faizabad 1966. As for *Darbār-i-akbarī*, Muḥammad Ibrāhīm, editor of the Lahore edition of 1910, claims in his preface that his text is more complete and more in keeping with Āzād's intentions than the original (1898) edition of Mīr Mumtāz ʿAlī. There is a Lucknow edition n.d., but *ca.* 1965. For *Nayrang-i-khayāl*, there is a Karachi edition of 1961. Āghā Muḥammad Bāḳir has edited selected articles by Āzād (*Maḳālāt Mawlānā M. Ḥ. Āzād*, Lahore 1966). *Ḳiṣaṣ-i-Hind* was reprinted in Lahore (1961) and Karachi (1962). Selected letters have been published: *Maktūbāt-i-Āzād*, Lahore 1907, and *Makātīb-i-Āzād*, Lahore 1966. The collected poetry was published as *Naẓm-i-Āzād*, Lahore 1910.

Among critical biographies, Muhammad Sadiq's *Muhammad Husain Azad—his life and work*, Lahore 1965, is of prime importance. The same author's shorter account in his *History of Urdu literature*, London 1964, 288-302, includes a conveniently brief analysis of Āzād's prose style (297-301), with extracts. In Urdu, there is Djahān Bānū Begum's *Muḥammad Ḥusayn Āzād*, Hyderabad Deccan, 1940. Among detailed studies of *Āb-i-ḥayāt*, mention must be made of Riḍāwī Masʿūd Ḥasan's *Āb-i-ḥayāt kā tanḳīd muṭālaʿa*, Lucknow 1953. Ḥālī's reviews of *Nayrang-i-khayāl* and *Āb-i-ḥayāt*, originally published in the ʿAlīgaṙh University Gazette, are available in *Kulliyyāt-i-nathr-i-Ḥālī*, Lahore 1968, ii, 176-83 and 184-94. (J. A. HAYWOOD)

ĀZĀDĪ (P.), freedom, synonymous with Arabic *ḥurriyya* [*q.v.*]. Deriving from the Avestan word *ā-zāta* and the Pahlavi word *āzāt* (noble), the word *āzādī* has as long a history as Persian literature itself. It was employed by Persian writers and poets such as Firdawsī, Farruk͟hī Sīstānī, Gurgānī, Rūmī, K͟hāḳānī, Nāṣir-i K͟husraw, and Ẓahīr Fāriyābī in a variety of meanings including, for instance, choice, separation, happiness, relaxation, thanksgiving, praise, deliverance, non-slavery, and so on (see Dihk͟hudā, art. *Āzādī*, in *Lug͟hat-nāma*, ii/1, 86-7). In modern times, the idea of social and political liberty has also been expressed by the term *āzādī* (and sometimes by the term *ik͟htiyār*), the latter sense of which will be dealt with below in reference to the Iranian world.

From its very nature, the modern connotation of *āzādī* has been associated with the process of Western impact on Persian culture and therefore its history. Considering the fact that the activities of the British East India Company (from 1600) coincided with the mass migration of Persian writers and poets to India, plus the information brought to India by travellers such as Iʿtiṣām al-Dīn, who recorded his impression of Europe in 1767, it would be logical to conclude that the Persian emigrants to India were among the first eastern people to have been exposed to European new ideas. It seems, however, that no noticeable Western influence can be observed in the Persian writings of the 17th century. The earliest favourable, but brief, account known to us of Europe is that of Muḥammad ʿAlī Ḥazīn (d. 1766), who wrote in 1732 that some of the European countries enjoyed laws, a better way of life, and more stable systems of government, and regretted not to have taken a trip to Europe, as was suggested to him by an English captain (Ḥazīn, *Taʾrīk͟h-i Ḥazīn*, Tehran, 1953, 92-3, 110-11).

One of the earliest, and relatively detailed, accounts in the Persian language of European social and political institutions belongs to a S͟hūs͟htarī-born émigré of India, ʿAbd al-Laṭīf Mūsawī D͟jazāʾirī, who learnt about the new ideas which had developed among the newly-born middle class of Europe and had been imported to India. Writing in 1801, ʿAbd al-Laṭīf dealt with modern topics such as freemasonry, equality, liberty and the function of the administration of justice in England. He also made reference to the British system of mixed government, i.e. the division of power among the king, the lords, and the subjects (*raʿāyā*), the latter being obviously considered as the propertied men who were entitled to elect and be elected.

For more detailed descriptions of modern ideas, including that of *āzādī*, one may look into the eye-witness accounts, the most widely quoted of which are those of Mīrzā Abū Ṭālib Iṣfahānī, son of another émigré to India, and Mīrzā Ṣāliḥ S͟hīrāzī of Iran. Both Abū Ṭālib, who travelled and lived in Europe from 1798 till 1803, and Mīrzā Ṣāliḥ, who studied in England from 1815 till 1819, wrote in detail about the type of liberty which then existed in England. Some differences, however, may be observed in their accounts: Abū Ṭālib seems more critical of the British system; he found, for instance, freedom of the press somewhat harmful, and refused to accept membership of freemasonry (cf. his *Maṣīr-i Ṭālibī*, Tehran 1974, 152, 195-6). Mīrzā Ṣāliḥ, on the contrary, called England with admiration *vilāyat-i āzādī* (land of freedom), and joined freemasonry with great interest (*Ṣafar-nāma-yi Mīrzā Ṣāliḥ S͟hīrāzī*, Tehran 1968, 189, 207, 374). As a matter of fact, most, if not all, of the Persians who went to Europe throughout the 19th century became freemasons, and learnt there to propagate the type of freedom which was understood by the masons and included in their famous slogan of *liberté, égalité, frate* (Ismāʿīl Rāʾīn, *Farāmūs͟hk͟hāna va Farāmāsūnrī Iran*, i-iii, Tehran 1968; Maḥmūd Katīrāʾī, *F māsūnrī dar Iran*, Tehran 1968).

In Europe, such ideas as liberty, equality, lai faire and so on, were developed in the course o struggles between the old feudal system and newly-born capitalism, so that for the "Third Est liberty meant freedom from the yoke of feuda and the freedom for private enterprise. Accordi this concept of liberty expressed could have little meaning for the Persian audiences who still experiencing their own type of "feudalism that time, and it must have appeared as an e taining fiction.

One of the consequences of the developmen capitalism in the West was the latter's need, an other things, of raw materials, cheap labour profitable investments in other parts of the w At the turn of the 19th century, Iran appeare the then great powers, i.e. England, France Russia, as important both strategically and nomically. Since Iran found itself too weak to sur Western encroachments, the Persian government it as indispensable to take certain measures strengthening of the country through modernisa so that students such as Mīrzā Ṣāliḥ were dispat to Europe to acquire modern sciences. Although internal and external forces supporting the régime of Iran were still strong, the proces modernisation did not come to a standstill. In dition to sending students abroad, there were sev diplomatic missions to Europe during the re both of Fatḥ ʿAlī S͟hāh (1797-1834) and Muḥam S͟hāh (1834-48). Missions such as those of Mīrzā 'l-Ḥasan Īlčī (England, 1814), K͟husraw Mīrzā (R sia, 1829), and Ād͟jūdānbās͟hī (Austria, France, England, 1834) helped the Iranian ruling circle obtain more information about the European i and institutions. A number of memoirs, such K͟husraw Mīrzā's, do indicate a misunderstan by some of the Iranian diplomats of the ide liberty. However, there appeared also intelli accounts of parliamentary systems in Europ countries.

In the outset of Nāṣir al-Dīn S͟hāh's reign (1848- a wide range of modernising measures were initi by the Amīr Kabīr. In 1858 Mīrzā D͟jaʿfar K Mus͟hīr al-Dawla formed his government, mode roughly on European cabinet systems. Believin D͟jaʿfar K͟hān's progressive thought, Mīrzā Malk another modernist, wrote to him a long letter ur him to reform the system of government and separate the powers. He declared the opinions of Iranian people to be free, *āzād*. Shortly after appearance of Malkam's letter, an anonymous au touched upon the necessity for free elections freedom of the press (MS. Mad͟jlis library, Teh No. 31856/4147, *Daftar-i Tanẓīmāt*, in *Mad͟jmūʿ āthār-i Mīrzā Malkam K͟hān*, Tehran 1948, 24 In the same year (1858), when an Italian nationa Orsini, attempted the life of Napoleon III, Farr K͟hān Amīn al-Dawla was on a diplomatic mis to Paris. He wrote not only of the French parliam but he also described with favour the remarks m in a letter to the Emperor by Orsini on patrioti liberty, and the freedom of Italy, for whose sake had taken that action; Farruk͟h included a Pers translation of that letter in his memoires (Ḥus b. ʿAbd Allāh Sarābī, *Mak͟hzan al-waḳāyiʿ: Sha maʾmūriyyat va musāfarat-i Farruk͟h K͟hān A al-Dawla*, Tehran 1965, 354-86).

ı866 an anonymous author wrote a treatise on . and political affairs, and paid special at- ɔn to the ideas of freedom and equality and their :ability to Islamic teachings. He classified mendable freedom" (*ikhtiyār-i mamdūḥ*) into ·pes which included freedom of speech, assembly publication (Ms. Madjlis Library 137; for an ınt of this exceptionally interesting work, see ıl Hossein Haeri, *Fihrist-i kitābkhāna-yi lis-i shūrā-yi millī*, xxi, Tehran 1974, 135-8).

e last few decades of the 19th century witnessed ımber of important changes from within and without; constitutional movements took place any European and some Asian countries; more :s were made by powerful and industrially ıced nations to colonise other countries; and ɔ-Russian rivalries in Iran were intensified. e developments, together with other factors, sed Iran to new ideas and predisposed towards stablishment of a new order involving a degree litical freedom for the subjects. The modernising ures undertaken by Mīrzā Ḥusayn Khān ısālār (d. 1881), and the appearance of news- rs such as *Īrān*, *Wakāyiʿ-i ʿadliyya*, *Waṭan*, *mī*, *ʿIlmī*, and *Mirrīkh* in the 1870s, and the gence of writers and social critics such as Mīrzā ʿAlī Ākhūnd-zāda (d. 1878), Yūsuf Khān ashār al-Dawla Tabrīzī (d. 1895) and Malkam ı (d. 1908), may be studied against the back- ıd of those developments. The critics fought stly for the establishment of a free enterprise m and the destruction of the old social structure, this involved agitation for a limited freedom of on, freedom of speech, etc. Some of the modern- ike Malkam and Sipahsālār went as far as not to advocate foreign investment in Iran, but also ed an active role in encouraging it. They seem ıve understood the concept of liberty as defined urope. Ākhūnd-zāda, for instance, propounded view that no reconciliation is possible between ty and Islam. He also saw freedom as preserved ıgh freemasonry activities (Farīdūn Ādamīyyat, *shahā-yi Mīrzā Fatḥ ʿAlī Ākhūnd-zāda*, Tehran , 148-9). Out of expediency, however, most of writers gave their definition of liberty some ıic colouring; they likened, for instance, free- of speech with the Islamic concept of *al-amr maʿrūf wa 'l-nahy ʿan al-munkar* (Abdul-Hadi i, *The idea of constitutionalism in Persian ıture prior to the 1906 Revolution*, in *Akten des Kongresses für Arabistik und Islamwissenschaft, ıgen, 1974*, Göttingen 1976, 189-207).

the same time, there appeared two more groups ıtellectuals who also wrote about freedom. ers such as Mumtaḥin al-Dawla (d. 1921), an rienced diplomat, and Mīrzā Ḥusayn Khān hānī, who visited Russia, Turkey, and the āz from 1884-5, found *āzādī* to be quite harmful. 870, while sitting at the place reserved for the ımatic corps in the British parliament, Mumtaḥin awla witnessed a serious attack waged by one e members on the Queen and the institution of archy in Britain. At this point, Mumtaḥin envied British members of parliament their freedom of ch, but did not believe that the Persians could the same privilege in the near future; ac- ingly, he flatly discredited the Iranians' struggles reedom during the Constitutional Revolution of -11 (Mahdī Khān Mumtaḥin al-Dawla Shakākī, *irāt-i Mumtaḥin al-Dawla*, Tehran 1974, 188-9, 11). To Farāhānī, freedom appeared to be a ructive element in history; he held that no system could survive unless it was based on one-man rule (*Safar-nāma-yi Mīrzā Ḥusayn Khān Farāhānī*, Tehran 1963, 139-46).

A third group of intellectuals, which also included some men from the first group, emerged in reaction to the intensification of foreign rivalries, the spread of governmental corruption and tyranny, and above all the concessions made to foreigners. The works of Ḥādjdj Sayyāḥ (d. 1925), Zayn al-ʿĀbidīn Marāghaʾī (d. 1911), Mīrzā ʿAbd al-Rahīm Tabrīzī Talibov (d. 1911), Mīrzā Āķā Khān Kirmānī (d. 1896), and some of the writings of Malkam and Afghānī (d. 1896), are the best representative expressions of the people's response to the existing political and eco- nomic situation in Iran. To Afghānī, freedom meant the replacement of the existing tyrannical régime by a benevolent government. Other writers especially Talibov, however, attached more meanings to the idea of freedom. The latter defined it in full details as involving the franchise and freedom of the press, assembly, and opinion. All of the men in this group opposed the existing "feudally" based social system and advocated a free enterprise system not dependent on foreign concessions, foreign goods, or foreign interventions.

It was during the same period that a number of reformist intellectuals, headed by Aḥmad Dānish (d. 1897), also began to emerge in Bukhārā. Dānish's most important political and philosophical work *Nawādir al-wakāyiʿ* (written 1875-82), was devoted to the necessity of social reforms and freedom of the people from the tyranny of the then Bukharān Amīr. His disciples such as Shāhīn, Sawdā, Asīrī, ʿAynī, and many others followed his steps (Jiri Bečka, *Tajik literature from the 16th century to the present*, in J. Rypka *et alii*, *History of Iranian literature*, Dordrecht 1968, 485-605). In a later period we also see revolutionary pieces of poetry such as "Surūd-i Āzādī" by ʿAynī and "Bi Sharaf-i Inkilāb-i Bukhārā" by ʿAkkāsbāshī (Ṣadr al-Dīn ʿAynī, *Namūna-yi adabiyyāt-i Tādjīk 300-1200 hidjrī*, Moscow 1926).

This period also coincided with some measures of modernisation in Afghānistān. To the Afghāns, be- cause of the Anglo-Russian rivalries throughout the 19th century, political *āzādī* simply came to mean the independence of their country from foreign en- croachments, in connection with which a number of short-lived periodical papers such as *Kābul* (1867) and *Shams al-Nahār* (1875) came into being. The Afghāns' approach to the idea of freedom was best represented in their first important weekly paper, *Sirādj al-Akhbār-i Afghāniyya* (1911), where prob- lems of modernisation and national independence were dealt with in a highly sophisticated manner. Its chief editor, Maḥmūd Ṭarzī, argued that "genuine national development and progress were possible only when a society enjoyed complete independence, sovereignty, and freedom" (Vartan Gregorian, *The emergence of modern Afghanistan*, Stanford 1969, 178). This type of argument about liberty was pursued by later papers such as *Amān-i Afghān*, *Ittiḥād-i mashrikī* and many others (Said Qassim Reshtia, *Journalism in Afghanistan*, in *Afghanistan*, ii (1948), 72-7).

In the course of the Persian Constitutional Revolu- tion of 1905-11, the idea of freedom was approached by the factions involved in the Revolution in three different ways. One of the groups, influenced prin- cipally by Islamic teachings, was in favour of free- dom, but a type of freedom consonant with Islam. Mīrzā Muḥammad Ḥusayn Nāʾīnī (d. 1936), for instance, defined freedom as an opposite to slavery, but like Montesquieu (*De l'esprit des lois*, i, l. iii, ch. viii) held that living under despotism was itself equal to slavery; therefore, freedom may be achieved only by the replacement of the existing tyrannical régime of Iran (Hairi, *Shīʿism and constitutionalism in Iran* [see *Bibl.*], 173-80, 218-19). The second group, to which belonged the Tabrīz revolutionaries, had a better insight into European ideas, together with a close association with the Russian revolutionaries, so that they interpreted freedom in a more western sense. In their approach both groups emphasised particularly the downfall of despotic rule in Persia and the ending of foreign intervention as being integral parts of freedom. The third group, i.e. the supporters of the old régime, under the leadership of Shaykh Faḍl Allāh Nūrī (d. 1909), opposed any principles of democracy, and especially the concepts of liberty and equality, which appeared to the Shaykh as detrimental to Islam (Abdul-Hadi Hairi, *Shaykh Fazl Allāh Nūrī's Refutation of the Idea of Constitutionalism*, to appear in *Middle East Studies*). The latter group even organised many mob demonstrations in which the people chanted: "We want no liberty; we want the Prophet's religion".

The Anglo-Russian agreements of 1907 and 1915, and the Anglo-Persian treaty of 1919 gave rise to a number of nationalist movements, such as those led by Kūčak Khān [*q.v.*], Khiyabānī [*q.v.*], and Muḥammad Taḳī Khān Pisyān. After the 1917 Russian Revolution, the Soviets withdrew the claims of the Tsars against Iran, so that freedom meant exclusively the abolition of the 1919 treaty and the freedom of Iran from any foreign intervention which could limit its independence. The newly-established Communist Party of Iran (1920), which co-operated with some of these movements, added a socialist colouring to the idea of freedom by propagating the idea of freedom of the peasants from the landowners through dividing up the latter's lands among the former.

Towards the end of the Ḳādjār dynasty, a number of poets and writers, such as Mīrzāda ʿIshḳī, Muḥammad Farrukhī Yazdī, Muḥammad Taḳī Bahār and Abu 'l-Ḳāsim Lāhūtī, wrote very critically about the freedom of the Persian people both from internal tyranny and from external influences; some of them met an untoward fate. Under Riḍā Shāh's reign (1925-41) the term *āzādī* was used only in rare cases; for instance, the newspaper *Iṭṭilāʿāt* used *āzādī* in the sense of the freedom from the Ḳādjār dynasty or from the movements and rebellions which had existed in Iran. In 1932 Riḍā Shāh outlawed the Communist Party, but the activities of some of the communists led by Dr. Taḳī Arānī (d. 1939) continued. In their literature, e.g. in *Dunyā*, social and political concepts, including liberty, were defined from the socialist point of view. Some other intellectuals such as the woman poet, Parwīn Iʿtiṣāmī (d. 1941), wrote about freedom in a symbolic and subtle way, but their general message was the freedom from the existing situation.

The period following Riḍā Shāh's abdication (1941-53) witnessed a campaign for the nationalisation of the Anglo-Persian Oil Company. The new Communist party, now calling itself *ḥizb-i tūda-yi Īrān* (founded in September 1941) held freedom to be the nationalisation of the oil However, it also saw freedom in the establishment of better relations with the Soviet Union so that Iran might evolve a Communist government. To the nationalists, on the other hand, freedom depended not only on the nationalisation of the oil but also on the extinguishing of Russian and all other foreign influences in Iran. These ideological conflicts culminated under Dr. Muḥammad M[…] diḳ's 28 month-rule, a period referred to by his [...] porters as *dawra-yi āzādī* ("the epoch of freed[…] during which for the first time popular involve[…] in politics was allowed to a certain extent an[…] activities of opposing political parties plus campaigns of the press belonging to different pol[…] wings were somewhat tolerated. This period […] to an end in August 1953 when Muṣaddiḳ's go[…] ment was overthrown by the army.

Bibliography: Abdul-Hadi Hairi, *Shīʿism […] constitutionalism in Iran: a study of the role p[…] by the Persian residents of Iraq in Iranian po[…]* Leiden 1976; idem, *European and Asian influ[…] on the Persian Revolution of 1906*, in *Asian Af[…]* N.S. vi (1975), 155-64; idem, *Why did the ʿU[…] participate in the Persian Constitutional Revol[…] of 1906-1909?*, in *WI*, xvii (1976), 127-54; i[…] *Afghānī on the decline of Islam*, in *WI*, xiii (1[…] 121-5, and xiv (1973), 116-22; idem, *Su[…] pīrāmūn-i vāzha-yi mashrūṭa*, in *Vaḥīd*, xii (1[…] 287-300; idem, *Sukhanī pīrāmūn-i vāzha-yi is[…] dar adabiyyāt-i inḳilāb-i mashrūṭiyyat-i Īrā[…] Vaḥīd*, xii (1974), 539-49; M. Riḍwānī, *Ḳadīm[…] dhikr-i dimokrāsī dar Niwishtahā-yi pārsī[…] Rāhnamā-yi Kitāb*, v (1962), 257-63, 36[…] ʿAbd al-Laṭīf Mūsawī Shūshtarī Djazā'irī, *T[…] al-ʿalam*, Ḥaydarābād 1846; Mudjtabā Mīr[…] *Awwalīn kārwān-i maʿrifat*, in his *Ta'rīk[…] farhang*, Tehran 1973; Ḥusayn Maḥbūbī Arda[…] *Ta'rīkh-i mu'assasāt-i tamaddunī yi djadīd Īrān*, i, Tehran 1975; idem, *Duwwumīn Kārw[…] Maʿrifat*, in *Yaghmā*, xviii (1965), 592-5; Mu[…] Afshār, *Safar-nāma-yi Khusraw Mīrzā*, Te[…] 1970; Muḥammad Mushīrī, *Sharḥ-i ma'mūriy[…] Ādjūdānbāshī*, Tehran 1968; Farīdūn Ādamiy[…] *Maḳālāt-i ta'rīkhi*, Tehran 1973; idem, […] *Kabīr va Īrān*, Tehran 1969; idem, *Fikr-i ā[…]* Tehran 1961; idem, *Andīsha-yi taraḳḳī va ḥ[…] mat-i ḳānūn: ʿĀṣr-i Sipahsālār*, Tehran 1[…] idem, *Andīshahā-yi Talibov*, in *Sukhan*, xvi (1[…] 454-64, 549-64, 691-701, 815-35; idem, *Andīsh[…] yi Mīrzā Āḳa Khān Kirmānī*, Tehran 1967; i[…] *Fikr-i dimukrāsī-yi idjtimāʿī dar nahḍat-i mas[…] iyyat-i Īrān*, Tehran 1975; Malkam Khān, *Maḍ[…] ʿa-yi āthār*, Tehran 1948; idem, *Ḳānūn*, 188[…] 1898; idem, [*Risālahā*], ed. Hāshim Rabīʿ-z[…] Tehran 1907; Hamid Algar, *Mirza Malkum K[…] a biographical study in Iranian modernism*, Berk[…] 1973; Fatḥ ʿAlī Ākhūnd-Zāda, *Alifbā-yi d[…] va maktūbāt*, Baku 1963; Yūsuf Mustashā[…] Dawla, *Yak kalima*, Paris 1870; Nikki R. Ke[…] *Sayyid Jamāl ad-Dīn "Afghani": a political […] raphy*, Berkeley 1972; M. M. Ṭabāṭabā'ī, *Na[…] Sayyid Djamāl al-Dīn Asadābādī dar bīdā[…] mashriḳzamīn*, Ḳum 1971; Āḳā Khān Kirm[…] *Hasht bihisht*, Tehran 1960; Mangol Bayat Phi[…] *The concepts of religion and government i[…] thought of Mīrzā Āqā Khān Kirmānī, a ninete[…] century Persian revolutionary*, in *IJMES*, v (1[…] 381-400; Manūčihr Kamālī Ṭāhā, *Andīsh[…] ḳānūnkhwāhī dar Īrān-i ṣada-yi nūzdah*, Te[…] 1974; Farzāmī, *Djang-i ʿaḳāyid*, Tehran 1[…] Mīrzā ʿAbd al-Raḥim Tabrīzī Talibov, *Safī[…] Ṭālibī yā Kitāb-i Aḥmad*, i-ii, Istanbul 1889, 1[…] idem, *Masā'il al-ḥayāt*, Tiflis 1906; idem, *Ma[…] al-muḥsinīn*, Tehran 1968; idem, *Īḍāḥāt khuṣūṣ-i āzādī*, Tehran 1906; idem, *Sīyā[…] Ṭālibī*, Tehran 1911; Zayn al-ʿĀbidīn Marāg[…] *Siyāḥat-nāma-yi Ibrāhīm Bayk*, i-iii, Tehran […] cutta 1906-9; *Ḥādjdj Sayyāḥ* (Muḥammad ʿ[…] *Khāṭirāt-i Ḥādjdj Sayyāḥ*, Tehran 1967; Mul[…]

.d Riḍā Fas͟hāhī, *Az Gāthā tā mas͟hrūṭiyyat: ārishī kūtāh az taḥawwulāt-i id͟jtimāʿī dar mīʿa-yi fiʾudālī-yi Īrān*, Tehran 1975; Sayyid .san Taḳī-zāda, *Akhdh-i tamaddun-i k͟hāriḏji āzādī, waṭan, millat, tasāhul*, Tehran 1960; m, *Taʾrīk͟h-i awāʾil-i inḳilāb va mas͟hrūṭiyyat-i in*, Tehran 1959; Yaḥyā Dawlātābādī, *Ḥayāt-i ḥyā*, i-iv, Tehran 1949-57; Aḥmad Kasrawī, *ʾrīk͟h-i mas͟hrūṭa-yi Īrān*, Tehran 1951; idem, *ashrūṭa bihtarīn s͟hakl-i ḥukūmat va ak͟hirīn ʾida-yi andīs͟ha-yi niz͟hād-i adamīst*, Tehran 56; idem, *Inḳilāb čist?*, Tehran 1957; Gholam oseyn Yousofi, *Dehkhoda's place in the Iranian nstitutional movement*, in *ZDMG*, cxxv (1975), 7-32; E. G. Browne, *The Persian revolution of 05-1909*, Cambridge 1910; idem, *The press and etry of modern Persia*, Cambridge 1914; Muḥam-ad Ḥusayn Nāʾīnī, *Tanbīh al-umma wa-tanzīh milla*, Tehran 1954; ʿAbd al-Raḥmān al-Kawā-ī, *Ṭabāʾiʿ al-istibād*, tr. ʿAbd al-Ḥusayn Ḳad͟jār, hran 1908; Mahdī Ḳulī Hidāyat, *K͟hāṭirāt va atarāt*, Tehran 1965; Riḍā Ṣafīnīyā, *Taʾrīk͟h-i ūr-i afkār-i mutaraḳḳīyāna-yi Īrāniyān ki ndjar bi āzādī va mas͟hrūṭiyyat gardīd*, in *lnamā-yi Dunyā*, v, 75-84; Aḥmad Ḳāsimī, *ish sāl inḳilāb-i mas͟hrūṭa-yi Īrān*, Milan 1974; B. Muʾminī, *Iran dar āstāna-yi inḳilāb-i as͟hrūṭiyyat*, Tehran 1973; idem, *Adabiyyāt-i s͟hrūṭa*, Tehran 1975; Muḥammad Nāẓim al-ām Kirmānī, *Taʾrīk͟h-i bīdārī-yi Īrāniyān*, i-ii, hran 1953, 1970; ʿAlī G͟harawī Nūrī, *Ḥizb-i mukrāt-i Īrān dar dawra-yi duwwum-i mad͟jlis-i ırā-yi millī*, Tehran 1973; Dāriyūs͟h Ās͟hārī and hīm Raʾīsnīyā, *Zamīna-yi iḳtiṣādī va id͟jtimā-yi inḳilābī-i mas͟hrūṭiyyat-i Īrān*, Tabriz 1953); ʿAlī Ād͟harī, *Ḳiyām-i kulunil Muḥammad ḳī K͟hān Pisyān*, Tehran 1965; ʿAlī Akbar ıs͟hīr Salīmī, *Kulliyyāt-i muṣawwar-i ʿIs͟hḳī*, hran 1971; ʿAbd al-Ḥusayn Zarrīnkūb, *Bahār āyis͟hgar-i āzādī*, in his *Bā kārwān-i ḥulla*, Tehran 64; Muḥammad Farruk͟h Yazdī, *Dīwān-i Far-k͟h*, ed. Ḥusayn Makkī, Tehran 1949; ʿAbd al-amīd ʿIrfān, *S͟harḥ-i aḥwāl va āt͟hār-i Malik S͟huʿarāʾ Muḥammad Taḳī Bahār*, Tehran 1956; ısayn Makki, *Taʾrīk͟h-i bīst sāla-yi Īrān*, i-iii, hran 1944-6; Mans͟hūr Gurgānī, *Siyāsat-i rawī dar Īrān*, i-ii, Tehran 1947; Ḥizb-i Tūda-yi in, *Inḳilāb-i Uktubr va Īrān*, 1967; Mazdak, *nād-i taʾrīk͟hī-yi d͟junbis͟h-i kārgarī-yi sūsīyāl mukrāsī va kumūnīstī-yi Īrān*, i-v, Florence 70-6; ʿAbd al-Ṣamad Kāmbak͟hs͟h, *Naẓarī bi inbish-i kārgarī va kumūnistī dar Īrān*, i-ii, assfurt 1972-4; Parwīn Iʿtiṣāmī, *Dīwān-i ḳaṣāʾid mat͟hnawiyyāt va tamt͟hīlāt va muḳaṭṭaʿāt*, Tehran 54; Abu ʾl-Faḍl Āzmūda, tr. *Haft maḳāla az ins͟hināsān-i s͟hūrawī*, Tehran n.d.; ʿAbbās asʿūdī, *Iṭṭilāʿāt dar yak rubʿ-i ḳarn*, Tehran 50; Yahyā Āriyānpūr, *Az ṣabā tā nīmā*, i-ii, hran 1971; Ḥusayn Kay Ustuwān, *Siyāsat-i awāzana-yi manfī dar mad͟jlis-i čahārdahum*, , Tehran 1948, 1950; R. W. Cottam, *Nationalism Iran*, Pittsburgh 1964; *Bāk͟htar-i imrūz*, 1950-3; ıṣtafā Raḥīmī, *Insānsālārī*, in his *Dīdgāhhā*, hran 1973; Aḥmad Dānis͟h, *At͟harhā-yi mun-k͟hab*, Stalinabad 1957; idem, *Pārčahā az Jawādir al-waḳāyiʿ"*, Stalinabad 1957; *Āriyānā ʾirat al-maʿārif*, i-iv, Kabul 1949-62; L. W. amec, *Afghanistan, 1900-1923*, Berkeley 1967; yyid D͟jamāl al-Dīn Asadābādī "Afg͟hānī", *aḳālāt-i d͟jamāliyya*, Tehran 1933; I. Spector, *e first Russian Revolution: its impact on Asia*, glewood Cliffs, N.J. 1962. See also ANDJUMAN, DUSTUR, D͟JAMʿĪYYA, D͟JARĪDA, ḤIZB and ḤUKŪMA.

(ABDUL-HADI HAIRI)

ʿAZAFĪ, BANU'L-, family of notables prominent in the annals of medieval Ceuta (Sabta [*q.v.*]) and descended from a Ceutan *faḳīh* by the name of Abu ʾl-ʿAbbās Aḥmad b. *al-ḳāḍī* Abī ʿAbd Allāh Muḥammad b. Aḥmad al-Lak͟hmī, whose ancestor Muḥammad al-Lak͟hmī was known as Ibn Abī ʿAzafa, whence "Azafī". There is no reason to suppose that the ʿAzafids were descended from Mad͟jkasa Berbers, as some 8th/14th-century Ceutans alleged. A gratuitous (but not wholly unreasonable) assumption of more recent date is that the family was of Andalusian origin.

Abu ʾl-ʿAbbās was born on 17 Ramaḍān 557/30 August 1162 and died on 7 Ramaḍān 633/16 May 1236. From all accounts he was a man of profound piety, and, throughout his adult life, he taught *ḥadīth* and *fiḳh* in the Great Mosque of Ceuta. It was on his initiative that the festival of the Prophet's nativity (*mawlid*; vulgar *mūlūd, mīlūd*) was introduced into the Mag͟hrib, and it was undoubtedly his example that in after times inspired his son Abu ʾl-Ḳāsim to adopt the custom of celebrating the *mawlid* as a public festival on a grand scale. At the time of his death, Abu ʾl-ʿAbbās was writing and had possibly almost completed his *K. al-Durr al-munaẓẓam fī mawlid al-Nabī ʾl-muʿaẓẓam*, the purpose of which was to promote his idea of celebrating the *mawlid* and putting an end to the celebration of non-Islamic festivals. The *Durr*, which is extant and has been carefully studied by F. de la Granja (see *Al-Andalus*, xxxiv (1969), 1-53) is ascribed by some to Abu ʾl-Ḳāsim, who actually seems only to have put the finishing touches to a largely completed work. Abu ʾl-ʿAbbās was also the author of a work entitled *Diʿāmat al-yaḳīn fī zaʿāmat al-muttaḳīn*. By the time of his death in 1236 both he and his family must already have achieved a position of eminence in Ceuta, for not long before the loss of Seville to Ferdinand III (end of 1248) one of that city's most notable families, the Banū K͟haldūn, anticipated the disaster by emigrating to Ceuta where they contracted matrimonial alliances with the sons and daughters of "al-ʿAzafī".

The First *Dawla*. For thirteen years after the death of Abu ʾl-ʿAbbās, the history of the ʿAzafid family is shrouded in obscurity. Not so the troubled history of their native Ceuta. The period was one of Almohad decline, Ḥafṣid intervention in the Muslim West and spectacular Christian triumphs in Spain which cost Islam both Cordova and Seville, to say nothing of Valencia, Murcia, Jaén and Játiva. In 1243 the governor of Ceuta, a certain Abū ʿAlī b. K͟halāṣ, withdrew his allegiance to the Almohad caliph and shortly afterwards acknowledged the sovereignty of the Ḥafṣid Abū Zakariyyāʾ. After the death of Ibn K͟halāṣ, which more or less coincided with the fall of Seville, the Ceutans were in no mood to tolerate his successor, Ibn S͟hahīd, an ineffectual cousin of Abū Zakariyyāʾ. The Sevillan disaster loomed large in their preoccupations: their ships had fought on the Guadalquivir, and their harbours had witnessed a sizeable influx of Sevillan refugees—among them S͟haḳḳāf, the hated *ḳāʾid* who had actually surrendered the keys of Seville to Ferdinand. There was, too, one aspect of Ḥafṣid administration which this mercantile people deeply resented—the exactions of its customs officer, Ibn Abī K͟hālid. Such was the position when news of Abū Zakariyyāʾ's death reached Ceuta (29 Rad͟jab 647/7 November 1249 or, more probably, 27 Ramaḍān 647/3 January 1250).

This was the signal for action. As the most widely respected notable, Abu 'l-Ḳāsim al-ʿAzafī was approached by Ceuta's *ḳāʾid al-baḥr*, Abu 'l-ʿAbbās Hadjbūn al-Randāḥī, and persuaded to consent to the overthrow of the regime and, in the event of success, to assume leadership of the community. The plan, as executed by al-Randāḥī, but not quite as envisaged by Abu 'l-Ḳāsim, resulted in the decapitation of Shaḳḳāf and Ibn Abī Khālid. Ibn Shahīd was deported, and the ʿAzafid, after assuming control, declared Ceuta's allegiance to the Almohad Caliph al-Murtaḍā (reg. 646-65/1248-66), who duly appointed a governor. The Almohad governor's stay was short: after only a few months in Ceuta, Abu 'l-Ḳāsim expelled him and sent the caliph a letter of explanation which he accepted.

What arrangement followed is unclear. We are only told that in 654/1256-7 the ʿAzafid became absolute ruler of Ceuta, which he took over and administered with great application and total devotion to the interests of its inhabitants. What is certain is that, despite his *de facto* autonomy, he remained loyal to the tottering throne of al-Murtaḍā and even defended his interests when the occasion demanded.

Considering that Abu 'l-Ḳāsim was, in his day, a key figure in the western Mediterranean, specific information on his life and rule is so sparse that most of what can be said of him must be deduced from his ascertainable policies. Born between 606/1209-10 and 609/1212-13, he was around forty when he came to power and seems to have had a maturity of judgment to match his years and such as to militate against rash ventures. His primary aim was to create and maintain a strong and prosperous Ceuta at a time when it was fast becoming not only a prime military objective for Castile, but also a target for ambitious Marīnids seeking control of Morocco. He therefore set about strengthening Ceuta's defences and evidently profited from a truce with Castile against handsome tribute over two consecutive two-year periods (? 1251-5). At the same time he aimed at stabilising, conserving and developing Ceuta's already extensive trans-Mediterranean trade, notably with Barcelona, Genoa and Marseille. Within about ten years, Ceuta seems to have gained real naval and economic strength. In 659/1261 her first real test came when the prospect of a Naṣrid Ceuta lured Ibn al-Aḥmar of Granada into launching a naval assault on the place—a venture that ended in disaster for Granada. As long as he lived, Abu 'l-Ḳāsim remained keenly alive to the dangers threatening Islam in the West and always took whatever measures were necessary to combat them. Thus, in 662/1263-4 we find him co-operating with the Marīnids as they launch their first *djihād* in Spain. In the years immediately following, we find him endeavouring to achieve and maintain stability between Ceuta and the Atlantic coast and, to that end, bringing a weak and divided Tangier (665/1266-7) under his control. Then, at the end of 1274 or early in 1275 we see him apparently sacrificing his autonomy to the Marīnid Abū Yūsuf, but in fact skilfully extricating him from an alliance concluded with Aragon and potentially dangerous to Islam. In practice he sacrificed little: a yearly "gift" to the Marīnid assured him virtual independence. Thereafter he made common cause with the ruler in prosecuting the *djihād* in Spain. Abu 'l-Ḳāsim died on 13 Dhu 'l-Ḥidjdja 677/27 April 1279, leaving Ceuta rich and powerful at sea.

Abu 'l-Ḳāsim was succeeded by his son Abū Ḥātim Aḥmad, an unambitious and self-effacing man, who was content to leave the administr of Ceuta to his elder brother Abū Ṭālib ʿAbd A Little is known of a third brother, Abū Muḥam Ḳāsim, but he may have been a senior military o since he commanded a Ceutan expeditionary in Spain in 1285. Abū Ṭālib carried his father's p of co-operation with the Marīnids a stage furth proclaiming all territory under ʿAzafid jurisdi to be Marīnid and by abandoning the trappin royal authority enjoyed by his father. He actively participated in the *djihād*, and in July at the relief of Algeciras, then blockaded by Al X, it was ʿAzafid ships that formed the backbo the Marīnid fleet which utterly routed the Casti But gradually the certain rewards of peaceful t notably with the Crown of Aragon, began to greater appeal than the uncertainties of the *dj* Marīnid setbacks in Spain in the 1290s and con ments in the Maghrib encouraged the ʿAzafids to withhold their dues to Fez and then, in 130 rebel against the sultan Abū Yaʿḳūb, who, wi Aragonese naval assistance, was powerless to in his will. But ʿAzafid independence was short-l in May 1305 Naṣrid forces were enabled by a affected garrison commander to seize Ceuta members of the ʿAzafid family were deporte Granada, where they remained, royally treate Muḥammad III until his deposition in March 1

The Second *Dawla*. In July 1309 Naṣrid C following an internal rising, capitulated to Marīnid Abu 'l-Rabīʿ, who then allowed the ʿAz to return from Spain and settle in Fez. There Y a son of Abū Ṭālib, met and found favour with Saʿīd ʿUthmān, the very prince who was to the throne on Abū 'l-Rabīʿ's death (November 1 In 710/1310-11 Yaḥyā was made governor of C and returned with the family to his native city brothers Abū Zayd ʿAbd al-Raḥmān and 'l-Ḥasan ʿAlī were appointed, respectively, *al-baḥr* and superintendent of the naval ship However, the temporary success of the su rebel son Abū ʿAlī resulted in their recall to late in 1314, and during their stay there the a Abū Ṭālib died. In 715/1315-16 Yaḥyā return Ceuta as Abū Saʿīd's governor, leaving his Muḥammad as a guarantee of his continuing giance to Fez, but accompanied by the rest o family. Soon after, Abū Ḥātim died and was sur by at least one son, Ibrāhīm.

Once back in Ceuta, Yaḥyā soon put himself a head of a council of notables (*shūrā*) and, wit aid of a Marīnid pretender, succeeded both i trieving his son and in proclaiming and mainta Ceuta's autonomy. In 719/1319, however, he to effect a reconciliation with Abū Saʿīd ar remit taxes in exchange for recognition as Ma governor. His motive in so doing was pro growing apprehension at the popularity, in C of an ambitious Ḥusaynid *sharīf* who bore h personal grudge and was, at the same time, resp by Abū Saʿīd. When Yaḥyā died at some date after 722/1322-3, he was succeeded by his appar ineffectual son, Abu 'l-Ḳāsim Muḥammad, governed under the tutelage of his cousin Muḥam b. ʿAlī, admiral of the fleet (*ḳāʾid al-asāṭīl*). D of the situation that in due course culminated i ʿAzafids' downfall are unclear; we know only their authority collapsed, that Abū Saʿīd ma on Ceuta in 728/1327-8, and that disaffected not surrendered the ʿAzafids to him. The reason the ʿAzafids' downfall are complex, but, as enemy, the Ḥusaynid *sharīf* Abu 'l-ʿAbbās Aḥ

. emerged as president of Ceuta's *shūrā*, it is hard to see in him one major cause of their undoing. rcumstantial evidence suggests that the ʿAzafids all taken to Fez where they were usefully em-ed—under surveillance—in the administration. Marīnids bore the family no ill will, and indeed ammad b. ʿAlī reappears as admiral of Abu asan's fleet which in 1340 almost annihilated the ilian fleet off Algeciras. Ten years later he was admiral of the fleet when he fell in action fighting ʿAbd al-Wādids [*q.v.*] in the Chélif plain.

Bibliography: J. D. Latham, *The rise of the zafids of Ceuta*, in *S. M. Stern memorial volume = Israel Oriental Studies*, ii (1972), 263-87); idem, *he later ʿAzafids*, in *Mélanges Le Tourneau* (= *ev. de l'Occident musulman et de la Mediterranée*, v-xvi (1973), 109-25) (on p. 125 the death of bū Zayd ʿAbd al-Raḥmān can now be given in e genealogy: 717/1317); M. Habib Hila, *Quelques ttres de la chancellerie de Ceuta au temps des zafides*, in *Actas II coloquio hispano-tunecino*, adrid 1972, 42-7. (J. D. Latham)

AZAMIYYA (*ṭarīḳa*) [see ABU 'L-ʿAZĀʾIM.].

-AZDĪ, *nisba* formed from the tribal name of and borne by a family of Mālikite *ḳāḍī*s of Bagh-, who will be treated under IBN DIRHAM, the name heir ancestor.

-AZDĪ, ISMĀʿĪL B. ISḤĀḲ B. ISMĀʿĪL B. ḤAMMĀD ZAYD, ABŪ ISḤĀḲ AL-ḲĀḌĪ (199-282/814-95), ikī *faḳīh*, originally from Baṣra, who in 246/860 eeded Sawwār b. ʿAbd Allāh as *ḳāḍī* of Baghdād t. After having been removed from office in 255-6/ 70, he was restored to office, transferred to hdād West in 258/871-2 and then given charge oth halves of the city from 262/876 till his death; vas then supreme *ḳāḍī* without having the official , although currently described as *ḳāḍī 'l-ḳuḍāt*. was also sent as an envoy to the Ṣaffārid who had aded the province of Ahwāz in 262/875-6.

his *ḳāḍī* was equally a specialist in the Ḳurʾān, *ith*, *fiḳh* and *kalām* and knowledgeable about mmar and *adab*. He was very opposed to all ovation, refuting al-Shāfiʿī and Abū Ḥanīfa and ading Mālikism through ʿIrāḳ. He was the author considerable number of works: the *K. Aḥkām Ḳurʾān*, *K. al-Ḳirāʾāt*, *K. Maʿānī 'l-Ḳurʾān*, *K. ḥtidjādj bi 'l-Ḳurʾān*, *al-Mabsūṭ fi 'l-fiḳh*, *K. mwāl wa 'l-maghāzī*, *K. al-Shafīʿa*, *K. al-Ṣalāt 'l-nabī* (ms. Köprülü, 428), *al-Farāʾiḍ*, *K. Uṣūl*, *Shawāhid al-Muwaṭṭaʾ*, *K. al-Sunan*, five snads, *K. al-Shufʿa* and several refutations.

His works were known in Spain, probably thanks is nephew Aḥmad al-Duḥaym b. Khalīl (278-338/ -949), and are often cited (see Ibn al-Faraḍī, *H*, vii, No. 110; Ibn Khayr, *Fahrasa*, *BAH*, ix, , 148, 247-8, 303-4). In particular, his *K. Aḥkam Ḳurʾān* (cited elsewhere only in the *Fihrist*, ed. o, 57) was copied by Ḳāsim b. Aṣbagh [*q.v.*]; see Pellat, in *al-And.*, xix/1 (1954), 77.

Bibliography: Ṭabarī, index; Masʿūdī, *Murūdj*, index; Khatīb Baghdādī, *Taʾrīkh*, i, 284-90; Dhahabī, *Ḥuffāẓ*, ii, 180 ff.; Ibn -ʿImād, *Shadharāt*, ii, 178; ʿIyāḍ, *Madārik*, d. Bakīr, iii, 168-81; Ibn Farḥūn, *Dībādj*, 92-3; Yāḳūt, *Udabāʾ*, vi, 129-40; Ṣūlī, *Akhbār al-Rāḍī a-'l-Muttaḳī*, tr. M. Canard, 107-8; Suyūṭī, *ughya*, 193; Brockelmann, S I, 273. (Ch. Pellat)

ZOV, Sea of- [see BAḤR MĀYUṬIS].

ZRŪ, Berber "stone", "pebble", and above all, ck", the name of numerous villages in North ica dominated by a rock or built at its foot, on its slopes or on its summit. One of these in Morocco, in the middle of the ancient province of the Fazāz and lying at 1,200 m. height, has become a small town of 15,000 inhabitants. In 1901, the Marquis de Segonzac estimated the population at only 1,400 (woodcutters, including 200 Ayt Mūsā Jews), and in 1940 there were still only 3,500.

Azrū is well-placed at the junction of two great imperial highways, now modernised: Fās to Marrakesh, and Meknès to the Tafilālt, and has become an important market for livestock. Two further facts have contributed to its growth: firstly, in 1914 a French military post was set up there to control the great Berber confederation of the Banī Mgild (who speak a Tamazight dialect and are of Ṣanhādja origin), and this made it an administrative centre; and secondly, in 1927 a "Berber" secondary college was founded there, confirming its demographic development and making it a lively and enduring cultural focus.

Azrū's strategic position has resulted in its frequent appearance on the pages of Moroccan history. In 534/1140 the Almohads, under the orders of the caliph ʿAbd al-Muʾmin and after a check which had scattered them, established themselves there firmly, and the *amīr* took a wife there, who was to be the mother of the prince ʿAbd Allāh, the future governor of Bougie. In 674/1274, under the Marīnids, one of the natural uncles of sultan Yaʿḳūb rebelled against him and entrenched himself in the Azrū mountain; the ruler besieged him there, reduced him to submission and pardoned him. In 1074/1663-4 Mawlāy al-Sharīf came to encamp at Azrū. The *ʿulamāʾ* and *shurafāʾ* of Fās came to him there and proclaimed him ruler; but the prince prudently remained at Azrū for that summer. In 1093/1684 Mawlāy Ismāʿīl journeyed in force into the Fazāz mountains in order to subjugate the Ayt Idrasen tribe who had been committing all sorts of depredations in the plain of the Sāʾis. On his approach, the tribe fled towards the upper part of the valley of the Wādī Mulūya, and the sultan profited by their absence to build at Azrū a *ḳaṣaba* garrisoned by 1,000 cavalrymen. Pushed back into the highlands, and cut off from their agricultural lands, the Ayt Idrasen sued for peace and obtained it in return for harsh conditions of *amān*. In 1226/1811 sultan Mawlāy Sulaymān, at the head of an army from all the provinces of the empire and of those Berbers who had remained faithful to him in his misfortunes, marched against the tribes of the Igerwān and the Ayt Yūsī. His ill-led troops suffered a bloody and humiliating defeat before Azrū, and were only kept safe through the protection of the Ayt Idrasen, the foes of 1093/1684. The "Azrū affair" had widespread repercussions throughout Morocco, and deprived the sultan of all his prestige; he never recovered, and died soon after.

The *ḳaṣaba* of Mawlāy Ismāʿīl is more or less in ruins today, but the modern town is developing rapidly, and is famous for its woollen carpets woven by a prosperous workers' co-operative. Thanks to the beauty of its location and to the magnificent cedar forests in the vicinity, Azrū has also become a flourishing tourist centre.

One should be careful not to confuse the above Azrū—as do the authors and interpolators of the *Ḳirṭās* and the *Dhakhīra*—with the place of the same name which dominates Tafarsit, in the country of the Banī Tūzīn in northern Morocco; it was here that, under the Marīnids, Ṭalḥa b. Yaḥyā took refuge and then left it after getting an authorisation to make the Pilgrimage to Mecca. See al-Bādisī, *al-Maḳṣad*,

Fr. tr. G. S. Colin, *Vie des saints du Rif*, in *AM*, xxvi (1926), 209 n. 4.

Bibliography: Zayyānī, *al-Turdjumān al-muʿrib...*, extract ed. and tr. O. Houdas, *Le Maroc de 1631 à 1812*, Paris 1886, index; Nāṣirī, *K. al-Istiḳṣā*, Cairo 1312/1894, tr. of vol. iv by E. Fumey, *Chronique de la dynastie Alaouie au Maroc*, in *AM*, ix-x, index; Marquis de Segonzac, *Voyages au Maroc (1899-1901)*, Paris 1903, index; E. Lévi-Provençal, *Documents inédits d'histoire almohade*, Paris 1928, 144-5; H. Terrasse, *Histoire du Maroc*, Casablanca 1950, index; and see arts. ATLAS, BERBERS and MOROCCO. (G. DEVERDUN)

BĀ ḤMĀD, Moroccan grand vizier whose real name was Aḥmad b. Mūsā b. Aḥmad al-Bukhārī. His grandfather was a black slave belonging to the sultan Mawlāy Sulaymān (1206-38/1792-1823), whose *ḥādjib* he had become [see ḤĀDJIB in Suppl.]. His father likewise became *ḥādjib* to Sayyidī Muhammad b. ʿAbd al-Raḥmān (1276-90/1859-73), and then became grand vizier during the reign of Mawlāy al-Ḥasan (1290-1311/1873-94); he enjoyed a miserable reputation, but his immense fortune allowed him to connect his name with the Bāhiya palace in Marrākush, whose building he undertook (inscription of 1283/1866-7, in G. Deverdun, *Inscriptions*, No. 206). He himself was said to be the offspring of a Spanish mother, and he had several children, amongst whom are mentioned Saʿīd, Idrīs—who both held important offices—and Aḥmad, called Bā Ḥmād. The latter was born in 1257/1841-2, and was first of all *ḥādjib* to Mawlāy Ismāʿīl who was the *khalīfa* in Fās of his brother Mawlāy al-Ḥasan. He then occupied the same office for that sultan. Since he had been responsible for the education of ʿAbd al-ʿAzīz b. al-Ḥasan, he favoured the accession to the throne of that prince, then 14 years old (1894); he took the title of grand vizier and, leaving the young sultan to amuse himself with childish pleasures, exercised real power in the state with sufficient political astuteness and authority to prevent Morocco falling into anarchy. Bā Ḥmād, whose strong personality has left behind a lasting impression, constructed in Marrākush the reservoir of the Agdal which bears his name, undertook various public works in the towns, and above all, continued his father's work; he enlarged the Bāhiya, apparently without any preconceived plan, on the site of some 60 houses and he purchased 16 gardens to form its parkland. He died on 17 Muḥarram 1318/17 May 1900, and was buried in the royal mausoleum of Mawlāy ʿAlī al-Sharīf (poetic epitaph in Deverdun, *Inscriptions*, No. 176).

Bibliography: Ibn Zaydān, *Itḥāf al-nās*, Rabat 1929 ff., i, 372-96, ii, 511, iv, 370-81; ʿAbbās b. Ibrāhīm, *Iʿlām*, Fās 1926-39, ii, 209-10, 255-61; L. Arnaud, *Au temps des Méhallas*, Casablanca 1951, 128; G. Deverdun, *Inscriptions arabes de Marrakech*, Rabat 1956; idem, *Marrakech des origines à 1912*, index. (ED.)

BĀBĀ NŪR AL-DĪN RISHĪ, the son of Shaykh Sālār al-Dīn, an Indian holy man, was born in the village of Bīdjbehāra, 28 miles south-east of Srīnagar, in about 779/1377. Although a Muslim, he has been called *rishī*, because he was more influenced by the ideas and practices of the Hindu Sadhūs and Rishīs than by those of Muslim Ṣūfīs and saints. From the age of thirty, Nūr al-Dīn began to withdraw to caves for meditation and prayers. He finally renounced the world and its pleasures and left his wife and children. In his last days he subsisted only on one cup of milk, and towards the end he took nothing except water, dying at the a 63 in 842/1438. He is the patron saint of the V and is greatly revered by its people. His sa and mystical verses, like those of Lallā Ded sung and recited all over Kashmīr. His tom Črār, 20 miles south-west of Srīnagar, att thousands of people, both Muslims and Hi every year.

The tendency to asceticism became more nounced among the followers of Nūr al-Dīn R called Rishīs after him. They did not marry; abstained from meat and subsisted on dry b and wild fruits; and they lived away from hu habitations, leading a life of piety, self-denial simplicity. They moved from place to place, plan shady and fruit-bearing trees for the benefit o people. According to Abu 'l-Faḍl, the Rishīs " looked upon as the most respectable class in Valley." But in recent years, owing to their wo ness and greed, respect for them has declined cept among the very ignorant.

Bibliography: Abu 'l Faḍl, *Āʾīn-i Ak* ii, tr. Blochmann, Calcutta 1927; Ḥādjdjī M al-Dīn Miskīn, *Taʾrīkh-i Kabīr*, Amritsar 1904; Mohibbul Hasan, *Kashmīr under the Sul* Calcutta 1959. (MOHIBBUL HASA

BĀBŪNADJ (Babūnak), from Persian *bābūn* the common camomile, primarily *Anthemis nc* L. (Compositae), also called Roman camomile, also *Matricaria chamomilla* L. (Comp.) and c varieties. The nomenclature is rather confuse can indeed hardly be expected that the various k of the camomile were kept apart with precision. term is derived from χαμαίμηλον ("apple of earth") and was known to the Arabs partly in a t scribed form (*khamāmālūn*, and variants), partl borrowed translation (*tuffāḥ al-arḍ*). The relati clearest determination is perhaps offered by anonymous pharmacobotanist of Spanish-Ar origin (very probably Abū ʿAbbās al-Nabāt al-Rūmiyya, 561-637/1166-1240): "There are t kinds of *al-bābūnadj*, the stalks, leaves and ger form of which are similar to each other. The dis tion between them is to be found in the colou the blossom-leaves which enclose the yellow, situ in the middle of the blossoms, for the blossom these three kinds are yellow in the middle. In white kind they are enclosed by small leaves w are white inside and outside, in the purple-colo kind by small leaves which are blue inside and side, and in the yellow kind by small leaves which yellow inside and outside. The distinction betw the white and the chrysanthemum (*al-ukḥuwān*) in the scent, for the chrysanthemum assumes traneous] scents, and all these kinds have a plea scent" (Nuruosmaniye 3589, fols. 108b, 23-109a In general, *bābūnadj* corresponds to the ἀνθεμί Dioscorides (*Materia medica*, ed. M. Wellmann Berlin 1906, 145-7 = lib. iii, 137), and app therefore also transcribed as *anthāmis* (and varia *Ukḥuwān* just mentioned, which is uncomm often equated with *bābūnadj*, is otherwise used the Arabs to render the παρθένιον (*barthāniyūn*, variants) of Dioscorides (*op. cit.*, lib. iii, 138), which we should probably understand the mec *Matricaria chamomilla*, still in use today. Ibn Bayṭār, on the other hand, says that the "wh kind of camomile described by Dioscorides and ca *ukḥuwān* by the Arabs, has been replaced by *bābū* (*Djāmiʿ*, i, 73, 11-13 = Leclerc no. 220, at beginning).

The blossoms of the camomile, which contai

at checks inflammations, were used as a medi-
for loosening spasms and for stimulating easily
peristaltic motion; infusions made from the
oms ("camomile tea") were utilised externally
aths, compresses and rinses at inflammations
in and mucous membranes, in both antiquity
n Islam in a manner similar to present practice.

Bibliography: for full information on camo-
e, see A. Dietrich, *Zum Drogenhandel im
mischen Ägypten*, Heidelberg 1954, 51-5, with
liography. Further see *La "Materia médica"
Dioscorides*, ii (Arabic tr. Iṣṭifan b. Basīl),
Dubler and Terés, Tetuán 1952, 299 f.; *The
dical formulary or Aqrābādhīn of al-Kindī*, tr.
Levey, Madison etc. 1966, no. 29; Bīrūnī,
ydala, ed. H. M. Saʿīd, Karachi 1973, Arabic,
61, Eng. 38-40 (*uḵẖuwān*); Ghāfiḳī, *Djāmiʿ,
. Rabat, Bibl. Gén. ḳ 155 i, fols. 83a-84a;
waydī, *Simāt*, Ms. Paris ar. 3004, fol. 34b;
a Biklārish, *Mustaʿīnī*, Ms. Naples, Bibl. Naz.
F. 65, fol. 20b; Ibn al-Djazzār, *Iʿtimād*, Ms.
asofya 3564, fol. 6a; Ghassānī, *Muʿtamad*,
irut 1975, 12 f.; Rāzī, *Ḥāwī*, xx, Ḥaydarābād
37, no. 1 (*uḵẖuwān*); Ibn Sīnā, *Ḳānūn*, Būlāḳ,
264 f.; Ibn Hubal, *Muḵẖtārāt*, Ḥaydarābād
52, ii, 35 f.; Dāwūd al-Anṭākī, *Tadhkira*, Cairo
71, i, 68 f.; Nuwayrī, *Nihāyat al-arab*, xi,
iro 1935, 286-91 (important, *uḵẖuwān* in the
ibihāt of Arabic poetry); H. G. Kircher, *Die
nfachen Heilmittel" aus dem "Handbuch der
irurgie" des Ibn al-Quff*, Bonn 1967, no. 30;
Schmucker, *Die pflanzliche und mineralische
teria medica im Firdaus al-ḥikma des ʿAlī
a Sahl Rabban aṭ-Ṭabarī*, Bonn 1969, no. 93.
                                    (A. DIETRICH)

ACTROMANCY [see ISTIḲSĀM].

ADAJOZ [see BAṬALYAWS].

ADGĪR (P.), literally "wind-catcher", the term
in Persia for the towers containing ventila-
shafts and projecting high above the roofs of
stic houses. They are also erected over water-
ge cisterns and over the mouths of mineshafts
der to create ventilation through the tunnels
. In domestic houses, cooler air is forced down
r to rooms at ground level or to cellars (the
zamīn), and it provides an early form of air
itioning. The towers are usually substantial,
e-sectioned structures with rows of apertures
four walls, and are divided internally by thin
brick or timber and mud-brick partitions and
es; but not enough of the surviving *bādgīr*s
h are mainly situated on the central plateau
rsia, e.g. around Yazd, or in the south near the
coastlands, and are now often falling into dis-
r with the advent of modern methods for
ng air and water) have been examined scien-
lly to ascertain exactly how the difference in
ressure required to create a down-draught is
ved. See H. E. Wulff, *The traditional crafts of
a*, Cambridge, Mass. 1966, 15, 106, and E.
ley, *Some vernacular buildings of the Iranian
au*, in *Iran, Jnal. of the British Inst. of Persian
es*, xv (1977), 100-1 (both with illustrations).
o Polo mentions the *bādgīr*s of Hormuz on the
an Gulf coast as the only things which make
earable there in summer, and other travellers,
as Pietro della Valle and Figueroa, have left
descriptions of them (see H. Yule, *The book of
Marco Polo the Venetian*, London 1871, ii,
).

e wind-shaft or wind-catcher was equally
n in the mediaeval Arab world and has con-

tinued in use to the present day. Indeed, it seems
that such contrivances were known in the buildings
of the Ancient Near East, such as those of Pharaonic
Egypt and Babylon. In mediaeval Arabic, the
device was known by the term *bādahandj* or *bādandj*,
arabised from the alternative Persian term to *bādgīr*,
bād-handj (see Dozy, *Supplément*, i, 47). Already in
the early ʿAbbāsid palace of Uḵẖayḍir in ʿIrāḳ [see
ARCHITECTURE I. (3). The ʿAbbāsid caliphate]
we find square-sectioned ventilation shafts in the
walls, and the word *bādgīr* appears in ʿIrāḳ as
bādjīr. It seems probable that ʿIrāḳ formed the
intermediate stage of the contrivance's spread westwards, in its new phase of life during Islamic times,
to Syria and Egypt. The *bādahandj* was already a
feature of the landscape in early Fāṭimid times,
for the astronomer Ibn Yūnus (d. 399/1008-9)
[*q.v.*]) discusses the correct orientation of what was
normally a single aperture at the top of the shaft,
since the prevailing cooler wind in Egypt is from
the north or north-west. ʿAbd al-Laṭīf al-Baghdādī
(d. 629/1231-2 [*q.v.*]) states that the large and ornate
wind-shafts of his time cost up to 500 *dīnār*s to
construct. The earliest surviving example from
Cairo seems to be the shaft in the *ḳibla* wall of the
mosque of al-Ṣāliḥ Ṭalāʾiʿ (555/1160), see K. A. C.
Creswell, *The Muslim architecture of Egypt*, Oxford
1952-9, i, 284-5. The *bādahandj* is mentioned in the
Thousand and one nights, and the littérateur ʿAlāʾ
al-Dīn al-Ghuzūlī (d. 815/1412-3 [*q.v.*]) devotes a
chapter of his anthology the *Maṭāliʿ al-budūr* to
the *bādahandj* in poetry and literature (see F.
Rosenthal, *Poetry and architecture: the Bādhanj*, in
Jnal. of Arabic Literature, viii [1978], 1-19). In
modern Egypt, the usual term for the contrivance
became *malḳaf* "[wind] catcher", noted by Lane in
his *Manners and customs of the modern Egyptians*,
ch. xxiv, and still in use (see S. Spiro, *An Arabic-
English dictionary of the colloquial Arabic of Egypt*,
Cairo 1895, 544: "ventilator, air-shaft, wind-sail");
in domestic houses, the air-shaft usually led down
to the public rooms of the *ḳāʿa* or *mandara*, or else
to another chamber used for sleeping (see A. Lézine,
*La protection contre la chaleur dans l'architecture
musulmane d'Égypte*, in *BEO*, xxiv [1971], 12-15).

Bibliography: in addition to references given
in the article, see A. Badawy, *Architectural provision against heat in the Orient*, in *JNES*, xvii
(1958), 125, 127-8 and Figs. 4, 6, 8; and see also
KHAYSH.   (C. E. BOSWORTH)

BĀDHĀM, BĀDHĀN, Persian governor in
the Yemen towards the end of the Prophet Muḥammad's lifetime. A Persian presence had been established in the Yemen *ca.* 570 A.D. when there had
taken place a Yemenī national reaction under the
Ḥimyarī prince Abū Murra Sayf b. Dhī Yazan [see
SAYF B. DHĪ YAZAN] against the Ethiopian-backed
governor Masrūḳ b. Abraha. The Persian Emperor
Khusraw Anūshirwān had sent troops to support
Sayf b. Dhī Yazan, and eventually, a Persian garrison, with a military governor at its head, was
set up in Ṣanʿāʾ. It was the progeny of these Persian
officials and soldiers, who intermarried with the
local Arab population, who became known as the
Abnāʾ [*q.v.*].

The Arab sources recount the story of the Persian
occupation of the Yemen and give the names of
the succession of Persian governors, beginning with
Wahrīz and his descendants and closing effectively
with Bādhām, who seems himself to have been un-
connected with Wahrīz's family (see al-Ṭabarī,
i, 945-51; al-Dīnawarī, *al-Aḵẖbār al-ṭiwāl*, Cairo

1960, 64; al-Mas'ūdī, *Murūdj*, iii, 162-7 = ed. Pellat, §§ 1015-20; Ibn al-Athīr, ed. Beirut, i, 447-51).

Bādhām seems to have been governor in Ṣan'ā' during Muḥammad's Medinan period, and when Muslim control began to be extended towards South Arabia at a time just after Heraclius's defeat of the Sāsānids, the Persian community's position must have become increasingly isolated and vulnerable; by now, they can have been little more than one of several local groups contending for mastery in the Yemen. Bādhām and the Abnā' may accordingly have been inclined to receive Muḥammad's overture sympathetically, but whether this involved anything more than an acknowledgement of distant political suzerainty is uncertain. The sources record Bādhām's conversion to Islam under the year 10/631-2, together with that of other Abnā' leaders such as Fīrūz al-Daylamī and the Abnāwī scholar Wahb b. Munabbih [*q.v.*] (al-Ṭabarī, i, 1763; Ibn al-Athīr, ii, 304; Caetani, *Annali*, ii/1, 358, 369). Western scholars have, however, been suspicious of this story of the conversion of Bādhām and the Abnā', and Caetani described it as "a pious fiction of the Muslim traditionists, in order to give a flavour of orthodoxy to Bādhām's nominal submission to Islam" (*ibid.*, ii/1, 371). The first *Ridda* War in the Yemen, under 'Ayhala b. Ka'b, called al-Aswad or Dhu 'l-Khimār [see AL-ASWAD], now supervened. Bādhām died at this point; his son Shahr succeeded temporarily to some of his power in the Yemen in 11/632-3 (al-Ṭabarī, i, 1864), but was killed by al-Aswad. Muslim political authority was probably not imposed in the Yemen by Abū Bakr's generals till 12/633-4. In any case, these events marked the end of any degree of Persian control in the Yemen, though the Abnā' continued as a distinct social group well into the early Islamic period (cf. al-Sam'ānī, *Ansāb*, facs. ff. 17b-18a, ed. Hyderabad, i, 100-2).

Bibliography: In addition to the references given in the article, see Nöldeke-Ṭabarī, *Geschichte der Perser und Araber*, 220 ff.; Caetani, *Annali*, ii/1, 358, 369-71, 661-85; idem, *Chronographia islamica*, i, 113, 123; A. Christensen, *L'Iran sous les Sassanides*², Copenhagen 1944, 368-70, 373; W. Montgomery Watt, *Muhammad at Medina*, Oxford 1956, 118, 128-30. (C. E. BOSWORTH)

AL-**BADHDH**, a district and fortress of northern Ādharbāydjān, famous as being the headquarters of the Khurramī rebel Bābak [*q.v.*] in the first decades of the 3rd/9th century. The exact site is uncertain, but it must have lain in the modern Ḳaradja-Dagh, older Maymad, the ancient Armenian region of P'aytakaran, to the north of Ahar and south of the Araxes River, near Mount Hashtād-Sar, at some spot between the modern districts of Hārand, Kalaybar and Garmādūz (V. Minorsky, *Studies in Caucasian history*, London 1953, 116 and Addenda et corrigenda slip). Bābak's fortress there was stormed by the caliphal general the Afshīn Ḥaydar [*q.v.*] in 222/837 (Ṭabarī, iii, 1198 ff., tr. E. Marin, *The reign of al-Mu'taṣim (833-842)*, New Haven 1951, 29 ff.). The only early Islamic geographer or traveller to give first-hand information about al-Badhdh is Abū Dulaf al-Khazradjī [*q.v.*], who travelled from Tiflis to Ardabīl via al-Badhdhayn (this ostensibly dual form reflecting an original Badhīn?), probably leaving the Araxes valley and going up the Kalaybar River. He speaks in his Second *Risāla* of a mine of red *Yamānī* alum there whose product was called *Badhdhī*; he also mentions that local traditions about Bābak were still strong a century or more later Khurramī sympathisers in the area expectin[g] return of a Mahdī (*Abū-Dulaf Mis'ar ibn Muh[alhil's] travels in Iran (circa A.D. 950)*, ed. and tr. Min[orsky,] Cairo 1955, § 15, tr. 35-6, comm. 75). A later s[ource] mentioning al-Badhdh, Ḳazwīnī's *Āthār al-[bilād]*, Beirut 1380/1960, 511, repeats Abū Dulaf's [infor]mation; and Yāḳūt's entry, *Buldān*, i, 529, is l[ate] and uninformative.

Bibliography: Given in the article.

(C. E. BOSWOR[TH])

BADHL AL-**KUBRĀ**, songstress and *rāwi[ya]* [of] early 'Abbāsid times, died before 227/842, pro[bably] in 224/839. She was born as a mulatto (*muwa[llada]* *ṣafrā'*) in Medina and brought up in Baṣra. Dj[a'far,] a son of the caliph al-Hādī, acquired her and, [in] 193/809, she became a favoured *djāriya* of al-[Amīn] and gave birth to a son of his. Being a pupil o[f] Djāmi', Fulayḥ and Ibrāhīm al-Mawṣilī she [pre]served the "classical" *ḥidjāzī* style of Arab m[usic,] preferring verses by *ḥidjāzī* poets also for her [own] compositions. She was a good songstress and lu[te] (*ḍāriba*), a *ẓarīfa*, and was famous for havi[ng a] répertoire of about 30,000 songs. For 'Alī b. Hi[shām] she compiled a *Kitāb fi 'l-aghānī* which cont[ained] 12,000 song texts (without musical indicat[ions]) and this became one of the sources of Abu 'l-F[aradj] al-Iṣbahānī (22 quotations). 'Alī b. Hishām [re]warded her with 10,000 *dīnārs*, and when she [died] she left a fortune, which was inherited by th[e de]scendants of 'Abd Allāh b. al-Amīn. Among [her] pupils were Danānīr and Mutayyam al-Hāshim[iyya].

Bibliography: *Aghānī*³, xvii, 75-80 (see indices); Shābushtī, *Diyārāt*¹, 28-9, 43; Nuw[ayrī,] *Nihāya*, v, 85-8; H. G. Farmer, *History of Ar[abian] music*, 134; K. al-Bustānī, *al-Nisā' al-'arabi[yyāt]*, Beirut 1964, 104-7; Kh. Mardam, *Djamhara[t al-]* *mughannīn*, Damascus 1964, 148-50.

(E. NEUBAU[ER])

AL-**BADĪ'** [see MARRĀKUSH].

BĀDIYA (A.) meant, in the Umayyad peri[od, a] residence in the countryside (whence the [verb] *tabaddā*), an estate in the environs of a settle[ment] or a rural landed property in the Syro-Jord[anian] steppeland.

For Musil, the *bādiya* was the successor t[o the] summer encampment called by the old S[yrian] Bedouin name of *al-ḥīra*. At the opening of the [present] century, the sense was restricted by archaeolo[gists] to the desert castles. They went so far as to cons[truct] theories about the attraction of the Bedouin w[ay of] life for the Umayyads and about the conserv[ative] role of the desert in upholding certain very persi[stent] traditions stronger than those of the nascent Is[lam]. Since the Umayyads were of urban Meccan o[rigin,] it is hardly necessary to look for an atavistic Bed[ouin]ism in order to explain their preferences for *bādiyas*. The new masters of Syria replaced, i[n the] towns as in the countryside, the old landhol[ders] whose territories, abandoned at the time of [the] Islamic conquest, were part of the plunder distrib[uted] to the great men. It was said that they sought [out]side Damascus, their official capital, purer air, [the] freshness of summer nights, protection against [epi]demics and vast, open spaces for hunting; in [fact] the Umayyads had a keen sense of the value o[f] land and the possibilities of financial return [from] fertile agricultural properties.

The agricultural development of Syria goes [back] well into Roman times. Exploitation of the [land] developed in regions where the water supply [was] difficult, necessitating an elaborate system of n and water conservation which could only be :taken with state aid or the injection of private al and which was not to survive the downfall : Umayyads. One very often finds an adaptation rlier Romano-Byzantine or Ghassānid instal-s as at Ḳaryatayn, the Byzantine Nazala, at yfa, Ptolemy's Atera, at the Roman station ays or at the classical and Byzantine centre of Rās [*q.v.*]. Alternatively, there were new ings erected, as at the two Ḳaṣr al-Ḥayrs or at Ḳaṣr al-Ḥallābāt. These were not "desert es" so much as "palace-towns", to be considered sentially Umayyad and constructed on the plan e small forts inherited from the *castra* of the , which had themselves been replaced by the foundations of the Ghassānids. There is vir-y no Umayyad construction which does not e classical structures or earlier foundations. No ence is to be found in the deep desert, and they l built in a zone within the *limes* which had been vated and populated since Hellenistic times and been protected against any possible occupation Bedouins who might damage the crops. After est, the sheep-raising tribes were allowed to ire their flocks on the cultivated lands, which benefited from their dung.

e *bādiya*s are generally to be found where there water supply, either on a line of transhumance, permitting contacts with the Bedouin tribes, se near some great artery of communication the routes from Damascus and Boṣrā towards nāʾ, the road from Damascus to Ḳarḳīsiyā , and the route which runs along the cultivable in of the *Hamad* from Ruṣāfa of al-Nuʿmān ar as Taymāʾ, passing through Tadmur or yra, Bakhrāʾ [*q.v.*], Djabal Says [*q.v.* below] Ḳaṣr Burḳuʿ [see BURḲUʿ below]. Their con-tion along the communication routes permits to attribute a function of *khān*s [*q.v.*] or caravan-s to them, in particular for certain constructions e Wādī ʿAraba listed by J. Sauvaget.

e Umayyads liked to stay to the south of ascus, on the Ghassānid sites of Djābiya and ik [*q.vv.*], and often spent the winter in the an valley at al-Sinnabra or in the palaces built Khirbat al-Minya and Khirbat al-Mafdjar [*q.vv.*]. r movements around were often dictated by need to visit agriculturally productive centres. y had a special liking for the region of the ḳāʾ [*q.v.*], where their residences among the mild s are numerous around Mshattā [*q.v.*], an un-hed work of the caliph al-Walīd II [*q.v.*], which ks the end of the architectural evolution of the yas.

idiya can be a synonym of *ḳaṣr* [*q.v.*], when it is a tion of a residence erected within a four-sided osure with dimensions recalling those of Roman l forts. The walls are provided with round towers, nown in Roman and Byzantine fortifications. re is a central courtyard within on to which open ns grouped in separate units and forming *bayts* backed by blind external walls which keep the ronment cool and increase the building's defen-potential. The disposition of internal arrange-ts is on the axes, and opposite the entrance gate ked by monumental towers is an audience cham-usually basilical in plan with apse at the end of ter or lesser importance. On the floors above lodging suites of rooms divided according to same plan as those on the ground floor. These are decorated with marble slabs, stucco work, coes and mosaics. In the immediate vicinity of the princely residence there may well be a mosque and a bath, as at Djabal Says. Certain *bādiya*s were used as centres for hunting (*mutaṣayyad*), like Abāʾir or Ḳuṣayr ʿAmra. A good picture of the architectural activities of the Umayyads in the *bādiya* is given by Abu 'l-Faradj al-Iṣfahānī in his *K. al-Aghānī*.

Bibliography: *Aghānī*, Tables alphabétiques; H. Lammens, *La «Bâdia» et la «Hîra» sous les Omayyades*, in *MFOB*, iv (1910), 91-112 = *Études sur la siècle des Omayyades*, Beirut 1930, 325-50; E. Herzfeld, *Mshattā, Ḥīra und Bādiya*, in *Jahrb. der Preuss. Kunstsammlungen*, xlii (1921), 104-46; Jaussen and Savignac, *Les châteaux arabes de Qeṣeir ʿAmra, Ḥarânah et Ṭûba*, Paris 1922; A. Musil, *Palmyrena*, New York 1928, Appx. ix, 277-89; A. Poidebard, *La trace de Rome dans le désert syrien*, Paris 1934; J. Sauvaget, *Remarques sur les monuments omeyyades*, in *JA* (Jan.-March 1939), 1-59; H. Stern, *Notes sur les châteaux omeyyades*, in *Ars Islamica*, xi-xii (1946), 72-97; O. Grabar, *Umayyad "palace" and the ʿAbbasid "revolution"*, in *SI*, xviii (1962), 5-18; U. Monneret de Villard, *Introduzione allo studio dell' archeologia islamica*, ch. ix, *L'abitazione omayyade*, Venice 1966, 233-48; A. Miquel, *L'Islam et sa civilisation*, Paris 1968, 504; D. and J. Sourdel, *La civilisation de l'Islam classique*, Paris 1968, 348-56; K. A. C. Creswell, *Early Muslim architecture*, i/2, Oxford 1969, 630. (N. ELISSÉEFF)

BADR-I ČĀČĪ, fully BADR AL-DĪN MUḤAMMAD Čāčī, poet of the 8th/14th century Dihlī Sultanate. A native of Čāč (Shāsh, Tashkent), he migrated to India and rose to favour at the court of Sulṭān Muḥammad b. Tughluḳ [*q.v.*], who conferred on him the style of *Fakhr al-Zamān*. His *ḳaṣāʾid*, which contain references to a number of contemporary events, with the dates often expressed in chronograms, constitute an important source for a period which is notoriously obscure and controversial. It is all the more unfortunate, therefore, that his *Shāh-nāma*, an epic chronicle of Muḥammad's reign completed in 745/1344-5, has not survived: it was still extant in the late 10th/16th century, when the Mughal historian Badāʾūnī (*Muntakhab al-tawārīkh*, ed. M. Aḥmad ʿAlī, Calcutta 1864-9, 3 vols., *Bibl. Indica*, i, 241) describes it as a "treasure".

Bibliography: Badr-i Čāčī, *Ḳaṣāʾid*, lith. ed. M. Hādī ʿAlī, Kānpūr n.d., lith. ed. and comm. M. ʿUthmān Khān, Rāmpūr 1872-3, 2 vols.; extracts tr. in Elliot and Dowson, *History of India*, iii, 567-73; Rieu, *Catalogue of the Persian MSS. in the British Museum*, London 1879-83, iii, 1032.
(P. JACKSON)

BADR AL-MUʿTAḌIDĪ, ABU 'L-NADJM, commander-in-chief of the armies of the caliph al-Muʿtaḍid (279-89/892-902). He was the son of one of al-Mutawakkil's *mawālī*, whose name cannot be established with certainty (Khurr or Khayr?), and was first in service as an equerry to al-Muwaffaḳ, gaining from that time the favour of the future caliph al-Muʿtaḍid, who, whilst still regent after al-Muwaffaḳ's death (Ṣafar 278/June 891), made him chief of police in Baghdād and then, after his accession, commander of all the forces. Badr led several expeditions into various regions (Fārs, al-Djazīra, ʿIrāḳ, etc.) in order to re-establish the military situation which had been rendered insecure by the Ḳarāmiṭa [*q.v.*]. At the same time, he played a political role of prime importance, for he became all-powerful, with a complete domination over the caliph, exercising a veto over everything. He gave one of his daughters in marriage to al-Muʿtaḍid's son, the future al-Muḳtadir, increasing his influence still further. He had the right to be addressed by his *kunya*, and the poets, and Abū Bakr al-Ṣūlī in particular, did not fail to include him in their eulogies of the caliph. It was because of his exceptional position that he acquired the name of "al-Muʿtaḍidi", distinguishing him moreover from several homonyms.

In 288/901 he pleaded in favour of al-Ḳāsim b. ʿUbayd Allāh [see SULAYMĀN B. WAHB] who was made vizier thanks to his intervention, but who failed to show him much gratitude for it. In fact, Badr refuse to take part in his machinations against the sons of al-Muʿtaḍid, so that al-Ḳāsim, fearing denunciation, took care immediately on the accession of al-Muktafī (289-95/902-8) to blacken Badr in the eyes of the new caliph and probably to profit also by the hostility towards Badr of certain other commanders. Badr fled to Wāsiṭ, but was invited to return to Baghdād under a guarantee of *amān*; in the course of his trip up the Tigris, he was attacked on the heights of al-Madāʾin by al-Ḳāsim's agents, who cut off his head whilst he was at prayer and sent it to al-Muktafī (6 Ramaḍān 289/14 August 902). His body was left on the spot and was later carried away by his family for burial at Mecca. This murder was denounced by the poets and imputed to the caliph, who might have been expected to heave a sigh of relief at seeing the head of the once-powerful general whom he had at first honoured on accession, but who seems however to have reproached his vizier for it.

Bibliography: Ṭabarī, iii, 2209-15 and index; Masʿūdī, *Murūdj*, viii, 114, 216 ff. = §§ 3242, 3360-6 and index; Hilāl al-Ṣābiʾ, *Rusūm dār al-khilāfa*, 94; idem, *Wuzarāʾ*, *passim*; Tanūkhī, *Nishwār*, Cairo 1392/1972, i, 172, 316-17, v, 110, viii, 114; Ghars al-Niʿma, *Hafawāt*, 206; Ibn al-Abbār, *Iʿtāb al-kuttāb*, Nos. 49, 50, 52; Ibn al-Athīr, vii, 170-1, 357-9; Ibn al-ʿImād, *Shadharāt*, ii, 201; Ibn Taghrībirdī, *Nudjūm*, iii, 129; Ibn al-Djawzī, *Muntaẓam*, vi, 34-6; Sourdel, *Vizirat*, index, and bibl. cited there. (CH. PELLAT)

BAGHR [see MĀRID].

BAHĀʾ AL-DAWLA WA-ḌIYĀʾ AL-MILLA, ABŪ NAṢR FĪRŪZ KHARSHĀDH B. ʿAḌUD AL-DAWLA FANĀ-KHUSRAW, Būyid supreme *amīr*, who ruled in ʿIrāḳ and then in southern Persia also from 379/989 to 403/1012) after 381/992 with the further honorific, granted by the caliph al-Ḳādir, of Ghiyāth al-Umma, and towards the end of his life, those of Ḳiwām al-Dawla and Ṣafī Amīr al-Muʾminīn). He was the third son, after Ṣamṣām al-Dawla Marzubān and Sharaf al-Dawla Shīrzīl, of the great *amīr* ʿAḍud al-Dawla [*q.v.*], who had built up the Būyid confederation into the mightiest empire of its time in the Islamic east.

On ʿAḍud al-Dawla's death in Shawwāl 372/March 983, Ṣamṣām al-Dawla, as the eldest son, succeeded as *amīr al-umarāʾ*, but his succession was disputed by Sharaf al-Dawla, and internecine warfare followed, in which the young Bahāʾ al-Dawla was also involved. Finally, in Ramaḍān 376/January 387 Ṣamṣām al-Dawla's position in Baghdād became parlous; he submitted to Sharaf al-Dawla, who now became the supreme *amīr*, and was partially blinded and imprisoned at Sīrāf. However, Sharaf al-Dawla died in Djumādā II 379/September 989, and Bahāʾ al-Dawla, whom Sharaf al-Dawla had nominated before his death as his successor, assumed power in Baghdād as *amīr al-umarāʾ* at the age of 19. He thus began a reign of 23 years, long by Būyid standards. This reign falls into two roughly equal p
the first filled with warfare against rivals lik
uncle Fakhr al-Dawla ʿAlī of Ray and Djibā
Ṣamṣām al-Dawla, now escaped from incarcera
until by *ca.* 1000 he had consolidated his pow
Fārs and Kirmān and was able to make Shīrā
father's old capital, the centre of his own domi
for the rest of his lifetime, acknowledged by a
Būyid princes as supreme *amīr*.

At the outset of his reign, Bahāʾ al-Dawla r
nised Ṣamṣām al-Dawla in Shīrāz as an equal
controlling Fārs, Kirmān and ʿUmān. In 38
he deposed the ʿAbbāsid caliph al-Ṭāʾiʿ [*q.v*
favour of his cousin al-Ḳādir [*q.v.*], whom he h
to find more tractable; this proved in fact the
and the new caliph agreed subsequently in 38
to become betrothed to Bahāʾ al-Dawla's
daughter, though she died before the marriage c
take place. The *amīr* also secured from the c
at this time a fresh grant of titles; and it is from
year that the ancient Iranian title *Shāhanshāh*,
unofficially by his father, appears on his coins
W. Madelung, *The assumption of the title Shāhā*
by the Būyids and "The reign of the Daylam (Da
al-Daylam)", in *JNES*, xxviii [1969], 174-5). B
al-Dawla now had to defend ʿIrāḳ and Ahwāz ag
the ambitions of Fakhr al-Dawla (who, urge
by his vizier the Ṣāḥib Ismāʿīl b. ʿAbbād [see
ʿABBĀD], had on ʿAḍud al-Dawla's death hi
assumed the title of *Shāhanshāh* and the im
headship of the Būyid family), and northern ʿ
against various local Arab and Kurdish c
Ṣamṣām al-Dawla, after his escape, took advan
of unrest in ʿIrāḳ and of Bahāʾ al-Dawla's
occupation with internal strife in Baghdād—the
sions of the Sunnī and Shīʿī populace and of
Turkish and Daylamī elements in the Būyid arm
and seized Ahwāz and Baṣra. Bahāʾ al-Dawla sec
the alliance of the ruler of the Baṭīḥa, Muhadh
al-Dawla ʿAlī b. Naṣr, and of the Kurdish p
Badr b. Ḥasanūya [see ḤASANAWAYH]. Even
his vizier and general Abū ʿAlī b. Ismāʿīl al-Muwa
could make little headway against Ṣamṣām
Dawla's skilful commander Abū ʿAlī al-Ḥasa
Ustādh-Hurmuz. After several oscillations in
fortunes of war, Ṣamṣām al-Dawla was in 388
assassinated near Iṣfahān by Abū Naṣr Shāh-F
a son of ʿAḍud al-Dawla's cousin and former
ʿIzz al-Dawla Bakhtiyār. Abū ʿAlī b. Ust
Hurmuz now came over to Bahāʾ al-Dawla's
with the remnants of Ṣamṣām al-Dawla's Day
troops. Once Abū Naṣr Shāh-Fīrūz had been k
in Kirmān, Bahāʾ al-Dawla was sole master of
southern provinces of Persia, Fārs and Kirmān,
of their dependency ʿUmān. Two years later,
implacable enemy Fakhr al-Dawla died, and
successors in Ray and Hamadhān, the young
inexperienced Madjd al-Dawla Rustam and Sh
al-Dawla Abū Ṭāhir respectively, acknowle
Bahāʾ al-Dawla's supreme overlordship, as c
minted at Ray from 400/1009-10 and at Hamad
from 401/1010-11 attest.

Bahāʾ al-Dawla now moved his capital f
ʿIrāḳ to Shīrāz, captured from the tempo
control of the sons of ʿIzz al-Dawla, and n
returned from it to Baghdād. The move eastw
showed that he regarded southern Persia as
heartland of the Būyid dominions, and except
the brief occupation in 390-1/1000-1 of Kirmān
the Ṣaffārid Ṭāhir b. Khalaf, the Persian la
remained generally peaceful. But the relinquisl
of Baghdād as capital meant a distinct relaxa

ontrol in ʿIrāḳ, which was henceforth entrusted ;overnors (for much of this period, until his h in 401/1010-11, to the ʿAmīd al-Djuyūsh Abū b. Ustādh-Hurmuz) at a time when powerful aies were rearing their heads there. Bahāʾ awla's departure for Fārs allowed the caliph ādir to enjoy more freedom of action and ten-vely to assert his authority, especially over the ection of Sunnī interests against Shīʿī policies ie Būyid *amīr* [see AL-ḲĀDIR BIʾLLĀH for details]. ve all, the confused situation in ʿIrāḳ after ıd al-Dawla's death and the squabbling of his in Fārs over control of the empire had allowed l Arab potentates in ʿIrāḳ to extend their power 3ūyid expense, so that direct Būyid authority to be for much of Bahāʾ al-Dawla's reign con-d to Baghdād and Wāsiṭ and their immediate nities. In northern ʿIrāḳ there were the ʿUḳaylids] of Mawṣil; Bahāʾ al-Dawla sent against the Abu ʾl-Dhawwād Muḥammad several expedi-s, but could not entirely quash his power, and r Abu ʾl-Dhawwād's death in 386/996, his hew Ḳirwāsh b. al-Muḳallad (after 391/1001) ied on the struggle. In central ʿIrāḳ, the Asadī ʿAlī b. Mazyad was ever ready to stir up the ouins of the Khafādja and Muntafiḳ groups v.] against Būyid rule, whilst in the south of country a rebel called Abu ʾl-ʿAbbās b. Wāṣil 393/1003 seized Baṣra and invaded Ahwāz, ing driven out from the Baṭīḥa Muhadhdhib Dawla. In 396/1006 a coalition of Badr b. Ḥasa-a's Kurds and Ibn Wāṣil's forces were able to iege Baghdād, but the capital was saved by Ibn ṣil's being captured and then executed (397/1006). attempt was made to conciliate the Arab *amīrs* Irāḳ, so that the ʿUḳaylid Ḳirwāsh b. al-Muḳallad in 396/1005-6 awarded the *laḳab* of Muʿtamid Dawla and the Mazyadid ʿAlī in 397/1007 that of ad al-Dawla. Also, the new governor for Bahāʾ Dawla in Baghdād after 401/1010, Fakhr al-Mulk ḥammad b. ʿAlī, defeated the ʿUḳaylids, drove off Khafādja and managed to make peace with the rds, who in fact ceased to be such a threat to Būyid position in ʿIrāḳ after Badr's murder in /1014-15.

n Djumādā II 403/December 1012 Bahāʾ al-Dawla d at Arradjān, probably en route for Baghdād. corpse was taken to Baghdād and then, like that his father, interred near the grave of the *Imām* b. Abī Ṭālib at Nadjaf near Kūfa. It appears t during his lifetime, Bahāʾ al-Dawla's (eldest?) Abū Manṣūr had been the *walī al-ʿahd*, for his ne, with the title of *amīr al-umarāʾ*, appears on inscription at Persepolis dated 392/1002, but this had died in 398/1008. Hence just before his th, he had nominated his 19-year old son Sulṭān Dawla Abū Shudjāʿ as supreme *amīr*; the latter er his accession appointed his brothers Djalāl Dawla and Ḳiwām al-Dawla as governors in ṣra and Kirmān respectively. The ensuing struggles ongst Bahāʾ al-Dawla's sons, combined with the bitions of the Arab *amīrs* in ʿIrāḳ and distant ssure from the Ghaznawids and then the Saldjūḳs the east, were soon to destroy the precarious unity the Būyid empire inherited by Bahāʾ al-Dawla m his father.

t is not easy to form a clear picture of Bahāʾ Dawla's character and personality, and he suffers the sources by comparison with his father. They cribe him as tyrannical to his entourage, avid for d and niggardly over its disbursement, but these es were not unfamiliar among other members of the Būyid family, and were in large part a reflex of the recurrent financial crises of the later Būyids and their desperate search for money and for fresh *iḳṭāʿ* land with which to pay their troops.

Concerning his cultural interests, little is known specifically, and the first half of his reign was in any case largely taken up with warfare. The historian and philosopher Miskawayh [*q.v.*] served as a secretary in his administration, and despite the absence of mention of outstanding poets in his circle at Shīrāz (Thaʿālibī in his *Tatimmat al-Yatima*, ed. Eghbal, i, 16-18, 26-30, mentions only two poets of note, Abū ʿAbd Allāh al-Ḥusayn al-Mughallis and Abū Saʿd ʿAlī al-Hamadhānī), there is reason to suppose that Bahāʾ al-Dawla continued the tradition of patronage of Arabic learning established by ʿAḍud al-Dawla before him. Certainly, Ṣamṣām al-Dawla had as his vizier for two years Abū ʿAbd Allāh al-Ḥusayn b. Aḥmad, Ibn Saʿdān [*q.v.* below], whose circle of scholars is known to us through the works of Abū Ḥayyān al-Tawḥīdī, and Sharaf al-Dawla was the patron of the distinguished astronomer Abū Sahl al-Kūhī [*q.v.*]. Abū Naṣr Shāpūr b. Ardashīr (d. 416/1025 [see SĀBŪR B. ARDASHĪR in *EI*[1]]), who served Bahāʾ al-Dawla as vizier on several brief occasions during the first part of his amīrate, seems to have been a scholar of outstanding calibre, considered by Thaʿālibī as worthy of a separate section in his anthology because of the amount of poetry dedicated to him by such figures as Abu ʾl-Faradj al-Babbaghā, Ibn Luʾluʾ and Abu ʾl-ʿAlāʾ al-Maʿarrī (*Yatīmat al-dahr*, ed. Damascus, ii, 290-7, ed. Cairo 1375-7/1956-8, iii, 129-36); whilst the governor for Bahāʾ al-Dawla in Baghdād (and subsequently for his successor Sulṭān al-Dawla) Fakhr al-Mulk was the patron of the poet Mihyār al-Daylamī [*q.v.*] and of the mathematician of Baghdād Abū Bakr Muḥammad al-Karadjī [*q.v.*; the *nisba* to be corrected thus from the "al-Karkhī" frequently found in western sources], the latter dedicating to the governor his treatise on algebra *al-Kitāb al-Fakhrī fi ʾl-djabr wa ʾl-muḳābala*.

Bibliography: Miskawayh's chronicle stops short of Bahāʾ al-Dawla's reign, but much detailed historical material is to be found in the *Dhayl* of Abū Shudjāʿ al-Rūdhrāwarī (up to 389/999) and in the surviving fragment of Hilāl al-Ṣābiʾ's *Taʾrīkh* covering 389-93/999-1003 (both sources forming vol. iii of Margoliouth and Amedroz's *Eclipse of the ʿAbbasid caliphate*, tr. vol. vi, the latter source being utilised by H. F. Amedroz for his study *Three years of Buwaihid rule in Baghdad, A.H. 389-393*, in *JRAS* [1901], 501-36, 749-86). These specifically Būyid sources can be filled out and supplemented by the general chronicles of Ibn al-Athīr, ix, Ibn al-Djawzī, vii, and Sibṭ Ibn al-Djawzī, the latter two especially important for events in Baghdād and ʿIrāḳ.

Of secondary literature, there are connected accounts of Bahāʾ al-Dawla's amīrate and of the cultural life of the period in Mafizullah Kabir, *The Buwaihid dynasty of Baghdad (334/946-447/1055)*, Calcutta 1964, 77-91, 179 ff.; in H. Busse, *Chalif und Grosskönig, die Buyiden im Iraq (945-1055)*, Beirut-Wiesbaden 1969, 67 ff. and index; and in idem, ch. *Iran under the Būyids*, in *Camb. hist. of Iran*, iv, ed. R. N. Frye, Cambridge 1975, 289-96. The extensive bibliography in Busse's book expands and brings up-to-date that of the article BUWAYHIDS [*q.v.*]. (C. E. BOSWORTH)

BAḤRIYYA. I. The navy of the Arabs up to 1250. Although Near Eastern writers in mediaeva times did not address themselves specifically to the subject of *baḥriyya*, references to seafaring activities made by Arab, Byzantine, southern and western European chroniclers, geographers and travellers, as well as pertinent details found in the Arabic papyri and the Geniza documents, provide a considerable body of information concerning the rise and fall of the Arab navy.

The naval requirements of the Arabs were dictated by the necessity of defending their Mediterranean territories—stretching from Cilicia and Syria in the East to the Spanish Levante seaboard in the West—and of protecting their shipping, as well as by their offensive operations against Christian enemies in the Mediterranean. Until the appearance of aggressive Italian fleets and the coming of the Crusaders, Muslim sea power, along with that of the Byzantines, constituted the dominant factor in mediaeval Mediterranean naval history.

The organisation and command structure of the *baḥriyya* were affected by the policy and strategy of the caliphate. In the beginning of the 2nd/8th century, the naval organisation involved several naval districts and distinct, self-controlled fleets. The naval districts, with their strategic ports (*th͟ag͟hr*, pl. *th͟ug͟hūr* [*q.v.*]) and warships, remained under the jurisdiction of commanders appointed by the caliph and responsible for the supervision of the construction and equipment of the ships; for their safety in the winter bases; for the selection of the entire naval personnel; for gathering and analysing naval intelligence; and for giving operational orders. With the decline of the caliphate, the organisational logistic, and operational responsibility for the *baḥriyya* rested with those dynamic régimes whose power was based on the coastal provinces, whether they enjoyed a sovereign status, as was the case of the Fāṭimids, or that of local dynasties, like the Ag͟hlabids, the Ṭūlūnids, the Ikhs͟hīdids and the Ayyūbids [*q.vv.*].

An essential feature of the *baḥriyya* were the *dūr al-ṣināʿa* (sing. *dār al-ṣināʿa* [*q.v.*]). These naval installations served not only as operational bases, but also as shipyards, naval arsenals and as the manpower centres supplying sailors and combat personnel. The number and activity of these installations depended on the degree of concern for naval matters of individual régimes. The latter ensured the operations of the installations by raising taxes specifically earmarked for naval expenditure; by procuring raw materials needed for the construction and fitting of warships; and by conscripting the necessary manpower. The Muslim naval inventory involved a great diversity of combat and supportive vessels. In fact "the Muslim navy not only had a variety of names for a single type, but a single name for a variety of types" (A. M. Fahmy, *Muslim naval organization*, 137).

A fleet (*al-usṭūl* [*q.v.*]) was commanded by the *rāʾis al-usṭūl* (commander of the fleet) selected from among the top naval officers (*al-ḳuwwād*), but the care of weapons and direction of naval action were discharged by the chief sailor (*ḳāʾid al-nawātiya*). The crews of the warships were made up of sailors (*nūtī*, pl. *nawātiya*); oarsmen (*ḳad͟hd͟hāf*); craftsmen and workmen (*d͟hawu 'l-ṣināʿa wa 'l-mihan*); as well as of the fighting men, such as the naphtha throwers (*al-naffāṭūn*) and the marines. The actual fighting involved both the bombardment with combustible projectiles, and the subsequent ramming, boarding and hand-to-hand combat of the marines. The latter were employed also for landing raids.

The early history of the *baḥriyya* was highlig by the raids against Cyprus in 28/649 and 33/ by the victory over a Byzantine armada in Battle of the Masts (D͟hāt al-Ṣawārī [*q.v.* in Sup in 34/655; and by the two sieges of Constantin in 54-69/763-9 and 98-9/717-18), during which Muslim fleets attempted to blockade maritime ac to the imperial capital, and supported logistic the Arab land forces. In that period Muslim squad raided Sicily in 32-3/652 and 46/666-7, tempora occupied Rhodes in 52/672 or 53/673 and Ar (Cyzikus) in 54/673, and raided Crete in 55/ In the first half of the 3rd/9th century, the posi of the *baḥriyya* was enhanced by the reassertio Muslim influence over Cyprus [see ḲUBRUṢ] and conquest of Crete [see IḲRĪṬIS͟H]; both these strat islands facilitated offensive operations aga Byzantine possessions. Regular Muslim fleets w stationed at Alexandria, Rosetta, Damietta, ʿAl Tyre, Sidon and Ṭarsūs. In the Western Medi ranean, the navy of the Ag͟hlabids engaged relentless attacks against Sicily [see ṢIḲILLIY and the southern and western shores of Italy f the naval base of Tunis.

The pursuit of ambitious political goals in Eg and Syria by Aḥmad b. Ṭūlūn (254-70/868 entailed both an expansion of naval installati especially those of ʿAkkā, and the strengthenin naval squadrons. His example was emulated Muḥammad b. Ṭug͟hdj al-Ikhs͟hīd (323-34/935- but neither the fleet of the Ṭūlūnids nor tha the Ikhs͟hīdids proved to be very effective. former was annihilated in 293/905 by a small ʿAbb fleet, the latter was unable to support Crete Cyprus against the resurgent Byzantine navy. the other hand, in 291/902 the Muslim *baḥri* achieved a great success when Ag͟hlabid naval fo conquered Sicily.

Following the Byzantine re-conquest of C (350/961) and Cyprus (352/963), the difficult t of upholding the prestige of the *baḥriyya* was ta over by the Fāṭimids. Having inherited strong na traditions from the Ag͟hlabids, the Fāṭimids un took a major expansion of the fleet. Their powe naval squadrons proved instrumental in contest supremacy in the western Mediterranean. Ma Sardinia, Corsica, the Balearic and other isla were attacked. In 324-5/934-5 a Fāṭimid fleet har the southern coast of France, took Genoa, coasted along Calabria, carrying off slaves and ot booty. In 344/955 another Fāṭimid fleet raided coasts of Umayyad Spain. In 358/969 a powe Fāṭimid armada participated in the conquest Egypt. Concerned with the offensive operations the Byzantines, as well as with the need for p serving the unity of their realm, which stretc from North Africa to Syria, the Fāṭimids attac great importance to the status of their navy. T founded a "Department of the Holy War or Maritime Constructions": (*Dīwān al-Djihād Dīwān al-ʿAmāʾir*). Ships were built in Alexand Damietta, at the island of Rawḍa, in Miṣr, and the new dockyards of al-Maḳs, which alone is credi with producing 600 vessels. Availability of services of the Syrian *th͟ug͟hūr*, such as Tyre Tripoli, extended the operational capacity of Fāṭimid fleet in the eastern Mediterranean.

In the 5th/11th century the power of the *baḥri* began to decline. The North African provin slipped away from the Fāṭimids. The fleets of Italian mercantile republics asserted their p ponderance in the western Mediterranean and be aid with virtual impunity the Algerian and sian shores. The dynamic Normans conquered y and Southern Italy, and then began preparing expansionist moves in Eastern Mediterranean. e first half of the 6th/12th century, the victories e Crusaders were facilitated by the decline of nid naval forces, and resulted in the loss of all nic coastal towns with the exception of ʿAsḳalān. the surrender of that fortress in 548/1153, the of Egypt became an easy target for Norman, an and Byzantine squadrons.

attempt to challenge the Christian naval r was made by Ṣalāḥ al-Dīn (567-89/1171-93), supplanter of the Fāṭimids. He increased the ies of the sailors, re-fortified Egyptian naval , and created a special office of the fleet (*dīwān ṭūl*), to which several branches of Egyptian nue contributed. In 574-5/1179 his fleet counted essels, of which 60 were galleys and 20 transports. ough the revitalised navy achieved some success ng Ṣalāḥ al-Dīn's struggle against the Crusaders uding an effective counter-attack in Dhu 'l-dja 578/February 1183 against a daring Frankish tration of the hitherto immune Red Sea waters), roved impotent to prevent the movement of stian fleets bringing new hosts of European iors eager to fight against the Muslim con-ors of Jerusalem. The Third Crusade (585-7/ -91) did not recover the Holy City, but it ered a mortal blow to the Egyptian navy, whose drons tried suicidally to support the garrison Akkā blockaded by a tremendous concentration uropean fleets. According to al-Maḳrīzī (766-845/ -1442), "After the death of Ṣalāḥ al-Dīn the rs of the fleet were given little attention ... ice in the navy was considered to be a disgrace ch an extent that to call at an Egyptian 'You r!' was treated as an insult. What a change the days when the names of the sailors were ked in the prayers of the people, and from the s when these very sailors had been called the ers of God, waging the Holy War against the of Allāh!"

Bibliography: A. M. ʿAbbādī, *Taʾrīkh al-ḥriyya al-islāmiyya fī Miṣr wa 'l-Shām*, Cairo 72; M. Canard, *Les expéditions des Arabes contre nstantinople dans l'histoire et dans la legende*, *JA*, ccviii (1926), 61-121; A. S. Ehrenkreutz, *e place of Saladin in the naval history of the editerranean Sea in the Middle Ages*, in *JAOS*, xv (1955), 100-16; E. Eickhoff, *Seekrieg und epolitik zwischen Islam und Abendland (650-40)*, Saarbrücken 1954; A. M. Fahmy, *Muslim val organization in the Eastern Mediterranean, m the seventh to the tenth century A.D.*, 1966; . Hoenerbach, *Araber und Mittelmeer, Anfänge d Probleme arabischer Seegeschichte*, in *Zeki Velidi gan Armağanı*, Istanbul 1950-5, 379-96; Dj. ankī, *Taʾrīkh al-baḥriyya al-miṣriyya*, Cairo 48; S. Māhir, *al-Baḥriyya fī Miṣr al-islāmiyya*, iro 1967; A. Lewis, *Naval power and trade in Mediterranean A.D. 500-1100*, 1951; al-Maḳrīzī, *Mawāʿiẓ wa 'l-iʿtibār*, Paris 1853, ii, 194; -R. Menager, *Amiratus-'Αμηρᾶς, l'Émirat et les igines de l'Amirauté (XIe-XIIIe siecles)*, 1960; udāma b. Djaʿfar, *Nuskhat ʿahd bi-wilāyat ghr al-baḥr*, in M. Hamidullah, *Muslim conduct state*, Karachi 1953, 319-21; M. A. Shaban, *lamic history, A.D. 600-750 (A.H. 132)*, Cam-idge 1971; M. Talbi, *L'Émirat aghlabide*, Paris 66, 384-524.

(A. S. EHRENKREUTZ)

, III [See Vol. I, 945 ff.].

BAKHĪT AL-MUṬĪʿĪ AL-ḤANAFĪ, MUḤAMMAD, *muftī* of Egypt from 1914 until 1921. He was born in the village of al-Muṭīʿa in the province of Asyūṭ on 10 Muḥarram 1271/24 September 1854. After completion of his studies at al-Azhar in 1292/1875, he remained attached to that institution as a teacher until 1297/1880, when he was appointed *ḳāḍī* of al-Ḳalyūbiyya province. This was the beginning of his career in the judiciary, in which he served as provincial judge in various resorts, as *ḳāḍī* of Alexandria, as *ḳāḍī* of Cairo, and in a number of other high positions such as the office of Inspector and the office of *muftī* in the Ministry of Justice, prior to his appointment as *muftī* of Egypt on 21 December 1914. In the course of his career he was involved, either directly or indirectly, in notable events of the day, such as the intrigues against reform in al-Azhar, as sponsored by Muḥammad ʿAbduh (cf. Aḥmad Shafīḳ, *Mudhakkirātī fī niṣf ḳarn*, Cairo 1936, ii, part 2, 35), the complications surrounding the marriage of ʿAlī Yūsuf (*ibid.*, 61), and the events of 1921, preceeding Egyptian independence (cf. Shafīḳ, iii, 275 ff.). He was a member of al-Rābiṭa al-Sharḳiyya [*q.v.*], but resigned from this association in 1925 in protest to the efforts of some of its members to bring about the annulment of the intended trial of ʿAlī ʿAbd al-Rāziḳ (cf. Aḥmad Shafīḳ, *Aʿmālī baʿd mudhakkirātī*, Cairo 1941, 183 f.). The latter's *Islām wa-uṣūl al-ḥukm* was severely criticised by Muḥammad Bakhīt in his *Ḥaḳīḳat al-Islām wa-uṣūl al-ḥukm*, Cairo 1344/1925-6. This book, as well as publications with suggestive titles such as *al-Murhafāt 'l-yamāniyya fī ʿunuḳ man ḳāla bi-buṭlān al-waḳf ʿalā 'l-dhuriyya*, Cairo 1344/1925-6; *Irshād al-ḳāriʾ wa 'l-sāmiʿ ilā anna al-ṭalāḳ idhā lam yuḍif ilā al-marʾa ghayr wāḳiʿ*, Cairo 1348/1929-30; *Ḥudjdjat Allāh ʿalā khalīḳatihi, fī bayān ḥaḳīḳat al-Ḳurʾān wa-ḥikam kitābatihi*, Cairo 1932, reflect Muḥammad Bakhīt's active intellectual involvement with the various issues of his time, such as the disputes pertaining to the translation of the Ḳurʾān, the position of women, and the campaign for abolition of the *waḳf ahlī*. Other publications such as his *Tanbīh al-ʿuḳūl al-insāniyya limā fī āyāt al-Ḳurʾān min al-ʿulūm al-kawniyya wa 'l-ʿumrāniyya*, Cairo 1344/1925-6; *Tawfīḳ al-Raḥmān li-tawfīḳ bayn mā ḳālahu ʿulamāʾ al-hayʾa wa-bayn mā djāʾ fī aḥādīth al-ṣaḥīḥa wa-āyāt al-Ḳurʾān*, Cairo 1341/1922-3; and *al-Djawāb al-shāfī fī ibāḥat al-taṣwīr al-fūtūghrāfī*, Cairo n.d.; and *Risāla fī Aḥkām ḳirāʾat al-fūnūghrāf*, Cairo 1324/1906-7, show his concern with problems arising out of the confrontation of Islam with the results of Western science and technology. Muḥammad Bakhīt died on 20 Radjab 1354/18 October 1935.

Bibliography: For biographies, see Zakī Fahmī, *Ṣafwat al-ʿaṣr fī taʾrīkh rusūm mashāhīr ridjāl Miṣr*, Cairo 1326/1908-9, 501 ff.; Ilyās Zakhūrā, *Mirʾāt al-ʿaṣr fī taʾrīkh rusūm akābir ridjāl bi-Miṣr*, Cairo 1916, ii, 467; Sulaymān al-Zayyātī, *Kanz al-djawhar fī taʾrīkh al-Azhar*, Cairo n.d., 172 ff.; and the weekly *al-Islām* (Cairo; ed. Amīn ʿAbd al-Raḥmān), iv (1935), 30, 38 f. (an obituary containing biographical data).

(F. DE JONG)

BĀḲĪ BI'LLĀH, KHWĀDJA, *Ṣūfi* saint of Muslim India, born in Kābul in 971/1563-4. His father, Ḳāḍī ʿAbd al-Salam Khaldjī Samarḳandi, was a scholarly *Ṣūfī*, and his mother a descendant of Shaykh ʿUbayd Allāh Aḥrār (d. 896/1491), the distinguished saint of the Nakshbandī order. [see AḤRĀR, KHWĀDJA, above]. He completed his early education and then studied the religious sciences under the guidance of Mawlānā Ṣādiḳ Ḥalwāʾī, who had stayed in Kābul at the persuasion of Mīrzā Ḥakīm in 978/1570-1 on his way back from the Ḥidjāz to Samarḳand. After some time, he accompanied Ḥalwāʾī to Transoxiana, and there he outshone other students of his in Islamic theology. As he was inclined towards piety and Ṣūfism, he visited the famous Ṣūfīs and developed a desire for spiritual perfection. Hence he turned to India and wandered about here and there in the Pandjāb, spending nights in vigil and performing mystical exercises, to the point that his health was adversely affected.

Having spent sometime in the Pandjab and Kāshmīr, Bāḳī bi'llāh again went to Transoxiana in 1000/1592 in search of a spiritual guide. In Samarḳand, he became the disciple of the Naḳshbandī saint Mawlānā Khwādjagī, who acquainted him with the teachings and philosophy of his order. He adopted the teachings of Shaykh Aḥrār and returned to India towards 1007/1599, settling down in Dihlī as a founder of the Naḳshbandī order there and gathering a number of disciples, including some of the leading grandees and scholars. Shaykh Farīd Bukhārī, one of Akbar's prominent nobles, also became his disciple, and met all the expenses of his *khānḳāh* in Dihlī. As regards his teachings, he emphasised the importance of right faith, strict adherence to the Islamic *Sharīʿa*, constant meditation and the service of man; to him, this was the essence of Ṣūfism, and no importance was attached to other mystic experiences. He considered Ibn al-ʿArabī's philosophy of *waḥdat al-wudjūd* ("unity of being") as a narrow lane, while ʿAlāʾ al-Dawla Simnānī's concept of *waḥdat al-shuhūd* he declared to be a wider road.

Bāḳī bi'llāh died in 1011/1603 leaving a number of distinguished disciples to further his work. It was largely due to him that the Naḳshbandī order subsequently gained popularity in India and became one of the important orders there, making an impact on the religious life of the Indian Muslims which can be felt even today.

Bibliography: Aḥmad Sirhindī, *Maktūbāt-i Rabbānī*, i, ed. Mawlānā Yār Muḥammad Djadīd Badakhshī, Kānpur 1877; Shaykh ʿAbd al-Ḥaḳḳ Muḥaddith, *Akhbār al-akhyār*, Dihlī 1914; Athar ʿAbbās Rizvī, *Muslim revivalist movements in India in the 16th and 17th centuries*, Lucknow 1965; Muḥammad Hāshim Badakhshānī, *Zubdat al-maḳāmāt*, Lucknow 1885. (I. H. SIDDIQUI)

BAKR B. **AL-NAṬṬĀḤ**, ABU 'L-WĀʾIL, minor poet of Baṣra, who belonged to the tribe of Bakr b. Wāʾil and who eulogised Rabīʿa; but it is not known for certain whether he was descended from Ḥanīfa b. Ludjaym or from his brother ʿIdjl (Ibn al-Kalbī-Caskel, Tab. 141), so that he is sometimes given the *nisba* of Ḥanafī and sometimes that of ʿIdjlī. He spent part of his life in Baghdād, and according to information given in the *Aghānī* (xix, 38), he is even said to have received for some time a stipend from the *dīwān* of al-Rashīd. However, he seems to have led a fairly restless life in search of patrons, being avid for rewards. He is moreover made into a *ṣuʿlūk*, a brigand of the highways, because he boasted of using his sword in order to earn his living; but the only relevant episode here mentioned in the sources is an attack by the hordes of Abū Dulaf al-Ḳāsim b. ʿĪsā al-ʿIdjlī (d. 225/840 [*q.v.*]) after the latter had remarked to Ibn al-Naṭṭāḥ that he was always boasting of his bravery but never put it to the test. For the rest, his relations Abū Dulaf are unclear; according to one tradi he was recruited into his army and received a sti until the end of his life, whilst another trad describes him as coming every year to the m of al-Karadj asking for money to buy an e allegedly adjacent to his own existing one. Wha the truth, he eulogised his benefactor, above all fine *ḳaṣīda* of 90 verses which has been prese by Ibn al-Muʿtazz. Abū Dulaf's brother, Maʿḳ ʿĪsā, interceded on his behalf for the prince to pa Ibn al-Naṭṭāḥ's indiscretions, which led to si eulogies on Maʿḳil and an elegy on his death. al-Naṭṭāḥ also mourned the death of Mālik b. al-Khuzāʿī, at whose side he had fought in paigns against the Khāridjīs of the district of Ḥul He is also found in Kirmān, where he receiv regular stipend, and at the side of Mālik b. Ṭ [see AL-RAḤBA], to whom he dedicated some p gyrics. However, the chronology of all these ev is far from certain, and it is most unlikely tha could have praised the latter person (who die 260/874), at least if he himself died in 192/808, w an allusion to his loss in the *Dīwān* of Abu 'l-ʿAtā (ed. Beirut 1964, 105, rhyme *-ātā*, metre *sarīʿ*) s to support.

The critics recognised that he handled with t the various poetical genres, though at the same criticising him for certain exaggerations on occa His eulogies and elegies remain within the Bed tradition, but several poems in which he hym *djāriya* called Durra have a more modernist f it was because these were set to music that Ba al-Naṭṭāḥ merited a notice in the *Aghānī*. O his total poetic production, which ran to a hun or so leaves (*Fihrist*, 232), Aḥmad b. Abī Ṭ Ṭayfūr made a selection (*Ikhtiyār shiʿr Bakr b Naṭṭāḥ*) which Yāḳūt cites (*Udabāʾ*, iii, 92).

Bibliography: Djāḥiẓ, *Ḥayawān*, iii, 196 232; Ibn Ḳutayba, *ʿUyūn*, index; Muba *Kāmil*, 561-2, 708-9, 853; Ibn al-Muʿtazz, *Ṭab* 99-103; Abū Tammām, *Ḥamāsa*, ii, 88-9; *Amālī*, i, 227; Bakrī, *Simṭ al-laʾālī*, 520; Mas *Murūdj*, vii, 140 = § 2824; Aghānī, xix, 3 Ibn ʿAbd Rabbih, *ʿIḳd*, ed. Cairo 1940, i, Tawḥīdī, *Imtāʿ*, iii, 50; Marzubānī, *Muwash* 298; ʿAskarī, *Ṣināʿatayn*, index; Ibn Khall *Wafayāt*, in the notice no. 511; Ibn Sh *Fawāt*, no. 62; Ibn Rashīḳ, *ʿUmda*, ii, 53, Khaṭīb Baghdādī, *Taʾrīkh*, vii, 90; Ḥuṣrī, *al-ādāb*, 596, 966-7, 1017; Nuwayrī, *Nihāya* 18; J. E. Bencheikh, *Les voies d'une créa* Sorbonne thesis 1971 (unpublished), in Wahhābī, *Marādjiʿ*, iii, 114-5; Bustānī, *DM* 105-6; Ziriklī, *Aʿlām*, ii, 46. (Ch. PELLA

AL-**BAKRĪ**, MUḤAMMAD TAWFĪḲ B. ʿALĪ MUḤAMMAD, Egyptian religious dignitary was born in Cairo on 27 Djumādā II 1287/24 Au 1870, and was appointed *naḳīb al-ashrāf* [*q.v.*], *sh mashāyikh al-ṭuruḳ al-ṣūfiyya* (head of the *ṭa* [*q.v.*]), and head of al-Bakriyya [*q.v.*] in January in succession to his deceased brother ʿAbd al- obtaining life-membership of the *madjlis shūr ḳawānīn* (Legislative Council) and of the *djamʿ al-ʿumūmiyya* (General Assembly) in that same year. During the period in which he held office of *shaykh mashāyikh al-ṭuruḳ al-ṣūfi* various regulations for the *Ṣūfī* orders in E were introduced. These regulations, which in force until 1976, allowed him to re-establish authority over the orders to which the head o Bakriyya had been legally entitled since 1812, ch had declined dramatically under his predeces- ʿAbd al-Bāḳī.

s *naḳīb al-ashrāf*, he was forced to abdicate in uary 1895 by the Khedive ʿAbbās Ḥilmī, who t have aimed at curbing al-Bakrī's aspirations political significance, as was suggested by Māhir an Fahmī (92 ff.; see bibliography). Following event, relations between al-Bakrī and the dive grew progressively worse when the latter ght to mobilise Ottoman support in his attempts assert his position over Lord Cromer, the British consul. This was totally unacceptable to al-Bakrī, e it ran counter to the unadulterated Egyptian ionalism which he advocated. In consequence, showed himself to be aggressively antagonistic Abbās Ḥilmī's policy, to a degree which brought close to being faced with legal prosecution for -majesté (cf. Aḥmad Shafīḳ, *Mudhakkirātī fī ḳarn*, Cairo 1936, ii/1, 248 f.; Muḥammad sayn, *al-Ittidjāhāt al-waṭaniyya fī 'l-adab al-ʿāṣir*, Cairo 1954, i, 94). When the Khedive nged his policy and turned to the Egyptian ionalists in his effort to achieve freedom from tish tutelage, relations improved considerably, in early 1903 Muḥammad Tawfīḳ was again called as *naḳīb al-ashrāf*, in succession to ʿAlī Biblāwī [*q.v.*], who had been appointed *Shaykh* al-Azhar. Concommitant to and as the result of *rapprochement* between the Khedive ʿAbbās mī and Muḥammad Tawfīḳ, the latter became dually more implicated in the Khedive's policy, ably in his efforts aimed at the deposition of the ftī of Egypt, Muḥammad ʿAbduh, who was a tégé of Cromer's, when the Khedive called upon for mediation on various occasions (cf. Shafīḳ, *dhakkirātī*, ii/1, 348, ii/2, 34 ff., 95 f.; Fahmī, ff.). On the political scene he manifested him- moreover, as an advocate of parliamentary ernment, for which he campaigned in the Legis- ve Council as well as in the Press. He was com- ted to pan-Islamism, and was actively involved the movement when he presided over the pre- inary meetings for the foundation of the Universal mic Congress (*al-Muʾtamar al-Islāmī al- mma*), proposed by Ismāʿīl Gasprinsky [*q.v.*], d in the palace of the Bakrīs in Cairo at the of 1907. From the latter year onwards, rela- ns between al-Bakrī and the Khedive again ome strained when Eldon Gorst, who had suc- ded Cromer to the proconsulate at the begin- g of that year, managed to win ʿAbbās Ḥilmī ay from the nationalists and obtained his sup- t for British policies. This caused the relation- p between al-Bakrī and the Khedive to deter- ate into one of the mutual distrust and hostility, ich must have contributed to the severe paranoia ich forced al-Bakrī to abdicate at the end of 1. In 1912, he left Egypt for Beirut, where he confined to a mental hospital until early 1928 en he returned. He died in Cairo in August 1932.

n addition to Muḥammad Tawfīḳ al-Bakrī's nificance for the *Ṣūfī* orders in Egypt, which e been under the lasting impact of an admini- ation which was at least partially designed by and which was instituted under his auspices, is also notable for his literary activities. He nded a short-lived predecessor of the Academy the Arabic Language, he compiled an anthology *radjaz* poetry (*Arādjīz al-ʿArab*, Cairo 1313/ 5-6)—about which it was rumoured that it had been compiled by him at all but by Aḥmad b. īn al-Shinḳīṭī (cf. *al-Muḳtaṭaf*, xix (Cairo 1895), 930 ff.; xx, 44 ff.)—and he published a selection from the works of eight poets from the ʿAbbāsid period (*Fuḥūl al-balāgha*, Cairo 1313/1895-6), in addition to a collection of poems and *maḳāmas* in the style of al-Ḥarīrī written by himself (*Ṣahārīdj al-luʾluʾ*, Cairo 1907. A selection from this work was published by ʿUthmān Shākir under the title *al-Luʾluʾ fi 'l-adab*, Cairo 1927). As a poet, he is considered as one of the last representatives of the classical tradition.

Bibliography: The most extensive biography is Māhir Ḥasan Fahmī, *Muḥammad Tawfīḳ al-Bakrī*, Cairo 1967, referred to in the article. It contains amongst others a lengthy discussion of his publishing activities and of his literary output, and gives further references. An autobiography is to be found in his *Bayt al-Ṣiddīḳ*, Cairo 1323/ 1905, 11 ff. For a discussion of the nature of his authority over the *Ṣūfī* orders in Egypt, and of the impact of the regulations introduced under his auspices and of his political activities, see F. de Jong, *Al-Mashāyikh al-Bakriyya and the transformation of their authority in 19th century Egypt*, in A. Dietrich (ed.), *Akten des vii. Kongresses für Arabistik und Islamwissenschaft*, Göttingen 1976, 224 ff.; and idem, *Ṭuruq and ṭuruq-linked institutions in 19th century Egypt*, Leiden 1978, ch. v, where additional references may be found.

(F. DE JONG)

BALANCE [see MINṬAḲAT AL-BURŪDJ; MĪZĀN].

AL-**BALAṬĪ, ABU 'L-FATḤ ʿUTHMĀN** B. ʿĪSĀ B. MANṢŪR B. MUḤAMMAD, TĀDJ AL-DĪN, grammarian, poet and *adīb*, originally from the town of Balad on the Tigris, which also had the name of Balaṭ (see Yāḳūt, i, 721), whence his *nisba* of al-Balaṭī, sometimes given in the diminutive form of al-Bulayṭī. Abu 'l-Fatḥ went first of all to teach in Syria, and then, when Saladin assumed power in Egypt (567/1171), he migrated to Cairo where the new sultan allotted to him a fixed stipend and appointed him to teach grammar and the Ḳurʾān in one of the mosques of the town. He remained there till his death on 19 Ṣafar 599/7 November 1202; his corpse was not discovered till three days after his death because the people of Cairo were preoccupied by the famine then raging and were unconcerned with each other.

Thanks to ʿImād al-Dīn al-Iṣfahānī (519-97/ 1125-1201 [*q.v.*]), who knew him personally, and to a *sharīf* called Abū Djaʿfar al-Idrīsī (apparently not to be confused with the famous geographer) who had been his pupil and who was in contact with Yāḳūt (d. 626/1129), we possess a very detailed physical description of this scholar and information on his habits. He was tall, corpulent, with a lofty forehead, a long beard and a ruddy complexion; he was very susceptible to cold, always wrapped himself up, took a thousand precautions when he went to the *ḥammām* and hardly went outside in winter. He had the reputation of being extremely learned in all the literary fields, but his personal conduct left something to be desired; he apparently sought the company of dissolute persons and sometimes got drunk.

The examples which have been preserved from his poetry show that it was of traditional type, and some poems show a special aptitude for verbal pyrotechnics in the vein of his time (all through one *ḳaṣīda*, a differing word in each verse which could be read equally well in the three grammatical cases; a rhyme in *-ūnū* which exhausts the lexicon's possibilities; a schema *mafʿala* arbitrarily constructed; etc.). Nevertheless, he also wrote a long poem in praise of al-Ḳāḍī al-Fāḍil [*q.v.*], in which Saladin's secretary is placed above al-Djāḥiẓ, Ibn ʿAbbād and Ibn al-ʿAmīd, as well as a *muwashshaḥa* whose *khardja* is not however in accordance with the rules, since it is in literary Arabic.

Al-Balaṭī is, in addition to his peetry, the author of various works: a *Kitāb al-ʿArūḍ al-kabīr*, a *K. al-ʿArūḍ al-ṣaghīr*, a *K. al-ʿIẓāt al-mūḳiẓāt*, a *K. al-Nayyir*, a *K. Akhbār al-Mutanabbī*, a *K. al-Mustazād ʿala 'l-mustadjād min faʿalat al-adjwād*, a *K. ʿIlm ashkāl al-khaṭṭ*, a *K. al-Taṣḥīf wa 'l-taḥrīf* and a *K. Taʿlīl al-ʿibādāt*.

Bibliography: Yāḳūt, *Udabā'*, xii, 141-67; idem, *Buldān*, i, 721, ii, 735; ʿImād al-Dīn, *Kharīdat al-ḳaṣr, Ḳism shuʿarā' al-Shām*, ii, 383; Kutubī, *Fawāt*, ii, no. 279; Ibn Ḥadjar, *Lisān al-Mīzān*, iv, 150-1; Suyūṭī, *Bughya*, 323-4; Ḥādjdjī Khalīfa, ed. Istanbul, *passim*; Brockelmann, S I, 530; Bustānī, *DM*, V, 24-5; M. Z. Enani, *Le muwaššaḥ en Orient*, Sorbonne thesis 1973 (unpublished), 90-1. (Ch. PELLAT)

BALBAN, GHIYĀTH AL-DĪN ULUGH KHĀN, the most prominent of the slave Sultans of Dihlī, was originally a Turkish slave of the Ilbarī clan. A member of the famous corps of Forty Slaves or *Čihilgānī* raised by Sulṭān Iltutmish, Balban rose, by dint of sheer merit and ability, to be the minister and deputy (*nā'ib-i-mamlakat*) of the ascetic king Nāṣir al-Dīn Maḥmūd Shāh (644-64/1246-65), to whom he had given his daughter in marriage. As *de facto* ruler during Maḥmūd's reign, he checked the forces of disintegration and infused vigour into the administration. The experience which he earned during his deputyship stood him in good stead when he inaugurated his own reign in 664/1266 as Ghiyāth al-Dīn Balban, following the death of the childless Maḥmūd. Many and varied were the problems which beset Balban as he set to administer the country ruined by internal anarchy and threatened with foreign invasion. The treacherous manoeuvrings of the Turkish nobility, the growing intensity of the Hindu resistance and the mounting menace of the Mongol inroads, combined to create a situation which called for realistic approach, coupled with a will to take bold action.

As a typical oriental monarch, he advocated the theory of the divine right of the king and rigidly insisted on the observance of court ceremonial. For refractory nobles, he thought the assassin's dagger or poison to be the only remedy and he got rid of most of them by a liberal use of both. With firm determination and concentrated drive, he brought the Mewati insurgents to their knees and suppressed the uprising of the Hindus of the Dōāb. For repelling the Mongol marauders, he put his able and trusted son Muḥammad Khān in command of an elaborate defence arrangement along the north-western frontiers, and as a result, the advance of the Mongols was effectively halted. At home, the army was re-organised, an efficient espionage system perfected and art and literature liberally patronised. The celebrated Amīr Khusraw [*q.v.*] was one of the literary luminaries of his court. As a result of this vigorous administration, perfect peace and prosperity prevailed over his kingdom, except for an insurrection in distant Bengal. After persistent flouting of the king's will by the governor of that province, Ṭoghrīl Khān, Balban had to take personal charge of a strong military expedition which resulted in the rebellious governor being caught and slain. His adherents were taken by the Sulṭān to Lakhnawtī [*q.v.*] where they were publicly punished by impalement. This exemplary chastisement was also intended to served as a stern warning to his son Bughrā Kh whom he appointed governor of Bengal before turning to Dihlī.

Balban's beloved son Prince Muḥammad, wh he had designated his heir, was killed early in 1286 in a fierce engagement with the Mongols. T bereavement eventually brought about his death a year later in 686/1287; this sounded death-knell of the Slave-King dynasty, for Khaldjīs took over the reins of the Dihlī sultan only three years later.

Bibliography: Ḍiyā al-Dīn Baranī, *Ta'rī Fīrūz Shāhī*, Calcutta 1860-6; Shams-i Sirādj *ʿA Ta'rīkh-i Fīrūz Shāhī*, Calcutta 1888-9; Elliott Dowson, *History of India*, iii; Sir Wolseley H *Cambridge history of India*, iii, Cambridge 19 A. B. M. Ḥabībullāh, *Foundation of Muslim in India*, Lahore 1945; A. L. Srivastava, *sultanate of Delhi*², Agra 1953; P. Hardy, *His ians of medieval India*, London 1960, ind G. Hambly, *Who were the Chihilgānī, the f slaves of Sulṭān Shams al-Dīn Iltutmish of Delhi Iran, Jnal. of the British Inst. of Persian Stud* x (1972), 57-62; Muḥammad ʿAzīz Aḥmad, *Polit history and institutions of the early Turkish em of Delhi (1206-1290)*, Indian edition, Delhi 197 (ABDUS SUBHAN

SĪDĪ **BALLĀ**, ABŪ MUḤAMMAD ʿABD ALLĀH ʿAZZŪZ AL-ḲURASHĪ AL-SHĀDHILĪ AL-MARRĀKUSH cobbler of Marrakesh to whom thaumaturgic g were attributed and who died in an odour of sanc in 1204/1789. His tomb, situated in his own reside at Bāb Aylān, has been continuously visited beca of its reputation of curing the sick. Although had not received a very advanced education, ʿAzzūz nevertheless succeeded in leaving behind abundant body of works, dealing mainly w mysticism and the occult sciences, but also w medicine. However, his works display hardly originality, and none of them has intereste publisher despite the success in Morocco of *Dhahāb al-kusūf wa-nafy al-ẓulumāt fī ʿilm al- wa 'l-ṭabā'iʿ wa 'l-ḥikma*, a popular collection therapeutic formulae (see L. Leclerc, *La chiru d'Abulcasis*, Paris 1861, ii, 307-8; H. P. J. Rena in *Initiation au Maroc*, Paris 1945, 183-4); his *K al-rumūz* concerning medicinal plants is equ well-known. Out of his three works on mystici the *Tanbīh al-tilmīdh al-muḥtādj* is perhaps the n original since it endeavours to reconcile the *sha* with the *ḥaḳīḳa* [*q.v.*]. Finally, in the field of occult sciences, his *Lubab al-ḥikma fī ʿilm al-h wa-ʿilm al-asmā' al-ilāhiyya*, of which at least manuscript survives, is a treatise on practical m and divinatory magic.

Bibliography: On the manuscripts of Ballā's works, see Brockelmann, S II, 704, M. Lakhdar, *Vie littéraire*, 253-6; see also Sūda, *Dalīl Mu'arrikh al-Maghrib al-A* Casablanca 1960, ii, 446, 449; ʿA. Gannūn, *Nubūgh al-Maghribī*², Beirut 1961, i, 304-5, 31 (ED

BALYŪNASH, also **B.NYŪN.SH** (in Africanus *Vignones*, in Marmol *Valdeviñones*), tuguese Bulhões, Spanish Bullones, site of a on important *ḳarya* 8 km. W.N.W. of Ceuta, bene Sierra Bullones (Djabal Mūsā). Its name is f the Spanish Romance *bunyólex* "vineyards", *not* or Benī Yūnus/-ash, etc. Surrounded on land mountains, Balyūnash lies in a small valley di ping sharply to a creek in a bay set in a narrow

:he Straits of Gibraltar. Bérard thought it the ıe of the Homeric Calypso's cave. Its Roman :ursor has been named as Exilissa.

n Islam the area's history may well have begun ı Mūsā b. Nuṣayr [*q.v.*], who is said to have ssed to Algeciras in 93/712 from what became :sā Mūsā, later within the orbit of Balyūnash. i-Provençal (*Hist. Esp. mus.*, ii, 260) associates emergence of Balyunāsh proper with a palace t among gardens by Ibn Abī ʿĀmir (Almanzor) protected by a fortress on the shore. In the 5th/ h century Balyunāsh was certainly known to the grapher al-Bakrī as a large, fertile and populous :e. Thereafter its importance grew with that of ta. In 1342 it witnessed a battle between ships n a Marīnid-Naṣrid fleet and vessels from a tilian fleet covering Alfonso XI as he besieged eciras. The heyday of Balyūnash—lauded as an n by poets from the 6th/12th century onwards— arently came with the 8th/14th century. Details its buildings, water resources, the range of its ticulture, arboriculture, etc. have been left by Anṣārī, a native of the area until 1415 when the tuguese occupation of Ceuta brought about its ertion. In 1418 Balyūnash was briefly the estate one João Pereira, a Portuguese courtier from ta.

Iediaeval Ceuta, a relatively barren, isolated and l peninsula, can be seen as the *raison d'être* of yūnash. A resort for princes and the rich, who fortified villas there, the latter was certainly ich source of fresh food and above all flowing ter, which, in Marīnid times at least, must have n fed directly to Ceuta as indeed it is today. ins still to be seen there bear marks of Andalusian hitectural and artistic influence.

Bibliography: L. Torres Balbás, *Las ruinas de Belyuneš*, in *Tamuda*, v (1957), 275-96 (contains ranslation of al-Anṣārī's description, for Arabic ext of which see *Hespéris*, xii (1931), *Tetuán* 1959), and ed. A. Ben Mansour, Rabat 1969; see lso J. Vallvé's tr. in *Al-Andalus*, xxvii (1962)); 3. Pavón Maldonado, *Arte hispanomusulmán en Ceuta*, in *Cuadernos de la Alhambra*, vi (1970), 9-107 plus plates; G. Ayache, *Beliounech et le lestin de Ceuta*, in *Hespéris-Tamuda*, xiii (1972), -36; R. Ricard, *Études sur l'histoire des Portugais u Maroc*, *passim*; G. S. Colin, *Étymologies maġribines*, in *Hespéris* (1926), 59 f. (on the name).

(J. D. Latham)

BĀNĪDJŪRIDS or Abū Dāwūdids, a minor nasty, probably of Iranian but conceivably of rkish origin, which ruled in Ṭukhāristān and dakhshān, sc. in what is now Afghan Turkestan, h a possible parallel branch in Khuttal, sc. in at is now the Tadzhik SSR, during the later /9th and early 4th/10th centuries.

The genealogy and history of the Bānīdjūrids are y imperfectly known, despite the attempts of Marquart, in his *Ērānšahr*, 300-2, and R. Vasmer, his *Beiträge zur muhammedanischen Münzkunde. Die Münzen der Abū Dā'udiden*, in *Numismatische tschr.*, N.F. xviii (1925), 49-62, to elucidate them ough the sparse historical references and the agre numismatic evidence. It seems that they ang from one Bānīdjūr, a contemporary of the ly ʿAbbāsid caliphs al-Manṣūr and al-Mahdī, o had connections with Farghāna, and his son shim (d. 243/857-8) was ruler of the mountain tricts of Wakhsh and Halāward on the upper us. But the first member of the family known h any certainty is Dāwūd b. al-ʿAbbās, who was governor of Balkh from 233/847-8 onwards, being still there when the Ṣaffārid Yaʿḳūb b. al-Layth captured the city temporarily in 258/872. Dāwūd fled to Samarḳand in Sāmānid territory (sc. to refuge with his suzerains?) but returned to Balkh shortly afterwards and died there in 259/873 (Barthold, *Turkestan down to the Mongol invasion*³, 77-8). It was probably this Dāwūd (thus according to Vasmer, *op. cit.*, 50, *pace* Marquart), and not the Dāwūd b. Abī Dāwūd of the Khuttal local rulers (see below), who at one point in his career made a raid south of the Hindu Kush against the local ruler Fīrūz b. Kabk, who was probably from the family of Zunbīls of Zābulistān (Ibn Khurradādhbih, 180; cf. Masʿūdī, *Murūdj*, viii, 42, 127-8).

Dāwūd b. al-ʿAbbās's kinsman (? nephew) Abū Dāwūd Muḥammad b. Aḥmad ruled in Balkh from 260/874 onwards, after having already controlled Andarāba and Pandjhīr in Badakhshān, the latter place important for its silver mines; during the years 259-61/873-5 Yaʿḳūb b. al-Layth took over Pandjhīr and minted coins there, but in 261/875 Abū Dāwūd Muḥammad was once more able to issue his own coins from there (Vasmer, *Über die Münzen der Ṣaffāriden und ihrer Gegner in Fārs und Ḫurāsān*, in *Num. Zeitschr.*, N.F. xxiii (1930), 133-4). If the information of the local historian of Bukhārā Narshakhī is correct, Abū Dāwūd Muḥammad was still ruling in Balkh in 285/898 or 286/899, when ʿAmr b. al-Layth summoned him, together with the Farīghunid *amīr* of Gūzgān and the Sāmānid Ismāʿīl b. Aḥmad, to obedience (*Ta'rīkh-i Bukhārā*, tr. Frye, *The history of Bukhara*, 87, cf. Vasmer, *Beiträge*, 54-5).

A parallel line of governors ruled north of the Oxus in Khuttal at this time [see khuttalān], and Ibn Khurradādhbih, *loc. cit.*, describes the ruler of Khuttal in *ca.* 272/885-6, al-Ḥārith b. Asad, as the kinsman of Dāwūd b. al-ʿAbbās, governor of Balkh; on the evidence of certain extant coins of his, he was still ruling in 293/906-7. Nevertheless, Vasmer thought that the apparentation of al-Ḥārith b. Asad's line to the main stock of the Bānīdjūrids was dubious. These Khuttal princelings minted coins in the early 4th/10th century, and the rebellious governor of Khurāsān Abū ʿAlī Čaghānī in 336/947 received help from the *amīr* Aḥmad b. Djaʿfar, whom Vasmer, however, attached to the direct offspring of Abū Dāwūd Muḥammad b. Aḥmad (*Beiträge*, 59 ff.), cf. Gardīzī, *Zayn al-akhbār*, ed. Nāẓim, 36, ed. ʿAbd al-Ḥayy Ḥabībī, 157, and Barthold, *Turkestan*³, 248. We do not know how long the power of these putative Bānīdjūrids in Khuttal lasted, although there was certainly a line of local rulers in Khuttal during the early Ghaznawid period, and a sister of Maḥmūd of Ghazna, the Ḥurra-yi Khuttalī of Bayhaḳī, was possibly married to one of these rulers, cf. Bosworth, *The Ghaznavids, their empire in Afghanistan and eastern Iran*, 138, 237, and idem, *The later Ghaznavids, splendour and decay. The dynasty in Afghanistan and northern India 1040-1186*, Edinburgh 1977, 148.

Bibliography: Given in the article. Vasmer, *Beiträge*, 53, has a conjectural genealogical table, followed by Zambaur in his *Manuel*, 202, 204.

(C. E. Bosworth)

BARBER [see čelebi; ḥallāḳ, in Suppl.].

BARDALLA, ABŪ ʿABD ALLĀH MUḤAMMAD al-ʿArabī b. Aḥmad al-Andalusī, prominent Moroccan *ḳāḍī* in the reign of Mawlāy Ismāʿīl [*q.v.*]. Born in Fās on 2 Djumādā II 1042/15 December 1632, he died there on 15 Radjab 1133/12 May 1721 and was interred outside Bāb Gīsa (al-Djīsa) on the left, or Ḳarawiyyīn, bank of the Wādi Fās.

Mainly because of its non-Arabic origin, "Bardalla" is vocalised differently in the Arabic sources, and, in some, one encounters corrupt forms such as in Bin Dalla. Understandably, we find inconsistencies in European spellings (Bordola, Bordala, Berdella, etc.). This last form most nearly represents the pronunciation of the family name as found in 20th century Fās, and it closely accords with the only two forms which—on the basis of scrutiny of manuscripts and inquiry from informed local sources—can be considered acceptable, viz. Bardalla, Burdalla. The Andalusian origin of Muḥammad al-ʿArabī's family suggests that the etymology is to be sought in a Romance diminutive in *-ello* of an epithet corresponding to, say, the modern Castilian *pardo* "brown", "dusky". Such a name is quite probable (see FILĀḤA, vol. iii, 901, col. 2, and cf. N.gh.rāl.h < Negrello, and on *-uh* > *a* (*tāʾ marbūṭa*), cf. also Ibn Sīda [*q.v.*] < Ibn Sīduh).

A respected jurist and teacher, Muḥammad al-ʿArabī seems to have been a popular and influential religious leader. During the first half of the 17th century and the first half of the 18th, notably between 1088/1677 and 1118/1706-7, we see him, against the background of the mosque of al-Ḳarawiyyīn [*q.v.*], serving in various religious capacities —*muftī*, superintendent of religious endowments (*nāẓir al-awḳāf/aḥbās*), *khaṭīb* and *imām*, and, last but not least, *ḳāḍī* of Fās (*ḳāḍī 'l-djamāʿa*). In this last office his career was somewhat erratic because of dismissals and reinstatements by the sultan. Thus from 1088/December 1677, when he replaced one Muḥammad b. al-Ḥasan al-Madjdjāsī, he had at least five or six separate terms of office. His initial troubles seem to have stemmed from the attempts of al-Madjdjāsī to cling to office and his later ones from the effects of local politics and rivalries. In 1116/1704 he was denounced to Mawlāy Ismāʿīl for performing the *ṣalāt* over his dead rebel son, Mawlāy Muḥammad al-ʿĀlim, but the sultan's wrath can have done him little harm, for we find him leading the Eclipse Prayer at al-Ḳarawiyyīn in 1118/1706. A man of evident integrity, he is described in one source as "the last just *ḳāḍī* of Fez".

Bibliography: In addition to Lévi-Provençal, *Chorfa*, 306 (see references in n. 1), 309, 312, 403, see the new edition and English translation, by Norman Cigar, of al-Ḳādirī's *Nashr al-mathānī* (= part I of a D. Phil. thesis, Oxford 1976 (details in *Bulletin of the British Society for Middle Eastern Studies*, 3 (1976), 43 f.)), i (tr.), 23 and n. 8, 26, 29, 30 f., 35, 46, 54 f.; ii, 94, etc.; Mawlāy Sulaymān, *K. ʿInāyat ūlī 'l-madjd bi-dhikr āl al-Fāsī b. al-Djadd*, Fās 1347, 27, 26, 40, etc.; al-Nāṣirī, *K. al-Istiḳṣāʾ*, vii, Casablanca 1957, 54, 91, 106, 107, 113. In Ibn Sūda, *Dalīl muʾarrikh al-Maghrib al-Aḳṣā* there are references to parts of two works preserved in the private library of Muḥammad b. Aḥmad Bardalla in Fās, one dealing with the early ʿAlawids, the other treating of the *ṣulaḥāʾ* of Fās, but they seem to be the work of Muḥammad al-ʿArabī's son despite the index reference (*Dalīl*, Casablanca 1960, 1965, i, 42 (no. 69), 145 (no. 525), ii, 608 (index), cf. ii, 441 (no. 2034)).

(J. D. LATHAM)

BĀRHA SAYYIDS (Bārha from the Hindī numeral *bārah* "twelve"), the name applied from Akbar's reign onwards to those in possession of a certain group of twelve villages in the Dōʾāb (Muẓaffarnagar district, U.P.).

After the establishment of the Īlkhānid Mo
kingdom in Persia and ʿIrāḳ in *ca.* 656/1258, m
Sayyid families migrated to India and obtai
grants of villages in the area extending from
Pandjāb to Bihār. Some of them were endo
with qualities of leadership and not only exerc
effective control over their own villages, but ra
the support of the neighbouring village lead
generally Hindus. The authenticity of their cla
to be Sayyids was always suspect, but their chiv
and heroic achievements made them indispens
to the Dihlī *sulṭāns*. The ancestor of the Bā
Sayyids, Abu 'l-Faraḥ, left his original home
Wāsiṭ [*q.v.*], in ʿIrāḳ, with his twelve sons at
end of the 7th/13th or in the 8th/14th century,
migrated to India, where he obtained four vill
in Sirhind [*q.v.*]. By the 10th/16th century som
Abu 'l-Faraḥ's descendants had taken over
Bārha villages in Muẓaffarnagar. In the reign
Akbar, the Bārha Sayyids occupied a place
distinction, and nine of them held *manṣabs* [
ranging from 2,000 to 250, the total family *ma*
being 8,550, a very high position in the Mu
hierarchy. Naturally, with the Bārha villages a
nucleus, the Sayyids owned extensive *djāgīrs* [
in the region. Their pride in their Indian birth gre
appealed to the local Hindu leaders, who hel
them to raise the strong contingents they led in
Mughal imperial wars. Occupying a distinguis
place in the vanguard, like many Rādjpūt warri
they preferred to fight as footsoldiers.

By the reign of Awrangzīb, although ostens
they maintained their traditional loyalty, they w
impelled by ambition to join in the scramble
political power. For example, Sayyid Ḥasan
(afterwards ʿAbd Allāh Ḳuṭb al-Mulk) and
younger brother Ḥusayn ʿAlī, known as the Say
brothers, by helping Farrukh-Siyar [*q.v.*] succ
to the throne in 1124/1712, obtained for themse
the highest civil and military positions in the gov
ment of their puppet emperor. They abolished
djizya and tried to conciliate the Rādjpūts; but
giving too much administrative power to t
favourite, Lāla Ratan Čand, a Vaishya, they
located the entire administrative machinery.
nally, in 9 Djumādā II 1131/29 April 1719, they
posed and strangled Farrukh-Siyar. They t
raised four puppet rulers to the throne, one a
the other. However, early in the reign of the fo
puppet emperor, Nāṣir al-Dīn Muḥammad S
[*q.v.*], they and their supporters were defeated
an opposition party under the leadership of Niẓ
al-Mulk [*q.v.*]. On 6 Dhu 'l-Ḥidjdja 1132/9 Octo
1720, Ḥusayn ʿAlī was assassinated, and, on
Muḥarram 1133/15 November 1720, ʿAbd Allāh
defeated near Āgra, taken captive and killed in
Dihlī prison on 1 Muḥarram 1135/12 October 172

The Bārha Sayyids were Shīʿīs, and many Su
Sayyid families, such as that of Shāh Walī A
Dihlawī [*q.v.*], who lived in their neighbourh
exerted themselves to ensure that the Bārha Say
did not recover their political power.

Bibliography: Besides the works cited
BAHĀDUR SHAH I, DJAHĀNDĀR SHĀH and FARRU
SIYAR, see Munawwar ʿAlī Khān (ed.), *Istiṣ
Sādāt-i Bārha*, India Office Ms. 4002; H. Bl
mann (tr.) and D. C. Phillot (ed.), *Āʾīn-i Akb*
Calcutta 1939, i; Shāh Walī Allāh, *Maktūb
Shāh Walī Allāh*, Raḍā Library, Rāmpūr (U.
Sulūk Fārsī no. 604; S. A. A. Rizvi, *Religious
intellectual history of the Muslims in Akbar's re*
Delhi 1975.

(S. A. A. RIZVI)

ĀRIZ, DJABAL, a mountainous and, in early ıic times, apparently wooded region of the nān province in Iran, described by the aeval historians and geographers as the haunt redatory peoples like the Kūficīs or Ḳufṣ and Balūč [see BALŪCISTĀN, KIRMĀN and ḲUFṢ]. It is steepsided granite chain running in a NW-SE tion from the mountain massif of central ān (sc. the massif which culminates in such s as the Kūh-i Hazār and the Kūh-i Lālazār), e south of the towns of Bam [*q.v.*] and Fahradj; geographers count it as amongst the *garmsīrāt* arm regions [see ḲĪSHLĀḲ] of Kirmān province. Djabal Bāriz rises to 12,450 feet, and the *Ḥudūd 'am* states that it possessed mines of lead, er and lodestone.

e actual name appears variously in the sources Bāriz, Bāridjān, etc., the modern form being -i Bāričī, and appears to be old. Herodotus ions Παρικάνιοι who paid tribute to Darius supplied infantry for Xerxes' army (cf. Marquart, *šahr*, 31), and Ṭabarī, i, 894, says that Khusraw shirwān re-established Sāsānid control over the le of al-Bāriz after the anarchy of Ḳubādh's years. Until the early ʿAbbāsid period, the al Bāriz remained a stronghold of Zoroastrian- The Kūfičīs or "mountaineers" of the region ted the attempts of Yaʿḳūb b. Layth to assert rid control over Kirmān, and it was probably after this time (sc. the later 3rd/9th century) Islam began to penetrate there. The geographers e following century describe the people of the ntain as savage robbers and brigands, whom punitive expeditions of Yaʿḳūb b. Layth, the ds Muʿizz al-Dawla and ʿAḍud al-Dawla, and Saldjūḳ Ḳāwurd b. Čaghrī Beg quelled only orarily (see C. E. Bosworth, *The Kūfichīs or in Persian history*, in *Iran. Jnal. of the British tute of Persian Studies*, xiv (1976), 9-17). Only villages, Kaftar and Dihak, are mentioned as et centres for the mountain. The Djabal Bāriz remained an inaccessible place, and Sir Percy s describes it as still being a haunt of thieves he was British Consul in Kirmān (*A fifth journey ersia*, in *Geogr. Jnal.*, xxviii (1906), 433).

Bibliography: In addition to the references en in the article, see Muḥammad b. Ibrāhīm, *'rīkh-i Saldjūḳiyān-i Kirmān*, ed. M. Bastānī-rīzī, Tehran 1964, 6, n. 1; *Ḥudūd al-ʿālam*, tr. norsky, 65, 125; Le Strange, *The lands of the stern Caliphate*, 316-17; *Admiralty handbook, rsia*, London 1945, 88, 95, 98, 106, 391. For ıropean travellers in the region, see A. Gabriel, *e Erforschung Persiens*, Vienna 1952.

(C. E. BOSWORTH)

-BARḲĪ, *nisba* of a Shīʿī family of which member, Abū Djaʿfar AḤMAD B. MUḤAMMAD b. id b. ʿAbd al-Raḥmān b. Muḥammad b. ʿAlī, ys a considerable renown in Imāmī circles. n the ancestor of the family, Muḥammad b. was imprisoned and put to death by Yūsuf b. ar al-Thaḳafī (governor of ʿIrāḳ from 120/738 26/744 [*q.v.*]) following the suppression of the t of Zayd b. ʿAlī (122/740 [*q.v.*]), his son ʿAbd ahmān escaped and established himself at Barḳa, ıe region of Ḳumm, whence the ethnic name arḳī, to which there is sometimes added, for the ose of avoiding confusion, the name al-Ḳummī ūt, *Buldān*, i, 572, s.v. "Barḳa", gives the *nisba* isely, but in the Egyptian edition of his *Muʿdjam abā'*, iv, 132, al-Barḳī becomes al-Raḳḳī). ʿAbd ahmān b. Muḥammad was accompanied by his son Khālid, who was still a child; the son of this last, Abū ʿAbd Allāh Muḥammad (correcting Yāḳūt, *Udabā'*, *loc. cit.*), would appear to be the first member of this family to participate in the transmission of Shīʿī tradition. A supporter of ʿAlī al-Riḍā (d. 203/818 [*q.v.*]) and of his son Muḥammad al-Djawād (d. 219/834) whom he certainly visited, he was the author, (if we are to believe Ibn al-Nadīm, *Fihrist*, Cairo ed. 309-10; cf. al-Ṭūsī, *Fihrist*, 153) of a number of works, sc. the *Kitāb al-ʿAwīṣ*, *K. al-Tabṣira*, *K. al-Ridjāl* (on transmitters of traditions ascribed to ʿAlī b. Abī Ṭālib) and the *K. al-Maḥāsin*, which poses an interesting problem of composition and attribution. If we are to judge by the details supplied by Ibn al-Nadīm this *K. al-Maḥāsin* would be a collection of "books" (*kutub*), that is, of chapters constituting a sort of encyclopaedia of knowledge which a good Shīʿī would be obliged to possess in order to conform to tradition: Kur'ān, history, geography, ethics, divination from dreams, etc. However, Ibn al-Nadīm, who probably did not have the opportunity to examine all these *kutub*, numbers about eighty of them and adds that the son of Muḥammad, Abū Djaʿfar Aḥmad, composed three works of his own: the *K. al-Iḥtidjādj* (a subject already dealt with by the preceding), *K. al-Safar* and *K. al-Buldān*, "more developed than that of his father."

Now the author of the *Fihrist* is, curiously, the only one to attribute a first version of the *K. al-Maḥāsin* to Muḥammad b. Khālid. Yāḳūt totally ignores this individual, whom he mentions neither in the *Muʿdjam al-buldān*, nor in the section of the *Muʿdjam al-udabā'* (iv, 132-6) devoted exclusively to Aḥmad b. Muḥammad and probably incomplete; basing himself, without admitting it, on the *Fihrist* of al-Ṭūsī (20-2), he lists a total of ninety-six titles, not specifying that they constitute the *K. al-Maḥāsin* mentioned above, but giving the impression all the same that the number of these *kutub* is variable and asserting that he has personal knowledge of those that he enumerates; he judges this Barḳī "worthy of credence, reliable" (*thiḳa*), although he reproaches him for relying on feeble transmitters (*ḍuʿafā'*) and for taking as a basis *ḥadīths* transmitted directly by representatives of the second generation (*marāsīl*).

The same reproach is directed at him—and in the same terms—by Shīʿī writers who describe how he was temporarily expelled from Ḳumm because of the defects of his methods; these authors ignore too the father of Aḥmad; they declare that this last was very wise and learned, composed verse and had many disciples (although the ones that they mention by name mostly belong to a later period); they make him an associate of Muḥammad al-Djawād (which would seem hard to accept) or of ʿAlī al-Hādī (d. 254/868) and a contemporary of al-Muʿtaṣim (218-27/833-42); they make no mention of his successors; and they suggest that he died in 274/887-8 or in 280/893-4.

The articles which the Shīʿī *ridjāliyyūn* devote to him are conveniently reproduced by Muḥsin al-Amīn al-ʿĀmilī in his *Aʿyān al-Shīʿa* (ix, 266) and most completely by al-Sayyid Muḥammad Ṣādiḳ Baḥr al-ʿUlūm, who was responsible for the second edition of the *Kitāb al-Maḥāsin* (Nadjaf 1384/1964, two volumes bound in one; the first edition, by Djalāl al-Dīn al-Ḥusaynī, Tehran 1370 (?) remained inaccessible to the author of the present article).

It must in fact be said that this celebrated *K. al-Maḥāsin*, which appears to have enjoyed great influence over a long period, has not survived in an integral form, although it has not totally disappeared, and eleven of its "books" have been preserved: (1) *al-Ashkāl wa 'l-karā'in* (11 *bābs*); (2) *Thāwab al-aʿmāl* (123 *babs*); (3) *ʿIkāb al-aʿmāl* (70 *babs*); (4) *al-Ṣafwa wa 'l-nūr wa 'l-raḥma* (47 *babs*); (5) *Maṣābīḥ al-ẓulam* (49 *babs*); (6) *al-ʿIlal* (1 *bab*); (7) *al-Safar* (39 *babs*); (8) *al-Ma'ākil* (136 *babs*); (9) *al-Mā'* (20 *babs*); (10) *al-Manāfiʿ* (6 *babs*); (11) *al-Marāfiḳ* (16 *babs*). These titles almost all appear, in the same form, in the ancient lists, where there is also reference to *kitābs* derived from *bābs* in the published chapters. So we possess one-sixth or one-seventh of the original work, which is essentially a collection of *ḥadīths* attributed to the Prophet and to the *Ahl al-Bayt*, in particular to al-Ḥusayn b. ʿAlī b. Abī Ṭālib, simply classified and reproduced without any interference on the part of the compiler. To judge by what has survived, the collection constituted a sort of *muṣannaf* of a particular type grouping together all the traditional elements that the Imāmī considered to be essential, both in matters relating to the faith and in questions of everyday life. All the same, a certain lack of order dominates the classification of traditions, so for example we find *ḥadīths* concerning bread in the chapter devoted to water (no. 9), whereas we would expect to find them in the preceding chapter (*al-Ma'ākil*), which is extensive and contains references to a long list of foodstuffs. The titles enumerated in the lists give the impression that the author did not neglect literary formation, poetry and other cultural fields, which makes the more regrettable the loss of so many chapters, no doubt considered less indispensable by posterity. It is probable that the *kitābs* formed independent fascicules, which would explain both how they could be so easily lost and why authors cannot agree either on their number or their order.

A comparison between Ibn al-Nadīm's list and all the others might perhaps allow an insight into the respective roles of the father and of the son in the compilation of the *Kitāb al-Maḥāsin*, but this would be a hazardous enterprise and ultimately of doubtful benefit. In other respects, the presentation of these lists is such that it is impossible to see clearly whether Muḥammad or his son wrote works that were not included in the composition of the *K. al-Maḥāsin*; it is however possible that one or the other left biographies of *ridjāl*, and al-Masʿūdī (*Murūdj*, i, 12 = § 8) mentions among the sources, attributing it to Aḥmad, a *Kitāb al-Tabyān* which no doubt had a historical or a hiero-historical character.

Bibliography: (in addition to references in the article): Khaṭīb Baghdādī, *Ta'rīkh*, v, 4; Ḳummī, *Ta'rīkh-i Ḳum*, 277; Ibn Ḥadjar, *Lisān al-Mīzān*, i, 262. Shīʿī authors (including those whose notices are given in the introd. of the *K. al-Maḥāsin*): Nadjāshī, *Ridjāl*, 55; Nūrī, *Mustadrak al-wasā'il*, iii, 552; Karbalā'ī, *Muntahā 'l-maḳāl*, lith. 1302, 41, 42; Mīrzā Muḥ. Astarābādī, *Manhadj al-maḳāl*, lith. Tehran 1307; Māmaḳānī, *Tanḳīḥ al-maḳāl*, 82-4; Khwānsārī, *Rawḍāt al-djannāt*, lith. Téhran 1306, 13. Modern biographers: Kaḥḥāla, ii, 97; Ziriklī, i 195; see also F. Rosenthal, *A history of Muslim historiography*², 501.

(Ch. Pellat)

BARṢAWMĀ AL-ZĀMIR, Isḥāḳ, famous flute player in early ʿAbbāsid times, died after 188/804. He was a dark-coloured *muwallad* of humble origin, son of a "Nabataean" woman from Kūfa. Ibrāhīm al-Mawṣilī brought him to Baghdād, gave him an education in "Arab music" (*al-ghinā' al-ʿarabī*) and introduced him to Hārūn al-Rashīd. He accompanied the singers in the concerts at court, belonging to the second class (*ṭabaḳa*) of court musicians, later on was promoted by the caliph to the class. Isḥāḳ al-Mawṣilī knew "nobody being competent in their profession than four per al-Aṣmaʿī as an expert in poetry, al-Kisā'ī in g mar, Manṣūr Zalzal as a lute player and Barṣa as a flautist".

Bibliography: *Aghānī*³, v, 176, 227, 241, vi, 164-5, 297, 303, 304, xix, 294, xx, 358; Dj *Ḥayawān*, vi, 17; Ibn ʿAbd Rabbih, *ʿIḳd* Cairo 1949, 31-2, 37; Pseudo-Djāḥiẓ, *Tādj* 41; Ibn al-Ḳifṭī, *Inbāh al-ruwāt*, ii, 27 H. G. Farmer, *History of Arabian music*, 116.

(E. Neubau

BASBĀS is the fennel (*Foeniculum vulg* belonging to the family of umbellal plants. term *bisbās*, used in the Maghrib for fennel, indi in the Eastern countries the red seed-shell of nutmeg (*Myristica fragrans*), known as Macis, the term *basbāsa*, not to be confused with the other terms, indicates only nutmeg in the e Arab world. The most often used synonym of *b* is *rāziyānadj*, borrowed from the Persian. The plete nomenclature, also taken from other ori languages, has been brought together by I. *Die Flora der Juden*, iii, 460-5. The Greek μάραθ(ρ)ον is found as *mārathūn* (and variant the Arabic medical inventories. Like in Dioscor this term indicates the garden fennel (*basbās bust* *Anethum foeniculum*, while ἱππομάραθον (*ibbūm thūn*, and variants, strictly speaking "horse fenn which is mostly mentioned in connection the garden fennel, apparently stands for the fennel. The term *basbās djabalī*, likewise usec the latter, is confusing, for the "mountain fen (Seseli) does not belong to the genus Foenicu Other kinds mentioned cannot as yet be determi

The volatile oil extracted from the fruits of fennel has a strongly fragrant scent and a bi camphor-like smell. It loosens phlegm and wa the form of fennel-tea or fennel-honey, used, as now, against coughs and flatulence. A decoctio the flower stalk was considered to be a diuretic to further menstruation; mixed with wine it used as a medicament against snake bites, v the pressed juice is praised as an ophthalmic rem The leaves and fruits were added to food as a s Aṣmaʿī counts them among the precious s (*Nabāt*, ed. Ghunaym, Cairo 1392/1972, 13 ff.). Ḥanīfa al-Dīnawarī praises their aroma, rem that the plant thrives on wild soil and proves observations with verses (*Nabāt. The Book of Pl* ed. B. Lewin, 59 f.). Fennel has been used as s from Old Egyptian times until today. Ibn al-ʿAw consecrates a special chapter to the cultivatio the fennel (*Kitāb al-Filāḥa*, tr. Clément-Mulle Paris 1866, 250 f.). Curious is the assertion of Nuw (*Nihāya*, xi, 82), that vipers and snakes, v leaving their holes in spring, rub their eyes at fennel shrub in order to be able to see again; same is mentioned repeatedly by Ḳazwīnī Wiedemann, *Aufsätze zur arab. Wissenschaf schichte*, ii, 336, 386).

Bibliography: Dioscurides, *Materia me* ed. Wellmann, ii, Berlin 1906, 81 f. (= lib. 70, 71); *La "Materia médica" de Dioscoride* (Arabic tr.) ed. Dubler and Terés, Tetuán 1 271; *The medical formulary or Aqrābādhīn al-Kindī*, tr. M. Levey, Madison etc. 1966, Suwaydī, *Simāt*, Ms. Paris ar. 3004, fols. 256a; Ibn Biklārish, *Mustaʿīnī*, Ms. Naples, I ız. iii, F. 65, fol. 82b; Ibn al-Djazzār, *Iʿtimād*, s. Ayasofya 3564, fol. 58a-b; Maimonides, *arḥ asmāʾ al-ʿuḳḳār*, ed. Meyerhof, no. 351; ıonymous [Abu 'l-ʿAbbās al-Nabātī b. al-Rūm-ya?], Ms. Nuruosmaniye 3589, fol. 102a-b; Ibn -Bayṭār, *Djāmiʿ*, Būlāḳ 1291, i, 93, ii, 134 f., tr. ɛclerc, nos. 286, 1019; Ghassānī, *Muʿtamad*, ed. . al-Saḳḳāʾ, Beirut 1975, 23 f. and 182-4; *Die ıarmakolog. Grundsätze des Abu Mansur ... arawi*, tr. A. Achundow, Halle 1893, 167, 210; *uḥfat al-aḥbāb*, ed. Renaud and Colin, Paris 34, no. 358; Rāzī, *Ḥāwī*, xx, Ḥaydarābād 1387, 5-9 (no. 378); Ibn Sīnā, *Ḳānūn*, Būlāḳ, i, 277, d 429 f.; Ibn Hubal, *Mukhtārāt*, Ḥaydarābād 62, ii, 178; Dāwūd al-Anṭākī, *Tadhkira*, Cairo 371, i, 74 f., 165; H. G. Kircher, *Die "einfachen eilmittel" aus dem "Handbuch der Chirurgie" des n al-Quff*, Bonn 1967, no. 34; W. Schmucker, *ie pflanzliche und mineralische Materia medica ı Firdaus al-ḥikma des ʿAlī ibn Sahl Rabban -Ṭabarī*, Bonn 1969, no. 318; F. A. Flückiger, *harmakognosie des Pflanzenreiches*, Berlin 1891, 8-50. (A. Dietrich)

ASHKARD, BASHĀKARD, Europeanised ı Bashkardia, a region of south-eastern n, falling administratively today within the 8th *n* or province of Kirmān and in the *shahrastān* istrict of Djīruft, of which it comprises one of nine constituent rural areas (*dihistānhā*), see *hang-i djughrāfiyā-yi Īrān*, viii, Tehran 1332/ 3, 49. It is the mountainous hinterland of western ɛrān, lying to the east of Mīnāb near the Straits Iormuz and bounded on the north by the southern ges of the Djāz-Muryān depression; the peaks of Māriz range within it rise to just over 7,000 feet. whole region has been, and still is, extremely ote and inaccessible, and only in recent decades a measure of control from Tehran been extended r a people formerly much given to raiding and ;andage. The main settlement is at Angohrān, the population is everywhere sparse; the *Ad-ılty handbook, Persia*, London 1945, mentions reeds huts at Angohrān, and a total population Bashkardia of an estimated 8,000 families; the *hang, loc. cit.*, mentions 108 settlements (*ābādī*), h a population of *ca.* 6,700.

'he people of Bashkardia are ethnically Iranian Shīʿī in *madhhab*; at least until very recently, social structure there included a slave element, h negroid and native Iranian. It was first specu-d by Tomaschek that the modern Bashkardīs ld be the descendants of the mediaeval Islamic ičīs or Ḳufṣ, the predatory people of Kirmān Makrān provinces often linked in the sources h the Balūč [see balūčistān and ḳufṣ]; for a ɔussion of this, see C. E. Bosworth, *The Kūfichīs Qufṣ in Persian history*, in *Iran. Jnal. of the ish Institute of Persian Studies*, xiv (1976), 9 ff. ɛ actual name Bashkard (Bashākard is a form ɔarently exhibiting a pseudo-Arabic broken plural) unattested till the mid-19th century, when the t Europeans, Col. E. Mockler and E. A. Floyer, ted the region; Dr. I. Gershevitch, who stayed in shkardia for some months in 1956, has never-less suggested that the name might derive from dominant Persian tribe, to which the Achaemen-themselves belonged, of the Pasargadae, located Ptolemy in Carmania (= Kirmān). The Bash-dī language is very aberrant from New Persian, l exists in two forms, a northern and a southern up of dialects. It contains certain old Iranian rds not surviving elsewhere, e.g. the hardwood *djag* or *djakh*, identifiable with the O. Pers. *yakā*-wood used in the construction of Darius's palace at Susa, see Gershevitch, *Sissoo at Susa* (*O. Pers. yakā = Dalbergia Sissoo Roxb.*, in *BSOAS*, xix (1957), 317-20, xx (1958), 174.

Bibliography: The main items in the exiguous bibliography of Bashkardia are given by Bosworth in *art. cit.*, 11, n. 13; of special note are the works of Floyer and A. Gabriel, and most recently, of Gershevitch, *Travels in Bashkardia*, in *Jnal. of the Royal Central Asian Society*, xlvi (1959), 213-24, and F. Balsan, *Étrange Baloutchistan*, Paris 1969. Linguistic material was collected by Gershevitch, but has not yet been published *in toto*; for sections of it so far accessible in print, see Bosworth, *art. cit.*, 13, n. 20. (C. E. Bosworth)

BASHKUT, Djewād Fehmī, modern Turkish Cevat Fehmi Başkut, Turkish playwright and journalist (1905-71). He was born in Edirne and educated at an Istanbul high school, choosing journalism as his career when he was still a very young man. He began to write plays in the early 1940s and became very popular. Of his 23 plays, most of which were performed in the city theatre (*Şehir tiyatrosu*) of Istanbul, the best known are *Küçük şehir* ("Little town") 1946; *Paydos* ("Break") 1949; *Harput'ta bir Amerikalı* ("An American in Kharput") 1956; and *Buzlar çözülmeden* ("Before the thaw") 1964. His plays are sentimental and unsophisticated renderings of human dramas and comic situations, with an edifying approach. He writes in an easy style at times tending to be somewhat literary and pedantic.

Bibliography: Metin And, *Elli yılın Türk tiyatrosu*, Istanbul 1973, 438 and index; Behçet Necatiğil, *Edebiyatımızda isimler sözlüğü*[9], 1975, s.v. (Fahir İz)

BASQUES [see bashkunish].

BATRIYYA or **BUTRIYYA**, the pejorative designation for a group of moderate Shīʿīs in the time of Muḥammad al-Bāḳir (d. 117/735) and for the moderate wing of the early Zaydiyya [*q.v.*] who did not repudiate the caliphates of Abū Bakr and ʿUmar. Their position was opposed to the more radical Shīʿī stand of the Djārūdiyya [*q.v.*], who considered ʿAlī the only legitimate immediate successor of the Prophet. The name is most often derived in the sources from the nickname *al-Abtar* of Kathīr al-Nawwāʾ and explained as referring to their "mutilating" (*batr*), either of the legitimate rights of the family of the Prophet, or of the recitation of the *basmala* in the prayer which they performed only with a subdued voice, or of the caliphate of ʿUthmān, which they repudiated for the last six years of his reign. The first of these explanations is clearly the most plausible one and points to an origin of the name in internal Shīʿī controversy.

Imāmī sources name the Kūfans Kathīr al-Nawwāʾ, Sālim b. Abī Ḥafṣa (d. 137/754-5), al-Ḥakam b. ʿUtayba (d. 112/730 or 115/733), Salama b. Kuhayl (d. 122/740), and Abu 'l-Miḳdād Thābit al-Ḥaddād as the chiefs of the Batriyya in the time of Muḥammad al-Bāḳir, and describe them as not recognising his full rank as *imām* and sole authority in religion and as criticising him for ambiguities in his teaching. ʿUmar b. Riyāḥ, who at first recognised the imāmate of al-Bāḳir, later also renounced him and joined the Batriyya after he had found al-Bāḳir contradicting a previous statement and proffering *taḳiyya* as an excuse.

Though only a few of the leaders of the Batriyya are expressly mentioned as participants in the rising of Zayd b. ʿAlī in 122/740, it may be assumed that the early Batriyya generally inclined towards supporting him, as his attitude toward the first caliphs was close to their own. The Zaydī Batriyya held that ʿAlī was the most excellent of men after the Prophet, but admitted the legitimacy of the imāmates of Abū Bakr and ʿUmar, since ʿAlī had voluntarily pledged allegiance to them. Concerning ʿUthmān, they either abstained from judgment or renounced him for the last six years of his reign. Unlike the Djārūdiyya, they did not ascribe a superior knowledge in religious matters to the descendants of ʿAlī, but accepted the *ḥadīth* transmitted in the Muslim community and admitted the use of individual reasoning (*idjtihād*, *raʾy*) in order to close gaps in the *Sharīʿa*. Thus they did not adopt the specifically Shīʿī theses in various points of the ritual and law and belonged to the traditionalist school of Kūfa in their *fiḳh* doctrine. A leader of the Batriyya in the revolts of Zayd and of Ibrāhīm b. ʿAbd Allāh (145/762-3) was the traditionist and *faḳīh* Hārūn b. Saʿīd al-ʿIdjlī, whose supporters, known as the ʿIdjliyya, were probably recruited from among his tribesmen. Equally prominent among the Zaydī Batriyya was the traditionist and theologian al-Ḥasan b. Ṣāliḥ b. Ḥayy [*q.v.*] (d. *ca.* 168/784-5), who supported the candidacy of Zayd's son ʿĪsā to the imāmate and concealed him from the ʿAbbāsid authorities. ʿĪsā b. Zayd, in spite of his preference of the Shīʿī position in some ritual matters (see L. Veccia Vaglieri, *Divagazioni su due Rivolte Alidi*, in *A Francesco Gabrieli*, Rome 1964, 328 ff.), generally inclined to Batrī views. A son of al-Ḥasan b. Ṣāliḥ b. Ḥayy led a group of Kūfan Batriyya in the revolt of Yaḥyā b. ʿAbd Allāh in the mountains of Daylamān [see DAYLAM] (*ca.* 176/792), but was soon alienated by Yaḥyā, who, espousing strictly Shīʿī ritual, disapproved of some of his practices. Also to be counted among the chiefs of the Batriyya is the *kalām* theologian Sulaymān b. Djarīr al-Raḳḳī [*q.v.*], although his supporters were often mentioned as a group separate from the Batriyya. He participated in the debate about the imāmate in the circle of the Barmakids, and a community of his followers survived in ʿĀnāt for some decades. In the 3rd/9th century, the Batriyya quickly disintegrated as the Kūfan traditionalist school was absorbed in Sunnism, while within the Zaydiyya, the Djārūdī views concerning the imāmate prevailed and Zaydī *fiḳh* was elaborated on the basis of the doctrine of the family of the Prophet.

Bibliography: Al-Nāshiʾ, *Masāʾil al-imāma*, ed. J. van Ess, Beirut 1971, 43-5; al-Nawbakhtī, *Firaḳ al-shīʿa*, ed. H. Ritter, Istanbul 1931, see index; al-Ashʿarī, *Maḳālāt al-islāmiyyīn*, ed. Ritter, Istanbul 1929-31, 68 f.; al-Kashshī, *Ikhtiyār maʿrifat al-ridjāl*, ed. Ḥasan al-Muṣṭafawī, Mashhad 1348/1969, 232-8, 390-2; Abu 'l-Faradj al-Iṣfahānī, *Maḳātil al-ṭālibiyyīn*, ed. Aḥmad Ṣaḳr, Cairo 1368/1949, 468; Nashwān al-Ḥimyarī, *al-Ḥūr al-ʿīn*, Cairo 1367/1948, 150 f., 155; Shahrastānī, 120 f.; R. Strothmann, *Das Staatsrecht der Zaiditen*, Strassburg 1912, 31-4; idem, *Kultus der Zaiditen*, Strassburg 1912, 56 f.; C. van Arendonk, *Les débuts de l'imāmat Zaidite au Yémen*, tr. J. Ryckmans, Leiden 1960, see index; W. Madelung, *Der Imam al-Qāsim ibn Ibrāhīm*, Berlin 1965, see index.

(W. MADELUNG)

AL-BATTĪ [see ABU 'L-ḤASAN AL-BATTĪ, in Suppl.].

BAWRAĶ (*būraḳ*) is natron, sesqui-ca nate of soda, a compound of various salts taining mainly sodium carbonate (soda). Der from the Persian *būra*, the term does not indi borax in the modern sense (Natrium biboracic but has given its name to it. The Arabic lexi raphers know the *bawraḳ māʾī*, *b. djabalī*, *b. arm* *b. miṣrī* (= *naṭrūn*), *b. al-ṣāgha* ("borax of goldsmiths", Chrysocolla), *b. al-khabbāzīn* (or: *khubz*) and *b. ifrīḳī*. Since unbiased elucidation these terms are almost completely lacking, enumeration is almost valueless. Al-Khwāra (*Mafātīḥ*, ed. van Vloten, 260) mentions, furt more, the *bawraḳ zarāwandī* and also the *ti* which is made artificially; both are known as ti until today. Further information about the non clature, also in other languages, is given in Moat *Ismāʿīl Ğorğānī* (see *Bibl.*). In his cosmogra Dimashḳī distinguishes between *bawraḳ* and *tin* he says that both have a natural and an artif kind and that both kinds of the latter were use melting and purifying minerals (Wiedemann, *sätze zur arab. Wissenschaftsgeschichte*, i, 713). fact that there existed a class of borax-tra (*bawraḳī*) indicates that trade in these var sodium compounds required specialised knowle This trade was apparently lucrative: Ibn Ḥawḳ 346 (tr. Kramers-Wiet, ii, 339) mentions a bo (*milḥ al-bawraḳ*) which was delivered from Lake to the bakers in ʿIrāḳ and Mesopotamia (*baw al-khabbāzīn*, see above); this denomination co from the bakers who used to coat the bread borate dissolved in water before putting it into furnace, in order to give it a prettier and more sh appearance. The particularly valuable *bawraḳ ṣāgha* (see above) was exported with great pr from Kabudhān to ʿIrāḳ and Syria.

The books on mineralogy mention the nume find-spots and kinds of *bawraḳ*. Like salt it is fo either as a liquid in water or as a solid on the sur of the soil. It is white, grey or red, and causes kinds of solid substances to melt. *Naṭrūn*, a k of *bawraḳ*, cleanses the body and beautifies skin; it is also used in chemistry as a reagent aga impurities (J. Ruska, *Das Steinbuch des Aristot* Heidelberg 1912, Arab. text 118, tr. 173).

In antiquity *bawraḳ* (*naṭrūn*) was known as νίτ which is different from our saltpetre (Nitrum). that time, as in Islamic times and nowadays, it gained from lakes which have no discharge, in wh it was left behind as a gleaming crust as a resul evaporation. According to Ghassānī and Ibn al-B (see *Bibl.*), *naṭrūn* is "Armenian borax", but t also say that the best *naṭrūn* comes from the Egyp saltlakes. It was widely used in therapeutics, es ially to treat skin-diseases like itching, scaly er tions, scabies, pimples and boils, and also to clea fresh wounds. Dissolved in wine, honey or wate purifies dirty and purulent sores. Taken interna it has a loosening effect, softens the bowel mot and dispels flatulence. In al-Kindī's collection prescriptions, it is an ingredient of various to powders. Spread on the eyes, it removes the so-ca hard white spot (*bayāḍ al-ʿayn al-ghalīẓ*); howe especially in the treatment of the eyes, quacl took possession of this substance (according Djawbarī, *al-Mukhtār fī kashf al-asrār*, cf. Wi mann, *Aufsätze*, i, 765 ff.).

Bibliography: Dioscurides, *Materia med* ed. Wellmann, iii, Berlin 1914, 83 f. (= lib 113); *La "Materia médica" de Dioscorides* (Arabic tr.) ed. Dubler and Terés, Tetuán 1

26 f.; *The medical formulary or Aqrābādhīn of l-Kindī*, tr. M. Levey, Madison etc. 1966, 248; Bīrūnī, *Ṣaydala*, ed. H. M. Saʿīd, Karachi 1973, rab. 102 f., and 363, tr. 79, 322; Ibn Biklārish, *Iustaʿīnī*, Ms. Naples, Bibl. Naz, iii, F. 65, fol. 5b; Maimonides, *Sharḥ asmāʾ al-ʿuḳḳār*, ed. leyerhof, no. 51; Ibn al-Bayṭār, *Djāmiʿ*, Būlāḳ 291, i, 125-7, tr. Leclerc, no. 381, with many uotations from sources; Ghassānī, *Muʿtamad*, Beirut 1975, 41 f.; F. Moattar, *Ismāʿīl Ǧorǧānī nd seine Bedeutung für die iranische Heilkunde nsbesondere Pharmazie*, Marburg 1971, 299 f. 10. 135): *Die pharmakolog. Grundsätze des Abu Iansur . . . Harawi*, tr. A. Achundow, Halle 1893, 62 f., 316; *Tuḥfat al-aḥbāb*, ed. Renaud and Colin, Paris 1934, no. 92; Rāzī, *Ḥāwī*, xx, Ḥaydarābād 387, 134-7; Ibn Sīnā, *Ḳānūn*, i, Būlāḳ, 267 f.; Dāwūd al-Anṭākī, *Tadhkira*, Cairo 1371, i, 87 f.; *l Libro Agregà de Serapiom*, ed. G. Ineichen, ii, Venice 1966, 77; H. G. Kircher, *Die "einfachen Heilmittel" aus dem "Handbuch der Chirurgie" des bn al-Quff*, Bonn 1967, no. 39; W. Schmucker, *Die pflanzliche und mineralische Materia medica m Firdaus al-ḥikma des ʿAlī ibn Sahl Rabban t-Ṭabarī*, Bonn 1969, no. 153; M. Berthelot, *La himie au moyen-âge*, i-iii, 1893 (new impression 967), with many references (see Indices).

(A. Dietrich)

BAYʿAT al-RIḌWĀN, the name given to an th exacted by the Prophet from some of his owers during the Medinan period.

During the expedition to al-Ḥudaybiya [*q.v.*] in u 'l-Ḳaʿda of the year 6 (March 628), a report ched Muḥammad that the Meccans had killed hmān b. ʿAffān, who had gone into Mecca to otiate a truce. Muḥammad realised that he uld lose face unless ʿUthmān's death was avenged, l summoned the members of the expedition to e an oath of allegiance to himself. There are erent versions of the content of the oath. Some d it was a pledge not to flee; others that it was ledge "to the death" (*ʿalā 'l-mawt*); and one man ān) is said to have pledged himself to do "what s in Muḥammad's mind" (*ʿalā mā fī nafsika*). To t the Meccans would have been very dangerous e the Muslims, as pilgrims, were lightly armed, l this was doubtless why Muḥammad asked for pledge and why it is described as a pledge "not flee" or "to the death". If the third version is rect, it indicates a formal increase in Muḥammad's ocratic power, which is known to have been in- asing informally about this period. One man, Djadd b. Ḳays, refused to take the oath and ears to have shortly afterwards been deposed Muḥammad from being chief of the Anṣārī clan Salima. The incident is mentioned in Ḳurān, iii, 18: "God was well pleased (*raḍiya*) with the ievers when they pledged themselves to you ler the tree." From this is derived the name *yʿat al-riḍwān* which may be translated "the dge of good pleasure" or "the pledge which ased (God)". It is also known as "the pledge of tree", and those who made the pledge here e later honoured as the *Aṣḥāb al-shadjara*, "the n of the tree". It has been suggested that the e might have been a sacred one in pre-Islamic es. At a later period, there was a mosque on the t (Bukhārī, iii, 113 = *Maghāzī*, 35; Wellhausen, *te*², 104).

Bibliography: Ibn Hishām, ed. Wüstenfeld, 746; al-Wāḳidī, ed. Marsden Jones, ii, 603 f.; W. Montgomery Watt, *Muhammad at Medina*, Oxford 1956, 50 f., 234; A. J. Wensinck, etc. *Concordance*, s.v. *bāyaʿa, bayʿa, shadjara*, etc.

(W. Montgomery Watt)

BAYHAḲĪ SAYYIDS, a religio-political group active in the political life of early Islamic Kashmīr. The Bayhaḳī Sayyids migrated to Kashmīr from Dihlī in the time of Sulṭān Sikandar (791-816/1389-1413), and played a very important part in the social and political life of the Valley until its conquest by the Mughals in 996/1588. Owing to their descent from Prophet Muḥammad, through his daughter Fāṭima, they were treated with great respect by the Sulṭāns, who gave them *djāgīr*s and high offices and entered into matrimonial relations with them. At first they were unpopular and aroused both the anger and jealousy of the Kashmīrī nobles, because, conscious of their high birth, they behaved arrogantly and joined those elements who were critical of Hindū practices and ceremonies and wanted the enforcement of the *Sharīʿa* and the Islamic way of life. But gradually they began to identify themselves with the aims and aspirations of the Kashmīrīs, who, thereupon, accepted them as their leaders on account of the abilities they displayed as soldiers and administrators.

The chronicles give such exaggerated accounts of the exploits of the Bayhaḳī Sayyids in Kashmīr that it is difficult to disengage fact from fiction. The first Bayhaḳī Sayyid, however, about whom any reliable evidence exists was Sayyid Muḥammad, who gave his daughter, Tādj Khātūn, in marriage to Sulṭān Zayn al-ʿĀbidīn (823-74/1420-70); and later his grandson, Sayyid Ḥasan, was married to the Sulṭān's daughter. On the death of Zayn al-ʿĀbidīn's son and successor Ḥaydar Shāh (874-6/1470-72), Ḥasan Shāh, who succeeded him, made Sayyid Ḥasan his *Wazīr*; and since Sayyid Ḥasan succeeded in setting up Muḥammad Shāh, Ḥasan Shāh's minor son, as Sulṭān in 889/1484, he continued as *Wazīr*. But his arrogance and his opposition to Hindū customs and practices aroused the anger of the Kashmīr nobles, who plotted against him, and early one morning they entered the fort of Nawshahr in Srīnagar, where they were holding court, and killed him and his thirteen followers. His two sons, Sayyid Hāshim and Sayyid Muḥammad, who were not in the fort at the time, carried on the struggle against the enemies of their father, but they were defeated and exiled from the country along with their followers. But after two years the Sayyids were recalled, and under the leadership of Sayyid Muḥammad, they once again became active in the struggle for the throne between Muḥammad Shāh and Fatḥ Shāh, intriguing with and making alliances with different groups as suited their interests. In the end, Sayyid Muḥammad succeeded in 898/1493 in becoming *Wazīr* of Muḥammad Shāh, but in 910/1505 he was defeated and killed by his rivals. This, however, did not demoralise the Sayyids. Instead, when Mīrzā Ḥaydar Dughlāt established his power in Kashmīr (948-58/1541-51), Sayyid Ibrāhīm, the son of Sayyid Muḥammad, joined the Kashmīr nobles in overthrowing him.

Under the Čak Sulṭāns also, the Bayhaḳī Sayyids continued to play an important part. ʿAlī Shāh Čak (978-86/1570-78) appointed Sayyid Mubārak the son of Sayyid Ibrāhīm as *Wazīr*, and took his advice on all important matters. But on Alī Shāh's death, Sayyid Mubārak set aside the latter's son Yūsuf Shāh on grounds of incompetence and declared himself Sulṭān (986/1578). Yet, after a few months he was overthrown by the nobles, who were

denied by him any share in the government. In spite
of this, he joined Yaʿḳūb Shāh, Yūsuf Shāh's son
and successor, in the struggle against the Mughal
armies sent by the Emperor Akbar to conquer Kashmīr. Finding resistance to the Mughals fruitless, he
submitted to the Mughal commander Ḳāsim Khān
Mīr Baḥr on 27 Dhu 'l-Ḥidjdja 994/9 December 1586,
and was sent to Āgra. Akbar wanted Sayyid Mubārak
to accompany Yūsuf Khān Riḍwī, who was ordered
by him to proceed to Kashmīr to relieve Ḳāsim
Khān. But Sayyid Mubārak refused; so he was
imprisoned and sent to Bengal. His son, Abu 'l-Maʿālī,
also fought side by side with Yaʿḳūb Shāh against
the Mughals, but he was taken prisoner. This was
the end of the significant role which the Bayhaḳī
Sayyids had played for over 150 years of Kashmīr
history.

Bibliography: G.M.D. Ṣūfī, Kashīr, i, Lahore
1948-9; Mohibbul Hasan, Kashmīr under the
Sulṭāns, Calcutta 1959; Bahāristān-i Shāhī, anonymous ms. I.O. 509.   (MOHIBBUL HASAN)

BAYRAĶ [see ʿALAM].

AL-BAZDAWĪ [see AL-NASAFĪ].

BEDOUINS [see BADW].

BEERSHEBA [see BĪR AL-SABʿ].

BEHZĀD. [see BIHZĀD].

BEKAA. [see BIĶĀʿ].

BELOMANCY [see ISTIĶSĀM].

BELUCHISTAN. [see BALŪČISTĀN].

BENĪ MELLĀL, formerly Ḳaṣaba Benī Mellāl
(from the name of the tribe living around it), or
sometimes Ḳaṣaba B. Kush, a town of Morocco
roughly equidistant from Casablanca, Marrakesh and
Fās. It lies on one of the slopes of the Dīr [q.v. in
Suppl.], at an altitude of 620 m./1,980 feet, in this
piedmont region between the Middle Atlas and the
wide, historic plain of the Tādlā, of which it has
recently become the official chef-lieu.

The town is built around the fortress or ḳaṣaba
built towards 1099/1688 by Mawlāy Ismāʿīl, restored
in the 19th century by Mawlāy Sulaymān and since
once again restored. The Vauclusian spring of
Asardūn to the south of the town leads one to think
that Benī Mellāl, like all the other centres of the
Dīr, e.g. Aghmāt, Damnāt [q.vv.], etc., goes back
to ancient times, but no traces of prehistoric life
have as yet been discovered there. It is possible
that Benī Mellāl is Ḥiṣn Daī, the little capital which
Yaḥyā b. Idrīs inherited in the 3rd/9th century at
the time of the division of his father's kingdom.
It is mentioned by the Arab geographers as a fortress
and an important market centre. In 534/1140 or
535/1141 it was occupied by the Almohads.

The demographic explosion of the town has been
remarkable. In 1918 it had an estimated 3,000
inhabitants; now it has 60,000, and the increase
between the 1952 and 1960 censuses has been 81%.
This undoubtedly stems from its administrative role
today, one of the results of agricultural development of the great alluvial plain of the Tādlā or else
of the very important hydraulic reservoir works
and irrigations improvements made over the last
30 years. Benī Mellāl's importance has grown still
further from its role as a market centre for provisions of the Berber tribes in the Middle Atlas valleys,
and also those of the central Grand Atlas (especially
the Wādī Tadghat). A very lively fair is held in the
town centre every week, where curious coverlets
of thin rugs (ḥanbal) in gaudy and evanescent shades
of colour are sold, and are much appreciated.

Superb gardens, rich olive-groves and flourishing
orchards of mulberry trees, oranges and pome-

granates, extend as far as the scarp out of w[ ]
gush six abundant and pure springs of water.
the midst of this oasis is the zāwiya of Sīdī Aḥ[ ]
b. Ḳāsim, whose minaret is attributed to the g[ ]
Almoravid Yūsuf b. Tashfīn (it is more prob[ ]
that it was the work of his grandson Tashfīn, [ ]
passed through Benī Mellāl before going on to
in Orania). The town has now become a centre
tourist excursions into the mountains, and
promise of a great future.

Bibliography: al-Bakrī, ed. and tr. de Sl[ ]
Description de l'Afrique Septentrionale, Alg[ ]
1913, index; H. Terrasse, Histoire du Ma[ ]
Casablanca 1949, index; P. Ricard, Guide B[ ]
Maroc[7], 1950, index; J. Pourtauborde, L'offic[ ]
l'irrigation aux Beni Amir-Beni Moussa, in E[ ]
clopédie d'Outre-Mer, Paris (June 1954), docum[ ]
No. 28; H. Awad, Djughrāfiyyat al-mudun
maghribiyya, Rabat 1964, index.
                                        (G. DEVERDUN

BESTIARY [see ḤAYAWĀN].

THE BEYOND [see ĀKHIRA].

AL-BIBLĀWĪ, ʿALĪ B. MUḤAMMAD, 26th sha[ ]
of al-Azhar. He was born in the village of Bib[ ]
near Dayrūṭ in Upper Egypt in Radjab 12[ ]
November 1835. After a period of study and tea[ ]
ing at al-Azhar [q.v.], he was employed at the Kh[ ]
vial Library and became its Director (nāẓir) fc[ ]
short period in 1881 and 1882. In the wake of
ʿUrābī insurrection in 1882, he was removed fr[ ]
this office, to which he had been appointed tha[ ]
to the help of his friend Maḥmūd Sāmī al-Bār[ ]
[q.v.], one of the insurrection's principal protagon[ ]
Subsequently he held the office of khaṭīb, and fr[ ]
2 Ṣafar 1311/14 August 1893 onwards the office
shaykh khidma of the Ḥusayn mosque in Ca[ ]
In addition to the latter office he was appoin[ ]
naḳīb al-ashrāf [q.v.] on 6 Shawwāl 1312/1 April 18
following the abdication of the former naḳīb, Muḥa[ ]
mad Tawfīḳ al-Bakrī [q.v.]. During his term [ ]
office, which was to last until the end of 1[3]
March 1902, a set of regulations was promulga[ ]
the so-called lā'iḥat niḳābat al-ashrāf (cf. al-Waḳ[ ]
al-Miṣriyya, 17 June 1895, no. 67), which m[ ]
the incumbent to this office virtually an offi[ ]
within the Ministry of Waḳfs and a subordinate
its nāẓir. His appointment as shaykh of al-Azhar
2 Dhu 'l-Ḥidjdja 1320/1 March 1903 in succession
Salīm al-Bishrī, who had been deposed because
his efforts to frustrate implementation of the
forms provided for in the law of 20 Muḥarram 1[3]
1 July 1896, was the result of a compromise betw[ ]
the Khedive and his ministers, who had origina[ ]
favoured other candidates. Only two years la[ ]
on 9 Muḥarram 1323/15 March 1905, he found him[ ]
compelled to resign when his inability to deal w[ ]
the obstruction of his efforts to implement refo[ ]
had reduced his authority to a unacceptably [ ]
level. He died shortly afterwards on 30 Decem[ ]
1905.

Bibliography: Biographies may be found[ ]
Aḥmad Taymūr, Tarādjim aʿyān al-ḳarn
thālith ʿashar wa-awā'il al-rābiʿ ʿashar, Cairo 19[ ]
81-5; and Maḥmūd b. ʿAlī al-Biblāwī, al-Taʾr[ ]
al-Ḥusaynī, Cairo 1324, 57 ff. The biographies
Khayr al-Dīn al-Ziriklī, al-Aʿlām, v, 171 f., [ ]
by Muḥammad Zakī Mudjāhid, al-Aʿlām
sharḳiyya, Cairo 1950, ii, 140, are mainly ba[ ]
upon Taymūr's. For additional data see ʿAbd
Mutaʿāl al-Ṣaʿīdī, Taʾrīkh al-iṣlāḥ fi 'l-Azhar [ ]
ṣafaḥāt min al-djihād fi 'l-iṣlāḥ, Cairo n.d., 6[7]
and Aḥmad Shafīḳ, Mudhakkirātī fī niṣf ḳa[ ]

airo 1936, ii, part 1, 214; part 2, 65 f.; *Aʿmāl Madjlis Idārat al-Azhar min ibtidāʾ taʾsīsihi sana 312 ilā ghāyat sana 1322*, Cairo 1323/1905-6, 19 ff. gives an overview of the controversies nd disturbances which occurred in al-Azhar uring al-Biblāwī's term of office and the way in hich he dealt with these. His *al-Anwār al-ḥusayiyya ʿalā risālat al-musalsil al-amīriyya*, Cairo 305/1887-8, was a text studied at al-Azhar; cf. l-*Azhar fī 12 ʿām*[an], Cairo n.d. (1965).

(F. DE JONG)

IBLIOMANCY [see ḲURʿA].

IGHĀʾ, the Ḳurʾānic term (XXIV, 33) for stitution. "Prostitute" is rendered by *baghiyy baghāyā*), *mūmis* (pl. *-āt*, *mayāmis/mayāmīs*, *vāmis/mawāmīs*), *ʿāhira* (pl. *ʿawāhir*), *zāniya* (pl. *ānī*). etc.; a more vulgar term, although we e here a euphemism, is *ḳaḥba* (pl. *ḳiḥāb*), which lexicographers attach to the verb *ḳaḥaba* "to gh", explaining that professional prostitutes d to cough in order to attract clients.

lthough M. Gaudefroy-Demombynes (*Mahomet*², is 1969, 48) saw in the legend of Isāf and ila [*q.v.*] the "reminiscence of sacred prostitu-", no such custom seems to have existed amongst pagan Arabs; T. Fahd considers moreover t the legend in question is edifying in its aim "has as its intention putting pilgrims on guard inst sacred prostitution as it was practised in Syrian temples". However, it is quite possible t vestiges of pagan ceremonies continued sporady in islamised regions, in particular, amongst ain Berber tribes.

n any case, pre-Islamic Arabia certainly was iliar with the world's oldest profession which , at least in the larger centres of population, ied on by free women, spinsters, widows or orced women, reduced by misery to trafficking heir own bodies, but mainly by slaves "working" their masters. These women were recognisable, elsewhere, by the banners which they flew at doors of their dwellings; they accepted all ers as clients; if they produced a child, the er was entrusted to the official responsibility the man whom the physiognomists (*ḳāfa* [see ĀFA]) designated as the father, the latter not ing the right to refuse. These items of informa- are given, on the authority of ʿĀʾisha, by al-khārī (*Ṣaḥīḥ*, *K. al-Nikāḥ*, *bāb* 36, vii, 19-20; tr. Houdas, *Les traditions islamiques*, iii, 565-6), mentions the preceding usages as one of the e forms of *nikāḥ* forbidden by the Prophet, the others being the *istibḍāʿ* and a kind of polyry. *Istibḍāʿ* consisted of a man who feared that himself could not sire a robust offspring placing wife in the hands of a better progenitor. In the *āḥ al-raḥt*, the woman in question takes a group husbands (less than ten) and, if she has a child, ibutes the paternity to one of this group, who nable to refuse it. Al-Bukhārī does not in this sage cite temporary marriage, *mutʿa* [*q.v.*], which likewise prohibited. In his *K. al-Bukhalāʾ* (ed. djirī, 112, tr. Pellat, 179), al-Djāḥiẓ uses the ression *zawdj nahārī* "husband by day", the se of which is hard to determine, but may allude a very fleeting type of temporary marriage.

form of more or less disguised prostitution was ays the fate of the lower level of singing girls ḲAYNA] attached to haunts of pleasure and erns (it should be noted that the modern Arabic n for "brothel", *mākhūr*, comes from Persian y-*khūr* "wine-drinker"). It was indeed a tavern-keeper (*khammār*) who is said to have procured for Abū Sufyān the woman who was to give birth to Ziyād b. Abīhi; the traditions concerning the recognition of the latter's collateral affiliation (*istilḥāḳ*) by Muʿāwiya reveal the existence in al-Ṭāʾif of a quarter of the courtesans (*ḥārat al-baghāyā*) inhabited in particular by slave girls belonging to the famous "physician of the Arabs", al-Ḥārith b. Kalada [*q.v.* below], to whom they had to pay a tax (see e.g. al-Masʿūdī, *Murūdj*, v, 21 ff. = §§ 1778 ff.), as was the usual practice for slaves working on their own account or employed by third parties. The Medinan ʿAbd Allāh b. Ubayy [*q.v.*] is also said to have practised this same form of exploitation, this being allegedly the origin (see the Ḳurʾān commentaries on xxiv, 33; al-Ṭabarī, *Tafsīr*, xviii, 132-4, al-Ḳurṭubī, *Tafsīr*, xii, 254-5, etc.) of the verse condemning this practice: "And do not constrain your maidservants (*fatayāt*) to prostitution (*bighāʾ*), if they wish to live in reputable marriage (*taḥaṣṣun*), in order that you may seek the chance gains of this present life; if anyone compels them thus [he will bear the sole responsibility for it], for God, who is merciful and compassionate, will pardon them after compulsion has been laid upon them". Thus the Ḳurʾān does not expressly condemn prostitution, and is content to forbid any woman being compelled to practise it.

For his part, the Prophet must certainly have spoken about the prostitutes, examples of whom he must have seen in Mecca and Medina (see Wensinck, *Concordances*, s.v. *baghiyy*, i, 204), but the most significant *ḥadīth* seems to be the one in which he forbids payment for the services (if the word *mahr* is correctly interpreted here) of the prostitute and the gains (*kasb*) from prostitution (al-Bukhārī, *Ṣaḥīḥ*, *K. al-Ṭalāḳ*, *bāb* 51; tr. Houdas, iii, 642). It was a roundabout way of prohibiting what was considered as a dishonourable activity, but one in the end adjudged by posterity as a necessary evil.

In practice, despite pious persons who inveighed from time to time against an institution which was regarded as incompatible with Muslim ethics, prostitution has always flourished in Muslim lands, keeping itself, under necessity, discreet, as in Fās, where at certain periods the police authorities suppressed it severely, shaving the heads of women thus misbehaving, parading them through the streets of the town and then expelling them, and insisting on their being buried in a special part of the cemetery (R. Le Tourneau, *Fès avant le Protectorat*, Casablanca 1949, 580). This seems to have been a special case, and the severity does not always seem to have been completely successful. Although travellers and historians are sparing of details, there are pieces of information testifying to the existence of more or less free-lance prostitutes as well as the existence of brothels in the various Islamic cities. Thus al-Muḳaddasī (*Aḥsan al-taḳāsīm*, 407) saw a brothel at Sūs, near the mosque, whilst Leo Africanus speaks of taverns at Fās with whores residing in them (tr. Épaulard, 191) and prostitution at Tunis (385). According to al-Ḳifṭī (*Ḥukamāʾ*, ed. Lippert, 298), the *muḥtasib* of Latakia put up for auction the favours of the public women and issued to the successful bidders a ring which they had to show if they were met at night with one of the women.

Indeed, at all times prostitution was not merely tolerated but even recognised officially and very often was subject to a tax payable to the public treasury. At Fās, the headman of the quarter had the task of supervising the courtesans and of preventing disorders, but in general, it was the *muḥtasib* who fulfilled this function (see P. Chalmeta, *El "señor del zoco" en Espana*, Madrid 1973, index, s.v. prostitutas). However, the manuals of *ḥisba* do not mention the existence of a precise regulatory scheme, and Ibn ʿAbdūn, for instance, is content to forbid the denizens of places of public resort to show themselves bareheaded outside the house (E. Lévi-Provençal, *Trois traités hispaniques de ḥisba*, Cairo 1955; idem, *Séville musulmane*, Paris 1947, § 168). In al-Andalus, the tax imposed on them was curiously called *kharādj* ("land tax" [*q.v.*]) and the brothels called *dār al-kharādj* (or *dār al-banāt*), whilst the prostitutes themselves were called *kharādjiyyāt* (Ibn Bassām, *Dhakhīra*, i/1, 207, where the text should be corrected) or even *kharādjayrāt* (Lévi-Provençal, *Hist. Esp. Mus.*, iii, 445-6). It is further known that ʿAḍud al-Dawla [*q.v.*] imposed a tax on the whores of Fārs (al-Muḳaddasī, 441) and that the Fāṭimids did likewise in Egypt (al-Maḳrīzī, *Khiṭaṭ*, i, 89).

As in many other lands, various categories of women might be distinguished. At the bottom of the scale were the somewhat wretched women who hired rooms in caravanserais by the town gates or near the centre, and in addition to the rent, paid a due to the keeper of the caravanserai; but there were also procurers who brought them clients, mainly strangers visiting the town; peasants, seasonal workers, soldiers, etc. Some of these women certainly sank to the level of the rogues and vagabonds whose various activities have been described by C. E. Bosworth in his *The mediaeval Islamic underworld* (Leiden 1976, 2 vols.). At a higher level, brothels proper catered for a more affluent clientele. As in pre-Islamic al-Ṭāʾif, special quarters were reserved for prostitution, which the authorities were thereby more easily able to control. This system has remained down to our own time, and a visit to these localities, which are sometimes picturesque, may even be recommended to tourists, male and female, by guides and travel agents; this is especially the case in regard to Bousbir (< Prosper) at Casablanca and the street of "dancing girls" of the Ouled Naïl at Bou Saada (Algeria).

The practice of early marriage among the Muslims, who can take four legitimate wives and as many concubines as they can afford to keep, ought in the natural course of things to have set bounds to venal love-making. However, many young men from the modest levels of society were unable to find their sexual initiation otherwise than by recourse to prostitutes, and legal marriage entailed financial burdens which men from the masses of people were not always in a position to undertake, especially if they had to migrate away from their original home. Furthermore, the Ḳurʾānic prohibition could always be easily circumvented by procurers and procuresses lured on by the prospect of gain, whilst the easy facilities for husbands in regard to the repudiation of their wives [see ṬALĀḲ] threw on to the streets women who did not always have the possibility of returning to their families.

Bibliography: There does not seem to have been produced any monograph on prostitution in mediaeval Islam. In the list of writings of Abu 'l-ʿAnbas al-Ṣaymarī [*q.v.* above] a *K. Nawādir al-ḳuwwād* (?) and a *K. al-Rāḥa wa-manāfiʿ al-ḳiyāda*, which may possibly have dealt with pimps, are to be found, but these have not survived. In addition to sources cited in the article, see A. Mez, *Renaissance*, Eng. tr. 361-4; A. Mazahéri, *La vie quotidienne des Musulmans au mo[yen] âge*, Paris 1947, 64-5; R. Le Tourneau, *Fès a[vant] le Protectorat*, Casablanca 1949, 557-9 and ind[ex]; al-Markaz al-ḳawmī li 'l-buḥūth al-idjtimāʿiy[ya], *al-Bighāʾ fi 'l-Ḳāhira*, Cairo 1961; a fairly w[ell] developed study by a sociologist is that of [A.] Bouhdiba, *La sexualité en Islam*, Paris 19[75], 228-39 and the bibl. cited there. On male p[ros]titution, see LIWĀṬ. (ED.)

BIHBIHĀNĪ, ĀḲĀ SAYYID MUḤAMMAD BĀḲ[IR], Shīʿī *mudjtahid* and proponent of the Uṣūlī [*q.v.*] *madhhab*, often entitled Waḥīd-i Bihbihānī or Muḥ[aḳ]ḳiḳ-i Bihbihānī, and commonly regarded by Shīʿī contemporaries as the "renewer" (*mudjadd[id]*) of the 12th Hidjrī century. He was born in Iṣfa[hān] some time between the years 1116/1704-5 and 11[18]/1706-7. After a brief period spent in Bihbihān, [he] was taken to Karbalāʾ by his father, Mullā Muḥa[m]mad Akmal, whose principal student he beca[me] while studying also under Sayyid Ṣadr al-[Dīn] Ḳummī. Mullā Muḥammad Akmal had stud[ied] under Mullā Muḥammad Bāḳir Madjlisī, the gr[eat] divine who had dominated Iranian Shīʿism in [the] late 11th/17th century, and had also married [his] niece. The young Bihbihānī, who came to exercis[e a] similar dominant role at the end of the 12th/1[8th] century, was thus both spiritually and genealogica[lly] related to Madjlisī. It is related that after complet[ing] his studies in Karbalāʾ, Bihbihānī intended to le[ave] the city, but was dissuaded from doing so by [the] appearance of the *Imām* Ḥusayn to him in a drea[m] instructing him to stay (Muḥammad Bāḳir Khʷā[n]sārī, *Rawḍāt al-djannāt fī aḥwāl al-ʿulamāʾ wa 'l-sād[āt]*, Tehran 1304/1887, 122). In obedience to the drea[m] he stayed on, and engaged in fierce controversy w[ith] adherents of the Akhbārī school of *fiḳh*, which [at] that time was predominant in Karbalāʾ as well [as] the other *ʿatabāt* [see AKHBĀRIYYA above]. T[he] controversy between the Akhbārīs and the Uṣū[līs], centering on various questions of *uṣūl al-fiḳh* a[nd] particularly on the permissibility of *idjtihād*, was [an] ancient one, but had become particularly acute [in] the late Ṣafawid period and the middle part of [the] 12th/18th century. Before the appearance of Bih[bi]hānī, the Akhbārīs were so assured in their do[mi]nance of the *ʿatabāt* that anyone carrying with h[im] books of Uṣūlī *fiḳh* was obliged to cover them for fear of provoking attack. By the end of his li[fe], however, Bihbihānī had been able almost complet[ely] to uproot Akhbārī influence from the *ʿatabāt* and [to] establish the Uṣūlī position as normative for all the Twelver Shīʿa. He accomplished this cha[nge] partly by debate, polemic and the composition [of] written refutations of the Akhbārī school, the m[ost] important of which was *Kitāb al-idjtihād wa 'l-akhb[ār]*. Hardly less effective was the demonstration of [the] prerogatives of *mudjtahid* that he provided. One [of] his pupils, Shaykh Djaʿfar Nadjafī (d. 1227/181[2]) records that he was constantly accompanied by [a] number of armed men who would immediat[ely] execute any judgement that he passed. The exam[ple] that he thus gave was to be followed by numer[ous] Iranian *ʿulamāʾ* of the Ḳādjār period. Anot[her] target of Bihbihānī's hostility was the Niʿmatall[āhī] Ṣūfī order; such was the enmity that he nurtu[red] for them that he gained the title of *ṣūfīkush* (Ṣū[fī]-killer). He died in 1206/1791-2 or 1208/1793-4, a[nd] was buried near the tomb of the *Imām* Ḥusayn [in] Karbalāʾ. Bihbihānī is credited with more th[an] sixty works; the titles of twenty of them are list[ed] in Muḥammad ʿAlī Mudarris, *Rayḥānat al-ad[ab]*, new ed., Tabriz n.d., i, 52, and a further fourte[en] s are preserved in autograph in the library of ›ihānī's descendants in Kirmān͟shāh (see Muḥsin mīn, *Aʿyān al-s͟hīʿa*, Beirut 1378/1959, xliv, 96). s said that his writings on *uṣūl al-fiḳh* were piled into a single work by one of his pupils, yid Mahdī Ḳazwīnī. The number of his pupils very large; among the most influential we may tion his sons, Āḳā Muḥammad ʿAlī, who settled Kirmān͟shāh and inherited his father's violent ed of the Ṣūfīs, and Āḳā ʿAbd al-Ḥusayn; ykh Dj̲aʿfar Nad̲jafī, author of a number of ortant works on Uṣūlī *fiḳh*; and three *mud̲jtahids* dominated the life of Iṣfahān in the first quarter he 19th century—Ḥād̲jd̲j Muḥammad Ibrāhīm bāsī, Sayyid Muḥammad Bāḳir S̲haftī, and yid Mahdī Baḥr al-ʿUlūm. But his influence nded far beyond the generation of *mud̲jtahids* trained; through his theoretical vindication of Uṣūlī position and his practical demonstration he function of *mud̲jtahid*, he was in effect the stor of all those *mud̲jtahids* who have sought e his time to assert a guiding role in Iranian ety.

Bibliography: Muḥammad b. Sulaymān Tunu-ābunī, *Ḳiṣaṣ al-ʿulamāʾ*, Tehran 1304/1887, 147-8; uḥammad Bāḳir K̲h^w^ānsārī, *Rawḍāt al-d̲jannāt* 23; ʿAbbās b. Muḥammad Riḍā Ḳummī, *Hadiyat -aḥbāb*, Nad̲jaf 1349/1930, 100; Mīrzā Muḥammad Alī Mudarris, *Rayḥānat al-adab*, i, 51-2; Muḥam-ad ʿAlī Bīdābādī, *Makārim al-āt̲h̲ār dar aḥwāl-i d̲jāl-i dawra-yi ḳād̲jār*, Iṣfahān 1337/1958, i, 20-5; Muḥsin al-Amīn, *Aʿyān al-s͟hīʿa*, xliv, 94-6; uḥammad Ḥirz al-Dīn, *Maʿārif al-rid̲jāl fī rād̲jim al-ʿulamāʾ wa 'l-udabāʾ*, Nad̲jaf 1384/ 964, i, 121-3; H. Algar, *Religion and state in Iran, 785-1906: the role of the Ulama in the Qajar period*, erkeley & Los Angeles 1969, 34-6; ʿAlī Dawwānī, *stād-i kull Āḳā Muḥammad Bāḳir Bihbihānī b. uḥammad Akmal maʿrūf ba Waḥīd-i Bihbihānī*, umm n.d.; H. Algar, *Religious forces in the ghteenth and nineteenth centuries*, in *Cambridge istory of Iran*, vii, ch. xiv (forthcoming).

(H. Algar)

BIHRANGĪ, Ṣamad, Persian prosewriter 39-68). Bihrangī's birth in a lower-class, Turkish-aking family in Tabrīz and his eleven-years' em-yment as a primary schoolteacher in rural arbāyd̲jān are attested in the greater part of *fārsī* writings. These, both fictional and non-ional, largely deal with village life in his native vince and with the specific problems of a cultural ority region. His concern for the plight of Ād̲h̲ar-d̲jānī peasant youth prompted a series of educa-al essays, as well as some twenty children's ies, the chief foundation of his present fame. able for their "ideological" content rather than strictly literary merits, Bihrangī's children's ies no longer recommend the conventional virtues obedience, cleanliness and modesty, but aim at arting "a correct view of the dark, bitter realities adult society". Accordingly, his stories picture needy, powerless village children, their search freedom and their revolt against ignorant parents, l landlords or urban aristocracy. The political mitment felt in most of these stories contributed Bihrangī's considerable popularity among the ident intelligentsia; at the same time, it gave to an increasingly restrictive censorship of his tings by the Iranian authorities and to a vast ve of rumours at his sudden death in September 8, reportedly a drowning accident. More explicit ws on society and literature are present in Bihrangī's essays, notably the insistence on straightforward, firmly committed writing and contempt for the "defeatist pseudo-intellectualism" of westernised Tehran. The tenets of his educational criticism are roughly similar to those earlier voiced by the author Āl-i Aḥmad [*q.v.* above], both a schoolteacher and a writer like himself; rejecting the unquestioned adoption of American teaching methods and finding the current textbooks inapplicable in a classroom with Azeri Turkish-speaking pupils, Bihrangī designed an alternative "textbook for village children": the completed but yet unpublished *Alif-bā barā-yi kūdakān-i rūstāʾī*.

Bibliography: The greater part of Bihrangī's writings first appeared in newspapers and periodicals under various pseudonyms, such as Ṣād, Ḳārānḳūs̲h̲, Bihrang, Bābak, etc. Thirteen of his children's stories were posthumously collected in *Mad̲jmūʿa-yi ḳiṣṣahā*, Tabrīz 1348 s̲h̲., which also contains a chapter on *Adabiyyāt-i kūdakān* (originally published as part of a review-article in *Rahnamā-yi Kitāb* xi (1347-53 sh.), 48-5), outlining the author's conception of children's literature. Not included in this volume are his most successful story, the internationally awarded *Māhī-yi siyāh-i kūčulū*, separately published in Tehran 1347 s̲h̲., and the collection *Talk̲h̲ūn wa čand ḳiṣṣa-i dīgar*, Tehran 1349 s̲h̲. A number of his educational essays appeared as *Kand-u-kāw dar masāʾil-i tarbiyatī-yi Īrān*, Tabriz 1344 s̲h̲.[2], while other articles on various subjects were posthumously edited as *Mad̲jmūʿa-yi maḳālahā*, Tabrīz 1348 s̲h̲.; this collection contains several chapters on Ād̲h̲arbāyd̲jānī culture and language, including the four articles listed in Afs̲h̲ār's *Index iranicus* ii, Tehran 1348 s̲h̲., 84, 415. An anthology of translated folktales was separately edited in collaboration with B. Dihḳānī: *Afsānahā-yi Ād̲h̲arbāyd̲jān*, i: Tabrīz 1344 s̲h̲., ii: Tehran 1347 s̲h̲. Finally, Bihrangī prepared some Persian translations from modern Turkish poetry and prose.

A valuable secondary source is the special Bihrangī issue of *Āras̲h̲*, ii/5 (Ād̲h̲ar 1347 s̲h̲.); for additional information, cf. ʿA. A. Darwīs̲h̲iyān's short monograph *Ṣamad d̲jāwidāna s̲h̲ud*, Tehran 1352 s̲h̲.[2] and G. R. Sabri-Tabrizi, *Human values . . .*, in *Correspondance d'Orient*, xi (1970), 411-8. Bihrangī's political role as a "totally involved revolutionary artist" is stressed by Th. Ricks in *The little black fish and other modern stories*, Washington, D.C. 1976, 95-126; his folklore studies are passingly mentioned by L. P. Elwell-Sutton in *Iran and Islam, in memory of the late Vladimir Minorsky*, Edinburgh 1971, 253-4. Of the children's stories, a German translation has appeared in B. Nirumand ed., *Feuer unterm Pfauenthron*, Berlin 1974, 19-35; English translations include two different renderings of *Māhī-yi siyāh . . .* in *The Literary Review*, xviii/1 (Rutherford, N.J. 1974), 69-84, and in *The little black fish. . .*, *op. cit.*, 1-19. For other translated stories, cf. M. C. Hillmann, ed., *Major voices in contemporary Persian literature*, and M. A. Jazayeri, ed., *Literature East and West*.

(G. J. J. de Vries)

BINN, a term of the Druze religion. In this, the Binn were conceived of as one of a number of earlier races or sects whose names are also mentioned in the Druze writings, such as the Rimm and the Ṭimm. The Binn were said to have been a group of inhabitants of Had̲jar in the Yemen who believed in the message of S̲h̲aṭnīl, the incarnation of Ḥamza in the Age of Adam. According to the Druzes, the city was originally called Ṣurna (meaning "Miracle" according to Ḥamza), and S͟haṭnīl came there from India. He called on the people to renounce polytheism and worship al-Ḥākim bi-Amr Allāh [*q.v.*] as their sole deity. Those who accepted his message he commanded to "be separate" (*yabīnūn*) from the polytheists; as a consequence they were known as al-Binn. This etymology is clearly unsatisfactory, and it is possible that a Persian origin should be sought for this term.

One of the Druze *dāʿīs*, al-Ḥārit͟h b. Tirmāḥ of Iṣfahān refused to obey S͟haṭnīl, and was expelled from the number of the *dāʿīs*, being dubbed "Iblīs". He became the *imām* of the polytheists in Ṣurna (the *d͟jinn* in the Druze account). When one of the Binn met another, he would say: "Flee from (*uhd͟jur*) Iblīs and his party!". As a result, Ṣurna acquired the name of Had͟jar.

Bibliography: H. Guys, *Théogonie des Druses*, Paris 1863, 35 and n. 70, 104; C. F. Seybold, *Die Drusenschrift*: *Kitāb Alnoqaṭ waldawāir. Das Buch der Punkte und Kreise*, Kirchhain 1902, 71; Muḥammad Kāmil Ḥusayn, *Ṭāʾifat al-Durūz*, Cairo 1962, 116; D. R. W. Bryer, *The Origins of the Druze Religion*, in *Isl.*, liii (1976), 8.

(R. Y. Ebied and M. J. L. Young)

BISĀṬ (a.), pls. *busṭ*/*busuṭ*, *absiṭa*, which implies the general meaning of extensiveness (thus in Ḳurʾān, LXXI, 18), is a generic term for carpet, more specifically, one of fairly large dimensions. Any kind of carpet with a pile is called a *ṭinfisa*; if it is decorated with multicoloured bands, a *zarbiyya* (*zirbiyya*, *zurbiyya*, pl. *zarābī*; cf. Ḳurʾān, LXXXVIII, 16); if it is decorated with a relief design, a *maḥfūra*; whilst a prayer carpet is called a *sad͟jd͟jāda* (modern Turkish *seccade*), and the collective *sad͟jd͟jād* is sometimes used as a generic term (on the numerous Arabic terms, see W. H. Worrell, *On certain Arabic terms for "rug"*, in *Ars Islamica*, i (1934), 219-22, ii (1935), 65-8). The word *kilīm*, applied to a woollen rug generally long and narrow in shape, is often taken to be of Turkish origin (see e.g. Lokotsch, No. 1176), but seems rather to be Iranian (Persian *gilīm*). Sumak, not far from Bakū, and the districts of Verne and Sile in the southern Caucasus, have given their name to a type of flatwoven carpets. The etymology of *ḳālī* (vars. *g͟hālī*, *k͟hālī*, modern Turkish *hali*) is unclear; Yāḳūt, *Buldān*, iv, 20, remarks that the carpets (*busuṭ*) called *ḳālī* are manufactured at Ḳālīḳalā (= Erzerum [*q.v.*]), but since this word was difficult to pronounce, the *nisba* has been shortened. Although this particular term is generally considered to be Turkish in origin, it is unattested in ancient Turkish texts; it is, however, used by Gardīzī [*q.v.*] and may therefore be of Iranian origin (detailed study in Doerfer, No. 1405). (Ed.)

i. Carpets of the central and eastern Islamic lands

1. Technique

For the manufacture of oriental carpets, sheep's wool, cotton, silk, goat-hair and camel-hair are used, which are prepared, spun and partly wound. The foundation consists of warp-threads (Fr.: *chaîne*, Ger.: *Kette*) stretched the length of the loom, and weft-threads (Fr.: *trame*, Ger.: *Schüsse*) run in horizontally. For knotted carpets which form the bulk of the products, one or several weft rows are inserted between knot rows, the latter forming the pile. In Turkey, the Caucasus and the regions of northwestern Persia inhabited by the Kurds, Turkish or Gördes knot (so called after the Tur town of Gördes [*q.v.*]), has been commonly u But whilst the Persian or Senneh-knot (so-ca after the Persian town of Senneh, today ca Sanandad͟j [*q.v.*]) is commonly associated with Pe India and Turkestan, the Gördes knot is also fc in Persian rugs and the commonly-accepted graphical demarcation must be treated with res (for diagrams of these two knots see *İA*, v/1, Kilims, and Sumak, Verne and Sile rugs are woven, with no pile. Until aniline and chror dyes were introduced in the eighties of the century, only natural dyes were used (see C. F Tattersall, *Notes on carpet-knotting and weav* Victoria and Albert Museum, 1961; A. N. Land and W. R. Pickering, *From the Bosporus to Sa kand, flat-woven rugs*, The Textile Muse Washington 1969).

2. History

a. Early Stages

The oldest known knotted carpet was discov in 1949 in the tomb of a local prince in Pazy in the Altai Mountains. By means of other find the tomb, it may be dated to the 4th century There are as yet no indications as to the place o manufacture, but the suggestion of its manufac in Achaemenid Persia has been put forward. technique (3,600 Turkish knots to the square d metre) and its design, in Achaemenid style, are remarkable perfection; it is one of, and the m important of, the three extant pieces of evid for a highly-developed art of knotting of this e date. It shows in a developed form the composi of a central field surrounded by borders, wh consist of a wide main border and several subsid or guard borders, characteristic of all orie carpets.

Very small fragments of carpets, conjectur dated between the 3rd and 6th centuries A were discovered by Sir Aurel Stein during his Tur expeditions (at Lop Nor). These, however, are knotted carpets but napped fabrics, in which pile is produced by the wefts, introduced first loops and later split (see A. Stein, *Ruins of de Cathay*, London 1912, 380, plate 116, 4). The "Spa knot", on the other hand, always tied aroun single warp, is used in a fragment discovered Le Coq in Kucha during the fourth Turfan exp tion, the earliest possible date of which is the 5th- century (see F. Sarre, *Ein frühes Knüpftepp Fragment aus chinesisch-Turkestan*, in *Berliner Mus* (1920-1), 110). The piece is too small and the des too faint to permit any conclusions about the car of this period. The many small fragments of knot carpets from Fusṭāṭ can hardly be dated (see M Dimand, *An early cutpile rug from Egypt*, in *Me politan Museum Studies*, iv (1933), 151 ff.; S. Rudenko, *The world's oldest knotted carpets fabrics*, Moscow 1968 (in Russian); R. B. Serjea *Material for a history of Islamic textiles up to Mongol conquest*, in *Ars Islamica*, ix (1942), 54 xv-xvi (1951), 29).

b. Turkey

Konya carpets.

The development of oriental knotted carpets be traced to a certain extent only from the 7th/1 century onwards. The oldest coherent group co from Anatolia. In 1907 F. R. Martin discove three large and several small fragments in

ʾ al-Dīn mosque at Konya, to which were n the generic name "Konya carpets". Shortly rwards, smaller fragments of the same type e found in the Eşrefoğlu mosque at Beyşehir. date of the enlargement of the ʿAlāʾ al-Dīn que, 1218-20, provides a date *post quem* for se carpets, but they do not necessarily belong he 7th/13th century. Their designs and technical ution are simple and the knots are not very e. Where they survive, the borders with their vy Kūfic character or large stars predominate r the inner motifs, which have small, all-over, at patterns. See F. R. Martin, *A history of ntal carpets before 1800*, i, 113, ii, plate xxx; Erdmann, *Siebenhundert Jahre Orientteppich*, ford 1966, 117; R. M. Riefstahl, *Primitive rugs he "Konya" type in the mosque of Beyshehir*, in *Art Bulletin*, xiii/2 (1931), 16 ff.; E. Kühnel, *mic art and architecture*, London 1966, 94 and 37b; and Pl. I.

natolian animal carpets.

he styles of Anatolian carpets of the 8th/14th 9th/15th centuries are attested by reproductions talian paintings of the period. They are charac- sed by a series of square or octagonal motifs d with stylised animals. The best known frag- t of such a carpet, which is in the Islamic Museum Berlin, shows on a yellow ground two octagons, in squares, in which are found a dragon and a enix, the pair borrowed from Chinese mythology ihnel, *Islamic art*..., 109-10 and pl. 42b). A fresco Domenico di Bartolo, dated between 1440 and 4, shows a carpet with a corresponding motif ated in an almost similar way. Another carpet n a church in Marby, preserved in the Statens toriska Museet in Stockholm, is closely connected design, technique and colouring with the Berlin gment. See C. J. Lamm, *The Marby rug and some gments of carpets found in Egypt*, in *Svenska entsållskapets Årsbok*, 1937, 51 ff.; K. Erdmann, *Türkische Teppich des 15. Jahrhunderts*, Istanbul [1957]; R. Ettinghausen, *New light on early mal carpets*, in *Aus der Welt der islamischen nst, Festschrift E. Kühnel*, Berlin 1959, 93; and II.

"Holbein" and "Lotto" carpets.

On the portrait of the merchant Gisze, painted by ns Holbein the Younger in 1532 and kept in the ture Gallery of the Staatlichen Museen, Berlin, be seen a carpet that serves as table-cloth. It resents a further group of Anatolian carpets ich appear frequently on paintings from the ddle of the 15th century until the end of the h century; these are characterised as "small- tterned Holbein carpets", and a fair number of m have survived. Their design, too, is based on ares with inset octagons in vertical and hori- tal rows. The octagons are formed by bands otted several times and the corners of the squares filled by stylised arabesque leaves, which, joined ether, merge into diamond-shaped linking motifs. riety of colours within the squares of some speci- ns produces a kind of chessboard effect. In the ails, these carpets correspond with the so-called ge-partitioned Holbein-carpets, the pattern of ich is limited to a few broad, clearly separated tifs which are ranged only lengthwise. The decora- n of the borders is mostly based on Kūfic charac- s. In the earlier designs the vertical strokes which ve been directed to the edging of the carpet are clearly recognisable. Later on they develop into a twined band without definite orientation. Red, with brownish shades, blue, yellow, white and green are dominant. The large-partitioned Holbein-carpets are believed to have been made in Bergama, the small partitioned ones in Uşak. See Pls. III, IV.

The fourth type of early Ottoman carpets is also localised in Uşak. These are the so-called Lotto-carpets, because they appear among others, on the paintings by the Italian painter Lorenzo Lotto. They are also called "carpets with arabesque ten-drils", since all specimens of this group show a red foundation covered with a yellow net of tendrils, arabesque leaves and palmettes. As is the case with the small patterned Holbein-carpets, their arrange-ment is basically determined by a system of octagons set in squares, while the fillings of the spandrels form also diamond-shaped figures. More often than the Kūfic-borders, those of the Lotto-carpets are made up of undulating tendrils, multifoiled lozenges and later on, alternating cloud bands. See Pl. V.

Medallion and Star Uşaks.

In the 11th/17th century the early Ottoman pat-terns are replaced by Persian-influenced arrange-ments of motifs which characterise the Medallion and Star-Uşaks. The centre of the Medallion-Uşaks is usually marked by a pointed oval-shaped medallion with a flamboyant outline and a floral inner-design. Lengthwise on both sides shield-shaped pendants are attached to the medallion. In the corners of the field quadrants of a differently shaped medallion appear. The composition can be understood as being a part of a system of staggered rows of medallions. Examples showing greater parts of the pattern prove this. The usually red ground colour between the medallions is traversed with entangled, angularly drawn tendrils. The Star-Uşak, with staggered star-shaped medal-lions, connected by lozenges, is a variant of the Medallion-Uşak. Both types occur frequently on Dutch 17th century paintings. Like the Lotto-carpets, the Uşaks were manufactured in coarse, misconstrued versions far into the 18th and 19th century (see K. Erdmann, *Weniger bekannte Uschak-Muster*, in *Kunst des Orients*, iv, 79 ff.; and Pls. VI, VII).

"Bird" and "Tschintamani" carpets.

Uşak-carpets with a white ground both in field and border are rare. Two simple patterns can here be distinguished: the "Tschintamani" and the "Bird" motifs. The first, in all-over repeat, consists of two parallel undulating lines and three balls arranged in a triangle over them. This motif is un-doubtedly of Far Eastern origin. From the 15th century onwards it is known as a pattern for clothing in Persian and Turkish miniatures, and from the 16th century it was popular on Turkish textile fabrics. The "Bird"-motif consists of horizontal and vertical running stripes crossing each other, and is composed of rosettes and leaves, the form of which superficially looks like birds. Both patterns have often been copied in the 20th century.

Transylvanian carpets.

An important group of small-sized Anatolian carpets from the 17th to 19th centuries, showing analogy with the Uşak-carpets, are the Transyl-vanian carpets, so-called because they have survived in great number in the churches of Transylvania. Besides some smaller versions of the Lotto-, Bird- and Tschintamani-patterns, they are mainly prayer-rugs, the inner-fields of which are arch-shaped to represent the *miḥrāb*, often in connection with one or more pairs of columns. They form a link with the Turkish prayer rugs of the 18th and 19th centuries from Gördes, Ladik and Milas (see E. Schmutzler, *Altorientalische Teppiche in Siebenbürgen*, Leipzig 1933; J. de Vegh and Ch. Layer, *Tapis turcs provenant des églises et collections de Transylvanie*, Paris 1925; M. Mostafa, *Turkish prayer rugs*, Cairo 1953; Turkish Rugs, *The Washington Hajji Baba*, The Textile Museum, Washington 1968).

c. Egypt

Mamlūk, Ottoman and Chess-board carpets.

Fifteenth-century Mamlūk Egypt saw the origin of clearly recognisable carpets with a kaleidoscopic design, consisting of stars, rectangles and triangles, filled with small leaves, shrubs and cypresses. Their wool is soft and glossy, and the colours normally range between cherry-red, vivid green and bright blue. The many-sided star-like ornaments and the arrangement of the motifs towards the centre show a stylistic connection with the inlaid metal-work, the wood and the leather fabrics and the book-illuminations of the Mamlūk period. Only a few large-sized Mamlūk carpets have survived, among which one with a silk pile counts as one of the most beautiful carpets in the world (Vienna, Museum für Angewandte Kunst). More numerous are small specimens with a medallion that takes up the entire width of the carpet, to the upper side and bottom of which a tightly patterned rectangular field is attached. An essential distinction between the Mamlūk and the Anatolian carpets lies in the fact that the former are characterised by groups of patterns and not by regular repeat patterns from which, within a constant internal relation as far as size is concerned, variable formats can be chosen. In the borders rosettes usually alternate with oblong cartouches. European and Oriental sources mention Cairo as an important centre of the knotting industry at least from 1474 onwards.

After Egypt was conquered by the Ottomans in 1517, the Mamlūk carpets were replaced by carpets manufactured in the Ottoman court-style. Their luxuriant floral decoration presents a sharp contrast to the geometrical patterns of the Mamlūk carpets. The palmettes and rosettes, the feathered lanceolate leaves and the naturalistically treated tulips, pinks and hyacinths are also to be found on the contemporary textiles and on pottery and tiles of Iznik. It would therefore seem obvious to deduce that the carpets also were manufactured in Turkey. However, in their fineness, technique and colour-scheme, they differ completely from the rest of the Anatolian carpets, but match to a considerable extent the Mamlūk carpets. It is therefore plausible that they were manufactured in the Cairene workshops after models made by Ottoman artists. This theory is supported by some hybrid types, *i.e.* Mamlūk carpets with elements of Ottoman carpets, and vice versa. The products of the Cairene workshops were of a special quality, as may be seen from the fact that Murād III in 1585 summoned eleven master carpet-makers together with their materials from Cairo to Istanbul. It is as yet unknown whether they carried out there a special order or established a local weaving-industry. Among the Ottoman carpets are some prayer rugs. Ewliyā Čelebi mentions the use of Egyptian prayer rugs in Anatolia in the middle of the 17th century. See Pls. VIII, IX.

The chess-board carpets hold an intermediate position between the Mamlūk and the Anato[lian] carpets. Their basic motifs are clearly Mamlūk[-like in] character: a star with eight rays on which sm[all] cypresses, blossoms and rosettes are radially direc[ted] stands in a hexagon or octagon which is itself pla[ced] in a square. The way in which this motif is d[ealt] with, the use of various-sized sections of the patt[ern,] the coarse wool, and the weft (which is always r[ed)] point however at Anatolia. The colours are restric[ted] to bright blue, vivid green and red, and thus co[me] near to the Mamlūk carpets. Moreover, these ch[ess-]board carpets have the Persian knot in comm[on] with the Mamlūk and Ottoman carpets. As t[he] place of origin E. Kühnel proposed the area aro[und] Adana in Anatolia; Rhodes and Damascus have a[lso] been suggested. They can be considered to h[ave] originated between the middle of the 10th/16th a[nd] the end of the 11th/17th centuries (see E. Küh[nel] and L. Bellinger, *Cairene rugs and others technica[lly] related, 15th-17th cent.*, Washington 1957; K. E[rd]mann, *Kairener Teppiche*, i, *Europäische und is[la]mische Quellen des 15.-18. Jh.*, in *Ars Islamica*, [v] (1938), 179; idem, *Mamluken- und Osmanenteppic[he]*, in *Ars Islamica*, vii (1940), 55; idem, *Neuere Un[ter]suchungen zur Frage der Kairener Teppiche*, in *A[rs] Orientalis*, iv (1961), 65).

d. Persia

α. Tīmūrid carpets.

The oldest Persian carpets which have be[en] preserved date from the first half of the 10th/16[th] century. They represent culminating points of [the] art of carpet knotting which are inconceiva[ble] without earlier stages. Tīmūrid miniatures of [the] 9th/15th century represent indeed with great [ac]curacy various genres of carpets. Roughly, two ba[sic] types can be distinguished. First a small-patt[ern] group with geometrical design, consisting of repeat[ed] squares, stars and crosses, hexagons, octagons [and] circles. They resemble contemporary tile-patter[ns.] The motifs are framed by bright, small bands wh[ich] interlace into stars or crosses and in between in[to] knots. The central field is monochrome or is divid[ed] in chess-board style with contrasting colours. In t[he] borders a Kūfic-like writing stands out from a da[rk] background. The relation to the small-pattern[ed] Holbein carpets is unmistakable.

This type is replaced by arabesque and flow[er] patterns towards the end of the 9th/15th centu[ry.] The finest specimens are to be found in the miniatu[res] of the painter Bihzād [*q.v.*]. He belonged to t[he] school of Herāt and was in 1522 entrusted with t[he] direction of the library of Shāh Ismāʿīl I in Tabr[īz.] A direct influence on the royal carpet manufactur[e] is thus possible. In this new style with arabesq[ue] patterns, construed lines cross the field—symmetri[c] to both axes—and outline semi-circles, circles, mul[ti]foils, cartouches and ellipses. These forms interse[ct] creating segments which are emphasised by th[eir] colour and by their arabesque tendril decoratio[n.] There are also carpets in which medallions are a[r]ranged over arabesques, and others with a simp[le] decoration of scrolls on a monochrome groun[d.] Instead of the stiff Kūfic borders, elegantly twist[ed] tendrils are used. These general principles and in[]dividual motifs form the bases of the Ṣafawid carp[ets] of the 10th/16th and 11th/17th centuries (see [M.] Briggs, *Timurid carpets*, in *Ars Islamica*, vii, [1] and xi-xii, 146).

β. Ṣafawid carpets.

Dating. Four carpets with a date inserted and so[me]

.ments provide the basis for dating the carpets h were manufactured in the 10th/16th and /17th centuries under the Ṣafawids: (1) the et with the hunting scene, designed by Ghiyāth in Djāmī and now in the Museo Poldi Pezzoli, n, with the date 929/1522, occasionally also 949/1542; (2) the famous Ardabīl carpet by ṣūd Kāshānī, dated 946/1539-40, manufactured ther with one or even two others for the tomb que of Shaykh Ṣafī; then, after a gap of more 100 years, (3) a "vase" carpet in the museum arajevo, 1067/1656, by Ustādh Muʾmin b. Ḳuṭb in Māhānī; and finally (4) a silk carpet by nat Allāh Djawshakānī, dated 1082/1671, from mausoleum of Shāh ʿAbbās II in Ḳum. Other riptions are of a literary character.

group of silk carpets with larger fields, executed gold and silver threads, the so-called "Polish"-ets, represent the style prevalent around 1600 and ie first half of the 17th century (Pl. XV). With the of documentary evidence they can be dated as ws. In 1601 the Polish king Sigismund Vasa III red such a carpet in Kāshān. In 1603 and 1621 h ʿAbbās I had five specimens sent as gifts ac-panying an embassy to the Signoria of Venice. des, contemporary reports of European travellers ain many references to these carpets. European tings, which contribute to the dating of Anatolian ets, are of no help in this respect as far as the sian carpets are concerned. Only the "Herāt" ets occur frequently on Dutch paintings of the n century. The Ṣafawid miniatures show that at beginning of the 10th/16th century the basic es of carpets had been developed. The repro-tions are, however, not sufficiently differentiated conclusions to be drawn from the schools of nting about periods of their origin and localisa-. Dates are to a high degree determined by istic aspects, the quality of the design and isation and the shape and various degrees of elopment of the singular forms being weighed against another. The margin for a subjective gment remains thus relatively large.

ocalisation. Because of their patterns and techni- singularities, the Ṣafawid carpets, with some ex-tions, can be divided into clearly discernible ups. It is however difficult to see the relations of se groups with the historically-established knotting tres. Undoubtedly the successive capitals Tabrīz m 1502), Ḳazwīn (from 1548) and Iṣfahān (from 6-7) had their court weaving manufactories. It is sible that the early Ṣafawid carpets came into ng in Tabrīz under the influence of Bihzād. It is prising that no attempts have been made to localise pets at Ḳazwīn. The work-shops of Iṣfahān are ficiently documented. Jean-Baptiste Tavernier cribes even their exact locality in the *Maydān* a. The manufacturing of silk so-called "Polish pets" and woollen carpets is proved to have taken ce in Iṣfahān. Apparently Kāshān was known ore Iṣfahān for its silk weaving. Pedro Teixeira ntions already in 1604 carpets from Kāshān with d and silk, beautiful brocades and velvets, and the ie of the town was evident in 1601 when King ismund Vasa III ordered from there silk carpets, rked with gold. So late as 1670 Chevalier Chardin s Kāshān the centre of the silk-industry. See Pl. V.

The woollen carpets, however, cannot be classified ce they are only very summarily dealt with in vellers' accounts. In his appraisal of the quality Persian carpets, Pedro Teixeira, who left Goa in 1604 and travelled to Europe through Persia, puts those from Yazd in the first place, those from Kirmān—further characterised in 1684-5 by Engelbert Kaempfer as carpets with animal patterns made from the best wool—in the second place, and those from Khūrāsān in the third. Thadäus Krusinski mentions the provinces of Shīrwān, Ḳarabāgh, Gīlān, the towns of Kāshān, Kirmān, Mashhad, Astarābād and the capital Iṣfahān as localities in which court weaving manufactories were erected under Shāh ʿAbbās I. Tabrīz was important during the 16th century, but in the 17th century it is hardly mentioned any more. Indications of the regions of origin, like north-western Persia (Tabrīz), southern Persia (Kirmān) and eastern Persia (Herāt etc.), which have become quite current in the literature on oriental carpets, represent rather a description of a particular type than a concrete localisation. The discovery of oriental sources like town chronicles, descriptions of weaving manufactories or patterns for designs, might clear up this problem.

Compartment rugs. The "Compartment rugs" of the Ṣafawids are derived from the carpets with arabesque pattern of the Tīmūrid period. The early specimens resemble their painted examples so closely that one is tempted to give them an earlier date. A Compartment rug in the Metropolitan Museum, New York, and its companion in the Musée historique des tissus, Lyons, thus belong entirely to the Tīmūrid tradition; the net-like pattern consisting of eight-lobed rosettes surrounded by shield-shaped motifs formed by interlaced bands and the East Asian motifs which fill these fields, such as the dragon, the phoenix and cloud bands as well as the arabesque tendrils in the background and the vertical arranged cartouches of the borders can easily be connected with Tīmūrid miniatures. If dated to the beginning of the Ṣafawid period, both carpets could have been manufactured in Tabrīz. To this pair of carpets belong some later variants with a raised medallion, establishing the transition to the medallion carpets of North-West Persia, and other variations with shields and quatrefoils in alternating rows. The overlapping fields, found in the carpets in Bihzād's miniatures, are seen again on several 17th century "Polish" carpets.

Carpets with hunting scenes and animals. The influence of miniature-painting is most evident on the carpets with hunting scenes and animals. Except for a few carpets with figures arranged asymmetrically, the scenes are adjusted symmetrically on the background, both in horizontal and vertical directions. An arrangement of medallions is put above this, usually with one medallion in the centre and quarters of medallions in the corners of the field. The hunters, on foot or horseback, attack lions, leopards, gazelles, deer and hares with spears, swords and arrows. Together with a great variety of birds, these animals appear also on the carpets with only animals, on which fights between deer or bull and lion, or between the *chʾi lin* or Chinese unicorn and dragon are in the foreground. The "Chelsea" carpet of the Victoria and Albert Museum, London (pl. X), with its net of medallions connected by diagonally arranged pointed ovals, holds a middle position between the Compartment rugs and the traditional carpets with medallions and animals. An upward and downward string of arabesque leaves divides the border in interlocking parts of contrasting colours. As "reciprocal pinnacle border", it was, in a simpler form, very popular on the later Ṣafawid carpets. Among the carpets which are close to the miniatures, two large, silk carpets with hunting scenes, in Vienna and Boston (see below), are conspicuous. To these are closely connected some silk woven carpets and about 12 woollen carpets (the so-called "Sanguszko" group).

Carpets with figures flourished in the 10th/16th century under Shāh Ṭahmāsp I. Apart from the mastery of the designs, their technical realisation is exemplary. They are an expression of court luxury. Such carpets were undoubtedly manufactured in Tabrīz, but the stylistic and technical differences point to other weaving centres as well. Under Shāh ʿAbbās I carpets with figures lose their importance, so that the few specimens of the 11th/17th century are mere offshoots of the 10th/16th century carpets.

North-west Persian Medallion-carpets. Together with a series of medallion carpets with figures, a restricted group of carpets which have in common a medallion on a background that is filled with tendrils is localised in north-western Persia, including Tabrīz. The most conspicuous specimen is the Ardabīl carpet, according to its inscription dated 946/1539-40. A star-shaped medallion, with corresponding quarter medallions in the corners of the field, appears above a fourfold symmetrical double system consisting of elegant spiral tendrils (see Rexford Stead, *The Ardabil carpets*, J. Paul Getty Museum, California 1974). More characteristic is a simpler class of carpets with medallions on a continuous, somewhat clumsily designed pattern of scrolls with small repeat. Here too the medallions are star-shaped and, as in the case with all medallion carpets of the 10th/16th century, they clearly stand out from the pattern of the background. Often secondary designs are added of a vertical cartouche and a shield-pendant, mostly to be found lengthwise on both sides. Border patterns consist of alternating cartouches and rosettes or a continuous, mirrored repeat of short, interlaced arabesque tendrils. Particularly striking in these carpets is their relatively long format. See Pl. XI.

Herāt carpets. The Herāt carpets normally have no medallion. They are characterised by a variety of large palmettes with flamboyant contours, which cover the points where most delicate spiral scrolls split and touch the symmetrical axes. The colour of the field is almost always purple, that of the borders dark green or deep blue. On the specimens of the 10th/16th century the spiral scrolls are tightly connected. The design is dense, with many bizarre cloud bands and often intermingled with animals and scenes of animal fights. The rich use of East Asiatic motifs has led scholars to localise these carpets in eastern Persia; it is indeed proved that high-quality carpets were manufactured in Khurāsān and its capital Herāt.

In a later type, the arrangement of tendrils is looser and wider, the cloud bands are less frequent and more clumsy, and animals are completely absent. The pattern is determined by palmettes and long, often two-coloured lanceolate leaves, also simplified. The details and borders show parallels with the "Polish" carpets, and therefore this type of Herāt carpets too can be dated to the 11th/17th century. It is as yet undetermined whether these are identical with the woollen carpets manufactured in Isfahan. Such "Herāt" carpets were exported to India and there imitated. It is difficult to distinguish between Persian and Indian workmanship. So far unambiguous criteria are lacking (see below). These carpets are the only type of classical Persian carpets which appear frequently on European paintings, especially the Dutch genre-paintings of the 17th century. These "Herāt" carpets were evidently a valuable comm ity to Europeans, for they have been preserve great quantity mainly in Portugal and Holl countries which through their East India Compa had close commercial relations with Persia India. See Pl. XII.

"Vase" carpets. In contrast with the medallion "Herāt" carpets, the "vase" carpets have most rising pattern which is mirrored only with respec the longitudinal axis. The direction is determine blossoming shrubs and, on many of these carp by receptacles which have the form of vase Chinese porcelain, filled with flowers, from w the name of this group of carpets is derived. Typ is the division of the field by means of oval lozen Three groups of lozenges, pushed one against other, are mostly intersected. They arise from dulating pairs of tendrils which touch each o and retreat behind magnificent flowers. The loze may however also be outlined clearly by tendril broad lanceolate leaves and be filled up with var colours. Occasionally, the arrangement of lozeng absent and there remain entangled rows of flo vases or shrubs arranged in a staggered patt Sometimes also patterns of arabesques occur, in mingled with shrubs and in connection with me lions. Striking are the wealth of colours, especi conspicuous in large-sized rosettes and palmet and the combination of these stylised flowers w naturalistic bushes. The borders are relatively s and the inner or outer guards are often lacking.

Opinions differ about the date of the "va carpets. Some fragments with very luxuriant de and vivid lineation recall stylistically the "Polish" carpets, with which they can be date the beginning of the 17th century. It is still ur discussion whether the pieces of the main gro which are designed in a clearer and stiffer way, o nated before or after these fragments. Some are later date, as is shown by the impoverishment the pattern. More difficult is the decision ab others, which are rich in details notwithstanc the rather simple pattern. The "vase" carpet of museum of Sarajevo, dated 1656, is not typi Its extraordinary well-executed design and the that figurative motifs are in general lacking, favo the opinion that most of the "vase" carpets origina in the 11th/17th century. Southern Persia (Kirm is regarded as the region of their manufacture K. Erdmann, review of *A survey of Persian art Ars Islamica*, viii, 174 ff.). See Pl. XIII.

Garden carpets. Ṣafawid gardens with their g metrical division by rectilinear canals, as e.g. Ha Djarīb near Iṣfahān, and the garden at Ashraf, out by Shāh ʿAbbās I in 1612, are reflected in garden carpets. With their canals and basins with and ducks, bordered by trees and bushes in wh birds and other creatures frolic, these carpets rep sent "portable gardens" which are accessible all y round. The earliest specimen is probably a gar carpet in the Jaipur Museum. According to an scription on the back, this "foreign carpet" arri at the palace in Jaipur on 29 August 1632, proba by order or as a gift. Apart from this one, only other garden-carpets from the Ṣafawid period h survived. The type lives on in a later, restric group which can be distinguished from its Ṣafa predecessors by the schematic outline of the det although the general principle remains the sa They may have been manufactured in north-west Persia from the second half of the 18th cent until sometime in the 19th century (see M. S. Dima *'ersian garden carpet in the Jaipur Museum*, in *Islamica*, vii (1940), 93; and Pl. XVI, no. 17).

'ortuguese" carpets. The ten to fifteen "Portu-e" carpets all go back to the same model and form the most coherent group. They owe their name to representations of sailing ships with European-sed persons on board and a man who emerges from water among fishes and sea monsters. The repre-ation is repeated four times in the corners, and lls the ornamental motifs on European maps. One ie interpretations of that scene is that it depicts arrival of Portuguese ambassadors in the Persian :. From the combination of oriental and European ifs it was further concluded that these carpets intended for Portuguese in Goa. The rest of filling of the fields is also unusual. It consists lozenge-shaped middle field with four small, ted oval medallions and irregularly notched and hered outline, surrounded by concentric inter-ig stripes of various colours. In the earlier speci-is these stripes are vivid and irregularly forked, he later ones they are rectilinear, parallel and lar. While there is no doubt about dating them he 17th century, their place of origin still remains ertain. Formerly these carpets were considered ave originated in southern or central Persia, but some scholars have proposed India. Neither othesis is supported by convincing proofs (see . Ellis, *The Portuguese carpets of Gujarat*, in *mic art in the Metropolitan Museum of Art*, ed. Ettinghausen, New York 1973, 267).

ilk carpets. The change in style which the Ṣafawid ets underwent between the 10th/16th and the 1/17th centuries, is especially recognisable in the carpets. The most famous and largest carpet of kind is the so-called Vienna hunting carpet which in the possession of the Austrian imperial house is now in the Museum für angewandte Kunst in nna. The use of silk for pile, warp and weft luces a very fine texture and gives the possibility an extremely precise design. So it is not only use of its costly material that this carpet heads figurative medallion carpets oriented towards miniature painting and dating from the period of h Ṭahmāsp. Its size of 6.93 × 3.23 m. corresponds 1 that of the large, woollen, knotted carpets. iy details are executed in gold and silver brocade. s said to have originated from Tabrīz or, more bably, from Kās̲h̲ān, known for its silk industry. ilk hunting carpet from the collection of Baron de Rothschild, which can be compared with the nna carpet, is now in the Museum of Fine Arts in ton. Some thirteen small-sized silk carpets, which Erdmann called the "small silk carpets of Kā-n" (*Siebenhundert Jahre Orientteppiche*, 143), are ted to these two. Apart from four carpets with nals and animal fights in a rising, symmetrical ingement, they also represent the type of the y medallion carpets. Representations of persons peris are lacking. They return on some woven carpets, also mostly of small size, which fit in istically with the figurative woollen carpets of "Sanguszko" group, and among which a frag-itary hunting carpet in the Residenzmuseum at nich stands out. Because of its size, theme and lity of delineation it is directly related to the nnese hunting carpet. It must, however, be taken account that the technique of a woven carpet s not permit the elegant lineation of a knotted . All these woven carpets have pointed oval dallions with transverse cartouches, borders with rnating cartouches and quatrefoils. In comparison with the knotted silk carpets the use of gold and silver brocade on large fields is new, and not only with respect to the emphasising of details. If the making of the Vienna hunting carpet, which undoubtedly figures at the beginning of the development, is dated to about the middle of the 16th century, then the "small silk carpets of Kās̲h̲ān", the figurative woven carpets and the woollen carpets of the "Sanguszko"-group present the style of the second half of the 16th century.

Contrasting with the new figurative woven carpets, there is a large group of woven carpets with purely floral decor, in which a coarsening of the lineation is recognisable. In two of these carpets—one completely preserved in the Residenzmuseum in Munich (Pl. XI) and the lengthwise half of another in the Textile Museum in Washington—the arms of the Polish king Sigismund Vasa III have been woven. As is known from documents, the king ordered in 1601 silk carpets worked with gold from Kās̲h̲ān. In a bill of 12 September 1602 pairs of carpets are mentioned, together with the sum of five crowns for the weaving of the royal arms. In 1642 an undefined number of carpets came as dowry into the possession of the Elector Philip William of the Palatinate by his marriage to princess Anna Catherina Constanza, a daughter of Sigismund III. Among these carpets were undoubtedly not only the woven carpets with the arms but certainly also the other woven carpets and the "Polish" carpets, now in the Residenzmuseum. The carpets with the arms thus illustrate the style of woven carpets about 1600. They form the starting point for a chronological order of the floral woven carpets, which with their latest specimens may reach as far as the second half of the 17th century. In the shape of their medallions, however, they remain related to the early Ṣafawid carpets.

The view that carpets with figurative representations were no more in fashion in the 17th century is confirmed by the knotted silk carpets, the large fields of which are brocaded with gold and silver threads, and the manufacturing of which flourished under S̲h̲āh ʿAbbās I. At first these carpets were thought to be of Polish origin and therefore were called "Polish carpets". The group includes now about 230 specimens, which came into the possession of European courts or churches as gifts of ambassadors or on order. They were however not only intended for export but were also in Persia a sign of wealth and luxury, and bear witness to the court taste in the beginning of the 17th century. Since these "representation" carpets, in contrast to the woollen carpets, evoked again and again the admiration of European travellers, they form rich source material, much more so than any other kind of Ṣafawid carpets. And thus it can also be ascertained that the main group was produced in the court manufactory in the *Maydān* area of Iṣfahān. In the "Polish" carpets the relaxation of the 16th century rules for the form of the carpets is unmistakable. This is shown by the shifting from lines to fields, which finds expression in the abandoning of the monochrome foundation and in the loss of the clear delineation of the medallions against the background. Characteristic is further a luxuriant, merely floral décor.

Production in great quantities brought about a rationalisation of the design, as can easily be shown from the many specimens known. This kind of production necessitated also economy in the material, as may be seen from the preference for smaller sizes and above all from the use of cotton besides silk in the weft.

The patterns can be reduced to about a dozen basic systems, mostly present in the few large-sized carpets. Variety is brought about by a difference in choice of various details, by different medallions and borders and by variations of colours. Apparently these carpets were preferably knotted in pairs, because until today 25 exact pairs are known, harmonising even in the borders and the division of colours. Continuing the tradition of Kās͟hān. where the earliest of these carpets may have originated, the uniform style of the "Polish" carpets was probably developed in Iṣfahān at the beginning of the 17th century, after the court was transferred there in 1005/1596-7. The "Polish" carpets, characterised by an obvious negligence in the discipline of the drawing, may date from the second half of the 17th century. The destruction of the Ṣafawid dynasty by the Afg͟hāns in 1722 put an end to the manufacture of brocade textile (see K. Erdmann, *Persische Wirkteppiche der Safawidenzeit*, in *Pantheon* (1932), 227; F. Spuhler, *Der figurale Kaschan-Wirkteppich aus den Slgn. des regierenden Fürsten von Liechtenstein*, in *Kunst des Orients*, v/1 (1968), 55; T. Mánkowski, *Note on the cost of Kashan carpets at the beginning of the 17th century*, in *Bull. of the American Inst. for Persian Art and Archaeology*, iv (1936), 152; M. S. Dimand, *Loan exhibition of Persian rugs of the so-called Polish type*, Metropolitan Museum New York 1930; F. Spuhler, *Ein neuerworbener "Polenteppich" des Museums für Islamische Kunst*, in *Berliner Museen*, N.F., xx/1, 27; idem, *Seidene Repräsentationsteppiche der mittleren bis späten Safawidenzeit*, inaugural thesis, Berlin 1968, to be published by Faber and Faber, London).

γ. *18th and 19th Centuries.*

The few carpets from the 18th century abandon to a great extent the tradition of the two preceding centuries. Simpler repeated patterns with plant motifs like trees, shrubs, forked leaves, palmettes and rosettes are preferred. In the 19th century production revives. The old centres of Tabrīz, Iṣfahān, Kās͟hān, Kirmān and K͟hurāsān with Herāt gain new importance with mostly large carpets. In Tabrīz and Kās͟hān small-sized silk carpets are knotted too, also as prayer rugs. The arrangement of the medallions on a monochrome or small-patterned background is preferred. A typical design of the 19th century is the "Herātī" pattern, spread all over Persia. The main element of its repeat is a lozenge with four lanceolate leaves which run parallel to the sides and a rosette in the centre. The *boteh* or almondstone pattern is equally popular. The figural carpets have their origin in the hunting and animal carpets of the 10th/16th century and came mainly from Tehran and Kirmān. Elements of the classical pattern are geometrised and distorted. Peculiarity and liveliness cannot be denied to the products of the 19th century. This is especially true for the carpets from the surroundings of the town of Bid̲j̲ār, which are, moreover, of outstanding quality. Characteristic is an extremely fine carpet, dated 1209/1794 (formerly in the McMullan collection, now in the Metropolitan Museum, New York), which in colouration and structure belongs to the Bid̲j̲ār carpets and for the drawing of which a pattern of a "vase" carpet was used. A series of later Bid̲j̲ārs can be connected to this one.

In contrast with the preceding centuries, there have been preserved from the 19th century not only carpets from the manufactories, but also ca that were made by tribes and villages for personal use, and village products of cottage ir tries, marketed in the larger towns. They are us small-sized. Their charm lies in their origina To these belong carpets from the towns of Hama Saruḳ, Bid̲j̲ār, Herīz, Senneh and Kirmāns͟hāh from the Kurdish tribes in the neighbourhood. S of the patterns of the Bak͟htiyāris living to west of Iṣfahān are based on the Iṣfahān-style. Ḳas͟hḳāʾī nomads around S͟hīrāz use both p geometrical forms and flowers and animals A. C. Edwards, *The Persian carpet*, London 1 (see further on tribal carpets, Section iii below).

e. India

During the 16th and 17th centuries carpets s times of very high perfection were manufacture the towns of Āgra, Lahore and Jaipur, evide without any preceding Indian tradition in this of handcraft. The stimuli surely came from Pe Under the Mug͟hal Akbar I (1556-1605), a st tendency towards Ṣafawid taste was develo This led to the summoning of Persian artists craftsmen and affected all the artistic activities u Akbar's successors D̲j̲ahāngīr, S͟hāh D̲j̲ahān Awrangzīb until about 1700. Between 1625 and European influences too made themselves felt the present state of research it is not possib establish a chronology of the Indian carpets of Mug͟hal period. It is plausible that the sep groups did not replace one another but existed temporaneously. Some fragments with grote animal patterns which are rooted in Indian my ogy are to be placed at the beginning of the dev ment and dated perhaps as early as the 16th cent The miniatures in the *Akbar-nāma* of Abu 'l- [*q.v.*], dated 1602-5, give us an idea of the ca *ca.* 1600. With their ogival medallions, scrolls cloud-bands, they correspond to the Persian ca of the 16th century, so that the actual origin rem obscure. In the same way the Indian carpets of later "Herāt" type cannot with certainty be separ from their Persian predecessors. A group pattern of scrolls stands out more clearly; characterised by lanceolate leaves at the end the scrolls, formed by leaves of blossoms w overlap like scales. This group is represented a carpet which was ordered in Lahore and prese in 1634 by Mr. Robert Bell, now in the possessic the Girdlers' Company of the City of London. authentically Indian is a carpet with scenes of an fights, carrying the arms of the Fremlin family in the Victoria and Albert Museum in Lond which helps to distinguish the Indian animal ca from the Persian ones. R. Skelton has proved vincingly that a naturalistic flower style arise miniature painting between 1620 and 1627, tow the end of the reign of D̲j̲ahāngīr. This style, couraged by the import of European bota works, spread to carpets and textile fabrics and not hesitate to employ plastic effects in its de produced by gradations of colour. A carpet rows of blossoming shrubs lies underneath rangzīb's throne on a portrait painted arc 1660. A date *post quem* is thus available for c a number of extant carpets of this kind, with che red background and a fine arrangement of colc Such a date is valid too for the extraordinarily t knotted prayer rugs with a central blossoming b standing out from a flat landscape. Apparently types did not originate before the second quart

17th century and may have reached their peak popularity about the middle of that century. ir differing quality indicates that they were ufactured in various centres. In the 18th and centuries the Indian carpets seem to have been le only for export and are artistically without sequence (see R. Skelton, *A decorative motif in ghal art*, in *Aspects of Indian Art, Papers presented in mposium at the Los Angeles Country Museum of Art*, ober 1970, Leiden 1972, 147; and Pls. XVI, XVII).

The Caucasus

he stylised, archaising representations of pairs of nals, dragons, trees, bushes, etc. on the Caucasian gon and tree carpets caused F. R. Marquart in 3, in the first chronology of Oriental carpets, to e these carpets at the beginning of the developt and to date them to the 13th/14th centuries. s opinion however is contradicted by the evident uence the Ṣafawid carpets have had on these agon" carpets, as is shown by the floral motifs, nals and scenes of animal fights. These carpets their name from the dragons which are mostly orted until they are unrecognisable. The dragons inserted into a rising lozenge-shaped design, made n diagonal stripes. This arrangement and the row borders point to a relation with the "vase" oets. According to modern opinion, only a few these carpets date back to the 17th century. ether with their Caucasian versions, most of m are derived from the 18th century tree-carpets floral carpets with spiral tendrils and have their in in the Shirwān/Ḳarabāgh area. Some of the casian carpets of the 17th and 18th centuries of considerable size, which indicated that they e manufactured in urban manufactories. In aclance with the sense of decoration of the rural ulation, a profusion of bright patterns with large ds in lively colouration developed in the 19th tury from the above-mentioned wealth of forms. h their geometrical design these small carpets runners—there are no more large-sized carpets this period—stand out clearly from the Persian oets of the 19th century. The most important tting centres were Ḳazaḳ, Shirwān, Dāghistān, rabāgh, Mūghān, Tālish, Gandja and Ḳuba (see Sakisian, *Nouveaux documents sur les tapis arméns*, in *Syria*, xvii (1936), 177; M. Ağaoğlu, *Dragon s, a loan exhibition*, The Textile Museum Washing- 1948; U. Schürmann, *Teppiche aus dem Kaukasus*, nswick n.d., Eng. tr. Grainge, Basingstoke 1974; alogues: *Kaukasische Teppiche*, Museum für nsthandwerk Frankfurt 1962; C. G. Ellis, *Cauan carpets in the Textile Museum*, in *Forschungen Kunst Asiens*, in *Memoriam Kurt Erdmann*, nbul 1969, 194; and Pl. XVII, no. 20).

. Spain

n a survey of knotted carpets as expressions of mic handicraft, the early Spanish carpets should be mentioned. The so-called synagogue carpet he Islamisches Museum, Berlin (I, 27), is probably oldest and may belong to the 14th-15th centuries. y are often large-sized pieces in a style which figures the later "Holbein" carpets. The colours he Spanish carpets are marked by stronger consts. The "Turkish" group may date from the h/16th centuries and is succeeded by works with aissance elements. Alcaraz, Letur, Cuenca and encia are known as knotting centres. The technical uliarity of the Spanish carpets consists in the that the knot is always twisted about a warp (see J. Ferrandis Torrés, *Exposición de alfombras antiguas españolas*, Madrid 1933; E. Kühnel, *Maurische Teppiche aus Alcaraz*, Pantheon 1930, 416; E. Kühnel and L. Bellinger, *Catalogue of Spanish rugs, 12th cent. to 19th cent.*, The Textile Museum, Washington 1953).

h. Turkestan

The varieties of the Turkoman productions are determined by the use that is made of them, especially as furnishing of the tent [see KHAYMA, iv, Central Asia]. Small carpets serve as floor-coverings, as curtains for the entrance, corresponding in format and design with a prayer rug, as tent-bands which border the upper edge of the round *yurt*. Various bags to store supplies, saddlebags and camel-ornaments are also knotted. They all have in common a deep-red to dark-purple ground and an all-over, geometric, repeat design in bright red, blue, white and (rarely) green and yellow. The way in which the *gül*, the star-shaped to octagonal leading motif which has the function of a tribal sign, is executed, may indicate the particular nomadic tribes: Tekke Turkomans, Yomuts, Čavdïrs (Tchodovs), Ersarïs and Sarïḳs, to whom can be linked the Balūč in the west and the Afghāns in the south. The way in which transposed rows of principal and subordinate *güls* are arranged, already existent on carpets to be seen on Tīmūrīd miniatures and on "Holbein" carpets, suggests a long tradition in the knotting art. Since, however, any support for an accurate dating is lacking, one hesitates to date single specimens to the 18th century (see A. Bogolubow, *Tapisseries de l'Asie centrale faisant partie de la collection réunie par A. Bogolubow*, St. Petersburg 1908 (new edition: A. A. Bogolyubov, *Carpets of Central Asia*, ed. J. M. A. Thompson, London 1973); H. Clark, *Bokhara, Turkoman and Afghan rugs*, London 1922; A. Thacher, *Turkoman rugs*, New York 1940; U. Schürmann, *Zentral-Asiatische Teppiche*, Frankfurt 1969, Eng. tr., *Central Asian rugs*, London 1970; V. G. Moshkova, *Kovry narodov sredney Asii Konza 19-20 vv.*, Tashkent 1970, Ger. tr., *Die Teppiche der Volken Mittelasiens*, Hamburg 1974.

3. Public Collections of Oriental Carpets

Europe. The most important collections are in Vienna, Österreichisches Museum für angewandte Kunst; London, Victoria and Albert Museum; Istanbul, Türk ve Islâm Eserler Müzesi; Berlin, Islamisches Museum, Staatliche Museen zu Berlin (East Berlin) and Museum für Islamische Kunst, Staatliche Museen, Stiftung Preussischer Kulturbesitz (West Berlin). Also in Amsterdam, Rijksmuseum; Florence, Museo Bardini; Hamburg, Museum für Kunst und Gewerbe; Leningrad, Hermitage; Lisbon, Fondation Calouste Gulbenkian; Lyons, Musée Historique des Tissus; Milan, Museo Poldi Pezzoli; Munich, Residenzmuseum and Bayerisches Nationalmuseum; Paris, Musée des Arts Décoratifs.

U.S.A. The most important collections are in New York, The Metropolitan Museum of Art, and Washington, The Textile Museum. Also in Boston, Museum of Fine Arts; Cleveland, The Cleveland Museum of Arts; Detroit, The Detroit Institute of Arts; Los Angeles, County Museum; Philadelphia, Philadelphia Museum of Art; St. Louis, City Art Museum of St. Louis.

4. Bibliographies.

The most extensive bibliography is in K. Erdmann, *Der orientalische Knüpfteppich*, Tübingen 1955 (several editions) arranged according to areas and within these chronologically by the year of publication (English tr. C. G. Ellis, *Oriental carpets*, London 1960, 2nd impression, Fishguard 1976); K. A. C. Creswell, *A bibliography of the architecture, arts and crafts of Islam to 1st Jan. 1960*, London 1961, Oxford 1973, 1139-1204, alphabetically arranged by authors (Supplement, Jan. 1960 to Jan. 1972, Cairo 1974 (329-37)); J. D. Pearson, *Index islamicus*; R. Ettinghausen art. *Ḳālī*, in *EI*[1] Suppl.

Bibliography: in addition to the works mentioned in the article, see *Tafelwerk zur Ausstellung orientalischer Teppiche, Orientalische Teppiche, Wien, London, Paris 1892-1896*, 3 vols.; Supplement, *Altorientalische Teppiche*, Leipzig 1908, ed. A. von Scala; F. R. Martin, *A history of oriental carpets before 1800*, Vienna 1908; *Die Ausstellung von Meisterwerken muhammedanischer Kunst in München 1910*, ed. F. Sarre and F. R. Martin; F. Sarre and H. Trenkwald, *Altorientalische Teppiche*, i, Vienna and Leipzig 1926; ii, 1928; *A survey of Persian art*, London, New York 1938, ed. A. U. Pope (reprint 1967).

Exhibitions and Museum publications: *L'Art de l'Orient Islamique, Collection de la Fondation Calouste Gulbenkian*, Museu Nacional de Arte Antiga, Lisbon 1963; *Meisterstücke orientalischer Knüpfkunst, Collection A. Danker*, Städtisches Museum Wiesbaden, 1966; *The Kevorkian Foundation collection of rare and magnificent oriental carpets, Special Loan Exhibition, a guide and catalogue*, by M. S. Dimand, Metropolitan Museum of Art, New York 1966; *Islamische Teppiche, The Joseph V. McMullan collection, New York*, Museum für Kunsthandwerk Frankfurt 1968, catalogue by U. Schürmann; *Alte Orient-Teppiche*, Museum für Kunst und Gewerbe Hamburg 1970, ed. R. Hempel and M. Preysing; *Arts de l'Islam des origines à 1700*, Orangerie des Tuileries, Paris 1971; *Islamic carpets from the collection of Joseph V. McMullan*, Hayward Gallery, London 1972; M. S. Dimand and Jean Mailey, *Oriental rugs in the Metropolitan Museum of Art*, New York 1973.

Private collections and handbooks: J. V. McMullan, *Islamic carpets*, New York 1965; M. H. Beattie, *Die orientalische Teppiche in der Sammlung Thyssen-Bornemisza*, Castagnola 1972; P. M. Campana, *Il tappeto orientale*, Milan 1962; G. Cohen, *Il fascino del tappeto orientale*, Milan 1968; R. Hubel, *Ullstein Teppichbuch*, Berlin, Frankfurt, Vienna 1965; K. Erdmann, *Siebenhundert Jahre Orientteppich*, Herford 1966 (Eng. tr. M. H. Beattie and H. Herzog, *Seven hundred years of oriental carpets*, London 1970). (F. Spuhler)

ii. In the Muslim West

In the Muslim West, the term *bisāṭ*, pl. *busuṭ* is attested, notably by Ibn Khaldūn, *Muḳaddima*, who uses it to describe the revenues paid every year by the Aghlabids to the ʿAbbāsid caliphs; under the caliphate of al-Maʾmūn, there is mention of 120 carpets (*busuṭ*). It may thus be supposed that these were precious objects of real artistic value and one's natural inclination is to think of "the carpet on which the sovereign and his ministers are seated" (Dozy, *Suppl.* i, 85, col. 2). Unfortunately, nothing is known of these carpets which were presumably manufactured in the large cities, al-Ḳayrawān and its satellites ʿAbbāsiyya or Raḳḳāda, in particular. Does the fact that these products were intended for the highest dignitaries permit us to suppose that, as early as this period, there was at least one *ṭirāz* [*q.v.*] in Ifrīḳiya? A workshop of this kind is attested at Mahdiyya in the period of the Fāṭimid al-Ma (*Djawdhar*, tr. Canard, 75), and there is mentio the manufacture of carpets there. It would s legitimate to suppose that, under the Aghlab there was the capacity for weaving luxury car (no doubt inspired by the carpets of the E intended for the caliphs and for the most se officials of the Muslim world.

The term *bisāṭ* is also employed by Yāḳūt (13th century), who mentions *busuṭ* in the regio Tebessa and describes them as sumptuous, v made and long-lasting. Should these carpets be s as the ancestors of the lock-stitched carpets wh until recently, still constitued one of the princ items of tent furniture, especially in the regio Tebessa: the tribes of the Nememsha, the Ḥara the Mahadba and the Ḥamāma? The most anc of these products, with strictly geometric decorat appear to perpetuate the old local traditions s are still to be found in the Djebel Amour, as wel in the Moroccan Middle and High Atlas.

Bisāṭ is not at the present time employed in part of North Africa, where various other Ar words are used to designate these long, polychro woven fabrics: *ḳṭīf* or *ḳaṭīfa*, *maṭraḥ*, *frāsh*, *farrashi* while in Morroco, Berber or Berberised words also used (P. Ricard, *Corpus*); as for the car manufactured in the towns (al-Ḳayrawān, Guerg Nedroma, Rabat, Mediouna), they are called *biyya*, pl. *zrābī*, or *sadjdjāda*, pl. *sadjdjādāt*. Th carpets are strongly influenced by the carpets Anatolia and of old Andalusia.

The existence of *busuṭ* carpets in Muslim Spai attested by various authors, in particular at Mur These products were much valued in the Or (al-Maḳḳarī, *Nafḥ al-ṭīb*, i, 123). Yāḳūt speaks the *busuṭ* of Elche (Alsh) (i, 350); but the expres *waṭāʾ* is preferred when describing the carpets Chinchilla or of Baza, the reputation of wh extended as far as the Orient.

In the modern and contemporary period, centres of traditional lock-stitch weaving in No Africa are distributed as follows:

(1) Carpets woven usually by men (*reggā* generally within the tent:

Tunisia: the Ḥamāma, the Mahadba, the Dura the Ouled bou Ghanem tribes.

Algeria: the Nemensha, the Ḥarakta, the Maa the Hodna tribes. See Pl. XVIII.

All these carpets are characterised by anci essentially geometric patterns, with compositi that vary little, and a colour scheme reduced two or three shades, and by apparently more rec patterns inspired by the carpets of Anatolia, ch acterised by one or several central polygonal mo (*miḥrāb*) framed by orthogonal fillets. The mu plication of *miḥrāb*s permits the creation of car of large dimensions. They are all polychrome, being the dominant background colour.

The carpets of the Djebel Amour (Algeria) h remained faithful to geometric décor and to anci local compositions; there are only two domin colours, red for the background and dark blue the motifs (recently replaced by black). At edges there are fringes woven with a polychro geometric design. These carpets are compara with certain Moroccan woven products of Middle Atlas. See pl. XIX.

Morocco: carpets of the High Atlas: Haouz Marrakesh, Ouled bou Sbaa, Aït Ouaouzguit, e carpets of the Middle Atlas: Zemmour, Zaian, B

1. Sal̲dj̲ūḳ. Ḳonya carpet. Türk ve Islâm eserleri Müzesi, Istanbul, No. 685.
Publ. by K. Erdmann, *Der orient. Knüpfteppich*, fig. 2.

2. Carpet with "dragon-phoenix" pattern, Anatolia, 14th century, Islamisches Museum, East Berlin, No. 74.

3. Ottoman. "Holbein" carpet, large type. Museum für Isl. Kunst, Berlin, No. I, 5526.

4. Ottoman. "Holbein" carpet, small type. Museum für Isl. Kunst, No. 82,894.

5. Ottoman. Lotto carpet, Museum für Isl. Kunst, Berlin, No. 82,707.

6. Ottoman. Medallion pattern ʿUs͟hāḳ carpet. Victoria and Albert Museum, London, No. T 71/1914. Publ. in *Guide to a collection of carpets*, V. and A. Museum, 1920, pl. XVI.

7. Ottoman. Star pattern ʿUs͟hāḳ carpet. Metropolitan Museum of Art, New York, Acc. No. 58.63. Gift of Joseph McMullan, 1958. Publ. by J. V. McMullan, *Islamic carpets*, 1965, No. 67.

8. Mamlūk. Silk carpet, Österreichisches Museum für angewandte Kunst, Vienna. Publ. by S. Troll, *Altorientalische Teppiche*, 1951, pl. 40.

9. Ottoman. Collection de la Bibliothèque des Arts Décoratifs, No. 7861.
Publ. in *Arts de l'Islam*, exposition août 1971, No. 5.

10. Ṣafawid. "Chelsea" carpet, V. and A. Museum, No. 589/1890.

ıd. Medallion pattern carpet from north-
ersia. Museu Nacional de Arte antiga, Lisbon.
n *L'Art de l'orient islamique*, 1963, No. 72
llection of the Gulbenkian Foundation).

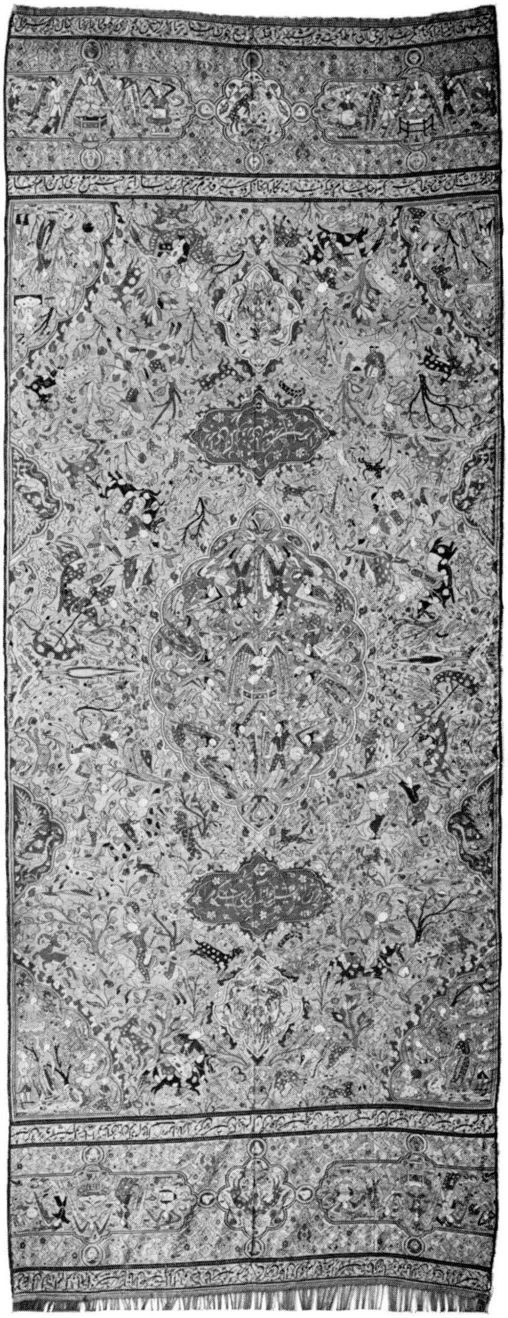

12. Ṣafawid. Woven silk carpet (389 × 152 cm., fragment), Residenzmuseum, Munich. Publ. by K. Erdmann, *Siebenhundert Jahre Orientteppiche*, 1966, pl. 1, fig. 24 (complete view).

13. Ṣafawid. Herāt carpet, Österreichisches Museum für angewandte Kunst. Publ. by Troll, *op. cit.*, No.

14. Ṣafawid. Carpet with "vase" pattern, V. and A. Museum (17′ 1″ × 10′ 10″).
Publ. by A. U. Pope, *A survey of Persian art*, pl. 1227.

15. Kā<u>sh</u>ān. Silk carpet, Museu Nacional de Arte antiga.
Publ. in *L'Art de l'orient islamique*, No. 70 (Collection of the Gulbenkian Foundation).

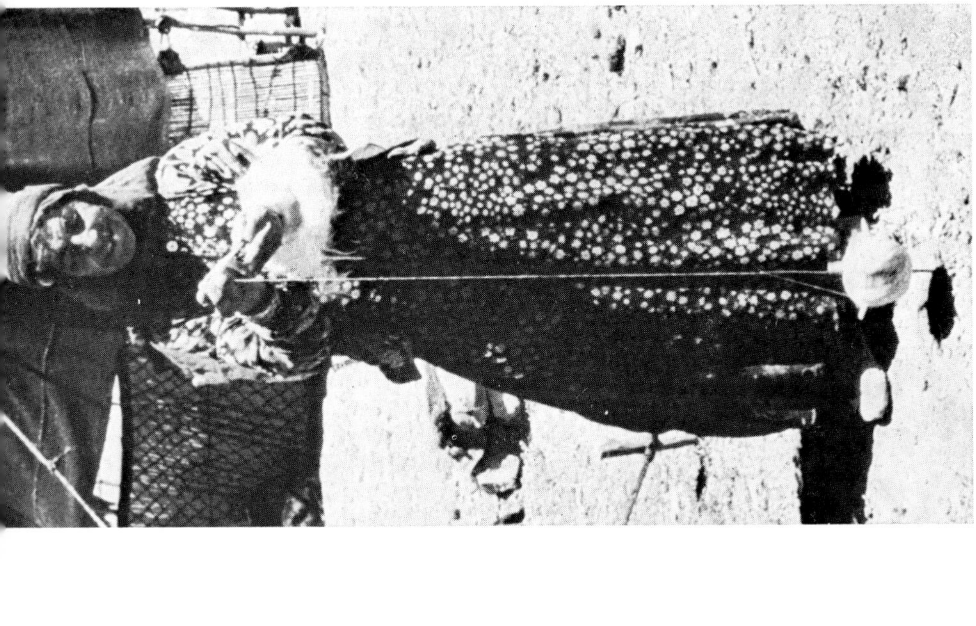

27. Carpet knotting at the Tribal Weaving School, Shīrāz (Photo: J. Allgrove).

28. Packing down the wefts (Photo: P. Wallum).

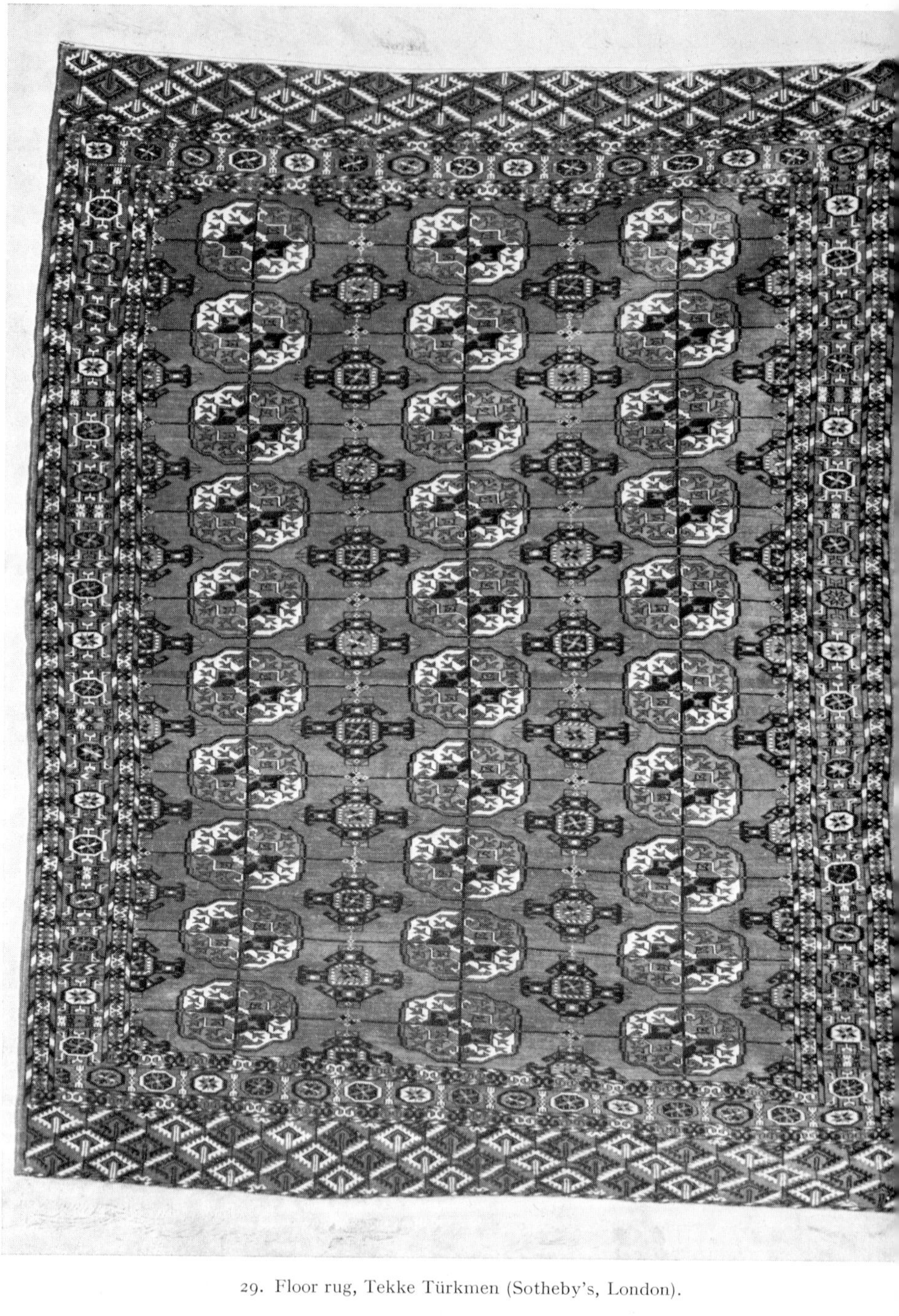

29. Floor rug, Tekke Türkmen (Sotheby's, London).

30. *Asmalïk* (camel flank hanging), Yomut Türkmen (Whitworth Art Gallery, Manchester University).

31. Floor rug, Ḳas͟hḳāʾī, Raḥimlu of the Ṣafī K͟hānī *Ṭāʾifeh* (Private collection).

32. a, b. Saddle-bag faces, Ḳas͟hḳāʾī (David Black Oriental Carpets).

r, Beni Mguild, Aït Youssi, Marmoucha, Aït arouchen, Beni Alaham, Beni Ouaraïn, etc.
ll these carpets manufactured among Berber es are of geometric design and employ only a ted range of colours.

) Carpets of urban manufacture showing atolian influence (woven by women):

unisia: al-Ḳayrawān, Tunis, and various coastal s where the influence of al-Ḳayrawān has been tive for about a century, there being sometimes l types with a fair degree of originality, (Bizerta articular).

lgeria: Cuergour and Sétif (at this present time in process of disappearing), Souf, Ḳalʿa of the ū Rached (influenced by Andalusian products).

orocco: Rabat-Salé, Casablanca, Mediouna (also ienced by Andalusia).

ll these carpets were, or still are, woven in the e, as a family business.

the contemporary period, the manufacture of ets, an export product, is tending to become ndustry, especially in the major cities such as ayrawān, Tunis, Tlemcen, Rabat-Salé, Casaca, and also in the more modest towns such as eul, Bizerta, Tebessa, Cherchel, etc.

Bibliography: Giacobetti, *Les tapis et tissages Djebel Amour*, 1932; P. Ricard, *Corpus des pis marocains*, 4 vols. 1923-24; L. Poinssot and Revault, *Tapis tunisiens*, 4 vols. 1937-57; . Golvin, *Les arts populaires en Algérie*, 6 vols. 950-6. (L. Golvin)

iii. Tribal rugs

Nomenclature. Until the 1960s few writers on et history except, perhaps, A. C. Edwards (*The sian carpet*, London 1975), distinguished between output of cities, villages and tribal groups, and in the past twenty-five years has the ancient style of Central Asia's pastoral nomads attracted ropologists, making it possible to isolate and ly their artefacts.

he custom of marketing an area's rugs in the l town has obfuscated classification—for ince, Bergama has lent its name to rugs made by gers and tribes in its hinterland, while Bukhara ill the popular label for the rugs of the Tekke kmen. Such misleading nomenclature, coined in last century, is now being superseded by more ise classification. Similarly, confusing technical s, with variants in different countries, are being aced by clearer terminology, based on I. Emery's k (*The primary structure of fabrics*, Washington, . 1966). In the past the words *carpet* and *rug* in French the word *tapis*) have been used nymously, leading to difficulty in the study of mentary evidence. *Carpet* is now used to define otted article of some size, say, 300 by 240 cm. upwards, while a *rug*, also of knotted pile, is ller, measuring up to about 300 by 200 cm. Both ds have been used to define flat-weave articles ell, and these are now named after their technique, nstance, *kilīm* or *gelīm*, which is tapestry-woven, *sumak*, after *sumak* weft-wrapping. Only knotted work is discussed here.

. Technique. There are a number of knots of h, as noted in Section i. 1 above, the two most mon are the Gördes or Turkish knot and the neh or Persian knot. Both are of known anti-y; the Pazyryk rug, dating from the 4th to 3rd ury B.C., was made with the Turkish knot, while Basadar fragments, possibly a century older, show the Persian knot. Again, these terms have proved confusing. The second was named after Senneh, in northwestern Iran, but in the area of modern Sanandadj the Turkish knot predominates. Consequently, although the so-called Turkish knot is the most commonly used in Turkey, both knots are found in Iran and both have been found in the same rug. Classification by knot only, therefore, should be regarded with caution. Each has different characteristics: the Turkish knot is symmetrical, the two tufts lying evenly on either side of the warps, and it is suited to a longer pile, while the Persian knot is asymmetrical, the tufts slanting to the left or right of the warps, and is favoured where clear definition of a complex pattern is required. Some scholars have now adopted the term *symmetrical* for the Turkish knot and *asymmetrical* for the Persian.

Description of designs is also prone to variation and many names have been arbitrarily coined by Europeans. A floor carpet can be described as follows: first, the central field and its ornament (some German writers, however, use the word *field* to define the motifs), while the borders are numbered starting from the inner one and specifying the main, or largest, border and the guards or narrow bands which divide them. This system may be adapted to describe saddle-bags, tent-bags and animal trappings.

In city workshops, fixed vertical looms make large pieces possible, and women knotters work from a cartoon under male supervision. Villagers use both vertical and horizontal looms, while among the tribes the latter is normal. The tribal loom (Pl. XX), evolved into streamlined simplicity, consists of wood warp beams, pegged into the ground. It is light, easily transported and flexible since it can be used to weave tapestry or, with the addition of a tripod supporting heddle rods, can be adapted for knotting or various compound weaves. It is necessarily small, and tension is difficult to control since it may be moved while a rug is being made. While cotton warps are favoured in cities and villages, tribal rugs until recently were knotted on wool warps, or a mixture of wool and goat hair, giving them their characteristic suppleness. Tribal wool is of fine quality, carefully selected and dyed. Vegetable dyes were retained longer by the tribes than by settled weavers, and a much-admired feature is the variations in tone, known as *abrash*, due to the dyeing of small batches of wool as required. Most of the dye plants like madder, weld and indigo are common, and it is the recipes which give colours their individuality.

The technique of knotting varies. In southern Iran knots are tied with the fingers and cut with a knife, while up in the north-west the wool is pulled through the warps with a hooked tool, at the other end of which is the cutting-blade. Having begun with up to 20 cm. of flat-weave, known as an "end", the weaver ties one, two or more rows of knots and between these inserts a row or two of plain-weave wefts, packing them down firmly with a carpet comb (Pl. XXI) to hold the knots in position. The cording at the sides is put in as the work progresses. Tribal weavers will use an old rug as a model and are free to improvise, especially on detail. The rug is finished with another "end" and the excess warps form the fringes. Clipping of the pile, requiring great skill, is done by tribeswomen as they go along, while in city workshops the knots are roughly slashed and the finished carpet, looking like an unkempt hedge, is clipped by a specialist. Tribal knotting varies from the coarse, shaggy pile of

Yürük rugs to the fine, velvety surface of Türkmen bags. Each has its own attraction, since the design is evolved to enhance the quality of the wool.

3. History. The carpet from Barrow 5 at Pazyryk (see S. I. Rudenko, *Naseleniya gornogo Altaya v Skifskoe Vremya*, Moscow-Leningrad 1953. Eng. tr. M. W. Thompson, *Frozen tombs of Siberia*, London 1970, 298-304) pushed back the beginnings of carpet history from the 6th century A. D. to the late 3rd century B. C. It is, however, a sophisticated piece, both in technique and design, arguing a long-developed tradition. It is unlikely that it was made by the Altai people, and it more plausibly reflects an eclectic taste for exotic imports. The Pazyryk burials, however, provide invaluable evidence of the life style of these Central Asian pastoral nomads, putative ancestors of later tribal groups, which was notable then, as now, for the major part played by textiles in their economy and cultural heritage. With their wealth based on their animals, and their sources of conflict pasturage and water, they made seasonal migrations, as do the Bakhtiyārī, the Ḳashḳā'ī and Khamseh in Iran today. They produced a class of mounted warriors who revolutionised warfare for both the Romans and the Chinese, gave rise to innumerable legends and bred distrust and fear among urban dwellers. It is likely that the women undertook the spinning and weaving, and even today these activies are considered effeminate by tribesmen with the memory of an élite warrior caste (Pl. XX). It can be surmised that knotting originated among even earlier pastoral nomads living in a harsh winter climate who were naturally reluctant to slaughter their animals and, as an alternative to fleeces, evolved a warm, tufted fabric. K. Erdmann and others believed that knotting may have developed among Turkic peoples in West Turkestan, (Erdmann, *Der orientalische Knüpfteppiche*, Tübingen 1955, Eng. tr. C. G. Ellis, *Oriental carpets*, Fishguard 1976, 14-16) and it would seem likely that it arrived in Anatolia with the Saldjūḳs in the 11th century A.D., where it was established by the 13th century as is attested by the Saldjūḳ pieces from the mosque of ʿAlā' al-Dīn in Konya (now in the Türk ve İslam Müzesi, Istanbul, illustr. in O. Aslanapa, *Turkish art and architecture*, London 1971). Also, Marco Polo, writing of his visit to Anatolia in 1271-2, says that the finest carpets in the world were made in Konya, Sivas and Kayseri, while Abu 'l-Fidā, quoting Ibn Saʿīd, who died in 1274, says that Aḳsarāy's carpets were exported "to all countries", and Ibn Baṭṭūṭa in the 14th century mentions that Turkish carpets were widely exported. Since many tribes surviving into modern times claim Turkic descent, it is no surprise to find design elements which are traceable to Saldjūḳ pilework. The all-over geometricised repeat, found in the Konya pieces, is a characteristic of Türkmen floor rugs, while octagons, hooked medallions and eight-pointed stars, together with border motifs (always the most conservative element in rug design), like the angular scrolling stem, key fret and arrowhead, are ubiquitous in tribal rugs and village rugs from Turkey, the Caucasus and Iran. Some of the creatures which appear frequently on Akstafa, Ḳashḳā'ī and Khamseh rugs also have a long pedigree, for their distant ancestors appear in Italian paintings of the 13th to 15th centuries, copied from rugs imported to Italy from Asia Minor (for a detailed discussion of painting evidence see *Bibl.*) *The marriage of the Virgin*, painted in the early 14th century by Niccolo di Buonacorso, in the National Gallery, London, shows a carpet with repeating octagons, each closing a large-tailed bird, precursor of the fanta birds knotted into 19th century rugs from so western Iran; while of surviving knotted examp similar birds appear in one of the Konya fragme and the Marby rug, of early 15th century date, in the Statens Historiska Museet, Stockholm, two octagons, each enclosing a pair of crested b on either side of a stylised tree (see C. J. La *The Marby Rug and some other fragments of car found in Egypt* (see above section i. 2. 6. for ref.).

Since they were subjected to continuous w very few tribal rugs of a pre-19th century date h survived (although notable exceptions are the T men rugs in the Ethnographic Museum, Lening unpublished in the West), making it impossibl write a coherent history. It can be inferred, howe that these ancient patterns persisted in spite of revolutionary changes in 16th century Iran u royal patronage, emulated in Ottoman court w shops, where the influence of illuminators and b binders emphasised the centre of the carpet introduced a large new répertoire of motifs. village and tribal traditions seem to have develc independently of the cities but, although they inevitably more conservative, there is evidenc borrowing and of organic growth; and 19th cen rugs show considerable diversity in the treatn of old themes.

The 19th century, which saw the earliest Europ documentation of the Central Asian tribes, marked a watershed, for the definition of the tional frontiers of Iran, Russia and Afghanis dealt a major blow to pastoral nomadism, and century has seen wholesale settlement.

The ethnically most homogeneous tribal confe acy was the Türkmen, who retained their exclusi until their territory on the Trans-Caspian ste was split up in the 1880s. Modern study has d onstrated major shifts of influence within confederacy, however, with tribes like the S and Sarïḳ, powerful in the 17th and 18th centu being overtaken in the 19th by the Tekke and bec ing extinct as tribal entities (see S. Azadi, *T menische Teppiche*, exhibition cat., Hamburg, I tr. 1970, *Turkoman carpets*, London 1975, 13-14 detailed lists of tribes and *ṭā'ifeh*s).

Türkmen pilework is justly famous for its h glossy wool, excellent vegetable dyes and knotting, normally using the asymmetrical Persian knot (but see M. H. Beattie, in *The Turco of Iran* [see Bibl.], 38-41, for exceptions), and T men rugs are unmistakable with their ground borders of the same colour, always red, but var from the clear tones of Salur and Tekke to ox-blood of the Sarïḳ and aubergine of the Yo and having in the central field an all-over repea *gül*s which, when used as primary ornament, se as a tribal totem, *tamgha*, exclusive to the tribe w used it. Tekke floor rugs (Pl. XXII) have octag *gül*s quartered by a lattice to enclose trifo forms identified by Moskova as birds (see Az *op. cit.*, 20-41) and also of totemic significa while the Yomut owned a number of *gül*s inclu the *kepse*, based on plant forms, and the *dïr* a hooked diamond enclosing birds (illustr. in Az *op. cit.*, and U. Schurmann, *Central Asian car* London 1969, pls. 15-25). It is known, however, the Sarïḳ and Tekke used older forms of the than those featuring in 19th century rugs, w secondary *gül*s and border patterns pose com blems, since it is now suggested that these may the ornaments originally belonging to another al group which was subjugated or absorbed. eover, a subjugated tribe, having lost its right ts primary ornament, possibly transferred it to ll items like bags, while the victorious group ht incorporate the weaker tribe's primary orna- t in its own smaller pieces. Ersarî rugs are sual in showing strong outside influences and, ddition to classic Türkmen motifs, large central lallions are introduced to bags while floor rugs prayer rugs may have floral patterns, treated i-naturalistically and in a higher tonal key str. in Azadi, *op. cit.*, pls. 7, 9, and 36, and urmann, *op. cit.*, pls. 41-56). As well as floor s, the Türkmen women used to knot many cles for their own use, including the tent-band, mi, *bu*, *yup*, which encircled the tent lattice the knotted pattern on a white plainweave and facing inwards; the *engsi* or *ensi*, a handsome with a cruciform design which acted as a tent r; the *kapunîk*, a fringed decoration hung over inside doorway; and a variety of bags, from dle-bags, *khordjin*, large storage bags, *čoval*, to ller ones, *torba*, for specific purposes like storing d, spindles, etc., These articles performed the ctions of storing the household equipment, sporting it on the migration and giving the rior of the round, felt-roofed tent an appearance apestry-hung splendour.

he finest knotting was reserved for covers, *aktsha*, for the much-valued horses, and the nut, who made the widest variety of articles patterns, used to knot a set of trappings for bridal camel, consisting of pentagonal flank gings, *asmalîk* (discussed in detail in R. Pinner M. Franses, *Turkoman studies*, i, London 1979), uently patterned with hooked stems or lozenges XXIII), and matching knee-hangings, *diyah ik*, while the two bundles of tent-poles lashed to a el when on the move would each have a bag- ped cover, *uk bash*, fitted over their protruding s.

ürkmen patterns have been influential, the two ıps which have borrowed most substantially n them being the Afghān and the Balūč. Modern hān rugs are knotted in the towns of Pakistan. ones, however, made by tribes related to the arî in northern Afghānistān, had qualities of r own. With a medium high pile, using the nmetrical or Persian knot, their central fields w an adaptation of the Tekke *gül*, without the ice, although the squarish octagons are quartered enclose trifoliate stems and leaves. They have e minor ornament than modern examples, and r colours, which include blues, yellows and wns on a red ground, are in a higher key. Borders ude geometricised plant forms, also borrowed n the Türkmen, and angular ribbon. Commercial ess has resulted in the standardisation of patterns colours, and rugs are often chemically washed roduce the "golden Afghans" popular in the West.

black-tented people, the Balūč nomadise in arid ıtry now forming parts of Iran, Afghanistan and istan. They utilise the good but undurable wool their sheep and undyed camel hair for warps, s and knotting, the Turkish or symmetrical t being more favoured, to produce a long, medium se pile. Distinctive features are the elaborately utiful ends in a variety of flat-weaves, and a ted range of dark colours: blues, blackish browns, ral reds and white. Their patterns reflect borrowing from Türkmen, Caucasian and Afshār sources, absorbed and reproduced in a characteristic manner. Floor rugs show octagons and Yomut borders, or all-over floral repeats treated semi-naturalistically and resembling Ersarî-Beshir rugs, this type being more commonly made in Iran. Their most typical product is the small prayer-rug with a stylised "Tree of Life" on an undyed camel hair ground.

Among the several tribes of Lur origin in western Iran, the Bakhtiyārī still migrate twice-yearly over difficult country in the Zagros mountains, in the proximity of other Lurs and of Mamassānī, Ḳashḳāʾī and Khamseh. Few of the so-called "Bakhtiyārī" rugs are tribal pieces, but were made by villagers in the Čahār Maḥall area, near Iṣfahān (see Edwards, *op. cit.*, 309-12, pls. 354-64). The Bakhtiyārī do very little weaving now, but still make a type of bag which is unique to them, the front and back of which are in flat-weave, usually *sumak* weft-wrapping with, along the bottom and up the sides, a strip of rather coarse, shaggy pile in the Turkish or symmetrical knot. This gives durability and is visually pleasing when the bags are stacked in the tent. Favourite motifs are 8-pointed stars in octagons, rosettes, the *Z-boteh* and borders of scrolling stem, while the flat-weave areas share these motifs and often have animals as well. Sizes vary from a very large saddle-bag, *talīs*, and bedding-bag, *mafrash*, and storage bags which can be loaded on to pack animals, *rū-kati*, to small, lavishly decorated bags, *namak-dān*, with narrow necks for pouring. Colours are rich dark reds, browns and blues, with white cotton in the flat-weave areas. These bags, hardly known in the West, are often bought by the Khamseh and Ḳashḳāʾī and can be seen in their tents.

The Afshārs, another tribe of Turkic descent, are believed to have been deported from Ādharbāydjān to Kirmān province by Shāh Ismāʿīl in the 16th century. Surrounded by Persian villagers, their tribal identity became blurred, so that it is difficult to distinguish a nomad from a village Afshār rug. Both knots are found. Old tribal pieces show a colour scheme of rich mid-blues, a clear red, yellow and ivory, and favour the diamond medallion layout, but the Persian *boteh* is often used as an all-over repeat, known as *dehadj*, and the chicken, *murghī*, found all over Fārs, is a favourite, while more naturalistic floral designs have been borrowed from Kirmān carpets. Borders, which are finely organised, range from rosettes, medallions and angular scrolling stem to Iṣfahānī floral ornament.

The tribal situation in Fārs province in south-western Iran has long been a complex one, since it is nomad country *par excellence*, with the Zagros mountains and hill valleys in the north and warmer plains south of Shīrāz, so that the migration routes of a number of tribes have impinged on one another. The two largest tribal confederacies, the Ḳashḳāʾī and the Khamseh, were founded for political reasons, the Ḳashḳāʾī during the 18th century and the Khamseh in 1861-2. The major *ṭāʾifeh*s of the Ḳashḳāʾī are Turkic, with some Lurs, Afshārs and Persians, while the Khamseh consists of five tribes of Turkic, Persian and Arab stock. Some tribes-people, however, are settled in villages, while of other groups like the Bolvardi, small sections belong to the Ḳashḳāʾī and the rest are villagers with no tribal allegiance. There has been wholesale borrowing of patterns and, since both knots are used, consequent difficulty in rug classification. The Ḳashḳāʾī have a reputation for the finest rugs. Their most typical composition, three stepped or hooked medallions in the central field, is shared by the Khamseh and other tribes, but in Ḳashḳāʾī pieces each medallion encloses a motif described as a crab or a stretched sheepskin but more likely a stylised plant form (Pl. XXIII). This simple scheme is garnished with detail: hooked octagons, rosettes, the Persian *boteh*, the Chinese knot and flower sprigs, as well as a menagerie of creatures like stylised peacocks, porcupines, gazelles, goats, (Pl. XXIVa), hawks, chickens and bees, powdering the ground with a nice sense of space. Another type has repeating *boteh*s all over the central field, a layout shared by the Afshārs. Main borders include the calyx and scrolling stems of city carpets (Pl. XXIII), but the narrow guard bands often retain older forms like the oblique stripe and reciprocal diamond. Skilled dyeing, for which the Shesh Bolūḳī Reshkūlī and Bullū were renowned, produced a sharp, clear red, several blues, a rich, creamy yellow, apricot, and soft dark brown and green, skilfully juxtaposed against ivory. Rug patterns are repeated on saddlebags of fine workmanship (Pl. XXIVb), chickens are shown here drinking at a fountain. Tent bags are generally made in flat-weave, but the Ḳashḳāʾī have lavished sumptuous trappings on their horses, including saddle covers and horse-cloths to cover the animals when they are tethered, which have knotted patterns on a plain-weave ground, while fringed chest and rump bands are still made, often embellished with blue beads against the Evil Eye.

Some attributions of designs to specific *ṭāʾifeh*s have been made (J. Allgrove, in *The Qashqāʾi of Iran*, exhibition cat., Manchester 1976, 64-95, pls. 5-8, 37-46), but the ethnic complexity of all the Fārs tribes and the eclectic nature of their patterns are barriers to precise classification.

The role of the tribeswomen who have always been responsible for the textile crafts extends into other areas for, since their rugs are the visual manifestation of tribal culture, the women have been the artists of the tribe and custodians of tribal traditions, a phenomenon unknown in the West; similarly, in this situation artists are not a specialist class, but have made for their own use artefacts both functional and of great beauty, bringing to mind Rudenko's comment concerning the Pazyryk textiles on the "astonishing skill and care lavished on the most trifling of articles". These are powerful reasons for studying tribal knotting in its own context.

Bibliography: (in addition to references given in the text and in the Bibl. to Section i above):

1. General. W. von Bode and E. Kühnel, *Vorderasiatische Knüpfteppiche*, Leipzig 1901, revised ed. and tr. C. Grant Ellis, *Antique rugs from the Near East*, London 1970; W. Grote-Hasenbalg, *Die Orientteppich, seine Geschichte und seine Kultur*, Berlin 1922; C. J. D. May, *How to identify Persian and other oriental rugs*, London 1969; H. Hubel, *A book of carpets*, London 1971.

2. Technique. H. Ling Roth, *Studies in primitive looms*, Halifax 1950; H. L. Wulff, *The traditional crafts of Persia*, Cambridge, Mass. 1966.

3. Early carpets. O. Aslanapa and Y. Durul, *Selçuklu halıları*, Istanbul 1973.

4. Carpets in paintings. J. von Lessing, *Altorientalische Teppiche*, Berlin 1877.

5. General works on the tribes of Persia, Afghānistān and Central Asia (see also the Bibls. to IRAN. ii. Demography and ethnography, ḲASHḲAY, TURKISTĀN, TÜRKMEN and TURKS. History and ethnography). H. Pottinger, *Travels in Belochistan and Sinde*, London 1816; A. Burnes, *Travels into Bokhara*, London 1834; C. Masson, *Narrative of various journey. Balochistan, Afghanistan and the Punjab*, Lon 1842; idem, *Narrative of various journeys Balochistan, Afghanistan, the Punjab and Ka* London 1844; J. Wolff, *Narrative of a missio Bokhara*, London 1845; A. Vambéry, *Travels Central Asia*, London 1864; idem, *Das Türkn volk*, Leipzig 1885; F. Burnaby, *A ride to Kh* London 1877; E. O'Donovan, *The Merv oa* London 1882; A. T. Wilson, *Report on Fars*, Si 1916; O. Garrod, *The nomadic tribes of Pe today*, and *The Qashqai tribe of Fars*, in *J Royal Central Asian Soc.*, xxxiii (1946); M. Ullens de Schooten, *Lords of the mounta southern Persia and the Kashkai tribe*, Lon 1956; G. E. Markov, *Die Wirtschaft der Türkme vor ihrer Übersiedlung in die Mittelasiatisc Oasen im 18. und 19. Jahrhundert*, in *Ethno phisch-Archäologische Forschungen*, Berlin 1(iv/1-2, 163 ff.; F. Barth, *Nomads of South Per the Basseri tribe of the Khamseh confederacy*, (1961; W. Barthold, *A history of the Turk people*, in *Four studies on the history of Cen Asia*, iii, Leiden 1962; P. Oberling, *The Tu peoples of southern Iran*, Cleveland 1964; id *The Qashqaʾi nomads of Fars*, The Hague 19 K. Jettmar, *Die frühen Steppenvölker*, Bac Baden 1964, tr. A. E. Keep, *Art of the step* London 1964; V. Monteil, *Les tribus de Fars e sedentarisation des nomads*, Paris 1966; E. Sun land, ch. *Pastoralism, nomadism and the so anthropology of Iran*, in *Camb. history of Iran* Cambridge 1968; D. Marsden, *The Qash nomadic pastoralists of Fars province*, in *Qashqāʾi of Iran*, exhibition cat., Manchester 1(9-18.

6. Tribal rugs. A. N. Ponomerev, *Motif Turkoman ornament* [in Russian], in *Turkm ovedenie*, No. 7-9, Ashkabad 1931; A. L *Turkestan and its textile crafts*, in *C. I. B. A. Rev.* Basle 1941, and Basingstoke 1974; V. G. Mosko *Tribal göls in Turkoman carpets* [in Russian] *SE* (1946), 145-62, Ger. tr. A. Kuntschik, *Göls türkmenischen Teppiche*, in *Archiv für Volkerku* iii (Vienna 1948), 24-43; M. S. Dimand, *Peas and nomad rugs*, exhib. cat., New York 19 C. D. Reed, *Turkoman rugs*, exhib. cat., Cambri Mass. 1966; A. N. Pirkulyeva, *Turkoman wo carpets of the central Amu Darya valley* [in F sian], in *USSR Academy of Sciences*: *Materia the culture of the peoples of Central Asia and zakstan*, Moscow 1966; S. A. Milhofer, *Zent asiatische Teppiche*, Hanover 1968; H. Mc Jones, *The Ersari and their weavings*, exhib. c Washington D.C. 1969; idem and J. W. Bouc *Rugs of the Yomud tribes*, *ibid.*, 1970; id *Weavings of the tribes of Afghanistan*, *ibid.*, 19 idem and R. S. Yohe, *Village and nomadic weav of Persia*, *ibid.*, 1971; Abbot Hall Gallery, Ken *The Turcoman of Iran*, exhib. cat. (contribs. P. and M. Andrews, M. H. Beattie and othe Kendal 1971; J. Franses, *Tribal rugs from Af nistan and Turkestan*, London 1973; A. de Fran and J. Housego, *Tribal animal covers from I* exhib. cat., Tehran 1975; idem, *Lori and Ba tiari flatweaves*, exhib. cat., Tehran 1976; Beresnova, ed., *The decorative and applied of Turkmenia*, Leningrad 1976; D. Black and Loveless, eds., *Rugs of the wandering Balu* London 1976; J. Housego, *Tribal rugs*, Lon 1978. (J. ALLGROVI

BITUMEN [see ḲAṬRĀN]

ıIYĀR, AL-BIYĀR (A. "wells, springs"), modern ārdjumand, a small town on the northern edges he Great Desert, the Dasht-i Kavīr, of Persia. mediaeval geographers describe it as being e days' journey from Bisṭām and 25 *farsakhs* ı Dāmghān, and as falling administratively hin the province of Ḳūmis [*q.v.*], although in ıānid times (4th/10th century) it seems to have ı attached to Nīshāpūr in Khurāsān. It was the ninus of an only-moderately frequented route ss the northeastern corner of the desert to shīz in Ḳūhistān.

/e have in Muḳaddasī, 356-7, 372, an especially ıiled description of the town, considering its lerate size and importance, lying as it did off great highway connecting western Persia with ırāsān; this is explicable by the fact that Mudasī's maternal grandfather had emigrated thence Jerusalem. He mentions that Biyār had good ivated fields and orchards, and grazing grounds sheep and camels; the rather scanty water supply carefully controlled in irrigation channels. There an inner citadel approached through a single ɜway, but there were three iron gates in the er walls. There was no Friday mosque, and the ıbitants were all Ḥanafīs, strongly opposed to Karrāmiyya [*q.v.*]; nevertheless, Muḳaddasī tes elsewhere (365) that the Karrāmiyya had a *nakāh* in Biyār. He further stresses the building ls of the Biyārīs, above all in the medium of mud ık. Politically it came within the Sāmānid domin- s at this time, and coins in the name of the nānid *amīrs* were minted there between 298/ -11 and 369/979-80; a coin is also extant of the ıznawids, from the year 426/1035, the eve of the sing of the provinces of Khurāsān and Ḳūmis Saldjūḳ hands (E. von Zambaur, *Die Münzgungen des Islams, zeitlich und örtlich geordnet*, Viesbaden 1968, 83). Yāḳūt, *Buldān*, ed. Beirut 17, mentions several scholars produced by Biyār, ongst whom were some noted Ḥanafī ones. stawfī, *Nuzhat al-ḳulūb*, tr. Le Strange, 148, refers the town's good cereals, but apart from these ıtions we possess little information on the place. few European travellers, beginning with Forster vards the end of the 18th century, began to cross northern edge of the Great Desert and to pass ough Biyār, by now known as Biyārdjumand (the earjemund" of Capt. C. Clerk, in *Jnal. of the graphical Soc.*, xxxi (1861), 53). There were in rk's time some 200 houses there, with a good ter supply from *ḳanāts* and gardens and fields; in nearby hills, the Kūh-i Biyārdjumand, copper, ena and marble were obtained, cf. W. Tomaschek, *historische Topographie von Persien. II. Die ge durch die persische Wüste*, in *SBWAW*, Phil.-t. Cl., cviii (1885), 632-3. At the present day, ārdjumand is the chef-lieu of the *bakhsh* of the ıe name, in the *shahrastān* of Shāhrūd, in the ond *ustān* of Iran; its population is *ca.* 2,600, see zmārā, *Farhang-i djughrāfiyā'-yi Irān*, iii, 54.

Bibliography: (in addition to references given n the article): Le Strange, *The lands of the Eastern Caliphate*, 366, 368; Schwarz, *Iran im Mittelalter*, 23-6; A. Gabriel, *Durch Persiens Wüsten*, Stuttgart 1935, 119-20; idem, *Die Erforschung Persiens*, Vienna 1952, 303; H. Halm, *Die Ausbreitung der Šāfiʿitischen Rechtsschule von der Anfangen bis um 8./14. Jahrhundert*, Wiesbaden 1974, 123.

(C. E. Bosworth)

BİYİḲLİ [see MEḤMED PASHA].

BLAZON [see RANK].

BLESSING [see BARAKA].

BOAT [see SAFĪNA].

BÖLÜKBASHĪ, RİḌĀ TEWFĪḲ, modern Turkish orthography RIZA TEVFİK BÖLÜKBAŞI, Turkish poet and writer (1866-1949). He was born in Djisr-i Muṣṭafā Pasha in Rumelia (Dimitrovgrad in present-day Bulgaria, formerly Čaribrod) while his father Khōdja Meḥmed Tewfīḳ Efendi, a civil servant and teacher, was *ḳāyimaḳām* there. His mother, a Circassian slave girl, died when Riḍā was eleven years old. His grandfather Aḥmed Durmush Bölükbashī was a guerilla leader from Debra in Albania who had fought against the Greeks during the rising in the Morea ([Feridun] Kandemir, *Kendi ağzından Rıza Tevfik* ("Rıza Tevfik from his own mouth"), Istanbul 1943, 94-7, 109). After attending various schools (including the Alliance Israélite school and Galatasaray) in Istanbul, he finished in the *rüshdiyye* (high school) of Gelibolu (Gallipoli), his family town, and entered the school of political science (*Mekteb-i Mülkiyye*), whence he was however expelled for political activities and insubordination. He switched to medicine, and after several temporary suspensions, graduated in 1899. He worked as government doctor at the Customs Office in Istanbul until the restoration of the Constitution in July 1908, when he joined political life. An enthusiastic member of the ruling Committee of Union and Progress (CUP) [see ITTIḤĀD WE TERAḲḲĪ DJEMʿIYYETI], he was elected deputy for Edirne, but soon broke with the CUP leaders and joined the opposition and became one of the leading figures of the Liberal Union [see HÜRRIYYET WE IʾTILĀF FİRḲASĪ] (Refik Halid Karay, *Minelbab ilelmihrab*, Istanbul 1964, *passim*). He taught philosophy at the University of Istanbul and Turkish literature at the American Robert College. He served as Minister of Education in 1918 and was made president of the Council of State (*Shūrā-yi Dewlet*) in 1919. As a member of the collaborationist Ottoman government, he signed the treaty of Sèvres (10 August 1920), which sealed his fate in the eyes of the Nationalists. Student protests forced him to give up his chair in the University (1921) and he fled the country following the Nationalist victory in Anatolia (September 1922). His name was later included in the list of the 150 undesirables [see YÜZELLİLİKLER]. After a brief stay in Egypt, he served for seven years in the government of *Amīr* ʿAbd Allāh (a former fellow-deputy in the Ottoman Parliament) in Jordan, spent a year in the USA and eventually settled in Djūniyya in Lebanon, where he lived with his wife in retirement until he returned to Turkey in 1943, five years after the general amnesty of 1938. He died in Istanbul on 31 December 1949. Although Riḍā Tewfīḳ is known by the nickname *Feylesof* ("The Philosopher") on account of his numerous publications on philosophical topics (see below), which are mainly works of compilation (but which greatly contributed to the teaching of modern philosophy in Turkey), his real contribution to Turkish literature is as a poet. In the late 1890s a young poet, Meḥmed Emīn (Yurdakul) [*q.v.*], suddenly appeared on the literary scene and made a sensation by his use of spoken Turkish, syllabic metre and the use of popular subjects. He was greeted as a guide and innovator, but did not have any following as his poetry was uninspired, awkward in style and totally lacking in musical effect. In contrast, Riḍā Tewfīḳ, who started his career in the same period by writing poems on the line of ʿAbd al-Ḥaḳḳ Ḥāmid and Tewfīḳ Fikret [*q.vv.*] found, in the early 1900s, the key to a regeneration of Turkish poetry; he was able to capture the style, language and inner warmth of leading poets and popular mystic (dervish) poets without blindly imitating them, but re-creating their warm and lively atmosphere in a modern garb [see ḲARADJAOGHLAN, ḲAYGHUSUZ ABDĀL and YŪNUS EMRE]. His success ushered in a new trend which was later moulded into a school by Ḍiyā᾽ (Ziya) Gökalp, that of the *Millī edebiyyāt* ("National literature"). Riḍā Tewfīḳ did not abandon the *ʿarūḍ* like most of his younger colleagues of the new school, but used it in parallel with the *hedje*. His influence on succeeding generations of poets continued in the 1920s and early 1930s and his style began to date only with the appearance of Orkhan Welī (Orhan Veli) Kanık and Fāḍil Ḥüsnī (Fazıl Hüsnü) Dağlarca, who revolutionised all concepts in Turkish poetry.

Riḍā Tewfīḳ Bölükbashî is the author of the following major works: *ʿAbd al-Ḥaḳḳ Ḥāmid we mülāhaẓāt-î felsefiyyesi* ("A.H. and his philosophic reflections"), Istanbul 1329 *rūmī*/1913; *Felsefe dersleri* ("A course of philosophy"), i, Istanbul 1330 *rūmī*/1914; *Mufaṣṣal Ḳāmūs-î felsefe* ("A comprehensive dictionary of philosophy"), i, Istanbul 1330 *rūmī*/1914; *Étude sur la religion des Hoûroufîs*, in Cl. Huart, *Textes persans relatifs à la secte des Hoûroufîs*, Leiden 1909; *Serabı ömrüm* ("Mirage of my life"), Lefkose (Nicosia) 1934, 2nd ed. Istanbul 1949, (contains all his poems, except some political satires); *Ömer Hayyam ve rübaileri*², Istanbul 1945, Introd.

Bibliography: Rūshen Eshref, *Diyorlarki* (interviews with leading writers) Istanbul 1918, 133-54 and *passim*: Halide Edib, *Memoirs*, New York 1926, *passim*; R. Gökalp Arkin, *R.T.B.*, *hayatı ve siirleri*², Istanbul 1939; Vahyi Ölmez, *R.T.*, Istanbul 1945; R. C. Ulunay, *R.T.*, *siirleri ve mektupları*, Istanbul n.d. [1943]; Hilmi Yücebaş, *Bütün cepheleriyle R.T.*, Istanbul 1950; Hilmi Ziya Ülken, *Türkiye'de çağdas düşünce tarihi*, i, Istanbul-Konya 1966, 406-24. (FAHIR IZ)

BOOTY [see FAY᾽, GHANĪMA].

BORNEO, a large island (area 292,000 sq. miles/ 755,000 km²) straddling the equator in the Indonesian archipelago, and mainly covered with tropical rain forest. The spinal range of mountains rises to 13,455 ft./4,100 m. in Mount Kinabalu in the northeastern tip of the island. Politically, the greater part of the island has since 1949 formed the Indonesian region of Kalimantan (a name which Indonesia also applies to the whole island); along the northern coast lie Sabah, the former British crown colony of British North Borneo and Sarawak, both of whom joined the Malaysian Federation in 1963, and the British-protected sultanate of Brunei [*q.v.* in Suppl.]. The following article deals only with the Indonesian part of the island; see also BORNEO in *EI*¹.

Indonesian Kalimantan is divided into four provinces (*daerah tingkat I*): Kalimantan Barat (Western Kalimantan, 157,066 sq. km., 2,019,936 inhabitants, capital: Pontianak), Kalimantan Tengah (Central Kalimantan, 156,552 sq. km., 699,589 inhabitants, capital: Palangka Raya), Kalimantan Selatan (Southern Kalimantan, 34,611 sq. km., 1,699,105 inhabitants, capital: Banjarmasin), and Kalimantan Timur (Eastern Kalimantan, 202,619 sq. km., 733,536 inhabitants, capital: Samarinda). South and Central Kalimantan originally formed one province, until on 23 May 1957, the area was divided because of the opposition of the Dayak people against the "Malays" (Muslims) in the southern parts.

1. *Earlier History*. In Sambas (north-western Kalimantan), which had been a Buddhist cult centre already in the 6th century A.D., a descend of the sultan's family of Johore established a sultan at the time of Brunei's conversion to Islam (betw 1514 and 1521), and Malays began to settle in area. Chinese workers were brought to work in gold mines, but in 1770 they revolted and forr semi-independent "republics" (*kung si*). Islam little influence on them, and only after 1965, w they were required to confess one of the ackn ledged religions in Indonesia, did a few of th become Muslims. Sambas has remained a strongh of Malay culture. The area of Lawei, an old Javan colony, and Matan on the Pawan river, turned Islam soon after the conversion of the sea ports northern Java. Sukadana, having—like Samba experienced the influence of Buddhist Sri Vija was islamised mainly by Malay and Arab trad from Palembang, which at that time (first half 16th century) was under the rule of Demak. 1608-9 Surabaya imposed its dominance, until 1622 Sultan Agung of Mataram wiped out influence of his main rival. Only in these areas south-western Kalimantan Barat, did class Javanese (*Kawi*) remain "the sultan's languag in Ketapang e.g. until this century, although this place only a *panembahan* resided. The 1 century saw the rise of the sultanate of Pontian founded in 1771 by an Arab adventurer, Sh ʿAbd al-Raḥmān, the son of a Ḥaḍramawtī an princess of Matan. Pontianak always stressed Arabic background and claimed that its und standing of Islam was a notably pure one.

According to tradition, Demak initiated the spr of Islam in southern Kalimantan, seizing the opp tunity for this when at the beginning of the 1 century a conflict occurred between two pretende Pangeran Samudra and Pangeran Tumenggung, the course of which the former appealed to the h of Demak. This was granted, and Samudra beca the founder of the Muslim sultanate of Banjarmas acknowledging the supremacy of Demak (1520). successors ruled until 1860, when the Dutch colon government abolished the sultanate after the rev of Hidāyat, the legal heir to Sultan Adam (d. 185 Like other revolts in 19th century Indonesia, movement was inspired by the idea of *djihād*. present, the area of the former sultanate is part the province of South Kalimantan, with the *ka paten* of Hulu Sungai (east of the Barito river) one of the strongest Muslim areas on the island. the earlier days of the sultanate, its ruler exercis his influence in most of the trading centres on southern coast, like Sampit, Kota Waringin, e which became centres for the propagation of Isl among the neighbouring Dayak tribes; some them, however, further withdrew to the interi Although the impact of Javanese customs and ma ners was strong, the literary language was Mal influenced by local idioms and Javanese. J. J. F emphasises that in spite of its particularities, ev *basa Banjar* (Banjarese colloquial) should be count among the numerous Malay dialects (*Hika Bandjar*, 7-12). This explains also why the Banjar Muslims and above all their *ʿulamā᾽*, felt a spec obligation to present themselves as authen teachers of Malay Islam after the *bahasa Indone* was proclaimed the offical medium of communicati in the archipelago (1928). On the other hand, th distinctively separated themselves linguistically ar as a consequence, culturally, from the Dayak trib for whom the term "Malay" and "Muslim" beca tical. Becoming a Muslim (= Malay) means for Dayak to loose his social relationships. Only a Dayak tribes became Muslims, e.g. the Bakum- a former sub-tribe of the Ngaju Dayak (Danand-, 139, in consent with Mallinckrodt).

n East Kalimantan, Pasir and Kutai [*q.v.*] saw rise of colonies of Buginese traders and ship-ders from South Sulawesi, soon after their neland had turned over to Islam (1605-11). ording to tradition, the first teacher of Islam in ir was an Arab, while Makassarese preachers, ong them the miraculous Tuan Tunggang Pa-gan, were active in Kutai. Like in South Sula-i, Islam in Kutai seems to have been mixed n many animistic survivals and remained weak oughout the 18th century. The sultans had their *on* in Tenggarong, between Samarinda where t of the Buginese settled, and the Dayak area. ir story is told in the *Salasila Kutai*, written in ay.

. *Modern developments*. As the sultans both in t and West Kalimantan during the times of ch supremacy were relatively independent in ir internal jurisdiction, Islamic law, more or less lified by the local customary (*adat*) law, played a ificant role. Courts were closely attached to the ace. After independence, the Indonesian govern-nt tried to bring these "religious courts" under authority of the local branches of the Ministry Religious Affairs (Lev, *Islamic courts*, 78 f.). On other hand, Islamic law has also influenced the *t* law of the non-Muslim Dayaks.

ince the beginning of the century, Sambas, Pon-ak and Banjarmasin have been caught up in mic modernist movements. The Malay periodical *'mām* (since 1906), partly inspired by Rashīd ā's *al-Manār*, was distributed in Pontianak and nbas. The "Serikat Islam", the oldest nationalist vement, held a congress in Kalimantan in 1923. 1930, the traditionalist "Nahdlatul Ulama" blished its first branches in Banjarmasin and rtapura, and South Kalimantan remained, besides t Java, a stronghold of this party until 1942. modernist "Muhammadiyah" became active in 7, its first branch being opened in Banjarmasin. *balligh̲ūn* or propagandists from Java and angkabau were sent there, some of them being ner attendants of the "Thawalib" schools in st Sumatra. Their progress seems to have been v; at the Muhammadiyah's national congress in 9, no participant from Kalimantan was noted. 1935, the movement had 29 branches on the nd. It is active in *daʿwa* or missionary and cational work by building schools, clinics, and tributing pamphlets and books, its activities ching now the Hulu (up-river) areas and the der districts between West Kalimantan and awak. In Banjarmasin, a government-related stitut Agama Islam Negeri" (I.A.I.N.) has been blished, whereas in Pontianak a branch of *Fukuctas Tarbiyah* of the I.A.I.N. Jakarta utat is active. A branch of the same I.A.I.N.'s *ultas Ushuluddin*, now in Singkawang, is to be ved to Pontianak.

Bibliography: Remarks on Islam in Kaliman-an are found in general works on Islam in In-lonesia [see bibliography to INDONESIA V. - SLAM IN INDONESIA]; further B. J. Boland, *The truggle of Islam in modern Indonesia* (= *Verandelingen van het Koninklijk Instituut voor Taal-, Land- en Volkenkunde*, 59), The Hague 1971; Deliar Noer, *The modernist Muslim movement in Indonesia 1900-1942*, Singapore—Kuala Lumpur 1973;—Historiography: A. A. Cense, *De Kroniek van Banjarmasin*, Santpoort 1928; C. A. Mees, *De Kroniek van Koetai*, Santpoort 1935; W. Kern, *Commentaar op de Salasilah van Koetai* (= VKI 19), The Hague 1956; J. J. Ras, *Hikajat Bandjar. A study in Malay historiography* (= Bibliotheca Indonesia, I), The Hague 1968 (with extensive bibliography);—Languages: A. A. Cense and E. M. Uhlenbeck, *Critical survey of studies on the languages of Borneo* (= Bibliographical Series 2), The Hague 1958 (Malay dialects pp. 7-13); A. B. Hudson, *A note on Selako: Malayic Dayak and Land Dayak languages in Western Borneo*, in *The Sarawak Museum Journal*, xviii (1970), 301-18;—Law: *Adatrechtbundels*, ed. by Kon. Instituut voor de Taal-, Land- en Volkenkunde, The Hague, xiii (1917), xxvi (1926), xxxvi (1933), xliv (1952); M. Mallinckrodt, *Het Adatrecht van Borneo*, Leiden 1928; Daniel S. Lev, *Islamic courts in Indonesia*, Berkeley-Los Angeles-London 1972;—Islam and the culture around it: F. Ukur, *Tuaiannja sungguh banjak*, Bandjarmasin-Djakarta 1960 (especially 121 ff.); J. Danandjaja, *Kebudajaan penduduk Kalimantan tengah*, in Koentjaraningrat (ed.), *Manusia dan Kebudajaan Indonesia*, Djakarta 1971, 119-44; A. B. Hudson, *Padjua epat: the Ma'anyan of Indonesian Borneo*, New York 1972; *200 Tahun Kota Pontianak*. Diterbitkan oleh Pemerintah Daerah Kotamadya Pontianak, Pontianak 1971; J. E. Garang, *Adat und Gesellschaft. Eine sozioethnologische Untersuchung zur Darstellung des Geistes- und Kulturlebens der Dajak in Kalimantan* (= Beiträge zur Südasien-Forschung, Südasien-Institut der Universität Heidelberg, 9). Wiesbaden 1974 (especially pp. 109-28);—for a short account of the development of Muslim Higher education until the foundation of the I.A.I.N. at Banjarmasin, see Analiansyah, *Proses Lahirnya IAIN Antasari*, in *Panji Masyarakat* No. 148 (1 April 1974);—Statistics: *Statistik Indonesia 1970-1971*, ed. by Biro Pusat Statistik, Djakarta 1972. (O. SCHUMANN)

BRAHMANS. [see BARĀHIMA].

BRICK [see LABIN].

BRIGAND [see FALLĀḲ, ḲAZAḲ, LIṢṢ, ṬARĪḲ].

BRUNEI, a sultanate on the northern coast of Kalimantan (Borneo [*q.v.*]), 5,765 sq. km. (2,226 sq. miles) in area with *ca.* 145,000 inhabitants. The capital is Bandar Seri Begawan (before 1970 called Bandar Brunei or Brunei Town), with *ca.* 45,000 inhabitants. Its principal landmark is the great Mesjid Omar Ali Saifuddin, built after World War II. Since the 6th century A.D., trade relations existed with China. Occasionally tribute was paid, not only to China but also to Buddhist Sri Vijaya (South Sumatra) and Majapahit (Java), where it was mentioned among other Bornean tributaries in *ca.* 1365. *The Sh̲āʿir Awang Semaun*, probably the oldest legendary account of Brunei's history, narrates how the 14 sons of "sultan" Dewa Emas Kayangan, who was of celestial origin, founded the empire of Brunei. The youngest brother was the warrior Semaun, their leader Awang Alak Betatar. When the sultan of Johore sent his daughter to be married to the sultan of Sulu, she was abducted and married to Alak Betatar. The sultan of Johore finally agreed to this state of affairs and installed Alak Betatar as the first Muslim sultan of Brunei, bestowing on him the regalia of Johore (Brown, 134 f.). As Sultan Muḥammad he is said to have reigned from 1405 to

1415. His successor Aḥmad married his daughter to an Arab from al-Ṭā'if, and their son Sulaymān became the ancestor of the later sultans of Brunei.

There seems to have existed, however, a rival pagan kingdom besides the Muslim sultanate, which gave the impression, in 1514, to the Portuguese that Brunei was still heathen. When Antonio Pigafetta, an Italian member of Magellan's expedition, visited Brunei in 1521, he mentioned that the sultan (Bulkiah I, the fifth of his dynasty) was waging heavy warfare against a rival pagan kingdom in the same harbour. Finally, Sultan Bulkiah succeeded in safeguarding his supremacy and brought Brunei to the climax of its glory, ruling over most of "Borneo" (hence its name), the Sulu Islands and parts of Mindanao and Luzon. It was the Spaniards, however, who, since 1578, from their stronghold in Manila, successfully began to confine Brunei's strength to the northern coasts of Borneo, from where, in their turn, pirates intimidated the Spanish, and other, fleets. During the 19th century, the territory of Brunei was encircled decisively. In 1841 most of Sarawak was ceded to Sir James Brooke. In 1888, Brunei became a British protectorate. Later, in 1906, the sultan was granted the right to supervise matters which concern Religious (Islamic) and Customary Law (*adat*-law). In 1959, however, when a new constitution was introduced—the first written one in Brunei's history — his juridical functions were turned over to the courts. Nevertheless, his internal position was also strengthened considerably, as a number of rights of the former resident were transferred into his hands. Brunei became "an internally self-governing Islamic Sultanate under British protection". Only security and foreign affairs were still handled by the British, who from now on were represented by a High Commisionary.

New perspectives for Brunei's future opened when in May 1961, Tengku Abdul Rahman as the Prime Minister of the Malayan Federation, forwarded the plan for a new federation, Malaysia, which was to include, besides the Malayan Federation, Singapore, Sarawak, British North Borneo (now Sabah), and Brunei. At the beginning, Sultan Sir Omar Ali Saifuddin's attitude was a positive one, in the hope that he would be able to join the *collegium* of the nine Malayan sultans who were to elect the Yang Dipertuan Agung from among themselves as the nominal Head of State for a period of five years. In a memorandum, prepared by the Malaysia Consultative Committee in February 1962, it was further stated that Islam was to be the official religion in the Federation (Gullick, 64), another matter favourably received by Brunei with its outspoken Malay tradition, contrasting to the other North Bornean territories where Islam is followed only by minorities and where the Malays were not acknowledged as *bumiputera* (indigenous).

But the sultan met with opposition from the "Party Ra'yat" (People's Party), led by Shaikh A. M. Azahari, which had gained 22 out of 23 possible seats when the Legislative Council of Brunei was elected in October 1962. Azahari himself had not run for a seat, and there is some doubt whether he is a Brunei citizen (Brown, 127); he is known to have fought against the Dutch in the Indonesian Independence War. On 6 December 1962, his followers staged a revolt, somewhat untimely, because Azahari at that time happened to be in Manila. His aim was to form a Negara Kalimantan Utara ("State of North Borneo"), including Sarawak, Brunei and Sabah, with the sultan as nominal ruler and himself, Azahari, as Prime Minister. W British help, however, the revolt was soon suppres Azahari stayed in exile abroad, but the strong position of Indonesia and the Philippines aga the formation of Malaysia, which probably insp Azahari's policy, now came into the open. Fin the sultan in July 1963 decided that Brunei sh not join Malaysia, officially because of his dis with Sarawak about the Limbang valley w nearly divides his territory into two enclaves; problems about the distribution of the profit Brunei's rich oil fields (exploited since 1929 by British Shell Company) may also have affected decision.

Since 1974, the question of Brunei's independe has become acute again. Sultan Sir Hassanal Bulk ruling since his father's abdication in 1967, is a opposed by Azahari who opts for a more democr and completely independent Brunei (now with Sarawak and Sabah), with the sultan as the m symbolic head of state. Azahari, still in exile, the future of Brunei based on a *Trisila* ("Th Pillars", obviously in distinction to Malaysia's Indonesia's *Pančasila* or "Five Pillars") of (a) Islamic Religion, (b) Nationalism, and (c) Democr The national colours he proposes are still thos the former "State of North Borneo", sc. red white (like Singapore and Indonesia), with a gr triangle symbolising Islam.

Bibliography: J. M. Gullick, *Malaysia and neighbours*[3], London 1967; D. G. E. Hall, *A Hist of South-East Asia*, New York 1968; D. E. Bro *Brunei*: *the structure and history of a Born Malay sultanate*, Monograph of the Brunei Muse Journal, ii/2, Brunei 1970 (with extensive bib graphy). (O. Schumann)

BŪ ʿAZZA [see abū yaʿazza].

BUBASHTRU (BOBASTRO), also s Bub.sh.t.r., Bāb.sh.t.r. and, frequently from 5th/11th century, Bash.t.r. or Bush.t.r., a mo tain stronghold famed as the headquarters, fi of ʿUmar b. Ḥafṣūn [*q.v.*], leader of Andalus resistance, mainly south of Cordova, to the Umayy from 267/880-1 until his death in 305/917, a then, of his sons until 315/928. The precise locat of Bobastro, often confused (as in *EI*[2] i, 1250) w Barbastro (Barbashturu) in Huesca province, proved a thorny problem. Erroneously identified Dozy with Castillón, near Teba (Málaga provin it was believed by Simonet to be situated 6 k east of Ardales in the Mesas of Villaverde (Mál province). His view prevailed, and in the 1920s was identified with a site excavated above the H de Chorro near the railway running from Cord to Málaga via Bobadilla. This identification accepted by Lévi-Provençal (*Hist. Esp. mus.* 303 n. 1), and it remains acceptable to some. It h however, been challenged by J. Vallvé Bermejo, w after meticulous examination of all available evider some of it new, has cogently argued that the facts the Bobastro campaigns as reported by our sour point to a site much further to the south-east. T site, he submits, is to be sought not far from present Cortijo de Auta in the Sierra del R north of Ríogordo (Málaga province) and the na Bobastro to be seen in a toponym recorded in 15th-century source, viz. Postuero, otherwise Co del Encina (Repartimiento de Comares). The ori of the name — which survives in one form or anot elsewhere in Spain — is very likely Iberian.

During the anti-Umayyad rebellion, Bobas was frequently the scene of military activity, a

›d it was there that the *amīr* al-Mundhir died 75/888 while pressing a siege. In 278/891 his ›ssor ʿAbd Allāh tried to take the place, but l. Subsequent attempts made by his sons ›rrif (280/894) and Abān (291/904 and 294/907) :tain the same objective also came to nothing. until 316/928 was Bobastro finally subdued a decade of slow but sure policy pursued by . al-Raḥmān III. So far as we can glean, Bobastro ›after remained an important Umayyad garrison it fell to the Berbers who defeated Muḥammad :roops on the banks of the Guadiaro in 400/1010. the years 1039 and 1047 we have passing ›ences to Bobastro under the Ḥammūdid "party s" of Málaga, and in 1147 we find it sheltering ›ahdī's brothers after a rising in Seville against Almohads who had just occupied the city. By 7th/13th century the fortress was in ruins.

Bibliograph: All the main references are ›ntained in J. Vallvé Bermejo, *De Nuevo sobre bastro*, in *Al-Andalus*, xxx (1965), 139-74. Apart ›m a study of the boundaries of Rayya (roughly ›ilaga province), this monograph provides a ›d index of place-names. (J. D. Latham)

›DŪḤ, an artificial talismanic word formed the elements of the simple three-fold magic ›re

9	2
5	7
1	6

expressed in *Abdjad* by

د	ط	ب
ج	ه	ز
ح	ا	و

›r groups of letters from that square are similarly, ›not see generally, used, e.g. بطد, زهج, واح, and ›her بطدزهج واح. From some, also, larger ›res are built up, as a four-fold on بدوح and ›-fold on بطدواح. In the older Arabic ›s on magic (e.g. *Shams al-maʿārif* of al-Būnī in Suppl.], d. 622/1225) this formula plays a ›aratively minor part; but after it was taken y al-Ghazālī and cited in his *Munḳidh min al-* (ed. Cairo 1303/1886, 46, 50, tr. W. Montgomery ›t, *The faith and practice of al-Ghazālī*, London , 77, 79-80,) as an inexplicable, but certain, ›tance in cases of difficult labour, it came to be ›ersally known as "the three-fold talisman, or or table of al-Ghazālī" (*al-wakf, al-khātam, al-*›*val, al-muthallath li'l-Ghazālī*) and finally has ›me the foundation and starting point for the e "Science of Letters" (*ʿilm al-ḥurūf*). Al-›ālī is said to have developed the formula, under ›e inspiration (*ilhām*), from the combinations of rs كهيعص and حمعسق which begin Sūras and XLII of the Ḳurʾān, and which by them-s are also used as talismans (Reinaud, *Monu-s musulmans*, ii, 236). For the process, see the *ātiḥ al-ghayb* (ed. Cairo 1327/1909, 170 ff.) of ›ad Mūsā al-Zarḳawī, a contemporary Egyptian ›cian, and on the subject in general, the sixth seventh *Risālas* in that volume. Others trace ›formula back to Adam, from whom it passed ı to al-Ghazālī (cf. the *al-ʿInāya al-rabbāniya*, ›nd *al-Asrār al-rabbāniya*, 16 of Yūsuf Muḥam- al-Hindī, an early 20th century Egyptian ›r on magic). In all this, al-Ghazālī's established ›tation as a custodian of mystical knowledge and ›cially of the book *al-Djafr*, evidently played a part (*JAOS*, xx, 113; Goldziher, *Le livre de Ibn Toumert*, 15 ff.). Another suggested origin is the Arameo-Persian name of the planet and goddess Venus, *Bīdukht* ܒܝܕܘܟܬ, بيدخت G. Hoffmann, *Auszüge aus syrischen Akten persischer Märtyrer*, 128 ff.). But though this name appears in the *Fihrist*, I, 311, 7, with magical and diabolical associations and is quoted very occasionally in connection with Zuhara (e.g. Maḳrīzī, *Khiṭaṭ*, 1324/1906, i, 8; Thaʿlabī, *Ḳiṣaṣ al-anbiyāʾ*, 1314/1896-7, 29—both with misprints) it appears to be totally unknown in magical or *Djinn* literature. Yet the name evidently passed early into South Arabic, became used there as a feminine proper name and as a feminine epithet, "fat" and was confused with the root بدخ (*LA*, iii, 484, *sub* بدخ). Other standing in Arabic it does not have. Further, when Budūḥ is associated with a particular planet, it is with Saturn (*Zuḥal*) and its metal is lead (Zarḳāwī, *Mafātīḥ*, 170), not copper as Venus would require. Hardly worthy of mention is Von Hammer's fancy that Budūḥ is one of the names of Allāh (*JA*, 1830, 72) though it may have a Turkish basis (and see, too, de Sacy, below), and the derivation he suggests or the story told by Michel Sabbagh to de Sacy (*Chrest. arabe*, iii, 364 ff.) that it was the name of a pious merchant whose packages and letters never went astray, though that may well be a popular Syrian explanation. In magical books there are few cases even of personifying the word (e.g. *Yā Budūḥ* in *al-Fatḥ al-raḥmānī* by Ḥādjdj Saʿdūn, 21), but for the popular mind Budūḥ has become a *Djinnī* whose services can be secured by writing his name either in letters or numbers (*JA*, Ser. 4, xii, 521 ff.; Spiro, *Vocabulary of colloquial Egyptian*, 36; Doutté, *Magie et Religion*, 296, with *Ḳayyūm* as though a name of Allāh; Klunzinger, *Upper Egypt*, 387). The uses of this word are most various, to invoke both good and bad fortune. Thus, in Doutté, [*op. cit.*], against menorrhagia (234), against pains in the stomach (229), to render one's self invisible (275) and against temporary impotence (295). Lane's Cairo magician also used it with his ink mirror (*Modern Egyptians*, ch. xii), and so in several magical treatises. It is also engraved upon jewels and metal plates or rings which are carried as permanent talismans, and it is inscribed at the beginning of books (like *Kabīkadj*) as a preservative, e.g. in *al-Fatḥ al-djalīl*, Tunis 1290. But by far the most common use is to ensure the arrival of letters and packages.

Bibliography: (in addition to references given in the article): Ibn Khaldūn, *Muḳaddima*, ed. Quatremère, iii, 131, 135, 139-40, 142-3, 157, tr. Rosenthal, iii, 163-4, 168-9, 174, 176-8, 193; Reinaud, *Monuments musulmans*, ii, 243 ff., 251 ff., 256; W. Ahrens, *Studien über die "magischen Quadrate" der Araber*, in *Isl.*, vii (1917), 186-250; idem, *Die "magischen" Quadrate" al-Būnī's*, in *Isl.*, xii (1922), 157-77; E. Wiedemann, *Zu den magischen Quadraten*, in *Isl.*, viii (1918), 94-7; G. Bergsträsser, *Zu den magischen Quadraten*, in *Isl.* xiii (1923), 227-55; T. Canaan, *The decipherment of Arabic talismans*, in *Berytus*, iv (1937), 100 ff.; W. Pax, *Der magische Kreis im Spiegel der Sprache*, in *Forschungen und Fortschritte*, xiii (1937), 380; Carra de Vaux, *Une solution arabe du problème des carrés magiques*, in *Revue de l'histoire des sciences*, i (1948), 206-12; L. Fischer, *Zur Deutung des magischen Quadrates in Durers MELENCOLIA I.*, in *ZDMG*, ciii (1953), 308-14;

H. Hermelink, *Arabische magische Quadrates mit 25 Zellen*, in *Sudhoff's Archiv für Geschichte der Medizin*, xliii (1959), 351-4.

(D. B. Macdonald*)

BUFFALO [see djāmūs, in Suppl.].

BUGHĀT [see mārid].

BUḲʿA means etymologically "a patch of ground marked out from adjoining land by a difference in colour, etc." or "a low-lying region with stagnant water" (see Lane, *s.v.*); the latter sense is obviously at the base of the plural Biḳāʿ [*q.v.*] to designate the (originally) marshy valley between the Lebanon and Anti-Lebanon ranges in Syria, and doubtless at that of the name al-Buḳayʿa for a settlement near the Lake of Ḥimṣ [*q.v.*] (see Le Strange, *Palestine under the Moslems*, 352). From these senses it acquires the broader one of "province, region, tract of land", as in the classical Arabic geographers (for Muḳaddasī, 31, tr. Miquel, 70, *buḳʿa* is a simple synonym for *mawḍiʿ*), and this seems to have been the farthest development of the term in the Muslim West (see Dozy, *Supplément*, i, 103b, who registers this latter sense only).

However, in the central and eastern parts of the Islamic world, *buḳʿa* acquired, apparently during the Saldjūḳ period, the sense of "dervish convent", "mausoleum", or in general "a building for pious, educational or charitable purposes". The transition here in sense clearly arises from the Ḳurʾānic phrase *al-buḳʿa al-mubāraka* (XXVIII, 30), traditionally interpreted as "the blessed hollow", the place where God spoke to Moses from the burning bush. From Saldjūḳ times onwards, *buḳʿa* appears in epigraphic phraseology. Thus an inscription of Yaghī-basan b. Ghāzī b. Dānishmand (537-60/1142-65) from Niksar and dated 552/1157-8 describes the construction of a *buḳʿa mubāraka*, probably to be interpreted as a dervish convent (see M. Van Berchem, *Épigraphie des Danishmendides*, in *ZA*, xxvii [1912], 87 = *Opera minora*, Geneva 1978, ii, 703, with further references to *CIA*, i. *Égypte*, nos. 44, 459, and iii. *Asie Mineure*, 24). It was likewise used in the Syro-Palestinian region from Ayyūbid times onwards, e.g. in 595/1198 to describe at Jerusalem a school (*maktab*) originally endowed by Saladin, and Van Berchem noted that in this same city, a Djāmiʿ al-Nisāʾ adjacent to the *Ḥaram* was still called al-Buḳʿa al-Bayḍāʾ, perhaps from its white rough-cast walls (*CIA*, ii. *Syrie du Sud, Jérusalem Ville*, i/2, 110, 112, no. 39, ii/1, 130, no. 176). Some three-and-a-half centuries later, we find the Ottoman Sultan Süleymān I described on a restored fortress at Jerusalem as *khādim al-ḥaramayn wa 'l-buḳʿa al-aḳdasiyya* (*ibid.*, i/2, 147, no. 45). In these instances, there still appears to be an ambivalence of meaning, with the double sense of the land on which the building stood and that of the building itself, one intended for religious or charitable uses.

Nevertheless, in the Turco-Iranian world the connection of the term *buḳʿa* with dervish convents and with mausolea, especially those of Ṣūfī saints, seems certain; such structures, whatever their precise architectural form and plan, would always be felt as "blessed places" in the Ḳurʾānic sense. In the biography of the Ṣūfī Shaykh Abū Saʿīd al-Mayhanī, the *Asrār al-tawḥīd* of Muḥammad b. al-Munawwar (written in the last quarter of the 6th/12th century), *buḳʿa*, in one place *buḳʿa-ī az khayr*, is synonymous with *khānaḳāh* [*q.v.*] in the sense of "dervish convent" (ed. Dhabīḥ Allāh Ṣafā, Tehran 1332/1953, 44, 146, 331, cf. F. Meier, *Abū Saʿīd-i Abū l-Ḫayr* (*357-440/967-1049*), *Wirklichkeit und Legende*, Teh Liège 1976, 305, n. 75, 310 and n. 115). B. O'K has gathered together instances of buildings descr usually in their inscriptions, as *buḳʿas*, from Anatolian region (after the Dānishmandid insta see above, for the periods of the Rūm Saldjūḳs the *beyliks*) and from the Iranian one (8th-9th/1 15th centuries, extending as far eastwards as Tīmūrid Shāh-i Zinda in Samarḳand), and noted that the term seemed eventually found favour in those regions than in the Arab one, his *Tāybād, Turbat-i Jām and Timurid vaultin, Iran, Jnal. of the British Institute of Persian Stu* xvii (1979), 94-6.

Bibliography: given in the article.

(C. E. Boswort

BUḲRĀṬ, Hippocrates, the most fa physician of antiquity, was born *ca.* 460 B.C. or island of Cos, and died *ca.* 375 in Larissa (Thess He sprang from the Asclepiads, an old native fa of physicians, where the name Hippocrates occu repeatedly. Already in antiquity he was consid an exceptional and model physician. This pre was due to Galen [see djālīnūs] in the first p who brought to its culmination the "Hippocra revival" which had started in the 2nd century and thus determined the image of Hippocrates the whole period to come; in Islam as in Eur Hippocrates became the symbol of "the true p sician". It is the more astonishing that hardly of the many writings transmitted under his n can be traced back to him with full certai Dependent on the classification, the size of "Corpus Hippocraticum" varies, but it comprise least 60 writings. To the Arabs Hippocrates well-known; his name appears as Buḳrāṭ, suppression of the Greek ending like in Su (Socrates) and Dīmuḳrāṭ (Demokritos), and als Ibuḳrāṭ and Abuḳrāṭ. The forms Ibuḳrāṭīs, A ḳrāṭīs, etc. are older; Syriac influence is still pre in Hīfūḳrāṭīs, Īfūḳrāṭīs.

There is no lack of biographical informa about Buḳrāṭ among the Arabs; the longest sec is found in Ibn Abī Uṣaybiʿa, *ʿUyūn al-anbā* 24-33. Buḳrāṭ's teachers are mentioned here ll. 16-17), his father Īraḳlīdis (Heracleides) and grandfather Buḳrāṭ; besides his father, the anc sources name also others, like Herodicos of Sel bria (Pauly-Wissowa-Kroll, *Real-Encyklopädie class. Altertumswissenschaft*, viii, 1912, 978 f.). is said to have lived up to the age of 95. The A biographers, to be sure, often present mislea information, e.g. Ibn Abī Uṣaybiʿa (*op. cit.*, i, ll. 22-3) says that Buḳrāṭ was trained on Rho Cnidos and Cos, while Ibn al-Ḳifṭī (*Ḥukamāʾ*, Lippert, 90 at the end to 91, 1) makes him stay a while in Fīrūhā (i.e. Βέροια = Aleppo, in the identified with Ḥimṣ; see also Barhebraeus, *Taʾ Mukhtaṣar al-duwal*, ed. Cheikho, 85) and Damas both pieces of information perhaps mean no m than that Buḳrāṭ travelled far and wide, as already known in antiquity. On the other hand, may assume that the Arabs retained scattered graphical data which are not found elsewhere. T were also right in stating that the Corpus Hip cratium does not go back to one single author that there have been several physicians of this na the mathematician Thābit b. Ḳurra names *Baḳāriṭa* or *Buḳraṭūn* ("Hippocraticians", one m say), the first of whom (in fact the second) wo have been the famous Buḳrāṭ (Ibn al-Na *Fihrist*, ed. Flügel, 293 f.; Ibn al-Ḳifṭī, *op. cit.*, 1

Arabs also knew about the unconfirmed state- of Galen according to which Hippocrates ıed a lucrative offer of Artaxerxes I to come e Persian court (P. Bachmann, in *NAWG*, Phil.- Kl. 1965, 20 f.). Again and again he is com- ed for his care of the sick and his personal tion; he allegedly was the first to found a tal (Ibn Abī Uṣaybiʿa, i, 27, ll. 1-2). Evidently, "Hippocratic oath" was also known to the ms, naturally in a somewhat different form; it be found in Ibn Abī Uṣaybiʿa, i, 25 f. and has translated by F. Rosenthal, *Das Fortleben der e im Islam*, Zurich 1965, 250-2. But Buḳrāṭ admired not only as the great physician but as the master of alchemy, astrology and magic Ullmann, *Die Natur- und Geheimwissenschaften slam*, Leiden-Cologne 1972, 155, 288 f., 389); as he gave his name to the handbook of Hellenistic c which has become famous and notorious under ame *Picatrix* (distorted from *Biḳrāṭis* "Hippo- s").

is impossible to say to what extent the Arabic on of Hippocratic writings coincides with the k one. We would probably have more accurate mation if had come down to us Galen's work, lost, Περὶ τῶν γνησίων καὶ νόθων 'Ιπποους συγγραμμάτων, which existed in Isḥāḳ unayn's translation as *Kitāb fī kutub Buḳrāṭ al- a wa-ghayr al-ṣaḥīḥa* (G. Bergsträsser, *Ḥunain sḥāq über die syrischen und arabischen Galen- etzungen*, in *AKM*, xvii/2, Leipzig 1925, no. We know several bibliographical compilations arious size. The first to be mentioned is the ble survey of the following 10 works, *ca.* 259/ compiled by the historian al-Yaʿḳūbī (*Taʾrīkh*, Houtsma, i, 107-29): *K. al-Fuṣūl* Αφορισμοι, *-Buldān wa-'l-miyāh wa-'l-ahwiya* Περὶ ἀέρων ων τόπων, *K. Māʾ al-shaʿīr* Περὶ πτισάνης, *Taḳdimat al-maʿrifa* Προγνωστικόν, *K. al- īn* Περὶ γονῆς. Περὶ φύσιος παιδίου, *K. al- n* (or: *K. Ṭabīʿat al-insān*) Περὶ φύσιος ἀνθρώ- *K. al-Ghidhāʾ* Περὶ τροφῆς *K. al-Asābīʿ* Περὶ μάδων, *K. Awdjāʿ al-nisāʾ* (Γυναικεῖα; cf. ver, M. Ullmann, *Zwei spätantike Kommentare er hippokratischen Schrift "De morbis mulie- s"*, in *Medizin-historisches Journal*, xii [1977], 2), *K. Abīdhīmiyā* 'Επιδημίαι. This text has cific value in so far as Yaʿḳūbī has added more ss detailed indices to six of these titles, so that identification can be assured through com- on with texts that have been preserved (cf. Klamroth, *Über die Auszüge aus griechischen ftstellern bei al-Jaʿqûbî*, in *ZDMG*, xl [1886], 03).

nother canon of 10 works, all commented upon alen, is given by Ibn al-Nadīm, *Fihrist*, 288, also names the translators. They partly coincide those given above, but instead of *K. Māʾ al- r, K. al-Djanīn, K. al-Ghidhāʾ, K. al-Asābīʿ* and *wdjāʿ al-nisāʾ*, we find here: *K. al-ʿAhd* "Ορκος, *l-Amrāḍ al-ḥādda* Περὶ διαίτης ὀξέων *K. al-* Περὶ ἀγμῶν, *K. al-Akhlāṭ* Περὶ χυμῶν and *Kāṭāṭiyūn* (read: *Kāṭyaṭriyūn*) Κατ' ἰητρεῖον. ebraeus (*Duwal*, ed. Cheikho, 35) names 9 ocratical works, all of which appear in both of nventories given above, while there is added the *hidjādj al-raʾs* Περὶ τῶν ἐν κεφαλῇ τρωμά-

e by far most detailed classification is found in Abī Uṣaybiʿa, i, 31-3; a corpus of *ca.* 61 titles, nearly the same number as in the Greek list. nd 30 of them are considered authentic by Ibn Abī Uṣaybiʿa. However, only 12 of these are marked as important; they are found in the lists given so far; for the others, see Ullmann, *Medizin*, 31-5; Sezgin, *GAS*, iii, 38-47. From the indications given on the title-pages and colophons of the manuscripts as well as in the lists of titles, it cannot always be established with certainty who were the Arabic translators of the works. In any case, Ḥunayn b. Isḥāḳ and his school were at the head. But there is no inventory of translations from Hippocrates's works drawn up by Ḥunayn himself, as is the case for his translations from Galen's writings. Buḳrāṭ is extremely frequently quoted by the Arab physicians. The following works of the Arabic corpus have been published so far: 1. *K. al-Fuṣūl. The Aphorisms of Hippocrates*, translated into Arabic by Honain Ben Ishak, ed. J. Tytler, Calcutta 1832; 2. *K. Taḳdimat al-maʿrifa*, ed. M. Klamroth in *ZDMG*, xl (1886), 204-33; 3. *K. Tadbīr al-amrāḍ al-ḥādda. Hippocrates: regimen in acute diseases*, ed. and tr. M. C. Lyons (*Arabic Technical and Scientific Texts*, i), Cambridge 1966; 4. *Kāṭyaṭriyūn. Hippocrates: In the Surgery*, ed. and tr. by Lyons (ibid., iii), Cambridge 1968; 5. *K. Ḥabal ʿalā ḥabal. Hippocrates: On superfoetation*, ed. and tr. J. N. Mattock (*ibid.*, iii), Cambridge 1968 (cf. Ullmann, *Die arabische Überlieferung der hippokratischen Schrift "De superfetatione"*, in *Sudhoffs Archiv*, lviii [1974], 254-75); 6. *K. Ṭabīʿat al-insān. Hippocrates: on the nature of man*, ed. and tr. Mattock and Lyons (*ibid.*, iv), Cambridge 1968; 7. *K. fi 'l-amrāḍ al-bilādiyya. Hippocrates: on endemic diseases (airs, waters and places)*, ed. and tr. Mattock and Lyons (*ibid.*, v), Cambridge 1969; 8. *K. fi 'l-Akhlāṭ. Hippocrates: de humoribus*, ed. and tr. Mattock (*ibid.*, vi), Cambridge 1971; 9. *K. fi 'l-Ghidhāʾ. Hippocrates: de alimento*, ed. and tr. Mattock (*ibid.*, vi), Cambridge 1971. 10. *K. al-Adjinna. Hippocrates: on embryos (On the sperm and on the Nature of the child)*, ed. and transl. M. C. Lyons and J. N. Mattock (*ibid.* vii), Cambridge 1978.

An effort should be made to establish a Corpus Hippocraticum Arabice, an aim which is admittedly still rather far away, but to which the above-mentioned editions form important preliminary studies. To this corpus should certainly be joined the Arabic translations of Galen's commentaries as well as the most important commentaries and paraphrases of the Arab physicians.

Bibliography: The Arabic sources for the life and works of Hippocrates, the new material in manuscripts which has become widely known, especially after the last World War, and the relevant secondary literature have been put together by M. Ullmann, *Die Medizin im Islam*, Leiden-Cologne 1970, 25-35, and F. Sezgin, *GAS*, iii, Leiden 1970, 23-47. Further important are: M. Steinschneider, *Die arab. Übersetzungen aus dem Griechischen*, new impression Graz 1960, 298-318; H. Diels, *Die Handschriften der antiken Ärzte*. First part: *Hippokrates und Galenos*, in *Abh. Pr. Ak. W.*, Phil.-Hist. Kl. (1905), Abh. iii; G. Bergsträsser, *Ḥunain ibn Isḥāḳ und seine Schule. Sprach- und literargeschichtliche Untersuchungen zu den arabischen Hippokrates- und Galen-Übersetzungen*, Leiden 1913; H. Ritter and R. Walzer, *Arabische Übersetzungen griechischer Ärzte in Stambuler Bibliotheken*, in *SBPr. Ak. W.*, Phil.-Hist. Kl. (1934), xxvi. — General: L. Leclerc, *Histoire de la médecine arabe*, i, Paris 1876, 231-6; *Handbuch der Geschichte der Medizin*, begr. von Th. Puschmann, hg. von M. Neuburger und J. Pagel, i, Jena 1902, 196-268; P. Diepgen, *Geschichte der Medizin*, i, Berlin 1949, 77-94.

(A. DIETRICH)

AL-**BULAYṬĪ** [see AL-BALAṬĪ, in Suppl.].

BULBUL SHĀH, *Ṣūfī* saint of mediaeval India. Bulbul Shāh, whose real name was Sayyid Sharaf al-Dīn, was a Mūsawī Sayyid and a disciple of Shāh Niʿmat Allāh Fārsī, belonging to the Suhrawardiyya order. He entered the Valley of Kashmir in the reign of Rādjā Suhādeva (1301-20) from Turkistān with 1,000 fugitives, fleeing before the Mongol invasion. Rinčana, a Ladakhi prince, who seized power from Suhādeva, possessed an inquisitive and a restless mind and was dissatisfied with both Buddhism, his own religion, and Hinduism, the religion of his subjects. Having come into contact with Bulbul Shāh, and learning from him about Islam, he was so much impressed by its teachings which, unlike those of Buddhism and Hinduism, were simple and free from caste, priesthood and ceremonies, that he became a Muslim and adopted the name of Ṣadr al-Dīn on the advice of the saint. The next person to embrace Islam was Rawančandra, Rinčana's brother-in-law; and according to one tradition Bulbul Shāh was able to convert nearly 10,000 people to his faith.

Rinčana built for Bulbul Shāh a *khānaḳāh* [*q.v.*] on the bank of the river Jehlam and endowed it with a number of villages, from the income of which a *langar* (free kitchen) was opened. Bulbul Langar has disappeared, but a quarter of Srīnagar, bearing the name of the hospice still exists. Rinčana also built near the hospice a mosque, the first ever to have been built in Kashmīr. It was destroyed by fire, and a smaller mosque was built in its place. Bulbul Shāh died in 728/1327 and was buried near it.

Bibliography: Mohibbul Hasan, *Kashmīr under the Sultans*, Calcutta 1959; R. K. Parmu, *History of Muslim rule in Kashmīr*, Delhi 1969; Muftī Muḥammad Shāh Saʿādat, *Bulbul Shāh Ṣāḥib* (Urdu), Lahore 1360/1941; Hādjdjī Muʿīn al-Dīn Miskīn, *Taʾrīkh-i Kabīr*, Amritsar 1322/1904.

(MOHIBBUL HASAN)

AL-**BŪNĪ**, ABU 'L-ʿABBĀS AḤMAD B. ʿALĪ B. YŪSUF AL-ḲURASHĪ AL-ṢŪFĪ MUḤYĪ 'L-DĪN (variants Taḳī al-Dīn, Shihāb al-Dīn), Arab author who wrote around forty works on magic. Hardly anything is known about his life; the date of his death (622/1225) was found by the present writer only in Ḥādjdjī Khalīfa (*Kashf al-ẓunūn*, *passim*, cf. Kaḥḥāla, *Muʿdjam al-muʾallifīn*, ii, 26; Bağdatlı İsmail Paşa, *Hadiyyat al-ʿārifīn*, i, 90 f.). He came originally from Būna (ʿAnnāba [*q.v.*]). It is doubtful that he transmitted information on the construction in 425/1033 of the Sīdī Bū Marwān mosque in that place, in a work called *al-Durra al-maknūna* (cf. G. Marçais, in *Mélanges William Marçais*, Paris 1950, 234), since this work does not appear in the catalogues of his writings. He is said to have died in Cairo and to have been buried in the Ḳarāfa cemetery near the tomb of ʿAbd al-Djalīl al-Ṭaḥāwī (d. 649/1251) (Ibn al-Zayyāt, *al-Kawākib al-sayyāra fī tartīb al-ziyāra fi 'l-Ḳarāfatayn al-kubrā wa 'l-ṣughrā* [written in 804/1401], Baghdad n.d., 268).

Al-Būnī's main work is the *Kitāb Shams al-maʿārif wa-laṭāʾif al-ʿawārif*, published in 4 volumes, Cairo n.d. [1905]. In 40 chapters, the headings of which are clearly arranged in Ahlwardt's Catalogue no. 4125, it contains a collection both muddled and dreary of materials for the magical use of numbers and letters-squares, single Ḳurʾān-verses, the names of God and of the mother of Mūsā, indications for the production of amulets, for the magical u scripts etc., all matters belonging to the field o *ḥurūf* [*q.v.*] or *awfāḳ*. In ch. 7 appear even the w with which Jesus is supposed to have resuscit the dead. The work exists in three forms, a s one which is the oldest, a long one and a mi sized one (cf. H. A. Winkler, *Siegel und Chara in der muhammedanischen Zauberei*, Berlin 67; *ibid.*, 68-86 contains the translation with mentary of the chapters on the "seven seals" the "highest name of Allah"). The number of m scripts which became known in the course of ti considerable; the oldest—if the colophon is aut tic—dates from 618/1221, thus from the aut lifetime (Manisa, Genel Küt., 1445, cf. T. Fahd *divination arabe*, Leiden 1966, 230-3). The work compilation based rather on current popular cus than on literature transmitted from Hellen superstition, since sources are hardly mentic Like all magic, these practices serve to realise w and longings and to ward off hardships, by tr to influence "supernatural" powers which ca be grasped by the intellect or the senses. At the of the work, al-Būnī therefore states that the teries of the letters (*al-ḥurūf*) cannot be prove logical intellect, but only by insight into di wisdom. He expresses himself in the same wa another work, the *Kitāb Laṭāʾif al-ishārāt fī al-ḥurūf al-ʿulwiyyāt* (the title is variable; I did have access to the lithography of Cairo 1 quoted by Ibn Khaldūn, *Muḳaddima*, iii, 140 (I tr. Rosenthal, iii, 174; Fr. tr. Monteil, iii, 1106 his *Risālat al-Shifāʾ li-adwāʾ al-wabāʾ* (cf. M. mann, *Die Medizin im Islam*, Leiden 1970, Ṭāshköprüzāde (d. 968/1560) copied much of Būnī's magic to warding off the plague.

Most of the other works circulating under name of al-Būnī seem to be more or less accu extracts from the *Shams al-maʿārif*; their relatio one another and to the main work is still to b vestigated. We may mention here the *Kitāb Uṣūl wa 'l-ḍawābiṭ*, a kind of introduction to secret sciences; the *Kitāb Sharḥ sawāḳiṭ al-F al-sharīfa* on the consonants *th*, *dj*, *kh*, *z*, *sh*, which do not occur in the first Sūra; the *al-L al-nūrāniyya* on the highest names and sev writings on the divine names (enumerated in F *op. cit.*, 237 f.). In addition to Goldziher's ea studies, G. Vajda has pointed to Jewish and pse Jewish elements in the *Shams al-maʿārif*, espec with regard to the names of God, the angels idea of *thaḳūfa* (from Hebrew *teḳūfā*, something "quarter of a year" and several other der meanings): *Sur quelques éléments juifs et pse juifs dans l'encyclopédie magique de Bûnî*, in *ziher Memorial Volume*, i, Budapest 1948, 38 J. Ruska deserves the credit for having dr attention to the abstruse chapter on alchemy in *Shams* and its sources; since this chapter fits so what unnaturally in the work, it may indeed been added by a later author who was familiar al-Rāzī's *Kitāb al-Asrār* (cf. *Isl.*, xxii [1934], 10).

Bibliography: (in addition to the w quoted in the article): the excellent stud W. Ahrens, *Die "magischen Quadrate" al-Bū* in *Isl.*, xii (1922), 157-77; in addition, G. B strässer, *Zu den magischen Quadraten*, in *I* xiii (1923), 227-35, and again, Ahrens, *ibid.*, (1925), 104-10; E. Doutté, *Magie et religion l'Afrique du Nord*, Algiers 1909, *passim*; Bro mann, I², 655 f., S I 910 f.; M. Ullmann, *tur- und Geheimwissenschaften im Islam*, iden 1972, 234, 390 f., 415. (A. DIETRICH)

·BURAK AL-ṢARĪMĪ (Ṣuraymī in Ibn al-i), (AL-)ḤADJDJĀDJ B. ʿABD ALLĀH (d. 40/660), ,āridjī who is said to have been the first to aim that "judgement belongs only to God" *im*; cf. al-Mubarrad, *Kāmil*, Cairo edn., 917), who is famed in history because of his being of the three plotters sworn to kill simultaneously). Abi Ṭālib [see IBN MULDJAM], ʿAmr b. al-ʿĀṣ, and Muʿāwiya b. Abī Sufyān. Al-Burak dingly proceeded to Damascus and stabbed wiya whilst he was praying, but only managed ound him in the hip. According to tradition, the k had two consequences: firstly, the "marriage " (*ʿirḳ al-nikāḥ*) was severed, so that Muʿāwiya unable to beget any more children, and secondly, atter decided that in future he would pray inside *ḳṣūra* (but see the ironical remark of al-Djāḥiẓ, *iwān*, ii, 161, where a dog is said to have led to take this precaution).

hen al-Burak was arrested, he immediately told wiya about the plot hatched against the three ns. He asked him to await news of the attack on and proposed to Muʿāwiya that he should go kill the caliph if Ibn Muldjam had failed and return and throw himself on Muʿāwiya's mercy. this point, the accounts diverge. According to , Muʿāwiya had him executed on the spot; rding to others, he threw him into prison and him when he heard of ʿAlī's death. According e apparently most current account, he had his s and feet (or one hand and one foot) cut off sent him to Baṣra, where Ziyād b. Abīhi put to death when he learnt that he had had a born to him whilst Muʿāwiya remained hence-sterile.

Bibliography: Mubarrad, *Kāmil*, 993; Ṭabarī, 3456-7, 3463; Djāḥiẓ, *Bayān*, ii, 206; Ibn al-albī-Caskel, *Djamhara*, ii, 229; Masʿūdī, *Murūdj*, 427, 436-7 = §§ 1730, 1739. (CH. PELLAT)

URḲUʿ or ḲAṢR BURḲUʿ, a ruin situated northern Jordan about 25 km. northwest of pumping-station H 4, now a small village on road from Mafraḳ to Baghdād. Here one of the est Islamic inscriptions, dated 81/700, is pre-d. A *ḥarra*-plain of about 650 m. altitude sur-ds the ruin, which lies on the northeast bank he Wādī Minḳād. About 2 km. northwest of uʿ, the wādī is blocked by a modern dam ing a small lake which contains water from late mn until summer. The alignment of the foun-ns of the southwest-part of the *ḳaṣr* suggests a similar dam existed there in the 7th century

ie building was first visited in 1928. An archaeo-al report on the site was published in 1960 Field, *North Arabian desert archaeological survey -1950*, Cambridge Mass. 1960, 94-9). The building re-studied in 1974 by H. Gaube, *An examination e ruin of Qaṣr Burquʿ*, in *Annual of the Depart- of Antiquities of Jordan*, xix, (1974), 93-100 and 14.

ie remains consist of a plain enclosure-wall at northwest and the southwest sides, and ranges ooms at the southeast (five rooms) and the heast sides (six rooms), enclosing a courtyard e there is a rectangular tower. Enclosure and is show traces of repeated repairs, plan alter-is and reconstructions. The masonry of the cture is of poor Hauranian style (basalt blocks he inner and outer faces, with a filling of lumps of basalt and clay). However, a thorough technical examination permits the isolation of five different stages of building-activity which can partly be connected with chronological evidences provided by inscriptions found at the spot. These inscriptions are: a Greek inscription from the 3rd century A.D. (Field, *op. cit.* 161 ff.); a Greek inscription from Byzantine times (Gaube, *op. cit.* 97); an Arabic inscription with the name of the *Amīr al-Walīd* (the later caliph Walīd I), dated 81/700 (*RCEA*, no. 12; Field, 154 f.; Gaube, 97); an Arabic inscription dated 782/1380 (Gaube, 97), and an Arabic inscription dated 812/1409 (Gaube, 97 f.).

In the course of its centuries-long use, Ḳaṣr Burḳuʿ served different purposes. The nucleus of the site, the rectangular tower in the courtyard, was a Roman-Byzantine watch-tower controlling one of the main caravan-roads from Arabia to Syria. All installations to secure the water supply of the place (the artificial lake and two reservoirs) are most probably contemporary with the tower. In the 5th or the 6th century A.D. this advanced post was transformed into a monastic settlement and some rooms were built to the southeast of the tower. By Walīd's order, rooms northeast and southeast of the tower and the enclosure were added. At this time Burḳuʿ served as a modest country-residence. It proves that in Umayyad times important members of the ruling family erected even small and rather primitive buildings. Later, in the Ayyūbid period, the building was restored and was most probably used as a *khān*.

Bibliography: Given in the article.

(H. GAUBE)

BURNOUS [see LIBĀS].

BURŪDJIRDĪ, ḤĀDJDJĪ ĀḲĀ ḤUSAYN ṬABĀ-ṬABĀʾĪ (1875-1961), the greatest religious authority (*mardjaʿ-i taḳlīd-i muṭlaḳ*) of the Shīʿī world in his time. He belonged to a well-established and wealthy clerical family from which emerged distinguished figures such as Sayyid Mahdī Baḥr al-ʿUlūm (d. 1797). After primary education in his home town, Burūdjird, he moved to Iṣfahān in 1892 and studied *fiḳh*, *uṣūl*, philosophy and mathematics under several specialists including Sayyid Muḥammad Bāḳir Durčaʾī. In 1902 he went to Nadjaf and attended the lectures of Khurāsānī [*q.v.*] and others until 1910, when he went back to Burūdjird with the intention of returning to Nadjaf, but the death both of his father and Khurāsānī in 1911 made him remain in Burūdjird. Despite the fact that Burūdjirdī was closely associated with Khurāsānī during the Persian Constitutional Revolution of 1905-11, we do not know of any co-operation between Burūdjirdī and Khurāsānī in the latter's constitutionalist campaign. This is an indication of Burūdjirdī's conservatism in the field of politics, which continued to present itself during Burūdjirdī's sole leadership from 1947-61.

While in Burūdjird he was recognised as a respected religious authority in the western part of Iran. He was so popular in his region that in 1926, when he was temporarily living in Ḳum, he was urged by the Burūdjirdīs to return to Burūdjird; he lived there until 1944. At this time the Ḳum Circle for Religious Studies which had been founded by Shaykh ʿAbd al-Karīm Ḥāʾirī [*q.v.* in Suppl.] in 1921 was being run by three men (Ṣadr, Ḥudjdjat, and Khwansārī [*q.v.*]). It was envisaged that due to his priority in age, experience and background in religious leadership, Burūdjirdī would be able to reorganise the Circle which, under the government's pressures, and especially after Ḥāʾirī's death in 1937, had been greatly diminished. To this end Burūdjirdī was cordially invited to Ḳum in December 1944. After the death of Sayyid Abu 'l-Ḥasan Iṣfahānī and Ḥādjdjī Āḳā Ḥusayn Ḳummī in Nadjaf in 1946 and 1947 respectively, Burūdjirdī was unquestionably acknowledged as the sole *mardjaʿ-i taḳlīd* in the whole Shīʿī world and held this title until his death.

During his leadership, many religious activities were undertaken: several libraries, hospitals, mosques, and religious schools were established or revived in different locations in Iran and other countries, including ʿIrāḳ and Germany; the publication of a number of religious books were subsidised; religious emissaries were dispatched to Europe, USA, Pakistan, Saudi Arabia and Africa. The Ḳum Circle for Religious Studies, which had become only a convenient alternative to that of Nadjaf during Ḥāʾirī's leadership, now proved to be the most important clerical centre in the Shīʿī world. Thanks to this centrality, many students and specialists of Shīʿism formerly living in Nadjaf and elsewhere joined the Ḳum Circle, to the extent that their number exceeded 5,000, and for the first time the Nadjaf Circle looked to Burūdjirdī for assistance, financial or otherwise.

In the field of scholarship, Burūdjirdī made noticeable contributions; in addition to regular teaching and handling religious affairs, Burūdjirdī wrote a number of books on *fiḳh* and *uṣūl*, several of which were never published; one speciality of his was *ḥadīth*. He has been widely acknowledged as the initiator of a new scheme which facilitates the process of determining the number and the extent of authority of the *ḥadīth* transmitters; it determines the time gap existing along the chain of transmitters, so that the classification of the *ḥadīth*s into *mursal* and *musnad* becomes easy. His scheme also helps to identify the identical names which appear in the chain of *ḥadīth* transmitters and to disclose any distortions or alterations there. Finally, it classifies the transmitters into 36 groups, each with distinguishable characteristics.

Another area of Burūdjirdī's concern was Sunnī-Shīʿī relations; to this end, Burūdjirdī closely cooperated with the Cairo *Dār al-Taḳrīb bayn al-Madhāhib al-Islāmiyya* and entered into correspondence with the Azhar rectors such as Shaykh Maḥmūd Shaltūt. This relationship, it is believed, resulted in the issuing of a *fatwā* in which Shaltūt declared Shīʿism to be as true a Muslim creed (*madhhab*) as other *madhhab*s which have been followed by the Sunnīs, and invited all Muslims to recognise it (see the Peer Mahomed Ebrahim Trust, *Shiaism explained*, Karachi 1972, pp. x ff.).

In the arena of politics Burūdjirdī remained rather inactive. At times, however, he favoured the Shāh of Iran and some of the factions tied to the Royal Court. On a certain occasion, the Shāh even went to Ḳum and visited Burūdjirdī at home. In 1952, during the general election for the 17th Iranian Parliament, Burūdjirdī was considered as a supporter of a Ḳum feudal candidate, Abu 'l-Faḍl Tawliyat, who was also supported by the Court. In the Shāh-Muṣaddiḳ struggles, Burūdjirdī was widely recognised as being opposed to some of the measures taken by the latter and was happy over Muṣaddiḳ's downfall in 1953. In 1952 a member of the *Fidāʾiyyan-i Islām* [*q.v.*] and then a friend of Muṣaddiḳ, Khalīl Ṭahmāsbī, who was accused of the assassination of the former prime minister ʿAlī Razmārā, went to Ḳum to visit Burūdjirdī, but he refus[ed to] meet with Ṭahmāsibī. In other political ma[tters] which did not form Burūdjirdī's immediate con[cern] he was very reluctant to interfere. During [the] Palestine movement of 1947-8, for instanc[e, a] demonstration was organised in front of his [house] urging him to condemn Israel, to which he di[d not] respond; however, in the end he prayed fo[r the] victory of the Palestinians and anathematised [the] Israelis (according to a leaflet picked up by [the] present writer on the street in Ḳum at the t[ime]).

Bibliography: Abdul-Hadi Hairi, *Sharḥ-i Āyat Allāh al-ʿUẓmā Ḥādjdjī Āḳā Ḥusayn bāṭabāʾī Burūdjirdī*, in *Madjalla-yi Muslim* (1951); Mahdī Bāmdād, *Sharḥ-i ḥāl-i ri[djāl-i] Īrān*, i, Tehran 1968; Muḥammad *Ḥusayn* [...] *al-Sharīʿa, Taʾrīkh-i Ḳum*, Ḳum 1971; Muḥam[mad] Ḥusayn Ṭabāṭabāʾī *et alii*, *Baḥthī dar bā[ra-yi] mardjaʿiyyat va rūḥāniyyat*, Tehran 1962; Wāʿiẓ Khiyābānī, *Kitāb-i ʿUlamāʾ-i muʿā[ṣirīn]*, Tabrīz 1947; Abū Muḥammad, *Wakīlī*, *Ḥaw[za-yi] ʿilmiyya-yi Ḳum*, Tehran 1969; Ṣāliḥ al-S[h]rastānī, *Ḳum wa djāmiʿatuhā al-ʿilmiyya* [...] *dīniyya wa-sayyiduhā al-Mardjaʿ al-Akbar Burūdjirdī*, in *al-ʿIrfān*, vi (1968), 729-60; A. [...] Lambton, *A reconsideration of the position o[f the] Marjaʿ al-Taqlīd and the religious institutio[n]*, *SI*, xx (1964), 115-35; Muḥammad [Sharīf] [...] *Āthār al-ḥudjdja*, i, Ḳum 1954; idem, *Gandjī[na-yi] dānishmandān*, i-ii, Tehran 1973; ʿAlī Daw[...] *Zindigānī-yi Āyat Allāh Burūdjirdī*, Ḳum 1[...]; ʿAlawī Burūdjirdī, *Khāṭirāt-i zindigānī-yi ḥ[...] Āyat Allāh al-ʿUẓma Āḳā-yi Burūdjirdī*, Te[hran] 1961; al-Shaykh Kāẓim al-Ḥalfī, *al-Sayyi[d] Burūdjirdī*, Nadjaf, 1961; R. W. Cottam, *Na[tion]alism in Iran*, Pittsburgh 1967; Khānbābā Mu[...] *Muʾallifīn-i kutub-i čāpī-yi fārsī va ʿarab[ī]*, Tehran 1961. See also IṢLĀḤ, ii. Iran.

(ABDUL-HADI HAI[RI])

BURUSHASKI is the language of [the] Burūsho, who form the majority of the popul[ation] of the isolated principalities of Hunza and N[agir] [*q.v.*] in the western Karakoram. It is prob[ably] used by about 20,000 persons. A closely rel[ated] dialect, called Werčikwār, is spoken in the Y[asin] valley further west towards Čitrāl. The language [was] no doubt formerly current over a larger terr[itory] than at present. Although it shares much vocabu[lary] with the Dardic languages Shiṇa of Gilgit [and] Khowār of Čitrāl (see DARDIC and KĀFIR LANGUAG[ES]), Burushaski has no known genetic relation[ship] either with the neighbouring Aryan, Turkic [or] Sino-Tibetan languages or with any other gr[oup], e.g. Causasian, Dravidian, etc. This may be sh[own] by the numerals 1-10: *hi, ālti, īski, wālti, ts[...] mišin, tale, āltam, hunti, tōrimi*. Character[istic] features are (i) the division of nouns into [four] classes, approximately: human, (hm) masculine [and] (hf) feminine, (x) non-human animate and ob[jects] conceived as units, and (y) inanimate, amorp[hous] and abstract, (ii) the occurrence of a plethor[a of] plural suffixes, and (iii) the pervasive use of "[pos]sessive" personal pronoun prefixes with both n[ouns] and verbs.

Bibliography: D. L. R. Lorimer, *The B[uru]shaski language*, 3 vols., Oslo 1935-8; idem, *We[rči]kwar-English vocabulary*, Oslo 1962; G. A. Kl[...] and D. I. Édel'man, *Yazïk Burushaski*, Mo[scow] 1970; H. Berger, *Das Yasin-Burushaski*, W[ies]baden 1974.

(D. N. MACKENZ[IE])

AL-**BŪṢĪRĪ**, SHARAF AL-DĪN ABŪ ʿABD A[LLĀH] MUḤAMMAD B. SAʿĪD B. ḤAMMĀD AL-ṢANHĀDJ[Ī] ptian poet of Berber origin, born on 1 Shaw- 608/7 March 1212 at Būṣīr [*q.v.*] or near to ṣ (see Yāḳūt, *s.v.*) in Upper Egypt. He was in known also by the *nisba* of Dalāṣī, it being said one of his parents originated from Dalāṣ and ther from Būṣīr; he also had a composite *nisba*, lāṣīrī, but this last was never very current. He ved the courses of the Ṣūfī Abu 'l-ʿAbbās Aḥmad ırsī (d. 686/1287; see al-Shaʿrānī, *al-Ṭabaḳāt brā*, Cairo n.d., ii, 12-18; P. Nwyia, *Ibn ʿAṭā'*, Beirut 1972, index) and was also involved e first developments of the Shādhiliyya order . He spent ten years in Jerusalem, and then ed at Medina and Mecca before settling at ys [*q.v.*], where he held a minor administrative *mubāshir*; see al-Ḳalḳashandī, *Ṣubḥ*, i, 451). He at Alexandria, at a date which varies in the es between 694 to 696/1294-7, and was buried e foot of the Muḳaṭṭam, near to al-Shāfiʿī [*q.v.*]. Būṣīrī was a skilled calligrapher, a traditionist a celebrated reciter of the Ḳur'ān, but his name been immortalised by a poem of his in praise of Prophet, the *Burda* ode [*q.v.*], upon which a of commentaries have been written and which njoyed up to the present time an extraordinary ss. It has not, however, thrown wholly into shade another work of his on the same theme, *ıṣīda al-hamziyya fi 'l-madā'iḥ al-nabawiyya* or *ı al-Ḳurā fī madā khayr al-warā*, printed and nented upon several times. Al-Būṣīrī is further- the author of a *Lāmiyya* in praise of the Prophet, *'-Ḳaṣīda al-muḍariyya fi 'l-ṣalāt ʿalā khayr al-ya*, of the *Dhukhr al-maʿād ʿalā wazn Bānat d*, of a *Yā'iyya*, of *al-Ḳaṣīda al-khamriyya* and ome secular pieces more or less written for ous occasions.

Bibliography: Kutubī, *Fawāt*, no. 411; yūṭī, *Ḥusn al-muḥāḍara*, Cairo 1293/1876, i, o; R. Basset, Introd. to his tr. of the *Burda*, ris 1894, I-XII; Ibn al-ʿImād, *Shadharāt*, v, 2; G. Gabrieli, *al-Burdatayn*, Florence 1901, -9; Brockelmann, I, 264-5, S I, 467-72. (Ed.)

-BUSTĀNĪ, name of a Lebanese family nguished in the field of Arabic literature, which the *muʿallim* Buṭrus al-Bustānī to Saʿīd S. al- ānī represents the various stages of the *nahḍa* marks the contribution of the Lebanon to the literary renaissance. Also, from the old *Ency- edia* of Buṭrus al-Bustānī to the present-day *rat al-maʿārif* of F. E. al-Bustānī, a period of a ury embraces the wide range of activities red by Lebanese and Arab scholars in the re of general culture. A detailed comparison of two generations of writers and of their methods vestigation and erudition shows more plainly by any other means, the long road that the nese travelled in their quest to acquire and to fit from the knowledge and the methods of the t. The Bustānīs, in waves that were successive intense, took turns in the service of the Arabic uage.

Maronite family, whose cradle was in northern non, it was drawn, at the end of the 16th cen- , in the time of the *amīr* Fakhr al-Dīn II, towards al-Ḳamar, to take advantage of the Maʿnid e and the commercial prosperity of the region. descendants of this prolific family were not to settle in other districts of the Shūf, such as iyya, Ibkishtīn and Mardj.

a period of less than a hundred years, we see dozens of representatives of this family have pied posts of supreme importance in the administration, the bar, the judiciary, the civil service and most of all in education, in the press and in literature. It was their idea to found a National School for the purpose of grouping together all the children of the country without religious segregation. Also, it was they who took the initiative in the sphere of encyclopedias and modern dictionaries. It was to one of them finally that the Lebanese government entrusted, in 1953, the task of founding the Lebanese University. In the following pages we shall confine ourselves to mentioning, by way of example, and in alphabetical order, some famous names among the Bustānīs of the past who have done service to Arabic letters.

1. ʿAbd Allāh al-Bustānī (1854-1930), eminent teacher and lexicographer, born at Dibbiya, studied at the National School of Beirut under two distinguished *shaykhs*: Nāṣīf al-Yāzidjī and Yūsuf al-Athīr. After founding, in Cyprus, with Iskandar ʿAmmūn, a review *Djunaynat al-akhbār* which had little success, he devoted his energies to education. In a career spanning forty years, he acquired high renown and formed, at the College of Wisdom and the Patriarchal College, an élite of poets (Wadīʿ ʿAḳl, Bishāra al-Khūrī, Shiblī al-Mallāṭ, Amīn Taḳī al-Dīn, etc.) and of journalists (Dāwūd Barakāt, Yūsuf al-Bustānī, etc.) and of writers (Shakīb Arslān, Isʿāf Nashāshībī, etc.). It was in the course of this career, and mainly for the benefit of his disciples, that ʿAbd Allāh al-Bustānī composed the majority of his writings. To assist in the teaching of Arabic, he prepared a dictionary, *al-Bustān* (2 vols. Beirut 1927-30), and an abriged version *Fākihat al-Bustān*. It was also for their benefit that he composed a number of plays, some inspired by French dramatic art (*La Guerre des deux Roses*, *Brutus*, etc.), some taken from the storehouse of Arab history (*Djassās, assassin de Kulayb*, *ʿUmar al-Ḥimyarī*, etc.) In recognition of his versatile achievements, he was elected a member of the Arab Academy of Damascus, and president of the short-lived Lebanese Academy.

Bibliography: M. al-Bustānī, *Kawthar al-nufūs*, 398-419; *al-Salsabīl*, Djounieh 1968, 154-8; Y. A. Dāghir, *Maṣādir al-dirāsa al-ʿadabiyya*, ii, 193-5; A. al-Djundī, *Aʿlām al-ʿadab*, ii, 253-4; ʿU. R. Kaḥḥāla, *Muʿdjam al-mu'allifīn*, vi, 148-9; Kh. Ziriklī, *al-Aʿlam*, iv, 285; and see *Munāẓara lughawiyya*, Cairo 1936; *Tadhkār al-yūbīl*, Beirut 1928.

2. Buṭrus b. Būlus al-Bustānī (1819-83) was born at Dibbiyya and first attended the village school, then the college of ʿAyn Warḳa, where he spent ten years, between 1830 and 1840. In order to help his mother, who had just lost her husband, in the task of raising and supporting his brothers, he refused the offer of a scholarship and went to Italy to complete his religious training at the Maronite College in Rome. It seems that he applied himself to learning English while at ʿAyn Warḳa, which was to serve him well in his future contacts with the Protestant missionaries. He settled finally in Beirut where he lived for forty-three years, and pursued a most distinguished career. His arrival coincided with the troubles caused by the departure of the *amīr* Bashīr II and the withdrawal of Egyptian troops. He made the acquaintance of some American missionaries, with whom he formed a friendship that grew stronger in time and contributed to his conversion to Protestantism. It was at this period that he met the doctor Cornelius Van Dyck, who was then a young physician working with the missionaries; he had just established himself in Beirut

and was eager to learn the language of the country. From 1846 to 1848, having temporarily left the city, he helped his friend in the school at ʿUbey, which the latter founded and which enjoyed a high reputation in this period. It was there, for the benefit of his pupils, that Bustānī composed his two educational manuals *Kas͟hf al-ḥid͟jāb fī ʿilm al-ḥisāb* and *Bulūg͟h al-arab fī naḥw al-ʿArab*; it was also there that his eldest son Salīm was born. On his return to Beirut in 1848, the American Consulate employed him as an interpreter, a post that he held until 1862. During this period, he continued to educate himself, to learn European and Semitic languages with the object of assisting Dr. Smith in his venture of translating the Protestant Bible. His energy was also reflected in a large corpus of lectures, articles and pamphlets. In 1860, he published his magazine *Nafīt Sūriyā* ("The Syrian bugle"); then in 1863 he founded his famous National School which continued to operate until 1875 and rendered the country very valuable service. In 1870, he undertook the publication of his two periodicals *al-D͟jinān* and *al-D͟janna*, followed a year later by *al-D͟junayna*. The major achievements of Buṭrus al-Bustānī were, besides his school and his reviews, his contribution to the translation of the Bible, his large dictionary *Muḥīṭ al-muḥīṭ*, edited in 1870 and the *Encyclopaedia*, the first volume of which appeared in 1876. He died while involved with this task, and he was able to produce only six volumes. His son Salīm applied himself to this work and added two further volumes. The encyclopedia in question came finally to a halt with the eleventh volume and was never completed.

The influence of al-Bustānī at his apogée was very deep. Lucid, far-sighted and sincere, he made accurate judgements of the state of his country from a national, cultural and moral point of view; then he set to work, applying himself to projects the achievement of which would seem impossible for one man alone. He saw clearly, in a setting of considerable obstacles, of a confused political situation, of intolerance and of opposition to Turkish rule, the long path that must be travelled in the quest for an authentic social and cultural renaissance. An indefatigable craftsman, of bold and progressive spirit, he devoted himself to his work and was involved with it to the very last days of his life.

Bibliography: M. ʿAbbūd, *Ruwwād al-nahḍa al-ḥadīt͟ha*, Beirut 1952; P. Andraos, *al-Muʿallim B. al-Bustānī* (dissertation submitted to the Lebanese University, 1970); F. E. al-Bustānī, *al-Rawāʾiʿ*, no. 22, Beirut 1950; M. al-Bustānī, *al-Salsabīl*, Djounieh 1968, 142-8; *al-Hilāl* of 15th January 1896 ʿU. Kaḥḥāla, *Muʿdjam al-muʾallifīn*, iv, 48-9; S͟h al-K͟hūrī, *Mad͟jmaʿ al-Masarrāt*, Beirut 1908; *al-Muḳtaṭaf*, of 1st August 1883; N. Naṣṣār, *Naḥwa mud͟jtamaʿ d͟jadīd*, Beirut 1969; M. Ṣawāyā, *al-Muʿallim Buṭrus al-Bustānī*, Beirut 1963; L. S͟haykhū, *al-Ādāb al-ʿarabiyya*, ii, Beirut 1910; Ph. Ṭarrāzī, *Taʾrik͟h al-ṣiḥāfa*, i and ii, Beirut 1913; D͟j. Zaydān, *Tarād͟jim mas͟hāhīr al-S͟harḳ*, ii, Cairo 1911.

3. Buṭrus b. Sulayman al-Bustānī (1893-1969), born at Dayr al-Ḳamar where he barely completed his primary studies, and went to live in Beirut with his brother Karam (see below, 4). Self-taught, his thorough linguistic and literary education was the fruit of assiduous personal effort. He first achieved distinction with his grammatical knowledge and his understanding of ancient texts which he analysed and annotated to make them accessible to his readers. In 1923 he founded his review *al-Bayān* which he edited until 1930. Here he ... with literary and social themes, analysed new w... appearing in the Lebanon and in the Arab coun... and encouraged the study of comparative litera... In the course of its publication, *al-Bayān* was a magnet and a support for young Lebanese wr... The world economic crisis forced Buṭrus to gi... different direction to his vocation. Henceforwa... devoted his efforts to education and to all might facilitate his task as teacher. It was to i... duce his pupils from the Brothers and the Colle... Wisdom to Arabic literature that he compose... three volumes, his valuable text-book *Les au... arabes*. The first of these volumes (1931) covers period from the pre-Islamic age to the Umayy... the second (1934) deals with the ʿAbbāsid age, third with al-Andalus and the *nahḍa*. Late... 1943, this series was crowned by a fourth vol... an anthology. Even though scientific method is respected scrupulously in his writings, Bu... excels through the purity of his style and the curacy of his comments. The last years of his c... were spent at the Lebanese University.

Bibliography: M. al-Bustānī, *al-Sals...* 199-206.

4. Karam al-Bustānī (1888-1966) was bo... Dayr al-Ḳamar, studied in the Jesuit school t... then went and settled in Beirut with his bro... Buṭrus (see above, 3.); here he applied hi... simultaneously to a number of tasks: teac... journalism and critical editing of ancient texts. ... a number of years, he was associated with Cat... missionary establishments (Jesuits, Francis... Sacre Coeur, Friars, etc.), where he taught A... literature. At this time he was collaboratin... various Lebanese reviews and journals that then in fashion (*al-Barḳ, Lisān al-ḥāl, al-Arz, Maks͟hūf*, etc.) and he gave generous assistanc... his brother Buṭrus in the editing of his review *Bayān*. His thorough knowledge of Arabic and erudition are shown in his study and editin... Arabic manuscripts and most of all in a serie... collections of poetry (*Dīwān Ibn Zaydūn, Dī... Ibn K͟hafād͟ja, Dīwān Ibn Hāniʾ al-Andalusī, ...zūmiyyāt al-Maʿarrī, Dīwān al-K͟hansāʾ*, etc.)... regards original production, the work of Kara... confined to a small number of works of a histo... social nature (*Légendes orientales, Princesses... Liban, Femmes arabes*).

Bibliography: M. al-Bustānī, *al-Sal...* 196-8.

5. Saʿīd b. Salīm al-Bustānī (1922-77) ... at Mard͟j (in the S͟hūf), studied in Beirut at College of Jesuit Fathers, then at the Institut... Oriental Literature, and pursued his studies France, where he obtained a State Diplom... Arabic and a Doctorate of Letters. On his retur... Lebanon, he occupied some important posts at Lebanese University. In 1974, he was appoi... Dean of the Faculty of Administration, then 1977, Dean of the Faculty of Literature. In course of his brief university career, he publi... his thesis *Ibn ar-Rūmī, sa vie et son oeuvre* (B... 1967). In addition, he contributed to the *Enc... paedia of Islām* and to the *Dāʾirāt al-maʿāri...* F. E. al-Bustānī. In university circles, Saʿīd Bustānī was associated with bilingualism western culture, and he defended his position principle vigorously. The hope of the Leba... élite, he died in mid-struggle, carried off sudd... by an incurable disease, leaving a number of im... tant works unfinished.

Salīm b. Buṭrus (1846-84) journalist and ɔlist, born at ʿUbey. He studied in the centres blished in the north of the Lebanon by Protestant ionaries recently arrived from America to pete with the propaganda diffused over two uries by the Catholic missionaries. As teachers, lso had his father Buṭrus and Nāṣīf al-Yāzidjī, introduced him to the subtleties of Arabic. At age of sixteen (in 1862) he entered the service he American Consulate in Beirut as an inter- er, a post that he held for ten years. Then his er called upon him to collaborate with him in many projects, especially in the running of the ional School, the editing of his reviews and the oration of the *Encyclopaedia*. Thanks to his wledge of foreign languages, his civic sense and literary and philosophical training, Salīm gave w impetus to the Renaissance, and turned it in ctions other than those pursued by the genera- of his father, of N. Yāzidjī, Athīr, Aḥdab and rs. The West influenced his thinking and his eption of society. He went far beyond the cul- l level deemed sufficient by his contemporaries tackled new and original genres in vogue in the t. He displayed this tendency towards innovation several spheres. First, in participating in the vities of literary societies and cultural asso- ions, in particular in belonging to the Syrian ntific Society in which he played a significant ; he occupied the post of vice-president, and for benefit of members and friends, he composed e plays, most notably *Madjnūn Laylā*, in six , performed on the 11th May 1869, and greeted Beirut audiences as a masterpiece. Later, he tempted to pursue this line of activity further he composed more plays in which prose and ry lie side-by-side and blend harmoniously. er, he found in his father's various reviews a ul medium for dealing with subjects fashion- in the western press. The columns of *al-Djinān* 'o-86) discussed moral and civic questions never t with before in Arabic journals of this period. obsequious journalist, the flatterer of power and authority (and such men were the general rule hat time), came under attack in Salīm's articles a thinker fired with civic concern and patriot- believing sincerely in his mission as social rmer. The titles of his surveys and articles suf- by themselves to reveal the breadth of the trum of social, moral, economic and political blems that he studied. We shall quote, by way xample, the following titles: *Birth and evolution ations*, *Factors of progress*, *Methods of education*, *role of economics in the evolution of society*, etc. ddition, he blazed the first trail of the modern bic novel. Taking the ancient heritage as a base, ackled subjects with a historical theme and thus ched the path later to be followed by Nakhla ludawwar and Dj. Zaydān.

mong his works we shall mention the following:

Nine novels published in serial form in *al-Djinān* veen 1870 and 1879;

Some twenty short stories composed directly in bic or translated from French or English (pub- ed at the same period in the same review);

A history of France;

l history of Napoleon Bonaparte in Egypt and Syria;

Statesmen.

hese three last were also published in *al-Djinān*.

Volumes vii and viii of the *Encyclopaedia* (and able participation in the editing of the first volumes).

Bibliography: Dj. Ayyūb, *Index alphabétique contenant noms d'auteurs et titres d'articles insérés dans al-Djinān, au cours de sa publication (1870-1886)*, see in particular articles signed by Salīm (typescript thesis, the Lebanese University); M. al-Bustānī, *al-Salsabīl*, 152-3; Y. Dāghir, *Maṣādir*, ii, 186; Dj. Khaṭṭār, *Salīm al-Bustānī: vie et oeuvre* (manuscript essay submitted to the Lebanese University, 1970). See also *Lisān al-ḥāl*, no. 712 (1884); *al-Muktaṭaf*, i (1884); Ṭarrāzī, *Ta'rikh al-ṣiḥāfa*, i, ii; Kaḥḥāla, *Muʿdjam*; Zaydān, *Mashāhīr*, i; Ziriklī.

7. Sulaymān b. Khaṭṭār al-Bustānī (1856-1925), politician and writer, born at Ibkishtīn, a small village in the neighbourhood of Dibbiyya (Shūf). He studied at the National School, attending the Arabic classes of Nāṣīf al-Yāzidjī and Yūsuf al-Athīr, and gaining a knowledge of the French, English and Turkish languages, as well as the sciences that were then in vogue. His artistic temperament was noticed by Buṭrus, his illustrious father, who took care of him and invited him to collaborate in his educational work, the editing of his reviews *al-Djinān*, *al-Djanna* and *al-Djunayna*, and the preparation of the *Encyclopaedia*. Invited to Baṣra, Sulaymān founded there a modern-style educational establishment, then he spent eight years in Baghdād where he occupied some very important administrative posts. A tireless traveller, Sulaymān visited many countries, notably Turkey, Egypt, India and Iran, as well as European and American states. Resuming his work on the *Encyclopaedia*, he settled in 1896 in Cairo and he contributed substantially to the editing of the tenth and eleventh volumes. In 1904, he accomplished his greatest work, a translation of the *Iliad* into Arabic verse (1260 pages of introduction and text). From this time onward he devoted his energies to politics, participating in the activities of various parties that were then proliferating in the Arab countries. His attitude was, initially, favourable towards the Ottomans, and this earned him, in 1908, when the Constitution was put into effect, election as representative of the *vilāyet* of Beirut in the Ottoman parliament, and later, in 1913, appointment to the post of Minister of Agriculture, Commerce and Industry. The change in policy on the part of the Sultan ʿAbd al-Ḥamīd II (1876-1909), and the opposition of Sulaymān to Turkey's entry into the First World War against the Allies, obliged him to retire from the government and leave Istanbul, going into exile first in Switzerland (1914-19) then in Egypt (1919-24) and finally in New York where he died a year later, totally blind.

In general, the literary output of Sulaymān is hardly extensive and does not appear to equal that of Buṭrus or Salīm; but thanks to his political involvements, his participation in the activities of literary circles and reformist parties, and his innumerable articles in the Arabic press, his work had a profound influence on the development of Arab aspirations and democratic views in regard to Ottoman rule. Setting aside his translation of the *Iliad*, the thorough research that he conducted by way of introduction to the translation, reveals to the Arabic reader, for the first time, a cultivated mind, familiar with Greek, Latin and modern sources, and involved in considerations related to comparative literature, something totally ignored at that time in Arab literary circles.

In *ʿIbra wa-dhikra*, or *l'État ottoman avant et après la Constitution*, published in Egypt (1908),

Sulaymān shows himself as a reformer, following the path blazed by his predecessors, and he expresses, in a clear and direct style, his ideas concerning different styles of government, liberty, tyranny, and the means of exploiting the resources of the Ottoman caliphate, as well as various procedures to be adopted for the modernisation of the state. In addition, a number of manuscript works are attributed to him, including *l'Histoire des Arabes*, and a book of *Memoirs* in English. In the Lebanese civil war of 1975-6, the house where Sulaymān was born in Ibkis͟htīn was not spared; it was plundered and partially destroyed, and his library suffered the same fate.

Bibliography: G. Bāz, *Sulaymān al-Bustānī*, Beirut n.d.; F. al-Bustānī, *ar-Rawāʾiʿ*, nos. 44-6; G. G͟hurayyib, *Sulaymān al-Bustānī et l'introduction de l'Iliade*, Beirut n.d.; D̲j̲. al-Hās͟him, *Sulaymān al-Bustānī et l'Iliade*, Beirut 1960; M. Sawāyā, *Sulaymān al-Bustānī et l'Iliade d'Homère*, Beirut 1948; A. Hamori, *Reality and convention in Book Six of Bustānī's* Iliad, in *JSS*, xxiii (1978), 95-101. See also the other authors mentioned in articles concerning the Bustānīs.

8. Wadīʿ al-Bustānī (1836-1954), born at Dibbiyya, studied at the American school of Sūḳ al-G͟harb, then at the American University of Beirut where he obtained his B.A. in 1907. He was involved in an astonishing range of activities. Following in the tracks of previous and contemporary members of the Bustānī family, he applied himself to literature and to travels in Arabia, especially to the Yemen (1909) and to the Far East (1912) where he became a friend of Tagore. He returned to Egypt, then, after 1917, occupied some very important administrative posts in Palestine, at that time under British Mandate. In 1953, he left Haifa to return to his native country and there he spent the last year of his life. Two major principles dominated his long career. The first was reflected in his participation in all the efforts to preserve the Arab identity of Palestine. The second, more important, and more fortunate in its results, consisted essentially in a long list of Hindu or Western books translated from English, a language which he knew thoroughly. Thanks to him, the major works of Lord Avebury came to be known in Arabic, notably *The pleasures of life* (Khartoum 1904), *The meaning of life* (Beirut 1909), *The fruits of life* (Cairo 1910) and *The beauties of nature* (Cairo, 1913). Other authors, too, attracted his attention; he translated *The Quatrains of K͟hayyām* (Cairo 1912), and some poems of Tagore which he published under the title *The sardine fisher* (Cairo 1917). His most remarkable and successful achievement was without doubt the translation of the Sanskrit epic of the *Mahābhārarata* (Beirut 1952), as well as other epic or semi-epic works from ancient India.

Other than translations, his principal works are: (a) *Lyrics of the War* (Poems, Johannesburg 1915); (b) *The absurdity of the Palestine Mandate* (Beirut 1936); (c) *Palestinian poems* (Beirut 1946); (d) *The Quatrains of Abu 'l-ʿAlāʾ* (manuscript).

Bibliography: M. al-Bustānī, *Kawt͟har nufūs*, 362-75; idem, *al-Salsabīl*, 189-96; Y. Dā *Maṣādir*, ii, 196-9; A. al-D̲j̲undi, *Aʿlām al-wa'l-fann*, ii, 263-5; ʿU. Kaḥḥala, *Muʿdjam*, 163; Y. Sarkis, *Muʿd̲j̲am al-maṭbūʿāt*, 561; S͟haykhū, *Taʾrīkh al-ādāb al-ʿarabiyya*, Zirikli, *Aʿlām*, ix, 127-8. (J. Abdel-Nou

BUṬRUS KARĀMA, Christian Arab offi and writer, the son of Ibrāhīm Karāma, born in Ḥimṣ in 1774. Together with his fathe was converted from the Greek Orthodox fait the Karāma family to Greek Catholicism. A result they were forced to migrate to Acre, w Buṭrus entered the service of the Pas͟ha ʿAl Asʿad (1806). In 1811 he moved to Lebanon, w he was employed by the *amīr* Bas͟hīr al-S͟hi [see bas͟hīr s͟hihāb ii] as a tutor to his sons as head of his chancellery. After Bas͟hīr's deposi in 1840, Buṭrus accompanied him to Malta, later to Constantinople, where he became a secre of the Sultan and court interpreter, thanks to mastery of both Arabic and Turkish. He die Istanbul in 1851.

Buṭrus composed many poems in Arabic, majority of which were collected in his *dīwān* ent *Sad̲j̲ʿ al-ḥamāma fī Dīwān al-Muʿallim Bu Karāma*.

When one of his Arabic compositions was atta by a Muslim critic, he replied with a spirited *maḳ* in which he maintained the proposition that e lence in Arabic letters and mastery of the Ar language was not dependent on being a Mus Notwithstanding the point of this dispute, it conducted along thoroughly Islamic lines, opposing views being expressed in verse, and Bu himself uses forms of expression which differ little from standard Islamic formulae, e.g. *maḳāma* begins "In the name of God, the Com sionate, the Merciful. Praise be to God, the Lor the worlds: Ruler of the Day of Judgement . .

Fair-minded Muslim critics appreciated the w of Buṭrus's poetry, and one, ʿAbd al-D̲j̲alīl al-I (1776-1854), composed a poem in which he judicated between Buṭrus and his chief detra finding in favour of the former.

Bibliography: D̲j̲urd̲j̲ī Zaydān, *Tarā mas͟hāhīr al-s͟harḳ fi 'l-ḳarn al-tāsiʿ ʿas͟har*, C 1903, ii, 189-92; L. Cheikho, *al-Ādāb al-ʿarab fi 'l-ḳarn al-tāsiʿ ʿas͟har*, in *Al-Machriq*, x (19 946-8, 1039-44; Sarkis, *Muʿd̲j̲am*, cols. 155 G. Graf, *Geschichte der christlichen arabis Literatur*, iv, 303-5; Kaḥḥāla, *Muʿd̲j̲am al-allifīn*, iii, 47-8; R. Y. Ebied and M. J. L. Yo *The "Khāliyyah" ode of Buṭrus Karāmah nineteenth-century literary dispute*, in *JSS*, (1977), 69-80.

(R. Y. Ebied and M. J. L. Youn

BUZZARD [see bayzara].

C

ČAČ-NĀMA, a Persian history of the Arab incursions into Sind in the 1st/7th and 8th centuries, with an introductory chapter concerning the history of the province on the eve of the Arab conquest Dāʾūdpota, New Delhi 1939, 14-72) and an epil describing the tragic end of the Arab comma ammad b. al-Ḳāsim and of the two daughters āhir, the defeated king of Sind (*ibid.*, 243-7). rding to the author, ʿAlī b. Ḥāmid b. Abī Bakr (about whom see Storey, i, 650), the *Čač-Nāma* translation of an Arabic book which Kūfī found time after 613/1216-17 in the possession of the of Alōr, Ismāʿīl b. ʿAlī ... b. ʿUthmān al-afī (*ibid.*, 9-10). No details about the author name of that book are given. However, a com-on between the *Čač-Nāma* and Arab historians as Balādhurī (*Futūḥ*, 431-46) bears out the provenance of those parts of the book that ibe the battles leading to the conquest of Sind; might well have used Madāʾinī's *Kitāb Thaghr al-* and *Kitāb ʿUmmāl* (or *Aʿmāl*) *al-Hind* (*Fihrist*, Yāḳūt, *Udabāʾ*, v. 315; cf. A. Schimmel, *ic literatures of India*, Wiesbaden 1973, 12). *Čač-Nāma* seems to have preserved Madāʾinī's tion concerning India in a much fuller fashion classical Arab histories. On the other hand, the also comprises a considerable amount of rial which probably reflects a local Indian rical tradition. The part dealing with the rise e Čač dynasty (14-72), the story of Darōhar, sinha and Djanki (229-234), and some tradi-attributed to a Brahman called Rāmsiya (179) to "some Brahman elders" (*baʿḍī mashāyikh-i ima*) (197; cf. also 206[14]) deserve to be mentioned is context.

e extensive account of the relationship that loped between the Arab conquerors and the population, which may well reflect a local im Indian tradition, is perhaps the most mean-l and fascinating part of the *Čač-Nāma* (208 ff.). Muḥammad b. al-Ḳāsim is said to have given nqualified blessing to the social characteristics dia and to have sanctioned both the privileges e higher classes and the degradations of the r ones. He upheld the central and indispensable ion of the Brahmans and confirmed the privi-accorded to them by ancient tradition. As for ower classes, represented in the *Čač-Nāma* by Djaṭs [*q.v.*] (al-Zuṭṭ in Arab historiography), ammad b. al-Ḳāsim confirmed the disabilities sed upon them by the deposed Čač dynasty ff.). Some of these disabilities bear a striking arity to the discriminatory measures employed st the *ahl al-dhimma* according to Islamic law. fascinating to observe the way in which the *ī* injunctions were transposed into the Indian u and probably blended with local custom. more fascinating is the transformation of the ctions themselves: they are not applied to all Muslims, irrespective of class, because of their al to embrace Islam; they serve rather as an ument to demonstrate and perpetuate the ior social status of an ethnic group. The *Čač-a* occasionally sounds like a document intended ccord Islamic legitimacy to the Indian social ture, to sanction the privileges of the Brahmans to confirm the degraded status of the lower es. It seems to be a historical and even religious fication of the persistence, under Islam, of a l system which is in sharp conflict with the ic world view. It may be considered an illustra-of Imtiaz Ahmad's statement that "... if the al Islamic ideology rejects caste, the actual fs held by the Muslims not only recognise caste ctions but also seek to rationalise them in ous terms" (*Caste and social stratification among Muslims*, New Delhi 1973, p. xxviii).

Bibliography: The *Čač-Nāma* was published by Dāʾūdpota, New Delhi 1939. Manuscripts: British Library Or. 1787; India Office, Ethé 435; cf. Storey, 650-1. Translations: M. K. Fredunbeg, *The Chach Namah, an ancient history of Sind giving the Hindu period down to the Arab conquest*, Karachi 1900; Elliot and Dowson, *The history of India as told by its own historians*, London 1867, i, 131-211 (description and partial translation); Makhdūm Amīr Aḥmad and Nabī Bakhsh Khān Balōč, *Fatḥ-Nāmayi Sind*, Ḥaydarābād (Sind) 1966 (Sindī translation and commentary; not used by the present author); cf. Storey, i, 651. Analyses: I. H. Qureshi, *The Muslim community of the Indo-Pakistan subcontinent*, The Hague 1962, 37 ff.; F. Gabrieli, *Muhammad ibn Qāsim ath-Thaqafī and the Arab conquest of Sind*, in *East and West*, xv (1964-5), 281-95; P. Hardy, *Is the Chach-Nāma intelligible to the historian as political theory?* in Hamida Khuhro (ed.), *Sind through the centuries*, Karachi 1978; Y. Friedman, *A contribution to the early history of Islam in India*, in M. Rosén-Ayalon, ed., *Studies in memory of Gaston Wiet*, Jerusalem 1977, 309-33; idem, *The origins and significance of the Chach Nāma* (forthcoming).

(Y. Friedmann)

ČAD, Chad, a region of Inner Africa. The Republic of Chad (area: 1, 284,000 km^2; population: about 4,000,000 in 1975) is one of the four states which emerged from the former French Equatorial Africa. The country stretches over 1,600 km. from south of latitude 8° N. to the north of latitude 23° N. Consequently, climate and vegetation vary from savannah woodland with an annual rainfall of more than 1,000 mm. in the south to the arid desert of the Sahara in the north. Chad is torn between two conflicting orientations, between North and Equatorial Africa.

Islam has created a measure of cultural unity in the northern and central parts of Chad, but it has also contributed to the alienation of the region south of latitude 11° N., which remains almost untouched by Islam.

About one million members of the Sara tribe form the main element among the Bantu population of the better-watered south. The Sara are also the largest single ethnic group in Chad as a whole. For centuries the Sara, together with other peoples of the south, were the target for slave raiding from the north.

Farther north the open country between latitudes 12° and 15° N. attracted waves of migrants, mainly nomads, from the north (the Tubu) and from the east (Arabs and Arabised groups). The nomads played an important role in the history of that region which saw the emergence of islamised African states.

Kānim, the earliest state in this region [see KANEM], was first mentioned by al-Yaʿḳūbī (*Taʾrīkh*, ed. Houtsma, 219) in the second half of the 3rd/9th century. The state of Kānim and its Kanembu people evolved as a result of an interaction between rulers of nomad origin (probably Tubu from Tibesti) and the indigenous population at the north-eastern corner of Lake Chad. An interpretation of the Arabic sources (Ibn Saʿīd, ed. Vernet, 1958, 28; al-Maḳrīzī, ed. Hamaker, 1820, 206; a *maḥram* in Palmer, *Sudanese memoirs*, iii, 3) suggests that the rulers of Kānim became converted to Islam in the 5th/11th century, undoubtedly through the influence of Muslims who moved along the trade route from Tripoli via Fazzān [*q.v.*] to Lake Chad. By the 7th/13th century Islam had spread to other sectors of the population. People from Kānim went on pilgrimage to Mecca and came to study in Cairo, where a *madrasa* for Kānimī students was established in the 640s/1240s (al-Maḳrīzī, *Khiṭaṭ*, ed. Wiet, 1922, iii, 266).

The ruling dynasty of Kānim claimed descent from Sayf b. Dhī Yazan [*q.v.*], and became known as the Saifawa. In the second half of the 8th/14th century the Saifawa were forced to evacuate Kānim because of harassment by the Bulala. The Bulala were probably an offshoot of the same dynasty who had mingled with one of the earliest Arab nomad groups coming from the east. The Saifawa moved to Bornu [*q.v.*] at the south-western corner of Lake Chad (now in Nigeria). After a transitory period the Saifawa rebuilt a state in Bornu, which towards the end of the 10th/16th century, under the reign of Idrīs Alawōma, regained its hegemony over the Chad basin. Kānim was reconquered by the Saifawa, who preferred to stay in Bornu. The Bulala rulers of Kānim became vassals to Bornu. About the middle of the 17th century the Bulala were removed from Kānim by the Tundjur, who had been themselves pushed out of Wādāy [*q.v.*]. Authority over Kānim rested with the *alifa* (from the Arabic *khalīfa*), who was nominally a deputy of the Saifawa rulers of Bornu. In the first half of the 19th century the *alifa* paid allegiance to the *sulṭān* of Wādāy, but in the second half of the century he came under the patronage of the Arab Awlād Sulaymān.

Arab nomads made their impact on Chad since the 14th century, when offshoots of Arab tribes which had penetrated the Nilotic Sudan advanced westwards across Kordofan and Dār Fūr. In the Chadian *sāḥil*, on the fringes of the Sahara, the Arabs maintained their traditional way of life as camel breeders, but those who had to seek pasture farther south abandoned the camel and became cattle pastoralists (*baḳḳāra*). They mixed with the local population but retained their Arabic dialect. Though they are divided into many tribes, these Chadian Arabs are generally referred to as Shuwa Arabs [*q.v.*]. To the south, the Arabs reached as far as 11° N., and through their contact with the local population contributed to the spread of Islam. In most cases the Arabs accepted the authority of local rulers though they became involved in intra-state and inter-state politics.

Wādāy, on the western boundary of Dār Fūr [*q.v.*], lay on the route of the Arab nomads. The first Muslim rulers of Wādāy were the arabised Tundjur, but they did little to spread Islam among the local population. The spread of Islam is associated with ʿAbd al-Karīm b. Djāmiʿ, of the Arab Djaʿaliyyīn [*q.v.*]. He had propagated Islam among the Maba of Wādāy and then mobilised them in a *djihād* against the Tundjur rulers. The Tundjur had been ousted and ʿAbd al-Karīm established a new dynasty which has survived to the present time. Until the middle of the 18th century Wādāy had been considered vassal to Dār Fūr, but then its *sulṭāns* asserted their independence and expanded south and west to reach the peak of their power in the 19th century. In 1850 the capital of Wādāy moved from Wara to Abeshe (Abeché). In 1851 H. Barth (*Travels*, 1857, iii, 566) wrote: "The Wadawy faqihs and *ʿulamāʾ* are the most famous of all the nations of the Sudan for their knowledge of the Kuran, the Fulbe or Fellani not excepted."

In its westward expansion, Wādāy came into conflict with Bornu, mainly over the kingdom of Baghirmi [*q.v.*]. The latter emerged at the beginning of the 16th century southeast of Lake Cha[d] the right bank of the Shari river, in a region w[hich] had formerly been raided for slaves. Under th[e in]fluence of Bornu, its rulers adopted Islam, bu[t] islamisation of the population of Baghirmi w[as a] longer process, as remarked by Barth (*Travels*, 1[857], ii, 561): "Their adoption of Islam is very recent, the greater part of them may, even at the pr[esent] day, with more justice be called pagans than [Mo]hammedans". During the 18th century, when [the] power of Bornu declined, Baghirmi prospered m[ainly] on trade in slaves procured in raids to the south [and] the south-east. But in the 19th century both B[ornu] (which had recovered under the *shaykh* Muḥam[mad] al-Amīn al-Kānimī) and Wādāy claimed Bagh[irmi] as tributary. Pressed between her two pow[erful] neighbours and exposed to raids and exactions [from] both directions as well as from Fazzān, the king[dom] of Baghirmi disintegrated. Its destruction [was] completed in 1892 and 1897 by Rābiḥ.

Rābiḥ b. Faḍl Allāh [*q.v.*], one of the flagbe[arers] of the slave trader Zubayr Pasha in the Su[dan,] retreated westwards after his master had [been] defeated by Gessi Pasha. At the head of a [...] army he skirted the powerful Wādāy and occu[pied] the disintegrating Baghirmi in 1892. He then inv[aded] Bornu, which had been caught unaware, sacke[d its] capital Kūkawa [*q.v.*] and became master of [the] whole Chad basin. He wrought destruction by [his] slave raids and punitive expeditions until he [was] overcome in 1900 by the advancing colonial tr[oops] of France, Germany and Britain. Though R[ābiḥ] had considered himself for some time a follow[er of] the *mahdī* of the Sudan, he had little interes[t in] religious affairs. Only in one corner of Chad [does] he seem to have contributed to the spread of Is[lam.] Dār Runga, south of Wādāy, had been for cent[uries] a hunting ground for slaves, separated from [the] Muslim north by a hostile boundary. The abs[ence] of Muslim settlements or even itinerant tra[ders] beyond this boundary inhibited the sprea[d of] Islam. Rābiḥ made Dār Runga a base for [...] raiding farther to the south, and it was during [this] period that people adopted some Arab cust[oms,] Arabic garb and rudiments of an Arabic dia[lect.] This process of acculturation, which brought [...] the spread of Islam, was most evident among c[...] and in the trading villages which developed at [that] time.

Most of the Arab tribes in Chad came from [the] Nilotic Sudan. The northern approaches thr[ough] the Sahara had always been blocked by the T[ubu] and the Tuareg. But in 1842 a section of the A[wlad] Sulaymān, who had been defeated by the Otto[mans] in Fazzān, migrated south to the region just n[orth] of Kānim. During the second half of the 19th cen[tury] the Awlad Sulaymān fought against the Tubu [and] Tuareg. Feuds among those nomads were some[what] mitigated towards the end of the century when [the] Sanūsiyya [*q.v.*] became established among both [the] Tubu and Awlad Sulaymān as well as in Wādā[y.]

In 1835 Muḥammad al-Sharīf, who later be[came] the *sulṭān* of Wādāy, met Muḥammad b. ʿAl[ī al-]Sanūsī [*q.v.*] in Mecca. Closer relations between [the] leaders of the Sanūsiyya and the *sulṭāns* of W[ādāy] developed during the reign of ʿAlī b. Muḥamma[d al-]Sharīf (1858-74), when the two parties co-oper[ated] in reviving trade along the route from Bengha[zi to] Wādāy via Kufra. Sanūsī traders enjoyed virtua[lly a] monopoly over this trade, and the influence of [the] Sanūsiyya among the Saharan nomads contrib[uted] to greater security for the caravans. Succe es of the Sanūsiyya—Djaghbūb (1856-95), a (1895-9) and Ḳūrū in Borku (1899-1902)— along this route. The southward shift of the es of the Sanūsiyya indicates the growing rtance of this region for that order.

1874 the Sanūsī leader Muḥammad al-Mahdī)-1902) exerted his influence to settle a succes- dispute in Wādāy. The successful candidate f (1874-98) became a devoted adherent of the siyya. In 1909 the Sanūsīs encouraged the *n* of Wādāy to resist the French colonial oc- tion. In Kānim, the Sanūsī *zāwiya* of Biʾr ī led resistance to the French from November to June 1902. Because of their involvement in colonial resistance, the activities of the Sanūsiyya to an end after the French occupation. The siyya still have some adherents in Kānim and āy, but the predominant *ṭarīḳa* in Chad is the iniyya. The rulers of Wādāy and Baghirmi, as as the *alifa* of Mao (Kānim), are Tidjānīs. The siyya, however, still maintain their influence ng the Tubu of Tibesti.

ough the Tubu had been nominally Muslims for g period, Islam had had little impact on their intil their exposure to the Sanūsiyya. The Tubu had successfully resisted outside cultural and ical influences, accepted the Sanūsī traders and ers. Traditionally the Derde, the spiritual and oral head of the Tubu in Tibesti, had only ed authority over his tribesmen, and Derde (d. 1939) believed that greater commitment to n and the application of the *Sharīʿa* would nce his personal authority. He invited Sanūsī hers to teach the Tubu the ways of Islam. ugh there is still considerable laxity in observing nic rituals and customs, the Tubu have become e of their Islamic identity. Tubu elders often to the pre-Sanūsiyya period as their *djāhiliyya*. e Tubu are divided into two main groups: the whose centre is in Tibesti and the Daza who in Borku and Ennedi. The latter were exposed he influence of *ʿulamāʾ* from Bornu and Wādāy seem to practise Islam with greater conformity. h greater security under colonial rule, traders teachers were able to move more freely and er away. The growing number of pilgrims from ria and other parts of West Africa who passed ugh Chad as well as foreign merchants from ria, Fazzān and the Sudan who operate in d, added to the impact of Islam on public and ate life.

ome ethnic groups which in the past had sought ge from the agression of the islamised states ually came out of their isolation, mixed with r groups and adopted Islam. In 1910 Islam had hed only a few notables among the Buduma on islands of Lake Chad, but in the middle of the ury all the Buduma were considered Muslims. ugh there are no exact figures, it is estimated more than half of the population of Chad are lims.

had was of great strategic importance for France he link between its African possessions of French atorial Africa, French West Africa and French th Africa. In the heartland of Africa and remote, e than any other territory in Africa, from sea- s, the conquest of Chad, and subsequently its inistration and development, posed numerous stic problems. Only in 1920 did the French plete the "pacification" of Chad, when they rcame the resistance of the Tubu, who had been ired by the Sanūsiyya.

In 1920 Chad was also constituted into a separate territory. In the delineation of its boundaries a crucial decision was made to include the Sara and other Bantu tribes south of 11° N. in Chad rather than in Oubangui-Chari (the present Central African Republic), where culturally-related ethnic groups live. It was this decision which gave Chad its bipolar structure of the non-Muslim Bantu south and the Muslim, partly arabised, north. Hence Chad is internally divided—there are no clear boundaries with its neighbours. Ethnic groups in Chad often feel closer to their own kins, or to related groups beyond the international boundary, than to other ethnic groups in Chad. In the colonial period and after independence, the authorities had to withstand powerful centrifugal tendencies.

In 1929 the French introduced the cultivation of cotton as a cash crop in the south, and the Sara were the first to integrate into the modern sector of the economy and to reap its benefits. It was also among the Sara that the French recruited troops to their colonial army, and the Sara continue to dominate the army also after independence. Protestant and Catholic missionaries opened schools in the south and an educated élite emerged among the Sara.

The Muslims in the central and northern parts of Chad had their own system of Islamic education and were reluctant to send their children to French schools, or even to government (non-missionary) schools. Only a few sons of Muslim chiefs were sent to study in French schools in the first years of colonial rule. They returned to hold positions in the administration and were able to articulate support for the traditional authorities. Young Muslims preferred to go for advanced studies to Cairo and Khartum, but on their return they discovered that because of their lack of French education they could not be employed by the administration. This frustration, combined with Islamic militancy which they had acquired in the Arab countries, led to their being considered a threat both to the colonial administration and to their own traditional authorities. As a remedy, an Arabic-French school was opened in Abeshe in 1952, under the patronage of the sultan of Wādāy, in order to keep students away from Arab countries and to give them both an Islamic and French education.

The French preferred to rule the central and northern provinces of Chad through their *sulṭān*s and chiefs. Following their initial resistance to colonial encroachment, the *sulṭān*s of Wādāy, the *alifa* of Mao, the Derde of the Tubu and lesser rulers, co-operated with the French administration and were able to retain, and sometimes even to strengthen, their political and religious authority. Only in the 1950s did the French introduce a series of reforms in local government which imposed some limitations on the power of the traditional rulers. But the latter faced an even greater threat with the introduction of elections to representatives assembies and with the emergence of political parties. With the support of the administration, the *sulṭān*s were able for some time to send their own men to the territorial assembly. But in 1957, with an almost universal franchise, the neutrality of the administration and the decline of the chief's powers, the radical *Parti Progressiste Tchadien* (PPT), which had been engaged in grassroots politics, became dominant. The PPT's basis of power was among the Sara who were better educated, more advanced economically and more articulated politically. The PPT exploited divisions among Muslim politicians, some of whom represented the interests of the traditional rulers while others, who had been exposed to influences from Cairo, North Africa and the Sudan, followed a more radical orientation.

When the Republic of Chad became independent in August 1960, the PPT had a marginal majority in coalition with minor political groups and individual politicians. Its leader, François Tombalabaye, became the first president of the republic. In the following years, Tombalabaye consolidated his power by gradually eliminating political rivals as well as ambitious allies. He relied on the support of the Sara, his own tribesmen, who dominated the armed forces. Most of the university graduates in Chad were also from among the Sara and they were appointed to senior political and administrative positions. But Tombalabaye sought also the co-operation of the traditional rulers, such as the *sulṭān* of Wādāy and the *alifa* of Mao. In order to appease them, he restored some of the powers that the *sulṭāns* had lost in the reforms during the last years of colonial rule. In order to maintain a semblance of national unity, he had Muslim ministers in his cabinet, some of whom were brought back to the government after periods of isolation in prison or in the political wilderness.

Muslims in Chad felt humiliated when they found themselves ruled by the people of the south, whom they had considered for centuries savage infidels and a fair game for slave raids. The Muslims found it hard to adjust to the change in the balance of powers, and resentment increased when Sara officials replaced the French not only in the capital but also in the territorial administration.

Since 1966 sporadic clashes between the government forces and dissidents spread from the south-eastern provinces of Salamāt to the provinces of Wādāy, Ba<u>th</u>a and Ba<u>gh</u>irmi. Disturbances occurred simultaneously also farther north in Borku, Ennedi and Tibesti. Widespread unrest was channelled into a co-ordinated rebellion by the FROLINAT (*Front de Liberation Nationale*), a radical movement which sought to overthrow the régime of Tombalabaye, to eradicate survivals of French colonialism and to foster closer relations with the Arab countries. Though couched in ideological terms, the rebellion was really an escalation of the conflict between north and south, in which the historical, cultural and religious background had current economic and political implications.

Until February 1972, FROLINAT operated almost freely from Libyan and Sudanese territories. Since then the Sudan has effectively sealed its border with Chad. In the middle of 1972 Libya also agreed to withdraw its support from the rebels, but it still harbours the leaders of FROLINAT and does not stop the supply of provisions and arms into Chad from Libya. French troops were sent to Chad, and they succeeded in establishing a measure of security in the eastern and central provinces. But following the withdrawal of the French troops the government's control of the countryside remained rather fragile.

In Tibesti there is not a clear line between Tubu tribesmen who support FROLINAT and those who fought in the name of the Derde, their spiritual and temporal leader. Through most of the colonial period the Tubu nomads of the farthest north were under French military administration. By agreement with President Tombalabaye this military administration continued after independence until 1964, when French troops have been replaced by Chadian tr who were mainly from among the Sara. These tr had hardly been prepared for the subtle tas governing the non-compliant Tubu nomads, anc situation has been aggravated by mutual dist Following a violent confrontation between troops tribesmen, the military command resorted to lective punishment and detained for some time Derde and his sons. In defiance of the governn the Tubu nomads deserted the oases and m with their herds into the desert, as they had also in the first years of colonial rule. The Derde his sons took refuge in Libya, and from there dire the resistance of the Tubu.

On 13 April 1975 a military coup brought to p General Malloum who, like the deposed Presi Tombalabaye, was a member of the southern tribe. The new government had only a pa success in achieving national reconciliation wh the military situation deteriorated even fur In February 1978 a northern offensive extended area controlled by FROLINAT to a point 250 km from the capital Ndjamena (the fo Fort Lamy). Their advance was checked only French troops who had hastily been flown in. internal conflict had international implicat and Libya, together with Chad's two other n bours—Niger and Sudan—brought the repre tatives of FROLINAT and the Chadian governi to agree on a cease-fire. For the first time, twelve years of fighting, there were at least fo arrangements for negotiations aiming at the building of Chad on the basis of equality betw the north and the south. These negotiations, ever, are bound to be difficult and lengthy [See the Addenda and Corrigenda].

Bibliography: al-Yaʿḳūbī, al-Muha (quoted in Yāḳūt), al-Idrīsī, Ibn Saʿīd, Faḍl Allāh al-ʿUmarī, Ibn <u>Kh</u>aldūn, al-ḳa<u>sh</u>andī, and al-Maḳrīzī are the most impor Arabic sources for the study of the histor Kānim. They are to be collated with local Ar documents (like the *maḥrams*) and chron For a scholarly analysis of these sources, se Marquart, *Die Benin-Sammlung des Re museums für Völkerkunde in Leiden*, Leiden 1 H. R. Palmer, *The Bornu, Sahara and Su* London 1936; Y. Urvoy, *Histoire de l'empir Bornou*, Paris 1949; J. S. Trimingham, *A his of Islam in West Africa*, London 1962; A. Sm *The early states of the Central Sudan*, in Ajayi Crowder, eds., *History of West Africa*, Lor 1971, i, 120-221; D. Lange, *Le Dīwān des su de [Kānem-]Bornū. Chronologie et histoire royaume africain*, Wiesbaden 1977.

On the peoples of Chad and their colonial history see M. el-Tounsy, *Voyag Ouadāy*, trad. de l'arabe par Perron, Paris 1 H. Barth, *Travels and discoveries in North Central Africa*, London 1857-8; G. Nacht *Sahara und Sudan*, Berlin and Leipzig 187 Eng. tr. A. G. B. Fisher and H. J. Fisher, i an London 1971-4; H. Carbou, *La région du Tch du Ouadai*, Paris 1912; E. E. Evans-Pritch *The Sanusi of Cyrenaica*, Oxford 1949; J. Char *Nomades noirs du Sahara*, Paris 1957; A. M Lebeuf, *Les populations du Tchad nord du parallèle*, Paris 1959; M. J. Tubiana, *Un docu inédit sur les sultans du Waddāy*, in *Ca d'Études Africains*, ii (1960), 49-112; A. Le vreur, *Sahariens et Sahéliens du Tchad*, Paris 1 M. J. Tubiana, *Survivance pré-islamique en* ighawa, Paris 1964; J. C. Zeltner, *Histoire des rabes sur les rives du lac Tchad*, in *Annales de Université d'Abidjan*, ii (1970), 101-237; D. D. ordell, *Eastern Libya, Wadai and the Sanūsiya, tarīqa and a trade route*, in *J. of African History*, viii (1977), 21-36.

On modern Chad: V. Thompson and R. dloff, *The emerging states of French Equatorial frica*, Stanford 1960; J. Le Cornec, *Histoire olitique du Tchad 1900-1972*, Paris 1963; C. asteran, *La rébellion au Tchad*, in *Rev. Fr. d'Ét. olitiques Africaines*, no. 73 (Jan. 1971), 35-53; M. Cuoq, *Les musulmans en Afrique*, Paris 75, 275-304; see also the annual record of ents in the volumes of *Africa Contemporary ecord*, ed. C. Legum. (N. Levtzion)

AKS, a tribal group which emigrated to hmīr from Dardistān under their leader Lankar during the reign of Rādjā Sūhadeva (1301-20). ns al-Dīn (739-42/1339-42), the founder of the anate in Kashmīr, made Lankar Čak his com-der-in-chief, patronising the Čaks in order to nteract the power of the feudal chiefs.

uring the early part of Sulṭān Zayn al-ʿĀbidīn's n, Pāndū, the leader of the Čaks, organised a ce as a protest against corvée labour, and set to the Sulṭān's palace and some government dings. As a punishment, the Sulṭān ordered the ruction of all the houses of the Čaks in Trahgām, miles north-west of Bārāmūla. Pāndū escaped, was captured and executed along with all the nbers of his family fit to bear arms. Thus sup-sed, the Čaks remained quiet for some years. taking advantage of the weakness of Zayn al-idīn's successors, they recovered their position, engaged themselves in the struggle for power nst their rivals, the Māgres. When Mīrzā Ḥaydar hlāt (845-55/1441-51) established his rule in hmīr, they suffered an eclipse. But by making mon cause with the nobles against him, they ight about his downfall; and in the struggle ch followed his death, they succeeded in securing themselves large *djāgīrs* and the *wizārat* from the ning Sultans. They became so powerful that in 1561 Ghāzī Khān Čak set aside Ḥabīb Shāh, declared himself king, becoming the first Čak ān. He was a good administrator, generous, rant and just, but also at times ruthless; he was first Kashmīr Sultan to introduce the practice blinding and mutilating the limbs of political onents.

he Čaks ruled Kashmīr from 968/1561 to 996/ 8. The outstanding ruler of the dynasty was ayn Shāh, who was generous, and although a d Shīʿī, liberal towards both the Sunnīs and dūs. A man of cultured tastes, he wrote verses Persian and enjoyed the society of poets, artists learned men of all religions. His brother ʿAlī h succeeded him, following his policies and ng from 978/1570 to 987/1579.

he weakest ruler among the Čak Sulṭāns was uf Shāh. It was he who surrendered to Rādjā gwān Dās, Emperor Akbar's commander, hout offering any resistance (24 Ṣafar 994/14 ruary 1586), and made a treaty with him, ording to which his kingdom was to be restored him. But Akbar denounced the treaty and im-oned him. Later, Yūsuf Shāh was given a *manṣab* oo and sent to Bihār. He died on 14 Dhu 'l-Ḥidjdja o/22 September 1592, and was buried at Biswak he Patna district.

aʿḳūb Shāh, the son of Yūsuf Shāh, denounced the treaty and declared himself sultan. He carried on the struggle against the Mughals, and inflicted defeats on the Mughal commander, Ḳāsim Khān. Meanwhile, Yaʿḳūb's intolerance towards the Sunnīs, who were compelled to recite the name of ʿAlī in the public prayers, antagonised their leaders, who appealed to Akbar for help. The emperor sent Yūsuf Khān Riḍwī to Kashmīr, accompanied by some Kashmīr chiefs who acted as guides. Yūsuf Khān, by adopting a policy of conciliation won over many Kashmīr nobles, and at the same time sent a force against Yaʿḳūb. The latter continued to resist, but finding himself alone and isolated, he surrendered when Akbar arrived in the Valley early in Radjab 996/June 1588. He was imprisoned and died in Muḥarram 1001/October 1592 and was buried, like his father, in Biswak.

Although leaderless, the Čaks continued to resist the Mughals, but were ruthlessly crushed. Djahāngīr's governor of Kashmīr, Iʿtiḳād Khān (1032-7/ 1623-7) hunted them down and killed them; eventually, they escaped to the hills and remote villages, taking up agriculture and other peaceful pursuits.

The Čak rule, though short-lived (968-96/1561-88), was culturally important, for the Čak Sultans, like the shāh Mīrs, encouraged education, patronised poets and scholars and promoted arts and crafts. Two outstanding poets and scholars of the period were Bābā Dāwūd Khākī and Shaykh Yaʿḳūb Ṣarfī; and the most noted calligraphist was Muḥammad Ḥasan, who entered Akbar's service and was given the title of *zarrīn ḳalam*. Under Djahāngīr and Shāh Djahān also, the most prominent calligraphists were those of Kashmīrī origin.

Bibliography: Niẓām al-Dīn, *Ṭabaḳāt-i Akbarī* iii, ed. B. De and Hidayat Hosain, *Bibl. Ind.*, tr. in the same series B. De and Barni Prashad; Abu ʾl-Faḍl, *Akbar-nāma*, iii, *Bibl. Ind.*, tr. in the same series by H. Beveridge; Muḥammad Aʿẓam Didāmarī, *Waḳiʿāt-i Kashmīr*, lith. Srinagar 1952; Pir Ghartām Ḥasan, *Taʾrīkh-i Ḥasan*, ii, ed. Ḥasan Shāh, Srinagar 1954; Mohibbul Hasan, *Kashmīr under the Sulṭāns*, Calcutta 1959; G. M. D. Ṣūfī, *Kashīr*, Lahore 1948-9. (Mohibbul Hasan)

ČAMLİBEL, Fārūḳ Nāfidh modern Turkish Faruk Nafiz Çamlibel, Turkish poet and playwright (1898-1973). He was born in Istanbul, the son of Süleymān Nāfidh, a civil servant in the Ministry of Forests and Mining (Orman we Maʿādin Neẓāreti). After high school he began to study medicine, but soon abandoned it to turn to journalism and teaching. He taught Turkish literature in Kayseri (1922-4), Ankara (1924-32) and Istanbul high schools and the American Robert College (1932-46). He was elected a deputy for Istanbul of the Democratic Party (DP) and served 14 consecutive years (1946-60) in Parliament until his arrest with other DP deputies by the Committee of National Unity (*Milli Birlik Komitesi*) which carried out the Revolution of 27 May 1960. He was detained on a Marmara island (*Yassıada*) until his acquittal 16 months later. He died on 8 November 1973 on board ship during a cruise in the Mediterranean. Fārūk Nāfidh (as he was known until 1934 when he added Čamlıbel) began to write poetry at the age of 17 using the traditional *ʿarūḍ* metre. His early works *Sharḳīñ sulṭānlarî* ("The Sultans of the East"), Istanbul 1918, and *Gönülden gönüle* ("From heart to heart"), Istanbul 1919, reveal the strong influence of Yaḥyā Kemāl [*q.v.*], who was the dominant literary figure of the period. The impact upon him of Ḍiyāʾ (Ziya) Gökalp's teaching was most marked, and from then on he wrote in the line of the popular bards (*saz shāʿirleri*), becoming the most important member of the group called *Besh hedjedji shāʿir* (five poets using syllabic metre, the others being Yūsuf Ḍiyāʾ, Orkhan Seyfī, Enīs Behīdj and Khālid Fakhrī): *Dinle neyden* ("Listen to the flute"), Istanbul 1919, and *Čoban česhmesi* ("Shepherd's fountain"), Istanbul 1926. But he did not completely abandon the *ʿarūḍ*, which he used (like his contemporaries) whenever he thought the subject matter lent itself better to this metre, as his *Suda ḥalḳalar* ("Circles on the water"), published in 1928 in *ʿarūḍ*, shows. In 1933 Fārūḳ Nāfidh published a selection of his poems under the title *Bir ömür böyle geçti* ("A whole life gone by like this"). He collected his humorous poems *Tatlı sert* ("Bitter sweet") in 1938, and his epic poems *Akıncı türküleri* ("Raider's songs") in 1939. Then followed a long silence until the publication of his *Zindan duvarları* ("Prison walls") in 1967. These are impressions of his prison days, in a rather outdated and hackneyed style, in the form of *ḳiṭʿa* (and not *rubāʿī* as stated by Mehmed Kaplan, *Cumhuriyet devri Türk şiiri*², Istanbul 1975, 31-3, *passim*). An anthology selected from all his works was published by the Ministry of Education in 1969, *Han duvarları* ("Inn walls", which is the title of his most popular poem). A master of form, Čamlîbel wrote unsophisticated romantic and sentimental poems of love, with no particular depth of feeling, but in an easy, flowing, polished and harmonious style which made him one of the most popular poets of the 1920s. Following the trend of the period, he also wrote patriotic and epic-historic poems, and many poems eulogising Anatolia (and its people), these being increasingly popular subject-matter for literature under the inspiration of the Nationalist movement following the First World War. Čamlîbel is also the author of a number of verse plays, mostly inspired by political motives (e.g. *Akın* ("Raid"), Istanbul 1932), except for his powerful *Djānawār* ("The monster"), Istanbul 1926, a vivid portrayal of the chronic conflict between peasants and landowners in Anatolia. Čamlîbel also attempted one novel, *Yıldız yağmuru* ("Rain of stars"), Istanbul 1936.

Bibliography: Kenan Akyüz, *Batı tesirinde Türk şiiri antolojisi*³ Ankara 1970, 842, 876; Mehmed Kaplan, *op. cit.*, 13-33 (should be used critically, since it is often politically biased); Behçet Necatiğil, *Edebiyatımızda isimler sözlüğü*⁸, Istanbul 1975; Cevdet Kudret, *Türk edebiyatından seçme parçalar*, Istanbul, 1973, 367-74. (Fahir İz)

CAMONDO, Avram, financier, philanthropist, and reformer active amongst Istanbul's Jewish community (d. 1873). Born in Venice, he arrived in Istanbul and entered the banking business midway through the reign of Sultan Maḥmūd II (1808-39). As his influence and power increased, Camondo became the *ṣarrāf* (personal banker) of a number of Ottoman officials, most notably of the Grand Vizier Muṣṭafā Reshīd Pasha, with whom he established extremely close ties. Camondo later became financial representative of the Baron Hirsch interests and at times acted in concert with the firms of Rothschild and Bleichröder.

In 1854 Camondo became a member of the *Intiẓām-ĭ Shehir* Commission, a body charged with advising the central government on measures necessary for the modernisation of Istanbul [see baladiyya]. To carry out the extensive plans of this commission, the Ottoman government in 1858 created an autonomous municipal council in Ghalaṭa [*q.v.* in Suppl.], the European district of the capital. From 1858 until 1861 Camondo was a lea member of this council, which marked the systematic effort to provide Istanbul with services and amenities of a modern European

Camondo's efforts at modernisation were directed toward the Jewish community of Istan which by the 19th century was marked by extr ignorance and fanaticism. In 1854 he founde modern school at Pīrī Pasha, where Turkish French were studied in addition to scripture. resulting attempt by conservatives to exc municate him provoked a serious conflict in Jewish community, which was resolved in favou the liberal faction only because of the interven of the Ottoman government. Camondo then bec head of the Jewish Community Council and tinued the task of educational reform. In 187 took up permanent residence in Paris, but tinued to provide Istanbul's Jewish commu with synagogues and educational institutions. A his death, his body, in accordance with his will, returned to Istanbul and buried in Sütlüdje.

Bibliography: M. Franco, *Essai sur l'his des Israélites de l'empire Ottoman depuis les orig jusqu'à nos jours*, Paris 1897, 153-5, 162-6, 187; ʿOthmān Nūrī (Ergin), *Medjelle-i Um Belediyye*, i (Istanbul 1922), 1412-13; Abra Galanté, *Histoire des Juifs d'Istanbul*, i, Ista 1941, 31, 63, 78, 185-6, 206. Similar informa can be found in idem, *Rôle économique des J d'Istanbul*, Istanbul 1942, 20-1, 44-5. (S. Rosentha

ČAWDOR, or Čawdîr, one of the major tri of the Turkmen [*q.v.*].

It appears already in the lists of 24 Oghuz tr given by Maḥmūd al-Kāshgharī (i, 57; Djuwal and Rashīd al-Dīn (ed. A. Ali-zade, Moscow 1 80, 122: Djāwuldur). The tribe participated in Saldjūḳ movement; the famous *amīr* Čaḳa, founded an independent Turkmen principality the Aegean coast at the end of the 11th century said to be a Čawdor. The tribal name (in the f Čawundur) was registered in Anatolia in the century (see F. Sümer, *Oğuzlar*, Ankara 1967, 17). The main part of the tribe, however, remai in Central Asia or returned to it from the west the *Shadjara-yi Tarākima* by Abu 'l-Ghāzī [(ed. A. N. Kononov, text 61, Russian tr. 68), Čawdor are mentioned among those tribes w came to Mangîshlak [*q.v.*] after disturbances in Oghuz *īl*. It remained on Mangîshlak till the century, longer than any other Turkmen tribe. his *Shadjara-yi Turk* (ed. Desmaisons, text, 210 224) Abu 'l-Ghāzī mentions the Čawdor only o in the account of the Turkmen tribes which tribute to the Uzbek khāns of Khʷārazm at beginning of the 16th century. The Čawdor mentioned in this connection together with ano old Oghuz tribe, the Igdir (in a form "Igdir Djāw dur"); together they are said to pay three-fou of the tribute imposed on Ḥasan-ili. The t Ḥasan-ili (Esen-ili in the Turkmen pronunciat also Esen-Khān-ili) has continued to exist till present time, but its exact meaning is not q clear; it seems that latterly it has been app mainly to the Čawdors themselves and someti only to one of their main clans, the Ḳara-Čaw Besides the Čawdor and the Igdir, the Ḥasa group included also the tribes of the Abdāl, Bū (Boz Ḥādjī), Burundjîḳ and Soyinadji (Soyin Ḥā In the 19th century all of them, except the last were mostly considered only as different clans of tribe Čawdor; in some descriptions, however, appear as separate tribes.

the 16th and 17th centuries, the dwellings of Čawdor were located mainly in the northern of Mangi̊shlaḳ, where the Būzači peninsula still rves the name of one of the above-mentioned . From the early 17th century, they were sed to a strong pressure both from the north, he Kalmuks [*q.v.*], and from the south, by the nate of Khīwa. As a result of this pressure in the 17th and the early 18th century, a part of the lor and the Igdir as well as all the Soyinadji ated to the region of the Volga Kalmuks, and, her with the Kalmuks, they became Russian cts (see V. V. Bartol'd, *Sočineniya*, ii/1, 613-14). he end of the 18th century, they moved to the hern Caucasus, and now they live on the rivers č and Kuma in the region (*kray*) of Stavropol'; 60 their total number was estimated as more 5,000. The greater part of the Čawdor moved ver in the first half of the 18th century to ārazm. At the end of this century their main e, Čawdor-ḳala, was in Arāl, in the north of ārazm, and they were the allies of the indepen- Uzbek rulers of the town of Ḳungrat in their with the khāns of Khīwa. After the victory of va over the Ḳungrat [*q.v.*] in 1810, part of the lor returned to Mangi̊shlaḳ, but in the 1830s 1840s they finally left Mangi̊shlaḳ for Khwārazm r the pressure of the Aday Ḳazaḳs, and since their centre has become the town of Porsi̊ Kalinin), about 30 miles to the east from Old nč. Only an insignificant number of Čawdors remain on Mangi̊shlaḳ.

Mangi̊shlaḳ the Čawdor were nomads, though number of their cattle was relatively small and nportant part of their economy was fishing and hunting on the Caspian sea. In Khwārazm they me sedentarised farmers. Their exact number nknown; the estimations of the late 19th and early 20th century vary between 3,500 and 0 families.

Bibliography: A. Čuloshnikov, in *Materiali̊ istorii Uzbekskoy, Tadžikskoy i Turkmenskoy SR*, Leningrad 1932, 73-5; Yu. Bregel', *Khoәmskiye turkmeni̊ v XIX veke*, Moscow 1961, -5, 29-31 *et passim* (see index); G. E. Markov, *erk istorii formirovaniya severni̊kh turkmen*, oscow 1961; R. Karutz, *Unter Kirgisen und rkmenen*, Leipzig 1911, chs. 1-2; K. Niyazkličev, *Očerki̊ po istorii khozyaystva i kul'turi̊ turkmen*, hkhabad 1973, 87-98; A. Džikiev, in *Trudi̊ stituta istorii, arkheologii i étnografii Akademii uk Turkmenskoy SSR*, vii (Ashkhabad 1963), 7-201. On the relations between the Čawdor on angi̊shlaḳ and Russia in the 18th and early th century, see *Russko-turkmenskiye otnosheniya XVIII-XIX vv.*, Ashkhabad 1963, esp. 67, 115, 8, 142, 159, 194. On the Čawdor in Northern ucasus, see P. Nebol'sin, in *Žurnal Ministerstva utrennikh del*, xxxix/7 (1852), 50-71; and A. A. lodin, in *Sbornik materialov dlya opisaniya stnostey i plemen Kavkaza*, xxxviii (1908), pt. i, 98. (Yu. Bregel)

ĀY-KHĀNA, lit. "tea-house", a term covering nge of establishments in Iran serving and light refreshments, and patronised mainly by working and lower middle classes. The term *va-khāna*, "coffee-house", is used almost synnously, though coffee is never served. This latter e, however, tells us something of the history of institution, for most of which we have to rely on the accounts of the European travellers. One of the earliest references occurs in Chardin's *Voyages* (ii, 321), where in his description of Iṣfahān in about 1670 he speaks of "les cabarets à café, à tabac, et pour ces boissons fortes qu'on fait avec le suc du pavot.". There is no mention of tea here, nor in Hanway's *Journal of Travels*, written nearly a hundred years later, nor even in Malcolm's *History of Persia* compiled at the beginning of the 19th century. Up to this point it seems that coffee remained the popular drink, but by 1866 Lycklama a Nijeholt was able to write that tea "forme la boisson ordinaire des divers habitants de la Perse" (ii, 105), though elsewhere he mentions that coffee as well as tea was served to him by the Imām Djumʿa of Iṣfahān. Yet even he does not use the term *čāy-khāna*, though he does mention that the word *ḳahwa-khāna* was applied to part of the servants' quarters in a large Persian house. E. G. Browne in 1887 records a stop at "a little roadside tea-house" near Tehran, and adds, "Many such tea-houses formerly existed in the capital, but most of them were closed some time ago by order of the Shah. The reason commonly alleged for this proceeding is that they were supposed to encourage extravagance and idleness, and, as I have also heard said, evils of a more serious kind. Outside the town, however, some of them are still permitted to continue their trade and provide the '*bona fide* traveller' with refreshment, which, needless to say, does not include wine or spirits." (*A year amongst the Persians*, 82). Elsewhere Browne mentions frequently the serving of tea at private entertainments, but never coffee.

Evidently, then, a fairly sudden change of habit took place during the first half of the 19th century, though why tea should suddenly have been preferred to coffee (neither of which grew in Īrān at that time) is not clear. It is not even certain when tea first became known to the Iranians. Bīrūnī's *Kitāb al-Ṣaydana*, written in the first half of the 5th/11th century, gives a detailed account of *čāy*, but only as a plant grown and used in China. According to a Ṣafawid manuscript referred to without quotation by Farīdūn Ādamiyyat in his *Amīr-i Kabīr wa Īrān*, tea was drunk in Īrān in Ṣafawid times; but the same author suggests that the widespread introduction of tea-drinking into Īrān was due to Amīr-i Kabīr [*q.v.* in Suppl.], who in 1849 received gifts of silver samovars from the Russian and French governments on the occasion of the coronation of Nāṣir al-Dīn Shāh, and encouraged the craftsmen of Iṣfahān to copy them. From then on, tea began to be imported in significant and increasing quantities, mainly the black tea of India, which was preferred to the milder Chinese. Tea was not actually grown in Īrān, and specifically in the Caspian area, until 1896.

The first dictionary appearance of the word *ḳahwa-khāna* is in Francis Johnson's, published in 1852; but the word *čāy-khāna* does not appear until the most recent dictionaries (e.g. Dihkhudā, pt. 41, 1338/1959). Even the omniscient Haim (1935) does not list it, but under *ḳahwa-khāna* adds the definition "[in Persia] a tea-house". However, the word *čāy-khāna* was certainly in common use by that time; indeed A. V. Williams Jackson met it as early as 1903, when he found along his route "mud cabins which served as tea-houses (*chāi khānah*)" (*Persia past and present*, 34).

At the present time the terms *čāy-khāna* and *ḳahwa-khāna* are to some extent interchangeable, but the former tends to be used for the small wayside establishments catering primarily for travellers (cf. Dihkhudā's definition "places on the highways and caravan routes where formerly carriage horses were changed"). Since the coming of motor transport most of these have disappeared, while others have acquired a degree of sophistication appropriate to the bus passengers who now constitute their main clientèle. By contrast the word *ḳahwa-khāna* usually designates the tea-shops in the towns and large villages, which serve as meeting-places for the local (male) community (a very few have curtained-off compartments for women). Both types of establishment serve much the same fare—tea, prepared with the aid of a large samovar, bread and cheese, eggs, perhaps *āb-i gūsht* or some other such simple dish, and of course the *ḳalyān* (water-pipe). (Coffee is obtainably only in the more sophisticated, European-style café (*ḳāfa*), patronised by wealthier clients, where tea, ice-cream, soft drinks, and French pastries are also to be had). For entertainment, there is the *takhta-yi nard* (backgammon board), and often the *naḳḳāl*, who recites long dramatic episodes from the *Shāh-nāma*, or traditional epics and folk-tales in prose or verse. In Ādharbāydjān a similar role is often filled by the *ʿāshiḳ*, who recites mystical poetry in Turkish, Arabic or Persian, accompanying himself on a stringed instrument. Dervish fortune-tellers (*rammāl*) are also commonly to be seen. In times of high political activity the *ḳahwa-khāna* may serve as a centre for the dissemination of news and views. Browne, in *The Persian revolution*, 143, quotes an unnamed Persian correspondent, writing on 19 June 1907: "In many of the *Qahwa-khánas* professional readers are engaged, who, instead of reciting the legendary tales of the Sháh-náma, now regale their clients with political news."

Many of the older *ḳahwa-khānas* are decorated with paintings and frescoes dating from Ḳādjār times. These may depict religious scenes (the martyrdom of Ḥusayn, for instance, or the *Miʿrādj* of the Prophet), *Shāh-nāma* episodes (the death of Rustam, the court of Ḍaḥḥāk, the fight between Bīzhan and Hūmān), love-stories (Laylā and Madjnūn, Shīrīn bathing), and dancing girls, musicians and entertainers at the royal court.

Bibliography: al-Bīrūnī, *Kitāb al-Ṣaydana*, ed. and tr. Hakim Mohammed Said, Karachi 1973, i (introduction), 84-5, ii, (translation), 128-9 (Arabic), 105-6 (English); *Voyages du Chevalier Chardin en Perse*, Paris 1686; Jonas Hanway, *An historical account of the British trade over the Caspian Sea with a journal of travels*, London 1753; Sir John Malcolm, *The history of Persia*, London 1815; *ibid.*, *Sketches of Persia*, London 1828; T. M. Chevalier Lycklama a Nijeholt, *Voyage en Russie, au Caucase et en Perse*, Paris 1872; Farīdūn Ādamiyyat, *Amīr-i Kabīr wa Īrān*, Tehran 1323/1944, ii, 248-50; E. G. Browne, *A year amongst the Persians*, London 1893; *idem*, *The Persian revolution*, Cambridge 1910; A. V. Williams Jackson, *Persia past and present*, New York 1906; Īradj Nabawi, *Tāblū-hā-yi ḳahwā-khāna'ī*, Tehran N.D. (*ca.* 1973). (L. P. Elwell-Sutton)

ČAYLAḲ TEWFĪḲ, modern Turkish Çaylak Tevfik, Turkish writer and journalist (1843-92). A self-taught man, he was born in Istanbul and became a civil servant. He started his career in Bursa and continued in Istanbul where he published the papers *ʿAṣir* ("Century", later renamed *Leṭā'if-i āthār*) and *Teraḳḳī* ("Progress"). In February 1876 he published his best-known paper, the humorous *Čaylaḳ* ("The Kite"), which became his nick-name and which ceased publication in June 1877 162 numbers. In 1877 he went, with a delegatic Hungary for a month and on his return he publ his impressions as *Yādigār-i Madjaristān* ("Sou of Hungary"). Čaylaḳ Tewfīḳ is the author o following works: *Ḳāfile-i shuʿarā'*, alphabeti arranged biographies of poets (which stop at letter *dāl*); *Istanbul'da bir sene* ("A year in Istanb Istanbul 1297-9 Rūmī/1881-3, his best known v the general title of a series of five books, consi of realistic descriptions of everyday life in Ista The subtitles of the work are (1) *Tandīr*; (2) *Ma ḳahwesi*; (3) *Kāghidkhāne*; (4) *Ramaḍān gedj* and (5) *Meykhāne*. Čaylak Tewfīḳ pioneered Naṣr al-Dīn Khōdja literature in modern Tur and published three volumes containing about stories on him, *Leṭā'if-i Naṣr al-Dīn*, *Bu* (1883) and *Khazīne-i Leṭā'if* (1885).

Bibliography: *Türk Ansiklopedisi*, xi (1 3), 407-8; Behçet Necatiğil, *Edebiyatım isimler sözlüğü*[8], Istanbul 1975. (Fahir İ

ČEH, the Ottoman term for the inhabit of present-day Czechochoslovakia, mainly hemia and Moravia, but partly also Slovakia. Arabs did not use this term, although the terri was known to them at least since the end of 3rd/9th century. In the so-called "Anony relation" on East European and Turkish peo preserved by a group of early and later Mu geographers (Ibn Rusta, *Ḥudūd al-ʿālam*, Gar al-Bakrī, Marwazī, ʿAwfī), the name of Svato (spelled variously as Sw.n.t.b.l.k., Sw.y.t.m etc.) ruler of the Great Moravian Empire (871 is mentioned. The name of his land (Mirwāt, M.r. is also given in some sources, but its localisati erroneously shifted too far to the east (cf. Rusta, 142-5, tr. Wiet, 160-3; *Ḥudūd al-ʿālam* Minorsky, §§ 42, 46; Gardīzī, ed. Barthold, 99- ed. ʿAbd. al-Ḥayy Ḥabībī, Tehran 1347/1968, Marwazī, ed. Minorsky, 22, 35).

Al-Masʿūdī must have had an excellent inform (probably a Slavonic slave from this region) on ethnic and political situation in Central Eu since his relation is entirely independent of c sources and rich in detail not to be found elsew In the list of Slavonic tribes and their rulers find also the name of Wenceslaus (Prince of hemia, 926-35), spelled as Wān.dj Slāw, but onl ruler of the Dudlebs (Dūlāba), one of the m Czech tribes at this period (*Murūdj*, iii, 62-3 = §§ 6; Marquart, *Streifzüge*, 102 ff., wanted to another ethnic name in the list Ṣāṣīn as Čāhīn Czechs], but this is unlikely as the context p rather to the Saxons). In his *Tanbīh*, 62, al-Mas describes the Danube (Danuba) and the Mo (Malawa) rivers and mentions also the Slav peoples Bāhmīn (Bohemians; this can be read as Nāmdjīn, the Slavonic term for the Germ and Murāwa (Moravians).

The most copious and detailed information a the territory of Czechoslavakia and its peoples i be found in Ibrāhīm b. Yaʿḳūb's [*q.v.*] narra who visited these countries in the sixties of the century and could well be called the discovere Central Europe. He names the successor and bro of Wenceslaus, Boleslav I (935-67) as the ru prince over Prague (Frāgh), Bohemia (Būyāma) Cracovia (Krakūwā). His detailed account is fu precious information about the economic and c mercial situation, and brings many facts about life, manners and customs of the people, as well few Slavonic words. His description of Pragu oldest extant in the literature, and the whole unt belongs to the most valuable sources of · Czech history. Unfortunately his relation is conserved in its entirety, but only in excerpts l-Bakrī's *al-Mamālik wa'l-masālik*; some fragts are preserved by al-Ḳazwīnī and by the late ribī geographer Ibn ʿAbd al-Munʿim al-Ḥimyarī is *Kitāb al-Rawḍ al-miʿṭār* (Bibl. Nat. Rabat, no. 238).

ter the 4th/10th century, the country of the hs and Slovaks wanes from the horizon of Arab Persian geographers. The only exception is al-ī, who in two sections (vi, 2 and 3) mentions miyya (Bohemia), but under this name he rstood two different countries, as is to be seen the list of towns belonging to it. His first miyya represents Slovakia (and partly northern gary) with the towns of Bāṣū (either Bratislava, erly Poszon, or Vácov), Aḳrā (Jager, Erlau), sh or * -nṣīn (either Bíteš in Moravia, or Trenčín lovakia), Shubrūna (Sopron), Niṭram (Nitra), The second Bū'āmiyya, in which the towns of ḳāṭ (Prague) and Māsla (Meissen) are located, s, according to al-Idrīsī, a part of his Allamāniyya many). All this shows that he had rather vague vledge about this part of Europe, borrowing his rmation from various sources and being unable armonise it (cf. Lewicki, *Polska*, part 2, *im*).

e next time the Muslim peoples came into con-with the territory of modern Czechoslovakia was r the Ottoman Empire. The Ottoman expansion e 11th/17th century touched also some southern ons of present-day Czechoslovakia, these regions forming a part of the Hungarian kingdom. owing the Battle of Mohács in 1526, the Turks essively conquered Buda in 1541 and Esztergom 543 and occupied the village of Kakat (today ovo), where they built a small fortress, called rdelen Parkani; this was the beginning of Otto-rule over Czechoslovak territory. In 1544 they uered the fortress Fil'akovo in eastern Slovakia Nógrad and Szécsény in northern Hungary. territory was then organized into four *sandjaks*, e of Esztergom, Nógrad, Szécsény and Fil'akovo, re more than 90 villages and hamlets on territory of present-day Czechoslovakia were ted.

uring the so-called Fifteen-Years' War of 1593-, the Ottomans lost the larger part of this region, hat afterwards only about 200 villages remained r their rule.

e greatest military enterprise of the 11th/17th ury, the campaign of Köprülü Aḥmed Pasha nst the Hapsburg monarchy in 1663-4, touched n Czechoslovak territory. In 1663 the Turkish y conquered the important fortresses of Nové ky (Uyvar, Neuhäusel, Érsekújvár), Nitra and ice as well as many smaller fortifications. After peace of Vasvár of 14 August 1664, the fortress Nové Zámky, together with 786 villages and lets in southern Slovakia, remained in Ottoman ds (cf. *Defter-i mufaṣṣal-i eyālet-i Uyvar*, Baş-anlık Arşivi, Tapu Defterleri, Nos. 115-698). of this territory a new *eyālet* was constituted its headquarters in Uyvar. Ottoman rule ed here until the reconquest of Nové Zámky in , whereas in the eastern regions of Slovakia it isted till a year later, when the township of avská Sobota paid for the last time taxes to the omans.

nce the treaties between the Ottomans and the Hapsburg monarchy were frequently infringed, the frontiers remained unstable and underwent many changes. The Ottoman administration considered all villages inscribed in the tax-registers or *defters* as its own territory and insisted firmly on this view, whereas the opposite party was not willing to accept this state of affairs. There thus emerged a wide frontier zone under the fiscal jurisdiction of both parties, i.e. a condominium. The inhabitants were forced to pay taxes to both sides; the levy of taxes on the disputed territory led to incessant fighting, to punitive expeditions for non-payment, to raids and plunderings of villages as well as to dragging-away of peoples into captivity or slavery. The main raids occurred against Rožňava and Jelšava in 1556, Gemer in 1569, Vráble in 1584 and 1630, Krupina in 1654, Žarnovice in 1654, etc. The marauding raids, chiefly by Tatar troops, devastated many times the whole region of the Váh and Nitra rivers (1543, 1552, 1575), as well as eastern Moravia (1530, 1599, 1663).

The only Turkish traveller who visited the territory of Czechoslovakia was Ewliyā Čelebi, who travelled in the southern regions in 1660-6 and also took part in the campaign of 1663-4. He visited and described the following towns and fortresses: Nové Zámky (Uyvar), Komárno (Komaran), Parkán-Štúrovo (Cigerdelen Parkanî), Šurany, Košice (Kashsha), Fil'akovo (Filek), Hlohovec (Galgofča) and Bratislava (Podjon), cf. *Seyāḥat-nāme*, vi, 46-51, 278-392; vii, 133-6, 335-45.

Two participants in the same campaign have also left accounts: Muṣṭafā Zühdi in the *Ta'rīkh-i Uyvar* (Halis Efendi Ktph., No. 2230) and Meḥmed Nedjātī in the *Ta'rīkh-i sefer-i Uyvar* (Revan Ktph., No. 1308), both written in 1665. In the Turkish historical literature the events of war on Czechoslovak territory were described in some detail by Ibrāhīm Pečewī (conquest of Fil'akovo, *Ta'rīkh*, i, 139-40; of Sobotka, ii, 140; the siege of Komárno, ii, 154-6). Kātib Čelebi gave an account of events of the Fifteen-Years War in his *Fedhleke*, i, 19-20, 132-6, 261-2.

Bibliography: Arabic accounts: J. Marquart, *Osteuropäische und ostasiatische Streifzüge*, Leipzig 1903, 95-160; T. Kowalski, *Relacja Ibrāhīma ibn Jaʿḳūba z podroży do krajów słowiańskich v przekazie al-Bekrī-ego*, Cracow 1946; T. Lewicki, *Polska i kraje sasednie w świetle "Ksiegi Rogera" geografa arabskiego z XII w. al-Idrīsī-ego*, 2 parts, Cracow-Warsaw 1945-54; I. Hrbek, in *Magnae Moraviae fontes historici*, iii, Brno 1969. Ottoman period: L. Fekete, *Az Esztergomi szandszak 1570. évi adóösszeiirńsa*, Budapest 1943; J. Blaškovič, *Some notes on the history of the Turkish occupation of Slovakia*, in *Acta Univ. Carol., Orientalis Pragensia*, Prague 1960, 41-57; idem, *Rimavská Sobota v case osmanskotureckého panstva* (*Rimavská Sobota at the time of Ottoman Turkish rule*), Bratislava 1975 (= Turkish documents, translation and commentary).

(I. Hrbek - J. Blaškovič)

CITRUS [see MUḤAMMADĀT].

ČOBĀN-OGHULLARÎ, a family of *derebeys* [*q.v.*] in Ottoman Anatolia, who controlled the districts (*nāḥiyes*) of Tiyek, Ekbez and Hacılar in the eastern parts of the Amanus Mountains or Gâvur Daği (in the hinterland of Iskenderun [see ISKANDARŪN] in modern Turkey). They claimed hereditary power in the area from the time of Sultan Murād IV (1032-49/1623-40), when the latter, in the course of his campaign against the Persians in

Baghdād, granted these districts to a local shepherd (*čobān*). By the 19th century, the family was divided into two branches, one controlling Tiyek and Ekbez and the other Hacilar. The Čobān-oghullarî played a part in the attempts of the more powerful *derebey* families of the Cicilian region to maintain their local autonomy against the Porte in Istanbul, were at times allied with e.g. the Kücük ʿAlī-og larî [*q.v.*].

Bibliography: see A. G. Gould, *Lord bandits? The derebeys of Cilicia*, in *IJMES*, (1976), 491. (Er

D

DABBĀGH (A.), "tanner", frequent as a *nisba* in mediaeval and modern Arabic. In pre-Islamic Arabia, the tanners were Jewish craftsmen. During the lifetime of the Prophet, his Companions, such as al-Ḥārith b. Ṣabīra, Sawda, Asmāʾ bint ʿAmīs and others, were associated with tanning. Saʿd b. ʿĀʾidh al-Ḳaraẓ, one of the Companions of Muḥammad, was busy trading in fruit of the acacia (*ḳaraẓ*) which was widely used as a material for the processing of leather. During the Umayyad, ʿAbbāsid and Mamlūk periods, there were many Jewish and Arab tradesmen engaged in tannery. Djāḥiẓ mentions Jewish tanners; al-Samʿānī and Ibn al-Athīr, on the other hand, cite numerous names of Arabs who were well-known not only as *dabbāghs*, but also as transmitters of traditions and religious lore.

The tanners worked and lived in the suburbs of towns and villages, and had their separate lanes (*darb*) in the markets known as *darb al-dabbāghīn*. They had their shops close to the camel-market of Mirbad in Baṣra during the Umayyad period. The shops of *dabbāghūn*, together with those of fishmongers, were situated in the markets of Karkh in Baghdād, away from the shops of the perfumers (*ʿaṭṭārūn*). The *muḥtasib* supervised the artisans' works and prevented the *dabbāgh* from using oak galls (*ʿafṣ*) instead of acacia fruits (*ḳaraẓ*) for leather processing, and cautioned the tanners not to mix hides of ritually-slaughtered cows with those of animals like horses, mules and donkeys which had died natural deaths without being properly slaughtered.

The *dabbāgh* does not appear prominently in Arabic anecdotes and humorous tales, whereas the weaver (*ḥāʾik*) and the cupper (*ḥadjdjām*) was often portrayed as a comic character in Arabic literature. The relative silence of Arabic *udabāʾ* about tanners was partly due to the social isolation in which the *dabbāghūn* worked and lived. Al-Rāghib al-Iṣfahānī expresses the accepted view about the *dabbāgh*, the *ḥāʾik* and the *ḥadjdjām*, that they are *siflat al-nās*, men of mean status. The ʿAbbāsid government, from time to time, imposed extraordinary taxes (*maks*) on skilled artisans, including tanners, but these fiscal measures were temporary. We find some evidence which suggest that the witness (*shahāda*) of craftsmen of low status like the sweeper (*kannās*), tanner, cupper and weaver was not acceptable in law; some Mālikī jurists, however, pleaded in favour of the waiving of this restriction and the acceptance of their *shahāda*. Ibn ʿĀbidīn and some other jurists, while discussing the law of *kafāʾa*, debated the question whether the tanners were eligible to contract marriages outside their own social group, and Arab prejudices against the *dabbāghs* clearly hindered upward social mobility among tanners through marriages with families of higher status.

Bibliography: Djāḥiẓ, *Thalāth rasāʾil*, J. Finkel, Cairo 1926, 17; Abū Ṭālib al-Ma *Ḳūt al-ḳulūb*, Cairo 1310/1892, ii, 279; Ibn Djawzī, *Manāḳib Baghdād*, Baghdād 1342/1 4, 28; idem, *al-Muntaẓam*, Hyderabad 1358, x, al-Rāghib al-Iṣfahānī, *Muḥāḍarāt al-udabāʾ*, Be 1961, ii, 459-60; Ibn Bassām, *Nihāyat al-r fī ṭalab al-ḥisba*, Baghdad 1968, 204-6; Ibn Ukhuwwa, *Maʿālim al-ḳurba*, London 1938, 229 al-Samʿānī, *al-Ansāb* (s.v. *al-dabbāgh*) Hydera 1966, v, 300-2; Ibn al-Athīr, *al-Lubāb fī tahdhīb ansāb*, (s. vv. *al-dabbāgh* and *al-ḳaraẓ*) Beirut i, 488-9, iii, 26; ʿAlāʾ al-Dīn al-Lubūdī, *Faḍ iktisāb*, Chester Beatty Ms. 4791, f. 57b; Ibn ʿ dīn, *Radd al-Muḥtār ʿalā durr al-Mukhtār*, C 1877, ii, 496-7; al-Kattānī, *Niẓām al-ḥukūma nabawīyya*, known as *al-Tarātib al-idāriyya*, Be n.d., ii, 56-7, 64, 92; A. Mez, *Renaissance of Is* Eng. tr. 39; R. Brunschvig, *Métiers vils en Is* in *St. Isl.*, xvi (1962), 48, 58. (M. A. J. Be

al-**DABBĀGH, ABŪ ZAYD ʿABD RAḤMĀN** b. Muḥammad b. ʿAlī b. ʿAbd Al al-Anṣārī al-Usaydī, b. 605/1208-9, d. 699/1 was, according to the eyewitness and prob interested testimony of al-ʿAbdarī, the unique scholar in al-Ḳayrawān of his time. If one believe an anecdote which states that he owed cognomen of al-Dabbagh to the fact that his gr grandfather disguised himself as a tanner in o to avoid the office of *ḳāḍī*, he must have stem from an ancient family of Ḳayrawānī *faḳīhs*. ʿAbdarī, who visited him in 688/1289 and rece from him a general *idjāza* for the transmission o whole work, praises his hospitality, fine appeara amiability, lofty mind and breadth of knowledge. was well-versed in all the traditional Islamic scien was a felicitous poet and excelled above all in *ḥa* His masters had been numerous (over 80), and devoted to them, in the fashion of the time, a *ba madj* or catalogue, which has survived. He also w a work on *ḥadīth*, *al-Aḥādīth al-arbaʿīn fī ʿu rahmat Allāh li-sāʾir al-ʿālamīn*, a history, *Taʾ Mulūk al-Islām* and a collection of edifying *v Djalaʾ al-afkār fī manāḳib al-anṣār*; none of th works has come down to us.

However, al-Dabbāgh owed his reputation ab all to his *ṭabaḳāt* devoted, in a chronological orde dates of death, to the saints and scholars who either lived in al-Ḳayrawān or had visited it. Acc ing to al-ʿAbdarī, this was called *Maʿālim al-ī wa-rawḍat al-riḍwān fī manāḳib al-mashhūrīn ṣulaḥāʾ al-Ḳayrawān*, and was in two big volu He drew substantially on the oldest sources, especially on the *Ṭabaḳāt* of Abu 'l-ʿArab and *Riyāḍ* of al-Mālikī. Al-Dabbāgh's work was in copied and enlarged firstly by Ibrāhīm al-ʿAw (d. *ca.* 719/1320), and above all by another Ḳa

, Ibn Nādjī (d. after 839/1435), who completed adding biographical notices of the scholars of own century and by interpolating all through earlier texts personal remarks generally introdu- by the verb *ḳultu* "I say". Hence al-Dabbāgh's is only known to us through this definitive in four volumes given to us by Ibn Nādjī with title *Maʿālim al-īmām fī maʿrifat ahl al-Ḳayra-*. In sum, we have here a collective work which, neans of anecdotes and edifying stories, brings fe before our very eyes and in successive layers, highly diverse world of piety and *fiḳh*. The Tunis on of this (1320-5) is very poor, but has been lited in a more critical way by Ibrāhīm Shabbūḥ airo 1968), which has however now stopped after first volume and seems unlikely to continue. For part, M. H. al-Hīla has made a very useful index h is unfortunately only available in roneotyped and has had little circulation.

l-Dabbāgh was buried in al-Ḳayrawān at the is Gate, in the enclosure reserved for his ancestors called the Silsilat al-Dhahab ("Golden chain"). was in fact the descendant of a famous line of ir.

Bibliography: ʿAbdarī, *al-Riḥla al-maghribiy-a*, ed. M. al-Fāsī, Rabat 1968, 66-7; Ibn Nādjī, *Maʿālim*, iv, 89-92; al-Wazīr al-Sarrādj, *Ḥulal*, l. M. H. al-Hīla, Tunis 1970, i, 262-70 (largely peats ʿAbdarī); R. Brunschvig, *Ḥafṣides*, Paris 947, ii, 382-3. (M. TALBI)

ABĪR (P.) "scribe, secretary", the term rally used in the Persian cultural world, including Indo-Muslim one (although in the later centuries it led to be supplanted by the term *munshī*, so that e-Burnell, *Hobson-Jobson, a glossary of Anglo-an colloquial words and phrases*, London 1886, record "dubeer" as being in their time "quite olete in Indian usage"), as the equivalent of bic *kātib* and Turkish *yazidji*. The word appears *dipīr/dibīr* (Pahlavi orthography *dpy(w)r*, see N. MacKenzie, *A concise Pahlavi dictionary*, don 1971, 26) in Sāsānid Persia to denote the etaries of the government departments, an in-ntial body in the state, and a chief secretary, *n-dibīrpat* or *dibīrān-mehisht* is mentioned in such ces as the *Kārnāmag-i Ardashīr*; see, for instance, ʿūdī, *Tanbīh*, 104, tr. Carra de Vaux, 148, giving *dafīrbadh* as the fourth of the five great dignita- in the Sāsānid state. A knowledge of writing and etaryship was considered part of a gentleman's cation, and the *Kārnāmag* records that Ardashīr nt *dibīrih* at Bābak's court (see M. Boyce, *The thian* gosān *and Iranian minstrel tradition*, in *AS* [1957], 32-3). From Sāsānid usage it passed Armenia, where we find mentioned a chief secre-, *drapet Areacʿ* (H. Hübschmann, *Armenische mmatik*, i, Leipzig 1897, 145). The origin of the d is seen in Old Iranian **dipibara* "bearer of ing", and this originally Iranian word passed ing pre-Islamic times into more westerly lan-ges, such as Aramaic and Armenian; for etymolog- details, see W. Eilers, *Iranisches Lehngut im ischen Lexikon: über einige Berufsnamen und l*, in *Indo-Iranian Jnal.*, v (1961-2), 216-17.

or the functions of *dabīrān* in Islamic times, see IB, ii and iii, and also DIWĀN, iv and v.

Bibliography (in addition to references given the article): Nöldeke-Ṭabarī, *Geschichte der erser und Araber zur Zeit der Sasaniden*, Leiden 879, 444-5; Christensen, *L'Iran sous les Sassani-es*², Copenhagen 1944, index. (C. E. BOSWORTH)

ḌABUʿ, ḌABʿ (A. *ḍubʿ*, *ḍubuʿ*, *ḍibāʿ*, *aḍbuʿ*, *maḍbaʿa*), grammatically feminine singular nouns designating the hyena (Persian: *kaftār*, Turkish: *ṣirtlan*, Berber: *ifis*, pl. *ifisen*) irrespective of sex or species (see Ch. Pellat, *Sur quelques noms d'animaux en arabe classique*, in *GLECS*, viii, 95-9). From this vague generic term, additional forms have been derived to differentiate the sexes: *ḍibʿān*, pl. *ḍabāʿīn* for the male (alongside *dhīkh*, pl. *dhuyūkh*) and *ḍibʿāna*, pl. *-āt*, for the female. The word *ḍabuʿ* (preferable to *ḍabʿ*) is of Sumero-Akkadian origin and is found in several languages of the Semitic group, most notably in Hebrew with *ṣebūʿa* (Jeremiah, xii, 9) and its plural (*ṣebūʿīm* in the Biblical toponym of the "Valley of the Seboim" or "Valley of the Hyenas" (I Samuel, xiii, 18), currently the valley of the Wādī Abū Ḍabʿa, tributary of the Wādī al-Ḳilt, to the west of Jericho. The Arabic dialects of the present day have all retained the original name of the animal in the forms *ḍbaʿ* and *ḍabᵃʿ* (fem. *ḍabʿa*, pl. *ḍbūʿa*).

The hyena family comprises four species, distributed geographically throughout Africa and from Arabia to Bengal; this means that the majority of Muslim peoples, and especially all Arabic and Berber speakers, have always been familiar with this repulsive carrion-eater, closely related to the dog family. The species that is most widely distributed, from the Atlantic coast of North Africa to India, is the striped hyena (*Hyaena hyaena* or *Heaena striata*) which lives a solitary life, occasionally in pairs, at altitudes of up to 1,500 metres and is essentially nocturnal. It is distinguished by its hide, varying in colour from grey to a dingy shade of yellow, and by its erect dorsal mane (*marāfīl*) which accounts for *ʿarfāʾ*, one of the many epithets applied to the animal. Its den (*widjār*, *ḥidn*, *rudjma*, *ʿirān*) is usually a deep, vaulted burrow under an outcrop of rock. Litters consists of five or six cubs (*furʿul*, *furʿulān*, pl. *farāʿil*, and in poetry, *bahdal*, *fartanā*, *hubayra*, *hinbar*, *hinnabr*, *hunbuʿ*). In Africa, the southern limit of its habitat is the mid-Sahara, where it is called, in Tamahaḳ, *erkeni/terkenit*, pl. *erkeniten/terkenitin*. The Arab nomads of the Sahara regions, for reasons of superstitious euphemism, refer to it as *bāb marzūḳ* "lucky door". The second species, found only in Africa, is the spotted hyena (*Hyena crocuta*), in Arabic *ḍabuʿ raḳṭāʾ*. Stronger and more ferocious than the former, this hyena has no mane and its hide is reddish with black speckles. It is found throughout Africa south of the Sahara, and its habitat overlaps that of its striped cousin in the central desert regions, where it is called *tahūri*, pl. *tihūryawin*; it is common in the Sudan and Eritrea under the name *marfaʿīn/marfaʿīl/marfaʿīb*. Its behaviour differs considerably from that of the striped hyena; a strong gregarious instinct causes it to live in packs (in dialect: *mḍabʿa*, pl. *mḍābiʿ*), each one of which may include more than a dozen members. Hunting in groups, both by day and night, the members of a pack pose a formidable threat to cattle and deer, and they have been known to attack isolated travellers; within the pack, a strict law regulates the distribution of captured prey. Much less prolific than the striped hyena, the spotted hyena has no more than one or two cubs to a litter. The other two species of hyena, the brown hyena (*Hyaena brunnea*) and the aard-wolf (*Proteles cristatus*), an insectivore, are virtually unknown in the Arab countries, being confined to central and southern Africa.

The Greeks, who knew of the hyena through the writings of Aristotle (*Hist. Anim.*, vi, 32) and Herodotus (iv, 192), had only two words for the animal: ὕαινα and γλάνυς, while the Arabs, many centuries before Islam, employed a wide vocabulary of terms to describe both the physical appearance and behaviour of the hyena (see Ibn Sīduh, *Mukhaṣṣaṣ*, viii, 69-72); ancient Arabic poetry contains the bulk of this terminology, which has virtually disappeared from contemporary speech. The first thing which struck the Bedouin about the appearance of the hyena was its swaying and limping gait (*hanbala, hunbuʿa*), owed to the fact that its forequarters are higher and more powerful than its hindquarters. This trait earned the animal a whole range of pejorative epithets with the general sense of "lame", such as: *dhayʾal/djayal, ʿardjāʾ, mathʿāʾ, khāmiʿa, khutaʿ, khalaʿlaʿ, khazʿal*, etc. The effect of this ignominious gait is aggravated by the animal's bandy forelegs, on account of which it was called *ʿaythūm, ʿathāmi, fashāhi* and *naʿthal*, while its thick, matted and mangy coat gave rise to the names *bāḳiʿ, aʿthāʾ/ʿathwāʾ/ʿithyān, umm ʿithyāl* and *ghunāfir*. Because of its black jowls and muzzle, it was known as *rashmāʾ* and *umm rasham*, and because of its ungainly and misshapen body, *ḥadādjir, ʿafshalīl, umm riʿm* and *umm dabkal*. Its nocturnal habits and appetite for carrion earned it a number of epithets with the general sense of "vileness", "filth", such as *djayʿar/djaʿāri, ḳutham/ḳathāmi, ḳashʿ, khanʿas* and *madrāʾ* It has always inspired disgust, with its necrophagous instinct and its habit of raiding cemeteries and unearthing and consuming freshly-interred corpses; as a result of this repugnant behaviour, the hyena earned uncomplimentary nicknames such as *umm al-ḳubūr* "mother of the tombs", and *nabbāsh al-ḳubūr* or *naḳāthi*, "grave-digger".

Al-Djāḥiẓ amassed a considerable quantity of information on the hyena by collecting legends relating to the animal in Bedouin circles, and he mentions this reprehensible behaviour, without himself believing in it, in connection with the coupling with swollen, unburied corpses of enemies slain in battle or of executed criminals (*Ḥayawān*, v, 117, vi, 450). He also mentions the fact that, like the hare, the hyena was alleged to be a hermaphrodite. Furthermore, this hermaphroditism was believed to be alternate, not simultaneous, the same individual being male one year, female the next. In reality, such legends may have arisen from the fact that the female hyena is seen to possess a strangely hypertrophied external genital organ, allowing it to be mistaken for a male. On account of its contact with corpses and its menstrual cycle, the hyena was regarded in the superstitious minds of the nomads as something essentially unclean, and for this reason could not serve as a mount for the genies (*Ḥayawān*, vi, 46). According to another fable, it was believed that by penetrating the shadow cast by a dog in the moonlight, the hyena could make the animal fall from the wall or the terrace where it was standing; the dog would then be eaten.

All in all, the hyena was regarded as a totally reprehensible and ill-omened beast, as is suggested by epithets with the sense of "mother of calamity" (*umm ḳashʿam, umm khinnawr, umm nawfal*), while its nocturnal rallying cry (*khaff, khafkhafa*), resembling a sardonic laugh, and its raucous growl of anger (*nawf, ḳushaʿ*), have always been of a type calculated to terrify the traveller stranded in the countryside, looking anxiously for the reassuring lights of an encampment or a village. To meet at night the animal known in different regions as "the crier" (*al-khaffūf*), "the growler" (*umm ʿattāb*), "the host of the road" (*umm al-ṭarīḳ*), "mother of the sands" (*umm al-ri*
and "the mother of the hill" (*umm al-kalada*)
sign of bad luck; striking a light is the only wa
banishing this unwelcome companion, this an
which joins forces with the wolf (*akhū nahs*
the jackal and the vulture in consuming the sc
left behind by the lion, the panther, the leo
or the caracal lynx. Another, more empirical m
of protecting oneself against any possibility of at
from the hyena was to carry on one's person p
of colocynth (*ḥanẓal*) or sea-onion (*ʿunṣul*) or to
the skin with black nightshade (*ʿinab al-thaʿ*
plants whose smell is repellent to the hyena. On
other hand, the underground cave where the hy
sleeps during the day is often shared by some s
or other large reptile with which it coexists peacea
this explains the hyena's most widely-spread
name *umm ʿāmir* "mother of the serpent".

In spite of its ferocious and formidable appeara
the hyena is, in fact, characterised by cowar
once captured and muzzled and seen in dayl
the animal is so terrified that it gives the impres
of total bewilderment and stupidity. This well-kn
behaviour led the Bedouin to coin the phrase *ah*
min ḍabuʿ "more foolish than a hyena" and
epithet *ḍabaʿṭa/ḍabaghṭa/dabaghṭarā* "stupid",
cribed the animal before being used as a wor
reproof for silly or mischievous children. In
Maghrib, a brutal or foolish person is contemptuo
described as *maḍbūʿ* or *mḍabbaʿ*, implying that, ir
words of the proverb *klā rās ḍbaʾ*, "he has eat
hyena's head". Although the young of the speci
caught before the age of weaning, is easily dom
cated and proves very much attached to its ma
the adult is quite untamable, as is shown by the tr
story of the kind Bedouin who gave refuge
hunted hyena and was eaten in his sleep as a rev
for his benevolence, an episode which gave ris
the proverbial expression *mudjīr umm ʿāmir* "prc
tor of the hyena", applied to excessive hospit
shown towards a stranger. The incorrigible and
sociable temperament of the adult hyena and it
tent malevolence gave rise to the metaphorical s
of the word *ḍabuʿ*, as used by the Arabs to desc
years of drought and the distress and misery w
accompanied them (*Ḥayawān*, vi, 446-7). Still r
explicit was the old adage *khariʾat bayna-hum al-ḍ*
"the hyenas have defecated between them", use
reference to rival tribes divided by implac
hatred. Comparison to the hyena, as to the mor
[see ḲIRD] and the pig [see KHINZĪR], was a grie
insult in Arabic as in Persian; in the latter, *r*
kaftār "face of a hyena" was used to describe repu
features inspiring distrust (*Ḥayawān*, vi, 452).

Belief in hybrid forms produced by mating
the hyena and the wolf was firmly entrenched in
Arab mentality, and al-Djāḥiẓ was the first to
to refute it categorically (*Ḥayawān*, ii, 18
According to the latter, copulation of a male hy
with a she-wolf would have produced the *simʿ*, a c
ture renowned for its agility (see al-Damīrī, *Ḥa*
ii, 27-8), identified by modern naturalists with
Cape hunting-dog (*Lycaon pictus*), a canine. Ar
verse crossing would have produced the *ʿisbār*
al-Damīrī, *op. cit.*, ii, 115-6), probably to be i
tified with the aard-wolf, a species of hyena r
tioned above, According to another legend da
from the early years of Islam, the *simʿ* and the *ʿi*
offspring of the hyena and the wolf were, in
the progeny of two tax-collectors, transformed
these two carnivores by Allah as a punishment
their greed (*Ḥayawān*, v, 80, 148-50); this alleged

ment gives historical force to the unfortunate
tation for usury acquired in this period by tax-
ctors and money-changers. Still more extrava-
was the idea of the evolution of the giraffe (*zarā-*
ccording to the following process: in Abyssinia, a
hyena mates with a "wild" she-camel, producing
brid (unknown and unnamed!) which, mating
s turn with, according to its sex, a male or a
le oryx, gives birth to the giraffe as a definite
uct. Although this comical explanation defies
e laws of genetics, it does, for the simple-minded,
unt for the physique of the giraffe; it has the low
quarters of the hyena, the long neck of the camel
the thin legs and cloven hooves of the antelope.
ng into consideration the colour of its hide,
ge speckled with black, we can understand its
pound name in Persian: *ushturgāv-i palang* "ca-
bovine-panther" and its current scientific name,
owed from the preceding, *Giraffa camelopardalis* L.
pre-Islamic Arabia the hyena does not seem
ve been the object of a taboo. It was considered
me-animal and there was no objection to its
being eaten in times of hardship; there was
a trade in the animal, and according to some
pilers of tradition (see al-Damīrī, *op. cit.*, ii,
nd al-Ḳazwīnī, *ʿAdjāʾib*, same edition, ii, 235),
s sold between al-Ṣafā and al-Marwa, on the Pil-
s' Route. In later times, the question of the
ity of the consumption of the meat of this canine-
ned carnivore was answered differently by the
judicial schools of orthodox Islam. This is under-
dable, since the Prophet Muḥammad, when asked
ve a ruling on this vexed question, replied in an
iguous fashion, saying that he himself did not eat
ut that it was a form of game (*ṣayd*) and could
efore be consumed. The exegetes expounded this
ce at some length, arguing that the hyena does
hunt living prey as predatory animals do, an ar-
ent which holds good only for the striped hyena,
sole species known in Arabia. As a result, con-
ption of the meat of the hyena is regarded as per-
ible by the Shāfiʿīs and the Ḥanbalīs (see H.
ust, *Le précis de droit d'Ibn Qudāma*, Beirut 1950,
al-Ḳalḳashandī, *Ṣubḥ al-aʿshā*, ii, 47-8; E. Gräf,
beute und Schlachttier im islamischen Recht, Bonn
, 143, 233). Mālik b. Anas and his followers were
reticent, considering the consumption of the
of this scavenger "worthy of reproof" (*makrūh*).
or Abū Ḥanīfa, he maintains categorically that
meat is absolutely impermissible, on the basis
e formal prohibition applying to all carnivores
pped with canine teeth.

hatever the motive, consumption or destruc-
the capture of the hyena was a practice that al-
s had enthusiasts, using the best means available
rding to the time and the place. In Islamic coun-
, the simplest and oldest method of hunting, no
t dating back to prehistoric times, was to trap
nimal with cords in the burrow itself. The brave
who had the audacity to confront this adversary,
pite of its terrible bite, was obliged, as a pre-
nary, to undress and to arm himself with cords
into slip-knots; he would then approach his
ry as stealthily and silently as possible and
zle and hobble the creature without, apparently,
untering any resistance. In this delicate opera-
the hunter relied not only on his own courage,
also, and most of all, on the magic power of for-
e proclaimed in a loud voice at the moment of
act with the beast; in the East, the most effica-
s formula was: *Umm ʿĀmir nāʾima*! "Umm ʿĀmir
leep!" Another injunction was more distateful (see *LA* under *ʿm-r*): *khāmirī Umm ʿĀmir abshirī bi-djarād ʿazlā wa-kamarⁱ ridjāl ḳatlā.* "Go back Umm ʿĀmir, go and play with mating grasshoppers and the penis of slain men!" In the Maghrib, the hunter, having invoked the local saint, said, with more delicacy: *hāti yeddek nehennīhā.* "give me your foot and I shall dye it with henna." It should be emphasised that the first condition for success was, before embarking on the enterprise, to seal up the smallest fissure capable of shedding light into the burrow; the hunter was obliged to operate in total darkness, as in indicated by al-Djāḥiẓ (*Ḥayawān*, vi, 48); he could, for his personal safety, arm himself with a short dagger (see L. Mercier, *La chasse et les sports chez les Arabes*, Paris 1927, 29-30). Arab authors who have described hunting, like the poet Kushādjim [*q.v.*] in his *Kitāb al-Maṣāyid wa 'l-maṭārid* (ed. A. Talas, Baghdād 1954, 103, 213-15) from the 4th/10th century, or the encyclopaedist of fieldsports ʿĪsā al-Asadī, in his monumental *Djamhara fī ʿulūm al-bayzara* from the 7th/13th century (ms. Escurial 903, fols. 162b-163b), have given accounts of various procedures, other than that described above, for the capture of the hyena; these include the hunting-trap, using a ditch fenced in with stakes, the kennel-trap with a guillotine-style door (*ridāḥa, ridāʿa*) or the snare (*kiffa*) with a running knot to catch the paw. Each of these devices was accompanied by a bait (*rimma*) consisting of the carcase of some animal. In more recent periods, metal traps with tongues have replaced all devices previously in use. Such traps should be large and very powerful, because in many case the hyena's vice-like jaws are strong enough to bend steel. The Mamlūk Ibn Manglī, summarising the works of al-Asadī in his *Kitāb Uns al-malāʾ bi-waḥsh al-falā*, in the 8th/14th century, gives the following advice, the fruit of his personal experience, to the mounted hunter: "When pursuing the hyena on horseback, the animal should be approached from the left-hand side; an archer, if right-handed, should overtake it on the left flank. If the hunter is armed with a lance or a sabre, he should attack at very close quarters. Nevertheless, it is said that if the hyena charges at you from the right, you will be unable to strike it, although if it approaches you on the left, it is vulnerable and you will have it at your mercy, if Allah wills." With much less style and finesse, the general practice in the Maghrib is simply to stun the hyena with a club, having first smoked it out of its lair, the same procedure as is used in Europe for the fox, the badger and the polecat. Heavy and sudden rainfall can sometimes force the hyena to evacuate its flooded burrow; a fact illustrated by the old Arabic expression used to describe torrential rain *sayl djārr al-ḍabuʿ* "a flood to drive the hyena outside".

The truth is that the hyena has never enjoyed any kind of favour on the part of Muslim communities because the animal, while alive, is of absolutely no use to them. At the very most, in ancient Arabia the shepherd could hope for its presence when his flock was threatened by a wolf since, according to his not illogical reasoning, so long as these two carnivores were in violent competition with each other, his sheep were safe, which explains the shepherd's prayer *Allahumma ḍabʿan wa-dhiʾban*! "Oh Allah, [send me at the same time] a hyena and a wolf." There was a time when, in certain regions, the hyena could play the role of the Hebrew scapegoat; in cases of persistent drought where all other propitiatory rites had failed, the procedure of last recourse was to tie the hyena to a wall by its tail and to set dogs on it, torturing it for three days before killing and burying it; with the evil destiny thus exorcised, rain was sure to come soon. Such is the interpretation laid on these obscure ritual practices by the mythologists.

In spite of everything, the hyena should not be unjustly abused because, wherever it lives in proximity to man it is, with the jackal and the vulture, a factor in biological equilibrium, contributing to the elimination of decomposing organic matter, the source of all diseases and epidemics. In Islamic countries, the rural populations willingly accept the presence of the hyena in spite of its unpleasant instinct for digging (*d̲j̲ayyāf*); at night, the animal is present in large numbers on the outskirts of encampments and villages, disposing of the garbage and waste products thrown out without any regard for hygiene.

In ancient medicine, as practised by the Greeks and later by the Arabs, the hide of the hyena, in all its forms, offered a wide range of therapeutic properties, the most valued being the supposed aphrodisiac quality of its brains and genital organs when dried and made into powder; but this drug only had a generative effect on the man and induced frigidity in the woman. Bearing in mind the mutual hostility between the live hyena and the dog, it was quite logical to extend this hostility beyond death and to use the remains of the former to repel the latter; also, carrying in one's person a piece of hyena's skin or its dried tongue gave protection against dog-bites and, consequently, rabies. Similarly, anointing oneself with grease from a hyena would prevent dogs from barking at one's approach; this practice was well-known to burglars. Applying the same grease to a placid dog would immediately transform it into a ferocious animal. A hyena skin buried at the entrance to a house was a permanent means of denying access to all dogs and, hung up outside a village, it kept all pestilence at bay. Wrapped round the sieve or the measure used in the handling of grain, this skin preserved the seed against depredation by grass-hoppers and birds; with fruit trees, the same effect could be achieved by the use of the animal's claws. In addition, the head and the tongue of the hyena were lucky talismans; the former promoted fertility in a dovecote and the latter, hung in a room where a banquet or a wedding feast was to take place, guaranteed enjoyment and was a protection against unpleasantness. On the basis of the hyena's power of vision in the darkness, its gall, used as an eyewash, was believed to prevent cataract and make nyctalops. Finally, the dried heart of a hyena, hung as a talisman round at a child's neck, was a sure means of improving spirit and intelligence; and the right paw of the animal, attached to the arm or the leg of a woman in labour, assuaged the pains of childbirth and guaranteed a successful birth. To this list of major qualities a large number of secondary properties could be added, and one might conclude that the hyena, for which the Arabs had no sympathy in its lifetime, the outlaw al-S̲h̲anfarā excepted (see his *Lāmiyyat al-ʿArab*, vv. 5, 59), was reconsidered and enjoyed a measure of favour after its death, on account of its numerous beneficial contributions to medicine and magic, two areas which were then regarded as being one.

Bibliography: (in addition to references given in the article): A. Maʿlūf, *Muʿd̲j̲am al-ḥayawān*, Cairo 1932, 129 (Hyaena); E. Ghaleb, *al-Mawsūʿa fi ʿulūm al-ṭabīʿa*, Beirut 1965, ii, 83; P. Bourgouin, *Animaux de chasse d'Afrique*, Paris 1955, 170-3; J. Ellerman and T. C. S. Morrison, *Checkl… Palaearctic and Indian mammals*, London 195… Hyaenidae; Fīrūz Iskandar, *Rahnamā-yi pist… rān-i Īrān. Guide to mammals of Iran*, Tehran … L. Guyot and P. Gibassier, *Les noms des ani… terrestres*, Paris 1967, 19-20; L. Lavauden, … *vertébrés du Sahara*, Tunis 1926, 35-6; iden… *chasse et la faune cynégétique en Tunisie*, Tunis … 10; V. Monteil, *Faune du Sahara occidental*, … 1951; J. Renaud and G. S. Colin, *Tuḥfat al-a…* Paris 1934, 146, no. 332. See also DHIʾB, IBN … and IBN ʿIRS.

(F. Vi…

DABŪSIYYA, a town of mediaeval T… oxania, in the region of Soghdia, and lying … canal which led southwards from the Nahr Ṣ… and on the Samarḳand-Karmīniyya-Buk̲h̲ārā … The site is marked by the ruins of Ḳalʿa-yi D… near the modern village of Ziyaudin (= Ḍiyā… Dīn), according to Barthold, *Turkestan*[3], 97. I… in a prosperous and well-watered area, say… mediaeval geographers, and Muḳaddasī, 324… R. B. Serjeant, *Islamic textiles, material for a h… up to the Mongol conquest*, Beirut 101, mentio… particular the brocade cloth known as Wa… produced there.

Dabūsiyya's main significance in history w… the place of a victory in 394/1094 of the last Sām… Ismāʿīl al-Muntaṣir [see ISMĀʿĪL B. NŪḤ] ove… Ḳarak̲h̲ānids before his final defeat and death, … also the scene of a sharp but indecisive battl… tween the Ḳarak̲h̲ānid ʿAlītigin or ʿAlī b. Ḥ… Bug̲h̲ra K̲h̲ān [see ILEK-K̲H̲ĀNS] and his Sa… allies on one side and the G̲h̲aznawid govern… K̲h̲ʷārazm, Altuntas̲h̲ [*q.v.* and also K̲H̲ʷĀRAZM-S̲… on the other, in which the latter was mortally w… ed (see Barthold, *op. cit.*, 270, 295-6). Dabū… apparently flourished at this time and was a … town of the early Ḳarak̲h̲ānids (see Zambaur… *Münzprägungen des Islams zeitlich und örtlich geo…* i, Wiesbaden 1968, 110). During the Mongol p… Dabūsiyya and Sar-i Pul both opposed Čingiz K̲… hordes in early 617/1220 (D̲j̲uwaynī-Boyle, i, … 107, 117), and operations around it between wa… Ozbeg princes are recorded by Bābur in the op… years of the 10th/16th century (*Bābur-nāma…* Beveridge, 40, 124, 137).

Bibliography: (in addition to references … above): Le Strange, *The lands of the eastern … phate*, 468, 471; *Ḥudūd al-ʿālam*, tr. Minorsky, …

(C. E. Boswor…

DACTYLONOMY [see ḤISĀB AL-ʿAḲD].

DĀGH U TAṢḤĪḤA, "branding and ver… tion", a term used in Muslim India for the bran… of horses and compilation of muster … for soldiers. The system of *dāg̲h̲* (horse bran… was first introduced in India by ʿAlāʾ al-Dīn K̲… (695-715/1296-1316), and was revived by S̲h̲ēr … Sūrī (947-52/1540-5). The system of double … (*d̲h̲āt* and *suwār*) made its appearance durin… second half of Akbar's reign. The motive pro… was to compel every *manṣabdār* actually to mai… the number of horses and cavalry men expect… him for imperial service. But dishonesty amon… nobles was found to be so widespread that a … paper edict could not remove it. Therefore, to … all evasions of military obligations, Akbar intro… *dāg̲h̲* (branding) for the horses and the *čihra* … criptive rolls) for the men. Detailed rules … framed for *dāgh u taṣḥīḥa*. Each *manṣabdār* h… bring his horses and men every year for bra… and inspection; in case of delay, assignment of… tenth of his *d̲j̲āgīr* was withheld. Nobles …

irs were remote were not expected to bring their es to the muster before twelve years, but after years since the last muster, one-tenth of their me was withheld. If a *manṣabdār* was promoted higher *manṣab* and three years elapsed since he presented his horses at a muster, he received a onal increase of salary, but was allowed to draw allowances for the increased number of his men after the first muster. He then obtained assign-ts against his old and new men.

he entire machinery of branding and inspection controlled by the *Bakhshī-yi mamālik* (or *Mīr shī*) in the central administration. He had under *bakhshīs* posted at the capitals of *ṣūbas* or provin- The actual work of branding and inspection was by an officer known as the *Dārūgha-yi dāgh u īḥa*, who reported to the *bakhshīs*. This depart-t was very important for maintaining the Mughal y up to prescribed standards, and the decline he quality of Mughal troops in the 12th/18th ury was widely ascribed to the collapse of the *u taṣḥīḥa* system.

Bibliography: Abu 'l-Faḍl, *Āʾīn-i Akbarī*, i, ibl. Ind., Calcutta 1867-77; *Selected documents Shah Jahan's reign, Daftar-i Dewani*, Hyderabad 950; M. Athar Ali, *The Mughal nobility under urangzeb*, Bombay 1966; Ibn Hasan, *The central ructure of the Mughal empire and its practical orking up to the year 1657*, Oxford 1936; and see STIʿRĀḌ. (M. ATHAR ALI)

ĀḤIS, the name given to a pre-Islamic war ed during the latter half of the 6th century . between two closely related tribes of Ghaṭafān, Banū ʿAbs and the Banū Dhubyān, or more rately the Banū Fazāra, a sub-tribe of Dhubyān. war took its name from a stallion called Dāḥis, which the quarrel arose, and which became verbial for bad luck.

he real reasons for the war are probably to be ht in the enmity generated by the domination Abs of all Ghaṭafān, as well as Hawāzin, which reached its peak around the middle of the century had begun to decline with the death of Zuhayr b. dhīma, the chieftain of ʿAbs [see GHAṬAFĀN]. war, which is said to have lasted forty years, con-ed until some years after the Day of Shiʿb Djabala, which ʿAbs joined with ʿĀmir against Dhubyān Tamīm; this battle is traditionally dated in the of the Prophet Muḥammad's birth.

he major events of the war, as well as their proper ence, are clear from our sources, although many ils are uncertain, since the main primary source ws signs of a tendentious recasting to give added ninence to the two leaders, Ḳays b. Zuhayr b. dhīma al-ʿAbsī and Ḥudhayfa b. Badr al-Fazārī Dhubyān.

he most detailed study of the first part of the war n to the Day of al-Habāʾa is by E. Meyer, *Der orische Gehalt der Aiyām al-ʿArab*, Wiesbaden 1970, 5, who gives a full bibliography. The main prima-ource is the commentary on the *Naḳāʾiḍ*, i, 83-108, ch is a continuous narrative on the authority -Kalbī (probably the son Hishām, d. 206/821-2), *ānī*[1], xvi, 24-33; [3]xvii, 187-208, gives the same unt almost verbatim on the authority of Muḥam- b. Ḥabīb (d. 245/860), Abū ʿUbayda (d. 209/824- Muḥammad b. Saʿdān (*fl.* 3rd/9th century), but s with the death of Ḥudhayfa on the Day of the of al-Habāʾa, omitting the latter half of the and the final conclusion of peace. Other accounts those of al-Mufaḍḍal b. Salama, *al-Fākhir*, o 1380/1960, 219-35 (quoted verbatim by Maydānī, *Madjmaʿ al-amthāl*, Cairo 1959, ii, 110-21), and Ibn al-Athīr, Beirut 1965, i, 566-83, neither of whom cites his authorities. The latter version is considerably curtailed and at the same time is eked out by the addition of dialogue and transitional passages to make the story more interesting and to fill in gaps in the narrative. A much shorter account also from Abū ʿUbayda, in Ibn ʿAbd Rabbih, *al-ʿIḳd al-farīd*, v. Cairo 1946, 150-60, is divided into *ayyām*.

All the primary accounts differ considerably one from another. We shall first summarise the main events of the war as they are related in the *Naḳāʾiḍ* and then point out the more important differences in the other sources.

Dāḥis was ill-omened even before his birth, since the owner of his sire tried but failed to recover the seed deposited in the womb of the dam, because the pair had mated without his knowledge or consent. The stallion grew up to be a swift runner and eventually became the property of Ḳays b. Zuhayr of ʿAbs, who seized him in a raid (83-5).

Different reasons are given for the ill-will between Ḳays and Ḥudhayfa, but whatever the cause, it eventually culminated in a horse-race arranged between the two. Each agreed to run a stallion and a mare. Ḳays ran Dāḥis and al-Ghabrāʾ and the entries of Ḥudhayfa were al-Khaṭṭār (or Ḳurzul) and al-Ḥanfāʾ. To make sure of winning, Ḥudhayfa stationed men along the course who seized and held Dāḥis until the other horses passed. When released, Dāḥis overtook the two horses of Ḥudhayfa and would have come in second behind al-Ghabrāʾ, but again the Banū Fazāra intervened and beat off the leaders, preventing them from finishing first. Both sides claimed victory, and the wager was not paid (85-8).

First blood in the conflict was drawn by Ḳays, who while on a raid killed ʿAwf b. Badr, the brother of Ḥudhayfa. The bloodwit of 100 camels was paid by al-Rabīʿ b. Ziyād al-ʿAbsī. Despite this, Ḥudhayfa retaliated by sending a group of men, among whom was his brother, Ḥamal b. Badr, against Mālik b. Zuhayr, the brother of Ḳays, who was married to a woman of Fazāra and living in the vicinity. Ḥamal kills Mālik, and when al-Rabīʿ hears of this, he leaves the *djiwār* of Ḥudhayfa, which he had enjoyed up to this time, and joins Ḳays (88-92).

At this point there is a digression to explain an estrangement that had occurred between Ḳays and al-Rabīʿ, who had stolen a coat of mail belonging to Ḳays. The murder of Mālik, however, reconciles the two men, who combine their forces against Ḥudhayfa (90). They demand the return of the camels that had been paid as blood money for ʿAwf, but Ḥudhayfa refuses. Then another brother of Ḥudhayfa, Mālik b. Badr, is killed by a certain Djunaydib akhū Banī Rawāḥa, a distant relative of Ḳays (93-4).

Peace is then sought by al-Aslaʿ b. ʿAbd Allāh al-ʿAbsī, who gives several young boys to Fazāra as hostages. Ḥudhayfa, however, is implacable. He gets possession of the boys and kills them one by one, forcing them to call on their fathers for help as he shoots them to death with arrows. Among the boys were Wāḳid b. Djunaydib and ʿUtba, the son of Ḳays b. Zuhayr (93-4).

Next follows a series of battles in which ʿAbs are victorious. On the Day of Khāthira, at which Ḥudhayfa was not present, Fazāra lost several prominent men, among them al-Ḥārith, another brother of Ḥudhayfa (94). Ḥudhayfa mustered his forces and set out in pursuit of ʿAbs, but fell into a trap laid by Ḳays, who sent off the animals and non-combatants in one direction, and together with his warriors went in another. As he expected, Ḥudhayfa and Dhubyān followed the animals, and, as they scattered to gather in the plunder, ʿAbs fell on them unexpectedly and wreaked such slaughter that al-Rabīʿ b. Ziyād and his brothers begged him to desist. This battle was known as the Day of Dhū Ḥusā (94-5). Ḥudhayfa and his brother Ḥamal escaped the carnage, and with a few companions came to the Well of al-Habāʾa, where they were finally hunted down by a group of ʿAbs, among whom was Shaddād, the father of the poet ʿAntara. Both Ḥudhayfa and Ḥamal were killed. The *Naḳāʾiḍ* adds as an afterthought that it was said that Ḥudhayfa killed the mother of Ḳays, whom he found among the animals, on the Day of Dhū Ḥusā (95-6).

From this point, the fortunes of war change. The rest of the chronicle is given over to the wanderings of ʿAbs, who, hard-pressed by the combined forces of Dhubyān, leave their homeland in an attempt to find allies or *djiwār* among the Arabs who were not of Ghaṭafān. They first defeat the Banū Kalb on the Day of ʿUrāʿir; then they go to the Banū Saʿd b. Zayd Manāt, who give them a pledge of security for three days, but attack them later and are defeated on the Day of Farūḳ. Then ʿAbs go to the Banū Ḥanīfa in al-Yamāma, but find no support with them. They finally find *djiwār* with ʿĀmir b. Ṣaʿṣaʿa, but it is given grudgingly and ʿAbs are subjected to indignities. It is during this period that they participate in the Day of Shiʿb Djabala referred to above. Thereafter they leave ʿĀmir and go to the Banū Taghlib. Taghlib react favorably to their request and send a delegation to consult with ʿAbs, but among the delegates Ḳays recognises an old enemy, Ibn Khims al-Taghlibī, who had killed al-Ḥārith b. Ẓālim, the man who had avenged the murder of Ḳays's father. Ḳays slays Ibn Khims and the chances for *djiwār* with the Banū Taghlib are ruined (98-104).

Thereafter, weary of war, Ḳays sends his tribe home to try to make peace with Dhubyān. After some difficulties this is accomplished, but Ḳays himself refuses ever again to be a *mudjāwir* of any house of Ghaṭafān and departs for ʿUmān, where he later dies. Peace is concluded with Dhubyān by al-Rabīʿ b. Ziyād and the rest of the Banū ʿAbs (104-8).

It is clear that whoever put together this account of the war—al-Kalbī or his informants—was a partisan of ʿAbs. Ḳays is made to appear as a paragon of forbearance (*ḥilm*) and Ḥudhayfa an unmitigated villain. Ḳays in the beginning attempts to call off the wager, which was made without his consent, because he realises that it can only lead to trouble. Ḥudhayfa insists on running the race, and then wins it only by cheating. He later on sends Ḥamal to kill Mālik b. Zuhayr, although he had previously accepted the bloodwit for his brother ʿAwf, and now refuses to return the camels. Ḳays lets one of his sons go as a hostage in an effort to bring about peace, and Ḥudhayfa kills him with the other children in a barbarous manner. Later on he kills Ḳays's mother. Finally, at the end, at the Well of al-Habāʾa, Ḥudhayfa shows himself a coward and has to be pushed into the fray by his brother Ḥamal. Ḳays, who was not present, expresses in verses his regret at the incident and refers to Ḥamal as "the best of men", and says he would weep for him forever, were it not that he had behaved unjustly.

In the other sources, Ḳays does not appear in such a good light, nor is Ḥudhayfa so wicked. According to *ʿIḳd*, v, 151, Dāḥis and al-Ghabrāʾ raced against each other and not as a team. The wager was betv
Ḳays and Ḥamal b. Badr, the owner of al-Ghal
who arranged the deception, and thus appear
instigator of the war instead of his brother.

Ḳays is said to have killed not the brother,
Mālik (or Nadba), the son of Ḥudhayfa, whom
father had sent as a messenger to ask for payn
of the wager. As a messenger his person should l
been sacred, but Ḳays said grimly, "I'll pay
later", and then thrust his spear through his l
(*ʿIḳd*, v, 152; Ibn al-Athīr, i, 572).

The killing of the children is told in two sepa
episodes. Rayyān b. al-Aslaʿ is taken prisc
but is released by Ḥudhayfa and gives his two
and nephew as hostages. Ḳays kills Mālik b. Badr
only then does Ḥudhayfa in retaliation kill the
sons of Rayyān, who die calling for their father.
is prevented from killing the nephew by the b
maternal uncles, who were apparently of Fazāra
al-Athīr, i, 576). Later, ʿAbs agree to pay Ḥudh
ten bloodwits for his losses and give as hostag
son of Ḳays and a son of al-Rabīʿ b. Ziyād. Ḥudh
is only able to get his hands on the son of Ḳ
but captures two other ʿAbsīs and kills the t
of them together. It is not actually stated that
last group were children (*ibid.*, 577). In still ano
account of this incident, Ḳays is made to bear
blame for foolishly insisting on giving host
against the advice of al-Rabīʿ b. Ziyād, who wi
to stand and fight (Maydānī, ii, 114). In general,
other sources give much more importance to al-R
than does the narrator in the *Naḳāʾiḍ*.

According to the *Naḳāʾiḍ*, Ḳays was not preser
al-Habāʾa when Ḥudhayfa and Ḥamal were slain,
he is there in the other versions, egging his comr
on with the cry *labbaykum* in answer to the
of the children as they were murdered (*ʿIḳd*, vi,
Ibn al-Athīr, i, 579).

ʿAbs and Dhubyān were permanently reconc
and the war of Dāḥis had no political aftermath
affected the course of events after the adven
Islam. For later Muslims, the most important re
of the war were literary, since it is the best-d
mented of all the wars of the pagan Arab tr
Several famous poets participated in it or allud
it in their poetry. Among them are ʿAntar
Shaddād, Nābigha al-Dhubyānī, Labīd, w
mother was of ʿAbs, and the ʿAbsī leaders K
and al-Rabīʿ. The memory of the major events in
struggle was doubtless still fresh when scholars b
to collect the poetry and anecdotal material conne
with it, though it is likely that the minor incide
the personalities of the participants, and the
causes of the quarrel had already been invested
an aura of romanticism. Probably the very quan
of data facilitated this process which is appa
in the surviving accounts. Even as late as the Um
yad period, the war was exploited for *fakhr* and *h*
themes; several Arabic proverbs and prover
expressions are said to have originated in the dial
between Ḥudhayfa and Ḳays (Maydānī, nos.
613, 821, and 1530), and Dāḥis became a perma
part of Arabic folklore and literature as a symb
bad luck and enduring enmity, embodied in
proverbs *ashʾam min Dāḥis* and *ḳad waḳaʿa bayna*
ḥarb Dāḥis wa 'l-Ghabrāʾ (*ibid.*, nos. 2033, 2925).

Bibliography: in addition to the w
mentioned in the text, see al-Mufaḍḍal al-Ḍa
Amthāl al-ʿArab, Istanbul 1300, 26 ff. (not se
al-Nuwayrī, *Nihāyat al-arab*, xv, Cairo 1949,
63 (copies *ʿIḳd*); G. W. Freytag, *Arabum prover*
ii, 275-83 (= Maydānī); Abū Tammām, *Ham*

rmina, ed. Freytag, i, 222-3, 232, 449, 450-1 ll quite brief); Ibn al-Kalbī, Hishām b. Muḥam-ad, *Nasab al-khayl*, ed. G. Levi della Vida, ›iden 1928, index (genealogies of Dāḥis and the her horses); W. Caskel, *Ǧamharat an-nasab*, i, ıfeln 130, 132 (genealogies of Dhubyān-Fazāra ıd ʿAbs); idem, *Aijām al-ʿArab*, in *Islamica*, iii *upplement*, 1930) 1-99 (literary aspects of *ayyām*-erature). (J. A. Bellamy)

Ā'IRA SANIYYA, the term used for the ıinistration of crown lands in the Ottoman ›ire during the last quarter of the 19th century. *yya* lands were the *mulk* (private freehold) of Sultan. They were administered by a well-nised establishment, the *Dā'ira Saniyya*, h had branch offices in areas where these lands abundant. After the revolution of 1908, Sultan l al-Ḥamīd II ceded his private properties to the e. The lands continued to be called *saniyya*, but were transferred to the newly-formed depart-t of *al-Amlāk al-mudawwara*.

'ithin months of the accession to the throne of l al-Ḥamīd II, vast areas of the richest agricul-l lands in ʿIrāḳ had been registered as his pri-property. Most of these lands were in the Ḥilla-āniyya, ʿAmāra, and Baṣra districts. They were ıired by all possibles means, from expropriation mperial order to *bona fide* purchases with the ın's money. The *Saniyya* Land Department in ḳ had close ties with the army, the only source rained engineers and surveyors able to collect revenues. The lands continued to be farmed out *ltizām*; tribes occupying *saniyya* lands persisted onsidering them as their tribal *lazma*. The Sultan ived from *saniyya* lands both the *mallākiyya* ıer's share) and the tithes. Tenants were granted ain privileges in order to induce them to remain hese lands.

ı Egypt, the term was related to the Mu-mad ʿAlī dynasty. Land given by Muḥammad and his successors to themselves or to members their family originally was called *djiflik* (pl *ālik*), and Ismāʿīl adopted the term *djafālik yya* or *djafālik al-dā'ira al-saniyya*. By 1880 the *ra Ṣaniyya* lands amounted to 503,699 feddans, of them in Upper and Middle Egypt. This land pledged as security for two loans contracted by īʿīl in 1865 and 1870 and consolidated and ied in 1877 and 1880. After Ismāʿīl's deposition in the course of the liquidation of Egypt's debt, *Dā'ira* lands passed into the control of the state, only a small part was later restored to the princes final settlement in 1893 or repurchased by them. bulk was sold to land companies and private ons. In 1898 British capital formed the syndicate :h later became the Daira Sanieh Company and osed of all *Dā'ira* lands on behalf of Egypt's itors. The operation was completed by March , resulting *inter alia* in a considerable increase he area owned in large estates.

Bibliography: A. Jwaideh, *The Sanīya lands Sultan Abdul Hamid II in Iraq*, in G. Makdisi d.), *Arabic and Islamic studies in honor of Hamil-n A. R. Gibb*, Leiden 1965, 326-36; ʿAlī Pasha ubārak, *al-Khiṭaṭ al-tawfīḳiyya al-djadīda*, Būlāḳ 304-5/1887-8; *Rapport présenté par le Conseil de irection de la Daïra Sanieh à S. A. Le Khedive ır la situation de l'année 1880*, Cairo 1881; G. Baer, *history of landownership in modern Egypt 1809-)50*, London 1962. (G. Baer)

AKAR, the capital of Senegal, is situated he tip of the Cape Verde peninsula. Its position is the westernmost outpost of the ancient world (its longitude reaches 17° 16′ W. at the point of the Almadies). The region of Dakar, which covers almost the whole of the peninsula, is subdivided into three parts: (1) An eastern highland area (more than 100 m. in altitude); the N'Diass range rises some 70 m. above lake Tanma; to the east, the relief consists of hills or low plateaux with very gentle slopes not exceeding 40 to 50 m.; (2) the tip of the peninsula; from Fann Point to Bel-Air Point, the coastline is very jagged; numerous capes (Fann Point, Cape Manuel, Bel-Air Point) define the bays (Soumbedioune, the Madeleines, Bernard, Port of Dakar, etc.); the altitude is very modest, except at Cape Manuel (40 m.); (3) In the north-west of the region, the coast-line is more or less jagged, with a series of capes; the Cape of Yoff, Cape of the Almadies. Here, by contrast, the contours are higher, with the Mamelles (100 m.), and with plateaux at altitudes of between 30 and 50 m. A vast plain links the two mountainous regions of the Cape Verde peninsula. The centre of this plain is a marshy area with stable dunes. In the north, a strong cordon of dunes forms a distinct barrage for seafarers and isolates a whole series of lakes: lake Yovi, lake Tanma, lake Retba, lake Mbebeusse, etc. To the south there is a cordon of shifting dunes.

The peninsula of Cape Verde has a special climate totally different from that of the interior of the country. During the "bad season" or rainy season, which lasts from mid-June to October, temperatures reach 25° to 27° C., the air is humid, and there is an average of 600 to 650 mm. of rainfall, the maximum being in the month of August. The singular feature of the climate is the length of the "good season", or dry season, which lasts from November to mid-June. Temperatures are mild (19° to 23°), owing to the proximity of the sea, but especially to the cold current of the Canaries, which hugs the Senegal-Mauretanian coast, and to the *alizé*, the sea-wind of the Azores, which bars the way to the *harmattan* (a hot and dry wind).

Historically, the peninsula of Cape Verde was part of the kingdom of Kayor. It was visited in 1444 by the Portuguese Denis Diaz. While Gorée, an island lying 3 km. to the east provided a transit centre for European navigators and for the slave trade, and was the residence of governors controlling the whole of the coastline as far as Gabon, Dakar was nothing more than a tiny village occupied by fishermen of the Lebou tribe (a branch of the Wolof). It was on 25 May 1857 that the captain of the vessel *Protet*, in agreement with the leaders of the theocratic Republic of the Lebou, officially hoisted the French flag at Dakar, which henceforward became a port of call on imperial communications routes to south America. In 1895, a general government was formed charged with co-ordinating the policy of the governments of the different colonies constituting French West Africa (A.O.F., l'Afrique Occidentale Française). The governor of Senegal was, however, actually installed at Saint-Louis, capital of the A.O.F.

It became a naval base in 1898, the capital of the A.O.F. in 1902 with a governor-general, the focal point of the major axes of communication between the A.O.F. and metropolitan France, and the seat of the Grand Federal Council in 1957. Dakar also became the capital of the colony of Senegal from 1957 onwards, then that of the Federation of Mali (comprising Senegal and the former French territories of the Sudan), and finally that of Senegal after the accession of the country to international sovereignty in 1960.

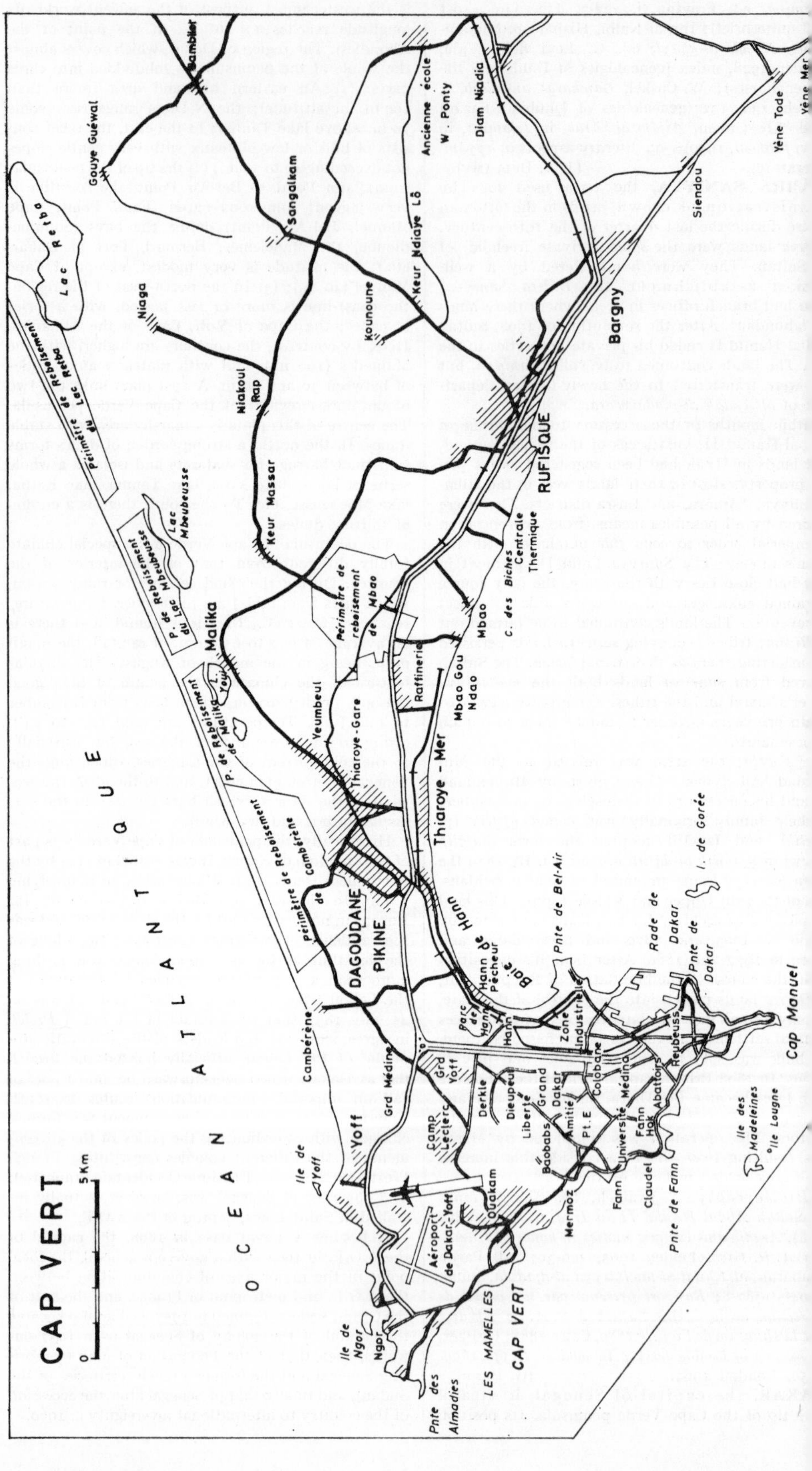
CAP VERT
0
5Km
OCEAN
ATLANTIQUE
Gouye Guéwal
Lac Retba
Périmètre de Reboisement du Lac Retba
Niaga
Bambilor
Sangalkam
Niakoul Rap
Kounoune
Keur Ndiaye Lô
Ancienne école W. Ponty
Diam Niadio
Siendou
Yène Todé
Yène Mer
Bargny
RUFISQUE
Lac Mbeubeusse
P. de Reboisement du Lac Mbeubeusse
Keur Massar
Malika
P. de Reboisement de Malika
Périmètre de rebolsement de Mbao
C. des Biches
Centrale Thermique
Mbao
Raffinerie
Mbao Gou Ndao
Yeumbeul
Thiaroye-Gare
Thiaroye-Mer
Périmètre de Reboisement de Cambérène
DAGOUDANE PIKINE
Baie de Hann
Pnte de Bel-Air
Hann Pêcheur
Parc de Hann
Hann
Zone Industrielle
Rade de Dakar
I. de Gorée
Pnte de Dakar
Cambérène
Grd Yoff
Grd Medina
Derkle
Dieupeul
Grand Dakar
Liberté
Amitié
Baobabs
Pt. E
Colobane
Université
Medina
Fann Hock
Abattoirs
Reubeuss
Cap Manuel
Ile de Yoff
Yoff
Camp Leclerc
Ouakam
Aéroport de Dakar-Yoff
Mermoz
Fann
Claudel
Pnte de Fann
Ile des Madeleines
Ile Lougne
Ile de Ngor
Ngor
Pnte des Almadies
LES MAMELLES
CAP VERT

:ficially the administrative, economic and reli-
; capital, Dakar comprises urban sectors with
arkably clear-cut divisions, regulated by the
s of 1946 and 1961. The former established four
s: (1) A mixed African and European residential
on the western sea-board as far as Yoff (the
ort); (2) A commercial and administrative zone
red on the southern region, bordering on the
mercial port; (3) An industrial zone, from the
jetty to Thiaroye; and (4) Finally, a group
served territories, *non aedificandi* sectors.
ie 1961 plan modified the earlier very little;
only changes were the specialisation of the in-
rial zone, the constitution of an important uni-
ity centre, and the designation of the new urban
re of Dagoudane-Pikine as the co-ordination
re for the direct plan.
ith reference to the urban structure, the town
akar occupies the south-eastern extremity of the
of the peninsula. It is the region which has
loped round the port, on the south-eastern pla-
x and on the southern part of the plain where is
ated the Medina. The essential characteristic of
urban zone is that it is almost the only area
ng buildings of solid construction. Grouped with-
: are the national organisations of a political
re, the administrative services, the entire
lesale trade, almost all the banks, insurance comes and real-estate organisations. The plan of
town is not a homogeneous unity; the port sector,
nost ancient, is in the form of rectangles, squares
iangles; the south-eastern sector is of the radio-
ric type with a series of roundabouts; the central
is of chequer-board form with narrow streets,
st in the south, urbanisation is least advanced.
ie town of Dakar comprises several quarters:
business quarter, an ancient nucleus, having
s centre the Kermel market, with several old
inistrative buildings, the main post- office, the
1-hall, an area which is very busy in the morning
deserted at night; the western quarter
red on the Place de l'Indépendance, very modern
full of activity (banks, estate agencies, travel
cies and insurance offices); the heterogeneous
tral quarter which consists rather of services
blishments and of wholesale houses, and is a
re of the textile trade and of traditional commer-
the human population is very mixed there, with
anese and Syrians, French, Portuguese Cape
leans, Moors, Toucouleurs, etc.; and the ad-
istrative quarter with high-rise public build-
: the National Assembly, the Presidency of the
ublic, the government ministries building, the
assies, hospitals, the Palais de Justice. It is
a residential quarter.
ie northern sector of the town of Dakar comprises
eastern section with some buildings of solid con-
ction in an area of insalubrious shanties (Re-
s) a central section, with waste-ground and some
e buildings (Colis Postaux, the École Malik Sy,
Great Mosque, the Institut Islamique, the Poly-
que) and some industrial establishments: Hui-
Petersen, Brosette, Air Liquide, etc.
he third industrial zone contains export and im-
industries (oil-works, large mills, maritime
stries and light industries). This zone is not
t up: it is mostly waste-ground with some market-
lens and shanty-towns (Darou Kip, Maka-
bane, etc.).
he *Grande-Médina* comprises several quarters: the
ule-Tapée, relatively urbanised with many solidly-
t houses, and some large modern establishments (the Mandel maternity hospital and dispensary, municipal nursery, etc.); *Fas*, barely urbanised, with very few asphalted roads, dotted with shanties giving place more and more to modern developments (the O. H. L. M. Centre). It is there that the Independence monument and the Kennedy girls' lycée are situated; *Colobane*, a quarter identical to Fas; *Gibraltar*, entirely residential, with some stylish villas constructed by the O. H. L. M.

Grand-Dakar constitutes the most recent, the most extensive and the most populous zone of urban development of Dakar. A very modern urbanisation exists alongside patches of shanty-town. It consists of the following quarters: Fann-Hock, Fann-Residence, Mermoz, Point E and Zone B, a superior residential zone (the University, the École normale supérieure, the École nationale d'économie appliquée, the Blaise Diagne and Delafosse Lycées, numerous embassies and luxury villas for governement ministers). In the centre of Grand-Dakar there are some small self-contained estates: Zone A, Cité du Port de Commerce et des Douanes, the estates of Bopp and of Wâgouniaye.

The allotments of the north encompass, between the Avenue Bouguiba and the Route du Front de Terre: the Cité de Police, the Karak, the simple or multistoreyed villas of the Sicap, the quarters of the Castors, of *Derkle* and of the *Cité des Eaux*, some villas of the O.H.L.M. I and II.

The *Grand-Dakar* with its shanty-towns is the quarter with the densest population (500 to the km²). The dominant characteristic is insalubrity. It lies between streets 10 and 13. SICAP and the O. H. L. M. are beginning to apply there a modern urbanisation policy.

Dakar and its suburbs. In the immediate hinterland of the town is a zone where the influence of Dakar is shown by certain characteristic features; installation of industrial establishments as far as MBao where there is a petrol refinery and where there begins the free industrial zone of Dakar-marine; the military camps of Quakam and of Camberene, the international airport of Yoff and its technical buildings; the major telecommunications establishments grouped at Yeumbel and to the north of Rufisque, a military conglomeration situated 30 km. from the capital; the presence of residential estates accommodating the workers of Dakar; the estates of the Almadies, of Ngor, of the airport, of Sabe, of Grand-Yoff, of the Patte d'Oie, the villas of the O.H. L.M., Guediawaye, Pikine, Thiaroye and Diaksaw.

Dakar also maintains reciprocal trading relations with certain villages in its close vicinity, providing the villages with fish and vegetables and furniture in exchange for various types of merchandise. These villages are Hann-Pêcheur, Oukam, Ngor and Yoff.

Demography. Dakar, which had only 20,000 inhabitants at the beginning of the century, today numbers more than 350,000. The census of 1961 gave a total population of 302,920 for the town of Dakar and 71,780 for the surrounding area. The same investigation listed 45,000 non-Africans, of whom 29,180 were French, 9,900 Lebano-Syrians, 5,800 Métis, 500 Antillese and about a hundred North Africans. With the exception of the Lebanese community, this non-African population has tended to diminish as a result of the Africanisation of cadres and the reduction of the French military presence.

The African population in 1961 numbered in total 398,060, or 9/10 of the population of Cape Verde (443,560). There are some thirty tribes represented, but five predominate: the Wolof (203,840 or 51.2%), the Toucouleurs (50,480 or 12.6%), the Lebou (36,860), the Sereres (25,980), and the Peul and Foula (23,900), a total of 341,060.

The Lebano-Syrians deal in commercial activities. The Africans practise fishing and agriculture (the Lebou), or are agents in public services (functionaries and members of the security forces), workers in personal services (the Toucouleur, Peul, young Sereres and Diola) or members of the liberal professions (lawyers, bailiffs, experts in various fields). Industries employ as many people as do the services. Commerce involve the employees of European commerce (clerks, bookkeepers, administrators), tradesmen based in the African quarters and vendors in the markets with a strong colony of Foula from Guinea (Konakry).

Religions. The two main religions practised in Senegal are Islam and Christianity (both Catholic and Protestant), and it is at Dakar that they are officially represented.

The primary religion of Senegal, after the virtual disappearance of animism, is Islam. In fact, 90 % of Senegalese are Muslims, as are 4/5 of the population of Dakar. Unlike Christianity, Islam in Senegal takes on a traditional, even local, character. The Muslims of Senegal, of the Mālikī rite, belong, in a general sense, to a religious fraternity (*ṭarīḳa*) led by a marabout, their spiritual chief. As a result of the rural exodus, Dakar is the meeting-point of all the fraternities existing in the country. From Dakar thousands and thousands of pilgrims travel once a year towards Touba, capital of Murīdism [*q.v.*], a fraternity founded by Shaykh Aḥmadu Bamba Mbacké in *ca.* 1895, or towards Tivaouane, capital of the Tīdjāniyya order. These two towns are certainly religious capitals, but it is at Dakar that contacts between the temporal (the secular state) and the spiritual take place. Periodically, the various religious leaders leave their respective capitals to meet the governmental authorities in Dakar.

The different fraternities represented in Dakar are: (a) The Tīdjāniyya [*q.v.*], of which the present spiritual chief is the "caliph" (*khalīfa*) El-Hadji Abdoul Aziz Sy, the third son of the late El-Hadji Malick Sy (1850-1922). The *khalīfa* has his official residence at Tivouane, a *zāwiya* founded by his father; however, he possesses houses in Dakar which provide him with a *pied à terre* and serve as accomodation for the *ṭālib*s, disciples who generally conduct Ḳurʾānic schools. These residences are constantly changing when the *khalīfa* is moving through the capital. A large number of the members of the Sy family reside in Dakar, and each one, in his home, has his following of *ṭālibs*.

While speaking of the Tīdjāni at Dakar, one cannot ignore El-Hadji Seydou Nourou Tall, grandson of El-Hadji Omar Tall (1796-1864), a man of the first importance both in the religious and the political sphere, whose residence is constantly full of Senegalese Toucouleur and Malian disciples.

(b) The Murīds. With the rural exodus of the peasants from the Baol, where are situated Touba and the *zāwiya* of *Shaykh* Aḥmadu Bamba, Dakar contains a significant number of Murīds, who every year make the Magal, or pilgrimage to Touba. Almost all the members of the MBacké family reside either at Touba, at MBacké, at Diourbel or in the neighbouring villages, and to our knowledge, only Serigne Shaykh MBacké, grandson of Shaykh Aḥmadu Bamba, representing the industrialist tendency of Murīdism, resides permanently in Dakar. He owns many houses there and a quarter bears his name (Sicap Serigne Cheikh); his residence is remarkable for the crowds of *ṭālibs* and of dependents. When the *kh* is on his way to Dakar, the crowds become numerous, each man pressing forward to ex his allegiance to his spiritual leader; the *ṭālibs* poems by the founder of Murīdism or recite Ḳurʾān for the whole length of the jou Dakar becomes a sort of Touba during entire visit of the *khalīfa*, the Shaykh Abdul A MBacké.

(c) The Ḳādiriyya, who have several impor centres in Senegal. Senegalese pilgrims often trav Baghdād, where there is the tomb of Shaykh ʿAb Ḳādir al-Djīlānī [*q.v.*], founder of the frater but every year thousands of Ḳādirī adherents their way to Nimzat, in Mauretania, where the o arose. NDiassâne in Senegal is the most impor centre of the Ḳādirī fraternity. As in the cas the others, many associations of Ḳādirī *ṭālibs* in Dakar. They are very active, especially du visits of their *khalīfa*, grandson of Shaykh Buh, one of the propagators of the sect in Sen In Dakar, the Ḳādiriyya has its own quarter in Gueule-Tapée on street 6.

(d) Of recent creation (1890), the fraternity the Lâye is less widespread than the previous t groups. The Lâyes take their name from Libas corruption of al-ʿAbbās), better known as Limâ Lâye (Imām Allāh) (1843-1909), marabout and fo er of the order whose influence remains limited to Cape Verde peninsula, more particularly among Lebou. It was from a base at Yoff that the fou preached his doctrine.

The present *khalīfa* is Shaykh Sidinā Mand Lâye; he lives in Camberence, a village not far f Dakar.

(e) The Tīdjānī sub-group of the Niassene based at Kaolack. In Dakar, Maryama Ni (daughter of the late El-Hadji Ibrahima Nia founder of the sub-sect) lives in Malik Sy Ave and receives visitors coming from all parts of Sene as well as from Nigeria, Egypt, Ghana, Dahon etc. Her brother, also in Dakar, supervises an portant Ḳurʾānic school whose renown stretc beyond the frontiers of the country.

In addition to its role as a capital, Dakar is meeting-point of all the fraternities existing Senegal, where the Muslim religion, because its importance, enjoys a number of official inst tional benefits conferred by the secular state.

At the University of Dakar, in the Faculty Literature, there is an Arabic section, and ther a department of Islamology at the I.F.A.N. (Inst Fondamental d'Afrique Noire).

The Great Mosque of Dakar is a religious inst tion of an official nature. Its construction 90 % financed by the state. The *Imām* is appoin by the Lebou community, but paid and housed by government. The Friday prayer in the Great Mos is transmitted only by the radio-masts of the O.R.T and on the occasion of major Muslim festivals, head of state is always officially represented the Prime Minister. In the precinct of the Great M que is the Islamic Institute of Dakar, which was augurated in 1974 by the President of the Repu and which has as its purpose basic research, edu tion and Islamic instruction.

Catholicism is under by a Senegalese archbis who has his seat in Dakar, the centre of the activi of the Catholic Church in Senegal. The Chu contributes very effectively to education; it admi ters infant, primary and secondary schools wh officially recognised by the Government and ive valuable subsidies from it.

rotestantism is poorly represented in Senegal; Protestants administer some infant schools which also recognised by the State.

ducational, sporting, cultural, artistic, manu- uring and touristic institutions are almost all ralised on Dakar. The only Senegalese University ith its Faculties and Institutes, the I.F.A.N. its major schools, of which the Ecole Normale érieure provides higher education, basic research the formation of higher cadres—is situated)akar. The Institutes of Applied Research (In- te of Nutritional Technology, the O.R.S.T.O.M., Institute of Development and of International anisations, the Institute of Oceanographic Studies 'hiaroye, the B.A.N.A.S., the Pasteur Institute, Institute of Psychiatric research, the Institute pplied Leprology and the National Institute of , are also based on the capital. There are in ar 12 centres of technical, professional, indus- and catering training, 112 primary and secondary ols and centres of General Education, without ting the Customs Service, Military Health, darmerie and Police training schools. All the eums are situated in Dakar or in Gorée.

n administrative, economic, human, cultural and ious focus, forced brutally into contact with radictory elements generating conflict between modern and the traditional, anxious to overcome e contradictions and reduce these tensions so as to ress towards an integral and harmonious develop- t, Dakar tends to be concerned not only with its destiny, but more realistically, with that of whole of Senegal.

Bibliography: A. P. Angrand, *Les lébou de Presqu'île du Cap-Vert*, Dakar 1946; A. Hauser, *es industries de transformation de Dakar*, IFAN tudes sénégalaises No. 5, Dakar 1954; J. Richard olard, *Villes d'Afrique Noire*, France Outre-mer o. 255, Présence Africaine, Paris 1958; R. Pas- uier, *Les villes du Sénégal au 19e siècle*, in *Revue histoire des colonies* (1960); M. Jodoin, *Les dustries manufacturières de la region dakaroise*, .E.S. University of Montreal 1963; Assane Seck, *akar, mètropole ouest-afraicaine*, IFAN Mémoire . 85, Dakar 1970; A. Samb, *Essai sur la contribu- on du Sénégal à la littérature d'expression arabe*, FAN Mémoire No. 87, Dakar 1972; *Annuaire ficiel de la République du Sénégal*, ed. La Société frica, Dakar 1976; J. Charfy, *La fondation de akar (1845-1857-1889)*, Paris N.D.

(Amar Samb)

AKHALIEH [see dakahliyya].

-DALĀL, Abū Zayd Nāḳid, *mawlā* of the Fahm e, musician and *ẓarīf* in Medina, born about 90, died about 145/762. Like his teacher Ṭuways 92/710) he was a *mukhannath*—hence the proverb re effeminate than al-Dalāl" — and is said to e been castrated by order of one of the caliphs, er Sulaymān or Hishām [but see Khaṣī]. His ical gifts and ready wits he used as an entertainer)uraysh women and a singer at weddings, accom- ying himself on a tambourine (*duff*). He composed ly artistic (*kathīr al-ʿamal*) melodies in a style ed *ghināʾ mudʿaf*, most of them on verses by temporary poets. Yūnus al-Kātib recorded one, hīm al-Mawṣilī 19, and Abu 'l-Faradj al-Iṣbahānī of his song texts in their *kutub al-aghānī*, the er using sources like the songbooks of al-Hishāmī Ḥabash and the *Akhbār al-Dalāl* by Isḥāḳ al- wṣilī.

Bibliography: *Aghānī*³, iv, 269-99 (main source, see indices); Ibn Khurradādhbih, *Mukhtār min Kitāb al-lahw wa'l-malāhī*, ed. I. ʿA. Khalīfa, Beirut 1961, 30-1; Djāḥiẓ, *Ḥayawān*, i, 121; Ibn ʿAbd Rabbih, *ʿIḳd*, vi, Cairo 1949, 27, 29; *Fihrist*, 141; *Tādj al-ʿarūs*, vii, 324-5; H. G. Farmer, *History of Arabian music*, 57-8.

(E. Neubauer)

DALMATIA (Dalmacija in Serbocroat), a historic province of Yugoslavia, formerly covering parts of the Federal Republics of Croatia (the territory of contemporary Dalmatia), of Montenegro and a very small section of Bosnia-Herzegovina.

I. Generalities

Skirted by the Adriatic Sea, Dalmatia stretches in a north-west-south-east direction at the foot of the Dinaric mountain ranges (Velebit, Svilaja, Bio- kovo) from the peninsula of Istria (according to some authors, only from the island of Pag) to the Albanian frontier, marked by the river Bojana.

But in fact, the territory designated by historians and geographers under the name Dalmatia is an area without strictly defined borders; these borders have indeed changed a number of times over the centuries. During the periods when the hinterland was controlled by powerful states (Croatia, Zeta, Bosnia, Hungary under the Angevins and the Otto- man Empire at its zenith), the territory of Dalmatia was limited to the Adriatic islands and to a few strongly fortified towns. In times of disintegration among the continental states, Dalmatia extended further into the interior of the Balkan Peninsula.

At the present day, the term broadly covers the central part of the Yugoslav Adriatic coast, that is, the coast-line from west of Velebit to the source of the river Zrmanja, and from there, in a south- easterly direction, to the frontier of Montenegro. The two other parts of the Yugoslav littoral are on one side *Severno Primorje* (the northern littoral): the peninsula of Istria, the gulf of Kvarner, as well as part of the coast in a south-easterly direction; and on the other side *Crnogorsko Primorje* (the Montene- grin littoral): the coast between Herceg Novi and the Albanian frontier.

Dalmatia comprises three geographical regions:

(a) the littoral, flat in places, steeply sloping in others, indented with deep gulfs and well sheltered anchorages;

(b) the interior of the country, with poorly defined limits; and

(c) the numerous islands which make up the Dal- matian archipelago.

The climate of Dalmatia is Mediterranean, al- though it is colder to the north of Split on account of the wind known as *bura* (called βορέας or βορρᾶς by the Greeks, *aquilo* by the Romans).

In the past, the economy depended most of all on fishing, on the rearing of sheep, the growing of cereals, olives, vines and fruit-trees; today, addi- tional sources of income are industry, shipbuilding and tourism. Ports worthy of mention include Split, Šibenik, Zadar, Ploče, Gruž (the port of Dubrovnik, formerly Ragusa) and with regard to the Montenegrin littoral, Bar (for the contemporary period), without forgetting the bay of Kotor, with Tivat, Kotor, Perast, Risan and Herceg Novi; whereas Rijeka (formerly Fiume), the principal port of Yugoslavia, situated at the end of the gulf of Kvarner, is not generally regarded as a city of Dalmatia (the territory of which, as stated above, is reckoned to lie further to the south) but as a city of "the Adriatic coast".

II. History

A. The pre-Ottoman period.

Inhabited since Neolithic times, Dalmatia was populated in the Bronze Age by Illyrian tribes, one of which would seem to have born the name Delmates/ Dalmates. (This was in any case the name given by the Romans, after the 1st century, to their province of Illyricum or Hilluricum.)

From the time of the 5th and 4th centuries B.C., the Greeks began establishing trading-posts (and later, colonies) on a number of islands (Vis, Hvar, Korčula, etc.) as well as in some of the coastal towns (Solin, Trogir, etc.). In the 3rd century B.C., there are records of raids by Celtic tribes.

The Illyrians of Dalmatia subsequently underwent conquest by the Romans, a conquest which was accomplished in stages, provoking wars of resistance and numerous revolts on the part of the indigenous population against the invader. Six centuries later, in 297 A.D., the enormous Roman province of Dalmatia (which stretched from Istria to Skadar, and from the Adriatic to Sava, Kolubara and Zaprada Morava) was divided by Diocletian into two regions: *Dalmatia* and *Praevalis* (*Provincia Praevalitana*), the latter approximately covering the territory of present-day Montenegro, with part of Albania, of Macedonia and of Serbia.

Under Byzantine rule from the 5th century onwards, Dalmatia also suffered invasion and temporary subjugation at the hands of various barbararian peoples, first the Ostrogoths, then the Avars; subsequently, it was swamped by the influx of Slavic tribes, who arrived in the Balkans in the 6th and 7th centuries.

During the following centuries, the various regions of Dalmatia passed successively (although belonging effectively, or nominally at least, to the Byzantine Empire) under the domination of the Franks, the different Croatian and Serbian states (Hrvatska, the Principality of Neretva, Zahumlje, Travunija, Duklja, etc.) and the Normans.

In the intervening period (in the 3rd/9th century), there are records of raids by the Arabs against the Dalmatian coast, in particular an unsuccessful siege of Ragusa (Dubrovnik), which seems to have lasted fifteen months, in 252/866-7 (cf. Theophanes Continuatus, *Historia de vita et rebus gestis Basilii . . .*, ed. I. Bekkeri, Bonnae 1838, 289-90; G. Musca, *L'emirato di Bari* (847-871)², Bari 1967; U. Rizzitano, art. ITALIYA, in *EI²*).

From the 11th century onwards, domination of the northern part of Dalmatia was contested by the Venetians, the Croats (*Regnum Croatiae et Dalmatiae*), and the Hungarians, and domination of the southern part by the various local Bosnian and Serbian principalities and kingdoms.

Between 1205 and 1358 a large portion of Dalmatian territory was held by Venice. During this period, there was a raid by the Mongols, who, while in hot pursuit of King Béla of Hungary, devastated the suburbs of Split and ransacked the town of Kotor in March 1242 (cf. R. Grousset, *L'Empire des steppes*, Paris 1948, 332-3).

Between 1358 and 1409 Dalmatia fell under the domination of Angevin Hungary (*regna Dalmatiae et Croatiae*), then under that of Venice (1409 and 1420-1797), although for a long time previously, many of the towns had often existed in a more or less (or totally) autonomous state, as was the case of Dubrovnik in particular (cf. M. Novak, *Autonomija dalmatinskih Komuna pod Venecijom*, Zadar 1965).

B. The Ottoman period.

(For the Republic of Dubrovnik, see RAGU for the history of the coastal region to the s of Dubrovnik, see KARA DAGH, i.e. Monten (Crnogorsko Primorje).

The conquest of the Balkan Peninsula by Ottomans, and their break-through in the directio Vienna, changed the map of Dalmatia yet again fact, throughout the period of the Ottoman Emp greatest power, Venice controlled only the Adri islands, the cities of the coast and a narrow coa strip stretching as far as Omiš, while the litt between the rivers of Cetina and Neretva (Maka Primorje), and the entire hinterland, were in hands of the Turks (*sandjak Lika, sandjak Klis, sandjak Hercegovina*). It was only after the begin of the decline of Ottoman power (end of the century), that Venetian Dalmatia began once n to extend into the interior of the peninsula.

Venetian rule in Dalmatia in the 15th and centuries operated on a feudal pattern. The land longed to the nobility, the majority of whom wer foreign stock. In the towns the artisans and trades were not permitted to take part in municipal coun There are records of numerous popular rebell against the feudal landlords. Maritime commerce reduced to the advantage of that of Venice. Agri ture, on the other hand, became rather more p perous (especially on the islands), mainly as a re of the influx of peoples fleeing from the Turks. In course of the next two centuries, there is evidenc a major transformation of Dalmatian society transformation which coincided with the declin Venice. Finally, we should take note of the emerge of a Dalmatian culture of a very high level.

(a) *From the arrival of the Turks to 1570.*

The first Ottoman raids against northern Cro began in 820/1417, those against Dalmatia a little la In 1432 the Turks invaded the region of Zadar, soon after 1463 that of Senj; subsequently, in S tember 1468, they mounted attacks against Za Sibenik and Split, then they once more devasta the region of Zadar in 1470, those of Split and Trogir in 1471, of Modruša (in the region of Lika far from Senj) in 1486, etc. But it was the regio Makarska (at the foot of the mountain of Biokc which was most exposed to the Ottoman atta From the years 1465-70 onwards, the Turks wer control of the entire hinterland, with the town Ljubuški, Vrgorac and Imotski. A little further the north, Omiš (which was to keep up a val resistance throughout the Ottoman period) repe the first attack, that of 1498. (On the frontier Venice in Dalmatia in the 15th century, see Šunjić, *Pomjeranje mletačkih granica u Dalmaci odnosi sa susjedima tokom XV stoljeća*, in *Godišn Društva Istoričara B.i.H.*, xv [1964], 47-62.)

The pressure on Dalmatia became still more inte after the decisive defeat inflicted on the Croats the Turks (*cladis croatica*) at Krbavsko Polje r Udbina (1493), and especially during the Veneti Turkish war of 1499-1503. Having once again dev tated the territories of Split, Trogir, Šibenik, Za and Nin, the Ottomans took control of the wh of Makarsko Primorje (from Cetina to Neret (on the conquest of Makarska, see V. Trpko *Vilajet Primorje*, in *Godišnjak Društva Istorič B. i. H.*, xiv [1963], 229-37), as well as the salien Bosiljina (Busoljina?) lying between Trogir Šibenik (1501).

The peace treaty signed at the beginning of 1

little effect on the situation on the ground, Turkish troops continuing to attack and devas- Dalmatian territories: an attack on Split in 1507, miš in 1509, on Skradin in 1512; the capture of ina (in Posušje) of Nutjak (on the river Cetina) of Vir (near Imotski) in 1513; in 1514 attacks kradin and Knin, and the capture of Karin; in an attack on the fortress of Klis; in 1520 the der of the region of Split; in 1522 a fresh siege is (by Khosrew Beg [*q.v.*], the illustrious *sandjak-* Bosnia), the capture of Knin (cf. V. Klaić, *Knin rskoga vladanja (1522-1688)* in *Serta Brunsmi-*, 1928, 257-62) and of Skradin; in 1523 the ire of Ostrovica (an important strong-point, rolling secondary strategic areas to the south elebit), the destruction of Nadin and of Vrana; 524 the capture of Sinj (according to some ors the town of Sinj was taken in May-June 1513. I. Šabanović, *Evlija Čelebi, Putopis*, Sarajevo, tlost 1967, 151 n. 14); in 1526 the capture of la, etc.

us, after the year 1524, the Turks held all he hinterland between the rivers Cetina and anja, with the exception of the fortresses of Klis eged again in 1531, finally taken in 1537) and brovac (taken in its turn in 1527), while Venetian natia was limited to the islands, a narrow coastal to the south of Velebit, and the territory lying een Omiš and Novigrad (minus the salient of jina).

so to be noted in this period are a number of lar revolts (revolts of the *pučani* against the al landlords), which we may add to the long list milar revolts of the preceeding centuries. Worth tioning are the revolt at Šibenik of 1510, and most rtant of all the great rebellion of the island of r (1510-14) which had repercussions not only in , Šibenik and Zadar, but also in many other ns of Dalmatia.

e Venetian-Turkish war of 1537-40, which fol- d the capture of the fortress of Klis (1537) and siege of Omiš by the Turks, brought ruin once n to the regions of Split (which was henceforth to the river Jadro as its frontier) Trogir, Šibenik Zadar, and led to the destruction of Vrana (on town of Vrana under the Ottoman domination, S. M. Traljić, *Vrana pod turskom upravom*, in *vi JAZU*, ix [Zadar 1962], 337-58; idem, *Vrana i gospodari u doba turske vladavine*, in *Radovi . . .*, [Zadar 1971], 343-77) and of Nadin (1537-8), e the Venetians briefly regained control of din and ransacked the town. Shortly after, in , the territory (*župa*) of Poljica passed into man hands, and was granted special status (cf. ućeska, *O položaju Poljica u Osmanskoj državi, rilozi za orijentalnu filologiju*, xvi-xvii [Sarajevo -7 (1970)], 77-91; idem, *O državno-pravnom polo- Poljica pod turskom vlašču*, in *Zbornik Pravnog teta u Zagrebu*, xvii/3-4 [1967], 386-94; idem, *oložaju Poljica u osmanskoj državi*, in *Poljički nik*, ii [Zagreb 1971], 61-72; idem, *O posjedovnim sima u Poljicama u svjetlu poljičkih turskih va*, in *Godišnjak Pravnog Fakulteta*, xxii [Sarajevo], 411-22). It was probably in the same period, inly during the first half of the 16th century, the little town of Jablanac (to the south of Senj, site the island of Rab) was razed to the ground. as not until the following century that the ed town began to recover (on the general situa- , see G. Stanojevic, *Dalmacija i crnogorsko pri- e u vrijeme mletaćkoturskog rata 1537-39 godine, storijski Glasnik*, Belgrade 1960/3-4, 87-112).

The peace, signed in October 1540 (after a suspension of hostilities for three months in 1539), had the effect of ceding to the Ottomans all the territories which they had previously occupied. In addition, the Turks were given war reparations.

The truce lasted for thirty years. During this period efforts were made to heal the ravages caused by a near-century of devastation and misery. Agriculture and stock-rearing, which had been very severely affected, improved, mainly as a result of the influx of people fleeing the occupied regions. Fishing also prospered, but commerce and craftsmanship were not so fortunate.

But it was a fragile truce, broken daily by the raids of the famous *Uskoci* on Ottoman territory. These were commando bands of guerrillas, based in Dalmatia (principally in Senj) and conducting military operations within the conquered territories; at sea they committed acts of piracy which did not only affect the Turks. In addition, they did not hesitate to engage in conflict with the Venetians, who hunted them most energetically, but would appeal to them for help when the occasion arose (cf. V. Vinaver, *Senjski Uskoci i Venecija do Kiparskog rata*, in *Istorijski Glasnik*, 1954/3-4, 43-66; G. Stanojević, *Prilozi za istoriju Senjskih Uskoka*, in *Ist. Gl.*, 1960/1-2, 111-141; idem, *Jedan dokumenat o senjskim Uskocima*, in *Vesnik Vojnog Muzeja JNA*, vi-vii [Belgrade 1962], 97-108; and naturally the same author's major work *Senjski Uskoci*, Belgrade 1973, as well as the two volumes of archive material published by B. Desnica, *Istorija Kotarskih Uskoka*, Belgrade, SANU, 1950-1; and S. Pavičić, *Raseljavanje staroga stanovnistva Senja i okolice, nastanjivanje uskoka i njihovo djelovanje*, in *Senjski Zbornik*, iii [Senj 1967-8], 324-70).

In the towns there was a remarkable florescence of Dalmatian culture, of literature especially, written either in Latin or in the language of the country, the most significant writers being Marko Marulić (1450-1524), Hanibal Lucić (1485-1553), Petar Hektorović (1487-1572) and others. Three other authors, equally celebrated, deserve greater attention, because they devoted many of their works to study of the Turks, and may therefore be regarded as the ancestors of "Yugoslav orientalism". They are: Feliks Petančić (Felix Brutus Petancius, de Petanciis, Petancius, Ragusinus Dalmata) (*ca.* 1455 - *ca.* 1517) of Ragusa; Ludovik Crijević Tuberon (Ludovicus, Aloysius de Cerva, de Crieva, Cervarius, Tubero) (1459-1527) also of Ragusa; and Antun Vrančić (Verantius, Vrantius, Wrantius, Vrancich) (1504-73) of Šibenik,

The writings of the first of these include a *Historia imperatorum regni Turcici* (or *Historia Turcica*) the manuscript of which is in Nuremberg; *De itineribus in Turciam . . . . .* (or . . . *Quibus itineribus Turci sint aggrediendi . . .*), ed. Vienna 1522; *Genealogia turcorum imperatorum . . .* (or *Descriptio Turcicae*) the manuscript of which is in Budapest (see D. Kniewald, *Feliks Petančić i njegova djela*, Belgrade, SANU, 1961; M. Kurelac, *Enciklopedija Jugoslavije*, vi, 474).

The writings of the second include: *De Turcarum origine, moribus et rebus gestis commentarius*, ed. Florence 1590; *Commentariorum de rebus, quae temporibus eius in illa Europae parte, quam Pannonni et Turcae eorumque finitimi incolunt, gestae sunt, libri xi*, 1st ed. Frankfurt 1603, 2nd ed. (under the title *Syndromus rerum Turcico-Pannonicarum*) Frankfurt 1627, 3rd ed. in J. G. Schwandtner, *Scriptores rerum Hungaricum*, ii, 107-381, 4th ed. Dubrovnik 1784 (see K. Krstić, in *Enc. Jug.*, ii, 390-1).

The third (who personally visited Turkey on a number of occasions and lived there for four years) wrote: *Iter Buda Hadrianopolim anno MDLIII . . .* ed. Venice 1774; *Diarium legationis nomine Maximiliani II . . . ad portam ottomanicam suscepta a.C. 1567,* ed. in M. G. Kovacich, *Scriptores rerum Hungaricarum,* Budae 1798; *Ratio itineris in Turciam facti per Danubiam,* ed. in *ibid.*; *Expeditionis Solymani in Moldaviam et Transylvaniam . . .* ed. Budapest 1934 (see M. Kurelac, in *Enc. Jug.*, viii, 534-5).

(b) *From the Cyprus War (1570-3) to the Cretan War (1645-69)*

Having refused to cede the island of Cyprus to the Ottoman Empire in 1569, Venice found itself engaged in another war against the Turks, which lasted from 1570 to 1573. The effects of this war were to the detriment of Dalmatia, in spite of the crushing defeat inflicted on the Ottoman fleet at the battle of Lepanto (October 1571), a battle in which a number of Dalmatian ships, with local crews, also took part (see *Lepantska bitka. Udio hrvatskih pomoraca u Lepantskoj bitki 1571 godine,* Zadar JAZU, 1974). In fact, Venetian successes in Dalmatia were ineffectual; Klis was besieged in 1571 and occupied briefly in 1572, as was Skradin, which the Venetians evacuated after demolishing part of its fortifications. Makarska was also besieged, but without success.

The Ottomans, on the other hand, ransacked the island of Mljet (1572), attacked the island of Korčula (cf. V. Foretić, *Turska opsada Korčule godine 1571,* in *Vesnik Vojnog Muzeja,* v/2 [Belgrade 1958], 61-91), burned the island of Hvar (1571) devastated the region of Split on a number of occasions (taking Solin and Kamen (according to H. Šabanović, *op. cit.*, 155, n. 37, the city of Kamen was taken as early as 1537), also the regions of Trogir, of Šibenik and of Zadar where they took Zemunik (which according to other sources had been captured in 1539, cf. H. Šabanović, *op. cit.*, 162, n. 92), besieged Novigrad, and occupied Nin for some time (for the town of Nin, see S. M. Traljić, *Nin pod udarom tursko-mlatčkih ratova,* in *Radovi . . .*, Zadar 1969, 529-48). The peace treaty of March 1573 restored the situation that had existed before the hostilities, but the Turks retained Zemunik and strategic positions around Solin. Mention should also be made of the unexpected capture of the fortress of Klis by a combined group of *Uskok*s and people of Split (7 April-31 May 1596), an exploit which had significant repercussions throughout Dalmatia.

After these distressing events, and in spite of continual border skirmishes, relations between the two Dalmatian territories (Turkish territory and Venetian territory), became gradually more correct and increasingly normalised. Trade with the Turkish-occupied hinterland developed, as did an important trans-Balkan commerce, in which, especially after 1592, the port of Split played a dominant role (see V. Morpurgo, *Daniel Rodriguez i osnivanje splitske skele u XVI stoljeću,* in *Starine JAZU,* liii [1966] 364-415)

But there were other towns, Trogir and Zadar for example, which established close commercial relations with the Ottomans, for the most part selling salt, and buying wheat, meat, cheese and wool (see S. Traljić, *Trgovina Bosne i Hercegovine s lukama Dalmacije i Dubrovnika u XVII i XVIII stoljeću,* in *Pomorski Zbornik,* i [Zadar 1962], 341-71). This normalisation of relations lasted more than seventy years, from 1573 to 1645, in other words, until the war of Crete.

(c) *From the War of Crete (1645-69) to 1683.*

This long period of peace was broken in the spring of 1645 by a new Venetian-Turkish war which l a quarter of a century. Many things had chang the meantime, both within the Ottoman Empire heyday of which was now long past), and in Eu But the outcome of the war was once again favou to the Ottomans, except however in Dalmatia.

On Dalmatian soil, the most significant mil actions took place between 1646 and 1649. In the Ottomans mounted a lightning raid into nort Dalmatia, in the regions of Šibenik and Zadar. town of Novigrad was taken (3 July 1646) as were grad and Nin, but an attack on Šibenik was rep (October 1646). In the course of their counter-at the Venetians and Dalmatians laid siege to Skr and recaptured it briefly in 1647. In 1646 the r of Poljica, and, in February 1647, that of Maka Primorje (the littoral between the rivers Cetina Neretva), severed their ties with the Ottoman En and allied themselves to Venice (Poljica neverth was compelled for some time to pay a *kharādj* t Ottomans). (On the position of Poljica in the century, see V. Mošin, *Poljičke konstitucije iz 1 1688,* in *Radovi Staroslovenskog Instituta JAZ* [Zagreb 1952], 175-206.)

In 1647 the Venetians (the bulk of whose a was made up of Dalmatians and of Slavs who fled from the regions under Ottoman rule) recapt the towns of Zemunik, of Novigrad, of Vrana an Nadin, before inflicting a further defeat on the T outside Šibenik (August 1647). Recovering Ostro Obrovac, and for a brief period Drniš (where al Turkish fortifications and monuments were dem ed), the Venetians attacked Knin and Vrlika, regained definitive control of Biograd (1648), most significant of all, of the famous strонghol Klis (30 March 1648). The Ottoman reaction was slow in coming; shortly afterwards, Turkish tr devastated the region of Poljica and that of R Kotari in the vicinity of Biograd.

Finally, in 1649, major military operations c to an end, when there was an outbreak of plagu Dalmatia, especially in Šibenik and in Zadar, fol ed by a period of widespread famine (see G. Sta vić, *Dalmacija u doba Kandijskog rata 1645-1* in *Vesnik Vojnog Muzeja JNA,* v [Belgrade 1 93-182; idem, *Trgovina robljem u doba Kandijshog 1645-1669,* in *Istorijski Glasnik,* 1958/3-4, 105- D. Kečkemet, *Dva odlomka iz "Povijesti Kandij rata u Dalmaciji" Šibenicanina Franje Divnića* (*nika*) in *Mogućnosti,* xx [Split 1973[, 876-88; S. Traljić, *Turskomletačke granice u Dalmaciji u X XVII stoljeću,* in *Radovi Inst. JAZU,* xx [Z 1973], 447-58).

For some time previous to this, there are rec of a large-scale migration of Slavic peoples kn as *Vlasi* (sing. *Vlah*) or *Morlaci* (sing. *Mor* —these are clearly to be understood as being ar men—towards Dalmatian territory, daily swelling ranks of the guerrilla commando bands (*hajduci,* s *hajduk,* and *uskoci,* sing. *uskok*). The latter m constant invasions of Ottoman territory (L Bosnia, Herzegovina), mounting attacks and bushes far into the interior, pillaging, killing, bur and kidnapping on their way. At the same ti Hadjuci and Uskoci conducted a policy someti favouring Venice, sometimes Austria, but m often the latter. A state of permanent minor war thus perpetuated on both sides of the fronti situation well described in Yugoslav popular poetry (from both the Christian and the Mu side), with a full gallery of heroes, all of whom well-known historical figures. (There are a g y publications dealing with the *hajduks*. Par-arly worth mentioning are the works of D. Popo-*O hajducima*, Belgrade 1930-1, 2 vols., and amardžić, *Hajdučke borbe protiv Turaka u XVI i I veku*, Belgrade 1952.)

the context of larger-scale battles, mention be made of the defeat of a Venetian-Dal-an force outside Knin (1654), and the ravages etrated by Ottoman troops in 1657-8 in the ns of Split, Šibenik and Zadar, with a raid on the d of Brač, following an attack on Split (1657). ie peace treaty was signed in 1671. In Dalmatia, position of the Venetians was then more favour-, since they retained Klis and its surrounding , the region of Poljica, and the littoral to the h of Omiš (Makarsko Primorje) (it may be noted *de jure*, this last territory should have remained r Ottoman control, but it belonged *de facto* to ce). The whole of Dalmatian territory under tian rule was henceforward known as *acquisto io*, and the frontier with Turkey became a forti-line called *linea Nani* (1671) (see I. Grčić, *a mletačka agrarna operacija u Dalmaciji*, in *rska Revija*, ii [Zadar 1953], 65-76; V. Omašić, *ačko-tursko razgraničenje na trogirskom području n Ciparskog i Kandijskog rata i njegove posledice*, ir 1971).

ie brief period of peace which followed lasted fifteen years. It was not long enough to allow iatia to recover from the ruin caused by long s of war, nor to revive its shattered agriculture commerce, not to mention the epidemics and nes which had weakened the country to a con-able extent. Split quickly regained its status as eading port for commerce between Italy and the ans. The port of Zadar was then of secondary rtance.

ie Ottoman military operations and the situa-in Dalmatia in this period are documented in ietimes whimsical but entirely first-hand account en by the famous Turkish traveller Ewliyā i, who visited these areas in about 1660; the *hat-nāme*, v, 458-72, 476-78, 480-91, 494-500 the excellent annotated translation by H. Šaba-ć, *E. Č., Putopis*, Sarajevo, Svjetlost 1967, 149-75-91, 195-204).

From 1683 to the Treaty of Sremski Karlovci anuary 1699)

ie decisive defeat of the Ottomans beneath the of Vienna (September 1683) signalled the end ieir presence in Dalmatia, where a large-scale ilar insurrection broke out. The Muslims of the panicked and fled towards the interior of the re. Within a short time the whole of northern iatia had been liberated; even before the end of year 1683, Skradin, Karin, Vrana, Benkovac, vac and Drnič were in the hands of the rebels, Turks retaining only the cities of Knin and Sinj. nice entered the war in the spring of the follow-year (1684), and Dalmatia was the scene of a number of military operations; Sinj was recap-l from the Ottomans in September 1686, Knin, a and Zvonigrad in 1688, Vrgorac between 1690 1694, Gabela in 1693, while the territories of ir, Šibenik and Zadar were finally liberated.

ie peace treaty was signed at Sremski Karlovci nuary 1699. Venice retained the areas she had uered, and her territory in Dalmatia (which the name *acquisto nuovo*) extended as far as the fortified frontier (*linea Grimani*), in other words, -Vrlika-Sinj-Zadvarje-Vrgorac-Gabela. In addi-each of these strategic points was surrounded by a neutral zone covering the range of a day's march. In return, Venice ceded to the Ottomans the territories conquered in Herzegovina. In turn, the Republic of Dubrovnik was enabled, with Austrian support, to free itself from Venetian influence; Turkey thus had access to the Adriatic Sea in the form of two narrow corridors, that of Sutorina (near Herceg Novi) in the south, and that of Neum-Klek in the north. The latter, nine kilometres long, is nothing more than a tiny gulf, situated to the south of the mouth of the river Neretva (on this period in general, see G. Stanojević, *Dalmacija u doba Morejskog rata 1684-1699*, Belgrade, Vojno Delo, 1962; on the new frontier between Dalmatia and the *pashalik* of Bosnia, see E. Kovačević, *Granice bosanskog pašaluka prema Austriji i Mletačkoj republici prema odredbama Karlovačkog mira*, Sarajevo 1973.)

(e) *From 1699 to the Peace of Požarevac* (*21 July 1718*).

At the end of the 17th century and the beginning of the 18th one, Venetian Dalmatia witnessed a spate of popular uprisings (such as, for example, that of the region of Vrana in 1692, and that of Bukovica and Ravni Kotari in 1704), caused in part by the penurious economic state of the peasantry, in part by the aggressive policy of the Roman Catholic church towards the Orthodox one.

On the military level, a new war against the Turks broke out in December 1714. Thanks largely to indirect aid from Austria, Venice scored a number of successes in Dalmatia; in 1715 Sinj repulsed the final siege by the Ottomans, and in 1717 Venetian-Dalmatian troops definitively recaptured the town of Imotski. These victories were augmented by successes achieved in Herzegovina, where the Venetians took the town of Mostar in 1717 (cf. G. Stanojević, *Dalmacija za vreme mletačko-turskog rata 1714-1718*, in *Istorijski Glasnik*, 1962/1-4, 11-49; S. M. Traljić, *Tursko-mletačko susjedstvo na Zadarskoj Krajini XVIII stoljeća*, in *Radovi JAZU*, iv-v [Zadar 1959], 409-24; M. Perojević—T. Macan, *Odjek Bečkog rata na Makarskom Primorju i u Hercegovini 1683-1723*, in *Historijski Zbornik*, xxiii-xxiv [Zagreb 1970-1], 179-214).

The peace treaty of Požarevac (July 1718) obliged Venice to give up all her conquests in Herzegovina, including the town of Gabela. In Dalmatia, however, her territory was enlarged through the addition of the region of Imotski, which led to some minor adjustments to the frontier of 1699. Thus the whole of Dalmatia was liberated from the Ottomans and came under Venetian control, with the exception of the two corridors of Neum-Klek and Sutorina (see the monograph by G. Škrivanić, *Dnevnik Dubrovčanina Mihajla Pešića o Požarevačkom mirovnom kongresu 1718 godine*, Belgrade 1952; L. Katić, *Prilike u splitskoj okolici poslije odlaska Turaka*, in *Starine JAZU*, xlvii [1957], 237-77).

The new frontier, *linea Mocenigo* (1721-3), passed to the east of the cities of Metković, Imotski, Sinj, Vrlika and Knin and extended as far as Klek and Žabska Gora, and all Dalmatian territory belonging to Venice was henceforward knowns as *acquisto nuovissimo*.

The Muslim inhabitants who had not succeeded in leaving Dalmatian territory in time were very soon forcibly converted, mostly by the Franciscans (cf. J. Cvijić, *Balkansko Poluostrvo*², Belgrade 1966, 337 which gives details borrowed from S. Zlatović, *Franovci države presvetog otkupitelja i Hrvatski puk u Dalmaciji*, Zagreb 1888, 233-4, 236-7, and from M. V. Batinić, *Djelovanje franjevaca u Bosni i Hercegovini za prvih šest viekova njihova boravka*, Zagreb 1881-7, ii, 147). On the Muslim inhabitants of Dalmatia who emigrated to Bosnia-Herzegovina, see M. Petrić, *O migracijama stanovništva u Bosni i Hercegovini Doseljavanja i unutrašnja kretanja*, in *Glasnik Zemaljskog Muzeja*, xviii (Etnog.) [Sarajevo 1963], 10-11.

C. After the Ottomans

Dalmatia remained under Venetian rule until the dissolution of the Republic in 1797. It was subsequently part of the Austrian Empire (1797-1805), the French Empire (1805-9), then one of the Illyrian Provinces (1809-13), before returning to the Austrian Empire (1815-1918).

After 1878 a number of Muslims from Herzegovina (which in that year became part of the Austro-Hungarian Empire) came and settled in Dalmatia. After a certain period of time they had grown considerably in number, and as a result the Muslim religious community (Ḥanafī rite) of Dalmatia was officially recognised by the Austro-Hungarian government, on 15 July 1912 (see *Reichgesetzblatt für Oesterreich 1912*, 875, paras. 1-7; M. Begović, *Organizacija Islamske verske zajednice u Kraljevini Jugoslaviji*, in *Arhiv za pravne i društvene nauke*, god. xxiii, drugo kolo, knjiga xxvii (xliv) br. 5, 25 November 1933, p. 379; the same, *Islamka verska zajednica*, in *Enciklopedija Jugoslavije*, iv, 372).

From 1920 to 1941 Dalmatia was part of the Kingdom of Yugoslavia, then from 1941 to 1945 it was divided between fascist Italy and the Ustachi Croatian State (*Nezavisna Država Hrvatska*), finally, since 1945, it has belonged to the People's Federal Republic of Yugoslavia (as part of the People's Republic of Croatia).

In 1971, there were roughly 4,000 Muslims in Dalmatia (the total number of Yugoslav Muslims at the time was a little over three million, of whom 18,457 lived in Croatia; see K. Hadžić, *Brojnost i rasprostranjenost muslimana u Jugoslaviji*, in *Takvim* [Sarajevo 1975], 119-34).

Bibliography: There has as yet been no study of Dalmatia in the Ottoman period (15th to 18th century) which takes into account simultaneously local, Turkish and Venetian sources. It is true that the existing documentation is indeed enormous, and that a large portion of this (archive documents in particular) is accessible only to a very small number of specialised researchers. Naturally, emphasis should be laid on the writings of Yugoslav historians and Turcologists who have in the past produced an impressive number of studies, monographs and articles on this subject. It should be noted however that the bulk of these publications have been primarily concerned with the Republic of Dubrovnik, and that consequently it is most difficult to present a bibliography concentrating exclusively on the history of the territory of Dalmatia as strictly defined.

An excellent general survey by J. Tadić is to be found in *Istorija naroda Jugoslavije*, ii, Belgrade 1960, 247-74, 519-30, 595-601, 1145-60. This work also contains a wise and intelligent analysis of the sources (the Ottoman sources are simply mentioned) and the entire bibliography available at that date (cf. 266 ff., 528 ff., 1159 ff.).

For a convenient list of Yugoslav publications on Dalmatia since 1945, see J. Tadić (ed.), *Dix années d'historiographie yougoslave 1945-1955*, Belgrade 1955 (see especially 217-55. 268-71, 374-84, 410-15, 540-54, 566); J. Tadić (ed.), *Historiographie yougoslave 1955-1965*, Belgrade 1965 (especially 113-42, 201-20 and *passim*); D. Janković (ed.), *The historiography of Yugoslavia 1965-1*
Belgrade 1975, (esp. 136-59, 185-96 and *pas*

In addition to the Ottoman historians (Nā
Reshīd, Pečewī, etc.) and the major histori
the Ottoman Empire (those of von Hammer, Z
eisen, Iorga, etc.), special attention shoul
drawn to the following works: G. Cattali
Storia della Dalmazia, 3 vols., Zadar 18
Š. Ljubić, *Pregled hrvatske povijesti*, Rijeka 1
V. Lago, *Memorie sulla Dalmazia*, Venice 1
V. Lamansky, *Secrets d'État de Venise*, St. Pe
burg 1884; J. N. Tomić, *Grad Klis u 1596 go*
Belgrade 1908; J. Tadić, *Španija i Dubrovn*
XVI veku, Belgrade 1932; L. Voinovitch, *His*
de Dalmatie, 2 vols., Paris 1934; J. Ravlić, *Ma*
ska i njeno Primorje, Split 1934; B. Pop
Povijest senjskih uskoka, Zagreb 1936; G. No
Prošlost Dalmacije, 2 vols., Zagreb 1944; A
Benvenuti, *Storia di Zara*, 2 vols., Milan 1
53; J. Radonić, *Rimska Kurija i južnoslove*
zemlje od XVI do XIX veka, Belgrade 195
Božić, *Dubrovnik i Turska u XIV i XV veku*,
grade 1952; A. Ujević, *Imotska Krajina*, Split 1
G. Praga, *Storia di Dalmazia*[3], Padua 1
L. Katić, *Solin od VII do XX stoljeća*, Split 1
G. Novak, *Povijest Splita*, 2 vols., Split 1957
V. Vinaver, *Dubrovnik i Turska u XVIII*
Belgrade 1960; R. Samardžić, *Veliki vek Dubro*
ka, Belgrade 1962; B. Djurdjev and M. V
Jugoslovenske zemlje pod turskom vlašću do k
XVIII stoljeća, Zagreb 1962; G. Novak, *Jadra*
more u sukobima i borbama kroz stoljeća, Belg
1962; E. Albrecht, *Das Türkenbild in der rag*
nisch-dalmatinischen Literatur des XVI. J
hunderts, Munich 1965; *Grad Zadar, presjek*
povijest, Zadar 1966; M. Šunjić, *Dalmacija u*
stoljeću, Sarajevo 1967; G. Stanojević, *Jug*
venske zemlje u mletačko-turskim ratovima X
XVIII veka, Belgrade 1970; T. Popović, *Turs*
Dubrovnik u XVI veku, Belgrade 1973.

Finally, one should add those articles alre
cited in the present article: A. Strgačić, *U*
osmanskih gusara u predjele Zadarskih otoka
Zadarska Revija, ii/4 (1953), 195-204, iii/1 (19
44-53; S. M. Traljić, *Zadar i turska pozadina od*
do potkraj XIX stoljeća, in *Grad Zadar* (Zadar 19
206-28; A. J. Soldo, *Prilozi proučavanju agra*
društvenih odnosa u Gornjem primorju od XV
polovine XIX stoljeća, in *Makarski Zbornik* (19
337-80; A. Rube-Filipi, *Biogradsko-vransko*
morje u doba mletačko-turskih ratova s osvrtom
povijest naselenja, in *Radovi Inst. JAZU*
(Zadar 1972), 405-98. (A. Popovi

DAM (A.), pl. *dimā*ʾ "blood", also "bl
guilt" [see diya, ḳatl]. In the present artic
will be appropriate to mention the numerous b
sacrifices offered by the Muslims, but we will
concern ourselves with the theory, nor is it
intention to list them [see dhabīḥa, ḥadjdj,
al-aḍḥā]. We will confine ourselves to a brief
vey of the beliefs relative to blood and the
to which it is put or to which it may be put
Muslims in the various circumstances where the
crifice of an animal is required, and the role
tributed to it in magic and therapy.

Arabic texts of the Middle Ages speak of
cardinal humours: black bile (*sawdāʾ*), phlegm (*ba*
am), yellow bile (*ṣafrāʾ*) and blood, associa
this last with joy and with the second string (*mat*
of the lute (see al-Djāḥiẓ, *Tarbīʿ*, § 152), and asser
that it is dominant in March, April and May
Masʿūdī, *Murūdj*, iii, 425 = § 1313). But these i

ate and unknown to the Ḳur'ān, which, setting the story of the creation of man represented by ›t of blood (*ʿalaḳa*, XXII, 5, XXIII, 14, XL, ', LXXV, 38) and the dietary prohibition (see v), makes only one brief reference (VII, 130/133) e miracle of the river turned into blood (Exodus, 17-21) and does not even mention the bleeding e nose (*ruʿāf*) among the sufferings inflicted by upon the ancient peoples of Arabia as punish- for their impiety (see al-Djāḥiẓ, *Tarbīʿ*, § 47 index). The Ḳur'ān gives no information as to place occupied by blood during the Djāhiliyya e, however, gory sacrifices were not lacking J. Chelhod, *Sacrifice, passim*), nor as to the eption that the Arabs had of it. However, for , as for the Hebrews (Genesis, ix, 4; Leviticus, 11, 14), the soul of all flesh was in the blood, oaths were sworn on the *dam* or the *dimā'*, as as on the pagan deities (see *LA*, s.v. *d. m. y.*). stinction was drawn between *rūḥ*, air circulating n the body, and *nafs*, the soul for which blood, sometimes designated by the same word (cf. asʿūdī, *Murūdj*, iii, 309-10 = §§ 1190-1; *LA*, *n. f. s.*), is the vehicle: only animals possessing a *sā'ila*, that is to say blood, render impure the r in which they die. The soul of a murdered man, ng the body with the spilt blood (see Chelhod, *ud.*, 102-3), then took the form of a bird (*hāma*, which did not cease to haunt the tomb of the n and could not be set at rest until the blood enemy had been shed there; thus J. Chelhod also in blood-vengeance a human sacrifice owed to pirit of the deceased. An analogous belief per- sts in various parts of the Mediterranean area: ving stones upon the scene of the crime has the t of covering the voice of the blood appealing vengeance and contributes to the immobilising e soul of the deceased (cf. Westermarck, *Ritual*, 19; Jaussen, *Moab*, 335-6; Servier, *Portes de ée*, 33-4 [see also KARKŪR, RADJM]. If blood has been spilt thus appeals for vengeance, it cause the earth has no longer absorbed it since murder of Abel (Ḳur'ān, V, 30-5/27-32) and the punishments that it incurred for hiding him from (cf. al-Djāḥiẓ, *Ḥayawān*, iv, 201); the earth efore feels the utmost aversion for blood, except aps for that of the camel, (*ibid.* iii, 136, iv, 201), this last idea is borrowed from Aristotle. And if, some sacrifices, the blood that has been shed ppears the next day, it is because it has been k by errant souls (Servier, *op. laud.*, 325). Even e view of Muslims who do not believe in the , the blood of the victims of an unjustified ler does not cease to stop seething until proper eance has been taken; that of John the Baptist become proverbial in this respect (al-Djaḥiẓ, *ta*, in *AIEO* Alger, x (1952), 312; Balʿamī- nberg, i, 569).

nce the blood is the vehicle for the soul, it is rstandable that among the Hebrews, its con- ption was forbidden (Genesis, ix, 4; Leviticus, 7, vii, 26, xvii, 10, 12, xix, 26; Deuteronomy, 6, xv, 23; I Samuel, xvi, 33), and it is probable even before the prohibition enunciated by the 'ān (II, 168/173, V, 4/3, VI, 146/145, XVI, 15), the pagan Arabs —but not the Christians— rally abstained from it. Nevertheless, if we ve the commentators, they used to eat a sort lack pudding made from camels' blood (al- lawī, on Ḳur'ān, II, 173; Chelhod, *op. laud.*, 175) according to al-Djāḥiẓ (*Hayawān*, iv, 96), they to drink as a tonic the blood extracted by the phlebotomist, the free-thinkers asserting that meat is only blood transformed. In this regard, it will be recalled that one of the reason invoked as a justification for the refusal to pay a salary to the blood-letter is that before Islam he used to sell the blood to third parties and that this type of sale was forbidden by a *ḥadīth* (cf. R. Brunschvig, *Métiers vils en Islam*, in *St. Isl.*, xvi (1962), 47). In another connection, a group of Ḳuraysh was given the name *Laʿaḳat al-dam* [*q.v.*] "lickers of blood" because of their practice of licking their fingers after dipping their hands into a receptacle containing the blood of a camel, as a means of sealing an alliance. There are scarcely any attestations of the practice consisting, in cases of the adoption by the tribe of a foreign element, of mixing the blood of the adopted man with that of a representative of the group, but in southern Turkey there still exists the "fraternity of blood", effected by the making on the wrist a gash which is sucked by the contractants (J.-P. Roux, *Traditions*, 324).

The ancient Arabs considered the blood of kings to be a specific remedy for rabies (*kalab*) and possession (*khabal*), and it may have happened that it was preserved for this purpose (cf. al-Djāḥiẓ, *Ḥayawān*, i, 5, 310; idem, *Tarbīʿ*, § 69; al-Masʿūdī, *Murūdj*, iii, 192-3 = § 1049; see also the legend of Djadhīma [*q.v.*] in which blood plays a certain role); this belief is still alive (cf. Wellhausen, *Reste*², 139-40; Doutté, *Magie et religion* 85).

Al-Djāḥiẓ mentions (*Bukhalā'*, ed. Ḥādjirī, 198, 200), somewhat as an exception, the practice of Bedouins who, dying of thirst in the desert, were constrained, after exhausting the contents of the first stomach of a camel, whose purpose was ultimately to provide them with water, to slaughter another; they collected its blood, which they beat carefully so as to separate the sediment (*thufl*) from the serum (called *mā'* = water); this alone they drank; this drink was called *maddūḥ* (cf. *LA*, s.v. *dj. d. ḥ.*; Chelhod, *Sacrifice*, 175).

Drinking the blood of an enemy does not seem to have been a current practice, in spite of the hatred which tribes sometimes held for one another; there is indeed a recent attestation of it (Jaussen, *Moab*, 177, n. 1), but it is exceptional. On the other hand, an arrow stained with the blood of an enemy (*sahm mudamm^an^*) and returned to the archer who had dispatched it was retained as a lucky talisman (*tabarruk^an^*) by the latter (*LA*, s.v. *d. m. y*).

Without being obsessed by blood, the ancient Arabs were especially superstitious about menstruation [see ḤAYḌ] and considered the woman thus indisposed (*ḥā'iḍ*) as impure and disqualified from performing certain acts. After Islam, the notion of impurity remained, but the Ḳur'ān (II, 222) confined to sexual relations the prohibition affecting women during the period of menstruation: and it is said that if this prohibition is infringed, Satan interposes between the partners. From another point of view, it is not impossible that the prohibition regarding the consumption of the hare and the rabbit, differently justified by Deuteronomy, xiv, 7, derives, in certain sects [see ARNAB in Suppl.] in part at least from the fact that the doe, which is believed to menstruate, naturally does not purify itself; the hyena is a similar case, and as a result these two animals cannot serve as mounts for the djinn (al-Djāḥiẓ, *Ḥayawān*, iii, 529, vi, 46).

Once it has left the veins of a living being, blood is at the same time impure and taboo, for it is through blood that a link is established between man and God, where it is a case of canonical sacrifices, between men and the invisible powers in the case of immolations which, although permitted, have retained a pagan character. Once it begins to flow, it is the blood which "gives to the ceremony its true sense of expiation, of purification and of protection" (Servier, *op. laud.*, 83).

Although the Ḳurʾān (XXII, 38/7) states with regard to sacrifices, "neither their flesh nor their blood shall reach Allāh, but only the piety coming from you shall reach Him" (cf. Amos, v, 21-2), a *ḥadīth*, retained only by al-Tirmidhī and Ibn Mādja (no. 3126) but often quoted, proclaims: "the blood [of the victim sacrificed for the Great Feast] finds its place in the presence of Allāh even before it has touched the ground" (al-Ghazālī, *Iḥyāʾ*, ed. 1278, i, 252; Westermarck, *Survivances*, 199; Chelhod, *Sacrifice*, 59), and such is doubtless the belief of the Muslims. The more abundant it is, the greater its power, and it is essential that the victim has been completely emptied of blood before dying (besides, it is this total effusion which renders legitimate the consumption of the butcher's animals, and the list of dietary prohibitions which figures in the Ḳurʾān (II, 168/173 and especially V, 4/3) is instructive in this regard, since it declares illicit all animals killed accidentally and not ritually bled to death, except in cases of necessity).

Independently of the role played by the blood of the sacrifice of the Great Feast in actually conveying the sacred offering from the Believer to God, it possesses protective and curative properties sometimes put to profitable use. It is thus that in Iran a piece of cotton is dipped in the blood of a sheep that has been immolated and allowed to dry; if a child has pains in the throat, a morsel of this cotton is put into water which he is made to drink (H. Massé, *Croyances*, 142). In Kabylia, blood is mixed with cattle dung which is smeared on a sheltered wall and administered in fumigations (*Fichier de Documentation berbère*, 1964/4, 12); in the same region a woman takes a little blood to mark the forehead of a child less than one year old (*ibid.*). In certain tribes, the mistress of the house still smears the posts and the lintel of the door with it to protect her home (Servier, *op. laud.*, 346); it is also poured over a ploughshare to consecrate it (*ibid.*, III-2; among the Zaghāwa (M.-J. Tubiana, 149) it is the hoes that are sprinkled with the blood of a he-goat, but in different circumstances). On the occasion of the feast of ʿĀshūrāʾ [*q.v.*] it is the practice to dip in the blood of a sacrificed animal branches of rose-laurel which are hung between the stable and the living-quarters (Servier 370); elsewhere blood is sprinkled on the threshing floor (Koller, 325).

In the few examples mentioned above, magical practices have come to be grafted on to rites considered orthodox; more numerous and more obvious are the vestiges of paganism which appear in the multifarious sacrifices offered to the djinn [see DJINN], those invisible powers whose existence orthodoxy was obliged to admit. Just as during the Djāhiliyya one became united with the divinity by pouring blood over the rocks which were their home (cf. T. Fahd, *Le Panthéon de l'Arabie centrale*, Paris 1968, 103, on Isāf and Nāʾila [*q.v.*]), similarly, one enters into communication with the protective genies or wards off the maleficent spirits by means of blood poured on the altar of the home or on high places especially frequented by spirits. Although it is difficult to arm oneself against the hostile attentions of the djinn which haunt the places, very dangerous for men, where blood flows abundantly, espe[c] abattoirs (see Doutté, *op. laud.*, 86; Westerm[arck] *Survivances*, 14, 165; Servier *op. laud.*, 60-1), very easy to protect oneself against invisible s[p] by means of the blood of sacrifices which, [while] attracting them, also annuls their maleficent p[ower]. This is why the life of superficially Islamised p[opu]lations is marked by immolations, often mode[st in] scale, which are followed by anointings and sp[rink]lings with the purpose of gaining protection [from] enemy spirits of the nether world, and of obta[ining] in some measure the goodwill of the protective g[enies] of the house or of the tent or of those who can a[ssure] the prosperity of fields and herds.

The threshold or the door (cf. Jaussen, *M*[...] 343), the central pole of a tent, the mill or [the] hearth (cf. J.-P. Roux, *Traditions*, 255) are true domestic altars; but every new object is [like]wise consecrated by offering the blood of an an[imal] to the protective genies of the home. When a [tent] is constructed, or an old one enlarged or a [part] of it replaced, the central pole is smeared [with] blood (Jaussen, 399). In Morocco, a woman sm[ears] a pole of the tent with the blood of an animal [when] her first child is born (E. Laoust, *Transhum*[...] 58) to assure herself of numerous progeny. In [the] land of Moab, marriages are the occasion f[or a] number of successive immolations, and in the c[ase] of the last at any rate, the bride is sprinkled [with] the blood of the victim. In the present day, in [...] [see KHAYR], masons still sacrifice an animal b[efore] starting to build, so that its blood may protect [them] against any accident which might cause their [blood] to be shed. There seems little purpose in reco[rding] further examples of this type which the ethnolo[gists] have noted in the course of their inquiries.

A problem of a different order is posed by blood sacrifices which, in agricultural areas, [ac]company all work in the fields: ploughing, harves[ting,] threshing, etc. It seems that blood is not encoun[tered] in rites designed to bring rain [see ISTISḲĀʾ], [and] the Zaghāwa who sprinkle it in the fields an[d] river beds (M.-J. Tubiana, index) can hardly be [the] only ones who do so. E. Laoust (*Mots et choses berb*[...] 315) has noticed in one Moroccan tribe an intere[sting] annual custom which takes place on a Wednesda[y or] a Thursday before ploughing begins: in a hole [dug] in the first piece of land to be sown and then ploug[hed] the farmer slaughters a sheep and smears wit[h its] blood his own right foot, then the left foot o[f the] *khammās* responsible for the ploughing; on t[he] pool which forms at the base of the hole, a little e[...] is thrown and on this the farmer scatters g[rain] which he thrusts into the ground with his h[...]; this place is henceforward sacred. E. Laoust sug[gests] two interpretations of this rite: to ward off the [evil] influences of the djinn, or to restore to the soi[l the] vital forces of growth. The two explanations a[re, it] seems, both to be accepted, for they are confir[med,] on the one hand, by the practice which co[nsists] of fixing with blood, after the harvest, the [...] liberated by the work in the fields, on the [other] hand the practice of sprinkling the sheaves [with] it, of spreading it in various places and of sme[aring] it on the clogs of the beasts that tread the [grain] on the threshing-floor (*ibid.* 391). After the har[vest] the jars containing the grain are also smeared [with] blood (Servier, *op. laud.*, 254). As for livesto[ck, it] too is protected by anointings, as is done in the [land] of Moab, to a newly-bought mare or to a new[born] filly (Jaussen, 354).

In the times when it was still possible to

ame, in the Moroccan Rīf, some of the blood ch animal killed was set aside to be offered e spirits of the rocks with the object of lessening rocity of the lions (Koller, 331).

ings are also haunted by djinn. At Sefrou, cco, in the autumn, a black or seven-coloured or a white cockerel is slaughtered beside one em, and the blood of the animal is poured into vater (H. Basset, *Grottes*, 89). In the case of springs, the bathers arm themselves against spirits by sprinkling the basin with the blood victim (Jaussen, 359-360).

well as djinn, deceased saints must be appeased nmolations (See Servier, *op. laud.*, 179). In the of Moab, for example, blood is cast on to the of a sanctuary (Jaussen, 356). Blood still serves e vehicle for the conditional malediction im- l upon a saint or another man, or for the transfer sponsibility in the practice of *ʿār* [*q.v.* in Suppl.] on the contrary, for the honour done to the for whom an animal has been slaughtered hod, *Sacrifice*, 185).

another context, it plays a particular role e taking of virginity, and it is well known on the day after a wedding, a cloth stained the blood of the bride must be exhibited. In lia, the water used to wash it is poured out e foot of a pomegranate tree, the symbol of ity (Servier, *op. laud.*, 144).

e preceding topic brings us back to menstrual l, which possesses particular properties. In medicine, it is recommended as an antidote log-bites, scurvy and freckles and serves also reserve the firmness of the breasts, but it also sses a magical power since seafarers can protect selves against the dangers of tempests and st the threat of a sea monster called expres- y *ḥūt al-ḥayḍ* "fish of the menses", by fixing e stern of their ship a cloth stained with this l. Al-Damīrī, in his *Ḥayāt al-ḥayawān*, from n these details are borrowed (s.v. *insān*) pro- in every account, under the heading of *khawāṣṣ* perties" data concerning the use of the blood imals in magic and medicine. By its very nature, ses in the preparation of philtres are fairly ed in number. These are a few examples: the l of the parrot (*babbaghā*ʾ), dried, powdered and d between friends transforms their friendship hatred. Sprinkling a mixture of the blood of a el (*ibn ʿirs*) and of a rat or a mouse (*faʾr*) and r brings discord to families. The blood of a she- (*baghla*) buried under the threshold of a house ents rats and mice from entering. If a man can about his person a quantity of the blood of a (*thaʿlab*), he is safe from all forms of trickery. rility can be improved or restored thanks he blood of the *tinnīn* (*sic* [*q.v.*]), of the frog a*ʿ*) of the sparrow (*ʿuṣfūr*) or of the hedgehog *fudh*), while that of the cat (*sinnawr*) and of a of pigeon (*shafnīn*) is a guarantee against nine infidelity; that of the swallow (*khuṭṭāf*) deprives a woman of all sexual desire. If the d of the frog prevents the growth of hair and es the teeth to fall out, that of the fox encourages th of the children's hair, and that of the lizard d *sāmm abraṣ* prevents loss of hair; against the owth of eyebrows (though al-Damīrī speaks of ashes), the blood of the chameleon (*ḥirbā*ʾ), e bear (*dubb*) and of the jerboa (*yarbūʿ*) is effi- ous.

folk-medicine, again, the blood of the tortoise *hfāt*) is effective against pains in the joints and stiffneck. That of the hare (*arnab*) causes scurvy and freckles to disappear; like that of the horse (or of the mare, *faras*), it has contraceptive properties. To cure maladies of the eyes, the blood of the viper (*afʿā*), of the mole (*khuld*), of the cockerel (*dīk*) or of the wood-pigeon (*warshān*) may be used; that of the cockerel is also a remedy for insect-bites and that of the mole or the weasel seems to be supremely efficacious against scrofula. The blood of the stag (*ayyil*) is efficacious against bladder-stones and that of the bull against haemorrhages; that of the pigeon (*ḥamām*) cures styes, stops nose-bleeds and, with oil, soothes the pain caused by burns; the effects of a dog-bite are alleviated by means of the blood of the hedgehog. Deafness can be cured with the blood of the wolf (*dhiʾb*), while that of the monkey (*ḳird*) has salutary effects in treating dumbness. A leper benefits from anointing himself with the blood of a ewe (*ḍaʾn*) or of a ringed pigeon (*fākhita*); abscesses are treated with the blood of the peacock (*ṭāwūs*), when they are serious, of the starling (*zurzūr*) if they are benign. The blood of the beaver (*ḳundus, kalb al-māʾ*) is effective against incontinence of urine, that of the ichneumon (*nims*) restores lucidity to a man who is possessed and finally, that of the crow (*ghurāb*) cures habitual drunkenness if it is mixed with wine, for which it inspires a definitive distaste. This is one of the few cases where the blood of an animal is imbibed; in the majority of cases mentioned above, it is used in the form of ointments, but whatever the manner in which it is utilised, it must, in principle at least, for this is not the case with some of the animals mentioned, come from a licit animal, which has been ritually slaughtered (al-Ḳayrawānī, *Risāla*, ed. and tr. Bercher, Algiers 1949, 321).

Bibliography: Wellhausen, *Reste arabischen Heidentums*², Berlin 1897; E. Doutté, *Magie et religion dans l'Afrique du Nord*, Algiers 1909; W. Robertson Smith, *Kinship and marriage in early Arabia*, London 1903; idem, *Lectures on the religion of the Semites*², London 1927; A. Jaussen, *Coutumes des Arabes au pays de Moab*, Paris 1908, ²1948, E. Laoust, *Mots et choses berbères*, Paris 1920; H. Basset, *Le culte des grottes au Maroc*, Algiers 1920; E. Westermarck, *Ritual and belief in Morocco*, London 1926; idem, *Pagan survivals in Mohammedan civilisation*, London 1933 (Fr. tr. *Survivances païennes dans la civilisation mahométane*, Paris 1935); H. Massé, *Croyances et coutumes persanes*, Paris 1938; A. Koller, *Essai sur l'esprit du Berbère marocain*², Fribourg 1949; J. Chelhod, *Le sacrifice chez les Arabes*, Paris 1955 (very important); idem, *Les structures du sacré chez les Arabes*, Paris 1964; J. Servier, *Les portes de l'année*, Paris 1962 (very important); M.-J. Tubiana, *Survivances préislamiques en pays zaghawa*, Paris 1964; Fichier de Documentation berbère, No. 94 (1964/4), *Valeur du sang*; J.-P. Roux *Les traditions des nomades de la Turquie méridionale*, Paris 1970.

(CH. PELLAT)

AL-DĀMAGHĀNĪ, ABŪ ʿABD ALLĀH MUḤAMMAD B. **ʿALĪ** B. MUḤAMMAD B. ʿALĪ B. MUḤAMMAD B. AL-ḤUSAYN B. ʿABD AL-MALIK B. ʿABD AL-WAHHĀB B. ḤAMMŪYA B. ḤASANAWAYH, Ḥanafī jurist who, as Chief Ḳāḍī of Baghdād, stands at the head of a family dynasty holding the positions of *ḳāḍī* or *ḳāḍī 'l-ḳuḍāt* down through the years. The following sketch is based mostly on *al-Djawāhir al-muḍiyya fī ṭabaḳāt al-Ḥanafiyya* by ʿAbd al-Ḳādir b. Abi 'l-Wafāʾ al-Ḳurashī (d. 775/1373). The best way to distinguish between them is by the use of their patronymic (*kunya*) and first name (*ism*). Among the eighteen identifiable members of this family, three distinguished themselves from among the others; namely, the eponym Abū ʿAbd Allāh Muḥammad (no. 1), his son Abu 'l-Ḥasan ʿAlī (no. 2), and one of their last descendants Abu 'l-Ḳāsim ʿAlī (no. 15). The eponyms *kunya* and *ism* are also those of the latter's brother (no. 16), and for this reason, the eponym was referred to—not it seems, in the contemporary documents, but later—as *al-Kabīr*, the Elder; this was in order to distinguish him from all the rest, not merely from his much later descendants who were too far removed to cause confusion and who had the same *kunya* and *ism* (nos 4 and 16), but of whom none was referred to as *al-Ṣag͟hīr*.

1. Dāmag͟hānī the Elder was born in 398/1007 in Dāmg͟hān in the province of Ḳūmis [*qq.v.*], where he was first educated and pursued his initial studies in law. He then came to Bag͟hdād in 419/1029 at the age of 21. Here he continued his studies of law under the two great masters of Ḥanafī law, al-Ḳudūrī (d. 428/1037) and al-Ṣaymarī (d. 436/1045). The jurisconsult Ḳudūrī, famous for his work on law, known especially by his name, *Muk͟htaṣar al-Ḳudūrī*, with numerous commentaries (see a list in *GAL*, I, 183, Suppl. I, 295), was also one of his teachers of *ḥadīt͟h* (see the certificate or *samāʿ* dated D͟hu 'l-Ḳaʿda 423 in the Köprülü Library (Istanbul) no. 1584, fol. 41b).

Coming from humble beginnings, Abū ʿAbd Allāh experienced material difficulties in pursuing his studies in the great capital. The *madrasas* had not yet begun to flourish in Bag͟hdād, with their endowments for the benefit of students as well as the teaching staff. He had therefore to work, as other needy students did, and pursue his studies at the same time. He took a job as night guard which also allowed him to study by the light of the guard's lamp. He studied hard and learned by heart the current text-books on law. One night he was surprised by a son of the caliph al-Muḳtadir, now an old prince who, admiring his knowledge of the law, invited him to come to his residence on Thursdays and aided him materially.

When the Chief *Ḳāḍī* of the caliph al-Ḳāʾim died in 447/1055, the year that the Saldjūḳs defeated the Buwayhids, the caliph consulted with the wealthy Ḥanbalī merchant Abū Manṣūr b. Yūsuf [*q.v.*] regarding his replacement. He wanted someone who was more knowledgeable in the field of law than the deceased. Abū Manṣūr suggested al-Dāmag͟hānī, who was thus qualified, but whose appointment would also please the *wazīr* of the Saldjūḳ Ṭog͟hrīl Beg, ʿAmīd al-Mulk al-Kundurī [*q.v.*]. Previously, the post of chief magistrate had been particularly reserved for adherents of the S͟hāfiʿī law school. Assigning it to a member of the Ḥanafī school, which was also that of the Saldjūḳ Sultan and his *wazīr*, was an act dictated by political expediency, not by al-Dāmag͟hānī's superior knowledge of the law; for there were other jurisconsults of the S͟hāfiʿī school, from which previous chief magistrates were chosen to serve, who were more highly qualified than he was, namely Abu 'l-Ṭayyib al-Ṭabarī (d. 450/1058), the great S͟hāfiʿī jurisconsult of the period; al-Māwardī (d. 450/1058), the celebrated author of *al-Aḥkām al-sulṭāniyya*; Abū Isḥāḳ al-S͟hīrāzī (d. 476/1083), disciple of Abu 'l-Ṭayyib al-Ṭabarī, his repetitor (*muʿīd*), and first professor at the Madrasa Niẓāmiyya of Bag͟hdād; and Abū Naṣr b. al-Ṣabbāg͟h (d. 477/1084), disciple of Abu 'l-Ṭayyib al-Ṭabarī, classmate and later colleague and rival of Abū Isḥāq al-S͟hīrāzī, and believed by Ibn K͟hallikān to be more knowledgeable in S͟hāfiʿī law than al-S͟hīrā

After his appointment, the fortunes of al-D g͟hānī changed. Only three years after his app ment, his residence was rich enough to attrac attention of burglars, and again later, in 493/ when his son Abu 'l-Ḥasan ʿAlī was the occupa

Dāmag͟hānī the Elder was considered in his as one of the leaders of his legal school, with reputation in the field of disputation (*munā* He continued in his post as *Ḳāḍī 'l-Ḳuḍāt* for t years, under the caliphs al-Ḳāʾim (d. 467/1075 al-Muḳtadī (d. 487/1094). He served as a substi *wazīr* under both caliphs, refusing to accep vizierate itself and not wanting to exceed his pos as *Ḳāḍī 'l-Ḳuḍāt* (Ibn al-Djawzī [also *apud* ʿAqīl], *Muntaẓam*, ix, 210, ll. 15-16: *fa-abā taʿa rutbati 'l-ḳaḍāʾ*). This genuine modesty was pe due to a gentle personality as well as to his hu beginnings. The period of his life when he liv poverty, hardly having enough to eat, was perhaps the cause of his becoming a voracious when he could afford to buy all the food he wa One anecdote (*Muntaẓam*, ix, 24, ll. 3 ff.) te his finishing off a thirty-pound (*raṭl*) plate of p at the end of a copious meal at a banquet give the caliph's *wazīr* Fak͟hr al-Dawla b. Djahīr. He in 478/1085.

Only one work on law has come down to us al-Dāmag͟hānī, the *Kitāb Masāʾil al-ḥīṭān wa 'l-* (Berlin Ms. 4982). His biographers do not cite works for him. Among his students was Abū Ilyās al-Daylamī (d. 461/1069), who was the professor of law at the great Madrasa of Abū H founded the same year as the Niẓāmiyya of Bag (see *GAL*, I, 460, Suppl. I, 637, and bibliogr cited; G. Makdisi, *Ibn ʿAqīl*, 171 ff. n. 6, and ir s.v. Abū ʿAbd Allāh al-Dāmag͟hānī).

Here follows a list of his descendants wit names, according to the enumeration in the sl below, all of whom were known by the *nisb* al-Dāmag͟hānī.

2. Abu 'l-Ḥasan ʿAlī b. Muḥammad below].

3. Abū Djaʿfar ʿAbd Allāh b. Muḥam Muhad͟hd͟hib al-Dawla (d. 518/1124); becan *s͟hāhid*-notary under his father (no. 1); appoint *ḳāḍī* of the East Side quarter of Bāb al-Ṭā Bag͟hdād, and of the stretch from upper Bag͟hd Mawṣil, by his brother (no. 2) when the latter be *Ḳāḍī 'l-Ḳuḍāt* (23 S͟haʿbān 488/28 August (*Djawāhir*, i, 287-8).

4. Abū ʿAbd Allāh Muḥammad b. ʿAlī, al-Ḳuḍāt (d. 516/1122); became *s͟hāhid*-notary u his father (no. 2), who appointed him as his r sentative magistrate in Bag͟hdād and elsew when his father died, he was put up as candidat the post of *Ḳāḍī 'l-Ḳuḍāt* to succeed his father was not appointed; was sent as ambassador o caliph to Transoxania and died during the mi at 38 years of age (*Djawāhir*, ii, 96).

5. Abu 'l-Ḥusayn Aḥmad b. Alī (d. 540/1 was appointed *ḳāḍī* of the West Side quart Kark͟h in Bag͟hdād, and later of the whole of West Side quarter of Bāb al-Azadj (*Djawāhir*, i al-Tamīmī al-Dārī al-G͟hazzī, *Muntaẓam*, ix, *al-Ṭabaḳāt al-saniyya fī tarādjim al-ḥanafiyy* 473).

6. Abū Naṣr al-Ḥasan b. ʿAlī (d. 555/1 substituted for his brother (no. 5) as *ḳāḍī* of the Side quarter of Kark͟h (*Djawāhir*, i, 199-200).

7. Abū ʿAbd Allāh al-Ḥusayn b. ʿAlī (d.

) (see *Djawāhir*, i, 214-5, where the year of h is given as 461, erroneously, because (a) the of death is given as Friday 11 Radjab, and 11 jab was a Friday for 561, but a Wednesday for and (b) the biographical notice cites him as a her of "Abū Naṣr al-Ḥasan" (no. 6), who died in 1160. One more discrepancy appears at the end he notice where the author of the *Djawāhir* es Ibn al-Nadjdjār (d. 643/1245) as citing the er (no. 2) of this Dāmaghānī as his informant rding the son, which is not possible).

Abū Manṣūr Djaᶜfar b. ᶜAbd Allāh (d. 568/ -3); born in 490/1097, he studied *ḥadīth* under two Ḥanbalīs Abu 'l-Khaṭṭāb al-Kalwadhānī 510/1116), known for both *ḥadīth* and *fiḳh*, and yā b. Manda (d. 511/1118), the great *ḥadīth*-rt (*Djawāhir*, i, 179).

Abū Saᶜīd al-Ḥasan b. ᶜAbd Allāh (d. 575/); studied *ḥadīth* under the great *ḥadīth*-expert 'l-Ḳāsim Hibat Allāh b. Muḥammad al-Shaybānī aghdādī (d. 524/1130) (*Djawāhir*, i, 196).

. Abu 'l-Muẓaffar al-Ḥusayn b. Aḥmad 579/1183); his brother (no. 12) accepted him as *id*-notary in 552/1157 and appointed him as his esentative magistrate in the quarter of the hal Palace on the East Side of Baghdād *wāhir*, i, 207-8).

. Abu Muḥammad al-Ḥasan b. Aḥmad 582/1186); his brother (no. 12) accepted him as *id*-notary in 552/1157 and appointed him *ḳāḍī* in West Side quarter of Karkh in Baghdād, then in Wāsiṭ; he spent a lifetime in his career as *ḳāḍī*, Wāsiṭ and Baghdād, between dismissals and pointments (*Djawāhir*, i, 188-89).

. Abu 'l-Ḥasan ᶜAlī b. Aḥmad (d. 583/1188); appointed *ḳāḍī* in the Karkh quarter of Baghdād's t Side in 540/1145 following his father's (no. 5) b. Then when the *Ḳāḍī 'l-Ḳuḍāt* Abu 'l-Ḳāsim b. al-Ḥusayn al-Zaynabī died in 543/1149, he was ointed *Ḳāḍī 'l-Ḳuḍāt* in his place, at the age of thirty, by the caliph al-Muḳtafī. He was confirmed in his appointment under the caliph al-Mustandjid, who then dismissed him. The caliph al-Mustaḍīʾ reappointed him, and, the appointment being confirmed later by the caliph al-Nāṣir, Abu 'l-Ḥasan continued to serve until he died. When he was dismissed by al-Mustandjid, he kept to his home, where he pursued his study of the religious sciences, considering himself as still the *Ḳāḍī 'l-Ḳuḍāt*, and all the *ḳāḍīs* as his authorised representatives, "because a *ḳāḍī*, unless guilty of moral depravity, may not be dismissed" (*li-anna 'l-ḳāḍiya idhā lam yaẓhar fisḳuh, lam yadjuz ᶜazluh, Djawāhir*, i, 351, 11. 9-10) (Ibn Kathīr, *al-Bidāya wa 'l-nihāya fi 'l-tārīkh*, xii, 329; *Djawāhir*, i, 350-2; Ibn Taghrībirdī, *al-Nudjūm al-zāhira*, vi, 104).

13. Abu 'l-Fatḥ Muḥammad b. ᶜAlī (d. 575/ 1180); was accepted as *shāhid*-notary by his father (no. 12) on Monday, 12 Radjab 575/Thursday 13 December 1179), who made him his assistant magistrate in the city of Baghdād; he died at the age of 29, less than three months after his appointment (*Djawāhir*, ii, 91).

14. Abu 'l-Faḍl Muḥammad b. al-Ḥasan (d. 592/1196); was accepted as *shāhid*-notary by his uncle (no. 12) on 12 *Shawwāl* 575/Tuesday 11 March 1180), three months after his cousin (no. 13), and was entrusted with the controllership of the caliphal burial grounds in the East Side quarter of al-Ruṣāfa. He died young (*Djawāhir*, ii, 40).

15. Abu 'l-Ḳāsim ᶜAbd Allāh b. al-Ḥusayn (died Sunday 30 Dhu 'l-Ḳaᶜda 615/17 February 1219); was appointed *ḳāḍī* in 586/1190, and dismissed in 594/1198; was reappointed as *Ḳāḍī 'l-Ḳuḍāt* in 603/ 1207, and dismissed once again in 611/1214; was highly esteemed for his knowledge of the law according to the various schools of juridical thought, as well as for belles-lettres (Abū Shāma, *Tarādjim ridjāl al-ḳarnayn al-sādis wa 'l-sābiᶜ*, 110-11; Ibn Kathīr, *al-Bidāya wa 'l-nihāya fi 'l-tārīkh*, xiii, 82;

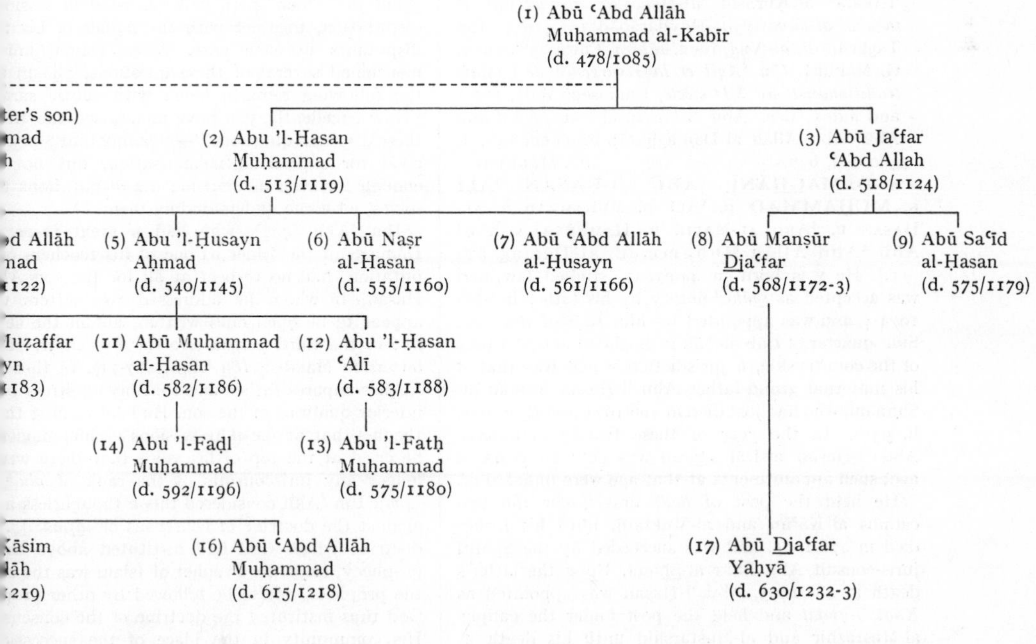

Djawāhir, i, 273-4; Ibn Taghrībirdī, *al-Nudjūm al-zāhira*, vi, 223).

16. Abū ʿAbd Allāh Muḥammad b. al-Ḥusayn died Wednesday 16 Shaʿbān 615/7 November 1218, three and-a-half months before his brother (no. 15); was accepted as *shāhid*-notary by his brother (no. 15) on 20 Shawwāl 603/20 May 1207, who appointed him as his representative magistrate in Baghdād, a post he kept until his brother's dismissal on 12 Radjab 611/17 November 1214 which entailed his own dismissal; he died four years later without reappointment (*Djawāhir*, ii, 48).

17. Abū Djaʿfar Yaḥyā b. Djaʿfar (d. 630/1232-3); he is known to have learned *ḥadīth* from his father (no. 8) and to have taught the subject, according to al-Mundhirī (Abū Muḥammad ʿAbd al-ʿAẓīm b. ʿAbd al-Ḳawī, d. 656/1258), who received authorisation (*idjāza*) by correspondence from Abū Djaʿfar, on more than one occasion, to teach on his authority, one in particular arriving from Aleppo in Shawwāl 620/October-November 1223). (*Djawāhir*, ii, 211).

The author of the *Djawāhir* gives the orthography of the ethnic name al-Dāmaghānī and says that it is the name of *Ḳāḍī 'l-Ḳuḍāt* Abū ʿAbd Allāh al-Dāmaghānī (no. 1) and of a group of his descendants (see *ibid.*, ii, 306). The author cites a nephew (the son of a sister) of Dāmaghānī (of no. 1), ʿUbayd Allāh b. Muḥammad b. Ṭalḥa b. al-Husayn, Abū Muḥammad al-Dāmaghānī (d. 502/1108), who was accepted by the uncle as a *shāhid*-notary (*Djawāhir*, i, 340-1).

Another Dāmaghānī (fl. 494/1102), ʿAbd Allāh b. al-Ḥusayn b. ʿAbd Allāh, was also accepted as *shāhid*-notary by Abū ʿAbd Allāh (no. 1), but his identification as a member of the family is not certain (*Djawāhir*, i. 274).

There are other persons noted with this name, but with no apparent relationship to this family.

Bibliography: Ibn al-Djawzī, *al-Muntaẓam*; Abū Shāma al-Maḳdisī, *Tarādjim ridjāl al-ḳarnayn al-sādis wa 'l-sābiʿ*, Cairo 1366/1947; Ibn Kathīr, *al-Bidāya wa 'l-nihāya*; ʿAbd al-Ḳādir b. Abī 'l-Wafāʾ al-Ḳurashī, *al-Djawāhir al-muḍiyya fī ṭabaḳāt al-ḥanafiyya*, Ḥaydarābād 1332/1914; Ibn Taghrībirdī, *al-Nudjūm al-zāhira*, Cairo 1383/1963; G. Makdisi, *Ibn ʿAqīl et la résurgence de l'Islam traditionaliste au XIᵉ siècle*, Damascus 1963, 172-5 and index, *s.vv.* Abu 'l-Ḥasan al-Dāmaghānī and Abū ʿAbd Allāh al-Dāmaghānī; Brockelmann, I, 460, S I, 637. (G. MAKDISI)

AL-**DĀMAGHĀNĪ, ABŪ 'L-ḤASAN ʿALĪ B. MUḤAMMAD** B. ʿALĪ B. MUḤAMMAD B. AL-ḤASAN B. ʿABD AL-MALIK B. HAMMŪYA, son of Abū ʿAbd Allāh Muḥammad al-Dāmaghānī [*q.v.*]. He was born in 449/1057, studied law, and was accepted as *shāhid*-notary by his father in 466/1073-4, and was appointed by him *ḳāḍī* of the East Side quarter of Bāb al-Ṭāḳ in Baghdād and of a part of the countryside, a jurisdiction which was that of his maternal grand-father Abu 'l-Ḥasan Aḥmad al-Simnānī, who had just died in 466/1074 (see *Djawāhir*, ii, 95-6). In the year of these two appointments, Abu 'l-Ḥasan al-Dāmaghānī was only 16 years of age; such appointments at that age were unheard of.

He held the post of *ḳāḍī* first under the two caliphs al-Ḳāʾim and al-Muḳtadī, until his father died in 478/1085, and was succeeded by the Shāfiʿī juris-consult Abū Bakr al-Shāmī. Upon the latter's death in 488/1095, Abu 'l-Ḥasan was appointed as *Ḳāḍī 'l-ḳuḍāt* and held the post under the caliphs al-Mustaẓhir and al-Mustarshid until his death in 513/1119. He held also the post of substitute- under these two caliphs, sharing the post with o

There are some anecdotes regarding Abu 'l-Ḥ al-Dāmaghānī which shed light on how he regarded by some of his contemporaries amon jurisconsults. In one of these, he is said to refused to accept the testimony of a person came to him at the behest of the caliph al-Must When the latter asked for an explanation, he re that on the Day of the Last Judgment God v hold him responsible for his actions, not the c who appointed him. Another anecdote concern Shāfiʿī jurisconsult Abū Bakr al-Shāshī (d. 504/ who came to Dāmaghānī to pay him a visit. *Ḳāḍī 'l-ḳuḍāt* did not show him respect by risin him, so Shāshī turned on his heels and left. Tha in the 480s. It was not until after the year 500/1 that they came together again on the occasion ceremony for mourning over a fellow juriscon death. Shāshī arrived first and took his seat. the *Ḳāḍī 'l-Ḳuḍāt* entered, everyone rose e Shāshī, who did not budge. Dāmaghānī wrote caliph Mustaẓhir complaining that Shāshī di respect the representative of the religious law caliph wrote back: "What do you expect me t to him? He is your senior in age, a more exc [jurisconsult], and more pious. Had you rise him, he would have done the same for you". S also wrote to the caliph complaining of Dāmag disdainful treatment of men of religious science included the following two verses: "A partiti screen, conceit, and excessive vainglory/ and staking reaching for the heights / If all this had as a result of ability / it would be easy to accep it comes as a result of coming from behind (me that he succeeded his father, riding on his tails)". The caliph finally brought the two consults together and they made up their qu But the anecdote ends on a note which shows Shāshī had not quite forgiven the magis Dāmaghānī sat with Shāshī, presumably in presence of other learned men, and began to g list of the questions of law that his father, D ghānī the Elder [*q.v.*], had discussed in sessic disputation, together with the names of his disputants in each case. When Dāmaghānī mentioned several of these questions, Shāshī the following remark, laden with subtle sar "How excellently you have memorised the tit these disputed questions!"—meaning that Shāsh good for superficial memorisation, but not enough for even memorising the disputations selves, let alone understanding them.

Ibn ʿAḳīl [*q.v.*], who had a great respec Dāmaghānī the Elder as one of his teachers c putation, had no respect at all for the son A Ḥasan, to whom he addressed two letters appear to be open ones written, not in the se but in the third person (see the French tr. of letters in Makdisi, *Ibn ʿAqīl*, 467-71). In these ʿAḳīl compares father and son, laying stress c inferior qualities of the son. He held against th the fact that, at one of his sessions as chief magis he cried at the top of his voice that there we longer any jurisconsults of the rank of *mu* [*q.v.*]. Ibn ʿAḳīl considered this a thoughtless against the doctrine of consensus or *idjmāʿ* [*q* doctrine which God had instituted above th prophecy, since the Prophet of Islam was the s the prophets, not to be followed by other pro God thus instituted the doctrine of the consen His community in the place of the success hets. He also held against Abu 'l-Ḥasan his ect of the learned men of Baghdād in favour of e from Khurāsān. He accused him of doing so the purpose of gaining a broader reputation, umably because these men would spread his e far and wide on their travels back and forth to home provinces.

n al-Djawzī (d. 597/1200), who gives a lengthy raphy of Abu 'l-Ḥasan and is our source for Ibn l's two letters, nevertheless speaks well of him, ng that he was a religious man, with a sense of our, with generosity and integrity, and that he knowledgeable in the field of *shurūṭ*, i.e. the ng of formal documents. Among his teachers, Ḥanbalī *Ḳāḍī* Abū Yaʿlā b. al-Farrāʾ (d. 458/), Abū Bakr al-Khaṭīb (d. 463/1071), al-Ṣarīfīnī 469/1076), and Ibn al-Naḳūr (d. 470/1078) are as those who taught him *ḥadīth*, and is said to related traditions in turn. He studied law under father and his brother [see under DĀMAGHĀNĪ, ʿABD ALLĀH, Nos. 1 and 3].

ou 'l-Ḥasan died in 513/1119 after having served lose on 30 years as magistrate and chief magis-. He was buried at his home in the quarter of al-Ḳallāʾīn on the West Side of Baghdād where ather was buried. and the remains of his father transferred to the shrine of Abū Ḥanīfa on the Side. (G. MAKDISI)

AMASCENING [see MAʿDIN].

ANDĀNḲĀN, DANDĀNAḲĀN, a small town in sand desert between Marw and Sarakhs in aeval Khurāsān and 10 *farsakh*s or 40 miles from ormer city. The site of the settlement is now in Turkmenistan SSR, see V. A. Zhukovsky, *alinî Starago Merva*, St. Petersburg 1894, 38. geographers of the 4th/10th century mention it was well-fortified and was surrounded by a 500 paces in circumference, the baths and a or caravanserai lying outside this wall (Ibn ḳal², 436-7, 456, tr. Kramers-Wiet, 422, 440; *ūd al-ʿālam*, tr. Minorsky, 105). When Yāḳūt it in the early 7th/13th century, it was ruinous abandoned, with only the *ribāṭ*, the minaret and walls outstanding, apparently because of the oaching sands, though he quotes a work of ʿānī's, the *Kitāb al-Taḥbīr*, that its ruin dated a sacking by the Ghuzz in Shawwāl 553/ ember 1158 (*Buldān*, ed. Beirut, ii, 477). Both it and Samʿānī (*Ansāb*, ed. Hyderabad, v, 381-3) many scholars who stemmed from Dandānḳān. e place's main claim to historical fame arises the fact that, outside Dandānḳān's walls in the ned and largely waterless desert, there took place of the decisive battles of eastern Islamic history. amaḍān 431/May 1040 a force of highly-mobile mens under the Saldjūḳ leaders Toghrïl and rī Beg defeated a more heavily-armed but ly demoralised Ghaznawid army under Sulṭān ūd b. Maḥmūd, and this victory gave the Sal-s control of the former Ghaznawid province of rāsān (see B. N. Zakhoder, *Dendanekan*, in *ten*, xviii (1954), 581-7, and Bosworth, *The navids, their empire in Afghanistan and eastern*, index).

Bibliography: Given in the article.

(C. E. BOSWORTH)

ANIEL [see DĀNIYĀL]

ĀR AL-ḤADĪTH.

I. Architecture.

e first *dār al-ḥadīth* [*q.v.*] founded by Nūr al-Dīn Damascus served as a prototype for similar establishments set up in Syria, ʿIrāḳ, Egypt and Palestine during the Zangid, Ayyūbid and Mamlūk periods. Unfortunately, this particular building is now virtually a ruin. The façade is completely disfigured by little shops built on the site of the rooms situated to the north of the courtyard. Of the building as a whole, some traces still exist: the walls of a prayer room with some vestiges of the *miḥrāb* decoration; the façade of this prayer room, made up of three bays; the courtyard on to which it opened; and the basin in its centre. These few remains have nevertheless allowed Jean Sauvaget to reconstruct the plan of the building (*Le Dār al-ḥadīth de Nour al-dīn*, in *Les monuments ayyoubides de Damas*, i, Paris 1938, 15-25). This plan fitted into a small, almost square rectangle (16.30 × 17.20 m. overall). It comprised a room with a *miḥrāb* ranging all along the south wall, which opened on to a central, square courtyard through a large, high central bay flanked by two other bays of more modest dimensions. Each of these bays was made up of a rectangular opening surmounted by a lintel and a curved, pointed arch. The central arch was supported on two rectangular pillars, whilst the lateral ones were supported on the piers of the doorway. Two rectangular and symmetrical rooms, one of them communicating with the prayer room, opened on to the lateral façades of the courtyard, and each communicated with a little vaulted room making up the east and west angles of the northern façade of the buildings as a whole. The central part of this last was made up of a passage way which led both to the central courtyard and also to two further small, vaulted rooms which themselves led to the courtyard. In the centre of the courtyard was a basin for ablutions.

The arrangement here, simple and functional, allows one to identify exactly the role of each of the various rooms: the prayer room at the end, teaching rooms at the sides, and possibly, the janitor's lodgings in the rooms along the façade.

Sauvaget has emphasised the relationship between the plan above and those of the oldest *madrasas* in Damascus, the difference being essentially in a reduction of the dimensions and the replacement of the *īwāns*—specific features of *madrasas*—by lateral rooms. Even so, the distinction between the two types of building was not always clearly made. To cite only one example, the Ḍiyāʾiyya, founded in Damascus by Ḍiyāʾ al-Dīn al-Maḳdisī before 643/1245, is given as a *dār al-ḥadīth* by Ibn Ṭūlūn (*al-Ḳalāʾid al-djawhariyya fī taʾrīkh al-madāris*, Damascus, 1949, 76) and as a *madrasa* by al-Nuʿaymī (*al-Dāris fī taʾrīkh al-madāris*, Damascus 1948, i, 80).

The opening of the first *dār al-ḥadīth*, was followed by the founding of numerous similar institutions based on Nūr al-Dīn's building; unfortunately, these have almost all disappeared. Of the 16 establishments listed by al-Nuʿaymī, Damascus has now only the remnants of Nūr al-Dīn's *dār al-ḥadīth*; the fine doorway with stalactites of that of Tingiz, built in 739/1338 and whose interior has been completely rebuilt (cf. Sauvaget, *Les monuments historiques de Damas*, Beirut 1932, 69, no. 44); and a few remnants of walls incorporated in shops or houses. As a result, we are forced to go back to the written sources in order to get information about the architecture of the *dār al-ḥadīth*s; but these are very laconic on this particular aspect, and the passages on these institutions concern themselves almost wholly with the lives of the teachers there. Alone of them Ibn Ṭūlūn devotes a few lines to the buildings themselves, and from him we learn that certain of them were mere

II. Historical development [see ii, 125 6].

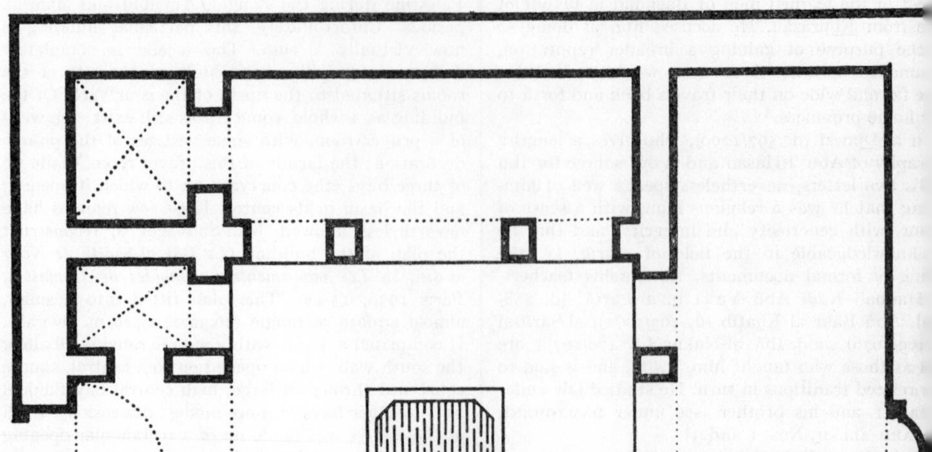

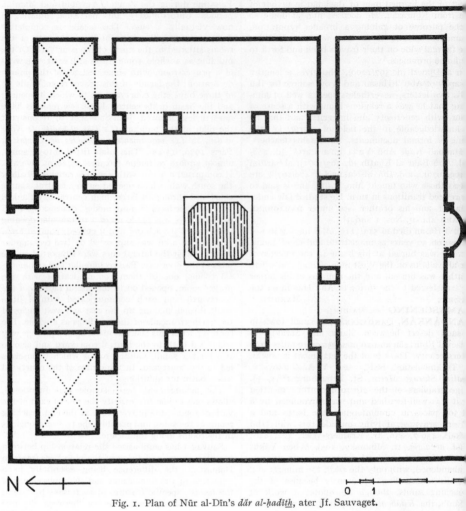

Fig. 1. Plan of Nūr al-Dīn's *dār al-ḥadīth*, ater Jf. Sauvaget.

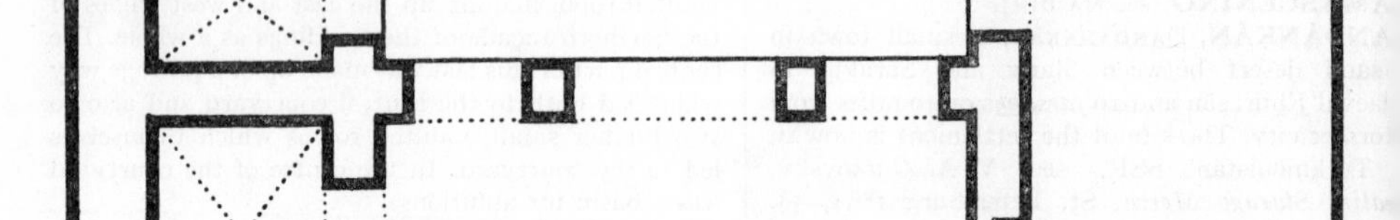

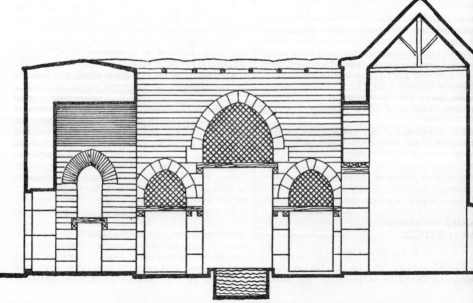

Fig. 2. Elevation of Nūr al-Dīn's *dār al-ḥadīth*, after J. Sauvaget.

s within the house of the *shaykh* who was giving ıstruction. Thus the Shaḳīshaḳiyya, founded in ıscus by Ibn Shaḳīshaḳa in 656/1258, was only ıodest dwelling of this master (cf. al-Nuᶜaymī, ;, i, 81). The Ḍiyāʾiyya (see above) had a plan ıbling that of the Nūriyya, but the rooms meant :udents were spread over two floors (Ibn Ṭūlūn, *ʾid*, 83). The Ḳalānisiyya, founded in *ca.* 729/ by the vizier Ibn al-Ḳalānisī (not to be confused the historian of the same name), had a very ısive hall, provided with three large windows ng on to the Nahr Yazīd, several doors giving s to it, a paved courtyard and a minaret (Ibn n, *op. cit.*, 86). The Niẓāmiyya, founded towards middle of the 9th/15th century by the *ḳāḍī ḍāt* Niẓām al-Dīn ᶜUmar, showed a structure more close to that of the *madrasas.* Three *īwāns* ed on to a court in whose centre was an ablutions n. The southern *īwān* had a *miḥrāb*, and the rn side was provided with a *riwāḳ* reserved for en (*ibid.*, 88).

metimes the *dār al-ḥadīth* had a *ribāṭ* or *khānḳāh* annexed to it, or else the founder's own tomb *rba* might be adjacent to it. This was the case the Nāṣiriyya, founded by al-Malik al-Nāṣir ıf on the southern slopes of Mount Ḳāsiyūn] some time before 659/1261, This imposing itectural complex, built on the banks of the Nahr d and decked out with yellow and white stones, topped by a minaret and also included a mill. rding to Ibn Ṭūlūn, *op. cit.*, 94, it was one of the t houses in Damascus; but by his time, it had entirely destroyed and even its site had vanished.

Aleppo, there are still some remains of the *dār ḥdīth* founded by Ibn Shaddād Yūsuf (the bioher of Ṣalāḥ al-Dīn) in 618/1221, as attested by ext of a foundation inscription carved on a stone k inserted in a modern wall of the reconstructed ling. According to the summary plan deduced Herzfeld, there remains a rectangular room ɔ × 6 m. overall, with a *miḥrāb* and three open- In the north-eastern corner, an entrance conɔus to the room's north wall and at the beginning ıother wall perpendicular to the latter gives on hat was possibly the *dār al-ḥadīth*'s courtyard zfeld, *Matériaux pour un Corpus Inscriptionum ɔicarum. Inscriptions et monuments d'Alep*, ii, pl. XVIIa).

ıe Kāmiliyya of Cairo, founded there by alk al-Kāmil Nāṣir al-Dīn in 622/1225 on the model ıe Nūriyya, is chronologically the second of the *al-ḥadīths* (cf. al Maḳrīzī, *Khiṭaṭ*, ed. Būlāḳ, ii, . Some remains of this building still exist, in icular, an *īwān*, whose pointed-arched vault is d in fired brick and is supported on the walls and stone piers (photograph by J. C. Garcin, in *ales Islamologiques*, vii [1967], pl. XII).

ıese various examples suffice to show how the itecture of the *dār al-ḥadīth* remained dependent that of the *madrasa*, when indeed it was not ıded in it. (S. Ory)

II. History [see Vol. II, 125-6].

ĀR ṢĪNĪ, or Dārṣīnī (Persian *dār čīnī* "Chinese d") is the Chinese cinnamon (*Cinnamomum ia*), next to the Ceylonese cinnamon (*Cinn. ınicum*) the most valuable spice from plants of cinnamon species, of the family of the Lauraceae, aps the oldest spice altogether. The rind of the ıch of the cinnamon-tree was used in China as icine, aromatic substance and spice already in the millennium B.C., and reached the Near East and the Mediterranean countries in the 2nd millennium. It cannot be established with certainty with what original plant *dārṣīnī* is to be associated, since in the pharmacognostic texts *Cinn. cassia* is also rendered by *salīkha*, which allegedly is not identical with *dārṣīnī*. The Greeks (Dioscorides) called the class κιν(ν)άμωμον, and the rind of the Chinese κασσία; the Arabs speak accordingly of *ḳinnāmūmun* (and variants) and *ḳāsiyā* (*ḳassiyā*); in Spanish-Arabic texts it even appears in the Romance form *djinnamū* (*cinamomo*), cf. M. Asín Palacios, *Glosario de voces romances*, Madrid Granada 1943, no. 196. Since Ceylonese cinnamon was exported rather late from the island, hardly before the 14th century A.D., *dārṣīnī*, according to its name, can only indicate Chinese cinnamon during the whole previous period.

The older Arab botanists (Abū Ḥanīfa al-Dīnawarī, *The book of plants*, ed. B. Lewin, Wiesbaden 1974, no. 814) did not know what to do with the term *ṣīnī* and associated it with an unidentified drug *ṣīnīn* mentioned by al-Aᶜshā (*Dīwān*, ed. Geyer, 201). Isḥāḳ b. Sulaymān al-Isrāʾīlī (d. *ca.* 320/932) was perhaps the first to perceive that cinnamon came indeed from China, see al-Ghāfiḳī [*q.v.* below], *al-Adwiya al-mufrada*, Ms. Rabat, Bibl. Gén. ḳ 155 i, fol. 130a, 11. Like the numerous other Asiatic spices, cinnamon was imported mainly by the sea route, the most important transit-port being ᶜAdan (W. Heyd, *Histoire du commerce du Levant au Moyen Âge*, Leipzig 1885-6, index s.v. Cannelle).

The Arabs knew a whole range of kinds of *dārṣīnī* which cannot be determined more closely: the "real Chinese cinnamon" (*dārṣīnī al-Ṣīn*), an inferior kind (*dār ṣūṣ*), the "real cinnamon rind" (*al-ḳirfa ᶜalā 'l-ḥaḳīḳa*), the "clove-rind" (*ḳirfat al-ḳurunful*), the "pungent cinnamon" (*al-ḥādd al-madhāḳ*), etc. As spice for food, there served not only the tubular rind of the cinnamon-tree, but also its leaves, blossoms and unripe berries. The pleasant scent is caused by the volatile oil extracted from the rind. Taken as a medicine, cinnamon reduces and softens thick substances, strengthens the stomach, liver and spleen and counteracts their sluggishness, quickens the activity of the heart, invigorates the eyesight and is effective against poisonous bites and stings of scorpions. Spread on excrement and urine, it does away with their nasty smell.

Bibliography: Dioscurides, *De materia medica*, ed. M. Wellmann, i, Berlin 1907, 18-20 (= lib. i, 14); *La 'Materia médica' de Dioscorides*, ii (Arabic tr. Iṣṭafan b. Basīl), ed. C. E. Dubler and E. Terés, Tetuán 1952, 22 f.; *The medical formulary or Aqrābādhīn of al-Kindī*, tr. M. Levey, Madison etc. 1966, 265 f. (no. 96); Bīrūnī, *Ṣaydala*, ed. Ḥakīm Muḥ. Saᶜīd, Karachi 1973, Arab. 189 f., Engl. tr. 156; Barhebraeus, *The abridged version of "The Book of simple drugs" of . . . al-Ghâfiqî*, ed. M. Meyerhof and G. P. Sobhy, Cairo 1932, no. 232; Suwaydī, *Simāt*, Ms. Paris ar. 3004, fol. 71b; Ibn Biklārish, *Mustaᶜīnī*, Ms. Naples, Bibl. Naz. iii, F. 65, fol. 32b; Ibn al-Djazzār, *Iᶜtimād*, Ms. Ayasofya 3564, fols. 66b-67a; Zahrāwī, *Taṣrīf*, Ms. Beşir Ağa 502, fol. 503a-b; Maimonides, *Sharḥ asmāʾ al-ᶜuḳḳār*, ed. Meyerhof, Cairo 1940, no. 95; Ibn al-Bayṭār, *Djāmiᶜ*, Būlāḳ 1291, ii, 83-5, tr. Leclerc, no. 841, with many quotations from sources; Ghassānī, *Muᶜtamad*, ed. M. al-Saḳḳāʾ, Beirut 1395/1975, 145-7; *Die pharmakolog. Grundsätze des Abu Mansur Muwaffak bin Ali Harawi*, tr. A. Ch. Achundow, Halle 1893, 305; *Tuḥfat al-aḥbāb*, ed. Renaud and Colin, Paris 1934, no. 112; Rāzī, *Ḥāwī*, xx, Ḥaydarābād 1387, 490-6 (no. 345); Ibn Sīnā, *Ḳānūn* (Būlāḳ), i, 288 f.; Dāwūd al-Anṭākī, *Ta<u>dh</u>kira*, Cairo 1371, i, 149; Ibn ʿAbdūn, *ʿUmdat al-ṭabīb*, Ms. Rabat. Bibl. Gén. 3505 D, fols. 61b-62a; *El Libro Agregà de Serapiom*, ed. G. Ineichen, ii, Venice 1966, 89 f.; F. Moattar, *Ismāʿīl Ǧorǧānī und seine Bedeutung für die iranischen Heilkunde*, Diss. rer. nat. Marburg 1971, no. 64; H. G. Kircher, *Die "einfachen Heilmittel" aus dem "Handbuch der Chirurgie" des Ibn al-Quff*, Bonn 1967, no. 99; W. Schmucker, *Die pflanzliche und mineralische Materia medica im Firdaus al-ḥikma des ʿAlī ibn Sahl Rabban aṭ-Ṭabarī*, Bonn 1969, no. 292; F. A. Flückiger, *Pharmakognosie des Pflanzenreiches*^{3}, Berlin 1891, 592-8; I. Löw, *Die Flora der Juden*, ii, 1924, 107-13.

(A. Dietrich)

DARAK (A.), *ḍamān al-darak*, in Islamic law the guarantee against a fault in ownership. As the most important of the various guarantees aimed at protecting the new legal status brought about by the conclusion of a contract of sale, the *ḍamān al-darak* ensures that the seller will make good should the buyer's title be contested by a third party. It is possible, for instance, that prior to the conclusion of the contract and without the knowledge of the two contracting parties, a third party had inherited all or part of the property sold, it had been given in *waḳf*, a neighbour had exercised his right of pre-emption, or a creditor had claimed the property in settlement of a debt against the seller. Thus the *darak* rises from a rightful claim of ownership (*istiḥḳāḳ*) before the contract has come into being, while a claim established after this (because a defect is discovered, or the object sold perishes before delivery, for instance) is not covered by the *darak* guarantee. Further, the seller is liable to the buyer only and not to another person to whom the property may have been transferred.

There is a difference of opinion on how the seller discharges his obligation; return of the price was the norm, but arguments are made for the return of the property itself, or its equivalent, if it is fungible, or its value together with the value of such improvements as had been made by the buyer at the time the claim was raised. The *ḍamān al-darak* is usually confined to contracts for the sale of immovable property, but in the formularies for written contracts we see that the guarantee could be given for movables of value as well, such as slaves, walls (considered movable because they could be dismantled for their materials), and palm trees (sold separately from the land and perhaps uprooted). It is not included in contracts in which the property is delivered at a later date, but rather, a separate witnessed document containing the guarantee is drawn up after delivery takes place. Nor is the guarantee given in conveyances in which the alienor receives no consideration, as in a deed of gift. The importance of this guarantee and the variety of formulas employed to express it reflect the concern of Islamic law for the protection of ownership and bona fide acquisition.

Bibliography: The term *darak* is defined in Lane, iii, 874; Dozy, *Suppl.*, i, 436-7; J. Schacht, *An introduction to Islamic law*, London 1964, 139; al-Sara<u>kh</u>sī, *K. al-Mabsūṭ fi'l-furūʿ*, Cairo 1324-31/1906-13, xxx, 173-4, 180, 183, 187-8. Discussion of various aspects of the legal status and the formulae is to be found in the <u>sh</u>*urūṭ* works, e.g., J. A. Wakin, *The function of documents in Islamic law: the chapters on sale from Ṭaḥāwī's "Kitāb al-Shurūṭ al-Kabīr"*, New York 1972, index, s.v.; al-Ṣayrafī, *al-Mukātabāt al-badīʿa fīmā yuktab min umūr al-Sharīʿa*, in al-Nuwayrī, *Nihāyat al-ara*[b fī] *funūn al-adab*, ix, 12; Mar<u>gh</u>īnānī, *al-Fa*[tāwā] *al-Ẓahīriyya*, MS British Museum, Rieu Su[ppl.] 4305, fol. 19a; *al-Fatāwā al-ʿĀlamgīriyya*, Calc[utta] 1251, vi, 424-6. Since this guarantee is a promi[nent] feature of the contract, examples of its us[e in] practice are found frequently in the extant d[eeds] of sale. For examples, see A. Grohmann, *Arabic papyri in the Egyptian Library*, i, 146, 169, 175, 182, 187 and *passim*; J. Sourdel-Tho[mine] and D. Sourdel, *Trois actes de vent damascain*[s du] *début du IV/X siècle*, in *JESHO*, viii (1965), W. Hoenerbach, *Spanisch-islamische Urkunden* [aus] *der Zeit der Nasriden und Moriscos*, Berkeley 1[965,] 41-2, 272; for earlier Near Eastern parallels, R. Yaron, *On defension clauses of some ori*[ental] *deeds of sale and lease, from Mesopotamia* [...] *Bibliotheca Orientalis*, xv, 15-22. See also ḌA[MĀN].

(J. A. Waki[n])

DARB ZUBAYDA, the pilgrim high[way] running from al-ʿIrāḳ to the Holy Cities of [the] Ḥi<u>dj</u>āz, named after Zubayda bint <u>Dj</u>aʿfar [*q.v.*], wife of Hārūn al-Ra<u>sh</u>īd.

The main section of the Darb Zubayda, from K[ūfa] to Mecca, is something over 1,400 km. in length. [A] branch to Medina leaves the main road at Ma[ʿdin] al-Naḳira, which is also the point at which the r[oad] from Baṣra joins it. From Maʿdin al-Naḳira to M[ecca] the distance is about 500 km., and from the s[ame] point to Medina it is about 250 km. Between Ma[ʿdin] al-Naḳira and Mecca, the section of the road l[ying] between Maʿdin Banī Sulaym and al-Mislaḥ has [an] alternative route which runs: Maʿdin Banī Sula[ym-] Ṣufayna-Ḥā<u>dh</u>a-al-Mislaḥ. This latter route [runs] across the Ḥarrat Rahaṭ, and was used for the s[ake] of its superior water resources. For the most part, [the] preparation of the track of the road consiste[d of] clearing the ground of boulders, rocks, etc., bu[t at] least one stretch (near Baṭn al-A<u>gh</u>arr) was paved [at] the expense of <u>Kh</u>āliṣa, the lady-in-waiting of [the] mother of al-Ra<u>sh</u>īd (al-Ḥarbī, *K. al-Manā*[sik], Riyāḍ 1389/1969, 305).

Fayd, the midway station of the road, was [the] seat of the *amīr al-ḥa<u>dj</u><u>dj</u>* and the road superinten[dent] (*ʿāmil al-ṭarīḳ* or *wālī al ṭarīḳ*) [see further, FA[YD] below] and was provided with fortifications (*ḥu*[*ṣūn*]) and markets. The main route of the Darb Zuba[yda] had 54 recognised stations (*manāzil*). Stopping pl[aces] for the evening meal were known as *mutaʿa<u>sh</u><u>sh</u>ā*.

There is no archaeological evidence for the us[e of] the Darb Zubayda route before the Umayyad per[iod,] but it must have been in use at least from the t[ime] of the foundation of Kūfa in the reign of ʿUma[r.] Al-Ḥarbī (*al-Manāsik*, 309) states that ʿU<u>th</u>[mān] had wells dug at Fayd, and Ṭabarī mentions [that] among the places at which ʿAlī stopped on his [way] from Medina to Kūfa in 36/656 were al-Raba[<u>dh</u>a,] Fayd and al-<u>Th</u>aʿlabiyya. Similarly, Ḥusayn b. [ʿAlī] stopped at *inter alia* al-Ḥā<u>dj</u>ir, Zarūd, Zubāla [and] al-ʿAḳaba. These are all major stations of the D[arb] Zubayda.

The ʿIrāḳ-Mecca road was a leading concern of [the] ʿAbbāsid caliphs, to the extent that as a w[ell-]maintained, reliable highway it may be regarde[d as] an ʿAbbāsid foundation. Al-Saffāḥ set up mileste[ones] and established fire-beacons (*manār*) along the wh[ole] route from Kūfa to Mecca (Ṭabarī, iii, 81; Ibn [al-]Athīr, Cairo edn., iv, 344), and he also constru[cted] forts (*ḳuṣūr*) along the northern section from [al-]Ḳādisiyya to Zubāla. Al-Manṣūr provided the r[oad] with hostels, and under this caliph the first r[oad] superintendent was appointed. The names of

21 of these superintendents have been preserved. ʿahdī enlarged the forts, constructed water tanks, wells and renewed the milestones. It was during eign that Yaḳṭīn b. Mūsā, the most outstanding e road superintendents, was appointed (161/777). incumbency lasted ten years, during which time pilgrim road was noted for its convenience, ort and safety (Ibn Kathīr, *al-Bidāya wa 'l-ya*, Beirut and Riyāḍ 1966, x, 133).
-Rashīd constructed cisterns, sunk wells and forts along the road, but he was outshone in e works by his wife Zubayda, whose contribution entioned in laudatory terms by many mediaeval ers. Al-Ḥarbī refers to at least eleven places h were provided with water facilities and rest-es or fortifications at her instigation, and states a cistern of a circular type (*birka mudawwara*) known as a "Zubaydiyya" (*al-Manāsik*, 288). h of Zubayda's work was devoted to the smaller ons at intermediate points between the larger ping places, which suggests that her objective to minister to the needs of poorer pilgrims who to make their long journey on foot. For the eep of the water installations in Mecca she left owments with a yield of 30,000 *dīnārs* per annum, it is probable that she provided funds for the eep of the road itself in the same way. It may be d that the mediaeval writers record the names of y wealthy individuals, both men and women, made the upkeep of the road the object of their factions.
mong the later caliphs, al-Wāthiḳ, al-Mutawakkil al-Muḳtadir were particularly active in main-ing and improving the road. Evidence of the tribution of al-Muḳtadir is provided by a Kūfic ription on stone, dated 304/917-17, which refers mprovements being carried out under the super-on of ʿAlī b. ʿĪsā [*q.v.*].
rom the 3rd/8th century, the security of the road increasingly disturbed by tribal raids, beginning that of the Banū Sulaym in 230/844. In 294/906 irred the first of many attacks on pilgrim traffic the Ḳarmaṭīs [*q.v.*], and these were to continue over thirty years. The last pilgrim caravan nised under an ʿAbbāsid caliph was that of 641/ 3, when al-Mustaʿṣim's mother performed the rimage, taking with her 120,000 camels (al-rawālī, *K. al-Iʿlām bi-aʿlām bayt Allāh al-Ḥarām*, Wüstenfeld, in *Die Chroniken der Stadt Mekka*, Leipzig 1857, 178).
fter the fall of Baghdād in 656/1258, pilgrim fic was often diverted through Damascus, but the b Zubayda continued to be used intermittently ater centuries, the frequency of traffic depending ely upon the presence or otherwise of a stable ninistration in Baghdād. The use of the road in the 1 century is attested by European travellers such ady Anne Blunt, Huber and Musil.
he coming of motor transport in the 20th century led to the final abandonment of the Darb ayda, although its cleared track is still everywhere ble, as are many of the waymarks (*aʿlām*), which ally consist of cairns of stones of over 2 m. in ht. Two undamaged milestones from the ʿAbbāsid iod have survived, and are now preserved in the āḳ Museum of Antiquities. One of these uses the em of the post-stage (*barīd* [*q.v.*]), the other that niles. Most of the water facilities of the road can be identified, even though many of these are ded up; they include square, rectangular and ular tanks, some of which are connected with ling tanks and flood diversion walls. Many of the wells are still in use by local tribesmen. The foundations of rest-houses and forts may still be seen at many points along the road, and in several cases (e.g. Ḳaṣr Zubāla, Ḥiṣn Fayd and al-ʿAḳīḳ) more substantial ruins testify to the high level of workmanship bestowed on the public facilities of the road.

Bibliography: see, in addition to the works mentioned in the text: Ibn Khurradādhbih, 125-8 131-2; Ibn Rusta, 174-80; al-Yaʿḳūbī, *Mushākalāt al-nās li-zamānihim*, ed. W. Millward, Beirut 1962, 24-6; Ibn Djubayr, *Riḥla*, ed. de Goeje, Leiden 1907, 203-13; ʿArīb al-Ḳurṭubī, *Ṣilat Taʾrīkh al-Ṭabarī*, Leiden 1897, 54, 59, 123-4, 130-1; Lady Anne Blunt, *A pilgrimage to Nejd*, repr. 1969, 32, 64, 57-8, 70-1, 84; C. Huber, *Voyage dans l'Arabie Centrale, Hamâd, Šammar, Qaçîm, Hedjâz*, in *Bull. Soc. Géographie*, VIIe série (1885) No. 6, 104-48, A. Musil, *Northern Neğd*, New York 1928, 205-36 and *passim*; N. Abbott, *Two Queens of Baghdad*, Chicago 1946, 238-9, 245-6, 250, 258-9; Saad A. al-Rāshid, *A critical study of the Pilgrim Road between Kufa and Mecca* (*Darb Zubaydah*), *with the aid of fieldwork*, Leeds Ph.D. thesis, unpublished (includes plans and illustrations).

(SAAD A. AL-RASHID and M. J. L. YOUNG)

ḌARĪBA (1)—(6): See Vol. II, 142-58.

(7)—Indonesia. The classical Malay chronicles are not very eloquent about matters of taxes and tolls, and the collections of *undang-undang*, or laws, are more concerned with court rituals than with legal or fiscal questions. More materials are available for the tax regulations under the Dutch administration. Thus F. de Haan's eminent work on *Priangan. De Preanger Regentschappen onder het Nederlandsch Bestuur tot 1811*, 4 vols., Batavia-The Hague 1911 ff., contains a lot of valuable information. But with regard to the Islamic kingdoms and sultanates in the archipelago which flourished in the 16th and 17th centuries, similar detailed studies, although probably less voluminous, are still a desideratum. In this article, the official orthography for Malay and Indonesian is used, except in quotations and the more generally known term of *shahbandar* (not: *syahbandar*).

The rise of the Islamic kingdoms and sultanates developed in two different settings: there are (a) the maritime centres, starting with Pasai (1202) and Malakka (1403), later being continued by Aceh (early 16th century), Demak (1478-1546), Banten (1525), Ternate (end of 15th century), Tidore (idem), Makassar (1605), Banjarmasin (begin of 16th century) and Pontianak (1771) which based their economics mainly on sea trade, whereas (b) Mataram (1582) retained an outspoken agrarian character, although, in the course of time, it gained suzerainty over a number of important seaports in Java and some oversea provinces on other islands.

(a) For the maritime sultanates, the backbone of their welfare was the harbour, and its administration had to be handled with special care. The most important functionary in the harbour administration was the *shahbandar*, or harbour master. He was usually appointed by the local ruler or sultan and chosen from among the foreign traders who had settled in the port. No salary was given to him. In big harbours, more than one *shahbandar* were sometimes active. Thus Malakka is reported to have had four of them at the same time during the period of its florescence before the Portuguese conquest (1511). The same holds true for Banda Aceh Darussalam during the reign of Iskandar Muda (1607-36). In such a case, each *shahbandar* was responsible for certain national groups, including the one from which he originated himself. In Malakka, one *shahbandar* had to take care of the Gujarati traders, another one looked after the other "western" traders from India, Persia, Arabia, Pegu (Burma) and North Sumatra, a third one dealt with those originating "east" of Malakka like Palembang, Java, the Moluccas or the Philippine islands, and the fourth one was responsible for the Chinese.

The *shahbandar* had to supervise the merchandise, take care of its transport and storage, inspect the markets and guarantee the security of the ships and the well-being of their crew, passengers, and tradesmen. When a ship entered the harbour, he had at once to inspect it and estimate the value of the goods. Based on his estimation, tolls were fixed and those objects chosen which had to be presented as gifts to the sultan or ruler and other high officials. The owner of the chosen gift, however, had to give his consent. Otherwise, according to the *Navigation and commercial law of Amanna Gappa* (Codex 130, chapter xxxv, see below), this gift would have a personal character and the captain had to pay for it. The collected tolls had to be handed over by the *shahbandar* to the *tumenggung* who headed the civil administration of the whole city, including the harbour.

The import tax which was demanded in Malakka was not the same for all traders. Those originating "from above the wind", i.e. the West, had to pay 6% of the value of their merchandise. Only food supplies from Siam, Pegu (Burma), the western coast of the Malay peninsula and northern Sumatra were exempted.

Besides this import tax, 1 to 2% of the value had to be presented to the ruler, the *bendahara* (treasurer), and the *tumenggung*. After the *shahbandar* had reached agreement with the captain and the traders, he was to bring his gifts to their destinates. Tomé Pires observed that the Gujarati traders in particular, who were sailing with considerably sized vessels, used another procedure to pay their taxes. They asked a delegation of ten traders to re-estimate the whole merchandise loaded on their boat, take 6% of its total value and present it directly to the *tumenggung*. Thus all duties were paid at once, including the different kinds of gifts for the ruler and his officials. On the other side, the *shahbandar* responsible for the Chinese, Siamese and the people from Liu Kiu, on his turn, sometimes freed his clients from all kinds of taxes, but then he expected an appropriate "gift", choosing himself those goods he thought to be suitable.

If a trader wanted to settle at Malakka, he had to pay 3% as taxes, and in addition to this another 6% as royal taxes. For Malays, however, this latter sum was reduced to 3% only (Tjandrasasmita, 74 ff.).

Other regulations were valid for tradesmen originating from lands "below the wind", i.e. in the East. Formerly, they seem to have been free from any kind of taxes. It was just expected that their gifts to the ruler and high officials should be appropriate and this could mean at least as high as the official taxes and tolls for the traders from the West. Later on, they also had to pay 5% for their goods, except again for food supplies.

In Banda Aceh, the *shahbandars* together with their secretaries (*keureukön*, Malay: *karkun*) and other personnel were responsible to the *Balai Furdah*. This was a special office for levying the harbour dues, linked to the *Bayt al-Māl* (Z. Ahmad, 92), which was headed by the Sri Maharaja Lela and the *penghulu kawal*, or supervisor of the guard. These officials,
too, were not real employees of the sultan, bu
was expected that they should gain their living f
the gifts the merchants had to deliver.

In relation to sea trade, the following kind
tolls and taxes (*adat wasé*) were known in Aceh:
hadia langgar: a gift for the permission to cast
anchor; the *adat lhôk*, for those ships anchorin
the harbour; the *adat memohon kunci*, to "ask
the key", i.e. to get permission for disembarkn
after the other taxes have been paid; the
mengawal, a donation for those Acehnese who gua
the ship during its stay in the harbour; the
ḥakk al-ḳalam, a kind of registration fee; the
kuala, demanded by the *shahbandar* for disembarl
or loading certain goods, for preserving the w
supply for departing ships, and help for t
stranded; the *adat cap*, to be paid with goods o
money to get the seal or permission of the sultan
sailing; the *adat kain*, a roll of textiles to be preser
by the Indian and European merchants when get
the *adat cap*; the *adat kain yang ke dalam*, i.e. tex
destined for the court; etc. (Tjandrasasmita, 77
Hoesin, 116 f.).

From the time of Iskandar Muda, every merch
had to pay an additional tax, the *usur* (A. ʿ*us*
for the sultan. Differences between the taxes to
paid by Muslim and Christian merchants are m
tioned but not explained.

Of equally high importance for the income of
ruler and his functionaries was the market. Here,
hariya was in charge of securing the payment
number of duties claimed by the *adat*; the *adat har*
a rent to be paid by merchants who kept their go
in a storehouse which had to be prepared by
hariya; the *adat kamsen*, to be taken from mercha
as an insurance against robbery; the *adat tandi*, a
for the clerk weighing the goods in the market;
the *adat peukan*, demanded from people going to
market.

All these taxes and tolls mentioned above had
be transferred either by the *shahbandar* or
hariya to the *ulëè balang*, or district chief, who
the same time served as the local military comm
der. He distributed part of this money to some
his civil servants, whilst another part had to
presented annually to the court. Like the *shahban*
hariya, or other senior officials, the *ulëè balangs*
not receive a salary.

For the people living in the villages, some ot
kinds of taxes were known. Those farmers w
received irrigation waters for their rice fields had
pay the *adat blang*, or *adat buèt umong*. Rent rates
be paid by tenants ranged from 50% to 20% of
yields and depended on the situation of the land
someone had a cause to be settled, he had first
pay the *adat peutoè* which permitted him to br
his cause to the court (*hak ganceng*). The judge (*k*
ḳāḍī) and other elders sitting in the court sess
were entitled to receive the *adat tuha*.

Besides paying their taxes either in kind or mon
the villagers had also to give their services volunta
to the *ulëè balang* or the *keutjhik*, or village ch
e.g. in preparing their rice fields. This had to be d
in *gotong royong* (cooperation) by the villag
without receiving any compensation but be
provided with food.

Taxes which were not under the competence
the *ulëè balang* were those levied on forest produ
(*adat glé*) and the *adat peutuha* for bringing the pep
to the market; trade with pepper was a ma
concern of the sultan himself.

Complementary to these duties, which were m

s based on customary law (*adat*), the obligations sed by the *sharīʿa* according to the Shāfiʿi *hab* had also to be fullfilled. Special attention given to the handing-over of *zakāt*. If someone reluctant, he had to be admonished either by *keutjhik* or the *teungku meunasah* who was fically in charge of supervising those aspects of ge life related to the *sharīʿa*.

the port of Banten, West-Java, which was, es Jambi, one of the main trading places for er, taxes were usually fixed incidentally, varying ship to ship. Chinese traders usually had to 5% of the value of their goods, but the Dutch in particular often were faced with discrimi- ry high fees, which *inter alia*, stimulated them rengthen their own new port of Batavia (1619). les the import taxes, a fee for anchoring had to aid. Two-thirds of the whole sum were to be ered to the sultan, the rest was for the *shah- ar*. Export taxes for local products, including er, were lower than those for products of foreign n.

ice the rise of the first Muslim kingdom in Java its centre in Demak (1478/1546), the seaport of ra became the dominant trading centre of the d. It was able to maintain this position under rule of the first rulers of Mataram, who were lly not too much interested in sea trade, con- rating their main interests in the agrarian ior of Java. Under Sultan Agung (1613-46) and *usuhunan* Amengku Rat I (1646-77), Japara was ome time the capital of Mataram's East-coast ince, headed by the *wedana bupati*, with the *tumenggung*. The city itself, as well as the other , was governed by the *kyai lurah*. It is not whether it was to him or to the *wedana bupati* the *shahbandar* and another official met by a h visitor in 1631, the *petiat-tanda* "who super- all fiscal offices and dominated all the river hs", were responsible. At all events, it was in nd the main task of the *wedana bupati* to collect ıstom duties from the ports, all taxes from his al province and those overseas tributaries *ah upeti*) which were directly under the super- n of one of the *bupatis* in his province, e.g. nbang which was under Demak, Sukadana r Semarang, or Jambi which was directly under ra. Part of the collected deliveries, especially from the export trade of rice, which was the opoly of the *susuhunan* himself and until 1657 allowed to be traded only in Japara, had to be sferred to the court.

the later years of Amengku Rat's I reign, and ially after the introduction of his policy of alisation, the higher provincial functionaries displaced, and the ports directly ruled by the *andars* as *quasi*-governors. They were now tly responsible to the court, i.e. to the *wedana g* as the royal treasurer and storekeeper and had end much of their time there, which made it r to control them. Simultaneously, Amengku Rat roduced a new form of taxation, i.e. money tion, in exchange for the formerly-used system xation which was based on natural and craft ucts. To increase the income of the court, he farmed out the provincial revenues out to the als and then demanded a specific annual sum e delivered. In the course of time, the whole gn trade, not only the export of rice, became te monopoly (Schrieke, i, 184 f.).

ice the days of the Hindu empire of Majapahit, olls to be paid in the central and east Javanese ports on the north coast had been very low, and were sometimes completely unknown, as in Gresik before 1612. Only Tuban formed an exception, and this was severely criticised by the Chinese. Moreover, certain nationalities could be exempted from fees, like the Dutch in Japara under Sultan Agung, or the Chinese, the latter certainly profiting from the fact that a number of *shahbandars* in the north Javanese port were of Chinese descent. But again, gifts were expected to be forwarded by them.

Another commercial centre attractive for merchants from the East as well as from the West was Makassar (Ujung Pandang), which since pre-Islamic days was known too for its free and open attitudes towards trade and its small demands of tolls. Although not directly dealing with questions of taxes and tolls, the *Navigation and commercial law of Amanna Gappa*, a Buginese codex compiled around 1676 and edited by Ph. O. L. Tobing in 1962 ([2]1977), gives interesting hints about the financial obligations and rewards of the community living together for some time on the same ship. During the journey, the traders are not considered as passengers, but are divided into three or four classes of crew members with special tasks and duties given to each of them. Those categorised as "regular crew" may leave the vessel only after having bailed the water from the vessel and paid a fee for "descending" from the ship. The "casual crew" members, however, are free to leave the vessel whereever they want, without paying anything. For each class, the volume of merchandise as well as the part of the hold in which to put their goods are fixed. The freight rate is determined by the distance between the home port and the port of destination, for which detailed data are given.

The sum collected with the freight rates determines the income of the owner of the ship and its senior crew, i.e. the captain, the coxswain, and the *jurubatu* who has to take soundings and cast the anchor: if neither the captain nor the other two are friends of the owner of the ship, than the proceeds have to be divided into two equal parts, one for the owner and one for the other three. If one of them is a friend of the owner, than two-thirds are for the owner.

A number of regulations deals with the sharing of profit or loss between the dealer and the owner of the goods. According to the principle of *bagi laba*, profit or loss have to be divided equally between both of them, if, in case of a loss, this is not due to negligence on part of the dealer. Otherwise, he has to compensate for it. Another principle states that the family of the dealer, if the goods get damaged because of his negligence, cannot be claimed to participate in compensating for the loss (ch. vii). The principle of *bagi laba* knows, however, some modifications. When the dealer has not yet returned and the owner has good reason to assume to that his partner is dead, he may claim a certain sum from his partner's family, but not more than half of the original capital. After that, he loses any right on the goods, even if his partner eventually reappears and has been succesful. If the dealer in fact has died and suffered a loss by his own fault, then his family has to compensate in full (ch. xii).

Debts, too, demand special regulations. If a debtor has sold his properties but cannot yet repay his debts, he has for some time to serve as a slave with his creditor until his debts are extinguished. After that, no claim may be made, even if the debtor becomes a wealthy man (ch. xiv).

If a passenger-tradesman dies on the way and his

heirs cannot be found, his goods have to be turned over to the captain who may trade with them and enjoy the profits. Returning to the domicile of the deceased, however, his property must be handed over to his family, either in money or in kind (ch. xvi).

All these regulations are very similar to those relating to land tenure in the village (*desa*), and as a matter of fact, during its voyage the vessel is considered as a microcosmos in the same way as is the *desa* ashore, representing the cosmic order which has to be preserved through harmonious relationships among its inhabitants. The "owner" of this microcosmos stays outside of it, but he is represented by his deputy and his deputy's helpers. This deputy does not receive a salary, but has to live, like his helpers, from what he collects as rent, or taxes.

(b) Mataram, as the most powerful Islamic kingdom in Indonesia, did not base its economics on sea trade but on the products of its agrarian interior in Java. It continued the main spiritual and administrative traditions of the last Hindu empire of Majapahit which was destroyed by Demak in 1478. The student of its taxation system has to note with regret, however, that the late B. Schrieke did not live to implement his plan of writing a history of Javanese taxation (Schrieke, i, 26). The data collected and evaluated in such a study would not only have been helpful in obtaining a clearer picture about the fiscal and economic development of the Javanese kingdoms, and especially of Mataram, but might also have provided a well-documented basis for studies on the religio-cultural currents in Javanese society which continually gave rise to millenarian movements among the peasantry, caused by the deteriorating economic situation which again was mainly the result of the burden of taxes levied on the farmers.

Basically, the structure of the village (*desa*) and the kingdom were not much different. The village chief, and similarly the ruler in the greater context, were considered as the representatives of the deity and thus entitled to consider the land of the *desa*, or the main lands of the kingdom, as their own property, which they then rented out to the people. In some village societies, this conviction was modified: not the village chief himself, but the village community, owned the land, and the council of the elders had to decide who of the villagers might farm a certain piece of land. Thus in Kediri, East Java, all the land was named *haqullah*, whereas in Banten and Krawang, West Java, only uncultivated land was considered as *haqullah*, whereas cultivated land became *haquladam* (Kartohadikoesoemo, 238). If someone died or moved to another *desa* without leaving an heir behind, his land fell back under the authority of the *desa*. In some places, land was redistributed after a certain time cycle. Someone who wanted to sell "his" land had to notify the village government and pay the *uang paseksèn*.

The communal understanding of land ownership is evident in the Law Codex of Majapahit, which was, on the whole, still used in Mataram. Para. 259 states that anyone who had asked for permission to farm a rice field but afterwards leaves it uncultivated, has to restore by other means the value of the rice he might have yielded. In para. 261, anyone who leaves an already cultivated rice field on its own, with the result that the crop get spoiled or is eaten by animals, is categorised as a thief, and that could mean capital punishment (Slametmuljana, 37, 165).

The relationship between the village and the central authority was maintained mainly via the taxes and labour obligations. As the land was n in fact considered as being the property of the far he had to pay the *upeti*, which means tribute. tax might rise to 50% of the harvest, but it c always be changed, according to the general situa Besides this, a capitation tax, housing taxes, for different kinds of offences against the laws, were known. Special taxes had to be delivere occasions like child birth, wedding ceremonies services for a deceased person. These could someti if they coincided with warfare or other disas bring the villagers to the edge of ruin (cf. the re by C. van Maseyck, quoted by Schrieke, ii, The special war tax which Sultan Agung ra mainly among the foreigners during his mili operations in East Java (Surabaya) in 162 recorded as follows: all married Chinese had to $22^{1}/_{2}$ reals, unmarried Chinese 18 reals, ma Javanese in the coastal regions who had been subjects for many years $4^{1}/_{2}$ reals, unmarried young men $4^{1}/_{2}$ reals, all recently-acquired sl from Madura and Surabaya $^{1}/_{4}$ real. This tax repeated in the following year (Schrieke, ii, 14 At times it was compulsory to purchase some k of spices, rattan, and cotton, and above all rice, trade with which was, as already mentioned, a monopoly under Amengku Rat. I. A major occa to deliver the collected taxes at the court was *ʿĪd al-Fiṭr*.

Labour obligations due to the ruler included building of the *kraton* (palace), important stree other state projects, and, in times of war, help army mainly as carriers. The village chief and c district potentates, too, were entitled to sum the villagers for forced labour. Thus the princip *gotong royong*, or cooperativeness, became more more abused. Eventually, a *desa* could also exempted from taxes but instead it was cha with the maintenance of a sanctuary.

Another source of income for the district r were the toll gates on streets and rivers wh especially since the middle of the 18th century v their number increased enormously, did great da ge to inland trade, and therefore time and a contributed to the rise of social unrest.

Upeti, or tribute, had also to be delivered b vassal or a dependency as a sign of loyalty, or b ally as reward for any kind of help received be It could be delivered in kind or money and c also comprise beautiful girls, rare animals or pl Another way of fulfilling the duties towards ruler was to send man-power. The annual tri imposed, e.g., on Palembang in 1668, was one dollar *per capita* (Daghregister 1668-9, quotec Schrieke, ii, 227).

Bibliography: C. Snouck Hurgronje, *De jehers*, Leiden 1893-4; J. D. van Leur, *The I nesian trade and society. Essay in Asian social economic history*, The Hague-Bandung 1 B. Schrieke, *Indonesian sociological studies*, Hague-Bandung 1955-7; W. P. Groeneveldt, *torical notes on Indonesia and Malaya com from Chinese sources*, Jakarta 1960; M. A. P. link-Roeloefsz, *Asian trade and European infl in the Indonesian archipelago between 1500 about 1630*, The Hague 1962; G. W. J. Dre *Atjehse douanetarieven in het begin van de v eeuw*, in *BKI*, cxix (1963), 406-11; Soeta Kartohadikoesoemo, *Desa*, Bandung² 1965; tono Kartodirdjo, *The Peasants' revolt of Ba in 1888*, The Hague 1966; idem, *Protest m ments in rural Java*, Oxford-Singapore 1973; i alii (eds.), *Sejarah Nasional Indonesia*, iii. *man Pertumbuhan dan Perkembangan kerajaan-ajaan Islam di Indonesia*, ed. Uka Tjandrasas-ta. Jakarta 1975; D. Lombard, *Le sultanat Atjeh au temps d'Iskandar Muda, 1607-1636*, ris 1967; Slametmuljana, *Perundang-undangan ajapahit*, Jakarta 1967; Ailsa Zainu'ddin, *A rt history of Indonesia*, Melbourne 1968; ehammad Hoesin, *Adat Atjeh*, Aceh 1970; A. Sutjipto, *Some remarks on the harbour city Japara in the seventeenth century*, in *Procs. of Fifth Conference of Asian History*, Manila 1971; karia Ahmad, *Sekitar Keradjaan Atjeh dalam un 1520-1675*, Medan 1972; Philip O. L. Tobing, *ıkum pelayaran dan perdagangan Amanna Gappa he navigation and commercial law of Amanna ppa)*, with an abbreviated English version, ung Pandang ²1977; Onghokham, *Penelitian mber-sumber gerakan mesianis*, in *Prisma* (Ja-rta), vi (1977, no. 1), 10-23.

(O. Schumann)

RYĀ KHĀN NOHĀNĪ, local governor hār under the Dihlī sultans. His original name t known, Masnad-i ʿĀlī Daryā Khān being his rific title. He was the third son of Masnad-i Mubārak Khān Nohānī, Sultan Bahlūl's *muḳtaʿ* vernor of the province of Karā and Manīkpūr. ā Khān Nohānī attached himself to Prince m Khān (later Sultan Sikandar Shāh) during eign of Sultan Bahlūl Lōdī. The first important t of his life was the battle of Ambāla, fought een Prince Niẓām Khān and Tatār Khān Yūsuf l, the rebel *muḳtaʿ* of the Pandjāb in 890/1485. 95/1490 he again fought on the side of Sultan ıdar Shāh against his own father, who had d the camp of the rival prince, Bārbak Shāh, in 901/1496, Sikandar Lōdī appointed him as *aʿ* of Bihār in reward for his services.

Bihār, Daryā Khān found that the Afghāns' ıre of the eastern territories was easier than ning control over them, for the rule of the over-wn Sharḳī dynasty [*q.v.*] had struck deep roots, the Muslim *ʿulamāʾ*, the Hindu *zamīndārs* and ommon people had been deeply attached to the ḳī house for generations. But he gradually eded in consolidating Afghān rule there, taking ures to win over local support. He extended rous patronage to the scholars and made generous grants to the Ṣūfīs and *Sayyids*; and the old ational institutions were maintained, while s and mosques were repaired. Thus the town of r grew into a metropolitan centre under his rnorship.

ring the reign of Sultan Ibrāhīm Lōdī, certain ical events caused an estrangement between him the sultan, although he had fought against his son-in-law, Islām Khān Sarwānī, the rebel in in 925/1519. In 930/1524, Nāṣir Khān Nohānī, elder brother of Daryā Khān, rebelled against ultan in the Ghāzīpur *sarkar*, and his flight to r turned the sultan against Daryā Khān. In an npt to save himself, Daryā Khān himself rebelled st the sultan and strengthened the defences of r fort; but soon afterwards he died, leaving his Bahār Khān, as his successor. His son and lson ruled over Bihār till the year 936/1530, Shēr Khān Sūr supplanted the Nohānī rule by wn.

Bibliography: ʿAbd Allāh, *Taʾrīkh-i Dāwūdī*, Shaykh ʿAbd al-Rashīd, Aligarh 1969; ʿAbd Ḳādir Badāʾūnī, *Muntakhab al-tawārīkh*, Bibl. d., Calcutta 1869; Shaykh Kabīr Batinī, *Afsāna-yi Shāhān-i Hind*, MS British Museum, Niʿmat Allāh Harawī, *Taʾrīkh-i Khān-i Djahānī*, ed. ʿImām al-Dīn, Dacca 1950; Niẓām al-Dīn Aḥmād, *Ṭabaḳāt-i Akbarī*, i, Bibl. Ind., Calcutta 1927; Shaykh Rizḳ Allāh Mushtāḳī, *Wāḳiʿāt-i Mushtāḳī*, British Museum MS. Add. 11, 633; *Epigraphia Indica*, Arabic-Persian Supplement 1965, ed. Z. A. Desai, Dihlī 1966.

(I. H. Siddiqui)

DASHT-I ḲĪPČAḲ, the Ḳīpčaḳ Steppe, was the Islamic name of the territory called Comania by Christian writers: the great plains of what is now Southern Russia and Western Kazakhstan. Both names were given while this region was still dominated by the Ḳīpčaḳ or Comans (the Dasht-i Ḳīpčāḳ is mentioned in the *Dīwān* of Nāṣir-i Khusraw, who died between 465/1072 and 470/1077): they were retained when it passed under the control of the Golden Horde [see batu'ids], who subjected and absorbed the Ḳīpčaḳ whilst adopting their speech in place of their native Mongolian. John de Plano Carpini and William of Rubruck travelled through the Dasht-i Ḳīpčaḳ during the reign of Batu [*q.v.*]. Carpini, who traversed it from end to end, supplied for the first time the modern names of the great rivers he crossed: the Don and the Volga. Rubruck, who entered the steppe via the Crimea, described it as a "vast wilderness" extending in places over thirty days in breadth, in which there was "neither forest, nor hill, nor stone, but only the finest pastur-age". Ibn Baṭṭūṭa's visit to the region occurred during the reign of Özbeg (712-42/1313-41). Like Rubruck he approached it from the south, through the Crimea; from Saray he proceeded in a westerly direction until he reached Byzantine territory. What little we know about social conditions in the Dasht-i Ḳīpčaḳ is derived almost entirely from Rubruck and Ibn Baṭṭūṭa.

Bibliography: W. W. Rockhill, *The journey of William of Rubruck to the eastern part of the world*, London 1900, 8-9, 12-13, 91-94; Ibn Baṭṭūṭa, *Riḥla*, ii, 356 ff., tr. Gibb, ii, 470 ff.; B. Spuler, *Die Goldene Horde*², Wiesbaden 1965, 5-6, 274-80.

(J. A. Boyle)

DATES [see tamr].

DAVID [see dāwūd].

DAWĀT, ink holder, a synonym for *miḥbara*, "inkwell". The term is also used for *miḳlama*, a place for keeping the *ḳalam* or pen, and more generally for *ḳalamdān*, penbox.

Islamic treatises describe the various ways of preparing ink and give different accounts of ink-wells, *miḥbara* or *dawāt*, that were used in their time. The *dawāt* is, according to al-Ḳalḳashandī, "the mother of all writing tools", and "a scribe without an inkpot resembles a man who enters a fight without a weapon". Following traditional religious relationships between the art of writing, meaning the transcribing of the "Word of God", the Ḳurʾān and the tools used for writing, various Islamic writers prohibit the use of inkwells made of precious metals, and call for the omission of human and animal forms in their decoration. However, the 4th/10th century poet al-Kushādjīm already accused the learned men of his time of being proud of their gold-and-silver-decorated inkpots. The religious prohibition of depicting human and animal forms was also disregarded.

The use of glass pots and the preference for the round shape, as suggested by al-Ḳalḳashandī, are documented by some 3rd/9th to 4th/10th century inkpots that have been preserved (Baer, *Inkwell*, n. 4; *The arts of Islam*, Hayward Gallery, 1976, nos. 117-8, with octagonal outer form). A fragmentary cylindrical cast-bronze vessel found at Nī<u>sh</u>āpūr suggests that this type of inkwell was used in Eastern Iran as early as the Sāmānid period.

In the course of the 6th/12th century, particularly during its second half, cylindrical bronze inkwells were produced in different Iranian workshops. They were of comparatively small size, and each was originally covered with a separate lid with a domed centre. Lid and body were generally provided with small loops or handles for fastening the pot to the hand of the scribe, and they were decorated with traced and inlaid silver and copper ornaments. Several signed inkwells from the mid-6th/12th to the early 7th/13th centuries, including some of Khurāsānian workmanship, have been preserved. On two of them the decoration includes a human figure, presumably the owner of the inkwell, proudly presenting a cyclindrical object of the same type as the vessel itself (Toronto, Royal Ontario Museum, ex-Kofler collection, and London, Victoria and Albert Museum). The covers of the Iranian inkwells are surmounted by a lobed dome that rests on a flat cylindrical collar. In the Syrian specimen, a hemispherical dome rests directly on the horizontal rim, and is surmounted by a pear-shaped finial terminating in a round knob. Both traditions blend in an early 7th/13th century inkpot in the Metropolitan Museum of Art (Baer, *Inkwell*). Three West-Iranian, early Ṣafawid inkpots signed by Mīrak Ḥusayn Yazdī point to the continuation of this type in the 10th/16th century. Apart from cylindrical caskets with small glass receptacles for ink and other writing implements, penboxes with a separate compartment for the *ḳalam* were used since early times. The earliest known so far is a bronze *ḳalamdān* dated 542/1148 in the Hermitage which has the shape of a parallelepiped. It is closed and has two openings on opposite ends, one for the ink and the other for the *ḳalam*. More common is the open, originally East-Iranian, wedge-shaped type made in two parts, in which the inner, compartmented box could be entirely removed. These penboxes were probably placed in a belt, and were commonly used in the Ottoman empire.

Rectangular open boxes with a hinged or separate cover are apparently based on wooden models. The earliest known metal penboxes from the middle of the 6th/12th century are round-ended, and these continued to be popular after the Mongol conquest; but in Mamlūk and Ottoman times, the rectangular penbox was more common. It was imitated by the Chinese in blue and white porcelain for export to the Near East and by Iznik potters working in the early 10th/16th century. A good example of its kind, decorated with a pseudo-Kūfic inscription and floral scrolls in pale blue on white, is kept in the Godman collection in England.

Dawāt and *ḳalamdān* are depicted in miniatures as early as the late 6th/12th century (*K. al-Diryāḳ*, Bishr Farès, *Le livre de la thériaque*, Cairo 1953, Pls. VII-IX). A round-ended penbox is shown in the *Djāmiʿ al-tawārīkh* copy in the University Library on Edinburgh (*Survey*, Pl. 827 A), while a small inkpot attached to a penbox of the easily portable type is painted by Behzad in a mosque scene of the *Bustān* of Saʿdī in Cairo, dated 893/1488 (*Prop. Kunstgeschichte*, no. 333).

Bibliography: General information based on literary sources can be found in A. Grohmann, *Arabische Paläographie*, i, Vienna 1967, 117-27. There is no comprehensive study of the *dawāt* in visual art. For a short survey, see E. Kül *Islamische Schriftkunst*, Berlin-Leipzig 1942, 8 One type of inkwell has been studied by E. B *An Islamic inkwell in the Metropolitan Mus of Art*, in R. Ettinghausen (ed.), *Islamic ar the Metropolitan Museum of Art*, New York 1 199-211. The writer is preparing a comprehen study of the *dawāt* in Islamic art and civilisat Representations of the different types are inclu in general books on Islamic and Persian art in exhibition catalogues: A. U. Pope (ed.), *survey of Persian art*, London-New York, 1 64; J. Sourdel-Thomine and B. Spuler (e *Die Kunst des Islam*, Propyläen Kunstgeschic Bd. 4, Berlin 1973; *The arts of Islam*, Hayw Gallery, 8 April - 4 July 1976, The Arts Cou of Great Britain, 1976; A. S. Melikian-Chirv *Le bronze Iranien*, Musée des Arts Decora Paris 1973. Signed metal inkwells and penb are listed in L. A. Mayer, *Islamic metalwor and their works*, Geneva 1959 (incomplete).

(E. Bae

DĀWIYYA and **ISBITĀRIYYA**, the Ar name for the Knights Templars and the Knig Hospitallers respectively. With the partial very late exception of the Teutonic Knights below), the other military orders established Syria during the Crusades went unnoticed (o least unnamed) by Arabic writers. Since it is possible to give here even a summary histor these extraordinary organisations, which in case belong more to European than to Isla civilisation, we shall restrict our consideratior two questions: (1) when and by what channels the terms *dāwiyya* and *isbitāriyya* enter the Ar language; and (2) how fully did Muslim histor understand and attempt to describe the orders

Isbitāriyya and its common variant *isbitār* simply arabised forms of Latin *hospitalis*, "lodg place for wayfarers", perhaps influenced by *hos larius*, "hospitaller" in a literal sense. (For the L terms, see J. Riley-Smith, *Knights of St. John*, n. 5 *et passim*.) Two other variants, *istibār istibāriyya*, which seem especially characteristi later writers beginning with Ibn Wāṣil [*q.v.*], pla represent the assimilation of a foreign word to Arabic *maṣdar* pattern *iftiʿāl*. Though the etymo is clear, we do not however know precisely when Muslims of Syria first became aware of the Hosp lers as a distinct group in the Frankish army. first recorded mention of them is in Ibn al-Ḳal (*Dhayl taʾrīkh Dimashḳ*, ed. Amedroz, 339), simply lists them without further explanatio members of a Frankish force overwhelmed Bāniyās in 552/1157. We must therefore assume by this date the term *isbitāriyya* was in com use among Syrian Muslims. It had doubtless bec current only recently, since the Hospitallers not play a major military role before 530/1136, w they were assigned the stronghold of Bayt Dj (Bethgibelin) by King Fulk, while the real f dations of their power were laid only in 539/ with the cession to them of Ḥiṣn al-Akrād [(Crac des Chevaliers) by Count Raymond I Tripoli.

In the passage just mentioned, Ibn al-Ḳal also names the Templars as members of the defe Frankish detachment; as with the Hospitallers, is the oldest Arabic reference to the Templars, again the term used for them, *Dāwiyya*, is left explained. Hence we must assume that by 1157 the Templars also were commonly perce

ig. 1. Inkwell with domed cover. Bronze, engraved and decorated with interlacings, the signs of the
odiac and blessings. East Iran, probably late 6th/12th century. Philadelphia Museum of Art, no. 30.1.
45 A & B. Photograph E. Baer.

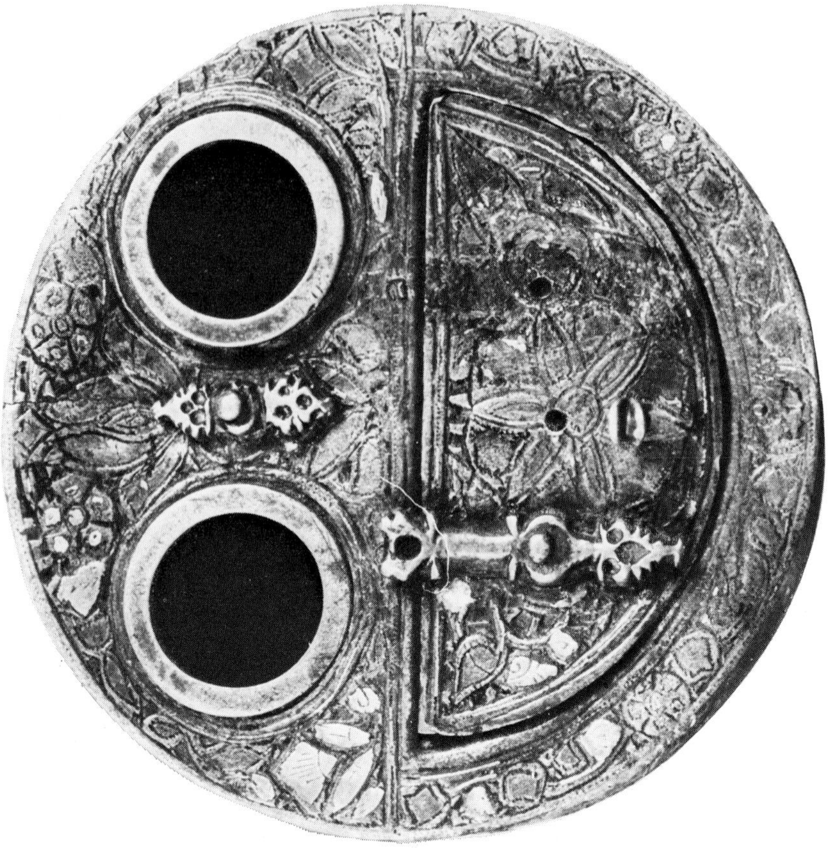

Fig. 2 a and b. Cylindrical inkpot with receptacles for ink and writing implements. Bronze, incised and inlaid

Fig. 3. Rectangular penbox. Brass, incised and inlaid with silver and copper. Decorated with the signs of the zodiac. 7th/13th century. London, British Museum, given by A. W. Franks, 1884. Photograph courtesy L. A. Mayer Memorial, Jerusalem.

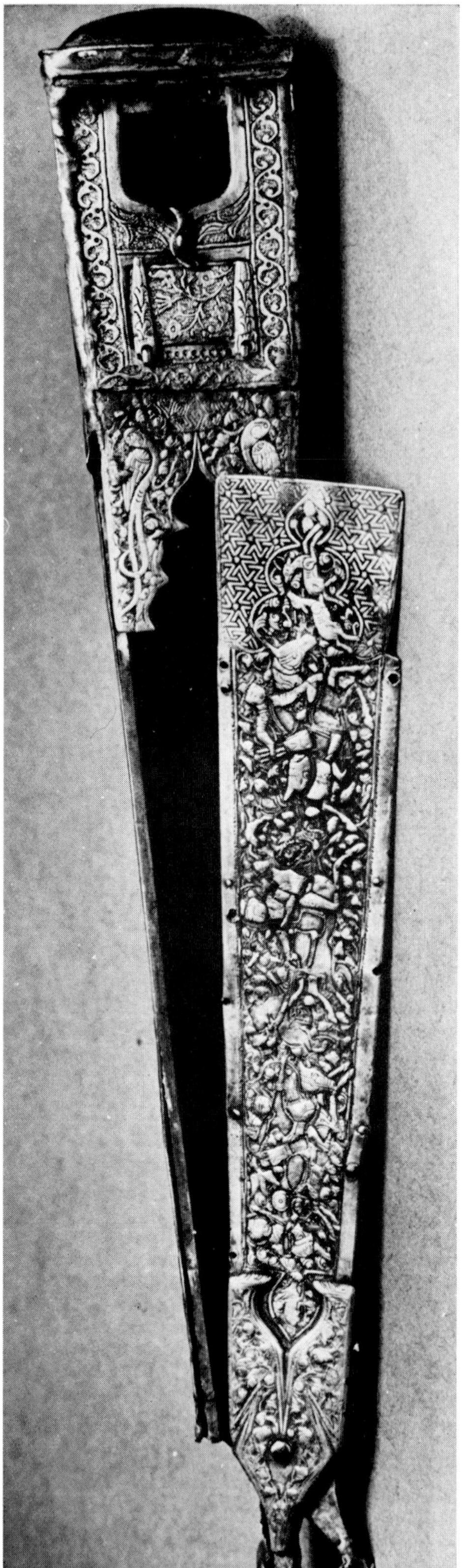

Fig. 4. Wedge-shaped penbox. Brass, incised and inlaid with silver and gold. Perhaps north-west Iran, mid-7th/13th century. Baltimore, Walters Art Gallery, no. 54.509. Photograph courtesy L. A. Mayer Memorial, Jerusalem.

Fig. 5. Penbox. Brass, engraved. Syria, 14th/15th century

familiar and distinct element within the Frankish y. Indeed, Usāma b. Munḳidh, writing some e decades after the event, records a visit to the i Mosque in Jerusalem in the years 532/8-1138- it was then partially occupied by the Templars, m he calls "my friends" (*aṣdiḳāʾī*). (*K. al-ār*, ed. Hitti, Princeton 1930, 134-5). At the of Usāma's visit, the Templars had been formally gnised as an order of the Church for only ten s or so (at the Council of Troyes, 1128), and : origins went back only to 1119. As in the case ne Hospitallers, therefore, the Muslims of Syria not slow to become aware of this new element 'rankish society.

n the other hand, the use of the word *Dāwiyya* the Templars raises real problems. For many ons, one cannot accept Hitti's suggestion that *iyya* is a "corruption of a Syriac word for 'poor', original name of the order in Latin being Pauperes militones Christi" (*History of the Arabs*[8], 644 . Rather, it seems best to derive the word from n *dēvōtus*, Old French *devot*, "one who has ed himself to God's service". Phonetically, this nology seems to fit both *dāwiyya* and its variant *viyya* reasonably well. Moreover, though it is that the Templars did not ordinarily call nselves *dēvōtī*, this term accurately characterises : status and outlook, and may well have been way in which they were described to the Muslims ocal informants. (Cf. the descriptions of them Villiam of Tyre, *RHC*, *hist. occ.*, i, 520; *Chronique Iichel le Syrien*, ed. and tr. J. B. Chabot, Paris -1914, iii, 201-3, 207-8).

s to the understanding of the orders displayed he Muslim writers of the 6th/12th and 7th/13th uries, we should not expect any full or accurate riptions, for this would have required an in- t into the corporate nature of Frankish society as the Muslims did not possess (cf. CRUSADES IFRANDJ). The Franks are often perceived and acterised as individuals in the Arabic texts, they are very rarely seen as members of a socio- omic class, nationality, or corporate entity; the rvations of Usāma b. Munḳidh, Ibn Djubayr, Ibn Wāṣil (*Mufarridj*, iv, 248-51) represent the hest limit of Muslim knowledge and concern in period. Nevertheless, it remains curious that Templars and Hospitallers were perceived early as a group apart from other Frankish warriors yet their precise nature was never investigated. hroughout the Saldjūḳ and Zangid periods ces on the orders are extremely rare in the oic texts; it is only in the time of Ṣalāḥ al-Dīn, cially in the years of the reconquest and the d Crusade (583-8/1187-92), that they become y common. This new prominence is certainly in part to the orders' greatly increased military political importance during and after the 1170s, it is equally owed to the writings of ʿImād al- al-Kātib al-Iṣfahānī, which were the chief ce for Ṣalāḥ al-Dīn's reign even for his own temporaries (e.g. Ibn Abī Ṭayyiʾ, Ibn al-Athīr). ād al-Dīn's *al-Fatḥ al-ḳussī* shows him to be er well-informed on the orders and suggests e progress in the Muslims' understanding of n; he knows which castles belong to which, he give an accurate description of their buildings cre and Jerusalem, he seems to have some sense their internal organisation (though he never usses it explicitly). He respects the military ities of both orders, but reserves his fiercest ective for the Templars. One of the ugliest passages in Arabic literature, unique in its gloating and brutality, is surely that which he devotes to Ṣalāḥ al-Dīn's massacre of Templar and Hospitaller prisoners after Ḥiṭṭīn. Ibn al-Athīr uses ʿImād al-Dīn's information to make a point of his own—the orders' boldness and fanaticism make them a standing threat to the Muslims, and sound public policy requires their extermination. Indeed, he sharply criticises Ṣalāḥ al-Dīn on those occasions when he decides to release Templar and Hospitaller prisoners instead of summarily executing them. (Ibn al-Athīr [Beirut reprint, 1966], xi, 531, 538, 558; xii, 22-3).

For the Ayyūbid period after Ṣalāḥ al-Dīn (589-658/1193-1260), there are only scattered reports on the orders, but the language used suggests a rising level of knowledge and sophistication. In a long report on al-Manṣūr Muḥammad of Ḥamāt's campaign against the Hospitallers in 599/1203 (*Mufarridj*, iii, 141-50), Ibn Wāṣil refers to them for the first time as *bayt al-istibār* (*domus hospitalis*), an expression which is henceforth common for both orders and which seems to imply some sense of their corporate nature. Likewise, for the first time they are called *al-ikhwa* (*fratres*), a term suggesting a similar conclusion. Finally, all officers of the orders had previous been named simply *muḳaddam*, whatever their real rank; now, however, Ibn Wāṣil distinguishes two subordinate officers, *muḳaddam al-turkubliyya* (Turcopolier) and *ḳūmiṣ min al-baḥriyya* (perhaps Commander of the Ship; cf. Riley-Smith, *op. cit.*, 329-30). Though Muslim writers never display a systematic knowledge of the orders' internal structure, this passage at least signals increased contact and familiarity. On a different level, there is a remarkable passage in Ibn al-Athīr (xii, 465-6, *anno* 623) which suggests some comprehension of the special tie which bound the Templars and Hospitallers to the Papacy, and which also demonstrates that Muslim authors had access to Christian informants for their information about such things.

The Mamlūk chronicles *per se* seem to add little that is new to the Ayyūbid texts, but they do reproduce a number of treaties between the Mamlūk sultan and various European rulers which reveal a sound assessment of the place of the orders in the Mediterranean balance of power, and whose precise terminology suggests a fairly accurate knowledge of their internal organisation. Thus in a treaty of 686/1287 between al-Manṣūr Ḳalāwūn and the King of Aragon, the orders are identified as potential enemies of Egypt and Aragon equal to the Papacy, to the Genoese and Venetians, and to the Byzantines (Amari, *Biblioteca arabo-sicula*, Leipzig 1857, 345). Again, when Ḳalāwūn dictated the terms of a truce with Acre in 682/1283, he recognised that the royal *bailli* could no longer command the obedience of all the Franks there, and so the chiefs of the orders were included among the signatories to the treaty. Especially striking is the precise and accurate titulature assigned to these men (*ḥaḍrat al-muḳaddam al-djalīl ifrayr* [Templars]; *al-muḳaddam ifrayr* [Hospitallers]; *al-marshān al-adjall ifrayr . . . nāʾib muḳaddam* [Teutonic Knights]). It is in this document that the Teutonic Knights appear to be identified for the first time as a separate entity, under the name *bayt al-isbitār al-amn* (the last word doubtless being an error for *al-almān*) (Maḳrīzī, *Sulūk*, i, 985-6, 995). Whatever knowledge of the orders may be ascribed to the historians and chancery of the early Mamlūk period, however, it would develop no further. For with the fall of Acre (690/

1291), the dissolution of the Templars (1307-14), and the transfer of Hospitaller headquarters to Rhodes (1306-10), Syro-Egyptian Muslims no longer had any real reason to take note of the orders. Henceforth, only the Hospitallers of Rhodes were to play any part in Islamic history, sc. that of the Ottomans.

Bibliography: The literature and published documentation on the orders is of course overwhelming, but the bulk of it refers to their European branches rather than to Syria. (This is especially true of the Templars, whose central archives were destroyed when the order was abolished in the years 1307-14.) The best general history of the orders remains H. Prutz, *Die geistlichen Ritterorden*, Berlin 1908. For the Hospitallers in Syria, we have an excellent recent study by J. Riley-Smith, *The Knights of St. John in Jerusalem and Cyprus, c. 1050-1310*, London 1967. For the Hospitallers in Rhodes (1306-1523), the most recent overviews are the chapters by A. Luttrell and E. Rossi in K. M. Setton, ed., *A history of the Crusades*, Madison, Wisc. 1975, iii, 278-339. Due to the lack of archival materials, there is no serious modern work which focuses on the Templars in Syria; however, A. J. Forey, *The Templars in the Corona de Aragón*, London 1973, is a detailed study of their role in Spain during the *reconquista*. The political and diplomatic role of the orders in the East is of course presented in the standard works on the Crusades. Archival materials can be approached through two major collections: *Cartulaire général de l'ordre des Hospitaliers de St-Jean de Jérusalem* (1100-1310), ed. J. Delaville le Roulx, Paris 1894-1906; and *Cartulaire général de l'ordre du Temple*, 1119?-1150, ed. Marquis d'Albon, Paris 1913. An extremely rich source for the Hospital's Rhodian period is the *Catalogue of the records of the Order of St. John of Jerusalem in the Royal Malta Library*, ed. J. Mizzi, V. Borg, A. Z. Gabarretta, Malta 1964. As suggested in the text, the Arabic sources all but ignore the orders during the Saldjūķ and Zangid periods. For the Ayyūbid period, the most interesting references are in ʿImād al-Dīn al-Kātib al-Iṣfahānī, *al-Fatḥ al-ķussī fi 'l-fatḥ al-Ķudsī*, ed. Landberg, Leiden 1888; tr. H. Massé, Paris 1972; Ibn al-Athīr, *Kāmil*; Ibn Wāṣil, *Mufarridj al-kurūb*, ed. al-Shayyāl *et al.*, Cairo 1953. In the early Mamlūk period, valuable information is yielded by Ibn ʿAbd al-Ẓāhir, *al-Rawḍ al-zāhir* (on Baybars), ed. A. A. Khowaiter (SOAS thesis, 1960); idem, *Tashrīf al-ayyām* (on Ķalāwūn), ed. M. Kāmil, Cairo 1961; al-ʿAynī, *ʿIkd al-djumān*, fragments publ. in *RHC, Hist. or.*, ii; Baybars al-Manṣūrī, *Zubdat al-fikra*, unpubl. (see Brockelmann, II, 44, S II, 43). In general, Ibn al-Furāt, *T. al-duwal wa'l-mulūk*, vii-viii, ed. Zurayķ and ʿIzz al-Dīn, Beirut 1936-8, gives the most reliable extracts of unpublished 7th/13th century materials. Maķrīzī, *Sulūk*, i, ed. M. M. Ziyāda, Cairo 1934, though late and of little use in itself, is important because of the editor's careful indexes and cross-references. Among Eastern Christian sources, Kinnamos (Greek), Matthew of Edessa (Armenian), Bar Hebraeus and (of highest importance) Michael the Syrian (Syriac) may be mentioned.

(R. STEPHEN HUMPHREYS)

DAWLAT KHĀN LODĪ, 27th ruler of the Dihlī sultanate, was the son of Maḥmūd Khān Lodī and a cousin of Mallū Iķbāl Khān. Native Persian chroniclers say nothing about the early history of this Afghān nobleman of Dihlī emerged as a dominant figure during the early
of the 9th/15th century when Tughluķid auth
was on the verge of dissolution. He served S
Nāṣir al-Dīn Maḥmūd II, the last ruler of the dyn
both as private secretary with the title *ʿAzī
Mamālik* ("Great one of the State") and as mi
governor of the Dōʾāb. On the death of the S
in 815/1412, the *amīr*s offered the throne of
to Dawlat Khān Lodī, who thus assumed power
without the honours of royalty, as incorrectly
tioned by Firishta, ii, 292; for the Tughluķid
narchy after Fīrūz Shāh's death in 790/1388
become a moribund institution, as evidence
Badāʾūnī in his *Muntakhab al-tawārīkh*, i, 266, v
he speaks of Sulṭān Maḥmūd's writ as exter
only from Dihlī to Palam, a suburb of the ca

The first act of Dawlat Khān Lodī on beco
ruler was to move out of the capital towards Ka
where he received the allegiance of Narsingh
and other Hindu landlords. But he had to retreat
Kalpi in the face of fierce onslaughts by Ibr
Shāh, the Sharķī ruler of Djawnpūr [see SHARĶ
Dawlat Khān's downfall came at the hands o
arch-rival Khiḍr Khān of Multān, who t
advantage of the prevailing disorder in and ar
Dihlī, attacked the capital in 816/1414. D
Khān took refuge in the fortress of Siri, which
invested by Khiḍr Khān for four months. At
he capitulated, and was sent prisoner to H
Fīrūzshāh, where he soon died. The Dihlī Sult
henceforth enjoyed a fresh lease of life for a
more than a century, with Khiḍr Khān becomin
first ruler of the Sayyid dynasty.

Bibliography: Mahdī Ḥusayn, *The Tu
dynasty*, Calcutta 1963; E. Thomas, *The chro
of the Pathan Kings of Delhi*, 2nd enlarged ed
Delhi 1967; Yaḥyā al-Sarhindī, *Taʾrīkh-i
bārakshāhī*, Calcutta 1931.

(ABDUS SUBHA

DAWR (A. pl. *ādwar*), "revolution, peri
the periodic movement of the stars,
coupled with *kawr* (pl. *akwār*), "great period"
Risāla no. 35 of the *Rasāʾil Ikhwān al-Ṣafāʾ*, [
Fi'l-adwār wa 'l-akwār). In the doctrines of
extreme Shīʿī sects, the period of manifesta
or concealment of God or the secret
dom.

The Ismāʿīliyya [*q.v.*]; According to the ea
Ismāʿīlī doctrine, history is composed of s
adwār of seven "speaking" (*nāṭiķ*) prophets, ea
whom reveals a new religious law (*sharīʿa*): A
Noah, Abraham, Moses, Jesus, Muḥammad an
Mahdī or Ķāʾim. Each *nāṭiķ* has his trustee (
who reveals the inner (*bāṭin*) meaning of the re
tive *sharīʿa*. The seventh *nāṭiķ*, the *Ķāʾim*,
abrogate Muḥammad's *sharīʿa* and restore the
tawḥīd [*q.v.*] of the times before Adam's fall.
period between each two *nāṭiķ*s is called "the
period" (*al-dawr al-ṣaghīr*). The whole cycle
Adam to the Ķāʾim (*al-dawr al-kabīr*) is also c
"period of the concealment" (*dawr al-satr*), be
the gnosis (*ʿilm*) is concealed by the outward (
law and is only known by the initiates. During
period of concealment, the seven planets rule
world. Before the *dawr al-satr*, there was a p
of manifestation or revelation (*dawr al-kashf*) d
which the twelve angels of the Zodiac kept
unadulterated pure *tawḥīd*; at the end of time
Ķāʾim will bring forth a new *dawr al-kashf*. I
literature of the Ṭayyibiyya [*q.v.*], an et
alternation of *satr* and *kashf* is supposed.

The Druzes [see DURŪZ]: In the Druze c

periods of reincarnation of the Divine Creator called *adwār*. The 13th treatise counts 70 *adwār*, of 70 × 70 × 1000 years.

ıe Nuṣayrīs [*q.v.*]: Like the Ismāʿīlīs, the ıyrīs assume a cycle of seven *adwār*, in which Divine "Sense" (*maʿnā*) incarnated himself in , Seth, Joseph, Joshua, Āṣaf (the vizier of non), Simon Peter and ʿAlī, while his "Name" , i.e. his prophet, was incarnated in Adam, ı, Jacob, Moses, Solomon, Jesus and Muḥam- .

ıe conception of the seven periods of revelation ıs to derive from old Jewish-Christian traditions those preserved in the Pseudo-Clementine ılies; it is a well-known topic in the speculations ertain Gnostics and Manichaeans (see T. Andrae, *Person Muhammads in Lehre und Glauben seiner einde*, Stockholm 1918, 322 ff.; H. H. Schaeder, *islamische Lehre von vollkommenen Menschen*, *DMG*, lxxix (1925), 213 ff.).

Bibliography: Abū Yaʿḳūb al-Sidjistānī, *. Ithbāt al-nubuwwāt*, ed. ʿĀ. Tāmir, 181 ff.; F. Seybold, *Die Drusenschrift Kitab Alnoqat aldawair*, Kirchhain 1902, 84; R. Dussaud, *istoire et religion des Noṣairîs*, Paris 1900, 42 f.; . Corbin, *Le temps cyclique dans le mazdéisme et ıns l'ismaélisme*, in *Eranos Jahrbuch*, xx (1952), 9 ff.). (H. Halm)

AYN (A.), like *obligatio* in Latin, means literally bt", but also expresses the idea of "claim". predominance of the passive aspect makes it ssary to specify the sense of the relationship; e when one says *lahu dayn*, this means that an gation is due to someone, i.e. he is a creditor, reas with *ʿalayhi dayn*, this means someone has obligation to fulfil, i.e. he is a debtor. Claim and btedness are thus two aspects of the obligation, rding to whether the active or the passive side mind, and this is why it seems more exact to k of "obligation" for *dayn*.

he obligation (*dayn*) which is a personal right is osed to that in an object (*ḥaḳḳ fi 'l-ʿayn*). The of *dayn* rests on that of *dhimma*, a word which a very wide sphere of applicability: it is the acity of being subject to the law, in fact the s of an obligation. Hence patrimony and *dhimma* e together in practice. It is thus easily under- dable why the *dayn* is classified by Muslim ıors among goods or chattels (see al-Māwardī, *b al-ḳāḍī*); in effect, it is an incorporeal possession nging to the creditor and existing in the patri- y or personal estate of the debtor, so that this ession makes necessary an "action" on the tor's part (see Abū Ḥanīfa's definition of the n: that it is an action required (*muṭālaba*)). But connecting obligation, this link, is often thrust the background, and authors confuse the right the thing which is the object of the right (cf. analogy of the distinction of *Schuld* and *Haftung* erman for the obligation, and *dayn* and *muṭālaba* Arabic). The obligation (*dayn*) must be distin- hed from its object (*ʿayn*) or personal action *mma*). The obligation which has as its object a -fungible, determinate thing (*dayn fi 'l-ʿayn*) is erent from the obligation which has as its object ersonal action (*dayn fī dhimma*). In regard to gations which have a determinate thing (*ʿayn*) bject, the expression *dhimma* is not used; if the tor refuses to hand it over, his personal patrimony ot responsible for it.

he sources of obligation (*dayn*). Obligation *dayn* can arise out of a contract (loan, sale, surety, transaction or marriage), or out of a tort requiring reparation.

The elements of obligation (*shurūṭ al-dayn*). Obligation necessarily presupposes (a) at least two persons, i.e. a person who is required to perform a certain act, the debtor (*madīn, maṭlūb*), and a second person to whom the fulfilment of this performance is due, the claimant (*rabb al-dayn, ṭālib*). The word *gharīm* indicates the two of them (Latin *reus*). But there can be several principals involved, claimant or debtors, as when there is joint responsibility for the obligation. (b) An object, i.e. the performance which is obligatory and which the other party is legally entitled to exact; a multiplicity of objects is possible (the case of alternative obligation). (c) A cause; Muslim authors often understand by this the origin of the obligation.

The effects of the obligation. This last can be completed or not completed. Where it is completed, see below, there results the extinguishing of the obligation. If it is not completed, the claimant has a right to recover damages because of loss suffered through the non-completion of the obligation. A formal notice is not necessary: *Dies interpellat pro homine*. From the very fact of non-performance, the debtor is presumed to be at fault, and must prove either force-majeure or act of God (*amr al-sulṭān, ḍarūra, ʿudhr* or *āfa samāwiyya*).

Modalities of the obligation sc. settlement and stipulations. In principle, only monetary claims can be affected by a settlement. This last is always presumed in the interest of the debtor. The stipulations can be suspensive or resolutory, but there is a reluctance to validate conditional obligations.

Extinguishing of the obligation. The usual method here is through payment, but there are other ways, e.g. dation in payment (*istibdāl*), extinction of the debt through one debtor or creditor succeeding to the estate of another, substitution of a new obligation, compensation, etc.

Modern legal phraseology translates *dayn* by "claim", and to this are added several epithets: an assigned or assignable claim, a certain one, an unsecured, simple one, a commercial one, a contested one, a dubious one, one which is due, a guaranteed one, etc. (see the translations of these terms in the *Dictionnaire des termes juridiques et commerciaux, Français-Arabe*, by Mamdouh Hakki, s.v. "créance".

Bibliography: Chafik Chehata, *Théorie générale de l'obligation en droit musulman*, i, Cairo 1936; Ibn ʿĀṣim al-Mālikī al-Gharnāṭī, *al-ʿĀṣimiyya*, 117; al-Ḳayrawānī, *Risāla*, 133, 210, 211, 267; Kāsānī, vii, 174. For modern works in Arabic, see Ṣubḥī Maḥmaṣānī, *al-Naẓariyya al-ʿāmma li 'l-mūdjabāt wa 'l-ʿuḳūd*, Beirut 1948.

(A. M. Delcambre)

DEBT [see dayn].

DECLAMATION [see shiʿr].

DECLENSION [see iʿrāb].

DECORATION [see fann].

DEED (juridical) [see ʿaḳd].

DEFAULT OF HEIRS [see mīrāth].

DEHKHUDĀ, ʿAlī Akbar (1297-1375/1879-1955), poet, satirist and lexicographer of modern Iran. During the constitutional revolution (1905-9), he acquired a reputation as poet and satirist. But later, with the rise of Riḍā Shāh Pahlavī [*q.v.*], he gave up all political activities, devoting himself to literature and philology. Besides the satirical pieces, the so-called *Čarand u parand*, in which his very sarcastic humour secured vast popularity for the journal *Ṣūr-i Isrāfīl*, his literary output includes a Persian translation of Montesquieu's *Esprit des Lois* (unpublished), a review of Nāṣir-i Khusraw's *Dīwān* (ed. S. N. Taḳawī and M. Minūwī, Tehran 1307/1928), a four-volume collection of Persian proverbs and aphorisms, called *Amthāl u ḥikam* (*Madjmāᶜ al-amthāl*, as cited in E. E. Bertels's *Očerki*, is not the correct title of the published volumes), and the extensive lexicon, *Lughat-nāma*, which has had to be published mainly as a posthumous work and is still in progress. While Dehkhudā is generally considered a pioneer in modern, simple prose-writing, his poetical work—except for a few pieces published in popular periodicals—seems rather of a turgid and pedantic character, though often well-spiced with humour.

Bibliography: The *Lughat-nāma-yi Dehkhudā*, of which 203 fascicules in about 22,796 pages, in folio, of 3 columns each, have so far (March 1976) been published), contains an introductory volume (fascicule 40) in which more details on the author's life and work are given, (cf. also *Dīwān-i Dehkhudā*, ed. M. Muᶜīn, Tehran 1334/1955; Dehkhudā, *Amthāl u ḥikam*, 4 vols., Tehran 1308-10/1929-30; Y. Āryan-Pūr, *Az ṣabā tā nīmā*, Tehran 1350/1931, ii, 77-105; Browne, *LHP*, iv, 469-82; idem, *The press and poetry of modern Persia*, Cambridge 1914, index; E. E. Bertels, *Očerki istorii persidskoy literaturi* (with penetrating critical remarks), Leningrad 1928, 125-27); P. Avery, *Modern Iran*, London 1965, 129-30; A. Bausani and A. Pagliaro, *Storia della letteratura persiana*, Milan 1960, indices; J. Rypka *et alii*, *History of Iranian literature*, Dordrecht 1968, index; Gh. Youssofi, in *ZDMG* (1975), 117-32. (A. H. Zarrinkoob)

DEMESNE [see ḌAYᶜA].

DEMIRDĀSHIYYA, a branch of the Khalwatiyya [*q.v.*] Ṣūfī order named after Muḥammad Demirdāsh al-Muḥammadī, an Azeri Turk as is suggested by his name. According to ᶜAbd al-Wahhāb al-Shaᶜrānī, *al-Ṭabaḳāt al-kubrā*, Cairo 1954, ii, 147 ff. (cf. Maḥmūd Rabīᶜ and Ḥasan Ḳāsim (eds.), Abu 'l-Ḥasan Nūr al-Dīn al-Sakhāwī, *Tuḥfat al-albāb wa-bughyat al-ṭullāb fi 'l-khiṭaṭ wa 'l-mazārāt wa 'l-tarādjim wa 'l-baḳāᵓ al-mubārakāt*, Cairo 1937, 15 f.), he had belonged to the community of mystics which had gathered around ᶜUmar al-Rūshānī (d. 892/1486), a protégé of the Aḳ Ḳoyūnlu [*q.v.*] ruler Uzun Ḥasan and a *khalīfa* [*q.v.*] of the second *pīr* [*q.v.*] of the order Yaḥyā al-Shirwānī (d. 869/1464).

The biographies written in the late 19th and early 20th century by Yūsuf b. Ismāᶜīl al-Nabahānī, *Djamiᶜ karāmāt al-awliyā*, Cairo 1329, ii, 9 f., and Muḥammad Zāhid al-Kawtharī, *Nabrās al-muhtadī fī idjtilāᵓ anbāᵓ al-ᶜĀrif bi-Allāh Demirdāsh al-Muḥammadī*, Cairo 1364/1944-5, state that Muḥammad Demirdāsh had originally been a *mamlūk* of the Sultan al-Ashraf Sayf al-Dīn Ḳāyit Bāy [*q.v.*] and the *murīd* [*q.v.*] of Aḥmad b. ᶜUḳba al-Ḥadramī (d. 895/1489-90) before he joined the disciples of al-Rūshānī in Tabrīz, from where he is said to have returned to Egypt towards the end of Ḳāyit Bāy's reign. This version is in accordance with the contents of the official biographies published on behalf of the *ṭarīḳa* [*q.v.*] at the beginning of the 20th century (appended to Muḥammad Demirdāsh al-Muḥammadī, *Risāla fī maᶜrifat al-ḥaḳāᵓiḳ wa 'l-maᶜānī min ḳawlihi "Wa laḳad ātaynāka sabᶜan min al-mathānī"*, Cairo n.d., 27-34 and 55-63), which are mainly based upon unpublished sections of ᶜAbd al-Raᵓūf al-Munāwī's *al-Kawākib al-durriyya fī tarādjim al-sāda al-ṣūfiyya*.

Muḥammad Demirdāsh was an adherent o[f] al-ᶜArabī's metaphysics, and he must have influenced by the teachings of the Shādhi[liyya] order in which he had been initiated by his spiritual master Aḥmad b. ᶜUḳba (cf. Demir[dāsh] *Risāla fī Maᶜrifat al-ḥaḳāᵓiḳ*, 32 f., 62), as ap[pears] in his treatises *al-Ḳawl al-farīd fī maᶜrifat al-ta*[...] Cairo n.d., and in *Risāla fī Maᶜrifat al-ḥa*[...] mentioned earlier in the article. The liturgy o[f the] order refers in no way to any special kind of my[stical] theology, as was noted by E. Bannerth, in *WZ*[*KM*] lxii (1969), 20, who described the *ṭarīḳa*'s [...] [*q.v.*]—*maḥyā* in the terminology of the or[der] and the ceremonial surrounding the yearly occ[asion] of retreat (*khalwa*) for a period of three days a[t the] end of Shaᶜbān, as it was practiced in the 1960s [...] bibliography). It is not unlikely, however, tha[t the] liturgy may have mirrored the influence of Ib[n] ᶜArabī's thinking upon Muḥammad Demirdās[h at] an earlier stage, since we have no evidence [of a] fixed ritual until about a century after his dea[th in] 929/1524, when his great-grandson and *khalīfa* [Mu]ḥammad al-Ṣaghīr composed a treatise in *r*[...] metre, entitled *Tuḥfat al-ṭullāb al-rāᵓimīn ḥadr*[...] *wahhāb wa-uṣūl al-ṭarīḳ*, Cairo n.d., which coc[...] the ritual and has been the principal manual o[f the] order ever since.

Among others, this manual gives the rules fo[r the] so-called *hūwiyya*, the most characteristic pa[rt of] the ritual in which the head of the order, a nu[mber] of *nuḳabāᵓ* (sing. *naḳīb* [*q.v.*]) and some men[...] form a circle turning anti-clockwise (or occasio[nally] two circles, one moving clockwise and the [...] circle moving anti-clockwise), while calling "*hū*, [...] This part of Demirdāshī ritual has been subje[ct to] outside criticism in the past (cf. ᶜAbd al-Ḳād[ir] Muḥyī al-Dīn al-Arbilī, *Ḥudjdjat al-dhākirīn wa* [...] *al-munkarīn*, Alexandria 1299/1881-2, 43 ff., ᶜAbd al-Ghanī al-Nābulusī, *Kitāb al-Ḥaḳīka* [...] *'l-madjāz fī riḥlat al-Shaᵓm wa-Miṣr wa 'l-Ḥi*[...] ms. Berlin 6146, fols. 242a ff.).

From the days of Muḥammad Demirdāsh [al-] Muḥammadī until the present, ceremonial gathe[rings] have been confined to the only existing *zā*[*wiya*] [*q.v.*] of the order, situated in the present ᶜAbbāsiyya quarter of Cairo. The original estab[lish]ment and the surrounding land had been do[nated] to Muḥammad Demirdāsh by Sultan Ḳāyit [Bāy] (cf. *Risāla fī Maᶜrifat al-ḥaḳāᵓiḳ*, 59). It was vi[sited] by Ewliyā Čelebi (cf. *Seyāḥat-nāme*, Istanbul [...] xiv, 206) as well as by ᶜAbd al-Ghanī al-Nāb[ulusī] (cf. *Kitāb al-Ḥaḳīḳa*, fol. 224) towards the en[d of] the 17th century, which suggests that the estab[lish]ment must have been of some importance at [that] time. The *zāwiya* complex with its *khalwa* cells [has] been described by ᶜAlī Mubārak, *Khiṭaṭ*, iv, 1[...] as it was in the 1860s and by E. Bannerth a cen[tury] later.

The order experienced a severe setback at [the] end of the 18th century when it was plundere[d by] French troops (cf. ᶜAbd al-Raḥmān al-Djab[artī,] *ᶜAdjāᵓib al-āthār*, Cairo 1297/1879-80, iii, 95), [but] continued to rank among the less prominent *ṭarīḳ*[*as* of] Cairo until the 1880s, when it experienced a re[vival] under the leadership of ᶜAbd al-Raḥmān Mu[ṣṭafā] al-Demirdāsh Bāshā, the founder of the Ca[iro] hospital named after him. After his death in 19[...] dispute about the succession occurred, in whic[h the] then *muftī* of Egypt ᶜAbd al-Madjīd Salīm interv[ened] (cf. Maḥmūd Abū Rayya, *al-Sayyid al-Ba*[...] Cairo n.d. 182). This dispute ended in the fo[rmal] investiture of ᶜAbd al-Raḥīm's six-year old gran[dson] ly named ʿAbd al-Raḥīm, and the appoint- of the principal *naḳīb*, Amīn al-Ṣayyād, as *vakīl* or regent, specifically charged with the of managing the *ṭarīḳa*'s affairs. The latter's Iusayn was head of the order in the 1970s.

tive membership of the order has never spread de Cairo. This has been the direct consequence e requirements set upon the potential *murīd*. ne desiring membership had to attend the y *ḥaḍra*s of the order held near the shrine of under for a period of at least two years. During period he had to be under the surveillance of f the order's *nuḳabāʾ*, who were always residents iiro. The latter had to judge the personality e candidate, and could propose him for initiation e head of the order (cf. Zakī Muḥammad Mudjā- *al-Aʿlām al-sharḳiyya*, iii, 110).

dditionally there were never more than twelve *bāʾ* at one time. New *nuḳabāʾ* were elected by ead of the order in consultation with the *nu-* already in office (cf. Muḥammad Sulaymān al- ārī, *Tuḥfat al-albāb wa-hidāyat al-ṭullāb fīmā bu ʿalayhim min al-ādāb*, Cairo 1322/1904-5, .

e mosque and shrine of Demirdāsh are the of an important weekly *ziyāra*-day (cf. F. De , *Cairene Ziyāra-days. A contribution to the of saint veneration in Islam*, in *WI*, xvii (1976),), and of *mawlid* celebrations in the second of Shaʿbān (cf. J. W. McPherson, *The Moulids gypt* Cairo 1940, 257 f. and E. Bannerth, in *'M*, lxii (1969), 129).

Bibliography: For further detail and ad- ional references, see E. Bannerth, *La Khal- tiyya en Égypte. Quelques aspects de la vie ne confrérie*, in *MIDEO*, viii (1964-6), 3-7; m, *Über den Stifter und Sonderbrauch der mirdāšiyya Sufis in Kairo*, in *WZKM*, lxii 69), 116-32 (which contains a German trans- ion of the section about *khalwa* in the *ṭarīḳa*'s nual *Tuḥfat al-ṭullāb*); idem, *Islamische Wall- rtsstätten Kairos*, Cairo 1967, 74 f., and M. senan, *Saint and Sufi in modern Egypt. An ay in the sociology of religion*, Oxford 1973, *ssim*. The section on al-Demirdāshiyya in G. Martin, *A short history of the Khalwatī 'er of dervishes*, in N. R. Keddie (ed.), *Scholars, nts and sufis. Muslim religious institutions ce 1500*, Berkeley-London 1972, 290-5, is gely based upon Bannerth's work.

The treatises by Muḥammad Demirdāsh al-Mu- nmadī and by Muḥammad Demirdāsh al- ghīr mentioned in the article have been published, ether with another treatise by the *ṭarīḳa*'s nder, *Kitāb al-Daradja al-ʿulyā fī maʿāridj al- liyāʾ*, by Muḥammad Nūr Ṣāliḥ al-Sirdjānī der the title *al-Madjmūʿa al-Demirdāshiyya*, iro 1348/1929-30. This collection contains also ection with biographical data on a number of *ykhs* of the order and a biography of ʿAbd al- ḥīm Muṣṭafā al-Demirdāsh Bāshā compiled by ṣṭafā Adham Bek Munīr, 52 ff.

For other biographies of ʿAbd al-Raḥīm, see kī Muḥammad Mudjāhid, *al-Aʿlām al-sharḳiyya*, 'ro 1955, iii, 109 ff., which gives also additional ormation about the order's religious practice, d Muḥammad Sulaymān Badawī, *Nabdha yasīra n ḥayāt ustādhinā al-fāḍil . . . ʿAbd al-Raḥīm ṣṭafā al-Demirdāsh Bāshā*, Cairo n.d. Other blications of the order, containing historical a, liturgical texts and rules, are *al-Nafaḥāt al- dsiyya fī awrād al-ṭarīḳa al-Demirdāshiyya*, Cairo n.d.; Muḥammad Labīb al-Ḥalabī and Ḥu- sayn Muḥammad al-Ḥalabī (eds.), *al-Fuyūḍāt al- nūrāniyya fī maḥyā al-ṭarīḳa al-Demirdāshiyya*, Cairo n.d.; and Muḥammad Nūr Ṣāliḥ al-Sirdjānī, *Risālat al-Silsila al-dhahabiyya fī tarādjim ridjāl al-sāda al-Khalwatiyya al-Demirdāshiyya*, Cairo 1319/1901-2.

On the position of al-Demirdāshiyya in 19th century Egypt, see F. De Jong, *Ṭuruq and ṭuruq-linked institutions in 19th century Egypt* Leiden, 1978, *passim*. Additional data on the history of the order may be found in F. De Jong, *Two anonymous manuscripts relative to the Ṣūfī orders in Egypt*, in *Bibliotheca Orientalis*, xxxii (1975), 186-90. Enver Behnan Şapolyo, *Mezhepler ve tarikatlar tarihi*, Istanbul 1964, 193, is full of conflicting detail. (F. De Jong)

DEMOGRAPHY. Demographers who study Islamic nations are concerned with population numbers and population change in those nations. Their works have, with a few exceptions, been recently written. This is due to the nature of the study. Though many of the basic principles of demography have been known for centuries demography as a field of study is relatively new. It is also dependent on statistical sources—records of population from censuses, surveys, and registration lists—that did not exist in many Muslim countries until very recent times. Because of this late development, many demographic topics have been little studied and for some Muslim countries no adequate demography has been written.

There are few demographic studies of Muslim population as such, and demographers have most often not been concerned with religion. Thus in the indexes of books of the demography of Islamic countries the words "Islam" or "religion" either do not appear or only a few references are cited. In addition, some countries with significant Muslim populations have become officially indifferent or even hostile to religion. The communist countries of Eastern Europe and Asia do not list any association by religion in their censuses. This makes historical or comparative analysis of Muslim population extremely difficult. Those in the "Muslim" category in the 1897 Russian Imperial census, for example, cannot be traced in the 1926 Soviet census, which only lists ethnic and linguistic groups, not religions.

For countries such as Saudi Arabia, Turkey, or Iran, of course, Total Population and Muslim Population are, in effect, the same. For other countries, however, especially those in South Asia and Africa, differential studies of the Muslim population would be valuable, though they are seldom done. Religion is usually not a consideration. This is especially true of the modern demographic sample surveys, which produce high-quality information on fertility, mortality, and marriages, but which often do not even ask the informants' religion.

For these reasons, much of the demographic material discussed below is not data or analyses of Muslim population, but of the population of Muslim countries. The distinction is real and important.

In historical documents and colonial records, terms such as "census", "survey", and "population estimate" are often used in a confusing manner. It is thus valuable to define exactly what is meant by the words used to describe basic demographic statistics. The following are definitions of the four sources of demographic data as they are usually defined and as the terms are used here:

Estimates. Estimates are not actual counts of the population. They range from wild guesses on the populations of entire nations to well-reasoned analyses based on incomplete or slightly inaccurate census returns.

Registration. In Muslim lands, registration data have always been kept by governments. Ideally, a population register records a person by age and sex and lists his date of birth and death and, perhaps, events such as marriage and conscription. More usually, births, deaths, and other events are registered separately, total numbers of births, deaths, etc. are published, and no attempt is made to keep a record of each individual. The former is usually called a Population Register, the latter a Register of Vital Events.

Sample surveys. Surveys ask demographic questions of a scientifically selected sample of the population, often 5 % to 10 %. The surveys take various forms, but are usually intended to find information on demographic variables, particularly fertility, in a detailed manner not possible in a census. Surveys are normally used to supplement information gained through a census. In countries such as those in the Sahel in Africa, though, in which taking censuses long proved impossible, "sample censuses" were taken instead.

Censuses. The census is the basic source of quality demographic data. To be a census, an enumeration must be intended to be an actual count of the members of the population of an area. It must be held in a short period of time. Every census should ask age, sex, and residence of all inhabitants, and questions on marital status, occupation, religion, and others are usually included also. Collections of registration data are not censuses.

Though the census and registration practices of each Muslim country have differed, some phenomena have been universal. In a Muslim nation's early census or registration records, females are undercounted. Children are also undercounted, and a person seldom knows his exact age, so age-specific data is incorrect. As education, economy, and experience with national statistics grows, these problems lessen.

With few exceptions, completeness and reliability of a nation's population statistics improve as time advances. Few Muslim nations have accurate historical statistics. For this reason, in Muslim nations historical demography depends on modern demography. Only by examining modern and accurate demographic data can an historical demographer gain the basic knowledge of fertility and mortality that he needs to evaluate historical records.

What follows are descriptions of the demography of nations with a Muslim majority or a large Muslim minority. They are arranged by geographic region and nation and two sorts of works are considered—government statistics and analytical/descriptive studies. Censuses are listed by year in which they were taken, not by issuing agency or publication year, for reasons of space. The articles and books cited deal with population and demography as a whole, not with specific subjects such as migration or fertility. Those interested in studies of specific demographic topics will find ample resources in the bibliographies of the works discussed below.

I. Mediaeval Islam

There is no reliable demography of Medieval Islam. Materials from which demographic calculations could be made, such as tax registers and military payrolls [see DĪWĀN] were kept by mediaeval Islamic governments, but have not survived.

Like the mediaeval Europeans, Muslims were little interested in population numbers for own sake. Furthermore, the Muslim world f need to keep religious statistics, and so it pos no analogies to the baptismal and marriage r of Western Europe. Though the great geogra and travellers of mediaeval Islam often men the "great size" of cities, the "large numbe people in an area, or gave fanciful estimates size of armies, they did not often offer even estimates of population numbers. This was reaso because there was no way geographers, tra or others could have known population nun No one had counted the population and, as has proven by the multitudes of erroneous "estim of population made in all areas of the worl only way accurately to know the size of a popu is to count it. The enumerations needed for p tion analysis were not made in the Islamic or at least have not been found, prior to the s great period of Islamic expansion, the T empires. In the empires, the keeping of popu statistics was the province of the state. Beg in the late 14th century, the Ottoman gover began to keep accurate counts of households Empire for taxation purposes. Similar counts taken by the emperor Akbar in Mughal Indi may have been taken in Ṣafawid Iran.

Non-statistical sources. While demog is essentially a statistical study, non-stat sources can be used to illuminate areas of popu history for which statistics are unavailable most obvious area in which this is true is mig Large-scale migration of Arabs, Mongols, and in Islamic times were recorded by geographe historians. The populations of cities can be at roughly estimated through archaeological ev and through measurements of contemporaries as Ibn Baṭṭūṭa, who simply measured the s city walls to gain a picture of the city's siz (by analogy) its comparative population. evidence of this sort is available in Le St *Lands*.) There are numerous quasi-statistical s for specific demographic events. An example type of material is al-Maḳrīzī on the plague famines of Egypt, whose material is analyse Michael Dols (*The Black Death in the Middle* Princeton 1977); for a translation of al-Ma work, see G. Wiet, in *JESHO*, v/1 (1962). sources give estimates of numbers dying, being or leaving a city or an area. It should be st that such sources can be used to gain an impr of the scope of demographic events, no more. population numbers are usually suspect. Mu formation may be available from analyses o graphers' accounts of the amenities of towns — mosques, etc.—but this research remains to be As to accuracy, the Muslim commentators, wh knew well the areas of which they spoken, are m be preferred to European sources.

One source of mediaeval Islamic demogra the system of records of Islamic law. The of the schools and fragmentary surviving judic cisions can at least give an impression of wha religiously-accepted in marriage and divorce matters that affect fertility, such as lact polygamy, and contraception. Basim Musalla made good use of this type of material in his w contraception (*Sex and society in Islam. The sa and medieval techniques of birth control* (diss., H University 1973). Unfortunately, legal code court decisions do not necessarily reflect practice of the majority of Muslim society, a reason legal matters have limited usefulness as ographic sources.

he fact that demographic evidence on mediaeval m is almost non-existent has not meant that nates have not been made. Josiah Cox Russell been in the forefront of those using materials as estimates of city sizes and poll tax revenues rrive at population totals. (See *Late ancient and ieval population*, Philadelphia 1958; *Late medieval an and Asia Minor population*, in *JESHO*, iii/3 o], 265-74; *The population of medieval Egypt*, in *rnal of the American Research Center in Egypt*, v 6], 69-82; and others.) Russell's work is often d, however, on unverifiable secondary sources, ue estimates of army sizes and taxation by histo- s who lived centuries after the fact, the calm ptance of population figures drawn without exa- ation from sources such as *La Grande Encyclopédie Encyclopaedia Brittanica*, and incredible logical ps that conveniently provide estimates when not poor data is available. Russell does show that nates are possible from fragmentary evidence, this evidence must be much more carefully ysed than he and those who have followed him e done.

he use of non-demographic evidence to find ulation totals seems to work better for urban than l areas. A good example of this type of analysis, gh for a later period than mediaeval Islam, is ré Raymond's *Signes urbains et étude de la popu- n des grandes villes arabes à l'époque ottomane, EO*, xxvii (1974), 183-93. Ch. Pellat has made a ographic study out of unusual material in *Peut-on aître le taux de natalité au temps du Prophète, ESHO*, xiv/2 (1971) 107-35, which shows that xceptional amount of information can be drawn limited data. Also, his *Quelques chiffres sur la noyenne d'une categorie de Musulmans*, in *Mélanges lamologie*, Leiden 1974, 233-46, is a pioneering ly in the use of biographical references for acting demographic information

Iany works on mediaeval Islamic history have ritically used population estimates as part of r descriptions. For examples of this, see two ies by Eliyahu Ashtor, *Histoire des prix et des ires dans l'orient médiéval*, Paris 1960, esp. 237, 272, and 273, and *A social and economic history he Near East in the Middle Ages*, Berkeley-Los eles-London 1976, esp. 290 and 291, see also his *mouvement migratoire au haut Moyen Âge: rations de l'Irak vers les pays méditerranéens*, in *ales E.S.C.* (1972/1), 185-214.)

II. Ottoman Empire

he 16th and 17th century Ottoman population sters (*defters*) were among the first European e records that can be used as population sources. e the records were not kept primarily as data on ulation, however, they must undergo considerable ipulation before they can yield total population mates, and they do not provide information on r demographic variables, such as fertility and tality.

he study of Ottoman *defters* was effectively un by Ömer Lutfi Barkan, who analysed the regis- for total population, city size, and economic nge (see especially, *Essai sur les données statis- es des registres de recensement dans l'empire man aux xve et xvie siècles*, in *JESHO*, i/1 (1957),). Many other scholars have used the *defters* d in the Ottoman archives and local collections rmer Ottoman possessions, and the registers have yielded population data on the empire as a whole, on provinces and on cities. Only a few of these studies can be listed here:

General studies. Barkan, *Osmanlı imparator- luğunda büyük nüfus ve arazi tahrirleri ve hakana mahsus istatistik defterleri*, in *Istanbul Üniversitesi Iktisat Fakültesi Mecmuası*, ii (1940), 20-59, 214-57; idem, *Tarihî demografi araştırmaları ve Osmanlı tarihi*, in *Türkiyat Mecmuası*, x (1951), 1-27; idem, *Research on the Ottoman fiscal surveys*, in *Studies in the economic history of the Middle East*, ed. M. A. Cook, London 1970.

Regional studies. Cook, *Population pressure in rural Anatolia, 1450-1600*, London 1972; W.-D. Hütteroth and Kamal Abdulfattah, *Historical geo- graphy of Palestine, Transjordan and southern Syria in the late 16th century*, Erlangen 1977; A. Cohen and B. Lewis, *Population and revenue in the towns of Palestine in the sixteenth century*, Princeton 1978; B. McGowan, *Defter-i Mufassal-i Liva-i Sirem: an Ottoman revenue survey dating from the reign of Selim II*, diss., Columbia University 1967; Halil Inalcik, *EI*² art. ARNAWUTLUK; Leila Erder and Suraiya Faroghi, *Population rise and fall in Anatolia*, in *Middle Eastern Studies*, xv/3 (1979), 322-45.

Urban studies. H. Lowry, *The Ottoman tahrir defters as a source for urban demographic history: the case study of Trabzon (ca. 1486-1583)*, diss., UCLA 1977; İnalcık, *EI*² art. ISTANBUL. R. Jennings. *Urban population in Anatolia in the sixteenth century, a study of Kayseri, Karaman, Amasya, Trabzon, and Erzurum*, in *IJMES*, vii/1 (1976), 21-57.

The *defters* themselves are described and discussed in DEFTER-I KHĀKĀNĪ. Facsimiles and translations of *defters* are given by Cohen and Lewis, Cook, and İnalcık, *Hicri 835 tarihli suret-i defter-i sancak-i Arnavıd*, Ankara 1954.

Ottoman *defters* were primarily kept as financial and military records and it would be a mistake to consider them to be highly reliable demographic sources. Certain groups were not counted (Barkan, *Essai*, 20-1), certain ones undercounted (C. Issawi, *Comment on Professor Barkan's estimate of the popu- lation of the Ottoman Empire in 1520-30*, in *JESHO*, i/3 [October 1958], 329-33). The registers were usually household counts, and comparisons between house- hold numbers in two time periods may be confused because of changing household sizes. Nevertheless, the Ottoman *defters* are an incomparable source for the historical demography of the Middle East, es- pecially when they are used as part of a detailed investigation of local, as opposed to empire-wide, population, society and economy.

After *ca.* 1700 the *defter* records cease, this being probably a sign of diminished central authority in the Empire.

In the reign of Sultan Maḥmūd II, the Ottoman empire once again began to collect population statistics. Unlike the 16th and 17th century *defters*, the new registration was the base of a system of mili- tary conscription. Each male in the empire was to be recorded in population registers (*taḥrīr-i nüfūs*), at first by general age group ("youth" and "adult" or "youth", "adult", and "aged"-categories corres- ponding to one's availability for military service). By the 1840s, though, the registers were being kept, at least in some areas, in much greater detail; each male was recorded by age, household, and his relationship to the head of the household. The *taḥrīrs* were perio- dically updated through "events" (*wuḳūʿāt*) registers in which were recorded births, deaths, conscriptions, and migration. During the reign of ʿAbd al-Ḥamīd II, registrations of females were kept, as well as those of males, but female registration was only successful in northern and western Anatolia and in the European sections of the empire (see Enver Ziya Kural, *Osmanlı imparatorluğunda ilk nüfus sayımı*, Ankara 1940; Fazila Ikbal, *1831 tarihinde Osmanlı imparatorluğunda idarî taksimat ve nüfus*, in *Belleten*, xv, no. 60, 617-28; and J. McCarthy, *Age, family and migration in nineteenth-century Black Sea provinces of the Ottoman Empire*, in *IJMES*, x [1979], 309-23).

The totals collected from the Ottoman registration system in provinces were published at intervals in the provincial yearbooks (*sāl-nāmes*), listing population by province, sub-province, and district, and often by religious group and sex. At various times the central government updated the data across the empire and published the data in what have been erroneously been called "censuses". Three of the "censuses" have been translated and reproduced (Kural; Kemal Karpat, *Ottoman population records and the census of 1881/82-1893*, in *IJMES*, ix [1978], 237-74; McCarthy, *International historical statistics: the late Ottoman empire*, Boston 1981). It should be noted that the Ottoman population totals by province uniformly underestimate the number of women and children in the province, and thus totals must be augmented by from 10 % to 30 %, depending on the province.

The uses of Ottoman figures for the study of the historical population of the Middle East are obvious. Simply stated, no one but the Ottoman government counted the population and no one but the Ottoman government even remotely knew what the population was. Data on total population from *sāl-nāmes* and "censuses" is increasingly being used in population studies. It is, however, the archival records of population that hold the greatest promise. When these records are available and utilised, accurate studies on fertility, mortality, and population change in the Ottoman Empire will be possible.

The 19th century Ottoman registration system has been described by Karpat (*Ottoman population*) and S. J. Shaw (*The Ottoman census system and population, 1831-1914*, in *IJMES*, ix/3 [1978], 325-37). For examples of the uses of *sāl-nāme* and "census" population records, see Vedat Eldem, *Osmanlı imparatorluğunun iktisadi şartları hakkında bir tetkik*, Ankara 1970; Leila Erder, *From trade to manufacture in Bursa*, diss., Princeton University 1976; and McCarthy, *The Muslim population of Anatolia, 1878-1927*, diss., UCLA, 1978.

Contemporary European sources on Middle Eastern population in Ottoman times will only be mentioned briefly here. Those that were accurate were drawn from Ottoman data, and thus are only valuable if they provide population statistics of areas for which the original Ottoman data is unavailable. The most valuable of the European sources are the books of Cuinet (*La Turquie d'Asie*, 4 vols., Paris 1890-4; *Syrie, Liban, et Palestine*, Paris 1896). Cuinet collected, amended, and published Ottoman population statistics, as well as data on the social and economic life of Ottoman Asia. No other European source can in any way compare with Cuinet. (Those interested in European sources should consult N. Michoff, *La population de la Turquie et de la Bulgaria au XVIIIe et XIXe siècles, recherches bibliographico-statistiques*, 4 vols., Sofia 1919-35, and the various volumes of *Die Bevölkerung der Erde*, a supplement of *Petermanns Mitteilungen*, Gotha, especially vol. xi, 1901, 3-23.)

Nineteenth and early 20th century Ottoman geographers were not greatly superior to the Europ
Though they often used data from Ottoman go
ment records, the geographers had little appreci
of the proper use of population statistics. Th
exception is the *Ḳāmūs al-aʿlām* of S͟hams a
Sāmī Fras͟heri (6 vols., Istanbul 1889-99), wh
demographically superior to the others.

III. Middle East

Demography is dependent on government s
tics, which are produced by individual pol
units. Perhaps for that reason, there have bee
works on Middle Eastern demography that cro
tional boundaries in their analysis and even fewe
treat the Middle East, or even the Arab world,
unit. Volumes on Middle Eastern demography
as J. I. Clarke and W. B. Fisher, *Populations*
Middle East and North Africa New York 1972
usually collections of chapters or articles that
each country individually. This is unfortunate,
many phenomena such as nomadism, polygamy
beliefs on contraception, and fertility levels wou
best studied for the Middle East in general, as w
for individual areas. (Two examples of the br
approach illustrate its benefits: *Muslim atti*
toward family planning, ed. Olivia Schieffelin,
York 1967; Oladele Olawayi Arowolo, *Correla*
fertility in Muslim populations, dissertation, Un
sity of Pennsylvania 1973.)

Some studies of the population of the Arab W
have been made, though these are usually divide
ternally by national boundaries. Of them, st
by G. Baer, *Population and society in the Arab*
Westport, Conn. 1964, and M. A. el-Badry, *Tren*
the components of population growth in the Arab
tries of the Middle East, in *Demography*, ii (1
140-86, are valuable, but now out of date. A
recent article by Youssef Courbage and Philippe
gues is an introduction to the demography o
Arab states, *La population des pays arabes d'O*
in *Population*, xxx, no. 6 (Nov.-Dec. 1975), 111
K. C. Zachariah has compared the accuracy
availability of data from the Arab states, *The*
graphic measures of Arab countries. A compa
analysis, in Cairo Demographic Centre, *Demogr*
measures and population growth in Arab coun
Cairo 1970, 279-326. (See also the internat
analysis of demographic problems in Part
Demographic aspects of socio-economic developme
some Arab and African countries, ed. S. A. Huz
and T. E. Smith, Cairo 1974, and G. Sabagh,
demography of the Middle East, in *MESA Bu*
iv/2 [15 May 1970], 1-19.)

Population studies for Middle Eastern na
are published in the international sources
below and, for 1968 and 1973, in the *Popu*
bulletin of the United Nations Economic Commi
for Western Asia, nos. 10 and 11 (January to
1976, Beirut 13-26).

Greater Syria. Issawi has collected Euro
statements on the population of Greater Syria i
19th century (*The economic history of the M*
East, 1800-1914, Chicago 1966, 209-10), the be
which were based on Ottoman figures. For the p
prior to 1918, the best sources on Syrian popul
are the state records of Ottoman Syria. Of
the printed population records of Ottoman Gr
Syria have been analysed by J. McCarthy (*Po*
tion of the Ottoman Fertile Crescent, in *Procs.*
Congress on the Economic History of the Middle
1800-1914, Haifa 1980). After 1918, Greater
was divided into Syria, Lebanon, and Palestine

statistical histories of the three new nations ·ged.

Syria, the French mandatory powers made ·pulation count in 1922, which they updated published in 1926. This count cannot be called ısus, since much of it was based not on actual ıeration, but on population totals given by village ·rs. Its totals are too low, as were those of the census of independent Syria in 1947, which did count nomads. Modern censuses were taken in and 1970. (The Syrian government printed, in tion to the results of the census of 1970 itself, mes of analysis of the census results by K. E. yanathan.) For an analysis of modern Syrian ılation and demographic variables, see Mouna ne Samman, *La population de la Syrie, étude émographique*, Paris 1978; Samman makes ısive use of Izzat Nouss, *La population de la e, étude démographique*, Paris 1951.

ıe population of Lebanon in the 19th century been analysed by Youssef Courbage and Ph. ;ues, *La situation démographique au Liban*, ıt 1974, ii, ch. I. European estimates are de-d in D. Chevallier, *La société du Mont-Liban à que de la révolution industrielle en Europe*, s 1971. Both studies are marred by their lack of ideration of Ottoman statistics, except insofar ıose statistics appeared in French works such as et's *Syrie, Liban, et Palestine*. The bulk of the bage and Fargues' work is, however, a good study odern Lebanese population. The French manda-administration attempted to enumerate the ılation of Lebanon in 1921, 1932 and 1941. Even best of these counts, that of 1932, was deficient undercounted the Muslim population. For ical reasons, no modern census has been taken, only limited evidence exists on demographic ıbles such as fertility and mortality (see D. key, *Fertility differences in a modernizing country*, ceton 1961). What data exist come from demo-hic surveys, which are described in *Available ›graphic data in the Lebanese Republic*, in *Popula-Bulletin* of the United Nations Economic Com-ion for Western Asia, nos. 10-11 (Jan.-July), 240-3. J. Chamie, *Religion and population ımics in Lebanon*, Ann Arbor, Mich. 1977, has ribed the unusual religious-demographic situa-in Lebanon.

. Palestine, the British took an incomplete census 922 and a more complete count in 1931. They recorded migration, an important phenomenon ?alestine, but probably missed much Muslim ılation movement, especially that of Bedouin. e the 1948 War and the division of Palestine, el has taken censuses in 1961 and 1972, begun gistration system in 1948 (often listed as "the ·us of 1948"), and held numerous sample surveys e population. Jordan has taken censuses in 1952, :, 1971, and 1979 and a fertility survey in 1976. results of the 1952 Jordanian census are very ·ient, and those that came from the 1948 Israeli ·tration count somewhat deficient.

stimates and census data for Palestine have been ented in great detail by R. Bachi, *The population ·rael*, Jerusalem 1976. Bachi's volume, which is ·xtremely valuable source, must be used with for the period 1880-1922. For that period, he ds using actual Ottoman population statistics substitutes British and other estimates without ification. Certain other events with large demo-hic implications, such as the 1948 and 1967 Wars, also incompletely and, as regards demography, inaccurately covered. The book is very good, however, on the analysis of Israeli statistics. See also, D. Friedlander and C. Goldscheider, *The population of Israel*, New York 1979, and various analytical volumes published by the Israeli government as part of its census publications.

A. Thavarajah, *Mid-decade demographic parameters of Jordan and population growth*, in *Demographic measures*, 55-75, has adjusted reports on population found in Jordanian censuses and registration records. He provides a good brief introduction to the problems of Jordanian data collection from 1952 to 1965. A much more detailed analysis comes in the Jordanian government's *Analysis of the population statistics of Jordan*, Amman 1966, which describes in detail the country's vital registration system, as well as its censuses, and the accuracy of both.

ʿIrāḳ. M. S. Hasan wrote the first study of the population of ʿIrāḳ in the 19th century, *Growth and structure of Iraq's population, 1867-1947*, in *Bulletin of the Oxford University Institute of Statistics*, xx (1958), 339-52. Hasan, however, accepted as accurate and reliable three types of data—Ottoman statistics as presented by Cuinet, European estimates, and the ʿIrāḳī census of 1947—and none of these can be considered accurate without extensive revision. Three Ottoman provinces made up the area of present-day ʿIrāḳ—Mawṣil, Baghdād, and Baṣra. Only in Baghdād were Ottoman population statistics fairly accurate, and even in Baghdād there was a significant undercount of women and children, an undercount reflected in Cuinet. European sources had no idea what the population was. Even the 1947 ʿIrāḳī census was an undercount. As a result, Hasan's figures must be rejected. The best source of total population numbers for Ottoman ʿIrāḳ is the series of estimates published by the Ottoman government in the *sāl-nāmes* of the ʿIrāḳī provinces (McCarthy, *Population of the Ottoman Fertile Crescent*)

The ʿIrāḳī government took censuses in 1927, 1934 and 1947. While the completeness of the censuses improved over time, each one produced an undercount. This was in part due to the use of census records as conscription records. K. C. Zachariah has found numerous errors in the early censuses, *Use of census data for estimating demographic measures of Iraq*, in *Demographic measures*, 27-54. The censuses taken in 1957, 1975, and 1977 are more reliable. See also Fāḍil al-Anṣārī, *Sukkān al-ʿIrāḳ*, Damascus 1970.

Arabian Peninsula. The best sources on the population of early 20th century Arabia are three geographic works: Shams al-Dīn Sāmī Frasheri, *op. cit.*; ʿAlī Djewād, *Memālik-i ʿOthmāniyyeniñ djughrāfyā lughātī*, Istanbul 1895; and J. G. Lorimer, *Gazeteer of the Persian Gulf*, Calcutta 1908-1915. The first two offer estimates based on the reports of Ottoman government officials, the third offers the estimates of British consular and intelligence officers, travellers, and merchants. None of the three is useful for anything but rough approximations of population numbers.

In 1947, Nello Lambardi published what he stated were population figures taken from Yemeni government records, *Divisioni amministrative del Yemen con notize economiche e demografiche*, in *OM*, xxvii/7-9 (July-Sept. 1947), 143-62. The statistics appear to have been part of a tax register of men and animals. Women and children were surely undercounted, but no figures by age and sex were kept, so the extent of the undercount cannot be determined. The Yemeni data are the only data for South Arabia before the

1970s. The British did keep a register of births and deaths in Aden, but the undercount, especially of mortality, was great.

In most parts of the Arabian Peninsula, no accurate census was taken before the 1970s. Only Kuwait and Bahrain were statistically advanced at an earlier date. The Gulf States have held censuses in the following years: Kuwait—1957, 1961, 1965, 1970, 1975; Bahrain—1941, 1950, 1959, 1965, 1971; Qatar —1970; United Arab Emirates—1968, 1975. Oman expects to take a census in 1981. South Yemen took a census in 1973, followed by North Yemen in 1975. Saudi Arabia discarded as under-enumerations the results of a census taken in 1962-3 and has never published the results of its 1974 census (though figures from the census were printed in Abdel Rahman al-Madani and Muhamed al-Fayez, *The demographic situation in the Kingdom of Saudi Arabia*, in *Population Bulletin*, 185-89). See also Zachariah, *Trends and components of population growth in Kuwait*, in *Demographic measures*, 81-114; Fisher, *Southern Arabia*, in Clarke and Fisher, *op. cit.*, 274-90; A. G. Hill, *The demography of the Kuwaiti population of Kuwait*, in *Demography*, xii/3 (Aug. 1975), 537-48, and *The demography of the population of Kuwait*, in *Population Bulletin*, xiii (July 1977), 42-55; Population Division of the United Nations Economic Commission for Western Asia, *An overview of the population situation in Bahrain*, in *Population Bulletin*, xiv (June 1978), 57-69.

Turkey. Rather than continue the Ottoman registration system, the Turkish Republic decided to draw its population enumerations from a system of censuses which followed the Western model. In this it emulated the Balkan countries, each of which had taken a census when it became independent from the Ottoman Empire.

Turkey held its first complete census in 1927 and has held quinquennial censuses since 1935. (For a description of the Turkish censuses, see *A critical review of demographic data obtained by Turkish population censuses*, in *Turkish demography: Proceedings of a Conference*, ed. C. Shorter and Bozkurt Güvenc, Ankara 1969.) The 1927 census is deficient, especially for the eastern provinces of Turkey, but provides useful information and can be adjusted (McCarthy, *Muslim population*, 185-223). From 1935 the Turkish censuses are, along with the Egyptian censuses, the best source of demographic information in the Middle East. Turkey has also held a series of sample demographic surveys, of which the most valuable is the Turkish Demographic Survey. See Nusret Fişek, *Demographic surveys in Turkey*, in *Turkish demography*, 1-18, and the volumes of the Turkish Demographic Survey, Ankara 1965- . The modern Turkish registration system has only produced published statistics for births, deaths, and marriages in the central cities of provinces and these are incomplete due to under-registration and migration.

The best short introduction to Turkish demography is an article by Shorter, *Information on fertility, mortality, and population growth in Turkey*, in *Turkish demography*, 19-42, and in *Population index*, xxxiv/1. More detailed coverage is in Figen Karadayı *et alii*, *The population of Turkey*, Ankara 1974. Turkey's demographers have produced a large and detailed literature in Turkish, French, German and English on Turkish demography. This work is listed and sometimes annotated in the fine bibliographies edited by Behire Balkan, *Türkiye nüfus bibliyografyası*, Ankara 1967, continuing. See also Necdet Tunçdilek and Erol Tü[illegible] tekin, *Türkiye nüfusu*, Istanbul 1959; Yakut B[illegible] toğlu, *La structure par âge et la mortalité de la pop[illegible] tion de la Turquie*, Paris 1970; and Ilhan Te[illegible] *Evolution of spatial organization in the Otto[illegible] Empire and Turkish Republic*, in *From Medin[illegible] Metropolis*, ed. L. Carl Brown, Princeton 1[illegible] 244-73.

Iran and Afghānistān. There are no reli[illegible] demographic statistics extant for Iran until [illegible] into the 20th century. In fact, the only contempo[illegible] statements on Persian population before World [illegible] I that have been published are European estim[illegible] mainly dating from *ca.* 1900. The Ṣafawī and Ḳā[illegible] registers have not been found, or at least not anal[illegible] and published. However, G. G. Gilbar has stu[illegible] critically European estimates of the populatio[illegible] Ḳādjār Iran and the effects of epidemics and [illegible] on the population and has made projection[illegible] population size, in his *Demographic development [illegible] late Qajar Persia, 1870-1906*, in *Asian and Afr[illegible] Studies*, xi (Haifa 1976), 125-56. See the comm[illegible] and reports on Iranian population by Issawi in *Economic history of Iran, 1800-1914*, 26-35, an[illegible] his *Population and resources in the Ottoman Em[illegible] and Iran*, in *Studies in eighteenth-century Isla[illegible] history*, ed. T. Naff and R. Owen, London 1977, [illegible] J. Bharier, *A note on the population of Iran*[illegible] *Population Studies*, xxii, 274-5.

The Iranian government made unsuccessful [illegible] tempts at population registration from 1928 [illegible] wards, and carried out an urban "head cou[illegible] between 1939 and 1941 in 25 cities (B. D. Cl[illegible] *Iran: changing population patterns*, in Clarke [illegible] Fisher, 68-96). Censuses were held in 1956 and 1[illegible] but the censuses, while providing the first fa[illegible] reasonable population data on many parts of I[illegible] included significant undercounting of women [illegible] of certain geographic areas and minority gro[illegible] especially nomadic Kurds and Turks.

Bharier has projected the population of I[illegible] from 1900 to 1970 in his *Economic developmen[illegible] Iran, 1900-1970*, Oxford 1971, 24-8, which incorp[illegible] tes material from his *A note* and other articles [illegible] Bharier. Djamchid Momeni, *The population of I[illegible] a dynamic analysis*, Tehran 1975, 25-30, give[illegible] slightly different set of estimates for the same per[illegible] Of the two, Bharier's analysis and estimates [illegible] superior. His estimates of total population [illegible] rural and urban populations, and migration giv[illegible] broad idea of population change in Iran from 1[illegible] Given the paucity of the data, no more can [illegible] expected.

The following can serve as an introduction to [illegible] modern population and demography of Iran: [illegible] *population of Iran, a selecion of readings*, ed. Dj[illegible] shid A. Momeni, Honolulu 1977; Djamshid Behr[illegible] and Mehdi Amani, *La population de l'Iran*, P[illegible] 1974; and various publications of the Instit[illegible] for Social Studies and Research in Tehran.

Afghānistān's geographical features and [illegible] nomadic nature of many of its people have made e[illegible] the rough estimation of population in Afghānis[illegible] a great task. Population sample surveys of Afg[illegible] nistān were taken in Afghānistān in 1960 and 196[illegible] the latter providing detailed information on de[illegible] graphic variables.

These surveys have been described by L. Dup[illegible] *Population review 1970: Afghanistan*, in *Ameri[illegible] Universities Field Staff Reports*, South Asia Se[illegible] xv/1 (Dec. 1970), and Hamidullah Amin and Gor[illegible] B. Schilz, *A geography of Afghanistan*, Oma[illegible] 'aska 1976, 153-64. Amin and Schilz print useful ts of the surveys, but they too readily accept ey and registration data in questionable areas, as records of female population and complete- of registration, and thus their work must be with care.

ghānistān conducted a more complete sample ey of sedentary population in 1971-3 (*National ographic and family guidance survey of the settled lation of Afghanistan*, 4 vols. 1975). The survey ided the first accurate data on the majority of oopulation. It was followed by a census in 1979, results of which are not available. Government tration of males was begun in Afghānistān in , but has produced no useful statistics and is y incomplete. The best analysis of the Afghān lation appears in the analytical volumes (1, 2, 4) of the 1971-3 National Demographic and Fam- uidance Survey. See also two articles by Dupree, *ılation dynamics in Afghanistan*, in *Field Staff rts*, South Asia Series, xiv/7 (April 1970), and *ement and migration patterns in Afghanistan: a tive statement*, in *Modern Asian Studies*, ix/3 7 1975), 397-413. J.-Ch. Blanc, *L'Afghanistan s populations*, Brussels 1977; J. Trussel and Ele- Brown, *A close look at the demography of Af- istan*, in *Demography*, xi/1 (Febr. 1979), 137-51. Russian articles on Afghānistān, see T. I. Kukh- *Bibliografiya Afganistana*, Moscow 1965.

IV. North Africa

ie populations of North Africa, like those of Middle East, are usually studied individually, on by nation. Only a few works have drawn to- er statistics from various nations into a picture North African population as a whole. See, for nple, Mahmoud Seklani, *Croissance démographi- comparée des pays du Maghreb, 1950-1960*, in *e Tunisienne des Sciences Sociales*, vi/17-18 (June), 29-51, and J. Vallon, *Les populations de l'Afri- au Nord du Sahara: Maroc, Algérie, Tunisie, e, Égypte*, in *Populations*, xxv/6 (Nov.-Dec.), 1212-35. Amor Benyoussef, *Population du hreb et communauté économique à quatre*, Paris ', uses population as a basis for analysis of social economic similarities of the Maghrib countries. nlike the Middle East, there are few good sources istorical population statistics for the Maghrib. se that do exist do not go farther back than the century, though one can hope for the future overy and use of Ottoman registers for earlier ods.

orocco. The political and statistical situation of nial Morocco was so fragmented that no reason- accurate statistics for the entire country exist re 1960. Prior to Morocco's independence and ication in 1956, the Spanish colonial power only mpted one census, in 1950, while the French in zone took counts in 1921, 1926, 1936, 1947, and -2. All except the French 1947 "census" were un- ounts. In 1947 the government counted ration 's to establish population numbers, and war-time alities seem to have caused an actual overcount, G. H. Blake, *Morocco: urbanization and concen- on of population*, in Clarke and Fisher, 404-5. The occan censuses of 1960 and 1971 gave more rea- ble totals, and the undercount of women and dren seen in other censuses of Muslim countries slight in Morocco in 1971. Two sample surveys Moroccan population have been held, in 1961-3 1971-3.

a population rurale du Maroc by D. Noin (2 vols., Paris 1970) gives full analyses of all demographic phenomena, including historical estimates of the population and an excellent bibliography. The work is essential to an understanding of Moroccan demography and demographic history. K. Krotki and R. Beaujot have analysed the accuracy of Moroccan population statistics and arrived at revised figures in *La population marocaine: reconstitution de l'évolution de 1950 à 1971*, in *Population*, xxx/2 (March-April 1975), 335-67. *La population du Maroc* (by the Institut National du Statistique et d'Économie Appliquée of Morocco, Rabat n.d.) is a reasonable summary of basic demographic measures on Morocco, but is disappointing in its lack of detailed analysis or bibliography.

Algeria. Algeria has one of the longest series of censuses of any developing country. The French began enumerating settled Algerian population and nomads (by "tent", not by person) in the entire country in 1856. Before 1886, a certain amount of estimation was used for remote areas, and it was only in 1886 that the French attempted actually to count the entire population. Even then, however, distrust of the colonial government and the difficulties of counting nomads and certain other parts of the population produced a serious under-enumeration; see G. Negadi, *Les sources de la démographie en Algérie*, in *La population de l' Algérie*, Algiers 1974 (?), 1-3. From 1886 to 1911 and from 1921 to 1936 the French held quinquennial censuses of Algeria. After the Second World War, censuses were taken by the French, then by the Algerian government in 1948, 1954, 1960, 1966, and 1977.

Despite their long series, the Algerian censuses only gradually improved in completeness and produced significant undercounts in all censuses prior to 1966. Added to the ubiquitous problems of under-enumeration of women and children, census-takers in Algeria experienced special problems with nomads and with migration to Europe. (For a detailed description of the first reasonably-accurate Algerian census and the problems mentioned above, see Abdelaziz Bouisri, *Technique, méthode, et résultats du recensement de la population Algérienne*, in *Revue Tunisienne*, vi/17-18 (June 1969), 95-125.)

Algeria's vital registration system was begun by the French, but under-registration was extremely high, perhaps 30 %. Since independence this figure has improved to 10-15 % of vital events unregistered; see M. L. Fares, *Population growth and socio-economic development in Algeria*, in *Demographic aspects*, 398-9). The country took a major National Demographic Survey in 1969-71 which has provided the best estimates of fertility and trends available.

In addition to the articles mentioned above, the following can be consulted as basic descriptions of Algerian population and demography: A. M. Bahri *Population et politique en Algérie*, in *Revue Tunisienne*, vi/17-18, 65-88; Zachariah, *Basic demographic measures of Algeria*, in *Demographic measures*, 1-25; A. Bouisri and F. de Lamaze, *La population d'Algérie d'après le recensement de 1966*, in *Population*, xxvi, numéro spécial (March 1971), 25-46; G. Negadi *et alii*, *Situation démographique de l'Algérie*, and the other articles and the bibliography in *La population de l'Algérie*, in *Population*, xxviii/6 (Nov.-Dec. 1973), 1079-1107.

Tunisia. Both the Ottoman government and the Tunisian Beylik kept registers of population, mainly as taxation records. J. Ganiage has examined these registers and deduced from them the population of Tunisia *ca.* 1860; see *La population de la Tunisie vers 1860. Essai d'évaluation d'après les registres fiscaux*, in *Études Maghrebines*, Paris 1964, 165-98, and in *Population*, xxi/5 (Sept.-Oct. 1966), 857-62). As is usually the case, the local records are far superior as sources of demographic information than any estimates by travellers or consuls. (For a brief summary of early estimates, see Mahmoud Seklani, *La population de la Tunisie*, Tunis 1974, 13-22.)

The French government of Tunisia and later the Republic held censuses in 1921, 1926, 1931, every ten years from 1936 to 1966, and in 1975. (Censuses of the European population of Tunisia were held earlier than 1921.) The first census seems to have undercounted the population due to the enumerators' dependence on tax registers (Clarke, *Tunisia: population patterns, pressures, and policies*, in Clarke and Fisher, 350; Seklani, *op. cit.*, 18-19), so it is perhaps not proper to call it an actual census. The latter censuses have shown the usual undercount of women and younger children. Various surveys have provided a more detailed demographic picture than seen in the censuses, especially the Tunisian Demographic Survey of 1968 (J. Vallin and G. Paulet, *Quelques aspects de l'enquête nationale démographique tunisienne*, in *Revue Tunisienne*, vi/17-18, 227-48).

Though death registration in Tunisia is very incomplete, since 1958 births seem to have been better recorded; see S. Zaghloul, *Demographic parameters of Tunisia*, in *Demographic measures*, 231, 233.

Tunisia has a well-developed statistical system. M. Picouet describes the system and gives an overview of available data in *Les sources de la démographie tunisienne à l'époque contemporaine*, Tunis 1972. The population itself is described, from the 19th century to 1990, in Seklani's *La population de la Tunisie*. See also: Hachemi Chtioui, *La croissance de la population et des resources en Tunisie pendant la période coloniale*, in *Revue Tunisienne*, vi/17-18, 53-64; A. Marcoux, *La croissance de la population de la Tunisie*, in *Population*, xxvi, numéro spécial (March 1971), 105-24; and the various publication of the Centre d'Études et de Recherches Économiques et Sociales of the University of Tunis and of the Tunisian Institut National de la Statistique.

Libya. The first population statistics for Libya were the Ottoman registration (males only) records for the Provinces of Benghazi and Tripoli. The Italians took censuses in 1931 and 1935 which underenumerated the nomadic population, but counted the city regions with greater accuracy, see Pan Chia-Lin, *The population of Libya*, in *Population Studies*, iii/1, 100-25. Independent Libya has held three censuses: 1954, 1964, and 1973. Statistics have improved with time, and an undercount in 1954 had greatly improved by 1973, though the 1973 census was still probably incomplete in coverage of nomads.

Compared to the other North African countries, very little has been written on the demography of Libya. R. G. Hartley, *Libya: economic developments and demographic responses*, in Clarke and Fischer, 315-47, describes population and economy, but provides very little analysis of Libyan demographic data. The best descriptions of the Libyan demography are the short *Demographic parameters of Libya*, by S. Zaghloul, in *Demographic measures*, 115-36, and a monograph by the Libyan census department, *Population growth, fertility, and mortality based on the 1973 Populations Census*, Addis Abbaba (UNECA) 1979.

Egypt. Egyptian population before 1800 has been estimated on the basis of taxes paid, land cultivation, and contemporary statements on city sizes, none of which have resulted in anything but very rough [ap]proximations. On these estimates, see W. Clel[and], *The population problem in Egypt*, Lancaster, P[a.] 1936, 3-6. The first attempt at scientifically coun[ting] the Egyptian population was made by members o[f the] French Expedition in 1800. It was followed b[y an] enumeration, based on tax registers, made [by] Muḥammad ʿAlī in 1821. Both of these early atte[mpts] resulted in considerable undercounts. The first [rela]tively accurate population count in Egyptian his[tory] was taken by Muḥammad ʿAlī in 1846, this [was] drawn from household registers similar to t[hose] mentioned above for the Ottoman Empire in [the] same period. A census along modern lines was ta[ken] in 1882, but its figures were once again too low. [See] J. McCarthy, *Nineteenth century Egyptian popula[tion]*, in *Middle Eastern Studies*, xii/3 (Oct. 1976), 1[...] which includes correction factors for the 1882 fig[ures].

The British took decennial censuses from 189[7 to] 1947. Except for a large undercount in the [...] wartime census, the British censuses are good p[opu]lation records. The amount of undercounting [di]minished as the census series went on. Attempt[s to] take a census of the new Egyptian Republic [were] frustrated in 1957 by war conditions, though [pre]liminary results were reported. The Egyptian gov[ern]ment carried out successful censuses in 1960 and 1[976] and a sample census in 1966. Registration of bi[rths] and deaths has been done since the middle of the [19th] century and, though it has never been complete, [the] registration of vital events in the 20th century [has] been accurate enough to provide a general pictur[e of] fertility and mortality patterns. By the stand[ards] of the developing world, Egypt has an excel[lent] series of demographic statistics.

An article by A. B. Mountjoy, *Egypt: popula[tion] and resources*, in Clarke and Fisher, 291-314, [is a] readable and non-technical summary of the E[gyp]tian population after 1966. For more analytic tr[eat]ments, see M. S. Khodary, *Use of census age di[stri]butions for estimating basic demographic param[eters] of the U.A.R.*, in *Demographic measures*, 249-78, [and] V. G. Valaoras, *Population analysis of Egypt (1[...]-1970)*, Cairo Demographic Centre, *Occasional P[aper]* no. 1, Cairo 1972. Atef M. Khalifa, *The popula[tion] of the Arab Republic of Egypt*, Cairo 1973, is the [most] comprehensive description of the population. [See] also Issawi, *Population and wealth in Egypt*, [in] *Demographic analysis: selected readings*, ed. [J. J.] Spengler and O. D. Duncan, Glencoe, Ill. 1[956]; Egypt, Central Agency for Public Mobilisation [and] Statistics, *The increase of population in the Un[ited] Arab Republic and its impact on development*, C[airo] 1969, esp. 1-30; Janet L. Abu-Lughod, *Cairo*, Pri[nce]ton 1971; Egypt, D̲j̲ihāz tanẓīm al-Usra wa 'l-Sukk[ān], *al-Aṭlas al-sukkānī li-D̲j̲umhūriyyat Miṣr al-ʿAra[bi]ya*, Cairo 1977.

The general works on Middle Eastern popula[tion] cited above usually include the demography [of] Egypt among their studies. Many monogra[phs] on the populations of the Middle East [and] Egypt are published by the Cairo Demogra[phic] Centre.

V. Sub-Saharan Africa

Islam is dominant across North-Central Af[rica] from Mauritania to Somalia, and there are sig[nifi]cant Muslim minorities in both East and West Afr[ica]. Demographic knowledge of this area only begins w[ith] the period of colonial domination. Though a few [tra]veller's accounts of the populations of small a[reas] exist for an earlier period, there are no accu[rate]

›s for the total populations of large areas un-
ıll into the 20th century.
e type of demographic statistics available b-Saharan African countries depends on whether olonial ruler of a nation was England or France. ınd was generally more able to take census sta- s of its sub-Saharan possessions than was France. at the very end of colonial rule, though, were English censuses remotely successful counts of lation. Before that time, numerous censuses were of the non-native populations, or of the popu- ıs of cities, or of selected areas, but the first ıl censuses of entire countries were only taken World War II.

fore the War the British did produce a wealth stimates of African population. These range simple estimates based on observation to com- approximations made by comparing the charac- ics of areas that had been enumerated with that had not and estimating that similar areas imilar population numbers. Both estimates and ses made in British Africa are considered in and thoroughly analysed by R. R. Kuczynski, *ographic survey of the British Colonial Empire*, s., Oxford 1948. Kuczynski collected censuses, ates, and other data and drew trom them accu- stimates of total population, fertility, mortality, nigration. While more recent studies have ques- d certain sections of his analyses, Kuczynski's still stands as a monument to careful scholarship.

e first reliable population data from East can censuses come from the British East an censuses of 1948. These were followed by ises taken in Kenya in 1962, 1969, and 1979, nzania in 1957-8, 1967, and 1978, and in Uganda 959 and 1969. Sample surveys have not been ıportant in East Africa as in West Africa and ahel and population registration has not proved tive.

r an introduction to the demography of East a, see Simeon Ominde, *The population of Kenya- ıda-Tanzania*, Nairobi 1975. Melte Monsted and een Walji, *A demographic analysis of East Africa*, ala 1978, go more deeply into analysis and inter- tion of demographic phenomena. An article by . C. Bleeker, *Demography*, in *East Africa: its e and resources*, ed. W. T. W. Morgan, Nairobi, on and New York 1972, 41-58, and the ch. on lation in R. M. A. van Zwanenberg and Anne , *An economic history of Kenya and Uganda*, obi 1975, 3-22, are both brief summaries of the n population history of the area. To date, the complete and detailed analyses of any country in Africa are in *The demography of Tanzania*, ed. di A. Henin, Dar es Salaam n.d., whose articles yse the results of the demographic survey of ania. On pre-1970 censuses and registration of s and deaths in the area, see the brief description bibliography by D. A. Lury, *Population data of Africa*, in *The population of Tropical Africa*, ed. Caldwell and Chukuka Okonjo, New York 44-70.

West Africa, no complete census was ever ı in Nigeria, Ghana, or Sierra Leone while were under British colonial rule, though in- t counts were taken in Ghana in 1948. Ghana held decennial censuses since 1960 and Sierra e censuses in 1963 and 1974. In Nigeria, wing upon a series of population estimates and al censuses beginning in 1866, the British took sus in 1952-3 that was relatively reliable. Since , each Nigerian census has proved to be more unreliable than the last. See R. K. Udo, *Population and politics in Nigeria*, in Caldwell and Okonjo, 97-105. Nigeria has held censuses in 1952-3, 1962, 1963, and 1973.

Unlike Nigeria, the censuses of Ghana and Sierra Leone have proved to be reliable. Sierra Leone censuses have exhibited only a slight, *ca.* 5 %, undercount and the Ghana censures are of a similar level of reliability. See T. E. Dow Jr. and E. Benjamin, *Demographic trends and implications*, and S. K. Gaisie, *Population growth and its components*, in *Population growth and socioeconomic change in West Africa*, ed. Caldwell, New York 1975, 427-54, and 346-66.

S. K. Gaisie and K. T. de Graft-Johnson, *The population of Ghana*, Legon, Ghana 1976, have summarised the demography of modern Ghana, but they mention little on historical population. For historical data, see Marion Johnson, *Census, map, and guessestimate: the past population of the Accra Region*, in *African historical demography*, Edinburgh 1977. See also T. E. Hilton, *Ghana population atlas*, London 1960; *Symposium on population and socioeconomic development in Ghana*, ed. N. O. Addo, *et alii*, Legon 1968; *Interdisciplinary approaches to population studies*, Proceedings of the West African Seminar on Population Studies, Legon 1972; and the three articles by Gaisie in *Population growth*.

Any studies of Sierra Leone should begin with G. M. K. Kpedekpo and G. John, *A bibliography on population and development planning in Sierra Leone*, Freetown 1979. The best short description of the Sierra Leone population are J. I. Clarke, *Population growth in Sierra Leone*, in Caldwell and Okonjo, 270-7, and M. F. Harvey, *The nature of movement of the population*, in *Population growth*, 455-72.

P. O. Olunsaya has briefly summarised historical and modern data on Nigeria in his *Population growth and its components: the nature and direction of the population*, in *Population change*, 254-74. It is symptomatic of the deficiences of the Nigerian census system that the only general book on Nigerian population is mainly a study of sample surveys (F. L. Mott and Olanrewaju J. Fapohunda, *The population of Nigeria*, Lagos 1975). I. I. Ekanem, *The 1963 Nigerian census: a critical appraisal*, Benin City 1972, has a good, brief introduction (30-45) to the statistical history of Nigeria. See also H. O. Emezi, *Nigerian population and urbanization, 1911-1974, a bibliography*, Occasional Paper no. 10 of the UCLA African Studies Center, 1975.

The Sudan has held three demographic sample surveys—1955-6, 1964-6 and 1967-8—and one census, in 1973. (The 1955-6 survey is often erroneously called a census.) Registration of births and deaths is extremely deficient. Despite increasing accuracy over time, all statements on Sudan's population have been undercounts, especially undercounts of nomads. Because of flaws in census and survey materials, much of what is known of Sudan's population comes from demographic analyses of defective data. For such analyses, see especially P. Demeny, *The demography of the Sudan*, in W. Brass, *et alii*, *The demography of Tropical Africa*, Princeton 1968, 466-514, and Zachariah, *Use of population and housing survey data of the Sudan for estimating its current demographic measures*, in *Demographic measures*, 169-93. The most complete picture of the Sudanese population is given in *The population of Sudan*, Khartoum 1958, but the book too often relies on defective data from the 1955-6 survey and even this data is out-of-date. The articles listed above and K. S. Seetharam and A. Farah, *Population trends and economic development in Sudan*, in *Demographic aspects*, 149-69, give a more accurate picture of the population.

That the French in Africa were not as active as the British in taking censuses was largely a function of the type of colonial territory which they held. The countries of the Sahel—Chad, Niger, Mali, and Mauritania—are ones in which holding an accurate census historically proved to be near impossible. Complete counts of population were hindered by the problems of counting nomads, lack of trained census takers, and the prohibitively high costs of censuses in what were extremely poor nations. Chad has never had a census, and the other three countries only held their first censuses in 1976-7, with uncertain results. Instead of censuses, demographers of the Sahel have relied on "sample censuses" of 5 to 10 % of the population. These have yielded the only fairly reliable data on fertility and mortality of the area. See S. P. Reyna, *Chad*, and Issaka Pankoussa, *et alii*, *Niger*, in *Population growth*. A similar, though more statistically reliable, set of sample surveys and post-1975 censuses has been held in other areas of formerly French Africa. Pre-independence "censuses" of French Equatorial Africa were actually either estimates or what are called administrative censuses. The latter are counts drawn from tax registers, administrative records, or attempts to assemble the population at market towns to be counted and have proved to be uniformly incorrect.

L. Verrière has described Senegal in 1965 (*La population du Sénégal*, Dakar 1965), basing his work on the 1960-1 sample survey, which was highly deficient. See also P. Metge, *Le peuplement du Sénégal*, Dakar 1966. The article by B. Lacombe, B. Lawry, and J. Vaugelade, *Senegal*, in *Population growth*, 701-19, is a better description of the population. A. Podlewski has described the population of Cameroon in *Population growth*, 543-64, but little else has been written on the country's population. See also J.-M. Cohen *et alii*, *Afrique Noire, Madagascar, Comores—Démographie comparée*, Paris 1967; *Demographic transition and cultural continuity in the Sahel*, ed. D. I. Pool and S. P. Coulihaly, Ithaca, N.Y. 1977.

Historical demography of Africa is necessarily hindered by the lack of sources. Unfortunately, the Muslim areas of Africa are often those with the worst potential for historical population statistics, since no "parish registers" or missionary records of conversions exist for African Muslims. Nevertheless, the application of sophisticated techniques of demographic and historical analysis is producing data on African Muslim populations of the past, particularly in the 19th century. An example of scholarly effort on African population, *African historical population*, Proceedings of a Seminar at the University of Edinburgh 1977, includes studies on the Sudan, the Ivory Coast, and French Equatorial Africa, all areas of significant Muslim population, and analyses of population statistics of East and West Africa. G. Ayoub Balamoan, *Migration policies in the Anglo-Egyptian Sudan, 1884-1956*, Cambridge, Mass. 1977, has demonstrated that limited African data can be used to establish sound historical knowledge on migration, demographic change, Muslim topics such as the Pilgrimage, and even political events. Many of the works mentioned above on modern African demography have sections on historical demography as well. The volumes by Kuczynski are particularly important for identifying historical statistics and their sources.

Most of the new nations of Africa have taken [...]suses since independence. F. Gendreau has publi[...] a list of censuses, and sample surveys, take[...] all the countries of Africa between 1946 and [...] see *La démographie des pays d'Afrique, revue et thèse*, in *Population*, xxxii/4-5 (July-Oct. 1[...] 930-1 (Some of the censuses listed by Gendreau [...] not complete or accurate enough to be listed as [...]suses by the United Nations.) More recent cen[...] are listed in the United Nations Demographic [...] book (described below).

There are not many general works on the d[...]graphy of sub-Saharan Africa. *The demograph[...] Tropical Africa*, ed. Brass *et alii*, Princeton [...] is a pioneer work, not only in African demogra[...] but in the study of the populations of develo[...] nations. E. van de Walle's *Characteristics of Af[...] demographic data* in the volume (12-87) is an [...]cellent summary of the types of errors foun[...] African censuses and surveys. Gendreau lists [...] populations of cities and countries in his a[...] *La démographie*, and considers the accuracy of va[...] types of data-gathering techniques—censuses, [...]ministrative censuses, and surveys. For a geogra[...] approach to African population, see W. A. Ha[...] *Population, migration, and urbanization in Af[...]* New York 1970. The best source on West Afri[...] *Population growth and socioeconomic change in [...] Africa*, the articles of which consider first the [...]mographic variables for the region as a whole, [...] for specific nations. Nigeria, Sierra Leone, [...] Ghana are particularly well represented.

For a brief introduction to sub-Saharan Afr[...] population, see the chapter by J. C. Caldwe[...] *General history of Africa*, ed. A. H. Boahele, [...] 1975, or Chantal and Yves Blayo, *The size [...] structure of African populations*, in *Populatio[...] African development*, ed. P. Cantrelle, Liège [...] (The other articles in the Cantrelle volume, pa[...] from a 1971 conference, are detailed studies of [...]cific problems in African demography.) The Un[...] Nations Economic Commission for Africa (A[...] Ababa) publishes continuing series on African de[...]graphy, especially the *Demographic handbook [...] Africa* and the African Population Studies Se[...] The bibliography by the United States Librar[...] Congress, *Islam in Sub-Saharan Africa* (Washin[...] 1978) mentions few articles specifically on pop[...]tion, but a number of articles cited as ethnogra[...] have demographic uses. See also: *Essays on Afr[...] population*, ed. K. M. Barbour and R. M. Proth[...] London 1961, which should be used only as a so[...] of references on early data, since the articles ac[...] inferior, usually colonial, data in their analy[...] *Population growth and economic development [...] Africa*, ed. S. H. Ominde and C. N. Ejiogu, Lon[...] Nairobi, Ibadan 1972; D. Morrison *et alii*, *B[...] Africa, a comparative handbook*, New York [...] London 1972.

VI. Caucasus and Central Asia

There are no accurate statistics of the nu[...] of Central Asian Muslims in what is today [...] U.S.S.R. until the 19th century. Barthold, *Turke[...]* ch. 1, mentions a few Chinese and Arab statem[...] on the populations of cities and numbers in arm[...] but these are no more than improbable guesses, [...] the city of Samarkand having 500,000 citizens [...] the late 19th century, travellers such as Cu[...] (*Russia in Central Asia*, London 1889) and Schu[...] (*Turkistan*, New York 1877) occasionally repo[...] city sizes, taken from Russian records, fairly a[...]

', though not figures on total population. See ki Velidi Toğan, *Bügünkü Türkili ve yakın tari-* tanbul 1942-7, 27-8.

e first census of Central Asia was taken in by the Russian government. The vassal states īwa and Bukhārā were not included in this cen- since they were nominally not included in the an Empire, and the populations of the two states ccordingly only known from contemporary esti- s. See Timur Kocaoğlu, *The existence of a Bukh- nationality in the recent past*, in *The nationality on in Soviet Central Asia*, ed. E. Allworth, York 1973, 151-8. Estimates of the population ukhārā and Khīva have been discussed and sed by F. Lorimer in *The population of the So- Union: history and prospects*, Geneva 1946, 129, more completely by L. Kroder, *Peoples of Central* Bloomington, Ind. 1963, 172-3. Like all cen- of traditional areas, the 1897 census figures ncomplete, especially for Muslim women and g children. Nevertheless, its data are excellent compared to the type of poor estimates that serve for previous periods.

e first complete census of Russian (Soviet) al Asian Muslims was taken in 1926, followed nsuses in 1939, 1959, 1970, and 1979. Official ates of the Central Asian population were also by the imperial government in 1911 and the So- government in 1956 (Kroder, 178, 190).

ce the Soviet state is atheistic, it does not re- se religious distinctions and the category lim" does not appear on the Soviet censuses. dent of Muslim population in the Soviet Union consider instead the population of multitudinous ic groups" whose antecedents were Muslims. parison of Imperial statistics on Muslims with t statistics on "ethnic groups" is very difficult, nalysis of Soviet Muslim population. Most demo- ic analyses of Central Asia or the Caucasus are by region or republic, i.e., multi-ethnic or i-religious subdivisions, or by ethnic or linguistic s, not religion.

M. Matley's *The population and the land*, in *al Asia: a century of Russian rule*, ed. All- n, New York and London 1967, is a good general e on Imperial and Soviet Central Asian popu- , as is ch. 7, *Demography*, of Krader's *Peoples ntral Asia*. General volumes such as *The natio- question in Soviet Central Asia*, and R. A. s *et alii*, *Nationality and population change in ia and the USSR*, New York 1976, contain large ons on Muslim populations and helpful biblio- ies. The best analyses of demographic variables ntral Asia and the Caucasus are in A. J. Coale *i*, *Human fertility in Russia since the nineteenth ry*, Princeton 1979, ch. 3. Though not a demo- ic text, A. Bennigsen and Ch. Lemercier-Quel- y, *Islam in the Soviet Union*, New York 1967, d be consulted for material on the Muslim fa- and bibliography. Demographic information, ly on total population, is scattered throughout rticles on the Turkish peoples of Central Asia the Caucasus in *Türk dünyası el kitabı*, Ankara Articles on population and modern demography ar in the journal *Vestnik Statistiki* (Moscow). r sources of demographic information and graphy, see U.S.S.R., Akademiya Nauk, Geo- eskoe Obshestvo Soyuza SSR, *Geografiya niya v SSSR, osnovnie problemi*, Moscow 1964, 2-4; G. J. Demko, *Demographic research on ia and the Soviet Union: a bibliographic review evaluation*, in *Demographic developments in Eastern Europe*, ed. L. A. Kosinski, New York 1977, 94-119. Barbara Anderson has compiled an excellent detailed list of Russian and Soviet statistical publications, *Data sources in Russian and Soviet demography*, in *Demographic developments*, 23-63.

VII. Indian Subcontinent

The Indian subcontinent, comprising the modern states of Bangladesh, India and Pakistan, has a long and detailed statistical history. The Mughals instituted a population, land, and tax registration system, and much demographic information from the Mughal period, and perhaps earlier, exists in local archives in the subcontinent (Ajit Das Gupta, *Study of the historical demography of India*, in D. V. Glass and R. Revelle, *Population and social change*, London 1972, 425). Little use has been made, however, of anything but population estimates as they appear in histories and chronicles, which sometimes themselves drew on contemporary government records. The first to make use of these population estimates was W. H. Moreland, *India at the death of Akbar*, London 1920, who based his population estimates on the relation of total population to reports of the area of cultivated land and to reports of the sizes of armies. His figures for total population have been improved on and generally supported by J. M. Datta, *Re-examination of Moreland's estimate of the population of India at the death of Akbar*, in *Indian Population Bulletin*, i/1 (Delhi April 1960), whose historical and demographic methodology was far superior to that of Moreland. K. Davis, *The population of India and Pakistan*, New York 1951, 24, raised Moreland's figures, as did Das Gupta, 425-30.

Estimates of mediaeval Indian Muslim population have been carefully catalogued by K. S. Lal, *Growth of Muslim population in medieval India, A.D. 1000-1800*, Delhi 1973. He has demonstrated that painstaking analysis of all types of sources—geographers' accounts, government records, histories, and censuses and registration records from small areas—can provide useful demographic statistics. Despite the completeness of Lal's work, his conclusions remain rough estimates only, many on the level of informed guesses.

British residents of the East India Company, and later the Empire, made numerous population reports in the 19th century. At first they resorted to devices such as counting houses, ploughs or villages and multiplying by set number, but later censuses of certain areas such as Bombay and Madras were taken, and these formed the basis of British population estimates for wider areas (Das Gupta, 419-35). Lal (224-52) has listed a number of early 19th century British censuses and estimates, but the most complete listing is in E. Thornton, *Gazeteer of the territories under the Government of the East India Company and of the Native States*, 4 vols., London 1854.

The first complete British census of the Indian subcontinent was taken in 1881, following an incomplete census in 1871. Figures in the 1881 census were too low, but have been adjusted by P. C. Mahalonobis and D. Bhattacharya, *Growth of the Population of India and Pakistan, 1801-1961*, in *Artha Vijñāna*, xviii/1 (March 1976), 1-10, and by K. Davis, ch. 4. Up to 1931, British censuses of the subcontinent gradually improved, until by the 1931 and 1941 censuses they were among the best in the colonial world.

On early Indian subcontinent population, see

also Zachariah, *An historical study of internal migration in the Indian sub-continent*, New York 1964; Government of India, *Report on the population estimates of India, 1820-1930*, Delhi 1975; T. G. Kessinger, *Historical demography of India*, in *Peasant Studies*, v/3 (July 1976), 2-8.

After independence, the Indian and Pakistani governments continued the censuses. India kept to the British decennial census plan and held censuses in 1951, 1961, 1971, and is planning a 1981 census. Pakistan took censuses in 1951, 1961, and 1972; Bangladesh in 1974. Of the three countries, India's census totals seem to be the closest to correct. Pakistan's census probably undercounts by 7-8 %. D. Natarajan, *Indian census through a hundred years*, New Delhi n.d., gives a detailed view of the Indian censuses. All three countries have held sample surveys which have been especially valuable in evaluating fertility. See, for example, Bangladesh, Census Commission, *Report on the 1974 Bangladesh retrospective survey of fertility and mortality*, Dacca 1977, and World Fertility Survey, *Pakistan fertility survey*, First report, Karachi? 1976.

India's size and economic situation, as well as its long series of available statistics, makes it the developing country most studied by demographers. Hundreds of articles are written each year on facets of Indian demography, and it is impossible to consider this vast literature here. Kingsley Davis's volume, mentioned above, is a good introduction to the demography of India up to independence. The Indian Registrar General's Office has published a general introduction to Indian population, *The population of India*, Delhi 1974, and a *Bibliography of census publication of India*, Delhi 1972. For a more complete review of the Indian statistical tradition, population, and demography, see Asok Mitra, *India's population: aspects of quality and control*, 2 vols., New Delhi 1978. See also R. H. Cassen, *India: population, economy, and society*, New York 1978.

Information on modern censuses and surveys of Pakistan and its demography is well summarised in Mohammad Afzal, *The population of Pakistan*, Islamabad 1974. L. Bean has written a short introduction to the subject in *The population of Pakistan, an evaluation of recent statistical data*, in *MEJ*, xxviii/2 (1974), 177-84. Though the area of Pakistan has been included in studies on the historical demography of India, studies of purely Pakistani historical demography have been done as well: A. S. M. Mohiuddin, *The population of Pakistan: past and present*, diss., Duke University 1962, and Pakistan Institute of Development Economics, *District Boundary changes and population growth for Pakistan, 1881-1961*, Dacca n.d. Earlier studies of Pakistani demography all include Bangladesh as East Pakistan.

See also *Studies in the demography of Pakistan*, ed. W. C. Robinson, Karachi 1965; A.D. Bhatti, *A bibliography of Pakistan demography*, Karachi 1965; Sultan S. Hashmi, *Main features of the demographic condition in Pakistan*, Karachi 1963; T. P. Schultz and Julie da Vanzo, *Analysis of demographic change in East Pakistan*, United States Agency for International Development Report by the Rand Corporation, Santa Monica, Cal. 1970; K. J. Krotki and Khalida Parveen, *Population size and growth in Pakistan based on early reports of the 1972 census*, in *The Pakistan Development Review*, xv/3 (Autumn 1976), 290-318.

VIII. Southeast Asia

Indonesia. In the late 18th and early 19th centuries, European colonial agents estimated the p
lation of Java, basing their figures on records c
Dutch East India Company. These estimates,
first of their kind, were gross underestimates.
first attempts at accurate enumeration of the po
tion were made by the British during their
rule in Indonesia (1811-16), when population regi
were made. The Dutch seem to have maintained
registers fitfully until 1880. At that time they enf
more complete registration, to be used as cons
tion records for compulsory labor. Probably bec
all who could do so naturally avoided such a regi
tion, these registers also produced a large u
count of population. Widjojo Nitisastro has ana
early material on the population of Indonesia i
Population trends in Indonesia, Ithaca and Lo
1970, and has concluded that the Dutch figure
total population are generally useless. Their
use should be as part of complete analyses of s
demographic areas. Bram Peper has concurre
Widjojo Nitisastro's analysis and has used altern
demographic methods to calculate the populati
19th century Java; see his *Population growth in*
in the 19th century, in *Population Studies*, x
(March 1970), 71-84.

The Dutch colonial government took a cens
1920 in Java, but included few other areas o
donesia and undercounted Java. Another col
census was held in 1930, with wider coverage
better results. Independent Indonesia has t
censuses in 1961 and 1971. Some areas were estim
rather than enumerated in 1961 and the 1971 ce
is superior. A number of sample surveys have
been taken in the 1960s and 1970s.

Widjojo's volume is the most complete descri
of the Indonesian population (to 1970), but it
depend on the 1961 census. *The population of*
donesia by the Demographic Section of the Unive
of Indonesia (Lembago Demografi) is more com
for the later period. G. McNeill and Si Gde
Mamus, *The demographic situation in Indon*
Papers of the East-West Institute, no. 28, Hon
1973, accurately summarise the available d
graphic information on the country.

See also J. M. van der Kroef, *The Arabs in I*
nesia, in *MEJ*, vii/3 (Summer 1953), 300-23
der Kroef too readily accepts Dutch colonial est
tes of population as accurate); J. N. Bhatta, *A s*
science bibliography of Indonesia, Djakarta 1
N. Iskandar, *Some monographic studies on the p*
lation of Indonesia, Djakarta 1970; and Masri S
rimbun, *The population of Indonesia: a bibliogra*
Yogyakarta 1974.

Singapore-Malaysia. The British begar
take population counts in the areas of Singa
Malaysia in 1824, and made 14 enumerations bet
1824 and 1860, none of which can be called reli
Modern censuses were taken in Singapore in
and 1881 and in both Singapore and the Mal
territories decennially from 1891 to 1931. As Br
colonial power expanded over new areas of Mala
the new areas were brought into the census;
Saw Swee-Hock, *The development of Popul*
statistics in Singapore, in *Singapore Statistical B*
tin, 1/2 (Dec. 1972), 87-93. After World War
the British took censuses in 1947 and 1957.
independent federation of Malaysia held a ce
in 1970, as did Singapore, which had seceded
the federation in 1965. Though registration of de
and births in Malaysia has only been reason
complete since *ca.* 1970, the census results since
have been reliable. On registration data, see J

ore, *et alii, The demographic situation in Malay-*
n *Population and development in Southeast Asia,*
. F. Kanter and L. McCaffrey, New York 1975,
Sample surveys have been taken in the 1960s
1970s.
w Swee-Hock has briefly described changes
pulation sizes in Singapore in *Population trends*
ngapore, 1819-1967, in *Journal of Southeast Asian*
ory, x/1 (March 1969), 36-49, and given a more
plete description of Singapore's demography in
apore, population in transition, Philadelphia
. Saw's analysis of population by "race" offers
ccurate picture of Muslim demography, i.e. the
ography of the Muslim peoples of Singapore.
thy Z. Fernandez *et alii, The population of*
aysia, is a good introduction to demographic
stics on Malaysia, though it contains little ana-
of the population. Those interested in historical
lation should consult C. A. Vlieland, *A report*
e 1931 census and certain problems of vital statis-
London 1932, esp. chs. 3, 13.
e also T. E. Smith, *Population growth in Malaya:*
nalysis of recent trends, London 1952; L. W. Jones,
population of Borneo, London 1966. Many mono-
hs and articles on modern Southeast Asian
lation are published by the United Nations
nomic and Social Commission for Asia and the
fic.

IX. General

e populations of Muslim lands have been ined as part of the estimates in works on world
rical population. The more detailed volumes,
as A. M. Carr-Saunders' *World population: past*
th and present trends, Oxford 1936, or M. Rein-
's *Histoire générale de la population mondiale*
h A. Armengaud and J. Dupaquier, 3rd ed., Paris
), contain fairly extensive statements on the
lations of Muslim lands. It must be remembered
these estimates have mainly collected and re-
uced scholarship that has been done on the va-
s geographic areas of the world by others, so
researchers might be better served by consulting
more primary works, which contain more detailed
yses. The authors of studies of world population
ory are forced to provide estimates for regions
times for which population numbers are actually
own. As has been seen above, Muslim lands are
among those whose historical populations are
own, so estimates of the populations of those
s in world population books must be used with
ion. In addition to Carr-Saunders and Reinhard,
the summary article by J. D. Durand, *Historical*
nates of world population: an evaluation, Uni-
ity of Pennsylvania Population Studies Center,
adelphia 1974, and United Nations, Department
Economic and Social Affairs, *The determinants*
consequences of population trends, 1, New York
3, ch. 2 (vol. ii is a bibliography on world
ulation).

General bibliographies. Many articles on
e demography of the Islamic World do not
ppear in the standard bibliographies on Islam,
ch as *Index islamicus*, since the bibliographies
not usually include technical demographic
urnals within their purview. The best source of
formation on works on any facet of demography
Population index (Princeton, quarterly), one
the most thorough and valuable bibliographies
the social sciences. In addition to hundreds of
urnals, the *Index* examines all relevant bibliogra-
hies from other disciplines for materials on demography. See also *Bibliographie internationale de la démographie historique* (Paris); *Review of population revues* (Paris); and *International population census bibliography*, 6 vols. and suppl., Austin, Texas 1965-8, new vols. in preparation.)

General statistics. The best source of recent demographic statistics on a country is usually the published census, sometimes updated by intercensal estimates in the nation's statistical yearbook. The United Nations *Demographic yearbook* (New York, annual) summarises statistics on population, fertility, mortality, and other demographic topics for all nations. Each year's edition of the *Demographic yearbook* also features detailed statistics on special topics such as marriage or international migration. See also the United Nations *Population and vital statistics report*, published quarterly (New York), which contains topical information.

From 1969 to 1978, the Population Council of the United States published short descriptions and statistics on the demography of various nations in its *Country profiles* (New York 1969-78). The United States Bureau of the Census publishes brief descriptions of selected nation's demography in the series *Country demographic profiles*.

(J. McCarthy)

DEMON [see DJINN, SHAYṬĀN].

DERBOUKA [see DARABUKKA].

DERIVATION [see ISHTIḲĀḲ].

DESERT [see BADW, ṢAḤRĀʾ].

DESK, WRITING [see KITĀBA].

DESTINY, FATE [see AL-ḲAḌĀʾ WA-ʾL-ḲADAR].

DEVIL [see IBLĪS, SHAYṬĀN].

DHABĪḤA means both the sacrifices of a victim and the victim itself. In addition to the religious sacrifices studied in the art. DHABĪḤA, there exist a host of others, meant for special occasions (*dbīḥa* in Maghribī Arabic; Berber *taməghrust*; etc.), which have been treated at length in the art. DAM above. On the blood sacrifices practised before the advent of Islam, see in particular ʿATĪRA and NADHR, and also J. Chelhod, *Le sacrifice chez les Arabes*, Paris 1955, and the bibliography cited there.

(Ed.)

DHĀT AL-ṢAWĀRĪ, Dhū ʾl-Ṣawārī, Ghazwat al-Ṣawārī, "the Battle of the Masts", the names given in the Arabic sources to a naval battle between the Arabs and Byzantines in the latter part of ʿUthmān's caliphate. The locale of the engagement is not wholly certain, but was probably off the coast of Lycia in southern Anatolia near the place Phoenix (modern Turkish Finike, *chef-lieu* of the *kaza* of that name in the *vilayet* of Antalya).

As governor of Syria, Muʿāwiya [*q.v.*] seems to have inaugurated a policy of building up Arab naval power in order to counter Byzantine control of the Eastern Mediterranean, and in 28/648-9 Cyprus had been attacked [see ḲUBRUS]. The Muslim fleet at Dhāt al-Ṣawārī comprised ships from the Syrian coastal ports and from Alexandria, and was under the command of either the governor of Egypt ʿAbd Allāh b. Abī Sarḥ [see ʿABD ALLĀH B. SAʿD] or of a certain Abu ʾl-Aʿwar; the Byzantine fleet was commanded by the Emperor Constans II Pogonatus in person. The exact date of this is unsure, but was either 31/651-2 or 34/654-5 (both dates in al-Ṭabarī, i, 2865, but 34/655 in al-Balādhurī, *Ansāb*, v, 50); nor are the details of the battle clear, whilst those which we do possess have been given many semi-legendary touches. However, the Muslim forces gained a decisive victory, and Constans had to flee to Sicily, where he was assassinated in 668. That the Arabs failed immediately to follow up this triumph, and did not attack Constantinople itself until Muʿāwiya's reign (in 52-8/672-8), was probably the consequence of mounting *fitna* within the caliphate, culminating in ʿUthmān's murder in 35/656 although they were able to sack Rhodes in 33/653-4, just after Dhāt al-Ṣawārī, if we adopt the earlier chronology for the battle.

Bibliography: For the Arabic, Syriac and Greek sources, see Caetani, *Chronographia islamica*, ii, 360. See also J. Wellhausen, *Die Kämpfe der Araber mit den Römern in der Zeit der Umaijiden*, in *Nachrichten der Königl. Gesell. der Wiss. zu Göttingen*, Ph.-Hist. Kl., iv (1901), 414-47; C. H. Becker, in *Cambridge mediaeval history*, ii = *Islamstudien*, i, 96-7; M. Canard, *Les expeditions des Arabes contre Constantinople dans l'histoire et dans la légende*, in *JA*, ccviii (1926), 61-121; P. K. Hitti, *History of the Arabs*, 200-1; G. F. Hourani, *Arab seafaring in the Indian Ocean in ancient and early mediaeval times*, Princeton 1951, 57-9; Y. ʿA. Hāshmī, *Dhātu 'ṣ-Ṣawārī, a naval engagement between the Arabs and Byzantines*, in *IQ*, iv (1961), 55-64; E. Eickhoff, *Seekrieg und Seepolitik zwischen Islam und Abendland, das Mittelmeer unter byzantinischer und arabischer Hegemonie (650-1040)*, Berlin 1966, 18-21. For the Byzantine point of view, and especially for the effect of this defeat on subsequent Byzantine naval policy, see H. Ahrweiler, *Byzance et la mer: la marine de guerre, la politique et les institutions maritimes de Byzance aux VIIᵉ-XVᵉ siècles*, Paris 1966, 17 ff. (C. E. BOSWORTH)

DHIKRĪS, ZIKRĪS, a Muslim sect of southern Balūčistān, especially strong amongst the Balūč of Makrān [*q.v.*], but also with some representation amongst the Brahūīs of further north. The sect's name derives from the fact that its adherents exalted the liturgical recitations of formulae including the name and titles of God, sc. *dhikr* [*q.v.*], above the formal Muslim worship, the *ṣalāt* or *namāz*.

The Dhikrīs were believed by Hughes-Buller to stem from the North Indian heterodox movement of the Mahdawiyya, the followers of Sayyid Muḥammad Mahdī of Djawnpūr (847-910/1443-1505), who claimed to be an *imām* with a revelation superseding that of Muḥammad the Prophet [see AL-DJAWNPŪRĪ and *EI*¹ art. MAHDAWĪS]. Adherents of the Mahdawiyya would have brought their doctrines to the remote region of Makrān via Farāh in eastern Afghānistān, where Muḥammad Mahdī Djawnpūrī was buried. The rise of the Dhikrīs in Makrān is apparently contemporaneous with that of the local line of Bolēday Balūč *maliks* in Makrān (early 17th century); both they and their successors after *ca.* 1740, the Gičkīs, were strong adherents of the Dhikrīs, and their heterodoxy brought down upon them several attacks by the orthodox Sunnī Khān of Kalāt, Mīr Naṣīr Khān (d. 1795) [see KILĀT and G. P. Tate, *History of the Ahmadzai Khans of Kalāt*].

Because, as with other unorthodox sects in Islam, its opponents spread slanderous reports about the immorality of the Dhikrī sect (incestuous practices, community of goods, etc.), the Dhikrī adherents were often driven to practice dissimulation in religion or *taḳiyya* [*q.v.*], and it is accordingly not easy to obtain a clear picture of their doctrines and practices. It seems that these were consolidated in the early 18th century by Mullā Gičkī and that they included the idea of *taʾwīl* of the Ḳurʾān by the Mahdī, whose interpretation had replaced Muḥammad of Mecca's literal one; the non-necessity of observing the R[...] ḍān fast; and the superiority of *dhikr* over [...] These formulae of *dhikr* are to be recited six [...] daily in special huts called *zikrānas* which ar[...] orientated towards the *ḳibla*. Instead of pilgri[...] to Arabia, the Dhikrīs established a Kaʿba or s[...] of their own at the Koh-i Murād near Turb[...] the district of Kēč in central Makrān, with a s[...] well of its own, the *čāh-i zamzam*. British obse[...] noted that the *mullās* of the Dhikrī commu[...] had considerable influence.

Hughes-Buller's information relates to the [...] decades of this century, when he noted that th[...] seemed to be on the decline, and it is diffic[...] ascertain the present status of the sect, if inde[...] survives at all in Balūčistān now; the 1961 Pak[...] population census reports mention the existen[...] Dhikrīs in Makrān and Las Bēla [*q.v.*], but they [...] be repeating information stemming from B[...] Indian times.

Bibliography: R. Hughes-Buller, *Baluch[...] District gazeteers series*. vii. *Makrān*, Bombay [...] 48-50, 116-21, 304; *Imperial gazeteer of Indi[...]* 276-80; and see M. Longworth Dames, *EI*¹ [...] *Balōčistān. Religion, education*, etc.
(C. E. BOSWOR[...])

DIALECT [see ʿARABIYYA and other langua[...]

DIAMOND [see ALMĀS].

DICTIONARY [see ḲĀMŪS, MUʿDJAM].

DIGITAL COMPUTER [see ḤISĀB AL-ʿAḲ[...]

DIKE [see MĀʾ].

AL-**DĪKDĀN**, a fortress situated on that [...] of the eastern shore of the Persian Gulf calle[...] Sīf ʿUmāra, not far from the island of Ḳays [...] and famous in the 4th/10th century. It was k[...] under three designations, Ḳalʿat al-Dīkdān, [...] Dikbāya and Ḥiṣn Ibn ʿUmāra, as well as the Pe[...] one Diz-i Pisar-i ʿUmāra (*Ḥudūd al-ʿālam*, tr. [...] It stood guard over a village of fishermen and a[...] which could shelter some 20 ships, and accordi[...] Ibn Ḥawḳal (tr. Kramers and Wiet, 268-9), follo[...] Iṣṭakhrī (140), no-one could get up to it una[...] since one had to be hoisted up by means of c[...] and a kind of crane or hoist. He adds that it [...] for the Banū ʿUmāra, an observation post [...] which they could watch the movement of shi[...] the sea: "when a vessel approaches, they bri[...] to a halt and demand a percentage of its cargo" [...] name of this fortress (= "tripod", "trivet" [...] Ibn Khurradādhbih, Glossary, 211), which al-Ma[...] considered as one of the wonders of the [...] (*Murūdj*, ii, 69 = § 501), is to be explained b[...] configuration of the land on which it was perch[...]

The geographers connect it with al-Djulan[...] Kanʿān (Ibn Ḥawḳal) or K.rk.r (*Ḥudūd*, tr. [...] cf. Abu 'l-Ḳāsim al-Azdī, *Ḥikāya*, 138 l. 3; b[...] is probable that these two names are a deform[...] of al-Mustakīr, see Ibn al-Kalbī-Caskel, Tab. [...] and ii, 264). The Banū ʿUmāra claimed to be de[...] dants of al-Djulandā and stated that their ance[...] had established themselves in the district in [...] time of Moses. Now al-Djulandā and his famil[...] known to have been kings in Yemen (Muḥamm[...] Ḥabīb, *Muḥabbar*, 265, 266; Ibn Ḥadjar, *Iṣāba* [...] 1295; M. Hamidullah, *Le Prophète de l'Islam*, i[...] etc.); on this basis, they levied dues on all merc[...] dise and probably indulged too in piracy, since [...] Ḳurʾānic verse (XVII, 78/79) "... a king who [...] behind them, taking every ship by force" [...] applied to them. In reality, the Banu ʿUmara [...] probably a family of the Azd [*q.v.*] of ʿUmān [...] had settled in Fārs at an unknown date and who[...]

-d the Sīf ʿUmāra during a period difficult -efine precisely. Yāḳūt (ii, 711) certainly states the Āl al-Djulandā (the name of several lords -ārs) were still powerful in his own time, but -nly cites (ii, 966), after al-Masʿūdī (*loc. cit.*), Allāh b. ʿUmāra who died in 309/921-2 after -ng reigned over the island of Zīrbādh for 25 years; -rother (?) Djaʿfar b. Ḥamza who reigned six -ths; and his son Baṭṭāl b. ʿAbd Allāh who suc- -ed his uncle (?), who had been assassinated by -*hilmān*. At all events, the fortress was in ruins -e time of al-Ḳalḳashandī (*Ṣubḥ*, iii, 242).

Bibliography: In addition to the sources -entioned above, see Marquart, *Ērānšahr*, 45; -hwarz, *Iran*, 77; Le Strange, 256-7; Barthold -d Minorsky, *Ḥudūd al-ʿālam*, 39-40, 377, 396.

(CH. PELLAT)

-DILĀʾ, an ancient place in the Middle -s region of Morocco which owed its existence -e foundation in the last quarter of the 10th/16th -ury of a *zāwiya* [*q.v.*], a "cultural" centre meant -eaching the Islamic sciences and Arab letters, and -e same time spreading the doctrine of the Shādh- -a [*q.v.*] order, more precisely the branch known -e Djazūliyya [see AL-DJAZŪLĪ, ABŪ ʿABD ALLĀH -AMMAD], and also sheltering the needy and tra- -rs. In 1048/1638, the *zāwiya dilāʾiyya* or *bakriyya* -n the founder's name, Shaykh Abū Bakr Ibn -ammad) was moved a dozen kilometres and gave - to a new complex, enjoying a certain importance, spot now occupied by the *zāwiya* of the Ayt -ḳ, 35 km. southwest of Khnīfra and 64 km. north- of Ḳaṣbat Tādlā. Impelled by the founder's -e, who belonged to a family possessing vast -tes and rich revenues, the *zāwiya* developed -iderably, especially after 1012/1603, for during -troubled period which followed the death of the -id sultan al-Manṣūr [*q.v.*], it provided a safe -n for students coming from the traditional urban -res and, thanks to its library and to the members -he Dilāʾiyyūn family, aided by scholars from -ide seeking refuge and staying at al-Dilāʾ, -llectual resources which were quite appreciable. subjects taught there comprised, in addition -ūfism, the Ḳurʾānic readings, *ḥadīth*, *fiḳh*, logic, -mar, *adab* and a little astronomy for determining -hours of prayer.

-bū Bakr (d. 1021/1612) seems to have limited -elf to dispensing his teaching to students of the -*ya*, but his descendants have left behind a fairly -ortant work which has been partly reviewed by -Iadjdjī (*al-Zāwiya al-dilāʾiyya*, 251-3). His succes- -Maḥammad b. Abī Bakr (d. 1046/1636) was in -icular the author of a *Fahrasa* (of which one ms. -ts in a private library) and of a collection of -*ths*, *Arbaʿūn ḥadīth^an^* (ms. Rabat 1295 Dj.). -nis death the direction of the *zāwiya* passed to -son Maḥammad al-Ḥādjdj (d. 1082/1671), who - soon transferred the centre to its new site and -ght it to its full development. Scholars and -ary figures like al-Maḳḳarī and Ibn al-Ḳāḍī -.] had already stayed at al-Dilāʾ, but the new -*ya* attracted quite a numerous group of scholars, -ng whom the most remarkable was certainly -ūsī [*q.v.*].

-aḥammad al-Ḥādjdj took part in the renaissance -rabic culture in Morocco which was owed to the -*ya dilāʾiyya*, although he did not participate very -vely in this intellectual movement. Already in -ather's lifetime he had undertaken minor expedi- -s which had been crowned with success, and he - turned resolutely towards military action, taking advantage of the decadence of the Saʿdids [*q.v.*]. Operations began in 1048/1638, and the head of the *zāwiya* combatted, in this same year and on the banks of the wādī al-ʿAbīd, a Saʿdid army sent from Marrakesh. Two years later, after various adventures, he had managed to establish his authority over the northwestern quarter of Morocco and, on 1056/1646, he reached as far as Tāfīlālt. In 1061/1651 he proclaimed himself sultan of Morocco and established diplomatic relations with various European powers. However, countermovements soon followed in various towns, and after some successes over other claimants to power and over the Spanish, he was finally beaten in 1079/1668 by the ʿAlawī sultan Mawlāy al-Rashīd [*q.v.*]. He was forced to submit to the latter, who merely exiled him with his family to Tlemcen, but allowed his troops to plunder the riches of the *zāwiya dilāʾiyya* and then had the complex—whose site has only recently been identified—razed to the ground.

The Dilāʾiyyūn later established themselves at Fās, where they soon came to form a kind of religious and intellectual aristocracy whose prestige was only surpassed by that of the Fāsiyyūn [see AL-FĀSĪ in Suppl.]. Only a grandson of Maḥammad al-Ḥādjdj, Aḥmad b. ʿAbd Allāh (d. 1091/1680) tried in 1088/1677 to rebel against Mawlāy Ismāʿīl [*q.v.*] in the region of al-Dilāʾ, but he was defeated in the next year on the banks of the wādī al-ʿAbīd. Some of Abū Bakr's descendants still live today in various towns of Morocco, in particular, at Fās, Casablanca and Rabat (see Ḥadjdjī, *op. cit.*, 255-6, and E. Lévi-Provençal, *Chorfa*, 299, with genealogical tables).

After Maḥammad b. Abī Bakr (see above), his son Aḥmad al-Ḥārithī (d. 1051/1641) composed a grammatical commentary which seems to have been lost, but it was another of his sons, Muḥammad, called al-Murābiṭ from his ascetic way of life, who was apparently the first to enjoy a wide audience beyond the confines of Morocco; he was indeed the author of various works which were in some demand in their time, amongst which have been preserved *al-Maʿridj al-muntaḳāt ilā maʿānī al-waraḳāt* (*fiḳh*; Ms. Rabat 276 K), *Natāʾidj al-taḥṣīl fī sharḥ al-Tashīl* (of Ibn Mālik; grammatical commentary in 4 vols. known as far as Egypt), *Fatḥ al-Laṭīf ʿalā 'l-basṭ wa 'l-tarīf fī ʿilm al-taṣrīf* (grammar; lith. Fās 1316), and other works (see G. Vajda, in *Hespéris*, xlviii [1956], 215-16). This grammarian survived the destruction of al-Dilāʾ and died in Fās in 1089/1678. Two other members of the family became especially well-known in Fās. The first, Abū ʿAbd Allāh Muḥammad al-Masnāwī b. Aḥmad b. Muḥammad al-Masnāwī b. Abī Bakr b. Muḥammad b. Maḥammad b. Abī Bakr (1072-1136/1661-1724), was a preacher and *imām* at the Abū ʿInāniyya *madrasa*, *muftī* and *shaykh al-djamāʿa* (i. e. dean of the professors). He has left behind several works, notably a genealogical treatise on the descendants of ʿAbd al-Ḳādir al-Djīlānī [*q.v.*], the *Natīdjat al-taḥḳīḳ fī baʿḍ ahl al-sharaf al-wathīḳ* (lith. Fās 1309/1891; ed. Tunis 1296/1879; partial Eng. tr. T. H. Weir, *The first part of the Natijatu 'l-tahqiq*, Edinburgh 1903); his output comprises, in addition to treatises on genealogy, law and mysticism, a poem of 40 verses written just before his death in order to seek God's pardon and recited at Fās at burials, and finally *al-Maḳāma al-fikriyya fī maḥāsin al-zāwiya al-bakriyya* (see Lévi-Provençal, *Chorfa*, 301-2; M. Lakhdar, *Vie littéraire*, 152-8 and bibl.). The other Dilāʾī worthy of note is Abū ʿAbd Allāh Muḥammad al-Ḥādjdj b. Muḥammad b. Abd al-Raḥmān b. Abī Bakr, who died accidentally between Mecca and Medina after having made the Pilgrimage (1141/1729). Several of his works have been preserved: poems glorifying the Prophet; *Zahr al-ḥadāʾik* (ms. Rabat 306 K) and *al-Zahr al-nadī fi 'l-khuluḳ al-muḥammadī* (ms. Rabat 157 D), an *urdjūza* on the Chorfa *Durrat al-tīdjān* (mss. Rabat 498, 522, 1180, 1244 K; lith. Fās), etc. (see Lakhdar, 166-8).

Bibliography: The basic Arabic sources are still unpublished: Yāzighī, *Ḥadāʾiḳ al-azhār al-nadiyya fi 'l-taʿrīf bi-ahl al-zāwiya al-dilāʾiyya al-bakriyya* (*urdjūza*; ms. Rabat 261 D); Tāzī, *Nuzhat al-akhyār al-marḍiyyīn fī manāḳib al-ʿulamāʾ al-dilāʾiyyīn al-bakriyyīn* (ms. Rabat 1264 K); Ḥawwāt, *al-Budūr al-ḍāwiya fi 'l-taʿrīf bi'l-sādāt ahl al-zāwiya al-dilāʾiyya* (ms. Rabat 261 D). These sources, the Moroccan historians in general and the documents of various origin which are concerned with the political, diplomatic and military events, during the period of Maḥammad al-Ḥādjdj, have been utilised by M. Ḥadjdjī for his excellent monograph, *al-Zāwiya al-dilāʾiyya wa-dawruhā al-dīnī wa 'l-ʿilmī wa 'l-siyāsī* (Rabat 1384/1964), to which one should in the first place direct the enquirer, who will find there both biographies of the main members of the Dilāʾiyyūn and also a detailed bibliography. In his thesis on *L'activité intellectuelle au Maroc à l'époque saʿdide* (Rabat 1976-7, 2 vols.), this same author has devoted a section to the *zāwiya* (551-7), and the index, s.vv. Dilāʾ, Dilāʾī and Dilāʾides, enables one to track down various items of scattered information. For the period after the destruction of the *zāwiya* at al-Dilāʾ, see E. Lévi-Provençal, *Les historiens des Chorfa*, Paris 1922, 298-303, and M. Lakhdar, *La vie littéraire au Maroc sous la dynastie ʿalawide*, Rabat 1971, index s.v. Dilāʾī.

(CH. PELLAT)

DINET, ALPHONSE, *Etienne* (1861-1929), French painter of oriental subjects and writer who assumed the name NACIR ED DINE (Nāṣir al-Dīn) when he became a convert to Islam.

He was born in Paris on 28 March 1861, and studied under several well-known painters (Galland, Bouguereau, Robert-Fleury). After a first trip to Algeria (1884), he won a scholarship which allowed him to return there in 1885, and from then onwards he led a nomadic life there for several months of each year, until he settled at Bou Saada (Bū Saʿāda) in 1907. It was in this region of the southern part of Constantine province that he met in 1889 an educated Algerian, Sliman ben Ibrahim (d. 1953), who having rescued him, at the risk of his own life, during a local disturbance, became an inseparable friend and constant collaborator of his, even in Paris. Contact with Muslims gradually detached Dinet from the Christian faith, which he renounced in 1913 and discreetly embraced Islam; he renewed publicly his profession of faith in the New Mosque of Algiers in 1927.

His artistic output, considerable in quantity and of high quality, comprises mainly Algerian and Arab scenes and landscapes, which very quickly brought him wide celebrity, even beyond the ranks of the Société des Orientalistes founded in 1887 by Léonce Benedite, which he immediately joined. Before the end of the 19th century, several of his tableaux were on display at various museums: *Les terrasses de Laghouat* (Luxembourg Museum), *Vue de M'sila* (Pau Museum), *Charmeurs de serpents* (Sydney Museum), etc. After having illustrated the 1898 edition of Devic's *Les aventures d'Antar*, he enhanced
with his own compositions texts gathered tog
or edited by Sliman ben Ibrahim and translat
his own hands, in particular, *Rabia el-Kc*
[*Rabīʿ al-ḳulūb*] *ou le printemps des coeurs*
Saharan legends, Paris 1902); *Tableaux de*
arabe (Paris 1904, 1928), which contain fin
productions of 24 oil paintings (including his
portrait and that of Sliman) accompanied
presentation and commentary by the latter trans
into French; *Mirages, scènes de la vie arabe,*
1960; *El Fiafi oua el-Kifar* [*al-Fayāfī wa 'l-*
ou le désert (Paris 1911); and *Khadra, dai*
Ouled Nail (Paris 1909, 1926). His most fa
work, again written in collaboration with Slima
published simultaneously in two parallel ver
French and English, at Paris in 1918, re
nevertheless *La Vie de Mohammed, Prophète d'*
The Algerian painter Mohammed Racim (R
also contributed to illustrating this luxury
which has never been re-published in its en
(a recent reimpression only has some colour
and one of Racim's aquarelles; a standard e
unillustrated, has appeared in Paris 1927,
1947, 1961, 1975 and 1977).

Two years after his official conversion, Dine
Sliman ben Ibrahim made together the Pilgri
to the holy places of Islam. Although he cl
to have taken "no notes, no drawing, no p
graphs" during his stay in Arabia, there app
magnificent plates showing scenes of the Pilgri
as illustrations for the *riḥla* which appeare
French from "El Hadj Nacir ed-Dine E. Din
El Hadj Sliman ben Ibrahim Baâmer" and
the double title *al-Ḥadjdj ilā Bayt Allāh al-Ḥ*
(in Arabic script) and *Le Pèlerinage à la M*
Sacrée d'Allah, together with the date 134
fact, this narrative, written on the return fro
pilgrimage of 1347 and completed on 6 (*sic*; rea
Rabīʿ II 1348/30 September 1929, came of
press in Paris at the beginning of 1930 (2nd
1962), just a few weeks after its principal au
death (24 December 1929). His funeral took pla
28 December at the Great Mosque in Paris (in w
foundation he had himself been concerned) i
presence of leading personalities and of the repr
tatives of several Muslim governments. His c
was taken to Bou Saada and buried in the
which he had made there, and which tourist
still today invited to visit (see Guides Bleus, *A*
s.v. Bou Saada); the house there he lived has
made into a Dinet Museum by Sliman ben Ibr

This highly-talented painter of oriental
deserves a notice in the *Encyclopaedia of Isla*
only because he died a Muslim, but also becau
can be considered as a fervent apologist fo
faith which he had assumed. Several of his w
works caused a certain stir in the Islamic w
especially in Egypt, thanks to his friend R
Rustum, who in 1929 published at Cairo *A*
khāṣṣa min nūr al-Islām, the translation of a le
by Dinet called *Rayons de lumière exclusive*
islamiques (2nd edn. Paris 1966). Tawfīḳ A
was to translate, in the *Madjallat Djamʿiyy*
Shubbān al-Muslimīn, the latter part of his *Pèler*
and ʿUmar Fākhūrī was to issue at Damascu
Ārāʾ gharbiyya fī masāʾil sharḳiyya, a versi
his *L'Orient vu de l'Occident* (Paris n.d.) unde
title *al-Sharḳ kamā yarāhu al-Gharb*. This last
very detailed critique of the studies of Lam
Nöldeke, De Goeje, Sprenger, Snouck Hurg
Grimme, Margoliouth, etc., which was subsequ
to be extensively used by the Azharī *shaykh*

.alīm Maḥmūd in the substantial introduction aced to his translation of *La Vie de Mohammed, ʰhète d'Allah,* made, in conjunction with his son ammad, from the original edition as *Muḥammad ıl Allāh* (Cairo 1956). It is rather surprising Dinet's *Sīra* which, as we have seen, had a y success among French-reading circles, did not v the attention of the Egyptians during the ›s, at a time when Haykal was in part in- ›d, in his *Ḥayāt Muḥammad,* by *La Vie de ›omet* of E. Dermenghem published at Paris ›929; possibly, like this last author (p. IV), regarded it as too traditionalist. It is a fact Dinet and Sliman ben Ibrahim affirmed that had based themselves exclusively on the works bn Hishām, Ibn Saʿd, etc. and on the *Sīra ›iyya,* and they remark that "the study of vations" introduced by "modern orientalists" the Prophet's biography have led them "to ›t that, at times, they were inspired by an mophobia hard to reconcile with science and worthy of our age".

can easily be seen that the detailed criticism :h makes up essentially *L'Orient vu de l'Occident* ʿAbd al-Ḥalīm Maḥmūd valuable arguments ınst the "orientalists" and in favour of a *sīra* of itional character which must have been pleasing s readers, since a second edition of his translation ›ared in 1958. The translator analyses Nāṣir ›īn's apologetical methods and, basing himself the latter's writings, demonstrates the super- y of Islam over Christianity. As opposed to the ‹s of the Arabists whose researches tend only to orth the reality of Islam, without any polemical ıtions, Dinet's principal Islamological works ı to have as their aim less a scientific study of new religion than a glorification of it and an ›uragement to the whole world to follow his ıple. His viewpoint is very clearly summed up paragraph of his *Pèlerinage,* where he affirms Islam responds "to all the aspirations of dif- ıt kinds of believers. Having a supreme simplicity Muʿtazilism, wildly mystical with Sufism, it gs a sense of direction and a consolation to the opean or Asian scholar, without stepping on the ›lute freedom of his thought, as much as to a anese negro whom it snatches away from the ›rstitious worship of fetishes. It exalts the soul the practically-minded English merchant, for m "time is money", as much as that of the deist osopher, and that of the contemplative of the t as much as that of the Westerner carried y by art and poetry. It will even seduce the ern medical man by the logic of its repeated ıtions and the rhythm of its bowings and pros- ions equally salutary to the care of the body as he health of the mind. The freethinker himself, is not inevitably an atheist, will be able to ›ider the Islamic revelation as a sublime mani- ıtion of that mysterious force called 'inspiration' will admit it without difficulty, since it :ains no mysterious element inadmissible by on".

Bibliography: F. Arnaudiès, *E. Dinet et el- adj Sliman ben Ibrahim,* Algiers 1933; J. Dinet- ollince (the painter's sister), *La vie de E. Dinet,* aris 1938 (with ills.); Rāshid Rustum, obituary t. in *al-Ahrām* of 29 December 1929; introd. to e Arabic tr. of *La vie de Mohammed.* See also E. Dinet, *Les fléaux de la peinture,* Paris 1904, ›05, 1926; as an official hommage to Dinet *n maître de la peinture algérienne, Nasreddin Dinet* (Ar. and Fr. texts, numerous ills.) was published in Algiers in 1977.

(Ch. Pellat)

ḌIRĀR b. **ʿAMR**, Abū ʿAmr al-Ghaṭafānī al-Kūfī (*ca.* 110-200/*ca.* 728-815), important Muʿtazilī theologian, disciple of Wāṣil b. ʿAṭāʾ (d. 131/749). In contrast to many other early Muʿtazilīs, he was of pure Arab extraction; he belonged to the ʿAbd Allāh b. Ghaṭafān in Kūfa. He founded his prestige, however, through his teaching in Baṣra where Wāṣil had lived. By profession he is said to have been a *ḳāḍī*. After 170/786 we find him in Baghdād in the circle of the Barmakids, where he took part, together with Hishām b. al-Ḥakam, the Ibāḍī scholar ʿAbd Allāh b. Yazīd, the Zaydī Sulaymān b. Djarīr, and others, including non-Muslim theologians, in the famous debates arranged by Yaḥyā b. Khālid al-Barmakī, the *wazīr* of Hārūn al-Rashīd. This position exposed him to certain suspicions: the *ḳāḍī* Saʿīd b. ʿAbd al-Raḥmān al-Djumaḥī (d. 174/790 or 176/792) outlawed him because of *zandaḳa*. But, in the presence of Barmakī protection, this seems to have been a mere verbal menace. In reality, Ḍirār had attacked the *zanādiḳa* and the *mulḥidūn* in several books; he seems to have lent intellectual support to the governmental measurements against the Manichaeans since the time of al-Mahdī (158-69/775-85). He not only applied the methods of dialectical theology (*kalām*); he also analysed them and tried to propagate them among the masses, through a *risāla ilā 'l-ʿāmma* (cf. Malaṭī, *Tanbīh,* ed. Dedering 31, ll. 10 ff.), which may have been identical with his *K. Ādāb al-mutakallimīn* or his *K. ilā man balagha min al-muslimīn.* He was an extremely prolific writer: 57 titles of books are listed in the *Fihrist,* more than those of any other Muʿtazilī.

This is all the more astonishing as neither Kaʿbī in his *Maḳālāt al-islāmiyyīn* nor the *ḳāḍī* ʿAbd al-Djabbār in his *Faḍl al-iʿtizāl* (nor, consequently, Ibn al-Murtaḍā in his *Ṭabaḳāt al-Muʿtazila*) allow him a biography; they did not consider him a Muʿtazilī. Nor did al-Khayyāṭ, when Ibn al-Rāwandī identified the Muʿtazila with Ḍirār's ideas. But Ibn al-Rāwandī is in line not only with non-Muʿtazilī writers like al-Nawbakhtī or al-Bazdawī and al-Dhahabī, but also with Muʿtazilī authors like Ibn al-Nadīm and al-Nāshiʾ al-akbar, who count Ḍirār among those numerous Muʿtazilīs who did not exactly correspond to the canonical school dogma established in the *uṣūl al-khamsa.* These five principles were apparently first formulated by Abu 'l-Hudhayl, and it is with Abu 'l-Hudhayl and Bishr b. al-Muʿtamir that opposition against Ḍirār emerged. Their verdict determined the later school tradition, but it did not succeed in suppressing Ḍirār's writings. Those who avowed their indebtedness to his ideas are therefore mostly found outside the Muʿtazila: Ḥafṣ al-Fard in Egypt and other Ḥanafīs in Baṣra and elsewhere. A Ḍirāriyya group is attested in Armenia by Nashwān al-Ḥimyarī (*al-Ḥūr al-ʿīn,* 212, l. 3). His influence in theology as well as in jurisprudence (*uṣūl al-fiḳh*) can be ascertained during at least two generations, although the opposition, Muʿtazilī as well as non-Muʿtazilī, frequently preferred, in such cases, to talk about "Djahmīs" instead of Ḍirārīs.

This was an old reproach: Bishr b. al-Muʿtamir had claimed, in his *Urdjūza* written in prison under Hārūn al-Rashīd, that Ḍirār and his school had succumbed to the influence of Djahm b. Ṣafwān. What was true in this was that Ḍirār had reacted against Djahm's rigid determinism: he had conceded that God creates (*khalaḳa*) everything including man's actions, but he also insisted that man, in order to be responsible for his actions, simultaneously does them himself, either immediately or through "generation" (*tawlīd*). In order to describe man's share in them, he used the Ḳurʾānic term *kasaba* or *iktasaba* which does not yet mean "acquisition" here, but rather the mere performance of the act (cf. M. Schwarz in *Islamic philosophy and the classical tradition, essays presented to R. Walzer*, Oxford 1972 367 f.); he stressed man's freedom of choice (*ikhtiyār*) by assuming a capacity (*istiṭāʿa*) already *before* the act. The concept is clearly synergistic; Ḍirār openly talked about two "agents", God and man. This is where Abu 'l-Hudhayl and Bishr b. al-Muʿtamir saw a sin against the spirit of the school; they eliminated the idea that God "creates" anything in human actions. Ḍirār could, however, argue convincingly with an example like the Ḳurʾān: when somebody recites the Ḳurʾān, not only his recitation, *ḳurʾān*, is heard, but also the Ḳurʾān as created by God. The equivocalness of the word (*ḳurʾān* and Ḳurʾān) added to the suggestiveness of the theory.

Outside the sphere of man, Ḍirār supported God's omnipotence by an elaborate metaphysical system based on the exclusively accidental structure of the creation. Each body consists of a network of indispensable accidents, i.e. qualities without which it would not exist, but which may be realised in a spectrum of varieties best described by their extremes: temperature ("hot or cold"), extension ("long or short"), weight ("light or heavy"), consistence ("humid or dry"), nature of its surface ("rough or soft"), colour, taste, odour, etc. In their agglomeration (*taʾlīf* or *idjtimāʿ*), they form its nucleus; there is nothing like a "substance". But they do not have a separate existence either; isolated, they are a mere abstraction. Other accidents which are not indispensable like movement, pain (in human beings) etc. may occur, but they do not form "part" of the body. They do not possess any endurance (*baḳāʾ*) and are therefore created anew in every moment (cf. Ashʿarī, *Maḳālāt al-islāmiyyīn*, 305, ll. 11 f. and 359, ult. ff.). A body for long does not lose its individuality, as less than half of its basic qualities have been replaced by their contrary. Change of any kind may be explained through this process; here Ḍirār and his adherents seem to have absorbed certain Aristotelian ideas, especially the concept of ἀλλοίωσις (*istiḥāla*, cf. *Isl.*, xliii (1967), 254 ff.). The entire model is, of course, not Aristotelian; Ḍirār criticised Aristotle for his doctrine of substances and accidents in a separate treatise (cf. *Fihrist*, ed. Fück, in *Shafi comm. volume*, 69, title no. 14). The system does not allow for any self-determining and independent nature of things (*ṭabīʿa*); this is why it was rejected offhand by Ḍirār's contemporary Muʿammar and later on by an-Naẓẓām, who joined a tradition which was more coloured by Stoic ideas [see KUMŪN]. The consequences were especially visible in the definition of man: he is a conglomerate of "colour, taste, odour, capacity, etc.", but there is no independent and immortal soul.

Using two surprisingly elaborate philosophical terms which were never applied again by the Muʿtazila, Ḍirār differentiated in everything which exists between its *anniyya* "existence" and its *māhiyya* "quiddity". Opposition arose when he transferred this distinction to God: we know God's *anniyya*, but we ignore the plenitude of His *māhiyya*. For we can infer the aspects of his essence only through rational conclusion; but we know from ourselves that outsider is never able to explore the hidden s of our nature to the same extent that we are aw of them ourselves. This is why we must be satis with negative theology: "God is omniscient" me means that He is not ignorant. Full knowledge be attained only in the Hereafter; then God's ess will be recognised, not through the *ruʾya bi 'l-a* as many non-Muʿtazilī theologians believed, through a sixth sense created for this purpose God. This theory seems to have been prepared Abū Ḥanīfa and was taken over by a numbe Ḥanafīs during the following two generations. L Muʿtazilīs may have seen in it too strong a limita of revelationary evidence and of the intellec potential of *kalām*; the theory still depended Djahm's concept of the total transcendence of G

They may have felt more familiar with Ḍir idea to differentiate between two aspects of G will: "God's will" may be identical with w happens, but also with what He only wants happen, in His commandments. The latter al native leaves room for man's *iktisāb*; sin, the cru problem of Ḍirār's theory of the two "creato seems to have been explained by him thro *khidhlān*, "abandonment (by God")) (ἐγκατάλειψ On the other hand, God would always be abl make all unbelievers believe, by His grace (*luṭf* Ibn Ḥazm, *Fiṣal*, iii, 165, ll. 7 ff. and iv, 192 9 ff.). This may have been a mere theoretical sumption. The idea was given up by most l Muʿtazilīs in favour of the concept of *al-aṣ* but Ḍirār was still followed in it by Bishr b. Muʿtamir.

Djahmī spirit may also survive in Ḍirār's de of the punishment in the tomb; already Shaḥḥ Abu 'l-Hudhayl's youngest disciple, could pret that no Muʿtazilī ever shared this radicalism (cf. al-Murtaḍā, *Ṭabaḳāt al-Muʿtazila*, 72, ll. 3 f.; *Ḳāḍī* ʿAbd al-Djabbār, *Faḍl al-iʿtizāl*, ed. Fu Sayyid, 201, ll. 17 ff.). Ḍirār's doctrine, howe that Paradise and Hell do not yet exist, but be created during the Last Judgment, and Adam therefore lived in a terrestrial garden, accepted by many later Muʿtazilīs like Hishām Fuwaṭī, ʿAbbād b. Sulaymān, Abū Hāshim, etc looks like an inversion of Djahm's thesis that P dise and Hell are finite *a parte post*; but its immed intention may have been to avoid certain destinarian arguments which inferred from actual existence of Hell the predetermined neces of Evil (cf. *Mélanges d'Islamologie, Volume déd A. Abel*, Leiden 1974, 108 ff., with reference t longer passage of Ḍirārī theology preserved in Hishām's *K. al-Tīdjān*). Ḍirār's thesis created ficulties not only in Ḳurʾānic exegesis, but also respect to several well-known *aḥādīth*, for insta about the nocturnal ascension (*miʿrādj*) of Prophet or about the martyrs entering Para immediately after their death.

This latter point, however, did not bother very much: he did not accept isolated tradit (*akhbār āḥād*) as a proof in theological quest (*aḥkām al-dīn*), and in his time most *aḥādīth* had this character of *āḥād*. The only epistemolog criterion which, besides the Ḳurʾān, he found enough to base upon it religious truth after death of the Prophet, was consensus (*idjmāʿ*) this he was followed by al-Aṣamm (*q.v.*], who t over the Muʿtazilī circle in Baṣra after him. Ḍir attack against *ḥadīth* had been formulated in *K. al-Taḥrīsh wa'l-ighrāʾ*; he had pointed to

that all sects used to rely on different and ıally contradicting *aḥādīth*. It is possible, gh unprovable, that the beginning of Ibn ıyba's *Taʾwīl mukhtalif al-ḥadīth* reflects Ḍirār's mentation (cf. *Der Orient in der Forschung. chrift O. Spies*, Wiesbaden 1967, 184 f.).
lief was, according to Ḍirār, closely linked to lectual understanding; it begins therefore only mental maturity (*kamāl al-ʿaḳl*). Simple people do not rationalise their convictions may always in unrecognised unbelief (cf. Ashʿarī, *Maḳālāt*, ll. 2 ff.). But true belief from a Nabataean ts higher than from an Arab, because the Arabs distinguished by the fact that the Prophet was ed from among them, whereas the Nabataeans ys have to transgress the barrier of contempt for having produced any prophet. If a Nabataean fore ever entered into competition with a ıshī concerning the caliphate, preference should iven to the Nabataean as the more appropriate l) candidate. This would have the additional ntage that a Nabataean does not have a power- clientèle and could therefore more easily be sed if necessary. The Ḳuraysh thus do not ess the monopoly of the caliphate, according to r; long before him the superiority of neo- ims had been defended by similar arguments A. Noth in *Isl.*, xlvii (1971), 178 f.). Nevertheless, r did not doubt that the first four caliphs were in the moment of their election. Judgment mes difficult only with the Battle of the Camel. ıis case, renowned Companions with equally good tation stood against each other. The result was both factions for ever lost their trustworthiness, if met separately. Ḍirār compared this situation two believing Muslims entering a house and of them being heard from outside pronouncing a ula of blatant unbelief, but both of them being d dead afterwards; there would be no criterion to find out the unbeliever among them, and of them would have to be treated as such. In context of the simile, the death of the two nents stood for the impossibility of getting ble historical information about the events of First Civil War. This neutralistic attitude had prepared by Wāṣil b. ʿAṭāʾ and was continued, slight variations and a different comparison, Abu 'l-Hudhayl (cf. al-Nāshiʾ al-akbar, *Uṣūl al- l*, § 90 and introduction, 46). The Shīʿa under- d it as a critique of ʿAlī; in later times, they smitted reports about discussions in which r had been defeated concerning the problem of *ıa* by Hishām b. al-Ḥakam or ʿAlī b. Mītham al-Sharīf al-Murtaḍā, *al-Fuṣūl al-mukhtāra*,[2]9, ff., [3]9, ll. -6 ff.).
ırār rejected ʿAbd Allāh b. Masʿūd's and Ubayy Kaʿb's recension of the Ḳurʾān on the ground their *ḥarf* was not revealed (cf. Nöldeke- vally, *Geschichte des Qorans*, iii, 107).

Bibliography: Sources and further detail are ven in J. van Ess, *Ḍirār b. ʿAmr und die "Cah- ıya"* in *Isl.*, xliii (1967), 241 ff. and xliv (1968), ff. Scattered reports are also found in *Ḳāḍī* ʿAbd Djabbār, *Faḍl al-iʿtizāl*, ed. Fuʾād Sayyid, ınis 1974, index s.v.; Yaʿḳūbī, *Mushākalat al-nās zamānihim*, ed. W. Milward, Beirut 1962, 25, 4; Abū Rashīd al-Naysābūrī, *Fi'l-tawḥīd*, ed. ɔū Rīda, Cairo 1385/1965, 591, 11. 5 ff.; Abū aʿlā b. al-Farrāʾ, *al-Muʿtamad fī uṣūl al-dīn*, ed. addād, Beirut 1974, 101, ll. 8 ff.; al-Ṣābūnī, *Bidāya min al-kifāya*, ed. Khulayf, Cairo 1969, 7, 11. 7 ff.; Murtaḍā b. al-Dāʿī, *Tabṣirat al-ʿawāmm*, ed. Iḳbāl, index s.v. None of them brings new material. For studies see also M. Horten, *Die philosophischen Systeme der spekulativen Theologen im Islam*, Bonn 1912, 139 ff.; L. Massignon, *La Passion de Hallâj*, new ed. Paris 1975, index s.v.; A. S. Tritton, *Muslim theology*, London 1947, 69 ff.; W. M. Watt, in *JRAS* (1943), 234 ff.; idem, in *MW*, xl (1950), 97 ff.; idem, *The formative period of Islamic thought*, Edinburgh 1973, 189 ff. and index s.v.; W. Madelung, *Der Imam al-Qāsim ibn Ibrāhīm*, Berlin 1965, index s.v.; L. Gardet, *Études de philosophie et de mystique comparée*, Paris 1972, 102 ff.; H. Daiber, *Das theologisch-philosophische System des Muʿammar ibn ʿAbbād as-Sulamī*, Beirut 1975, index s.v. (J. van Ess)

DISSOLUTION [see faskh].

DITCH [see khandaḳ].

DIVINE DECREE [see al-ḳaḍāʾ wa-'l-ḳadar].

DĪWĀN-BEGI, the title of high officials in the Central Asian khānates in the 16th-19th centuries.

The title appears first, apparently, in the Tīmūrid period, when its bearer, a Turkic *amīr* of one of the tribes of the Čaghatāys, was in charge of military affairs and of the affairs of the Turkic subjects, and stood at the head of *dīwān-i imārat* (or *dīwān-i aʿlā*) (see H. R. Roemer, *Staatsschreiben der Timuridenzeit*, Wiesbaden 1952, 169-71). The title had the same meaning in the state of the Aḳ Ḳoyunlu [*q.v.*] (see J. E. Woods, *The Aqquyunlu*, Minneapolis-Chicago 1976, 11). In the Ṣafawī state in Iran, the *dīwān-begi* was one of the seven *arkān-i dawlat* (members of the *madjlis-i aʿlā*) and was the high justiciar, who tried, jointly with the *ṣadr al-ṣudūr*, the major crimes, as well as civil cases, controlled all *Sharīʿa* courts and was a court of appeal for the whole kingdom (see *Tadhkirat al-mulūk*, ed. V. Minorsky, text, 20b-22b, tr. 50-1, comm. 119-20). There is very little information about the *dīwān-begi* in the Shaybānid [*q.v.*] state in the 16th century, besides the fact that this title did exist; in the *ʿAbd Allāh-nāma* by Ḥāfiẓ Tanīsh [*q.v.* below] it appears very rarely and without definition of its functions.

More detailed information comes only from the time of the Ashtarkhānids [see djānīds]. The *Baḥr al-asrār* by Maḥmūd b. Walī (second quarter of the 17th century) mentions the *dīwān-begi* in a description of the ceremonial at the court of the Ashtarkhānids in Balkh as being among the officials who were sitting on the left side of the khān, near the tripod (? *si pāya*; see V. V. Bartol'd, *Sočineniya*, ii/2, 391, 396; cf. M. A. Abduraimov, *Očerki agrarnîkh otnosheniy v Bukharskom khanstve v XVI — pervoy polovine XIX veka*, i, Tāshkent 1966, 73, where a reference is made to an account of a Russian ambassador to Bukhārā in the 17th century, who mentions that the throne of the khān of Bukhārā was raised above the level of the floor of the reception room by six steps; probably, the throne of the ruler of Balkh was raised above the level of the floor by three steps, and the expression *ba-ḳurb-i si pāya* can mean "near the three steps [leading to the throne]". This interpretation, however, remains dubious. Cf. also Quatremère, in *Notices et extraits*, xiv/1, 496, where *si pāya* is explained as "une charpente"). In the administrative manual *Madjmaʿ al-arḳām* compiled in Bukhārā in 1212/1798, the *dīwān-begi-yi kalān* is described as an official second in the rank after the *atalīḳ* [*q.v.* above]; he was entrusted with the state finance, mainly with the collection of *kharādj* [*q.v.*], as well as with the supervision of the irrigation in the region of Ḳara-ḳul (see facsimile in *Pis'mennîye *pamyatniki Vostoka* 1968, Moscow 1970, 55; Russian tr. by A. A. Semenov, in *Sovetskoye vostokovedeniye*, v [1948], 147). Russian ambassadors in Bukhārā in 1669 also describe the *dīwān-begi* as the second high-ranking official after the *atalīḳ* and mention that he received the credentials from the ambassadors and passed them to the khān (see *Nakaz Borisu i Semenu Pazukhinīm* ..., St. Petersburg 1894, 49, 55, 76). The Ashtarkhānid chronicles confirm that one of the duties of the *dīwān-begi* was the reception of ambassadors (see *Taʾrīkh-i Muḳīm-Khānī* by Muḥammad Yūsuf Munshī, Russian tr. by A. A. Semenov, Tāshkent 1956, 89). In the 19th and early 20th centuries, under the Mangït [*q.v.*] dynasty in Bukhārā, the *dīwān-begi* had similar functions, though he was now the second figure after the *ḳosh-begi* [*q.v.*], and not the *atalīḳ*. He was called also *ḳosh-begi-yi pāyān* ("the lower *ḳosh-begi*"), because his residence was at the foot of the *ark* (the citadel) of Bukhārā, and *zakātči-yi kalān* ("head of the collectors of *zakāt*" [*q.v.*]). He was the deputy of "the great *ḳosh-begi*" (*kull-i ḳosh-begi*), and in the absence or during an illness of the *amīr* he governed the country together with the *ḳosh-begi*. Both under the Ashtarkhānids and the Mangïts, besides this *dīwān-begi* residing in Bukhārā, there were also *dīwān-begi*s of main provincial rulers, such as those of Balkh, Čārdjūy, Ḥiṣār, with similar functions. Under the Mangïts, the honorary rank of *dīwān-begi* (the third from the top in the hierarchy of Bukhārā) was given also to various officials not necessarily connected with financial affairs, such as governors of some towns. In Ḳaratigin [*q.v.*], both under the independent *shāhs* and under the domination of Bukhārā, *dīwān-begi* was the first deputy of the ruler, and he was in charge of state finance as well as of the ruler's estate (see N. A. Kislyakov, *Očerki po istorii Karategina*, Stalinabad-Leningrad 1941, 183). In the semi-independent principality of Ura-Tubā [*q.v.*] in the 19th century, *dīwān-begi*s were low officials—local tax-collectors, subordinate to the *sarkār*, who was in charge of the collection of *kharādj* and of irrigation in the principality (see A. Mukhtarov, *Očerk istorii Ura-Tyubinskogo vladeniya v XIX v.*, Dushanbe 1964, 53). The title *dīwān-begi* could be given also to supervisers of finance in large private estates, such as those of the Djūybārī *shaykh*s in the 16th century (cf. P. P. Ivanov, *Khozyaystvo džuybarskikh sheykhov*, Moscow-Leningrad 1954, 60).

In the Khānate of Khīwa, the post of *dīwān-begi* was probably established only in the early 19th century. In any case, neither the local historian Muʾnis [*q.v.*] in his *Firdaws al-iḳbāl* nor other sources mention this title earlier, and it is not included in the list of 34 dignitaries (*ʿamaldār*) established by Abu 'l-Ghāzī Khān [*q.v.*] (cf. *Firdaws al-iḳbāl*, MS of the Leningrad Branch of the Institute of Oriental Studies, C-571, f. 65b). This title is mentioned by Muʾnis for the first time in his account of the events of 1222/1808, when two *dīwān-begi*s appear simultaneously (*ibid.*, f. 272a). Also later, there were at least two *dīwān-begi*s in Khīwa. They are mentioned among the high officials of the state along with the *ḳosh-begi* and the *mehter* [*q.v.*]; they were usually of mean origin, often Persian slaves. N. Murav'yev (1821) mentions *dīwān-begi*s as unimportant officials subordinate to the *ḳosh-begi* and the *mehter* (see N. Murav'yev, *Puteshestviye v Turkmeniyu i Khivu*, Moscow 1822, ii, 63); none of other Russian descriptions of the khānate compiled in the first half of the 19th century mentions them at all. In the reign of Allāh-Ḳulī Khān (1240-58/1825-42), the chief *dīwān-begi* was entrusted wit collection of *zakāt* and customs (see N. Zaleso *Voyenniy sbornik*, xxii [1861], No. 11, 65), a remained his main duty till the end of the century. Besides him, there was a *dīwān-beg* charge of khān's estates and a *dīwān-begi* of governor of Hazārasp (a senior relative of khā his heir). In the reign of Sayyid Muḥammad Ra Khān II (1281-1328/1864-1910), the chief *dīwān* Muḥammad Murād ("Mat-Murad" of Ru sources) became the most influential person an the Khīwan dignitaries and was considered as a minister by Western observers (cf. e.g. H. M *A travers l'Asie centrale*, Paris 1885, 238).

In the Khānate of Khoḳand [*q.v.*], the title *dī begi* is also attested, though no explanation is a able about the duties of its bearer. It seems, howe that it was more a rank than an administrative and its position was the same as that of *dīwān* in the hierarchy of Bukhārā (between the ran *parwānači* [*q.v.*] and *atalīḳ*). Radjab Dīwān- executed in 1236/1820, is said to have had highest title in the khānate, *wazīr al-wuzarāʾ* V. P. Nalivkin, *Histoire du khanat de Khok* Paris 1889, 140-1), which indicates, apparently, he was considered the head of the civil adminis tion; but before that he is mentioned as a gove (*ḥākim*) of Tāshkent (*ibid.*, 125, 135).

Bibliography: in addition to the works in the text, see: A. A. Semenov, in *Materia istorii tadžikov i uzbekov Sredney Azii*, ii, Stalin 1954, 57, 61, 66; M. Yu. Yuldashev, *K khanlïgïda feodal yer egalïgï wa dawlat tuzïlïsh* Uzbek], Tāshkent 1959, 263-4. (Yu. Brege

DJABAL SAYS, the name of a volc mountain in Syria situated *ca.* 105 km. so east of Damascus. Around its west and south runs a small valley opening to the southeast in large volcanic crater. In years with normal rai this crater is filled with water for about eight mo A reservoir near its centre makes Djabal Says o the few secure waterplaces in the region, w sometimes more than a hundred nomad fam camp in autumn. At the mouth of the valley on southeast-slope of Djabal Says and opposite t on the fringe of another slope, remains of nume buildings are preserved. The site was first visite 1862 by M. de Vogüé and excavated from 196 1964 by K. Brisch. The ruins consist of a consider number of houses, a mosque, a church, a *ḥamm* some storehouses for provisions, *khān*s a barracks, and a palace.

The *palace* is situated on the south side of valley. It consists of a rectangular enclosure, 67 m. × 67 m., from which eight towers (four a corners, one in the middle of each side) pro Entrance is given through a door in the ce tower of the north-side. Behind the door one e a tunnel-vaulted vestibule at the back of whi a doorway, opening into a great entrance hall w leads to a courtyard, *ca.* 31 m. × 31 m. This c yard is surrounded by ranges of rooms (54 exclu the small rooms in the hollow towers and the trance hall) most of which are organised into groups (*buyūt*) of five or six rooms. In additio this, there are three pairs of rooms and four isol rooms, two of which served probably as stairc An arcade ran around the paved courtyard in of the rooms. In the centre of the courtyard cistern. The lower parts of the walls consis basalt blocks on the inner and outer faces fillings of lumps of basalt and mortar rising u ɜ places to a height of *ca.* 2 m. The upper parts ıe walls were built of mud bricks. An exception ıe entrance tower, the upper parts of which are of basalt. Most of the basalt sections and some ıe brick sections of the walls are preserved. No ɜs of ceilings were found. De Vogüé, who visited ɔal Says more than a hundred years ago, saw ‹ vaultings. The building had originally two ːs and is stylistically linked with two other ces, Minya (see KHIRBAT AL-MINYA] and Kharrāna].

ıe *ḥammām, ca.* 150 m. east of the palace, sures *ca.* 16 m. × 17 m. It consists of a large room, *ca.* 10 m. × 4.5 m., with a semicircular ra in the north. Its south side opens into two ıs, *ca.* 3.5 m. deep. The east room can be entered door from the east. At its west side, it is con- ed with four smaller rooms, three of which ed as the apodyterium, tepidarium and darium of the bath. The lower parts of the s resemble those of the palace. The upper ions are built of burnt brick. All rooms with exception of the west room seem to have been ɜred by vaultings or domes of burnt brick. The t room was probably not covered at all. The ding resembles closely Ḥammām al-Ṣarākh [*q.v.*] ordan.

he *mosque, ca.* 70 m. west of the palace, is a are building measuring *ca.* 9.5 m. × 9.5 m. The erved lower sections of its walls are built of ılt. It can be entered by two doors from the ːh and the east. The interior of the building is ded into two equal parts by two arches running -west and resting on a pier in the centre and on piers. Here, as in the palace, the upper parts of walls seem to have been built of mud bricks. If was the case, they could only have carried a den roof.

ther buildings. Probably the most interesting fea- ɜ of Djabal Says is that, in addition to the above- ıtioned buildings, a considerable number of more lest structures is preserved. At the south-side of valley in an area stretching from the *ḥammām* ɜ easternmost structure), *ca.* 300 m. to the west, traces of more than 15 other buildings can be ı. The majority of them are of almost square pe and consist of ranges of rooms around three four sides of a central courtyard. They are of rer architectural quality than the palace, the *ımām* and the mosque. Some of these buildings e doubtlessly built at the same time as the ace and served as storehouses and barracks or *ns*, whereas some are obviously later. The latter n to be contemporary with a few smaller buildings ɔse plans resemble those of simple farmhouses e range of rooms with a courtyard in front of it). posite the valley, at the southeastern foot of ıbal Says, in an area stretching *ca.* 400 m. from thwest to northeast and *ca.* 100 m. from south- t to northwest, some thirty other buildings are be found. Almost all of them have courtyards h rooms at one, two, three or four sides. The st conspicuous structures among them are: a lding with towers at its corners looking like a ace in miniature, a structure next to it, which sch thinks was a mosque, and a one-naved church embling the large room of the *ḥammām.*

Literary sources (al-Bakrī and Yāḳūt) tell us that caliph al-Walīd (86-96/705-15) had a residence at ays, a waterplace east of Damascus, which is ıbtlessly identical with our site. This conclusion supported by inscriptions found on the spot. One of them bears the name Usays, in some others the names of sons of al-Walīd are mentioned. Hence the palace, the *hammām,* the mosque (which Brisch thinks to be later than the palace) and some of the buildings next to the palace, can be attributed to al-Walīd. Some other buildings are definitely later than the palace, because building material from the palace was used in their construction. It is hard to determine whether there were only two periods of building activity or more. Around the south side of the church a group of very small houses with rather irregular plans is clustered. These differ from the plans of most of the buildings at Djabal Says and might represent a third period of building activity, earlier or later than the two already isolated. A pre-Islamic date is suggested by the church (but we also find a church in the Umayyad settlement of ʿAndjar [see ʿAYN AL-DJARR] in Lebanon), by an inscription found at Djabal Says with the name of the Ghassānid ruler Ḥārith b. Djabala, dated 528, and by a Roman coin.

Bibliography: K. Brisch, *Das omayyadische Schloss in Usais. I.* in *Mitteilungen des Deutschen Archäologischen Institutes,* Abteilung Kairo, ix (1963) 141-87; *II.* in *ibid.,* xx (1965) 138-77; K. A. C. Creswell, *Early Muslim architecture,* Oxford 1969, 472-7; M. de Vogüé, *Syrie centrale,* Paris 1865-77, 71, figs. 26-8, pl. 25; J. Sauvaget, *Les Ruines omeyyades du Djebel Seis,* in *Syria,* xx (1939), 239-56; Yāḳūt, *Muʿdjam,* i, 272.

(H. GAUBE)

DJABALA B. AL-**ḤĀRITH**, Ghassānid chieftain [see GHASSĀN] of the pre-Islamic period, who made his début in Ghassānid - Byzantine relations *ca.* 500 A.D., when he mounted an offensive against Palestina Tertia but was beaten by Romanus, the *dux* of that province. Shortly afterwards in 502, Byzantium concluded a treaty with the Ghassānids and recognised them as its new allies (*foederati*). Throughout the remaining part of the reign of the emperor Anastasius (491-518), the sources are silent on Djabala, who was probably not yet the Ghassānid king but was acting as the general of his father, al-Ḥārith b. Thaʿlaba.

In the reign of the emperor Justin (518-27), Djabala came into prominence, now as the king of the Ghassānid federates, whom he ruled from al-Djābiya [*q.v.*], his seat in the Djawlān. By that time, the Ghassānids had been won over to Monophysite Christianity and had become its staunch supporters. However, the return of Byzantium to the Chalcedonian position and Justin's expulsion of the Monophysite bishops alienated the Ghassānids and their king, who consequently would not take part in the defence of the oriental provinces against the Persians and their Lakhmid allies, and could not come to the succour of their coreligionists in South Arabia during the reign of Yūsuf Dhū Nuwās [*q.v.*]. But in all probability, it was he who enabled al-Aws and al-Khazradj of Medina to achieve an ascendancy over the Jewish tribes there, Abū Djubayla of the Arabic sources being none other than Djabala himself or one of his relatives.

With the accession of the emperor Justinian (527-65), there was a reconciliation with the Monophysites; the Ghassānids under Djabala returned to service to fight the wars of Byzantium against the Persians and the Lakhmids, but Djabala was not destined to live much longer. His more illustrious son, al-Ḥārith b. Djabala, is attested as king already in 529, and the presumption is that Djabala died at the battle of Thannuris in Mesopotamia in 528, commanding the Ghassānid contingent in the

Byzantine army against the Persians; the Syriac authors remember him under the nickname of Aṭfar.

In the list of Ghassānid buildings, three are attributed to Djabala, sc. al-Ḳanāṭir, Adhruḥ, and al-Ḳasṭal.

Bibliography: Theophanes, *Chronographia*, ed. de Boor, i, 141; Procopius, *History*, i, xvii, 47; Malalas, *Chronographia*, ed. Bonn, 441-2; Zachariah Continuatus, *Ecclesiastical history*, *CSCO*, lxxxviii, 64; Ibn al-ʿIbri, *Taʾrīkh Mukhtaṣar al-duwal*, ed. A. Ṣālḥānī, Beirut 1890, 87; Yāḳūt, *Muʿdjam al-buldān*, iv, 463-5; Ḥamza al-Iṣfahānī, *Taʾrīkh*, Beirut 1961, 100; Th. Nöldeke, *Die Ghassānischen Fürsten aus dem Hause Gafna's*, 1887, 7, 8, 10; I. Shahīd (Kawar), *The last days of Salīḥ*, in *Arabica*, v (1958), 145-58; idem, *Ghassān and Byzantium: a new terminus a quo*, in *Isl.*, xxxii/3, 232-55; idem, *The Martyrs of Najrān*, Subsidia Hagiographica, xlix, Brussels 1971, 272-6 and index, 296. (I. A. Shahid)

DJĀBIR b. **ʿABD ALLĀH** b. ʿAmr b. Ḥarām b. Kaʿb b. Ghanm b. Salima, Abū ʿAbd Allāh (or Abu ʿAbd al-Raḥmān, or Abū Muḥammad) al-Salamī al-Khazradjī al-Anṣārī, Companion of the Prophet. His father, ʿAbd Allāh, was one of the seventy men of Aws and Khazradj who gave the Prophet the oath of allegiance at the ʿAḳaba Meeting [see al-ʿAḳaba] and committed themselves to defend him. His father is also recorded in the list of the twelve *nuḳabāʾ*, the chosen group from among the seventy; Djābir himself had attended the Meeting as a very young boy, and is therefore counted in the list of "the Seventy" and in the honourable list of those who embraced Islam together with their fathers. His father prevented him from taking part in the two encounters at Badr and Uḥud, leaving him at home to look after his seven (or nine) sisters. A report according to which he attended the battle of Badr and drew water for the warriors is denied authenticity by al-Wāḳidī and marked by him as an ʿIrāḳī tradition. On the Day of Uḥud, Djābir lost his father, his mother's brother ʿAmr b. al-Djamūḥ and his cousin Khallād. Djābir's father distinguished himself in the fight and was the first Muslim warrior killed in this battle. The Prophet did not object to Djābir mourning for him, and gave him permission to uncover his face. ʿAbd Allāh was buried according to the Prophet's ruling as a martyr on the spot where he fell, clad in his garment, with his wounds still bleeding. The Prophet personally suggested that he should act as father to Djābir and put ʿAʾisha in his mother's place. On the day following the battle of Uḥud, Djābir asked, and was granted permission to join the force dispatched by the Prophet to Ḥamrāʾ al-Asad. After that, Djābir accompanied the Prophet on 18 or so expeditions.

The Prophet showed great concern for Djābir and his family and often came to his dwelling. Djābir's family, who were familiar with his tastes, used to prepare for the Prophet his favourite kind of meal. On one such visit the Prophet blessed the family of Djābir and their abode, on another he cured Djābir of fever by sprinkling on him water which he had used for ablution. The Prophet gave his approval for Djābir to marry a woman who was not a virgin, and who would take care of his sisters. By his blessing, he helped Djābir to pay a debt which his father owed to the Jew Abū Shaḥma, and he invoked God's forgiveness for him when he bought his camel (*laylat al-baʿīr*).

After the death of the Prophet, ʿUmar appointed Djābir chief (*ʿarīf*) of his clan. During the military
operations of the conquest of Damascus he was
as a member of an auxiliary force dispatche
Khālid b. al-Walīd. On another occasion he
dispatched by ʿUmar with a small group to al-I
When the rebellious Egyptian troops advance
Medina in order to besiege the house of ʿUth
Djābir was among the group sent by the calip
negotiate with them and appease them. He is
to have fought on the side of ʿAlī at Ṣiffīn (37
and then to have returned to Medina. During
expedition of Busr b. Arṭāt (40/660), Djābir
compelled to swear allegiance to Muʿāwiya; th
did in precautionary dissimulation (*taḳiyya* [q
after having consulted Umm Salama, the wife o
Prophet. This is a new trait of character, indic
Shīʿī sympathies, and is one of the earliest cas
taḳiyya mentioned in the texts. As an indicati
Djābir's attachment to Medina and to the reli
the Prophet, one may adduce the report that he
Abū Hurayra prevailed upon Muʿāwiya to leave
minbar of the Prophet in Medina and not to tra
it to Syria. He is said to have visited the cou
ʿAbd al-Malik and to have asked him for
grants for the people of Medina. When the force
by Yazīd b. Muʿāwiya against Medina (63
entered the city, Djābir openly voiced his objec
circulating an utterance of the Prophet about
punishment which would befall people who
frighted the city. He was saved from death
Marwān when a man, enraged by his words, atta
him intending to kill him. After the victory o
Ḥadjdjādj over Ibn al-Zubayr (73/692), al-Ḥadj
ordered the hands of some of the opponents o
Umayyad rule to be stamped in the same wa
was done to the *dhimmīs* and Djābir was an
those opponents. Djābir's sharp criticism and un
words with regard to the rulers, especially
Ḥadjdjādj, provoked the latter's caustic re
that Djābir displayed the same pride as the
(by which, of course, the Anṣār were meant).

Djābir died at 78/697 at the age of 94 (other rep
however, give varying dates). He is said to
been the last survivor of the group of 70 Anṣār
attended the ʿAḳaba Meeting, thus fulfillin
prediction of the Prophet. The prayer over his g
was performed by the governor of Medina, A
b. ʿUthmān, or according to another tradition
al-Ḥadjdjādj b. Yūsuf when he came to Medina
his victory over ʿAbd Allāh b. al-Zubayr.

Djābir is noted as a most prolific narrato
traditions from the Prophet. The number of t
going back to him is estimated at 1,540; al-Buk
and Muslim recorded 210 *ḥadīths* transmitted
him in their compilations, and the subject-rang
his transmission is extremely wide. Of special
terest are Djābir's reports about events which
witnessed and details furnished by him about e
ditions in which he took part. Djābir was hi
respected by the scholars of *ḥadīth* and is cou
in the lists of reliable transmitters and the *a*
al-futyā. He used to recite his traditions in
mosque of Medina; his sessions of *ḥadīth*-transmis
were attended by a wide circle of students,
would discuss the traditions of their master a
leaving the mosque. A composition known as *ṣa*
Djābir contained a great number of traditions rec
ed by him. Scholars of *ḥadīth* were eager to circu
traditions on his authority, without always obser
the necessary rules of *ḥadīth* transmission. Eve
distinguished pious scholar like al-Ḥasan al-B
was suspected of reporting some traditions on
direct authority of Djābir, although he never

disciple. The impressive list of those who trans-
:ed his traditions includes the names of three of
sons: ʿAbd al-Raḥmān, ʿAḳīl and Muḥammad.
descendants are said to have settled in North
ica, in a place called al-Anṣāriyya.
n Shīʿī tradition, Djābir was granted an excep-
ally high rank. The *ḥadīth*s recorded in Shīʿī
rces on his authority touch upon the fundamental
ıts of Shīʿī belief: the mission of ʿAlī, his qualities,
authority over the believers, the graces granted
by God, the divine virtues of his descendants
the duties of allegiance and obedience incumbent
n the believers. It was the *imām* al-Bāḳir who
ed Djābir about the Tablet which God sent
n to Fāṭima and which Djābir got permission to
y. In this Tablet God named the *imām*s and
blished their order of succession. It is note-
thy that, according to some versions, the *imām*
pared the copy of Djābir with the Tablet in
possession and stated that the copy is a reliable
accurate one. In another story, Djābir confirms
accuracy of the unusual report about the *hidjra*
old him by the *imām*. Djābir is credited with the
ith about the appointment of ʿAlī as *waṣī*, which
ns the base of the Shīʿī interpretation of Sūra
I, 1-4. It was he who reported the utterance of
Prophet that ʿAlī is the *ṣirāṭ mustaḳīm*, the
ıt path to be followed. The *imām* al-Bāḳir stressed
t Djābir was privileged to possess knowledge of
correct interpretation of Sūra XXVIII, 85,
ich, according to him, refers to the *radjʿa*, the
appearance of the Prophet and ʿAlī. Among
her Shīʿī traditions reported on Djābir's authority
he one which states that there are two weighty
gs left by the Prophet for the Muslim community:
Ḳurʾān and his Family (*al-ʿitra*). Another
dition has it that the angel Djibrīl bade the Prophet
claim the vocation of ʿAlī and his descendants,
imāms, and tell the Muslim community about
ī's distinguished position on the Day of Resur-
tion and in Paradise. The Sunnī version of Djābir's
ort that the first thing created by God was the
ht of Muḥammad had its Shīʿī counterpart,
ed back to Djābir, which said that this Light
split into two parts: the Light of Muḥammad
the Light of ʿAlī, and that it was later transferred
the succeeding *imāms*. It is on the authority of
bir that the significant tradition which states
t the last persons to be with the Prophet when
died were ʿAlī and Fāṭima is reported. Some of
traditions relate the miracles of ʿAlī. ʿAlī ascended
Heaven in order to put down the rebellion of the
ked *djinn*, who denied his authority and a
inous angel prayed in his place in the mosque.
other miracle happened when ʿAlī walked with
bir on the bank of the Euphrates: a very high
ve covered ʿAlī; when he reappeared completely
after a short time, he explained that it had
n the Angel of the Water who greeted and
braced him.
Djābir is distinguished in the Shīʿī tradition by a
nificant mission entrusted to him by the Prophet:
was ordered to meet the *imām* al-Bāḳir and to
vey to him the greetings of the Prophet, which
did. This created a peculiar relationship between
elderly bearer of the good tidings and the young
ipient, the *imām* al-Bāḳir. According to tradition,
two used to meet, and some of the traditions
nsmitted by al-Bāḳir are told on the authority of
bir and traced back to the Prophet. It is evident
t the idea that the *imām* might have derived his
owledge from a human being is opposed to the principles of the Shīʿa. It had thus to be justified that it was merely done in order to put an end to the accusations of the Medinans, who blamed al-Bāḳir for transmitting *ḥadīth*s on the authority of the Prophet, whom he had never seen. As the traditions reported by Djābir and those independently reported by the *imām* and revealed to him by God were in fact identical, the insertion of Djābir's name between the name of the *imām* and that of the Prophet was quite a formal act, with no significance. A few traditions are indeed reported with names of some Companions inserted between the *imām* and the Prophet. In one of the traditions it is explained that this insertion may make the *ḥadīth* more acceptable to people, although it is obvious that the *imām*s knew more than that Companion whose name was inserted between the *imām* and the Prophet.

The close relationship of Djābir with the family of ʿAlī is also exposed in the story relating that Fāṭima bint ʿAlī asked Djābir to intervene and to persuade Zayn al-ʿĀbidīn to cease his excessive devotional practices which might be harming for his health. It was a sign of respect and faith that, when Ḥusayn asked his enemies on the battle-field of Karbalāʾ to save his life, quoting the utterance of the Prophet that he and his brother were the lords of the youths of Paradise (*sayyidā shabāb ahl al-djanna*), he referred to Djābir who would vouch for the truth of the utterance. Djābir is said to have been present at the grave of Ḥusayn shortly after he was killed and to have met there the family of Ḥusayn who were sent back by Yazīd b. Muʿāwiya. Another Shīʿī tradition reports about his visit to the grave of Ḥusayn and his moving speech over the grave.

Djābir had intimate relations with the family of ʿAlī and especially with the two *imām*s Zayn al-ʿĀbidīn and al-Bāḳir. There are some Shīʿī attempts to link him with Djaʿfar al-Ṣādiḳ and to fix the date of his death at the beginning of the 2nd century A.H.

Finally, the high position of Djābir in Shīʿī tradition is expressed by the fact that he was placed in the list of the four persons who clung to the true faith and in the list of the nine persons to whom ʿAlī promised that they would be in Paradise.

Bibliography: Ibn Ḳudāma al-Maḳdisī, *al-Istibṣār fī nasab al-ṣaḥāba min al-anṣār*, Cairo 1392/1972, index; ʿAbd al-Malik b. Ḥabīb, *al-Taʾrīkh*, Ms. Bodl. Marsh 288, p. 126; Abū ʿAbd Allāh al-Ṣūrī, *Djuzʾ*, Ms. Leiden Or. 2465, fols. 4b-5a; Abu 'l-ʿArab, *K. al-Miḥan*, Ms. Cambridge Oq 235, fol. 162a; ʿAbd al-Ghanī al-Nābulusī, *Dhakhāʾir al-mawārīth fī 'l-dilāla ʿalā mawāḍiʿ 'l-ḥadīth*, Cairo 1352/1934, i, 125-76, nos. 1139-1599; Aḥmad b. ʿAlī al-Ṭabarsī, *al-Iḥtidjādj*, Nadjaf 1386/1966, i, 84-8, 291; Aḥmad b. al-Ḥusayn al-Bayhaḳī, *al-Sunan al-kubrā*, Hyderabad 1344, i-x, index; Akhṭab Khʷwārizm, *al-Manāḳib*, Nadjaf 1385/1965, 27, 36, 60, 62, 80, 82, 88, 106-7, 195, 219, 227, 266; Aḥmad b. Ḥanbal, *K. al-ʿIlal wa-maʿrifat al-ridjāl*, ed. Talat Koçyiğit and Ismail Cerrahoğlu, Ankara 1963, i, index; idem, *Musnad*, Būlāḳ, iii, 292-400; al-Madīnī, *al-ʿIlal*, Beirut 1392/1972, index; anon., *Taʾrīkh al-Khulafāʾ*, ed. P. A. Gryaznyevič, Moscow 1967, fol. 42a, l. 1, 213b, ll. 4-5; Abū Nuʿaym, *Ḥilyat al-awliyāʾ*, repr. Beirut 1387/1967, ii, 4-5, iii, 189-91, 200-2; al-Balādhurī, *Ansāb*, i, ed. Ḥamīdallāh, Cairo 1959, index, v. ed. S. D. Goitein, Jerusalem 1936, index, Ms. fol. 1215b; al-Dhahabī, *Siyar aʿlām al-nubalāʾ*, Cairo 1956 f., i, 235-7 (ed. Ṣalāḥ al-Dīn al-Munadjdjid), iii, 126-9 (ed. Asʿad Ṭalas);

idem, *Taʾrīkh al-Islām*, Cairo 1367, iii, 143-5; idem, *Ḥuffāẓ*, Hyderabad 1375/1955, i, 43-4; al-Faḍl b. al-Ḥasan al-Ṭabarsī, *Iʿlām al-warā bi-aʿlām al-hudā*, ed. ʿAlī Akbar al-Ghaffārī, Tehran 1338, 58, 210, 253, 262-3; Furāt al-Kūfī, *Tafsīr*, Nadjaf n.d., 77, 101, 174, 175, 176, 192-3, 205, 220; al-Ḥākim, *al-Mustadrak*, Hyderabad 1342, iii, 202-4, 564-6; Hāshim b. Sulaymān al-Baḥrānī al-Tawbalī al-Katakānī, *al-Burhān fī tafsīr al-Ḳurʾān*, Ḳumm 1394, i, 305, 522, 563, ii, 127-8, 442, iii, 146-7, 239-40, iv, 148, 245, 490, 491; Ibn ʿAbd al-Barr, *al-Istīʿāb*, Cairo 1380/1960, i, 219-20, no. 286; Ibn Aʿtham al-Kūfī, *K. al-Futūḥ*, Hyderabad 1391/1971, iv, 57; Ibn ʿAsākir, *Taʾrīkh* (*tahdhīb*), Damascus 1329 f., iii, 386-91; Ibn al-Athīr, *Usd al-ghāba*, Cairo 1280, i, 256-8; Ibn Bābawayh, *Amālī*, Nadjaf 1389/1970, 16, 19-20, 47, 68, 79, 85, 108, 110, 119, 215-16, 244, 297, 315-16; Ibn Ḥadjar, *Tahdhīb al-Tahdhīb*, Hyderabad 1325, ii, 42-3, no. 67, vi, 153, no. 309, vii, 253, no. 461, ix, 90, no. 117; idem, *al-Iṣāba*, Cairo 1392/1972, i, 434-5, no. 1027, iv, 189-90, no. 4841; Ibn Hishām, Cairo 1355/1936, indices; Ibn Ḥazm, *Djawāmiʿ al-sīra*, ed. Iḥsān ʿAbbās and Nāṣir al-Dīn al-Asad, Cairo n.d., index; idem, *Djamharat ansāb al-ʿarab*, Cairo 1962, 359; Ibn al-ʿImād, *Shadharāt al-dhahab*, Cairo 1350, i, 84; Ibn Saʿd, *Ṭabaḳāt*, index; Ibn Ḳutayba, *Maʿārif*, Cairo 1960, index; Pseudo-Ibn Ḳutayba, *al-Imāma wa 'l-siyāsa*, Cairo 1378/1967, i, 183; Ibn Shahrāshūb, *Manāḳib āl Abī Ṭālib*, Nadjaf 1376/1956, *passim*; Ibn Ṭāwūs, *al-Luhūf ʿalā ḳatlā 'l-ṭufūf*, Tehran 1348, 196; Ibrāhīm b. Muḥammad al-Bayhaḳī, *al-Maḥāsin wa 'l-masāwī*, Cairo 1380/1961, index; Ibrāhīm b. Marʿi al-Shabrakhītī, *Sharḥ ʿalā 'l-arbaʿīn ḥadīth*(!) *al-nawawiyya*, Beirut n.d., 86; Ismāʿīl b. Muḥammad al-ʿAdjlūnī al-Djarrāḥī, *Kashf al-khafāʾ wa-muzīl al-ilbās ʿammāʾshtahara min al-aḥādīth ʿalā alsinat al-nās*, Cairo 1351 (repr.), i, 265, no. 827; al-ʿIṣāmī, *Simṭ al-nudjūm al-ʿawālī*, Cairo 1380, ii, 331, 423, 475, 482, 485, 492, iii, 91-2, 144; al-Khaṭīb al-Baghdādī, *Mūḍiḥ awhām al-djamʿ wa'l-tafrīḳ*, Hyderabad 1378/1959, i, 395, 398; Khalīfa b. Khayyāṭ, *Taʾrīkh*, ed. al-ʿUmarī, Nadjaf 1386/1967, index; Khalīl b. Aybak al-Ṣafadī, *Nakt al-himyān*, Cairo 1329/1911, 132-3; al-Kishshī, *Ridjāl*, Nadjaf n.d., 42-5, 113-4; al-Kulaynī, *al-Kāfī* (*al-uṣūl*), Tehran 1388, i, 242, 442-4; al-Māmaḳānī, *Tanḳīḥ al-maḳāl fī aḥwāl al-ridjāl*, Nadjaf 1349, 199-200, no. 1569; al-Madjlisī, *Bihar āl-anwār*, Tehran 1385 f., *passim*; al-Masʿūdī, *Ithbāt al-waṣiyya*, Nadjaf 1374/1955, 165-6, 173; al-Djahshiyārī, *K. al-wuzarāʾ wa'l-kuttāb*, Cairo 1938, 21; Muḥammad b. Aḥmad al-Ahdal al-Ḥusaynī al-Marāwiʿī, *Bughyat ahl al-athar fīman ittafaḳa lahu wa-li-abīhi ṣuḥbat sayyid al-bashar*, Cairo 1347, 36, l. 2; Muḥammad b. al-Fattāl al-Naysābūrī, *Rawḍat al-wāʿiẓīn*, Nadjaf 1386/1966, 202-3, 206, 271; Muḥammad b. Ḥabīb, *al-Muḥabbar*, Hyderabad 1361/1942, index; Muḥammad b. al-Ḥasan al-ʿĀmilī, *al-Djawāhir al-saniyya fī 'l-aḥādīth al-ḳudsiyya*, Nadjaf 1384/1964, 201-9, 242-3, 256-7, 265-6, 304 (see the tradition on p. 304 in Daylamī's *Firdaws al-akhbār*, Ms. Chester Beatty 3037, fol. 167a, ll. 8-9); Muḥammad b. Abī 'l-Ḳāsim al-Ṭabarī, *Bishārat al-muṣṭafā li-shīʿat al-murtaḍā*, Nadjaf 1383/1963, 19-20, 23, 40, 65, 66-7, 74, 101, 133, 137-9, 145, 158, 183, 187, 190-2; Muḥammad Nawawī b. ʿUmar al-Djāwī, *Targhīb al-mushtāḳīn li-bayān manẓūmat al-sayyid al-barzandjī Zayn al-ʿĀbidīn*, Cairo n.d., 40; Muḥammad b. Yaḥyā al-Mālaḳī, *al-Tamhīd wa 'l-bayan fī maḳtal al-sh* *ʿUthmān*, Beirut 1964, index; al-Muḥibb Ṭabarī, *al-Riyāḍ al-naḍira fī manāḳib al-ʿash* Cairo 1372/1953, ii, 203, 222, 265, 296; ic *Dhakhāʾir al-ʿuḳbā fī manāḳib dhawī 'l-ḳu* Cairo 1356, 66, 70-1, 85, 91, 95, 96, 119, 129, Nūr al-Dīn al-Haythamī, *Madjmaʿ al-zawāʾid manbaʿ al-fawāʾid*, Beirut 1967 (reprint) ix, 7, 12, 87, 88, 172, 317, x, 9-10; Ṣafī al-Dīn Khazradjī, *Khulāṣat tadhhīb Tahdhīb al-kamā asmāʾ al-ridjāl*, Cairo 1391/1971, i, 156, no. al-Shaykh al-Mufīd, *al-Ikhtiṣās*, Nadjaf 1390/1 2, 56-7, 195, 196, 205-6; idem, *al-Irshād*, Na 1381/1962, 254 inf., 262; idem, *al-Amālī*, Na n.d., 39, 41, 48, 74, 98, 100, 111, 112; al-Ṭal *Taʾrīkh*, index; al-Ṭayālisī, *Musnad*, Hydera 1321, 232-48, nos. 1667-1801; al-Waḳidī, *Magh* ed. Marsden Jones, Oxford 1966, index; Yaʿḳū Sufyān al-Fasawī, *al-Maʿrifa wa 'l-taʾrīkh*, Esad Ef. 2391, fols. 5b, 13b; al-Yaʿḳūbī, *Taʾ* index; E. Kohlberg, *An unusual Shīʿī isnād* *Israel Oriental Studies*, v (1975), 142-9; U. Ru *Pre-existence and light*, in *ibid.*, 99, n. 86, 11 22; Sezgin, *GAS*, i, 85, no. 3. (M. J. Kiste

DJĀBIR AL-DJUʿFĪ, Abū ʿAbd Allāh or Muḥammad b. Yazīd b. al-Ḥārith, Kufan S traditionist of Arab descent. His chief tea seems to have been al-Shaʿbī [*q.v.*] (d. 100/718- Among other well-known traditionists, from wh he related, were ʿIkrima, ʿAṭāʾ b. Abī Rabāḥ Ṭāwūs. Initially, he held the moderate Shīʿī vi widespread among the Kūfan traditionists. Late joined the more radical Shīʿī circles looking Muḥammad al-Bāḳir (d. *ca.* 117/735) and his Djaʿfar al-Ṣādiḳ for religious guidance. Accordin some Sunnī heresiologists, he became the leade the extremist Shīʿī followers of al-Mughīra b. S after the latter was killed by Khālid al-Ḳ governor of Kūfa, in 119/737. Imāmī sources, on other hand, report a statement of Djaʿfar al-Ṣā commending him for having said the truth about *imāms* while condemning al-Mughīra for lying ab them. This makes it appear unlikely that Dj actually belonged to the Mughīriyya, who cognised the Ḥasanid Muḥammad b. ʿAbd Allāh their *imām*, but does point to some relation between him and al-Mughīra. According to ano Imāmī report, Djābir first aroused the suspicion Yūsuf b. ʿUmar, governor of Kūfa (120-6/738-44), then incited the people of Kūfa against his succes Manṣūr b. Djumhūr (126/744). According to n sources, he died in 128/745-6. Other death d given for him are 127/744-5 and 132/749-50.

Sunnī *ḥadīth* criticism was divided concerning trustworthiness. His transmission was evide accepted at first as reliable and highly accurate later, as his Shīʿī attitude became more radical, was shunned. Thus Sufyān al-Thawrī and Shu related on his authority and noted his reliabil though critical judgments are also reported f them. Abū Ḥanīfa is said to have condemned as a notorious liar who claimed to have a *ḥadīth* every legal question. Among the authors of canonical collections of *ḥadīth*, Abū Dāwūd, Tirmidhī, and Ibn Mādja quoted a few traditi in which he appears in the chain of transmit Al-Bukhārī and Muslim excluded him, the la quoting negative reports about him in the in duction to his *Ṣaḥīḥ* (Cairo [1963?], i, 15). standard accusations against him were that believed in the *radjʿa* [*q.v.*] and that he clai secret knowledge of many thousands of *ḥadīths* wh

ʼould not divulge. The Imāmī attitude to him also ambiguous. While he was considered a loyal ›orter of the *imāms* al-Bāḳir and al-Ṣādiḳ, he was ribed as "mixed-up" (*mukhtaliṭ*) by scholars sed to extremist tendencies. Several Imāmī :tionists who related from him, ʿAmr b. Shimr, ıḍḍal b. Ṣāliḥ, Munakhkhal b. Djamīl and Yūsuf ʼaʿḳūb, were accused of extremism and con-ed weak transmitters. The *ghulāt*, on the other , recognised him as the most intimate disciple uḥammad al-Bāḳir, who was fully initiated into mysteries of the gnostic knowledge and super-an nature of the *imām*, and they ascribed mira-ıs qualities and powers to him. It is uncertain ʼhat extent reports later circulating under his e among the *ghulāt* go back to Djābir, whatever elations with the contemporary Shīʿī extremists. arly Imāmī source states that ʿAbd Allāh b. al-ṯh, leader of the extremist followers of ʿAbd ı b. Muʿāwiya [*q.v.*], after the latter's death in 748-9, spread extremist doctrines about metem-hosis, pre-existence of the human souls as shadows *a*) and cyclical history (*dawr* [*q.v.* in Suppl.]), bing them to Djābir b. ʿAbd Allāh al-Anṣārī Djābir al-Djuʿfī "who were innocent of them" al-Nawbakhtī, *Firaḳ al-shīʿa*, ed. H. Ritter, ıbul 1931, 31).

ıe Imāmī scholar al-Nadjāshī (d. 450/1058) men-, the following books of Djābir as still available im: *K. al-Tafsīr*, *K. al-Nawādir*, *K. al-Faḍāʾil*, *-Djamal*, *K. Ṣiffīn*, *K. al-Nahrawān*, *K. Maḳtal al-Muʾminīn*, and *K. Maḳtal al-Ḥusayn*. ir occasionally appears in al-Ṭabarī's Ḳurʾān nentary and his *Taʾrīkh* as a transmitter of ʾān exegesis and in the latter work also as a smitter of reports on the caliphate of ʿAlī and death of al-Ḥusayn (see Ṭabarī, index s.v. ir al-Rāwī). It is unlikely, however, that al-.rī was quoting directly from any works of ir. Extensive quotations of his reports con-ng the battle of Ṣiffīn and the caliphate of are contained in the *K. Waḳʿat Ṣiffīn* of Naṣr uzāḥim. Naṣr's authority for them was, how-ʿAmr b. Shimr, who is accused by the Shaykh ısī of having made additions to Djābir's s.

Bibliography: Ibn Saʿd, vi, 240; al-Bukhārī, *Taʾrīkh al-kabīr*, Ḥaydarābād 1360-77/1941-58, , 210 f.; al-Ashʿarī, *Maḳālāt al-islāmiyyīn*, ed. Ritter, Istanbul 1939-31, i, 8; al-Kashshī, *tiyār maʿrifat al-ridjāl*, ed. Ḥasan al-Muṣṭafawī, ıshhad 1348/1970, 191-8, 373; al-Mufīd, *al-tiṣāṣ*, ed. Ḥasan al-Kharsān, Nadjaf 1390/1971, ; al-Ṭūsī, *Fihrist kutub al-shīʿa*, ed. A. Sprenger, lcutta 1853-5, 73; al-Nadjāshī, *al-Ridjāl*, Tehran l., 99-101; Nashwān al-Ḥimyarī, *al-Ḥūr al-ʿīn*, iro 1367/1948, 168; al-Dhahabī, *Mīzān al-ʿdāl*, ed. ʿAlī Muḥammad al-Bidjāwī, Cairo 1382/63, i, 379-84; Ibn Ḥadjar, *Tahdhīb al-tahdhīb*, .ydarābād 1325-7/1907-9, ii, 46-51; al-ʿĀmilī, *yān al-shīʿa*, xv, Damascus 1359/1940, 199-226. r the Djābir tradition among the *ghulāt* and ışayrīs, see *K. al-Haft wa 'l-aẓilla*, ed. ʿA. mir and Ign.-A. Khalifé, Beirut 1960, 28, 128; Ṭabarānī, *Madjmūʿ al-aʿyād*, ed. R. Stroth-ınn, in *Isl.*, xxvii (1946), index; *Umm al-Kitāb*, W. Ivanow, in *Isl.*, xxii (1936), index; Gold-er, *Muh. St.*, ii, 112 f. Eng. tr., ii, 110-11; gin *GAS*, i, 307; T. Nagel, *Rechtleitung und lifat*, Bonn 1975, 216 f. (W. MADELUNG)

ʼABR (A.), compulsion in marriage exer-upon one or other of the prospective partners, under conditions which vary according to the judicial schools. The right of *djabr* is foreseen neither by the Ḳurʾān nor by the *Sunna*, and a *ḥadīth* (al-Bukhārī, *Nikāḥ*, *bāb* 42) actually declares that neither the father nor any other person may give in marriage without her consent a virgin or a woman who has already been under the authority of a husband; the Prophet himself consulted his daughter Fāṭima before giving her in marriage to ʿAlī, but it seems that the majority of early Muslim jurists preferred to follow an ancient Arab custom. Later traditions confirm their point of view, and all the schools made *djabr* a point of doctrine, without always employing this term, which does not appear with this particular sense in the classical dictionaries.

In general, this right belongs to the master when applied to slaves of both sexes, on condition that they suffer no damage (see ʿABD), or to the father, grandfather or testamentary guardian (*waṣī*) in other cases; in principle, the *walī* [see WILĀYA] is only considered to exercise this right by the Ḥanafīs, and by the Mālikīs in the case of an orphan girl who does not have a *waṣī*. Except when subject to impediment [see ḤADJR], boys normally acquired the right to consent to their marriage after puberty [see BĀLIGH], so that they escaped from *djabr* at an early age, in the legal sense at least. So it is upon girls that the arrangements relative to matrimonial compulsion have the most relevant effect in classical Muslim law.

According to the Ḥanafīs, even the *walī* may arrange a marriage in the name of children of either sex who are below the age of puberty, and in the case of the girl in particular, this applies whether she is a virgin or not. On attaining puberty boys and girls enjoy a right of choice (*khiyār*) if they have been married by their *walī mudjbir*, who according to this school may be chosen from among a wide range of agnatic relatives; if it is the father or the grandfather who has exercised the right of *djabr*, however, no annulment is possible. A slave woman given in marriage by her master against her will may also annul her marriage if she is enfranchised.

According to the Shāfiʿīs, the *walī* may not give a virgin girl in marriage without her consent, at least tacit; only the father or the grandfather in fact exercises the right of *djabr*, but in this school, it is the notion of virginity which is crucial, the loss of virginity, whether legal, accidental or illegal, conferring upon the interested party the right to consent to her marriage (or re-marriage) even if she is still below the age of puberty.

For the Ḥanbalīs, the conditions for the exercise of the right of *djabr* approximate to those of the Mālikīs, who show themselves the most rigorous in combining the notions of impuberty and of virginity. In fact the father has the right to give his daughter in marriage without her consent, not only if she is subject to impediment, as in the other schools, but also, with certain restrictions, if she is a virgin, whether past the age of puberty (she may even be an old maid) or below it; he exercises the right of *djabr* equally over a pre-pubescent girl deflowered after a legal marriage, and over a post-pubescent girl deflowered accidentally or illegally. There is no right of choice, but the father is obliged to respect the principle according to which the partners must be well-suited [see KAFĀʾA]. So in order to escape the paternal *djabr*, the daughter must be past the age of puberty and legally deflowered (*thayyib*) or, if she has preserved her virginity after the age of puberty, she must be emancipated in respect of property, or married for a year or less and divorced, or a widow whose marriage has not been consummated. The *walī* other than the father is never *mudjbir*, that is to say that he only has the right to give a girl in marriage when she is past puberty, but her consent, more or less tacit, is then required; having become *thayyib*, she must give an explicit consent through the intermediary of her *walī*.

Among the Imāmī Shīʿīs, the right of *djabr* belongs to the father, and, with certain reservations, to the grandfather. In early times, it was applied to the virgin daughter whatever her age, but ultimately it was decided that the post-pubescent virgin is no longer subject to it.

Such is the theory. In practice, the governments of the majority Muslim states, whether independent or under foreign protectorate, have long ago attempted to curb the right of *djabr* by fixing the age of marriage at twelve and above for girls and by forbidding the *ḳāḍīs* to conduct unduly premature weddings; but is has not always been possible to exercise a very strict control. In the states which have modern legal systems, this right has been totally abolished or restrained by the necessity of the mutual consent of the parties, even if the mediation of the *walī* is still required (if the latter refuses, it is possible to have recourse to the judge). There remain, however, vestiges of it in the most modern legal codes, such as that of Morocco which provides (art. 12) that the judge has the right to use compulsion in a case where it is feared that a girl will misbehave if allowed to remain a spinster.

Bibliography: The *fiḳh* works, chs. on marriage, notably, for the Ḥanafīs, Ḳudūrī, *Mukhtaṣar*, ed. and tr. G. H. Bousquet and L. Bercher, Tunis n.d.; for the Shāfiʿīs, Shāfiʿī, *K. al-Umm*, Cairo 1325, vii, 181-5; for the Mālikīs, Mālik, *Muwaṭṭaʾ*, Cairo 1951, ii, 525; Khalīl b. Isḥāḳ, *Mukhtaṣar*, tr. Bousquet, ii, Algiers-Paris 1958, 17 ff.; for the Shīʿīs, Kulaynī, *Kāfī*, Tehran 1391, v, 391 ff.; al-Sharīf al-Murtaḍā, *Intiṣār*, Nadjaf 1971, 119-21. See also Ibn Ḥazm, *Muḥallā*, Cairo 1351, ix, 459 ff.; A. Querry, *Droit musulman*, Paris 1871-2, i, 650; G. Stern, *Marriage in early Islam*, London 1939, 32-3; J. Roussier-Théaux, *La neutralisation du droit de djebr*, in *Rev. Afr.*, lxxxi (1938) 161-8; E. Desportes, *Le droit de djebr*, in *Rev. de Legisl. alg.*, 1949/1, 109-19; G. H. Bousquet, *Le droit de djebr et la cour d'Alger*, in *ibid.*, 1950/1, 211-15; idem, *La morale de l'Islam et son ethique sexuelle*, Paris 1953, 90 ff.; L. Milliot, *Introduction à l'étude du droit musulman*, Paris 1953, 295 ff.; R. Brunschvig, *Considérations sociologiques sur le droit musulman*, in *SI*, iii (1965), 65-6; J. Schacht, *Islamic law*, Oxford 1964, 161-2; Linant de Bellefonds, *Traité de droit musulman comparé*, Paris-The Hague 1965, index; M. Borrmans, *Statut personnel et famille au Maghreb de 1940 à nos jours*, Sorbonne thesis 1971, index. See also NIKĀḤ. (CH. PELLAT)

DJABRIDS, a dynasty based in al-Aḥsāʾ [*q.v.*] in eastern Arabia in the 9th-10th/15th-16th centuries. The Banū Djabr descended from ʿĀmir b. Rabīʿa b. ʿUḳayl

The founder of the dynasty was Sayf b. Zāmil b. Djabr, who supplanted the Djarwānids of ʿUḳayl [see AL-ḲAṬĪF]. Sayf's brother and successor Adjwad was born in the desert in the region of al-Aḥsāʾ and al-Ḳaṭīf in Ramaḍān 821/October 1418. Adjwad in his fifties was strong enough to become involved in the politics of Hormuz on the other side of the He told the Medinan historian al-Samhūdī ho had visited the tomb of Kulayb, the hero o saga of the war of al-Basūs, in Ḥimā Ḍariyya [a tomb revered by a Bedouin cult. Adjwad exte his authority westwards into Nadjd and tov ʿUmān in the east, where he gathered tribute won fame as a captain who had suffered wounds in battle. At the same time he was tinguished for his piety; he diligently coll books of the Mālikī law school to which he adh a school with many followers in eastern Ar Some of the Mālikī judges whom he appointed converts from the Shīʿa. He made frequent grimages, the last being in 912/1507, when he said to have led a throng of 30,000. His gener was such that the Bedouins of eastern Arabia remember him as a sort of latter-day Ḥātim al- The traces of a fort near the village of al-Muna in al-Aḥsāʾ are known as Ḳaṣr Adjwad b. Zan

With the arrival of the Portuguese in the Pe Gulf in 913/1507, Albuquerque learned of the p of the Djabrids. Adjwad had just died, leaving sons, the eldest of whom was Muḳrin. The fa pilgrimage in 926/1520 by Muḳrin, whom Egyptians visiting Mecca regarded as "the lo the Bedouins of the East", is described in ḲAṬĪF.

Back from al-Ḥidjāz, Muḳrin in Shaʿbān July 1521 encountered a Portuguese force that descended on the island of al-Baḥrayn. Ha married a daughter of the Amīr of Mecca, M had brought with him Turkish craftsmen sailors to build and man a fleet to oppose Christian enemy and had strengthened his with 400 Persian archers and 20 Ottoman sh shooters. The battle took place on land. Aft heroic resistance, Muḳrin fell gravely wounded died three days later.

In 928/1521 Ḥusayn b. Saʿīd, the Djabrid commander in ʿUmān, joined the Portugues expelling the Persian garrison from Ṣuḥār on coast of the Gulf of ʿUmān, and the Portu recognised Ḥusayn as the new governor t describing him as master of the whole stretc territory southwards to Ẓafār on the Arabian

As the 10th/16th century wore on, the Dja grew weaker in the face of an Ottoman adv from the north and incursions by the Shar Mecca from the west. Rāshid b. Mughāmis of Muntafiḳ, an Ottoman subject, dealt the Djabr crippling blow in 931/1524-5. An inscriptio Masdjid al-Dibs in al-Hufūf, the capital of al-A bears the name of the first Ottoman g nor, Meḥmed Farrūkh Pasha, and the date 1556.

In 986/1578-9 the Sharīf Ḥasan b. Abī Num while besieging Miʿkāl in the oasis of al-R captured a number of the leading figures t among whom there may have been membe Banū Djabr. Three years later the same Sharīf towns and forts in al-Khardj and al-Yamāma the way home, the Sharīf was attacked by Bed of Banū Khālid, whom he routed. This inc lends credence to the likelihood of a direct nection between the Djabrids and this tribe, p cularly its section named the Djubūr.

Bibliography: al-Samhūdī, *Wafāʾ al-w* Cairo 1326; al-Sakhāwī, *al-Ḍawʾ al-lāmiʿ*, i, 1353; ʿUthmān b. Bishr, *ʿUnwān al-madjd*, 1391; A. de Albuquerque, *Comentarios*, Coi 1923; J. de Barros, *Decades da Asia*, Lisbon

. von Oppenheim, *Die Beduinen*, iii/i, ed. W. ıskel, Wiesbaden 1952; W. Caskel, *Ein "unkannte" Dynastie in Arabien*, in *Oriens*, ii 949), 66-71; ʿAbd al-Laṭīf Nāṣir al-Ḥumaydān, -*Taʾrīkh al-siyāsī li-imārat al-Djubūr fī Nadjd a-sharḳ al-djazīra al-ʿarabiyya, 820/1417-931/525*, in *Madjallat Kulliyyat al-Ādāb, Djāmiʿat -Baṣra*, No. 16 (1980) (detailed study; includes nealogical table); idem, *Nufūdh al-Djubūr fī arḳ al-djazīra al-ʿarabiyya baʿd zawāl salṭatihim -siyāsiyya, 931/1525-1288/1871*, in *op. cit.*, o. 17 (1980). (G. Rentz)

JĀDJARM, a town in the western part of liaeval Khurāsān in Persia, now a town and a *bakhsh* or sub-district in the *shahrastān* or :ict of Budjnurd in the Khurāsān *ustān*. It lies at western end of the elongated plain which tches almost from Bisṭām in the west almost to āpūr in the east, which is drained by the largely ıe Kāl-i Shūr stream, and which is now traversed the Tehran-Nīshāpūr-Mashhad railway.

he mediaeval geographers, up to and including nd Allāh Mustawfī (see Le Strange, *The lands of Eastern Caliphate*, 392-3, 430), advert to the lity of the region of Djādjarm, which they ribe as a well-fortified town, with cereals and :, and with water from springs which was con-ed to the field by *ḳanāt*s. The *Ḥudūd al-ʿālam* /982), tr. Minorsky, 102, describes it as "the orium of Gurgān, Ḳūmis and Nīshāpūr". It lay n important caravan route which ran westward Nīshāpūr through Djuwayn, along the plain then by the Dīnār-Sārī defile through mountains n to the Caspian lowlands; it was this route h Masʿūd of Ghazna's army took in 426/1035 n that ruler marched against the Ziyārid prince urgān and Ṭabaristān Manūčihr b. Ḳābūs, see haḳī, *Taʾrīkh-i Masʿūdī*, ed. Ghanī and Fayyāḍ, 9. In the Mongol and Il-Khānid periods this e was particularly well-traversed, and the Spanish y Clavijo gives a detailed account of his journey Djādjarm, see *Embassy to Tamerlane 1403-1406*, e Strange, London 1928, 176.

. Ṣafawid and Ḳādjār times. Djādjarm clearly ined, and the earlier fertility largely disappeared; region doubtless suffered until the later 19th ury from the insecurity engendered by Türkmen rsions into northern Khurāsān. C. E. Yate in the s estimated that Djādjarm had 500 houses; pooner in 1961 estimated that the town had households or *ca.* 5,500 persons. It seems, there- that the town has received a modest amount of perity in recent decades; the main cash crop of listrict today is cotton.

Bibliography: In addition to the references ven in the text, see B. Spooner, *Arghiyān. The ea of Jājarm in western Khurasan*, in *Iran, Jnal. the British Inst. of Persian Studies*, iii (1965), -107, and J. Aubin, *Réseau pastoral et réseau avanier, les grand'routes du Khurassan à l'époque ongole*, in *Le monde iranien et l'Islam*, i, Geneva-ıris 1971, 105-30 (corrects certain errors of Le range and Spooner, especially the wrongful entification of the mediaeval district of Arghiyān th Djādjarm). For the *ʿulamāʾ* of Djādjarm, see mʿānī, *Ansāb*, ed. Hyderabad, iii, 160-1, and ıḳūt, *Buldān*, ed. Beirut, ii, 92.

(C. E. Bosworth)

ĀDJARMĪ, a *nisba* referring to Djādjarm [*q.v* e] in western Khurāsān, the name of two Per- poets, father and son, who flourished in the gol period.

1. The elder, Badr al-Dīn b. ʿUmar, made his career under the patronage of the Djuwaynīs [*q.v.*], a clan originating from the same area, which came to political power under the early Il-Khāns. He was in particular connected with the governor of Iṣfahān, Bahāʾ al-Dīn Muḥammad Djuwaynī (d. 678/1279). The contemporary poet Madjd-i Hamgar, who also belonged to the circle of this patron, is said to have been his teacher. Badr al-Dīn used as his pen-name either Badr or Badr-i Djādjarmī. He wrote elegies on the death of Bahāʾ al-Dīn, of Shams al-Dīn Ṣāḥib-Dīwān and on the death of the mystic Saʿd al-Din Hammūʾī, another close relation of the Djuwaynīs. His own death occurred in Djumādā II 686/August 1287. Fragments of his poetry have been preserved in the anthology compiled by his son, but he also retained the attention of the *tadhkira*-writers (cf. e.g. Dawlatshāh, 219 ff.; see further Ṣafā, *Taʾrīkh*, 558). Although the pretentious title *malik al-shuʿarāʾ* has become attached to his name, his works represent the average of the poetry of his age. Notable are two poems of a didactic nature: a short *mathnawī* in the metre *khafīf* on palmoscopy (*ikhtilādj* [*q.v.*]), and a *kaṣīda* dealing with prognostics (*ikhtiyārāt* [*q.v.*]) based on the position of the moon in the various *burūdj* (cf. *Muʾnis*, ii, 861-75 and 1218-21).

2. Muḥammad b. Badr, the son, is only known through his extensive anthology of poetry entitled *Muʾnis al-aḥrār fī daḳāʾiḳ al-ashʿār*, which was completed in Ramaḍān 741/February-March 1341. It is distinguished from the works of the *tadhkira* type by the lack of any biographical data concerning the poets whose works are represented in the collection, as well as by its method of arrangement. The collection contains poems of about 200 different poets from various periods, but the emphasis is on the 7th-8th/-13th-14th centuries. The anthologist frequently quotes his father, and has inserted some specimens of his own work as well. Apart from that, the Iṣfahānī poet Kamāl al-Dīn Ismāʿīl [*q.v.*], one of the early masters of the so-called "ʿIrāḳī style", appears to be a distinct favourite. The poems have been arranged into thirty chapters according to their subject-matter, genre or poetical form. Most of them are unabridged. This anthology constitutes a valuable source for the study of mediaeval Persian literature in many respects. It has preserved much material from the Il-Khānid period, but also from earlier periods, that otherwise would have been lost. Chapter xxvii, on *rubāʿiyyyāt*, contains a special section devoted to ʿUmar Khayyām, with a group of thirteen quatrains (added as an appendix to the edition of the *Robaʿiyyat-e Hakīm ʿOmar Khayyām* by Fr. Rosen, Berlin 1925). The nature of its arrangement provides a number of starting-points for the investigation of poetical genres.

The *Muʾnis al-aḥrār* has already been used as a source by Riḍā Ḳulī Khān Hidāyat (cf. *Madjmaʿ al-fuṣaḥāʾ*, lith. Tehran 1295, i, *muḳaddama*). But it became widely known only through the discovery of an autograph, dated Ramaḍān 741/February-March 1341, which formerly belonged to the Kevorkian Collection. This manuscript at first attracted the attention of art historians on account of a series of pictures illustrating, firstly, a poem entitled *ashʿār-i muṣawwar*, especially composed for illustration by *ustād* Muḥammad al-Rāwandī, and, secondly, the *ikhtiyārāt-i ḳamar* by Badr al-Dīn. The miniatures have been attributed to the Īndjū school of painting at Shiraz. The manuscript has been described in detail in the catalogue of the *Exhibition of the Kevorkian Collection . . . exhibited at the Galleries of Charles of London . . . New York, March-April 1914*, no. 264. After the auction of the collection in 1927, the six folios containing these paintings were dispersed to several public and private collections (cf. K. Hilter, *Zentralblatt für Bibliothekwesen*, liv (1937), no. 48, and H. Buchtal, O. Kurz and R. Ettinghausen, *Ars Islamica*, vii (1940), 155, no. 48; see also Basil Gray, *La peinture persane*, Geneva 1961, 60 ff., but the interpretation of the pictures there is to be corrected). The literary contents of the manuscript were examined by M. Ḳazwīnī (*Bīst maḳāla*, ed. by ʿAbbās Iḳbāl, Tehran 1313/1934[1], 138-55; ed. Tehran 1332/1953[2], ii, 184-206; in English in *BSOS*, v (1928-30), 97-108). Several other copies, all, however, of a much later date, have since come to light (cf. e.g. A. J. Arberry, in *JRAS* (1939), 380-1; M.-T. Dānishpazhūh, *Madjalla-yi dānishkada-i adabiyyāt-i Tihrān* viii (1339/1960), 504 ff.; Ṭabībī in the introduction to the second volume of his edition). The text has been edited by Mīr Ṣāliḥ Ṭabībī (2 vols., Tehran 1337-50/1958-71), who has supplied most of the lacunae in the autograph from the later manuscripts as well as from other sources.

Bibliography: In addition to the works quoted in the article, see F. Meier, *Die schöne Mahsati*, Wiesbaden 1963, 117 f.; G. Lazard, *Les premiers poètes persans*, Tehran-Paris 1964, 6; Dh. Ṣafā, *Taʾrīkh-i adabiyyāt dar Īrān*, iii/1, Tehran 1353/1974[2], 558-67; Sotheby's Spring Islamic Catalogue, Monday 23rd April 1979, 84, no. 144. (J. T. P. de Bruijn)

DJAʿFAR b. ABĪ YAḤYĀ, SHAMS al-DĪN ABU 'l-FAḌL b. Aḥmad b. ʿAbd al-Salām b. Isḥāḳ b. Muḥammad al-Buhlūlī al-Abnāwī, Zaydī, scholar and *ḳāḍī*. His ancestors, including his father, were Ismāʿīlī *ḳāḍīs* of Ṣanʿāʾ under the Ṣulayḥids and Ḥātimids. His brother Yaḥyā (d. 562/1167) served the Ismāʿīlī Zurayʿids of ʿAdan as a panegyrist and judge. Djaʿfar converted to Zaydism at an unknown date and at first adhered to the doctrine of the Muṭarrifiyya [*q.v.*]. After the arrival of the Khurāsānian Zaydī scholar Zayd b. al-Ḥasan al-Bayhaḳī in Ṣaʿda in 541/1146, Djaʿfar studied with him. Al-Bayhaḳī represented the doctrine of the Caspian Zaydiyya and, with the support of the Zaydī *Imām* al-Mutawakkil Aḥmad b. Sulaymān (d. 566/1170), who also studied with him, vigorously fought the Muṭarrifī heresy. In 545/1151, when al-Mutawakkil temporarily succeeded in wresting Ṣanʿāʾ from Ḥātim b. Aḥmad, he appointed Djaʿfar *ḳāḍī* of the town. *Ḳāḍī* Djaʿfar accompanied al-Bayhaḳī, when he left the Yaman, in order to pursue further studies with him and, after al-Bayhaḳī's unexpected death in al-Tihāma, continued his journey alone. He is known to have studied and received authorisation for the transmission of books in Mecca, in Kūfa, where he was present in Dhu 'l-Ḥidjdja 550/February 1156, and in Rayy, where he received an *idjāza* on 1 Djumādā I 552/13 June 1157. His chief teacher in Rayy was the Zaydī scholar Abu 'l-ʿAbbās Aḥmad al-Kannī, from whom he later transmitted numerous works in the Yaman. In 554/1159 he returned to the Yaman and renewed his service to the *Imām* al-Mutawakkil. In this year he stirred up Sunnī antagonism in Ibb by propagating Muʿtazilī theology. He settled in Sanāʿ near Ṣanʿāʾ and taught in his *madrasa*, attracting numerous students as well as the strong opposition of the Muṭarrifiyya, who built their own *madrasa* next to the mosque of the town. In Waḳash, the centre of Muṭarrifī learning, he debated with the prominent Muṭarrifī scholars Muslim al-Laḥdjī and Yaḥyā b. al-Ḥusayn al-Yaḥirī. In Djumādā I 556/May 1161 he preached at funeral of the son of the *Imām*, who continue support him in his struggle against the Muṭarrif He died in 573/1177-8 and was buried in Sanāʿ.

Ḳāḍī Djaʿfar played the most conspicuous ro the introduction of the religious literature of Caspian Zaydī community to the Yaman. Throug transmission of this literature as well as throug own works, said to number more than thirty, i fields of religious learning, he became the fou of a school which recognised the Caspian Zaydī *Ir* as being equally authoritative teachers with Yamanī *Imāms*, and he espoused the Baṣran M zilī doctrine in theology and legal methodolog ready adopted by most Zaydīs outside the Ya thus restoring ideological unity within the Zayd His school became predominant in the Yamanī munity under the *Imām* al-Manṣūr ʿAbd Allā Ḥamza (d. 614/1217), who supported its view his own many writings and waged a war of e mination against the Muṭarrifiyya.

Bibliography: Anonymous Yamanī chro ms. Ambrosiana H 5, fols. 21b, 23b, 40b, 43b Ibn Samura, *Ṭabaḳāt fuḳahāʾ al-Yaman*, ed. F Sayyid, Cairo 1957, 180; Ibn Abi 'l-Ridjāl, *M al-budūr*, i, ms. Ambrosiana B 130, fol. 139; Y b. al-Ḥusayn b. al-Ḳāsim, *Ghāyat al-amānī* Saʿīd ʿAbd al-Fattāḥ ʿĀshūr, Cairo 1388/19 302; al-Siyāghī, *al-Rawḍ al-naḍīr*, Cairo 134 1928-30, i, 12-14; al-Djundārī, *Tarādjim al-r* in Ibn Miftāḥ, *al-Muntazaʿ al-mukhtār*, i, 1332/1913, 9 f.; Brockelmann, I, 508, S. I 699 f.; W. Madelung, *Der Imam al-Qāsim Ibrāhīm*, Berlin 1965, 204, 212-16. (W. Madelun

DJAʿFAR b. MANṢŪR al-YAMAN, Ism author and partisan of the Fāṭimids [*q.v.*]. He the son of the first Ismāʿīlī missionary in Yama Ḥasan b. Faraḥ b. Ḥawshab b. Zādān al- known as Manṣūr al-Yaman [*q.v.*]. When in the 286/899 the chief of the Ismāʿīlī propaganda, ʿU Allāh, claimed the imāmate, Manṣūr al-Y acknowledged him; the letter by which ʿUbayd tried to prove his ʿAlid descent has been preserv Djaʿfar's *al-Farāʾiḍ wa-ḥudūd al-dīn* (see H. F. dani, *On the genealogy of Fatimid caliphs*, Cairo 1 When after the death of Manṣūr al-Yaman 914-15) his sons were excluded from the leade of the community in Yaman, they fell away from giance to the Fāṭimids, except Djaʿfar (see al-Yamānī, *Kashf asrār al-Bāṭiniyya*, ed. al-Kaw 217). He came to the Maghrib during the rei the second Fāṭimid caliph al-Ḳāʾim (322-34/934 and under al-Manṣūr (334-41/946-53) he f against the Khāridjī rebel Abū Yazīd [*q.v.*]. merits of his father secured him the financial port of the caliph al-Muʿizz (341-65/953-75), he was forced to pledge his house in al-Manṣū (Ṣabra) to a creditor (see *Sīrat al-Ustādh Djaw* ed. M. Kāmil Ḥusayn and M. ʿA. Shaʿīra 126 f.) date of his death is not known; possibly he com his *Taʾwīl al-zakāt* only in the last year of al-M (see W. Madelung, *Imamat*, 96). The date 28 for his *Asrār al-nuṭaḳāʾ* has certainly no solid (see Madelung, *loc. cit.*); there is therefore no r to take him for a grandson of Manṣūr al-Y and all sources agree that he was his son.

Djaʿfar's works (see W. Ivanow, *Ismaili liter* Tehran 1963, 21 f.; P. Kraus, in *REI*, vi (486 f.; F. Sezgin, *GAS*, i, 578 f.) mostly tre the allegorical exegesis (*taʾwīl*) of the Ḳurʾā of the ritual duties (e.g. *al-Riḍāʿ fi 'l-bāṭin*;

rūf al-muʿdjama; Taʾwīl al-farāʾiḍ; Taʾwīl al-; Taʾwīl sūrat al-Nisāʾ). His Asrār al-nuṭaḳāʾ collection of legends of the prophets from Adam uḥammad. The gist of the "Book of the intervals conjunctions" (K. al-Fatarāt wa 'l-ḳirānāt) bed to him, which P. Kraus (loc. cit.) incorrectly ns to the later Ṭayyibiyya [q.v.] literature, sts of prophecies which expect as the Mahdī "the Fourth, the Seventh of the second heptad" f the three hidden Imāms and the four Fāṭimid hs), i.e. al-Muʿizz. The Kitāb al-Kashf ascribed jaʿfar contains six older treatises from early nid times which have been clearly put together e time of al-Ḳāʾim (see Madelung, op. cit., 52 ff.).

Bibliography: (in addition to the works cited the article): Djaʿfar b. Manṣūr al-Yaman, tāb al-Kashf, ed. R. Strothmann, London-mbay 1952; W. Madelung, Das Imamat in frühen ismailitischen Lehre, in Isl., xxxvii 961), 94-7; H. Halm, Zur Datierung des ismāʿī-schen "Buches der Zwischenzeiten und der zehn njunktionen" (Kitāb al-fatarāt . . .), in Welt des ients, viii (1975), 91-107. (H. HALM)

AGHATAY [see ČAGHATAY].

ALĀL AL-DĪN MANGUBIRTĪ [see DJALĀL ĪN KHWĀRAZM SHĀH].

ALĀLĀBĀD, a town of eastern Afghani-, situated in lat. 34°26′ N. and long. 70°27′ E. altitude of 620 m./1, 950 ft. It lies in the valley e Kābul River some 79 miles from Peshāwar e east and 101 miles from Kābul city to the west, is on the right bank of the river. As well as roughly midway along the historic route ecting Kābul with the beginning of the plains orthern India, Djalābād is also strategically ted to command routes into Kāfiristān [q.v.] ern Nūristān) and today, routes run northwards it up to the Kānur and Alingār River valleys. e area around Djalābād is that of the ancient rahar (contemporary pronunciation, Nungrihar ngrahar; the name has now been revived, in the version, as the name of a modern Afghān nce, see below), which was a flourishing region rally and religiously, forming part of the hara of the Sakas and then Kushans. Buddhism strong there, and the early 7th century Chinese hist pilgrim Hsüan-Tsang records it as Na-ka- = * Nagarahāra; cf. G. H. Macgregor, in JASB, 1844), 867-80, T. Watters, On Yuan Chwang's s in India, 629-645 A.D., London 1904, 182-90, Ḥudūd al-ʿālam, tr. Minorsky, comm. 252-3. Buddhist antiquities of the region have been ited and looted since the 19th century; serious eological investigation dates from the work e Délégation Archéologique Française en Afgha-n 1923-8 at Hadda a few miles south of Djalālā- mainly at Tepe Kalan stupa (J. Barthoux, ouilles de Haḍḍa, Méms. DAFA, iv, Paris 1933, vi, Paris 1930), and this has recently been nued by Sh. Mustamandī (Nouvelles fouilles dda (1966-1967) par l'Institut Afghane d'Arché-, in Arts Asiatiques, xix (1969), 15-36, cf. upree, Afghanistan, Princeton 1973, 306). This n of Nangrahar has also at times been included e eastern part of that of Lamghān or Lamghānāt.

e comparatively low-lying and sheltered valley of the Kābul River gives Djalābād what Dupree alled a "Mediterranean, dry-summer, sub-cal climate" (this is in fact more accurate than lum's term "monsoon climate"). Rain falls ly in the three winter months, and the mild climate has meant that Djalālābād has for long been a winter residence place for many Kābulīs and a winter haven for tribesmen of the climatically harsh slopes of the Safīd Kūh to the south of the river valley and of the Kāfiristān fringes. At present, Djalālābād is the centre of a rich area for the growing of sugar cane by irrigation, rice, fruits, etc., and a Ningrahar irrigation project, built around a dam in the Darunta gorge, has recently been undertaken. Ethnically, the Djalālābād region comprises some Tādjīk villagers but mainly Pushtūns of the Ghilzay, Shinwari, Khugiyani, Mohmand and Safi tribes.

The actual town of Djalālābād only appears in Islamic history during the Mughal period, and Akbar is said to have founded it in ca. 978/1570. Nādir Shāh Afshār campaigned in the district, and defeated the Pushtūn tribes at nearby Gandamak. It is during the 19th century that the town really comes into prominence. The American traveller Charles Masson was there in ca. 1826-7, and states that he discerned the ruinous mud walls of two earlier towns on the site, the contemporary town being the smallest of the three. The then governor of Djalālābād was Nawāb Muḥammad Zamān Khān b. Asʿad Khān, a nephew of Dōst Muḥammad [see DŪST MUḤAMMAD], and the revenue of the whole province of Djalālābād, including that from the Tādjīk villages and from Laghmān, amounted to three lakhs (i.e. 300,000) of rupees (Narrative of various journeys in Balochistan, Afghanistan and the Panjab, London 1842 (repr. Karachi 1974), i, 174-80; Sir Thomas Holdich, The gates of India, London 1910, 352 ff.).

Shortly after Masson's visit, Djalālābād was seized and sacked by Dōst Muḥammad in his expansion from Kābul (1834). It then played a crucial role in the First Afghan War (1839-42). It was occupied by Major-General Sir Robert Sale's brigade of the British forces ("the illustrious garrison") from November 1841 till April 1842 against the attacking Afghān army of Muḥammad Akbar Khān, and fortified by the British troops, despite a severe earthquake there in February 1842 which damaged the defences. It was Djalālābād that the remnants of Major-General William Elphinstone's ill-fated army straggled back from Kābul in January 1842, the town being only relieved three months later by Major-General George Pollock (see J. A. Norris, The First Afghan War 1838-1842, Cambridge 1967, 371 ff.). During the Second Afghan War (1879-80), Djalālābād was again occupied by British troops, who built a defence post, Fort Sale, one mile to the east of the town. It had now become a favoured winter residence of the amīrs of Kābul, and in 1892 ʿAbd al-Raḥmān Khān [q.v.] built a palace and garden near the western gate of the walled town. When in 1919 the amīr Ḥabīb Allāh [q.v.] was assassinated in the Laghmān district, his brother Naṣr Allāh was briefly proclaimed king at Djalālābād, but abdicated in favour of his nephew Amān Allāh b. Ḥabīb Allāh. During the Third Afghan War, which followed these events almost immediately, Djalālābād was bombed from the air by the British (cf. L. W. Adamec, Afghanistan 1900-1923, a diplomatic history, Berkeley and Los Angeles 1967, 107-8, 117, 122). It was amongst the Shinwaris and other Pushtūn tribes of the Djalālābād region that the amīr Amān Allāh [q.v., in Suppl.] endeavoured in 1928 to exert his centralised authority and to end the extortion of protection money (badraḳa) from caravans travelling to Peshāwar, provoking a rising of the Shinwaris in which, amongst other things, the rebels sacked the British consulate in Djalālābād; this rising, and the poor performance of the royal Afghān army against it, were contributory causes of Amān Allāh's downfall and abdication in 1929 (cf. L. B. Poullada, *Reform and rebellion in Afghanistan, 1919-1929, King Amanullah's failure to modernize a tribal society*, Ithaca and London 1973, 162 ff.).

The modern town has since 1964 been the provincial capital of Ningrahar; its population was estimated by J. Humlum at 20,000-30,000, swollen during the winter by the influx of Kābulīs and others (*La géographie de l'Afghanistan, étude d'un pays aride*, Copenhagen 1959, 140). It has by now lost the protective wall and the bazaars of the old city, and the modern town has expanded towards the west. Djalālābād also possesses a military airport, originally built with US aid for civil purposes.

Bibliography: (in addition to sources given in the article): *Imperial gazetter of India*, Oxford 1908, xiv, 11-13; *Area handbook for Afghanistan*, Washington D.C. 1973, index; and the general histories of Afghānistān (Fraser-Tytler, Masson and Romodin, Klimburg, etc.), especially for the events of the 19th century.

The name Djalālābād occurs elsewhere in the Central Asian and Indo-Afghān worlds. For the Djalālābād in the modern Kirghiz SSR, see the article s.v. in *EI*². For the Djalālābād in Sīstān (= Dōshak), see Holdich, *op. cit.*, 335, 497. For the Djalālābād in the Shāhdjahānpūr District of Uttar Pradesh in India, situated on the Ganges and in lat. 27° 43′ N. and long. 79° 40′ E., said to have been founded by the Tughlukid Djalāl al-Dīn Fīrūz Shāh, and the Djalālābād in the Muzaffarnagar District of Uttar Pradesh, in lat. 29° 37′ N. and long. 77° 27′ E., said to have been founded by one Djalāl Khān under Awrangzīb, see *Imperial gazetteer of India*, xiv, 13-14.

(C. E. Bosworth)

DJALĀLĪ, a term in Ottoman Turkish used to describe companies of brigands, led usually by idle or dissident Ottoman army officers, widely-spread throughout Anatolia from about 999/1590 but diminishing by 1030/1620. The term probably derives from an earlier (925/1519) political and religious rebellion in Amasya by a Shaykh Djalāl. Official Ottoman use appears in a petition (*ʿarḍ*) as early as 997/1588 (Divan-i Kalemi 997-8-C), where the term identifies unchecked rebels (*ashkiyā*ʾ) engaging in brigandage. Analysis of the three-decade period of *Djalālī* revolts indicates that these leaders had in common certain objectives which arose through deteriorating social and political conditions in Anatolia.

First, constant warfare for decades on the Ottoman boundaries expended men and treasure, leaving large areas of the Anatolian heartland without proper protection from local outlaws. By the later 10th/16th century, the Ottomans found themselves unable to move militarily beyond the lines generally established by Sulṭān Sulaymān Ḳānūnī, both in Hungary and is Persia. Hostilities continued with the Habsburgs from 1002/1593 until the Treaty of Zsitvatorok (11 November 1606); war in the east with the Ṣafawid Shāh ʿAbbās [*q.v.*] continued from 1012/1603 until the Treaty of Amasya in 1021/1612.

Second, deterioration in the economic stability of the Empire brought about serious imbalances. Monetary inflation, due largely to Mexican silver from Europe, caused a rapid increase in prices which affected daily-wage soldiers who, when pay was in arrears, increasingly either refused to fight or revolted. When the central government found itself without funds to disperse, it devised new sources of cash: sale of offices to wealthy purchasers, [de]mands for increased tribute from subject nat[ions], the sale of lands formerly administered by cav[alry]men (*tīmārs* [*q.v.*]), debasement of the coinage, [and] the increase of peasant taxes. Food shortages, [and] widespread famine, occurred due to limited agr[icul]tural technology, a decade of drought (985-157[7 to] 993/1585), increase in population, heavy dem[ands] by Ottoman armies in both Europe and Pe[rsia], scorched-earth policies by the Ottoman and Pe[rsian] armies in eastern Anatolia, and illegal sale of g[rain] to European markets.

Third, as in other areas of the Mediterran[ean], Ottoman lands experienced unrest and band[itry] among classes normally quiescent. Peasants (*reʿ*[*āyā*]) on cavalry lands sold as *iltizām* [*q.v.*] found their absentee landlords interested more in profits [than] traditional patronage. Legally tied to their la[nd], peasants felt the oppression of the new landow[ners] whose excesses could not be bridled, and tha[t of] the tax collectors, many of whom could hardl[y be] differentiated from brigands. With technolo[gical] changes in warfare, increased numbers of Mu[slim] *reʿāyā* enlisted as daily-wage musketeers (*sekb*[*ān*]) returning to Anatolia after their campaigns jo[bless] but expert in the military arts. Another norm[ally] tranquil group were students training in *madr*[*asas*] [*q.v.*] for positions in the Ottoman bureaucr[acy]. Frustrated especially because their number far [ex]ceeded available positions, they wandered in gr[oups] across rural Anatolia, some preaching religious [re]vival, and most of them participating in anti-s[ocial] violence against small villages and lonely trav[ellers] (Akdağ, *Celâlî isyanları*, 85-100).

Fourth, misguided leadership within the Otto[man] government kindled the great *Djalālī* rebell[ions]. After the astonishing Ottoman victory over the H[abs]burgs at Ḥāč Owasî (Mezö-Keresztes [*q.v.*]) in Hun[gary] on 23 October 1596, the newly-appointed grand v[izier] Čighāla-zāde Sinān Pasha [*q.v.*] declared fo[rfeit] the property and the lives of all who deserted (*fi*[*rārīs*]) from the battle. The *Firārīs*, whose several thous[ands] included many high-ranking officers, fled to Ana[tolia] where they joined the forces of the *Djalālī* le[ader] Ḳarāyazîdjî ʿAbd al-Ḥalīm and fought success[fully] against Ottoman armies for several years. The successful actions of important Ottoman gene[rals], including Naṣūḥ Pasha against the *Djalālī* Ṭ[awīl] Khālīl at Bolvadin (1014/1605), and Farhād Pas[ha's] [*q.v.*] anti-*Djalālī* campaign of 1015/1606, demon[stra]ted the need for greater military organisation [and] discipline in recognition of the seriousness of [the] rebellions.

Where Ottoman leadership often failed becau[se of] personal incompetence, bureaucratic sluggish[ness] and court intrigue, local *Djalālī* chiefs proved th[em]selves master strategists and attractive lea[ders] with objectives in many ways unique in Ottoman [his]tory. Unlike most rebels, they did not attemp[t to] establish a bureaucratic state and a taxation [sys]tem, to coin money, or to have their names rea[d in] the Friday mosque prayer (*khuṭba*). The *Dj*[*alālī*] leaders primarily desired a place for themselves in [the] established Ottoman order, usually accepting a [par]don from the weak government, leading to the off[er of] positions as *sandjaḳ begis* or *beglerbegis*. At su[ch a] time, their rank and file became salaried and *ʿaskerīs* [*q.v.*], non-taxed. When they failed to [ob]tain governmental recognition, both leaders and [men] lived on plunder, pillaging villages or outl[ying] city districts, demanding enormous ransoms of urban dwellers and incurring the hatred of the c le. Djalālī bands ruled wide areas of Anatolia, unicated with one another, and occasionally in unity. Though commonly branded as pro-ts of the Persian Shāh ʿAbbās and of Shīʿa, sectarian fervour played little part in their ties. Neither the Persian monarch nor any foreign power gave them official recognition. different kind of rebellion occurred contempo-usly in northern Syria and is often erroneously lered to be a Djalālī revolt, possibly because short-lived alliance with some Djalālī leaders yāḳ, Akhbār al-aʿyān, 133). Djānbūlādoghlī Pasha based his revolt on the power of his well-n Kurdish family and Turkoman retainers, as s on regional loyalties in Aleppo and Damascus. al recognition came in the form of an alliance the Grand Duke of Tuscany (Fondo Archivisto eo, No. 4275 is the Italian copy of the treaty) a vague understanding with the Ṣafawid Shāh tī, Talkhīṣāt, f. 11b).

e dangerous international implications of Djān-oghlī's revolt were not missed by the newly-nted (1015/1606) grand vizier, the nonagenarian dju Murād Pasha. On the occasion of peace in ary, he immediately marched toward Aleppo, lished military discipline, used a variety of loyal Anatolian as well as dewshirme [q.v.] forces, he paid promptly, and smashed the Syrian Djānbūlādoghlī at Oruč Owasī near Lake ʿAmīḳ /1607). Six months later he turned against the Djalālīs, took advantage of their fickle indivi-sm, pardoned some, executed most, and routed army of Ḳalenderoghlī Meḥmed at Göksün sī, though the rebel leader fled to Persia. A later Murād Pasha executed the last great lī leader, Muslu Čawush.

the years following Ḳuyudju Murād Pasha's (1020/1611), though Djalālī faded from official n the Mühimme defterleri, the term remained ttoman historical writing to identify certain olian rebels. Ewliyā Čelebi in the mid-11th/ 7th century mentions the "Djalālī Pashas" hat-nāme, viii, 104), and Naʿīmā (Taʾrīkh, v, describes the activities of a 12th/18th-century as Djalālīlik ("like a Djalālī"). Today, the ry of the Djalālīs remains only in the folk of the Anatolian hero Köroghlu [q.v.].

Bibliography: Official documents found in Baş Vekalet Arşivi, Istanbul, contain Mühimme teri, lxx-lxxx, zeyl 7 and 8, and Kâmil Kepeci snifi lxxi, covering the years 1000-22/1591-1617, with a hiatus between 1005-11/1596-1603; Emiri Tasnifi, nos. 455-9, 465, 616; Fekete snifi, Bab-i Asafi, Divan-i Kalemi nos. 997-1014; ül-Emin Tasnifi nos. 29, 200-2, 504, 506, 586, , 688. Eye-witness accounts include Wāsiṭī, khīṣāt dār ʿahd-i Sulṭān Aḥmad Khān, Esad ndi Kütüphanesi, Süleyman Kütüphanesi, 2236 ff. 5a-30a; Topdjular Kātibi ʿAbd al-dir, Tawārīkh-i āl-i ʿOthmān, Vienna Staats-liothek, no. 1053, ff. 216b-262b, passim; de Gontaut Biron, Ambassade en Turquie de n de Gontaut Biron, Baron de Salignac, 1605 à o (Correspondance diplomatique et documents dit), in Archives Historiques de la Gascogne, fasc. Paris 1889; M. Brosset (ed. and tr.), Collection istoriens Arméniens. Th. Ardzrouni, Xe s., toire des Ardzrouni; Arakel de Tauriz, XVIIe s., toire de l'Aghovanie, St. Petersburg 1874, i, -314; Iskandar Beg Munshī, Taʾrīkh-i ʿālam-yi ʿAbbāsī, Tehran 1335/1957, ii, 764-805, sim; O. Burian, The report of Lello, third English ambassador to the Sublime Porte, Ankara 1952. General histories of the rebels may be found in Naʿīmā, Taʾrīkh, Istanbul 1280/1863, i, 231-474; ii, 1-50; Pečewi, Taʾrīkh, Istanbul 1283/1866, ii, 246-335, passim; Ḥādjdjī Khalīfa, Fedhleke-i Kātib Čelebi, Istanbul 1286/1869, i, 270-310, passim; Ṣolāḳ-zāde Meḥmed Hamdānī, Taʾrīkh, Istanbul 1298/1880, 670-96; and Muṣṭafa Pāshā, Natāʾidj al-wuḳūʿāt, Istanbul 1294/1877, ii, 14-31. The major modern study is M. Akdağ, Büyük Celâlî karı-şıklıklarının başlaması, Erzurum 1963, and Celâlî isyanları, Ankara 1963, as well as art. Kara-yazıcı, in IA, vi, 339-43; M. A. Cook, Population pressure in rural Anatolia, 1450-1600, London 1972; F. Braudel, La Méditerranée et le monde Méditerranéen à l'époque de Philippe II, 2nd rev. ed., Paris 1966, i, 517-48, ii, 62-8, 75-92; G. Berchet, Relazioni dei Consoli Veneti nella Siria, Turin 1866, 105-20; L.-L. Bellan, Chah ʿAbbas I, sa vie, son histoire, Paris 1932, 133-47; İ. H. Danişmend, İzahli osmanlı tarihi kronolojisi, iii, Istanbul 1950, 219-46 passim; H. Inalcik, The Ottoman empire, London-New York 1973, 46-52; idem, The heyday and decline of the Ottoman Empire, in The Cambridge history of Islam, i, The Central Islamic lands, London 1970, 342-50; A. Rāfiḳ, Bilād al-Shām wa-Miṣr min al-fatḥ al-ʿOthmānī ilā ḥamlat Nābili-yūn Bunābart, 1516-1798, Damascus 1968, 200-8; A. S. Tveritinova, Vosstanie Kara Iazydzhi—Deli Hasana v Turtsii, Moscow 1946; C. Orhonlu, art. Murad Paşa, Kuyucu, in IA, viii, 651-4; H. D. Andreasyan, Polonyalı Simeon'un seyahat-nâmesi, 1608-1619, Istanbul 1964, passim; S. Shaw, History of the Ottoman empire and modern Turkey, i, Empire of the Gazis: the rise and decline of the Ottoman empire, 1280-1808, Cambridge 1976, 171-91; references to the rebellion of Djānbūlā-doghlī ʿAlī Pasha may be found in Fondo Archi-visto Mediceo, no. 4275, ff. 113-117b; Tannūs al-Shidyāḳ, Akhbār al-aʿyān fī Djabal Lubnān, Beirut, 1276/1859, 130-35; Muḥammad b. Faḍl Allāh al-Muḥibbī, Khulāṣat al-athar fī aʿyān al-ḳarn al-ḥādī ʿashar, Cairo 1284/1867, iii, 266 ff.; Venezia, Archivio di Stato, Campo dei Frari, Filze 64 (1607), 65 (1607), and 66 (1608); al-Ḥasan b. Meḥmed al-Būrīnī, Tarādjim al-aʿyān min abnāʾ al-zamān, Vienna Staatsbibliothek Codex Arab 1190, Mixt. 136, 150a-152b; and a modern study, P. Carali, Fakhr ad-Dīn II, principe del Libano e la corte Toscana, 1605-1635, Rome 1936, i, 139-49.

(W. J. Griswold)

DJAMĀL AL-DĪN IṢFAHĀNĪ, Muḥammad b. ʿAbd al-Razzāḳ, Persian poet of the later Saldjūḳ period, and father of a better-known poet Kamāl al-Dīn Ismāʿīl [q.v.]. A goldsmith and miniature painter in his early years, he left his workshop, as his son tells us, to study, acquiring extensive theo-logical knowledge, traces of which are to be found as characteristics in his ʿIrāḳī-styled poetry. Con-tinuous eye troubles, a speech impediment, a large family of at least four sons, and a short tour through Ādharbāydjān and Māzandarān, very likely in search of more generous patrons, constitute all the details we know from his personal life. Besides local grandees of the Āl-i Ṣāʿid and Āl-i Khudjand, to whom he dedicated flattering ḳaṣīdas, his other patrons in-cluded some Saldjūḳ princes of ʿIrāḳ and a number of local rulers of Ādharbāydjān and Māzandarān. Among contemporary poets, he paid equivocal lip-service to Khāḳānī [q.v.], held friendly correspondence with Ẓahīr-i Fāryābī, and wrote mordant satires against Mudjīr-i Baylaḳānī. He also paid homage to

Anwarī and Rashīd-i Waṭwāṭ [*q.vv.*], who seem to have ignored him rather disdainfully. Djamāl al-Dīn's ascetic ideas—including the idea of renunciation—are best presented in the *ḳaṣīdas* which he wrote in the fashion of Sanāʾī, though these are far inferior to Sanāʾī's ones. His *Dīwān*—comprising *ḳaṣīdas*, quatrains, and *ghazals*—contains no less than 10,000 verses and displays the lucid and flowing ʿIrāḳī style. Djamāl al-Dīn is said to have died either in 588/1192 or in 600/1203, the former being more likely.

Bibliography: Waḥīd-i Dastgirdī, *Dīwān-i Ustād Djamāl al-Dīn Muḥammad b. ʿAbd al-Razzāḳ Iṣfahānī* (with biographical introduction), Tehran 1320/1941; ʿAwfī, *Lubāb al-adāb*, ed. Saʿīd Nafīsī, Tehran 1335/1956, 759-60; Badīʿ al-Zamān Furuzān-Far, *Sukhan va sukhanvarān*,[2] Tehran 1350/1971, 547-54; J. Rypka *et alii*, *History of Iranian literature*, Dordrecht 1968, 213-14; idem, in *Cambridge history of Iran*, v, 584-5.

(A. H. ZARRINKOOB)

DJAMĀL ḲARSHĪ, sobriquet of ABU 'L-FAḌL DJAMĀL AL-DĪN MUḤAMMAD B. ʿUMAR B. KHĀLID, scholar and administrator in Turkestān during the Mongol era. He was born at Almalïgh around 628/1230-1, his father a *ḥāfiẓ* of Balāsāghūn and his mother originating from Merw. He enjoyed the patronage of the local Turkish dynasty founded at Almalïgh [*q.v.*] by Būzār (or Uzār), and obtained a position in the chancellery there. In 662/1264, however, he was obliged to leave Almalïgh, and for the remainder of his life resided at Kāshghar, though travelling widely in western Turkestān.

In 681/1282 he composed a Persian commentary (*ṣurāḥ*) on the great lexicon *al-Ṣiḥāḥ* of Djawharī [*q.v.*], subsequently adding to it a historical and biographical supplement. Djamāl Ḳarshī's *Mulḥaḳāt al-Ṣurāḥ* is in fact the only historical source we possess emanating from the Central Asian state founded by Ḳaydu [*q.v.*]. Extracts of the work, which includes particularly valuable sections on the Ḳarakhānids [see ILEK-KHĀNS] and the Mongol rulers of Turkestān [see ČAGHATAY KHĀNATE], surveys of various Central Asian cities, and biographies of local divines, were edited by Barthold in *Turkestan*, Russ. ed., i, 128-52. The *Mulḥaḳāt* was completed soon after the accession of Ḳaydu's son Čapar [*q.v.*] in 702/1303, the latest date mentioned.

The date of Djamāl Ḳarshī's death is unknown. The surname is due to his connection with the rulers of Almalïgh (*ḳarshī* = "palace"), and is not a *nisba* from *Ḳuraysh* as was formerly supposed.

Bibliography: V. V. Barthold, in *Zapiski Vostočnogo Otdeleniya Imperatorskogo Russkogo Arkheologičeskogo Obshčestva*, xi (1897-8), 283-7; idem, *Turkestan*[3], 51-2; Brockelmann, I, 296, S I, 528; H. F. Hofman, *Turkish literature*, iii/1, 3, Utrecht 1969, 84-9, with full MS references.

(P. JACKSON)

AL-**DJĀMIʿA** AL-**ʿARABIYYA**, the Arab League. Established at the end of the Second World War, this reflects the desire to renew the original unity, a desire which has continued to be active in Muslim communities following the decline and subsequent collapse of the Arab-Islamic empire.

It was during the final years of the 19th century and before the First World War that Arab nationalists became aware of their national homogeneity, based on a common language and destiny, and on a similar way of life and culture (*ḳawmiyya* [*q.v.*]).

Egypt, reverting to the cause of Arabism between the two World Wars, in order to put an obstacle in the way of Hāshimite designs (a plan for a Gr Syria conceived at ʿAmmān, or for a Fertile cent, put forward by Baghdād) took the initi of assembling in Alexandria representatives o Arab States regarded as being independent. meeting, marked by the signing of a protocol (7 ber 1944), laid the foundations of a unity whicl ratified the following year in Cairo, where on 22 M 1945 the Pact of the Arab League was signe Saudi Arabia, Egypt, Iraq, Lebanon, Syria, T Jordan and Yemen.

Subsequently, the League has been joined b following countries: Libya (1953), Sudan (1 Tunisia and Morocco (1958), Kuwait (1961), A (1962), South Yemen (1967), the United Arab E tes, Ḳaṭar, Baḥrayn and ʿUmān (1971), Mauri and Somalia (1974) and Djibouti (1977). Further the Palestine Liberation Organisation has bee mitted, first in the capacity of an observer (1 then as a full member (1976).

The text adopted by the founders after lon cussion, is remarkable for its flexibility and its plicity. It specifies that the object of the L is "the forging of links between the member S and the coordination of their policies" with th of fostering collaboration in respect of each of them.

The components of the Organisatio currently the following:

— The Council of the League, the supreme which can meet at the level of Heads of State, I Ministers or Foreign Ministers. Summit mee composed of Heads of State since 1964 have

1. Cairo (13-17 January 1964).
2. Alexandria (5-11 November 1964).
3. Casablanca (13-18 January 1965).
4. Khartoum (29 August-2 September 1967).
5 Rabat (21-23 December 1969)
6. Algiers (24-29 November 1973).
7. Rabat (26-29 October 1974).
8. Cairo (25-26 October 1976).

The council decides questions of administrati a simple majority, but in all important cases, sions are only binding if they have been taken u mously. Conversely, they are binding only o States that have voted for them (art. 7).

— Five other councils, at ministerial level (co defence, economics, information, health, youth) instituted in 1950.

— Ten permanent committees are charged studying various questions entrusted to them submitting in various cases projects for resolut recommendations.

— An administrative tribunal and a commit financial control are directly responsible to the cil of the League.

— Seventeen specialised agencies have been inst by particular agreements to investigate co technical problems.

— The permanent Secretariat-General, whi directed by a Secretary-General elected by a thirds majority, himself assisted by a numb additional secretaries, comprises several depart and controls specialised bureaux, institutes and centres. Three Egyptians have successively he office of Secretary General of the Arab League

— ʿAbd al-Raḥmān ʿAzzām Pasha (March October 1952),

— ʿAbd al-Khāliḳ Ḥassūna (October 1952-May

— Maḥmūd Riyāḍ (since 1 June 1972).

The Secretariat-General maintains perm delegations to the United Nations in New Yor ɘva, as well as Information Offices in the princi- oreign capitals (Washington, New York, Ottawa, s, London, Bonn, Geneva, Brussels, Rome, rid, Buenos-Aires, Brasilia, Tokyo, New Delhi, ar, Lagos, Nairobi and Addis Ababa).

nce the creation of the Organisation various s for reform have been proposed by different ɘs: Syria (1951), Iraq (1954), Morocco (1959,), Algeria, Iraq and Syria (1964). These projects never come to fruition. Since June 1967 this ect has only been tackled by experts.

onflicts between member States have not been ing, leading to almost constant disputes between or more of the partners. These have been moti- d by various factors: frontier disputes, local ersion, differences over the choice of foreign y, differences of approach concerning the manner onducting the war or of obtaining peace in the eli-Arab conflict, abortive attempts at union, logical rivalries, personal antagonisms and a per- ent struggle for supremacy. Generally, the States erned have avoided referring their quarrels to Council of the League. They have preferred to e their differences by seeking the arbitration er of bilateral diplomacy or of other, larger or- sations, such as the U.N.O. or, since its incep- in 1963, the O.A.U. In a number of cases, cer- members have failed to attend meetings. Some- s the tactics adopted by Egypt, by the very fact the latter is host to the League, paralyse its ac- y. But to this day no decisive schism has inter- d with its workings.

he League, which has supplied a considerable ntity of aid to liberation movements and has as- ed the emancipation of Arab nations, serves in as a forum where mutual aggressions and rival- may be diminished, and where, after the con- tation, a measure of co-existence develops.

n the economic sphere, it has given birth in 8 to a bureau for the boycott of Israel, in 1950 he Union of Chambers of Arab Commerce, Indus- and Agriculture and in 1957 to the Council of b Economic Unity. It has played a not inconsider- role in the matter of oil, organising congresses providing facilities for meeting and observation nded by experts from all parts of the world, ses- s which have themselves led to the establishment roups of producing States such as O.P.E.C. (Or- isation of Petroleum Exporting Countries) in 1960 O.P.E.A.C. (Organisation of Petroleum Export- Arab Countries) in 1968.

is in the name of the League that attempts have n made since 1964 to organise an Arab Common ket, which has never got beyong the stage of a free- e zone limited to Egypt, Iraq, Syria and Jordan. ore recently there have been founded the A. F. D. (Arab Fund for Economic and Social Develop- t), (1973), the Union of Arab Banks (1975), the b Institute for the Guarantee of Investments 5) and the Arab Bank for Economic Development frica (1975). Since 1973 the League has played a or role in the Arab-European dialogue and in b-African co-operation.

andicapped by the weight of mentalities whose ution remains very slow, paralysed by the poli- l rivalry of member States, affected by the tur- ence of an unstable international world, the Lea- nevertheless plays a role that often goes unno- d as a centre for contacts, exchanges and studies re Arabs may meet, learn to understand one ther, overcome their difference and arrive at com- n solutions [See also the Addenda and Corrigenda].

Bibliography: Studies on the League are numerous but often partial. As the basis for a bibliography, one may consult A. M. Gomaa, *The foundations of the League of Arab States. War-time diplomacy and inter-Arab politics, 1941 to 1945*, London-New York 1977. R. W. McDonald, *The League of Arab States, a study in the dynamics of regional organization*, New Jersey 1965; A. el-Telawi, *Le Secrétariat-général de la Ligue des États Arabes*, Paris II thesis (goes up to 1971); The activities of the League may be followed in specialist journals like *Cahiers de l'Orient contemporain*, Paris 1945-69; *Orient*, Paris 1957-69; and *Maghreb-Machrek*, Paris, since 1964. An overall view is given in the *Fiches du monde arabe*, Beirut. A recent publication by the League in Cairo is the monthly bulletin in Arabic, *Djāmiʿat al-duwal al-ʿarabiyya*, from January 1978. (R. Santucci)

DJAMMĀL (A.) camel-driver or cameleer, also an owner of and hirer of camels (hence synonymous here with *mukārī*) and a dealer in camels; Persian equivalent, *ushturbān*.

During the pre-Islamic and post-Islamic periods camel caravans travelled enormous distances between the main centres of population and trade. Our sources indicate that relatively high wages were earned by the *djammālūn* during the ʿAbbāsid period. The *djammāl*, it also seems, came under the jurisdiction of *ḥisba* [*q.v.*] officials in Islamic towns. The conduct of the camel-men came under some criticism from writers like Djāḥiẓ and Ibn al-Djawzī. Ibn Saʿd cites a tradition that ʿUmar b. al-Khaṭṭāb chastised a *djammāl* for overburdening a camel. However, the great expansion of international trade between regions during the ʿAbbāsid period gave the camel-men a significant role to play in Arab society, and they were one of the most important groups of transport-workers. It was during this epoch of greatness of Islamic civilisation that we find some *djammālūn* among the transmitters of the Prophetic traditions (*aḥādīth*). Ibshīhī [*q.v.*] tells a tale that the caliph al-Muʿtamid awarded a pious *djammāl* a monthly allowance of 30 *dīnārs*, besides a royal gift of 500 *dīnārs* in cash. In contrast to their mediaeval glory, the modern camel-men's trade is regarded as demeaning and low (*danīʾ*), and on some of the pilgrim roads to Mecca, one could hear a lot of critical comments about the conduct of the *djammālūn* until very recent times.

Bibliography: Ibn Saʿd, *Ṭabaḳāt*, Beirut 1958, vii, 127; al-Shaybānī, *al-Makhāridj fi'l-ḥiyal*, Leipzig 1930, 12; Djāḥiẓ, *Ḥayawān*, iii, 307-8; Thaʿālibī, *Laṭāʾif al-maʿārif*, Cairo 1960, 128; Ibn al-Djawzī, *Ṣifat al-ṣafwa*, Cairo 1970, ii, 341, 408; Samʿānī, *Ansāb*, Hyderabad 1963, iii, 319-25; Ibshīhī, *Mustaṭraf*, Cairo 1952, ii, 81; Ḳalyūbī, *Ḥikāyāt*, Calcutta 1856, 168; M.S. al-Ḳāsimī, *Dictionnaire des métiers damascains*, Paris 1960, i, 83. (M. A. J. Beg)

DJAMMŪ, a region of northern India, lying between lat. 32° and 33° N. and long. 74° and 76° E. and extending east of the Čenāb. It is bounded on the south by the Sialkōt district of the Pandjāb and on the north by Kashmīr, of which it now constitutes a province, covering an area of 12, 375 sq. miles. Its capital, the town of the same name, is situated on the right bank of the Tavī.

The original name of this ancient principality, which lay in the valleys of the Tavī and the Čenāb, was Durgara, from which is derived the ethnic term Dogrā for its mountaineer inhabitants. Even the name Durgara, however, figures for the first time only in copper-plate grants of the early 10th century, and Djammū appears to be referred to in Kalhana's *Rādjatarangiṇī* as Babbapūra (Babor). During the reign of the great Kashmīr king Kalaśa (1063-89), Djammū was tributary to Kashmīr, and his subordination continued into the 12th century, when the decline of their powerful neighbour enabled the *rādjās* to assert their independence.

At this time, Čakradeva, ruler of Djammū, played a part in the struggle between the last Ghaznawid sultan in the Pandjāb, Khusraw Malik b. Khusraw Shāh (555-82/1160-86) and the rising power of the Ghūrids [*q.v.*]. Čakradeva allied with the Ghūrid Muʿizz al-Dīn Muḥammad against Khusraw Malik and his Khokar allies, who had been harrying Djammū and refusing allegiance to its ruler, their suzerain (see C. E. Bosworth, *The later Ghaznavids, splendour and decay: the dynasty in Afghanistan and northern India 1040-1186*, Edinburgh 1977, 129-30).

The *vamśāvalī* of the *rādjās* of Djammū supplies a long list of rulers, often with very few details of their reigns, and the chronology can only occasionally be fixed by reference to external sources. Tīmūr, in the course of his invasion of this region in 801/1398-9, forcibly converted the *rādjā* of Djammū to Islam, and this is probably the Bhīm-dēv (d. 1423) whom we find on the throne over the next few decades; but his successors reverted to Hinduism. This did not preclude co-operation with Ḥasan Shāh of Kashmīr in resisting the invasion of Tatar Khān Lūdī, governor of the Pandjāb, around 1480, while during the troubled reign of Muḥammad Shāh (1484-7), Parasramdēv of Djammū intervened in Kashmīr's internal politics, putting to death a great number of *sayyid*s.

In the 16th century Djammū was divided into two states, Djammū and Bahū (Bao), separated by the Tavī. Both principalities, which were reunited in the next century, followed the other hill states in accepting the suzerainty of the Mughal emperor Akbar, and remained subject to his successors until the 18th century. With the transfer of power in the Pandjāb after 1165/1752 to the Afghāns, whose authority was weaker, the hill chiefs were able to recover a certain independence. Under Randjit-dēv (d. *ca.* 1780), who reduced Kishtwār to subjection, Djammū extended as far as the Ravī in the east and in the west even beyond the Čenāb. Randjit-dēv himself, however, was obliged to pay tribute to the Sikhs, and after his death the disputes among his sons enabled him to consolidate their hold upon the region. In 1819 the Sikh ruler Randjit Singh conquered Kashmīr, and for his services during the campaign Dulāb Singh, a descendant of Randjit-dēv's brother, was in the following year made Rādjā of Djammū. He embarked on an energetic programme of conquest, reducing Ladākh (1834) and Baltistān (1841). With the death of Randjit Singh in 1839, the Sikh empire fell into decline, and Gulāb Singh stood aloof from the first war with the British (1845-6), acting subsequently as mediator. By the treaty of Amritsar of 16 March 1846 he received from the British, for the sum of 75 *lakhs*, Kashmīr and all the mountainous territory between the Indus and the Ravī. For the later history of Djammū, see KASHMĪR.

Bibliography: F. Drew, *The Jummoo and Kashmir Territories*, London 1875; *Imperial gazetteer of India*, Oxford 1907-9, xv, 94 ff.; J. Hutchison and J. P. Vogel, *History of the Panjab hill states*, Lahore 1933, ii; G. M. D. Sufi, *Kashīr: a history of Kashmīr*, Lahore 1949, ii; R. K. Parmu, *A history of Muslim rule in Kashmir 1320-1*
New Delhi 1969. (P. JACK

DJĀMŪS (Ar., fem. *djāmūsa*, pl. *djawāmīs*) d nates the Indian buffalo or water buf (*Bubalus bubalis*), with, in other regions, the sp *arni*, *fulvus* and *kerabau*; it is the βοῦς ἄγριο βούβαλος mentioned by Aristotle as found ir wild state in Arachosia, the present-day Balūč (see *Hist. Anim.*, ii, 1 (4) and French transl by J. Tricot, Paris 1957, i, 115-6). The Af buffalo (*Syncerus caffer*), which is unsuitable domestication and which the Sudanese call *dj al-khalā*ʾ "Buffalo of the wilderness", is quite known to the Arab writers. The term *djāmū* Berber *talhamust*, pl. *tilhamusin*) is an arabis from the Islamic period of the Persian comp noun *gāv-i mīsh* "bull-sheep" (which al-Djāḥiẓ t cribes as *kāwmāsh*/*kāwmīsh* in *Ḥayawān*, i, 15 182, v, 459, vii, 243), given to this domestic bovine whose facial profile is reminiscent of th the ram, with the short and upturned muzzle, narrow and slightly arched forehead and the flat, ringed horns, set very far apart and cur horizontally towards the rear; the long tail has ea the beast, in some localities, the dialectical nan *dhunbūb* (from *dhanab* "tail").

The domestication of the Indian buffalo place relatively recently in the historical era, we note that Aristotle speaks of it as a wild sp which corresponded to the bull as the wild boar responds to the pig. As for Europe, the hist Paul Warnefrid, according to Paul the Deacon, s that it was in 596, during the reign of the Lom king Agilulf, that the first buffaloes appeare Italy, in the Pontine marshes; they had already introduced some time previously into Eastern Eu notably in the lower Danube valley, whence rapidly spread towards the North. In the tim Albert the Great, who describes them perfectly, were to be found not only in Hungary where they remained, but in all the Slavonic regions and in neighbouring Germanic provinces. As for the A they did not really discover the animal until the 1st/7th century, with the Islamic expansion Persia and Afghānistān. As soon as the Muslim quest reached India, the new rulers were quic exploit the buffalo, a creature in which they covered special qualities not possessed by the qualities which contributed to a great extent to cultivation of vast tracts of low-lying and ma ground that were hitherto unexploitable. The s aquatic nature of the Indian buffalo, whose na habitat is marshland, added to a powerful phy constitution and a strong herd instinct, made it ideal instrument for clearing these impenetr areas of the ferocious animals, lions especially, w infested them. In fact, as al-Djāḥiẓ so rightly (*Ḥayawān*, vii, 119-120), the buffalo, the elep [see FĪL] and the rhinoceros [see KARKADDAN] the three "great herbivores" (*ruʿasāʾ al-bahā* daring to confront and overpowering the "carnivo lords" (*sādāt al-sibāʿ*). In groups, buffaloes bec formidable, posing to the danger that threatens t the moving rampart of their massed horns, formi protective ring around the females, the calves, even their human masters (see al-Damīrī, *Ḥay* 183). Moreover, the buffalo is an extremely dist ful creature with a vigilance that cannot be chea to such an extent that the ancients claimed th never slept on account of a worm lodged in its b (see al-Ḳazwīnī, *ʿAdjāʾib* ..., in the margin o Damīrī, *op. cit.*, ii, 203). The intrepid resistance p the buffalo to the lion, defined by the admiring Djāḥiẓ as "stout-heartedness" (*shadjā'at al-ḳalb*, *awān*, vii, 142) very soon came to the attention he herdsmen, then to that of the Muslim rulers , taking advantage of this fighting instinct, reрced it by sheathing the horns of the animals in per or iron, thus improving their armament besending them out against the great beast (see uwayrī, *Nihāyat al-arab*, x, 124).

he earliest introduction of buffaloes into the r East is attributed to the powerful governor of a Mu'āwiya b. Abī Sufyān [*q.v.*] who used his poal skill to transfer *en masse* the Zuṭṭ [*q.v.*], their large herds of buffalo, from the eastern tiers of the Tigris, to which point they had ally penetrated, into the region of the 'Awāṣim] and of the 'Amḳ [*q.v.*] of Antioch which was ined by lions. These Zuṭṭ or Djat [*q.v.*] (pl. Djitān, *Ḥayawān*, v, 407, n. 2), semi-nomadic Indoans from Sind, a people highly rebellious in the of any constraint, were at that time essentially ders of buffaloes, and their steady progress westd was to be an important factor in the prolifera- of these Indian bovines around the Mediterra- n basin. The northern frontier region of Syria ived a second influx of buffaloes, 4,000 according bn al-Faḳīh (see *Abrégé du Livre des pays*, French H. Massé, Damascus 1973, 137), under the calite of al-Walīd I and for the same reason, sc. ger and instability caused by lions. Then the ph Yazīd II repeated the operation for the efit of Cilicia and the lower Orontes (see AL-'ĀṢĪ). ally, it was again from these same regions that the bāsid caliph al-Mu'taṣim was obliged, in 222/837, deport the entire Zuṭṭ nation, which was settled ng with its buffaloes in the vast Mesopotamian land region of al-Baṭīḥa [*q.v.*]; this draconian asure came as a result of the raids and acts of gandage indulged in by these turbulent and perually rebellious Indo-Aryans, a large number of m had been transplanted thither by the energetic ayyad governor al-Ḥadjdjādj b. Yūsuf al-Thaḳafī, transported them by sea from Daybul [*q.v.*], after r capture in 94/712 by the general Muḥammad b. Ḳāsim al-Thaḳafī. They were to give their name he Nahr al-Zuṭṭ, one of the marshes situated been Wāsiṭ and Baṣra (see Yāḳūt, *Mu'djam*, iv, 840, *Ḥayawān*, v, 399); these are the same people who, en centuries later, arrived in western Europe and e nicknamed, according to the various countries, iganes", "Bohemians", "Egyptians/Gypsies/Gita- ", "Romanies", etc. After this deportation, buffa- did not however disappear from Lower Mesopo- ia since, following the Zuṭṭ, Arab tribes, including Bāhila [*q.v.*] and the Banu 'l-'Anbar [see TAMĪM], tinued to breed them; this species of bovine psered exceedingly and, in the 4th/10th century, Mas'ūdī could write (*Murūdj*, ii, § 870): "As for faloes, in the Syrian border region, they draw riots of the greatest size; like the bulls ... [of Rayy/Rages] ... they bear in their nostrils a g of iron or of copper. The same custom is obved in the province of Antioch ... large numbers buffalo are also found in 'Irāḳ, and especially the *ṭufūf* of Kūfa and of Baṣra, in the *Baṭā'iḥ* and neighbouring regions." In our own times, some 'ī Arab tribes, including the Āl Bū Muḥammad and Ma'dān, still make their livelihood through the ring of the buffalo to the south of al-'Imāra nara) on the approaches to the Hawr al-Ḥammār, the butter which they produce supplies the rket of Baghdād.

In Egypt, the domesticated buffalo (in dialect *gāmūs*, *gāmūsa*) guaranteed the prosperity of agriculture in the Nile valley from the Delta to Aswān. Its introduction into the ancient kingdom of the Pharaohs was owed to the Muslims, and seems to have been contemporary with that experienced by Syria and the 'Awāṣim; the major Arab historians make no mention of the question, but it may be supposed that the first creatures arrived there carrying or drawing equipment in the rearguard of military contingents coming to take up garrison duties. Whatever the case may be, the fellah whose livelihood was bound up with the periodic flooding and subsiding of the great river found in the buffalo the ideal partner for the efficient agricultural exploitation of the muddy soil left by the receding of the water; there, as in the rice swamps of the Far East, the buffalo manoeuvres easily and its docility makes it the best draught-animal for this kind of terrain. Furthermore, it is able to defend itself against the irritations of mosquitoes by wallowing in the mud of the tributaries in the manner of the pachyderms, and it spends the hottest hours of the day agreably, submerged up to the nostrils in the tidal waters; its presence along the banks of the Nile proved decisive in the elimination of the crocodiles which infested them (see al-Ḳazwīnī, *op. cit.*, ii, 203). The number of buffaloes in Egypt grew so quickly and so extensively that in the 7th/13th century, al-Maḳrīzī tells us (*Khiṭaṭ*, i, ch. xxxix) certain sultans, in their constant quest for increased revenue, imposed an excessive annual tax of three to five *dīnār*s per head, which at that time represented half of the value of the animal; this crushing burden on the fellah was furtunately abolished in the following century. It was in the course of the 8th/14th century that the intrepid Moroccan traveller Ibn Baṭṭūṭa became acquainted with and appreciated, first at Damietta and then in the Indies, the excellent milk of the buffalo (*Riḥla*, Cairo 1928, i, 17, ii, 12). In Ceylon (*ibid.*, ii, 136) he consumed buffalo steaks, then, putting into port at Kaylūkarī (ii, 158) while on his way to China, he was offered, among other presents, two female buffaloes by the local princess.

To the many advantages offered by the buffalo to the peasantry dependent on the great rivers of Islam, an additional asset that should be mentioned was the use by craftsmen of its hide, which was particularly resistant and ideal for the manufacture of shields (see *Ḥayawān*, vii, 86). It was much in demand by the savage Bedjā herdsmen [*q.v.*] for their nomadic journeys between the Upper Nile and the Red Sea (see *Khiṭaṭ*, ii, ch. xxxii); from terms such as "buffleterie" (French), "buff-belts" (English) we know of the high value placed upon this leather for the equipment of European soldiers up until the last century. In mediaeval oriental medicine, fumigations making use of this leather were recommended for the elimination of house-bugs, while the salted fat of the animal was held to be an ointment effective in the prevention of scabies and leprosy.

In the Maghrib, the buffalo (in dialect: *zāmūs*) is hardly known except in one small herd of about fifty animals living wild on the banks of the Tunisian lake of Ischkeul. The origin of this herd is obscure; the general opinion is that these buffaloes were imported from Italy at the beginning of the 13th/19th century, during the reign of Aḥmad Bey [*q.v.*]. But the studies of L. Joleaud and L. Lavauden (see *La chasse et la faune cynégétique en Tunisie*, Tunis 1920, 14) tend to show that these animals are the last remnants, having reverted to the wild, of the buffaloes once the property of the Carthaginians; such a thesis seems extremely hazardous, in spite of everything. In Algeria, finally, where the buffalo is not present, the term *djāmūs* (or *zāmūsh*) designates women's bracelets carved from the horns of the animal. In reference to this term, it is to be noted that some authors have given the title *djāmūs al-baḥr* "river buffalo" to the hippopotamus (see FARAS AL-MĀ').

Bibliography: Besides the sources quoted in the article, see R. Thévenin, *L'origine des animaux domestiques*, Paris 1960, 78; L. Guyot and P. Gibassier, *Les noms des animaux terrestres*, Paris 1964, 38-9; Yarkin Ibr., *Büffelzucht und Büffeltype in Anatolien*, in *Ann. Univ. Ankara*, iii (1948-9), 209-40. (F. VIRÉ)

AL-**DJANBĪHĪ**, MUḤAMMAD B. ʿABD AL-NABĪ (other forms are Djinbayhī and Djunbayhī), Egyptian author of a variety of tracts of which the majority have as a central theme the denunciation of what is seen as the various manifestations of decay of Islamic civilisation in Egypt.

He was born in 1842 in the village of Djinbāwāy (Djinbawāy, Djimbaway) in the *markaz* of Itāy al-Bārūd in al-Buḥayra province. After a period of study at al-Azhar, he held the office of *khaṭīb* in al-Muṭahhar mosque in Cairo. He resigned from this office at an early age and returned to his village (cf. *I'tilāf al-maʿānī wa 'l-mabānī fī takhmīs ḳaṣīdat Abī Firās al-Ḥamdānī*, Cairo n.d., 16), where he devoted himself to what he saw as his mission: to struggle for the victory of Truth, i.e. of Islam as conceived by him, and to exhort the Islamic world to this end (cf. *Tasliyat al-ṣadāra wa 'stinhāḍ al-wizāra*, Cairo n.d., 13). These exhortations were set forth in a number of books and pamphlets permeated with a strong mystical strain, and supported by quotations from authors belonging to the Shādhiliyya order [*q.v.*] into which al-Djanbīhī himself had been initiated. They were directed against Christian missionary activity (cf. *Taṣḥīḥ al-tardjīḥ bayn Muḥammad wa 'l-Masīḥ*, Cairo 1321/1903-4; *Muthabbit al-ʿaḳl wa 'l-dīn fī 'l-radd ʿalā sufahā' al-mubashshirīn*, Cairo n.d.; and *Masmūm al-asinna wa 'l-shihām fī 'l-radd ʿalā man shawwashū al-afkār bi-daʿwā tanwīr al-afhām*, Cairo n.d.), against journalism (cf. *Kashf al-izār ʿan mushawwahāt al-awzār*, Cairo 1902, *passim*; *al-Sirādj al-wahhādj fī 'l-dalāla ʿalā ashraf minhādj*, Cairo n.d. 73 f; *Aṣdaḳ al-naṣā'iḥ al-nahī ʿan al-mūbiḳāt wa 'l-ḳabā'iḥ*, Cairo n.d., 159), against the foundation and character of the Egyptian University (*Balāyābūz al-ʿaṣriyya tanshuruhā al-Djāmiʿa al-Miṣriyya*, Cairo n.d.), and against Western science and scholarship (cf. *Risālat al-Ḥabīb wa-dalālat al-ṭabīb*, Cairo n.d., 68, 99; *al-Razāyā al-ʿaṣriyya li-shubbān al-umma al-Miṣriyya*, n.p., n.d. (approx. 1923), 32). In addition, he denounced the *ʿulamā'* for not being able to counter the decay envelopping Islamic civilisation (cf. *Aṣdaḳ al-naṣā'iḥ*, 13; *Ḥāfiẓat al-ādāb wa-mawḳiẓat al-albāb*, Cairo 1316/1898-9, 30), and condemned demands for independence as un-Islamic and political demonstrations as *bidaʿ* to which in the past only the Khawāridj [see KHĀRIDJĪS] had delivered themselves (cf. *al-Razāyā al-ʿaṣriyya*, 52 f.). At the same time, he criticised Lord Cromer (cf. *al-ʿAmal al-mabrūr fī radaʿat ahl al-ghurūr*, Cairo n.d., 136; *Risālat al-Ḥabīb*, 29), whom he saw as not just aiming at maintaining political domination, but as directed in the final resort at establishing religious domination (cf. *Aṣdaḳ al-naṣā'iḥ*, 147); wrote against the calls for *iṣlāḥ* of those belonging to the reformist movement—which he saw as being different from al-Wahhābiyya [*q.v.*; cf. *Razāyā al-ʿaṣriyya*, 60 ff., 147]—and attacked denounced its inspirers Djamāl al-Dīn al-Afg[hānī] and Muḥammad ʿAbduh (cf. *Zaḥzaḥat al-zā'ighīn munāwasha al-mutawassilīn*, preceeding *Irshād Shaykh Maḥmūd Khaṭṭāb*, mentioned below, 18, *Aṣdaḳ al-naṣā'iḥ*, 120 ff.; *al-Razāyā al-ʿaṣri[yya]* 46 ff.), as well as its representatives such as Ḳā[sim] Amīn and Muḥammad Farīd Wadjdī (cf. *Irshād umam ilā yanbūʿ al-ḥikam*, Cairo 1338/1919-20, *al-ʿAmal al-mabrūr*, 49 f.; *Aṣdaḳ al-naṣā'iḥ*, 11[0]. The most provocative of his publications (which still awaiting a proper evaluation) is a book enti[tled] *Irshād al-Shaykh Maḥmūd Khaṭṭāb ilā ṭarīḳ al-i[...] wa 'l-maṭāb*, Cairo 1336/1817-8. It contains a leng[thy] and profound attack upon Maḥmūd Khaṭṭāb al-Su[bkī] [*q.v.*], the founder of the Djamʿiyya al-Sharʿi[yya] li-Taʿāwun al-ʿĀmilīn bi'l-Kitāb wa 'l-Sunna Muḥammadiyya, commonly known as al-Subkiy[ya]. It must be considered as one of the more signific[ant] treatises written against al-Subkī's conception of [Is]lam (cf. F. De Jong, *Ṭuruq and ṭuruq-oppositio[n in] 20th century Egypt*, in F. Rundgren (ed.), *Proceed[ings] of the VIth Congress of Arabic and Islamic Stu[dies]*, Stockholm-Leiden 1975, 87 f.). Muḥammad Djanbīhī died in 1927.

Bibliography: A biography by Badawī Ṭ[...] ʿAllām is prefaced to Muḥammad al-Djanb[īhī] *Hamm baṭnī ʿabaṭanī*, Cairo 1954 (2nd. ed.). [See] also the biographical notes by ʿAbd al-Ka[...] Salmān in the postscript to the edition of *I'[tilāf] al-maʿānī* mentioned in the article. This boo[k] is the only one of al-Djanbīhī's publicati[ons] mentioned by Brockelmann, S I, 440. To [the] works referred to in the article and the ones lis[ted] by Sarkīs, 714 f. must be added *Karam al-rubūbi[yya] wa-sharaf al-ʿubūdiyya*, Cairo 1927; and *Nashr asrār al-bashariyya min ṭawāyā al-akhlāḳ muḥammadiyya*, Cairo 1319/1901-2. (F. DE JONG)

DJAND, a mediaeval town on the lower reac[hes] of the Sīr Daryā in Central Asia, towards its bouchure into the Aral Sea, in what is now Kazakhstan SSR; its fame was such that the A[ral] Sea was often called "the Sea of Djand".

Djand is first mentioned by certain Muslim g[eo]graphers of the mid-4th/10th century, in particu[lar] by Ibn Ḥawḳal, and following him, by the anonym[ous] author of the *Ḥudūd al-ʿālam* (wrote 372/982). Ḥawḳal mentions three settlements on the lower [Sīr] Daryā amongst the Oghuz Turks of that regi[on]: Djand; the "New Settlement", (al-Ḳarya al-ḥadī[tha], appearing in the Persian sources as Dih-i Naw, [and] in later Turkish contexts as Yengikent (Kāshgh[arī], tr. Atalay, iii, 149-50: Yenkend) or Shahr-kent (in the *K. al-Tawassul ila 'l-tarassul*, Nasawī's *S[īrat] Sulṭān Djalāl al-Dīn* and on certain coins); [and] Khuwāra. Of these, al-Ḳarya al-ḥadītha was [the] largest, being provisioned with corn from Tra[ns]oxania when there was peace between the Turks [and] Muslims, and lying on the left bank of the rive[r] 10 stages from Khʷārazm across the Ḳizil Ḳum [*q.v.*] at two stages from the Aral Sea shore, and 20 sta[ges] from Fārāb or Pārāb, the later mediaeval town [of] Otrār [see FĀRĀB]. This town was the winter reside[nce] of the ruler of the Oghuz, the Yabghu. The ruins of Ḳarya al-ḥadītha probably lie at the modern Dj[an]kent-ḳalʿa, near the old Khīwan fort of Djān-ḳa[lʿa] and 22 km./14 miles downstream from Kazalin[sk]. Djand lay further upstream, on the right bank of [the] river, not far from the modern Qyzyl-Orda (

ɔvsk of Tsarist Russian times); the Russian ar-əologist P. Lerch and the American traveller Schuyler identified its site with an old Kirghiz etery and the ruins at Khorkhut, a station on Orenburg-Tashkent postroad (now the track of the railway), but this identification is not rely certain (see Schuyler, *Notes of a journey in sian Turkistan, Khokand, Turkistan. Bukhara, Kuldja*, London 1876, i, 62-3; E. Bretschneider, *liaeval researches from eastern Asiatic sources*, don 1910, ii, 95-6). The site of Khuwāra is totally nown, and it disappears from mention after the of the 4th/10th century.

he three settlements were important as entrepôts trade with the Inner Asian steppes, and Gardīzī l-5th/11th century) mentions the route which ran n Fārāb to Yengi-kent and thence to the lands of Kimäk [*q.v.*] on the banks of the Irtysh (*Zayn khbār*, ed. Ḥabībī, 258). All three settlements a population of Muslim traders in the 4th/10th tury. Barthold assumed that these Muslims had nselves founded the settlements as trading-posts, pendent of any policy on the part of the Sāmā- to extend their power into the pagan Turkish pes (cf. his *Histoire des Turcs d'Asie Centrale*, and *Four studies on the history of Central Asia. A history of the Turkmen people*, 92). Recently, ever, the results of investigations by Soviet aeologists in the lower Sīr Daryā area have gested that these places had a pre-Islamic his-; S. P. Tolstov has spoken of these in his *Goroda ov*, in *SE*, iii (1947), 55-102, as "Hunno-Turkish" lements, resettled and refortified in the 4th/ 1 century, whence the name "New Settlement". well as these three places on the lower Sīr Daryā, e is mention in the sources of other Turkish ns on the middle course of the river, such as rān and Sīghnāḳ (the latter on the site of the ent-day ruins of Sunaq-qurghan), and Idrīsī, sibly utilising information of over two centuries re from Djayhānī, names over ten settlements of Oghuz on the Sīr Daryā; other sources mention the Oghuz already in the 4th/10th century in-led both nomads and sedentaries (see Tolstov, *Auf Spuren der altchoresmischen Kultur*, Berlin 1953 4; O. Pritsak, *Der Untergang des Reiches des zischen Yabǧu*, in *Fuad Köprülü armağanı*, nbul 1953, 399-401; Bosworth, *The Ghaznavids, r empire in Afghanistan and eastern Iran*, 211-13).

t all events, Djand was an important centre of Oghuz towards the end of this century, and it s a rôle in the semi-legendary accounts of Saldjūḳ ins, those called in Mīrkhwānd the *Malik-nāma*. eponymous founder of the family, Saldjūḳ b. ḳāḳ, is said to have come to Djand with his follow- to have become a Muslim and to have relieved Muslim population of the town of the tribute ed on them by the still-pagan Oghuz Yabghu; lly, he was buried there. From these events ed the hostility between the two branches of the uz, that of Saldjūḳ and that of the Yabghu (Ibn thīr, Mīrkwānd, etc., utilised in Barthold, *Turke- down to the Mongol invasion*[2], 178, 257, Cl. Cahen, *Malik-Nameh et l'histoire des origines seldjukides*, *Oriens*, ii (1949), 43-4, and Bosworth, *op. cit.*, 219- The conversion of the Yabghu nevertheless fol-ed *ca.* 390/1000, and he assumed the Islamic e of ʿAlī; Gardīzī records this conversion under year 393/1003 and states that ʿAlī contracted a riage alliance with the last Sāmānid Ismāʿīl Iuntaṣir [*q.v.*] (*Zayn al-akhbār*, ed. Nāẓim, 64, Habībī, 176; Pritsak, *op. cit.*, 405-6).

Djand now became for some 50 years the centre of an Oghuz principality which played an important part in the diplomatic and military policies of the great powers of the region, sc. of the Ghaznawids, who after 408/1017 controlled Khwārazm, and the Ḳarā-Khānids or Ilek-Khāns [*q.v.*] of Transoxania. As for Yengi-kent, the original seat of the Yabghu, we can only assume that it must have passed into the hands of the Ḳipčaḳ [*q.v.*], who were at this time expanding their power within the steppes and who came to control much of the middle Sīr Daryā as far up as the Isfīdjāb-Shāsh region, which accordingly long remained a pagan area. The Ghaznawid historian Bayhaḳī in his *Taʾrīkh-i Masʿūdī*, and a later source like Abu 'l-Ghāzī's *Shadjara-yi Tarākima*, mention the ruler in Djand Shāh Malik b. ʿAlī, sc. the son and successor of the Yabghu, and the local historian of Bayhaḳ, Ibn Funduḳ, gives him the full name of Abu 'l-Fawāris Shāh Malik b. ʿAlī al-Barānī (concerning this *nisba*, see Z. V. Togan, *Umumî türk tarihine giriş*, i, Istanbul 1946, 181), with the honorifics of Ḥusām al-Dawla and Niẓām al-Milla. The hostility between the two branches of the Oghuz, the line of the Yabghu in Djand and the Saldjūḳs in Transoxania and the northern fringes of Khurāsān, made Shāh Malik the natural ally of Masʿūd of Ghazna against his rebellious governors in Khwārazm and against the Ḳarā-Khānids, and in 429/1038 the sultan appointed Shāh Malik as his governor in Khwārazm; but when, in Shaʿbān 432/April 1041, the latter was triumphant and occupied Khwārazm, Masʿūd had already been deposed and was dead (see Barthold, *Turkestan*, 297-303; Cahen, *Le Malik-Nameh*, 49-55; Bosworth, *The Ghaznavids*, 238-9, 241).

The fortunes of the Saldjūḳs were, however, in the ascendant after their victory at Dandānḳān in 431/1040. By 435/1043-4 they had secured Khwārazm, and Shāh Malik was forced to flee from Djand, which also passed under Saldjūḳ control. Yet the subsequent pre-occupations of the Saldjūḳs in Persia and the west apparently allowed Djand to slip from their hands, doubtless into those of the local Ḳipčaḳ. In 457/1065 Alp Arslan had to lead an expedition to Djand and Ṣawrān; the ruler of Djand submitted, and was confirmed there as governor on behalf of the Saldjūḳs (Barthold, *op. cit.*, 298, 302; Pritsak, *Der Untergang des Reiches des Oğuzischen Yabğu*, 408).

Under the Khwārazm-Shāhs [*q.v.*], Djand and the middle Sīr Daryā reaches, together with the Manghishlaḳ peninsula [*q.v.*] to the east of the Caspian Sea, were regarded as important frontiers (*thughūr*) against the pagan Ḳipčaḳ. Atsïz led a campaign from Djand into the steppes early in his reign, probably *ca.* 527/1133. Because of Atsïz's humiliation at the hands of his suzerain, the Saldjūḳ sultan Sandjar, who in the winter of 542/1147 had invaded Khwārazm, Djand was lost to the Shāhs, and passed to Kamāl al-Dīn b. Arslan Khān Maḥmūd, the grandson of Sandjar's Ḳarā-Khānid nephew Arslan Khān Muḥammad, ruler of Samarḳand. According to Djuwaynī, Atsïz and his army appeared at Djand in the spring of 547/1152, on pretext of organising an expedition against the Ḳipčaḳ, and Kamāl al-Dīn was seized and deposed. The Shāh's eldest son Il Arslan was now appointed governor of Djand, an indication of the importance attached to it, and the allotting of this governorship to a Khwārazmian prince became henceforth frequent; Tekish was governor at his father Il Arslan's death, and under Tekish, the prince Malik Shāh was governor. Various expeditions from Djand against the Ḳipčaḳ are recorded in the later 6th/12th and early 7th/13th centuries, e.g. in the winter of 577/1181-2 by Malik Shāh b. Tekish, in the winter of 591/1194-5 by Tekish himself against Ṣighnāḳ and Ḳayïr Buḳu Khān, chief of the Oran tribe of the Ḳïpčaḳ, and in the autumn of 606/1209 by the Shāh ʿAlāʾ al-Dīn Muḥammad (Barthold, *Turkestan*, 324, 328-9, 337, 340, 361-3). It was during the course of an expedition northwards from Djand into the Ḳïpčaḳ steppes that Khwārazmian troops first clashed accidentally with Čingiz Khān's Mongols, according to Nasawī, in 612/1215-16, although the exact chronology is uncertain here (see Barthold, *op. cit.*, 369-71).

In the strategy of their invasions, the Mongols regarded Djand as an important point. The Khwārazm-Shāh's governor in Djand and Shahr-kent or Yengikent was Ḳutlugh Khān, who had 10,000 cavalrymen in the latter town. The Mongol commander Čin-Temür was at first repulsed from Djand, but returned in the spring of 617/1220. Djand surrendered peacefully, but was sacked, and the official of the Mongols ʿAlī Khwādja from Ḳizhduwān near Bukhārā was appointed governor, retaining this office, according to Djuwaynī, till his death. Yengi-kent (the Iankint of John of Plano Carpini) was likewise taken, apparently without resistance, as was the town of Barčlïgh-kent or Barč-kent (Carpini's Barchin) at a so-far unidentified spot on the Sïr Daryā between Djand and Sïghnāḳ. Čingiz's eldest son Djoči then used Djand as a base for the attack on Gurgāndj in Khwārazm in the next year (Djuwaynī-Boyle, i, 83, 86-90; Barthold, *Turkestan*, 415-16; Bretschneider, *op. cit.*, i, 277-8). It was around this time that Yāḳūt wrote about Djand, mentioning that its population was of the Ḥanafī *madhhab* and that one of its famous men was the poet and stylist, resident in Khwārazm, the *Ḳāḍī* Yaʿḳūb b. Shīrīn al-Djandī, pupil of Zamakhsharī and contemporary of Samʿānī (cf. Samʿānī, *Ansāb*, ed. Hyderabad, iii, 350); Yāḳūt noted that the town was now in the hands of the Tatars, and nothing was known of the fate of its inhabitants (*Buldān*, ed. Beirut, ii, 168-9).

In fact, Djand continued to enjoy a modest prosperity under the Mongol Great Khāns and then under the Čaghatayids, and it appears on an early 14th century Chinese map as Jan-di. An 8th/14th century Čaghatay source attributes the construction of mosques, *madrasas*, etc. in Djand, Barč-kent, Otrār and Ṣawrān to the Özbeg Khān Ergen, son of Sasï Buḳa; but Djand and Barč-kent apparently ceased to exist as towns towards the end of that century (see Barthold, *Four studies*. ii. *Ulugh Beg*, 101).

Bibliography: Given in the article.

(C. E. Bosworth)

DJANDJĪRA, the Marāṭhā corruption of the Arabic word *djazīra* "island", is the name of a former native state in the heart of the Konkan on the west coast of India. It actually owes its name to the fortified island of Djandjīra (lat. 17° 45′ N. and long. 73° 05′ E.), lying at the entrance of the Rajapuri creek, half a mile from the mainland on the west and 48 km. south of Bombay. The impregnable fort, which has an excellent command over the Arabian Sea, rose to prominence under the Niẓām Shāhī [*q.v.*] rulers of Aḥmadnagar towards the end of the 9th/15th century when a Ḥabshī or Abyssinian adventurer named Sīdī Yāḳūt, in the service of Aḥmad Niẓām Shāh (892-915/1487-1509), was made commander of the fortress island, which was also consequently called Ḥabsān. The ruler of the island used to be a Sunnī Muslim known as Sīdī, but later on he came to be known also as Wazīr and Nawāb. The Sīdīs of Djandjīra were a prosper community of skilled seamen, noted for their tena and fighting spirit, expressed in the warfare activities of a long and chequered career exten over four-and-a-half centuries.

By the middle of the 11th/17th century, the S of Djandjīra were firmly established as an effect though small, naval power on the west coast m taining on behalf of the Sulṭān of Bidjāpūr a pov ful fleet for protecting the maritime trade for providing transport for Muslim pilgrims bo for Mecca. Later on, the Sīdīs transferred t fleet to the service of the Mughals, who were n willing than the Sulṭāns of Bidjāpūr to offer t protection against the mounting menace of the M ṭhās. Hence in 1080/1670 Awrangzīb made the Admiral of the Mughal navy and gave him an an grant of four lakhs of rupees (400,000) for the m tenance of the fleet.

The most remarkable aspect of Djandjīra's his was its invincibility in the face of determined slaughts by the Marāṭhās under three generation their chieftains, i.e., Sāhādjī, Sīvādjī and S bhadjī—father, son and grandson—to whom quest of the tiny Djandjīra was a matter of prest The concerted attempts of the Peshwa and Angres in the early 18th century failed to dimi Djandjira's power of resistance. It survived all na challenges and continued to hold its own even as country passed under the British paramoun which adopted a policy of non-interference in Sīdī's administration. Moreover, the Djandjīra ru power obtained possession of the port of Djaʿfarā on the south coast of Kathiawar. This singular dependent status of the state continued till 1287/1 when, following a breakdown in law and order th the Sīdī had to conclude a treaty with the Bri government, resulting in the introduction of a sident British Officer.

The erstwhile state of Djandjīra, which consi of three municipalities—Murud, Shriwardhan Djaʿfarābād—merged with the state of India w the sub-continent attained independence in 1947 present, Djandjīra proper is included in the Mu municipality of the Kolaba district of Maharas state.

Bibliography: D. R. Banaji, *Bombay and Sidis*, London 1932; ʿAlī Muḥammad Khān, *Mi i-Aḥmadī*, Baroda 1927-30; *Maharashtra S Gazetteer* (*Kolaba District*), Bombay 1964.

(Abdus Subha

AL-**DJARĀDATĀN**[1] "the two locusts", the n given to two slave singing girls who, accor to legend, lived in the time of the people of [*q.v.*] and belonged to a certain Muʿāwiya b. Bak ʿImlāḳī (see al-Ṭabarī, i, 235-6 and al-Masʿ *Murūdj*, index). When the delegates of the peopl ʿĀd came to make the pilgrimage to Mecca in o to obtain rain, the two girls so charmed them Muʿāwiya had to make up some verses to re them to the object of their mission; but they fo in the end to make the *ṭawāf*, and it was this fai of duty which led to the destruction of the pe of ʿĀd. The names of these two legendary s girls vary considerably in the sources. Accor to al-Ṭabarī (*Tafsīr*, Cairo 1315, ii, 250-1), one called Warda and the other Djarāda; accordin Ibn Badrūn (65), they were called Ḳaʿādi Thamādi (or Nafādi and Taʿādi), but the sole p of interest in these indications is the form $C^1a\,C^2$ characteristic of a certain number of feminine nar It is possible that just one of them was called Djar

: al-Djafādjī (*Shifāʾ*, 85) says that this name was applied to all singing girls [see ḲAYNA], and the dual was formed according to a well-known :iple (cf. al-Baṣratān[i], etc.).

Bibliography: Djāḥiẓ, *Tarbīʿ*, § 151; Ṭabarī, 234-6; Masʿūdī, *Murūdj*, index; Ibn ʿAbd abbihi, *ʿIḳd*, vii, 28; Kisāʾī, *Ḳiṣaṣ*, 107; Maydānī, 138-9 (three proverbs arising out of the girls); *ghānī*, index; Maʿarrī, *Ghufrān*, index; Nāṣir -Dīn al-Asad, *al-Ḳiyān wa 'l-ghināʾ fi 'l-ʿaṣr al-āhilī*[2], Cairo 1968, 73-5.

lso, ʿAbd Allāh b. Djudʿān [*q.v.*] is said to have essed two singing girls known as al-Djarādatān[i], d Ẓabya and al-Ribāb. Ibn Djudʿān allegedly : them to Umayya b. Abi 'l-Ṣalt [*q.v.*] as a reward :he poet's addressing eulogies to him.

Bibliography: Djāḥiẓ, *Tarbīʿ*, index; Caussin : Perceval, *Essai*, i, 351; Nāṣir al-Dīn al-Asad, . *cit.*, 84-5 and index. See also ḲAYNA.

(CH. PELLAT)

JARĪDA

i-vi. — See Vol. II.

vii. — INDIA AND PAKISTAN

his article defines the Muslim press as those spapers both owned and edited by Muslims. The nition does not include either newspapers in uages normally associated with Islam, for in-.ce Persian and Urdu, with which Muslims have nothing to do, or newspapers edited by lims but owned by men of other faiths.

he Muslim press originated in the government private newsletters of the Mughal period. There the *waḳāʾiʿ*, a confidential letter by which the eror was informed of developments in his domi-.s, and the *akhbār*, a semi-public gazette by which rmation was transmitted to the court. Amongst :r groupings in Indian society, based on common tical or commercial interests, private newsletters ılated. They were handwritten and several copies ach were produced. Large numbers were noted ing Dihlī in the 1830s and they were influential)udh (Awadh) up to 1857.

uslim newspapers in modern form began to emer-ı the 1830s. Among the first were the *Samachar-harajandra*, a weekly in Bengali and Persan pu-ıed by Shaykh ʿĀlim Allāh from Calcutta between :-5, and the *Ṣayyād al-akhbār* published in Urdu ı Dihlī in 1837 by Syed Mohammad Khan (Sayyid ıammad Khān), the elder brother of Syed Ahmed .n (Sayyid Aḥmad Khān [*q.v.*]). The introduction 'rdu lithography in 1837 gave a boost to the deve-ıent of the press in north India, and by the 1840s ral Muslim newspapers were being published.

ı the second half of the 19th century, the Muslim s grew steadily. It flourished primarily in north ia, though it had outposts in the Madras and ıbay Presidencies. Its major centres were La-, Dihlī, Lucknow and Calcutta, and its major uages Urdu and Bengali. Very few specifically lim newspapers were published in English, though *Punjab Observer* is worthy of note. Most leading spapers were weeklies, and only the *Paisa Akhbār* ıded in Lahore in 1888 sustained daily publication : a long period. Among the most influential news-ers, though not those with the largest circulation, the two edited by Syed Ahmed Khan from ʿAlī-ı, the *Tahdhib al-Akhlāḳ* and the *Aligarh Institute ette*. The former educated its readers primarily :he religious and social aims of the ʿAlīgaṛh 'ement, and the latter instructed them in its edu-onal and political aims. The range of subjects which these publications covered indicated a general trend; newspapers were becoming less concerned with literary exercises and sectarian religious polemic, and more with local, national and international affairs.

During the 19th century, the Muslim press, like the Indian press generally, grew in response to the increasing activity of government and the citizen's increasing awareness of the world beyond his locality. Nevertheless, nothing contributed more to the foundation of new Muslim publications, and to major increases in the circulation of newspapers already in existence, than upheavals in the world of Islam. Indian Muslims had powerful pan-Islamic sympathies. This point is made graphically by the striking expansion of the Muslim press which coincided with the last years of the Ottoman empire, in fact from the Italian invasion of Tripoli in 1911 to the abolition of the caliphate in 1924. Newspapers were founded: in 1911 Muḥammad ʿAlī's *Comrade*, in 1912 Abu 'l-Kalām Āzād's *al-Hilāl*, Ḥamīd al-Anṣārī's *Madīna* and ʿAbd al-Bārī's *Hamdam*, in 1913 Muḥammad ʿAlī's *Hamdard*. These new publications and established ones sold on a hitherto unknown scale; the weekly *al-Hilāl* achieved a circulation of 25,000, while Ẓafar ʿAlī Khān converted his *Zamīndār* from a weekly selling 2,000 copies into a daily selling 30,000. There was a dramatic improvement in the quality of production; both *al-Hilāl* and *Hamdard* were printed rather than lithographed. There was a similar improvement in journalism; *al-Hilāl* was written in new and forceful Urdu, while *Comrade* was the equal of any contemporary Anglo-Indian weekly. These newspapers greatly stimulated and even created political agitations, and government acknowledged their influence by gagging them. They also brought their editors, men such as ʿAbu 'l-Kalām Āzād and Muḥammad ʿAlī, to the forefront of Muslim politics.

During the 1920s and 1930s the Muslim press, though never as strong or as vociferous as the Congress or Hindu press, continued to grow. Some of the great newspapers of the pan-Islamic era died, for instance *al-Hilāl* and *Comrade*, but others such as *Zamīndār* and *Madīna* continued. Fresh newspapers were founded; in 1922 *Muslim Outlook*, the first English-language Muslim daily of importance, and in 1927 *Inḳilāb*, the leading Urdu daily of the 1930s. Both were published in Lahore.

It was not until the 1940s that the Muslim press began to compete on equal terms with that of the Congress. Muslim newspapers played a major role, a role which still has adequately to be evaluated, in winning support for the All-India Muslim League's campaign for Pakistan. As in the pan-Islamic era, it showed that it was most effective when religious and political issues were combined. Among the leading League newspapers were *Andjām* in Urdu and *Dawn* in English from Dihlī, *Nawāʾ-i Waḳt* in Urdu from Lahore, *Hamdam* in Urdu from Lucknow, and *Āzād* in Bengali and *Star of India* in English from Calcutta. Not all Muslim newspapers supported the League, for instance *al-Djamʿiyyat*, the voice of *Djamʿiyyat al-ʿulamāʾ*, and *Madīna* were distinctly pro-Congress, but by the 1940s pro-League newspapers both in numbers and in circulation far outstripped their Congress Muslim rivals.

The partition of the subcontinent in 1947 in large part destroyed the Muslim press as it had existed. In India, despite the country's vast Muslim population, a specifically Muslim press has been unimportant; among the leading Muslim newspapers are *Radiance* and *al-Djamʿiyyat*. Pakistan, on the other hand, has developed a press of considerable dimensions both in English and in the various regional languages. In West Pakistan the leading newspapers in English are *Dawn* and *Pakistan Times* and in Urdu *Nawāʾ-i Waḳt* and *Mas̲h̲riḳ*; in East Pakistan up to 1971 the leading English newspaper was *Morning News* and the leading Bengali newspaper *Āzād*. By the late 1960s the Pakistan press was producing 800,000 newspaper copies daily, of which more than three-quarters were in languages other than English. This vigorous newspaper industry existed in spite of heavy restrictions upon press freedom imposed by government and in spite of growing competition from commercial radio and television.

Bibliography: There is no work devoted specifically to this subject. The newsletter is dealt with by J. N. Sarkar in S. P. Sen, ed., *The Indian press*, Calcutta 1967. A. S. Khurshid examines the growth of the Pakistan press in his contributions to A. S. Khurshid, ed., *Press in Muslim world*, Lahore 1954, and J. A. Lent, ed., *The Asian newspapers' reluctant revolution*, Iowa 1971. Aspects of the provincial Muslim press are treated in N. Gerald Barrier and Paul Wallace, *The Punjab press 1800-1905*, Ann Arbor 1970, and M. N. Islam, *Bengali Muslim public opinion as reflected in the Bengali press 1901-1930*, Dacca 1973. For the Indian press generally, see J. Natarajan, *History of Indian journalism*, Part ii of the *Report of the Indian Press Commission*, Dihlī 1955; and M. Chalapathi Rau, *The press*, Dihlī 1974.

(F. C. R. Robinson)

viii. — East Africa

The history of the press and its development and use among East Muslims is very brief. The Muslim intelligentsia, however, have received and read newspapers and journals from other parts of the Muslim world, particularly from Egypt, from the closing years of the 19th century until the present.

It was such connections that helped develop the first interest in establishing local media. The first Muslim to do so was S̲h̲ayk̲h̲ al-Amīn b. ʿAlī b. Nāfʿi Al-Mazrūʿī [see kenya, muslims in,], a Muslim scholar of Mombasa who was familiar with the works and publications of al-Afg̲h̲āni, Muḥammad ʿAbduh and Ras̲h̲īd Riḍā. Newspapers and journals like *al-Manār* were regularly read by S̲h̲ayk̲h̲ al-Amīn and a coterie of Muslim scholars on the East African coast. Concerned about the low status of Muslims and Islam in this region, S̲h̲ayk̲h̲ al-Amīn decided to use the press to raise the level of Muslim religious, cultural and political consciousness, very much along the lines of the Middle Eastern reformers.

First he founded a modest-sized paper called simply *al-Ṣaḥīfa*. Shortly afterwards, in 1932, he established a more substantial paper, appropriately called *al-Iṣlāḥ*. The paper was financed by the founder, with contributions from well-wishers, and was published in two parts, a Swahili one and an Arabic one, the former being often a virtual translation of the latter. Thus a wider readership was achieved through the use of Swahili, the *lingua franca* of Eastern Africa. It discussed issues relevant to the political, economic and religious situation of the East African coast and regularly included news from the rest of the Muslim world, with which the editor of the paper often called for greater solidarity.

In 1932, S̲h̲ayk̲h̲ al-Amīn was appointed *Ḳāḍī* of Mombasa. His new duties compelled him to hand over the running of *al-Iṣlāḥ* to another Muslim scholar, S̲h̲ayk̲h̲ ʿAbd Allāh al-Ḥas. There developed a noticeable difference in approach and style in the pa
which was not now as popular and effective, so
the paper declined and its publication ended
afterwards. S̲h̲ayk̲h̲ al-Amīn had continued to w
and published booklets on Islam after his appo
ment as *Ḳāḍī*, and, in 1937, as Chief *Ḳāḍī* or *S̲h̲*
al-Islām of Kenya. One such booklet was a repro
tion of selected articles from *al-Iṣlāḥ* which
published under the title of *Uwongozi* (Sw
"Guidance").

Even so, it was left to the Aḥmadiyya sect [
and see kenya, muslims in,] to expand the pub
ing of newspapers. Their arrival in the 1930s
earned them the immediate hostility of the orth
Muslim communities, and S̲h̲ayk̲h̲ al-Amīn hi
carried out a campaign to discredit them in
Africa. Nevertheless, in Tanzania they founded
newspapers, one in Swahili, *Mapenzi Ya M*
("The Love of God") and one in English,
African Times. Both papers reflected the cha
teristic militant defence of Islam, lengthy expos
of its teachings and their relevance to mo
society, and regular theological challenges to C
tians and Christianity. It is certain that these
papers have contributed to the relative suc
of the Aḥmadī sect in Tanzania.

It was in Tanzania also that a Muslim mon
journal, *The Light*, was founded in the 1960s by
It̲h̲na ʿAs̲h̲arī community, modestly printed and c
pletely financed by members of the communit

A general comment to be made about these p
cations, including the other journal irregul
produced by the Ismāʿīlī community, *Africa Ism*
is that each one of them has a limited distribu
The two journals hardly go beyond the commun
concerned. The two Aḥmadī newspapers are rega
as heretical propaganda, and thus not appreci
by other Muslims as representing authentic relig
views or the ideal way of reflecting the imag
Islam in East Africa. An acceptable, popular Mu
press has yet to emerge. (A. I. Sali

ix. — South Africa

The implantation of Islam in the extreme so
of the African continent took place in three sta
The first Muslims arrived there in 1667, Mala
slaves whom the Dutch had imported as ma
labour to improve their new colony of the C
Their slave status prevented these Malays f
practising their Islamic religion and from posses
land, and they only obtained a place of wor
in 1797. They were unable also freely to move a
and were compelled to stay in the Cape, so
Islam was unable to expand beyond this limit.

However, the importation after 1860 of a sec
wave of manual labourers was necessitated by
growing development of new crops in the territo
of the white settlers (Boers) at the time of
"great Trek" or migratory movement of 183
Hence from 1860 until the beginning of the 20th
tury, the owners of sugar cane plantations, a
which was very prosperous in Natal, brough
Indian farm workers, some of whom were Musl
Islam was thus implanted at two points in w
became after 1910 the Union of South Africa,
in the south and one in the west. The econ
crisis which began in 1929 threw a consider
number of Indian farm workers out of a job
compelled them to seek another living. Some
them settled in Durban, the capital of Natal, w
the remainder spread throughout the land tow
the Cape, Johannesburg, Pretoria, Port Elisa

other South African towns. Thus the third and phase of the implantation of Islam in South ca was completed.

ıe opening of the 1960s was an important period the Muslim community there, and it marks the nning of its organisation and its expansion. This ess was inaugurated by certain Indian Muslim ers, who aimed at stimulating the feelings of diverse ethnic elements of the Muslim community a consciousness that they were above all Muslims that, in the light of this, they should work for progress of the Muslim community. In effect, the ay and Indian Muslims had previously thought of nselves as belonging rather to their own ethnic munity, and their activities, above all those of very active Indians, had taken place within the nework of their original communities.

his movement brought about the creation after of several Muslim organisations, such as the ciation of South African Muslim women or even association of South African Muslim butchers. It also during this period of intense activity that Muslim press came into being, thanks to its ching by a Muslim of Indian origin, M. Sayyed, he shape of a fortnightly called *Muslim News*. irst number appeared at the beginning of January 1, and had 12 pages, eight in English and four Jrdu, and was edited and printed at Athlone, a rict on the eastern edge of Cape Town where many lims live. In 1971 the four Urdu pages disappear- and since that date, *Muslim News* has contained eight pages in English. It styles itself the only th African Muslim newspaper; however, there t two bulletins, the *Ramadan Annual* and the *slim Digest*, published both by one press group, Makki one.

Iuslim News was meant essentially to inform th African Muslims about religious and cultural vities of the community, and likewise to give ortation on the practices of the Islamic faith. hout departing from these original aims, it evol- in 1973 in another direction by assuming a inct political aspect. Condemnation of *aparthei* of white domination was expressed in the course rticles which became more and more specific and ent in tone, a condemnation which arose from a ly denunciation of the very difficult living con- ons of the non-white population of South Africa. er the publication of articles criticising govern- ıt policy on these topics, the direction and editor- of *Muslim News* were in December 1975 and in in March 1976 brought before the courts in the e; but the journal has nevertheless continued ppear.

perusal of *Muslim News* allows one to appreciate efforts made by the Muslim community of South ica to improve their precarious conditions of ng. Great improvements have actually been ieved in various fields, such as health and educa- . An orphanage has been built, health services e been set up in districts where they were lacking, finally, numerous mosques and *madrasas* have n constructed and a programme of Islamic studies anised. All this has come to fruition from contri- ions and from the gifts of a few very rich Muslims. inally, *Muslim News* at times highlights in its ımns the lack of unity within the Muslim com- nity of South Africa, one mainly due to dissensions ween the three great national Muslim associa- s, the Muslim Judicial Council, the Muslim As- bly and the Ashura (< *s̲h̲ūrā*). These are essen- ly quarrels between personalities trying to assert their own pre-eminence. They have no effect at all on the South African Muslim community's sense of solidarity, and are in fact tending now to disappear; this can only strengthen the community's determination, for despite its numerical smallness (200,000 members out of a total population of 22 millions) it is certainly one of the most vigorous Muslim communities of the southern hemisphere.

(P. Gorokhoff)

x. — The Ḳumuḳ [see ḳumuḳ].

D̲J̲ĀWARS (< Persian *gāwars*) is millet, *Panicum miliaceum* L. (Gramineas), one of the oldest cultivated plants. While in Europe it is now almost only used as fodder, millet plays a prominent role as cereal and victuals in many areas of Asia and Africa. Although the ancient Spartans ate millet, Dioscorides considers millet as the least nutritious of all cereals (*De materia medica*, ed. Wellmann, i, 1907, 173 f. = lib. ii, 97). This is adopted by the Arab translator (*La "Materia médica" de Dioscorides*, ii, ed. Dubler and Terés, Tetuan 1952, 179), who renders the Greek κέγχρος with *kank̲h̲arūs* (and variants). But already Ibn Māssa, a contemporary of Ḥunayn, says that millet, cooked in milk, or broth mixed with millet flour and fat, is an excellent food (see Ibn al-Bayṭār, *D̲j̲āmiʿ*, Būlāḳ 1291, i, 156, 15-16). On the nomenclature, the following can be remarked: occasionally, *kank̲h̲arūs* is understood as both *d̲j̲āwars* and *d̲h̲ura*, and the first of these is equated with the Mozarabic *banīs̲h̲uh*; cf. Anonymous (Ibn al-Rūmiyya?) Nuruosmaniye 3589, fol. 89b, 21; on *banīs̲h̲uh* (Romance *panizo*), see M. Asin Palacios, *Glosario de voces romances*, Madrid-Granada 1943, no. 406. Others consider *d̲j̲āwars* as a kind of *duk̲h̲n* (also *alūmus* < ἔλυμος), by which may be meant the small sorghum (Pennisetum spicatum), widespread in the Sudan and also called Moorish millet, while *d̲h̲ura*, also called *d̲j̲āwars hindī* "Indian millet", indicates the great sorghum (*Sorghum vulgare*). In his book on plants, Abu Ḥanīfa equates *duk̲h̲n* with *d̲j̲āwars* and considers it as a kind of *d̲h̲ura* (*The book of plants*, ed. B. Lewin, Uppsala-Wiesbaden 1953, no. 405). In the course of time, *d̲h̲ura* has become the leading expression for millet. Bīrūnī knows already the Turkish term *dārī* for this (*Ṣaydala*, ed. Ḥakīm Muḥ. Saʿīd, Karachi 1973, Arab. 130, Engl. 106), and names the Indian synonyms.

As a foodstuff, *d̲j̲āwars* has the inconvenience of causing constipation, of being hard to digest and of promoting urine, but the constipation effect can be removed by adding fat or purgatives, and also by diluted wine or by baths. On the other hand, when applied in a warm compress, it proves to be a good remedy against gripes and cramps. It has an astringent effect and is therefore suitable to be used as nourishment for those suffering from dropsy, whose stomachs should be contracted and whose bodies should be "desiccated".

Bibliography: (apart from the titles already mentioned): Rāzī, *Ḥāwī*, xx, Ḥaydarābād 1387/1967, 248-51 (no. 207); *Die pharmakolog. Grundsätze des Abu Mansur ... Harawi*, tr. A. Ch. Achundow, Halle 1893, 177; Zahrāwī, *Taṣrīf*, Ms. Beşir Aga 502, fol. 502a, 7-8; Ibn Sīnā, *Ḳānūn* (Būlāḳ), i, 288; Ibn ʿAbdūn, *ʿUmdat al-ṭabīb*, Ms. Rabat, Bibl. Gén. 3505 D, fols. 33a, 5-6; 36a, 16-19; Ibn Biklāris̲h̲, *Mustaʿīnī*, Ms. Naples. Bibl. Naz. iii, F. 65, fol. 29b; G̲h̲āfiḳī, *al-Adwiya al-mufrada*, Ms. Rabat, Bibl. Gén. ḳ. 155 i, fol. 116a; P. Guigues, *Les noms arabes dans Sérapion*, in *JA*, 10ème série (1905), v, s.v. *Ieuers* (no. 285); Maimonides, *Sharḥ asmāʾ al-ʿuḳḳār*, ed. Meyerhof, Cairo 1940, no. 70; Ibn al-Bayṭār, *Djāmiʿ*, i, 156, tr. Leclerc, no. 460; Yūsuf b. ʿUmar, *Muʿtamad*³, ed. M. al-Saḳḳā, Beirut 1395/1975, 63; Suwaydī, *Simāt*, Ms. Paris ar. 3004, fol. 59a (cf. also A. Dietrich, in *Mélanges d'islamologie dédiés à A. Abel*, Leiden 1974, 105); Dāwūd al-Anṭākī, *Tadhkira*, Cairo 1371/1952, i, 102 f.; *Tuḥfat al-aḥbāb*, ed. Renaud and Colin, Paris 1934, no. 96; I. Löw, *Die Flora der Juden*, i, 1928, 738-46; *El Libro Agregà de Serapiom*, ed. G. Ineichen, ii, Venice 1966, 137, s.v. *iocuers*. (A. Dietrich)

AL-DJAWBARĪ, ʿABD AL-RAḤĪM (not ʿAbd al-Raḥmān) b. ʿUmar b. Abī Bakr Djamāl al-Dīn al-Dimashḳī, dervish and alchemist from Damascus who travelled and wrote in the first half of the 7th/13th century. He spent some time in Egypt (before 613/1216, and in 620/1223, 623/1226 and 624/1227) and in Northern Syria (Āmid, Anṭākiya, Ḥarrān, Konya, al-Ruhāʾ) and travelled through the Biḳāʿ and the Ḥidjāz (Djidda, al-Madīna). He claims to have been also in Cyprus, Baḥrayn and India.

Al-Djawbarī wrote between 629/1232 and 646/1248-9 upon the request of the Artuḳid al-Malik al-Masʿūd (in 629/1232 ruler of Āmid and Ḥiṣn Kayfā) his book *al-Mukhtār fī kashf al-asrār* ("The selection in the unveiling of Secrets"). This is a concise encyclopedia of tricks, practices and devices used by fraudulent Ṣūfīs, false alchemists, beggars, impostors, drugsellers, jugglers, quacks etc. i.e. the mediaeval Islamic underworld, known as the Banū Sāsān [see sāsān, banū]. The book is modelled after the *Kashf al-dakk wa-īḍāḥ al-shakk* of Ibn Shuhayd [*q.v.*], which is lost. Al-Djawbarī lived himself by some of these practices, and the *Mukhtār* is a colourful mine of first-hand information for the social and cultural history of the Islamic Middle Ages. Al-Djawbarī's entertaining personality also caught the interest of some of the political rulers of his time; he proudly relates that he blackmailed a fraudulent alchemist from the Maghrib out of ʿIzz al-Dīn Aybak al-Muʿaẓẓamī's (died 646/1248-49) court by threatening to divulge the secret of his competitor's method to make gold. The book combines realism and psychological insight, a certain knowledge of mechanics medicine and botany with a familiarity with alchemistic and hermetic writings and an enlightened, if naive, scepticism towards many things miraculous.

The *Mukhtār* falls outside the scope of traditional mediaeval Islamic literature and scholarship and is written in careless "Middle-Arabic", full of jargon and dialectical expressions. It has been printed several times (Damascus 1302/1885; Istanbul n.d., Cairo 1316/1898 and several times n.d.). All printings are incomplete, expurgated and unreliable. The author of this article is preparing an edition, based on the available manuscripts. Two further books of al-Djawbarī, a treatise on geomancy and *al-Ṣirāṭ al-mustaḳīm fī ʿilm al-rūḥāniyya wa 'l-tandjīm*, a work on the occult sciences and astrology, are lost. The *Kitāb al-Siḥr al-ḥalāl fi'l-alʿāb al-sīmawiyya wa-baʿḍ fawāʾid ṣināʿiyya mudjarraba*, printed after some of the Cairo editions, has been erroneously ascribed to al-Djawbarī, and is in reality a translated extract of a 19th century French treatise on "magie naturelle".

Bibliography: All information concerning al-Djawbarī has to be gathered from his *Mukhtār*. Al-Djawbarī's importance has already been noted by M. Steinschneider, *Ǵauberi's "entdeckte Geheimnisse, eine Quelle für orientalische Sittenschilderung*, in *ZDMG*, xix (1865), 562-77; idem, *Polem und apologetische Literatur in arabischer Spr zwischen Muslimen, Christen und Juden*, Anl II: *Ǵauberi's "entdeckte Geheimnisse"*, in *Abh lungen für d. Kunde des Morgenlandes*, vi/3, Le 1877; and M. J. de Goeje, *Ǵaubari's "entd Geheimnisse"*, in *ZDMG*, xx, (1866), 484- A considerable part of the *Mukhtār* has translated by E. Wiedemann, who stressed, haps overmuch, al-Djawbarī's importance Islamic natural sciences, cf. the list of transl passages in S. Wild, *Jugglers and fraudulent S* in *Proceedings of the VIth Congress of Arabic Islamic Studies. Visby 13-16 August, Stock 17-19 August 1972 = Kungl. Vitterhets His och Antikvitets Akademiens Handlingar, Filolo filosofiska serien 15*, Uppsala 1975, 58-63. further C. E. Bosworth, *The mediaeval Isl underworld. The Banū Sāsān in Arabic so and literature*. Part One. *The Banū Sāsān in A life and lore*, Leiden 1976, 14-15, 24, 106-18, M. Ullmann, *Die Natur- und Geheimwissensch im Islam* (*Handbuch der Orientalistik*, 1. Abteil Ergänzungsband VI, 2. Abschnitt), 254, 367. (S. Wil

DJAWHAR

(i) Substance. [see Vol. II].

(ii) Jewel, jewelry

Whether or not *djawhar* had the meaning "je from the beginning of this word's usage in the Ar language is uncertain, but this meaning is attested from early in the Islamic era. For exam both *djawhar* and the plural *djawāhir* are used in Paris manuscript of the *Kitāb al-Aḥdjār li-A ṭāṭālīs* (publ. with tr. and comm. in 1912 by J. Ru as *Das Steinbuch des Aristoteles*—see p. 92 for above-mentioned terms), a work which Ruska da to some time before the middle of the 3rd/9th cent The Arabic lexicographers from at least as earl the 4th/10th century give "jewel" as a meaning *djawhar* (e.g. in the *Tahdhīb al-lugha* of al-Az [*q.v.*]). This usage continues throughout the centu to the present day, traceable both in histo literature and in, for example, the 12th/18th cent dictionary *Tādj al-arūs* (for a more complete lis of the definitions by the Arabic lexicographers, Lane's *Lexicon*, s.v. *dj-h-r*).

The word *djawhar* makes no appearance in Ḳurʾān, even though there are specific reference both jewelry (gold bracelets, XVIII, 31 and XL 53; silver bracelets, LXXVI, 21; bracelets of and pearls, XXII, 23 and XXXV, 33) and prec stones (*yāḳūt*, ruby, LV, 58; *mardjān*, small pear coral, LV, 22 and LV, 58; and *luʾluʾ*, pearls, X 23, XXXV, 33 and LV, 22). In four of the passages mentioning the wearing of bracelets verb *yuḥallawna* is used. From its root, which m "to adorn", another common word for jewelr general (*ḥaly*) is derived (see Lane, s.v. *ḥ-l-y*). H ever, *djawhar* was clearly the most important si term for jewelry or jewels in the Arabic langu during its reign as the *lingua franca* of the Isla world.

Let us now turn from the consideration of w used for jewels to an attempt to form a pictur the objects themselves. That is, what kinds of je did the peoples of the regions under considera make, collect, wear or otherwise use in the var historical periods in which they lived? This historical question, an extensive, as opposed intensive, definition of the word *djawhar*, s itute our main concern in what follows. This nark the first attempt ever made at a survey lamic jewelry, and thus must be regarded as sional in certain respects.

arly Islamic jewelry (1st-4th/7th-10th centuries)

y history of Islamic jewelry ought to begin examples from the earliest centuries of Islām. ever, to the best of our knowledge, there are few extant pieces datable to before the first of the 5th/11th century in either the eastern stern parts of the Muslim world. Consequently, empting to reconstruct a picture of the jewelry gue during the first three hundred and seventy-years of the Islamic period we are forced to to pictorial or sculptural representations in ion to literary descriptions.

e available representations show that the ry and other body-adorning and costume ele-s worn during the period were very strongly enced by the Roman, Byzantine and Sāsānid nents found current in the countries conquered he Muslims. A few examples should suffice to rate this point.

e ball-shaped earrings depicted on the sculpture Khirbat al-Mafdjar (R. W. Hamilton, *Khirbat afjar*, Oxford 1959, Pl. XXII, 4) and the tear-shaped examples in the paintings at Sāmarrāʾ Herzfeld, *Die Ausgrabungen von Samarra*, n 1927, Pl. LXXI, top) compare very closely those found on Sāsānid rock reliefs and coins Fukai and K. Horiuchi, *Taq-i-Bustan*, Tokyo , ii, Pl. IX and A. U. Pope, *A survey of Persian* London and New York 1938, iv, Pl. 251 F, H, , N, O). Sāsānid prototypes (Fukai and Horiuchi, *it.*, i, Pl. XX) can also be found for some of the ornaments depicted in a manuscript of al-Ṣūfī 9/1009 (E. Wellesz, *An early al-Ṣūfī manuscript e Bodleian Library in Oxford*, in *Ars Orientalis*, ig. 10) and for the belt fittings in a wall painting Nīshāpūr datable to before 1000 A.D. (Fukai Horiuchi, *op. cit.*, i, Pl. LXIV, and W. Hauser C. K. Wilkinson, *The Museum's excavations at apur*, in *Metropolitan Museum of Art Bulletin* il 1943], Fig. 45).

estern influence, on the other hand, can readily en in some of the jewelry depicted in the wall tings at Ḳuṣayr ʿAmra. The heart-shaped ants worn by one of the female figures (M. Al-o, L. Caballero, J. Zozaya and A. Almagro, *yr ʿAmra*, Madrid 1975, Pl. XXVII, top) bear close comparison to Roman pieces (*Allen orial Art Museum Bulletin*, xviii/2-3, Oberlin, —hereinafter abbreviated *Allen*—Fig. 68), as the shorter necklace of oval elements worn by same figure (L. Pollak, *Klassisch-Antike Gold-iedearbeiten*, Leipzig 1903, Pl. XVI, No. 396). alloped and jewelled necklace worn by one of nale figures as well as one consisting of a series endant elements adorning a female figure (Al-o *et alii*, *op. cit.*, Pls. XI and IX) have close ntine parallels (A. Greifenhagen, *Schmuck-ten in Edelmetall*, i, Berlin 1970, Pl. 49, and opolitan Museum of Art No. 17. 190.1667).

e vogue for breast ornaments held in place by ed straps, seen so often on the figures in Ḳuṣayr ra, (Almagro *et alii*, Pl. XVII, top) probably red the Islamic repertoire from the West also a Greek example, see H. Hoffman and P. David-*Greek gold*, 1965, Fig. D), although the earliest nple known to these authors is from 2nd century B.C. India, the country which also seems to be the ultimate source for the waist ornaments seen in the paintings in our late 1st/early 8th century Jordanian bath (S. Swarup, *The arts and crafts of India and Pakistan*, Bombay 1957, Pl. 88, left and 104 left).

Thus during the earliest centuries of the Muslim era, the jewelry traditions of the Roman, Byzantine and Sāsānid realms seem to have been important as models for Islamic jewelry. Having seen how close the Islamic representations often are to their apparent models, one is tempted to speculate that, to some extent, the scarcity of early Islamic jewelry may be due to our ignorance, and that many of the pieces now classified as Roman, Byzantine and Sāsānid are in fact Islamic in date. Another major factor accounting for the "disappearance" of jewels, especially when it comes to the larger and more valuable stones and pearls, was their re-use in new stringings or settings in accord with the taste of the times. From the remarkable series of large stones, especially diamonds and spinel "rubies", which were inscribed with the names of Persian and Mughal rulers, we know that such stones had considerable histories (discussed in greater detail below); for example, the inscriptions in the name of Nādir Shāh in two large spinels and a teardrop-shaped emerald show concretely how in these cases stones from one treasure were re-used by a subsequent owner (in one case as an armband, and in the other, on a string of prayer beads—see V. Ball, *A description of two large spinel rubies, with Persian characters engraved upon them*, in *Proceedings of the Royal Irish Academy*, iii/3, 380-400 and Pl. X; V. B. Meen and A. D. Tushingham, *Crown jewels of Iran*, Toronto 1968, 46, 64-5 and 67).

We know from a number of literary accounts concerning the period at present under discussion not only that early Islamic rulers collected precious stones, but that they also used them in ways similar to those which we can verify from much later periods.

In one of the most informative and detail-laden works among those which deal with notable treasures, the *Kitāb al-Dhakhāʾir wa 'l-tuḥaf* of al-Ḳāḍī al-Rashīd b. al-Zubayr (ed. M. Hamidullah, Kuwait 1959), we have in § 18 the following: "al-ʿAlāʾī recounted in the *Kitāb al-Adjwāb* that Ṣabīḥ, the secretary, said that ʿUmar b. Yūsuf (i. e. Yūsuf b. ʿUmar) al-Thaḳafī sent to Hishām b. ʿAbd al-Malik a red ruby which was bigger than his palm and a pearl of the greatest possible size. The messenger came in to him. He could not see the face of Hishām because of the height of his throne and the number of cushions. He took the stone and the pearl from him and said: Has he written down their weight? Then he said: Where are the likes of these two to be found?" What is particularly interesting about the above account is that it is such large stones and pearls which were considered appropriate for the ruler and that he was fully aware that the real way of recording such items was by weight. Hishām's questions become even more meaningful when we know that, according to al-Bīrūnī [*q.v.*], al-Rashīd, who also received many comparable gifts, was a great admirer of valuable stones and that he sent the jeweller Ṣabāḥ, the grandfather of al-Kindī [*q.v.*], to Ceylon to buy stones (see Mohammad Jahia al-Haschmi, *Die Quellen des Steinbuches des Berūnī*, Bonn 1935, 14). Not so incidentally, these gifts (sc. the ruby and the pearl) were appropriate to kings not only because of their size but also because they were among the most valued gems in the Islamic world from earliest to latest times, although one often suspects that the huge red rubies, *yāḳūt*, cited are either red tourmalines or spinels, even though there were those competent to differentiate. For an example of methods used for such differentiation, we may point to al-Bīrūnī who recorded the specific weights of stones in relation to sapphire, which he gave the arbitrary value of 100. Thus the pearl "is 65 and a third and a quarter" (see F. Krenkow, *The chapter on pearls in the book on precious Stones by al-Berūnī*. Part II, in *IC*, xvi/1 [1942], 26-7).

Specific literary accounts and numerous recorded gifts and purchases as well as pictorial evidence exist which establish the prevailing hierarchy of value in stones. According to al-Bīrūnī in his *Kitāb al-Djamāhir fi 'l-djawāhir* (as cited by E. Wiedemann, *Über den Wert von Edelsteinen bei den Muslimen*, in *Isl.*, ii [1911], 348), there are three outstanding precious gems, the ruby (*yāḳūt*), the emerald (*zumurrud*) and the pearl. Wiedemann (*op. cit.*, 348 n. 1) also informs us that in f. 5a of the *Steinbuch des Aristoteles* it says that the pearl, the *yāḳūt* and the *zabardjad* (topaz) and their kind are preferred by people over other precious stones. For a concrete example, we may cite another passage from the *K. al-Dhakhā'ir* (§ 33) which recounts gifts given to al-Mutawakkil by a favourite slave girl consisting of twenty tamed gazelles, with twenty Chinese saddles with small saddle-bags containing musk and ambergris and other perfumes, "And each gazelle had a female slave attendant with a golden belt, having in her hand a golden rod, at whose tip was a jewel, a ruby or an emerald or some other from the jewels of high value."

It is hardly possible to estimate real prices; thus that given for the famous Djabal (see al-Masʿūdi, ed. Pellat, index) varies considerably according to the sources. Wiedemann states, in *op. cit.*, 346, and following al-Dimashḳī, that it must have weighed 14½ *mithḳāl*s (according to Kahle's conversion figures, in *Die Schätze der Fatimiden*, in *ZDMG*, N.F. xxxiv [1935], 336, this would amount to about 64 gr. or 320 carats) for 80,000 *dīnārs*. Furthermore, according to the same source, al-Rashīd is said to have paid 90,000 *dīnārs* for a pearl named *al-Yatīma*, "the Orphan". The weight is not given, although weights for pearls of this name are mentioned in several other accounts of the early Islamic period. In the light of the comments of al-Bīrūnī as cited by Krenkow (*art. cit.*, Part I, 407) and of the passage, also from al-Bīrūnī, cited below, it would seem that this name, along with *Farīda*, "Unique" ,was given to any large pearl, perhaps especially to those pear- or teardrop-shaped, for which no match could be found.

Further accounts of the early Islamic period indicating the value placed on certain stones are the following, all taken from the above-cited *K. al-Dhakhā'ir*:

(i) In the time of the caliph Hishām b. ʿAbd al-Malik, the "king of India" sent as a present to Djunayd b. ʿAbd al-Raḥmān, the then governor of Sind, a jewel-studded camel mounted on a silver, wheeled under-carriage, and its udders were full of pearls and its throat was full of rubies, both of which could be made to pour forth. Djunayd sent this on to Hishām, who appreciated it highly. "It amazed Hishām and everyone who was in his company, and it remained in the Umayyad treasury until it passed to the ʿAbbāsids" (§ 15).

(ii) There is an account (§ 27) of a gift sent to al-Rashīd, by "one of the kings of India", of "an emerald rod longer than a cubit. At its head was the image of a bird of red rubies, and it was invaluable." We are told that this bauble passed down through the ʿAbbāsid family, serving for at least part of the tir a plaything for royal children, to al-Muʿtaṣim, ordered a search for the (at that point) missing r encrusted bird (valued, we are told, at 100,000 d by one ʿAbd Allāh b. Muḥammad) which had be separated from it but which was found, under th of punishment, by the treasurers.

(iii) We read (§ 29) that al-Ma'mūn correspo and exchanged gifts with a king of India, and the Indian king's letter to al-Ma'mūn mentione gifts he was sending: "And the gifts were a cu red ruby, the opening of which was one span by one finger thick, full of pearls, each of w weighed a *mithḳāl*. They totalled 100 pearls . . ."

For the actual use of precious stones in jew there is considerable evidence that in this Islamic period, as in the previous Roman Byzantine periods as well as in much later pe such as the Mughal one in India, many of the l precious stones were bored and strung on c chains, wires or whatever was appropriate. Rem ably graphic literary confirmation of this is affo by al-Bīrūnī's treatment of the emerald, as cite Wiedemann (*op. cit.*, 351), when he says that em jewels or beads (*kharaza*) are called reeds or t (*ḳaṣaba*) because of their long form and because bores through them. This has a remarkable rir veracity because of what we know of the longish talline formation of the emerald, as well as great number of presumably Byzantine neck which incorporate just such bored sections of eme crystals. This practice of boring and stringing pre stones as beads was not confined to emeralds. following passage from the *K. al-Dhakhā'ir* (§ does not furnish certain proof of this, but give indication of its likelihood. We are told that whe Mutawakkil was returning from Damascus, in 858, he was met by his mother's servant, with from "al-Sayyida" Ḳabīḥa, the mother of al-Muʿ Their amount was 400,000 *dīnārs*." This enorm treasure included "a string of beads of jewels c unknown value." From the same work (§ 14) hear again of "beads of great jewels" in a caske jewels which had been brought by the Fāṭimid ca al-Muʿizz when he came to Cairo from his prev capital in Tunisia.

Occasionally we are fortunate enough to passages which describe or unconsciously indi not only the precise kind of gem involved, but the arrangement or manner of stringing of these wels. Once more from the *K. al-Dhakhā'ir* (§ 22 learn that "Mu'nisa, the slave girl of al-Ma'mūn lāh, gave to Mutayyam, the slave girl of ʿA Hishām . . . with the knowledge of al-Ma'mūn, a n lace whose central pearl was like an egg of a spar and black beads whose value was 10,000 *dīnārs* this value the only imaginable black beads are b pearls of fine quality—we know that, accor to al-Bīrūnī, on the authority of al-Ḥasan and Ḥusayn of Rayy, court jewellers to Maḥmū Ghazna, Maḥmūd's treasury included black pear see Haschmi, *op. cit.*, 15), and four stones of rubies and four stones of emeralds on its right left, between them the precious beads of gold. continuing necklace had dates (*balaḥ*—here su meant to indicate the shape of the beads) anoi with perfume (*ghāliya*). Mutayyam found the d anointed with perfume (*ghāliya*) elegant and deli ful; her joy could not be increased by the remai jewels." Although we cannot be absolutely cer of the arrangement here, the general picture is q clear; that called up in the imagination by this assage to follow is amazingly like that which one rom the accounts of the likes of Tavernier (see ·ls in *India*, tr. V. Ball, London 1889, ii, 150) as is what one actually sees being worn by Mughal ; in their miniature paintings (see below in on on Mughal India). Another very graphic ge from the early Islamic period is found in ūnī's chapter on pearls (Krenkow, *op. cit.*, 5), in a section discussing the egg-shaped pearl: pearl called al-Yatīma weighed three *mithkāls* it was called al-Yatīma (orphan) because its had gone before a sister [pearl] could be born t]. Likewise, a similar one was called Farīd ue) when its equal could not be found and it necessary to make it the centre of a necklace is called qilāda." Elsewhere in the same work nkow, *op. cit.*, Part II, 33), al-Bīrūnī is arguing st "coral" and for "small pearls" as being the ct understanding of the term *mardjān*, and we n idea of his sense of what is proper as regards combination of stones with pearls. He quotes ssage from Abū Nuwās and then comments: owned with pearls and marjān like a rose be-: red anemones.' So he thinks that the white is adorned in the necklace between two reds, ing the ruby and the coral. Such a necklace d be uncommon and of bad taste. On the ary, the small pearls are put between every pearl and two encompassing rubies filling the between them, holding them apart; then on nt of their polish, the redness of the ruby ns and can be compared with the redness of "

her such accounts about the combination of s, emeralds and pearls of various sizes could ven, but perhaps those cited above are sufficient dicate something of the nature of a type of je-y that seems to have had currency throughout enturies in most of the Islamic world and of h we have nothing but the literary accounts and rial representations, together with some of the s (in such repositories as the Iranian crown s and the Topkapi in Istanbul). What we do left to us in something of its original form, al-gh of less intrinsic value, is of greater historical rtance, for it provides us with a better picture e changes in artistic taste from period to period. regards those few objects datable to the early nic period, they fit very well into the pattern lished for those adornments found in the ings and reliefs discussed at the outset, i.e. exhibit a dependence on Roman, Byzantine or Sāsānid models. However, these objects also a development away from the older objects in s of decorative motifs or principal designs, an nisation of their pre-Islamic models. Perhaps the striking example of this is an amulet case ex-ted at Nīshāpūr which can be dated before A.D., on the basis of its epigraphic decoration 1). Sāsānid as well as Byzantine prototypes for the general shape (M. Negro Ponti, *Jewelry small objects from Tell Mahuz* (*North Mesopo-a*), in *Mesopotamia*, v-vi [1970-1], Fig. 85, No. 36, W. and E. Rudolph, *Ancient jewelry from the tion of Burton Y. Berry*, Bloomington, Indiana Fig. 153), but its elaborate yet beautiful in-tion of form and decoration are peculiarly nic, as is its nielloed Kūfic inscription.

so datable to the same period on epigraphic nds are two belt fittings excavated at Nīshāpūr, f which is shown in Fig. 2. Unlike the smooth-l and undecorated fittings on the depiction of the horseman in the Nīshāpūr wall painting discussed earlier, these two sculpted and decortéd objects may have been part of a set like that in Fig. 3. The latter should be dated to the 3rd/9th century on the basis of its close comparison with the fittings depicted in a painting from Sāmarrā᾽ (E. Herzfeld, *op. cit.*, Pl. LXV, right).

Some of the finger rings from Nīshāpūr also seem to be datable to this period. The silver as well as the gold ring pictured in Fig. 4a and b both show a dependance on Roman models (E. H. Marshall, *Catalogue of the finger rings, Greek, Etruscan and Roman, in the Departments of Antiquities*, British Museum London 1907, Pl. XV, 526, Pl. XIII, 469), and as will be discussed later, the silver ring can be seen as a precursor of a type of Saldjūk Persian ring.

2. Early mediaeval jewelry (5th-7th/11th-13th centuries)

Once we move into the early mediaeval period, not only do we have many more extant jewelry examples than we did for the early Islamic period, but we are also able to establish firmer dates for them. The reasons for the survival of these relatively large groups of objects, as well as the explanations of the lines of development which brought the art to this brilliant flowering during the early mediaeval period. continue to elude us. The jump from the few early objects just discussed to the objects we are about to present is often a very large one indeed.

Pivotal pieces for the study of early mediaeval jewelry in greater Iran are a pair of bracelets, which are illustrated in Fig. 5a-b. Each of the four hemispheres flanking the clasp of each bracelet bears a flat disk of thin gold at its back, which was decorated by pouncing it over a coin, in this case a coin bearing the name of the ʿAbbāsid caliph al-Ḳādir billāh (381-422/991-1031). The late Dr. George Miles was of the opinion that the style of the coins used was that of those minted in 390/1000, 397/1007 and 419/1028, during the rule of Maḥmūd of Ghazna, and that they were probably struck in the mint of Nīshāpūr. As the gold discs were most probably embossed over relatively new coins, a dating to the first half of the 5th/11th century seems quite secure.

There are a large number of extant bracelets in both gold and silver which are analogous to these, although none are as fine or as elaborate. The main characteristics of this group of bracelets are the four hemispheres flanking the clasp, the tapering of the shank toward the clasp and the twisted effect of the former; or alternatively, a non-tapered shank is subdivided into ball-shaped sections.

Pre-Islamic jewelry has again served as a model for these bracelets, which show a continued conservatism and traditionalism in the medium. Examples of coins and imitation coins on jewelry are quite numerous in the Byzantine period; and the twisted effect of the shank must ultimately derive from Greek bracelets with similar shanks (Metropolitan Museum of Art No. 45. 11.10—see Hoffman and Davidson, *op. cit.*, Fig. 61b). Those with shanks subdivided into ball-shaped sections must have had as their ultimate models Roman rings and bracelets as well (*Allen*, Fig. 107).

The hollow gold and silver rings from Nīshāpūr with stone settings which we saw earlier seem to have given rise to the type of ring seen in Fig. 6. Its epigraphic and vegetal decoration in niello place it very neatly in the early mediaeval period, more particularly in the 6th/12th or 7th/13th centuries; and furthermore, the type of setting with its heavy claws is very typical for Persian jewelry of this period. The bracelet illustrated in Fig. 7a-b, whose mate is in the Boston Museum of Fine Arts, shares many of the features seen in the last object discussed. Four of its elements take the form of truncated pyramids (as does the bezel of the ring), and bear the heavy claws to hold the now-missing stones. It also prominently features epigraphic decoration in niello.

The granulated treatment of the border on the obverse of the pendant in Fig. 8a-b, the settings with heavy claws and the niello-like decoration, relate this object to the bracelet just discussed. A feature we have not met with before, however, is that found on the reverse—a double twisted wire decoration laid on the gold sheet. This method of decorating a plain gold surface was very popular in Iran during the period in question and can be seen on a pair of earrings, one of which is shown in Fig. 9, which bear close comparison with a pair found in Russian excavations (in the region between the Sea of Azov and Moscow) whose finds can be dated between the 1170s and 1240 (G. F. Korzukhina, *Russkie kladî IX-XIIIvv*, Moscow 1954, pl. LX). The open-work beads decorating the upper part of these earrings were also an important feature of Iranian jewelry at this time. Another pair of earrings, seen in Fig. 10, are composed of three such beads. There are many variations of such three-bead earrings from 6th/12th and 7th/13th century Iran, and a large number of similar ones were found in the Russian excavations already mentioned (for example, Korzukhina, *op. cit.*, pls. XLV, XLVIII, XXXI, XXXIII, etc.).

Fig. 11a-b illustrates a type of ring which seems not to have been in vogue in the Islamic world before the second half of the 6th/12th century. However, once introduced, it enjoyed great popularity and variety. The most essential features of this ring type are a cast shank, often with anthropomorphic terminals, and polygonal bezels. The prototypes, again, are to be found in Greek as well as Roman rings (Marshall, *op. cit.*, fig. 61, and pl. XVI, 552). The ring chosen to illustrate the type is a particularly fine example, with four of the six corners of the bezel decorated with human heads, the crown itself consisting of a repeating geometric pattern executed in openwork filigree and the shank bearing harpies and terminating in double-bodied harpies. Although not as elaborate as our example, many rings of this type were found in the Russian excavations mentioned above whose finds can be dated between the 1170s and 1240 (Korzukhina, pls. XXXVII, 3, XXXVIII, 3, XLV, 4, etc.). The style of the animals as well as the technique employed on the belt fittings in Fig. 12 relate this object very closely to the above ring.

Because the geometrical design and its mode of execution on the two hair ornaments in Fig. 13 are identical to that on the ring in Fig. 11a-b, these objects must be dated to the same time, if not to the same workshop. Between the bronze core and the gold exterior of these ornaments there was a textile which was probably brightly coloured, and this must have heightened the impact of these striking pieces. Hair ornaments had a long pre-Islamic history, and tubular ones are still current in the Middle East today.

The earrings featuring polyhedral beads in Fig. 14 must also be similarly dated, since two hair ornaments with closely related beads were found in the Russian excavations mentioned above (Korzukhina, pl. LIX). Their sophisticated and ingenious transformation of the spherical bead into a pentagonal dodecahedron is quite in keeping with the e[...] ordinary amount of sophistication at the time i[...] usage of geometric solids as the forms of b[...] weights, etc., especially notable in the finds fro[...] Metropolian Museum's excavations at Nīshāp[...]

A cache of jewelry and 82 gold coins foun[...] Tunisia about 50 years ago allows us to est[...] relatively firm dates for certain types of je[...] executed in the Fāṭimid realms (G. Marçais a[...] Poinssot, *Objets kairouanais, notes et documents,* Tunis 1952, 467-93, and Marilyn Jenkins, *Fā[...] jewelry, its sub-types and influences*, in *Kuns[...] Orients*, in press); and this in turn allows us to[...] certain closely related objects from the F[...] Crescent.

Marçais and Poinssot have shown that the je[...] in this cache was made before the end of the 436/1045, and Jenkins has demonstrated th[...] was very likely produced in Egypt. She has delineated a number of characteristic featur[...] this jewelry, thus permitting a considerable b[...] ening of the group. On the basis of these wor[...] seems likely that the gold objects about to be[...] cussed, as well as many others closely relate[...] them, were all produced in a relatively short p[...] of time before 436/1045.

Each sub-type enumerated below will be i[...] duced by one or more Fāṭimid objects datab[...] means of the Tunisian cache. These groupings out of Marc Rosenberg's theory of "the batt[...] granulation and filigree", in which he sugges[...] historical progression proceeding from those [...] on which granulation, consisting of grains of than one size—most often set on paired wires-[...] the dominant decorative device, to those on [...] grains are also placed on paired wires but on [...] the granulation and filigree could be said to be [...] equal footing. The third sub-type incorporates a small amount of granulation; and the final [...] shows the complete displacement of granulatio[...] filigree (see Rosenberg, *Geschichte der Goldschm[...] kunst auf technischer Grundlage, Granulation* Frankfurt 1918, 96-104). The closely simi[...] among the objects comprising the various sub-g[...] makes it highly likely that the "battle" was a [...] one, at least in the case of Fāṭimid Egypt.

Examples of the finest and most decorat[...] complex type of Fāṭimid gold work are the open[...] biconical and spherical beads in Fig. 15 exhib[...] filigree work and granulation with grains of more one size. Another example of this particular [...] of Fāṭimid jewelry is a gold bracelet with a ta[...] tubular shank and heart-shaped terminals in th[...] chaeological Museum, Istanbul (G. Breitling *et Das Buch vom Gold*, Lucerne and Frankfurt 1975[...] No. 6). The area where the shank meets the term[...] bears three large grains, or more properly, shot. bracelet bears close comparison with one in th[...] mascus Museum, also with heart-shaped terminal[...] with a twisted-wire shank (*Catalogue du Musée[...] tional de Damas*, Damascus 1969, Fig. 119, r[...] The latter may in turn be compared with se[...] excavated in Russia in finds datable to the 5th[...] and turn of the 6th/12th centuries (Korzukhin[...] *cit.*, pl. XIV). All this confirms that this gro[...] bracelets with tubular or twisted-wire shanks heart-shaped terminals, whether made in Egy[...] somewhere in the Fertile Crescent (as is pro[...] the case with the bracelet in the Damascus Mus[...] were contemporary with the beads illustrate[...] Fig. 15 (which are datable by means of the Tu[...] cache) and consequently must date before 436/[...]

nother bracelet which must be placed in this t and decoratively most complex phase is that in Fig. 16 a-b, which has a mate in the Da-us Museum. The twisted effect of its tapered k and the four hemispheres flanking its clasp, ell as the treatment of the area where the shank s the clasp, relate it very closely to the Persian elet illustrated in Fig. 5a-b, which is probably ble to the early 5th/11th century. However, the of bosses on the clasp, the style of wirework he back of the clasp and the treatment of the k relate the Freer bracelet more closely to con-orary objects made in Egypt. We therefore at-te this bracelet to a workshop in the Fertile cent, most probably in Syria, where both Egyp-and Persian influences would very likely be found. so contemporary and made either in Egypt or Fertile Crescent are a group of six bracelets twisted-wire shanks whose clasps bear granules o triangular arrangements, flanked on two sides roups of three contiguous shot, on either side set stone (*Catalogue du Musée National de Damas*, 119, second from right; *Collection Hélène Sta-s*, iv, *Bijoux et petits objets*, Pl. XI, and p. 73, 11 and 12; and the European art market). manner of usage of the grains on the clasps of bracelets is closely related to that on the np-shaped" beads on the necklace in Fig. 15.
e next Fāṭimid sub-type is illustrated in 17a-b. Unlike the beads discussed above, this ant bears grains of only one size, and the fili-and granulation can be said to be equally im-ant.
ose objects exhibiting filigree with only a very e use of granulation, such as the bracelet in 18 with repousséed shank, are examples of the sub-type. Bracelets with repousséed shanks ng geometric designs, sometimes filled with an figures, were a later development of such elets (Metropolitan Museum of Art No. 58.37, A. de Ridder, *Collection de Clercq catalogue*, vii/1, II, No. 1279).
nother example of this phase is the pair of ngs in Fig. 19. However, the use of undecorated w hemispheres as well as the tapering of the s to a point take them out of the Egyptian milieu as was the case with the bracelet in Fig. 16 a-b several other objects mentioned above, perhaps venance in the Fertile Crescent should be sug-d for them (cf. Zakiyya ʿUmar al-ʿAlī, *Islamic ry acquired by the Iraq Museum* [in Arabic], in r, xxx, Pl. 8; Paris, Grand Palais, *L'Islam dans ollections nationales*, Paris 1977, No. 363; and opolitan Museum of Art, No. 95.16.2-3). Closer Egyptian prototypes than the above, but incor-ing Persian elements as well, is another earring n also must have been made in the Fertile Cres-(Hayward Gallery, *The arts of Islam*, London No. 239).
we have said, the final phase in Fāṭimid jewelry presented by those objects with no granulation ll, their decoration being executed solely in ee or in filigree combined with a technique than granulation, such as cloisoné enamelling. examples can be seen in Figs. 20 and 21. The may be compared with the biconical bead g. 15 (see also L. A. Mayer Memorial Institute slamic Art, Jerusalem, No. J75, the wirework of n is closely related to that on the back of the of the bracelet in Fig. 16a-b), but here three ical beads are combined to form a necklace spa-type of combination also seen in the material from Ur (C. L. Wooley, *Ur excavations*, ii. *The Royal Cemetery*, Oxford 1934, pl. 146a), as well as from Cyprus of the first half of the first millenium B.C. (Metropolitan Museum of Art, No. 74.51.3297). Another type of tripartite spacer can be seen on the necklace in Fig. 15.

In the medium of silver, the earring shown in Fig. 22 has a shape and the box-like construction which we have seen often in the jewelry from the Fertile Crescent. These features, in addition to the style of its nielloed vegetal and epigraphic decoration, place it in the early part of the period under discussion.

Towards the end of what we have called the early mediaeval period, one of the Islamic lands west of Iran (probably Syria) produced the silver and gilt bronze belt illustrated in Fig. 23, other elements of which are in the Benaki Museum, Athens. According to Mr. Benaki's records (see Berta Segall, *Museum Benaki, Katalog der Goldschmiede-Arbeiten*, Athens 1938 No. 323, and p. 190) the inscription on the buckle is in the name of al-Malik al-Ṣāliḥ ʿImād al-Dīn Ismāʿīl, who was twice the Ayyūbid ruler of Damascus and who was killed in battle at Cairo in 648/1250 (mistakenly said in Segall to have taken place in 1266). Although there was a Mamlūk sultan of the same name who ruled in the 8th/14th century (743-6/1342-5), the titular formulae which one can read on the buckle do seem closer to those of the Ayyubid ruler than of the Mamlūk one.

3. Late mediaeval jewelry (8th-11th/14-17th centuries)

For reasons still largely unclear to us, when attempting to deal with the jewelry art of the late mediaeval period, we are faced with a situation similar to that in the early Islamic period. That is, there are very few extant pieces from any part of the Muslim world datable to this period, and therefore we are again forced to turn to pictorial representations in addition to literary descriptions for our main picture of the jewelry of this important four-hundred-year period.

It is probable that the representations of jewelry in Persian miniatures do not give us a full and adequate picture of the jewelry in vogue at the time, even for the upper classes. This is partly due to the very limitations of the Persian miniature art itself in terms of what it could show; and one gets the feeling that convention played some part in what jewelry the painter chose to decorate his figures, just as painters' conventions had a part in the architectural forms and decoration represented in these miniatures. However, it does seem on the other hand that the representations do reflect in a general way the types and, as will be seen, the changing styles of jewelry worn. With Mughal miniatures, the representations are more detailed, and give a feeling of being less fanciful, more indicative of a specific time, place and object.

The necklace in Fig. 24a-b is one of two extant pieces of 8th/14th century gold jewelry known to the present authors (the other is a head ornament in the Staatliche Museen, Berlin -Dahlem, No. 565, which is very closely related to the gilded silver head ornament found in a 14th century tomb at Novorossiisk, for which see R. Zahn, *Sammlungen der Galerie Bachstitz*, ii Berlin 1921, pl. 123). The shapes used in the wire and stone work on the obverse of the necklace's two principal elements, as well as the contours of these elements themselves, relate it closely to the crown of Anūshirwān in a page from the Demotte Shāh-nāma (Metropolitan Museum of Art No. 52.20.2, see I. Stchoukine, *La peinture iranienne sous les derniers ʿAbbasides et les Il-Khans*, Bruges 1936, ms. no. XV, no. 24), and the style of the chased design as well as the motifs on the reverse of these elements clearly point to the same period. In addition, the overall Chinese feeling is in line with what we might expect at this time.

To come back to the miniature mentioned above, we might point out that both of the principal figures wear simple gold hoop earrings and that this fashion can be seen in other representations of the period. For example, in a miniature probably painted in ʿIrāḳ in *ca.* 771-81/1370-80 (R. Ettinghausen, *Arab painting*, New York 1962, 178) we see very similar earrings worn by the Archangel Isrāfīl.

We may take this occasion to say that the wearing of earrings by men is a custom with a very long history in the Near East, being well-attested in for example, Assyrian, Achaemenian and Sāsānid reliefs. We have already referred in section 1 above to a man wearing earrings in a wall painting from Sāmarrāʾ, and we have literary evidence that earrings were worn by pre-Islamic Arabs: al-Bīrūnī in his chapter on pearls (Krenkow, *op. cit.*, I, 407) quotes an extract from al-Aswad b. Yaʿfur [*q.v.*] which contains the phrase "... runs a man with two pearls [in the lobes of his ears] ...". This custom continued in the Islamic world, although not universally, until the beginning of the modern period, as attested by, for example, paintings of the Mongol, Tīmūrid, Ṣafawid and Mughal schools.

A belt of gilded silver consisting of 62 elements was found in the 14th century tomb at Novorossiisk mentioned above (R. Zahn, *op. cit.*, pls. 121, 122). The overall style of the belt, as well as the decoration on the triangular and rectangular pieces, relate it to two earlier belts illustrated in Figs. 12 and 23.

Turning to the more western part of the Muslim world, several gold bracelets can be quite securely placed in 8th/14th century Mamlūk Egypt or Syria. Continuing the bracelet tradition in this part of the world as discussed above, these have hollow shanks—plain or giving a twisted effect—but they now terminate in animal heads. The clasp is round and tabular, and the one in the Benaki Museum, Athens, is decorated with an Arabic inscription (B. Segall, *op. cit.*, No. 319, and Cairo, *Islamic art in Egypt 969-1517*, April 1969, No. 20).

At the turn of the 8th/14th and 9th/15th century in Iran we not only see the continued use of the type of belt already discussed (M.S. Ipsiroğlu, *Painting and culture of the Mongols*, New York n.d., fig. 47) but we also begin to see the use of a new belt type consisting of a large gold roundel or roundels on a cloth or leather strap, a type which appears soon to have superseded the older style and which was to remain in vogue in Iran for centuries to come (Metropolitan Museum of Art, No. 57.51.20, *MMA Bulletin*, N.S., xvi [1957], 56, and No. 33. 113, *MMA Bulletin*, xxix [April 1934], 59-60, fig. 2).

One of these latter miniatures (57.51.20) also shows a new fashion in the decoration of the female visage: strings of beads framing the face, being secured by the headcloth at the top of the head and passing under the chin. As we shall see, this type of ornament was still in vogue in Iran in the Ḳādjār period. This popular Tīmūrid fashion is also in evidence in two other miniatures, one from *ca.* 829/1426 and the other from between 1470 and 1480, which also show us examples of Tīmūrid earrings. These appear to be either plain gold hoops, hoops with a single pendant tear-drop pearl (seen earl[ier in] paintings from Sāmarrāʾ) or gold hoops with pendant paired pearls (Metropolitan Museu[m of] Art, No. 13.228.13, fol. 17b; see New York, House Gallery, *Muslim miniature paintings fro[m] XII to XIX century*, 1962, 58, no. 41, and No. 5 24; *MMA Bulletin*, N.S., xvi [April 1958], 232)

As regards the fashion in bracelets during Tīmūrid period, a miniature from a *Haft pa[ykar]* manuscript shows bathing women wearing si[ngle] strings of beads at their wrists (Metropolitan Mu[seum] of Art, No. 13.228.13, fol. 47a, *MMA Bulletin*, xxv [May 1967], 325, fig. 16). One of a pair of silver bracelets with dragon-headed terminals bearing on the top an Arabic inscription can be in Fig. 25. At least two other examples of this are extant, and it may represent a simpler and version of the Mamlūk bracelets discussed a with animal heads flanking their clasps.

The cast gold and jade seal ring illustrate Fig. 26 may have developed out of the type of illustrated in Fig. 11a-b, as they have several portant features in common: the technique of cas followed by a significant amount of chasing; sh which have anthropomorphic terminals and whic decorated with designs on two levels; and a lo adorning the centre of the shank (for the univ importance and use of the seal ring throughou lamic history, see KHĀTAM and MUHR).

The necklace seen on the woman in the det a miniature from a manuscript dated 853/14 in Fig. 27 points both backward and forward in The central element is related to one of those o necklace in Fig. 24a-b, whereas the overall com rion is identical to what we shall see is the popular type of Ṣafawid necklace represented ir niatures, although the rosettes here are two-di sional elements instead of spherical beads as ir case of the Ṣafawid necklace.

Naṣrid Spain is better represented by ex jewelry than other areas during this period. The r lace illustrated in Fig. 28 consists of five per elements and five beads. The pendant elements an indebtedness to Fāṭimid jewelry in their box construction, the use of gold loops on their cir ference for stringing pearls or semi-precious st and their combination of gold and cloisonné en as well as of filigree and granulation. However, are not as laboriously executed as the best Fāṭ pieces, and the work has been further decrease simply pouncing a gold sheet over the decorated side of the pendant to produce the decoration o back, a peculiarity of Naṣrid jewelry.

As indicated earlier, the vogue for beads fra the face continued in the Ṣafawid period bu addition, two other types of head ornament—w sources of inspiration were probably earlier crow were very popular during this period. Exam are to be seen in Figs. 29 and 30, both of w appear to be of gold set with stones.

The necklace shown in Fig. 27 was the imme precursor of that worn by the woman in Fig The elements and their arrangement are iden except that the flat rosettes set with a single s in the 853/1450-51 miniature have, seventy-five later, become what appear to be granulated sp set with multiple stones. The central element also changed from an apparently carved or pa piece to a gold pendant set with stones. Another of necklace which we see represented in Ṣaf paintings, worn as a choker or close to the th consisted of a central triangular, sometimes bej

2

4a

4b

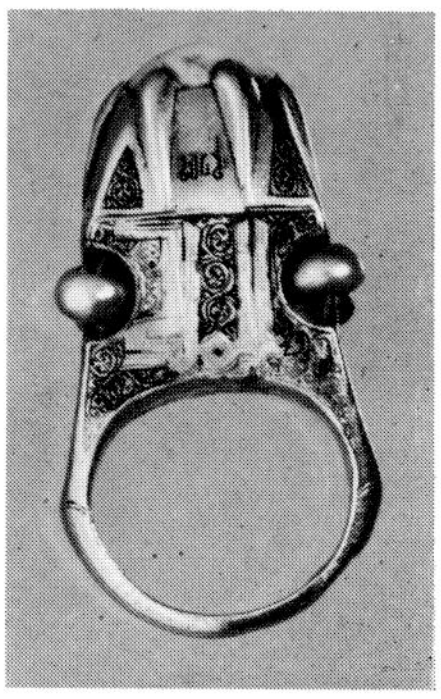

6

ilver amulet case worked in repoussé with cast elements and niello inlay. From the excavations of the opolitan Museum of Art at Nīshāpūr, Rogers Fund, 1939. Probably Nīshāpūr, probably 4th/10th century. Tehran, Mūzeh-i Īrān-i Bāstān.

Bronze belt fitting, cast, from the excavations of the Metropolitan Museum of Art at Nīshāpūr, Rogers l, 1939. Probably Nīshāpūr, probably 4th/10th century. The Metropolitan Museum of Art, No. 40.170.214, Rogers Fund 1939.

Bronze belt fittings, cast. Probably ʿIrāḳ or Iran, 3rd/9th century. Collection of Mr. and Mrs. Everett ı, St. Thomas, V.I.* (Illustrations marked with an asterisk are photographs by courtesy of Patti Cadby Birch.)

(a) Silver ring, hollow, fabricated from sheet. From the excavations of the Metropolitan Museum of t Nīshāpūr, Rogers Fund, 1939. Probably Nīshāpūr, probably 4th/10th century. Tehran, Mūzeh-i Īrān-i Bāstān.

old ring, hollow, fabricated from sheet. From the excavations of the Metropolitan Museum of Art at āpūr, Rogers Fund, 1939. Probably Nīshāpūr, probably 4th/10th century. The Metropolitan Museum of Art, No. 40.170.156.

old ring, decorated with niello and set with turquoise and pearls. Iran, 6th-7th/12th-13th centuries. Gallery of Art, No. 57.3. Courtesy of the Smithsonian Institution, Freer Gallery of Art, Washington, D.C.*

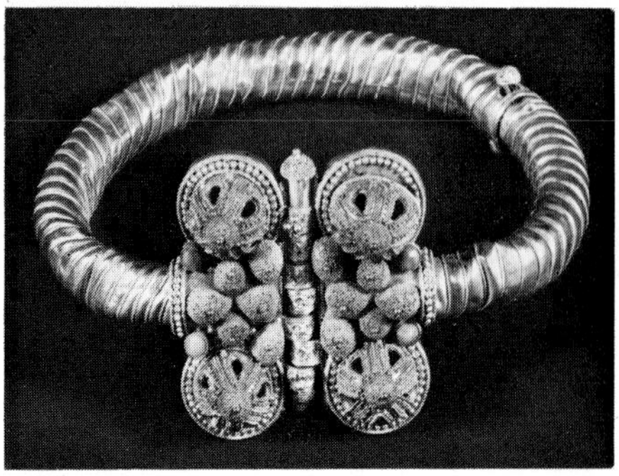

5a

5b

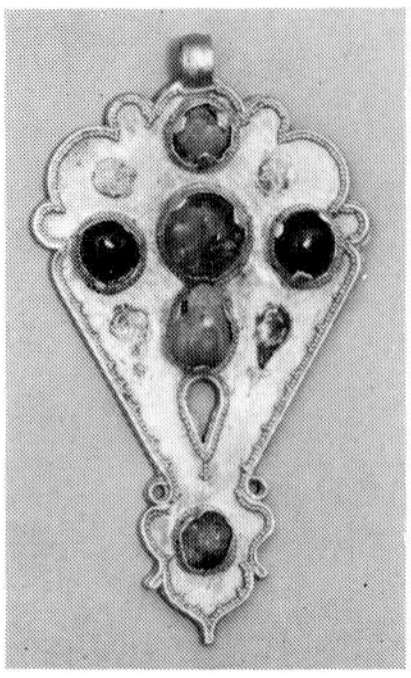

8a

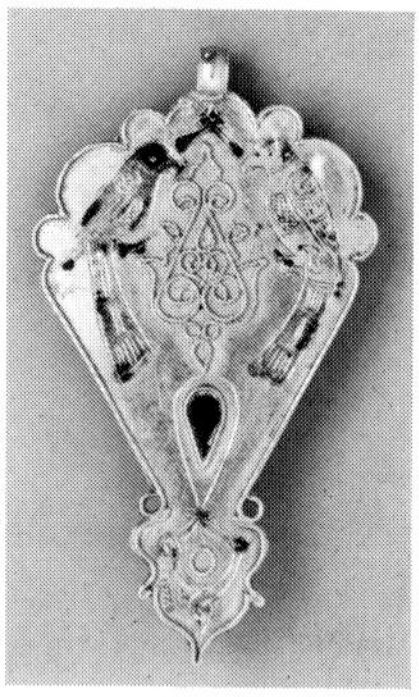

8b

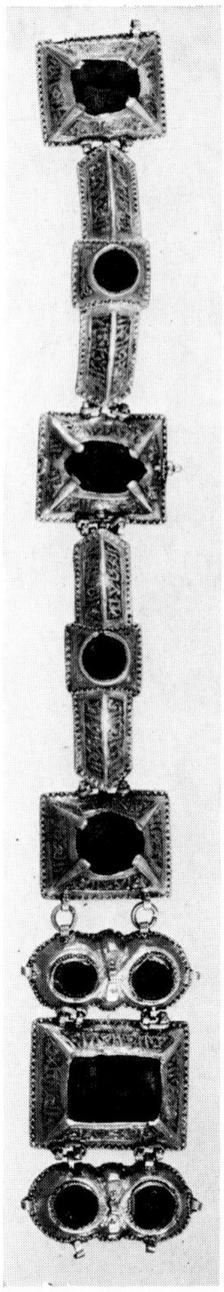

7a

7b

9

5a-b. Pair of gold bracelets, fabricated from sheet with applied twisted and granulation. Eastern Iran, probably early 5th/11th century. (a) Gallery of Art, No. 58.6. Courtesy of the Smithsonian Institution, Freer Ga of Art, Washington D.C.
(b) Metropolitan Museum of Art, No. 57.88, Harris Brisbane Dick Fund, (detail of underside of clasp).

7a-b. Gold bracelet, hollow, fabricated from sheet, decorated with niello granulation. Iran, 6th-7th/12th-13th centuries. Freer Gallery of Art, No. 5 Courtesy of the Smithsonian Institution, Freer Gallery of Art, Washington, I

8a-b. Gold pendant, fabricated from sheet, decorated with engraving, tw wire and granulation, set with garnets, turquoise and other precious st Iran, 6th-7th/12th-13th centuries. The Metropolitan Museum of Art, No. 19 Purchase, Richard Perkins Gift, 1977.

9. Gold earring, one of a pair, fabricated from sheet, decorated with tw wire and granulation and incorporating loop-in-loop chains. Iran, 6th 12th-13th centuries. Staatliche Museen, Preussischer Kulturbesitz, Museum Islamische Kunst, Takustrasse 40, 1 Berlin 33-Dahlem, No. J 57/71.

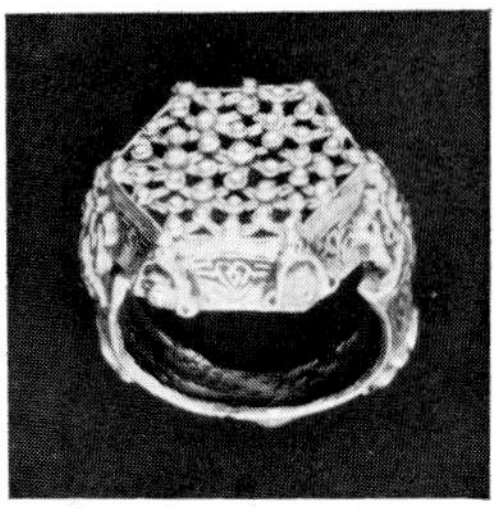

11a

11b

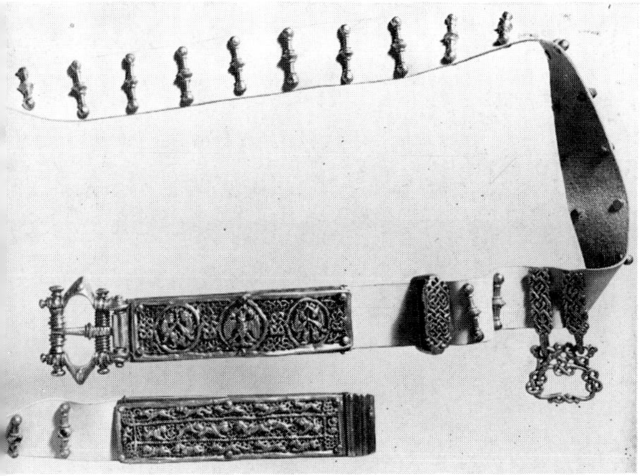

13

Pair of gold earrings, fabricated entirely from wire and granules. Iran, 6th-7th/12th-13th centuries. The Metropolitan Museum of Art, No. 52.4.5-6, Rogers Fund, 1952.

-b. Gold ring, cast, fabricated and engraved. Iran, 6th-7th/12th-13th centuries. The Metropolitan Museum of Art, No. 1976.405, Gift of Mr. and Mrs. Everett Birch, 1976.

Set of silver-gilt belt fittings, cast and chased. Iran or Anatolia, 6th-7th/12th-13th centuries. Reproduced by courtesy of the Trustees of the British Museum, No. 1959 7-22 1-5.*

Pair of gold hair ornaments with bronze core, decorated with twisted wire and granulation and (formerly) ›ured cloth. Iran, 6th-7th/12th-13th centuries. The Metropolitan Museum of Art, No. 52.32.9,10, Rogers Fund, 1952.

14. Pair of gold earrings, fabricated from sheet, decorated with twisted wire and granulation. Iran, 6th-7th/12th-13th centuries. The Metropolitan Museum of Art, No. 1979.7.3ab, Purchase Richard S. Perkins Gift, Rogers Fund, Louis E. and Therea S. Seley Purchase Fund for Islamic Art, Norbert Schimmel, Jack A. Josephson, and Edward Ablat Gifts.

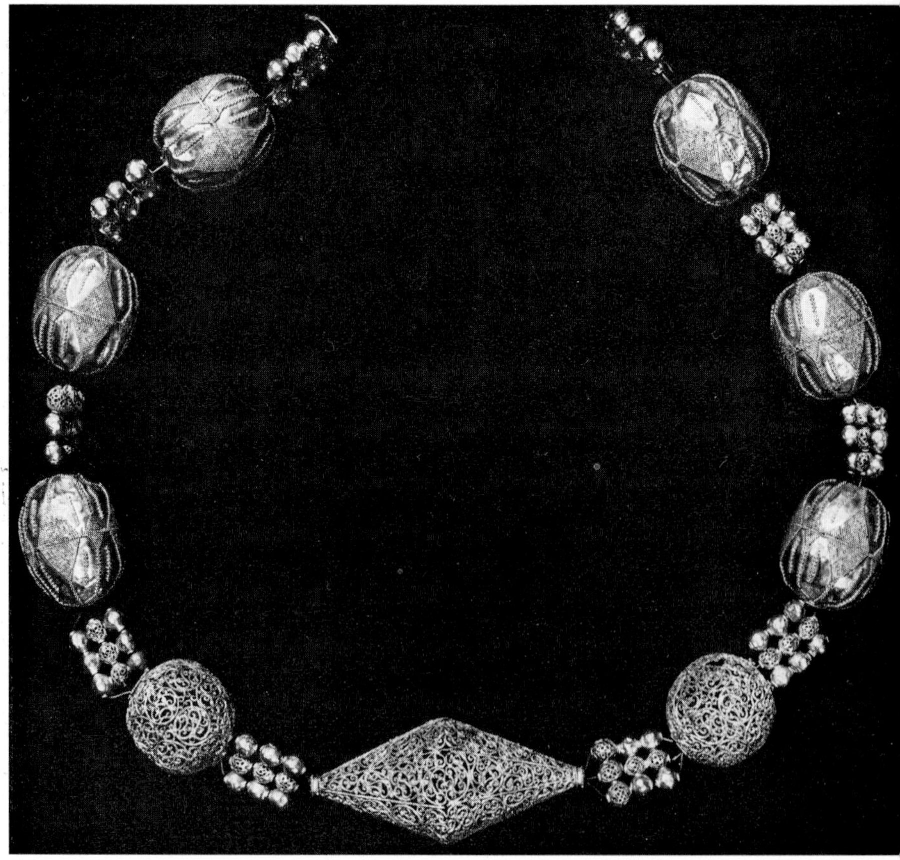

15. Group of gold beads, fabricated from sheet, and/or twisted wire decorated with granulation. Egypt, 5th/11th century. Israel Museum, Jerusalem.

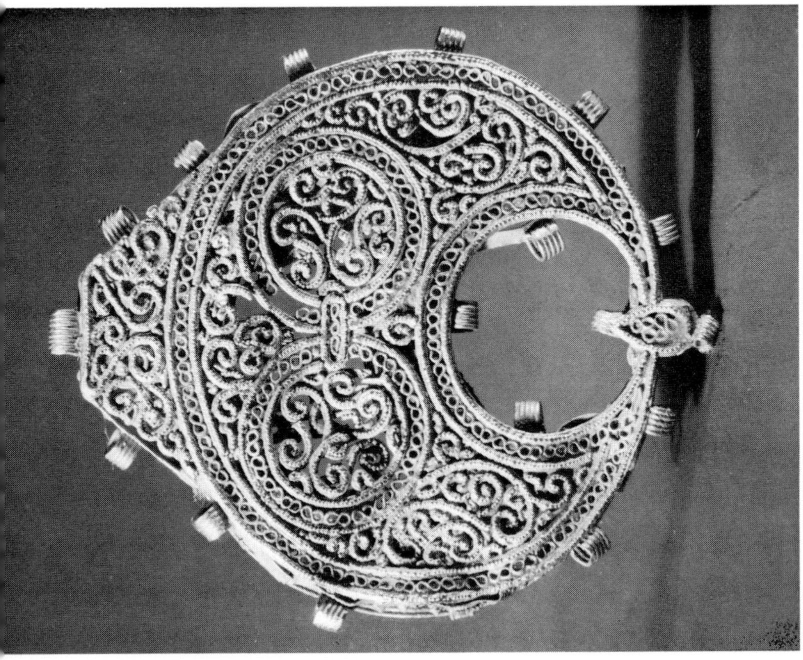

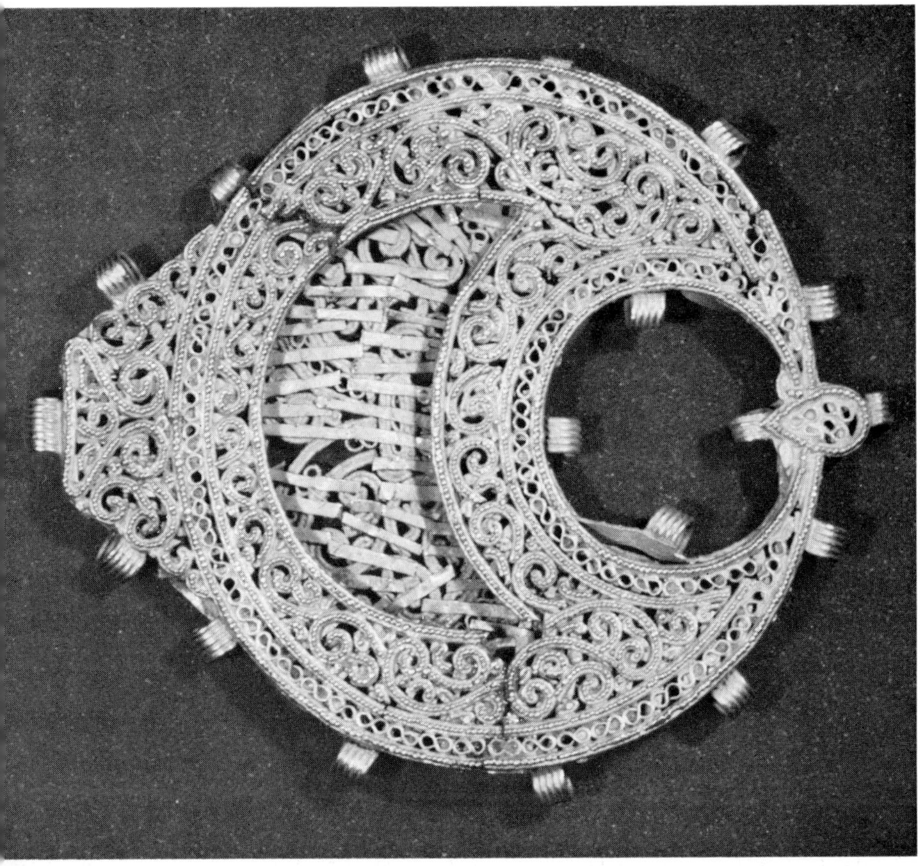

17a-b. Gold pendant, constructed of twisted wire on flat strips of gold, decorated with granulation and (formerly) cloisonné enamel and pearls and/or semi-precious stones. Egypt, 5th/11th century. The Metropolitan Museum of Art, No. 1974.22, Purchase, The Friends of the Islamic Department Fund, 1974.

16a

16b

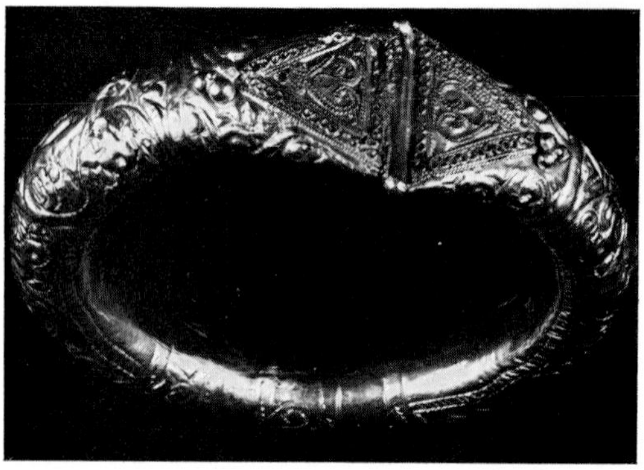

18

19

20

16a-b. Gold bracelet, fabricated from sheet and twisted wire, decorated in repoussé and granulation. Probably Syria, 5th/11th century. Freer Gallery of Art, No. 48.25. Courtesy of the Smithsonian Institution, Freer Gallery of Art, Washington, D.C.*

18. Gold bracelet, fabricated from sheet and decorated with twisted wire, repoussé and shot. Egypt, 5th/11th century. L. A. Mayer Memorial Institute for Islamic Art, Jerusalem.

19. Pair of gold earrings, fabricated of wire and decorated with shot and hollow hemispheres. Probably S or ʿIrāḳ, 5th/11th century. The Metropolitan Museum of Art, No. 39.157.1,2, Rogers Fund, 1939.

20. Gold pendant, fabricated from wire and strips of sheet, set with cloisonné enamel and unidentified g stone. Egypt, 5th/11th century. The Metropolitan Museum of Art, No. 30.95.37, The Theodore M. D Collection, Bequest of Theodore M. Davis, 1915.

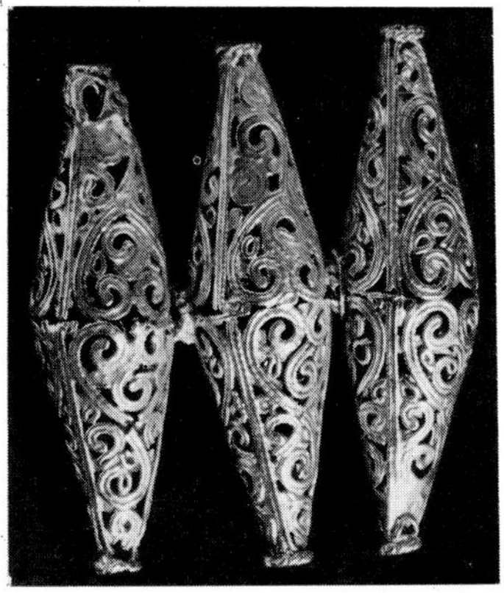

21

22

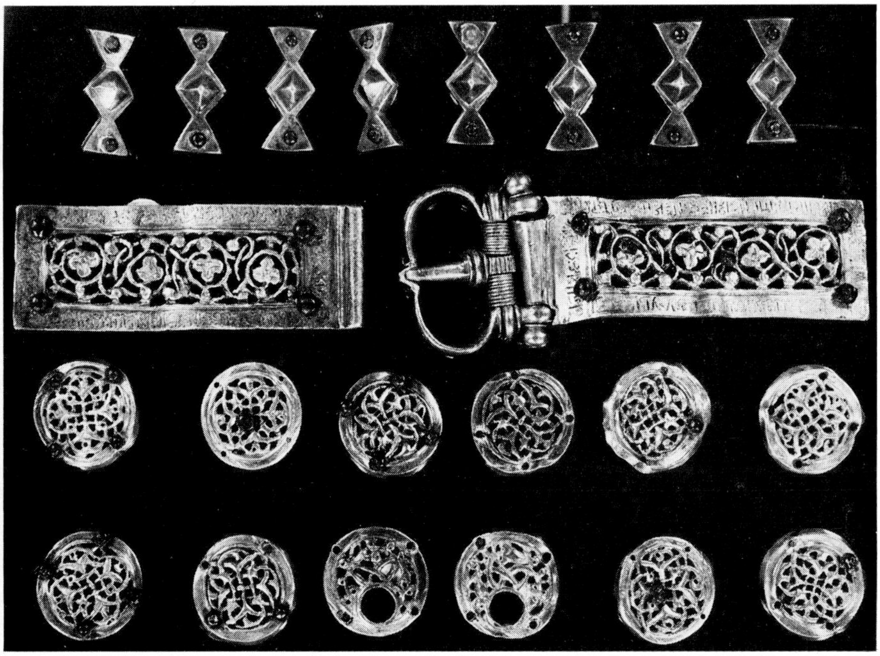

23

21. Gold "spacer" bead, constructed of wire. Egypt, 5th/11th century. Israel Museum.

22. Silver earring, fabricated and decorated with niello. Syria or Egypt, probably 5th/11th century. Israel Museum.

23. Set of silver and gilt bronze belt fittings. Cast, fabricated and *ajouré*. Probably Syria, 7th/13th century. L. A. Mayer Memorial Institute for Islamic Art.

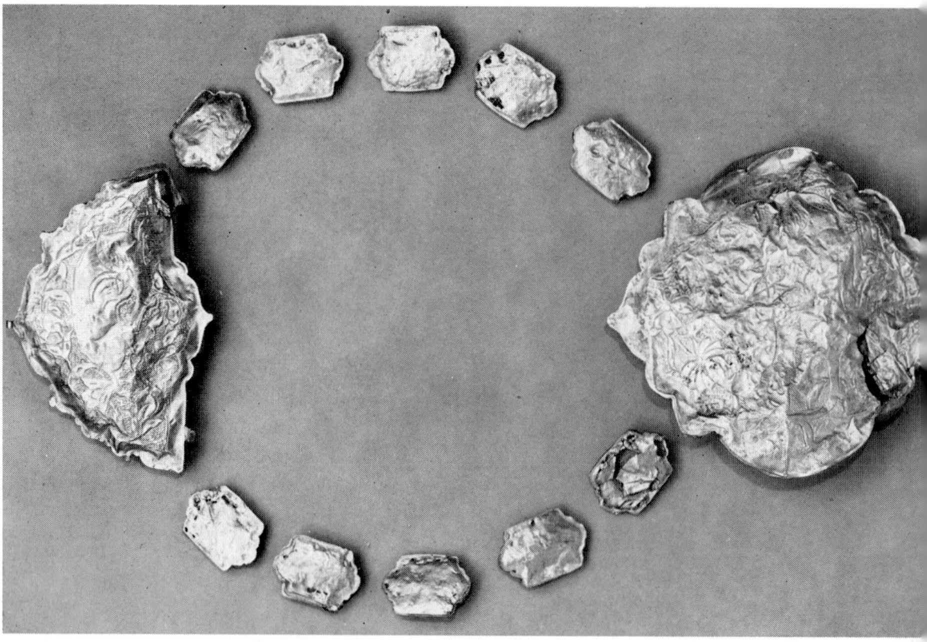

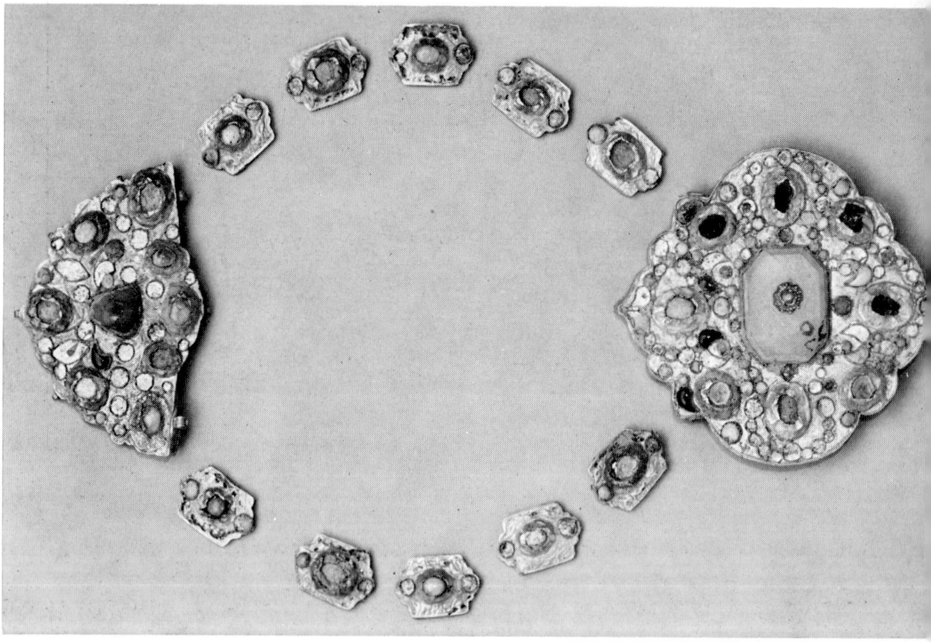

24a-b. Gold necklace, fabricated from sheet, embossed and set with turquoise, glass and unidentified stones. Iran, 8th/14th century

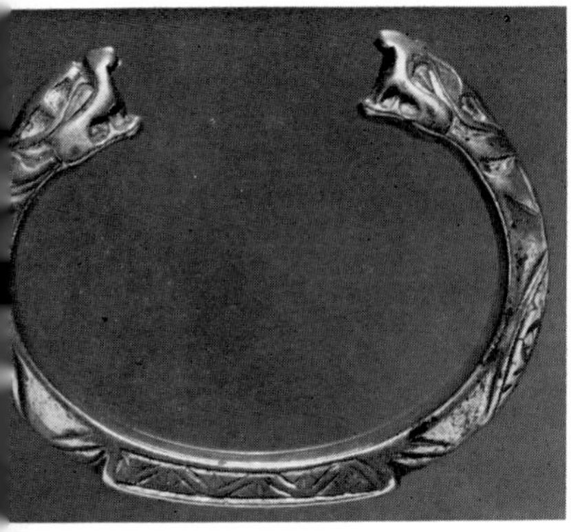

26

29

27

Silver bracelet, cast and chased. Iran or Transoxiana, probably 9th/15th century. The Metropolitan Museum of Art, No. 64.133.3, Fletcher Fund, 1964.

Gold ring, cast and chased, set with jade sealstone. Iran or Transoxiana, probably 9th/15th century. The Metropolitan Museum of Art, No. 12.224.6, Rogers Fund, 1912.

Detail from a miniature from a manuscript of the *Khāwar-nāma*, 1450-51. The Metropolitan Museum of Art, No. 55.125.2, Rogers Fund, 1955.

Detail from "Bahrām Gūr in the Red Palace", page from the *Khamsa* of Niẓāmī, 931/1524-5. The Metropolitan Museum of Art, No. 13.228.7, fol. 220a, Gift of Alexander Smith Cochran, 1913.

28. Elements from a gold necklace, fabricated from sheet and wire, decorated with granulation and cloisc enamel. Spain, probably 9th/15th century. The Metropolitan Museum of Art, No. 17.190.161, Gift of J. Pier Morgan, 1917.

30

31

32

Detail from "Bahrām Gūr in the Yellow Palace", page from the *Khamsa* of Niẓāmī, 931/1524-5. The Metropolitan Museum of Art, No. 13.228.7, fol. 213a, Gift of Alexander Smith Cochran, 1913.

31. Detail from arm of statue, Čihil Sutūn, Iṣfahān, Ṣafawid period.

Detail from "An old woman complains to Sulṭān Sandjar", page from the *Khamsa* of Niẓāmī, 931/1524-5. The Metropolitan Museum of Art, No. 13.228.7, fol. 17a, Gift of Alexander Smith Cochran, 1913.

PLATE XL DJAWHAR

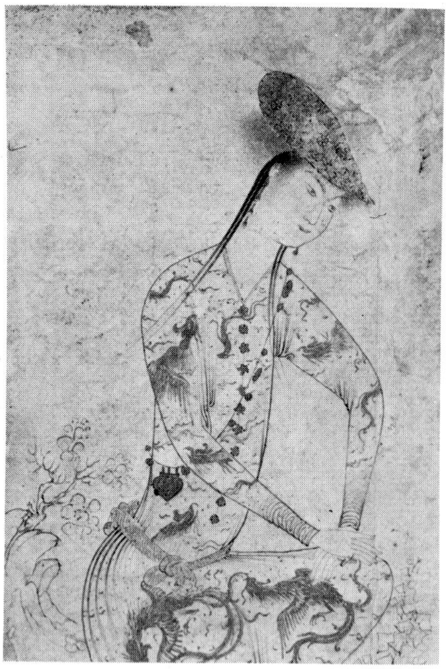

33

35

33. Detail from a drawing of a youth. Ḳaz̲
ca. 988/1580. The Metropolitan Museum of Art,
1973.92, Fletcher Fund, 1971 and Rogers Fund, ▸

34. Detail from a miniature painting depic
Sh̲āh Djahān and his son S̲h̲udjāʿ, from the
Djahān Album, India, period of Djahāngīr (101
1605-27). The Metropolitan Museum of Art,
55.121.10.36, Rogers Fund and the Kevor
Foundation gift, 1955.

35. Detail from a miniature painting depicting "The glorification of Akbar", from the S̲h̲āh Djahān Alb
India, period of Djahāngīr. The Metropolitan Museum of Art, No. 55.121.10.22, Purchase, Rogers Fund
the Kevorkian Foundation gift, 1955.

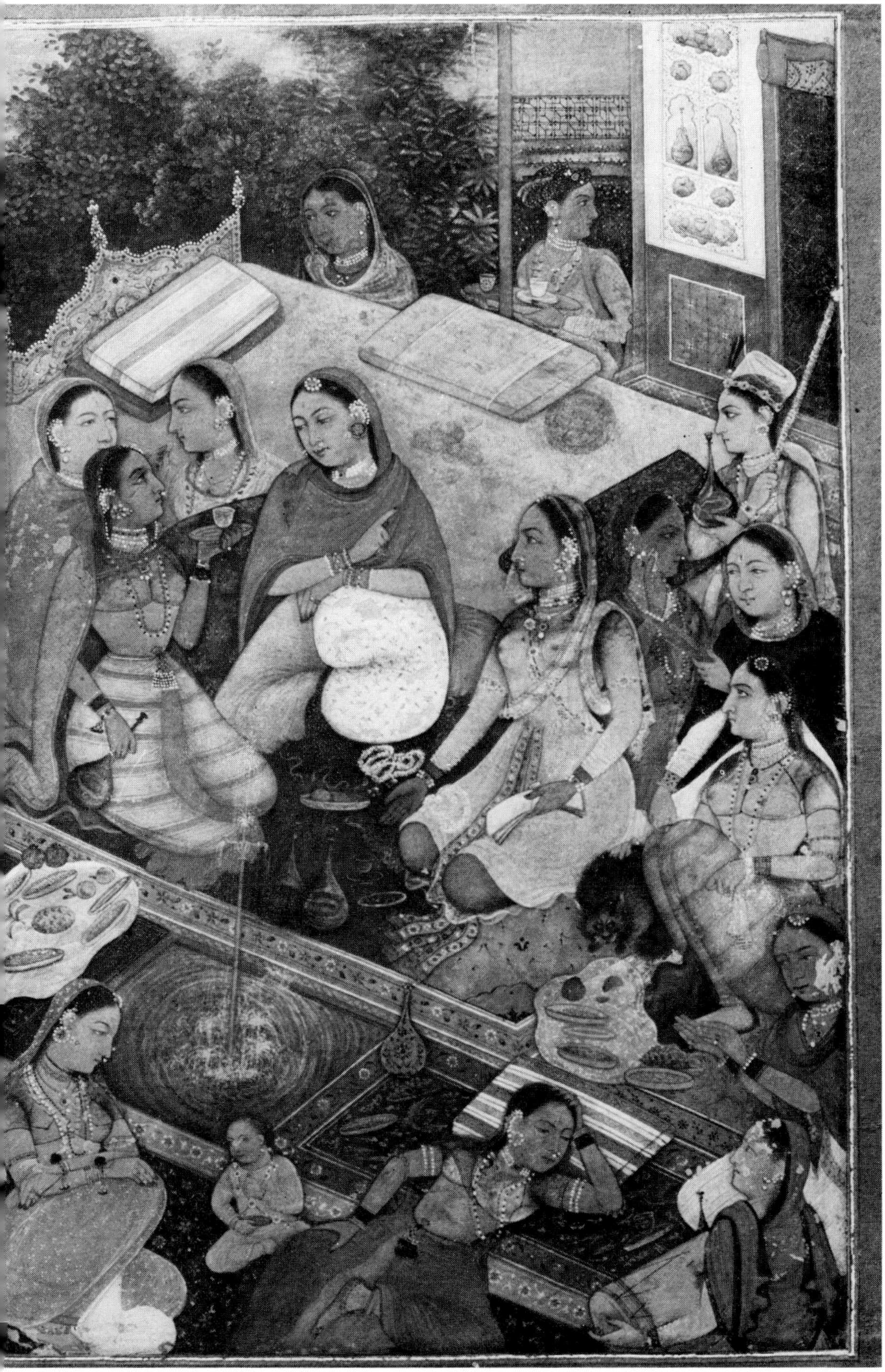

Ḥarīm scene, from an album, Mughal India, Period of Shāh Djahān (1037-68/1628-57). The Metropolitan um of Art, No. 30.95.174, no. 26, The Theodore Davis Collection, Bequest of Theodore M. Davis, 1915.

37a

37b

38

40a

40b

37a-b. Gold head ornament, fabricated of wire and sheet, decorated with granulation and set with various stones. Northwestern India, 18th-19th centuries. The Metropolitan Museum of Art, No. 15.95.105, Kennedy Fund, 1915.

38. Gold necklace set with various stones, back enameled, probably Jaipur work, 18th century. The Metropolitan Museum of Art, No. 19.111.3, Rogers Fund, 1919.

40a-b. Gold head ornament, set with precious stones and pearls, back enamelled. Iran, 19th century. Collection of Joseph Benyaminoff, New York.

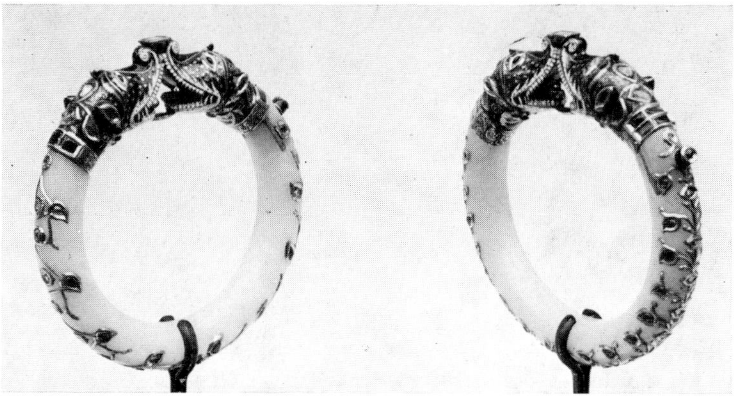

39

41b

39. Pair of bracelets, shanks of white jade, inlaid with gold and set with precious stones, terminals gold with enamel, India, 11th-12th/17th-18th centuries. The Metropolitan Museum of Art, No. 02.18.770,771, Gift of Heber R. Bishop.

41a-b. Gold head ornament fabricated from sheet, shot and wire, back worked in repoussé, set with precious stones. Bukhārā, 19th century. Collection of Joseph Benyaminoff.

42. Pair of gold earrings, enamelled and with pendant pearls. Iran, 19th century. Collection of Joseph Benyaminoff.

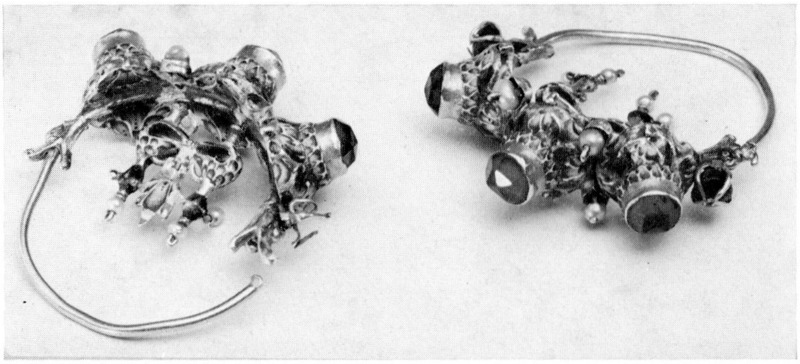

43

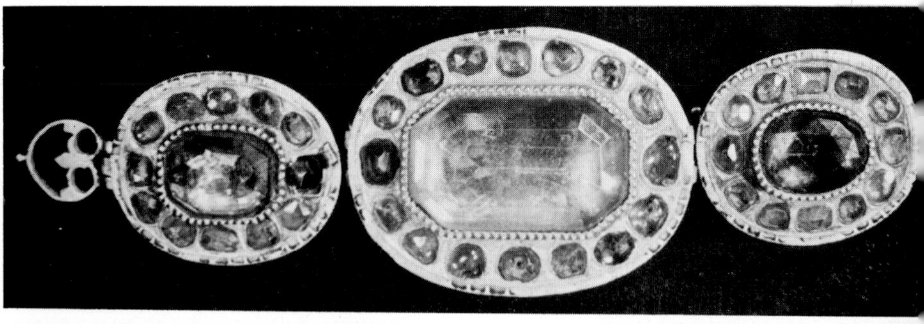

44a

44b

43. Pair of gold earrings, enamelled and set with facetted, coloured glass "stones". Iran, 19th centu
Collection of Joseph Benyaminoff.

44a-b. Gold armband, set with precious stones, back enamelled. Iran, 19th century. Negārestān Museu
Tehran.

45

45. Pair of gold head ornaments, set with precious stones and pearls. Morocco, 18th-19th centuries. Collection of Joseph Benyaminoff.

46. Gold necklace, with enamelled elements and strung with (probably original) pearls, set with precious stones. Morocco, 18th-19th centuries. Collection of Joseph Benyaminoff.

47a

47b

47a-b. Gold necklace, decorated with enamel and set with precious stones. Morocco, 18th-19th centurie
Collection of Joseph Benyaminoff.

gold element flanked by two smaller gold ele-
ıts on a string of pearls; and we see Iranian women
aintings of this period wearing a series of strings
eads, plain or bearing a single pendant (Metro-
tan Museum of Art No. 52.20.6, unpublished,
a wall painting from the Čihil Sutūn (1057/1647)
ṣfahān, unpublished). These paintings also show
ntinued vogue for bracelets consisting of simple
ngs of beads.
lso at the Čihil Sutūn, we encounter on the
ues at the edge of the pool an early example of
bejewelled tripartite armband which was to have
h popularity in the Ḳādjār period (Fig. 31).
he new belt type, which was first observed in
sian miniatures dating to around 1400 A.D., was
her elaborated upon in the Ṣafawid period. The
nents are jewelled and the number represented on
iven belt is increased (Fig. 32). Two complete
awid belts and a buckle are extant (Pope, *Survey
Persian art*, vi, pl. 1394a-c).
he types of earrings current in Ṣafawid Iran
w, for the most part, a continued conservatism
east as far as the representations are concerned.
find gold hoop earrings and gold hoops with
ngle shot at the bottom or at the bottom and two
s. There are also variations on the type of earring
sisting of a gold hoop with a pendant pearl which
ne case consists of three pendant stones, blue,
te and red (Fig. 33). In addition to these, we
see more complex pendant earring varieties
posed of gold, pearls, rubies or garnets and eme-
s or in some cases composed of the aforementioned
es, but depicted in the miniatures in a way that
ot detailed enough to permit a description.
ome of the ring types represented in the minia-
es of this period include: archer's rings, usually
icated in black; seal rings and others represented
h white and green stones (we may mention the
depicted with a white stone—in Metropolitan
seum of Art No. 1970.301.7, unpublished—which
y much resembles in style that illustrated in
. 26); plain gold rings with rectangular bezels;
gold thumb rings.
nother Ṣafawid fashion seen depicted is the
ring of bandoliers, an example of which can be
n in Fig. 33. This one incorporates gold beads,
lets, a rosette and a gold pendant. Others of the
iod bear jewelled elements (Metropolitan Museum
Art No. 12.224.4, miniature unpublished).
ecognisable representations of jewelry in Otto-
n miniatures are almost non-existent. A rare
ance shows Meḥemmed II wearing a white
her's ring and a ring set with a blue stone (N.
soy and F. Çağman, *Turkish miniature painting*,
nbul 1974, pl. I). A hint of the kinds of treasures
hand in Tavernier's time (in addition to arms,
nsils and the like enriched with diamonds, rubies,
eralds and other precious stones), can be had
n the following:
But what is most precious in that Chamber
transcends all the rest, is a strong Coffer all
ronwork, which contains another, of about a foot
a half square, wherein there is a vast Treasure.
en this Coffer is open'd you see a kind of Gold-
iths Jewel Box, wherein are ranked all sorts of
vels of highest value, as *Diamonds*, *Rubies*,
eralds, a huge number of excellent Topazes,
four of those Gems, call'd *Cats-eyes*, which are
beautiful, that they are not to be valu'd. Having
isfy'd your curiosity with the former, you come
t to certain little Drawers full of several Jewels,
at Roses of Diamonds, Pendants, other Roses
of Rubies and Emeralds, Strings and Chains of Pearls and Bracelets. There stands aside by itself a Cabinet, where are the Sorgouges, or the things wherein are fasten'd the Heron-tops, which the Grand Seignor wears in this Turbant. They are as it were little handles, made in the fashion of Tulips, cover'd over with the most precious Stones of the Seraglio, and 'tis into this that the Heron-top enters, that rich Plume of Feathers ... Of these Handles, some are higher and more precious than others: and my Oversear of the Treasury assur'd me, that, of all sorts of them, great and small, there are above a hundred and fifty. The lesser ones serve only for the Campagne, and the great ones, which are the richest, are reserv'd for the Pomps and Magnificences of the Court, and when the Grand Seignor marches in Ceremony to *Constantinople*. If he has a desire to satisfie his sight with the lustre of his precious Jewels, he Orders the Coffer to be brought into his own Chamber; but if he calls for some particular Piece of the Treasury, he gives order to the *Chasnadarbachi*, to fetch it, and that Chief Officer of the Treasury cannot enter it, without abundance of mysterious precautions" (*The six voyages of John Baptista Tavernier* ... (and) ... *The description of the Seraglio*, made English by J. P., London 1678, ch. viii, "A relation of the Grand Seignor's Seraglio", 46-8). Aside from the familiar strings of pearls, it is of interest to note that the treasury contained at this time a number of rose-cut diamonds, rubies and emeralds.

One such rose-cut diamond adorns the top of an hexagonal box, at present in the Hazine, the body of which is formed from a huge hollowed-out emerald crystal. According to an inscription on a mounting for one of its suspension hooks, this box was made by order of Sultan Aḥmed I in 1025/1616. The settings employed in this piece are extremely similar to those used in contemporary western Europe, while other objects in the Topkapı Hazine bear close comparison with Persian and Indian objects as regards techniques employed. For example, a dagger with a solid emerald handle which purportedly was presented to Meḥemmed IV by his mother Turkhān Sulṭān during the consecration of the Yeñi Djāmiʿ in 1073/1663 exhibits not only enamelling very similar to that which we associate with Ḳādjār Iran, but also the type of thickly encrusted surface which gives the impression of the stones having been pushed through the thin gold sheet from the back. A further closer study of the jewel treasures in the Topkapi would no doubt prove instructive regarding the nature if not the origins of the Ottoman style in jewelry.

Although few major pieces of Mughal jewelry from before the late 18th century remain extant, we are for a number of reasons in a better position to formulate an idea of the jewelry art of the earlier centuries of the Mughal period than we were in attempting to arrive at some picture of the jewelry of, for example, Tīmūrid and Ṣafawid Iran or of Ottoman Turkey. First of all, there is a large body of extant material dating from the late 18th to the 20th centuries, which, given the amazing tenacity of forms and traditions in Indian jewelry, gives us a rich context in which to consider the bits of evidence for the jewelry of the earlier centuries of the Mughal period. Secondly, for those curious about the jewels of this period, the miniatures produced under the Mughals are almost invariably much more detailed and therefore contain much more information for those who study the objects depicted. And thirdly, we have a wealth of precise verbal accounts of the jewels, thrones, etc., of the Mug͟hal court, especially those of the sharp and knowledgeable J. B. Tavernier.

One real disadvantage for the would-be student of Mug͟hal jewelry is the lack of available information about the jewelry of India during a very long period prior to the one with which we are here concerned. It may have been noticed that this article has not include any discussion of jewelry made under the Dihlī Sultanate. Pieces must exist, perhaps unrecognised or unpublished, in Indian museums or private collections; but we do not know definitely about such jewelry and have no real notion from any source as to its nature. Despite the absence of extant pieces from some extensive periods of time, it seems safe to say, on the basis of observation of recent and contemporary work and of study of such pictorial records as the highly detailed sculptures, that India has the longest unbroken jewelry tradition of any nation on earth, as well as the greatest variety of jewelry forms, functions and techniques. For the period from the beginning of British domination to the present, there are many studies of particular regional and/or technical types and styles, and we will make no attempt to survey or summarise this material here. We shall content ourselves rather with a presentation of some of the notable features of the adornment associated with the period of the glory of the Mug͟hal Empire, and their continuation into the later period, namely the 18th and 19th centuries.

Aside from whatever may have been the tradition at the time of the Mug͟hal conquest in the 10th/16th century, we may safely assume that a considerable amount of Tīmūrid tradition passed southward with the royal family, its treasures and entourage, and that Tīmūrid tradition in turn represented an amalgamation of other Islamic, and to some extent Central Asian and Chinese traditions.

Our best evidence for the jewelry styles of the periods of the emperors Akbar until Awrangzīb (963-1119/1556-1707) are the miniatures painted under their patronage. A striking confirmation of the veracity of these paintings is afforded by a statement of Tavernier concerning what he saw during the reign of Awrangzīb (*Travels in India*, ii, 150), that there is "no person of any quality that does not wear a Pearl between two color'd stones in his Ear." Although the following paintings are somewhat earlier (e.g. Metropolitan Museum of Art No. 30.95.174, no. 11, "Akbar giving audience ...," *ca.* 1590-1600, unpublished; and Metropolitan Museum of Art No. 55. 121.10.29, portraits of three nobles, all of whom have this type of earrings, and a huntsman, from the Shāh D͟jahān Album, period of D͟jahāngīr, 1014-36/1605-27, unpublished), they invariably show earrings with a precious stone (ruby or emerald) between two pearls, confirming the style of earring described by Tavernier. The discrepancy of detail may be due to a change in the arrangement by Awrangzīb's time, or may result from a confusion on Tavernier's part, as he had just been describing a pearl in the emperor's collection, the largest perfectly round one he had ever seen and one for which the emperor was unable to find a mate. If he could have paired it, Tavernier says, he would have made of them earrings, each with a pair of rubies or emeralds on each side, "according to the custom of the Country" (*loc. cit.*). This preference for the combination of pearls, rubies and emeralds coincides with what was said above in section 1, and one sees the combination everywhere in Mug͟hal (as indeed, in Tīmūrid, Ṣafawid and Ḳād͟jār) pa ings. The only other colour commonly seen is b (sapphire), but this latter occurs much less of than the other three.

Of course, we know that from ancient times Ir was the land of precious stones, and that e stones which did not originate in India itself, s as the rubies of Burma, often found their way to ot countries by way of India. Furthermore, India i self was a major market for stones from early tin even for those stones which had to come from c siderable distance, such as the emerald (coming fr Egypt). India and her immediate neighbours s as Ceylon, "Indo-China" and the mountains Badak͟hs͟hān produced an amazingly large var consisting of most of the precious stones known to this day. The *Ratnaparīkṣa*, or "Apprecia of gems", a compilation of Indian tradition ab gemstones, their varieties, qualities, sources, e which was apparently compiled as a technical gu before the 6th century A.D. (L. Finot, *Les lapidaires diens*, Paris 1896), exhibits a surprising degree knowledge and a surprisingly systematic approach dealing with a wide variety of stones. In it, we find canonisation of the "nine gems": the ruby, diamond, the cat's-eye (chrysoberyl), the "hyacin (zircon?), the topaz, the sapphire, the pearl, coral and the emerald (Finot, *op. cit.*, 171). Des this great variety, there is already expressed in t compilation a strong hierarchy of preferences, w the diamond considered first among gems. The or of treatment of our other major stones is: pe ruby, sapphire, and emerald.

Thus it is not at all surprising that we see Mug rulers and noblemen represented as wearing earrin turban ornaments, bracelets and necklaces of variety of lengths and arrangements consisting most solely of large pearls, rubies, sapphires a emeralds. For example, in Fig. 34 we see a paint from the Shāh D͟jahān Album which depicts D͟jah with his son S͟hud͟jāʿ. Aside from the jewelry w by the pair, which consists of pearls, emera and rubies, the painting is of additional inter as it shows D͟jahān with a ruby between the fing of his right hand and other rubies and emeralds a dish held in his left hand. We are making no sumptions in interpreting the red stones as rub the green as emeralds, etc., as the following pass from Tavernier (*loc. cit.*) shows. He describes a offers a line drawing of a large pearl belonging Awrangzīb: "Numb. 4. Is a great perfect pearl, well for its Water as for its form, which is like Olive. It is in the midst of a Chain of Emeraulds a Rubies, which the Great Mogul wears; which be put on, the Pearl dangles at the lower part of Breast."

Perhaps something should be said here about diamond, in light of its mention in connection w the *Ratnaparīkṣa* as well as Tavernier's ample te mony not only to the presence of diamonds in Ottoman Treasury (see above), but the great amo of mining, cutting and use of diamonds in India his time (*op. cit.*, ii, *passim*).

As is well known, India was *the* great source diamonds up until their discovery in Brazil a South Africa, and as the *Ratnaparīkṣa* and ot early Indian texts indicate, the Indians were us the diamond as a jewel well before Muḥammad's ti Indeed, even as early an author as Pliny (Book xxx 15) seems to speak of the diamond under the te *adamas* and he calls it the most valued of human p sessions, having been for long only known to kin he also seems to confuse it with other stones; his assertion that it cannot be broken even by ımer blows on an anvil has the status of mere ›nd. He does speak of its use to engrave other ıes and such usage probably has a more ancient .ory than we shall ever be able to establish.

.ccording to Finot (*op. cit.*, p. xxx), certain of early Indian texts with which he deals indicate t it is undesirable to cut diamonds and that ideal form is the perfect octahedral crystal (*op.* p. xxvii). What is most important to notice ;, however, is that the practice of cutting the nond was known to them. Even as late as Taıier's time (see ii, 56, of Ball's translation), such expert on gems as he could say of cleaving diaıds (to avoid wastage by simply grinding away terial) that the Indians "are much more accomhed than we are."

.l-Bīrūnī, cited by Wiedemann (*op. cit.*, 352), ns to offer contradictory information regarding use of the diamond in the early Islamic period. says on the one hand, that the people of Khurāsān . ʿIrāḳ only use the diamond for drilling (and ting) and poisoning, and on the other, that a achme" of diamond in one piece costs one thou-l *dīnār*s, whereas if in small pieces the price is one ıdred *dīnār*s. This price quotation seems to clearly ıcate a gemstone usage, not an abrasive one, where y small pieces are used anyway. In any case, ac-ling to al-Bīrūnī in another place in his stone k (as cited in Haschmi, *op. cit.*, 28-9), the diaıd is mentioned by poets of the Djāhiliyya and the ıayyad period (Imruʾ al-Qays and Abu 'l-Nadjm ›ectively). Again from al-Bīrūnī (Haschmi, *op. cit.*, . in citing a treatise by Naṣr b. Yaʿḳūb al-Dīnawarī ıes much more solid and detailed information, ac-ling to which the Buwayhid Muʿizz al-Dawla nad b. Buwayh (ruler in ʿIrāḳ 334-56/945-67) gave brother Rukn al-Dawla a ringstone of diamond .ch weighed three *mithḳāl*s. Furthermore, he says . *cit.*) that Manṣūr b. Nūḥ al-Sāmānī (either ıṣūr I 350-65/961-76 or Manṣūr II 387-9/997-9) had ›ral ringstones, of which one was a diamond, and t "one never saw a larger diamond".

'hus it seems fairly certain that the diamond , known as a gemstone throughout the Islamic ldle Ages. How these diamonds were cut and set do not know. Even the Mughal miniatures show hing which to our knowledge can be identified as .amond. The earliest inscription on a diamond of .ch we are aware is one in the name of Niẓām Shāh h the date 1000/1591-2, now in the Iranian crown 'els (Meen and Tushingham, *op. cit.*, 46, unpictured ›e-cut" diamond, 22.93 ct.).

'o return to our discussion of the forms of Mughal ›els, another ubiquitous item in Mughal paintings inger rings which come in some variety, although ir details are generally not possible to ascertain, ›ept for the colour (and by deduction, the type) :he gemstones. One well-known type of ring that dentifiable is the archer's ring (discussed above ler Ṣafawid Iran), which we know from many ant examples, usually of jade and often inlaid h gold and precious stones. Another form of jewel ally associated with men is the *subḥa* or string ›rayer beads. These beads were of course made of ry variety of material from wood and bone to ıes of all sorts. The passage cited above (in section about the inscribed stones in the Iranian crown ›els shows that Nādir Shāh had a *subḥa* with ›ralds, and there are in fact representations in ghal miniatures of precious stone *subaḥ*. For example, a painting of Akbar done in the period of Djahāngīr (1014-36/1605-27), a detail from which is seen in Fig. 35, shows Akbar fingering a string of prayer beads consisting of large rubies, sapphires and pearls. Although the number of beads is not correct for Muslim prayer beads (being neither 33 nor 99), this must be attributed to a mistake, casual or otherwise, on the part of the artist.

Certain fashions already noted in 9th/15th to 13th/19th century Iran are also to be seen in the Mughal miniatures. Among these are the bandolier, which passes over one shoulder and down under the opposite arm, on which is strung various jewelled charms, including amulet cases of a form similar to that from Nīshāpūr (Fig. 1) and those in Iranian miniatures (see Fig. 33) and of which numerous Mughal examples from the 18th and 19th centuries exist (e.g. Metropolitan Museum of Art No. 15.95.137 and 138, unpublished).

In another miniature in which we can observe such bandoliers (Fig. 36), we see a profusion of clearly-depicted jewelry. Most of the ladies shown have chokers fitting high on the neck which consist of a central jewel (a large ruby or emerald set in a square or rectangular gold "box") held by three rows of pearls which complete the circuit of the neck. Another type of choker seen is one consisting of a series of closely-placed rectangular gold and stone jewels forming a continuous band bordered on top and bottom by a single row of pearls. Most persons also have intermediate-length pendants, apparently held by silk cords, which also consist of large central stones (rubies or emeralds) set in a simple rectangular or elliptical gold box, with pendant pearls. In addition, one sees the strings of large and small stone beads and pearls which are universally represented and described. We see here also a lady wearing the type of jewelled tripartite armband discussed above as seen on a statue from the Čihil Sutūn (extant Mughal examples from the 18th and 19th centuries include Metropolitan Museum of Art No. 15.95.40, 41 and 41.100.118, both unpublished). Other types of arm decorations seen in this rich miniature include: apparently solid gold armbands which fit at the elbow; a wide tapered close-fitting bracelet set with pearls, sapphires and rubies; another bracelet very similar to a choker described above, with a large ruby set in gold and held by two rows of pearls; and an upper-arm band which is similar to another of the chokers, with a series of stones set in rectangular gold settings and bordered with rows of pearls. Finally, we may mention some of the types of ear and more nose rings seen. There are several examples of the type of earring with the stone between two pearls discussed above, but there they have also a pendant teardrop-shaped pearl. The same type of ring, but without the pendant pearl, occurs as a nose ring. The other major type of earring is a large, disc-like one of gold set with stones large and small and sometimes with a pendant pearl. Some of these (particularly that on the lady in the centre) bear a rather close resemblance to the star-like element on the head-ornament (Fig. 37a). The position also was similar since this element rested at the side of the head at the ear.

The detail of this piece (Fig. 37b) shows that granulation was an art which continued at a high technical and artistic level in India. This technique has existed in India from at least the 1st-2nd centuries A.D., as the jewelry excavated at Sirkap, Taxila, now in the Central Asian Antiquities Museum, Dihlī, shows (see *The art of India and Pakistan*, catalogue of an exhibition held at the Royal Academy of Arts, London 1947-8, ed. Sir Leigh Ashton, New York [1948?], figs. 180 and 186).

The way in which the elements in the necklace from Taxila (Ashton, *op. cit.*, fig. 180) fit together almost in the manner of a jigsaw puzzle has striking parallels in any number of 18th and 19th century Indian necklaces, (one example of which is shown in Fig. 38). In these and a myriad of other ways, the jewelry art of India displays an astounding tenacity for the preservation of traditions.

Another striking demonstration of this traditionalism is to be found in the pair of bracelets in Fig. 39. Bracelets of this type are well-known and exhibit an ingenious type of pivoting clasp closed with a threaded pin. The universally-used type of clasp pin in Islamic jewelry outside India and in one or two isolated examples of the 8th/14th century, is one which is held in place by friction. But a pair of bracelets found at Puszta Bakod in Hungary (now in the National Museum, Budapest, see Franz M. Feldhaus, *Die Technik der Antike und des Mittelalters*, Potsdam 1931, 221-2 and Figs. 252 and 254; and M. Rosenberg, *op. cit.*, i, 123 and Figs. 141-3) and dating from the period of the tribal migrations (perhaps 5th-7th centuries A.D.), displays not only terminals of snout-to-snout beasts in a manner very reminiscent of our Indian ones, but they, like the Indian ones, are closed by a counter-clockwise threaded screw. This type of screw closure is found on a variety of types of Indian jewelry, and almost invariably the threads are made not by cutting but, like those on the much earlier bracelets just mentioned, by soldering on to the pin and into the hole which receives it coils of wire with regular spaces between (Feldhaus, *op. cit.*, 221-2, traces the screw closure in jewelry back to at least the 5th century A.D., as it is found in a fibula from the grave of Childerich, d. 481). It should be noted that all of the above mentioned jewelry found in Europe which exhibits the screw closure is of the type with hammered-in garnets, a type which was widespread in Europe and Asia between about the 4th and (depending on the region) the 10th or 11th centuries. The screw pin may have come to India with some of these migrating peoples.

Our pair of bracelets exhibits two other features for which Mughal and post-Mughal India is justly celebrated. The white jade shanks are inlaid with gold forming graceful floral patterns, the leaves and flowers of which are formed by stones set into the gold. Although sporadically practised in Turkey and Iran, possibly under Mughal influence, this art in those areas did not rival that in India either in level of technique and artistry or in longevity.

The gold terminals of these bracelets are covered with brilliant enamels which demonstrate a masterful control of the medium. Jaipur is best known for this type of enamelling, which is perhaps best described as "encrusted", in which three-dimensional forms are covered. Additionally, details are sometimes cut into the metal under transparent enamels to contribute to the liveliness of the effect. The literature on the subject of Indian arts and crafts from the 18th to the present century contains much information on Indian enamelling, and we will not dwell upon it, beyond saying that the art here reached one of its greatest consummations. These enamels, of course, like other precious techniques from time immemorial, adorned and bejewelled a whole array of objects which were not jewelry in the modern sense such as arms, thrones, utensils and the like, and as such they constitute a branch of jewelry.

As we suggested at the outset, the subject of dian jewelry is an enormous and complex one, pecially because of the wealth of evidence in sculptures and paintings and the variety of recent contemporary forms. And this situation, combi with the great dearth of known pre-18th cent pieces, leaves one in a great state of puzzlem about where all the older pieces went. We can course explain this to some extent by remember that even within families it was customary to re stones in the latest style, especially after pass from one owner to another, and in the process melt down the precious metals for re-use. To a particularly notorious case of radical and wholes change of ownership, that of the Mughal ro treasures, we know that most of what was on ha when Nādir Shāh took Dihlī was immediat transformed into ingots for ease of transport (M and Tushingham, *op. cit.*, 11); and of course stones and pearls were hauled away, either to be mounted or simply deposited in the Iranian treasu Such "radical and wholesale changes of ownersh have of course been taking place throughout Isla (and other) history, and we can well imagine t many of the stones that were in the Mughal treas at the time of Nādir Shāh's visit had in turn form part of the treasuries of various earlier hous The Mughal treasury may for instance have inclu stones that had once belonged to some ʿAbbāsid Fāṭimid caliph. Such would be impossible to prove the absence of inscriptions on the stones; but th are tantalising bits of information to be found. example, when one compares the weight repor (23 *mithḳāl*s, which by Kahle's precise formula of *mithḳāl* = 4.414 gr.—and not 4.5 gr., to which rounds it off—gives 101.5 gr. or 507.5 carats) a large balas ruby which was part of the enorm loot dispersed from the Fāṭimid treasury during chaotic period in al-Mustanṣir's reign (see Kah *op. cit.*, 336, 356) with that of the largest kno balas ruby in the world, now in the Iranian cro jewels (reported as 500 ct. by Meen and Tushingha *op. cit.*, 46, 47, 67), one is struck by the agreem in weight. Of course it may be a coincidence, but embers of hypothesis are fanned when we know t Nāṣir al-Dīn Shāh told Dr. Feuvrier, his physic in the 1890s, that "the hole . . . was pierced to ta a cord by which it hung around the neck of the Gol Calf" and that "this ruby came from a king Abyssinia, and had been brought back from India Nādir Shāh" (Meen and Tushingham, *op. cit.*, 6

Despite the various reasons for and the me nisms of the transformation and transfer of jew from one period and region to another, one is s left in a quandary. In the case at hand, where all the pieces of the period which were not in Mughal royal treasury? Surely some were kept family heirlooms or got buried, to be found late

We must believe that future excavations, in c junction with heightened awareness on the part researchers in museums and on historical texts, w continue to provide information on this as well other periods where we are faced with these hard- explain lacunae.

4. The final phase of the tradition (18th and 19th centuries)

The conservatism in style which has been not as a major characteristic of the three broad peri covered so far continues in the final phase of Islamic jewelry tradition which is to be treated he

In Ḳādjār Iran, bandoliers were still fashiona

men and women (S. J. Falk, *Qajar paintings*, ɴdon 1972, pls. 2, 26, 46, 47), although instead ie metal amulets and pendants sometimes set with ,es seen on the Ṣafawid examples, the Ḳādjār ones ı to have consisted solely of pearls or of elements .posed of pearls and/or precious stones. The style :he belts in Iran during this period remained ntially the same.

trings of beads were still worn on the wrists (Falk, 26 and 43), in addition to bracelets composed precious stones set into square bezels hinged to the other, as well as plain gold bangles (Falk, 17, 23, 25).

ne of the latter paintings referred to above ıt in pl. 17) also shows a continuation of the ue for a string of pearls framing the face. In the ljār period, however, the pearls only appear to e extended from ear and the strings are longer ıs to serve as necklaces (Falk, pls. 19, 20). There also an elaboration of jewelled head ornaments, ecially for women, in the Ḳādjār period. These e worn either pendant from their head cloths or in ıbinations serving as simple or elaborate headdres- (Falk, pls. 5-7, 18-21). An example of one of these .dant elements can be seen in Fig. 40a-b. The small large elements are hinged together and a ring is ıched to the top of the former. The two projecting aments are removable, for decorating the top of eather (Falk, pls. 5, 20). A similar object, in ; case used to decorate the foreheads of Jewish Muslim brides in the region of Bukhārā, can be ı in Fig. 41a-b. Influence from the Indian sub-tinent is very obvious on this subject, as on much djār jewelry, particularly in the manner of setting stones.

ı very popular type of earring in Iran during 18th and 19th centuries consisted of a series hemispheres or cones, hung one below the other, h pendant elements (Falk, fig. 1). These were cuted in enamel, sheet metal or in filigree, with er pendant pearls or balls, repoussé- or wire-orated metal sheets of a combination of both (see . 42). A prototype for this kind of earring is to found in 1st or 2nd century India (The Royal ıdemy of Arts, London, *The art of India and kistan*, pl. 22, No. 185). Another popular earring e can be seen in Fig. 43. This variety consists of a ıi-circular lower part often decorated with dragon-ıded terminals and spherical or knob-like pro-.sions around its circumference (Falk, figs. 3, 4). ain, these were executed alternatively in enamel, et metal and filigree.

\ very fine example of the ubiquitous Ḳādjār ıband, referred to earlier in connection with the awid example, can be seen in Fig. 44a-b, here cuted in gold, enamel and precious stones.

Aside from a continued vogue for strings of beads the neck (Falk, pls. 14, 38), pendants or roundels with precious stones on strings of pearls or beads re a popular necklace type during the Ḳādjār riod (Falk, fig. 7, pls. 17-19). The last painting o shows a necklace bearing a central element very nilar in shape to that seen in Fig. 27.

To the best of our knowledge, aside from the new ces in the Topkapı Hazine (most of which are either ban ornaments or belt buckles of well-known pes), very little Ottoman jewelry of any significance ıde and used in Turkey itself has survived from the riod in question. However, we can learn a consider-le amount about fine Ottoman jewelry of this riod from that made in the more distant regions the Ottoman empire and even from Morocco. When one compares pieces which can be attributed to Istanbul (*Collection Hélène Stathatos. ii. Les objets byzantins et post byzantins*, Limoges 1957, pl. XI, nos. 79, 80, 82 and pl. XIII, nos. 107-9) with the gold jewelry from Morocco of the same period, one feels quite justified in stating that the provincial craftsmen were drawing at least some of their inspiration from the Turkish capital. The similarity is so great, in fact, that one can safely use such Moroccan pieces to fill in the large gaps in the Istanbul jewelry.

The style of the gold work on the Moroccan head ornaments in Fig. 45 is very close to that on the diadem and the oval pendant in the Stathatos collection. That iconography was also shared can be seen on the necklace in Fig. 46. The double-headed bird, whose body is set with stones and from whose tail extend pendants of pearls and precious stones, is very close to a pendant in the Stathatos collection. The two enamelled cylindrical beads on this necklace, however, are descendants of those seen on the Naṣrid necklace in Fig. 28.

The necklace in Fig. 47a-b combines precious stones on the obverse with enamelling on the reverse, which is another feature of the Istanbul jewelry.

The largest body of Muslim North African material, however, has a series of styles all its own assuming a myriad of forms and drawing its inspiration from a variety of periods and areas. There is a rather detailed literature on the subject which can be studied by those with a particular interest (see *Bibl.* below). A study of the literature on this jewelry, which extends into the 20th century, as well as the later Indian jewelry, provides insights into the ways various earlier pieces and types were worn, and gives an idea of their overall effect. The same can be said for ethnographic studies, which often provide the best documentation of recent and contemporary jewelry from the various regions whose earlier jewelry productions have been discussed above.

Bibliography: (in addition to references given in the article): Cl. Cahen, *Documents relatifs à quelques techniques iraqiennes au début du onzième siècle (L'Hotel de l'Or de l'Iraq)*, in *Ars Islamica*, xv-xvi (1951), 23-8; D. M. Dunlop, *Sources of gold and silver in Islam according to al-Hamdānī*, in *SI*, viii (1957); A. S. Ehrenkreutz, *EI*² art. DHAHAB; H. C. Beck, *Classification and nomenclature of beads and pendants*, in *Archaeology*, lxxvii; A. Lucas, *Ancient Egyptian materials and industries*⁴, revised J. R. Harris, London 1962; H. Maryon, *Metalwork and enamelling, a practical treatise on gold and silversmith's work and their allied crafts*⁵, New York 1971; O. Untracht, *Metal techniques for craftsmen*, New York 1968; R. Webster, *Gems: their sources, descriptions and identification*, Washington 1962; H. E. Wulff, *The traditional crafts of Persia*, Cambridge, Mass. and London 1966; J. G. Hawthorne and C. S. Smith, trs., *On divers arts: the treatise of Theophilus*, Chicago 1963; R. Hendrie, tr. and notes, *An essay upon various arts ... by Theophilus ...*, London 1847; Sir John Hill, and ed., *Theophrastus's History of stones*, London 1774; J. H. F. Notton, *Ancient Egyptian gold refining: a reproduction of early techniques*, in *Gold Bulletin*, vii/2 (April 1974); V. Ball, *The true history of the Koh-i-Nur*, in *The English Illustrated Magazine* (1891); B. K. Ismail, and M. Tosi, *A turquoise neckstone of King Ninurta-Apal-Ekur*, in *Sumer*, xxxii (1976); al-Bīrūnī, *al-Djamahir fī maʿrifat al-djawāhir*, ed. F. Krenkow, Ḥaydarābād 1936; G. F. Kunz, *The curious* *lore of precious stones*, Philadelphia and London 1913; B. Laufer, *Notes on turquoise in the East*, Chicago 1913; N. F. Moore, *Ancient mineralogy*, New York 1859; Pliny, *Natural history*, (English tr. D. E. Eichholz) vol. x, Libri XXXVI-XXXVII, London 1962; H. Ritter, *Orientalische Steinbücher*, in H. Ritter, J. Ruska, F. Sarre and R. Winderlich, *Orientalische Steinbücher und Persische Fayencetechnik*, Istanbul 1935; J. Ruska, *Die Mineralogie in der arabischen Literatur*, in *Isis*, i (1913-14); idem, *Über Nachahmung von Edelsteinen*, in *Quellen und Studien zur Geschichte der Naturwissenschaft und Medizin*, 1933; E. Wiedemann, *Beiträge zur Mineralogie usw. bei den Arabern*, in *Festgabe Lippmann*, 1927, 48-54; idem, *Zur Mineralogie bei den Muslimen*, in *Archiv Gesch. Naturw. Techn.*, i (1909), 208-11; idem, *Zur Mineralogie im Islam*, in *SPMSE*, xliv (1912), 205-56; P. Ackerman, *Jewellery in the Islamic period*, in Pope, *Survey of Persian art*, iii, Oxford 1938-9, 2664-72; M. Ağa-Oğlu, *Remarks on the character of Islamic art*, in *Art Bulletin*, xxxvi (1954) (esp. 180-90, "Opposition to luxury"); J. Allan, *EI*² art. KHĀTAM; *Allen Memorial Art Museum Bulletin*, xviii/2-3; *Catalogue of the Melvin Gutman collection of ancient and medieval gold*, Oberlin, Ohio n.d.; P. Amandry, *Collection Hélène Stathatos. i. Les bijoux antiques*, Strasbourg 1953; idem, *Collection Hélène Stathatos. iii. Objets antiques et byzantins*, Strasbourg 1963; J. Besancenot, *Bijoux arabes et berbères du Maroc*, Casablanca n.d.; J. B. Bhushan, *Indian jewellery, ornaments, and decorative designs*, Bombay 1964; P. C. Birch, *Ancient Persian necklaces*, Pforzheim n.d.; W. Born, *Small objects of semiprecious stone from the Mughal period*, in *Ars Islamica*, vii (1940), 101-4; M. Boyer, *Mongol jewellery*, Copenhagen 1952; A. P. Charles, *A monograph on gold and silver ware produced in the United Provinces*, Allahabad 1905; O. M. Dalton, *Franks Bequest. Catalogue of the finger rings, early Christian, Byzantine, Teutonic, Medieval and later . . .*, British Museum, London 1912; J. Deny, *EI*² art. MUHR; M. S. Dimand, and H. E. McAllister, The Metropolitan Museum of Art, *Near Eastern jewelry, a picture book*, New York 1944; R. Ettinghausen, *Originality and conformity in Islamic art*, in *Individualism and conformity in classical Islam*, A. Banani and S. Vryonis, eds., Wiesbaden 1977 (esp. 104-5); P. Eudel, *Dictionnaire des bijoux de l'Afrique du Nord*, Paris 1906; idem, *L'orfèvrerie algérienne et tunisienne*, Algiers 1902; F. Falk, *Jewelry from Persia: the collection of Patti Birch*, (Catalogue of an exhibition at the Schmuckmuseum Pforzheim n.d., privately printed); M. Gerlach, ed., *Primitive and folk jewelry*, New York 1971; M. Gómez-Moreno, *Joyas árabes de la Reina Católica*, in *al-Andalus*, viii (1943), 473-5; Ruy de Gonzáles de Clavijo, *Embassy to Tamerlane, 1403-1406*, tr. G. Le Strange, London 1928; J. Goudard, *Bijoux d'argent de la "Tache de Taza"*, in *Hespéris*, viii (1928), 285-94; O. Grabar, *The Umayyad Dome of the Rock in Jerusalem*, in *Ars Orientalis*, iii (1959) (esp. 46-52); Z. M. Hasan, *Kunūz al-Fāṭimiyyīn*, Cairo 1356/1937; J. Herber, *Note sur l'influence de la bijouterie soudanaise sur la bijouterie marocaine*, in *Hespéris*, xxxvii (1950), 5-10; W. L. Hildburgh, *A Hispano-Arabic silver-gilt and crystal casket*, in *The Antiquaries' Journal*, xxi (1941), 211-31; idem, *Medieval Spanish enamels*, London 1936; S. S. Jacob and T. H. Hendley, *Jeypore enamels*, London 1886; J. L. Kipling, *The industries of the Punjab*, in *The Journal of Indian Art*, ii (London 1888); C Lamm, *EI*² art. BILLAWR, BALLŪR; A. Lar Müller, *La vie juive au Maroc*, Musée d'Is Jerusalem 1973, Catalogue no. 103 [in Hebr idem, *Bokhara* (Israel Museum cat. no. 39) Jer lem 1967; E. W. Lane, *An account of the man and customs of the modern Egyptians*,⁵ London 1 Appendix A, Female ornaments; S. Lane-P *A history of Egypt in the Middle Ages*⁴, Lon 1925 (esp. 110-11, 145-9); R. J. Mehta, *The ha crafts and industrial arts of India*, Bombay 1 R. N. Mukharji, *Art-manufactures of India*, Delhi 1974; M. Rosen-Ayalon, *A silver ring Medieval Islamic times*, in *Studies in memor Gaston Wiet*, Jerusalem 1977, 195-201; M. C. R *An Egypto-Arabic cloisonné enamel*, in *Ars mica*, vii (1940), 165-7; Ch. Schefer, *Sefer Nan relation du voyage de Nassiri Khosrau*, Paris 1 J. B. Tavernier, *Travels*; S. Weir, *The Bed* (see "Jewellery", 59-72) London 1976; L. Willia *The arts and crafts of older Spain. i. Gold, s and jewel work*, London and Edinburgh 1 K. Benda, *Mittelalterlicher Schmuck*, Prague 1 (Slavic finds highly comparable to media Islamic jewelry); O. von Falke, *Der Mainzer G schmuck der Kaiserin Gisela*, Berlin 1913.

(M. KEENE and M. JENKIN

DJAWHARĪ, ṬANṬĀWĪ, modernist Egyp theologian. He was born in 1278/1862 in village of Kafr ʿAwaḍ Allāh Ḥidjāzī in the Delta to the south-east of al-Zaḳāzīḳ. He stu at al-Azhar [*q.v.*] and at Dār al-ʿUlūm [*q.v.*] f 1889 until 1893 when he graduated. After his duation, he worked as a school-teacher at var primary and secondary schools until his retirem in 1922, except for the period between 1908 1914 when he taught at Dār al-ʿUlūm (eth *tafsīr*, *ḥadīth* and grammar) and at the Egyp University (Islamic philosophy).

He is the author of an impressive oeuvre of ne thirty published books—some of which were tra lated into a number of other Oriental language and numerous articles on a variety of subj published in different periodicals throughout Islamic world. The majority of his writings c stitute an effort to show how the teachings Islam, and in particular, the contents of the Ḳur were in accordance with human nature, and w method, theory and findings of Western mod (19th and early 20th century) science, with wh he had familiarised himself mainly through popu accounts in English.

His principal work is his Ḳurʾān commentary, *Djawāhir fī tafsīr al-Ḳurʾān al-karīm*, Cairo 19 35, in 26 volumes, which was analysed extensively J. Jomier, *Le Cheikh Ṭanṭāwī Jawharī (1862-194 son Commentaire du Coran*, in *MIDEO*, v (19 115-74. The scope and nature of Ṭanṭāwī's writi and the extensive learning displayed by him, d the attention of European orientalists like Santillana, M. Hartmann and Carra de Vaux, w gave mostly eulogising analytical accounts of so items (cf. Carra de Vaux, *Les penseurs de l'Isla* Paris 1926, v, 275-284; M. Hartmann, *Scha Ṭanṭāwī Dschauharī. Ein moderner egyptischer The und Naturfreund*, in *Beiträge zur Kenntnis des Orie* xiii (1916), 54-82; D. Santillana, *Kitāb ayna 'l-in* (review), in *RSO*, iv (1911), 762-3).

Throughout his life, Ṭanṭāwī Djawharī showe theoretical as well as practical interest in spiritis as appears from passages in many of his writi and in particular from his books *Kitāb al-Arw*

:o 1910, 1920, 1931, *Barā'at al-ʿAbbāsiyya Ukht ʾashīd*, Cairo 1936, which is a defence of al-bāsa's innocence of adultery, in defiance of the tentions presented by Djirdjī Zaydān in his ilarly-named novel, written upon instruction n the spirit of Harūn al-Rashīd, and *Aḥlām fi ʿyāsa wa-kayfa yataḥakkak al-salām al-ʿāmm*, :o 1935, in which he presents in a series of reve-ons an all-enfolding view of the fundamental er, in accordance with which human existence uld ideally be. Ṭanṭāwī Djawharī was an active nber of the spiritistic association of Aḥmad mī Abu 'l-Khayr (d. 1960) known as *Djamʿiyyat lhrām al-Rūḥiyya*. Decause of this profound nmitment to spiritism, his writings were criticised shunned by Azhar circles (cf. ʿAbd al-Laṭīf ḥammad al-Dimyāṭī, *al-Wisāṭa al-rūḥiyya*, Cairo 8/1949, 57-9), but no formal action aimed at the hibition of any of his books has ever been taken. :side Egypt, however, his works were forbidden for e time at the end of the 1920s by the Dutch sor in the Netherlands Indies (cf. *Mir'āt al-ḳ, Madjalla adabiyya akhlāḳiyya idjtimāʿiyya* okjakarta), iv-v (Oct.-Nov. 1928), 63-5), while his onventional Ḳur'ān commentary was banned in di Arabia (cf. Muḥammad Ḥusayn al-Dhahabī, *ʿafsīr wa 'l-mufassirūn*, 3 vols., Cairo 1961-2, iii,).

Ie was the official Egyptian candidate for the oel Prize (cf. *al-Risāla* (Cairo), vii (1939), 188,) when he died in January 1940.

Bibliography: In addition to the references iven in the text, see the literature mentioned in he article by Jomier. The latter article contains biography of Ṭanṭāwī pieced together from the iographical material scattered throughout the *ıfsīr* and supplemented by oral information btained by Jomier from members of Ṭanṭāwī's amily in the early 1950s. See for additional bio-raphical material, F. de Jong, *The works of ʿanṭāwī Jawharī (1862-1940). Some bibliographical nd biographical notes*, in *Bibliotheca Orientalis* xxiv/5-6 (1977). This article also gives details bout Ṭanṭāwī's books not mentioned by Brockel-ıann, *GAL*, S III, 329 ff. and in the article by omier. In addition, see Ilyās Zakhūrā, *Mir'āt l-ʿaṣr fī ta'rīkh wa-rusūm akābir ridjāl Miṣr*, :airo 1897, ii, 225-8; C. C. Adams, *Islam and nodernism in Egypt. A study of the modern reform novement inaugurated by Muḥammad ʿAbduh*, ondon 1933, 245-7 (based upon M. Hartmann's rticle mentioned in the text). ʿAlī al-Djanbalāṭī, *ʿī dhikrā Ṭanṭāwī Djawharī*, Cairo 1962, and ʾa'ūf ʿUbayd, *al-Insān rūḥ lā djasad*, Cairo n.d., 99 ff. (F. de Jong)

JĀWĪDHĀN KHIRAD (P.) "eternal wisdom", title of a kind of Iranian *Fürstenspiegel* ose earliest known mention, occurs in a work by ʾjāḥiẓ, now lost, containing the memorable ings of wise men and poets (see al-Khafādjī, *āz*, 108), the *Istiṭālat al-fahm*. Judging by an ract which has been preserved, this author ounts, on the authority of al-Wāḳidī, the con-ions in which the *Djāwīdhān khirad*, the spiritual tament written "just after the Flood" by the thical king Hūshang [*q.v.*] for his sons and cessors, was allegedly rediscovered. When al-'mūn was proclaimed caliph in Khurāsān, the g of Kābulistān sent to him a *shaykh* called ūbān bearing a letter in which the ruler stated t he was sending him the most magnificent sent in the world in the person of this wise man who, adds al-Djāḥiẓ, used the *sadjʿ* of the diviners (!) and gave apposite replies to questions put to him. When al-Ma'mūn arrived in Baghdād, Dhūbān pointed out to him the hiding-place at Ctesiphon/al-Madā'in of a casket of black glass containing a piece of brocade in which were preserved one hundred leaves. Dhūbān informed the caliph's secretary, al-Ḥasan b. Sahl [*q.v.*], that it was the *Djāwīdhān khirad* translated from the language of Hūshang into Persian (= Pahlavi) by Gandjvar b. Isfandiyār, vizier of the king of Īrānshahr. Al-Ḥasan b. Sahl had each leaf read out and explained, one after the other, by a certain al-Khiḍr/al-Khaḍir b. ʿAlī, then put the text into Arabic. However, since the leaves as given to him were in a state of disorder, he had to pass by a great part of them. The tradition adds that al-Ma'mūn, when he heard about this translation, could not prevent himself from expressing his admiration.

Such is the legend concerning the discovery of the *Djāwīdhān khirad*, the fate of whose Pahlavi original is unknown. Neither is anything known about what happened to al-Ḥasan b. Sahl's Arabic text, which must have been in circulation for a certain period before being itself translated into Persian. R. Henning (in *ZDMG*, cvi [1956], 73-7) thinks that it could possibly have been preserved in the *Yatīmat al-sulṭān* attributed to Ibn al-Muḳaffaʿ (ed. Kurd ʿAlī, in *Rasā'il al-bulaghā'*[2], Cairo 1365/1946, 145-72) which displays several points in common with the *Djāwidhān khirad* of the historian-philosopher Miskawayh [*q.v.*].

The latter avers that, after having been struck, when a youth, by the enthusiastic judgment on the *Djāwīdhān khirad* by al-Djāḥiẓ, he felt compelled to bring it to light again, and that his untiring researches at last enabled him to find a copy with a *mōbedhān mōbedh* of Fārs. Even conceding that this information has a base in reality, it is regrettable that Miskawyh gives no indication as to what language it was written in. It might be supposed *a priori* that it was a copy of the Pahlavi original, but such a hypothesis seems hardly plausible if one gives attention to the complete harmony, in Arabic, between the wording of an important number of sentences of the *Yatīmat al-sulṭān* and this author's own *Djāwīdhān khirad*, for in this latter case, Miskawayh certainly did not retranslate a Pahlavi text, even though he was capable of this, as his usage of other Iranian texts inacessible in Arabic demonstrates.

The interest of this anthology of Miskawayh (ed. ʿA. Badawī, Cairo 1952, under the title *al-Ḥikma al-khālida*) consists essentially in the author's clearly-manifested intention of inculcating that "among all the nations, intelligences concur in following the same way, and neither differ according to the countries involved nor change with the elapsing of time", after having pinpointed many resemblances between the wisdom of the ancient Iranians, illustrated by the document which he claims to have rediscovered and the Pahlavi texts which he has utilised, and that of the Indians, Arabs and Greeks. In order to achieve his aim, he conveys to the reader "a rambling succession of moral reflections or philosophical discourses borrowed from various sources" to which the libraries of Ibn al-ʿAmīd and ʿAḍud al-Dawla [*q.vv.*] had enabled him to find easy access (on these sources, see M. Arkoun, *Contribution à l'humanisme arabe au IVe/Xe siècle: Miskawayh philosophe et historien*, Paris 1970, 146-58; from a more general point of view,

Arkoun has devoted an extended study to Miskawayh's work, *Introduction à la lecture du Kitâb "Jâvîdân khirad"*, as a preface to the Persian version of Shushtarī, in *Wisdom of Persia*, xvi, Tehran 1976, 1-24). Miskawayh's extensive readings provided him with a rich documentation on the wisdom of the Persians (5-88), the Indians (89-100), the ancient Arabs (101-208), the Greeks (282-4) and the "modern Muslims" (285-342). Especially worthy of note is the Table of Cebes (229-62), and this Arabic adaptation has since a long time back attracted the attention of orientalists (Span. tr. P. Lozano y Casela, *Parafrasis árabe de la Tabla de Cebes*, Madrid 1793; ed. and tr. Suavi, *Le Tableau de Cébès ou l'image de la vie humaine*, Paris 1873; R. Basset, *Le Tableau de Cébès*, Paris 1898; and see Arkoun, *Contribution à l'humanisme arabe*, 158-60).

Bibliography: (in addition to works cited above): S. de Sacy, *Mémoire sur le Djavidan Khired*, in *Mém. Acad. des Inscrs. et B.-L.*, ix (1831), 1-31; Ethé, in *Gr. Iran. Phil.*, ii, 346; ʿAbd al-ʿAzīz Maymanī, in *MMIA*, ix (1929), 129-39, 193-200 (reprinted in Kurd ʿAlī, *op. cit.*, 469-85); Brockelmann, I, 242, S I, 584; A. J. Arberry, *Javidhan khiradh*, in *JSS*, viii (1963), 145-58; for a more detailed analysis, see MISKAWAYH. (CH. PELLAT)

DJAWZ is the nut in general, and in particular the class of the walnut (*Juglans regia* L.), rich in varieties. Term and object are of Persian origin (*gawz*), as correctly recognised by the early Arab botanists (Abū Ḥanīfa al-Dīnawarī, *The book of plants*, ed. B. Lewin, Uppsala-Wiesbaden 1953, 86, l. 14). They also relate that the walnut-tree is widespread in the Arab peninsula, especially in the Yemen, and that its wood is appreciated because of its firmness; shields made from wood of the walnut-tree are mentioned also in poetry because of their hardness: *ṣaḥīfatu tursin djawzuhā lam yuthakkabi* (*op. cit.*, 16, l. 2 and 86, l. 17; *Dhayl Dīwān Ibn Muḳbil*, ed. ʿIzzat Ḥasan, Damascus 1381/1962, no. 4). In Islamic times, Iran remained an important area for the cultivation of the walnut-tree. Geographers occasionally describe the differences in climate in view of the trees that are found: walnut-trees grow in cold regions, date-palms in hot regions, according to Muḳaddasī, 459, 463. For the cultivation areas in particular, see P. Schwarz, *Iran im Mittelalter nach den arabischen Geographen*, new impr. Hildesheim 1969, 29, 38, 72, 98, 159, 272, 421, 882, and B. Spuler, *Iran in früh-islamischer Zeit*, Wiesbaden 1952, 402, 406. In Andalusia the walnut was also called by the Romance term *nuez* = *nuwādjī* in Anonymous, Nuruosmaniye 3589, fol. 88a, l. 24, *nūdj(ī)* in M. Asīn Palacios, *Glosario de voces romances*, Madrid-Granada 1943, no. 383.

Since the walnut had allegedly been imported by the Persian kings, the Greeks called it κάρυα βασιλικά (plur.), *ḳāriyā bāsiliḳā* (and variants) in the Arabic translation of Stephanos. It was considered hard to digest and noxious to the stomach; when taken on an empty stomach, it causes nausea, expels tape-worms and, when taken with figs and rue, it is effective against deadly poisons. In the course of the centuries, the Arab physicians and pharmacists acquired considerable new knowledge about the healing power of the nut; the fresh fruit, crushed and mixed with honey, is a proved collyrium against the dimness of the eyesight; shell and leaves are astringent and therefore effective against the trickling of urine. By applying a mixture of walnuts and onions, the poison introduced by the bite of a rabid dog can be extracted. Blonde hair can be d black by a mixture of pulverised iron and the f nut shells, crushed while still green. Other prep tions are effective against psoriasis; by washing mouth with decoctions, soft gums are strengthe The juice of the leaf removes suppurations of ear, the ashes of the shell staunch internal external bleedings, and the fruit pulp of old, gr nuts is effective against boils on the head. Wa oil acts as a solvent and alleviates pain. Cer noxious secondary effects of the walnut, such headaches and yellow gall, can be avoided by ta oxymel or by sucking sour pomegranates, etc was generally believed that sleeping under a tree had a slimming effect.

In a more general sense, *djawz* is synonymous *thamar* and indicates the fruits of a whole rang plants of oriental origin. The latin *nux* may taken this meaning from Arabic pharmacology in same way as *granum* took the meaning of *ḥabb*; might compare the combinations of these term Dozy, *Suppl.*, i, 233 and 239-41 respectively. may be enumerated, after Ibn al-Bayṭār, *Djāmi* 175-8, tr. Leclerc, nos. 526-38, only the fruits frequently combined with *djawz*: 1. *Djawz bauw djawz al-ṭīb*, the nutmeg, *Nux moschata*.—2. *Dj māthil*, the thorn-apple, *Datura stramonium* 3. *Djawz al-ḳayʾ*, the nux vomica.—4. *Djawz ruḳaʿ*, another kind of nux vomica, *Elcaia iemane Forsk.*—5. *Djawz al-khums*, an Indian nut whic not further definable.—6. *Djawz ʿabhar*, undefine 7. *Djawz al-ḳaṭā*, a kind of succulent herb, *Se cepaea*.—8. *Djawz al-zandj* (perhaps to be read a because it is said that the fruit is effective agains *ḳawlandj al-rīḥī*, the windy colic), probably *culia acuminata*.—9. *Djawz al-anhār*, prob synonymous with *djawr al-ḳaṭā*, above no. 7.— *Djawz al-shark*, the Abyssinian nut, *Unona aet pica* (?).—11. *Djawz al-kawthal*, an Indian *Gardenia dumetorum* (?).—12. *Djawz armāniyūs*, Abyssinian nut, = 10 (?).—13. *Djawz djund* fruit of the *Garcinia mangostana*. For fur material, see Dozy, i, 233; M. Meyerhof's c mentary on Maimonides, *Sharḥ asmāʾ al-ʿuḳḳār*, 82; F. A. Flückiger, *Pharmakognosie des Pflan reiches*³, Berlin 1891, Index s.v. Nux.

Bibliography: (besides the titles alre mentioned): Dioscurides, *De materia medica*, Wellmann, i, Berlin 1907, 114 = lib. i, 125; "*Materia médica*" *de Dioscorides*, ii (Arab. tr.) Dubler and Terés, Tetuán 1952, 118; ʿAlī Rabban al-Ṭabarī, *Firdaws al-ḥikma*, ed. Ṣidd Berlin 1928, 383; Rāzī, *Ḥāwī*, xx, Ḥaydarā 1387/1967, 267-71; *Die pharmakolog. Grunds des Abu Mansur . . . Harawi*, tr. A. Ch. Achund Halle 1893, 178, 198; Ibn Sīnā, *Ḳānūn* (Būlāḳ 280 f.; Bīrūnī, *Ṣaydala*, ed. H. M. Saʿīd, Kar 1973, Arab. 144, Engl. 114; Ibn Biklārish, *Mu ini*, Ms. Naples, Bibl. Naz. iii, F. 65, fol. Ghāfiḳī, *al-Adwiya al-mufrada*, Ms. Rabat, Gén. ḳ 155 i, fols. 114a-115a; Ibn Hubal, *M tārāt*, Ḥaydarābād 1362, ii, 50; P. Guigues, *noms arabes dans Sérapion*, in *JA*, 10ème s (1905), vi, s.v. Leuz (no. 337); Maimoni *Sharḥ asmāʾ al-ʿuḳḳār*, ed. Meyerhof, Cairo 1 no. 82; Ibn al-Bayṭār, *Djāmiʿ*, Būlāḳ 1291, i, 17 tr. Leclerc, no. 525; Yūsuf b. ʿUmar, *Muʿta* ed. M. al-Saḳḳāʾ, Beirut 1395/1975, 76; Ibn al-Ḳ *ʿUmda*, Ḥaydarābād 1356, i, 226; Nuwa *Nihāya*, xi, Cairo 1935, 89 f.; Dāwūd al-Anṭ *Tadhkira*, Cairo 1371/1952, i, 109 f.; I. Löw, *Die F der Juden*, ii, 1924, 29-59. (A. DIETRIC

-DJAWZĀʾ [see MINṬAḲAT AL-BURŪDJ]

-DJAYHĀNĪ, surname of viziers of the ānids [*q.v.*], of whom one at least wrote a ous *Kitāb al-Masālik wa 'l-mamālik* which has r been found in spite of the hopes raised by anicsek (*al-Djaihani's lost* Kitab al-masalik val-nalik: *is it to be found at Mashhad*? in *BSOS*, v/l 6), 14-25; see also V. Minorsky, *A false Jayhānī*, *SOAS*, xiii (1949), 89-96). The identity of the ıor of this work poses a problem difficult to solve. Ibn Faḍlān (*Risāla*, ed. A. Z. V. Togan, *Ibn lāns Reisebericht*, Leipzig 1939, text § 4, tr. 6, M. Canard, in *AIEO Alger*, xvi (1958), 54) relates a Djayhānī, who bore the title *al-shaykh al-īd*, obtained for him an audience with the young ānid Naṣr b. Aḥmad (301-31/913-43 [*q.v.*]) and nged for his lodging at the time of his journey Bukhārā in 309/922; he refers only to the *nisba* this individual and makes no mention of any rary activity whatsoever. In 336/947, when sing the *Murūdj*, al-Masʿūdī as yet had no wledge of the *Kitāb al-Masālik*, but he mentions n the *Tanbīh* (ed. Ṣāwī, 65) some years later ore 346/957), and summarises its contents: a cription of the world, marvels, cities, capitals, , rivers, peoples and the places that they inhabit, hout reference to the relevant itineraries (cf. ḳūt, *Buldān*, i, 7), and without passing judgment; him, the name of the author is Abū ʿAbd Allāh ḥammad b. Aḥmad.

bn al-Nadīm, in 377/987-8, four times mentions Djayhānī (*Fihrist*, Cairo ed. 198², 219, 473). In the t passage, Abū ʿAbd Allāh b. Muḥammad b. ṣr, vizier of an unspecified ruler (*ṣāḥib*) of Khurā-, is the author of the *K. al-Masālik*, of a *K. al-sāʾil* written wholly on behalf of a secretary of te, and of two other works, the titles of which are lear; without doubt the titles that should be ected (cf. Dodge's translation, i, 302) are: *K. al-ūd li 'l-khulafāʾ wa'l-umarāʾ* (which was ap-ently a formulary) and *K. al-Ziyādāt fī K. al-shiʾ fi 'l-Maḳālāt* (which might have been a plement to the *Maḳālāt* of al-Nāshiʾ al-Akbar, a t of which has been published and annotated by van Ess in *Frühe muʿtazilitische Häresiographie*, rut 1971). Immediately after, Ibn al-Nadīm otes to al-Balkhī (d. 322/934 [*q.v.*]) quite a long icle in which he describes the circumstances under ich the latter lost the protection of the vizier of ṣr b. Aḥmad, Abū ʿAlī al-Djayhānī, who was a alist (but Abū ʿAlī was no longer vizier at the e of the death of al-Balkhī; see below); D. M. nlop, (*EI*² art. AL-BALKHĪ) makes this Djayhānī e son of the geographer". Subsequently (219) Ibn Nadīm accuses Ibn al-Faḳīh [*q.v.*] of having pla-rised al-Djayhānī's book; apparently it is the *al-Masālik* which is in question, but this source not mentioned in the *K. al-Buldān*, which is ant, and it is impossible to assess the degree of th in an assertion of this kind. Finally, in the rth passage (473), it is Muḥammad b. Aḥmad al-ayhānī who appears among those ostensible slims who were secretly *zindīḳ*s [*q.v.*]; it is not possible that this Djayhānī is the same as the e previously described as a dualist and also the ne as the one whom al-Tawḥīdī (d. 414/1023) otes (*Imtāʿ*, i, 78-90) in order to refute the opinions lently hostile to the Arabs which this writer had pressed "in his book".

So far, we possess only a date (309/922), two nyas, Abū Allāh and Abū ʿAlī, and two names, uḥammad b. Aḥmad and Aḥmad b. Muḥammad. With the same *kunya* and the same name as those in the *Tanbīh* of al-Masʿūdī, Yāḳūt (*Udabāʾ*, xvii, 156-9) introduces the Djayhānī who exercised to some extent the functions of regent at the court of the Sāmānid Naṣr b. Aḥmad from the time of his accession in 301/913; it is evidently of this vizier that Ibn Faḍlān speaks (see above). Yāḳūt, who was well acquainted with the *K. al-Masālik* (*Buldān*, i, 7 and 394, with reference to Soghdia), does not mention its title and confines himself to indicating the *kunya* of the author, Abū ʿAbd Allāh; it is in any case remarkable that, in his article on Djayhān (ii, 181), he mentions only one Djayhānī, Abū ʿAbd Allāh Muḥammad b. Aḥmad, vizier of the Sāmānids at Bukhārā and the author of works, in regard to which he refers the reader to his *K. al-Akhbār*. It is never-theless under the name of Abū ʿAbd Allāh Aḥmad b. Muḥammad b. Naṣr that, copying Ibn al-Nadīm, he places, in his *Muʿdjam al-udabāʾ* (iv, 190-2), the biographical article regarding the Djayhānī who wrote the *K. al-Masālik*; he borrows from a *K. Farīd al-taʾrīkh* on the history of Khurāsān some verses composed against this vizier, of whom he says that after having served under Manṣūr b. Nūḥ (350-65/961-76 [*q.v.*]), he was dismissed by Nūḥ b. Manṣūr (366-87/977-97 [*q.v.*]) in 367/978. For the first time, we have two dates: 301 and 367. Al-Ṣafadī (*Wāfī*, ii, 80-1, no. 389, and viii, 53-4, no. 3463) copies, under the same headings (in other words, respectively, Aḥmad and Muḥammad) the two articles of Yāḳūt which he nevertheless considers suspect; the correct reading seems to him to be Aḥmad b. Muḥammad. Ḥādjdjī Khalīfa (no. 1664) opts for Abū ʿAbd Allāh Aḥmad b. Muḥammad, but Kaḥḥāla, while following this last biographer (*Muʿdjam al-muʾallifīn*, ii, 165) and attributing to Aḥmad, who was still alive in 367/978, the *K. al-Masālik*, the *K. al-Rasāʾil* and the *K. al-ʿUhūd*, has no scruples about a contra-diction and makes Abū ʿAbd Allāh Muḥammad b. Aḥmad (ix, 25) the author of the *Rasāʾil* and the *Masālik*, following the *K. Hadiyyat al-ʿārifīn* of Ismāʿīl Pasha al-Baghdādī.

It is not unusual for the commonness of names such as Muḥammad and Aḥmad to lead writers and their copyists astray, but here, we have the clear impression that the Sāmānids employed three viziers bearing the *nisba* of al-Djayhānī: the first (I), who served in the entourage of Naṣr b. Aḥmad at his accession, must have been called ABŪ ʿABD ALLĀH MUḤAMMAD B. AḤMAD B. NAṢR; he was replaced, no doubt in about 310/922, by Balʿamī [*q.v.*], Abu 'l-Faḍl Muḥammad b. ʿUbayd Allāh, whose successor was ABŪ ʿALĪ MUḤAMMAD B. MUḤAMMAD AL-DJAYHĀNĪ (II); this last was vizier from 326 to his death in 330/937-42 (Ibn al-Athīr, viii, 283), that is, at the end of the reign of Naṣr b. Aḥmad, and there is no reason to suppose that he was not the son of (I); no doubt it was his own son, ABŪ ʿABD ALLAH AḤMAD B. MUḤAMMAD B. NAṢR (III) who was deprived of his office, according to Yāḳūt, in 367/978, and replaced by al-ʿUtbī.

Among these three individuals, who clearly seem to belong to the same family, one should attempt to ascertain which is the author of the *K. al-Masālik* (the other three works mentioned are too little known to be taken into consideration). V. Minorsky (preface to the *Ḥudūd al-ʿālam*, xvii), V. V. Barthold (*ibid.*, 16, 23) and A. Miquel (*La géographie humaine du monde musulman*², Paris-The Hague 1973, xiii-xxiv) opt, with D. M. Dunlop and Sarton (*History of science*, i, 635-6), for no. I, which seems however unlikely, since it is probable that his book would have been known to al-Masʿūdī—who is in fact the only one to refer to the name of Muḥammad b. Aḥmad—before the revision of the *Murūdj* (332/943). The association of no. II with al-Balkhī would incline us to attribute the *K. al-Masālik* to him, but his *kunya* of Abū ʿAlī rules out such an identification, since the author of this work is always Abū ʿAbd Allāh.

In these circumstances, it is legitimate to suggest, as a hypothesis, that the *K. al-Masālik* is a family work, perhaps begun by Muḥammad b. Aḥmad (I), continued by his son Muḥammad b. Muḥammad (II) and completed by his grandson Aḥmad b. Muḥammad (III) in the years immediately following 330/941-2. Examples of this kind are not rare in Arabic literature (see AL-BARḲĪ in Suppl., IBN SAʿĪD AL-MAGHRIBĪ, etc.) and it is probably the plurality of authors which gives rise to confusions which the other exploitable sources do not enable us to solve, although they supply some information regarding the work in question.

Ibn Ḥawḳal (writing in *ca.* 375/985) declares (*Ṣūrat al-arḍ*², text 329, tr. Kramers-Wiet, 322) that he took with him in the course of his travels, which certainly began in 331/943 but stretched over a long period, the books of Ibn Khurradādhbih, of al-Djayhānī and of Ḳudāma, but he regrets possessing the first two which have monopolised too much of his attention, and he does not seem to rate them very highly, although he does not hesitate to exploit al-Djayhānī (453/438) insofar as regards Khurāsān, visited by him in the third quarter of the 4th century. Al-Muḳaddasī (375/985), who also utilises him on a number of occasions, is more explicit; in his *Aḥsan al-taḳāsīm* (3-4; tr. Miquel, Damascus 1963, §§ 10-11), he describes Abū ʿAbd Allāh al-Djayhānī (without further qualification) as a philosopher, astronomer and astrologer and adds that he gathered together people "who were acquainted with foreign countries in order to inquire from them concerning the different states, their resources, their access routes, the height at which the stars revolve there, and the position occupied there by the shadow . . . For him this was a means of conquering these countries, of getting to know their resources and of perfecting his knowledge of the stars and of the celestial sphere". While acknowledging his merits, al-Muḳaddasī seems subsequently to reproach al-Djayhānī for having developed at length the physical geography of the countries described, thus neglecting some important facts. Finally, Gardīzī, who was writing between 440 and 443/1049-52, confirms al-Muḳaddasī's suggestion by declaring (*Zayn al-akhbār*, ed. Nāẓim, Berlin-London 1928, 28-9) that al-Djayhānī was in contact with correspondents residing in areas stretching from Byzantium to China, obtaining written information and making selective use of the material.

The *K. al-Masālik* perhaps consisted of seven volumes (cf. note on ms. C. of al-Muḳaddasī, tr. Miquel, *op. laud.*, 14), but the information supplied by this note is confusing and should be treated with all the more caution seeing that it is hardly likely that Ibn Ḥawḳal would have encumbered himself with such a voluminous work (unless, of course, it was an abridged version that he carried about with him). It must in fact have supplemented the *K. al-Masālik* of Ibn Khurradādhbih, with which moreover it appears sometimes to be confused. On account of this, some authors attribute to this work a particular political stamp, but the information consists above all of purely geographical data, unpublished and difficult to obtain otherwise, which must been of interest to other writers, and we cannot be astonished as the disappearance of a wor widely exploited. The debt of the author of *Ḥudūd al-ʿālam*, of Gardīzī and others to al-Djay has been the object of scholarly speculation on part of Minorsky and of Barthold (see prefaces to *Ḥudūd*, xvii-xviii and 23-6), but it is clear that many uncertainties remain for absolutely conclusions to be reached.

Bibliography: in addition to the sou mentioned in the article, see also Marq *Streifzüge*, xxxi-xxxii and *passim*; A. Mi *Géographie humaine*, xxiii-xxv, 92-5, and in

(CH. PELLA

AL-**DJAZARĪ**, BADĪʿ AL-ZAMĀN ABU 'L- ISMĀʿĪL B. AL-RAZZĀZ, engineer who worked i Djazīra during the latter part of the 6th/12th tury. His reputation rests upon his book, *Kitā maʿrifat al-ḥiyal al-handasiyya* (ed. and tr. D. Hill, *The book of knowledge of ingenious mecha devices*, Dordrecht 1974), which he composed in 1206 on the orders of his master Nāṣir al-Dīn Maḥm a prince of the Artuḳid dynasty [*q.v.*] of Diyār B All that we know of his life is what he tells us in introduction to his book, namely that at the tim writing he had been in the service of the ru family for twenty-five years. The book is div into six categories (*nawʿ*), the first four of wh each contains ten chapters (*shakl*), but the last only five each. The categories are as follows: water-clocks and candle-clocks; (2) vessels pitchers for use in carousals; (3) vessels and ba for hand-washing and phlebotomy; (4) fountains musical automata; (5) water-lifting machines; (6) miscellaneous. There are many illustrations, b of general arrangements and detailed drawings, these are of considerable assistance in understan the text, which contains many technical express that have since fallen into disuse. Some thirt manuscript copies, made between the 7th/13th the 12th/18th centuries, are extant to bear wit to the widespread appreciation of the book in Islamic world (listed in Hill, 3-6; to which must added Topkapı Saray mss. H 414 and A 33 There are, however, no references to al-Djazar the standard Arabic biographical works of Middle Ages, and there is no known translation i a European language before the 20th century.

Only one of the complete machines, a tw cylinder pump driven by a paddle-wheel, can said to have direct relevance to the developmen mechanical technology. Many of the devices, h ever, embody techniques and mechanisms that of great significance, since a number of them ente the general vocabulary of European engineering various times from the 7th/13th century onwa Some of these ideas may have been received direc from al-Djazarī's work, but evidence is lack Indeed, it seems probable that a large part of Islamic mechanical tradition—especially wa clocks and their associated mechanisms and au mata—had been transmitted to Europe before Djazarī's book was composed [see ḤIYAL, in Supp Even leaving aside the question of direct tra mission, we still have a document of the great historical importance. First, it confirms the existe of a tradition of mechanical engineering in Eastern Mediterranean and the Middle East fr Hellenistic times up to the 7th/13th century. Djazarī was well aware that he was continuing t tradition and was scrupulous in acknowledging k of his predecessors, including Apollonius of antium (?), the Pseudo-Archimedes, the Banū ıā (3rd/9th century), Hibat Allāh b. al-Ḥusayn (d. '1139-40), and a certain Yūnus al-Asṭurlābī. er writings and constructions, whose originators e unknown to al-Djazarī, are also mentioned. ndly, his use of and improvement upon the ier works, together with his meticulous des- tions of the construction and operation of each ice, enables us to make an accurate assessment of level of achievement reached by the Arabs in hanical technology by the close of the 6th/12th ury.

Bibliography: Eight valuable articles on l-Djazarī's work were published in the early ears of this century by E. Wiedemann and . Hauser, listed in *Der Islam*, xi (1921), 214; see lso Wiedemann, *Aufsätze zur arabischen Wissen- chaftsgeschichte*, Hildesheim 1970, ii, index, 846. he miniature paintings from two of the manu- cripts are discussed in A. K. Coomaraswamy, *'he treatise of al-Jazarī on automata*, Boston 1924. ee also Brockelmann, S I, 902. For the other riters mentioned, see ḤIYAL, in Suppl.

(D. R. HILL)

L-DJAZARĪ, SHAMS AL-MILLA WA 'L-DĪN ABŪ ADĀ MAʿADD B. NAṢR ALLĀH, ʿIrāḳī composer *maḳāmāt*; a native of Djazīrat al-ʿUmar, he l in 701/1301. His *al-Maḳāmāt al-Zayniyya*, ch were written in 672/1273 for the author's son n al-Dīn Abu'l-Fatḥ Naṣr Allāh, are a good mple of the imitations of the *Maḳāmāt* of al- īrī. The external form of the work follows that l-Ḥarīrī precisely: there are 50 *maḳāmāt*, most of ch are named after towns. The various episodes linked together by a common hero, Abū Naṣr lisrī, and a common narrator, called al-Ḳāsim Jjiryāl al-Dimashḳī. The narratives of al-Djazarī's *ıāmāt* are overwhelmed with the ingenious puns, oorate rhymes and other forms of wordplay for ch they provide the vehicle. The lavish use of words to provide long series of phrases ending he same rhyme makes an immediate understand- of the *maḳāmāt* difficult. They copy the form of r famous model to the point of exaggeration, do not have the inspired wit of its contents. rockelmann records six surviving MSS of *al- ḳāmāt al-Zayniyya* (II, 205, S II, 199). In ad- on there are 13 selections from al-Djazarī's work the Leeds Ar. MS 169, whose principal contents the *Maḳāmāt al-Ḥarīrī*. The selections from al- zarī are from the following *maḳāmāt*: *al-Ḳudsiyya, Āniyya, al-Djīmiyya al-Shīrāziyya, al-Iskan- iyya al-Khayfā', al-Dimashḳiyya, al-Ḍabṭā', al- māliyya al-Djūniyya*.

Bibliography: Ḥadjdjī Khalīfa, ii, col. 1785; rockelmann, *loc. cit.*; for some specimens of Djazarī's rhymed prose and verse, together with nglish translations, and a full list of the 50 itles of his *maḳāmāt*, see R. Y. Ebied and M. J. L. 'oung, *Shams al-Dīn al-Jazarī and his Al-Maqā- ıāt al-Zayniyyah*, in *The Annual of Leeds Univer- ity Oriental Society*, vii (1975), 54-60.

(R. Y. EBIED and M. J. L. YOUNG)

JAZZĀR (A.), "slaughterer", of camels, sheep, ts and other animals. These formed a distinct up of workers in mediaeval Arab society, te apart from the *ḳaṣṣāb* and *laḥḥām*, the two ns used for the butcher. In modern times, how- r, the *djazzār* is synonymous with the latter ns. Djāḥiẓ and other writers use the words *zzārūn* and *ḳaṣṣābūn* alongside each other to show them as separate groups; there were *dār al-djazzārīn* in Medina and Mecca during the 1st century A. H.; while there were many *sūḳ al-djazzārīn* as well as *sūḳ al-ḳaṣṣābīn* in Baghdād and other Islamic cities throughout the Middle Ages. The word *djazzār* seldom appears as a *nisba* with Arabic names, though *ḳaṣṣāb* is often used as an occupational surname among the Arabs.

The *djazzār* was required to be an adult (*bāligh*) and a sane (*ʿāḳil*) Muslim who would utter the name of God at the time of each slaughter. The *muḥtasib* saw to it that the *djazzār* slaughtered animals free from illness or defects. The non-Muslim (*dhimmī*) butchers practised their trade side-by-side with their Arab colleagues in the Middle East and North Africa. Friday was the weekday when most slaughtering of animals took place, according to Djāḥiẓ.

Unlike craftsmen of low prestige like tanners and cuppers, the slaughterers and butchers were not socially ostracised in Arab society. The Prophet forbade one of his relatives to employ a *khādim* [*q.v.*] in the trades of a slaughter (*djazzār*), or butcher (*ḳaṣṣāb*), cupper (*ḥadjdjām*) or goldsmith (*ṣā'igh*), (al-Kattānī, *al-Tarātib*, ii, 106). The *djazzār* was usually a free person (*ḥurr*). The slaughterers were disliked by Arabs for the uncleanliness (*nadjāsa*) of their work. Ibn al-ʿImād cites a case of an unscrupulous *djazzār* who utilised a dead animal for selling its meat, and the case was perhaps not untypical. Some Arab *udabā'* discussed the professions of the nobility (*ṣināʿāt al-ashrāf*) and cited the names of many Ḳuraysh [*q.v.*] like al-Zubayr b. al-ʿAwwām, ʿAmr b. al-ʿĀṣ, ʿĀmir b. Kurayz, and Khālid b. Asīd, among *djazzārūn* in their early careers. The *djazzārūn*, according to Djāḥiẓ, could never be rich, and their economic condition remained unchanged in Arab society over a long period. During the Buwayhid period, the slaughterers, butchers and other tradesmen had to pay additional imposts (*maks*), although they were usually exempt from taxation. The daily earnings of a *djazzār* in Egypt during the reign of al-Ḥākim bi-Amr Allāh (386-411/996-1020) was one *dīnār*, which was an exceptionally high income for a worker.

The slaughterers and butchers are portrayed in Arabic history books as groups of persons with violent tempers. The butchers were expelled from the Round City of Baghdād by Abū Djaʿfar al-Manṣūr for their tendency towards violence. Ṭabarī records that the *djazzārūn* rioted in Mecca in 262/875-6, producing 17 casualties and jeopardising the pilgrimage of many people. For this and other reasons, a minor Arab poet echoed the sentiments of the public by saying that he did not wish to live in a locality where a slaughterer would be his neighbour. Al-Lubūdī, a jurist of the Mamlūk period, came to the conclusion that the occupation of the *djazzār* was undesirable (*makrūh*), because it bred hard-heartedness among men. Despite these criticisms, however, one gets the impression that the slaughterers were not generally despised in Islamic society.

Bibliography: Djāḥiẓ, *al-Ḥayawān*, Cairo 1938-40, iv, 430-2; v, 389; idem, *al-Bukhalā'*, Cairo 1963, 111; Ibn Ḳutayba, *al-Maʿārif*, Beirut 1970, 249-50; Abū Ḥayyān al-Tawḥīdī, *al-Baṣā'ir wa'l-dhakhā'ir*, Damascus 1966-7, ii/1, 41-5; Ṭabarī, *Ta'rīkh*, iii, 1908; al-Wakīʿ, *Akhbār al-ḳuḍāt*, Cairo 1947, i, 102; al-Bayhaḳī, *al-Maḥāsin wa'l-masāwī*, Beirut 1960, 103; al-Khaṭīb al-Baghdādī, *Ta'rīkh Baghdād*, Cairo 1931, i, 80; idem, *al-Bukhalā'*, Baghdād 1964, 188; Ibn al-Djawzī, *al-Muntaẓam*, vii, 15; viii, 181; al-Samʿānī, *al-*

Ansāb, Hyderabad 1963, iii, 268; Ibn al-Athīr, *al-Lubāb fī tahdhīb al-ansāb*, Beirut n.d., i, 276; Ibn Bassām, *Nihāyat al-rutba fī ṭalab al-ḥisba*, Baghdād 1968, 34-36; Ibn al-Ukhuwwa, *Maʿālim al-ḳurba*, London 1938, 97-105; Ibn al-ʿImād, *Shadharāt al-dhahab*, iv, 208; al-Samhūdī, *Wafāʾ al-wafāʾ*, Beirut 1971, ii, 765; al-Kattānī, *Niẓām al-ḥukūma al-nabawiya* (known as *al-Tarātib al-idāriyya*), Beirut n.d., ii, 105-6; H. H. Abdul Wahab, *Waraḳāt*, Tunis 1965, i, 238-41 (writes about a Banu 'l-Djazzār, of Tunis, in the 4th/10th century, who bore the *nisba* of *al-djazzār*, but they ceased to be slaughterers; instead they became famous by practising medicine (*ṭibb*)); ʿAbbās al-Azzāwī, *Taʾrīkh al-ḍarāʾib al-ʿIrāḳiyya*, Baghdād 1959, 25-7; *Alf layla wa-layla*, Beirut 1909, iii, 16-19; ʿAlāʾ al-Dīn al-Lubūdī, *Faḍl al-iktisāb*, Chester Beatty Ms., 4791, f. 57b. (M. A. J. Beg)

AL-**DJAZZĀR PASHA**, AḤMAD, the dominant political figure in southern Syria (the *eyālets* of Sidon and Damascus) during the last quarter of the 18th century and the early years of the 19th. A Bosnian by origin (some sources assert that he was of Christian parenthood), he was born *ca.* 1722; the story of his early life is confused with legend. He apparently began his career at the age of sixteen as a soldier of fortune in Istanbul, where he entered the service of the Grand Vizier Ḥakīm-Oghlū ʿAlī Pasha. In 1756, when his master was sent to attend to the affairs of Egypt for two years, he accompanied him there and stayed behind to attach himself to the local Mamlūk military system. His Mamlūk patron, ʿAbd Allāh Bey, was administering the Buḥayra district in the Delta region as *kāshif* when he was murdered by the local Bedouins in the course of a rising. The *shaykh al-balad* ʿAlī Bey (1760-73) appointed Djazzār to succeed his master as *kāshif* of the district, raising him to the rank of Bey. It is alleged that Djazzār came to be so-called (*djazzār* = "butcher") as a result of the ferocity with which he proceeded to subdue the Bedouins of the Delta; it is possible, however, that Djazzār was his original surname, or that it was a *nom de guerre* which he adopted at the start of his career to promote his image as a competent professional soldier.

Djazzār remained attached to ʿAlī Bey in Egypt for several years. By 1768, however, he had become dangerously compromised in Mamlūk political intrigues. Fleeing Cairo, he returned for a short while to Istanbul; it was probably then that he first became officially attached to the Ottoman state as an agent. He then proceeded to settle in Syria, where he set out to establish for himself a large *mamlūk* household and a private army of Bosnian, Albanian, North African and other mercenaries which became the basis of his personal power.

Between 1768-74 the Porte was involved in a war with Russia; in the course of the hostilities, a Russian naval squadron appeared in the eastern Mediterranean, and Russian agents were sent to Acre (ʿAkkā) to encourage the powerful chieftain of Galilee, Ḍāhir al-ʿUmar, to join ʿAlī Bey of Egypt in a revolt against the Porte (Ḍāhir had successfully usurped power in the southern parts of the *eyālet* of Sidon, with Ottoman acquiescence, since the 1730). It was after Ḍāhir rose in revolt that Djazzār was sent in 1772 by the governor of Damascus to defend Beirut, which had shortly before been bombarded and pillaged by Ḍāhir's Russian allies. Since 1749, Beirut had been controlled by the Shihāb *amīrs* of Mount Lebanon; technically, however, it was part of the *eyālet* of Sidon (as was, indeed, the whole of
Shihāb domain). The ruling Lebanese *amīr*, Y
Shihāb (1770-88), was opposed to Ḍāhir, and ha
at first to see Djazzār established in Beirut. Howe
when Djazzār refused to honour the Shihāb clai
suzerainty over Beirut, Yūsuf Shihāb turned to
old adversary Ḍāhir for help, and the latter s
moned the services of the Russian squadron aga
Djazzār. Beirut was bombarded for a second tim
1773 and besieged by land and sea for four mo
before its garrison was starved into surrender. Dja
fled the town and was given refuge for a time
Ḍāhir in Acre. Betraying his host at the first
portunity, he fled to Damascus, smuggling out
him a convoy of Ḍāhir's munitions. Delighted by
persistent loyalty, the Porte raised him to the r
of Pasha and appointed him *beylerbeyi* of Rum
then *müteṣarrif* of the *sandjaḳ* of Ḳarā Ḥiṣā
Anatolia in 1775. Later in that same year, w
Ḍāhir al-ʿUmar was finally defeated and killed
his own men, Djazzār was appointed *beylerbeyi* of
eyālet of Sidon, and established the seat of
government in Acre. In the following year, he
confirmed in the government of the *eyālet* with
rank of *wazīr*, and continued in the office and r
until his death in 1804.

In Acre, Djazzār used his *mamlūk* household
his private army to set up a régime of remark
stability; his policy of ruthless repression, and
cruelty with which he meted out punishments, m
him the object of general fear. On one occasion
1790, a group of his officers and *mamlūks*, suppo
and possibly prompted by his political enemie
Istanbul and by the French traders in Acre, st
a rebellion against him which was almost succes
but the rebellion was crushed by a surprise ac
and never repeated. Despite the constant intri
against him in Istanbul, Djazzār's mandate in
eyālet of Sidon was annually renewed, without in
ruption, for twenty-nine years—a record witl
precedent in the history of Ottoman provin
administration. On four different occasions (in 1
1790, 1799 and 1803), the *eyālet* of Damascus
also entrusted to his care. At a time when
general decline of the Ottoman state was encoura
rebellion and the usurpation of power in the pro
ces, an efficient and loyal governor in Syria, w
was an area particularly prone to insubordinat
was badly needed, and Djazzār was just the man
the job. In the coastal *eyālet* of Sidon, which
already overshadowing the inland *eyālet* of Dama
in importance because of the increasing Europ
(and particularly French) maritime trade with
Levant, Djazzār suppressed the unruly Mitw
(Twelver Shīʿīs) and other tribes of the hill cou
of Galilee and northern Palestine, and established
administration firmly in the area. While he was
able to destroy the Shihāb emirate in Mount Leba
he did manage to exploit the Maronite-Druze
fessional jealousies and the political factional
prevailing there to reduce the Shihāb *amīrs*, who
once fought successful wars against the governor
Damascus, into docile and subservient fiscal age
In Acre, Sidon and Beirut, he was careful to k
the lucrative commercial activity going, but at
same time took strict measures of control to de
the maximum profit from it for himself. He establis
a personal monopoly over the cotton and grain tr
in his territory, and also made heavy imposition
the silk trade; as a result, he amassed a huge fort
which contributed to the perpetuation of his po
His payments of the required tribute to the Otto

ury, though at times unpunctual, were always ct. In 1799, when General Bonaparte advanced wards from Egypt to occupy Syria, Djazzār, ed by the British, successfully repelled his k on Acre and forced him to retreat; he thereby he seal on the failure of Bonaparte's eastern ure, and paved the way for the final expulsion e French from Egypt two years later.

spite the great power which he came to wield in ıern Syria, Djazzār administered the *eyālet* of ı in strict loyalty to the Porte, and not in the ıer of the *mutaghalliba*—the tribal chieftains and ary adventurers who seized the opportunity of man decline to establish autonomous principa- in the provinces. In Syria, the *mutaghalliba* Ḍāhir in Galilee, and the Shihābs in Mount non) normally sought to promote their power atering politically to the fierce particularism of ocal tribes and sects, of whom the Maronites Druzes of Mount Lebanon and the Mitwālī ther tribesmen of Galilee and northern Palestine prime examples. They also tended to identify selves with the interests of the new and pre- nantly Christian merchant class which thrived ıe import-export trade with Europe. In Mount non and Beirut, the close association of the āb *amīrs* with the Maronite silk merchants was cted by the conversion of an increasing number e *amīrs* from Sunnī Islam to Christianity; in Ḍāhir had favoured the Christians generally, surrounded himself with Christian agents and sers. Like Ḍāhir, Djazzār by necessity employed etent Christians (of the Sakrūdj, Iddī, Ḳālūsh Mārūn families) as secretaries, treasurers and ards; he was careful, however, not to pamper the stians as a community, and most Christians who d him ended up in prison, in the torture cham- or on the gallows, with their fortunes confis- and their families reduced to destitution. wise, Djazzār cared little for the support of the smen and peasants of the mountain hinterland, n he knew to be venal and fickle, and ultimately pendable. Instead, he appears to have sought larity among the Sunnī Muslim populace of towns by appealing to their instinctive senti- s. At a time when the Ottoman state, as the ersal Muslim state, was suffering repeated ts and humiliations at the hands of Christian rs, the high-handed manner in which Djazzār with the local Christian bourgeoisie, and with French and other European traders in Acre and ı, could only have met with strong approval g the urban Muslims, particularly those of the classes. The Pasha's repressive policy towards crypto-Maronite Shihābs and the heterodox es and Mitwālīs must certainly have had the effect. As governor of Beirut in 1772-3, Djazzār armed the Sunnī Muslims of the town to help in efence against the Russians. As ruler of the of Sidon, his unwavering championship of the man cause, which was the cause of Islam, ably secured for him some popularity among ower Muslim classes of the coastal towns. What- the extent of this popularity was, it has remained corded, because the available accounts of his ıe were not written by his supporters but by Christians, the foreigners and the Muslim bles who, as communities and sometimes possibly dividuals, had suffered at his hands and were imous in branding him as a bloodthirsty tyrant. the whole, the Djazzār régime represents the reassertion of the Ottoman imperial prerogative in the traditional manner against the particularist tendencies in Syria, before the radical social and political changes of the 19th century. His determined efforts to break the stubborn local autonomies fore-shadowed the policy of centralisation of the *Tanẓīmāt* period.

Bibliography: ʿAbd al-Razzāḳ al-Bīṭār, *Ḥulyat al-bashar fī taʾrīkh al-ḳarn al-thālith ʿashar*, Damascus 1961-3; Muḥammad Kurd ʿAlī, *Khiṭaṭ al-Shām*, Beirut 1969; Ṭannūs al-Shidyāḳ, *Akhbar al-aʿyān fī Djabal Lubnān*, Beirut 1954; Ḥaydar Shihāb (al-Shihābī), *Taʾrīkh Aḥmad Bāshā al-Djazzār*, Beirut 1955; idem, *al-Ghurar al-ḥisān fī taʾrīkh ḥawādith al-zamān* (published as *Lubnān fī ʿahd al-Umarāʾ al-Shihābiyyīn*, Beirut 1933); E. Lockroy, *Ahmed le Boucher; la Syrie et l'Égypte au 18e siècle*, Paris 1888; Volney, *Voyage en Égypte et en Syrie*, Paris 1959; Amnon Cohen, *Palestine in the eighteenth century; patterns of government and administration*, Jerusalem 1973; H.A.R. Gibb and Harold Bowen, *Islamic society and the West*, i/1 and 2, London 1950-7; P. M. Holt, *Egypt and the Fertile Crescent, 1516-1922*, London 1966.

(KAMAL S. SALIBI)

DJEBEDJI (T. "armourer"), the name given to a member of the corps of "Armourers of the Sublime Porte" (*Djebedjiyān-i dergāh-i ʿālī*), a *Ḳapî Ḳulu* [*q.v.*] Corps closely associated with the Janissaries [*q.v.*]. Their function was to manufacture and repair all arms, ammunition and other equipment belonging to the Janissaries and, on campaign, to transport this equipment to the front, distribute it to the Janissaries and to collect it at the end of the campaign, keeping a record of losses and repairing damaged items.

The Corps was presumably founded shortly after the Janissaries and, until the late 10th/16th century, its recruits came from the *pendj-yek*, the principle by which the state took one in five of prisoners of war and the *dewshirme* [*q.v.*]. However, the system broke down when the *djebedjis*, like the Janissaries, received permission to marry and recruit their own children and native Muslim to the Corps.

Like the other *Ḳapî Ḳulu* Corps, the *djebedjis* were divided into thirty-eight divisions (*orta*), the first of which was divided into 59 sections (*bölük*). Each *orta* represented a different craft in the repair or manufacture of guns, gunpowder and other war materials. The chief officer of the Corps was the *djebedji bashî*, under whom came the *bash ketkhudā*, who usually succeeded him if his post fell vacant, and four other *ketkhudās*. Another officer was the *djebekhāne bash čawushu*. A *bölük bashî* commanded each *orta*, and under him was the *oda bashî*, and the chief craftsmen, called *usta*. The central barracks of the Corps was in Istanbul, but its members served in turn in the frontier fortresses of the Ottoman Empire. A group of *djebedjis* would always accompany a Janissary garrison. Their total strength varied according to the size of the Janissary Corps; there were about 500 *djebedjis* in the mid-10th/16th century and their numbers fluctuated between about 2,500 and 5,000 in the 12th/18th century.

The Corps was abolished, together with the Janissaries, in 1241/1826.

Bibliography: see İ. H. Uzunçarşılı, *Osmanlı devleti teşkilâtında kapukulu ocakları*, ii, 3-21, of which the foregoing is a summary. (ED.)

DJEBEL [see DJABAL].

DJELAL ED-DIN ROUMI [see DJALĀL AL-DĪN RŪMĪ].

DJEZZAR [see DJAZZĀR].

AL-DJILDAKĪ, ʿIzz al-Dīn Aydamir b. ʿAlī b. Aydamir, Egyptian alchemist, who died in 743/1342 or later. He was the last outstanding Muslim adept of his art, of encyclopaedic, though rather uncritical, learning. Almost nothing is known of his life; he himself, however, tells that he spent more than 17 years on extensive travels, which lead him to ʿIrāḳ, Asia Minor, the Maghrib, Yemen, Ḥidjāz, Syria, and Egypt, where he ultimately settled. Al-Djildakī represents the mystical and allegorical trend in Muslim alchemy, but there is evidence that he had real experience in practical operations and chemical substances. His interests extend also to the *khawāṣṣ*, i.e. the magic properties of things, and to pharmacology, medicine and astrology, especially the attribution of metals and other substances to the seven planets. He often reflects on the parallels between natural and alchemical processes, and he attacks Ibn Sīnā who denied the possibility of artificial transmutation (see *Avicennae De congelatione et conglutatione lapidum*, ed. E. J. Holmyard and D. C. Mandeville, Paris 1927, 6-7). His very numerous works, which still exist in many manuscripts, are valuable for the history of alchemy through his philologically-accurate quotations from his predecessors. He is familiar with Djābir b. Ḥayyān's theory of balances as well as with his biography (see P. Kraus, *Jābir ibn Ḥayyān*, in *Mém. de l'Inst. d'Égypte*, xliv (1943), xlv (1942), indexes). Among other Greek, Indian and Persian authorities he refers to Hermes [see HIRMIS], Cleopatra (see M. Ullmann, in *WZKM*, lxiii-lxiv (1972), 161-73), the caliph ʿAlī and Khālid b. Yazīd [*q.v.*], and he also composed lengthy commentaries on writings of Apollonius (see BALĪNŪS), Ibn Umayl [*q.v.*], Ibn Arfaʿ Raʾs, and al-Sīmāwī.

Bibliography: Brockelmann, II, 173-4, S II, 171-2; E. Wiedemann, *Zur Alchemie bei den Arabern*, Erlangen 1922, 17-8, 20-4, 29-31; E. J. Holmyard, *Aidamir al-Jildakī*, in *Iraq*, iv (1937), 47-53; idem, *Alchemy*, Harmondsworth 1957, 100-1; J. Ruska and W. Hartner, *Katalog der orientalischen und lateinischen Originalhandschriften ...*, in *Quellen u. Stud. z. Gesch. d. Naturw. u. d. Medizin*, vii (1940), 263-8; A. Siggel, *Katalog der arabischen alchemistischen Handschriften Deutschlands*, Berlin 1949, 1950, 1956 (valuable analysis of many works); A. A. Semenov, *Sobranie vostočnīkh rukopisei akad. nauk Uzb. SSR*, i, Tashkent 1952, no. 536; F. Sezgin, *GAS*, iv, Leiden 1971, index; M. Ullmann, *Die Medizin im Islam*, Leiden-Cologne 1970; idem, *Die Natur- und Geheimwissenschaften im Islam*, Leiden 1972, indexes; idem, *Katalog der arabischen alchemistischen Handschriften der Chester Beatty Library*, i, Wiesbaden 1974, index.

(G. Strohmaier)

DJISR MANBIDJ [see ḲALʿAT NADJM].

DJIRGA (Pashto; cf. H. G. Raverty, *A dictionary of the Pukhto, Pushto, or language of the Afghāns*, London 1867, 330b), an informal tribal assembly of the Paṭhāns in what are now Afghānistān and Pakistan, with competence to intervene and to adjudicate in practically all aspects of private and public life among the Paṭhāns.

In the course of his abortive mission to Shāh Shudjāʿ and the Durrānī court of Kabūl in 1809 [see AFGHĀNISTĀN. v. History (3) (A)], Mountstuart Elphinstone described the *djirga* system as alive and vital, with assemblies at various levels, from the village at the bottom up through the clan or *khēl* to the tribe or *ulus* at the top, with a *djirga* of subordinate chiefs around the tribal *khān*; but he observed that it was a model frequently mod or disrupted rather than a neat hierarchy o stitutions. He noted too that the *djirga* was principal means of administering criminal jus where an offended party had not already ave his wrongs in blood, and of determining amoun compensation due to a victim; and he adjudg a useful and tolerably impartial institution *account of the kingdom of Caubul*[3], London 18 215-26). At the very apex of the system, the of Afghānistān might summon a "great (*djirga*" of leading chiefs for consultation at cri junctures.

The political division of the Paṭhāns in the c of the 19th century into those to the east of became the Durand Line and in British India those to the west in the independent kingdo Afghānistān eliminated the *loya djirga* as an e tive expression of feelings of the whole Pa nation, although the institution was event incorporated into the political structure of mc Afghānistān as a representation of all ethnic social groups with the state, and not merely o Paṭhāns; for the *djirga* in Afghānistān of the two centuries, see MADJLIS.. 2. Afghānistān.

On the British side of the Frontier, the *djirga* continued as an instrument of democratic t expression; it was, for instance, tribal *djirgas* w in November 1947 signified the adhesion of North-West Frontier Province to the nas Pakistan, and in February 1980 a *djirga* of Pa and Balūč chiefs and notables met at Sībī in n ern Balūčistān to affirm opposition to fu Soviet Russian encroachment after the l power's occupation of Afghānistān towards the of 1979. As far back as the second half of the century, a modified and less authentic typ *djirga* had been made part of the Frontier Cr Regulations, originally promulgated in 1872. U this arrangement, cases involving tribal ho blood feuds and women could be withdrawn the magistrates' courts and arbitrated upon *djirga*, which was however in this case a grou tribal elders appointed by the magistrate and ceptable to both parties. Here the *djirga* wa ancillary of British Indian law, though after *ca.* in the recently-pacified parts of northern Balūč and the newly-administered tribal areas of North-West Frontier Province, the *djirga* adopted as a substitute for the formal legal sys thus in effect enshrining Paṭhān custom.

Bibliography: (in addition to references g in the article): Sir Olaf Caroe, *The Pathans 550 AD 1957*, London 1958, 353-6, 435; J. W. S *The Pathan borderland*, The Hague 1963, 6 145-7.

(C. E. Boswort

DJUDHĀM (A.), leprosy or Hansen's dise

I. *Terminology*. A number of Arabic terms may refer to leprosy were created on the basis o symptomatology of the disease. Aside from distinctive symptoms of advanced lepromа leprosy, various terms were adopted that descriptive of leprous lesions, but they were restricted exclusively to leprosy. No clinical cas leprosy are reported in the mediaeval me literature that might clarify the terminology. T can be little doubt, however, that *djudhām* refe to leprosy, particularly of the lepromatous type. term was used in pre-Islamic Arabia; it was de from the Arabic root of the word, meaning mutilate" or "to cut off," and is descriptive o rious disfigurement that occurs in cases of l us leprosy. Thus, *adjdham* (pl. *djadhmā*) may . "mutilated" from having an arm or foot cut r "leper" and "leprous" (al-Murtaḍā, *Ghurar vā'id*, Cairo 1954, i, 5). Conversely, the use of oot would strongly suggest that the lepromatous of the disease existed in pre-Islamic Arabia. .derable confusion exists concerning terms other *djudhām*; the difficulty is certainly due to the rous forms that leprosy may take, particularly s early stages and its mimicry of other skin ses. The term *baraṣ* was definitely used to leprosy, but it could be applied to other skin ders. This term was also used in pre-Islamic ia. It was derived from the Arabic root that mean "to be white or shiny." Emphasis on the ness of the skin in the Arabic medical accounts *raṣ* and *bahak* may have referred to the hypoentation occurring in the early stages of dihous leprosy or the macules and infiltrated is of tuberculoid leprosy. Depending on the xt, white and black *baraṣ*, white and black *ḳ*, *wadaḥ*, and *ḳawābī* were often used to name us symptoms. In addition, the following terms l apply to leprosy, but they were rarely used ne are clearly euphemistic: *abḳaʿ*, *aḳshar*, , *aslaʿ* (*sulʿ*), *barash*, *bayāḍ* (*bayḍā'*), *dā' al-asad*, *l-ḳuʿṭāl*, *muraḳḳaʿ*, *sū'* (*aswā'*).

Medical history. There is no persuasive nce that true leprosy occurred in ancient Egypt, potamia, or Persia before the time of Alexander Great. It must have existed much earlier in i, the Far East, and probably central Africa. *ʿat*, the so-called leprosy of Leviticus, does not spond to any modern diagnosis of the disease; s a non-specific condition and essentially a noncal notion. The *lepra* (Gr. *leprós*, "scaly") ioned in some of the Hippocratic writings was a skin ailment that cannot be identified and probably not related to leprosy. It was not e 300 B.C. that true leprosy entered the sphere edical science. At that time, physicians of andria became acquainted with its lepromatous and named it *elephantiasis* because of the ening and corrugation of the skin. The tuberd type, however, was not yet clearly distinguished other, non-specific skin eruptions. Galen [see INŪS], in the 2nd century A.D., inadequately ibed what he called *elephantiasis graecorum* and (*Ad glauconem*). The earliest and best desion of leprosy was given by a contemporary alen, Aretaeus of Cappadocia (*Extant works*, ed. tr. F. Adams, London 1856, 123-9/366-73, 2364-7); Aretaeus' pathology and treatment of the se were important because they strongly influd later Greek physicians whose works were lated into Arabic. With the single exception of aeus, however, the pathogenesis of leprosy was ined in late Roman medicine by the theory of ours. Leprosy was due primarily to a prenance of black bile, the melancholic humour, he body. The disease was considered by the k doctors to be both contagious and hereditary. victims were believed to be unclean and speilly marked by strong venereal desires. There an increasing recognition of the polymorphous acter of leprosy, particularly of the milder culoid type. The disease in advanced stages considered incurable. All the ancient authors d to mention the loss of sensation, which is a picuous symptom of the disease. The treatment e diseased consisted of bloodletting, cauterisation, ation, baths, fomentations, diets, and invariably the theriac of vipers. Together with the classical descriptions of leprosy, the various treatments entered into Arabic medical science.

The earliest indisputable proof of leprosy in the Middle East has been found by Møller-Christensen in two skeletons from Egypt (Aswān) that date from about A.D. 500. Therefore, there can be little doubt that genuine leprosy existed from the early Islamic period and that Muslim doctors had sufficient opportunity to observe it. Practically every Arabic writer on medicine discussed leprosy. The earliest account seems to have been the *K. fi 'l-djudhām* by Yūḥannā b. Māsawayh [*q.v.*]. The work is apparently lost, but it was frequently quoted by later Arabic authors; an anonymous treatise does exist that contains the opinions of Ibn Māsawayh as well as those of al-Rāzī and Ibn Sīnā (A. Z. Iskandar, *Catalogue of Arabic manuscripts*, London 1967, 70 f., 126). The first full account of leprosy in Arabic medicine is to be found in al-Ṭabarī's *Firdausu 'l-Ḥikmat* (ed. Siddiqi, Berlin 1928, 318-25); the pathology and therapeutics of the disease are largely consistent with the earlier Greek medical texts. Arabic writers who discussed leprosy include the following: al-Kindī (*Fihrist*, tr. Dodge, New York 1970, ii, 621; *Medical formulary*, tr. Levy, Madison 1966, 60, 158, 233 *et passim*), Yūḥannā b. Sarābiyūn, Thābit b. Ḳurra (*K. al-Dhakhīra*, ed. Sobhy, Cairo 1928, 7, 29, 138-41; M. Ullmann, *Die Medizin im Islam*, Leiden 1970, 124), al-Rāzī (*K. al-Ḥāwī*, Hyderabad 1970, iv, 59 f., 65, 73, 93, xxiii/2, 1-33, 47-72, 88-120), Ibn Abi 'l-Ashʿath (Ullmann, *Die Medizin*, 139), ʿAlī b. al-ʿAbbās al-Madjūsī (*Kāmil*, Cairo 1877, i, 310 f., ii, 194-6), Abū Manṣūr Ḳumrī, Abu 'l-Ḳāsim al-Zahrāwī, Ibn Sīnā (*Ḳānūn fi 'l-ṭibb*, Būlāḳ 1877, iii, 140-6, 281-7), al-Djurdjānī, Ibn Abi 'l-ʿAlā' Zuhr (Albucasis, *On surgery and instruments*, ed. and tr. Spink and Lewis, Berkeley and Los Angeles 1973, 142-9), Ibn al-Ḳuff (*K. al-ʿUmda*, Hyderabad 1356/1937, i 155 f., ii, 48-51), Ibn Masʿūd al-Shīrāzī, al-Azraḳī (*Tashīl al-manāfiʿ*, Cairo 1304/1887, 275 f., 291-4), Nafīs b. ʿIwaḍ and Ghiyāth b. Muḥammad.

The medical textbook of al-Madjūsī [*q.v.*] is quite important because it was one of the first Arabic works to be translated into Latin (*Liber pantegni*). Its translation by Constantinus Africanus [*q.v.*] was decisive for the Western terminology of leprosy. The translator could not use the word *elephantiasis* in translating al-Madjūsī's account of leprosy because in Arabic the term (*dā' al-fīl*) was already used for the present-day disease of that name. In this situation, Constantinus seized upon Biblical usage, where the Latin translation of Hebrew and Greek was *lepra*; he therefore translated *djudhām* as *lepra* rather than *mutilatio*, which would have been more precise and would have avoided the stigma attached to *lepra*. As it was, the use of *lepra* for leprosy in general caused confusion with the Hippocratic use of the word and extended the application of the name with its evil connotations to a wider range of skin disorders. Al-Zahrāwī's work was also translated into Latin and became well-known in Europe. In his discussion of leprosy, al-Zahrāwī made a significant contribution to medicine by describing, for the first time apparently, the neurological symptoms of the disease. It is difficult to believe that local anaesthesia had not been observed among lepers much earlier. In the Middle East, the loss of sensation caused by leprosy was noticed by Ibn al-Ḳuff; the source of his observation is unclear. (The leprosy of Baldwin IV [d. 1206], king of the

Latin Kingdom of Jerusalem, is described by William, bishop of Tyre; the narrative contains the only incontrovertible clinical evidence of the anaesthetic symptoms of leprosy in the Middle East [*A history of deeds*, tr. Babcock and Krey, New York 1934, ii, 296, 460].) The description of insensitivity by al-Zahrāwī was repeated in the Western medical literature, at least from the 12th century. It served as a means of distinguishing lepers and excluding them from society. As opposed to the Galenic tradition of the other works, al-Azraḳī's work may be regarded as a good example of "Prophetic medicine" (*al-ṭibb al-nabawī*). Al-Azraḳī's quasi-medical discussion of leprosy may well reflect popular beliefs and practices that persisted throughout the mediaeval period alongside those of professional medicine. Moreover, it was a common practice during the mediaeval period to attribute to stones the ability to ward off disease; for leprosy, topaz (*zabardjad*) was reputed to have this property (M. Ullmann, *Neues zum Steinbuch des Xenokrates*, in *Medizinhistorisches Journal*, vii [1973], 71).

In sum, the Arabic medical writers borrowed heavily from Hellenistic sources, but their works were not entirely imitative. The description of leprosy in the Arabic medical textbooks followed the encyclopaedic form of ancient manuals; the descriptions of leprosy were brief, non-clinical, and largely theoretical. The Muslim understanding of the disease was most clearly indebted to the earlier sources in its adoption of the humoural theory to explain the illness. Care and treatment were also consistent with Hellenistic practices; however, Arabic medicine introduced a greater variety of simple and compound medications. Furthermore, the Arabic doctors adopted the view that leprosy was contagious and hereditary. Yet they did not view the disease as fiercely contagious, and their writings lack any element of moral censorship of the diseased. Moreover, the medical texts did not recommend flight from the leper or his isolation from the community. The influence of this non-condemnatory attitude toward the disease and its victims in Muslim society is impossible to gauge, but it would be reasonable to assume that through the activity of Muslim doctors it weighed against the selective discrimination and segregation of lepers. Generally, the Arabic writers paid greater attention to leprosy than the Hellenistic doctors. In the classification and description of the disease Muslim doctors made significant advances. The earlier writers distinguished, for the most part, between *elephantiasis* and leprosy. The Arabic writers tended to regard *elephantiasis-djudhām* as one form of leprosy. Concerning the symptomatology of leprosy, the Arabic doctors refined the description of the skin lesions and called attention to the neurological signs. Despite its own inherent difficulties, the Arabic terminology was more appropriate and detailed than that of the classical authors. It is probable that Arabic terminology influenced Byzantine nomenclature. Finally, Arabic medical understanding of leprosy was important because it was conveyed to the West and formed the basis for European knowledge of the disease until the 17th century.

III. *Social history*. The Arabs in pre-Islamic Arabia were afflicted by leprosy, along with a large number of other communicable diseases. Leprosy is attested by the famous Arabic poets of the period. The first important figure in the history of the Arabs before Islam who probably suffered from some form of leprosy was Djadhīma al-Abrash [*q.v.*] or al-Waḍḍāḥ, the king of al-Ḥīra, who play dominant role in the politics of Syria and ʿIr the second quarter of the 3rd century A.D. famous pre-Islamic poets may also have been str by the illness. The first, ʿAbīd b. al-Abraṣ, o basis of his name, may have been leprous. Le would account for his wife's aversion from which is mentioned in his poetry (C. Lyall, *Dīwān*, Leiden-London 1913, 6, 33-6, 38 f.). second and more famous was al-Ḥārith b. Ḥ al-Yashkurī [*q.v.*], who wrote the seventh o *Muʿallaḳāt.*

The Ḳurʾān mentions in two places the heali the lepers (*al-abraṣ*) by Jesus (III, 48 and V, More important for their influence on M society are the *aḥādīth* that were attributed t Prophet concerning leprosy. The best-known of traditions is the statement that a Muslim sh flee from the leper as he would flee from the Similarly, another familiar tradition asserts a healthy person should not associate with l for a prolonged period and should keep a sp distance from them (Wensinck, *Handbook*; Bukhārī, *al-Ṣaḥīḥ*, Būlāḳ ed., viii, 443; Ibn Ḳuta *ʿUyūn al-akhbār*, Cairo 1925-30, iv, 69; *LA*, 354 f.). The two pious traditions are prescrip for social behaviour and appear to deal with moral and medical difficulties posed by the l The traditions may have strengthened the desi Muslims to avoid those individuals who were spicuously afflicted by the disease because it morally as well as physically offensive. Le was believed by some to be a punishment by for immorality. Consequently, leprosy was invoked as a curse on a Muslim for his imm behaviour. Medically, both traditions seem to ex an implicit belief in contagion. The idea of conta is also found in other traditions that are unre to leprosy and in the medical and non-me literature. Nevertheless, the belief in contagion denied by the Prophet in a number of other tradi which state that disease comes directly from The tradition advising flight from the leper i fact, preceded by a complete denial of contagic the collection of al-Bukhārī. Thus the issue of tagion is quite contradictory; it was the su from an early time of religio-legal discussion attempted to harmonise these traditions. contradiction was not resolved; it would ap that many witnessed contagion and found justi tion for it in the traditions, while the more religic inclined may have adhered to the principle of contagion. The latter were partially justified in case of leprosy because it is only moderately tagious and some individuals are not predisp to it at all. There were also traditions that commended supplication to God for relief leprosy, for the matter should not be left ent to fate.

The legal status of the leper was directly rel to the pious traditions. Leprosy is not discusse the Arabic legal texts as a separate subject, b is treated as a disability within such broad a as marriage, divorce, inheritance, guardianship, interdiction of one's legal capacity [see ḤA Because leprosy was considered a mortal illness, leper was limited in his legal rights and obligatio along with the minor, the bankrupt, the insane, the slave. The leper's status seems to have particularly close to that of the insane in matters, especially in regard to marriage and divc a marriage could be dissolved by either pe

.use of the disease. In Mālikī law, a man in an ınced state of leprosy should be prevented from ıbiting with his slave wives and still more so his free wives, which is consistent with a belief e hereditary nature of the malady. Also, Mālikī allowed an automatic guarantee of three days, he expense of the seller of slaves, against any lts" in a slave; the guarantee was extended to year in case of leprosy. In addition, the develop-t of leprosy in a slave might be a cause for his umission.

general, the differing religio-legal traditions ed as the bases for various interpretations of the ıse. These traditions account for the wide spec- of behaviour by and toward the leper, ranging his total freedom of action to segregation in ɔsaria. The range of popular responses to the : is reflected in early Arabic literature that s with leprosy and other skin irregularities.)jāḥiẓ and Ibn Ḳutayba [*qq.v.*] collected poetry narrative accounts on this subject. Al-Dj̲āḥiẓ's pilation of material is to be found in his *al-Burṣān l-ʿurdj̲ān* (Cairo 1972, 8-110), which is concerned a large number of physical infirmities and onal characteristics. The author's objective is how that physical infirmities and peculiarities ot hinder an individual from being a fully active ber of the community or bar him from im-ant offices. Al-Dj̲āḥiẓ maintained that such ents are not social stigmas but are what may be d signs of divine blessing or favour. The afflicted spiritually compensated by God and special t should be attached to their lives. Thus he tered the contrary opinion that the infirm ıld be disparaged or satirised for their afflictions. of the poets quoted by Ibn Ḳutayba also ar to say that skin disorders should not be the e of scorn and revilement but should prompt the rer to repentance (*ʿUyūn al-akh̲bār*, iv, 63-7). Ibn ıyba and al-Dj̲āḥiẓ cite numerous references to sy in Arabic poetry, as in the fierce poetic s of Dj̲arīr and al-Farazdaḳ, and mention those s who were themselves leprous, such as Ayman h̲uraym [*q.v.*]. There are other historical reports robable instances of the disease in early Islamic ry, such as that of Ibn Muḥriz [*q.v.*].

e most important political figure in early Islam was probably afflicted by leprosy was ʿAbd al-z b. Marwān [*q.v.*]. It is reported that he suffered "lion-sickness" i.e. *dj̲udh̲ām*. He was given y medications for the ailment, but they were ective. Therefore, his physicians advised him to e to Ḥulwān [*q.v.*] because of the sulphurous ıgs there, and he built his residence there (Abū , *The churches and monasteries of Egypt*, ed. and 3. Evetts in *Anecdota Oxoniensia*, vii, Oxford , 154). Shortly after the time of ʿAbd al-ʿAzīz, ıave the brief but significant statement of al-arī that the caliph al-Walīd I was in Syria, ably Damascus, in 88/707 and conferred a ber of benefits upon the people. Al-Ṭabarī says awarded the lepers [*al-mudj̲adh̲dh̲amīn*] and : 'Do not beg from the people.' And he awarded y invalid a servant and every blind man a er "(*Taʾrīkh̲*, vi, Cairo 1964, 496). As with the lids and the blind, the caliph apparently made isions for the lepers in some manner. The passage nbiguous, but it seems that he had the lepers rated from the rest of the population (E. Browne, ɔian *medicine*, repr. Cambridge 1962, 16 f.). This of al-Walīd is traditionally considered by Arabic ɔrians to be the institution of the first hospital in Islam (cf. S. Hamarneh, *Development of hospitals in Islam*, in *Journal of the History of Medicine and Allied Sciences*, xvii [1962], 367). The first hospital is alleged by al-Maḳrīzī to have been built by al-Walīd in the year 88/707, and the caliph "provided for doctors and others in the *māristān*, and he ordered the restraint of the lepers [*al-dj̲adh̲mā*] lest they go out, and stipends for them, and provisions for the blind." (*al-K̲h̲iṭaṭ*, repr. Cairo 1970, ii, 405; see also BĪMĀRISTĀN and A. ʿĪssā, *Histoire des Bimaristans*, Cairo 1928, 95). One may well imagine that the caliph created a hospice—*dār al-marḍā*, later called a *māristān* or *bīmāristān* in the ʿAbbāsid period—for the afflicted of the city, comparable to Byzantine practice (see D. Constantelos, *Byzantine philanthropy and social welfare*, New Brunswick, N.J. 1968, 78 *et passim*). The later hospitals of the ʿAbbāsid period treated leprosy and other chronic ailments in special quarters (S. Hamarneh, *Medical education and practice in mediaeval Islam*, in *The history of medical education*, ed. C. O'Malley, Berkeley and Los Angeles 1970, 41).

Leprosy certainly existed in the Middle East during the mediaeval period, but there is no way of determining its extent. Individual cases of leprosy are occasionally mentioned in the historical literature, such as that of Abu 'l-Barakāt al-Bag̲h̲dādī [*q.v.*], who died of leprosy about 560/1164. We know as well that leprosy afflicted the Jews because there is considerable material about lepers in the Geniza, especially in letters from Tiberias, where they sought healing in the hot springs and the air of the place (J. Mann, *The Jews in Egypt and in Palestine*, Oxford 1920-2, i, 166 f., ii, 192-5). According to Ibn al-Uk̲h̲uwwa (*Maʿālim al-ḳurba*, ed. R. Levy, 1938, ch. xlii), the *muḥtasib* or market inspector [see ḤISBA] must not allow people suffering from leprosy to visit the baths. Also from Egypt, a *waḳf* of the Mamlūk sultan Barsbāy [*q.v.*] states that those afflicted especially with leprosy (*dj̲udh̲ām aw baraṣ*) should not be employed (A. Darrag, ed., *L'acte de waqf de Barsbay*, Cairo, 1963, 56). The specific discrimination against lepers in these two instances appears to show that the theological proscription of contagion had very little practical effect (see M. Ullmann, *Islamic medicine*, Edinburgh 1978, ch. vi). Furthermore, lepers commonly begged in the streets of the cities, despite the pious endowments on their behalf and laws against mendicancy. While many must have been genuinely leprous, it was not unusual during the mediaeval period for men and women to feign the disease by intentional disfigurement in order to receive public charity (C. E. Bosworth, *The mediaeval Islamic underworld*, i, Leiden 1976, 24, 84, 100). Deception of the opposite kind was also common in the slave market, where a buyer had to be on his guard against the concealment of leprous sores on the bodies of slaves. During the later Middle Ages, the reappearance of plague must have destroyed large numbers of lepers because of their exceptional vulnerability to diseases other than leprosy. The Black Death in the mid-8th/14th century and the serious recurrences of plague thereafter may account for the particular depopulation of lepers among a generally-diminished population.

In the Islamic West, leprosaria were established and special quarters were designated for lepers. The quarters seem generally to have been located outside the walls of many Muslim cities, often in conjunction with leper cemeteries (Leo Africanus, *Description de l'Afrique*, ed. and tr. A. Épaulard, Paris 1956, i, 60 f., 229, ii, 399; E. Lévi-Provençal,

Histoire de l'Espagne musulmane, i, 188, iii 335, 382, 434). The first Muslim hospital appears to have been built in al-Ḳayrawān, and near it was situated a separate building called the *dār al-djudhamā*, where lepers received medical treatment (Hamarneh, *Development of hospitals*, 375). Further west, the Almohad sultan Yaʿḳūb al-Manṣūr founded hospitals for lepers (see BĪMĀRISTĀN and R. Le Tourneau, *Fès avant le Protectorat*, Casablanca 1949, 72, 110). Sulphur springs were considered to be particularly beneficial for lepers in North Africa as they were in the Middle East (E. Westermarck, *Ritual and belief in Morocco*, London 1926, ii, 44, 484 ff., 497 ff.; Legey, *Essai de folklore marocain*, Paris 1926, 158; C. Grey, ed. and tr., *Travels of Venetians in Persia*, London 1873, 144; Leo Africanus, *op. cit.*).

In Anatolia, the Ottomans built hospitals in the later Middle Ages, similar to the Byzantine *xenodochia*. A leper house was built at Edirne in the time of Murād II (d. 855/1451) and functioned for almost two centuries. Before this foundation, the Turks had constructed others in Sivas, Kastamonu, and Kayseri. In 936/1530 Sulaymān II built a leprosarium in Scutari, which survived until modern times. An important leper house was founded as a *waḳf* by Sultan Selīm I in 920/1514 near Istanbul, which operated until 1920; it is described by A. Süheyl Ünver in his article, *About the history of the leproseries in Turkey*, in *Neuburger Festschrift* (1948), 447-50.

The traditional ways of dealing with lepers in Muslim society lasted well into the 19th century. Lepers and leprosaria were particularly noticed by Western travellers, and their accounts add to our knowledge about the plight of the diseased (*Ulrich J. Seetzen's Reisen*, Berlin 1854-9, i, 120 f., 277 f.; Klingmüller, *op. cit.*, 49; D. L. Zambaco, *Voyages chez les lépreux*, Paris 1891; *Aus einem Briefe des Herrn Consul Wetzstein an Prof. Fleischer*, in *ZDMG*, xxiii (1869), 309-13). There is no reliable observation of true leprosy by Western travellers in the Middle East during the mediaeval or early modern periods. The only exception is the report of leprosy in Egypt by Prosper Alpini in his *Medicina Aegyptorum* [1719], 56). Europeans' concern about the disease was often heightened by their belief in its highly contagious nature (M. Clerget, *Le Caire*, ii, Cairo 1934, 16; *Description de l'Égypte*, i, Paris 1809, 492-8, ii/2, Paris 1822, 697; Clot-Bey, *Aperçu général sur l'Égypte*, ii, Paris 1840, 356 f.). Leprosy was also probably common in the countryside, but most of our documentation comes from the urban centres. Leprosy as well as syphilis and elephantiasis frequently occurred in Egyptian villages in the 19th century and were poorly treated (J. Walker, *Folk medicine in modern Egypt*, London 1934, 23). Today leprosy remains a health problem in the Middle East and North Africa.

Bibliography:

I. Terminology: The technical vocabulary for leprosy has been discussed by mediaeval and modern scholars: E. Seidel, *Die Medizin im Kitāb Mafātīḥ al ʿUlūm*, in *SBPMS* Erlg., xlvii (1915), 10, 16 f.; *LA*, iii, 474 ff., viii, 151, 270, xi, 311, xiv, 353-7; Lane, *Lexicon*, 188, 267, 298; P. Richter, *Beiträge zur Geschichte des Aussatzes*, in *Südhoff's Archiv für Geschichte der Medizin*, iv (1911), 328-52; F. Adams, *The Seven Books of Paulus Aegineta*, London 1846, ii, 12-5, 21-3; C. Elgood, *On the significance of al-Baraṣ and al-Bahaq*, in *JASB*, xxvii (1931), 177-81; A. Stettler-Schär, *Leprologie im Mittelalter und im der frühen Neuzeit*, in *Beiträge zur Geschichte der L* Zurich 1972, 55-72.

II. Medical history: In addition to the w cited above, see: *Galeni opera omnia*, ed Kühn, 1821-33, xiv, 757; Caelius Aurelianus *acute diseases*, ed. and tr. I. Drabkin, Ch 1950, 816-9; Oribasius, *Collectio medica*, t Daremberg, Paris 1851, iv, 59 ff.; H. Carlo *Der Lepraabschnitt aus Bernard von Go "Lillium medicinae"*, Leipzig 1913, 9; D Zambaco, *La lèpre a travers les siècles et les con* Paris 1914; V. Klingmüller, *Die Lepra*, B 1930; H. A. Lichtwardt, *Leprosy in Afghan* in *International Jnal. of Leprosy*, ii (1935), M. el-Dalgamouni, *The antileprosy campaig Egypt*, in *IJL*, vi (1938), 1-11; L. Rogers E. Muir, *Leprosy*, Baltimore 1946; R. Coch and T. Davey, eds., *Leprosy in theory and prac* Bristol 1964; V. Møller-Christensen, *Eviden leprosy in earlier peoples*, in D. Brothwell A. Sandison, eds., *Diseases in antiquity*, Sp field, Ill. 1967, 295-306; idem, *Evidence of t culosis, leprosy and syphilis in Antiquity an Middle Ages*, in *Proceedings of the 19th I national Congress of the History of Med (Basel 1964)*, Basel-New York 1966, 22 H. Koelbing and A. Stettler-Schär, *Aussatz, L Elephantiasis Graecorum — zur Geschichte der L in Altertum*, in *Beiträge zur Geschichte der L* 34-54; O. Skinenes, *Notes from the histor leprosy*, in *IJL*, xli (1973), 220-37; E. Kol T. Hushangi, B. Azadeh, *Leprosy in Iran*, in xli (1973), 102-11.

III. Social history: In addition to the w cited above, see: Ibn Ḥawḳal, *Configuration terre*, tr. Kramers and Wiet, Paris-Beirut 196 30, 35; C. Niebuhr, *Travels*, Edinburgh 179 276 f.; C. Doughty, *Travels in Arabia Des* London 1936, i, 436 f., 655, ii, 18; W. Wittm *Travels*, repr. New York 1971, 352, 446, 4 K. Opitz, *Die Medizin im Koran*, Stuttgart 1 22 f., 27, 39 f.; E. Seidel, *Die Lehre von der C gion bei den Arabern*, in *AGM*, vi (1912), 8 K. Grön, *Lepra in Literatur und Kunst*, in K müller, *op. cit.*, 806-42; Y. L. de Bellefo *Traité de droit musulman comparé*, Paris 1 245-69; R. Eshraghi, *Social aspects of lep* in *Meshed Medical Journal*, iii (1969), 3 N. A. Stillman, *Charity and social service medieval Islam*, in *Societas*, v (1975), 10 M. W. Dols, *The Black Death in the Middle* Princeton 1977, 23 *et passim*. (M. W. Do

DJUHAYNA [see ḲUḌĀʿA].

DJULFĀ (in Armenian, J̌ułay), a town on River Araxes, on the northern border Ādharbāydjan, once in Armenia and now in U.S.S.R. Also, in 1014/1605, Shāh ʿAbbās I fou a suburb of Iṣfahān bearing the same nam accommodate the Armenians transferred by him the original town.

I. Djulfā in Ādharbāydjan is situated in 38° 58′ N, long. 45° 39′ E, and is built on the nort bank of the Araxes besides an old bridge (Shara Dīn ʿAli Yazdī, *The history of Timur-Bec*, Lo 1723, 265-6); it lies in the ancient canton of Go mentioned in Armenian literature as early as *History* of Moses of Khoren (J. A. Saint-Ma *Mémoires historiques et géographiques sur l'Arm* Paris 1818, i, 1267, 133, 237, ii, 365, 423). Lyin the edge of a volcanic belt extending south-east Iran, the surrounding land is rocky and ba although suitable for the cultivation of the vi ses of Khoren refers to Gołtʿn as *ginewēt* ("wine ı"). On the main route northwards from Tabrīz Nakhidjevan and Tiflis, in the 10th/16th century ılfā became the centre of a flourishing community Armenian merchants, trading as far afield as rope, India and Central Asia, and with a special erest in the traffic of silk. According to Cartwright, the end of the century the population was 10,000, h 2,000 houses (John Cartwright, *The Preachers avels* . . ., London 1611, 35-6).

After his successful campaigns against the Ottoman rks, Shāh ʿAbbās I resolved to depopulate eastern nenia and to create an empty tract between nself and his enemy. To this end, he transferred major part of the population to Persia, estimated some 60,000 families, including numbers of orgians and Jews besides Armenians. The exodus described by the Armenian chronicler Arakʿel of briz, who refers to it as the great *sürgün* ("exile, oulsion") (Arakʿel of Tabrīz, *Livre d'histoires*, St. tersburg 1874, tr. M. Brosset); it was considered astrous in the eyes of the Armenians, who com-ed many bitter folk-songs lamenting their ction from a prosperous area. Shāh ʿAbbās I tured Djulfā in 1013/1604, and recognising the ful role that the merchants might play in his n economy, transferred them to Iṣfahān; he gave m three days to gather their possessions, and then troyed the town and bridge. Although Djulfā was ned, a few Armenians made their way back later the 11th/17th century. Remains of churches and ancient cemetery still survive. The extension of Russian railway system to Tabrīz through ılfā, and its establishment before the first World ır as a stage on the Indo-European telegraph e, led to an increase in its importance; it now ves as a frontier post between Iran and the U.S.S.R.

II. New Djulfā (in Armenian, Nor J̌ułay) is uated in lat. 32° 40′ N, long. 51° 41′ E, and forms uburb of Iṣfahān built on the south bank of the yanda-rūd river, linked to the Čahār Bāgh in ahān by the Allāhwardī Khān bridge. It was ated in 1014/1605 by Shāh ʿAbbās I, to house Armenians transferred from old Djulfā on the axes. Other Armenian emigrants were settled in ahān itself, but subsequently moved to New ılfā in 1065-6/1654-5, where the mixed geo-aphical origin of the population was reflected in names of the different quarters, such as *Hirvanli* revan), *Nakshivanli* (Nakhidjevan) (Chardin, ii,). The population of New Djulfā has been estimated 15,000-20,000 to start with, rising to 30,000 by 30. Some 50,000 more Armenians were settled in villages in the countryside around Iṣfahān. The iritual head of the community was a Bishop, ing allegiance to the Catholicos at Etchmiadzin, d responsible for Armenians throughout Persia, well as those in Baṣra and Baghdād (Gregorian, *cit.*, 667).

Shāh ʿAbbās I helped the newcomers to establish emselves in New Djulfā, even assigning Persian asons and engineers to assist them. His support the Djulfā merchants in international trade was immense consequence, both of the Persian economy d their own good fortune. The strength of their sition was assured in 1027/1618, when the Ar-enian merchants secured the monopoly of the silk ade abroad, wresting the privilege from the British. measure of the significance of this monopoly is e estimated volume of the silk crop in Persia, ore than 4 million pounds in the early 11th/17th ntury rising to 6 million pounds by the 1670s (C. Issawi, *The economic history of Iran: 1800-1914*, Chicago 1971, 12). A further advantage was gained in Russia in 1078/1667, when Czar Aleksei Mikhail-ovich granted the Armenians special privileges, including the right to travel north from Astrakhan and deal directly with European buyers. The main advantage to Shāh ʿAbbās I was the skill of the merchants in foreign trade, coupled with their reputation for honesty and diligence. With New Djulfā at the centre, an international trade network was established, with Armenian merchants settled as far afield as Tonkin, Siam, Java, the Philippines, India, the Near East, Holland, France, England, Germany, Italy, Poland, Sweden and Spain. Spices, cotton goods and porcelain were brought from the Far East and India; silk was exported from Persia to Europe; in return, a large variety of European goods was imported into Persia, including cloth, glass, clocks and watches, metal-work and oil paintings. As one traveller observed, "All the com-modities of the East were made known to the West, and those of the West serve as new ornaments for the East . . . in the midst of Persia is now (*ca.* 1112/1700) seen everything that is curious throughout all the countries where the merchants have extended their correspondence" (J. P. de Tournefort, *Relation d'un voyage du Levant*, Paris 1717, iii, 232-3).

Shāh ʿAbbās I accorded the Armenians something close to equal status with his Muslim subjects; New Djulfā was organised as a separate entity within the city, under the jurisdiction of its own *kalāntar* [*q.v.*], responsible for the collection of taxes, and a *kadkhudā* for the maintenance of civic order [see Iṣfahān, Vol. IV, p. 103]. Foreign embassies and missions were generally housed in New Djulfā; as the Armenians were skilled linguists and often acted as interpreters and intermediaries, this gave them a double advantage in the conduct of exchanges between the foreigners and the Persian court. Foreign missionaries, such as the Jesuits, Dominicans and Carmelites, were also established in New Djulfā; so were foreign craftsmen, like jewellers, gunsmiths and watchmakers, who often took Armenian wives. Shāh ʿAbbās I took a personal interest in the affairs of the Armenian community, visiting them in New Djulfā and even attending religious festivals, such as Christmas and Easter. In 1029/1619, he took part in a special ceremony on the banks of the Zāyanda-rūd, afterwards dining and spending the night with his Armenian hosts (P. della Valle, *Voyages*, iii, 100-13).

The increasing wealth of the Armenian com-munity was reflected in the erection of numerous churches and private houses erected in New Djulfā in the first half of the 11th/17th century. The churches, of which thirteen still survive, combine Armenian plans with Persian construction, brick replacing the Armenian traditional use of dressed stone; two of the churches have onion-shaped domes with double shells. The decoration is an eclectic mixture of Armenian, European and Persian ele-ments. The interiors of the two largest churches, Surb Amenaperkitch (All Saviour's Cathedral) and Meydani Betghahem (Bethlehem Church), contain carved gilt stucco, *cuerda seca* tile panels, and wall-paintings in European style; the paintings are probably the work of Western artists and Armenian assistants. New Djulfā was also a centre for copying and illuminating manuscripts; a number of these are among the collection of almost 700 Armenian manuscripts in the Museum adjacent to the Cathe-dral, which also contains other items of historical interest. A few private houses still survive of the Ṣafawid period, either built round a central courtyard, or in the middle of a walled garden, with separate quarters for men and women. Several are decorated with wall-paintings in European manner, as well as in more conventional Persian style. When Sir Thomas Herbert visited the house of the *kalāntar* Khwādja Naẓar in 1038/1628, the impropriety of the wall-paintings earned his disapproval.

The Armenians were responsible for introducing a number of Western innovations, the most significant of which was the printing-press using cast metal type; the first Armenian work printed in New Djulfā was the Book of Psalms (*Saghmos*), which appeared in 1638.

Shāh ʿAbbās I's friendly policy towards the Armenian minority continued under his successors, Shāh Ṣafī and Shāh ʿAbbās II, but by the second half of the 11th/17th century, during the reign of Shāh Sulaymān, relations between the Persians and the Armenians became strained. In the 12th/18th century under Nādir Shāh, the Armenians suffered excessive taxation and other penalties, and many Armenians emigrated, particularly to India. At present the Armenian community is reduced to less than 500 families. A large Armenian cemetery, with several thousand carved gravestones, including those of a number of Europeans, lies to the south of the town.

Bibliography: I. Old Djulfā. The Armenian sources include a description of the area attributed to Moses Khorenacʿi (Moses of Khoren), *Géographie de Moïse de Corène d'après Ptolémée*, Venice 1881, Armenian text, tr. A. Soukry: see also V. Langlois, *Collection des historiens anciens et modernes de l'Arménie*, Paris 1869-80, ii. The major source for the 17th century is the chronicler Arakʿel Davrizhetzi (Arakʿel of Tabrīz), *Livre d'histoires*, in *Collection d'historiens Armeniens*, i, tr. M. Brosset, St. Petersburg 1874; a ms. by Père Badjétsi gives details of the forced migration, see *JA* (1837), tr. Brosset; see also R. Gulbenkian, *L'ambassade en Perse de Luis Pereira de Lacerda, et des Pères Portugais de l'Ordre de Saint-Augustin, Belchior dos Anjo's et Guilherme de Santo Agostino 1604-1605*, Lisbon 1972, and L. Alishan, *Siunikʿ kam Sisakan*, Venice 1893. For a description of the bridge across the Araxes in the 14th century, Sharaf al-Dīn ʿAli Yazdī, *The history of Timur-Bec* ..., London 1723. Various European travellers mention the town in the 17th and 18th centuries: J. Cartwright, *The Preachers Travels* ... London 1611; A. de Gouvea, *Relation des grandes guerres et victoires obtenues par ... Chah Abbas* ..., Rouen 1646; J. B. Tavernier, *Les six voyages* ..., Paris 1682; Sir John Chardin, *Voyage en Perse et aux Indes Orientales* ..., Amsterdam 1686; Père J. Villotte, *Voyages d'un missionaire ... en Turquie, en Perse, en Arménie, en Arabie et en Barbarie*, Paris 1730. In the 19th century, the ruined town is described by Sir W. Ouseley, *Travels in various countries of the east* ..., London 1819-23, iii; Sir R. Ker Porter, *Travels in Georgia, Persia, Armenia, Ancient Babylonia* ..., London 1821-2; F. Dubois de Montpéreux, *Voyage autour du Caucase* ..., Paris 1839-43, iv; idem, *Atlas*, Neuchâtel 1843, ii, Plate XXXVII; E. Brayley Hodgetts, *Round about Armenia*, London 1896. The most recent historical study is that of V. Gregorian, *Minorities of Isfahan: the Armenian community of Isfahan, 1587-1722*, in *Studies on Isfahan. II*, in *Jnal of the Society for Iranian Studies* vii (1974). See also *Russian embassies to the Georgian Kings* (1 1605), ed. W. Allen, tr. A. Mango, Cambr 1970. For Armenian remains in the area, Jurgis Baltrušaitis, *Études sur l'art médiéva Géorgie et en Arménie*, Paris 1929; Muham Javad Mashkur, *Naẓarī bih tārīkh-i Ādharbāy va āthār-i bāstānī va djamʿiyyat-shināsī ān*, Teh 1349 sh.; L. Azarian and A. Manoukian, *Khatch documents of Armenian architecture*, 2, Milan 1

II. New Djulfā. The leading Armenian so is Y. Tēr Yovhaniantz, *Patmutʿiwn Nor Julay yAspahani* (*History of New Djulfā in Iṣfah* New Djulfā 1880; see also V. Gregorian, *op.* On the special dialect of Djulfa, see K. Patka *Izsledovanie o dialektakh armiyanskago yazïka*, Petersburg 1869, 76-103. Ismāʿīl Rāʾīn, *Īrānī armanī*, Tehran 1350 sh., gives a general his of Armenians in Iran. The history of the c munity in New Djulfā is richly documented in works of European travellers; in addition to t already mentioned, see Pietro della Valle, *L conditioni di Abbàs Rè di Persia*, Venice 1(idem, *Viaggi de P. della V* ..., Venice 1661; de Silva y Figueroa, *L'ambassade de D. G. de S y Figueroa en Perse*, Paris 1667; Sir Tho Herbert, *A relation of some yeares travaille* London 1634, and 3rd ed. 1665; Adam Olear *The voyages and travels of the Ambassadors sen Frederick Duke of Holstein* ..., London 16 Père Rafaël Du Mans, *Estat de la Perse en 1660* Paris 1890; Gabriel de Chinon, *Relations nouve du Levant: ou traités de la religion, du gouvernem et des coutumes des Perses, des Armeniens et Gaures* ..., 1671; Jean de Thévenot, *Rela d'un voyage fait au Levant* ..., Paris 1664- André Daulier Deslandes, *Les beautez de la P* ..., Paris 1673; Jan Struys, *Drie aanmerkelijke seer ramspoedige Reysen door Italien, Griekenla Lijflandt, Moscovien, Tartarijen, Meden, Pers Oost-Indien, Japan* ..., Amsterdam 1676; J Fryer, *A new account of East-India and Pe* ..., London 1698; Sir William Hedges, *The di of W.H. ... during his agency in Bengal* Hakluyt Society, London 1887; Cornelius Bruyn, *Reizen van C. de Bruyn* ..., Delft 16 Important material concerning the Cath missions and the Armenians is contained in *chronicle of the Carmelites in Persia*, London 19 For Armenian trade, R. W. Ferrier, *The menians and the East India Company in Persia Econ. Hist. Rev.*, 2nd ser., i (1973); N. Steensgaa *Carracks, caravans and companies*, Copenha 1973. For the 18th century and later history New Djulfā, *The chronicles of Petros di Sa Gilanentz*, tr. C. Minasian, Lisbon 1959; and Lockhart, *The fall of the Safavī dynasty and Afghan occupation of Persia*, Cambridge 19 For Djulfāites abroad, see M. Seth, *The Ar nians in India*, Calcutta 1937; and J. M. I Santos Simões, *Carreaux céramiques Holland au Portugal et en Espagne*, The Hague 1959. the churches, domestic architecture, and cra see John Carswell, *New Julfa, the Armen churchrs and other buildings*, Oxford 1968; Karapetian, *Isfahan, New Julfa: le case de Armeni/The houses of the Armenians*, Rome 19 A. U. Pope, ed. *A survey of Persian art*, Oxf 1939; T. S. R. Boase, *A seventeenth-century ty logical cycle of paintings in the Armenian Cat dral in Julfa*, in *Journal of the Warburg a Courtauld Institutes*, xiii (1950). For details of cemetery, see T. W. Haig, *Graves of Europeans* e Armenian cemetery at Isfahan, in *JRAS*, xi 919). (J. CARSWELL)

JULLANĀR is the blossom of the pomenate (<Persian *gul-i anār*), in Greek βαλαύσ-, accordingly *bālawusṭiyūn* (with variants) in the hanos-Ḥunayn translation. It is the blossom of wild pomegranate tree (*rummān barrī*), also d *al-maẓẓ* by the Arab botanists. It is mentioned assing by Aṣmaʿī (*K. al-Nabāt*, ed. ʿAbd Allāh hunaym, Cairo 1392/1972, 36) and described in il by Abū Ḥanīfa al-Dīnawarī (*Le dictionnaire nique*, ed. M. Hamidullah, Cairo 1973, no. 1028). ording to this source, the tree grows in the nen highlands, puts forth blossoms (*djullanār*) does not bear fruit and has a hard, inflammable d. The outer layers of the seedshell—and not blossoms themselves, as the texts have it—yield lly-like, tasty juice which produces a satisfying t and is used as a medicine. *Djullanār al-arḍ* is sionally put together or compared with the okistis (*hibūḳistīdhās* = ὑποκιστίδος), a pulpy growing in the roots of the Cistus and also used extracting juice. Both also largely correspond as as healing effect is concerned, as was already hasised by Dioscorides in the respective sections: have an astringent effect and are good for ric complaints, dysentery and enteric ulcers; they together fresh wounds, staunch venous and rial blood and secure loose teeth (*al-asnān al-aḥarrika*); applied on the head in compresses n vinegar, they check congestion of the blood to brain. In the absence of blossoms, one can also the shells of the pomegranate.

Bibliography: Dioscurides, *De materia medica*, d. Wellmann, i, Berlin 1907, 104 f. = lib. i, 111; a "*Materia médica*" *de Dioscorides*, ii (Arabic tr.), d. Dubler and Terés, Tetuán 1952, 108; Rāzī, *āwī*, xx, Ḥaydarābād 1387/1967, 254-6, no. 210; *ie pharmakolog. Grundsätze des Abu Mansur ... arawi*, tr. A. Ch. Achundow, Halle 1893, 361, 73; Ibn al-Djazzār, *Iʿtimād*, Ms. Ayasofya 3564, l. 61a-b; Zahrāwī, *Taṣrīf*, Ms. Beşir Ağa 502, l. 502a, 4; Ibn Sīnā, *Ḳānūn*, Būlāḳ, i, 284 f.; bn Biklārish, *Mustaʿīnī*, Ms. Naples, Bibl. Naz. , F. 65, fol. 29b; Ghāfiḳī, *al-Adwiya al-mufrada*, s. Rabat, Bibl. Gén. ḳ 155 i, fol. 113a-b; Ibn ubal, *Mukhtārāt*, Ḥaydarābād 1362, ii 54; . Guigues, *Les noms arabes dans Sérapion*, in *A*, 10ème série (1905), v, s.v. *Iulinar* (no. 293); aimonides, *Sharḥ asmāʾ al-ʿuḳḳār*, ed. Meyerhof, airo 1940, no. 75; Ibn al-Bayṭār, *Djāmiʿ*, Būlāḳ 291, i, 164, tr. Leclerc, no. 494; Yūsuf b. ʿUmar, *Iuʿtamad*³, ed. M. al-Saḳḳāʾ, Beirut 1395/1975, 9 f.; Ibn al-Ḳuff, *ʿUmda*, Ḥaydarābād 1356, i, 26; Suwaydī, *Simāt*, Ms. Paris ar. 3004, fol. 65b; uwayrī, *Nihāya*, xi, Cairo 1935, 100-5 (with nany examples from poetry); Ghassānī, *Ḥadīḳat -azhār*, Ms. Ḥasan Ḥusnī ʿAbd al-Wahhāb, fol. 2a-b; Dāwūd al-Anṭākī, *Tadhkira*, Cairo 1371/ 952, i, 106; *Tuḥfat al-aḥbāb*, ed. Renaud and olin, Paris 1934, no. 94; I. Löw, *Die Flora der uden*, iii, 95; *The medical formulary or Aqrābādhīn f al-Kindī*, tr. M. Levey, Madison etc. 1966, 53 f. (no. 65). (A. DIETRICH)

L-DJURDJĀNĪ, ABŪ BAKR ʿABD AL-ḲĀHIR ABD AL-RAḤMĀN (d. 471/1078), philologist and rary theorist, was born in Gurgān where he nt his entire life, about which very little is known. studied grammar with Muḥammad b. al-Ḥasan ārisī, a nephew of Abū ʿAlī al-Fārisī. Yāḳūt ne (*Irshād*, v, 249) reports that he was also ored by al-Ḳāḍī al-Djurdjānī, but later on (vii, 3) asserts that al-Fārisī was his only teacher.

To his contemporaries, al-Djurdjānī was famous mainly as a grammarian whose work included such popular manuals as *Miʾat ʿāmil* and *K. al-Djumal*, as well as *al-Mughnī* (a commentary in 30 volumes on Abū ʿAlī al-Fārisī's *K. al-Īḍāḥ*) and a short version of it called *al-Muḳtaṣad*. He also wrote on *iʿdjāz* (the inimitability of the Ḳurʾān), etymology and prosody, and he compiled an anthology of the poetry of Abū Tammām, al-Buḥturī and al-Mutanabbī.

However, to later generations and especially to modern scholars, al-Djurdjānī's reputation rests on his powerful and sophisticated theoretical work on stylistics, syntax, poetics and poetic imagery, which many critics have compared with modern literary theory, demonstrating that he anticipated a number of the most recent trends in the study of poetic structure. His books *Dalāʾil al-iʿdjāz* and *Asrār al-balāgha* have won him wide acclaim as the founder of the two "sciences" *ʿilm al-maʿānī* and *ʿilm al-bayān*. He himself does not, however, use these phrases as technical terms designating two independent branches of literary analysis.

Al-Djurdjānī's exploration of poetic structure originated as an inquiry into the mysteries of *iʿdjāz*, but soon developed into a comprehensive theory on the nature of language, meaning, the imagination and poetic imagery. Going beyond the dualism of *maʿnā* (meaning) and *lafẓ* (words), he argues that eloquence and expressiveness are functions neither of meaning nor of words but of the construction (*naẓm*) of linguistic elements into harmonised syntactic patterns determined by a set of rules which form the grammar of the language. In other words, construction is nothing but *murāʿāt maʿānī al-naḥw* (lit. "observing the meanings of grammar").

At the roots of al-Djurdjānī's theory of construction lies a psychological view of the nature of literary creation. He believes that the linguistic structure of a literary composition is underlined by a structure of experience and that the order of words in the former follows the order of meanings in the psyche (*nafs*) which is presupposed by the intellect (*ʿaḳl*). Identifying some of the basic syntactic structures in Arabic, he explores the correspondence in them between the structure of language and the structure of thought. He then outlines a symbolic theory of language according to which language is a system of relations (a concept fundamental to modern linguistics) governed by two principles: the arbitrary nature of linguistic signs and the conventional nature of language itself. The first principle means that there is no inherent relation between a word and its referent and, therefore, a word in isolation does not possess any qualities which render it better or worse than any other word. In fact, a word does not mean much until it has entered into a set of syntactic relations with other words. Consequently, the same meaning cannot be expressed in two different ways. Any syntactic change in a composition generates changes on the semantic level. Thus the unit of linguistic analysis ceases to be the single word and becomes the fully meaningful formulation in which every element is an organic part of the total structure. No element is extraneous or superfluous. This applies to all aspects of structure, including imagery.

Al-Djurdjānī identifies two distinct ways of expression, one direct, the other indirect. The content of the first he calls "meaning", that of the second the "meaning of meaning". Meaning is conveyed by literal statement, the meaning of meaning by metaphorical language, *kināya* and one type of *tamthīl*. An image is thus viewed not as an alternative to, or ornamentation of, literal statement (as widely believed in both Arabic and western criticism until this century), but as a distinct act of imaginative creation which expresses a meaning otherwise impossible to express.

The *Asrār* is devoted to the study of imagery, its nature, function, relationship to thought and various forms. Al-Djurdjānī identifies two types of *madjāz*, one pertaining to language (*lughawī*), the other to the intellect (*ʿaḳlī*) and differentiates the types of *madjāz* based on transference from those involving no transference, distinguishing sharply between two fundamental relationships, contiguity and similarity. The latter he asserts to be the *raison d'être* of *istiʿāra* [*q.v.*]. Refining the concept of *istiʿāra* further, he denies the dominant view that *istiʿāra* involves transference. One type of *istiʿāra* he shows clearly to be based on proportional analogy and to involve no transference of a single word at all, the other type (involving the usage of a single word) he defines in contextual terms. *Istiʿāra*, he believes, consists in using a word to refer to a thing other than its original referent, on the basis of some similarity revealed between the referents, while however still possessing its original meaning and thus becoming a double-unit underlined by tension. In this fashion he anticipates I. A. Richard's work which has revolutionised the study of metaphor.

All types of imagery, except *kināya*, originate in similarity, and similarity, al-Djurdjānī argues, is a sharing (*ishtirāk*) of an attribute, or set of attributes, between two entities, which may occur either in the attribute itself (*fi 'l-ṣifa nafsihā wa-ḥaḳīḳat djinsihā*, or in something presupposed by or resultant from the attribute (*fī ḥukm*in *lahā wa-muḳtaḍā*). Similarity also varies in its remoteness and intensity from one image to another. Al-Djurdjānī uses these basic distinctions to classify the various types of imagery and explore their imaginative and stylistic role. He thus establishes two inseparable criteria to define an image: the imaginative basis underlying it and the linguistic apparatus in which it is formulated. *Tashbīh* is thus differentiated from *tamthīl* and *istiʿāra*, and the ambiguous structure involving the copula "Zaid is a lion" is described as an intensified simile (*tashbīh balīgh*) rather than an *istiʿāra* (a distinction not yet made sufficiently clearly in modern European criticism). Consequently, al-Djurdjānī denies the interchangeability of *tashbīh*, *tamthīl* and *istiʿāra*.

The central piece of al-Djurdjānī's work on *istiʿāra* is his classification of its types according to the nature of the dominant trait or point of similarity in each type. This fundamentally anti-Aristotelian classification represents one of the latest developments in the analysis of metaphor in European studies (cf. K. Abu Deeb, *Al-Jurjānī's classification of istiʿāra with special reference to Aristotle's classification of metaphor*, in *Journal of Arabic Literature*, ii (1971)).

Throughout his analysis, al-Djurdjānī uses psychological criteria of a strong Gestaltian nature. He also hints at an organic approach to poetry according to which a poem is to be studied as an organic whole whose parts interact with, and modify, each other, their interaction being determined by the dominant emotion underlying the poem. His practical criticism is a fine example of the power of this approach to illuminate aspects of the poem which would remain otherwise hidden.

Bibliography: 1. al-Djurdjānī's p lished works: *Asrār al-balāgha*, ed. H. Ri Istanbul 1954; *Dalāʾil al-iʿdjāz*, ed. Rashīd R Cairo 1366/1946; *Kitāb al-Djumal*, ed. ʿAlī Ḥay Damascus 1972; *Miʾat ʿāmil* (also known a *ʿAwāmil al-miʾa*, Būlāḳ 1247/1831; *al-Mukhtār shiʿr al-Mutanabbī wa 'l-Buḥturī wa-Abī Tamm* in *al-Ṭarāʾif al-adabiyya*, ed. A. A. al-Maym Cairo 1937; *al-Risāla al-shāfiya fī iʿdjāz al-Ḳu* in *Thālāth rasāʾil fī iʿdjaz al-Ḳurʾān*, ed. Khalafalla and M. Z. Sallām, Cairo 1956.

2. Works with biographical infor tion on al-Djurdjānī: al-Bākharzī, *Du al-ḳaṣr*, ed. al-Ḥilū, Cairo 1388/1968; Ibn Anbārī, *Nuzhat al-alibbāʾ*, Baghdād 1294/1 al-Ḳifṭī, *Inbāh al-ruwāt*, Cairo 1955; Brockelm I, 114, 287; S I, 503.

3. Modern studies on al-Djurdjā K. Abū Deeb, *Al-Jurjānī's theory of poetic ima* London 1978; idem, *Studies in Arabic lite criticism; the concept of organic unity*, in *Edeb* iii, Philadelphia 1977; M. Z. al-ʿAshmāwī, *Ḳa al-naḳd al-adabī wa 'l-balāgha*, Cairo 19 A. A. Badawī, *ʿAbd al-Ḳāhir al-Djurdjānī*[2], C 1962?; M. Khalafalla, *ʿAbd al-Ḳāhir's theor his "Secrets of Eloquence", a psychological appro* in *JNES*, xiv (1955); N. Mandūr, *Fi 'l-mīzān djadīd*[2], Cairo n.d.; A. Maṭlūb, *ʿAbd al-Ḳ al-Djurdjānī*, Beirut 1973; Ritter, Introd. to edn. of the *Asrār al-balāgha*. (K. Abu Dee

DOG [see KALB].

DOGMA [see ʿAḲĪDA].

DOMAIN [see ḌAYʿA].

DOME OF THE ROCK [see ḲUBBAT AL-ṢAKH

DONATION [see HIBA].

DOVE [see ḤAMĀM].

DRAFSH-I KĀWIYĀN [see KĀWA].

DRAGOMAN [see TURDJUMĀN].

DRAGON [see TINNĪN].

DROMEDARY [see IBIL].

DRUGGIST [see ʿAṬṬĀR].

AL-**DUWAYḤĪ**, IBRĀHĪM AL-RASHĪD B. Ṣ AL-DUNḲULĀWĪ AL-SHĀʾIḲĪ, Ṣūfī shaykh Nubian extraction and belonging to the Shā liyya order, and a disciple and *khalīfa* [*q.v.* Aḥmad b. Idrīs [*q.v.*]. He was born in 1228/181 Duwayḥ near Dunḳulā (Dongola) on the Nu Nile and belonged to the tribe of the Shāʾiḳiyya. joined the religious community of Aḥmad b. I in 1246/1830 in the town of Ṣabyā in ʿAsīr [*q* where the latter had sought refuge from prosecu for heresy by the Meccan *ʿulamāʾ*, and succee him as leader of the Aḥmadiyya (al-Idrisiy *ṭarīḳa* upon his death in 1254/1837. Rivalries al the *ṭarīḳa* leadership, which involved the two n notable of Aḥmad b. Idrīs's disciples, Muḥamm ʿUthmān al-Mīrghanī [*q.v.*] and Muḥammad b. al-Sanūsī [*q.v.*], caused him to leave Ṣabyā. He w first to Egypt and later to the Sudan where propagated the order. Finally, he settled in M where he faced charges of heresy on two occasion 1273/1856-7 brought against him at the instiga of competing factions from among Aḥmad b. Id disciples. These charges were dropped due to in vention by the Ottoman governor of the Ḥidjāz, on the second occasion due to intervention by *shaykh al-ʿulamāʾ* of Mecca. Le Chatelier (see Bib raphy) reports that he was one of the most pop *shaykh*s of Mecca, in particular with Indian pilg who flocked to his *zāwiya* [*q.v.*] and from whom received substantial donations. After his death 1291/1874, when the *ṭarīḳa*, which had by t me known as al-Rashīdiyya and had obtained embership in Syria, Egypt, Sudan and Yemen, passed under the leadership of his successor ammad b. Ṣāliḥ (d. 1909), his nephew, a decline in. A distinct branch, al-Ṣāliḥiyya [*q.v.*] devel- in Somalia under the latter's disciple Muḥam- Gūlēd al-Rashīdī (d. 1918; cf. E. Cerulli, *alia. Scritti vari editi ed inediti*, Rome 1957, i, f.) and allegiance to the Meccan *zāwiya* as the *a*'s principal centre ceased to be paid by Ibrā- 's *khulafā*ʾ in Egypt. In the latter country, an pendent branch known as al-Dandarāwiyya rged under the leadership of the son of one of hīm al-Rashīd's *khulafā*ʾ, Abu 'l-ʿAbbās al- darāwī (d. 1950), which obtained membership in pt and in Somalia in particular (cf. al-Mīrghanī Irīsī, *Daʿwat al-ḥaḳḳ fi 'l-ṭarīḳa al-Dandarā- ya al-Idrīsiyya*, Cairo 1952, *passim*).

he claims by members of al-Rashīdiyya that *ṭarīḳa* embodied the purest form of Aḥmad b. s's teachings were disavowed by Āmīn al- ānī, *Mulūk al-ʿArab*, Beirut 1951³, i, 285 ff., based his conclusions upon personal observations eligious practice of a Rashīdiyya group in Aden.

Bibliography: In addition to the references ven in the article, see J. S. Trimingham, *Islam the Sudan*, Oxford 1949, 230 f.; idem, *Islam in thiopia*, Oxford 1952, 235, 243 f.; idem, *The ufi orders in Islam*, Oxford 1971, 120 f., who raws heavily upon the account given by A. Le hatelier, *Les confréries musulmanes du Hedjaz*, aris 1887, 92-7; Muḥammad Khalīl al-Hadjrasī, *al-Ḳaṣr al-mushīd fi 'l-tawḥīd wa-fī ṭarīḳa Sīdī Ibrāhīm al-Rashīd*, Cairo 1314/1896-7, contains the most extensive biography in Arabic and biographical data on some of his *khulafā*ʾ in Egypt (98 ff.). This biography may be found back in an abbreviated form in Muḥammad al-Bashīr Ẓāfir, *al-Yawāḳīt al-thamīna fī aʿyān madhhab ʿālim al-Madīna*, Cairo 1324-5/1906-7, 94. For names of Ibrāhīm al-Rashīd al-Duwayḥī's *khulafā*ʾ in Somalia, see also ʿAydarūs b. ʿAlī al-ʿAydarūs al-Naḍīrī al-ʿAlawī, *Bughyat al-āmāl fī taʾrīkh al-Sūmāl*, Mogadishu 1954, 223 f. Ibrāhīm al-Rashīd himself wrote a biography of his teacher Aḥmad b. Idrīs entitled *al-ʿIḳd al-durr al-nafīs* of which only sections were published by Ṣāliḥ b. Muḥammad al-Madanī, in *al-Muntaḳā al-nafīs fī manāḳib ḳuṭb dāʾirat al-taḳdīs ... Aḥmad b. Idrīs*, Cairo 1960, 39 ff.

For publications of the order, see Muḥammad b. Aḥmad al-Dandarāwī, *Sanad al-ṭarīḳa al-Aḥmadiyya al-Idrīsiyya al-Rāshīdiyya al-Muḥammadiyya*, Alexandria, n.d.; Mūsā Āghā Rāsim (ed.), *Awrād ... Ibrāhīm al-Rashīd*, Alexandria 1309/1891-2. Publications of al-Rashīdiyya al-Dandarāwiyya are Muḥammad Ibrāhīm Naṣr al-Ḥarīrī (ed.), *Awrād al-Aḥmadiyya*, Cairo n.d.; Farādj Aḥmad al-Salīmī, *al-Durar al-naḳiyya fī awrād al-ṭarīḳa al-Dandarāwiyya al-Idrīsiyya*, Alexandria n.d.; ʿAbd Allāh al-Yamanī, *al-Awrād al-Aḥmadiyya al-Rashīdiyya al-Dandarāwiyya*, *al-ṣalāt al-ʿaẓīmiyya*, Beirut 1387/1967-8. (F. DE JONG)

DYNASTY [see DAWLA].

E

AGLE [see ʿUḲĀB].

BONY [see ABANŪS].

BLIS [see IBLĪS].

BRO [see IBRUH].

CLIPSE [see KUSŪF].

CONOMIC LIFE [see FILĀḤA, MĀL, ṢINĀʿA, ĀRA, etc.].

DICT [see FARMĀN].

KINČI B. ḲOČḲAR, Turkish slave comman- of the Saldjūḳs and governor for them in ʷārazm with the traditional title of Khʷārazm- h [*q.v.*] in 490/1097. He was the successor in this e of Anūshtigin Gharčaʾī, the founder of the sequent line of Khʷārazm-Shāhs who made r province the centre of a great military empire the period preceeding the Mongol invasions. ording to Ibn al-Athīr, x, 181-2, Ekenči was one Sultan Berk-Yaruḳ's slaves (but according to waynī, ii, 3, tr. Boyle, i, 278, one of Sandjar's es), and was appointed to Khʷārazm by Berk- uḳ's representative in the east, the Dād-Beg ashī, probably when Berk-Yaruḳ came himself Khurāsān early in 490/1097. Ekinči did not enjoy er there for long, however, being killed later year by a conspiracy of *ghulām*s, his successor Khʷārazm-Shāh then being Anūshtigin's son b al-Dīn Muḥammad. Ekinči's son Ṭoghrīl-tigin ientioned also by Ibn al-Athīr as a subsequent l against Ḳuṭb al-Dīn.

kinči came from the Ḳun tribe [*q.v.*] of Turks, Minorsky surmised that he was the transmitter of information about that group in Marwazī's *Ṭabāʾiʿ al-ḥayawān* (*Sharaf al-Zamān Ṭāhir Marvazi on China, the Turks and India*, London 1942, tr. 29-30, comm. 98, 101-2), noting that he must have been a person experienced in and knowledgeable about Central Asian affairs in order to have been appointed governor in Khʷārazm.

Bibliography (in addition to works cited in the article): Marquart, *Über das Volkstum der Komanen*, 48-52, 202; Barthold, *Turkestan*³, 324; I. Kafesoğlu, *Harezmşahlar devleti tarihi* (*485-617/1092-1229*), Ankara 1956, 37-8; C. E. Bosworth, in *Cambridge history of Iran*, v, 107, 142-3. (C. E. BOSWORTH)

ELECTUARY [see ADWIYA].

ELIČPUR, ILIČPUR, modern AČALPUR, a town of the mediaeval Islamic province of Berār [*q.v.*] in southern Central India, lying near the headwaters of the Purnā constituent of the Tāptī River in lat. 21° 16′ N. and long. 77° 33′ E. Up to 1853, Eličpur was generally regarded as the capital of Berār, after when Amraotī became the administrative centre.

The pre-Islamic history of Eličpur is semi-legendary, its foundation being attributed to a Jain Rādjā called Il in the 10th century. By Baranī's time (later 7th/13th century), it could be described as one of the famous towns of the northern Deccan. The Dihlī Sultan ʿAlāʾ al-Dīn Khaldjī captured it in 695/1296 during his first expedition against the Rādjā of Deogīrī Ramačandra [see DAWLATĀBĀD], who was made tributary to the Sultans; and when

Deogīrī finally fell in 719/1318, Eličpur and Berār came under direct Muslim rule. Under the Bahmanīs [*q.v.*], it was the capital of Berār province, and featured prominently in the campaignings of the Khaldjī ruler of Mālwa [*q.v.*], Maḥmūd Shāh (839-65/1436-62) against the Bahmanīs, being sacked in 870/1466, so that the Bahmanī Sultan Muḥammad III Lashkarī was compelled to cede to Mālwa Berār as far as Eličpur [see also KHĒRLA]. From 890/1485 to 980/1572 Eličpur was under the Bahmanīs' epigoni, the ʿImād-Shāhīs [*q.v.*]. Under the Mughals, it was at first placed in the shade by the new centre of Bālāpur, but soon regained its importance as the capital of the *ṣūba* of Berār, with a fort being built there of brick and stone; according to the *Āʾīn-i Akbarī* of Abu 'l-Faḍl, the revenue of Eličpur (which came within the *sarkār* of Gāwil, see below) amounted to 14 million *dāms* (ii, tr. H. S. Jarrett, Calcutta 1949, 237, 240).

But after the rise of the first independent ruler in Ḥaydarābād, the Āṣaf Djān Niẓām al-Mulk (d. 1161/1748 [see ḤAYDARĀBĀD. b. Ḥaydarābād State], Eličpur sank to only local significance under governors of the Niẓāms. The governor Salābat Khān erected various public buildings in the town in the early years of the 19th century, and he and his son Nāmdār Khān held the title of Nawwāb of Berār till the latter's death in 1843 and the subsequent extinction of the line.

In later British India, Berār was taken over in 1853 from the Niẓām as the "Hyderabad Assigned Districts", nominally on perpetual lease, and then it became *de facto* part of the Central Indian Province. Eličpur, by now the largest town in Berār (population in 1901, 26,082, including 18,500 Hindus and 7,250 Muslims), gave its name at first to one of the Districts of Berār, but in 1905 it was incorporated in the Amraotī (Amravati) District. In the present Indian Union, Eličpur is now called Ačalpur and falls within the Amravati District of the Nagpur Division of Maharashtra State. The 1971 census gave population figures of 43,326 for Ačalpur town and 24,125 for Ačalpu camp.

The monuments of Eličpur include a famous shrine or *dargāh* of the Muslim warrior ʿAbd al-Raḥmān Ghāzī, described as a kinsman of Maḥmūd of Ghazna (like the much more celebrated Sālār Masʿūd, buried at Bahrāič in Uttar Pradesh [see GHĀZĪ MIYĀN]), but more probably a commander of Fīrūz Shāh Khaldjī's. To the south of Eličpur is the hill fortress of Gāwilgaṛh [*q.v.*], and there is a group of Jain temples at Muktagīrī nearby.

Bibliography: *Cambridge history of India*, iii, index; *Imperial Gazetteer of India*², xii, 10-21; A. C. Lyall, ed., *Gazeteer for the Haidarabad Assigned Districts, commonly called Berar*, Bombay 1870, 144-8; s.v.; Fitzgerald and A. E. Nelson, eds., *Central Provinces District Gazeteers, Amraoti District*, Bombay 1911, 30-100 *passim*, and 394-401.

(C. E. BOSWORTH)

ELLORA [see ELURĀ].

EMANCIPATION [see TAḤRĪR].

EMERALD [see DJAWHAR, ZUMURRUD].

ENCYCLOPAEDIA [see MAWSŪʿA].

ENSIGN [see ʿALAM].

EPITHET [see NAʿT, ṢIFA].

ERG [see ṢAḤRĀʾ].

ERGUN, SAʿD AL-DĪN NÜZHET, modern Turkish SADETTİN NÜZHET ERGUN, Turkish scholar and literary historian (1901-46). Born in Bursa, he was educated at the Faculty of Letters of Istanbul University and taught Turkish literature in va secondary schools in Anatolia and later in Istar where he also worked as a librarian. He startec career as a scholar while he was a teacher in Konya lycée, with a book on the folk-lore of Ko A hard-working and prolific scholar, his works based on first-hand research into what is m original manuscript material, this being prese with only limited criticism. He is the author great number of studies and monographs on n classical and folk poets and on some modern wri His major works are *Konya khalkiyyat we harthiy* (with Meḥmed Ferīd), Istanbul 1926; *Khalk shāʿi* 3 vols, Istanbul 1926-7; *Karacaoğlan, hayat şiirleri*, Istanbul 1932 (a pioneer work on the g folk poet); *Baki divanı*, Istanbul 1935; *Türk şai* 3 vols., Istanbul 1936-45 (his most important w published in fascicules comprising alphabe biographies of poets, together with exam which stopped at the letter F, in the 96th fascic *Türk musikisi antolojisi* 2 vols, Istanbul 1 *Cenap Şehabettin*, Istanbul 1934 (a pioneer wor C. Ş., whose poetical works are put together fo first time in this monograph); and *Bektaşi şa ve nefesleri*, Istanbul 1944.

Bibliography: Ibrahim Alaettin Gövsa, *T meşhurları*, Istanbul n.d. (1946) s.v.; *Türk siklopedisi*, Ankara 1968, s.v.; Behçet Neca *Edebiyatımızda isimler sözlüğü*⁸, Istanbul 197

(FAHİR İ

ERMINE [see FARW].

ERSARÎ, one of the major tribes of Turkmen [*q.v.*] in Central Asia.

The name is not mentioned in the lists of Oghuz tribes by Maḥmūd al-Kāshgharī and Ra al-Dīn. It appears for the first time in histo works of Abu 'l-Ghāzī [*q.v.*] written in the century. According to the Turkmen traditio rendered by Abu 'l-Ghāzī (*Shadjara-yi Tarāk* ed. A. N. Kononov, text, 67-9, Russian tr., 7 Ersarî Bay (the eponym of the tribe?) was great-grandson of Oghurdjik Alp, a descendan Salur Ḳazan (cf. on this personage, *Kitāb-i D Korkud, passim*), who left ʿIrāḳ after a quarrel Bayandur Bek and came to Mangîshlaḳ [*q.v.*] a part of the Salur tribe. Thus this tradition indic the genealogical kinship of Ersarî with the known Oghuz tribe Salur (Salghîr of Maḥmūd Kāshgharī). In another place of the same v (text, 73-4, tr., 75), Abu 'l-Ghāzī tells that E Bay, who lived in the Balkhān [*q.v.*] mountains, a contemporary of Shaykh Sharaf Khwādja Urgenč, who wrote for him, on his request, *Muʿīn al-murīd*, a religious and didactic treatis verse, in Turkī (about the book, written in 1313-4, and the author, see: A. N. Samoylovič *Mir-Ali-Shir*, Leningrad 1928, 138; A. Z. V [Togan], in *Türkiyat mecmuası*, ii [1928], 315 J. Eckmann, in *Philologiae turcicae fundamenta* 279 f.). Ersarî Bay appears also in another plac *Shadjara-yi Tarākima* (text, 78, tr., 77-8) as ancestor (*ulugh ata* "great-grandfather") of tribe Ersarî, which owned a number of spring the Great and Little Balkhān mountains. The T men tradition, as related by Abu 'l-Ghāzī, places story in the middle or the second half of the century (after the death of the khān of the Go Horde Berdi Bek, 1359); the same tradition sh that the tribe Ersarî was already rather nume by that time, so that its origin must be relate some earlier period rather than the beginning o same century, when Ersarî Bay allegedly li rī Bay was probably an historical figure; his ɔ, known as Ersarī Baba, is situated near the h-eastern corner of the Ḳara-Boghaz gulf, on ıeights bearing the same name Ersarī Baba, and described by Russian traveller N. Murav'yev in early 19th century, as well as by modern arche- ists. The latest archeological researches in ern Turkmenia, apparently, confirm also the men genealogical tradition connecting the rī with the Salur (see S. P. Polyakov, *Etničeskaya iya Severo-Zapadnoy Turkmenii v sredniye veka,* cow 1973, 122-3, 102-4).

t the beginning of the 16th century, the Ersarī spread over a vast territory in western Turk- ia, from Mangīshlaḳ to the Little Balkhān ntains. Not only the tribe itself, but also its 1 clans are mentioned in the *Shadjara-yi Turk* Abu 'l-Ghāzī (ed. Desmaisons, text, 237, 267, tr., 254, 286, 337) in connection with the his- of the Khānate of Khīwa in the 16th century. the beginning of this century, the Ersarī were e head of the tribal group known as the "outer r" (*Tashkī Salur, ibid.*, text, 209, tr., 223), h included also the tribes Teke [*q.v.*], Sarīḳ] and Yomut [*q.v.*], nomadising between Man- laḳ and northern Khurāsān, while the "inner r" (*Ički Salur*), or the Salur proper, remained in north-west of Mangīshlaḳ. However, already by end of the same century, the Ersarī began to e eastwards, partly as a result of pressure from north by the Mangīt [*q.v.*], but mainly because growing desiccation of western Turkmenia, ıisation of wells and shortage of pasture. At the inning of the 17th century, at least part of arī returned to Mangīshlaḳ, but in the second rter of the same century they were finally driven of this region, this time by the Kalmuks [*q.v.*]. a short time, during the reign of Isfandiyār n (1032-52/1623-42), Ersarī apparently played e role, together with the Salur, in the Khānate Khīwa, but they had to leave it as a result of the tary campaigns of Abu 'l-Ghāzī and his son sha against the Turkmens described in *Shadjara- Turk*. Apparently, at that time the Ersarī mi- ted to the middle course of the Āmū Daryā .], the Labāb (cf. A. Vámbéry, *Travels in Central a*, London 1864, 231), where they have re- ned till the present time. There are also, probably, e indications of another route of their migration, ough Marw (either directly from Mangīshlaḳ and khān or from Khwārazm) and Marūčak to the hān Turkestan. In 1740 they fled before the y of Nādir Shāh which marched on Bukhārā ıg the Āmū Daryā, and came again to Mangīshlaḳ hammad Kāẓim, *Nāma-i ʿālam-ārā-yi Nādirī*, simile ed., Moscow 1965, ii, f. 257a), but in the t year they returned to their homes.

On the Āmū Daryā, the Ersarī became mostly entarised and settled in a narrow strip of land m 4 to 20 miles wide) along the river, mainly ts left bank from Denau in the north to Kalīf in south, where they were occupied with farming ed on irrigation. This territory formed a part of *wilāyats* of the Khānate of Bukhārā, those of djūy [see ĀMUL] and Karkī; now it forms the djou region (*oblast'*) of the Turkmen Soviet public. Shortage of land suitable for cultivation sed permanent emigration during the 19th tury, especially to Afghān Turkestan, where arī settled in the regions of Andkhūy [*q.v.*], a and Mazār-i Sharīf [*q.v.*]. It seems that cattle- eding was for these groups of Ersarī of greater importance than for their kinsmen on the Āmū Daryā.

The exact number of Ersarī has never been known. Figures given by 19th century travellers vary greatly (from 25 to 110 thousand families); at present, neither in the Soviet Union nor in Afghānistān are there any statistical data on individual Turkmen tribes.

Bibliography: in addition to the works cited in the text, see Capt. Bīkov, *Očerk dolinī Amu-Dar'i*, Tashkent 1880; A. V. Komarov, in *Sbornik geografičeskikh, topografičeskikh i statističeskikh materialov po Azii*, xxv (St. Petersburg 1887), 278-93; M. V. Grulev, in *Izvestiya Turkestanskogo otdela Imp. Russkogo Geografičeskogo obshčestva*, ii/1 (Tashkent 1900), 65-7; G. Jarring, *On the distribution of Turk tribes in Afghanistan*, Lund 1939, 45-7; A. Karrīyev, V. G. Moshkova, A. N. Nasonov, A. Yu. Yakubovskiy, *Očerki iz istorii turkmenskogo naroda i Turkmenistana v VIII-XIX vv.*, Ashkhabad 1954, esp. 130-2, 167-8, 181, 184-5, 188, 192-3, 198, 206-8, 217-21, 223-7, 232-3, 236, 246; Yu. Bregel', in *Kratkiye soobshčeniya Instituta étnografii Akademii nauk SSSR*, xxxi (Moscow 1959), 14-26 (abridged English tr. in *Central Asiatic review*, viii/3 [1960], 264-72); Ya. R. Vinnikov, in *Trudī Instituta istorii, arkheologii i étnografii Akademii nauk Turkmenskoy SSR*, vi (Ashkhabad 1962), 5-22, 42-9, 101-10; M. Annanepesov, *Khozyaystvo turkmen v XVIII-XIX vv.*, Ashkhabad 1972, 40-2, 87-90, 94-103.

(YU. BREGEL)

ESʿAD PASHA, SAḲĪZLĪ AḤMED, twice Ottoman Grand Vizier and holder of various high offices, military and civil, born in Scios (Tkish. Saḳīz) in 1244/1828-9, son of Meḥmed Agha, locally known as *Ḳule aghasī*. A graduate of the War College at Istanbul (Ḥarbiyye [*q.v.*]), Esʿad was appointed aide-de-camp to Fuʾād Pasha [*q.v.*], who, when Grand Vizier, appointed him as director of the Ottoman military school in Paris as well as military attaché. Esʿad in 1868 became lieutenant-general (*ferīk*) commanding Bosnia-Herzegovina and governor-general (*wālī*) of Scutari (Ishkodra). His career, military and civil, was a succession of appointment, dismissal and reappointment, characteristic of this period: field-marshal or commander (*mü<u>sh</u>īr*) of the First Army (Istanbul), *wālī* of Yemen, minister of war and commander-in-chief (*serʿasker*), commander-in-chief of the Fourth Army and *wālī* of Erzurum, *wālī* of Ankara (for one day only), *wālī* of Sivas, Minister of Marine, again *serʿasker*, Grand Vizier from 15 February till 15 April 1873, *wālī* of Konya, field-marshal commanding the Fifth Army in Syria and *wālī* of Damascus, again Minister of Marine, and from 26 April till 29 August 1875 again Grand Vizier, then Minister of Works, and *wālī* of Aydìn. He visited his birthplace Scios again, and he died at Izmir in the same year of 1875. Esʿad Pasha was chosen for the suite of Sultan ʿAbd al-ʿAzīz on his European tour in 1867. But his lack of political experience caused him to stay only a short while at the top; thus he could not deal effectively with the revolt in Herzegovina (July 1875). In politics, Esʿad seems not to have belonged to a leading group. He was a young military man enjoying the Sultan's favours up to a point, but was a mere figurehead in politics.

Bibliography: Sāmī, *Ḳāmūs al-aʿlām*, ii, 910; *Sidjill-i ʿOthmānī*, i, 342 f.; İ. H. Danişmend, *Izahlı Osmanlı tarihi kronolojisi*, Istanbul 1971,

iv, 243 f., 247 f., 249 f., 251, v, 86 f., İbnülemin Mahmud Kemal İnal, *Osmanlı devrinde son sadriazamlar*, Istanbul 1940-53. For the general background, see F. Bamberg, *Geschichte der Orientalischen Angelegenheit* ....., Berlin 1888, 424-44, 448; E. Z. Karal, *Osmanlı tarihi*, vii, 72, 74 ff., 133 f., 136; R. H. Davison, *Reform in the Ottoman empire 1856-76*, Princeton 1963 (repr. New York 1973), 168, 292 ff., 297, 306 f.; *Tanzimat I*, Istanbul 1940, 974, 976, portrait on plate 53.
(A. H. DE GROOT)

ESENDAL, MEMDŪḤ S̲H̲EWKET, modern Turkish MEMDUH ŞEVKET ESENDAL, Turkish short story writer and politician (1883-1952). He was born in Čorlu in Eastern Thrace, the son of Kahyabeyog̲h̲lu S̲h̲ewket, a modest farmer of an immigrant (*göčmen*) Turkish family from the Balkans. He did not have any regular schooling but was self-taught; then when his father died in 1907, he looked after the family until 1912 when the Balkan War broke out and the family moved to Istanbul. He had joined the Committee of Union and Progress (CUP) in 1907; at the outbreak of the First World War he was appointed inspector of the CUP, so that he was able to get to know at first-hand conditions of life in Anatolia and in Thrace. In 1919 he fled to Italy to avoid arrest by the occupying forces, but soon after he was invited to Ankara by Muṣṭafā Kemāl Pas̲h̲a, who sent him as the representative of the Nationalist government to Ād̲h̲arbāyd̲j̲ān. He continued with mainly a diplomatic career (with short intervals as teacher or member of Parliament) and served as ambassador in Tehran (1925-30), Kabul (1932) and Moscow (1932-8), and as Secretary-General of the Republican People's Party for four years (1941-5). He was elected deputy for Bilecik in 1946 and served until 1950. He died in Ankara on 16 May 1952.

Because of his absorbing political and diplomatic engagements, he wrote very irregularly and at lengthy intervals and generally signed his writings with the initials M. S̲h̲. and later (after 1934) M. Ş. E.; occasionally he used pen-names such as Mustafa Yalınkat and M. Oğulcuk. Although a contemporary of the pioneer short story writer ʿÖmer Seyf al-Dīn [*q.v.*], he did not begin to publish his short stories (written mostly much earlier) until 1925 in the periodical *Meslek*. Esendal's short stories differ substantially, in subject matter, plot and style from the "classical", Maupassant-type short stories preferred by most of his contemporaries. There is hardly any plot in them; they are character studies or sketches of the moods of ordinary people with emphasis on women, written in spoken Turkish, in a most natural and spontaneous manner, without any elaboration or embellishment, and imbued with human warmth and optimism. Only a small number of his short stories have been published in book form. Some remain in the collection of periodicals and newspapers, some have never been published and are in the hands of his heirs. The published volumes are *Hikâyeler I* and *II* (1945). Some stories, with the addition of new ones, were posthumously published under the titles *Temiz sevgiler* (1965) and *Ev ona yakıştı* (1972). Esendal is the author of three novels which have the same characteristics of his short stories: *Mīrāt̲h̲*, serialised in *Meslek* (1925) but not published in book form; *Waṣṣāf Bey*, never published; and *Ayaşli ve Kıracıları* (1934), an interesting and realistic series of sketches of characters in the early days of Ankara as the new capital.

Bibliography: Tahir Alangu, *Cumhuriyetten*

sonra hikâye ve roman, ii, Istanbul 1965, 106; S. K. Karaalioğlu, *Resimli Türk edebiyatı sözlüğü*, Istanbul 1974, 143-4; *Türk ansiklope* xv, Ankara 1967, s.v. (FAHİR İ

ES̲H̲REF, MEḤMED, modern Turkish MEḤ Eṣref, Turkish satirical poet (1846-19 He was born in Gelenbe, near Manisa, in Wes Anatolia the son of Ḥāfiẓ Muṣṭafā, of the Usuoǧ larī family. He attended for a while a *madras* Manisa, where he learnt Arabic and Persian, after serving as a government official in n bouring provinces, went to Istanbul (1878), w he passed the required examination to becom Ḳāyīm-maḳām and served as such in various ṛ of Anatolia, including in distant ḳaḍās in the ḷ and Eastern Black Sea region. By this time, virulent satires imbued with anger against injustice, tyranny and corruption of the Ḥamī régime, which were known all over the coun reached the ears of the Palace. When he was ser at Gördes, near Manisa, following a z̲h̲urnal (rep house in Izmir was searched and he was arre (1902), brought to Istanbul and detained for s months and then sentenced to one year's impri ment. On the completion of his term, he was allo to go to Izmir (1903) where he became a very pop character, although under strict supervision. 1904 he fled to Egypt where he continued to w his satirical poems against ʿAbd al-Ḥamīd II his régime.

Es̲h̲ref is the author of the following works, published in Cairo: *Dedjdjāl* ("Antichrist"), 2 v 1904-7; *Istimdād* ("S.O.S."), 1906; *Ḥasb-i* ("Friendly talk"), 1908; *S̲h̲āh we pādis̲h̲āh*, 19 and *Īrānda yangīn var* ("Iran is burning"), 1 Returning to Istanbul after the restoration of Constitution in July 1908, Es̲h̲ref began to publi weekly humorous paper *Es̲h̲ref*, where he re-ṛ lished poems of his Egyptian period as well as ones. He died in Ḳara-ag̲h̲ač near Manisa on May 1912.

Es̲h̲ref had a passionate temperament an boundless satirical power, but he lacked a sens balance in his literary expression and skill in v technique. His satires, like those of the 17th cent poet Nefʿī [*q.v.*], are often unrefined and even vul However, he wrote many unforgettable satir lines which are still frequently quoted with s faction, even though the language and style antiquated.

Bibliography: Mustafa Şâtim (Es̲h̲ref's s *Meşhur şair Eşref'in hayatı*, Izmir 1943; Cev Kudret, *Eşref, hicviyeler*[3], Istanbul 1970; *1 ansiklopedisi*, xv, Ankara 1967, 473; Tahir Alar *100 Ünlü Türk eseri*, s.v. (FAHİR İz

ESPARTO [see ḤALFĀʾ].

ES̲H̲REFOG̲H̲LU ʿABD ALLĀH, also known Es̲h̲ref-i RŪMĪ, Turkish poet and mys the founder of the Es̲h̲refiyye branch of the Ḳa iyya Ṣūfī ṭarīḳa (d. 873/1469). His father Es̲h̲ref Egypt as a young man and settled in Iznik (Nic Es̲h̲refog̲h̲lu himself was educated in Bursa wl he was introduced to the famous 9th/15th cent saint Emīr Sulṭān [*q.v.*], on whose recommenda he went to Ankara where he joined the fam s̲h̲ayk̲h̲ and mystical poet Ḥād̲j̲d̲j̲ī Bayram, liked him and gave him his daughter in marri On Ḥad̲j̲d̲j̲ī Bayram's instructions, Es̲h̲refog̲h̲ went first to Izmit, and then to Ḥamā, where worked with Ḳādirī s̲h̲ayk̲h̲s, and then returne Iznik, where he set up a convent. His reputaʿ soon spread as far as Istanbul, and Maḥmūd Pa

) (d. 878/1474), the famous *wazīr* of Meḥemmed
ecame one of his disciples. Es͟hrefog͟hlu died in
, where he is buried. The Es͟hrefiyye *ṭarīḳa*
 he founded is a blend of the Ḳādiriyya [*q.v.*]
 the Bayramiyya, with special emphasis on
ion and asceticism.

hrefog͟hlu's poems are written in a warm and
ng style where both *ʿarūḍ* and *hed͟je* metres are
 following the poetic and mystic traditions of
s Emre [*q.v.*]. His *dīwān* was printed in Istanbul
80/1864 and in Roman script in 1944 (edited
 an introduction by Asaf Halet Çelebi). A
er popular edition was published in 1972.

hrefog͟hlu is also the author of many popular
ic works on an edifying nature, the most
us of which is *Muzakkī 'l-nüfūs* ("The Purifier
uls"), which remained a practical manual of
sh life for centuries and is a masterpiece of
5th century Turkish prose; it was printed in
bul in 1281/1865 (for a good MS., see Konya,
eol. Libr. no. 5452; for specimens based on
 see Fahir İz, *Eski Türk edebiyatında nesir*,
bul 1964, 70-92).

Bibliography: Ismet Parmaksızoğlu, in *Türk
siklopedisi*, xv, 1967, 477-8; A. Gölpınarlı,
ırkiye'de mezhepler ve tarikatlar, 1969, *passim*
ith further bibliography). (Fahir İz)

SRĀR DEDE, Turkish Mewlewī poet of
 18th century, a close friend and protégé of
great poet G͟hālib Dede [*q.v.*]. Born in Istanbul,
 was trained as a Mewlewī dervish in the
ta convent, under the supervision of G͟hālib
, its *s͟hayk͟h*. He died in 1211/1796-7 before his
er (who wrote a famous elegy for him) and was
d in the convent cemetery.

rār wrote mystical poems in the line of G͟hālib
. His little *Dīwān* has not been edited. Esrār
 is also the author of an incomplete *Ted͟hkire-yi
ırāʾ-i mewlewiyye* which contains the biographies
ore than 200 Mewlewī poets. The work, which
also not been edited, is based on Ṣāḥib Dede's
ie-i mewlewiyye and was published in a shortened
 by ʿAlī Enwer under the title of *Semāʿk͟hāne-i*
(Istanbul 1309 Rūmī/1893).

Bibliography: Gibb, *HOP*, iv, 207-11;
 Gölpınarlı, *Mevlana'dan sonra mevlevilik*, Is-
anbul 1953, *passim*; S. N. Ergun, *Türk şair-
i*, s.v. (Fahir İz)

THICS, ETHOLOGY [see ak͟hlāḳ].

TYMOLOGY [see is͟htiḳāḳ].

UBOEA [see eğriboz].

ULOGY [see madīḥ].

XCHANGE VALUE [see ʿiwāḍ].

XPIATORY OFFERING [see kaffāra].

YYŪBOG͟HLU, Bedrī Raḥmī, modern Turkish
ri Rahmi Eyuboğlu, Turkish poet, writer
 painter (1913-75), younger brother of the
wing. He was born in Görele, near Trabzon on
Black Sea. Educated at Trabzon lycée and the
nbul Academy of Fine Arts, he spent two years
aris for further study in painting. On his return
3) he was appointed to the staff of the Istanbul
demy of Fine Arts, where he taught until his
h from cancer on 21 September 1975.

is writings and sketches began to appear in *Yeni
n* in 1933. As a painter he became interested in
 arts and crafts and studied popular motifs in
, scarves, socks and colour patterns, and was
tly inspired by them. In his predominantly de-
ptive poetry, which brought a new tone to con-
porary Turkish verse, he used the same colourful
nique, strongly influenced by folk poetry and
music. His first volume of verse was published in 1941: *Yaradana mektuplar* ("Letters to the Creator)", followed by *Karadut* ("Black mulberry") in 1948. Then several volumes followed which were all put together in *Dol karabakır dol* (1974). His essays, written in an informal small-talk style, were posthumously published in book form, *Delifişek* (1975) and *Tezek* (1976).

Bibliography: Asım Bezirci, *Dünden bügüne türk şiiri*, Istanbul 1968; Behçet Necatigil, *Edebiyatımızda isimler sözlüğü*[9], Istanbul 1978, s.v. (Fahir İz)

EYYŪBOG͟HLU, Ṣabāḥ al-Dīn Raḥmī, modern Turkish, until 1934 Sabahattin Rahmi, afterwards Sabahattin Eyuboğlu, Turkish essayist, writer and translator (1908-73). Born in Akçaabat (Polathane) near Trabzon, the son of Raḥmī Eyyūbog͟hlu, a civil servant, he was educated in Trabzon. He then went to France on a government scholarship and studied French literature and aesthetics in Dijon, Lyon and Paris universities (1928-32). Becoming lecturer (*doçent*) in French literature in the University of Istanbul (1933-9), he was invited, together with some of his colleagues, by Ḥasan ʿĀlī Yüd͟jel (Yücel), the reforming Minister of Education (1938-46), to Ankara where he served respectively as member of the Advisory Board (*Talim ve terbiye kurulu*) deputy chairman of the Office of Translation [of world classics], and teacher at the Hasanoğlan Higher Village Institute [see köy enstitüleri]. Back in Istanbul after one year's study leave in France, he taught in Istanbul Technical University (1951-8). Because of his liberal ideas, he was arrested and detained for several months in 1971, during the emergency régime of 1971-2. He died in Istanbul of a heart attack on 13 January 1973.

Ṣabāḥ al-Dīn Eyyūbog͟hlu developed a theory of nationalism which is mainly based on Kemalism, with particular emphasis on secularism and "populism" (*halkçılık*) and with the addition of the notion of an "Anatolian" people accepting as "ours" all the peoples, arts and cultures which have flourished on Anatolian soil (without distinction of race, language and faith). Many of his essays elaborate on this theme, rejecting rival ideologies like Turkism, Turanism, Islamism and Westernism. His numerous essays were published in various periodicals, particularly *Varlık*, *İnsan*, *Yaprak* and regularly in *Yeni ufuklar*, and they cover a great range of subjects from literature, language and cultural change to art, folklore and politics. He always laid special emphasis on the need for the fusion and identification of intellectuals with ordinary people in order to develop an original culture.

Eyyūbog͟hlu writes in a simple straightforward style and is considered, together with Atač, as a master of contemporary Turkish prose. However, he lacks Atač's originality and conciseness and is often shallow and repetitive. His major contribution is his translations from the French, some of which are masterpieces of the genre (see below). Ṣabāḥ al-Dīn Eyyūbog͟hlu is the author of the following major works: *Mavi ile kara* ("Blue and Black"), Istanbul 1961, enlarged edition 1967, a selection of his essays; *Sanat üzerine denemeler* ("Essays on art"), Istanbul 1974, published posthumously, contains most of the essays omitted from the previous work; *Yunus Emre*, Istanbul 1971, an impressionistic study of the 13th century Turkish poet; and *Turan yolunda* ("On the way to Turan"), Istanbul 1967, which satirises Pan-Turanism and is based on a misreading of the allegory in André Malraux's autobiographical work *Les noyers de l'Altenberg*. Among more than fifty titles of his translations, the following are outstanding: Montaigne's *Essais*, Rabelais' *Gargantua*, verse translations of La Fontaine's *Fables* and ᶜUmar Khayyām's *Rubāᶜiyyāt* (mainly based on a Turkish paraphrase). Eyyūboghlu collaborated in the preparation of several art books and in the ma of films on early Anatolian culture.

Bibliography: Mehmed Seyda, *Ede dostları*, Istanbul 1970 (contains autobiograp notes); *Yeni ufuklar*, special number, March 1 *Milliyet san'at dergisi*, no. 17 (26 January 1 (complete list of his works and translations).

(FAHIR

F

FABLE [see MATHAL].

AL-**FAḌL** B. AL-**ḤUBĀB** B. ABI KHALĪFA MUḤAMMAD b. SHUᶜAYD B. ṢAKHR AL-DJUMAḤĪ, (d. 305/917-18), littérateur, poet, traditionist and *ḳāḍī* of Baṣra. He was a *mawlā* of Djumaḥ of Ḳuraysh and the nephew, on his mother's side, of Ibn Sallām [*q.v.*]. He was born in and died at Baṣra, where he made himself the transmitter of a fairly extensive number of religious, historical, literary and genealogical traditions. He also received a legal training sufficient for him to act as the *ḳāḍī* of Baṣra towards 294/907 with functions delegated by the Mālikī *ḳāḍī* Abū Muḥammad Yūsuf b. Yaᶜḳūb b. Ismāᶜīl al-Azdī, whose seat of office was in eastern Baghdād (L. Massignon, in *WZKM* [1948], 108) but who also had jurisdiction over southern ᶜIrāḳ (Wakīᶜ, *Akhbār al-ḳuḍāt*, Cairo 1366/1947, ii, 182).

At this time, Abū Khalīfa was already famous in his native town, where he was in contact with well-known personages, especially the Tanūkhīs [*q.v.*]; he had a particularly deep knowledge of Arabic poetry, taught the works of his maternal uncle and was himself the author of a *Kitāb Ṭabaḳāt al-shuᶜarā' al-djāhiliyyīn* and a *Kitāb al-Fursān*. He also gathered into a *dīwān* the poetry of ᶜImrān b. Ḥiṭṭān [*q.v.*], which brought him accusations of Khāridjī sympathies, but Shīᶜī tendencies were also imputed to him, and one verse implies that in *fiḳh* he was a Ḥanafī. His works do not seem to have survived, and his verses only exist in part, but his name is often cited in *adab* works. He is, moreover, the hero of a certain number of anecdotes in which his tendency to express himself in rhymed prose is ridiculed. One of these, if it is authentic, allows one to affirm the survival at the end of the 3rd century of a Baṣran tradition which sent as delegates to the caliphal court orators charged with expressing, in rhymed prose, the people's complaints, who had always cause to lament the hardness of the times and the arbitrary ways of the local authorities. Abū Khalīfa, as the mouth-piece of a delegation sent to al Muᶜtaḍid (279-98/892-902), was able to obtain satisfaction through provoking his audience to mirth because of the affected nature of his speech (al-Masᶜūdī, *Murūdj*, viii, 128-34 = §§ 3264-70). His biographers classify him amongst the blind scholars.

Bibliography: *Fihrist*, Cairo edn., 165; Ṣūlī, *Akhbār al-Rāḍī wa 'l-Muttaḳī*, tr. M. Canard, Algiers 1946-50, 29, 208; Tanūkhī, *Nishwār*, ii, 27-8, iv, 183; Masᶜūdi, *Murūdj*, index; Ibn al-Djazarī, *Ṭabaḳāt al-ḳurrā'*, ii, 8, no. 2557; Khaṭīb Baghdādī, *Ta'rīkh*, ii, 429; Ḥuṣrī, *Zahr al ādāb*, 825; Zubaydī, *Naḥwiyyīn*, index; Yāḳūt, *Udabā'*, xvi, 204-14 and index; Ṣafadī, *Nakt al-himyān*, 226; Suyūṭī, *Bughya*, 373; Ibn Ḥadjar, *Lisān al-Mīzān*, iv, 373, Ibn al-ᶜImād, *Shadharāt*, ii, Bustānī, *DM*, iv, 285.

(CH. PELLA

FAḌL AL-SHĀᶜIRA, AL-YAMĀMIYYA AL-ᶜAB YA, MAWLĀT AL-MUTAWAKKIL, Arab poetess, in 257/871 (or 260/874). Born probably as a *muwa* and brought up in Baṣra, she was presented to later on freed by al-Mutawakkil. She was called "most gifted poetess of her time" by Ibn al and, being a good songstress and lute player held a famous literary circle in Baghdād. Amc her admirers were the poet Saᶜīd b. Ḥumayd the musician Bunān b. ᶜAmr al-Ḍārib. Ibn Djarrāḥ (quoted by Ibn al-Nadīm) knew a s collection of her poetry. Her verses were se music by several contemporary court musicians.

Bibliography: *Aghānī*[3], xix, 300-13 (see indices); Ibn al-Muᶜtazz, *Ṭabaḳāt*[3], 426-7; *Fih* 164; Ibn al-Sāᶜī, *Nisā' al-khulafā'*[2], 84-90; Kut *Fawāt*, ii, Cairo 1951, 253-5; Suyūṭī, *Musta* 50-6; Cl. Huart, *La poétesse Fadhl*, in *JA*, sé xvii (1881), 5-43; F. Sezgin, GAS, ii, 623-4; Stigelbauer, *Die Sängerinnen am Abbasidenhof die Zeit des Kalifen Al-Mutawakkil*, Vienna 1 31-4.

(E. NEUBAUE

FAITH, BELIEF (in God) [see ᶜAḲĪDA].

FAKHR-I MUDABBIR, the *shuhra* of FA AL-DĪN MUḤAMMAD B. MANṢŪR MUBĀRAK SHĀH ḲURASHĪ, Persian author in India during time of the last Ghaznawids, the Ghūrids and first Slave Kings of Dihlī (later 6th/12th cent early 7th/13th century).

His birth date and place are both unknown, he was a descendant, so he says, on his father's from the caliph Abū Bakr and on his mother's f the Turkish *amīr* Bilgetigin, the immediate decessor in Ghazna of Sebüktigin and father-in of Maḥmūd of Ghazna; he may well have been b and reared in Ghazna itself. He first appears Multān as a youth during the reign of the Ghaznawid sultan in the Pandjāb Khusraw M b. Khusraw Shāh. After the defeat and deposi of this last in 582/1186 by the Ghūrid Muᶜizz al- or Shihāb al-Dīn Muḥammad b. Sām, Fak Mudabbir went to Lahore and undertook genealog researches there for thirteen years. The fruits o this work were his extensive genealogical tal extending from the Prophet to the Ghūrids' s commanders in India, the *Shadjara-yi ansāb*, ext in a unique British Museum ms.; this book brought to the attention of Ḳuṭb al-Dīn Ay [*q.v.*], and led to Fakhr-i Mudabbir becoming *pers grata* in court circles. It was to the Dihlī su Shams al-Dīn Iltutmish [see ILTUTMISH] that dedicated his other great Persian prose work, *Ādāb al-ḥarb* (see on this, below), and since he

; himself as being by then an infirm old man *ḍaʿīf*), he probably died before the end of that n's reign in 633/1236.

ere is some uncertainty over the possible ification of our Fakhr-i Mudabbir with a Fakhr wla wa'l-Dīn Mubārak Shāh b. al-Ḥusayn al-arrūdhī mentioned by the literary biographer in his *Lubāb al-albāb*, ed. Saʿīd Nafīsī, Tehran 1956, 113-17, as a good poet in Arabic and an and a *nadīm* or confidant of the Ghūrid ith al-Dīn Muḥammad b. Sām (558-99/1163-. E. Denison Ross, in his edition of the intro-on and early part of the *Shadjara-yi ansāb*, on 1927, accepted this identification. Storey, ver, rejected this, despite a similarity of names, cing detailed arguments in his *Persian literature*, 56-7, and his reasoning seems conclusive; the Mubārak Shāh al-Marwarrūdhī seems to have the author also of works on astronomy and s.

e main claim of fame of Fakhr-i Mudabbir elf is his authorship of the *Ādāb al-ḥarb wa'l-īʿa*, or as the name appears in one of the extant the *Ādāb al-mulūk wa-kifāyat al-mamlūk* on by Aḥmad Suhaylī Khwānsārī, Tehran 1967, unfortunately based on the shorter mss. not on the fuller India Office one, which has *wāb* or chapters as opposed to only 36). This th a treatise on kingship and statecraft (hence king of the "Mirrors for princes" genre) and a rather theoretical and idealised consideration e art of war. In addition to advice on tactics, rganisation of troops, the use of various weapons, the book is liberally interspersed with historical lotes, giving it a distinct value as a historical nent, above all for the development of the rn Islamic world. The eighteen anecdotes ng to the Ghaznawids have been translated English by Miss Iqbal M. Shafī as *Fresh light e Ghaznavīds*, in *IC*, xii (1938), 189-234; they sh useful information on the dynasty not found here. A translation of the whole work into a rn language would be welcome.

Bibliography: Storey, i, 1164-7; C. E. Bos-rth, *Early sources for the history of the first four znavid sultans (977-1041)*, in *IQ*, vii (1963), also in *The medieval history of Iran, Afghanistan l Central Asia*, London 1977; idem, *The znavids, their empire in Afghanistan and tern Iran 994-1040, Edinburgh* 1963, 20-1.

(C. E. Bosworth)

ḲĪR OF IPI, the name given in popular nce to Ḥādjdjī Mīrzā ʿAlī Khān, Pathan *ah* and agitator along the Northwestern tier of the Indo-Pakistan subcontinent in both ater British Indian and the early Pakistani ds, d. 1960.

member of the Torī Khēl group of the ʿUth-ay Wazīrs of North Wazīristān, probably one e most unreconciled of the Pathan tribes of the tier in British times, he came to especial inence in 1936-7, inflaming the Tōrī Khēls and lahsūds of the Tochi valley against the British ary presence, and then retreating to a series of at Gorwekht near Razmak, not far from the an frontier, which served as his headquarters e rest of his life. In 1941 he was apparently cted by Axis agents from the German and n embassies in Kabul with a view to raising frontier against Britain, but nothing much ialised. After the Partition of 1947 between and Pakistan, the Faḳīr actively identified himself with the Afghān-sponsored "Pashtūnistān" movement, and after 1950 became president of a southern "Pashtūnistān" local assembly based on Gorwekht, where stocks of food and arms and a small Pashto printing press were kept. He died in 1960.

Bibliography: J. W. Spain, *The Pathan borderland*, The Hague 1963, 51, 76, 160, 184-6, 202, 237; W. K. Fraser-Tytler, *Afghanistan, a study of political developments in Central and Southern Asia*³, London 1967, 310.

(C. E. Bosworth)

FAMILY [see ʿĀʾila].

FAʾR (A., pl. *fiʾrān, fiʾara, fuʾar*) masculine substantive with the value of a collective (noun of singularity *faʾra*) designates, like the Persian *mūsh*, firstly, among the Rodents (*ḳawāriḍ, ḳawāḍim*), the majority of types and species of the sub-order of the Myomorphs (with the Dipodids, Glirids, Murids, Spalacids and Cricetida), secondly, among the Insectivores (*ākilāt al-ḥasharāt*), the family of the Soricids. The term is applied equally well to the largest rats as to the smallest shrews and gerbils. The adjectives of abundance *faʾir, faʾira, mafʾara* and *mufʾira* which are derived from it contain the same general idea, so that, in texts, *faʾr* and *fiʾrān* always present a problem of discrimination between rats and mice; this lack of precision persists with the dialectal form *fār* pl. *fīrān*, as well as with its Berber equivalent *agherda* pl. *igherdayen*.

However, jointly with this collective of broad semantic extent, several more precise nouns fortunately help towards a skeleton classification of all this prolific world of mammals which flee the light and whom humanity treats, in general, as undesirables, by reason of the depredations to which their way of life forces them. Without pretending to be able to apply, with the existing Arabic philological resources, a scientific system which proves most complicated, it is, nevertheless, possible to give a glimpse of all the known species of the Muslim populations by dividing these species under one of the four following most significant rubrics: *djuradh*, *faʾra*, *khuld* and *yarbūʿ*.

A. Djuradh (pl. *djirdhān, djurdhān*) and its derivative *djirdhawn*, with the dialectal forms *djred*, *djūred* in the Maghrib and *djardūn* in Syria, defines all rats of a large size without distinction of species. Among the numerous strains of rats, the ordinary man of every people has for long recognised two categories according to their ethology, the town-dwellers and the rustics, and the fable of the meeting between the town rat (*ḥaḍarī*) and the country rat (*rīfī*) remains one of the themes of fables common to all literatures. The majority of rats whose life is linked with towns are of a large size (*ʿaḍal* pl. *ʿidlān*), the Brown rat (*Mus decumanus*) or "Sewer rat", which is grey-brown, hence his name *marnab* (Maghrib: *ṭubba*, Tamahak *taghūlit*, pl. *tighūlitin*) and the Black rat (*Mus rattus*), both of which owed their rapid extension of their area of distribution to the maritime commercial traffic in the Mediterranean basin since the high Middle Ages. It was the same for the Alexandrian rat (*Mus alexandrinus*) also called "palm rat" or "roof rat" (*Mus tectorum*) and whose chosen habitat is in high places (granaries, terraces, the tops of date-palms) and not in the infrastructure of buildings. Proper to Egypt, this rat was introduced into Italy by merchant shipping; it makes a nest at the top of palms and, when it is hunted, is able to let itself fall to the ground without injury by blowing himself up like a balloon. In the large oases it is confused with the "palm rat" (Saharan: *ṭunba*, Tamaḥaḳ *akkolen*), an erroneous name of a small ground squirrel (*Euxerus erythropus*) which feeds on dates. Still included among the "true rats", so the naturalists say, there must also be cited the large burrower rat of Egypt and Arabia called the Fat sand rat (*Ps. obesus*) which is cream-coloured. All the Maghrib used to know the Striped rat or "Barbarian rat" (*Arvicanthus barbarus*) by the name of *zurdānī* (Tamaḥaḳ *akunder*, pl. *ikunderen*). Numerous geographical strains, such as the *Mus calopus* and *Mus peregrinus*, still remain to be studied in Morocco.

In the vast group of country rats, scourge of farmers and habitual nourishment of nocturnal predators, the Voles and Field-mice (types *Arvisola*, *Microtus* and *Apodemus*), confused under the name of *ʿakbar* (Hebrew *ʿakbār*, in I. Sam. vi, 4-5; Isaiah ii, 20, lxvi, 17; Levit. xi, 29), have had since the most ancient antiquity the just reputation of being terribly harmful. The most common, the Common vole (*Microtus arvalis*) *ʿakbar ḥaḳli, faʾrat al-ghayṭ*, is present in all the cultivated zones, along with the strains *Mus micrurus* in Persia and *Hypudoeus syriacus* in Syria; a close neighbour in Egypt is the semi-aquatic "Nile rat", *djuradh al-Nīl* (*Arvicanthis niloticus*), while the Sudan has its opposite number in the "Khartoum rat", *djuradh al-kharṭūm* (*Arvicanthis testicularis*). The Field mouse (*Apodemus sylvaticus*), *dathīma, faʾrat al-ḥirādj* (in Syria, *djurdhān*) prefers living in trees, and is found in company with the Dormouse, the Garden dormouse (types *Glis*, *Myoxus*, *Eliomys*), *djuradh sindjābī*, *ḳarḳadūn*, and the Small dormouse (*Muscardinus*), *zughba*. On the Saharan borders lives Munby's dormouse (*Eliomys munbianus lerotinus*), *thadghagath* in Berber, which the Tuareg eat on occasion, as well as the Goundis (types *Ctenodactylus* and *Massouteria*), *ḳundī/gundī*, Tamaḥaḳ *telūt*, *taralemt*, large, very suspicious, burrowing rodents rather similar to the Cobaye (*Cavis porcellus*). It is perhaps to the latter as well as to the Hamsters that the Arab philologists attribute the name of *yahyarr*, defined as being "the largest of all the rats".

Al-Djāḥiẓ was happy to record all the information that he had been able to glean on the subject of rats (*Ḥayawān*, v, 245 ff. and *passim*). Regarded as noxious creatures, he tells us that in Khurāsān and Antioch the rats are particularly aggressive, holding their own against cats and going as far as nibbling the ears of sleeping persons; the frightful trench wars with their train of rats which our century has known, alas, only confirm these sayings. Their depredations and their less engaging aspects arouse in every man repulsion, as nothing resists their inexorable incisors, unless it is metal. On the other hand, al-Djāḥiẓ shows, out of concern for justice, a positive aspect in the presence of these parasite hosts; if they invade a dwelling, it is because they find there something to satisfy their appetites and so it is a sign that it enjoys a certain prosperity. Hence the wish expressed in this old adage is understandable: *akthar*[a] *'llāh*[u] *djurdhān*[a] *baytik*[a] "may Allah multiply the rats of your house". With the same intention, a storyteller of Medina used to offer up this prayer: *Allahumm*[a] *akthir djurdhānanā wa-aḳill*[a] *ṣibyānanā* "O Allah, give us many rats and few children", evoking implicitly the danger of misery which overpopulation could bring about. On the contrary, the expression *tafarraḳat djirdhān*[u] *baytihi* "the rats of his house have dispersed" may be an image of being wrecked by poverty; i
days and with the same idea, sailors may see
of the inescapable loss of the ship when th
desert it. Furthermore, rats often show pr
ingenuity; faced with an oil container, the ra
know how to sample the contents by dipping
tail a number of times. Caught in a cage, it
manages to escape with the help of its sharp
In the countryside, rats take care not to dig
hole (*khabār*) on roads in order to avoid the d
of being trampled by beasts of burden. Som
may be attracted, like the so-called "thie
Magpie (*ʿaḳʿaḳ*), by anything which shines
steal jewels and money, and the adage *asraḳ*
djuradh "more thieving than a rat" is truly sp
al-Damīrī records, with reference to this, (
al-ḥayawān, i, 191-2) the discovery, in the ti
the Prophet, of a cache concealing several
thanks to a rat, and the one who discovered i
full possession of the find, which was attribut
divine intervention.

Before Islam, certain rats, especially the co
ones, were hunted for their flesh, as were th
mastix lizard [see ḌABB], the hedgehog and th
cupine [see ḲUNFUDH] and the jerboa (see b
These primitive tastes did not disappear immed
with Islam since, according to Abū Zayd al-N
(*Ḥayawān*, iv, 44, v, 253, vi, 385), the fa
radjaz poet Ruʾba b. al-ʿAdjdjādj [*q.v.*], of the
8th century, used to feast on roasted rats cau
his own house.

In the Ḥidjāz, the palm rat used to be so co
that the expression *umm djirdhān* "mother of
designated metaphorically the top of the date
where the animal chose to live, and *djur*
became the name of a variety of date. Fi
authorities on horses gave the name *al-djura*
"the two rats "to two symmetrical dorsal m
of the horse because of their shape.

B. FAʾRA, while being the noun of singular
faʾr, designates more especially the mouse
every small rodent which resembles it. The Co
mouse or "grey" mouse (*Mus musculus*),
al-bayt, present wherever there is man, nu
numerous geographical strains, of which *M.*
gentilis, *algirus*, *far* and *Hayii* are to be found
Maghrīb, *M. m. variegatus* in Egypt, *M. m. pre*
in Syria and *M. m. flaviventris* in Arabia.

At every time, the mouse was at the orig
misdeeds, seen as catastrophes, coming unexpe
to disturb daily life. Already in the Ark of
according to the legend, its depredations excite
complaints of the women, from which resulte
creation of the pair of cats, then that of the p
pigs [see KHINZĪR]. The Prophet Muḥammad
self had set a trap to get rid of this "little ra
(*fuwaysiḳa*) which, according to several tradi
had only just missed setting fire to his hou
pulling, in order to nibble it, the wick of the li
lamp; thanks to the immediate intervention
master of the house, the only damage it did
to make a hole in his prayer carpet. From
episode, which was no doubt authentic an
the first of its kind, an irrevocable curse fell
the mouse, which was then added to the list
four execrable species (*fawāsiḳ*), i.e. the crow
GHURĀB], the kite, *ḥidāʾ*, the scorpion [see ʿA
and the biting dog [see KALB], a list to
Mālik b. Anas added the lion [see ASAD], the pa
namir, *nimr*, the leopard [see FAHD] and the
[see DHIʾB], to be destroyed at all times and e
where in Islam, even by the pilgrim in a sacr

. It was, furthermore, enjoined on the young nunity to extinguish every lamp at night, in homes and in the mosques, and not to do as Christians who imprudently left permanently ed a sanctuary night-light in their churches and els (*Ḥayawān*, v, 121, 269, 319).

fore Islam, the mouse scarcely enjoyed, among Arabs, any greater credit, since it passed as g the metamorphosis of a Jewish sorceress to and that of a dishonest crow to others (*Ḥayawān*, 77). In addition, some proverbs such as *alaṣṣ faʾra* "more thieving than a mouse", *aksab min* "more hoarding than a mouse" presented it pilferer and an inveterate miser. In the climate ch a reputation one can understand the energetic tation with which al-Djāḥiẓ opposes (*Ḥayawān*, 98 ff.) the words of the Avesta which propose the mouse was a creation of Ormuzd, genius of l, while the cat was that of Ahriman, genius of

e words *faʾra* and *birr* include, apart from the mon mouse, all the other species of small nts such as the Dwarf mouse (*Micromys minutus*) called *zubāna*, the Arian mouse (*Mus arianus*) d *siktim*, the Desert mouse (*Mus barbarus*) or ʾ and *faʾrat al-ṣaḥraʾ* and all the representatives e *Acomys* type or Spiny mouse, *ḳunfuʿ/ḳinfiʿ*, *A. viator* in Tripolitania, *A. Cahirinus* in pt, *A. Chudeau* in Mauritania and *A. dimidiatus* ran. *Faʾra* also extends to cover the small in-vores with a very elongated snout which form Shrews (of types *Sorex*, *Crocidura*, *Suncus*, *hantulus*). More precisely, the Shrew is called *ba* and the Arab authors speak of it as deaf use of the absence in it of an external ear *yawān*, vi, 317). It bears in addition the names *t al-bīsh* "wolf's-bane mouse" and *faʾrat al-n* "poison-mouse" by reason of its supposed tance to the poison of venomous plants, whose s it nibbles at the time when insects are in t supply.

rab poets and prose writers have often dealt the atavistic hostility of the cat towards the se, which it makes its favourite prey; the ances-cat-and-mouse antagonism is well set in relief the old expression *lā yaʿrifu hirran min birrin* doesn't know a cat from a mouse" being applied ne who is completely ignorant.

here should also be mentioned an extension of use of *faʾr* and *faʾra* to designate other animals ng the appearance of rats and mice. Also to be d is *faʾr al-būṣ* "cannaies rat" given to the aul-e (*Aulacodus*) as well as *ḳubāʿ*; the *faʾr al-khayl* ses' rat" is the Polecat, the *faʾrat al-khayl* "the es's mouse" is the Weasel [see IBN ʿIRS], the *firʿawn* "Pharaoh's rat" is the Ichneumon s) and the *faʾr al-thayyil* "Scutch-grass rat" is Golunda, a countryside predator of the rice-tations. Finally, by contamination between the s *F-ʾ-R* and *F-W-R*, *faʾra* is wrongly substituted *fāra* "odour" in the names *Faʾrat al-ibil* (for *al-ibil*), a special odour which camels emit they are watered, after being satiated with rant plants, and *faʾrat al-misk* "odour of musk", not "musk rat"), a name given to the contents he musk vesicle (*nāfidja*) of a "small animal" *aybba*) hunted in Tibet and which, despite its name *djuradh al-misk* "musk rat", is not a rat *yawān*, iii, 514, v, 301-4, vi, 27, vii, 210-11). Djāḥiẓ adds that the name of *faʾr al-misk* is given rtain house rats which emit a characteristic odour lar to musk.

C. KHULD (pl. *khildān* and dial. *khlūda*) and its doublet *djuldh* (pl. *madjālidh*, *manādjidh*), of Aramaic origin (Hebrew *ḥōled* in Levit. xi, 29), is the name of the Mole rat or Blind rat (*Spalax typhlus*) a vegetarian rodent and burrower widespread in Egypt, in the Near East and in Arabia, especially in Yemen; it there takes the place of the common mole (*Talpa europaea*) which does not exist there. This Mole rat is also called *abū aʿmā*, *faʾr aʿmā* "blind rat" because its very small eyeball disappears beneath a cutaneous fold; similarly, the absence in it of an external ear made it said (*Ḥayawān*, ii, 112, iv, 410; *Ḥayāt al-ḥayawān*, i, 297 ff.) that it was also deaf and that it only guided itself underground by its sense of smell. Furthermore, its great distrust is at the origin of the proverbial expression *asmaʿ min khuld* "with hearing finer than that of the Mole rat". So believing it blind, deaf and an insectivore, the ancients supposed that it fed itself by staying with its mouth open at the entrance of its hole and swallowing the flies which came to settle on its tongue (*Ḥayawān*, ii, 112).

Known since the most ancient antiquity, the Blind Mole rat (the ἀσπάλαξ of Aristotle) was however more familiar to the Arabs as it was, according to the sayings of all the Muslim authors, the direct agent of Allāh in the breaking of the famous dam of Maʾrib [see MAʾRIB] around the year 542 A.D. It was said to have provoked by its labyrinth of galleries the fatal fissures through which the mass of devastating waters burst forth, the *sayl al-ʿarim* mentioned in the Ḳurʾān (XXXIV, 15-16). With the word *ʿarim*, probably of Ḥimyarite origin, the Arab philologists tentatively saw in it a plural (sing. *ʿarima*) signifying at once "dikes", "rats" and "torrential rains" (*LA*, s.v. *ʿ-R-M*). Although archaeologists have established the majority of the combined causes of this catastrophe (poor maintenance, silting up and hence raising of the level, flooding of the wadi and perhaps simultaneous earth tremors) which brought about a diaspora of the local tribes, it is the Mole rat which, in the general opinion, remains the instrument of this divine chastisement. It is not, however, to be ruled out that it played its part in the collapse of the gigantic earth dike, magnificently linking the works at the two ends of the dam, for this eager borer of the soil lives in sizable colonies and is particularly prolific; the proverb *afsad min khuld* "more ravaging than a Mole-rat" is there to confirm its misdeeds.

As for the mole (of the two strains *europaea* and *romana*), it is only known in the Maghrib, and it is to the Latin *talpa* that it owes its names *ṭawbīn/ṭūbīn* in Hispano-Moorish (cf. Spanish *topo*) and *ṭūbba* in the modern dialects; compared to a rodent, it is also named *fāra ʿamyā* "blind rat". By failing to distinguish between the mole and Mole rat, the majority of Arab lexicographers, with *khuld*, maintained the confusion between these two quite different species. For a good system, it seems that in modern Arabic *khuldiyyāt* defines clearly the Spalacids and *ṭawbiyyāt* the Talpids.

D. YARBŪʿ (fem. *-a*, pl. *yarābīʿ*) having passed to *djarbuʿ* pl. *djrābī* in dialects (Pers. *mūsh dō pā*, Tamaḥaḳ, *edewi*, pl. *idewan*), designates at once the jerboa in general (types *Dipus*, *Jaculus*, *Alactagalus*, *Alactaga*), and the gerbil and the jird (types *Gerbillus*, *Meriones*, *Psammomys* and *Pachyuromys*). All these small rodents and leapers of desert and steppe are very similar in appearance, gait and ways; each of them can be compared with a miniature kangaroo with a long tail ending in a brush rather like a spear and its head, hence its ancient name of *dhu 'l-rumayḥ* "with the small spear" given to every species. The Arabs, nevertheless, distinguished the jerboa and gerbil, calling the former *yarbūʿ shufārī* "the great" and the latter *yarbūʾ tadmurī* "the small"; in our own time, the Marāzīg of Tunisia make the same difference with *shāḥī* and *fār aḥmar*. From Africa to Arabia, as many geographical strains of jerboas are enumerated as of gerbils and jirds, but, without attempting a system for the most part complicated, it is to be maintained that the most common jerboa is that said to be of Egypt (*Jaculus jaculus* or *Jaculus aegyptius*) which is to be found from Mauritania to the Arabo-Persian Gulf; it is this of which the Arab authors speak and al-Djāḥiẓ (*Ḥayawān*, v, 260, v, 385) then al-Damīrī (*Ḥayāt* . . ., ii, 409) mention some similarities between its behaviour and that of the hare [see ARNAB, above], notably in their common ruse of *tawbīr* or *zamūʿ* consisting of only resting, in light soil, on the shaggy pads (*zamaʿāt*) of the heels in order to leave the faintest possible tracks. But it is especially for its genius at escaping (*nifāḳ*, *tanfīḳ*) when it is hunted that the jerboa is famous among the Bedouins who, at all times, eagerly hunted it as choice game. By day, the jerboa lies asleep at the bottom of its underground lair with many obstructed outlets, with a small pile of spoil earth showing them on the outside. The hunter who, in order to dislodge it, sounds the corridors of the burrow with a long stick cannot divine the exit from which the animal is going to spring out; if it finally comes out, it is with such bounds and such abrupt swerves that it very often keeps in check the most alert saluki. After tens of metres of frantic running, it soon seeks to plunge back into the ground. These retreat outlets of the jerboa bear the names *nāfiḳāʾ*, *ḳāṣiʿāʾ*, *rāhiṭāʾ*, *dāmmāʾ* (see Ibn Sīduh, *Mukhaṣṣaṣ*, viii, 92), and it is from the first of these words (root *N-F-Ḳ*) that there is derived (according to the philologists and exegetes) the Ḳurʾānic meaning of *nifāḳ* "dissimulation, duplicity, hypocrisy" in the matter of faith (al-Damīrī, *Ḥayāt* . . ., ii, 408-9).

In the pre-Islamic period, the Bedouins used to refrain from hunting the jerboa by night for, like the hedgehog and porcupine [see ḲUNFUDH], it passed for a mount of the *djinn*. Jerboas, gerbils and jirds live in small societies, of which each one colonises a sector (*arḍ marbaʿa*), and it was also believed that, as with the monkeys [see ḲIRD], they each had a chief in the role of nocturnal sentinel of the group and ensuring a permanent surveillance for the security of the young (*dirṣ*, pl. *adrāṣ*, *durūṣ*) who could easily stray, as the proverb says *aḍall min walad al-yarbūʿ* "straying more than the young of the jerboa"; if the chief relaxed his vigilance, he was hunted and replaced.

Finally, the great round, jet black eye of the jerboa is used as an image in the Maghrib, where *ʿayn al-djarbūʿ* designates a large buck-shot for shooting large game and, in Tunis, the colour "mouse grey" is called *djarbūʿī* "jerboa grey".

Of all these small creatures of the soil (*ḥasharāt al-arḍ*) which *faʾr* represents, only the jerboa, in Ḳurʾānic law, was recognised as legal for consumption by three of the four juridical schools of orthodoxy, the Ḥanafīs contesting this legality. For all the other rodents, the prohibition of consumption relates not only to their flesh, but also to every commodity in which they have put their teeth (*suʾr al-faʾr*) "rats, mice scraps") and every alimentary liquid (oil, milk, honey, vinegar, etc.) in which one of them has fallen (*faʾir*); also any pr
"contaminated" cannot be put on sale.

In urban areas, the destruction of invading
and mice has always been a permanent nece
and the means employed, in mediaeval Islam,
very varied, but their absolute efficacy was r
assured. The most widespread method was pois
with the aid of baits prepared for the purpose
poisons which they contained were either of vege
or chemical origin. As toxic plants they used
sea-onion (*scilla maritima*), *ʿunṣul baḥrī* called
al-faʾr "rat onion", the rose bay (*nerium olea*
diflā, *samm al-ḥimār* "donkey's poison" and
hyoscyamus (*hyoscyamus albus*), and *bandj*. A
chemical products they had vitriol (*ḳalḳand*), su
of arsenic (*shakk*, *shubha*, *rayb*, *rahadj*) or "ratsb
(*samm al-faʾr*), called in ʿIrāḳ *turāb hālik* "
earth", which was extracted in Khurāsān,
litharge (*murtaḳ*, *murdāsandj*); oxgall, don
urine and iron filings were also included in
preparations. Another practice was to smoke
the holes of the rodents by burning cumin, ho
horse's hoof and natron (*naṭrūn*). Cages were
with several systems of fall-traps and box-tra
pottery, whose patterns are still in use, but
simplest and most effective was that which al-
(*Djamhara*, . . . ms. Escurial, Ar. 903, fols. 1
166a) advocates in the 7th/13th century and w
consists of a basin filled with water and on w
is placed a rolling-pin (*shawbak*), baited in
middle with some dripping or cheese; attracted
greedy rodent, creeping along this unsteady
makes it shake unavoidably with its own weight
one side to the other and ends up by drow
Complementing all these stratagems, a perma
hunt was assured in homes and shops by s
domestic carnivores such as the cat, the afore
tioned weasel, the civet (*zabād*) and the genet (
nīṭ). The protection of doves [see ḤAMĀM] ag
the rats which preyed on the eggs consists, in
own time still, of encircling the outside of the f
grilles with a covering of completely varni
ceramic squares at the bottom of a slope; somet
the exit holes consisted of pottery pipes going
outside in order to place an insurmountable obs
in the way of every climber, and this is a me
constantly employed in the pigeon-houses w
adorn the Nile Valley. To all these direct mea
defence must be added the rich arsenal of m
formulas, talismans and conjuring practices w
serve to reinforce in the imagination the chanc
success; of these, one of the most widespread w
kill a mouse, cut off its tail and bury it in the
munal room of the house.

In ancient healing, the specific virtues attrib
to the corporeal elements of rodents were relati
limited. The head of a mouse placed in a linen
and applied to the head was used to dispel mig
and headache. The eye of a rat carried as a talis
allayed malaria; the upper lip of a Mole rat had
same effect, while the blood of the latter w
beneficial eye-lotion for all ocular troubles.
spoil earth of its galleries and its brain mixed
rose water made a good plaster against gout. Fin
one of the most curious and useful properties
that of the urine of a mouse which, it app
perfectly erases ink on parchments. It is to be
posed that the difficulty was in procuring a litt
this precious liquid, but it could be achieved
capturing in a small cage-trap, one or a numb
mice and rigging up at the bottom of the devi
small spout leading to a bottle. It was then s

t to provoke a sudden irruption of the house cat rder to achieve, under the effect of the terror, ng the captives, the awaited physiological reac- of urination; it is this, at least, which al-Damīrī *cit.*, ii, 2009 suggests, who seems to have ex- mented with this stratagem with the aim of ing parchments, this material being always very ly valued in the Middle Ages.

rom this glimpse of the manner in which Muslim ion treated rats and mice, these terrible carriers lague and cholera, it is evident that in Islam scarcely enjoyed any more credit than in stianity and that there was no good to be ex- ed from this race of parasites on the fruits of 's labour; the experience which this old Moroccan e conceals: *el-fār mā ka-yūled g͟hēr ḥaffār* "the nouse can only beget a grave-digger" sums up this general contempt.

Bibliography (apart from the references ted in the text): Amin al-Maʿlūf, *Muʿd͟jam al-yawān. An Arabic zoological dictionary*, Cairo 32; E. Ghaleb, *al-Mawsūʿa fī ʿulūm al-ṭabīʿa, ictionary of natural sciences*, Beirut 1965; L. vauden, *Les vertébrés du Sahara*, Tunis 1926; . Lhote, *La chasse chez les Touareg*, Paris 1951; rūz Iskandar, *Rāhnamā-yi pistāndārān-i Īrān, ide to mammals of Iran*, Tehran 1977.

(F. Viré)

-**FĀRĀBĪ**, Abū Ibrāhīm Isḥāḳ b. Ibrāhīm, cographer. The early sources are sparse in rd to him. Only Yāḳūt gives him a whole notice bāʾ, vi, 61-5 = *Irs͟hād*, ii, 226-9); al-Suyūṭī oduces a few extracts from this, adding nothing hya, i, 437-8); and al-Ḳifṭī speaks of him only entally in his *Inbāʾ* (i, 52-3), in his notice on 'l-ʿAlāʾ al-Maʿarrī.

is date of birth is unknown, but he probably died 50/961 (the date given by Brockelmann, I², 133, Kraemer, 212). He was the maternal uncle -D͟jawharī, author of the *Ṣiḥāḥ* (d. *ca.* 400/1009]), which keeps al-Fārābī within the 4th/10th ury and exludes the date of 450/1058 (Yāḳūt, vi, cf. al-Ḳifṭī, *Inbāʾ*, i, 53). He lived in his natal of Fārāb [*q.v.*]. Yāḳūt, *loc. cit.*, reports, how- on the authority of the *ḳāḍī* Yūsuf b. Ibrāhīm iftī (father of the author of the *Inbāʾ*) from the en, where he resided, that al-Fārābī went to the en, lived in Zabīd, composed there his *Dīwān lab* and died there also, before he had been able ach it, at a date *ca.* 450 A.H.; but Yāḳūt him- on the basis of all the historical details which he brought together (vi, 63-5), rejects the reports of ḳāḍī Yūsuf (vi, 65). Yāḳūt bases himself here on, articular (vi, 63), the fact that he had read as ws, written in al-D͟jawharī's own hand, *ḳaraʾ- ʿalā Ibrāhīm, raḥimahu Allāh, bi-Fārāb* "I read c. the *Dīwān al-adab*] at Fārāb with [Abū] nīm [the author]". Elsewhere Yāḳūt says (vi, notice on al-D͟jawharī), "I found at Tibrīz a of the *Dīwān al-adab*, written in al-D͟jawharī's (*bi-k͟haṭṭ al-D͟j.*) in the year 383". It is also opriate to consider the old mss. to be mentioned er on.

r his part, al-Ḳifṭī (*Inbāʾ*, i, 52) repeats an dote which brings in Abu 'l-ʿAlāʾ al-Maʿarrī in to explain how the Yemenis were able to ve that al-Fārābī had come to the Yemen, as asserted; this anecdote has pungency, but y any value.

e *Dīwān al-adab*'s editor, Aḥmad Muk͟htār ar, in his sketch of the author (i, 3-10), also ts this alleged trip to Yemen (6) and considers it reasonable to think that he went to Buk͟hārā and Bag͟hdād, especially as he would only have been able to find in the latter city the necessary material for the composition of the *Dīwān al-adab*; hence it is very probable that it was put together in Bag͟hdād. All this, however, is a question only of probabilities. For al-Fārābī's sources, see *ibid.*, i, 31.

He taught his book at Fārāb and it became known in neighbouring regions (i, 7), and it was there that the earliest study on his work appeared, in the shape of the *Tahd͟hīb Dīwān al-adab* of al-Ḥasan b. al-Muẓaffar al-Naysābūrī, a *lug͟hawī* who lived in K͟hʷārazm and died in 442/1050-1 (*ibid.*).

The *Dīwān al-adab* [*fī bayān lug͟hat al-ʿArab*], according to the complete title in the Oxford ms. (Kraemer, 212) is an original dictionary. The vocabulary is set forth according to the forms (*wazn*); under each *wazn*, in the alphabetical order of the *last* radical consonant. This innovation had a great renown in Arabic lexicography; al-D͟jawharī adopted this arrangement for his *Ṣiḥāḥ*, and it became widespread. Al-Fārābī nevertheless retained something of al-K͟halīl's way: he divided the subject-matter up into six *kutub* (1) the *Kitāb al-sālim*; (2) the *K. al-muḍāʿaf*; (3) the *K. al-mit͟hāl*; (4) the *K. d͟hawāt al-t͟halāt͟ha* [the *ad͟jwaf*]; (5) the *K. d͟hawāt al-arbaʿa*; and (6) the *K. al-hamza*. In each *kitāb* there came first the nouns and then the verbs, strictly separated.

This dictionary arranged by *wazn* is a precious aid for Arabic philological studies, for it permits one to study these *wazns*. But for practical consultation it is not easy. Aḥmad Muk͟htār ʿUmar's edition is with the *murād͟jaʿa* of Ibrāhīm Anīs, who opens the first volume with a *taṣdīr*. So far, three volumes have appeared at Cairo (1394/1974 and each following year), and a fourth will give the *Kitāb*s 5 and 6 and indices. Brockelmann lists 30 mss. (I², 133, S I, 195-6, III, 1196); the editor cites 23 of these (i, 31-2), but has based his text on five, and especially on the two oldest, from 391 and from before 390 (i, 57-60).

Ḥād͟jd͟jī K͟halīfa in his *Kas͟hf al-ẓunūn* confused the *Dīwān al-adab* with al-Zamak͟hs͟harī's *Muḳaddimat al-adab*, see the editor's *muḳaddima* (p. *ṭ*), and there is also a confusion between al-Fārābī the lexicographer and al-Fārābī the philosopher (*ibid.*).

The *Dīwān al-adab* had a deep influence on al-D͟jawharī's dictionary, which not only followed the arrangement by the last radical, but also took over the same subject matter, making Kopf observe justty [see al-d͟jawharī] that the latter's own contribution was minimal. Al-Fārābī's work also had an influence, in regard to method, on the *S͟hams al-ʿulūm* of Nas͟hwān al-Ḥimyarī, according to the editor (i, 52-3), and on two Arabic-Persian dictionaries, those of Abū ʿAbd Allāh al-Ḥusayn al-Zawzanī (d. 486/1093) and of Abū D͟jaʿfar Aḥmad al-Bayhaḳī (d. 504/1110-11). It was further the model, in regard to form, of the Turkish dictionary by Maḥmūd al-Kās͟hg͟harī, the *Dīwān lug͟hāt al-turk* (Kraemer, 212).

Lost works of al-Fārābī include a *Bayān al-iʿrāb* and a *S͟harḥ Adab al-kātib*, mentioned by Yāḳūt (vi, 63). Al-Suyūṭī, *Muzhir*³, i, 211, gives an extract from a *K. al-Alfāẓ wa 'l-ḥurūf* on the value of the tribes for their *ʿarabiyya*. He begins it thus: *ḳāla Abū Naṣr al-Fārābī*, which was the *kunya* of the philosopher, and the editor, following Ibrāhīm Anīs, sees here an error by al-Suyūṭī (as earlier by Abū Ḥayyān) and prefers to connect the work with Abū Ibrāhīm al-Fārābī the lexicographer. Both these scholars are unaware of the *K. al-Ḥurūf* of Abū Naṣr al-Fārābī, published in Beirut 1969

(Recherches, Série 1, vol. 46) and edited by Muḥsin Mahdī. *K. al-Ḥurūf* is the oldest title by which the work has been known, but since Ibn Abī Uṣaybiʿa it has been known as the *K. al-Alfāẓ wa 'l-ḥurūf* (*muḳaddima*, 34). Al-Suyūṭī's citation is indeed there (147, and not at the beginning), but not word-for-word; it seems that al-Suyūṭī made a résumé of what al-Fārābī said and then added something of his own, according to the editor's explanation (*muḳaddima*, 40). Hence there is no reason for attributing to the lexicographer al-Fārābī an allegedly lost *K. al-Alfāẓ wa 'l-ḥuruf*.

Bibliography: J. Kraemer, *Studien zur altarabischen Lexikographie*, in *Oriens*, vi (1953), 201-38; al-Ḳifṭī, *Inbāʾ al-ruwāt ʿalā anbāh al-nuḥāt*, i, Cairo 1369/1950; al-Suyūṭī, *Bughyat al-wuʿāt fī ṭabaḳāt al-nuḥāt*, i, Cairo 1384/1964. There is a description of the *Dīwān al-adab* by Ḥusayn Naṣṣār, in *al-Muʿdjam al-ʿarabī, nashʾatuhu wa-taṭawwuruhu*, i, Cairo 1375/1956, 176-81, exposition by the editor at i, 10-53. See also the authors cited in the text.

(H. Fleisch)

FARĀMŪSH-KHĀNA (P. *farāmūsh* "forgotten" and *khāna* "house"), the word used in Iran to designate a centre of masonic activities. The term seems to have originated in India, where a masonic lodge was first founded by the British in 1730. The earliest known references in Persian sources to the idea of freemasonry in general and to Indian masonic activity in particular can be found in the writings of ʿAbd al-Laṭīf Shūshtarī Djazāʾirī, a Persian émigré to India. Writing in 1801, ʿAbd al-Laṭīf believed that the reason why the Indians and the Persian-speaking people of India call the freemasons *farāmūsh* was that whatever questions were put to them—many of whom were Muslim—they answered: "It is not in my memory" (*Tuḥfat al-ʿālam*, Ḥaydarābād 1846, 292). The usage might have easily passed from India to Īrān, as, in the opinion of ʿAbd al-Ghanī Mīrzāyev, it also passed from there to the Persians of Central Asia, where Aḥmad Makhdūm Dānish of Bukhārā saw elements of absolute happiness for mankind in the idea of a *farāmūsh-khāna*, see his *Asnād-i djadīd rādjiʿ bi farāmūsh-khāna va baʿḍī az maḳāṣid-i ahl-i ān*, in *Djashn-nāma-yi Muḥammad Parwīn Gūnābādī*, ed. Muḥsin Abu 'l-Ḳāsimī, Tehran 1975, 409-20).

One of the early Persian-speaking travellers to Europe who gave an account of freemasonry was Mīrzā Abū Ṭālib Iṣfahānī, son of another Persian émigré to India. He travelled and lived in Europe from 1798 till 1803. While in London (21 January 1800 to 7 June 1802), Abū Ṭālib, who was in close association with a number of distinguished English men and women, was urged to join "the freemasons who are being called *farāmūshān* by foreigners". Being somewhat critical of freemasonry, Abū Ṭālib claims to have refused the offer, but he describes in detail a high-class and colourful party to which "no one but the freemasons" were invited (*Maṣīr-i Ṭālibī*, Tehran 1973, 151-2).

The first Iranian person known to have joined freemasonry in Europe was ʿAskar Khān Afshār Arūmī, a high-ranking dignitary of the Ḳadjār royal court. ʿAskar Khān, who was on a diplomatic mission to the court of Napoleon, was initiated into the lodge of the Philosophic Scottish Rite in Paris in 1808. The second initiate is known to have been Mīrzā Abu 'l-Ḥasan Khān Īlčī, the first Iranian ambassador to England. He was initiated in London in 1810 under the guidance of Sir Gore Ouseley who, after Īlčī's initiation became the British Ambassador to Iran. Īlčī's friendly relations with the British were so close that he received a mon[thly] payment from the East India Company from [...] till his death in 1846. Another early Iranian ma[n] have been happily initiated into freemasonry [...] Mīrzā Ṣāliḥ Shīrāzī, one of the students sen[t to] England in 1815. Mīrzā Ṣāliḥ joined the *farām[ūsh-]khāna* in London in 1817. A "Mr. Harris" who [was] known to Mīrzā Ṣāliḥ as "the chief of the *farām[ūsh-]khāna*" had honoured him with two masonic ra[nks.] A week before his departure from London, M[īrzā] Ṣāliḥ was urged by Mr. Harris to attend t[he] masonic lodge in order to receive the rank [of] master in masonic hierarchy; "otherwise", H[arris] said to Ṣāliḥ, "you will go back to Iran with defe[ct]" (Mīrzā Ṣāliḥ, *Safar-nāma*, Tehran 1968, 189, [...] 374).

Generally speaking, almost all the Iranian nota[bles] who went abroad in the 19th century, eithe[r as] exiles like Riḍā-ḳulī, Nadjaf-ḳulī, and Taymūr, t[he] Ḳādjār princes (in 1835), or as diplomatic repre[sen]tatives such as ʿAbd Allāh Garmrūdī (in 18[...]) Farrukh Khān Amīn al-Dawla (in 1857), and m[any] others, were initiated into freemasonry lo[dges.] According to some reports, the Iranians were [...] curious to find out about freemasonry; they [were] given the impression that freemasonry had [an] oriental origin and that the Persians should re[vive] this ancient tradition. Masonic activity particul[arly] appealed to Iranian modernist thinkers becaus[e of] the attachment of the impressive and gene[rally] misleading slogan "liberté, égalité, fraternité" [of] continental freemasonry. Thus we see spokesme[n of] modernism such as Sayyid Djamāl al-Dīn Asadā[bādī] "Afghānī" and Mīrzā Fatḥ ʿAlī Ākhūnd-Zāda [...] inclined to freemasonry. It seems, however, [...] Ādjūdānbāshī, who believed that the *farām[ūsh-]khāna* "lacks anything which may bring benef[it to] religion and state", was one among few except[ions] (Muḥammad Mushīrī, *Sharḥ-i maʾmūriyyat-i Ā[dju]dānbāshī*, Tehran 1968, 398).

Despite their existence in Īrān, the Iranian ma[sons] do not seem to have carried on any notice[able] masonic activity during the first half of the [19th] century. However, in 1858 Mīrzā Malkam K[hān] Nāẓim al-Dawla who had been initiated into [the] *Sincère amitié*, a masonic lodge in Paris, in 1[...] established for the first time a *farāmūsh-khān[a in]* Tehran. Malkam had reportedly secured Nāṣir [al-]Dīn Shāh's full consent for this, but his *farām[ūsh-]khāna* was not recognised by any internation[ally] known masonic lodge. Many distinguished [in]dividuals joined the *farāmūsh-khāna*. Account[s of] the motives behind the establishment of the *f[arā]mūsh-khāna* are abundant, but it seems clear [that] through this secret organisation, Malkam was [able] to introduce his audiences to modern social [and] political ideas. However, some internal fo[rces] including traditionalist conservatives, and exte[rnal] elements such as the Russians, turned Nāṣir al-[Dīn] Shāh against it, so that he declared its abolitio[n in] 1861 in these words: "From now on, if the ph[rase] *farāmūsh-khāna* comes out of anyone's mouth, [let] alone his possible involvement in its organisa[tion,] he will be most severely punished by the gov[ern]ment" (Maḥmūd Katīrāʾī, *Farāmāsūnrī dar Ī[rān]*, Tehran 1968, 74).

Malkam Khān's *farāmūsh-khāna* was accordi[ngly] closed, but the secret activities did not enti[rely] die out. Those who were acquainted with the *f[arā]mūsh-khāna* gathered together secretly and, after [the] assasination in 1896 of Nāṣir al-Dīn Shāh, [...]

ıded a secret society called the *Djāmiʿ-i ādamīy-* ("League of Humanity") on the basis of Malkam's *mūsh-khāna* and propagated Malkam's ideas. s secret society was headed by ʿAbbās-ḳulī ın Ādamiyyat and composed of distinguished ıians; it was actively involved in the Persian stitutional Revolution of 1906. Certain members his society organised a masonic lodge (*ibid.*, 95), , according to Ismāʿīl Rāʾīn, the society itself tributed to the forwarding of British policy in ı (*Farāmūsh-khāna va farāmāsūnrī dar Īrān*, i, ıran 1968, 576-7). This society was banned by ıammad ʿAlī Shāh in 1908. The *andjuman-i uwwat* which began to operate openly in 1899 was active in the Constitutional Revolution is known to have been formed of members obedient the international masonic lodges.

Although Sir Arthur Hardinge speaks of a certain ount of masonic activity in Īrān at the turn of present century (Ismāʿīl Rāʾīn, *Andjumanhā-yi ī dar inḳilāb-i mashrūṭiyyat-i Īrān*, Tehran 1967, f.), it seems that the first internationally-recised masonic lodge was established in Tehran in 7 by the Grand Orient de France and called ge du Réveil de l'Iran". Some of the men initiated this lodge were among the most active particits in the Persian Constitutional Revolution, and e of them, like the Sardār Asʿad (Ḥādjdjī ʿAlī Khān Bakhtīyārī) were regarded as pro-British dul-Hadi Hairi, *Why did the ʿulamāʾ participate the Persian Revolution of 1906-1009?*, in *WI*, (1976), 127-54). Later on, more masonic lodges e established in Shīrāz (1919), Ābādān (1920), djid-i Sulaymān (1924), and Tehran (1951, 1957).), an American lodge was founded in Tehran in 2; to this lodge were reportedly affiliated the ary Club, World Brothers' Club, and Moral armament (Rāʾīn, *Farāmāsūnrī*, iii, 11-477).

Due to the secret character of freemasonry, rature on Persian masonic experience was quite ıty and fragmentary until recently. Some tises were written for and against the Malkam āmūsh-khāna* in the 1860s, but they were not ı published (for the text of two such treatises, sult Katīrāʾī, *op. cit.*, 159-93). Apparently the Persian book which was wholly devoted to the ject was published in India in 1874. For more orate accounts of Persian freemasonry, we have had wait until the 1960s, when a number of rmative books and articles appeared, although t of them were largely inaccurate and poorlyumented. The most informative of all is Rāʾīn's ve-quoted three-volume work (1968) which tains, among other things, the names of many ıg Iranians who have been affiliated to masonic ges. The author's own name, however, was tted "despite his alleged membership of an erican affiliated lodge" (Hamid Algar, *An introion to the history of Freemasonry in Iran*, in *dle Eastern Studies*, vi (1970), 293).

Bibliography: Abu 'l-Ḳāsim b. Zayn al-ʿĀbidīn, *Fihrist-i kutub-i ... Shaykh Aḥmad ḥsāʾī wa sāyir-i mashāyikh ...*, Kirmān n.d.; iridūn Ādamīyyat, *Fikr-i āzādī va muḳaddima-yi ahḍat-i mashrūṭiyyat*, Tehran 1961; idem *Andīsha-i taraḳḳī va ḥukūmat-i ḳānūn: ʿAṣr-i Sipahsālār*, ehran 1972; Adīb al-Mamālik Farāhānī, *Dīwān*, ehran 1933; Īradj Afshār, *Asnād-i marbūṭ-i bi arrukh Khān*, in *Yaghmā*, xviii (1956); Fatḥ ʿAlī khūnd-Zāda, *Alifbā-yi djadīd va maktūbāt*, Baku 963; Hamid Algar, *Mīrzā Malkum Khān: a study the history of Iranian modernism*, Berkeley and Los Angeles 1973; A. Bausani, *Un manoscritto persiano inedito sulla ambasceria di Ḥusein Ḫān Moqaddam Āǧūdānbāšī in Europa negli anni 1254-55 A.H. (A.D. 1838-1839)*, in *Oriente Moderno*, xxxiii (1953), 485-505; W. S. Blunt, *Secret history of the English occupation of Egypt*, London 1903; R. W. Cottam, *Nationalism in Iran*, Pittsburgh 1964; Yaḥyā Dawlatābādī, *Taʾrīkh-i muʿāṣir yā ḥayāt-i Yaḥyā*, i, Tehran 1957; ʿAbd al-Razzāḳ Maftūn Dunbulī, *Maʾāthir al-sulṭāniyya: taʾrīkh-i djanghā-yi Iran va Rus*, Tehran 1972; J. B. Fraser, *Narrative of the residence of the Persian princes in London in 1835 and 1836*, repr. New York 1973; idem, *Narrative of a journey into Khorasan in the years 1821 and 1822*, London 1825; Comte de Gobineau, *Les religions et philosophies dans l'Asie Centrale*, Paris 1928; R. F. Gould, *History of Freemasonry throughout the world*, iv, New York 1936; Abdul-Hadi Hairi, *Shīʿīsm and constitutionalism in Iran: a study of the role played by the Persian residents of Iraq in Iranian politics*, Leiden 1977; Sir Arthur Hardinge, *A diplomatist in the East*, London 1928; Mahdī-ḳulī Hidāyat, *Safar-nāma-yi tasharruf bi Makka-yi muʿaẓẓama az ṭarīḳ-i Čīn, Zhāpun, Āmrīkā*, Tehran 1945; idem, *Khāṭirāt va khaṭarāt*, Tehran 1965; S. Hutin, *Les Francs-Maçons*, Paris 1961; Maḥmud ʿIrfān, *Farāmāsūnhā*, in *Yaghma*, ii (1949); Muḥammad Ḥasan Iʿtimād al-Salṭana, *Rūz-nāma-yi khāṭirāt*, Tehran 1966; Ḥasan Iʿẓām Ḳudsī, *Kitāb-i Khāṭirāt-i man*, i-ii, Tehran 1963-4; A. K. S. Lambton, *Secret societies and the Persian Revolution of 1905-6*, in *St. Antony's Papers*, no. 4, *Middle Eastern Affairs*, no. 1 (1958), 43-60; idem, *Persian political societies 1906-11*, in *St. Antony's Papers*, no. 16, *Middle Eastern Affairs*, no. 3 (1963), 41-89; A. Lantoine, *Asrār-i Farāmūsh-khāna*, tr. Djaʿfar Shāhīd, Tehran n.d.; A. G. Mackay, *Encyclopedia of freemasonry*, Philadelphia 1905; Ḥusayn Maḥbūbī Ardakānī, *Taʾrīkh-i Muʾassasāt-i tamaddunī-yi djadīd dar Īrān*, Tehran 1975; Aṣghar Mahdawī and Īradj Afshār, *Madjmuʿa-yi asnād va madārik-i čāpnāshuda dar bāra-yi Sayyid Djamāl al-Dīn mashhūr bi Afghānī*, Tehran 1963; Maḥmūd Maḥmūd, *Taʾrīkh-i rawābiṭ-i sīyāsī-yi Īrān va Ingilīs dar ḳarn-i nūzdahum-i mīlādī*, vi-vii, Tehran 1952-3; Mahdī Malik-Zāda, *Taʾrīkh-i inḳilāb-i mashrūṭiyyat-i Īrān*, i, Tehran 1949; Malkam Khān, *Ḳānūn*, 41 issues from 1889 onwards; idem, *Madjmūʿa-yi āthār*, Tehran 1948; idem, *[Risālahā]*, Tehran 1907; Murtaḍā Mudarrisī Čahārdihī, *Zindigānī va falsafa-yi idjtimāʿī va sīyāsī-yi Sayyid Djamāl al-Dīn Afghānī*, Tehran 1955; Saʿīd Nafīsī, *Nīmarāhi bihisht*, Tehran 1953; Muḥammad Nāẓim al-Islām Kirmānī, *Taʾrīkh-i bīdārī-yi Īrāniyān*, Tehran 1953; Fereshteh M. Nouraie, *Taḥḳīḳ dar afkār-i Mīrzā Malkam Khān Nāẓim al-Dawla*, Tehran 1973; Pīr-Zāda Nāʾīnī, *Safar-nāma*, Tehran 1964; J. E. Polak, *Persien, das Land und seine Bewohner*, i, Leipzig 1865; Djahāngīr Ḳāʾimmaḳāmī, *Taʾrīkh-i taḥawwulāt-i sīyāsī va niẓāmī-yi Īrān*, Tehran n.d.; idem, *Čand sanad marbūṭ-i bi taʾrīkh-i farāmūsh-khāna dar Īrān*, in *Yaghma*, xvi (1963); Ismāʿīl Rāʾīn, *Mīrzā Malkam Khān: zindigī va kūshishha-yi sīyāsī-yi ū*, Tehran 1971; ʿAlī Riḍā Ṣabā, *Iṭṭilāʿātī dar bāra-yi Maḥmūd Khān Malik al-Shuʿarāʾ*, in *Rāhnamā-yi kitāb*, xii (1969); Ḥusayn b. ʿAbd Allāh Sarābī, *Makhzan al-waḳāʾiʿ*, Tehran 1966; Khān Malik Sāsānī, *Sīyāsatgarān-i dawra-yi Ḳādjār*, i-ii, Tehran 1959-66; A. Sepsis, *Quelques mots sur l'état religieux actuel de la Perse*, in *Revue de l'Orient*, iii (1844); ʿAlī Asg͟har S͟hamīm, *Īrān dar dawra-yi salṭanat-i Ḳād͟jār*, Tehran 1963; Sir Percy Sykes, *A history of Persia*, ii, London 1963; Ibrāhīm Taymūrī, *ʿAṣr-i bīk͟habarī yā tāʾrīk͟h-i imtīyāzāt dar Iran*, Tehran 1953; Vahid, ii (1965) (a series of articles on Riḍā-ḳulī Mīrzā's mémoirs); Masʿūd Mīrzā Ẓill al-Sulṭān, *Sarguzas͟ht-i Masʿūdī*, Tehran 1907; see esp. on the "Loge du Réveil de l'Iran", P. Sabatiennes, *Pour une histoire de la première loge maçonnique en Iran*, in *Revue de l'Univ. de Bruxelles*, special issue, 1977, 414-42. See also FARMĀSŪNIYYA, below.

(ABDUL-HADI HAIRI)

FARANGĪ MAḤALL, a family of promiment Indian Ḥanafī theologians and mystics flourishing from the 12th/18th century to the present day. The family traces its ancestry through the great scholar and mystic K͟hʷād͟ja ʿAbd Allāh Anṣārī of Harāt to Ayyūb Anṣārī, the Prophet's host in Medina. It is not known when the family migrated to India but, according to the family biographers, one ʿAlāʾ al-Dīn settled in Sihālī of the Awadh [*q.v.*] province of north India during the 8th/14th century. His descendant, Mullā Ḥāfiẓ, was acknowledged as a distinguished *ʿālim* by the emperor Akbar who made a generous *madad-i maʿas͟h* grant in his favour in 967/1559 (Anṣārī, *A very early farmān of Akbar*, see *Bibl.*). In 1103/1692 the great-great-grandson of Mullā Ḥāfiẓ, Mullā Ḳuṭb al-Dīn, who was also hailed as a leading *ʿālim* of his time, was murdered in a squabble over land and his library burned. The emperor Awrangzīb recompensed his four sons by assigning to them a European indigo merchant's palace in Lucknow and by granting pensions to support their scholarly work. Around 1106/1695 the family moved from Sihālī to the palace which was known as Farangī Maḥall.

The descendants of Ḳuṭb al-Dīn made Farangī Maḥall into a centre of learning which for 250 years attracted scholars not only from all parts of India but also from places as far away as Arabia and China. Teaching was the profession of most Farangī Maḥallīs and the man who first established their reputation was Mullā Niẓām al-Dīn [*q.v.*], the third son of Ḳuṭb al-Dīn. In the early 12th/18th century he made Farangī Maḥall into the biggest centre of learning in north India. Students from outside Lucknow were boarded at the city's Tīla mosque, which had room for 700, and the expenses involved were met in part by the Mug͟hal emperors (Anṣārī, *Bānī-i Dars-i Niẓāmī*, 88-9). Yet there was at this time no *madrasa* in Farangī Maḥall, and no central organising institution; members of the family simply taught in their homes those who came to them. This remained the pattern of teaching for over 200 years. Attempts were made to found a *madrasa* in the 19th century, but only in 1323/1905 did one Farangī Maḥallī, ʿAbd al-Bārī [*q.v.* in Suppl.], coordinate the efforts of his relatives and bring them within an institutional framework. This Madrasa-yi ʿĀliya Niẓāmiyya continued its work until the 1380s/1960s.

Although Farangī Maḥall always remained their base, many of the descendants of Ḳuṭb al-Dīn travelled widely as teachers. Some like ʿAbd al-Bārī and ʿAbd al-Bāḳī (b. 1286/1869-70) taught in Medina; others taught and set up *madrasas* in India. Notable amongst these are: the great logician, Mullā Ḥasan (d. 1209/1794-5), who left a reputation in Rampūr capable of winning respect and support for the teaching efforts of the Farangī Maḥall family nearly 200 years later; the extremely succes Malik al-ʿUlamāʾ Mullā Ḥaydar (d. 1256/184c who established the Hyderabad branch of family and brought Farangī Maḥall into a continu association with India's most powerful Mus state; but most important of all, ʿAbd al-ʿAlī B al-ʿUlūm [*q.v.*] who in the sixty years before death in 1225/1810-1 taught in Lucknow, S͟hāhd͟jah pūr, Rampūr, Buhār and finally in Madras wh through his teaching and through the *madrasa* wl he set up in the Wālād͟jāhī mosque, he inspire revival of learning in South India.

In Lucknow and wherever they travelled, Farangī Maḥall family pioneered a new curricul known as the *Dars-i Niẓāmiyya*. Till recently curriculum has formed the basis of most *madr* courses in India, including that of the *Dār al-ʿu* at Deoband. The *Dars-i Niẓāmiyya* was crea by Mullā Niẓām al-Dīn. It is designed to direct student only to the most difficult or most comp hensive books on each subject, so that he is b forced to think and has a chance of finishing education by the age of sixteen or seventeen. T curriculum has been criticised for placing to m emphasis on the rational sciences. This seems justified. It stipulates no specific bias and insists no particular books. It is at bottom a way of teach and the emphasis is left to those who use it.

Members of the Farangī Maḥall family also wr much, and amongst the most prolific were M Mubīn (d. 1225/1810-11) and ʿAbd al-Bārī w wrote 111 books. Of course, many of their bo were glosses and super-glosses on the classical te they taught, but there were also works on mystici and collections of poetry; there were biograph like ʿInāyat Allāh's *Tad͟hkira-yi ʿulamāʾ-i Fara Maḥall* which is the major source of family histo and then there was a variety of work from versa scholars like Walī Allāh (1182-1270/1768-1853) w ranged from a commentary on the Ḳurʾān in f volumes to a treatise on government, *Ādāb salāṭīn*. Works which should be noted in particu are: Mullā Ḥasan's text on logic which has b popular for nearly 200 years amongst those teach the *Dars-i Niẓāmiyya*, Baḥr al-ʿUlūm's study Rūmī's *Mat͟hnawī*, and Mullā Niẓām al-Dīn's w on the life and deeds of his friend and *pīr*, Say ʿAbd al-Razzāḳ of Bānsa, *Manāḳib-i Razzāḳiy* The works of one prolific scholar, who wrote alm entirely in Arabic, stand before all. ʿAbd al-Ḥa al-Lak͟hnawī's *al-Siʿāya fī kas͟hf mā fī s͟harḥ wiḳāya*, his al-*Taʿlīḳ al-mumad͟jd͟jad* and his *Ẓa al-amānī* establish him as one of the greatest schol of recent times [see ʿABD AL-ḤAYY]. These boo together with his collection of *fatāwā*, are still mu used by Muslims both inside and outside India a have led to Lucknow being known as the "city ʿAbd al-Ḥayy".

The scholarship of the Farangī Maḥall fam placed particular emphasis on jurisprudence a logic, which was to be expected from *ʿulamāʾ*, ma of whose pupils were initially destined to beco government servants and who with this in mi were patronised by the Mug͟hal emperors. Th represented a distinctly different tradition to t founded by S͟hāh Walī Allāh [*q.v.*] of Dihlī in 12th/18th century and sustained by the Deoba school from the 13th/19th century. The Fara Maḥallīs fostered the skills designed to supp Muslim states; the followers of Walī Allāh w concerned to develop the resources to enable Musli to cope with the loss of political power. They look

: to classical Islam emphasising in their scholar- the Ḳur'ān and the *Ḥadīth*. Followers of the traditions of course crossed swords. ʿAbd al- y had a notable exchange with Nawwāb Ṣiddīḳ an Khān [*q.v.*], the leader of the Ahl al-Ḥadīth edullah, 93-101), while ʿAbd al-ʿAlī debated so essfully with ʿAbd al-ʿAzīz of Dihlī, Shāh Walī h's son, that ʿAbd al-ʿAzīz felt compelled to ress him as Baḥr al-ʿUlūm or "Sea of knowledge" ayāt Allāh, *Tadhkira*, 141). A further feature of Farangī Maḥall tradition was tolerance, and gh Lucknow is renowned for its Shīʿī-Sunnī rrels, many Shīʿīs sat at the feet of these learned nīs. Their independence of mind was another acteristic. Mullā Niẓām al-Dīn, for instance, *fatāwā* at variance with many of those in the t legal guide of his time, the *Fatāwā Ālamgīrī* ṣārī, *Bānī-i Dars-i Niẓāmī*, 163-4), while the t strength of ʿAbd al-Ḥayy as a scholar was his acity to cast aside precedent and go back to principles in promoting an understanding of m. Much work needs to be done before the larly achievement of the Farangī Maḥall family be fully appreciated, but Shiblī Nuʿmānī did exaggerate when, after visiting Farangī Maḥall 313-14/1896, he summed it up in these words: is is the Cambridge of India" (Shiblī, 99).

he Farangī Maḥallīs, however, were not just lars; they were also, to a man, mystics. Even d al-Ḥayy, whose grave is one of bare earth open the skies, stressed the benefits of visiting the ne at Bānsa and in his will urged his relatives tudy Imām al-Ghazālīs's *Iḥyā' ʿulūm al-dīn*. As heir scholarship, the mysticism of the Farangī allīs with its heavy concentration on the saint's b and the celebration of *ʿurs* contrasted strik- y with the later Walī Allāh-Deobandī tradition ch eschewed such practices. Moderate supporters he doctrine of *waḥdat al-wudjūd*, they continued tudy and to teach the works of Ibn al-ʿArabī up he 20th century. Sayyid ʿAbd al-Razzāḳ (d. 5 wwāl 1136/27 June 1724), the illiterate *pīr* of Ḳādirī order, was the saint to whom all members his learned Farangī Maḥall family looked. They rded their association with ʿAbd al-Razzāḳ as ial to their spiritual well-being, while the *sadj- das* of his shrine at Bānsa some 30 miles from know were careful to pay the scholars of Fa- gī Maḥall especial respect. There are also three ortant centres of devotion within the family. shrine of Mullā Niẓām al-Dīn in Lucknow, ch is renowned for the benefit it can bring the ntally disturbed and scholars in difficulty; the ne of Shāh Anwār al-Ḥaḳḳ, and his successors followers, which is also in Lucknow; and the ine of Mawlānā ʿAbd al-ʿAlī Baḥr al-ʿUlūm which n the Wālādjāhī Mosque at Triplicane, Madras. re are, furthermore, three important *silsilas* ch run through the family: the Ḳādirī flowing n Sayyid ʿAbd al-Razzāḳ of Bansa, the Čishtī- āmī from Shāh Ḳudrat Allāh Niẓāmī of Ṣafīpur, the Čishtī-Ṣābirī which goes back through llā Ḳuṭb al-Dīn to Shaykh Muḥibb Allāh of āhābād, the great proponent of Ibn al-ʿArabī, to h Aḥmad ʿAbd al-Ḥaḳḳ of Radawlī.

By the present century, the springs of Indian sticism were failing, but where they still flowed, Farangī Maḥall family were often prominent. ey had connections with many of the major ines in North India. They taught the sons of ny *sadjdjādas* at the Madrasa-yi ʿĀliya Niẓāmiyya, calendar of which was arranged to enable students to attend important *ʿurs*. Consequently, the Farangī Maḥallīs were given much respect. The last important *pīr* of the family was ʿAbd al-Bārī. His influence was ramified widely throughout North Indian society, where his disciples ranged from the cadets of great landed families to politicians such as Muḥammad and Shawkat ʿAlī and to relatives of the *sadjdjādas* of the most important shrine in India, that of Muʿīn al-Dīn Čishtī at Adjmīr. His influence, and that of Farangī Maḥall, was demonstrated when at the *ʿurs* of Muʿīn al-Dīn Čishtī in 1334/1916 he played the leading role in founding the Bazm-i Ṣūfiyya-yi Hind, which aimed to revive and to reform Indian mysticism.

From the time when they were established in Farangī Maḥall, the descendants of Ḳuṭb al-Dīn, through the expansion of the family, through teaching, through writing, through giving *fatāwā* and through providing spiritual leadership, made wide connections throughout Indo-Muslim society. As modern politics developed, these connections represented a significant network of influence reaching from Lucknow to Madras and from Karachi to Chittagong. When the Farangī Maḥallīs wished to organise an India-wide movement, as in the campaign to protect the holy places of Islam embodied in the Andjuman-i Khuddām-i Kaʿba [*q.v.* in Suppl.] founded in 1331/1913, or in the campaign to support the Sharīf Ḥusayn against Ibn Saʿūd in 1343-4/1925-6, their activities were based on this network. Moreover, it played a similar role when Farangī Mahallīs joined "modern" politicians in the great religio-political movements of the period. They were in the forefront of those driving forward the Indian *Khilāfat* movement up to the end of 1338/1920, while they were again prominent in the revival of the All-India Muslim League after 1356/1937. In all these campaigns Farangī Maḥall *ʿulamā'* promoted policies which, as in most other things, Deobandi *ʿulamā'* either found difficult to support or opposed outright. This Deobandi opposition only serves to illuminate the point that the Farangī Maḥallīs were the first *ʿulamā'* to enter modern Indian politics. Men such as ʿAbd al-Bārī, Salāmat Allāh and ʿInāyat Allāh, orators, writers and builders of organisations, were important channels through which modern politicians based in Dihlī and Lucknow made contact with the Muslim masses.

The contributions of the Farangī Maḥallīs to Muslim education, learning and politics over three centuries make them remarkable among Indo-Muslim families. Family tradition itself helps to explain this record of sustained achievement. Each generation has placed great emphasis on maintaining the family's standards of learning and mystical knowledge. And this process has been helped by the way in which the family has kept together; however far Farangī Maḥallīs strayed in search of a living, most returned to Lucknow to marry, to find solace in times of difficulty and to die. Moreover, the family has remained united except for one division which developed over the succession to Baḥr al-ʿUlūm in Madras. Only from the middle of the present century, as Islamic education has retreated before western education and as the partition of the subcontinent has divided the family between India and Pakistan, has the hold of family tradition weakened, and the record of achievement declined.

Bibliography: Much biographical material relating to members of the Farangī Maḥall family may be found in: Walī Allāh Farangī Maḥallī, *al-Aghṣān al-arbaʿa*, Nadwa ms., Lucknow;

Mawlawī Ḥafīẓ Allāh, *Kanz al-barakāt*, n.d.; Alṭāf al-Raḥmān Ḳidwāī, *Aḥwāl-i ʿulamāʾ-i Farangī Maḥall*, 1907; ʿAbd al-Bārī, *Āthār al-uwal*, n.d.; Mawlawī ʿInāyat Allāh, *Tadhkira-yi ʿulamāʾ-i Farangī Maḥall*, Lucknow 1928; Mawlawī ʿInāyat Allāh, *Risāla-i ḥasrat al-āfāḳ ba wafāt madjmūʿat al-akhlāḳ*, Lucknow 1929; Ṣibghat Allāh Shahīd Anṣārī, *Ṣadr al-mudarrisīn*, Lucknow 1941. The following works offer information primarily on the educational activities of the family: Muḥammad Raḍā Anṣārī, *Bānī-i Dars-i Niẓāmī*, Lucknow 1973; Shiblī Nuʿmānī, *Maḳālāt-i Shiblī*, Aʿẓamgaṙh 1955, 91-123; Alṭāf al-Raḥmān Ḳidwāī, *Ḳiyām-i niẓām-i taʿlīm*, Lucknow 1924; G. M. D. Sufi, *Al-Minhaj*, Lahore 1941, chs. ii and iii. For the Farangī Maḥallī interest in mysticism, in addition to the biographical works above, see: Nūr al-Ḥasan Adjmīrī, *Khādimāna guzārish*, Lucknow 1923; ʿAbd al-Bārī, *ʿUrs Ḥaḍrat Bānsa*, Lucknow n.d.; and for their political activities, see: F. Robinson, *Separatism among Indian Muslims: the politics of the United Provinces' Muslims 1860-1923*, Cambridge 1974 chs. vii-ix. Light is shed on other aspects of the family's history and activities by Muḥammad Raḍā Anṣārī, *A very early farmān of Akbar*, cyclostyled paper, Centre of Advanced Study, Aligarh Muslim University, and Saeedullah, *The life and works of Muhammad Siddiq Hasan Khan Nawab of Bhopal 1248-1307/1832-1899*, Lahore 1973. 93-101. (F. C. R. ROBINSON)

FARAS AL-MĀʾ (A., pl. *khayl al-māʾ*, *khuyūl al-māʾ*) and synonyms *faras*, *al-bahr faras al-nahr*, *faras nahrī*, *ḥiṣān al-baḥr*, denoting the hippopotamus, are nothing other than Arabic translations of its Greek name ὁ ἵππος ὁ ποτάμιος in the works of Herodotus, then ἱπποπόταμος in the works of Galen and Aristotle; Herodotus also calls it ὁ ἵππος τοῦ Νείλου, whence *faras al-Nīl* "horse of the Nile" and Pliny simply translated the Greek as *equus fluviatilis*. In Nubia it bears the name *birnīḳ* and in the Touareg country, *agamba* (pl. *igambaten*) and *bango* (pl. *bangōten*). The epithets *khinzīr al-māʾ* (Kazimirski) and *djāmūs al-baḥr* (Amīn al-Maʿlūf) attributed to the hippopotamus seem to be errors of definition.

Belonging to the order of non-ruminant artiodactylae, this bulky African pachyderm (*Hippopotamus amphibius*) forms, with its dwarf relative from Liberia, the recently-discovered pygmy hippopotamus (*Choeropsis liberiensis*), the family of hippopotamids, which is closely related to the suids and whose habitat at the present stretches over central and south-eastern Africa, from Senegal to Ethiopia and the Transvaal. In the mid-Quaternary period it was present in large numbers in Europe and North Africa, as is proved by fossile remains. It was widespread throughout the Sahara in the Neolithic period and at the dawn of recorded history; Hannon, in the course of his famous journey, came across the animal in a river which was probably the Saguiet-el-Hamra flowing to the north of the Rio de Oro. The Nile was a home for these creatures the whole length of its course, including the Delta, until very recent times, since the Neapolitan doctor Zerenghi captured a pair of them in a ditchtrap, in 1609, near Damietta. At the beginning of the 19th century, according to Rüppel, the hippopotamus was still common in Nubia, but today, in order to find it, one must travel down the Nile to a point well beyond Khartoum; the shrinking of its habitat and the rapid drop in its numbers are due to the combined action of the progressive drying-up of the Sahara and associated regions and uncontrolled destruc on the part of man, black as well as white.

The first mention of the hippopotamus appea be Biblical, since exegetes identify it with *Behemoth*, the brute beast (arabised as *bahī* associated with the root *B-H-M*) described in Book of Job (xl, 10-19), as being one of the works of God and as embodying blind force al side the "Leviathan" (possibly the crocod whatever the case may be, it is very probable the waters of the Jordan were acquainted with creature in those remote times. Common throug ancient Egypt, the hippopotamus, the wal scourge of crops, was the incarnation, in mythology, of the maleficent goddess Thou partner in evil to the crocodile god Sobek; a statu in varnished blue ceramic (Paris, Museum of Louvre) dating from the 11th Dynasty, or al two thousand years before the Christian definitely constitutes one of the most anc representations of the pachyderm. After the Bi it is in the works of Herodotus (*Histories*, ii, 71) we find the oldest description of the "horse of Nile" based on information, now lost, given Hecate of Miletus (6th century B.C.); Aristotle to reproduce this account (*Natural history*), tr Tricot, Paris 1957, i, 127) and after him, a num of authors including Plutarch, Diodorus of Si Strabo, Pausanias and Pliny. For all of them, image of the hippopotamus is that of a clo footed beast like the cow, with a mane and wit horse's whinny, but with a very large and s nose, and with the tail and tusks of the wild b It kills and eats the crocodile and devastates c on the banks of the river; it is the size "of a donk and its hide, impenetrable so long as it is kept dr used to make javelins, shields and helmets. In s of the exhibition of hippopotami at Rome on occasion of triumphs, and especially at that Augustus after his victory over Cleopatra, in s of the presence of a specimen in the menagerie Heliogabalus, and in spite, finally, of a pre description of the animal given by Achilles Ta and repeated, in the year 325 of the present by Eusthatus of Cappadocia, the western w was to remain until the Renaissance in aln complete ignorance of the hippopotamus, to extent that in his *Treasury*, the Florentine Brun Latini (13th century) could still write: "l'ypopot est un peissons qui est apelez cheval fluviel po que il naist el flun de Nile." The creature c began to be known with the accounts, in 1544 P. Gilles and P. Belon who were able to observe leisure, in Constantinople, one of these animals l in captivity. In the East, Arab authors, cosmo phers and encyclopaedists, while retaining assertions of Aristotle, were able nevertheless collect, from Nubia and Abyssinia, more pre information. Thus al-Djāḥiẓ, without him knowing the animal, reproduces on the sub (*Ḥayawān*, vii, 129-45, 250) some interesting det supplied by travelling merchants. He decl notably that the traces left by the hippopotamus the course of its nocturnal sorties, on the mu banks of the Nile, shows to the river farmers farthest limit to which the river will rise when flood, and that, if captured young, the hippopota is easily domesticated and used to be kept in ho in close proximity to women and children; this said to be an effective means of protecting them f the jaws of the ever-lurking crocodile. When leaves the river to graze, adds al-Djāḥiẓ, the hip mus goes a considerable distance and only ts browsing while returning to the water, as if as calculated in advance the quantity of food will be necessary for it during the night. Its h had the power, among the Nubians, to soothe r frequent stomach ailments, caused by their le diet of raw fish and their habit of drinking dy water; the invalid would wear one of these h over his stomach. Besides, the internal organs he hippopotamus were regarded by them as a l remedy against the periodical seizures of epi- ics at the time of new moons (*ṣarʿ al-ahilla*). these observations, al-Masʿūdī adds (*Murūdj*, 5) that while feeding, the hippopotamus deposits excrement here and there and that the intact s that it contains ensure a regrowth of the tation. However, this manner of restitution did e to compensate for the havoc wreaked in the ted fields, whose owners were often obliged to press the creatures that were to blame for the age; in order to do this, they did not hesitate sacrifice generous portions of lupins (*turmus*, *is*) offered to the greedy pachyderms, which ld gorge themselves with them before returning he water and soon after burst with meteorism. hose who, after these two authors, made mention he hippopotamus were content to repeat what previously been said. It is, however, curious to that al-Idrīsī, describing the Nile and Nubia *zhat*, climate I, section 4), devotes only two lines he animal, stating that it has webbed feet. Still e astonishing is the lack of attention paid to it al-Maḳrīzī (*Khiṭaṭ*, ch. xx) in the context of nders of the Nile"; repeating al-Masʿūdī, he s only that the animal is present in large numbers he mining district of the Shankīr, on the double d of the river. Al-Damīrī completes all the pre- ng with his customary rubrics about the per- sibility of eating it, the particular qualities of organs and the animal's role in oneiromancy. s we know (*Ḥayāt al-ḥayawān al-kubrā*, Cairo 5/1937, ii, 221-2) that according to the scheme Ḳurʾānic law, the flesh of the hippopotamus may consumed because it is a wild herbivore "resem- g" a horse. We also learn that the skin of the hyderm, buried in the middle of a village, protects latter from every scourge; that after burning, ashes of this skin mixed in a paste with flour of vetch (*kirsanna*) makes a plaster which, in three s, cures abcesses; and that the gall, after prolonged king, is dried to make a powder for treating eyes cted with the dark cataract (*al-māʾ al-aswad*). at al-Damīrī omits to mention is the high value orded to the ivory of the teeth and tusks of the popotamus. In fact, this ivory was exported from t Africa along with that of the elephant [see J and FĪL] and the "horn" of the rhinoceros [see KADDAN], but at a higher price because of the eriority of its grain, of which the pure white s not grow yellow in the course of time; con- d with the ivory of walrus-tusks under the ne *rohart* (Nordic in origin), the West imported s a high-quality material for craftsmen of inlaid ds, of high-class cutlery, and, most of all, of ficial dentures; the production of synthetic terials with resin base destroyed this market to e extent.

n short, all these mediaeval texts relating to the popotamus are nothing more than echoes of ounts where imagination frequently prevails over lity; also, the only true Arab testimony of real umentary value concerning the animal remains that of the indefatigable Moroccan globe-trotter Ibn Baṭṭūṭa, who saw it with his own eyes in its Nigerian habitat. In fact, having left Sidjilmāsa and crossed Mauretania and the vast desert of the Touaregs, he came, in the course of the year 754/1353, to the Muslim kingdom of Mali [*q.v.*] on the Niger which, like all men at that time, he believed to be a branch of the Nile. There he was in the very heart of hippopotamus country, since *mali* is its name in Bambara, in Malinka and in Mandingo. His first encounter with the animals took place in the vicinity of a broad bay (*khalīdj*) in the river (possibly Lake Debo) which he had to cross by boat with his caravan (*Riḥla*, Cairo 1346/1928, ii, 201). "... There were there," he tells "sixteen enormous quadrupeds which astonished me and which I took to be elephants in view of their large numbers in this same place. Then I saw them plunge into the water of the river and I consulted Abū Bakr b. Yaʿḳūb (the caravan guide) about these huge creatures. They are, he explained to me, "horses of the river" (*khayl al-baḥr*) that have left the water to graze on dry land. They are larger than horses, but they have the mane, the tail and the head, although their foot is that of the elephant. I had occasion to see these hippopotami again when we travelled down the Nile (= the Niger) in canoes from Timbuktu (*Tunbuktū*) to Gao (*Kūkū*, formerly called Gogo); they were swimming in the middle of the river, lifting their heads above the surface and breathing noisily. For fear of these animals the canoists moved closer to the bank lest they capsize us. The natives have a cunning method for fighting these beasts; they use javelins of which the (barbed) iron tip is pierced with a hole through which they thread strong cords. They attack the animal with these throwing-weapons and, if the spear strikes the foot or the withers, the iron becomes deeply embedded; all the hunters then have to do is drag the victim to the bank with the ropes; they then dispatch him and feed on his flesh. Hence the abundance of bones strewn the whole length of the banks of the river." We may add that, since then, the massacre has not ceased and has intensified with the coming of the Whites to Africa; the hippopotamus provided, to a considerable extent, the subsistence of the armies fighting in the Cameroons at the time of the First World War, and it has since paid a heavy tribute to suppliers of shipyards and to local militia chiefs, without counting "safari" enthusiasts in search of spectacular trophies. Some partial measures towards the protection of the animal have fortunately intervened in some modern African states, for there can be no doubt, as an English explorer has written, "... that once civilization has driven the hippopotami away from an African river, that river loses one of its greatest charms and one of its major ornaments."

Bibliography: in addition to references given in the article, see L. Blancou, *Géographie cynégétique du monde*, Paris 1959, 96; P. Bourgoin, *Animaux de chasse d'Afrique*, Paris 1955, 73-5; R. Fiasson, *L'homme contre l'animal*, Paris 1957, 77; L. Guyot and P. Gibassier, *Les noms des animaux terrestres*, Paris 1967, 74-6; Th. Haltenorth and W. Trense, *Das Grosswild der Erde*, Bonn-Munich-Vienna 1956; B. Heuvelmans, *Sur la piste des bêtes ignorées*, Paris 1955, ii, 115-16; L. Lavauden, *Les grands animaux de chasse de l'Afrique Française* (collection *Faune des colonies françaises*, v/7), Paris 1934, 416-20; H. Lhote, *La chasse chez les Touaregs*, Paris 1951, 68-9; I. T. Sanderson, *Living mammals of the world*,

Fr. tr. *Les Mammifères vivants du monde*, Paris 1957. (F. Viré)

FARMĀSŪNIYYA (A.), freemasonry (also in Arabic: *Firmāsūniyya*, *Māsūniyya* and *Bināya Ḥurra*; in Turkish, *Franmasonluk*, *Farmasonluk*, *Masonluk*).

I. In the Ottoman empire and its successor states.

Freemansonry first penetrated the Empire via lodges (Arabic *maḥfil*; Turkish *mahfel*, *loca*) established by Europeans. As many of the lodges were established without the authority of organised freemasonry, they were frequently short-lived. Several lodges were reported in Aleppo, Izmir and Corfu in 1738, in Alexandretta in the early 1740s, in the Armenian parts of Eastern Turkey in 1762 and in Istanbul in 1768 or 1769. Individual freemasons—although not lodges—were reported in Tunisia in 1784 (Jews of Livornese origin) and a year later in Algeria (local Muslims). In Egypt, lodges were allegedly set up by French officers during the Napoleonic Occupation. Despite the small number and limited activities of freemasons in the 18th century, the Ottoman authorities restricted them, with only moderate success, as early as 1748. More information is available on masonic activity since the 1820s, especially among foreigners and local Christians and Jews in Istanbul, Izmir, Syria, Thrace, Macedonia, Epirus and other parts of the Empire. From the mid-19th century onwards, more and more international freemasonic organisations founded lodges in the main population centres of the Empire, through their European residents. The spread of freemasonry was indeed a facet of European influence; it progressed more rapidly in areas under European political control, e.g. in Algeria after 1830 (1851: 842 freemasons in 14 lodges), Tunisia after 1881 (1910: more than 300 freemasons) and Egypt after 1882. European economic penetration had an impact as well; the first lodge in Jaffa was set up by French railway engineers in 1891. Robert Morris, an American freemason who toured Asia Minor in 1868 and founded the first lodge in Jerusalem, in that year calculated that 17 English, 15 French and 8 Italian lodges were active throughout the Empire. Actually there were more; by the end of the century, there was hardly a city or town of importance without at least one lodge. Christians, Muslims and Jews mingled freely in these lodges (although certain lodges were preponderantly of one faith, such as Sion's Lodge, founded among the Izmir Jews in 1870), which were among the few meeting-places for members of different faiths, as well as for foreigners and natives. This created a language problem, and the ritual was sometimes performed in more than one language. Membership figures were generally modest—between approximately one dozen and one hundred per lodge—but the importance of freemasonry was enhanced by such important persons as the Algerian *amīr* ʿAbd al-Ḳādir (1864), Meḥmed Rashid, *wālī* of Syria (1868), Djamāl al-Dīn al-Afghānī [*q.v.*], Muḥammad ʿAbduh [*q.v.*] and several members of the Khedivial family (from the 1860s onwards). Moreover, many local freemasons were people-of-means—generally of the upper middle classes—because of the relatively high membership dues. This remains true, to a great extent, to this very day.

It was perhaps inevitable that the lodges would serve, at times, as nuclei for anti-establishment and even revolutionary political activity. owing to their clandestine nature. Prince Ḥalīm, Grand Master of the Grand Orient of Egypt in 18… attempted to use the freemasons in his stru… against the Khedive Ismāʿīl. In 1876, the dep… Sultan Murād V unsuccessfully sought to enlist… assistance of the freemasons in Istanbul to en… his safety from ʿAbd al-Ḥamīd II's designs… probably even for launching a counter-coup. I… in the 20th century, masonic lodges, mostly tho… Salonica, served as a cover for the meeting… leaders of the Young Turks, of whom at least… Ṭalʿat, was an active freemason. There is, how… no conclusive evidence that freemasonry as… played a role in the preparation and implementa… of the Young Turk Revolution. True, freemas… could—and did—operate more freely in the … Ḥamīdian era (it had been proscribed during ʿ… al-Ḥamīd II's reign), although only for a s… period, as Enwer forbade its activities soon … World War I broke out. Persistent rumours a… freemansonry have nonetheless discredited i… Republican Turkey and some of the Arab state… Syria and Egypt freemasonry is prohibited… several others, it is severely limited). This is ha… due to the number of freemasons: There were a… 500 freemasons in Turkey in 1923 and *ca.* 2… 2400 between 1930 and 1935—when all lodges … closed down. They reopened in 1948 as an Associa… of the Masons of Turkey (Türkiye Mason Dern… which has been publishing since January 19… periodical, *Türk Mason Dergisi*, renamed *M…* *Dergisi* in July 1973. Turkish membership rea… 2,367 in 1966; figures for other Middle Eas… states are not available, but seem to be equ… modest (e.g. in 1931, there were *ca.* 1500 in Pales… and *ca.* 1000 in Tunisia) and declining since… disappearance of the Mandates and Protector… Rather, freemasonry's universalist and internati… character, partly beyond the state's immed… control, awakened suspicion in nationalist cir… while the non-Muslim origins of its founders and… marked secularist spirit in many of the lo… aroused animosity among devout Muslims. F… masonry's social and educational philanthropy… been resented, as well, which may explain why m… if not most published works on freemasonry, in … Arabic and Turkish, tend to attack rather … defend it. Several of those printed in the Arab st… link freemasonry and Zionism (without tang… proof), denigrating both. Such works have b… published in Turkey, too, where the most pro… exponent of anti-freemasonry was Cevat R… Atilhan. Recently, Turkish organs sympathetic to… Nationalist Action and National Salvation Pa… have systematically been presenting freemasonr… evil and hostile to both Turkey and Islam. Th… attitudes notwithstanding, masonic activity … tinues in Turkey and nearly all the Arab states, … varying degrees of success.

Bibliography: *Précis des travaux de la R.·. amis de Napoléon le Grand à l'O.·. d'Alexan… relatifs à une fête de la paix, célébrée le 19 j.·. 9. m. de l'an de la V.·. L.·. 5809*, Alexandria 1… De Bélisaire, *Orient d'Alger. Procès verbal de … auguration du nouveau temple, 8e jour du 9e … de l'an de la V.·. L.·. 5837*, Marseilles 1838; Morris, *Freemasonry in the Holy Land, or the h… marks of Hiram's builders*, New York 1872; Raff… Scarozza, *Alla massoneria universale generalm… ed a tutte le potenze massoniche particolarmente s… legale regolare esistenza del Grande Oriente Egiz… contra la guerra fatta degli oppositori questo po… lavoro a tutti inditiuta-imente un massone ded…*

exandria 1874; Ed. St. J. Fairman, *Prince Halim* *cha, of Egypt—a freemason*, London 1884; R. F. uld, *The history of freemasonry: its antiquities,* *nbols, constitutions, customs, etc.*, iii, London 87, esp. 320 ff.; D. Cazès, *Essai sur l'histoire* *Israélites de Tunisie*, Paris 1888, 140-1; F. G. Nichichievich, ed., *Annuaire maçonnique uni-* *sel pour 1889-1890*, Alexandria 1889; Djurdjī ydān, *Ta'rīkh al-māsūniyya al-ʿāmm mundhu* *sh'atihā ilā hādhā 'l-ʿām*, Cairo 1889; Ilyās unsī, *Dustūr al-maḥāfil al-miṣriyya al-waṭaniyya* *tābiʿa li-ʿashīrat al-bannā'īn al-abrār dhawī* *ʿahd al-ḳadīm wa 'l-rāya al-ʿāmma al-muṣaḥḥaḥa*, iro 1893; Shāhīn Makāriyūs, *Kitāb al-ādāb al-* *isūniyya*, Cairo 1895; idem, *Kitāb al-asrār al-* *afiyya fi 'l-djamʿiyya al-māsūniyya*, Cairo 1900; yā 'l-Ḥādjdj, *al-Khulāṣa al-māsūniyya*, Cairo oo; anon., *al-Ḥaḳīḳa al-djaliyya fi 'l-shīʿa al-* *isūniyya*, Cairo 1907; N. Nicolaides, *L'Empire* *oman, une année de constitution*, Brussels 1909, o-3; L. Shaykho, *al-Sirr al-maṣūn fī shīʿat al-* *masūn*, Beirut 1909-11; Grand Orient Ottoman, *struction pour le premier grade symbolique*, tanbul 1910; idem, *Règlement général du Grand* *ient Ottoman pour les ateliers du 1er au 3me degré*, tanbul n.d. [1910]. Joseph Sakakini, *Incident* *ec la grande loge d'Égypte. Rapport du* (sic) *seph Sakakini, de l'irrégularité de la grande loge* *Égypte présidée par Idris Ragheb Memphitique*, tanbul 1910; R. F. Gould *et alii*, eds., *A library* *freemasonry*, iv, London 1911, 124-6, 145-7; on., *Le livre noir: l'anarchie dans la grande loge* *tionale d'Égypte*, Caire n.d. [1912-13]; Djūrdj shkar and Wadīʿ Ḥannā, *al-Ḳānūn al-ʿumūmī li* *maḥfal al-akbar al-Iskūtlāndī 'l-ʿāmil bi-ṭarīḳat* *bannā'īn al-aḥrār al-ḳadīma al-maḳbūla*, Beirut 26; Kemalettin Apak, *Türkiye masonluk tarihi*, mir 1932; Eugen Lennhoff and Oskar Posner, *ternationales Freimaurerlexikon*, Munich 1932; on., *Türkiye büyük meşrıkının 1935 bütçe* *zamnamesi projesi*, Istanbul 1934; R. Chajim sef David Asulai, *Maʿgal ṭōb ha-šalem: Itinera-* *um (1753-1794)*, ed. Aron Freiman, Jerusalem 34, 61; Yūsuf al-Ḥādjdj, *Fī sabīl al-ḥaḳḳ: haykal* *laymān aw al-waṭan al-ḳawmī li 'l-Yahūd*, eirut 1934; Süleyman Kulçe, *Türkiye'de mason-* *k*, Izmir 1948; ʿAbd al-Raḥmān Sāmī ʿIṣmat, *Ṣahyūniyya wa 'l-māsūniyya*[2], Alexandria 1950; . Raif Ogan, *Türkiyedeki masonluk iç yüzü ve* *ları*, Istanbul 1951; J. M. Landau, *Parliaments* *d parties in Egypt*, Tel-Aviv 1953, 80-3 (= rabic tr., Cairo 1975, 84-6); Z. H. Velibeşe, *urkiyede franmasonluk*, Ankara 1956; E. E. amsaur, *The Young Turks: prelude to the revolution* *1908*, Princeton 1957, 103-10; Kemalettin Apak, *na çizgiteriyle Türkiyedeki masonluk tarihi*, tanbul 1958; Sayf al-Dīn al-Bustānī, *Awḳifū* *dhā 'l-saraṭān: ḥaḳīḳat al-māsūniyya wa-ahdā-* *hā*, n.p. [Damascus], n.d. [1959]; Cevat Rifat tilhan, *Farmasonluk insanlığın kanseri*, Istanbul 60; B. Lewis, *The emergence of modern Turkey*, ondon 1961, 172-4, 207-8; J. M. Landau, *Prole-* *mena to a study of secret societies in modern* *gypt*, in *Middle Eastern Studies*, London, 1 (Jan. 65), esp. 4 ff.; Aḥmad Ghalwash, *al-Djamʿiyya* *-māsūniyya: ḥaḳā'iḳuhā wa-khafāyāhā*, Cairo 66; X. Yacono, *Un siècle de franc-maçonnerie* *gérienne (1785-1884)*, Paris 1969; Mehmet Vedat nat, *Yakın tarihimizde masonluk üzerine bir* *neme*, Istanbul 1971; Cevat Rifat Atilhan, *Türk,* *le düşmanın*, Istanbul 1971; Necdet Sevinç, *dular, masonlar, Komünistler*, Istanbul 1971; E. Kedourie, *Young Turks, freemasons and Jews*, in *Middle East Studies*, vii (1971), 89-104; Sultan Abdülhamit, *Siyasî hatırlarım*, Istanbul 1974, 97-8; Daniel Ligou, ed., *Dictionnaire universel de la franc-maçonnerie*, i-ii, n.p. [Paris] 1974; J. M. Landau, *Radical politics in modern Turkey*, Leiden 1974, 182-96, 277 (= Turkish tr., Ankara 1978, 261 ff.); Necdet Sevinç, *Ordular, masonlar, Komünistler*[3], Istanbul 1975; anon., *Masonik faaliyetler üzerindeki perdesi kalkınmalıdır*, n.p. 1975; Hasan Cem, *Dünyada ve Türkiyede masonluk*, Istanbul 1976; Hikmet Tanyu, *Tarih boyunca Yahudiler ve Türkler*, i-ii, Istanbul 1976-7; Feroz Ahmad, *The Turkish experiment in democracy 1950-1975*, London 1977, 235, 367, 376-8, 384; M. Ertuğrul Düzdağ, *Türkiye'de masonluk meselesi*, Istanbul 1977; İlhami Soysal, *Türkiye ve dünyada masonluk ve masonlar*, Istanbul 1978, 165 ff.; David Farhi, *Yĕhudey Sālōnīḳī bĕ-mahpekhat ha-Tūrkīm ha-tsĕʿīrīm* ("The Jews of Salonica in the Young Turk revolution"), in *Sĕfūnōt*, Jerusalem, xv (1978), 135-52; anon., *Uṣūl al-bināya al-ḥurra*, Acre n.d.; Cevat Rifat Atilhan, *Masonluk nedir?* n.p., n.d.

(J. M. Landau)

2. In Persia. For this, see farāmūsh-khāna, above.

FAROUK [see fārūḳ].

FARRUKHĀN, the name of two *iṣpahbadhs* of Ṭabaristān: Farrukhān Djīlānshāh, ancestor of the Dābūyid dynasty of Ṭabaristān and of the Bādhuspānid dynasty of Ruyan, and Farrukhān the Great, his great-grandson and the second Dābūyid *iṣpahbadh* of Ṭabaristān.

1. Farrukhān Djīlānshāh, *iṣpahbadh* of Ṭabaristān at the time of the Arab conquest, in about 22/643. He claimed to be the great-grandson of Djāmasp, brother of the Sāsānid king Kawādh I (488-531), at least according to Ibn Isfandiyār, 97, who asserts that he ruled over the south-Caspian provinces (Ṭabaristān, Djīlān, Daylam) and the land of the Khazars and the Slavs; but his titles contradict these assertions, in fact, according to Balʿamī, iii, 493; Ibn Khurradādhbih, 119, tr. 91; al-Ṭabarī, i, 2659, he adopted the pompous titles: Djīl Djīlān, Iṣpahbadh Iṣpahbadhān, Iṣpahbadh Khurāsān, Padhishkhwārdjarshāh, which are to be translated as: King of the people of Djīlān, chief of the *iṣpahbadhs* (of Ṭabaristān), (holding his office from the) *iṣpahbadh* of Khurāsān, king of the mountain regions (of Ṭabaristān). If then control of the land of the Khazars and Slavs is to be excluded, there is no reason to suppose that Farrukhān exercised effective control of Daylam and Djīlān, in spite of his title of Djīlānshāh, which simply indicates that he was a native of Djīlān, as is confirmed by Balʿamī, iii, 493. In fact, Daylam and Djīlān are not mentioned among Farrukhān's possessions in the treaty of capitulations which he concluded with the general Suwayd b. Muḳarrin, in 22/643 (al-Ṭabarī, i, 2659-60). All that is attested by the sources is that Farrukhān, profiting from the decline of the central Sāsānid power, enjoyed autonomy over Ṭabaristān, and occupied a senior position with regard to the other local chieftains. His allegiance to the Sāsānids is shown by the fact that he sent military contingents to the battle of Nihāwand (21/642) which decided the fate of the Iranian plateau (al-Balādhurī, 280; al-Dīnawarī, 141).

After their victory, the Arab armies marched against the northern provinces of Persia and took control of al-Rayy (in spite of the intervention of troops sent from Ṭabaristān, Balʿamī, iii, 489), of

Dunbāwand, Ḳūmis and Djurdjān, thus encircling Ṭabaristān. Also, "when the *iṣpahbadhs* of Ṭabaristān became aware of these facts, they went to consult their suzerain, upon whom they all depended, and who lived at Āmul, in the centre of the province. This was a powerful man, a Gīlānī, his name was Farrukhān and he was called *iṣpahbadh* of the *iṣpahbadhs* ..." (Balʿamī, iii, 493). Farrukhān advised submission with the payment of a meagre 500,000 *dirhams* in tribute for Ṭabaristān (Balʿamī, iii, 493-4; al-Ṭabarī, i, 2659-60), which was far less than the sum paid to the Sāsānids, according to Ibn Isfandiyār, 118. This submission was to prove purely formal, hence this led in 30/651 to an expedition by Saʿīd b. al-ʿĀṣ, which initially met with fierce resistance (al-Ṭabarī, i, 2836, ii, 1322; Balʿamī iv, 334-5; al-Balādhurī, 334-5; Ibn Isfandiyār, 98). The local historians indicate neither the length of the reign of Farrukhān, nor the date of his death, but state that his son Djīl Djāwbara seized control of Daylam and Djīlān (which were reckoned to form part of the possessions of Farrukhān Djīlānshāh), raised an army there and threatened to invade Ṭabaristān (another of his father's territories). The King of Kings Yazdgird III (632-51) was obliged to accept the *fait accompli* and to invest Djīl Djāwbara with the title Djīl Djīlān, Padhish-khwārdjarshāh (Ibn Isfandiyār, 97; Ẓahīr al-Dīn, 42).

Now these events are placed in the 35th year of the new Persian era, which corresponds to 667 A.D., if the era in question is that of Yazdgird III, who fled from his capital, Ctesiphon-Seleucia, in 637 A.D., and was assassinated in 31/651. One might suppose that Farrukhān Djīlānshāh had been deposed, which would explain the reconquest by his son, but the strangest thing is that Ibn Isfandiyār, 97, claims that Djīl Djāwbara established his capital at Fūman, in Djīlān, reigned 15 years and divided his territories among his elder son Dābūya (eponymous ancestor of the Dābūyids) and his younger son Bādhuspān (eponymous ancestor of the Bādhuspānids [*q.v.*]; the Dābūyids continued to dominate the other local princes of Ṭabaristān (the Zarmihrids of Miyāndurūd near Sāriya; the Ḳārinids of the Ḳarīn mountains; Bāwandids of the Sharwīn mountains; the Marzbāns of Ṭamīsha; etc.) and had their capital at Āmul, while the Bādhuspānids controlled Rūyān. On the other hand, the death of Djīl Djāwbara is placed by the local historians in the year 50 of the new era of the Persians, which corresponds to 682 A.D., if the era in question is that of Yazdgird III. Now Ṭabaristān inaugurated its own era on the 1st Farvardīn I/27th Shawwāl 31/11th June 652, and the year 50 of the era of Ṭabaristān corresponds to 82-3/701-2. This shows that the exploits attributed to Djīl Djāwbara are probably a legendary account, inspired by the etymology of his name Djāwbara, which means "he who rides a bull"; according to the local sources, Djīl Djāwbara disguised himself, for a reconnaissance of Ṭabaristān, by pushing in front of himself two cows from Djīlan (Ẓahīr al-Dīn, 39; Rehatsek, in *JBBRAS* (1876), 438). As for the new era of the Persians, it is the era of Ṭabaristān (since the length of the reigns of the Dābūybid *iṣpahbadhs*, as given by the local historians, corresponds within a few years to the dates shown by the Dābūyid coinage discovered up to the present) rather than that of Yazdgird III (which differs by 20 years from the era of Ṭabaristān). So we have a reign of Farrukhān Djīlānshāh lasting until roughly 61/680; his successors were his son Djīl Djāwbara who reigned 15 years (*ca.* 62-77, 681-96), then Dābūya who "reigned over Ṭabaristān in a severe an flexible manner" (Ibn Isfandiyār, 98) for 16 y that is *ca.* 77-92/696-710, and finally Farrukhā Great, surnamed *Dhu 'l-Manāḳib* ("the Virtuc who reigned for 17 years according to the sources.

2. Farrukhān the Great, great-grandso Farrukhān Djīlānshāh, and second *iṣpahbadh* o Dābūyid dynasty of Ṭabaristān. His reign b with the issue of coinage in the name of the Dāb *iṣpahbadhs*, dating from the year 60 of the e Ṭabaristān 93/711. The coinage consists of s half-drachmas, of the same type as the Sā dirhams of Khusraw II (590-628), but their origin lies in the fact that they are dated by the e Ṭabaristān, which begins on the 1st Farvardī of the era of Yazdgird III, corresponding to the June 652 (according to Mordtmann, in *ZDMG* (1854), 173-4, and not 651 as is supposed by quart, *Ērānšahr*, 133). The year of issue is indic on the left on the reverse side of the coins, in Pal of which the writing is ambiguous, which exp how its interpretation may be difficult and s times uncertain. It is thus that Unvala insists there are two princes: Farroxᵛ (the Farrukhān Great of the local sources) who reigned 10-11 y from 60 to 70 T., and another prince, whom he Farroxᵛān, who would be the son of Farroxᵛ, who would have reigned 8-9 years, from 72 to 7 (reproduction of the coinage of Farrukhān Great, of the years 60, 63 65-70 75, 77 T. in Un Plate). To justify this distinction, he stresses difference in the orthography of the names: Far and Farroxᵛān, which is also found in Ibn Isfand 114. This historian mentions in the reign of last Dābūyid, Khurshīd, a Fakhrān and a Farruk both sons of Djusnas. Furthermore, Unvala dec that the coins of Farroxᵛ have no marginal inscrip on the right, whereas those of Farroxᵛān bear words *apd* and *nwak* (= "miraculous, marvel good"), after the year 72 T. (Unvala: 7, § 3; 8, 5, 7, 9, 10; 30, § 10; n. 6; 31, § 11, 15). These a ments did not convince J. Walker (accordin Unvala, 7-8, § 4), who thinks that the referen to the same individual, Farrukhān the Great whom the local historians speak (reproduction of coinage from 60-2, 65-70, 75, 77, in Walker, i, xxiii), but does not give reasons.

In our opinion, there are important objection Unvala's hypothesis: seeing that Ibn Isfandiyār tinguishes so carefully the sons of Djusnas, t is no reason why he should confuse Farroxᵛ Farroxᵛān. On the other hand, Unvala (8, § 4; § 15) makes Farroxᵛān the son of Farroxᵛ "as patronymic indicates", which is not conclusive, Fakhrān and Farrukhān are two brothers, and father and son. Finally, the supplementary marg inscriptions do not imply *ipso facto* the existenc two persons: in fact the coins of the governc Ṭabaristān Hāniʾ b. Hāniʾ have marginal ins tions on the right, which vary (reproductio Walker, i, Pl. xxv, 12-15, xxxviii, 12-15); som them mention only the name of the governor, o bear the initial ع of عدل (= "justice") above name (according to Unvala: 12, § 6). There is question here in Unvala's mind of two dis governors.

On the other hand, the anonymous coinage 134 T., 135 T., and 137 T. are of three varie the first are marked *nwak(u)*, *nwak*, ععع (= "v good"); the second *Djarīr*, *nwak(u)*, ع; the third *nwak(u)*, *apd* and *nwak*, *apd* and ع (according ɪvala: 12, § 9; 10, § 25; reproduction in Walker, 'l. xxvi, 15-17, xxvii, 1-9, 13, xxxviii, ii, 14). Pahlavi words *apd* and *nwak* are thus homologues e initial ع of عدل, and it is clear therefore that rrox^{v} and a Farrox^{v}ān cannot be distinguished e manner employed by Unvala.

cording to Ibn Isfandiyār, 27, Farru<u>kh</u>ān the t took control of the territories lying between ristān and Nī<u>sh</u>āpūr, and put an end to the sions by the Turks of Dihistān with whom he a truce. This respite was put to advantage in orcing his realm, so well that when hostilities resumed, the Turks were crushed at Tūrān-čar ırī<u>sh</u>a. This narrative in fact recalls an episode e reign of <u>Kh</u>usraw I (Christensen, *Sassanides*, which was associated elsewhere with the grand- r of Farru<u>kh</u>ān the Great, <u>D</u>jīl <u>D</u>jāwbara. This is not to be believed, especially since Ibn diyār states elsewhere (105) that Farru<u>kh</u>ān tained friendly relations with the governor of āsān, Ḳutayba b. Muslim (86-96/702-15) [*q.v.*]. hese errors are explained by the fact that the historians claim that the Dābūyids ruled over ristān, Gīlān and Daylam because they bore the Gīl Gīlān, Iṣpahba<u>dh</u> Iṣpahba<u>dh</u>an (king of the Iṣpahba<u>dh</u> of the Iṣpaba<u>dh</u>s). Now, neither nor Daylam was under the rule of Farru<u>kh</u>ān Great, for Ibn Isfandiyār, 99-100, mentions an k made by the Daylamīs against Ṭabaristān, tack which was frustrated by a trick. Similarly, Yazīd b. al-Muhallab tried to conquer Ṭaba- ı in 97/717, Farru<u>kh</u>ān the Great "appealed elp to the King of Daylam who sent him 10,000 " (Balʿamī, iv, 228). These Daylamī reinforce- s and the nature of the terrain, suitable for ıshes, saved the *iṣpahba<u>dh</u>* from annexation of erritory, but he was obliged to consent to a y tribute to obtain the withdrawal of Yazīd's s (al-Ṭabarī, ii, 1320-1, 1327-9; al-Balā<u>dh</u>urī, ; Ibn Isfandiyār, 105-7, presents a different on, which cannot be accepted). Farru<u>kh</u>ān the t concerned himself with the development of ristān until his death, *ca.* 110-12/728-30. He succeeded by his son Dā<u>dh</u>burzmihr who ed for 12 years (Ibn Isfandiyār, 108) until 22/739.

Bibliography: In addition to the Arabic ırces (Balā<u>dh</u>urī, *Futūḥ*; Ibn al-Faḳīh; Yaʿḳubī, *'rīkh*; Ṭabarī; Ibn al-A<u>th</u>īr) and the Persian es (Balʿamī; Ibn Isfandiyār, abridged tr. E. G. owne; Ẓahīr al-Dīn, *Ta'rī<u>kh</u>-i Ṭabaristān*, ed. Dorn, St. Petersburg 1850; E. Rehatsek, *The w and Gāobārah Sepahbuds along the southern res of the Caspian*, in *JBBRAS*, xii (1876), 410- there should be added J. Marquart, *Ērānšahr*; rdtmann, *Erklärung der Münzen mit Pehlevi genden, iii. Abteilung, Münzen von Tabaristan*, *ZDMG*, viii (1854), 173-80; H. L. Rabino di rgomale, *Les dynasties de Māzandarān de l'an H. à l'an 1006 H (672-1597/98) d'après les rces locales*, in *JA*, ccxxviii (1938); J. M. vala, *Numismatique du Ṭabaristān*, Paris 1938; Walker, *A catalogue of the Arab-Sassanian coins the British Museum*, London 1941; M. Rekaya, *s provinces sud-caspiennes de la conquête arabe milieu du IIIe siècle de l'H./642-864*, typed moire, Paris-Sorbonne 1968, abridged in *RSO*, iii (1973-4), 117-52. (M. Rekaya)

RŪḲ, King of Egypt, son of King Fu'ād -36) [see fu'ād al-awwal] and Queen Nazlī (*née* Ṣabrī), grandson of the Khedive Ismāʿīl (1863-79) [see Ismāʿīl Pa<u>sh</u>a], was born in Cairo on 21 <u>D</u>jumādā al-ūlā 1338/11 February 1920. He was proclaimed Crown Prince on 13 April 1922, officially named Prince of the Ṣaʿīd (Upper Egypt) on 12 December 1933, and proclaimed King of Egypt on 28 April 1936 in succession to his father who died on that day. He officially ascended the throne on 6 May 1936. On 20 January 1938 he married Ṣafīnāz <u>Dh</u>u 'l-Fiḳār, daughter of Judge Yūsuf <u>Dh</u>u 'l-Fiḳār, Vice-President of the Alexandria Mixed Court of Appeals. Ṣafīnāz was given the name and title of Queen Farīda of Egypt. There were three daughters from the marriage, before it was dissolved in November 1948, when Fārūḳ divorced Farīda. On 6 May 1951 Fārūḳ, at thirty-one, married Nārimān Ṣādiḳ, the seventeen-year old daughter of Ḥusayn Fahmī Ṣādiḳ, who was already betrothed to Zakī Hā<u>sh</u>im, an Egyptian official of the United Nations Secretariat. She bore him a son, Crown Prince Aḥmad Fu'ād, who was born in Cairo on 16 January 1952.

Fārūḳ's intended education was suddenly cut short at sixteen when his father died. It is, however, unlikely that he would have taken to serious study in preparation for his royal duties even had his father lived longer. Until he was fifteen, Fārūḳ was tutored at home. His English governess, Mrs Ina Taylor, was generally in charge. She tried to impart the main features of a typically English formative education into a prince living in ornate, European-modelled palaces, but in which much of court life, practice and behaviour remained a mixture of imported European formalities and native Ottoman oriental standards. His father tried gradually to introduce the young prince to his future royal duties. Thus Fārūḳ was made Chief Scout of Egypt in 1933 at the tender age of thirteen. A year before that he had made his first appearance in a public function. The following year, 1934, he deputised for his father at the Air Force celebrations in Heliopolis. At fourteen and fifteen he cut a dashing young figure of a handsome, polite prince. King Fu'ād, however, was a politically-involved monarch. Between 1930 and 1935, crucial years in Fārūḳ's life, Fu'ād was involved in one constitutional or political crisis after another, an economic depression, and mounting opposition from the so-called popular political parties such as the Wafd. He hardly had much time to devote to his son. Consequently, Fārūḳ spent those crucial formative years mostly with his three sisters, his governess, his mother and her female relatives. His only frequent male companions were palace servants, guards and his French gymnastics master. It is not known, for instance, if during those formative years, he had any male friends of his age.

Fārūḳ failed to gain a place at Eton. Nevertheless, his father sent him to England in 1935 with a view to entering the Royal Military College, Woolwich. He was accompanied by his officially-designated tutor Aḥmad Ḥasanayn (Pa<u>sh</u>a), a Balliol man, champion fencer and famous explorer, who was later to have a great influence over the young king, especially in the period from 1941 to 1945. The notoriously anti-British General ʿAzīz Alī al-Maṣrī accompanied Fārūḳ as his military tutor. Fārūḳ failed the entrance examination to Woolwich, but he was allowed to attend some lessons two afternoons a week. The rest of the time he spent at Kenry House, Kingston Hill, Surrey, where he settled with his entourage in October 1935. Sgt.-Major W. H. Parker looked after his physical fitness training, including fencing. Fārūḳ's six-month sojourn in England was short and of limited education value since he attended no formal or regular course of study. He did, however, acquire a taste for London's attractions, particularly its famous shops.

Returning to Egypt upon the death of his father, Fārūḳ could not assume his full royal duties until he had attained his majority which, by the Hijra calendar reckoning, was to be in August 1937. Until then a Regency Council, consisting of his uncle Prince Muḥammad ʿAlī, ʿAzīz Pasha ʿIzzat and his maternal uncle Sharīf Pasha Ṣabrī, acted for him. ʿAlī Māhir, a man close to King Fuʾād, had been Prime Minister since January of that year, and generally exerted a direct influence over the new young monarch. Subsequently, as Chief of his Royal Cabinet and Prime Minister again in 1939-40, he was to complicate Fārūḳ's relations with the more popular leader of the Wafd, Muṣṭafā Naḥḥās Pasha, embroil him in contacts with the Axis powers and thus further exacerbate his relations with the British Ambassador Sir Miles Lampson especially, and the British generally. Another early, dubious influence on the young inexperienced king was that of Shaykh Muṣṭafā al-Marāghī, Shaykh of the Azhar, a man who was also close to his father and who harboured anti-Wafdist, anti-British sympathies. Both these men, as well as others among his courtiers, were to involve Fārūḳ in the treacherous shoals of Egyptian politics from 1936 to 1952. They seemed to counter the influence of his mentor, Aḥmad Ḥasanayn, an ambitious though dexterous and consummate politician, who somehow tried to smooth relations between the king, the political parties and the British.

Fārūḳ, however, began his reign quite auspiciously as a highly-popular young monarch. His month's tour of Upper Egypt in January-February 1937 was a great success and the envy of the politicians. A second tour of Europe in April-July 1937 seemed to initiate Fārūk into the less edifying delights of European capitals. By 1940, before he was 21, the men around him, led by ʿAlī Māhir, had fully acquainted him with the need jealously to guard his political prerogatives against the Wafd and the British. Thus he tacitly approved of Māhir's use of certain new radical youth movements, such as the Young Egypt Society, and of the Azhar in order to push forward his leadership of a national Islamic regeneration. When, at the insistence of the British, ʿAlī Māhir was dismissed as Prime Minister in June 1940, Fārūḳ was left at the mercy of the politicians and Britain's war needs. In fact, as early as 29 November 1937, Sir Miles Lampson, who did not particularly like Fārūḳ and whose relationship with him resembled that between Cromer and the young Khedive ʿAbbās (Ḥilmī) II [*q.v.*] from 1892 to 1914, cabled to the Foreign Office in London:

> HM by all indications is shaping for the role of traditional oriental despot . . . His ultimate overthrow will occur when Nahhas goes . . . .

Lampson was forty years older than Fārūḳ and his opinion of the young Egyptian king may have been influenced accordingly. What is certain, however, is that Lampson did not appreciate Fārūḳ's flouting of British war interests in his persistence with appointed governments of his choice, his refusal to deal firmly with several crises in 1940-1, occasioned by Italy's entry into the war and the collapse of France, and his continued connections with ʿAlī Māhir and his anti-British agitation through the use of extremist political groups such as the Nat party, the Muslim Brethren, the Young E Society and the Azhar. It seems that he took A Ḥasanayn's advice in appointing both the I Ṣabrī and Ḥusayn Sirrī coalition governments 1940-January 1942). But neither of these go ments was strong enough to deal with the exige of war. Both were open to the machinations o palace and to the attacks of the majority party. Actually, the latter began to agitate ag them in order to recapture the initiative in th tionalist cause. Naḥḥās Pasha in June 1941, the British were being pressed by Rommel's f practically at the gates of Alexandria, appro the British with a view to his returning to p The timing was crucial, for Britain was in a difficult military position in Greece and the We Desert. When Naḥḥās threatened to foment po agitation in the country, Lampson felt he act. It was the concatenation of these events suggested vigorous British intervention in Egy affairs. The intervention was to prove fateful fo career and future of Fārūḳ.

Amidst anti-government and anti-British de strations in January 1942, largely inspired organised by pro-ʿAlī Māhir elements, the procrastinated over severing diplomatic rela with Vichy France. When his Prime Minister H Sirrī, did so, the King dismissed his Foreign Min a move against which the British protested mently, leading to the resignation of the government on 1 February. A British request Naḥḥās be invited to form a government wen heeded for three days, while Fārūḳ gathere leaders of all the political parties in his pala discuss the crisis. As Lampson did not speci his Note to the King what kind of govern Naḥḥās might lead, Fārūḳ invited him to le national coalition government. But Naḥḥās in on a purely Wafdist cabinet, which the King w not accept.

When Lampson marched into ʿĀbdīn Pala 9 p.m. to confront Fārūḳ, accompanied by Ge Stone, GOC British Land Forces, and backed u a battalion of armoured troops that had surrou the Palace, he did not do so with the intenti imposing on the King a purely Wafdist governi Rather, the ultimatum he read to the King dema his abdication. Fārūḳ, however, on Ḥasan advice, offered with alacrity the compromise for of a purely Wafdist government headed by Na

The so-called Palace Incident of 4 February had paradoxical consequences. It made F temporarily at least, very popular with Egy nationalists as well as with the Egyptian o corps, but created a permanent rift between and Naḥḥās of the Wafd, whom he planned to miss at the earliest opportunity. It also deep the incurable antipathy between him and Lam In fact, Fārūḳ acquired a deep resentment fo British in general. A motor accident in al-Ḳaṣ on 15 November 1943 added to his fears, fan and resentments. Yet after the Battle of Ala he had no choice but to affect an overtly pro-B attitude.

Immediately after the War, Fārūḳ faced se political problems in the country, made even difficult by the greatly strengthened violent m ment of the Muslim Brethren [see AL-IKHWĀ MUSLIMĪN], army officer conspiracies, Comm and other extremist groups. He escaped ann to Cyprus or Europe on prolonged summer holi

:ew corpulent, lazy and coarse. He seemed to most of the day and wander at night, accom- d by his trusted servants Antonio Pulli, Ernesto ci, Pietro Garo, his ADC ʿUmar Fatḥī and banian bodyguards. He divided his time between uberges des Pyramides and the Helmia Palace clubs, his various private garçonnières in and Alexandria, and the Royal Automobile gambling table in the centre of modern Cairo. nsecurity and unhappiness of his childhood, is interrupted or nonexistent education, added s inferiority complex and inability to concen- He was estranged from his wife and mother sought escapist pleasures in the company of n procured for him by his servants. He became ted to all kinds of pills, hormonal preparations, ety of elixirs, food and gambling. He acquired nia for collecting coins, stamps, pornographic ture, aids and ephemera. He became more e, unpunctual and socially impossible, with oarse practical jokes, kleptomania, compulsive ing and bad sportsmanship, characterised by ak of cruelty. He could neither lead—and thus ate the internecine warfare between Egyptian cians—nor be led by anyone other than by hantic courtiers like his Press Adviser, Karīm t, or his Business Adviser, Elias Andrawus. He in the gilded cages that were ʿĀbdīn, Ḳubba, azah and Raʾs al-Tīn palaces, or in his fortress- state at Inshāṣ, 35 miles from Cairo, where *feddān*s of the best agricultural land produced fruits and housed a model poultry farm. He ed everything which he did not own, including men's women and possessions.

ūḳ's scandalous European holiday from August tober 1950 prompted a petition signed by most sition party leaders and politicians protesting st his shameful behaviour. At the same time, nist groups led by Young Egypt, and other ground organisations such as the new Free rs and the Marxists, openly called for the hrow of his régime. Considered widely to have nitted the ill-equipped and unprepared Egyptian to the war in Palestine in order to indulge his y with King ʿAbd Allāh of Jordan, and openly ed of having profited from arms purchases cted with that war, his marriage to Nārimān 51 and the birth of the Crown Prince in January did not improve Fārūḳ's image or fortunes. ot was too advanced. By autumn 1951 Fārūḳ et on a collision course with the stirring forces e country, chief among them the Free Officers. ppointed the pro-British Ḥāfiẓ ʿAfīfī Pasha as of his Royal Cabinet and recalled his ambas- to Britain, ʿAbd al-Fattāḥ ʿAmr, to serve as olitical adviser. More significant was his attempt ck senior military posts with his own men, as General Ḥaydar, the Chief of Staff, and al Husayn Sirrī ʿĀmir, who replaced General mmad Nadjīb (Naguib) as Commander of the ier Defence Force.

e violent events which accompanied the prob- of Anglo-Egyptian relations since 1946 cul- ed in the Wafd's demagogic but fateful uni- l abrogation of the 1936 Anglo-Egyptian y in October 1951 and the explosion of the that burned the centre of modern Cairo on nuary 1952, Black Saturday, and these gave the pretext to dismiss Naḥḥās and the Wafd power. A succession of palace-appointed neral governments, including one led by his entor ʿAlī Māhir, were unable to deal with the drifting, explosive political situation. In the mean-time, Fārūḳ had himself proclaimed a *Sayyid*, or descendant of the Prophet, a most unlikely genea-logical claim in view of his Macedonian-Albanian forefathers. Neither Lampson nor his successors were able or willing either to deal with Fārūḳ firmly or to conjure up a formula to resolve the impasse. Nor was a Conservative government in London after 1951 willing to play an imperial role in Cairo, barely four years after leaving India.

Yet Fārūḳ's security agents had uncovered the real threat to his throne, namely, the Free Officers. His courtiers, however, were suspicious of each other as always, ever-solicitous and sycophantic, but were incapable of concerted action. Equally, the politi-cians were sunk in their petty quarrels, all anxious to keep the Wafd, by now weakened and relatively corrupt, out of power at any cost. On the very day when Fārūḳ in Alexandria ordered the arrest of the Free Officer conspirators at 9 p.m. (22 July 1952), the latter seized power three hours later.

Fārūḳ believed that the British were behind the army conspiracy. Even though he tried to contact British GHQ in the Canal for help, he did not trust them. Instead he sought the help of the Americans with a view to saving his and his family's lives. Ironically, his father's old friend and his own erst-while mentor and adviser, ʿAlī Māhir, brought Fārūḳ the army officers' demands, signed by Naguib, requiring the dismissal of his immediate entourage of courtiers. Two days later on 26 July ʿAlī Māhir returned as Prime Minister of the new military régime with the order for Fārūḳ to abdicate in favour of his infant son, Crown Prince Aḥmad Fuʾād, and to leave the country permanently by 6 p.m. Less than a year later in June 1953, the monarchy in Egypt was abolished in favour of a republic.

Like his grandfather the Khedive Ismāʿīl, Fārūḳ sailed off to Naples on the Royal Yacht "Maḥrūsa" with his family, gold ingots and over two hundred pieces of luggage. He had been depositing money in Switzerland, Italy and the United Stated for many years, at least since the end of the Second World War. What he could not take with him were the vast tracts of land (over 30,000 *feddāns*) and palaces, and his remarkable coin, stamp and porno-graphic collections. He finally settled in Rome. His daughters from his marriage to Farīda were packed off to Switzerland, and his second wife Nārimān soon returned to Egypt with her mother. She was divorced from Fārūḳ and remarried a Dr. Adham Naḳīb. Fārūḳ reverted to his life of girlfriends and nightclubs, a familiar massive and rotund figure in the bistros and nightspots of Rome, interspersed with occasional visits to Switzerland and to the gambling tables of Monaco, which principality had granted him citizenship.

Two weeks after he had left a heart clinic in Switzerland, he drove one of his Italian girl friends to a roadside inn, the "Île de France", for dinner around midnight. He suffered a heart attack while just starting to enjoy the Havana cigar which he had lit after a gargantuan dinner. He died two hours later at 2.08 a.m. on 18 March 1965 in a Rome hospital, aged 45 years, 2 months and 7 days. At the request of his family and according to his will, he was buried in Cairo two days later very quietly and in the dead of night, alongside his forefathers. His was the last effective reign of the Muḥammad ʿAlī dynasty, founded by that soldier of fortune from Kavalla in 1805.

Bibliography: J. Bernard-Derosne, *Farouk, la déchéance d'un roi*, Paris 1953; T. E. Evans (ed.), *The Killearn diaries*, London 1972; B. St. C. McBride, *Farouq of Egypt, a biography*, London 1967. (P. J. VATIKIOTIS)

FASĀʾĪ, ḤĀDJDJĪ MĪRZĀ ḤASAN, Persian scholar of the 19th century and author of a historical-geographical work on his native province of Fārs, the *Fārsnāma-yi Nāṣirī* (the latter part of the book's title being a reference to the Ḳādjār sultan Nāṣir al-Dīn Shāh, in whose reign Ḥasan Fasāʾī wrote).

He was born, according to the autobiography inserted into his book, in 1237/1821-2 in the small town of Fasā [*q.v.*] in Fārs, of a family which had been prominent in the intellectual and religious life of Shīrāz for at least four centuries; various members of it had been famed for their scholarship or their administrative expertise, and one of his forebears, Niẓām al-Dīn Mīrzā Aḥmad, had been vizier to the Ḳuṭb-Shāhī ruler of Golconda in the Deccan, ʿAbd Allāh b. Muḥammad (1020-83/1611-72) [see ḲUṬB-SHĀHĪS]. Ḥasan Fasāʾī himself studied theology and then medicine, practising in Shīrāz as a physician and becoming involved in a protracted legal dispute over his family's ancestral pious foundations or *awḳāf*.

In 1289/1872 the governor of Fārs, Mīrzā Masʿūd Ẓill al-Sulṭān, commissioned him to use earlier cartographical work of his to make a general map of the province. Subsequently, he came to enjoy the favour and patronage of another governor, the reformist Farhād Mīrzā Muʿtamad al-Dawla (on whose draconian measures in Fārs see E. G. Browne, *A year amongst the Persians*[3], London 1950, 115-18, and also Storey, i, 204), travelling extensively around southern Persia in the entourage of the governor's son Iḥtishām al-Dawla. Then in 1296/1879 Farhād Mīrzā ordered him to compose a geography of Fārs on the basis of his maps. This eventually became the *Fārsnāma-yi Nāṣirī*, in two volumes, one on the history of Fārs from the beginning of Islam till his own days (in fact, up to 1300/1883), and one on its geography and topography. A lithographed edition was printed at Tehran in 1313-14/1895-6; the author's own death took place at some unknown date after this. The historical section is written on the traditional Islamic annalistic pattern. The author utilises earlier histories of Persia and of Fārs, and for his especially valuable treatment of the Ḳādjār period, he quotes archival material, including diplomatic letters and treatises, as well as eyewitness accounts of events. All in all, the *Fārs-nāma-yi Nāṣirī* may be regarded as the culmination of the long tradition of annalistic historiography in Persia, much as Djabartī's chronicle was for that science in Egypt.

Bibliography: The *Fārs-nāma-yi Nāṣirī* has been recently reprinted at Tehran in 1965; the section on the Ḳādjār dynasty and Fārs under its rule has now been translated into English by H. Busse, *History of Persia under Qājār rule*, New York 1972, with a useful introduction. See also Storey, i, 353, and Storey-Bregel, ii, 1031-5. (C. E. BOSWORTH)

AL-**FĀSĪ**, individual *nisba* of the members of a prominent family of Moroccan scholars. Descended from the Ḳurayshite clan of the Banū Fihr, originally established in Spain but settling in Fās at the end of the 10th/16th century, this family is known collectively under the name Fāsiyyūn, while the citizens of the town are called rather Ahl/Āl Fās. In view of the fact that the article AL-FĀSIYYŪN in Volume II of the *EI* deals wit population of Fās in general, it has been consi useful to collect in this Supplement the basic relating to the members of this line who have co uted the most actively, over the last four cen to religious, intellectual and literary life, wi limiting themselves simply to passing on a v and still highly appreciated, form of teaching

In general, the genealogical tree drawn by E. Provençal (*Chorfa*, 242) continues to be valid we shall confine ourselves to referring the reac it; the accounts devoted by the learned histori the most notable personalities of the Fāsiyyūn lost none of their value, but they can be conside enlarged and made more accurate in the lig documents, mostly manuscripts, that are available. The work of Muḥammad al-Fāsī ar Hajji in Arabic or in French, of ʿA. Gann Arabic, of M. Lakhdar in French and of still o enables us to acquire an increasingly clear vi the merits of a group of eminent scholars who c however, be better served by a detailed mono in view of the extensive documentation provid biographical sources, whether long-establishe recently discovered.

I. — ABU 'L-MAḤĀSIN [*q.v.*] Yūsuf (d. 18 R 1013/14 August 1604) was the founder, in F the district of the Ḳalḳaliyyūn (see Le Tour *Fès*, Casablanca 1949, index), of the *zāwiya* c Fāsiyyūn, which was given the name Sīdī ʿAb Ḳādir al-Fāsī.

II. — His brother Abū Zayd ʿABD AL-RAḤM Muḥammad (d. 1036/1626) founded a second *z* in the same district and wrote commentaries annotations of religious works; a number of have been published, notably *al-Anwār al-lām sharḥ Dalāʾil al-khayrāt*, lith. Fās 1317/1899.

III. — Among the four sons of Abu 'l-Ma AḤMAD AL-ḤĀFIẒ (971-1021/1564-1612) also commentaries on works relating to liturgical (*al-djahr bi 'l-dhikr*, lith. Fās) or ecstatic da (*ḥukm al-samāʿ wa 'l-raḳṣ*, lith. Fās).

IV. — The brother of the latter, Abū ʿAbd Ḥāmid MUḤAMMAD AL-ʿARBĪ (988-1052/1580- was the author of a number of works, among the *Mirʾāt al-maḥāsin min akhbār al-Shaykh 'l-Maḥāsin* (lith. Fās 1324) is important fo account that it gives of his father and the history of the family.

V. — The following generation is represented notably by ʿABD AL-ḲĀDIR (1007-91/1599- [*q.v.*], b. ʿAlī (960-1030/1553-1621) b. Abi 'l-Ma who left only some *responsa*, but whose prodi scholarship and teaching inspired his son ʿAb Raḥmān (no. VI) to write two hagiographic (*Tuḥfat al-akābir fī manāḳib al-Shaykh ʿAb Ḳādir* and *Bustān al-azāhir*) and a treatise re to his disciples (*Ibtihādj al-baṣāʾir*); this las been studied by M. Ben Cheneb, in *Actes du Congrès des Orient.*, vi, Paris 1907).

VI. — The son of the preceding, Abū Zayd AL-RAḤMAN (1042-96/1631-85), has been mad subject of an article in vol. I of the *EI*; add t bibliography M. Lakhdar, *La vie littéraire*, 8 and bibliography cited; see also ʿAMAL, 3.

VII. — Another great-grandson of Abu 'l-Mah Abū ʿĪsā/ʿAbd Allāh MUḤAMMAD AL-MAHDĪ (1109/1624-98) b. Aḥmad (d. 1062/1653) b. ʿA Yūsuf, was the author of a number of impo works some of which have survived, on the Ḳu readings, the *Sīra*, law, mysticism etc. and notably of a biography of Abu 'l-Maḥāsin *ihir al-ṣafiyya* (ms. Rabat D 1234), an abridge-of his *Rawḍat al-maḥāsin al-zahiyya*.

.I. — Abū ᶜAbd Allāh MUḤAMMAD AL-ṬAYYIB 13/1701) b. Muḥammad (d. 1116/1704) b. ᶜAbd dir (no. V) left no works of importance, but usin Abū ᶜAbd Allāh MUḤAMMAD (1058-1134/ 1722) b. ᶜAbd al-Raḥmān (no. VI) was the r of several works, among which attention d be drawn to a *fahrasa* [*q.v.*]. entitled *al-ḥ al-bādiyya fi 'l-asānīd al-ᶜāliyya* and used by ānī [*q.v.*] (ms. Rabat K 1249; see also al-āsī, *Ahamm maṣādir*, 121-2).

. — ABŪ MADYAN MUḤAMMAD (1112-81/1701-. Aḥmad b. Maḥammad b. ᶜAbd al-Ḳādir V), preacher and teacher at the Ḳarawiyyīn, , besides conventional commentaries, some ry compositions of which the titles are suf-tly revealing: *al-Muḥkam fi 'l-amthāl wa ım*, *Tuḥfat al-arīb wa-nuzhat al-labīb* (ms. t D 590, fols. 81 b - 144 b; summarily edited ranslated into Latin by Fr. de Dombay, Vienna , *Madjmūᶜ al-ẓuraf wa-djāmiᶜ al-ṭuraf* (ms. t K 1717, fol. 2-93); these are *adab* compilations.

— Abū ᶜAbd Allāh MUḤAMMAD (1118-79/ 65) b. Aḥmad b. Maḥammad, brother of the ding, was the author of biographical works of ı only one, a short treatise on the Chorfa of cco, would appear to have survived.

. — The son of the preceding, Abu l'-ᶜAbbās AD (1166-1213/1753-99) composed, on his n from the Pilgrimage (1211/1796) a *riḥla* of a number of manuscripts exist and which has tly been published by M. El Fasi (Rabat); story of a journey is remarkable among works genre on account of the simplicity of the style, letail of the description and the accuracy of vation.

I. — His brother Abū Mālik ᶜABD AL- WĀḤID -1213/ 1758-99)was a poet who wrote a *fahrasa* ally in verse, a monograph on the Ṣiḳilliyyūn a (ms. Rabat G 97) and an *urdjūza* on the iyyūn (ed. Tunis).

II. — A descendant of Muḥammad al-ᶜArbī IV), Abū Ḥafṣ ᶜUMAR (1125-88/1713-74) b. Allāh b. ᶜUmar b. Yūsuf b. Muḥammad al- was a polygraph who composed various com-aries, annotations, letters of a judicial nature a *Dīwān* containing numerous imitations of or less well-known poems on subjects generally mystical flavour.

V. — A distant cousin of the preceding, Abū Allāh MUḤAMMAD (1130-1214/1718-99) b. al-Salam b. Maḥammad b. ᶜAbd al-Salām b. ımmad al-ᶜArbī (no. IV) specialised in the ānic readings, to which he devoted a number of ngs that have in part survived.

. — Abū ᶜAbd Allāh MUḤAMMAD AL-ṬĀHIR -85/1830-68) b. ᶜAbd al-Raḥmān is considered one of the most brilliant members of the y, although he went against the example of his its and entered government service; as Palace tary he was a member, in 1276/1860, of a matic mission sent to London, to the court of n Victoria, by Sultan Sīdī Muḥammad (1276-59-73) and, on his return, composed an account s journey which has just been published by l Fasi. As usual, the traveller expresses his ler at the novelties that he has seen and relates experiences in language that is simple and d of all pretension.

VI. — Finally, one should mention ᶜABD AL-IR (d. 1296/1879) b. al-Madjdhūb (d. 1260/1844) b. ᶜAbd al-Ḥāfiẓ b. Muḥammad (no. IX) a preacher of Fās who is said to have been the author of a chronological index entitled *Tadhkirat al-muḥsinīn bi-wafayāt al-aᶜyān wa-ḥawādith al-sinīn*, which is still missing.

Were one to attempt to assess the contribution of the Fāsiyyūn to Arabic culture and literature, it would appear from their impressive corpus of writings that they contributed most of all, as much by their teaching as by the commentaries and annotations that they composed, to the maintenance of the classical tradition in the intellectual capital of Morocco; some of them were composers of verse, but not one of them proved to be a true poet. Hence we can doubtless declare without injustice that their most tangible contribution consists in their *fahrasas*, their accounts of journeys, and their monographs on their family or on certain of its members.

Bibliography: In addition to the general biographical works, see especially Muḥammad al-Fāsī (no. IV), *Mirʾāt al-maḥāsin*, lith. Fās 1324; Sulaymān al-ᶜAlawī, *ᶜInāyat ūlī 'l-madjd bi-dhikr āl al-Fāsī b. al-Djadd*, Fās 1347/1928; E. Lévi-Provençal, *Chorfa*, index; M. El Fasi, in *Hespéris*, xxix (1942), 65-81; ᶜA. Gannūn, *al-Nubūgh al-maghribī*², Beirut 1961, index; M. Lakhdar, *La vie littéraire*, index; M. Hajji, *L'activité intellectuelle au Maroc à l'époque saᶜdide*, Rabat 1976-7, index. (CH. PELLAT)

FAṢṢĀD, ḤADJDJĀM (A.), two terms denoting blood-letter (*faṣṣād*, lit. "phlebotomist" and *ḥadjdjām*, lit. "cupper"). Al-Djāḥiẓ indicates that *ḥidjāma* (cupping) and *faṣd* (phlebotomy) are similar professions. Some pseudo-scientific books on phlebotomy and blood-letting were written by reputable physicians in ᶜAbbāsid Baghdād and Aghlabid Ḳayrawān in the 3rd/9th century, e.g., Yuḥannā b. Māsawayh (d. 243 H./857) wrote a *Kitāb al-Faṣd wa'l-ḥidjāma* ("Book of phlebotomy and blood-letting"), and Isḥāḳ b. ᶜUmrān (d. 279/ 892) wrote in Ḳayrawān a medical treatise called *Kitāb al-Faṣd* (cf. Ibn Djuldjul, *Ṭabaḳāt al-aṭibbāʾ wa'l-ḥukamāʾ*, Cairo 1955, 65, 85). The phlebotomist was required by customary law to be learned and reliable in the anatomy of organs, veins, muscles and arteries, and he practised his craft in consultation with a physician. They bled veins of the human body and also performed circumcision (*khitān*) for men as well as women in Arab society. Phlebotomy involved some hazards. Many persons actually died as a result of improper venesection, according to Ibn Bassām al-Muḥtasib. Arab customary law made the *faṣṣād* liable to pay compensation in the event of injury or death of a patient resulting from careless opening of veins. This was probably the reason why the *muḥtasib* stipulated that the *faṣṣādūn* should practise their craft in public places and that they must keep a number of their instruments, including lancets, in good condition. Among Muslim jurists, Abū Ḥanīfa reckoned phlebotomy as a recommendable practice (*sunna*), and not a compulsory duty, but others regarded it as a compulsory duty. Available evidence suggests that the *faṣṣād* had a better social position than the *ḥadjdjām*, and that there was no stigma attached to the phlebotomist's profession.

Ḥidjāma (cupping) was a less hazardous profession than *faṣd*, but it was also a less popular work than phlebotomy. The *ḥadjdjām* existed in pre-Islamic Arabian society and continued to render service to Islamic society until recent times. The cupper is a much-satirised character in Arabic tales, and had a very low status. Unlike the phlebotomist, the cupper practised blood-letting on parts of the human body other than veins, and used his cup for relief of pain or itching.

Abū Ṭayyiba was a *ḥadjdjām* who served the Prophet Muḥammad and was much honoured in early Islamic society. He performed *ḥidjāma* on men as well as women. Although *ḥidjāma* was permitted by the *sunna*, there are conflicting Islamic traditions about it. A saying attributed to the Prophet described the earnings of a cupper as evil (*khabīth*), analogous to the earnings of a whore. Some other traditions state that the cupper was paid in cash and kind by the Prophet. The anti-*ḥadjdjām* traditions are likely to be apocryphal and they only express the prejudices of the Arabs of the Umayyad and ʿAbbāsid periods. Arab writers cite instances of cuppers, including the poet Abu 'l-ʿAtāhiya, who did not accept any fee for *ḥidjāma* from their clients. Tuesday and Saturday were regarded as auspicious days of the week for *ḥidjāma*, according to an Arab taboo of the ʿAbbāsid and Mamlūk periods.

A proverbial saying of the 3rd/9th century crystallised public opinion: "A look in the mirror of the *ḥadjdjām* is demeaning (*dana'a*)." The cupper was said to be given to gossip, and the allegation was illustrated by anecdotes about Abū Ḥanīfa [*q.v.*] and a cupper, and also about Hārūn al-Rashīd [*q.v.*] and a talkative *ḥadjdjām*. The social isolation of cuppers probably led some of them to narrate traditions (*aḥādīth*) on chains of narrations from one *ḥadjdjām* to another only, says al-Samʿānī. The prejudice against the cupper may be explained in part by the fact that body services were generally considered repugnant, and also partly by the fact that most cuppers were men of inferior social origins, such as *mawālī* and slaves. The cupper was disqualified from giving valid testimony (*shahāda*) in a court of law, and the *ḥadjdjām* was deemed unfit to marry a woman from a social group outside his profession; one source further states that the son of a *ḥadjdjām*, irrespective of his merits, was automatically unsuitable to be a boon-companion (*nadīm*) of the sovereign.

Bibliography: Aḥmad b. Ḥanbal, *Musnad*, Cairo 1313/1896, iii, 464; Aslam b. Sahl al-Razzāz al-Wāsiṭī, known as Baḥshal, *Ta'rīkh Wāsiṭ*, ed. Gurguis ʿAwwād, Baghdād 1967, 171; al-Djāḥiẓ, *Rasā'il*, ed. Sandūbī, Cairo 1933, 127; idem, *al-Bukhalā'*, Cairo 1963, 118; idem, *Ḥayawān*, Cairo 1938, iii, 32; Ps.-Djāḥiẓ, *Kitāb al-Tādj*, Cairo 1914, 23-4; Wakīʿ, *Akhbār al-ḳuḍāt*, Cairo 1947, ii, 54; al-Tanūkhī, *Nishwār al-muḥāḍara*, London 1921, i, 174; al-Thaʿālibī, *Khams rasā'il*, Istanbul 1301/1883, 131; idem, *Arbaʿ rasā'il*, Istanbul 1883, 204; al-Khaṭīb al-Baghdādī, *Kitāb al-Taṭfīl*, Damascus 1346/1927, 83-4; Badīʿ al-Zamān al-Hamadhānī, *Maḳāmāt*, Beirut 1924, 180; al-Samʿānī, *al-Ansāb*, Hyderabad 1964, iv, 69; al-Zamakhsharī, *al-Mustaḳṣā*, Hyderabad 1962, i, 40, 270; Ibn Bassām, *Nihāyat al-rutba fī ṭalab al-ḥisba*, Baghdād 1968, 110-18; Ibn al-Ukhuwwa, *Maʿālim al-ḳurba*, London 1938, 159-64; al-Rāghib al-Iṣfahānī, *Muḥāḍarāt al-udabā'* (basic), Beirut 1961, ii, 462-3; Bar-Hebraeus, *The laughable stories*, tr. E. A. W. Budge, London 1897, 122-8, Syriac text, 98-103; Ibshīhī, *al-Mustaṭraf*, Cairo 1308-10/1890-2, i, 66; Ibn Ṭūlūn, *Rafʿ al-malāma ʿāmma ḳīla fi'l-ḥidjāma*, Chester Beatty ms., 3317, ff. 59a-66b; Aḥmad Ibrāhīm al-Sharīf, *Makka wa'l-Madīna fi'l-djāhiliyya wa-ʿahd al-Rasūl*, Cairo 1965, 38, 221-2; R. Brunschvig, *Métiers vils en Islam*, in *SI*, xvi (1962),
(M. A. J. B

FATE [see AL-ḲAḌĀ' WA-'L-ḲADAR].

FAYD, an important settlement in N during mediaeval times, now a village, situat lat. 27° 8′ N. and long 42° 28′ E. It lies on a in the borderlands between the two regions c Djabal Shammar to the north-west and al-I [*q.v.*] to the south-east, some 80 miles/130 south-east of Ḥā'il [*q.v.*]. The early Islamic graphers locate it in the territory where the pa grounds of the B. Ṭayyi' and the B. Asad ma together, near to the frequently-mentioned mountains of Ṭayyi'", sc. Salmā and Adjā'. I followed by Samhūdī, describes it as a famous [*q.v.*] of pre-Islamic times, and they and I mention that when the chief of Ṭayyi' Zayd al-I b. Muhalhil became a Muslim, the Prophet ren him Zayd al-Khayr and awarded him Fayd *ḳaṭīʿa*. Apparently there was a popular belief its full name was Fayd b. Ḥām b. ʿAmalīḳ afte first dweller there. Accordingly, the settle probably existed in some form during the Djāhil especially as it is mentioned in early poets Zuhayr b. Abī Sulmā and al-Shammākh (Ibn b. Isḥāḳ al-Ḥarbī, *K. al-Manāsik wa-amākin al-ḥadjdj wa-maʿālim al-djazīra*, ed. Ḥamac Djāsir, Riyadh 1389/1969, 306-9; Bakrī, *Muʿ mā 'staʿdjam*, iii, 1032-5; Samhūdī, *Wafā' al-v* iii, 1102).

Fayd's importance under Islam came fron position being roughly half-way along the pilgri route from Kūfa in ʿIrāḳ to Mecca and Medina, route known subsequently as the Darb Zubayda in Suppl.]. Already in the earliest decades of I the caliph ʿUthmān is said to have done irrig works there (Ḥarbī, *op. cit.*, 309; Samhūdī, *loc.* in the early ʿAbbāsid period, similar charitable w are attributed to al-Manṣūr, al-Mahdī and the al-Faḍl b. al-Rabīʿ; whilst in the 4th/10th cen the Būyid *amīr* ʿAḍud al-Dawla made furthe provements, according to Muḳaddasī (see belov now became a place of fair importance, and Arabic geographers and travellers describe i possessing two well-fortified citadels, a bat Friday mosque and many other amenities. It ample supplies of running water from springs from wells, used to irrigate date palm groves stored in cisterns. Supplies of food and fodder kept there for the pilgrims, and heavy bag could be deposited there with reliable agents recovered when the pilgrims returned from Ḥaramayn. It was consequently the headquarte the state-appointed warden of the pilgrimage its route across Arabia, the *amīr al-ḥadjdj* or *al-ṭarīḳ*, and his contingent of guards (see Ḥ *loc. cit.*; Ibn Khurradādhbih, 127; Ibn Rusta, tr. Wiet, 204; Yaʿḳūbī, *Buldān*, 312, tr. Wiet, Muḳaddasī, 108, 254; Ibn Djubayr, *Riḥla*, 2 tr. R. J. C. Broadhurst, 214; Yāḳūt, *Buldān*, B 1374-6/1955-7, iv, 282-3). The arts of peace also have been cultivated to some extent, Yāḳūt, *loc. cit.*, lists certain *ʿulamā'* stemming Fayd.

The stationing of the *amīr al-ḥadjdj* at Fayd vital, for travel along the pilgrimage route always fraught with dangers from the preda Bedouins or from schismatics, and the histo annals abound with accounts of attacks [see ḤA iii. The Islamic Ḥadjdj]. Thus in 294/906-7 Ṭayyi' besieged al-Muktafī's *amīr al-ḥadjdj* Was Ṣuwārtigin in Fayd for three days (Ṭabarī, iii, 2 al-Athīr, Beirut 1385-7/1965-7, vii, 553); in)24 the Carmathians under Abū Ṭāhir al-nābī massacred near there a large part of the image caravan of the East and elsewhere (ʿArīb, T. *al-Ṭabarī*, 118-19; Hamadānī, *Takmilat -Ṭabarī*, ed. A. Y. Kanʿān, Beirut 1961, i, 43); st in 412/1021-2 the Nabhān of Ṭayyiʾ, under chief Ḥammād b. ʿUdayy, besieged in Fayd pilgrimage from Khurāsān financed by Maḥmūd hazna, after receiving already a payment of ɔ *dīnārs* as protection-money [see khuwwa], but finally repelled (Ibn al-Djawzī, *al-Muntaẓam*, 2; Ibn al-Athīr, ix, 325). Ibn Djubayr, *loc. cit.*, Ibn Baṭṭūṭa, *Riḥla*, i, 409-10, tr. Gibb, i, 252-3, d that in their time, the pilgrims entered Fayd arlike array in order to ward off the Bedouins. later times, Fayd began to lose its importance vour of Ḥāʾil when the pilgrimage route began ass through the latter town and caravans went the oasis of al-ʿAdwa (cf. A. Musil, *Northern , a topographical itinerary*, New York 1928, 66). first described in its more modest circumstances European travellers in the later 19th century. G. Palgrave passed through it en route from to al-Ḳaṣīm (*Narrative of a year's journey gh Central and Eastern Arabia (1862-63)*, London Cambridge 1865, i, 227-30), as did C. M. Doughty, Fayd was in the territories of Ibn Rashīd, *amīr* āʾil (*Travels in Arabia Deserta*, London 1921, 9). Musil says that it comprised only 35 huts, bited by Tamīmīs. It is now a large village, with palms, pasture for beasts and a good supply of water. The mediaeval settlement lies about mile/1 ½ km. to the north, and has remains of ings and cisterns, and possibly of a mosque, ther with deep wells; these constructions have much reduced in recent times by stone-plun-rs.

Bibliography: Given substantially in the ticle, but see the survey of earlier historical and ographical information in Musil, *loc. cit.*, Appx. , The station of Fejd in history, 216-20, and w the doctoral thesis of S. ʿA. ʿA. al-Rashīd, *critical study of the Pilgrim Road between Kufa d Mecca (Darb Zubaydah), with the aid of field-rk*, Leeds 1977 (unpublished), with a full scription and plan of the site.

(C. E. Bosworth)

YḌ-I KĀSHĀNĪ, the pseudonym by which ammad b. Murtaḍā, called Mawlā Muḥsin, one he most prolific Shīʿī theologians of his , is better-known. He was a poet, philosopher, rt on *ḥadīth* and skilled authority on Shīʿī his mind dominated most of the religious ces of his time, and his writings touched on al differing domains.

e exact date of his birth is unknown, but he in 1091/1680 at an advanced age, so that he have been born, in the town of Ḳum(m), in 007/1598. After initial studies in his natal town, ft for Shīrāz to hear the lectures of the famous sopher Ṣadr al-Dīn Shīrāzī, who gave to him of his daughters in marriage. His incisive mind ed him to assimilate a large range of subjects, he was generally recognised as one of those ogians especially attached to the traditions of Prophet and the *Imāms*, and as a traditionalist ar, was the adversary of the philosopher and der of the Shaykhī trend of thought, *Shaykh* ad Aḥsāʾī [*q.v.*]. However, he incurred equally hostility of some traditionalist theologians who sed certain of his mystical ideas. He was, in fact, a poet who also excelled at the philosophical sciences. His main work is undoubtedly the *Abwāb al-djinān* ("Gates of paradise"), written in 1055/1645; as a philosophical mystic, his intuition and incisive mind made him close to al-Ghazālī. His other works include the *ʿIlm al-yaḳīn fī uṣūl al-dīn*, which is an exposition of the principles of Shīʿī faith, apparently modelled philosophically on Ibn Sīnā's *Ishārāt*, since it is made up of a series of *uṣūl* or principles just as Ibn Sīnā's work is a series of *ishārāt* or indications. His second important work here is the *Minhādj al-nadjāt*, in which Kāshānī deals with the practice of the principles of Shīʿī faith. It is divided into chapters corresponding to the five articles of faith, (1) the divine unity; (2) the divine justice; (3) prophethood; (4) the imamate; and (5) the resurrection.

Kāshānī's abundant output comprises over 90 works in Persian and Arabic, in all of which is discernible his predilection for poetry; all of his prose is sprinkled with his own verses or with those of the great Persian and Arabic poets, e.g. the Arabic text of his *Kalimāt maknūna* is full of Arabic and Persian quatrains. Several others of his family were noted as scholars, and especially his brother, the author of several works on ethics.

Bibliography: Khwānsārī, *Rawḍāt al-djannāt*, 522-42; Fayḍ-i Kāshānī, *Mirʾāt al-ākhirāt*, introd., 1; Maʿṣūm ʿAlī Shāh, *Ṭarāʾiḳ al-ḥaḳāʾiḳ*, i, 177, 179, 181, 183.

(M. Achena)

FAYOUM [see al-fayyūm].

FAYṢAL b. **ʿABD** al-**ʿAZĪZ** b. ʿAbd al-Raḥman Āl Suʿūd (*ca.* 1323-95/*ca.* 1906-75), king of Suʿūdi Arabia (regn. 1385-96/1964-75). His mother was Ṭurfa Āl al-Shaykh. Educated traditionally, the young prince rode in battle at the age of 13 and soon became his father's stalwart commander; at the same age, he began his diplomatic career when, in 1337-8/1919, his father deputed him to congratulate the English king on the defeat of Germany. Abroad, he made characteristically acute independent observations of Western society and, most exceptionally, ultimately learned English and French privately. Soon after ʿAbd al-ʿAzīz [*q.v.* in Suppl.] conquered al-Ḥidjāz (1345/1925), he appointed Fayṣal viceroy of the new province and foreign minister. He lived most of the next thirty years in al-Ḥidjāz, but diplomacy took him to Europe frequently, and, following the establishment of diplomatic relations with the United States (1359/1940), to that country also.

Fayṣal had a total of four wives. First was Sulṭāna b. Aḥmad al-Sudayrī, by whom he had ʿAbd Allāh. In 1350-1, he married ʿIffat b. Aḥmad Āl Thunayyān, a relative raised in Turkey. They had six sons: Muḥammad, Suʿūd, Turkī, Saʿd, ʿAbd al-Raḥmān, and Bandar. Around 1359/1940 he married Ḥayya b. Turkī b. Djalwī, and they had Khālid. All the sons were educated in the United States and England as, reportedly, were several of his six (?) daughters. Of his wives, two were divorced years before his death, and one died; ʿIffat remained his constant helpmate and encouraged him to more liberal attitudes toward women.

Before King ʿAbd al-ʿAzīz died in 1373/1953, he had arranged that his eldest living son, Suʿūd, should succeed him, and he had designated Fayṣal as Suʿūd's successor. Fayṣal served as prime minister for part of Suʿūd's reign as well as foreign minister. The reign did not prove successful. In 1376-7/1957 Fayṣal had several stomach operations in the United States, and when he returned home, he found the kingdom in some disorder and near bankruptcy. Senior members of the royal family decided to ease out Suʿūd, who in 1377/1958 "voluntarily" surrendered power to Fayṣal while remaining king nominally. By 1379-8/1960 Suʿūd reasserted himself, but the family will prevailed, and in 1384/1964 Fayṣal was proclaimed king.

Intelligent and equally at home in Bedouin tent or Western capital, King Fayṣal proved a masterful ruler. Domestically, he faced with considerable success the challenge of leading a very conservative traditional society, propelled by unprecedented oil-based revenues, into the modern world. Externally, he opposed Israel and communism, headed the conservative Muslim bloc, and maintained friendship with the United States. After ʿAbd al-Nāṣir's [*q.v.* in Suppl.] death in 1390/1970, Fayṣal reached an understanding with the new Egyptian leader al-Sādāt, financed Egypt and Syria in the Arab-Israeli war of 1393/1973 and participated fully in the subsequent oil embargo and in the phenomenal OPEC-sponsored oil price increases.

When shot down in *madjlis* [*q.v.*] on 26 March 1975 at the age of 70 by a youthful royal assassin, King Fayṣal's country had been set on a peaceful course of modernisation and was a major force in Arab and world affairs. Personally, he enjoyed wide respect for his astute politics, his piety, and his simple ways. He was succeeded by his brother Khālid.

Bibliography: H. St. J. Philby, *Saʿudi Arabia*, London 1955, *passim* (also other works by Philby); Amīn Saʿīd, *Fayṣal al-ʿAẓīm*, Beirut 1385/1965; G. de Gaury, *Faisal: King of Saudi Arabia*, London 1966; M. Khadduri, *The traditional (idealistic) school – the moderate: King Faysal of Saudi Arabia*, in *Arab contemporaries: the role of personalities*, Baltimore and London 1973; ʿĪd Masʿūd Djuhānī, *al-Malik al-Baṭal*, Cairo 1974; P. L. Montgomery, *Faisal ... led Saudis ...*, in *The New York Times*, 26 March 1975, 10; Faisal: *monarch, statesman and patriarch: 1905-1975*, in *Aramco World Magazine*, xxvi/4 (1975), 18-23; V. Sheean, *Faisal: the King and his kingdom*, Tavistock, England 1975 (not serious); H. Ṭanṭāwī, *al-Fayṣal: al-insān wa 'l-istarātīdjiyya*, Cairo 1975; *al-Dāra*, i/3 (1395/1975), 1-293 ("memorial number", devoted to memorials, documents, speeches, and appreciations of Fayṣal); *al-Dāra*, i/4 (1395/1975), 210-62 (an index of all Fayṣaliana in the gazette *Umm al-Ḳurā*). See also Procs. of the conference held at Santa Barbara under the auspices of the Univ. of Southern California, May 1978. (R. BAYLY WINDER)

AL-**FAZĀRĪ**, ABU 'L-ḲĀSIM (?) MUḤAMMAD, Sunnī poet of al-Ḳayrawān and contemporary of the first four Fāṭimids. His life, like that of many of his contemporaries in Ifrīḳiya, is very little known. Thus there is no notice of him in the ancient sources, unlike his grandfather Ibrāhīm (?), classed by al-Khushanī amongst the Muʿtazila; convicted of *taʿṭīl*, the "stripping away of God's attributes", he was executed for it. As for his father, ʿĀmir, ʿAbd Allāh or ʿAlī, he is classed by al-Zubaydī amongst the grammarians of the Ifrīḳiyan capital; he is said to have appropriated the sums of the *kharādj* which he had collected in the Sahel of Tunisia on behalf of the Shīʿī caliphs and to have taken refuge in Egypt. These two "stains" on Abu 'l-Ḳāsim's lineage brought him the gibes of a certain Muḥammad al-Tūnisī, who may have been, we think, his pro-Shīʿī compatriot al-Iyādī [*q.v.*]. Nearer our own time, H. H. Abdul Wahab has g a brief notice of him, from which it appears tha poet was born and lived at al-Ḳayrawān and he died in 345/956, but these are pieces of informa of little reliability since they are not based on explicit source.

Some 112 verses only of al-Fazārī's po scattered in the *Riyāḍ al-nufūs* of al-Mālikī, been recovered and put together by M. Yalao *ḳaṣīda* against the "ʿUbaydīs", but largely mad of a lively eulogy of al-Ḳayrawān and its scho a fragment of another satire against the Fāṭi but more violent in its language; and an eleg memory of al-Mammasī, one of the "85 mart of al-Ḳayrawān who fell in the ranks of Abū Y [*q.v.*]. To these gleanings should be added th verses of the *Ḳaṣīda Fazāriyya* dedicated to Manṣūr [*q.v.*] after his victory over the Khā This poem seems to owe its fame not so much to originality of its laudatory themes as to its cu prologue, viz. 33 verses in which the poet pass review the legendary heroes of the Arabic knig tradition, in a laboured parallel between these names and that of the dedicatee, as if the ashamed of his palinode, were reducing to a s minimum the eulogy of a recent adversary.

In sum, al-Fazārī is a minor poet, but a re sentative one, at the side of his compatriot Sah Warrāḳ, of the Mālikī current in urban Ifrī divided between his hatred of the Fāṭimids an distrust of the revolutionary tendencies of the " on the donkey", Abu Yazīd.

Bibliography: The poetry of al-Fazārī been edited by Yalaoui in the *Annals of University of Tunis* (*Ḥawliyyāt* [1973], 119 see also al-Khushanī, *Classes des savants de l' qiya*, ed. Ben Cheneb, 220; al-Mālikī, *Riyā nufūs*, B. N. Paris ms. 2153; Ibn Nādjī al- bāgh, *Maʿālim al-īmān*, Tunis 1320; al-Zuba *Ṭabaḳāt al-naḥwiyyīn wa 'l-lughawiyyīn*, C 1954, 272; al-Ḳifṭī, *Inbāh al-ruwāt*, No. Brockelmann, S I, 148; Sezgin, *GAS*, ii, H. H. Abdul Wahab, *Mudjmal taʾrīkh al- al-tūnisī*. (M. YALAOU

FEISAL [see FAYṢAL].

FENNEC [see FANAK].

FERGHANA [see FARGHĀNA].

FIBRE, NET [see ṢAYD].

FIDĀʾ (A., pl. *afdiya*) "redemption, repurc ransoming". The dictionaries give several mea for *fidāʾ* and its derivatives, amongst which *f* offers especial interest [see FIDĀʾĪ, FIDĀʾIYY ISLĀM]. Another word derived from the same *fidya*, appears in the Ḳurʾān to denote the which compensates for the days of Ramaḍā which fasting has not been practised (II, 180 192/196) or the impossibility of purchasing a p in paradise (LVII, 14/15). The verbal forms *tafādā* and *iftadā* are more common there *fadaynā-hu* in regard to the ransoming of Ism XXXVII, 107), but the sole occurrence of (XLVII, 4-5/4) concerns the ransoming of cap of war taken from Muḥammad's enemies: "W you come up against the infidels, smite their n then, when you have made wide slaughter an them, tie fast the bonds; then either set them as an act of grace or by ransom until the war down its burdens". The present article deals the ransoming of Muslims, prisoners or slaves by unbelievers, in the West. For the East, LAMAS-ṢU. (E

The most perfect form of *fidāʾ*, recommende

West by the Mālikī *fuḳahāʾ* as a means of redeem- believers held captive in Christian territory, is payment of this ransom in the form of pigs and ; previously submitted by *dhimmīs* to the nic community, this contribution then being oned acceptable as an element of the payment he *djizya* owed by these tributaries. But this not often happen.

ore frequently, *fidāʾ* operates on a financial s. In principle, it is the Muslim state which has obligation to provide the necessary money, icting it from public funds; however, the ransom sually put together by relations or friends of the ives, and it consists of contributions made for purpose by individuals. In 578/1182, for example, the time of the Almohad caliph Abū Yaʿḳūb uf, the town of Seville ransomed, at a price of o *dīnārs*, seven hundred of its citizens who had captured by Alfonso VIII of Castille; this ey had been raised by appeals made for this ʾ in the mosques of Seville.

ne devout individual who devotes himself lly or episodically to the ransoming of Muslims captive by infidels is called *al-fakkāk*. It is often that such an agent is able to travel alone spontaneously in Christian territory for the pose of arranging the release of captives; the idel" power tends to be uncooperative. In 1318, example, the king of Aragon rejected a request his subjects in Lorca, asking him to grant conducts authorising the free movement of *aqueques moros*" across his estates (*Registre de ncellerie* no. 244, of the *Archives de la Couronne ragon*, Barcelona, fo. 234).

practice, *fidāʾ* is often linked to a reciprocal of compensation; the liberation or ransom of stian prisoners or slaves in the hands of Muslims. act, in a case where the infidel refuses to allow Muslims whom he holds to be ransomed in any r way, Islam permits these men to be exchanged Christian captives, even if the latter are sub- ently likely to take up arms against the *dār slām*.

t the same time, one should note the appearance Christian context of an equivalent of the Muslim leemer": he is called *alfaqueque* in Castillian, in Catalan (from the Latin *exire* "to go out"). some extent, members of the Trinitarian and cedarian religious orders, of which the former e at the end of the 12th century, the latter at beginning of the 13th, may be regarded as istian *alfaqueques*. The term *al-fakkāk* thus comes enote not only the Muslim who ransoms one of brothers, but, in a more general sense, the man liberates a captive.

principle, every *fakkāk* is respected by the osing side: neither his liberty of his dignity is promised. Sometimes, however, this rule is not wed. In 772/1371, for example, a Catalan *aquech*" or "*exea*", from the island of Ibiza, was ined in Granada, although he arrived there ed with a safe-conduct from the Naṣrid sover- ; he was acting as guide to a group of Granadans m he had ransomed in the Balearic Isles and m he was in the process of returning to their patriots. The sultan ordered his release once he satisfied as to the authenticity of the official -conduct with which had been given to the alan, but he refused to set free some other istians, who had accompanied this accredited *'aquech*" to Granada.

n the liberations thus effected, the *fidāʾ* is clearly supplemented by a commercial enterprise, where the operative is inspired by the profit-motive. The agents who used their own funds to ransom Muslim slaves held in Christian lands and subsequently negotiated their return to Muslim territory, sought to profit by the operation; on their return, they repeated the process elsewhere, in the opposite direction. Very often, Jews took on the role of commercial *alfaqueques*: in 1004, for example, the Count of Barcelona granted to four Jews the right to ransom and to restore to Islamic territory Muslim captives held in Catalonia.

Most often, liberations were effected in the course of diplomatic transactions, claims and exchange of ambassadors; normally, an ambassador acted as "redeemer", where necessary retaining a specialist *fakkāk* in his entourage. Examples of liberations by exchange made in the context of these missions and negotiations are: in 713/1313, between Bougiots held as slaves in Majorca, and Majorcan slaves in Bougie; in 1321, between Catalan slaves in the Naṣrid king- dom and Granadans held captive in the lands of the Crown of Aragon; also, in 837/1434-5 between sub- jects of Alfonso the Magnanimous, King of Aragon and Sicily, held prisoner in Ḥafṣid territory, and Tunisian slaves in the lands of King Alfonso; etc.

There were other ways in which the *fidāʾ* could operate; sometimes, a Muslim captive sends for a number of co-religionists from his own land and makes them hostages, as a guarantee for the ransom which he has promised and which he himself goes to raise. This was the course followed by, for example, in Oviedo, *ca.* 287/900, by an important member of the court of Cordova, who left in his place one of his sons, two of his brothers and a nephew, who had come to the Asturias for this purpose. Sometimes, a slave concludes a "contract of liberation" (contract of "talliage") with his proprietor: either because he is authorised to collect money, or because he is hired out to a third party and is allowed to keep the supplementary payments given him by the latter when the occasion arises, or because he makes his living in one way or another, or because he receives money from home, such a captive is free from the day that he succeeds in remitting to his master the sum required within a period determined under the contract. In 703/1303, for example, two Muslim slaves in the kingdom of Valencia were authorised by their proprietor to travel round the country to raise a certain sum within ten months, demanding from their co-religionists (the free Muslims of the kingdom) "alms of precept" and "supplementary gifts". This fact is known to us from a deed drawn up by a *ḳāḍī* of Valencia in Rabīʿ I 703, preserved in the archives of the Kingdom of Aragon in Barcelona; this is a document designed to facilitate fund- raising on the part of slaves who were bearers of it, introducing them to all *fuḳahāʾ*, *ʿulamāʾ*, *imāms*, *shaykhs*, administrators, notables and other Muslims living in the territory of the King of Aragon.

Bibliography: Alarcón Santon and Garcia de Linares, *Los documentos árabes diplomáticos del Archivo de la Corona de Aragón*, Madrid-Granada, 1940, doc. 157, 402-3; Ch.-E. Dufourcq, *Catalogue du Registre 1389 de la Chancellerie de la Couronne d'Aragon (1360-1386)*, in *Miscelánea de textos medievales*, ii, Barcelona 1974, doc. nos. 151, 163, 167 and 169; idem, *La vie quotidienne dans les ports méditerranéens au moyen âge*, Paris 1975, ch. vii; Gazulla, *La redención de cautivos entre los musulmanes*, in *Boletín de la Real Academia de Buenas Letras* (Barcelona 1928), 321-42; Verlinden, *L'esclavage dans l'Europe méditerranéenne*, i, Bruges 1955; ii, Ghent 1977.

A remarkable work inspired by a ransom mission is that of Ibn ʿUthmān [*q.v.* in Suppl.], *al-Iksīr fī fikāk al-asīr*, ed. Muḥammad al-Fāsī, Rabat 1965. (Ch.-E. Dufourcq)

FIGS [see tīn].

FÎNDÎḲOGHLU, Ḍiyāʾ al-Dīn Fakhrī, modern Turkish Ziyaeddin Fahri Findikoğlu (1901-74) (he also occasionally used his original name Aḥmed Khalīl), Turkish sociologist and writer. He was born in Tortum near Erzurum in Eastern Anatolia, and graduated from the School of Posts and Telegraph (*Posta-Telgraf mekteb-i ʿālīsi*) in 1922, and also from the Department of Philosophy of Istanbul University (1925). He taught philosophy and sociology in various schools in Erzurum, Sivas and Ankara, until in 1930 he went to France on a government scholarship and obtained a Ph.D. in philosophy from the University of Strasbourg (1936), being then appointed lecturer (*doçent*) in the University of Istanbul. In 1937 he transferred to the Faculty of Economics, where he became Professor in 1941. He died in Istanbul on 16 November 1974.

Fîndîḳoghlu became interested at an early stage in literature and folk-lore, and published poems and studies on folk poets (e.g. *Bayburtlu zihni*, 1928). Later, he concentrated on research about Ḍiyāʾ (Ziya) Gökalp and Ibn Khaldūn and on problems of social change in their legal and sociological implications, and also on the co-operative movements, making considerable contributions to both these fields. From being a moderate liberal, he developed into an extreme conservative and traditionalist, and in his many articles in various periodicals, particularly in his own *İş* ("Action"), he waged a relentless war against reformist tendencies and against all innovations (e.g. he signed Fındıkoğlu Ziyaeddin Fahri instead of Ziyaeddin Fahri Fındıkoğlu, as the former was more in keeping with old Turkish usage). He joined the opponents of the language reform movement and carefully avoided all neologisms in his writings.

Fîndîḳoghlu is the author of the following major works: *Ziya Gökalp, sa vie et sa sociologie*, Nancy 1935; *Essai sur la transformation du code familial en Turquie*, Paris 1935; *Ibn Haldun'un hukuka ait fikirleri ve tesiri* ("Ibn Khaldūn's ideas on law and their impact"), 1939; *Ahlak tarihi*, 3 vols., 1945-6; *Sosyalizm*² (1965); *Kooperasyon sosyolojisi* (1967).

Bibliography: *Fındıkoğlu bibliyoğrafyası 1918-1958*, Istanbul 1959; Hilmi Ziya Ülken, *Türkiye'de çağdaş, düsünce tarihi*, ii, Konya 1966, 804-9; *Türk Ansiklopedisi*, xvi, 1968, 287. (Fahir İz)

FINDIRISKĪ, Mīr Abu 'l-Ḳāsim b. Mīrzā Ḥusaynī Astarābādī, known in Persia as Mīr Findiriskī, Persian scholar and philosopher. He was probably born in Iṣfahān, where he studied and spent much of his life. He also travelled extensively in India, and died in Iṣfahān in 1050/1640-1. His tomb is located in the Takht-i Fūlād cemetery, and this shrine is visited by many devotees throughout the year. Mīr Findiriskī was one of the most famous of the philosophers and scientists of the Ṣafawid period, respected by both Shāh ʿAbbās and the Mughal court in India, yet little is known of the details of his life. In Iṣfahān he taught the sciences, and especially the philosophy of Ibn Sīnā, above all the *Shifāʾ* and the *Ḳānūn*, and such well-known figures as Āḳā Ḥusayn Khʷansārī, Muḥammad Bāḳir Sabzawārī, Radjab ʿAlī Tabrīzī, and possibly Mullā Ṣadrā, studied with him. Yet he was far from being merely a rationalistically-orie[nted] philosopher; he was also a Ṣūfī, an alchemis[t,] profound student of Hinduism, a gifted poet and who was believed by his contemporaries to pos[sess] supernatural powers. Besides being, along with Dāmād and Bahāʾ al-Dīn ʿĀmilī, one of the m[ain] figures of the "School of Iṣfahān", Mīr Findi[riskī] was also the most notable intellectual link betw[een] the tradition of Islamic philosophy in Persia the movement for the translation of Sanskrit t[exts] into Persian in India which is usually associ[ated] with the name of Dārā Shukōh [*q.v.*].

Few works survive from Mīr Findiriskī's pen, those which do are all of exceptional inte[rest]. Perhaps the most important of his works, whic[h is] also unusual in both its theme and treatment in annals of Islamic philosophy, is the Persian *Risāl[a-yi] ṣināʿiyya*, which concerns the metaphysical s[tatus] of human society. In this work, various occupat[ions] and professions in society are placed in a hierar[chy] corresponding to the hierarchy of knowledge also of being. Another of this treatises, *Risāl[a-yi] ḥarakat*, again in Persian, deals with a refutatio[n of] the Platonic ideas upon the basis of Aristote[lian] physics. This is quite surprising, because Mīr [Fin]diriskī is the author of one of the most fam[ous] philosophical *ḳaṣīda*s of the Persian langu[age] beginning with the verse:

> Heaven with these stars is lucid,
> pleasing, and beautiful;
> Whatever exists in the world above,
> has in the world below a form.

These verses clearly confirm the reality of archetypal world.

As a matter of fact, this *ḳaṣīda* is the best-kn[own] of Mīr Findiriskī's works in Persia, and one u[pon] which his philosophical reputation rests. It [was] commented upon by such later figures as Muḥamm[ad] Ṣāliḥ Khalkhālī and Ḥakīm ʿAbbās Dārābī. In Persian answer to the question of Āḳā Muẓa[ffar] Kāshānī on whether there is analogy in quiddi[ty] he follows those who believe in the principality [of] quiddity, and is far from the position of a m[eta]physician of being such as Mullā Ṣadrā. Mīr F[in]diriskī, this contemporary of Michael Meier [and] Robert Fludd, was also widely known as an [al]chemist, and in fact was buried in an iron coffin [to] prevent his body from being stolen. He is thus author of an Arabic treatise on alchemy, as wel[l as] a Persian poem on the royal art, both of which h[ave] been discovered recently but remain unedi[ted]. Finally, he is the author of a summary of the Y[oga] *Vasiṣtha* and a voluminous commentary upon Persian translation of this work by Niẓām al-[Dīn] Pānipātī, both of which are also still unedited. T[his] commentary is without doubt one of the peaks [of] the intellectual encounter between Islam [and] Hinduism. Although only these few works surv[ive] from Mīr Findiriskī, and the manuscript of the *U[ṣūl] al-fuṣūl* on Hinduism and a history of the Ṣafaw[ids] attributed to him have never been discovered, [he] remains a vivid and lively figure in the later hist[ory] of Islamic philosophy in Persia and survives to [this] day, even in the consciousness of the common peo[ple] as one of the greatest sages of the Ṣafawid period.

Bibliography: H. Corbin and S. Dj. Āshtiy[ānī], *Anthologie des philosophes iraniens*, i, Tehr[an-] Paris 1972, 62-97 (Persian and Arabic text), 31 (French text); Riḍā Ḳulī Khān Hidāyat, *Ri[yāḍ] al-ʿārifin*, Tehran 1344 A.H.S., 267-9; Mīr F[in]diriskī, *Risāla-yi ṣināʿiyya*, ed. ʿA. Shih[ābī] hran, 1317 A.H.S.; idem, _Sharḥ-i Ḳaṣīda_, with mmentary by M. S. <u>Kh</u>al<u>kh</u>ālī, Tehran 1325/ 07; F. Mu<u>dj</u>tabāʾī, Ph.D. thesis on the comentaries of Mīr Findiriskī upon the _Yoga Vasiṣṭha_, nter for the Study of World Religion, Harvard niversity, 1976 (unpublished); S. H. Nasr, _The hool of Isfahan_, in M. M. Sharif, ed., _A history of uslim Philosophy_, ii, Wiesbaden 1966, 922-6; uḥammad ʿAlī Tabrīzī, _Rayḥānat al-adab_, hran 1311-3 A.H.S., iii, 231-2; M. Fi<u>sh</u>ārakī, ʾīr Findiriskī_, in M. Abu ʾl-Ḳāsimī (ed.), _Dja<u>sh</u>nima-yi Muḥammad Parwīn Gunābādī_, Tehran 75, 343-58. (SEYYED HOSSEIN NASR)

IRDOUSI [see FIRDAWSĪ].

IROUZ [see FĪRŪZ].

IRRĪM, PIRRĪM, a stronghold in the Elburz intains mentioned in mediaeval Islamic times eld by the Iranian native princes of the Caspian on, firstly the Ḳārinids and then the Bāwandids .]. Its exact position is unfortunately not fixed ie itineraries of the geographers, and an authority Ibn Ḥawḳal, ed. Kramers, 377, tr. Kramerst, 367, following Iṣṭa<u>kh</u>rī, merely mentions it as capital of the Ḳārinids since pre-Islamic times, re their treasuries and materials of war were ed; Yāḳūt adds to this information that it was stage from Sārī, the town of Ṭabaristān in the tal region (iii, 890; ed. Beirut, iv, 260). The rmation that Firrīm was the fortress of the inids was anachronistic by these geographers' es, since the execution of Māzyār b. Ḳārin in 840 meant the extinction of that dynasty; it ably passed soon after then to the Kāwūsiyya of the Bāwandids, who were certainly installed e in the 4th/10th century.

a the _Ḥudūd al-ʿālam_ (372/982) we have quite a iled description of the Kūh-i Ḳārin, the district hich Firrīm was situated, and of the town itself, some interesting sociological and folkloristic rvations. Much of the population of the district still Zoroastrian, but Firrīm contained Muslim igrants, merchants and artisans; the Bāwandid hbads' military camp was half-a-_farsakh_ outside town itself (tr. Minorsky, 135-6). A certain unt of Muslim settlement may have taken place early ʿAbbāsid times onwards, since Ibn Isliyār in his _Taʾrī<u>kh</u>-i Ṭabaristān_, abridged tr. G. Browne, Leiden-London 1905, 122-3, records al-Manṣūr's governor Abū <u>Kh</u>uzayma aliīmī (143-4/760-1) placed a garrison in Firrīm 00 men under <u>Kh</u>alīfa b. Bahrām. It is also rded that Māzyār established a mosque in Firrīm al-Faḳīh, 306, tr. Massé, 362). From mentions he sources on the confused fighting in northern sia amongst Daylamī and other adventurers ing the Būyid period, it seems that the Bāwandids tinued to hold Firrīm. They minted coins there legends of <u>Sh</u>īʿī type, usually acknowledging them the ʿAbbāsid caliphs and the Būyids of as their suzerains, during the second half of 4th/10th century (coins of Rustan b. <u>Sh</u>arwīn, ned ca. 353-69/ca. 964-80, and of <u>Sh</u>ahriyār b. ā, reigned ca. 358-96/ca. 969-1006, the first aps with his power contested), though their nt issues from 499/1105 onwards are all from Sārī mint (see G. C. Miles, _The coinage of the vandids of Ṭabaristān_, in _Iran and Islam, in nory of the late Vladimir Minorsky_, ed. C. E. worth, Edinburgh 1971, 443-60, and idem, in ibridge history of Iran_, iv, 373, 375).

Ione of these pieces of information enables us to with sureness the exact location of Firrīm.

P. Casanova, in _Les Ispehbeds de Firîm_, in _ʿAjabnáma, A volume of oriental studies presented to Edward G. Browne_, ed. T. W. Arnold and R. A. Nicholson, Cambridge 1922, 117-21, argued for an identification with the mediaeval and modern town of Fīrūzkūh [_q.v._] on the Tehran-Sārī highway. Minorsky, on the other hand, in _Ḥudūd al-ʿālam_, comm. 387, thought that Firrīm must have lain on the western branch of the Tidjīn-Rūd, to the south-south-east of Sārī and north of Simnān. Certainly, the geographers were not sure whether it should be attached administratively to Sārī and Ṭabaristān or to Ḳūmis [_q.v._] on the southern slopes of the Elburz, cf. Ḥamd Allāh Mustawfī, _Nuzhat alḳulūb_, ed. Le Strange, 162, tr. 158. The fact that in early 20th century Persia there was a _bulūk_ or district called Farīm in the larger division of Hazārdjarīb (H. L. Rabino di Borgomale, _Mázandarán and Astarábád_, London 1928, 56-7) may strengthen the latter identification, but is is probably only really archaeological exploration which can finally decide.

Bibliography: In addition to references given in the text, see for the coins minted at Firrīm, E. von Zambaur, in _Wiener Numismatische Zeitschr._ xlvii (1914), no. 472 (discusses all issues then extant), and idem, _Die Münzprägungen des Islams zeitlich und örtlich geordnet_, Wiesbaden 1968, i, 185-6 (coins from 225-840 (ʿAbbāsid) to 746/1345-6 (Il-<u>Kh</u>ānid)). (C. E. BOSWORTH)

FĪRŪZ <u>SH</u>ĀH <u>KH</u>ALDJĪ [see <u>KH</u>AL<u>DJ</u>IS].

FISH [see SAMAK].

FLOOD [see MĀʾ].

FLUTE [see NĀY].

FONDOUK [see FUNDUḲ].

FOSTAT [see AL-FUSṬĀṬ].

FOUAD [see FUʾĀD].

FOULBÉ [see FULBÉ].

FREEDOM [see <u>DJ</u>UMHURIYYA, ḤURRIYA].

FREEMASONRY [see FARĀMŪ<u>SH</u>-<u>KH</u>ĀNA, FARMĀSŪNIYYA].

FRIEZE [see <u>KH</u>IRḲA, ṢŪF].

FŪDHANDJ (_fawdan<u>dj</u>, fawtan<u>dj</u>_, etc.) is mint _Mentha_ L. (Labiatae). The term is of Persian, and ultimately of Indian origin (_pūdana_), which explains the various ways of transcription in the Arabic rendering. Under the name _ḥabaḳ_ mint was well-known to the Arab botanists (Aṣmaʿī, _K. al-Nabāt_, ed. ʿAbd Allāh al-<u>Gh</u>unaym, Cairo 1392/1972, 17). They describe it as a fragrant plant with an acrid taste, square-sectioned stalk and leaves similar to those of the willow. It often grows near water and resembles the water-mint, called _nammām_. The Beduins considered it as a means to check in both man and animal the longing for coitus (Abū Ḥanīfa al-Dīnawarī, _The book of plants_, ed. D. Lewin, Uppsala-Wiesbaden, 1953, no. 247, and _Le dictionnaire botanique_, ed. M. Hamidullah, Cairo 1973, no. 840).

The Arabic nomenclature of the mint is abundant, as was already the Greek one, but it is rather confused, and so the identification of the individual kinds is made considerably difficult. Ibn Dju<u>l</u>djul [_q.v._] of Cordoba equates the καλαμίνθη of Dioscorides, which appears as _ḳālāminthī_ (and variants) in Stephanos-Ḥunayn, with _fū<u>dh</u>an<u>dj</u>_ (see Anonymous, Nuruosmaniye 3589, fol. 99a-b) and knows the following three kinds of it: (a) _fū<u>dh</u>an<u>dj</u> nahrī_, the "river-mint", also called _ḍawmarān_, apparently _Mentha aquatica_ L.; (b) _fū<u>dh</u>an<u>dj</u> djabalī_, the "mountain-mint", also called _nābuṭa_ (< Latin _nepeta_, cf. F. J. Simonet, _Glosario de voces ibéricas y latinas usadas entre los mozárabes_, Madrid 1888, 397 f., with Mozarabic complementary forms), probably _Mentha_ *tomentella* Link; (c) *fūdhandj barrī*, the "wild mint", also known as *ghalīkhun* (γλήχων), *Mentha pulegium* L.

This simple basic pattern was completed and differentiated by later pharmacologists. For the river-mint there appear the Arabic terms *nammām*, *ḥabaḳ al-māʾ* and *ḥabaḳ nahrī*, in Egypt *ḥabaḳ al-timsāḥ*, in Andalusia the Mozarabic *mantarāshtaruh* (*mastranto*, etc., see Simonet, *op. cit.*, 359); the last term indicates in fact another kind, namely *Mentha rotundifolia* L. In the literature of translations the river-mint probably corresponds with σισύμβριον = *sisinbaryūn* (and variants). The mountain-mint is later mostly equated with the "rocky" (*al-ṣakhrī*) and with the wild mint (according to Ibn al-Waḥshiyya in Nuwayrī, *Nihāya*, xi, Cairo 1935, 69, 7). In Mozarabic the wild mint is called *bulāyuh*, *fulāyuh* (*poleo* < Latin *pulegium*, German *Polei*, see Simonet, *op. cit.*, 452), and also *ghubayrāʾ* or *ʿirmiḍ*. To this should be added above all the "cultivated mint" (*fūdhandj bustānī*), that is, the pepper-mint, *Mentha piperita*, the ἡδύοσμον *īdiyāsmun* of the literature of translation, well-known and favoured as *naʿnaʿ* or *nuʿnuʿ*. Other kinds are also mentioned, which can be omitted here; they are not at all to be connected with the genus mint (like *fayṭal*), or only with some restriction (like *ṣufayrāʾ*).

As still today, mint had a many-sided medicinal effect, above all from the menthol contained in the volatile oil of the leaves of the peppermint. For the preparation of fragrant peppermint tea, Ibn Waḥshiyya (in Nuwayrī, *op. cit.*, 70) recommends a method which is based upon all kinds of superstitious notions. The juice of the river-mint, taken with honey, has a strong heating and sweat-producing effect; taken with water, it helps against shooting pains and sciatica, promotes menstruation, drives off the tape-worm and is useful against jaundice since it opens up the sluggishness of the liver. Mountain-mint dilutes thick and stickly fluids which accumulate in the breast or lungs, and secretes them. Peppermint, taken with vinegar, does away with nausea and vomiting and checks haemorrhages. On the specific effect of menthol is based its use, common until now, for diarrhoea, gripes, flatulence and, above all, catarrh of the respiratory tubes. A few verses praising the fragrant peppermint tea are found in Nuwayrī, *op. cit.*, 71 f.

Bibliography: (besides the titles already mentioned): Dioscorides, *De materia medica*, ed. Wellmann, ii, Berlin 1906, 40-8 = lib. iii, 31-5; *La "Materia médica" de Dioscorides* (Arabic tr. and ed. Dubler and Terés, Tetuán 1952, 253-6; Rāzī, *Ḥāwī*, xxi, Ḥaydarābād 1388/1968, 243-51 (no. 621), with many quotations and recipes; *Die pharmakolog. Grundsätze des Abu Mansur ... Harawi*, tr. A. Ch. Achundow, Halle 1893, 238 f.; Ibn al-Djazzār, *Iʿtimad*, Ms. Ayasofya 3564, fols. 83a-84a; Zahrāwī, *Taṣrīf*, Ms. Beşir Ağa 502, fol. 508b, 29-32; Ibn Sīnā, *Ḳānūn* (Būlāḳ) i, 409 f.; Bīrūnī, *Ṣaydala*, ed. H. M. Saʿīd, Karachi 1973, Arab. 296, Engl. 256; Ibn ʿAbdūn, *ʿUmda*, Ms. Rabat, Bibl. Gén. 3505 D, fols. 130a, 19-131a, 2; Ibn Biklārish, *Mustaʿīnī*, Ms. Naples, Bibl. Naz., iii, F. 65, fol. 78b; Ibn Hubal, *Mukhtārāt*, Ḥaydarābād 1362, ii, 157 f.; P. Guigues, *Les noms arabes dans Sérapion*, in *JA*, 10ème série (1905), v, s.v. *fandenegi* (no. 175); Maimonides, *Sharḥ asmāʾ al-ʿuḳḳār*, ed. Meyerhof, Cairo 1940, no. 309; Ibn al-Bayṭār, *Djāmiʿ*, Būlāḳ 1291, iii, 170-2, tr. Leclerc, no. 1712; Yūsuf b. ʿUmar, *Muʿtamad*, ed. M. al-Saḳḳāʾ, Beirut 1395/1 372-4; Suwaydī, *Simāt*, Ms. Paris ar. 3004, 221a-b; Ghassānī, *Ḥadīḳat al-azhār*, Ms. Ḥ Ḥusnī ʿAbd al-Wahhāb, fol. 93a; Dāwūd al-An *Tadhkira*, Cairo 1371/1952, i, 252 f.; *Tuḥfa aḥbāb*, ed. Renaud and Colin, Paris 1934, no. 325; F. A. Flückiger, *Pharmakognosie des Pfla reiches*³, Berlin 1891, 722-9; I. Löw, *Die Flor Juden*, ii, 1924, 75-8; *The medical formular Aqrābādhīn of al-Kindi*, tr. M. Levey, Mac etc., 1966, 312 f. (A. DIETRIC

FUḲAHĀʾ AL-MADĪNA AL-SABʿA, the se "jurists" of Medina, to whom tradition tributes a significant role in the formation of J. Schacht, who was especially interested in t *fuḳahāʾ*, wrote (*Esquisse d'une histoire du musulman*, Paris 1952, 28; cf. idem, *An introdu to Islamic law*, Oxford 1964, 31): "The Medinans traced back the origin of their special brand of teaching to a number of ancient authorities, died in the final years of the first and the early y of the second century of the Hegira. In a later pe seven of them were chosen as representatives; t are the 'seven jurisconsults of Medina' ... Al none of the doctrines attributed to these anc authorities can be considered as authentic. transmission of the judicial doctrine of Medina becomes historically verifiable at the same pe approximately, as in Iraq, with Zuhrī (died in year 124 of the Hegira)." It may further be no in this context, that the name of al-Zuhrī [figures prominently in the enumeration, by the ographers, of those who supposedly formed audience of the seven *fuḳahāʾ*. J. Schacht (*origins of Muhammadan jurisprudence*, Oxford 1 22 ff.; 243 ff.) is also able to show that the lis these jurisconsults, to some extent variable, finally fixed *ne varietur*, rests on no foundation, he considered that in fact it is a question of a ventional group of *tābiʿūn* mentioned for the time in definitive form by al-Ṭaḥāwī (d. 321/933 his *Sharḥ maʿānī l-āthār* (Lucknow 1301-2, i, 1 then by Abu 'l-Faradj al-Iṣfahānī (d. 356/967) in *Aghānī* (ed. Beirut, ix, 136, 145). He recogni however, that this list was definitely drawn up a earlier date, although he cites no reference in context. Now the *Fihrist* (ed. Cairo, 315) ment a work of Ibn Abi 'l-Zinād (d. 174/790-1 [*q.v* Suppl.]) entitled *Raʾy al-fuḳahāʾ al-sabʿa min al-Madīna wa-mā' khtalafū fīhi*, which creates impression that this group—whose composition been probably already fixed—was felt, towards middle of the 2nd century A. H. not only as a torical reality, but also as early evidence of doctrinal pluralism accepted by Islam, since it possible to find out divergencies of opinion f among equally-respected "scholars". The remains, however, that the seven *fuḳahāʾ* ch would appear above all else to be purveyors tradition, for whom the sources are, in the natur things, almost all the same. In addition, it justifiably be supposed that their reputation established considerably later than the time of t disappearance, since the date of death of the majo of them is not known with certainty; one m however expect it to be fixed in the year 94/712 designated precisely by the name *sanat al-fuḳa* since according to tradition a number of them said to have died in that year.

Whatever the case may be, the definitely-adop list comprises the following personalities, with reg to whom it has not been judged beneficial, follow studies of J. Schacht, to undertake researches the works of *fiḳh*:

— Abū Bakr b. ʿAbd al-Raḥmān b. al-Ḥārith ...ishām b. al-Mughīra al-Makhzūmī, a prominent ...ayshite who became blind and was surnamed ...āhib or Rāhib Ḳuraysh on account of his piety. ...abarī (ii, 272) is the only one to give him the ...e of ʿUmar, and Ibn al-Kalbī-Caskel (Tab. 23) ...tions only two other sons of ʿAbd al-Raḥman b. ...ārith. Too young to serve as a combatant at the ...tle of the Camel [see al-djamal], he remained ...ledina, where he became intimate with ʿAbd al-...ik b. Marwān, who commended him to the care ...is son al-Walīd. He passed on some *ḥadīth*s of ... Hurayra and of the wives of the Prophet to a ...ber of traditionists, among whom the most ...able would appear to be al-Zuhrī. He died in ...12-13.

Bibliography: Muṣʿab al-Zubayrī, *Nasab ...uraysh*, 303-4; Ibn Ḳutayba, *Maʿārif*, 282, 588, ...99; Ibn Khallikān, *Wafayāt*, ed. Iḥsān ʿAbbās, ...eirut, no. 117; Ibn Saʿd, *Ṭabaḳāt*, ed. Beirut ...388/1968, ii, 383; Masʿūdī, *Murūdj*, v, 132-4 = § 1889-90; Ibn al-ʿImād, *Shadharāt*, i, 104; ...awawī, *Tahdhīb*, 672-3; Ibn Ḥadjar, *Tahdhīb al-...ahdhīb*, xii, 30-2; Ṣafadī, *Nakt al-himyān*, 131.

...— Khāridja b. Zayd b. Thābit al-Anṣārī, ... Zayd (d. 99 or 100/717-19) son of the Prophet's ...etary. Appointed *muftī* of Medina, he collected ...itions from his father and passed them on, most ...bly to al-Zuhrī.

Bibliography: Ibn Saʿd, *Ṭabaḳāt*, index; ...n Khallikān, no. 211; Nawawī, *Tahdhīb*, 223; ...n Ḥadjar, *Tahdhīb al-Tahdhīb*, iii, 74-5; idem, ...*āba*, no. 2136; Ibn ʿAsākir, *Taʾrīkh Dimashḳ*, ..., 24-5; Ibn al-ʿImād, *Shadharāt*, i, 118.

...I. — ʿUrwa b. al-Zubayr b. al-ʿAwwām, ... ʿAbd Allāh (b. *ca.* 23/644, d. between 91 and ...09-18), grandson of the first caliph through ...āʾ bint Abī Bakr [*q.v.*]. He was considerably ...nger than his brother ʿAbd Allāh [*q.v.*], in whose ...vities he played no part; in fact, he avoided ...olvement in politics, but is was he who is said ...have brought to ʿAbd al-Malik b. Marwān, in ...92, the news of the defeat and death of the anti-...ph. He lived subsequently in Medina, where he ...aid to have written, on the instruction of ʿAbd ...Ialik, a series of epistles on the beginnings of ...m. He collected traditions from his aunt ʿĀʾisha, ...n his mother, from his father (?) and from Abū ...ayra and passed them on notably to his own ..., to Sulaymān b. Yasār (see below) and to al-...rī. The biographers tell that he was most cou-...ous and that he endured in silence the amputation ... foot.

Bibliography: Muṣʿab al-Zubayrī, *Nasab ...uraysh*, 245 and index; Ṭabarī, i, 1180, ii, 1266; ...n Saʿd, *Ṭabaḳāt*, index; Ibn al-Kalbī-Caskel, ...ab. 19 and ii, 575; Ibn Khallikān, no. 416; ...awawī, *Tahdhīb*, 420-1; Ibn Ḥadjar, *Tahdhīb al-...ahdhīb*, vii, 180-5; Ibn Ḳutayba, *Maʿārif*, index; Goldziher, *Muh. Studien*, ii, 20.

...V. — Sulaymān b. Yasār al-Hilālī, Abū ...ūb/Abū ʿAbd al-Raḥman/Abū ʿAbd Allāh (d. *ca.* ...718-9) *mawlā* of Maymūna, wife of the Prophet, ... passed on traditions acquired from ʿĀʾisha, Ibn ʿAbbās, Abū Hurayra and others and whose ...ience included notably al-Zuhrī.

Bibliography: Ibn Ḳutayba, *Maʿārif*, 459; ...abarī, index; Balādhurī, *Futūḥ*, 266; Ibn Saʿd, ...*abaḳāt*, index; Ibn Khallikān, no. 270; Nawawī, ...*ahdhīb*, 302-3; Ibn Ḥadjar, *Tahdhīb al-Tahdhīb*, iv, 228-30; Masʿūdī, v, 462 = § 2214; Ibn al-ʿImād, *Shadharāt*, i, 134.

V. — ʿUbayd Allāh b. ʿAbd Allāh b. ʿUtba b. Masʿūd al-Hudhalī, Abū ʿAbd Allāh, great-nephew of ʿAbd Allāh b. Masʿūd [*q.v.*], who collected traditions from his father, from Ibn (al-) ʿAbbās, from Abū Hurayra and other Companions and had a number of transmitters, in particular al-Zuhrī. He was extremely learned, according to his biographers, and he is said to have been the teacher of ʿUmar b. ʿAbd al-Azīz at Medina. He is known as a Murdjiʾite. He owes to his skill as a poet his inclusion in the *Aghānī* (ed. Beirut, ix, 135-47) and it is in the chapter devoted to him that Abu ʾl-Faradj enumerates twice (135, 145) the seven *fuḳahāʾ*, the second time with reference to a passage in which ʿUbayd Allāh is supposed to cite his six colleagues; Schacht (*Origins*, 244) believes with some justification that this is a fabrication invented for the requirements of circumstances; it seems in fact to have a mnemonic quality, like two verses (with rhyme-*djah*) quoted by Ibn Khallikān in the article on Abū Bakr b. ʿAbd al-Raḥmān ʿUbayd Allāh, who was blind, died in about 98/716-7 and was buried at al-Baḳīʿ.

Bibliography: Djāḥiẓ, *Bayān*, i, 356 and index; idem, *Ḥayawān*, i, 14 and index; Ṭabarī, index; Abū Tammām, *Ḥamāsa*, ii, 126-7; Ibn Ḳutayba, *Maʿārif*, 250, 251, 588; Ibn Saʿd, *Ṭabaḳāt*, index; Masʿūdi, *Murūdj*, v, 376 = § 2129; Ḥuṣrī, *Djamʿ al-djawāhir*, 4; Harawī, *Ziyārāt*, 94/215; Ibn Khallikān, no. 356; Nawawī, *Tahdhīb*, 400-1; Ibn Ḥadjar, *Tahdhīb al-Tahdhīb*, vii, 180-5; Dhahabī, *Tadhkirat al-ḥuffāẓ*, i, 74; Abu Nuʿaym, *Ḥilyat al-awliyāʾ*, ii, 188; Ṣafadī, *Nakt*, 197-8; Ibn al-ʿImād, *Shadharāt*, i, 114; Ziriklī, iv, 360.

VI. — Saʿīd b. al-Musayyab b. Ḥazn al-Makhzūmī, Abū Muḥammad. A true Kurayshite, this oil merchant collected traditions from his father-in-law Abū Hurayra and from other Companions and acquired a great reputation for piety and knowledge in the domain of *ḥadīth*, of *fiḳh*, and of *tafsīr*. Given the title Sayyid al-Tābiʿīn, he seems to have been preferred to the other *fuḳahāʾ* by the Medinans, who subsequently abandoned his doctrine, which was different from that of Mālik (cf. Schacht, *Origins*, 7) but was judged sufficiently important to merit a monograph by al-Dhahabī. Politically, he affirmed his desire for independence by refusing to recognise Ibn al-Zubayr, which cost him sixty strokes of the lash, then refusing to pay allegiance to the sons of ʿAbd al-Malik, al-Walīd and Sulaymān, which earned him a second flogging. His biographers also speak of his ability to interpret dreams. The date of his death varies considerably in the sources, but it is possible to pinpoint the year 94/712-13. He was buried at al-Baḳīʿ.

Bibliography: Ibn al-Kalbī-Caskel, Tab. 22 and ii, 501; Ibn Ḳutayba, *Maʿārif*, index; Ibn Hishām, *Sīra*, index; Ṭabarī, index; Balādhurī, *Futūḥ*, index; Ibn Saʿd, index; Muṣʿab al-Zubayrī, *Nasab Ḳuraysh*, 345; Yaʿḳūbī, *Historiae*, ii, 276; Masʿūdī, *Murūdj*, iv, 148, 254, 255, v, 118 = §§ 1479, 1581, 1874; Ibn Ṭiḳṭaḳā, *Fakhrī*, ed. Derenbourg, 167, 168; H. Laoust, *Ibn Baṭṭa*, 51; Harawī, *Ziyārāt*, 94/125; Maḳdisī, *Création*, index; Ibn Khallikān, no. 262; Nawawī, *Tahdhīb*, 283-5; Ibn Ḥadjar, *Tahdhīb al-Tahdhīb*, iv, 84-8; Dhahabī, *Tadhkirat al-ḥuffāẓ*, i, 51-3; Ibn al-ʿImād, *Shadharāt*, i, 102-3; Ibn Taghrībardī, *Nudjūm*, i, 228; Goldziher, *Muh. Studien*, ii, 31, 97.

VII. — al-Ḳāsim b. Muḥammad b. Abī Bakr, Abū ʿAbd al-Raḥmān/Abū Muḥammad. Grandson of the first caliph, and, as the story goes, of the last Sāsānid, because his mother was allegedly one of the three daughters of Yazdadjird (see al-Masʿūdī, *Murūdj*, index, s.v. Shahrbanū), he was adopted by his aunt ʿĀʾisha after the death of his father in 38/658. He transmitted to al-Zuhrī and to a number of other recipients traditions from his aunt and from several Companions, including Abū Hurayra. He died in *ca.* 106/724-5 at Ḳudayd and was buried at al-Abwāʾ [*q.v.*].

Bibliography: Djāḥiẓ, *Bayān*, ii, 322; Ibn Ḳutayba, *Maʿārif*, 175, 588; Muṣʿab al-Zub *Nasab Ḳuraysh*, 279; Ibn al-Kalbī-Caskel, 21; Ibn Saʿd, index; Abū Nuʿaym, *Ḥilya awliyāʾ*, ii, 183; Masʿūdī, *Murūdj*, v, 463 = § 2 Maḳdisī, *Création*, vi, 80; Ibn Khallikān, no. Harawī, *Ziyārāt*, 89/205; Nawawī, *Tahdhīb*, 5 Ibn Ḥadjar, *Tadhīb al-Tahdhīb*, viii, 3 Ṣafadī, *Nakt*, 230; Ibn al-ʿImād, *Shadharāt*, i,

(CH. PELLA

FUNERAL OBSEQUIES [see DJANĀZA].

FUR [see FARW].

G

GADĀʾĪ KAMBŌ, SHAYKH, Ṣūfī saint of Muslim India.

He was the eldest son of Shaykh Djamālī Kambō (d. 941/1535), an important Suhrawardī Ṣūfī saint, who enjoyed the status of poet-laureate at Sikandar Lōdī's court and later served the Mughal emperors, Bābur and Humāyūn as their courtier. Having completed the customary education, Shaykh Gadāʾī perfected himself in the exoteric as well as esoteric sciences of the Ṣūfī. His father then made him his *khalīfa* or spiritual successor, with permission to enrol *murīd*s or disciples in the Suhrawardī order. On Shaykh Djamālī's death, he inherited half of his father's huge fortune as the remaining half going to his younger brother, Shaykh ʿAbd al-Ḥayy, known as Ḥayātī. In recognition of his father's services, Humāyūn made Gadāʾī his courtier in place of Djamālī. Gadāʾī was also a gifted poet and musician, composing verses both in Persian and Hindi, his musical compositions in Hindi being famous during Akbar's reign.

After Humāyūn's defeat by Shēr Shāh Sūr near Ḳanawdj in 947/1540, Gadāʾī fled to Gudjarāt out of fear of the Afghāns, for the Indian allies of the Mughals had to be punished, and from there went to Arabia for the pilgrimage. On his return he remained in Gudjarāt where he was joined by his *murīd*s, some of whom belonged even to Afghān families, and he became famous in Gudjarāt for his opulent sessions of *samāʿ*.

With the restoration of Mughal rule in India in 962/1555, the political situation changed, and Gadāʾī again joined Akbar's court in the Pandjāb some time before the second battle of Pānīpat took place in Muḥarram 964/November 1556. Bayram Khān Khān-i Khānān, who had become the regent, appointed Gadāʾī as *Ṣadr* of the Mughal empire for old friendship's sake as well as for political reasons, hoping that Gadāʾī would act as a liaison between the Mughals and the Indian élite. But the Mughal historians of Akbar's reign, who generally compiled their works after the fall of Bayram Khān, are critical of Shaykh Gadāʾī, accusing him of arrogance, high-handedness and favouritism in the distribution of land-grants and stipends among the Shaykhs, Sayyids, scholars and other deserving persons. Akbar also complains in his *farmān* to Bayram Khān, issued at the time of the latter's dismissal, that one of his misdeeds was the elevation of Shaykh Gadāʾī to the *Ṣadārat* in preference to Sayyids and *ʿulamāʾ* of nobler origin. In fact, all such complaints and grievances were concocted to provide Akbar with a pretext for removing Bayram Khān f power.

According to Shaykh Rizḳ Allāh Mushtāḳī, earliest source, Gadāʾī played an important rol the beginning of Akbar's reign, and the re consulted him on every matter because of familiarity with Indian affairs. The Tūrānī nc got annoyed with him when he did not join h with them against the Shīʿī Bayram Khān, in s of the fact that he himself was an orthodox Su He retired largely from politics after Bay Khān's dismissal and settled in Djaysalmer. A a few years, Gadāʾī came back to Dihlī and s his last years as a Ṣūfī there. On his return, Al showed him much respect, most probably for past services at the crucial time of his reign, his land was also restored to him. Being weal Gadāʾī led a luxurious life; he was very fon participating in the *ʿurs* ceremonies of the saints of Dihlī, and spent much money on arran *samāʿ* sessions. He also acquired a numbe beautiful slave girls and enjoyed their compan his old age. He died at Dihlī in 976/1568-9 and buried inside the tomb of Shaykh Djamālī in I rawlī.

Bibliography: ʿAlāʾ al-Dawla Ḳazwīnī, *Na al-maʾāthir*, MS. Mawlānā Āzād Library, Alig ʿĀrif Ḳandahārī, *Taʾrīkh-i Akbarī*, also kn as the *Taʾrīkh-i Ḳandahārī*, ed. Imtiyāz ʿArshī, Rampur 1962; ʿAbd al-Ḥaḳḳ, *Akhbā akhyār*, Delhi 1914; ʿAbd al-Ḳādir Badaʾ *Muntakhab al-tawārīkh*, Bibl. Ind., Calcutta 1 Abu 'l-Faḍl, *Akbar-nāma*, ii, Bibl. Ind., Calcu Niʿmat Allāh Harawī, *Taʾrīkh-i Khān-i Djah* ii, ed. Imām al-Dīn, Dacca 1950; Niẓām al- *Ṭabaḳāt-i Akbarī*, ii, Bibl. Ind., Calcutta; I Allāh Mushtāḳī, *Wāḳiʿāt-i Mushtāḳī*, MS. Bri Museum Add. 11,633; S. A. A. Rizvi, *Relig and intellectual history of the Muslims in Akb reign*, New Delhi 1975, 53-4, 233, 228.

(I. H. SIDDIQU

GALENA [see AL-KUḤL].

GALLEY [see SAFĪNA, SHĀNIYA].

GANGES [see GANGĀ].

GANGŌHĪ, ʿABD AL-ḲUDDŪS, a promi Ṣūfī saint of Gangōh (Sahāranpūr district, U Pradesh, India). Ḳuṭb al-ʿĀlam ʿAbd al-Ḳuddū Ismāʿīl b. Ṣafī al-Dīn Ḥanafī Gangōhī was born 860/1456 and received his Ṣūfī formation at Ruda a Čishtī centre (*khānḳāh*) in the region of Aw that was organised by Aḥmad ʿAbd al-Ḥaḳḳ dawlawī (d. 837/1434) and is supposed to derive

tion from ʿAlāʾ al-Dīn ʿAlī b. Aḥmad al-Ṣābir 90/1291) of Kalyar, the founder-figure of the iyya branch of the Čishtiyya. Though nominally isciple and successor (*khalīfa*) of his brother-in-Muḥammad b. ʿĀrif b. Aḥmad ʿAbd al-Ḥaķķ, al-Ķuddūs appears to have been initiated into practices by Shaykh Piyārē, an old servant at *hānķāh*. In 896/1491 ʿAbd al-Ķuddūs migrated āhābād (midway between Sirhind and Pānīpat) e suggestion of Sikandar Lōdī's *amīr* ʿUmar Kāsī. When Bābur sacked Shāhābād in 932/ ʿAbd al-Ķuddūs moved across the Djamnā r to Gangōh where he died in 944/1537 (not in 543 as noted in *Āʾīn-i Akbarī*), and is venerated s shrine until today.

s most important disciples are his son, Rukn n Muḥammad (d. 982/1574) who collected the lotes about his father in the *Laṭāʾif-i Ķuddūsī* 1311/1894; including the reminiscences of the ān soldier Dattū Sarwanī); his chief *khalīfa*, l al-Dīn Muḥammad b. Maḥmūd Thānēsarī (d. 582), the author of *Taḥķīķ arāḍī al-Hind* ačī 1383/1963), to whom Akbar paid a visit ey, i, 17, no. 25; 1198); and ʿAbd al-Aḥad (d. 578), the father of Aḥmad Sirhindī [*q.v.*]. His lson ʿAbd al-Nabī b. Aḥmad (d. 990/1582), n as the author of two Arabic treatises (*GAL* 602), held for some time the office of *ṣadr al-* at Akbar's court. ʿAbd al-Ķuddūs wrote nentaries on Suhrawardī's *ʿAwārif al-maʿārif* Ibn al-ʿArabī's *Fuṣūṣ al-ḥikam*. The scope of his ence as a spiritual guide during the period of ition from Lōdī rule to the Tīmūrid empire is cted in the collection of his letters, *Maktūbāt-i ūsiyya* (Dihlī 1287/1870; abridged, Dihlī 1312/), some of which were addressed to Sikandar , Bābur and Humāyūn as well as to various ān and Mughal nobles. His works also include *Anwār al-ʿuyūn fī asrār al-maknūn* (Lakhnaʾū 1878; ʿAlīgaṛh 1323/1905; Lakhnaʾū 1327/) which records the sayings of Aḥmad ʿAbd al-ķ Rudawlawī; a Ṣūfī tract, *Gharāʾib al-fawāʾid* hdjdjar 1314/1897?); and two mystical treatises led *Nūr al-hudā* and *Ķurrat al-aʿyun* (MS Ethé , 14 and 16). His brief compendium of Ṣūfī iples, *Rushd-nāma* (Djadjdjar 1314/1897), ad-tes a popularised version of *waḥdat al-wudjūd* , alludes to Nathapanthī Yogic practices and des a series of Hindī verses (added in the in of MS Princeton 113). ʿAbd al-Ķuddūs was wned for mystic states under the spell of *dhikr*] which were induced by his fervent practice of ʿ [*q.v.*] and *ṣalāt-i maʿkūsa* [*q.v.*].

Bibliography: Abu 'l-Faḍl ʿAllāmī, *Āʾīn-i kbarī*, tr. Jarrett, Calcutta 1948, iii, 417; ʿAbd Ḥaķķ Dihlawī, *Akhbār al-akhyār*, Dihlī 1332/ 14, 221-4; Muhammad b. Ḥasan Ghawthī andawī, *Gulzār-i abrār* (= *Adhkār-i abrār*, tr. dū), Lāhawr 1395/1975, 239-40; Muḥammad āshim Kishmī Badakhshānī, *Zubdat al-maķāmāt*, ānpūr 1308/1890, 96-101; Dārā Shikōh, *Safīnat awliyāʾ*, Kānpūr 1301/1884, 101 (no. 118); bd al-Raḥmān Čishtī, *Mirʾāt al-asrār*, *ṭabaķa* ; Muḥammad Akram Barāsawī, *Iķtibās al-wār* (= *Sawāṭiʿ al-anwār*), Lāhawr 1313/1895, . 30; Ghulām Sarwar Lāhawrī, *Khazīnat al-fiyāʾ*, Kānpūr 1312/1894, i, 416-18; Muḥammad usayn Murādābādī, *Anwār al-ʿārifīn*, Bareilly 90/1873, 349-58; Lakhnaʾū 1293/1876, 411-20; orey, i, 967 f., no. 1279; S. Nūrul Ḥasan, *Laṭāʾif-i uddūsī, a contemporary Afghān source*, in *edieval India Quarterly*, i (1950), 49-57; Iʿdjāz al-Ḥaķķ Ķuddūsī, *Shaykh ʿAbd al-Ķuddūs Gangohī awr unkī taʿlīmāt* [Urdu], Karači 1961; S. Digby, *Dreams and reminiscences of Dattū Sarwanī*, in *The Indian Economic and Social History Review*, ii (1965), 52-80; 178-94; ʿAzīz al-Raḥmān, *Tadhkira Makhdūm ʿAlī Aḥmad Ṣābir Kalyarī*, Dihlī 1391/1972 (quoting an anonymous *Sawāniḥ-i Ķuddūsī*); S. Digby, *ʿAbd al-Ķuddūs Gangōhī*, in *Medieval India: a miscellany*, iii, ʿAlīgaṛh 1975, 1-66. (G. Böwering)

GARDEN [see bustān].

GAZ, a measure of length in use in Muslim India, considered equal to the *dhirāʿ*, which was treated as a synonym for it. Sixty *gaz* formed the side of the square *bīgha*, a traditional measure of area. Five thousand *gaz* made the length of a *kuroh* (Persian) or *krosa* (Sanskrit), the traditional measure of road-length.

The length of the *gaz* varied, often according to locality and also according to the subject of measurement (land, cloth, etc.). There is no way of knowing the standard length of the *gaz* under the Dihlī Sultans. But under Sikandar Lōdī (894-923/1489-1517) the measure known as *gaz-i Sikandarī* was about 30 inches long. The Mughal Emperor Humāyūn increased it to 30-36 inches. This measure continued in use until 994/1586, when Akbar instituted the *gaz-i ilāhī*, equal to *ca.* 32-32½ inches.

The *gaz-i ilāhī* was the standard unit of measurement during the reign of Akbar, and continued to be so during the reign of Djahāngīr. During the reign of Shāh Djahān, a slightly longer measure, the *dhirāʿ-i Shāh Djahānī*, of about 32.80 inches, was introduced for calculating road lengths; while a much smaller *gaz* was brought into use for measuring area.

Bibliography: Abu 'l-Faḍl, *Āʾīn-i Akbarī*, i, Bibl. Ind., Calcutta 1867-77; Irfan Habib, *The agrarian system of Mughal India*, Bombay 1963, Appendix A; W. H. Moreland, *India at the death of Akbar*, London 1920, 54; see also dhirāʿ.

(M. Athar Ali)

GEHENNA [see djahannam].

GEMINI, TWINS [see minṭaķat al-burūdj, nudjūm].

GENESIS [see takwīn].

al-**GHĀFIĶĪ**, Abū Djaʿfar Aḥmad b. Muḥammad b. Aḥmad Ibn al-Sayyid, Spanish-Arabic pharmaco-botanist, native of the fortress Ghāfiķ near Cordova. His dates are not known, but he may have died around the middle of the 6th/12th century. He was considered to be the best expert on drugs of his time; he elaborated thoroughly the material transmitted from Dioscurides and Galen and presented it in a concise, but appropriately complete form in his *Kitāb al-Adwiya al-mufrada*. According to Ibn Abī Uṣaybiʿa (*ʿUyūn al-anbāʾ*, ii, 133, 14), Ibn al-Bayṭār was accustomed to take this work continuously with him on his scientific journeys, together with a few others. Other writings of al-Ghāfiķī are not known.

M. Meyerhof repeatedly expressed as his belief that al-Ghāfiķī was the most important pharmaco-botanist of the Islamic Middle Ages (latterly expressed in *Sharḥ asmāʾ al-ʿuķķār. Un glossaire de Matière médicale composé par Maïmonide*, Cairo 1940, introd., xxix f.). In accordance with our actual knowledge, Ibn Samadjūn and Ibn al-Rūmiyya, both also Spaniards, will have to be put on the same level as al-Ghāfiķī. The three of them, especially Ibn al-Rūmiyya, were primarily not pharmacists but botanists; because of their exact description of plants they were copied by Ibn al-Bayṭār, not entirely—as Meyerhof thought—but to a great extent. The Arabic text of al-Ghāfiḳī has become known only in recent times; until then one had to depend on a Latin translation from which M. Steinschneider compiled a list of drugs, *Gafiki's Verzeichnis einfacher Heilmittel*, in *Virchow's Archiv für pathologische Anatomie und Physiologie*, lxxvii (1879), 507-48; lxxxv (1881), 132-71. To the manuscripts enumerated in M. Ullmann, *Medizin im Islam*, 277, should be added a valuable copy, found in Tamgrut and now preserved in Rabat, which contains the first part of the work (up to the letter *zāy*) (cf. Shaykh Muḥammad al-Fāsī, in *Trudy 15. Meždunarodnogo Kongresa Vostokovedov*, ii, Moscow 1963, 19).

Al-Ghāfiḳī arranged his collection according to the *abdjad* alphabet. Names of drugs beginning with the same letter appear twice under this letter: firstly as heading of a *ḳism fi 'l-kalām ʿalā 'l-adwiya*, in which the drugs are described in detail and the sources relating to this are mentioned, then again in a *ḳism fī sharḥ al-asmāʾ*, i.e. a short list of synonyms from various languages. As sources are mentioned Dioscurides, Galen, al-Rāzī, Abū Ḥanīfa al-Dīnawarī, Ibn Samadjūn, Isḥāḳ b. ʿImrān, Masīḥ (al-Dimashḳī), al-Ṭabarī (ʿAlī b. Rabban), Ibn Wāfid, Ibn Sīnā, an unknown person (*madjhūl*, often), Ibn Māssa, Ibn Māsawayh, al-Isrāʾīlī (Isḥāḳ b. Sulaymān), *al-Filāḥa al-nabaṭiyya*—to name only those who occur most; personal observations of the author often form the conclusion. The status of the manuscripts now known is sufficient to justify a critical edition of this important work.

A century after al-Ghāfiḳī, Barhebraeus [see IBN AL-ʿIBRĪ] composed an extract from his book on drugs under the title *Muntakhab Kitāb Djāmiʿ al-mufradāt li-Aḥmad ... al-Ghāfiḳī*, available in an edition, with translation and valuable commentary, by M. Meyerhof and G. P. Sobhy, that unfortunately reaches only as far as the letter *dhāl*, *The abridged version of "The book of simple drugs" of Ahmad ibn Muhammad al-Ghâfiqî by Gregorius abu 'l-Farag (Barhebraeus)*, fascs. 1-3, Cairo 1932, 1933, 1938. The discovery of the Ghāfiḳī manuscripts was the reason for the interruption of the edition of the *Muntakhab*.

Bibliography: (apart from the works mentioned in the article): Ibn Abī Uṣaybiʿa, *ʿUyūn*, ii, 52; Ṣafadī, *al-Wāfī bi 'l-Wafayāt*, vii, ed. I. ʿAbbās, Wiesbaden 1969, 350; al-Marrākushī, *al-Dhayl wa'l-takmila li-kitābay al-Mawṣūl wa'l-Ṣila*, ed. Muḥammad b. Sharīfa, i/1, Beirut n.d., 389; Maḳḳarī, *Nafḥ al-ṭīb, Analectes ...*, ed. Dozy *et alii*, Leiden 1855-61, i, 934, l. 14, ii, 125, 18 = ed. I. ʿAbbās, Beirut 1968, ii, 691, iii, 185; Dimashḳī, *Nukhbat al-dahr*, ed. Mehren, St. Petersburg 1866, 242; Brockelmann, I² 643, S I 891; M. Levey, *Early Arabic pharmacology*, Leiden 1973, 109-12, 152-4; M. Ullmann, *Die Medizin im Islam*, Leiden 1970, 276 f., with a bibliography of Meyerhof's numerous studies.

(A. DIETRICH)

AL-GHĀFIḲĪ, ABU 'L-ḲĀSIM [see AL-KABTAWRĪ].

GHALAṬA, a district, now called Beyoğlu, of Istanbul [*q.v.*], which occupies the broad angle of land between the lower northern shore of the Golden Horn (Khalīdj) and the Bosphorus. Historically, Ghalaṭa comprises more particularly (a) the quarters *intra muros*, i.e. the site of the (formerly) walled Genoese colony of Pera which surrendered on terms (*vire ile*) to Meḥemmed II in 1453; and (b) the post-conquest area of la "Frankish" and Greek settlement *extra m* known to the Ottomans from the early 16th ce as Beyoghlu and to non-Muslims as Pera. "Gre Ghalaṭa—i.e. the area of at least partial "Fran settlement—in the 16th to 18th centuries and sequently was bounded by what were comr regarded as its suburbs: on the Golden Hor Muslim quarter of Ḳāsīm Pasha, the site o Ottoman arsenal (*tersāne-yi ʿāmire*) and, or Bosphorus, that of Ṭopkhāne, which deve after the conquest around the state cannon-fo (*ṭopkhāne-yi ʿāmire*) outside the Porta de li barde/Ṭopkhāne ḳapīsī.

Ghalaṭa (from the quarter "of the Galat in the early Byzantine settlement of Sykai) w little significance until the aftermath of the F Crusade and the restoration of Byzantine ru Constantinople. The original concession situat a *locus apud Galatham*, granted to Genoa in lay along the lower shore of the Golden between the present-day Atatürk bridge an ferry terminus at Karaköy, with its land limits marked by what is now Voyvoda Dja and Yanīḳ Ḳapī Ṣoḳaghī. This settlement burned by the Venetians in 1296; rebuilt and rounded by a ditch; delimited by an Imperial of 1 May 1303 (translation in Belin, *Latinité*, destroyed once more by fire in 1315 (*accessi igne accidentali quasi tota Peyre combusta est*); despite a Byzantine interdiction, fortified or land side and rebuilt in the following year. established, Ghalaṭa *intra muros*, the "communi Peyre", self-governing under the authority *podestà* sent out annually from Genoa, deve rapidly to reach its final form and extent i years immediately preceding the Ottoman con of Constantinople. The first extension to the ori *enceinte* was constructed in 1348-9, enclosi triangle of steeply rising ground with its base fo by the eastern half of the long land-wall an apex marked by the massive circular Tor Christi, i.e. the Ghalaṭa Kulesi which has since been the major landmark and symbol o district.

From this time, i.e. from the middle of the 14th century, the Republic of Genoa and its c of Pera cultivated close relations with the r power of the Ottomans—cf. the letter of the Sig dated 21 March 1356 to "Messer Orcham, gr amiraio (*i.e. amīrī kabīrī*) de la Turchia", from w it is clear that the Genoese of Ghalaṭa—"li nost Peyra che sum vostri figi e servioi e veraxi"— already closely involved in commercial rela with the Ottomans and acting as their po allies against Venice and Byzantium. By the part of the same century, if not earlier, M merchants must have been a familiar sight o streets of Pera: the agreement concluded in 1387 between Murād I and Genoa (Belgrano, 1 provided for the partial exemption from cus dues of "Turks" who were engaged in comm activities in Ghalaṭa, and in the reign of Bāye Ottoman envoys were received by the *podestà*, members of leading Perote families were sent t Ottoman court as ambassadors (Belgrano, 153,

In the late 14th/early 15th centuries, al certainly in response to the first Ottoman sie Constantinople by Bāyezīd I, Ghalaṭa *intra m* took on its final form. The districts which lay in diately to the west of the original concession an extension of 1348-9 were enclosed by a wall w rom the Tower to the Golden Horn, and slightly the entire eastern quarter of Ghalaṭa, fronting Bosphorus, was also enclosed by a wall. The area of Ghalaṭa *intra muros* was thus brought pproximately 370,000 square metres, the circuit e outer wall being approximately 2,800 metres J. Gottwald, *Die Stadtmauern von Galata*, in *orus*, N.F. iv [1907], 22).

e fortifications of Ghalaṭa were further gthened and improved by the efforts of succes- *podestàs* in the last decades of Genoese rule. of the surviving or recorded inscriptions date this period (cf. the collections, made from the century onwards, by Covel, de Mas Latrie, ano, Gottwald, etc., listed in the *Bibliography*). Genoese colony at this time played an ambiguous between the Ottomans and the Christian powers, in 1444 field-guns ("canons et cullevrines") supplied from Ghalaṭa to Murād II (Wavrin, *eil de chroniques*, v, 49). Even at the last hour, the fate of Constantinople was sealed, the orities in Pera made desperate attempts to l the inevitable conquest by the Ottomans. In a semi-circular curtain-wall was built on the l side of the Tower in order to provide pro- on from artillery bombardment, but in the new of gunpowder and greatly-improved siege guns, aṭa and its defences were vulnerable from the ts to the north of the Tower. On 30 May 1453, ay following the fall of Constantinople, Ghalaṭa ndered. The last *podestà* and the principal ns were allowed to depart and the colony d into Ottoman hands.

e preliminary agreement to surrender Ghalaṭa been concluded in the Ottoman camp on 28 or ay; by the terms of the capitulation itself (cf. orga, *Le privilège de Mohammed II pour la ville Péra (1er juin 1453)*, in *Académie Roumaine, tin de la section historique*, ii [1913-14], 11-32; l'Allegio d'Alessio, *Traité entre les Génois de a et Mehmet II (1er juin 1453)*, in *Echos d'Orient*, x [1940], 161-75), Ghalaṭa, *urbem nostratium ierrimam et singularem* (Adam de Montaldo, *ensis*, "de Constantinopolitano excidio", ed. esimoni, *Atti Soc. Ligur. Patria*, x [1874], 342), placed under the authority of an Ottoman *oda*. The inhabitants were permitted to retain ir property and houses; their shops and their yards; their mills and their ships; their boats their merchandise entire; and their women and ren according to their wishes". The property e inhabitants who had fled was confiscated by state. The inhabitants were given freedom to e in the Ottoman Empire and to come and go and and sea without paying any taxes except poll-tax. The existing churches were to remain e hands of the inhabitants, who might hold ces in them, but without sounding bells or ers. No new churches were to be built. Further itions excluded the male children of the inhab- s of Ghalaṭa from the *devshirme* [*q.v.*]: "we not take their children as janissaries", and ibited the settlement of Muslims in Ghalaṭa.

der Ottoman rule, "greater" Ghalaṭa came to onstituted one of the three important *ḳāḍīlīḳs* of *bilād al-thalātha*, i.e. Eyyūb, Ghalaṭa and Üs- r; much of the area appears rapidly to have established as *waḳf*. The topography of Ghalaṭa *muros* in the Ottoman period has received derable attention (cf. in particular A. M. eider and M. Is. Nomidis, *Galata. Topographisch- iologischer Plan*, Istanbul 1944; W. Müller-Wiener, *Bildlexikon zur Topographie Istanbuls*, Tübingen 1977, *passim*), and both western and Islamic literary sources are largely known (for a survey of the latter see E. Rossi, *Galata e i geografi turchi*, in *Studi bizantini*, ii [1927], 67-74). Detailed work on the demographic, social and administrative history of Ghalaṭa in the high Ottoman period must await the full exploitation of the relevant Turkish archival materials (cf. the list for Istanbul generally in *EI*², iv, 244-5 by H. İnalcik).

The four centuries between the Ottoman conquest and the late Tanẓīmāt period were marked in Ghalaṭa by a slow but steady process of demographic change, cf. in particular, K. Binswanger, *Untersuchungen zum Status der Nichtmuslime im osmanischen Reich des 16. Jahrhunderts*, Munich 1977, 128-46. The guarantees given by Meḥemmed II for the security of the churches and the reservation of the area *intra muros* to non-Muslims were soon disregarded (e.g. by the conversion of the church of S. Paolo (e S. Domenico) *ca.* 880-3/1475-8 and the subsequent (late 9th/15th century) settlement around what thereby came to be called the ʿArab Djāmiʿi of large numbers of Muslim refugees from Spain (B. Palazzo, *Arap Djami ou Eglise Saint-Paul à Galata*, Istanbul 1946; Müller-Wiener, 79 f.). Partly-Muslim quarters also rapidly came into existence in the parts of Ghalaṭa which were not covered by the capitulation of 1453, i.e., the strips of land outside the walls along the Bosphorus and the Golden Horn and the hilly area to the north of the Tower. Two centuries after the conquest, Ewliyā Čelebi noted (*Seyāḥat-nāme*, i, Istanbul 1314, 426-36) that in the reign of Murād IV, Ghalaṭa possessed 60,000 Muslim and 200,000 non-Muslim inhabitants, divided amongst eight Muslim, seventy Greek, three "Frank", i.e. Latin, and two Jewish quarters (*maḥalle*).

Simultaneously with the establishment and growth of Muslim settlement occurred changes in the composition of the Christian population of Ghalaṭa. Elements of the Latin population were enumerated in 1580-1 as 500 *kharādj*-paying subjects of the sultan; 5,000 liberated slaves; 2,000 slaves "of all nationalities"; five or six hundred "étrangers de passage", mostly from Spain, Sicily and Venice; one hundred staff of embassies and a further six or seven thousand slaves (? including the labour corps of the arsenals at Ṭopkhāne and Ḳāsim Pasha). Many of these post-conquest Latin elements in Ghalaṭa later came to claim a more exalted pre-conquest lineage.

After 1453 the walls of Ghalaṭa lost most of their significance, and from the early 10th/16th century, settlement on the heights of Pera, e.g. by the "bey's son" Luigi Gritti, son of a doge of Venice and confidant of the Grand Vizier Ibrahīm Pasha, from whom the district took its name of Beyoghlu, increased. The envoys of Venice established themselves there early in the reign of Süleymān I, sending their despatches "da li vigne di Pera". Pera in this period was thinly populated, a salubrious locality forming an easy refuge from the plague-infested alleys within the walls (cf. T. Bertelé, *Il Palazzo degli ambasciatori di Venezia in Costaninopoli*, Bologna 1932, 81). In the building of an embassy in this quarter, Venice was to be followed in the 16th century by France and England and, later, by Holland and other European states which sent envoys to reside at the Ottoman court, a fact which, above all others, gave to Beyoghlu its special character until the 20th century.

The greatest change since the conquest to affect

Ghalaṭa occurred in the middle of the 19th century. In 1844 de Mas Latrie could still describe Ghalaṭa as "une ville franque, qui existe en entier avec son donjon, ses tours, ses églises, ses crénaux". Within twenty years, the walls, with the exception of the Tower and some fragments, were demolished and the land-wall ditch filled in. This act, together with the construction of one, later two bridges across the Golden Horn, the rapid expansion of Pera/Beyoghlu to the north in the latter part of the 19th century; the granting of a degree of municipal autonomy to Beyoghlu and the construction of a short underground railway (1884) from Karaköy to the heights of Pera and of tramways, began the final effacement of Genoese and Ottoman Ghalaṭa *intra muros* as an identifiable entity. Since then, the process has accelerated, and the development of a new economic centre of gravity in Beyoghlu on the axis of Taksim-Harbiye, when coupled with the decline into insignificance of the non-Muslim indigenous population of Beyoghlu and the demolition of older quarters for urban renewal and road-widening, has tended to erase further the differences between Ghalaṭa and the rest of Istanbul.

Bibliography: Besides the bibliography of works on Istanbul, many of which deal incidentally or in part with Ghalaṭa, cf. in particular: F. W. Hasluck, *Dr. Covel's notes on Galata*, in *Annual of the British School at Athens*, xi (1904-5), 50-62; E. d'Allegio d'Alessio, *Galata et ses environs dans l'antiquité*, in *Revue des études byzantines*, iv (1946), 218-37; idem, *Traité entre les Génois de Galata et Mehmet II (1er juin 1453)*, in *Echos d'Orient*, xxxix (1940), 161-75; idem, *La communauté latine de Constantinople au lendemain de la conquête ottomane*, in *Echos d'Orient*, xxxvi (1937), 309-17; J. Sauvaget, *Notes sur la colonie génoise de Péra*, in *Syria*, xv (1934), 252 ff.; J. M. J. L. de Mas Latrie, *Notes d'un voyage archéologique en Orient*, in *Bibl. de l'École des Chartres*, ii/2 (1845-6), 489-544; J. Gottwald, *Die Stadtmauern von Galata*, in *Bosporus: Mitteilungen des deutschen Ausflugvereins "G. Albert"*, N.F. iv (1907), 1-72; V. Promis, *Statuti della colonia Genovese di Pera*, in *Miscellanea di storia italiana*, xi (1870), 513-780; E. Rossi, *Galata e i geografi turchi*, in *Studi bizantini*, ii (1927), 67-80; Cornelio Desimoni, *Memoria sui quartieri dei Genovesi a Constantinopoli nel sec. xii*, in *Giornale ligustico di Archaeologia, storia e belle arti*, i (1874), 137-80 (in Constantinople proper); idem, *I Genovesi e i loro quartieri in Constantinopoli nel secolo xiii*, in *ibid.*, iii (1870), 217-76 (deals with the original Genoese concession in Ghalaṭa); V. Promis, ed., *Continuazione della Cronaca di Jacopo di Voragine*, in *Atti Soc. lig. di storia patria*, x (1874), 493 ff.; Rossi, *Le lapidi genovesi delle mura di Galata*, in *ibid.*, lvi (1928), 143-67; M. de Launay, *Notices sur les fortifications de Galata*, Constantinople 1864 (not seen); idem, *Notice sur le vieux Galata*, in *Univers* (Constantinople), Nov. 1874; Dec. 1974; Feb. 1875; Mar. 1875 (not seen); G. I. Bratianu, *Recherches sur le commerce génois dans la mer noire au xiiie siècle*, Paris 1929, 89-114; idem, *Actes des notaires génois de Péra et de Caffa de la fin du xiii s.*, Bucharest 1927; L. T. Belgrano, *Documenti riguardanti la colonia di Pera. Prima serie*, in *Atti soc. lig. di storia patria*, xiii (1877-84), 97-336; *2a serie*, 931-1004; G. Hofman, S. J., *Il Vicariato apostolico di Constantinopoli, 1453-1830*, Rome 1935 (*Orientalia Christiana Analecta*, no. 103); M. A. Bélin, *Histoire de la Latinité de Constantinople*, Paris 1894; Djelāl Esad, *Eski Gh*[...] Istanbul 1913; S. Eyice, *Galata ve Kulesi*, Ist[...] 1969; A. M. Schneider and M. Is. Nomidis, *G*[...] *topographisch-archäologischer Plan*, Istanbul [...] Ö. L. Barkan and E. H. Ayverdi, *Istanbul vak*[...] *tahrir defteri 953 (1546) tarihli*, Istanbul *passim*; Ewliyā Čelebi, *Seyāḥat-nāme* i, Ist[...] 1314, 426-36; Ḥüseyn Aywānsarāyī, *Ḥadīk*[...] *djawāmi*ʿ, Istanbul 1282, ii, *passim*; W. M[...] Wiener, *Bildlexikon zur Topographie Ista*[...] Tübingen 1977; *EI*², art. *Istanbul* (H. İna[...] *İA*, art. *Istanbul: Galata* (S. Eyice), both extensive bibliographies. Historical plan[...] Ghalaṭa in de Launay (reproduced in Belg[...] *Atti*, xiii, *ad finem*), Schneider and Nor[...] Djelāl Esād and Müller-Wiener, 321.

(C. J. Heywo[...]

GHANAM (a.), a femine singular noun [...] the value of a collective (with the plurals *agh*[...] *ghunūm* and *aghānīm*) designates the clas[...] small livestock with a predominance, acc[...] to the countries, of either sheep (*shā*ʾ *al-shiyāh al-ḍaʾn, ḍāʾina*), or goats (*shiyāh al-māʿiza*). Like the two other collectives *ibil* "camelidae" and *khayl* [*q.v.*] "equidae", *gh*[...] defines one of the three aspects of nomadic p[...] ral life covered by the term *badw* [*q.v.*] as[...] as an important activity of the sedentary [...] culturalist countryfolk [see filāḥa], who ma[...] periodic migrants; small livestock constitute fo[...] one group a direct and unique source of subsis[...] (*kanī al-ghanam*) with the milk, fleece, hide[...] rarely the meat and, for the others, an extra pr[...] negotiable in the fairs through the intermedia[...] the sheep merchant (*djallāb*).

The root *gh-n-m* implies the acquisition of [...] by means other than those of barter and purc[...] the synonyms *ghunm* and *ghanīma* [*q.v.*] "b[...] war trophy" set in relief this idea, excluding [...] it any allusion to the means of illegal and im[...] appropriation. Also, *ghanam* (dialect. *ghnem/g*[...] is understood in the sense of "sheep-goat [...] mony" (see Ḳurʾān, VI, 146/147, XX, 19/18, [...] 78) completing with *baḳar* [*q.v.*] "cattle" the[...] meaning of *naʿam* "livestock" (pl. *anʿām*, use[...] times in the Ḳurʾān). In Arabic, it is the equiv[...] of the Latin nouns *peculium* and *pecunia*, de[...] from *pecus* "herd". Parallel with *ghanam* and [...] the same meaning, one finds, especially in[...] Maghrib, the terms *māl* [*q.v.*] and *kasb/kisb* [...] whence the dialectal *ksība/ksīb* "flock of s[...] (cf. Berber *ulli*, from the radical *l* "to possess"[...]

Although the Ḳurʾānic verse (VI, al-Anʿām, 143) saying: "[Allah has provided you] with [...] species of animals in pairs, two for the sheep[...] two for the goats . . ." does not make any discri[...] tion between the two species, a long polemic bet[...] intellectuals reported by al-Djāḥiẓ (*Ḥayawā*[...] 455 ff.) brought into opposition the partisans o[...] sheep and those of the goat. However, this s[...] goat duality was not new, since echoes of it are f[...] in the two monotheistic religions prior to Isla[...] fact, to the degradation of the goats, the Jew[...] their rite of the "scapegoat" at the time of [...] Festival of Atonement, while Christian demon[...] saw in this animal an incarnation of the devi[...] contrast, sheep enjoyed the favour of the two [...] munities, as they were favourites of God; th[...] the ram of Abraham, the paschal lamb, the sy[...] of the mystical lamb applied to Christ and the pa[...] of the "good shepherd" wisely leading his "s[...] (Vulgar Latin *ovicula*, from *ovis*). The Arabs, e Islam, used to sacrifice a ewe (*ʿatīra*) to their ities, in the month of Radjab, whence its name *djabiyya*, by way of prayer and as an act of sgiving; while in the Maghrib and Tunisia in ular, the cult of the ram was widespread, iscent of the Egyptian cult of Ammon Ra, and s only definitively abolished by the energetic ssions of the Aghlabid *amīrs*, in the 3rd/9th ry (see T. Lewicki, *Culte du bélier dans la ie musulmane*, in *REI* [1935], 195-200; G. Ger- *Le culte du bélier en Afrique du Nord*, in *ris*, xxxv [1948], 93-124). In veneration for ıam, Islam preserves the rite of the sacrifice sheep on the 10th of the month of Dhu 'l-Ḥidj- he day of the pilgrimage [see ḤADJDJ], culmi- g at Minā [*q.v.*] called *yawm al-naḥr* "day of nter"; for all the Muslim countries it is the t of the sacrificial victims" (*ʿīd al-aḍḥā*) or t of the offerings" (*ʿīd al-ḳurbān*) and, in the rib, "the great feast" (*al-ʿīd al-kabīr*). Engaging torico-religious arguments, the apologist for the would point out the superiority of the former the goat on account of its wool, its milk and sh; furthermore, in grazing, the sheep does not the "acid tooth" of the goat which uproots the s, damages the bushes by devouring the buds reaks down buildings by its need to climb over thing, whence the proverb *al-miʿzā tubhī wa-lā* "the goat destroys and does not build". ly, the sheep with his thick fleece and covering decently conceals his posterior, whereas the p of tail of the goats, shamelessly raised, is a ıce to modesty, not to mention the goatish which makes the company of the *tayyās* -herd" shunned. Linguistically, to call some- *tays* (pl. *tuyūs*, dialect. *tīs*) was a great insult notably, in the expression *mā huwa illā tays fī* "he is only a goat in a boat", alluding to the ous and persistent smell which the animal s wherever it has stayed. On the contrary, the ame *kabsh* "ram" was eulogistic and flattering, ially in the metaphor *huwa kabsh min al-kibāsh* a chief ram", synonymous with *huwa faḥl min ūl* "he is a chief stallion", i.e. "he is a champion". st these notions is the defender of the goats *al-māʿiz*, in whom one should see, at the time, the Ḥidjāzī or the Yemenī, their respective lands being particularly abundant in goats; ch a person, the goat outclasses the sheep as by the varied products which it supplies as s vitality and resistance. In the society of herds one would say of an energetic man: *māʿiz min al-ridjāl* "he is a goat among men", as one would snub the incapable weakling *mā huwa illā naʿdja min al-niʿādj* "he is only f the ewes". Apart from the important place ied by goats' hair, as smooth (*sabad*) as flock *zz*), the equal of wool (*labad, ṣūf*) among ers, goats' hide was and still is the principal ial for containers, bags, straps, shoes, cloths overs (see the list in *Ḥayawān*, v, 485); although -breeders, the tribesmen of Muḍar remained ul to their red tents of goats' hide.

fact, this polemic, puerile as it may appear, ot solely literary, for it was the reflection of d antagonism dividing the tribes according to nds of husbandry that they practised; a series ore or less authentic Prophetic traditions es to this antagonism between breeders (see mīrī, *Ḥayāt*, s.vv. *shāt*, ii, 41-8; *ghanam*, ii, 2; *maʿz*, ii, 326-7; *ḍaʾn*, ii, 76-80, and *Ḥayawān*, 3-8) and one of the most typical says "Pride (*fakhr*) is characteristic of the owners of horses, brutal roughness (*djafāʾ*) of the owners of camels, and serenity (*sakīna*) of the owners of small live-stock". Among the great nomadic camel-breeders scorn for the small nomadic sheep-breeders was expressed by degrading proverbs such as *al-ʿunūḳ baʿd al-nūḳ* "the she-goats after the she-camels", stigmatising the misfortune of a group forced by poverty to give up camels for small livestock, for, to them, this meant really a descent, since *al-ẓilf lā yurā maʿ al-khuff* "the cloven hoof [of the small livestock] is not seen alongside the hoof [of the camel]". All these tribal oppositions arising from the kinds of husbandry were to vanish with Islam, for the position of the Prophet in favour of small livestock was very clear; having been a shepherd himself, he was pleased to say "Among all things, small livestock is an invitation to modesty and an incitement to choose poverty, leaving aside grandeur and pomp; prophets and just men were pastors of small livestock". In his eyes, the sheep-goat association was for man a divine gift and he used to say, moreover, "I recommend you to have the greatest care for sheep, clean their mucus (*rughām*) and clear their enclosure of every thorn and stone, for these animals are also to be found in Paradise", advising the shepherd to perform his prayers near the fold. Small livestock also provide him with a metaphor to express his aspirations for the Islamisation of the conquered regions by encouraging the crossing of beasts with a black fleece (= the Persians) with those with a white fleece (= the Arabs, of superior race).

In the linguistic domain, sheep and goats were defined by a considerable number of terms which the great Arab philologists of the 2nd/8th and 3rd/9th centuries attempted to gather together in specialised works, of which very few have been preserved for us. One of the first seems to be al-Naḍr b. Shumayl (d. 203/818) [*q.v.*] with his *Kitāb al-Ghanam*, the fourth volume of his huge encyclopaedia of Bedouin life, the *Kitāb al-Ṣifāt*. At a later date there are a *Kitāb Naʿt al-ghanam* and a *Kitāb al-Ibil wa 'l-shāʾ* of Abū Zayd al-Anṣārī (d. 214/829) [*q.v.*], a *Kitāb al-Ghanam* ascribed to al-Akhfash al-Awsaṭ (d. *ca.* 215/830 or 221/835) [*q.v.*], the *Kitāb al-Shāʾ* (ed. Haffner, 1895) of al-Aṣmaʿī (d. 213/828) [*q.v.*] and, finally, a *Kitāb al-Ghanam wa nuʿūtihā* of Abū ʿUbayd al-Ḳāsim b. Sallām (d. 224/838) [*q.v.*]. Ibn Sīduh gives an idea of the extent of ancient terminology concerning goats and sheep in his *Mukhaṣṣaṣ* (vii, 176-95; viii, 2-20) in the chapter *kitāb al-ghanam*, consisting of about forty pages. To this ancient base must be added the other mass of material contained in the different Arab and Berber dialects, from ʿIrāḳ as far as the Atlantic Ocean, of the tribes devoted to the husbandry of small livestock. The scanning of several lexicons dedicated to these dialects, such as that of G. Boris for South Tunisian (*Parler arabe des Marazig*, Paris 1958) or that of Cl. Denizeau (*Parlers arabes de Syrie, Liban et Palestine*, Paris 1960) allows the evaluation of a minimum of two hundred terms, the elementary word-store which each tribal group uses in the exercise of its pastoral activity; this approximate figure still remains well below the reality for some sections. Such an abundance of vocabulary sets in relief the vital character which the husbandry of sheep and goats presents for a mass of Muslim populations, sedentary as well as nomadic; this linguistic richness is not specifically that of the Arabic language, but is to be found among Turkish-speaking shepherds as well as Persian-speaking ones and Berber speakers.

In spite of this plethora of terminology, it remains hard to define precisely the many strains of sheep and goats belonging to the Arabs and other Islamised peoples, just as in the West the zoötechnicians have had some difficulty in unravelling the skeins of the domestic strains of the sheep (*Ovis aries*), undoubtedly descended from an oriental wild sheep (*Ovis ammon*), as well as those of the goat (*Capra hircus*), possibly a descendant of the Aegagrus or Pasang (*Capra ibex aegagrus*), as these two species are naturally polymorphs. Among the sheep one can distinguish, according to the language and in a very general manner, the strains with a large fatty tail (*alya*) or Barbary sheep (= from Barbary or the Maghrib), those with a long, non-fatty tail, those with long hoofs peculiar to India and Guinea and from which derive the strains of Northern Europe and, finally, those of Spain with the "merinos" introduced from the Maghrib under the dynasty of the Marīnids whose Hispanicised name it has kept. All these strains are subdivided, according to the desired aim of their breeding, into wool sheep and dairy sheep; the sheep kept for its meat, despite the absolute legality of the consumption of its flesh, has not attained in the lands of Islam the importance that it has attained in feeding Western Christendom.

On the subject of zoological strains, the Arab authors and al-Djāḥiẓ in particular (*Ḥayawān*, v, and vi, *passim*, see index), speak only of a few, especially in Arabia, the most widespread being distinguished by some typical anatomical anomaly such as dwarfishness. Also among the species with a very foreshortened shape there is the *ḥadhaf* "the docked one" of the Ḥidjāz and Yemen with a black fleece and almost without a tail and ears; similar was the *ḳahd*, but with a russet-coloured fleece. Baḥrayn had the *naḳad* "puny beast", a stunted sheep, but a good wool producer, whose small size gave rise to the image *adhall min al-naḳad* "slighter than the dwarf sheep". In Yemen the *ḥaballaḳ* is still bred, itself a dwarf, and the *ṭimṭim* with shorn ears and with a woolly dewlap under the throat; whereas the *sādjisī* was large and its wool of a pure white, while the *djalam* of Ṭā'if, very high on its hooves, had a fleece so smooth that it appeared bald; it was of African origin. Among the strains with a fatty caudal wen, apart from the Barbary sheep (dial. *mazmūzī*), the "Caracul" [see ḲARĀ KÖL] of Central Asia cannot be omitted, with its long wavy black fleece whose lambs were frequently sacrified for their precious coat called ("breitschwanz" or "astrakhan" [see ASTRAKHĀN].

As for the goats, it can be maintained that the majority of the strains of Arabia and the Near East were of African origin. The *nūbiyya* "Nubian" and the *ḥabashiyya* "Abyssinian" goat were distinguished from each other, both large with broad, hanging ears and a short fleece. Quite similar was the *ḥaḍaniyya* (from Mount Ḥaḍan) in Nadjd and whose hair was black or deep red. The *shāmiyya* "Syrian" strain was long-haired, being related to the strains of Asia whose most renowned representative across the centuries remains the "angora" (*anḳarī*) [see ANḲARA] from the name of the great Turkish commercial centre where its "flock" (*mirʿizz, mirʿizzā, mirʿizzā'*, see *LA* under *r-ʿ-z*; *Ḥayawān*, v, 483; *Kitāb al-Tabaṣṣur*, tr. in *Arabica*, i [1954], 158, §§ 10-11) was woven (*thawb mumarʿaz*) and exported, but which came, in fact, from the herds of Armenia and the Causacus of Tibetan stock. The success which the textile "mohair" (an Arabo-English term derived from *mukhayyar* "chosen" with the co[…] ment of "hair") still has on the world marke[…] the different "camelots" (diapered, waved, […] and watered) testifies to the high quality o[…] goat fleeces and confers on them an equal ra[…] value to that of the best sheep's wools. It i[…] same with the goats of Kashmir and Tibet, w[…] silky down covered with long gander is col[…] daily by carding and woven and gives the shaw[…] India their renown.

Among the pastoral peoples, nomadic and se[…] tary, the methods of husbandry of each species […] hardly varied since antiquity, having attaine[…] experience a degree of adaptation which wou[…] hard to improve upon. For the former, the rh[…] of the seasons unfolds in a permanent ques[…] even only slightly green pastures (*marāʿī*) […] unpolluted watering places, in the steppes bord[…] the great deserts, for access to the luxuriant, jealo[…] guarded oases is forbidden to them just as th[…] the private *ḥimā* was forbidden to them in pre-Is[…] times. In Africa as well as in the East and in […] these movements are apparently organised, […] codified, according to ancestral agreements i[…] manner of customary right based on group […] cedence; there is no need to dwell on the intermi[…] conflicts which these questions of pasturage ca[…] to, especially in the period of drought. At th[…] ginnings of the agricultural zones and afte[…] cereal harvests, contracts of location of pa[…] (*sarḥa*) on the stubble and fallow can be conc[…] between cultivating owners and wanderin[…] migratory shepherds (*ʿuzzāb*). The encampme[…] *dawār* [*q.v.*] "circle of tents" is placed as ne[…] possible to a well [see BI'R], a spring or a pool of[…] the watering place (*mawrid*) indispensable fo[…] animals. The circular area delimited by the […] (*murāḥ*), whose enclosure is completed by a b[…] of thorny brushwood, assures the flock of a re[…] nocturnal security reinforced by the vigilan[…] these half-wild dogs called with precision "[…] dogs" [see KALB]. The twice-daily milking […] place after the separation of the unweaned y[…] before the morning departure of the flock for […] turage and in the evening on its return from […] watering place; in the East it is mostly the […] who perform it, whereas in the Maghrib it i[…] of the numerous women's chores (see G. S. […] *Chrestomathie marocaine*, Paris 1939, 214-18). […] fresh milk (*ḥalīb*) is immediately churned by swi[…] in the goatskin container (*shakwa*) hung on […] there is derived from it, on the one hand, butte[…] (*laban*) consumed immediately either as a dri[…] as a food or put to curdle with the rennet (*in*[…] to make a mild cheese (*djubn*) whose residual […] (*mā' al-djubn*) is given to the lambs and ki[…] incorporated in culinary preparations. On the […] hand, the fresh butter (*zubda*), unwashed […] separated from the buttermilk, is immediatel[…] in the goatskin, sometimes salted, to obtain, […] it has become rancid, preserved butter (*sam*[…] substance based on the fat and used in all […] [see GHIDHĀ']. To consume the fresh milk an[…] butter as it comes from the churn would be, i[…] eyes of the Bedouin, an unthinkable waste in […] of the three or four sub-products present i[…] milk; hence comes the interest shown in the goa[…] churn and its contents in this dialectal met[…] from the Maghrib *yeddoh fī sh-shekwa idhā mā el-lben yedjbed ez-zebda*! "He has his hand i[…] churn; if he does not draw out buttermilk, h[…] draw out butter!" to describe someone whc[…]

. a situation which is very lucrative and not tiring, and parallel to the French image "avoir é un bon fromage" (cf. American English "He ie a big cheese").
art from the two daily necessities of the watering the milking, the shepherd's year numbers al major activities for the life and survival of and beasts. First, at the beginning of winter, is the shearing (*djazza*) of the wool-bearers and earer (*djazzāz*) has to know how to manage the s (*djalam*) with dexterity and rapidity on the al, while it is held on the ground; the mass of obtained (*djazīza*) will serve as exchange ncy in the oases for utensils and durable food- (dates, sugar, flour etc.). Another crucial l and, perhaps, the most harrassing for those nsible for the flock who have to stay awake day ight, is that of the parturition (*nitādj*) of the ant females with all the care demanded by ers and newborn, lambs and kids being confused e beginning under the names *sakhla* (pl. *sakhl*, ', *sukhlān*) and *bahma* (pl. *baham, bihām*). The , as they grow, take on different names whose n of nomenclature will not be treated exhausti- here, as it varies from one region to another. If th threatens to be difficult and may endanger fe of the female in labour and that of the young, is no hesitation in practising a Caesarian n and the offspring saved is called *ḥullān*, *n*. In ancient terminology, the distinction en lamb and kid only appeared clearly at the f weaning (*fiṭām*) around four or five months. then, the young lamb-kid (*badhadj, farīr, furār*, *r*), is left to its mother, but when it is over months, the teats are progressively taken from ding by their being forbidden it, the maternal maries being enclosed in a bag (*shamla, shımāl*), may be made of a hedgehog skin [see ḲUN-]; a gag (*faṭṭāma*) is also used, applied to the le of the young in the company of its mother. e hours of milking the young are kept apart. weaning, the kid becomes a *djafr* (pl. *djifār*) the lamb *kharūf* (pl. *khirfān*) and, before it is year old, the sex is distinguished, with *djady* *ʿuṭʿuṭ* for the he-kid, *ʿanāḳ* for the she-kid, *l* and *immar* (dial. *ʿallūsh*) for the he-lamb and and *immara* for the she-lamb. When one year assed, with the goats, the male is the *ʿatūd* e *ʿarīḍ*, then, around two years, the *djadhaʿ* or whereas the female becomes *ʿanz* or *ṣafiyya*; essively each of them are called *thanī, rabāʿī*, and after seven years, *sāligh*. The he-goat s, in the dialects, the *ʿatrūs*. As for the sheep, similar terminological graduation, one arrives e *kabsh* for the ram and the *naʿdja* for the repro- ve ewe; castration of the males is not always ised, for it is proscribed by Ḳurʾānic law and e-lambs and kids remaining are taken, in the of the *djallāb*, to the abattoirs (*madjzar* pl. *īzir*) of the urban centres or delivered directly e butcher (*ḳaṣṣāb*) of the nearest village. Those supply the feasts and ceremonies of the tribal are only an infinitesimal part.
cording to the social organisations peculiar to Muslim people, the groupings of sheep and can be very variable as to the number of heads estock; also, the term "troupeau" (French) and k" (English), without numerical precision, do ave a direct correspondent in Arabic. The small y flock of ten to forty animals (*ḳaṭīʿ*, dial. , *ḳaṭʿa, nūba*) is called *fizr*, if there are only p, and *ṣubba*, if there are only goats. With the hundred, one speaks of *ḳīnā* of sheep and *ghīnā* or *ḳawṭ* of goats. With two hundred, it is the *khiṭr* and above that the *waḳīr* without distinction of species. The joining together, for common needs, of several *waḳīr* with their dogs and carrier donkeys forms a *firḳ* or a *mughnam*, which may number several thousand head; such a moving mass can be described further as a *ghanam mughannama* (comp. "a sea of sheep and goats") and with this idea of multitude it will be said, *aḍʿana 'l-ḳawm wa-amʿaza* "the group is very rich in sheep and goats".

Equally highly variable is the condition of the pastor (*rāʿī*, dial. *sāriḥ*, Berber *ameksa, amaḍan*), shepherd or goatherd, or most often, both at once, according to the framework of the society in which he is integrated. Among the sedentaries, a youth suffices to guard the few beasts of the family circle, but, in some villages, the livestock of each is gathered into a single flock which may be quite large, each animal bearing the mark of its owner, and they also have recourse to a professional shepherd. He is engaged under a renewable seasonal contract covering two seasons (*kamāla*, either summer-autumn, or winter-spring) and he is paid mainly in kind. On the day of his engagement he receives a small sum as a deposit, the outer garment (*ʿabāʾ, burnus*, Morocco *selhām*) indispensable against inclement weather, a large woollen haversack (*kurz, ʿamāra*) to carry his personal possessions and, also, for those of the newborn who may arrive during the journey for pasture, and a crook (*ʿukkāz, ḥanfa*) which can be a strong club as a defensive weapon. He is assured of daily food and at the expiry of his contract, he has the right to twenty lambs and kids (*riḍāya*). In the case of his contract not being renewed, he gives back the deposit, the cloak and the haversack. In fact, the good shepherd is automatically re-employed and his services for the same employer can last a lifetime (see Colin, *Chrestomathie marocaine*, 216 ff.).

However small a flock may be, the shepherd has to be vigilant at all times; he must prevent the animals from trespassing on the cultivated lands, round up the stragglers, ward off every danger from predatory carnivores and thieves, assist a female in her labour and take care of the newborn. He is bound to compensate for every animal that dies through his negligence, but if a wolf or lion or panther kills it despite his intervention, he is cleared, if he can bring the carcase (*biṭāna*) to justify himself. This last clause hardly functions nowadays where governments have practically eliminated the insecurity reigning in the isolated regions, but the danger from thefts has not entirely disappeared. In addition to his dog, the shepherd may have the help of a youngster (*rassāl*) to keep the young apart while their mothers are milked or to lead the animals in small groups to the watering place. It is in this school that the boys learn the craft. Even among his flock the shepherd finds auxiliary help with, on the one hand, the "leader" (*dalūl, marīʿ, marīr*) wearing the chief's alfa collar (*shabbāḥ, shaband*), and old ram or billy-goat whom the flock follows blindly in ranks fleece against fleece and, on the other hand, the "haversack bearer" (*karrāz*), whose solid horns scarcely suffer from this extra burden. In the evening, the flock having returned to its covered or open fold (*zarb, zarība, marḳad, ḥaẓīra, ṣīra*), the shepherd goes to eat with his master and returns to sleep among his animals. They, confident in the man, obey his orders expressed by fixed onomatopaeic calls such as *birbir*! to gather them together, *sikk*!, *ikht*!, *ḥerr*!, *tītī*!, *terr*! to urge them on, *hish*!, *ḳahḳah*!, *taḥtaḥ*!, to stop them and *hirhir*! to invite them to the water. Contrary to the usage in Christendom, the animals of flocks, in Islam, do not wear bells.

In the mountainous regions (the Atlas, Lebanon, Sinai, etc.) an annual migration takes place following the periods of the growth of herbage at high altitude. For these fixed migrations the flocks of several clans or villages are joined together and the long line of horns and undulating chines slowly climbs the slopes accompanied by the cohort of dogs, mules and donkeys charged with the food and necessary impedimenta for camps of several months. For this occasion, each owner delegates a man in charge (*ḳaʿʿād*) to coordinate and control the movements of the group and to ensure the feeding of the shepherds. This putting out to grass (*tarbīʿ*) can be prolonged for four or five months according to the atmospheric conditions encountered at the high altitudes. During the hot hours and the night, the animals are put under cover in caves (dial *ḳaṭṭīn*, *maʿzab*, *shaḳīf*) and other natural shelters.

Among the small sheep nomads, all the men are shepherds and their life is much harder than that of the sedentary shepherds, for it is linked to a constant quest for pastures and drinkable water, while having to face the merciless competition of the great camel nomads.

The condition of the shepherd of small livestock, nothwithstanding the eulogistic Prophetic traditions, concerning him, seems always to have been the object of disrepute in general Muslim opinion; to be a *shāwī* still retains a pejorative nuance (see W. Marçais and A. Guiga, *Textes arabes de Takroûna*, i, Paris 1925, 257-9, nn. 37 and 39). In the eyes of the cultivator, the shepherd passes for a pilferer, when he is not reproached with particularly shameful practices with his animal (*Ḥayawān*, v, 458). In pre-Islamic Arabia the protection of the livestock was often the task of slaves and, in the Middle Ages, this scorn for the pastor might also be reinforced by racial oppositions (see Ibn Khaldūn, *Berbers*, i, 106). Al-Djāḥiẓ cites (*Bukhalāʾ*, French tr. Ch. Pellat, *Le livre des avares*, Paris 1951, 198) this Bedouin's curse hurled at his adversary: "If you lie, may you draw milk seated" (= may Allah change your noble she-camels into vile ewes). In the Maghrib, the shepherd is in the lowest rank of the country proletariat, writes W. Marçais (*op. laud.*), lower than the *khammās* and the jobbing workman and, in the mouth of the countrywomen with their unpolished language, the supreme insult hurled at a rival is that of "maid for shepherds".

In spite of so much disgrace and by force of circumstances, the pastor of small livestock remains, in all the lands of Islam, one of the indispensable artisans, ensuring the subsistence of the rural and civic populations. Furthermore, the shepherds, constantly observing nature and the sky, and this since the domestication of the goat and sheep (the verb *raʿā* means at the same time "to pasture the flock" and "to observe the stars"), have made a great contribution through their experience acquired in the progress of the astronomy and meteorology proper to each season. To be convinced, one has only to consider the sum of precise evidence preserved, in a concise form, in the rhymed sayings that these contemplators of the heavenly vault composed for each of the twenty-eight *anwāʾ* of the year (see Pellat, *Dictons rimés, anwāʾ et mansions lunaires chez les Arabes*, in *Arabica*, ii [1955], 17-41); these sayings mention the notable influences on the flocks of the

evolution of time in the course of the twelve mo
for the craftsman, their laconicness is very te
By way of example, two of these sayings taken
the fifty best known will suffice to sketch the
contrasts of climate which the shepherd ha
endure. The first evokes the dog-days and
scarcity of water (Pellat, No. 14) in these
terms, "When Sirius rises [at the end of Jun
the morning (*safarā*), if you do not see rain (*ma*
do not give food to the she-lambs or he-l
(*immarā*) . . ." [for they will risk dying of th
The second relates to mid-December when
water becomes ice (Pellat, No. 32),"When *al-Na*
("the Ostriches", i.e. γ, δ, ε, η, σ, φ, τ, ζ, Sagi
rise, the animals stay motionless (*al-bahāʾim*) be
of the constant (*al-dāʾim*) ice, and the cold aw
every sleeper (*nāʾim*)". With this monthly gui
the constellations the shepherds regulate
migrations which, far from straying, lead
where their flocks will find the best conditio
subsistence.

Apart from the vicissitudes arising from the
weather to which the animals of the flock ar
posed, they can also be the victims of accidents
individual or collective illnesses. In the past,
the lack of effective therapeutics, the shepherds
to lament a percentage of certainly high lo
Epidemics (*wabāʾ*, *mawtan*) would occur periodi
with their terrible consequences; spontan
abortion (*ikhdādj*, *iskāṭ*, *ikhfād*), agalactia (*sh*
and sterility (*ʿuḳr*). The causes were attribu
especially to many neighbouring viruses of the
cella type entailing brucellosis or Maltese
(*ḥummā māliṭiyya*) and foot-and-mouth di
(*djilākh*, *ḥummā ḳulāʿiyya*). The sheep pox (*a*
nabkh) also ravaged them, as did coccidiosis (*dju*
bringing on diarrhoea and anaemia. Sarc
mange or "blackmuzzle" (*naghaf*), psoroptic m
(*ḳuḥāl*, dial. *bū ṭagga*), gastro-intestinal strong
and flukeworm due to the small fluke of the
(*Dicrocoelium lanceolatum*), all leading to aqu
or dry cachexia, also destroyed a good numb
animals. Microbial infections of the feet and ho
such as foot rot (*iltihāb al-fawt*) and hoof inf
mation (*ḳuwām*), which could lead to the drop
off of the horn cover and decalcification of
instep (*ʿuḳāb*, *khumāl*), condemned their immob
victims to enforced slaughter. Infections of
respiratory tubes were endemic, with pleurop
monia of goats (*ḳaṣaba*, dial. *bū farda*), pulmo
strongylosis provoking sneezing (*kudās*, *nathīr*)
mucus or glanders (*mukhāt*, *zikhrīṭ*, *rughām*)
tested by the Prophetic tradition cited ab
Finally, cases of cenurosis or turnsick (*thawal*,
bū nshīnīsh) were frequent, as were swellings (*h*
and convulvus of the oesophagus (dial. *farrās*)
to dehydration. Against this cohort of inv
enemies constituted by the microbes, the shep
would find himself totally unarmed, attemp
despite everything, some empirical treatments
the external infections. Purulent sores were
terised with a red-hot iron (*kayy*), and m
(*djarab*) and ringworm (*ḳarāʿ*) are, even nowa
treated by the application of tar (*ḳaṭrān*, *ḳir*
is with tar also that the waters of the bracki
magnesian watering place are purified (*mashadj*)
in Syria, a billy-goat or ram carries around his
a cow-horn (*baṭṭāl*) full of this substance to pr
for the hour of watering. Many other therape
sometimes extravagant, mixed with conjur
magical practices take place everywhere in I
as in Christendom, and the list would be very

while, in modern times, veterinary science is ⸱gated under the auspices of the authorities of ⸱ state, and competent services periodically ⸱ effective prophylactic measures, to the coun-⸱e by means of vaccination (talḳīḥ), disinfection ⸱r) of contaminated sites and by injection (ḥaḳn) ⸱werful medications absorbed into the body of ⸱ick patients; it can also be confirmed that at ⸱nt the flocks of sheep and goats of the Muslim ⸱tries are almost freed from the scourge of the epidemics.

⸱n has very often known how to exploit to his ⸱t the natural gentleness and docility of sheep ⸱goats, and the servility in which he keeps them ⸱s them the object of griefs with which the ram ⸱aches him in the course of the whole philo-⸱cal "colloquium" which the Iḵhwān al-Ṣafāʾ ⸱ hold with the domestic animals in their mem-⸱e Epistles (see Rasāʾil, ed. Beirut 1957, ii, 215). ⸱ct, sheep and goats had not only to feed their ⸱nator, but also to amuse him; jugglers and ⸱s performers would be seen distracting the ⸱et crowds with their "knowledgeable" (laḳina) ⸱ and goats in association with dogs and monkeys ⸱ḴIRD] in turns of balance and dance, and the ⸱an sheep (s̲h̲āt makkiyya) passed as particularly ⸱l in this kind of exercise (Ḥayawān, vii, 218). ⸱e East and the Near East the public still shows ⸱defatigable taste for ram fights (niṭāḥ), giving ⸱o bets which can reach large sums; the organ-⸱n of these fights is the affair of the kabbās̲h̲, ⸱er-selector of rams, whose lucrative profession ⸱not besmirched with the disfavour of that of ⸱goatherd (maʿāz), for it satisfied the innate ⸱on of orientals for the game.

⸱e names taken from the vast Arabic terminology ⸱rning small livestock are numerous in the ⸱ of zoology and astronomy. In the former are ⸱ ʿanz/ʿanza, designating at the same time the ⸱les of the vulture, the eagle and the houbara ⸱rd; it is also the name of the reef heron (Egretta ⸱is), while the glossy ibis (Plegadis falcinellus) ⸱knamed ʿanz al-māʾ and maʿazat al-māʾ "water ⸱". ʿAnz al-māʾ is also the trigger fish (Balistes ⸱scus) and ʿannāz "goatherd" used to designate ⸱black stork (Ciconia nigra), one of fourteen ⸱logous birds (ṭuyūr al-wād̲j̲ib) for the sporting ⸱s of crossbow shooters (rumāt al-bunduḳ) until ⸱th/13th century. As for the naʿd̲j̲a "the sea ⸱(naʿd̲j̲at al-baḥr) represents both the turn-⸱(Arenaria interpres) and the oyster-catcher ⸱natopus ostralegus), which are generally con-⸱. The great white oryx and addax antelopes ⸱MAHĀ] are nicknamed niʿād̲j̲ al-raml "ewes of ⸱ands" and the diminutive nuʿayd̲j̲a is applied ⸱rood ibis (Ibis ibis). The manatee (Manatus) is ⸱ "sea lamb" and, finally, the cattle egret ⸱ılcus ibis) is nicknamed abū g̲h̲anam because of ⸱mbiosis with the flocks which it clears of flies ⸱parasites of the fleece.

⸱astronomy, "the shepherd" is the constellation ⸱phiuchus (or Serpentarius) with the star Katf ⸱ı "the shepherd's shoulder" (= β Ophiuchi) ⸱ wrongly "Celbalrai" (kalb al-rāʿī "the shep-⸱s dog"). A similar error is that of some authors ⸱named rāʿī and kalb al-rāʿī the stars γ Cephei ⸱p, κ Cephei; the same applies to "Rigel" (β ⸱is) which is rid̲j̲l al-d̲j̲awzāʾ "Orion's foot" ⸱ot rāʿī al-d̲j̲awzāʾ. By contrast, rāʿī al-naʿāʾim ⸱ shepherd of the ostriches" corresponds to λ ⸱tarii. The constellation of the Coachman ⸱ga) is named ʿannāz "goatherd", a name

confused with ʿanāḳ al-arḍ "ground lynx" or caracol designating the star γ Andromedae. In the Coach-man, the star "Capella" (α Aurigae) answers to the names al-ʿayyūḳ "the she-kid" (= Alhayoc), al-ʿanz "the she-goat" and al-ʿatūd "the young ram" (= Alhatod). In the same constellation belong al-d̲j̲adyān¹ "the two kids" (ζ, η Aurigae) with the former (muḳaddam) and the latter (muʾak̲h̲k̲h̲ar). The first zodiacal constellation, the Ram (al-ḥamal), com-prises al-naṭḥ or al-nāṭiḥ "that which butts" (= α Arietis) which with β Arietis represents "the two horns of the Ram" (karnā ʾl-ḥamal). Finally, al-d̲j̲ady "the kid" applies, on the one hand, to the tenth zodiacal constellation, Capricorn, with the star "Algiedi" (= α Capricorni) and, on the other, to the polar star or "Algedi" (= α Ursae minoris), an abbreviation of d̲j̲ady al-farḳadayn "kid of the two young oryx" i.e. the kid of the region of β and γ Ursae minoris. One must not forget that for a thou-sand years the Pole Star was, not λ, but β Ursae minoris (for all these stars, see A. Benhamouda, Les noms arabes des étoiles, in AIEO, Alger, ix [1951], 76-210; P. Kunitzsch, Untersuchungen zur Stern-nomenklatur der Araber, Wiesbaden 1961).

Bibliography: Apart from references cited in the text, see: A. General. Les débuts de l'élevage du mouton (Colloque d'Ethnozootechnie), Ethno-zootechnie No. 21, Paris-Alfort 1977, 130 pp. B. North Africa. Le pays du mouton (public. General Government of Algeria), Alger 1893; J. Ballet, Laitage, in IBLA, xii (Tunis 1949), 203-7; L. de Barbier, Le Maroc agricole, Paris 1927; P. Bardin, Les populations arabes du contrôle civil de Gafsa, in IBLA, Tunis 1944; idem, La vie d'un douar (essay on rural life in the great plains of the High Med̲j̲erda) (Rech. Mediter., doc. 2), Tunis 1965; A. Bernard L'élevage dans l'Afrique du Nord d'après H. G. Saint-Hillaire, in Ann. Geogr., xxviii (1919), 147-50; idem, L'élevage du mouton dans la région d'Oued Zem, in Rens. Col. (1927), 349-61; J. Berque, Structures sociales du Haut Atlas, Paris 1955; idem, Aspects du contrat pastoral a Sidi-Aissa, in R. Afr., lxxix (1936), 899-911; G. Boris, Documents linguistiques et ethnographiques sur une région du Sud Tunisien (Nefzaoua), Paris 1951; R. Capot-Rey, Le no-madisme dans l'Afrique du Nord-ouest d'après P. G. Merner, in Ann. Geogr., xlviii (1939), 184-90; J. Caro Baroja, La historia entre los nomadas saharianos, in AIEA viii/35 (1955), 57-67; J. Celerier, La transhumance dans le Moyen Atlas, in Hespéris, vii (1927), 53-68; R. Chudeau, L'élevage et le commerce des moutons au Tidikelt, in Ann. Geogr., xxvi (1917), 147-9; J. Clarke, Summer nomadism in Tunisia, in Econ. Geogr., xxxi (1955), 157-67; J. Despois, La fixation des Bédouins dans les steppes de la Tunisie Orientale, in RT (1935), 347-59, and R. Afr., lxxvi (1935), 71-4; A. Djedou, L'élevage du mouton dans la région de Bou-Saada, in AIEO Alger, xvi (1958), 257-351; idem, Le travail de la laine à Bou Saada, in R. Afr., ciii (1959), 348-55; G. Douillet, Lexique des activités pastorales d'une confédération tribale du Sud Oranais (unpubl. memoir); E. F. Gautier, Nomad and sedentary folks of Northern Africa, in Geogr. Rev. xi (1921), 3-15; Native life in French North Africa, in Geogr. Rev., xiii (1923), 27-39; A. Geoffroy, Arabes pasteurs nomades de la tribu des Larbas (Algerian Sahara), Paris 1887; Hamy, Laboureurs et pasteurs berbères (29th Conference session of the Assoc. Frçse. Avancement Sciences) Paris 1900; J. Huguet, Les Oulad Nail, nomades *pasteurs*, in *Rev. Ec. Anthrop.*, xvi (1906), 102-4; A. Leriche, *Coutumes maures relatives à l'élevage*, in *BIFAN*, xv (1953), 1216-30; W. Marçais and A. Guiga, *Textes arabes de Takroûna*, Paris 1925, 257-9 nn. 37, 39 and p. 337 n 2; H. Menouillard, *Moeurs indigènes en Tunisie: la tonte des moutons*, in *RT* (1906), 117-21; idem, *L'année agricole chez les indigènes de l'extrême Sud Tunisien*, in *ibid.* (1911), 428-33; Dr. Miègeville, *Le problème du mouton au Maroc*, in *Rens. Col.* (1929), 505-20; A. de Montalembert, *L'agriculture et l'élevage au Maroc*, in *ibid.* (1910), 71-6; E. Payen, *Le mouton et la laine de l'Afrique du Nord*, in *ibid.* (1927), 349-61; A. Roux, *La vie berbère par les textes* (*Parlers du sud-ouest marocain*), Paris 1955; C. Della Valle, *L'allevamento del bestiame nel Marocco francese*, in *Boll. Soc. Geogr. Ital.* ser. 8-9 (1956), 158-79; C. Egypt. L. Keimer, *Les moutons arabes à grande queue d'Hérodote* (*iii, 13*) *et ceux d'Egypte, in BFA*, xii/2 (1950), 27-33; D. Syria. A. de Boucheman, *Note sur la rivalité de deux tribus moutonnières de Syrie, les "Mawali" et les "Hadidyin"*, in *REI*, viii (1934), 11-58; L. Krader, *The ecology of nomadic pastoralism*, in *Bull. Inst. Soc. Scient.*, xi (1959), 499-510; T. Lewicki, *Medieval Arab and Persian sources on the keeping of domestic animals among the early Slavs* [in Russian], in *Kwartalnik historii kultury materialney*, ii (1954), 444-68; E. Iran. C. G. Feilberg, *L'élevage et l'agriculture d'autrefois en Lourestan* (Cong. Inst. Scient. Anthrop. Ethnol. 2), 1939, 239-41; W. Haas, *The transformation of the nomadism of the Iranian tribes into sedentary life* (Cong. Inst. Scient. Anthrop. Ethnol. 2), 1939, 238-9; F. Turkey. Bilgemre Kadri, *Sheep raising in Turkey*, in *Ann. Univ. Ankara*, iii (1948-9), 245-73. (F. Viré)

GHANĪMAT KUNDJĀHĪ, Muḥammad Akram, poet of Mughal India and exponent of the "Indian style" (*sabk-i hindī* [*q.v.*]) in the Persian poetry of the subcontinent.

He was born at an unknown date in the first half of the 11th/17th century at Kundjāh, a small village in the Gudjrāt district of the northern Pandjāb (now in Pakistan). He was an adherent of the Ṣūfī order of the Ḳādiriyya [*q.v.*], but apart from stays in Kashmīr, Dihlī and Lahore, did not go very far from his native village, where he died in *ca.* 1106/1695. His works comprise a *Dīwān*, mainly of *ghazal*s, and a *mathnawī* poem written in 1092/1681 called the *Nayrang-i ʿishḳ* "Talisman of love", a romance set in contemporary India with mystical and symbolical overtones (*Dīwān*, ed. Ghulām Rabbānī ʿAzīz, Lahore 1958; *Nayrang-i ʿishḳ*, ed. idem, Lahore 1962, replacing Nawal Kishore texts). Aziz Ahmad has detected in the *mathnawī*'s sensuousness and sentimentality signs of Mughal decadence (*Studies in Islamic culture in the Indian environment*, Oxford 1964, 227). A. Bausani, whilst conceding this charge, has pointed out the interest of Ghanīmat's poetry as examples of the peculiarly "Indian style", and has suggested that his fondness for lengthy compound expressions echoes the enormous compound epithets of Sanskrit poetry of the *Kāvya* style, especially as Ghanīmat's century was one of considerable Muslim-Hindu cultural interaction, in which, for instance, several Sanskrit works were translated into Persian at the Mughal court (*Indian elements in the Indo-Persian poetry: the style of Ġanimat Kunǧāhī*, in *Orientalia hispanica sive studia F. M. Pareja octogenario dicata*, ed. J. M. Barral, Volumen I *Arabica-Islamica*, pars prior, Leiden 1974, 105-19).

Bibliography: (in addition to references above): Bausani, *Le letterature del Pakistane letteratura Afgane*[2], Florence-Milan 1968. (E

GHĀRŪḲA, a system whereby a debtor owner transfers part of his plot, and the rig cultivate it, as security on a loan until redemp Other Arabic terms for the same system were *ḥiyāzī* and *bayʿ bi'l-istighlāl*, and in Ottoman Tu *istighlāl* (Pakalın, ii, 97). This is the French *chrèse*. It is not identical with *al-bayʿ bi'l-wafāʾ* French *vente à rêméré*), i.e. a "conditional sale" t lender to be nullified as soon as the debt is redee a system preferred by fellahs who hesitate to with the material possession of their land. In however, the difference was small, since accordi the latter contract too the creditor often "lea the land to his debtor, i.e. the yield of the served as interest on the loan in the form of "r Both systems were rather common prior to the century because Islamic and Ottoman law dic provide for mortgages, but they did not disap after the introduction of mortgages, becaus administrative difficulties involved in the latter.

Ghārūḳa is a form of usury, and as such hibited by the *sharīʿa*. According to all four schools or *madhāhib*, a profit derived from a p belongs to the debtor and the creditor is not all to gain from it. A Mālikī Azharī has even st explicitly *wa-mā tafʿaluhu al-ʿāmma min al-ghā ḥarām* (Shenouda, 39 n. 1). The Ḥanafī sc however, has created a loophole by making it la for the debtor to cede of his own free will the p from the pledge to the creditor (*Multaḳā al-a faṣl* entitled *rahana radjulun ʿaṣīran*; *Hidāya*, xlviii, ch. 4).

Early this century, *ghārūḳa* seems to have common usage in Egypt. One of the custo systems of pledging land in ʿIrāḳ was identical the Egyptian *ghārūḳa* (S. M. Salīm, *al-Čibā* Baghdād 1957, ii, 281).

Bibliography: J. F. Nahas, *Situation é mique et sociale du fellah égyptien*, Paris 1901, 1 W. Shenouda, *De l'expropriation par voi saisie immobilière*, Cairo 1914, 36-9; G. Bae *history of landownership in modern Egypt 1 1950*, London 1962, 34-5. (G. Ba

GHASSĀL (A.), lit. "a washer of clothes also of the dead", is nearly synonymous wit word *ḳaṣṣār* (al-Khaṭīb, cf. *Taʾrikh Baghdād*, vi, In classical Arabic there are a number of term corpse-washer such as *ghassāl al-mawtā*, *g al-mawtā* and simple *ghāsil*. The modern Arabic for a washer of clothes is *ghassāl*, but the co washer (*ghāsil*) in Syria is also called *mugh*

The act of washing the corpse, putting a sh on it, attending the funeral prayers and buryin deceased are some of the obligations on all Mus according to the *Sharīʿa*. The minimum qualific of the *ghāsil* is that he must be well-versed i *Kitāb al-Djanāʾiz* (the book of funeral ritual Islamic jurisprudence. The corpse-washer is req to wash the dead body three times accordin standard Islamic practices. In the case of a fe corpse, the daughter of the deceased, a near rel or a female corpse-washer (*ghāsila*) is employe ritual washing. The corpse-washer must not loo the genitals of the deceased or divulge any know of physical deformities of the *mayyit*. It is, there necessary that the *ghāsil* should be a trusted (*a* reliable (*thiḳa*) and an honest (*ṣāliḥ*) Muslim, Ibn Ḳudāma. A tradition of the Prophet reads: the trustworthy persons wash your corpse"

hnī, ii, 379). Some individuals performed the : of corpse-washing out of an inner sense of ʼ (waraʿ), asceticism (zuhd) and observance of unna, wrote Khaṭīb al-Baghdādī.
nder normal circumstances, the male as well as le corpse-washers performed their work without interference from government officials. But ng the Fāṭimid rule in Egypt, the caliph al-im imposed a number of restrictions on outdoor vities of women, who were prevented from going of their house, from entering a public bath mām) and from asking a cobbler to make shoes hem. Consequently, every female corpse-washer sila) had to seek a special permission or license the *ṣāḥib al-maʿūna* and judicial authorities to tise her trade from the year 405/1014 onwards *al-Muntaẓam*, vii, 269). However, some writers to suggest that a similar ban on female corpse-ers was enforced for the first time in the year 867 in Egypt under ʿAbbāsid administration. *ghāsil*'s work was probably a part-time occupa-; it usually earned him an adequate wage which, ourse, varied according to capability of payment irers, who naturally came from all strata of ty. At least in one untypical case, a *ghāsil* sold garments like a *ḳamīṣ* and a *djubba* worn by a ased person and thereby earned an extra sum ght *dīnār*s, besides his usual wage, in the late lūk period (*ca.* 905/1500). The profession of the se-washer has tended to become hereditary in e countries of the Middle East until very recent s, but in non-Arab Muslim countries we do not the existence of a professional group of corpse-ers.
he *ghassāl*, washer of clothes, has been one of a p of manual workers since early Islamic civilisa-serving mostly the middle and the upper classes ociety. He had to adhere to a code of conduct ned by *ḥisba* officials. The washerman was asked to beat more than one set of clothes on his wash-stone and not to press garments against wooden s, in order to avoid damage. They were advised ash clothes in clean water and not to mix up one omer's garments with another's. However, the herman (*ghassāl*) and the bleacher often ignored code of conduct and gained widespread notoriety their untrustworthiness in mediaeval Arab ety, according to one *ḥisba* official and writer. *ghassāl*, it appears, not only washed clothes of omers but also cleaned up dilapidated sites of ʿAbbāsid city of Baghdad. During the Buwayhid od, Fakhr al-Dawla bought at a price of three rs some old stones from rings from a *ghassāl* who found the precious objects while cleaning up the ed sites of the city. One of these stones turned to be a ruby and another a turquoise and both set into a gold ring which fetched 20,000 *dīnārs* Ṭiḳṭaḳā, *al-Fakhrī*, Beirut 1966, 293-4). During Saldjūḳ period, some *ghassālūn* were arrested for alleged dishonesty. The *ghassāl*, says Djāḥiẓ, not have any surplus income, but he lived on his gre earnings, all of which he spent daily.
the modern period, the work of washing clothes been performed in Syria and Egypt by the washer-an, *ghassāla*. These poor women workers visit houses of the wealthy to wash and clean clothes earn between three and six piasters (*ḳirsh*) for garment they wash. They supply soap, washing s and their labour and in return get a cash wage well as food from their employers. The wages of ssālāt in Egypt were lower than those of Syria ing the early decades of the 20th century.

The social position of the corpse-washer (*ghāsil*) has been higher than that of the washer of clothes (*ghassāl*). This difference has been influenced by Arab and Islamic traditions. A number of statements attributed to the Prophet Muḥammad describe corpse-washing as a meritorious work which delivers the *ghāsil* from sin (cf. *al-Mughnī*, ii, 379). In contrast with this favourable position of corpse-washer, the washer of clothes had a low status, due to the servile nature of his work. The word *ghassāl* was rarely used as a name indicating profession during the classical period of Islamic civilisation. Moreover, the *ghassāl*, like other workers of despised status, such as the cupper (*ḥadjdjām*), the veterinarian (*bayṭār*), the sweeper (*kannās*), the watchman (*ḥāris*), the fishmonger (*sammāk*) and the tanner (*dabbāgh*), were denied the honour of being addressed by their patronymic (*kunya*) in Arab society (cf. Tawḥīdī, *Baṣāʾir*, Damascus 1964-6, i, 355).

Bibliography: Ibn Saʿd, *Ṭabaḳāt*, Beirut 1958, vii, 503; Djāḥiẓ, *al-Bayān wa'l-tabyīn*, Cairo 1950, iii, 191; Yaʿḳūbī, *Taʾrīkh*, Beirut 1970, ii, 281; Abū Nuʿaym, *Akhbār Iṣbahān*, Leiden 1934, ii, 299; Ibn al-Djawzī, *al-Muntaẓam*, vii, 269, x, 68; Ibn Ḳudāma, *al-Mughnī*, Cairo n.d., ii, 378-82; Ibn Bassām al-Muḥtasib, *Nihāyat al-rutba fī ṭalab al-ḥisba*, Baghdad 1968, 81, 83, 179; Ibn al-Ukhuwwa, *Maʿālim al-ḳurba*, ed. Levy, London 1937-8, 36-51; Ibn Taymiyya, *al-Ḥisba fi'l-Islām*, Cairo n.d., 22; al-Bundārī, *Zubdat al-nuṣra*, Cairo 1900, 202; Ibn Ṭūlūn, *Mufākahat al-khillān fī ḥawādith al-zamān* (*Taʾrīkh Miṣr wa'l-Shām*), Cairo 1966, i, 301-2; Djamāl al-Dīn al-Ḳāsimī — Khalīl al-ʿAẓam, *Dictionnaire des métiers Damascains*, Paris 1960, ii, 239, 459; al-Kattānī, *al-Tarātib al-idāriyya*, Beirut n.d., i, 64 (sic) (citing al-Khuzāʿī); A. Mez, *Die Renaissance des Islams*, 341-42, Eng. tr. 362; Lane, *Arabic-English lexicon*, vi, 2259; R. Le Tourneau, *Fès*, 551. (M. A. J. Beg)

GHAWTH (A.), literally "succour, deliverance", an epithet of the *Ḳuṭb* [*q.v.*] or head of the Ṣūfī hierarchy of saints. It is used of him only when he is thought of as one whose help is sought, but that, from the nature of the *Ḳuṭb*, is practically always; thus it is a normal sequent to *Ḳuṭb*. Other, however, say that the *Ghawth* is immediately below the *Ḳuṭb* in the Ṣūfī hierarchy. In Sunnī Islam, such a figure as al-Ḥasan al-Baṣrī [*q.v.*] came to be thought of as the institutor of Sunnism and the *Ghawth* of his time; and we also find an allusion to the term in the title of one of the pseudepigraphia of ʿAbd al-Ḳādir al-Djīlānī [*q.v.*], sc. the *Ghawthiyya* or *Miʿrādjiyya*, a questionnaire on Ṣūfī terminology.

Bibliography: Djurdjānī, *Taʿrīfāt*, Cairo 1321/1903-4, 109; *Dictionary of technical terms*, 1091, 1167; Lane, *Lexicon*, s.v.; T. P. Hughes, *A dictionary of Islām*, 139, s.v. *Ghauṣ*; Hudjwīrī, *Kashf al-maḥdjūb*, tr. Nicholson, 214; L. Massignon, *Essai sur les origines du lexique technique de la mystique musulmane*[2], Paris 1954, 133, 199; J. S. Trimingham, *The Sufi orders in Islam*, Oxford 1971, 160, 164. (D. B. Macdonald*)

GHAZAL.

i, ii. — See Vol. II, s.v.

iii. In Ottoman Turkish literature.

After their conversion to Islam, the Turks adopted and assimilated Arabo-Persian cultural institutions, but in literature they tended to follow the Persian type. Thus it was the Persian *ghazal* rather than the Arabic one which became a model both in Eastern (Čaghatay) and Western (Ottoman) Turkish literature. The Turkish *ghazal*, which became the most popular poetical form after the *mathnawī* [*q.v.*], is very similar to the Persian *ghazal* from the point of view of technique [see GHAZAL. ii. In Persian literature]. It is a short poem of 5-15 *bayts*, with a single rhyme. In the first *bayt*, called the *maṭlaᶜ*, both *miṣrāᶜ*s rhyme together; the last *bayt*, in which the author mentions his *makhlaṣ* ("pen-name") is called *maḳṭaᶜ*. The content is of love, mystical or real, the joys of life, wine, the beauties of nature, etc. There are also edifying and didactic *ghazals* which concentrate on *ḥikmet* [see ḤIKMA], philosophical statements on the world, human destiny and actions, such as the majority of the *ghazals* of the 11th/17th century poet Nābī [*q.v.*]. Each *bayt* of a *ghazal* is an independent unit in content, and need not be connected with the preceding and following *bayt* except by rhyme. Occasionally a *ghazal* may have a unity of subject, in which case it is called *yek-āvāz* ("one harmony"). The most commonly-used metres in the Turkish *ghazal* are *hazadj*, *ramal*, *radjaz*, *muḍāriᶜ* and *mutaḳārib*. One shortcoming of Turkish poets writing in *ᶜarūḍ* is particularly striking in the *ghazal* form. This is *imāle* (*imāla*) (the reading of a short vowel as a long one in Turkish, which has no long vowels, simply for the sake of metre), which no master of versification ever succeeded in completely avoiding, so much so that the *imāle* (considered by some as a proof of the existence of long vowels in Turkish, see *Bibl.*) ended up by being considered as an embellishment during the post-classical period. Most folk poets (*Sāz shāᶜirleri*), with rare exceptions [see ḲARADJAOGHLAN] occasionally used *ᶜarūḍ* and also wrote *ghazals* in imitation of *dīwān* poets (M. Fuad Köprülü, *Saz şairleri*², Istanbul 1962, Introd.). The *ghazal* form was cultivated in Turkish literature from the 7th/13th century until the second half of the 19th one, and then only sporadically by some modernist and neo-classicists (see Köprülü-zāde Meḥmed Fuʾād, TURKS III. *Ottoman Turkish literature*, in *EI*¹). Turkish biographies of poets (*tedhkire-yi shuᶜarāʾ*) list the names of several hundred poets who each produced a *dīwān* (the bulk of which, as a rule, consists of *ghazals*), but only half a dozen outstanding and about a dozen minor poets wrote *ghazals* which rise above the level of mediocrity and have a claim to art. Although Turkish poets (both Čaghatay and Ottoman) were inspired and influenced by classical Persian poets, it would be a superficial judgment to consider the former as blind imitators of the latter, as is often done. A common technique and limited vocabulary, and the same world of imagery and subject matter based mainly on Islamic sources, were shared by all poets of Islamic literatures (see Fahir İz, *Eski Türk edebiyatında nazım*, ii, Istanbul 1967, Introd.), and a mere parallelism of these in poets of the same or diverse languages might easily tempt one to draw easy and misleading conclusions (as e.g. by Hasibe Mazıoğlu, *Fuzuli-Hafız*, Istanbul 1962). A closer study reveals that outstanding Turkish poets of the early periods such as Ḳāḍī Burhān al-Dīn, Nesīmī [*q.v.*], ᶜAlī Shīr Newāʾī, Nedjātī, and many of the classical era like Fuḍūlī, Bāḳī, Shaykh al-Islām Yaḥyā, Nefᶜī, Nāʾilī and particularly Nedīm [*q.vv.*] and others, wrote, under common conventions, many original *ghazals* with a strong personal flavour (for a chronological selection of Ottoman Turkish *ghazals*, see Fahir Iz, *op. cit.*, i). Many Turkish *dīwān* poets, particularly Nefᶜī and Nedīm, were conscious of this originality and they expressed their own feelings in many of their *ghazals* and *fakhriyyes*. It is fair to say that outstanding Turkish classical authors manage retain their personal and their Turkish chara even though using Persian set themes, fig conceits and imagery, in the same way that Cor and Racine remained French in spite of their u Greek and Latin poetical conventions, characters plots. During the literary *Tanẓīmāt* movement o mid-19th century, the *ghazal* continued to be c vated partly by modernists like Ḍiyāʾ (Ziyā) Pa Nāmiḳ Kemāl and others, and exclusively by "neo-classicists" of the so-called *Endjümen-i shu* group (Leskofčalī Ghālib, Yeñishehirli ᶜAwnī, etc contemporary Turkish literature the *ghazal* form revived by Yaḥyā Kemal Beyatlī (1884-1958 [q who from 1918 until his death wrote a numbe *ghazals* in the language and style of some 17th 18th century poets (particularly Nāʾilī and Ne which were posthumously collected in a boo *Eski şiirin rüzgâriyle* ("With the breath of poetry"). These very popular and successful past did not go beyond being curiosities, and the *gh* form was not practised after the 1920s except b occasional traditionalist or for humourous satirical purposes (e.g. in Khalil Nihād Bozte *Sihām-i ilhām* (1921) and Faruk Nafız Çamlı *Tatlı sert* (1938).

Bibliography: M. Fuad Köprülü, art. in *İA*; Ahmed Ateş, art. *Gazel*, in *İA*, Muᶜa Nādjī, *Iṣṭilāḥat-i edebiyye*, Istanbul 1307 r 1894, 166-78; Gibb, *HOP*, i, 80; Aḥmed Ṭa *Khalḳ shiᶜirleriniñ shekil we newiᶜleri*, Ista 1928; Talât Tekin, *Ana Türkçede aslî uzun ünl* Ankara 1975. (FAHIR İ

GHĀZĪ KHĀN, Indo-Muslim milit leader. Known to Kashmīr chroniclers as Su Ghāzī Shāh Čak, he was the son of Kādjī Čak, leader of the Čaks [*q.v.*] and a powerful chief. Not is known of Ghāzī Khān's early life except tha 933/1527 Ghāzī with other chiefs defeated Mughals sent by Bābur to help Sikandar, so Sulṭān Fatḥ Shāh, against Muḥammad Shāh reigning Sulṭān of Kashmīr. Next year, however, Čaks were defeated, and Ghāzī Khān, who fo under his father, was taken prisoner. In the mi of 959/1552, he joined the Kashmīr nobles to de Haybat Khān Niyāzī and his Afghān follow Towards the end of 962/1555, he became *Wazī* Sulṭān Ismāᶜīl Shāh by setting aside his co Dawlat Čak and blinding him. Early in 963/1 Abu 'l-Maᶜālī, a turbulent Mughal noble, hav escaped from the wrath of Akbar, invaded Kash but Ghāzī Khān defeated him, and then suppre the rebellion of Kashmīr nobles, who were aga him. In the summer of 967/1560, Akbar sent K Bahādur, a cousin of Mīrzā Ḥaydar Dughlāt, w an army to invade Kashmīr, but the latter defeated at Radjaurī and then at Danaor.

In 968/1561, under the pretext that Ḥabīb Sh (964-8/1557-61), grandson of Muḥammad Shāh his own nephew, was incompetent, Ghāzī Khān him aside and himself ascended the throne, assum the title of Sulṭān Naṣir al-Dīn Ghāzī Čak and t laying the foundation of the Čak dynasty. He brave, able and a man of strong will. He suppres rebellions, established law and order and successf defended Kashmīr against the Mughals. He wa cultured man and a poet and patronised lear men; but he was also the first Kashmīr ruler introduce the practice of blinding his political ri and cutting off their limbs. In his old age he suffe from leprosy, which impaired both his health eyesight; hence he entrusted the work of the gove to his brother, Ḥusayn Khān. Later, he changed ıind and tried to recover power, but Ḥusayn deposed him and himself ascended the throne. Shāh died after four years in 974/1566-7 at the f 58.

3ibliography: the best accounts of Ghāzī ih are in the anonymous *Bahāristān-i Shāhī*, lia Office ms. 509, and in Ḥaydar Malik's *ʾrīkh-i Kashmīr*, I. O. ms. 510; see also Mohibbul san, *Kashmīr under the Sulṭāns*, Srinagar 1974; M. D. Sufi, *Kashīr*, Lahore 1948-9.

(MOHIBBUL HASAN)

ĮĀZĪPŪR (area, 1.473 sq. m.), a District e easternmost part of the state of Uttar lesh in India. It lies in the great alluvial plains ıe Ganges and extends in equal portions on r side of the river. Though one of the smallest e, it is one of the most thickly-populated and ly-cultivated districts of the state. For ad- strative purposes, it is divided into four *taḥṣīls*, ly Ghāzīpūr, Muḥammadābād, Saʿīdpūr and iniyya. Paddy, wheat, cotton, sugar and co are the traditional products of the district. āzīpūr is obviously a name of Muslim origin, the Hindu tradition, which ascribes the founda- of Ghāzīpūr town to the eponymous hero ā Gādhī, who called his stronghold Ghāzīpūr, ıo historical basis whatsoever. Though the ter- y constituting the modern District has a long ry going as far back as the days of early Indo- n colonisation, the town was not really founded about the middle of the 8th/14th century. rding to reliable local records, during the reign ultān Fīrūz Shāh, one Čakāwa Mandhāta, a ndant of the famous Rādjā Prithiwīrādj of , obtained a large tract of land at Kathāwat the present village of Ghausegunj in the *taḥṣīl* Iuhammadābād and later, building a fortress , declared himself independent of the Dihlī in. It is said that once his nephew and heir d a Muslim girl, whose widowed mother ap- d to the Sulṭān for the redress of the affront. onding promptly, the then ruling Sulṭān Mu- mad Tughluḳ despatched a band of 40 warriors r one Sayyid Masʿūd, who reached the place in 330, and in a battle fought on the site of Ghā- r town, Masʿūd slew the rebellious Rādjā. The in thereupon granted Masʿūd the estates of his uished enemy, with the title of Malik al-Sādāt ī, which gave the name to the newly-founded Masʿūd Ghāzī left behind six sons, one of whom, id Ḳuṭb al-Dīn, was married to the daughter of id Muḥammad and had himself two sons, id Dūst Muḥammad and Sayyid Yaḥyā; the endants of the former settled in the village of , while those of the latter in Nonhera, both ted in the *taḥṣīl* of Ghāzīpūr.

ɔr the greater part of the 9th/15th century, zīpūr remained part of the dominions of the ḳīs [*q.v.*] of Djawpūr, after whose decline it rted to the possession of the Dihlī Sulṭān. After battle of Pānīpāt in 932/1526, the Mughal em- r Bābur [*q.v.*] annexed Ghāzīpūr to his conquests orthern and eastern India. Ten years later, it t out of Mughal hands, following Humāyūn's at by Shīr Shāh in the decisive engagement ht at Baxar, close to the southern borders of the ict. Ghāzīpūr remained under the peaceful inistration of the Afghāns till it was recovered the Mughals in 974/1569 by ʿAlī Ḳulī Khān n-i Zamān, governor of Djawnpūr, from whom town Zamāniyya derives its name. Abu 'l-Faḍl in his *Āʾīn-i Akbarī* speaks in detail of Ghāzīpūr as being a flourishing *sarkār* in the *ṣūba* of Allāhābād. Sādāt Khān, the first Nawwāb-Wazīr of Awadh or Oudh [*q.v.*], placed Ghāzīpūr in charge of ʿAbd Allāh Khān, a native of the district, who has left his imprint on the city by his magnificent buildings, whose ruins still exist. With the taking over of the district by the British in 1781, Ghāzīpūr enjoyed undisturbed peace till the outbreak of the Sepoy Mutiny of 1857 which took a heavy toll of life and property in the eastern part of the district, bordering Bihār. Normalcy could not be restored until five months of complete confusion had elapsed.

Ghāzīpūr town, which is the headquarters of the District of the *taḥṣīl* of the same name, stretches along the north bank of the Ganges for nearly four km. Before the introduction of the railways, it used to be a centre for trade and river-traffic. Among the antiquities of the town, the most notable are the ruins of the Čihil Sutūn or "Hall of the Forty Pillars", which was the palace of the above-mentioned ʿAbd Allāh Khān, who lies buried in the garden known as *Nawāb kī Čahār Dīwārī*. Another landmark is the tomb of Lord Cornwallis, who died there in 1805; this consists of a domed structure supported on twelve Doric pillars, with a marble bust executed by Flaxman.

Bibliography: *The imperial gazetteer of India*, xii, 1908; *Ghazipur District gazetteer*, Allahabad 1909; *Census of India* 1961, xv/4, Delhi 1965.

(ABDUS SUBHAN)

AL-**GHAZZĀL**, ABU 'L-ʿABBĀS AḤMAD B. AL-MAHDĪ AL-GHAZZĀL AL-ANDALUSĪ AL-MALAḲĪ, the secretary of the sultan of Morocco Sīdī Muḥammad b. ʿAbd Allāh (1171-1204/1757-89), who entrusted to him various diplomatic missions. In 1179/1766 he was the head of a delegation sent to negotiate an exchange of captives with Charles III of Spain; he was received with great honour in Madrid, and was able to return to Morocco with a Spanish mission which made a peace treaty with the sultan and an agreement about the exchange of prisoners. In 1182/1768 he was sent to Algiers to oversee the exchange of Algerian with Spanish prisoners and accomplished this with success. However, the Spanish king, after the sultan had besieged Melilla in 1185/1771, had to renounce the terms of the treaty made between the two rulers and drawn up by al-Ghazzāl, so that the latter fell into disgrace. He retired to Fās, where he died in 1191/1777 and was buried in the *zāwiya* of ʿAbd al-Ḳādir al-Fāsī [see AL-FĀSĪ, above].

This diplomatist left behind an account of his journey to Spain called *Natīdjat al-idjtihād fi 'l-muhādana wa 'l-djihād*, of which numerous mss. are extant; a résumé was made by Bodin in *AM*, iii (1918), 145-85, and it was published by A. Bustānī at Tetuan in 1941. Al-Ghazzāl's *riḥla* is doubly interesting. From the historical aspect, it is a valuable document since the author gives details about the aim of his mission and lists the names of the Muslim prisoners; from the literary point of view, although it is written in rhymed prose, it describes the stages of the journey and gives a picture of Spain under Charles III. He notes, like other travellers in Europe, the things which were new to him, but shows himself somewhat partial, insisting on the superiority of his own country.

He is, furthermore, the author, notably, of epistles in praise of his sultan and of a biography of the head of the ʿĪsāwa religious order, *al-Nūr al-shāmil* (ed. Cairo 1348/1929).

Bibliography: E. Lévi-Provençal, *Chorfa*, 327-30; H. Pérès, *L'Espagne vue par les voyageurs musulmans*, Paris 1937, 23; Ibn Sūda, *Dalīl muʾarrikh al-Maghrib al-akṣā*, Casablanca 1960, i, 124, 167, 174, 234, ii, 366-7; Brockelmann, S II, 712; M. Lakhdar, *Vie littéraire*, 249-52 and bibl. given there.   (ED.)

AL-GHAZZĪ, ABŪ ISḤĀḲ IBRĀHĪM [B. YAḤYĀ?] B. ʿUTHMĀN B. ʿABBĀS AL-KALBĪ AL-ASHHABĪ (441-524/1049-1129), Arabic poet of the Saldjūḳ period.

He was born in Ghazza [*q.v.*] at a time when that town was still under Fāṭimid rule, but as a Shāfiʿī Sunnī and as a person especially proud of emanating from the Imām al-Shāfiʿī's own birthplace, his life was to be orientated towards the East, where the establishment of the Saldjūḳs favoured a resurgence of Sunnī orthodoxy. He was studying in Damascus in 481/1088 as a pupil of the traditionist Naṣr b. Ibrāhīm al-Maḳdisī (d. 490/1096, see Brockelmann, S I, 603), but then left for ʿIrāḳ. Disappointed at Ḥilla in his expectations of the Mazyadid Sayf al-Dawla Ṣadaḳa, he spent some time at the Niẓāmiyya *madrasa* in Baghdād during the caliphate of al-Mustaẓhir, but then departed for Persia, where he spent the remainder of his long life, travelling extensively in search of congenial patrons.

He was in Ādharbāydjān and Shīrwān, where he was again disappointed, this time by the Yazīdid Shīrwān-Shāh Farīburz b. Sālār; in Iṣfahān, where he stayed with a member of the Banū Faḍlūya, the Shabānkāraʾī Atabegs of Fārs; in Kirmān, where he enjoyed the patronage of the vizier of the local Saldjūḳ *amīr*s Nāṣir al-Dīn Mukram b. ʿAlāʾ; and also in Khurāsān, where he journeyed as far as Samarḳand and the court of the Ḳarakhānids. Here in the farther east of the Saldjūḳ empire he seems to have found favour with the Sulṭān Sandjar at Marw, and it was there that the scholar ʿAbd al-Karīm b. Muḥammad al-Samʿānī [*q.v.*] met him at the end of al-Ghazzī's life when he had, so al-Samʿānī says, reached 90 years of age but had apparently fallen into poverty. Al-Samʿānī, in his *Mudhayyal* to the *Taʾrīkh Baghdād* of al-Khaṭīb [*q.v.*], cited by ʿImād al-Dīn al-Iṣfahānī, met him in Marw, where al-Ghazzī was staying at the local Niẓāmiyya *madrasa*. When al-Ghazzī left for Balkh on his last journey, he sold about ten *riṭl*s' weight of the autography manuscripts of his poems, which al-Samʿānī was subsequently able to acquire and to copy out from them over 5,000 verses; the remainder of his verses, however, al-Ghazzī also sold, and these later perished in a fire at Balkh. Al-Ghazzī died before he could reach Balkh, and his body was taken there for burial.

Nearly 5,450 verses of his *dīwān* survive, in a considerable number of manuscripts, but clearly in the course of a long life as a panegyric poet al-Ghazzī must have written much more than this; al-Samʿānī says that he was "sparing" (*ḍanīn*) of recording his poetry. It seems probable that the extant manuscripts stem ultimately from al-Samʿānī's copy. The great majority of his verses are in the genre of eulogy, addressed to 58 different *mamdūḥūn*; it seems that al-Ghazzī was willing to travel anywhere in the hope of reward. The rest of his poetry can be classified as satire, *ʿitāb*, etc., with some erotic poems addressed *more temporis* to boys. Al-Ghazzī enjoyed considerable contemporary renown, at a time when Arabic poetry was still in its post-ʿAbbāsid period of florescence, so that ʿImād al-Dīn could say that his poetry became proverbial in its time and that he was one of the quadrumvirate

of great contemporary poets, together with friend and correspondent Abū Ismāʿīl al-Ḥ al-Tughrāʾī and with Abu 'l-Muẓaffar Muḥar al-Abīwardī and Abū Bakr Aḥmad al-Arra [*q.v.*].

Bibliography: ʿImād al-Dīn al-Iṣfa *Kharīdat al-ḳaṣr, ḳism shuʿarāʾ al-Shām*, Shukrī Fayṣal, Damascus 1375/1955, i, 3-75 principal source); Sibṭ b. al-Djawzī, *Mirʾāt* 133-4; Ibn al-Djawzī, *Muntaẓam*, xi, 15-16 Khallikān, ed. Iḥsān ʿAbbās, i, 57-62, No. 1 de Slane, i, 38-42; Ziriklī, *Aʿlām*, i, 44; Bro mann, I², 294, S I, 448; ʿAlī Djawād Āl ʾ *al-Shiʿr al-ʿarabī fi 'l-ʿIrāḳ wa bilād al-ʿAdj 'l-ʿaṣr al-saldjūḳī*, Baghdād 1961, i, 177-84.   (C. E. BOSWOR

AL-GHIṬRĪF B. ʿAṬĀʾ AL-DJURASHĪ, ʿAbb governor. He was the brother of the fa Khayzurān [*q.v.*], the Yemeni girl of slave origin married the caliph al-Mahdī and was mother c two successive caliphs al-Hādī and al-Ra Al-Ghiṭrīf is also given the *nisba* of "al-Kind the biography of him by Gardīzī (probably stem from al-Sallāmī's lost *Taʾrīkh Wulāt Khurāsān* by al-Samʿānī, and may accordingly have a *mawlā* of the great South Arabian tribe of F [*q.v.*] (*Zayn al-akhbār*, ed. ʿAbd al-Ḥayy Ḥ Tehran 1347/1968, 96, 129-30). From com obscurity, as a slave who watched over vineyar Djurash in the Yemen, his fortunes rose Khayzurān's great influence in the state and his position as *khāl*, maternal uncle, of the cal A daughter of his, ʿAzīza, married Hārūn al-Ra In 170/786-7 he was appointed governor of the Y (Khalīfa b. Khayyāṭ, *Taʾrīkh*, ed. Zakkār, ii, al-Yaʿḳūbī, *Historiae*, ii, 481; *Aghānī¹*, xiii, 13) then in 175/791-2 governor of Khurāsān, Sīstān Gurgān in succession to al-ʿAbbās b. Djaʿfar office which he held until he was replaced in 17 by Ḥamza b. Mālik al-Khuzāʿī (Khalīfa, ii, al-Yaʿḳūbī, ii, 488; al-Dīnawarī, *al-Akhbār al-ṭ* Cairo 1960, 387; al-Ṭabarī, iii, 590-1, 612, 626, Ḥamza al-Iṣfahānī, *Taʾrīkh sinī mulūk al* Beirut 1961, 164-5; al-Azdī, *Taʾrīkh Mawṣil*, Establishing himself at Bukhārā in order to with the disturbed situation in Transoxania, internal threats and threats from the Turks o Central Asian steppes (cf. Barthold, *Turkestan to the Mongol invasion³*, 198 ff.), al-Ghiṭrīf despat an expedition in 175/791-2 under ʿAmr b. D into Farghāna against the *Yabghu* of the Ḳa [*q.v.*] and one under his deputy Dāwūd b. Yaz Ḥātim against the Khāridjite rebel in Sīstān Ḥudayn of Ūḳ (Gardīzī, 129-30; *Taʾrīkh-i Sī* 153-4, tr. M. Gold, Rome 1976, 121-2; Bosw *Sīstān under the Arabs...*, Rome 1968, 85). sources are silent concerning al-Ghiṭrīf's career his dismissal from Khurāsān, but a scion of his Muḥammad b. Aḥmad al-Ghiṭrīfī, is mentione one later source on Transoxanian history, R. N. Frye, *City chronicles of Central Asia Khurasan: a history of Nasaf?*, in *Fuad Köp armaǧanı*, Istanbul 1953, 167 = *Islamic Iran Central Asia (7th-12th centuries)*, London XXXII; presumably this last is the traditionist Aḥmad Muḥammad b. Aḥmad b. al-Ḥusayr Ribāṭī al-Ghiṭrīfī of Gurgān mentioned by Samʿānī, *Ansāb*, f. 410a.

The most enduring legacy of al-Ghiṭrīf's gover ship in the East was, however, his role in introdu a new coinage into Bukhārā. The story is give detail by Narshakhī in his *Taʾrīkh-i Bukhārā* arris Riḍawī, Tehran 1939, 42-5, tr. Frye, bridge, Mass. 1954, 35-7, and more briefly by .mʿānī, *loc. cit.*, cf. also Barthold, *Turkestan*[3], 5. The old silver coinage of the pre-Islamic ian rulers of the city, the Bukhār-Khudās, had ly disappeared from circulation, and Khwāraz- silver coins had had to be imported. Hence at request of the local people, al-Ghiṭrīf coined *ıms* from an alloy of six metals, henceforth vn as "black" or Ghiṭrīfī/Ghidrīfī *dirhams*, and nt only for local circulation. Taxation requisitions now fixed at the rate of six of these Ghiṭrīfī *ıms* for one silver *dirham*, but the exchange equently fluctuated, causing hardship for those ng *kharādj* at the revised rate. The position was he end stabilised, for alloy *dirhams*, Ghiṭrīfī, ammadī (after a financial official, Muḥammad Dahda) and Musayyabī (after a preceding rnor of Khurāsān, al-Musayyab b. Zuhayr al-bī) ones, continued to be used sporadically in soxania for a long time to come. Ibn Ḥawḳal, Kramers, 490, tr. 470, describes Ghiṭrīfī *dirhams* irculating in the region of Hayṭal, i.e. Bactria the eastern fringes of Khurāsān [see HAYĀṬILA]; uḳaddasī, 340, speaks of them as circulating in hārā and certain other localities of Transoxania; the translator into Persian of Narshakhī's ory states that in his time (522/1128), 100 pure r *dirhams* equalled 70 Ghiṭrīfī *dirhams*, and the *mithḳāl* equalled 7½ Ghiṭrīfī *dirhams*. See further , *Notes on the early coinage of Transoxania*, r. Numism. Soc. Notes and Monographs 113, York 1949, 41-9.

Bibliography: Given in the article, but note at Zambaur, *Manuel*, 48, gives al-Ghiṭrīf's name d the date of his governorship wrongly.

(C. E. BOSWORTH)

HIYĀTH AL-DĪN BALBAN. [See BALBAN, in ol.].

HUBAYRĀ, site of an early Islamic city irmān Province in Iran. It is situated some 70 km. h of Kirmān, the provincial capital, in the Bard 'alley, at the confluence of the Čārī and Ghubayrā s. At the time of the Arab conquest the provin- capital was at Sīrdjān, some 200 km. to the h. The main caravan route from Sīrdjān to runs considerably to the south of Kirmān Ibn Khurradādhbih, 49, describes the stations this route, and Ghubayrā is mentioned as the from Sīrdjān towards Bam. According to khrī, the stations between Sīrdjān and Bam were ollows: Shāmāt, Ghār, or Bahār, Khannāb, bayrā, Kūghūn, Rāyin, Sarvistān and Darčīn, ern Darzīn (ed. Īradj Afshār, Tehran 1961, 140 f. map facing p. 139). A detailed account of the is given by Muḳaddasī, 462-3, who writes that is a small town surrounded by villages, with a ess in its midst, while outside was the market ntly built by Ibn Ilyās. Both this place and hūn have fine mosques and the water comes from *its*". During the 8th/14th century Ghubayrā nged to the Muẓaffarid realm. The town was ed and destroyed by Tīmūr's army in 795/1393. ppears that Ghubayrā as a town ceased to exist that time, although archaeological evidence cates that there was a small settlement on the in Ṣafawid times.

he ruins of Ghubayrā were first reported in ern times in J. R. Caldwell's excavation report Tall-i Iblīs (Caldwell, Chase and Fehérvári, in *stigations at Tal-i Iblīs*, ed. J. R. Caldwell, ngfield, Ill. 1967, chs. vi, viii). Subsequently, four seasons of excavations were conducted on the site under the direction of A. D. H. Bivar and G. Fehérvári (brief excavation reports were published by A. D. H. Bivar and G. Fehérvári in *Iran*, under "Survey of excavations", x (1972), 168-9, pls. II-III; xi (1973), 194-5, pls. IV-VIb; xiii (1975), 180-1, pls. V-VI; and xv (1977), 173-4, pls. IIa-b; also in the *Proceedings of the 1st, 3rd and 4th Annual Symposia of Archaeological Research in Iran*, Tehran 1972, 1974, 1975. The first interim report was published in *JRAS* (1974), 107-41.

Bibliography: given in the article.

(G. FEHÉRVÁRI)

GHULDJA [see ḲULDJA].

GIAFAR [see DJAʿFAR].

GIFT [see HIBA].

GILGIT, a town in the northwest of Pakistan, with a population of 4,671, situated on the right bank of the Gilgit river, a tributary of the Indus, 4,890 ft. above sea level. Owing to its geographical position, being near the borders of several countries and because roads radiate from it into the surrounding valley and beyond to Sinkiang and Transoxiana, it has always been an important trading centre and of considerable strategic significance.

Gilgit's ancient name was Sargin, which, owing to reasons unknown, was changed to Gilgit. But its people call their country Shīnakos and their language Shīnā. They are of Aryan origin, of fair complexion, well-built but unwarlike, cheery, honest, frugal and industrious, given to polo and dancing.

Gilgit was noticed by the Chinese travellers Fa-hien and Hiuen-Tsang as well as by the Muslim scholar al-Bīrūnī, who says that its ruler's name was Bhattā-Shāh. However, Gilgit's early history is legendary. In 751 A.D. the Chinese, who had occupied it, were defeated and driven out by the Arabs. Early in the twelfth century Shamshīr, the youngest son of Azar, a Yārḳandī Turk belonging to the Trākāne (Tārā Khān) family, invaded Gilgit and, having overthrown its Buddhist ruler, Shrī Budat, established his family's rule. It was during his reign that, according to tradition, six Ṣūfī saints, whose tombs still exist, converted the Buddhist inhabitants of Gilgit to Islam. Later, Tārā Khān (689-735/1290-1335) tried to introduce the Ismāʿīlī creed, but Mīrzā Khān (972-1008/1565-1600) rejected it in favour of Imāmī Shīʿism, which is still the majority faith of Gilgit.

The Trākāne family's rule came to an end in 1822 with ʿAbbās Khān, after which Gilgit was in turn ruled by the chiefs of Punīāl, Nagar and Yasīn. In 1842 Karīm Khān of Nagar, having seized Gilgit from Gawhar Amān of Yāsin with the help of the Sikhs, became their tributary. But when in 1846 Kashmīr was transferred to Mahārādjā Gulāb Singh of Djammū by the British, claims to Gilgit were also made over to him. In 1889, however, the British, in face of Russian aggression, took control of Gilgit and the surrounding area and placed it under a British Agent. But before the grant of independence to the subcontinent in August 1947, it was restored to Mahārādjā Harī Singh. In November 1947 the local people, with the support of the Gilgit Scouts, imprisoned his governor, Gansārā Singh, and proclaimed Gilgit's accession to Pakistan, which readily took control of the area. Recently, the Chinese have constructed a road which links it with Rāwalpindī and Sinkiang. This has enhanced Gilgit's both military and commercial importance.

Bibliography: Major C. E. Bates, *A gazeteer of Kashmir and the adjoining districts of Kishtāwar, etc.*, Calcutta 1873; E. F. Knight, *Where three empires meet*, London 1893; F. Drew, *The Djammu and Kashmir territories*, London 1875; G. J. Adler, *India's northern frontier*, London 1963; Mawlvī Ḥashmat Allāh Khān, *Taʾrīkh-i Djammū va riyāsathā-i maftūḥa Mahārādjā Gulāb Singh*, Lucknow 1939. (MOHIBBUL HASAN)

GIRL [see ḲĪZ].

GLOBE, TERRESTIAL [see KURRAT AL-ARḌ].

GLOSS [see ḤĀSHIYYA].

GOAT [see MAʿZ].

GOD [see ALLĀH].

GORGAN [see GURGĀN].

GOURARA (Gurāra), oasis group of the central Sahara, in Algerian territory, contained within the southern fringe of the Great Western Erg to the north (the border on this side may be located at the furthest centres of permanent settlement), the north-west flank of the plateau of Tadmait to the south-east, and Oued Saoura to the west (the border on this side being the last centre of Berber-speakers, Baḥammou, as opposed to the exclusively Arabic-speaking population of the Saoura). To the south, on the Touat side, the border was traditionally imprecise, the oases allying themselves to Timimoun (Gourara) or to Adrar (Touat) by means of *ṣoff* agreements. The French administration created an artificial border here, definitively fixed in 1944.

Physical geography. Between the plateaux of the *reg* of Meguiden to the east (altitude 325 m.), a mound of clays and red sandstones of Continental Intercalary, and the Villefranchian *hamada* (silicified limestone) of Ouled Aissa to the west (350 m.), the heart of Gourara is constituted by a depression, the base of which is occupied by plains of salinated clay (*sebkha*), unsuitable for any crop other than palm-trees, of which the biggest is the *sebkha* of Timimoun, a huge channel 80 km. in length and varying in width between 2 and 15 km., lying on a north-north-east to south-south-west axis at the foot of the Meguiden, the base of which dips to an altitude of 192 m. At its extremities, the *sebkha* adjoins sectors of more abundant vegetation, bearing the name "oued", which seems to be synonymous with "pasturage". The *sebkha* corresponds to an ancient water-course flowing towards the south, founded on the hamadian surface along a pre-tertiary rib, but the erosions of the quaternary periods of humidity have eaten more deeply than pre-tertiary erosion. No importance need be attached to the remarks of Ibn Khaldūn (*Histoire des Berbères*, tr. de Slane, 2nd ed., Paris 1925, i, 196), who did not know the region personally, on a river "flowing from west to east". No doubt this arises from a confusion with the Saoura. Between the *sebkha* and the plateau of Ouled Aissa, there stretches a complex morphological zone, where the substratum of carboniferous sandstone and limestone, modified by interwoven pleats giving rise to appalachian reliefs (the mound of Timimoun, east-west), partially fossilised by deposits of Continental Intercalary and Tertiary formed into projecting hillocks, is invaded by various dunary formations, branches of erg and lesser forms.

Human geography. In severe climatic conditions (15 mm. annual rainfall), there has persisted a sedentary population, descendants of an ancient stock of judaised Zenatas, which remains for the most part Berber-speaking. In 1952, out of a total of 25,000 habitants, the Gourara consisted of 61% Berber-speakers and 39% Arabic-speakers. The Arab elements, of Hilālian origin (Meharza and Khenafsa) arrived in the 6th/12th century, and it is this period which saw the first appearance of the Ar speaking *ksour*, present only in the north in Tinerkouk and in the south in the Deldoul an Aouguerout, although the recent settlemen Chaanba nomads has joined an important nucleus to the old Berber centre of Timimoun. settlement process is actively continuing at present day, and the sedentary population, w has grown steadily over the past three decad spite of a considerable level of emigration toward Tell, must currently be approaching the figu 40,000, with a proportion of Arabic-speakers tainly superior to that of 1952. In addition, dark-skinned Ḥarātīn (see ḤARṬĀNĪ), either Be speaking or Arabic-speaking according to language of their masters, in 1952 constituted n a half (46%) of the population (compared estimates of 29% "Zenatas" and 25% "Arabs")

This population lives today in concent groups in villages (*ksour*), of which the large Timimoun (5,000 inhabitants), often dominate a *kasba* containing the individual granaries w the people's crops are preserved (in other c granaries are attached to private houses). It s that the habitat was formerly more dispersed, indicated by the existence of numerous small r in a period of domination on the part of large s nomadic Zenata or Arab tribes on whom the se tary population was strictly-speaking depen The progressive concentration of the habitat w testify simultaneously to a trend towards seder living and to a renewal of instability in the century. The economic basis is provided by p trees (about 400,000), of which the surplus pro tion (5 to 6,000 tonnes of dates) partially compen for the inadequacy of cereal production (300 to of wheat and barley), and permits the purchas wool used in the weaving of *dokkali*, dyed mate manufactured by the women (350 looms) and tially marketed abroad. Small-holding is the and indirect exploitation is common. Palms gardens are irrigated largely by subterranean drai channels (*foggara*) in the *sebkha* of the east, somet combined with hoisting machinery to raise the v of the channel when the level is too low for irriga purposes, and with wells whose water is raise balanced arms in the northern region at the fr of the Erg.

Bibliography: K. Suter, *Timimun. Anthropogeographie einer Oase der Algeris Sahara*, in *Mitteilungen der Geographischen sellschaft Wien*, xciv (1952), 31-54; R. Capot- *Le Sahara français*, Paris 1953, *passim*; J. Bi *Le Gourara, étude de géographie humaine*, Al 1956 (*Université d'Alger, Institut de Reche Sahariennes, Mémoire no. 3*), 222 pp. (b contains all the preceding bibliography and r to the sources), to be supplemented by H. Schi (ed.), *Die Sahara und ihre Randgebiete*, Mu 1971-3, *passim*. (XAVIER DE PLANHO

GÖVSA, IBRĀHĪM ʿALĀʾ AL-DĪN, modern Tu İBRAHİM ALAETTİN GÖVSA, Turkish author, grapher and poet (1889-1949), was born in Is bul, the son of Muṣṭafā ʿĀṣim, a civil servant, fro Turkish family of Filibe (Plovdiv in present Bulgaria). Educated at the Wefā lycée, Istanbul, in Trabzon, where his father was chief secre (*mektūbdju*) of the province, he studied in Ista University (1907-10), subsequently taught in Tra lycée and in 1913 went to Switzerland with a gov ment scholarship, where he studied psychology pedagogics at the University of Geneva and at

-Jacques Rousseau Institute. On his return 5), he taught at the Istanbul Teachers' Training ge (*Dār al-muʿallimīn*), where later he also me Director. Appointed in 1926 as a member of Advisory Board (*Taʿlīm we terbiyye dāʾiresi*) of Ministry of Education in Republican Turkey, he later elected a member of Parliament (1927), e he served until 1946, with a brief interval in when he was an inspector for the Ministry of cation. He died in Ankara on 29 October 1949. vsa started his career as a poet, published his poems in the traditional *ʿarūḍ* metre in the *wet-i fünūn* [*q.v.*] (1908), but later switched to bic metre (*hedje wezni*) following the new literary l in *Yeñi medjmūʿa* (1917 onwards). One of the eers of children's verse (*Čodjuḳ shiʿirleri*, 1910), sa continued to write poetry until 1940 on lyric epic (*Čanaḳḳale izleri*, 1926) topics, using al-ately both metres. Though not outstanding as a , he occasionally reaches a level above the age when he is inspired by an unusual event (e.g. amous elegy for Atatürk, *Tavaf*, 1938). He also e humorous verse and prose and successful iches (e.g. *Nazif'ten Hamid'e ahiretten mektuplar*,). But Gövsa is particularly known as a biog-er and encyclopaedist. A meticulous and onsible collector of materials from written and sources, he contributed greatly to contemporary raphical literature in Turkey. Apart from his t share in the planning and preparation of the kish Encyclopaedia (*İnönü Ansiklopedisi*, later *Ansiklopedisi*) from 1941 onwards, of which he also Secretary-General (1943-5), Gövsa is the or of the following major works in this field: *hur adamlar* ("Famous men"), 4 vols., 1933-8; *ifler ve mucitler* ("Explorers and inventors"), ; *Türk meşhurları ansiklopedisi* ("Encyclopaedia amous Turks"), n.d. [1946]; and *Resimli yeni ve ansiklopedi* ("New illustrated encyclopaedic onary"), 1947-9 (up to the letter L).

Bibliography: *Türk ansiklopedisi*, xvii, An-ara 1970, s.v.; Behçet Necatigil, *Edebiyatımızda imler sözlüğü*[8], Istanbul 1975, s.v. (Fahir İz)

UIDE [see zaʿīm].

UILD [see ṣinf].

UITAR [see kītāra].

UJARAT, GUJERAT [see gudjarāt].

UJARATI, GUZARATI [see gudjarātī].

UL KHĀTŪN, the queen of Sultān Ḥaydar ı of Kashmīr (874-6/1470-2). The chronicles do say whether she belonged to a Muslim family of gn origin or to a Kashmīrī family. It is more likely that she was the daughter of a Bayhaḳī id [*q.v.*], for the Kashmīr rulers were always very r to marry in the family of these descendants ne Prophet, and regarded such an alliance with e. However, strangely enough, unlike the royal es of foreign origin, Gul Khātūn, according to narādja's *Rādjataranginī*, favoured Hindū customs ceremonies. Gul Khātūn was active in the tics of the kingdom and played an important role ecuring the throne for her son, Ḥasan Shāh. She also interested in girls' education and established *rasas* at her own expense. She was much re-ted and loved by her son, who constructed a ge of boats in her memory over the Djehlam rinagar.

Bibliography: anon., Bahāristān-i Shāhī, dia Office ms. 509; Ḥaydar Malik, *Taʾrīkh-i ashmīr*, I. O. ms. 510; Djonarādjā, *Rādjatavan-nī*, tr. J. C. Dutt, *Kings of Kashmir*, Calcutta 377-98; Mohibbul Hasan, *Kashmīr under the Sulṭāns*, Srinagar 1974; G. M. D. Sufi, *Kashīr* Lahore 1948-9. (Mohibbul Hasan)

GŪMĀL, Gomal, a river of the Indus valley system and the North-West Frontier region of the Indo-Pakistan subcontinent. It rises in eastern Afghānistān some 40 miles/62 km. east of the Āb-i Istāda lake. Flowing eastwards, it is joined from the south by the Kundar and Zhōb rivers, and forms the southern boundary of the South Wazīristān tribal agency of the former North-West Frontier Province of British India (now Pakistan). Below the settlement of Murtaḍā, it leaves the mountains and enters the lower-lying lands of the Dēra Ismāʿīl Khān district [see dēradjāt], and is diverted into many irrigation channels; from this point also it is known as the Lūnī River. The bed of the river is often largely dry in rainless periods, and only in times of flooding do its waters actually reach the Indus itself.

Where the river emerges from the northern end of the Sulaymān Mountains into the lower terrain we have the Gomal Pass, a defile some four miles long and one of the routes from Afghānistān to the Indus valley; although much used by nomadic Ghalzays [*q.v.*] and other Pathan tribes bringing merchandise down to the plains, its comparative iso-lation and wildness have not made it such a historic route for the passage of armies as the routes further north of the Kurram [*q.v.*] valley and the Khyber Pass [see khaybar], although in the spring of 910/1505 Bābur used part of the track along the swollen Gomal River when travelling from Bannū to Ghazna (*Bābur-nāma*, tr. Beveridge, 235-6).

During the 19th century, Sarwār Khān, chief of Tank in Bannū, dammed the Gomal River just below where it emerges to the plains (see H. B. Edwardes, *A year on the Punjab frontier in 1848-9*, London 1851, i, 414-15). Towards the end of the century, Sir Robert Sandeman, the pacifier of Balūčistān, planned to open up the Gomal Pass for general access and thus gain an alternative route to the one from Multān into the Zhōb valley of north-eastern Balūčistān, occupied in 1889. In that same year, as part of the "Forward Policy", the Viceroy of India Lord Lansdowne authorised subsidies for the Wazīrīs and other tribesmen. Tribal *malik*s and *djirga*s were summoned to a durbar at Apozai in Zhōb, and military posts established in the Gomal valley in order to command the route and in the hope to exerting some influence in Wazīristān. The system worked for some time, but in the long run hopes of making the Gomal Pass generally accessible have proved vain for both the Government of India and its successor Pakistan.

Bibliography: Mountstuart Elphinstone, *An account of the kingdom of Caubul*[3], London 1839, i, 135-6; T. H. Thornton, *Colonel Sir Robert Sandeman, his life and work on our Indian frontier, a memoir*, London 1895, 223-4, 230-, 241; C. Collin Davies, *The problem of the North-West Frontier 1890-1908*[2], London 1975, 71-3 and index; Sir Olaf Caroe, *The Pathans 550 B.C.-A.D. 1947*, London 1958, 375-6; J. W. Spain, *The Pathan borderland*, The Hague 1963, 26-7; D. Dichter, *The North-West frontier of West Pakistan, a study in regional geog-raphy*, Oxford 1967, index. (C. E. Bosworth)

GÜMÜLDJINE, the Ottoman Turkish form of the Greek Komotene, Komotini, a town of over 30,000 inhabitants in Western Thrace, the modern Greek province of Rhodope, which from the sixties of the 14th century until 1912 was without interruption a part of the Ottoman Empire.

The name Komotene is the academic version of

Koumoutsinas, which was already used by Cantacusinos in the mid-14th century. The *Destān* of Ümür Pas̲h̲a (ed. Mélikoff, 101, 124) appears to be the first Turkish source to use the form "Gümüld̲j̲üne" when relating Ümür Aydïnog̲h̲lu's actions in Thrace in and after 745/1344.

Komotene emerged as a small urban centre (*polisma*) after the Bulgarian invasion of Czar Kaloyan in 1207, during which the old city of Mosynopolis was thoroughly destroyed. The remaining inhabitants of Mosynopolis fled within the walls of an uninhabited but rather well-preserved stronghold, Komotene. This new town is mentioned in connection with the actions of the Emperor Andronicus III against the Turkish pirates and during the Byzantine civil war of the 14th century, which were catastrophic for the lowland population of Thrace.

The old Ottoman chroniclers (ʿĀs̲h̲ïḳpas̲h̲azāde, Nes̲h̲rī, Oruč, Anonymus Giese, Idrīs-*Destān* IV) unanimously place the conquest of Komotene by the Ottomans in or around 762/1361, after the capture of Zag̲h̲ra (Stara Zagora) and Filibe (Plovdiv) and before the conquest of Biga. Ferīdūn Aḥmed Beg, in his *Müns̲h̲eʾāt al-selāṭīn*, has a letter from the ruler of Ḳaramān to Murād I, congratulating him on the conquest of Filibe, Zag̲h̲ra and Gümüld̲j̲ine, and also the answer of Murād, dated 764/1362-3. Almost all the sources mention G̲h̲āzī Ewrenos Beg as conqueror. Between 763/1361-2 and 785/1383 (capture of Serres or Siroz), Komotene was the seat of an *ud̲j̲* confronting Serbian-controlled Macedonia, and stood under command of Ewrenos Beg. Somewhere in these two decades, Ewrenos Beg erected in his residence a large domed *mesd̲j̲id*, an *ʿimāret*, a *ḥammām* and a large number of shops, and added the revenue of the villages of Anbarköy and Küčük Köy to this *waḳf*. These buildings formed the nucleus of Islamic life in Western Thrace. The buildings were situated outside the old walled enclosure of Koumoutsinas, where the original Greek population continued to live. The colonisation of Muslim Turkish citizens in Komotene, and of large numbers of Turkish farmers in the deserted plains around the town, appears to be also connected with Ewrenos Beg. The toponymy of villages, hills, meadows and brooks is overwhelmingly Turkish, which may be an indication that the newcomers found little or no autochthonous inhabitants to transmit the existing toponyms. The fragmentarily-published registers of the 9th/15th and 10th/16th century Ottoman censuses point in the same direction, and show clearly the heavy preponderance of the Muslim Turkish population in these districts.

When in 785/1383 Ewrenos Beg moved the seat of his *ud̲j̲* closer to the chief field of action (Western Macedonia), Komotene remained a relatively small town with a predominantly Muslim population. The Burgundian knight Bertrandon de la Broquière passed "Caumussin" in 1433 on his way to Serres. He called it a "fairly good little town", which was "well-enclosed by walls and situated on a little river in a lovely country and good plain near the mountains".

According to the census of 925/1519, Komotene numbered 393 Muslim households, 197 unmarried Muslims, 42 Christian households, six unmarried Christians and eight Christian widows, as well as 19 Jewish households and five unmarried Jews. This gives a total of 2,500 souls, which is roughly the average of a local Balkan town of that time. It was by then the second urban centre in size of Western Thrace (after Xanthi or Iskeče). According to the census of 936/1530, Komotene had 17 *maḥalle*s which all bore Turkish names. The same s[...] mentions the names of all religious and educat[...] institutions of the town: one mosque, 16 *mes*[...] four *zawiya*s, four schools and one church. Wh[...] the middle of the 16th century the French tra[...] Pierre Belon du Mans (*Observations des plus singularités*, etc., Paris 1588, ch. lx) passed "petite bourgarde Commercine", he mentions "ruines d'un petit chastelet, dedans leque[...] l'Église Grecs Chrestiens". His remark that [...] town was "habité des Grecs, et peu de Turc[...] curious and certainly not in accordance with th[...] situation. The Ottoman geographer Meḥ[...] ʿĀs̲h̲ïḳ visited Komotene in *ca.* 998/1590 and [...] that "There are there [in Komotene] Friday mos[...] baths and markets. The *ḥād̲j̲d̲j̲i* and *g̲h̲āzī* Ew[...] Beg constructed in Gümüld̲j̲ine a public kitche[...] dining hall for the travellers (sc. an *ʿimā*[...] Shortly afterwards, in the first decade of the [...] century, Komotene shared the attention of [...] *defterdār* of Aḥmed I, Ekmekd̲j̲izāde Aḥmed P[...] who dotted most of Thrace with buildings fo[...] promotion of Islamic culture. In Komoten[...] erected a small but exquisite mosque, a d[...] *ḥammām*, a domed and lead-covered *mekt*[...] *medrese* and an *ʿimāret*. The mosque is the [...] Ottoman structure on Greek territory which [...] number of multi-coloured tile panels dating [...] the best period of the Iznik kilns (988-98/158[...]

Most of the information on Ottoman Komot[...] contained in vol. viii of the *Seyāḥat-nāme* of E[...] Čelebi, who visited the town in 1078/1667-8. By [...] the place had apparently enjoyed a great expan[...] Ewliyā numbers "4,000 prosperous, stone-[...] houses", 16 *maḥalle*s and 5 Friday mosques[...] *mesd̲j̲id*s, two *ʿimāret*s, two *ḥammām*s, five *med*[...] seven *mekteb*s, 17 *k̲h̲ān*s and 400 shops. A numb[...] his figures can still be checked and are cor[...] others look suspiciously high (viz. the figure fo[...] houses). This source especially sings the prais[...] the pious foundations of Ewrenos and Aḥmed P[...] His description of the latter's mosque is very accu[...] and in no way exaggerated.

In the 18th century, epidemics of plague rav[...] the Thracian lowlands and led to the disappear[...] of whole villages. (A lonely minaret in the [...] 4 miles/7 km. of Komotene pathetically marks [...] site of the village of Eski Gümüld̲j̲ine.) In the [...] century, the town witnessed again a conside[...] revival. Entire new quarters arose on its perip[...] and especially on the eastern side. During [...] century, a number of Ottoman buildings [...] restored and new ones erected. The Eski D̲j̲āmiʿ [...] old *mesd̲j̲id* of Ewrenos Beg) was greatly enla[...] by enveloping it by a spacious prayer hall in [...] Ottoman "empire" style. The Yeñi D̲j̲āmiʿ [...] Ekmekd̲j̲izāde Aḥmed) was enlarged in the s[...] manner. In the time of ʿAbd al-Ḥamīd II the [...] was linked with Istanbul and Salonica by a rail[...] The same sultan erected a large clock tower in [...] town as well as a *medrese*. Ottoman inscript[...] still preserved, record these actions.

Since the reorganisation of the provincial [...]ministration of the empire in the sixties of the [...] century, Komotene was the chef-lieu of a *sand̲j̲*[...] the *wilāyet* of Edirne. In the eighties of the [...] century, the town is reported to have conta[...] 13,560 inhabitants, ten Friday mosques, 15 *mesd̲*[...] two Greek and one Armenian churches, one s[...]gogue, four *medrese*s, two schools for higher ed[...]tion, ten *mekteb*s and various schools for the educa[...] of the non-Muslim part of the population.

...me of the *wilāyet* of Edirne of 1310/1892 has ...antially the same numbers, but adds details on ...idual buildings.

...ring the First Balkan War (1912), Komotene ...ed a Bulgarian occupation. In the few months ...een Balkan War II and World War I, Komotene ...the capital of a short-lived Muslim "Republic of ...üldjine", as no Balkan power was then master ...e territory. It was again occupied by the Bul-...ns in World War I. After the Treaty of Lausanne ...), town and territory were ceded to Greece, ...h promised to respect the ethnic-religious ...osition of its population (around 1900, 149,230 ...s (including a group of 20,000 Bulgarian-...king Muslims, the Pomaks); 58,357 Greeks; and ...2 Bulgarians). Under Greek administration, ...Muslim element dwindled down to 112,665 in ..., but the Greek element had mounted to 243,889 ...all of Western Thrace. The Bulgarians disap-...ed during and after the two world wars.

...day Komotene is a mixed Muslim Turkish-...k Orthodox town, roughly fifty-fifty between ... groups. In 1961 the total number of inhabitants ...28,355. The town is the largest urban centre of ...tern Thrace. It is the seat of the *muftī* of all ...ims in Greece and has a Turkish high school, ...ty mosques and *mesdjids*, and is the place where ... Turkish and Islamic periodicals and newspapers ...issued. Among the preserved monuments of ...man architecture are both mosques mentioned ...e, the Clock Tower, the *turba* of Fāṭima Khānīm, ... of the Grand Vizier Rusčuḳlu Sherīf Ḥasan ...a, dating from 1195/1781, and the *ʿimāret* of ...ī Ewrenos. The latter was confiscated by the ...ks after 1923 and used as an electric power ...on till 1974, when some minor repairs were ...ed out, and a new purpose was sought for it (as ...useum of Turkish Folklore). In the time of the ...nels (1970), the *ḥammām* of Ghāzī Ewrenos was ...royed by dynamite; its 8th/14th-century Arabic ...iption was already smashed in 1923. On the ... of the town is the Poshposh Tekke with a ...eyard with a number of interesting steles ...nging to local *aʿyān* and members of various ...ish orders (Naḳshbandī, Rifāʿī etc.). Until the ...y seventies, the town faithfully preserved its ...man physiognomy from the Ḥamīdian age.

Bibliography: For a survey of the early ...story, see G. I. Theocharides' summary of three ...ctures on *The history of the Thracians and the cities ...Komotine and Xanthi as given by Stilpon Kyria-...des*, in *Balkan Studies*, ii (Salonica 1961), 323-9. ...For the material from Ottoman census materials ...ncerning town and district, see Ö. L. Barkan, ...s *déportations comme méthode de peuplement et ...colonisation dans l'Empire Ottoman*, in *Revue ...la Faculté des Sciences Économiques de l'Uni-...rsité d'Istanbul*, No. 11 (1956), with map, giving ...e ethno-religious composition of the area in ...tail; *Turski Izvori za Bâlgarskata Istorija*, ii, ...fia 1966, 468-80; *Turski Izvori*, iii, Sofia 1972, ...-42, 359-74, 412-26, 474-83; Muhiddin Kocabıyık, ...*imülcine târih hakkında bir araştırma*, in A. Dede, ...*umeli'nde bırakılanlar*, Istanbul 1975, 13-51, ...th numerous details on 10th/16th century ...omotene; Meḥmed-i ʿĀshıḳ, *Menāẓırü 'l-ʿawālım*, ...tograph ms., Halet Efendi no. 616, vol. ii f. 20 v. ...For the description of Thrace by Ewliyā, ...yāḥat-nāme*, viii, Istanbul 1928, 85-90, see also ... J. Kissling, *Beiträge zur Kenntnis Thrakiens im ...Jahrhundert*, in *Abhandlungen für die Kunde des ...orgenlandes*, xxxii/3, Wiesbaden 1956.

For the *Tanẓīmāt* period, see H. H. Kornrumpf, *Die Territorialverwaltung im östlichen Teil der europäischen Türkei vom Erlass der Vilayetsord-nung bis zum Berliner Kongress nach amtliche osmanischen Veröffentlichungen*, Freiburg 1976.

The numbers given for the inhabitants, and for the ethnic-religious composition of the town's population, vary in various publications. Compare Adil Özgüç, *Batı Trakya Türkleri*, Istanbul 1974, and K. G. Andreadis, *The Moslem minority in Western Thrace*, Salonica 1956, where the Turkish and the Greek views are set forth. For the minutes of the Lausanne Conference, see for example *Lozan Barış konferansı (tutanaklar, belgeler)*, in *Siyasal Bil. Fak. neşr.* Ankara 1969.

For the monuments of Ottoman architecture and epigraphy, see for the time being M. Kiel, *Observation on the history of Northern Greece during the Turkish rule*, in *Balkan Studies*, xii/2 (Salonica 1971), 415-62, and also in Abdurrahim Dede, *Rumeli'nde bırakılanlar*, 53-74. A more comprehensive account is forthcoming by Kiel, *The Ottoman Balkans, a survey of monuments of Turkish architecture in Albania, Bulgaria and Greece*.

For the Republic of Gümüldjine, with illustra-tions of its flag, stamps and coins, see Adil Özgüç, *op. cit.* (M. Kiel)

GŪRAN, Shaykh Abu 'l-Fatḥ b Shaykh Mu-ḥammad, official and commander in 10th/16th century Muslim India. An Indian-born Muslim (*shaykhzāda*), he took service under Ibrāhīm Lōdī (923-32/1517-26) and was posted at Koyl [*q.v.*] (modern ʿAlīgaŕh). After the battle of Pānīpāt [*q.v.*] (932/1526), Bābur sent Mullā Apāḳ to Koyl for enlisting troops. Shaykh Gūran came over with two to three thousand men. He subsequently occupied Sambhal on behalf of his new master, and shortly afterwards seized Gwālior from Tatār Khān. In the Battle of Kānwa (933/1527) he was one of the com-manders of the right wing, and after the battle, he was sent to Koyl to expel the rebel Ilyās Khān. In Muḥarram 934/October 1527), at the invitation of Shaykh Gūran, Bābur paid a visit to his house at Pīlakhna (12 miles south of Koyl) and was enter-tained there hospitably. He participated in the siege of Čandīrī (934/1528). In 936/1529-30 he was ap-pointed Ḳilʿadār or castellan of Gwālior, a post which he held till Bābur's death (937/1530).

During the reign of Humāyūn, he was appointed governor of Mālwa, and held this post till his death in 943/1536-7. He died in Mandsore and his dead body was brought from Mandsore to Koyl, where he lies buried in an identified grave.

Shaykh Gūran is said to have been an accomplished musician. He was usually referred to as Hindustānī Beg.

Bibliography: *Bābur-nāma*, tr. A. S. Beveridge, London 1922, index; Rizk Allāh Mushtāḳī, *Wāḳiʿāt-i Mushtāḳī*, Br. Mus. MS. Add. 11633 and Or. 1929 (see on this, Storey, i, 512-13); Rāḍī Muḥammad Kolvī, *Akhbār al-djamal*, MS. Habib Ganj Collection, No. 22/30, Aligarh Muslim Uni-versity. (M. Athar Ali)

GURĀRA [see gourara, in Suppl.].

GURČĀNĪ, a Balūč tribe of modern Pakistan, living partly in the Indus valley plains of the Dēra Ghāzī Khān District of the Pandjāb [see dēradjāt], and partly in the Mārī and Drāgal hills of the Sulay-mān Mountains range and the upland plateaux of Sham and Paylāwagh, extending as far west as the modern Loralai District of northeastern Balūčistān.

The tribe is of mixed origin, some sections being Dōdāīs of mingled Balūč-Sindh Rādjpūt extraction, whilst others are pure-blooded Balūč of the Rind and Lāshārī groups; the chief's family belongs to one of the Dōdāī sections.

In the early 19th century, the Gurčānīs had a reputation for turbulence and bellicosity, so that Edwardes could call them "troublesome" and "a vain and captious race, ever ready to take offence and never to be relied on". After 1819 the Sikh ruler Randjīt Singh extended Sikh power across the Indus and by 1827 had overrun all the Dēra Ghāzī Khān district, this last being from 1832 to 1844 under the governorship (*kārdārī*) of Dīwān Sāwan Mal of Multān. He experienced much trouble from the Gurčānīs, and was compelled to build a fort in their country at Harand. This fort was in fact successfully defended for the Sikh cause by Muḥkam Čand against Lt. (afterwards Sir) H. B. Edwardes during the Second Sikh War of 1848-9, although the Gurčānīs, who controlled the surrounding countryside, joined the Balūč and Pathan levies of the British forces against their old opponents the Sikhs. Subsequently, in British India, the eastern part of the Gurčānī country came within the tribal area of Dēra Ghāzī Khān administered from the Pandjāb, and the western part within the tribal agency areas of Balūčistān and the khanate of Kalāt [see KILĀT]; a complaint of the Gurčānīs in the later part of the 19th century was that these administrative divisions weakened the unity of the tribe and exposed them to depredations of their enemies in the adjacent territory of Kalāt, the Bugtīs and the Marrīs (see T. H. Thornton, *Colonel Sir Robert Sandeman, his life and work on our Indian frontier, a memoir*, London 1895, 337-8).

Bibliography: H. B. Edwardes, *A year on the Punjab frontier in 1848-9*, London 1851, ii, 6-7, 275 ff., 294-5, 305-6; M. Longworth Dames, *The Baloch race, a historical and ethnological sketch*, London 1904, 49, 58, 64-6, 84; *Imperial gazeteer of India*², xi, 251.

(C. E. BOSWORTH)

GWĀDAR, a town and district on the Makrān coast, formerly a dependency of the sultanate of ʿUmān and since 1378/1958 a territorial possession of Pākistān. The district of Gwādar extends for 40 miles along the shoreline of Gwādar West Bay, from Cape Pishkān to Gwādar Head, and some 14 miles inland. The town stands on a sandy isthmus, about a mile wide, at the foot of a seaward, hammer-head promontory rising to 400 feet. Its inhabitants, numbering perhaps 5,000, are mostly Makrānī tribesmen of the Bulayday Maliki and Gički groups, along with small groups of Balūčīs, Arabs, Khōdjas and descendants of African slaves. They live mainly by fishing.

Until the mid-12th/18th century Gwādar, like rest of Makrān, was in the hands of tribes who sel recognised any paramount authority. There Makrān fell under the sway of Mīr Naṣīr Khā Kalāt (regn. 1168-1209/1750 to 1794-5), the hea the Brahūi confederation of the Balūč, who in acknowledged the Durranī Shāh of Afghānistā his suzerain [see KILĀT]. Nasīr Khān gave Gwāda Sayyid Sulṭān b. Aḥmad of Masḳaṭ in 1198/1784 w the latter sought refuge at his court after b driven from ʿUmān. Whether the grant wa perpetuity is unclear; for while the Āl Bū S apparently continued to pay tribute for Gwāda successive *khāns* of Kalāt, in the form of occas gifts of slaves, until *ca.* 1274/1857-8, in 1277/18 the ruling *khān* suggested that the governmen India might purchase Gwādar from ʿUmān and r it over to him.

The completion in 1279/1862-3 of the first se of the Indo-European telegraph from Karach Gwādar coincided with the assertion of Pe claims to Makrān, including Gwādar, and led government of India to depute Colonel F. J. Gold to investigate the nature of the ʿUmāni tit Gwādar. He reported the right of possession t prescriptive and indefeasible and the Persian c to be groundless. The frontier of Persia with B was subsequently (1288/1871) fixed as startin Gwāṭar Bay, some 50 miles west of Gwādar t

The incorporation of Gwādar into Kalāt, w was under British protection, was suggested by viceroy, Lord Curzon, in 1320/1902, both to pre the smuggling of arms through the port to Persia Afghanistan, and to preclude any possible Fren Russian designs upon it. The suggestion was acted upon lest it contravene the Anglo-Fr declaration of 1278-9/1862 on the integrity of ʿUmāni dominions. Gwādar remained an ʿU possession until it was ceded to Pākistan in 1 1958, reputedly for the sum of 3 million ster

Bibliography: Capt. N. P. Grant, *Journ a route through the western parts of Makra JRAS*, v (1839); Capt. E. C. Ross, *Memoran on Mekran*, in *Selections from the Bombay Go ment Records*, cxi, Bombay 1868; Col. F. J. G smid, *Notes on Eastern Persia and Western luchistan*, in *JRGS* (1867); J. A. Saldanha, *P of Mekran Affairs*, Calcutta 1905, 87-117 Hughes-Buller, *Baluchistan District Gazeteers*, s vii, vii A, *Makrán and Khárán*, Bombay 1 25-6, 46, 51, 53-4; J. G. Lorimer, *Gazetteer o Persian Gulf, ʿOman and Central Arabia*, Calc 1908-15, i, 601-22, 2150-2204, ii, 585-90.

(J. B. KELL

GYROMANCY [see RAML].

H

ḤABBA KHĀTŪN, Kashmīrī singer and poetess. Called Zūn ("moon") before her marriage, she is a semi-legendary figure in the Valley of Kashmīr. Daughter of a peasant of the village of Čandahār, near Pāmpūr, 8 miles to the south-east of Srīnagar, she was unhappy with her husband who ill-treated her, so she left him. Bīrbal Kāčrū in his *Wāḳiʿāt-i Kashmīr*, which he wrote in the middle of the century, says that, being a good singer and poss of a melodious voice, she captivated the hea Yūsuf Shāh Čak (986-94/1578-86), who married But this account appears to be apocryphal, for not supported by any earlier authority. Neithe historian Ḥaydar Malik nor the author of the I

-i S̲h̲āhī, who were contemporaries of Yūsuf
, refer to her, although they mention all the
inent queens of the mediaeval period. This,
ver, does not mean that she did not exist, as
writers have begun to say in recent years. In
first place, there is a strong tradition, which is
ssible to ignore, in Kas̲h̲mīr that Ḥabba Khātūn
in the second half of the 10th/16th century;
n the second, there is a large body of her songs
poems in Kas̲h̲mīrī which are attributed to her
to no one else. What seems more probable is
she was a mistress of Yūsuf S̲h̲āh (Taʾrīk̲h̲-i
n, ii, 296), and Bīrbal wove round her all kinds
mantic stories. After Yūsuf S̲h̲āh surrendered
kbar's general, Rādjā Mān Singh, at the end of
994/middle of February 1586, and he left
mīr with Rādjā Mān Singh, never to return,
a Khātūn retired to the village of Pandac̆uk,
t 5 miles to the south-east of Srīnagar. She
nued to live quietly in a cottage close to the
ue, both of which she had built, and died at the
f about 55 years.

bba Khātūn appears to have been a cultured
an interested in music and the education of girls,
hom she opened madrasas. She was a poetess
ntroduced lols or love lyrics in Kas̲h̲mīrī poetry.
songs which she composed are even to this day
by the common people of Kas̲h̲mīr; and it was
ho is said to have introduced the melody known
st Kas̲h̲mīrī.

Bibliography: Bīrbal Kāc̆ru, Madjmaʿ al-
ārīk̲h̲ (mss. in Punjab University Library,
hore; Kas̲h̲mīr University Library, Srīnagar;
d Bodleian Library, Oxford); Pīr G̲h̲ulām
san, Taʾrīk̲h̲-i Ḥasan, ii, ed. Ḥasan S̲h̲āh,
nagar 1954; G. M. D. Sufi, Kas̲h̲īr, ii, Lahore
9; Mohibbul Hasan, Kas̲h̲mīr under the Sulṭāns,
nagar 1974; R. K. Parmu, History of Muslim rule
Kas̲h̲mīr, Delhi 1969.   (Mohibbul Hasan)

ABSIYYA, a poem dealing with the theme
mprisonment. The term occurs in the Persian
ion for the first time about the middle of the
2th century in Niẓāmī ʿArūḍī's Čahār maḳāla
Ḳazwīnī-Muʿīn, Tehrān 1955-7, matn 72). It is
ed there to poems that were written by Masʿūd-i
i Salmān [q.v.] more than half-a-century earlier
which were still greatly admired as the sincere
ssion of the poet's sufferings. Although several
an poets have composed poetry of this nature,
absiyyāt of Masʿūd have remained both excep-
and exemplary. Not only was he the first to
them, but the theme itself was a characteristic
work. It is developed by Masʿūd to an extent
has not been equalled by any imitator of later
.
ere is a very close link between the prison-
y of Masʿūd and the story of his life. Twice in
ourse of his career he became involved in the
cal downfall of his patrons at the provincial
of the G̲h̲aznawids at Lahore. Consequently, he
o spend almost two decades, 480/1087-8 to 500/
7, banished to a number of remote fortresses
. E. Bosworth, The later Ghaznavids, splendour
ecay. The dynasty in Afghanistan and Northern
1040-1186, Edinburgh 1977, 16, 67-8, 72, 74,
he ḥabsiyyāt are, therefore, first of all topical
s, by means of which the poet tried to evoke
emency of the Sulṭān of G̲h̲azna, either directly
rough the intermediary of influential friends.
ms of various forms could serve this purpose.
tructure of the panegyrical ḳaṣīda offered the
oility to take the theme as the subject of the

prologue (cf. e.g. Dīwān, 19, 335 f., 356 f., 515).
More often, however, a section especially devoted to
an account of the poet's condition (ḥasb-i ḥāl) was
added to the panegyrical address of the patron (Dīwān, 58 f., 93 f., 107 f., 312 ff., 349 f., 489 f., 526 f.).
In one instance, the two variants are combined
(Dīwān, 427 ff.). There are also several non-pane-
gyrical ḳaṣīdas among the ḥabsiyyāt of Masʿūd
(e.g. Dīwān, 63 f., 67 ff., 106, 329 f., 331 f., 351 ff.,
354 ff., 486 ff., 493, 503 f., 552 f.). Sometimes the
characteristic ḥabsiyya motifs only occur incidentally
in poems dealing mainly with other themes. Other
forms besides the ḳaṣīda lent themselves for the
use of a prison-poem.

The contents of the poems vary from complaints
of the prisoner's misery in more or less general terms,
hardly to be distinguished from the wider category of
poetical complaints about any grievance whatsoever,
to the specific portrayal of his life in the dungeon.
In spite of the close relation between these latter
poems and the reality to which they refer, there is
a certain amount of conventionalisation to be noticed
in the representation of the poet's condition. Recurrent motifs are the description of the physical and
mental state of the prisoner, of the dungeon, the
chains and the jailers, of the darkness and the long
sleepless nights during which the poet contemplates
the stars through the narrow window of his cell, and
of the suffering on account of his long separation
from relatives and friends. Mostly, the heavenly
powers, instead of the Sulṭān, are blamed for the
misfortune that has befallen the poet. But Masʿūd
sometimes admits that the real cause is to be sought
in the fact that he, being only a poet, has aspired to
political and military office (cf. especially Dīwān,
153 f., a ḳaṣīda addressed to a certain Muḥammad-i
Khaṭībī who had met with a similar fate).

The ḥabsiyya elements are in these poems often
connected with passages in which the poet speaks
about his profession. These statements usually
contain the conventional boast about the artistic
abilities of the author, undoubtedly intended as an
argument in favour of his release. But there are also
utterances that are more specifically related to the
ḥabsiyya theme: writing poetry is the sole comfort
left to the prisoner; the poet resents the favours
bestowed in his absence on worthless flatterers; and
he becomes disgusted with the poetry of the court
and pronounces his intention to abandon it altogether after he will be released (e.g. Dīwān, 109, 516,
526). Religious elements are only rarely mingled
with these ruminations.

The models for prison-poetry set by Masʿūd-i
Salmān have continuously influenced other poets who
for one reason or another have had to undergo a
period of confinement. Two poets of S̲h̲irwān,
Falakī and Khāḳānī [q.v.], who both flourished in
the middle and later part of the 6th/12th century,
are among the earliest imitators of Masʿūd's ḥabsiyyāt. Khāḳānī's most celebrated prison-poems are
the two odes in which he addressed Christian princes,
although in these poems the display of the poet's
exceptional knowledge of Christian terms and concepts overshadows the ḥabsiyya-elements (cf.
V. Minorsky, in BSOAS, xi [1945], 550-78). With
Khāḳānī, the motif of imprisonment is often only a
metaphor. He likes to refer to S̲h̲irwān as his "place
of imprisonment" (ḥabsgāh) where he has to stay
against his will like a "captive" (s̲h̲ahrband). This
is particularly evident in a ḳaṣīda written on the
occasion of Sulṭān Sandjar's capture by the G̲h̲uzz,
which scattered the poet's hopes of a career in

Khurāsān (cf. *Dīwān*, 155 ff.; see also 45, 282 and *Tuḥfat al-ʿIrāḳayn*, ed. by Yaḥyā Ḳarīb, Tehrān 1333/1954, 29[3], 30[7], 108[5-6] (*dāmgāh-i Shirwān*), 212[3]).

The close connection with actual experiences of imprisonment has made the conventional pattern of the Persian *ḥabsiyyāt* adaptable for use in later centuries, in spite of changing circumstances. In the Indian tradition of Persian poetry, prison-poems have been written up to the present day. Among the poets who resorted to it was Mīrzā Ghālib [*q.v.*], who composed a few poems at the occasion of an imprisonment in 1848. *Ḥabsiyyāt* have also been written in Urdu (cf. Annemarie Schimmel, *The Islamic literatures of India*, Wiesbaden 1973, 11).

As far as modern Persian poetry in Iran is concerned, the best examples of prison-poetry are to be found in the works of Muḥammad-Taḳī Bahār [*q.v.*], who was imprisoned for political reasons on three occasions. Most of his *ḥabsiyyāt* came into being during the last two periods, which occurred respectively in 1929 and 1933-4. It is evident that Bahār was inspired directly by the mediaeval *ḥabsiyyāt*, although he introduced many contemporary elements, such as a complaint about the traffic noise outside his Tehran prison. Like Masʿūd-i Saʿd-i Salmān, he used various forms of poetry. His most interesting work of this kind is a *mathnawī* entitled *Kārnāma-i zindān* (*Dīwān-i ashʿār*, ii, 2-126) in which the theme of the *ḥabsiyyāt* is combined with a wide range of other subjects. The poem has been designed to the model of ancient Persian didactical poetry. Bahār has made this influence explicit by inserting the narration of a dream about a meeting with the poet Sanāʾī [*q.v.*].

Modern Persian prose has also become a vehicle for the expression of the experiences of political prisoners. Outstanding examples of this new branch of the *ḥabsiyyāt* are *Ayyām-i maḥbas* by ʿAli Dashtī and *Waraḳpārahā-yi zindān* by Buzurg ʿAlawī.

Bibliography: Masʿūd-i Saʿd-i Salmān, *Dīwān*, ed. Rashīd Yāsimī, Tehran 1330/1951, *passim*; Falakī-i Shirwānī, *Dīwān*, ed. Hādī Ḥasan, London 1929, 57 f.; Khāḳānī, *Dīwān*, ed. Ḍiyāʾ al-Dīn Sadjdjādī, Tehrān 1338/1959, 23-8, 60-2, 155-8, 173-4, 320-4; Mīrzā Asad Allāh Khān Ghālib, *Ḳiṭaʿāt*, etc., ed. Ghulām-Rasūl Mihr, Lahore 1969, 184-92; idem, *Ḳaṣāʾid*, etc., ed. Mihr, Lahore 1969, 441-6; Muḥammad-Taḳī Bahār Malik al-Shuʿarāʾ, *Dīwān-i ashʿār*[2], Tehran 1344-5/1965-6, *passim*. See further M. Dj. Maḥdjūb, *Sabk-i Khurāsānī dar shiʿr-i fārsī*, Tehrān 1345/1966, 656-9; F. Machalski, *La littérature de l'Iran contemporain*, ii, Wrocław-Warszawa-Kraków 1967, 45, 48-51; H. Kamshad, *Modern Persian prose literature*, Cambridge 1966, 69 f., 116-19; ʿAbd al-Ḥusayn Zarrīnkūb, *Bā kārwān-i ḥulla*, Tehran 2535/1976[3], 83-95. (J. T. P. de Bruijn)

al-ḤADDĀD, al-ṬĀHIR, nationalist and reformist Tunisian writer, considered as the pioneer of the movement for feminine liberation in his country.

Born in Tunis *ca.* 1899 into a family of modest status originally from the Ḥāma of Gabès, he studied at the Zaytūna [*q.v.*] from 1911 to 1920 and gained the *taṭwīʿ* (corresponding to the diploma for completing secondary education). He then took part in the trade union movement and was put in charge of propaganda in an organisation founded in 1924, the *Djāmiʿat ʿumūm al-ʿamala al-tūnisiyya*, whose chief promoters were hunted down and banished in 1925. His experiences and his reflections inspired him to write an important work, *al-ʿUmmāl al-tūnisiyyūn wa-ẓuhūr al-ḥaraka al-niḳābiyya* (Tunis 1927; ed. Tunis 1966), in which he gave an hist characterisation of trade unionism in Tunisia of the *Djāmiʿa* mentioned above, studied at l the social situation in Tunisia (but without t to apply Marxian analyses, since his own countr too different from Europe and moreover foreign domination), and put forward certain ref

However, he very soon affirmed that the reform which should be put into practice cerned woman and the family, and in 1930 publ *Imraʾatunā fi 'l-sharīʿa wa 'l-mudjtamaʿ* (2n Tunis 1972), in which he endeavoured to prove his own liberal ideas were not in contradicti the teachings of Islam, which had been the fi give dignity to the Arab woman, but should develop progressively further. In this work inveighs against polygamy, the wearing of (assimilated to muzzles), the marriage of Tu males with foreigners, divorce, which is a cala and finally, the ignorance in which women are The first remedy for the ills of society is thu education of girls and consequently, the setti of schools in which they can receive an educ complete in every sphere, so that once they adult years, they will be on the way to orga more rationally the life of their family and to sh in national activities just like the menfolk. Inevit there were criticisms. The main one directed a was that of Muḥammad al-Ṣāliḥ b. Murād, i *al-Ḥidād ʿala mraʾat al-Ḥaddād aw radd al-khaṭ 'l-kufr wa 'l-bidaʿ allatī ḥawāhā Kitāb "Imraʾat 'l-sharīʿa wa 'l-mudjtamaʿ"* (Tunis 1931), see ʿUmar b. Ibrāhīm al-Barrī al-Madanī, *Sayf al ʿalā man lā yarā al-ḥaḳḳ*, Tunis 1931.

Al-Ṭāhir al-Ḥaddād, who died at Tunis on cember 1935, left also behind a certain amou poetry in which he expressed some of his social Finally, in 1975 a collection of his reflections published in Tunis under the title of *al-Kha*

Bibliography: The personality and wo al-Ṭāhir al-Ḥaddad are beginning to be the su of studies and monographs, since he is now sidered to some extent a figure of national See in particular al-Djīlānī b. al-Ḥādjdj Y and Muḥammad al-Marzūḳī, *al-Ṭāhir al-Ḥa ḥayātuhu, turāthuhu*, Tunis 1963 (in whic poetry is to be found, already gathered tog by Zayn al-ʿĀbidīn al-Sanūsī, *Taʾrīkh al al-tūnisī fi 'l-ḳarn al-rābiʿ ʿashar*, Tunis 1 Aḥmad Khālid, *al-Ṭāhir al-Ḥaddād wa al-tūnisiyya fi 'l-thuluth al-awwal min al al-ʿishrīn*, Tunis 1967; Djaʿfar Mādjid, *al- al-Ḥaddād*, Tunis 1979 (study, followed b lected passages and verse and some of the *wāṭir*); Mutafarrij [= L. Bercher], in *REI* (201-30; J. Berque, in *Études d'orientalism Lévi-Provençal*, ii, Paris 1962, 487-8; C. mourette, *Polémique autour du statut de la f musulmane en Tunisie en 1930*, in *BEO D* xxx (1978), 12-31. (E

al-ḤĀDĪ ILA 'l-ḤAḲḲ, Abu 'l-Ḥusayn Y b. al-Ḥusayn b. al-Ḳāsim b. Ibrāhīm al-Ḥa the founder of the Zaydī imāmate in Ya was born in al-Madīna in 245/859. His mothe Umm al-Ḥasan Fāṭima bint al-Ḥasan b. Muḥa b. Sulaymān b. Dāwūd b. al-Ḥasan b. al-Ḥasa excelled early in religious learning and by the seventeen is said to have reached the level o dering independent judgments in *fiḳh* and comp treatises. Because of his erudition, physical stre bravery, and asceticism he soon came to be consi

s family, including his fathers and uncles, as
ıost suitable candidate for the Zaydī imāmate.
een 270/884 and 275/889 he visited with his
y Āmul in Ṭabaristān, then under the rule of
aydī ʿAlid Muḥammad b. Zayd, evidently in
to seek the support of the adherents of the
ine of his grandfather al-Ḳāsim b. Ibrāhīm
there. His activity soon aroused the suspicions
uḥammad b. Zayd and he was forced to leave
pitately. He also seems to have visited Baghdād
y. In 280/893-4 he came to northern Yaman for
irst time, invited by tribes in the region of
who were hoping that he might put an end to
feuds. He led a campaign as far south as al-
fa near Ṣanʿāʾ, but meeting much disobedience
g his followers, decided to return to al-Faraʿ,
y's trip southwest of al-Madīna. Three years
he was again urgently invited and on 6 Ṣafar
5 March 897 entered Ṣaʿda which became his
al and permanent base of operation. Shortly
his arrival, he issued his formal call (*daʿwa*) for
ort as the *imām* and assumed the title *amīr al-*
ınīn with the caliphal name al-Hādī ila 'l-Ḥaḳḳ.
er consolidating his control over the area of
, he extended his rule over Nadjrān in Djumādā
4/July 897, where he concluded a special treaty
the large community of Dhimmīs. In the
ving year he conquered the towns of Khaywān
Athāfit south of Ṣaʿda. His efforts to gain
ssion of Ṣanʿāʾ were only temporarily successful.
town was voluntarily turned over to him by its
Abu 'l-ʿAtāhiya of the Āl Ṭarīf, who had
dy previously supported him, and he occupied
the first time on 22 Muḥarram 288/19 January
and then pushed his conquests south as far as
ıār and Djayshān. The opposition of the Āl
r and the Āl Ṭarīf, who had been entrenched in
regions, was strong, and he quickly lost them
and definitely relinquished Ṣanʿāʾ in Djumādā
9/May 902 in a state of severe illness. A year later,
w campaign to take the town ended in failure
he capture of his son Muḥammad by the enemy.
Djumādā II 293/April 906 he again entered
ı̄ʾ, invited by a coalition of Yamanī chiefs
sed to the Ḳarmaṭī leader ʿAlī b. al-Faḍl. After
ırrel with Asʿad b. Abī Yuʿfir, he left voluntarily
uḥarram 294/November 906, and the Ḳarmaṭīs
possession of the town. Only during a campaign
lī b. al-Faḍl to Tihāma, an army of al-Hādī once
occupied Ṣanʿāʾ from 19 Radjab – 12 Shawwal
April – 23 June 910. Also abortive was a
paign of al-Hādī to Tihāma, probably early in
autumn 905. Even his rule in northern Yaman
shaken by numerous tribal rebellions, especially
adjrān, where the Banu 'l-Ḥārith revolted on
occasion. In 296/908 they succeeded in killing
overnor, and al-Hādī, already plagued by illness,
apparently unable to restore his rule over the
ince. His most loyal supporters were, besides
bers of his family and various other ʿAlids, a
troop of "Ṭabarīs", i.e. Zaydī volunteers
Daylamān and Kalār who arrived in two groups
5/898 and 289/902. He died on 19 Dhu 'l-Ḥidjdja
8 August 911. His tomb in the mosque of
a became a place of pilgrimage for the Zaydīs.
-Hādī's doctrine in *fiḳh*, laid down chiefly in
nfinished *K. al-Aḥkām* and the *K. al-Muntakhab*
cted by his follower Muḥammad b. Sulaymān
ūfī, became authoritative among the Zaydīs in
an as well as part of the Caspian Zaydī com-
ity. It was based on the doctrine of his grand-
er al-Ḳāsim b. Ibrāhīm, though in some points
al-Hādī adopted more strictly Shīʿī views, and was further elaborated, in Yaman, by al-Hādī's sons Muḥammad al-Murtaḍā (d. 310/922) and Aḥmad al-Nāṣir (d. 322/934), and, in the Caspian community, by the *imāms* al-Muʾayyad bi'llāh (d. 411/1020) and Abū Ṭālib al-Nāṭiḳ (d. 424/1033). In his theological works, al-Hādī generally espoused the doctrine of the Muʿtazilī school of Baghdād rather than that of his grandfather. It is unlikely, however, that he ever was a student of Abu 'l-Ḳāsim al-Balkhī, the contemporary head of this school, as some late sources state. Concerning the imāmate, he took a radically Shīʿī position, sharply condemning Abū Bakr and ʿUmar as usurpers.

Bibliography: ʿAlī b. Muḥammad b. ʿUbayd Allāh, *Sīrat al-Hādī ila 'l-Ḥaḳḳ Yaḥyā b. al-Ḥusayn*, ed. Suhayl Zakkār, Beirut 1392/1972; short biographies of al-Hādī are also contained in the following, unedited works: Abu 'l-ʿAbbās al-Ḥasanī, *al-Maṣābīḥ*, Abū Ṭālib al-Nāṭiḳ, *al-Ifāda*, and al-Muḥallī, *al-Ḥadāʾiḳ al-wardiyya*, ii; *Fihrist*, 194; Yaḥyā b. al-Ḥusayn b. al-Muʾayyad bi'llāh, *Ghāyat al-amānī*, ed. Saʿīd ʿAbd al-Fattāḥ ʿĀshūr, Cairo 1388/1968, i, 166-201; R. Strothmann, *Das Staatsrecht der Zaiditen*, Strassburg 1912, 53 f., 58 f.; C. van Arendonk, *Les débuts de l'imāmat zaidite au Yémen*, tr. J. Ryckmans, Leiden 1960, 127-305; W. Madelung, *Der Imam al-Qāsim ibn Ibrāhīm*, Berlin 1965, esp. 163-6; Sezgin, *GAS* I, 563-6. Several theological treatises of al-Hādī have been edited by Muḥammad ʿImāra in *Rasāʾil al-ʿadl wa'l-tawḥīd*, Cairo 1971, ii.

(W. MADELUNG)

HADJ [see ḤADJDJ].

ḤADJDJĀM [see FAṢṢĀD, in Suppl.]

HADJI [see ḤĀDJDJĪ].

ḤĀDJDJĪ AL-DABĪR, sobriquet of ʿABD ALLĀH MUḤAMMAD B. SIRĀDJ AL-DĪN ʿUMAR AL-NAHRWĀLĪ B. KAMĀL AL-DĪN MUḤAMMAD AL-MAKKĪ AL-ĀṢAFĪ ULUGH KHĀNĪ, historian in Gudjarāt under the Muẓaffarid dynasty. He was born in Mecca in 946/1540, the son of a Gudjarātī official who had been sent there in 941/1535 with the treasure of the Muẓaffarid Bahādur Shāh Gudjarātī [*q.v.*] and who returned to India in 962/1555, settling in Aḥmadābād. In 965/1559 Ḥādjdjī al-Dabīr entered the service of Muḥammad Ulugh Khan, a noble in the party of ʿImād al-Mulk, who opposed Iʿtimād al-Mulk [see GUDJARĀT]. After the invasion and conquest of Gudjarāt by Akbar in 980/1572-3, his father was entrusted with the *waḳf*s under the Mughal administration, and Ḥādjdjī al-Dabīr himself with the duty of conveying the funds to Mecca and Medina. He lost this post, however, in 983/1576, the year of his father's death. Subsequently we find him in the employ of another Gudjarātī noble, Sayf al-Mulūk, in Khāndesh, and finally in that of the Khāndesh noble Fūlād Khān, who died in 1014/1605.

This is the latest date mentioned in his Arabic chronicle, *Ẓafar al-wālih bi-muẓaffar wa-ālih*, in two *daftars*: (1) an account of the Muẓaffarids of Gudjarāt and of the neighbouring rulers in Khāndesh and the Deccan, and (2) a general history of Muslim rule in northern India. Of the lost authorities he quotes, the most important is the *Taʾrīkh* (or *Ṭabaḳāt*)-*i Bahādurshāhī* of Ḥusām Khān, which covered the period down to 940/1535. The date of composition of Ḥādjdjī al-Dabīr's own work is problematical, since he mentions the *Mirʾāt-i Sikandarī*, which was presented to the world only in 1020/1611. Ross therefore hypothesised that he began to write in 1015/1606.

Bibliography: *Ẓafar al-wālih bi-muẓaffar*

wa-ālih, ed. Sir E. Denison Ross, *An Arabic history of Gujarat*, London 1910-28, i, pp. vii-viii, and ii, pp. xvii ff.; Brockelmann, S II, 599-600.

(P. JACKSON)

ḤĀDJDJĪ IBRĀHĪM KHĀN KALĀNTAR, Persian statesman, was the third son of Ḥādjdjī Hāshim, the headman, or *kadkhudā-bāshī*, of the Ḥaydarīkhāna quarters of Shīrāz in the reign of Nādir Shāh. His ancestors were said to have been converts to Islam from Judaism. One of them emigrated from Ḳazwīn to Iṣfahān and is said to have married into the family of Ḥādjdjī Qawām al-Dīn Shīrāzī. Ḥādjdjī Maḥmūd ʿAlī, Ḥādjdjī Ibrāhīm's grandfather, was a wealthy merchant of Shīrāz. After the death of Mīrzā Muḥammad, the *kalāntar* of Shīrāz in 1200/1786, Djaʿfar Khān Zand made Ḥādjdjī Ibrāhīm *kalāntar* of Shīrāz, which office he continued to hold under Djaʿfar Khān's successor, Luṭf ʿAlī Khān. He appears to have enjoyed a position of considerable influence in the city and among the tribal leaders and governors of the surrounding districts. Although his relations with Luṭf ʿAlī Khān were disturbed by mutual suspicion already in 1204/1789-90, when Luṭf ʿAlī set out to attack Iṣfahān in 1205/1790-1 he left Ḥadjdjī Ibrāhīm in charge of affairs in Shīrāz. The latter seized the city during Luṭf ʿAlī's absence. Disorders meanwhile broke out in Luṭf ʿAlī's camp. He escaped and fled to Shīrāz, thinking that the city was still in his hands. After Ḥādjdjī Ibrāhīm had refused him access, he retired to the south. Ḥādjdjī Ibrāhīm sent an army after him, but this was defeated in Tangistān. Meanwhile, Ḥādjdjī Ibrāhīm entered into negotiations with Āḳā Muḥammad Khān Ḳādjār and was appointed *beglarbeg* or governor of Fārs. Zand resistance, however, continued and was not finally overcome until 1208/1794 [see ḲĀDJĀR].

In 1209/1794 Āḳā Muḥammad Khān made Ḥādjdjī Ibrāhīm *ṣadr-i aʿẓam*, in succession to Mīrzā Shafīʿ Māzandarānī, with the title Iʿtimād al-Dawla, which office he held for seven years, first under Āḳā Muḥammad Khān and then under Fatḥ ʿAlī Shāh. He appears to have been a competent administrator and virtually to have presided over every department of state. His brothers and sons also held governments. His power, however, aroused jealousy. His enemies persuaded Fatḥ ʿAlī Shāh that he was plotting to overthrow him, and on 1 Dhu 'l-Ḥidjdja 1215/15 April 1801 he was arrested in Tehran. Those of his relatives who held provincial governments were also seized. He was blinded and exiled to Ḳazwīn, where he died, and his estates were confiscated. Only two of his sons, twins, ʿAlī Riḍā and ʿAlī Akbar Ḳawām al-Mulk (b. 1203/1788-9), survived.

Bibliography: Ḥādjdjī Mīrzā Ḥasan Fasāʾī, *Fārsnāma-yi nāṣirī*, Tehran lith.; Mihdī Bāmdād, *Sharḥ-i ḥāl-i ridjāl-i Īrān dar ḳarn-i dawāzdahum wa sīzdahum wa čahārdahum-i hidjrī*, Tehran 1968-9, i, 21-8; Muḥammad Ḥasan Khān Iʿtimād al-Salṭana, *Ṣadr-i tawārīkh*, ed. Muḥammad Mushīrī, Tehran 1349, 12-44; idem, *Khalsa*, ed. Maḥmūd Katīrāʾī, Tehran 1348, 22-3; Riḍā Ḳulī Hidāyat, *Taʾrīkh-i Rawḍat al-ṣafā-yi nāṣirī*, Tehran 1339, ix, 367-70, x, 114-15, and index; ʿAbd Allāh Mustawfī, *Sharḥ-yi ḥāl zindagī-yi man*, Tehran 1945-6, i, 38-9, 50-2; Sir John Malcolm, *History of Persia*, London 1829, ii, 107 ff., 184, 206-9, 213-14, 309; idem, *Sketches of Persia*, London 1845, 202-6, 217-18, 222-4; Sir Harford Jones Brydges, *The dynasty of the Kajars*, London 1833, cxlii ff., 22, 25, 28, 128-33; C. R. Markham, *A general sketch of the history of Persia*, London 1874, 330 ff., 369-70; E. Scott Waring, *A tour to Sh* London 1807, 93-4.

(A. K. S. LAMBT

ḤĀDJIB.

i-v. — See Vol. iii.

vi. — IN MOROCCO.

This office, which existed already in the Alm organisation, though with a very modest role, ap again under the Marīnids (J. Temporal, translat Leo Africanus, calls the *ḥādjib* "chief of the men and A. Epaulard, another translator, makes hi chamberlain", head of the "court attendants" was still alive under the Saʿdids.

Under the ʿAlawids, the *ḥādjib* was for lon most important official of the Sharīfian palac was specifically designated as the interme between the sovereign and the high officials o *Makhzan* [*q.v.*], and it was through him that were given their orders and commissioned for sions. He kept the seal or stamp for fixing t official documents emanating from the ruler, ar had under his command all the internal profess groups (*ḥinṭa*, pl. *ḥnāṭi*) of the palace servants, tapestry-weavers, cooks, etc. In the protocol lis chief minister came after him, and he himself the place immediately behind the ruler, whor followed like a shadow. The office seemed so nece that the pretender al-Hība [*q.v.* in Suppl.], al immediately when he was proclaimed sultan ir Sūs in 1912, nominated someone as his *ḥādjib*. Ḥādjib Aḥmad b. Mūsā known as Bā Ḥmād above] was remembered as a great man in Mo at the end of the 19th century.

However, since the recovery of independen 1956, the *ḥādjib* has lost his importance, and n of his responsibilities have passed into the h of the Director of Protocol appointed by the Mi of the Royal Palaces.

Bibliographie: Leo Africanus, *Descriptio l'Afrique*, tr. Temporal, Paris 1896, tr. Epau Paris 1956, indices; L. Massignon, *Le M d'après Léon l'Africain*, Paris 1906; H. Gail *Le Makhzen*, in *Bull. de la Soc. de Geogr. d'A* (1908), 438-70; E. Lévi-Provençal, *Les histo des Chorfa*, Paris 1922, Appx. II, Liste des tionnaires impériaux des dynasties cherifier al-ʿUmarī, *Masālik al-abṣār*, tr. Gaude Demombynes, Paris 1927, index; G. S. C *Chrestomathie marocaine*, Paris 1939, par 208-9 (on the internal services of the pal G. Deverdun, *Inscriptions arabes de Marra* Rabat 1956, index. Ibn Zaydān, *al-ʿIzz wa 'l fī maʿālim naẓm al-dawla*, Rabat 1961, index also BĀ ḤMĀD above.

(G. DEVERDU

ḤAḌRAMAWT

The opportunity is taken of prefixing to the body of the article, on Ḥaḍramawt in the Isl period, some important recent items of informa on the region in the pre-Islamic time.

i. PRE-ISLAMIC PERIOD

In 1974 a French archaeological mission under direction of J. Pirenne began work at Shabwa, w is still continuing. The most significant result been the tracing of a very extensive town site to northeast of the rectangular sacral enclosure w the earliest visitors had noted; included in this some impressive ruins of what was probably royal place, and there were large tracts of cultiv ground in the wadi.

In 1973 Muṭahhar al-Iryānī published a seri Sabaean votive texts from Maʾrib which add mu

:nowledge of relations between Saba and Ḥaḍra-. These were sometimes peaceful, as in the case . a Sabaean mission was sent to Shabwa to take in the festival of the Ḥaḍramite national deity ı'rīkh al-Yaman, 184). At other times relations hostile, and the most striking text of this kind 13) shows that while the main Sabaean and amite armies were engaged in battle in the Bayḥān, a small Sabaean flying column, l at "rescuing" the queen of Ḥaḍramawt who sister to the Sabaean king, managed to capture oyal palace in Shabwa and hold out there for ays until relieved by the arrival of the main ean army after it had decisively defeated the amite force; the king of Ḥaḍramawt was sent as a prisoner to Ma'rib. Subsequently, the ean forces raided the port of Cane and destroyed aber of ships there—evidence that the later fame e Ḥaḍramīs as seafarers goes back to early times.

1974-6 Garbini has plausibly argued that the (up to then almost universally accepted) of the :e of the South Arabian pantheon is devoid of ıs evidence in favour of it, and exposed to vital nce contradicting it. Hence the reference in the r entry to "the astral triad of moon, sun and s-star", and the identification of the Ḥaḍramite nal deity as a moon god, must be treated now as f-date. Garbini's re-evaluation of the Sabaean nal deity as essentially a Dionysiac vegetation , having also affinities with a Herakles figure olar associations, must extend to the Ḥaḍramite as well.

:nificant new facts are now available about :oundation of a Ḥaḍramite settlement on the east of Salāla; this Pirenne identifies as the cal Moscha.

is opportunity may also be taken of saying that pelling of the name of the sand-desert between ib and Shabwa as Sab'atayn (a spelling deriving Philby) seems to be mistaken; modern maps d it in the spelling Sabʿatayn, It is what Yāḳūt other mediaeval Arab geographers call the ad desert.

3ibliographie: A. F. L. Beeston, *Warfare in :ient South Arabia*, London 1976; idem, *The myarite problem*, in *Procs. of the Seminar for abian Studies*, v (1975), 1-7; idem, *The settlement Khor Rori*, in *Jnal. of Oman Studies*, ii (1976), 42; Muṭahhar al-Iryānī, *Fī ta'rīkh al-Yaman*, nʿā' 1973; G. Garbini, *Il dio sabeo Almaqah*, in O, xlviii (1974), 15-22; idem, *Sur quelques oects de la religion sud-arabe pré-islamique*, in *h. G. W. Gött.*, Phil.-Hist. Kl., iii. Folge, Nr. (1976), 182-8; J. Pirenne, *The incense port at oscha, Khor Rori*, in *Jnal. of Oman Studies*, i 975), 81-96.

(A. F. L. Beeston)

ii. In the Islamic Period

lamic tradition, the name is derived either from ersonal name Ḥaḍramawt b. Ḥimyar, or from *mayyit*, or some such expression.

e name is applied to the wādī, the area and *abīla* of South Arabia. The wādī runs roughly east along the 16° line about 48° 15′ to 49° 15′, ıich point it becomes the Wādī al-Masīla, as it south-east and then due south to flow into the between Ḥayrīdj and Sayḥūt on the Indian n coast.

e area of Ḥaḍramawt begins in the west at a rawn between Shabwa in the north to the sea at aʿ on the Wādī Ḥadjr and extends south of Wādī amawt as far as Wādī al-Masīla in the east. The main towns of the area, which covers the territories of the pre-independence Ḳuʿayṭī and Kathīrī sultanates and now falls within the fourth and fifth governorates of the People's Democratic Republic of Yemen, are, in the north and along the Wādī, Shabwa, Ḥurayḍa, Shibām, Say'ūn, Tarīm, ʿĪnāt [*q.v.* below] and Ḳabr Hūd. The chief southern coastal towns are al-Mukallā, al-Shiḥr (though see below, on history) and Ghayl Bā Wazīr. Ḥaḍramawt is thus bounded by the sea in the south, Mahra country, the sixth governorate, in the east, the desert, the Empty Quarter, in the north and the western half of the fourth governorate in the west.

The tribal group named Ḥaḍramawt is supposed to inhabit the east and central areas of the Wādī itself, Shibām being described as the beginning of its territory. Its members are descended through Saba' al-Aṣghar from Ḥimyar.

1. History.

It is difficult to build up a comprehensive picture of the early and mediaeval history of Ḥaḍramawt. This is due to the relative inaccessibility and lack of exploitation of local Ḥaḍramī chronicles, still with few exceptions in manuscript, and to the extremely cursory treatment of the area in the Yemenī histories, in which Ḥaḍramawt appears only as a distant province of the Yemen.

First contacts with Islam were made directly with the Prophet, rather than through the Yemen, however, and there was correspondence between him and the local Kinda leaders of Ḥaḍramawt, resulting in the visit of al-Ashʿath b. Ḳays (or perhaps Wā'il b. Ḥadjr) to Medina. There he was well received by the Prophet, who acceded to his request and appointed Ziyād b. Labīd al-Anṣārī as ruler of Ḥaḍramawt. The latter remained there until after the Prophet's death. There can be no doubt that the conversion of the Ḥaḍramīs to Islam was not carried out as simply and as speedily as the Muslim sources insist, and the role of Ziyād and his successors in the area must have been more one of religious propagandist than of political leader. Indeed, Ḥaḍramawt, like the Yemen with its appallingly difficult problems of communication, must have entered the Islamic fold very gradually over an extended period of time.

The Prophet, the Orthodox, Umayyad and ʿAbbāsid caliphs until the 3rd/9th century, all appointed governors to Ṣanʿā', al-Djanad and Ḥaḍramawt. It is clear that the governor of the first always reported directly to the seat of Islamic government and that occasionally the latter two did also. For the most part, however, the governor of Ḥaḍramawt was merely a junior assistant of the governor of Ṣanʿā', and thus Ḥaḍramawt became a province (*mikhlāf*) of the Yemen. It should be mentioned at this juncture that al-Shiḥr, perhaps because of the independence of strong local rulers, during the early and mediaeval periods invariably figures as a separate political entity, not part of Ḥaḍramawt at all and always mentioned alongside it. Probably due to the steady exodus of many prominent Ḥaḍramīs from their native land to other parts of the empire during the Orthodox caliphate, the area sank into relative obscurity in the Umayyad and ʿAbbāsid eras.

The year 130/747 saw the introduction into Ḥaḍramawt of Ibāḍī doctrines by Abū Ḥamza al-Mukhtār b. ʿAwf al-Azdī al-Ḥarūrī, a close follower of ʿAbd Allāh b. Ibāḍ, from whom the Ibāḍiyya derived its name, and a Ḥaḍramī, ʿAbd Allāh b. Yaḥyā al-Kindī. Khāridjī ideas had in fact penetrated Ḥaḍramawt as early as 66/685, when a party of

Na**dj**diyya, the followers of Na**dj**da b. ʿĀmir al-Ḥanafī, arrived. It is possible therefore that the area was still receptive to Ibāḍī ideas in the 2nd/8th century. Al-Mu**kh**tār b. ʿAwf was a native of Baṣra and met ʿAbd Allāh b. Yaḥyā during the pilgrimage of 128/745. He was persuaded to return to Ḥaḍramawt with ʿAbd Allāh two years later. To what extent the Ibāḍiyya managed to control Ḥaḍramawt is not at all clear, though al-Masʿūdī, writing of the position in 332/943, states that they were predominant in the area and that there was no difference between them and the Ibāḍīs of ʿUmān. Certainly, the final blow to the movement in Ḥaḍramawt did not come until the intervention from the Yemen of the Ṣulayḥids, staunchly **Sh**īʿī and maintaining close ties with Fāṭimid Egypt, in the mid-5th/11th century.

It is evident that the Ibāḍiyya did not exercise political control over the entire area of Ḥaḍramawt, however. The Banū Ziyād, originally ʿAbbāsid representatives in the Yemen in the early 3rd/9th century, operating from their headquarters in Zabīd, conquered Tihāma and ruled independently. They then for some unknown reason became involved in Ḥaḍramawt also. The founder of the dynasty himself, Muḥammad b. Ziyād, had been appointed governor of the Yemen by the ʿAbbāsid caliph al-Maʾmūn. It was he who brought about Ziyādid rule in Ḥaḍramawt, rule which was to continue after his death in 245/859 until after the fall of the Ziyādids in 407/1016.

In fact, Ḥaḍramawt fell into Ṣulayḥid hands after their capture of Aden in 454/1062. Aden, Laḥ**dj**, Abyan, al-**Sh**iḥr and Ḥaḍramawt were all at the time in the hands of the Banū Maʿn, the little-known descendants of Maʿn b. Zāʾida [*q.v.*], who were at first left to administer the territories on behalf of their conquerors. In 473/1080, however, after the Maʿnids' refusal to pay the agreed *kharādj* to the Ṣulayḥids, the latter installed their **Sh**īʿī protégés, the Banū Zurayʿ, to run the affairs of the area, including Ḥaḍramawt, on their behalf. Thus the situation remained until after the entry of the Ayyūbids into the Yemen in 569/1171.

It is difficult at this stage to work out the exact chronology of events in Ḥaḍramawt. Certainly, with Ṣulayḥid control of Ḥaḍramawt through their clients, the Zurayʿids, lost, three powerful local dynasties appeared on the scene. Centred on Tarīm, the Banū Ḳaḥṭān took over much of the area, while the remainder fell to the Banu 'l-Daʿʿār in **Sh**ibām and the Āl Iḳbāl on the coast in al-**Sh**iḥr. The greater part of Ḥaḍramawt was taken by ʿU**th**mān al-Zan**dj**īlī, the Ayyūbid *nāʾib*, in 576/1180 after the departure for the north of the first Ayyūbid ruler, Tūrān-**Sh**āh b. Ayyūb, however, though pockets of local rule continued into the 10th/16th century, for the Ayyūbids were never in a position to pay much attention to Ḥaḍramawt; the demands of the troubled local situation on the Ayyūbid administration in the Yemen proper were too great to allow the luxury of firm control there. Other local dynasties followed: the Āl Yamānī, for example, from 621/1224 in Tarīm, surviving into the 10th/16th century.

The Ayyūbids' efforts in pacifying almost the whole of the Yemen proper and in putting an end to all local dynasties, with the exception of the Zaydīs north of Ṣanʿāʾ, ensured for their successors, the Rasūlids, a peaceful and stable country. The brilliant Rasūlid administration, which had assumed power through bloodless change, was not only able to consolidate the efforts of their erstwhile masters, the Ayyūbids, but was also able to think of eastwards expansion and the recapture of Ḥaḍramawt, ir case a province of the Yemen. There was, ther considerable Rasūlid activity along the south c even during the reign of the first sultan, al-] al-Manṣūr ʿUmar who died in 647/1249. During of his son and successor, al-Muẓaffar Yūsuf, whc in 694/1295, Rasūlid power was first emplanted along the coast as the port of Ẓafār, which unde Rasūlids marked the eastern limit of their cont

Possibly the only, and certainly the gre challenge to Rasūlid authority in Ḥaḍramawt that of the Ḥabūḍīs. Though originally from Ḥa in Ḥaḍramawt, the dynasty was founded in by Muḥammad b. Aḥmad (d. 620/1223). The fa continued on the coast through Aḥmad b. Muḥan (d. 628/1230) and Idrīs b. Aḥmad (d. 670/1271) latter's son, Sālim b. Idrīs, seized the opportuni take Ḥaḍramawt in 673/1274. Despite the cri help to the Rasūlids from the local populatic Ḥaḍramawt, it took the plundering by the Ḥal of a Rasūlid ship off Ẓafār and the Ḥabūḍīs' u the Rasūlid vassals of al-**Sh**iḥr to cast off allegiance to their masters to bring the latter all speed eastwards from their Yemenī ca Taʿizz. Ẓafār was recaptured and Ḥaḍrar recovered. The Ḥabūḍī house was destroyed.

It was the Ṭāhirids who succeeded in the 9th/15th century to most of the territories hel the Rasūlids, particularly those in the south east, though they were never strong in the Y north of Taʿizz. Although much less is known o dynasty than of the Rasūlids, their predecesso is possible to assert that Ḥaḍramawt for a time under their control. By the latter half of the 9th century, however, the Ka**th**īrīs, a tribal group inating from Ẓafār, had taken over some of interior of the country. They also controlled al- which they had at first held for the Ṭāhirids. Pos as early as the beginning of the 10th/16th cen a new political force was introduced into the for with the Ka**th**īrīs quarrelling among themse one faction brought into Ḥaḍramawt to assist group of Yāfiʿīs, a large tribal unit inhabiting area to the north-east of Aden. Yāfiʿī influ lingered on after this dispute, particularly in seaports of al-Mukallā and al-**Sh**iḥr. From no down to the 20th century, the political histor Ḥaḍramawt is nothing more than the chronic disputes between the Ka**th**īrīs and at least Yāfiʿī tribal factions, though of course from early 10th/16th century both the infidel Portug and the Turks had shown an interest in the sea along the South Arabian coast and had at t attacked and even occupied them.

In the 20th century, under the British Pr torate Ḥaḍramawt was divided between the Ka sultanate with its capital in Sayʾūn and the Ku sultanate, originally a Yāfiʿī tribal group, cen on al-Mukallā. Both sultanates were thus part o Eastern Aden Protectorate until the independen the whole of South Arabia in 1967.

2. Social organisation.

In general terms Ḥaḍramī society can be div into four classes: the *sayyids*, the *ma**sh**āyi**kh***, *ḳabāʾil* (tribesmen) and the *masākīn* or *ḍu* ("poor").

It is interesting to note that the pre-Isl South Arabian inscriptions refer to an aristoc group of *musawwads*, a word used to this da Ḥaḍramawt to denote the *sayyids*. The latter are descendants of the Prophet, while the *ma**sh**āyik*

noble families with the right to the hereditary
of *shaykh*, a word denoting class distinction,
a tribal chief. The *sayyid*s reached Ḥaḍramawt
ie early 6th/12th century, where they found
7 scholars, particularly in Tarīm and mainly of
mashāyikh class. Petty jealousies and quarrels
een the *sayyid*s and *mashāyikh* have continued
the time of the arrival of the former in Ḥaḍra-
t, though these have never prevented the trans-
on of knowledge and learning between the
social strata. By the close of the 6th/12th
ry only the ʿAlawī group of *sayyid*s remained
ive their name to them—the ʿAlawī *sayyids*.
an area of constant warfare and hostilities,
nstitution of the neutral territory was essential.
in Ḥaḍramawt the *ḥawṭa* [*q.v.*] came into
; at an early date. A saint in his own life-time
d demarcate the area of the *ḥawṭa* and arrange
he agreement of the tribes and, if necessary,
uthorities in the area, that a particular *ḥawṭa*
d remain inviolate and under the control of a
ab. Before the arrival of the *sayyid*s in Ḥaḍra-
t, the *ḥawṭa*s were in the hands of the *mashāyikh*.
as only then the *sayyid ḥawṭa*s were grad-
established, leading to the general decline of
mashāyikh ones.

3. Geography.

adramawt is a hot and, with the exclusion of the
al strip, dry land. The coastal plain is naturally
emely humid, as well as hot. Again if one excludes
coastal areas, it is mountainous too, and this,
her with the extremely low rainfall throughout
rea, means that very little of the total can be
e over to agriculture, the chief industry. Dates
traditionally formed the main crop, though in
recent times cotton has been an important
nodity also. Local grain crops include maize
oats. Tobacco is also found in places. Agriculture
tered either by the perennial flow of water in
vādīs (*ghayl*) or by wells.

4. The people.

e inhabitants of Ḥaḍramawt are Shāfiʿī Sunnīs.
s not surprising in such a poor area, they have
ys been prepared to travel abroad in search of
ing their livelihood. Many travelled to the East
es, in particular to Java, and their financial
s remitted home have always been the mainstay
e local economy.

Bibliography: Ṣāliḥ b. Ḥāmid al-ʿAlawī, *ʾrīkh Ḥaḍramawt*, Jedda 1968; Government of mbay, *An account of the Arab tribes in the inity of Aden*, Bombay 1909; A. S. Bujra, *The litics of stratification*, Oxford 1971; Hamdānī, *fat djazīrat al-ʿArab*; H. C. Kay, *Yaman, its ly medieval history*, London 1882; Comte de ndberg, *Études sur les dialectes de l'Arabie méri- onale*. i. *Ḥaḍramoût*, Leiden 1901; O. Löfgren, *abische Texte zur Kenntnis der Stadt Aden in ittelalter*, Uppsala 1936-50; Sir J. Redhouse and hammad ʿAsal, *El-Khazrajī's history of the súlí dynasty of Yemen*, *GMS*, Leyden-London 06-18; R. B. Serjeant, *The Portuguese off the uth Arabian Coast*, Oxford 1963; idem, *The iyids of Ḥaḍramawt*, London 1957; idem, *South abian Hunt*, London 1976; G. R. Smith, *The yyūbids and early Rasūlids in the Yemen*, *GMS*, ndon 1974-8; Yāḳūt, *Buldān*, s.v.; T. Lewicki, *s Ibāḍites dans l'Arabie du Sud au moyen âge*, *Fol. Or.*, i (1959), 3-17. (G. R. Smith)

iii. Language and dialect

The chief language of Ḥaḍramawt is, of course, Arabic. Until the most recent times, however, the literary Arabic of most regions of Arabia would include some non-literary vocabulary. These items were for the most part technical words of various trades and professions and, indeed, even at the present day there are often no literary equivalents for such technical words and expressions, except in the domain of commerce. Landberg and Serjeant have well documented the technical vocabulary of such trades as fishing and building. Some dictionnaires of Classical Arabic, such as the *Tādj al-ʿarūs* and Nashwān's *Shams al-ʿulūm* give southern Arabian terms not appearing in the earlier lexical sources.

The Ḥaḍramī dialect does, however, have a limited literary application in various genres of popular poetry. This dialect is in any case fairly close in phonology, morphology and syntax to literary (that is to say modern Classical) Arabic. This poetry has been difficult to record in the past, though Serjeant made a most useful collection, because it is often of such a satirical or personal nature that the poet would prefer its circulation to be circumscribed. It may be, nevertheless, that this kind of poetry will find its way increasingly into print, in much the same way as *nabaṭī* poetry is now widely printed and read in northern Arabia.

The Mahra [*q.v.*] make up a considerable linguistic minority in Ḥaḍramawt, in that part adjoining Dhofar (Ẓafār), and it is undoubtedly true that Mahrī [*q.v.*] or an earlier form of this Semitic language was the principal language of the whole or most of the South, though even in pre-Islamic times Arabic would seem to have been an important language for the composition of formal works such as poetry.

The Mahrī of Ḥaḍramawt is fairly well-documented in the publications of the Austrian South Arabian Expedition, which are, to all intents and purposes, confined to this dialect of Mahrī. The Ḥaḍramī dialect of Mahrī is less conservative than that of Dhofar and a good deal more penetrated by Arabic. Indeed, many Mahra in Ḥaḍramawt now speak only Arabic, and this is particularly true of the settled elements. In Dhofar, on the contrary, many Mahra have adopted Djibbālī (or Śherí), the language of the mountain area.

Most of the dialects of Mahrī, or languages closely related to it, are spoken in Dhofar, but there is in Ḥaḍramawt, close to the border, a language spoken, namely Hōbyōt, whose existence has not previously been reported. On the basis of the little information available, Hōbyōt seems to be a Mahrī dialect with a considerable intermixture of Djibbālī. Another hitherto unreported language or dialect spoken not far over the Dhofar border, called Whēbyōt, may in fact be the same as Hōbyōt, with perhaps a greater admixture of Djibbālī.

Bibliography: C. Landberg, *Études sur les dialectes de l'Arabie méridionale*. i. *Ḥaḍramoût*, Leiden 1901; idem, *Glossaire datînois*, i-iii, Leiden 1920-42; R. B. Serjeant, *Prose and poetry from Ḥaḍramawt*, London 1951 (for his many articles on related topics, see J. D. Pearson, *Index islamicus*); al-Zubaydī, *Tādj al-ʿarūs*, Kuwait 1965-74; ʿAẓīmuddīn Aḥmad, *Die auf Südarabien bezüglichen Angaben Naśwān's im Śams al-ʿulūm*, Leiden and London 1916; D. H. Müller, *Südarabische Expedition, ix. Mehri- und Ḥaḍrami-Texte . . .*, Vienna 1909 (and iii by A. Jahn; iv, vi, vii by D. H. Müller); M. Bittner, *Studien zur Laut- und Formenlehre der Mehri-Sprache in Südarabien*, in *SBWAW* (1909-15); A. Jahn, *Grammatik der Mehri-Sprache in Süd-Arabien*, Vienna 1905. E. Wagner gives a useful bibliography for Southern Mahrī in his *Syntax der Mehri-Sprache*, Berlin 1953. (T. M. Johnstone)

ḤĀFIẒ TANÎSH b. Mīr Muḥammad al-Bukhārī, with the poetical name Nakhlī, historian of ʿAbd Allāh Khān [*q.v.*], the Shaybānid ruler of Bukhārā.

His father was close to ʿUbayd Allāh Khān (940-6/1533-40). Ḥāfiẓ Tanîsh mentions in his historical work that he began to write it, being 36 years old, when ʿAbd Allāh Khān established his rule over Transoxania and made Bukhārā his capital. It was believed for a long time (including by the present author) that he means the official accession to the throne of ʿAbd Allāh Khān, which took place in 991/1583, and therefore the date of his birth was supposed to be 956/1549 (36 years before the date of the beginning of his work, cf. below). However, Ḥāfiẓ Tanîsh mentions also that he wrote a *ḳaṣīda* on the accession to the throne of Iskandar Khān, the father of ʿAbd Allāh Khān (968/1560), which must place the date of his birth much earlier—probably, in the 1530s or even 1520s. In that case, Ḥāfiẓ Tanîsh may have meant by the establishment of the rule of ʿAbd Allāh Khān over Transoxania the capture of Bukhārā (964/1557), or the accession of Iskandar Khān (under whom ʿAbd Allāh was the actual ruler), or the capture of Samarḳand (986/1578). Ḥasan Nithārī in his anthology *Mudhakkir al-aḥbāb*, written in 974/1566-7 (see Storey, 802, no. 1102), mentions a poet Nakhlī among those poets who had not yet reached an advanced age and lived in Bukhārā (MS. of the Leningrad Branch of the Institute of Oriental Studies, B-4020, ff. 126-7); this person may very probably be Ḥāfiẓ Tanîsh.

He began to write probably his Persian history of ʿAbd Allāh Khān in the 1570s or 1560s; it was known already in 993/1585, when his contemporary Mīr Sayyid Muḥammad praised it in his *Adhkār al-azkiyāʾ* (see B. Aḥmedov and K. Munirov, *Ḥāfiẓ Tanîsh Bukhārī* [in Uzbek], Tashkent 1963, 55). After ʿAbd Allāh Khān had been proclaimed the supreme khān of all the Uzbeks (991/1583), Ḥāfiẓ Tanîsh was introduced to his court by the historian's patron, an influential *amīr* Ḳul-Bābā Kökältāsh, and became an official historiographer, usually also accompanying the khān in his numerous military campaigns. In 992/1584 he began to re-write his history according to a new plan, and gave it the title *Sharaf-nāma-yi Shāhī* (a chronogram = the date 992); both in Central Asian historiography and in modern scholarly literature it became known also as the *ʿAbd Allāh-nāma*. According to the initial plan of this second version, as laid down in author's preface, it was to be divided into a *muḳaddima* (the genealogy of ʿAbd Allāh Khān and a short history of the Djučids and the Shaybānids, his predecessors); two *maḳāla*s (1) from ʿAbd Allāh Khān's birth in 940/1533 to his accession and (2) from his accession onwards; and a *khātima* (on the outstanding qualities of the khān, the famous people of his reign, his buildings, etc.). The first *maḳāla* was apparently finished not earlier than 995/1586-7 (mentioned as the current date in the text) and before 998/1589-90 (mentioned as the current date in the preface to the second *maḳāla*, found only in one of the existing manuscripts). He carried his work up to 997/1588-9 (the date of the last event which he mentioned, the conquest of Harāt by the Uzbeks), but then the plan of the work was changed, and Ḥāfiẓ Tanîsh included the whole material in the first *maḳāla*. The *khātima*, absent in all existing manuscripts, was most pro[bably] not written at all. It is not known when the a[uthor] finished the work in its existing form.

The *Sharaf-nāma-yi Shāhī* is based mainly o[n per]sonal observations of the author, reports of eyewitnesses and official documents. In his *m[uḳad]dima*, Ḥāfiẓ Tanîsh used various literary so[urces] which he partially named, as well as oral trad[ition]. The work is written in ornate prose, with exte[nsive] use of *sadjʿ* and numerous verses (their total nu[mber] is 4,760), both by Tanîsh himself and other p[oets]. The main deficiency of the work, besides its pom[pous] style, is the frequent absence of precise d[ates]. Nevertheless, it is one of the major works of Ce[ntral] Asian historiography and the most important hi[stori]cal source for the Shaybānī period.

The further career of Ḥāfiẓ Tanîsh is not [known]. Nothing is known about his life in the last se[veral] years of the reign of ʿAbd Allāh Khān, nor durin[g the] short reign of his son ʿAbd al-Muʾmin. Some so[urces] mention a poet with the same poetical nam[e] Nakhlī at the court of the Ashtarkhānid Imām-[Ḳulī] Khān (1020-51/1611-42) (see *Tadhkira-yi Ṭ[āhir] Naṣrābādī*, Tehran 1316-17/1937-8, 435; *Tadhk[ira-yi] Muḳīm-Khānī* by Muḥammad Yūsuf Mu[nshī], Russian tr. by A. A. Semenov, 83, 90); accordi[ng to] Naṣrābādī, after the death of Imām-Ḳulī [Khān] (1054/1644-5) this Nakhlī went to Balkh, whe[re he] died. Two manuscripts of the *dīwān* of Nakh[lī are] preserved in Tashkent and Dūshanbe; one o[f the] *ḳaṣīda*s in this *dīwān* is dated 1045/1635-6. If Nakhlī is identical with Ḥāfiẓ Tanîsh, it must [mean] that the latter was still active at an age of abou[t] or more. Even more doubts are thrown upon [this] identification by the fact that none of the p[oems] belonging to Ḥāfiẓ Tanîsh and cited in *Sharaf-nā[ma-yi] Shāhī* is included in the *dīwān* of Nakhlī. [Some] scholars, nevertheless, accept the identific[ation] without reservations.

Bibliography: biographical information a[bout] Ḥāfiẓ Tanîsh is discussed especially in the follo[wing] works: B. Aḥmedov, in his preface to the [first] volume of the Uzbek translation of the *Sh[araf-] nāma-yi Shāhī* (see below) and in his work, tog[ether] with K. Munirov, cited above; V. P. Yudi[n], *Materialî po istorii kazakhskikh khanstv XVIII vekov*, Alma-Ata 1969, 237-40; M. A. [Sala]khetdinova, in *VII godičnaya naučnaya se[ssiya] LO IVAN* (*kratkiye soobshčeniya*), Moscow [1971], 111-3, and in *VIII godičnaya naučnaya se[ssiya] LO IVAN*, Moscow 1972, 48-52; N. D. Miklu[kho-]Mayklay, *Opisaniye persidskikh i tadžik[skikh] rukopisey Instituta Vostokovedeniya*, vîpus[k] Moscow 1975, 295-6. The text of the *Sharaf-nā[ma-yi] Shāhī* remains unpublished. Concerning the m[anu]scripts and publications of short extracts, as [well] as Russian translations of extracts, see St[orey-] Bregel, 1130-3, no. 990. The publication of a[n] Uzbek translation begun in 1966 is still [not] finished: only two volumes (out of four) [were] published in 1966-9 (see Storey-Bregel, 1[...]).

(Yu. Bregel)

HAGIOGRAPHY [see manāḳib].

HAIFA [see ḥayfā].

ḤĀʾIK (a.), pl. *ḥāka*, also *ḥayyāk* (synonym, *sādj*), weaver. Given the supreme importanc[e of] textiles in mediaeval Islamic life and economy [see e.g. ḥarīr and bisāṭ in Suppl.], the class of wea[vers] was probably the most numerous and certainly [one] of the most important groups of artisans. [The] weavers of Damascus, Baghdād, Egypt, the Ye[men] and a host of other towns throughout the Isl[amic]

l wove fabrics ranging from the coarse and aday types to the finest and most delicate (cf. . Serjeant, *Islamic textiles, material for a history o the Mongol conquest*, Beirut 1972, *passim*). cially highly-skilled workers were to be found in *irāz* [*q.v.*] factories producing for the court and he state during the Umayyad, ʿAbbāsid and nid periods, and these were probably somewhat r-paid than the mass of textile workers. The whelming majority of these last worked in their homes for dealers or middlemen or in small shops situated in the markets of cloth merchants. he whole, the weavers were, as in the ancient classical societies of the Near East, an exploited ill-paid class, working in vile conditions, and fact no doubt contributed to their image in aeval Islamic times as a turbulent and socially-ile group, easily swayed by heterodox religious political doctrines; one recalls the similar e of weavers in mediaeval France, Flanders and and, when in the first two regions at least, *and* was at times almost synonymous with etic". Certainly, at the beginning of the 3rd/ entury, the Coptic weavers of the Nile delta in ɔt earned only half-a-*dirham* per day, "insuffi- for the bread of their mouths", as they com-ed to the Patriarch Dionysios of Tell-Mahré Mez, *Renaissance*, 433-4, Eng. tr. 461).
e materials used included cotton, wool, linen silk. Some jurists recommended that a weaver ld not weave silken cloth, which is forbidden for s' wear. The legality of whether a cloth should be n in silk mixed with other material forms the ect of juristic discussion. If the warp of the c (*sadā*) is *ibrism* and its weft (*luḥma*) is *kuṭn* or (floss silk), it was permissible (cf. Ibn Ṭūlūn, *d al-ṭālib*, Chester Beatty Ms. 3317, fol. 50). ving was carried on by men as well as women, spinning was done by womenfolk only.
mediaeval Islamic times, opinion was in general lemnatory of the manners and habits of the vers. Typical anti-*ḥāʾik* opinions are as follows: most silly persons are the weavers"; "When a ver is asleep, he is worthless and harmful; when s awake, his companionship brings disgrace"; intelligence of a woman is equal to that of nty weavers"; and the like. According to a d, told by many Arab and Syriac writers, s' mother Mary (*Maryam*) once lost her way in h of her son and she asked the weaver to guide to the Sepulchre; but the *ḥāʾik* misguided her; then asked a tailor (*khayyāṭ*), who showed her right path. Thereupon Mary cursed the weaver blessed the tailor. This is why the weaver is ed to be damned for ever. This legend served as basis for prejudice against weavers. Arab senti-t about the weavers is further epitomised in iẓ's words, "The weavers in every age and in y country possess in equal measure foibles such ort temper, stupidity, ignorance and iniquity."
. Islamic tradition literature (*ḥadīth*), the trade e *ḥāʾik* is often linked with other noisome and easant callings, sc. those of the cupper [see ĀD in Suppl.], the tanner [see DABBĀGH in Suppl.] the sweeper. This condemnation was noted by lziher, who pointed out that the *textor* in Roman s was despised, and that in the early Islamic ɔd, many of the weavers, both male and female, slaves (*Die Handwerke bei den Arabern*, in *us*, lxvi [1894], 205 = *Gesammelte Schriften*, iii, esheim 1969, 318). R. Brunschvig subjected the status of the weaver to a detailed examination in his *Métiers vils en Islam*, in *SI*, xvi (1962), 50 ff. He demonstrated that this could not be from the unpleasant and polluting nature of the trade, as with tanning and sweeping, but must rather have arisen on religious grounds, from the many traditions in circulation, attributed to ʿAlī and to other prominent dignitaries of early Islam, condemning weavers as the offspring of Satan (cf. also the story of Mary and the *ḥāʾik*, above). However, the gradual spiritualisation of Islamic society by the ʿAbbāsid period, the notion of the equality of all believers, and the evident high economic value of the textile trade, did eventually contribute to an amelioration of attitudes towards weavers.

Thus Islamic society adopted paradoxical attitudes towards the weaver and his craft. The weaver is despised, but weaving (*ḥiyāka*) as a handicraft is praised. Ibn Ḳutayba, Thaʿālibī, and Bayhaḳī include *ḥiyāka* in a list of the crafts of the nobility (*ṣināʿāt al-ashrāf*), and Ibn Taymiyya, Ibn Ṭūlūn and other scholars uphold the theory that weaving is one of the obligatory duties of the collective body of the Muslims (*farḍ kifāya* [see FARḌ]). Ghazālī and al-Lubūdī say that weaving is a highly beneficial and indispensable craft. "Weaving and tailoring are two essential crafts in civilisation, because humanity is in need of them for comfort", argued Ibn Khaldūn also. In spite of these pronouncements on the importance of weaving, public invectives against the weavers persisted in traditional Islamic societies.

The legal status of weavers and other despised professions was weak, and there was discussion over their *ʿadāla*, their probity and their admissibility as bearers of legal testimony (*shahāda*) in courts of law [see ʿADL]. The attitudes of the law schools varied somewhat. The Ḥanafīs were inclined to admit the *ʿadāla* of the despised trades, if their practitioners displayed superior religious and moral qualities; the Mālikīs were the most rigorous, only admitting it where necessity had compelled adoption of the trade in question; the Shāfiʿīs and Ḥanbalīs took up intermediate positions. The Imāmī Shīʿī attitude was more liberal than the Sunnī one on matters like *ʿadāla* and on the doctrine of *kafāʾa* [*q.v.*], comparability of status in marriage. Social restraints notwithstanding, early Islamic civilisation produced learned men among sons of weavers, e.g., Abū Ḥamza Madjmaʿ b. Samʿān al-Ḥāʾik, an Islamic traditionist, and Ibn al-Ḥāʾik, the author of *Kitāb Djazīrat al-ʿArab*.

Bibliography: In addition to references given in the article: Djāḥiẓ, *Ḥayawān*, Cairo 1948, ii, 105; idem, *Rasāʾil*, Cairo 1933, 127; Ibn Ḳutayba, *Maʿārif*, Beirut 1970, 249-50; Bayhaḳī, *al-Maḥāsin wa 'l-masāwī*, Beirut 1960, 103; Shaybānī, *Kitab al-Kasb*, in *Kitāb al-Mabsūṭ*, Cairo 1906-13, xxx, 260; Thaʿālibī, *Arbaʿ rasāʾil*, Istanbul 1883-4, 203; idem, *Laṭāʾif al-maʿārif*, Cairo 1960, 129; Abū Nuʿaym, *Akhbār Iṣbahān*, Leiden 1934, ii, 117; al-Khaṭīb al-Baghdādī, *Taʾrīkh Baghdād*, iii, 67; idem, *al-Taṭfīl*, Damascus 1346, 83; Tawḥīdī, *Baṣāʾir*, Damascus 1966, iv, 146-7; Ghazālī, *Iḥyāʾ ʿulūm al-dīn*, Cairo 1346, i, 12; Rāghib al-Iṣfahānī, *Muḥāḍarāt*, Beirut 1961, ii, 459-61; Ibrāhīm b. ʿAlī al-Shīrādjī, *al-Tanbīh fi 'l-fiḳh*, Leiden 1879, 236-7; Ibn al-Djawzī, *Akhbār al-ḥamḳā*, Damascus 1345, 112; al-Samʿānī, *Ansāb*, Hyderabad 1964, iv, 32; Bar-Hebraeus, *The laughable stories*, tr. E. A. W. Budge, London 1897, 123; al-Lubūdī, *Faḍl al-iktisāb*, Chester Beatty Ms., 4791, fol. 57a; Ibn Taymiyya, *al-Ḥisba fi 'l-Islām*, Cairo n.d., 21; Yāḳūt, *Irshād*, vi, 1, 9; Ibshīhī, *al-Mustaṭraf*, Cairo 1952, i, 65; Ibn Ṭūlūn,

Ḍawʾ al-sirādj fī-mā ḳīla fi ʾl-nassādj, Chester Beatty Ms. 3317, fols. 127-9; Ibn Khaldūn, *Muḳaddima*, Cairo n.d., 266-7, 400, 411; M.S. al-Ḳāsim, *Dictionnaire des métiers damascains*, Paris i, 86-8; Kattānī, *Tarātib*, Beirut n.d., ii. 58-60. (M. A. J. Beg)

ḤĀʾIRĪ, Shaykh ʿAbd al-Karīm Yazdī (1859-1937), a Persian religious leader with whom the history of the Shīʿī clergy entered a new phase.

After preliminary education in Ardakān and Yazd, Ḥāʾirī left for ʿIrāḳ in 1877 and studied mainly under Sayyid Muḥammad Fishārakī (d. 1898) in Sāmarrāʾ and Nadjaf. In 1900, upon the invitation of his colleague, Sayyid Muṣṭafā and the latter's father Ḥādjdjī Āḳā Muḥsin, Ḥāʾirī moved to Arāk (Iran) and established the Arāk Circle for Religious Studies. Ḥāʾirī argued that politics in the Muslim world were being controlled by Western powers and were consequently hostile to Islam. In order to prevent the extinction of Islam, therefore, a responsible religious leader must not interfere in politics. This type of approach by Ḥāʾirī to politics, which was pursued throughout his life, began to be noticed in Arāk and resulted in his departure from that city, where his host, Ḥādjdjī Āḳā Muḥsin, was fighting against the Persian Constitutional Revolution of 1906 (Aḥmad Kasravī, *Tārīkh-i Mashrūṭa-yi Īrān*, Tehran 1951, 281-5, 409) and naturally expected Ḥāʾirī's cooperation. Ḥāʾirī then went to Nadjaf, but he found it also seriously involved in the Persian Revolution; therefore he moved to Karbalā where he limited himself to religious activities, including teaching *fiḳh* and *uṣūl*. Ḥāʾirī again moved to Arāk and lived there 1913-22, during which time he enjoyed a large body of disciples.

Meanwhile, in 1920, because of the death of two great *mudjtahids*, Mīrzā Muḥammad Taḳī Shīrāzī and Shaykh al-Sharīʿa Iṣfahānī, the office of *mardjaʿ-i taḳlīd* was divided among Sayyid Abu ʾl-Ḥasan Iṣfahānī and Mīrzā Muḥammad Ḥusayn Nāʾīnī in Nadjaf and Ḥāʾirī in Iran. By then, Ḥāʾirī's apolitical character was widely known, and turned out to play a role not only in his own life but also in the fate of the clerical world of the Shīʿa. To see this role, one must keep in mind that the British, having a variety of interests in the Shīʿī world, had faced many difficulties caused by the Shīʿī *ʿulamāʾ* of ʿIrāḳ, such as their involvement in the Persian Revolution, their declaration of *djihād* in World War I, and their struggle for the independence of ʿIrāḳ in 1919-22. After the imposition of the British mandatory rule in ʿIrāḳ in 1920, efforts were made to curtail the influence of the *ʿulamāʾ*. This policy resulted, among other things, in the banishment in 1923 of Nāʾīnī, Iṣfahānī, Shaykh Mahdī Khāliṣī and many other *ʿulamāʾ*, which injured the prestige and centrality of the Shīʿī institution of ʿIrāḳ.

In the meantime, we see Ḥāʾirī receiving particular attention in Iran. Upon the invitation of the notables of Ḳum, Ḥāʾirī, in March 1922, went to Ḳum to establish the Circle for Religious Studies of that city, where he received a warm reception; the then monarch, Aḥmad Shāh, personally went to Ḳum to greet him. Through Ḥāʾirī's efforts, the attention of the Shīʿa was directed to the Ḳum Circle; solutions for religious problems were sought in Ḳum and the students of religion, whose number at a time exceeded 1,000, found Ḳum a convenient alternative to Nadjaf and Karbalā. The latter development bore fruits favourable to the British policy in the area; the clerical institution of ʿIrāḳ was partially transferred to Iran, whose then strongest man, the S Sipah (later Riḍā Shāh), was in fact to curta there was created in Iran a strong religious which would by its nature weaken the young Pe Communist movement; and finally (perhaps most important of all), clerical leadership came in to the hands of Ḥāʾirī who, unlike his Nadjaf leagues, would not intervene in politics. Ḥāʾirī once was drawn into these: in 1924 the Sardār S attempted a republican form of government w gave rise to a popular uprising and involved clergy, including the banished *ʿulamāʾ* then resi in Ḳum. On this subject, meetings were held by *ʿulamāʾ* of the exodus and chaired by Ḥāʾirī in (F.O. 416/74, 26 March 1924, no. 126) and finall terminate the confusion, Ḥāʾirī and other *ʿul* were urged to declare that they requested the Sa Sipah to dispense with republicanism. In c cases, however, Ḥāʾirī rejected politics; he did fully identify his position with that of the *ʿul* of the exodus. Measures taken by Riḍā Shāh aro clerical opposition led by Ḥādjdjī Āḳā Nūr A Iṣfahānī in 1927 and Ḥādjdjī Āḳā Ḥusayn Ḳu in 1935, to neither of which Ḥāʾirī gave a no able response. Even the Circle founded by Ḥ became the target of governmental pressures, to extent that his special assistant, Shaykh Muḥam Taḳī Bāfḳī, was arrested in 1927 (Muḥammad I *Risālat al-Taḳwā wa-mā adrāka mā al-taḳwā: Sh ḥāl-i Shaykh Muḥammad Taḳī Bāfḳī*, Tehran 19 but no reaction was elicited from Ḥāʾirī.

Ḥāʾirī's biographers give him credit for his typ approach to politics at that specific period: protected religion in the light of his patience, dence, and wisdom" (Āghā Buzurg Ṭihrānī, *Ṭab aʿlām al-Shīʿa*, i/3 Tehran 1962, 1161-4). T pressures, however, did not preclude Ḥāʾirī undertaking with great interest cultural activ such as establishing a library, hospital, relig schools, public cemetery and mortuary, housing the poor, and so on. It is interesting to note tha trained many disciples who later on became relig leaders, some of whom, unlike Ḥāʾirī, undert political activities; Āyat Allāh Sayyid Rūḥ A Mūsawī Khumaynī, who was living in exile in P until his return to Iran in January 1979, may mentioned as the best-known example.

Bibliography: Abdul-Hadi Hairi, *Shī and constitutionalism in Iran: a study of the played by the Persian residents of Iraq in Ira politics*, Leiden 1977; Muḥammad ʿAlī Muda *Rayḥānat al-adab*, i, Tabrīz 1967; Mullā Wāʿiẓ, *Kitāb-i ʿUlamāʾ-i muʿāṣirīn*, Tabrīz 19 Muḥammad Rāzī, *Āthār al-ḥudjdja*, i-ii, K 1954-5; Sayyid ʿAlī Riḍā Rayḥān Yazdī, *Āʾīn dānishwarān*, Tehran 1967; Muḥammad Ḥirz Dīn, *Maʿārif al-ridjāl*, ii, Nadjaf 1964; Ma Bāmdād, *Sharḥ-i ḥāl-i ridjāl-i Īrān*, ii, iv, Teh 1968; Sayyid Muḥammad Mahdī al-Mūs *Aḥsan al-wadīʿa*, ii, Nadjaf 1968; Amīr Mas Sipihrūn, *Taʾrīkh-i barguzīdagān*, Tehran 19 Ghulām Ḥusayn Muṣāḥib, ed., *Dāʾira al-maʿā fārsī*, i, Tehran 1966; Yaḥyā Dawlatābādī, *Ḥay Yaḥyā*, iv, Tehran 1952; Ḥasan Iʿẓām Ḳu *Kitāb-i khāṭirāt-i man*, ii, 1964; Muḥamn Ḥusayn Nāṣir al-Sharīʿa, *Taʾrīkh-i Ḳum*, K 1971; Ḥusayn Makkī, *Taʾrīkh-i bīstsāla-yi Ī* ii-iii, Tehran 1944-6; ʿAbd Allāh Musta *Sharḥ-i zindigānī-yi man*, iii, Tehran 1964; Ā Buzurg Ṭihrānī, *al-Dharīʿa ilā taṣānīf al-Shīʿa*, Tehran 1941; Ḥādjdjī Sayyid Aḥmad Shub Zandjānī, *al-Kalām yadjūr al-kalām*, i, Ḳum 19

tuwār, spring 1950; *Iṭṭilāʿāt*, 1934; Sayyid
hammad Ḥusayn Ṭabāṭabāʾī, *et alii*, *Baḥthī*
bāra-yi mardjaʿiyyat va rūḥāniyyat, Tehran
52; Mahdī Ḳulī Hidāyat, *Khaṭirāt wa khaṭarāt*,
hran 1965; ʿAbbās Fayḍ, *Ḳum wa rūḥāniyyat*,
Ḳum 1938; Abbās Masʿūdī, *Iṭṭilāʿāt dar yak*
ʿ-i ḳarn, Tehran 1950; Muḥammad Ḥasan
rāvī, *al-Ḥadīḳa al-raḍawiyya*, Mashhad 1947;
assan R. Atiyyah, *Iraq 1908-1921: a political*
dy, Beirut 1973; ʿAbd Allāh Fahd al-Nafīsī,
wr al-Shīʿa fī taṭawwur al-ʿIrāḳ al-siyāsī
ḥadīth, Beirut 1973; [Muḥammad al-Khāliṣī],
aẓālim-i Ingilīs, Tehran, n.d. For divergent
ws on the republican movement, cf. *inter*
a, Ḥusayn Kūhī Kirmānī, *Bargī az taʾrīkh-i*
ʿāṣir-i Īrān yā ghawghā-yi djumhūrī, Tehran
52; *Shafaḳ-i surkh*, Jan. 22, 1924; *Ḥabl al-matīn*,
t. 6, 13, 27, and Nov. 3, 1924; *Īrānshahr*, ii, nos.
7 (1924), 274-7, 372-4, 432; ʿAlī Akbar Mushīr
līmī, *Kulliyyāt-i muṣawwar-i ʿIshḳī*, Tehran
71; Sayyid Mahdī Farrukh, *Khāṭirāt-i siyāsī-yi*
rrukh, Tehran 1968; Abu ʾl-Ḳāsim ʿĀrif Ḳaz-
nī, *Kulliyyat-i Dīwān*, Tehran 1963; Munīb al-
hmān, *Post-revolution Persian verses*, Aligarh
55; Iʿzāz Nīkpay, *Taḳdīr yā tadbīr: khāṭirāt*,
hran 1969. For an incomplete picture of the
oblem, see with caution, D. N. Wilber, *Riza Shah*
hlavi, New York 1975. (ABDUL-HADI HAIRI)

AKARI [see ḤAKKĀRĪ].

-ḤĀKIM AL-DJUSHAMĪ, ABŪ SAʿD AL-SIN B. MUḤAMMAD B. KARĀMA AL-BAYHAḲĪ ARAWḲANĪ, Muʿtazilī, later Zaydī, scho- was born in Ramaḍān 413/December 1022 Djusham (Persian: Djishum), a village in the n of Bayhaḳ. According to Ibn Funduḳ, he was scendant of Muḥammad b. al-Ḥanafiyya, but family was not known by the *nisba* of al-ʿAlawī. first teacher was Abū Ḥāmid Aḥmad b. Mu- mad al-Nadjdjār, a student of the Muʿtazilī ʿAbd al-Djabbār, who taught him Muʿtazilī logy, *uṣūl al-fiḳh*, and *ḥadīth*. After Abū Ḥāmid's h in 433/1041-2, he continued his studies with ʾl-Ḥasan ʿAlī b. ʿAbd Allāh (d. 457/1067), ident of the Zaydī *imām* Abū Ṭālib al-Nāṭiḳ, in haḳ. He also studied and taught in Naysābūr, re he read Ḥanafī *fiḳh* works with the famous afī scholar Abū Muḥammad al-Nāṣiḥī, *ḳāḍī* *ḍāt* of Bukhārā, in 434-6/1043-5. Other well- vn scholars whom he heard in Naysābūr were *mīr* Abu ʾl-Faḍl al-Mīkālī, Abū ʿAbd al-Raḥmān lamī, and ʿAbd al-Ghāfir al-Fārisī. Later he ht in the mosque of his native village Djusham, re he read the sixty lectures contained in his *Djalāʾ al-abṣār*, in the years 478-81/1086-8. ng his students was Aḥmad b. Muḥammad b. ḳ al-Khʷārazmī, the teacher of al-Zamakhsharī. lied in Mecca in Radjab 484/May 1101, allegedly d by religious opponents because he had written ctitious "Epistle of the devil to his fatalist hren" (*Risālat Iblīs ilā ikhwānihī al-mudjbira*) because he publicly propagated Zaydī doctrine. uring most of his life, al-Ḥākim al-Djushamī vely supported the Muʿtazilī theology of the ol of ʿAbd al-Djabbār and adhered to the Ḥanafī ol of *fiḳh*. Though expressing philo-ʿAlid sen- nts and recognising the imamate of the Zaydī *ms*, he did so on the basis of Muʿtazilī doctrine he imāmate, and equally espoused the legitimacy he imāmate of Abū Bakr, ʿUmar and ʿUthmān. late in his life does he appear to have completely ed to Zaydism and to have written works on the dī doctrine of the imāmate and on Zaydī *fiḳh*. He is said to have composed 42 books, several of them in Persian. Many of his writings were brought to the Yaman, where they gained high esteem among the Zaydī scholars, who frequently referred to the author merely as al-Ḥākim. His extant Ḳurʾān commentary *al-Tahdhīb*, in nine volumes, supports Muʿtazilī doctrine more consistently than al-Zamakhsharī's *al-Kashshāf* and contains numerous quotations from earlier, lost Muʿtazilī commentaries. It was later twice abridged. His continuation of ʿAbd al-Djabbār's *Ṭabaḳāt al-Muʿtazila*, contained in his *Sharḥ al-ʿuyūn*, has been edited (by Fuʾād Sayyid, *Faḍl al-iʿtizāl wa-ṭabaḳāt al-Muʿtazila*, Tunis 1393/1974, 365-93). His *K. Djalāʾ al-abṣār*, a collection of wide-ranging lectures and narrations, was quoted by Ibn Isfandiyār for its reports on the Caspian ʿAlids (see *Taʾrīkh-i Ṭabaristān*, ed. ʿAbbās Iḳbāl, Tehran [1320/1942], i, 101).

Bibliography: al-Ḥākim al-Djushamī, *Sharḥ al-ʿuyūn*, i, ms. Leiden Or. 2584, fols. 151b-152a; Ibn Funduḳ al-Bayhaḳī, *Taʾrīkh-i Bayhaḳ*, ed. A. Bahmanyār, Tehran 1317/1938, 212 f.; Ibn Shahrāshūb, *Maʿālim al-ʿulamāʾ*, ed. ʿAbbās Iḳbāl, Tehran 1353/1934, 83; al-Ṣarīfīnī, *al-Muntakhab min kitāb al-siyāḳ li-taʾrīkh Naysābūr*, in R. N. Frye, *The histories of Nishapur*, The Hague 1965, fol. 133b; Ṣārim al-Dīn Ibrāhīm b. al-Ḳāsim, *Ṭabaḳāt al-Zaydiyya*, ms. photocopy no. 290 Cairo, *Dār al-Kutub* pp. 344 f.; al-Djundārī, *Tarādjim al-ridjāl*, in Ibn Miftāḥ, *al-Muntazaʿ al-mukhtār*, i, Cairo 1332/1913, 32; M. Ḳazwīnī, *Yāddāshthā-yi Ḳazwīnī*, ed. Īradj Afshār, Tehran 1333/1954, ii, 157-62; Brockelmann, I, 524, S I, 731 f.; M. T. Dānishpazhūh, in *Rev. Fac. Lett. Tabriz*, xvii (1344/1965), 299 n. 3; W. Madelung, *Der Iman al-Qāsim ibn Ibrāhīm*, Berlin 1965, 186-91; F. Sayyid, *Faḍl al-iʿtizāl*, Tunis 1393/1974, 353-8. (W. MADELUNG)

ḤĀL (pl. *aḥwāl*; *ḥāl* is normally fem. but often in Ashʿarī texts is taken as masc.; the form *ḥāla* is occasionally found in both Muʿtazilī and Ashʿarī sources), a technical term of philosophy employed by some of the Baṣran *mutakallimūn* of the 4th/10th century and the 5th/11th one to signify certain "attributes" that are predicated of beings. The term was taken over from the grammarians first by Abū Hāshim al-Djubbāʾī [*q.v.*] and subsequently used in two basic ways, one by Abū Hāshim and his followers in the Baṣran Muʿtazila and the other by al-Bāḳillānī and al-Djuwaynī [*q.vv.*] in the Ashʿarī school. The treatment of the *ḥāl* within the contexts of the two school traditions differs to such an extent that one must recognise two distinct concepts. The discussion of the *aḥwāl* by later Ashʿarī writers (e.g. al-Shahrastānī and Fakhr al-Dīn al-Rāzī), though they tend to focus primarily on the preoccupations of their own predecessors in the Ashʿarī tradition, does not keep the two conceptions clearly distinct, and certain modern studies based chiefly on these sources have tended to misconstrue the problem, particularly in regard to the Muʿtazilī tradition.

A. *The Muʿtazila*. For Abū Hāshim and the Baṣran Muʿtazila following him, the expression *ḥāl* designates the "attribute" (*ṣifa*) as the latter is conceived to be an ontologically real and distinguishable perfection of a being or essential entity (*shayʾ*, *nafs*, *dhāt*). In the works of the classical Muʿtazila, accordingly, the *ḥāl* is most commonly designated by the term *ṣifa* (*ṣifa*$_2$ as defined below). In order to understand the concept it is necessary to clarify the verbal and conceptual context of its formulation and of its occurrence within the texts. Most importantly, there occurred in the development of the Baṣran *kalām* from the 3rd/9th century until the 5th/11th an accretion of new formal meanings for the terms *ṣifa, waṣf*, and *ḥukm* (some of them peculiar to the Muʿtazila or to the Ash̲ʿarīs, and others shared by the two schools) that must be distinguished if the ontology of the *aḥwāl*, as treated in the texts, is to be understood.

So far as concerns the discussion of the nature of things, the teaching of the Baṣran *kalām* was from the outset explicitly cast in terms of an analysis of the predicates that are said of them: of the predicates (the Arabic nouns and adjectives: *al-asmāʾ wa 'l-awṣāf*) that are predicated of beings and those particularly that are said of God in the Ḳurʾān. The word *ṣifa*, in its first and probably original sense in the theology of the Baṣrans, is taken over and adapted from its use by the grammarians with the meaning "a descriptive term". In this sense, then (*ṣifa*$_1$), it refers to any general or descriptive predicate term and so combines the grammarians' categories of noun and adjective (verbs being paraphrased into adjectives) (see e.g. ʿAbd al-D̲j̲abbār, *al-Mughnī*, v, 198). *Ṣifa*$_{\_}$ is thus virtually synonymous with *waṣf*$_1$: the expression (*ḳawl*) employed in describing (*waṣafa*) something, i.e. in formulating the sentence in which the particular word is predicated of a subject noun which is taken to denote some concrete entity (*s̲h̲ayʾ*). In another sense (*ṣifa*$_2$), the predicate expression (*ṣifa*$_1$) may be considered from the standpoint of its meaning (*al-maʿnā*$_1$: what is meant as opposed to the word or material utterance: *al-ʿibāra, al-lafẓ*) and so as signified by any of several expressions (*awṣāf*$_1$, *asmāʾ*) that are considered to be synonymous in their strict sense (*ḥaḳīḳa*) as they are said of a particular entity (e.g. "*ḳādir*" = "*ḳawī*" = "*ʿazīz*", as said of God). A proposition affirming a particular *ṣifa*$_2$ as true of something may be thus formulated, employing any one of a number of *ṣifāt*$_1$ (= *awṣāf*$_1$, *asmāʾ*) (see e.g. ʿAbd al-D̲j̲abbār, *al-Mad̲j̲mūʿ al-muḥīṭ bi 'l-taklīf*, 172). Within the Baṣran tradition of the *kalām*, then, the question, whether to affirm a given predicate as true of an entity (*waṣafahū bihā*), is or is not to assert (*at̲h̲bata*) the reality of an "attribute" belonging to it and that of the ontological status of such an attribute, if any is held to be asserted by the *ṣifa*$_1$, are questions in terms of their various responses to which the major schools may be distinguished, and on the basis of which their conceptions of the *aḥwāl* are divided.

For Abū ʿAlī al-D̲j̲ubbāʾī, an entity (*s̲h̲ayʾ*) or essence (*nafs, d̲h̲āt*) is an object of knowing (*maʿlūm*) that strictly speaking exists (*wud̲j̲ida*) or does not exist (*ʿudima*) and which, as an object of knowing, may be directly referred to (*d̲h̲akara*) and may be made the subject of a predication (*uk̲h̲bira ʿanhū*) (see, e.g. al-As̲h̲ʿarī, *Maḳalāt al-Islāmiyyīn*, ed. H. Ritter, Istanbul 1929-30, 519). It is not, however, said of something else. *Ṣifāt*$_1$ are employed in describe entities, i.e. to express what is known about them. According to the mature teaching of al-D̲j̲ubbāʾī and of the Baṣran Muʿtazila after him, *ṣifāt*$_1$ are those expressions that name the "essence" or essential entity as such or that describe it as it is in some particular way distinguished from entities essentially similar to it. Generic terms, i.e. those which designate broader classes of beings, embracing several kinds of essential entities, they do not consider to be *ṣifāt*$_1$ in the strict sense but rather as quasi-*alḳāb* (terms whose use to name or describe something is in part arbitrary). As predicate expressions or terms (thus excluding the use of an expression to name an entity and to refer to it as the subject of the p[r]osition), the *ṣifāt*$_1$ are not, as such, directly [refer]ential. They are, however, understood to [have] implicit reference when said of a particular b[eing]. That is to say, when predicated of a particular b[eing] most *ṣifāt*$_2$ implicitly assert the entitative re[ality] either of the being denoted by the subject term [or of] another being, and accordingly the various pred[icate] expressions are systematically paraphrased in [order] to make explicit what ontological assertion (*iṯ*[*bāt*]) is implicit in each particular affirmation. Thu[s, for] example, to say "Zayd strikes" is to assert that [there] exists an act of striking (*ḍarb*) that has occurre[d on] his part (*ḍārib* = *waḳaʿa minhū ḍarb*^{un}) or to [say] "Zayd knows" is to assert that there exists an a[ct of] knowing that belongs to him (*ʿālim* = *lahū ʿil*[*m*]). In these instances, the entities whose reali[ty is] asserted in the affirmation of the proposition[s are] termed the "cause" (*ʿilla*, pl., *ʿilal* or *maʿnā*$_2$, [pl.] *maʿānī*) of the proposition or judgement (*ḥu*[*km*]) that the thing is so, and the predicate term co[mes], therefore, to be called *ṣifat*$_1$ *maʿnan* (i.e. a [predicate] whose affirmation of the subject implies the re[ality] of a *maʿnā*$_2$; *maʿnā* originally meant the "se[nse]" of the predicate or judgement: *ḥukm* the "se[nse]" or "meaning" being contextually understood by [the] Baṣran *mutakallimūn* as the reality of that e[ntity] the presence of which, in a given relationship t[o the] subject, is asserted by the particular predicate. [By] the time of al-D̲j̲ubbāʾī, the two words *ʿilla* [and] *maʿnā* are employed as synonyms, being used i[nter]changeably in most contexts, and within a cen[tury] the semantic origin of this sense of *maʿnā* seem[s to] have been forgotten). As conceived by the Ba[ṣran] *mutakallimūn*, the *maʿānī*$_2$ are not, however, a[ttri]butes. They are, rather, entities in the strict se[nse], beings that are themselves distinct objects and [which] as such are not predicable of something else. I[n al-] D̲j̲ubbāʾī's analysis, then, since God is absol[utely] one and undivided, when one says "God kn[ows]" (*Allāh*^{u} *ʿālim*) there is no assertion of the re[ality] of any entity other than God's self (*nafsuhū*) [and] accordingly the predicate term is, in this insta[nce], called an "essential predicate" (*ṣifat*$_1$ *nafs*^{in}, [a] predicate expression whose affirmation of the sub[ject] implicitly refers to and asserts the reality onl[y of] the self or essence of the entity denoted by the [sub]ject term). All terms that name or describe the [self] or essence of a thing as such are, when used pre[dic]atively, *ṣifāt*^{9} *nafs*. Thus al-D̲j̲ubbāʾī now[here] speaks of attributes, if we understand "attrib[ute]" in its usual sense (as, e.g. a property, characteri[stic] or quality of a thing, as when we speak of a fig[ure's] "being triangular" or "triangularity" as a prop[erty] belonging to it); he has no term for such a con[cept] and uses no formal expression that would imply [the] reality of such a thing.

The concept of the attribute as an ontologi[cally] real perfection, property, or state of the bein[g of] an entity was introduced into the Baṣran *kalām* [by] Abū Hās̲h̲im. Though most often referred to in Muʿtazilī texts by the term *ṣifa*$_3$, the attribute, [so] conceived, is also referred to by the word *ḥāl* (st[ate]). This latter term Abū Hās̲h̲im apparently took [from] the grammarians of the Baṣran school (the Kū[fans] employ a different expression reflecting their [own] grammatical analysis), and it is likely that he for[med] the philosophical concept partially in terms [of] reflection on the significance of *ḥāl* expression[s as] these are understood and analysed by them. W[hen] explicitly discussing Abū Hās̲h̲im's conceptio[n of] the attribute (*ṣifa*$_3$, *ḥāl*) for the purpose of refu[...]

e Ashʿarīs (e.g. al-Bāḳillānī and al-Shahrastānī) often speak of it as ḥāl, probably to avoid the valence of the word ṣifa, though in other con- where the doctrine of Abū Hāshim and his vers is discussed, one often finds ṣifa in the arī texts and occasionally also waṣf, the latter senting more peculiarly Ashʿarī usage.

ie attribute (ṣifa₃, ḥāl) is not an essential entity ⁾, dhāt) as this is strictly defined and understood. not therefore considered to be an object or y that can be known in isolation (bi-nfirādihā, idjarradihā). Rather, the entity of which it is ttribute is known as qualified by it (yuʿlam ʿalay- ʿcf. ʿAbd al-Djabbār, Sharḥ al-uṣūl al-khamsa, 9-14 and 366, 9-11). Thus though not a distinct t of knowing and so not "known" (maʿlūma) in trict sense of this term, the attribute or state is theless grasped and understood (maʿḳūla) as one vs a thing is specifically qualified by it (mukh- bihā). Furthermore, since the attribute or state ot an entity, it cannot be said to be existent vdjūda) or non-existent (maʿdūma) because these icates are properly used only of entities. In that , however, an ontologically real perfection or of the being of an entity, the attribute (ṣifa₃) have actuality (taḥṣul) and so is said to be ac- (ḥāṣila) as also one may properly speak of its presence (zawāluhā) or non-actuality (intifāʾuhā) thing. Likewise, one does not speak of its coming e (ḥudūthuhā) since "coming to be" (al-ḥudūth) s properly to the initiation of existence (tadjad- al-wudjūd); one speaks, rather, of the initiation e attribute (tadjadduduhā). In concrete instances, , the attribute (ṣifa₃, ḥāl) is indicated by the ession "the thing's being thus and so", as one ks, for example, of "its being existent" (kawnuhū djūdᵃⁿ) or of "its being living" (kawnuhū ḥayyᵃⁿ) a body's "being in motion" (kawnuhū mutaḥar-). Propositions such as "he is alive" (huwa ḥayy) hus considered by Abū Hāshim and his followers e Muʿtazilī school to assert the actuality of the bute (ḥuṣūl al-ṣifa₃, ḥuṣūl al-ḥāl), viz. in this in- ce of his being alive or being living or the body's g in motion, and it is to the attribute or state that such a predicate (ṣifa₁) implicitly refers. ough they disagree in certain matters of detail e of which are philosophically important) Abū ṇim and his successors classify the attributes ₃, aḥwāl) into five basic categories according ie grounds to which their actuality is, in each , to be ascribed. (Note that we are not here erned with the classification of predicates in ral, but only those that assert the actuality of ₃, aḥwāl.) These are:

ie Attribute of the Essence (most often termed al-dhāt, though other expressions are frequently loyed; cf. Frank, Beings, 80 n. 1); this is the ʒ's being itself what it is in itself. It is asserted, xample, in the statement "the atom is an atom" jawhar djawhar). What is referred to here is way the thing is in itself" (mā huwa ʿalayhī fī ihī). The attribute of the essence is, thus, ir- cible (cf. e.g., ʿAbd al-Djabbār, al-Madjmūʿ uḥīṭ bi ʾl-taklīf, 61, 9 ff. and Abu Rashīd, Ziyādāt arḥ, 192, 11 ff. and 278, 11 ff.), and is actual la) even in the possible, for to posit the entity ⁾ posit the actuality of the Attribute of the nce. That is to say, God knows, out of an infinite ber of beings of every class, each particular vidual that He can create; thus although an vidual entity whose existence is possible (al- z wudjūduhū) is non-existent and as non-existent

(bi-kawnihī maʿdūmᵃⁿ) has no ontologically real state (ḥāl), it has nevertheless reality as a possible existent (it is thābit al-djawāz) in that it is a particular and distinguishable object of God's power (i.e. in- sofar as it is maḳdūr ʿalayhī).

2. The essential attributes (commonly termed ṣifāt₃ al-nafs, al-ṣifāt₃ al-dhātiyya, or al-muḳtaḍā ʿammā huwa ʿalayhī fī dhātihī, i.e. "the attribute that is entailed by the way the thing is in itself"); these attributes are those whose actuality is entailed by the Attribute of the Essence (by the way the thing is in itself) given the actuality of its existence. These are the manifest (ẓāhira) attributes that reveal the nature of the essential entity as it is in itself (tunbiʾ ʿammā huwa ʿalayhī fī dhātihī), as for example, the atom's occupying space (kawnuhū mutaḥayyizᵃⁿ or God's being existent, living, knowing, etc.

3. The attributes whose actuality flows immediate- ly from (ṣadara ʿan) an entitative, determinant cause (ʿilla, maʿnā₂) and which are, accordingly, termed simply li-ʿilla or li-maʿnā₂ and are said to be "caused" (maʿlūla). Included under this category is, for ex- ample, a human individual's being knowing (kawnuhū ʿālimᵃⁿ), an attribute whose actuality is asserted in the sentence "Zayd knows" (Zayd ʿālim) and whose actuality arises immediately from the presence of the act of knowing (al-ʿilm) that exists as a concrete entity in his heart. The attribute (ṣifa₃, ḥāl) in this instance is a perfection that specifically qual- ifies (takhtaṣṣ) not its immediate physical locus (al-maḥall), but rather the living corporeal whole (al-djumla al-ḥayya) that is the individual, and it is for this reason that Abū Hāshim and his successors say that the predicate "knowing" is said of the whole and not of the organ or substrate. "Moving", on the other hand, is predicated only of the material sub- strate (al-maḥall) since the attribute of "being in motion" (kawnuhū mutaḥarrikᵃⁿ) belongs only to the locus of the entitative cause of its actuality.

4. Attributes whose actuality depends upon the agent that effects the existence of the thing and which, therefore, are said to be bi ʾl-fāʿil. Though many characteristics (aḥkām₂) of temporal entities are ascribed to an agent as their source, either immedi- ately to his agency as such or mediately through the manner of the act's occurrence (li-wadjh wuḳūʿihī), the only true attribute (ṣifa₃, ḥāl, in the strict sense) that is said to be "due to the agent" is that of a temporal entity in its being existent (kawnuhū mawdjūdᵃⁿ).

5. Attributes whose actuality in the thing is due "neither to its essence nor to an entitative cause" (lā li ʾl-nafs wa-lā li-ʿilla/li-maʿnā₂); the desig- nation of a class of predicates (ṣifāt₁, awṣāf₁, asmāʾ) as lā li ʾl-nafs wa-lā li-ʿilla would seem to have originated with Abū ʿAlī al-Djubbāʾī. Because of the basic difference of his analysis and ontology from that of the later school, however, the predicates that he so classed are not the same as those so classed by Abū Hāshim and his successors. What predicates (ṣifat₁) and what attributes (ṣifāt₃) Abū Hāshim may have classed under this heading, if any, indeed, is at present uncertain. His followers, however, assign the attribute (ṣifa₃, ḥāl) of "being perceiving" (kaw- nuhū mudrikᵃⁿ) to this category, since perception, ac- cording to their view, arises directly from the per- ceiver's being living on the condition of the appro- priate presence of the perceptible. (Perceiving is here distinguished from sensation—al-ḥiss—since the predicate "sensing"—muḥiss—is taken to in- dicate not a true attribute but only the functioning of the sense organ.) It may be that "being per- ceiving" is the only true attribute which they class

thus; predicates (*ṣifāt*$_1$) which are implicitly negative are said to be *lā li 'l-nafs wa-lā li-ʿilla*, but they do not indicate ontologically real attributes.

For us the essential reality of a thing (its *ḥaḳīḳa*) is its essential attributes, for what we understand and refer to when we speak of it is its being as it is known to us in these attributes. Predications, according to the classical Muʿtazila, are said of essential entities that are known (*maʿlūma*) and distinguished as such; the predicates that refer to a thing's essential attributes (*al-ṣifāt*$_1$ *al-dhātiyya*) are those which we employ to define it. According to Abū Hāshim and his followers in the Baṣran Muʿtazila, it is thus that through their essential attributes we know entities, i.e. in that they are so manifested to us as belonging to the same essential class (*djins*) or to different classes, for beings that share (*ishtaraka*) in one essential attribute must be alike (*tamāthala*) in that which entails (*iḳtaḍā*) the actuality of the attribute, and so must share in all their essential attributes. (See, e.g., ʿAbd al-Djabbār, *Sharḥ al-uṣūl al-khamsa*, 108, 9-12 and 199, 3-5; *al-Mughnī*, iv, 270 f. and 252, 8-10).

One speaks also of the "modality" of an attribute (*kayfiyyat al-ṣifa*$_3$). Existence (a thing's being existent: *wudjūduhū* = *kawnuhū mawdjūd*^{an}), for example, is an attribute that is common to all existent entities. Some entities, however, (sc. God) are eternally existent (*lam yazal mawdjūda*^{an}) while others (sc. all beings other than God) are temporally existent (*muḥdath*). The terms "eternal" (*ḳadīm*) and "temporal" (*muḥdath*) refer to the modality of the attribute of being existent. Similarly the term "inherent" (*ḥāll*) used of the accident's inherence in its substrate (*kawnuhū ḥāll*^{an} *fī maḥallihī*) refers to a modality of its existence. (See e.g., ʿAbd al-Djabbār, *al-Madjmūʿ al-muḥīṭ bi 'l-taklīf*, 163, 4-7 and Abū Rashīd, *Ziyādāt al-sharḥ*, 384, 14 f.).

Not all predicates that may be affirmed as true of an object imply the presence of an ontologically real attribute (*ṣifa*$_3$, *ḥāl*). Some terms, for example, refer to the "characteristics" (*aḥkām*$_2$) of attributes; others (e.g. ethical terms) refer to contingent characteristics (*aḥkām*$_2$) of acts which, determined by one or another of the states of the agent (*aḥwāl al-fāʿil*) (see, e.g., ʿAbd al-Djabbār, *al-Mughnī*, viii, 159 and *al-Madjmūʿ al-muḥīṭ bi 'l-taklīf*, 352), derive immediately from the manner of its coming to be (*wadjh al-ḥudūth* = *wadjh wuḳūʿihī*) and others to the modality (*kayfiyya*) of an attribute. Some, viz. those that describe a thing in its perceptible qualities, refer not to *ṣifāt*$_3$ (*aḥwāl*) but to dispositions (*hayʾāt*) of the material substrate; some descriptive terms are implicitly negative (e.g. "inanimate", "other", "dissimilar" and the like) and so refer to no real attribute; some refer primarily to a being other than that denoted in the subject, viz. the "derived predicates" (*al-ṣifāt*^{9} *al-mushtaḳḳa*) (see, e.g., ʿAbd al-Djabbār, *al-Mughnī*, vii, 58, 3-7 and for the term of Ibn Fāris, *al-Ṣāḥibī fī fiḳh al-lugha*, ed. M. el-Chouémi, Beirut 1383/1964, 86 ff.), i.e. those that assert the actuality of an action performed by the subject and those that assert the actuality of the state (*ḥāl*) or act of another (e.g. "known" or "commanded"). Generic terms, finally, are not considered to be truly descriptive terms (*ṣifāt*$_1$) by the Baṣran Muʿtazila, as was noted above. Accordingly, one must distinguish those instances where the expression *kawnuhū* ... ("its being ...") is employed to denote an ontologically real attribute (*ṣifa*$_3$, *ḥāl*) and those in which it is employed merely as a nominal periphrasis for a sentence (e.g. *kawnuhū aswad* as a periphrasis for *huwa aswad* "it is black") that does not assert the actu of an attribute (*ṣifa*$_3$, *ḥāl*) of the being that is den by the subject term. The differences in the underst ing of these terms by the Muʿtazila and the Ashʿar characteristic of those in their conception of the *a*

B. *The Ashʿarīs.* Among the Ashʿarīs, the con of the "attribute" (*ḥāl*) as conceived by Abū Hā was borrowed, adapted, and employed by al-Bāḳ and al-Djuwaynī and, it would seem, by no ot (see, e.g., al-Shahrastānī, *al-Nihāya*, 131.) Al-B lānī's acceptance and use of the concept was, ever, inconsistent; in some works (among them two published compendia, *al-Inṣāf* and *al-Tamhī* expressly denied the validity of the concept (th it implicitly underlies the discussion in a numb important passages in both *al-Inṣāf* and *al-Tam* while in others, including his last major *kalām* w *al-Hidāya*, he is reported to have asserted its val and to have integrated it into his treatment of predicates of being and of the divine attrib (see, e.g., al-Djuwaynī, *al-Shāmil*, 294, 629). Djuwaynī, on the other hand, seems to have pressly employed the concept in most if not all c *kalām* works, though he is reported to have reje it in his late juridical writing. (See, e.g., Ab Ḳāsim Sulaymān b. Nāṣir al-Anṣārī, *Sharḥ al-Ir* Princeton University ms. ELS 634, fol. 356.) In present absence of any direct, adequate evid concerning al-Bāḳillānī's treatment and use of *aḥwāl* concept, the present outline reflects str only the discussion and terminology of al-Djuwa The sources, however, indicate no major differ between al-Djuwaynī's understanding and us the concept and those of al-Bāḳillānī; one therefore suppose that their teaching in this res was substantially the same.

Like Abū Hāshim, the Ashʿarīs who employed concept of the "attribute" as *ḥāl* describe it as thing's being such and so" (*ḳawn al-shayʾ*). The text to which the concept was adapted and whose overall structure it had to be integrated dif however, in several important respects from th the Muʿtazilī tradition of Basra, even though Ashʿarī analysis of the predicates that are sai beings is in some ways analogous to that of al-D bāʾī. Omitting those predicates that refer to ac (*ṣifāt*$_1$ *al-afʿāl*) and so to an entity essentially trinsic to that denoted by the subject term, Ashʿarī and his followers, in contrast to the Muʿta recognise only two categories of descriptive predic (*asmāʾ*, *awṣāf*$_1$, *ṣifāt*$_1$), since they divide the ent which constitute the ontological basis for the t of the predication (*istiḥḳāḳ al-waṣf*: the th "deserving to be so described") and whose rea accordingly is asserted (*muthbat*) as that w requires its affirmation (*mā awdjaba 'l-waṣf*) (1) the "self" (*nafs*) of the being denoted by subject, as when one says of a being that it is "e ent" (*mawdjūd*) or "temporal" (*muḥdath*) or "colour" (*lawn*) or of God that He is "eter (*ḳadīm*) or "majestic" (*ʿaẓīm*); and (2) those assert the reality of an entitative, determi cause (*maʿnā*$_2$, *ʿilla*) subsistent in the subject when one says of a being that it is "living" ("liv = "life belongs to it": *ḥayy* = *lahū ḥayāt*) or "k ing" ("knowing" = "an act of knowing belong it": *ʿālim* = *lahū ʿilm*) and the like. In additio the words *maʿnā*$_2$ and *ʿilla*, the Ashʿarīs often in some contexts almost always) refer to t entities (*al-maʿānī*$_2$) as *ṣifāt*$_4$. (This, in fact, is only sense in which al-Ashʿarī himself employs word *ṣifa*.) Against al-Djubbāʾī and others, arīs insist that predicates such as "living", wing" and the like always imply the presence ı entitative determinant (*maʿnā*$_2$, *ʿilla, ṣifa*$_4$) e subject, whether they be said of a material ; or of God, who is immaterial. Again, whereas ıasters of the Baṣran Muʿtazila take descriptive cates to be said of individual entities which, n and recognised as particular essences, are ibed by the predicate (*waṣf*$_1$, *ṣifa*$_1$), the Ashʿarīs rstand the subject term to denote an individual y simply as an object: as an existent (*mawdjūd*) e existence is its "self" (*nafs*). (Thus *shayʾ* = *ljūd* = *wudjūd* = *nafs*, *dhāt*, whilst the non-exist- s simply the unreal subject spoken of in a neg- proposition: "it is not true that there exists an t such that ...".) Thus, where the Baṣran Muʿta- fter al-Djubbāʾī distinguished expressions that consider to be descriptive (*ṣifāt*$_1$) strictly ing, i.e. those which name the essence as such scribe it in some particular way, from those consider to be quasi-*alḳāb*, i.e. those which we oy to assign an essence to various broader, ic classes and which, therefore, are said uni- ly of beings that are essentially different, the arīs make no such distinction, but rather consider kinds of terms to be truly descriptive, classing econd of the Muʿtazilī categories amongst the ntial predicates" (*al-ṣifāt*$_1$ *al-nafsiyya*), viz. that assert as the basis of the validity of their nation of the subject only the reality of the t (*nafs al-mawdjūd* = *wudjūduhū*) of which are said. No more than al-Djubbāʾī, however, al-Ashʿarī speak of "attributes" as this word is ıonly understood, nor does his analysis, or that ost of his followers in the two centuries imme- y succeeding, make place for such a concept. *ifa*$_4$ is simply a *maʿnā*$_2$ (*ʿilla*). They agree that eing of God's *ṣifāt*$_4$ differs from that of those ging to creatures and there is some question the exact ontological status of the former, i.e. whether God's *ṣifāt*$_4$ are validly termed *ashyāʾ* *ıwdjūda* or if they are denumerable; but it is theless clear that *ṣifāt*$_4$ are entities of some (more precisely, of two kinds) though not of a that nowadays we should term attributes. (Al- lānī, cited in al-Kiyā al-Harāsī, *Uṣūl al-dīn*, 114a and 123a, says that, in contrast to the , they are entitative objects or beings, *dhāt*, , *maʿnā*.) One notes that with but two or three tions, common also to the Muʿtazila, abstract ; are not employed in the writings of al-Ashʿarī f the majority of his followers until the 5th/11th ry and that the expression *kawnuhū* ... is st everywhere shunned, chiefly for accuracy of ssion but also, no doubt, in order to avoid the lance of accepting Abū Hāshim's ontology.

Djuwaynī rejects the common Ashʿarī thesis all the "essential predicates" (*ṣifāt*$_1$ *al-nafs*, *īt*$_1$ *al-nafsiyya*) assert simply the being of the ʾ of the subject and that what is asserted (*al-* *₁*) in affirming one of the *ṣifāt*$_1$ *al-maʿānī*$_2$ *fāt*$_1$ *al-maʿnawiyya*) is simply the reality of eing of the *maʿnā*$_2$ (*ṣifa*$_4$) as belonging to the ct. For every positive predicate (*waṣf*$_1$, *ṣifa*$_1$) cognises an "attribute" (*waṣf*$_2$, *ṣifa*$_5$), which signates by the expression *kawnuhū* ..., e.g. the 's "being an atom" (*kawnuhū djawhar*^{an}), "its an entity" (*kawnuhū shayʾ*^{an} *wa-dhāt*^{an}), "its existent" (*kawnuhū mawdjūd*^{an}), "its occupying " (*kawnuhū mutaḥayyiz*^{an}), etc.; and so also with *fāt*$_1$ *maʿnawiyya*, the attributes (*ṣifāt*$_5$) signified e latter being commonly termed *aḥkām*$_3$ as well as *ṣifāt*$_5$, *awṣāf*$_2$, (see e.g. *al-Irshād*, 30, *al-Shāmil*, 308, *et alibi*). He holds, moreover, in regard to those predicates which do not refer simply to the existent as such (to its existence as its "self": *nafs*) that one must posit the reality (*thubūt*) of the attribute (*waṣf*$_2$, *ṣifa*$_5$, *ḥukm*$_3$) as a state (*ḥāl*). This, he says, is necessary in order to have an ontological basis for the true sense of the common or universal predicate terms and their definitions (viz. *al-ḥaḳāʾiḳ wa 'l-ḥudūd*) (see e.g. *al-Shāmil*, 633, and the citation of al-Bāḳillānī in al-Kiyā al-Harāsī, *op. cit.*, fols. 115a and following), as also in order to explain what is known and asserted to be true in the case of the *maʿānī*$_2$ (*aḥkām al-ʿilal*), i.e. in order to explain what is known and asserted to be true (*al-ḥukm*$_1$) of the entity to which the *maʿnā*$_2$ (*ʿilla*) belongs as the effect (*maʿlūl*, *mūdjab*) of the latter (see e.g. *al-Shāmil*, 629 ff. and *al-Irshād*, 80 ff.) In these cases what is known (*ʿulima*) of something is not the thing itself (*al-nafs* = *wudjūduhū*) but an ontologically real attribute (*ṣifa*$_5$ *thābita*) or state (*ḥāl*) of it, and it is this that the descriptive predicate strictly speaking refers to and asserts as real (*thābit*). Regarding the "essential attributes", al-Djuwaynī says "Every attribute (*waṣf*$_2$) that is not understood negatively and the ignorance of which is not contradicted by the knowledge of the existence of the being that is denoted by the subject (*al-mawṣūf*), is a state (*ḥāl*)" (*al-Shāmil*, 630, 17 f.; cf. also *al-Irshād*, 80). Thus when one says of a being that it is a (unit or quantum of) black (*sawād*) or that it is a colour (*lawn*) or an accident (*ʿaraḍ*) or that it is inherent in a substrate (*ḥāll fī maḥāll*), the reference is to "its being black" (*kawnuhū sawād*^{an}), "its being a colour" (*kawnuhū lawn*^{an}, "its being an accident" (*kawnuhū ʿaraḍ*^{an}), and "its being inherent" (*kawnuhū ḥāll*^{an}): its "blackhood" (*as-sawādiyya*), "accidentality" (*al-ʿaraḍiyya*), etc. Each of these attributes (*aḥwāl*, *ṣifāt*$_5$, *awṣāf*$_2$) is a distinct object of knowing (*maʿlūm*). Likewise the knowledge of an entity's being knowing (*kawnuhū ʿālim*^{an}) is distinct from the knowledge that the act of knowing (*al-ʿilm*) by virtue of whose subsistence in it is knowing, exists (*kawnuhū mawdjūd*^{an} = *nafsuhū*) and is an act of knowing (*kawnuhū ʿilm*^{an} = *al-ʿilmiyya*); each of these attributes (*ṣifāt*$_5$), as an ontologically real state (*ḥāl*) or characteristic (*ḥukm*$_3$) of the subject, is a distinct object (*maʿlūm*), known in a distinct act of knowing (*ilm*). As the attribute (*ḥāl*, *ṣifa*$_5$) is other than the entity to which it belongs (the *ṣifa* is other than the *mawṣūf*), so al-Djuwaynī holds that existence (*al-wudjūd* = *nafs al-mawdjūd*) is not a *ḥāl* (see e.g. *al-Irshād*, 31). Though it is an object insofar as it is known (*maʿlūm*), the *ḥāl* is not an entity (*shayʾ*) (*al-Shāmil*, 640, 679) and so is not described as existent (*mawdjūd*) or non-existent (*maʿdūm*, *muntafī*). (See also the citations of al-Bāḳillānī in al-Kiyā al-Harāsī, *op. cit.*, fols. 114a and 115a.)

The "self" as such is understood and conceived not as an essence but as an object, and the predicates which assert the entitative reality of the "self" as such (e.g. *shayʾ*, *dhāt*, *nafs*, *mawdjūd*) neither are synonymous with those which assert the actuality of its *aḥwāl* (e.g. *djawhar*, *ʿaraḍ*, *lawn*, *ʿilm*, *ḥaraka*) nor do they imply the assertion of its *aḥwāl*. Since, then, the *aḥwāl* are neither identical with nor derived from the "self" as such of the being of which they are attributes and are known separately from the knowledge of its existence, that a being should have one essential attribute (*ṣifāt*$_5$ *nafs*) does not necessarily entail its having another. Beings that are essentially diverse (*mukhtalifa*) may share (is̲h̲taraka) in common essential attributes, as for example a human act of knowing (ʿilm) and a motion of an atom share in accidentality (al-ʿaraḍiyya, i.e. kawnuhumā ʿaraḍayn) and a human act of knowing (a maʿnā₂ which is an accident) and God's eternal act of knowing (a maʿnā₂ which is not an accident, i.e. is not a contingent entity inherent in a material substrate) have in common (id̲j̲tamaʿā fī) their being acts of knowing (kawnuhumā ʿilmayn = al-ʿilmiyya) and so are, both, correctly denoted and described by ʿilm. Like entities (al-mit̲h̲lān, al-mutamāt̲h̲ilān) are alike in and by virtue of their selves (li-anfusi-himā) (see e.g. al-S̲h̲āmil, 312); they are therefore those beings that are analogous (sadda aḥaduhumā masadda 'l-āk̲h̲ar) or are equivalent (mustawiyān) in all their essential attributes (ṣifāt₅ al-nafs, al-ṣifāt₅ al-nafsiyya) (cf. e.g. al-S̲h̲āmil, 292, 313 f.).

In no sense does al-D̲j̲uwaynī take up the ontology of Abū Hās̲h̲im and his Muʿtazilī followers. No-where does al-D̲j̲uwaynī treat the attribute (ḥāl, ṣifa₅) as an ontologically real perfection of a being in terms of which other perfections, properties, char-acteristics, qualities, or operations are to be un-derstood and explained. He does not speak of an at-tribute's entailing (iḳtaḍā) the actuality of another attribute or of its effecting (at̲h̲t̲h̲ara) a charac-teristic or quality of a thing, nor does he regard any attribute as constituting the immediate ground of the possibility (ṣaḥḥaḥa) of some qualification of an entity or as the condition (s̲h̲arṭ) of its actuality. Similarly, he does not speak of attributes (ṣifāt₅, aḥwāl) as having modality (kayfiyya) nor of the char-acteristics (aḥkām₂) of attributes. Finally, where the Muʿtazilīs distinguish four categories of maʿānī₂, one as effecting no ḥāl whatsoever, either of its immediate substrate of inherence or of the whole of which the latter is a part, and others as producing one or another qualification (ḥāl) either of the imme-diate substrate or of the whole composite (al-d̲j̲umla), al-D̲j̲uwaynī makes no distinction whatsoever, assert-ing simply that every maʿnā₂ causes a ḥāl (those of material entities only in their immediate substrate of inherence) (see e.g. ʿAbd al-D̲j̲abbār, al-Mug̲h̲nī, vi/2, 162 and ix, 87, and al-D̲j̲uwaynī, al-S̲h̲āmil, 629 ff.). Though there may be found sometimes a certain parallelism of argumentation (cf. e.g. ibid., 637 f. and ʿAbd al-D̲j̲abbār, al-Mad̲j̲mūʿ al-muḥīṭ bi 'l-taklīf, 188 f.) the conception of the aḥwāl and their role within the integrated contexts of the systems is significantly different in the teaching of the As̲h̲ʿarīs and in the thought of Abū Hās̲h̲im and his followers. Al-D̲j̲uwaynī employs Abū Hās̲h̲im's distinction between the Attribute of the Essence and the essen-tial attribute (categories 1 and 2 in A above) to-gether with the concept of the ḥāl in order to found a distinction in the As̲h̲ʿarī essential predicates in terms of their denotation. Thus although he speaks of "attributes" in both instances, he distinguishes those predicates (awṣāf₁, ṣifāt₁) that denote or assert simply the existence (i.e. the "self") of an entity as such from the rest, which assert distinct attributes that are states (aḥwāl). Similarly, he posits the reality (t̲h̲ubūt) of the "states" as real attributes (ṣifāt₃ t̲h̲ābita) or characteristics (aḥkām₃ t̲h̲ābita) as the effect (maʿlūl, mūd̲j̲ab) of the maʿānī₂, in order to distinguish ontologically the assertion of the ṣifāt₁ maʿnawiyya from that of those expressions which refer to the maʿānī₂ and describe them as such (e.g. to distinguish the reference of ʿālim from that of ʿilm), a distinction effectively denied by most of the earlier As̲h̲ʿarīs (see e.g. al-Bāḳillānī, al-Tamhīd, § 97, and al-D̲j̲uwaynī, al-S̲h̲āmil, 631). Al-D̲j̲uwaynī,

in short, (and the same is clearly true of al-Bāḳ when he used the aḥwāl) posits the aḥwāl on order to supply referents for certain predicates concomitantly to resolve certain difficultie logical reference and extension, particularl predicates that are said both of God and creat the aḥwāl serve no other function within the sy Whereas the concept of the ḥāl constitutes the foundation and core of the metaphysics of Baṣran Muʿtazila from the time of Abū Hā al-Bāḳillānī and al-D̲j̲uwaynī employ it wi introducing any essential alteration into the tion of As̲h̲ʿarī metaphysics. Finally, by the ex introduction of purely intentional referents (viz. cepts thematically understood as entia rationis) the As̲h̲ʿarī kalām along with the Aristotelian al-G̲h̲azālī [q.v.] was able to resolve in a much les kward manner the problem that his master, al-waynī, had sought to deal with by means of the a

Bibliography: ʿAbd al-D̲j̲abbār al-Hamad al-Mug̲h̲nī, various editors, Cairo 1959-65, pa. idem, al-Mad̲j̲mūʿ al-muḥīṭ bi 'l-taklīf, ed. ʿAzmī, Cairo n.d., passim; idem, S̲h̲arḥ a k̲h̲amsa, ed. A. ʿUt̲h̲mān, Cairo 1384/1965, pa. Abū Ras̲h̲īd al-Nīsābūrī, K. al-Masāʾil, A. Biram, Berlin 1902, passim; idem, Ziyād sharḥ (an extensive fragment of the first part o work published by M. Abū Rīda under the Fi 'l-Tawḥīd, Cairo 1969), passim; al-Bāḳi al-Tamhīd, ed. R. McCarthy, Beirut 1957, §§ 44, 200-3 et alibi; al-D̲j̲uwaynī, al-Irs̲h̲ād M. Mūsā and A. ʿAbd al-Ḥamīd, Cairo 1369/ 79-84 et alibi; idem, al-S̲h̲āmil, ed. A. S. al-Na Alexandria 1969, 629-42 et alibi; al-Kiyā al-H. Uṣūl al-dīn, Cairo ms. Kalām 290, passim, esp. fols. 114a-120b; al-S̲h̲ahrastānī, Nihāy ikdām fī ʿilm al-kalām, ed. A. Guillaume, O 1934, 131-49; Fak̲h̲r al-Dīn al-Rāzī, al-Muḥ Cairo 1323, 41-2; R. Frank, Abu Hashim's t of "states", its structure and function, in Act Congresso de Estudos Arabes e Islâmicos, Co Lisboa 1 a 8 de setembro de 1968, Leiden 85-100; idem, Beings and their attributes, Alb N.Y. 1978; D. Gimaret, La théorie des aḥwāl d Hâs̲h̲im al-Ǧubbâʾî d'après des sources aš̲ʿarite JA (1970), 47-86; M. Horten, Die Modus-Th des Abu Haschim, in ZDMG, lxiii (1909), 3
(R. M. Fran

HALIḲARNAS BALÍ̲ḲČÍSÍ pseudonym D̲j̲ewād S̲h̲ākir, modern Turkish form C S̲h̲āḳir Kabaağaçli, Turkish novelist short story writer (1886-1973).

Born in Istanbul, the son of the general, dipl and writer Meḥmed S̲h̲ākir Pas̲h̲a (1855- (brother of the grand vizier Aḥmed Pas̲h̲a [he stemmed from a prominent family from A karahisar. He was educated at the American R College in Istanbul and at Oxford University, v he graduated in Modern History in 1908. He st his career as a short story writer, translator, gr artist and a cartoonist contributing to various s lived periodicals which mushroomed following restoration of the Constitution. He spent several in prison for killing his father in a crime passi in Afyonkarahisar (1914). During the turbulent years of the Republic, a short story about the ha of deserters without trial, based on his prison niscences, which he published, under the pen-Ḥüseyn Kenʿān, in the Resimli hafta ("The W Illustrated", No. 35, 13 April 1925) got him trouble. He was arrested and tried by the Tribu Independence (Istiḳlāl maḥkemesi) of Ankara, v nced him to three years banishment in the for-sea port of Bodrum (ancient Halicarnassus), for nilitary and defeatist propaganda (because at uncture, troops were being sent to quell a large-revolt in the eastern provinces). When his term over, Djewād Shākir decided to settle in this town which had captured his heart, and he red inceasingly to develop it. He assumed the ame of Haliḳarnas Balîḳčîsî ("The Fisherman alicarnassus"), living there until 1947 when he d to Izmir to work as a journalist and expert st guide and for his children's education. He died nir on 13 October 1973 and is buried in Bodrum, ured by its people for his opening-up of this ed city to the world.

liḳarnas Balîḳčîsî began to write regularly in um after the age of fifty, and devoted his entire the sea and to seamen. He spent his daily life g sea folk, fishermen, sponge fishers, divers and nen and shared their lives, struggles, worries and most of the characters in his short stories and s are real people whom he had met in the Aegean . Exuberant and expansive by temperament, he s with uncontrolled romantic impetus works defy all sense of discipline in technique and But he captured his reader with his *joie de vivre*, sense of humanity and deep understanding of llow-men. Haliḳarnas Balîḳčîsî is the author of ollowing major works. Short stories: *Merhaba niz* (1947), *Ege'nin dibi* (1952), *Yaşasın deniz*). Novels: *Aganta, burina burinata* (1946), *in, çocuğu* (1956), *Uluç Reis* (1962), *Turgut* (1955), *Deniz gurbetçileri* (1969). Memoirs: *sürgün* (1961). He also wrote several popular s on Anatolian mythology and made many lations (For a bibliography of his publications, *'eni yayınlar* of October 1974).

Bibliography: Tahir Alangu, *Cumhuriyetten ra hikâye ve roman*, ii, Istanbul 1965, 301-26; vdet Kudret, *Türk edebiyatında hikâye ve roman*, Istanbul 1970, 352-61; idem, *Mavi sürgün olayi, Nesin Vakfı yıllığı*, 1966, 567-92; M. Zekeriya tel, *Hatırladıklarım*, Istanbul 1968, 134-7; hçet Necatigil, *Edebiyatımızda isimler sözlüğü*[8], anbul 1975 s.v.; Azra Erhat, *Mektuplariyle likarnas Balıkçısı*, Istanbul 1976. (Fahir İz)

LĪLADJ is myrobalanus, the plum-like of the Terminalia chebula-tree, a Combratacea uth-Asia and the Malayan archipelago. Being ful and cheap substitute (*badal*) for gall or oak-s (*ʿafṣ*), they were used already in antiquity xtracting tannic acid and as a medicine. The appears also as *ahlīladj* or *ihlīladj* and goes gh Persian *halīla* back to Sanskrit *harītakī*. Syn-s are *hārsar* (indicated as "Indian" and proba-be derived from the Sanskrit term mentioned), and *mufarfaḥ* (with variants). These fruits allegedly unknown to the earlier Greeks: the νος μυρεψική of Dioscorides (*De materia medica*, . Wellmann, ii, Berlin 1906, 301 f. = lib. iv, is the fruit of a kind of Meringa, known to the s as behen-nut (*bān*). The later Greeks called μυροβάλανος ("salve-acorn"), and when the s imported from India the real myrobalanus were confounded, notwithstanding their com-y different medical effect.

e Arabs knew five kinds of myrobalanus, all of had reached Europe perhaps already at the of the School of Salerno, but they were imported at quantities and used in the Western pharma-nly through the trade of the Portuguese. The ing kinds are under discussion: (1) the yellow myrobalanus (*halīladj aṣfar*, *Terminalia citrina*). Its juice has an aperient effect and purges yellow gall. As an ointment, it dries up wound-boils, and pulver-ised and diluted with rose-water, it heals burns; (2) the myrobalanus of Kābul (*halīladj kābulī*), the ripe fruit of *Terminalia chebula*, is considered as the finest. Its effect is like that of the first one and, besides, it has the property of conferring a lucid intellect; (3) the black myrobalan (*halīladj aswad*), the unripe fruit of the *Terminalia chebula*, as large as a small olive; (4) *balīladj*, *Terminalia bellerica*; and (5) *amladj*, useful against haemorrhoids, in the Eastern and Western Middle Ages considered as a kind of myro-balanus, in fact, however, the fruit of a completely different family of plants, namely the *Phyllanthus emblica* (Euphorbiaceae). However, the nomen-clature is not established with certainty.

The fruits were harvested at various stages of ripeness: small, unripe, dried, they served as medi-cine; the ripe fruits of the size of walnuts were used for the preparation of tannin, which was in high demand. In India, where the myrobalanus tree is indigenous, the fruits were widely used as medicine, especially as stomachics and purgatives; the Tirphala or Triphala ("tri-juiced medicine"), consisting proba-bly of three of the kind mentioned above, was in particular esteemed (cf. al-Khʷārazmī, *Mafātīḥ al-ʿulūm*, ed. van Vloten, Leiden 1895, 186: *tarī abhal ay thalāthat akhlāṭ wa-hiya ahlīladj aṣfar wa-balīladj wa-amladj*). The Arabs mixed the fruits with spices in order to increase their digestive effect. The myro-balanus has now disappeared from the pharmaco-poeias in the West, but may still be used here and there in the East; only for the preparation of tannin is it still to be found on the market.

In mathematics the various forms of the term, especially *ihlīladj*, were also used to designate an ellipse (M. Souissi, *La langue des mathématiques en arabe*, Tunis 1968, Nos. 35, 37).

Bibliographie: ʿAlī b. Rabban al-Ṭabarī, *Firdaws al-ḥikma*, ed. Ṣiddīḳī, Berlin 1928, 417, see W. Schmucker, *Die pflanzliche und mineralische Materia medica im Firdaus al-ḥikma des ... aṭ-Ṭabarī*, Bonn 1969, no. 787; Rāzī, *Ḥāwī*, xxi, Ḥaydarābād 1388/1968, 636-8 (no. 898); *Die pharmakolog. Grundsätze des Abu Mansur .. Harawi*, tr. A. Ch. Achundow, Halle 1893, 145 f., 337 f.; Ibn al-Djazzār, *Iʿtimād*, Ms. Ayasofya 3564, fols. 4b-5a; Zahrāwī, *Taṣrīf*, Ms. Beşir Ağa 502, fol. 512a, *ll.* 3-4; Ibn Sīnā, *Ḳānūn*, Būlāḳ i, 297 f.; Bīrūnī, *Ṣaydala*, ed. H. M. Saʿīd, Karachi 1973, Arab. 377 f., Engl. 329 f.; Ibn Biklārish, *Mustaʿīnī*, Ms. Naples, Bibl. Naz. iii, F. 65, fol. 37b; Ghāfiḳī, *al-Adwiya al-mufrada*, Ms. Rabat, Bibl. Gén. ḳ. 155 i, fols. 152b-154b; Ibn Hubal, *Mukhtārāt*, Ḥaydarābād 1362, ii, 68 f.; P. Guigues, *Les noms arabes dans Sérapion*, in *JA*, 10ème série (1905), v, 496 (no. 71) *Bellileg*, 530 (no. 226) *Halilig*; Maimonides, *Sharḥ asmāʾ al-ʿuḳḳār*, ed. Meyerhof, Cairo 1940, no. 112; Ibn al-Bayṭār, *Djāmiʿ*, Būlāḳ 1291, iv, 196-8, tr. Leclerc, no. 2261 (with many quotations from sources); Yūsuf b. ʿUmar, *Muʿtamad*[3], ed. M. al-Saḳḳāʾ, Beirut 1395/1975, 536-9; Ibn al-Ḳuff, *ʿUmda*, Ḥaydarābād 1356, i, 125 f., see H. G. Kircher, *Die "einfachen Heilmittel" aus dem "Handbuch der Chirurgie" des Ibn al-Quff*, Bonn 1967, no. 23; Suwaydī, *Simāt*, Ms. Paris ar. 3004, fol. 80b; Barhebraeus, *The abridged version of "The Book of simple drugs" of ... al-Ghâfiqî*, ed. Meyerhof and Sobhy, Cairo 1932, no. 264; Ghassānī, *Ḥadīḳat al-azhār*, Ms. Ḥasan H. ʿAbd al-Wahhāb, fols. 123b-124a; Dāwūd al-Anṭākī,

Tadhkira, Cairo 1371/1952, i, 62; *Tuḥfat al-aḥbāb*, ed. Renaud and Colin, Paris 1934, nos. 43, 126; W. Heyd, *Histoire du commerce du Levant au moyen-âge*, ii, Leipzig 1886, 640-3; F. A. Flückiger, *Pharmakognosie des Pflanzenreiches*³, Berlin 1891, 269 f.; *The medical formulary or Aqrābādhīn of al-Kindī*, tr. M. Levey, Madison, etc. 1966, 342 (no. 314); F. Moattar, *Ismāʿīl Ǧorǧānī und seine Bedeutung für die iranische Heilkunde*, Diss. rer. nat. Marburg 1971, no. 115. (A. Dietrich)

HALKEVI [see KHALḲEVI].

ḤALLĀḲ (A.), lit. "barber", "hairdresser", synonymous with *muzayyin*; the *ḥadjdjām* ("cupper") [see FAṢṢĀD, in Suppl.] also used to be a part-time barber. The *ḥallāḳ*s formed a group of skilled workers, of mixed social origins. The well-known barber in the Islamic society of Medina was Khirāsh b. Umayya, who shaved the Prophet Muḥammad's hair. The Prophet had his hair shaved at Minā at the time of the *ḥadjdj*, and Muslims have followed this practice during the Greater and Lesser Pilgrimages ever since.

Some barber's work at the time of the Pilgrimage received attention from the Arab writers, who recorded unusual events. For instance, a *ḥallāḳ* while shaving the hair of Abū Sufyān [*q.v.*], accidentally cut the wart (*thulūl*) on his head, and this reportedly caused his sickness and death in 20/640, says al-Samhūdī. During the Umayyad period, another *ḥallāḳ* became widely known at the time of the *ḥadjdj* of Yazīd b. al-Muhallab [*q.v.*], who paid 5,000 *dirham*s to the *ḥallāḳ* after ritual shaving of his hair. The event illustrates that some barbers received charity from pilgrims in addition to their usual fee. Some Muslims used to have a yearly hair-cut on the Day of Sacrifice (*yawm al-naḥr*), as was the practice of al-Ḥasan al-Baṣrī [*q.v.*], and Muslims even today observe this custom.

The *ḥallāḳ* worked at market places and also in public baths in Islamic cities or specific days of the week. During the ʿAbbāsid period, the hairdresser was one of the five regular attendants at every *ḥammām*. The *muḥtasib* demanded expertise from each *ḥallāḳ*, who could neither shave a child's hair without his guardian's permission nor cut a slave's hair without his master's approval. Usually a *ḥallāḳ* received a *dāniḳ* or a *dirham* for each hair-cut. It was also customary for the *ḥallāḳ* to give free hair-cuts to the poorer members of society during the Mamlūk period, writes al-Ibshīhī. In spite of their useful services, the barber was a person of very humble status, ridiculed by writers. A *ḥallāḳ* could marry only within his own social group, according to the customary law of *kafāʾa*, which imposed similar restrictions on sweepers, weavers, cuppers and grocers. Seldom did a barber attain prominence in early Islamic society, either by acquiring knowledge of Islamic sciences or otherwise. The only known exception to this was Abu 'l-Ḥasan ʿAlī b. Muḥammad al-Ṣūfī al-Muzayyin, the barber who distinguished himself as a practising mystic and a close friend of al-Djunayd [*q.v.*].

Bibliography: al-Rabīʿ b. Ḥabīb, *al-Djāmiʿ al-ṣaḥīḥ*, Jerusalem 1381/1961, 40; Ibn Saʿd, *Ṭabaḳāt*, Beirut 1958, vii, 176; viii, 139, 429 (basic source); Abū Nuʿaim, *Geschichte Iṣbahāns*, Leiden 1934, i, 17; al-Ṣābiʾ, *Rusūm dār al-khilāfa*, Baghdād 1964, 19-20; *Rasāʾil Ikhwān al-ṣafāʾ*, Cairo 1928, i, 213, 215; al-Sulamī, *Ṭabaḳāt al-Ṣūfiyya*, Cairo 1969, 382-5; al-Khaṭīb al-Baghdādī, *Kitāb al-Taṭfīl*, Damascus 1346/1927, 83-4; Ibn Bassām, *Nihāyat al-rutba fī ṭalab al-ḥisba*, Baghdād 1968, 71; Ibn al-Ukhuwwa, *Maʿālim al-ḳurba*, London 1938, 156; Ibn al-Athīr, *al-Lubāb fī tahdhīb al-ansāb*, Beirut n.d., iii, 205; ider *Nihāya fī gharīb al-ḥadīth wa 'l-āthār*, Cairo i, 426-8; al-Ibshīhī, *al-Mustaṭraf*, Cairo 19 143, 161 (useful source); al-Samhūdī, *Waf wafāʾ bi-akhbār dār al-Muṣṭafā*, Beirut 197 911; Ibn ʿĀbidīn, *Radd al-muḥtār ʿalā du mukhtār*, Cairo 1877, 496-7; al-Kattānī, *Niẓa ḥukūma al-nabawiyya*, Beirut n.d., ii, 104- also M. Abdul Jabbar Beg, *Workers in the māmāt in the Arab Orient in the early Middle* in *RSO*, xlvii (1972), 77-80. (M. A. J. B

AL-**HAMADHĀNĪ**, ʿAyn al-Ḳuḍāt [see al-Ḳuḍāt, in Suppl.].

ḤAMĀDISHA, or **ḤMĀDSHA** as they are l called, are the members of a loosely and div organised religious confraternity or "p (*ṭarīḳa*) which traces its spiritual heritage back t Moroccan saints (*walī*s or *sayyid*s) of the late and early 18th centuries, Sīdī Abu 'l- Ḥasan ʿ Ḥamdush (d. 1131/1718-9 or 1135/1722-3), pop called Sīdī ʿAlī and Sīdī Aḥmad Dghughī (?

Although little is known historically of the saints, their lives, like the lives of other pc North African saints, are rich in legend. legends stress the saints' acquisition, possession passing on of blessing or *baraka* [*q.v.*]. Sīdī ʿAlī is generally recognised as the master of Sīdī Aḥ is thought to have derived his teachings from al-Salām b. Mashīsh [*q.v.*] and his student A Ḥasan al-Shādhilī. (Members of the confrate recite on occasion a *ḥizb* which they trace t Shādhilī.) Sīdī ʿAlī spent years at the Ḳaraw University in Fās, and, according to the *Salw anfās* of Djaʿfar al-Kattānī, he is to be classed a the *shaykh*s of the mystical tradition in whic trance (*ḥāl*) is powerful. He would occasionall into lion-like rages. Both Sīdī ʿAlī and Sīdī Aḥm buried on the south face of the Djebel Zarhūn sixteen miles from the city of Miknās; Sīdī ʿ the village of Banī Rashīd, Sīdī Aḥmad in Warād. Their sanctuaries (*ḳubba*s), which are the charge of their (putative) descendants (*awl sayyid*), are the object of individual and coll pilgrimages. The latter, the *mūsem* (*mawsim*), place each year on the sixth and seventh day the *mūlūd* (*mawlid*), the Feast of the Pro Birthday, and is attended not only by the Ḥm but by tens of thousands of devotees of the s

The Ḥmādsha are in fact members of one o other of two distinct confraternities which closely related and often confused. The ʿAlla are the followers of Sīdī ʿAlī and the Dghugh of Sīdī Aḥmad. Both brotherhoods have a netw lodges (*zāwiya*s) and teams (*ṭāʾifa*s) that ex throughout the principal towns and cities or nor Morocco and through the Gharb and Zarhūn The Ḥmādsha brotherhoods, which have neithe membership nor the fame of such popular ord the ʿĪsāwā [*q.v.*], do not extend across the Mor frontier. In a figure that is undoubtedly too Draque estimated their membership in 1938 at Today, despite a marked decrease in the popu of the confraternities in Morocco, the Ḥmādsha's ber is considerably greater than Draque's esti

The members themselves fall into three di classes: the *awlād al-sayyid*, who trace their cent back to their ancestral saint, live princi in the village in which he is buried, and do not ally participate in his ecstatic ceremonies; *fuḳarāʾ* who are members of lodges (*zāwiya*s) or t (*ṭāʾifa*s); and the devotees, or *muḥibbūn* wh simply attracted to the saint and his cult. Ea rotherhoods is in the charge of the head, the *ār*, of its respective *awlād al-sayyid*.

e Ḥmādsha are notorious for their practice g trance of slashing their heads with knives or rds (*shaḳria*) or beating them with water jugs, balls, or clubs studded with nails. The princi- remony (*ṣadaḳa, layla*, or *ḥadra*) of the brother- is not dissimilar in form to the ceremonies of Īsāwā, the Djilāla [see ḲĀDIRIYYA], and other ar Maghribī brotherhoods. (It tends to be more y organised, and more frenetic, in the shanty s and countryside than in the urban *zāwiyas*.) ceremony usually begins with at least a per- ory chanting of popular litanies—there is no ard *dhikr* or *ḥizb* for the brotherhood—and nues with the *ḥadra* or trance-dance. Men and n dance first to the music of drums (*ṭabl* and and oboe (*ghayṭa*) and then to that of the drums ither a reed recorder (*nīra*) or a guitar (*ganbrī*); fall first into a light, somnambulistic trance *ḥāl* and then into a deeper, wilder trance *djedhba*. It is during *djedhba* that acts of self- ation (by men, rarely by women) are performed animals (pigs and camels) imitated (see Ā).

e *ḥadra* is not understood in terms of a mystical or communion with God. Rather, the *baraka* of aint is held responsible for the *ḥāl*; *djedhba* ually interpreted as possession by a *djinn* ī) or more frequently by a *djinniyya*. The most on possessing spirit is the *djinniyya* or *ghūla* a Ḳandīsha [*q.v.* above] who is said to manifest f as either a beauty or a hag, always with the of a camel or some other hooved animal. The ssing spirit is thought to respond to a particular al phrase (*rīḥ*), often accompanied by words, it finds pleasing. The Ḥmādsha themselves primarily as curers of the *djinn*-struck and the -possessed. Their aim is less to exorcise per- ntly the possessing spirit than to establish a iotic relationship between the spirit and its n. Often membership in the brotherhood occurs a Ḥmādsha cure. Their ceremonies are thought to bring *baraka* to their sponsor, to those in dance, and to the ceremonial area itself.

Bibliography: J. Herber, *Les Hamadcha et les loughiyyin*, in *Hespéris* (1923); G. Draque, *uisse d'histoire religieuse du Maroc*, Paris n.d.; Dermenghem, *Le culte des saints dans l'Islam ghrébin*, Paris 1954; V. Crapanzano, *The Ha- dsha*, in N. Keddie (ed.), *Saints, scholars, and is*, Berkeley, 1972; idem, *The Ḥamadsha: a dy in Moroccan ethnopsychiatry*, Berkeley 1973; m, *Mohammed and Dawia*, in V. Crapanzano V. Garrison (eds.), *Case studies in spirit posses- n*, New York 1976. (V. CRAPANZANO)

ḤAMAL [see MINṬAḲAT AL-BURŪDJ].

MĀSA, the epic genre in Islamic litera-

vi. IN SWAHILI LITERATURE.

Swahili literature, the word *hamasa* occurs rarely has the meaning of "virtue, courage, energy". normal words for "courage, valour" in Swa- literature are *ushujaa, ujasiri, uṣabiṭi* and *ri*, all words of Arabic version, and so is the for virtue, *fadhila*. There are only a few non- tive heroic poems known in Swahili literature, of them self-praises in true African fashion. most famous of these is the Ukawafi of Liongo, ng himself, and at the same time an Ode to om: "I am a young eagle. When this iron is broken, I will soar up into the skies, higher than all". [see MADĪḤ. 5. In Swahili].

The vast majority of heroic poetry in Swahili is narrative and composed in the *utenzi* metre of lines of eight syllables; every four lines form a stanza *ubeti* (the word is formed on the basis of *bayt*). The rhyme scheme is *a a a b*, in which *b* represents the rhyme of the last line of every stanza throughout the whole poem; there are in Swahili more than a thousand words ending in *ya, ri*, etc. Rhyme in Swahili means the identity of the last syllable, so that *amba, imba, omba, umba* are rhyme-words.

About the life of the semi-mythical poet-hero Liongo we possess a few epic fragments which however, are certainly not contemporary (he lived presumably *ca.* 1010/1600). The oldest datable Swahili epic in Swahili is also the finest ever written in it; the ms. in Hamburg is dated 1141/1728. Its theme is the myth of the Prophet Muḥammad's expedition to Tabūk where according to this legend, he encountered and defeated the Emperor of Con- stantinople, Heraclius I, hence the epic's title, *Utendi wa Herekali*, or *Chuo cha Tambuka*. The published text (1958) has 1,145 stanzas. The sophisti- cated structure, the compact language, the intense style and the rich imagery show that it stands at the end of a long evolution of epic poetry of which we have no documentation. All we know is that the *Herekali* had many imitators, none of whom ever reached the powerful diction and the visionary heights of this first epic. The author, Bwana Mwengo b. Athumani, worked for a time at the court of the sultan of Pate, who requested him to versify the Arabic legend (*hadithi*), in "Swahili." Mwengo's son Abu Bakari composed at least one epic on the theme of an other *maghāzī* [*q.v.*] tradition, the *Katirifu*, i.e. the expedition of Muḥammad against king Ghiṭrīf (ms. in SOAS, undated, but probably *ca.* 1750-60). Here follows a list of the major heroic-narrative poems in Swahili. *Abdu-Rahmani*. This adventurous son of Abū Bakr, whose bride is a daughter of the infamous Abū Sufyān, fights numer- ous battles which made him so popular that there are two epic poems about him in Swahili.

Ali. ʿAlī is by far the most popular hero in Swahili epics literature, but so far no complete epic about his life has come to light. His exploits are celebrated in the *Utenzi wa Anzaruni* in which he defeats the *shayṭān* Anẓurnī (cf. Ḳurʾān, VII, 14); in the *Utenzi wa Herekali*; in the *Katirifu*; in the *Rasi'l-Ghuli* (*ca.* 1870), a Swahili versification of the *Futūḥ al- Yaman*, one of the longest Swahili epics (4,300 stan- zas) and of course in the epic of Haibara, on the battle of Khaybar [*q.v.*], of which only an incomplete ms. survives. The *Utenzi wa Muhamadi* contains among others the episode of the Battle of the Trench (*Handaki* [see KHANDAḲ]); this epic of the life of Muḥammad is the longest in Swahili literature, and with that, the longest epic ever composed in an African language. The *Utenzi wa Badiri*, the Epic of the Battle of Badr [*q.v.*] is the next in length, with 4,500 stanzas; yet it is not length that makes an epic great literature.

Hajji Chum of Zanzibar (*fl. ca.* 1920) wrote an epic on the Battle of Uḥud which contains some beautifully dramatic scenes; it was edited by H. E. Lambert (East African Literature Bureau in Nairobi; 739 stanzas). Hemedi b. Abdallah al-Buhriy (d. 1922) wrote, apart from the long version of the Abdu- Rahmani mentioned above, an equally long epic about the German conquest of the Swahili Coast in 1884. For the pious Swahili, this was a Holy War against "Christian" invaders who bombed women and children from their safe warships. It is by far the best modern epic, i.e. one that deals with recent historical events instead of the mainly mythical events set during the life of the Prophet. The only epic set after his life are the three known versions of the life and death of Huseni (i.e. al-Ḥusayn [*q.v.*]), which shows (as do the Swahili traditions about ʿAlī) that there must have been considerable S͟hīʿī influence on the East African Coast. The epics that deal with the lives of the prophets before Muḥammad (Ādam, Ayyūb, Mūsā, Yūnus, Yūsuf), and those on the lives of the first Muslim women (K͟hadīd͟ja, Fāṭima, ʿĀʾis͟ha) are not heroic in the true sense of chivalresque and are left outside the scope of this article.

Bibliography: A complete list of titles, mss. and editions can be found in Knappert, *The canon of Swahili literature*, in B. R. Bloomfield, ed., *Middle East Studies and Libraries ... for Prof. J. D. Pearson*, London 1980, 85-102. Epic poetry is discussed in Knappert, *Four centuries of Swahili verse*, London 1979, chs. 3, 5, 8; idem, *Traditional Swahili poetry*, Leiden 1967, ch. 3; text editions: idem, *Swahili Islamic poetry*, Leiden 1971, iii; *Utenzi wa Miiraji*, see *Afrika und Uebersee*, xlviii (1964), 241-74; *Katirifu*, in *ibid.*, liii, 81-104, 264-313. The two great works on the Swahili epic are: E. Dammann, *Dichtungen in der Lamu Mundart des Suaheli*, Hamburg 1940, and: J. W. T. Allen, *Tendi*, London 1971. (J. Knappert)

al-**ḤAMDAWĪ**, Abū ʿAlī Ismāʿīl b. Ibrāhīm b. Ḥamdawayhī, better known as al-Ḥamdūnī (this *nisba* being due to a defective reading, cf. al-Samʿānī, *Ansāb*, ed. Hyderabad, iv, 241), minor poet of Baṣra in the 3rd/9th century. From his profession (that of *kātib*, Ibn Ḳutayba, *ʿUyūn*, iv, 89) and his origin, he belonged to the class of high officials of Persian origin in the ʿAbbāsid administration; his grandfather had been *ʿarīf al-zanādiḳa* under al-Mahdī from 168/784-5 (Goldziher, *Ṣâliḥ b. ʿAbd al-Ḳuddûs und das Zindîḳthum während der Regierung des Chalifen al-Mahdî*, in *Trans. Congress of Orientalists*, London, ii, 1892, 108).

Nothing is known of his youth; the *Ag͟hānī*[1], xii, 61-2, mentions his relations with the libertine poets of Baṣra ʿAbd al-Ṣamad b. al-Muʿad͟hd͟hal and Madraṭān. Like them, he does not seem ever to have left Baṣra to seek his fortune in Bag͟hdād. Amongst his patrons, especially notable was Muḥammad b. al-Mug͟hīra b. Ḥarb (genealogy in Ibn Ḥazm, *D͟jamhara*[2], 369), known as Ibn Ḥarb. This scion of the Muhallabids, governor of Nahr Tīrā and a lover of bacchic sessions, offered a slightly worn *ṭaylasān* to the poet, who was angered and launched a series of ten epigrams at Ibn Ḥarb. Their success—al-Mubarrad's circle seems to have appreciated them, according to al-Ḥuṣrī, *Zahr al-ādāb*, 550—led al-Ḥamdawī to make the *ṭaylasān* the central motif of his poetry. Other fragments of his attack a descendant of Sulaymān b. ʿAlī, the governor of Baṣra and outstanding patron, al-Ḥusayn b. D͟jaʿfar (*Ag͟hānī*[1], xx, 37) and al-Ḥasan b. Rabāḥ, an aristocratic Baṣran of whom al-D͟jāḥiẓ thought highly.

Towards the end of al-Ḥamdawī's life there took place the episode of Saʿīd b. Sabandād; a skinny and bony ewe triggered off an incident similar to that of the *ṭaylasān*. The only biographical detail attested is provided by a particularly rancorous distich directed against Saʿīd b. Ḥumayd after his appointment in 248/862 as head of the Correspondence Department (al-Ṭabarī, iii, 1515). But after this date, al-Ḥamdawī is no more mentioned.

Al-Ḥamdawī was essentially a satirist. One epi of his was so boldly drawn that it was attributed, its high quality, to Abū Nuwās (Ibn al-Hi *Taʾhīl al-g͟harīb*, ii, 249; Abū Nuwās, *Dīwān* Wagner, ii, 152). The interest of his poetry lies treatment of themes: here we have a *ṭaylasān* a ewe raised to the level of literary types (al-T͟haʿ *T͟himār al-ḳulūb*, Cairo 1965, 376, 601, 673) and viding points of reference for scholars. Ibn al-I Ibn Sukkara and Ibn Ṣārah evoke this famous *sān*, and in the 9th/15th century, al-Suyūṭī, fc the same path in his *al-Aḥādīt͟h al-ḥisān fī faḍl a lasān* (ms. Escurial 1972, fols. 27b, 29b-30a-b). *hid͟jāʾ* of insinuation is thrown into relief by a fort of poetic style which is extremely bravura *mīn* and metaphors (Ibn Abī ʿAwn, *Tas͟hbīhāt*, him twelve times) brought great delight to scholars (al-D͟jurd͟jānī, *Kināyāt*, 123).

Bibliography: As well as references above, see Ibn al-Muʿtazz, *Ṭabaḳāt*, index; ʿAbd Rabbihi, *ʿIḳd*, index; Masʿūdī, *Murūd͟j* 89 = § 3213 and index s.v. Ḥamdūnī; I *D͟jamʿ al-d͟jawāhir*, index; Ibn al-D͟jarrāḥ, *Wa* 62; Bayhaḳī, *al-Maḥāsin wa 'l-masāwī*, 304, ʿAskarī, *Maʿānī*, index; al-K͟hālidiyyān, *Tuḥaf wa 'l-hadāyā*, index; ʿAbd Allāh b. Mu mad al-ʿAbdalkānī, *Ḥamāsat al-ẓurafāʾ*, ms. I bul University 1455, fol. 111a; Ibn Ḥam *Tad͟hkira*, ms. Raʾīs al-kuttāb 769, v. 154a, 1 161 a; Aydamīr, *al-Durr al-farīd wa-bayt al-ḳ* ms. Fātiḥ 3761, 26 b, 193 a, 354 a; Ḥusayn S al-ʿAllāḳ, *al-S͟huʿarāʾ al-kuttāb fi 'l-ʿIrāḳ fi 'l al-t͟hālit͟h al-hid͟jrī*, Beirut 1975, index; Ibn K kān, Būlāḳ, ii, 472-3, ed. Iḥsān ʿAbbās, vii, 95 Ṣafadī, no. 3994. The poet's *dīwān* has been brc together and published in the Iraqi journa *Mawrid*, iii/1 (1974) (additions in iv/1, 197 A. D͟j. al-Nad͟jdī; it has been studied by A. A *Thèmes et style d'al-Ḥamdawī*, in *JA*, cc (1979), 261-307. (A. Ara

ḤAMDŪN IBN al-**ḤĀD͟JD͟J** [see ibn al-ḥā

ḤAMĪD ḲALANDAR, Ṣūfī mystic and of Muslim India.

He was born in Kilōg͟harī (Dihlī) some time tow the close of K͟hald͟jī period. His father, Mawlānā al-Dīn, was a devout disciple of S͟hayk͟h Niẓām a Awliyāʾ, and Ḥamīd Ḳalandar visited the S͟h along with his father when he was a mere child father made proper arrangements for Ḥamīd's e tion, and he completed his studies according to traditions of his age. When Muslim families forcibly transplanted by the order of Sultan Mu mad b. Tug͟hluḳ from Dihlī to Deogīrī, Ḥamīd had to move to the Deccan. In Dawlatābād (De he benefited from the company of Mawlānā Bu al-Dīn G͟harīb, the *k͟halīfa* of S͟hayk͟h Niẓām a Awliyāʾ, and then in 753/1352-3 returned to I In 754/1353 he paid a visit to S͟hayk͟h Naṣīr al the successor of Niẓām al-Dīn Awliyāʾ. Bein formed about his father's association with his m S͟hayk͟h Naṣīr showed him much regard, a "Mawlānā, how can I address you as Ḳaland (sc. because he was a scholarly man). He told him once Niẓām al-Dīn Awliyāʾ had told his father th child would live in the fashion of a Ḳalandar [*q.v* accordingly shaved his head, eye-brows, mousta beard, and wore saffron clothes like the Ḳalan

Ḥamīd Ḳalandar compiled the *Malfūẓāt* or sa of S͟hayk͟h Naṣīr al-Dīn of Dihlī in Persian, depi the great S͟hayk͟h, *inter alia*, as talking to diff people who belonged to the various strata of so and came to the S͟hayk͟h's *k͟hānḳāh* with their ma lems. The work is characterised by clarity of ght and is free from miracles and other mystical orations. He also left a *Dīwān* of poetry which is extant, although Shaykh ʿAbd al-Ḥaḳḳ Muḥad- says that his verses were of poor quality and portant. The *Madjmūʿa-yi laṭāʾif wa-safīna*, an 9th/15th century anthology (B.M. Or. 4110), ains a number of *ḳaṣīdas* composed by Ḥamīd ndar in praise of Sultan Fīrūz Shāh of Dihlī, ing that he was a courtier also. The statement of id Muḥammad Gīsū Darāz [*q.v.*] contains some that Mawlānā Ḥamīd and his companions, ānā Ādam, Mawlānā Lādhū Shāh and Mawlānā af al-Dīn had no genuine aptitude for Ṣūfism, it is nevertheless correct that Ḥamīd possessed er a house, nor a wife or a child, and always as a Ḳalandar.

Bibliography: ʿAbd al-Ḥaḳḳ, *Akhbār al-hyār*, Dihlī 1914; Ḥamīd Ḳalandar, *Khayr al-djālis*, ed. K. A. Nizami, Aligarh 1960; Sayyid ḥammad Ḥusaynī, *Djawāmiʿ al-kalim* (sayings Shaykh Muhammad Gīsū Darāz) ed. Muhammad mid Siddiqui, Kānpur 1356/1937-8; Mīr Khurd, *yar al-awliyāʾ*, Dihlī 1302/1885. (I. H. Siddiqui)

ḤAMĪD al-DĪN ḲĀḌĪ NĀGAWRĪ, Muḥammad ṬĀʾ, Ṣūfī saint and scholar of Muslim a. On becoming a Ṣūfī he came to be known as kh Ḥamīd al-Dīn. Having travelled to different m countries, he came to Dihlī during the reign tutmish (607-33/1211-36 [*q.v.*]) and soon devel- an intimacy with Shaykh Ḳuṭb al-Dīn Bakhti- Kākī, the leading Čishtī saint of Dihlī. He himself ged to the Suhrawardī order and was the *khalīfa* ief disciple of Shaykh Shihāb al-Dīn Suhrawardī 632/1145-1234). Being fond of *samāʿ* (songs sung the spiritual entertainment of the Ṣūfīs), he it popular in Dihlī. He is reported to have d in Nāgawr as *ḳāḍī*, thereby acquiring the of Nāgawrī. Towards the end of his life he to Dihlī and died there in 641/1244, being buried the grave of his friend, Shaykh Ḳuṭb al-Dīn Kākī. mīd al-Dīn Nāgawrī was learned in both Arabic Persian and wrote a number of popular books on on and Ṣūfism, as well as composing verses. Shaykh Niẓām al-Dīn Awliyāʾ quoted to his ples the opinion of a certain leading scholar of the 3th century who used to tell his pupils "What- you study is available in these pages [sc. in works of the *ḳāḍī*], and whatever you do not know o contained herein. Whatever (knowledge) I have ired is based on (his works) and what I do not is also in his (works)." Amongst his numerous s, only the *Ṭawāliʿ al-shumūs* and *Sharḥ-i Arbaʿīn* of both in the Ḥabīb Gandj Collection, Mawlānā Library, Aligarh) are extant. The former ex- s the meanings of the names of God, while the r is a commentary on the selected forty tradi- of the Prophet relating to gnosis and the love od. There are extracts from his famous works, *awāʾiḥ* and the *Lawāmiʿ*, contained in the *Akh-l-akhyār*, and there is a quatrain composed by kh Ḥamīd al-Dīn in praise of Shaykh Farīd n Gandj-i Shakar of Adjōdhān quoted in the *kh-i Muḥammadī* of Biḥamad Khānī.

Bibliography: ʿAbd al-Ḥaḳḳ Muḥaddith Dih-ī, *Akhbār al-akhyār*, Dihlī 1309/1891-2; Ghawthī aṭṭārī, *Gulzār-i abrār* (a 17th century work), Ḥabīb Gandj Collection, Mawlānā Āzād orary, Aligarh; Muḥammad Mubārak Kirmānī, own as Mīr Khurd, *Siyar al-awliyāʾ*, Dihlī 1302/85; Muḥammad Bihāmad-Khānī, *Taʾrīkh-i uḥammadī*, ms. British Museum Or. 137; Mīr Ḥasan Sidjzī, *Fawāʾid al-fuʾād* (collection of the table talk of Shaykh Niẓām al-Dīn Awliyāʾ), Newal Kishore 1302/1885; Storey, i, 5. (I. H. Siddiqui)

ḤAMĪD al-DĪN ṢŪFĪ NĀGAWRĪ SIWĀLĪ, Ṣūfī saint of Muslim India. He was the posthumous son of Shaykh Muḥammad al-Ṣūfī, and allegedly the first child to be born in a Muslim family associated with the ruling class in Dihlī after its conquest by the Turks. When he was a grown-up young man, he became fond of a voluptuous life, but soon became disgusted with it and then decided to devote himself to religion and piety. He entered the circle of the disciples of Shaykh Muʿīn al-Dīn Čishtī in Adjmer and soon became a devoted Ṣūfī, repenting of his past sins and adopting a life of poverty. Being impressed by his sincerity and devotion, his *pīr* gave him the title of *Sulṭān al-tārikīn* "monarch of recluses", and he was also given a *khilāfat-nāma*, i.e. permission to enrol disciples.

Shaykh Ḥamīd al-Dīn finally settled down in Siwāl, a small village adjacent to Nāgawr, where he lived in a thatched house and dressed himself like a peasant, using two sheets of cloth to cover the upper and the lower parts of the body; he lived frugally and earned his livelihood by ploughing the land, never establishing any contact with the members of the ruling class nor accepting any aid from the state. He owned a cow that he milked himself, and was a strict vegetarian. His death took place in 674/1276 at an advanced age.

He was of the early Čishtī saints who made the order popular and widely-known in India. It is interesting to note that he lived and worked as a Ṣūfī in rural surroundings, while all the leading Ṣūfīs tended to live in the urban centres. He composed verses and wrote on religious problems, and his letters, addressed to Shaykh Bahāʾ al-Dīn Zakariyyāʾ Suhrawardī of Multān and other persons were very famous during mediaeval times. He wrote treatises also on Ṣūfism, the extracts from which are to be found in Shaykh ʿAbd al-Ḥaḳḳ Dihlawī's *Akhbār al-akhyār*.

Bibliography: ʿAbd al-Ḥaḳḳ Muḥaddith Dihlawī, *Akhbār al-akhyār*, Dihlī 1309/1891-2; Sayyid Muḥammad Mubārak Kirmānī, known as Mīr Khurd, *Siyar al-awliyāʾ*, Dihlī 1302/1885; *Surūr al-budūr*, an anonymous work, but certainly written by one of the grandsons of Ḥāmīd al-Dīn Ṣūfī Nāgawrī, as the contents reveal, ms. Habīb Gandj Collection, Mawlānā Āzād Library, Aligarh; Storey, i, 6, 1192. (I. H. Siddiqui)

ḤAMZA MAKHDŪM, Ṣūfī saint of the Kubrawiyya. He was the son of Bābā ʿUthmān, of Rādjpūt descent, and was born in about 900/1494-5. He studied in the famous *madrasa* in Srīnagar known as Dār al-Shifāʾ, which was founded by Sulṭān Ḥasan Shāh (876-89/1472-84). He studied the Ḳurʾān, *ḥadīth*, *fiḳh* and Ṣūfism under able teachers like Bābā Ismāʿīl Kubrawī, the principal of the *madrasa* and a great scholar of his time, his son Mullā Fatḥ Allāh Shīrāzī and Mullā Luṭf Allāh. After completing his education, Ḥamza Makhdūm became a follower of the Kubrawī order. He exhorted the Muslims to adhere to the *Sharīʿa* and to give up all un-Islamic beliefs and practices which they had borrowed from the non-Muslims. He was also one of the leaders of the movement against Shīʿism, which had begun to spread in the Valley in the first half of the 10th/16th century due to the efforts of Mīr Shams al-Dīn ʿIrāḳī and his followers. Ḥamza Makhdūm, therefore, undertook tours in the Valley to prevent the spread of Shīʿism and also to propagate Islamic fundamentalism. Ghāzī Shāh Čak (968-70/1561-3), the first ruler of the Čak dynasty, being a staunch S̲h̲īʿī, banished him from Srīnagar to Bīrū, a village 20 miles away. He was allowed to return to Srīnagar by Sulṭān Ḥusayn S̲h̲āh (970-8/1563-70), who was a liberal ruler. But Ḥamza Mak̲h̲dūm did not give up his anti-S̲h̲īʿī activities and was a party to inviting the Emperor Akbar to conquer Kas̲h̲mīr and save Sunnism. He died at the age of 84 and was buried on the slope of the Harīparbat hillock in Srīnagar, below Akbar's fort. He is greatly revered by the Kas̲h̲mīrīs, who hold his anniversary every year and visit his tomb in large numbers.

Bibliography: G. D. H. Ṣūfī, Kas̲h̲īr, Lahore 1948-9; Mohibbul Hasan, Kashmir under the Sulṭāns, Calcutta 1959; K̲h̲ʷādja Isḥāḳ Ḳārī, Ḥilyat al-ʿārifīn, ms. B.M. Or. 1868, a life of S̲h̲ayk̲h̲ Ḥamza Makhdūm; Ḥādjdjī Muʿīn al-Dīn, Tāʾrīk̲h̲-i kabīr, Amritsar 1322/1904. (Mohibbul Hasan)

HANAFITES [see ḤANAFIYYA].

HANDASA [see ʿILM AL-HANDASA].

HANDŽIĆ (AL-**K̲H̲ĀNDJĪ**), MUḤAMMAD B. MUḤAMMAD B. ṢĀLIḤ B. MUḤAMMAD, a leading Bosnian Muslim and Arabic author who was born in Saray Bosna about 1909. He received his early education in Bosnia, and his higher education at al-Azhar in Cairo, where he was admitted to the degree of al-ʿālimiyya. After this he performed the ḥadjdj with his father, and returned to his native country to teach. He belonged to the Ḥanafī mad̲h̲hab, and followed the teachings of Ibn Taymiyya in fiḳh. He died at Saray Bosna on 29 July, 1944.

During his short literary career he contributed both to the international literature of Islam, with his various works on theology, and to the Arabic literature of Yugoslavia with his poetry, his works dealing with various aspects of the local history of the Muslims in Bosnia, and his literary study al-Djawhar al-asnā fī tarādjim ʿulamāʾ wa-shuʿarāʾ Būsna. In addition to the latter work his published writings include a commentary on Risālat Ḥayāt al-anbiyāʾ by Aḥmad al-Bayhaḳī, a commentary on al-Kalim al-ṭayyib of Aḥmad b. Taymiyya and Risālat al-Ḥaḳḳ al-ṣaḥīḥ fī it̲h̲bāt nuzūl Sayyidinā al-Masīḥ. A number of his works remain unpublished, including some Arabic poems and a supplement to Ḥadjdjī K̲h̲alīfa's Kas̲h̲f al-ẓunūn.

Bibliography: Zakī Muḥammad Mudjāhid, al-Aʿlām al-s̲h̲arḳiyya fi 'l-miʾa al-rābiʿa ʿas̲h̲ra al-hidjriyya, ii, Cairo 1950, 174; ʿUmar Riḍā Kaḥḥāla, Muʿdjam al-muʿallifin, xi, Damascus 1960, 280; for his unpublished works, see K. Dobrača, Fihris al-makhṭūṭāt al-ʿarabiyya wa'l-turkiyya wa'l-fārisiyya, i, Sarajevo 1963, passim; R. Y. Ebied and M. J. L. Young, An exposition of the Islamic doctrine of Christ's Second Coming, as presented by a Bosnian Muslim scholar, in Orientalia Lovaniensia Periodica, v (1974), 127-37.

(R. Y. Ebied and M. J. L. Young)

AL-**ḤĀRITH** B. **KALADA** B. ʿAMR B. ʿILĀDJ AL-T̲H̲AḲAFĪ (d. 13/634-5), traditionally considered as the oldest known Arab physician.

It is nevertheless difficult to pin down his personality. He came originally from al-Ṭāʾif, where he was probably born a few years after the middle of the 6th century A.D., and is said to have been a lute-player (trained in Persia?) before studying medicine at Gondēs̲h̲āpūr [q.v.] and, adds Ṣāʿid al-Andalusī (Ṭabaḳāt al-umam, ed. Cheikho, Beirut 1912, 47, tr. Blachère, Paris 1935, 99) with small probability, in the Yemen. He became the "physician of the Arabs", acquiring great fame, and according to some late sources had relations with the Persians, even to the

point that he is supposed to have had with one of Kisrās—unhesitatingly identified with K̲h̲u Anus̲h̲irwān, who however died in 579 A.D.—a conversation in the course of which he was led revealing to the monarch the principles behin medical treatments (see especially, Ibn K̲h̲al Wafayāt, ed. I. ʿAbbās, Beirut 1965, vi, 373-6 Abī Uṣaybiʿ, Aṭibbāʾ, ed. Müller, i, 110-11). A ment of this kind, which leads one to believe tha Kalada was the author of a treatise on hygien also al-G̲h̲uzūlī, Maṭāliʿ al-budūr, ii, 101-3), is cl apocryphal, but it undoubtedly contains some o aphorisms current among the Arabs of the tim membrance of which has not entirely disappeare is mainly a question of pieces of advice on foo sexual hygiene which investigators of the 2nd 8th-9th centuries were able to gather together

Since al-Ḥārith also practised at Mecca, on va occasions he tended Muḥammad, it is related, b his mission, and there are naturally attribute him some spectacular cures of a patently fol nature. Among these figures his treatment of a y whose illness, difficult to diagnose, was simpl impossible love which he felt for his sister-i (Ibn Ḳayyim al-Djawziyya, Ak̲h̲bār al-nisāʾ, 1319, 21-2, citing al-Aṣmaʿī; cf. R. Basset, Mille contes, etc., Paris 1926, ii, 74-5, who brings for several variants of this tale and points out i semblance to the intervention of the physician sistratos with Antiochus). According to a lege anti-Umayyad origin, when the wife of Yūsuf al kafī, who had had al-Ḥārith as her first husl brought al-Ḥadjdjādj [q.v.] into the world, S appeared amidst the family in the form of Ibn K and made the baby drink some blood because h refusing his mother's breast; this was the orig the bloodthirsty nature of the great governo Masʿūdī, Murūdj, v, 288-9 = §§ 2052-3).

The biographers also lay emphasis on one o cures which had far-reaching consequences, tha formed at al-Ṭāʾif on a person described as a of Yemen called Abu 'l-K̲h̲ayr (Ibn Ḳutayba, Ma 288) or else al-Nūs̲h̲adjān [b. Wahrīz] (Yāḳūt Zandaward), or even simply a Yas̲h̲kurī of Kask Balād̲h̲urī, Ansāb, iv/a, 163); the sick man, now of leprosy, showed his gratitude by presenting Ḥārith the famous Sumayya, who came orig from Zandaward and had belonged to the Pe emperor. This explicatory story is already suspect, but may contain a basis of truth; it is cult to make out subsequent events because o anti-Umayyad traditions which have obscured tl This Sumayya, who is moreover sometimes r up with the mother of ʿAmmār b. Yāsir [q.v.], mayya bint K̲h̲ubāṭ (Ibn Ḳutayba, Maʿārif, had several children: the third one, Ziyād gave rise to the well-known controversies; the se Nufayʿ, known historically by his kunya of Bakra [q.v.], was not recognised by al-Ḥārith, gave out that his father was one his slaves o Masrūḥ; as for the first child, Nāfiʿ, several so (in particular, al-Balād̲h̲urī, loc. cit.) make hir son of al-Ḥārith, but Ibn al-Kalbī (-Caskel, Tab only mentions a Nāfiʿ b. Kalada, who woul cordingly be the brother of the physician. Wi becoming aware of a contradiction, since he a that al-Ḥārith was childless, Ibn Ḳutayba (loc attributes to him a daughter Azda who was th of ʿUtba b. G̲h̲azwān [q.v.]; the latter broug three brothers-in-law to Baṣra and employed as a secretary (see also al-Balād̲h̲urī, Ansāb, 164). Complicating the situation even further ib (*Muḥabbar*, 460) further cites another daughter -Ḥārit͟h, Ḳilāba, who married a distant cousin, r b. ʿUmayr b. ʿAwf (Ibn al-Kalbī-Caskel, Tab.

can be seen that this family history is very cult to disentangle, and it offers a character- example of the confusions brought about by the ts of many *mawālī* to provide themselves with an genealogy and, in this particular case, by the e political propaganda aimed at blackening the yyad's names. According to the information men- ed above, Sumayya was apparently married at once, since it was her husband ʿUbayd who the alleged father of Ziyād. Now the historical ces reflect, in regard to Muʿāwiya's recognition iyād's position as collateral relative (*istilḥāḳ*), anti-Umayyad tradition according to which ayya was a prostitute, which makes this "physi- of the Arabs" a procurer, since she had been lled at his instigation in the *ḥārat al-bag͟hāyā* -Ṭāʾif in return for paying him a share of her ings (al-Masʿūdī *Murūd͟j*, v, 22, 24 = § 1778,). Logically, the physiognomists ought to have vened and pronounced upon the father of each er children [see BIG͟HĀʾ, above], but the sources nothing about this.

-Ḥārit͟h b. Kalada probably gave up this latter rity—if indeed the information about it is entic—after he was converted to Islam and had ired the status of one of the Prophet's Compan- According to a tradition which has clearly been aped (see al-Ṭabarī, i, 2127-8; al-Masʿūdī, *ūd͟j*, iv, 184 = § 1518; cf. *al-Fak͟hrī*, ed. Deren- g, 133), Abū Bakr was poisoned by the Jews, al-Ḥārit͟h, who had shared his meal, lost his sight died soon afterwards.

ne discerns that, if the historical existence of the ysician of the Arabs" cannot be put in doubt, personality is surrounded by a host of legends h have secured a foothold in the historical and raphical literature and which make very difficult ttempts to disentangle the true from the false. s well as the treatise on hygiene attributed to there are some verses given under his name, bly the following (al-ʿAskarī, *Sināʿatayn*, 123): ere are some people who shower strangers with beneficence, whilst they afflict their relatives unhappiness right till death".

Bibliography: (in addition to references given the article): D͟jāḥiẓ, *Buk͟halāʾ*, ed. Ḥād͟jirī, 98, Pellat, 159; Ibn Ḳutayba, *ʿUyūn*, index; lād͟hurī, *Futūḥ*, 343; Ibn D͟juld͟jul, *Ṭabaḳāt aṭibbāʾ*, Cairo 1955, 54; Ḳifṭī, *Ḥukamāʾ*, ed. ppert, Leipzig 1903, 161-2; Ibn Abī Uṣaybiʿa, *ibbāʾ*, i, 109-13; Ibn al-Athīr, ii, 231, iii, 370; Ibn bd Rabbih, *ʿIḳd*, index; Marzubānī, *Muʿd͟jam*, 2; Ibn Ḥad͟jar, *Iṣāba*, no. 1475; Tabrīzī, *S͟harḥ Ḥamāsa*, 252; Leclerc, *Médecine arabe*, i, 26-8; amidullah, *Le Prophète de l'Islam*, 41, 317, 505; Massignon and R. Arnaldez, *La science arabe*, ris 1957, i, 444; D. M. Dunlop, *Arabic science the West*, Karachi n.d., 2; M. S. Belguedj, *La édecine traditionnelle dans le Constantinois*, rasbourg 1966, 9. (CH. PELLAT)

-ḤĀRIT͟HĪ, ṢĀLIḤ B. ʿALĪ (1250-1314/1834-96), inent Ibāḍī leader of the second half of the century and paramount *s͟hayk͟h* (*tamīma*) of the ederation of tribes of Eastern ʿUmān known as S͟harḳiyya Hināwīs.

nis regional grouping began to crystallise under h leadership during the civil war that marked ollapse of the Yaʿāriba Imāmate in the first half of the 18th century and continued to develop as one of the major political groupings around which the loyalties of the tribal moiety divisions within ʿUmān tended to polarise in times of crisis, the so-called Hināwī and G͟hāfirī *s͟haffs* (alliances). Within the Ḥirt͟h clan itself, leadership was shared by three family groupings, the senior to which Ṣāliḥ belonged, with its "capital" (*ʿāṣima*) at al-Ḳābil; a cadet branch (the Āl Ḥumayd) at nearby al-Muḍayrib; and the third controlling the original clan settlement of Lower Ibrā (whence the *nisba* Barwānī, var. Barvānī, in East African sources). These divisions were particularly important in the politics of Zanzibar where members of the Ḥirt͟h tended to dispute the leadership of the old-established ʿUmānī settlers (most of whom originated in the S͟harḳiyya); but at home, the paramount leadership of the Ḳābil branch seems to have been firmly established by at least the beginning of the 19th century, for ʿĪsā b. Ṣāliḥ, Ṣāliḥ's great-grandfather, is mentioned in the sources as being leader of the S͟harḳiyya Hināwīs from the beginning until the middle of the century.

In the latter part of his life, ʿĪsā joined the opposition to Sayyid Saʿīd b. Sulṭān (sultan *ca.* 1804-56) in ʿUmān. His grandson, ʿAlī b. Nāṣir (Ṣāliḥ's father), on the other hand, was a strong supporter of Sayyid Saʿīd in his East African domain; at one time he was Saʿīd's governor in Mombasa, later his envoy to England. He was killed in Saʿīd's service at the battle of Siu during the campaign against the Mazārīʿ of Pate (winter 1844-5).

Ṣāliḥ himself seems to have come strongly under the influence of his great-grandfather and was brought up in the tribal environment at al-Ḳābil. It was ʿĪsā who was also presumably responsible for sending him to study with Saʿīd b. K͟halfān al-K͟halīlī (1820?-71), one of the Ibāḍī *ʿulamāʾ* with whom he had been involved in the abortive attempts to promote Ḥumūd b. ʿAzzān as *Imām* during the mid-1840s. Following the death of Sayyid Saʿīd, the Ibāḍī movement profited from the succession disputes and tended to cultivate the aspirations of members of the Ḳays b. al-Imām Aḥmad branch of the Āl Bū Saʿīd from Rustāḳ in ʿUmān and of Sayyid Barg͟has͟h b. Saʿīd in Zanzibar. Ṣāliḥ's first appearance in this political scene was during his sole recorded visit to Zanzibar in Sayyid Mād͟jid b. Saʿīd's time (sultan 1856-70); there he became involved in Sayyid Barg͟has͟h's attempt to depose his brother with the help of the Ḥirt͟h and other Ibāḍī leaders. After the failure of this coup in 1859, Ṣāliḍ took refuge in Somalia for a couple of years, during which time he completed his formal studies.

Upon his return to ʿUmān, he immediately became involved in the increasingly complex political situation which revolved around the Āl Bū Saʿīd dynastic struggle, by now exacerbated by the Canning award of 1861 which divided Zanzibar from ʿUmān, the Ibāḍī movement which tended to look for tribal support from the Hināwī faction in central ʿUmām, Wahhābī expansionism and increasing British intervention in ʿUmānī affairs. Eventually, in September 1868, the parricide sultan, Sālim b. T͟huwaynī (sultan 1866-8), was evicted from Muscat by a tribal force drawn from the Rustāḳ and Bāṭina Hināwīs under ʿAzzān b. Qays and the S͟harḳiyya Hināwis led by Ṣalīḥ b. ʿAlī; thereupon ʿAzzān was elected an *Imām* with limited power (a *ḍaʿīf Imām*) under the sponsorship of the then leading *ʿulamāʾ*, Saʿīd b. K͟halfān al-K͟halīlī (who was also paramount leader of the Hināwī Banī Ruwāḥa), Muḥammad b. Sulaysim al-G͟hāribī (from the Bāṭina Yāl Saʿd) and Ṣāliḥ.

In 1871 Turkī b. Saᶜīd re-established the sultanate with a G͟hāfirī tribal army, encouraged by the British and financially aided by his brother Mād͟jid from Zanzibar. ᶜAzzān was killed in the siege of the capital and Saᶜīd b. K͟halfān al-K͟halīlī murdered after he had eventually been persuaded to surrender by the British Agent in Muscat. From then onwards, Ṣāliḥ directed the Ibāḍī movement until his death in 1896.

In the Ibāḍī literature Ṣāliḥ is described as *al-Imām al-muḥtasib*, that is, an *ᶜālim* with the dependability and integrity to lead and advise the Muslim community until such time as an *Imām* can be properly elected. It was in this guise that he continued his attacks, with the support of the S͟harḳiyya Hināwīs and their *badw* Wahība allies, on the sultans in Muscat (1874, 1877, 1895), and against dissident tribesmen, notably the campaign in 1894 against the Banī S͟huhaym of the Wādī Damā, who were the shaikhly clan of the Masākira, the Ḥirt͟h's great rivals in Ibrā, and in 1896 against the Banū D͟jābir, leaders of the G͟hāfirī confederation of central ᶜUmān who were harrying the Raḥbiyyān allies of the S͟harḳiyya Hināwīs. It was during the latter attack that he met his death, struck by a bullet in the thigh at al-D͟jayla.

During the first part of this period, Ṣāliḥ's main aim seems to have been that of undermining the position of Turkī b. Saᶜīd (Sultan 1871-88), but after the failure of the 1877 attack he largely confined his activities to intriguing against the régime at Muscat and in maintaining his political authority in the interior. In Fayṣal b. Turkī's time, on the other hand, he does seem to have had ideas of sponsoring Saᶜūd, a son of ᶜAzzān b. Ḳays, as a candidate for the Imāmate. Ṣāliḥ was succeeded by his eldest son ᶜĪsā (d. 1946) who, with another of his former pupils, ᶜAbd Allāh b. Ḥumayd al-Sālimī (d. 1914), were to play a major part in restoring the Imāmate in central ᶜUmān in 1913.

Ṣāliḥ's surviving literary work is a collection of *d͟jawābāt*, arranged in 1916-17 by A. Walīd Saᶜīd b. Ḥumayd b. K͟halīfayn al-Ḥārit͟hī, later *ḳāḍī* of the *Imām* Muḥammad b. ᶜAbd Allāh al-K͟halīlī (*Imām* 1920-54), under the title *ᶜAyn al-maṣāliḥ* (see Bibliography).

Bibliography: 1. ᶜUmānī sources: al-Ḥārit͟hī, ᶜIsā b. Ṣāliḥ b. ᶜAlī, *K͟hulāṣat al-wasāʾil fī tartīb al-masāʾil*, Damascus n.d., introduction; al-Ḥārit͟hī, Ṣāliḥ b. ᶜAlī, *ᶜAyn al-maṣāliḥ*, Damascus n.d.; Ibn Ruzayḳ/Razīḳ, tr. G. P. Badger, *History of the Imâms and Seyyids of 'Omân* ..., Book 3, Hakluyt Society 1871; al-Sālimī, ᶜAbd Allāh b. Ḥumayd, *Tuḥfat al-aᶜyān bi-sīrat ahl ᶜUmān*, Cairo 1961, ii, 218-97; al-Sālimī, Muḥammad b. ᶜAbd Allāh, *Nahḍat al-aᶜyān bi-ḥurriyyat ᶜUmān*, Cairo n.d., 71-4; al-Siyābi, Sālim b. Ḥumūd, *Isᶜāf al-aᶜyān fī ansāb ahl ᶜUmān*, Beirut 1965, 21-2, 114-15. 2. Works incorporating most of the relevant contemporary European source material: R. Coupland, *East Africa and its invaders*, Oxford 1938; idem, *The exploitation of East Africa 1856-1890*, London 1939; J. B. Kelly, *Britain and the Persian Gulf 1795-1880*, Oxford 1968; R. G. Landen, *Oman since 1856* ..., Princeton 1967; J. G. Lorimer, *Gazetteer of the Persian Gulf, ᶜOman and Central Arabia*, Calcutta 1908-15; C. S. Nicholls, *The Swahili Coast* ..., London 1971. See also J. C. Wilkinson, *The Ibāḍī Imāma*, in *BSOAS*, xxxix (1976). (J. C. WILKINSON)

HARNESS, TRAPPINGS [see KHAYL].

HARPOON [see ṢAYD]

AL-**ḤASAN** B. AL-**ḲĀSIM** B. AL-ḤASAN B. ᶜALĪ B. ᶜABD AL-RAḤMĀN B. AL-ḲĀSIM B. AL-ḤAS[A]
ZAYD B. AL-ḤASAN B. ᶜALĪ B. ABĪ ṬĀLIB, AL-[DĀᶜĪ]
ILA 'L-ḤAKK ABŪ MUḤAMMAD, Zaydī rule[r of]
Ṭabaristān, was born in 263 or 264/876-8, pro[b]
in north-western Iran.

Nothing is known about his life before he joine[d the] Zaydī *imām* al-Ḥasan al-Uṭrūs͟h [*q.v.*] al-Nāṣir [li 'l-] Ḥaḳḳ while the latter was active in convertin[g the] Daylamīs and Gīlīs east of the Safīd-rūd to I[slam.] He was commander of the vanguard of al-N[āṣir's] army in the great victory over the Sāmānid [army] under Abu 'l-ᶜAbbās Ṣuᶜlūk on the river Būr[...] west of S͟hālūs in D͟jumādā II 301/January 914 [which] led to the conquest of Ṭabaristān by al-Nāṣir [...] Ḥasan b. al-Ḳāsim pursued the fleeing enemy [and] on his return ordered the massacre of some [...] K͟hurāsānian soldiers descending from the fortr[ess of] S͟hālūs, denying knowledge of a promise of s[afety] which al-Nāṣir had given them. During the [rule] of al-Nāṣir in Ṭabaristān, he remained in c[ommand] of the army, though a rivalry and enmity deve[loped] between him and al-Nāṣir's son Abu 'l-Ḳāsim D͟j[aᶜfar,] especially after the latter was appointed gov[ernor] of Sāriya in 302/914-15. Al-Ḥasan conspire[d to] depose al-Nāṣir with some Gīlī and Daylamī c[hiefs] whom he had been sent to recruit with their t[roops.] When they arrived in Āmul, he arrested al-Nāṣi[r and] imprisoned him in a castle in Lārid͟jān. Shortly a[fter]wards, however, the Gīlī chief Līlī b. al-Nu[ᶜmān] arrived from Sāriya calling for support of al-N[āṣir,] and al-Ḥasan was deserted by most of his suppo[rters.] As al-Nāṣir was restored to the rule, he tried t[o flee] but was apprehended and brought before the i[mām,] who pardoned him and permitted him to leav[e for] Gīlān. Some time later al-Nāṣir, upon the interce[ssion] of his son Abu 'l-Ḥusayn Aḥmad, recalled [him,] granted him the title *al-Dāᶜī ila 'l-Ḥaḳḳ* and ma[rried] a daughter of Aḥmad to him. Earlier he had appa[rent]ly been married to a daughter of al-Nāṣir. The[n al-] Nāṣir appointed him governor of Gurgān and or[dered] his son D͟jaᶜfar to assist him. The latter, how[ever,] worked against him and deserted him when he [was] attacked by a (Sāmānid?) army of Turks. Al[-Ḥasan] was forced to retreat and then besieged in a fo[rtress] near Astarābād, probably in winter 304/91[6-17.] Eventually he escaped with a handful of men [and] went to Āmul and from there to Gīlān.

After the death of al-Nāṣir in S͟haᶜbān 304/Feb[ruary] 917, Aḥmad, in accordance with the wishes o[f his] father, recalled him from Gīlān and surrendere[d the] rule to him. D͟jaᶜfar, however, reproached his br[other] for this and defected, first joining the Sāmānid [gov]ernor of Rayy and then going to Gīlān to gathe[r sup]porters. Aḥmad remained loyal and subdued [the] Bāwandid Ispahbad S͟harwīn b. Rustam and [the] Ḳārinid S͟hahriyār, rulers of the highlands of Ṭ[aba]ristān, forcing them to pay a higher tribute [to al-] Dāᶜī, but he prevented him from putting the[m to] death. Then he was sent against the Sāmānid ge[neral] Ilyās b. Ilyasaᶜ, who had seized Gurgān, and def[eated] him. Al-Dāᶜī and Aḥmad occupied Gurgān but [were] forced to withdraw to Tamīs͟ha before an[other] Sāmānid army under Ḳarātakīn. Aḥmad now d[eser]ted al-Dāᶜī and joined D͟jaᶜfar in Gīlān. On 5 [Dhu] 'l-Kaᶜda 306/12 April 919 D͟jaᶜfar defeated al[-Dāᶜī] and took possession of Ṭabaristān, whilst al[-Dāᶜī] sought refuge with the Ispahbad Muḥamma[d b.] S͟hahriyār in the mountains. The latter seized [him] and sent him to the D͟justānid ᶜAlī b. Wahsū[dān, the] ᶜAbbāsid governor of Rayy, who imprisoned hi[m in] the fortress of Alamūt. He was released afte[r the] murder of ᶜAlī b. Wahsūdān by the latter's br[other] raw Fīrūz and went to Gīlān to seek support. jumādā II 307/November 919 he retook Āmul the two sons of al-Nāṣir were absent in Gurgān. efeated Aḥmad near Astarābād and then won over by offering to share the rule with him. ar, who had remained in Gurgān and was ted by his army, fled to Gīlān. In 308/921 Līlī b. ʿmān, al-Dāʿī's governor of Gurgān, conquered ghān, Nīshāpūr and eventually Marw, intro- g the *khuṭba* for the ʿAlid. He was defeated by e Sāmānid army and killed near Ṭūs in Rabīʿ I uly-August. When the defeated army returned urgān, a group of Daylamī and Gīlī leaders pired to depose al-Dāʿī and to put Aḥmad on hrone. Informed about the plot, al-Dāʿī hastened urgān and during a reception killed seven of , among them Harūsindān b. Tīrdādh, the king e Gīl. This ruthless punishment of the plotters o a defection of many Daylamīs and Gīlīs to the inids and eventually caused his downfall.

310/922-3 al-Dāʿī and Aḥmad were defeated by Sāmānid general Sīmdjūr al-Dawātī at Djalāyīn e region of Gurgān and were forced to retreat to isha. Aḥmad recovered Gurgān on 1 Dhu 'l- dja 310/22 March 923 and was entrusted with government of the town while al-Dāʿī ruled in l. Shortly afterwards, however, Aḥmad made common cause with his brother Djaʿfar who revolted in Gīlān against al-Dāʿī. Aḥmad attacked āʿī in Āmul but was defeated and joined Djaʿfar īlān. The two brothers then invaded Ṭabaristān, orted by several Daylamī and Gīlī leaders, ng them Mākān b. Kākī [*q.v.*] and Asfār b. iya [see ASFĀR B. SHĪRAWAYHĪ]]. Al-Dāʿī fled, to Sāriya and then into the highlands while ad took over the rule in Āmul on 28 Djumādā I 11 September 923. After Aḥmad's death two ths later and the succession of Djaʿfar, al-Dāʿī cked Āmul but was deserted by his supporters sought again refuge in the mountains and later īlān. Only after Mākān, having been involved conspiracy, was expelled from Ṭabaristān, did āʿī gain again a powerful supporter. Early in spring 926 Mākān seized Āmul, expelling the g ʿAlid, Aḥmad's son Abū Djaʿfar Muḥammad, brought al-Dāʿī from Gīlān to restore him to er. At this time the Sāmānid Aḥmad b. Naṣr to invade Ṭabaristān, but was encircled in the ntains and forced to pay a ransom of 20,000 rs to al-Dāʿī for his release. Disapproving of conduct of Mākān, al-Dāʿī once more left for n. Mākān kept urging him to return and, on his est, immediately released Abū Djaʿfar Muham- , al-Dāʿī's brother-in-law, whom he had seized imprisoned. Eventually al-Dāʿī rejoined Mākān mul, and in 316/926 they set out on an ambi- s campaign of conquest and took Rayy from its ānid governor early in Shaʿbān/latter half of tember. Their absence from Ṭabaristān was used sfār, who was ruling Gūrgān under Sāmānid over- ship, to invade that country. Al-Dāʿī quickly rned to Āmul with 500 men, but failed to get the port of the people there on which he had counted. was defeated outside Āmul and on his flight was d by Mardāwīdj b. Ziyār, who thus avenged the h of his uncle Harūsindān, on 24 Ramaḍān 11 November 928.

l-Dāʿī was popular as a ruler in Ṭabaristān and clearly preferred to his rivals of the descen- ts of al-Nāṣir. He is highly praised in the account bn Isfandiyār and in other sources for his jus- for restraining the Daylamī and Gīlī army from transgressions, for patronising scholars and poets and for building *madrasas* and *khānaḳāhs*. The Kūfan Zaydī supporters of al-Nāṣir also preferred him to the sons of the *imām*, and pressed the latter to ap- point him as his successor. He never gained, however, recognition as a Zaydī *imām*, evidently because he lacked the necessary qualifications of religious schol- arship. The renunciation of any claim to the Zaydī imāmate may have been expressed in the title *al-Dāʿī ila 'l-Ḥaḳḳ* which was chosen for him by al-Nāṣir (see W. Madelung, *Der Imam al-Qāsim ibn Ibrāhīm*, Berlin 1965, 154 f.).

Bibliography: Masʿūdī, *Murūdj*, ix, 5-8; Abū Isḥāḳ al-Ṣābī, *K. al-Tādjī*, ms. Ṣanʿāʾ, fols. 9a-11b; Abū Ṭālib al-Nāṭiḳ, *al-Ifāda*, mss., in the biography of al-Uṭrūsh al-Nāṣir; Ibn Isfandiyār, *Taʾrīkh-i Ṭabaristān*, ed. ʿAbbās Iḳbāl, Tehran 1941, i, 269, 272-92; Ibn al-Athīr, viii, 62, 74, 90 f., 121 f., 138 f.; Ibn ʿInaba, *ʿUmdat al-ṭālib*, ed. Muḥammad Ḥasan Āl al-Ṭāliḳānī, Nadjaf 1380/1961, 83 f., 91, 309; R. Strothmann, *Das Staatsrecht der Zaiditen*, Strassburg 1912, 55 f.; W. Madelung, *Abū Isḥāq al-Ṣābī on the Alids of Ṭabaristān and Gīlān*, in *JNES*, xxvi (1967), 31-41; S. M. Stern, *The coins of Āmul*, in *NC*, 7th ser., vii (1967), 216-20. (W. MADELUNG)

AL-ḤASAN B. MUḤAMMAD B. AL-ḤANAFIYYA, grandson of ʿAlī and half-brother of Abū Hāshim [*q.v.*], important member of the Hāshimī clan in Medina, author of the two earliest texts so far known of Islamic theology.

During the final crisis of Mukhtār's revolt in Kūfa (67/687) he decided to join the movement; he arrived, however, too late and went on to Nisibis where a certain Abū Ḳārib Budayr b. Abī Ṣakhr directed the last pocket of "Khashabī" resistance against the troups of al-Muhallab b. Abī Ṣufra, who supported Muṣʿab b. al-Zubayr (cf. for this episode, *Aghānī*[2], vi, 50, ll. 9 ff., where the name of Budayr is misread as Yazīd, and the Syriac author John of Phenek, in A. Mingana, *Sources syriaques*, Leipzig 1907, i[2], 183* ff.; also the sources given by W. al-Ḳāḍī, in *Akten des VII. Kongresses für Arabistik und Islamwissenschaft Göttingen 1974*, 297, n. 9). He was captured and imprisoned by ʿAbd Allāh b. al-Zubayr, but managed to escape to his father Muḥammad b. al-Ḥanafiyya in Minā. When, after the collapse of Ibn al-Zubayr's anti-caliphate, Muḥammad b. al-Ḥanafiyya decided to pay allegiance to ʿAbd al-Malik in 73/693, al-Ḥasan, amongst all members of the clan, drew the most spectacular consequences from this step: he wrote an open letter, later on known as his *K. al-Irdjāʾ*, in which he implicitly declared Mukhtār's allegiance to his father to have been nothing more than intrusion and imposture and where he pleaded for postponing (*irdjāʾ*) any judgment upon "those who first participated in the schism of the community" (*ahl al-furḳa al-uwal*), i.e. upon ʿUthmān and his own grandfather ʿAlī. This astonishing attitude against the claims of his family seems to have been born out of the insight that ʿAbd al-Malik's reconciliatory policy towards dissident political groups deserved some recognition and that the daemonising view of history proferred by the few remaining followers of Mukhtār at Kūfa, who were known as Sabaʾiyya at this time (and not yet as Kaysāniyya), was too sectarian in order to have any future. Whether the caliph exerted any pressure, especially with respect to the weak financial situation of the ʿAlids, is difficult to substantiate. Al-Ḥasan had his letter recited in different places by ʿAbd al-Wāḥid b. Ayman, a Meccan *mawlā* with whom he was on friendly terms, but he also personally made propaganda for his ideas in Kūfa. In spite of a certain success, he could not avoid criticism, and only a few years later those who were considered to be "Murdji'ites" in Kūfa gave up the political passivity intended by al-Ḥasan's notion of *irdjā'* and joined the uprising of Ibn al-Ash'ath, especially in its final phase (82/701). Al-Ḥasan seems, however, to have been responsible for the invention of this term, which was to have a rather multifacetted history in early Islam.

In addition to the *K. al-Irdjā'*, he appears as the author of an extensive refutation of the Ḳadariyya which may have been composed only shortly afterwards, perhaps during the religious discussions preceding and accompanying the revolt of Ibn al-Ash'ath. The treatise does not yet refer to the *Risāla* written by al-Ḥasan al-Baṣrī to 'Abd al-Malik, and it is ignorant of certain Ḳadarī doctrines developed there, but it presupposes the existence of a rather elaborate Ḳadarī theology, which it attacks on rational as well as on exegetical grounds. Against his opponents, al-Ḥasan b. Muḥammad b. al-Ḥanafiyya stresses the omnipotence of God also with respect to human actions, but he does not say that God forces man to act against his will (only this would be *djabr* in his view). With al-Ḥasan al-Baṣrī and other Ḳadarīs, he shares a synergistic concept, but whereas the Ḳadariyya interpreted God's "leading astray" as a mere secondary reaction which is justified by man's sin, al-Ḥasan b. Muḥammad b. al-Ḥanafiyya sees sin as the result of the withdrawal of God's "support" (*tawfīḳ*). In his discussion of omnipotence he does not yet differentiate between divine predestination and divine foreknowledge. The treatise is structured in the form of hypothetical questions and answers (*in ḳāla ... ḳulnā*) and as such represents the earliest example of *kalām* literarure in Islam. It is not preserved in its entirety, but in extensive fragments embedded in a later refutation written by the Zaydī *imām* al-Hādī ila 'l-Ḥaḳḳ (245-98/859-911; cf. the edition in Muḥammad 'Imāra, *Rasā'il al-'adl wa 'l-tawḥīd*, Cairo 1971, ii, 118 ff.).

Al-Ḥasan b. Muḥammad b. al-Ḥanafiyya also enjoyed a high reputation as a jurist. A few *fatwās* of his are mentioned in later sources: on the appropriate distribution of the *khums* (which was a political problem because of the definition of the *dhu 'l-ḳurbā*), on *mut'a* marriage (which he prohibited, in contrast to later Imāmī opinion), on the unlawfulness of having more than four wives at the same time (cf. Makḥūl al-Nasafī, *al-Radd 'alā ahl al-bida'*, Ms. Oxford, Pococke 271, fol. 45a, ll. 4 ff.), and on the unlawfulness of eating the meat of the domesticated donkey (against 'Abd Allāh b. 'Abbās). Ibn Isḥāḳ [*q.v.*] took over from him some traditions about the life of the Prophet; al-Zuhrī seems to have been closely associated with him. He died at an uncertain date; but this must have been either during the caliphate of 'Abd al-Malik (i.e. before 86/705), in 95/714 or during the caliphate of 'Umar II (99-101/717-20) at the latest.

Bibliography: W. Madelung, *Der Imam al-Qāsim ibn Ibrāhīm*, Berlin 1965, 228 ff.; Wadād al-Ḳāḍī, *al-Kaysāniyya fi 'l-ta'rīkh wa 'l-adab*, Beirut 1974, index s.v.; J. van Ess, *Das Kitab al-Irǧā' des Ḥasan b. Muḥammad b. al-Ḥanafiyya*, in *Arabica*, xxi (1974), 20 ff. (cf. the additions in *Arabica*, xxii [1975], 48 ff.); idem, *The beginnings of Islamic theology*, in J. E. Murdoch and E. D. Sylla (eds.), *The cultural context of medieval learning*, Dordrecht 1975, 87 ff.; idem, *Anfänge muslimischer Theologie*, Beirut 1977: edition, translation, and commentary of the fragments of al-Ḥāsan's re[futa]tion of the Ḳadariyya, and collection of the [bio]graphical material (with further references).

(J. VAN ES[S])

ḤASAN B. NŪḤ B. YŪSUF B. MUḤAMMA[D B.] ĀDAM AL-BHARŪČĪ AL-HINDĪ, Musta'lī-Ṭay[yibī] Ismā'īlī savant.

According to his own statement he was born [and] brought up in Khambhāt (Cambay) in India, [and] received his early education there. It is not kn[own] when and by whom the surname "Bharūčī", from Bharūč or Broach, [see BHAROČ], was g[iven] to him. Urged on by a thirst for knowledge, he st[...] he renounced family, left his country, travelle[d to] Yaman, and became a student of Ḥasan b. Idrīs, twentieth *dā'ī muṭlaḳ*. The books read by him wit[h his] teacher in various branches of the *'ulūm al-da'wa* [are] fully described in the introduction to his *Kitāb [al-]Azhār*. He was also closely associated with 'A[lī b.] Ḥusayn b. Idrīs and Muḥammad b. Ḥasan b. I[drīs], who later became the twenty-second and twe[nty-]third *dā'ī muṭlaḳs*. He was the mentor of Yūsu[f b.] Sulaymān, the twenty-fourth *dā'ī muṭlaḳ*, and [died] on 11 Dhu 'l-Ḳa'da 939/4 June 1533.

His claim to fame is rightly based on his vol[umi]nous work *Kitāb al-Azhār wa-madjma' al-anwār [al-]malḳūṭa min basātīn al-asrār*. It is a chrestomath[y of] Ismā'īlī literature in seven volumes wherein m[any] earlier works, otherwise lost, are preserved eithe[r in] full or in part. It also contains extensive exce[rpts] from Sunnī and Zaydī works, especially on the life [and] character of 'Alī b. Abī Ṭālib [*q.v.*]. Volume one [was] edited by 'Ādil al-'Awwā in *Muntakhabāt Ismā'īli[yya]*, Damascus 1958, 181-250, whereas the remai[ning] volumes are in manuscript. Major subjects of e[ach] volume are described in I. Poonawala, *Bibliogra[phy] of Ismā'īlī literature*, Malibu, Calif. 1977, 178-8[...]

Bibliography: The main biographical so[urce] is the author's own work *Kitāb al-Azhār*, i, 186[...] Ismā'īl b. 'Abd al-Rasūl al-Madjdū', *Fihrist*, [ed.] 'Alī Naḳī Munzawī, Tehran 1966, 77-88.

(I. POONAWAL[A])

ḤASAN, MĪR GHULĀM (1140-1201/1727-[...]), Urdu poet noted for his *mathnawīs*, was bor[n in] Dihlī, the son of Mīr Ḍāḥik, a poet of modest att[ain]ments who was satirised by Sawdā. Mīr Ḥasan h[ad a] liberal education, which included the Persian [lan]guage, but apparently not Arabic. He learned [the] poetic art from his father and from Mīr Dard. A[fter] the sack of Dihlī in 1739 by Nādir Shāh, he emigra[ted] with his father to Faizabad (or Fayḍābād [*q.v.*]), the capital of Oudh or Awadh [*q.v.*]. En route, t[hey] stayed at Dig, near Bharatpur, and joined the [pil]grimage procession to the festival of the saint S[hāh] Madār at Makanpur. The poet was to describe [this] journey and festival in a colourful *mathnawī*, *Gulz[ār-i] Iram*, composed about nine years before his de[ath]. In Faizabad, Mīr Ḥasan joined the service of [the] Nawwāb. In 1189/1775 the new Nawwāb, Āṣaf [al-]Dawla, transferred the capital to Lucknow, so [the] poet moved there also. Here he composed his lon[gest] and best-known *mathnawī*, *Ṣiḥr al-bayān* ("[The] enchantment of eloquence"), which won immed[iate] acclaim, and is frequently known merely as "[Mīr] Ḥasan's *Mathnawī*". This was finished in 1199/1[785], less than two years before the poet's death.

Mīr Ḥasan's complete poetical works do not s[eem] to have been published. He is known to have wri[tten] both *ghazals* and *marthiyas*, and he was the gra[nd]father of Anīs [*q.v.*], the famous Urdu elegist. Bu[t it] is for his *mathnawīs* that he is chiefly remembe[red]. Yet of the eleven with which he is credited, c[...]

al-bayān is widely known, and it may justly escribed as the original model of the Urdu narra- *mathnawī*, and one of the two or three greatest nples of the form. It runs to about 2,000 couplets *utaḳārib* metre, and tells, in some detail, a story oyalty, love and magic of the kind current in a. The central plot concerns the love between ce Bīnaẓīr and Princess Badr-i Munīr. There is a idiary love plot involving Nadjm al-Nisā', the īr's daughter, and Fīrōz Shāh, son of the King ne Jinn. A magic flying horse plays an important in the events of the story. But the supernatural ents in the story are no more important than say—Central European *Zauberoper* or *Zauber- e* in the 18th and 19th centuries. The elements ch raise an incredible story to the level of great ature are many and varied, but they include characterisation, which relates the characters rdinary human beings; the vivid and colourful ription of people and places; the effective use hetorical devices such as word-play; the timeless guage, which seems remarkably up-to-date two uries later; and the numerous examples of omic" verse which embody simple philosophising lend themselves to quotation in everday life. In , few Urdu poets since have had his facility for ng things so simply yet effectively, often with rnal rhyme. *Siḥr al-bayān* has been adversely icised chiefly for its unnecessary length. But apart n the series of introductions devoted to God, the phet, the *Imām* ʿAlī and others, ending with one he Nawwāb Āṣaf al-Dawla, the length is duly fly to the detailed description, without which it ld lose most of its charm.

rom what the poet says about his poem in the few couplets, he clearly regarded it as a new e of *mathnawī*, and as his chief claim to fame. says:

t is a new type, and the language is new.
t is not a [normal kind of] *mathnawī*, it is the enchantment of eloquence.
rom it my fame will endure throughout the world,
'or wherever these words are is a memorial.

dence of the immense popularity of the work be seen in the various verse translation into er Indian vernaculars, and also in the dramatic sions. Thus in Bengali there is a verse translation 863, and a play entitled simply *Mathnawī* of 1876. Bahādur ʿAlī's Urdu prose version, completed er the auspices of Fort William College, Calcutta, printed there in 1803, and has since been frequent- eprinted. It contains many poetical quotations n Mīr Ḥasan's original. The story provided a ourite plot for early Urdu drama in the late h century.

he qualities found in *Siḥr al-bayān*—apart from involved story—are present in his other *math- īs*. Thus *Gulzār-i Iram* includes a vivid description crowded market; another, *Rumūz al-ʿārifīn*, has ūfī background.

Iīr Ḥasan's other claim to fame is his account, in sian, of Urdu poets, including his contemporaries, *Tadhkira-yi-shuʿarā'-yi-Urdū*, which has become andard reference work.

Bibliography: There are numerous editions, s well as manuscripts of *Siḥr al-bayān*. That dited by ʿAbd al-Bārī Āsī (*Mathnawiyāt-i-Mīr Ḥasan*, Lucknow 1945, is recommended because also includes *Gulzār-i Iram* and *Rumūz al- ʿārifīn*, and has a useful introduction, with numer- us footnotes explaining difficult vocabulary. *Mathnawī-yi-Mīr Ḥasan*, ed. Ḥāmid Allāh Afsar, Allahabad 1925, has a short introduction which discusses the poem's good and bad qualities (11-14), and a glossary. Mīr Ḥasan's *Tadhkira-yi-shuʿarā'-yi-Urdū* was published at ʿAlīgaṛh in 1922.

For accounts of Mīr Ḥasan, particularly *Siḥr al-bayān*, mention must first be made of R. Russell and Khurshidul Islam, *Three Mughal poets: Mir, Sauda, Mir Hasan*, London 1969, 69-94. This account is devoted chiefly to re-telling the story, but also includes a useful critical assessment. Saksena gives a general account of the poet in his *History of Urdu literature*, Allahabad 1927, 67-70. See also Muhammad Sadiq, *History of Urdu literature*, London 1964, 108-11. Urdu accounts of the poet include the following: Muḥammad Ḥusayn Āzād, *Āb-i-ḥayāt*, Lahore ed. 1950, 249-51; Maḥmūd Fārūḳī, *Mīr Ḥasan awr khāndān kē dusrē shuʿarā*, Lahore 1952; Waḥīd Ḳurayshī, *Mīr Ḥasan awr un kā zamāna*, Lahore 1959. For Mīr Bahādur ʿAlī's prose version, see Major Henry Court's English tr., *The naṣr-i Benaẓīr*, Calcutta 1871, 2nd ed. 1889. (J. A. Haywood)

ḤASAN BEDR al-DĪN, later Pasha (1851-1912), Ottoman Turkish soldier and playwright, chiefly famed as the collaborator during the years 1875-9 of his fellow-officer and friend, the author and dramatist Manāstirli̊ Meḥmed Rifʿat [*q.v.*], in the writing of some 16 plays, some translations from the French and some original, which were produced at the Gedik Pasha Theatre in Istanbul (see manāstirli̊ meḥmed rifʿat for full details).

He was born at Sīmāw near Kütahya, the son of an army officer, was educated at the military school (*Iʿdādī*) in Damascus and then at the Istanbul War College (*Ḥarbiyye*), where he graduated the first of his class and was the contemporary and classmate of his future collaborator Manāstirli̊ Meḥmed. He served briefly in the Imperial Guards, but in the increasingly repressive atmosphere of Sultan ʿAbd al-Ḥamīd II's reign he was soon banished from Istanbul to the eastern provinces, and served in Syria and Palestine with the rank of colonel. However, he was soon stripped of this rank, presumably as the result of a *zhurnal* or delatory report, and taught in Damascus schools for a living. After the restoration of the Constitution in 1908, he returned to Istanbul, was rehabilitated under the Young Turk régime, promoted to brigadier-general and then general of a division, and was finally appointed commander and governor of Ishkodra [*q.v.* in Suppl.] or Scutari (modern Shkodër in northern Albania). After a brief spell of service, he resigned on the grounds of ill-health, returned to Istanbul and died there in 1912.

Bibliography: See that for manāstirli̊ meḥmed rifʿat. (Fahir İz)

ḤASAN NIẒĀMĪ, historian of the Dihlī sultanate in Muslim India.

He was the son of Niẓāmī ʿArūḍī Samarḳandī, the famous Persian littérateur [*q.v.*], but left his hometown, Nīshāpūr, sometime towards the close of the 6th/12th century because of political instability there. In Dihlī he made friends with high officers of Sultan Ḳuṭb al-Dīn Aybak (602-7/1206-10 [*q.v.*]), including the Ṣadr Sharaf al-Mulk. Impressed by his learning, his friends advised him to produce a literary work so that he might get royal patronage; hence Ḥasan Niẓāmī decided to compile the history of Aybak's achievements in Arabic. But his friends persuaded him to write it in Persian, since there were in India few people literate in Arabic. In the meantime, the royal *farmān* was proclaimed that Aybak's conquests in India should be recorded by scholars, along with those of his master, Sultan Muʿizz al-Dīn Muḥammad b. Sām [see GHŪRIDS]. Hence the compilation of the *Tādj al-maʾāthir*.

The first part contains a description of Sultans Muʿizz al-Dīn Muḥammad and Ḳuṭb al-Dīn Aybak. On Sultan Aybak's death Ḥasan Niẓāmī continued his work under Iltutmish, and according to Sir Henry Elliot, brought it up to the year 626/1229; but the extant copies of the work end with the description of the occupation of Lahore by Iltutmish in 614/1217. Since Iltutmish was his last patron, the author is not impartial in his criticism of his master's rivals, such as Tādj al-Dīn Yildiz and Sultan Nāṣir al-Dīn Ḳubāča. He omits mention of Ārām Shāh, the son of Ḳuṭb al-Dīn Aybak, because Iltutmish has usurped the throne and killed him. Moreover, there is no space devoted to the description of the nobles of the early sultans of Dihlī, who had helped the sultans in stabilising Muslim rule in northern India at its very beginning. In fact, Ḥasan Niẓāmī fails to produce a history in the real sense of the word; his work reads like a mere *Fatḥ-nāma*.

It was, moreover, written in an ornate and florid style, full of verbosity and rhetorics. The historical details are interspersed with the Ḳurʾānic verses and Arabic and Persian poems; more than half of the work comprises only verses. Despite these defects, the *Tādj al-maʾāthir* enjoyed fame because of its bravura style, much to contemporary literary taste, and much imitated subsequently.

Bibliography: Storey, i, 493-5, 1310; H. M. Elliot and J. Dowson, *The history of India, as told by its own historians*, ii, 204-43; Ḥasan ʿAskarī, *Tāj al-Maʾāthir of Ḥasan Niẓāmī*, in *Patna University Journal*, xviii/3 (1963).

(I. H. SIDDIQUI)

ḤASRAT MOHĀNĪ, SAYYID FAḌL AL-ḤASAN, prominent Indian journalist, poet and politician, was born most probably in 1297/1880 in the small town of Mohān in Uttar Pradesh. His family, which numbered many scholars, physicians and mystics, claimed descent from Sayyid Maḥmūd who migrated from Nīshāpūr in Iran and founded Mohān in 615/1218. One recent ancestor had been royal physician to the Kings of Awadh, another had been minister of religious affairs in the Hyderabad state. Ḥasrat was educated at government schools and privately in Arabic and Persian. In 1316/1899 he headed the provincial list in the matriculation examination and won a government scholarship to the Muḥammadan Anglo-Oriental College at Aligarh.

From his student days Ḥasrat was a prominent figure in the political and cultural activities of North Indian Muslims. He fought for Islamic causes in India and abroad. In 1903 he started an Urdū weekly, *Urdū-i muʿallā*, which appeared intermittently until 1938: its pan-Islamist and virulently anti-British views strongly influenced young educated Muslims. In 1909 he was jailed for a year for publishing an article critical of British educational policy in Egypt, and he was prominent in the explosion of pan-Islamic protest which preceded World War One. In 1916 he was interned for the duration of the War after he was found to be connected with ʿUbayd Allāh Sindhī's [*q.v.*] plan, the "Silk Letters Conspiracy", to raise the Frontier tribes against the British. During the *Khilāfat* movement he associated increasingly with the *ʿulamāʾ*, coming to be called our "mad mullā" by Muḥammad and Shawkat ʿAlī [*q.v.*], and tried continually to drive the agitation more extreme: striving to make non-co-operation with government the policy of the *Khilāfat* movement at its conference of November 1919, declaring support for an Afghān invasion of India at Congress-*Khilāfat* meetings of June 1920, and atte ing to make complete independence for India aim of the Congress and the Muslim League at t sessions in 1921. He was imprisoned from 192 1924. On his release he startled many by decla himself a Communist as well as a Muslim, and chaired the reception committee of the first In Communist Conference at Kānpur in 1925. F this point Ḥasrat's influence in Indian po declined. He remained notable but could no lo find support amongst many. From 1937 he was ac in the Muslim League, of which he had been a mer from its foundation and President in 1921, bu was out of harmony with the direction it was tak He opposed the League's demand for Paki and devoted much of his time from 1942 to to promoting his own plan for a three-tiered In confederation to solve the communal problem 1946 he was elected as a Muslim League candi to the UP Legislative Council and to the In Constituent Assembly. He died in Lucknow in 1

Although vigorously engaged in politics, Ḥa maintained a considerable literary output. His r important prose works are his commentary on 13th/19th century poet Ghālib, *Sharḥ-i Ghālib*, his discussion of the conventions of Urdū poe *Nikāt-i sukhān*. Primarily, however, he was a p He contributed much to the refinement of the U *ghazal* and was the only *ghazal* writer of mo times to become a "classic" while still alive. Dja Miyān Farangī Maḥallī has edited the most comp edition of his works, *Kulliyāt*, 2nd. ed., Lahore 1

Evidently, several somewhat contradictory the mingle in Ḥasrat's life. There is his faith, as evi in his private life as in his public actions. A pun ious observer of prayer and fasting, he also perfor the *Ḥadjdj* at least eleven times between 1932 his death. He was, moreover, in the traditio his ancestors, a mystic and a follower of the Far Maḥall family [*q.v.* above] of Lucknow, becomi *murīd* of Mawlānā ʿAbd al-Wahhāb (d. 1321/190 in 1894 and being made a *khalīfa* in both Ḳādirī- zāḳī and Čishtī-Niẓāmī *silsilas* by Mawlānā ʿAb Bārī [*q.v.* above] in 1917. There is his impervious to the communal attitudes which influenced so m of his contemporaries; hence he opposed Pakis admired Hindus of a revolutionary caste of mind Tilak, Aurobindo Ghose and Subhas Bose, and w poems in Hindi praising Krishna and expres his longing for Hindu holy places. Then the his Communism, though it is unlikely that understanding of Communist theory and pra would have withstood rigorous examination. attractions, it seems, stemmed in part from a Muslim love of egalitarianism, in part from a ha of British imperialism and in part from the that it took no account of communalism. Invaria Ḥasrat propounded his position with sincerity without fear. Such independence of mind inv conflict with others. He was expelled two times Aligarh College, imprisoned at least three time the British, had memorable confrontations with Gandhi and Jinnah, led the party which stormed Congress session at Kānpur in 1925, and refuse sign the Indian constitution because he did not t it brought the freedom for which Indians had fou Above all things a rugged individualist, he wa ceived with great respect throughout his life th heard increasingly by few.

Bibliography: Khālid Ḥasan Ḳādirī, *Ḥ*

hānī: a study of his life and poetry, London versity Ph. D. thesis, 1971 (unpublished); ncis Robinson, *Separatism among Indian slims: the politics of the United Provinces' slims 1860-1923*, Cambridge 1974.

(F. C. R. ROBINSON)

SSANI [see ḤASANĪ]

SSŪ TAYLI "the oilman", a religious tee of Muslim India, was born at an unknown some time in the 10th/16th century, at Makhi- n the bank of the Chenab, in the Pandjāb. ritical change in Hassū's life came when he was . He met one of the living "nine naths of hnath". The latter recognised in him his sixty- nd premier disciple, who had spent 82 years in austerities before his birth. Hassū now em- d on his career as a saint. He went to Lahore he worked as a porter, but subsequently be- a grain merchant and opened a grain store at i Mandi. A devout admirer of his, Sūrat Singh, him as a merchant of a curious type—knowing thing about the future prices, he bought dear old cheap! He died at Lahore in 1104/1603. mb still survives, an object of some veneration; pot is also remembered where he used to sell

his death, Hassū Tayli appears to have re- d formally a Muslim, though he did not follow ve basic observances of Islam. For this latter, sciple Sūrat Singh has ready explanations: he d all the time, so why should he have prayed in ? Why should he have paid *zakāt*, or kept daily when he never had anything stored up, and broke his fast? Why should he have gone on mage, to circumambulate the Kaʿba, when nt round the Kaʿba of his heart a hundred times e breath? His chief disciple, Shaykh Kamāl, the term *Malāmatiyya* [*q.v.*] to designate his r's school, with considerable aptness.

e significance of this religious sect lies in the that it openly drew its disciples from amongst Hindus and Muslims, and declared its connec- with ascetic and mystic predecessors in both ons. Nor did the followers of this sect make any npt to hide the rather modest origins of their er.

Bibliography: Sūrat Singh, *Tadhkira-yi Pīr ssū Tayli*, unique Ms. in Department of History, garh Muslim University; M. Athar Ali, *Sidelights ideological and religious attitudes in the Punjab ing the 17th century*, in *Medieval India—a scellany*, ii, Bombay 1972. (M. ATHAR ALI)

-ḤĀTIMĪ, ABŪ ʿALĪ MUḤMMAD B. AL-ḤASAN -MUẒAFFAR, literary critic and philolo- of the 4th/10th century, who died inBaghdād Rabīʿ II 388/26 April 998.

ough the name of his father is sometimes given Ḥusayn, the testimony of Abū ʿAlī al-Muḥassin nūkhī (*Nishwār al-muḥāḍara*, ed. ʿA. al-Shālidjī, t 1391-3/1971-3, iii, 14) and of al-Khaṭīb al- dādī, who received traditions from al-Ḥātimī gh Abū ʿAlī's son, Abu 'l-Ḳāsim al-Tanūkhī (see *kh Baghdād*, ii, 214, 356, xi, 231) can probably usted. All biographers agree that he was a pupil hulām Thaʿlab [*q.v.*], but fail to mention other ers, except Yāḳūt (*Udabāʾ*, vi, 501), who states al-Ḥātimī was born early enough to have been a of Ibn Durayd [*q.v.*]. Since Ibn Durayd died in 33, this information, if correct, would indicate al-Ḥātimī was born around 310/922 or even ear- Yāḳūt however also quotes an autobiographical from al-Ḥātimī's [*Taḳrīʿ*] *al-hilbādja*, a book which al-Ḥātimī wrote for the vizier, Abū ʿAbd Allāh [al-Ḥusayn b. Aḥmad] b. Saʿdān [see IBN SAʿDĀN below], who held office from 373/983 till 374/985 (see Ibn Miskawayh, *Tadjārib al-umam*, iii, 85, 102, 107). In this note, al-Ḥātimī claims that he served Sayf al-Dawla at the age of nineteen. If we assume that al-Ḥātimī did not join the circle of Sayf al-Dawla before the latter had established himself firmly in Aleppo in 336/947, he could not have been born before 317. The question is whether al-Ḥātimī's autobio- graphical report can be trusted, since both the des- cription of his character by contemporary authors (see Abū Ḥayyān al-Tawḥīdī, *al-Imtāʿ wa 'l-muʾānasa*, i, 135, iii, 126-7) and the tone of many of his own re- marks in the *Mūḍiḥa* (see below) suggest that he was given to unbridled self-glorification. A further reason for questioning the report in the *Hilbādja* is that he quotes in the *Ḥilya* (see below) ʿAlī b. Sulaymān al-Akhfash who died as early as 315/927 (cf. Bone- bakker, *Materials for the history of Arabic rhetoric*, in *AIUON*, Suppl. no. 4, xxxv [1975], fasc. 3, p. 88). The autobiographical report quoted by Yāḳūt goes on to say that at the court of Sayf al-Dawla, al-Ḥātimī was treated as the equal of the grammarians Abū ʿAlī al-Fārisī, Ibn Khālawayh [*q.vv.*] and Abu 'l-Ṭayyib al-Lughawī [*q.v.* above]. Since Abū ʿAlī al-Fārisī joined Sayf al-Dawla in 341, al-Ḥātimī cannot have given up his career with Sayf al-Dawla before that date, again assuming that his report can be trusted. It is also likely that al-Ḥātimī left Aleppo not later than Dhu 'l-Ḳaʿda 351/December 962, the date of the attack on Aleppo by Nicephorus Phocas (Abu 'l-Ṭayyib al-Lughawī died in the massacre that fol- lowed, according to the editor of Abu 'l-Ṭayyib's *Marātib*, Cairo 1375/1955, 5-6). In any case, we find him in Baghdād in the summer of 352/963 (or possibly 351/962, cf. M. S. Kiktev in *Literatura Vostoka* [1969], 81 note) involved in a discussion with the poet al- Mutanabbī, whom he may well have known already at the court of Sayf al-Dawla. The *Yatīmat al-dahr* of Thaʿālibī (ed. M.M. ʿAbd al-Ḥamīd, Cairo 1375- 7/1956-8, iii, 108-11, 131-3) quotes verses by al- Ḥātimī on the Ziyārid ruler Shams al-Maʿālī [Ḳābūs b. Wushmagīr] [*q.v.*], on the Buwayhid vizier Sābūr b. Ardashīr and on the caliph al-Ḳādir bi 'llāh, but these do not throw any light on al-Ḥātimī's career during the second half of his life (the *Yatīma* text suggests that these poems were composed by a son of al-Ḥātimī; unless one follows the text in Yāḳūt vi, 501-2, assuming at the same time. that this text contains, in a brief parenthesis, two lines by al- Ḥātimī's father and that Yāḳūt should have read *li'bnihi* as in the *Yatīma* ed.).

From the introduction of a story in al-Tanūkhī's *al-Faradj baʿd al-shidda* (Cairo 1903, ii, 85 = Cairo 1375/1955, 305), it appears that al-Ḥātimī visited Egypt, but unfortunately there is no indication at which period of his life this visit took place. Nor do we know any details about his career as a *kātib*, though he is qualified as such by several biographers.

Al-Ḥātimī chiefly owes his fame to two *risāla*s on the poet al-Mutanabbī which go under various names. The first of the two is known as *al-Risāla al- mūḍiḥa* [*fī dhikr sariḳāt Abi 'l-Ṭayyib al-Mutanabbī wa-sāḳiṭ shiʿrih*], *Djabhat al-adab*, *Munāẓarat Abī ʿAlī al-Ḥātimī li-Abi 'l-Ṭayyib*, or simply *al-Risāla al- Ḥātimiyya*. The correct title, at least of the longer version of this *risāla* which is preserved in the ms. Escurial 772 (and quoted in part by Ibn Khallikān and, following him, al-Yāfiʿī, *Mirʾāt*, Hyderabad 1337-9, repr. Beirut 1390/1970, ii, 437-41), is undoubt- edly *al-Mūḍiḥa*. This title is explained by the author as referring to a type of wound inflicted on the head (Lane, s.v. *shadjdja*), and may be a *double entendre*, since *mūḍiḥa* means also "making apparent", "disclosing", i.e. the defects of al-Mutanabbī's poetry. The title *Djabhat al-adab* must be the result of a wrong interpretation of a sentence in the preface, though it appears in several mediaeval biographies (see the ed. of the *Mūḍiḥa* by M.Y. Nadjm, Beirut 1385/1965, 3, ll. 12-3, 4, l. 18, and 6, note 1 of the introduction). The *risāla* is a caricature of al-Mutanabbī and a condemnation of his poetry, in the framework of a discussion between the poet and al-Ḥātimī. The attack was instigated by the Buwayhid vizier al-Muhallabī and reflected the rivalry between the Buwayhid Muʿizz al-Dawla and the Ḥamdānid Sayf al-Dawla (see R. Blachère, *Un poète arabe du IVeme siècle de l'Hégire*, Paris 1935, 223-5, 228). It ended, according to al-Ḥātimī, in al-Mutanabbī's flight to Kūfa. A shorter version of the same *risāla* exists in Yāḳūt's *Udabā'* (vi, 504-18), in Yūsuf al-Badīʿī's *al-Ṣubḥ al-munabbī* (ed. M. al-Saḳḳā *et alii*, Cairo 1963, 128-42), in the MS Cairo, Dār al-Kutub 2039 (ed. I. al-Dasūḳī al-Bisāṭī, Cairo 1961, as an appendix to the *Ibāna ʿan sariḳāt al-Mutanabbī* of Abū Saʿd Muḥammad b. Aḥmad al-ʿAmīdī) and in at least two other manuscripts. There is a Russian translation in the above mentioned article by Kiktev. An even shorter version is preserved in Shihāb al-Dīn al-Khatādjī (ed. ʿA.M. al-Ḥulw, Cairo 1386/1967, ii, 421-7), which does not make any mention of Muhallabī and Muʿizz al-Dawla. These shorter versions end in a reconciliation, after which al-Mutanabbī and al-Ḥātimī part as good friends. Al-Badīʿī's text, Khatādjī and the text published by al-Bisāṭī (but not the text in Yāḳūt) even add a last sentence to the effect that al-Ḥātimī became so much convinced of al-Mutanabbī's merits as a poet that he decided to write another *Risāla Ḥātimiyya*. This second *Risāla Ḥātimiyya* to which the shorter versions of the first allude may be the list of parallels between verses by al-Mutanabbī and pseudo-Aristotelian sententiae which is preserved not only in a considerable number of manuscripts, but also in the *Kitāb al-Badīʿ fī naḳd al-shiʿr* by Usāma b. Munḳidh (ed. A. A. Badawī *et alii*, Cairo 1380/1960, 264-83) and in quotations in the Mutanabbī commentary by al-ʿUkbarī (see Blachère, *op. cit.*, 268-9, and the examples translated by F. Rosenthal in *Das Fortleben der Antike im Islam*, Zürich 1965, 352-4, and cf. 118). Yet there may be some doubt about the authenticity of this second *risāla*, since biographies such as those by Yāḳūt and al-Suyūṭī, which offer a detailed list of al-Ḥātimī's oeuvre, do not mention it. An accurate description of the *risāla* appears in *al-Muḥammadūn min al-shuʿarā'* by Ibn al-Ḳifṭī (ed. H. Maʿmarī, Cairo 1390/1970, 231), though Ibn al-Ḳifṭī fails to mention it in his Ḥātimī biography in the *Inbāh al-ruwāt*. A second description occurs in al-Ṣafadī's *Wāfī bi 'l-wafayāt*, ii, 343; but several unpublished manuscripts of the *risāla* have only a descriptive title with no indication of the origin of the work. Nor does al-Ḥātimī's name (as far as the author of the article knows) appear in the above-mentioned Mutanabbī commentary and in Usāma's *Badīʿ*. Mention should be made of a curious manuscript in the Ambrosiana (F 300) which brings together a somewhat more elaborate rendering of the short version of the first *Risāla* and the second *Risāla* claiming (not very convincingly) that both were based on a verbal account given by al-Ḥātimī in 369/979-80. The best edition of the second *Risāla Ḥātimiyya* is that by F.A. al-Bustānī in *Machriq*, xxix (1931), 132-9, 196-204, 273-80, 348-55, 461-4, 623-32, 759-67, 925-34, and in a separate ed. published in the year. A facsimile edition with translation was pub by O. Rescher in *Islamica*, ii (1926), 439-73; editions can be disregarded.

As a document of mediaeval Arabic li criticism, the longer version of the *Mūḍiḥa* is the most interesting of the three texts, not on cause of its penetrating and often rightful cri of al-Mutanabbī's poetry, but also because of its analysis of the distinction between slavish imi of themes from ancient poetry and the subtle morphosis of such themes as he finds it in the w truly gifted poets. This analysis goes beyon original aim of the *risāla*, which sets out to be a against al-Mutanabbī and a grotesque picture character and habits. The first encounter betwe Ḥātimī and al-Mutanabbī is followed, in the *M* but not in its shorter version, by a descripti three further encounters at the house of al-Muh in the presence of scholars of note, such as Abū al-Sīrāfī, ʿAlī b. ʿĪsā al-Rummānī and ʿAlī b. I al-Munadjdjim. In the preface to his edition (1 Nadjm raises the question whether the meetir the home of al-Muhallabī actually took place anc not invented in order to find a suitable form f elaboration of the theme of discussion of the meeting. It is indeed unlikely that al-Muta would have allowed himself to be publicly humi on four different occasions.

Al-Ḥātimī is frequently quoted in mediaeval books on literary theory as an authority on d tions of figures of speech by early critics. Ma these quotations can be traced in al-Ḥātimī's *I al-muḥāḍara*. The *Ḥilya* is not, however, a wo literary theory, but rather an anthology on p with short sections on literary theory. A specifically dealing with this subject is quoted Ḥātimī himself in the *Ḥilya* and was known to U (see *Badīʿ*, 8) and perhaps to others (see *Mat* 14-6, 20, 27). The survival of the *Ḥilya* in Maghribī manuscripts (one of which has a mar note indicating that a small portion of the bool already circulated in Spain before the rest arı and Ibn Ḥazm's [*q.v.*] recommendation of "the of al-Ḥātimī" as manuals on poetry (*al-Taḳr ḥadd al-manṭiḳ*, ed. I. ʿAbbās, Beirut 1959, 20 well as other evidence (see *Materials*, 18) indicate al-Ḥātimī enjoyed a considerable reputation in S

Other writings by al-Ḥātimī have not appar survived. As far as one can judge from the given by Yāḳūt and by others, al-Ḥātimī's interest was literary criticism, though he wrote books on lexicography and grammar.

Bibliography: in addition to the texts studies mentioned in the article, see *Ta Baghdād*, ii, 214; Ibn al-Ḳifṭī, *Inbāh al-r* Cairo 1369-93/1950-73, iii, 103-4; Ibn Khal ed. M.M. ʿAbd al-Ḥamīd, Cairo 1367/1948 482-6 (no. 621); al-Suyūṭī, *Bughya*, Cairo 35-6; Ḥādjdjī Khalīfa, ed. Flügel, iii, 112, 312, v, 79, vi, 166 (there are numerous other biogra but they do not add anything of substance t above); Brockelmann, G I, 88, S I, 141, M. ʿA. Shuʿayb, *al-Mutanabbī bayn nāḳidīhi*, 1964, index; I. ʿAbbās, *Ta'rīkh al-naḳd al- ʿind al-ʿArab*, Beirut 1391/1971, 243-70 *et pa* A. Maṭlūb, *Ittidjāhāt al-naḳd al-adabī fi 'l-ḳar rābiʿ li 'l-hidjra*, Beirut 1393/1973, 258-65; Se *GAS*, ii, 488; S. A. Bonebakker, *A biograp sketch of Abū ʿAlī Muḥ b. al-Ḥasan al-Ḥātir AIUON*, forthcoming. (S. A. BONEBAKK

WKING [see BAYZARA]

WSAM, the earlier Arabic name of the mod-own of Rūdisar in eastern Gīlān on the coast Caspian Sea. It is an Arabisation of the local , which appears to have been Khosham or ıam. Thus the name is given by al-Muḳaddasī 55, 360) and probably by Abū Dulaf b. Muhalhil Minorsky, *Abū-Dulaf Mis'ar b. Muhalhil's ls in Iran*, Cairo 1955, 23) as Kh-sh-m; by al-ī (*al-Ḳānūn al-Mas'ūdī*, Hyderabad 1954-6, ıs Khawsam; and by Aṣīl al-Dīn Zawzanī (ed. Rabino, in *JA* (1950), 327, 330) as Hawsham. endering of the initial *kh* as *h* in Arabic corre-ed to the pronunciation of Arabic *hā'* by the *khā'* and the shift of Persian *shīn* to Arabic curred frequently. The identity of al-Muḳad-Kh-sh-m with Hawsam, rejected by Muḥam-Ḳazwīnī and Minorsky, is ascertained by his nce to it (360) as "the town of the *dā'ī*." The ary given by him elsewhere (372), which places sh-m at a two days' trip west of the Safīd-rūd, ırs to refer to a different town also mentioned ıl al-Dīn Zawzanī (332).

wsam is generally described as the eastern-town of Gīlān, located at the border between the ıd the Daylam, whose territories extended west to the coast. It is first mentioned as a resi-of the Zaydī *imām* al-Ḥasan al-Uṭrūsh [*q.v.*] al-li'l-Ḥaḳḳ, who was active in the region during ıst decade of the 3rd century/903-13 converting l and Daylam to Islam. After the collapse of the 'Alid reign in Ṭabaristān in 316/928, it became hief seat of 'Alid rule in the Caspian region he centre of scholarship of the Nāṣiriyya, the l of al-Nāṣir in *fiḳh* and theology. It was ruled *ca.* 319/931 to 350/961 by Abu 'l-Faḍl Dja'far al-r fi 'llāh [see AL-THĀ'IR FI 'LLĀH], grandson of ther of al-Nāṣir and, through his mother, of al-himself. His descendants remained in control of wn during much of the time until and beyond nd of the century, though often in contention descendants of al-Nāṣir and other 'Alids, which nvolved efforts by the Ziyārids and Buwayhids cure their suzerainty over the region. The rids, though Zaydīs of the Nāṣiriyya school, as *amīrs* without claiming the Zaydī imāmate. 53 or 354/964-5, the Zaydī *imām* Abū 'Abd al-Mahdī li-Dīn Allāh took the town from al-ı Amīrkā, son of Abu 'l-Faḍl al-Thā'ir, and ruled , with a short interruption, until his death in 70. *Ca.* 380/990 the *imām* Aḥmad b. al-Ḥusayn ı'ayyad bi'-llāh stayed in Hawsam for a year, ome time later for another period of over two . He eventually took his residence in Langā, west ıwsam, leaving that town to the Thā'irid Kiyā 'l-Faḍl who nominally recognised his imāmate. e early 5th/11th century, Abū Dja'far al-Haw-the most famous collector and commentator of orks of al-Nāṣir, was active there. *Ca.* 432/1041-2 āṣirī *'ulamā'* of Hawsam set up al-Ḥusayn al-, a descendant of al-Uṭrūsh al-Nāṣir, as *imām*, e reigned in the town until his death in 472/1079-.e was buried next to Abū 'Abd Allāh al-Mahdī, their tombs became a place of pilgrimage for aspian Zaydīs. Thereafter, Hawsam came under ıle of the *imāms* Abū Riḍā al-Kīsumī (d. after 100) and Abū Ṭālib al-Akhīr (502-20/1108-28), gh they did not take their permanent residence . The town evidently declined in the latter part 5th/11th century and lost its rank as the chief of eastern Gīlān to Lāhīdjān [*q.v.*]. Around the of the century, the Bāwandid Ispahbad Ḥusām al-Dawla Shahriyār, after surrendering control of Ṭabaristān to his son Nadjm al-Dīn Ḳārin, retired to Hawsam, where he built a *khānaḳāh* for himself. He bought much land in the region and ordered the construction of a market and shops. After he fell ill and was brought back to Ṭabaristān by his son, he put a former servant in charge of his property in Hawsam (Ibn Isfandiyār, *Ta'rīkh-i Ṭabaristān*, ed. 'Abbās Iḳbāl, Tehran 1941, ii, 37 f.). The report reflects both the decline of the town and its continued attraction as a religious centre. The general decline continued during the following century. In a letter sent to the Yaman in 607/1210-11, a Zaydī scholar of Lāhīdjān mentioned the deplorable condition of the two shrines of Abū 'Abd Allāh al-Mahdī and al-Ḥusayn al-Nāṣir in Hawsam, expressing his hope that the Yamanī *imām* al-Manṣūr 'Abd Allāh b. Ḥamza would restore them. In the early 8th/14th century, Hawsam seems to have regained some importance as an administrative centre, for a coin was minted there for the Ilkhān Abū Sa'īd between 733/1332 and 736/1335 if the restoration of the name of the mint proposed by Fraehn, *De Ilchanorum seu Chulaguidarum numis*, in *Mém. Acad. Imp. Sciences* St. Pétersbourg, 6th ser., ii [1834], 530, 548, is correct. Ẓahīr al-Dīn Mar'ashī (*Ta'rīkh-i Gīlān*, ed. M. Sutūda, Tehran 1347, 143 f.), however, describes the town as having long fallen into ruin when Sayyid Raḍī Kiyā (789-829/1387-1426) of the Amīr Kiyā'ī dynasty of Lāhīdjān ordered its rebuilding and gave it the name Rūdisar. Raḍī Kiyā granted tax exemptions in order to attract people to the town, brought shipbuilders to the harbour, built a congregational mosque in a large square, a market with shops, a bath, palace, stable and hotel. The shrine and cemetry of al-Ḥusayn al-Nāṣir were preserved from the former town, and several royal personages were buried there in the 9th/15th and 10th/16th centuries.

Bibliography: In addition to the references given in the article, see *Ḥudūd al-'ālam*, 136, 388; Yāḳūt, iv, 996; H. L. Rabino, *Le Guîlân*, in *RMM*, xxxii (1916-17), 336-9; Muḥammad Ḳazwīnī, notes to edition of Djuwaynī, iii, 422-4; S. M. Stern, *The coins of Āmul*, in *NC*, 7th ser., vii (1967), 269-78; W. Madelung, *Abū Isḥāq al-Ṣābī on the Alids of Ṭabaristān and Gīlān*, in *JNES*, xxvi (1967), 20f., 45-51; idem, *The Alid rulers of Ṭabaristān, Daylamān and Gīlān*, in *Atti del III Congresso di Studi Arabi e Islamici*, Naples 1967, 488-90; idem, *The minor dynasties of Northern Iran*, in *Cambridge History of Iran*, iv, Cambridge 1975, 219-22; Manučihr Sutūda, *Az Āstārā tā Astarābād*, ii, Tehran 1351, 216-9, 304-8.

(W. MADELUNG)

ḤAYDAR-I ĀMULĪ, BAHĀ' AL-DĪN ḤAYDAR B. 'ALĪ B. ḤAYDAR AL-'UBAYDĪ (719/1319 or 720/1320 — after 787/1385), early representative of Persian theosophy and commentator on Ibn 'Arabī.

Our knowledge about his life is based on two autobiographical passages written in 777/1375-6 and 782/1380 respectively. He originated from a family of Ḥusaynī *sayyids* in Āmul, Māzandarān, whose population had been known for its Shī'ī leanings for a long time. During his studies he left his home-town for Astarābād and Iṣfahān. But in his late twenties he returned and became a confidant, and afterwards a minister of Fakhr al-Dawla Ḥasan b. Shāh Kaykhusraw b. Yazdagird, the last ruler of Ṭabaristān belonging to the Kīnakhwāriyya branch of the Bāwandid dynasty [*q.v.*]. This period seems to have been rather short, because in 748/1347 he was still in Khurāsān, as is attested by a vision which he had there and which he reports in his works, whereas two years later, in 750/1349, shortly before Fakhr al-Dawla's assassination by members of his own family, he experienced a religious crisis which made him give up his courtly life, in spite of his reverence for his master, and perform the *ḥadjdj*. For the rest of his life, at least during the documented part of it, he stayed in ʿIrāḳ. In Baghdād he studied with Naṣīr al-Dīn al-Kāshānī al-Ḥillī (d. 755/1354) and Fakhr al-Dīn Muḥammad b. Ḥasan, the son of the famous ʿAllāma al-Ḥillī, two Shīʿī scholars who enjoyed the patronage of the Djalāʾirids [*q.v.*]. With the latter one he exchanged a theological and juridical correspondence which is preserved in an autograph (*al-Masāʾil al-Āmuliyya*, dated 762/1361; ms. Tehran University no. 1022, fols. 71b-76b). He also wrote for him his *Risālat Rāfiʿat al-khilāf ʿan wadjh sukūt Amīr al-Muʾminīn*, an apology for ʿAlī's passive attitude towards the first caliphs.

The number of Ḥaydar-i Āmulī's works which are known to us, by title at least, amounts to 34. The earliest book preserved is his

(1) *Djāmiʿ al-asrār wa-manbaʿ al-anwār*, an exposition of the deeper meaning of the *sharīʿa* by means of *taʾwīl* (ed. Osman Yahya and Henri Corbin, in Sayyed Haydar Amoli, *La philosophie shiʿite*, Bibl. Iran. 16, Tehran-Paris 1969, 2 ff.; for an analysis of its contents, cf. Corbin in *Eranos-Jahrbuch*, xxx, (1961), 90 ff. and xxxi (1963), 80 ff., also in *En Islam iranien*, Paris 1972, iii, 149 ff.; P. Antes, *Zur Theologie der Schiʿa. Eine Untersuchung des Ǧāmiʿ al-asrār* . . ., Freiburg 1971). It was finished about 752/1351; in the introduction, eight other works, obviously of smaller size, are mentioned, some of which may date back to the time before Āmulī settled in Irak. In one of them, his *Risālat al-arkān*, he had treated the same subject as in his *Djāmiʿ*, restricted only to the five "pillars" of Islam. — After 760/1359 he wrote his

(2) *Risālat al-Wudjūd fī maʿrifat al-maʿbūd* which in itself has not been rediscovered yet, but a summary of which, finished at Nadjaf in 768/1367 under the title *Risālat Naḳḍ al-nuḳūḍ fī maʿrifat al-wudjūd*, has been edited by Yahya and Corbin (*ibid.*, 620 ff.). The problem of being is treated under the aspects of its unity and multiplicity (i.e. its epiphany, *ẓuhūr*), more in correspondence with the ideas of Ibn ʿArabī than with the tradition of Ibn Sīnā. — In 777/1375-6 he finished his

((3) *al-Muḥīṭ al-aʿẓam*, a huge commentary on the Ḳurʾān in seven volumes written after the model of the *Baḥr al-ḥaḳāʾiḳ wa 'l-daḳāʾiḳ*, the *tafsīr* by Nadjm al-Dīn-i Dāya (d. 654/1256). For its structure, cf. H. Corbin, in *La philosophie shiʿite*, French introd., 46 ff. — Between 781/1379 and 782/1380 he wrote

(4) *Naṣṣ al-nuṣūṣ*, a commentary on Ibn ʿArabī's *Fuṣūṣ al-ḥikam* to which he added, after the model set by earlier commentators like Dāwūd b. Maḥmūd al-Ḳaysarī (d. 751/1350), voluminous prolegomena (ed. Yahya and Corbin, in *Bibl. Iran.* 22, Tehran-Paris 1975). In them, he proved the insuperability of Muḥammad among the prophets and of Ibn ʿArabī among the mystics. Muḥammad and Ibn ʿArabī are connected historically by the *revelatio continuata* through the Shīʿī *imāms* and phenomenologically by the *mundo imaginalis* (*ʿālam al-mithāl*), the world of spiritual being from which emanated the vision in which Ibn ʿArabī claimed to have received the *Fuṣūṣ* from the Prophet himself during his stay in Damascus in 627/1230. In spite of all reverence, however, Āmulī deviates from Ibn ʿArabī in the question of the *khātam al-wilāya*, the "seal of sainthood". Whereas Ibn ʿArabī saw this ideal realised in an absolute sense in Jesus (= *wilāya muṭlaka*), whereas many of his adherents believed that, in mentaneous limitation, it had been represente Ibn ʿArabī himself (= *wilāya muḳayyada*), Ḥay Āmulī puts ʿAlī and the twelfth *imām* in their his originality thus merging with his Shīʿī convic He criticises Dāwūd al-Ḳaysarī, who had be Anatolian descent and had lived in Sunnī Egyp his unclear, i.e. non-Shīʿī, attitude in this pro (which came closer to Ibn ʿArabī's intention). other commentators, both of them of Iranian o Muʾayyad al-Dīn al-Khudjandī (d. 690/1291) Kamāl al-Dīn ʿAbd al-Razzāḳ al-Kāshānī (d. 1330) are mentioned with respect. Complicated nu ical speculations concerning the *imāms* and prophets are clarified through diagrams (tr by Corbin in *Eranos-Jb.*, xlii [1973], 79 ff.). — Ān latest attested work is his (5) *Risālat al-ʿUlūm ilāhiyya* which he composed in 787/1385 at th of 65. The autograph is preserved in Nadjaf. — A list of Āmulī's works is found in *La philos shiʿite*, French introd. 37 ff. (H. Corbin), A introd. 19 ff. (O. Yahya).

Ḥaydar-i Āmulī combined Shīʿī convic hereditary in his family with an ʿIrāḳī and Pe Ṣūfī tradition strongly imbued with the ideas o ʿArabī [*q.v.*]. In this high esteem for the *shayk akbar* he follows earlier mystics of Persian des like Saʿd al-Dīn-i Ḥammūya (587-650/1191-1252), Nadjm al-Dīn-i Dāya (d. 654/1256), both of who quotes quite frequently. Like them, he was a spe tive type; in contrast to two other famous Ira Ṣūfīs who were his exact contemporaries, ʿA Hamadhānī (714-86/1314-85), equally origin from a family of *sayyids*, and the Sunnī Bahā Dīn al-Naḳshbandī (717-91/1318-89), he did found a separate *ṭarīḳa* nor did he adhere to a them. More strongly than anybody else before he insisted on the common origin of Shīʿism Ṣūfism, thus laying the ground for a dogma he Iranian mystical orders until today. This is wh pleaded for a transcending of the normal juri approach to Islam by a union of *sharīʿa*, *ṭa* and *ḥaḳīḳa*; the Muslim who combines these aspects is not only a believer (*muʾmin*), but a be put to test (*muʾmin mumtaḥan*), equally remote literalist Shīʿism as from antinomian Ṣūfism. Sh is thus understood as the esoteric side of Islam not in an extremist sense. It may be noted, in connection, that the term *muʾmin mumtaḥan* was used by extremists like the Nuṣayrīs; Ḥaydar Ā may have reinterpreted it in opposition to ra tendencies in popular Islam.

All knowledge (*maʿrifa*) is derived from the *im* they represent the Shīʿī *nūr Muḥammadī* as as Ibn ʿArabī's *ḥaḳīḳa Muḥammadiyya*, this latt tity being understood by Āmulī as consisting light aeons which correspond to the metaphy persons of the 14 "sinless ones" (*maʿṣūm*): Muḥam Fāṭima, and the 12 *Imāms*. The 12 *Imāms* an 7 Prophets are summed up in the mystical nu 19 which pervades revelation and universe *Basmala* has 19 letters; the universe consists o Universal Intellect + the Universal Soul + 9 sp + 4 elements + 3 realms of nature + man; about numerical speculations of this kind in article by Corbin in *Eranos-Jb.*, xlii [1973], 7 God as the *mubdiʿ* of the universe is ὑπερούσιος can only be recognised in His epiphanies. This to a metaphysics of the divine names and attrib the normal monotheism propagated by Muḥam is differentiated, as *tawḥīd ulūhī*, from the *ta idī* administered by the *imāms*, i.e. the insight God alone *is* in the real sense of the word. In ining these elements, Ḥaydar-i Āmulī's thinking sents an "open" system which is based on tation and pneumatic exegesis more than an rsive reasoning.

Bibliography: Given in the article, but see o amongst sources, Nūr Allāh al-Shushtarī, *adjālis al-muʾminīn*, Tehran 1375/1955, ii, 51 ff.; ḥammad b. ʿAlī al-Tabrīzī, *Rayḥānat al-adab*, 30 (no. 54), and ii, 498 (no. 892); Khwansārī, *wḍāt al-djannāt*, Tehran 1306, 203 f.; Maʿṣūm ī Shāh, *Ṭarāʾiḳ al-ḥaḳāʾiḳ*, ed. Muḥammad aʿfar Maḥbūb, i-ii, indexes, s.v.; ʿĀmilī, *Aʿyān Shīʿa*, xxix, 25 ff.; Kaḥḥāla, *Muʿdjam al-ʾallifīn*, iv, 91; Brockelmann, S II, 209 and , 1266 *ad* 209. Studies: H. Corbin, in *Mélanges rientalisme offerts à Henri Massé*, Tehran 1963, ff.; idem, in *École Pratique des Hautes Études*, section, *Annuaire 1961-62*, 75 ff.; *1962-63*, ff.; *1963-64*, 77 ff.; *1973-74*, 283 ff.; Kamāl ṣṭafā al-Shaybī, *al-Fikr al-shīʿī wa 'l-nazaʿāt al-iyya ḥattā maṭlaʿ al-ḳarn al-thānī ʿashar al-hidjrī*, ghdād 1386/1966, 120 ff.; R. Gramlich, *Die iitischen Derwischorden Persiens*. Zweiter Teil: *ube und Lehre*, Wiesbaden 1976, index s.v.

(J. van Ess)

AYDAR KHĀN ʿAMŪ UGHLĪ, originally n as Tariverdiov (1880-1921), Persian revolu-ary and activist. He was born into a Persian y living in Armenia and brought up there. egan his education in Alexandropol (Leninakan), nia, and studied at a higher level in Erivan and , receiving a degree in electrical engineering 99 from the latter place. He then began to work company in Baku. In 1900 Ḥaydar joined the asian Social Democratic Party led by Nariman nanov, and soon afterwards he helped to estab-he Committee for the Persian Social Democrats ucasia.

1902, at the invitation of the Persian govern-, Ḥaydar went to Mashhad to supervise the r Station installed for the Shrine of Imām Riḍā, e he however stayed for only eleven months, g it as unfertile ground for political activism and ng both the governor of Khurāsān and the custo-of the Shrine oppressive. During his short stay, rtheless, Ḥaydar played a part in an uprising st the Shrine custodian, Sihām al-Mulk, who was ved to have been a grain hoarder. He then left ad for Tehran in 1903.

hile working for the railway and later on for Amīn al-Ḍarb Power Station in Tehran, Ḥaydar agated constitutionalism, and when there was spread opposition to the Belgian financial ad-, M. Naus, Ḥaydar encouraged the clerical nts of the Sipahsālār Mosque to take refuge in British Legation at Tehran by giving each of a certain amount of money.

ter the first parliamentary election in Tehran, lar established the first branch there of the l Democratic Party, the aim of which was red to be "uprooting the existing despotism". the Party believed in armed struggle, Ḥaydar ned a number of bomb explosions. In June 1907 imself exploded a bomb at the house of Mīrzā ad Khān ʿAlāʾ al-Dawla, a prominent member he *andjuman-i khidmat*, and the party also tened ʿAlī Aṣghar Khān Atābak, the Grand r. Thus in September 1907 Atābak was killed Abbās Āḳā Ṣarrāf, a party comrade of Ḥaydar. ards the end of 1907 Ḥaydar planned the assassination of Muḥammad ʿAlī Shāh, who was then attempting to extinguish the Persian constitutional system established in 1906. This plan, however, misfired; the Shāh himself remained safe, and Ḥaydar was arrested, though released subsequently.

Upon Muḥammad ʿAlī Shāh's bombardment of the Persian Parliament in 1908 and his repression of the constitutionalists, Ḥaydar fled to Baku. While in Russia, he continued his campaign by publishing articles in the Georgian press against the Shāh's régime. He also recruited some 700 Georgian volunteers for the constitutionalists' camp in Tabrīz, and later he himself joined the Tabrīz movement led by Sattār Khān. Ḥaydar took an active part in the constitutionalists' victorious actions in Marand and Khuy, and he also helped to establish a school and a newspaper in Khuy, where he appeared as a hero in the poetry produced at that time.

When he heard about the rise of the constitutionalists in Gīlān and Iṣfahān he went to the latter city and closely co-operated with the anti-Shāh forces. In 1909, together with Shaykh Muḥammad Khiyābānī and others, he established the Democrat Party in Tehran. He also founded a branch of the same Party in Mashhad in 1910. In the meantime, Ḥaydar was accused of the assassination on 15 July 1910 of Sayyid ʿAbd Allāh Bihbahānī, a clerical leader of the Persian Constitutional Revolution, who was believed to have turned against the revolutionary factions; Ḥaydar was interrogated but released later. In retaliation for Bihbahānī's murder, some members of the *Iʿtidāliyyūn* Party made an attempt on Ḥaydar's life (Mahdī Malik-zāda, *Taʾrīkh-i Inḳilāb-i mashrūṭiyyat*, vi, Tehran 1953, 219).

In 1910 Sattār Khān and his fellow *mudjāhidīn* moved to Tehran. The various revolutionary factions now fell into confused, internecine struggles; there ensued several assassinations among the *mudjāhidīn* and other revolutionary groups, and finally the government forces defeated Sattār Khān. In this bloody warfare, Ḥaydar, at one time a good friend of Sattār Khān, is said to have fought against him.

Meanwhile, Ḥaydar undertook a secret mission among the Bakhtiyārīs, but no longer feeling safe in Iran, fled the country and joined Lenin, the Russian Bolshevik leader, in Europe in 1911. On his way to Europe, Ḥaydar, through his friend, Sadekov, received a sizable amount of money from Muḥammad ʿAlī, the ex-Shāh of Iran, having falsely promised him help to regain his throne. Later, Ḥaydar excused himself by saying that he took the money in order to reduce the source of the ex-Shāh's power and corruption (ʿAbd al-Ḥusayn Nawāʾī, *Ḥaydar ʿAmū Ughlī va Muḥammad Amīn Rasūl-zāda*, in *Yādgār*, v/1-2 (1948), 43-67).

While in Europe with Lenin, Ḥaydar was also in touch with the Iranian exiles in Paris and Berlin. In 1915, he joined the anti-Allied Committee organised by Sayyid Ḥasan Taḳī-zāda and others, and was commissioned by the committee to go to ʿIrāḳ and organise an armed force against the British; this mission was not however successful. He then returned to Berlin, and shortly afterwards went to Moscow where he took part in the 1917 Soviet Revolution. In September 1920, Ḥaydar participated in the Congress of the People of the East held in Baku and, together with Avetis Sulṭān-zāda, represented Iran in the Publicity Council of the Congress.

Aiming at profound structural changes in Iran, Ḥaydar wrote an essay analysing the political and social situation of Iran and proposing certain revolutionary measures to be carried out by the newly-born Communist Party of Iran; this essay, which was written in January-March 1921, is known as "Ḥaydar Khān ʿAmū Ughlī's theses" (Mazdak, *Asnād-i taʾrīkhī-yi djunbish-i kārgarī, sūsiyāl dimukrāsī va kumūnīsti-yi Īrān*, iii, Florence 1972, 45-53.).

He now made an unsuccessful attempt to unite all the anti-British revolutionary forces organised by Muḥammad Taḳī Pisyān in Khurāsān, by Khiyābānī in Ādharbāydjān, and by Kūčak Khān in Gīlān, and also made a strenuous effort to create peace between the rival factions within the Djangalī movement in the north of Persia [see KŪČAK KHĀN DJANGALĪ]. He then was invited by Kūčak Khān and other Djangalīs to Gīlān, and joined the revolutionary Republic of Gīlān as Foreign Commissioner. However, factional hostilities and ideological conflicts within the Djangalī forces finally resulted in the murder of Ḥaydar and in the extinction of the Djangalī movement in 1921.

Bibliography: For Ḥaydar Khān's own writings and political speeches, consult Mazdak, *Asnād*, i, iii, vi, 1970-6, and Nasrollah Saifpour Fatemi, *Diplomatic history of Persia 1917-1923*, New York 1952. Ḥaydar's autobiography was dictated to Ibrāhīm Munshī-zāda, a Russian dissident in Iran, and appeared in ʿAbbās Iḳbāl, *Ḥaydar Khān ʿAmū Ughlī*, in *Yādgār*, iii, no. 5 (1947), 61-80; an English translation of the autobiography is given in A. Reza Sheikholeslami and Dunning Wilson, *The memoirs of Ḥaydar Khān ʿAmū Ughlū*, in *Iranian Studies*, vi (1973), 21-51. Because of Ḥaydar's involvement in the Persian Constitutional Revolution of 1906-11 and subsequent political developments in Iran, all the works concerned with the period provide extensive information and ample references about Ḥaydar. See especially the articles: DJAMʿIYYA; DUSTŪR; ḤUKŪMA; KHIYĀBĀNĪ, Shaykh Muḥammad; KHURĀSĀNĪ, Mullā Muḥammad Kāẓim; KŪČAK KHĀN DJANGALĪ, Mīrzā; (in Suppl.) ĀḲĀ NADJAFĪ, Ḥadjdjī Shaykh Muḥammad Taḳī Iṣfahānī; ĀZĀDĪ; ḤĀʾIRĪ, Shaykh ʿAbd al-Karīm Yazdī. See also ʿAbd al-Ḥusayn Nawāʾī, *Inḳilāb-i Gīlān čigūna āghāz shud?*, in *Yadgar*, iv, no. 3 (1947), 41-55; idem, *Sattār Khān Sardār-i millī Kahramān-i Ādharbāydjān*, in *Iṭṭilāʿāt-i Māhāna*, no. 9 (1948); ʿAbbās Iḳbāl, *Ḳātil-i ḥaḳīḳī-yi Mīrzā ʿAlī Aṣghar Khān Atābak*, in *Yadgar*, iii, no. 4 (1946), 47-51; Raḥim Riḍāzādā Malik, *Čakīda-yi inḳilāb Ḥaydar Khān ʿAmū Ughlī*, Tehran 1973; Ḥasan Malik-zāda Hīrbud, *Sarguzasht-i ḥīratangīz*, Tehran 1949; Hafez Farman Farmayan, *Kitābshināsī-yi Mashrūṭa*, Tehran 1966; Ismāʿīl Rāʾīn, *Ḥaydar Khān ʿAmū Ughlī*, Tehran; *Bisūyi āyanda*, April-May 1951; Muḥammad Ḳazwīnī, *Wafayāt-i muʿāṣirin*, in *Yādgār*, iii (1947), 38-49; Aḥmad Ḥisābī, *Mudjāhid-i buzurg Ḥaydar ʿAmū Ughlī*, Tehran 1949; Mahdī Bāmdād, *Sharḥ-i ḥāl-i ridjāl-i Īrān*, i, Tehran 1968 (under *Ḥaydar*). (ABDUL-HADI HAIRI]

ḤAYDAR MALIK, Kashmīrī soldier, scholar and engineer. He was the son of Ḥasan Malik of Čādura, a village about 10 miles south of Srīnagar, and descended from Rāmčandra, the commander-in-chief of Radja Suhādeva (1301-20). His family seemed to have gone into eclipse during the early period of the Sultanate, but with its conversion to Shīʿism early in the 10th/16th century, it became active in the social and political life of Kashmīr. Ḥaydar Malik's grandfather, Malik Muḥammad Nādjī, played an important role in bringing about the overthrow of Mīrzā Ḥaydar Dughlāt in 958/1551; and his father, Ḥasan Malik fought against the Mughal army sent by Emperor Akbar to conquer Ka
Ḥaydar Malik also took up arms against the Mu
He served Yūsuf Khān Čak, son of Sulṭān Ḥ
Shāh (970-8/1563-70), for 24 years, and accom
him in exile to Hindustan. He fought side-b
with Yūsuf Khān, who was sent by Akbar to su
the refactory *zamīndārs*; and when Djahāngī
Yūsuf Khān with Ḳuṭb al-Dīn, governor of Ben
suppress Shīr Afkan, who held a *djāgīr* in Bur
for being in league with the Afghān rebels, an
Afkan was killed, Ḥaydar Malik gave prot
to his widow, Mihr al-Nisāʾ, the future Nūrd
and sent her safely to Āgra. On Yūsuf Khān's
Ḥaydar Malik entered the service of Djah
who conferred upon him the titles of *Čaghata*
Rāʾis al-Mulk.

Ḥaydar Malik was versatile, being not o
soldier but also a historian, an architect a
engineer. His *Taʾrīkh-i Kashmīr*, written in s
lucid Persian in 1031/1620-1, describes the h
of Kashmīr from the earliest times to 1027/161
twelfth year of Djahāngīr's reign. Although a
he wrote objectively, and his work is an imp
source for the history of the Sultanate in Ka

When the Djāmiʿ Masdjid of Srīnagar w
stroyed by fire, Ḥaydar Malik's father was accu
having set fire to it. Djahāngīr sent Ḥaydar Ma
rebuild it, which he did at his own expense. H
rebuilt the tomb of Shams al-Dīn ʿIrāḳī, the Nūr
shiyya saint, which had been destroyed by the S
as a reprisal for the destruction of the Djāmiʿ M
Later, Ḥaydar Malik constructed by order of
hāngīr a canal from the river Sind to irrigate th
Afzā garden. He was also entrusted with the s
vision of the construction of the waterfall at V
He died in Kashmīr at a ripe old age in the re
Shāhdjahān, who had in 1036/1627 appointed h
superintendent of buildings to be built around V

Bibliography: Mohibbul Hasan, *Ka*
under the Sulṭāns, Calcutta 1959; idem, *A n*
the assassination of Shir Afkan, in *Ghulam Ya*
commemoration volume, ed. H. K. She
Hyderabad 1966; R. K. Parmu, *History of M*
rule in Kashmīr, Delhi 1969; Haydar M
Taʾrikh-i Kashmīr, ms. India Office 510, s
unpublished. (MOHIBBUL HAS

ḤAYS (A.; noun of unity, *ḥaysa*), an Arab
made from dates (of the variety called *barnī*) cr
and then kneaded with some preserved butte
this is added skimmed, dried and crumbly ca
milk cheese, or some flour, or even some crum
bread. The invention of this mixture of ingre
is attributed traditionnally (see al-Djāḥiẓ, *Buk*
ed. Ḥādjirī, 211; tr. in *Arabica*, ii/3 [1955], 336
prominent member of Makhzūm called Suway
Haramī (Ibn al-Kalbī-Caskel, *Djamhara*, Tab.
who is also said to have been the first to serve
as a drink in Mecca (Muṣʿab al-Zubayrī, *N*
Ḳuraysh, 342).

Judging by some anecdotes (e.g. in *Buk.*
65, 112, 163, tr. 106, 180, 259) and by a frequ
cited verse (metre *kāmil*, rhyme *-bū*; *Bukhalāʾ*,
Ibn Ḳutayba, *ʿUyūn*, iii, 19; al-Marzubānī, *Muʿ*
215; al-Ḳālī, *Amālī*, iii, 86; al-Baghdādī, *Kh*
ed. Būlāḳ, i, 242 = ed. Cairo, ii, 32; *LA* and
root *ḥ - y - s*), it was a much-appreciated food
especially suitable for travellers (al-Baghdādī,
al-Ṭabīkh, Mawṣil 1353/1934, 82), but equally fa
ed by sedentary peoples. However, this dish wa
considered worthy of "being included in the
cuisine" (M. Rodinson, *Recherches sur les docu*
arabes relatifs à la cuisine, in *REI* [1949], 148)

ırthermore, the idea of a mixture or mélange ined in the root led to the word *ḥays* being used pejorative sense. Indeed, there was a saying *i 'l-amr ḥays* "this is a wretched affair", and a ›rb, *ʿāda 'l-ḥays yuḥās* "the *ḥays* has been re-d", that is to say, "it was already bad, but has become worse", uttered when someone criticises ›nd person who has performed his task badly, but ›lf fails to do it any better (al-Maydānī, *Madjmaʿ* ›*thāl*, i, 484).

Bibliography: In addition to references given the article, see De Goeje, *BGA*, iv, 222.

(Ed.)

ıZĀRADJĀT, a region of central Af-istan spanning the modern (post-1964 re-ısation) provinces of Bāmiyān, Wardak, Ghaznī, and Uruzgān. The region is almost wholly ıtainous, its northern backbone being formed by Kūh-i Bābā range [*q.v.*] and its outliers. There ›nsequently very few towns and these tend to lie e river valleys, e.g. Dawlatyār on the upper Herī and Pandjāb or Pandjāō on the Pandjāb tribut-›f the upper Helmand. The sedentary agricultur-.azāras [*q.v.* below] are the main ethnic element e region, but there are also Pashtūn or Afghān ıds, e.g. Ghalzays [*q.v.*], who have moved in the east and who have clearly-defined grazing ıds.

Bibliography: J. Humlum, *La géographie de* ı*fghanistan, étude d'un pays aride*, Copenhagen 59, 86-8, 114-16, 156-7. (C. E. Bosworth)

AZĀRAS, the name of a group of peoples .biting the central mountains of Afghā-ān; they form one of the principal population ents of the country, amounting perhaps to ›oo.

ıe Hazāras are almost certainly an ethnically d group, whose components may or may not be ed to each other. In appearance, Hazāras are ›minantly brachycephalous, with Mongoloid l features, though this is by no means universal. e is therefore much in favour of Schurmann's ›thesis that the Hazāras of the core region, the ıradjāt [*q.v.* above], at least, are a mixed popula-formed from a fusion of an aboriginal Iranian ıtain people with incoming Mongol-Turkish ents. The Hazāras early attracted the attention 9th century western travellers and scholars use of persistent legends that the Hazāras are endants of Mongol soldiers, the human débris ıngiz Khān's campaigns in the early 13th century hese traditions were retailed, for instance, by ıtstuart Elphinstone at the beginning of the century — and because it was believed, on the ; of linguistic material collected in the 1830s ıgst the Aymāḳs by E. Leech, that the Hazāras substantially spoke Mongol at that time. It now ıs more probable that Mongol-Turkish elements trated into central Afghānistān, via the more low-; and open river valleys of the south and west er than across the mountain barriers to the north, he Čaghatayid and Tīmūrid periods, mingling the indigenous Iranian population there; st the vestigial communities of ethnic and lin-tic Mongols have now been shown to be centred he Ghōrāt region to the west of the Hazāra ones, churmann, *The Mongols of Afghanistan*. The name āra "group of 1,000 men" (P. *hazār* "1,000") is ainly reminiscent of the military-tribal system ıe Mongols, with its contingents of 1,000 cavalry-(Mgl. *mingan* "1,000", Tk. *biñ*/*miñ*), but the āras themselves must have become essentially Iranian speakers by *ca.* 1500; their language does, it is true, include a considerable admixture of Turkish and Mongol words [see IRAN. iii. Languages, in Suppl.].

Various sub-groups can conveniently be distinguished amongst those peoples included under the blanket designation of Hazārās. The main body is that of the Hazāradjāt or Dāy Kundī Hazāras, who are sedentary agriculturists with only small herds, living in fortified stone villages (*ḳalʿas*). Their agriculture is necessarily a limited, irrigation one, restricted by the altitude and the climate, with short summers and snow for 4-6 months of the year. Until the later 19th century and the extension to the Hazāradjāt of the central power in Kābul (see below), the power of the Dawlat-Begs, an upper class of landowners, was dominant, and still remained strong after that time. The Kūh-i Bābā Hazāras live to the north of that range, and stock rearing, with transhumance to summer pastures of *yaylaḳ*s, plays a great part in their economy. The Shaykh ʿAlī Hazāras occupy the region around Bāmiyān and the Ghōrband valley northwards to the foothills of Afghān Turkistān, and are unusual among the Hazāras for their use of summer *yurt*-type tents, whereas the tents used by the more southerly Hazāra groups are of the "black tent" variety [see KHAYMA. iv. In Central Asia]. There is a little-known group of Hazāras in Badakhshān; amongst the Taymannīs of the Ghōrāt is a small group of Hazāras; and there are the Berberī Hazāras in northeastern Persia, in the Turbat-i Djam district south of Mashhad, apparently immigrants from Afghānistān during the disturbances of the 19th century. Finally, there are the so-called Hazāra Aymāḳs of northwestern Afghānistān, in the western section of the Paropamisus Mountains, including the mediaeval Islamic regions of Bādghīs and Gūzgān. These are mainly semi-nomads, with *yurt*-type tents, but with some non-irrigation agriculture; they are Persian-speaking, but their Persian has affinities with Khurāsānī Persian, whereas that of the Hazāradjāt and the more easterly Hazāras is close to the Darī of Kabul and other Tādjīk groups of the north and east of Afghānistān. Also, they and the Taymannī Hazāras are distinguished from other Hazāra groups by their adherence to the Sunnī *madhhab*. Perhaps one should note, too, the place-name Hazāra [*q.v.*] for a district in the North-West Frontier Province of Pakistan.

The Shīʿism of the majority of the Hazāras distinguishes them from the predominant, strongly Sunnī milieu of the rest of Afghānistān. The Hazāradjāt Hazāras are Imāmī or Twelver Shīʿīs, and it has been suggested that this intrusive Shīʿism came during the Ṣafawid period of Persian history, when the expanding Ṣafawid state intermittently controlled Ḳandahār and southern Afghānistān; the remnants of the Mongols in the Ghōrāt are Sunnīs. Today, these Hazāras have no mosques in their villages, but *takiya-khāna*s instead. Amongst the northeastern Hazāras, the Shaykh ʿAlīs and Badakhshān ones, Ismāʿīlī Shīʿism is widespread; there were doubtless connections between these groups and the Ismāʿīlism of the upper Oxus districts and the Hunza-Gilgit region.

Within Afghānistān, the Hazāras have tended to suffer discrimation on account of their Shīʿism and supposedly Čingizid origins, and they still suffer today from imputations of stupidity and simple-mindedness. As an isolated and independent-minded mountain people under their own *khān*s and *mīr*s, they resented the centralising policies of the Afghān rulers of Kabul. Dūst Muḥammad [*q.v.*] whipped up Sunnī sentiment against the Hazāras; in 1888 the Hazāras rebelled against the authority of ʿAbd al-Raḥmān Khān [*q.v.*], and in 1891 the Khān organised the suppression of Hazāra unrest as a *djihād* by Sunnī fighters for the faith or *ghāzīs* against Shīʿī political enemies. It was after this fierce fighting that many Hazāras emigrated to Persian Khurāsān and the Quetta region of British Balūčistān, and many Hazāras were also resettled in Afghān Turkistān. Already Elphinstone noted that there were many Hazāras in Kābul, including 500 in the royal guard, and in the early 20th century, Ḥabīb Allāh Khān recruited a labour force of several thousand Hazāras for his road-building and public works policies. Today, there are Hazāra immigrant colonies in all the main towns of Afghānistān, sending remittances back to their families; in Kābul, they are, in particular, building and general labourers and wood sellers.

Bibliography: Mountstuart Elphinstone, *An account of the Kingdom of Caubul and its dependencies*[2], London 1842, ii, 203-14, and see also the other 19th century writers and travellers in Afghānistān, such as Ferrier and Bellew; Elizabeth E. Bacon, *An inquiry into the history of the Hazara Mongols of Afghanistan*, in *Southwestern Jnal. of Anthropology*, vii (1951), 230-54; H. F. Schurmann, *The Mongols of Afghanistan, an ethnography of the Moghôls and related peoples of Afghanistan*, The Hague 1962; K. Ferdinand, *Ethnographical notes on the Chahar Aimaq, Hazara and Moghuls*, in *AO*, xxviii (1964-5), 175-203; M. Klimburg, *Afghanistan, das Land im historischen Spannungsfeld Mittelasiens*, Vienna 1966, 130-1; W. K. Fraser-Tytler, *Afghanistan*[3], London 1967, 56-7; V. Gregorian, *The emergence of modern Afghanistan, politics of reform and modernization, 1880-1946*, Stanford 1969, 77, 79-80; L. Dupree, *Afghanistan*, Princeton 1973, 56, 58, 161. On language, see now G. K. Dulling, *The Hazaragi dialect of Afghan Persian*, Central Asian Monographs No. 1, London 1973.

(C. E. Bosworth)

HEART [see ḳalb]

HEDJAZ [see al-ḥidjāz]

HELM [see safīna]

HELMEND [see hilmand]

HEMP (Indian) [see ḥashīsh]

HERCULES, PILLARS OF [see ḳādis]

al-**HĪBA** [see aḥmad al-hība, above]

HIDJRA in *fiḳh*. For Muslims residing in the *Dār al-Ḥarb*, emigration to the *Dār al-Islām* (*hidjra*) is a recommendable act. If they cannot perform their religious duties in freedom, emigration becomes obligatory. These prescriptions are founded on Ḳurʾān, IV, 97-100 and some traditions, like Muḥammad's saying: "I have nothing to do with Muslims residing amongst the polytheists" (Abū Dāwūd, *djihād*, 95; Nasāʾī, *ḳasāma*, 27). The Mālikīs hold that emigration is always obligatory and that the tradition: "No emigration after the Conquest [of Mecca]" (Bukhārī, *djihād*, 1, 27, *īmān*, 41, *ṣayd*, 10, *maghāzī*, 35; Muslim, *imāra*, 85-6; Abū Dāwūd, *djihād*, 2; Tirmidhī, *siyar*, 32; Nasāʾī, *bayʿa*, 15**), which other *madhhabs* consider as an abrogation of the general command to emigrate, only applied to the Muslims abiding in or around Mecca, who were no longer obliged to emigrate, as their territory had become *Dār al-Islām*. During the 19th and the beginning of the 20th century, as a reaction against colonial expansion, some Islamic politico-religious movements gave this doctrine a new lease of life, inducing their followers to leave Islamic territory which had fallen under foreign domination; see e.g. khilāfa, khilāfat movement.

Bibliography: Muḥammad b. Aḥma Sarakhsī, *Sharḥ Kitāb al-siyar al-kabīr*, ed. al-Dīn al-Munadjdjid, Cairo 1971, i, 94-5; Abū b. ʿAlī al-Rāzī al-Djaṣṣāṣ, *Aḥkām al-Ḳurʾā* Muḥammad al-Ṣādiḳ Ḳamḥāwī, Cairo n.d 262; Abū Bakr Muḥammad b. ʿAbd Allāh ʿArabī, *Aḥkām al-Ḳurʾān*, ed. ʿAlī Muḥamm Badjāwī, Cairo 1387/1967, ii, 876; Abu 'l- Muḥammad b. Rushd, *Kitāb al-Muḳadd* Cairo 1325/1907, ii, 285; ʿAbd al-Ḥamīd al wānī, *Ḥāshiya ʿalā tuḥfat al-muḥtādj*, Mecca 5/1886-8, viii, 62; Abū Muḥammad ʿAbd All Aḥmad b. Ḳudāma, *al-Mughnī*, ed. Ṭāhā ḥammad al-Zaynī, Cairo 1388-9/1968-9, ix, 2 Muḥammad Rashīd Riḍā, *al-Hidjra wa-ḥukm limī 'l-Būsna fīhā*, in *al-Manār*, xii (1909), 41 Rudolph Peters, *Dār al-Ḥarb, Dār al-Islām u Kolonialismus*, in *XIX. Deutscher Oriental tag. Vorträge*, Wiesbaden 1977, 579-89; ʿUm Naqar, *The pilgrimage tradition in West A* Khartoum 1972, 82-92.

(R. Pete

HIERARCHY OF SAINTS [see abdāl, ik al-ṣafāʾ]

HIEROGLYPHS [see barbā]

ḤIKR, one of the various forms of long- lease of *waḳf* property. Originally, the ai these contracts was to give tenants an incenti maintain and ameliorate dilapidated *waḳf* prope which are inalienable. In exchange, the tena granted—according to different schools of la interpretations—priority of lease, the right of pe nent lease, the usufruct of the property or eve proprietorship with the *waḳf*. *Ḥikr* contracts, v were common in Egypt and Syria, are perp or made for a long duration. The tenant may buildings or plant trees, which become his full pr property. He is entitled to transfer and sel property and the right of perpetual lease to other person and they are inherited according t *Sharīʿa*. The tenant pays a yearly rent which v according to the current value of the land (*ad mithl*). According to the prevalent view, *ḥikr waḳf* property has to be authorised by a *ḳāḍī*, ar is supposed to do so only if there is no other w accordance with *waḳf* law to secure income fo *waḳf*.

Theoretically, *ḥikr* rights may be acquire *mulk* property as well, and indeed there seem to been such cases (cf. Mubārak, *Khiṭaṭ*, iii, 11), in general, *ḥikr* was confined to *waḳf*—probabl cause the interest shown by private owners in property generally was greater than the admini tors' interest in their *waḳfs*.

A similar system, *idjāratayn*, was commo Anatolia and in all countries formerly part of Ottoman Empire, apparently since the 16th or century (for Ottoman Egypt see, e.g. ʿAbd al-Ra al-Djabartī, *ʿAdjāʾib al-āthār*, Būlāḳ, 1297/188 94; M.-A. Lancret, *Mémoire sur le système d'impos territoriale, Description de l'Égypte, État mod* i, Paris 1809, 239). *Idjāratayn* contracts inv immediate payment of a lump sum, *muʿadjdja* well as yearly, variable, rather low rents, *muʾad* For repairs and setting up of installations in E and Palestine, a system called *khuluww al-i* was used, whose main features were a loan made t *waḳf* (*murṣad*) and the right of the *waḳf* at any to repurchase the property and repay the tenan added value. *Khuluww*, according to Mālikī law, i geria and Tunis, was rather like *ḥikr* and invo perpetual usufruct or even "co-proprietorship" the *waḳf*. The same is true for the Tunisian *enzel* which was found not only on *ḥubūs* but also on properties. In Morocco, the prevalent system of tual lease by the *ḥubūs* of dilapidated shops workshops was the *djalsa* (*guelsa*), also called or *zīna* (cf. Dozy, *Suppl.*, i, 207). The tenant s the necessary repairs, pays an annual rent and acquires the perpetual usufruct of the property. *a* in Tunis and *gedik* in Egypt were similar arments in volving, in addition to perpetual lease, ownership and use of tools and installations ps and workshops. However, there was a major ence between all the Mālikī—North African ms and those which were prevalent in Egypt, , and Turkey, according to Ḥanafī law: in the rib the lessee paid a fixed annual rent, while early rents paid in the East were supposed to according to market fluctuations (*adjr al-mithl*). these and various other systems, see Pröbster, .; Milliot, 55 ff., 126-6; Abū Zahra, 107 ff.)

Egypt, *ḥikr* has existed at least since the 12th ry (cf. S. D. Goitein, *Cairo: an Islamic city in ght of the Geniza documents*, in I. M. Lapidus, *'e Eastern cities*, Berkeley and Los Angeles 1969, Iassanein Rabie, *Some financial aspects of the system in medieval Egypt*, in *al-Madjalla al-khiyya al-Miṣriyya*, xviii [1971], 1-24). *Ḥikr* imilar practices of perpetual lease flourished periods of decline in the power of the central ment which involved deterioration of *waḳf*s. is what happened in various parts of Cairo the decline of the Fāṭimids (Mubārak, *Khiṭaṭ*, 102), and in the Maghrib with the decline Marīnid dynasty and the disorders under the ians which brought about the dilapidation *waḳf*s (Milliot, 43). The recurring fires in Istan- d other Anatolian towns have been considered primary reason for the spreading of *idjāratayn* acts in Ottoman Turkey. The *ḥikr* served as a expedient to develop deteriorated *waḳf* s in periods of economic prosperity. In the d half of the 19th century in Egypt, ʿAlī Mubārak, the Minister of Awḳāf, granted a amount of *ḥikr*s to private persons to develop Ṭanṭā and others towns (Mubārak, *Khiṭaṭ*, ii, x, 53).

other reason for the increase in *ḥikr* was the pt by debtors to save their estates from the en- ment of their creditors. This they achieved lling the *raḳaba* of the estate to a mosque at inal price while keeping the usufruct and paying nual *ḥikr*, equivalent to the interest on the originally paid by the mosque. Thus they re- the right to transfer their property, but it not be touched by their creditors (J. H. Scott, *Law affecting foreigners in Egypt*, Edinburgh 120-1). *Ḥikr* has often been used as a way to ch upon *waḳf* property. Frequently administra- eglected to collect the rent, and after some time state became known as the lessee's property. ers even claimed to be entitled to become pro- rs by prescription (cf. ʿAzīz Khānkī, *al-Wakf ḥikr wa 'l-taḳādum*, in *Madjallat* al-*Ḳānūn wa ṣād*, vi [1936], 779-829).

eover, in all periods *ḥikr* and similar practices been used by dishonest *nāẓir*s as a convenient of fraud. In Palestine, "the conversion of held as ijare wahide into ijaretein proceeded rapid rate in the nineteenth century, mainly gh the dishonesty of the local Kadis and s of Awkaf, who were often interested parties h transactions. It was an easy matter for a to advance the plea that a property had been incorrectly registered ... vast tracts of land were converted about this period into ijaretein, the Wakf being the sole loser, whilst the mutawali received a considerable accession to his income. The Law of 19 Jemaz-ul-Akhir, 1280, categorically forbade conversion unless there is the sanction of the Sherʿ, and an Imperial Irade had been obtained" (J. B. Barron, *Mohammedan Wakfs in Palestine*, Jerusalem 1922, 32).

As a result, the number of perpetual leases of *waḳf* property in Islamic countries grew tremendously. At the end of the 19th century, the number of persons who had made *ḥikr* contracts in Egypt was estimated at 20-25,000 (*Madjmūʿat al-ḳarārāt wa 'l-manshūrāt*, Būlāḳ 1899, 236 f.), and in the 1930s, the Ministry of Awḳaf alone administered more than 11,000 *ḥikr*s (Abū Zahra, 135). *Ḥikr* contracts were made predominantly on *khayrī* (public) *waḳf*s, i.e. those whose income was dedicated to hospitals, mosques, the poor, etc. (Pröbster, 141-2; Milliot, 36). Many of Cairo's public baths (*ḥammām*) had to pay yearly *ḥikr* rents to various *waḳf*s (to whom, apparently, the property had originally belonged) (Mubārak, *Khiṭaṭ*, ii, 28, 38, 113, 116; iv, 45; vi, 66-71). Recently-discovered documents have shown that very large parts of Cairo were *ḥikr* which for years had been considered private property. However, income from *ḥikr* was extremely small. According to Mubārak's data on some Cairo mosques, their income from *ḥikr* in the third quarter of the 19th century was between 0.4 % and 1.31 % of their total income (Mubārak, *Khiṭaṭ*, iv, 45, 59, 60; v, 99). In the course of the first half of the 20th century, the percentage of income from *ḥikr* in the total income of the Ministry of Awkāf from *awḳāf* declined from 2.59 % in 1899 and 1.88 % in 1904 to about 1 % from 1908 onwards (with few exceptions of lower or higher percentages). The highest percentage was obtained in the Waḳf al-Ḥaramayn category and a somewhat lower one in *khayrī waḳf*s, while *ahlī waḳf*s had the lowest percentage (1.91, 1.30, and 0.07 respectively in the 1928-9 budget). Percentages of *ḥikr* income in the total *waḳf* revenue in Palestine were similar: in 1927 the Supreme Moslem Council estimated *ḥikr* income at 1.95 % of its budget, and in fact received a sum which constituted only 1.10 % of the total *waḳf* revenue (Israel State Archives, K/102/34, 24). Though legally there should be no difference between *ḥikr* rates and the rent of the same land prior to the improvements made by the lessee, the report of an official committee appointed in Egypt in the 1930s put average rents on *ḥikr* lands at one-third of usual rents. *Sharīʿa* Courts calculated the value of *waḳf* lands encumbered with *ḥikr* as one-third of the value of similar lands free of *ḥikr* (Abū Zahra, 129-51).

Since the beginning of the 20th century, attempts have been made to abolish *ḥikr*. The Egyptian Awḳāf Administration had declared as early as 1898 that its aim was to sell the *ḥikr*s, since their revenue was too small compared with the cost of collecting it. The problem was that theoretically it is forbidden to sell *waḳf* property and that it was too complicated to exchange the great number of *ḥikr*s. Attempts made to do this during the first years of the century had failed. *Ḥikr* on *waḳf ahlī* was abolished together with such *waḳf*s in Egypt in 1952 by art. 7 of Law no. 180 of that year, and Law no. 649 of 1953 and no. 295 of 1954 provided for the voluntary sale and termination of *ḥikr*s on *waḳf khayrī*. The owner of the *raḳaba* (the *waḳf*) was to receive three-fifths of the price paid and the holder of the *ḥikr* the rest. Apparently these laws were not effective, and in 1960 a new law (no. 92) was enacted, according to which all *ḥikr*s were to be liquidated: the holder was given the option to buy the property from the *waḳf* for three-fifths of its value, otherwise it would be put for auction and the proceeds divided between the *waḳf* and the holder in a ratio of 3 to 2. In Turkey, *idjāratayn* and *muḳāṭaʿa* (= *ḥikr*) were liquidated by the Vakıflar Kanunu of 5 June 1935. According to this law, the establishment of such arrangements in future was prohibited and existing ones were dissolved. Lessees were made owners of properties they held and required to pay compensation amounting to twenty times the yearly rent, according to a scheme of easy terms (Köprülü, 246 ff.). In ʿIrāḳ, the 1929 Law of Waqf Administration had already abolished *ḥikr* and *idjāratayn*, but apparently not effectively. In 1960 and 1962 new laws called *Iṭfāʾ ḥaḳḳ al-ḥikr* were enacted, according to which administrators and other people concerned were entitled to apply to a law court for the dissolution of *ḥikr*, *idjāratayn*, *muḳāṭaʿa*, and similar systems of perpetual lease. The law court would fix the value of the property and the share of the *waḳf* and the lessee (Muḥammad Shafīḳ al-ʿĀnī, *Aḥkām al-waḳf*, Baghdād 1965, 60, 244-6).

Bibliography: In addition to the literature on *waḳf* in general, see in particular Eug. Clavel, *Le wakf ou habous*, Cairo 1896, ii, ch. 12; U. Pace and V. Sisto, *Code annoté du Wakf*, Alexandria 1946, 138-59; J. Abribat, *Essai sur les contrats de quasi-aliénation et de location perpétuelle auxquels l'institution du hobous à donné naissance*, in *Revue Algérienne et Tunisienne de Législation et de Jurisprudence*, xvii (1901), 121-51; L. Milliot, *Démembrements du habous*, Paris 1918; E. Pröbster, *Privateigentum und Kollektivismus im mohammedanischen Liegenschaftsrecht, insbesondere des Maghrib*, Leipzig 1931; ʿAlī Pasha Mubārak, *al-Khiṭaṭ al-tawfīḳiyya al-djadīda*, Būlāḳ, 1304-5, *passim*; Muḥammad Abū Zahra, *al-Ḥikr*, in *Madjallat al-Ḳānūn wa 'l-Iḳtiṣād*, x (1940), 93-151; B. Köprülü, *Evvelki hukukumuzda vakıf nev'iyetleri*, Fasıl IV: *Icareteynli vakıflar*, in *Istanbul Universitesi, Hukuk Fakültesi Mecmuası*, xviii (1952), 215-57; *al-Ahrām*, 3 August 1954; 6 May 1962.

(G. Baer)

AL-HILĀLĪ, Abu 'l-ʿAbbās Aḥmad b. ʿAbd al-ʿAzīz b. Rashīd al-Sidjilmāssī, Moroccan scholar who owned his *nisba* to Ibrāhīm b. Hilāl (d. 903/1497; see Brockelmann, S II, 348), the ancestor of a family of intellectuals in Sidjilmāssa. He was born in that town in 1113/1701, and began his studies there, going on to Fās for them, and then returning to the Tāfilālt, where he gathered round himself numerous pupils. He also obtained *idjāza*s from various eastern scholars on the occasions of two pilgrimages. He died at Madaghra (Tāfilālt) on 21 Rabīʿ I 1175/20 October 1761.

Al-Hilālī owed his fame to the quality of his teaching and to a fairly abundant output of works which entitle him to be considered as one of the greatest Moroccan scholars of the 12th/18th century. His work is partially preserved (see the list of mss. in Lakhdar), and includes some *fahrasa*s; a *riḥla*, which appears to be lost; some commentaries on works of *fiḳh*, on the subject of the Ḳurʾānic *ḳirāʾāt*, on lexicography and on logic; and finally, some poetry. His piety is displayed in a *ḳaṣīda* on the *asmāʾ ḥusnā* [*q.v.*] and above all in a poem of 129 verses in which he sums up the rule of life for the true believer, and recommends this latter to prepare for the next life in this present one, to fight against evil tendencies and desires and to conform to the o[bliga]tions of Islam. This poem enjoyed a very great [vogue] in Morocco.

Bibliography: Ḳādirī, *Nashr al-mathānī*, 1310/1892, ii, 273-5; Kattānī, *Fihris al-fa[hāris]*, Fās 1346-7/1927-8, ii, 421-3; Mukhtār Sūs[ī], *Maʿsūl*, Casablanca 1370/1950, iv, 32-52; Ma[ḵ]... *Shadjarat al-nūr al-zakiyya*, Cairo 1349/1930, 355; E. Lévi-Provençal, *Chorfa*, 316-17; Bro[ckel]mann, II, 456, S. II, 390; M. Lakhdar, *Vie [litté]raire*, 221-4 and bibl. given.

(E...)

HINDIBĀʾ, endive, *Cichorium endivia*, cultivated form of a species of the ligulate ch... family. Through Syriac *anṭūbiyā*, both terms *hin[dibāʾ]* and "endive" go back to Greek ἴντυβος, whi[ch is] recorded only sporadically; normally the pla[nt is] called σέρις, in the Arabic translations *sāris* or ... The nomenclature, rich and confused, can be [sum]marised as follows: the wild endive (*hindibāʾ b...*) was already known to the earlier Arab bota[nists] under various names: *ʿalath* or *ghalath* (Abū Ḥ[anīfa] al-Dīnawarī, *Le dictionnaire botanique*, ed. M. Ḥ[amī]dullah, Cairo 1973, nos. 735, 804), further *ya...* *baḳla murra*, *ṭarkhashḳūḳ* and variants (*op.* ... no. 1115). As indicated by the last but one nam[e, it] is a "bitter vegetable" and is therefore also c[alled] *amarūn* (and variants). The latter term is n[ot of] Greek origin, as the books on medicine have it, [but] is to be derived from Latin *amarum*. The cultiv[ated] endive, usually called *hindibāʾ* (also by al-Dīna[warī], *op. cit.*, nos. 1103, 1104), is the popular, tasty s[alad] plant, particularly widespread in the Arab ... and known there under the Mozarabic name *sharr...* or its arabicised form *sarrākh* (Castilian *sarraj...*; F. J. Simonet, *Glosario de voces ibéricas y latinas*, Madrid 1888, 584), while in Morocco the Berber *tīfāf* is mainly used.

The medicinal effect of endive was exceptio[nally] extensive, as can be seen in Ibn al-Bayṭār's article, where numerous older sources are indic[ated]. It is above all effective against eye-diseases and [pois]oning, in minced form also against boils wh[en in] their initial stage, and it strengthens the liver [and] stomach. The root helps against scorpion-stings, the juice against jaundice, constipation, persis[tent] fever and suppurations. The *ṭarkhashḳūḳ* menti[oned] above is *taraxacum*, the dandelion used in po[pular] medicine because of its bitter substance. On [the] cultivation of endive in Spanish agricultur[e, in] particular on sowing, planting out and irriga[tion,] ample information based on several sources is g[iven] by Ibn al-ʿAwwām, *K. al-Filāḥa*, tr. J.-J. Clém[ent-]Mullet, ii, Paris 1866, 146-9.

Bibliography: Dioscurides, *De materia me[dica]*, ed. M. Wellmann, i, Berlin 1907, 203 f. (= li... 132); *La "Materia médica" de Dioscorides*, ii, A... tr. Iṣṭafan b. Basīl, ed. C. E. Dubler and E. T[erés], Tetuán 1952, 200 f.; ʿAlī b. Rabban al-Ṭa[barī], *Firdaws al-ḥikma*, ed. Ṣiddīḳī, Berlin 1928, ... Rāzī, *Ḥāwī*, xxi, Ḥaydarābād 1388/1968, ... (no. 896); *Die pharmakolog. Grundsätze des ... Mansur ... Harawi*, tr. A. Ch. Achundow, ... 1893, 282, 408; Ibn al-Djazzār, *Iʿtimād*, Ms. ... sofya 3564, fol. 19a-b; Zahrāwī, *Taṣrīf*, Ms. ... Ağa 502, fol. 512a, 4-6; Ibn Sīnā, *Ḳānūn*, Būl[āḳ] ... 298; Bīrūnī, *Ṣaydala*, ed. H. M. Saʿīd, Ka[rachi] 1973, Arab. 378, Engl. 330; Ibn ʿAbdūn, *ʿUmd[at al-]ṭabīb*, Ms. Rabat, Bibl. Gén. 3505 D, fols. ... 14-168a, 22; Ibn Biklārish, *Mustaʿīnī*, Ms. Na[ples], Bibl. Naz. iii, F. 65, fol. 36b; Ghāfiḳī, *al-Ad[wiya] al-mufrada*, Ms. Rabat, Bibl. Gén. ḳ 155 i, ... 151a-152b; P. Guigues, *Les noms arabes dans* ...

n, in *JA*, 10ème série (1905), v., s.v. *Dundebe* . 165); Maimonides, *Sharḥ asmāʾ al-ʿuḳḳār*, ed. yerhof, Cairo 1940, no. 114; Ibn al-Bayṭār, *imiʿ*, Būlāḳ 1291, iv, 198-200, tr. Leclerc, 2263; Yūsuf b. ʿUmar, *Muʿtamad*, ed. M. al-ḳāʾ, Beirut 1395/1975, 539-41; Ibn al-Ḳuff, *nda*, Ḥaydarābād 1356, i, 264; Suwaydī, *Simāt*, Paris ar. 3004, fol. 81a-b; Nuwayrī, *Nihāya*, xi, ro 1935, 67-9; Ghassānī, *Ḥadīḳat al-azhār*, Ms. san Ḥ. ʿAbd al-Wahhāb, fols. 122b-123a; Dāwūd Anṭākī, *Tadhkira*, Cairo 1371/1952, i, 335 f.; *ḥfat al-aḥbāb*, ed. Renaud and Colin, Paris 1934, 124; I. Löw, *Die Flora der Juden*, i, 1928, 433-9; Asín Palacios, *Glosario de voces romances . . . los xi-xii*), Madrid-Granada 1943, no. 523; *El ro Agregà de Serapiom*, ed. G. Ineichen, ii, nice 1966, 121; *The medical formulary or ʾābādhīn of al-Kindī*, tr. M. Levey, Madison 1966, 244 (no. 40), 301 (no. 188).

(A. Dietrich)

NN, an inferior species of *djinn* [*q.v.*]. ıdī (*Murūdj*, iv, 11 = § 1340) states that many e believe that the Ḥinn are a sub-species of *inn* who are of a weaker and lowlier kind, but mns the belief in them as a delusion. Belief in inn, is, however, accepted by the Druzes (see uys, *Théogonie des Druses*, Paris 1863, n. 78, ; *Taḳsīm Djabal Lubnān* (Leeds Arab. MS 178, 4b); C. F. Seybold, *Die Drusenschrift: Kitāb aṭ Waldawāir. Das Buch der Punkte und Kreise*, hain 1902, 71), and they are occasionally men- elsewhere in Arabic literature, e.g. al-Djāḥiẓ, *ılāʾ*, Beirut 1960, 58.

Bibliography: in addition to the works men- ıed in the article, see D. R. W. Bryer, *The ins of the Druze religion*, in *Der Islam*, liii 76), 8, and the literature there cited.

(R. Y. Ebied and M. J. L. Young)

PPOCRATES [see buḳrāṭ, above]

PPOPOTAMUS [see faras al-mā, above]

ḤIṢĀFĪ, Ḥasanayn, founder of the al- ıyya al-Shādhiliyya *ṭarīḳa*. He was born in 1848-9 in the village of Kafr al-Ḥiṣāfa, Ḳalyū- province, Egypt.

ginally he was a *khalīfa* [*q.v.*] of an offshoot of adaniyya branch of the Darḳāwa [*q.v.*], known Makkiyya al-Fāsiyya. He had been initiated into *rīḳa* by its founder, Muḥammad b. Muḥammad ī (d. 1288/1872), when in Mecca for the pilgrim- n the year of the latter's death. He defied as ful certain forms of *dhikr* [*q.v.*] characteristic *ṭarīḳa* and introduced into it certain elements ching and ritual peculiar to al-Tidjāniyya [*q.v.*]. brought about a conflict within al-Makkiyya ıiyya which resulted in the formation of an endent and distinct *ṭarīḳa* which became known Ḥiṣāfiyya al-Shādhiliyya.

er Ḥasanayn's death in 1910, when the *ṭa-* position of supreme leadership had passed to n Muḥammad ʿAbd al-Wahhāb (d. 1949), vari- ctions emerged under local leaders who paid ominal allegiance to the successor of the *ṭarīḳa*'s er. One of these factions in Banī Suwayf, led by mmad Aḥmad al-Tukhāwī (d. 1361/1942), ped into an independent and distinct *ṭarīḳa* n as al-Ṭukhāwiyya. Another faction in al- ūdiyya (Buḥayra province) led by Aḥmad al- rī was virtually severed from the main body *ṭarīḳa* when it was organised into the Djamʿiyya āfiyya al-Khayriyya, an organisation which he root and forerunner of the Ikhwān al- nūn [*q.v.*].

Ḥasanayn al-Ḥiṣāfī was buried in Damanhūr, where his shrine is venerated; a *mawlid* [*q.v.*] is celebrated there yearly.

Bibliography: ʿAlī al-Djaʿfarāwī, *al-Manhal al-ṣāfī fī manāḳib al-sayyid Ḥasanayn al-Ḥiṣāfī*, Cairo 1330/1911-12, contains the principal biography in addition to a number of his sermons (71-87) and a short treatise in which he gives instruction in the fundamentals of *taṣawwuf* and elaborates his position with respect to *dhikr* (61-109). This section may be found also in a much more expanded form in the principal manual of the order, which is Ḥasanayn al-Ḥiṣāfī's *al-Sabīl al-wāḍiḥ*, Cairo 1951. Other writings of al-Ḥiṣāfī are mentioned in a biography by Muḥammad Zakī Mudjāhid, *al-Aʿlām al-sharḳiyya*, 4 vols., Cairo 1949-63, iii, 101 f., which is largely based upon the biography by al-Djaʿfarāwī. A discussion of the early history of the order and of its exceptional position among the *ṭarīḳas* in the 19th century Egypt may be found in F. de Jong, *Ṭuruq and ṭuruq-linked institutions in 19th century Egypt*, Leiden 1978, 101-3.

(F. de Jong)

ḤIYAL (a.), with the basic meaning of "devices, subterfuges", has had its sense considerably extended, and in particular, denotes in Classical Arabic ingenious contrivances, automata, various pieces of machinery, and finally, the science of mechanics. Since the article Ḥiyal in Vol. III deals mainly with legal fictions and ruses and with casuistic processes, the present article is especially concerned with automata, with the Arabic works describing them and with the tradition of which they are the most remarkable expression.

The mediaeval Arabic books on machines are often called "automata treatises" by modern writers, but the designation is somewhat misleading. The books deal with *ḥiyal* [*q.v.*], which in one of its senses denotes mechanical contrivances and covers a much wider field than that of automata. The descriptions in the treatises, supplemented by references in histories and by archaeological evidence, enables us to list the following constructions: water-clocks and candle-clocks; trick vessels and liquid dispensers, measuring devices; fountains, lamps; water-raising machines; musical automata; locks. According to Abū ʿAbd Allāh al-Khwārazmī [*q.v.*], who compiled his scientific encyclopaedia *Mafātīḥ al-ʿulūm* towards the end of the 4th/10th century, trebuchets (*mandjanīḳ*) are also *ḥiyal* (ed. van Vloten, Leiden 1895, 247). The word therefore means virtually any mechanical contrivance from small toys to large machines. *Ḥiyal* may indeed be automata, as in the case of trick vessels; they may display a variety of automata, for instance on the monumental water-clocks; or the automatic element may be completely lacking. The closest Arabic word for automaton is in fact simply "movement" (*ḥaraka*), which is used frequently by the writers, e.g. al-Djazarī [*q.v.* above] and Ibn al-Nadīm (*Fihrist*, 397). Often a variety of *ḥarakāt* is described for the more complex devices, and the craftsman is instructed to select those that suit his tastes and purposes. The concern of this article is mainly with the contrivances that incorporated automatic effect.

Several treatises composed in Arabic are known to us, including: *Kitāb al-Ḥiyal* by the Banū Mūsa, written in Baghdād *ca.* 236/850 (Hauser; Wiedemann and Hauser - W.H. 1); *Kitāb ʿAmal al-sāʿāt wa 'l-ʿamal bihā*) by Riḍwān, written in 600/1203, describing the repairs of a monumental water-clock built by his father Muḥammad al-Sāʿātī in Damascus *ca.*

545/1150 (W.H. 2); *Kitāb fī maʿrifat al-ḥiyal al-handasiyya* by al-Djazarī, written in 602/1206 (Hill 1); and a treatise on clocks written by Taḳī al-Dīn b. Maʿrūf (932-72/1526-65), namely *al-Kawākib al-dawriyya* (ed. and tr. with commentary by S. Tekeli, *The clocks in [the] Ottoman Empire in [the] sixteenth century*, Ankara 1966). A second work by Taḳī al-Dīn, dealing with various types of machines, entitled *al-Ṭuruḳ al-saniyya fī 'l-ālāt al-ruḥāniyya* has recently been edited in Arabic (Aḥmad Y. al-Ḥasan, Aleppo University 1976).

Almost certainly there are manuscripts yet to be discovered, and there are known manuscripts that await close study. Perhaps the most important of these is a manuscript in the Biblioteca Medicea Laurenziana in Florence. Numbered 152 (formerly 282) it is catalogued as *anonymi tractatus de mechanicis*. The section of the work that concerns us here is entitled *Kitāb al-Asrār fī natāʾidj al-afkār* and occurs amid a number of mathematical treatises attributed to Abū ʿAbd Allāh, known as Ibn Muʿādh, who worked in Cordoba in the 5th/11th century. (For Ibn Muʿādh, see the article *al-Jayyānī* in the *Dictionary of Scientific Biography*.) It has not yet been possible to make a close study of this treatise, which is dated 664/1266. It is unfortunately in poor condition, with several of its pages torn, but it is written in a clear Maghribī script and it may be possible to decipher large parts of it. An examination of photographs of some of the leaves indicates that it describes water-clocks, and other machines. The drawings are well-executed and suggest considerable sophistication—for instance, they incorporate geartrains in the main parts of the machinery. This work, even if its authorship cannot be established with certainty, may prove to be of considerable importance for the study of mediaeval Islamic mechanical technology.

Apart from the treatises themselves, there are other attestations to support the existence of a thriving tradition of machine technology in mediaeval Islam. Al-Djazarī mentions a candle-clock built by a certain Yūnus al-Asṭurlābī (Hill 1, 87) and a musical automaton constructed by Hibat Allāh b. al-Ḥusayn (Hill 1, 170), otherwise known to us as an astrolabist (Suter, 117). There are also references to be found in the works of geographers and historians concerning mechanical devices which they had seen: for instance, the striking water-clock with automata presented to Charlemagne by vassals of Hārūn al-Rashīd (Eginhard, *Annales Francorum* in *Monumenta German. Script.* i, 194), and the silver tree with whistling birds in the garden of the Caliph al-Muḳtadir [see BAGHDĀD, History]. Remains of two water-clocks built in the 8th/14th century are still to be seen in Fās (D. de Solla Price, *Mechanical water clocks of the 14th century in Fez, Morocco*, in *Ithaca*, 26 VIII-2 XI [1962], 599-602). It cannot be doubted, therefore, that there was a tradition of mechanical engineering in Islam that probably originated in the 2nd/8th century and continued until it merged with the developing European engineering in the 10th/16th century. It was a tradition that was concerned mainly with devices to provide amusement and aesthetic pleasure, with some utilitarian elements, and almost certainly reached the peak of its achievements in the work of al-Djazarī.

One impetus for the establishment of this tradition was undoubtedly the availability in Baghdād in the 3rd/9th century of Arabic translations of Greek treatises, especially those of Philo (*ca.* 230 B.C.) and Hero (*fl. ca.* 60 A.D.). The works of Hero, in particular, were highly regarded in mediaeval Islam—several, including one on automata, are mentione[d by] Ibn al-Nadīm (*Fihrist*, 397). A number of the [Banū] Mūsā's devices closely resemble devices des[cribed] by Philo and Hero, and there seems little [doubt] that the brothers had access to the Greek tre[atises]. It would be incorrect, however, to assume that [Philo] and Hero were the sole inspiration for the Banū [Mūsā] and their successors, or even the most importan[t].

From the time of Archimedes onwards, it seems certain that a tradition of mechanical [engi]neering, more practical than that represented b[y the] known works of Philo and Hero, had spread thr[ough]out the eastern Mediterranean and western [Asia]. Monumental water-clocks, for instance, had [been] built in Syria in Byzantine times (H. Diels, *Üb[er die] von Prokop beschriebene Uhr von Gaza*, in *Abh. P[reuss.] Akad. Wiss. Berlin*, Phil.-Hist. Klasse [1917], N[o. ...]). According to Riḍwān (W.H. 2, 179-80), this tra[dition] was continued in Damascus in the Umayyad p[eriod] and remained unbroken up to the time of his f[ather]. Riḍwān, in the same passage, also mentions a [two-]way transmission of ideas between Byzantium [and] Sāsānid Iran. It is indeed highly probable tha[t me]chanised technology developed in Iran in the Sā[sānid] period and continued into Islamic times: fro[m the] Banū Mūsā onwards many of the technical expre[ssions] used are of Persian origin. Nor can a similar [ex]change between Iran and India be left out of acc[ount].

Activity also continued in Byzantium. A tr[eatise] on a complicated musical automaton, pro[bably] written in Byzantium in the 1st/7th or 2nd/8th [cen]tury, was described by al-Djazarī (Hill 1-170[;] E. Wiedemann, *Aufsätze zur arabischen Wissensc[hafts]geschichte*, Hildesheim 1970, ii, 50). Three A[rabic] versions of this treatise, ascribed to a certain A[pollo]nius, are extant. A most important work, attri[buted] to Archimedes, and describing the construction [of a] water-clock, exists in several Arabic mss. [Both] Riḍwān and al-Djazarī acknowledge that the water-machinery of their monumental clocks [was] derived from the "Archimedes" treatise (H[ill 1;] W.H. 3). The origins of this work are still some[what] obscure. It may have contained basic ideas [of] Archimedes, developed by Philo, with later accre[tions] from Byzantine and Islamic writers. Indeed, [the] treatise exemplifies the problems that arise whe[n we] try to identify the various cultural elements i[n the] Arabic "translations". The "Philonic" corpu[s, to] cite another example, has been transmitted in [two] versions, a Greek fragment, and a late Arabic [ver]sion. The last-named certainly includes later [Hel]lenistic and Islamic additions, and it is dif[ficult] to isolate Philo's own contributions.

For the present, we can make the following [hy]potheses for the origins and development of Isl[amic] mechanical technology: (1) At the time of the Isl[amic] conquests, there was an established tradition f[or the] manufacture of water-clocks and other mechanica[l de]vices in an area that stretched from the eastern [Me]diterranean to India. Chinese influence cann[ot be] excluded. This tradition was recorded not only in [doc]umentary form, but in the experience of crafts[men] and in the existence of earlier constructions. (2) [This] tradition was continued in Islam, but no re[cords] were committed to writing before the Banū Mū[sā in] the 3rd/9th century. The Banū Mūsā drew [on] translations from Greek treatises, and from th[e ex]perience of craftsmen, adding many refinen[ents] of their own. (3) Later writers, such as al-Dja[zarī,] were able to exercise an eclectic judgement, [taking] elements from Greek works and from the establ[ished] Islamic corpus as they saw fit. Because al-Djaza[rī]

ular was a fine engineer, he made significant
vements on the work of his predecessors. (4)
as essentially practical engineering, and the
ic writers derived much of their knowledge
the works of other craftsmen—astrolabists, mill-
ts, irrigation specialists, metalworkers, jewel-
and the makers of articles for domestic use and
nent.
mic mechanical engineering was based upon a
sticated, if empirical, use of the principles of
tatics, hydrostatics and mechanics. Their
ials included timber, sheet brass and copper,
bronze, iron (for small components, nails and
, iron and copper wire, rope and string. From
they fashioned the devices and mechanisms
oduce the desired effects: vessels of various
s, figures of men and animals, tanks, air-vessels,
tube and concentric siphons, pulleys, tipping-
ets, axles and bearings, pipes, conical valves,
with multiple borings, gears, and special
anisms designed for individual machines.
es, graduated for a given flow, were made from
s of onyx.
ghty-five of the Banū Mūsā's one hundred
es, and about twenty of al-Djazarī's fifty, are
vessels of various kinds. They demonstrate a
dering variety of effects. For example, wine and
r were poured into a jar and issued in succession
the same tap; a pitcher would not accept any
liquid once inpouring was interrupted; several
ls could be withdrawn separately from the same
when tilted, a pitcher could be allowed to dis-
ge or not, according to the wish of the pourer
revent discharge he covered a concealed air-hole
his finger). These effects were obtained by using
ertoire of about ten basic motifs, together with
onents designed for individual machines. These
onents were assembled inside the main con-
r, often with great ingenuity. In all the cases, the
l itself was the automaton, and the visible ef-
was the discharge of liquid. The fountains des-
d by the Banū Mūsā and al-Djazarī, in which the
arge changes shape at regular intervals, are es-
ally large versions of the trick vessels, but with
ch greater aesthetic content.
doubtedly, the large water-clocks are the most
rtant constructions of the Islamic engineers,
he engineering skills that went into their manu-
re, for their beauty, and for their relevance to
istory of mechanical engineering. Two of al-Dja-
s clocks (category I, 3, 4) are operated by a
ersible float, the *tardjahār*, a bowl with a grad-
d orifice in its underside that submerges in a
period. The *tardjahār* is an ancient device for
uring time, but these clocks are the only instance
now of in which the *tardjahār* is incorporated in
ing machinery. They have the additional feature
at some of the automata are not simply for dis-
, but also form an essential part of the operational
. The standard type of monumental clock, how-
, is exemplified by the first two described by al-
arī, and by the clock constructed by Muḥammad
ʿātī. Apart from its use of masonry for its
g, al-Sāʿātī's clock is very similar to al-Djazarī's
umental clock (category I, ch. 1), which may be
n to exemplify this type of timepiece. This clock
reconstructed in the Science Museum, London,
the 1976 World of Islam Festival; it is quite
tiful, and works perfectly. The display screen
out 3.50 metres by 1.60 metres in width. At the
om of the machine are the figures of five musi-
s—two trumpeters, two drummers and a cymbalist—who perform at the sixth, ninth and twelfth hours. Above these figures is a semicircle of glass roundels, at the side of which are the figures of brass falcons. Above the apex of the semicircle are two rows of twelve doors each, in front of which a small representation of the moon moves at a steady speed. The clock operates on "solar" or "temporal" hours, obtained by dividing the hours of daylight by twelve. Every hour one upper door opens to reveal a standing figure, one lower door revolves to show a different colour, each of the falcons drops a bronze ball from its beak on to a cymbal, and one of the glass roundels becomes fully illuminated. The clock is crowned with a Zodiac circle, painted with the appropriate signs, and having glass discs representing the sun and moon set to their correct positions in the Zodiac. The circle rotates at a constant speed throughout the day. All the automata, except the musicians, are operated by the steady sinking of a heavy float in a cylindrical reservoir—a string from the top of the float passes through a pulley system to the actuating mechanisms. The outflow from the reservoir is kept constant by a sophisticated system of feed-back control and flow-regulation. The musicians are made to perform by the sudden release of the outlet water, which is collected in a special tank.

Taken as a whole, one may distinguish the work of the Islamic engineers from that of their predecessors by their greater pre-occupation with automatic control. For example, their confident use of conical valves in flow systems, the use of a crank in a machine, segmental gears, etc. They also used manufacturing techniques that were unknown in earlier times, notably the use of closed mould-boxes with green sand for casting metals. Many of the components and techniques of this identifiably Islamic engineering were later incorporated into European machine technology, but we have as yet little certain knowledge of how and when the transmission took place. As far as we know, none of the Arabic machine treatises was translated into a European language before modern times, but the dissemination of engineering ideas and practices has always been fairly rapid and, until recently, without documentary assistance. Traveller's reports, contacts between craftsmen, and inspection by craftsmen of machines built by their predecessors, were the usual means for the transmission of mechanical knowledge. Al-Djazarī, for instance, mentions several times that he had inspected machines made by earlier craftsmen, or that their constructions had been described to him (Hill 1-83, 170, 199). It seems likely that the passage of information occurred at different times and places, although the designs may not have been put to immediate use, but have lain dormant until their usefulness became apparent to later generations of engineers. It seems probable, however, that the most important transmission took place in the Iberian peninsula towards the close of the 6th/12th century, with the adoption by Christian Spain of Islamic ideas, particularly the monumental water-clock, which itself incorporated most of the techniques and components used by Islamic engineers. The large clocks of al-Sāʿātī and al-Djazarī do not incorporate gears in their main operating mechanisms, but the "Archimedes" clock and the clocks in the "Ibn Muʿādh" treatise do so. These clocks are the direct ancestors of the mechanical clock; if one replaces the steadily descending float with an escapement-controlled weight; then the mechanical clock, with its driving mechanisms, and automata, does not differ essentially from its predecessor. The mechanical clock exercised a potent influence upon the development of machine technology, and the waterclock is therefore directly relevant to this development. Islamic components and techniques were also incorporated into European engineering from the 7th/13th century onwards and were an important element in the establishment of modern machine design, particularly in the fields of delicate mechanisms and control systems.

There were less tangible influences of the Islamic automata tradition. Culturally, they are related to the "live" puppets of western literature and folklore, such as Pinocchio and the doll Olympia in one of the *Tales of Hoffman.* The cultivation of aesthetic delight, exemplified by the fountains of the Banū Mūsā and al-D̲j̲azarī, was continued in Europe by men such as Tomaso da Siena, who created the water gardens at the Villa d'Este and Bagnaia. More importantly, the representation of cosmological and biological phenomena was one of the factors that led men to adopt a rationalistic, mechanistic view of the universe, an attitude that has been immensely fruitful in the development of modern science.

Bibliography: (in addition to works mentioned in the text): There are as yet no Arabic editions of any of the *ḥiyal* treatises and one must therefore have recourse to translations. (An edition of al-D̲j̲azarī's work is however being prepared by A. Y. Ḥasan and will be published by Aleppo University.) (In the works cited the location of the Arabic ms. is given.) Descriptions of thirteen of the Banū Mūsā devices, with illustrations and notes are given by E. Wiedemann and F. Hauser in *Über Trinkgefässe und Tafelaufsätze*, in *Isl.*, viii (1918), 268-91 (W.H. 1); the remainder are dealt with by Hauser in *Über das Kitāb al-Ḥiyal — das Werk über die sinnreichen Anordnungen der Benū Mūsā*, in *Abhandl. zur Gesch. der Naturwissenschaften und der Medizin*, Erlangen 1922. (A fully annotated English translation of the entire work is currently being prepared by the writer.) For al-D̲j̲azarī, see D. R. Hill, *The Book of knowledge of ingenious devices*, Dordrecht 1975, a fully annotated English version (Hill 1). Riḍwān's treatise is available in an abbreviated translation with notes and illustrations, by Wiedemann and Hauser, *Über die Uhren in Bereich der Islamischen Kultur*, in *Nova Acta der Kaiserl. Leop.-Carol Deutschen Akad. der Naturforscher*, c (Halle 1915), 169-272 (W.H. 2). Two translations of the pseudo-Archimedes are available, both with notes and illustrations: Wiedemann and Hauser, *Uhr des Archimedes and zwei andere Vorrichtungen*, in *Nova Acta*, ciii (1918), No. 2, 164-202 (W.H. 3); D. R. Hill, *On the construction of water-clocks*, London 1976 (Hill 2). For the Arabic version of Hero's *Mechanics* and Philo's *Pneumatics*, there are edited Arabic texts with French translations, both by Carra de Vaux: *Les mécaniques ou l'élevateur de Héron d'Alexandrie sur la version arabe de Qostà ibn Lûqâ*, in *JA*, 9e Série (1893), i, 386-472; ii, 152-92, 193-269, 420-514; and *Le livre des appareils pneumatiques et des machines hydrauliques par Philon de Byzance*, in *Académie des Inscriptions et Belles Lettres*, xxxviii (1903), Pt. 1. A recent work on Philo is F. D. Prager, *Philo of Byzantium*, in *Pneumatica*, Wiesbaden 1974; there is useful discussion of the Latin and Greek versions, but the Arabic section is inadequate, and inferior in every way to Carra de Vaux's edition. For Hero's pneumatics, there is an English translation, B. Woodcroft, *The Pneumatics of Hero of Alexandria*, London 1851, re-issued with an introduction by M. B. Hall, London 1971. The studies of A. G. Drachmann are of the greatest value for the [cut off] cal tradition, notably *The mechanical techn[cut off] of Greek and Roman antiquity*, Copenh[cut off] Madison-London 1936; and *Ktesibios, Philo[cut off] Heron; a study in ancient pneumatics*, in *Historica Scientarium Naturalium et Medicina[cut off]* Bibliotheca Universitatis Hauniensis, Copenh[cut off] iv (1946), 1-197. For automata in genera[cut off] A. Chapius and E. Droz, *Automata*, tr. A. [cut off] Neuchatel-London 1958; D. de Solla [cut off] *Automata and the origins of mechanism and me[cut off] istic philosophy*, in *Technology and Culture* (1964), 9-23. On the influence of the Greek [cut off] tion, there is a valuable survey by Price in *from the Greeks*, Science History Publications, [cut off] York 1975, 51-62. The Indian tradition of mec[cut off] cal devices and its connections with Greek [cut off] Islamic ideas is described by V. Raghav[cut off] *Yantras or mechanical contrivances in Ancient I[cut off]* in *The Indian Institute of Culture*, Basavan[cut off] Banglalore, Transaction No. 10 (1952) 1-31. [cut off] index to J. Needham's *Science and civilisati[cut off] China*, iv/1, Cambridge 1965, should be cons[cut off] for transmission from and into China, partic[cut off] the entries under "Automata", "Clocks", "C[cut off] work" and "Water-power". (D. R. Hi[cut off]

HOESEIN DJAJADININGRAT, PANG[cut off] ARIA, Muslim scholar and Indonesian st[cut off] man, historian and linguist (1886-1960).

Born at Kramat Watu, the chief town of a [cut off] district in the residence Bantam (Bantĕn) in [cut off] Java, where his father was a government off[cut off] he sprang from an old prominent family which [cut off] related to the former Sultans of Bantam [see I[cut off] NESIA, iv]. In his early youth, Hoesein's hist[cut off] interest must have been evoked by reminisc[cut off] of the period of the Bantam Sultans, kept [cut off] through stories and legends and through old buil[cut off] such as the monumental mosque in the former [cut off] of Bantam, the remains of the Sultan's resi[cut off] (Kraton) and pleasure gardens. More than any [cut off] region of Java, Bantam is also the area of cent[cut off] old Muslim piety; there are many *pĕsantrèns* [cut off] gious schools), where the Muslim sciences are st[cut off] industriously from Arabic text-books, and in e[cut off] village there are people who have performed [cut off] pilgrimage to Mecca at least once. At an early [cut off] Hoesein was destined for a European education [cut off] academic career by his progressive father, who [cut off] been promoted to be Regent of Serang. After prev[cut off] training in Batavia and at the gymnasium in Lei[cut off] Hoesein was matriculated into Leiden Universi[cut off] 1905 as the first Indonesian student of the se[cut off] "Languages and Literatures of the East-In[cut off] Archipelago". He read Sanskrit with J. S. Sp[cut off] and Arabic, first with M. J. de Goeje and, from [cut off] onwards, with the latter's successor C. Sn[cut off] Hurgronje. When a prize was offered for the [cut off] essay on data preserved in Malay works concer[cut off] the history of the sultanate of Atjèh, he was [cut off] tinguished with a golden medal of honour. In [cut off] he received his Ph. D. degree for the thesis *Crit[cut off] beschrijving van de Sadjarah Banten* ("Critical ex[cut off] nation of the Sajarah Bantĕn"), a Javanese chro[cut off] dealing with the history of Bantĕn, but contai[cut off] also traditions concerning the earlier history of [cut off] and the period of its conversion to Islam. Bac[cut off] Indonesia, Hoesein was appointed to the acad[cut off] function of "official for the study of Indian [cut off] Indonesian) languages" and commissioned to de[cut off] himself to the Achinese language. At the begin[cut off] of 1914 he went to Atjèh and, after his retur[cut off]

.via by mid-1915, continued his studies with aid of the material collected, the extensive .nese literature preserved in manuscript, and the assistance of Achinese informants. His *ısch-Nederlandsch Woordenboek* ("Achinese-Dutch ionary") was published in two volumes in .

ɔing the only Indonesian Ph.D., he several times to sit on various official committees, and in he was appointed as assistant to the then govern-tal commissioner for Native Affairs, G. A. J. eu, and as such he was mainly in charge of Islamic irs. From 1920 till 1924 he was Assistant-Adviser Native Affairs to the Government, and then ived an appointment as a professor at the Uni-ity of Law, newly-erected in Batavia, where he ht Muslim Law and Indonesian languages. n this period date a number of articles on Indo-an languages and literature, Islamic and Indo-an history; as monographs were published: *Mohammedaansche wet en het geestesleven der ɔnesische Mohammedanen* ("Muslim law and itual life of the Indonesian Muslims") (1925), and: *magische achtergrond van de Maleische pantoen* he magical background of the Malay pantun") 3).

[oesein turned his attention to statesmanship, n, in 1935, he became a member of the Council Dutch East India, the highest government mittee. As such, he had a great part in the rm of religious Muslim judicial administration in a, which led to such institutions as the panghulu-rts (religious courts) and in 1938, to the Court of mic Affairs (the higher religious court) at Batavia. ile Hoesein was holding for one year the office Director of the Department of Education and rship, the first Indonesian Faculty of Letters opened (4 December 1940). During the war 42-5) and the first disturbed years afterwards, mostly remained inactive, reading and studying membership of the Council of Dutch East India ed in 1946). When in 1948 the provisional Federal ernment was formed, he became Secretary of te for Education, Arts and Sciences. As such, was present at the Round Table-Conference at Hague in 1949. When the Republic of Indonesia ame independent on 27 December 1949, Hoesein his office, but his scholarly qualities were rec-ised in 1951, when he was invited to take the ir of Arabic and Islamology at the University of onesia in Jakarta (formerly Batavia). Now over enty, he was free to teach the subject of his pref-nce; he chose the history of Indonesia's conver-1 to Islam. He published some more articles and ɔte the chapter on "Islam in Indonesia" in Kenneth Morgan, *Islam—the Straight Path: Islam inter-ted by Muslims* (New York 1958), in which are ated the origin of Islam in Indonesia, religious ıcation, the actual situation of Islam in Indonesia, anged according to the concepts *sharīʿa*, dogma, ism and reform, and finally a characterisation Indonesian Islam. He died in 1960.

A Javanese aristocrat by origin and through his rriage to a daughter of the Javanese royal house of ngkunagara, and the first Indonesian to devote nself to the study of Islam after a Western acade-c education, Hoesein Djajadiningrat remained a vout Muslim throughout his life and as such en-ed the confidence of his co-religionists. Through uprightness and justice he was hold in reverence Indonesians, Arabs and Dutch alike.

Bibliography: given in the article. A list of Hoesein's writings, compiled by Atja, has been published in *Bahasa dan Budaja*, viii/5-6 (1960).

(G. F. Pijper)

HOGGAR [see AHAGGAR].

HOMONYM [see AḌDĀD].

HOMS [see ḤIMS].

HOOPOE [see HUDHUD].

HORN [see BŪḲ].

HORSEMAN [see FĀRIS].

HORTICULTURE [see BŪSTĀN].

HOSPITALERS, KNIGHTS [see DĀWIYA, above].

HOURI [see ḤŪR].

ḤUBAYSH B. AL-ḤASAN AL-DIMASHḲĪ, surnamed al-Aʿsam "the one with the withered limbs", translator of Greek medicinal writings into Arabic. He was a Christian and a nephew of the master-translator Ḥunayn b. Isḥāḳ [*q.v.*], who esteemed him highly as a collaborator and considered him very talented but not particularly assiduous. The quality of his translations was so high that later they were held often for Ḥunayn's work; because of the similarity of the consonant ductus, uncritical users are even said to have been of the opinion that the name Ḥubaysh—the real translator—should be changed into Ḥunayn. His dates are not known; he may have lived at the ʿAbbāsid court towards the end of the 3rd/9th century. He belonged to those prominent translators who had been awarded by the Banu 'l-Munadjdjim a fixed monthly salary of *ca.* 500 *dīnārs* (*Fihrist*, ed. Flügel, 243, 18-20).

Ḥubaysh had only a very scant knowledge of Greek, or none at all; with the exception of the Hippocratic oath and the herb-book of Dioscurides, he translated Galen's works exclusively, 35 of them from Arabic into Syriac, and three from Syriac into Arabic (cf. *Ḥunain ibn Isḥāq über die syrischen und arabischen Galen-Übersetzungen*, ed. and tr. G. Bergsträsser, *AKM*, xvii/2, Leipzig 1925, index, 45). His language is that "of a scholar who aims only at clear-ness, who is little trained linguistically and does not care much for linguistic beauty, but on the other hand sets himself to some kind of correctness" (G. Bergsträsser, *Ḥunain ibn Isḥāḳ und seine Schule*, Leiden 1913, 41). On the basis of the then known translations, Bergsträsser (*ibid.*, 28-46) classified the linguistic peculiarities of Ḥubaysh; additions are given by M. Meyerhof and J. Schacht, *Galen über die medizinischen Namen*, in *Abh. Preuss. Akad. Wiss.*, Phil.-hist. Kl., Berlin 1931, 4-7. In view of the tight relation between teacher and pupil, the many similarities in language of Ḥunayn and Ḥubaysh are not surprising.

Besides the translated works, Hubaysh is also the author of original writings. They are completely based on his knowledge of Greek medicine, but, as far as pharmacology is concerned, they often reach further back and prove that already in those days other sources were used or that personal observations were introduced. Mention should be made firstly of his additions (*ziyādāt*) to Ḥunayn's *Kitāb al-Masāʾil al-ṭibbiyya*, which became extraordinarily widely dif-fused, cf. A. Dietrich, *Medicinalia arabica*, Göttingen 1966, 39-44; this enlarged edition became a standard work which was to occupy quite a number of com-mentators and epitomists. Other works of Ḥubaysh preserved in manuscript are: (1) *Kitāb Iṣlāḥ al-adwiya al-mushila*; (2) *K. al-Aghdhiya*; (3) *K. fi 'l-Istisḳāʾ* and (4) *Maḳāla fi 'l-nabḍ*. Only from quotations are known: (5) *K. al-Adwiya al-mufrada* (often cited by Ibn al-Bayṭār); (6) *Taʿrīf amrāḍ al-ʿayn*, quoted in Khalīfa's *al-Kāfī fi 'l-kuḥl* (see J. Hirschberg, etc. in *Anhang der Abh. Preuss. Akad.*

Wiss., Berlin 1905, 13, 20 f., and idem, *Die arabischen Augenärzte*, ii, Leipzig 1905, 158); and (7) a dispensatorium (*aḳrābādhīn*), possibly composed not by Ḥubaysh but by Ḥunayn.

Bibliography: (besides the works quoted in the article): Ibn al-Nadīm, *Fihrist*, ed. Flügel, 297; Ibn al-Ḳifṭī, *Ḥukamā'* 177; Ibn Abī Uṣaybiʿa, *ʿUyūn*, i, 202 and *passim*; Barhebraeus, *Duwal*, ed. Ṣālḥānī, Beirut 1890, 252 f.; idem, *Chronicon syriacum*, ed. P. Bedjan, Paris 1890, 163; M. Meyerhof, in *Isis*, viii (1926), 690-702, 708; H. Ritter and R. Walzer, *Arabische Übersetzungen griechischer Ärzte in Stambuler Bibliotheken*, in *Abh. Preuss. Akad. Wiss.*, Phil.-hist. Kl., Berlin 1934, 829; G. Bergsträsser, *Neue Materialien zu Ḥunain ibn Isḥāq's Galen-Bibliographie*, in *AKM*, xix/2, Leipzig 1932, 32 (lists) and *passim*; L. Leclerc, *Histoire de la médecine arabe*, i, Paris 1876, 154-7; M. Steinschneider, *Die arabischen Übersetzungen aus dem Griechischen*, new impression Graz 1960, 266; G. Graf, *GCAL*, ii, 1947, 130 f.; Brockelmann, I², 227 f., S I, 369; M. Ullmann, *Die Medizin im Islam*, Leiden 1970, 119 and *passim*; F. Sezgin, *GAS*, iii, Leiden 1970, 265 f.

(A. Dietrich)

ḤUD̲H̲AYFA b. **ʿABD** b. Fuḳaym b. ʿAdī [see al-ḳalammas]

ḤUDŪD al-**ʿĀLAM**, "The limits of the world", the title of a concise but very important anonymous Persian geography of the world, Islamic and non-Islamic, composed towards the end of the 4th/10th century in Gūzgān [*q.v.*] in what is now northern Afg̲h̲ānistān. The work exists in a unique manuscript of the 7th/13th century (the "Toumansky manuscript") which came to light in Buk̲h̲ārā in 1892. The Persian text was first edited and published by W. Barthold at Leningrad in 1930 as *Ḥudūd al-ʿālem, rukopisī Tumanskago*, with an important preface (this last reprinted in his *Sočinenya*, viii, 504-46; an English tr. of this was included by Minorsky in his translation of the whole work, see below), and subsequently by D̲j̲alāl al-Dīn Ṭihrānī, Tehran 1314/1935, and Manūčihr Sutūda, Tehran 1340/1962. Soon after Barthold's edition appeared, V. Minorsky produced an English translation, together with a lengthy commentary of immense erudition, *Ḥudūd al-ʿĀlam, "The regions of the world", a Persian geography 372 A.H. — 982 A.D.*, GMS, N.S. xi, London 1937. A second edition (London 1970) includes Minorsky's own "Addenda to the *Ḥudūd al-ʿĀlam*", originally published in *BSOAS*, xvii (1955), 250-76, and also a second series of addenda.

The authorship of the work still remains a puzzle, though it was dedicated to the *amīr* of Gūzgān, of the Farīg̲h̲ūnid line, Abu 'l-Ḥārit̲h̲ Muḥammad b. Aḥmad b. Farīg̲h̲ūn [see farīg̲h̲unids]. Minorsky suggested the possibility, though the evidence is indirect and requires further investigation, that the author might have been the S̲h̲aʿyā b. Farīg̲h̲ūn [see ibn farīg̲h̲ūn below] who wrote an early encyclopaedia of the sciences, the *D̲j̲awāmiʿ al-ʿulūm*, for an *amīr* of Čag̲h̲āniyān [*q.v.*] on the upper Oxus in the middle years of the 4th/10th century; cf. his *Ibn Farīghūn and the Ḥudūd al-ʿĀlam*, in *A locust's leg, studies in honour of S. H. Taqizadeh*, London 1962, 189-96, reprinted in his *Iranica, twenty articles*, Tehran 327-32.

The form of the *Ḥudūd al-ʿālam* is concise and pithy. Unlike such contemporary geographers as Ibn Ḥawḳal and Muḳaddasī, the author does not personally seem to have been a traveller, but he relied instead on earlier sources and reports, such as those of Ibn K̲h̲urradād̲h̲bih [*q.v.*] and, apparently, Allāh Muḥammad al-D̲j̲ayhānī [see al-d̲j̲ayh above], except for the immediate region of his in northern Afg̲h̲ānistān. Its archaic language style are interesting pieces of evidence for Persian prose, cf. G. Lazard, *La langue des plu ciens monuments de la prose persane*, Paris 1963, Original features of the author's approach ar concern for exact enumeration of physical fea (the seven seas, rivers, lakes, islands, etc.) of inhabited world; his division of this last into t main parts, Asia, Europe and "Libya" (= Afr his enumeration of 45 distinct countries (*nāḥ* lying to the north of the equator; and the unus large proportion of space allotted to the non-Isl lands, even though the Muslim ones, surveyed rou from east to west, naturally occupy the greater of the work. The information on the local topogra of Afg̲h̲ānistān is probably first-hand, with sp emphasis on Gūzgān, G̲h̲arčistan, G̲h̲ūr, etc.; material on the Eurasian and Turkish steppes their peoples is likewise very significant. Fin the author furnishes useful details about local ducts and trade movements.

Bibliography: In addition to references g in the article, see I. Y̲u̲. Kračkovskiy, *Arabsk geografičeskaya literatura*, in *Sočineny̲a̲*, iv, Mos Leningrad 1957, 224-6, partial Arabic tr. C 1963, 223-4; A. Miquel, *La géographie humain monde musulman jusqu'au milieu du XI*ᵉ *s* Paris 1967, xxxiii, 398-9; see also d̲j̲ug̲h̲rāf iv, c, i.

(C. E. Boswort

HUNAYN, site of a mediaeval seaport western Algeria, not far west of Beni-Saf (B. and, as the crow flies, about 45 km. N. W. of Tlem Within a walled area (41,000 sq. m.) are ruins *ḳaṣba* and traces of a mosque's, and possibly al *ḥammām*'s, foundations. On dry land below the *ḳ* lie the remains of a rectangular interior dock (4,25 m.), once protected by rampart and towers and tered, seemingly via achannel, by a large arc carved stone of the kind characteristic of cer parts of Muslim Spain. Most of what remains is in Marīnid architectural tradition and thought a butable to the sultan Abu 'l-Ḥasan.

Words in Ibn Abī Zarʿ's *Rawḍ al-ḳirṭās* must be taken as implying the existence of Hunayn the port of Tlemcen in 237/851-2. Hunayn finds place in Ibn Ḥawḳal's 4th/10th century descrip of the Oran-Melilla coast, but it was known to Bakrī in the 5th/11th century as a fortress (*ḥ* with a good and busy anchorage. Inhabited by miyya Berbers, it had more orchards and varie of fruit than any neighbouring coastal *ḥiṣn*. A cent later al-Idrīsī's description is "a charming and p perous small town with solid wall, market trace." *Extra muros*, large tracts of land were farm Under the Almohads its importance grew, for only was ʿAbd al-Mu'min [*q.v.*] from the Kūmiy but he also championed the *d̲j̲ihād* in Spain. so he made Hunayn—only two days' sailing a from Alberia—a naval shipyard. Thereafter gradually emerged as the new port of Tlem wholly ousting Ars̲h̲gūl, the old. In the 7th/1 century Tlemcen became the capital of the ʿAbd Wādids [*q.v.*] and a great commercial metrop As the northern terminal of the major trans-Saha trade axis running from sub-Saharan Africa, it ideally placed for exchanges with Mediterran Europe. In its brisk trade with Christian and Mus Spain and elsewhere, Hunayn played a major and prospered, even during the long ʿAbd al-Wād

‌id struggle. In 698/1298 it wisely submitted e Marīnid Abū Yaʿḳūb and emerged unscathed his eight-year siege of Tlemcen ended with his in 1307. In 736/1335-6 it again fell into Marīnid s, this time for ten years under Abu 'l-Ḥasan, hen to a Kūmiyya rebel from whom the ʿAbd ‌did Abū Thābit recovered it in 1348. It was ‌unayn that Ibn Khaldūn was arrested by ‌ids in 1370 and to Hunayn that he was deported Spain in 1374.

er the Spanish seizure of Oran in 1509, Venetian was diverted thence to Hunayn. Around the time the port became a haven for corsairs, a which eventually led to its seizure in 1531 by paniards, who chose, however, to abandon it in presumably after rendering the port unservice- Hunayn never regained its old prosperity.

ibliography: G. Marçais, *Honaïn*, in *RAfr*, ‌c (1928), 333-50 (contains most of the references Arabic sources; illustrated); R. Basset, *Nedro-h et les Traras*, Paris 1901, 95-105 (useful for t-mediaeval history); R. von Thoden, *Abū Ḥasan ʿAlī: Merinidenpolitik zwischen Nord-ka und Spanien... 1310-1351*, Freiburg-im-‌isgau 1973, index (for mediaeval European lings of Hunayn, see 185, n. 3); Ch.-E. Dufourcq, *spagne catalane et le Maghrib au xiiie et xive les*, Paris 1966, index; R. Arié, *L'Espagne sulmane au temps des Naṣrides*, Paris 1973, ex. (J. D. LATHAM)

ḤUSAYMA is the name which, since the in-dence of Morocco in 1956, has been given to a and small archipelago on the coast of Rīf between the Cape of Quilates on the East ne More headland to the West. It is known also e name of Alhucemas as well as by that of ‌urjo, the town founded by the Spaniards in today, it is the capital of the province.

origin of the old place name as well as the ne poses unsolved problems. In classical anti- the bay seems to have had no particular for the *Itinerary* of Antonius merely indicates vo groups of three islets: *ad sex insulas*. The uis de Segonzac in 1901 passed through the terri- f the Banī Waryāghal (Uryaghəl) and speaks of ay of Nukūr [see NAKŪR, NĀKŪR], a town and s principality which have been destroyed l times in the past but of which traces seem to been found on the banks of the *wādī* of the same five miles from the sea. This seems acceptable, se the Arab geographers and the Moroccan nment have always given the name Ḥadjrat kūr to the small archipelago, and another h traveller in 1904, Ch. René Leclerc, confirms ‌istence of the name then. Although in Spanish rd *alhucema* "lavender", is derived from Arabic *zāmā*, with the same meaning, the place name derived from the plant name. *Al-Khuzāmā* ver encountered in ancient geographical or ical texts in the Western Arabic sources, old maps of the strait of Gibraltar. However, ly al-Būʿayyāshī, with some other scholars rting him, admits that the name Alhucemas n unquestionably Arabic origin and that the name al-Ḥusayma which has been adopted Moroccans is no more than an arabised form Hispano-Arabic word. Others, like the author voluminous encyclopaedia *Espasa-Calpe*, say the name Alhucema is a corruption of al-‌ma, but this suggestion needs further dis-n, see below.

largest islet of the archipelago, which is 170 m. long and 75 m. broad, is about 1300 m. from the coast; it was ceded with the others to Spain in about 1554 by the Saʿdid Mawlāy ʿAbd Allāh [*q.v.*]. This was to prevent the Turks, who had temporarily taken the Peñon de Velez from Spain, from seizing them in a similar manner. But Spain did not consider it necessary to follow up this action by even a symbolic occupation of these strategic islands. The affair was conducted so well that France was not aware of the cession, and in 1665, a French commercial company, which was intent on exploiting the possibilities of the coast of the Rīf, decided to set up an establishment in the bay of Nukūr under the name of the Compagnie d'Albouzème. In contemporary sources sometimes the term "Albouzème" is used, but otherwise it is "Les Albouzèms", or variants. The first term denotes the earlier town (called in Arabic al-Mazimma) which the ʿAlawī sultan Mawlāy Rashīd [*q.v.*] was to destroy. The second term denotes the town together with its port and its islands, but the words are often interchanged. There are frequent references to the name al-Mazimma in ancient and modern texts, especially in the *Description of Africa* of Leo Africanus, who devotes an interesting chapter to it.

But where is al-Mazimma? Al-Bādisī, writing at the end of the 19th century in his *Maḳṣad*, speaks of ramparts with gates overshadowed by a rock. At the beginning of the 20th century, René Leclerc noted the existence of a village on the side of a hill amongst several ruins; this was probably Nukūr, and al-Mazimma seems to have been the port associated with it. Wherever the town and the port may have been exactly, it was Cardinal Mazarin who first planned to set up a commercial establishment "on the islands of Albouzème". He went as far as appointing a consul for it, but when the cardinal died, the project was abandoned. However, the plan was not forgotten and on 4 November 1664 a decree from the French Conseil d'État authorised the creation of a company to be conducted by two brothers from Marseilles, Michel and Roland Fréjus. Roland did not reach Morocco until 1666 and, although his journey across the Rīf delighted him, one made in order to see Mawlāy Rashīd at Tāzā, it did not produce the expected results and he returned to France. The company was declared bankrupt, and was replaced by the Compagnie du Levant (on all this episode, see J. Caillé, *Representative diplomatique*, 31).

It was not until 1673 that Spain occupied these islands (*peñons*); on one of them, the largest, she set up a *presidio* (penitentiary) and a cemetery on another one nearby. Concerning life on this waterless archipelago, see J. Cazenave, *Présides espagnols*, 457-507. The Peñon d'Alhucemas, like Melilla and the Peñon de Velez, was besieged by the troops of Muḥammad the Great in December 1774. The Spanish resisted the bombardments bravely, and on 19 March 1775, the siege was lifted. It was also in the bay of Alhucemas that Spanish troops disembarked on 8 September 1925 to end the violent revolt of ʿAbd al-Karīm [*q.v.*] whose headquarters were at Adjdir, 8 kms. away.

The archipelago, like the rest of the Spanish zone of the protectorate, was returned to the Moroccan authorities after Morocco regained her independence. The new provincial capital, al-Ḥusayma (pop. 5,000) is a young modern city, aiming at becoming a prosperous tourist centre and seaside resort.

Bibliography: F. de la Primaudée, *Les villes maritimes de Maroc*, in *R. Afr.*, xvi (1872), §§ 12-13;

A. Moulieras, *Le Maroc inconnu, vingt deux ans d'exploration*, i, Paris 1895, 91-101, "Tribu des Beni Ouriarel", 91-101 with map; Marquis de Segonzac, *Voyages au Maroc*, Paris 1903, 56; B. Meakin, *The Land of the Moors*, London 1901, 336-9; M. Besnier, *Géographie ancienne du Maroc*, in *AM*, iii (1904); C. R. Leclerc, *Le Maroc Septentrional, souvenirs et impressions*, Algiers 1905; E. Doutté, art. *Alhucemas*, in *EI*[1]; I. Bauer, *El Rif y la kabila de Beni Urriaguel*, in *Memorias de la Societad española de antropologia, etnografia y prehistoria*, i (Madrid 1921-2); Col. H. de Castries, *Sources inédites, Filaliens*, i, Paris 1922, 86; J. Cazenave, *Les Présides Espagnoles d'Afrique, leur organisation au XVIII*e *siècle*, in *R. Afr.*, 1922/2, 255-69, and 1922/3, 457-507; A. Steiger, *Contribución a la fonética del hispano-arabe y de los española*, Madrid 1922; al-Bādisī, *El-maqṣad* (*vies des saints du Rif*), annotated French tr. G. S. Colin, in *AM*, xxvi (1926); *Rif et Jbala* (a communication), in *Bulletin de l'enseignement public du Maroc*, lxxi (Jan. 1296) (with bibl.); Ibn Zaydān, *Itḥāf*, Rabat 1931, 346-7 (*Ḥadjrat al-Nukūr*); J. Caillé, *La représentation diplomatique de la France au Maroc*, PIHEM, Notes et Documents, viii, Paris 1951, with a complete bibl. of the Compagnie d'Albouzème; Leo Africanus, *Africae descriptio*, French tr. A. Épaulard, Paris 1956, 277-8; P. Schmitt, *Le Maroc d'après la géographie de Ptolémée*, Centre de Recherches Piganiol, Tours 1973; A. al-Būʿayyāshī, *Ḥarb al-Rīf al-taḥrīriyya*, Tangier 1974, i, 112-4. (G. Deverdun)

ḤUSAYN b. ʿALĪ b. ḤANZALA [see ʿAlī b. Ḥanzala, above].

ḤUSAYN DJAJADININGRAD [see Hoesein Djajadiningrat, above].

al-**ḤUSAYNĪ**, Ṣadr al-Dīn Abu 'l-Ḥasan ʿAlī b. Nāṣir b. ʿAlī, author of the late Saldjūḳ period and early decades of the 7th/13th century, whose work is known to us through its incorporation within an anonymous history of the Saldjūḳs and succeeding Atabegs of Ādharbāydjān, the *Akhbār al-Dawla al-saldjūḳiyya* (ed. Muhammad Iqbal, Lahore 1933; Tkish. tr. Necati Lugal, Ankara 194[illegible]; Brockelmann, I[2], 392, Suppl. I, 554-5). Al-Ḥu[illegible] apparently composed the *Zubdat al-taw[illegible] akhbār al-umarāʾ wa 'l-mulūk al-saldjūḳiyya*, [illegible] forms the first part of the longer, anonymous [illegible] The *Zubda* was in turn based on the history [illegible] Saldjūḳs by ʿImād al-Dīn al-Kātib al-Iṣfahānī [illegible] continued up to 590/1193-4, the date of the [illegible] of the last Great Saldjūḳ sultan, Ṭoghrīl III. [illegible] author of the *Akhbār al-dawla al-saldjūḳiyya* continued his own work with the history of the [illegible] begs of Ādharbāydjān, either up to 620/1223 [illegible] 622/1225-6, the latter being the date of the d[illegible] of the caliph al-Nāṣir [*q.v.*] and of Özbeg b. Pah[illegible] [see Ildeñizids].

There are considerable problems regarding [illegible] al-Ḥusaynī and the anonymous author and the[illegible] spective works, which have been discussed by K. [illegible] heim, *Prolegomena zu einer Ausgabe der im Brit[illegible] Museum zu London verwahrten Chronik des [illegible] schuqischen Reiches*, Leipzig 1911, by M. T. Hou[illegible] *Some remarks on the history of the Saljuks*, in *A*[illegible] (1925), 145 ff., by Lugal in the Introd. to his [illegible] lation of the *Akhbār*, by Cl. Cahen, *Le Malik-n[illegible] et l'histoire des origines seljukides*, in *Oriens*, ii ([illegible] 32-7, and by Angelika Hartmann, *an-Nāṣir l[illegible] Allāh (1180-1225), Politik, Religion, Kultur i[illegible] späten ʿAbbāsidenzeit*, Berlin 1975, 17-18.

It seems that al-Ḥusaynī's name became att[illegible] to the *Akhbār* through a copyist's mistake, th[illegible] author being, in Hartmann's view, an official i[illegible] administration at Baghdād. As for al-Ḥusayn[illegible] remains an enigmatic figure; he was apparent[illegible] ʿAlid, and may conceivably be identical wit[illegible] "al-Ṣadr al-Adjall, Ṣadr al-Milla wa 'l-Dīn" of N[illegible] pūr, historian and poet, whom ʿAwfī [*q.v.*] men[illegible] and knew personally in the early 7th/13th cen[illegible] see his *Lubāb al-albāb*, ed. Saʿīd Nafīsī, T[illegible] 1335/1956, 125-7.

Bibliography: Given in the article.

(C. E. Boswor[illegible]

HUT [see sukna]

HYDROMANCY [see istinzāl]

I

IATROMANCY [see firāsa, istikhāra]

ʿIBĀDAT KHĀNA, literally "House of Worship", the name of the chamber or building where religious discussions among theologians were held under the patronage of the Mughal Emperor Akbar. It was constructed by Akbar at Fatḥpūr Sikrī [*q.v.*] the seat of his court, in 983/1575. He was then interested in finding a common interpretation of Muslim law, and invited Muslim jurists and theologians to hold discussions with a view to resolving their disputes; he was himself present at many of these. It was discovered, during the course of discussions, that Muslim orthodoxy was divided not only on the fine points of law but also on basic principles. Akbar's subsequent disenchantment with Muslim orthodoxy were ascribed by Badāʾūnī to the effects of the open and bitter theological disputes of the ʿIbādat Khāna. Akbar then enlarged the scope of the debate by inviting non-Muslim divines to discussions in the ʿIbādat Khāna, and Hindus, Christians and Parsees could now explain a[illegible] of their faith and engage in controversy with M[illegible] divines. The *Dabistān-i madhāhib* contains a[illegible] teresting record of these discussions among [illegible] sentatives of various religions.

With the *maḥḍar* of 987/1579, when Muslim [illegible] logians set forth high claims for Akbar as an [illegible] preter and enforcer of Muslim law, the ʿI[illegible] Khāna sessions seem to have ended. The *maḥḍ[illegible]* not win much support among Muslims; and A[illegible] himself began to hold larger religious views. [illegible] over, he left Fatḥpūr Sikrī soon afterwards, ar[illegible] sessions with such religious divines as appear[illegible] his court were held elsewhere.

The actual building of the ʿIbādat Khā[illegible] Fatḥpūr Sikrī has not been properly identifie[illegible]

Bibliography: Abu 'l-Faḍl, *Āʾīn-i Akbar[illegible]* Blochmann, Bibl. Ind., Calcutta 1867-77; *Akbar-nāma*, Bibl. Ind., Calcutta 1873-87; al-Ḳādir Badāʾūnī, *Muntakhab al-tawārīkh*, d., Calcutta 1864-9; anonymous, *Dabistān-i* *dhāhib*, Nawal Kishore, Lucknow 1904; Sri ım Sharma, *The religious policy of the Mughal* *nperors*, Bombay 1962; Aziz Ahmad, *Studies in* *'amic culture in the Indian environment*, Oxford 64, 168-9; idem, *An intellectual history of Islam* *India*, Edinburgh 1969, 29; S. A. A. Rizvi, *ligious and intellectual history of the Muslims in* *:bar's reign*, New Delhi 1975, 111 f. and index.

(M. Athar Ali)

ᶜĀDIYYA or Abᶜādiyya (pl. *abāᶜid*) was the used in 19th century Egypt for land surveyed 813 under Muḥammad ᶜAlī, but not included e cadaster and not taxed because it was un- vated. These lands extended over an area of to 1.0 million *feddāns* (a *feddān* amounted, at nd of Muḥammad ᶜAlī's rule, to 4,416.5 square es). To increase the country's wealth he made grants of *ibᶜādiyya* to high officials and notables, pting them from taxes on condition that they oved the land and prepared it for cultivation. first relevant decree was issued on 1 December , after which grants rapidly increased. At first ients only enjoyed usufructuary rights, but der to encourage investment, Muḥammad ᶜAlī compelled in 1836 to decree these lands as being itable by eldest sons and, on 16 February 1842, ant almost complete rights of ownership, includ- he right of sale and transfer. Saᶜīd, who needed ey to implement the modernisation policy begun uḥammad ᶜAlī, imposed on 30 September 1854 a (ᶜ*ushr*) on *ibᶜādiyya* and similar categories of granted as private property, all of which were ified from then onwards as ᶜ*ushūriyya* lands. He orced, however, property rights to these lands. se 25 of his 1858 Land Law explicitly stated that were "the full property of whomsoever received . . . and that he might deal with them in every ct as a property owner". *Ibᶜādiyya* owners were entitled, from then onwards, to endow these s as *wakf* or to bequeath them in their wills. ajor expansion in grants of *ibᶜādiyya* land after ammad ᶜAlī's rule occurred under Ismāᶜīl, 1863 to 1876, mainly in the northern part of the a. After that grants of *ibᶜādiyya* discontinued. ltivators residing on *ibᶜādiyya* lands were pted from the *corvée*, i.e. forced labour for pub- orks, such as strengthening dikes and for fighf- locusts. This attracted the fellahs of neigh- ing lands, thus enriching even more the notables ng *ibᶜādiyya*s and encouraging differentiation ndownership.

Fayyūm, *ibᶜādiyya* lands were granted to tern Desert Bedouin tribes in order to encourage settlement. In contrast to other *abāᶜid*, the s did not receive legal title to their land, but d exemption from taxes, forced labour, and con- tion, by cultivating it. The experiment did not ys meet with success, and many Bedouins farmed land out to fellahs for half the yield. Decrees d in 1837, 1846, and 1851 outlawing this prac- and many threats issued to the tribes that they d lose their *ibᶜādiyya*, were not implemented. turned Bedouin *abāᶜid* into *kharādjiyya* (not *iriyya*) land and thus refrained from granting Bedouin full private ownership. Full ownership achieved by Bedouin owners of *abāᶜid*, together other owners of *kharādjiyya* land, at the end e century.

ᶜ*ādiyya*s were also freely granted by Mu- mad ᶜAlī to foreign subjects, although Muslim did not allow strangers (*musta'man*) to settle permamently in a Muslim country and thus debarred them from acquiring landed property without becoming *dhimmī*s. Problems arising from foreigners owning land under the Capitulations [see imtiyāzāt] were solved by *Tanẓīmāt* legislation and the establishment of the Mixed Courts in Egypt in 1876.

Bibliography: Y. Artin, *La propriété foncière en Égypte*, Cairo 1883; ᶜAlī Pasha Mubārak, *al-Khiṭaṭ al-tawfīḳiyya al-djadīda*, Būlāk 1304-5; G. Baer, *A history of landownership in modern Egypt 1800-1950*, London 1962. (G. Baer)

IBEX [see ayyil]

IBN ABI 'L-ASHᶜATH, Abū Djaᶜfar Aḥmad b. Muḥammad b. Muḥammad, Arab physician. According to a statement of the Syro-Arab physician ᶜUbayd Allāh b. Djibrīl b. Bakhtīshūᶜ, given by Ibn Abī Uṣaybiᶜa, Ibn Abi 'l-Ashᶜath originated from Fārs. Having been originally an administrative official, he hurriedly left the country after his income had incurred *muṣādara*, and reached Mosul in a wretched condition. There he treated with success a son of the Ḥamdānid Nāṣir al-Dawla, who had been taken ill. Having thus risen to distinction, he stayed in Mosul where he had many pupils and where he died at a very advanced age, shortly after 360/970. He was considered to be an excellent specialist on Galen [see djālīnūs]; like him he had presented his knowledge in a logical and systematic way, rather than on the basis of personal observations; the statement, e.g., according to which he tested repeatedly the results of medicines, is a rather informal topos which is often found in the introductions to pharmacopoeias.

Apart from a theological work, finished in 355/966 and only known by its title (*Kitāb fi 'l-ᶜilm al-ilāhī*), and apart from the explanation of unnamed Aristotellian works, Ibn Abi 'l-Ashᶜath wrote books on medicine, zoology and veterinary science, some of which have been preserved in manuscript but none of which has been published so far. There are in the first place revisions of some of Galen's works: (1) Περὶ τῶν καθ' Ἱπποκράτην στοιχείων *K. al-Usṭukussāt ᶜalā ra'y Abuḳrāṭ*; (2) Περὶ κράσεων *K. al-Mizādj*; (3) Περὶ ἀνωμάλου δυσκρασίας *Maḳāla fī Sū' al-mizādj al-mukhtalif*; (4) Περὶ ἀρίστης κατασκευῆς τοῦ σώματος ἡμῶν *Maḳāla fī Afḍal hay'āt al-badan*; (5) Περὶ εὐεξίας *Maḳāla fī Khiṣb al-badan*. Among his own works, there should be mentioned above all: (6) *K. Ḳuwā al-adwiya al-mufrada*, a book on the powers of simple medicaments, written in 353/964 at the request of some pupils and preserved in several good manuscripts. It is mainly based on Galen's Θεραπευτικὴ μέθοδος (*Ḥīlat al-bur'*), has an instructive arrangement and would deserve an edition. Further have been preserved: (7) "On food and those who feed themselves" (*K. al-Ghādhī wa 'l-mughtadhī*), a dietary work written in Armenia in 348/960; (8) "On sleeping and being awake" (*Maḳāla fi 'l-Nawm wa 'l-yaḳẓa*); and (9) a *K. al-Ḥayawān*, evidently remarkable because of its precise zoological observations. A dozen other writings are only known by title or from isolated quotations; mention should be made of a book on dementia and pleurisy (*K. fi 'l-Sirsām wa 'l-birsām*) in three chapters, written in 355/966, and further of commentaries on Galen's Περὶ αἱρέσεων *K. al-Firaḳ* and Περὶ διαφορᾶς πυρετῶν *K. al-Ḥummayāt*, and also of an explanation of the famous synopsis of sixteen works of Galen (*al-kutub al-sitta ᶜashar*, alias *al-Djawāmiᶜ*).

Bibliography: Ibn Abī Uṣaybiᶜa, ᶜ*Uyūn*, i, 245-7; Brockelmann, I², 272, S I 422; A. Dietrich, *Medicinalia arabica*, Göttingen 1966, 143-5;

M. Ullmann, *Die Medizin im Islam*, Leiden 1970, 138 f.; idem, *Die Natur- und Geheimwissenschaften im Islam*, Leiden 1972, 25. (A. DIETRICH)

IBN ABĪ DJUMʿA [see KUTHAYYIR].

IBN ABĪ DJUMHŪR AL-AḤSĀʾĪ, MUḤAMMAD B. ʿALĪ B. IBRĀHĪM B. ḤASAN B. IBRĀHĪM B. ḤASAN AL-HADJARĪ, Imāmī scholar, was born in al-Aḥsā *ca.* 837/1433-4 into a family with a scholarly tradition. He studied first in al-Aḥsā with his father and later in al-Nadjaf with various scholars, among them al-Ḥasan b. ʿAbd al-Karīm al-Fattāl. In 877/1472-3 he visited Karak Nūḥ in Syria in order to hear traditions from ʿAlī b. Hilāl al-Djazāʾirī. After a pilgrimage to Mecca, a visit to his home country and to the shrines of the *Imāms* in Baghdād, he travelled to Mashhad in 878/1473-4 where he stayed in the house of the Sayyid Muḥsin b. Muḥammad al-Riḍawī al-Ḳummī and engaged in debates with a Sunnī scholar from Harāt described in an extant *Risāla*. During the next two decades, he seems to have mostly been teaching in Mashhad, al-Nadjaf and al-Aḥsā. He is known to have been in Mashhad in 888/1483 and, for a third visit, in 896-7/1490-2. In 893/1488 he was in al-Aḥsā and, after a visit to Mecca, he taught in al-Nadjaf in 894-5/1493-4 where he completed his *K. al-Mudjlī*. In 898-9/1493-4 he stayed in the region of Astarābād and dedicated one of his works to the Amīr ʿImād al-Dīn. A commentary on al-ʿAllāma al-Ḥillī's creed *al-Bāb al-ḥādī ʿashar* was completed by him on 25 Dhu 'l-Ḳaʿda 904/4 July 1499 in Medina. The date and place of his death are unknown.

Ibn Abī Djumhūr's numerous extant writings, mostly still unpublished, include treatises and books on ritual, law, legal methodology, tradition, theology, and controversy about the imamate. His fame rests, however, on his *K. al-Mudjlī* or *Mudjlī mirʾāt al-nūr al-mundjī* (lith. eds. Tehran 1324 and 1329). Formally a supercommentary on his own *kalām* work *K. Maslak (masālik) al-afhām fī ʿilm al-kalām*, it offers a theosophic synthesis of Imāmī scholastic theology, philosophy of the school of Ibn Sīnā, illuminationist thought of al-Suhrawardī and Ṣūfism, chiefly of Ibn al-ʿArabī and his school. His work anticipated the endeavours of the philosophical school of Iṣfahān of the Ṣafawid age to synthesise the thought of the same school traditions, though it seems to have had little direct influence on them. Later Imāmī opinion about Ibn Abī Djumhūr was generally favourable, though some criticised his *K. al-Mudjlī* as excessively Ṣūfī in tone.

Bibliography: Nūr Allāh Shushtarī, *Madjālis al-muʾminīn*, Tehran 1299/1882, 250-4; al-Ḥurr al-ʿĀmilī, *Amal al-āmil*, ed. Aḥmad al-Ḥusaynī, Baghdad 1385/1965, ii, 253, 280 f.; al-Baḥrānī, *Luʾluʾat al-Baḥrayn*, ed. Muḥammad Ṣādiḳ Baḥr al-ʿUlūm, Nadjaf 1386/1966, 166-8; al-Khwānsārī, *Rawḍāt al-djannāt*, ed. Asad Allāh Ismāʿīliyān, Ḳumm 1390-2/1970-2, vii, 126-34; al-Nūrī al-Ṭabarsī, *Mustadrak al-wasāʾil*, Tehran 1318/1900, iii, 361-5, 405; H. Corbin, *L'idée du Paraclet en philosophie iranienne*, in *La Persia nel Medioevo*, Rome 1971, 53-56; W. Madelung, *Ibn Abī Jumhūr al-Aḥsāʾī's synthesis of kalām, philosophy, and Ṣūfism* (forthcoming). (W. MADELUNG)

IBN ABI 'L-ZINĀD, ABŪ MUḤAMMAD ʿABD AL-RAḤMĀN B. ʿABD ALLĀH B. DHAKWĀN, Medinan traditionist and jurist of the 2nd/8th century, who came from a *mawālī* family. His father Abu 'l-Zinād (d. 130/747-8) had been made head of the *kharādj* of ʿIrāḳ, and he himself was appointed to a similar office at Medina. He then went to Baghdād, where he died in 174/790-1 at the age of 74. His brother Abu 'l-Ḳāsim and his son Muḥammad transmitted *ḥadīth*s. Goldziher (*Muh. Studien*, i 32-3, Eng. tr. i, 31, 38) noted that ʿAbd al-Rah was one of those who, if they did not invent i least spread, in order to buttress the prohibitic wine, a tradition which said that ʿAbd Allā Djudʿān [*q.v.*] abstained from wine. He was contemporary and also opponent of Mālik (d. 795-6 [*q.v.*]), and seems to have tried to fou personal legal rite. The *Fihrist*, ed. Cairo 315, at uted to him two works of *fiḳh*, one on success (*K. al-Farāʾiḍ*) and the other on the divergenci the *fuḳahāʾ* of Medina [*q.v.* above], the *Raʾy fuḳahāʾ al-sabʿa min ahl al-Madīna wa-mā khte fīhi*; this last would doubtless have been of rate importance for the study of the origins o lamic law.

Bibliography: Ibn Ḳutayba, *Maʿārif*, 464-6; idem, *ʿUyūn al-akhbār*, i, 44; Djahshi *Wuzarāʾ*, 20, 54-5; Khaṭīb Baghdādī, *Taʾrīkh* 228; Nawawī, 718-19; Ibn Ḥadjar, *Tahdhīb Tahdhīb*, vi, 170-2; Bustānī, *DM*, ii, Zi *Aʿlām*, iv, 85. (E

IBN AL-ADJDĀBĪ, ABŪ ISḤĀḲ IBRĀHĪM ISMĀʿĪL AL-ṬARĀBULUSĪ, Arab philologist a family originally stemming from Adjdā (Libya); he himself lived at Tripoli, where he at an uncertain date, probably in the first half of 7th/13th century. Hardly anything further is kn about his life, and the biographers limit themselv emphasising the breadth of his knowledge and contribution to the technical literature of schola his time. They attribute to him some eight w whose titles show that he was interested in lexi raphy, metrics, the *anwāʾ* [*q.v.*] and genealogies is, in particular, the author of an abridgement of *Nasab Ḳuraysh* of Muṣʿab al-Zubayrī [*q.v.*]). F amongst his writings, Yāḳūt (*Udabāʾ*, i, 130, and *dān*, s.v. Adjdābiya) and al-Suyūṭī (*Bughya*, 178) serve the titles of only two, the *Kifāyat al-m ḥaffiẓ wa-nihāyat al-mutalaffiẓ fi 'l-lugha al-ʿarab* and the *Kitāb al-Anwāʾ*, and it may be that these the only ones to have survived. The first on lexicographical compendium, seems to have enj wide success, to judge by the number of survi manuscripts (cf. Brockelmann, I, 308, S I, 541 was even put into verse and several editions have appeared (in particular, Cairo 1285/1868 Beirut 1305/1887).

The second work was apparently lost until ʿI Ḥasan discovered, in Ankara University Libr a manuscript which he published in 1964 at Dama (in the collection *Iḥyāʾ al-turāth al-ḳadīm*, ix). work, which has the title *K. al-Azmina wa 'l-an* is often mentioned in the list of *kutub al-anwāʾ* c piled by the Arab philologists (cf. Ch. Pellat, *Dict rimés* ..., in *Arabica*, ii/1 [1955], 37). It is slend in size than Ibn Ḳutayba's book (ed. Hamidu Pellat, Ḥaydarābād 1956), but is more system and less involved. It deals with the various calen (Arabic, Roman, Syriac), describes the main sta asterisms as well as the planets, defines the seas the zodiac signs and the lunar mansions, explains to calculate the hours for prayer and to deter the direction of Mecca, and lists the various wi It then goes on to define the *nawʾ* and follows order of the months of the Julian calendar, giving Syro-Arabic and Latin names, in order to point the varying astronomical phenomena which show way to them [see ANWĀʾ], without forgetting to note the beginning of the corresponding Co month. Its details on the agricultural round

tional in nature, as are its maxims and sayings, gh these are sometimes different, it is true, from which the present author of this article has ered together. One peculiarity worth mentioning e indicating of the star or asterism which passes e meridian at sunset, midnight and the time of morning prayer. Altogether, this little treatise opular astronomy and meteorology, although nologically quite late and marred by numerous s, has a very honourable place in the series of *al-anwāʾ*.

Bibliography: In addition to the sources entioned in the article, see ʿIzzat Ḥasan's rod. to his edition; Ḥādjdjī Khalīfa, v, 54; riklī, *Aʿlām*, i, 25; Bustānī, *DM*, ii, 328.

(CH. PELLAT)

N AL-AKFĀNĪ (a *nisba* referring to the seller rouds, *akfān*), cf. al-Samʿānī, *K. al-Ansāb*, f. Several persons were known by this name, ngst which three deserve some mention.

AL-ḲĀḌĪ ABŪ MUḤAMMAD ʿABD ALLĀH B. AMMAD B. ʿAbd Allāh b. Ibrāhīm b. ʿAbd Allāh -Ḥusayn b. ʿAlī b. Djaʿfar b. ʿĀmir b. AL-ĀNĪ AL-ASADĪ, jurist. Born in 316/928, and g in 405/1014 in Baghdād, he was *ḳāḍī* in al-na, then in Bāb al-Ṭāḳ, then in Sūḳ al-Thulāthāʾ in Baghdād), and from 396/1005-6 *ḳāḍī* for whole of Baghdād. He was weak in relating tions, but a liberal patron to traditionists al-Khaṭīb al-Baghdādī, *Taʾrīkh Baghdād*, x, 2, no. 5284).

HIBAT ALLĀH B. AḤMAD b. Muḥammad al-rī al-Dimashḳī, ABŪ MUḤAMMAD AL-AKFĀNĪ, orian, who died in 524/1129 as an octogenarian amascus and was the author of biographical s: *Djāmiʿ al-wafayāt* (now lost), and *Tatimmat ikh Dārayyā wa-tasmiyat man ḥaddatha min ā* (cf. Ṣ. al-Munadjdjid, *Muʿdjam al-muʾarrikhīn mashḳiyyīn* ..., Beirut 1978, 31-2, and the es quoted there, especially Ibn al-ʿImād, *harāt*, iv, 73, and also Makkarī, *Nafḥ al-ṭīb*, Dozy *et alii*, i, 562).

MUḤAMMAD B. IBRĀHĪM b. Sāʿid, Shams al-Abū ʿAbd Allāh al-Anṣārī, known as IBN AL-ĀNĪ, physician and encyclopaedist. Born ndjār, he died in 749/1348 in Cairo of the plague. holar of many talents, he was employed in al-iristān al-Manṣūrī (see BĪMĀRISTĀN) in Cairo influential position, and wrote many books and ises. A contemporary account on him is given l-Ṣafadī in *al-Wāfī bi 'l-wafayāt*, ii, 25-7, and s *Aʿyān al-ʿaṣr* (ms. Atif Efendi 1809, s.v., a exaggerated biography full of laudatory re-s); and letters by Ibn al-Akfānī are quoted in fadī's *Alḥān al-sawādjiʿ* (ms. Berlin, cat. Ahl-t, 8631, iii, 33a ff.). Other biographical accounts Ḥadjar, *Durar*, iii, 279-80; al-Maḳrīzī, *al-Muḳaffā*, Leiden Or. 1366a, ff. 38b-40a; al-Shawkānī, *al-al-ṭāliʿ*, ii, 79-80; al-Ziriklī, *al-Aʿlām*, vi, 189) ll, directly or indirectly, derived from al-Ṣafadī's nt.

me 22 books or treatises by Ibn al-Akfānī are n to have existed, more than half of these being erned with medicine and related sciences. rs treat of logic, *tafsīr*, *firāsa* [see AFLĪMŪN], nomy, the *arbaʿīn*, mathematics and gemmol-None of these is remarkable for great originality. l-Akfānī's fame rests mainly on his encyclopae-*rshād al-ḳāṣid ilā asnā al-maḳāṣid*. In this he with 60 sciences, along the lines of al-Fārābī's *al-ʿulūm*. After two introductory chapters ducation in general and the division of the sciences, Ibn al-Akfānī treats of *al-adab* (10 subdivisions), *al-manṭiḳ* (9 subdivisions), *al-ilāhī* (9 subdivisions, with heresiology), *al-ṭabīʿī* (10 subdivisions), *al-handasa* (10 subdivisions), *al-hayʾa* (5 subdivisions), *al-ʿadad* (7 subdivisions, the last of which is *al-mūsīḳā*). Added to these are *al-siyāsa*, *al-akhlāḳ*, and *tadbīr al-manzil*, comprising the practical sciences (*al-ʿulūm al-ʿamaliyya*). All sections have a bibliography. The book concludes with a short list of philosophical terms and their definitions. The *Irshād al-ḳāṣid* stood as a model for the *Miftāḥ al-saʿāda* by Ṭāsh-köprüzāda [*q.v.*], as can be seen easily from the table of contents of both works and from the arrangement of the material in the sections.

Bibliography: in addition to references given in the article, note that there are some 40 mss. of the *Irshād al-ḳāṣid*, dispersed in libraries from Rabat to Rampur. Editions: A. Sprenger, Calcutta 1849, and Maḥmūd Abu 'l-Naṣr, Cairo 1900 (both unsatisfactory). For a survey of the life, works and influence of Ibn al-Afkānī, see the introduction of the forthcoming edition of *Irshād al-ḳāṣid* by J. J. Witkam; the work was an important source for E. Wiedemann, the historian of Arabic science, cf. his *Aufsätze zur arabischen Wissenschaftsgeschichte*, ed. W. Fischer, Hildesheim 1970, index s.v. Afkānī. The chapter on music was published and translated by A. Shiloah, in *Yuval*, i (1968), 221-48. See also Brockelmann, II², 171, S II, 169-70.

(J. J. WITKAM)

IBN ʿAMR AL-RIBĀṬĪ, ABŪ ʿABD ALLĀH MUḤAMMAD B. MUḤAMMAD B. ʿAMR AL-ANṢĀRĪ, Moroccan poet and *faḳīh*, of Andalusian origin, who was born at Rabat, fulfilled the office of *ḳāḍī* for some time, and from 1224/1809 taught at Marrākush. Whilst making the Pilgrimage, he stopped at Tunis, and received there some *idjāza*s; he died in the Ḥidjāz on 10 Rabīʿ I 1243/1 October 1827.

Ibn ʿAmr was neither a great *faḳīh* nor a great poet. His works, which include in particular a *dīwān*, a *fahrasa* and a *riḥla*, have not been preserved *in toto*, and his fame rests essentially on an imitation of the *Shamaḳmaḳiyya* of Ibn al-Wannān [*q.v.*], a *ḳāfiyya* known by the name of *al-ʿAmriyya* which enjoyed a celebrity mainly because of the religious sentiments expressed in the last verses. In this *ḳaṣīda*, of classical mould, the author piles up rare words of the type that one can often describe as *ḥūshī* [see ḤŪSH] and resorts to rhetorical devices in order to arrive at a eulogy of the Prophet who, according to tradition, had supposedly cured him of gout.

Bibliography: Marrākushī, *al-Iʿlām bi-man ḥalla Marrākūsh*, no. 509; Kattānī, *Fihris al-fahāris*, Fās 1346/1927, i, 202-5; Sāʾiḥ, *al-Muntakhabāt al-ʿabḳariyya*, Rabat 1920, 95-100; M. Lakhdar, *Vie littéraire*, 306-9, and bibliography cited.

(ED.)

IBN ʿASKAR, MUḤAMMAD B. ʿALĪ B. KHAḌIR B. HĀRŪN AL-GHASSĀNĪ, an Andalusian *faḳīh*, philologist, poet and man of letters, who wrote a history of Málaga. Born in a village near this important sea-port *ca.* 584/1188-9, he was later to hold high judicial office there. Between 626/1229 and 631/1234 he served as deputy of Ibn Hūd's [see HŪDIDS] *ḳāḍī*, Abū ʿAbd Allāh b. al-Ḥasan al-Judhamī. In 635/1238 he was appointed *ḳāḍī* of Naṣrid Málaga by Muḥammad I, and he continued in that office until his death on 4 Djumādā II 636/12 January 1239. As a young man Ibn ʿAskar was a pupil of Abu 'l-Ḥadjdjādj b. al-Shaykh (d. 604/1207), author of the *K. alif bāʾ*, to which M. Asín Palacios devoted the well-known study *El "Abecedario" de Yusúf Benaxeij* (Madrid 1932). His own pupils included his nephew, biographer and continuator, Abū Bakr b. al-Khamīs, and the celebrated Ibn al-Abbār [*q.v.*].

Ibn ʿAskar's history of Málaga is frequently mentioned and quoted by Andalusian authors of the 7th/13th and 8th/14th centuries. Its title is *al-Ikmāl wa 'l-iʿlām fī ṣilat al-Iʿlām bi-maḥāsin al-aʿlām min ahl Mālaḳa al-kirām*, suggesting that it is a continuation of the *Iʿlām* of the Málagan scholar Aṣbagh b. al-ʿAbbās (d. 592/1196). By Ibn al-Khaṭīb [*q.v.*], however, for whom the work was a main source of the *Iḥāṭa*, it is called *Maṭlaʿ al-anwār wa-nuzhat al-abṣār*, etc. There are other variants, including the simple and commonly used title *Taʾrīkh Mālaḳa*. At the time of the author's death the work was unfinished, and the task of completing it fell to Ibn Khamīs (see above), who seems to have flourished somewhere around the middle of the first half of the 7th/13th century. The one extant manuscript which we have of the *Ikmāl* (in private hands) is incomplete, but a large part has fortunately survived, and from this an assessment can be made of its literary and historical value. The biographies of Málagan notables included in it have a distinct literary value in that they offer, in addition to biographical data, worthwhile specimens of biographees' poetry (unfortunately, no account is taken of *muwashshaḥāt* and the *zadjal*). On the historical side it contains material that can be utilised to supplement, complement and control our existing accounts from the 8th to the 13th centuries A.D.

Ibn ʿAskar was the author of a number of other works, namely (i) *al-Mashraʿ al-rawī*, a supplement to al-Harawī's works on unusual terms in the Ḳurʾān and *ḥadīth*; (ii) *Nuzhat al-nāẓir fī manāḳib ʿAmmār b. Yāsir*, a work dedicated to the Banū Saʿīd of Alcalá la Real and devoted to the life of the first member of the family to come to Spain (Ibn ʿAskar was a close friend of the family); (iii) *al-Djuzʾ al-mukhtaṣar ... ʿan dhahāb al-baṣar*, a work on blindness written to console a blind friend; (iv) *Idhdhikhār al-ṣabr*, an ascetic work; (v) *al-Arbaʿīn al-ḥadīth*; and (vi) *al-Takmīl wa 'l-itmām li-Kitāb al-Taʿrīf wa 'l-iʿlām*, a commentary on and supplement to a work by al-Suhaylī of Fuengirola (507-81/1113-85) on proper names not occurring in the Ḳurʾān.

Bibliography: All important references are given in J. Vallvé Bermejo, *Una fuente importante de la historia de al-Andalus: la "Historia" de Ibn ʿAskar*, in *Al-Andalus*, xxxi (1966), 237-80 (includes translations of some of the most notable historical passages). (J. D. LATHAM)

IBN ʿAZZŪZ, called **SĪDĪ BALLĀ**, ABŪ MUḤAMMAD ʿABD ALLĀH AL-ḲURASHĪ AL-SHĀDHILĪ AL-MARRĀKUSHĪ, a cobbler of Marrakesh to whom thaumaturgic gifts were attributed and who died in an odour of sanctity in 1204/1789. His tomb, situated in his own residence at Bāb Aylān, has been continuously visited because of its reputation of curing the sick. Although he had not received a very advanced education, Ibn ʿAzzūz nevertheless succeeded in leaving behind an abundant body of works, dealing mainly with mysticism and the occult sciences, but also with medicine. However, his works display hardly any originality, and none of them has interested a publisher, despite the success in Morocco of his *Dhahāb al-kusūf wa-nafy al-ẓulumāt fī ʿilm al-ṭibb wa 'l-ṭabāʾiʿ wa 'l-ḥikma*, a popular collection of therapeutic formulae (see L. Leclerc, *La chirurgie d'Abulcasis*, Paris 1861, ii, 307-8; H. P. J. Renaud, in *Initiation au Maroc*, Paris 1 183-4); his *Kashf al-rumūz* concerning medi plants is equally well-known. Out of his three v on mysticism, the *Tanbīh al-tilmīdh al-muḥtā* perhaps the most original, since it endeavou reconcile the *sharīʿa* with the *ḥaḳīḳa* [*q.v.*]. Fin in the field of the occult sciences, his *Lubāb al-ḥ fī ʿilm al-ḥurūf wa-ʿilm al-asmāʾ al-ilāhiyya*, of w at least one manuscript survives, is a treatis practical magic and divinatory magic.

Bibliography: On the manuscripts of Ballā's works, see Brockelmann, S II, 704, M. Lakhdar, *Vie littéraire*, 253-6; see Ibn Sūda, *Dalīl muʾarrikh al-Maghrib al-A* Casablanca, 1960, ii, 446, 449; ʿA. Gannūn, *Nubūgh al-Maghribī*[2], Beirut 1961, i, 304-5, (E

IBN BĀBĀ AL-KĀSHĀNĪ [see AL-ḲĀSHĀNĪ].

IBN AL-BALKHĪ, Persian author of Saldjūḳ period who wrote a local history topographical account of his native province the *Fārs-nāma*. Nothing is known of him save w can be gleaned from his book, nor is the exact of his name known, but his ancestors came Balkh. His grandfather was *mustawfī* or accoun for Fārs under Berk-yaruḳ b. Malik Shāh's gove there, the Atabeg Rukn al-Dawla or Nadjm al-D Khumārtigin, and Ibn al-Balkhī acquired his tensive local knowledge of Fārs through accomp ing his grandfather in his work. He was accordi asked by sultan Muḥammad b. Malik Shāh compose a historical and geographical acc of the province; since he mentions the Atabe Fārs Fakhr al-Dīn Čawlī as being still alive, composition of the *Fārs-nāma* must be placed tween Muḥammad's accession in 498/1105 Čawlī's death in 510/1116.

The first two-thirds of the *Fārs-nāma* on the Islamic history of Persia and the Arab conques Fārs are entirely derivative, being based on Ḥa Iṣfahānī, but the remainder is a very impor account of the province's topography and notab concluding with a section on the Shabānkāra K and containing details of contemporary happeni This last third of the book was much used in 8th/14th century by Ḥamd Allāh Mustawfī [*q.v.*] the geographical part of his *Nuzhat al-ḳulūb*.

Bibliography: G. Le Strange and R. Nicholson edited the last third of the Per text, *The Fársnáma of Ibnu'l-Balkhí*, *GMS*, N. London 1921; Le Strange had previously tr lated this in *JRAS* (1912), also as a sepa monograph, *Description of the province of Far Persia*, London 1912. See also Storey, i, 35 and Storey-Bregel, ii, 1027-8. (C. E. BOSWORTH

IBN AL-BAZZĀZ AL-ARDABĪLĪ, TAWAKK (TŪKLĪ) B. ISMĀʿĪL, *murīd* of Shaykh Ṣadr al- al-Ardabīlī (d. 794/1391-2), son and first successo Shaykh Ṣafī al-Dīn al-Ardabīlī (d. 735/1334), founder of the Ṣūfī order of the Ṣafawiyya and ancestor of Shāh Ismāʿīl I (d. 930/1524 [*q.v.*]), eponym of the Ṣafawids [*q.v.*; see also ARDABĪL]. exact dates of Ibn al-Bazzāz are unknown. At stimulus of Shaykh Ṣadr al-Dīn he compose biography of Shaykh Ṣafī al-Dīn, with the *Ṣafwat al-ṣafāʾ* or *Mawāhib al-saniyya fī mana al-ṣafawiyya*. Written in a simple style with rhetorical ballast, this voluminous work gives of all information on the miracles (*karāmāt*) Ṣūfī doctrine of the Shaykh, but describes also i vivid way daily life in the sanctuary of the or ives an account of the relations of the Shaykh the secular rulers in the period of the Ilkhāns m the colophon of the manuscript India Office 842 (Ethé, *Cat. of Pers. mss.*, i, col. 1008), bly erroneously described as an autograph, it s that Ibn al-Bazzāz finished his work in ān 759/July-August 1358. The numerous scripts of the *Ṣafwat al-ṣafā*ʾ, among which exist also Turkish translations, prove the arity of this important hagiographic work. tical edition is not yet available; a lithograph published by Aḥmad b. Karīm Tabrīzī in ay in 1329/1911.

the 10th/16th century, the chroniclers of the id dynasty used the *Ṣafwat al-ṣafā*ʾ as their source for the early period of the Ṣafawiyya and for the genealogy of the Ṣafawids, who ed descent from the seventh Imām Mūsā al-n. This genealogy is, however, very much ted, because the pedigree of the Ṣafawids, at in its complete form, was apparently inserted he work only by Abu 'l-Fatḥ al-Ḥusaynī, who d the *Ṣafwat al-ṣafā*ʾ (Storey, i/1, 13 ff. and 196 ff.) at the order of the Ṣafawid Shāh Tah-I (d. 984/1576).

ibliography: Storey, i/2, 939 ff.; Browne, *P*, ii, iv, 34-40; Nikitine, *Essai d'analyse du wat-uṣ-ṣafa*, in *JA* (1957), 385-94; Z. V. Togan, *l'origine des Safavides*, in *Mélanges Massignon*, Damascus 1957, 345-57; Hanna Sohrweide, *Sieg der Ṣafaviden in Persien und seine Rückkungen auf die Shiʿiten Anatoliens im 16. rhundert*, in *Isl.*, xli (1965), 97 ff.; Mahmud a-Motlagh, *Scheich Safi von Ardabil*, diss. ttingen 1969, 19-22 and *passim*; Erika Glassen, *frühen Safawiden nach Qāżī Aḥmad Qumī*, amkundliche Untersuchungen, 5, Freiburg i. Br. o, 18 f., 21-52; M. M. Mazzaoui, *The origins of Ṣafawids, Shīʿism, Ṣūfism and Ġulāt*, Freiburger amstudien 3, Wiesbaden 1972, 47 ff. A critical tion of the *Ṣafwat al-ṣafā*ʾ is being prepared by oint team working at the Universities of Utah Freiburg-im-Breisgau under the direction of zzaoui. (E. Glassen)

N BIKLĀRISH, Yūsuf (Yūnus?) b. Isḥāḳ rāʾīlī, Judaeo-Arab physician and pharist who lived in Almeria *ca.* 1100 A.D. There rote the *K. al-Mustaʿīnī* for al-Mustaʿīn billāh Djaʿfar Aḥmad b. Yūsuf al-Muʾtamin billāh ed 478-503/1085-1109), the Hūdid ruler of ossa [see hūdids], after whom the work was d.

e book must have attracted attention immely, for it is often quoted by al-Ghāfiḳī [*q.v.*], a younger contemporary of Ibn Biklārish, in *. al-Adwiya al-mufrada*; in the Latin version of atter under the name Buclaris or Boclaris (i.e. Biclaro?). It is also remarkable that both rs quote almost the same sources. After a etical explanation of pharmacology which is tially based on Galen, the *Mustaʿīnī* contains cial table-like section, arranged in five unequal ns. The first two small columns give the names ?), and characteristics (*ṭibāʿ*) of the simple cines, the third (*tafsīruhā bi-'khtilāf al-lughāt*) ins their explanation together with their Greek, c, Persian, Latin and Mozarabic synonyms, the h the Succedanea (*abdāl*) and the fifth their y, specific effect and region of application āfiʿuhā wa-khawāṣṣuhā wa-wudjūh istiʿmālihā*). covering text on the upper and lower margin contains further details, and above all the sources. The order of the total of 704 drugs follows the *abdjad* alphabet in its Maghribī form. In Europe, attention has been given so far almost exclusively to the third column (synonyma): it contains important vocabulary material, especially of the Romance languages, and was used abundantly by Simonet for his *Glosario* and in particular by Dozy for his *Supplément*. H. P. J. Renaud made several investigations into the *Mustaʿīnī*, the last in *Hespéris*, x (1930-1), 135-50; he planned an edition with translation and commentary, but this did not come to fruition; such a work is, however, long overdue.

Of other writings of Ibn Biklārish, only one work on dietetics is known by its title; in the introduction to the *Mustaʿīnī* it is quoted twice as *Risālat al-Tabyīn wa 'l-tartīb*.

Bibliography: Ibn Abī Uṣaybiʿa, *ʿUyūn*, ii, 52; M. Steinschneider, *Die arabische Literatur der Juden*, 147 f.; M. Meyerhof, *Un glossaire de matière médicale composé par Maïmonide*, Cairo 1940, xxviii; Brockelmann, I^2, 640, S I, 889; M. Ullmann, *Die Medizin im Islam*, Leiden 1970, 201, 275. (A. Dietrich)

IBN DAḲĪḲ al-ʿĪd, Taḳī al-Dīn Abū 'l-Fatḥ Muḥammad b. ʿAlī b. Wahb b. Muṭīʿ b. Abi 'l-Ṭāʿa, jurist and traditionist who was born in Shaʿbān 625/July 1228 in Yanbuʿ in the Ḥidjāz (not in Lower Egypt as stated by Brockelmann), although his parents came from Manfalūṭ in Upper Egypt. He was brought up in Ḳūṣ in Upper Egypt, and travelled to Cairo and Damascus to hear *ḥadīth*s. He later taught jurisprudence according to the Mālikī and Shāfiʿī schools. He became a judge in 675/1295, and died in Cairo on 11 Ṣafar 702/6 October 1302.

He wrote a number of books on *fiḳh* and *ḥadīth*, including a work in twenty volumes entitled *al-Ilmām fī aḥādīth al-aḥkām*, and he also left some poetry and a collection of sermons. He was deeply interested in alchemy, a fact mentioned by Ṭāshköprüzāde in his *Miftāḥ al-saʿāda wa-miṣbāḥ al-siyāda*, i, Hyderabad 1911, 281, although he appears to have left no writings on this subject. However, an anonymous writer (in the short treatise *Fī bayān ʿamal al-fiḍḍa wa 'l-dhahab*) has preserved a record of the methods used by Ibn Daḳīḳ al-ʿĪd in attempting to transmute quicksilver and sulphur into gold, and quicksilver and arsenic into silver.

Bibliography: Dhahabī, *Ḥuffāẓ*, iv, 262 ff.; Kutubī, *Fawāt*, Būlāḳ 1283, 305 f.; Ziriklī, *al-Aʿlām*, iii, 949; Brockelmann II, 75, S II, 66; Kaḥḥāla, *Muʿdjam al-muʾallifīn*, xi, 70 f.; R. Y. Ebied and M. J. L. Young, *An anonymous Arabic treatise on alchemy*, in *Isl.*, liii (1976), 100-9.

(R. Y. Ebied and M. J. L. Young)

IBN DĀRUST, Tādj al-Mulk Abu 'l-Ghanāʾim Marzubān b. Khusraw-Fīrūz Shīrāzī (438-86/1046-93), high official in the Great Saldjūḳ administration under Sultan Malik Shāh [*q.v.*], tand hat ruler's last vizier.

Born of a secretarial family in Fārs, he began his official career in the service of the slave commander Sāwtigin, who eventually recommended him to the sultan as a person of promise. Malik Shāh made him superintendent of the education and possessions of various of his sons, then overseer of the royal palace and its ancillaries, and finally head of the Saldjūḳ chancery, the *Dīwān al-Inshā*ʾ *wa 'l-Ṭughrā* [see dīwān, iv. Īrān].

Much of the internal history of Malik Shāh's reign reflects a struggle for authority in the administration (the *dīwān*s) and at court (the *dargāh*), in which various officials were ranged against the great vizier Niẓām al-Mulk [*q.v.*], his sons and his partisans, the so-called Niẓāmiyya; in this Ibn Dārust placed himself on the side of the vizier's enemies. Hence when Niẓām al-Mulk was assassinated in Ramaḍān 485/October 1092, many contemporaries assumed that the real instigators of the murder, in which the Ismāʿīlī *fidāʾī* was a mere tool, were Ibn Dārust and even the sultan himself, suspicious of the vizier's commanding power and presence in the state.

Malik S͟hāh now appointed Ibn Dārust as his vizier, but the latter's triumph was short-lived, for the sultan himself died next month (mid-S͟hawwāl 485/mid-November 1092). Ibn Dārust now allied with Malik S͟hāh's wife, the Ḳarak͟hānid princess Terken K͟hātūn, to place the latter's son Maḥmūd on the throne in Bag͟hdād, even though Maḥmūd was only a small child, and on grounds of experience and potential, was obviously inferior to Berk-yaruḳ, Malik S͟hāh's son by another wife and, at twelve or thirteen years old, on the threshhold of adulthood. Although Ibn Dārust and Terken K͟hātūn managed to seize Iṣfahān, their forces were defeated by those of Berk-yaruḳ's partisans, with the Niẓāmiyya as their driving-force, at the battle of Burud͟jird at the end of D͟hu 'l-Ḥid͟jd͟ja 485/end of January 1093. Ibn Dārust was captured, and although Berk-yaruḳ, mindful of Ibn Dārust's administrative expertise, was inclined to take him as his own vizier, the Niẓāmiyya insisted on exacting vengeance for their dead leader, and secured his execution in Muḥarram 486/February 1093.

Ibn Dārust was the *mamdūḥ* of various Sald͟jūḳ poets like Muʿizzī, and he was also one of several great men in the Sald͟jūḳ state, both civilian and military, who were active in founding colleges and other charitable and educational works; his Tād͟jiyya *madrasa* was begun in 480/1089 in Bag͟hdād at the Bāb Abraz as a S͟hāfiʿī college, rivalling Niẓām al-Mulk's own more famous foundation; the celebrated scholars Abū Bakr al-S͟hās͟hī and Abū Ḥāmid al-G͟hazālī's brother Abu 'l-Futūḥ taught there.

Bibliography: There are very brief biographies in Ibn al-D͟jawzī's *Muntaẓam*, ix, 74, and Sayf al-Dīn Faḍlī ʿUḳaylī's *Āt͟hār al-wuzarāʾ*, ed. Urmawī, Tehran 1337/1959, but for the rest, see scattered references in the historical sources for the Sald͟jūḳ period (Ṣadr al-Dīn Ḥusaynī, Rāwandī, Bundārī, Ibn al-D͟jawzī, Sibṭ Ibn al-D͟jawzī, Ibn al-At͟hīr), utilised in Bosworth, *Cambridge history of Iran*, v, 74 ff., 82, 93, 102-5, 216; M. F. Sanaullah, *The decline of the Saljūqid empire*, Calcutta 1938, 9, 40-1, 83; İ. Kafesoğlu, *Sultan Melikşah devrinde Büyük Selçuklu imparatorluğu*, Istanbul 1953, 169, 200 ff.; Abbas Eghbal, *Wizārat dar ʿahd-i salāṭīn-i buzurg-i Sald͟jūḳī*, Tehran 1338/1959, 93-100; C. L. Klausner, *The Seljuk vezirate: a study of civil administration 1055-1194*, Cambridge, Mass. 1973, 28-9, 52. For Ibn Dārust's educational foundations, see G. Makdisi, *Muslim institutions of learning in eleventh-century Baghdad*, in *BSOAS*, xxiv (1961), 25-6, and idem, *Ibn ʿAqīl et la resurgence de l'Islam traditionaliste au XIᵉ siècle*, Damascus 1963, 137-41, 209-10, 225-6.

(C. E. Bosworth)

IBN DIRHAM, seldom-used patronym of an eminent family of Mālikī jurists and *ḳāḍīs*, originally of Baṣra, who bear the ethnic name AL-AZDĪ in some sources; but since the members of this family are most often cited under their personal name or simply by their *kunya*, and since the line of parentage which connects them is consequently difficult to determine, it has been judged expe to assemble them here under this somewhat art appellation, following the example of F. al-B who, in the *Dāʾirat al-maʿārif* (iii, 61), adopted one of them, the tenth of those listed below. ḳāḍīs, who for the most part held office in Bag in the 3rd and 4th/9th and 10th centuries, are by L. Massignon (*Cadis et naqibs baghdadien* *WZKM*, li/1-2 [1948], 108, where Ismāʿīl b. should be read in place of b. Ḥammād), followin articles devoted to them by al-K͟haṭīb al-Bag (*Taʾrīk͟h Bag͟hdād*), after Wakīʿ (*Ak͟hbār al-ḳ* and especially al-Tanūk͟hī, who gives them con able space in *al-Farad͟j baʿd al-s͟hidda* and partic in the *Nis͟hwār al-muḥāḍara*.

The following table, which cannot be regard exhaustive, contains the names mentioned ir principal sources for the period until the mid 10th century; it is unlikely that the family c to exist at this time, but it does not seem to given any more eminent practitioners to the profession.

I. - Abū Ismāʿīl ḤAMMĀD B. ZAYD B. DI (98-179/717-95) is the first member of the fami have made a mark on history. A blind sla Ḥāzim b. Zayd al-D͟jahḍamī (Azd), he was a chised by his two sons, D͟jarīr and Yazīd (see Ḳutayba, *Maʿārif*, index), devoted himself to study of *ḥadīt͟h* and passed on his knowledge number of traditionists, including Bis͟hr al- [*q.v.*]. He is to a certain extent regarded as the fou of an independent *mad͟hhab* and accorded the status as al-T͟hawrī in Kūfa, Mālik in the Hi and al-Awzāʿī in Damascus; he thus represe Baṣra, his home-town, but in spite of the re with which he was treated he does not seem to founded a school, since his descendants were t selves Mālikīs.

Bibliography: Ibn Saʿd, *Ṭabaḳāt*, vii/2, Balād͟hurī, *Futūḥ*, 283; Ibn Ḳutayba, *Ma* 502-3, 525; Ṭabarī, index; Masʿūdī, *Murūd͟j* 294 = § 2500; Ibn Baṭṭa-Laoust, index; Ib D͟jazarī, *Ḳurrāʾ*, i, 258; Maḳdisī, *Création*, ii 145; Abū Nuʿaym, *Ḥilyat al-awliyāʾ*, vi, 25 ʿIyāḍ, *Tartīb al-madārik*, index; Nawawī, *Ta al-asmāʾ*, 217-8; D͟hahabī, *Tad͟hkirat al-ḥuffā* 211-2; Ibn al-ʿImād, *S͟had͟harāt*, i, 292; Ṣa *Nakt al-himyān*, 147; Massignon, *Lexique techn* 168, 197, 243.

II. - Abū Yaʿḳub ISḤĀḲ B. ISMĀʿĪL B. ḤAM (176-230/792-845), grandson of the preceding, responsible for *maẓālim* in Egypt under the calip of al-Maʾmūn (in 215/830), then in Baṣra under of al-Muʿtaṣim (ʿIyāḍ, *Madārik*, ii, 558-9; Tag͟hrībardī, *Nud͟jūm*, ii, 212).

III - Abū Yūsuf YAʿḲŪB B. ISMĀʿĪL B. ḤAM (d. 246/860), brother of Isḥāḳ, was, it seems, first *ḳāḍī* of the family; having served in this o at Medina, he made his way to Bag͟hdād wher frequented the court of al-Muʿtaṣim and transmi *ḥadīt͟hs*. Subsequently, al-Mutawakkil appointed for the second time *ḳāḍī* of Medina, then of I where he resided until his death (al-Tanūk͟hī, *Nis͟h* vii, 16-18; ʿIyāḍ, *Madārik*, ii, 560).

IV. - Abū Ismāʿīl ḤAMMĀD B. ISḤĀḲ B. ISM (199-267/815-81) was described in a general sens being *ḳāḍī* of Bag͟hdād (K͟haṭīb Bag͟hdādī, viii, 1 but there can be no doubt that the area in ques was the Round City of al-Manṣūr (in 251/ according to Massignon, *Cadis*, 108). He is mentic among the companions of al-Muwaffaḳ, and to are attributed a *Kitāb al-Muhādana* and a *Radd*

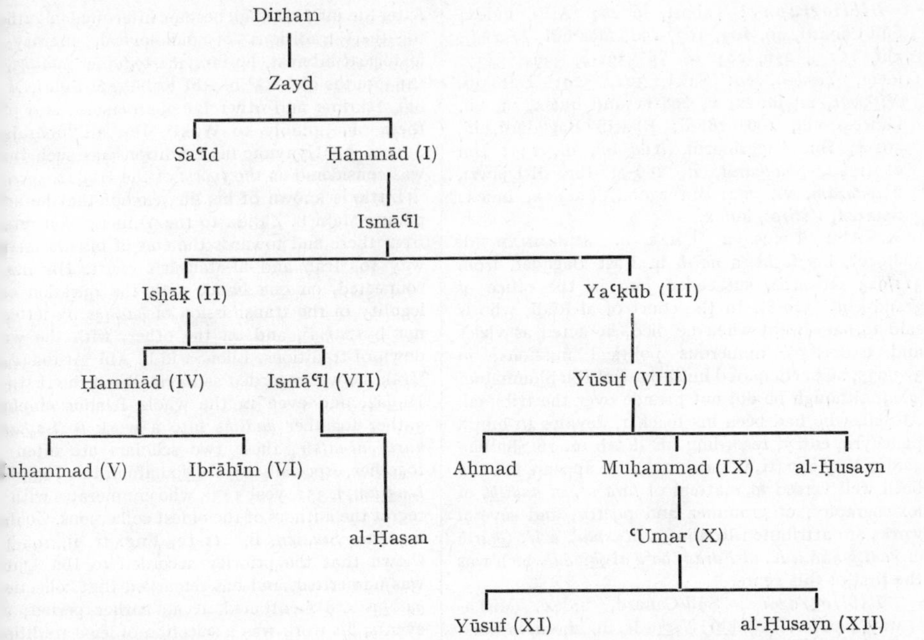

ᶜīᶜī (al-Tanūkhī, *Nishwār*, vi, 21, vii, 51; , *Madārik*, iii, 181-2).

- Muḥammad b. Ḥammād b. Isḥāḳ (d. 276/889) ppointed *ḳāḍī* of Baṣra by al-Muwaffaḳ (Wakīᶜ, -2).

. - Abū Isḥāḳ Ibrāhīm b. Ḥammād (240-323/854- who survived his brother by many years, is dered principally as a traditionist. According to aṭīb al-Baghdādī (vi, 61-2), he was also a *ḳāḍī*, t what date, or in what town, is not known; he however, in Baghdād (al-Ṣūlī, *Akhbār ar-Rāḍī*, tr. M. Canard, Algiers 1946, 107; see also Ibn in, *Dībādj*, 85; Ibn Taghrībardī, *Nudjūm*, iii,

. - Abū Isḥāḳ Ismāᶜīl b. Isḥāḳ b. Ismāᶜīl b. ĀD [see al-Azdī, in Suppl.]. his son Abū ᶜAlī al-Ḥasan, who was a celebrated nd an *adīb*, see Tanūkhī, *Nishwār*, vi, 326; b Baghdādī, vii, 284.

I. - Abū Muḥammad Yūsuf b. Yaᶜḳūb b. īl b. Ḥammād (208-97/823-910), was the first er of the other branch of the family to serve as Baghdād, where he first assumed charge of the (271/884-5) and of the *nafaḳāt* of al-Muwaffaḳ. atter, on the death of Muḥammad b. Ḥammad V), appointed as his successor Yūsuf b. Yaᶜḳūb, emained titular *ḳāḍī* of Baṣra, of Wāsiṭ and of istricts of the Tigris from 276/883 to 296/909, e was represented there by a deputy, for he was living in Baghdād, where the jurisdiction of *im* was entrusted to him in 277. On the death āᶜīl b. Isḥāḳ (No. VII), he was given the post of of East Baghdād, which he combined with that aṣra, having as *nāʾib* in the capital his son mmad from 289/902 onward. When in 296/908 tter gave his support to Ibn al-Muᶜtāzz [*q.v.*], ther was dismissed and he spent the last year of ng life in retirement. He passed on some *ḥadīths* ed down by his cousin Ismāᶜīl b. Isḥāḳ (No. VII) rote a number of works: *Faḍāʾil azwādj al-Nabī*, *-Ṣiyām wa 'l-duᶜāʾ wa 'l-zakāt* and a *Musnad* of a b. al-Ḥadjdjādj [*q.v.*].

ibliography: Wakīᶜ, ii, 182; Tanūkhī, *Nishwār*, v, vi, vii, viii, indices; ᶜIyāḍ, *Madārik*, iii, 182-7; Ibn al-ᶜImād, *Shadharāt*, ii, 227; Ibn Taghrībardī, *Nudjūm*, iii, 171.

IX. - Abū ᶜUmar Muḥammad b. Yūsuf b. Yaᶜḳūb (243-320/857-932) is the most celebrated member of the entire family, and his *kunya* alone is sufficient to identify him. Born in Baṣra, he followed his father to the capital and held the office of *ḳāḍī* over the Round City of al-Manṣūr from 284/897 to 292/905, then over al-Sharḳiyya from 292 to 296. Dismissed after the Ibn al-Muᶜtazz affair, he remained unemployed for a few years, but was reinstated in 301/914 in East Baghdād and al-Sharḳiyya, where he remained until his death, after receiving, in 317/929, jurisdiction over the entire capital and being given the title of grand-*ḳāḍī*. Abū ᶜUmar played an important political rôle under the caliphate of al-Muḳtadir; in particular, it was he who, in 309/922, issued a *fatwā* against al-Ḥallādj [*q.v.*], whom he ultimately condemned. L. Massignon paints a severe portrait of the man and accuses him of having given too much servile obedience to the authorities: "An accomplished courtier", he wrote, "with a magnificent command of manners which will always be legendary, and curiously devoted to the use of perfumes, he was able to contradict himself with the most disconcerting cynicism; he compensated for the imperfect subtlety of his Mālikī rite in matters of *ḥadīth* and of *ḳiyās* with a fastidious concern for the form in canonical casuistry; he must have been very proud of having finally succeeded, for the 'common good', in concluding such an arduous case with such an ingenious solution" (*Le cas de Ḥallāj*, in *Opera minora*, ii, 181). It is a known fact that he had drawn from the doctrine of al-Ḥallādj concerning the seven turns around the Kaᶜba of the heart "an argument to make him one with the Carmathian raiders who sought to destroy the Temple of Mecca" (*ibid.*, 178).

In 310, his name was also put forward for the post of vizier and, in 317, he officiated when al-Muḳtadir agreed to abdicate, although he destroyed the records of the abdication.

Bibliography: Ṭabarī, index; ʿArīb, index; Ṣūlī-Canard, 40, 103, 107, 150; Masʿūdī, *Murūdj*, viii, 217-9, 256, 284 = §§ 3361-2, 3394, 3437; idem, *Tanbīh*, ed. Ṣāwī, 322, 329; Tanūkhī, *Nishwār*, iii, index, v, 208-11 and index, vi, vii, indices, viii, 106, 186-8; Khaṭīb Baghdādī, iii, 401-4; Ibn Taghrībardī, *Nudjūm*, iii, 235; Ibn al-ʿImād, *Shadharāt*, ii, 286-7; Ibn al-Djawzī, *Muntaẓam*, vi, 222; Massignon, *Passion*, index; Sourdel, *Vizirat*, index.

X. - Abu 'l-Ḥusayn ʿUMAR B. MUḤAMMAD (d. 328/940), his father's *nāʾib* in East Baghdād from 311/923 onwards, succeeded him in the office of grand-*ḳāḍī* (320-8). In the court of al-Rāḍī, who is said to have wept when he died, he acted as vizier and undertook numerous political missions; in 323/935, he participated in the case of Ibn Shannabūd [*q.v.*], although he did not preside over the tribunal. Al-Ṣūlī, who had been his teacher, devotes to him a panegyric entry, recording his death on 16 Shaʿbān 328/27 May 940 (tr. Canard, 219). He appears to have been well versed in matters of *farāʾiḍ*, of *ḥadīth*, of lexicography, of grammer and poetry, and several works are attributed to him: a *Musnad*, a *K. Gharīb al-ḥadīth* and a *K. al-Faradj baʿd al-shidda* which was the first of this genre.

Bibliography: Ṣūlī-Canard, index; Miskaway, *passim*; Tanūkhī, *Nishwār*, iii, vi, vii, indices; Khaṭīb Baghdādi, vii, 284; Yāḳūt, *Udabāʾ*, xvi, 67-70; Ibn al-Djawzī, *Muntaẓam*, vi, 307; Suyūṭī, *Bughya*, 364-5.

XI. - Abū Naṣr YŪSUF B. ʿUMAR (305-56/918-67) was already deputising for his father and astonishing the public with the extent of his knowledge when he sat for the first time as *ḳāḍī* in the mosque of al-Ruṣāfa (East Baghdād) on 25 Muḥarram 327/22 November 938. As *ḳāḍī* of West Baghdād in 328/940, it was he who recited the prayer for the dead over al-Rāḍī on 16 Rabīʿ I 329/19 December 940. He was retained in office by al-Muttaḳī, then dismissed and reinstated on 24 Shaʿbān 329/24 May 941, but the sequence of events is not clear; there is no doubt that he was soon dismissed once more, making his way to Iṣfahan; at his death, he was *ḳāḍī* of Yazd. In the meantime, he had adopted the Ẓāhirī doctrine.

Bibliography: Ṣūlī-Canard, 177, 220; Tanūkhī, *Nishwār*, iv, 23-5 and index, v, 261, vi, 14, vii, 16-8; Khaṭīb Baghdādī, xiv, 322-4; Ibn al-Djawzī, *Muntaẓam*, vi, 300, vii, 42.

XII. - Abū Muḥammad AL-ḤUSAYN B. ʿUMAR (d. after 360/971) succeeded his father together with his brother and was given East Baghdād in 328, then, the following year, he took on the duties of Abū Naṣr, but it seems that he did not retain them for long, since all trace of him is soon lost.

Bibliography: Ṣūlī-Canard, 227; Tanūkhī, *Nishwār*, iv, 203-4, vi, 74, vii, 17-18.

It would certainly be very interesting to pursue further study of this eminent family and to examine in a more exhaustive manner its links with authority on the one hand, and on the other, with the contemporary Banū Abi 'l-Shawārib. (CH. PELLAT)

IBN DJUMAYʿ, ABU 'L-MAKĀRIM HIBAT ALLĀH B. ZAYN B. ḤASAN: see the article IBN DJĀMIʿ, where should be read IBN DJAMIʿ; at present IBN DJUMAYʿ is generally considered as the right form of the name.

IBN DJURAYDJ, ABU 'L-WALĪD/ABŪ KHĀLID ʿABD AL-MALIK B. ʿABD AL-ʿAZĪZ B. DJURAYDJ AL-RŪMĪ AL-ḲURASHĪ AL-MAKKĪ (80-150/699-767), Meccan traditionist of Greek slave descent (the ancestor being called Gregorios) and probably a *mawlā* of the family of Khālid b. Asīd. After having first of all become interested in gath together traditions of philological, literary historical interest, he brought together *ḥadīths* the mouths of ʿAṭāʾ b. Abī Rabāḥ, al-Zuhrī, M hid, ʿIkrima and other famous persons, and p them on, notably to Wakīʿ, Ibn al-Mubārak Sufyān b. ʿUyayna; his erudition was such th was considered as the *imām* of the Ḥidjāz.

Little is known of his life, except that he ac panied Maʿn b. Zāʾida to the Yemen, soon ret from there and towards the end of his life mad way to ʿIrāḳ and al-Manṣūr's court. His na connected, on one hand, with the question c legality of the transmission of *ḥadīths* by lette not by *samāʿ*, and on the other, with the w down of traditions. Like Saʿīd b. Abī ʿArūba [*q.* ʿIrāḳ, he was regarded as having been the first i Ḥidjāz, and even in the whole Islamic empi gather together *ḥadīths* into a work *fi 'l-atha ḥurūf al-tafsīr*; these two scholars are often together, especially by al-Dhahabī in Ibn Taghrī *Nudjūm*, i, 351, year 143), who enumerates with regret the authors of the oldest collections. Gold in *Muh. Studien*, ii, 211-12, Eng. tr. ii, 196-7 shown that the priority accorded to Ibn Dju was unmerited, and has remarked that collectic *ḥadīths* are mentioned at an earlier period; a events, his work was a selection of legal traditic classified form, as the *Fihrist*, ed. Cairo 316, r grouped by chapters on legal purity, the praye *zakāt*, etc.

Bibliography: Djāḥiẓ, *Bayān*, iii, 283; i *Ḥayawān*, index; Ibn Ḳutayba, *Maʿārif*, 4 519; Ibn Khallikān, *Wafayāt*, no. 348, ed. ʿAbbās, iii, 163-4; Khaṭīb Baghdādī, *Taʾrīk* 400-7; Ibn Taghrībirdī, *Nudjūm*, i, 351; Ib ʿImād, *Shadharāt*, i, 226-7; Nawawī, *Tahdhīb*, Ibn Ḥadjar, *Tahdhīb al-Tahdhīb*, vi, 4 Dhahabī, *Tadhkirat al-ḥuffāẓ*, i, 160; Gold *Muh. Studien*, index; Brockelmann, S I, and bibl. given there; Bustānī, *Dāʾirat al-ma* ii, 404-5; Ziriklī, iv, 305. (CH. PELL

IBN FARĪGHŪN, SHAʿYĀ (?), author i 4th/10th century of a concise Arabic e clopaedia of the sciences the *Djawām ʿulūm* "Connections of the sciences". The a wrote in the upper Oxus lands, and dedicate work to the Muḥtādjid *amīr* of Čaghāniyān Abū ʿAlī Aḥmad b. Muḥammad b. al-Mu (d. 344/955). Minorsky surmised from his nam this has been interpreted correctly) that he v scion of the Farīghūnids [*q.v.*] in northern Afgh tān, rulers of the district of Gūzgān [*q.v.*] as utaries of the Sāmānids, and latterly, of the Gh wids; a connection too with the unknown auth the Persian geography, the *Ḥudūd al-ʿālam* above], is not impossible, though as yet unp (see V. Minorsky, *Ibn Farīghūn and the Ḥud ʿĀlam*, in *A locust's leg, studies in honour of Taqizadeh*, London 1962, 189-96).

The author of the *Djawāmiʿ* was first iden by D. M. Dunlop in his article *The Ğawām ʿulūm of Ibn Farīġūn*, in *Zeki Velidi Togan'a arm* Istanbul 1950-5, 348-53. He was clearly a pu Abū Zayd al-Balkhī, presumably the author c geography *Ṣuwar al-aḳālīm* re-edited and com by al-Iṣṭakhrī [see AL-BALKHĪ and DJUGHRĀFIY c, ii], d. 322/934, who had himself written a *K. A al-ʿulūm* "Book of the divisions of the scier Ibn Farīghūn used the *tashdjīr* system in h rangement of the sciences, i.e. that of "trees" "branches" for the groups and sub-groups.

ımi^c resembles the slightly later *Mafātīḥ al-* of Abū ʿAbd Allāh al-Khwārazmī [*q.v.*] in that livided in the first place into two *maḳālas*, one e Arabic sciences and one on the non-Arabic but it is not so clearly arranged as the *Mafātīḥ*. evaluation of the work must await publication text, for which several mss. exist.

Bibliography: In addition to references en above, see H. Ritter, *Philologika XIII*, in *ens*, iii (1950), 83-5; F. Rosenthal, *A history of slim historiography*², Leiden 1968, 34-6; ockelmann, S I, 435; Sezgin, *GAS*, i, 384, (reading the author of the *Djawāmiʿ*'s name "Mutaghabbī (?Mubtaghā) b. Furayʿūn"). (C. E. Bosworth)

N GHIDHĀHUM (usual French spelling: Ben ahem), ʿAlī b. Muḥammad, leader of the revolution in Tunisia.

rn around 1815 as the son of a Badawī doctor *ādī* of the Mādjir tribe in the district of Thala, said to have studied at the Great Mosque, ne secretary to the *ḳāʾid* of his tribe, al-ʿArbī i) Bakkūsh, then *ḳāḍī*, but was dismissed by the . When the Khaznadār government decided mber 1863) to double the *madjbā* tax, a revolt, ng in the south of March 1864, soon engulfed of the country. Ibn Ghidhāhum was proclaimed of the People" by the Mādjir and recognised by neighbouring tribes, probably thanks to his ous prestige (as an alleged *sharīf* and marabout e Tidjāniyya), as well as to his promises. He the *ḳāʾid* Bakkūsh and his entourage, yet aled to the tribes for moderation. His movement authority having declined by July, he accepted fer of amnesty and obtained an estate for him- nd tribal commands for his aides. On 26 July, *haykhs* and notables surrendered in the north- after the government had promised to halve *ushr* tax, appoint native *ḳāʾids* instead of Mam- and abolish the constitution. Yet, the Khaznadār ng merely played for time, Ibn Ghidhāhum up arms again in the autumn, but in January orces were crushed near Tebessa. He crossed Algeria and was interned till January 1866. The of the Tidjāniyya recommended him to the ch as one of his best *aḥbāb* and as a learned man had never mixed in politics. Hoping for the inī's intercession with the Bey, Ibn Ghidhāhum ed back to Tunisia, but was caught and died in n (10 October 1867). The significance of the ion and the personality and role of Ibn Ghidhā- have been reconsidered since the thirties. merit sees the former as an "episode in the nial struggle of the Badū against the settled lation and beylical authority in general" (*RT*], 227). In A. Temimi's view, Ibn Ghidhāhum d vision, resolve and a plan; he was carried by the events rather than shaped them, and l to embody the aspirations of the revolution; etrayed them and dealt the latter a death blow *MM*, vii [1970], 176).

Bibliography: further to references in the xt: Ch. Monchicourt, *La région du Haut Tell en nisie*, Paris 1913, 230, 298, 318; M. Gandolphe, *s évènements de 1864 dans le Sahel, etc.* in *RT* 918), 138-53; P. Grandchamp, *Documents atifs à la révolution de 1864 en Tunisie*, Tunis 35; J. Ganiage, *Les origines du protectorat nçais en Tunisie (1861-1881)*, Paris 1959, 6 f., 232, 248 f., 251, 262 f., 267 f.; Ibn Abi Ḍiyāf, *Itḥāf ahl al-zamān bi-akhbār mulūk tūnis wa-ʿahd al-amān*, Tunis 1964, 5, 112-33, 136, 168-71; B. Salāma, *Thawrat Ibn Ghidhāhum*, Tunis 1967; Kh. Chater, *Insurrection et répression dans la Tunisie du XIXe siècle: la mehalla de Zanouk au Sahel 1864)*, Tunis 1978. (P. Shinar)

IBN AL-ḤĀDJDJ, Ḥamdūn b. ʿAbd al-Raḥmān al-Sulamī al-Mirdāsī al-Fāsī (1174-1232/1760-1817), "one of the most outstanding scholars of the reign of Mawlay Sulaymān" (1206-38/1792-1823), according to E. Lévi-Provençal, *Les historiens des Chorfa*, Paris 1922, 342, n. 5).

As the *faḳīh* appointed to the Moroccan sultan, he filled the office of *muḥtasib* of Fās, then of *ḳāʾid* of the Gharb, before devoting a great part of his activities to literature. He is the author of several commentaries and glosses, of epistles of a religious character and of an account of the pilgrimage which he made, but also the author of a *maḳṣūra* [*q.v.*], of a poetic version of the *Ḥikam* of Ibn ʿAṭāʾ Allāh al-Iskandarī [*q.v.*], of a poem of nearly 4,000 verses in praise of the Prophet (with a commentary in 5 volumes) and a series of eulogies of the sultan. Some of his writings have been preserved in manuscript at Rabat (see Lévi-Provençal, *Les manuscrits arabes de Rabat*, Paris 1921, nos. 292 (5), 305, 337, 338, 434, 497 (11-12), and part of his poetic output (mss. 337 and 338 above; now K 963 and K 2707) has been gathered together into a *Dīwān* lithographed at Fās and containing notably a certain number of *muwashshaḥāt*. This versifier, who still enjoys a certain celebrity, sometimes gave himself up to some curious pyrotechnics. M. Lakhdar (*Vie littéraire*, 283-4) sets forth a poem in 26 verses rhyming in *-dī* and in the metre *basīṭ*, of which each hemistich is divided into four sections written successively in red, black, blue and black; if the blue column is removed, the metre *munsariḥ* results, if the blue and the red, *muḳtaḍab*, and if the red alone, *madīd makhbūn*.

The genealogy and the *manāḳib* [*q.v.*] of Ḥamdūn Ibn al-Ḥādjdj were the subject of a monograph by his son Muḥammad al-Ṭālib (see Lévi-Provençal, *Chorfa*, 342-5) called the *Riyāḍ al-ward* (ms. Rabat 396).

Bibliography: Nāṣirī, *K. al-Istiḳṣā*, vi, 151; Kattānī, *Salwat al-anfās*, lith. Fās 1316/1898, iii, 4; Fuḍaylī, *al-Durra al-bahiyya*, lith. Fās 1314/1896, ii, 327; Sāʾiḥ, *al-Muntakhabāt al-ʿabḳariyya*, Rabat 1920, 83; ʿA. Gannūn, *al-Nubūgh al-maghribī*, Beirut² 1961, i, 296-7, ii, 257, 282-7; Ibn Sūda, *Dalīl muʾarrikh al-Maghrib al-aḳṣā*, Casablanca 1960, i, 215, ii, 349, 390, 421-2; ʿA. al-Djirārī, *Muwashshaḥāt maghribiyya*, Casablanca 1973, 182-5; M. Lakhdar, *Vie littéraire*, 281-4. (Ed.)

IBN ḤĀTIM, Badr al-Dīn Muḥammad al-Hamdānī, state official and historian under the second Rasūlid sultan of the Yemen, al-Muẓaffar Yūsuf (647-94/1249-95).

Ibn Ḥātim's name appears nowhere in the biographical literature of mediaeval Yemen, and neither the date of his birth nor that of his death is known. The last reference to him falls under the year 702/1302-3. However, from his history of the Ayyūbids and early Rasūlids in the Yemen, *al-Simṭ al-ghālī al-thaman fī akhbār al-mulūk min al-Ghuzz bi'l-Yaman* (ed. G. R. Smith, *The Ayyūbids and early Rasūlids, etc.*, GMS, N.S. xxvi/1, *The Arabic text*, London 1974), it is possible to cull some information concerning the man and his official life. He belonged to the Banū Ḥātim of Yām of Hamdān, who at the time of the Ayyūbid conquest of the Yemen in 569/1173 controlled the area of Ṣanʿāʾ, the country's chief town. He was thus an Ismāʿīlī, though this proved no handicap to his rise to a high position in the staunchly Sunnī Rasūlid state under al-Muẓaffar Yūsuf. He was a member of the small cadre of some four or five officials employed by the sultan in the capacity of roving ambassador, personally representing him wherever in the country he was needed, now negotiating with recalcitrant tribes, now conveying a personal message from the sultan, at times even participating in military operations.

His official state position, however, did not restrict or hamper his historical writing in any way. His account of the Ayyūbid and first two Rasūlid sultans is a refreshingly impartial one, perhaps slightly biased towards his own family, the Banū Ḥātim, but containing much otherwise unknown information on this crucial period of Yemenī history, when the country was beginning to form a political unit after centuries of rule by numerous petty dynasties. He writes in the *Simṭ* of al-Muẓaffar Yūsuf's reign as a dispassionate eye-witness. We know too that he wrote *al-ʿIḳd al-thamīn fī akhbār mulūk al-Yaman al-mutaʾakhkhirīn*, though this remains undiscovered. It was clearly a more general history of the Yemen, covering a longer time-span than the *Simṭ*.

Bibliography: see the edition mentioned above and Smith, *The Ayyūbids, etc.*, Part 2, London 1978; idem, *The Ayyūbids and Rasūlids—the transfer of power in 7th/13th century Yemen*, in *IC*, xliii (1969), 175-88; Sir J. Redhouse and Muhammad Asal, *el-Khazrajī's History of the Resúlí Dynasty of Yemen*, GMS, iii, Leyden and London 1906-18. (G. R. Smith)

IBN HISHĀM al-**LAKHMĪ** al-Sabtī, Abū ʿAbd Allāh Muḥammad b. Aḥmad b. Hishām b. Ibrāhīm b. Khalaf, lexicographer, grammarian, *adīb* and versifier. He was probably born at Seville, and certainly died in that city in 577/1182, after having lived for a long time at Ceuta.

We know very little of his life, but his biographers list his masters and his pupils and indicate the titles of his works, amongst which one notes several commentaries; one may merely remark that these included a *sharḥ* on the *Maḳṣūra* of Ibn Durayd, which was especially appreciated by al-Ṣafadī (*Wāfī*, ii, 1301) and al-Baghdādī (*Khizāna*, Būlāḳ, i, 490 = Cairo, iii, 105), *al-Fawāʾid al-maḥṣūra fī sharḥ al-Maḳṣūra* (of which several mss. exist; see Brockelmann, S I, 172; partial ed. by Boysen, in 1828 [see maḳṣūra]) and a *sharḥ* on the *Faṣīḥ* of Thaʿlab which already shows up Ibn Hishām's taste for the purity of the language (cf. al-Suyūṭī, *Bughya*, 20). There are extant a small quantity of verses on the various senses of the word *khāl* and above all, a treatise on the *laḥn al-ʿāmma*, given this title by Ibn al-Abbār and al-Suyūṭī (for *m.h.n.* read *laḥn*), but otherwise called *Taḳwīm al-lisān* by al-Marrākushī, and given two different titles in the Escorial ms. 46, *K. al-Radd ʿalā 'l-Zubaydī fī laḥn al-ʿawāmm*, and ms. 99, *K. al-Madkhal/al-Mudkhal ilā taḳwīm al-lisān wa-taʿlīm al-bayān*. This work, which provides precious information on Spanish and Moroccan Arabic, comprises two basic sections: in the first one, the author makes critical remarks on the parallel books of al-Zubaydī and Ibn Makkī [*q.vv.*], defending at the same time actual usages with arguments drawn from the old lexicographers. The transitional part is brought about by means of an exposition of the terms which provide dialectical variants (*lughāt*), amongst which speakers have a tendency to choose the less good one and thus end up committing f[aults]. The second section, now thereby introduced, [deals] with current faulty expressions caused by pho[netic], morphological or semantic changes; unnece[ssary] borrowings are mercilessly tracked down [and] replaced by the corresponding Arabic words[;] correct forms are introduced by the formula "[one should not] say . . .", followed by "whilst the correct [usage] requires one to say . . ." or by an equivalent for[m]. The treatise ends with a series of proverbs d[rawn] from classical poetry, but corrupted and defo[rmed] by the *ʿāmma*; the use of this latter term pose[s,] in all analogous works, a difficult problem, conce[rning] which one should refer to the article Laḥn [al-]ʿĀmma.

The last chapter has been edited by ʿAbd al-[ʿAzīz] al-Ahwānī in *Mélanges Taha Husain* (Cairo [1962],) 273-94); this same scholar had already publish[ed a] study on the work and its author followed [by a] selection of western terms (*alfāẓ maghrib[iyya]*) appearing in the second section (see *RIMA*, [ii] [1376/1956], 133-57, and iii/2, 285-321). The [re]mainder of this same section has been edited [criti]cally, with abundant annotation, and presente[d by] M. El-Hannach as a *thèse du 3e cycle* at the Unive[rsity] of Paris IV in 1977, but this has not yet been [pub]lished.

It may be of interest to note that the *Madkha[l]* [was] put together as part of a fairly common proce[ss] which it is possible, for once, to follow the de[tails]. Thus the treatises of al-Zubaydī and Ibn M[akkī] inspired in Ibn Hishām various observations w[hich] he communicated to his pupils without act[ually] putting them together in the form of a book; notes which he left behind or which his pupils [took] were brought together in 607/1210 for a man na[med] Ibn al-Shārī under the title of *K. al-Madkh[al ilā] taḳwīm al-lisān*; at the beginning of the 8th/[14th] century, Muḥammad b. ʿAlī b. Hāniʾ al-Lak[hmī] al-Sabtī (d. 733/1332; see al-Suyūṭī, *Bughya*, [...] and Pons Boigues, *Ensayo*, 319) arranged all [the] materials and "published" them under the tit[le] *Inshād al-ḍawāl(l) wa-irshād al-suʾʾāl*; in the c[ourse] of this same century, this latter work was i[n] turn worked on by Ibn Khātima (d. 770/1365 [q.v.]) who called the résumé which he had made *Īrād al-laʾāl min Inshād al-ḍawāl(l)*; finally, [an] unknown author extracted from this last avat[ar a] section which G. S. Colin thought worthy of pub[lica]tion as a document (in *Hespéris*, xii/2 [1931], 1[...]); it is the introduction of this extract which allow[s us] to trace back this chain.

Bibliography: In addition to works alr[eady] mentioned, see Ibn al-Abbār, *Takmila*, no. 1[...]; Ibn Diḥya, *Muṭrib*, Cairo 1954, 183; Ibn ʿAb[d al-]Malik al-Marrākushī, *al-Dhayl wa 'l-takmila*, B. N. Paris 1256, f. 25; Suyūṭī, *Bughya*, [...]; H. Derenbourg, *Catalogue*, i, 58; Pons Boig[ues,] *Ensayo*, 280; Brockelmann, I, 308, I², 113, S I, 541. (Ch. Pella[t])

IBN KABAR, Abu 'l-Barakāt, Shams al-Ri[yāsa] al-Naṣrānī, Copt from Egypt (d. between [...] and 727/1320-7) who was secretary to Baybar[s al-]Manṣūrī [*q.v.*], author of the *Zubdat al-fikra*. Cer[tain] historians, e.g. al-Ṣafadī, followed by Ibn Ḥa[jar] and al-Maḳrīzī, allege that Ibn Kabar helped [to] compile his book. It is difficult, impossible even[, to] evaluate the importance of this help, for Bay[bars] undeniably had a talent as historian and a [...] lively taste for books and chronicles, as attests cle[arly] al-Mufaḍḍal b. Abī Faḍāʾil, Ibn Kabar's conten[...]

and co-religionist, and this view is shared by l-Maḥāsin Ibn Taghrībardī.

reover, it is certain that Ibn Kabar made a ıé of Baybars al-Manṣūrī's history, the *Mukh--akhbār*, the ms. of which is preserved in the osiana collection of Milan (Ms C 45 Inf.). The n of the Fāṭimids, together with part of the of al-Manṣūr Ḳalāwūn, is lacking in this manu-, and the text stops abruptly in the year 702/

ı Kabar's main work is a book on the eccle-cal sciences of the Copts, *Kitāb Miṣbāḥ al- wa-īḍāḥ al-khidma*. This has been edited and lated by Dom Louis Villecourt, with the col-ıtion of Mgr. E. Tisserant and Gaston Wiet, in *logia Orientalis*, xx/iv, Paris 1928. Ibn Kabar eft behind a Coptic-Arabic dictionary, published thanasius Kircher under the title *Scala magna.* others of his works remain unpublished.

Bibliography: al-Mufaḍḍal b. Abi 'l-Faḍa'il, *Manhadj al-sadīd*, ed. Blochet, *PO*, xiii, xiv, xx, is 1919-28; Maḳrīzī, *Sulūk*, ed. Ziyāda, ii/1, ; Ibn Ḥadjar, *al-Durar al-kāmina*, Cairo 1966, 43; Ibn Taghrībardī, *al-Manhal al-ṣāfī*, BN is ms., Fonds arabe 2069, f. 106a; Sakhāwī, *in*, tr. F. Rosenthal, in *A history of Muslim oriography*, Leiden 1952, 418; *Lingua aegyp-a restitua*, Rome 1643, 41-272; Brockelmann, , 55 (correct Bekr to Kabar); E. Tisserant, Villecourt and G. Wiet, *Recherches sur la sonalité et la vie de Abul Barakat Ibn Kubr*, in *C*, xxii (1921-2), 373-94; Graf, *GCAL*, ii, 438- O. Löfgren and Renato Traini, *Arabic manu-ipts in the Bibliotheca Ambrosiana*, i (Antico ndo and Medio Fondo), Vicenza 1975, 71.

(ABDEL HAMID SALEH)

N AL-ḲAṬṬĀN, a name well-known to histo-of the mediaeval Muslim West and, as such, thought to have been borne by only one person. is, however, no doubt that it was the name vo different people who, in all probability, father and son. Since nothing further can be of this putative relationship, it seems prudent eak of the two persons as the "Elder" and the nger".

IBN AL-ḲAṬṬĀN THE ELDER. This person is to entified with one Abu 'l-Ḥasan ʿAlī b. Muḥam-b. ʿAbd al-Malik b. Yaḥyā al-Kutāmī al-Fāsī, ligious scholar and jurist from Fās, for ı we have only the date of his death, viz. ıʿ I 628/7 January 1231. As all his biographers that he died in A.H. 628, he can hardly have the author (as supposed by Lévi-Provençal and s after him) of the *K. Naẓm al-djumāna* (see), since the author of this work served the had caliph al-Murtaḍā (*reg.* 646-65/1248-66). e early background of this Ibn al-Ḳaṭṭān, all now is that he was of Cordovan origin. We can assume that either he or his father and family emigrated from Andalusia to Fās. In later life portance seems to have lain in the prominence position in the Almohad hierarchy, for we are that he was head of the *ṭalaba* in Marrakesh and he enjoyed great prosperity in the service of the (on the *ṭalaba* as a high-ranking class of Almohad taries, and on Ibn al-Ḳaṭṭān in particular, see kins, *Medieval Muslim government in Barbary*, , and 108, respectively). After the death of the h Abū Yaʿḳūb Yūsuf al-Mustanṣir, Ibn al-ān the Elder fell victim to the Almohad power gle which ended in the victory of Muḥammad Allāh (al-ʿĀdil) over the caliph ʿAbd al-Wāḥid after only eight months' rule. Leaving Marrakesh in 621/1224, Ibn al-Ḳaṭṭān was able to return later, but in fact he seems never again to have been able to make a secure and permanent home there or indeed to lead a settled life. When he died, he was *ḳāḍī* of Sidjilmāsa, a city then in rebellion against the reigning caliph. Among writings attributed to this Ibn al-Ḳaṭṭān are a commentary on the *K. al-Aḥkām* of ʿAbd al-Ḥaḳḳ al-Ishbīlī (confused with the *K. al-Aḥkām* of Ibn al-Ḳaṭṭān the Younger), a *Maḳāla fi 'l-awzān* and *al-Naẓar fī aḥkām al-naẓar*.

2. IBN AL-ḲAṬṬĀN THE YOUNGER, otherwise Abū ʿAlī (and/or Abū Muḥammad) al-Ḥasan (or al-Ḥusayn) b. ʿAlī b. al-Ḳaṭṭān, historian, jurist and traditionist. Unlike the Elder, this Ibn al-Ḳaṭṭān has, surprisingly, found no place in known biographies. If "b. ʿAlī b. al-Ḳaṭṭān" is any guide, we may be right in supposing him to have been a son of the preceding Ibn al-Ḳaṭṭān. The dates of his birth and death are unknown; the most we can say is that he flourished in the reign of al-Murtaḍa (see above), whose favour he enjoyed and for whom he is said by Ibn ʿIdhārī to have written a history entitled *K. Naẓm al-djumān wa-wāḍiḥ al-bayān fīmā salafa min akhbār al-zamān* (there are variants of the title) as well as a number of other works, viz. *K. Shifā' al-ghalal fī akhbār al-anbiyā' wa 'l-rusul*, *K. al-Aḥkām li-bayān āyātihi ʿalayhi 'l-salām* (on *ḥadīth*), *K. al-Munādjāt*, and *K. al-Masmūʿāt*. Of all these writings, only a part of the *Naẓm* seems to have survived. Until this part was discovered, the work was only known through the use which other Maghribī writers had made of it, notably Ibn ʿIdhārī. The complete *Naẓm* was, so far as can be gleaned, a large encyclopaedic work covering the history, and to some extent the geography, of North Africa and Spain from the Arab conquest to the author's own time. The extant portion, dealing with the period 500-33/1106-7 to 1138-9, bespeaks a tendentious "palace" chronicle, but it is valuable as it not only reproduces original official documents and quotes authors whose works are no longer known to us, but it also reports on the Fāṭimids in Egypt, giving information not to be found elsewhere.

Bibliography: J. F. P. Hopkins, *Medieval Muslim government in Barbary*, London 1958, loc. cit.; Maḥmūd ʿAlī Makkī, *Djuz' min Kitāb Naẓm al-djumān* (Muhammad V University Publications), Rabat n.d., but *ca.* 1966 (almost all the main references may be found in Makkī's introduction to this edition); on Abu 'l-Ḥasan, see I. ʿAbbās, *Contributions to the material on the history of the Almohads, as portrayed by a new biography of Abū al-Ḥasan Ibn al-Ḳaṭṭān (628/1230)*, in *Akten des VII. Kongresses für Arabistik und Islamwissenschaft*, Göttingen 1976, 15-38.

(J. D. LATHAM)

IBN KAYSĀN, ABU 'L-HASAN MUḤAMMAD B. AḤMAD B. IBRĀHĪM, Baghdādī philologist who according to all the known sources, died in 299/311-12; this date is nevertheless challenged by Yāḳūt who, believing that al-Khaṭīb al-Baghdādī is in error, opts for 320/932.

He was the pupil of al-Mubarrad and Thaʿlab [*q.vv.*], and is said to have brought together the doctrines of the grammatical schools of both Baṣra and Kūfa, though his own preference was for the former; he was moreover the author of a work, no longer surviving, a *K. al-Masā'il ʿalā madhhab al-naḥwiyyīn mimmā khtalafa fīhi al-Kūfiyyūn wa 'l-Baṣriyyūn*. Abū Ḥayyān al-Tawḥīdī relates in his *Imtāʿ* (iii, 6) that he had written over his door "enter and eat". In another, unspecified work, the same author (cited in particular by Yāḳūt and al-Suyūṭī) describes the programme of his lecture courses and describes the crowd which surrounded him, leaving about a hundred mounts in front of the gate of the mosque where he was teaching, but Yāḳūt does not seem to take Abū Ḥayyan's account at its face value. In addition to the *K. al-Masāʾil*, Ibn al-Nadīm attributes the following works to Ibn Kaysān: *al-Muhadhdhab fi 'l-naḥw*, *K. al-Shādhānī fi 'l-naḥw*, *al-Mudhakkar wa 'l-muʾannath*, *al-Maḳṣūr wa 'l-mamdūd*, *Mukhtaṣar al-naḥw*, *al-Mukhtār fī ʿilal al-naḥw*, *al-Hidjāʾ wa 'l-khaṭṭ*, *al-Waḳf wa 'l-ibtidāʾ*, *al-Ḥaḳāʾiḳ*, *al-Burhān*, *al-Ḳirāʾāt*, *Maʿānī al-Ḳurʾān* and *Gharīb al-ḥadīth*, to which one should perhaps add *Ghalaṭ adab al-kātib*, *al-Lāmāt*, *al-Taṣārīf*, *al-Fāʿil wa 'l-mafʿūl bihi*, cited by Yāḳūt, *Sharḥ al-ṭiwāl* (al-Anbārī) and a *Talḳīb al-ḳawāfī wa-talḳīb ḥarakātihā*, which is doubtfully authentic. The *Kitāb Maṣābīḥ al-kitāb* (read the latter word thus) ascribed by A. J. Arberry, *Chester Beatty Library. Handlist of the Arabic manuscripts*, Dublin 1955, to Ibn Kaysān seems to be in fact by an author of Shīʿi sympathies, the well-known Abu 'l-Ḳāsim al-Ḥusayn al-Wazīr al-Maghribī [see AL-MAGHRIBĪ]; see U. Y. Ismail, *A critical edition of* al-Maṣābīḥ fī tafsīr al-Qur'ān al-ʿaẓīm *attributed to Ibn Kaysān al-Naḥwī* ..., Manchester Ph.D. thesis 1979, unpublished.

Bibliography: Ibn al-Nadīm, *Fihrist*, 81 (ed. Cairo 120); Khaṭīb, Baghdādī, *Taʾrīkh Baghdād*, i, 325; Ḳifṭī, *Inbāh*, ed. Cairo 1369-74/1950-5, iii, 57-9; Zubaydī, *Ṭabaḳāt al-naḥwiyyīn*, ed. Cairo 1373/1954, 170-1; Anbārī, *Nuzha*, ed. A. Amer, Stockholm 1963, 143; Yāḳūt, *Udabāʾ*, xvii, 137-41; Suyūṭī, *Bughya*, 8; F. Bustānī, *Dāʾirat al-maʿārif*, iv, 484; Brockelmann, I², 111, S I, 170.

(CH. PELLAT)

IBN KHALAF, the name of a family, of whom the best-known two members are:

1. ABŪ GHĀLIB MUḤAMMAD B. ʿALĪ B. KHALAF, called Fakhr al-Mulk, vizier of the Būyids, born at Wāsiṭ on Thursday 22 Rabīʿ II 354/27 April 965, and killed by Sulṭān al-Dawla Abū Shudjāʿ Fanā-Khusraw on 27 Rabīʿ I 407/3 September 1016. The poets and scholars, to whom he had been extremely generous, composed for him a great number of poetic eulogies, and al-Karadjī [*q.v.*] dedicated his *Fakhrī* and his *Kāfī* to him.

2. ABŪ SHUDJĀʿ MUḤAMMAD AL-ASHRAF B. MUḤAMMAD B. ʿALĪ B. KHALAF, son of the preceding, whose date of birth is unknown, but he was killed in 466/1073-4 by Badr al-Djamālī [*q.v.*], at the time when this latter arrived in Egypt at the summons of the Fāṭimid caliph al-Mustanṣir. Abū Shudjāʿ was this caliph's minister on two occasions: firstly, for two days only, in Muḥarram 457/December 1064-January 1065, and secondly, at the end of the same month in the same year, and this tenure of office lasted till mid-Rabīʿ I of the same year/February 1065.

It seems that this minister should not be confused with ʿAlī b. Khalaf al-Kātib [see the following article], despite some recent attempts at this identification which are conjectural and unjustifiable.

Bibliography: Ibn Khallikān, *Wafayāt*, ii, 85; Ibn al-Ṣayrafī, *Ishāra*, 53; Ṣābiʾ, *al-Wuzarāʾ*, ed. Farradj, *passim*; Ibn Muyassar, *Taʾrīkh Miṣr*, ed. Massé, ii, 15, 23, 33; Suyūṭī, *Ḥusn al-muḥāḍara*, ii, 203; Dawadārī, *Kanz al-durar*, vi, 382; Maḳrīzī, *Ittiʿāẓ*, ii, 271, 313, 333; Ibn al-Ḳalānisī, *Dhayl*, 64; Ṣafadī, *Wāfī*, iv, 118; Yāḳūt, *Udabāʾ*, xiii, 260, xviii, 234; idem, *Buldān*, v, 350; Ibn Saʿīd, *Mughrib*, section al-Ḳāhira, ed. Naṣṣār, 35[…] Taghrībardī, *Nudjūm*, iv, 242, 257; G. Sh[…] *Madjmūʿa*, i, 114-5; A. H. Saleh, *Une sou[…] Qalqašandī*, Mawādd al-Bayān, *et son a[…] ʿAlī b. Ḫalaf*, in *Arabica*, xx/2 (1973), 19[…]

(ABDEL HAMID SAL[…]

IBN KHALAF, ABU 'L-ḤASAN ʿALĪ B. K[…] B. ʿABD AL-WAHHĀB AL-KĀTIB, one of the […] secretaries (*kuttāb*) of the Fāṭimids of […] (al-Ḳalḳashandī, *Ṣubḥ*, vi, 432; idem, *Ḍawʾ*, […] The date of his birth is unknown, but it is l[…] that in 437/1045-6 he was living in Egypt, wh[…] wrote his work for the secretaries of the *dīw[…] inshāʾ*, his manual called the *Mawādd al-[…]* which contains in particular model letters and o[…] documents. An incomplete manuscript of this[…] has recently been identified in the Süleym[…] Library in Istanbul (Fatih 4128).

Ibn Khalaf was also the author of two […] which he cites in his *Mawādd*, the *Ālat al-[…]* (fols. 162b and 166a) and a *Kitāb al-kharādj[…]* 16a and 25b), but these have not come to ligh[…] date of his death is uncertain. Al-Ḥabbāl al[…] records, in his *Wafayāt al-Miṣriyyīn fi 'l-ʿa[…] Fāṭimī*, in Shawwāl 455 the death of a certai[…] 'l-Ḥasan ʿAlī b. Khalaf al-Zayyāt (cf. *RIMA[…]* [1956], 336-7), who could be our secretary.

Bibliography: In addition to references […] in the article, see Ḥādjdjī Khalīfa, ii, 55[…] Shayyāl, *Madjmūʿāt*, i, 14-15; S. M. Stern, *F[…] decrees*, 105; A. H. Saleh, *Une source de Qalqa[…]* Mawādd al-Bayān, *et son auteur*, *ʿAlī b. Ḫa[…]* *Arabica*, xx/2 (1973), 192-200.

(ABDEL HAMID SAL[…]

IBN KĪRĀN, ABŪ ʿABD ALLĀH MUḤA[…] AL-ṬAYYIB B. ʿABD AL-MADJĪD B. ʿAB[…] SALĀM B. KĪRĀN (1172-1227/1758-1812), *faḳīh* littérateur of Fās. He received a traditional e[…] tion from the local scholars, and himself t[…] rhetoric to numerous pupils, including Ibn al-Ḥ[…] [*q.v.*], Ḥamdūn, Ibn ʿAdjība, al-Kūhin [*q.vv.*] the sultan Mawlāy Sulaymān (1205-38/1792-[…] who continually showed his high opinion o[…] Kīrān by consulting him and by entrusting to[…] with other *fuḳahāʾ*, the applying of his ordin[…] His work is largely preserved, and comprises […] mentaries on various sūras and other writings […] Rabat K 1373, K 1379, K 1673, K 2534), n[…] *al-Murshid al-muʿīn ʿalā 'l-ḍarūrī min ʿilm al-[…]* Ibn ʿĀshir (lith. Fās 1296; ms. Rabat K 81)[…] also an *urdjūza* on the logic of his pupil Ib[…] Ḥādjdj (ms. Rabat 434). He also wrote gloss[…] Ibn Hishām's commentary on the *Alfiyya* o[…] Mālik (Fās 1315) and, in collaboration with […] other scholars, a commentary on the forty *ḥadī[…]* al-Nawawī (ms. Rabat 55). Amongst his o[…] works, one might mention two short gramm[…] works on *law* (ms. Rabat D 938) and *ḳāla* (K 1373); an *urdjūza* on metaphor (Fās 1310; the[…] mentary of al-Būrī in ms. Rabat D 921); and a […] work meant to exhort the faithful (K 1072 […] some *responsa*).

His brother Muḥammad b. Abd al-Madjī[…] 2 Muḥarram 1214/6 June 1799) has left behi[…] *urdjūza* on *iʿrāb* (ms. D 1348, with comm.), a[…] son Abū Bakr (d. 4 Djumādā II 1267/16 April […] was an *imām* at Fās.

Bibliography: Nāṣirī, *Istiḳṣā*, iv, 149; […]tānī, *Salwat al-anfās*, lith. Fās 1316/1898, iii, […] E. Lévi-Provençal, *Chorfa*, index; Ibn […] *Dalīl muʾarrikh al-Maghrib al-Aḳṣā*, i, […] Brockelmann, S II, 875; Bustānī, *DM*, iii,[…]

Lakhdar, *Vie littéraire*, 275-7 and bibl. given ›re. (ED.)

›N AL-ĶUFF, AMĪN AL-DAWLA ABU 'L-FARADJ ›UWAFFAĶ AL-DĪN YAᶜĶŪB B. ISḤĀĶ, known as ›ALIKĪ AL-MASĪḤĪ (the Melkite Christian) AL-›AKĪ, physician and surgeon.

› was born at Karak [*q.v.*] in 630/1233. His ›r, Muwaffaḳ al-Dīn Yaᶜḳūb, was a learned clerk under the Ayyūbids, who excelled his in Arabic philology, literature, calligraphy, ›y and history. Ibn Abī Uṣaybiᶜa, in his *ᶜUyūn ›bā'*, Cairo 1882, ii, 273-4, gives the first and complete, contemporary biography of Ibn al-› brief though it is. From it we learn that the ›y moved from al-Karak to Sarkhad in south-›rn Syria, whither the father was transferred to for the state, possibly *ca.* 643/1245. Becoming ›ainted with Ibn Abī Uṣaybiᶜa, the father's ›onship with the latter soon developed into a ›ng friendship. Upon request, Ibn Abī Uṣaybiᶜa ›y accepted to be Abu 'l-Faradj's first medical ›er, finding the latter a very intelligent student. ›r this master, Abu 'l-Faradj mastered first of all ›asic courses and doctrines of the healing art. ›hen took the advanced subjects of therapeutics ›clinical medicine. When towards the middle of ›century, the father again moved to Damascus new job there, Abu 'l-Faradj accompanied the ›y and continued his education at the Syrian ›al. Besides medicine, he studied philosophy and › natural history, metaphysics and mathematics. also, no doubt, he obtained medical training at ›ity's hospitals. During the reign of the Ayyūbid ›ṣir Ṣalāḥ al-Dīn Yūsuf (648-58/1250-60), Ibn ›ıff was appointed as the first known military ›cian-surgeon at ᶜAdjlūn [*q.v.*]. There he stayed ›everal years, until he was summoned during the of the Mamlūk al-Ẓāhir Baybars (658-76/1260-›o become the physician-surgeon at the Damas-›itadel.

›ı al-Ḳuff's fame seems to have spread widely, ›he gained the respect of his colleagues and ›cal students. Upon requests from a number of ›, he composed several works, including his ›known manual on surgery, *ᶜUmdat al-iṣlāḥ fī ›l ṣināᶜat al-djarrāḥ*, ed. Hyderabad 1356/1937. ›r works still extant in manuscript include his ›on the healing art, *al-Shāfī fi 'l-ṭibb*; his com-›ary on Ibn Sīnā's *al-Ḳānūn* on medicine' ›*ı al-Ḳānūn*; his commentary on Hippocrates' ›*risms*, *al-Uṣūl fī Sharḥ al-fuṣūl*, which deserves ›dependent investigation; and his compendium ›ealth care and the treatment of diseases, *Djāmiᶜ ›araḍ fī ḥifẓ al-ṣiḥḥa wa-dafᶜ al-maraḍ*. He died ›amascus in 685/1286 at a relatively early age.

›*Bibliography*: In addition to Ibn Abī Uṣay-›a's *ᶜUyūn al-anbā'*, see Ḥādjdjī Khalīfa, *Kashf*, Istanbul 565, 1023; Leclerc, *Histoire*, ii, 203-4; ›ockelmann, *GAL*, I, 649, S, I, 899; E. Wiede-›nn, *Beschreibung von Schlangen bei Ibn Kaff*, ›*SPMSE*, xlviii-xlix (1916-17), 61-4; G. Sobhy, ›*ı 'l-Kuff, an Arabian surgeon of the VII century ›Higra*, in *Jnal. of the Egyptian Medical Asso-›tion*, xx (1937), 349-57; O. Spies, *Beiträge zur ›abischen Zahnheilkunde*, in *Sudhoffs Archiv*, ›i (1962), 153-77; G. Kircher, *Die einfachen ›ilmittel aus dem Handbuch der Chirurgie des ›ı al-Quff*, diss. Bonn 1967; S. Hamarneh, *The ›ysician, therapist and surgeon Ibn al-Quff*, ›iro 1974; idem, *Catalogue of Arabic manuscripts medicine and pharmacy at the British Library*, ›iro 1975, 189-93. (S. K. HAMARNEH)

IBN KULLĀB, ᶜABD ALLĀH B. SAᶜĪD B. MUḤAM-MAD AL-ĶAṬṬĀN AL-BAṢRĪ (died 241/855?), foremost representative of a compromising theology during the time of the *miḥna* [*q.v.*]. Nothing is known about his life. He contradicted the Muᶜtazilī doctrine of *khalḳ al-Ḳur'ān* by introducing a distinction between the speech of God (*kalām Allāh*) and its realisation: God is eternally speaking (*mutakallim*), but he can only be *mukallim*, addressing himself to somebody, if this addressee exists. Speech is a permanent and unchangeable attribute (*ṣifa* or *maᶜnā*) which subsists in God; but when, in revelation, it becomes speech to somebody, it is subject to alteration: it may be represented in various languages and must adapt itself to various situations by taking the form of an order, a statement etc. The expression *khalḳ al-Ḳur'ān* is thus misleading: it is true insofar as the "trace" (*rasm*) of God's speech is concerned, its reproduction (*ḥikāya*) in historical reality, especially in a Holy Scripture, and its subsequent recitation (*ḳur'ān* = *ḳirā'a*), which is a meritorious action (*kasb*) performed by man; but it does not allow for the conclusion drawn by the Muᶜtazila that God is only speaking through temporal speech and not *per se*. That there is uncreated speech is proved by the word *kun* "Be", by which God created everything else and which can therefore not be created itself. This uncreated speech does not yet consist of letters and sounds; it can therefore not be heard by anybody (in contradiction to sūra IX, 6 which had to be interpreted metaphorically). The only exception was Moses, to whom God said: "I have chosen thee, so *listen* to what is suggested" (XX, 13); he heard God speak to him directly. But we do not have any information about how Ibn Kullāb explained this kind of perception.

God's speech is eternal not by itself (which would mean that one attribute or "accident", namely eternity, were to subsist in another one, namely speech), but by the eternity of God's essence. God's attributes are related to each other in a most intimate way: they are "neither identical nor not identical". They share common features, but they are not interchangeable. The same must therefore be said with regard to their relationship with God's essence: *lā hiya huwa wa-lā hiya ghayruhū*. They are not entirely different from Him, but also not completely identical with Him, i.e. no mere "names" in the sense of ᶜAbbād b. Sulaymān [*q.v.*], the Muᶜtazilī with whom Ibn Kullāb held frequent discussions. There was no necessity, in this context, for a distinction between *ṣifāt al-dhāt* and *ṣifāt al-fiᶜl*: God's will, which was considered a "factual quality" and as such temporal by the Muᶜtazilīs, is eternal according to Ibn Kullāb, likewise His kindness (*karam*) and His generosity (*djūd*), His friendship (*walāya*) and His enmity (*ᶜadāwa, sakhṭ*). The formula was also applied to the *ṣifāt khabariyya*, attributes which are only accepted because they form part of revelation, i.e. the anthropomorphisms: God's face, His hands, His eye, etc., are "neither identical with Him nor not identical with Him". We do not know what this meant exactly, but we hear that God is "sitting on His throne" with His essence, not as a body and not in a definite place.

Ibn Kullāb did not restrict God's attributes to those mentioned in the Ḳur'ān. An attribute may be inferred from any description (*waṣf*) given about God. But there are some of them which do not fit into the "formula". God is eternal and thus possesses eternity (*ḳidam*, which does not belong to the

Ḳurʾānic vocabulary), but this eternity must be directly identical with Him because nothing eternal exists besides Him. Similarly, His being can in no way be "not identical" with Him. The character of God's divinity was discussed among Ibn Kullāb's followers.

In other theological problems, Ibn Kullāb supported the view of the *aṣḥāb al-ḥadīth*. He believed in the *ruʾya bi'l-abṣār*, in the final salvation of all Muslims in spite of their sins, and in a moderate form of predestination. Man has no immanent capacity of acting (*ḳudra*); he only receives it in the moment of the performance. He may use it for the contrary of his action, i.e. for sin as well as for obedience, but this freedom of choice does not influence the salvational status determined by God from the beginning.

Ibn Kullāb's *ṣifāt* theory was prepared by earlier speculations inside and outside the Muʿtazila, especially by discussions between Abu 'l-Hudhayl [*q.v.*] and Hishām b. al-Ḥakam [*q.v.*] and by the ideas of the early Zaydī theologian Sulaymān b. Djarīr al-Raḳḳī (for whom cf. W. Madelung, *Der Imām al-Qāsim ibn Ibrāhīm*, 61 ff.). He was, however, the first to elaborate them into a coherent system which corresponded to the tenets of the *aṣḥāb al-ḥadīth*. He also apparently put them on a broader basis by adding, e.g., a theory of human speech which worked with the same differentiation between speech as such and its reproduction through letters and sounds. He wrote several books, among them a *K. al-Ṣifāt* and a refutation of the Muʿtazila. Only a small fragment of one of them has been found up to now (cf. *Oriens*, xviii-xix [1965-6], 138 f.). Among his adherents in Baghdād was the mystic al-Ḥārith al-Muḥāsibī (died 243/857); in Nīshāpūr his doctrine seems to have been supported by al-Ḥusayn b. al-Faḍl al-Badjalī, a contemporary who was mainly known as a commentator of the Ḳurʾān. The orthodox reaction under al-Mutawakkil and the prohibition of *kalām* in 238/852-3 seriously hampered the expansion of the school. Theologians who held similar ideas were attacked by Aḥmad b. Ḥanbal and his disciples as *Lafẓiyya*, people who believed in the createdness of the pronunciation (*lafẓ*), i.e. the recitation of the Ḳurʾān. But two generations later, Ibn Kullāb's ideas were renewed by Aḥmad b. ʿAbd al-Raḥmān al-Ḳalānisī from Rayy and by his contemporary al-Ashʿarī (died 324/936 [*q.v.*]). The Ḳāḍī ʿAbd al-Djabbār (died 415/1025) still polemicises much more against the Kullābiyya than against al-Ashʿarī, and seems not always to distinguish sharply between them. But al-Muḳaddasī notes already in *ca.* 375/985 that the Ashʿariyya school was superseding its predecessor. The last traces of the school disappear in the 5th/11th century.

Bibliography: The main information about Ibn Kullāb's doctrine is found in Ashʿarī's *Maḳālāt al-Islāmiyyīn*, cf. index s.v. ʿAbd Allāh b. Saʿīd, cf. also Ibn al-Nadīm, *Fihrist*, ed. R. Tadjaddud, Tehran² 1973, 230, ll. 6 ff. These and other sources are analysed in J. van Ess, *Ibn Kullāb und die Miḥna*, in *Oriens* xviii-xix (1965-6), 92 ff. See also M. Allard, *Le problème des attributs divins*, Beirut 1965, 146 ff.; W. M. Watt, *The formative period of Islamic thought*, Edinburgh 1973, 286 ff.; F. E. Peters, *Allah's Commonwealth*, New York 1973, index s.v.; H. Daiber, *Das theologisch-philosophische System des Muʿammar ibn ʿAbbād as-Sulamī*, Beirut 1975, index s.v.; H. A. Wolfson, *The philosophy of the Kalām*, Cambridge, Mass. 1976, 248 ff.; J. Peters, *God's created speech*, Leiden 1976, index s.v.; R. M. Frank, *Beings and attributes*, Albany 1978, index. (J. van E

IBN MANGLĪ, Muḥammad al-Nāṣirī, a Ma[mlūk] officer of the guard [see Ḥalḳa] of Sulta[n] Malik al-Ashraf Shaʿbān (764-78/1362-77 [known as the author of several works on art of war and of a treatise on hunting.

According to a laconic item of information [by Ibn Manglī himself, he must have been bo[rn in] Cairo at the opening of the 8th/14th century, bet[ween] the years 700 and 705/1300-6. As his arabised [name] shows (perhaps originally Möngli), his father w[as a] Ḳîpčaḳ [*q.v.*], who had been brought at a tende[r age] to the Mamlūk training school and recruited t[o the] corps of the Baḥriyya [*q.v.*] under Sultan al-M[alik] al-Nāṣir Nāṣir al-Dīn Muḥammad [*q.v.*], who [had] three separate periods of power between 693/ and 741/1341; this is the origin of the title of af[filia]tion, al-Nāṣirī, applied to him. Our author [came] therefore into the class of *awlād al-nās* [*q.v.*] "so[ns of] the people of high rank", which allowed hi[m to] become a member of the sultan's guard of ho[nour]. After having undergone the wide-ranging mil[itary] education of the "youths of good family", he e[nded] his long career as a military man, in this same corps, with the high rank of *muḳaddam* (= co[lonel] or brigadier?), ensuring him comfort of life [and] respect. To his cultural interests, Ibn Manglī a[dded] a deep religious sense, almost asceticism; at the [end] of his treatise on hunting, he thanks God for allo[wing] him not to take a wife, the source of unhappiness. [It is] unknown whether his own death preceded or foll[owed] the ignominious end of his master, strangled to d[eath].

Ibn Manglī's works on the art of war an[d] military and naval tactics are only known t[o us] through titles and citations, but his treatis[e on] hunting, put together in 773/1371-2, is prese[rved] in a unique manuscript (Paris, B.N., Ar. 283[2], 53) called *Uns al-malā bi-waḥsh al-falā* "The soc[ial] contact of the élite people with the wild beast o[f the] open desert". The author did not intend to co[mpose] an original work, but, so he says, conceived the [plan] of it as an abridgement (*mukhtaṣar*) of the [great] encyclopaedia on venery *al-Djamhara fī ʿulūm al-bayzara* "Compendium on the arts of falco[nry]" (Escurial, Ar. 903; Istanbul, Aya Sofya [;] Calcutta, Asiatic Soc., Ar. 865 M9) written in [ ] 1240 by the Baghdādī author Abu 'l-Rūḥ ʿĪsā b. [ ] b. Ḥassān al-Asadī. To the basic fabric of al-As[adī's] work Ibn Manglī was able to add, in addition t[o the] fruits of his own long experience on the sub[ject,] references to the best authors, such as al-Da[mīrī,] al-Djāḥiẓ, Ibn Ḳutayba, Ibn Waḥshiyya, Ibn [ ] al-Rāzī and many others. One is grateful to hi[m for] not having conceived of it as an *adab* [*q.v.*] w[ork;] his clear, precise and curt style reflects the mil[itary] man, whilst certain dialectical expressions [ ] the contemporary language.

In 1880 one Florian Pharaon, a person of [Le]vantine origin, brought out an edition and t[rans]lation, under the title *Traité de vénerie* ([ ] pp. 154 text, 143 tr.), of Ibn Manglī's work; the manuscript which he used, very lacking [and] defective, is not the Paris one. As a result, [one] wonders whether this Pharaon knew Arabic [or] anything about hunting at all, since the work o[f the] Mamlūk author is so mangled.

As well as the great interest which Ibn Ma[nglī's] treatise holds for the devotee of the chase an[d the] specialist on animals, the historian can glean [from] it a host of details on the horses, the style of r[iding] and the handling of weapons as known am[ong]

Mamlūks of the 8th/14th century, for whom .ng served as a school for war.

Bibliography: Brockelmann, II, 136, S II, 7; G. Zoppoth, *Muhammad ibn Mänglī, ein yptischer Offizier und Schriftsteller des 14. Jhr.*, *WZKM*, liii (1957), 288-99; *EI²* art. Bayzara; Möller, *Studien zur mittelalterlichen arabischen lknereiliteratur*, Berlin 1965; F. Viré, *Abrégé cynégétique d'Ibn Manglī*, annotated tr. (forthming). (F. Viré)

N MATTAWAYH, Abū Muḥammad al-an b. Aḥmad, Muʿtazilī theologian. Virtually ing certain is known about his life beyond that as a student of Ḳāḍī ʿAbd al-Djabbār (d. 415/) in Rayy and survived him. His grandfather awayh has been erroneously identified, on the of the title page of Houben's edition of his *adjmūʿ fi 'l-muḥīṭ bi 'l-taklīf*, as ʿAlī b. ʿAbd b. ʿUtba (read ʿAṭiyya) b. Muḥammad b. ad al-Nadjrānī, who was rather the scribe of of the manuscripts of this book. The death dates 1, without mention of a source, by Houben 1076) and by ʿAbd al-Karīm ʿUthmān (468/1075) ot appear reliable. There is no evidence in his it works that he survived his teacher for over a century. His *Ḳ. al-Tadhkira* was evidently posed soon after ʿAbd al-Djabbār's death, for of the latter's students except Abū Muḥammad -Labbād is mentioned in it, while Abū Rāshid aysābūrī (who cannot have survived ʿAbd jabbār very long) quotes it in his *Ḳ. Ziyādāt arh*. There is a possibility that he is identical , or related to, the Ibn Mattawayh or "Sibṭ ūya" lampooned by the vizier al-Ṣāḥib b. ād (d. 385/995), ʿAbd al-Djabbār's patron in y, in some obscene verses, especially since one e verses seems to allude to his belonging to the azila (see al-Thaʿālibī, *Yatīma*, iii, 101 f.; Yāḳūt, bāʾ, ii, 342).

n Mattawayh generally set forth the doctrine is teacher ʿAbd al-Djabbār, whose *Ḳ. al-Muḥīṭ -taklīf*, a comprehensive Muʿtazilī theology, he phrased, commented upon and, in a few points, cised in his Ḳ. *al-Madjmūʿ fi 'l-muḥīṭ bi 'l-taklīf* i edited by J. J. Houben, Beirut 1965, and by ar al-Sayyid ʿAẓmī, Cairo 1965). Also extant s *Ḳ. al-Tadhkira*, a work in two volumes on the re of substances and accidents (vol. i edited by ī Naṣr Luṭf and Fayṣal Badīrʿūn, Cairo 1975). ommentary on it by an anonymous author ing *ca.* 570/1174-5 is preserved in manuscript S. M. Dānishpazhūh, in *Nashriyya-yi Kitābkhāna-Iarkazī-yi Dānishgāh-i Tihrān*, ii [1341/1962], 156 His *Ḳ. al-Kifāya* is quoted in Ibn Abi 'l-Ḥadīd's *h Nahdj al-balāgha*. In it he argued at length for superior excellence of ʿAlī over Abū Bakr. Going ond any previous Muʿtazilī position, he affirmed impeccability (*ʿiṣma*) of ʿAlī but maintained, nst the Imāmī Shīʿī doctrine, that impeccability no prerequisite for the validity of the imāmate. *. al-Taḥrīr* by him is quoted in Maḥmūd b. alāḥimī's *K. al-Muʿtamad fī uṣūl al-dīn*.

Bibliography: al-Ḥākim al-Djushamī, *Sharḥ -ʿuyūn*, in *Faḍl al-iʿtizāl wa-ṭabaḳāt al-Muʿtazila*, 1. Fuʾād Sayyid, Tunis 1393/1974, 389; Ibn -Murtaḍā, *Ṭabaḳāt al-Muʿtazila*, ed. S. Diwald-Vilzer, Wiesbaden 1961, 119; Sezgin, *GAS*, i, 627; Abd al-Karīm ʿUthmān, *Ḳāḍī 'l-ḳuḍāt ʿAbd al-jabbār b. Aḥmad al-Hamadhānī*, Beirut 1386/1967, . (W. Madelung)

BN MIḲSAM, Muḥammad b. al-Ḥasan b. ḳūb b. al-Ḥasan b. al-Ḥusayn b. Muḥammad b. Sulaymān b. Dāwūd b. ʿUbayd Allāh b. Miḳsam, Abū Bakr al-ʿAṭṭār al-Muḳriʾ al-Naḥwī, who lived from 265/878-9 until 354/965, was one of the most learned experts in *ḳirāʾa* [*q.v.*] and also noted for his knowledge of Arabic grammar as practised in the school of Kūfa. According to his contemporaries, his only fault was that he, when teaching the Ḳurʾān, instructed in various readings (*ḳirāʾāt*) which were not agreed upon by the majority of scholars of his days (*idjmāʿ*). Thus, instead of *nadjiyyan* in XII, 80, he read *nudjabāʾa*, which did not make sense in the context. He tried to justify his controversial readings with grammatical arguments. This evoked the scorn of other Ḳurʾān teachers, and the matter was brought to the attention of the sultan who demanded that he recant. Ibn Miḳsam yielded to the pressure, but in other reports it says that he abided by his readings until his death. Apparently this caused some concern with the theologians of his days in regard to those ignorant people who were taken with his teachings and, subsequently, led astray. The whole episode bears a strong resemblance to what happened one year later to Ibn Shanabūdh (d. 329/939 [*q.v.*]). Yāḳūt mentions the titles of eighteen books attributed to Ibn Miḳsam, mainly dealing with Ḳurʾān and the Arabic language, but also including a refutation of the Muʿtazila. All of these seem to have been lost.

Bibliography: Nöldeke-Schwally, *Gesch. des Qorans*, index s.v.; al-Khaṭīb al-Baghdādī, *Taʾrīkh Baghdād*, ii, 206 ff.; Yāḳūt, *Udabāʾ*, vi, 498-501; Ibn al-Djazarī, *Ghāyat al-nihāya*, ii, 123 ff.; Ibn al-Anbārī, *Nuzhat al-alibbāʾ*, 360-3; Ibn Ḥadjar, *Lisān al-mīzān*, iv, 130 f. (G. H. A. Juynboll)

IBN MĪTHAM, Abu 'l-Ḥasan ʿAlī b. Ismāʿīl b. Shuʿayb b. Mītham (often read as al-Haytham) b. Yaḥyā al-Tammār (whence the less common name for him, Ibn al-Tammār), al-Asadī (al-Ṣābūnī, according to Ibn Ḥazm, *Fiṣal*, iv, 181), *Imāmī theologian* of the 2nd/8th century.

Mītham was a Companion of the Prophet (Ibn Ḥadjar, *Iṣāba*, no. 8472) who had adopted the cause of ʿAlī b. Abī Ṭālib and had settled at Kūfa, where his great-grandson was born at an uncertain date; nor is the date of his death known. Having left his natal town for Baṣra, ʿAlī b. Ismāʿīl frequented the great Muʿtazilī scholars of the time, especially Abu 'l-Hudhayl and al-Naẓẓām [*q.vv.*], with whom he engaged in controversy, but apparently without great success (cf. al-Khayyāṭ, *Intiṣār*, index, who states that he was under the influence of the young (*aḥdāth*) Muʿtazilīs). Al-Masʿūdī, in *Murūdj*, vi, 369 = § 2566, mentions him at the head of the theologians who took part in a colloquium organised by Yaḥyā b. Khālid b. Barmak on *ʿishḳ* [*q.v.*], and records (vi, 371 = § 2569) the presence there of Hishām b. al-Ḥakam [*q.v.*]. The latter, who died in 179/795-6, is considered as the main representative of Imāmī theology in his time, and Ibn Mītham did not enjoy a parallel fame; but it is probable that Ibn Mītham was his elder, since he is cited before him by Ibn al-Nadīm, *Fihrist*, ed. Cairo, 249, who states that he was the first to formulate the doctrine of the imāmate, and attributes to him a *Kitāb al-Imāma* (called *al-Kāmil*) and a *K. al-Istiḥḳāḳ*. If al-Nawbakhtī (*Firaḳ al-Shīʿa*, 9) is to be believed, this political doctrine may be summed up in the following manner: ʿAlī was the most meritorious (*afḍal*) after the Prophet, and the community committed an error in choosing Abū Bakr and ʿUmar, but did not however fall into sin; on the other hand, ʿUthmān was to be rejected (*takfīr*). For his part, al-As͟hʿarī, *Maḳālāt*, 42, 54, 516, delineates the main outlines of his theological doctrine: the Divine Will is, for him, as for His͟hām, a moving force (*ḥaraka*), but for him, a moving force external to God, which moves Him. In regard to faith, this consists essentially in respect for the divine obligations; whoever infringes them loses the quality of *muʾmin* and becomes a *fāsiḳ*, without however being wholly excluded from the community, since he can marry within it and inherit.

Bibliography: In addition to the sources mentioned above, see Ṭūsī, *Fihrist*, 212, no. 458; Nad̲j̲ās͟hī, *Rid̲j̲āl*, 176; Abū ʿAlī al-Karbalāʾī, *Muntahā ʾl-maḳāl*, 207-8; Māmakānī, *Tanḳīh al-maḳāl*, ii, 270; Bag͟hdādī, *Hadiyyat al-ʿārifīn*, i, 669; Kaḥḥāla, *Muʿd̲j̲am*, vii, 37; W. M.Watt, in *St. Isl.*, xxi, 289, 291; idem, *The formative period) of Islamic thought*, Edinburgh 1973, 158-9, 188. (Ed.)

IBN al-MUBĀRAK al-LAMAṬĪ [see al-lamaṭī]

IBN MUḲBIL, Abū Kaʿb (Abu ʾl-Ḥurra in Ibn Durayd's *Is͟htiḳāḳ*, 12) Tamīm b. Ubayy b. Muḳbil b. al-ʿAd̲j̲lān al-ʿĀmirī (i.e. the ʿĀmir b. Ṣaʿṣaʿa; see Ibn al-Kalbī-Caskel, Tab. 101), Bedouin poet of the *muk͟haḍram*, who is said, like many other people of his age, to have lived 120 years (although al-Sid̲j̲istānī does not cite him in his *K. al-Muʿammarīn*). He died after the battle of Ṣiffīn (37/657), to which he alludes in one of his poems (*Dīwān*, 345), probably in Muʿāwiya's reign and in any case, at a time when al-Ak͟hṭal [*q.v.*] had already made himself known to him.

Ibn Muḳbil seems to have led the rather monotonous life of the Bedouins of his time, and his biographers, eager for pieces of information, record hardly any striking facts. They give prominence to his marriage to his father's widow, al-Dahmāʾ, whom he had to divorce in conformity with the laws of Islam (Ibn Ḥabīb, *Muḥabbar*, 325-6), but he long regretted this, judging by the numerous verses where her name is mentioned (see *Dīwān*, index). When he had reached an advanced age, he asked for hospitality from a certain ʿAṣar al-ʿUḳaylī, who had two daughters; these last mocked him, because he was blind in one eye, so their father compelled one of them, Sulaymā, to marry him (*Dīwān*, 76-7). As a good Bedouin poet, Ibn Muḳbil mentions several women in the *nasīb* of his poems, and in particular a certain Kabs͟ha/Kubays͟ha (see *Dīwān*, index), but of course, no precise information can be drawn from this. Although Ibn al-Kalbī does not mention any progeny of his, he is said to have had a dozen children (Ibn Ras͟hīḳ, *ʿUmda*, ii, 291), all poets in their turn, and al-Bakrī (*Muʿd̲j̲am mā staʿd̲j̲am*, i, 131) adds the name of an Umm S͟harīk who is said to have transmitted her father's verses.

Another fact lacking from his life story is an exchange of *hid̲j̲āʾ* [*q.v.*] verses with a poet who was a partisan of ʿAlī b. Abī Ṭālib, al-Nad̲j̲ās͟hī [*q.v.*]; the latter had attacked his tribe in the time of ʿUmar b. al-K͟haṭṭāb, and the dispute was brought before the caliph, who first of all shrank back from delivering a judgment but was subsequently forced to throw al-Nad̲j̲ās͟hī into jail (this happening is recorded by numerous authors, in particular, Ibn Ḳutayba, *S͟hiʿr*, 290; al-Bakrī, *Faṣl al-maḳāl fī s͟harḥ Kitāb al-amthāl*, Beirut 1391/1971, 310-11; Ibn Ras͟hīḳ, *ʿUmda*, i, 37-8; al-Ḥuṣrī, *Zahr al-ādāb*, i, 19-20; al-Bag͟hdādī, *K͟hizāna*, Būlāḳ, i, 113 = Cairo, i, 214-15; etc.). The two poets exchanged insults over a period of years, and once again one sees Ibn Muḳbil replying to his enemy, who had attacked Muʿāwiya after the battle of Ṣiffīn (*Dīwān*, No. 42). He had previously expressed pro-Umayyad s[...] ments in an elegy inspired by the murder of ʿUt͟h[...] (*Dīwān*, no. 3), but apart from his polemics [...] al-Nad̲j̲ās͟hī, he seems to have been uninterest[...] political affairs and to have held aloof from ad[...] sing eulogies to highly-placed personages. Her[...] *madīḥ* [*q.v.*] is little represented in his *dīwān*, boa[...] poetry (*fak͟hr*), personal or tribal, abound or[...] other hand. As a Bedouin poet, he defends natu[...] the Bedouin qualities such as generosity, cont[...] for riches, courage and endurance; the main ch[...] teristic of his work is indeed description (*w*[...] of the desert, atmospheric phenomena, the c[...] wild animals, and especially, the arrows (*ḳ*[...] used in the gambling game called *maysir* [...] to such a point that he became proverbial for [...] and one spoke of the *ḳidḥ Ibn Muḳbil* (Ibn Ḳut[...] *S͟hiʿr*, 427). His work was exploited by the p[...] ogists (Sībawayh cites him ten times; see also, al-Mubarrad, *Kāmil*, 498; al-Bag͟hdādī, *K͟hi*[...] Būlāḳ, i, 111-13 = Cairo, i, 211-15, *s͟hāhid* 32, [...] and because of the number of place names i[...] poetry, he was a source for the compilers of [...] graphical dictionaries (Yāḳūt cites him 142 [...] in the *Muʿd̲j̲am al-buldān*).

He was reproached basically because he regr[...] too much the pre-Islamic times and found hi[...] ill at ease (Ibn Sallām, *Ṭabaḳāt*, 125; see *Dī*[...] 129-41), and it may be because of this that [...] judgments of the critics on him differ consider[...] Ibn Sallām, 119, places him in the fifth class o[...] D̲j̲āhiliyya poets with K͟hidās͟h b. Zuhayr, al-A[...] b. Yaʿfur and al-Muk͟habbal b. Rabīʿa, who ar[...] remarkable as poets. Most curiously, al-Ak[...] whom he had in fact attacked (*Dīwān*, 10[...] 312-14), is said to have delivered a very favou[...] verdict on him (T͟haʿlab, *Mad̲j̲ālis*, 481; Ibn Ra[...] *ʿUmda*, i, 80), whilst al-Aṣmaʿī [*q.v.*] did not con[...] him at all as one of the *fuḥūl* (al-Marzubānī, *was͟hs͟hāḥ*, 80); this severe judgment did not how[...] prevent this same scholar from collecting tog[...] his *Dīwān*, of which other recensions were mad[...] Abū ʿAmr al-S͟haybānī, al-Ṭūsī, Ibn al-Sikkīt [...] al-Sukkarī (*Fihrist*, ed. Cairo, 224) and a commen[...] written by Muḥammad b. al-Muʿallā al-Azdī (Yā[...] *Udabāʾ*, xix, 55). One at least of these recen[...] was known in Ifrīḳiya, as the *ʿUmda* of Ibn Ra[...] and the *Masāʾil al-intiḳād* of Ibn S͟haraf [...] adjudged Ibn Muḳbil's poetry as archaic and so[...] constructed) attest in particular, and also in[...] Andalus (see Ibn K͟hayr, *Fahrasa*, 397), but [...] only recently that there has been discovere[...] Çorum [see čorum] the manuscript of an uniden[...] recension. A very careful edition of the *Dīwān* [...] been done by ʿIzzat Ḥasan (Damascus 1381/1[...] to which he has appended a *D̲h̲ayl* and va[...] highly useful indices; another ed. by Ahme[...] Türek, Ankara 1965.

Bibliography: The main sources have [...] given in the article; ʿIzzat Ḥasan's introdu[...] to the *Dīwān* contains the sparse biograp[...] details which are known and a study of [...] Muḳbil's works. See further Ziriklī, *Aʿlām*, [...] Wahhābī, *Marād̲j̲iʿ*, i, 123-5, where some [...] references may be found. (Ch. Pella[...])

IBN NĀD̲J̲Ī, Abū ʾl-Ḳāsim/Abu ʾl-Faḍl b. [...] b. Nād̲j̲ī al-Tanūk͟hī, *ḳāḍī*, preacher [...] biographer, who was born and who died a[...] Ḳayrawān (*ca.* 762-837 or 839/*ca.* 1361-1433 or 1[...]. He studied in his natal town and in Tunis, and [...] filled various posts as *ḳāḍī* and as *k͟haṭīb* (in D̲j̲a[...] Beja, Lorbeus, Sousse, Gabès, Tebessa and al-Ḳa[...]

, and put together commentaries on *fiḳh* works, articular, on the *Risāla* of Ibn Abī Zayd al-Ḳay-nī (this *sharḥ* was printed at Cairo 1914, 2 vols.). ever, his fame stemmed especially from a colle- of biographies of religious scholars of his natal from its origins till the 9th/15th century, the *ālim al-īmām fī maʿrifat ahl al-Ḳayrawān*, only part with the notices on the 8th/14th century g completely from his own pen; all the opening reality a borrowing from a collection by a ecessor, al-Dabbāgh [*q.v.* above].

Bibliography: Aḥmad Bābā, *Nayl al-ibtihādj*, 3; Ibn al-Ḳāḍī, *Durrat al-ḥidjāl*, No. 1330; trod. to Ibrāhīm Shabbūḥ's ed. of the *Maʿālim*; e also the *Bibl.* to AL-DABBĀGH. (ED.)

IBN NĀṢIR, the name, nowadays replaced by ĀṢIRĪ, of a Moroccan family who founded branch of the Shādhiliyya order [*q.v.*] known as riyya and founded its headquarters at the ya of Tamgrūt [*q.v.*] in southern Morocco. The erous biographical sources, published and lited, as well as a monograph on the family, the at *al-mushtarī* (Fās 1309) by Aḥmad al-Nāṣirī lāwī, allow its history to be traced easily and a genealogical tree to be constructed; the er will find information on this in the article ĀṢIRIYYA, and there will merely be given here e information on those members of the Banū r who took part in a conspicuous fashion in ary and intellectual life over the last four uries.

AL-ḤUSAYN B. MUḤAMMAD b. Aḥmad b. ammad b. Ḥusayn b. Nāṣir b. ʿAmr b. ʿUthmān arʿī (d. 1091/1680) succeeded his father (d. /1642) as head of the *zāwiya* of Ighlān (a few s from Zagora). This *zāwiya* was, however, itively abandoned after an outbreak of plague h broke out in 1091/1680, of which al-Ḥusayn himself a victim; he had made three journeys he East and had composed a *Fahrasa* extant at at (ms. 506J).

His elder brother, Abū ʿAbd Allāh MAḤAMMAD UḤAMMAD (1015-85/1606-74) had left the Ighlān ya in 1040/1631 in order to settle in the one at grūt, which he now headed; according to the t reliable tradition, it was he who founded the iriyya order. He wrote several works of *fiḳh*, e poetry, letters and *adjwiba* on points of law.

Maḥammad's son AḤMAD (1057-1129/1647-1717) eeded his father as head of the order. He made pilgrimage four times, and utilised these occasions establish branches of the order in various parts North Africa, as far as Egypt, and composed cerning his pilgrimage of 1121/1709-10 a volumi- *Riḥla* (lith. Fās 1320; partial tr. A. Berbrugger, *Exploration scientifique de l'Algérie*, ix, 1846, ff.); this travel account has a certain interest ause the author adds his personal observations he regions which he passed through and records its of some importance, in addition to his mention is itineraries and the religious personnages whom net en route. Since Aḥmad left behind no children, headship of the *zāwiya* passed to the descendants is brother Muḥammad al-Kabīr.

Abū ʿAbd Allāh MUḤAMMAD (al-Makkī) B. ĀA b. Muḥammad (al-Kabīr) b. Maḥammad eeded his father, who died in 1142/1729. The of inspecting the order's branches in the various ns of Morocco led him to write a travel narrative, *ayāḥin al-wardiyya fi 'l-riḥla al-Marrākushiyya* Rabat 88 G, 1-83), but he also left behind some try and several biographical works, amongst which may be noted the *Fatḥ al-malik al-Nāṣir fī idjāzāt marwiyyāt Banī Nāṣir* (ms. Rabat 323 K) on the *idjāzāt* received by his forebears, and above all, *al-Durar al-muraṣṣaʿa fī akhbār aʿyān Darʿa* or the *Kashf al-rawʿa fi 'l-taʿrīf bi-ṣulaḥāʾ Darʿa* (mss. Rabat K. 265 and 88 G, 84-116), finished in 1152/1739, which traces the history of the Nāṣiriyya order. He died after 1170/1756.

5. Abū ʿAbd Allāh MUḤAMMAD B. ABD AL-SALĀM b. ʿAbd Allāh b. Muḥammad (al-Kabīr), who died in 1239/1823. He made the pilgrimage to Mecca twice and wrote two accounts of these. The autograph ms. of the first, *al-Riḥla al-kubrā*, is extant in the Royal Library at Rabat (no. 5658); the author adds his own personal observations and is not afraid to contradict his predecessors (notably al-ʿAyyāshī and al-ʿAbdarī [*q.vv.*]). He further left behind *al-Mazāyā fī-mā ḥadatha/uḥditha min al-bidaʿ bi-Umm al-Zawāyā*, a *Fahrasa* (ms. Rabat 3289 K), a commentary on the 40 *ḥadīth*s of Maḥammad al-Djawharī (ms. Rabat 137 Q) and some *responsa* on some cases in point, the *Ḳatʿ al-watīn min al-marīḳ fi'l-dīn* (ms. Rabat 1079 D, fols. 107-15).

6. It is convenient, finally, to note that the famous author of the *K. al-Istiḳṣā*, AḤMAD AL-NĀṢIRĪ [see AL-SALĀWĪ] was a direct descendant of Ibn Nāṣir.

Bibliography: To the works by members of the family cited above, one should add the great biographical collections of Moroccan authors like Ifrānī, *Ṣafwat man intashar*, lith. Fās n.d.; Ḳādirī, *Nashr al-mathānī*, Fās 1310/1892; Muḥammad al-Kattānī, *Salwat al-anfās*, lith. Fās 1316; ʿAbd al-Ḥayy al-Kattānī, *Fihris al-fahāris*, Fās 1346-7/1927-9; the manuals of Moroccan literature; Ibn Sūda, *Dalīl muʾarrikh al-Maghrib al-Aḳṣā*, Casablanca 1960-5; Lévi-Provençal, *Chorfa*, index s.v. Ibn Nāṣir; M. Lakhdar, *La vie littéraire au Maroc sous la dynastie ʿalawide*, Rabat 1971, index s.v. Ibn Nāṣir and the bibl. cited there. (ED.)

IBN NĀẒIR AL-DJAYSH, TAḲĪ 'L-DĪN ʿABD AL-RAḤMĀN, *ḳāḍī*, official and author of the Mamlūk period in Egypt. His precise dates are unknown, but he was apparently the son of another *ḳāḍī* who had been controller of the army in the time of Sultan al-Nāṣir Nāṣir al-Dīn Muḥammad b. Ḳalāwūn, and he himself served in the *Dīwān al-Inshāʾ* under such rulers as al-Manṣūr Ṣalāḥ al-Dīn Muḥammad (762-4/1361-3) and his successor al-Ashraf Nāṣir al-Dīn Shaʿbān (764-78/1363-76). His correspondence was apparently collected into a *madjmūʿ*, for al-Ḳalḳashandī [*q.v.*] quotes four letters from it, to external rulers, in his *Ṣubḥ al-aʿshā*. Ibn Nāẓir al-Djaysh was also, in a well-established Mamlūk tradition, the author of a manual for chancery secretaries, the *Tathḳīf al-Taʿrīf*, an improved version of the well-known guide of Shihāb al-Dīn Ibn Faḍl Allāh al-ʿUmarī [see FAḌL ALLĀH], *al-Taʿrīf bi 'l-muṣṭalaḥ al-sharīf*; the *Tathḳīf* has survived in at least four manuscripts (not however recorded in Brockelmann) and is again quoted several times by al-Ḳalḳashandī.

Bibliography: M. Gaudefroy-Demombynes, *La Syrie à l'époque des Mamelouks d'après les auteurs arabes*, Paris 1923, pp. XII-XIII; W. Björkman, *Beiträge zur Geschichte der Staatskanzlei im islamischen Ägypten*, Hamburg 1928, 69, 75, 129; C. E. Bosworth, *Christian and Jewish religious dignitaries in Mamlûk Egypt and Syria: Qalqashandî's information on their hierarchy, titulature and appointment*, in *IJMES*, iii (1972), 67.

(C. E. BOSWORTH)

IBN AL-RĀHIB, Coptic polygraph, born between 1200-10 and died between 1290-5. Known principally as a historiographer on account of the *Chronicon orientale*, which has been falsely attributed to him since the 17th century, Nushū᾽ al-Khilāfa (or simply al-Nushū᾽) Abū Shākir b. al-Sanā (abbreviation of Sanā᾽ al-Dawla) al-Rāhib Abu 'l-Karam (alias Abu 'l-Madjd) Buṭrus b. al-Muhadhdhib in fact represents, with Abū Isḥāḳ b. al-ʿAssāl [*q.v.*] and Abu 'l-Barakāt Ibn Kabar [*q.v.*], the leading encyclopaedist of the golden age of Christian Arabic literature, in the 7th/13th century. He wrote about all the disciplines of human knowledge which an Arab Christian of the period was in a position to cultivate: chronology and astronomy, history, philology and hermeneutics, philosophy and theology (in the full spectrum of their ramifications). But it is not this fact alone which confers upon his work an encyclopaedic character; such versatility was not unusual in his milieu. The decisive factor is most of all his method of working, the very dimensions of his studies, and finally, the abundant wealth of textual sources, Greek and patristic, Muslim Arab and Christian, which he quotes or incorporates to a large extent in his own works. It is in this work of compilation, besides, even more than in original thought, that the value of his writings seems to reside.

Ibn al-Rāhib was born into a large and distinguished Coptic family of Old Cairo, all of them churchmen as well as senior officials of the Ayyūbid state. His father, known at the time under the name al-Sanā al-Rāhib or al-Rāhib Anbā Buṭrus (he became a monk at an advanced age), enjoyed a considerable reputation both in public administration, where for two periods he was responsible for state finance, and in ecclesiastical circles, where he virtually played the role of interim patriarch in the latter part of the long period during which the diocese of Alexandria was vacant (1216-35), before becoming spokesman for the opposition under the much-contested patriarchate of Cyrillus b. Laḳlaḳ (1235-43). His son, al-Nushū᾽ Abū Shākir, was, for his part, deacon of the renowned church of al-Muʿallaḳa and played a senior role in the administration, apparently in the *dīwān al-djuyūsh* [*q.v.*].

It was relatively late, probably after leaving public service in the wake of political repercussions which accompanied the rise to power of the Mamlūks, that he began his literary activity. It is in fact confined to the period between the years 655/1257 and 669/1270-1. Beyond the latter date, Ibn al-Rāhib limited himself to reproducing and improving his works. Extremely extensive and hitherto unedited, these are, in chronological order:

(a) *K. al-Tawārīkh*. Recently identified in three manuscripts, this is the work on which, in reality, Ibn al-Rāhib's renown is based. It comprises three distinct parts, unequally divided into fifty-one chapters: a study of astronomy and chronology (chs. 1-47); a history of the world (ch. 48), of Islam (ch. 49) and of the Church (in the form of a history of the patriarchs of Alexandria—ch. 50); and finally, a brief account of the Seven Ecumenical Councils of the Orient (ch. 51). The celebrated *Chronicon orientale* represents, in fact, only a mediocre abstract of the long chronographical section (chs. 48-50). The *K. al-Tawārīkh* was, in addition, exploited to a large extent by the Christian historiographer, al-Makīn b. al-ʿAmīd [*q.v.*] and—through the latter, apparently—constantly mentioned by al-Maḳrīzī and Ibn Khaldūn [*q.vv.*]. In the first half of the 16th century it was translated into classical Ethiopic (Geʿez) by no less a person than the Etcheguié Enbaqom, whic[h] quired for it a position of considerable eminen[ce] Ethiopian literature. For this the manual of ecclesiastical year and of universal chronology titled *Abushākĕr*, is not the least of the evid[ence].

(b) The study of Coptic philology, comp[osed] in 1263, includes a rhymed vocabulary (*su mukaffā*) according to the method used by the lexicographers, preceded by a grammar (*muḳad* [*q.v.*]) which, through its originality, is distingui[shed] from the series of Coptic prefaces of the Middle A[ges]. Although the vocabulary itself hitherto seems t[o be] lost, an attentive reading of the prologue—w[hich] is available to us along with the grammar an[d in] which the author sets out his project in det[ail] enables us to see there a work of lexicograph[y] superior to the *Scala rimata* of his contemp[orary] Ibn al-ʿAssāl [see SULLAM].

(c) *K. al-Shifā* (1267-8). A work of Bi[blical] Christology, of an exclusively exegetical chara[cter]. Conceived according to massive proportions, it originally structured on the basis of the ima[ge of] the Tree of Life, consisting of a triple trunk each part bearing three branches (*farʿ*) loaded innumerable fruits (*thamara*). The abundance an[d] variety of patristic and other commentaries (esp[ecial]ly the *Firdaws al-naṣrāniyya* of the Nestorian al-Ṭayyib [*q.v.*], which are dotted throughout work, make it an interesting Arabic florilegiu[m] Biblical commentaries relating to the perso[n of] Christ.

(d) *K. al-Burhān* (1270-1). An extensive theolo[gico-]philosophical summa in fifty chapters (*mas*[...] dealing with almost all the questions of philoso[phy,] theology, ethics and culture likely to be of int[erest] to an educated Copt of the period. It is particu[larly] to be noted that the theodicy of the *K. al-Bu*[*rhān*] (chs. 28-40) hinges entirely on that of the *K* *Arbaʿīn* of the great Persian theologian F[akhr] al-Dīn al-Rāzī [*q.v.*].

Bibliography: Graf, *GCAL*, ii, 428-35; Y. Sidarus, ***Ibn al-Rāhibs Leben und Werk.*** *koptisch-arabischer Enzyklopädist des 7./13. J*[*ahr*]*hunderts* (Islamkundliche Untersuchungen Freiburg 1975, with detailed analysis of so[urces] and complete bibl. (A. SIDARU[S])

IBN AL-RŪMIYYA, ABU 'L-ʿABBAS (sporadic[ally] Abu Djaʿfar) AḤMAD B. ABĪ ʿABD ALLĀH MUḤAM[MAD] B. MUFARRIDJ B. ABI 'L-KHALĪL ʿABD ALLĀH UMAWĪ AL-ḤAZMĪ AL-ẒĀHIRĪ AL-NABĀTĪ AL-ʿASHS[HĀB], Spanish-Arabic pharmacobotanist. He was in Seville in 561/1166 (according to others, 567/1[171-2]) and died there in 637/1240. His allegedly Byza[ntine] origin on the maternal side may have procured the nickname by which he became known, but w[hich] he did not like hearing. In any case, he was a f[ree]man of the Umayyads. He was educated as a M[āliki] traditionist and jurist, but then joined the Ẓāhi[rīs] and became an ardent adherent of Ibn Ḥazm [...] None of his writings bearing upon this activity s[eem] to have survived; some *ridjāl*-works may be menti[oned] here: *al-Muʿlim bi-zawā᾽id* (or: *bi-mā zād*[*a*]) *al-Bukhārī ʿalā Muslim*, *Ikhtiṣār Gharā᾽ib ḥ*[...] *Mālik* (*li-l-Dāraḳuṭnī*), *Naẓm al-darārī fī-mā tafa*[*rrada*] *bihi Muslim ʿan al-Bukhārī*, further an abs[tract] from Ibn al-Ḳaṭṭān's (d. 360/971) *K. al-Kām*[*il fi*] *'l-ḍuʿafā᾽ wa 'l-matrūkīn*, and a supplement to [this] work under the title *al-Ḥāfil fī tadlīl al-K*[...] finally legal investigations on the performance o[f] prayer, like *Ḥukm al-duʿā᾽ fī adbār al-ṣalawāt* *Kayfiyyat al-adhān yawm al-djumʿa*. The knowl[edge] related to these subjects he acquired durin[g] nsive study-tour, made in connection with the image which he undertook in 613/1216, and h led him through North Africa, Egypt, al-āz, Syria and ʿIrāḳ. His extraordinary long raphy in Marrākus̲h̲ī's Dhayl (see Bibl.) can xplained by the fact that this author cites most, ot all, of the traditionists and jurists whose res Ibn al-Rūmiyya attended and who were his orities in ḥadīth.

is real renown, however, is based on his achieve-ts as a pharmacobotanist. As he himself relates, /as initiated into pharmacology in 583/1187 in āku s̲h̲ by ʿAbd Allāh b. Ṣāliḥ, one of Ibn ayt̤ār's teachers. With him he studied three ks: (1) the Materia medica of Dioscorides; (2) work by Ibn D̲j̲uld̲j̲ul [q.v.] in which the latter ains the simple medicines named by Dioscorides sīr asmāʾ al-adwiya al-mufrada min kitāb Diyus-lis); and (3) the brief treatise of the same author medicines not mentioned by Dioscorides (Maḳāla ikr al-adwiya allatī lam yad̲h̲kurhā Diyuskūrīdis). Seventeen years later (600/1204), Ibn al-iyya in his turn taught the works mentioned, in Marrākus̲h̲. The shortcomings and inaccuracies h meanwhile had struck him in the works of Ibn d̲j̲ul induced him now to write a corresponding by himself, namely Tafsīr asmāʾ al-adwiya al-ada min kitāb Diyuskūrīdis (the title thus being tical with that of Ibn D̲j̲uld̲j̲ul). In all probability, ering on certainty, it is this work which exists a anonymous text of the mad̲j̲mūʿa Nuruosma-3589; the present writer is preparing a text-on together with an annotated German transla-Ibn al-Rūmiyya shortened considerably the ents of Dioscorides' work, to the extent that he out almost completely the therapeutic uses of medicinal herbs; instead, he did, however, give h space to their botanical description. The enclature of the herbs is also particularly im-ant: it offers significant material for the know-e of Mozarabic [see ALJAMÍA] and of the Berber cts in Morocco at that time. Above all, it is worthy that the author makes a sharp distinction een the certain and the uncertain, especially een what was transmitted and what he had seen elf. If one bears in mind that ancient natural ce already at an early stage abandoned personal stigation in favour of compilation and came to more and more on written sources, the endeavour, gnisable here, to gain a solid basis, particularly xamining nature itself, has to be rated highly. is reasonable to assume that Ibn al-Rūmiyya e down the Tafsīr before he started on the jour-o the Orient mentioned above. The second botan-work, however, al-Riḥla al-mas̲h̲riḳiyya, more prehensive but only known to us through nu-us extracts by Ibn al-Bayt̤ār, turns out to be the y scientific result of this journey which lasted t two years. Of particular interest for the history vilisation is the description of the manufacture apyrus, the oldest one since Pliny (for this and other Arabic accounts, see A. Grohmann, All-ine Einführung in die arabischen Papyri, Vienna , 35 f.). The Riḥla is of high quality and has led L. Leclerc (Histoire de la médecine arabe, ii 244) M. Meyerhof (Maïmonide, xxxiii) to the judge- that Ibn al-Rūmiyya is the botanist par ex-ace among the Arabs and that he can only be ared with al-G̲h̲āfiḳī [q.v. above] as far as pendence of scientific method is concerned. the latter, Ibn al-Rūmiyya found moreover y faults; his work al-Tanbīh ʿalā ag̲h̲lāt̤ al-G̲h̲āfiḳī

fī adwiyatihi (quoted by Marrākus̲h̲ī, Dhayl, 1/2, 513) has been unfortunately lost, as is also a treatise on compound drugs (Maḳāla fī tarkīb al-adwiya), mentioned by Ibn Abī Uṣaybiʿa.

Bibliography: Ibn Abī Uṣaybiʿa, ʿUyūn, ii, 81; Ibn al-Abbār, al-Takmila li-Kitāb al-Ṣila, Cairo 1955, i, 121; Abū S̲h̲āma, Tarād̲j̲im rid̲j̲āl al-ḳarnayn al-sādis wa 'l-sābiʿ, Cairo 1366/1947, 170; Ibn Saʿīd, Ik̲h̲tiṣār al-ḳidḥ al-muʿallā fi 'l-taʾrīk̲h̲ al-muḥallā, ed. Ibr. al-Ibyārī, Cairo 1959, 181; al-Marrākus̲h̲ī, al-Dhayl wa 'l-takmila, ed. S̲h̲arīfa, i/2, 487-518; Dhahabī, Tad̲h̲kirat al-ḥuffāẓ, Ḥaydarābād 1377/1958, iv, 210; Ṣafadī, al-Wāfī bi 'l-wafayāt, viii, 45 (no. 3451); Ibn Rāfiʿ, Muntak̲h̲tab al-Muk̲h̲tār, Bag̲h̲dād 1357, 8; Ibn al-K̲h̲at̤īb, al-Iḥāta fī ak̲h̲bār G̲h̲arnāt̤a, Cairo 1319, i, 88-93; Ibn Farḥūn, Dībād̲j̲, Cairo 1351, 42 f.; Maḳḳarī, Nafḥ al-t̤īb, ed. I. ʿAbbās, ii, 596, iii, 135, 139, 185; Ibn al-ʿImād, S̲h̲ad̲h̲arāt al-d̲h̲ahab, v, 184; A. Dietrich, Medicinalia arabica, Göttingen 1966, 183-7; idem, in Acc. Naz. Lincei, Convegno Internaz. 9-15 Aprile 1969 (Oriente e Occ. nel Medioevo: Filosofia e scienze), Rome 1971, 375-90; M. Ullmann, Die Medizin im Islam, Leiden 1970, 279 f. (A. DIETRICH)

IBN RUS̲H̲D, ABU 'L-WALĪD MUḤAMMAD B. AḤMAD, AL-D̲J̲ADD ("the grandfather" of the celebrated philosopher Averroes or Ibn Rus̲h̲d [q.v.]), the most prominent Mālikī jurist of his day in the Muslim West, whose very real merits as an exponent of Mālik have been eclipsed by his grandson's fame as an exponent of Aristotle. Born in 450/1058-9, he died on 21 Dhu 'l-Ḳaʿda 520/8 December 1126 and was buried in the cemetery of (Ibn) ʿAbbās in east Cordova, his native city.

From 511/1117 until 515/1121 Ibn Rus̲h̲d was, as ḳāḍī 'l-d̲j̲amāʿa in Cordova, holder of the highest office in the Andalusian judiciary. For some reason that is not very clear, he either resigned or, less probably, was dismissed. What is clear is his impor-tant political role following the defeat, on 13 Ṣafar 520/19 March 1126, of Alfonso I of Aragon (El Batal-lador) at Arniswāl (? Anzul). Until his defeat, Alfonso had made rapid progress in his attempt to recover al-Andalus for Christendom and had gained wide-spread Mozarab sympathy and collaboration. Quick to perceive the danger that still threatened Islam from within, Ibn Rus̲h̲d hastened to Marrakesh on 30 March 1126 to warn the Almoravid ruler ʿAlī b. Yūsuf b. Tās̲h̲ufīn [q.v.] and to advise him. Ex-pressing his legal opinion that the Mozarabs had, by their treachery, lost all right to protected status, he prevailed upon ʿAlī to have large numbers deported, and in consequence many were transported to Salé, Meknès and other places in Morocco. At the same time, he advised the construction of walls around Andalusian cities and towns as well as a wall around Marrakesh for the protection of the Almoravids against rivals on their own soil. He is also said to have recommended the replacement of ʿAlī's brother, Abū T̤āhir Tamīm, as Almoravid representative in Spain, possibly because of his inability to defend Islam there. Five months after his return to Spain he died—in the same year as his famous grandson was born.

Abu 'l-Walīd Ḳurt̤ubī, as our Ibn Rus̲h̲d was known, was a great teacher of Mālikī fiḳh and the author of commentaries and compendia of basic works. One of his most important commentaries was that on the Mustak̲h̲raja of al-ʿUtbī (d. 255/869), viz. K. al-Bayān wa 'l-taḥṣīl li-mā fi 'l-Mustak̲h̲raja, etc. (in 110 parts). Better known today is his K.

al-Muḳaddimāt al-mumahhadāt li-bayān mā 'ḳtaḍathu rusūm al-Mudawwana (Cairo 1324; Muthannā repr. Baghdād, n.d. but 1960s). To his pupil Ibn al-Wazzān (*not* -Warrāḳ) we owe an important—historically and otherwise—collection of *fatwā*s entitled *Nawāzil Ibn Rushd*, a selection of which, together with an illuminating introduction, has been published by Iḥsān ʿAbbās in *Al-Abḥāth*, xxii (Beirut 1969), 3-63). In such of Ibn Rushd's writings as have come down to us, one perceives an incisive and logical mind and clarity of thought matched by lucidity of expression.

Bibliography: All the essential references have been brought together in Iḥsān ʿAbbās's introduction to the *Nawāzil* cited above.

(J. D. LATHAM)

IBN SAʿDĀN, ABŪ ʿABD ALLĀH AL-ḤUSAYN B. AḤMAD, official and vizier of the Būyids in the second half of the 4th/10th century and patron of scholars, d. 374/984-5.

Virtually nothing is known of his origins, but he served the great *amīr* ʿAḍud al-Dawla Fanā-Khusraw [*q.v.*] as one of his two inspectors of the army (*ʿāriḍ al-djaysh*) in Baghdād, the *ʿāriḍ* responsible for the Turkish, Arab and Kurdish troops. Then when ʿAḍud al-Dawla died in 372/983 and his son Ṣamṣām al-Dawla Marzubān assumed power in Baghdād as supreme *amīr*, he nominated Ibn Saʿdān as his vizier. He occupied this post for two years, and seems to have made it his policy to reverse some of the trends of the previous reign; thus according to Abū Ḥayyān al-Tawḥīdī [*q.v.*], he favoured the release in the new reign of the historian Ibrāhīm b. Hilāl al-Ṣābiʾ [see AL-ṢĀBIʾ] and took charge of the proper burial of the corpse of Ibn Baḳiyya [*q.v.*], the former vizier of ʿIzz al-Dawla Bakhtiyār executed by ʿAḍud al-Dawla. However, his enemy Abu 'l-Ḳāsim ʿAbd al-ʿAzīz b. Yūsuf [*q.v.* above], formerly *kātib al-inshāʾ* to ʿAḍud al-Dawla, secured his dismissal on what was, according to Rūdhrāwarī, a trumped-up charge of complicity in the military revolt in Baghdād of Asfār b. Kurdūya in support of Ṣamṣām al-Dawla's brother and rival for power, Sharaf al-Dawla Shīrzīl. Ibn Saʿdān was accordingly imprisoned and then executed in 374/984-5.

The sources say of him that he was liberal to his dependants, but kept himself inaccessible from the populace of Baghdād—in Rūdhrāwarī's phrase, *bādhilan li-ʿaṭāʾihi, māniʿan li-liḳāʾihi*—thus incurring unpopularity to the point that his personal boat on the Tigris (*zabzab*) was once stoned. His claim to lasting fame lies in his role as a Maecenas—he renewed the pensions of scholars which had lapsed on ʿAḍud al-Dawla's death—and as the organiser of a circle of literati in Baghdād embracing both Muslims and Christians and at which all kinds of speculative and philosophical questions were discussed. He was the friend and patron of Tanūkhī (see the latter's *Nishwār al-muḥāḍara*, ed. ʿAbbūd al-Shāldjī, Beirut 1391-2/1971-2, iv, 96-7). Tawḥīdī was one of his *nudamāʾ*, and dedicated to Ibn Saʿdān his epistle on friendship, the *K. al-Ṣadāḳa wa 'l-ṣadīḳ*, although this was not completed for another 30 years (cf. M. Bergé, *Une anthologie sur l'amitié d'Abū Ḥayyān al-Tawḥīdī*, in *BEO*, xvi [1958-60], 15-60). He was intimate enough with Ibn Saʿdān to address to the vizier an epistle on statecraft (in his *K. al-Imtāʿ wa 'l-muʿānasa*, ed. Aḥmad Amīn and Aḥmad al-Zayn, Cairo 1953, iii, 210-25, tr. by Bergé, *Conseils politiques à un ministre. Epître d'Abū Ḥayyān al-Tawḥīdī au vizir Ibn Saʿdān al-ʿĀriḍ*, in *Arabica*, xvi [1969], 269-78). In both the *K. al-Imtāʿ* and the *K. al-Ṣadāḳa* Tawḥīdī gives us a picture of these scholarly sessions; the participants included the Muslim philosopher Sulaymān al-Manṭiḳī [*q.v.*], the Christian ones Y… b. ʿAdī and ʿĪsā b. Zurʿa [see IBN ZURʿA], Ibr… al-Ṣābiʾ, Miskawayh [*q.v.*], the engineer and m… matician Abu 'l-Wafāʾ al-Būzadjānī [*q.v.*], the m… poet Ibn al-Ḥadjdjādj [*q.v.*], and several other… was at the request of Abu 'l-Wafāʾ that Taw… composed a record of 37 of the sessions, formin… *K. al-Imtāʿ*; and Tawḥīdī's collection of philosop… discussions, his *K. al-Muḳābasāt*, derives also … considerable extent from these meetings.

Bibliography (in addition to references g… in the text): For the scanty details of Ibn Saʿ… life, see Abū Shudjāʿ al-Rūdhrawarī's *Dha…* Miskawayh, ed. Amedroz, in *Eclipse of the ʿAb… caliphate*, iii, 40, 85, 102-3, 107, and Ibn al-Athī… 27, 29. Concerning Tawḥīdī's information, cf. … Margoliouth, *Some extracts from the Kitāb al-I… wal-Muʾānasah of Abū Ḥayyān Tauḥīdī*, *Islamica*, ii (1926), 380-90. For the text of a l… of Ibn Saʿdān's to the Būyid Fakhr al-D… [*q.v.*], see Ḳalḳashandī, *Ṣubḥ al-aʿshā*, viii, … Of secondary literature, see Ibrahim Kei… *Abū Ḥayyān at-Tawḥīdī, essayiste arabe du … s. de l'Hégire*, Beirut 1950, 42-3; Mafizullah K… *The Buwayhid dynasty of Baghdad*, Calcutta 1… 156, 179; J. Chr. Bürgel, *Die Hofkorrespon… ʿAḍud al-Daulas*, Wiesbaden 1965, 118-19; Busse, *Chalif und Grosskönig, die Buyiden im … (945-1055)*, Beirut-Wiesbaden 1969, 65, … 509-10.; M. Bergé, *Pour un humanisme … Abū Ḥayyān al-Tawḥīdī*, Damascus 1979, in… s.v. al-ʿĀriḍ.

(C. E. BOSWORT…)

IBN AL-SARRĀDJ, appellative of a far… prominent in the 9th/15th century history of … Naṣrid kingdom of Granada. Passing … Spanish literature as "Abencerraje" in the … century ("Bencerraje" may date from the end o… 15th), the name appears more than a century … in French as "Abencérage" (which, *pace* … Provençal (*Hist. Esp. Mus.*, i, 351) does not d… from Sirādj), and finally in English as "Abence… age".

The patronymic "b. al-Sarrādj" is known … before the 9th/15th century. It is borne, for exam… by an Abū ʿAbd Allāh Muḥammad of Málag… 5th/11th century panegyrist of the Ḥammū… [*q.v.*], and in the 7th/13th century both by a g… marian of Pechina living in Almería and by another Abū ʿAbd Allāh Muḥammad, a *faḳīh* … *khaṭīb* of the Great Mosque of Granada. Early in … next century we find an Abū ʿAbd Allāh Muḥam… b. Ibrāhīm b. al-Sarrādj, a Granadan doctor … botanist whose works, now lost, were esteeme… their day.

Up to the beginning of the 8th/14th century … patronymic is borne by isolated figures whose … nexions with one another are really indetermi… If, as claimed, the B. al-Sarrādj were of noble … lineage—seemingly of old Yemenī stock—it is str… to find no mention of them in the great Hispano-… genealogical treatises.

From the mid-8th/14th century we begin to dis… in Granada the emergence of a clearly defi… family, militarily successful and increasingly … fluential. One notable member was Abū I… Ibrāhīm b. Abī ʿAbd Allāh b. al-Sarrādj (d. 766/1… commander of the *ḳaṣaba* of Ronda and govern… its highly important military district. By the … 9th/15th century the family was playing a vital … in defending Naṣrid frontiers and enjoyed a re… tion for valour in the *djihād*. Before mid-centu…

dy constituted a powerful and ruthlessly am-
ıs political party.
1419 the party staged its first rebellion through
bers in command of Guadix and Illora. Resentful
lī al-Amīn, then regent for the Naṣrid minor
mmad VIII *El Pequeño*, they slew the former
eplaced the latter by Muḥammad IX *El Zurdo*, a
lson of Muḥammad V. The grand vizierate fell to
'l-Ḥadjdjādj Yūsuf b. al-Sarrādj, organiser of
oup, and thereafter for eight years the Aben-
jes held sway in Granada.
ıen, in October 1427, Muḥammad was restored
yalists led by Riḍwān Bannigash (Banegas),
f b. al-Sarrādj and his followers opted not to
v their sultan into exile at the court of the
d Abū Fāris in Tunis, but to lie low and spy a
ce for pardon. This once gained, they plotted
achieved the restoration of Muḥammad IX with
aid of Juan II of Castile and Abū Fāris. By
mber 1429 Yūsuf b. al-Sarrādj and his sultan
back in power in Granada and so remained till
mber 1431, when the former fell at Loja fight-
joint Castilian and loyalist Granadan force,
e success put Yūsuf IV on the throne. But
f's reign was brief: by April 1432 Muḥammad IX
back on the throne and Yūsuf dead. Throughout
ammad IX's third reign—up to 1445—prominent
ions were assigned to the sons of Yūsuf b.
rrādj (Muḥammad and Abu 'l-Ḳāsim) and other
bers of their family and party. The period
-60, on the other hand, was one of vicissitudes
e Naṣrid throne fell successively to Muḥammad
l Cojo and Yūsuf V, and then reverted first to
ammad X and then to Muḥammad IX, who
ed till the end of 1453 or early 1454.
ıce the sultan Saʿd (*Ciriza/Muley Zad/Çah*; *reg.*
-62, 1462-4) owed his throne to the B. al-Sarrādj
w led by one Abu 'l-Surūr al-Mufarridj—the
y enjoyed his favour for a time. In 1460 we
the son of Abu 'l-Ḳāsim (above), another Abu
djdjādj Yūsuf, as one of the most influential
's of the realm, and yet another Yūsuf b. al-
dj as a *wazīr* in Mufarridj's administration. But
came a rift: resentful of tutelage, perhaps, and
nant at covert attempts to have his son Abu 'l-
n ʿAlī (Muley Hacén) supplant him, Saʿd had
rridj and the *wazīr* Yūsuf summarily executed
e Alhambra (July 1462). Muḥammad and ʿAlī b.
rrādj fled to Málaga and set up Yūsuf V (Aben
ël)—who was assured of Castilian support—as
ter-claimant. His premature death brought
'l-Ḥasan ʿAlī to the fore again, and in August
the latter, in concert with the B. al-Sarrādj,
threw Saʿd and seized the throne. The B.
rrādj were back in power: an Ibrāhīm b.
shʿar, an influential *ḳāʾid* who had married into
amily, became grand *wazīr*, and his administra-
included Abū ʿAbd Allāh Muḥammad, son of Mu-
mad b. Yūsuf al-Sarrādj (above). A strange
mstance was soon to undo them. In 1419 ʿAlī
married Fāṭima, daughter of Muḥammad IX.
is death, the veneration in which they held him
heir patron shifted to Fāṭima. And so ʿAlī's
marriage to a Christian renegade was seen as a
onal affront, and they drifted into rebellion.
ge retribution followed. Those who escaped with
lives fled, some to asylum in the noble houses
Medina Sidonia and Aguilar, other to various
ilian border towns. In 1482 they then slipped
to supplant ʿAlī by his eldest son—by Fāṭima—
ʿAbd Allāh Muḥammad (XII), the famous
odil. Till the end of Boabdil's reign and of Muslim Granada, the family's party held supreme political power. Granada once in Christian hands (1492), the Abencerrajes sold up and moved to the Alpujarra, then in March 1493 emigrated almost en masse to the Maghrib. Ironically, the family that had once defended Islam in Spain so well, had, by their part in ruinous civil wars, done so much to bring about its downfall.

Their story as told in Pérez de Hita's *Historia de los vandos de Zegries y Abencerrajes* (1595, 1619) is fiction born of a few grains of truth. In this celebrated novel, which moulded most subsequent literary treatment of "moros de Granada", the Abencerrajes are the model of all chivalry, valour and charm. Their rivals are the brave but jealous and brutally perfidious Zegríes—from *thaghrī* "borderer", a term seemingly applied to Maghribī *mudjāhidūn* in Spain (who were in fact politically a spent force well before the 9th/15th century). Falsely and secretly accused of dishonouring Boabdil and plotting against him, the leading Abencerrajes are unsuspectingly summoned to the Alhambra and assassinated. Not all perish; the word gets out, and insurrection follows. After a fierce struggle Muley Hacén is proclaimed, but finally the rebels are pacified, and Boabdil is restored. The Abencerrajes are banished and take refuge in Castile where they convert to Christianity. The honour of Boabdil's wife—besmirched by the Zegríes at the beginning of the whole saga to turn Boabdil against the Abencerrajes—is finally vindicated and the accusers slain by Christian knights. During the 17th and 18th centuries the theme of the Abencerrajes was taken up by other European authors, notably Chateaubriand in his *Les aventures du dernier Abencérage*.

The *Sala de los Abencerrajes*, in the *Cuarto de los Leones* of the Alhambra, derives its name from various assertions that thirty-odd Abencerrajes were slain there by Muḥammad X or, as others say, Muley Hacén or Boabdil. The fiction appears to have its roots in (a) Saʿd's assassination of Mufarridj and Yūsuf (above), and (b) Hernando de Baeza's account of the murder of Muḥammad IX and his sons by Saʿd and Abu 'l-Hasan ʿAlī in the Cuarto de los Leones.

Bibliography: L. Seco de Lucena Paredes, *Los Abencerrajes: leyenda e historia*, Granada 1960 and bibliography (73-5); R. Arié, *L'Espagne musulmane au temps des Naṣrides*, Paris 1973, 130 ff.

(J. D. LATHAM)

IBN SHAKRŪN (pronounced Shukrun) **AL-MIKNĀSĪ**, ABŪ MUḤAMMAD or ABŪ NAṢR ʿABD AL-ḲĀDIR B. AL-ʿARABĪ AL-MUNABBAHĪ AL-MADAGHRĪ, Moroccan physician and poet who was contemporary with sultan Mawlāy Ismāʿīl (1082-1139/1673-1727) and who died after 1140/1727-8. He received a traditional education at Fās, studied medicine under Ādarrāḳ [*q.v.* above] Aḥmad b. Muḥammad, performed the pilgrimage and profited by the opportunity to follow courses in medicine at Alexandria and Cairo. He then returned to settle at Meknès, where he entered the sultan's service, but led a fairly austere and cloistered life.

As well as a commentary on a grammatical work and various poems which reveal a certain talent for versifying, Ibn Shaḳrūn owes mainly his fame to an *urdjūza* of 673 verses on food hygiene, the *Shaḳrūniyya*, which has always been highly popular among the people; it gives interesting pieces of information on food practices of the time (ed. Tunis 1323/1905; lith. Fās 1324/1906; ms. Rabat K 1613). He was also the author of a *risāla* called *al-Nafḥa al-wardiyya fi 'l-ʿus͟hba al-hindiyya* on sarsaparilla and the treatment of syphilis; this text has been studied and made use of H. J. P. Renaud and G. S. Colin in their *Documents marocains pour servir à l'histoire du "mal franc"*, Paris 1935, index.

Bibliography: Ibn Zaydān, *Itḥāf aʿlām al-nās*, Rabat 1347-52/1929-33, i, 264, v, 320-30; ʿAlamī, *al-Anīs al-muṭrib*, lith. Fās 1315, 193; Lévi-Provençal, *Chorfa*, 297; Renaud, *Médecine et médecins marocains*, in *AIEO Alger*, iii (1937), 90-9; M. Lakhdar, *La vie intellectuelle au Maroc*, Rabat 1971, 161-6 and bibl. cited there. (Ed.)

IBN AL-ṢUḲĀʿĪ (vars. Suḳāʿī, Ṣaḳāʿī, Ṣaḳḳāʿī), AL-MUWAFFAḲ FAḌL ALLĀH B. ABI 'L-FAK͟HR AL-KĀTIB AL-NAṢRĀNĪ, official of the Mamlūk administration, who died almost a centenarian in Damascus in 726/1325, leaving behind the reputation of having been a good Christian and a chronicler worthy of trust. He composed a Harmony of the four gospels (a work which corresponds to the description of ms. 1029 in the Sbath collection, at present inaccessible) in Hebrew, Syriac, Coptic and Latin, and as well as a biographical work on singers (*Wafayāt al-muṭribīn*), three historical works: a continuation of the *Taʾrīk͟h* of al-Makīn Ibn al-ʿAmīd, a résumé of the *Wafayāt al-ʿayān* of Ibn K͟hallikān whose title is unknown to us, and a continuation of this last, the *Tālī Kitāb Wafayāt al-aʿyān*. The historian al-Ṣafadī acquired for his personal library the copy of the *Tālī* at present in the Bibliothèque Nationale in Paris as arabe 2061.

The *Tālī* is thus the sole work of Ibn al-Ṣuḳāʿī which has survived. It is in the conventional form of a biographical collection containing entries, arranged in alphabetical order, of persons who died between 657/1258 and 725/1324. Beyond the apparently monotonous nature of the compilation, it is from the choice of persons covered, the terms used to describe them and the anecdotes retailed about them, that the personality of the author emerges. He appears as a Christian firmly attached above all to moral standards, a skilful diplomat who knew how to retain the friendship of his contemporaries at a time of violent changes when the Mongol invasions led to a deterioration of relations between Muslims and *D͟himmī*s, and a trusty official who held the posts of *kātib* in the *dīwān al-murtadjaʿ*, the *dīwān al-birr* and the *dīwān al-mawārit͟h*. The exercise of his functions in the matter of frauds and inheritances gave him access to the records of several financial scandals which the authorities had probably stifled, since the chroniclers contemporary with Ibn al-Ṣuḳāʿī, although very fond of retailing these matters, do not mention them. However, his frequenting of Damascene intellectual circles where tasty anecdotes were passed round by word of mouth, gave him the subject-matter for several stories which he gives and which can also be found, with variants, in al-D͟hahabī, al-Yunīnī and al-D͟jazarī, and which al-Ṣafadī was to insert in his own work after the text of the *Tālī*.

Ibn al-Ṣuḳāʿī's moderation in depicting his contemporaries was not merely dictated by prudence. One should see in it rather the indulgence of a person who had reached an advanced age and who, although he allowed himself some lively and ironical comment on those who had, either at close hand or from a distance, made up part of his life, prided himself that in the eventide of his life he had as a Christian been able to come to terms with his Muslim environment, to gain confidence and attract confidences, and to behave as a well-balanced individual without losing any of his personal dignity and without compr[o]ing his faith.

Bibliography: Ibn Ḳāḍī S͟huhba, *al-I… bi-taʾrīk͟h al-Islām*, ms. Oxford, Or. Marsh… fol. 200b; Ibn Ḥadjar, *Durar*, iii, No. 591; … al-ʿImād, *S͟had͟harāt*, vi, 75; Brockelmann… 400 (with the name given incorrectly); S. al-M… djdjid, in *RIMA*, ii/1 (1956), 99; Ziriklī, *A…* v, 358; Kaḥḥāla, *Muʿdjam*, viii, 76; *Tālī K… Wafayāt al-aʿyān* (*un fonctionnaire chrétien… l'administration mamelouke*), ed. and tr. J. Su… Damascus 1974. (J. Subli…

IBN AL-TAMMĀR [see IBN MĪT͟HAM, abov…

IBN ʿUḲDA, ABU 'L-ʿABBĀS AḤMAD B. … ḤAMMAD B. SAʿĪD B. ʿABD AL-RAḤMĀN B. IBR… B. ZIYĀD B. ʿABD ALLĀH (B. ZIYĀD?) B. ʿAD… AL-HAMDĀNĪ AL-ḤĀFIẒ, Kufan traditio… was born on 15 Muḥarram 249/10 March … His ancestors, ʿAdjlān and Ziyād were clien… ʿAbd al-Raḥman b. Saʿīd b. Ḳays al-Sabīʿ… Hamdānī (d. 66/686) and ʿAbd al-Wāḥid b. … b. Mūsā al-Hās͟himī respectively. His father… a Kūfan Zaydī making a living by copying b… and teaching the Ḳurʾān, literature and g… mar, and was given the nickname ʿUḳda bec… of his knowledge of the intricacies of Arabic g… mar and inflection. Ibn ʿUḳda visited Bag… three times. The first time, in his youth before… 886, he heard *ḥadīt͟h* from a number of reno… traditionists. The second time, most likely in… first decade of the 4th century (913-22 A.D.)… incurred the enmity of the popular traditi… Yaḥyā b. Ṣāʿid (d. 318/930) by contesting the… ability of the *isnād* of one of his *ḥadīt͟h*s. Acco… to one account, he was briefly imprisoned by… vizier ʿAlī b. ʿĪsā [*q.v.*] at the instigation of… followers of Ibn Ṣāʿid until his criticism was pr… correct. This detail is not confirmed by ano… more elaborate account. A third time, he vi… Bag͟hdād towards the end of his life and taug… the mosque of al-Ruṣāfa, where he is known to … transmitted *ḥadīt͟h* in Ṣafar 330/November … and in the S͟hīʿī mosque of Barāt͟hā. His only c… trip was to the Ḥidjāz. Thus he transmitted m… from Kūfans and visitors to Kūfa. He died … D͟hu 'l-Ḳaʿda 332/1 July 944 in Kūfa.

Ibn ʿUḳda was generally recognised as the gre… traditionist of Kūfa in his time. Fabulous st… were related about his prodigious memory and… hundreds of thousands of traditions collected… memorised by him and the camel-loads of books w… his library contained. His transmission spanned… whole gamut of Kūfan traditions, Sunnī, Im… and Zaydī, and Sunnī and S͟hīʿī traditionists … equally eager to hear from him. Among his promi… Sunnī students were al-Dāraḳuṭnī, Ibn ʿAdī, … Ṭabarānī, and Abū ʿUbayd Allāh al-Marzub… Though he was criticised for relating objection… (*munkar*) *ḥadīt͟h*s, reports on the blemishes (*m… lib*) of Abū Bakr and ʿUmar, and traditions f… newly-discovered books (*widjāda*), and on … basis was accused of having spoiled the *ḥadīt…* Kūfa, he was considered a faithful transmi… Among the Imāmīs, Hārūn b. Mūsā al-Tallaʿuk… and Aḥmad b. Muḥammad b. al-Ṣalt transmi… from him. He appears frequently as the only K… transmitter of early Kūfan Imāmī traditions in… time complementing the common Imāmī trans… sion of the school of Ḳumm. The Imāmī r… books hold him in high esteem as a transmi… though emphasising that he remained a Djā… Zaydī until his death. Actually, he seems to …

orted the views of the Ṭālibiyya, who considered inciple all descendants of Abū Ṭālib as suited he imāmate, rather than those of the sectarian iyya of his time, who restricted it to the descen- s of ʿAlī and Fāṭima, He appears as an important mant of Abu 'l-Faradj al-Iṣfahānī in his *K. ātil al-Ṭālibiyyīn*, to whom he transmitted in cular the *K. Nasab Āl Abī Ṭālib* of the ʿAlid ā b. al-Ḥasan b. Djaʿfar.

n ʿUḳda's own works, whose titles are listed e Imāmī *ridjāl* works, included a book on the ts of Kūfa (*K. Faḍl al-Kūfa*), an enormous *l-Sunan*, a Ḳurʾān commentary, books on the mitters from ʿAlī, al-Ḥasan, al-Ḥusayn, ʿAlī al-ʿĀbidīn, Muḥammad al-Bāḳir, Zayd b. Djaʿfar al-Ṣādiḳ, Abū Ḥanīfa, as well as *musnads* lī, Zayd b. ʿAlī, and Abū Ḥanīfa. A fragment s *K. Dhikr al-nabī* has been published from a rus (N. Abbott, *Studies in Arabic literary ri, i*, Chicago 1957, 100-8). His book on the smitters from Zayd b. ʿAlī was the chief source n extant similar work by the Kūfan Zaydī ʿAbd Allāh Muḥammad b. ʿAlī al-ʿAlawī 45/1053).

Bibliography: al-Ṭūsī, *Fihrist kutub al- īʿa*, ed. A. Sprenger, Calcutta 1853-5, 42-4; em, *Ridjāl al-Ṭūsī*, ed. Muḥammad Ṣādiḳ Āl hr al-ʿulūm, Nadjaf 1381/1961, 441 f.; al- djāshī, *al-Ridjāl*, Tehran n.d., 73 f.; *Taʾrīkh ghdād*, v, 14-23; Ibn Shahrāshūb, *Maʿālim al- amāʾ*, ed. ʿAbbās Iḳbāl, Tehran 1353/1934, 13 f.; n al-Djawzī, *al-Muntaẓam*, vi, 336 f.; al-Dha- bī, *Tadhkirat al-ḥuffāẓ*, Haydarābād 1334/1915, 55-7; idem, *al-ʿIbar*, ii, ed. F. Sayyid, al- uwayt 1961, 230; idem, *Mīzān al-iʿtidāl*, ed. lī Muḥammad al-Bidjāwī, Cairo 1382/1962, i, 6-8; Ibn Ḥadjar, *Lisān al-mīzān*, Ḥaydarābād 29-31/1911-13, i, 263-6; al-Ṣafadī, *al-Wāfī*, i, ed. Iḥsān ʿAbbās, Wiesbaden 1969, 395 f.; Khwānsārī, *Rawḍāt al-djannāt*, ed. A. Ismā- iyān, Ḳumm 1390-2/1970-2, i, 208 f,; R. Stroth- ann, *Das Problem der literarischen Persönlichkeit id b. ʿAlī*, in *Isl.*, xiii (1923), 15 f.; Muḥsin al- nīn, *Aʿyān al-Shīʿa*, Damascus 1935-, ix, 8-45; W. Madelung, *Der Imam al-Qāsim ibn āhīm*, Berlin 1965, 47, 59. (W. MADELUNG)

N ʿUMĀRA [see AL-DĪKDĀN, above]

N ʿUTHMĀN AL-MIKNĀSĪ, ABŪ ʿABD ALLĀH AMMAD B. ʿABD AL-WAHHĀB B. ʿUTHMĀN, a occan diplomat and vizier of the 12th/18th ury, who played a prominent role in the forging es between his country and Spain. At the start s career he followed his father as preacher in of the mosques of Meknès; here he came to the ntion of the Sultan, Sīdī Muḥammad b. ʿAbd h (1171-1204/1757-89) who, at a date difficult etermine, took him into his service as a secretary. 193/1799, he was sent to the court of King Charles f Spain with the object of obtaining the redemp- of Algerian captives and of renewing friendly ions between the two states; this mission met success and led to the treaty of Aranjuez h was signed in 1780 (see V. Rodríguez Casado, *mbajada del Talbe Sidi Mohamed Ben Otomán 780*, in *Hispania*, xiii (1943), 598-611; idem, *ica marroqui de Carlos III*, Madrid 1946, 285- M. Arribas Palau, *El texto árabe del Convenio ranjuez de 1780*, in *Tamuda*, vi (1958); idem, *a árabes de Mawlay Muḥammad b. ʿAbd Allāh ivas a la embajada de Ibn ʿUṯmān de 1780*, in *éris-Tamuda*, ii/2-3 (1961), 327-35), and Ibn mān has left a detailed account of his mission, *al-Iksīr fī fikāk al-asīr* published by M. El Fasi in Rabat in 1965, with a long introduction describing the life and work of the diplomat.

On his return, he was appointed vizier, but the success of his first mission induced the sultan to entrust him with a second, to Malta and Naples, to secure the redemption of more captives; this mission, carried out in 1196/1782, was also made the subject of an account entitled *al-Badr al-sāfir fi 'ftikāk al-asārā min yad al-aduww al-kāfir* (this has been summarised by Ibn Zaydān, *Itḥāf*, iii, 320-9, and a number of manuscripts exist in Rabat and Meknès).

Three years later, Ibn ʿUthmān was entrusted with a new mission, this time to the court of ʿAbd al-Ḥamīd I in Istanbul, with the object of resolving with the Ottoman sultan a conflict provoked by Turkish soldiers on the borders of Algeria and Morocco. The diplomat set out on the 1st Muḥarram 1200/4th of November 1785 and did not return to Morocco until 29th Shaʿbān 1202/4th of June 1788; he had in fact taken advantage of his stay in the Orient to make the Pilgrimage, which provided him with the material for a third *riḥla*, with a more elaborate title than the preceding two: *Iḥrāz al-muʿallā wa 'l-raḳīb fī ḥadjdj Bayt Allāh al-ḥarām wa-ziyārat al-Ḳuds al-sharīf wa 'l-Khalīl wa'l-tabarruk bi-ḳabr al-Ḥabīb* (see Ibn Zaydān, *Itḥāf*, iii, 30-5; an edition by M. El Fasi has been in the course of preparation for a considerable length of time).

On his return, he was sent to escort to Algeria the captives released by Spain. On the death of Muḥammad b. ʿAbd Allāh, he continued in the service of Mawlāy al-Yazīd (1204-6/1789-92) who sent him on to the court of Charles IV of Spain; setting out at the end of December 1790, he was received by the sovereign in Madrid on the 27th of January 1791, but his mission was unsuccessful and he set out for home on the 18th of August; the following day, Charles IV declared war on Morocco; Ibn ʿUthmān was however permitted to return to Madrid, where he lived as a private citizen until April 1792. Some very interesting documents concerning his stay in Spain have been discovered and published by M. Arribas Palau (*La estancia en España de Muḥammad ibn ʿUṯmān (1791-1792)* in *Hespéris-Tamuda*, iv/1-2 (1963), 120-92; cf. the same *Cartas árabes de Marruecos en tiempo de Mawlay al-Yazid (1790-1792)*, Tetuan 1961). On the death of al-Yazīd, Ibn ʿUthmān returned to Morocco and entered the service of Mawlāy Sulaymān (1206-38/1792-1823), who had already written to him in Spain entrusting him with a diplomatic mission. The new sultan did not hesitate to appoint him governor of Tetuan, as well as his representative in dealings with foreign consuls in residence in Tangier (see M. Arribas Palau, *Muḥammad ibn ʿUṯmān designado gobernado de Tetuán a finales de 1792*, in *Hespéris-Tamuda*, ii/1 (1961), 113-27). Because of his talents as a diplomat, he was also given the task of resolving internal problems; one of his major achievements was persuading, in 1797, the governor of Safi, ʿAbd al-Raḥmān b. Nāṣir, to support the new administration; the latter had previously refused to recognise Mawlāy Sulaymān. His last important diplomatic act was the signing on 22 Ramaḍān 1212/2 March 1799 of the treaty between Morocco and Spain (see M. Arribas Palau, *El texto árabe del tratado de 1790 entre España y Marruecos*, in *Tamuda*, vii (1959), 9-51). He died soon after at Marrakesh, where he was travelling in the Sultan's entourage (beginning of 1214/mid-1799) and it was his rival al-Zayyānī [*q.v.*] who was entrusted with the task of returning his belongings to Meknès.

In addition to descriptions of journeys, which are also historical documents of great value, Ibn ʿU<u>th</u>mān is the signatory of a considerable corpus of diplomatic correspondence which has for the most part been published and translated by M. Arribas Palau. He has also left a number of poems which bear witness to a considerable poetic talent and confirm what one might be entitled to expect of a Moroccan with a strong grounding in traditional culture. His account of the journey to Istanbul and the Holy Places also reflects the education that he had received, and it often gives the impression of a stylistic exercise in rhymed prose, rich with religious and literary reminiscences. On the other hand, his other writings are composed in a simpler and more natural style; a number of dialectical forms are encountered here, and the author does not hesitate to transcribe Spanish words when he talks about Spain and describes, not without precision and colour, the novelties that he has observed in that country.

Bibliography: In addition to the fundamental works of M. Arribas Palau given in the article, see Marrāku<u>sh</u>ī, *al-Iʿlām bi-man ḥalla Marrāku<u>sh</u> wa-A<u>gh</u>māt min al-aʿlām*, Fās 1355-8/1936-9, v, 142-3; Ibn Zaydān, *Itḥāf aʿlām al-nās*, Rabat 1347-52/1929-33, iii, 301-5, 318-30, iv, 159-68; Zayyānī, *Turd<u>j</u>umān*, ed. and tr. O. Houdas, *Le Maroc de 1631 à 1812*, Paris 1886, index; H. Pérès, *L'Espagne vue par les voyageurs musulmans*, Paris 1937, 17-29; M. al-Fāsī, *Muḥammad b. ʿU<u>th</u>mān al-Miknāsī*, Rabat 1961-2; M. Lakhdar, *Vie littéraire*, 266-71, and bibl. cited there.

(ED.)

IBN WAHB, ABU 'L-ḤUSAYN ISḤĀḲ B. IBRĀHĪM B. SULAYMĀN B. WAHB AL-KĀTIB, scion of an old and distinguished secretarial family and author of a remarkable <u>Sh</u>īʿī work on Arabic rhetoric, style and the secretary's art, the *K. al-Burhān fī wud<u>j</u>ūh al-bayān*. His grandfather Sulaymān was vizier to al-Muhtadī and al-Muʿtamid, fell in disgrace under al-Muwaffaḳ and died in his prison in 292/905. About his father and himself we know almost nothing. His *floruit* belongs to the first half of the 4th/10th century. His book must have been composed in or after 335/946-7, since it mentions the vizier ʿAlī b. ʿIsā [*q.v.*] as already dead. He is thus a contemporary of Ḳudāma b. D<u>j</u>aʿfar [*q.v.*], under whose authorship the work was placed by the editors of the truncated Escorial ms., ʿA.Ḥ. ʿAbbādī and T. Ḥusayn, despite strong doubts of the latter, and published under the title *Naḳd al-na<u>th</u>r* (Cairo 1351/1933). The discovery by ʿAlī Ḥasan ʿAbd al-Ḳādir of a complete copy of the work in the Chester Beatty Collection (ed. A. Maṭlūb and <u>Kh</u>. Ḥadī<u>th</u>ī, Ba<u>gh</u>dād 1387/1976) made possible the correct identification of author and title.

The *Burhān* represents an interesting attempt to apply Greek, Muʿtazilī and Imāmī doctrines to Arabic rhetoric. The latter trend is evidenced by positive references to some *imāms* of the Twelver line, including the eighth, and by the use of principles such as *taḳiyya*, *ʿisma*, *ẓāhir/bāṭin*, *taʾwīl*, *rumūz* (in the Ḳurʾān), *kitmān* and *badāʾ*. It also shows some influence of D<u>j</u>āḥiẓ's *Bayān*, but is strongly critical of it. Whether he was also influenced by Ḳudāma has not yet been conclusively proved. The author also cites four writings of his own, the *K. al-Ḥud<u>j</u>d<u>j</u>a*, *K. al-Īḍāḥ*, *K. al-Taʿabbud* and *K. Asrār al-Ḳurʾān*. None of these seems to have survived, nor has any mention of them been found in the sources so far.

Bibliography: T. Ḥusayn and ʿA. Ḥ. ʿAbbādī (eds.), *K. Naḳd al-na<u>th</u>r*, Cairo 1941, Introd. ʿA. H. ʿAbd al-Ḳādir in *al-Risāla*, xvi (1 1257 ff. and in *RAAD*, xxiv (1949), 73-81 Tabāna, *Ḳudāma b. D<u>j</u>aʿfar wa 'l-naḳd al-a* Cairo 1373/1954, 94-108; S. A. Bonebakker *K. Naḳd al-<u>sh</u>iʿr*, Leiden 1956, 16-20; <u>Sh</u>. *al-Balā<u>gh</u>a taṭawwur wa-taʾrī<u>kh</u>*, Cairo 93-102; Maṭlūb and Ḥadī<u>th</u>ī (eds.), *K. al-Bu* Introd., 1-41. (For his conception of the *bayān*, see art. *s.v.* in i, 1115a). (P. SHIN

IBN WARSAND, ʿALĪ B. AL-ḤUSAYN BAD<u>J</u>ALĪ, founder of a <u>Sh</u>īʿī sect in the Ma known as the Bad<u>j</u>aliyya [see AL-BAD<u>J</u>ALĪ]. books (*kutub*), in which he gathered <u>Sh</u>īʿī traditions, are quoted by the Ḳāḍī al-Nuʿmā his *K. al-Īḍāḥ*. These quotations indicate tha wrote in the first half of the 3rd/9th century belonged to the Mūsawī <u>Sh</u>īʿa, who recog Mūsā al-Kāẓim as their last *imām* and as the M He lived and taught in Nafṭa in Ḳasṭīliya. doctrine seems to have been propagated firs his son al-Ḥasan [see AL-BAD<u>J</u>ALĪ] in Darʿa and still before 280/893, by a Muḥammad Ibn War quite likely a son of al-Ḥasan, in the Sūs al- There the Bad<u>j</u>aliyya come to constitute one o two factions into which the population of Tārū was divided and engaged in constant fighting the other, Sunnī Mālikī, faction. They suppo and were led by the Idrīsid *amīrs* of the region were themselves converts to their doctrine. close association with them probably lies behind evidently mistaken, assertion of some sources they restricted the imāmate to the Ḥasanid de dants of ʿAlī to the exclusion of Ḥusaynids. Bad<u>j</u>aliyya were wiped out in Tārūdānt after Almoravid conquest of the town in 458/1066. sect survived, however, in Tiyūywīn, the se major town of the Sūs. It was most likely absc or extinguished after the middle of the 6th century by the Almohad movement originatin the same region.

Bibliography: (in addition to the so mentioned in the article on al-Bad<u>j</u>alī): al-I *Description de l'Afrique septentrionale et sahari* ed. H. Pérès, Algiers 1957, 39; Ibn Abī *Rawḍ al-ḳirṭās*, ed. C. H. Tornberg, Uppsala 82; M. Talbi, *L'Émirat Aghlabide*, Paris 571-3; W. Madelung, *Some notes on non-Isn Shiism in the Maghrib*, in *Stud. Isl.*, xliv (1 87-97; Widād al-Ḳāḍī, *al-<u>Sh</u>īʿa al-Bad<u>j</u>aliy 'l-Ma<u>gh</u>rib al-Aḳṣā*, in *A<u>sh</u>ghāl al-muʾt al-awwal li-taʾrī<u>kh</u> al-Ma<u>gh</u>rib wa-ḥaḍāratih* Tunis 1979, 165-94. (W. MADELUN

IBN ZAKRĪ, a name of at least two Magh scholars, one from Tlemcen, of the 9th/15th cen the other from Fās, of the 12th/18th century well as Zakariyāʾ in the Ḳurʾan (III, 37, 38, 85, XIX, 2, 7, XXI, 89, 90), an Arabic form o Zacharias of Luke (i, 5-25), Ma<u>gh</u>ribī nomencl recognised and still recognises, among Muslims Jews, the name Zakrī (orthography Zekri, and, patronym, Benzekri, Benzecri and Ibnou-Z

These two scholars are:

1. IBN ZAKRĪ (Abu 'l-ʿAbbās Aḥmad b. Muḥan al-Ma<u>gh</u>rāwī al-Tilimsānī) born at the beginnir the 9th/15th century and died in Ṣafar 900/14 Tlemcen, whence his *nisba*. Brosselard (31 put an end to the uncertainties of the Arabic graphical sources which placed the date of his sometimes in 899/1493 and sometimes in 906/ and to the errors of oral tradition which lo his burial place at Yabdar three leagues

·cen, by publishing the epitaph of his tomb vered by him at Tlemcen "three hundred s from that of Sanūsī", also corroborating the tion of al-Warthīlānī (1121-93/1710-79) who he had "visited his tomb, at al-ʿUbbād, in the ity of those of Abū Madyan, al-Sanūsī, the ·ānīs, Ibn Marzūḳ and the two sons of the n".

ter losing his father at an early age and being ght up by his mother, Ibn Zakrī was placed e age of twelve as an apprentice weaver. With t for study, the young Ibn Zakrī made his way, he was able, to the mosques and *madāris* of cen (al-ʿUbbād, al-Yaʿḳūbiyya) to hear the res of the *ʿulamāʾ* of the age, among others Zāghū (Aḥmad b. Muḥammad, d. 845/1441; see ad Bābā, 78, 308; al-Ḥafnāwī, ii, 42), who was a weaver; al-ʿUḳbānī (Ḳāsim b. Saʿīd, d. 450; see Ibn Maryam, 147; Aḥmad Bābā, 85; afnāwī, ii, 85); Abū ʿAbd Allāh Muḥammad b. bbās b. ʿĪsā al-ʿUbbādī (d. 871/1467; see Ibn am, 223). On his relations with his masters on his character, the biographical accounts t some anecdotal details which show him as ous, obliging and, moreover, gifted with a voice.

ving become in his turn a doctor of religious engrossed in the sources of *fiḳh*, jurisprudence, ānic exegesis, theology and Arabic grammar, xercised successfully the functions of *ḳāḍī*, and professor, and had future masters as ples, including Zarrūḳ (Aḥmad b. Muḥammad b. al-Burnusī al-Fāsī, 846-79/1442-93; see Ben eb, no. 51; Brockelmann, S II, 361), who was a er; Ibn Marzūḳ (Aḥmad b. Muḥammad *ḥafīd al-* [*q.v.*], d. 925/1519); Abū ʿAbd Allāh Muḥammad uḥammad b. al-ʿAbbās (d. 920/1513; see Ibn am, 259); Aḥmad b. Muḥammad b. al-Ḥādjdj al- āwī (d. 930/1521; see Ibn Maryam, 8, 17, 23).

s biographers have also noted that he had a orable controversy, doubtless theological, with val al-Sanūsī (Muḥammad b. Yūsuf b. ʿUmar b. ayb 830-95/1427-90 [*q.v.*]), and that he is the or of the following writings:

ughyat al-ṭālib fī sharḥ ʿAḳīdat Ibn al-Hādjib 2, 1538; Fās, Ḳarawiyyīn, 1594; see Brockel- , I, 539);

l-Manẓūma al-kubrā fi ʿilm al-kalām, a theo- al treatise of more than 1500 verses in *radjaz* , also entitled *Muḥaṣṣil* (or *Mukammil*) *al- ṣid* (Esc. 2, 1561; Rabat, 89; Fās, Ḳarawiyyīn, 1571, 1587), which was made the object of a nentary in two versions, one long and one short, led *Naẓm al-farāʾid wa-mubdī 'l-fawāʾid li- ṣṣil al-maḳāṣid* by Aḥmad al-Mandjūr (926-95/ 87 [*q.v.*]);

omm. on *al-Waraḳāt fī uṣūl al-fiḳh* of al-Dju- ī (Abu 'l-Maʿālī ʿAbd al-Malik b. ʿAbd Allāh, Imām al-Ḥaramayn [*q.v.*], entitled *Ghāyat rām bi-sharḥ muḳaddimat al-imām*, Cairo i, see Brockelmann, S I, 672, who gives a list of ther commentaries on this work and S II, 85;

l-Masāʾil al-ʿashr al-musammāt bi-bughyat al- ṣid wa-khulāṣat al-marāṣid, Cairo 1344/1925;

certain number of *fatāwī* reproduced in the *ār* of al-Wānsharīshī (the above lith., Fās 1899 in 12 volumes);

Iasāʾil al-ḳaḍāʾ wa 'l-futyā on which there is formation;

rdjūza fī ḥisāb al-manāzil wa 'l-burūdj on which formation is available.

Ḥādjdjī Khalīfa attributes to him erroneously some works of his homonym from Fās.

Tlemcen had a mosque bearing his name (called Djāmiʿ Sīdī Zegrī [*sic*]) to which Brosselard devoted a study, publishing an inventory of its endowments contained in an act of *ḥubs* dated 1154/1741. For its part, popular belief made of him a *walī* or saint and a Ṣūfī, capable of performing miracles (*karāmāt*) and of overcoming, by the gift of ubiquity, terrestrial distances (*ṭayy al-arḍ*). Finally, speaking of the *ʿulamāʾ* of Tlemcen, an Andalusian author said "Knowledge is with al-Tanasī, virtue with al-Sanūsī and pre-eminence (*riyāsa*) with Ibn Zakrī", whom another described as *ibn dhirāʿi-hi* ("son of his arms" or "son of his works").

It should be added that Ibnou-Zekri (Muḥammad al-Saʿīd b. Aḥmad al-Zawāwī al-Djannādī, professor of *fiḳh* in the upper division of the Algiers *madrasa* and *muftī* of Algiers, originally from the tribe of Ayth Zekrī of Great Kabylia (1267-1322/1851-1914), author of *Awḍaḥ al-dalāʾil ʿalā wudjūb iṣlāḥ al-zawāyā bi-bilād al-Ḳabāʾil*, Algiers 1321/1903, used to say that he was a descendant of Ibn Zakrī al-Tilimsānī, as al-Ḥafnāwī remarks, who, with a note of scepticism, declares "In the matter of genealogy, people have to be taken at their word".

Bibliography: Ibn Maryam, *al-Bustān fī dhikr al-awliyāʾ wa'l-ʿulamāʾ bi-Tilimsān*, Algiers 1326/1908; Aḥmad Bābā, *Nayl al-ibtihādj bi-taṭrīz al-dībādj*, Cairo 1351/1932, 170; Ibn al-Ḳāḍī, *Djadhwat al-iḳtibās fī man ḥall min al-aʿlām madīnat Fās*, lith. Fās 1309/1891; Ibn ʿAskar, *Dawḥat al-nāshir*, lith. Fās 1309/1891, i, 88; Ifrānī, *Ṣafwat man intashar*, ed. Ḥādjdjī, Rabat 1396/1926, 119-21; Ḳādirī (Muḥammad b. al-Ṭayyib), *Nashr al-mathānī*, lith. Fās 1310/1892; Warthīlānī, *Nuzhat al-anẓār*, Algiers 1326/1908; Brosselard, *Les inscriptions arabes de Tlemcen*, in *RA* (1858-61); Abbé Bargès, *Complément à l'histoire des Béni Zeiyan, rois de Tlemcen*, Paris 1887; Hafnawi, *Taʿrīf al-khalaf bi-ridjāl al-salaf*, Algiers 1324/1906, i, 38-41; Ben Cheneb, *Étude sur les personnages mentionnés dans l'Idjāza du Cheikh ʿAbd El Ḳādir el-Fāsy*, Paris 1907, 218, 244.

2. Ibn Zakrī (Abū ʿAbd Allāh Muḥammad b. ʿAbd al-Raḥmān al-Fāsī), born at an unknown date in Fās where he always lived and where he died in 1144/1731, was at first a young apprentice tanner (*dabbāgh*) in the service of his father with whom he used, after his manual work was done, to attend classes given by the latter's friend Abū ʿAbd Allāh Maḥammad b. ʿAbd al-Raḥmān b. ʿAbd al-Ḳādir al-Fāsī [see al-fāsī in Suppl.]. He also followed the lectures given by Abū ʿAbd Allāh Muḥammad, otherwise known as al-Ḥādjdj al-Khayyāṭ al-Ruḳʿī (d. 1115/1703; see al-Ḳādirī, ii, 172, al-Kattānī, i, 230), always staying shyly at the rear of the auditorium. One or the other, or both, of these two *shaykh*s noticed the pertinence of the questions that he asked them and the active part that he took in discussions, and they immediately suggested to his father that he be given leave of absence from the tannery and encouraged to study, offering to take upon themselves the cost of his tuition. Their advice was followed. The young man completed his education with other teachers, including: Abū ʿAbd Allāh Maḥammad b. ʿAbd al-Ḳādir al-Fāsī [see al-fāsī in Suppl.]; Aḥmad Ibn al-Ḥādjdj (d. 1109/1697, see Lakhdar, 107-8 and Index); Abū ʿAbd Allāh Muḥammad b. Aḥmad al-Masnāwī (1072-1136/1661-1724, see al-Ḳādirī, ii, 204; al-Kattānī, iii, 44; Ben Cheneb, §

13; al-Nāṣirī, iv, 44; Lévi-Provençal, 301). He soon
became *imām* of a small mosque in the jewellers'
quarter (*ṣāg̲h̲a*), where he gave, every Thursday and
Friday, lectures on Ṣūfism according to the *Ḥikam*
of Ibn ꜥAṭāʾ Allāh [*q.v.*] with such success that the
place became too small for his rapidly-growing audience. It is true that in this context his biographers
are unanimous in saying that he was unrivalled, and
that he was well versed in other branches of scholarship current at the time: Arabic grammar, lexicology, metrics, rhetoric, epistolary art, genealogy,
biography, history, etc. He also used the practice
and technique of *id̲j̲tihād*, in the sense of rational
effort at explanation and deduction in the judicial
sphere.

Among those who attended his lectures were:
his own master al-Masnāwī, mentioned above;
Masꜥūd al-Ṭāhirī al-D̲j̲ūṭī (d. 1150/1737, see al-
Kattānī, i, 326); Abu'l-Ḥasan ꜥAlī b. Muḥammad
al-Manālī al-Zabādī (d. 1163/1750, see al-Kattānī,
ii, 187); al-Wazīr al-G̲h̲assānī (1063-1146 / 1653-1733,
Lakhdar, 122-5) who wrote his biography in a
pamphlet entitled *al-ꜥArf al-siḥrī fī baꜥd faḍāʾil
Ibn Zakrī*, of which a manuscript copy is to be found
in the Aḥmadiyya library in Fās (see Ibn Sūda, i,
no. 724, p. 189); Gannūn, 288, attributes it,
probably mistakenly, to the above-mentioned
al-Zabādī.

In 1140/1727 he performed the duty of *ḥad̲j̲d̲j̲*
and noticing, while passing through Cairo, the
people's addiction to tobacco, he took it upon himself
to embark on a campaign for the prohibition of this,
which he regarded as a vice. The result of this
campaign was the convening, at the University of
al-Azhar, of a colloquium in the course of which
his arguments commanded respect, although the
objection was raised that he was speaking as a
Mālikī, whereas in Egypt one was either a Ḥanafī
or a S̲h̲āfiꜥī. He asked his opponents: "Would you
smoke in the presence of the Prophet?"—"No,"
was the reply, "abstinence would be imposed by
decency and by respect for the Prophet".—"Well
then," he added abruptly, "should not anything
that cannot be done in the presence of the Prophet
be forbidden? To abstain from the performance of a
duty is a *bidꜥa* (culpable innovation) and *bidꜥa*
and its agent are condemned to the fires of Hell.
Furthermore, to practise indecency outside the view
of the Prophet and believe oneself blameless is
hypocrisy!" Disconcerted, the *ꜥulamāʾ* of al-Azhar
made no reply.

Ibn Zakrī al-Fāsī enjoyed visiting the *chorfa* of
Wazzān, in particular Mawlāy al-Ṭayyib (d. 1089/
1679), and was associated with their disciple and
biographer al-Ḥād̲j̲d̲j̲ al-K̲h̲ayyāṭ al-Rukꜥī, whose
pupil he was. He was ultimately regarded as a
miracle-worker who believed that, when wide-awake,
he had seen the Prophet. It is also said that, endowed
with a considerable fortune, he used it to render aid
to the disinherited.

His writings, dealing with various subjects, were,
it is said, "numerous, read and studied to advantage
almost everywhere." These are, on the one hand,
commentaries on works of grammar, theology and
mysticism composed by Muslim authors of East
and West, and annotations and glosses which have
for the most part been left incomplete, and on the
other hand, didactic poems concerning various
matters, and at least one original prose work. Kattānī,
i, 158, supplies the following list:

S̲h̲arḥ al-Farīda fī 'l-naḥw wa'l-taṣrīf wa'l-k̲h̲aṭṭ of
al-Suyūṭī (lith. Fās 1319/1901); *S̲h̲arḥ al-Ḥikam*

al-ꜥaṭāʾiyya, ms. Paris 1351, on the programm
his teaching and the object of more than tw
glosses by Zarrūḳ (Aḥmad b. Aḥmad b. ꜥIs
Burnusī al-Fāsī (846-99/1442-93 [*q.v.*]), no
mention other commentaries, of which the
important would seem to be that of the Sp
mystic Ibn ꜥAbbād al-Rundī entitled *G̲h̲ayt̲
mawāhib al-ꜥaliyya*, Būlāḳ, 1285/1868; see Bro
mann, G II, 143-4; S II, 145-7, IBN ꜥABBĀ
RUNDĪ and IBN ꜥAṬĀʾ ALLĀH; *S̲h̲arḥ al-ḳawā*
'l-taṣawwuf by Zarrūḳ, considered the most impo
and the best known of the latter's writings,
1318/1900 (see Brockelmann, S II, 326); *S̲
al-Naṣīḥa al-kāfiya li-man k̲h̲aṣṣa-hu Allāh
ꜥāfiya* by the same Zarrūḳ (see Brockelmann,
361, who gives a list of other commentaries on
work); *S̲h̲arḥ Ṣalāt ꜥAbd al-Salām b. Mas̲h̲īs̲h̲*,
known as *al-Ṣalāt al-mas̲h̲īs̲h̲iyya* (see its tex
al-Fāsī (Abū ꜥAbd Allāh and Abū Ḥāmid Muḥan
al-ꜥArabī b. Yūsuf, 988-1052/1580-1643), 63
Gannun, 356, and in Ḥād̲j̲d̲j̲ī, 175) which has bee
object of a number of other commentaries
al-Kattānī, i, 146; Lévi-Provençal, 312); *
(*taꜥālīḳ*) on al-Buk̲h̲ārī's compilation, exeges
Ḳurʾānic verses, an incomplete marginal
(*ḥās̲h̲iya*) on the commentary by Ibn His̲h̲ām
the *Alfiyya* of Ibn Mālik, poems on various subj
miscellanea mentioned by al-Ḳādirī and al-Ka
whose continued existence cannot be verifie
Hamziyya in praise of the Prophet, modelle
that of al-Būṣīrī [*q.v.* in Suppl.], with a commen
in two volumes (mss. Rabat K. 1372 and 1
an original work which, after his death, seem
have caused a sensation in Morocco and w
bears two titles, *al-Sayf al-ṣārim fi'l-radd ꜥ
mubtadiꜥ al-ẓālim* and *al-Fawāʾid al-mutt
fi'l-ꜥawāʾid al-mubtadaꜥa*; in these he propo
the thesis according to which "merit is a matt
piety, not of genealogy." This work exists
manuscript volume in the library of ꜥAbd
Raḥmān b. Zaydān at Meknès (see Ibn Sūd
no. 418, p. 118). It aroused among the Moro
ꜥulamāʾ a polemic which lasted for almost a cen
on the problem of racism and anti-racism.
Ḳādirī, who could have known Ibn Zakrī at th
of twenty, since he died only forty-two years
than him, at the age of sixty, claims that he h
a very widespread rumour (*mustafīḍa*) that
latter had been responsible for the publication
book in support of the *S̲h̲uꜥūbiyya*, which ass
the superiority of non-Arabs over Arabs; he adds
all the contemporary men of religion reproa
him for this and vilified him ruthlessly and ju
In the long biographical notice which he de
to him, al-Ḳādirī invokes the authority of
than twenty teachers, and derives support
many Ḳurʾānic verses and *ḥadīt̲h̲*s in the atte
first to give a definition of the *S̲h̲uꜥūbiyya*, t
who put non-Arabs and Arabs on the same level
those who put non-Arabs above Arabs, and
to lay emphasis on the merits of the Arabs, who
birth to the Prophet Muḥammad and suppo
him in his noble mission, finally concluding
as regards Muslim law, all Muslims, irrespe
of race and irrespective of the period in which
embraced Islam, enjoy equal rights. Howeve
careful reading of this article gives the impre
that, according to al-Ḳādirī, Ibn Zakrī had appo
himself the spokesman of Muslims of Jewish o
then very numerous in Fās, who did not car
the Arabs, to whom they denied any distin
merit, making no exceptions in this regard eve

Anṣār, the Ḳuraysh and the parents of the
het, to whom a great many authentic *ḥadīth*s
citly gave a privileged status. Furthermore,
neo-Muslims prided themselves on being the
ndants of the Banū Isrāʾīl and of the prophets
, Hārūn, Zakariyyā, and others, and on this
nt they considered themselves superior to the
s. By his action, again in the words of al-Ḳādirī,
Zakrī had committed a reprehensible deviation
cut himself off from the faith, thus deserving
punishment laid down for those who allow
selves to be led astray by passion." Moreover,
ne not spent his time "among groups of men of
wn kind, men living in ease and opulence, who
ged performances of musical entertainment in
presence, and whose sympathy he made great
ts to gain, putting forward ideas of the type
n have been attributed to him, so well and to
an extent that all his associates ultimately
ne his disciples"?
re than half a century before, Mayyāra al-Akbar
ʿAbd Allāh Muḥammad al-Fāsī, 999-1072/
1662, see al-Ḳādirī, 235; al-Kattānī, i, 165;
Provençal, 259, n. 4, 7°) had also written a
dealing with this problem and entitled *Naṣīḥat*
ghtarrīn fi'l-radd ʿalā dhawī 'l-tafriḳa bayn
uslimīn (Royal Lib., Rabat ms. 7248, fols. 71a-
; its author, according to al-Ḳādirī, had a
excuse and did not deserve reproach because,
s time, the neo-Muslims were the victims of
ssment and even persecution on the part of
m Arabs. Mayyāra took their part, arguing
vour of the unity of the Muslim community.
nety years after Ibn Zakrī, Abu 'l-ʿAbbas
ad b. ʿAbd al-Salām b. Muḥammad al-Bannānī
234/1818)—the Bannānī family is known to
been of Jewish origin—took up the defence
-Zakrī and, with the object of dismissing al-
rī's accusations, wrote two books which,
een them, bear no fewer than eight different
, as follows: *Taḥliyat al-ādhān wa'l-masāmiʿ*
srat al-ʿallāma al-djāmiʿ; *al-Nūr al-lāmiʿ*
nz ruwāt al-madjāmiʿ; *al-Manhal al-ʿadhb al-*
i fī nuṣrat al-ʿallāma Ibn Zakrī; *Bustān al-*
ʾid al-muḥdathāt al-badāʾiʿ; *Rashf al-ḍarab*
dīl Banī Isrāʾīl wa'l-ʿArab (these five titles
those of the first book, which comprises two
nes, the first of which still exists, in private
s, in Fās; see Ibn Sūda, no. 256, p. 84); *al-*
ih al-mughrī ʿalā nuṣrat al-ʿallāma Ibn Zakrī;
dhyīl wa-shifāʾ al-ghalīl wa-izālat dāʾ al-ʿalīl;
djāla al-mūfiya bi-muḥtādj al-manẓūma al-
ya, for the second book, completed in 1222/
in one volume, which still exists in the form of
utograph manuscript by Muḥammad b. ʿAbd
llām Bannānī, and which was apparently a
of commentary on a *ḳaṣīda* of about three
red verses composed by Abū ʿUmar ʿUthmān
Alī al-Yūsī (d. 1084/1674; see al-Ifrānī, 113;
adirī ii, 13; al-Yūsī, *in fine*; Ben Cheneb, § 5);
reply to those who denigrate the merits of the
i Isrāʾīl and who maintain, wrongly, that Islam
them nothing" (see Ibn Sūda, no. 427, and
, pp. 120 and 426).
is controversy over racism and anti-racism,
he end of the 12th/18th century and at the
nning of the 13th/18th century, throws an
pected light on the ideas and pre-occupations
e Moroccan thinkers of that time and on their
ude towards non-Arabs and Jews converted to
n.

Bibliography: Fāsī (Muḥammad al-ʿArabī), *Mirʾāt al-maḥāsin min akhbār al-shaykh Abi' l-Maḥāsin*, lith. Fās 1324/1906; Yūsī, *Muḥāḍarāt*, lith. Fās 1317/1899; Ifrānī, *Ṣafwat man intashar*, lith. Fās n.d.; al-Ḳādirī, *Nashr al-mathānī*, lith. Fās 1310/1892; al-Kattānī, *Salwat al-ʿanfās*, lith. Fās, 3 vols. 1316/1898; al-Nāṣirī, *K. al-Istiḳṣā li-akhbār al-Maghrib al-Aḳṣā*, Cairo 1312/1894 and Casablanca 1956; Ben Cheneb, *Étude sur les personnages mentionnés dans l'Idjāza du Cheikh ʿAbd al-Ḳādir al-Fāsī*, Paris 1907; Lévi-Provençal, *Chorfa*, Paris 1922; Gannūn (ʿAbd Allāh), *al-Nubūgh al-maghribī fi 'l-adab al-ʿarabī*, Tetuan 1356/1837, 3 vols.; Ibn Sūda, *Dalīl muʾarrikh al-Maghrib al-Aḳṣā*, Casablanca, i, 1960, ii, 1965; M. Ḥadjdjī, *al-Zāwiya al-dilāʾiyya*, Rabat 1384/1964; M. Lakhdar, *Vie littéraire*, 169-71 and index.

3. H. al-Kattānī (i, 161) devotes a brief biographical notice to another IBN ZAKRĪ (Abu 'l-ʿAbbās Aḥmad, d. 1154/1741 in Fās) who is none other than the son of the preceding and who lived an ascetic life in the *khalwa* of the well-known Moroccan saint Sīdī Būshta (Abu 'l-Shitāʾ).

(M. HADJ-SADOK)

IBRĀHĪM SHĪRĀZĪ, better known as ḤĀDJDJĪ IBRĀHĪM SHĪRĀZĪ, was a Persian Prime Minister of the early Ḳādjār period, and a most influential agent in the transfer of power from the Zand dynasty to the Ḳādjārs.

His father, the one-eyed Ḥādjdjī Hāshim, reportedly of Jewish stock, had secured him a position of chief magistrate in the office of the *kalāntar* [*q.v.*] of Shīrāz. In the course of the chaotic period which followed the death of Karīm Khān Zand, the flattering attitude which he took towards his chief Mīrzā Muḥammad Kalāntar earned him the favour of the Zand ruler Djaʿfar Khān, who subsequently, on the withdrawal and death of Mīrzā Muḥammad, offered him the office of the *kalāntar* of Shīrāz (1200/1782). Luṭf ʿAlī Khān Zand, the youthful son and successor of Djaʿfar Khān, added his rather unthinking support to this parvenu's career, and, in the course of his ensuing struggle against the Ḳādjār Āḳā Muḥammad Khān, he entrusted the holding of his capital to this rather dubious *kalāntar*.

Ḥādjdjī Ibrāhīm, however, either in order to protect his fellow-citizens against the consequences of the dynastic wars, or just to dissociate himself from a losing cause, was brought to betray his brave but tyrannical sovereign. Thus in 1205/1791, while Luṭf ʿAlī and his soldiers had camped outside Shīrāz, and the capital was entrusted to Ḥādjdjī Ibrāhīm, an incident in the Zand camp plotted by the Ḥādjdjī, together with a surprise coup d'état which the latter staged against the Zand party in Shīrāz, resulted in Luṭf ʿAlī's fleeing, upon which Shīrāz was lost for ever to the Zand. Meanwhile, as Ḥādjdjī Ibrāhīm, probably due to his fear of a Zand revanche, made an appeal to the Ḳādjārs, Āḳā Muḥammad Khān occupied Shīrāz and appointed —not without some reservation—the old *kalāntar* as the Governor-General of the whole province of Fārs (1206/1791). Nevertheless, when after the extirpation of the Zands, and probably in order to curb the local influence of Ḥādjdjī Ibrāhīm, Shīrāz and the whole province of Fārs were granted to the Ḳādjār Crown Prince Bābā Khān (i.e. the later Fatḥ ʿAlī Shāh), the Ḥādjdjī was given an honorific title of Iʿtimād al-Dawla [*q.v.*], with a rather nominal premiership, to keep him as an attendant in the Shāh's retinue (1209/1795).

Under Fatḥ ʿAlī Shāh, who owed his accession

partly to the wise arrangements made by the old Ḥādjdjī Ibrāhīm, the latter's prestige and fortune increased rapidly, and his sons, brothers, and relatives obtained vast tracts of land with important positions throughout the Persian provinces. However, his own arrogance, along with the offensive behaviour of his relatives, caused considerable administrative hostility, and some of his opponents presented to the Shāh convincing documents—forged or authentic—to prove his involvement in treasonable activities. A royal decree, issued in great secrecy, directed the royal emissaries to seize and prosecute Ḥādjdjī Ibrāhīm and all his relatives at one time, on a previously fixed date, in Tehran and the provinces (1215/1801). Of all his male descendants, only two small boys were spared.

Ḥādjdjī Ibrāhīm's downfall, in which his rival Mīrzā Shafīʿ Māzandarānī had an important rôle, was later deplored by Fatḥ ʿAlī Shāh. His political opponents, however, did not cease to criticise him severely for his so-called treacherous character, his selfish impetuosity and his lack of tact in diplomatic affairs.

Bibliography: ʿAbd al-Razzāḳ b. Nadjaf-Ḳulī, *Maʾāthir-i sulṭāniyya*, 71-4; *Dhayl-i Mīr ʿAbd al-Karīm va Āḳā Muḥammad Riḍā bar taʾrīkh-i Gītī-Gushāy*, ed. Saʿīd Nafīsī, Tehran 1319, 339-95; Iʿtimād al-Salṭana, M. Ḥasan Khān, *Ṣadr al-tawārīkh*, Tehran 1349, 12-43; Ḥādjdjī Mīrzā Ḥasan-i Fasāʾī, *Fārs-nāma-yi Nāṣirī*, Tehran 1314, 249-50; Aḥmad Mīrzā ʿAḍud al-Dawla, *Taʾrīkh-i ʿAḍudī*, ed. H. Kūhī-i Kirmānī, Tehran 1328, 51; Riḍā Ḳulī Khān-ī Hidāyat, *Rawḍat al-ṣafāʾ-i Nāṣirī*, new ed. Tehran 1339, ix, 367-70; Mahdī-yi Bāmdād, *Taʾrīkh-i ridjāl-i Īrān, Ḳarn-i 12, 13, 14*, Tehran i, 21-8; Sir J. Malcolm, *History of Persia*, London 1861, ii, 217-24; Sir H. J. Brydges, *The dynasty of the Kadjars*, London 1833, p. cxli; R. G. Watson, *A history of Persia*, London 1886; P. Horn, *Geschichte Irans in islamischer Zeit*, in *Gr. Ir. Phil.*, ii, index; Sir P. Sykes, *A history of Persia*³, London 1930, ii, 295-6, 302; see also the Bibl. to KARĪM KHĀN ZAND.

(A. H. ZARRINKOOB)

IBRĪḲ (in Islamic art), a term used for any kind of ewer, irrespective of function or material, but generally a vessel for pouring water or wine. Together with a basin, it is also used for washing hands and feet. Other terms for specific kinds of ewers are *kubra* or *bulbula* (see Abū Nuwās, *Diwān*, ed. Wagner, i, Beirut 1958, 54, 3).

The chronology and geographical origin of early metal ewers up to the 4th/10th century have not yet been definitely established. They can be classified typologically into five groups, representing a slow departure from mainly Sāsānid and Soghdian prototypes towards the formation of truly Islamic shapes. The most characteristic features are: a tendency towards heavier bodies, with an emphasis on the lower part of the body in the earlier phases, shifting to the formation of shoulders; a development of shapes in which the transition between body, neck, mouth and foot is clearly marked and set off; and a preference for faceted shapes. One group is characterised by a bipartite neck which is contracted in its lower part and is cylindrical and faceted in the upper half. The ovoid or cylindrical body rests on three small feet (*Survey*, Pl. 244A). Another group is best known from the "Marwān" ewer in Cairo (*Survey*, Pls. 245-6), but its traditional association with the Umayyad caliph Marwān has to be discarded. The chronologically latest type has an body, a low footring and a straight, slightly f neck with a flat lip. It is well-balanced in propc and its shape was retained up to Saldjūḳ t Except for one group (the "Marwān" ewer) handles meet the neck by its lip. Popular typ thumb rests are a pomegranate or a full paln

Between the early 5th/11th and the begi of the 7th/13th century, workshops in Khurāsā Transoxania produced bronze ewers which car oil lamp-shaped spout. Early examples have found in Akhsīkath, in ancient Farghāna, ar Shahrastān, ancient Ushrūsana. Late 6th/12 early 7th/13th century specimens are inlaid silver and copper. One ewer in Paris is dated 1190-1 (*Survey*, Pl. 1309A). Khurāsānian work active in the late 5th/11th and 6th/12th cen also produced ewers with a high, raised s Some have spherical bodies, while in other case body is either melon-shaped, faceted or fl One of the fluted ewers is signed by Maḥmī Muḥammad al-Harawī and dated 577/1181 (M *Islamic metalworkers*, 1959, 59; for the whole see Abu 'l Faradj al-ʿUsh, *A bronze ewer with a spout*. The dates suggested by the author are d able).

In the 7th/13th century, Mosul, Damascus Cairo workshops produced richly decorated i brass ewers with a pear-shaped, plain or fa body, cylindrical neck and straight spout. I and signed specimen are the "Blacas" ewer in British Museum (Barrett, *Islamic metalwork*, pls. 12-13), and two ewers in Paris (Rice, *I brasses*, appendix, nos. 16 and 21). The pear-sh body and straight spout remain characte features of 8th/14th century Mamlūk ewers. have a high body, which is contracted in its part, and the neck is surmounted by a top-h cup (*The arts of Islam*, Hayward Gallery no. 216). Ewers with a strongly swelling b curving spout and handle, a contracted or fu shaped neck and a high splayed foot occur in 15th century Egypt and Iran simultaneously Carswell, *Six tiles*). Their occurrence on painted from Cairo and Damascus suggests a wider dist tion than that attested to by preserved obj Ewers depicted on contemporary and later minia seem to point to a continuation of this type in 10th/16th and later centuries.

Ceramic ewers follow the metal shapes very clo Some early ceramic renderings even imitate sold marks. Ewers with a fluted or cylindrical body a raised spout are particularly common among Pe monochrome glazed relief wares of the 6th/ and 7th/13th centuries.

Wine ewers and washing services are freque depicted in miniatures and other media (for 8th/ century washing sets, see M. S. Ipşiroğlu, *S alben*, Diez'sche Klebebände aus den Ber Sammlungen, Wiesbaden 1964, pls. XVII XVIII).

Bibliography: General books: A. U. (ed.), *A survey of Persian art*, Oxford 19 G. Wiet, *Objets en cuivre*. Cat. Gén. du M Arabe du Caire, 1932. Monographs on si objects: K. Erdmann, *Islamische Giessge des 11. Jahrhunderts*, in *Pantheon*, xxii (July-1938), 251-4; D. S. Rice, *Studies in Isl metalwork. II*, in *BSOAS*, xv/1 (1935), 6 idem, *An unpublished "Mosul" ewer dated 1229*, in *BSOAS*, xv/2 (1953), 229-32; i *Inlaid brasses from the workshop of Aḥmad al-D*

Mawṣilī, in *Ars orientalis*, ii (1957); U. Scerrato, *getti metallici di età Islamica in Afghanistan, II: Ripostiglio di Maimana*, in *AIUON*, N.S. /2, Naples 1964; A. S. Melikian Chirvani, *ivres inédits de l'époque de Qā'itbāy*, in *Kunst Orients*, vi/2 (1969), 119-24; B. Marshak, *onze ewer from Samarkand*, in A. A. Ivanov and S. Sorokin (eds.), *Srednyaya Aziya i Iran* Central Asia and Iran"), Leningrad 1972, -90 (with English summary); Abu 'l Faradj al-sh, *A bronze ewer with a high spout in the Metropolitan Museum of Art*, in *Islamic Art in the etropolitan Museum of Art*, ed. R. Ettinghausen, w York 1972, 191 ff.; J. Carswell, *Six tiles*, *ibid.*, 101 ff. For a systematic discussion of the velopment of Islamic ewers with illustrations, E. Baer, *Metal work in Islamic art and civilizan* (forthcoming). (EVA BAER)

HTHYOLOGY [see SAMAK].

OGLAN [see IČ-OGHLANĪ].

RĪS B. AL-ḤASAN, ʿIMĀD AL-DĪN, the last t exponent of the Ismāʿīlī *daʿwa* [*q.v.*] aman, came from a prominent al-Walīd family Kuraysh which headed the Mustaʿlī-Ṭayyibī *a* since the beginning of the 7th/13th century. vas born in 794/1392 in the fortress of Shibām, h peak of Mount Ḥarāz and a stronghold of the ʿīlīs. In 832/1428 he succeeded his uncle ʿAlī b. Allāh as the nineteenth *dāʿī*. Besides being a tile author, he was also a politician and a ior; he fought several battles against the Zaydīs ʿda, thereby regaining control of several Ismā-ortresses. He died on 19 Dhu 'l-Ḳaʿda 872/10 1468.

e is considered the most celebrated historian of *laʿwa*. His three historical works are the main es for the history of the Ismāʿīlīs from the 1th century until the second half of the 9th century. The first, *ʿUyūn al-akhbār*, in seven mes, is the most comprehensive work on the ry of the Ismāʿīlī *imām*s and the Fāṭimid sty. It also contains valuable information on beginning of the *daʿwa* in Yaman and on the yhids [*q.v.*]. The second work, *Nuzhat al-afkār*, vo volumes, deals with the Ismāʿīlī history in an, especially after the collapse of the Ṣulayḥids, the year 853/1449, and is considered to be the important source for the three-hundred-year ry of the *daʿwa* there. The third work, entitled *lat al-akhbār*, is a continuation of the preceding , wherein the events are brought up to the year 1465. Both the latter works are of great impor-e, since they deal with contemporary events and light on an obscure period of Yamanī history. addition to panegyrics of the *imām*s and the , his poetic *Dīwān* contains some historical mation. His work on Ismāʿīlī doctrine entitled *al-maʿānī* is regarded as the highest achievement *akāʾik* [*q.v.*] ever reached by the Yamanī *daʿwa*. also composed several refutations of Sunnī, lī and Muʿtazilī doctrines. Most of his works have ived and have been preserved in private collec-.

Bibliography: The main biographical sources e the author's own works mentioned above; e also Ismāʿīl b. ʿAbd al-Rasūl al-Madjdūʿ, *hrist*, ed. ʿAlī Naḳī Munzawī, Tehran 1966, 34, , 73-7, 85, 97, 103, 150-1, 239-42, 270, 275-7; r a detailed description of his works and sources e Ismail Poonawala, *Bibliography of Ismāʿīlī erature*, Malibu, Calif. 1977, 169-75.

(I. POONAWALA)

IDRĪS B. AL-ḤUSAYN B. ABĪ NUMAYY, ABŪ ʿAWN, Sharīf of Mecca in the early 11th/17th century. He was born in 974/1566, and became *Sharīf* and governor of the Ḥidjāz in 1011/1602-3 after his brother Abū Ṭālib and in conjunction with his nephew Muḥsin. This division of power ended, however, in a fierce internal family dispute, apparently over Idrīs's retinue and followers (*khuddām*), and in 1034/1624-5 the family deposed Idrīs from the governship of the Ḥidjāz in favour of Muḥsin. The conflict was resolved by a truce, during the time of which Idrīs promised to leave Mecca altogether. He now fell ill, and died and was buried at Yāṭib in the Djabal Shammar (17 Djumādā II 1034/25 February 1625). Muḥibbī quotes extensively from the eulogistic poetry addressed to him in his heyday of power.

Bibliography: The main biographical notice is in Muḥibbī, *Khulāṣat al-athar*, Cairo 1284/1867-8, i, 380-4; see also ʿUthmān b. Bishr al-Nadjdī, *ʿUnwān al-madjd fī taʾrīkh Nadjd*, Riyadh 1385-8/1965-8, i, 32; Aḥmad b. Zaynī Daḥlān, *Khulāṣat al-kalām fī bayān umarāʾ al-balad al-ḥarām*, Cairo 1305/1887-8, 64-6; Ziriklī, *al-Aʿlām*, i, 266.

(ED.)

AL-IDRĪSĪ, DJAMĀL AL-DĪN ABŪ DJAʿFAR MUḤAMMAD, B. ʿABD AL-ʿAZĪZ B. ABI 'L-ḲĀSIM (d. 649/1251), upper Egyptian author of Moroccan background who wrote, under the Ayyūbid sultan al-Malik al-Kāmil, his monograph on the monuments of Djīza (Gīza), the *K. Anwār ʿuluww al-adjrām fi 'l-kashf ʿan asrār al-ahrām*. The oldest extant version of this text is preserved in a copy commissioned by the Ottoman philologist ʿAbd al-Ḳādir b. ʿUmar al-Baghdādī (d. 1093/1682) [*q.v.*], who compiled—on the basis of Idrīsī's writing—his own *K. Maḳṣad al-kirām fī ʿadjāʾib al-ahrām*.

Idrīsī's tract on the Pyramids is distinguished from the copious earlier and later writings on the subject by its systematic and concise structure, its comprehensiveness and the rigorous application of the techniques and standards of *ḥadīth* scholarship to his presentation. Each of the six chapters of the book is a complete short monograph. Ch. 1 deals with the genre of the pagan *ʿadjāʾib* and their compatibility with the tenets of Islam; considerable space is devoted to the question why the Pyramids are not, or are only summarily, mentioned in the Ḳurʾān. Idrīsī vigorously defends the protection of the Pharaonic monuments. He names as witnesses for his standpoint the *Ṣaḥāba* who wrote pious graffiti on the Pyramids, settled and died in Djīza in the shadow of these pagan structures and "whose hands were not stretched out to them (sc. the Pyramids) in bad intent" (ms. Munich, Aumer 417, fol. 32a). He even contrives to declare Djīza, by virtue of the *Ṣaḥāba*'s presence, a "holy land" (*arḍ muḳaddasa*), and ranks the *ziyāra* to these *ʿadjāʾib*—tokens of God's majesty and warning—as obligations incumbent upon every scholar coming to the area (*ṭalab al-ʿadjāʾib*). More than once the book betrays signs of a strong local pro-Egyptian, quasi-Shuʿūbī bias: Idrīsī takes up the *topos* of the legendary intelligence of the Egyptians and skilfully intertwines it, firstly with the tradition (from a *Kitāb Masīsūn al-Rāhib*) that the dust of Djīza and of Anṣinā/Antinoe, another old Egyptian sanctuary, constitute a talisman which gives the people of Egypt their unique mental gifts; and secondly with the role of Hermes [see HIRMIZ], whom he introduced as the Greek warden of sagacity and wisdom, apart from his function as one builder of the Pyramids. In the late 13th and the 14th century, we observe the dramatic widening of this chasm between iconoclastic Muslim zealots and the moderates of Idrīsī's kind who point at the unadulterable place of these *ʿadjāʾib* within Muslim *Heilsgeschichte*.

In chs. 2 to 6, Idrīsī gives valuable data on the sites of Djīza, many of which are not repeated by later compilers. He gives a detailed description, also architectural, of the way the traveller takes from the Bāb Zuwayla, the south gate of the Fāṭimid city of Cairo, to the Pyramids. He mentions all the holders of high office who, between the days of al-Maʾmūn and his own, came to the Pyramids, often in search for treasures, *maṭālib*, as the Egyptians say. The Fāṭimid period saw the apogee of activities around the Pyramids; in al-Afḍal b. Badr al-Djamālī's days fires were lit on top of the Great Pyramid in certain nights. Idrīsī gives a list of contemporary scholars who saw, or wrote on, the Pyramids, among them Ibn al-Djawzī, ʿAbd al-Laṭīf al-Baghdādī (whose description of the Pyramids and the Sphinx he faithfully reproduces) and Ibn Mammātī (who composed a book on the Pyramids which Idrīsī counts among his sources), but also, *min ghayr ahl al-ḳibla* "from among the non-Muslims", the envoy of Frederick II to al-Kāmil (Count Thomas of Acerra?), who showed great zeal in deciphering a Latin inscription on the Pyramid of Cheops.

Idrīsī devotes extensive space to the controversial issue whether the Pyramids were built before or after the Deluge. He presents the arguments of those who held the latter position (among them a Jewish author who claims Aristotle as builder of the two great Pyramids), yet in an uncompromising fashion refutes their theories for the other, antediluvian, even pre-Adamite, theory. Unfortunately, the sphinx, *Abu 'l-Hawl* [*q.v.*], is given only passing mention. Too many stories circulated about it, as he complains.

Bibliography: Brockelmann, I, 478-9, S I, 879 f.; Ḥādjdjī Khalīfa, *Kashf al-ẓunūn*, i, 1833, 482, § 1412; U. Haarmann, *Die Sphinx. Synkretistische Volksreligiosität im spätmittelalterlichen islamischen Ägypten*, in *Saeculum* (1978), passim; idem, *Der Schatz im Haupte der Sphinx*, in *Die islamische Welt zwischen Mittelalter und Neuzeit*, Beirut 1979, *passim*. (U. HAARMANN)

AL-ʿIDWĪ AL-ḤAMZĀWĪ, ḤASAN, one of the principal protagonists of the events preceeding the British occupation of Egypt in 1882, was born in the village of ʿIdwa near Maghāghā in al-Minya province, Upper Egypt in 1221/1806.

He studied at al-Azhar [*q.v.*] and taught there from 1242/1826-7 onwards. He was a man of considerable wealth, which allowed him to spend generously on pious works and the publication of his writings. However, his inability adequately to regulate his financial affairs led to solvency problems and to a case raised against him in Court by the owner of the printing press, al-Maṭbaʿa al-Kāstiliyya, where he had most of his books printed (cf. al-Afūkātū Kātīskī (ed.), *Risāla*... *ʿan al-daʿwā allatī bayn* ... *Mūsā Kāstilī wa 'l-Shaykh Ḥasan al-ʿIdwī*, Cairo 1287/1870-1). In these works, which are listed in Brockelmann, *GAL*, II, 486, S II, 729, he concerns himself mainly with *fiḳh* and related issues, while in addition he wrote on *ḥadīth*, *tawḥīd* and *taṣawwuf*. His writings pertaining to the latter field reflect his adherence to al-Shādhiliyya order [*q.v.*]. He had been initiated into various branches of this *ṭarīḳa*, amongst others into al-ʿAfīfiyya [see AL-ʿAFĪFĪ above].

He was among the religious notables who ac supported the Khedive Ismāʿīl in his effor counter the danger of increasing interna control, and played a significant role in the e preceeding the Khedive's deposition in 1879.

His role during the ʿUrābī [*q.v.*] insurre when he sided with the ʿUrābiyyūn and pu demanded the deposition of the Khedive Ta caused his arrest following the British occupati Cairo in September 1882. He was set free i course of the subsequent court proceedings ag those involved in the insurrection, on condition he return to his native village of ʿIdwa. He in Cairo on 17 Ramaḍān 1303/19 June 1885 an buried in the now-demolished mosque which been constructed by him near the mosque Ḥusayn (cf. ʿAlī Mubārak, *Khiṭaṭ*, v, 48) and to the newly-erected mosque named after where his shrine may be found today (cf. the mo *al-Muslim*, xix (Cairo 1969), 9, 4).

Bibliography: For biographies, see Mubārak, *Khiṭaṭ*, xiv, 37, where al-ʿIdwī's in the ʿUrābī insurrection is omitted (cf. G. *Studies in the social history of modern E* Chicago-London 1969, 243); Zakī Muḥar Mudjāhid, *al-Aʿlām al-sharḳiyya*, Cairo ii, 98; Muḥammad al-Bashīr Ẓāfir al-Azhar *Yawāḳīt al-thamīna fī aʿyān madhhab ʿāli Madīna*, Cairo 1324-5/1906-7, i, 126 f.; al-Dīn al-Ziriklī, *al-Aʿlām*, ii, 214. For addi biographical data, see Ilyās al-ʿAyyūbī, *T Miṣr fi 'l-ʿahd al-Khidīw Ismāʿīl Bāshā min 1863 ilā sanat 1879*, Cairo 1923, i, 42 f.; and Broadley, *How we defended Arabi and his fr* London 1884, 365 ff., 369 f. On his *ṭarīḳa* alleg see Muḥammad Zakī Ibrāhīm, *Dalīl al-mu ilā al-ṭarīḳa al-Muḥammadiyya al-Shādhi* Cairo 1969, 49. For al-ʿIdwī's role in the e referred to in the article, see A. Schölch, *Äg den Ägyptern. Die politische und gesellscha Krise der Jahre 1879-1882 in Ägypten*. Z Freiburg i.Br., n.d. *passim*, where further refe may be found. (F. DE JO

ĪḲĀʿ (form IV from *w-ḳ-ʿ*), literally "to let the wand (*ḳaḍīb*) in order to mark the rhyt singing, a term denoting musical metri "rhythm" in the sense of measuring the qu of notes. The early Islamic *īḳāʿ* can be considere forerunner of mediaeval European mensura. on oriental practices inherited by the Ara shows elements of Greek rhythmos and simil to Indian *tāla*. According to Ṣafī al-Dīn al-Ur the roots of *īḳāʿ* go back to Sāsānid Iran, Indian musical presence is attested.

The internal structure of *īḳāʿ* is obvious Arab origin, being built up in analogy to the pr rules of Arab poetry. One *īḳāʿ* consists of two "c (*adwār*), each of them being composed of s "basic" notes (*uṣūl*) and a pause (*fāṣila*). In m ing the basic notes, the musician gets at the m patterns of the chosen "form" (*djins*) of *īḳāʿ* early music schools knew seven or eight namely *al-thaḳīl al-awwal*, *al-thaḳīl al-thānī*, *al-r al-hazadj* and their "quick" (*khafīf*) forms.

Al-Khalīl b. Aḥmad (d. 175/791), author of *Kitāb al-Īḳāʿ*, is regarded as the "inventor" c science. Citations in later sources or original give information about the *īḳāʿ*-theories of than ten authors up to the 5th/11th centur most important being al-Fārābī, who dedicate chapters of his *Kitāb al-Mūsīḳī al-kabīr* an remarkable monographs to this subject.

e īḳāʿ tradition of the Mawṣilī school, preserved e *Kitāb al-Aghānī* of Abu 'l-Faradj al-Iṣbahānī, sted for a long time in Spain, whilst the develop- in the Eastern caliphate had already given to more elaborate systems. The metres described afī al-Dīn al-Urmawī (d. 693/1294) led to the musical practice of the last "international" ol of ʿAbd al-Ḳādir al-Marāghī (d. 838/1435) ll as to the *uṣūl*, *awzān*, *ḍurūb* or *adwār* (*al-īḳāʿ*) e succeeding local traditions in Iran (disappear- there in the 12th/18th century), in Turkey re practice and theory continues up to our own and in the Arab countries (where the late and the early 20th centuries have brought ival of local metrical forms).

Bibliography: Almost all Arabic, Persian d Turkish musical treatises and most ency- paedias dealing with music contain a chapter on ʿ. For its early Arabian theory, see F. Dieterici, *e Propaedeutik der Araber im 10. Jahrhundert*, rlin 1865, 112-17; H. G. Farmer, *Saʿadyah on on the influence of music*, London 1943, -89; A. Shiloah, *L'épître sur la musique des hwān al-Ṣafāʾ*, in *REI*, xxxiv (1966), 176-8; Neubauer, *Die Theorie vom īqāʿ. I: Übersetzung Kitāb al-Īqāʿāt von Abū Naṣr al-Fārābī*, in *iens*, xxi-xxii (1968-9), 196-232; H. Avenary, *e Hebrew version of Abū l-Ṣalt's treatise on sic*, in *Yuval* (Jerusalem), iii (1974), 68-71. r later Arabian theories and modern practice, R. d'Erlanger, *La musique arabe*, Paris 1930-59. r Turkish forms, see Suphi (Ezği), *Nazarî amelî Türk musikisi*, Istanbul 1933-53; H.-P. del, *Studien zum usul "devri kebir" in den rev der Mevlevi*, in *Mitteilungen der Deutschen sellschaft für Musik des Orients*, xi (1972-3), 9; S. Heper, *Türk musikisinde usuller*, in *usiki mecmuası*, Istanbul, no. 344-7 (June-Sept. 78).

(E. Neubauer)

HTISĀN, Muḥammad Ṣadr ʿAlāʾ, secretary author under the Dihlī sultanate.

was the son of Aḥmad Ḥasan, a native of , and entered his ancestral profession of *dabīr* cretary in the *Dīwān al-Inshāʾ* or royal chancery time towards the close of the Khaldjī period. is accession to the throne in 720/1320, Sultan āth al-Dīn Tughluḳ Shāh raised him to the ion of *Dabīr-i khāṣṣ* in recognition of his learning t he was still in his early twenties, and in this city he accompanied the sultan on an expedi- to Bengal. After the conquest of Bengal, the n, on his way back to Dihlī, invaded the inde- ent territory of Tirhut, seized it and entrusted harge to Aḥmad Yalbugha. In Tirhut, Ikhtisān ll because of the overwhelming heat and was ned to bed for quite a long time; during this s he translated a Sanskrit romance into ornate an, completing it in 725/1325, and calling it the *īn al-uns*.

e *Basātīn al-uns* shows Ikhtisān's mastery e Persian language. It contains an introduction g us information about his own career and the leur of sultan Muḥammad b. Tughluḳ, so that introduction is a document of considerable rical significance, supplementing Baranī's *Ta- -i Fīrūz Shāhī* with regard to the radical views ultan Muḥammad b. Tughluḳ. Like Baranī, sān also belonged to the sultan's faction and ribed to his rationalist views about religion society. Being an intellectual, well-versed in ic sciences, the sultan emphasised the need for terpreting the Islamic *Sharīʿa* according to the requirement of the time. The orthodox *ʿulamāʾ* opposed the sultan, whilst liberal thinkers like Ikhtisān supported him in this respect; Ikhtisān calls Muḥammad b. Tughluḳ Nuʿmān-i Thānī, while the orthodox Ṣūfīs and *ʿulamāʾ* condemned him as a tyrant and oppressor (*djabbār* and *ḳahhār*).

On Muḥammad b. Tughluḳ's death, his confidants were either killed or thrown into jail. Fortunately, Ikhtisān happened to be in Iran at that time, having been sent there by the late sultan as an ambassador to the Ilkhānid Court. He may have got information of his patron's death and the acces- sion of Sultan Fīrūz Shāh III to the throne (752/1351) in Multān, then a border city. It was there that he fell ill and died after a short illness. Thus Ikhtisān escaped imprisonment, while Baranī, the author of the *Taʾrīkh-i Fīrūz Shāhī* underwent it as a result of the reaction against Muḥammad b. Tughluḳ's policies.

Bibliography: Rieu, *Catalogue of the Persian manuscripts in the British Museum*, ii; Ikhtisān, *Basātīn al-uns*, ms. British Museum Add. 7717; Sayyid Muḥammad Mubārak Kirmānī, known as Mīr Khurd, *Siyar al-awliyā*, Delhi 1302/1885; Muḥammad Bihāmad-Khānī, *Taʾrīkh-i Muḥam- madī*, ms. British Museum, Or. 137.

(I. H. Siddiqui)

IKHTIYĀRIYYA, the *élite* or veterans of an Ottoman guild or army unit (*odjaḳ*).

Ikhtiyār, "choice" in Arabic, had acquired the meaning of "old" both in Turkish and in modern Arabic, and thus came to designate the chosen and the elders of certain units, two attributes which in traditional society were virtually identical. The *odjaḳ ikhtiyārlarî* in Ottoman Egypt consisted of retired officers and veterans of the *odjaḳ*s, and their function was mainly ceremonial and advisory. They were headed by a *bāsh ikhtiyār*. In the guilds the informal group of *ikhtiyāriyya* was also designated by a large variety of other similar terms (cf. Baer, *Egyptian guilds*, 53, and *Structure of Turkish guilds*, 183). There were no rules to determine when and under what conditions an *usta* became a member of this group. Similarly, its members had no well- defined tasks. Originally, as long as *futuwwa* tradi- tions survived in the guilds, they played an important role in the ceremonies of initiation. Later, it was their principal function to support the head of the guild in his relations with the authorities and thus to demonstrate that he was acting in the guild's name. It was upon their recommendation that the head of the guild was appointed by the *ḳāḍī*, and the chief assistant of the *ketkhudā* [*q.v.*] of the Turkish guilds, the *yigit bashî*, was chosen from among them, and apparently by them, but their choice had to be confirmed by the authorities.

In 19th century Egypt, the traditional term for veteran masters in the guilds was replaced by the term *ʿumda* (pl. *ʿumad*), but the character and functions of this group remained the same. Docu- ments from that period show that they participated in the control of prices of comestibles and the distribu- tion of the tax burden among the members of the guilds.

Bibliography: H. Thorning, *Beiträge zur Kenntnis des islamischen Vereinswesens*, Berlin 1913, 113-14, 233-5; S. Shaw, *Ottoman Egypt in the 18th century*, Cambridge, Mass. 1962, 21, 30-5; idem, *Ottoman Egypt in the age of the French Revolution*, Cambridge, Mass. 1964, 38-40; G. Baer, *Egyptian guilds in modern times*, Jerusalem 1964, 53, 65-6; idem, *The structure of Turkish guilds and its significance for Ottoman social history*, in *Proceedings of the Israel Academy of Sciences and Humanities*, iv, 183-4, 186.

(G. Baer)

IKLĪL al-MALIK is the melilot, *Melilotus officinalis* (Leguminosae) (Greek μελίλωτος, French "mélilot", German "Honigklee"), a plant of the Papilionaceae family, of which about 16 kinds are or were used as medicine. The Arabic term ("royal crown") is a rendering of Syriac *k^e^līl malkā*; more infrequently-used synonyms are *nafal, ḥantam, shadjarat al-ḥubb* ("love-tree"), etc. In general, distinction is made between the yellow-blossomed plants, which grow one m. high, and the white-blossomed plants growing still higher. Both are slender biennial herbs which are indigenous to uncultivated lands in Europe and Asia, but not in the North. One of these kinds—or still another one?—is the *iklīl al-malik al-muʿaḳrab* "scorpion-like melilot", thus known because of the form of its blossom-pods which resemble the tail of a scorpion. Certain roots, introduced from Syria into the Arab West under the name *ʿirḳ al-ḥayya* ("serpent's root") and used there as antidote against poisonous snakebites, are said to be roots of the melilot. Finally, it may be remarked that the plant was known in Arabic Spain under the Romance name *ḳurunīlla* (= *coronilla*, cf. F. J. Simonet, *Glosario de voces ibéricas y latinas ...*, Madrid 1888, 135 f.). The Arab translators describe it, of course, under *mālīlūṭus*.

In conformity with its Greek name, it was already known in antiquity that the melilot is a honey-producing plant. The Arabs adopted its therapeutic use largely from the Greeks. The aromatic herb was—and still is—used in compresses to soften and ripen hot, hard boils and all kinds of calluses. In warm compresses it is also useful for articular pains, if before a successful "purification" of the body takes place (through purging, blood-letting and vomiting). Together with other ingredients, the melilot cures stomach, ear and head-aches. Taken internally, it procures the discharge of urine, menstruation and the foetus, and mitigates the irritation of itching with diseases of the testicles.

Bibliography: A full chapter on *iklīl al-malik* is given in A. Dietrich, *Zum Drogenhandel im islamischen Ägypten*, Heidelberg 1954, 49-51. See further Dioscurides, *De materia medica*, ed. M. Wellmann, ii, Berlin 1906, 52 f. (= lib. iii, 40); *La "Materia médica" de Dioscorides*, ii (Arab. tr. Iṣṭafan b. Basīl), ed. Dubler and Terés, Tetuán 1952, 258; Rāzī, *Ḥāwī*, xx, Ḥaydarābād 1387/1967, 125 f. (no. 140); *Die pharmakolog. Grundsätze des Abu Mansur ... Harawi*, tr. A. Ch. Achundow, Halle 1893, 150, 340; Ibn al-Djazzār, *Iʿtimād*, ms. Ayasofya 3564, fol. 12b; Ibn Sīnā, *Ḳānūn*, Būlāḳ, i, 243; Bīrūnī, *Ṣaydala*, ed. H. M. Saʿīd, Karachi 1973, Arab. 62 f., Engl. 41; Ibn Biklārish, *Mustaʿīnī*, ms. Naples, Bibl. Naz. iii, F. 65, fol. 12b; Ghāfiḳī, *al-Adwiya al-mufrada*, Ms. Rabat, Bibl. Gén. ḳ 155 i, fol. 21a-22a; Ibn Hubal, *Mukhtārāt*, Ḥaydarābād 1362, ii, 20; Anonymous [Abu 'l-ʿAbbās al-Nabātī Ibn al-Rūmiyya?] ms. Nuruosmaniye 3589, fols. 99b-100a (with precise description of the plant); Ibn al-Bayṭār, *Djāmiʿ*, Būlāḳ 1291, 50 f., tr. Leclerc, no. 128; Yūsuf b. ʿUmar, *Muʿtamad*, ed. M. al-Saḳḳā[3], Beirut 1395/1975, 6; Ibn al-Ḳuff, *ʿUmda*, Ḥaydarābād 1356, i, 211, cf. H. G. Kircher, *Die "einfachen Heilmittel" aus dem "Handbuch der Chirurgie" des Ibn al-Quff*, Bonn 1967, no. 3; Suwaydī, *Simāt*, ms. Paris ar. 3004, fols. 13-14; 164a, 3-8; Barhebraeus, *The abr version of "The Book of simple drugs" of .. Ghâfiqî*, ed. Meyerhof and Sobhy, Cairo no. 30; Dāwūd al-Anṭākī, *Tadhkira*, Cairo 1952, i, 55; I. Löw, *Die Flora der Juden*, ii, 465 f.; M. Asín Palacios, *Glosario de voces rom ...*, Madrid-Granada 1943, no. 168.

(A. Dietric

IKRĀH (a.), a legal term denoting "dure The jurists distinguish two kinds: unlawful (*ghayr mashrūʿ*), and lawful (*ikrāh bi-ḥaḳḳ*). the first of these is recognised by the Ḳurʾā *ikrāh fi 'l-dīn*, II, 256), and has legal effects.

Unlawful duress may be of two degrees, grave (*ikrāh tāmm* or *muladjdji*ʾ) if it involves s bodily harm, or slight (*ikrāh nāḳiṣ* or *muladjdji*ʾ) if it only involves verbal threats or n buffets. Lawful duress, which has no legal e may take the form, for example, of a judge exe duress on a debtor to discharge his debt by s property surplus to his personal needs.

The authorities differ regarding the degre validity in contracts agreed under duress, in general the effect of duress in civil law is to a declaration voidable by *khiyār*, i.e. the in party has the right unilaterally either to c or to ratify the contract. In criminal law, the of duress is to diminish responsibility to the of removing the penal sanction and making act itself allowable; thus drinking wine under t of death or mutilation is permissible.

Consequently, the attestation of absence of d is an important element in the drafting of dee sale and other legal documents involving contra obligations, and such absence of duress ma declared in phrases such as *bi-lā ikrāh wa-lā i*

Bibliography: Ṣubḥī Maḥmaṣānī, *al-Naẓa al-ʿāmma li'l-mūdjabāt wa'l-ʿuḳūd fi 'l-sh al-islāmiyya*, Beirut 1948; J. Schacht, *An intr tion to Islamic law*, Oxford 1964, 117-18; Mu Aḥmad al-Zarḳāʾ, *al-Fiḳh al-islāmī fī th al-djadīd*, Damascus 1968, and bibliography cited; R. Y. Ebied and M. J. L. Young, *Arabic legal documents of the Ottoman p* Leiden 1976 (see documents on pp. 15, 16, 24,

(R. Y. Ebied and M. J. L. You

ILĀHĪ ERA, also known as *Taʾrīkh-i* "Divine Era", was introduced by the M Emperor Akbar in 992/1584. The first year o era was the year of Akbar's accession, 963/15 and it was a solar year beginning with Na (the day of vernal equinox, about 20 March). names of the months were the same as those c ancient Persian calendar. The number of days month varied from 29 to 32. The calculations made, and rules for the era drawn up, by Allāh Shīrāzī. Abu 'l-Faḍl justified the introdu of Ilāhī era on the ground that the Islamic era, being ancient, should be replaced by some era commencing from a recent epoch-making e As the accession of Akbar was such an even the Ilāhī era was set to commence from that The Ilāhī era made it possible to keep a re account of the officers' allowances, of book-ke and of audit. In 1069/1658-9, Awrangzīb abolished the observation of the Nawrūz fes but did not prohibit the use of the Ilāhī m in the offical records. He ordered that the months and years should be written befor Ilāhī months. In 1079/1668-9 he prohibite publication of almanacs, but the officials pro vithout the use of almanacs it was not possible llow the Ilāhī calendar properly; and some pancy between the actual vernal equinox he initial day of the official solar year gradually red in course of time. Mīrzā Rādjā Djāʾī 's *zīdj-i Muḥammad Shāhī* in the next century n attempt to evolve a new solar calendar for l use, based largely on the same principles Ilāhī calendar.

ibliography: Abu 'l-Faḍl, *Akbar-nāma*, iii, l. Ind., Calcutta 1873-87; idem, *Āʾīn-i Akbarī*, Bibl. Ind., Calcutta 1867-77; Muḥammad shim Khwāfī Khān, *Muntakhab al-lubāb*, l. Ind., Calcutta 1860-74; S. H. Hodivala, *torical studies in Mughal numismatics*, The mismatic Society of India, Calcutta 1923; also TAʾRĪKH. (M. ATHAR ALI)

AḲ, the region of Transoxania lying within reat northwards bend of the middle reaches Jaxartes river and to the south of the right-affluent the Āhangarān (Russian form, Angren) It thus lay between the provinces of Shāsh TASHKENT] on the northwest and Farghāna on the east. The Arabic and Persian geographers 3rd-5th/9th-11th centuries describe it as a shing province, with its mountains producing and salt. They give the names of many towns the chief one being Tūnkath, whose ruins been identified by Soviet archaeologists 50 (90 km.) from modern Tashkent.

early Islamic times, Īlāḳ lay on the frontiers en the abode of Islam and the pagan Tur-steppes. During the Sāmānid period and just vards, its local princes (given the title of n) enjoyed considerable prestige, and minted own coins during the period of Sāmānid se, e.g. in 388/998 and 399/1008-9. The author *Ḥudūd al-ʿālam* describes the people of Īlāḳ herents of "those who wear white", pre-bly the supporters of the "veiled prophet" ḳannaʿ [*q.v.*], whose rising took place in the 2nd/8th century. This information may be ronistic for his own time, but we do read that period of the Sāmānid *amīr* Naṣr b. Aḥmad 1/914-43) the local *dihḳān* was sympathetic Ismāʿīlī propaganda current then.

ibliography: Le Strange, *The lands of the ern Caliphate*, 482-3; Barthold, *Turkestan n to the Mongol invasion*³, 162, 169-75, 233, 307; *Ḥudūd al-ʿālam*, tr. Minorsky, 117, -7. (C. E. BOSWORTH)

ČPUR [see ELIČPUR, above].

LAYSH, MUḤAMMAD B. AḤMAD B. MUḤAM-onetime Mālikī *muftī* of Egypt and one of rincipal protagonists in the events preceeding ritish occupation of Egypt in 1882. He was in Cairo in Radjab 1217/October-November into a family of Moroccan extraction. After a of study at al-Azhar [*q.v.*] from 1232/1816-7 1245/1829-30, he was engaged in teaching at nstitution, as well as at the Ḥusayn mosque. 70/1854 he was appointed to the office of *h al-sāda al-Mālikiyya* [*q.v.*] in succession to mmad Ḥubaysh, and remained in office until d of his life.

comitantly, he held supreme leadership of dhiliyya [*q.v.*] *ṭarīḳa*, that of al-ʿArabiyya, in position notable Azharī scholars such as Mu-ad al-Amīr al-Kabīr and Muḥammad al-Amīr hīr had been his predecessors.

wever, the mystical conception of Islam to he must have adhered is only incidentally manifest in his writings—the scope of which encompasses the majority of the fields of traditional Muslim learning—such as in his *Fatḥ al-ʿalī 'l-mālik fi 'l-fatwā ʿalā madhhab al-Imām Mālik*, Cairo 1319/1901-2, i, 5, where he supports the doctrine of *al-nūr al-muḥammadī* [*q.v.*]. He was opposed to the reforms introduced at al-Azhar by its *shaykh* Muḥammad al-Mahdī al-ʿAbbāsī. During the campaign for removal of the latter from office—which resulted in the appointment of Muḥammad al-Imbābī as *shaykh al-Azhar*—Muḥammad ʿIllaysh became the favourite candidate of the Azharī *ʿulamāʾ* and of the students for succession of al-ʿAbbāsī. His involvement with the ʿUrābiyyūn [see ʿURĀBĪ], his active support of their cause and his effort to mount resistance against the British invasion—he was among the first to call for the proclamation of *djihād*—resulted his arrest and detention following the British occupation of Cairo in September 1882. He died in prison on 9 Dhu 'l-Ḥidjdja 1299/22 October 1882.

Bibliography: Biographies may be found in ʿAlī Mubārak, *Khiṭaṭ*, iv, 41-44; Ilyās Zakhūrā, *Mirʾāt al-ʿaṣr fī taʾrīkh wa-rusūm akābir ridjāl Miṣr*, i, 196 f.; Khayr al-Dīn al-Ziriklī, *al-Aʿlām*, vi, 244; and prefaced to Muḥammad ʿIllaysh, *Fatḥ al-ʿalī 'l-mālik fi 'l-fatwā ʿalā madhhab al-Imām Mālik*, 2 vols., Cairo 1319-21/1901-4. See also Abu 'l-Wafā al-Marāghī, *Min aʿlām al-Mālikiyya al-Miṣriyya*, in *al-Hady al-Islāmī*, Bayḍāʾ, viii/1 (March 1969), 76-8. For a short discussion of the position of al-ʿArabiyya al-Shādhiliyya under the leadership of Muḥammad ʿIllaysh, see F. de Jong, *Ṭuruq and Ṭuruq-linked institutions in 19th century Egypt*, Leiden 1978, 113-14. For additional biographical data, see ʿAlī Mubārak, *Khiṭaṭ*, viii, 74; Amin Sāmī, *Taḳwīm al-Nīl*, iii, part 2, 519 f., 921 f.; Muḥammad Rashīd Riḍā, *Taʾrīkh al-Ustādh al-Imām*, i, 133 f.; Aḥmad Shafīḳ, *Mudhakkirātī fī niṣf ḳarn*, i, 152, 178; Muḥammad ʿAbd al-Djawād al-Ḳāyātī, *Nafḥat al-bishām fī riḥlat al-Shām*, Cairo 1319/1901-2, 6 f.; and Sulaymān al-Ḥanafī al-Zayyātī, *Kanz al-djawhar fī taʾrīkh al-Azhar*, Cairo n.d., 162 f. (F. DE JONG)

ʿILM AL-AKTĀF [see KATIF].

ʿILM AL-HANDASA (A.), geometry. From the 3rd/9th century onwards, the Arabs were introduced to geometry through the translation of Greek works, especially that of Euclid's *Elements*. They then adopted for this science the Greek name under the form *djūmaṭriya*. Subsequently, they came into contact with the applied geometry of Archimedes, of Hero of Alexandria, and with the Indian *Siddhantas* (in Arabic, *Sind Hind*), and definitively adopted the word *handasa* (borrowed, according to al-Khalīl, from the Persian *andāzah* = measure, size).

In the evolution of geometry among the Arabs, two important periods may be distinguished:

I. The period of translations and of initiation (3rd/9th century).

A. The first place belongs to the *Elements of Geometry* of Euclid (*Kitāb al-Uṣūl* or *K. al-Arkān*), one of the most translated and annotated books. (a) We may mention two translations owed to Ḥadjdjādj b. Yūsuf b. Maṭar, one entitled the *Hārūnī*, the other, more precise, known by the name of the *Maʾmūnī*. (b) A translation by Isḥāḳ b. Ḥunayn revised and corrected by Thābit b. Ḳurra of Ḥarrān (219-88/834-901). (c) al-ʿAbbās b. Saʿīd al-Djawharī (214/829) wrote a commentary on it, including, among other things, a number of figures and particular cases added to the first proposition of these *Elements*. (d) A commentary on the fifth proposition by Abū ᶜAlī Muḥammad b. ᶜĪsā al-Māhānī (between 239 and 270/853-84) comprises 26 figures and is concerned principally with proofs that do not make use of reasoning by absurdity. (e) A commentary by Abu 'l-ᶜAbbās al-Faḍl b. Ḥātim al-Nayrīzī (d. 310/922-3). (f) A commentary by Abū Djaᶜfar al-Khāzin of Khurāsān (d. 310/922-3). (g) Abu 'l-Wafāʾ al-Buzdjānī (323-88/934-98) has left an incomplete commentary on it. (h) al-Kindī (184-259/800-73) devotes a *risāla* to the "objectives of the work of Euclid" (*Aghrāḍ K. Uḳlīdis*); he comments here, in particular, that the work is, in reality, a compendium of ancient knowledge set in order and annotated by Euclid, and that one of his followers, Hypsicles, added on the fourteenth and fifteenth propositions.

B. The *Data* (*Muᶜṭayāt*) of Euclid, translated by Isḥāḳ and revised by Thābit.

We must mention at this point—and we shall have occasion to return to it—the criticisms made of Euclid's postulates by al-Nayrīzī in his *Risāla fi 'l-muṣādara al-mashhūra li-Uḳlīdis* "Letter relating to the famous postulate of Euclid"; by al-Hasan b. al-Haytham (354-430/965-1038); by ᶜUmar al-Khayyām (467-517/1074-1123) in his *Risāla fī sharḥ mā ashkala min muṣādarāt Uḳlīdis* "Letter explaining some difficulties raised by the postulates of Euclid"; and by Naṣīr al-Dīn al-Ṭūsī (597-672/1201-74) in his *Taḥrīr uṣūl Uḳlidīs* "Restatement of the Elements of Euclid", and his *Taḥrīr muṣādarāt Uḳlīdis* "Observations on the postulates of Euclid".

C. The *Conic sections* (*al-Ḳuṭūᶜ al-makhrūṭiyya*) of Apollonius, a work which apparently comprised 8 propositions; the first four were translated, under the supervision of Aḥmad b. Mūsa b. Shākir, by Hilāl b. Abī Hilāl al-Ḥimṣī (d. 218/833), and the last three by Thābit b. Ḳurra.

D. The *Elements of geometry* of Menelaus. Thābit translated three of its propositions. An unknown translator revised the chapters relating to triangles. The problem of transversals and their applications in the study of conic forms inspired Thābit to compose his work *al-Ḳawl fi 'l-shakl al-kaṭṭāᶜ wa 'l-nisba al-muʾallafa* ("Survey of the transversal and harmonic division"), a work translated into Latin by Gerard of Cremona (*Liber Thabit de figura alchata*). Naṣīr al-Dīn al-Ṭūsī also made this work the basis of his treatise *Kitāb al-Shakl al-ḳaṭṭāᶜ*, in which he set out to establish the fundamental principles of spherical trigonometry.

E. The work of Pappus (the *Collection of mathematics*), notably a translation by Thābit of his commentary on the Book of Ptolemy relating to the area of the sphere; and his commentary on the tenth proposition of Euclid.

F. The geometrical work of Archimedes: (a) His work *On the sphere and the cylinder*, translated by the Banū Mūsā, later by Thābit and by Isḥāḳ b. Ḥunayn. A translation by Kusṭā b. Lūḳā (299/912) served as the basis for the Hebrew translation of Ḳalonimos b. Ḳalonimos (728/1328). (b) *On the squaring of the circle* (*Fī taksīr al-dāʾira*; *Tarbīᶜ al-dāʾira*; *Misāḥat al-dāʾira*), translated by Thābit and by Ḥunayn b. Isḥāḳ, a translation revised by Naṣīr al-Dīn al-Ṭūsī (ed. Hyderabad 1359/1940). (c) The *Lemmata* (*al-maʾkhūdhāt*), translated by Thābit and annotated by Abu 'l-Ḥasan ᶜAlī b. Aḥmad al-Nasawī (370-431/980-1040); Ṭūsī makes use of it in his study published in 1940 at Hyderabad. (d) *Measuring the side of a regular heptagon inscribed in a circle* (*tasbīᶜ al-dāʾira*), a work which ins in particular, Abū Sahl al-Kūhī.

G. The work of Hero of Alexandria, notabl *K. Ḥall shukūk Uḳlīdis* ("Resolution of d concerning Euclid"); and the *K. al-Ḥiyal al-rūḥā* ("Pneumatics").

We may note, finally, the translation o *Sindhantas* which familiarised the Arabs with lems of surveying and of the measuring of su and volumes, and in a general manner, wit various applications of geometry.

II. The period of creativity (4th-9th/ 15th centuries).

The translated material was, as we have n progressively annotated, discussed and correct

From the 3rd/9th century, but especially the 4th/10th one, the specific contribution o Arabs became more important. The latter su mented the ancient works in a number of disci (astronomy, optics, algebra), with new proofs with the resolution of geometrical problems; applications came into being, especially in scul and in architecture; trigonometry was disco and codified; important theoretical questions raised; the authority of ancient masters was tested, and the way was open for the progre geometry in hitherto unknown directions.

But before reviewing certain of the most brated Arab contributions to geometry, here f century by century, the authors and the works may be mentioned:

3rd/9th century: al-Khʷarazmī (d. *ca.* 232/ *Bāb al-misāḥā* — al-Djawhari (214-15/839-30); *tafsīr K. Uḳlīdis* "Commentary on the Boo Euclid"; *K. al-Ashkāl allati zādaha fi 'l-m al-ūlā min Uḳlīdis* "On the figures that he added to the first proposition of Euclid"; *Zi fi 'l-maḳāla al-khāmisa min K. Uḳlīdis* "Supple to the fifth proposition of Euclid", cf. *Fihrist*, 1348/1930, 379; and Suter, 21. — the Banū b. Shākir (Muḥammad, d. 259/873), *Maᶜrifat mi al-ashkāl al-basīṭa wa 'l-kuriyya* "Informatio the surfaces of plane and spherical figures" Carullah 1475, 3; 1502, 9; Köprülü, 930, 14; 931 Rampūr 311; Bodl. i, 960); *Muḳaddimat a -makh* "Introduction to the conical forms" (mss. Bo 943, 5; Leiden 979; Sarton 193); *Ḳismat al-za bi-thalātha aḳsām mutasāwiya* "Trisection of an (cf. *Fihrist*, 379. — al-Māhānī, *Risālā fi 'l-* "Treatise on proportions" (*Fihrist* 379; mss. 6009; Paris 3467, 1°); *R. fi 'l-mushkil min al-* "Epistle on complex proportions" (ms. Paris 39); *R. fī 26 shaklan min al-maḳāla al-ūlā min U* (*Fihrist*, 379, Thābit b. Kurra; see D. above); *Shakl al-ḳaṭṭāʾ* (*Fihrist*, 380; mss. Paris 2457, 2467, 13; Esc. 971, 2; Algiers 1446, 5); *K. fi mi ḳaṭᶜ al-makhrūṭ alladhi yusammā 'l-mukāfiʾ* "Su of the conical form known as the parabola" Paris 2437, 25; Cairo vi, 197). — al-Battānī (244 858-929): we note in particular his contributic trigonometry and his elegant solutions to prob of spherical trigonometry by means of orthograp projection, solutions known and partially imi by Regiomontanus (1436-76).

4th/10th century: al-Nayrīzī, Sharḥ Uḳlīdis (*F* 389; S. 363); *R. fi 'l-muṣādara al-mashhūra li-Uḳ* — al-Buzdjānī, *K. fīmā yaḥtādj ilayhi al-ᶜu wa 'l-kuttāb min ṣināᶜat al-ḥisāb* "Elements of culus essential for the accountant and the secret 3rd part, *fī aᶜmāl al-misāḥa* "Methods relati surfaces". — al-Sidjzi (358-89/969-99) one of greatest Muslim geometrists, *R. fī ikhrādj al-ḳ awāʾir al-mawḍūʿa min al-nuḳaṭ al-muʿṭāt* "In en circle, to draw certain straight lines through points" (ms. Paris 2458, 1; Sédillot, *Notices traits*, xiii, 143); *R. fi 'l-djawāb ʿan al-masāʾil suʾila ʿanhā fī baʿḍ al-ashkāl al-maʾkhūdha min -maʾkhūdhāt li-Arshamidis* (ms. Paris 2458, 8; ot 116); *Taḥṣīl al-ḳawānīn al-handasiyya al-ūda* (ms. Paris 2458, 2; Sédillot, 139); al-Sidjzi particularly interested in circles and in conical ns.

11th century: Ibn al-Haytham is well-known s studies in optics (Problem of Alhazen). Among eometrical works we note the following (cf. *n al-anbāʾ*, ed. Beirut 1377/1957, iii, 154 ff.): *Uṣūl Uḳlīdis fi 'l-handasa wa 'l-ʿadad wa-ṣuhu* ("Commentary and summary of the nts of Euclid"; *K. al-Taḥlīl wa 'l-tarkīb al-siyyayni* ("Analysis and synthesis in geom-; *Maḳāla fī ḥall shakk, raddan alā Uḳlīdis fi ḳāla al-khāmisa kitābih fi 'l-Uṣūl al-riyāḍiyya* lysis of a doubt, in response to Euclid in the roposition of his work 'Elements of mathemat-; *Maḳāla fī misāḥat al-mudjassam al-mukāfiʾ* the surface of the paraboloid"; *Maḳāla fī īṣṣ al-ḳaṭʿ al-mukāfiʾ* "On the properties of the ola"; *Maḳāla fī khawāṣṣ al-ḳaṭʿ al-zāʾid* "On the rties of the hyperbola"; *Maḳāla fī ḥall shukūk ḳāla al-ūlā min K. Uḳlīdis* "Analysis of doubts rning the 1st proposition of the Book of Euclid". t be added that Ibn al-Haytham, besides his etical work, tried to find practical applications s results. It is sufficient to recall, in this context, necdote related by al-Ḳifṭī (iii, 149, 150) con-ng his attempt to construct a barrage on the acts of the Nile, near Aswān, with the object ulating the course of the river.

12th century: ʿUmar al-Khayyām, *R. fī sharḥ shkala min muṣādarāt K. Uḳlīdis* "Explanation ficulties raised by the postulates of the Book of d" (mss. Leiden 967; Paris 4946); *Maḳālā fi br wa 'l-muḳābala* (mss. Leiden 1020; Paris 7, 2461): in particular, geometrical solutions cond-degree equations.

13th century: Naṣīr al-Dīn al-Ṭūsī, *R. al-shakl ṭāʿ*; here he expounds the theory of transversals which he deduces original connections enabling to lay the foundations of spherical trigonom- *Taḥrīr ʿUṣūl Uḳlīdis* "Examination of the ents of Euclid" (mss. Tunis 56R, 58R, Latin tr., e 1594); *Taḥrīr muṣādarāt Uḳlīdis* (ms. Tunis ; the method employed in these studies is ted by a number of commentators on Euclid, ding, especially, Shams al-Dīn al-Samarḳandī, *īl al-taʾsīs*, and the commentary by Mūsā b. ammad Ḳāḍī-zāda al-Rūmī (815/1412) (mss. 2705, 223R, 2746; Esc. 952, Paris 6853); nentary by Ḥasan b. Muḥammad Naẓẓām sābūrī (811/1408) in his *Tawḍīḥ* of the *Tadhkira* ṣī (ms. Tunis 236, copy dating from 860/1398).

15th century: Al-Kāshī (d. 832/1429): *al-Risāla ḥīṭiyya fi 'stikhrādj muḥīṭ al-dāʾira* "Determina-f the perimeter of the circle".

brief analysis of the contribution of the lims towards the progress of geometry: *Analysis*.—1. First one may note, in the guise troduction to books on various disciplines, a ber of geometrical questions, the solution of n is necessary for the explanation of the ideas ed subsequently in these works; this is the case the opening chapters of treatises on astronomy e the properties of circles drawn on spheres are ibed in detail and where there are solutions to problems of distances, volumes of solids, plane or spherical trigonometry.

On the other hand, in spite of the duality of origin of geometry and of arithmetic or of algebra, the two latter being initially discrete sciences, the former of continuous scope, the Muslims, since al-Khwarazmī, have used algebra for the solving of geometric problems; they have also made use of geometry for the solving of new algebraic problems. It is sufficient, in this context, to recall the solution by al-Khayyām of cubic equations by means of intersection of circles, parabolas or hyperbolas; we may also cite al-Māhānī's problem concerning the plane sections of the sphere, which led him to the third-degree equation $x^3 + b^2 = bx^2$.

2. It is impossible to overestimate the importance of the revolution brought about in astronomical calculations, in particular, or in physics, by a sister science of geometry, developed and codified by the Muslims who made of it an independent discipline, sc. trigonometry. Thanks to this new science, a whole range of problems was completely solved, and with a precision depending uniquely on tables (*zīdj*) established at an early stage.

In the 3rd/9th century, al-Battānī solved the equation sin x = a cos. x discovering the formula

$$\sin x = \frac{a}{\sqrt{1 + a^2}} \text{ (for the arcs of the 1st quadrant).}$$

Ḥabash compiled the table of tangents. In the 4th/10th century, Abu 'l-Wafāʾ brought real progress to trigonometry. He established the relations:

$$\sin (a + b) = \sin a \cos b + \sin b \cos a$$

$$2 \sin a = 1 - \cos 2a$$

$$\sin 2a = 2 \sin a \cos a$$

$$\sec a = \frac{1}{\cos a} = \sqrt{1 - tg^2 a}$$

He set out the formula of sines in a spherical triangle:

$$\frac{\sin a}{\sin A} = \frac{\sin b}{\sin B} = \frac{\sin c}{\sin C}$$

Ibn Yūnus (958/1009) author of the Ḥākimī table, demonstrated the formula:

$$\cos a \cos b = 1/2 [\cos (a + b) + \cos (a - b)],$$

permitting the passage from a sum to a product, an operation which was to be of importance in the logarithmic system of calculation invented later.

In the 6th/12th century, Djābir b. Aflaḥ knew the equation cos b = cos B sin c. In short, Arabic trigonometry was already a long-established science when Fibonacci used it, *ca.* 1220, for the measuring of surfaces and when, *ca.* 1464, Regiomontanus, putting al-Ṭūsī's work to good use, composed the first treatise on trigonometry published in Europe in 1485.

3. Geometry was further applied by the Arabs in geodesic measurements, executed to check the ancient proportions and to verify the conclusions of the *Almagest* of Ptolemy (scientific expeditions by the Banū Shakir, *ca.* 212/827, in the region of Palmyra and Raḳḳa, then in the neighbourhood of Sindjār, the Latin *Singara*, with the object of measuring the earth's inclination). Al-Battānī fixed the geographical coordinates of 310 locations, including 30 in the West; al-Ḥasan al-Marrākushī gave the co-ordinates of 135 locations, of which 71 belong to the western Mediterranean. Al-Bīrūnī dealt with the problem of cartography and of the representation, on a plane surface, of the celestial or terrestial sphere. He reviewed various methods of projection, conical, cylindrical, orthographical or

stereographical, the lines of the sphere being represented by ellipses, parabolas or hyperbolas.

4. "Geometry", wrote the Ikhwān al-Ṣafā', "has as its principal field of application the measurement of surfaces, measurement which is essential for surveyors, accountants, tax agents, landowners, in their various operations or transactions, such as the collection of property tax, the drainage of water-courses, the postal service, etc."

5. An important area in the application of geometry is that of architecture and sculpture; Muslim art, inspired by geometry, invented the extended arch, cupolas resting on regular polygons, corbellings, stalactites, groups of polyhedrons of stucco and light. The work of the sculptor in stone or in stucco was designed by the mathematician.

B. *Works.*—Among the works of pure geometry written by the Muslims, Suter mentions only two treatises, in the 3rd/9th century the book by the Banū Shākir (*Maᶜrifat al-ashkāl al-basīṭa wa 'l-kuriyya*), and in the 4th/10th century, the *Geometry* of Abu 'l-Wafā which has come down to us in a Persian edition owed to one of his pupils (cf. F. Woepcke, in *JA* [1855], 218-56 and 309-59).

However, it is possible to take account of other writings which in our view are of great importance: The ms. of Thābit b. Ḳurra mentioned above *Fī misāḥat ḳaṭᶜ al-makhrūṭ alladhī yusammā 'l-mukāfiᶜ*, where, following the example of Archimedes, the former uses a method of integral calculus in the quest for the limit of the equivalent on "integral sums" for the determination of the surface of a segment of a parabola, or the volume of a paraboloid revolving around its axis or around any other straight line passing through the focus.

An important fact deserves to be remembered; this is the attitude of a group of Muslim scholars towards the principle of authority and the enormous prestige enjoyed by the name of Euclid since ancient times, a prestige which has not ceased to be immense up to a period close to the present day. In the list which we have presented, it is notable that, since the 3rd/9th century, scholars have not refrained from expressing serious reservations in regard to certain of Euclid's postulates, and in particular the famous 5th postulate concerning parallel lines.

In a closely-argued discussion, they first insist on the fact that Euclid himself, not entirely convinced by his proposition, does not see it as a "first truth" or an axiom, but a postulate which he simply invites the reader to adopt. Thus they attempt to go further and construct the theory of parallels by using other axioms and postulates, and employing the methods of Eudox and Archimedes.

The most remarkable works are those of Djawharī (3rd/9th century), of Abharī, of Nayrīzī (4th/10th century), of Ibn al-Haytham and Khayyām (5th/11th century) and of Ṭūsī (7th/13th century). These works were translated into Latin and Hebrew; their influence is evident in the work *Commentaries to the introduction of Euclid's elements* by Levi ben Gerson (14th century), in *Rectifier of wrong* by Alfonso (14th-15th century) and in the commentaries on the Elements of Euclid by Clavius (16th century).

The demonstration of the 5th postulate by Ṭūsī (published in Rome in 1594 and in London in 1657) was known to John Wallis (1616-1703) and to Saccheri (1667-1733). The essential point of the demonstration of Khayyām and of Ṭūsī rests on the possibility of constructing a quadrilateral ABCD (made famous later through the work of Saccheri) such that $AB = CD$, $A\hat{B}C = 1D$, $B\hat{C}D = 1D$, thus entailing that $B\hat{A}D = A\hat{D}C$. Three cases are th cally possible for these angles: they can be angles, acute or obtuse. Khayyām and Ṭūsī con that only the first case is really practicable known that subsequently, the basic theore non-Euclidian geometry of Lobachevski a Bolyai rest essentially on the hypothesis acute angle; the obtuse-angle hypothesis corres to the geometry of Riemann.

In conclusion, it may be said that the s of the Muslims constituted an important mi in the sequence of progress of geometry; they some essential questions, from a scientific a as from a philosophical point of view. They h excellent idea of not limiting geometry to cont scales. They were remarkably adept at holdi balance between theoretical abstract though practical art, i.e. concrete application. If they to a great extent the disciples of Euclid a other masters of Greek geometry, they ha courage to criticise the works that they h herited and to express serious doubts on their su and their theoretical scruples were great. They prepared the way for the subsequent develo of geometry.

Bibliography: Alfonso, *Meyasheriqub*, ms. Add 26894, Russian tr. in preparati G. M. Gluskina; Chr. Clavius, *Euclidis El torum libri XV*, Cologne 1596; *Euclidis E torum geometricorum libri tredecim ex trac doctissimi Nassiriddini Tusini nunc primum a impressi*, Rome 1594; J. Wallis, *De postulato et definitione quinta lib. 6 Euclidis*, in *Opera matica*, ii, Oxford 1693, 669-73; G. Sac *Euclides ab omne naevo vindicatus*, Milan F. Woepcke, *L'Algèbre d'Omar Alkhay* Paris 1851; Sarton, *Introduction*; D. E. S *Euclid, Khayyam and Saccheri*, in *Scripta matica*, ii/1 (Jan. 1935), 5-10; A. Mieli, *La s arabe*, Leiden 1938; E. B. Plooij, *Euclid's ception of ratio and his definition of propor magnitudes as criticized by Arabian comment* Rotterdam 1950; B. A. Rosenfeld and Yushčkevič, *Omar al-Khayyam*, Moscow Rosenfeld, *The theory of parallel lines i Medieval East*, in *Actes du XIe congrès interna d'histoire des sciences*; Yushčkevič, *Gesc der Mathematik im Mittelalter*, Basle 1964, 28 idem, *Les mathématiques arabes*, tr. M. Caz and K. Jaouiche, Paris 1976; R. Taton, *H générale des sciences*, i, Paris 1966, 440-525 Jaouiche, *De la fécondité mathématique: d' Khayyam à G. Saccheri*, in *Diogène*, lvii (97-113; S. H. Nasr, *Islamic science, an illus survey*, London 1976. (M. Souis

ᶜIMĀD AL-DĪN ᶜALĪ, FAḲĪH-I KIRM Persian mystical poet of the 8th/14th cen was born at Kirmān about 690/1291-2.

In the *Ṣafā'-nāma* he relates that when his f died in 705/1305, he and a brother took ove direction of a *khānaḳāh* which had been found Kirmān by his father's *shaykh*, Niẓām a Maḥmūd, for the benefit of the followers o *ḳuṭb al-aḳṭāb* Zayn al-Dīn ᶜAbd al-Salām Ka Through this line of mystical tradition, ᶜ al-Dīn was connected with the teaching of Ḥafṣ ᶜUmar al-Suhrawardī [*q.v.*]. Besides his pation as the *shaykh* of a convent, he was a doctor of Islamic law, as his *laḳab* suggests. reliable information concerning his life can be d from the traditional biographies. According frequently retold anecdote appearing for the

in the *Ḥabīb al-siyar*, the cat of ʿImād al-Dīn
ḍ imitate his master in the performance of his
ers. The origin of the story can be traced to a
in one of the poems of Ḥāfiẓ, which has been
preted as a reference to a rivalry between the
poets for the favours of the Muẓaffarid ruler
Shudjāʿ (cf. Humāyūn-Farrukh, Introduc-
81 ff.). Many panegyrical references in the
ıs of ʿImād al-Dīn indicate that he was on good
ıs with the rulers of his age and several of their
sters. His most important patrons were the
affarids. Though Shāh Shudjāʿ favoured him in
icular, ʿImād al-Dīn already wrote poems dedi-
ḍ to Mubāriz al-Dīn Muḥammad. Occasionally,
praised their opponent, Abū Isḥāḳ Indjū of
āz, as well and it is possible that he stayed some
at Shīrāz himself. His poetry was also appre-
ḍ at the court of the Īl-Khān Abū Saʿīd.
ost of ʿImād al-Dīn's life was apparently spent
Kirmān where, according to Dawlat-Shāh, he
in 773/1371-2. The alternative, but less probable,
of 793/1391 is mentioned by Taḳī Kāshī (cf.
nger, *Oudh catalogue*, Calcutta 1854, 436-8).
convent and the tomb of ʿImād al-Dīn were
visited in the late 9th/15th century.
ıe known works of ʿImād al-Dīn consist ex-
vely of poetry. As a pen-name he used the form
ıd, or more rarely, ʿImād-i Faḳīh. The *Dīwān*
ains predominantly *ghazals*. His place in the
lopment of the Persian *ghazal* is an interesting
as he was among the most prominent writers
cultivated the genre during the interval between
ives of Saʿdī and Ḥāfiẓ. The former is named by
ıd as an admired predecessor. The latter was a
ıger contemporary who must have been ac-
nted with ʿImād's work. Not only did ʿImād
Ḥāfiẓ share a number of patrons; their poetry
vs that they made use of many similar motives.
ings of these common elements have been made
ome modern researchers (e.g. Ibn Yūsuf Shīrāzī,
ammad Muʿīn and Humāyūn-farrukh). On
other hand, the style of ʿImād is clearly dis-
uishable from that of Ḥāfiẓ on account of the
ıer's greater simplicity of language and the more
rent structure of his *ghazals*. The central theme
ıe longing of the lover for the transcendental
ved. Anacreontic and *ḳalandarī* elements, though
lacking, are only subordinate motives. The
tical intention of ʿImād's *ghazals* cannot be
aken, even in those cases where the poem serves
the prologue to a short panegyrical address.
poet used to recite and discuss poems of his
in his *khānaḳāh*, as Djāmī tells us in the *Bahā-
ın*. From this notice, the conclusion may be
vn that he used them as a tool for this mystical
hing. The *ghazals* of ʿImād have been analysed
K. Stolz, *Der Dīwān des ʿImāduddīn Faqīh*, in
KM, xlix (1942), 31-70.
he second part of ʿImādī's literary output con-
of a series of *mathnawiyyāt*. Apart from a few
short pieces, there are five poems of an inter-
iate size:
The *Ṣafāʾ-nāma*, or *Muʾnis al-abrār*, is a
ıctic poem written in imitation of Niẓāmī's
khzan al-asrār, with which it has the metre *sarīʿ*
common. It was completed in 766/1364-5 and
icated to Shāh Shudjāʿ. One of its original
ures is a description of Shīrāz. The text has been
ed by Muḥammad Iḳbāl in *Oriental College
gazine*, v-viii (1929-32), *passim*.
. The *Ṣuḥbat-nāma*, or *Ṭarīḳat-i ṣuḥbat-nāma*,
he same metre as the *Būstān* of Saʿdī, was completed in 731/1330-1. It was dedicated to the *wazīr* of the Īl-Khān, Ghiyāth al-Dīn Muḥammad b. Rashīd al-Dīn Faḍl Allāh. In ten discourses, the manners are described of the rulers, the saints, the students, the scholars, the anchorites, the travellers, the *ahl-i futuwwat*, the beautiful ones, the lovers and the singers and musicians. To each discourse, one or more illustrative stories are added. The seventh chapter has been edited and translated by H. W. Duda, *ʿImāduddīn Faqīh und die Futuwwa*, in *ArO*, vi (1934), 112-24.

3. The *Maḥabbat-nāma-i ṣāḥibdilān*, a short *mathnawī* preceded by a prose introduction containing the dedication to the Īl-Khānid *wazīr* Khwādja Taḳī al-Dīn ʿIrāḳī. The metre used in the second part is *hazadj-i musaddas-i maḥdhūf*. The theme of love, studied here in all the realms of nature, is treated in the form of a series of ten disputations, between the soul and the body as well as between a number of entities which belong to the mineral, the vegetable and the animal kingdom. The illustrative stories, added in each case, deal with famous pairs of lovers (cf. H. W. Duda, *Ferhād und Schīrīn*, Prague 1933, 98-100, where the story of the fifth disputation is discussed). The title of the poem is a chronogram indicating that it was completed in 732/1331-2.

4. The *Ṭarīḳat-nāma*, composed in the same metre as the preceding poem, was completed in 750/1349-50 according a chronogram hidden in one of the lines, but Humāyūn-Farrukh regards the line as corrupt and dates the work between 754-9, i.e. during one of the last years of the reign of Mubāriz al-Dīn Muḥammad, to whom it is dedicated. The subject of the poem is an adaptation of the *Miṣbāḥ al-hidāya*, the Persian translation by ʿIzz al-Dīn Maḥmūd Kāshānī (died 735/1334-5) of the *ʿAwārif al-maʿārif* of Abū Ḥafs ʿUmar al-Suhrawardī (for a list of the ten chapter headings, see Munzawī, iv, 2994-5).

5. The *Dah-nāma* (in the ms. Aya Sofya no. 4131, dated 841 A.H., the work is called *Naṣīḥat-nāma*) belongs superficially to a genre of *mathnawīs* in the metre of the preceding poems which consists of collections of ten letters exchanged between an imaginary pair of lovers. ʿImād has introduced several changes into the conventional pattern: he uses other metres as well, alternates between the forms of the *mathnawī* and the *ḳaṣīda*, and even deviates from the basic theme by inserting letters to some of his patrons instead of love-letters. See further T. Ganjeï, *The genesis and definition of a literary composition, the Dahnāma* ("*Ten love-letters*"), in *Isl.*, xlvii (1971), 59-66.

Contrary to the relative oblivion that has become the fate of the works of ʿImād in later centuries, they seem to have been held in high esteem during his own lifetime and the immediately-following century. Several early manuscripts have been preserved, one of which (Madjlis no. 1030) may be an autograph. Among the writers of the beginning of the 9th/15th century, Bushāḳ and Ādharī highly praised the poetical talents of ʿImād.

Bibliography: the *Dīwān-i ʿImād-i Faḳīh-i Kirmānī* has been edited by Rukn al-Dīn Humāyūn-Farrukh, Tehran 1348/1969, with an extensive introduction; the aforementioned *mathnawiyyāt*, together with a short poem entitled *Humāyūn-nāma*, have been edited by the same in *Pandj gandj*, Tehran 2537/1978. For descriptions of the most important manuscripts, see further Sir G. Ouseley, *Biographical notices of Persian poets*, London 1846, 195-200; Sachau-Ethé,

Catalogue of the Persian manuscripts in the Bodleian Library, Part i, Oxford 1889, cols. 572-3; Maulavi Abdul Muqtadir, *Catalogue.... Bankipore, Persian poets: Firdausî to Hâfiz*, Patna 1908, 217-9; Blochet, *Catalogue des manuscrits persans de la Bibliothèque Nationale*, iii, Paris 1928, 217-8; H. W. Duda, *Ferhād und Schīrīn*, Prague 1933, 191-2; idem, in *ArO*, vi (1934), 113-4; Ibn Yūsuf Shīrāzī, *Fihrist-yi kitābkhāna-yi madrasa-yi ʿAlī Sipahsālār*, ii, Tehran 1318/1939, 643-4; idem, *Fihrist-i kitābkhāna-i Madjlis-i Shurā-yi millī*, iii, Tehran 1321/1942, 359-63; Ahmed Ateş, *Istanbul kütüphanelerinde farsça manzum eserler*, i, Istanbul 1968, 273-8; *Nuskhahā-yi khaṭṭī*, vi, Tehran 1348/1969, 683; A. Munzawī, *Fihrist-i nuskhahā-yi khaṭṭī-yi fārsī*, iii, Tehran 1350/1971, 1886, 2450 f.; iv, Tehran 1351/1972, 2819, 2985 f., 2990, 2994 f., 3174, 3327. The main biographical sources are Dawlat-Shāh, 254-6; Djāmī, *Bahāristān*, Vienna 1846, 101; Khwāndamīr, *Ḥabīb al-siyar*, Bombay 1857, iii/2, 37 (see also ʿAbd al-Ḥusayn Nawāʾī, *Ridjāl-i Kitāb Ḥabīb al-siyar*, Tehran 1324/1945, 83); Amīn Aḥmad Rāzī, *Haft iḳlīm*, Tehran 1340/1961, i, 275-7; Luṭf-ʿAlī Beg Ādhar, *Ātashkada*, Tehran 1337/1958, 124; Riḍā-Ḳulī Khān Hidāyat, *Riyāḍ al-ʿārifīn*, Tehran 1305/1887-8, 109-10. See also Browne, *LHP*, iii, 258-9 and *passim*; Īradj Afshār, *Fihrist-i maḳālāt-i fārsī*, i, Tehran 1339/1960, 460, 5916.

(J. T. P. de Bruijn)

ʿIMĀDĪ is the pen name of a Persian poet of the 6th/12th century whose personal name has not been transmitted. Sometimes the title Amīr is added to it, presumably referring to his prominence as a poet of the court in his own days. Another *nisba* often attached to the name ʿImādī is Shahriyārī. The biographical sources interpret the latter differently. According to some, it is derived from the name of a district of Rayy, implying that ʿImādī originated from that area, which is not unlikely. Others, however, have connected it with the founder of the Islamic branch of the Bāwandid dynasty [*q.v.*] of Māzandarān. It is certain, anyhow, that the former *nisba* refers to the poet's allegiance to a member of that family, Sayf al-Dīn ʿImād al-Dīn Farāmurz, designated as *shāh-i Māzandarān* (*Rāḥat al-ṣudūr*, 210), although he cannot be identified definitely with any ruler known from other historical sources (cf. M. Ḳazwīnī, *Mamdūḥ-i ʿImādī*, in *Bīst maḳāla*[2], Tehran 1332/1953, ii, 343-51). ʿImādī apparently started his literary career under the protection of this ruler, on whose death he wrote an elegy (*Rāḥat al-ṣudūr*, 371-2, cf. especially the note by the editor). Afterwards, ʿImādī went over to the service of the Saldjūḳ court and composed several panegyrics for Sulṭān Rukn al-Dīn Ṭoghrïl II (526-9/1132-4). Many other patrons are mentioned in the poems of ʿImādī, one of the latest may have been the Eldigüzid *atābak* Djihān-Pahlawān Muḥammad (570-81/1175-86) (cf. the different opinion of Ḳazwīnī, *op. cit.*, 348). It is less certain that he also praised Sulṭān Ṭoghrïl III (571-90/1176-94), as is sometimes asserted (for the full list of the patrons of ʿImādī, see S. Nafīsī, *Taʿlīḳat-i Lubāb al-albāb*, 724 f.). Of the two dates mentioned for his death, 573/1177-8 (Taḳī Kāshī) and 582/1186-7 (*Ātashkada*), the former seems to be the most probable.

ʿAwfī has entered a few of ʿImādī's poems under the name of ʿImād al-Dīn Ghaznawī. This has led to speculations about an eastern origin of ʿImādī. Later biographers mention the Ghaznawid poet Mukhtārī as his father. According to a notice given by Taḳī Kāshī, ʿImādī studied treatises on *taṣa*[...] with Sanāʾī at Balkh. The same writer propose[...] possibility that there might have been two diffe[...] but contemporaneous, poets by this name. [...] assumption was rejected already in the *Haft i*[...] There is no evidence known from his own works [...] could corroborate the theory of his connection [...] Ghazna.

Although ʿImādī was first of all renowned [...] poet of the court, he also wrote religious po[...] He recites poems of this nature during the ses[...] held by the famous preacher Ibn ʿAbbādī (*R*[...] *al-ṣudūr*, 209). In one of his *ghazals*, ʿImādī cl[...] refers to the transcendental meaning that shoul[...] read into the conventional imagery (cf. e.g. D[...] armī, *Muʾnis al-aḥrār*, ii, Tehran 1350/1971, 110[...]

There are some indications that point to a f[...] high esteem for ʿImādī's poetry in his own t[...] Ḥasan Ghaznawī Ashraf even recommended [...] work as good material for the study of tyro [...] (*Rāḥat al-ṣudūr*, 57). ʿImādī exchanged poems [...] of mutual praise with another poet of Rayy, Ḳiw[...] Both poets were in many respects imitators of [...] style of Sanāʾī. ʿImādī even went so far tha[...] adapted one of Sanāʾī's poems for his own [...] (Shams-i Ḳays, 464 ff.). A modern critic (Furū[...] farr) has praised ʿImādī's ability to maintain a [...] balance between subtlety of concepts and simpl[...] of language.

Quite soon, however, ʿImādī's poetry app[...] to have lost the interest of the public. No comp[...] copy of his *Dīwān* is now known to exist. The lar[...] collection now extant is the British Museum ms. [...] 298 containing more than 1400 lines, most of w[...] belong to *ḳaṣīdas*. More material is scattered [...] a great number of sources, but a comprehen[...] collection is still lacking.

Bibliography: Rāwandī, *Rāḥat al-ṣudūr*, [...] Muḥammad Iqbál, London 1921; ʿAwfī, [...] Browne, ii, 257-67, ed. S. Nafīsī, 430-6; cf. *Taʿl*[...] 722-8; Shams-i Ḳays, *al-Muʿdjam fī maʿ*[...] *ashʿār al-ʿadjam*, Tehran 1338/1959, *pas*[...] Taḳī Kāshī, *Khulāṣat al-ashʿār* (cf. Bloc[...] *Catalogue des manuscrits persans de la Biblioth*[...] *Nationale*, iii, Paris 1928, 50 and Nafīsī, *op. c*[...] Amīn Aḥmad Rāzī, *Haft iḳlīm*, Tehran 1340/1[...] iii, 23-31; Luṭf-ʿAlī Beg Ādhar, *Ātashk*[...] Tehran 1337/1958, 33, 117, 170, 220; Riḍā-[...] Khān Hidāyat, *Madjmaʿ al-fuṣaḥāʾ*, Te[...] 1295/1878, i, 350-2; Ch. Rieu, *Catalogue of* [...] *Persian Manuscripts in the British Mus*[...] London 1881, ii, 557-8; Badīʿ al-Zamān Furū[...] farr, *Sukhan wa sukhanwarān*[1], Tehran 1312/1[...] ii, 166-77, [2]Tehran 1350/1971, 517-32; Dh. S[...] *Taʾrīkh-i adabiyyāt dar Īrān*, ii, [3]Tehran 1339/[...] 743-50; A. Munzawī, *Fihrist-i nuskhahā-yi khaṭ*[...] *fārsī*, iii, Tehran 1350/1971, 2451.

(J. T. P. de Bruij[...])

al-IMĀRĀT al-ʿARABIYYA al-MUTTA[...] DA (the United Arab Amirates), the federat[...] of seven shaykhdoms of the lower G[...] formerly known as the Trucial States, inaugur[...] on 14 Shawwāl 1391/2 December 1971. The mem[...] states are Abū Ẓabī (Abū Dhabī), Dubayy, [...] Shāriḳa (Shārdja), ʿAdjmān, Umm al-Ḳayw[...] Raʾs al-Khayma and Fudjayra. The federati[...] total area is about 30,000 square miles and its po[...] lation (180,226 at the 1968 census) has been vari[...] ly estimated, in the absence of reliable statistics [...] anything between 320,000 and 700,000, mo[...] concentrated in Abū Ẓabī and Dubayy shaykhdo[...]

Until December 1971, the seven shaykhdoms w[...]

d to Great Britain by a series of treaties, the t dating back to 1236/1820, whereby Britain ised responsibility for the conduct of the shaykh- s' foreign relations and ensured their observance e engagements they had entered into over the to respect the maritime truce and to abstain piracy and slave-trading. It was generally ac- d that an implicit reciprocal obligation devolved Britain from these engagements to defend the ial Shaykhdoms against their enemies. A first towards promoting some form of association g the shaykhdoms was taken in 1371-2/1952 the establishment of the Trucial States Council, up of the rulers of the seven shaykhdoms. her steps were the setting up of the Trucial s Development Council to assist economic, specially agricultural, progress, and the organi- n of the Trucial Oman Scouts (first formed as Trucial Oman Levies in 1950 on the model of Jordanian Arab Legion) to keep the peace ghout the shaykhdoms and along their borders. definition of these borders was, for the most accomplished in the years between 1374-5/1955 380-1/1961.

Shawwāl 1387/January 1968 the British govern- announced that it intended to withdraw from pecial position in the Gulf by the end of 1971 'l-Ḳaʿda 1390), and at the same time to termi- its treaty relationship with the Trucial States, ayn and Ḳatar. A month after the statement made the rulers of Abū Ẓabī and Dubayy an- ced (on 19 Dhu 'l-Ḳaʿda 1387/18 February) that they were forming a union of their two khdoms with the intention of co-ordinating foreign and defence policies, and of co-operating such matters as internal security, education, h services and immigration. At their instigation nference of the Trucial Shaykhs and the rulers aḥrayn and Ḳatar was held at Dubayy the wing week, and on 28 Dhu 'l-Ḳaʿda/27 February ision was reached in principle to create a federa- of the nine shaykhdoms. Ultimate power in the ation would reside in a supreme council made f the nine rulers, while executive authority d be vested in a federal council. The agreement tablish the federation, which was to be called "Federation of Arab Amirates" (*Ittiḥād al- āt al-ʿArabiyya*), was to come into force on the day of Dhu 'l-Ḳaʿda 1387/30 March 1968.

er the next two years, little discernible progress made towards the creation of the federation. of the preliminary work—on a common ncy, a unified educational system, federal com- ications, integrated medical and social services, —was delegated to committees, whose effective- was hampered by their lack of authority and dilatoriness. The chief obstacles, however, political. For nearly two centuries the shaykh- s concerned had been at odds—and frequently pen conflict—with one another over territorial ites, dynastic rivalries and tribal dissensions. e underlying and enduring sources of discord d an outlet during the negotiations towards ation in acrimonious disagreements over the of the provisional federal capital, the selection term of office of the federation's president, and, seriously of all, the distribution of power in the eme and federal councils and representation in proposed consultative assembly.

hrayn and Ḳatar were insistent that they, Ẓabī and Dubayy should have one vote each on supreme council, while the remaining five Trucial States were to be confined to one collective vote. They further insisted that all decisions taken by the council should be unanimous. For their part, the Trucial States wanted equality of voting rights, though they were divided over the question of unani- mous or majority decisions, with Abū Ẓabī pushing most strongly for the principle of majority decisions. Perhaps the greatest disagreement of all was over the allocation of seats in the proposed consultative assembly. Baḥrayn wanted representation to be on the basis of population, which would have given her twice as many seats as the other eight states com- bined. They in turn, and for this very reason, wanted equal representation for all states. Fear of Baḥrayn's predominance in the federation, not only because of her numerical strength but also because of the superior skills and educational attainments of her people, was perhaps the most potent single reason why the federation of nine shaykhdoms languished and eventually expired.

Another important reason was the uneasiness engendered among some of the shaykhdoms' rulers by the overhanging threat of major territorial claims against two of their number—the Persian claim to sovereignty over Baḥrayn, and Saʿūdi Arabia's claim to a considerable portion of Abū Ẓabī shaykhdom, in- cluding the Buraymī oasis on its border with ʿUmān. It was her desire for support in resisting the Per- sian claim that had greatly influenced Baḥrayn's de- cision to participate in the federation. The other states, however, were reluctant to risk offending Persia by according Baḥrayn the support she sought. Dubayy, for instance, because of her close commercial ties with Persia, was most averse to becoming em- broiled in the dispute. There was a similar aversion on the part of most of the shaykhdoms to being drawn into Abū Ẓabī's frontier disagreement with Saʿūdi Arabia. Ḳatar's relations with the Saʿūdis had been intimate for many years, whereas those with Abū Ẓabī had been distant, and at times hostile, for generations. Baḥrayn was counting upon Saʿūdī diplomatic help against the Persians, while Dubayy had for years been locked in a contest with Abū Ẓabī for political influence in Trucial ʿUmān.

A fateful stage in the negotiations towards a federation of the nine shaykhdoms was reached in Rabīʿ I 1390/May 1970, when a resolution of the Perso-Baḥraynī dispute was achieved. At the request of both parties, and of Britain as the protecting power, the UN secretary-general had appointed a personal representative in Muḥarram 1390/March 1970 to ascertain the wishes of the people of Baḥrayn regarding the future political status of the shaykhdom and its relationship to Persia. The secretary-general's representative reported at the beginning of May that the Baḥraynīs were "virtually unanimous" in want- ing a fully independent, sovereign state, and that "the great majority" desired it to be an Arab state. The UN security council unanimously endorsed the report on 11 May, and later that month (Rabīʿ I 1390) the Persian government accepted it. The renunciation of the Persian claim to Baḥrayn, although it was henceforth to determine Baḥrayn's attitude to the Federation of Arab Amirates, had no effect upon the other threats to the federation's territorial integrity. In the first week of May, Saʿūdi Arabia reasserted her claim to the western and southern areas of Abū Ẓabī and to the Buraymī oasis. A fortnight later Persia put forward a claim to the islands of Abū Mūsā and the Greater and Lesser Tūnbs (Tūnb-i Buzurḳ and Naḥiyy Tūnb), situated a few miles inside the Gulf to the west of the Straits of Hurmuz. Abū Mūsā had up to this time been regarded as a possession of the Trucial Shaykhdom of al-S̲h̲āriḳa, and the Tūnbs as belonging to Raʾs al-K̲h̲ayma.

Having secured the abandonment of the Persian claim, the Baḥraynīs had no wish to create a fresh source of friction with the Persians by taking the part of al-S̲h̲āriḳa and Raʾs al-K̲h̲ayma in the controversy over Abū Mūsa and the Tūnbs. This caution, combined with the resentment felt over what was considered to be the insufficient weight given to Baḥrayn's interests and importance in the projected federation and the aversion to siding with Abū Ẓabī in its resistance to the Saʿūdis, served to set Baḥrayn after May 1970 on a political course that took it steadily away from the federation and towards independence. Where Baḥrayn led, Ḳatar was bound to follow, as much for reasons of *amour propre* (its ruling family had been at feud with that of Baḥrayn for over a century) as out of considerations of political advantage and prudence. The final spur was applied by the decision of the Conservative government in Britain, which had been elected to power in June 1970, to adhere to its predecessor's policy of withdrawal from the Gulf by the end of 1971. (The decision was announced in March 1971 but there is evidence that it had been reached some time previously.) Baḥrayn declared its independence on 22 D̲j̲umāda II 1391/14 August 1971, and Ḳatar followed suit on 11 Rad̲j̲ab 1391/1 September 1971.

A few weeks earlier, six of the seven Trucial States, having concluded that a federation of the nine shaykhdoms was no longer feasible, had decided to form a federation of their own. The Trucial federation, entitled the "United Arab Amirates" (*al-Imārāt al-ʿArabiyya al-Muttaḥida*), was proclaimed at Dubayy on 25 D̲j̲umāda I 1391/18 July 1971. The ruler of Raʾs al-K̲h̲ayma, S̲h̲aykh Ṣaḳr b. Muḥammad al-Ḳāsimī, refused to join the federation, partly because its members showed no anxiety to assist him actively in opposing the Persian claim to the Tūnbs, partly because of his jealousy of the position and power which the rulers of Abū Ẓabī and Dubayy commanded within the federation. His fellow Ḳāsimī ruler, S̲h̲ayk̲h̲ K̲h̲ālid b. Muḥammad of al-S̲h̲āriḳa, proved more pliable over the extension of Persian authority over Abū Mūsā Island. His acquiescence in a Persian occupation was obtained in late November in return for an annual subsidy and an equal share in the exploitation of the submarine oilfields located off Abū Mūsa. On 12 S̲h̲awwāl 1391/30 November 1971, the day before Britain's special treaty relationship with the Trucial States was due to end officially, Persian troops occupied Abū Mūsa and the Tūnbs, meeting with armed resistance on the Greater Tūnb from the retainers of the ruler of Raʾs al-K̲h̲ayma. There were a number of repercussions from the Persian occupation of the islands, among them the expulsion of several thousand Persians from ʿIrāḳ and the nationalisation by the Libyan government of the British Petroleum Company's assets in Libya. The most violent individual reprisal was the murder in D̲h̲u 'l-Ḥid̲j̲d̲j̲a 1391/late January 1972 of the ruler of al-S̲h̲āriḳa, S̲h̲ayk̲h̲ K̲h̲ālid b. Muḥammad al-Ḳāsimī, by his cousin the ex-ruler, S̲h̲ayk̲h̲ Ṣaḳr b. Sulṭān al-Ḳāsimī, ostensibly in revenge for the alienation of Abū Mūsā to Persia. S̲h̲ayk̲h̲ Ṣaḳr b. Muḥammad of Raʾs al-K̲h̲ayma was so shaken by the assassination that at the end of D̲h̲u 'l-Ḥid̲j̲d̲j̲a 1391/mid-February 1972 he joined the federation.

The treaties between Britain and the Trucial States were abrogated on 13 S̲h̲awwāl 1391/1 De ber 1971, and the United Arab Amirates was forr inaugurated the following day. Its president S̲h̲ayk̲h̲ Zāyid b. Sulṭān al-Nihayyān, the rul Abū Ẓabī, and the vice-president, S̲h̲ayk̲h̲ R b. Saʿīd al-Maktūm, the ruler of Dubayy. Unde terms of the provisional constitution drawn up the previous two years in consultation wit Egyptian jurist, Dr Waḥīd al-Rifāʿat, they we hold office for five years and be eligible fo appointment at the end of that time. The ca of the UAA was temporarily established at Abū until a permanent capital had been built on a si the border of Abū Ẓabī and Dubayy.

The *fons et origo* of executive and legislative p within the federation is the supreme federal cou composed of the rulers of the seven consti shaykhdoms or amirates. Decisions of the co are by majority vote, with Abū Ẓabī and Du both possessing the power of veto. The pres appoints the prime minister, the deputy ministe the other ministers (some two dozen) who tog make up the federal council or cabinet. The cabi prime function is to carry into effect the deci of the supreme council and the instructions o president. The provisional constitution, which to 152 articles, also established a federal nat council to serve as a consultative assembly. It sists of forty delegates appointed for a term of years by the rulers of the amirates, Abū Ẓabī Dubayy each having eight delegates, al-S̲h̲āriḳa Raʾs al-K̲h̲ayma, six, and the other three amir four. Although the constitution would appea empower the national council to initiate legisla its principal task is clearly to discuss and app the budget and draft legislation presented to i the council of ministers. The constitution also vides for the establishment of a supreme cour the federation and a number of courts of firs stance. Responsibility for the defence of the fe tion is vested in a higher defence council, heade the president and consisting of the vice-presi the prime minister, the minister of defence and interior, and the commander of the Union Def Force, which has been formed around the nucle the Trucial Oman Scouts.

The constitution of the UAA, both in its provis and in its operation, reflects the primacy wi the federation of Abū Ẓabī and Dubayy, the wealthiest and most populous amirates. At the of their term as president and vice-president in 1 1976, S̲h̲ayk̲h̲ Zāyid of Abū Ẓabī and S̲h̲ayk̲h̲ Rā of Dubayy were re-elected to their respective of for a further five years. Members of their fam and close adherents hold the chief portfolios in council of ministers. The federal budget is prov almost exclusively by Abū Ẓabī from its large oil enues. (Dubayy, although deriving a substantia come from oil and commerce, refuses to contri more than a token amount.) Abū Ẓabī also h defence force considerably larger and better equi than that of the union. Naturally, the wealth political predominance of the two shaykhdoms inspired envy and some resentment among the fortunate members of the federation, with exception perhaps of al-S̲h̲āriḳa, which enjoy moderate degree of affluence from oil rever The arbitrariness of fortune which has blessed Ẓabī and Dubayy has tended to perpetuate and to intensify the longstanding rivalries and anin ties among the shaykhdoms, more particul those between the northern Ḳāsimī tribal confe and the southern Banī Yās confederation. re are other strains within the federation besides e caused by the imbalance of wealth and by old al and dynastic vendettas. Social and economic ıges in recent years have been rapid and pro-dly unsettling. A huge influx of immigrants of inds has broken the traditional mould of society. arned affluence of an unreal magnitude has oded customary morals, values and restraints. n ideological notions have undermined the old tical certainties, with what eventual consequences impossible to foretell. The basis of the UAA was, remains, a coalition of interests among its nber states, especially the need for some kind nutual security against the larger Gulf powers. ether the federal structure erected thus far will e sturdy enough to withstand the fissiparous sures within it remains to be seen.

Bibliography: Waḥīd al-Rifāʿat, *The Union Arabian Gulf Amirates*, in *Revue égyptienne de oit international*, xxvi (1970); *Constitution of the AA*, in *Middle East Journal*, xxvii/3 (1972), 307-; J. D. Anthony, *Arab states of the Lower Gulf*, ashington, D.C. 1975, 97-122; *Middle East Record*, (1968), Jerusalem 1973, 667-7, and v (1969-70), erusalem 1977, 992-1004. (J. B. KELLY)

MPECCABILITY, SINLESSNESS [see ʿIṢMA].

MPROVISATION [see IRTIDJĀL].

NAḲ (spelt *ināḳ*, *ināgh* and *ināḳ*), a title which ted in various Turkic and Mongol states.

he word is evidently a deverbal noun from the kic verb *inan-* [**ina-*] "to trust, to rely on" etc., the basic meaning "close friend, confidant, tworthy person". (The spelling *ʿināḳ*, with al *ʿayn*, very often found in the Central Asian ces of the 19th century, is most probably only ndication of the initial back vowel; an explana- of this spelling given by A. A. Semenov, deriving word from Arabic *ʿināḳ* "embrace", is, at best, a literary invention.) A similar derivative from the e verb, *inanč* "reliance", "trust", is registered ıe Turkic texts of the 10th century and later as a or rank of persons belonging to the close retinue he ruler (cf. especially *inanč beg* in Maḥmūd ghari, i, 119, and *Ḳutadgu bilig*, Farghāna 293); this title was used through the whole jūḳ period (cf. also such titles as *inanč payghu*, *č bilge* etc.; see Sir G. Clauson, *An etymological onary of pre-thirteenth-century Turkish*, Oxford , 187). The same meaning, probably, had also title *inal* (another deverbal noun from the same ı), found already in the runic inscriptions of Yenisey (see *Drevnetyurkskiy slovar'*, Leningrad), 218; S. E. Malov, *Yeniseyskaya pis'mennost' kov*, Moscow-Leningrad 1952, 38, 45, 49). The s *inal*, *inal-tegin*, *inalčuk* (*inalčiḳ*) were also ly used during the Ḳarakhānid and Saldjūḳ ods (see G. Clauson, *op. cit.*, 184-5); there is, ever, another reading and explanation of this from *inäl* "deputy" [?], found in the Orkhon riptions and in Chinese sources of the same od (see *Drevnetyurkskiy slovar'*, 209, 218; G. rfer, *Türkische und mongolische Elemente im persischen*, iv, 196-9, No. 1900; cf., however, Pelliot, *Notes sur l'histoire de la Horde d'Or*, s 1949, 182-3, n. 2). The word *inaḳ*, which is not d in runic inscriptions and appears first only he texts written in the Uyghur characters, was owed into Mongolian from Turkic already before end of the 12th century; it existed in the time ingiz-Khān as a title of close companions (*nukers*]) of the khān.

After the Mongol conquests this title, probably under the Mongol influence, superseded other derivatives of *inan-* also among the Turks. It is mentioned in Persian historical sources of the Mongol and Tīmūrid periods, without a definition of its meaning, but clearly as a title of high-ranking persons especially close to the ruler (examples given by Quatremère, *Histoire des Mongols de la Perse*, i, pp. L-LI, n. 84; see also the *Ẓafar-nāma* by Niẓām al-Dīn Shāmī, ed. F. Tauer, i, 96, 142, ii, 109, 118, 148). Sometimes the *inaḳ*s (*ināḳān*, *ināḳiyān*) are mentioned in these sources as a special category of the retainers of the ruler (cf. such expressions as *umarāʾ wa ināḳiyān*, *muḳarribān wa ināḳān*, *khawāṣṣ wa ināḳān*, *farzandān wa nūkarān wa ināḳiyān* [of an *amīr*], etc.). The term had the same meaning also in the Aḳ Ḳoyunlu [*q.v.*] state, where one source mentions an *amīr* among the *inaḳ*s whose post was equal to that of a *mukrdār* (see V. Minorsky, in *BSOAS*, x/1 [1940-2], 170-1).

It seems that in the post-Tīmūrid period this title was used only in the Uzbek khānates of Central Asia. It is not mentioned by Maḥmūd b. Walī, the author of *Baḥr al-asrār*, in his description of the ceremonial at the court of the Ashtarkhānid ruler in Balkh (cf. V. V. Bartol'd, *Sočineniya*, ii/2, 390-3), though it certainly existed during the Ashtarkhānid period; according to the *ʿUbayd-Allāh-nāma* by Muḥammad Amīn Bukhārī (early 18th century; see Russian tr. by A. A. Semenov, Tashkent 1957, 33), a person in the rank of *inak* was keeper of the royal seal (cf. above, under the Aḳ Ḳoyunlu) in the reign of Subḥān-Ḳulī Khān (d. 1114/1702). A retainer of ʿUbayd Allāh Khān (1114-29/1702-11), a Kalmuk (i.e. a person of slave origin), was promoted simultaneously to the post (or rank?) of *inaḳ* and to the post of the first minister, *ḳosh-begi-yi kull* [see ḲOSH-BEGI] (see *ibid.*, 45, 191); he was also the keeper of the seal (*ibid.*, 204). His two successors, also of slave origin, were also given the rank of *inaḳ* together with the post of the great *ḳosh-begi* (*ibid.*, 230, 276). The administrative manual *Madjmaʿ al-arḳām* compiled in Bukhārā in 1212/1798 mentions two *inaḳ*s: first, "the great I." (*ʿināḳ-i kalān*), who was the third (after the *ḳosh-begi*) among the four dignitaries especially close to the sovereign, and whose duty was to pass the royal orders to persons under the rank of *amīr*; and second, "the little I." (*ʿināḳ-i khurd*), who kept the box with the royal seals and also had to receive all reports from the province and messages brought by foreign ambassadors, to open them and to pass them to the *munshī* for reading (see facsimile in *Pis'mennīye pamyatniki Vostoka 1968*, Moscow 1970, 56, 57). N. Khanīkov (*Opisaniye Bukharskogo khanstva*, St. Petersburg 1843, 183-5, 187) mentions only one *inak*, whose duty was to set his seal on the reverse of the diplomas granting the ranks of *mīr-i akhūr*, *ishik-āghāsī* and *čaghatāy-begi*; apparently, this was the office of the former *inaḳ-i khurd*. At the time of the last Mangīts [*q.v.*], however, the title *inaḳ*, as well as some other titles, became simply a honorary rank—the fifth from the top in the hierarchy of Bukhārā, between *dadkhʷāh* and *parwānači*—given to various officials.

In the Khānate of Khīwa, the title *inaḳ* was given to the leaders of the Uzbek tribes, and it was originally the second in importance after the title *atalïḳ* [*q.v.*, above]. The historian of Khīwa Muʾnis [*q.v.*], in his account of the administrative reform of Abu 'l-Ghāzī [*q.v.*] (1053-79/1643-63), mentions that the khān's council of 34 *ʿamaldārs* established by Abu 'l-Ghāzī included four *inaḳ*s and four "Čaghatāy *inaḳ*s" (*Firdaws al-iḳbāl*, ms. of the Leningrad Branch of the

Institute of Oriental Studies, C-571, f. 65b). There was one *ināḳ* from each of four *tupä*, into which all Uzbek tribes in Khwārazm were apparently divided already in the 16th century: Uyghur and Nayman, Ḳungrat and Ḳiyat, Mangït and Nukuz, Ḳanglï and Ḳïpčaḳ; the meaning of the title *Čaghatāy ïnaḳ* is not clear. Muʾnis (*ibid.*, f. 101a) claims that already in the reign of Abu ʾl-Ghāzī, Umbay Înaḳ, the ancestor of the Ḳungrat [*q.v.*] dynasty became the khān's powerful first minister in reward for the service rendered by him previously. In the concluding part of the *Shadjara-yi Turk* written on behalf of Abu ʾl-Ghāzī's son Anūsha (ed. Desmaisons, text, 327, tr., 351) there is mentioned a Yādigār Înaḳ brought by Abu ʾl-Ghāzī from Hazārasp to Khīwa and given the *inaḳlïḳ*, though he certainly already held the title *ïnaḳ* before (cf. *ibid.*, text, 326, tr., 349); this may be interpreted as a promotion of one of the Uzbek *ïnaḳ*s to the post of the "great I.", like that which Umbay Înaḳ held (later?). The reports of the Russian ambassadors, who were in Khīwa in the reign of Anūsha Khān, show, however, that the *ïnaḳ*s were still on the second place after the *atalïḳ*s (see *Nakaz Borisu i Semenu Pazukhinïm*..., St. Petersburg 1894, 43-4). Artuḳ Înaḳ, from the Mangït tribe, became actual ruler of the Khānate of Khīwa after its conquest by Nādir Shāh (1740).

In the third quarter of the 18th century, Muḥammad Amīn Înaḳ, chief of the Ḳungrat tribe, became the ruler of the khānate and the founder of the dynasty, which remained in power till 1920 and is called sometimes in scholarly literature "Inaḳids". The third ruler from this dynasty, Eltuzar Înaḳ, proclaimed himself khān in 1219/1804. After that, *ïnaḳ* became the highest title for the Uzbek nobility in Khīwa (the historians of Khīwa mention cases of promotion from the rank of *atalïḳ* to the rank of *ïnaḳ*, see e.g. *Firdaws al-iḳbāl* (ms. cit., ff. 317b, 578a). During the reign of Muḥammad Raḥīm Khān (1220-40/1806-25), his elder brother Ḳutlugh Murād had the title *ïnāḳ-bek* and was styled *amīr al-umarāʾ* (*ibid.*, f. 316a; but the *atalïḳ* was still considered as senior Uzbek *amīr*); he was called also *biy-ïnaḳ* and *ïnaḳ-āḳā*. In the middle of the 19th century, the title of *ïnaḳ-bek* (that is, senior I.) was given to the khān's heir, who was mostly governor of the town of Hazārasp; before the Russian conquest (1873), however, this title was applied not to the heir, but to one of senior relatives of the khān (cf. A. L. Kuhn's papers in the Archives of the Leningrad Branch of the Institute of Oriental Studies, file 1/13, ff. 36a-38b). Besides him and the four *ïnaḳ*s of the Uzbek tribes, the title was granted sometimes to the tribal chiefs of the Turkmens.

The title *ïnaḳ* existed also in the Khānate of Khoḳand [*q.v.*], where it was given to a court official (or officials) in charge of the provision for the court and for the khān's bodyguards; they supervised also the personal domains of the khān. At the same time, apparently, it was here also, as in Bukhārā, an honorary rank given to various dignitaries, such as provincial governors (cf. V. P. Nalivkin, *Histoire du khanat de Khokand*, Paris 1889, 104).

Bibliography: in addition to the works cited in the text, see B. Ya. Vladimirtsov, *Obshčestvennïy stroy mongolov*, Leningrad 1934, 93; P. Pelliot, *Notes sur l'histoire de la Horde d'Or*, Paris 1949, 182-3, n. 2; A. A. Semenov, in *Sovetskoye vostokovedeniye*, v (1948), 148-9; idem, in *Materialï po istorii tadžikov i uzbekov Sredney Azii*, ii, Stalinabad 1954, 61; A. L. Troitskaya, *Katalog arkhiva Kokandskikh khanov XIX veka*, Moscow 1968, 545; idem, *Materialï po istorii Kokandskogo kha[...] XIX v.*, Moscow 1969, 5, 21; Radloff, *Wörter[...]* i, 1361-3; G. Doerfer, *Türkische und mongol[...] Elemente in Neupersischen*, ii, 217-20, nos. 6[...] É. V. Sevortyan, *Étimologičeskiy slovar' tyurk[...] yazïkov*, Moscow 1974, 654-6. (Yu. Brege[...]

ʿÎNĀT, a town in Ḥaḍramawt, about 10 [...] 15 km. due east of Tarīm, and situated at the [...]fluence of the Wādīs ʿÎnāt and Ḥaḍramawt. [...] holy family of ʿÎnāt is the Āl Bū Bakr b. Shaykh [...] the illustrious *manṣab*, Shaykh Bū Bakr b. S[...] known as Mawlā ʿÎnāt, is buried in the town. [...] family has been subjected to severe criticism [...] other Sayyid groups because of its bearing a[...] ʿÎnāt has become one of the most important *ha[...]* [*q.v.*] in Ḥaḍramawt. It is famous for its own b[...] of hunting dogs which seem to be indistinguish[...] from the common "pie-dog". With these dogs [...] inhabitants participate in the ibex hunt under [...] direction of the Manṣab. The number of the inh[...]ants of the town was greatly reduced after the [...] time famine in Wādī Ḥaḍramawt, and a f[...] recent figure suggests a population of about 1[...] The old quarter organisation has in reality [...]appeared, though originally there were se[...] quarters. Landberg employs the spelling ʿE[...] (ʿAynāt), though it seems that all other Euro[...] forms proposed are erroneous.

Bibliography: H. von Wissmann, *Ma[...] Southern Arabia*, Royal Geographical Soc[...] London 1958; Le Comte de Landberg, *Arabic[...]* Leiden 1898, 206; R. B. Serjeant, *Saiyid[...] Ḥaḍramawt*, London 1957, 17-18; idem, *S[...] Arabian hunt*, London 1976, 32-3.

(G. R. Smit[...]

ʿINĀYAT KHĀN, a noble of the In[...] Mughal emperor Awrangzīb. He stemmed [...] Khwāf [*q.v.*] in Khurāsān, but no information a[...] his early career is available. In 1077/1666-7 he [...] appointed head of the *dīwān-i khāliṣa* (*dīwā[...]* crown lands). In 1079/1668-9 he was promote[...] the rank of 900 *dhāt* and 100 *suwār*. In 1080/166[...] he reported that the expenditure had incre[...] since the time of Shāh Djahān and that there [...] a large deficit; Awrangzīb thereupon ordered [...] enlargement of the *khāliṣa* lands and a reduc[...] in expenditure. In 1082/1671-2 he was appoi[...] *fawdjdār* [*q.v.*] (commandant) of Čakla Barēlī an[...] 1086/1675-6, *fawdjdār* of Khayrābād. In 1088/16[...] he was again appointed *pīshdast-i daftar-i khā[...]* and was promoted to the rank of 1000 *dhāt* [...] 100 *suwār*. In 1092/1681-2 he was promoted t[...] head of the *dīwān-i buyūtāt* (in charge of the Imp[...] Household accounts), and shortly after, at his [...] request, was appointed governor of Adjmēr. [...] took part in a campaign against the Rathors, [...] died in 1093/1682. He was not apparently implic[...] in the conspiracy of Pādshāh Ḳulī Khān, his [...] in-law, who was killed at about this time.

Bibliography: Mustaʿīd Khān, *Maʾāt[...] ʿĀlamgīrī*, Bib. Ind., Calcutta 1871; Shāh Na[...] Khān, *Maʾāthir-al umarāʾ*, Bib. Ind., Calc[...] 1888, ii; Khwāfī Khān, *Muntakhab al-lubāb*, [...] Ind., Calcutta 1860, ii. (M. Athar A[...]

ʿINĀYAT KHĀN, an obscure general of [...] Mughal Emperor Awrangzīb [*q.v.*]. He was the fat[...] in-law of Tahawwur Khān, one of the principal sup[...]ters of Awrangzīb's son Akbar during the rebellio[...] 1091-2/1680-1. When in Dhu ʾl-Ḥidjdja 1091/Jan[...] 1681 Awrangzīb advanced to Dō-rāha, in the Adj[...] region, ʿInāyat Khān was ordered to write to Tah[...]wur Khān inducing him to desert the prince's a[...]

at Kurkī; Tahawwur Khān complied, but on his
al in Awrangzīb's camp some confusion arose
hich he was killed.

Bibliography: Sir Jadunath Sarkar, *History
Aurangzib*[1], Calcutta 1912-24, iii, 411-12.
(P. Jackson)

[I]CENSE [see LUBĀN].

[IN]DEPENDENCE [see ISTIḲLĀL].

[IN]FALLIBILITY [see ʿIṢMA].

[IN]ḤIṢĀR, or in Ottoman Turkish also ḤAṢĬR,
the words used for monopolies and restric-
practices of Ottoman guilds, the full
being *inḥiṣār-i beyʿi ve shirā*. These monopolies
.ded restrictions concerning the number or
of people allowed to perform a trade or a pro-
on, as well as limitations imposed on production
ı commerce. Restrictions of this kind were con-
ed necessary and beneficial to society. As
ıst this, monopolistic hoarding or cornering
condemned and prohibited by the government.
[d]istinguish between the two kinds, the second
called in Turkey *iḥtikār*, but this term was
in Arabic for both kinds of monopolies (cf.
, *Monopolies*, 145-6; *Egyptian guilds*, 107 n. 11,
51).

[d]ocuments relating to Istanbul and Cairo dating
the 18th and 19th centuries show that a crafts-
or merchant who wanted to practice his craft or
e independently needed the agreement of the
l's head. In earlier periods, and in some smaller
ıs, economic activity seems to have been less
icted, though there is evidence that in the 17th
ıry Cairo craftsmen in various branches under-
: ceremonies of initiation in order to acquire
ljāza, without which they were not allowed to
tice their craft. One of the main purposes of
e restrictions was to limit the number of shops
eople occupied in a trade or craft. Such limita-
s are indeed documented for Istanbul from the
century onwards well into the 19th. In addition,
ts were made to prevent the establishment
[w]ildcat" enterprises, and especially to eliminate
llicit trade of hawkers and pedlars (*ḳoltuḳčular*).
ıother kind of restriction was the limitation
ıch guild to producing or selling specific goods
. The aim of such measures was to eliminate ex-
al and internal competition and thus to prevent
ıl upheavals and unrest. For the same purpose it
ordered, in some cases, that specific production
articular dresses was limited to specific commu-
s in order to maintain their distinctive cos-
e. Many trades or guilds were confined to specific
es or markets, which often bore the name of
craft or the trade.

ost of these restrictions were controlled by the
ɛ system. *Gedik* literally means "breach" and
e acquired the meaning of privilege. Thus a *gedik*
the right to exercise a craft or a trade, either
eneral or, more frequently, at a special place
ı a specific shop. Most *gedik*s included the right
ıe tools of a workshop or a business. The number
ediks in each craft was fixed, though it could
ıanged from time to time. Since nobody was al-
d to become a master or open a shop without
ıng a *gedik*, new masters could be accepted only
ı a vacancy occurred. *Gedik*s were inheritable if
ıeir fulfilled all other conditions for becoming a
ter in the craft; otherwise the rule was that they
ransferred to apprentices or journeymen of the
l, not to outsiders.

ıl monopolies and restrictions of the guild
ɛm were sanctioned by the authorities, decreed
as government orders and enforced by the officers of
the state. After some unsuccessful attempts to abolish them in Egypt in the middle of the 19th century,
they gradually disappeared, in Egypt as well as
in other parts of the Ottoman Empire, in the course
of the second half of the century. On 9 January 1890
it was decreed in Egypt that every person was free
to exercise any craft or occupation or profession
or trade, except for dangerous occupations or for
those which were government monopolies.

Bibliography: ʿOthmān Nūrī, *Medjelle-yi
umūr-i belediyye*, i, Istanbul 1922; C. White,
Three years in Constantinople, London 1845;
G. Baer, *Monopolies and restrictive practices of
Turkish guilds*, in *JESHO*, xiii/2 (1970), 145-65;
idem, *Egyptian guilds in modern times*, Jerusalem
1964, 105-12. (G. Baer)

INIMITABLENESS OF THE ḲURʾĀN [see
IʿDJĀZ].

INSPECTION OF TROOPS [see ISTIʿRĀḌ and
(above) DĀGH U TAṢḤĪḤA].

**INSTITUT DES HAUTES ÉTUDES MARO-
CAINES** (I.H.E.M.) *al-Maʿhad li 'l-ʿulūm al-ʿulyā
al-maghribiyya*, one of the most important
centres of intellectual life in Morocco over
a period of forty years, bearing in mind the fact
that it followed on from the École Supérieure de
Langue Arabe et des Dialectes Berbères opened in
Rabat in 1915 for the training of highly-qualified
civilian interpreters.

The I.H.E.M. was established, by decree of the
grand vizier, on 11 February 1920/20 Djumādā
I 1338, with "the object of instigating and encouraging scientific studies relating to Morocco, of co-
ordinating them and centralising the results." It
was replaced, in 1956, after Moroccan independence,
by the Faculté des Lettres et des Sciences Humaines
of Rabat.

If the École Supérieure had been directed by
interpreters of distinction like M. Nehlil and I.
Hamet, the I.H.E.M. was headed by a succession of
professors of high renown, sc. H. Basset, E. Lévi-
Provençal, L. Brunot and H. Terrasse. The staff of
directors of studies, lecturers and research super-
visors has included among its more distinguished
members now dead, F. Arin, A. Basset, E. Biarnay,
R. Blachère, H. Bruno, H. de Castries, J. Célérier,
P. de Cénival, L. Chatelain, G. S. Colin, J. de Cossé-
Brissac, R. Hoffher, M. Bendaoud, E. Laoust, C. Le
Cœur, R. Le Tourneau, V. Loubignac, G. and W.
Marçais, G. Marcy, P. Mauchaussé, J. Meunié,
R. Montagne, L. Paye, H. Renaud, P. Ricard, J.
Riche and A. Roux. Many of these have been con-
tributors to this Encyclopaedia.

The achievement of the I.H.E.M. has been considerable. Morocco has witnessed the emergence of a
strong school that has addressed itself with energy
and enthusiasm to the scientific study of the country
and has almost entirely re-evaluated our knowledge
of the Maghrib and Muslim Spain. The Institute first
published, as successor to the review *Les Archives
Berbères*, a *Bulletin de l'I.H.E.M.* which after the
first issue, took on the splendid title *Hespéris*, which
it kept until it ceased publication. The scientific
authority and exceptional documentary interest of
this publication were such that in 1972 a complete
facsimile edition was published (comprising the
Archives Berbères and the unique *Bulletin*).

Hespéris published among its articles a *Bibliographie Marocaine* of a very wide-ranging character
since it embraces, under some forty headings, all
that is known concerning Morocco and its successive

civilisations. Edited by specialists from the Bibliothèque Générale of Rabat, it has made an unrivalled contribution to any methodical study of the Maghrib. This bibliography was published between 1923 and 1953.

Hespéris merged in 1960 with the review *Tamuda*, born in Tetuan in the last years of the Spanish Protectorate, and it continues in this form to serve Morocco and the pursuit of knowledge.

Besides *Hespéris*, the I.H.E.M. has published several collections comprising the complete *Hesperis* (15 volumes); collected Arabic texts (12 volumes); Publications of the I.H.E.M. (62 volumes); collected articles of the Centres d'Etudes Juridiques (45 volumes); Proceedings of the Congresses of the I.H.E.M. (9 volumes); some extra-mural publications, including *Initiation au Maroc* (3 editions), a *Notice sur les règles d'édition des travaux* and some *Brefs conseils pratiques* for the transcription and printing of Spanish and Portuguese words (R. Ricard); collected Notes and Documents (21 volumes); and collected Moroccan Berber Texts (2 volumes).

In addition to research, publications, public sources in Arabic (classical and dialectal), in Berber and in Moroccan civilisation, the I.H.E.M. provided training for the various degrees in arts and the law degree awarded by French universities. It thus enabled many young people to start and complete their higher studies in Arabic and in law without the obligation to go to France.

Also worthy of mention is the Institut Scientifique Chérifien, founded in 1920, an institution of higher education devoted exclusively to the study of scientific problems related to Morocco. Very advanced for its time, it was awarded the patronage of the Académie des Sciences of Paris. It continues to produce admirable work and numerous publications.

Bibliography Direction générale de l'instruction publique, des beaux arts et des antiquités: *Historique (1912-1930)*, Rabat 1931, chs. ii, xii; *Bull. de l'Inst. des Hautes Études Marocaines*, No. 1 (Dec. 1920), text of the vizieral decree setting up the establishment and the inaugural speech of the first Congress of the I.H.E.M. delivered by G. Hardy, setting forth the scientific and humanistic programme of the Institute; *Publication de l'I.H.E.M. (1915-1935), tables et index*, suppl. to *Hespéris*, 1936, 3rd term (pp. 82); *Publications de l'I.H.E.M. et de la Section Historique du Maroc*, Rabat 1954 (pp. 17); M. Hosotte-Raynaud, *Publications de l'I.H.E.M., 1936-1954, Tables et répertoires*, Rabat 1956 (pp. 145); P. Morin, *Bibliography analytique des Sciences de la Terre. Maroc et regions limitrophes, depuis le début des recherches géologiques à 1964* (Notes et mémoires au Service Géologique No. 182), Rabat 1965, 2 vols.; A. Adam, *Bibliographie critique de sociologie, d'ethnographie et de géographie humaine du Maroc*, Mémoires du Centre de recherches anthropologiques, préhistoriques et ethnographiques d'Alger, Algiers 1972, Introd.

(G. Deverdun)

INSTITUT DES HAUTES ÉTUDES DE TUNIS, an institution of higher learning founded in 1945, by the amalgamation of the Centre d'Études Juridiques, a subsidiary of the University of Algiers, and the École Supérieure de Langue et Littérature Arabes. This Institute benefited from its inception from an administration arranged under the patronage of the University of Paris and supervised by the Department of Public Education of Tunis u the Protectorate, later by the Minister or Secreta State for National Education of the Tunisian gov ment. This administration was not altered by Franco-Tunisian Cultural Convention of 1 Septer 1955: the latter in particular maintained the pat age of the University of Paris. Thus the Insti has continued to prepare students for degrees diplomas offered by the French state and, sim neously, to award Tunisian diplomas.

The Institut des Hautes Études of Tunis directed by a president, assisted by a deputy p dent, resident in Tunis. The presidents have su sively been William Marçais and Jean Roche, deputy presidents Jacques Flour, Roger Jan Merlin and Pierre Marthelot. It comprised sections, later to become faculties: legal and econ studies, science, literature and arts, philology linguistics. Instruction was provided by Fr and Tunisian professors and lecturers, with qu cations entitling them to teach to the stand of French higher education, and by tutors, assist and course supervisors appointed on the recomn dation of the heads of section.

These studies were pursued by students regist in the normal way and also, after the independ of Tunisia, by the pupils of the École Norr Supérieure, of the École Nationale d'Administra and of the Centre d'Études Economiques, attendi number of joint courses. Thus, in 1958-9, the strength numbered 1,522, of whom 382 were g Tunisians numbered 44.7 % of the total.

Apart from routine education, the Institut Hautes Études included a number of laboratories study centres, providing and co-ordinating special equipment and research facilities for the student the various departments. Similarly, a univer library offered its resources to the students, resou that in time were added to the study facilities vided by the General Library of Sūḳ al-ʿAṭṭārī

Finally, the Institut des Hautes Études was sponsible for the creation of two reviews: the *Cah de Tunisie*, a quarterly review of the arts, repla the former *Revue tunisienne*, and the *Revue de d* also quarterly. A certain number of volumes published in the form of specialised collections Library of Law and Economics, Publications of Science Section and the Literature Section (P P.U.F.).

Thus there operated for some fifteen years institution of modern higher education, equiva to that of the French universities. The patrona the University of Paris, reinforced by numer visits from French professors, ensured that a h standard was maintained.

It was by virtue of these high standards t the Institut des Hautes Études of Tunis became University of Tunis, by the decree of 31 March 1

If the patronage of the University of Paris disappeared, along with an obsolete administra council, links with the French university have mained very strong, although not institutional, a naturally, not exclusive, since progressively their acquisition of State doctorates, Tunis professors have advanced in number and in respo bility in their own university. The guardianshi the Tunisian state was established with the l risk of friction when one of the heads of departm a Tunisian, Mahmoud Messadi, became Secret of State for National Education; the pro-rec for his part, was none other than a former profe of the Institute and director of the École Norm érieure, Ahmed Abdesselem, both of them in-ctuals, writers and academics of great distinc-

hus the University of Tunis, totally and pro-sively integrated with the country, and totally pendent in its fortunes, in the framework of the .tutions of independent Tunisia, has become ightaway, in spite of its relative youth and in e of (and to some extent, thanks to) its original s with the French university, one of the most nguished and effective universities of the Arab ld. (P. MARTHELOT)

NSULT [see SHATM].

NTERPRETER [see TURDJUMĀN].

NTERROGATION [see ISTIFHĀM].

NVECTIVE [see HIDJĀʾ].

NZĀL (French spelling: "enzel", from *anzala*, odge, give hospitality), traditional type of .e peculiar to Tunisia. Presumably a survival he Roman *emphyteusis*, it served as a means rcumventing the inalienability of pious founda-s. The Mālikis define it as a "lease in perpetuity ʾ *muʾabbad*) of a property to a person engaging self to build a house, or any other edifice, or .t trees on it and pay a perpetual rent calculated he year or month" (D. Santillana, *Istituzioni di to musulmano malichita*, Rome 1925, i, 441). Clavel's definition distinguished between the domanial aspects of the estate: "L'enzel est ontrat sui generis, par lequel le wakf ou le pro-taire d'un bien mulk se dépouille, à perpétuité, du domaine utile d'un immeuble, n'en conservant le domaine éminent, à charge par le tenancier de er un canon annuel fixe" (*Le Wakf ou Habous*, e 1896, 2, 188). The rights of the lessee are so as to place him in *loco domini*: he may build, .t, make improvements (which become his prop-), bequeath or transfer his rights, etc. The *inzāl* mbles the Tunisian *kirdār* and the Egyptian *ḥikr*, differs from both in four points: (1) it has lost its nal purpose, viz. to render *wakf* property pro-ive thus providing income to its beneficiaries; t is no longer limited to *wakf*, but includes pri-property as well; (3) it is annulled in case of payment of rent for two consecutive years; (4) amount of rent cannot be adjusted to the fluctu-ns of the rental value of the property. Under the ich protectorate, the practice of *inzāl* gained nentum, as it enabled the colons to acquire exten-land holdings without prior capital investment.

Bibliography (further to references in the xt): J. Abribat, *Essai sur les contrats de quasi-iénation et de location perpétuelle*, Algiers 1902; Del Matto, *Enfiteusi ed Inzal*, in *L'Africa aliana*, N.S. vi (1927), 16-21; H. de Montéty, *ne loi agraire en Tunisie*, Cahors 1927; F. Valenzi, *contratto di Enzel nel diritto musulmano*, in *ivista delle Colonie italiane* (1931), 83-91; A. emla, *Le contrat d'Enzel en droit tunisien*, thesis, aris 1935; G. Vittorio, *I beni "habous" in Tunisia*, *OM*, xxxiv (1954), 540-8. (P. SHINAR)

-ʿIRĀĶĪ, SAYYID SHAMS AL-DĪN, religious ler active in the evangelisation of Kash-He was the son of Sayyid Ibrāhīm, a Mūsawī yid, and was born in the small town of Kund-ān, situated near Tehran on the road to Ķazwīn. eceived a good education, and, while still young e under the influence of Sayyid Muḥammad Nūr hsh (795-869/1393-1464), the founder of the bakhshiyya Order [see KUBRĀ, NADJM AL-DĪN]. ressed by his eloquence and learning, Sultan ayn Mīrzā Bāyķarā (873-911/1469-1506) took him into his service and sent him as his envoy to Sulṭān Ḥasan Shāh (877-89/1472-84) of Kashmīr. On arriving in the Valley, where he stayed for eight years, he became the disciple of Bābā Ismāʿīl, a Kubrawī saint, and then secretly won over Bābā Alī Nadjdjār, one of his most devoted followers, to the Nūrbakhshiyya creed, which was a mixture of Shīʿa and Sunnī doctrines, leavened by Ṣūfī pantheism. But his success was limited because, being an envoy, he could not preach openly. Besides, the Sunnī *ʿulamāʾ* came to know of his religious beliefs and compelled him to leave Kashmīr. He returned to Harāt, but as he lost the favour of Sulṭān Ḥusayn Mīrzā on account of his unorthodox beliefs, he left for Ray to live with Shāh Ķāsim, the son of Sayyid Muḥammad Nūr Bakhsh.

While he was in Ray, Shams al-Dīn heard that those whom he had converted in Kashmīr had relapsed into orthodoxy; so, on the advice of Shāh Ķāsim, he decided to proceed to the Valley. He left Ray in Rabīʿ I 907/September 1501. Travelling via Mashhad-Ķandahār-Multān, he entered Kashmīr in the spring of 1502 through the Punč-Bārāmūla route. On arriving in Srīnagar, he again won over Bābā ʿAlī Nadjdjār. But the most important convert was Mūsā Rayna, a powerful noble, who supported him in his activities, and gave him money to build a *khānķāh* [*q.v.*] at Djaddibal in Srīnagar. But on account of the opposition of the orthodox *ʿulamāʾ* and of Sayyid Muḥammad Bayhaķī, the *wazīr* of Sulṭān Muḥammad Shāh, he left Kashmīr. He went to Baltistān, to the north-east of Kashmīr, and carried on missionary work among its Buddhist inhabitants with considerable success. He stayed there for over two months until the defeat and death of Sayyid Muḥammad Bayhaķī [see BAYHAĶĪ SAYYIDS above] in 911/1505, and returned to Srīnagar at the invitation of Mūsā Rayna, who had again become powerful. During the nine years that Mūsā Rayna was *wazīr*, Shams al-Dīn carried on his activities without any hindrance. The conversion of Tādjī Čak and other Čak nobles further enabled him to consolidate his work.

Meanwhile, a great change had come over the Nūrbakhshiyya which, under the influence of Ṣafawid Īrān, increasingly began to identify itself with Shīʿism by shedding those of its doctrines which it had borrowed from Ṣūfism and Sunnī Islām. Shams al-Dīn, too, felt the impact and, inclined as he had always been towards the doctrine of the Twelvers, he now openly preached it, so that by the time he died in 932/1526, Shīʿism had become well established in Kashmīr. In remote Baltistān, however, the Nūrbakhshiyya beliefs survived.

Bibliography: The only biography of Shams al-Dīn known to exist is a *Tuḥfat al-aḥbāb* by a contemporary of his whose exact name is not known. The manuscript of the work is with Sayyid Muḥammad Yūsuf, a Shīʿī *mudjtahid* of Kashmīr and a descendant of Shams al-Dīn. Other works to be consulted are: Pīr Ḥasan Shāh, *Taʾrīkh-i Ḥasan*, ii, Srīnagar 1954; Mīrzā Ḥaydar Dughlāt, *Taʾrīkh-i Rashīdī*, tr. E. D. Ross and N. Elias, London 1895; Nūr Allāh Shushtarī, *Madjālis al-muʾminīn*, Tehran 1299/1882; Mohibbul Hasan, *Kashmir under the Sultans*, Srīnagar 1974; *Oriental College Magazine*, Lahore (February and May 1925, and August 1929). (MOHIBBUL HASAN)

IRAN
iii. Languages

(a) Pashto [see afghān. (ii). The Pashto language]
(b) Kurdish [see kurds, kurdistān. v. Language]
(c) Zaza [*q.v.*]
(d) Khʷārazmian
(e) Sogdian and Bactrian in the early Islamic period
(f) New Persian
(g) New Persian written in Hebrew characters [see judaeo-persian. ii. Language]

(d) Khʷārazmian.

Khʷarazmian, last attested late in the 8th/14th century (before yielding to Turkish), belonged to the Eastern branch of the Iranian language family, being most closely related to Sogdian, its southeastern neighbour. Pre-Islamic records are limited to coin legends and other inscriptions in a regional, partly ideographic development of the Aramaic script, found on wooden tablets, ossuaries, and silver vessels, and some documents on leather. Surviving Islamic sources consist almost exclusively of (a) some 400 isolated sentences quoted in Arabic books of case-law, and (b) the Khʷārazmian glosses (in one case almost complete) in different copies of al-Zamakhsharī's Arabic dictionary *Muḳaddimat al-adab*. They use the Arabo-Persian script, augmented by two letters (*ḥ* and *f*) with triple dots above, producing *c* (for both affricates *ts* and *dz*, as originally in Pashto) and *β* (i.e. *v*, distinct from *w*) respectively. While *p*, *č*, *dj* (*ǰ*), *kh* (*x*), *gh* (*γ*), *sh* (*š*), *zh* (*ž*), *k* (*k* and *g*) and the emphatics ʿ, *ḥ*, *ḳ* (*q*), *ṣ*, *ḍ* (*ż*), *ṭ*, *ẓ* presumably had their Persian values, the remaining letters, including *th*, *dh* (fricative θ, δ), evidently kept their original pronunciation. The letters are, however, often unpointed and for the most part unvowelled. Remarkable is the distinct spelling of words in pause position, with a presumably stressed vowel *-y-* before the last consonant, e.g. *ʾwrk* [*urg] 'wolf', in pause *ʾwryk* [*urég]. The basic numerals exemplify some typical consonant developments: 1 *ʾyw* (< *aiwa-*), 2 *ʾδw* (< *duwa-*), 3 *šy* (as Christian Sogdian, < *θraya-*; also 30 *šys* < *θrisąs*, but 13 *hrδs* < **θridasa*, cf. Parthian *hryds*), 4 *cfʾr* (< *čaθβārō*, cf. Parth. *čfʾr*), 5 *pnc* (< *panča*), 6 *ʾx* (< *xšwaš*), 7 *ʾβd* (as Sogd., < **hafta*), 8 *ʾšt* (< *ašta*), 9 *šʾδ* (< **frāda* "increase", but 19 *nwʾδs*), 10 δs (< *dasa*), 20 *ʾwsc* (< *wīsati*), 100 *sd* (< *satam*).

The morphology was characteristically Eastern Middle Iranian. Nominal forms distinguished two grammatical genders, two numbers and, in combination with pre- and postpositions, five variously inflected cases: nominative-accusative, genitive-dative, possessive, ablative and locative. A complex system of personal and demonstrative pronouns included many suffixed forms. There was a definite article, masc. *ʾy*, fem. *yʾ*, plur. *ʾy*, often coalescing with prepositions. Adjectives mainly preceded nouns. Examples: *ʾy kʾm* "the mouth", *c-y kʾmʾ-h* "from his mouth", *f-y kʾmʾ-h* "in, into his mouth", *f-y pcwycc f-y kʾmʾn* "in the corner (**pcwyck*) of the mouth"; *yʾ (θ-zrywnk) βwm* "the (grassy) earth", *yʾ βwmyʾ-δʾr* "the earth (direct object)", *c-ʾ βwmy* "from the earth", *ʾy bfnynk ʾy βwmnʾn* "Creator of the earths"; *yʾ pšk* "the back", *ʾy bʾr yʾ pšky* "the load of the back", *pr-ʾ pškʾ-h* "on his back"; *wdnk pxtyk* "old wine (*pxtk*)", *yʾ wdnc bdw* "the old property"; *wdncy rʾc* "old veins (*rʾk*)". The verbal system was based on a present stem and an imperfect formed from it, marked in polysyllabic stems by an *ā* substituted for the vowel of the first syllable: verbs with an initial vowel took a prefix *m-* instead. Through the use of various stem or final suffixes four tenses (present, imperfect, injunctive and future), six moods (indicative, subjunctive, conditional, optative, potential and imperative) and a permansive aspect were all distinguishable. Compound tenses, formed with the past participle and the auxiliary *δʾry-* "to have", are only rarely attested. Notable, besides the third-person singular present endings in *-c* (< *-ti*), are the third-person plurals in *-ʾr*. The most striking syntactic feature was that of "anticipation", whereby the objects of verb or preposition appeared as pronominal suffixes early in the sentence, in a regular order, even when they appeared later as independent forms, e.g. *hyδdʾ-hy-nʾ-dʾ-br ʾy slʾm* "he recited the greetings before him" (literally, "he read-him-them-off-upon the greetings").

Bibliography: A.Z. Walīdī (Zeki Velidi Togan), *Ḫwārezmische Sätze in einem arabischen Fiqh-Werke*, in *Islamica*, iii (1927), 190-213; W.[B.] Henning, *Über die Sprache der Chvarezmier*, in *ZDMG*, xc (1936), *30*-*34* (= *Selected papers*, i, 401-5); Togan, *Documents on Khorezmian culture. I. Muqaddimat al-adab, with the translation in Khorezmian*, Istanbul 1951; Henning, *The Khwarezmian language*, in *Zeki Velidi Togan'a armağan*, Istanbul 1955, 421-36 (= *Sel. papers*, i, 485-500); idem, *The structure of the Khwarezmian verb*, in *Asia Major*, N.S. v (1956), 43-9 (= *Sel. papers*, ii, 449-56); idem, *The Choresmian documents*, in *ibid.*, x (1965), 166-79 (= *Sel. papers*, ii, 645-58); J. Benzing, *Das chwaresmische Sprachmaterial einer Handschrift der "Muqaddimat al-Adab" von Zamaxšarī*, Wiesbaden 1968; D.N. MacKenzie, *The Khwarezmian glossary. I*, in *BSOAS*, xxxiii (1970), 540-58, *II*, in xxxiv (1971), 74-90, *III*, 314-30, *IV*, 521-36, *V*, in xxxv (1972), 56-74 (= *Iranica diversa*, ii, 459-550); Henning, *A fragment of a Khwarezmian dictionary*, ed. MacKenzie, London 1971; M. Samadi, *Das chwarezmische Verbum*, Wiesbaden 1986; MacKenzie, *The Khwarezmian element in the* Qunyat al-munya, London 1990.

(D.N. MacKenzie)

(e) Sogdian and Bactrian in the early Islamic period.

1. Sogdian (or Soghdian) was the Middle Iranian language of Ṣughd [*q.v.*] and adjacent areas. As an Eastern Iranian language, Sogdian is related fairly closely to Choresmian (Khʷārazmian, see (d) above) and Bactrian, more distantly to Middle Persian (Pahlavī). The form of Sogdian known from texts seems to be based on the language of the capital Samarḳand, but the limited evidence available indicates that the dialects spoken in areas such as Bukhārā and Čāč (Shāsh, Tashkent) were quite similar and no doubt mutually comprehensible with Sogdian proper.

Most of the surviving Sogdian manuscripts date from the 4th to 10th centuries A.D.; in addition to secular texts such as letters and business documents, they include a mass of Buddhist, Christian and Manichaean literature, written in four different scripts. Almost all of this material was found far to the east of the Sogdian homeland, in areas where Sogdian merchants had founded trading colonies, in particular the Turfan [*q.v.*] oasis in Chinese Turkistan (Xinjiang) and Dunhuang in western China. The most important Sogdian texts found in Ṣughd itself are the so-called "Mug documents" (published by Livshits and Bogolyubov-Smirnova). These date from the period of the Islamic conquest of Ṣughd under Ḳutayba b. Muslim [*q.v.*] at the beginning of the 2nd/8th century and represent part of the administrative archives of its last independent rulers. Of particular interest is a letter in Sogdian from an Arab official named ʿAbd al-Raḥmān b. Ṣubḥ to the Sogdian king Dhēwāshtīč (see I. Yakubovich, *Mugh 1.I revisited*, forthcoming in

Studia Iranica, xxxi [2002], 215-30). The Sogdian documents from the eastern colonies also contain a few references to the people and events of the Muslim world: a life of the Christian saint John of Daylam mentions al-Ḥadjdjādj b. Yūsuf, the *amīr* of Khurāsān (d. 95/714) (see W. Sundermann, in *Acta Antiqua Academiae Scientiarum Hungaricae*, xxiv/1 [1976], 95-101), while the trilingual (Sogdian-Turkish-Chinese) inscription of Karabalgasun in Mongolia possibly alludes to events connected with the rebellion of Rāfiʿ b. Layth [*q.v.*] of Samarḳand in 190-4/806-10 (according to Y. Yoshida, in *Documents et archives provenant de l'Asie Centrale*, ed. A. Haneda, Kyoto 1990, 119-20).

As a result of the important role of the Sogdian merchants in the long-distance trade between China, India and the West, Sogdian came to be used as a *lingua franca* of the Central Asian trade routes and many Sogdian documents may have been written by and for non-native speakers. This is particularly obvious in the latest Sogdian documents (3rd-4th/9th-10th centuries), some of which display strong influence from Turkish. Soon after the beginning of the 5th/11th century, Sogdian seems to have gone out of use as a written language, having been superseded by Turkish and in Ṣughd itself by Persian. Although New Persian is in origin the language of the south-western Iranian province of Fārs, its development into a literary language had begun in the east of the Iranian world, especially in Transoxania, with the result that the language of the earliest Persian poets is full of Sogdian and other Eastern Iranian words (see W.B. Henning, *Sogdian loan-words in New Persian*, in *BSOS*, x/1 [1939], 93-106). A certain amount of Sogdian linguistic material is also preserved in the writings of Muslim scholars such as al-Bīrūnī, who gives both the standard Sogdian and the Bukhāran names of many months, festivals, plants, etc. (see Henning, *Mitteliranisch*, 84-6). Particularly remarkable is the philosopher al-Fārābī's discussion in his *Kitāb al-Ḥurūf* of the means for expressing the notion of existence in Sogdian (see A. Tafazzoli, *Three Sogdian words in the Kitāb al-Ḥurūf*, in *Bull. of the Iranian Culture Foundation*, i/2 [1973], 7-8).

The disappearance of Sogdian as a language of culture and administration did not immediately lead to its disappearance as a spoken language. Indeed, one Sogdian dialect has survived to this day as a result of its speakers' location in a remote mountain valley in northern Tajikistan. Now known as Yaghnōbī, this language was estimated in 1975 to be spoken by some 2,000 persons, mostly Sunnī Muslims.

Bibliography: I. Gershevitch, *A grammar of Manichean Sogdian*, Oxford 1954; W.B. Henning, *Mitteliranisch*, in *Hdb. d. Or.*, ed. B. Spuler, I/IV/1, Leiden-Cologne 1958, 20-130; *Sogdiyskie dokumentī̆s gory Mug. II. Yuridičeskie dokumentī i pis'ma* (ed. V.A. Livshits). *III. Khozyaystvennīe dokumentī*, ed. M.N. Bogolyubov and O. Smirnova, Moscow 1962-3; N. Sims-Williams, *Sogdian*, in *Compendium linguarum iranicarum*, ed. R. Schmitt, Wiesbaden 1989, 173-92; R. Bielmeier, *Yaghnōbī*, in *ibid.*, 480-8.

2. Bactrian was the Middle Iranian language of ancient Bactria with its capital Bactra, later Balkh [*q.v.*]. Bactrian is generally reckoned as an Eastern Iranian language, but it is now becoming clear that it has almost as much in common with Western Iranian, especially Parthian, as with Eastern Iranian languages such as Sogdian and Choresmian (Khʷārazmian).

Unlike other Middle Iranian languages, Bactrian was usually written in the Greek script, a legacy of the conquest of Bactria by Alexander the Great. It is chiefly known from short inscriptions on coins and seals from Afghānistān and the north-west of the Indian sub-continent; a few more substantial monumental inscriptions (mostly found in Afghānistān, but also in the neighbouring areas of Uzbekistan and Pakistan); a handful of manuscript fragments from Chinese Turkistan (Xinjiang), including a unique folio in Manichaean script; and a recently-discovered group of more than 150 documents, including letters, legal and economic documents and a couple of fragmentary Buddhist texts, most of which appear to originate from the principality of Rōb (al-Ṭabarī's Ru'b, modern Rūī in the northern Hindūkush). These documents now form by far the largest part of the surviving corpus of Bactrian, so that all surveys of the material written before they began to come to light in the 1990s must be regarded as seriously out of date.

The earliest Bactrian inscriptions date from the 1st to the 2nd centuries A.D., when Bactria was the centre of the Kushān empire, the latest to the 3rd/9th century. The documents belong to the intervening period, from the 4th century A.D. to the 2nd/8th century, during which time Bactria was subject to a succession of foreign rulers: the Sāsānid dynasty of Iran, the Chionites, Hephthalites (Arabic *Hayṭāl* [see HAYĀṬILA]), Turks and finally Arabs. By the middle of the 2nd/8th century, the area was substantially under Muslim control. Some of the latest Bactrian documents refer to the use of "Arab silver dirhams" and to taxes payable to the Arabs (the word used being *Tāžīg*), while the very last (dated in the year 549 of the local era, probably corresponding to 164/781) seems to have been written by a Muslim ruler, who prefaces the text with a Bactrian version of the *bismillāh*.

A number of Bactrian words and titles are cited by Muslim writers, who refer to the language as *al-balkhiyya* (the language of Balkh) or *al-ṭukhāriyya* (the language of Ṭukhāristān [*q.v.*], a term commonly used in Islamic sources but first attested in two Bactrian documents of the Hephthalite period, *ca.* 6th century A.D.). A list of Bactrian month-names is found in some manuscripts of al-Bīrūnī's *Chronology*, for example, though this does not seem to have the authority of al-Bīrūnī himself (see N. Sims-Williams and F. de Blois, *The Bactrian calendar*, in *Bull. of the Asia Institute*, x [1996 (1998)], 149-65).

Bibliography: N. Sims-Williams, *New light on ancient Afghanistan: the decipherment of Bactrian*, London 1997; idem, *From the Kushan-shahs to the Arabs. New Bactrian documents dated in the era of the Tochi inscriptions*, in *Coins, art and chronology. Essays on the pre-Islamic history of the Indo-Iranian borderlands*, ed. M. Alram and D.E. Klimburg-Salter, Vienna 1999, 245-58; idem, *Bactrian documents from Northern Afghanistan. I. Legal and economic documents*, Oxford 2000. (N. SIMS-WILLIAMS)

(f) New Persian.

i. General introduction: definition, position, periodisation, denominations
ii. History of the language, scripts
iii. Phonology, grammar, word formation, vocabulary
iv. History of grammar writing: Western-type and indigenous
  1. Studies on Persian in Europe
  2. Persian grammars by indigenous authors

i. *General introduction*

1. Definition

New Persian is the name given by Western scholars to the language written in modified Arabic script, which has been used roughly in the past millennium, from the 9th century A.D. up to the present day, that is, historically, in the Islamic period of the Persian-speaking population. Geographically, it was first spoken in western Iran, with the south-western province Pārs or Fārs (Arabicised form; Lat. Persis) acting as a centre in mediaeval times. However, the bulk of its earliest literary documents (9th-10th centuries) originated from the north-east (Khurāsān, including Nīshāpūr, Marw, Harāt, etc.) and Central Asia; but from the late 10th century, it became the literary language in Western Iran as well. In the subsequent centuries, parallel with the Islamisation of the neighbouring countries, Persian as a language of culture, administration and everyday communication dominated vast territories ranging from Anatolia to the Indian subcontinent (North India), including Transoxania and Afghānistān, developing various written and spoken standards and dialects. Shortly after its emergence, Classical Persian became the culturally-dominant language of the area in question. Its latest representative, Modern Persian, called *Fārsī* by native speakers, with its closely related dialects and variations is spoken by approximately 50 million people as their mother tongue or their second standard languae. Today, Modern Persian is the official language of Iran, spoken as a mother tongue by 50% of the population (*ca.* 30 million). Its closest relatives are *Tādjīkī* [*q.v.*], the official language of Tādjīkistān, written in modified Cyrillic script, and Afghān or Kābulī *Darī* [*q.v.*], the second official language after *Pashto* (which was declared to be the first in 1936) [see AFGHĀN. ii] in Afghānistān (*ca.* 5 million) and, in Central Asia, in the modern republics of the former Soviet Union (*ca.* 5 million). These three languages, Modern Persian, *Tādjīkī* and *Darī*, regard Classical Persian as their common ancestor with which unbroken continuity is supposed to have been maintained. Therefore the latter two are sometimes described as the varieties or dialects of Persian (see G. Lazard, *Le persan*, in *Compendium linguarum iranicarum* (= *CLI*), ed. R. Schmitt, Wiesbaden 1989, 289; J. Wei, *Dialectal differences between three standard varieties of Persian, Teheran, Kabul, and Tajik*, Center for Applied Linguistics of the Modern Language Association of America, Washington D.C. 1962; G.L. Windfuhr, *Persian*, in *The world's major languages*, ed. B. Comrie, London and Sidney 1987, 523). Small segregated Persian-speaking communities can be found in neighbouring multilingual areas as well.

2. The position of New Persian among the New Iranian languages

New Persian is a member of the South Western group of the New Iranian languages within the Indo-Iranian branch of the Indo-European language family. From among the Western New Iranian languages (e.g. Kurdish dialects, Balōčī, etc.) New Persian is the major representative, sharing a series of phonological and grammatical features with them while also exhibiting innovations. See, for instance, the preservation of the Old Iranian initial voiced plosives *b, d, g* both in the South-West Iranian New Persian *birādar* < Middle Persian *brādar* < Old Iranian **brātar-* "brother" and in the North-West Iranian Balōčī *brāt* vs. Eastern Middle Iranian Sogdian *βr't* and Eastern New Iranian Pashto *wror* (cf. D.N. MacKenzie, *Pashto*, in Comrie, *op. cit.*, 548). New Persian is the only New Iranian language which is documented in all three of its historical periods (Old, Middle and New Persian), displaying various local dialects as well. After an approximately two-century period of cultural and linguistic dominance of Arabic between the collapse of the Sāsānid empire (7th century) and the emergence of a new literary Persian language (*ca.* mid-9th century), it became the culturally dominant language in subsequent centuries. Its first documents appeared in the eastern provinces after its having supplanted Middle Persian and Arabic in the written medium and other Middle Western and Eastern Iranian languages such as Parthian in Khurāsān, and Sogdian, Bactrian and Khʷārazmian in Transoxanian (cf. Lazard, *The rise of the New Persian language*, in *CHIr*, iv, Cambridge 1975, 595-632).

Genetically, New Persian derives from Middle Persian, although not without breaks in the continuum. Geographically, the two preceding phases, Old Persian and Middle Persian, are linked to the regions of the southwest of Iran (i.e. the province of Pārs), while New Persian appears to have emerged first as a language of literature in the East. Typologically, however, the differences between Old Persian and Middle Persian are very considerable (especially in phonology and grammar), but less so between Middle Persian and New Persian (see H. Jensen, *Neupersische Grammatik*, Heidelberg 1931, 4; Lazard 1975, 596; idem, *Les modes de la virtualité en moyen-iranien occidental*, in *Middle Iranian studies*, ed. W. Skalmowski and A. van Tongerloo, Leuven 1984, 1-13). The changes concerned mainly the exponents of inflectional morphology which induced alterations in the language type. Old Persian, like many other old Indo-European (Greek, Latin) and Indo-Iranian (Sanskrit, Avestan) languages, was inflectional, while Middle and New Persian became a language of a mixed type displaying less inflectional and more agglutinative characteristics. That is to say, grammatical categories earlier expressed by inflection and conjugation were partially preserved, even though with significant restructuring in the verbal paradigm, but some of them were completely abandoned (see W. Sundermann, *Westmitteliranische Sprachen*, in *CLI*, 110-11). In nominal morphology, for instance, the old case system was supplanted by new ways of expressing grammatical categories such as by pre- and postpositions, *iḍāfa* structure or word order, supposedly due, among other factors, to stress placement. As a result, analytic structures began to be dominant in New Persian morphology, while inherited Old Iranian synthetic structures came to be gradually, but not completely, abandoned. Simultaneously, the vocabulary incorporated a large number of northwestern and eastern Iranian elements (see W. Lentz, *Die nordiranischen Elemente in der neupersischen Literatursprache bei Firdosi*, in *Zeitschrift für Indologie und Iranistik*, iv [1926], 251-316, and W.B. Henning, *Sogdian loan words in New Persian*, in *BSOAS*, x [1939-42], 93-106) and, in increasing proportion, Arabic lexical items. More recently, there has been considerable borrowing from various Turkic languages and neologisms from such Western languages as French, English and Russian.

3. Periodisation

New Persian, which spans more than a thousand years, has undergone considerable changes. Persian as it appears today is markedly different from the language of the classical authors, displaying considerable variations in both the spoken and written standards. Traditionally, the periods of Persian, especially those of its written variants, are linked to the alternation of the ruling dynasties (cf. Old Persian as the official language of the Achaemenids in the 6th-4th centuries B.C., or Middle Persian, the language of the Sāsānids in the 3rd-7th centuries, and further used by the Zoroastrian clergy in religious writings in the 8th-10th centuries; see J. de Menasce, *Zoroastrian literature after the Muslim conquest*, in *CHIr*, iv, 543-65.). Similarly, the emergence of New Persian is connected with the fall of the Sāsānid empire and the Arab conquest. The transition periods, however, appear to be the most tangible if they are accompanied by a change in the writing system, or in close connection with it, a change in faith. Nevertheless, neither Middle Persian and New Persian nor the various stages of the last thousand years' history of New Persian in the Islamic era can easily be separated. It is well known from the more recent periods of Persian how much written and spoken varieties can differ from each other. Certain spoken forms were used in Persian for centuries without being incorporated in the literary language, or else they were taken over with a certain delay, sometimes centuries later, under social pressure, as a result of literary and political movements. As a consequence, the various linguistic stages can only be set up *post hoc* and always with a certain degree of idealisation and oversimplification. This is the more so since the transmission of all ancient texts was very uncertain because the copyists often "normalised" them by introducing or abolishing archaisms and dialecticisms. Consequently, the actual use of the language, which must have been marked by individual features and plenty of idiosyncrasies, often fails to be accounted for.

According to generally accepted views, after its emergence in the spoken registers (*ca.* 7th-9th centuries) New Persian is divided into Early Classical (9th-12th centuries), Classical Persian (from the 13th century on), and Modern Persian (from the 19th century on), which is supposed to be based on the local dialect of Tehran. Windfuhr provides a classification into five periods such as "formative" (7th-10th centuries), "heroic" (10th-12th centuries), "classical" (13th-15th centuries), "post-classical" (15th-19th centuries) and finally "contemporary" Persian, following a predominantly literary periodisation (*Persian grammar. History and state of its study*, The Hague 1979, 166).

Other views, found especially in former Soviet studies written in Russian, ascribe the splitting of Classical Persian into three new, closely related literary languages such as the Modern Persian of Iran (*Fārsī*) and Afg̲h̲ān (or Kābulī) *Darī* and *Tād̲j̲īkī* to the beginning of the 16th century when the disintegration of the earlier common classical heritage and the first steps towards developing new local standards might have begun (see L.S. Peysikov, *Problema yazîka daru v trudak̲h̲ sovremennîk̲h̲ iranskik̲h̲ učonnîk̲h̲*, in *Voprosî yazîkoznaniya* 1960, 120-5; V.A. Yefimov, V.S. Rastorgueva and Y.N. S̲h̲arova, *Persidskiy, tad̲j̲ikskiy, dari* in *Osnovî iranskogo yazîkoznaniya* (= *OIY*); *Novoiranskiye yazîki, zapadnaya gruppa*, eds. V.A. Abaev, M.N. Bogolyubov, V.S. Rastorgueva, 1982, 7 *Tād̲j̲īkī*, by I. Steblin-Kamensky; Zs. Telegdi, *Beiträge zur historischen Grammatik des Neupersischen. I. Über die Partikelkomposition im Neupersischen*, in *Acta Linguistica Academiae Scientiarum Hungaricae*, v [1955], 68 n. 1). In earlier Soviet publications the denomination "klassičeskiy persidsko-(dari-)-tad̲j̲ikskiy" (*OIY* 1982, 20) or simply "*Tajik*" (Rastorgueva, *A short sketch of Tajik grammar*, Bloomington, Ind. 1963, 1) was used to refer to the common origin, claiming an unbroken continuity with the Classical Persian language and literature (*OIY*, 1982, 9, 13). Another periodisation marks off the last (19th-20th) centuries, when the emergence of the three modern languages was supposed to have begun (A. Pisowicz, *Origins of the New and Middle Persian phonological systems*, Cracow 1985, 9 n. 1; Lazard 1989, 289). The divergent opinions on the periodisation can be attributed to the different ways of evaluating spoken and written forms. The new written varieties, *Darī* and *Tād̲j̲īkī*, are obviously based on ancient local spoken dialects (Lazard, *La langue des plus anciens monuments de la prose persane*, Paris 1963, 15), but the characteristic features of these dialects were first observed in written media only in the last century (see W. Geiger, *Bemerkungen über das Tādschikī*, in *Grundriss der iranischen Philologie* (= *GIPh*), ed. W. Geiger and E. Kuhn, Strassburg 1895-1904, i, 2, 407-8; I.M. Oranskij, *Die neuiranischen Sprachen der Sowjetunion*, The Hague 1975, i, 22; A. Farhâdi, *Le persan parlé en Afghanistan: grammaire du Kâboli*, Paris 1955, 2; L.N. Dorofeeva, *Yazîk farsi-kabuli*, Moscow 1960, 9-10). Meanwhile, the overall cultural dominance of Persian, both as a common *Hofsprache* and as a spoken language continued also to prevail in the former Persian-speaking area.

4. Denominations

As the periodisation indicates, the division between the classical language and its modern continuations presents peculiar difficulties, reflected in the denominations of Persian in Western scholarship and in the native tradition. The two main varieties of New Persian are generally called Classical and Modern Persian in the West with further subdivisions into diachronic, local and style or register variants. In linguistic literature, both scientific and popular, New Persian is sometimes called Modern Persian (e.g. J. Darmesteter, *Études iraniennes*, 2 vols., Paris 1883; H. Paper, in *Current Trends in Linguistics* (= *CTL*), vi [1970], Introduction, or Windfuhr 1979, 7) vs. contemporary Persian or contemporary colloquial or Neo-Persian (see F. de Blois in *Persian literature. A bio-bibliographical survey begun by the late C.A. Storey* (= *PL*), v, part 1, London 1992, part 2, 1994 or in French, néopersan (Lazard 1989, 263). Native speakers use the name *Pārsī* or its Arabicised form, *Fārsī*, or both, without distinction (see M.T. Bahār, *Sabk-s̲h̲ināsī ya taṭawwur-i nat̲h̲r-i fārsī*, [2]Tehran 1337/1958, i, 2), denoting all varieties of New Persian. In scholarly publications, the denomination *fārsī-i bāstānī* vs. *fārsī-i naw* distinguishing an "old archaic" and a "new" variety of [New] Persian, can also be found in Iran (see *Lug̲h̲at-nāma* (= *LN*) by Dihk̲h̲udā). *Fārsī* is the name of the official language of today's Iran, which has come to be used as an equivalent of Modern Persian, or simply Persian in modern text and grammar books outside Iran as well (A.K.S. Lambton, *Persian grammar*, Cambridge 1967, p. xi n. 1; D. Crystal, *The Cambridge encyclopedia of language*, Cambridge 1987, 301; similarly Lazard, *Le persan*, 1989, 263). In native sources the name *Darī* [*q.v.*] or *Fārsī-i darī* is also used, referring to the oldest and most respected variety of the [Classical] literary Persian or, simply as an equivalent of *Pārsī* or *Fārsī*. The speakers of *Tād̲j̲īkī*, which is very closely connected to Persian, use also *Fārsī* to designate their mother tongue (*Fārsīwān, Fārsībān*, or *Fārsī-gū[y]*) *Tād̲j̲īk*.

ii. *History of the language*

I. The emergence of New Persian: *Pahlawī, Pārsī, Darī*

1. *The native tradition*

The complexity of the linguistic situation in Iran is clearly indicated by the wide range of names used for Persian since the time of its emergence, either as common names, synonyms or denominations, with or without clear distinctions being made. Therefore the history of the language starts here with investigations into the early native tradition as a source of language history. The early history of the names applied to the various forms of Persian and the alleged change of their references may elucidate the eclectic use of these denominations in more recent periods and the difficulties of the periodisation of the language history as well. It must be emphasised, though, that the authors of these early Islamic sources who spoke about the varieties of Persian were not linguists but historians, geographers and literary men, in most cases of the last category, poets. Hence the information they gave about the dialects once spoken or still spoken in the age they lived in was more "narrative" than "technical", and it was often embedded in myths with much folklore and obscure details. The picture one can gain from these texts is thus not always clear or coherent. A truly technical treatment of linguistic issues in Iran lies in the distant future.

2. *Mediaeval Arabic and Persian sources on Persian language*

The intricate problems of the transition period between Middle Persian and New Persian (7th-9th centuries) has been extensively treated by G. Lazard in a series of studies based on the analysis of mediaeval Arabic sources, Early and Classical New Persian texts as well as Persian and non-Persian dialects (see the summary in *La formation de la langue persane*, Paris 1995). One of the earliest sources mentioning the names *Pahlawī*, *Pārsī* and *Darī*, which denoted the languages used in Iran at the end of the Sāsānid period, was attributed to Ibn al-Muḳaffaʿ (d. 757 [*q.v.*]) by Ibn al-Nadīm (d. 987) in his *Fihrist* and repeated by K͟hʷārazmī (d. 985), and by Yāḳūt (d. 1229) through Ḥamza al-Iṣfahānī (d. 970) (see Bahār 1958, i, 19; Lazard, *Pahlavi, Pârsi, Dari. Les langues de l'Iran d'après Ibn al-Muqaffaʿ*, in *Iran and Islam. In memory of the late Vladimir Minorsky*, ed. C.E. Bosworth, Edinburgh 1971, 361-91; idem, art. *Darī* in *EIr*, vii, 1994, 34-5). These descriptions continued to be repeated by Persian lexicographers until the 19th century, albeit with certain modifications (cf. É.M. Jeremiás, *Pahlavī, Pārsī and Darī in Persian lexicography*, in *Acta Ant. Hung.*, xxxviii [1998], 175-83).

In the following, some shifts in the meanings of these terms will be shown through some characteristic passages quoted from this native tradition. After talking about *Pahlawī* as the language of Fahla (i.e. the ancient Media) the earliest informant, Ibn al-Muḳaffaʿ, says that *Darī* is "the language of the cities of Madāʾin; it is spoken by those who are at the king's court. [Its name] is connected with presence at court. Among the languages of the people of Khorasan and the east, the language of the people of Balk͟h is predominant." He continues on to say that *Pārsī* is "the language spoken by the *mowbeds* (priests), scholars and the like; it is the language of the people of Fārs" (translated by Lazard in his art. *Darī*, 34). This rather incoherent description can be better elucidated by Arabic and Persian sources originating from the subsequent (10th-11th) centuries, e.g. al-Masʿūdī and al-Muḳaddasī or Firdawsī, Balʿamī, Ḥakīm Maysarī, Kaykāwūs b. Iskandar, etc. As evidenced by these texts, the denominations *Pahlawī*, *Pārsī* and *Darī* may have changed their references to varying degrees during the first centuries of the Islamic era, denoting various written and spoken varieties depending on the text where they appeared. Accordingly, *Pahlawī* or *Pahlawānī* (literally meaning "Parthian" originating from Pahlaw < Parthava "Parthia"), appears to have referred at one time to Parthian and Middle Persian but also to the local dialect of the northern region called Fahla in an Arabicised form (see the poems written in this dialect and called *Fahlawiyya*, cf. *EIr*, ix, 158 and the most recent publications on this topic in *Mad͟jalla-i zabāns͟hināsī*, xv [1379/2000], no. 1). *Pārsī*, "the ancient language" first denoted Middle Persian (*Pārsīg*) as described by Ibn al-Muḳaffaʿ, but with a shift of meaning it came to mean New Persian and has continued to denote New Persian of whatever kind until today (see *LN*, art. *Pārsī/Fārsī*). *Darī* (etymologically, "belonging to the royal court") also denoted the Persian language which was supposed to be spoken both in the capital of the Sāsānid empire (Ctesiphon) and in the East. It was the name of the language of literature which appeared in the eastern part of Iran, sc. K͟hurāsān, and has been used in Persian texts since the 10th century. All the quotations in Arabic sources attributed to Persian kings or their subjects were thought to have been in *Darī* (cf. Bahār 1957, i, 19) and the language of all the ancient texts was called *Darī* or *Pārsī-i Darī* (Lazard 1989, 264), sometimes contrasted with *Pahlawī* when the latter denoted Middle Persian or *Pārsī* (Lazard 1994). The expression *Pārsī-i Darī* (in Arabic *al-fārsiyya al-dariyya*) indicates that occasionally, it might have been distinguished from *Pārsī* as a special variety, the *Darī* form of *Pārsī* (e.g. al-Muḳaddasī and Kaykāwūs b. Iskandar, *ca.* 1082-83; cf. Lazard 1994, 34). Other than that, it was often used as a synonym for *Pārsī*. The expression *Pārsī u Darī* (in the *S͟hāh-nāma* by Firdawsī, ed. Moscow, viii, 254) seems to be a "distortion" (see P.N. K͟hānlarī, *Tārīk͟h-i zabān-i fārsī*, 3 vols., new ed. Tehran 1365/1986, i, 273).

In his earlier studies, G. Lazard explained the linguistic situation of the post-Sāsānid period by contrasting *Pārsī* and *Darī* as the written and spoken form of the same language. According to his interpretation, it was the spoken language that spread to the eastern region, as Ibn al-Muḳaffaʿ's report suggested, after having gradually supplanted the local dialects (e.g. Parthian). As a spoken variety, it was supposed to have been used in the whole empire, but it was in K͟hurāsān that it was first used for literary purposes and became the new literary language of the subsequent centuries.

3. *Early dialectal sources (8th-11th centuries): the evidence of Judaeo-Persian texts*

Recently published sources on local dialects and on the Judaeo-Persian texts, however, have helped throw new light on the linguistic situation and the rise of the new literary language in the first centuries of the Islamic era, as described earlier (Lazard, *Lumières nouvelles sur la formation de la langue persane: une traduction du Coran en persan dialectal et ses affinités avec le judéo-persan*, in *Irano-Judaica*, ii, ed. Sh. Shaked and A. Netzer, Jerusalem 1990, 184-98 = 1995, 107-21). A manuscript discovered in Mas͟hhad which contained an anonymous and undated Ḳurʾān translation (*Ḳurʾān-i Ḳuds, kuhantarīn bargardān-i Ḳurʾān ba fārsī*, ed. ʿA. Rawāḳī, Tehran 1362/1984) was written in a local dialect of Sīstān in the 11th century, as supposed by Lazard. This text shares a series of dialectal features with Judaeo-Persian texts (mainly Bible translations and paraphrases), and both show common peculiarities with Middle Persian, mainly regarding words and certain morphological features. The properties which the two sources share are unknown in literary New Persian, which induced Lazard to develop a new hypothesis that at the beginning of the Islamic period "there were important differences between the common language spoken in the south and that in use in the north. The former, as represented by literary Middle Persian, retained most of its ancient forms; the latter evolved from the same Persian language, which had spread throughout the north, but evinced the influence of the dialects that it had supplanted there, particularly Parthian. It thus diverged noticeably from the original form. Both were called *Pārsī* (Persian), but it is very likely that the language of the north, that is, the Persian used on former Parthian territory and also in the Sasanian capital, was distinguished from its congener by a new name, *Darī* ([language] of the court). It was only natural that several centuries later, literary Persian, based on the speech of the Northeast, bore the same name" (1994, 35; see also 1989, 263 n. 1).

This hypothetical reconstruction might be extended in the future by investigating other Persian sources as well, the text editions of which are far from being completed, and these may help clarify some more details. True, there are other interpretations also. For instance, K͟hānlarī has developed the (unlikely) hypothesis, relying on al-Muḳaddasī's report (10th century), that *Darī*, the chancery language of Buk͟hārā, had been transported there from the royal court of the Sāsānids by the state officials (1986, i, 280-1).

4. *More recent native sources on the languages of Iran: lexicography and grammar from the 17th-19th centuries*

Extensive descriptions of the languages used in Iran, like those of Ibn al-Muḳaffaʿ and his compatriots, can only be found much later, in the huge Hindustānī lexicographic compilations written in and after the 17th century. These works, of which the most famous are the *Farhang-i D̲j̲ahāngīrī* (= *FD̲j̲*), 1608-9, ed. R. ʿAfīfī, Mas͟hhad 1351/1972; *Burhān-i ḳāṭiʿ* (= *BḲ*), 1652, ed. M. Muʿīn, Tehran 1341/1962; and *Farhang-i Ras͟hīdī* (= *FR*), 1654, ed. M. ʿAbbāsī, Tehran 1337/1958 (see ḲĀMŪS. 2. Persian lexicography), partly preserved the old heritage and partly added some more information on language varieties, grammar, style of letter writing, etc. These accounts about the grammar, dialects, history and vocabulary of Persian, which occasionally bear witness to fantasy at work, were collected in chapters and placed as an introductory part to the *farhangs*, serving as a kind of grammatical introduction. The very first chapters usually dealt with the varieties of Persian (*Pārsī*) which were supposed to be of seven *gūna* "species": four of them (*harawī, sagzī, zāwulī* and *sug͟hdī*) were regarded as obsolete (*matrūk*), in which "letter, book and verse cannot be written" (*FD̲j̲* 15; *FR* 46) and three others as currently used (*mutadāwil*), these being *Darī, Pahlawī* and *Pārsī*. Apart from the suprising fact that these languages were treated as the variations of *Pārsī* still in living use in Iran in the 17th century (e.g. *Pārsī* was described as the common language of Iran, with Iṣṭak͟hr as its capital), they covered slightly or markedly different notions as compared to earlier sources, but also contained ideas similar to those found in the first grammatical compilations that relied heavily on lexicography, e.g. ʿAbd al-Wāsiʿ Hānsawī's *Risāla* from 18th-century India (lith. Kānpūr 1872) or Irawānī's *Ḳawāʿid* (lith. [Tabrīz] 1262/1846; see Jeremiás, *Tradition and innovation in the native grammatical literature of Persian*, in *Histoire, Épistémologie, langage* (Paris), xv [1993], 51-68). The three denominations were treated fairly consistently in these recent sources, differences existing only in detail, emphasis and arrangement. In comparison with older sources, however, the authors of these compilations did not bother to reconcile the most contradictory and fabulous accounts in the description of the single languages; they simply quoted them as differing opinions on the same subject (e.g. on *Darī*: "some said that it was spoken in Bal͟kh, Marw, Buk͟hārā, Badak͟hs͟hān . . ., but according to others it was spoken in the Kayānian court, and then there were those who regarded it as the purest, unmixed language" (see *FR* 47; *FD̲j̲* 16; *BḲ* 20, 500). Entirely new motives also appeared in these descriptions: one was something like "ideological", and another might be called a "linguistic argument". Both concerned the reputation of Persian among the languages spoken by Islamic peoples. The eminence of Persian as the second language after Arabic was illustrated by various stories and supported by a *tafsīr* [*q.v.*] called *Daylamī* with the intention of symbolising the role of *Pārsī* as a common language in the whole empire (*BḲ* 500; Irawānī, fol. 4b, see Jeremiás 1998, 181). The superiority or dignity of the Islamic languages like Arabic, Persian or Ottoman Turkish appears to have been a matter of debate since the 15th century, enthusiastically treated by Mīr ʿAlī S͟hīr Nawāʾī and Kemāl Pas͟ha-zāda [*q.vv.*] (see R. Brunschvig, *Kemâl Pâshâzâde et le persan*, in *Mélanges d'orientalisme offerts à Henri Massé*, Tehran 1963, 48-64 (= *Études d'islamologie*, Paris 1976, i, 379-95); B.G. Fragner, *Mīr ʿAlī Shēr Navāʾī: the "Judgement" reconsidered*, in *Irano-Turkic cultural contacts in the 11th-17th centuries*, ed. É. Jeremiás, Budapest 2002; idem, *Die "Persophonie". Regionalität, Identität and Sprachkontakt in der Geschichte Asiens*, in *Anor*, v, Halle-Berlin 1999).

This linguistic argument was even more clearly spelled out in the 17th-century lexicography where *Darī* was treated. The compilators declared that "*Darī* is the language in which there is no deficiency (*nuḳṣānī*)" (see *FD̲j̲*, 16; *FR* 47; *BḲ*, 20). The idea of *nuḳṣānī* seemed to denote something missing from the "authorised" (*ṣaḥīḥ*) word form. As examples, the authors quoted two lists of doublets: nouns with the same meaning, but written with or without the initial *alif*, which represented the vocalic onset, e.g. *abris͟hum/baris͟hum* "silk", *ispīd/sapīd* or *sipīd* 'white', *is͟hkam/s͟hikam* "belly", *us͟htur/s͟hutur* "camel" etc. and imperative verbal forms with or without the verbal prefix *bi-*, e.g. *bi-raw/raw* "go"; *bi-šnaw/šnaw* "listen", etc. According to the commentary, the "defective" words are not correct *Darī* forms. The sources say almost unanimously that Persian is regarded as "correct, uncorrupted" (*faṣīḥ*) only if there is no *nuḳṣānī* in it.

This very peculiar interpretation of *Darī* goes back to the traditional treatment of lexical and grammatical doublets based on a peculiar analysis of the (morphological) structure of the word. Ancient lexicographers and prosodists listed all the so-called "meaningful letters" (*ḥurūf-i maʿānī*) occurring in different positions in the word, first at the end where rhymes appeared (see S͟hams-i Ḳays's rhyme science in *al-Muʿd̲j̲am fī maʿāyīr as͟hʿār al-ʿad̲j̲am*, ed. Mudarris Raḍawī, [2]Tehran 1338/1959, in the 13th century), and later, as an extension of this practice, at the beginning and in the middle of the word. The technical terms denoting the base (*aṣlī*) and the extension (*waṣlī* or *zāʾid*), were borrowed from the Arabic grammatical and literary tradition, but they were adapted to Persian with a special connotation. *Aṣlī* denoted the base which always appeared as a word, while *zāʾid* marked any additional element, mainly inflectional and derivational morphemes attached to this base form. Later, the term *zāʾid* came to be used in a somewhat different meaning in lexicography denoting any letter which was added to or removed from the base form without changing its meaning (cf. Jeremiás, *Zāʾid and aṣl in early Persian prosody*, in *JSAI*, xxi [1997], 167-86). All the sources from the 17th century seemed to agree that these doublets were used only in poetry as required by prosody but never in common speech. However, talking about *Darī*, the author of *FR* (47) added that the "defective" forms were also used in towns, by which he probably meant that these forms were used both in poetry and the spoken idiom. The problem with the doublets of the imperative forms is somewhat different. Imperative forms may appear with or without the verbal prefix *bi-* in literary texts. But it was obligatory for the imperative in genuine *ṣaḥīḥ darī* forms, as Shams-i Ḳays remarked (232). Prestigious authors such as Niʿmat Allāh (*ca.* 1540, cf. A.M. Piemontese, *Catalogo dei manoscritti persiani conservati nelle bibliotheche d'Italia*, Rome 1989, no. 403, fol. 296) or even earlier, Muḥammad b. Hindūshāh Nakhčiwānī [*q.v.*], the author of *Ṣiḥāḥ al-Furs* (1328), seems to share this opinion (cf. *ā* ["come" imperat.] *ba-maʿnī dar-ā wa bi-yā'*, ed. ʿA. Ṭāʿatī, Tehran 1341/1962, 19). Moreover, *BḲ* and *FDj* make a clear distinction between the two functions of the verbal prefix *bi-*: it was regarded as obligatory in the imperative but obsolete in past forms, where it was used as embellishment. This usage may have indicated a change in the language (see below, on grammar). In more recent native sources, however, this distinction seems to have become dimmed and the verbal prefix *bi-*, in both present and past forms, was called *zā'id* in most cases, that is, an element which only has an aesthetic function (cf. *FR*, 15; Hānsawī, 3; Irawānī, fol. 22b). This topic was also dealt with by Irawānī (1846), who used a strange "linguistic" argument proving the eminence of Persian against other Islamic languages; this argument rests on its [grammatical] simplicity: there is no *iʿrāb*, no dual and no feminine gender which would make the language difficult for beginners, says Irawānī (fol. 3b).

These scattered references on language and its different variations may help one to draw the following conclusions. It seems to be a *communis opinio* that from the very beginnings the most highly respected literary variety of Persian was called *Darī* in indigenous sources, sometimes as an extension, and sometimes as an equivalent of *Pārsī* or *Fārsī*, and this view continued to prevail in subsequent centuries. More recent sources, however, tend to talk about the "rules of *Pārsī*" or *Fārsī* (see Niʿmat Allāh, ʿAbd al-Wāsiʿ Hānsawī, Rawshan ʿAlī Djawnpūrī, Irawānī, Tālaḳānī, Ḥabīb Iṣfahānī, to mention only a few, cf. the references in *PL*, iii/1, 1984, 123ff.). But despite this preference for the name *Darī* in older sources, the denominations *Pārsī*, *Fārsī* or *Fārsī-i Darī* or *Darī* seem to have been used almost interchangeably. One must not forget that these eclectic sources did not use well-defined terms when they talked about language. On the contrary, literary persons (*ahl-i zabān*) usually thought of the language in terms of "ancient" or "modern" and "common (spoken)" or "dialectal" forms. The reason for that was quite obvious: there was no grammatical tradition in Persian, "no exact norm (*miḳyās*) of the rules (*ḳawānīn*) of Persian (*Darī*) on the basis of which the correct (*ṣaḥīḥ*) and corrupt (*fāsid*) usage could be defined and on which one could rely when defining what was right (*ṣawāb*) and wrong (*khaṭā*) in Persian speech (*kalām-i Pārsī*), to which one could turn in case of need", thus noted by Shams-i Ḳays in the 13th century (*op. cit.*, 205) and repeated almost word for word by Shams-i Fakhrī in the 14th century (*Lexicon persicum id est libri Miʿyâr i G'amâlî pars quarta*, ed. C. Salesmann, Kazan 1887, 3) and the author of *FDj* in the 17th century (4). But even if writers were unaware of the fine grammatical distinctions of social or historical dimensions, they must have had some knowledge of the differences between the usage of the "ancient" (*mutaḳaddimīn*) and "modern" (*muta'akhkhirīn*) poets (see Shams-i Ḳays, 208-9) or of the language of literary or common speech (*muḥāwarāt-i pārsī*, in *FDj* 40; *BḲ* 26; Ḥabīb Iṣfahānī, *Dastūr-i sukhan*, [Istanbul] 1289, 54) or poetry and prose (see ʿAbd al-Wāsiʿ Hānsawī, 41; Ḥabīb Iṣfahānī, 15). Scattered hints at some "virtual" norm in Shams's poetic manual, which never came to be institutionalised, or the lists of doublets and denominations such as *Furs-i ḳadīm* (*FDj* 8; *FR* 47), *Pārsī-i bāstānī* (*FDj* 4; *BḲ* 500) in lexicography might serve as proofs (cf. Jeremiás, *Grammar and linguistic consciousness in Persian*, in *Proceedings of the Third European Conference of Iranian Studies*, ii, ed. C. Melville, Wiesbaden 1999, 19-31). The literary model was but the poets' use of the language, which was far from being uniform. This discrepancy between linguistic and literary norms may be the very reason for the lack of clarity and the contradictions in the sources (see the definition of *Darī* in *LN*: *zabān-i fārsī-i rasmī-i maʿmūl-i imrūza* "the official Persian language used today"), which makes the separation of *Fārsī* and *Darī* almost impossible. Paradoxically, however, the lack of a strictly regulated norm preserved more of the linguistic reality of the previous periods in comparison with the Arabic grammatical literature which often dealt with an idealised construct which differed considerably from actual speech (see K. Versteegh, *Landmarks in linguistic thought. III. The Arabic linguistic tradition*, London 1997, 156).

II. The impact of Arabic

With a few exceptions (see below, V. Scripts, 2), all the sources discussed above were written in the Perso-Arabic script (the earliest manuscript dates from the beginning of the 10th century, cf. L.P. Elwell-Sutton, *Arabic influences in Persian literature*, in *EIr*, ii, 233-7). It was not only the script that was taken over, but Arabic became the medium of written expression, both in administration, science and literature in the eastern areas (Khurāsān and Transoxania) in the first two centuries after the Muslim conquest. As a consequence, the supreme dominance of the Arabic language and culture almost completely supplanted Persian in the written medium during this period. Even though the western part of Iran preserved longer the ancient culture, as the Pahlawī writings from the 9th-10th centuries attest, the knowledge of the "old" language, that is, Middle Persian, and its insurmountable script was a privilege of a few. However, Persian was never abandoned but was allowed to thrive in the spoken idiom and from the mid-9th century in the East, and from the end of the 10th century in the West, it began to regain its position in culture and literature (cf. IRAN. v. History (a)). Moreover, Persian not only survived as a spoken idiom, and began to appear in the written documents, but was also imported by Muslim conquerors into further eastern areas, unlike the other territories of the caliphate, and a considerable proportion of the Arab population which had settled in the towns of Iran were assimilated rapidly. In the subsequent centuries, in Transoxania, Afghānistān, North India (and later also westwards to Anatolia), Persian became the main literary language.

But this new literary language, which is called New Persian and was based on the spoken variety of the East, showed essentially new characteristics due to the impact of Arabic and the culture imported by this language. Despite the Persians' increasing national identity, Arabic as the language of science became gradually adopted and cultivated by a growing number of significant scholars of Iranian origin (cf. C.E. Bosworth, *The political and dynastic history of the Iranian world (A.D. 1000-1217)*, in *CHIr*, v, 4). Contemporaneously, models of Arabic scientific thinking began to be adapted to Persian. The sphere of literature adduces a good example of this development: although Iranians retained and cherished the ancient tradition in mind and memory, as Firdawsī's *Shāh-nāma* shows, Persian poets tried to follow the rules of the Arabic prosody from the early beginnings of New Persian poetry, in sharp contrast to the previous literary canons. As a consequence, the following centuries saw the infiltration of a large number of Arabic loan words into New Persian (*ca.* 30% in the 10th century and 50% in the 12th century: cf. Lazard, *Les emprunts arabes dans la prose persane du Xe au XIIe siècle: aperçu statistique*, in *Revue de l'École nationale des langues orientales*, ii [1965], 53-67; ʿA.A. Ṣādiḳī, *The Arabic element in Persian*, in *EIr*, ii, 229-31). As a result, Persian, as a new literary language "appears to have been from the start a mixed language, based on the Persian dialect but bearing marked traces of other Iranian dialects and infiltrated with Arabic words" (Lazard 1975, 597). This mixed nature of Persian, and the fact that their language is essentially different from those of their neighbours, was well known to the Iranians themselves from the start, as evidenced by the first works in literary sciences (prosody and lexicography), which made a clear distinction between the Arabic and Persian letters, words and word formation in most cases. Moreover, this knowledge subsisted until quite recently in the native tradition (see "the [*fārsī*] language is a mixture of two languages" (*murakkab az du zabān*), writ-ten by Ḥabīb Iṣfahānī, *op. cit.*, preface, 4, in the 19th century).

III. Classical Persian and its variants

The script, religion and literary models (e.g. the new system of versification) are the most decisive characteristics which distinguish the period of New Persian from the previous ones (see also W.B. Henning, *Die Schrift als Symbol der Einheit des Mitteliranischen*, in *Mitteliranisch*, Hdb. d. Or., I, iv, *Iranistik, Linguistik*, Leiden-Köln 1958, 21). Despite its bewildering variety at the outset—Khurāsān and Sīstān especially displayed markedly distinctive features—New Persian appears to have become a surprisingly "unified" literary language after the 13th century (Lazard 1963, 23-4) and continued to be regarded as such during the subsequent centuries, as the common name *Pārsī* indicates. But this was an *apparent homogeneity* which might be attributed to at least two main factors: the highly conservative script, which remained practically unchanged over the last thousand years, and the prestige of Classical Persian literature. Due to its Semitic character, the Arabic script by its very nature disguised changes in the pronunciation of words or in the meaning in most cases of the grammatical morphemes, giving the impression of a static language situation. On the other hand, the general respect and admiration surrounding the classical literature, especially poetry, helped keep the language of the classical authors alive for centuries until fairly recently.

It does not mean, however, that men of letters and scholars were or are not aware how significantly speech and writing differ in Persian (see, for instance, P.N. Khānlarī, *Zabān u lahdja*, in *Dar bāra-i zabān-i fārsī*, Tehran 1340/1961, 75-85; M.R. Bāṭinī, *Tawṣīf-i sākhtimān-i dastūr-i zabān-i fārsī*, Tehran 1348/1969, 11; ʿA.A. Ṣādiḳī, *Zabān-i fārsī wa gunahā-i mukhtalif-i ān*, in *Farhang u zindagī*, ii [1349/1970], 61-6; T. Waḥīdiyān, *Dastūr-i zabān-i ʿāmiyāna-i fārsī*, Tehran 1343/1964). However, the first attempts to include linguistic expressions closer to the colloquial style in text and grammar books (e.g. Ṣādiḳī, and Gh. Arzhang, *Dastūr, Sāl-i duwwum*, Tehran 2535/1976) were received with sharp criticism at first (see M.S. Mawlāʾi, in *Yaghmā*, xxx [2536/1977], 245-51), though it was common experience that the characteristic features of classical and modern standards, even the least formal or vulgar forms, could appear in literature either intermingled in the same work or clearly distinguished. This might also explain why the language is simply called *Fārsī*, that is, "Persian" implying all the variants. The differences between the diachronic ("les formes anciennes" Lazard 1989, 288) and synchronic variants (formal and colloquial standards, local usage or the new literary standards like *Tādjīkī* and Afghān *Darī*) in phonology, grammar and vocabulary came to be described by linguists, although much remains to be done. It must be emphasised, however, that the apparent variations in the grammar of Persian do not always reflect ongoing changes in the language but rather the standardisation process of the literary language. As the formation of the Classical Persian literary language clearly testifies, dialectal or colloquial forms may have disappeared or become incorporated in the written language, occasionally or else in varying degrees, depending on the literary genre. Poetry, for instance, preserved more of the earlier archaic forms, supposedly due to the requirements of prosody, while prose displayed considerable variation in the same genre (see, for instance, the early *tafsīrs*, in Jeremiás, *Some grammatical problems of early New Persian syntax*, in *Proceedings of the second European conference of Iranian studies*, Rome 1995, 325-34). This linguistic diversity was occasionally associated with divergent stylistic values. For instance, some recurrent patterns could be classified either as archaic, dialectal or colloquial or as social variants. This was mainly due to the lack of a firmly established linguistic norm based on a highly respected canon such as the Ḳurʾān in Arabic, on the basis of which the grammar of the language might have been worked out. Paradoxically, this diversity inside Classical Persian or between classical and modern usage, and the maintenance of the classical literary norm, causes difficulties in defining stages in the linguistic history of Persian (see A.V. Rossi, *Sprachübergänge und historische Übergänge in der iranischen Literatur*, in *Transition periods in Iranian history*, Studia Iranica, Cahier 5, 1987).

IV. Modern Persian: spoken and written variants

This phenomenon gives a special status to Persian: the fact that even today, native speakers can understand (though not always in the strictly linguistic sense of the word) ancient texts, and by reading and memorising them they become acquainted with some grammatical characteristics of the ancient language, sometimes dating from a thousand years back. The message of the novels or poems written occasionally (not typically) by modern authors in the style of the ancient language seems to be fully understood (see, for instance, *Parīzād u Parīmān* by Ṣādiḳ Čubak in the collection of short stories, *Čarāgh-i ākhir*, Tehran 1948). In these literary works, the ancient language is imitated by using "classicising" grammatical archaisms like obsolete prepositions or verbal forms. The maintenance of this very formal style as a literary norm has been backed by social institutions: this language was taught in school as the norm of Persian. The same divergence between the newly-arising spoken variant and its acceptance as a literary (written) standard is likely to have existed throughout the modern period, which makes it almost impossible to tell the exact point in time of the beginnings. But Modern Persian, as it appears today, is distinctly different from the classical language, displaying also a wide range of social, dialectal, diachronic and stylistic variations, which are consciously used by authors in most cases. *Style*, therefore, seems to be the most essential factor in the definition of Modern Persian (see C.T. Hodge, *Some aspects of Persian style*, in *Language*, xxxiii [1957], 355-69).

The crucial question is, therefore, in what sense the term Modern Persian is used. It is generally linked with the spoken dialect of Tehran (see ĪRĀN, vii, Literature; J. Towhidi, *Studies in the phonetics and phonology of Modern Persian*, Hamburg 1974; Peysikov 1960; Waḥīdiyān 1964; etc.). This view is a consequence of the periodisation which marks the beginning of the modern period with the rule of the Ḳād̲j̲ār dynasty, with the capital Tehran as a centre from the 19th century onwards. It must be emphasised, however, that, on the one hand, certain typical characteristics of Modern Persian's formal and informal standards began to appear centuries earlier in the written literature and, on the other, some typical colloquialisms can be traced back in other local dialects as well. That is, not all the typical features of Modern Persian can be restricted topographically to Tehran and chronologically to the 19th century, though there are many belonging to them. For instance, from the 15th century on, a set of "archaisms" (e.g. the verbal prefixes *hamī-* instead of *mī-* or *bi-* with past forms such as *bi-guft* and certain preposition like *farā, furū* or the combination of the pre- and postposition *mar . . . . rā*, etc.) were gathered in a separate chapter and labelled as embellishment (*zīnat, taḥsīn*) by native lexicographers (*Lug̲h̲at-i Niʿmat Allāh; FD̲j̲; BḲ; FR*), clearly indicating their archaic character. Similar lists were repeated time and again until recent times in native lexicography and grammar (see ʿAbd al-Wāsiʿ Hānsawī; Irawānī) as well. This shows that native scholars came to realise that grammatical forms such as certain prepositions or verbal forms, abundantly used in ancient texts, had ceased to belong to living usage. They became obsolete and served only as a "decoration" of style for their age (see Telegdi 1955, 134 n. 133; M. Bāḳir, *Bā-i zīnat bar sar-i fiʿl* ("The ornamental verbal prefix bi-"), in *MDATeh*, viii [1961], 1-10; Jeremiás 1993, 63, 1997, 183). Similarly, in some of the earliest descriptions of Persian in the West—though not in all of them—the verbal morpheme *bi-* prefixed to simple past forms was characterised as redundant or pleonastic (W. Jones, *A grammar of the Persian language*, 9London 1828, 49; J. Platts, *A grammar of the Persian language*, London 1894, 174; C. Salemann and V. Shukovski [Žukovskiy], *Persische Grammatik*, Berlin 1889, 60). Beyond doubt, these grammars were intended to describe the language of the Classical texts, but occasionally hints were made at the living usage, which might have differed from the classical forms in many ways. Early evidence for this may be the first collections of Persian and non-Persian spoken local dialects from the last century. Žukovskiy, one of the first dialectologists of Persian patois, immediately recognised the richness of the non-standard Persian local varieties during his first field trip (1883-86) along the Tehran-S̲h̲īrāz-Iṣfahān route. In his materials of Persian and non-Persian dialects, and in those of his later followers such as O. Mann (1901-3, 1906-7), K. Hadank and A. Christensen, a set of characteristic features which are the same or similar to those of the spoken (colloquial) language of Tehran appears. See some examples from the phonology and morphology: (a) *āN* > *u, o* (Žukovskiy, *Materialĭdlya izučeniya persidskikh narečiy*, i, St. Petersburg, 1888, 212; V.W. Geiger, *Kleinere Dialekte und Dialektgruppen*, in *GIPh*, i, 2, 357, 422; K. Hadank, *Die Mundarten von Khunsâr . . .*, in *Kurdisch-Persische Forschungen*, 1926, iii, 1, XXXIX; A. Christensen, *Iranische Dialektaufzeichnungen aus dem Nachlass von F.C. Andreas*, zusammen mit Kaj Barr und W.B. Henning, in *Abhandl. Göttingen*, Phil.-Hist. Kl., Dritte Folge, Nr. 11, 1939, 15; Lambton, *Three Persian dialects*, London 1938, 44; O.I. Smirnova, *Isfakhanskiy govor*, Moscow 1978, 13); (b) the colloquial variations of the verbal personal affixes in Sing. 3. *-ad* > *-e* (*-i, -ē*, etc.) (Geiger in *GIPh*, 411; Mann, *Die Mundart der Mukri Kurden*, in *Kurdisch-Persische Forschungen*, iv, III, 1, 1906, LXXV; idem, Die *Tâjîk-Mundarten der Provinz Fârs*, in *KPF*, i, 1909, 24; Christensen, *op. cit.*, 267), in Pl. 2. *-īd* > *-īn, -ī(t)* and in Pl. 3. *-and* > *-an, -in* (Mann, *op. cit.*, 1909, 25); (c) the progressive verbal forms constructed with the auxiliary *dās̲h̲tan* collected in Iṣfahān in 1885 (see Žukovskiy, *Osobennoe značenie glagola dâs̲h̲tan v persidskom razgovornom yazîke*, in *ZVORAO* iii [1888], 376-77; A.Z. Rozenfel'd, *Vospomogatel'naya funktsiya glagola dās̲h̲tan v sovremennom persidskom yazîke*, in *Sovetskoe Vostokovedeniye*, v ([1948], 305-310) and also used in the Central dialects and Māzandarānī (see the bibl. in Jeremiás, *On the genesis of the periphrastic progressive in Iranian languages*, in *Medioiranica* [1993], 104 n. 10); (d) colloquialisms in the nominal morphology: the omission of the *iḍāfa* vowel (Žukovskiy, 1888, 214) or the determinative morpheme, the stressed suffix *-ā* ~ *ä(h), -e* (Hadank, *op cit.*, 10-13, Christensen, *op. cit.*, 42), etc.

This selection of the relevant features seem to support the opinion that some essential characteristics of Modern Persian, both its literary written form (*fārsī-i kitābī*) and its oral variants (*fārsī-i muḥāwaraʾī*), must have existed centuries earlier. Its modern descriptions, however, are primarily based on the usage as it is written and spoken in Tehran (*fārsī-i ʿāmiyāna*), the present capital of Iran, which is becoming the common spoken standard all over Iran through the modern mass media (cf. Lazard 1989, 289; Pisowicz, 9).

V. Scripts

1. *Perso-Arabic script*

New Persian, including its chronological and dialectal variants used in Iran, Afg̲h̲ānistān and Central Asia (except Tād̲j̲īkī [*q.v.*]) in the 20th century), since the Islamic conquest has been written predominantly with the Arabic script augmented with four modified letters for denoting peculiar Persian phonemes (p پ, ch چ, zh ژ, g گ) which do not exist in Arabic. These "Persian letters" were created from their nearest equivalent letters (b ب, j ج, z ز, k ك), and both series continued to be used in the manuscript tradition until the 12th century and beyond (for the details of adaptation from the time of Sībawayhi (8th century [*q.v.*]) see P. Horn, *Neupersische Schriftsprache*, in *GIPh*, i/2, 12; Lazard 1963, passim; F. Meier, *Aussprachefragen des älteren neupersisch*, in *Oriens*, xxvii-xxviii (1981), 71; K̲h̲ānlarī, *Wazn-i s̲h̲iʿr-i fārsī*, Tehran 1354/1975, 117, etc.). The Arabic writing being a Semitic, consonantal alphabet, it was not designed for an Indo-European language like Persian, consisting as it did only of consonantal signs (*ḥarf*) representing the semantic load whereas, in Persian, consonants and vowels are of equal value. In this system vowels are represented only partially and in various ways: by consonantal letters, orthographic devices and superscript signs. In the script, therefore, there is no one-to-one correspondence between graphemes and phonemes (e.g. the geminated consonants are written with one *ḥarf* with the superscript sign called *tashdīd* as *ḥm'm* = *ḥammām* "bath" in most cases), although there is a regularity in denoting or omitting certain phonemes. The Persians, while having for the most part, adapted the letters and the principles of the Arabic writing, developed innovations in order to denote the peculiarities of the Persian language. In the Semitic system, three letters (*ḥarfs*), *alif, yā'* and *wāw* are used to mark long vowels *ā, ī, ū* and the sequences *ay, aw* (traditionally called diphthongs), whereas short vowels remain normally unwritten. Exceptions are the word intial and word final positions: word initial short vowels (*a, i, u*) are represented graphically by the letter *alif* and their long equivalents with *alif* and the corresponding *ḥarfs* (*yā'* or *wāw*). Furthermore, the letter *alif* is the sign of the glottal stop which is practically used as an orthographic device following the principles of the Arabic (Semitic) orthography which do not allow a syllable to start with vowels, and do not allow a sequence of two vowels (cf. G. Endress, *Die arabische Schrift*, in *Grundriss der arabischen Philologie*, i, ed. W. Fischer, Wiesbaden 1982, 165-97), e.g. *'knwn* = *aknūn* "now", *'ft'dan* = *uftādan* "to fall" and *'sfh'n* = *iṣfahān* "Iṣfahān", *'w* = *ū* "he/she" and *'yr'n* = *īrān* "Iran". Initial long *ā* is rendered with *alif* surmounted by the superscript sign *madd* آ.

The Perso-Arabic script gradually developed a special system of denoting word final short vowels (*a, i, u* in the Classical Persian transcription system and *e, o* in the Modern system) by the "silent" letters (*bayān-i ḥaraka*), e.g. *hā'*: *š'hn'mh* = *Shāh-nāma, kh* = *ki* (in ancient texts also written as *ky, k*) and *wāw*, e.g. *dw* = *du* "two" and *tw* = *tu* "you", but *tr'* = *tu-rā* "you (acc.)". Historically short vowels (*a, i, u*) can be denoted optionally in all positions by superscript signs (*zabar* or *zebar* in Modern Persian) = Ar. *fatḥa, zīr* = Ar. *kasra* and *pīsh* = Ar. *ḍamma*). In ancient manuscripts, the early classical long vowels (*madjhūl*) *ē* and *ō* were distinguished occasionally by special superscript signs on the letters *yā'* and *wāw* (e.g. *Codex Vindobonensis*, ed. F.R. Seligmann, Vienna 1859, and Bukhāran Jewish-Persian texts, cf. Horn, in *GIPh*, i/2, 33; the Lahore *Tafsīr (madjhūl ē)*, cf. MacKenzie, *The vocabularly of the Lahore Tafsīr*, in *Iran and Islam. In memory of the late Vladimir Minorsky*, 419 n. 7; and see further Meier 1981, 86, and Windfuhr 1979, 150). The orthography of *alif* and *hamza* representing phonemes or serving as orthographical devices display intricate problems both in Arabic and Persian. The complexity or sometimes confusion in their description can be ascribed to the double adaptation (first of the Nabatean Aramaic writing to Arabic in the late 7th century, then the Arabic script to Persian) and to its relatively late standardisation. Its orthography was not yet fixed in the 9th century (see Endress, 189). A Persian characteristic of the orthography is that *hamza*, the sign of the glottal stop in Arabic, does not necessarily appear as a separate letter, but it is used as a hiatus symbol (Windfuhr 1979, 139) on syllabic or morphene boundaries (there is a disagreement on this point; see HAMZA; Lazard 1957 = 1992, 48; Windfuhr 1987, 527). The Arabic loans, however, can follow or disregard the rules of the classical Arabic orthography (e.g. the vocalic restriction rules) according to registers and contexts where they appear.

The Perso-Arabic script, which is written from right to left, contains 32 letters: 28 letters are taken over from Arabic plus four special Persian letters supplied with three dots. But not all the letters distinguish phonemes in Persian (see below, iii. Phonology). These letters (allographs) came mainly, but not exclusively through Arabic loan words, e.g. ذ, ض, ظ = /z/, ث, ص = /s/, ط = /t/, غ, ق = /gh/, ح = /h/, أ; ع = ' (or zero). Some of these letters (ث, ذ, ص, ط, غ and ق) do occur in words of Persian origin due to various reasons, e.g. as reflexes of earlier linguistic periods or the unfixed and wavering orthography (see, for instance, *padhīruftan*, in Modern Persian pronunciation *paziroftan, Tahmūrath* vs. *Tahmūras/Tahmūrat, ṣad* or *sad* "hundred", *Ṭihrān* or *Tihrān* "Tehran" (see Horn, in *GIPh*, 12; Meier 1981, 105). The digraph kh^{w}/kh^{v} (= /kh/) is a remnant of the archaic spelling of a labialised fricative (Pisowicz, 121). Ancient manuscripts show sporadically the spellings of the early New Persian period. E.g. the triple-dotted letter *fā'* (ڤ ß) denoted the postvocalic spirant labiodental /v/ (see also some sparse examples in word-initial position in Lazard 1963, 137–8; idem, 1989, 264; Meier 1981, 72; Pisowicz, 119), and the dotted *dāl* (ذ) denoted the spirant pronunciation of the postvocalic *d* (commonly transcribed with the Greek letter δ) in words of Persian origin (see the wavering manuscript tradition in Meier 1981, 105). While the letter *fā'* was abandoned early, the use of the letter ذ, which appears to have been more widespread (except in Transoxania, Balkh and Ghazna, see Shams-i Kays, 221), continued to be preserved through the old poets' practice of selecting rhyme long after its disappearance from the living usage (*ca.* 13th century, see Rempis, in Lazard 1963, 144, n. 1). This phenomenon was included in the traditional lexicography as "the rule of *dhāl* and *zāl*" until the 19th century (see Shams-i Kays, 254-6; *BḲ*, 21; Irawānī, fol. 6b; cf. Lazard 1963, 143; Meier 103, 111; Pisowicz, 107). Some words have preserved the archaic spelling, but the pronunciation of this letter has merged with /z/ in Modern Persian, e.g. in *paziroftan*.

The first attempts to put Persian texts into Arabic script originate from the 9th century. After some fluctuation and instability (see Meier 1981; Lazard 1963, 4) a standard system of script appears to have developed by the 12th century and has remained almost unchanged until recently. The lack of punctuation and capital letters, the disguised pronunciation and an apparent inconsistency in the orthography of certain words and compounds can cause considerable difficulties in reading Persian texts. Although in the most recent period there are some attempts to improve orthography, this question is far from being settled (see Windfuhr 1979, 150).

For the various styles of handwriting, see KHAṬṬ. ii.

2. *Non-Arabic scripts used for New Persian texts* (for a summary, see Meier, 88-9; Lazard 1989, 264-5)

(a) Hebrew characters have been used from the 8th century onwards by Jewish communities to denote their own dialect called Judaeo-Persian [*q.v.*], related very closely to the southern dialect of early New Persian.

(b) An undated bilingual Psalm-fragment written by Christians in New Persian with Syriac characters has been preserved in the materials found in Chinese Turkestan (see F.W.K. Müller, *Ein syrisch-neupersisches Psalmenbruchstück aus Chinesisch-Turkestan*, in *Festschrift Eduard Sachau*, ed. G. Weil, Berlin 1915, 215-22; W. Sundermann, *Einige Bemerkungen zum syrisch-neupersischen Psalmenbruchstück aus Chinesisch-Turkestan*, in *Mémorial Jean de Menasce*, ed. Ph. Gignoux et A. Tafazzoli, Louvain 1974, 441-52).

(c) Among the fragments written in Manichean script there are also some New Persian texts (see M. Boyce, *A catalogue of the Iranian manuscripts in Manichean script in the German Turfan collection*, Berlin 1960, 150; W.B. Henning, *Persian poetical manuscripts from the time of Rūdakī*, in *A locust's leg. Studies in honour of S.H. Taqizadeh*, London 1962, 89-104).

(d) Religious writings and a fragmentary dictionary were written by Armenian Christians in their own script in the 15th century (see Pisowicz, 76).

(e) The Latin script was used by travellers and missionaries to describe Persian texts for centuries, the supposedly oldest one in the *Codex Cumanicus* written in the 13th century (see D. Monchi-zadeh, *Das Persische im Codex Comanicus*, Uppsala 1969; A. Bodrogligeti, *The Persian vocabulary of the Codex Cumanicus*, Budapest 1971; Pisowicz, 73 ff.). Glosses, grammars and vocabularies compiled especially for practical purposes, can be found abundantly from the 16th-17th centuries onwards (see P. Orsatti, *Sistema di transcrizione e fonetica neopersiana nel Dictionarium Latino-Persicum di P. Ignazio di Gesu*, in *AIUON*, xliv [1984], 41-81; Jeremiás, *Grammatical rule and standard in the first Persian grammars written in Latin (XVIIth c.)*, in *Italia ed Europa nella linguistica del Rinascimento*, ed. M. Tavoni, Ferrara 1996, 569-80). Though these texts can give some useful information on the pronuncation of Persian, as a whole they must be regarded as unreliable sources osn crucial points of the history of Persian phonology (see Pisowicz, 79).

(f) Apart from modern *Tādjīkī* the Cyrillic alphabet was used by a Russian traveller in his account of his journeyings, to denote some Persian words in the 15th century (see Pisowicz, 79).

iii. *Phonology, grammar, word formation and vocabulary*

I. Generalities

In spite of its apparent homogeneity owing to many factors, New Persian of the Muslim period underwent profound changes affecting all levels of grammar and vocabulary. The distinction, therefore, between the various stages of Persian is necessary, but, as the periodisation indicated (see above, i), it cannot easily be made. There are two main approaches to the description of linguistic phenomena in Iranian studies. Diachronic or historical studies trace the changes that took place between various phases, while synchronic description is concerned with the Persian used at a given time. But while Modern Persian can be described on the basis of its present use, the synchronic description of Classical Persian can only be carried out with limitations due to the absence of a standardised Classical Persian. Otherwise comparisons can be made between the language style used by Firdawsī (10th c.), Bayhaḳī (11th c.), Niẓāmī (12th c.), Saʿdī (13th c.) or Djāmī (15th c.), etc. Their varieties of Classical Persian share a set of common features but they also differ inasmuch as they display different language forms. In linguistic studies, the dominance of the diachronic approach is clearly felt, whereas synchronic studies have only recently begun to emerge.

II. Phonology

The phonemic status and the exact phonetic characterisation of Persian sounds can be established with certainty for the most recent period; the following analysis therefore starts with formal Modern Persian and aims to identify the characteristic features of the previous phases in comparison with it (cf. Windfuhr 1979, 7; Lazard 1989, 265; Pisowicz, 9).

The sound system of the formal Modern Persian consists of 6 vowels and 24 consonants. There is, however, a considerable disagreement on the phonemic status of certain phonetic sequences or the conditioned and optional allophonic variations, which can reduce or increase the number of phonemes depending on the currently applied theory of analysis or the register examined. The phonemic status of the glottal stop or that of the sequences [ei̯] and [ou̯] (traditionally called diphthongs) are such variables.

The six vowels of Modern Persian are the front /i/, /e/, /a/ and the back /u/, /o/, /â/ articulated with a high /i, u/, a mid /e, o/ or a low /a, â/ (or, according to others, with high, mid-high and mid-) tongue position. Historically there was a phonological opposition between long and short vowels in Classical Persian (/ā/ – /a/, /ī/ – /i/, /ū/ – /u/), but length ceased to be a phonemic characteristic in the modern period (/â/ – /a/, /i/ – /e/, /u/ – /o/), although it has been retained in certain positions as a redundant phonetic property. Therefore *â, i, u* are occasionally distinguished as long or "stable vowels" (*ā, ī, ū*) vs. short or "instable ones" (*a, e, o*) in the descriptions of Modern Persian (cf. Lazard 1989, 265). The diphthongs [ei̯] and [ou̯] occurring within one word are commonly analysed as the combination of two phonemes, a vowel and a consonant /e/ + /y/ and /o/ + /w/ in Modern Persian (see the summary, including the history of the monophonemic interpretation, in Windfuhr 1979, 137-8, Pisowicz, 22-7 and Lazard 1989, 265). The biphonemic interpretation of the sequence /ow/ entails the postulation of a phoneme /w/ in Modern Persian (cf. the phonemic inventory in Classical Persian), which appears in a certain style with a limited distribution, after /o/ and in word final position (see Pisowicz, 24). As for the distribution of vowels, there is no restriction except for the final position: there is no final /a/ (see Classical Persian final /a/ > /e/) except in two words (*na* "non-", *va* "and") and /o/ occurs rarely (see the studies on experimental phonetics in Lazard 1970, 67; esp. Š.G. Gaprindašvili and Dj.Š. Giunašvili, *Fonetika persidskogo yazîka*, Tbilisi 1964, i; J. Towhidi, *Studies in the phonetics and phonology of Modern Persian*, Forum Phoneticum 2, Hamburg 1974).

The most significant characteristics of the phonological development in New Persian are the loss of contrast between long and short vowels and the lowering of the historically short high vowels /i/ > /e/, and /u/ > /o/. Early Classical Persian contained two more long vowels /ē/, /ō/, which merged with /ī/ and /ū/ by the Classical period (see F. Meier, *Aussprachefragen des älteren Neupersisch*, in *Oriens*, xxvii-xxviii [1981], 70-176), but were preserved by the rules of classical rhyming long after their disappearance from living use. For allophonic variations and fluctuations in vowels, see M. Shaki, *The problem of the vowel phonemes in the Persian language*, in *ArO*, xxv [1957], 45-55; Pisowicz, 13-16; Lazard, *A grammar of contemporary Persian*, Costa Mesa 1992, 19-22.

The consonants of Modern Persian include the voiceless and voiced plosives and affricates /p/, /t/, /č/, /k/, /q/, /ʾ/, /b/, /d/, /j/, /g/, the voiceless and voiced fricatives /f/, /s/, /š/, /x/, /h/, /v/, /z/, /ž/, the nasals /m/, /n/, the liquids /l/, /r/ and the semivowels /w/, /y/. (See the transcription: /q/ = ḳ, /j/ = dj, /š/ = sh, /x/ = kh, /ž/ = zh, [γ] = gh.) The phoneme /q/ represents three conditioned allophones, the uvular voiceless plosive [q] in the (absolute) initial position (*ḳânun* [qânun] "law" or in the medial geminate sequence (*baḳḳâl* [baqqâl] "grocer"), the voiced fricative [γ] in intervocalic position (*maḳâle* [maγâle] "study") or in certain consonant clusters (*taghyir* [taγyir] 'change') and the uvular voiced plosive [G] after /n/. There is, however, a disagreement about the place of /q/ in the system of phonemes, whether it is a plosive /q/ or fricative /γ/, due to its considerable fluctuations in pronunciation (see the details in Pisowicz, 42-7).

The occurrence of the glottal stop /ʾ/ as a separate

phoneme is restricted to certain medial and final positions before and after consonants in careful speech represented with the letter *ʿayn* and the signs *hamza* or *alef*, such as *maʿlum*/maʾlum "known", *al-ʾân*/alʾân "now" or *robʿ* /robbʾ "quarter". It can also occur in intervocalic position in words of Arabic origin in place of the genuine *ʿayn* as in *sâʿat* /sâʾat "hour". Its rise was due to the impact of two separate Arabic phonemes /ʾ/ and /ʿ/ transmitted by loans, but the pronunciation of the Arabic voiced pharyngeal /ʿ/ merged entirely with the glottal stop. The phonemicity of the initial glottal stop is questioned (cf. Pisowicz, 50-1). Besides, there is a non-phonemic indigenous glottal articulation represented by the signs *hamza* or *alef* (which may have helped the incorporation of the glottal stop of Arabic origin into Persian), e.g. in a vocalic onset before any initial vowel after a pause /emruz/ → [ʾemruz] "today", before any internal vowel preceded by a vowel /pāiz/ → [pāʾiz] "autumn" or at a morpheme boundary between vowels /bi-ârâm/ → [biʾârâm] "restless". In various registers of Modern Persian the glottal stop can alternate with zero (hiatus) or an intrusive element like the glide *y* (rarely *w* or *h*), e.g. /xâen/ → [xâʾen] ~ [xâyen] "traitor" or /xâne-i/ → [xâneʾi] ~ [xâneyi] "a house", except when the glottal stop represents an etymological pharyngeal spirant. The latter can be replaced by a hiatus, but never by a glide, e.g. *sâʿat* /sâʾat/ → [sâat] (Pisowicz, 49). In general, its appearance or disappearance, occasionally with a compensatory lengthening of the preceding vowel or, more rarely, consonant (/maʾlum/ → [ma:lum], /dafʾe/ → [daffe]), or substitution by an intrusive element can vary according to register under certain conditions (see the details in Windfuhr 1979, 139-40; Pisowicz, 20-2, 47-51; Lazard 1992, 11-4, 31-4). In the spoken register, the glottal stop does not exist at all (Lazard 1992, 12), but according to others it is pronounced at a morpheme boundary after a consonant before the following vowel in all styles (see [mano] "I and . . ." vs. [manʾo] "prohibition and . . ." in Pisowicz, 48). For other characteristics of the colloquial style such as assimilation, contraction, the dropping of *h*'s, etc. see Hodge 1957; E. Provasi, *Some notes on Tehrani Persian phonology*, in *Iranica*, ed. Gh. Gnoli and A.V. Rossi, Naples 1979, 257-80; Pisowicz, 57-8; Lazard 1992, *passim*. On the impact of Arabic loans, see Ali-Ashraf Sadeghi, *L'influence de l'arabe sur le systeme phonologique du persan*, in *La linguistique*, ii (1975), 145-52.

Characteristic of Classical Persian is the full phonemic status of the semivowel /w/ with the labiodental fricative [v] as an allophone (preserved in Afghan Dari, cf. Farhâdi, 37-8). The reconstruction of phoneme /w/ for the early Classical Persian and the fact that there is no initial cluster in Persian (see syllable structure) make the postulation of the phoneme /x^w/ plausible. But the labial articulation disappeared gradually (/x^w/ > /x/) with an accompanying labialisation of the following short vowel (/x^waš/ > Mod. Pers. /xoš/ "happy", but /x^wāstan/ > Mod. Pers. /xâstan/ "to wish"), while the archaic spelling has been retained (cf. Meier, 75; Pisowicz, 121). Another characteristic of Classical Persian is that /q/ and /γ/ were separate phonemes, as they still are in certain modern dialects, such as Tā͟dj͟īkī. Another remarkable feature is the distinct spellings of certain allophones, such as the labiodental fricative [v] (written with the triple-dotted *f*), the spirant pronunciation of the phoneme /d/ in intervocalic or final postvocalic positions [δ] (written with the dotted *d*), originally a dialectal feature in central and southern Iran in early Classical Persian. The former disappeared early, but the latter seems to have been in use until the 13th century, as the spellings of the ancient manuscripts testify. The fluctuations of dialectal origin such as *b* ~ *f* (*abzār* – *afzār*) or *b* ~ *w* (*nabard* – *naward*) are also attested in manuscripts (cf. Lazard 1963, 137 and *passim*).

The syllable structures are V, CV, VC, CVC, VCC and CVCC, if initial glottal stop is disregarded. But their types are CV, CVC and CVCC if it is regarded as a separate phoneme. There are no genuine clusters in initial position in New Persian. Old and Middle Persian initial clusters were replaced by syllables containing prothetic or anathyptic vowels (Middle Persian *spēd* > Classical Persian *ispēd* or *sipēd* / *sifēd* > Modern Persian *sefid* "white"). For details, see J. Krámsky, *A study in the phonology of Modern Persian*, in *ArO*, xi [1939], 66-83; C.T. Scott, *Syllable structure in Tehran Persian*, in *Anthropological Linguistics*, v [1964], 27-30; Windfuhr 1979, 143-4; Lazard 1989, 266.

Stress in Modern Persian is expiratory and non-phonemic. In general it falls on the final syllable of non-verbal forms (nouns, adjectives, adverbs). Certain conjunctions, adverbs and particles have initial stress, such as *váli* "but", *ấri* "yes", *ấyâ* "whether", etc. Nouns (incl. infinitives, participles or verbal nouns) retain their final stress if the following suffixes are attached to them: the indefinite marker *-i*, the object suffix *-râ*, the connecting vowel of the *iḍāfa -e*, the conjunction *-o* "and", *ham* "also" or one of the pronominal clitics *-am, -at, -a͟sh, -mân, -tân, -͟shân* or, one of the clitical forms of the verb "to be" *-am, -i, ast, -im, -i, -and*). By contrast, the plural markers *-hâ* and *-ân* carry the stress (*ketâb-hấ* "books", *zan-ấn* "women") and forms in apostrophe (vocative) preserve an archaic initial stress (*pédar* (voc.) vs. *pedár* (nom.) "father". On the other hand, all verbal forms have non-final stress (except for the form of the 3rd person singular in the simple past, which carries the stress on the final syllable, e.g. *k͟haríd* "he bought"). It may fall on the stem (*k͟haríd-am* "I bought"), on the verbal prefixes (*mí-khar-am* "I am buying/I buy", *bé-khar-am* "[that] I buy"), on the preverbs (*bár mi-andāz-ad* "he abolishes") or on the nominal part of the verbal phrase (*ḥárf mi-zan-am* "I am speaking/I speak"). The verbal prefixes of negation or prohibition (*na-, ne-, ma-*) are always stressed (*némi-k͟har-am* "I am not buying/I do not buy", *ná-k͟harid-am* "I did not buy", *má-k͟har* "don't buy"). In true compounds or in compound nominal phrases, a secondary (weaker) stress may occur on the first nominal part in addition to the main or primary stress, e.g. *ằteš-parást* "fire-worshipper", *kètâb-e pedár* "the father's book".

As the examples attest, stress is relatively fixed in words and phrases. However, it may be weakened, shifted or completely disappear according to the speaker's purport, if there is emphasis upon one segment, e.g. *ḥárf mi-zan-am* vs. *ḥarf mí-zan-am*.

In a typical sentence, the primary stress falls on the last syntagm, which is normally a verb or verbal phrase. At the beginning, a conjunction, an adverb or a vocative may appear with initial accent followed by nominal phrases with final or nearly final accent. Affirmative sentences have a falling intonation, but in interrogative sentences the pitch rises.

Although stress is non-phonemic, certain phonemic sequences may appear as contrasting minimal pairs, such as *mâhí* "fish" vs. *mấh-i* "a moon" or *s͟hâh-í* "kingship" vs. *s͟hấh-i* "a king", but this contrast as a distinctive feature does not exist in the lexicon (cf. *mâhí* – *mấh, s͟hâhí* – *s͟hấh*/. In colloquial Persian there are several such minimal pairs originated from contracted forms, e.g. *kharidám* (< *kharidé am*) "I have bought" vs. *kharíd-am* "I bought".

For further details, see M. Lucidi, *L'accento nel persiano moderno*, in *Ricerche linguistiche*, ii [1951], 108-40; G.E. Nye, *The phonemes and morphemes of Modern Persian: a descriptive study*, Doct. Diss. Series no. 11, Ann Arbor 1955; Ch.A. Ferguson, *Word stress in Persian*, in *Language*, xxxiii [1957], 123-35; Towhidi 1974; Windfuhr 1979, 144-9; Lazard 1970, 67-8; 1992, 37-46; 1989, 266-7.

III. The problems of transliteration and transcription

Persian script disguises pronunciation, therefore a certain extent of interpretation in transcription with Latin (or Cyrillic, etc.) characters is necessary. More than one system has been conceived representing historical, etymological or stylistic factors. For instance, the differences between the phonological inventories of Classical and Modern Persian appear to be so essential that they may be represented by different systems of transcription. See the transcription of Classical Persian phonemes: *ā, ī, ū, (ē, ō), a, i, u, p, t* (or *ṭ*), *č, k, ḳ* (or *q*), *ʾ* (or *ʿ*), *b, d, dj, g, f, s* (or *ṣ, s̲* = Arabic *th*), *sh, kh, khʷ, h* (or *ḥ*), *z* (or *ẓ, ż* = Arabic *dh*), *zh, gh, m, n, l, r, w, y*, and that of Modern Persian: *â, i, u, a, e, o, p, t, č, k, ḳ* (or *q, gh*), *ʾ* (or *ʿ*), *b, d, dj, g, f, s* (or *ṣ, s̲*), *sh, kh* (or *khʷ*), *h* (or *ḥ*), *v, z* (or *ẓ, ż, ẕ*), *zh, m, n, l, r, w, y*. The transcription of Classical texts according to modern pronunciation is also justified because that is the way they are read today. For practical reasons, however, here the transcription of titles, names or grammatical terms follows the system used throughout in the *EI* which represents Classical Persian consonants in an Arabicised form reflecting the written forms closely (e.g. *iḍāfa*, but Class. Pers. *iżāfa*, Mod. Pers. *eżāfe*). Occasionally, Modern Persian pronunciation is indicated as well. Archaic and dialectal spellings (except for the digraph *khʷ*) are omitted and the morphological structures in the examples are phonemically represented, which means that non-etymological glides or intrusive elements (e.g. *khāna-i* "a house" in Classical Persian or *khāne-i* in Modern Persian) or aphaeresis (e.g. *dânešdju ast* > *dânešdju-st* "he/she is a student"), etc., normally remain unwritten.

IV. Grammar: morphology and syntax

In this section, first a formal classification of word classes will be given with occasional references to their occurrences in smaller and larger grammatical units (words, phrases) and then to their functional classification in larger constructions (clause, sentences).

1. *Verbs and verb phrases* (morphology, semantics of verb forms, colloquial and archaic features, etc.)

The morphology of verbs is clear and transparent, but their semantics gives rise to considerable difficulties. Verbal forms can consist of either one word or more than one word and can express a wide range of grammatical categories like number (singular, plural), person (first, second, third), tense (present, past, future, etc.), mood (indicative, conjunctive, imperative), aspectual nuances (imperfect, perfect, progressive, inferential, etc.) and voice (active, passive). Simple verbs have a clear-cut morphological pattern: the minimal verbal form consists of a stem and a personal suffix, but the majority of simple verbs have also a verbal prefix. These forms are based on two stems, i.e. present (I) or past (II). Past stems always end in dental plosives (after vowels, *n, r* in *-d*, otherwise in *-t*) and are derived from infinitives by dropping the ending *-an*. Present stems can be either regular or irregular. The first group can be obtained from past stems by cutting *-id-*, e.g. *kharidan* "to buy" → *kharid-* (II) → *khar-* (I). Present stems of irregular verbs are to be found in vocabulary, e.g. *kardan* "to do" → *kard-* (II), *kon-* (I) or *didan* "to see" → *did-* (II), *bin-* (I). Certain groups of irregular verbs share certain common features in deriving their present stems from past stems, e.g. *sâkhtan* "to make" → *sâkht-* (II), *sâz-* (II), *gorikhtan* "to flee" → *gorikht-* (II), *goriz-* (I) or *farmudan* "to order" → *farmud-* (II), *farmây-* (I), *sorudan* "to sing" → *sorud-* (II), *sarây-* (I), etc. (see more details in Lazard 1992, 131-5). Verbal stems can combine with two sets of personal suffixes: the first set is attached to the forms based on stem (I): 1. *-am*, 2. *-i*, 3. *-ad* in singular and 1. *-im*, 2. *-id*, 3. *-and* in plural; the second set attached to the forms constructed with the stem (II) is the same except sing. 3rd person (a zero morpheme ø). Complex (called also "compound" or "analytic" *vs.* "synthetic") verb forms consisting of more than one constituent are constructed on certain nominal forms of the main verb, i.e. the past participle (past stem + *-e*, e.g. *kharid-e, sâkht-e*) or the so-called short infinitive (which is formally equivalent with the past stem, e.g. *kharid*) plus auxiliary verbs like the various types of the verb "to be" (i.e. the full verb *budan, bâš-* or its clitic forms like *-am, -i, ast, -im, -id, -and*), *khʷâstan, khʷâh-* "to wish/will" or *šodan, šow-* "to become". The so-called progressive form has a special structure: both the main verb and the auxiliary (*dâštan, dâr-* "to have") are conjugated forms (*dâr-ad mi-kon-ad, dâšt-ø mi-kard-ø, dâšte mi-karde ast*) and can be separated from each other by other word(s). The use of this periphrastic progressive is restricted in several ways, e.g. it can be used only in indicative mood and in affirmative sentences (see for more details, below). The future tense is expressed with a special morphology of the auxiliary *khʷâstan, khʷâh-* "to wish" (the present form of the auxiliary without the verbal prefix *mi-* plus the short infinitive of the main verb, e.g. *khʷâh-ad kard* "he will do" cf. also the use of *khʷâstan* as a modal auxiliary, e.g. *mi-khʷâh-ad be-kon-ad* "he wants (would like, etc.) to do"). The majority of finite verb forms have one or two verbal prefix (*mi-, be-, na-, ma-*), which may express various meanings like mood, aspect, negation or prohibition. Their use is partly, but not wholly, exposed to the stylistic levels of their context. The verbal prefix *mi-* (< Classical Persian *hamī* < Early Classical and Middle Persian *hamē*) occur with both simple and complex forms constructed on present and past stems or on past participles: *mi-kon-ad, mi-kard-ø, mi-karde ast, dâšte mi-karde ast.* The prefix *be-* (< Classical < Middle Persian *be-*) or its allophonic variations *bi-* or *bo-* are used only with non-indicative forms in Modern Persian, based on the present stem such as subjunctive present (*be-kon-ad*) and imperative (*be-kon*). All simple and complex verb forms in the indicative are negated with *na-*. It is prefixed to the finite forms of simple main verbs (*na-kard-ø*) or to the participles of complex verbs (*na-karde ast, na-karde bude ast*, etc.), except for the future and passive forms where it is prefixed to the auxiliary (*na-khʷâh-ad kard, karde na-šod-ø*). In the prohibitive, the prefix *na-* (*na-kon, na-kon-id*) is used generally, except for very formal (literary) style where *ma-* (*ma-kon, ma-kon-id*) appear instead. Colloquial language does not use *ma-* at all. The prefixes *na-* and *mi-* may be used simultaneously (with the allophone *ne-* of the morpheme *na-* if it is followed by *mi-*, e.g. *ne-mi-kon-ad*), but *be-* and *mi-/na-/ma-* may not in Modern Persian (see the different usage in Classical Persian).

The paradigm of the verb *kardan, kon-* "to do": indicative mood: present *mi-kon-am* "I do, I am doing", preterite (simple or "aoristic" past) *kard-am* "I did", imperfect *mi-kard-am* "I was doing, I used to do", etc., progressive forms in the present and the past: *dâr-am mi-kon-am* "I am (in the act of) doing", *dâšt-am mi-kard-am* "I was (in the act of) doing", (present) perfect *karde-am* "I have done", etc., past perfect (or pluperfect) *karde budam* "I had done", etc.; there are three more ("double") complex forms based on the perfect, *mi-karde-am* "I have been doing (inferential)", *karde bude-am* "I had done" (inferential) and *dâšte mikarde-am* "I have been doing" (inferential); periphrastic future *khʷâh-am kard* "I will/shall do"; subjunctive mood: present *be-kon-am* "I may do", "that I do", subjunctive past *karde bâš-am* "I may have bought", "that I did", etc.; two imperative forms *be-kon* "do" (sing.), *be-kon-id* (pl.). Nominal forms (traditionally called participles, or participle adjective, used as modifiers or agential noun) are based on two stems: *nevis-ande* (present stem plus *-ande*) "writing (adj.), writer" (see *nevis-ande-gân* "writers"), *nevešt-e* (past stem plus *-e*) "written, writing" (see *nevešte-hâ, nevešte-jât* "writings"). Nominal forms derived from verbs are the full (or long) infinitive *kardan* which can be used in all functions where a noun can appear, but the occurence of the short infinite is strictly limited: apart from future forms it appears after impersonal expressions only (*bâyad raft* "one must go"). The two participles, *nevis-ande* "writing" or "writer" based on stem (I) plus *-ande* and *nevešt-e* (see above) can be used as verbal adjective, e.g. *sâl-e âyande* "the next (coming) year", or as noun, e.g. *nevešte-hâ-ye Bahâr* "B.'s writings". The participles *nevešte, karde,* etc., are suggested to have active meaning in modern Persian (see Telegdi, 1961, 186; Humāyunfarrukh, 78-9; see also *LN nevešte = nevešte šode*) in contrast to ancient usage in which it was regarded as having passive meaning. A homophone form of the past participle of certain transitive verbs (actually nonfinite verb forms) has been distinguished by Lazard (*gérondif*) expressing co-ordinated "circumstantial complementation" on the basis of their differing syntax (see *baste* "closed" used as "gerundive" in *baste ast* "it is closed" or *baste nist* "it is not closed" vs. the verbal form "perfect" like *baste ast* "he has closed" and *nabaste ast* "he has not closed" (cf. Lazard 1989, 273, 281; 1992, 168-9; see also *fiʿl-i waṣfī* in Humāʾī, in *LN, Muqaddima*, 120, and Humāyunfarrukh, 519). Similarly, forms derived from present stem with (nonproductive) *-ân* or *-â* with limited force, e.g. *ravân* "running" or *dânâ* "learned, wise" are suggested to be also called "gerund" (see *gérondif* in Lazard 1989, 273; idem 1992, 167-8). This distinction itself and the true nature of these forms, however, remain to be clarified. The participle of obligation or possibility is formed by the full infinite plus a suffix *-i* like *didan-i* "[things ought] to be seen".

Passive formation: certain verbs can express the passive with the fully conjugated forms of the auxiliary *šodan* (or *gaštan, gardidan* in formal style or *âmadan* in very formal style and in the classical language) attached to the past participle of the main verb, e.g. *kharide mi-šavad* "is being bought", *kharide šod* "was bought", *kharide šode ast* "has been bought", *kharide khʷâh-ad šode* "will be bought", *kharide šavad* "be bought" (subj.), etc. The agent of the action is rarely expressed by circumlocutions such as *be tavassoṭ-e* "by (lit. the intermediation of)", *az dast-e* "by (lit. by the hand of)", *az ṭaraf-e* "on behalf of", "by (lit. from the side of)", e.g. *Ḥasan az tavassoṭ-e Aḥmad košte šod* "Ḥ. was killed by Aḥmad", etc. The spoken style avoids passive formation. The place of passive forms in the verbal paradigm and the details of its morphology and semantics, especially those of verbal compound phrases (locutions) need further investigations (cf. *taqsim kard* "he divided (something among some persons)"—*taqsim šod* "it was divided (into sg.)", but *towżiḥ dâd* "he explained (sg.)"—*towżiḥ dâde šod* "explanation was given" (on the passive see J.A. Moyne, *The so-called passive in Persian*, in *Foundations of Language*, xii (1974), 249-67).

Note some additional features of verbal morphology: the so-called primary verbs like "to be", "to exist" or "to have" have a special, sometimes defected morphology, e.g.: the notion of the substantial verb is expressed with full forms (a), defective forms (b) or with clitics (c): a) forms based on *bud-* (II), *bâš-* (I) (or its archaic variant *bov-*) "to be", e.g. indic. present *mi-bâš-am* "I am" (lit.), past *bud-am* "I was" (it never takes the prefix *mi-* except in hypothetical clauses) and in present subj. *bâš-am* "may I be, etc.", imperative *bâš* "be" (these two forms never take the prefix *bi-*), old optative (used in formulas only) *bâd* or *bâdâ* "may it be!"; *hast* "exists" (*hast-am, hast-i, hast,* etc.), in negation *nistam, nisti, nist,* etc., but it has no infinitive); *dâštan* "to have" never takes the prefixes *mi-* and *be-* (it may take in certain verbal phrases, e.g. *dust mi-dâram* "I love (s.o.)"). For other defective forms of modal auxiliaries such as *khʷâstan, khʷâh-* "to wish, will", (*mi-*)*bâyest, bâyad* (inc. such archaic forms as (*mi-*)*bâyesti* 'it is necessary, one must", see Lazard 1992, 137-42. On the other hand, the auxiliary *tavânestan, tavân-* "can" has a regular conjugation. On the modern usage of auxiliary expressions, see Parwīz Nāṭil Khānlarī, *Dar bāra-i zabān-i fārsī*, Tehran 1340/1961 (*passim*); Bāṭinī, *Masāʾil-i zabānshināsi-i nawin*, Tehran 1354/1975, 191.

This rather poor inventory of verbal morphology does not reveal all the underlying semantic distinctions which verb forms can cover. The overlap of tense and aspect or mood and aspect cause considerable difficulties whose details have not been wholly explored. In addition, the syntactic realisation of aspect can be limited by further facts, e.g. by social context or lexical choice. Therefore, the main oppositions may differ to some extent in formal and informal standards: the use of the so-called progressive forms, for instance, can alter aspectual oppositions (on this novelty in colloquial Persian see Salemann and Shukovski, 1888; Rozenfel'd 1948; Lazard 1957, 151 = 1992, 160; K. Kishāvarz, *Mudāriʿ wa mādi-i malmūs*, in *Rāhnamā-yi kitāb*, v (1962), 687-94; S. Obolensky, *Persian basic course*, Washington 1963, 8, 253; M.R. Bāṭinī, *Sākhtimān-i dasturi-i zabān-i fārsī*, Tehran 1348/1969, 15; Jeremias, *Diglossia in Persian*, in *Acta Linguistica Acad. Scient. Hung.*, xxxiv (1983), 280-3). The most essential points of the semantics of verb forms are as follows: the present forms *mi-kon-am* "I do" and *be-kon-am* "that I do" (meaning obligation, possibility, etc.) express a clear opposition of moods between indicative and subjunctive expressed by verbal prefixes (*mi-, be-*). On the other hand, *mi-kon-am* "I do" and *dâr-am mi-kon-am* "I am (in act of) doing" are contrasted with reference to aspect: the first form is unmarked for aspect and *mi-* simply indicates indicative, but the periphrastic construction expresses a progressive ongoing action. This latter construction is stylistically marked: it occurs in the written and spoken informal standard only. In addition, its use is morphologically and also lexically limited: verbs form two disjoint sets according to their inherent aspectual properties: those which can appear in the progressive and those which cannot. The latter group called "stative" or "non-progressive" verbs, e.g. *istâdan* "to stand", *mordan* "to die", etc. expresses the present progressive by means of perfect (*nešaste-am* "I am sitting") and the past progressive by means of pluperfect (*nešaste budam* "I was sitting"). These "stative" verbs have also progressive forms conveying another modal implication, the so-called "ingressive": *dâr-am mi-nešin-am* "I am going to sit down" (cf. Ṣādiḳī-Arzang 2535/1976, 40; Waḥīdiyān, 68). Because of this restricted use of progressive forms, the present indicative *mi-kon-am* can also convey various imperfective (continuous, durative, iterative, progressive, etc.) values, but in formal Persian only ("I do" or "I am doing"); in Modern spoken Persian this "aoristic" form means "I do" only.

The past tense offers a larger scale for expressing aspectual nuances than the present. The past forms *kard-am* "I did" and *mi-kard-am* "I was doing" convey distinctions between perfective (traditionally called simple past or "aoristic") and imperfective. Here the verbal prefix *mi-* can cover various aspectual values, e.g. continuous, iterative, durative and also progressive in formal Persian. Similarly to the present forms, informal Persian has an additional form with progressive value *dâšt-am mi-kard-am* "I was doing" in the past. This latter verb contrasts with continuous but non-progressive within imperfective (*mi-kard-am*) as well as with non-continuous (perfective) past forms (*kard-am*). It means that both *mi-kon-am* and *mi-kard-am* can cover more aspectual values in the formal language than the same form in the informal register. On the other hand, *mi-kon-am* "I do" (and also "I am doing" in formal Persian) and *kard-am* "I did" can be in opposition with the perfect *karde-am* "I have done" which indicates the present relevance of a past situation (e.g. *nâme-râ nevešte-am* "I have written the letter"). Note that this phonological form of the perfect belongs to the formal language. In the spoken variety, contracted forms are used like *kardé-am* > *kardam* with an ultimate stress vs. *kard-am* in the simple past which has stress on the stem (cf. stress in (iii) Phonology, above). The past perfect (called also pluperfect) *karde bud-am* "I had done" indicates an anterior event completed before another action was taking place (*vaqt-i ke Ḥasan vâred šod Piruz rafte bud* "When Ḥ. arrived P. had (already) gone"). In fact, these perfect forms belong to a semantically complex category of fairly wide applicability expressing various aspectual features of resultative character. It also includes an aspectual nuance called "inferential", "distanced past" or "auditive", a well-known aspectual category in Tādjīk and Turkic languages ("non-evident" verb forms). These terms indicate that the speaker is reporting an event which he has not witnessed himself and his knowledge is from second hand ("reported speech"). A series consisting of four such verbal forms (*karde-ast, mi-karde ast, dâste mi-karde ast, karde bude ast*) began to be interpreted as "inferential" in the Modern Persian paradigm only recently (see Windfuhr, *The verbal category of inference in Persian*, in *Acta Iranica*, xxii (1982), 263-87; Lazard, *L'inférentiel ou passé distantié en persan*, in *Stud. Ir.*, xiv (1985), 27-42; idem, 1989, 273). It should be noted, however, that in earlier descriptions of Persian grammar (Horn, in *GIPh*, 154; Jensen 1931, 158; Rastorgueva 1964, 38; Lazard 1957 = 1992; idem, 1963, 295) the "double" compound verb forms (sometimes mentioned only cursorily) were interpreted on the basis of their morphology as extended forms of the perfect, the imperfect or the past progressive (see *mi-karde ast* "the compound imperfect" in Lazard, 1992, 154 or "perfect durative" in Rastorgueva 1964, 43, *rafte bude ast* "the double compound past" or "the completed past of the perfect" in Lazard 1992, 156, *dâšte... mi-karde ast* "the completed past" of the progressive in Lazard, 1992, 160) and accordingly, they were regarded as forms which combined certain nuances of the perfect ("completed time") with the durative meaning of the imperfect, etc. Their relationship with equivalent Tādjīk forms were expressly denied (cf. Lazard, *Caractères distinctifs de la langue tadjik*, in *Bulletin de la Société Linguistique*, lii (1956), 151; idem 1963, 295). On the other hand, in one of the earliest descriptions of the informal standard of Modern Persian, Waḥīdiyān (1964, 62-4) described these forms as *naḳlī* "narrative" verb forms by giving the following examples: [*be-ṭowri ke mi-guy-and*] *Vaḥid az safar bar gašte* [*ast*] "[it is said that] V. has returned from journey" in contrast to *Vaḥid az safar bar gašt* "V. returned from journey", *goft ẓohr-hâ mi-khʷâbide-i* "He said [that] you used to sleep at noon" and [*mi-guy-and*] *dâšte mi-khʷorde* "[it is told] he was eating (had been eating)" (cf. also Ṣādiḳī 2535, 60-6). It is emphasised that if there are expressions like *ẓâheran, guyâ* "apparently", *mi-guy-and* "it is told" or *šanide-ast* "it is heard (reported)", etc. the use of the inferential is obligatory, otherwise it is the language users' choice.

For compound or periphrastic verbs, see below, V. Word formation and vocabulary.

The characteristics of the verbal system in the early classical periods of Persian: The morphological structure of verbal forms (prefix + stem + verbal suffix) is the same in the earlier periods of Persian as in Modern Persian. There are, however, essential differences both in the behaviour of certain constituents of the verbal form and also in the set of grammatical devices, the use of which was abandoned in the subsequent periods or preserved only for conveying highly formalised archaic or "neo-classical" style. Such a difference between Modern and Classical Persian appears in the use of verbal prefixes: the meaning and rules of their order and combination with each other and the two stems (past and present) varied widely: e.g. the classical prefixes (*ha*)*mī-* and *bi-* expressed mainly aspectual differences and could combine with both stems, e.g. *bi-raft, bi-šud* "(he) went away, passed away" with perfect, resultative nuance vs. *(ha)mī-ravad* "(he) is going" with continuous, progressive, iterative, etc., aspectual meaning (note that *hamī* was still used as an adverb in early classical sources written separately). These verbal prefixes preserved certain features of their origin in ancient texts: *bi* < Middle Persian *be-* was a preverb attached inseparable to the verb, while *hamī* < early Classical and Middle Persian *hamē* "always", being an adverb, moved freely, and its place became fixed only in later periods.

On the other hand, the minimal verbal form consisting of the present stem joined by personal suffixes (*rav-ad*) was used widely as an "aoristic" unmarked neutral form. Thus, with some oversimplification, the set of prefixes and suffixes attached to verbal stems remained unchanged almost totally in the past millennium, but the meaning and ordering of morphemes, that is, the internal composition of verbal forms varied significantly throughout history. For the details of the combinations of the verbal prefixes (*ha*)*mī-* and *bi-* or *bi-* and the negation *na-* or (*ha*)*mī* prefixed to imperative and nominal forms, or *bi-* prefixed to forms in the simple past, complex verbal forms or nominal forms, etc. see Lazard 1963, 274-326; Aḥmadī Gīwī, *Dastūr-i tārikhī-i fiʿl*, passim; on the pre-classical use of the preverb *bi-*, see J. Josephson, *The preverb be and the verb kardan in Book Pahlavi Texts*, in *Proceedings of the Second European Conference of Iranian Studies*, ed. B.G. Fragner *et al.*, Rome 1995, 335-46.

Early Classical Persian texts have preserved a group of archaic elements of verbal morphology (see the ancient forms of personal suffixes or verb forms without any suffix, etc.). The most characteristic features of this early period are: the morpheme *-ī* < *ē(d)* attached to conjugated forms (incl. the clitic forms of the verb "to be" or rarely, stem forms) was used in differing functions in present and past forms expressing various values of mood (optative, conditional or irreal modality), but in the past it could also convey the habitual, durative, etc., nuances of aspect (similarly to *(ha)mī-*). In old prose it appears to have been a productive morpheme and was used simultaneously with the verbal prefixes *bi-* and *(ha)mē-*, but subsequently it fell into disuse and its function was taken over gradually by the verbal prefix *mī-* even though not completely—the morphology and semantic values of these forms or the differing use of *-ē* and *-ēd* have not been fully explored, see the examples in Aḥmadī Gīwī, 337-42, and Lazard 1963, 327-38, e.g. *agar man ānjā na-budam-ē* . . . "If I had not been there . . ." (irreal), or *čūn pēš-i payghāmbar āmad-ē guft-ē* "when he used to come to the Prophet he used to say . . ." (habitual). For other archaic elements occurring in ancient texts such as the old precative or optative (*dār-ād, rasān-ād, kun-ād*), the imperative formed by *-ē* (*dih-ē, bi-firist-ē*), the type of the perfect (*kardast-am*), or verbal (and also nominal) forms followed by the morpheme *-ā* conveying the vocative or exclamative (*guft-ā*), and for the verbal morphology and syntax of ancient texts, consult Lazard 1963; Bahār, *Sabk-shināsī*, Tehran [2]1337/1958; Aḥmadī Gīwī, Tehran 1380/2001.

2. *Nouns and noun phrases*

Generalities: Nouns, adjectives and partly adverbs are forms which do not exhibit any specific morphological feature (e.g. ending) that would indicate their word class individually. They easily enter into another word-class while materially they remain the same and may occur in various syntactic functions. See the examples *pir* "old" and "old man", *mard* "man" and "brave" (cf. *mard-tar* comp., *kheyli mard ast* "he is very brave"), or *bâlâ* used as an adverb (*bâlâ âmadan* "to come up(wards)") or as an attributive (*otâq-e bâlâ* "the upper room", cf. *bâlâ -tar* comp.) or as a noun (*bâlâ-ye khiyâbân* "the upper part of the street"); or *khub* "good" and "well" (*dokhtar-e khub* "good girl" and *khub mi-khʷânad* "he reads well").

The noun or noun phrase can function as subject, object and various complements expressed by prepositional phrases in the sentence. These syntactic roles or such grammatical categories as determination (definiteness and indefiniteness) are expressed by postponed markers (called sometimes exponents, suffixes, particles or post-positions) and by determiners of various types; occasionally they can also remain unmarked. The markers attached to the noun (phrase) display a set of stressed and unstressed grammatical morphemes of various natures (*iḍāfa*, plural- or object-markers and articles). A striking characteristic of Persian is that the noun and its marker(s) are not closely knit; markers do not constitute inseparable elements of the word they are joined to. They can move relatively freely, although to varying degrees, and can be attached to one noun, to a chain of nouns or a noun phrase as a whole. The sequence of these markers, their phonetic forms (allomorphs) or even the rules of their presence or absence are not always firmly fixed. Their use is governed by stylistic factors and vary also in different phases of Persian. In ancient texts their place and sequence were freer than in more recent sources, where they tend to move towards the end of the noun phrase in an ordered sequence (esp. the object marker *-râ*) if there is more than one marker. This sort of "group inflection" (a traditional, but not quite appropriate term) is a characteristic of New Persian which, in this point, differs significantly from the behaviour of the formatives of the agglutinating languages or from the nominal inflection of the ancient Indo-European languages. In the latter, word-classes, traditionally called parts of speech, are morphologically recognisable and the basic syntactic relations are expressed by case endings attached to specific stem-forms and only to those. In Persian this old type of nominal inflection was gradually abandoned and the new way of marking morpho-syntactic categories developed by the Islamic period (see Telegdi, *Zur Morphologie des Neupersischen*, in *AO Hung.*, xii (1961), 183-99; idem, *Beiträge zur historischen Grammatik des Neupersischen. I. Über die Partikelkomposition im Neupersischen*, in *AO Hung.*, v (1955), 75); Lazard 1992, 262-4.

Gender, number and other categories (the morphemes -i, -e, -râ): Gender is not marked morphologically in Persian. Female and male can be expressed lexically by the words *mâde* "female" and *nar(re)* "male" pre- or postponed (the latter, which is more colloquial, is constructed with *iḍāfa*), such as *mâde-šir* or *šir-e mâde* "lioness" and *nar-šir* or *šir-e nar* "(male) lion". The feminine ending of the Arabic loans *-at* > Class. Pers. *-a* > Mod. Per. *-e* (*malek* "king", *maleke* "queen", but also *-at* as in *sâ'at* "hour") is rarely used with words of Persian origin, such as *hamšir*—*hamšire* "brother—sister" (formal). In a very formal style an adjectival modifier following an Arabic broken plural may appear in an Arabicised feminine form (*mamâlek-e khâreje* "foreign countries" vs. standard *mamâlek-e khârej*).

Plural is expressed by two alternating stressed morphemes: *-hâ* with inanimates and *-ân* (variants: *-gân* or *-yân* according to the word's final vowel) with human beings, such as *ketâb-hâ* "books", *zan-ân* "women" or *bande-gân* "servants" (exceptions are numerous, e.g. *derakht-ân* "trees", *akhtar-ân* "stars", etc.). The stressed plural marker has a firmly fixed position immediately following the noun. Sometimes it may also be added to constructions consisting of two nouns in juxtaposition or adjectival phrase, such as [*kot-o šalvâr*]*-hâ* "coat-and-trousers = suits".

In Modern Persian, except in very formal styles, *-hâ* is widely used in place of *-ân*. In addition, certain Arabic loans have preserved their original plural formation, both regular (*-ât, -jât, -iyât, -in, -yun, -âlât*) or irregular ("broken plural"), such as e.g. *kalema* "word" and *kalemât* "words" or *vazir* "minister" and *vozarâ* "ministers". In the formal language, the plural marker *-ât* or *-jât* occur with non-Arabic words as well, e.g. *farmâyeš-ât* "instructions" or *mive-jât* "fruits". Arabic broken plurals were widely used in Classical Persian and continue to be retained in modern formal style. Sometimes Persian plural markers are also added to Arabic broken plurals cumulating the two types of plural formation, such as *zarf* "vessel", *zoruf* or *zoruf-hâ* "vessels". In the classical period, certain Persian words were re-borrowed from Arabic with their broken plurals modelled on patterns of Arabic morphology (where they are in use to this day), such as *farmân* "order" and *farâmin* "orders", *bostân* "garden" and *basâtin* "gardens", etc. Certain nouns have double plurals, each with its separate meaning, such as *sar-ân* "chiefs" and *sar-hâ* "heads" or *ḥarf-hâ* "letters" and *ḥoruf* "speeches". Selection from among the alternative plural forms is mainly governed by stylistic factors.

There is a special use of the plural marker *-hâ* occurring in adverbial expressions conveying a shade of meaning "approximation" (cf. *ba'd-hâ* "afterwards" in Lazard 1992, 93; *birun-hâ* "somewhere outside", *tu-hâ* "somewhere inside" in G. Hincha, *Beiträge zu einer Morphemlehre des Neupersischen*, in *Isl.*, xxxvii (1961), 143-60).

Historically, both *-ān* (< Old Iranian pl. gen. **-ānām*) and *-hā* (< Book Pahlavi *-īhā*) had their roots in Middle Persian. The former was older and more widely used with all sorts of nouns, but the latter took its place gradually (see W. Sundermann, *Mittelpersisch*, in *CLI*, 155). For further details cf. Jensen, 38-41; Lazard 1963, 195-9; idem 1992, 57-66; R. Humāyūnfarrukh, *Dastūr-i djāmi'-i zabān-i fārsī*, [2]Tehran n.d. ([1]1337/1958), 253-74; M. Mu'īn, *Mufrad wa djam'*, Tehran [5]1369/1991; Hincha 1961, 141-60.

Iḍāfa (*possessive and attributive constructions*): The modification of a noun with a following modifier is expressed by a clitic vowel *-e* or after vowels *-ye* (Class. Pers. *-i* or *-yi*) attached to the head noun(s). The construction is called *iḍāfa* (Class. Pers. *iżâfa*, Mod. Pers. *eżâfe*) "annexation" (cf. the similar but not wholly equivalent construction in Arabic). The head noun(s) in singular or plural is (are) followed by one or more modifiers, which can be an adjective (as in most cases) or a noun, a pronoun, or more complex spatial and temporal expressions consisting of nouns, adjectives, prepositions, etc. Two main types can be distinguished according to their inner structures: *ketâb-e bozorg* "the big book" and *ketâb-e pedar* "the book of the father" (called Ez. I and Ez. II by Hincha, 148-51, or *tarkib-e vasfi* "descriptive composition" and *tarkib-e eżâfi* "possessive c." by native grammarians). If the first type is extended by another adjective, the new modifier refers to the head noun ([*ketâb*]*-e bozorg-e fârsi* "the big Persian book"), while in the second case the new modifier refers to the second noun-member of the construction (*ketâb-e* [*pedar*]*-e fârsi* "the book of the Persian father" which itself functions as a head as well. More complex noun-phrase structures may contain a long chain of modifiers (*tadvin-e dastur-e zabân-e fârsi* "the codification of the grammar of the Persian language" or [Ferdowsi,] *sokhanguy-e piruzi-ye niki bar badi* "[F.,] an orator of the victory of goodness over badness"), sometimes representing a reduced relative clause (*kaleme-hâ-ye makhtum be hâ-ye gheyr-e malfuz-e fârsi* ("words with non-spoken final *h*"). Theoretically, noun phrases can be indefinitely extended, but their complexity is constrained by perception factors. Depending on the semantic relation between the head and its modifier(s), several subtypes can be listed: e.g. qualification by a noun indicating origin (*âb-e češme* "well-water") or material (*ketâb-e adabiyât* "the book of literature") or specification (*šahr-e Tehrân* "the city of T.", *mazhab-e eslâm* "the religion of Islam" etc.). Detailed descriptions of these types in rhetorical terms as *ḥaqiqi* "literal" vs. *majâzi* "metaphorical" etc., can be found in native literature (see Mu'īn, *Iżāfa* (*the genitive case*), Tehran [5]1370/1991). Titles and other designations may occur either with *iḍāfa* (*âqâ* "mister", *janâb*, *ḥazrat* "excellence, honour, dignity", *marḥum* "late") or without *iḍāfa* (*doktor, ḥakim, šeykh*). If a head noun is suffixed by the indefinite *-i*, the adjective attributive follows it without *iḍāfa* (*ketâb-i bozorg* "a big book"). This construction is characteristic of formal Modern Persian only, but it was commonly used in Classical Persian. Another characteristic of the ancient language is that modifiers (both nouns and adjectives) often precede the head noun. In this case there is no *iḍāfa* construction, the constituents stand in juxtaposition (*delir mard* "a brave man", *Irân šahr* "the empire of Iran", cf. Lazard 1963, 200-3). The connecting vowel *-e* (in classical transcription *-i*) may be dropped both in the classical poetry due to the requirements of prosody and in modern dialects or in colloquial styles (in rapid speech), especially in frequently used expressions (*pedar-bozorg* "grandfather", *janâb-'âli* "Sir", etc.).

Historically, the *iḍāfa* construction developed fully by the New Persian period (see the use of the partly equivalent and scarcely occurring Middle Persian relative particle *-ī* in Sundermann, *Mittelpersisch*, 158-9).

Several details, esp. the syntactic-semantic relations between the constituents of the multiple *iḍāfa* structures, which are characteristic of the formal written style, remain unresolved (see L.S. Peysikov, *Voprosi sintaksisa persidskogo yazîka*, Moscow 1959, 41-108 (the most detailed description); M.R. Bāṭini, *Tawṣīf-i dastūri-i zabān-i fārsī*, Tehran 1348/1969, 137-52; Lazard 1992, 66-71; idem 1989, 275).

Definiteness—indefiniteness: The unstressed clitic *-i* (< Class. Pers. *-ī*, < early Class. Pers. *-ē* < Old Persian *aiva-* "one") traditionally called "indefinite article" or "article of unity" is joined to a noun in singular or plural or to a noun phrase, e.g. *ketâb-i* "a book" or *ketâb-hâ-i* "some, certain books" (vs. *ketâb-hâ* "books") or *ketâb-e bozorg-i* "a big book". In the colloquial language indefiniteness is often expressed by the numeral *yek* "one" which precedes the noun (*yek ketâb* "a book") and may be used simultaneously with the clitic *-i* (*yek ketâb-i*). Although the expressions *yek ketâb* and *yek ketâb-i* appear to be equivalent in certain contexts, they may also have different stylistic values. There are, for instance, cases, where *-i* and *yek* are not interchangeable; see the terms "Kennzeichnung der Individualisierheit" ("the sign of individualisation") for *yek* and "Restriktion" ("restriction") for *-i* by Hincha, 169-70, e.g. *yek ruz* "eines (bestimmten) Tages" ("a particular day") vs. *ruz-i* "pro Tag, ein einzelner Tag" ("daily, every day"). Although the fine points of the use of the clitic *-i* have not been wholly explored, there can be a restricting function, which appears to make the reference of the noun phrase more precise. In addition, its relatively independent character are manifested in phrases like in the following examples by Ḥidjāzī (quoted from Telegdi, 1961, 192): *javân-e šekaste va nâkhoš-i* "a tired (lit. broken) and sick young man" (Hidâyat) or *har jâhel-e az donyâ bikhabar-i* "each ignoramus who does not understand the world", or *dar donyâ-i digar* "einer anderen Welt" "in a different world" (Cubak). This latter type was especially common in Classical Persian, where the clitic *-i* tended to be joined to the first head noun.

The same clitic morpheme *-i* with a restricting function can be attached to the antecedent of a restrictive relative clause (*mard-i ke tu-ye oṭâq ast* "the man who is in the room"). (This morpheme is called *yâ-ye ešâre* by native grammarians.) The antecedent noun may be preceded by a demonstrative pronoun and is compatible with the stressed object suffix *-râ* (*ân mard-i-râ ke . . .* "that man whom . . .") and the stressed morpheme *-e* which is used only in colloquial style (*ân mard-é-i ke . . .* "that man who . . ."). According to Hincha, the clitic *-i* is in complementary distribution with Ez. II and the pronominal possessive suffix *-aš* in each position (171). There is considerable disagreement, however, on whether these two functions of the clitic *-i* with different distributions are to be regarded as one or two morphemes. Native speakers seem to distinguish the two functions (cf. Lazard, *L'enclitique nominal -i en persan: un ou deux morphemes*, in *BSL*, li (1966), 249-64; idem, 1989, 275-6). For more details see Meier, 139-44; Windfuhr, 3-40; Ch. Lehmann, *Yā-ye ešārat. Zur Grammatik der persischen Relativsatzes*, in *Indogermanische Forschungen*, lxxxii (1977), 97-106.

A stressed morpheme *-e* is used after nouns in

singular (*hotel-é* "the hotel [in question])" as if it was a definite article (Hincha's term is "Punktualisierung", 176), but its use is restricted to the colloquial style in Modern Persian only. In formal language there is no direct way of expressing definiteness, but it is possible to indicate the definite or indefinite nature of the noun acting as an object in the sentence (see the object suffix *-râ*). The morpheme *-e* has a limited distribution as it may occur with demonstrative pronouns (*ân pesar-é*), but never with the so-called indefinite "article" *-i* (for a different view, see Hincha, 176). If the *-é* is joined to a noun phrase (Ez. I) the *eżâfe* vowel *-e* is dropped, e.g. *ketâb-bozorg-é* (cf. ʿA.A. Ṣādiḳī, *Dastūr. Sāl-i duwwum*, Tehran 2535/1976, 131). Apparently its occurrence is widespread in both Persian and non-Persian dialects (see Christensen 1939, 42, and also Windfuhr, 41).

The object marker -râ: The unstressed morpheme *-râ* (also called particle or postposition, which indicates its relatively independent or word-like character) is attached to a noun in singular or plural, or to a noun phrase of whatever length, indicating direct object under certain conditions. These "conditions" are a matter of debate and are impossible to grasp by hard and fast rules: its place, functions, appearance or disappearance seem to be dependent on grammatical, semantic and stylistic factors. In the sequence of the postponed morphemes which can follow a noun or a noun phrase, *-râ* is always the last in the sequence in Modern Persian (e.g. *ketâb-hâ-i-râ*). It is said to mark the direct object in the sentence if it is made "definite" by pre- and postponed determiners, modifiers or by context, e.g. *ân ketâb-râ* "that book (acc.)", *ketâb-e u-râ* "his book (acc.)", *ketâb-râ khʷândam* "I read the book". There are cases, however, where the direct object can also be followed both by the morpheme *-i* and by *-râ*. In these cases the morpheme *-i* appears to make the object not indefinite, but rather restrictive or "individuated", e.g. *ketâb-i-râ* "a certain book (acc.)". On the other hand, the object marker is not used if the object is generic, e.g. *šab-hâ ketâb mi-khʷân-am* "in the evenings I read book(s)" (cf. Lazard 1989, 280). The rationale for its occurrence is far from clear. It may be connected with the semantic nature of the noun acting as object or with the relationship between object and predicate ("caractère humain de l'objet" or "absence d'affinité sémantique entre le verbe et l'objet") or, with the complexity of the expression (cf. Lazard 1989, 280; idem 1992, 74-6, 183-90). Its use in the colloquial language is very unsteady: it is often missing where formal language would use it.

In Modern Persian *-râ* sometimes appears where a direct object marker is not expected to occur. Some of the instances of these "uncommon" uses of the morpheme *-râ* do occur in both formal and informal Modern Persian, while others may be seen only in the very formal (literary) style. The first group includes elliptic exclamative phrases, such as *khodâ-râ šokr* "thanks to God", *to-râ be-khodâ* "I swear you by God" or *khodâ-râ* "for God's sake!" or *qażâ-râ* (= *az qażâ*) "by chance". An emphatic use of the morpheme *-râ* introducing a topic at the beginning of the sentence occurs in the less formal style, such as *to-râ ce kâr konam*? "What am I to do with you?" (lit. "As for you, what shall I do?"). Sometimes it is used with adverbial expressions denoting time (*zohr-râ* "at noon" quoted by Lazard from Ṣādiḳ Hidāyaṭ). The second group whose construction is characteristic of the very formal (literary) style in Modern Persian consists of expressions where the noun followed by *-râ* features as indirect object, like *to-râ goftam* [= *be to goftam*] "I told you" or *šomâ-râ kâr dâram* [= *bâ šomâ kâr dâram*] "I have to speak to you". In these examples *-râ* is substituted by prepositions in the equivalent expressions which are equivalent grammatically but not stylistically. Another archaic and very formal use of this morpheme is the construction where *-râ* is attached to the complement of the existential verb "to be" expressing possession (that is, to the possessor noun), such as *u-râ pesar-i bud* "he had a son", an equivalent of the sentence *u pesar-i dâšt* (cf. Lazard 1992, 191; Hincha, 186). These latter two functions are obviously remnants of old usage. Not only these two points but the whole domain of its use (place, functions, distribution, etc.) show differences between Modern and Classical Persian displaying also dialectal variations (cf. its use with the proposed particle *mar*). See further details in Telegdi 1961, 194; Lazard 1963, 356-84; idem, *Le morpheme râ en persan et les relations actancielles*, in *BSL*, lxxvii (1982), 177-207; I.K. Ovts̱innikova, *Funkts̱ii posleloga rā v sovremennon literaturnom persidskom yazîke*, in *Trudi Instituta yazîkoznaniya*, vi (1956), 356-391; idem, *Ispol'zovanie posleloga* rā *v proizvedeniyakh tadjikskikh i persidskikh klassiceskikh avtorov (XI-XV vv.)*, in *TIY*, vi (1956), 392-408.

3. *Adjectives and adjective phrases*

Adjectives are invariable words in Persian showing no distinction of gender, number or case. Comparative adjectives are formed by the suffixes *-tar* and *-tarin* (*boland-tar* "high" *boland-tarin* "highest", note that the same suffix can be attached to adverbs as well). There are certain adjectives which have suppletive comparative and superlative forms, see *beh*, and *beh-tar* ("better"), *beh-tarin* ("best") in relation to *khub* "good" or *biš*, *biš-tar* ("more, numerous") in relation to *besyâr* "much, many", etc. These doublets can be used in different social contexts in Modern Persian. The comparison between two gradable adjectives are made by the preposition *az* (*in pesar az ân boland-tar ast* "this boy is taller than that"). Superlative forms usually precede the head noun (*qadim-tarin ketâb* "the oldest book"), similarly to certain adjectives with special semantic value (*khub pesar-i* ("a good boy", see Lazard 1989, 277). Adjectives may be preceded by adverbs or adverb phrases. The most commonly used premodifiers of this type are *besyâr, kheyli* "very", *ʿajab* "strange" (*masʾale-ye kheyli mohem(m)* "very important problem").

For ancient comparative and superlative forms like *meh, mehin* ("greater, greatest"), *beh, behin* ("better, best"), the doublets *khub-tar/beh-tar* and some additional points of their use or modes of intensification in both Modern and Classical Persian, see Lazard 1992, 81-9; idem 1963, 201-14.

Because of their "unmarked" nature, adjectives easily change their word-class membership without any morphological modification—for instance, a large part of them can be used as nouns or adverbs (see above, I. Generalities). The syntactic behaviour of these words, which obtain their new meaning via transposition, is similar to the other members of the same word-class even though their original word-class attributes do not disappear completely. For instance, nominalised adjectives take the same exponents as the noun proper while preserving some features of their own in certain constructions (e.g. in *iḍāfa* or in compounds such as *deltang* and *tangdel*, see Telegdi, *Zur Unterscheidung von Substantiv und Adjektiv im Neupersischen*, in *AO Hung.*, xv (1962), 325-36).

4. *Adverbs and adverb phrases*

This heterogeneous class overlaps with other word classes such as nouns, adjectives or prepositions, etc. The group of words which are traditionally regarded as adverbs are *konun/aknun* "now", *emruz* "today", *fardâ* "tomorrow", *zir* "under", *zebar* "above", *nazdik* or *nazd* "near", *dur* "far", *ʿaqab* "behind", *piš* "before", *pas* "after", *birun* "outside", *bâlâ* "up", *pâin* "down", *sakht* "very", etc., in addition to the morphologically derived adverbs (of manner in most cases) created from adjectives by the still creative suffix of Arabic origin *-an*, e.g. *ettefâqan* "by chance", *jeddan* "seriously", *jânan* "whole-heartedly", etc. The syntactic behaviour of certain simple adverbs, however, varies according to the constructions where they occur. For instance, *piš, pas, birun, bâlâ, pâin* used in combination with verbs of movement function as adverbs of space (*bâlâ raft* or *raft bâlâ* "he went up" in modern colloquial); used in noun phrase they appear as attributives (*oṭâq-e bâlâ* "the upper room, mansard", *šab-e piš* "the previous night"); used in adverb phrases, they behave as nouns (called "adverbes-substantifs" by Lazard 1957, 84 = 1992, 90; for a different view see Telegdi 1961, 187-9) displaying nearly all the properties nouns have though to varying degrees. That is, they may occur with or without prepositions, with certain determiners (e.g. demonstrative pronouns) and plural markers indicating "approximation" (cf. Telegdi 1961, 189; Lazard 1992, 65). They also occur in *iḍāfa* constructions, but they never appear with articles (see *bâlâ* "the upper part, top, height" in the examples *dar bâlâ-ye* "above, over s.th.", *bâlâ-ye kuh* "at the top of the mountain", etc. or *hamin aknun* "just now", *baʾd-hâ* "later" or more complex phrases such as *az emruz be-fardâ* "from today till tomorrow", cf. Telegdi 1961, 187-9). Actually, a large group of nouns may also occur in such adverb phrases either with or without prepositions (e.g. (*dar*) *pošt-e divâr* "behind the wall", *be manzel* [*raft*] *manzel* "he went home" (colloquial), see prepositional phrases). Similarly, most of the adjectives may function as adverbials (of manner in most cases, called "adjectifs-adverbes" by Lazard 1957, 79 = 1992, 90, e.g. *tond* "quick, quickly"). For various ways of intensifying or concretising the meanings of adverbial expressions, see *tanhâ* "alone", *ham* "also, even", *niz* "also", *ḥattâ* "even", *bâz-ham* "still, yet", etc. (see Lazard 1992, 90-5).

The manifold behaviour of certain adverbs might be explained by their historical development: e.g. *bâlâ* and *pâin* were originally nouns, but they became adverbs while preserving some features of their former class-membership. By contrast, some old adverbs (*bar, dar, foru, farâ*) became fixed in preverbal position used formally as verbal prefixes (and not as adverbs) and formed a single lexical item with the verb while abandoning their independent meaning as adverbs (e.g. MP *abar āmadan* > Class. P. *bar āmadan* "to rise [sun]" > Mod. P. *bar âmadan* "to cope, rise [dough]"). Note that some of them became obsolete already in the classical language and were substituted by "new" adverbs, e.g. *foru* by *pâin* "down" or *dar* by *tu* "in"; others merged into one single word (see the modern homophones of various origins, e.g. Class. Persian *andar* > *dar* "in" (adv.) and *dar* "door" (noun) in classical phrases such as *dar āmadan* "to come in" and (*ba-*)*dar āmadan* "to come out" > Mod. Pers. *dar âmadan* "to come out"—for substitution, see Class. Persian *bar âmadan* → Mod. Pers. *bâlâ raftan* "to rise, go up").

In addition, in the course of time certain adverbs had partly or wholly lost their ancient meaning, e.g. *piš* or *pas* were local-temporal adverbs in Classical Persian, but they have only temporal reference in Modern Persian, or *bar* in *bar ašoftan* = *ašoftan* "flare up, agitate" (see also the modern continuation of the old homophones: MP *abar* > Cl. Pers. *bar* "up, on" and MP *war* > Cl. Pers. *bar* "breast" [noun] > Mod. P. (*az*) *bar*(*-e*) "over, upon, on [prep.]"). For more details of these highly heterogeneous, sometimes obscure groups of words called adverbs or sometimes particles, see Telegdi 1955; idem, 1961.

5. *Prepositions or prepositional phrases*

There are only a few true prepositions in Persian such as *be* "to, at, in, with", etc., *dar* "in, into (litera.)", *bar* "on, to", *az* "from, since", *bâ* "with", *bi* "without", *tâ* "until", *joz* "except", *čun/čon* "as, like". They can precede the noun (*dar oṭâq* "in the room"), the noun phrase (*dar oṭâq-e bozorg* "in the big room") or the co-ordinated nouns (*dar oṭâq va âšpazkhâne* "in the room and the kitchen"). These prepositions are never followed by *iḍâfa*.

In addition, there are various types of "compound" prepositions: e.g. adverbs followed by prepositions (*piš az* "before (of time)", *qabl az* "before", *pas az* "after"), nouns (or substantivised adverbs) with or without prepositions connected to another noun via *iḍāfa* (*dar pošt-e divâr* "behind the wall", *az ṭaraf-e* "from the side of" *be-ṭaraf-e* "towards", *be tavassoṭ-e* "by (the intervening of)" (*dar*) *tu-ye* "in(side)", *az zir-e* "from under" etc., or adjectives followed by prepositions (*râjeʾ be* "concerning", etc.).

Both true prepositions and the connecting vowel of *iḍâfa* may be dropped in colloquial style (see Lazard 1992, 76-9).

There were some more prepositions in Classical Persian, but they became obsolete in post-classical Persian as early lexicographic sources indicate, e.g. *andar, foru, farâ*, etc. Another characteristic of Classical Persian was the joint use of certain prepositions (*be, bar*) and certain postpositions (*bar, (an)dar, bâz*), e.g. *be Yaman dar* "in Y." (cf. Lazard 1963, 399-421; Kh.Kh. Rahbar, *Dastūr-i zabān-i fārsī. Kitāb-i ḥurūf-i iḍāfa wa rabṭ*, [2]Tehran 1367/1988, 69-396).

6. *Numerals*

The cardinal numerals between 1 and 20 (*yek* "1", *do* "2", *se* "3", etc.), all tens (*si* "30", *čehel* "40", *panjâh* "50", etc.), hundreds (*ṣad* "100", *devist* "200", *siṣad* "300", etc.) and thousand (*hezâr*) are single words. The other numbers consist of either two or three or more words connected by *o* "and" (e.g. *bist-o yek* "21", *hezâr-o yek* "1001", *do hezâr-o bist-o yek* "2021", etc.). Nouns following the cardinal numerals are normally in singular (*do ketâb* "two books"). Characteristic of Persian is the use of so-called "numeratives" words, a certain type of classifiers, between the numerals and the head noun. The most used "numeratives" are *nafar, tan, tâ, dast*, etc. (*do nafar dânešju* "two (persons) students", *do tâ ketâb* "two (pieces) books"). Ordinals are derived from cardinals with the suffixes *-om* or *-omin* (*čahâr-om* or *čahâr-omin* "fourth"). If they consist of more than one member they are attached to the last member, e.g. [*yek hezâr-o panjâh-o hašt*]*-om* "1058". The two series of ordinal numerals (*panj-om* or *panj-omin* "fifth") display different syntactic and semantic characteristics. The first type used as an attributive follows the head noun with *iḍâfa* (*ketâb-e panjom* "the fifth book") but the second precedes it (*panjomin ketâb*). For their differing semantic values, see Lazard 1992, 101. The first cardinal numerals have a variety of forms (*yekom/avval/nokhost* "first", *dovvom/deyyom* "second", *sevvom/seyyom* "third"). For various numerical expressions, see Lazard 1992, 102-5.

7. *Pronouns: personal, possessive, reflexive, reciprocal, demonstrative, interrogative and indefinite*

Personal and some other pronouns can be expressed in two different ways: by stressed independent words or by clitic morphemes. The members of the two sets can substitute each other in certain, but not in all positions. The choice of clitic pronouns is heavily dependent on stylistic factors.

Stressed personal pronouns have the distinction of number (singular and plural), person (1st, 2nd and 3rd), and gender with a strictly limited force (animate and inanimate in the 3rd person): *man* "I", *to* "you", *u, vey* (lit.) or *ân* (denoting inanimate things in most cases) "he/she/it", *mâ* "we", *šomâ* "you", *išân* or *ânhâ* "they". There is a variety of forms and meanings in polite or colloquial usage. For instance, characteristic of modern colloquial is the occurrence of plural forms with a singular value or the forms *mâ-hâ* "we, us", *šomâ-hâ*" "you". *Išân* (coll. *išun*) is often used as a polite equivalent of the third person singular pronoun. Similarly, in polite speech, the first or second person pronouns in singular may be substituted by various forms, e.g. *bande* "servant", *in jâneb* "this side" (lit.), *janâb-e ʿâli/ʿâli janâb* "Your Excellency" (see further details, incl. concordance, below, in 8. *Syntax*).

Personal pronouns, as usual, share the functions of nouns, but not all of them. For instance, they may be preceded by prepositions, e.g. *bâ mâ* "with us", or postponed by object markers, e.g. *mâ-râ* "us (acc)" (but see *man-râ* > *ma-râ* "me (acc.)"). Having determining function they are used with *iḍāfa* (*ketâb-e mâ* "our book") acting as a quasi-possessive pronoun. But in this function pronouns do not exhibit exactly the same syntax as nouns or adjectives when they act as modifiers. For instance, they do not allow any further extension of the noun phrase, but they terminate the chain of noun(s) and adjective(s) (cf. *ketâb-e bozorg-e mâ* "our big books", *ketâb-e pedar-e mâ* "the book of my father" or *ketâb-e pedar-e bozorg-e mâ* "the book of my grandfather").

Clitic pronouns are: *-am, -at/-et* (coll.), *-aš/-eš* (coll.) in the singular and *-emân, -etân, ešân* in the plural. As a matter of fact, these clitic morphemes are personal suffixes used in two differing functions: if they are attached to the noun phrase acting as determiner they refer to the possessor as a kind of "determinative possessives" or, if they are used as complements in verbal phrases they refer to the direct or indirect object, rarely (and redundantly) the subject. These clitics, although their phonological shapes and allophones are the same in both functions, differ as for their modification or complementation: clitics used in determinative functions appear to be suffix-morphemes and the word so produced has a complex morpheme structure (*ketâb-aš* = *ketâb-e u* "his book") which can take the object marker (*ketâb-aš-râ* "his book (acc.)"). In the second case, where clitics are used to denote complements of verbs or verbal phrases, the verb and its complement appear to be rather a syntactic construction that cannot be extended (*didam-aš* [= *u-râ didam*] "I saw him", *dâdam-aš* [= *be-u dâdam*] "I gave him (s.th.)" or *nist-eš* [= *u nist*] "he is out (coll.)"). This construction itself is rather unique in that it can be expressive of both the predicate and the object or (more rarely) the subject (cf. É. Jeremias, *Some grammatical problems of early New Persian syntax*, in *Proceedings of the Second European Conference of Iranian Studies*, ed. Fragner *et alii*, Rome 1995, 325-34.)

Other more peripheral functions (partitive, anaphoric, emphatic or pleonastic) of these clitic pronouns (especially the form *-eš*) are very common in informal registers (see more details in Lazard 1992, 109-16). Certain constructions, e.g. if prepositions are followed by such clitics (*az-eš* = *az u* "from him") or they are attached to the non-verbal part of compound verbs (*dust-et dâram* = *dust dâram to-râ* "I love you"), occur hardly ever in formal style. The use of pronominal clitics in earlier periods of Persian was not exactly the same as in Modern Persian. Its occurrence as possessive affix is an innovation of New Persian shared by most of the West Iranian languages. The possessive affixes rigidly attached to the correlative words must have been fully developed in earliest prose. There is, however, a significant difference in frequency in comparison with modern usage. They are used less frequently and in most cases with a limited set of words (e.g. *pedar, mâdar, pesar, khodâ*).

On the other hand, their use as verbal complement continues an old tradition, which itself has not however remained unchanged. In old texts their place was not rigidly fixed; they appeared in various positions in the sentence, although a tendency can be seen to attach them to verbs or to the nominal part of verbal phrases. In some rare examples they appeared after words already extended by other grammatical morphemes (e.g. Class. Pers. *par-ē-š* "one of his feather(s)", cf. Jeremias 1995, 328). This very archaic usage disappeared later.

Reflexive pronouns are *khod, khištan* "oneself" and *khiš* "his, her". The first two are pronouns used in formal language having no distinction of number or person, but they can be constructed with prepositions, followed by the object suffix *-râ* or used as a determinative possessive word with *iḍāfa* (*bâ khod, khod-râ, pedar-e khod*). In colloquial language they are always used with determinative possessive affixes (*khod-am, khod-et, khod-eš*, etc.). *Khiš* is an adjective acting as determiner (*mâdar-e khiš-râ dust dârad* "she loves her mother") and in this function it may be regarded as a formal equivalent of *khod* and *khištan.* In Classical Persian *khiš* (< early Class. Pers. *khēš*) was also used as pronoun beside *khod* and *khištan* (cf. Lazard 1963, 230).

Reciprocal pronouns are *yekdigar, hamdigar* "each other, one another" with the same distinctions as the reflexive pronouns obtain (*yekdigar-râ dust dârand* "they love each other"). See also the independent use of *ham* (*bâ ham* "together"), which is not to be confused with the particle *ham* "also, even" or the copulative conjunction *ham . . . va ham* "and . . . and".

Demonstrative pronouns distinguish singular and plural and can be simple (*in* "this" and *in-hâ* "these", *ân* "that" and *ân-hâ* "those") or compounded with the particle *ham* "same, very" (*hamin* "this same one", *hamân* "that same one") or *čon-, čen-* < *čun* (*čonin, čenin, hamčenin* "like this", etc.). Simple demonstratives precede the noun and remain invariable in the plural if they are used as determiners (*in zan* "this woman", *in zan-ân* "these women").

Interrogative pronouns are: *ke/ki* (coll.) "who", *kehâ/ki(h)â* (coll.) (pl.), *če/či* (coll.) "what", *čehâ/čihâ*" (coll.) (pl.), *kodâm(hâ)* "which one(s)". The latter two pronouns can be used as adjectives as well. *Čand/čandom* "how much/many" shares the syntax with cardinals: it precedes the noun in singular (*čand ruz* "how many days"), but its other form follows it with *iḍāfa* (*ruz-e čandom*). Interrogative pronouns can act as determiners with definitive or indefinite references, but their syntax is still to be investigated.

Indefinite pronouns and determiners: There is a relatively small number of simple indefinite pronouns which can be compounded with various nominal morphemes, like *kas, šakhṣ* "person", *čiz* "thing", *jâ* "place", *qadr* "quantity" or the pronoun *kodâm* "which (one)" to produce a large set of expressions acting as determiners and fulfilling various syntactic functions. Occasionally they can be followed by the indefinite *-i*, but the syntax of its use is not wholly explored (*hič kas* or *hič kas-i* "no one", *hič čiz* "nothing", *hič vaqt* (determinative functions combined with the definite article *-i* or *yek*). Semantically they appear to belong to various classes (universal, assertive, negative, etc.) like *hame* "all", *ba'ẓi* "some", *kasi* "somebody", *hič kasi* (in interrogative or negative sentence) or *har kasi* (in affirmative sentence) "anybody", similarly "*čizi* "something", *hič čiz(i)* or *har čiz(i)* "anything", *hič yek, hič kodăm* "neither", etc. For further details, see Lazard 1992, 124-9.

8. *Syntax*

The simple sentence consists of a subject and a predicate. The predicate, which occurs at the end of the sentence in most cases, can be a (conjugated) verb, a noun, a pronoun, an adjective or a prepositional phrase acting in predicative function followed by various forms of the verbal copula. The subject, however, can be omitted and in this case the predicate alone constitutes a sentence of minimal size (e.g. *raftand* "[they] went away"). Characteristic of Persian are the various types of sentences constructed with so-called "impersonal" verbs or verb phrases, e.g. *momken ast* "it is possible", *'eyb na-dârad* "it does not matter", etc. In another common type of simple sentences the logical subject is expressed by the clitic pronoun attached to the predicative adjective, e.g. *sard-am ast* "I am cold". The concord (or agreement) between the subject and the predicate is normally simple: a singular subject requires a singular object. But there are exceptions, mainly due to semantic or stylistic factors: if the subject is a collective noun or a noun designating inanimate things, the predicate is in singular; in elevated style, honorific addresses are used with predicate in plural, e.g. *šomâ goftid* "you (sing.) told", *âqâ* (sing.) *nistand* (pl.) "the master is not at home" (for more details see above, 2, and Lazard 1992, 178-82; Mu'īn, *Noun. Singular and plural*, Tehran 1369/1991).

The two major constituents of the simple sentence can be further extended by direct or indirect objects and adverbial phrases (for the details of their use, see previous sections). General characteristics of the behaviour of the constituents in the smaller or larger units of the sentence are mobility and optionality even though the constituents show these features in varying degrees. This means that grammatical exponents can be easily omitted and the word order is rather flexible. Normally, the predicate is at the end of the sentence and the subject is at the beginning followed by the object (SOV). Other complements come either before or after the object, but temporal expressions often occur at the initial position (e.g. *šabhâ ketâb mi-khând* "in the evenings he used to read a book"). Generally, objects or space and time expressions move comparatively freely and their syntactic features vary considerably (see the unstable use of grammatical morphemes like the object suffix *-râ* or the dropping of prepositions in less formal styles in above, 4; cf. also Lazard 1992, 183-212). Interrogative sentences have the same word order as affirmative ones differing only in intonation.

Juxtaposed units (phrases or clauses) are coordinated by *va* (or by the clitic *-o* in special cases), *ham . . . (va) ham* "and, also" (*-ham* also used as a clitic, e.g. *šomâ-ham goftid* "you also told . . ."), *na . . . na* "neither . . . nor", *yâ* "or", *khʷâh . . . khʷâh* "either . . . or" and *vali(kan), ammâ* "but, however". Subordinate clauses of different types (object, subject, casual, temporal, etc.) are connected by the conjunction *ke* in most cases, esp. in informal styles, e.g. *goft ke pesar-aš âmad* "he said that his son arrived". Normally this conjunction simply indicates subordination. The most common conjunctions (consisting of one or more words) that introduce subordinate clauses are: *tâ, tâ barâ-ye in ke* "that, until that", etc. (object, final temporal, etc.), *čun, čon, čun ke, zirâ (ke)* "when, as, because", etc. (temporal, casual) and the conditional subordinator *agar* "if" (in negation *magar inke* "unless"). There is a relatively wide freedom in selecting the mood of the verb of subordinate clauses: it can be either in indicative or in subjunctive depending on the speaker's choice of modality. Tense, mode and aspect features of the predicate in conditional clauses are more (but not wholly) fixed: the selection of the verb form in the main (or "matrix") clause and in the conditional clause is directly connected with fulfilment of a real condition or a hypothetical one with present or past reference. See some examples by Ṣādiḳī: *agar Hušang kâr konad, movaffaq mi-šavad* "if H. works, he succeeds"; *agar Hušang bi-yâyad bâ u be gardeš mi-ravam* (or *khʷâham raft*) "if H. should come, I (will) go walk with him"; *agar diruz barf nemi-bârid, havâ sard nemišod* "if yesterday the snow had not fallen (or there had not been snow), the weather would not have become cold", etc. (see more examples in his *Dastūr*, 103-6). Relative clauses are constructed in a special way: due to the lack of relative pronouns such clauses are introduced by the conjunction *ke* and the head noun can be (optionally) repeated in the clause by a pronoun: *yek mard vâred šod ke man u-râ nemi-šenâkhtam* "a man entered whom (*ke u-râ*) I did not know". In restrictive relative clauses constructed with a definite head noun the antecedent is supplied by the morpheme *-i*, e.g. *mard-i ke âmad* "the man who came" (see Lazard 1992, 229-36). Spoken style is developing special syntactic and semantic characteristics of subordinate clauses (see A. Nadjafī, *Kārburd-i "ki" dar fārsī-i guftārī*, in *Nāma-i Farhangistān*, i [1374/1995], 7-19).

This short enumeration of the semantic and syntactical properties of simple and complex sentences does not cover all the possibilities that occur in Modern Persian (see more details in Lazarda 1992, 218-57, and for earlier usage, idem 1963, 455-92; Bahār, *Sabkshināsī, passim*). This field of Persian grammar, however, has remained unexplored.

V. Word formation and vocabulary

1. There are various ways of word formation in Persian such as transposition, derivation by suffixation or prefixation and composition, some cases of which have been already treated in the morphology of the verb, noun and prepositional phrase. Transposition is one of the most common and productive processes which makes new words without adding any morphological marker, e.g. adjectives from nouns or vice versa, or adverbs from adjectives (e.g. *khʷāb* "sleeping" in *khʷāb-i* "are you sleeping?", *šoluq* "tumult" → "tumultuous", *tond* "quick, quickly", etc. See more examples above, in iii. IV. 2. *Nouns and noun phrases, Generalities*). Similarly, certain verbal stems or conjugated forms can be used as nouns (e.g. *kharid* [stem II = simple past tense, 3rd person, sing.] "he purchased, purchase", *ma-gu* [prohib., 2nd person, sing.] "do not say, top secret"); see also more complex compound forms like composition made of the stems (II+I) of the same verb (*goft-o gu* "conversation") or the stems (II+II) of different verbs (*âmad-o raft* "intercourse, familiarity = lit. coming and going"), etc.

Word formation via derivation displays a large set of suffixes, some of which are still productive, whilst certain others are stylistically coloured (e.g. colloquial, obsolete or archaic). The most common suffixes of nominal derivations are: - *i* (or *-gi* after final *-e*) which creates abstract (rarely concrete) nouns from adjectives and nouns (*bozorg* "big, great" → *bozorgi* "bigness, greatness", *mard* "man" → *mardi* "manliness", *bande* "servant" → *bandegi* "servitude", *širin* "sweet" → *širini* "sweetness, sweets" [cf. pl. *širini-jāt*]); another *-i* forms adjectives from nouns (*Irân* "Iran" → *irâni* "Iranian"); *-ak* forms diminutives from nouns (*dokhtar* "girl" → *dokhtarak* "little girl"). The next series of derivations forming nouns and adjectives (*-či, -če, -bân, -dân, -estân, -in, -mand, -var,- vâr, -nâk*) has various levels of productivity in Modern Persian (*maʿdan-či* "miner", *kitâb-če* "booklet", *bâgh-bân* "gardener", *qalam-dân* "pen-holder", *nârenj-estân* "orangery", *pašm-in* "woollen", *arzeš-mand* "valuable", *nâm-var* "famous", *omid-vâr* "hopeful", *nam-nâk* "humid", etc.). Another group of nouns is derived from verbal stems (I or II) by the suffixes *-eš, -âk, -âr* (*raftan, row-* "to go" → *raveš* "method", *khordan, khor-* "to eat" → *khorâk* "nourishment", *raftan, rav-* "to go" → *raftâr* "behaviour", etc.). For other sorts of derivations by suffixation which are not productive anymore, see causative forms in verbal morphology (*šenâkhtan, šenâs-* "to recognise" → *šenâsân-/šenâsân(i)d-* "to make known", etc.).

The most common types of derivation by prefixation are: *nâ-* (*nâ-pâk* "impure", *nâ-mard* "[a] coward", *nâ-mâder* "step-mother"), *ham-* (*ham-vaṭan* "compatriot"), and *por-* (*por-ḥarf* "loquacious").

Composition is a frequently used process of word formation in Persian. The principal types of compound words, according to the syntactic and semantic relations between their two constituents and according to the word class produced by the composition, are: "determinative" (endocentric) compounds made up of two nominal parts (*kâr* "work" + *khâne* "house" → *kârkhâne* "work-shop, factory"); "possessive" (exocentric) compound (*fârsi* "Persian" + *zabân* "language" → *fârsizabân* "Persian-speaking, i.e. a person whose language is Persian"); a noun followed by a verbal stem (I), whose relation is equivalent to a verb and an object or a verb and another verbal complement and the compound so produced can have an active (or passive or locative, etc.) meaning, e.g. *âtaš* "fire" + *parastidan/parast-* "to adore" → *âtašparast* "fire-worshipper", *dast* "hand" + *neveštan/nevis-* "to write" → *dastnevis* "hand-written, manuscript (lit. written by hand)"; a noun followed by a verbal stem (II) forms a compound with passive or intransitive meaning, e.g. *khâne* "house" + *zâdan/zây-, zâd-* "to be born" → *khânezâd* "born at home". These compounds represent only a few of the possible types. In certain cases, however, one cannot judge with certainty whether they represent phonological sequences held together by stress and intonation, or whether they have become lexicalized compositions (see Lazard 1992, 261-91). Their exact nature and status, however, are still to be scrutinised although much has been done in this field (see the discussion of the types *deltang* "heart-tight(ened)" and *tangdel* "tight-heart(ed)" in Telegdi, *Zur Unterscheidung von Substantiv und Adjektiv im Neupersischen*, 325-36).

A particular type of verbal expression is represented by two large groups, called "verbs with preverbs" and "verbal phrases" (or "compound verbs", Fr. "locutions verbales"), whose use appears to be one of the main characteristics of Persian vocabulary since earliest times. The two sets present different types of lexical items with regard to their syntactic and semantic properties. The first group also consists of at least two subgroups which are very similar to each other, but only on the surface; they display two different types depending on their inner semantic structure: the first subgroup represents an ancient procedure of verbal composition, where verbs are preceded by true "living" adverbs of place (e.g. *piš* "before", *pas* "after", *birun* "outside", *bâlâ* "up", *pâ'in* (*pâyin*) "down") as in *bâlâ raftan* "to go up", *pa'in âmadan* "to come down", *birun bordan* "to take out". The meaning of such a phrase is made up of the meaning of the two constituents.

In the other subgroup, the first member is also an adverb of place, but in this kind of verbal phrase the adverb ceases to behave as an adverb (losing its original adverbial meaning), and the sequence acquires a new, secondary meaning, e.g. *farâ-gereftan* "to learn", *foru-raftan* "to plunge" (very formal), *bar-gaštan* "to return" (neg. *bar na-gašt*), *dar-yâftan* "perceive, understand" (note that *bar* and *dar* are formally identical to the prepositions *bar, dar*). In Classical Persian, this type of new verb formation was a living procedure, but over the course of time these verbs with preverbs have acquired a secondary meaning, e.g. *bar-âmadan* ("to overcome, result, rise (dough)"), and their original meaning began to be expressed by a new phrase, e.g. "to come up" > *bâlâ raftan* (see details in Telegdi, *Beiträge zur historischen Grammatik des Neupersischen. I. Über die Partikelkomposition im Neupersischen*, 67-183).

The most developed system of enlarging verbal vocabulary was, however, the formation of "compound" verbs. This heterogeneous group, including sometimes very peculiar verbal constructions, consisted of two, sometimes more words in addition to the "base" verb. The most common type is formed with verbs of exclusively Persian origin such as *kardan* "to do", *zadan* "to strike, cut", *dâdan* "to give", *dâštan* "to have" following a nominal form of Arabic origin in most cases (noun, adjective, etc.), e.g. *ḥarf zadan* "to speak", *dust dâštan* "to love", *bidâr kardan* "to waken", *bidâr šodan* "to wake up", etc. Even though this type of compound verb constitutes a semantically independent lexical item in the dictionary, whose components are not inflected separately, sometimes their sequence is broken up and the non-verbal parts follow the syntactic behaviour of their original word class, e.g. *ḥarf-i zad* "he spoke (s.th.)", *birun-eš kard* (informal) = *u-râ birun kard* "[he] expelled him". Therefore sometimes the question whether they should be regarded as free constructions, syntactic phrases or lexicalised items, is difficult to answer (see for more details, Lazard 1989, 285-87; idem 1992, 291-301).

2. *Loan words in Persian*

New Persian in the past millennium has absorbed a large amount of foreign words. During its first centuries these loans were borrowed from various northwestern and eastern Iranian dialects in most cases (see above, i. *General introduction*). Despite this relatively large group of loans (e.g. Parthian, Sogdian, etc.; see the citations of Henning, Lentz, Sundermann in the *General introduction*) which were taken over either via cultural channels or from substrata, the most effective and influential lenders were the Arabs. The infiltration of Arabic loans began in the earliest formative period (8th-9th centuries) of the Islamic period, increased heavily in the 10th-12th centuries and has continued until quite recently. Its linguistic influence is most clearly detectable in the lexicon, and somewhat less so in morphology. Loan words from Arabic constitute more than 50% of the contemporary Persian vocabulary, but in elevated styles it may exceed even 80% (Pisowicz, 19). Among these loans, for instance, words with the feminine ending (*tā' marbūṭa*), the largest class of Arabic borrowings in Persian, make up about 7% (see J.R. Perry, *Form and meaning in Persian vocabulary*, Costa Mesa 1991). Their quantity, however, varies according to media, literary genres and linguistic styles. The majority of these words, including also broken plurals or genitive structures, appear as lexical borrowings. That is, these loans, though their Arabic morphological structures are clear, have not usually become integrated into the morphology of Persian except in some rare cases, but have mostly remained part of the vocabulary, signalling a highly elevated style in the majority of cases. This means that, apart from some rare examples, the Arabic grammatical structures, e.g. the Arabic plural or nouns supplied with Arabic feminine ending *-e* (*malek-e* "queen", *hamšir-e* "sister"), or a feminine adjectival form governed by a broken plural, which are present in these loans, do not represent creative morphological categories in Persian. They do not generally function in order to create Persian structures analogically even though they occur sporadically in highly elevated style (see above, IV. 2.). Arabic lexemes, and especially participles used in Persian context, show some modification of various degrees in orthography, pronunciation and meaning. See Meier 1981, *passim*; Dj. Matīnī, *Taḥawwul-i talaffuẓ-i kalimāt-i fārsi*, in *Madjalla-i dānishkada-i adabiyyāt-i Mashhad* (1350/1971), 249-83; Ali-Ashraf Sadeghi, *L'influence de l'arabe sur le systeme phonologique du persan*, 145-52; Pisowicz, *passim* (esp. 67). See more details on general and specific problems of borrowings in Lazard, *Les emprunts arabes dans la prose persane du Xe au XIIe siècle: aperçu statistique*, in *Revue de l'École nationale des langues orientales*, ii (1965), 53-67; Telegdi, *Remarque sur les emprunts arabes en persan*, in *Acta Iranica*, ii (1974), 337-45; Peysikov, *Leksikologiya sovremennogo persidskogo yazïka*, Moscow 1975; W. Skalmowski, *Ein Beitrag zur Statistik der arabischen Lehnwörter im Persischen*, in *Folia Orientalia*, iii (1961), 171-5; Kh. Farshidard, *ʿArabī dar fārsī*, [5]1367/1988; M.D. Moinfar, *Le vocabulaire arabe dans le livre des Rois de Firdausī*, Wiesbaden 1970. For borrowings other than Arabic, see G. Doerfer, *Türkische und mongolische Elemente im Neupersischen*, i-iv, Wiesbaden 1963-75, and M.A. Jazayery, *Western influence in contemporary Persian: a general view*, in *BSOAS*, xxix (1966), 79-96; Windfuhr (incl. Arabic) 1979, 155-8 (for earlier literature, see Horn, in *GIPh*, i, 2, 2-9; Jensen, 4-5 and Bahār, *Sabkshināsī*, *passim*).

Persian, as the cuturally dominant language in the area, has influenced considerably both the narrower and larger surrounding territories. This influence has been exercised both by literature and through everyday communication. There is some information on the influence made upon Ottoman Turkish, but only scanty information concerning such languages as Urdu or Hindi (see Hardev Bahri, *Persian influence on Hindi*, Allahabad 1960, cf. Windfuhr 1979, 219; and see further the general bibliographies on linguistics and languages).

iv. *History of grammar writing: Western-type and indigenous*

1. Studies on Persian in Europe.

The first grammatical descriptions of Persian appeared from the 18th century onwards in Europe, although there were scattered references on Persian in the previous centuries as well (the oldest such source is the Persian part of the *Codex Cumanicus*, see D. Monchi-Zadeh, *Das Persische im Codex Cumanicus*, Uppsala 1969; A. Bodrogligeti, *The Persian vocabulary of the Codex Cumanicus*, Budapest 1971; P. Orsatti, *Prodromi degli studi europei sul persiano nel Rinascimento*, in *Italia ed Europa nella linguistica del Rinascimento*, ed. M. Tavoni, Ferrara 1996, ii, 551-67). These first descriptions written by missionaries, theologians, scholars or people of practical orientation (e.g. Ludovicus de Dieu [1628], John Greaves [1649], Ignazio di Gesù [1661]) were meagre collections of paradigms in most cases. Sometimes they offered some (not always reliable) hints about the spoken variety, but their subject of "linguistic" description was the written (literary or formal) language (cf. P. Orsatti, *Grammatica e lessicografia Persiana nell'opera di P. Ignazio di Gesù*, in *RSO*, lv (1981), 55-85; Jeremiás, *Grammatical rule and standard in the first Persian grammars written in Latin (XVIIth century)*, in Tavoni (ed.), *op. cit.*, ii, 569-80; eadem, *The impact of Semitic linguistics on the first Persian grammars written in Europe*, in *Irano-Judaica*, iv, ed. Shaul Shaked and Ammon Netzer, Jerusalem 1990, 159-71). However, the latest grammar of this century by J.B. Podesta (1691) stands pre-eminent in terms of quality and quantity (cf. Jeremiás, *The knowledge of Persian and a scholarly approach to the language: a Persian grammar by J.B. Podesta, 1691, Wien*, in *AO*, xlviii [1995], 71-86). On the famous "*Gazophylacium*", an early lexicographic work containing also a meagre description of Persian, see M. Bastiaensen, *La Persia Safavide vista da un lessicografo europeo. Presentatione del*, in *RSO*, xlviii (1973-4), 175-203. The earliest really good description written in a modern language was made by the famous Sir William Jones (see G.H. Cannon, *Sir William Jones's Persian linguistics*, in *JAOS*, lxxviii [1958], 262-73; Jeremiás, *The Persian grammar of Sir William Jones*, in *History of Linguistics*, ed. D. Cram *et al.*, Amsterdam 1999, 277-88). The 19th century saw a proliferation of Persian grammars written in various languages of Europe (see C. Salemann – V. Shukovski 1888, 106-9; Windfuhr, *passim*, and below, *Bibl.*).

2. Persian grammars by indigenous authors.

The earliest Persian sources offering data on linguistic thinking came from "scientific" works such as those on prosody, metrics or philosophy (logic), e.g. Shams-i Ḳays's *al-Muʿdjam fī maʿāyīr ashʿār al-ʿadjam*, Ibn Sīnā's *Dānishnāma*, Naṣīr al-Dīn Ṭūsī's *Kitāb Asās al-iḳtibās* or Sharīf Djurdjānī's logical works (see Jeremiás, *Arabic influence on Persian linguistics*, in *History of the language sciences*, ed. S. Auroux *et al.*, i, section IX. *The establishment of Arabic linguistics*, ch. 49, Berlin 2000, 329-34; eadem, *Rābiṭa in the classical Persian literary tradition: the impact of Arabic logic on Persian*, in *JSAI*, xxvii [2002], 550-74). After some abortive beginnings, the earliest description of Persian was written by Kemāl Pasha-zāda or Ibn Kemāl Pasha in the early 16th century in Arabic (see Brunschvig, *Kemâl Pâshâzâde et le persan*; Jeremiás, *Kamālpāšāzāda as a linguist*, in *Irano-Turkic cultural contacts in the 11th-17th centuries*, ed. Jeremiás, Budapest [2002] 2003, 79-110). In addition to lexicographic sources which contained chapters on issues of linguistic interest (see above *BQ*, *FDJ*, *FR*), one of the first Persian compilations based on such sources appeared in Tabrīz by Īrawānī (see Jeremiás, *Tradition and innovation in the native grammatical literature of Persian*, in *Histoire, Épistemologie, Langage* (Paris), xv [1993], 51-68). On the history of Persian, see Khānlarī, *Tārīkh-i zabān-i fārsī*, Tehran, and on the history of writing grammar in Iran, see Dj. Humāʾī, *Dastūr-i zabān-i fārsī*, in *Lughatnāma-i Dihkhudā*, *Muḳaddima*, Tehran 1337/1958, 110-47; Ī. Afshār, *Kitābshināsī-i dastūr-i zabān-i fārsī*, in *Farhang-i Īrānzamīn*, ii (1954), 19-45; M.B. Ṣanīʿ, *Sayrī dar dastūr-i zabān-i fārsī*, Tehran 1371/1992. On lexicography, see ḲĀMŪS. 2. Persian Lexicography; S. Nafīsī *et alii*, *Farhang-hā-ī fārsī*, in *Lughatnāma-i Dihkhudā*, *Muḳaddima*, 178-378.

Bibliography: Valuable grammatical studies on certain stages of the history of the language are numerous, but for some other fields research has only just begun. A concise descriptive grammar or a detailed and reliable description of the language history is still missing. In addition to the references given above, for a general orientation, see Lazard, *Persian and Tajik*, in *CTL*, vi, The Hague-Paris 1970, 64-96 (bibl. from 1950 until 1968 at 77-96); Ehsan Yar-Shater, *Iran and Afghanistan*, in *ibid.*, 669-89; Windfuhr 1979; *CLI*, ed. Schmitt, 1989. For the best bibliographical journal for Iranian studies, see *Abstracta Iranica*, supplement to *Studia Iranica* published by L'Institut Français de Recherche en Iran, Paris-Tehran. In Iran there is an increasing number of general and specific bibliography and periodicals, e.g. M. Gulbun, *Kitāb-shināsī-i zabān u khaṭṭ*, Tehran 2536; Afshār, *Zabānshināsī*, in *Fihrist-i maḳālāt-i fārsi*, iv, Tehran 1369/1990; see also the studies published in *Madjalla-i zabān-shināsī* (Iran University Press).

(Éva M. Jeremiás)

viii. Art and Architecture

(a) Art.

The arts of Iran will be analysed according to five broad periods; the first stretches from the Islamic conquest to the rise of the Saldjūḳids in the mid-11th century, a period characterised by the lingering effects of Sāsānid rule, and strong cultural, artistic and economic ties between Iran and ʿIrāḳ. The second, which encompasses the next two centuries when Iran was ruled by the Saldjūḳids and their successors, is characterised by an expansion in the quality and quantity of goods manufactured in the cities of Iran. The third, which stretches from the consolidation of Mongol conquests in the mid-13th century to the rise of the Ṣafawids in the early 16th century, is dominated by the artistic patronage of various courts. The fourth period coincides with Ṣafawid rule (1501-1722); their contribution was to unify Iran under a single government which facilitated a diffusion of court culture to a broader spectrum of the population. Some members of the dynasty also fostered a more commercial focus in the works of art produced within the court itself. The concluding phase of traditional Iranian art lasted from the fall of the Ṣafawids in 1722 to the end of the Ḳādjārs in 1925. During this time, Iran was subjected to new pressures that brought it into ever closer contact with other regions such as India and Europe. Some aspects of artistic culture suffered from external competition but others were reinvigorated, particularly court portraiture and the commercial production of carpets. The weaving, sale and collecting of carpets involved a wider spectrum of Iran's population than had earlier phases of artistic production and patronage.

1. *The Sāsānid heritage and the beginnings of Islamic art 650-1050*

The abrupt demise of the Sāsānid Empire in the mid-7th century A.D. helped to shape artistic development of Iran under Islam. The hasty departure of the Sāsānid court from the royal palace at Ctesiphon allowed the conquering Muslim armies to witness the sumptuous surroundings in which those rulers had lived. Sāsānid defeats between 637 and 642 led the Muslim victors to acquire gold and silver vessels, bejewelled crowns and ornaments, silken garments ornamented with gems and precious metals and a jewel-encrusted carpet. The actual booty was distributed among the troops and soon disappeared from view, but its description in literary accounts helped to preserve an association of the Sāsānids with an opulent court culture and in turn, generated later emulations. The court regalia or ceremonials of some Muslim rulers such as the Ziyārids [*q.v.*] and Būyids [see buwayhids] appear to have reflected Sāsānid traditions. The Islamic conquest's rapidity and the fact that it was not accompanied by large-scale destruction probably helped to maintain continuity of production among textile-, glass- and metalworkers in most regions of Iran. Popularised versions of Sāsānid court culture survived in aristocratic circles, particularly in the Caspian region. This broader tradition is evident in the continuity between the pre-Islamic and Islamic periods in the shape and decoration of objects used for festivals and feasts. These include ewers, boat-shaped drinking vessels and zoomorphic containers (A.S. Melikian-Chirvani, *Le rhyton selon les sources persanes*, in *St. Ir.*, xi [1982], 263-92; idem, *From the royal boat to the beggar's bowl*, in *Islamic Art*, iv [1990-1], 3-112).

The most public form of Sāsānid art, their rock-cut reliefs, were largely ignored in the Islamic era until the advent of the Ḳādjār dynasty in the late 18th century when they began to serve as models for reliefs portraying those rulers (see below, 5). Nevertheless, images depicting Sāsānid rulers in characteristic poses continued to be replicated in several media. Literary references mention the post-Sāsānid use of textiles bearing the likenesses of these monarchs, and depictions of "Bahrām Gūr at the hunt" appear on both metalwork and ceramic vessels of Islamic date (Maria Vittoria Fontana, *La Leggenda di Bahrām Gūre Āzāda*, Naples 1986). Memories of Sāsānid life were also transmitted through texts such as the *Shāh-nāma* of Firdawsī [*q.v.*] completed in 404/1010, describing the accomplishments of Iran's pre-Islamic rulers. Its themes were popularised through wall-paintings and eventually by illustrated copies.

In Iran there appears also to have been a substantial continuity in textile production between the pre-Islamic and Islamic era. The ties between a ruler and the textiles produced in his territory codified in the *ṭirāz* [*q.v.*] system continued from the Sāsānid to Islamic periods, although there was a shift from the figural designs that included portraits of the rulers themselves in the pre-Islamic period to inscriptions giving the titles and epithets of Muslim rulers. The production of figural textiles did not, however, end with the Sāsānids. Some silks ornamented with roundels containing birds or animals that survive in European collections, or have been discovered through archaeology, appear to postdate the Islamic conquest. Included among them are fabrics showing a composite creature that combines the legs and head of a feline with the wings and tail of a bird. One of these, made into a man's *khaftān* and now preserved in the Hermitage Museum, St. Petersburg, appears to date from the 10th century (Anna Jeroussalimskaja, *Soieries sassanides*, in *Splendeur des Sassanides*, Brussels 1993, 113-26, figs. 127-8). Melikian-Chirvani has identified this type of textile with a silk fabric known as *parand* that is associated with Khūzistān in Persian sources (Parand *and* Parniyān *identified*, in *Bull. of the Asia Institute*, N.S., v [1991], 175-9). Older textile practices may also have lingered along the southern coast of the Caspian, an area noted for both its conservatism and its production of silk fabrics. These included green silk brocades known as *ṭabarī* after their place of production, Ṭabaristān. They were highly valued as carpets and may have had both figural ornament and Arabic inscriptions (R.B. Serjeant, *Islamic textiles. Materials for a history up to the Mongol conquest*, Beirut 1972, 74-80).

Iran's integration into the wider Islamic polity ensured that major changes also occurred in other artistic media such as calligraphy, bookmaking and ceramics. In all three cases, Iranian developments mirror those in ʿIrāḳ at the centre of the ʿAbbāsid caliphate. The rise of local lines of rulers such as the Būyids of central Iran or the Sāmānids of Khurāsān and Transoxania (Mā warā' al-nahr [*q.v.*]) probably encouraged artistic production in their provincial capitals, but surviving examples testify more to the pervasive impact of ʿIrāḳī culture than to the strength of any independent cultural developments. This is particularly true of the arts associated with Būyid patronage. The theory that the Būyid dynasty represented an "Iranian" phase in the history of Islamic Iran, popularised in the 1940s and 1950s, was followed by the "discovery" of silks, metalwork, and even a manuscript, the *Andarz-nāma*, all attributed to Būyid patronage. Today much of this corpus of "Būyid" art has been identified as of modern origin (Sheila S. Blair, J.M. Bloom, and Anne E. Wardwell, *Reevaluating the date of the "Buyid" silks by epigraphic and radiocarbon analysis*, in *Ars Orientalis*, xxii [1992], 1-42). There are, nevertheless, objects produced during the period and region of Būyid domination such as a gold jug bearing the titles of Abū Manṣūr Bakhtiyār (*r.* 967-78), a Ḳur'ān copied at Iṣfahān in 972, and an early copy of ʿAbd al-Raḥmān al-Ṣūfī's *Ṣuwar al-kawākib al-thābita* ("Book of constellations") dated to 400/1009-10, in Oxford, all of which have a solid claim to authenticity (E. Wellesz, *An early al-Ṣūfī manuscript in Oxford*, in *Ars Orientalis*, iii [1959], 1-26).

The artistic currents manifested in Khurāsān during the 9th, 10th and early 11th centuries, and broadly associated with the Sāmānids [*q.v.*], combine local traditions linked to the region's pre-Islamic past with innovations deriving largely from ʿIrāḳ. The high quality of locally produced ceramics, metalwork and glass, known primarily through excavation, underscores the region's economic and cultural vitality. Glass excavated at Nīshāpūr exhibits close parallels to specimens found in ʿIrāḳ (J. Kröger, *Nishapur. Glass of the early Islamic period*, New York 1995). The collection of twenty glass objects excavated at the Famen Temple in Shaanxi province, China, that were buried before 874, is a notable case of objects with parallels among finds from Iran and ʿIrāḳ (An Jiyao, *Dated Islamic glass in China*, in *Bull. of the Asia Institute*, N.S. v [1991], 123-37).

Ceramics excavated at Nīshāpūr and other Sāmānid centres such as Samarḳand, are notable for their varied technique, shape and decoration. Some vessels emulate types popular in ʿIrāḳ which in turn reflect Chinese prototypes, whereas others exhibit local techniques, shapes and decoration. The most original, produced from the mid-9th to early 11th centuries, consist of plates, dishes and jugs embellished in slip-painting with both Arabic inscriptions, generally aphorisms, and patterns reflective of the local metalwork tradition. These handsome vessels with their well-written texts on a stark white ground often bear a striking resemblance to manuscript pages (C.K. Wilkinson, *Nishapur. Pottery of the early Islamic period*, New York [1973?]); *Terres secrètes de Samarcande. Céramiques du VIIe au XIIIe siècle*, Paris 1992). Although no dated manuscripts of this period appear to have survived, the Sāmānid ruler Manṣūr b. Nūḥ I (*r.* 961-76) initiated the translation of two major works in Arabic composed by Abū Djaʿfar al-Ṭabarī [*q.v.*]: his chronicle of early Islamic history, a task assigned to Abū ʿAlī al-Balʿamī [see BALʿAMĪ. 2], and his Ḳur'ānic commentary. The latter's abridged translation into Persian, accomplished by a group of religious scholars, must have been produced in bilingual manuscripts. Later examples of Ḳur'āns with interlinear translations and Persian commentaries produced in Khurāsān during the 11th and 12th centuries suggest that local calligraphers favoured variants of the "ʿAbbāsid" scripts used in contemporary ʿIrāḳ (F. Richard, *Splendeurs persanes*, Paris 1997, 33-8).

2. *Iranian art under the Saldjūḳids and their successors 1050-1220*

The gradual westward expansion of the Saldjūḳids (*r.* 1040-1194 [*q.v.*] during the 11th century allowed them to unify the eastern and western sections of Iran and to create a more homogeneous culture over the region as a whole. Paradoxically, even though these Turks were of tribal nomadic origin, the principal artistic consequences of their dominion appeared in Iran's urban centres. The Saldjūḳids ruled from a series of cities including Nīshāpūr, Rayy, Iṣfahān, Hamadān, Kirmān and Marw, but their zone of influence was also extended by alliances with other rulers including the Khʷārazm Shāhs and the Ghaznawids. In addition to the absence of a single administrative centre, the fissiparous character of the Saldjūḳid state stemmed from their tradition of dividing their domain among various family members, including minor princes who ruled with the assistance of a guardian or *atabeg* [see ATABAK]. After the dynasty's decline in the mid-12th century, effective power passed to a number of local rulers who had previously been Saldjūḳid tributaries or *atabegs* for various princes. Despite this political fragmentation, crafts flourished in towns from Harāt and Nīshāpūr in the east to Kāshān, Iṣfahān and Tabrīz in the west.

Members of the Saldjūḳid dynasty are known principally as patrons of architecture (see (b), below), but the relative stability and prosperity associated with their rule was also a stimulus to the development of the portable arts. Metalwork and ceramic objects produced between the mid-11th and mid-13th centuries are noted for their innovative decorative techniques and their excellent craftsmanship. The strong foundations of this period's artistic culture also allowed it to survive for several decades after the demise of the Saldjūḳid dynasty itself. Dated and inscribed objects suggest that several crafts, including metalworking and ceramics, reached a peak of quality in the first two decades of the 13th century just prior to the devastation brought about by the Mongol conquests of the 1220s (R. Ettinghausen, *The flowering of Seljuq art*, in *Metropolitan Museum Journal*, iii [1970], 113-31; R. Hillenbrand (ed.), *The art of the Saljuqs in Iran and Anatolia*, Costa Mesa 1994).

The practice of inlaying objects of brass or bronze with copper, silver and gold was developed with particular skill in eastern Iran and Khurāsān. During the 12th century this technique was associated with the city of Harāt, where some of the finest pieces are known to have been made, including a bath-bucket known as the "Bobrinsky Bucket" dated to 1186 and now in the Hermitage Museum. Objects given this distinctive and painstaking form of embellishment include ewers, bowls and trays intended for use in celebrations and implements such as pen cases and inkwells that were part of the paraphernalia of government officials. This technique was also practised by craftsmen in the western sections of Iran, and by the first quarter of the 13th century it had spread to the city of Mawṣil in ʿIrāḳ. Melikian-Chirvani has suggested that the pieces made in western Iran drew their inspiration from the Khurāsānian tradition, but it is unclear whether such connections would have been established through trade or because of the migration of craftsmen from east to west (*Metalwork from the Iranian world, 8th-18th centuries*, London 1982, 23-54, 136-42).

Although utilitarian ceramics continued to be produced in many places, the most ambitious objects are associated with the workshops of the central Iranian town of Kās̲h̲ān. This centre was well endowed with the raw materials needed for the production of a new type of body based on the use of crushed quartz and other forms of silicon which could be shaped to an unparalleled thinness and even to create white bodies that were translucent. Although the ultimate inspiration for these changes is thought to have derived from a desire to imitate the thin and translucent bodies of Chinese porcelain, the Kās̲h̲ān potters embellished their wares with painting executed in several different techniques (Ettinghausen, *Evidence for the identification of Kashan pottery*, in *Ars Islamica*, iii [1936], 44-75).

The best-known decorative mode employed by the Kās̲h̲ān potters is that of over-glaze painting in metal oxides and other pigments. The resulting "lustre-painting" [see KHAZAF] gave the objects a metallic sheen and brilliance. This technique had been applied to ceramics already in 9th-century ʿIrāḳ and in Egypt during the 10th and 11th centuries. Its use at Kās̲h̲ān appears to date from the late 12th century, and the technical secrets involved in its production may well have been carried there by emigré craftsmen fleeing the collapse of Fāṭimid rule in Egypt. Whatever the source from which this knowledge was obtained, the potters of Kās̲h̲ān made this technique their own, applying it both to vessels destined for household use and to tiles used in the embellishment of architecture. They also employed other decorative techniques such as the use of moulded ornament or painting in under- and over-glaze colours. The most laborious of these techniques known as "seven-colour ware" could be executed with great finesse and allowed the ceramics to bear designs of increasing intricacy. Notable examples decorated in this technique include cups which narrate heroic tales or a large platter that depicts the siege of a fortress (O. Watson, *Persian lustre ware*, London 1985; Marianna S. Simpson, *The narrative structure of a medieval Iranian beaker*, in *Ars Orientalis*, xii [1981], 15-24; J. Soustiel, *La céramique islamique*, Freiburg 1985, 77-105).

The 11th and 12th centuries also witnessed the expansion of manuscript production in Iran; proportioned scripts developed in ʿIrāḳ during the late 10th century and 11th century were adopted by calligraphers working in Iran (D. James, *The master scribes*, London 1992, 22-57). The most elaborate decoration occurs in Ḳurʾān manuscripts, such as the one copied and illuminated at Hamadān in 1164; but similar embellishments appear in a few secular manuscripts, and some illustrated books were produced in Iran and Sald̲j̲ūḳid Anatolia (Ettinghausen, *Manuscript illumination*, in *Survey of Persian art*, 1937-54; Melikian-Chirvani, *Le roman de Varqe et Golšāh*, in *Arts asiatiques*, xxii [1970]).

3. *Iranian art of the Mongol and Tīmūrid periods*

The initial devastation of the Mongol invasion of Central Asia and Iran (1218-23) was followed by a second, less destructive wave of conquests in the 1250s which brought the remainder of Iran under Mongol control. Although skilled craftsmen were usually exempted from the general slaughter that ensued when a city or town resisted Mongol forces, the population and artistic productivity of the most devastated regions, such as K̲h̲urāsān, plummeted and would not recover until the 15th century. By way of contrast, the cities and towns of western and southern Iran including Kās̲h̲ān, Tabrīz and S̲h̲īrāz not only escaped destruction but even provided the catalyst for a revival of artistic production in the later 13th and 14th centuries. Two major changes helped to transform the arts: increased connections between Iran and East Asia, especially China, and the growing importance of the princely courts as loci of artistic consumption and even at times of its production. This gave Iran's rulers a greater role in shaping its artistic traditions than they had previously exercised.

The first of the arts to revive may have been ceramics, led by the production of lustre-painted tiles and vessels at Kās̲h̲ān. An important group of such tiles was produced to embellish a palace constructed by Abaḳa K̲h̲ān (*r.* 1265-82) at Tak̲h̲t-i Sulaymān in north-west Iran (R. Naumann, *Die Ruinen von Tacht-e Suleiman und Zendan-e Suleiman*, Berlin 1977). Here for the first time vegetal and animal themes of Chinese origin such as lotus and prunus blossoms, many-clawed dragons and birds with extravagant plumage became part of the repertoire of Iranian craftsmen. Many of these same elements are also prominent in the luxurious silk textiles embellished with gold and produced under Mongol patronage in various sections of their domain, some of which have recently come to light among objects taken from Tibet. Even before their arrival in the Near East, the Mongols had demonstrated that they placed a high value on textiles, particularly those of silk brocaded with gold, and took pains to ensure their access to a steady supply. Those measures included seizing skilled weavers and moving them from one region to another to establish workshops where they would produce textiles for their Mongol masters (M. Rossabi, *The Silk trade*, in J.C.Y. Watt and Ann Wardwell (eds.), *When silk was gold*, New York 1997, 14-19). Although it is difficult to link surviving fabrics with any specific production centre, textiles depicted in Persian manuscripts of the late 13th and early 14th centuries demonstrate that textiles designs of Far Eastern origin were in use there as well.

The history of S̲h̲īrāz shows a different aspect of this era. Its rulers, the Salg̲h̲urids [*q.v.*], forged an alliance with the Ilk̲h̲ānid Mongols which ensured the city's survival, and local traditions helped to shape its artistic production. A long-standing association of the nearby monumental ruins of Persepolis with a mythical past, in which deeds of the Biblical ruler Solomon and the Iranian hero D̲j̲ams̲h̲īd were interwoven, provided the basis for a distinctive local titulature used by the city's Islamic rulers who declared themselves to be "heirs to the Kingdom of Solomon". These titles appear in a group of brass vessels inlaid with silver produced in S̲h̲īrāz during the 14th century. Although K̲h̲urāsānī typologies of shape and decoration from the pre-Mongol era appear in some of them, other metalwork from Fārs displays complex faceted, fluted and imbricated shapes. The new emphasis on figural compositions in their decoration is akin to those used in illustrated manuscripts of the period (Melikian-Chirvani, *Metalwork from the Iranian world*, 136-230).

G̲h̲azān K̲h̲ān's acceptance of Islam in 1295 helped to integrate the traditional arts of Islamic Iran with the new cultural modes of the Mongol period. This is evident in two main areas—the creation of sumptuous, large-scale Ḳurʾānic manuscripts and the preparation of illustrated copies of Persian texts. G̲h̲azān's interests included medicine and various scientific disciplines, and he commissioned the translation of Ibn Buk̲h̲tīs̲h̲ūʿ's *Manāfiʿ al-ḥayawān* into Persian. An illustrated copy of it dated to either 1297 or 1299, now in the Pierpont Morgan Library, New York, was probably prepared for him (Barbara Schmitz, *Islamic and*

Indian manuscripts and paintings in the Pierpont Morgan Library, New York 1997, 9-23). Ghazān also ordered his vizier Rashīd al-Dīn to compile a history of the Turks and Mongols, a project that during the reign of Ghazān's brother and successor, Öldjeytü (*r.* 1316-35) was expanded to encompass the history of the rest of Eurasia. Some copies of the resulting text, the *Djāmiʿ al-tawārīkh* ("Compendium of chronicles"), were illustrated. The earliest and most important of these, now divided between the Edinburgh University Library and the Khalili Collection, London, was completed in 1314, probably for presentation to Öldjeytü (Sheila S. Blair, *A Compendium of chronicles*, London 1995, 16-31). As befits the text's wide-ranging sources, its illustrations show the impact of the several pictorial traditions available in Mongol Iran, including illustrations executed in Byzantine, Nestorian and Armenian workshops, Chinese cartography, Chinese printing, as well as earlier Persian paintings.

The gradual assimilation of the Mongols to Islamic culture was also marked by the creation of large-scale richly illuminated copies of the Ḳur'ān. The most impressive, executed by the period's leading calligraphers and embellished with full-page illuminations, were commissioned by Öldjeytü, most probably for the religious complex at Sulṭāniyya which became his tomb. Copies were prepared for him simultaneously in three cities: one was made in Baghdād, another in Mawṣil, and the third in Hamadān. All shared with the manuscripts of Rashīd al-Dīn's history an unusually large size, measuring 50 × 37 cm, and all were adorned with extensive gilded ornamentation (D. James, *Qurans of the Mamluks*, New York 1988, 92-126). A number of impressive Ḳur'ān manuscripts were also produced at Shīrāz for local dignitaries, including female patrons such as Tāshī Khātūn, the mother of Abū Isḥāḳ Īndjū (*r.* 1343-57), and his sister Fārs Malik Khātūn. Their manuscripts combine well-executed gold calligraphy in ʿIrāḳī modes with a local style of illumination (*ibid.*, 162-73; James, *The master scribes*, London 1992, 122-35).

The Mongol period also marks the beginning of the creation of illustrated copies of Firdawsī's *Shāh-nāma*, a text often regarded as historical and a source of edification for rulers. Copies produced between the late 13th and mid-14th centuries exhibit diverse features, suggesting that they were commissioned by a variety of patrons. Some, although lavishly illustrated, are compact in size, whereas others are on the scale of large Ḳur'ān manuscripts. One such large copy has been linked to the reign of the last important Mongol ruler, Abū Saʿīd (*r.* 1316-35), and may have been commissioned either by him or by his vizier, Rashīd al-Dīn's son Ghiyāth al-Dīn Muḥammad (O. Grabar and Sheila Blair, *Epic images and contemporary history: the illustration of the Great Mongol Shahnama*, Chicago 1980).

The death of Abū Saʿīd in 1335, without an heir, set the stage for conflicts between rival Mongol factions for control of his domain. The most influential among these factions for artistic development were the Djalāyirids [*q.v.*]. They seized the region of Tabrīz as well as much of ʿIrāḳ including Baghdād, and embraced manuscript patronage with particular enthusiasm. Shaykh Uways (*r.* 1356-74) [see UWAYS. 1] and his son Sulṭān Aḥmad (*r.* 1382-1410) gave painting and manuscript production a high priority within their courts. The Muẓaffarids [*q.v.*], who ruled Kirmān, Shīrāz, Yazd and Iṣfahān, continued to patronise the metalworkers and the Ḳur'ānic calligraphers of Fārs, and also commissioned illustrated copies of important Persian texts, including Firdawsī's *Shāh-nāma* and Niẓāmī's *Khamsa*. The concern of these dynasties with artistic patronage was emulated by the Tīmūrid and Turkman dynasties that followed them.

Tīmūr's (*r.* 1370-1405) own relentless and destructive military campaigns left little time for cultivation of the arts, other than architecture which he apparently viewed as a tangible embodiment of his power, but many of his descendants made artistic patronage an integral part of their life. This activity came naturally to them, for it reflected an integration of craft production into the physical fabric of court life, a process which had begun with the mobile camp-cities of the Mongols. In the course of the 15th century, Tīmūr's feuding descendants gradually lost control over the territory which he had painstakingly assembled, but along the way they embraced the idea that a princely court should be a catalyst for connoisseurship in the visual arts. Craftsmen connected with Tīmūrid courts produced a variety of goods ranging from the accoutrements of nomadic prestige (tents, decorated saddles, embroidered silks, and jade drinking vessels) to manuscripts so lavishly ornamented that some were even written on gold-embellished paper and bound in bejewelled covers.

The list of Tīmūrid patrons of the book stretches from the incorrigibly rebellious Iskandar b. ʿUmar Shaykh to Shāh Rukh and his sons Bāysonghor and Ibrāhīm Sulṭān, who were both noted calligraphers who had their own book-producing workshops. This process reached a climax with the last major Tīmūrid ruler, Sulṭān Ḥusayn Bayḳara (1470-1506). His court at Harāt, enriched by the intellectual power of ʿAlī Shīr Nawā'ī, included the talented calligrapher Sulṭān ʿAlī Mashhadī and the painter Bihzād [*q.v.*], whose fame later reached legendary proportions. It is a fitting expression of the interlocking realms of personal experience and aesthetic pleasure at Tīmūrid courts that the patrons themselves were often portrayed in their own manuscripts either directly in a frontispiece, or indirectly in the guise of participants in a literary narrative (T.W. Lentz and G. Lowry, *Timur and the princely vision*, Washington, D.C. 1989).

Despite the relatively short duration and intrinsic fragility of Tīmūrid control over Iran, the dynasty's legacy of combining patronage of the arts with other more obvious forms of royal prestige was also adopted by several of their rivals among the Ḳara Ḳoyunlu and Aḳ Ḳoyunlu dynasties, notably Pīr Budaḳ Ḳara Ḳoyunlu and Yaʿḳūb Aḳ Ḳoyunlu. Relatively few works of art associated with these patrons are extant, but those manuscripts that have survived are notable for their intricate blue and gold illumination and expressionistic style of painting. Both of these features continued to be popular under the Ṣafawids.

It is generally believed that during the 15th century patterns and decorative schemes created by court workshops were first used in the design of textiles and carpets. Although literary references to carpets indicate that they were produced in Iran from the Sāsānid period onward, those descriptions are inadequate for reconstructing either their technical characteristics or their appearance. It seems that in Iran the production of knotted pile carpets only became common after the influx of Turkish nomads that began in the 11th century. Depictions of carpets in Persian manuscripts of the 14th and 15th centuries suggest that most had a central zone occupied by small-scale repetitive motifs similar to those used in Anatolian carpets of that period. During the 15th century, some carpets depicted in Tīmūrid paintings have designs focused on a central medallion that may be round, oval or star-shaped. Often the carpet's corners contain quarter-medallions while the remainder of its field is filled with vegetal ornament usually in the form of spiraling vines with a variety of blossoms placed along them at intervals (Amy Briggs, *Timurid carpets. I*, in *Ars Islamica*, vii [1940], *II.* in *ibid.*, xi-xii [1946]). These painted carpets resemble the finest extant 16th-century carpets as well as designs used in manuscript illumination and book bindings [see also BISĀṬ, in Suppl.].

4. *Iranian art of the Ṣafawid period*

The Ṣafawid creation of a kingdom whose boundaries resemble those of the modern Iranian state served to encourage a more homogenous artistic tradition within the region as a whole, a process also furthered by two of the dynasty's most influential rulers, S̲h̲āh Ṭahmāsp I (*r.* 1524-76) and S̲h̲āh ʿAbbās I (*r.* 1587-1629). S̲h̲āh Ṭahmāsp's approach to the arts is an extension of the cultural attitudes which characterised late Tīmūrid Harāt in the period of Sulṭān Ḥusayn Bayḳara, a connection that is understandable since Ṭahmāsp spent much of his youth in that city. The prince showed an aptitude for painting as well as calligraphy, so that when he returned to Tabrīz to ascend the throne, he gave a great importance to the book arts. During the first decades of his reign, the royal workshop was engaged in the production of manuscripts, particularly copies of the classics of Persian literature. The most important manuscript associated with his patronage is a copy of Firdawsī's *S̲h̲āh-nāma* which is almost a picture album, for its 759 folios contain 258 illustrations and most of these occupy almost the entire surface of a page. As might be expected from a project of this size, it gives evidence of having been executed by numerous painters and the paintings show a range of styles and quality. By and large, the most impressive paintings are those situated in the manuscript's earliest sections where some of them continue trends originating in Tīmūrid Harāt while others echo features of western Iranian art under the Turkmans. The most elaborate compositions depict complex architectural structures the divisions of which are used to separate an event into narrative components (M.B. Dickson and S.C. Welch, *The Houghton Shahnama*, 2 vols., Cambridge, Mass. 1981). The impact of court etiquette and activities on the illustrative programs of a manuscript is particularly striking in the case of a manuscript of Niẓāmī's *K̲h̲amsa* also prepared for S̲h̲āh Ṭahmāsp and now in the British Library (Welch, *Persian painting*, New York 1976, 70-97).

Ṭahmāsp I's enthusiasm for manuscript patronage was echoed by other members of the dynasty, notably his brothers Sām Mīrzā and Bahrām Mīrzā as well as his nephew Sulṭān Ibrāhīm Mīrzā. The last-named devoted considerable time and energy to artistic pursuits and employed a substantial number of calligraphers, painters and illuminators. A copy of D̲j̲āmī's *Haft awrang* produced for him between 1556 and 1565, and now in the Freer Gallery of Art, shows the manner in which an illustrated manuscript could become a "world unto itself". Every folio provides a feast for the eye, contrasting finely executed calligraphy with colourful gold-decorated borders, while its paintings draw the viewer into a self-contained universe inhabited by people of various ages and social stations (Marianna S. Simpson, *Sultan Ibrahim Mirza's Haft awrang*, New Haven 1997).

During the Ṣafawid era, the popularity of illustrated manuscripts spread beyond the confines of the court, and they were produced also in non-royal workshops for a widening circle of patrons. Workshops in the city of S̲h̲īrāz were particularly active in the book-trade. During the 16th century, in addition to the ever-popular poems by Firdawsī and Niẓāmī, texts by several writers active in the late Tīmūrid period continued to be both widely copied and frequently illustrated, including the poetry of D̲j̲āmī, Hātifī and the prose of Ḥusayn Gawzargāhī (F. Richard, *Splendeurs persanes*, Paris 1997, 157-204). By the early 17th century, however, the attention of artists and collectors had shifted to single-page paintings, especially portraits, which were often gathered in *muraḳḳa*ʿs [*q.v.*] (albums) (Sheila R. Canby, *The rebellious reformer*, London 1996).

The Ṣafawid court was also involved in the production of various other kinds of artifacts, particularly silk textiles embellished with gold and silver and carpets with complex patterns which echo the intricate designs of book illumination or even of book illustration. Annually on the occasion of Nawrūz [*q.v.*], following a well-established Islamic practice, Ṣafawid rulers were expected to provide their courtiers and retainers with garments appropriate to their status and position. Some garments worn by the ruler and his close associates were made of silk woven or embroidered in intricate patterns and embellished with gold and silver; used textiles were routinely destroyed in order to recover the metal which they contained. Ṣafawid rulers sent luxury textiles as diplomatic gifts to their rivals, the Ottomans and the Mug̲h̲als. Historical accounts confirm that several towns in Iran produced luxury textiles and rugs, including Kās̲h̲ān, Yazd, Kirmān and Iṣfahān, although it is difficult to link surviving examples with any particular centre (Carol Bier (ed.), *Woven from the soul, spun from the heart*, Washington, D.C. 1987; May Beattie, *The carpets of Central Persia*, Westerham 1976).

The few surviving rugs from 16th-century Iran follow designs created by professionally trained designers or painters. Some have elaborate figural and landscape compositions, whereas others are noted for their multi-level designs of vegetal scrolls. S̲h̲āh Ṭahmāsp I is known to have taken a personal interest in the production of carpets, and S̲h̲āh ʿAbbās I is even said to have practised the weaver's craft. During his reign, weavers worked in the grounds of the royal palace at Iṣfahān, although production of luxury textiles and rugs also continued in other centres. The intricate time-consuming designs and lavish use of silver and gold that characterise Ṣafawid court carpets and textiles preserved in shrines or sent as diplomatic gifts suggest that court production was viewed as an index of royal prestige, rather than as a commercial venture (M. Aga Oghlu, *Safawid rugs and textiles*, New York 1941; Bier and Bencard, *The Persian velvets at Rosenborg*, Copenhagen 1995; F. Spuhler *et al.*, *Denmark's coronation carpets*, Copenhagen 1987).

5. *Iranian art from 1722 to 1925: the Afs̲h̲ārid, Ẓand and Ḳād̲j̲ār periods*

Although the period from the effective end of the Ṣafawid dynasty in 1722 to the emergence of the Ḳād̲j̲ārs in 1794 was marked by chronic political instability, artistic patronage still continued on an intermittent basis largely echoing trends of the late 17th century. Lacquerwork (actually varnished watercolour paintings, usually on a papier-mâché surface), which had earlier been used for bookbindings, was also used for pen-boxes, mirror cases and caskets. A few paintings and luxury textiles can be linked to Nādir S̲h̲āh (*r.* 1736-47), and his seizure of Mug̲h̲al treasures during his invasion of India provided Iran's rulers with jewels later used with great effect by the Ḳādjārs in their court regalia. Karīm Khān Zand's reign (1751-79) is notable for a stress on large-scale figure paintings on canvas that were used to embellish buildings, a practice expanded under the Ḳādjārs. It was that dynasty's second ruler, Fatḥ ʿAlī Shāh, who made the most concerted and skillful use of pictorial imagery as an adjunct to state policy. He revived the use of rock-cut reliefs for heroic images of himself and of his court and similar compositions were also used on portable objects such as lacquerwork bookbindings or mirror cases. Enthusiasm for large-scale figural painting was not limited to the Ḳādjār court. Itinerant story-tellers used portable picture scrolls (sometimes identified as "Coffee-house paintings") as an adjunct to the recitation of stories and to performances of the passion play or *taʿziya* [*q.v.*] (see Layla S. Diba and Maryam Ekhtian (eds.), *Royal Persian paintings. The Qajar epoch 1785-1925*, Brooklyn 1999.

The second half of the 19th century witnessed a decline in most local crafts due to the competition created by imports from Europe and India. One exception was the production of carpets, which were much in demand both within Iran and abroad. The old system of court production was replaced by commercial workshops that drew on the skill of many segments of Iran's population. Large-scale enterprises, situated in major urban centres such as Iṣfahān, produced standardised carpets to the specifications of a mostly foreign clientèle. Smaller production centres, situated in villages, the homes of private citizens or even in nomadic encampments, created more varied wares which often combined traditional schemes with idiosyncratic embellishments. This broadly based "folk-art" provided a kind of democratisation of Iran's artistic tradition that carried it into the 20th century (A.C. Edwards, *The Persian carpet*, 1953).

Bibliography: *Survey of Persian art*; J.W. Allan, *Persian metal technology 700-1300*, London 1979; O. Grabar, *The art of the object*, in *Camb. hist. of Iran*, iv, 351-63; Grabar, *The visual arts, 1050-1350*, in *ibid.*, v, 641-58; B. Gray, *The pictorial arts in the Timurid period*, and *The arts in the Safavid period*, in *ibid.*, vi, 843-76, 877-912; F. Spuhler, *Carpets and textiles*, in *ibid.*, 698-727; B.W. Robinson, *Persian painting under the Zand and Qajar dynasties*, in *ibid.*, vii, 870-89; J. Scarce, *The arts of the eighteenth to twentieth centuries*, in *ibid.*, 930-58; R.W. Ferrier (ed.), *The arts of Persia*, New Haven 1989; A. Soudavar, *Art of the Persian courts*, New York 1992.

(PRISCILLA SOUCEK)

(b) Architecture.

The buildings erected in Iran during the Islamic period are some of the finest constructed anywhere in the Muslim lands. They are noteworthy for their sophisticated vaulting systems and their sublime use of coloured decoration on both interior and exterior. Both traits may have been encouraged by the materials available for construction. Although large supplies of wood grow near the Caspian Sea and good stone for masonry is found in Fārs and Ādharbāydjān, brick is the predominant building material in most of the region. Already in pre-Islamic times, builders in Iran had devised ways of roofing their structures with domes supported on squinches, arches thrown over the corner of a room. Builders in Islamic times maintained the tripartite elevation of wall, squinch and vault, but divided the zone of transition into increasingly smaller and more elaborate segments, culminating in the *muḳarnas* [*q.v.*]. At the same time, they carved and painted the stucco covering interior surfaces and developed several methods of glazing tiles in a full range of colours, so that brick surfaces covered with brilliantly coloured tiles became a hallmark of Iranian Islamic architecture.

The following discussion surveys the development of these trends in Iranian Islamic architecture in five chronological periods. Within each period, a short assessment precedes discussions of the major building types and of form, materials and decoration. The article considers Iran in the broadest sense, comprising the plateau between the Tigris and Oxus rivers, and occasionally includes sites beyond these confines, such as Baghdād or Samarḳand. Naturally, more buildings and more types of buildings survive from the later period, making it possible to sketch a fuller picture from the extant record. By contrast, relatively few buildings survive from earlier times, and the evidence for early Islamic architecture in Iran has to be pieced together from widely scattered remains and snippets of information gleaned from texts.

1. *Before 900*

Virtually nothing is known about buildings from the period of Umayyad rule when the Islamic capitals were in Syria, but, as befits Iran's position as one of the most important provinces in the ʿAbbāsid empire, most of the buildings erected there in the 3rd/9th century reflect the forms and styles used in the capital province in ʿIrāḳ. Compared to ʿIrāḳ, contemporary buildings in Iran are generally smaller, but show a wider variety of materials, including rubble and mortar, fired brick, mud brick (particularly in northeast Iran and the adjacent regions of Central Asia) and wood. Many are decorated with the styles of carved stucco development at the ʿAbbāsid capital of Sāmarrāʾ [*q.v.*].

The most important building type known from early Islamic times in Iran is the congregational mosque. Congregational mosques built in Iran resemble those constructed elsewhere in the ʿAbbāsid domains, for virtually all of them are (or were) large buildings with a central courtyard surrounded by porticos or arcades and a large covered prayer hall on the *ḳibla* side (in Iran, the southwest). The prayer hall was a hypostyle room, in which the roof was supported on a multitude of single supports, either piers or columns. The best standing example of a hypostyle congregational mosque is the one known as the Tārī Khāna, erected at Dāmghān in the 3rd/9th century. The remains of others have been excavated at several sites, including Sūsā in Khuzistān in southwestern Iran and at Sīrāf on the Persian Gulf (dateable A.D. 815-25), but the largest and most important of these hypostyle congregational mosques was the one erected at Iṣfahān. Founded *ca.* 771, it was expanded under the ʿAbbāsid caliph al-Muʿtaṣim (*r.* 218-27/833-42) and served as the basis for the present Friday Mosque (Masdjid-i Djumʿa) in the city.

In addition to the hypostyle congregational mosque, there were other types of small mosques. One type had an attached courtyard leading to a rectangular prayer hall (measuring between 5 and 10 m on a side) divided by one or more transverse arcades, with a projecting *miḥrāb* [*q.v.*] in a rectangular salient. At least ten examples were excavated in the residential quarters at Sīrāf, and some may date as early as the 3rd/9th century. Another type of small mosque is a square covered with nine domes. The one that survives at Balkh is about four times the area of the small mosques at Sīrāf (measuring *ca.* 20 m to a side) and was elaborately decorated on the interior with extravagantly carved stucco.

The same forms and decoration were used on a smaller scale in domestic architecture. Vaulted and domed houses excavated at Marw (now in Turkmenistan) were decorated with Sāmarrā'-style stucco. Houses excavated at Nī<u>sh</u>āpūr also had stucco dados elaborately carved in a similar style (several are now on display in the National Museum in Tehran and the Metropolitan Museum in New York).

Caravanserais [see KHĀN] erected along the major trade routes across Iran and Central Asia also reflect the plans of those found elsewhere in the ʿAbbāsid lands. Three mud-brick forts erected at Darzīn in Kirmān province, for example, are square buildings (25 m on a side) with round buttresses and tunnel-vaulted chambers.

2. *900-1250*

This was the most creative period in Iranian architecture, and all of the distinctive features of Iranian Islamic architecture—the use of fine-quality baked brick as the primary material of construction and decoration, the development of glazed tile as an important medium of both interior and exterior decoration, the four-*īwān* plan, mausolea, minarets, the tripartite elevation of dome chambers, the subdivision of the squinch into increasingly smaller units and the *muḳarnas*—appear for the first time during this period. Most of these features are commonly associated with the patronage of the Sal<u>dj</u>ūḳ dynasty (432-590/1040-1194), whose territories stretched from Central Asia to ʿIrāḳ, but many were introduced earlier and were not limited to the Sal<u>dj</u>ūḳ domains.

New congregational mosques were built to suit the need of the growing Muslim community. Those erected in the 4th/10th century, as at Nā'īn and Ardistān, continued to use the hypostyle plan, but the major feature of this period was the development of a new plan having a courtyard surrounded by arcades linking four *īwāns*, high vaulted rooms open to the court at one end. The transformation from the hypostyle to the four-*īwān* plan is best seen in the mosque at Iṣfahān, an early capital of the Sal<u>dj</u>ūḳ domains. In 485/1086-7, the twenty-four columns in front of the *miḥrāb* were replaced with a free-standing domed pavilion supported on giant polylobed piers. Then, later, probably in the early 6th/12th century, four *īwāns* were added around the court. This combination of four *īwāns* plus dome chamber was soon repeated in congregational mosques in nearby towns such as Ardistān, whose hypostyle mosque was revamped between 553 and 555 (1158-60).

Despite the occasional use of other types of congregational mosque, the four-*īwān* plan became the standard for congregational mosques erected all over Iran from this period onwards. Scholars have long debated why this change occurred. Although the reasons are not entirely clear, it may have been simple practicality and utility. This plan had already been used in many pre-Islamic buildings in ʿIrāḳ and Iran, ranging from the Parthian palace at Ashur (1st century A.D.) to Sāsānid houses at Ctesiphon (6th century A.D.). It provided a suitable setting of monumentality, without any rigid princely or cultic associations.

From the 6th/12th century the four-*īwān* plan also became standard for many other types of buildings. To judge from later examples, this plan may have been used for *madrasas*, which began to proliferate at this time. This plan was also used for caravanserais, such as Ribāṭ-i <u>Sh</u>araf, built in 508/1114-15 by the Sal<u>dj</u>ūḳ vizier <u>Sh</u>araf al-Dīn Ḳummī on the old route north from Nī<u>sh</u>āpūr to Marw. Building civil structures was considered an act of piety and a sign of sovereignty, and many local rulers embellished their domains in this way. The Kurdish prince Badr b. Ḥasanawayh (*r.* 370-404/980-1013), for example, erected a series of bridges along the pilgrimage route near <u>Kh</u>urramābād; Kākūyid *amīrs* added iron gates to the mud-brick walls around the city of Yazd in 432/1040-1, as did the <u>Sh</u>addādid *amīr* <u>Sh</u>āwūr I b. Faḍl at Gan<u>dj</u>a in 455/1063.

From the 5th/11th century onwards, minarets began to proliferate thoughout Iran. Most are tapering brick cylinders about 30 m tall, decorated with horizontal bands of elaborate brick patterns and elegant inscriptions. In earlier ʿAbbāsid times, minarets had been attached to congregational mosques and normally set opposite the *miḥrāb*. In this period they were erected by a broader spectrum of people, including viziers, judges and private individuals, and sometimes set as isolated, free-standing constructions. Their proliferation may also indicate a revolution in technique which made these tall baked-brick towers resilient to earthquakes.

The monumental tomb [see ḲUBBA; TURBA] was another major type of building erected in this period. Tomb towers were popular along the Caspian littoral, as exemplified by the Gunbad-i Ḳābūs (397/1006-7), the earliest and also the most spectacular example to survive. The classic example of the domed tomb is the mausoleum of the Sāmānids at Bu<u>kh</u>ārā (310s/920s), but its exquisite form and decoration in carved plaster and baked brick bespeak a long tradition. The domed tomb became the most popular type. Three fine examples were erected at Marā<u>gh</u>a in the 6th/12th century, but the largest and most splendid is the one built at Marw for the Sal<u>dj</u>ūḳ sultan San<u>dj</u>ar (*r.* 511-52/1118-57).

Larger tomb complexes also developed during the period. Some, such as those at Ma<u>sh</u>had or Ḳumm, surrounded the graves of <u>Sh</u>īʿī *imāms*. They were underwritten not only by wealthy <u>Sh</u>īʿīs but also by government officials seeking to garner the support of heterodox segments of the local population. Other complexes grew up around the graves of such learned figures as al-Ḥakīm al-Tirmi<u>dh</u>ī or such mystics as Abū Yazīd al-Bisṭāmī [*q.vv.*]. These shrine complexes were often agglomerative, and the specific stages of construction can only be revealed by detailed archaeological investigations, usually impossible because of the sacred nature of the sites.

Texts mention large palaces and elaborate houses for the upper classes in the Būyid capitals at Ba<u>gh</u>dād and <u>Sh</u>īrāz and the Sal<u>dj</u>ūḳ capitals at Iṣfahān, Ba<u>gh</u>dād and Marw. Excavations have revealed only tantalising fragments from minor sites, such as limestone panels from the palace of the Ḥasanawayhids at Sarma<u>dj</u> in southwest Iran or carved stucco panels from Tirmi<u>dh</u> on the Oxus. Contemporary houses excavated at Nī<u>sh</u>āpūr were lavishly decorated with painted stucco.

Domes were elaborated and articulated during this period. In order to lighten the domical mass, both physically and visually, builders developed the double dome, in which two shells of slightly varied profile are connected by intermittent ties. Niẓām al-Mulk's *Siyāsat-nāma* (ed. H. Darke, Tehran 1340/1962, 211, tr. idem, London 1978, 167) mentions that one of the 4th/10th-century tombs of the Būyids at Rayy already had such a double dome (*ba du pū<u>sh</u>i<u>sh</u>*), and extant examples survive from the end of the 5th/11th century (e.g. the tomb at <u>Kh</u>arraḳān dated 486/1093-4). Ribs were used to facilitate construction in a land where wood was unavailable for centring. As the dome was built, the ribs were bonded into the construction and often exploited for decorative effect. The inventiveness Iranian builders displayed in the manipulation of domed spaces is clear from the Friday Mosque at Iṣfahān, where over two hundred examples cover the individual bays, although the exact chronology of the vaults has not been established and it is still unclear what percentage can be assigned to this period.

Dome chambers typically show a tripartite elevation, with the dome supported on an octagonal zone of transition, in which four squinches alternate with four blind arches, in turn supported on four walls arranged in a square. In more elaborate examples, builders inserted an intermediary sixteen-sided zone or squinch net between the dome and the octagonal zone. In a single example, the north dome at Iṣfahān, the parts are aligned vertically. In all other cases, the three parts are distinguished visually.

In addition to vaults, builders also manipulated arches. *Miḥrāb*s from this period, the earliest to survive in the region, consist of concentric niches within rectangular frames, as at the 4th/10th-century congregational mosque at Nā'īn. Builders also developed the *pīs̲h̲ṭāḳ* [*q.v.*], an arched opening surrounded by a free-standing rectangular frame. The ruined building at Sarwistān, which Bier has recently re-attributed to the early Islamic period, had a *pīs̲h̲ṭāḳ* in the middle of the façade, and by the 4th/10th century builders used this form in Iranian mosques and mausoleums (e.g. the Arab-Ata mausoleum at Tim in the Zarafs̲h̲ān Valley dated 367/977). The *pīs̲h̲ṭāḳ* soon became one of the most distinctive features of Iranian architecture, used in a variety of building types including caravanserais (e.g. Ribāṭ-i Malik, rebuilt in 471/1078-9, and Ribāṭ-i S̲h̲araf) and mausolea (e.g. Uzgand and Sarak̲h̲s, 5th-6th/11th-12th centuries).

Builders in this period also displayed their inventiveness by varying the shape of the arch, from round to keel-shaped, trilobed and polylobed, and by combining squinches of different shape in the same building. Five different types of squinch, for example, are used at Ribāṭ-i S̲h̲araf. By further subdividing the squinch, builders seem to have developed the *muḳarnas*, tiers of niche-like elements that project out from the row below. Already at the Gunbad-i Ḳābūs, a few tiers of *muḳarnas* decorate the half-vault over the door, and *muḳarnas* corbels were used to support the cornices of tomb towers, as at the Gunbad-i ʿAlī (448/1056-7) in Abarḳūh or the balconies of minarets, as at Bisṭām (514/1120-1). *Muḳarnas* was clearly used to provide a visual transition, but its structural role remains to be documented.

During this period, fine baked brick was the pre-eminent material for the construction of important buildings, while mud brick, pisé and stone were used for subsidiary structures or in specific areas. By the 6th/12th century, a standard baked brick measuring *ca.* 25 × 25 × 5 cm had replaced the large rectangular bricks used in the early period and the smaller bricks associated with Būyid buildings in the Iṣfahān region. Bricks were laid in a variety of flush or basket bonds, from common and double bond to diaper patterns, or in combinations of recessed and projecting bricks.

Builders also exploited the spaces between the bricks for decorative effect. Builders in northeastern Iran often laid bricks in double bond so that the vertical joints created a pattern of light and shade across the wall. Builders sometimes filled the joints with plaster endplugs, which were stamped or carved with geometric, floral or epigraphic, patterns, or with pieces of glazed tile, which contrasted with the matte, reddish or yellowish brick. Holes in the brickwork on the earlier tomb tower erected at K̲h̲arraḳān in 460/1067-8 were probably filled with these glazed pieces, and small fragments are still preserved in the dome chamber in the congregational mosque at Gulpāyagān erected under the Sald̲j̲ūḳ Muḥammad b. Maliks̲h̲āh (*r.* 498-511/1105-18 [*q.v.*]). From the 6th/12th century onwards, builders commonly set out glazed bricks which spelled out sacred words and phrases in the technique known as *bannā'ī* "builder's [technique]".

Builders or decorators (the distinction is unclear in this period) also realised the potential of other methods for adding colour to their brick buildings. The most labour-intensive and therefore the most expensive method was to cut the glazed tiles into small pieces to form geometric designs, strapwork or inscriptions. The most common glaze was light or turquoise blue, easy to prepare from copper. The tomb chamber at Naṭanz (389/998-9) has small pieces of glazed tile inset in the plaster decoration. The minaret at Sīn (526/1132) has a complete inscription made up of pieces of glazed tile. Two tombs at Marāg̲h̲a, the Gunbad-i Surk̲h̲ (542/1147-8) and the Gunbad-i Kābūd (593/1196-7), have elaborate strapwork patterns. One monument erected shortly before the Mongol invasions, the *madrasa* at Zawzan (616/1219), displays two additional colours of glazed tile, white and dark blue.

From *ca.* 1200, builders also decorated the interior of buildings with expensive lustre tiles. At major shrines such as Ḳumm and Mas̲h̲had, hundreds of individual tiles, some specially made to fit the site, were used to cover the cenotaphs, *miḥrāb*s and walls of the tomb chambers. These tile revetments were signed by the most famous potters of the day, Muḥammad b. Abī Ṭāhir and Abū Zayd, both members of prominent lustre-potting families from Kās̲h̲ān, home to this speciality. As the city of Kās̲h̲ān, located near important mines, had a monopoly on tile production, the term *kās̲h̲ī* [*q.v.*] came to refer to glazed tile.

Similarly, builders often painted the stucco coating interior surfaces. Traces of red, blue and green paint are often visible on *miḥrāb*s, and walls were sometimes painted to imitate brick bonding patterns. Other subjects include geometric and vegetal ornament as well as figures, animals, and birds. The increased use of colour and the growing taste for covering up wall surfaces foreshadow later developments, but at this time structure and decoration were kept in balance.

3. *1250-1500*

This period marked the triumph of coloured decoration. Builders elaborated the technique of tile mosaic so that it covered the entire surface. They also expanded the palette to a full range of seven colours (dark and light blue, white, black, yellow and green, in addition to unglazed brick). They added other techniques of tile decoration, including *cuerda seca* and *lād̲j̲wardīna*, overglaze painting. This period also saw an increase in the height, verticality and size of buildings, and the enormous complexes ordered by Mongol and Tīmūrid rulers attest the wealth available in this period of trans-Asian trade. Individual buildings were often incorporated into complexes, which combined a mosque, *madrasa*, *k̲h̲ānḳāh* and other service buildings around a tomb, either for the founder (as in Öld̲j̲eytü's tomb at Sulṭāniyya [*q.v.*] or Tīmūr's tomb, the Gūr-i Mīr at Samarḳand) or for a Ṣūfī saint (as at Naṭanz, Bisṭām and Gāzur Gāh outside Herat).

Congregational mosques followed the standard

four-*īwān* plan. The one built at Warāmīn in the 1320s exemplifies Ilkhānid work, but the most impressive is the elephantine one erected by Tīmūr in his new capital at Samarḳand. Known as the Mosque of Bībī Khānum, after Tīmūr's favourite wife, it measures a gargantuan 100 × 125 m. Wherever space was available, as in these two examples, these congregational mosques had regular exteriors, but whenever they had to be shoehorned into the space available in a city, as in the one that Tīmūr's daughter-in-law Gawharshād added to the shrine of the Imām al-Riḍā in Mashhad in 821/1418-19, the exterior was irregular. As before, these mosques focus on the courtyard, and the one at Mashhad is truly magnificent, with dazzling tile mosaic and underglaze- and overglaze-painted tiles.

*Madrasa*s of the period are even more homogeneous than mosques and have a similar plan of a court surrounded by two stories of students' cells connecting four *īwān*s, as at the Madrasa Imāmī (755/1354) at Iṣfahān or the one built at Khargird in 846-8/1442-5 by the architect Ḳawām al-Dīn Shīrāzī, the first Iranian architect whose career and style can be delineated. The *madrasa*s built by Shāh Rūkh's son Ulugh Beg in Bukhārā and on the Rīgistān in Samarḳand (both 820-3/1417-21) are variations on the same theme.

A similar plan was also used for rural caravanserais, often erected along major trade routes as part of the flourishing overland trade. Caravanserais were also built within cities. One of the few urban commercial buildings to survive is the Khān al-Mīrdjān (or Khān al-Urtma) in Baghdād (758/1359); its sophisticated transverse-vaulted roofing system, which allows light to flood the interior, shows that the patron, the governor of Baghdād for the Djalāyirids, considered the caravanserai as important as the other parts of his complex.

Both the tomb tower and the domed square chamber continued to be used for funerary monuments. Mausolea built for lesser figures, such as descendants of the *Imām*s or minor princes or princesses, were relatively small, free-standing buildings (e.g. the Imāmzāda Dja'far at Iṣfahān, 725/1325). The most striking examples, notable for their fine tile decoration, are found in the necropolis outside of Samarḳand known as the Shāh-i Zinda, where many domed structures lining the street leading to the principal shrine were built for female members of Tīmūr's family. Since some orthodox scholars condemned the building of mausolea, the cenotaph was sometimes set in the open air in front of an *īwān*. Several Tīmūrid examples of this arrangement, which has been called a *haẓīra*, are found at Gāzur Gāh, Turbat-i Shaykh Djam and Ṭayyabād.

Richer patrons, mainly sultans and their chief ministers, built larger tombs as part of elaborate funerary complexes. The best example to survive from the Ilkhānid period is the mausoleum of the Khān Öldjeytü at Sulṭāniyya, but the foundations established by Ghazān Khān and his vizier Rashīd al-Dīn at Tabrīz were equally large. Large complexes were also built around the tombs of Ṣūfī saints. A few honoured contemporary *shaykh*s, such as the complex built at Naṭanz in the opening decade of the 8th/14th century for the Suhrawardī *shaykh* 'Abd al-Ṣamad (d. 699/1299-1300), but more commonly they honoured saints long since dead, as at the complex of Abū Yazīd Bisṭāmī, which underwent major restoration at the same time. These complexes, like mosques, had regular exteriors whenever space allowed, as at the gigantic shrine that Tīmūr erected on the steppe for Aḥmad Yasawī [*q.v.*] at Turkistān (799-801/1397-99) and the one that Shāh Rūkh erected for 'Abd Allāh Anṣārī [*q.v.*]) at Gāzur Gāh (829-32/1425-29).

A few palaces were permanent constructions. *Ca.* 1275, the Ilkhān Abaḳa, for example, constructed a summer residence at Saṭūrīḳ (now Takht-i Sulaymān [*q.v.*]) on the foundations of the Sāsānid sanctuary of Shīz. The quality and abundance of the architectural décor, particularly the marble carvings and the lustre and *lādjwardīna* tiles, show that the Mongol ruler spared no expense. Both the site, which has been identified as the place where the Sāsānid emperors had been crowned, and the decoration, including lustre tiles with quotations and scenes illustrating themes from the *Shāh-nāma*, may have been chosen for their association with pre-Islamic Iranian kingship. The ruins of the Aḳ Sarāy, Tīmūr's palace at Shahr-i Sabz (781-98/1379-96) show the same concerns for size and fine tile decoration.

More often, however, the Mongols lived in elaborate tents [see KHAYMA. iv]. Ghazān's summer palace, for example, was said to have been a tent of golden tissue which took two years to make, and the Spanish ambassador Ruy Gonzalez de Clavijo described the even more sumptuous pavilions inhabited by Tīmūr. These tents were often set in gardens, and the Tīmūrids constructed several canals outside Harāt to water their extensive suburban estates set in gardens with such evocative names as the Bāgh-i Djahān-ārā "(World-adorning garden"). Observatories are the most notable civil structures to survive from this period. The one ordered by Hülegü in 758/1258 for the celebrated astronomer Naṣīr al-Dīn Ṭūsī [*q.v.*] on a hill north of his capital at Marāgha served as the model for the one that Ulugh Beg built at Samarḳand in 823/1420 for Ghiyāth al-Dīn Kāshī [*q.v.*].

Builders in this period shifted their attention from structure to space, developing new and inventive ways of covering both square and rectangular areas. The solid walls of earlier buildings were pierced with openings and bays, and several types of transverse vaulting were developed to admit light and air. Experiments with transverse vaulting over rectangular spaces in the 8th/14th century led to the development of squinch-net vaulting in the 9th/15th. Builders transformed the traditional square room into a cruciform chamber with broad niches on the sides. Both the recesses and the central square are spanned with four broad arches. The intersection of these eight arches creates a smaller square which supports the traditional arrangement of four squinches, an octagon, a sixteen-sided zone and the dome. The interstices between the ribs and squinches are filled with faceted and painted plaster, hence the name "squinch net". This new system has many advantages: the vault itself is significantly smaller than the square room it covers; it is relatively light in weight; and the loads are concentrated on points rather than walls, as in Gothic architecture, so that the walls can be opened up with windows or filled with staircases and subsidiary rooms.

Builders also altered the proportions used in this period, making rooms taller, arches more pointed and minarets more attenuated. Typical of the new verticality and refinement of form are the monumental portals with soaring double minarets preserved in Iṣfahān, Yazd and Abarḳūh. Many of these soaring vaults are decorated with plaster *muḳarnas* shells that are suspended from the outer shell by ropes. Those used at Naṭanz in the early 8th/14th century are relatively simple, but the ones erected a century later at Turkestān are of unparalleled complexity.

Abarḳūh, Gunbad-i ʿAlī, 448/1056-7.

Tehran, Gulistān Palace, Shams al-ʿImāra, completed 1282-84/1865-67, view from the rear.

Iṣfahān, Masdjid-i Imām, formerly the Masdjid-i Shāh, begun 1020/1611, courtyard.

Sangbast, tomb and adjacent minaret, probably 6th/12th century.

Dāmghān, Congregational Mosque, known as the "Tārī-Khāna," 3rd/9th century, courtyard looking toward prayer hall (vaults restored 20th century).

Nāyin, Congregational Mosque, 4th/10th century, court façade showing brickwork added during the Būyid period.

Māhān, Shrine of Niʿmat Allāh, vaulted hall adjacent to the tomb, early 11th/17th century.

Yazd, Congregational Mosque, west prayer hall, late 8th/14th century.

Nāyin, Congregational Mosque, 4th/10th century, stucco *miḥrāb*.

Decoration, too, became more complex. Entire wall surfaces were often covered with *bannāʾī*, thereby enveloping the building in a web of pious phrases. Tile mosaic became more common, with floral and curved designs replacing the angular ones used earlier. Interior plaster surfaces were often covered with intricate moulded and painted designs, often derived from book painting and thereby suggesting the existence of a central design studio in this period.

4. *1500-1800*

The buildings erected during this period are some of the most alluring and attractive in all Iranian architecture, and for many viewers, their glittering web of glazed tile, soaring portals, bulbous domes, and slender minarets epitomise the essential qualities of Persian architecture. In part, their fame is a matter of survival, for a large and impressive ensemble of buildings is easily accessible in Iṣfahān [*q.v.*], the third capital of the Ṣafawids, and Shīrāz [*q.v.*], capital of the Ṣafawid regent Muḥammad Karīm Khān Zand (*r.* 1164-93/1751-79). In part, the attractiveness of this architecture is due to its open and easy design, with simple compositions based on addition and symmetry. These buildings show little structural or formal innovation, for builders needed to build and decorate vast structures in the shortest time; hence colourful tile revetments sometimes conceal structural banality. The greatest strength lies in the planning and execution of large urban ensembles, in which a variety of commercial, religious and political functions are integrated in harmonious compositions. This was also the period when builders, like contemporary painters, developed an interest in the history of their art, be it the Tīmūrid tradition of dynastic architecture in Khurāsān or the local building traditions of Iṣfahān and Shīrāz.

In general, buildings, especially religious ones, use the same type of plans found in earlier periods. The four-*īwān* plan, for example, continued to be standard for congregational mosques, as in the splendid one, now called the Masdjid-i Imām, that Shāh ʿAbbās (*r.* 995-1038/1587-1629) ordered for his new capital at Iṣfahān. The same plan was also used for *madrasas* and *khāngāhs*. So, too, the domed tomb remained popular. The tomb of Khʷādja Rābiʿ at Mashhad (1030/1620) is a domed octagon, whereas that for Ṭahmāsp's father Shaykh Djibrāʾīl, in the village of Kalkhurān near Ardabīl, is a square surmounted by a tall bulbous dome recalling Tīmūrid tombs of Central Asia.

In comparison with earlier times, much more civil architecture survives from this period, particularly from the reign of Shāh ʿAbbās, who saw architecture as a means of enhancing his economic policies. An extensive system of *ḳanāts* [*q.v.*], subterranean aqueducts directly linked to aquifers, were dug to supply new settlements. Bridges were set up along important roads, as in the superb examples over the Zāyanda Rūd [*q.v.*] at Iṣfahān. Different types of buildings for collecting and storing water were developed, such as the water storage tank (Pers. *āb-anbār*), usually a large domed cistern ventilated by means of pipes (Pers. *bādgīr* [*q.v.* in Suppl.]). To make and store ice, builders developed ingenious mud-brick structures (Pers. *yakhčāl*), often decorated with inventive brickwork. ʿAbbās also encouraged the construction of thousands of pigeon towers (Pers. *burdj-i kabūtar*) on the fertile plain around Iṣfahān so that he could heavily tax the guano harvest. Similarly, the city of Bukhārā, one of the Shaybānid capitals in Central Asia, was dotted with caravanserais (Pers. *tīm*) and domed markets (Pers. *čahār-sū*).

These many buildings were often integrated into fine ensembles centred around a large *maydān* [*q.v.*] or public square. In Iṣfahān, ʿAbbās had four new buildings strategically and symbolically positioned around the *maydān*: the bazaar entrance on the north faced the congregational mosque, and a small mosque known as the Masdjid-i Shaykh Luṭf Allāh on the east faced the ʿĀlī Ḳapu, the entrance to the palace precinct. Between 1596 and 1606, ʿAbbās's governor Gandj ʿAlī Khān laid out a similar complex in the provincial capital of Kirmān, with a bath, caravanserai, mint, water tower, mosque and other public buildings connected by a continuous portico around a large rectangular *maydān* (100 × 50 m). Many of these urban developments continued under Muḥammad Karīm Khān Zand at Shīrāz, who glorified his capital with broad avenues and more than 25 public buildings. As in Iṣfahān and Kirmān, the most important structures, including the citadel or *arg*, the congregational mosque known as the Masdjid-i Wakīl (begun in 1766), a public bath and a vaulted bazaar, were grouped around a *maydān*.

This was also the period when the major shrine complexes in Iran took on their definitive shape. To mark their claims of sovereignty and establish their legitimacy, the Ṣafawids expanded and rebuilt the family shrine at Ardabīl, making it one of the largest in the country, matched only by the shrine around the tomb of the eighth Imām al-Riḍā at Mashhad. Both shrines received substantial endowments, not only property and chattels but also precious objects, particularly books. ʿAbbās also endowed a staggering 1,162 pieces of Chinese porcelain to the shrine at Ardabīl, and had a new building, the Čīnī-Khāna, built to house it. Other shrines developed for Ṣūfī *shaykhs*. One of the most picturesque is that for Shaykh Niʿmat Allāh Walī at Māhān outside Kirmān, whose sequence of courtyards and richly-carpeted and splendidly-vaulted halls evokes the wealth and authority accorded these brotherhoods in Ṣafawid Iran.

Town planning and building on such a wide scale necessitated the employment of dozens of architects and master-builders assisted by calligraphers, tile-makers, plasterers, woodworkers and painters. The workforce, especially at the top, was highly mobile and dominated by the Iṣfahān school, which attracted the finest talent from throughout the Ṣafawid domains. The vast scale of architecture during this period led builders to standardise exteriors but to experiment with structure. They perfected the system of ribbed vaults developed during the 9th/15th century by empirical study of the strength of materials. For example, large rooms were spanned by ribbed arches with forked bases which distributed the weight on to piers concealed within the walls. These structural experiments have only been revealed during the course of restoration, as in the upper two floors of the ʿĀlī Ḳapu palace at Iṣfahān. New forms include the *tālār*, the pillared hall known from Achamaenid times and adopted during this period for audience halls.

Flat walls were often decorated with paintings of varied subjects. Some illustrate current events, such as the series of embassies and battles depicted on the walls of the Čihil Sutūn palace at Iṣfahān. Others evoked classic Persian themes, such as the romance of Khusraw and Shīrīn. A few, such as the murals in the Imāmzāda Shāh Zayd in Iṣfahān, depict religious scenes, and some others, such as a group of oil paintings, depict foreigners. In many cases, these wall paintings seem to be the work of the same artists who illustrated manuscripts and single-page paintings.

5. *1800 to the present day*

Architecture in this period can be seen as a struggle between tradition and innovation. Under the Ḳādjārs [*q.v.*], new Europeanising features were grafted on to traditional ones. Thus congregational mosques, erected at Ḳazvīn, Zandjān, Simnān and Tehran, followed the now-classic plan of an open court with two or four *īwāns*, but interior façades were articulated with such new features as kiosks, windcatchers or clocktowers. The increasing acceptance of European architecture, especially under Nāṣir al-Dīn S̲h̲āh (r. 1264-1313/1848-96 [*q.v.*]), is especially clear in secular architecture, exemplified by several palaces in and near Tehran, such as the Gulistān Palace and the Ḳaṣr-i Ḳādjār. Traditional forms such as the *tālār* are combined with such European elements as tall windows, engaged pilasters and grand staircases. The mixture of traditions is also evident in the decoration, in which tile mosaic, underglaze-painted tiles and mosaic mirror-work mingle with floral, figural and landscape scenes in the Victorian style.

These experiments with European modernism continued in the 20th century under the Pahlawīs, as the best architects linked an appreciation of traditional values with such modern requirements as waste disposal. Nader Ardalan's Centre for Management Studies in Tehran (1972) followed the form of a traditional *madrasa* and used local construction methods and labour (see further on modern buildings in the capital, TIHRĀN, I. 3(b), (c)). Similarly, the enormous tomb constructed at Rayy for Āyatullāh K̲h̲umaynī [*q.v.* in Suppl.] in 1989 used the traditional form of domed tomb surrounded by minarets, although it was executed using relatively inexpensive materials and techniques of industrial construction.

Bibliography: The bibliography on Iranian architecture is enormous and expanding rapidly. The following includes only books and other major studies. Ruy Gonzáles de Clavijo, *Embassy to Tamerlane 1403-1406*, tr. G. Le Strange, London 1928; E. Diez, *Churasanische Baudenkmäler*, Berlin 1918; *Survey of Persian art*; *Āthār-é Irān*, i-iv (1936-49); M. Siroux, *Caravansérails d'Iran et petites constructions routières*, Cairo 1949; D.N. Wilber, *The architecture of Islamic Iran. The Il Khânid period*, New York 1955; D. Hill (photographer), *Islamic architecture and its decoration, A.D. 800-1500*, Chicago 1964; A. Godard, *The art of Iran*, ed. J.M. Rogers, London 1965; Lisa Golombek, *The Timurid shrine at Gazur Gah*, Toronto 1969; Wilber, *The Masjid-i ʿAtiq of Shiraz*, Shiraz 1972; Nader Ardalan and Laleh Bakhtiar, *The sense of unity. The Sufi tradition in Persian architecture*, Chicago 1973; R. Naumann, *Die Ruinen von Tacht-e Suleiman und Zendan-e Suleiman*, Berlin 1977; Muhammad-Yusuf Kiani, *Iranian caravanserails with particular reference to the Safavid period*, Tokyo 1978; D. Whitehouse, *Siraf. III. The Congregational Mosque and other mosques from the ninth to the twelfth centuries*, London 1980; T. Allen, *Timurid Herat*, Wiesbaden 1983; E. Galdieri, *Isfahan. Masğid-i ğumʿa, III*, Rome 1984; C.K. Wilkinson, *Nishapur. Some early Islamic buildings and their decoration*, New York 1986; Abbas Daneshvari, *Medieval tomb towers of Iran. An iconographical study*, Lexington, KY 1986; L. Bier, *Sarvistan. A study in early Iranian architecture*, University Park, PA and London 1986; Sheila S. Blair, *The Ilkhanid shrine complex at Natanz, Iran*, Cambridge, MA 1986; R. Ettinghausen and O. Grabar, *The art and architecture of Islam. 650-1250*, Harmondsworth 1987; B. O'Kane, *Timurid architecture in Khurasan*, Costa Mesa, CA 1987; Golombek and Wilber, *The Timurid*

architecture of Iran and Turan, Princeton 1988; J.M. Bloom, *Minaret, symbol of Islam*, Oxford 1989; Grabar, *The Great Mosque of Isfahan*, New York 1990; Blair, *The monumental inscriptions from early Islamic Iran and Transoxiana*, Leiden 1992; eadem and Bloom, *The art and architecture of Islam, 1250-1800*, London and New Haven 1994; Barbara Finster, *Frühe iranische Moscheen, vom Beginn des Islam bis zur Zeit salğunqischer Herrschaft*, Berlin 1994; R. Hillenbrand, *Islamic architecture. Form, function and meaning*, Edinburgh 1994; idem (ed.), *The art of the Saljuqs in Iran and Anatolia: Proceedings of a symposium held in Edinburgh in 1982*, Costa Mesa, CA 1994; O'Kane, *Studies in Persian art and archiecture*, Cairo 1995; Muḥammad Karīm Pīrnīa, *Āshnā-yi bā miʿmārī-yi islāmī-yi Īrān*, Tehran 1374/1995; *Mosques. An encyclopedia of the Iranian historial monuments in the Islamic era*, 2 [in Persian], Tehran 1999.

(SHEILA S. BLAIR and J.M. BLOOM)

IRIČ, also ERIČ, ERAČ, on modern maps Erachh, a small town of north-central India, situated on the south bank of the Betwā river, 65 km/40 miles northeast of Jhansi and 100 km/62 miles southeast of Gwalior (lat. 25° 47' N., long. 79° 9' E.). It is now in the Jhansi District in the extreme southwest of Uttar Pradesh Province of the Indian Union.

Although now within a region largely Hindu, the area round Irič is rich in Indo-Muslim remains and monuments. It was in Muslim hands by 709/1309, when the K̲h̲aldjī commander Malik Kāfūr [*q.v.*] stayed at Irič, then renamed Sulṭānpūr, en route southwards for Warangal [*q.v.*]. The D̲j̲āmiʿ Masd̲j̲id there was built by G̲h̲āzī Ḍiyāʾ al-Dīn in 815/1412 during the time of the last Tug̲h̲luḳid Maḥmūd S̲h̲āh II, and was added to in the time of Awrangzīb. There is also a fort and five gates to the town. Under the Mug̲h̲als, it was the centre of a *sarkār* in the *ṣūba* of Agra, but by the mid-18th century was under Marāthā control until the region passed to the British.

Bibliography: D.L. Drake-Brockman, *District gazetteers of the United Provinces*, xxiv, *Jhansi District*, Allahabad 1909, 254-6; J.F. Blakiston, *The Jami Masjid at Badaun and other buildings in the United Provinces*, Memoirs ASI, xix, Calcutta 1926; S.H. Hodivala, *Studies in Indo-Muslim history*, i, Bombay 1939, 252-3; P. Jackson, *The Delhi Sultanate, a political and military history*, Cambridge 1999, 199.

(C.E. BOSWORTH)

IRTISH, conventionally Irtysh, a river of Siberia and the main left-bank affluent of the Ob [*q.v.*]. It rises from glaciers on the southern slopes of the Altai mountains near the modern frontier of the Mongolian Republic and Chinese Turkestan or Sinkiang [*q.v.*] through the Zaysan lake into the Kazakhstan Republic, then out of it into the Omsk *oblast* of the Russian Federation and joins the Ob at Khanty Mansiysk, its complete course being 3,720 km/2,312 miles, the greater part of it navigable.

The Irtis̲h̲ is mentioned, as *ärtis*, in the Ork̲h̲on inscriptions (Kültégin E37; Bilgä Kagan E27), where it is stated that the Kag̲h̲an's armies crossed the Altai and then the Irtis̲h̲, and attacked the Türges̲h̲ on its farther (i.e. western) side (cf. Barthold, *Zwölf Vorlesungen*, 46, 112). But the history of the Irtis̲h̲ basin in early Islamic times is very obscure; none of its peoples can have become Muslim before the post-Mongol, later mediaeval period. A geography like the Ḥudūd al-ʿālam mentions the Artus̲h̲ (ʾ.r.t.s̲h̲) as located between the Og̲h̲uz and Kimäk tribes, but the author was clearly describing a river further west (possibly the Yayïḳ [*q.v.*], which rises in the Urals and flows into the

Caspian), since he says that it emptied into the lower Volga (tr. Minorsky, 75, §6.42, comm. 215). Maḥmūd al-Kāshgharī mentions the *Ertish suwi* as a river in the Yemāk/Yemäk steppes which flows, so he says, after receiving many tributaries, into a lake; this error would appear to stem from the same source as the *Ḥudūd al-ʿālam*, since the Arctic Ocean, the *Baḥr al-Ẓulumāt* of Arabic travellers, can hardly be meant (*Dīwān lughāt al-turk*, tr. Atalay, i, 97, tr. Dankoff and Kelly, i, 129). The Islamic geographers seem to locate the Kimäk [*q.v.*] roughly between the (true) Irtish and the Ob, and Gardīzī writes of the trade route which led northwards from Transoxania to the land of the Kimäk, on the Irtish (cf. Barthold, *op. cit.*, 112-13; but the lower course of the river, beyond the Kimäk, must have been the home of Ugrian peoples, the ancestors of the peoples found there in the 16th century, the Ostyaks or Khanty). During these later mediaeval times, the former lands of the now-vanished Kimäk, were apparently occupied by the Tatars (perhaps including aboriginal Ugrians now Turkicised) and, to their south, the Kazakhs occupied this region (see J. Forsyth, *A history of the peoples of Siberia, Russia's North Asian colony 1581-1990*, Cambridge 1992, 10-16, 21-7).

It was on the banks of the Irtish that Čingiz Khān in 1208 defeated the remnants of his Mongolised Turkish rivals, the Nayman tribe; he halted in the summer of 1219 on the banks of the Irtish before his troops appeared in Transoxania; and towards the end of Čingiz Khān's life, his son Djoči established his *ordo* on the river (Barthold, *Turkestan*³, 361, 392-3, 403, 450; idem, *Zwölf Vorlesungen*, 165, 180). The Great Khān Ögedey was buried, when he died in 639/1241, on a mountain in Mongolia near the headwaters of the Irtish (Rashīd al-Dīn, in Barthold, *Turkestan*³, 473). Islam may have appeared amongst Turkish nomadic tribes in the region when the Blue (or White) Horde came to control its southern and western fringes. In 792/1390 Tīmūr despatched from Tashkent an army against a Khān called Ḳamar al-Dīn, and this marched north from the Issïk-Kul [*q.v.*], crossed the Ili and reached the Irtish (Sharaf al-Dīn Yazdī, *Ẓafar-nāma*, Bibliotheca Indica, i, 495); and at the end of the 15th century, the Khānate of Sibir [*q.v.*] moved its centre to Sibir or Kashlik or Isker near the confluence of the Irtish and its tributary the Tobol. The overwhelming of the Khānate of Sibir in the 1590s [see KUČUM KHĀN], however, brought the greater part of the course of the Irtish under Russian control.

Bibliography: Given in the article; and see OB and SIBIR. (C.E. BOSWORTH)

ISFĪDJĀB, a town and an extensive district of mediaeval Islamic Central Asia, identifiable with the later Islamic town of Sayram. Popular etymologising saw in the name the Persian component *sipīd, ispīd* "white". It lay on the Aris river, a right-bank affluent of the Sïr Daryā [*q.v.*], 14 km/8 miles to the east of the later town of Chimkent (lat. 42° 16' N., long. 69° 05' E.); Chimkent itself, now in the southernmost part of the Kazakhstan Republic, is mentioned in the historical sources from Tīmūrid times onwards, e.g. in Sharaf al-Dīn ʿAlī Yazdī.

Isfīdjāb apparently had a pre-Islamic history, though nothing is known of this; it may have had a local Iranian ruler, as did the adjacent regions of Īlāḳ [*q.v.* in Suppl.] and Usrūshana [*q.v.*]. The incursions into Transoxania of Ḳutayba b. Muslim [*q.v.*] are said to have reached as far as Shāsh and Isfīdjāb, but it appears more firmly in history with a report that, in 225/840, the Sāmānid governor of Samarḳand Nūḥ b. Asad subdued it and built a wall round its vineyards and cultivated lands (presumably as protection against raids by the steppe Turks) (al-Balādhurī, *Futūḥ*, 422; al-Samʿānī, *Ansāb*, ed. Ḥaydarābād, vii, 26). Being on the northernmost edge of the Islamic lands in Central Asia, Isfīdjāb was very much a frontier town, the resort of *ghāzī*s and other fighters for the faith, who congregated in *ribāṭ*s [*q.v.*] fortified against the infidel Oghuz and Kimäk Turks, and numbered by al-Muḳaddasī, 273, with palpable exaggeration, at 1,700. Many of these *ribāṭ*s were built and financed by the people of the Transoxanian towns well behind the frontier, and manned by them in relays; *ribāṭ*s of the men of Nakhshab, Bukhārā and Samarḳand are mentioned, and another *ribāṭ* was that financed by the Sāmānid commander Ḳaratigin al-Isfīdjābī, with Ḳaratigin and his son Manṣūr buried nearby (al-Muḳaddasī, *loc. cit.*; Ibn al-Athīr, ed. Beirut, viii, 492). That this Ḳaratigin—obviously a Turk—was the local ruler of Isfīdjāb in the early 4th/10th century, as Barthold assumed, is by no means sure. At all events, because of its role as a vital frontier post (*thaghr djalīl wa-dār al-djihād*) it was, unusually for Transoxania, exempt from taxation, and the local ruler paid only a token tribute and forwarded presents to the Sāmānid *amīr* in Bukhārā (Ibn Ḥawḳal, 510, tr. 488; al-Muḳaddasī, 340; cf. Barthold, *Turkestan*³, 175-6, 211-12, and idem, *A history of the Turkman people*, in *Four studies on the history of Central Asia*, iii, 77-8).

The geographers describe it at this time as thoroughly well defended, with a citadel (ruinous, however, in Ibn Ḥawḳal's time) and walls round the *shahristān* and *rabaḍ* respectively. As a place where the products of the steppes could be exchanged for those of the settled lands, its markets were flourishing, and al-Muḳaddasī mentions in particular the *sūḳ al-karābīs*, that of the cotton merchants, the rents from whose shops were a charitable *waḳf* that yielded 7,000 dirhams a month (Ibn Ḥawḳal, 510, tr. 487-8; al-Muḳaddasī, 273; cf. Le Strange, *The lands of the Eastern Caliphate*, 483-4, and Barthold, *Turkestan*³, 175-6).

We do not know what ultimately happened to the local rulers of Isfīdjāb, but in 382/992 the Ḳarakhānid ruler of Balāsāghūn, Bughra Khān Hārūn or Ḥasan, occupied the town as he advanced into the Sāmānid dominions, and it is mentioned that a certain Abū Manṣūr Muḥammad b. Ḥasan al-Isfīdjābī rebelled against Sāmānid authority in the very last days of the dynasty (387/997) and summoned help from the Ḳarakhānid Ilig Naṣr.

In the early 7th/13th century, the inhabitants of Isfīdjāb, together with those of Shāsh, Farghāna and Kāsān, were removed by the Khʷārazm Shāh ʿAlāʾ al-Dīn Muḥammad and the land laid waste because he was unable to protect them from the destructive raids of the Mongol Küčlüg [*q.v.*] (Yāḳūt, *Buldān*, ed. Beirut, i, 179; Ibn al-Athīr, xii, 271; Barthold, *Turkestan*³, 368-9). The second disaster which Isfīdjāb suffered, according to Yāḳūt, *loc. cit.*, was devastation by the Mongols of Čingiz Khān.

It is around this time that the name Sayram begins to replace Isfīdjāb, although already in the later 5th/11th century, Maḥmūd al-Kāshgharī, *Dīwān lughāt al-turk*, tr. Atalay, iii, 176, tr. Dankoff and Kelly, ii, 241, equated Sayram/Saryam with the older Isfīdjāb. As such, Sayram figures in the history of the western part of what became, from the 8th/14th century onwards, Mogholistān [*q.v.*], e.g. in the history of the later Čaghatayids as recounted by Mīrzā Muḥammad Ḥaydar Khān. Thus it is recorded that ʿĪsā Bugha Khān devastated Sayram, Turkistān and Tashkent in

855/1451, and later in the century, Sayram was governed by Yūnus Khān, the maternal grandfather of Bābur [*q.v.*]. The Čaghatayid Manṣūr Khān led an expedition against the Kirghiz [see ḲIRGĪZ] in 928/1522 because these Turks had been ravaging the lands from Sayram to Farghāna (*Tārīkh-i Rashīdī*, tr. Elias and Ross, 79, 358). Thereafter, Sayram passed substantially under the control of the nomadic kingdom of the Ḳazāḳ. In 1723 Sayram, Turkistān and Tashkent passed under the control of the Kalmucks [see KALMUK] and remained within their vast nomadic empire until the destruction of this by the Chinese in 1758. Thereafter, the region reverted to Ḳazāḳ rule, and then, in the first half of the 19th century, passed under Russian control; see ḲIRGĪZ.

Bibliography: Given in the article.

(C.E. Bosworth)

ISFIZĀRĪ, Muʿīn al-Dīn Muḥammad Zamčī, epistolary stylist and historian in Tīmūrid Khurāsān whose birth and death dates are unknown but who flourished in the second half of the 8th/14th century.

From what he says in his own works, he arrived in Harāt, probably from Isfizār in what is now western Afghānistān, in 873/1468-9, and was employed as a *munshī* at the court of Sultan Ḥusayn Bayḳara [see ḤUSAYN at Vol. III, 603a] under the patronage of the vizier Ḳiwām al-Dīn Niẓām al-Mulk (d. 903/1497-8). Isfizārī is most famous as the author of a history and compendium of information on the city of Harāt, its topography and its *faḍāʾil*, the *Rawḍāt al-djannāt fī awṣāf madīnat Harāt*, dedicated to Ḥusayn Bayḳara, begun in Muḥarram 897/November 1491 and completed two years later at the end of 899/autumn 1494. Noteworthy here is his use of earlier, lost sources, such as a history of the Kart or Kurt dynasty of Harāt by one Rabīʿī Bushandjī. The history was edited by Sayyid Muḥammad Kāẓim Imām, 2 vols., Tehran 1338-9/1959-60, also by Muḥammad Isḥāḳ, Calcutta 1380/1961 (*non vidi*); description and analysis of contents by Barbier de Meynard in *JA*, 5th ser., vol. xvi (July-Dec. 1860), xvii (Jan.-June 1861), xx (July-Dec. 1862). Isfizārī's *Risāla-yi Ḳawānīn*, an epistle in praise of Harāt and its ruler, is also extant, as is also an *inshāʾ* collection of his.

Bibliography: See also Browne, *LHP*, iii, 420-1; Storey, i, 355-6, 1296, iii, 256-7; Storey-Bregel, ii, 1045-8; Rypka *et alii*, *Hist. of Iranian literature*, 434, 447.

(C.E. Bosworth)

ISHKĀSHIM, a small settlement in the modern Afghān province, and the mediaeval Islamic region, of Badakhshān [*q.v.*].

It lies in lat. 36° 43' N., long. 71° 34' E., and should not be confused with Ishkāmish, further westwards in the Ḳunduz or Ḳaṭaghān district of Badakhshān. The historic Ishkāshim is on the left or southern bank of the Pandj or upper Oxus river (only in Soviet times did a smaller settlement on the other side of the river become the chef-lieu of the so-called Ishkāshim *tuman* or district of the Gorno-Badakhshān Autonomous Region within the Tādjīk SSR; cf. BADAKHSHĀN at Vol. I, 853b), and is at present connected with the provincial capital of the [Afghān] *wilāyat* of Badakhshān, Fayḍābād, by a road across the Sardāb pass. When Soviet Russia invaded Afghānistān, the Russian army in the early 1980s constructed a bridge across the Oxus at Ishkāshim for transporting troops and matériel. Ishkāshim has in fact played a part in history because of its position along the only winter route between Badakhshān and the trans-Oxus regions of Shughnān and Wakhān [*q.vv.*]; and it was here that the British traveller John Wood crossed the ice-covered river in 1837 (*A journey to the source of the River Oxus*, 2nd ed. London 1872, 204-6).

The place existed in early Islam, and the *Ḥudūd al-ʿālam*, tr. Minorsky, 121, makes Sikāshim the chef-lieu of Wakhān and the residence of its *malik*; the people comprised at that time (late 4th/10th century) both Muslims and infidels (*gabrakān*, ? Zoroastrians). Many of the local people, on both sides of the Pandj here, are Ismāʿīlīs, locally known as Mawlāʾīs (see F. Daftary, *The Ismāʿīlīs: their history and doctrines*, Cambridge 1990, 544). The people of villages in the vicinity of Ishkāmish, also in one place on the right bank of the Pandj, perhaps totalling in all some 2,000, speak a distinctive Eastern Iranian language of the so-called "Pamir group", Ishkāshmī (see the *Bibl.* to BADAKHSHĀN, and also J.R. Payne, in R. Schmitt (ed.), *Compendium linguarum iranicarum*, Wiesbaden 1989, 417-44).

Bibliography (in addition to references given in the article): L.W. Adamec, *Gazetteer of Afghanistan. Badakhshan province and Northeastern Afghanistan*, Graz 1972, 85-6; Muḥammad Nādir Khān, *Rāhnamā-yi Ḳaṭaghān wa Badakhshān*, ed. M. Sutūda, Tehran 1367/1988, index.

(C.E. Bosworth)

ʿISHḲĪ, Muḥammad Riḍā Mīrzāda, modernist poet, playwright, journalist and fervent Iranian nationalist (b. 5 June 1894, d. 3 June 1924 = 12 Tīr ASH 1303).

ʿIshḳī's life is shrouded in legend because of his ultra-patriotic pronouncements in his writings and speeches, his unconventional and often militant ideas in politics and literature, and above all, his tragic death at the early age of thirty from an assassin's bullet. He received his elementary education in his native Hamadān, attending the Ulfat and Ālyāns (Alliance) high schools, in the latter of which he learned French and was introduced to Western civilisation. His knowledge of French helped him to gain employment as a translator/interpreter for a merchant in Hamadān. However, before finishing school, he travelled around the provinces and towns, his eyes being thereby opened to the dismal social and economic conditions of his country and countrymen. At the beginning of the First World War, ʿIshḳī was back in Hamadān, where in *ca.* 1915 he started his career as a journalist by publishing *Nāma-yi ʿIshḳī*; from the start, he was an *engagé* journalist with leftist leanings. As Iran became a theatre of war with the movement of foreign armies, ʿIshḳī joined a group of expatriates and settled for several years in Istanbul. It seems that even before he left, ʿIshḳī was a Turcophile and was interested in the activities of the reformist and nationalist group of the Young Turks. According to some writers, while in Istanbul he attended the *Dār al-Funūn* for courses in science and philosophy.

ʿIshḳī's poetic gift now suddenly blossomed. This took place whilst travelling in Mesopotamia, in the midst of the ruins of the Sāsānid royal palace at Ctesiphon. The remains of the palace, with its huge *īwān*, triggered off a poetic rapture in ʿIshḳī, and he composed *Rastākhīz-i shahriyārān-i Īrān* ("The resurrection of Iranian kings"). It became the first opera in the Persian language, and was first staged in Iṣfahān on ʿIshḳī's return to his homeland, to the tumultuous reception of the audience. ʿIshḳī himself sang the part of the poet. This one-act opera play is a mixture of realism and fantasy, and is full of patriotic pathos, with *dramatis personae* including the poet (ʿIshḳī); Khusraw-dukht (the Sāsānid princess); Darius the Great; Cyrus the Great; Anūshīrwān; Khusraw Parwīz and his wife Shīrīn; and the prophet Zoroaster. The purpose of this opera was to juxtapose the glories of the ancient Iran with that of the land of ʿIs͟hḳī's own day; the ancient kings accuse contemporary Iranians of having no energy and will and of leaving the country in a state of apathy and lethargy. ʿIs͟hḳī's second poem inspired by the Sāsānid ruins was *Kafan-i siyāh* ("The black shroud"). This is an epic poem 427 verses long, composed in the *musammaṭ* form set in the time of K͟husrāw and S͟hīrīn, and what was meant to be a romantic epic turned out to be a powerful social commentary and criticism.

ʿIs͟hḳī's criticism of the Iranian polity was carried to its height upon his return to Iran from his self-imposed exile in Istanbul after the end of the War. He wrote his vehement opposition to the 1919 Anglo-Iranian treaty in a form of a patriotic *ḳaṣīda*, *Muk͟hālifat bā Ḳarārdād-i Īrān wa Inglīs* ("Opposition to the Iran-England treaty), in which he ridiculed the Prime Minister Wut͟hūḳ al-Dawla [*q.v.*] as well as the passivity of his compatriots, and this resulted in his being sent to prison. In 1920, he published a new journal *Ḳarn-i bīstum* ("The twentieth century"). His poetry and prose now became more and more inflammatory as he demanded radical reforms from the government, the Russian Bolshevik Revolution of October 1917 having had a clear impact on his ideas; in 1922, on the occasion of the Iranian New Year, he composed a poem *ʿĪd-i kārgarān* ("Festival of the Workers"). In his poetry, as in his journalism, he focused unrelentingly on Iran's national and social problems. In his satirical works, ʿIs͟hḳī came to use an increasingly malicious language, full of invectives, against members of the government as well as against deputies in the Mad͟jlis, and he rapidly moved to the extreme position of vigilantism, calling for an annual bloodbath in order to cleanse Iran of corruption. In 1924, he participated in a nationwide canvass for an ideal model (archetype) of each field of endeavour to which prominent thinkers were invited to write and publish. Answering that call, he wrote his revolutionary narrative poem *Sih tāblū-yi idiyāl* ("Three ideal tableaux"). Ahmad Karimi-Hakkak has written that this work was ʿIs͟hḳī's "solitary attempt to break through the constraints of poetic diction and to liberalize the concept of rhyme and meter . . .". Since, however, ʿIs͟hḳī ends his poem advocating a bloodbath "to cleanse the country of all traitors", Karimi-Hakkak adds that "*The Three Tableaux* must ultimately be seen as an angry young man's frustrated outburst against the political situation in Iran during the last years of Qajar rule." ʿIs͟hḳī's next angry outburst turned out to be fatal. It was the time when Riḍā K͟hān [see RIḌĀ S͟HĀH] was preparing to become the first President of the Iranian Republic, and ʿIs͟hḳī strongly opposed this idea for two reasons, being afraid that the president, Riḍā K͟hān, would establish a military dictatorship, and also that Iranians were not yet ready for a republican democratic polity. He opted therefore for the continuation of the Ḳād͟jār dynasty. A few days after the publication of his attack on Riḍā K͟hān, ʿIs͟hḳī was assassinated in Tehran.

ʿIs͟hḳī's contribution to Persian literature, journalism and political thought has yet to be fully examined and described, but there is no doubt that, had he lived longer, he would have been regarded as the writer who laid the foundation of modern Persian letters.

Bibliography: ʿAlī Akbar Mus͟hīr Salīmī, *Kulliyyāt-i muṣawwar-i Mīrzāda ʿIs͟hḳī*, Tehran 1324/1945 and subsequent eds.; F. Machalski, *ʿEshkī: le camp des modernistes*, in *La littérature de l'Iran contemporaine*, Cracow 1967, 132-53; J. Rypka *et al.*, *History of Iranian literature*, Dordrecht 1968, 385-6; Muḥammad ʿAlī Sipānlū, *Čahār s͟hāʿir-i āzādī*, Uppsala 1372/1994, 121-249; Ahmad Karimi-Hakkak, *Recasting Persian poetry. Scenarios of poetic modernity in Iran*, Salt Lake City 1995, 210-31; idem, *EIr*, art. *ʿEšqī*; Muḥammad Ḳāʾid, *Mīrzāda ʿIs͟hḳī*, Tehran 1377/1998.

(P. CHELKOWSKI)

IS͟HḲODRA, the Turkish form of the name of the town of Shkodër/Shkodra (Slavonic, Skadar) in the north of modern Albania.

The town is situated at an altitude of 16 m/52 feet near the banks of the lake of the same name, at the confluence of an arm of the Drin, the Buna/Bojana and the Kiri, and is dominated by the fortress of Rozafa and by Mt. Tarabosh. This ancient urban centre was founded in the 4th century B.C., in the Illyrian period, around the acropolis. It was successively dominated by the Romans (in 168 B.C.), Byzantines, Serbs (from 1043), Byzantines again, Serbs again, Ottomans (1393) and Venetians (from 1396). It became definitively Ottoman after two sieges (1474 and 1478-9). After the departure of the greater part of its population in accordance with the Ottoman-Venetian peace treaty, Is͟hḳodra (equally called Iskenderiyye or Skutari) became the centre of a *sand͟jaḳ* of the same name and was gradually repopulated and Islamised. The tax registers show that, in addition to the troops of the garrison and their families, there were in 1485 27 Muslim and 70 Christian hearths, in 1528 119 and 43 respectively, and in 1570-1 217 and 27 respectively.

The town owed its importance, right up to the early 20th century, to its politico-administrative role and also to its geo-strategic position, directly connecting it with the Adriatic Sea (some 20 km/12 miles away by water) and the Italian ports, plus its situation on important trade routes (northwards to Montenegro, eastwards to the centre of the Balkan peninsula (Is͟hḳodra-Prizren road) and southwards to the plains of the Albanian coastland. As the centre of a frontier *sand͟jaḳ* (comprising the modern regions of Montenegro and northern Albania), Is͟hḳodra enjoyed its greatest period of florescence from the mid-18th century onwards, when the office of *sand͟jaḳ-beyi* passed into the hands of a local *aʿyān* family, that of Bus͟hatlî. There they succeeded at the head of the town and *sand͟jaḳ*, which last they tried to enlarge: Meḥmed Pas͟ha, then his three sons Muṣṭafā Pas͟ha, Ḳara Maḥmūd Pas͟ha [*q.v.*] and Ibrāhīm Pas͟ha, and, finally, Muṣṭafā's grandson, also Muṣṭafā Pas͟ha [*q.v.*], who was in the end subdued by the Porte in 1831. In 1862 Is͟hḳodra became the centre of an *eyālet* with just one *sand͟jaḳ*, then from 1875 it was the capital of the smallest Ottoman *wilāyet*, with two *sand͟jaḳ*s, those of Is͟hḳodra and Drač [*q.v.*] (Durrës). Being on the frontier with Montenegro, the province retained a special character (*müstet͟hnā*) until the Young Turk revolution. Reforms were never completely introduced. The *wālī* was also the military commander. The Muslim population did not perform military service but went out on campaigns in *bayraḳ*s (there being 15 in the town). No population census was made. The Muslims and Christians of the adjacent mountain areas freely bore arms.

During the last century of Ottoman occupation, the town expanded towards the north. Because of epidemics, flood problems (the Drin changed its course in 1865) and earthquakes (notably in 1905), the old quarters within and around the fortress (Alibey, Tabak, Ayazma, etc.) were abandoned for new ones (Parutsa,

Rus, Pera<u>sh</u>, etc.). According to the *sālnāme* of 1310/1892-3, I<u>sh</u>ḳodra had at this time 12 Muslim quarters and 2 Christian ones, with a population of *ca.* 40,000 (almost all Albanians), two-thirds of these being Muslims and the rest Roman Catholic Christians. Some of the Muslims were *muhād<u>j</u>irūn* from Bosnia-Hercegovina and Montenegro [see MUHĀD<u>J</u>IR. 2.]. There was also a small community of Orthodox Christians (*ca.* 600 persons, Slavs and Vlachs) and a quarter of Muslim gypsies. Towards the end of the 19th century, the bazaar [see SŪḲ], which stretched between the fortress and the new town, and trade in general, lost their importance relative to that of Rumelia because of the development of Salonica and the construction of the Salonica-Mitrovica railway line.

The cultural and social development of I<u>sh</u>ḳodra was the product of oriental, western and local influences which met there. The importance of Islamic culture is attested by the rate of Islamisation, the existence of mosques (almost 30, without much architectural significance except for the "Leaden Mosque" in the Tabak quarter, south of the citadel), the presence of dervish *tekke*s (the Bektā<u>sh</u>īs are said to have been expelled at the opening of the 19th century by Muṣṭafā Pa<u>sh</u>a; the Rifāʿiyya and Ti<u>dj</u>āniyya [*q.vv.*] appeared there at the beginning of the 20th century) and the foundation of *medrese*s. Though remote from the great centres of Islamic culture, I<u>sh</u>ḳodra produced poets writing in the oriental tongues (notably, members of the Bu<u>sh</u>atlî family and numerous *ʿulamāʾ* who enjoyed great authority in the town. "Catholic-Italian" culture was brought by merchants and by missionary orders (Franciscans and also Jesuits from the second half of the 19th century onwards). The consuls of France, Britain, Russia, Greece and, above all, Austria-Hungary and Italy (who oversaw educational establishments) had an important influence; some of them, like A. Degrand and Th. Ippen, have left writings on the town and its region. As for local influences, these were the result of the weight of villagers of the plain and, above all, the mountain people (Malisos), mostly Christian and living according to customary law (*ḳānūn*) in the surrounding regions (in 1856 the Ottoman authorities installed a Commission for the Mountains (*<u>Dj</u>ibāl Komisyonu*) at I<u>sh</u>ḳodra). At the end of the 19th to the beginning of the 20th centuries there began to develop an Albanian literary culture under the impulse of certain members of the religious orders and the stimulus of the Austro-Hungarian and Italian consuls.

Ottoman domination ended in 1913 after a long siege by Montenegrin forces. After various occupations, the town and its region became part of the new Albanian state in 1919-20. Although it was the most important urban centre of the new state, Shkodër was not chosen as the capital, to the great chagrin of its people, because of its eccentric position on the Montenegrin border. Its development was adversely affected by this. It had only 28,500 people in 1942 and 71,000 in 1985. In this post-Ottoman period, the town has remained both the centre of Albanian Catholicism and of traditional Islam. Its *ʿulamāʾ* have been raised as opponents of the reforms introduced when the Islamic community was restructured in the new state. On the other hand, it was at Shkodër that, in November 1990, the first church and first mosque were re-opened after 23 years of the prohibition of all forms of religious activity by the Communist authorities who had seized power in 1944. Since then, several mosques have been restored or built. One of them, opened in the mid-1990s, is one of the biggest mosques in the Balkans. A *medrese* has opened and an Islamic centre supported by an organisation based on Birmingham is active. Hence Shkodër is today one of the most important centres of Islam in Albania.

Bibliography: Ewliyā Čelebi, *Seyāḥātnāmesi*, vi, 107 ff.; J.G. von Hahn, *Albanesische Studien*, i, Jena 1854, 94-111; <u>Sh</u>ems ül-Dīn Sāmī, *Ḳāmūs al-aʿlām*, ii, 977 ff.; A. Baldacci, *Scutari d'Albania*, Rome 1890; A. Degrand, *Souvenirs de la Haute-Albanie*, Paris 1901, 184 ff.; Th. Ippen, *Skutari und die Nordalbanische Küstenebene*, Sarajevo 1907; K. Jireček, *Geschichte der Serben*, Gotha 1911; idem, *Skutari und sein Gebiet im Mittelalter*, in L. von Thalloczy, *Illyrisch Albanische Forschungen*, i, Vienna-Liepzig 1916, 94-124; M. von Šufflay, *Städte und Burgen Albaniens hauptsächlich während des Mittelalters*, Vienna-Leipzig 1924; L. Rey, *Guide d'Albanie*, Paris 1930; Stavri N. Naçi, *Pashallëku i Shkodrës nën sundimin e Bushatllive në gjysmën e dytë të shekullit të XVIII (1757-1796)*, Tirana 1964; H.J. Kornrumpf, *Ahmed Cevdet Paşa über Albanien und Montenegro. Aus Tezkere Nr. 18*, in *Isl.*, xlvii (1971), 93-135; Selami Pulaha, *Le cadastre de l'an 1485 du sandjak de Shkodër*, Tirana 1974; Zija Shkodra, *Qyteti shqiptar gjatë rilindjes kombëtare*, Tirana 1984; art. *Shkodra*, in *Fjalori enciklopedik Shqiptar*, Tirana 1985; Naçi, *Pashallëku i Shkodrës (1796-1831)*, Tirana 1986; M. Kiel, *Ottoman architecture in Albania, 1385-1912*, Istanbul 1990, 226-42; N. Clayer, *L'Albanie, pays des derviches*, Berlin-Wiesbaden 1990; Hakan T. Karateke (ed.), *İşkodra şairleri ve Ali Emirî'ini diğer eserleri*, Istanbul 1995; N. Clayer, *Note sur la survivance du système des* timâr *dans la région de Shkodër au début du XXe siècle*, in *Turcica*, xxix (1997), 423-30; eadem, *Islam, state and society in post-communist Albania*, in H. Poulton and S. Taji-Farouki (eds.), *Muslim identity and the Balkan state*, London 1997, 115-38; Faik Luli, Islam Dizdari and Nexhmi Bushati, *Në kujtim të brezave*, Shkodër 1997; Hamdi Bushati, *Shkodra dhe motet*, 2 vols. Shkodër 1998. (NATHALIE CLAYER)

I<u>SH</u>TĪ<u>KH</u>ĀN, I<u>SH</u>TĪ<u>KH</u>AN, a town and district of mediaeval Islamic Transoxania. It lay seven *farsa<u>kh</u>*s north of Samarḳand and was administratively separate from it. There were many arable fields, irrigated by a canal taken off the Zaraf<u>sh</u>an river [*q.v.*]. In the 4th/10th century, the town had a citadel, a *<u>sh</u>ahristān* and a *rabaḍ* or suburb; a village of the same name exists on the site today.

When the Arabs took over Samarḳand in the second quarter of the 8th century A.D., the I<u>kh</u><u>sh</u>īds of Sogdia transferred their capital to I<u>sh</u>tī<u>kh</u>ān. In the 3rd/9th century the district furnished a body of troops for the ʿAbbāsid army, distinguished as *al-I<u>sh</u>ktī<u>kh</u>aniyya* in al-Tabarī, iii, 1362, and at Ba<u>gh</u>dād these were allotted, with other troops from the Iranian and Central Asia East, a special quarter, whilst at Sāmarrāʾ they were allotted land grants (*ḳaṭāʾiʿ*) (al-Yaʿḳūbī, *Buldān*, 248, 262-3, tr. Wiet, 30, 55). The revenue of the market in the town of I<u>sh</u>tī<u>kh</u>ān was granted to the ʿAbbāsid general ʿU<u>dj</u>ayf b. ʿAnbasa [*q.v.*], confiscated by the caliph al-Muʿtaṣim on ʿU<u>dj</u>ayf's fall in 223/838, and subsequently granted to Muḥammad b. Ṭāhir b. ʿAbd Allāh.

Bibliography: See also Yāḳūt, *Buldān*, ed. Beirut, i, 196; Le Strange, *The lands of the Eastern Caliphate*, 466 and Map IX; Barthold, *Turkestan*[3], 95-6; C.E. Bosworth (tr.), *The History of al-Ṭabarī. XXXIII. Storm and stress along the northern frontiers of the ʿAbbāsid caliphate*, Albany 1991, 49 n. 159.

(C.E. BOSWORTH)

AL-ISʿIRDĪ, NŪR AL-DĪN IBN RUSTUM, Muḥammad b. Muḥammad b. ʿAbd al-ʿAzīz, 7th/13th century

Syrian poet. Born in 619/1222 in Isʿird or Siʿird [*q.v.*] in Southeastern Anatolia, which he sentimentally remembers in his *Dīwān*, he lived in Baghdād and visited Egypt, but most of his adult life was, it seems, spent in Damascus (and al-Ṣāliḥiyya). There the *ḳāḍī* Ṣadr al-Dīn Ibn Sanī al-Dawla (590-658/1194-1260), for whom al-Isʿirdī expressed biting contempt, appointed him one of the official witnesses (attorneys) doing business under the famous clock of the great mosque. He won the favour of al-Malik al-Nāṣir Ṣalāḥ al-Dīn Yūsuf, ruler of Aleppo (since 634) and of Damascus (since 648) until his sad end in 658/1260, who made him his boon-companion. He was in contact with many of the littérateurs and other important men of his time, such as Djamāl al-Dīn Ibn Yaghmūr (599-663/1203-64) and the ambassador Nadjm al-Dīn al-Bādarāʾī (594-655/1198-1257). At the end of his short life, he suffered loss of vision. He died in 656/1258.

His *Dīwān* is so far known to be preserved only in ms. Escorial ar. 472 (with the title-page bound into ms. ar. 399), incomplete at the end. In addition to the many poems addressed to al-Malik al-Nāṣir on a large variety of personal and public events, it includes poems addressed to, among others, the caliphs al-Mustanṣir and al-Mustaʿṣim, and al-Malik al-Muʿaẓẓam, as well as fellow-poets, *dūbayts*, *ghazals*, riddles, and the like, as one would expect in a *dīwān* of the period. Wine-drinking plays throughout its customary large role. The *Dīwān* offers valuable sidelights on the political and cultural history of Syria and Egypt immediately before the coming of the Mongols. Another work, apparently lost, *Sulāfat al-zar(a)djūn fi ʾl-khalāʿa wa ʾl-mudjūn*, dealt, as the title indicates, with lewd verses of his own composition, and also by others. Most of the verses quoted by the biographers, including the *Rangstreit* poem of wine and *hashīsh* (cf. F. Rosenthal, *The Herb*, Leiden 1971, 6, 163-6), may well go back to this work, as only a couple of them can be traced in the extant manuscript of the *Dīwān*. The same applies to additional verses quoted by al-Ṣafadī in *al-Ghayth al-musadjdjam fī sharḥ Lāmiyyat al-ʿadjam*.

Al-Isʿirdī represents the lighthearted side characteristic of Syrian secular life and culture before "the end of the days of joy in Damascus" (Ibn al-Ṣuḳāʿī, ed. J. Sublet, 168, tr. 196) which came with al-Malik al-Nāṣir's downfall and the Mongol invasion. Little as we know about him, it seems clear that he, in common with numerous contemporaries, combined serious activity with a great zest for life and provided and enjoyed an atmosphere in which, despite all the political turmoil of the age, ease and elegance flourished as they were scarcely ever to do afterwards.

Bibliography: Ṣafadī, *Wāfī*, ed. H. Ritter, i, 188-92, who furnishes most of the information for later biographers, also, in a slightly shortened and rearranged form in his *Nakt al-himyān*, Cairo 1329/1911, 255-7; Kutubī, *Fawāt*, Cairo 1951, ii, 329-34, ed. I. ʿAbbās, Cairo 1973-4, iii, 271-6; Ibn Kathīr, *Bidāya*, xiii, 212; Ibn al-ʿImād, *Shadharāt*, v, 284; Ḥādjdjī Khalīfa, ed. Yaltkaya, 995; Brockelmann, I², 299 (where the wrong date of death, 652, goes back ultimately to Flügel's ed. of Ḥādjdjī Khalīfa). (F. Rosenthal)

ISKĀF, Iskāfī (a., pl. *asākifa*), "shoemaker", the tradesman who in pre-modern Islamic times produced ordinary shoes (*khuff*, pl. *khifāf*), nailed boots used by the common people (*lālaka*, pl. *lawālik*) and also *shamushkāt* (sing. *shamushk*), a type of boots of Coptic Arab origin (cf. al-Subkī, *Ṭabaḳāt al-shāfiʿiyya*, Cairo 1966, 360). The shoemakers' use of leather gave rise to a proverbial expression *bayt al-iskāf* "the shoemaker's house" which looked like a "house of hides" because of the pieces of leather everywhere. Like other trades, shoemakers were subject to the practices of the *ḥisba* [*q.v.*], enjoined to use good quality materials and to deliver goods on time.

The *asākifa*, like other artisan groups concerned with leather-working, such as the sandal-maker (*ḥadhdhāʾ*) and maker of leather bags (*kharrāz*), had a low social status because their work was regarded as unclean, and until modern times they worked hard for low wages; the proverb *al-iskāfī ḥāfī wa ʾl-ḥāʾik ʿuryān* "the shoemaker goes barefoot and the weaver is naked" expresses this succinctly. Often they worked on the street or at a street corner because of their inability to rent a shop. ʿAbbāsid Baghdād did, however, have a *darb al-asākifa*, a special lane for them to ply their trade. In Ottoman Istanbul, the shoemakers had their own guild like the tanners and other workers with leather, such as saddlers and cobblers.

Shoemakers often died in indigency. Al-Rāghib al-Iṣfahānī describes a shoemaker's legacy: "Madjnūn was asked, 'What do you say about an *iskāf* who dies, leaving behind his mother and sister?' He replied, 'His inheritance (*mīrāth*) belongs to the dogs and his [funeral] expenses are borne by the tanners (*dabbāghūn*); there remains nothing for his mother and sister except throwing dust and tearing their clothes (sc. in despair and anguish)'." There is little evidence of social mobility amongst shoemakers in pre-modern Islamic society, although there were in the ʿAbbāsid era secretaries and traditionists bearing the *nisba* of al-Iskāfī ([*q.v.*] and see the works of al-Samʿānī and Ibn al-Athīr given in the *Bibl.*, s.v.); whether the *nisba* relates to their own past or, more probably, to an ancestor who had plied this trade, is unclear.

Bibliography: Thaʿālibī, *Thimār al-ḳulūb*, Cairo 1326/1908, 193; Ṭālaḳānī, *Risālat amthāl al-baghdādiyya*, Baghdād n.d., 14; Ibn al-Djawzī, *Manāḳib Baghdād*, Baghdād 1342/1923, 14; Samʿānī, *K. al-Ansāb*, ed. Ḥaydarābād, i, 233-5, iv, 96-7, v, 68-9; Ibn al-Athīr, *Lubāb*, Beirut n.d., i, 57; al-Rāghib al-Iṣfahānī, *Muḥāḍarāt al-udabāʾ*, Beirut 1961, ii, 463; Ibn Bassām al-Muḥtasib, *Nihāyat al-rutba fī ṭalab al-ḥisba*, Baghdād 1968, 130; E. Fagnan, *Additions aux dictionnaires arabes*, Algiers 1923, 159; Muḥammad Saʿīd al-Ḳāsimī *et alii*, *Ḳāmūs al-ṣināʿāt al-shāmiyya, Dictionnaire des métiers damascains*, 2 vols. Paris-The Hague 1960, i, 38. (M.A.J. Beg)

ISKĀN (a.), lit. "coming into a peaceful state, settlement, the allocation of living quarters or space", hence in modern usage, "sedentarisation" as a stage after a migratory or nomadic existence.

Unlike *badw* [*q.v.*], "desert, people of the desert", and *ḥaḍar* "settled lands, people of the settled lands", *iskān* is not a concept often used in the Arabian peninsula and its fringes. In the recent past, the Bedouin of northern Arabia, when talking about the town of Shaykh Miskīn in the Ḥawrān [*q.v.*], ostensibly connected the term *miskīn* with the root *s-k-n* (when it is, in fact, derived from a quite separate, ancient Semitic usage, see miskīn]; these townspeople were said to be descendants of people who had been unable to cope with the rigours of Bedouin lifestyle and had therefore settled.

In fact, equating *iskān* with "sedentarisation" places an undue emphasis on a "nomad-settler" dichotomy, when town or village and countryside were generally enmeshed in multiple relationships. Hence in what follows, some separation of contexts is attempted in an otherwise generalised discussion.

The Arabian peninsula and its ancillaries include a great diversity of physical environments, habitats and natural resources. Urban and rural settlements differ, not only from each other but also between themselves, and over time. Movement patterns are similarly diverse and shift through time. Factors affecting settlement and nomadism over the region can be discussed in general terms only, with regional and historical examples indicated in the bibliographical references. Settling and settlement take place in economic and political—often administrative—contexts; religious reasons have been important at some times and places. The economic context changes from the traditional period when animals were an essential source of energy and the more recent one, starting about the 1850s or 1860s, and involving modern sources of energy culminating with oil from regional oilfields [see NAFṬ. 3] and electricity grids. In traditional political economies, governments or rulers got wealth from taxation, tribute and booty, most of which ultimately depended on localised agricultural production; modern nation states get wealth from oil, directly or indirectly, and participation in the global political economy.

Environmental factors necessitate some seasonal mobility in most modes of livelihood, agricultural, commercial, and administrative as well as pastoral. In most social groups, households were and are the productive and consuming units, which may or may not have all members present. They drew and draw resources from various directions, drawing on two or more components from herding, agriculture, commerce and services. Towns and countrysides continue to be enmeshed through a variety of networks which may change over time but have features that continue.

Iskān as "settling" has been a decision made by households and families throughout millennia all over the Arab world. For some groups, at some times and in some places, the settling was permanent; for others, it was temporary. The reasons for settling (and its reverse) by individual households and families are usually economic and social, but sometimes political. When households provided their own shelter and needs, moving or settling were not so different. The ability to defend household persons and property, which gives honour [see ʿIRḌ], could be achieved as a settled person and as a nomad. Changing from nomadic to settled status, and vice-versa, was managed through existing and long-standing networks and a variety of contracts or agreements, and some settling by households in the present continues to function in this manner.

With larger groups, "settlement" is more a response to significantly changing political, religious or economic events; governments may also decide on a policy of settlement to resolve perceived problems, while fiscal policies may encourage or discourage settlement. Whereas individual households decide all the time to settle or to be nomadic, decisions by groups of households to settle or by governments to settle nomads are more episodic. A well-known historical example of a government settling nomads as a policy is that of the early Islamic state, which recruited nomadic tribesmen into the armies as *muḳātila* and settled them in garrison towns (Donner 1981, 264-7; Kennedy 1986, 62-9) as a method of control, these troops to be financed by booty and tribute. Islam regards nomadic life as incompatible with a truly Muslim way of life [see TAʿARRUB]. A more recent example of government policy of settling nomads was the Ottoman empire's *Tanẓīmāt* [*q.v.*] reforms of the mid-19th century, which put legal, military and fiscal pressure on pastoralists to settle and grow grain in Syria, Transjordan and ʿIrāḳ in order to replace supplies from the former Ottoman lands in the Crimea and the Balkans. Between 1908 and 1914, ʿAbd al-ʿAzīz Ibn Suʿūd planted settlements of I<u>kh</u>wān [*q.v.*] among tribes unwilling to give their allegiance to him, and so extended his influence (Musil 1928, 283), although he was later unable to control I<u>kh</u>wān forces. During the 1920s to the 1940s, the Mandate governments [see MANDATES] together with the new Suʿūdī kingdom, required tribal sections to follow the government in whose territory each section had its summer water sources. As pastoral livelihood become untenable for many, these summer water points became the bases for settlements, first as storage depots and then as villages. All modern nation states of the region, with the exception of Oman/ʿUmān, apart from its Dhofar/Ẓufār region (Chatty 1996, 9, 188-9), regard settlement of nomads as a means of imposing or encouraging incorporation into the state and identity as citizens. States with potentially rich agricultural areas like ʿIrāḳ and Syria initially left the settlement of nomads to market forces, changes in land laws and the provision of hydraulic schemes. Later, their more revolutionary governments saw tribalism and nomadism as primitive survivals to be eradicated by social engineering. Saudi Arabia set up agricultural schemes in the 1960s to settle nomads and established the National Guard to provide employment for tribesmen after a long series of drought years in the 1940s and 1950s (H.H. Hamza 1982; W. and Fidelity Lancaster 1986, 1993). Later, state provision of water, electricity, health and education services, and subsidies for agriculture and housing, distributed oil wealth to rural areas (W. Lancaster 1997, 139-50, 166-80; ʿA.-R. al-Sudairi 1995). The UAE urged settlement in government-sponsored housing schemes and employment as a way of forming a modern society. Oman, after 1970, provided services to all citizens without requiring settlement.

Living quarters may be allocated by an individual family with the agreement of the heads of other families of the place, by a *<u>sh</u>ay<u>kh</u>* or headman, or by a government agent, depending on the nature of the living place. Tent sites of nomad encampments arrange themselves along lines of closeness and distance of members; links through women influence the siting of particular tents. Women's relationships similarly affect those who live in small villages and in house groups throughout the peninsula. Some recent settlements developed by state governments attempted to break up traditional residence patterns and to form new bonds of citizenship. Large hydraulic and agricultural developments in Syria had, along with economic objectives, the political aim of generating a "new class of socialist peasants". Between the late 1950s and early 1960s, rural people from more than a hundred villages wanting to acquire land poured into one development (Françoise Metral, 1984). The agricultural reform service scattered populations with shared common origins, settling individual families in housing along roads and canals. Twenty years later, these housing groups had not become communities; many households have rebuilt extended family structures inside a homogenous village, others have left the area and rent out their land. UAE government housing was allocated on strictly patrilineal lines, ignoring traditional practices of having neighbours who are closest through links through women.

Settlement by tribal groups occurred in the recent past as a result of government changes in the land law and of changing market forces. From the 1860s in ʿIrāḳ, Syria and what is now Jordan, as the value of transit trade and desert products declined, many nomadic and semi-nomadic groups moved to agriculture, or else to sheep-herding rather than camel herding. From the 1930s, there were mass movements from the ʿIrāḳī countryside to towns and cities, caused by debt among agricultural workers, repressive land laws and the uncertainties of agricultural production (H. Batatu 1978, 35). In Syria, after the Second World War, nomads, especially camel herders, had to adapt fast to the fully mechanised cultivation of grain and cotton (J. Hannoyer 1980, 294); later, more grazing lands were lost to irrigated vegetable and fruit growing for export to the oil states of Saudi Arabia and the Gulf.

Scholars frequently discuss settlement in terms of "the frontier of settlement" and make a positive correlation between strong government, commercial agriculture and settlement. It used to be assumed that from near the end of the ʿAbbāsid period, settlement declined in rural areas but increased in cities, and nomadism took over countrysides until the process was reversed from the middle of the 19th century onwards. Archaeological and historical research has shown that settlement continued, with fluctuations, in the countrysides of Syria, Jordan and ʿIrāḳ, although it appears that there was an urban demographic decline from the 15th century to the late 18th century (Beaumont, etc. 1988, 212-13). In the Arabian peninsula itself, the "frontier of settlement" thesis was not developed. It seems that there was here more rural settlement than had been previously thought; and that there was movement between settlement and nomadism, with some settlements disappearing and others being founded. The general thesis linking strong government, commercial agriculture and settlement is not wholly consistent with actual historical examples, since it ignores particular events and local circumstances along with governments' sources of revenue; what is meant by commercial agriculture; access to land, sources of labour and the established social processes utilising these; the service provision of pastoralism; distribution of goods by means other than an obvious market; and the nature of the household and multi-resource livelihoods. Such social practices negate ideas of settlement and nomadism as being absolutes.

At the present, the proportion of nomads to settled people in the states of the Arab Middle East has declined as compared with 150 years ago. Percentages are difficult, but for ʿIrāḳ, nomadic tribes were estimated at 35% in 1870, 17% in 1905, and 5% in 1947 (Samira Haj, quoting Hasan 1997, 157); for Saudi Arabia, about 40% of the population were nomadic in the 1950s, 11% in 1970, and under 5% now (Eickelman 1998, 74). The basic reason for this massive change is that the bases of nomadic livelihoods (herding, together with processing and trading dairy and animal products, supplying services like transport and protection; or crafts and animal products for groups like the Ṣulayb [*q.v.*], have all become less viable. Profitable herding has been made more difficult by the imposition of state borders, involving the loss of seasonal grazing areas and markets, and by the loss of grazing land to government agencies and non-governmental organisations. The demand for animals for riding, carrying and draught in agriculture has virtually gone; states have taken over protection and mediation services in rural areas; entry to participation in administrative and security agencies of government now comes from education, which usually means residence in a village or town, at least during term time. Since modern states need educated people, they provide schools in centres, together with health services and administrative functions throughout their territories. Oil-rich states encourage settlement by grants or by building housing with all modern services, and they provide schools and clinics. Throughout the whole region, many former herding tribespeople are employed by the state in security forces and other official employment; they or other members of their households may have irrigated land for vegetable or fruit cultivation, and/or sheep for meat or dairy products. Camels continue to be herded for milk, meat and racing in Saudi Arabia, the Gulf states and Oman.

Some authorities see a breakdown of traditional nomadic social structures arising out of settlement and its associated education and employment. Others consider that these structures come from tribal, rather than nomadic as such, customary social practice, and that these structures are resilient and adaptive.

Thus the fact that the terms "settled" and "nomadic" are of limited value has been indicated by some scholars (e.g. J.C. Wilkinson 1977, 189; Soraya Altorki and D.P. Cole 1989, 81; W. and Fidelity Lancaster 1999, 54-61), who regard them as simplistic. Linking "settled" and "nomadic" to the conceptual identities of *badw* and *ḥaḍar* is, according to these authorities, unsatisfactory, since here the crucial determinant is the ability to get one's living and security by one's own efforts and networks, rather than by accepting government employment and provision. Of course, there are many who do both at the same time, and are in fact "settled" and "nomadic". Movement is now important to households in order to link employment and traditionally-owned resources in the countrysides.

Bibliography: A. Musil, *Northern Nejd*, New York 1928; I. Lapidus, *Muslim cities in the later Middle Ages*, Cambridge 1967; W.-D. Hutteroth and K. Abdulfattah, *The historical geography of Palestine, Transjordan and Southern Syria in the late 16th century*, Erlangen 1977; J.C. Wilkinson, *Water and tribal settlement in South-East Arabia*, Oxford 1977; H. Batatu, *The old social classes and the revolutionary movements of Iraq*, Princeton 1978; J. Hannoyer, *Le monde rural avant les réformes*, in A. Raymond, *La Syrie d'aujourd'hui*, Paris 1980; F.M. Donner, *The early Islamic conquests*, Princeton 1981; U. Fabietti, *Sedentarisation as a means of detribalisation*, in T. Niblock (ed.), *State, society and economy in Saudi Arabia*, London 1982; H.H. Hamza, *Public land administration in Arabia*, London 1982; Frauke Heard-Bey, *From Trucial States to United Arab Emirates*, London and New York 1982, [2]1996; Françoise Metral, *State and peasants in Syria: a local view*, in *Peasant Studies*, xi (1984), 69-90; Dawn Chatty, *From camel to truck; the Bedouin in the modern world*, New York 1986; J. Janzen, *Nomads in the Sultanate of Oman. Tradition and development in Dhofar*, Boulder and London 1986; H. Kennedy, *The Prophet and the age of the Caliphates*, London 1986; W. Lancaster and Fidelity Lancaster, *The concept of territoriality among the Rwala Bedouin*, in *Nomadic Peoples*, xx (1986), 41-8; N. Lewis, *Nomads and settlers in Syria and Jordan, 1800-1950*, Cambridge 1987; P. Beaumont, G.H. Blake and J.M. Wagstaff, *The Middle East, a geographical study*, London 1988; Soraya Altorki and D.P. Cole, *Arabian oasis city: the transformation of ʿUnayza*, Austin, Texas 1989; papers, including that of W. and Fidelity Lancaster, *Sécheresse et stratégies de reconversion économique chez les bedouins de*

Jordanie, in R. Bocco, R. Jaubert and Françoise Metral (eds.), *Steppes d'Arabie. État, pasteurs, agriculteurs, et commerçants: le devenir des zones sêches*, Paris and Geneva 1993; papers in E. Rogan and T. Tell (eds.), *Village, steppe and state: the origins of modern Jordan*, London 1994; Chatty, *Mobile pastoralists. Development planning and social change in Oman*, New York 1996; Samira Haj, *The making of modern Iraq 1900-1963*, Albany 1997; W. Lancaster, *The Rwala Bedouin today*, [2]Prospect Heights, Ill. 1997; A. Meir, *As Nomadism ends*, Boulder and Oxford 1997; D.F. Eickelman, *The Middle East and Central Asia, an anthropological approach*, [3]New Jersey 1998; papers in J. Ginat and A. Khazanov (eds.), *Changing nomads in a changing world*, Brighton 1998; W. and Fidelity Lancaster, *People, land and water in the Arab Middle East*, Amsterdam 1999.

(W. and FIDELITY LANCASTER)

ISKANDAR KHĀN b. **DJĀNĪ BEG**, ruler in Transoxania, from his capital Bukhārā, of the Turco-Mongol Shībānid [*q.v.*] or Abu 'l-Khayrid dynasty, ruled 968-91/1561-83. Iskandar was in fact a weak and ineffective ruler. Real power was in the hands of his son 'Abd Allāh, who had shown his ability against rival families in Transoxania as early as 958/1551 and who became the greatest of the Shībānids; after his father's death he was to reign unchallenged for a further sixteen years [see 'ABD ALLĀH B. ISKANDAR]. For the course of events in these decades, see SHĪBĀNIDS and R.D. McChesney, *EIr* art. *Central Asia. vi. In the 10th-12th/16th/18th centuries*.

Bibliography: See those to the two arts. mentioned above, and also C.E. Bosworth, *The New Islamic Dynasties, a chronological and genealogical manual*, Edinburgh 1996, 288 no. 153. (ED.)

ISKĀṬ (A.), a legal term meaning "relinquishment", specifically of a right (*ḥaḳḳ*). In general, four conditions must be met to make the relinquishment of a right valid: (a) that the right should exist at the time it is relinquished (e.g. the right to collect a debt to be incurred in the future may not be relinquished); (b) that the right relinquished does not concern *milk al-ʿayn* (i.e. the ownership of the substance of a thing, whether movable or immovable, is not subject to relinquishment, but only to transfer, *naḳl*); (c) that the interest of the person entitled to the right should be absolute and not limited by other interests (e.g. it cannot be an interest such as that of a trustee in a *waḳf* property); and (d) that the relinquishment of the right does not involve an illegal result.

Iskāṭ may be of two kinds: *iskāṭ maḥḍ* (true relinquishment) and *iskāṭ ghayr maḥḍ* (quasi-relinquishment). The first kind includes divorce (*ṭalāḳ*), manumission of a slave (*iʿtāḳ*) and the relinquishment of the right of pre-emption (*shufʿa*). In the latter case, short clauses of relinquishment of the right of pre-emption are often added to deeds of sale of houses (e.g. *ḳad asḳaṭnā shufʿatanā min dhālik*), neighbours of the vendor in Islamic law having the right of pre-emption [see SHUFʿA].

The term *iskāṭ ghayr maḥḍ* includes legal transactions such as acquittance of debt (*ibrāʾ ʿan al-dayn*), which is not regarded as a pure relinquishment since it partakes of the nature of a donation (*tabarruʿ*).

Bibliography: Adnan Kouatly, *Étude comparative du droit de préemption*, Damascus 1948, 424-45; Muṣṭafā Aḥmad al-Zarḳāʾ, *al-Fiḳh al-islāmī fī thawbih al-djadīd*, Damascus 1968, and bibliography there cited; R.Y. Ebied and M.J.L. Young, *Some Arabic legal documents of the Ottoman period*, Leiden 1976 (see documents on pp. 15, 17, 23).

(R.Y. EBIED and M.J.L. YOUNG)

IṢLĀḤ.

v. CENTRAL ASIA

Central Asia (here basically understood in the sense of the pre-modern Mā warāʾ al-Nahr [*q.v.*]), notwithstanding its regional pecularities, historically is to be regarded as an integral part of the Islamic world. Hence, in one way or another, its Muslim community—at least until the Russian "October Revolution" of 1917—was influenced by and/or contributed to reformist trends and movements current in other Muslim regions, in particular, those of Russia, Ottoman Turkey, the Arab world and also India. Basic features of the religious discourse on *iṣlāḥ* in the 18th-20th centuries, as described in the previous sections of this article (see Vol. IV) are to be found in Central Asia as well. But, because of the impact of roughly seven decades of Soviet rule, our knowledge about the specific nature of *iṣlāḥ* in Central Asia, and about its various supporters, actual developments, exchange of ideas, etc., is still rather poor in comparison to that about other regions. The inaccessibility of relevant sources during the Soviet period, as well as the application of Marxist-Leninist concepts of history, have led to a somewhat eclectic picture.

As a result of the prolonged Soviet impact, reformism in Central Asia appears predominantly as a class-based (bourgeois), nation-cultural, and finally political (nationalist) movement among Muslim intellectuals emerging around the turn of the 19th to 20th centuries, and considerably gaining strength after 1905-7 when censorship in the Russian empire was loosened and the press could function more freely [see DJARĪDA. iv]. This reform movement was the so-called Djadīdism [see DJADĪD], but the usual self-designations of its representatives were different, e.g. *iṣlāḥātkhᵘāh* ("reformer"), *taraḳḳīparwar* ("progressive"), *munawwir* ("enlightener"), *yāsh* or *djawān* ("young"). It figures as a historically more or less isolated phenomenon, directly inspired by an identical movement which started somewhat earlier among Russia's Muslims. A key role in these endeavours, in the first place directed to renewing the Muslim educational system, disseminating Western-type knowledge, and fighting harmful social conditions and customs, falls to the well-known Crimean Tatar modernist Ismāʿīl Gasprali [*q.v.*] and the influential newspaper *Terdjümān* founded by him in 1883. The reformist or modernist efforts of the Djadīds, at least to a certain extent, are characterised according to the Soviet jargon as "progressive", in sharp contrast to a more or less obscure stereotype of "reactionary" Ḳadīmīs.

Even though such views of developments in *iṣlāḥ* in Central Asia cannot, of course, be called entirely wrong, they nevertheless neglect some important traits of this phenomenon that are essential to an appropriate understanding of it. This lack of coherence is especially revealed by recent research, and concerns in particular the questions of: (a) indigenous roots and precursors of the so-called Djadīdism; (b) interrelations with other Muslim and non-Muslim regions, with their influence on the background of individual thinkers; and (c) fundamentals, causes, contents and the course of the debate with traditionalist *ʿulamāʾ*, labelled by the modernists as Ḳadīmīs.

Far from our having comprehensive answers to these and related questions, some salient hints will have to suffice. Besides the oft-repeated statement that the Central Asia of the Khānates (Bukhārā, Khīwa and Khoḳand [*q.vv.*]) in the 18th-19th centuries represented a bulwark of intellectual stagnation, obscurantism and religious dogmatism, it must be noted that such eminent precursors of reformism and modernism in the Volga-Ural region as ʿAbd al-Naṣīr al-Ḳūrṣāwī (1776-1812) and Shihāb al-Dīn al-Mardjānī (1818-89) both finished their studies in Bukhārā, Central Asia's most famous centre of Muslim learning. A decisive role in their taking up positions against *taḳlīd* and favouring *idjtihād* was played by Bukhāran *mudarrisūn* who were affiliated with the influential Naḳshbandiyya (Mudjaddidiyya) [*q.v.*, and see AḤMAD SIRHINDĪ, its founder, who based his teachings rigorously on the Ḳurʾān and Sunna]. In this respect, it is worth mentioning that Central Asia, and particularly Bukhārā, was not an isolated region but was connected through extensive trade relations with China, India, Russia, and also Western Siberia where, besides Tatars, *bukhārlïḳ* played a major role in spreading Islam and building up Muslim institutions, thereby in some cases showing reformist approaches at a comparatively early date. "Critical erudition" also can be found in 19th-century Bukhārā itself, among what might be called the teachers' generation of its later modernists (the Young Bukhārans, emerging around the end of the first decade of the 20th century), such as Aḥmad Makhdūm Dānish (1827-97) [see ĀZĀDĪ, in Suppl.] who subsequently, under Soviet auspices, was praised as a [Tādjīk] "enlightener" (al-Ḳūrṣāwī and al-Mardjānī were removed from their Islamic context in a similar way); Mīrzā ʿAbd al-ʿAẓīm Sāmī (*ca.* 1835-1914?) who served as a *munshī* of the *amīrs* Muẓaffar (1860-85) and ʿAbd al-Aḥad (1885-1910); Dāmullā Muḥammad Ikrām(ča) (1847-1925) who was appointed in 1913 one of the twelve official Bukhāran *muftīs*; Muḥammad Sharīfdjān Makhdūm, named Ṣadr-i Ḍiyāʾ (1867-1932), from a well-known *ḳāḍī* family, himself being appointed 1917 for three months *ḳāḍī-yi kalān*, the highest judicial officer in Bukhārā. All of them, except Ṣadr-i Ḍiyāʾ, shared the characteristic of having stayed for some time abroad, either by travelling to Russia or by performing the *Ḥadjdj*.

To be sure, all this does not mean that Bukhārā in the 18th-19th centuries was a stronghold of *iṣlāḥ*. On the contrary, al-Ḳūrṣāwī, for example, already met with sharp opposition and even condemnation by the overwhelming majority of Bukhāran *ʿulamāʾ*, including the then ruling *amīr* Ḥaydar (1800-26), when he, in regard to the question of the divine attributes [see ṢIFA. 2], opposed the generally accepted doctrine that God possesses either seven or eight *ṣifāt* by arguing that the only way to formulate a qualification of God is His own word, the Ḳurʾān, in which the *ṣifāt* are not at all limited to a definite number of seven or eight. Leaving aside that kind of subtle debates, it can be stated at least that Bukhārā was in constant exchange with the outside world, and to some extent participated in current Islamic developments, thereby providing certain prerequisites for a more evident manifestation of reformist endeavours that was to happen only at the beginning of the 20th century, then taking shape in Djadīdism, current amongst Russia's Muslims. The main impetus to Djadīdism, the followers of which—beyond the basically regressive concept of *iṣlāḥ*—also believed in Western ideas of progress, thus came from outside. But in Central Asia it met with an already existing specific spiritual basis of genuine *iṣlāḥ*, namely, a critical attitude towards traditional ways of rule, social life and religious learning which, as their critics saw it, were incompatible with "true" Islamic principles.

Unlike the Muslims of the Volga-Ural region, who already for centuries had stood up against Russia's rule and various policies of Russification, Central Asia had to face the challenges of colonial rule only from the second half of the 19th century, when it was conquered by Russia (abolishing the Khānate of Khoḳand finally in 1876, and reducing Bukhārā in 1868 and Khīwa in 1873 to protectorates). At that time Russia's Muslim communities had for about one hundred years received a slightly more favourable administrative status through the institutions of a *muftiyyat* in Ufa (1782) and the "Spiritual Assembly" in Orenburg (1788), allowing them a certain self-determination which was channelled particularly into strengthening and developing the *Sharīʿa* and their own educational system (the *maktab* and *madrasa*). Within this framework, and by meeting the growing challenge of Western modernity, it soon happened that reformist and/or modernist trends gained ground. It also seems quite natural that they aimed at improvement according to "modern" requirements in fields like education, which had become fundamental to Muslim self-assertion. Given such a partly common goal of reformist and traditionalist forces on the one hand, and limited resources on the other hand—the Muslim educational system in Russia was not state-sponsored—conflict, beyond the level of the later, overemphasised purely ideological controversies between Djadīds and Ḳadīmīs, was inevitable.

Though Central Asia played no visible role in this process in Russia which finally led to Djadīdism, Central Asia had at least mediated the first reformist impulses in Russia which, roughly 200 years later, were re-imported in the form of developed concepts of Muslim modernism. These concepts met with a situation in Central Asia in which indigenous society and its traditional institutions had to cope with the serious setback of Russian conquest and rule. Hence, in addition to the existing traces of a "critical erudition" mentioned above, we find in the urban centres of Russian Turkistān and of the protectorates of Bukhārā and Khīwa, evidently from around the turn of the 20th century, small local circles of Muslim modernists who were in touch with one another and had a loose network of contacts with kindred spirits stretching as far as Russia, the Caucasus, Turkey, Egypt, the Ḥidjāz and India. The more or less simultaneous introduction of a Western infrastructure, involving railways, postal services and telegraph, increased mobility and enhanced communication.

The majority of outstanding Central Asian modernists, although of different social origins, belonged to the younger generation and had gone through a traditional *maktab* and *madrasa* education. Some had a Russian education, and finally, a considerable number of them had fruitful experience of the outside Muslim world. Another group of supporters of modernism, at least in Bukhārā, was made up of traders and entrepreneurs. Their business interests led them to welcome efforts towards reform oriented towards interpretations of Western standards of knowledge and civilization. At the same time, endeavours of this kind were combined with a more or less conscious harking back to the fundamentals of the "true", early Islam. This synthesis of both following the dictates of the Ḳurʾān and "keeping up with the times" in practice mainly resulted in activities to disseminate knowledge (the press, publications, textbooks, founding of charitable societies (*djamʿiyyat-i khayriyya*) and *uṣūl-i djadīd* ("new-method") *maktabs*), and to criticise "backward" administrative institutions (e.g. the judiciary, *awḳāf*) and social conditions (e.g. features of popular religion, certain activities of Ṣūfī brotherhoods, lavish festivities and moral decline—the latter, by the way, was a field in which the Djadīds largely shared the opinion of the Ḳadīmīs).

These general characteristics are mirrored in the basic biographical data of distinguished Central Asian modernists (their backgrounds and their entire work are, for the most part, not yet sufficiently studied), such as: (1) Sayyid Aḥmad Ṣiddīḳī, named ʿAdjzī (Samarḳand, 1864-1927, *madrasa* education, published the first textbook for "new method" *maktabs* [*Ustād-i awwal*, Tashkent 1901], *ca.* 1901-3 *Ḥadjdj* and residence in the Ḥidjāz, Egypt and Russia; then founding "new method" *maktabs*, writing textbooks and contributing to modernist press); (2) Maḥmūd Khʷādja Bihbūdī (Samarḳand, 1875-1919, *madrasa* education, 1900 *Ḥadjdj*, 1903-4 stay in Cairo, Istanbul, Ufa and Kazan; then founding a "new method" *maktab*, acting as *muftī*, publisher, editor of the newspapers *Samarḳand* [1913-4] and *Āʾina* [1914-5], writer of textbooks, theatrical plays); (3) ʿAbd Allāh Awlānī (Tashkent, 1878-1934, *madrasa* education, editor of newspapers *Shuhrat* [1907], *Āsiyā* [1908] and *Tūrān* [1917], founder of "new method" *maktabs* [1908, 1912], charitable society [1909], writer [textbooks, anthology, theatrical plays], organising [1913] a theatre group); (4) Munawwar Ḳārī ʿAbd al-Rashīd Khān (Tashkent, 1878-1931[?], editor of newspapers *Khūrshīd* [1906], *Ṣadā-yi Turkistān* [1914] and *Nadjāt* [1917], published textbooks); and (5) ʿAbd al-Raʾūf Fiṭrat [*q.v.*] (Bukhārā, 1886-1938[?], *madrasa* education, 1904 *Ḥadjdj*, *ca.* 1910-14 studying in Istanbul, the starting point of his career as an important writer and as theorist of Central Asian modernism).

Within the Central Asian context, the activities of these and other adherents of modernism represented a remarkable phenomenon that to some extent challenged traditional society and colonial rule. But these modernists were few in number and, beyond shared basic ideas and goals, they seem to have formed a rather disparate movement of limited success. They lagged behind the modernist debate in other parts of the Muslim world. Their influence did not apparently reach beyond the borders of Central Asia, and even in their homeland they had no firm socio-political grounding. When finally, in the course of the Russian Revolutions of 1917, some of the Central Asian modernists entered the political stage (striving for an autonomy of Turkistān within a Russian federation, or for an implementation of reforms in Bukhārā), they were quickly swept away and successively absorbed by various more firmly-based social and political forces and realities (ranging from Soviet power to the armed resistance of the Basmačīs [*q.v.*]).

Bibliography: In addition to the *Bibls.* of the articles mentioned in the text, see of more recent special studies, D.R. Brower and E.J. Lazzerini (eds.), *Russia's Orient. Imperial borderlands and peoples, 1700-1917*, Bloomington, Ind. 1997; S.A. Dudoignon, D. Is'haqov and R. Möhämmätshin (eds.), *L'Islam de Russie. Conscience communautaire et autonomie politique chez les Tatars de la Volga et de l'Oural, depuis le XVIIIᵉ siècle*, Paris 1997; M. Kemper, *Sufis und Gelehrte in Tatarien und Baschkirien, 1789-1889. Der islamische Diskurs unter russischer Herrschaft*, Berlin 1998; A. Khalid, *The politics of Muslim cultural reform. Jadidism in Tsarist Central Asia*, Berkeley 1998; A. von Kügelgen *et alii* (eds.), *Muslim culture in Russia and Central Asia from the 18th to the early 20th centuries*, i ff., Berlin 1996-; *Le réformisme Musulman en Asie Centrale. Du «premier renouveau» à la soviétisation, 1788-1937*, Paris 1996 (= *Cahiers du Monde Russe*, xxxvii/1-2 [Jan.-June 1996]). (R. Eisener)

ISMĀʿĪL ḤAḲḲĪ BALṬADJİOGHLU (1886-1978), Turkish sociologist, educator and author. He was born in Istanbul in 1886, the son of a government official, Ibrāhīm Edhem, and Ḥamīde. He finished his *Wefā Iʿdādisi* in 1903, and continued his education in the Department of Natural Science in the *Dār ül-fünūn*, graduating in 1908. During the same year, he started his career as a teacher of calligraphy in the *Dār ül-muʿallimīn-i ibtidāʾiyye* and was sent to Europe in 1910 by the Ministry of Education to do research in pedagogy and handicrafts. After his return to Turkey in 1911, Ismāʿīl Ḥaḳḳī lectured on handicrafts, calligraphy, aesthetics, pedagogy and psychology in several schools and worked in certain administrative posts whereby he initiated various reforms combating the traditional methods of education. He was elected Dean of the Faculty of Letters in the *Dār ül-fünūn* on several occasions between 1921-4 and was President of the school in 1923, resigning in 1927. He was removed from his position as a lecturer at the *Dār ül-fünūn* with its closure on 31 July 1933. Between 1941-2, Ismāʿīl Ḥaḳḳī worked as a professor of pedagogy in the Language and History-Geography Faculty of Ankara University. He was elected to the Parliament as the Afyon representative of the Halk Partisi in 1942 and the Kırşehir representative in 1946. From 1950 until his death in 1978, he continued his career as an author and publisher.

Besides publishing *Yeni Adam*, a journal mainly devoted to pedagogy and culture, he wrote many books and articles for various newspapers and journals such as *İkdam*, *Yeni Fikir*, *Akşam* and *Ulus* throughout his life. In his works, he mostly concentrated on sociological and pedagogical issues, but also showed an interest in writing plays.

Bibliography: 1. Selected works. *Taʿlīm ve terbiyede inḳilāb*, Istanbul 1912; *Terbiye-i ʿawāmm*, Istanbul 1914; *Umumi pedagoji*, Istanbul 1930; *Demokrasi ve sanat*, Istanbul 1931; *İçtimai mektep nazariyeleri ve prensipleri*, Istanbul 1932; *Andaval palas*, Istanbul 1934; *Felsefe*, Istanbul 1938; *Toplu tedris*, Istanbul 1938; *Dolap beygiri*, Istanbul 1940; *Kafa tamircisi*, Istanbul 1940; *Rüyamdaki okullar*, Istanbul 1944; *Pedagojide ihtilal*, Istanbul 1964.

2. Studies. H.Z. Ülken, *Türkiye'de çağdaş düşünce tarihi*, Istanbul 1992, 450-6; N. Tozlu, *Ismayıl Hakkı Baltacıoğlu'nun eğitim sistemi üzerine bir araştırma*, Istanbul 1989; Ilhan Akar, *İsmail Hakkı Baltacıoğlu'nun eğitim ve kültür görüşleri üzerine bir araştırma*, Ankara 1994; A. Ferhan Oğuzkan (ed.), *İ. Hakkı Baltacıoğlu yaşamı ve hizmetleri. Türk Eğitim Derneği IV. anma toplantısı 16 Ekim 1996*, Ankara 1996. (Aylin Özman)

ISMĀʿĪL ḤAḲḲĪ b. Ibrāhīm b. ʿAbd al-Wahhāb, **MANĀSTİRLİ** (1846-1912), Ottoman religious scholar and preacher. Born and raised in Manāstir in present-day Macedonia, he went to Istanbul as a young man, took *medrese* courses and taught at the Fatih Mosque. In 1874 he became preacher (*wāʿiẓ*) at the Dolmabahçe Mosque and then at the Aya Sofya, where he drew large crowds. He began his teaching career as professor of Arabic at the *ʿAskerī Rüshdiyye* in Eyüb, and in 1884 became teacher of jurisprudence in the *Ḥuḳūḳ Mektebi*, where he remained until he became a senator (*aʿyān aʿḍāsī*) after the 1908 revolution. He taught courses on religious matters at various institutions (*Mühendiskhāne, Mülkiyye, Dārülfünūn, ʿAskerī Ṭibbiyye*) and was also professor of exegesis at the recently founded Preachers' Seminary (*medreset ül-wāʿiẓīn*). On 5 December 1912 (25 Dhu 'l-Ḥidjdja 1330), still a senator, he died at his waterfront residence in Anadoluḥiṣār and was buried in the cemetery next to the Fatih Mosque.

In addition to Turkish, he knew Arabic, Persian and Bulgarian. His writings include a translation of, and commentary on, *al-Ḳaṣīda al-nūniyya* on the Islamic creed by Khiḍr Beg [*q.v.*]; *Beyyināt-i Aḥmediyye* (Istanbul 1329/1911), an annotated translation of *al-Risāla al-Ḥamīdiyya fī ḥaḳīḳat al-diyāna al-islāmiyya wa-ḥaḳḳiyyat al-risāla al-Muḥammadiyya* by Ḥusayn b. Muḥammad al-Djasr or al-Djisr al-Ṭarābulusī (d. 1327/1909, the teacher of Rashīd Riḍā [*q.v.*], cf. Brockelmann, S II, 776, S III, 321); and *Ḥaḳḳ we ḥaḳīḳat*, a critique of Reinhart Dozy's *Essai sur l'histoire de l'Islamisme* (traduit du hollandais par Victor Chauvin, Leiden and Paris 1879; originally published as *Het Islamisme*, Haarlem 1863), translated by ʿAbdullāh Djewdet. For his other works, see *Bibl.*; he also contributed numerous articles to journals and newspapers.

Bibliography: Ismāʿīl Pasha al-Baghdādī, *Hadiyyat al-ʿārifīn*, i, 222-3; İbrahim Alâettin, *Meşhur adamlar hayatları-eserleri*, Istanbul 1933-35, ii, 799; İbrahim Alâettin Gövsa, *Türk meşhurları ansiklopedisi*, Istanbul n.d. [*ca.* 1940], 193; Kaḥḥāla, ii, 266. Further works of Ismāʿīl Ḥaḳḳī: *Mewāʿiẓ*, Istanbul 1324/1906-7; *Ḳoṣowa ṣaḥrāsı mewʿiẓasi*, Salonica 1327/1909; *Uṣūl-u fiḳh*, Istanbul 1328/1910 [textbook]; *Mawāhib al-Raḥmān fī manāḳib al-imām Abī Ḥanīfa al-Nuʿmān*, Istanbul 1310/1892-3, a translation of Ibn Ḥadjar al-Haytamī [*q.v.*], *al-Khayrāt al-ḥisān fī faḍāʾil al-Nuʿmān*. (Ed.)

ISMĀʿĪL PASHA BAGHDĀDLİ, Ismāʿīl b. Muḥammad Amīn b. Mīr Salīm al-Bābānī al-Baghdādī, in modern Turkish orthography, Bağdatlı İsmail Paşa (1839-1920), Ottoman army officer and author of two important bio-bibliographical reference works.

He was born in Baghdād, in a family originating from Bābān, near Sulaymāniyya in ʿIrāḳ, hence his other *nisba* (variant: Bābān-zāde). In 1908, after the Young Turk Revolution, he became a general (*mīr liwā*) in the gendarmerie (*djandarma dāʾiresi*). On his death in 1920 he was buried in Bakırköy near Istanbul. The most extensive notice on his life and work is by Hulûsi Kılıç, in *Türkiye diyanet vakti islâm ansiklopedisi*, iv (1991), 447-8 (with portrait and a specimen of handwriting, and with further references, mostly to Turkish sources). A short mention is given by Khayr al-Dīn al-Ziriklī, *al-Aʿlām*, [4]Beirut 1979, 326.

The two works whereby Ismāʿīl al-Baghdādī is still remembered today are:

1. *Īḍāḥ al-maknūn fī ʾl-dhayl ʿalā Kashf al-ẓunūn ʿan asāmī al-kutub wa ʾl-funūn*. This work, written mostly in Arabic, was posthumously edited by Muḥammad Sharaf al-Dīn Yaltḳāyā (Şerefettin Yaltkaya) and Rifʿat Bilka al-Kilisī (Kilisli Rifat Bilge) and published in two volumes (Istanbul 1945-7, with a portrait in vol. i, several times reprinted) on the basis of the author's copy, which is now kept in the library of the Head Office of the Yapı ve Kredi Bankası in Istanbul. It is written in Arabic and is in fact an annotated list of titles of works, put in alphabetical order, just like its great example, the *Kashf al-ẓunūn*, by the author's famous predecessor Muṣṭafā b. ʿAbd Allāh Ḥādjdjī Khalīfa, Kātib Čelebī (d. 1067/1657 [*q.v.*]). The author's description of the books contain the title, the name and life span of the author, or the year of composition, reference to a printed version (if any), and occasionally the opening words of the text as well. If that latter feature is available, it shows that the author must have had a copy of the text at hand. If a text is a commentary (*sharḥ*), reference is made to its *matn*. There are numerous references to Persian and Turkish works as well, and the *Īḍāḥ al-maknūn* is useful in this respect as well. Its main use is for Arabic bibliography, however, which includes the extensive Arabic literature produced by non-Arabs. His work is in more than one respect a supplement to the *Kashf al-ẓunūn*. It not only bridges the time gap of two-and-a-half centuries between the previous work and the supplement, but it also adds to the bibliographical material which was not known or available to Ḥādjdjī Khalīfa. Although the bibliographical entries are not very extensive, the sheer size of the work, with its more than 10,000 titles, makes it an indispensable, and as yet unsurpassed, bibliographical tool for the literature of the late classical and early modern period. Its inclusion of Persian and Turkish works is witness to the scope of the literary interests of the Ottoman élite.

2. *Hadiyyat al-ʿārifīn. Asmāʾ al-muʾallifīn wa-āthār al-muṣannifīn*. This is the monumental biographical counterpart to the previous work. It is a list of approximately 9,000 authors of in all some 50,000 works (vol. i, which ranges from *alif* to *lām*, mentions 5,398 authors and *ca.* 25,000 works). It was edited by Kilisli Rifat Bilge and Ibnülemin Mahmud Kemal İnal (vol. i, Istanbul 1951) and Ibnülemin Mahmud Kemal İnal and Avni Aktuç (vol. ii, Istanbul 1955). It has been reprinted several times in Baghdād and Tehran. Nail Bayraktar has published a register of the *shuhra*s mentioned in the *Hadiyyat al-ʿārifīn* (*Hediyyetü ʾl-ârifîn, esmâü ʾl-müellifîn ve âsârü ʾl-musannifîn şohretlet indeksi*, Istanbul 1990). The work is arranged by *ism* of the author, followed by the patronyms and other name elements, with personal details, notably the year of demise, and it then provides the reader with the titles of the books composed by these authors.

Bibliography: Given in the article.

(J.J. Witkam)

İSMET İNÖNÜ (Ottoman form, ʿIṣmet), b. 1884, died 1973, Turkish military commander and statesman, who served on three occasions as Prime Minister in the Turkish Republic (October 1923-November 1924; March 1925-November 1937; and November 1961-February 1965) and once as President (1938-50). He played an important part in the Turkish War of Independence (1919-12), made significant contributions to the institutional framework of the new Turkish Republican state, initiated multi-party politics in 1945, acted as champion of the procedural rules of democracy as well as of secularism, and had a critical role in the relatively speedy return to civilian politics following the military interventions of 1960-1 and 1971-3.

The son of a lawyer in Izmir, ʿIṣmet made a career in the Ottoman army, and during the First World War served on the staff of Aḥmed ʿIzzet Pasha in Yemen, commanded the Fourth Army in Syria in 1916, and at the time of the armistice of 30 November 1918 was Under-Secretary for War in Istanbul. ʿIṣmet Pasha, as he had become, was in 1920 elected to the last Ottoman Parliament as member for Edirne, but soon afterwards joined the cause of Muṣṭafā Kemāl (the later Atatürk [*q.v.*]) in resisting the Allied occupation of Anatolia, and when the Greeks invaded western Anatolia, he became chief of the General Staff of the Nationalist army and repelled the invaders at the two battles of İnönü to the west of Eskişehir (January and April 1921), from which engagements he later took his European-type surname.

When the Grand National Assembly met in Ankara

in 1922, ʿIṣmet became Foreign Minister, and represented Turkey at the Lausanne peace conference, strongly opposing Britain and France and gaining most of what Muṣṭafā Kemāl wanted in the final Treaty of Lausanne of 24 July 1923. When the Turkish Republic was proclaimed on 29 October 1923, ʿIṣmet became Atatürk's Prime Minister, remaining in power thus for nearly fourteen years. On Atatürk's death on 10 November 1938, he became President and permanent chairman of the ruling Republican People's Party [see DJÜMHŪRIYYET KHALḲ FIRḲASÏ].

During this period, when westernising reforms were being imposed from above on Turkish society, and when in the 1920s there were rebellions in southeastern Turkey by traditionalist elements, İnönü adopted a rather authoritarian position, but then, in the 1939-45 period, he became much more flexible. He had a large measure of self-confidence in himself and in the future for Turkey. He believed that, together with Atatürk, a threatened resurgence of conservative Islam could be dealt with, when in 1930 many elements of the population seemed to sympathise with the Free Republican Party (*Serbest Cümhuriyet Fırkası* [see ḤIZB. ii] of Ali Fethi Okyar [*q.v.*]). mistakenly perceiving that party as a religiously-oriented one. Similarly, during the 1939-45 years he oversaw the eventual transition to a multi-party political system. Under his skillful leadership, Turkey remained neutral in the Second World War, but the country became strained internally and there were pressures from the victorious Western powers for a more democratic political régime. İnönü was now led towards the formation of a multi-party system, and in the reaction against the RPP's authoritarian rule, the Democrat Party [see DEMOKRAT PARTI], triumphed in the 1950 elections, entailing İnönü's replacement as President by Celal Bayar. He now became for a decade the leader of the opposition and defender of democracy in the in-creasingly authoritarian climate of Adnan Menderes' [*q.v.*] premiership in the late 1950s. After the military intervention of 1960, he formed three coalition governments between 1961 and 1965. However, the RPP suffered heavy defeats in the 1965 and 1969 elections, and İnönü was criticised by Kemalist and socialist elements within his party for the compromises he had made with his coalition partners and with conservative elements; but when he declared the ideology of the RPP as "left of centre", this led in 1967 to the secession of centrist elements in his party to form the Reliance Party (*Güven Partisi*). In 1972 he was replaced as RPP leader by the leader of its leftist faction, Bülent Ecevit, and he died in the following year.

İnönü was a pragmatist, always open to new experiences and ready to learn. He came to conceive of democracy as an exchange of views among the patriotic and knowledgeable sections of the population in order to discover the best public policies, and he thought that these last should be based on valued ideas and not on particularist interests. In this respect, he was an elitist. For him, the state as an entity representing the general interest had priority over a democracy perceived as responsiveness to the preferences of the people at large. Yet this elitism was tempered by a genuine belief in the common sense of the people and a belief in their potential for self-improvement. He did not identify harmony with unanimity, and regarded politics as ideally an adversarial process, since this produced exchanges of ideas and evolved good policies. He remains, therefore, a somewhat enigmatic figure.

Bibliography: 1. Sources. *İsmet Paşa'nın siyasi ve içtimai nutukları, 1920-1933*, Ankara 1933; H. Melzig (compiler), *İnönü diyor ki: nutuk, hitabet, beyanat, hasbihaller*, Istanbul 1944; K. Kop (comp.) *Milli Şef'in söylev, demeç ve mesajları, 1938-1945*, Ankara 1945; *İnönü'nün söylev ve demeçleri, T.B.M. Meclisi'nde ve C.H.P. kurultaylarında, 1919-1946*, Istanbul 1946; S. Erdemir (comp.) *Muhalefette İsmet İnönü*, 3 vols., Istanbul 1956-62; idem (comp.), *İhtilâlden sonra İsmet İnönü*, Istanbul 1962; A. İpekçi (comp.), *İnönü Atatürk'ü anlatıyor*, Istanbul 1976; S. Selek (comp.) *İsmet İnönü. Hatıralar*, 2 vols., Istanbul 1985-7; S. Özel (comp.), *Baba İnönü'den Erdal İnönü'ye mektuplar*, Ankara 1988; A.R. Cihan (comp.), *İsmet İnönü'nün TBMM-'ndeki konuşmaları, 1920-1973*, 3 vols., Ankara 1992-3; N. Kal (comp.), *Televizyona anlattıklarım*, Ankara 1993.

2. Studies. C. Bilsel, *İsmet İnönü. Büyük devlet reisi*, Istanbul 1939; N.A. Banoğlu, *İsmet İnönü*, Istanbul 1943; H. Melzig, *İsmet İnönü. Millet ve insaniyet*, Istanbul 1943; E.B. Şapolyo, *İnönü*, Ankara 1945; F. Unat, *İsmet İnönü. Biyografi*, Ankara 1945; İ.H. Tökin, *İsmet İnönü. Şahsiyeti ve ülküsü*, Ankara 1946; A.F. Erden, *İsmet İnönü*, Istanbul 1952; H. Göktürk, *İnönü*, Ankara 1962; S. Aydemir, *İkinci adam*, 3 vols. Istanbul 1966-8; A.R. Cihan and A. Tekin, *Çağdaş devlet adamı. İsmet İnönü*, Istanbul 1989; M. Toker, *Demokrasimizin İsmet Paşa'lı yılları, 1944-1973*, 7 vols. Ankara 1990-3; S. Kalkanoğlu, *İsmet İnönü, din ve laiklik*, Istanbul 1991; İ. Artuç, *İsmet Paşa: bir dönemin perde arkası*, Istanbul 1993; Gülsün Bilgehan, *Mevhibe*, Ankara 1994; H. Derin, *Çankaya özel kalemimi anımsarken*, Istanbul 1995; E. İnönü, *Anılar ve düşünceler*, 2 vols., Istanbul 1995-8; N. Uğur, *İsmet İnönü*, Istanbul 1995; Bilgehan, *Mevhibe-II. Çankaya'nın hanımefendisi*, Ankara 1998; M. Heper, *İsmet İnönü. The making of a Turkish statesman*, Leiden 1998; O.F. Loğoğlu, *İsmet İnönü and the making of modern Turkey*, Ankara n.d. [1999].

(METIN HEPER)

ISTANBUL.

VIII. MONUMENTS

The first and most important of the Ottoman monuments of Istanbul is Saint Sophia. The only church to be transformed into a mosque immediately after the conquest of the city (others followed later, mostly in the reign of Bāyezīd II), it remained symbolically the model of imperial religious architecture. From the reign of Selīm II onwards, it became a place of burial reserved exclusively for the Ottoman royal family and was restored on numerous occasions between 1572-3 and 1847-9.

Ottoman building activity dates from 1458, when Meḥemmed II built the mosque of Eyyūb and decided to construct his own imperial complex (Fātiḥ) at the square of the Holy Apostles, and the Ṭopḳapï Palace on the site of the ancient acropolis of Byzantium. This plan, added to other decisions taken in the course of the same reign—building of the *bezistān* (1456), of the first palace on the site of the Theodosian forum (1453-5), of the barracks of the Janissaries (Eski odalar), of the saddlers' market (Sarrādj Khāne, 1475), the markets of the major and the minor Ḳaramān (after 1467)—led to the formation of a monumental axis which, while initially retracing the route of the Byzantine Mesus (Dīwān Yolu) from Saint Sophia to the Old Palace, from this point follows a northerly direction, across the complex of Fātiḥ and extending as far as the Adrianople Gate (Edirne Ḳapïsï).

This activity also corresponded with the choice of architects of non-Muslim origin, apparently in contrast to what is known of the builders of the first period of Ottoman architecture, that of Bursa and of Edirne. This practice could also be linked with the policy of recruiting from among all the peoples of the Empire and even beyond, implemented broadly by Meḥemmed II in almost all sectors of public life, but also with the search for new stylistic and technical solutions. This appears to have been the case in choice of Sinān the Elder (ʿAtīḳ), a freedman of Byzantine origin, supposed to have built the Fātiḥ mosque on the model of Saint Sophia. This was also the time of the introduction into Ottoman architecture of the demi-cupola, as is mentioned in a passage from Tursun Beg (*Taʾrīkh-i Abu 'l-Fatḥ*, fol. 58), who applauds the outstripping of Saint Sophia, and another from the Anonymous Giese (99), who de-nounces the latter as sacrilege, inviting comparison with the imperial Byzantine model.

Parallel with the founding of these imperial edifices, Meḥemmed II encouraged his entourage to follow his example. This injunction was implemented to varying degrees: individuals such as Maḥmūd Pasha or Khāṣṣ Murād Pasha, of Byzantine origin and graduates of the Palace school, built some important mosques, their architecture, paradoxically, mirroring that of the first Ottoman mosques of Bursa; others like Gedik Aḥmed Pasha [see AḤMAD PASHA GEDIK] or Isḥāḳ Pasha, contented themselves with constructing secondary buildings in the capital and established their major projects in the towns of Anatolia.

The accession of Bāyezīd II in 1481 marks a halt in monumental construction in Istanful.

The sovereign initially built mosques and large religious complexes at Tokat, at Amasya and at Edirne, while other leading figures of the regime confined themselves to converting the churches of the capital into mosques. Seventeen of them are known to have been adapted for Muslim worship, as opposed to four during the reign of Meḥemmed II. The only monumental project completed during the last twenty years of the 15th century was the mosque built by Dāwūd Pasha (1485). It conforms to the model inaugurated by Bāyezīd II in the provinces, with a single cupola resting on a cube. With a diameter in excess of 18 m, this remains the largest cupola of all the vizieral mosques of the capital.

Deciding, at the opening of the 16th century (in 1500-4), to build a religious complex in the capital, Bāyezīd II borrowed the system of roofing of Saint Sophia, with two demi-cupolas flanking the central cupola, but also followed the model of the mosques of Bursa in adding *tāb-khāne* (lodgings for dervishes) on both sides of the prayer hall. The complex was built on land reclaimed in its entirety from the Old Palace and situated at the strategic point where the Dīwān Yolu joins the Great Bazaar and Usun Čarshî, the Makros Embolos of the Byzantines, linking the central axis of the city to the port. As is the case with the Fātiḥ mosque, this axis traverses the complex passing between the mosque and the *medrese*, thus accentuating its role as a triumphal thoroughfare. Other dignitaries of the period were to follow this example: thus ʿAtīḳ ʿAlī Pasha built a complex on both sides of the Dīwān Yolu (1506) on the site of the forum of Constantine, around the Burnt Column (Djemberli Tash).

The great earthquake of 1509, followed by the unrest in the latter part of Bāyezīd's reign, resulted in another interruption in the monumental construction of the capital. Similarly, Selīm I (1512-20) and his administration, too occupied in waging war, left no architectural vestiges, and it was Süleymān I who, on his accession in 1520, built a mosque in memory of his father. It was situated in a place chosen more for the view that it offers of the Golden Horn, overlooking the Greek quarter of Fener, than for its centrality, but the effect of monumental edifices on the panorama of the city, for purposes of seeing and being seen, seems henceforward to have been a decisive factor; it was to find its most absolute expression with the Süleymāniyye. The mosque known as that of Sultan Selīm (1522) is also the last imperial edifice to reprise the model of a single cupola resting on a cube; it is inspired directly by that of Bāyezīd II at Edirne.

This monument to filial piety apart, the first two decades of the reign of Süleymān I (1520-66) were niggardly in monumental constructions of religious character. On the contrary, the sovereign and his entourage were competing in the construction of palaces. Süleymān renovated the Ṭopḳapî Palace and built a palace on the hippodrome for his Grand Vizier Ibrāhīm Pasha [*q.v.*]. Monumental building activity was resumed with the appointment of Sinān to the post of chief architect in 1538 and was to continue without intermission during the half-century of his activity [see SINĀN].

The sovereign gave the signal for the start of this activity in 1539, ordering the construction of a complex for his wife Khürrem Sulṭāne [see KHURREM], built on the site known as ʿAwret Bāzārî (women's market), in the vicinity of the column of Arcadius. It consists of a mosque, progressively complemented by an *ʿimāret* and a hospital (*dār ül-shifāʾ*). It is probable that Süleymān subsequently decided, on his return from the Hungarian campaign in 1541, to begin a monumental assemblage situated on the triumphal axis, on the site of the Janissaries' barracks (Eski odalar) which he intended to appropriate. On the death of the prince Meḥemmed, in 1543, this mosque was dedicated to him, and the complex probably remained incomplete since it was situated exclusively on the northern part of the axis, the barracks situated to the south being retained. In this mosque, his first monumental project, Sinān took to the very limit the process in which Ottoman architecture had been engaged since 1453, proposing a system of roofing in perfect symmetry, with four demi-cupolas. But after the peace treaty concluded in 1547 with the Emperor Charles V, Süleymān decided to commission a new imperial complex, returning to the model of Saint Sophia and also attempting to attain its dimensions. This was to be the Süleymāniyye (1550-7), overlooking the Golden Horn and likewise built on land reclaimed from the Old Palace, competing with its rival for prominence in the vista of Istanbul. Similarly, the totality of religious and social institutions which surrounded it stole primacy from the Fātiḥ complex, since henceforward the *medrese* of the Süleymāniyye constituted the highest level of religious education in the Ottoman empire.

Members of the Ottoman royal family and their entourage shared in this construction frenzy. Mihr-i Māh Sulṭāne [*q.v.*], daughter of Süleymān and Khürrem, had her first complex, consisting of a mosque, a *medrese* and a caravanserai, built at the quay of Üsküdār, on the Asiatic bank, the place where the Bosphorus was crossed (1548). Twenty years later Sinān completed, again on behalf of Mihr-i Māh, a mosque with a courtyard *medrese* at Edirne ḳapî, at the point where the triumphal axis joins the land wall. In experimenting with the cupola on pendentives, which frees interior space entirely, Sinān here definitively outstripped the model of Saint Sophia, achieving the absolute unity and disengagement of interior space, more in accordance with the Muslim tradition.

The Grand Vizier Rüstem Pas̲h̲a (in office 1544-53, 1555-61 [*q.v.*]), husband of Mihr-i Māh, chose for his buildings the most densely populated areas of the city and found himself obliged, no doubt for this reason, to disperse them. He built a *k̲h̲ān* (*ca.* 1550) at G̲h̲alaṭa [*q.v.*, in Suppl.] on the site of the former Genoese cathedral dedicated to Saint Michael, a *medrese* with octagonal courtyard enclosed within a square, situated below the mosque of Maḥmūd Pas̲h̲a (1550) and a mosque facing the *ḥammām* of Taḥt al-ḳalʿa, completed after his death in 1562. This mosque, built on the site of that of ʿAṭṭār K̲h̲alīl, the most ancient attested in the city (1457), had interior surfaces entirely covered with magnificent ceramics from Iznik, used here on a massive scale for the first time. Sinān Pas̲h̲a, brother of Rüstem, Grand Admiral of the Ottoman fleet (1550-4), built in his turn a mosque with a courtyard *medrese* at Bes̲h̲iktās̲h̲, embarkation-point of the fleet.

Ḳara Aḥmed Pas̲h̲a, Grand Vizier 1553-5, drew up shortly before his execution in the latter year a *wakfiyye* in which he gave instructions for the construction of a mosque with the sums bequeathed. His steward, Ferruk̲h̲ Ketk̲h̲udā, undertook the search for a site and acquired a piece of land close to the land walls inside the gate of Ṭopḳapi̊, where in 1560 Sinān completed a mosque with a courtyard *medrese*.

While the successors of Süleymān, Selīm II (1566-74 [*q.v.*]) and Murād III (1574-95 [*q.v.*]) built their mosques respectively at Edirne and at Mag̲h̲nisa, Istanbul continued to be endowed with monumental constructions under the long vizierate of Ṣoḳollu Meḥmed Pas̲h̲a (1565-79 [*q.v.*]), benefiting from the energy of Sinān's workforce. Ṣoḳollu's first project in the capital was a funeral monument, built in 1568-9 at Eyyüb. This consisted of a mausoleum accompanied by a *medrese*, a combination which became standard from the end of the century onward, contributing to the transformation of the suburb of Eyyüb into a necropolis for the military and religious dignitaries of the empire. Ṣoḳollu subsequently built below the hippodrome, near the docks used by galleys (Ḳadi̊rg̲h̲a), a complex situated in proximity to his palace. This consisted of a mosque with courtyard *medrese*, completed in 1572, to which a *zāwiya* was added. Another mosque was built by the same Grand Vizier in 1577-8, outside the walls of G̲h̲alaṭa, beside the Arsenal, to commemorate his service at the head of the Admiralty (1546-50). Piyale Pas̲h̲a [*q.v.*], High Admiral 1554-68, commissioned from Sinān a mosque situated behind the arsenal, in an area populated by sailors and workers in the naval dockyards. For this building, completed in 1572, where solemn prayers were to be offered before the departure of the fleet, Sinān reverted to the hypostyle model with six cupolas, combined with open-air spaces for prayer capable of accommodating entire ships crews. It was without doubt the same problem of capacity which induced the architect to adopt for the mosque of the High Admiral Ḳi̊li̊d̲j̲ ʿAlī Pas̲h̲a (1571-87 [see ʿULŪD̲J̲ ʿALĪ]), built in 1581 at Ṭopk̲h̲āne, a revival of the model of Saint Sophia with lateral galleries.

In the mid-1570s, Nūr Bānū Sulṭāne [*q.v.*], mother of Murād III, undertook the construction of an important complex above Üsküdār [*q.v.*], a transit depot for caravans arriving from Anatolia. A caravanserai and a *zāwiya* enclosed a mosque and courtyard, with a *medrese* lower down. The whole was completed in 1583. In the meantime, Sinān also constructed a little architectural jewel for S̲h̲emsī Pas̲h̲a, on the banks of the Bosphorus at Üsküdar (1581), as well as a mosque accompanied by two *medreses* on different levels for Zal Maḥmūd Pas̲h̲a at Eyyüb (1580-81). Finally, among the last works of this architect, completed by his successor Dāwūd Ag̲h̲a, attention should be drawn to the mosque of Mesīḥ Meḥmed Pas̲h̲a [*q.v.*] (1586) at Ḳara Gümrük and that of Nis̲h̲ānd̲j̲i̊ Meḥmed Pas̲h̲a (1588) on the main axis between Fātiḥ and Edirne Ḳapi̊.

To complete the monumental landscape of Istanbul and its environs, also worth mentioning is the system of water supply completed between 1554 and 1563, comprising four monumental aqueducts upstream of the Golden Horn, as well as the bridge of Büyük Čekmed̲j̲e on the Edirne road.

The death of Sinān, in 1588, also coincided with the beginning of the exhaustion of the financial resources of the empire, embroiled in a protracted war against Persia and, before long, against Austria. Prestige constructions were to become more modest and their functions modified. A surfeit of mosques was to be succeeded by complexes composed of a mausoleum and a *medrese*, the latter accommodating a large number of rural immigrants drawn by the functions of religious education and the judiciary—virtually the only professions open to persons of Muslim birth.

In 1593-4 D̲j̲errāḥ Meḥmed Pas̲h̲a built the last vizieral mosque to be completed before the 18th century. The density of the city seems not to have permitted monumental constructions without costly expropriations. Thus in order to build her own mosque, on her acquisition of the title of queen-mother with the accession of her son Meḥemmed III in 1595, Ṣafiyye Sulṭāne [*q.v.*] made inroads on the Jewish quarters of the city's port. Hampered by the death of the architect Dāwūd Ag̲h̲a in 1598, by technical problems arising from the digging of foundations at a site close to the water, and by the death of Meḥemmed III in 1603, relegating Ṣafiyye Sulṭāne to the Old Palace, construction remained incomplete and was only to be resumed sixty years later by K̲h̲adīd̲j̲e Turk̲h̲ān Sulṭāne, the mother of Meḥemmed IV, being completed in 1663 (Wālide D̲j̲āmiʿ).

The new sultan, Aḥmed I (1603-17 [*q.v.*]), was the first since Süleymān to undertake the construction of an imperial complex. The latter, situated above the hippodrome, necessitated a massive expropriation of the vizieral residences which were situated there. The manner in which the buildings of the complex are dispersed is testimony to the difficulties of expropriation. The complex of the Blue Mosque, the name given to the mosque of Aḥmed I on account of its extensive decoration in ceramics of this colour, marks the end of the first period of monumental edifices of Istanbul.

G̲h̲aḍanfer Ag̲h̲a, senior eunuch of the palace, introduced into the capital the combination of a *medrese*, a mausoleum and a fountain. The latter, built in 1590-1 at the foot of the aqueduct of Valens (Bozdog̲h̲ān kemeri) rapidly started a trend. These more modest combinations were more easily integrated into the dense urban fabric and contributed to the vitality of the principal axes of the city. Thus the combinations of this type built by Sinān Pas̲h̲a (1592-3), Ḳuyud̲j̲u Murād Pas̲h̲a (1610), Köprülu Meḥmed Pas̲h̲a (1660-1 [see KÖPRÜLÜ]), Merzifonlu Ḳara Muṣṭafā Pas̲h̲a (1681-90 [see ḲARA MUṢṬAFĀ PAS̲H̲A]), Amd̲j̲azāde Ḥüseyin Pas̲h̲a (1700-1) and Dāmād Ibrāhīm Pas̲h̲a (1719-20 [*q.v.*]) were situated on the triumphal axis of the city, while that of Ekmekd̲j̲i-zadē Aḥmed Pas̲h̲a (before 1618) was located on the street joining this axis to Wefā and beyond to the Golden Horn. A more complete complex, also containing a *zāwiya*, was that of Bayram Pas̲h̲a (1634-5) situated in the vicinity of the complex of K̲h̲ürrem Sulṭāne.

These combinations were virtually the sole markers of the 17th century, when new imperial constructions—with the exception of the completion of the Wālide mosque and the small mosque built by Kösem Sulṭāne on the heights of Üsküdār—were nonexistent. The return of the sultans to Istanbul after a period of residence at Edirne, with the accession of Aḥmed III in 1703, marked the start of a new phase of architectural activity, responding to new needs and new styles. The needs resulted from the development of the city, where density of population led to increasingly frequent fires and epidemics. These induced the prosperous classes to take refuge in the periphery, such as the Eyyüb, the northern shore and the Bosphorus, where new residences were to be constructed, soon to be followed by new mosques. At the same time, the need to protect collections of precious manuscripts from fire required the construction of libraries as independent buildings, while the shortage of water resulting from overpopulation led to new projects of water provision, including monumental fountains. These secular buildings, less hampered by the weight of tradition, also gave opportunities for new stylistic experiments, often described as Ottoman baroque art, first coming to prominence in the "Tulip Period" (1718-30) [see LĀLE DEVRI].

The fountains and the *sebīl* (places for the distribution of water, see SABĪL) regularly accompanied combinations of a *medrese* and a mausoleum, but it was to them that the first stylistic innovations were applied. These were already perceptible in the *sebīl* of Amdjazāde Ḥüseyin Pas̲h̲a, at the turn of the 18th century and were developed in that of Dāmād Ibrāhīm Pas̲h̲a twenty years later. In another arrangement, where *sebīl* and fountain became the principal elements in a small complex also containing a mausoleum, as well as a school no longer in existence, built at Dolma Bag̲h̲če by Ḥadjdjī Meḥmed Emīn Ag̲h̲a (1741), the baroque elements attained their fullest expression. The *sebīl* or fountain was also to be found in association with a primary school (*ṣibyān mektebi*) situated on the upper level (fountain school of Reʾīs ül-Kuttāb Ismāʿīl Efendi at Ḳaraköy [1742] and *sebīl* school of Redjāʿī Meḥmed Efendi at Wefā [1775]), but this combination, frequently encountered in Ottoman Cairo, remained exceptional in Istanbul.

The monumental fountain standing alone in a covered space was first seen at the very end of the Tulip Period, the first five known examples being virtually contemporaneous. Dāmād Ibrāhīm Pas̲h̲a, responsible for the drawing of water from Üsküdār, built the first of these four-faced monumental fountains beside the harbour of this suburb in 1728-9. The same year, Aḥmed III built the monumental fountain before the main entrance of the Ṭopḳapī Palace. His successor, Maḥmūd I (1730-54) undertook the conveyance of water from the northern shore of the Golden Horn (waters of Taḳsīm) and three other monumental fountains were built in 1732-3 on this network: that of Ṭopk̲h̲āne by the sovereign himself, that of ʿAzap Ḳapī (in front of the Arsenal) by the queen-mother Ṣalīḥa Sulṭāne and that of Kaʿba Tās̲h̲ by the Grand Vizier Ḥekīm-og̲h̲lu ʿAlī Pas̲h̲a [see ʿALĪ PAS̲H̲A ḤAKĪM-OG̲H̲LU].

The first independent library was built by Köprülü Fāḍil Aḥmed Pas̲h̲a as an extension of the familial complex on the Dīwān Yolu (before 1676), and S̲h̲ehīd ʿAlī Pas̲h̲a also built a free-standing library behind the mosque of S̲h̲āh-zāde in 1715. This type of building nevertheless acquired a monumental nature—while retaining modest dimensions—with the library built in 1719-20 by Aḥmed III in the third courtyard of the Ṭopḳapī Palace. New architectural experiments were evident in that of ʿĀṭif Efendi at Wefā (1741) and were to be most fully expressed in the library of the Nūr-u ʿOt̲h̲māniyye complex (1755). Among later buildings, those of Rāg̲h̲ib Pas̲h̲a (1762) at Lāleli and of Dāmād-zāde Meḥmed Murād Efendi—known as Murād Mollā—(1775) at Čars̲h̲amba are worth mentioning.

A new type of building linked with projects for the provision of water consisted of dams, reservoirs placed in the Belgrade forest to the north-west of the city, a happy combination of utility and ornament. The oldest, a straight wall supported by four buttresses, is known by the name of the Dark Dam (Ḳaranlīḳ Bend); dating from 1620 it was located on the network set up by Sinān. The Topluzu Bend, built in 1750 on the network of Taḳsīm, introduced cut-off corners, more resistant to the pressure of water. By way of the Aywad Bendi (1765) and the Wālide Bend (1797), progress was made towards the vaulted dam, realised in 1839 with the dam of Maḥmūd II.

The 18th century also marked a renewal in the construction of religious buildings, but the first phase was slow and hesitant. The mosque built by Aḥmed III for his mother Emetüllāh Gülnūs̲h̲ Sulṭāne at Üsküdār (1708-10)—a place apparently reserved for the wives of the imperial family—revived the models of the 16th century, albeit with some adjustments to the lines of the *sebīl* typical of the Tulip Period. Similarly, it was again the *sebīl*, as well as the school placed above the entry-gate, rather than the mosque, which represented innovation in the monumental complex built by Hekīm-oghlu ʿAlī Pas̲h̲a in 1734-5. This makes even more surprising the full-scale renewal of architectural motifs in the Nūr-u ʿOt̲h̲māniyye complex, begun in 1748 by Maḥmūd I and completed in 1755 under ʿOt̲h̲mān III. Even though the daring solutions, such as the horseshoe-shaped courtyard, were not to be repeated in subsequent centuries, the Nūr-u ʿOt̲h̲māniyye marked a new phase in imperial building activity which was not to be discredited for as long as the empire lasted.

Muṣṭafā III (1757-74) built no fewer than three imperial mosques: that of Ayazma at Üsküdār, named after his mother, in 1758-61, that of Lāleli in 1760-3, and that of Fātiḥ, rebuilt in 1766-71 after the earthquake of 1765. His successor, ʿAbd ül-Ḥamīd I (1774-89) dedicated to the memory of his mother Rabīʿa Sulṭāne the mosque of Beylerbey on the Asiatic shore of the Bosphorus, and to the memory of his wife Hümās̲h̲āh Ḳadīn that of Emirgān on the European shore. He also built near the port his own funeral monument, consisting of a *medrese*, an *ʿimāret*, a *sebīl* and a mausoleum. In this complex, constructed in stages between 1775 and 1789, what is observed is the transition from baroque in the *sebil* to Ottoman neo-classicism in the mausoleum.

The reign of Selīm III (1789-1807 [*q.v.*]) marked the zenith of a flamboyant baroque which was expressed essentially through funereal monuments: the complex composed of an *ʿimāret*, a *sebīl* and a mausoleum of the queen-mother Mihr-i S̲h̲āh Sulṭāne, built at Eyyūb in 1792-5, and the mausoleum was accompanied by a school and a *sebīl* of the sovereign's sister S̲h̲āh Sulṭāne, also at Eyyūb (1800). The tendency continued beyond the reign with the mausoleum and *sebīl* of Naks̲h̲idil Sulṭāne built by Maḥmūd

II in memory of his mother in the cemetery of Fātiḥ in 1818. Finally, baroque and rococo decoration, abundantly present in those parts of the Ṭopḳapi̊ Palace dating from the second half of the 18th century, also infiltrated the *zāwiya*, but it was only in the mosque-*zāwiya* of Küčük Efendi, completed in 1825, that the oval form of the plan supplemented the decorative effects. Selīm III also built in 1802-5 a mosque in the proximity of the barracks designed to accommodate the new army which was to replace that of the Janissaries. Built in the centre of a chequer-shaped plot, it perpetuated the model of the Nūr-u ʿOthmāniyye while developing in the form of an annexe the imperial pavilion which seems henceforward to have corresponded to new formal functions, the sovereign receiving dignitaries here after the Friday prayer.

During the reign of Maḥmūd II (1808-39), baroque was maintained but attempts were made to adopt a more imperial style. This was manifested particularly in imperial edifices: a pavilion of ceremonies (Alāy köshkü) in the angle of the wall of the Ṭopḳapi̊ Palace (1810), a school of Djewri Kalfa on the Dīwān Yolu (1819) and, above all, the sovereign's mausoleum on the same axis (1839). However, in the second half of his reign the ascendancy of the Balyan family imprinted on monumental Ottoman architecture a style that, despite its boundless eclecticism, remained deeply original in its capacity for syntheses and infinitely varied interpretations of the historical forms of Ottoman architecture.

The first work that can be attributed with confidence to the Balyans is the Nuṣratiyye mosque, situated in the quarter of Ṭopkhāne, to the north of the Golden Horn, whither architectural activity was progressively transferred. Thus the mosque of Khi̊rḳa-yi̊ Sherīf, built in 1851 to accommodate the mantle of the Prophet, and that of Pertew Niyāl Sulṭāne, built in 1869-72 at the crossroads of Aḳ Sarāy, could be considered the last *intra-muros* religious monuments of the city.

The activity of the Balyans was manifested essentially through the imperial palaces built on the shores of the Bosphorus: Dolma Baghče (1846-55), Küčük Su (1856), Beylerbey (1863-65), and Čirāghān (1864-72), as well as the pavilion of Ihlamur (1855) in the valley of the same name. The mosques erected during this period beside the Bosphorus (Dolma Baghče, 1855, Ortaköy, 1853), or in the vicinity (Medjīdiyye, 1848), belonged to same aesthetic movement, with interiors reminiscent of ballrooms. The first buildings of the palace of Yi̊ldi̊z on the heights of the Bosphorus and the mosque built close by (1877) are the last manifestations of this architecture.

New functions resulting from the reforms of the *Tanẓīmāt* (1839 onwards [*q.v.*]) entailed new architectural forms most often undertaken by foreign or Levantine architects. The Swiss brothers Gaspare and Giuseppe Fossati, sent from St. Petersburg to build the new Russian embassy, also worked for the Ottoman administration; Alexandre Vallaury, son of a French émigré, constructed a number of public buildings, from the Archeological Museum, in neo-classical style (1891-1907), to the office of the Ottoman National Debt (1897) and that of the Ottoman Bank (1890-2). Finally, the Italian Raimondo d'Aronco was invited by ʿAbd ül-Ḥamīd II to become the quasi-official architect of the reign, constructing the last buildings of the palace of Yi̊ldi̊z, and introducing the Viennese Secessionist style to the Ottoman capital with the astonishing mausoleum of Sheykh Ẓāfir at Beshiktāsh. The Young Turk revolution of 1908 put an end to the activity of these architects, and a national style was imposed. The latter is manifested in modern buildings such as the main Post Office or the office building built for the benefit of *waḳfs* (the fourth Wāḳif Khān) as much as it is in mosques seeking classical inspiration from the 16th century (mosque of Bebek, 1913).

Bibliography: Aḥmed Efendi, *Tārīkh-i Djāmiʿ-i sherīf Nūr-u ʿOthmānī*, in *TOEM Suppl.*, Istanbul 1335/1916-17; G. Martiny, *Die Piale Pascha Moschee*, in *Ars Islamica*, iii (1936); A. Saim Ülgen, *Topkap'da Ahmed Paşa heyeti*, in *Vakflar Dergisi*, ii (1942); D. Kuban, *Türk barok mimarisi hakkında bir deneme*, Istanbul 1954; M. Erdogan, *Mimar Davud Ağa'ın hayat ve eserleri*, in *Türkiyat Mecmuası*, xii (1955); E.H. Ayverdi, *Gazanfer Asa manzumesi*, in *Istanbul Üniversitesi Edebiyat Fakültesi Tarih Dergisi*, iii (1957); R.M. Meric, *Bâyezid câmii mimâr. II. Sultan Bâyezid devri mimarlar ile baz binalar*, in *Ankara Üniversitesi Ilâhiyat Fakültesi Türk ve Islâm Sanatlar Tarihi Enstitüsü, Yıllık Araştırmalar Dergisi*, ii (1957); Ş. Akalin, *Mi'mar Dalgic Ahmed Paşa*, in *Istanbul Üniversitesi Edebiyat Fakültesi Tarih Dergisi*, xiii (1958); D. Kuban, *Besiktaşt'a Sinan Pasa camii*, in *Mimarlik ve Sanat* (1961); M. Erdoğan, *Son incelemelere göre Fatih Cami'inin yeniden inşa meselesi*, in *Vakflar Dergisi*, v (1962); A. Kuran, *Türk barok mimarisinde bat anlamında bir teşebbüs: Küçük Efendi manzumesi*, in *Belleten*, xxvii/107 (1963); S. Eyice, *Atik Ali Paşa camii'nin türk mimarisindeki yeri*, in *İÜEFTD*, xiv/19 (1964); P. Karahasan, *Istanbul Sultan Selim camii hakkında*, in *Sanat Tarihi Yıllığı*, i (1965); A. Kuran, *The mosque in early Ottoman architecture*, Chicago 1968; D. Kuban, *An Ottoman building complex of the sixteenth century: the Sokollu Mosque and its dependencies in Istanbul*, in *Ars Orientalis*, vii (1968); Ö. Aksoy, *Osmanlı devri Istanbul sıbyan mektepleri üzerine bir inceleme*, Istanbul 1968; E. Yücel, *Amcazade Hüseyin Paşa külliyesi*, in *Vakıflar Dergisi*, viii (1968); C. Palumbo-Fossati, *I fassati di Morcote*, Bellinzona 1970; G. Goodwin, *A history of Ottoman architecture*, London 1971; I.B. Alpay, *I. Sultan Abdulhamid külliyesi ve Hamidiye medresesi*, in *Sanat Tarihi Yıllığı*, viii (1972); N. Atasoy, *İbrahim Paşa sarayı*, Istanbul 1972; Ö.L. Barkan, *Süleymaniye cami ve imareti inşaat*, 2 vols., Ankara 1972, 1979; A. Kuran, *Mimar Sinan'ın ilk eserleri*, in *Belleten* (1973); idem, *Zâl Mahmud Paşa Külliyesi*, in *Boğaziçi Üniversitesi Dergisi–Humaniter Bilimler*, i (1973); G. Güreşsever, *Haseki Darüşşifası*, in *Sanat Tarihi Yıllığı* (1973); E.H. Ayverdi, *Osmanlı mi'mârîsinde Fâtih devri 855-886 (1451-1481)*, 2 vols., Istanbul 1973-4; S.H. Eldem, *Köşkler ve kasırlar*, 2 vols., Istanbul 1974; A. Kuran, *Haseki külliyesi*, in *BÜDHB*, ii (1974); idem, *Üsküdar'da Mihrimah Sultan külliyesi*, in *ibid.*, iii (1975); A. Arel, *18. yüzyıl İstanbul mimarisinde batılılaşma süreci*, Istanbul 1975; Z. Nayir, *Osmanlı mimarisinde Sultan Ahmet külliyesi ve sonrası, 1609-1690*, Istanbul 1975; idem, *İstanbul Ḥaseki'de Bayram Paşa külliyesi*, in *Ord. Prof. Dr. İsmail Hakkı Uzunçarşılı ya armağan*, Ankara 1976; W. Denny, *Ceramics of the mosque of Rüstem Paşa*, New York-London 1977; W. Müller-Wiener, *Bildlexikon zur Topographie Istanbuls*, Tübingen 1977; A. Kuran, *Tophane'de Kılıç Ali Paşa külliyesi*, in *BÜDHB*, vi (1978); S.K. Yetkin, *Şemsi Pąsa külliyesi*, in *Sanat Dünyası*, xix (1980); P. Tuglac, *Osmanlı mimarliğında batılılaşma dönemi ve Balyan ailesi*, Istanbul 1981; Y. Yavuz, *Mimar Kemalettin ve birinci ulusal mimarlık dönemi*, Ankara 1981; D. Kuban, *Tarih-i Cami-i Şerif-i Nur-i Osmanî ve 18. yy Osmanlı yap tekniğe üzerine gözlemler*, in *Türk ve Islam Sanat üzerine denemeler*, Istanbul 1982; J.M. Rogers, *The state and the arts in Ottoman Turkey. Part 1. The stones of Süleymaniye. Part 2. The furniture and decoration of Süleymaniye*, in *IJMES*, xiv

(1982); S.H. Eldem and F. Akozan, *Topkapı Sarayı bir mimarî araştırma*, Istanbul 1982; İ.A. Yüksel, *Osmanlı mimârîsinde II. Bayezid Yavuz Selim devri (886-926/1481-1520)*, Istanbul 1983; M. Cezar, *Typical commercial buildings of the Ottoman classical period and the Ottoman construction system*, Istanbul 1983; A. Kuran, *Üsküdar Atîk Valide külliyesinin yerleşme düzeni ve yap tarihi üzerine*, in *Suut Kemal Yetkin'e armağan*, Ankara 1984; H. Stierlin, *Soliman et l'architecture ottomane*, Paris 1985; G. Necipoğlu, *The Süleymaniye complex in Istanbul*, in *Muqarnas*, iii (1985); A. Kuran, *Mimar Sinan*, Hürriyet Vakf, Istanbul 1986; Z. Çelik, *The remaking of Istanbul*, Seattle 1986; H. Crane (ed.), *Risāle-i miʿmāriyye*, Leiden 1987; K. Çeçen, *Mimar Sinan ve Kırkçeşme tesisleri*, Istanbul 1988; G. Erol, *Çinili cami ve külliyesi*, in *Sanat Tarihi Araştırmalar Dergisi*, iii (1988); S. Yerasimos, *Sinan and his patrons. Programme and location*, in *Journal of the Islamic Environmental Design*, v (1987), Rome 1990; idem, *La fondation de Constantinople et de Sainte-Sophie dans les traditions turques*, Paris 1990; S. Eyice, *Istanbul'da Sultan II. Bayezid külliyesi*, in *STAD*, viii (1990); H. Crane, *The Ottoman Sultans' Mosques. Icons of imperial legitimacy*, in *The Ottoman city and its parts*, ed. I. Bierman, D. Preziosi and R. Abou al-Haj, New York 1991; G. Necipoğlu, *Architecture, ceremonial and power. The Topkapi Palace in the fifteenth and sixteenth centuries*, New York 1991; K. Çeçen, *Üsküdar sular*, Istanbul 1991; idem, *Taksim ve Hamidiye sular*, Istanbul 1992; S. Ögel, *18. ve 19. yüzyıldan osmanlı camilerinde geleneksel anlama katkılar*, in *Semavi Eyice armanğan, İstanbul yazelar*, Istanbul 1992; A. Egemen, *İstanbul'un çeşme ve sebilleri*, Istanbul 1993; H.O. Barişta, *İstanbul çeşmeleri. Kabataş Hekimoğlu Ali Paşa meydan çeşmesi*, Ankara 1993; idem, *İstanbul çeşmeleri. Azapkapi Saliha Sultan çesmesi*, Ankara 1995; D. Barillari and E. Godoli, *Istanbul 1900*, Istanbul 1997; S. Yerasimos, *Istanbul, la mosquée de Soliman*, Paris 1997; C. Kafescioğlu, *Heavenly and unblessed, splendid and artless: Mehmed II's mosque complex in Istanbul in the eyes of its contemporaries*, in *Essays in honour of Aptullah Kuran*, ed. C. Kafescioğlu and L. Thysenocak, Istanbul 1999; Yerasimos, *Constantinople, capitale d'empires*, Paris 2000; idem, *Osmanlı İstanbul'unun kuruluşu*, in *Osmanlı mimarığının 7. yüzyıl "Uluslarüstü bir miras"*, Istanbul 2000; A.H. Polatkan, *Kılıç Ali Paşa camisi ve Ayasofya: bir historisist deneme*, in *ibid.*; A.Y. Kubilay, *18. ve 19. yüzyıl İstanbul vakf kütüphaneleri üzerine tipolojik bir değerlindirme*, in *ibid.*; Vakıflar Genel Müdürlüğü, *Istanbul Yeni Cami ve Hünkar Kasır*, n.p., n.d.

(S. Yerasimos)

ISTILḤĀḲ (A.), the verbal noun of Form X of the verb *laḥiḳa* "to reach, catch up with," having the meaning of "to try to reach, attach, adopt, affiliate s.o. to s.th." (see *WbKAS*, letter lām, 330). In early Islamic history, it was especially used for the attempt in 44/665 of the Umayyad caliph Muʿāwiya I [*q.v.*] to attach the very able official Ziyād b. Abīhi [*q.v.*] to his own, ruling clan of Umayya. Ziyād was of dubious parentage, his mother Sumayya being apparently a slave, and Muʿāwiya aimed at linking Ziyād to his own family as the putative son of his own father, Abū Sufyān [*q.v.*]. For details of this *istilḥāḳ* process, see ZIYĀD B. ABĪHI, with full references.

(Ed.)

ITHM (A.), a term of Islamic theology meaning "sin", used in Ḳurʾān, II, 216/219, V, 32/29, XLIX, 12, amongst various other terms denoting sin and sinfulness in varying degrees, such as *dhanb*, pl. *dhunūb*, used in Ḳurʾān, III, 129/135 and *passim*. For a discussion of the concept of sin and its consequences, see KHAṬĪʾA.

IʿTIṢĀM AL-DĪN B. SH. TĀDJ AL-DĪN, SHAYKH, a resident of Tādjpur, in the Nadiya district of Bengal, who went to England on a diplomatic mission in 1180/1769 and wrote an account of his journey in his *Shigarf-nāma-yi wilāyat* or *Wilāyat-nāma*. Iʿtiṣām al-Dīn began his official career as a *munshī* in the service of Mīr Djaʿfar [see DJAʿFAR, MĪR]. During the time of Mīr Ḳāsim [*q.v.*] he joined the service of Major Yorke. In 1177/1763 he fought on the British side against Mīr Ḳāsim. He served General Carnac (1765-6) for a short period and later entered the service of the Mughal Shāh ʿĀlam. In 1180/1769 he went to England with Captain Archibald Swinton bringing a letter (copy available in the Library of Royal Asiatic Society, no. 134; W. Morley, 128) from Shāh ʿĀlam to George III. Munīr al-Dawla, who, according to Sarkar (*Fall of the Mughal empire*, ii, 402), was a devoted partisan of the British at Shāh ʿĀlam's court, insisted on paying Iʿtiṣām al-Dīn 2,000 rupees towards his expenses. In this letter, Shāh ʿĀlam sought British help in conducting him to Dihlī and placing him on the Mughal throne. Iʿtiṣām al-Dīn returned from England in 1883/1769. In 1189/1775 he helped the East India Company's negotiations with the Marāthās [*q.v.*].

The *Shigarf-nāma* is one of the earliest accounts of a journey to England written by an Indian. In about 86 chapters he gave his impressions about the various aspects of English society—religious life, clubs, the judicial system, public schools, sports, etc. He also visited Oxford University and the Bodleian Library. He describes London and its principal buildings, as also agricultural methods and farming. Some autobiographical references are also given. It appears that his relations with Swinton did not remain cordial to the last (ʿAlīgaṙh ms. fols. 100-5).

For mss. of the *Shigarf-nāma*, see Storey, i, 1143; also ʿAlīgaṙh, Ḥabīb gandj Collection 35.7. An abridged Hindūstānī version of it was made by Munshī Shamshīr Khān and was published by J.E. Alexander with an English translation, London 1827.

Bibliography: Storey, i, 1142-3; Rieu, *B.M.* Catalogue i, 383, ms. Or. 200; Garcin de Tassy, *Histoire de la litterature hindoue*, i, 463; *Swinton family records*, privately printed, Edinburgh 1906.

(K.A. Nizami)

IYĀS B. **ḲABĪṢA** AL-ṬĀʾĪ, a pre-Islamic individual who played a certain role in the relations between Arabs and Persians, but whose biography is not absolutely clear. According to Ibn al-Kalbī-Caskel (*Ǧamharat an-nasab*, Tab. 252, and ii, 361), his genealogy appears to be as follows: Iyās b. Ḳabīṣa b. Abī ʿUfr/ʿAfrā b. al-Nuʿmān b. Ḥayya b. Saʿna b. al-Ḥārith b. al-Ḥuwayrith b. Rabīʿa b. Mālik b. Safr b. Hinʾ b. ʿAmr b. al-Ghawth b. Ṭayyiʾ (thus his *nisba* is to be amended in the article DHŪ ḲĀR).

This Arab chieftain succeeded in gaining the favour of Khusraw Aparwīz (Kisrā Abarwīz), who apparently entrusted to him some months before the accession of al-Nuʿmān III b. al-Mundhir [*q.v.*], the administration of al-Ḥīra (al-Ṭabarī, i, 1017). It is difficult to establish exactly in which period the king granted him as a life possession 30 villages on the banks of the Euphrates and appointed him administrator of the region of ʿAyn Tamr, since the traditions are inconsistent. It is possible that Khusraw rewarded him in this way for services rendered when he was attacked and forced to flee by the usurper Vahrām Čūbīn (Bahrām [*q.v.*] Djūbīn). Al-Nuʿmān III [*q.v.*], the king of al-Ḥīra at this time, did not come to the aid of his suzerain, although a certain Ṭāʾī had given him his horse to enable him to escape at a time when he was in a perilous situation on the banks of the Nahrawān. According to some (e.g. al-Ṭabarī, i, 1029), the hero of this story is Iyās; for others (Levi della Vida, *Livres des Chevaux*, Leiden 1928, 32; al-Masʿūdī, *Murūdj*, ii, 216-7 = § 636), it was his nephew, Ḥassān b. Ḥamẓala al-Ṭāʾī, who gave the king his horse, al-Ḍubayl, and subsequently received as a land grant the *ṭassūdj* of Khuṭarmiyya. The chronicles mention a victory won by Iyās over the Byzantines near Ṣatīdamā, but the most important event of his life was his appointment to succeed al-Nuʿmān III after the Emperor of Persia had taken his revenge by putting the latter to death. Although the date of this appointment is hard to establish, it may be located between A.D. 602 and 604/5; Khusraw Aparwīz appointed to serve at his court a Persian official whose title of Nakhwīraghān appears in various forms in the Arabic sources (cf. A. Christensen, *Sassanides*², 452). According to the same sources, Iyās governed al-Ḥīra for nine years, and it was in the eighth year of his reign that the prophetic mission of Muḥammad began. He died probably in the year A.D. 611 or 612.

It was during the period when he governed al-Ḥīra that there took place the famous battle of Dhū Ḳār [*q.v.*], in which he participated as leader of the Arab warriors; the Arabo-Persian troops were defeated, but Iyās was spared drastic punishment and retained his responsibilities. He was, essentially, the last Arab "king" of al-Ḥīra since the town was subsequently placed in the hands of exclusively Persian officials until the Islamic conquest. Finally, the sources consider him a talented poet, but very few of his verses have been preserved (see, however, Abkāryūs, 46-9).

Bibliography: Ṭabarī, i, 1029-32 and index; Balādhurī, *Futūḥ*, 243; Ibn Ḳutayba, *Maʿārif*, 605; Abū Tammām, *Ḥamāsa*, 73; Masʿūdī, *Murūdj*, ii, 212 = § 1073; idem, *Tanbīh*, ed. Ṣāwī, 158, 208; Maḳdisī, *al-Badʾ wa ʾl-taʾrīkh*, iii, 169 ff., 208; Ibn ʿAbd Rabbih, *ʿIḳd*, index; *Aghānī*, ed. Beirut, xxiii, 220-41, *passim*; Nöldeke, *Geschichte der Perser und Araber*, 311 ff.; Cheikho, *Shuʿarāʾ al-Naṣrāniyya*, 135-8; Rothstein, *Laḥmiden*, 107 ff.; *Bibl.* to the art. DHŪ ḲĀR.

(CH. PELLAT)

IZMĪD, modern form İZMIT, a town of north-western Turkey, lying at the head of the Gulf of Izmit (Izmit Körfezi) in lat. 40° 47' N., long. 29° 55' E.

It is the classical Nicomedia, named after Nicomedes I of Bithynia, who in 264 B.C. founded it as his new capital. The Roman emperor Diocletian made it in the late 3rd century A.D. his capital in the east; it was there that he abdicated in 305 (see W. Ruge, art. *Nikomedeia*, in *PW*, xvii/1, cols. 468-92). The spelling Nikumīdiyya appears in such Arabic geographers as Ibn Khurradādhbih and al-Idrīsī, and subsequently, forms like Iznukumīd and Iznikmīd are found in Islamic sources.

It was captured from the Byzantines by the Saldjūḳs when they swept through Asia Minor under Sulaymān b. Ḳutulmish (d. 479/1086 [*q.v.*]) towards the end of the 5th/11th century. Sulaymān made his capital at nearby Nicaea [see IZNĪḲ], but shortly after his death Nicomedia was recaptured by Alexius I Connenus, and apart from the brief period when the Latin emperors of Constantinople held the town (1204-7), it remained in Byzantine hands until captured after a long siege by the Ottomans under Orkhan. The dates for this vary in the Greek and Turkish sources, the former placing this in 1338; at all events, it must have been soon after the fall of Nicaea in 731/1331 (cf. Pitcher, *An historical geography of the Ottoman empire*, 38). In 1402 the Turkish town was sacked by a group of Tīmūr's troops. In Ottoman times Izmid, in the *sandjaḳ* of Ḳodja-eli [*q.v.*], became especially important as a naval arsenal, reportedly founded by the Köprülüs, and for building small merchant vessels using timber supplied by the extensive forests of the vicinity.

In the earliest register so far known, an *idjmāl* dated 937/1530, the settlement is on record as one of the five towns (*nefs*) of the province. As it is mentioned first in the list, it must have been the residence of the local governor. The town contained 589 men of tax-paying age, 86 of whom were exempted from certain dues. Of the remainder, 351 were heads of households and 152 were bachelors. These figures indicate a settlement of about 2,000-2,500 inhabitants. In the *ḳaḍā*, there were two *medreses* and two children's schools, as well as two Friday mosques, in addition to five public baths (Ahmet Özkılınç *et alii* (eds.), *438 numaralı muhâsebe-i vilâyet-i Anadolu defteri (937/1530), dizin ve tıpkıbasım*, Devlet Arşivleri Genel Müdürlüğü 1994, ii, 65-6).

In 962-3/1555, Hans Dernschwam saw a fortress on a hill with a new mosque, which supposedly had been built in place of a previous church. A sizeable part of the town also was located on this hill. At the time of Dernschwam's passage, the classical ruins were being quarried for stone. This was sawn locally into the sizes required by Istanbul builders, presumably for use in the construction of the Süleymāniyye, then in progress (*Tagebuch einer Reise nach Konstantinopel und Kleinasien (1553/55)*, ed. F. Babinger, Munich and Leipzig 1923, 153-4). The area's abundant water resources also served for the operation of mills grinding flour for the consumption of Istanbul, including the Janissary bakeries. Due to its functional link with the capital, Izmīd formed an exception to the rule that towns were to feed themselves from the product of their own *ḳaḍās*. For the hinterland was heavily forested rather than agricultural, with high-quality pine trees suitable for ships' masts abundant. As late as the second half of the 11th/17th century, the French ambassador was permitted to export a certain number for the use of the French navy (R. Mantran, *Istanbul dans la seconde moitié du XVII*ᵉ *siècle. Essai d'histoire institutionelle, économique et sociale*, Paris and Istanbul 1962, 445).

The only surviving register enumerating individual taxpayers (*mufaṣṣal*) and covering Izmīd dates from 1034/1624-5. At this time, the town consisted of 29 fully-fledged town quarters or, in some cases, recent accretions to older urban wards. The total tax-paying population numbered 849; no data on bachelors being available, our estimate of total population cannot be very precise, but probably the number of inhabitants had about doubled since 937/1530. One of the quarters was named for the local Friday mosque. Since another urban ward was called Djumʿa, it is likely that the town possessed two structures suitable for Friday prayers; possibly one of these was the Süleymān Pasha mosque which, according to a rescript dated 1171/1758, was recorded in the official registers of the time but has not been located in the surviving *taḥrīrs* (Ahmet Kal'a *et alii* (eds.), *İstanbul ahkâm defterleri İstanbul vakıf tarihi*, Istanbul 1998, i, 238). Near the port there was a Christian quarter; this may well have grown in later years, as in 1165/1752 the town boasted a *metropolid*, albeit one who resided in Istanbul (*ibid.*, i, 338-9). During this same period, the town also possessed some Jewish residents (*ibid.*, i, 164). As the non-Muslim quarter is described as lying "under the town", we may assume that most of the Muslim wards lay on the hill, as they had done in Dernschwam's time (Ankara Tapu ve Kadastro Genel Müdürlüğü, Kuyudu Kadime, no. 49, fol. 12b).

Ewliyā Čelebi visited Iznikmīd about 1050/1640, describing the ruined fortress, which in his opinion had been destroyed by Sultan ʿOthmān to prevent its use by the Byzantine nobles with whom this ruler was at war. Among the notable buildings, Ewliyā mentioned a mosque built by Pertew Pasha on the seashore, a work of Mimʿār Sinān, along with a public bath and *kerwānsarāy* by the same vizier. A garden palace with an extensive park had been built for Murād IV. The town contained 23 quarters, three of which were inhabited by Christians while one was settled by Jews. There was no *bedestān*, normally the hallmark of a major commercial centre, but the extensive depots located near the port seem to have served similar purposes. Timber merchants formed a significant part of the urban élite *Seyahatnamesi, Topkapı Sarayı Bağdat 304 yazmasının transkripsyonu dizini*, Istanbul 1999, 39-40).

In the 12th/18th century, woodworking crafts, such as the manufacture of combs and spoons, appear to have been of some significance. However, the Iznikmīd craftsmen did not supply themselves with wood directly from the forest villages, but purchased it in Istanbul. Yet there must have been economic opportunities available in the town itself, as toward the end of the century, Izmīd supposedly held 30,000 people. A.D. Mordtmann Senr., who saw the town shortly after the end of the Crimean War, claims that it was inhabited by 2,000 Turkish, 1,000 Armenian and 200 Greek families, which means that he estimated a population size of about 15,000 (*Anatolien, Skizzen und Reisebriefe aus Kleinasien (1850-1859)*, ed. Babinger, Hanover 1925, 282-3). According to Mordtmann, a small salt pan, already mentioned by Ewliyā, was in operation, the local harbour was still of some importance and the arsenal was, at the time, building a warship for the Ottoman navy. Further development of the town was, however, impeded by the prevalence of malaria. In the closing years of the 19th century, Izmīd formed the centre of the *müteṣarriflik* of the same name (V. Cuinet, *La Turquie d'Asie*, Paris 1890-4, iv, 301-400). Urban growth had probably been promoted by the railroad linking Istanbul to Ankara, and the town's population now amounted to about 25,000, living in 5,857 houses and purchasing their daily needs in 1,140 shops. Stone quarries and a sawmill were still active: two state-owned factories had been established, making fezzes and woollen cloth for uniforms; another such factory, producing fine silk fabrics and located in Hereke, administratively was situated in the *wilāyet* of Istanbul but geographically much closer to Izmīd. In the immediate vicinity, the townlet of Armach (Cuinet's spelling) was inhabited by Armenians who in 1019-20/1611 had immigrated from Iran. Housing a seminary for Gregorian priests, this locality specialised in silk cultivation.

However, Izmit's transformation into a major industrial centre has come under the Republic, and especially, after the Second World War, with the town benefiting from its easy access to Istanbul. Until 1970, a state-owned paper mill opened in 1936 produced practically all the paper used in Turkey (art. *Kocaeli*, in *Yurt ansiklopedisi*, Istanbul 1982-3, vii, 5037). Since the 1960s, car tyres, petrochemicals and liquid petrol gas (the major fuel for cooking in Turkey) have been developed there, and since there is now an autoroute along the northern shore of the Gulf of Izmit, the area between Izmit and Istanbul is becoming the major coherent industrial area of Turkey. Izmit itself is now a city of over 300,000 which attracts migrants; its factory workers, now organised, were major participants in the labour unrest of summer 1970. It suffered badly from the 1999 earthquake, when amongst many others, buildings of the recently-established provincial university were destroyed. Yet despite this industrialisation, away from the coastline, some of the area's agricultural potential remains, including the cherries of Yarımca, known to Ewliyā Čelebi, and also tobacco, sunflowers and sugar beet.

Bibliography: In addition to references in the article, see J.B. Mordtmann's *EI*[1] art. s.v.; Cuinet, *op. cit.*, iv, 357 ff.; Naval Intelligence Division. Admiralty Handbooks, *Turkey*, London 1942-3, ii, 555 and index. (Suraiya Faroqhi)

IZMĪR, the Turkish form of the ancient Greek name Smyrna, one of the great mercantile cities of the Eastern Mediterranean. It lies in western Anatolia at the head of the Gulf of Izmir, and the pre-modern city lay mainly on the small delta plain of the Kızılcullu (ancient Melas) river.

Izmir has a history going back five millennia, archaeological excavations having revealed the earliest level of occupation as contemporary with the first city of Troy at the beginning of the Bronze Age (*ca.* 3,000 B.C.). Greek settlement is indicated from *ca.* 1,000 B.C., and Herodotus says that the city was founded by Aeolians but then seized by Ionians. It became a fine city, possibly re-founded by Alexander the Great in 334 B.C. Under the Romans it was the centre of a civil diocese of the province of Asia, and was one of the early seats of Christianity. In Byzantine times it continued as a metropolitan see and was the capital of the naval theme of Samos.

With the invasions of Turkmens across Anatolia towards the end of the 11th century, the Turkish chief Čaḳa/Tzachas established himself at Smyrna in 1081 and from there raided the Aegean islands. But after the Turks were driven out of Nicaea in 1097 [see izmīd, in Suppl.], Smyrna reverted to Byzantine rule in 1098. It was over two centuries before it passed under Turkish control again, when it was conquered by the Aydînoghullarî [see aydîn-oghlu] (716-17/1317: Ḳadīfe Ḳalʿe; 729-30/1329: Ashaghî Ḳalʿe) (Tuncer Baykara, *Izmir şehri ve tarihi*, Bornova-İzmir 1974, 28; for slightly variant dates, see Irène Mélikoff-Sayar, *Le destān d'Umur Pacha*, Paris 1954, 40). On his visit in *ca.* 731/1331, Ibn Baṭṭūṭa found a largely ruinous place, whose upper fortress was held by the Aydînoghullarî and which possessed at least one *zāwiye* (*Riḥla*, ii, 310-12, tr. Gibb, ii, 445-7). The city was captured by the Knights of Rhodes on 28 October 1344, although the Aydînoghullarî and later the Ottomans held on to the citadel or upper fortress. The Knights were finally expelled by Tīmūr in 804-5/1402, when he took the lower fortress, and the Aydînoghullarî briefly reinstated.

However, in 817/1414-15, Izmir became an Ottoman possession, after the last Aydînoghlu to rule, Djüneyd, known as Izmīr-oghlu, had been defeated by Sultan Meḥemmed I (Himmet Akın, *Aydınoğulları tarihi hakkında bir araştırma*, Ankara 1968, 80; for a later date of the final Ottoman conquest, namely 828-9/1425, see D. Goffman, *Izmir. From village to colonial port city*, in Ethem Eldem, Goffman and B. Masters, *The Ottoman city between East and West*, Cambridge 1999, 86). As the new governor, an Islamised son of the former Bulghar Tsar Shishman, was appointed, but the first extant *taḥrīr* describing the town only dates from 935/1528-9 (physical damage to earlier registers accounts for this absence: Başbakanlık Arşivi, Istanbul, Tapu Tahrir no. 148).

In the 9th-10th/15th-16th centuries, Izmir was a small settlement; in 937/1530, 304 adult males, both tax-paying and tax-exempt, were on record; 42 of these were Christians (İsmet Binark *et alii* (eds.), 166 *numaralı muhâsebe-i vilâyet-i Anadolu* (*937/1530*), Ankara 1995, 392). There were no more than five urban wards, one of them situated in the immediate vicinity of the port, rather active in spite of the town's small size. By 983/1575-6, Izmir had grown to house 492 taxpayers in eight urban wards; in addition, a group of former Izmirlis had settled in the nearby village of Boynuzsekisi, but continued to pay their taxes with the town's population (Tapu ve Kadastro Genel Müdürlüğü, Ankara, Kuyudu Kadime no. 167, fols. 3b ff.). One of the port's major functions was the supply of Istanbul with grain, raisins, cotton and other agricultural products (Zeki Arıkan, *A Mediterranean port. Izmir in the 15th and 16th centuries*, in *Three ages of Izmir, palimpsest of cultures*, ed. Enis Batur, tr. Virginia T. Saçlıoğlu, Istanbul 1993, 59-70).

But Izmir's remarkable growth really begins in the later 10th/16th century, when the cotton, cotton yarn and other products of the region began to attract French, English, Dutch and Venetian traders. Izmir thus took over the role of mediaeval Ayat̲holug̲h (Ephesus, Altiluogo), which was losing its commercial significance due to the silting up of its port (D. Goffman, *Izmir and the Levantine world, 1550-1650* (Seattle and London 1990). At first illegal, the exportation of cotton was legalised in 1033/1623 (Suraiya Faroqhi, *Towns and townsmen of Ottoman Anatolia*, Cambridge 1984, 136-7). In the 11th/17th century Izmir and the surrounding region were settled by numerous migrants from other provinces, including Jews from Salonika who fled the mounting exactions and diminishing rewards of the Macedonian woollen industry (Goffman, *op. cit.*, 97-102). Toward the century's end, J.-B. Tavernier estimated the population at about 90,000 (*Les six voyages en Turquie & en Perse*, ed. St. Yérasimos, Paris 1981, i, 138; for a general overview of the descriptions of Izmir by 17th-century Europeans, see Sonia Anderson, *An English consul in Turkey*, Oxford 1989, 1-18). Turks formed the vast majority (about 60,000), while there were also 15,000 Greeks, 8,000 Armenians and 6,000 to 7,000 Jews. A major earthquake destroyed the city in 1099/1688, with the heaviest damage in the seaside quarter, but it was soon rebuilt (N.N. Ambraseys and C.F. Finkel, *The seismicity of Turkey and adjacent areas: a historical review 1500-1800*, Istanbul 1995, 90-1). To a large extent, the exportation of Persian raw silk to Europe passed through Izmir; thus this port had entered into a successful competition with the much older mart of Aleppo (Necmi Ülker, *The emergence of Izmir as a Mediterranean commercial center for French and English interests, 1698-1740*, in *Internat. Jnal. of Turkish Studies*, 1 [1987], 1-37). However the regular passage of caravans through a plague-infested mountain area on the Ottoman-Persian border meant that the city was exposed to contagion not only through ships' crews and cargoes, but also on account of overland trade (D. Panzac, *La peste à Smyrne*, in *Annales E.S.C.* [1973], 1071-93).

In the early 18th century, Persian silk was less frequently seen in Izmir, as wars accompanying the decay of the Ṣafawids impeded cultivation; moreover, English traders gained access to alternative sources in Bengal and China. While English merchants, specialised in the commercialisation of silk, largely gave up trading in the Levant, French merchants, in particular, continued their activities. At the beginning of the 17th century, Izmir and Iskenderun constituted the major exporting centres as far as the Marseilles trade was concerned, while at the century's end, Iskenderun had fallen far behind, and Izmir uncontestably handled the vast majority of French exports (Elena Frangakis-Syrett, *The commerce of Smyrna in the eighteenth century* (*1700-1820*), Athens 1992, 257-9). In certain years, over 45% of all Ottoman goods shipped to Marseilles passed through Izmir. Exports included mohair yarn from Ankara, silk, cotton, both spun and raw, and wool. Among imports, the only manufactured item were Languedoc woollen fabrics, produced exclusively for the Ottoman market (Cl. Marquié, *L'industrie textile carcassonnaise au XVIIIe siècle* . . ., Carcassonne 1993). In addition, Izmir imported coffee from the Caribbean, sugar and indigo.

Of the numerous public buildings of Ottoman Izmir, very little survives. Ewliyā Čelebi, who visited the town in 1081-2/1671 and admired the relief of a female face at the entrance to the seaside fortress, praises the Bïyïḳlïog̲h̲lu D̲j̲āmiʿi, later destroyed in the earthquake of 1099/1688, and also mentions the Fāʾiḳ Pas̲h̲a D̲j̲āmiʿi, one of the oldest mosques in town (*Seyāḥatnāmesi*, Istanbul 1935, ix, 88-100). His descriptions in part reflect the data collected by the officials who, in 1068/1657-8, put together a *taḥrīr* under the orders of a certain Ismāʿīl Pas̲h̲a (for further information on this document, see Faroqhi, *Towns*, 276). At different times in Izmir's history, 25 *medreses* were active (Münir Aktepe, *Ottoman medreses in Izmir*, in *Three ages of Izmir*, 85-99). Ewliyā also mentioned the multitude of *k̲h̲ān*s (Aktepe, *İzmir hanları ve çarşıları hakkında ön bilgi*, in *Tarih Dergisi*, xxv [1971], 105-54; W. Müller-Wiener, *Der Bazar von Izmir*, in *Mitteilungen der Fränkischen Geographischen Gesellschaft*, xxvii-xxviii, [1980-1], 420-54). In the late 18th and early 19th centuries, certain Izmir buildings were decorated with elaborate reliefs, featuring slightly stylised views of local mosques and other buildings. The popularity of this decoration may indicate the donors' pride in the prosperity of their city (Ayda Arel, *Image architecturale et image urbaine dans une série de bas-reliefs ottomans de la région égéenne*, in *Turcica*, xviii [1986], 83-118).

An active trade resulted in the residence of foreign consuls, the English historian Paul Rycaut officiating as Charles II's representative between 1077-8/1667 and 1089/1678 (Anderson, *An English consul*, *passim*). By contrast, the Ottoman central administration was merely represented by the *ḳāḍī* and the tax farmers collecting customs and other dues. Unlike in many other Ottoman commercial centres, foreign traders were not obliged to reside in the *k̲h̲ān*s but could inhabit houses by the seashore, many of them with landing stages of their own. Houses for rent, known as *frenk k̲h̲āne*, were built by Ottoman notables as an investment and sometimes passed on to pious foundations. Thus the seaside quarter became known as the "street of the Franks". The latter also were permitted their own churches, the French worshipping at St. Polycarpe, whose parish registers survive from the 18th century onwards (Marie Carmen Smyrnelis, *Colonies européennes et communautés ethnico-confessionelles à Smyrne: coexistence et réseaux de sociabilité*, in *Vivre dans l'Empire ottoman*, ed. F. Georgeon and P. Dumont, Paris 1997, 173, 194). Entertainments might take on a semi-public character, with plays performed in the French consulate even in the 11th/17th century, while a hundred years later, the Jewish community also staged plays (Eftal Sevinçli, *Theater in Izmir*, in *Three ages of Izmir*, 370). Officially speaking, neither French nor English merchants were expected to bring their wives, much less marry local Christian women, for this would have made them subjects of the Sultan; sojourn in the Ottoman Empire was expected to be a temporary affair. In practice, certain French and English families lived in the city for generations, and marriages of Frenchmen to Roman Catholics of Greek or Armenian background were common enough.

Ewliyā Čelebi vaunted the enormous revenues which the *ḳāḍī* of Izmir enjoyed in his own time, partly due to regular emoluments and partly due to the presents which he could expect (ix, 89). But in the 18th century, the major Ottoman presence in the area was not the *ḳāḍīs* but a family of tax farmers and dues collectors acting for absentee governors and known as the Ḳara ʿO<u>th</u>mānog<u>h</u>ullarî. The economic power of these personages derived from the fact that they marketed the cotton and other agricultural produce they collected from local peasants to foreign exporters (G. Veinstein, *"Ayân" de la région d'Izmir et le commerce du Levant (deuxième moitié du XVIIIe siècle)*, in *ROMM*, xx [1975], 131-46; for a contrary position, emphasising the role of the family as actual landholders, see Yuzo Nagata, *Tarihte ayânlar, Karaosmanoğulları üzerinde bir inceleme*, Ankara 1997, 89-142). Political power and status allowed the Ḳara ʿO<u>th</u>mānog<u>h</u>ullarî to drive hard bargains, so that peasants also entrusted them with the goods they wished to sell on their own behalf. Socio-political status also was documented by the numerous pious foundations this family established in the region, for which the two *<u>kh</u>āns* constructed in Izmir by different Ḳara ʿO<u>th</u>mānog<u>h</u>ullarî were meant to produce revenue (Inci Kuyulu, *Kara Osman-oğlu ailesine ait mimari eserler*, Ankara 1992, with extensive bibl.).

In the 19th century, Izmir continued to function as a city specialising in foreign trade. However with the Ottoman Empire's increasing integration into a transcontinental economy dominated by Europe, the character of this trade changed, while its volume continuously expanded. Grain, sesame, figs, raisins (at the end of the century by far the single most valuable crop), the tanning agents sumach and valonia, and opium, all arrived in the depots of Izmir's "gentlemen traders", many but not all of them non-Muslims. Ottoman merchants operated as middlemen, dependent on exporting European merchants (Halit Ziya Uşaklıgil, citing a passage from *Kırk yıl*, 5 vols., Istanbul 1936, cited in English tr. in C. Issawi, *The economic history of Turkey 1800-1914*, Chicago and London, 1980, 72-3; V. Cuinet, *La Turquie d'Asie*, Paris 1892-4, iii, 362 ff.).

Izmir's role as a centre of export trade encouraged investment in the construction of railroads; thus one of the first Anatolian railways linked Izmir to Turgutlu, then known as Kasaba, and another line connected Aydın and Izmir. However, the orientation of these railways according to the needs of import and export merchants limited their overall economic usefulness (Orhan Kurmuş, *İmperyalizmin Türkiye'ye gelişi*, Istanbul 1974). Between 1867 and 1875, the port of Izmir was modernised, with quays and a breakwater constructed (Mübahat Kütükoğlu, *İzmir rıhtımının inşaatı ve işletme imtiyazı*, in *Tarih Dergisi*, xxxii [1979], 495-558). A few industrial enterprises served the preparation of agricultural goods for export. While most of the olive, sesame and other vegetable oils were still pressed in old-style mills, there were a few ventures, undertaken by members of the Ottoman minorities but also by the occasional Englishman, to found modern-style factories (Abdullah Martal, *Değişim sürecinde İzmir'de sanayileşme, 19. yüzyıl*, Izmir 1999, 144-5). In the import sector, textiles assumed a greater importance after about 1840. At that time, the output of English cotton factories began to flood the Izmir market, unimpeded by any protective duty since the Anglo-Ottoman commercial treaty fixed custom dues at a low level and prohibited monopolies (Martal, *Sanayileşme*, 123-5). This did not, however, prevent the emergence of a flourishing textile industry specialising in home furnishings (Cuinet, iii, 429).

Moreover, rising standards of living among the European middle classes, as well as the stylistic preferences of the Victorian age, led to an increased demand for carpets. What had previously been a luxury trade expanded to cater for mass markets which around 1900, came to include the more affluent sectors of the working class. While these carpets were manufactured in small towns of the Aegean region, notably Uşak [see ʿUS<u>H</u>ĀḲ], they became known as Smyrna rugs in Europe, not only because they came out through the city's port but also because the merchants organising this venture, British traders occupying a prominent position, were frequently based in Izmir (D. Quataert, *Machine breaking and the changing carpet industry of western Anatolia 1860-1908*, repr. in *Workers, peasants and economic change in the Ottoman Empire 1730-1914*, Istanbul 1993, 117-36.

Trade and an active public administration had by the end of the 19th century stimulated urban growth, the population of Izmir proper reaching the 200,000 mark. About 89,000 were Muslim Turks and 59,000 Orthodox Greeks, while over 36,000 inhabitants carried foreign passports (Cuinet, iii, 440; for further statistical information, largely culled from the *sālnāmes*, see the anonymous art. *Izmir*, in *Yurt ansiklopedisi, Türkiye il il, dünü, bugünü, yarını*, 4271-87). Steamboat lines and a tram assured intra-urban communication and, in 1905, electricity was introduced. The city became an educational centre, with nine state schools on the secondary level. For the Greeks, there was the "Evangelical School" famed for its high level of instruction, in addition to numerous foreign, especially French educational establishments.

Izmir was not directly affected during World War I, although many young men were drafted into the army or into labour bataillons. But in 1919, with the Ottoman Empire defeated and Istanbul occupied by the Allies, the Greek government, with the backing of the British Prime Minister Lloyd George, landed troops in Izmir and occupied the city until 1922, when the invaders were driven out by the Nationalist army under the command of Muṣṭafā Kemāl [Atatürk]. Both the Greek occupation and the later withdrawal of the Greek forces were accompanied by large-scale flight from Izmir, which in September 1922 was moreover destroyed by a major conflagration (M.L. Smith, *Ionian vision, Greece in Asia Minor 1919-1922*, rev. ed. London 1998). The exchange of populations decided upon in the Treaty of Lausanne (1923) involved the exodus of the remaining Greek population, whose places were taken by Turks who had been forced to vacate Greek territory.

In the 1960s, Izmir began to add new functions to its traditional role as an export-import centre serving an agricultural hinterland. Small-scale industry developed, and in automotive transportation, numerous minute undercapitalised entrepreneurs were also active. As in all large Turkish cities, migration from rural areas led to the hasty construction of shantytown housing and the emergence of a large "informal sector" (Mübeccel Kıray, *Örgütleşemeyen kent, İzmir'de iş hayatının yapısı*, Ankara 1972). By 1980, Izmir had developed into a city of over half a million inhabitants, surrounded by highly urbanised suburbs. Apart from the beginnings of an investment goods industry, factories processing tobacco, olives and fruits continue to be a local specialty, and tourism also plays an important role in the urban economy. With two universities, the city also has become one of the educational centres of Turkey.

Bibliography: Given in the article. See also J.H. Mordtmann, *EI*[1] art. s.v. (Suraiya Faroqhi)

ʿIZZET HŌLŌ (al-)ʿĀbid, Aḥmad b. Muḥyī 'l-Dīn Abu 'l-Hawl b. ʿUmar b. ʿAbd al-Ḳadir, popularly known as **ʿARAB ʿIZZET** Pas̲h̲a (1272-1343/1855-1924), late Ottoman statesman and close counselor of Sultan ʿAbd al-Ḥamīd II [*q.v.*].

Born in Damascus (hence his nickname "ʿArab") as the son of a wealthy local notable, Hōlō Pas̲h̲ā, he was educated in his hometown and in Beirut and became proficient in Turkish and French. Counted among the reformers, he edited a weekly in Arabic and Turkish, named *Dimas̲h̲k*. Moving to Istanbul, he eventually joined the ranks of the chamberlains (*kurenā*) of ʿAbd al-Ḥamīd and then became a Second Secretary (*ikind̲j̲i kātib*) of the *Mābeyn* [*q.v.*]. He gained great influence at court and was finally appointed Vizier. In May 1900 he was made head of the supervisory committee for the Ḥid̲j̲āz Railway [*q.v.*]. From gifts of the Sultan and from kickbacks paid to him by foreign companies he acquired great wealth, and became the object of public outrage. The then famous satirist S̲h̲āʿir Es̲h̲ref (1847-1912), in a lampoon against ʿAbd al-Ḥamīd, wrote:

Besmele gūs̲h̲ eyleyen s̲h̲eyṭān gibi,
Ḳorḳuyursun "höt" dese bir ed̲j̲nebī.
Pādıs̲h̲āhım öyle alçaksın ki sen
ʿIzzet-i nefsin ʿArab ʿIzzet gibi!

Like Satan, when he hears the *bismullāh*,
you panic, if a foreigner says "hum".
My Lord, you are so lowly that your soul's nobility is like unto ʿArab ʿIzzet.

At the outbreak of the 1908 revolution he fled to London and thenceforward lived outside his own country, mainly in England, Switzerland and France. He died in Egypt, where he had gone for medical treatment, and was buried in Damascus.

Bibliography: İbrahim Alâettin Gövsa, *Türk meşhurları ansiklopedisi*, İstanbul n.d. [*ca.* 1940], 198; Ziriklī, *Aʿlām*[3], i, 163; H. Yücebaş, *Şair Eşref bütün şiirleri ve 80 yıllık hatıraları*, Istanbul 1978, 5. (Ed.)

J

JAMIA MILLIA ISLAMIA (al-D̲j̲āmiʿa al-Milliyya al-Islāmiyya), a Muslim University, formerly in British India and now in the Indian Union.

In September 1920, the Indian National Congress adopted the non-cooperation resolution against the British government. The Jamia Millia Islamia (National Muslim University) was the "lusty child of the non-cooperation days", according to Jawaharlal Nehru, independent India's first Prime Minister 1947-64.

Mawlānā Maḥmūd Ḥasan (1851-1920), the *ʿālim* at the *Dār-al-ʿulūm* in Deoband, performed the opening ceremony on 29 October 1920. The Jamia's principal architects were the Oxford-educated Mawlānā Muḥammad ʿAlī (1878-1931), the pan-Islamic leader Dr. Muk̲h̲tār Aḥmad Anṣārī (1880-1936), an Edinburgh-trained medical doctor, and Ḥakīm Ad̲j̲mal K̲h̲ān (1863-1927), a leading practitioner of the *unani* system of education and one of Dihlī's well-known citizens. Among its prominent vice-chancellors have been Dr. Zākir Ḥusayn (1879-1969) and Muḥammad Mud̲j̲īb (1902-85).

In its nascent stages, the Jamia's *raison d'être* was to keep Muslim education free from government aid and control and to evolve a philosophy of education that would be in keeping with national characteristics and in consonance with the Islamic spirit. The founders believed that communal peace and religious understanding were the fruits of true education. Consequently, they devised a curriculum to end religious discord between all faiths, to familiarise youth with their own cultural heritage without rejecting what was true and useful in the culture of others, and to evolve an organic thesis of traditional and modern education. The first *Amīr-i D̲j̲āmiʿa* (Chancellor), Ḥakīm Ad̲j̲mal K̲h̲ān, expected students to know each other's culture: "The firm foundation of a united Indian nationhood depends on this mutual understanding."

M.K. Gandhi, the main inspiration behind the founding of the Jamia, hoped that this institution would interpret Muslim culture in a manner consonant with truth and the requirements of a people diverse in culture. He hoped that it would produce good Muslims who would be men of refinement and character, living according to the highest moral standards and serving the people with devotion and sincerity.

In 1935, Halide Edib Hanum, the Turkish author [see k̲h̲ālide edīb], lectured at the Jamia. According to her, the institution's chief objective was to create a harmonious nationhood, and she observed that, in its aim, if not always in its procedure, it was nearer to the Gandhian movement than any other Muslim institution she had come across in India. In 1943, W.C. Smith, the historian of Islam, commented that the Jamia "has been constantly growing, ever refurbishing its methods, and branching out from time to time to meet new needs.... Its education has aimed at being, and has been, progressive, Indian, and Muslim."

The pursuit of such ideals ran into rough weather owing to paucity of funds, and yet dedicated teachers kept the Jamia going under adverse circumstances. They did not have money, and worked amidst and through poverty. They did not even have the shelter of houses, so they taught under the open sky. Yet they cheerfully faced the hard trials in an atmosphere of enthusiasm and optimism. Zākir Ḥusayn, vice-chancellor from 1926 to 1948, remembered those years of deprivation as "days of joy".

In the 1930s, the All-India Muslim League staked its political claims as the sole spokesman of the Muslim community. Muḥammad Mud̲j̲īb, the historian at Jamia, told Muḥammad Iḳbāl (1876-1938 [*q.v.*]), the poet of Indian Islam, that his plea for a Muslim state in north-western India was opposed to their cherished ideal that Muslims live and work with non-Muslims in order to realise common ideals of citizenship. In March 1940, Muḥammad ʿAlī Djināḥ (1876-1948 [*q.v.*]) put forward the "two-nation" theory to legitimise his demand for a Muslim homeland. Unlike the university at ʿAlīgarh, which turned into an "arsenal of Muslim India", the "two-nation" theory found no supporters in the Jamia *birādarī* (fraternity).

An institution with a nationalist record could not escape the fury of the angry mobs that rioted in independent India's capital after the country's Partition. The Jamia's property was looted and destroyed. But it lived through this experience to provide the healing touch and was, in the opinion of Gandhi, "like an oasis in the Sahara".

The university, in search of moral and political support after independence in August 1947, could have turned into a quasi-religious or quasi-communal institution, but this did not happen, and the Jamia's historic character has remained unchanged. "I look on this," claimed Mudjīb, "as a secular school."

In the mid-1920s, the total enrolment of the schools and colleges was about eighty, with 25 to 30 teachers. Today, the Jamia is a central university, administered by an act of Parliament. Over 5,600 students receive education and training in social, physical and natural sciences, humanities, education, law, engineering and mass communication. From a few thousand rupees in the 1930s, its maintenance budget, in 2000-1, is approximately 36.11 crores.

Bibliography: Mushirul Hasan, *Legacy of a divided nation: India's Muslims since independence*, London 1997; idem, *A nationalist conscience: M.A. Ansari, the Congress and the Raj*, New Delhi 1987. See also W.C. Smith, *Modern Islam in India, a social analysis*, Lahore 1943; Halide Edib, *Inside India*, London 1936.

(Mushirul Hasan)

K

ĶĀBĀDŪ, Maḥmūd b. Muḥammad b. Muḥammad b. ʿUmar (1230-88/1815-71), poet, man of letters and religious figure, and one of the precursors of reform in Tunisia.

After having learnt the Ḳurʾān, Arabic language and the rudiments of *fiḳh*, he left the *kuttāb* or Ḳurʾān school and plunged into individual readings of the mystics, and especially, the writings of Ibn al-ʿArabī [*q.v.*]. Under this influence, he spent his youthful life as a dervish. At the age of 18, his wanderings took him as far as Libya, where at Misrāṭa he met a famed Ṣūfī master, the *shaykh* Muḥammad Ẓāfir al-Madanī (d. 1854). In this *shaykh*'s company, he regained his desire for study. Three years later, he left him with the license, *idjāza* [*q.v.*], to transmit his teachings. On his return to Tunis, he attended the lectures of several *shaykh*s of the Zaytūna [*q.v.*], including Muḥammad Bayram al-Thālith, Aḥmad b. Ṭāhir al-Luṭayyif and Muḥammad b. Mulūka. At the same time, he taught the Zaytūna students abridgements of grammar, logic and rhetoric. One of his masters recommended him to the minister Sulaymān Kāhiya as a tutor for his sons. The minister's death in 1838 led him into exile for a second time, and he went to Istanbul and remained there till 1842. According to Ibn Abī Ḍiyāf, who met him at the time of a mission to the Sublime Porte and who led him to return to Tunis, he spent these years in study and teaching, as he had done at the Zaytūna. One of his biographers, Zayn al-ʿĀbidīn al-Sanūsī, states that he followed courses in mathematics at the Military College in Istanbul.

Back in Tunis, Ḳābādū was appointed professor at the Military Polytechnic School of Bardo, the first Tunisian to teach thus in this institution, whose director and teachers had been till then exclusively Europeans. During the years spent there (1842-55), he played a decisive role in the education of an élite, which was to be a spearhead of the reforms achieved between 1840 and 1875. Amongst his students, who also became his friends and protectors, was the great statesman and reformer Khayr al-Dīn (d. 1889 [*q.v.*]), author of the celebrated *Aḳwam al-masālik fī maʿrifat aḥwāl al-mamālik*, and the general Ḥusayn (d. 1887), one of the authors of the *ʿahd al-amān* or Fundamental Pact, who functioned as, *inter alia*, minister of education and public works. His teaching at the Bardo School involved only Arabic language and literature, but he encouraged his best students to translate from French into Arabic manuals and scientific works that he thought necessary for the formation of an élite to guide the country along the path of reform and modernisation. He checked and corrected the Arabic versions of certain works and wrote prefaces for others.

As soon as he demitted his duties at the School, Ḳābādū was appointed to the Zaytūna, on the recommendation of the Ḥanafī *muftī* Bayram al-Rabīʿ, as a teaching *shaykh* of the first class, retaining this position till the year of his death in 1871, combining it with the offices of *ḳāḍī* of the Bardo and then that of Mālikī *muftī* (from 1868 onwards). These positions enabled him to retain his influence and even to enlarge his audience. Whilst teaching rhetoric and logic, he stimulated the formation of circles at the Zaytūna in which he introduced subjects relevant for the various disciplines. At the Bardo School, he encouraged students who had a scientific and technical education to take an interest in the literature and history of Arab Muslim civilisation. At the Zaytūna, he led students seeking a traditional education towards the modern sciences and the study of other civilisations, thus contributing to the forming of a generation of Zaytūna graduates open to the spirit of reforms which brought a religious legitimisation to the movement for modernisation by the Bardo-trained élite he had himself taught. His most notable disciples at the Zaytūna were the *shaykh* Sālim Būḥādjib (1828-1924) and Bayram al-Khāmis (1839-89). The first of these was hailed by Muḥammad ʿAbduh [*q.v.*] as one of the minds most open to the reform he and al-Afghānī preached; he later became Mālikī *muftī* and then *shaykh al-islām*, a post previously reserved for

Ḥanafīs, and president of the Consultative Council. The second held various offices with the reformist ministers before going into exile, after Khayr al-Dīn's fall, at Istanbul and then Cairo, where he instigated a reformist newspaper, *al-Iʿlām*, and a reform movement.

If Muḥammad Ḳābādū is considered as a precursor of reform in Tunisia, this stems mainly from his role in the education of a political and religious élite to which he remained close and which put into action the reform of institutions in 19th-century Tunisia. At the Bardo School, as at the Zaytūna, he inculcated those reformist ideas which had begun to be known within the Muslim world at the end of the 18th century. This spirit, which Ḳābādū defended in his writings and in his official duties, rested on the will to reconcile the Arab-Islamic heritage with the ideas and knowledge that had brought about progress in Europe.

Not all of his work has come down to us, and what he wrote before 1842 is essentially lost. Even of his later works, at least a commentary on the poems of al-Mutanabbī is lost. His extant work is available in three editions: by M. al-Sanūsī (1877); by the Tunisian Publishing Society (1972); and by the University professor Amor Ben Salem, based on scholarly research, and published by the CERES at Tunis (1984). His oeuvre contains a section on poetry (= Ben Salem's first vol.), which is more important than the prose works (= the second vol., with various annexes). His poetry reflects the different stages of his career. His political ideas are especially to be found in his eulogies of the three Beys whom he knew between 1842 and 1871, and of the viziers and influential figures of the same period, as also in his poems hailing such events as the promulgation of the Fundamental Pact in 1846 and the Constitution of 1861, the publication of Khayr al-Dīn's book, etc. His closeness to the ruling powers explains the limits of his reformist policies, as seen in certain poems, like those where he hails the suspension of the reforms after the rebellion of ʿAlī b. Ghidhāhum [see IBN GHIDHĀHUM, in Suppl.] in 1864. His religious feeling is reflected in his invocations, addresses to saints and poems composed to glorify the great Ṣūfī leaders, the Prophet and his descendants, to which his own sharīfian origins attached him. Filled with classical culture, he was interested in the various forms of the Arabic poetic tradition, and his style and the forms adopted by him show a respect for classical canons of literature. These characteristics surface also in his non-poetic works, within which rhymed prose is dominant. This part of his work includes his letters, the editorials of the first 25 numbers of the *Journal Officiel*, his articles within that journal, the preface of the Arabic translation of Jommier's book on war, an epilogue to the Official Press of Tunisia's edition of the *Muwaṭṭaʾ*, a panegyric addressed to Khayr al-Dīn's book and the prefaces to his poems.

Ḳābādū's life and work have attracted much attention from those who consider him as a precursor of reform in Tunisia; the most complete and the most rigorously scholarly edition of his work remains that of Ben Salem.

Bibliography: *Dīwān Ḳābādū*, i-ii, ed. Amor Ben Salem, University of Tunis 1984; *Dīwān Ḳābādū*, STD, Tunis 1972; *al-Rāʾid al-rasmī al-tūnisī* (Journal Officiel Tunisien), nos. 1-25, 1860-1; nos. 27-8, 1871; Ben Salem, *Ḳābādū, ḥayātuhu, āthāruhu wa-tafkīruhu al-iṣlāḥī*, University of Tunis 1975; idem, art. *Ḳābādū*, in *Dāʾirat al-maʿārif al-tūnisiyya*, fasc. 1, Carthage 1990, 47-52; Rashīd al-Daḥdāḥ, *Ḳimaṭrat tawāmīr*, Paris 1880; Ibn Abi ʾl-Ḍiyāf, *Itḥāf ahl al-zamān bi-akhbār mulūk Tūnis wa-ʿahd al-amān*, Min. Aff. Cult., Tunis 1963-6, iv, 36-7, 61, v, 46-50, 56; Muḥ. Makhlūf, *Shadjarat al-nūr al-zakiyya fī ṭabakāt al-mālikiyya*, Cairo 1929, i, 393; Muḥ. al-Nayfar, *ʿUnwān al-arīb ʿammā nashaʾa fī ʾl-mamlaka al-tūnisiyya min ʿālim wa-adīb*, Tunis 1932, i, 127-30. Other bibliographical sources. Ḥasan Ḥusnī ʿAbd al-Wahhāb, *Mudjmal taʾrīkh al-adab al-tūnisī*, 3Tunis 1968, 277-8; al-Hādī Ḥammūda al-Ghuzzī, *al-Adab al-tūnisī fī ʾl-ʿahd al-ḥusaynī*, STD, Tunis 1972, 177-219; Muḥ. al-Khiḍr Ḥusayn, *Tūnis wa-djāmiʿ al-zaytūna*, Cairo 1971, 82-8; Muḥ. al-Fāḍil Ibn ʿĀshūr, *Arkān al-nahḍa al-tūnisiyya*, Tunis 1962, 5-10; *al-Ḥaraka al-adabiyya wa ʾl-fikriyya fī Tūnis*, Tunis 1972, 29 ff.; Muḥ. Maḥfūẓ, *Tarādjim al-muʾallifīn al-tūnisiyyīn*, 5 vols. Beirut 1986, iv, 47-52.

(M.Ch. Ferjani)

ḲABBĀNĪ, Nizār Tawfīḳ (1923-98), the most widely read and, with over 18,000 lines of verse, the most prolific 20th-century Arabic poet, an important innovator of form and content.

Ḳabbānī became a diplomat in 1945 after finishing his law studies in his native Damascus, but he left the service in 1966 so as to devote himself to full-time writing in Beirut, where he started his own publishing house (Dār Manshūrāt Nizār Ḳabbānī) in 1967. He died in London, where, after a short spell in Geneva, he had spent his last years. He was laid to rest in Damascus.

Ḳabbānī's highly poetical and persuasive language is eminently accessible and has been described as a "third language", neither lexicographically classical nor educated vernacular. His departure from classical norms is, in the poet's own words, a deliberate attack on the haughty history of Arabic rhetoric. Still, many of his poems are in a traditional Khalīlian metre with monorhyme and a fixed line-length (but often printed in a modern lay-out). However, more than a fifth of his poems (196 out of a total of 863) are non-metrical. In between are many poems in the tradition of *shiʿr ḥurr* (lit. "free poetry") with varied rhymes and variable line-length (brought about by the fact that the constituent metrical foot—or *tafʿīla*—is repeated a different number of times in different lines). An early example of this, already in his first *dīwān* *Ḳālat liya ʾl-samrāʾ* (1944), is the poem *Indifāʿ*.

Ḳabbānī's linguistic rebellion operates within a wider militant vision that defies a stagnant, underdeveloped and inhuman Arab society with its taboos on sexuality, religion and political power. This disposition is artistically expressed in hundreds of love poems, and some 140 overtly political poems. His "Notes on the book of the defeat" (*Hawāmish ʿalā daftar al-naksa*), "the angriest poem in contemporary Arabic" (S. Jayyusi), which appeared in the aftermath of the June 1967 defeat, ushered in a new stage, as underlined in the poet's own words "Ah my country! You have transformed me/from a poet of love and yearning/to a poet writing with a knife." Through the unity of his poetic vision, however, love and politics in Ḳabbānī are not compartmentalised. Much of his love poetry can in fact be read as political, and the political poems resonate with his love poetry.

His detractors tend to read his love poetry as a narcissistic Don Juanesque catalogue of amorous exploits and accuse the poet of superficiality. His social and political criticism has been read as sadistic nest fouling, and his writings have been banned more than once. Yet his poetry is popular with the masses and is memorised by millions, to which the sung versions of some twenty poems by singers such as Umm Kulthūm [*q.v.*], Fayrūz, ʿAbd al-Ḥalīm Ḥāfiẓ (d. 1977), Mādjida al-Rūmī (b. 1957), Kāẓim al-Sāhir, Nadjāt al-Ṣaghīra and others have also contributed.

His prose works include statements on poetry, and the autobiographical *Ḳiṣṣatī maʿa 'l-shiʿr* (1973) and *Min awrāḳī 'l-madjhūla: sīra dhātiyya thāniya* (2000; not seen).

Ḳabbānī's contacts with Spain (with a professional stay at the Syrian embassy from 1963 till 1966) have contributed to a focus on Andalusian themes, and several poems have been translated into Spanish, notably three volumes by P. Martínez Montávez: *Poemas amorosos árabes*, Madrid 1965, [3]1988; *Poemas políticos*, Madrid 1975; *Tú, amor*, Madrid 1987. An Italian collection *Poesie*, tr. by G. Canova *et al.*, was published in Rome 1976. Volumes in English are *Arabian love poems*, tr. by B. Frangieh and C.R. Brown, Colorado Springs 1992, with the original texts in the poet's own hand, and *On entering the sea: the erotic and other poetry of Nizar Qabbani*, tr. by L. Jayyusi *et al.*, New York 1996, with an introduction by Salma K. Jayyusi. Several translated poems are included in surveys of modern Arabic poetry.

Bibliography: 1. Works. The collected works (including poetry, prose and interviews) have been published in nine volumes, Beirut 1997. They lack a common name, and are entitled *al-aʿmāl al-shiʿriyya al-kāmila* (vols. i, ii, iv, v and ix); *al-aʿmāl al-siyāsiyya al-kāmila* (vols. iii and vi); and *al-aʿmāl al-nathriyya al-kāmila* (vols. vii and viii) [earlier editions in eight volumes]. Indexes of titles, first lines, metres and vocabulary are in Burhān Bukhārī, *Mudkhal ilā 'l-mawsūʿa al-shāmila li 'l-shāʿir Nizār Ḳabbānī*, [Kuwayt] Dār Suʿād al-Ṣabāḥ 1999.

2. Critical studies. G. Canova, *Nizār Qabbānī: poesie d'amore e di lotta*, in *OM*, lii (1972), 451-66; idem, *Nizār Qabbānī: "La mia storia con la poesia"*, in *OM*, liv (1974), 204-13; A. Loya, *Poetry as a social document. The social position of the Arab woman as reflected in the poetry of Nizār Qabbānī*, in *MW*, lxiii (1973), 39-52; Z. Gabay, *Nizār Qabbānī, the poet and his poetry*, in *MES*, ix (1973), 207-22; Muḥyī 'l-Dīn Ṣubḥī, *al-Kawn al-shiʿrī ʿinda Nizār Ḳabbānī*, Beirut 1977; Khrīstō Nadjm, *al-Nardjisiyya fī adab Nizār Ḳabbānī*, Beirut 1983; S. Wild, *Nizār Qabbānī's autobiography: images of sexuality, death and poetry*, in R. Allen, H. Kilpatrick and E. de Moor (eds.), *Love and sexuality in modern Arabic literature*, London 1995, 200-9; P. Martínez Montávez, *Al-Andalus y Nizar Kabbani: la tragedia*, in *Cuadernos 'Ilu*, i (1998), 9-24; *Nizār Ḳabbānī, shāʿir li-kull al-adjyāl* (= *Nizār Qabbānī, a poet for all generations*), i-ii, ed. by a committee under Suʿād Muḥammad al-Ṣabāḥ, Kuwayt 1998 (73 items, see review by S. Moreh in *JSS*, xlv [2000], 221-3). (W. STOETZER)

KABĪR, North Indian mystic and poet (d. *ca.* 1448). Although Kabīr is regarded as one of the most influential saint-poets of mediaeval Northern India, there is very little authentic information concerning his life. We can reliably state that he was born in Benares to a family of low-caste Muslim weavers called *djulāhā*s, probably in the opening years of the 9th/15th century. Beyond this, various hagiographies of Kabīr, depending on the authors' sectarian affiliation, make competing claims that he was a Muslim Ṣūfī, a Hindu with liberal Vaiśnava leanings or a champion of Hindu-Muslim unity who rejected institutionalised forms of both Islam and Hinduism. Kabīr's fame is based on the numerous couplets (*dohā*s) and songs (*pada*s) attributed to him and called *Kabīrvāṇī*s, or "words of Kabīr". Written in a caustic colloquial style in a mediaeval Hindi dialect and sung in folk melodies, these compositions have been an integral part of oral religious literature in North India, being recited by Muslims and Hindus alike. Selections of Kabīr's verses have been incorporated into the *Ādi granth*, the scripture of the Sikh community, as well as the *Pañčvāṇī*, the hymnal of the Dādūpanthī sect. The Kabīr Panthīs, "the followers of the path of Kabīr", have a compilation of his poetry called the *Bījāk*. Since Kabīr's verses, like most mediaeval Indian devotional poetry, were initially transmitted orally and recorded in writing only later, there are serious doubts concerning the authenticity of much of the corpus attributed to him.

Kabīr, who was influenced by various religious currents including forms of Ṣūfism and tantric yoga expounded by the Nāth yogis, is regarded as the pioneer poet of the *sant* movement that swept across North India in the 15th century. The *sant*s, or poet-saints, were participants in a grass-roots religious reformation that rejected the worship of multiple deities in favour of an esoteric form of religious practice whose goal was union with the one attributeless (*nirguṇa*) God. They also questioned the efficacy of religious rituals and validity of scriptural authority. Expressing themselves in vernacular poems, the *sant*s conceived of the human-divine relationship in terms of *viraha*, or yearning, longing love. Union with the Divine could be attained by anyone, regardless of caste, through meditation on the divine name and with the guidance of a *guru*. In poems attributed to him, Kabīr is particularly harsh in his attacks on the representatives of institutionalised religion, the Hindu *brāhmin* and the Muslim *mullā* or *ḳāḍī*, whose bookish learning and rituals he considered entirely useless in the spiritual quest. After his death, some of Kabīr's disciples organised themselves into a sect, the Kabīr Panth. Notwithstanding Kabīr's anti-institutional and anti-ritualistic stance, at the sect's central monastry in Benares, both monks and lay people engage in a ritualised recitation of Kabīr's poems and make offerings to an image of their master.

Bibliography: G.H. Westcott, *Kabir and the Kabir Panth*, Calcutta 1953; Aziz Ahmad, *Studies in Islamic culture in the Indian environment*, Oxford 1964, 143-7; Charlotte Vaudeville, *Kabīr*, Oxford 1964; eadem, *Kabir and the interior religion*, in *History of Religions*, iii (1964); Linda Hess and Sukhdev Singh, *The Bījak of Kabīr*, San Francisco 1983; J.S. Hawley and M. Juergensmeyer, *Songs of saints of India*, Oxford 1988; J.R. Hinnells (ed.), *Who's who of world religions*, London 1991, 204 (S.C.R. Weightman).

(ALI S. ASANI)

KABĪRA (A., pl. *kabāʾir*), a term of Islamic theology meaning "grave [sin]", occurring in Ḳurʾān, II, 42/39, 138/143 and *passim*. It was the stimulus for much discussion amongst theologians and sectaries like the Khāridjites [*q.v.*] on what constituted a grave sin and how committing one affected a man's salvation. For a discussion, see KHAṬĪʾA.

AL-**ḲABḲ**.

History.

1. For the early Islamic period up to the Mongol and Tīmūrid periods, see Vol. III, 343-50.

2. The period 1500-1800.

Compared to previous and later epochs, these three centuries are among the least studied periods in the history of the Caucasus. The main reason for that lies not in the unavailability of sources but rather in their inaccessibility until the recent past. The Russian archives, the most used ones, are far from having been fully scrutinised. In the Ottoman archives, only the surface has been scratched, chiefly due to the efforts of French scholars (A. Bennigsen, Ch. Lemercier-Quelquejay, G. Veinstein *et al.*). The rich local collections, or rather those that have survived wars, deportations, confiscation and deliberate destruction, have only begun to be intensively collected, catalogued and studied in the 1980s, mainly by Dāg͟hīstānī scholars (A. S͟hik͟hsaidov, K͟h. Omarov, G. Orazaev *et al.*). Their works, published mainly locally, are not easily obtainable, however. The result is that most of the information available on this period is from the viewpoint of the neighbouring Great Powers (above all, Russia) competing for mastery over the Caucasus.

Yet even the scant information at our disposal points to the importance of the internal processes that occurred during these three centuries. To start with, this seems to be the time when the Northern Caucasus was converted to Islam. In the 16th and 17th centuries, the Adīg͟he peoples (known collectively as Čerkes [*q.v.*]) and the Kabartay [see KABARAS] of the north-western and central Caucasus respectively, were Islamised by the Crimean Tatars and the Ottomans. In the east, the Islamisation of Dāg͟hīstān, as well as of the G͟humīḳs [see ḲUMUḲ] in the foothills to the north had been completed around the 16th century, to be followed by that of the Čečens [*q.v.*] (the Islamisation of the Čečens would be completed only in the first half of the 19th century). Contrary to the established view, Islam seems to have spread among the G͟humīḳs from the "Golden Horde" rather than from Dāg͟hīstān; and it was they, not the Dāg͟hīstānīs, who started to Islamise the Čečens. This is hinted at by the fact that these two peoples adhere to the Ḥanafī *mad͟hhab*, while the Dāg͟hīstānīs belong to the S͟hāfiʿī one.

This difference in *mad͟hhab* notwithstanding, Dāg͟hīstān, a major centre of Islamic scholarship since the 5th/11th century, supplied religious leadership to the north-eastern Caucasus well into the 20th century. This meant *inter alia* that, in this area, the main literary language had remained Arabic, which facilitated ties with the major S͟hāfiʿī centre of Zabīd in the Yemen (I. Yu. Kračkovskiy, *Dagestan i Iemen*, in *Izbrannïe sočineniya*, Moscow and Leningrad 1960, vi, 574-84). Nevertheless, the daily life of the Muslims in Dāg͟hīstān, as all over the Northern Caucasus, continued to be regulated by the local *ʿāda* (pronounced *ʿadát*) rather than by the *S͟harīʿa* (pronounced *s͟harʿát*). On some occasions the local *ʿādawāt* were written down, usually in the local idiom (for an example in Russian tr., see K͟h.-M.O. K͟hashaev (ed.), *Kodeks ummu-k͟hanna avarskogo (spravedlivogo)*, Moscow 1948). A serious attempt to inforce the *S͟harīʿa* and eradicate *ʿāda* would be made only in the 19th century.

Another major process was that of forming a new social structure in parts of the north-eastern Caucasus. The Adīg͟he and the Kabartay seem to have retained their stratified order, dividing society into nobles and commoners. The Čečens, on the other hand, seem to have forced out the nobility in the 16th century and established a society based on the equality of free men. Each community/clan was run by a council, *khel*, of its elders and pan-Čečen matters were discussed and decided in the *mehk khel* "the council of the land". In the eastern and northern parts of Dāg͟hīstān, all the principalities known from previous periods continued to exist, their rulers bearing different titles: the *S͟hāmk͟hāl* of Targhī, the *ʿUṣmī* (pronounced *ʿuts͟mī*) of Ḳaraḳytāḳ, the *Maʿṣūm* of Ṭabarsarān, the *Sulṭān* of Iliṣū and the *K͟hāns* of G͟hāzī G͟humuḳ, Mek͟htulī and Avaristān. The extent of their control, territory and influence depended on the personal qualities, power and charisma of each individual ruler. To this period belong, however, the first testimonies available to us concerning *d̲j̲amāʿas* (pronounced *d̲j̲amaʿát*) in the inner and western parts of Dāg͟hīstān, independent of the principalities to the east and north (and thus dubbed by Russian sources "free communities", *volʾnïe obs͟hčestva*).

The *d̲j̲amāʿa*, a community of several villages, usually confined within natural boundaries, was the basic political, social and economic unit in the country. It had most probably existed in previous times as well. Each *d̲j̲amāʿa* was headed by an elected *ḳāḍī*, who chaired the council of the elders. The most vital matters, however, were decided by a general assembly of the *d̲j̲amāʿa*. All men, whether noble, *uzdens* (free men) or *d̲j̲ankas* (descendents of noble fathers and common mothers) were equal members of the *d̲j̲amāʿa*. The principalities were, in fact, a confederation of *d̲j̲amāʿas*, each deciding whether to accept a ruler's authority. The free *d̲j̲amāʿas* did not recognise any outside authority over them, though on some occasions they formed permanent loose confederations. The most prominent of these was the confederation of ʿAḳūs͟ha (known also as Darg͟hī) which headed the alliance that defeated the troops of the Persian ruler Nādir S͟hāh Afs͟hār [*q.v.*].

The external affairs of the Caucasus have attracted relatively much more interest from scholars. The Caucasus was part of the last major realignment of Great Powers in the Muslim World, sc. that of the first two decades of the 16th century. In fact it became the main battle ground between two of them, the Sunnī Ottomans and S͟hīʿī Ṣafawids. After three Ottoman (1534-6, 1548-9 and 1554-5) and one Ṣafawid (1552) major campaigns, the peace of Amasya (1555) divided Trans-Caucasia between the two. Ottoman overlordship was recognised over the western part of Georgia (i.e. the kingdom of Imeretʾi and its "vassal" principalities of Guri, Svanetʾi and Abkhazia), while Ṣafawid overlordship was recognised over its eastern parts (the kingdoms of Kʾartlʾi and Kak͟hetʾi), and present-day Armenia (Erivān and Nak͟hd̲j̲ivān), Ād͟harbāyd̲j̲ān (S͟hīrvān, annexed in 1536) and the southernmost corner of Dāg͟hīstān (Derbend, annexed in 1509). This line of division would remain in force throughout the period with two notable exceptions (1578-1602 and 1723-35), when the Ottomans took advantage on the first occasion of internal struggles within the Ṣafawid house, and on the second occasion, of the disintegration of Ṣafawid power temporarily to seize control over the entire Caucasus.

North of the main mountain range, the Sunnī Muslims habitually recognised the Ottoman Sultan's authority. This, however, was far from constituting even a shadowy Ottoman rule. In the west and centre, the Ottomans exercised a very limited, indirect and ineffective control over the Čerkes and Kabartay, mainly via the Crimean K͟hāns. In the east, in the various polities of Dāg͟hīstān (remote, cut off and claimed by the Ṣafawids and their successors), the Ottomans usually enjoyed nothing more substantial than sympathy. Nevertheless, their Sunnī identity added to the obstinate resistance by some Dāg͟hīstānī polities to the *rawāfiḍ*, i.e. the S͟hīʿī Persians. Several fragments on the margins of manuscripts testifying of such acts of resistance in different places and times were published by S͟hik͟hsaidov in 1991 (in Russian tr., in A.A. Isaev (ed.), *Rukopisnaya i pečatnaya kniga v Dagestane*,

Ma<u>kh</u>ačḳala 1991, 128-9). On many occasions the mountain dwellers managed to beat the invading armies, the most resounding defeat being that dealt in 1744 to Nādir <u>Sh</u>āh's troops by the joint forces of the confederation of ʿAḳū<u>sh</u>a and other *d̲jamāʿas*. The futility of the attempts to conquer the mountains gave rise to a Persian proverb to the effect that "when Allāh wants to punish a <u>Sh</u>āh, He inculcates into his head the idea of campaigning in Dā<u>gh</u>istān."

The collapse of Nādir <u>Sh</u>āh's empire after his assassination in 1747 was not followed by any Ottoman attempts to seize the area. This granted the kings of eastern Georgia half a century of freedom, and allowed for *de facto* independent <u>kh</u>ānates to be established in Derbend, Ḳubbāh, Bāḳū, <u>Sh</u>ekkī, <u>Sh</u>īrvān, Gand̲ja, Ḳarābā<u>gh</u>, Erivān, Na<u>kh</u>d̲jivān and Ṭālī<u>sh</u>. The resulting vacuum on their southern borders permitted different Dā<u>gh</u>istānī communities and rulers to expand and raid the lowlands, mainly into eastern Georgia. The boldest raids were carried out by ʿUmar (pronounced ʿUmma), <u>Kh</u>ān of Avaristān (1774-1801). Once the Ḳād̲jārs started to bring together the lands of the Ṣafawids, they turned towards the Caucasus. In 1795, after the local rulers had ignored a series of demands to acknowledge his suzerainty, Āghā <u>Kh</u>ān Muḥammad, the founder of the dynasty, led a campaign into Trans-Caucasia, which culminated in the sack of Tiflīs. However, the Ḳād̲jārs' attempts to reincorporate the Caucasus into their empire met a new obstacle in the shape of Imperial Russia.

Muscovite Russia had shown interest in the affairs of the Caucasus already in the second half of the 16th century. Having seized control over the entire Itil (Volga) basin by conquering the <u>kh</u>ānates of Ḳāzān and Astra<u>kh</u>ān [*q.vv.*] (1552 and 1556, respectively), Tsar Ivan IV ("the Terrible") tried immediately to expand south into the Caucasus. For that purpose he pursued three goals: (1) the settlement of Cossacks on the Terek river; (2) alliances with local chiefs in the area, the most important of which was his marriage in 1561 to the daugther of a Kabartay prince; and (3) an attempt to help his coreligionists, the kings of Georgia, who had appealed for help to the new Orthodox power in the north. The Ottomans, though unsuccessful in capturing Astra<u>kh</u>ān (1569), were nevertheless strong enough to thwart the attempts by Ivan as well as by his two successors Feodor (in 1594) and Boris Godunov (in 1604).

Weakened by the "time of troubles" of the early 17th century, Russia was deterred for more than a century and a half by the might of both the Ottomans and the Ṣafawids from any initiatives in that direction. Nevertheless, additional Cossacks settled on the Terek and were incorporated by Peter I ("the Great") into a continuous line of defence facing the eastern Caucasus. It was he also who ventured a campaign to the south. In 1722, following the Af<u>gh</u>ān invasion of Persia he marched with an army and navy along the western and southern shores of the Caspian as far as Astarābād. Yet he did not dare to challenge the Ottomans by advancing inland beyond the littoral, and the campaign achieved nothing tangible. Only Catherine II ("the Great") successfully resumed Russia's advance southwards with a double-pronged policy.

In the Northern Caucasus, the erection of the fortress of Mozdok (1763) was the immediate cause of the 1768-74 war with the Ottomans and of a fourteen-year long struggle with the Kabartay. Following the peace of Küčük Ḳaynarča [*q.v.*], Cossacks were settled opposite the western Caucasus and a continuous line of defence established, to be known in the 19th century as "the Caucasian Line". These events were the trigger for the ten-year long resistance (1785-94) led by Manṣūr U<u>sh</u>urma [*q.v.*], a Čečen who assumed the title *al-Imām al-Manṣūr*, and called on all the Muslims of the Caucasus to return to the *<u>Sh</u>arīʿa* and to unite against Russian encroachment. In this he provided a foretaste of the events of the 19th century.

At the same time, Catherine re-established Russian ties with the king of K'artl'o-Ka<u>kh</u>et'i (i.e. Georgia; see AL-KURD̲J) and during the war of 1768-74, a Russian force crossed for the first time the Caucasus range and then operated against the Ottomans in Georgia. In 1783 the treaty of Georgievsk made K'artl'o-Ka<u>kh</u>et'i a Russian protectorate. A Russian force was stationed in Tiflīs and a paved road, "the Georgian military highway", was cut across the mountain range. However, the Russian force was soon withdrawn (1784), which left K'artl'o-Ka<u>kh</u>et'i exposed to the Ḳād̲jārs while the king, confident in Russian protection, provoked the 1795 sack of Tiflīs by his refusal to accept Ā<u>gh</u>ā <u>Kh</u>ān Muḥammad's overlordship. The Emperor Paul, Catherine's son and successor, was averse from involvement in the affairs of the Caucasus. Yet in 1799 he found himself obliged to protect K'artl'o-Ka<u>kh</u>et'i against the threats of Fatḥ ʿAlī <u>Sh</u>āh, Ā<u>gh</u>ā <u>Kh</u>ān Muḥammad's successor. Finally, on his deathbed, Giorgi XII, the last king of K'artl'o-Ka<u>kh</u>et'i, asked the Russian Emperor to take his kingdom under the Tsar's protection. On 30 December 1800 N.S., Paul issued a manifesto incorporating K'art'li and Ka<u>kh</u>et'i into the Russian Empire.

Alexander I, Paul's son and successor, confirmed his father's decision on 24 September 1801 N.S. Unlike Paul, Alexander used the annexation of K'art'li and Ka<u>kh</u>et'i as the first step in Russia's expansion into and beyond the Caucasus. Thus began the sixty-five years' long struggle to conquer the Caucasus, known in Russian historiography as "the Caucasian War", one that would drastically alter the political, religious, economic, social, ethnic and demographic composition of the Caucasus.

Bibliography: Some items have been mentioned in the text. Among the very few published Dā<u>gh</u>istānī chronicles is Mīrzā Ḥasan b. ʿAbd Allāh al-Ḳadarī al-Dā<u>gh</u>istānī, *Kitāb Ā<u>th</u>ār-i Dā<u>gh</u>istān*, Bāḳū 1903. For a list of Dā<u>gh</u>istānī sources published in the 1980s, usually in Russian translation, see the bibl. of A.A. Isaev (comp.) and A.R. <u>Sh</u>i<u>kh</u>saidov (ed.), *Rukopisnaya i pečatnaya kniga v Dagestane (Sbornik statei)* [Manuscript and printed books in Dā<u>gh</u>istān (a collection of articles)], Ma<u>kh</u>ačḳala 1991, 183-8.

V.N. Gamrekeli (ed.), *Dokumentī po vzaymootno<u>sh</u>eniyam Gruzii s Severnīm Kavkazom v XVIII v.* [Documents on the mutual relations of Georgia and the Northern Caucasus in the 18th century], Tbilisi 1968 is a collection of documents from the archives in Tbilisi.

Published documents from the Russian archives include: S.A. Belokurov (ed.), *Sno<u>sh</u>eniya Rossii s Kavkazom, 1578-1613* [Russia's relations with the Caucasus, 1578-1613], Moscow 1889; P.G. Butkov, *Materialī dlya novoy istorii Kavkaza s 1722 po 1803 g.* [Sources for the modern history of the Caucasus, 1722-1803], St. Petersburg 1869; <u>Kh</u>.-M.O. <u>Kh</u>ashaev (ed.), *Pamiatniki običnogo prava Dagestana XVII-XIX vv. Ar<u>kh</u>ivnīe materyalī* [Sources on the customary law of Dā<u>gh</u>istān, 16th-19th centuries. Archival sources], Moscow 1965; M.O. Kosven and

K͟h. V. K͟hashaev (eds.), *Istoriya, geografiya i etnografiya Dagestana XVIII-XIX vv. Ark͟hivnïe materyalï* [History, geography and etnography of Dāg͟hïstān in the 18th-19th centuries. Archival sources], Moscow 1958; T.K͟h. Kumïkov and E.N. Kusheva (eds.), *Kabardino-Russkie otnos͟heniya v XVI-XVII vv.* [Kabartay-Russian relations in the 16th-17th centuries], Moscow 1957; R.G. Mars͟haev, *Russko-Dagestanskie otnos͟heniya XVII–pervoy polovinï XVIII vv. (dokumentï i materiyalï)* [Russo-Dāg͟hïstānī relations in the 17th and first half of the 18th centuries (documents and sources)], Makk͟hač-ḳala 1958; K͟h.K͟h. Ramazanov and A.R. S͟hik͟h-saidov (eds.), *Očerki istorii yuz͟hnogo Dagestana. Materyalï k istorii narodov Dagestana s drevney s͟hik͟h vremen do načala XX veka* [An outline of the history of southern Dāg͟hïstān. Sources for the history of the peoples of Dāg͟hïstān from antiquity to the beginning of the 20th century], Mak͟hačḳala 1964.

Among the latest collections from the Ottoman archives is Mehmet Saray *et al.* (eds.), *Kafkas araştırmaları*, i, Istanbul 1988. (M. GAMMER)

3. The period 1800 to the present day.

a. *Introduction*

Any attempt to furnish a coherent and objective overview of the history of the Caucasus in the modern period is hampered by the scarcity of local sources and by the inherent biases of the historical accounts generated by its colonisers, the Ottomans, Persians and Russians, who, for more than a century, were vying with one another for sovereignty over this strategically important area. The same goes for European historiography of the region, which was likewise shaped by political agendas of the European states and their colonial designs. This is especially true of the works of 19th-century British writers, both lay and academic, who viewed Russia as its principal colonial rival in the East. Following the Russian Communist Revolution of 1917, Russian colonial prejudices and stereotypes were superseded by Marxist axioms of class struggle and of the five historical socio-economic formations and modes of production specific to each of them. After World War II, these axioms were further aggravated by the ideological clichés of the Cold War epoch. From the 1920s until the disintegration of the Soviet Union in 1991, the area remained practically inaccessible to Western researchers. Most, therefore, had to rely on Soviet studies of the area, which were shaped by the official Marxist views of history. With the fall of the Soviet régime, a large body of historiography has emerged produced by scholars of Caucasian background. Coloured by a wide spectrum of nationalist agendas, this new historiography offers drastic revisions of the Russian and Soviet conceptions of Caucasian history, and especially of the Russo-Caucasian wars of 1829-64. The present account will focus primarily on the historical evolution of the mountaineer communities of the northern Caucasus (Kabarda, Dāg͟histān, Čečnya, Ingus͟hetia, Circassia and Abk͟hāzia) with predominantly Muslim populations. Historical events in the Christian areas of the Caucasus (Georgia, Armenia and the Christian areas of Ossetia [see AL-KURDJ; ARMĪNIYA; OSSETES]) will be touched upon briefly only in so far as they are relevant to the history of their Muslim neighbours (for developments in Transcaucasia, see ĀDHARBĀYDJĀN; SHĪRWĀN; GANDJA).

b. *Russian expansion and Persian withdrawal*

In the late 18th and early 19th centuries, three major outside powers vied for control of the Caucasus: the Ottomans, who maintained (largely nominal) control of the northwestern coast of the Black Sea (Circassia [see ČERKES]), parts of present-day Georgia adjacent to the Black Sea and the western regions of Transcaucasia; Persia, which exercised sovereignty (often only nominal) over several k͟hānates in Ād͟harbāyd͟jān, Dāg͟histān and the eastern areas of Transcaucasia; and Russia. The first decades of the 19th century witnessed a steady Russian military expansion into the Caucasus regions formerly controlled by Russia's Muslim imperial rivals. A large part of present-day Georgia, the kingdom of Kartli-Kak͟heti, recognised the sovereignty of the Russian Empire in 1801, when its last independent ruler, George XII, handed the reins of government over to the Russians in the face of an impending Persian invasion. Soon afterwards, the Russian military authorities of the Caucasus began the construction of the Georgian Military Highway between the city of Vladikavkaz (presently the capital of the Autonomous Republic of North Ossetia) and Tiflīs [*q.v.*] (presently Tbilisi, the capital of the Republic of Georgia). This ambitious project was intended to consolidate Russia's hold on her new dependencies in the Central Caucasus. In December 1802, the Russians convened a meeting of the rulers of the mountaineer communities and principalities of the northeastern Caucasus at the Russian fortress of Georgievsk. During the meeting, the rulers agreed to sign a treaty granting Russia a special status in Dāg͟histān and adjacent lands. Some rulers, including the powerful k͟hān of Avaristān, recognised Russian tutelage over their lands and pledged to join forces with Russia in the event of a Persian invasion of their lands. Between 1804 and 1813, the k͟hānates of Gand͟ja, Bākū, Ḳarābāg͟h, S͟hīrwān, Darband [*q.vv.*] parts of Abk͟hāzia [see ABKHĀZ], the principalities of Imereti and Ak͟halk͟halaki, as well as several Muslim communities of Dāg͟histān, came under Russian rule. The intermittent hostilities between the Russian Caucasian Corps and Persian forces throughout 1804-13 were, as a rule, favourable in outcome to the Russians. Russian victories can be attributed at least in part to the dynastic struggles within the Persian ruling élite, which weakened its ability to resist Russian encroachments on Persia's former dependencies in the region.

Russian claims to its new domains in the Caucasus and Transcaucasia were formalised by the Gulistān Treaty of 1813. This document decisively redrew the map of the Caucasus in favour of the Russian Empire. In 1826, the Persian army led by the Ḳād͟jār Crown Prince ʿAbbās Mīrzā [*q.v.*] invaded Ḳarābāg͟h in an attempt to regain control of Persia's former dependencies in the central Caucasus and Transcaucasia. Despite initial successes, the Persian advance was eventually repelled by the Russian army under the command of Ivan Paskievič, who led the Russians to victory over ʿAbbās Mīrzā's forces at the battle of Gand͟ja (Elizavetpol) in September 1826. In 1828, after two years of hostilities in which the Russians scored one victory after the other, Persia was forced to sign the humiliating treaty of Turkomānčāy [see TÜRKMEN ČAY (i)]. This document all but eliminated Persia's influence in the northern Caucasus by denying it any direct contact with its potential Muslim allies in Dāg͟histān. On the Ottoman front, in 1828-9, Russian troops penetrated as far as Erzurum [*q.v.*] and Ad͟jaria (Ad͟jaristān) and blockaded the strategic Black Sea ports of Poti and Anapa [*q.v*]. The Russian military successes drastically reduced the Ottoman Empire's ability to exercise its influence over the Circassian (Adyg͟he [see ČERKES]) tribes of the northwestern Caucasus, which even at the height of Ottoman power were Ottoman vassals in name only. Under the treaty of Adrianople (Edirne [*q.v.*]) of 1829, the Ottomans had to cede to Russia many of their former territories along the Black Sea coast. These territorial losses deprived the Ottomans of direct access to Circassia.

c. *Ermolov and the consolidation of Russian power*

Much of the credit for Russia's success in the Caucasus goes to the talented general Alexei Ermolov (Yermolov). His military genius and diplomatic acumen helped the Russian Caucasian Corps to defeat the Persians and to bring most of their former dependencies in the Caucasus under Russian rule. Appointed by Tsar Alexander I as the military governor of the Caucasus in 1816, Ermolov consistently implemented what many Russian and Western historians view as "policies of terror" toward the mountaineer communities and local principalities. His brutal treatment of his Caucasian adversaries was deliberately aimed at breaking their will to resist Russia's rule and to cow them into submission. Granted full authority over the area by the Tsar (in the Russian sources of the age, Ermolov was often referred to as the "proconsul of the Caucasus"; his own personal memoirs of the Caucasus campaigns seem to have been consciously patterned on Caesar's *Commentaries on the Gallic Wars*, reflecting his desire to emulate his illustrious predecessor), Ermolov ruled over Russia's new colonies with an iron fist, sparing neither his new subjects, nor his own troops, nor even the Russian irregulars, known as "Cossacks". Parallel to his often merciless "pacification" of Caucasian tribes and principalities, Ermolov embarked on a series of ambitious administrative and military reforms that sought to consolidate Russian colonial authority over the region and encourage immigration of Russian settlers (Cossacks) to the area. In some regions (e.g. Kabarda), Ermolov also implemented a sweeping judicial reform. Thus in 1822 he replaced the local *S̲h̲arīʿa* and *ʿādāt* jurisdiction with civil courts staffed by Russian colonial officials. This measure undermined the positions of the local aristocracy and sparked several riots that had to be suppressed, with its usual brutality, by the Russian Caucasus Corps.

Controlling this vast and rugged area with just 49,000 troops (of which only 40,000 maintained at least some semblance of military readiness) proved to be a great challenge to Ermolov and his chiefs of staff. Their responses to the tremendous difficulties faced by the Russian colonial enterprise amounted to sustained social engineering, such as the forced resettlement of some tribes (Ossetes and Nog̲h̲ay Tatars [*q.v.*]), the brutal "pacification" of "hostile" mountaineer communities, and the imposition of corvée services on others, e.g. the Čečens [*q.v.*]. These measures disrupted the customs and lifestyles of the mountaineers, who retaliated by attacking Russian forts and settlements and carrying off prisoners and booty. Another source of resentment against the Russian military administration was its attempt to eliminate the widespread slave trade in the northern Caucasus. For many centuries this business had been an important source of income for many local tribes, which sold captives to Ottoman merchants. The captives were then re-sold in Ottoman slave markets. Initially, Russian efforts to eradicate the slave trade bore only limited results. It took the Russians several decades of thorough policing and enforcement of their anti-slavery edicts finally to put an end to this practice.

The mountaineers responded to Russia's interference in their traditional occupations with armed uprisings. They were brutally put down by the Russian Caucasus Corps. The rebels' villages and fields were burned to the ground. The "hostile" populations were chased into the inhospitable mountains. Such punitive campaigns, however, had only a limited impact, since the villages were easily rebuilt once Russian troops had left the area. At the same time, this brutal repression against a people unaccustomed to foreign rule bred and sustained hatred towards the Russian administration among the mountaineers. Ermolov soon realised the inadequacy of his policy, and embarked on military and administrative measures aimed at consolidating Russian presence in the region. The new policy consisted in the construction of fortified defence lines. They were formed by Russian fortresses and forts connected by networks of roads. Cut through the virgin forests of Čečnya, the roads were meant to separate "pacified" tribes and villages from those which continued to resist Russian rule. In the process, the "hostile" communities were pushed ever deeper into the barren mountains, where they faced hardship and starvation.

Throughout Ermolov's tenure as military governor of the Caucasus, mountaineer resistance (1816-27) in the eastern and central parts of the region remained spontaneous, unorganised and localised. Sporadic insurrections against Russian rule were easily suppressed by the better-equipped and disciplined Russian troops, which made good use of their superior firepower. Despite their personal bravery and intimate knowledge of the terrain, the mountaineer levies of Dāg̲h̲istān, Kabarda, Čečnya and Ingus̲h̲etia were unable to defeat the Russians due to a lack of co-ordination and organisation. The local ruling élites were usually unable to provide leadership, since they had been either bribed by the Russians or torn by internal strife. In other cases (e.g. in Čečnya and some "democratic" Čerkes (Adyg̲h̲e) tribes of the north-western Caucasus), the mountaineer élite had not yet been formed. Such "democratic" mountaineer societies posed an especially severe problem for the Russian authorities, which preferred to deal with local nobility rather than entire communities. Furthermore, Ermolov's cunning implementation of "divide and rule" policies led to the decimation of many ruling families, who tried to resist Russian rule, especially in Dāg̲h̲istān. Some historians of the Caucasus even argue that Ermolov, steeped in the idea of "progress" and "civilisation", viewed the local rulers as brutal and ignorant despots, who were inherently incapable of embracing Russia's "civilising mission" in the Caucasus. He therefore considered them irrelevant and dispensable.

Whether intentional or not, Ermolov's policies seem to have led to the considerable weakening and discrediting of the local élites, which may explain why most of the leaders of the mountaineer resistance to Russian rule in 1829-59 came from relatively humble backgrounds and relied for the most part on free peasant communities for their support. Be this as it may, it is obvious that Ermolov's rule permanently upset the earlier balance of power in the region. His draconian measures set the mountaineer resistance movement on its feet on an unprecedented scale. The movement derived its vitality from the idea of equality of all Muslims before the Divine Law and their duty to actively resist "infidel" Russian rule. Since the majority of the subjugated tribes and communities of the northern and central Caucasus professed Islam, it was only natural that resistance to Russian domination took the form of *d̲j̲ihād*, which, in the local tradition, is usually referred to as *g̲h̲azawāt*.

d. *The Caucasian* g̲h̲azawāt *and its leaders*

As with many contemporary Muslim movements, the leaders of Caucasian resistance often began their careers by preaching a strict adherence to the *Sharīʿa* and fighting against such widespread "vices" as wine drinking, smoking, lax observance of Islamic rituals, dancing, singing and the free mingling of the sexes. Simultaneously, these self-appointed enforcers of the *Sharīʿa* often sought to reduce the sphere of, if not to eradicate completely, the application of the customary law (*ʿādāt*), which usually favoured local élites. Such measures appealed to the poorer strata of the mountaineer population, who hoped that the rule of the *Sharīʿa* would improve their lot and reduce their dependence on the nobles. Once the reputation of the religious leader as an uncompromising enforcer and advocate of the *Sharīʿa* had become firmly established, he could use his popularity to rally his followers around a certain political cause. In the mountaineer communities, whose traditional values and lifestyle were threatened by Russian colonial advances, a call to a holy war against the infidel Russian enemy was likely to receive an enthusiastic response.

In any event, the careers of the Čečen Shaykh Manṣūr Ushurma [*q.v.*] and the three Dāghistānī *imāms* of the northern Caucasus [see SHĀMIL] unfolded according to this scenario. The extent of these leaders' affiliation with what the Russian writers of the age called *myuridizm*, namely, the Naḳshbandiyya-Mudjaddidiyya-Khālidiyya Ṣūfī order (in the case of Ushurma there is no historical evidence of his association with any Ṣūfī *silsila*, while the three *imāms* were at least nominally Naḳshbandī *shaykh*s) remains a moot point. However, many Russian and Western historians of the Caucasus continue to view *myuridizm*/Naḳshbandī Ṣūfism as the principal vehicle and source of inspiration for the movements in question.

The events of the thirty-year war led by the three *imāms* of Dāghistān and Čečnya, Ghāzī Muḥammad (Kazi Mullā), Ḥamzat (Gamzat) Bek and Shāmil (Shamwīl) are discussed in the article SHĀMIL and will not be detailed here. The war cost both sides dearly in casualties and material resources. Russia's initial military strategy, imported from the European theatre of war, was geared to winning victories in pitched battles through an orderly movement and deployment of large military contingents. Much value was placed by the Russian military command on besieging and capturing enemy strongholds and headquarters. Such strategic assumptions proved to be ineffective or outright counterproductive in the Caucasus, where the Russian army faced a highly mobile and elusive opponent. The headquarters of the mountaineer levies could be easily moved from one village to another without impairing their ability to effectively fight the Russians through swift night raids, ambushes, diversionary tactics, misinformation and other forms of guerilla warfare. These tactics were honed to perfection in Dāghistān and Čečnya under the talented leadership of the Imām Shāmil, who implemented it with remarkable success from 1834 to the late 1840s, when the Russians were finally compelled to reconsider their military doctrine. Nevertheless, in spite of repeated military setbacks, the Russian military command continued to cling stubbornly to the ineffective "one-blow" strategy for over ten years. Its flaws culminated in the disastrous expedition of 1845 against Shāmil's headquarters at Dargho (Darghiya, in present-day Čečnya). Led by the newly-appointed viceroy of the Caucasus Prince Mikhail Vorontsov, the Russian expeditionary force lost almost 1,000 men killed (including three generals), almost 2,800 wounded, 179 missing in action, three guns and all its baggage, including the army war-chest.

Vorontsov realised his error and convinced Tsar Nicholas I to implement the siege strategy that was first introduced by Ermolov but had been abandoned by his successors following his removal from office in 1827. Efforts were made to strengthen existing fortifications, to build new ones and to connect them with a network of improved roads. These defence lines cut through Shāmil's domains in Dāghistān and Čečnya, gradually reducing his sphere of influence and depriving him of provisions and manpower. This slow and less spectacular military strategy, which following Vorontsov's retirement in 1854 was continued by his successor, Prince Aleksandr Baryatinskiy, eventually bore fruit. Deprived of the resources to wage war against the superior Russian military machine and abandoned by the majority of his former followers, the third *imām* of the Caucasus surrendered to the Russians in the summer of 1859. The bloodiest episode of the Russo-Caucasian war came to an end, although armed resistance to Russian rule continued throughout the Caucasus for another decade.

e. *Circassia and Muḥammad Amīn*

Shāmil's long resistance to Russian conquest had wide-ranging repercussions for the mountaineer communities and tribes throughout the Caucasus, including those areas that remained formally under Russian rule or were contested by the Russian and Ottoman empires, namely, Kabarda, Balkaria, Ossetia and the western Caucasus (Circassia, Abkhāzia, Guria, etc.). Thirty-seven Kabardian princes and nobles went over to Shāmil in 1846, following his raid into Kabarda. At the same time, the majority (around 200) remained loyal to the Russians and were richly rewarded by the Russian administration for their refusal to support Shāmil's movement. Throughout Shāmil's imāmate, the Transkuban region and Circassia (Adygheya) remained, for the most part, outside his direct influence. However, news about his military successes against the Russian forces periodically reinvigorated local resistance. In 1840 four major Russian fortresses along the coast of the Black Sea were captured and destroyed by Čerkes tribes. In 1842, Shāmil sent his emissary, Ḥādjdjī Muḥammad, to Circassia instructing him to spread *ghazawāt* among the Muslim populations of the western Caucasus. After Ḥādjdjī Muḥammad's death in 1845, he was succeeded by Shāmil's *nāʾib* (military governor) named Sulaymān Efendi. On Shāmil's instructions, he began to preach *ghazawāt* against the Russian garrisons stationed in the area and attempted to recruit several Čerkes (Adyghe) tribes to Shāmil's cause. However, Sulaymān Efendi soon fell out with Shāmil and defected to the Russians.

At the end of 1848, Shāmil appointed Muḥammad Amīn as his next *nāʾib* in Circassia. The new *nāʾib*, who was not familiar with local realities, soon became embroiled in a power struggle between the aristocracy and free squires (*tfokotles*) of the Abadzekh, the largest Adyghe (Čerkes) tribe. After flirting for some time with the Abadzekh princes, Muḥammad Amīn eventually decided to throw in his lot with the peasants, promising them independence from their aristocratic masters and equality under the *Sharīʿa* law. His populist politics alienated the nobility, who turned to the Russians, hoping to retain their traditional privileges. Throughout the 1850s, Muḥammad Amīn was able to secure the loyalty of just one Adyghe tribe, the Abadzekhs. He later extended his rule to some other Adyghe (Čerkes) communities, such as the Natukhays and Shapsugs. Muḥammad Amīn modelled his administration of the nascent Čerkes (Adyghe) state on that of Shāmil's imāmate. The lands under his jurisdiction were divided into a number of territorial units called *maḥkama*. Each *maḥkama* consisted of around 100 households. The administrative centre of the *maḥkama* was located in a fortified Čerkes village (*aul*), which usually had a mosque, a court of law, a prison and a *madrasa*. The *maḥkama* was ruled by a religious official (*muftī*) and a council of three Muslim judges (*ḳāḍīs*). Each Adyghe (Čerkes) household was to supply one mounted warrior (*murtaziḳ*) for Muḥammad Amīn's military force. The *murtaziḳ*s constituted the military foundation of Muḥammad Amīn's rule. In all, Muḥammad Amīn's state at its height consisted of four *maḥkama*s among the Abadzekhs, one among the Shapsugs and two among the Natukhays.

f. *The Crimean War and its impact on the Caucasus*

The beginning of the Crimean War in 1853 galvanised the mountaineer resistance movement on both sides of the Main Caucasian Range. In the eastern and central Caucasus, Shāmil was preparing to invade Georgia, to cut the Russo-Georgian Military Highway and, finally, to effect a juncture with an invading Ottoman force at Tiflīs. The capital of the Caucasus was expected to fall to the allied Muslim army within a few days. In the western Caucasus, Muḥammad Amīn and his Čerkes levies, supported by an Ottoman sea-borne expeditionary force, were bound to disrupt Russian communications and capture the lands of the Turkic-speaking Ḳaračay [*q.v.*] on the northern slopes of the Main Caucasus Range. Muḥammad Amīn was then to march across Kabarda and Ossetia and to join Shāmil's forces there. In Guria (a part of present-day Georgia), which had been under Russian administrations since 1840, a large Ottoman force attacked the fortress of Shekvetili (St. Nicholas Port) on the Black Sea and wiped out its small garrison, which consisted of a Russian detachment and pro-Russian Gurid militia.

These developments awoke the Russian administration of the Caucasus to the possibility of a powerful military coalition between the invading Ottomans and their local supporters among the Adyghes. In response to the repeated pleas of his viceroy, Prince Vorontsov, Tsar Nicholas I agreed to send reinforcements to the Caucasus. In the hostilities that followed, the Ottomans' expeditionary force (the so-called Anatolian Corps) was defeated by the Russians in several pitched battles in the southern Caucasus. The Porte's plans suffered another major setback in the harbour of Sinop in November 1853, when a Russian naval force led by Admiral Nakhimov attacked and destroyed the Ottoman fleet that was to land at Sukhum-Ḳalʿe in order to join forces with the Čerkes levies. In March 1854, a joint Anglo-French naval squadron sailed into the Black Sea. Its appearance forced the Russian military command to dismantle or to blow up a number of Russian fortresses along the Circassian coast (the so-called "Black Sea Defence Line"), including Anapa. Only those fortresses deemed able to withstand a prolonged siege from the sea were preserved and received fresh reinforcements.

These measures and the absence of a Russian naval presence in the Black Sea gave the Anglo-French fleet full control of sea communications off the Circassian coast. The allies tried to establish direct ties with Shāmil and Muḥammad Amīn in order to better coordinate their military operations in the Caucasian theatre of war. While the Anglo-French emissaries failed to reach Shāmil, they succeeded in securing Muḥammad Amīn's commitment to participate in joint Ottoman and Anglo-French operations against the Russians. The allied plans were upset in the summer of 1854, when several Ottoman brigades were defeated by the Russian army in a series of bloody engagements. The Circassian tribes, which expected the Ottoman troops to help them in their unequal struggle against the Russians, were surprised to discover that their Ottoman allies were themselves in desperate need of assistance. These reversals may explain why Sefer (Safar)-bey (beg), an Adyghe prince of the Natukhay tribe, whom the Ottomans had appointed as governor of Sukhum-Ḳalʿe with the rank of *pasha*, was unable to recruit enough Čerkes fighters to form a separate corps under his command. The Abkhāz, who had both Christian and Muslim princes, were divided, with the Christian part of the population favouring the Russians. The Ottoman cause was not helped by Shāmil's inactivity. Burdened by the internal problems of his imāmate and incapable of undertaking any large-scale military operations due to the lack of resources and growing war fatigue among his followers, he was unable or unwilling to respond to the Ottoman and Anglo-French pleas for a more aggressive strategy against the Russians.

The next year (1855) of the Crimean campaign did not bring any dramatic changes to the stalemate on the Caucasian front. Shāmil remained inactive, while neither Sefer-bey nor Muḥammad Amīn were able to convince the Čerkes chiefs to form a separate corps under Ottoman command. Their efforts were hampered by their personal rivalry and their dependence on mutually hostile social groups within the Čerkes (Adyghe) communities. While Sefer-bey, a Čerkes prince, represented the interests of the mountaineer aristocracy, Muḥammad Amīn relied on the free Čerkes peasantry, which was anxious to minimise its feudal obligations *vis-à-vis* the nobles. As a result, the two leaders often worked at cross-purposes. The Russian military successes in Transcaucasia, such as the capture of Kars and Bayazet, and the lack of a decisive allied victory in the Crimea, hampered the efforts of Ottoman military commanders in the western Caucasus. With the fall of Sevastopol in September 1855, Muḥammad Amīn attempted once again to form a Čerkes corps under his command, but to no avail. The Čerkes tribes were not ready to relinquish their independence and to join the Ottoman-led military coalition, whose ultimate goals they did not share. Besides, the plans of the European allies to mount a massive offensive against the Russian troops stationed in the Caucasus never materialised. Without the support from their European partners, the Ottomans proved unable to dislodge the Russian forces from the western Caucasus. At the same time, with no major victories to their credit, they were unable to convince their potential allies among the Čerkes tribes of the necessity to launch an all-out attack against the Russians. ʿUmar (ʿÖmer) Pasha's initially successful campaign against a Russian force near Zugdidi (Georgia) in the autumn of 1855 failed to impress the Čerkes and Abkhāz enough to join his expeditionary force. In the end, the European powers' decision not to shift the centre of hostilities from the Crimean Peninsula to the western Caucasus, which would allow the Ottomans to make decisive advances in that area, worked to Russia's advantage. Despite the loss of its naval power in the Black Sea, Russia retained her overall strategic superiority in the region, which eventually enabled her to bring it firmly under control.

g. *The end of the Crimean War and the collapse of mountaineer resistance*

The allied plans to invade the Caucasus were shelved when the warring parties began peace negotiations and signed a peace treaty in Paris during the winter of 1856. The results of the Crimean War, although by no means favourable to the Russians, failed to reverse Russia's inexorable expansion in the Caucasus and to put an end to her domination over the areas already conquered by Russian troops. If anything, it confirmed for many mountaineer leaders the futility of resistance against Russian rule. If Russia was able to withstand the attack of the greatest European and Muslim powers of the age, how could their small levies have any hope of defeating her on their own? It is even more remarkable that, despite the growing war fatigue and despondency among his supporters and the overall devastation suffered by his realm, S̲h̲āmil was able to continue his struggle until August 1859, when he surrendered to the Russian forces at the village of Gunīb in Dāg̲h̲istān.

Following the collapse of S̲h̲āmil's movement, in November 1859, Muḥammad Amīn started negotiations with the Russian military command of the Kuban military district. He pledged allegiance to the Russian Empire, recognised its sovereignty over his lands, and was thus able to keep his position as the spiritual and political leader of the Abadzek̲h̲ tribes. With the death of Sefer-bey at the end of 1859, Čerkes resistance to Russian rule was reduced to a few sporadic and unorganised uprisings among the largest Adyg̲h̲e tribes—the Ubyk̲h̲s [*q.v.*], S̲h̲apsugs and Abadzek̲h̲s, who tried to forge a military alliance, albeit unsuccessfully. Their attempts to stem the Russian advance lasted until 1864, which is considered by many historians to be the final year of the so-called Great Caucasian War (as we have seen, it is probably more appropriate to speak of a series of military conflicts of various intensities throughout the Caucasus). At the beginning of that year, a Russian expeditionary force conquered the town of Tuapse, one of the last Čerkes strongholds on the Black Sea. In the following months, the remaining sparks of resistance were extinguished by the Russian expeditionary corps directed from Ekaterinodar, the capital of the Kuban military district. The Russian military conquest of the Caucasus came to an end.

During and after the Crimean War, Čerkes rebellions against Russian rule were encouraged and assisted by outside powers, especially Britain and, to a lesser extent, France. The provisions of the Paris Peace Treaty seriously impaired Russia's ability to control the Black Sea coast. In the absence of a Russian naval force to patrol the coastal area (under the Paris Treaty, Russia was allowed to have only six corvettes in the entire Black Sea area), Britain and France gained free access to the Čerkes populations of the western Caucasus. Some elements within the British government accepted the advice of the British diplomat and Turkophile, David Urquhart, to assist the Čerkes in establishing an independent state that would serve as a buffer between the Ottoman lands and the Russian colonial possessions in the western Caucasus. To this end, the British and the French enlisted the help of Polish emigrants to England and France who had fled their country after the Russian crackdown against Poland's bid for independence in 1830. In addition, there were many Polish deserters from the Russian Army stationed in the Caucasus who had joined the Čerkes tribes to take an active part in anti-Russian resistance. Throughout the late 1850s and early 1860s, several Polish-led contingents of European volunteers equipped by England and France landed on the Circassian coast in an effort to encourage the local tribes to rise against the Russians. However, they were not always welcomed by the Čerkes, who were wary of the motives of these self-appointed supporters of their independence. Moreover, the efforts of small foreign contingents were not enough to change the overall strategic situation in the Caucasian theatre of war, which was dominated by Russian military might. Faced with a lack of success and, consequently, a lack of support from the local populations, all foreign contingents gradually withdrew from the western Caucasus, leaving their Čerkes allies face-to-face with the Russian Empire.

h. *The tragedy of mass emigration*

In the early 1860s, the Russian administration of the Kuban military district (*oblast'*) embarked on a large-scale plan to resettle the Adyg̲h̲e tribes. These measures were proposed and implemented by the military governor of the Kuban region, General Nikolai Yevdokimov (Evdokimov), who was intent on preventing the Adyg̲h̲es from resuming their resistance to Russian rule by undermining their economic and geopolitical foundations. Unlike Dāg̲h̲istān with its barren mountains, the Kuban area with its extraordinary fertile arable lands was quite suitable for resettlement with Russian and Ukrainian peasants, who were considered to be much more "reliable" than the warlike Čerkes tribes with their long history of anti-Russian warfare. According to Yevdokimov's plan, the "hostile" Čerkes tribes were to be resettled from the mountains into the plains of Transkuban to live under the watchful eye of the Russian military administration. The lands vacated by the Čerkes were given to Russian settlers, mostly Cossacks from Russia and Ukraine, in return for their military service along Russia's new borders. Another objective of Russian colonial policy was to bar the Čerkes from any contacts with the Ottomans or any hostile European powers by removing them from the coastal areas, which were still easily accessible from the sea. From 1861 to 1864, the Russian authorities established 111 new Cossack settlements (*stanit̲s̲as*) with a population of 142,333 families.

These measures triggered a massive exodus of the dislocated mountaineer populations to the Ottoman lands. Encouraged and presided over by a few murky and unscrupulous adventurers of dual loyalties (such as Mūsā Kunduk̲h̲ov, a Russian general of Kabardian origin with connections at the Ottoman court) and some members of the local Čerkes and Kabardian nobility anxious to preserve their influence over their former bondsmen, the emigration turned out to be a terrible tragedy for the mountaineer peoples. The emigrants, known as *muhād̲j̲irūn*, came from practically every North Caucasian community: Kabardians, Čečens, Ossetes, Natuk̲h̲ays, Abadzek̲h̲s, S̲h̲apsugs, Ubyk̲h̲s, Bžeduk̲h̲s, Ābāzins, Ḳaračāys, Abk̲h̲āz, Temirgoys, Nog̲h̲ay Tatars and a few others. During the winter and spring of 1864 alone, 257,068 individuals departed for Anatolia from seven Black Sea ports under Russian control. The refugees were motivated by a variety of factors, such as the dislocation and resentment produced by the Russian resettlement schemes and oppressive rule, hopes for a happy life under friendly Muslim rule in Anatolia (inspired in part by Ottoman propaganda), and the religious rulings issued by Muslim religious authorities, which proclaimed living under infidel rule to be a grave sin for any Muslim who had other options. Once the emigrants found themselves on board ships headed for Ottoman Turkey, they were readily preyed upon by Ottoman slave-traders and greedy crews who charged their passengers by the head and therefore packed as many of them as possible into each ship.

Cramped conditions combined with various infectious diseases took a heavy toll on the human cargo. The ships, usually commercial craft not intended for carrying passengers, quickly turned into abodes of death. According to some chilling eye-witness accounts, they left hundreds of dead bodies in their wake. The survivors found themselves at the mercy of Ottoman authorities at the ports of destination, which, for the most part, were totally unprepared for such a massive influx of refugees. The makeshift refugee camps at Trabzon (Ṭarabzun [*q.v.*]), Samsun (Ṣāmsūn [*q.v.*]) and other Ottoman ports became abodes of human suffering. Reduced to starvation, parents sold their sons and daughters into slavery, driving the price of a child to all-time lows (30 to 40 roubles for a 10- to 12-year-old). Unmarried young men had the option of joining the Ottoman army, but, the majority of refugees, especially the sick and the elderly, were doomed to a life of misery and starvation. Estimates of the scale of the emigration and the death rate among the refugees vary dramatically depending on the political and ethnic background of historians. Some sources cite as many as 15 million emigrants, others speak of half a million souls, of whom only one half survived the tragedy of mass resettlement. The latter figure appears to be more realistic, although the real scale of this human tragedy is yet to be determined through a careful examination of Russian and Ottoman archives.

The causes of the Caucasian *hid̲j̲ra* remain a matter of debate, which has grown especially intense since the fall of the Soviet Union. It is clear that the Russian authorities did little to prevent the mountaineers from leaving their lands. Thus the Russian governor of the Kuban *oblast'*, writing in 1889, said that he saw "no particular harm to the interest of the state in the desire of the natives (*tuzemtsy*) to leave the area. On the contrary, [he saw] much benefit in the removal from the area of this troublesome element." No wonder that the Russian authorities not only did not try to prevent the mountaineers from emigrating, but on many occasions paid their sea-fare. The Ottomans, too, had a vested interest in the emigration since they hoped to resettle the mountaineers along the Ottoman-Russian border and to use them as border-guards and a military force in case of future hostilities between the two empires. To these imperial interests one may add the sheer human depravity of Ottoman slave-traders and the concerns of the mountaineer élites, especially the Kabardian ones, over the potential loss of their serfs after the expected implementation of the Russian anti-bondage laws. The end result, however, is obvious to everyone. The fertile plains south of the Kuban river and the coastal areas along the Black Sea lost most of their indigenous population. The land was gradually resettled by Cossacks, Armenians, Greeks and peasants from central Russia and Ukraine. Between 1867 and 1897, the Russian and Ukrainian population of the Kuban and Stavropol' *oblast's* had grown by 230% and 155% respectively, leaving the local population in the minority. At the turn of the 20th century, in the Kuban *oblast'* Russians constituted more than 90% of the population. By contrast, the number of "natives" had fallen to a miniscule 5.4%. According to a modern Western researcher, "the lands of the Circassians and the Abkhāz, once overwhelmingly Muslim, had become overwhelmingly Christian" (J. McCarthy, *The fate of the Muslims*, *apud* P. Heinze, *Circassian resistance to Russia*, in M. Bennigsen-Broxup (ed.), *The North Caucasus barrier*, London 1992, 104).

Those mountaineers who remained were transferred to the Transkuban steppes and resettled amidst the Cossacks under constant Russian surveillance. As envisioned by Yevdokimov, the resettlement effectively undermined their ability to launch large-scale resistance movements against Russian rule. The decree of 9 March 1873, issued by the Russian administration of the Caucasus, strictly prohibited any contacts between the Russian subjects of Čerkes background and their relatives in the Ottoman Empire. The former Adyg̲h̲e lands remained under Russian military administration until 1871, when the Russians felt safe enough to replace it with civil rule throughout the Kuban region and the Black Sea area, by now thoroughly Russified and practically cleansed of "hostile elements". Nevertheless, the Russian military authorities continued to play a major role in the everyday administration of the region. The movements of the Adyg̲h̲es were thoroughly monitored and restricted by the Russian police and the Cossacks, effectively confining the mountaineers to their *auls*. The *auls* were administered by an elected or appointed headman (*stars̲h̲ina*), who had to be approved by the local Cossack chief (*ataman*). At the same time, during the Russo-Ottoman war of 1877-8, Russian imperial authorities were sufficiently confident of the mountaineers' loyalty to the Russian government to enlist them as irregulars to fight against the Ottoman armies in Bulgaria, Romania and even Transcaucasia. The Russian expeditionary force in the Balkans and the southern Caucasus also included many irregular cavalry units from the central and eastern Caucasus, namely, Kabardia, Dāg̲h̲istān, Ingus̲h̲etia, Ossetia, and Čečnya. Many mountaineer fighters distinguished themselves in the battlefield and were decorated for their bravery by the award of Russian medals. At the same time, on the Caucasus front many Čerkes and Abk̲h̲āz emigrants and their descendants took an active part in the Ottoman offensive against the Black Sea ports of Batumi and Suk̲h̲umi (Suk̲h̲um-Ḳalʿe). They were driven in part by the desire to avenge themselves on the Russian Empire for the suffering inflicted upon them by its oppressive rule. While the Ottoman forces were able to make some important gains in the area, in the end, the Russian successes in the Balkans determined the favourable outcome of the war for the Russian Empire, which was reflected in the Treaty of Berlin signed in the summer of 1878 (see further, MUHĀD̲J̲IR. 2.).

i. *The rise of D̲h̲ikrism in Čečnya: Kunta Ḥād̲j̲d̲j̲ī Kis̲h̲iev, the man who preached peace*

In the late 1850s, not long before the fall of S̲h̲āmil's imāmate, Kunta Ḥād̲j̲d̲j̲ī, a poor Ḳumuḳ [*q.v.*] peasant (some sources consider him to be a Čečen) of Ilsk̲h̲ān-Yurt, began to disseminate a new spiritual teaching among the war-weary Čečens and Ingus̲h̲. Initially a follower of the Naḳs̲h̲bandī brotherhood, Kunta Ḥād̲j̲d̲j̲ī is said to have been initiated into the Ḳādiriyya *ṭarīḳa* [*q.v.*] during his visit to Mecca on the *ḥād̲j̲d̲j̲* in the late 1850s. The exact circumstances of his initiation into this brotherhood are obscure. According to some of his followers, he received the teaching of the Ḳādiriyya directly from its founder, S̲h̲ayk̲h̲ ʿAbd al-Ḳādir al-D̲j̲īlānī [*q.v.*], who appeared to him in a dream. Contrary to the activist precepts of S̲h̲āmil's *myuridizm*, which preached a holy war against the Russians, Kunta Ḥād̲j̲d̲j̲ī encouraged his followers to engage in acts of penitence (*tawba*) and individual self-purification through frugality, humility, abstention from worldly delights and withdrawal from this world. On the social plane, the new preacher emphasised solicitude for the needs of one's neighbours, mutual assistance and the necessity to share one's wealth with the poor and needy. Kunta Ḥadjdjī also advocated peaceful co-existence with the Russians as long as they allowed the Čečens and Ingush the freedom to practice their religion and follow their customs.

As mentioned above, Kunta Ḥādjdjī's pacifistic message ran counter to Shāmil's ideology of armed resistance to Russian rule. Moreover, Shāmil also saw in Kunta Ḥādjdjī a rival in the struggle for the loyalties of the mountaineers, a struggle that Shāmil was already losing due to the growing war fatigue and despondency among his supporters in the face of Russian military superiority. Shāmil is said to have summoned the young preacher to his headquarters and subjected him to a close interrogation. Upon witnessing the vocal *dhikr* and dance that Kunta Ḥadjdjī performed in accordance with the precepts of the Ḳādirī brotherhood, Shāmil allegedly declared it contrary to Naḳshbandī precepts and "orthodox" Islam. He then ordered the preacher of *zikrizm* (a Russified version of the Arabic *dhikr* [*q.v.*]) to leave the territory of his imāmate to perform a second pilgrimage and to gain a better knowledge of the intricacies of Islamic law.

Kunta Ḥādjdjī reappeared in Čečnya after the collapse of Shāmil's imāmate in either late 1861 or early 1862. With Shāmil no longer on the scene, his message received an eager hearing among the war-weary Čečens and Ingush. Accounts of Kunta Ḥādjdjī's sermons indicate that, in addition to pacifism, his teaching was tinged with millenarian expectations and a doomsday mentality. He called upon his audiences to prepare for the Day of Judgement by purifying their souls, renouncing the transient allures of this life and adhering strictly to the pious precepts of the Ḳādirī *ṭarīḳa*. Articulated in a simple language easily understood by the ordinary Čečens and Ingush, Kunta's teaching soon acquired a broad popular following. Initiation into the new *ṭarīḳa* was very simple. Kunta Ḥadjdjī or one of his lieutenants took the new member by the hand and asked him or her to acknowledge the spiritual authority of the *shaykh*, to repeat the *shahāda* [*q.v.*] one hundred times a day, and to participate in the ritual dance of the *ṭarīḳa*. Kunta Ḥādjdjī's followers recognised him as their spiritual master (*ustādh*) and considered themselves his faithful disciples (*murīdūn*). Seeking to spread his teaching among the masses, Kunta Ḥādjdjī sent emissaries to various Čečen and Ingush communities.

In the course of time, Kunta Ḥādjdjī's movement acquired institutional dimensions and administrative structure. Following Shāmil's example, he appointed a number of his foremost followers as his *nāʾib*s in various areas of Čečnya and Ingushetia. According to the Russian colonial authorities of the day, Kunta Ḥadjdjī divided Čečnya into five (according to some sources eight) *niyābat*s or *nāʾib*ships. Each *nāʾib* had under his command several lieutenants (*wakīl*s), who were entrusted with spreading the teaching of the new *ṭarīḳa* among mountaineer communities. Kunta Ḥādjdjī's inner circle included his brother Mowsar (who was the *nāʾib* of the Avturkhān district), Myačik (the *nāʾib* of the area between Urus-Martan and Ačkhoi-Martan), Bamat-Girey Mitaev and Čim-Mīrzā Taumurzaev. The latter two were to found their own branches of Kunta Ḥādjdjī's *ṭarīḳa* after his arrest and exile. In all, Russian sources estimated the number of Kunta Ḥādjdjī's followers to be around 6,000 men and women. Most of them resided in the villages of Shali, Gekhi, Shaladji, Urus-Martan and Avtury. Russian sources claim that, despite its pacifistic message, some of Shāmil's former fighters among the Čečens came to see Kunta Ḥādjdjī's teaching as a new version of Shāmil's *ghazawāt* ideology. The Russian authorities, ever suspicious of any popular religious teaching that could mobilise the mountaineers for a certain political cause, encouraged renowned local scholars, such as ʿAbd al-Ḳādir Khordaev and Muṣṭafā ʿAbdullaev, to condemn *zikrizm* as being contrary to the *Sharīʿa*. In particular, the scholars denounced Kunta Ḥādjdjī's loud *dhikr* techniques and musical instruments that induced ecstatic states in the participants. They also pointed out that Kunta Ḥādjdji had no scholarly qualifications to substantiate his claims to the spiritual leadership of the Čečens and Ingush. Kunta Ḥādjdjī responded with his usual humility. He readily acknowledged the authority of his learned critics as interpreters of the outward aspects of the Islamic revelation. However, he presented himself as an exponent of its true essence, which was hidden from the majority of believers. Later accounts, circulated by Kunta Ḥādjdjī's supporters, ascribe to him a number of miracles that allegedly demonstrated the superiority of his spiritual teaching over the dry scholasticism of his detractors.

In early January 1863, after some hesitation, the Russian authorities decided to put an end to Kunta Ḥādjdjī's preaching. On the orders of the viceroy of the Caucasus, the Grand Duke Mikhail Romanov, Kunta Ḥādjdjī and fourteen of his closest followers and *wakīl*s, including his brother Mowsar, were arrested and sent to the Russian city of Novočerkassk. Several months later, he was separated from his companions and exiled to the town of Ustyužno in the Novgorod province of northern Russia. There he spent the rest of his days in misery under police surveillance. Throughout his exile he balanced on the brink of starvation, as his daily six kopeks' allowance was barely enough to buy a piece of bread. The Russian authorities ignored his repeated requests for an increase in allowance; his letters with pleas for help addressed to his wife and family were intercepted by the Russian secret police and never reached their destination. In any event, by that time, his wife and other members of his family had already emigrated to Anatolia with thousands of other *muhādjirūn*. Kunta Ḥādjdjī died around 1867, his health undermined by a life of deprivation.

Kunta Ḥādjdjī's arrest in early 1863 triggered a rebellion of his followers that became known as "The Battle of Daggers" (Rus. *kinžal'nyi boi*). On 18 January 1863, a group of 3,000 to 4,000 of Kunta Ḥādjdjī's followers, armed only with daggers, sabres and sticks, charged against a Russian detachment near the Čečen village of Shali. As they found themselves within the firing distance of the Russian troops, dancing and singing Ḳādirī litanies, they were mowed down by Russian fire. The "*dhikr* army" dispersed, leaving behind some 150 dead, including several women dressed as men. The site of the Battle of Daggers near Shali has become one of Čečnya's most sacred places, along with the grave of Kunta Ḥādjdjī's mother at the village of Guni, in the Vedan district of Čečnya. It is said that Kunta Ḥādjdjī's *nāʾib* Myačik-Mullā had persuaded the attackers that their *ustādh* would miraculously protect them from Russian bullets and cannon-fire. Following the massacre, the Russian administration arrested and exiled to Russia many members of the *dhikr* movement. Some of them managed to escape and became *abrek*s (that is, bandits of honour, who vowed to fight the Russians to the death).

In May 1865, a Čečen shepherd of the Kharačoi *aul* named Taza Ekmirza(ev) proclaimed himself a new *imām* and attempted to raise the population of a mountainous part of Čečnya known as Ičkeriya. Taza claimed to have performed an ascension to heaven (*miʿrādj* [*q.v.*]), during which God himself had ordained him as the new *imām* of Čečnya in the presence of the Prophet and Shaykh Kunta Ḥādjdjī. Taza's claims were endorsed by a number of former followers of Kunta Ḥādjdjī, especially Myačik-Mullā. The Russian administration reacted strongly by sending three infantry detachments, led by Colonel Golovačev, against the rebels. Fearing Russian reprisals, the Čečen population of Ičkeriya seized Taza and his closest supporters and handed them over to the Russian command. Taza was convicted, sentenced to 12 years of hard labour and sent to Siberia. The spring of 1865 witnessed a massive exodus of the Muslim population, including many of Kunta Ḥādjdjī's former supporters, from Čečnya and Ingushetia to Ottoman Turkey. Scared by the rumours of impending forced resettlement and conversion to Christianity, some 23,000 Čečens boarded Ottoman ships bound for Anatolia. Of these, around 2,100 individuals later returned to the Caucasus, bringing with them stories of hardship and deprivation. These stories stemmed the tide of refugees, although some families continued to emigrate to the *Dār al-islām* in the decades leading up to the Russian Revolution of 1917.

j. *The Russo-Ottoman War of 1877-8 and beyond*

The *dhikr* movement, now effectively banned by the Russian authorities, was reduced to a semi-clandestine existence. To protect its leaders from Russian persecutions, the *ṭuruḳ* claiming descent from Kunta Ḥādjdjī and his lieutenants grew extremely secretive and fractious. In 1877-8, some of their members took an active part in the rebellion of ʿAlī-bek Ḥādjdjī Aldanov, during which, for the first time, the Ḳādirīs fought side by side with the members of the Naḳshbandī *ṭarīḳa* of Dāghistān led by Ḥādjdjī Muḥammad of Sogratl (Thughūr). His father, ʿAbd al-Raḥmān al-Thughūrī (d. 1882), also took an active part in the rebellion. A renowned scholar, ʿAbd al-Raḥmān was considered to be the chief Naḳshbandī *shaykh* of Dāghistān and Čečnya after the emigration to the Ottoman realm of Shāmil's spiritual preceptor, Djamāl al-Dīn al-Ghāzī Ghumuḳī. After the followers of Shaykh Muḥammad Ḥādjdjī proclaimed him *imām* of Dāghistān and Čečnya, he began to send his *nāʾib*s and *wakīl*s to various Dāghistānī communities, inviting them to fight the Russians in the name of "freedom and *Sharīʿa*". The revolt was triggered in part by the Russian policy aimed at limiting drastically the jurisdiction of the *Sharīʿa* and replacing it with the customary law (*ʿādāt* [*q.v.*]). This fact explains the large number of religious leaders among the rebels. Another important motive of the rebellion was Ottoman propaganda, which predicted an impending victory of the Ottoman army in the Caucasus and the Balkans. Some of the inflammatory flyers that circulated among the mountaineer communities were signed by Shāmil's second son, Ghāzī Muḥammad, now a general of the Ottoman army. The rebellion lasted for a whole year, until it was finally quashed by a Russian military force led by General Svistunov.

Following the suppression of ʿAlī-bek Aldanov's movement, the abolition of Ḥādjdjī Muḥammad's imāmate and the execution of twenty-eight of its leaders by the Russian military administration, their surviving supporters went underground. The early 1880s witnessed the emergence of three principal branches (known locally as *wird*s) of the Ḳādiriyya under the leadership of Bamat-Girey (Bamatgiri) Ḥādjdjī Mitaev and Čim-Mīrzā in Čečnya and of Baṭalḥādjdjī Belkhoroi(ev) in Ingushetia. Their influence on the mountaineer communities was of great concern for the Russian administration, which suspected the leadership of the new brotherhoods of trying to create an alternative power structure completely outside Russian control. Continual Russian surveillance and persecution turned the brotherhoods into secret societies, whose members often practiced endogamy and were suspicious of outsiders. This is especially true of the Baṭalḥādjdjī *wird*, which was characterised by particularly strict discipline and fear of outsiders. Each male member of this brotherhood carried a long dagger, which he did not hesitate to use to protect his honour or to retaliate against any attack on the honour of his *ustādh*. Each of the three *wird*s that emerged from the Kunta Ḥādjdjī movement practiced a distinctive type of *dhikr*. Thus the members of the Bamat-Girey *wird* are known for their high jumps (hence their Russian sobriquet, *pryguny* "jumpers"); the Baṭalḥādjdjī *dhikr* is distinguished by the intensive clapping of hands, while the Čim-Mīrzā brotherhood is characterised by the use of drums (hence their Russian name *barabanshčiki* "drummers"). Many members of the *abrek* movement, including the famous Čečen "bandit of honour" Zelimkhān, were associated with one or the other *wird*. Consequently, Russian attempts to crack down on the *abrek*s were often accompanied by persecutions against the Kunta Ḥādjdjī *wirds*. Thus in 1911, the *shaykh*s of the three Kunta Ḥādjdjī *wirds*, Bamat-Girey, Baṭalḥādjdjī and Čim-Mīrzā, together with their closest followers (thirty in all) were arrested and exiled to Kaluga.

These persecutions and the dire economic conditions in Čečnya and Ingushetia, which were suffering from chronic food shortages, triggered a new wave of emigration. In 1913 alone, some 1,000 Čečen families left their homeland for Anatolia in search of a better life. Paradoxically, similarly dire economic conditions in neighbouring Dāghistān did not prevent it from retaining its position as the major centre of Islamic learning and literacy in the northern Caucasus. In many areas of Dāghistān, even after the Russian conquest, Arabic remained the principal language of administration and correspondence among isolated mountaineer communities, whose multilingual inhabitants continued to use it as a *lingua franca* up until the late 1920s-early 1930s, when it was finally supplanted by Russian. Before the Russian Revolution there were, according to different estimates, from 800 to 2,000 Ḳurʾānic schools in Dāghistān alone, enrolling around 40,000 students. At the beginning of the 20th century, Dāghistān boasted five printing presses, including the Mavraev Publishing House at Temīr-Khān-Shūrā (Makhač-ḳalʿe [*q.v.*]), which specialised in Arabic books. It also produced books in major Dāghistānī languages: Avar, Darghin, Ḳumuḳ and Laḳ [*q.vv.*]. In 1911 alone, it published 256 titles in these languages.

The strong position of Islamic learning in Dāghistān was recognised by the Russian administration, which prohibited Russian Orthodox missionaries from proselytising in the area, fearing popular unrest among the local Muslim population. Russian attempts to replace local religiously-based education with Russian schools had only limited success. The so-called "new method" gymnasia and technical schools in the urban centres of Dāghistān, Čečnya and Ossetia were dominated by non-native, Russian-speaking students and faculty. At the same time, the last decade of the 19th century and first decade of the 20th century witnessed the steady growth of a small but active Russian-educated intelligentsia among the Caucasian ethnicities, which became an important vehicle in spreading Russian culture among their respective ethnic groups. Overall, however, the literacy level among the mountaineers remained relatively low throughout the Caucasus. The Russian census of 1897 shows Dāghistān to be in the lead with 9.2%, followed by Adygheya (7%), Ḳaračay (4.6%), Kabarda (3.2%), and Balkariya (1.4%).

k. *The Caucasus on the eve of the Russian Revolution*

Following the discovery of commercial amounts of oil in some areas of Čečnya in 1894, the region underwent a rapid economic and social transformation and by 1910 had become a major centre of oil production in the Caucasus, second only to Bākū. Radical changes in the social and economic landscape of the region were underway throughout the first decade of the 20th century, as Čečnya and its neighbours were becoming increasingly integrated into the world economy. This process is attested by the emergence of a number of local companies with links to major European and Russian entrepreneurs and banks. They presided over many local projects, including the creation of the oil industry and attendant infrastructure in and around Grozny. Several newly-built railways linked central Russia to the major urban centres of the Caucasus—Ekaterinodar, Vladikavkaz, Novorossisk (former Sudjuk-Ḳalʿe), Stavropolʾ and Bākū. These cities soon became centres of anti-government agitation spearheaded by, for the most part, Russian revolutionary intelligentsia and Russian-speaking industrial and railway workers. While the majority of the mountaineers of the northwestern and central Caucasus did not benefit from these developments (in fact, due to widespread land speculation, many local peasants lost their already tiny lots of agricultural land and were forced to migrate to the rapidly-growing cities), some members of the Čerkes, Čečen and Ingush élites, including some wealthy leaders of Ṣūfī *wirds*, profited from this economic boom. The growing economic inequality and abiding hostility between the Russian settlers (Cossacks) and the mountaineers fuelled rural unrest, especially in Čečnya and Ossetia. As usual, the Russian administration resorted to the tactic of deportation and exile to Russia and Siberia of real or imaginary "troublemakers". Among those deported from Čečnya and Ingushetia in the first decade of the 20th century were *shaykhs* of the Naḳshbandiyya (e.g. ʿAbd al-ʿAzīz Shaptukaev, also known as Dokku Shaykh and Deni Arsanov,) and *ustādhs* of the local Ḳādirī *wirds*, Baṭalhādjdjī Belkhoroev, Bamatgirey-Ḥādjdjī and their closest followers. The Russian revolution of 1905-6 galvanised local resistance movements, which were driven in part by the forced Russification of the rural population and the growth of the number of Russian settlers and landlords. In line with Marxist principles, the Russian Communist agitators, who, for the most part, were based in the industrial centres of the region, attempted to reach out to the mountaineer masses and to rally them to their cause. However, these attempts met with limited success among the majority of mountaineers, who remained suspicious of the goals of the agitators, many of whom espoused atheism. As a result, the revolutionary movement in the Caucasus was for the most part confined to the urban centres with a substantial Russian population. Local disturbances continued throughout the first decade of the 20th century, despite severe repression. In 1914-15, the hardships and shortages of World War I triggered another wave of anti-government protests both in cities and the countryside. The military defeats of Russian armies on the Western front and the wartime requisitions instituted by the Russian administration resulted in acts of sabotage and mass desertions among mountaineer recruits.

l. *The Russian Revolution and civil war*

The victory of the democratic revolution in Russia in February 1917 instilled in the Caucasian nations a hope to finally rid themselves of the oppressive imperial rule. In the heady days after the revolution, mountaineer leaders saw their chance to secure independence from Russia. Throughout the Caucasus, there mushroomed numerous "civil committees" and "revolutionary councils", which represented a wide spectrum of political views from "Muslim Communism" of various shades to bourgeois liberalism and parliamentary democracy. At the same time, many mountaineer communities remained committed to the more traditional religious values and leaders. Thus a "congress of the Čečen people" that spontaneously assembled in Grozny in March 1917 demanded the reinstatement of the *Sharīʿa* as the law of the land and the creation of the post of the chief *muftī* of the Terek *oblastʾ* with wide-ranging jurisdiction. Such demands were actively supported by local scholars, many of whom were leaders of the Caucasian Ḳādirī *wirds* and the Naḳshbandiyya, namely Sugaip-Mullā, ʿAlī Mitaev, Deni Arsanov and ʿAbd al-Wahhāb Ḥādjdjī Aksayskii. The spiritual authority and economic power (the individuals just mentioned were wealthy landowners and successful entrepreneurs) wielded by such traditional religious authorities made them indispensable for the new crop of local politicians, who represented the interests of the nascent mountaineer bourgeoisie. Thus the famous Čečen oil tycoon and politician ʿAbd al-Madjīd Čermoev was anxious to secure the support of the influential Ṣūfī *shaykhs* Yūsuf Ḥādjdjī and Deni Arsanov.

On 1 May 1917, the "First Congress of the Mountain Peoples" was convened at Vladikavkaz (North Ossetia). Presided over by the Balkar intellectual Basiyat Shakhanov, it lasted for ten days. Of its 400 participants many were authoritative religious scholars and Ṣūfī *shaykhs*, namely, Deni Arsanov and Sugaip-Mullā Gaysumov from Čečnya, Uzun Ḥādjdjī and Nadjm al-Dīn Efendi Gotsinskii from Dāghistān, Ḥamzat Ḥādjdjī Urusov from Ḳaračay, etc. The Congress called for the formation of the Union of the Mountain Peoples of the Caucasus, which, in turn, was supposed to be part of a larger political structure called the "All-Caucasus Muslim Union". The resolutions of the Congress included a demand for the establishment of the office of *Shaykh al-Islām* at the government of the Russian Federation, who would preside over a consultative council of six representatives of the three major schools of law on the territory of the former Russian Empire, namely, Shāfiʿī, Ḥanafī and Djaʿfarī (Shīʿī). Another resolution called for the creation of an "academy of *Sharīʿa* sciences" at Vladikavkaz and the declaration of the *Sharīʿa* as the only law of the land.

In June 1917, the famous Muslim scholar and Naḳshbandī *shaykh* of Dāghistān, Uzun Ḥādjdjī, arrived in Čečnya. He had already acquired a reputation there for piety and clairvoyance during his earlier sojourn at the Čečen village of Shatoi, whose inhabitants had given him shelter from the persecution of the Russian military police shortly before the Russian Revolution. At a meeting of the inhabitants of the Shatoi district, Uzun Ḥādjdjī declared Nadjm al-Dīn

Gotsinskii, a respected scholar of liberal leanings and son of a *nāʾib* of Imām S̲h̲āmil, as *imām* of Čečnya and Dāg̲h̲istān. The *s̲h̲ayk̲h̲* confirmed his nomination by a display of his miraculous powers. According to some "eye-witness" accounts, he performed his prayer on his felt coat (*burka*) which he had spread in the middle of lake Eyzen-Am.

In September 1917, the Second Congress of the Mountain Peoples was assembled at Andy, on the border between Dāg̲h̲istān and Čečnya. It attracted some 20,000 participants from all over the Caucasus. In addition to traditional religious and political leaders and members of the nascent mountaineer bourgeoisie, the Congress was attended by representatives of leftist political parties, including the Bolsheviks, and a number of political emissaries from the Provisional Government of Russia. Another congress took place at Temīr-K̲h̲ān-S̲h̲ūrā, in Dāg̲h̲istān. Its participants ignored Uzun Ḥād̲j̲d̲j̲ī's appointment of Gotsinskii as *imām* of Dāg̲h̲istān and Čečnya. Instead, they bestowed upon him the title of chief *muftī*, which carried less political authority. This event upset Uzun Ḥād̲j̲d̲j̲ī, since it nullified his earlier appointment of Gotsinskii as *imām*. Upon hearing the news, Uzun Ḥād̲j̲d̲j̲ī withdrew from Temīr-K̲h̲ān-S̲h̲ūrā together with some 10,000 of his supporters. Uzun Ḥād̲j̲d̲j̲ī's departure reflected his frustration with the growing influence of leftist, "socialist" groups on the events in Dāg̲h̲istān and Čečnya and their attempts to seize the initiative from the traditional mountaineer leadership and to use it to their advantage. Gotsinskii's authority was drastically reduced when a mass meeting of Dāg̲h̲istānī villagers (apparently orchestrated by the opponents of Gotsinskii) named the Naḳs̲h̲bandī *s̲h̲ayk̲h̲* ʿAlī Ḥād̲j̲d̲j̲ī of Akūs̲h̲a—a village in the Dargin region of Dāg̲h̲istān—as the second *muftī*.

Similar tensions between various tribal, ethnic and political factions, often working at cross-purposes, were in evidence in other areas of the northern Caucasus. Thus at a meeting of the Čečen National Council, the *murīds* of the Naḳs̲h̲bandī *s̲h̲ayk̲h̲* Deni Arsanov attacked and beat up the Council's chairman Aḥmad-K̲h̲ān Mutus̲h̲ev. As a result, Arsanov became chairman "by default". The breakdown of centralised authority resulted in chaos and political assassinations, which had begun shortly after the February revolution of 1917 and which continued uninterrupted throughout the rest of the year.

Against this background, the long-standing animosity between the Russian and Ukrainian Cossacks and the Čečens burst into the open, leading to a tit-for-tat warfare between the two groups. Several Čečen and Cossack settlements were plundered and put to the torch. In the course of these hostilities, a Cossack detachment murdered *s̲h̲ayk̲h̲* Deni Arsanov, along with his 35 *murīds*, after he had attempted to broker a peace agreement between the warring parties. This tragic episode led to a further escalation of violence. In December 1917 the members of the Čečen National Council were forced to flee from Grozny, which had fallen into the hands of revolutionary workers and soldiers, most of whom were of Russian or Ukrainian backgrounds. This event led to the isolation of the capital from the rest of the country and the emergence of two parallel power structures, the Russian-dominated *Sovdeps* (councils of representatives of workers and soldiers) and the one which was controlled by traditional Čečen leaders, such as *s̲h̲ayk̲h̲* ʿAlī Mitaev and the former chairman of the Čečen National Council, Aḥmad-K̲h̲ān Mutus̲h̲ev, both of whom were affiliated with different branches of the Kunta Ḥād̲j̲d̲j̲ī *ṭarīḳa*. Into this complex and near-chaotic political landscape came former officers of the "Wild Division" of the Tsarist army, who tried to form a political alliance with the traditional Čečen leaders against the Bolsheviks in Grozny.

The situation grew even further confused after the collapse in late October 1917 of the Provisional Government of Russia and the seizure of power in the Russian capital by the Bolsheviks and their radical political allies. In the Caucasus, the power vacuum created by the change of guard in St. Petersburg (Petrograd) was filled in the early months of 1918 by a series of short-lived "unions", "congresses" and "councils", which were usually organised by ethnicity. All these political bodies proved to be extremely fractious and incapable of reaching consensus on any given proposal or policy. Under the circumstances, leftist political parties, such as the Bolsheviks, Mensheviks, and Social Revolutionaries, which had been cemented by a strict party discipline and decades of struggle against the Russian imperial government, turned out to be the only viable alternative to the authority of the traditional religious leaders of mountaineer society. Steeped in the arts of political agitation and revolutionary demagoguery, the leftist parties soon gained the upper hand in the struggle to win over the masses. Their clear and catchy political slogans, promising social and ethnic equality and an equitable distribution of land, resonated with the aspirations of the impoverished Russian and mountaineer classes. To enhance their influence even further, in January 1918, a group of representatives of the leftist political parties of the northern Caucasus agreed to form the so-called "Socialist Bloc".

After a period of political jockeying, the Bolsheviks, led by Sergei Kirov, succeeded in wresting the leadership of the Bloc from their rivals, the Mensheviks and Socialist Revolutionaries. On 4 May 1918, the leaders of the Socialist Bloc declared the creation of the Terek Peoples' Republic, with its capital in Vladikavkaz. The new republic was to be part of the Russian Federation. It included Ossetia, Čečnya, Ingus̲h̲etia, Kabarda, Balkaria, and the lands of the Ḳumuḳs and Nog̲h̲ay Tatars. As Russia descended ever deeper into the chaos of civil war, many mountaineer leaders began to consider the possibility of creating an independent state. In the early months of 1918, a group of politicians led by Tapo Čermoev, Vassan-Girey D̲j̲abagi, Ps̲h̲emak̲h̲o Kotsev and several other mountaineer leaders of a liberal slant, formed the so-called "Mountain Government" at Tiflīs. On 11 May 1918, they declared an independent "Mountain Republic". The primary goal of the new state, as envisaged by its founders, was the immediate cessation of civil war on its territory and the construction of a new life on democratic principles.

This programme was, however, never implemented. Soon after the fall of the Bolshevik-dominated Terek Peoples' Republic, the country was occupied by the White Army of General Denikin. Since Denikin's political programme rested on the idea of the restoration of Russian imperial rule and revival of a "one and undivided Russia", he hurried to abolish the independent "Mountain Republic" and attacked its supporters in Kabarda and North Ossetia. When the White Army arrived in Čečnya and Ingus̲h̲etia, it unleashed a brutal punitive campaign against the local population, burning down dozens of villages and executing hundreds of their inhabitants. The protests of the Mountain Republic's leadership addressed to the Western powers, which had actively supported and equipped Denikin, went unheeded. In the meantime, the Bolsheviks of the Terek Peoples' Republic went underground. Many Bolshevik ministers (commissars) found refuge in the remote mountains of Ičkeriya (Čečnya). From there, they directed a campaign of sabotage and agitation against the Whites. Their calls to resist the White Army and expel it from the country found an eager reception among the mountaineers, who had realised that Denikin's victory would lead to the restoration of the oppressive Russian imperial rule over their lands. Playing on such fears, the Bolsheviks made a pact with the local religious leaders, such the Ḳādirī *shaykh* ʿAlī Mitaev and the Naḳshbandī elder *shaykh* Sugaip-Mullā, who enjoyed wide support among the mountaineer masses. The Bolsheviks did not hesitate to promise their allies, in the case of victory, full political autonomy and freedom to practice their religion and to implement the rule of the *Sharīʿa*.

In June 1919, the popular Čečen revolutionary Aslanbek Sheripov and the Dāghistānī leader Uzun Ḥādjdjī agreed to form a unified front against the occupying White Army. In September, Uzun Ḥādjdjī proclaimed himself *imām* and military commander (*amīr*) of the "North Caucasus Emirate" with the capital at Vedeno (Vedan), the Čečen village that some 80 years earlier had served as a headquarters of Shāmil's imāmate. Simultaneously, Uzun Ḥādjdjī declared a "holy war" (*ghazawāt*) against the White legionnaires. Uzun Ḥādjdjī's headquarters became the recruitment point of mountaineer fighters from all over the northern Caucasus, especially Kabarda, Balkaria, Ingushetia, and Dāghistān. Many volunteer detachments were led by Ṣūfī *shaykhs*, who often arrived in Vedeno accompanied by their *murīds*. Some of them were given ministerial posts in the Emirate government. The leaders of this new state, which they classified as a "*Sharīʿa* monarchy" (Rus. *shariatskaya monarkhia*), declared their primary aim to be full independence from Russia under the rule of the *Sharīʿa*. The territory of the Emirate was divided into seven provinces that were administered by Uzun Ḥādjdjī's *nāʾibs*. In addition, he sent his ambassadors to the neighbouring states, such as Ādharbāydjān, with which he maintained close ties throughout his political career.

Impressed by Uzun Ḥādjdjī's influence on the mountaineers of different ethnic and tribal backgrounds, the Bolsheviks endeavoured to secure his support in the struggle against their common enemy, the Whites. On 4 February 1920, the Bolsheviks formed a special "committee for the restoration of Soviet rule in the Northern Caucasus" under the chairmanship of Ordžonikidze with Kirov as his chief lieutenant. They succeeded in convincing the mountaineer leadership of the necessity to join forces against the White Army. From then on, the Caucasian Red Partisans and the Fifth Red Army led by the Bolshevik commander Nikolai Gikalo fought alongside the *murīds* of Uzun Ḥādjdjī and of other local *wirds*. Some members of the Čim Mīrzā *wird* of the Kunta Ḥādjdjī *ṭarīḳa* even decorated their sheepskin hats (*papakhas*) with red bands to demonstrate their solidarity with the Bolsheviks.

In March 1920, after having suffered a series of crushing defeats at the hands of the Muslim-Bolshevik coalition, the White Army abandoned the major cities of Čečnya and Dāghistān and began to withdraw to the coast of the Caspian Sea. The city of Darband was liberated after a nineteen-day, street-by-street battle, giving the Whites no alternative but to put their entire army on ships and sail from the port of Petrovsk. Their departure ushered in a new stage of the war, during which the former allies soon found themselves locked in a life-and-death struggle for control of the country they had just liberated. This, however, did not happen overnight, as the Soviets initially did not feel strong enough to turn against their Muslim comrades-in-arms. A cable from Vladimir Lenin addressed to the Bolshevik Revolutionary Committee (*revkom*) of Grozny instructed its members to respect the mountaineers' desire for religious and political autonomy and independence. This was, however, apparently only a temporary tactical manoeuvre that was to be supplanted by a more aggressive strategy on the part of the Bolshevik party leadership, which was determined to bring the entire Caucasus under communist rule.

m. *The anti-Soviet rebellion of 1920-1 in Upper Dāghistān*

The death of Uzun Ḥādjdjī in May 1920 did not lead to the dissolution of his Emirate. His functions as head of a theocratic state were taken up by a number of authoritative religious leaders, such as the Ṣūfī *shaykh* ʿAlī Mitaev, who had about 10,000 followers in Čečnya and Ingushetia. Like Uzun Ḥādjdjī, Mitaev maintained close relationships with Nadjm al-Dīn Gotsinskii, who was generally recognised as the new *imām* of Čečnya and Dāghistān. However, for reasons that are not entirely clear, ʿAlī Mitaev did not take an active part in Gotsinskii's bid for independence from Soviet Russia in the months that followed. Gotsinskii assembled under his command about 20,000 seasoned fighters, who were to become the core of his rebel army.

Throughout 1920, tensions were mounting between the former allies of the anti-White coalition in many parts of Dāghistān and Čečnya. They were fuelled by the highhandedness of the Red Army's commanders and political commissars, who were ignorant of the customs, religious beliefs and social institutions of the local populations and tended to dismiss them as contrary to Communist ideology. Steeped in atheistic propaganda, they viewed the mountaineers' attachment to the Islamic religion as a "reactionary superstition" that had to be discouraged, if not uprooted altogether. The constant influx of fervent revolutionary propagandists and atheistic-minded political representatives (*upolnomočennye*) from Rostov and other cities of southern Russia added to the growing discontent with Soviet rule among the mountaineers and their leaders. The disaffected political groups established their base in the rugged mountainous areas of western Dāghistān, from where they attempted to orchestrate resistance to the Bolshevik authorities.

In August 1920, Nadjm al-Dīn Gotsinskii and Colonel Kaitmas ʿAlīkhānov convened an assembly at the remote village of Gidatl, during which ʿAlīkhānov was proclaimed "war minister" of the newly formed "Sharīʿa Army of the Mountain Peoples". The uprising spread quickly among the mountaineers of Avaristān and the Andy range. The area's rugged terrain made it a natural fortress for the rebel army. In a matter of weeks, Soviet rule in Upper Dāghistān was effectively eliminated and replaced by authorities loyal to Imām Gotsinskii, including Saʿīd-bek (a great-grandson of Imām Shāmil, who had joined the rebellion at Gotsinskii's invitation), Colonel ʿAlīkhānov, a few traditional leaders affiliated with Ṣūfī *ṭuruḳ* and some former officers of the Tsarist army, including Colonel Djaʿfarov, who was appointed commander-in-chief of the rebel military forces. Food and supplies were provided by the local population, but each fighter had to have his own weapons. The army was divided into 100 strong infantry units, supported by small cavalry detachments. Throughout the rebellion, the rebels suffered from shortages of weapons and ammunition and had to rely heavily on the supplies captured from the Red Army. This disadvantage was counterbalanced in part by the rebels' intimate knowledge of the local terrain and their mastery of the art of mountain warfare.

The Bolsheviks' initial reaction to the rebellion was ineffective and confused. Their detachments stationed in the area suffered heavy casualties and had to abandon their base at Botli<u>kh</u>, which was occupied by the rebel troops. In less than six weeks, most of Upper Dā<u>gh</u>istān on the border with Čečnya was cleansed of Red Army units and their local allies, the Red Partisans, and fell under the control of the rebels. The only Red Army units that still remained in Upper Dā<u>gh</u>istān were trapped within their fortresses. To relieve them, during the first two weeks of October 1920, Red Army reinforcements were sent to Temīr-<u>Kh</u>ān-<u>Sh</u>ūrā from Ā<u>dh</u>arbāy<u>dj</u>ān. Upon arrival, they were dispatched to the rebel-controlled areas with the orders to occupy the strategic village of Arakany (Harakān). As a 700-strong Red Army expeditionary force led by the head of the Dā<u>gh</u>istān ČeKa ("Committee for Struggle Against Counter-Revolution, Sabotage and Speculation") was approaching Arakany, on 30 October 1920, it was enticed into a narrow gorge by the rebel levies under the command of <u>Sh</u>ay<u>kh</u> Muḥammad of Bala<u>kh</u>any and massacred to the last man.

Following this military disaster, which was a re-run of many similar ones suffered by the Imperial Russian army in the 19th century, the Bolshevik military command of the Caucasus began to prepare a massive military expedition into the mountains of Upper Dā<u>gh</u>istān with the mission to crush the rebellion once and for all. The new Red Army force under the command of Todorskii was supported by the pro-Russian and pro-Bolshevik mountaineer fighters (Red Partisans), who had distinguished themselves in the struggle against the White Army of General Denikin. The Red Partisans took an active part in the ensuing hostilities and were instrumental in relieving the Red Army garrisons besieged at <u>Kh</u>unza<u>kh</u> and Gunīb. Intent on quelling the rebellion at any cost, the Red Army command continued to pour more reinforcements into Dā<u>gh</u>istān. They were deployed against the rebel army at <u>Gh</u>imrāḥ (Gimry), Botli<u>kh</u> and Arakany, which counted some 3,500 fighters among its ranks. The Red Army detachments continued to suffer heavy casualties (almost 400 men) at the hands of the rebels throughout November 1920; during that month the Red Army garrisons were effectively reduced to holding their positions at Gunīb and <u>Kh</u>unza<u>kh</u>. Their occasional punitive forays into the mountains failed to suppress the rebels, instead arousing the hatred of the local population, which actively supported the rebels. The loss of the élite "First Model Revolutionary Discipline Rifle Regiment" near Botli<u>kh</u> in late November 1920 was a dramatic evidence of Red Army's inability to achieve its strategic objectives as well as the counterproductive nature of its scorched-earth policy against the civilian population. On the other hand, the reversals suffered by the Red Army infused the rebel forces with confidence, and gave them much-needed supplies and ammunition. In the end, the Red Army regiments led by Na<u>dj</u>m al-Dīn Samurskii were forced to seek refuge in their last remaining strongholds at Gunīb and <u>Kh</u>unza<u>kh</u>. Their siege by the rebel army lasted for two months, during which the Red Army fighters suffered terrible deprivations. At the end of 1920, the Red Army command made another attempt to quash the rebellion. Fresh Red Army divisions from Russia and Ā<u>dh</u>arbāy<u>dj</u>ān were dispatched into the region with the orders to cut the rebels off from their supply base in Čečnya, to punish the local population for their co-operation with the rebel force, and to surround and eliminate the enemy force. Valley after valley was occupied by the fresh Red Army troops and a renewed scorched-earth policy applied to the conquered villages, forcing the rebels to withdraw ever deeper into the barren mountains. Supported by armoured vehicles, the Red Army scored an important victory in early January 1921 at <u>Kh</u>od<u>zh</u>al-Ma<u>kh</u>i. The remaining rebels, some 1,000 men, retreated to the *aul* of Gergebil, where they took their final stand against the superior Red Army force. In the course of the all-out advance that began on 7 January, the Red Army forces suffered heavy casualties, and were still unable to capture the well-fortified *aul* until 26 January 1921. In the course of the siege, the Red Army units lost a total of 877 men, with the rebels' casualties probably twice, if not more that number. The remaining rebel forces evacuated the area around Gergebil and retreated to Arakany and <u>Gh</u>imrāḥ (Gimry). Arakany was captured by a Red Army unit on 14 February 1921 after a fierce hand-to-hand street battle, leaving most of Upper Dā<u>gh</u>istān under Soviet control. Gimry, an almost impregnable mountain fortress and the birthplace of <u>Sh</u>āmil, remained the last rebel stronghold. Due to its natural defences, it could only be forced to surrender by around-the-clock artillery fire. Within a week, 90% of the buildings in the *aul* were reduced to rubble. The rebels responded by lightning night raids against the artillery units positioned around the village.

After the capture of Gimry on 17 February 1921, its surviving defenders withdrew to western Dā<u>gh</u>istān. The Soviet victory was due in part to the fall to the Soviets of the independent Georgian Republic in late February 1921, which left the rebel forces exposed to Red Army attacks from Georgian territory, now firmly under Soviet control. The last rebel detachment led by Colonel <u>Dj</u>aʿfarov counted some 250 to 300 men, including a few surviving leaders of the rebellion, such as the "war minister" Colonel ʿAlī<u>kh</u>ānov and Lieutenant Abakarov. They assembled at the *aul* of Gidatl, the birthplace of their resistance movement, in April 1921. The *aul* fell in May after several days of fierce fighting. Some rebel commanders managed to escape, only to be hunted down, captured and executed by the Soviet interior troops within the next few years. Of the principal figures of the Dā<u>gh</u>istān rebellion, only Saʿīd-Bek, great-grandson of Imām <u>Sh</u>āmil, was able to make his way to Turkey.

The war between the Soviets and their Muslim opponents was accompanied by atrocities on both sides. The bodies of the fallen Red Army combatants were routinely mutilated by the rebels in response to their indiscriminate violence against the population of the *auls* suspected of supporting the guerrillas. As a result of several years of hostilities, most of Dā<u>gh</u>istān lay in ruins; it took more than a decade of strenuous effort to rebuild the country. The brutal suppression of Dā<u>gh</u>istān's bid for independence left a legacy of mutual hatred between the local population and the Soviets. This hatred manifested itself in the series of small-scale uprisings that continued throughout the late 1920s and early 1930s.

n. *"Class struggle" and Communist purges in Čečnya and Ingu<u>sh</u>etia, 1920-38*

In Čečnya and Ingu<u>sh</u>etia, now firmly under Soviet

control, the Muslim population was in no position to participate actively in the Dāg̲h̲istān rebellion, although some minor disturbances did take place on the border between Čečnya and the rebel-controlled parts of Dāg̲h̲istān. In Čečnya, tensions between traditional leaders and pro-Communist elements came to the fore in the course of public debates over the future of the Autonomous Mountain Soviet Socialist Republic, which was proclaimed on 17 November 1920. It included the territories of present-day Čečnya, Ingus̲h̲etia, Ossetia, Kabarda, Balkaria and Ḳaračay.

The government of the infant republic was dominated by revolutionary-minded intellectuals, who had supported the Bolsheviks from the early days of the February Revolution in Russia and were willing to co-operate with the Soviets in return for domestic autonomy. Under Lenin, the Russian political leadership was ready to accommodate their nationalist agendas and grant them independence *vis-à-vis* the Bolshevik régime in Moscow. The secularised revolutionary leaders of the Mountain Republic faced opposition from the more religiously-minded political factions, whom Bolshevik sources described as "supporters of the *S̲h̲arīʿa*" (*s̲h̲ariatisty*). At issue was the role and scope of the *S̲h̲arīʿa* legislation in the life of the new state. The *s̲h̲ariatisty* demanded the full and unconditional implementation of *S̲h̲arīʿa* legislation in all spheres of public life, whereas their leftist opponents sought to restrict it to the realm of private conviction and prohibit its public dissemination. The leftists eventually triumphed over the supporters of the *S̲h̲arīʿa* and declared Communist values and secular legislation to be the only law of the land. In August 1922, a decree issued by the Central Committee of the Soviet Mountain Republic officially abolished local *S̲h̲arīʿa* courts, although in Čečnya and Ingus̲h̲etia they remained active until 1926.

Gradually, the struggle against the *S̲h̲arīʿa* turned into a concerted political campaign against its learned exponents, the *ʿulamāʾ*. Since, by virtue of their special status in mountaineer society Muslim scholars continued to dominate local councils (soviets) in the Čečen and Ingus̲h̲ countryside, in September 1921 the Communist Central Committee based in Grozny issued a decree replacing local Soviets with Bolshevik-dominated revolutionary committees (*revkoms*). The anti-clerical campaign unleashed by the Bolsheviks was aimed at reducing the influence of traditional Muslim leaders on the masses and at isolating them politically. Some Muslim scholars sought to retain their social roles by cooperating with the Soviets. Among them was the Ṣūfī *s̲h̲ayk̲h̲* ʿAlī Mitaev. As the son of the renowned founder of the Bamatgirey *wird* (a branch of the Kunta Ḥād̲j̲d̲j̲ī *ṭarīḳa*), Mitaev enjoyed wide popularity among the Čečens and Ingus̲h̲. A veteran of the revolutionary war against the White Army, the Bolsheviks considered him reliable enough to appoint to the Revolutionary Committee of the Čečen *oblast'*. Once a month, he is said to have arrived at its meetings in Grozny accompanied by thirty mounted disciples (*murīd*s), who patiently waited for him outside the Communist Party headquarters until the end of the meeting. ʿAlī Mitaev's political agenda included the demand for an autonomous Mountain Republic under the rule of the *S̲h̲arīʿa*.

In 1924, the Bolshevik party, now headed by Stalin, embarked on a campaign to curtail national autonomies and subject them to the direct rule of the Central Committee of the Communist Party in Moscow. That year witnessed the dismantling of the Soviet Mountain Republic and the creation of a number of regional autonomies, Ḳaračay-Circassia, Kabarda-Balkaria, Adyg̲h̲ea, Čečnya, Ingus̲h̲etia and North Ossetia. This political manoeuvre was followed by a campaign to disarm the mountaineer communities, which was rightly seen by the mountaineers as a prelude to a new wave of repression. To forestall any possibility of rebellion, the communist security agency (OGPU, the forerunner of the KGB) accused many former members of the governing bodies of the Mountain Republic of disloyalty to the Communist party and of fomenting an armed rebellion against the Soviet authorities of Čečnya and Ingus̲h̲etia. Among those implicated in the "anti-party activities" was ʿAlī Mitaev. He was enticed into a trap by OGPU operatives, arrested and executed in 1925. The OGPU also arrested the prominent Naḳs̲h̲bandī elder and Islamic scholar Sugaip-Mullā Gaysumov. His life was spared, due in part to his old age and his active role in the struggle against the White Army. However, as with most members of the *ʿulamāʾ* class, he was to be kept under close police surveillance.

From that time on, the OGPU pursued a relentless campaign to isolate and neutralise the Muslim "clergy" of Čečnya, Ingus̲h̲etia and Dāg̲h̲istān as well as other autonomous republics of the northern Caucasus. Many prominent local scholars versed in Arabic and Islamic culture were arrested on trumped-up charges of conspiracy, espionage or membership in the parties and factions that had been condemned by the Central Committee of the Russian Communist Party as "deviant" or "dangerous". Later on, in 1926, the local party cadre, including the President of the Central Executive Committee of Čečnya, Tas̲h̲temīr Elderk̲h̲anov and his several aides, were accused of sympathising with the "reactionary clergy" and "bourgeois nationalists" and removed from their offices. They were replaced with Russian party apparatchiks, such as Ivanov and Černoglaz, whose wanton disrespect for local customs and beliefs and fervid implementation of anti-religious policies triggered several small-scale uprisings, which were brutally suppressed by the Soviet interior troops. Many participants of these movements, including those responsible for the assassination of Ivanov and Černoglaz, belonged to the local *wird*s, primarily those of Kunta Ḥād̲j̲d̲j̲ī and Baṭalḥād̲j̲d̲j̲ī. In a sense, the "*ṭarīḳat* conspiracy" was an invention of Černoglaz, who expected to receive substantial awards and promotion from the Central Committee of the Soviet Communist Party for "unmasking" it. His assassination at the hands of Kunta Ḥād̲j̲d̲j̲ī *ṭarīḳa* members was an act of revenge for his dogged persecution of its leaders and ruthless implementation of anti-religious policies.

This act triggered a series of new persecutions against the members of the implicated *ṭuruḳ* and their leaders, whom the Soviet authorities viewed as the bastions of "religious fanaticism" and "reactionary ideology". In less than one month, the OGPU forces arrested 300 Čečens, Ingus̲h̲ and Dāg̲h̲istānīs, including 39 religious leaders, and accused them of plotting an armed rebellion under "religious and nationalist banners". Simultaneously, the Soviet administration of the northern Caucasus sought to undermine the economic foundations of the *ʿulamāʾ* class by confiscating local religious endowments and prohibiting the collection of the *zakāt* [*q.v.*]. These measures, combined with the introduction of the hated *kolk̲h̲oz*s and crackdown on the *kulak*s (wealthy peasants) by the Soviet authorities, provoked a wave of local uprisings and unrest that continued throughout 1929-30. Some of the uprisings were led by the former Red Partisans, such as S̲h̲ita Istamulov and his brother Ḥasan of the village of S̲h̲ali in Čečnya. On 5 December 1936, the Čečen-Ingus̲h̲ Autonomous Region (*oblast'*) was "upgraded" to the status of an autonomous republic. This act was accompanied by another wave of reprisals against the so-called "anti-Soviet elements" of local societies. In the process, the NKVD (the Peoples' Commissariat of Internal Affairs) forces rounded up and imprisoned thousands of men and women. Most of the arrested were tried under Article 58 of the Soviet criminal code, which envisaged punishments by death and hard labour for such crimes as treason, espionage, fomenting an armed rebellion, sabotage, terrorism, anti-Soviet propaganda, etc. Hundreds of mountaineers were executed; others were sent to Siberia or concentration camps. Some Čečen and Ingus̲h̲ men escaped into the mountains, from where they launched revenge attacks against NKVD operatives and Communist Party functionaries. A decade of political purges left the Čečen and Ingus̲h̲ population demoralised and exhausted by the unequal struggle against the Soviet state and its giant apparatus of political repression. The ranks of the traditional religious leaders were decimated, while those who survived the horrors of Stalin's extermination campaigns were either forced underground or placed under the close surveillance of the Communist secret police.

o. *World War II and the mass deportation*

Against all odds, resistance to Soviet rule continued throughout the 1930s under the leadership of some members of the Soviet-educated intelligentsia, whose goal was to free their country of the Soviet yoke. Inspired by the Red Army reversals during the Finno-Soviet war of 1939-40, a former Čečen writer and party official, Ḥasan Israilov, started an armed insurrection in the remote mountain area of Galančož, near S̲h̲atoi.

His movement received a new impetus after Nazi Germany began a large-scale military operation against the Soviets on the eastern front and in the Caucasus. In February 1942, when the German troops approached the Russian city of Taganrog, approximately 350 miles from the Čečen-Ingus̲h̲ Republic, another rebel group headed by Mairbek S̲h̲eripov joined Israilov's insurrection. To suppress it, the Soviet military command resorted to an indiscriminate bombing of Čečen villages in the areas under rebel control. In 1943-4, Stalin and his Politburo, accomplished what some Russian military rulers (General Ermolov) and radical politicians (Pavel Pestel, a leader of the "Decembrist" movement) had only dreamed of a century earlier—a massive expulsion of the "hostile" mountain population to Russia and Siberia with the intention of eradicating its resistance to Russian rule. In 1943, a Communist Party decree abolished the Čečen-Ingus̲h̲ Republic, along with the neighbouring republics of Ḳaračay and Balkaria. The abolition was justified by the fact that the population of these republics had not only "co-operated" with the Nazis, but also "invited" them to conquer their lands and promised them full support. While the German troops had indeed occupied briefly the lands of the Ḳaračays and Balkars, they had never set foot on Čečen-Ingus̲h̲ territory. In any event, it made absolutely no legal sense to hold entire nations responsible for the "co-operation" with Germany of some of its representatives. However, the legal issues pertaining to the deportation of mountain nations were of no concern to Stalin and his henchmen (the deportation of the mountaineers was organised and executed by the NKVD chief Lavrentii Beria). They were determined

to punish the mountaineers for their long resistance to the cruel and arbitrary Communist rule and for their continuing struggle for freedom and independence. In late 1943-early 1944, the population of four Caucasian nations, Čečens, Ingus̲h̲, Balkars and Ḳaračays—men, women and children—were rounded up *en masse* by special Red Army detachments, placed in freight cars and transported to Central Asia. Only three-quarters (some say 50%) of the deported Čečens and Ingus̲h̲ are said to have reached their destination. The rest died *en route* of disease, crowded conditions and starvation. The survivors were placed in special settlements where they remained under the close surveillance of the forces of the Soviet Ministry of Internal Affairs until the end of exile in 1957. Those few Čečens and Ingus̲h̲ who were able to escape into the mountains, continued an *abrek*-style resistance to the Soviets by assassinating Red Army and police officers, robbing and burning down the farms of new settlers from Russia and neighbouring republics, engaging in sabotage, etc.

Deprived of the benefits of culture and education, many members of the exiled nations turned to Islam for consolation and guidance. For many, Islam became a badge of honour and a powerful source of identity and resistance to the Communist régime's attempts to erase any distinguishing ethnic and religious characteristics of its subjects. As a result, during the years of exile, the position of traditional religious leaders, which had been undermined by two decades of Communist rule and by competition from secular nationalists, was reinforced. This is especially true of the exiled Čečens and Ingus̲h̲, among whom the traditional Ṣūfī *wird*s remained active throughout the exile. Moreover, a new *wird* named after Vis (Uways) Ḥādjdjī, a branch of the Čim Mīrzā Ḥādjdjī *silsila*, is said to have come into being during this period. Ṣūfism survived also among the exiled Ḳaračays, many of whom were affiliated with the local branch of the Naḳs̲h̲bandiyya *ṭarīḳa*. At the same time, there is no evidence to support the oft-repeated claims that, in the 1960s, after the return from Central Asia, from 90% to 95% of the Čečen and Ingus̲h̲ believers were affiliated with a Ṣūfī *ṭarīḳa*. Given the fact that this period coincided with Khrus̲h̲čev's campaign to crack down on "religious superstitions" in all Soviet republics and that leaders of the atheist campaign tended to provide grossly inflated statistics in order to secure additional resources from the Communist Party authorities, such statements have to be treated with extreme caution.

The exile lasted for thirteen years for the Čečens and Ingus̲h̲ and fourteen for the Balkars and Ḳaračays. In January 1957, the Twentieth Communist Party Congress, presided over by Nikita Khrus̲h̲čev, declared the "rehabilitation" of the four deported mountain nations along with the other victims of Stalin's terror, namely, the Kalmuks, the Crimean Tatars and the Volga Germans. The Čečens, Ingus̲h̲, Ḳaračays and Balkars were allowed to return to their native lands and their autonomous republics were re-established by the Soviet government. Upon arrival, many exiles found their lands and houses occupied by the people who were resettled there on Stalin's orders. This created a fertile ground for conflicts over land between the new settlers and the returning indigenous population. Thus in Ingushetia, the lands that had been vacated by the exiled Ingush population were occupied by the settlers from neighbouring North Ossetia. With the weakening of the Soviet state in the late 1980s, the long-standing conflict between these two ethnic groups escalated into violence and bloodshed to the extent that the Soviet government was forced to send regular army units to the area in order to separate the combatants. In Čečnya, the majority of new settlers were Russian Cossacks from the neighbouring Stavropol' region (*krai*). The Russo-Čečen military conflicts of 1994-6 and 1999-2002 led to an upsurge of Čečen nationalism and anti-Russian sentiment. As a result, many Cossack families were forced to flee to Russia along with thousands of Russian and Ukrainian families that had resided in Čečnya's urban centres, especially in Grozny and Gudermes.

p. *Conclusion*

The developments in the Caucasus following the dissolution of the Soviet Union in December 1991 cannot be detailed here, especially since many aspects of local social and political life are still in flux and require a careful analysis. In the absence of precise data and opportunities for on-site research, any general conclusions are at best premature. The old biases and stereotypes of Soviet historiography are now being replaced by new ones. They spring from the proliferation of nationalist mythologies associated with the process of nation-building and forging new religious and national identities. Unfortunately, despite the opening up of the area to Western scholars in the aftermath of the collapse of the Soviet régime, the ongoing warfare and continuing hostage-taking in various parts of the Caucasus, most notably in Čečnya, Ingushetia, Dāghistān, Ḳarābāgh, Abkhāzia and Ossetia, make research trips to the area extremely dangerous. In many senses, the Caucasus has all the typical characteristics of the so-called "post-Soviet" political, social and economic space, i.e. general political instability, near-disastrous economic conditions resulting from a steep decline in industrial and agricultural output, high unemployment and crime rates, a feeling of nostalgia for the stability and certainties of the late Soviet era, corruption at all levels of the state apparatus, etc.

Since the disintegration of the Soviet Union, the political landscape of the area has been determined by several military conflicts, of which the two Russo-Čečen wars, the war between Abkhāzia and Georgia and the struggle for [Nagorno-]Ḳarābāgh [*q.v.*] between Armenia and Ādharbāydjān, deserve special mention. In all these cases, religion plays an important role, at least on the rhetorical level, as the parties to the conflict adhere to different religious traditions, i.e. "Christian" Russia versus "Muslim" Čečnya; "Muslim" Abkhāzia versus "Christian" Georgia; "Christian" Armenia versus "Muslim" Ādharbāydjān. As the political space in the new ethnic formations is being contested by multiple forces and factions, Islam has come to serve as a powerful source of rhetoric and legitimacy for the participants. Furthermore, different political factions uphold different interpretations of Islam, which further complicates the local discursive landscape.

So far, the most prominent and consequential divide has been between the supporters of "traditional" Islam and the so-called "Wahhābīs". The former emphasise loyalty to the local version of Islamic religion as explained and maintained by mountaineer *ʿulamāʾ* and Ṣūfī elders (*ustādhs*). The "traditionalists" encourage the reverence of local saints, the continuing use of the local customs (*ʿādāt*), participation in Ṣūfī rituals and respect for the traditional clan structure. The "Wahhābīs", who style themselves *salafiyyūn* [see SALAFIYYA], claim to follow the teaching of Ibn ʿAbd al-Wahhāb [*q.v.*] and its modernised version upheld by Suʿūdī-based scholars. They are particularly active in Čečnya and Dāghistān. In 1996-9, in the Buynaksk region of Dāghistān, several local "Wahhābī" groups attempted to create small enclaves of *Sharīʿa* rule. Their leaders declared their independence of the official Dāghistānī government at Makhač-ḳalʿe [*q.v.*]. In late 1999, they fought against Russian troops, which had been sent to suppress them, alongside the Čečen Wahhābīs led by the field commander, *Amīr* Shāmil Basaev. According to the Caucasian "Wahhābīs", their teaching represents the "pure and simple" Islam of the primaeval Muslim community. They demand that their followers and Muslims at large strictly adhere to their version of the "Islamic" dress code (described as "Arab" by its opponents) for men and women, carefully observe the basic Muslim rites and restrictions and participate in *djihād* against the "enemies" of the Muslim community worldwide. The supporters of Caucasian "Wahhābism" reject as *bidʿa* [*q.v.*] many key elements of "traditional" Caucasian Islam, namely, belief in the supernatural and intercessory powers of Ṣūfī *shaykhs* and *ustādhs*, the practice of *dhikr* and the use of the local *ʿādāt* alongside the *Sharīʿa*.

To what extent "Wahhābism" can be seen as a mere foreign import (as argued by its detractors), deliberately introduced into the Caucasus by missionaries and volunteer fighters (*mudjāhidūn*) from Suʿūdī Arabia, the Arab states of the Gulf, Afghānistān and Pākistān, and cultivated through an elaborate system of material incentives and sophisticated propaganda, remains unclear. One cannot deny that "Wahhābism" has found a wide following among the Čečen and Ingush youth, as well as some middle-aged men and women, whose lives have been shattered by the brutality of the Russo-Čečen wars. By infusing its followers with a sense of camaraderie and common cause that goes beyond the immediate goals of nationhood and independence, "Wahhābism" serves as a powerful source of identity and mobilisation that renders it especially well suited for the trying times of war. At the same time, by its sweeping rejection of local customs and practices, Caucasian "Wahhābism" inevitably creates a rift between different groups of mountaineers. Often, but not always, this rift is generational in its nature. The fact that "Wahhābism" has been embraced by the younger generation of Čečen military and political leaders (Shāmil Basaev, Mowladi Udugov, Arbi Baraev, etc.) in opposition to the "Ṣūfī" Islam of the supporters of President Maskhadov may indicate that the former are eager to free themselves from the traditional sources of legitimacy and authority in order to enter into a dialogue with, and perhaps secure assistance from, the Muslim community worldwide.

Bibliography: See the *Bibls.* to the articles referred to in the text. One may also consult the sources listed below:

1. General history. Muriel Atkin, *Russian expansion in the Caucasus to 1813*, in M. Rywkin (ed.), *Russian colonial expansion to 1917*, London and New York 1900, 139-87 (a standard Western survey of the early stages of the conquest); M. Autlev, *Adygi i russikie*, Krasnodar 2000 (a review of the history of the Čerkes-Russian relations over the past 400 years from a Communist vantage point); M. Bennigsen-Broxup (ed.), *The North Caucasus barrier*, London 1992 (a collective monograph on various aspects of the history of the northern Caucasus written from a viewpoint sympathetic to the struggle of the local population against the Russian advance); V. Degoev, *Bolʾshaya igra na Kavkaze*, Moscow 2001 (a revisionist view of the military conflicts in the Caucasus, which tries to place them

in a global context); A. Fadeev, *Rossia i Kavkaz v pervoi treti XIX v.*, Moscow 1960 (a general overview of the history of the Caucasus until 1840 that emphasises the role of European powers in supporting and perpetuating mountaineer resistance to Russian conquest); Ya. Gordin, *Kavkaz: zemlia i krov'*, St. Petersburg 2000 (an essay on the moral and ethical implications of the Caucasian war for Russia and Russian history by a liberal Russian thinker); G. Mirfenderski, *A diplomatic history of the Caspian Sea*, New York 2001 (a collection of essays pertaining to the Russo-Persian contacts in and around the Caspian Sea from the 18th century to the present day); Kh.M. Ibragimbekov, *Kavkaz v Krymskoi Voine (1853-1856)*, Moscow 1971 (a detailed account of the impact of the Crimean War on the Caucasus, which emphasises the role of the local population in thwarting the Ottoman advance and condemns the "plotting" of British agents in Circassia); V.N. Ratushniak *et al.* (eds.), *Kavkazskaia voina: uroki istorii i sovremennost'*, Krasnodar 1995 (an attempt to reassess the history of the Caucasus in the light of the political and ideological agendas of post-Communist Russian society); D. Makarov, *Ofitsial'nyi i neofitsial'nyi islam v Dagestane*, Moscow 2002 (an attempt to examine the current political situation in the north Caucasus through the prism of the conflict between the Salafīs and Ṣūfīs in post-Soviet Dāghistān); M. Mamakaev, *Čečenskii taip (rod) v period ego razlozheniya*, Grozny 1973 (a standard account of the social structure of Čečen society from a Marxist viewpoint); A. Naročnitskii (ed.), *Istoria narodov Severnogo Kavkaza (konets XVIII v.-1917 g.)*, Moscow 1988 (the most comprehensive Soviet account of the history of the area with special emphasis on "class struggle" within Caucasian societies and the "progressive" elements of Russian culture that influenced them); N. Pokrovskii, *Kavkazskie voiny i imamam Shamila*, Moscow 2000 (a comprehensive study of the Caucasian societies and Muslim struggle against the Russian conquest by an unorthodox Soviet historian, who treats Shāmil and his predecessors as heroes of a national liberation struggle); Y. Ro'i, *Islam in the Soviet Union*, New York 2000 (a well-documented study of the status of the Muslim minorities of the Soviet Union based largely on the NKVD/KGB archives; it is somewhat marred by the author's poor knowledge of Islam and its history); F. Shčerbina, *Istoria Kubanskogo kazač'iago voiska*, ii, Ekaterinodar 1913 (a detailed account of the Russian conquest of the northern Caucasus by a Kuban Cossack historian); A. Smirnov, *Politika Rossii na Kavkaze v XVI-XIX vekakh*, Moscow 1958 (a study of the Russian expansion in the Caucasus in the 16th-19th centuries from the perspective of a Stalinist historian); *Osada Kavkaza*, St. Petersburg 2000 (a collection of memoirs of seven Russian officers who took an active part in the conquest of the Caucasus); V. Tishkov, *Obshčestvo v vooruzhennom konflike*, Moscow 2001 (a rather impressionistic study of the recent Russo-Čečen conflict by the former Minister for the Nationalities of the Russian Federation; the author's promise, in his introduction, to provide new theoretical approaches to the conflict and its causes is not realised in the subsequent narrative).

2. Studies of individual personalities and movements. V. Akaev, *Shaykh Kunta Khadzhi: zhizn' i učenie*, Groznyi 1994 (a reassessment of the figure of Kunta Ḥādjdjī by a Čečen historian); T. Barrett, *Crossing the boundaries. The trading frontiers of the Terek Cossacks*, in D. Brower and E. Lazzerini (eds.), *Russia's Orient*, Bloomington and Indianapolis 1997, 227-48 (an illuminating study of the mutually beneficial trade relations between the Terek Cossacks and the mountaineers); V. Degoev, *Imām Shāmil: prorok, vlastitel', voin*, Moscow 2001 (an attempt to revise the traditional Russian/Soviet views of Shāmil's imāmate); L. Derluguian, *The unlikely abolitionists. The Russian struggle against the slave trade in the Caucasus (1800-1864)*, Ph.D. diss., SUNY Binghamton 1997, unpubl. (a thorough and informative examination of the slave trade in the Caucasus and the Russian attempts to abolish it); A. Knysh, *Sufism as an explanatory paradigm. The issue of the motivations of Sufi movements in Russian and Western historiography*, in *WI*, xlii/2, (2002), 1-35 (a critical examination of the role of Ṣūfism in the Muslim resistance to the Russian conquest of the Caucasus); Dž. Mesxidze, *Die Rolle des Islams beim Kampf um die staatliche Eigenständigkeit Tschetscheniens und Inguschetiens 1917-1925*, in A. von Kügelgen, M. Kemper and A. Frank (eds.), *Muslim culture in Russia and Central Asia from the 18th to the early 20th centuries*, ii, Berlin 1998, 457-81 (a study of the role of the learned classes of Čečen and Ingush societies in nation-building after the Russian revolution); G. Yemelianova, *Sufism and politics in the North Caucasus*, in *Nationalities Papers*, xxix/4 (2001), 661-88 (a recent attempt to explain the conflicts and power struggle in contemporary Dāghistān and Čečnya by the activities of the local Ṣūfī orders). (A. Knysh)

ḲABṬŪRNUH, Banu 'l-, a family of 5th/11th-century al-Andalus whose Arabic *nasab* was the Banū Sa'īd.

They comprised three brothers who were poets and also secretaries to the Afṭasid prince of Badajoz, Abū Ḥafṣ 'Umar al-Mutawakkil (464-88/1072-95 [*q.v.* and AFṬASIDS]), and then were subsequently in the chancery of the Almoravids. The *laḳab* of al-Ḳabṭūrnuh (according to other sources, al-Ḳabṭūrnah or al-Ḳubṭūrnuh) suggests an Hispanic origin, probably one stemming from the Low Latin **capiturnus* "having a large head". The first of the three brothers, Abū Muḥammad Ṭalḥa (Ibn al-Abbār, no. 259) is the author of several fragments, of an epicurean and festive type, as well as three fragments elegising his wife, Umm al-Faḍl. The second brother, Abū Bakr 'Abd al-'Azīz (Ibn al-Abbār, no. 1743), is the best known of them; he has left behind the most substantial written legacy, including a poem of 14 verses recounting nostalgically the days of his youth at Cordova, plus other poetic and prose fragments, including a short *risāla* in an artificial style (ed. Makkī, in *RIEIM*, vii-viii, 186-8). Only a few very rare verses remain from the third brother, Abu 'l-Ḥasan Muḥammad. The family's poetry is often considered as exemplifying the Andalusī poetry of the Taifas period [see MULŪK AL-ṬAWĀ'IF. 2], hedonist in tone and in a brilliant but rather mannered style.

Bibliography: Ibn Bassām, *Dhakhīra*, ed. Iḥsān 'Abbās, 8 vols. Beirut 1979, ii/2, 752-73; Ibn Khāḳān, *Ḳalā'id*, ed. M.Ṭ. Ibn 'Ashūr, Tunis 1990, 355-69 (both essential); Ibn al-Khaṭīb, *Iḥāṭa*, ed. 'A.A. 'Inān, 4 vols. Cairo 1973, i, 520-3; Maḳḳarī, *Nafḥ al-ṭīb*, ed. 'Abbās, 8 vols. Beirut 1968, i, 634-9; F. Velázquez, *Tres poetas de Badajoz: los Banū l-Qabṭūrnu, según la "Ihāṭa" de Ibn al-Jaṭīb*, in *Annuario de Estudios Filológicas (Universidad de Extramadura)*, xxi (1998), 441-6. (I. Ferrando)

ḲADAMGĀH (a. and p.), literally "place of the [imprint of the] foot", a village in Khurāsān, on the highway to Mashhad and some 20 km/12 miles east of Nī<u>sh</u>āpūr at the southern edge of the Kūh-i Bīnālūd (lat. 36° 07' N., long. 59° 00' E.). It is locally famed as a *ziyāratgāh* or place of pilgrimage, since the Eighth Imām of the <u>Sh</u>īʿa, ʿAlī al-Riḍā [*q.v.*], is said to have halted there and left the imprint of his foot on a stone, henceforth to be regarded with reverence; see Bess A. Donaldson, *The wild rue. A study of Muhammadan magic and folklore in Iran*, London 1938, 59, 148-9).

The concept of sacred imprints on rocks, on the roof and walls of caves, etc., is widespread across the Old World, certainly from the Middle East to South and South-East Asia (in the latter regions, with e.g. footprints of the Buddha, as at Adam's Peak, Ceylon). In the Islamic lands, imprints of the Prophet Muḥammad's foot are early found all over the Arab lands, and subsequently in Ottoman Turkey, and are especial objects of veneration in Muslim India (as likewise are imprints of holy men in non-Muslim India); see ḲADAM <u>SH</u>ARĪF and also Annemarie Schimmel, *And Muhammad is His Messenger. The veneration of the Prophet in Islamic piety*, Chapel Hill, N.C. 1985, 42-3.

There are in fact numerous similar *ḳadamgāhs* or shrines of saints and holy men, often but not always ʿAlids, apart from the one mentioned above near Nī<u>sh</u>āpūr, throughout Eastern Persia, Af<u>gh</u>ānistān and Northwestern India, including a footprint of the caliph ʿAlī b. ʿAbī Ṭālib at the (Sunnī) shrine of Mazār-i <u>Sh</u>arīf [*q.v.*] in northern Af<u>gh</u>ānistān. One should also mention *pan<u>dj</u>agāhs*, "places of the [imprint of the] palm of the hand", impressions of the hands of holy men. Thus in Kābul, to the east of the Bālā Ḥiṣār above the city, is the shrine of the Pan<u>dj</u>a-yi <u>Sh</u>āh Mardān ("Lord of Mankind", i.e. the Prophet Muḥammad) mentioned by the traveller Charles Masson (*Narrative of various journeys in Balochistan, Afghanistan, and the Panjab*, London 1842, ii, 236, iii, 93; and cf. R.D. McChesney, *Waqf in Central Asia. Four hundred years in the history of a Muslim shrine, 1480-1889*, Princeton 1991, 226).

Bibliography: Given in the article.

(C.E. BOSWORTH)

ḲĀḌĪ-ZĀDE RŪMĪ, ṢALĀḤ AL-DĪN MŪSĀ b. Muḥammad b. Maḥmūd al-Rūmī, usually referred to as Ḳāḍī-zāde al-Rūmī or Mūsā Ḳāḍī-zāde al-Rūmī, lived *ca.* 760-*ca.* 835/1359-1432, dates derived from an early work written in 784/1382-3 and from his having outlived <u>Gh</u>iyā<u>th</u> al-Dīn al-Kā<u>sh</u>ī (d. 832/1429 [*q.v.*]), noted astronomer/mathematician from Bursa who played a substantial role in the Samarḳand observatory [see MARṢAD] of Ulu<u>gh</u> Beg [*q.v.*] and whose commentaries were used extensively as teaching texts for mathematics and astronomy.

After studying for a time in his native Bursa, where his father Maḥmūd was a prominent judge at the time of Sultan Murād I, Ḳāḍī-zāde travelled to Persia to pursue an education in the philosophical and mathematical sciences. There he studied with the famous theologian al-Sayyid al-<u>Sh</u>arīf al-<u>Dj</u>ur<u>dj</u>ānī [*q.v.*], probably at the court of Tīmūr in Samarḳand; this was, however, an unhappy experience for both parties with al-<u>Dj</u>ur<u>dj</u>ānī complaining of his student's infatuation with the mathematical sciences while Ḳāḍī-zāde made it known that his teacher was deficient in those subjects. After Tīmūr's death, Ḳāḍī-zāde found both a student and patron in Tīmūr's grandson Ulu<u>gh</u> Beg, also in Samarḳand. He became the head of the large *madrasa* there and Ulu<u>gh</u> Beg himself sometimes attended his lectures. Sometime later, *ca.* 823/1420, he collaborated with <u>Gh</u>iyā<u>th</u> al-Dīn al-Kā<u>sh</u>ī under the directorship and patronage of Ulu<u>gh</u> Beg to build the famous Samarḳand observatory and undertake its observational programmes. After al-Kā<u>sh</u>ī's death in 1429, he no doubt assumed additional responsibilities. By then he was assisted by the talented young ʿAlī Ḳū<u>sh</u><u>dj</u>ī [*q.v.*], who continued the observational programme after Ḳāḍī-zāde's death. Ḳū<u>sh</u><u>dj</u>ī's daughter would marry Ḳāḍī-zāde's son <u>Sh</u>ams al-Dīn; a grandson of this union was the famous Ottoman astronomer/mathematician Mīrim Čelebī (d. 931/1525).

Ḳāḍī-zāde was not noted for his innovations or creativity, and his works reflect this. He was most famous for his commentaries on al-<u>Dj</u>a<u>gh</u>mīnī's [*q.v.*] astronomical compendium *al-Mula<u>kh</u><u>kh</u>aṣ fī 'l-hayʾa* (814/1412) and <u>Sh</u>ams al-Dīn al-Samarḳandī's [*q.v.*] geometrical tract *A<u>sh</u>kāl al-taʾsīs* (completed 815/1412); the large number of extant manuscripts of both commentaries indicates their enduring popularity as teaching texts. A work on determining the value of Sin 1° is heavily dependent on the more mathematically accomplished al-Kā<u>sh</u>ī. His supercommentary on A<u>th</u>īr al-Dīn al-Abharī's [*q.v.*] *Hidāyat al-ḥikma* seems to be his only philosophical or theological work, though he did intend to write a refutation of parts of al-<u>Dj</u>ur<u>dj</u>ānī's famous commentary on al-Īdjī's *Mawāḳif*. The common attribution to Ḳāḍī-zāde of Biblioteca Medicea Laurenziana or. MS 271, a commentary on Naṣīr al-Dīn al-Ṭūsī's astronomical work *al-Ta<u>dh</u>kira*, is incorrect; it is actually by al-<u>Dj</u>ur<u>dj</u>ānī.

Bibliography: Ṭa<u>sh</u>köprüzāde, *al-<u>Sh</u>aḳāʾiḳ al-nuʿmāniyya*, Istanbul 1985, 14-17 (main biographical source); Ḥa<u>dj</u><u>dj</u>ī <u>Kh</u>alīfa, Istanbul 1941-3, 105, 137, 139, 859, 1819, 2029; Brockelmann, I, 468, 473, 511, II, 212, S I, 850, 865; G.P. Matvievskaya and B.A. Rozenfeld, *Matematiki i astronomi musulmanskogo srednevekov<u>ya</u> i i<u>kh</u> trudi (VIII-XVII vv.)*, Moscow 1983, ii, 487-9; E. İhsanoğlu *et al.*, *Osmanlı astronomi literatürü tarihi*, Istanbul 1997, i, 5-21 (full bibl.); idem, *Osmanlı matematik literatürü tarihi*, Istanbul 1999, i, 3-18; H. Dilgan, art, *Qāḍī Zāda al-Rūmī*, in *Dict. of Scientific Biography*, xi, 227-9; E.S. Kennedy, *A letter of Jamshīd al-Kāshī to his father*, in *Orientalia*, xxix (1960), 191-213; A. Sayılı, *The observatory in Islam*, Ankara 1960.

(F.J. RAGEP)

KAFAN (A.), "shroud".

In the Islamic world, a dying person was often forewarned of imminent death by a dream, or by a dream that an inhabitant of his town had had during the preceding days, to the effect that the Prophet or some other great figure like Abū Bakr, ʿUmar or ʿAlī, was waiting for him and he should get ready for the meeting. Since death is the natural goal of life, its approach should be managed calmly. When the death agony is imminent, the dying person pronounces the *<u>sh</u>ahāda* or profession of faith, whilst raising one finger of the right hand to re-affirm for the last time his belief in the unity of God. If he is too weak, someone close to him murmurs in his ear just as his father murmured to him at his birth. The corpse is washed, unless the dying person has washed himself in preparation, and then wrapped in three cloths, white shrouds, or cloths of any other colour except red, fastened very tightly. A professional enshrouder, *kaffān*, takes charge of this process using cloths woven by an *akfānī*. The shroud has often been acquired long before death by the deceased, the sole piece of property which he retains after his death, since it does not figure in what he leaves behind as inheritance. Only the corpse of a martyr killed in the way of *<u>dj</u>ihād* is not washed, but buried where he has fallen and in his bloodstained garments.

For great persons, the number of shrouds and their

value could increase considerably. At his death, the Fāṭimid vizier Ibn Killis [*q.v.*] was buried, at the expense of the caliph al-ʿAzīz, in fifty perfumed shrouds and cloths of various fibres, with a total value of 10,000 dīnārs (see al-Maḳrīzī, *Ittiʿāẓ al-ḥunafāʾ*, ed. Dj. Shayyāl, Cairo 1387/1967, i, 268-9; see also the store of Fāṭimid shrouds mentioned by al-Musabbiḥī, *Akhbār Miṣr*, ed. A.F. Sayyid and Th. Bianquis, Cairo 1978, 107). The fibres used in spinning these costly shrouds, and also the inscriptions on them—a politico-religious content in Fāṭimid Egypt, and often poetical, on the theme of the inevitability of death, in Būyid ʿIrāḳ—have been studied by both archaeologists and museum specialists (R. Gayraud, *al-Qarāfa al-kubrā, dernière demeure des Fāṭimides*, in M. Barrucand (ed.), *L'Egypte, son art et son histoire*, Paris 1999, 443-64; bibl. and characteristic texts in E. Garcin, *Le textile dans l'Islam médiéval, productions būyides et fāṭimides*, diss. DEA, Lumière-Lyon 2 1999, unpubl., 59-60).

The corpse was borne, on the same day, but rarely at night, on a simple bier, *naʿsh* (*wa-ḥumila naʿshuhu ʿalā ayd*^{in}, al-Musabbiḥī, *op. cit.*, 108) by men who would sometimes run: "If I am good, bear me speedily to God, and if I am bad, get rid of me quickly." A prayer was pronounced over the corpse near a mosque. Everyone would stand as the corpse passed by, even for the corpses of Jews and Christians (it was usual to be present at the funerals of important members of the other religious communities), out of respect for the angels accompanying it. It was even more meritorious to bear a corner of the bier. Sometimes the dead person was borne along without a bier, like a package wrapped in a white shroud, or conversely, the corpse could be carried in an open wooden coffin (*ṣandūḳ*, *tābūt*, also meaning cenotaph). The chroniclers mention this fact as a sign of respect felt for someone of a distinguished social group.

The corpse, wrapped in the shroud, is lowered into a tomb dug out for this purpose (see the detailed description of the types of Muslim tombs in Y. Raghib, *Structure de la tombe d'après le droit musulman*, in *Arabica*, xxxix [1992], 395-403). The shroud is then loosened so that the dead person can be at his ease, and the face is turned towards Mecca (archaeologists have found skeletons with *post mortem* fractures of the cervical vertebrae). Three handfuls of earth are thrown over the corpse, whilst pronouncing the words "We created you with this [earth], We give him back to it, and We will resurrect him anew" (cf. the myths of ancient Mesopotamia and Ḳurʾān, XXII, 5, XXX, 19, etc.). The cavity is filled with earth and pebbles, with an orifice left for the deceased to get water. From this point onwards, and until the palms planted on the tomb become dried up, the deceased is given over to interrogation by the angels of death preparatory to the Last Judgement [see ʿADHĀB AL-ḲABR].

Bibliography: M. Galal, *Essai d'observations sur les rites funéraire en Egypte actuelle*, in *REI*, xi (1937), 131-299; H. Laoust (tr.), *Le précis de droit d'Ibn Qudāma*, Beirut 1950, 45-9, s.v. "Les pratiques funéraires", a very detailed description of the Sunnī ritual for washing the corpse, enshrouding and inhumation; a shroud depicted in a Christian illuminated ms. of the 13th century at Mawṣil, in R. Canavelli (ed.), *La Méditerranée des Croisades*, Milan 2000, 138; a bier and shroud depicted in the illustrations of a *Shāh-nāma* from Tabrīz 1330-6, in B. Gray, *Persian painting*, Geneva 1961, 32. See also DJANĀZA, ḲABR, MAḲBARA, MAWT, and their *Bibls*. (TH. BIANQUIS)

ḲAFES (A., T.) "cage", the popular term in Ottoman Turkish usage for the area of the harem of the Ṭopḳapï palace in which Ottoman princes of the blood (*sheh-zādeler*) were confined from the early 17th century onwards.

In a more abstract sense, historians apply the same term to the system whereby the rights of claimants to the Ottoman throne were determined, as opposed to the "law of fratricide" which it was gradually superseding during this period. In the sources, the term is of late usage only (d'Ohsson uses the word in the plural; *Tableau de l'Empire ottoman*, vii, 101; ʿĀṣïm, *Tārīkh*, Istanbul n.d., ii, 32). Earlier and more widely attested, however, is the appellation Shimshīrlik (or Čimshīrlik "the box shrub") or Shimshīrlik odasï ("the boxwood chamber"), a reference to the little courtyard planted with box, at the north-east corner of the courtyard of the Wālide Sulṭān (Silaḥdār, *Tārīkh*, Istanbul 1928, ii, 297; Uzunçarşılı, *Saray*, 91; Rāshid, *Tārīkh*, Istanbul 1282/1865-6, ii, 2-3; Necipoğlu, *Topkapi Palace*, figs. 94, 168, 178). It consisted of a set of pavilions (twelve, according to d'Ohsson, who presents each as "comprising several rooms and surrounded by a high wall"), surmounted by cupolas, fitted with chimneys and windows which, for the preservation of sexual segregation, did not overlook the harem. Some were decorated with the mural tiles typical of the 17th century and with marble niches (Necipoğlu, 178). Similar arrangements existed in the palace of Edirne: the princes were transferred thither when the Sultan made it his residence.

Adult *sheh-zādeler* began living in the interior (*enderūn* [*q.v.*]) of Ṭopḳapï from the time, in the second half of the 16th century, when the practice of entrusting them with provincial governorships in Anatolia was partially and then totally abandoned. This then became the exclusive prerogative of the son of the reigning sovereign. On the other hand, on the accession of Aḥmed I, while still a minor (1603), the leading dignitaries of the state allowed his younger brother Muṣṭafā to live installed in a niche within the palace. Furthermore, on the death of the same ruler (1617), they preferred this brother to succeed him rather than his eldest son ʿOthmān, who was still very young (Pecewī, *Tārīkh*, Istanbul 1283/1866-7, ii, 360-1; Kātib Čelebi, *Fedhleke*, Istanbul 1281/1864-5, i, 385). Having thus emerged from his confinement, Muṣṭafā I was deposed after an initial reign of three months, on account of mental disorders; he "returned to his former apartments" (Naʿīmā, *Tārīkh*, Istanbul 1281/1864-5, ii, 163). He was brought out once again to be restored to the throne after the insurrection which resulted in the assassination of his nephew ʿOthmān II (May 1622). No more successful than the first, this second reign lasted only sixteen months and Muṣṭafā returned to his prison, where he died in 1639.

These events were the harbingers of important changes: henceforward, despite continuing attacks mounted by ʿOthmān II and Murād IV against their respective brothers—outdated practices denounced by public opinion—the brothers of reigning sovereigns were allowed to live, but were politically neutralised by rigorous seclusion in the most secure and secret area of the Palace. In parallel, despite the inclination of numerous sultans to promote one of their sons to the succession, the principle of seniority, made possible by the survival of the sultan's brothers, led, by gradual stages, to the establishment of a successorial system in the Ottoman dynasty: in the early 18th century, the chronicler Rāshid presents the eldest of the brothers of Meḥemmed IV, Süleymān II, who succeeded the deposed sultan in 1687, as "the august person who in his turn took charge of the sultanate (*nöbet-i salṭanat*), according to the order of birth" (*tertīb-i sinn-i wilādet üzre*, Rās̲h̲id, ii, 3). Silaḥdār confirms that seniority had become the rule when, on the occasion of the replacement of Muṣṭafā II, deposed in 1703, Aḥmed III, son of Meḥemmed IV, was preferred by the arbiters of the situation, on account of the "order of succession" (*tertīb-i nöbet*), as well as the qualities of the candidate, over the prince Ibrāhīm, a son of Aḥmed II who, furthermore, was still a minor (*Nuṣret-nāme*, ed. İ. Parmaksızoğlu, Istanbul 1962, ii, 177).

Another consequence of the establishment of the *ḳafes* was to promote, by constituting a reserve of legitimate candidates to the throne, the notion that the solution to political crises was not to be found only in the sacrifice of a number of senior dignitaries, serving as a "safety-fuse" for the reigning sultan; there was also the option of a change of sultan, a new accession (*d̲j̲ülūs*): the sovereign himself became a safety-fuse to the benefit of the superior entity constituted by the dynasty, his throne, like other positions of eminence in the empire, being nothing more than "an ejectable seat".

This was indeed an eccentric preparation for an eventual reign: total seclusion which could last several decades (see in Alderson, 36, the table of periods spend in the *ḳafes*, before their accession and after their eventual dethronement, by the twenty-three sultans concerned, from Muṣṭafā I to ʿAbd ül-Med̲j̲īd II). However, a distinction should be drawn, following the lead of d'Ohsson, between two categories of *s̲h̲eh-zādeler*: on the one hand, the sons of the reigning sultan who, while stringently kept apart from any political activity (and barred from procreation), were not altogether excluded from public life: on the contrary they participated in festivals which, when the case arose, were dedicated to them (circumcisions, the beginnings of education, etc.; cf. S. Faroqhi, *Crisis and change*, in H. Inalcik and D. Quataert (eds.), *An economic and social history of the Ottoman Empire*, Cambridge 1994, 613-14), or in official functions (Aḥmed III received the French ambassador, Andrezel, surrounded by his four sons; illustration by J.-B. Van Mour, reproduced in A. Boppe, *Les peintres du Bosphore au XVIIIe siècle*, Paris 1989, 29); and on the other hand, the other princes of the blood. To the latter alone the régime of the *ḳafes* was applied in full rigour. Furthermore, as soon as their father ceased to reign, the princes of the first category were relegated to the second: thus on leaving the prison where he had just spent 39 years, to ascend the throne in place of his deposed brother Meḥemmed IV, Süleymān II issued a *k̲h̲āṭṭ-i humāyūn* ordering the transfer to the same place of his displaced brother, the latter's two sons Muṣṭafā and Aḥmed, as well as his own younger brother Aḥmed (the future Aḥmed II) who had previously shared his prison (Silaḥdār, *Tārīk̲h̲*, ii, 298). Reduced to the company of their pages, their eunuchs and concubines who were not permitted to give birth, to male children in any case (on Ak̲h̲īretlik K̲h̲ānïm, fathered by ʿAbd ül-Ḥāmid I in the *ḳafes*, see Uzunçarşılı, 115), these princes were strictly cut off from the exterior, deprived of any experience of the world and of any useful education, neglected and despised (on succeeding his brother, Süleymān II appeared wearing an old *ʿanterī* robe and shod in heavy cavalry boots; Silaḥdār, *Tārīk̲h̲*, ii, 298). Some coped with their boredom by practising various manual occupations (Ohsson, vii, 102). Added to these inconveniences was the fearful threat which the suspicions of the reigning sultan constantly posed to the lives of his potential rivals. The anxiety which could be thus aroused among the latter is well illustrated by the attitudes of Ibrāhīm or of Süleymān II when invited to take the throne; both were convinced that this was a trick on the part of their respective brothers, Murād IV and Meḥemmed IV, to have them executed, and they stubbornly refused to leave their prison (Naʿīmā, *Tārīk̲h̲*, iii, 450-2; Silaḥdār, *Tārīk̲h̲*, ii, 198). It may be noted to what an extent the shadow of fratricide, although in fact no longer practised, continued to hang over the dynasty (as late as 1730, on leaving the throne, Aḥmed III entrusted to his nephew and successor Maḥmūd I, as "a trustee of God" the protection of his children (Ferāʿīd̲j̲izāde, *Güls̲h̲en-i maʿārif*, Istanbul 1252/1836-7, ii, 1251; ʿAbdī, *1730 Patrona Halil hakkından bir eser. Abdi Tarihi*, ed. F.R. Unat, Ankara 1943, 42). The vigilance of the Janissaries, anxious to maintain the freedom of manoeuvre guaranteed to them by a plethora of possible sultans, was the best safeguard of the sequestered princes: in 1632, rebellious Janissaries compelled Murād IV to show them that his brothers were still alive (Uzunçarşılı, 227-8). According to Bobovius, adapted by Girardin, 30-1, "*la milice est toujours leur tutrice*".

Chroniclers have often stressed the negative effects of the system on the competence and mental health of the sovereigns produced by it (blaming it in particular for some of the psychological disorders associated with Muṣṭafā I or with Ibrāhīm), but this "black legend" is doubtless to be treated with caution: the stringency of confinement certainly varied according to reigns and circumstances: only Muṣṭafā I, after his first deposition, or Ibrāhīm after his dethronement, are presented as being immured alive, "already interred" (Naʿīmā, ii, 218, iii, 330). In other cases, the links of princes with their reigning parent, between themselves and even with the outside world were not entirely severed: "Sultan Soliman, brother of the current emperor, has acquired universal esteem throughout the empire . . . and his renown has induced all ranks of the militia to declare themselves his protectors," Bobovius noted (122-3), with regard to the future Süleymān, disparaged as he was in other respects. Worth noting, on the other hand, is the energy displayed by Aḥmed II when, on emerging from 43 years of the *ḳafes* he inaugurated his brief reign (1691-5) (Silaḥdār, ii, 576-80). More generally, in the course of time a progressive humanisation of the *ḳafes* is observable, associated no doubt with the individual personality of certain sultans, but especially with the stabilisation of the new successorial system; during his 39 years on the throne, Meḥemmed IV (1648-87) made no further attempts to harm his two brothers, even going sometimes to speak with them (Uzunçarşılı, 96; Bobovius evokes "a fairly comfortable prison"). Several decades later, Aḥmed III showed himself respectful and amicable towards his brother Muṣṭafā II (1695-1703) whose place he took, not that this prevented the latter dying 140 days later in the *ḳafes*, "of nostalgia for the crown and for the throne" (Defterdār Ṣarï Meḥmed Pas̲h̲a, *Zübde-i weḳāyiʿāt*, ed. Özcan, Ankara 1995, 815, 835). When in 1730 it was the turn of Aḥmed III to be overthrown, the transfer of power between him and his nephew Maḥmūd I took place very smoothly: he kissed him on the forehead, while the other kissed his hand (Ferāʿīd̲j̲izāde, 1251). But it was not until the end of the 18th century that the régime was definitively relaxed: on the death of his father Muṣṭafā III in 1774, the future Selīm III was granted a considerable degree of freedom by his uncle ʿAbd ül-Ḥāmid I, enabling him in particular to correspond with Louis XVI (Uzunçarşılı,

Selim III'ün Veliaht'iken Fransa Kralı Lüi XVI ile muhabereleri, in *Belleten*, ii [1938], 191-246; S. Munir, *Louis XVI et le sultan Selim III, in Revue d'Histoire diplomatique*, xxvi [1912], 516-48). Similarly, ʿAbd ül-Medjīd (1839-61) was to allow a free hand to his brother ʿAbd ül-ʿAzīz (he fathered a son before becoming sultan, Yūsuf ʿIzz ül-Dīn, born in 1857) and having ascended the throne (1861-76) the latter showed the same latitude towards his nephews, having two of them accompany him on his journey to Paris and London in 1867 (Alderson 34-5).

Bibliography (besides the chroniclers cited in the text): İ.H. Uzunçarşılı, *Osmanlı develetinin saray teşkilâtı*, Ankara 1945; A.D. Alderson, *The structure of the Ottoman dynasty*, Oxford 1956; G. Necipoğlu, *Architecture, ceremonial and power. The Topkapi Palace in the fifteenth and sixteenth centuries*, Cambridge, Mass. 1991; L.P. Peirce, *The Imperial harem. Women and sovereignty in the Ottoman Empire*, New York-Oxford 1993; A. Bobovius, *Topkapi. Relation du Sérail du Grand Seigneur*, ed. A. Berthier and S. Yerasimos, Arles 1999.

(G. Veinstein)

al-**KAFF** (a.), verbal noun of the verb *kaffa* in the sense of "to abstain, desist [from s.th.]," and "to repel [s.o. from s.th.]" (see *WbKAS*, i, *Letter Kāf*, 236-9), in a religio-political context refers to the quiescent attitude of some Khāridjite [*q.v.*] groups in early Islam, called *ḳaʿada* "those who sit down", i.e. stay at home, in abstaining from overt rebellion and warfare against the ruling authority. See further ḳuʿūd.

(Ed.)

KĀHĪ (late 9th century-988/late 15th century-1580), the *takhalluṣ* [*q.v.*] or pen-name of an Indo-Muslim poet, Nadjm al-Dīn Abu 'l-Ḳāsim Muḥammad, who wrote at the courts of the Mughal emperors Humāyūn and Akbar [*q.vv.*].

According to most writers he was born in Transoxania at Miyānkāl, a district situated between Samarḳand and Bukhārā, but stayed a long time in Kābul, whence he is also known as Kābulī. When fifteen years old he is said to have visited Djāmī (d. 898/1492 [*q.v.*]) at Harāt, and spent some seven years in the poet's company. Subsequently he went to India on two separate occasions, once in *ca.* 936/1530 and then in 961/1554. In his first visit he travelled to Bhakkar in Sind to meet the Ṣūfī mystic Shāh Djahāngīr Hāshimī (d. 946/1539-40) of Kirmān, author of the Persian *mathnawī Maẓhar al-āthār*, and lived in Gudjarāt writing for Bahādur Khān and Muḥammad Khān, who ruled that state from 932-43/1525-36 and 943-61/1536-53 respectively. In *ca.* 956/1549 he returned to Kābul and entered the service of prince Akbar. It was as a member of Akbar's entourage that he made his second visit to India, spending the remaining years of his life in that country. His patrons this time included, in addition to Humāyūn and Akbar, the noblemen of Banāras and Djawnpūr, Khān Zamān and his brother Bahādur Khān, who were both slain in their abortive revolt against Akbar in 975/1567. From 969/1561-2 onward he lived in Āgra, where he died in 988/1580 at an advanced age of 110 or 120 years.

Kāhī was an important figure of Akbar's reign, noted for his poetry as well as other attainments. Besides writing *ḳaṣīdas* and *ghazals*, he displayed special skill in composing chronograms and riddles. He is also said to have written a *mathnawī* on the model of Saʿdī's *Būstān* entitled *Gul-afshān*. His other accomplishments included the study of Ḳur'ānic exegesis, scholastic theology, music, astronomy and mysticism.

Bibliography: 1. Sources. Aḥmad ʿAlī Khān Hāshimī Sandīlawī, *Tadhkira-i makhzan al-gharā'ib*, Bodleian MS. 395; Abu 'l-Faḍl, *Ā'īn-i Akbarī*, i, tr. H. Blochmann, Calcutta 1868; Ghulām ʿAlī Khān Āzād Bilgrāmī, *Khizāna-i ʿāmira*, Cawnpore 1871; Mīr Ḥusayn Dūst Sanbhalī, *Tadhkira-i Ḥusaynī*, Lucknow 1875; Ṣiddīḳ Ḥasan Khān, *Shamʿ-i andjuman*, Bhopal 1876; Amīn Aḥmad Rāzī, *Haft iḳlīm*, iii, ed. Djawād Fāḍil, Tehran n.d.; ʿAbd al-Ḳādir Badā'ūnī, *Muntakhab al-tawārīkh*, iii, tr. Wolseley Haig, Calcutta 1925; Niẓām al-Dīn Aḥmad, *Ṭabaḳāt-i Akbarī*, ii, tr. B. De, Calcutta 1936; Muḥammad ʿAlī Mudarris Tabrīzī, *Rayḥānat al-adab*, iii, Tabrīz 1369/1949-50; Mīr ʿAlī Shīr Ḳāniʿ Tattawī, *Maḳālāt al-shuʿarā'*, ed. Ḥusām al-Dīn Rāshidī, Karachi 1957; Ḳudrat Allāh Gopāmawī, *Tadhkira-i natā'idj al-afkār*, Bombay 1336/1957-8; Luṭf ʿAlī Beg Ādhar, *Ātash-kada*, ed. Sayyid Djaʿfar Shahīdī, Tehran 1337/1958; Bindrāban Dās Khushgū, *Safīna-i Khushgū*, Patna 1959; Lachmī Narāyan Shafīḳ, *Shām-i gharībān*, ed. Akbar al-Dīn Ṣiddīḳī, Karachi 1977.

2. Studies. T.W. Beale, *An oriental biographical dictionary*, London 1894; *IC*, xxvii/2-4 (1953); *Indo-Iranica* (Calcutta), viii/1, 4 (1955), and xxi/4 (1968); J. Rypka, *History of Iranian literature*, Dordrecht 1968, 723-4.

(Munibur Rahman)

ḲAḤṬĀNITE, Qahtanite, a name which has been proposed for designating the ensemble of graffiti found in pre-Islamic South Arabia but whose use has not yet become generalised.

The numerous written documents found in Arabia and dated from pre-Islamic times, may be classed under three headings: (1) monumental inscriptions on stone or other durable materials, meant to be exposed and using varieties of the Arabian alphabet (South Arabian, Dedanite, Liḥyānite and Ḥasaean) or foreign scripts (Aramaic, Greek, Latin and Geʿez); (2) private documents (correspondence, contracts, lists or writing exercises), written in cursive South Arabian script on wooden sticks or palm stalks, all of these having been found in Yemen; and (3) very numerous graffiti written on rocks in various forms of the Arabian alphabet.

The monumental inscriptions and the documents in cursive South Arabian script can be divided into several groups, to be defined by ranging over provenance, dating and the political, linguistic, religious and tribal information given in the text. For designating these ensembles, Western scholars have devised names derived from the political groupings where these writings have originated, or failing that, from the region where they have been found. Thus in South Arabia, there have been accordingly classified the Sabaic inscriptions (from the kingdom of Saba' [*q.v.*]; the Madhābic (from the region of the Wādī Madhāb), previously called Minaean [see maʿīn]; Ḳatabānic (from the kingdom of Ḳatabān [*q.v.*]; and Ḥaḍramitic (from the kingdom of Ḥaḍramawt [*q.v.*]. In the oasis of al-ʿUlā (ancient Dedan) and of Madā'in Ṣāliḥ (ancient Ḥegra/al-Ḥidjr [*q.v.*] are recognised two successive ensembles, called Dadanitic (after the ancient name of the oasis) and Liḥyānite (after the ancient tribe [see liḥyān]), which Michael Macdonald has recently suggested should be grouped under the single term Dadanitic (Macdonald, 2000, 29). Finally, on the Arabian shores of the Perso-Arabian Gulf, a group of some 50 texts has been called Ḥasaitic, after the name of the region al-Ḥasā' [*q.v.*] or al-Aḥsā'.

It is more difficult to classify the graffiti, which number tens of thousands, because their content, often poor and uninformative, gives hardly any indications of their language or tribe or cults. Contributing to this difficulty is the fact that very few of them have been rigorously studied. Their typology is based mainly on adducing as evidence the various types of the Arabic alphabet and, additionally, on examining the distinct and homogeneous zones of their distribution.

It is further not very easy to give a name to the various groups of graffiti at present recognised, since the identity of their authors is unknown. At an early stage, specialists isolated two groups, called Ṣafaitic [*q.v.*] (from the Djabal al-Ṣafā to the southeast of Damascus) and Thamudic [*q.v.*], making a connection with the ancient tribe of Thamūd [*q.v.*]. But it soon became apparent that the Thamudic ensemble, in which were grouped all the non-classified graffiti, was a vast hold-all term for an extremely heterogeneous group. A first tentative step to devise a new order for them was made by F.V. Winnett, who adduced five sub-groups, each defined by a variety of the Arabian alphabet and called by letter of the Latin alphabet, A, B, C, D and E. Later researches by this same author, continued by those of M. Macdonald and G. King (Macdonald-King, 2000), have shown that two of these sub-groups belong to particular regions, Ḥismā' (southern Jordan and northern Ḥidjāz) and the district of the Taymā' oasis, whence the names Ḥismaic (former Thamudic A) and Taymanitic (former Thamudic E) have been proposed.

There remains to classify the numerous other Thamudic graffiti, notably those found in the region between the Ḥidjāz and Yemen, these being especially numerous in the regions of Nadjrān [*q.v.*] and Ḳaryat al-Fāw [see FĀʾW] (the latter 280 km/165 miles to the northeast of Nadjrān (Jamme, 1973). For these, the terms "Southern Thamudic" (see Macdonald-King, 2000, 44) or "Ḳaḥṭānite" (Robin, 1978, 106-7) have been proposed, but these terms remain provisional whilst a typology of the whole ensemble remains to be sketched out. The task is difficult because a number of these graffiti recall the proximity and prestige of the South Arabian states by mixing together, in varying proportions, the regular South Arabian script letters and those reflecting local graphic forms.

This name "Ḳaḥṭānite" stems from Ḳaḥṭān, the ancient eponym of the South Arabs, according to the purveyors of traditions on the beginnings of Islam (see especially, Ibn al-Kalbī's *Djamharat al-nasab*). The name of this eponym probably comes from a tribe established at Ḳaryat al-Fāw (the ancient Ḳaryat^{um} dhāt Kahl^{im}, sc. "the Ḳarya of Kahl", Kahl being the name of a god of the oasis). Two inscriptions mention this tribe. The first, found at al-Fāw, is the tombstone of "Muʿāwiyat, son of Rabīʿat, of the line of M. . . ., [the Ḳa]ḥṭānite, king of Ḳaḥṭān and of Madhḥig"; from the style of writing, this would date from the 1st century A.D. (Ansārī-Qaryat al-Fāw 2/1-2). The second inscription, stemming from the temple of Awwām at Maʾrib in Yemen, has a dedication to the Sabaean god Almaqah in which the writer evokes an expedition against "Rabīʿat of the line of Thawr^{im} king of Kiddat [= Kinda] and of Ḳaḥṭān", in the reign of the Sabaean king Shaʿr^{um} Awtar, *ca.* 220-5 (Ja 635/26-7). Ptolemy probably mentions the same tribe in the 2nd century A.D. in the form Κατανῖται (VI. 7, 20 and 23).

The reason why Ḳaḥṭān, the pre-Islamic tribe at Ḳaryat al-Fāw, associated in the first place with Madhḥidj [*q.v.*] and then dominated by Kinda [*q.v.*], has been chosen as an eponym for the South Arabs has not yet been solved. It is likely that we have here a tradition of Kindī origin, which would have been imposed when the tribe of Kinda had a dominant position in Central Arabia, in the 5th and 6th centuries A.D. This hypothesis underlines once more that Kinda is the source of the greater part of Arab traditions bearing the verifiable historical information on pre-Islamic South Arabia.

Bibliography: 1. Inscriptions. Ansārī-Qaryat al-Fāw 2 = ʿA.R. al-T. al-Ansārī, *Aḍwāʾ djadīda ʿalā dawlat Kinda min khilāl āthār Ḳaryat al-Fāw wa-nuḳūshihā*, in *Sources for the history of Arabia*, Pt. 1 (*Studies on the history of Arabia*), vol. 1, Univ. of Riyāḍ Press 1979 (A.H. 1399), 2-11 of the Arabic part; Chr. Robin, *L'Arabie antique de Karibʾīl à Mahomet. Nouvelles données sur l'histoire des Arabes grâce aux inscriptions*, in *RMMM*, lxi (1991-3), 121; Ja 635 = A. Jamme, *Sabaean inscriptions from Maḥram Bilqîs (Mârib)*, Publics. of the American Foundation for the Study of Man, iii, Baltimore 1962, 136-8.

2. General. Jamme, *Miscellanées d'ancient* [sic] *arabe*, Washington, private public. 1973 (this volume is almost entirely given over to the publication of the Ḳaryat al-Fāw graffiti, called "Sabaean" by the author); M.C.A. Macdonald, *Reflections on the linguistic map of pre-Islamic South Arabia*, in *Arabian Archaeology and Epigraphy*, xi (2000), 28-79; idem and G.M.H. King, *EI*² art. THAMUDIC; Robin, *Quelques graffites préislamiques de al-Ḥazāʾin (Nord-Yémen)*, in *Semitica*, xxviii (1978), 103-28 and pls. III-IV; J. Ryckmans, *Aspects nouveaux du problème thamoudéen*, in *Stud. Isl.*, v (1956), 5-17. (CH. ROBIN)

ḲĀʾIMĪ, ḤASAN BABA (d. 1102/1691), Bosnian Muslim poet of the 11th/17th century.

After the Ottoman conquest of the 9th/15th century, Slavs converted to Islam began to write in the Islamic languages of Turkish, Persian and Arabic, whilst some authors continued to write in Slavonic but in Arabic characters (*alhamiado*).

Ḥasan Baba, with the *makhlaṣ* of Ḳāʾimī, was the most celebrated poet of his time in Bosnia and the Balkans in general. Little is known of his life, but he seems to have been in easy circumstances and to have lived most of his life in Sarajevo [*q.v.*], where he was born by 1039/1630. He was apparently an adherent of the Ḳādiriyya *ṭarīḳa*, and *sheykh* of the *tekke* of Sinān Agha in Sarajevo, and he dedicated poems to the founder, ʿAbd al-Ḳādir al-Djīlānī. He seems to have left Sarajevo towards the end of his life, perhaps driven out of the Sarajevo rebellion of 1093/1682 and to have lived in Zvornik, where he died and where he has his *türbe*.

He is the author of two *Dīwāns* in Turkish, the first one of mystical poetry and the second, smaller one of *ḳaṣīda*s only called *Wāridāt* ("incomings, gains"), the whole comprising several thousand verses, extant in a hundred mss., mostly copied in the 19th century. In the *Wāridāt*, he touched upon political events, such as the long campaign by the Ottomans for the conquest of Crete from the Venetians, a war which also affected Dalmatia and its coastal towns. In the first *ḳaṣīda* of this *Dīwān*, comprising 174 *beyt*s, he correctly foretold the date of the end of the war (1079/1669), giving him great celebrity; and much of the enthusiasm for copying Ḳāʾimī's works arose after 1878 when the Austrians extended their protectorate over Bosnia and Hercegovina, since the poet had alluded to universal conquests by the Turks and the universal triumph of Islam. Modern Bosnian scholars, on the other hand, have claimed him as a Bosnian patriot (although the concept of "patriotism" did not exist in his time) or even as a proto-Marxist; at most, one can note his evident love for Bosnia and, especially, for Sarajevo.

Ḳāʾimī also wrote *alhamiado* poetry, including an

"ode against tobacco", written when Murād IV banned the use of tobacco [see TUTUN] in the Ottoman empire, and a second, shorter ode on the Cretan War in addition to the one in Turkish.

Bibliography: See for full references, Jasna Samic, *Le Dîwân de Ḳâ'imî*, Paris 1986, with bibl. at 251-80. (JASNA SAMIC)

ḲĀ'IN, conventionally Qayen, etc., a town of eastern Persia (lat. 33° 43' N., long. 59° 06' E.), now in the administrative province of Khurāsān but in mediaeval Islamic times falling within the region known as Ḳūhistān [*q.v.*]. It lies on the road connecting the urban centres of northern Khurāsān (Mashhad, Turbat-i Ḥaydariyya, etc.) with Birdjand, Persian Sīstān and Zāhidān.

Ḳā'in must be an ancient town, but virtually nothing is known of it before the descriptions of the 4th/10th century geographers. The 8th century Armenian geography attributes its foundation to Lōhrāsp, son of Wishtāsp, of Iranian legendary history (Markwart-Messina, *A catalogue of the provincial capitals of Ērānshahr*, Rome 1931, 12, 53). In the 4th/10th century it appears as the administrative centre of Ḳūhistān, with a citadel, also containing the *dār al-imāra* and congregational mosque, surrounded by a trench and rampart, and an outer wall with three gates. The water supply came mainly from *ḳanāt*s. Al-Muḳaddasī considered it a place of few amenities and harsh living conditions, but one which flourished as an emporium (*furḍa*) for the trade of Khurāsān passing southwards to the Gulf of Oman and the Arabian Sea shores (Ibn Ḥawḳal, 446, tr. Kramers and Wiet, 431; al-Muḳaddasī, 321; *Ḥudūd al-ʿālam*, tr. Minorsky, 103). Nāṣir-i Khusraw passed through it in 444/1052 and found it a large, fortified town; he marvelled at the great arch (*ṭāḳ*) of its mosque (*Safar-nāma*, ed. M. Dabīr-Siyāḳī, Tehran 1335/1956, 127, tr. W.M. Thackston, New York 1986, 102). In the ensuing Saldjūḳ period, Ḳā'in and fortresses in its surrounding district became known as haunts of the Ismāʿīlīs; an Ismāʿīlī presence, including within the town of Ḳā'in, has persisted until today (see F. Daftary, *The Ismāʿīlīs, their history and doctrine*, Cambridge 1990, 341, 387, 543; C.E. Bosworth, *The Ismaʿilis of Quhistān and the Maliks of Nīmrūz or Sīstān*, in Daftary (ed.), *Mediaeval Ismaili history and thought*, Cambridge 1996, 221-9; and ḲŪHISTĀN).

It has often been assumed that the name of the Persian principality *Tunocain* mentioned by Marco Polo is a conflation of Ḳā'in and the town of Tūn [*q.v.*] some 18 farsakhs north-north-west of it (see Yule-Cordier, *The Book of Ser Marco Polo*, London 1903, i, 83, 86, 127-8); certainly, Bābur, two centuries later, continued to link the towns thus (*Bābur-nāma*, tr. Beveridge, 296, 301). Two generations or so after the time of Marco Polo, the town was still large and flourishing, on the evidence of Ḥamd Allāh Mustawfī; he mentions how most houses had cellars from which they could tap into the adjacent subterranean *ḳanāt*s and how the men all carried arms and were ready to use them (*Nuzhat al-ḳulūb*, 145-6, tr. 144).

The subsequent history of Ḳā'in is substantially that of the local amirate, whose capital it was until this last was moved to the larger and more important town of Birdjand in the 19th century, of the Khuzayma family, which traced its origins back to early Islamic Arab governors of Khurāsān. It fully emerges into history in Nādir Shāh Afshār's time, when the monarch bestowed the governorship of the Ḳā'ināt, the region around Ḳā'in, on Amīr Ismāʿīl Khān Khuzayma. In the chaotic conditions after Nādir's assassination, Amīr ʿAlam Khān (d. 1753) briefly expanded his power beyond its traditional boundaries of Ḳā'ināt and Sīstān as far as Mashhad and Harāt in the north and Persian Balūčistān in the south (1748-53). In the Ḳādjār period, the family continued as guardians of the eastern frontier of Persia against Afghān and Balūč marauders. Curzon described Amīr Hishmat al-Mulk ʿAlam Khān III (d. 1891) as "probably the most powerful subject of the Persian crown" (*Persia and the Persian question*, i, 200), and C.E. Yate, who was at Ḳā'in in 1894, met his second son Shawkat al-Mulk Muḥammad Ismāʿīl Khān, who became Amīr of Ḳā'ināt (*Khurasan and Sistan*, Edinburgh and London 1900, 66 ff., 76-7). The Khuzayma family adopted the family name of ʿAlam when Riḍā Shāh Pahlavī introduced this requirement in the 1930s, and Asad Allāh ʿAlam (d. 1978) had a distinguished career under the last Shāh, Muḥammad Riḍā, beginning with his appointment as the youthful governor of Sīstān and Balūčistān in 1945 and ending as Minister of the Imperial Court in 1966-77; his memoirs, published in English as Assadollah Alam, *The Shah and I*, London 1991, are a prime source for the later years of the Shāh's reign. See for the history of the family and its role in the political and military history of Persia's eastern frontiers, Pirouz Moujtahed-Zadeh, *The Amirs of the borderlands and Eastern Iranian borders*, London 1995.

The region of Ḳā'ināt of recent times corresponded largely to the ancient Ḳūhistān, but was in the 1973 administrative reorganisation subdivided into two *shahrastān*s, that of Ḳā'in or Ḳā'ināt and that of Birdjand [*q.v.*]. This was modified in the 1980s under the Islamic Republic, when three *shahrastān*s were formed: Ḳā'ināt; Birdjand to its south; and Nihbandān in the further south, adjoining Sīstān and Kirmān. Thus the town of Ḳā'in is at present the chef-lieu of its *shahrastān* (which contains a single *bakhsh*, the Bakhsh-i Markazī, and eight *dihistān*s). The population of Ḳā'in itself was in 1986 15,955, and that of the whole *shahrastān* 122,149 (Moujtahed-Zadeh, 50-5; this information on administrative arrangements replaces that given in the arts. BIRDJAND, in Vol. I, 1233b, and ḲŪHISTĀN, in Vol. V, 355b).

Bibliography (in addition to references in the article): Le Strange, *The lands of the Eastern Caliphate*, 352-3; Razmārā (ed.), *Farhang-i Īrān-zamīn*, ix, 292-3; Barthold, *An historical geography of Iran*, Princeton 1984, 135-6. (C.E. BOSWORTH)

KĀKAṚ, a Gharghusht Pashtūn tribe concentrated in southeastern Afghānistān and Pākistānī Balūčistān. Though not prominent among Afghān [*q.v.*] groups migrating to India during the early Dihlī Sultanate [*q.v.*], Kākaṛs are noticeable among military and political élites during the Lōdī, Sūrī and early Mughal [*q.vv.*] periods. Ḥaybat Khān Kākāṛ, patron and collector of materials for Niʿmat Allāh's *Makhzān-i Afghānī*, demonstrates Kākaṛ participation in Mughal literary production.

Kākaṛistān designates territory on and between the Tūba and Sulaymān mountain ranges, including the microregions of Būrī, Pīshīn, Sībī [*q.v.*] and Zhūb/Zhōb [*q.v.*]. Within this area Kākaṛs incorporated non-Pashtūn minority groups such as Gadūn and Watensī speakers in *hamsāya* dependency relationships, and there is a lack of consensus about whether other local Pashtūn groups, including the Panṛī and Nagher, are Kākaṛs. Surrounding Ačakzay, Ghalzay [*q.v.*], Tarīn and Wazīr Pashtūns and various Balūč [*q.v.*] communities form the social boundaries of Kākaṛ territory, which is economically linked to the greater Indo-Islamic world through the markets of Ḳandahār, Kwaṭṭa, and the Dēradjāt [*q.vv.*].

Bibliography: Mountstuart Elphinstone, *An account of the Kingdom of Caubul*, London 1839, repr. Karachi 1992, ii, 161-73; B. Dorn, *History of the Afghans*, London 1829-36, repr. Karachi 1976 (= tr. of Niʿmat Allāh Harawī, *Makhzān-i Afghānī*), part I, pp. ix, 75, 93, 131, 167-8, part II, pp. iii-viii, 32, 34, 36-8, 53, 56, 57, 122, 129; C. MacGregor, *Central Asia. Part II. Afghanistan*, London 1871, 473-77; H. Priestly, *Afghanistan and its inhabitants*, Lahore 1874 (= tr. of S.M. Ḥayāt Khān, *Ḥayāt-i Afghānī*), 19, 76, 78, 148-56; H.G. Raverty, *Notes on Afghanistan and parts of Baluchistan*, Calcutta 1878, repr., Quetta 1982; Yu.V. Gankovski, *The peoples of Pakistan*, Lahore n.d. [1971], 11, 135, 196.

(Shah Mahmoud Hanifi)

ḲALANSUWA, Ḳulansiya (a), the name for a cap worn by men either under the turban proper or alone on the head.

The word, from which verbal forms are derived as denominative verbs, is apparently of foreign origin; while it used to be commonly connected with the Latin *calautica* (for which, however, the form *calantica* is difficult to quote and besides, it means a head-cloth for women), Fraenkel wished to derive it through the Aramaic *ḳ.w.l.ś* (cf. Arabic *ḳāliṣ*, *ḳālis*, Dozy, *Supplément*, ii, 395) from κῶνος (*conus*). The Arab grammarians and lexicographers found in the manifold formation of the broken plural and the diminutive a reason for using *ḳalansuwa* as a paradigm for substantives of more than three radicals with such peculiarities.

Caps of different shapes were called *ḳalansuwa*; varieties of the *ḳalansuwa* are *ṭurṭūr, burnus, urṣūṣa*, etc. While it is related of the Companions of the Prophet that they wore tight-fitting *ḳalansuwas*, later, a long peaked sugar-cone shape, supported within by pieces of wood, became fashionable, for which the name *ṭawīla* was usual. It seems to have come from Persia (cf. the head-dresses in the Dura-Ṣāliḥiyya 1st century A.D. paintings, in J.H. Breasted, *Oriental forerunners of Byzantine paintings*, Chicago 1924) for it was regarded by the pre-Islamic Arabs as a noteworthy feature of Persian dress (G. Jacob, *Altarabisches Beduinenleben*, ²Hildesheim 1967, 237) and is said to have been first adopted in the reign of the first Umayyad by ʿAbbād b. Ziyād from the inhabitants of the town of Ḳandahār, conquered by him (Yāḳūt, ed. Wüstenfeld, iv, 184). High, black *ḳalansuwas* were worn by the ʿAbbāsid caliphs from al-Manṣūr to al-Mustaʿīn and by their viziers and *ḳāḍīs*. The latter adhered longest to the *ḳalansuwa*, so that in the course of the 3rd/9th century—this headgear being also popularly known as *danniyya*, pot-hat, or *ṭawīla*—it became their regular official headgear, together with the neck-veil or *taylasān* [*q.v.*] and at times was strictly forbidden to other classes of the community (al-Kindī, *K. al-Ḳuḍāt*, ed. R. Guest, 460, 586). On the other hand, criminals had a *ḳalansuwa* put on their heads when they were led through the streets. The *ḳalansuwa* was also worn among the Umayyads in Spain, where *muḳallas* meant a *muftī* wearing the *ḳāliṣ*. A headdress introduced by Tīmūr into his army was also known as *ḳalansuwa*.

The name *ḳalansuwa* appears several times in Ibn Baṭṭūṭa, according to whom (ii, 378, tr. Gibb, ii, 481) the Ḳipčaḳs, for example, called their *ḳalansuwas* by the Persian name *kulāh*. Concerning the *futuwwa* [*q.v.*] societies in Anatolia (*akhiyyat al-fityān*), he says (ii, 264, tr. Gibb, ii, 421) that their members wore several *ḳalansuwas* above one another, a silk one on the head, above it a white woollen one, to the top of which was tied a strip of cloth two fingers broad and one ell long: at meetings, only the woollen *ḳalansuwa* was taken off, the silk one remaining on the head. A similar pendant strip of cloth is also part of the dress of the Coptic priests of modern Egypt and is there called *ḳallūsa* or *ḳalaswa*; here the name appears to have been transferred from the cap itself to its most striking and therefore better known part.

At periods when, as in the 2nd/8th century, both Muslims and Christians wore *ḳalansuwas*, the latter had to tie two knots of another colour to it (al-Ṭabarī, iii, 1389); but when the *ḳalansuwa* went out of fashion with the Muslims in the 3rd/9th century, it remained the mark of the Christians. The word is therefore frequently found in Arab authors meaning the headdress worn by Christian monks and hermits, Greek priests and even the Pope himself. Through the Crusades, the high cap with the veil seems to have found its way to Western Europe as a woman's dress.

The name *ḳalansuwa* was also given to other objects of similar shape: *ḳ. nuḥās* is the metal cap of the obelisk near Heliopolis (ʿAyn Shams [*q.v.*]); *ḳ. turāb* in modern Arabic is used for a chemical sublimating vessel; *ḳ. buḳrāṭ* is used by surgeons for a particular kind of head bandage; and *ḳāliṣ* (*ḳūlis*) is the name of a plant, which seemed to represent a human head with a high cap. *Ḳalansuwa* was also the name of a fortress near al-Ramla in Palestine, see G. Le Strange, *Palestine under the Moslems*, London 1890, 476.

Bibliography (in addition to references given in the article): Dozy, *Dictionnaire détaillé des noms des vêtements chez les Arabes*, Amsterdam 1843, 365-71; idem, *Supplément*, ii, 395, 401; S. Franekel, *Die aramäische Fremdwörter im Arabischen*, Leiden 1886, 53-4; H. Lammens, *Remarques sur les mots français dérivés de l'arabe*, Beirut 1890 (supposes an influence of the word *ḳalansuwa* on Fr. *calotte*); A. Mez, *Die Renaissance des Islâms*, Heidelberg 1922, 26, 45-6, 130, 217, 348-9, 367; Yedida Stillman, *Arab dress: a short history*, Leiden 2000, index and pls. 4, 14, 26, 44; and see further, libās.

(W. Björkman)

KALIKAT, locally Kōḻikōḍu (interpreted in Malayalam as "cock fortress", see Yule and Burnell, *Hobson-Jobson, a glossary of Anglo-Indian colloquial words and phrases*, ²London 1903, 148), conventionally Calicut and, in modern Indian parlance, Kozhikode, a town of the Western Deccan or Peninsular Indian coastland (lat. 11° 15' N., long. 75° 45' E.) in what was known in pre-modern times, and is still known, as the Malabar coast [see maʿbar]. In British Indian times it was the centre of a sub-district (*tālūk*) of the same name in the Malabar District of the Madras Presidency, later Province; it is now the centre of the District of Kozhikode in the Kerala State of the Indian Union.

In pre-Muslim times, the region around Kalikat fell within the powerful Hindu kingdom of the Čolas. The commander of the Khaldjī sultans of Dihlī, Malik Kāfūr [*q.v.*], broke through the Deccan to the Malabar coast for the first time in the opening years of the 8th/14th century, although this success was short-lived [see maʿbar]. It was, however, probably as a result of Muslim knowledge of the region that the traveller Ibn Baṭṭūṭa was able *ca.* 739/1338 to visit the Malabar coast and, specifically, Kalikat (which he spells as Ḳāliḳūṭ). He describes the ruler there as an infidel having the title of Sāmarī, a rendering of Malayalam *sāmūri* or *sāmūtiri*, a vernacular modification of Skr. *sāmandri* "sea king", which the Portuguese subsequently rendered as Samorin or Zamorin. There was already a substantial community there of Muslim traders, who had commercial connections with the Maldive Islands, Ceylon, Java and China. There was a *s̲h̲āhbandar* [*q.v.*] or head of the Muslim merchant community *vis-à-vis* the ruler, called Ibrāhīm, who came from Baḥrayn, and also a *ḳāḍī* and the *s̲h̲ayk̲h̲* of a Ṣūfī *zāwiya* or hospice in the town. Ibn Baṭṭūṭa noted a large number of Chinese ships in the busy harbour, and it was in one of these junks that he then embarked for China (*Riḥla*, iv, 88-94, tr. Gibb and Beckingham, iv, 812-14, cf. Yule-Cordier, *Cathay and the way thither*, London 1914-15, iv, 24-6; on the Chinese presence at Kalikat, see Yule-Cordier, *The Book of Ser Marco Polo*, ²London 1903, ii, 391-2 n. 5).

In 1370 the Malabar coast passed into the general control of the powerful Hindu kingdom of Vid̲j̲ayanagar [*q.v.*] and remained under non-Muslim rule with the exception of a short period towards the end of the 17th century when the Mug̲h̲al emperor Awrangzīb overran the Deccan. As in Ibn Baṭṭūṭa's time, Kalikat itself remained under the rule of its Zamorins till the 18th century.

Another Muslim, the historian ʿAbd al-Razzāḳ [*q.v.*] al-Samarḳandī, was sent as an envoy to the Zamorin of Kalikat by the Tīmūrid S̲h̲āhRuk̲h̲ in 846/1442, and mentions seeing ships from the Horn of Africa and Zanzibar in its harbour; the numerous local Muslim community had two mosques and a S̲h̲āfiʿī *ḳāḍī*. It was just after this, in 1444, that the first European to visit Kalikat, Nicolo Conti, came from Cochin. The Zamorins extended their authority with the help of the Muslim traders, and in the 15th century Kalikat became the most important town on the Malabar coast. Malabar was also a part of India where the Portuguese endeavoured to establish forts and trading factories, with Covilha at Kalikat in 1486 and Vasco da Gama there in 1498. A factory was set up in 1500, but immediately destroyed by the local Muslims, whose monopoly of trade was now seriously and, in the end, fatally challenged; a fort was built in 1511, but evacuated in 1525, the end of Portuguese activities at Kalikat. European settlements were more successful at Cannanore or Kannanūr [*q.v.*] and at Cochin, whose Rād̲j̲ās were enemies of the Zamorins, hence sought European help and support.

The English first appeared at Kalikat in 1615 when three ships under Captain William Keeling arrived. In 1664 the English East India Company opened a factory; in 1698 the French Company opened one; and in 1752 the Danish did likewise. The extensive trade in cotton cloths exported from Kalikat—Marco Polo mentions the fine textiles of Malabar—was the origin of the English term calico (see Yule and Burnell, *Hobson-Jobson*, 147-8). By the later 17th century, the power of the Zamorins was in decline, but they continued to be hostile to foreigners. Kalikat suffered badly in the Mysore Wars of the later 18th century, being sacked by the Muslim armies of Ḥaydar ʿAlī [*q.v.*] of Mysore in 1773, and those of his son Tīpū Sulṭān [*q.v.*] in 1788, who tried to establish a rival capital in Malabar on the south bank of the nearby Beypore river. In 1790 Kalikat was occupied by East India Company troops, and by the Treaty of Seringapatam of 1792, the town passed finally under British control.

A significant proportion of the town's population remained Muslim, under their Hindu and then British rulers, being part of the Māppiḷa community of Muslims on the Malabar coast [see MAPPILA]. In the 1901 census, they formed 40% of Kalikat's 77,000 population, with over 40 mosques, including the S̲h̲ēkkindē Paḷḷi, with the shrine and tomb of S̲h̲ayk̲h̲ Māmu Koyā, said to have come from Egypt to Kalikat in the 16th century. In 1970 the town had a population of 330,000, and in 2003, 453,700.

Bibliography: C.A. Innes, *Madras District gazetteers. Malabar and Anjengo*, Madras 1908, 45 ff., 380-9; *Imperial gazetteer of India*², ix, 289-91. For studies on the history of the Malabar coast and the European presence there, see the *Bibls.* to MAʿBAR and MAPPILA.

(C.E. BOSWORTH)

KALIMANTAN, PULAU KALIMANTAN, or KLEMANTAN, one of the pre-colonial names of the island of Borneo [*q.v.* in Suppl.], one of the larger Sunda Islands in present-day Indonesia and Malaysia. The name is officially used in Indonesia for the whole island, whereas in Malaysia the term Borneo, derived by the Portuguese from the name of the old and once powerful sultanate of Brunei [*q.v.* in Suppl.] in the north, is still in use. About three-quarters of the island is part of the Indonesian Republic, being divided into four provinces: West, Central, South and East Kalimantan. The northern states of Sarawak and Sabah [*q.vv.*] are part of the Federation of Malaysia (since 1963), while the Sultanate of Brunei re-obtained its independence from British protection in 1984.

The present article deals essentially with the ethnic and social structures of the whole island; for the Indonesian part of the island specifically, see BORNEO, in Suppl. The whole island covers an area of *ca.* 755,000 km^2. As most of the area is, or was, covered by tropical rain forest growing partly on swampy ground, particularly in the vast plains in the south, the population density was very thin; an average of 22 people per km^2 was counted. Bigger settlements are usually found on river shores not too far away from their mouths, thus presenting themselves as strategic places for rule and commerce. The people used to live in villages or longhouses on the shores of the huge rivers that, until recently, together with their tributaries, were almost the only ways of communication for most parts of the island, except in the mountainous areas where rapids and ravines made shipping almost impossible.

Ethnologists usually divide the indigenous population of Kalimantan into two major groups: the "Malays" and the "Dayaks". These terms, however, should not be taken necessarily to denote ethnic, or even cultural identities. In both groups, a large variety of ethnic, cultural, linguistic and tribal entities exist. In very general terms, "Malay" denotes those individuals or groups who *masuk Islam* ("became Muslims") and therefore either considered themselves to have taken over "Malay" religion and *adat* (customs), or who were considered by their former kinsfolk to have left their old relationships and adopted a new and strange identity, namely, the Malay one. "Dayak" then covers all those indigenous tribes and groups who did not become Muslim but either kept to their traditional religious and cultural identities or, later, became Christians.

Such "ethnic switching" of the "Malays" was not a general rule, however, as sometimes is taken for granted. Some of those groups who turned to Islam still maintained a number of their traditions, e.g. living in longhouses, or continuing their own nutrition habits. Thus e.g. the Bakumpai in the south Barito districts in South Kalimantan did not take over Malay habits, although they became strong propagators of Islam to the Dayaks in the interior. Other tribal entities maintained parts of their traditional social structure and habits after converting to Islam, e.g. the Bajau on the west coast of Sabah and the Bajau Laut

(Sea Bajau) in the Tawau region (who may, however, originate from the Southern Philippines). The Islamic Madurese who were transplanted from the island of Madura and Eastern Java to West Kalimantan by the Indonesian army after 1965 and settled there on land owned formerly by Chinese refugees living there since the fall of the Ming dynasty in 1644, met with the unanimous hostility of the Chinese (now partly Protestant, Catholic or traditional Chinese), the Dayaks (partly Christian or traditional), and the "Malays" from the former sultanate of Sambas. After the collapse of President Suharto and the power of his army who had sheltered them, they suffered a severe series of massacres.

The first strongholds of Islam on Kalimantan were those settlements that were already established as harbour and military watch stations under the Maritime Kingdom of Sri Vijaya which had its centre near Palembang [*q.v.*] in south Sumatra, and which vanished in the 14th century (particularly in West Kalimantan, like Sukadana, Sambas), or by the Javanese Empire of Majapahit which decayed at the end of the 15th century (e.g. Kutai [*q.v.*] in East Kalimantan). Muslim sultans established their power, and their seats of power continued their roles as trading and administrative centres. Other centres like Brunei and Banjarmasin [see BANDJARMASIN] followed suit, and these increased in importance for the "Malay" or regional traders when, first the Portuguese and later the Spaniards, and then the British and the Dutch, attempted to promote their trading interests. These traders, although only few among them were ethnic Malays, continued to use Malay as their *lingua franca* as they had done already in the times of (Buddhist) Sri Vijaya, and they were also the main communicators of Islamic teachings, first from a foothold in the coastal and sub-coastal settlements and from there penetrating into some of the up-river regions. The interior of the island remained, however, closed to them.

Bibliography: J.E. Garang, *Adat und Gesellschaft*, Wiesbaden 1974, esp. 109 ff., 178 ff.; Judith Nagata, *In defense of ethnic boundaries. The changing myths and charters of Malay identity*, in C.F. Keyes (ed.), *Ethnic change*, Seattle 1981, 88-116; R.L. Wadley, *Reconsidering an ethnic label in Borneo*, in *BTLV*, clvi/1 (2000), 83-101, esp. 85. (O. SCHUMANN)

KĀMILIYYA, an early Shīʿī sect which is normally mentioned for having criticised not only Abū Bakr and ʿUmar, as did the Rāfiḍa [*q.v.*], but also ʿAlī. The founder, a certain Abū Kāmil Muʿādh b. Ḥuṣayn al-Nabhānī, seems to have lived in Kūfa during the first decades of the 2nd century A.H., but has left no traces in later sources. He supported Zayd b. ʿAlī [*q.v.*] and therefore did not acknowledge anybody as *imām* who abstained from coming out for his rights. This verdict applied to ʿAlī as well as to his son Ḥasan; only Ḥusayn acted as an *imām* should do. Apart from that, Abū Kāmil seems to have shared some of the gnostic ideas proffered by Abū Manṣūr al-ʿIdjlī (executed under Yūsuf b. ʿUmar al-Thaqafī between 120/738 and 126/744 [see MANṢŪRIYYA]), e.g. metempsychosis. Among those who felt attracted to him was the father of the poet Bashshār b. Burd [*q.v.*]. His adherents followed Zayd b. ʿAlī's sons, Yaḥyā first and then ʿAlī, but when the latter joined al-Nafs al-Zakiyya (Muḥammad b. ʿAbd Allāh [*q.v.*]) and shared his defeat, they lost their orientation and faded away. Later heresiographers failed to recognise the identity of the sect; they had to entirely rely on a few lines of *hidjāʾ* poetry. Malevolent reporters like Maʿdān al-Shumayṭī changed the name into Kumayliyya. In Shīʿī tradition, the group sometimes appears as al-Ḥuṣayniyya (al-Nawbakhtī, al-Ḳummī, Ḳāḍī al-Nuʿmān).

Bibliography: Ashʿarī, *Maḳālāt al-Islāmiyyīn*, 17 ll. 4 ff.; Baghdādī, *al-Farḳ bayn al-firaḳ*, 39 ll. 3 ff.; Nawbakhtī, *Firaḳ al-Shīʿa*, 51 ll. 9 ff.; Saʿd b. ʿAbd Allāh al-Ḳummī, *al-Maḳālāt wa 'l-firaḳ*, 14 l. 10 and 74 §145; Ḳāḍī Nuʿmān, *al-Urdjūza al-mukhtāra*, ed. Poonawala, 210 vv. 2073 ff.; Ch. Pellat, in *Oriens*, xvi (1963), 102-3; J. van Ess, *Die Kāmilīya*, in *WI*, xxviii (1988), 141-53; idem, *Theologie und Gesellschaft im 2. und 3. Jh. Hidschra*, i, Berlin 1991, 269-72. (J. VAN ESS)

KANBŌ, KAMBŌ, SHAYKH DJAMĀLĪ, Suhrawardī Ṣūfī saint of early 10th/16th century Muslim India, who died in 941/1534-5 during the reign of the Mughal ruler Humāyūn [*q.v.*] and was buried at Mihrawlī. His son Gadāʾī [see GADĀʾĪ KAMBŌ, in Suppl.], whom Djamālī had in his lifetime made his *khalīfa* or spiritual successor within the Suhrawardī order, achieved equal religious influence at the courts of Humāyūn and then Akbar.

Bibliography: See that to GADĀʾĪ KAMBŌ. (ED.)

ḲANTIMĪR, DEMETRIUS (Cantemir, Kantimiroğlu) (1673-1723), Hospodar (Rumanian "lord") or tributary prince of Moldavia during Ottoman times, and renowned musical practitioner and theorist. Born on 26 October 1673 at Silişteni, he was the son of Constantin, Prince of Moldavia (1685-93). In 1687 he was sent as a princely hostage to Istanbul, and was to stay there until 1691 and then again from 1693 until 1710, when he was himself appointed *Boghdān beyi*, i.e. governor of Moldavia [see BOGHDĀN]. But he promptly formed an alliance with Peter the Great, and was forced to flee as a result of the unexpected Ottoman victory of 1711, thereafter living in Russia, attached to the court. In 1722 he took part in the Caucasian campaign, but fell ill, and died on 21 August 1723.

Whatever the importance of his political role, it is his prodigious scholarly and creative achievements that justify his reputation as a major figure. As familiar with Islamic as with classical and contemporary European culture, he was a polymath who had interests in architecture, cartography and geography, and also wrote on philosophy and theology. In Western Europe he was considered important above all as an authority on the history and current state of the Ottoman Empire, and his *Incrementa atque decrementa aulæ Othomanicæ*, first published in 1734-5 in an English translation, was to remain the standard source on the Ottomans for a century, and is still of interest for its personal observations. A further important work that remained undeservedly in its shadow is the *Systema de religione et statu Imperii turcicii.*

In Turkey, on the other hand, where he is known as Kantemiroğlu, it is for his musical accomplishments that he is renowned. He was an outstanding *ṭunbūr* [*q.v.*] player; his innovative treatise was to exert a major influence on theoretical writing down to the middle of the 19th century; and the modern repertoire preserves a considerable number of pieces attributed to him. Some are spurious, but it is evident from those he included in his collection of notations, itself invaluable as a comprehensive record of late 17th-century Ottoman instrumental music, that he was a skillful and innovative composer.

Bibliography: 1. Works of Cantemir. *Descriptio Moldaviæ*, in *Operele Principelui Demetriu Cantemiru*, i, Bucharest 1872; *The history of the growth and decay of the Othman Empire*, tr. N. Tindal, 2 vols., London 1734-5; *Systema de religione et statu Imperii turcicii (Sistemul sau întocmirea religiei muhammedane)*, tr. V. Cândea, Bucharest 1977; *Kitāb-i ʿIlm-i mūsīḳī ʿalā wedjh ul-ḥurūfāt*, ms. Türkiyat Enstitüsü Y. 2768.

2. Studies on Cantemir. T.T. Burada, *Scrierile ale lui Dimitrie Cantemir*, in *Analele Academiei Române*, xxxii (Memoriile secţ. literare) (1909-10); P.P. Panaitescu, *Dimitrie Cantemir. Viaţa şi opera*, Bucharest 1958; M. Guboglu, *Dimitrie Cantemir–orientaliste*, in *Studia et Acta Orientalia*, iii (1960); C. Măciucă, *Dimitrie Cantemir*, Bucharest 1962; E. Popescu-Judeţ, *Dimitrie Cantemir et la musique turque*, in *Studia et Acta orientalia*, vii (1968); E. Popescu-Judetz, *Dimitrie Cantemir, cartea ştinţei muzicii*, Bucharest 1973; idem, *Studies in oriental arts*, Pittsburgh 1981; idem, *Meanings in Turkish musical culture*, Istanbul 1996; G. Cioranesco, *La contribution de Démètre Cantemir aux études orientales*, in *Turcica*, vi (1975); İ.B. Sürelsan, *Dimitrie Cantemir (1673-1723)*, Ankara 1975; S. Faroqhi, *Kultur und Alltag im osmanischen Reich*, Munich 1995; W. Feldman, *Music of the Ottoman court. Makam, composition and the early Ottoman instrumental repertoire*, Berlin 1996.

(O. Wright)

ḲAPLAN MUṢṬAFĀ PASHA (d. 1091/1680), Ottoman vizier and *ḳapudan pasha* [*q.v.*]. Educated in the palace school at Istanbul, he made his early career in the private household of the sultan or *enderūn* [*q.v.*]. Launched afterwards into a military and administrative career, Ḳaplan Muṣṭafā Pasha was appointed *beglerbegi* of Damascus before 1076/1666. From 6 February 1666 to April 1672, he served as Grand Admiral (*ḳapudan pasha*). Under the Grand Vizier and Commander-in-Chief Fāḍil Aḥmed Pasha Köprülü, he commanded the main squadron during the War of Candia (*Girid Seferi* [see iḲrītish; ḳandiya]. In 1077/1666 his fleet of 47 galleys served to transport men and materials to Crete. On 30 October 1666, the Grand Vizier boarded the admiral's flagship (*bashtarda*) at Termis Iskelesi (the fortress of Ternis, Thermisia, present-day Ermioni), or at Monemvasia, Menekshe [*q.v.*], in order to go to the front in Crete. In the next year, he made a punitive raid on the Cyclades, sacking the island of Paros [see para]. In 1672 he was made *beglerbegi* of Aleppo and appointed *serʿasker* (commander of the field army) for the Sultan Meḥemmed IV's Polish campaign, and in the following year he was made *beglerbegi* of Diyār Bakr.

Muṣṭafā Pasha fought before Cehrin (Čyhyryn), the seat of the Ukrainian hetman Doroshenko, at that time an Ottoman ally, in 1674/1085 and again in 1089/1678, reconquering that fortress on 2-3 Redjeb 1089/20-1 August 1678. From 1678/1089, Muṣṭafā was Grand Admiral for the second time till his death in the harbour of Izmir on 10 Shawwāl 1091/5 December 1680 while cruising the Archipelago.

Bibliography: [Kemal Yükep,] *Türk silahlı kuvvetleri tarihi III c. 3.k. eki. Girit seferi (1645-1669)*, Ankara 1977, 65-8, 73-9; R.C. Anderson, *Naval wars in the Levant 1559-1853*, Liverpool and Princeton 1952, 178-81; İ.H. Danişmend, *Osmanlı tarihi kronolojisi*, Istanbul 1971-2, iv, 441-3, 448, v, 198-9; Hammer-Purgstall, *Histoire*, xi, 234, 296-8, 306, 338, 341, 387-9, 389-10, 399, xii, 27-9, 32, 46n; B.J. Slot, *Archipelagus turbatus*, Leiden-Istanbul 1982, i, 168, ii, 395-6.

(A.H. de Groot)

KARAM (a.), the qualities of nobility of character, magnanimity, generosity, all the virtues making up the noble and virtuous man (see *WbKAS, Letter Kāf*, Wiesbaden 1970, 142-3). For a discussion of honour and nobility, see ʿirḍ; murūʾa and sharaf.

KARAMANLIDIKA [see turks. II. vi, in Suppl.]

ḲARAṬĀY (or Ḳirṭāy) al-ʿIzzī al-Khāzindārī, an author of the Mamlūk period about whom very little is known.

His name would seem to indicate that he was a *mamlūk* of a *khāzindār* or treasurer. Three fragments of his chronicle, called *Taʾrīkh al-Nawādir mimmā djarā li ʾl-awāʾil wa ʾl-awākhir*, have been preserved, the most interesting being that covering the years 626-89/1228-90 (Gotha A 1655), in which the author says that he was writing between 1293 and 1341. This latter part is not free from faults (chronological errors, anecdotes which are hard to verify, and legends mixed with real events), hence should be used only with care, but its interest lies in the fact that it transmits oral sources contemporary with the author, certain information stemming from highly-placed personages of the final years of the Ayyūbid period, such as Djamāl al-Dīn Ibn Maṭrūḥ [*q.v.*], and likewise some fragments of the abridged, and little-known, history of al-Nāṣir Ḳalāwūn's reign composed by the *ḳāḍī* Sharaf al-Dīn Ibn al-Waḥīd. The author was, moreover, largely inspired by the well-known chronicle of Ibn Wāṣil [*q.v.*] and may have used a source common to himself and Ibn al-Dawādārī [*q.v.*].

Bibliography: Ed. by the late H. Hein, *Der Taʾrīḫ maǧmūʿ an-nawādir des Amīr Šihāb ad-dīn Qaraṭāy*, Bibl. Islamica, Beirut, in press; ed. and partial tr. G. Levi Della Vida, *L'invasione dei Tartari in Siria nel 1260 nei ricordi di un testimone oculare*, in *Orientalia*, N.S. iv (1935), 353-76; Brockelmann, II, 54, S II, 53; Cl. Cahen, *La chronique de Ḳirṭāy et les Francs de Syrie*, in *JA*, ccxxix (1937), 140-5; R. Irwin, *The image of the Byzantine and the Frank in Arab popular literature*, in *Mediterranean Historical Review*, iv (1989), 226-42; Linda S. Northrup, *From slave to sultan*, Stuttgart 1998, 33-4, 47.

(Anne-Marie Eddé)

ḲĀSIM ARSLĀN (?-995/?-1587), Indo-Muslim poet, court panegyrist of the Mughal emperor Akbar [*q.v.*] in the later 10th/16th century.

Details regarding his life and career are scanty. According to *Muntakhab al-tawārīkh*, he was originally a native of Ṭūs; but most other writers refer to him as Mashhadī, which would indicate that he might have lived in Mashhad. He was brought up in Transoxania and went to India during Akbar's reign. It is related that he took Arslān as his pen-name because his father claimed descent from Arslān Djādhib, a military commander of Maḥmūd of Ghazna. Ḳāsim Arslān is described as a man of broad religious views, enjoying a witty, sociable and generous disposition. Apart from his status as a poet, he was known in his time as a skilled calligrapher, specialising in the *nastaʿlīḳ* style. His *dīwān*, which is rare, comprises various kinds of poems. One of his *ḳaṣīdas* is addressed to the Eighth Imām ʿAlī al-Riḍā and expresses the poet's devotion to the Shīʿī leader. His *ghazals*, mostly short, describe amatory feelings in simple speech. His chronograms, for which he is especially noted, are useful in providing dates of certain historical events. He died, according to most accounts, at Lahore in 995/1587.

Bibliography: 1. Sources. *Dīwān*, Oriental Public Library, Bankipore, 249; ʿAlī Ḳulī Khān Wālih Dāghistānī, *Riyāḍ al-shuʿarāʾ*, B.M. Add. 16,729; Amīn Aḥmad Rāzī, *Haft iḳlīm*, ii, ed. Djawād Fāḍil, Tehran n.d.; Ṣiddīḳ Ḥasan Khān, *Shamʿ-i andjuman*, Bhopal 1876; ʿAbd al-Ḳādir Badāʾūnī, *Muntakhab al-tawārīkh*, iii, tr. Wolseley Haig, Calcutta 1925; Niẓām al-Dīn Aḥmad, *Tabaḳāt-i Akbarī*, ii, tr. B. De, Calcutta 1936; Abu ʾl-Faḍl, *Āʾīn-i Akbarī*, i, tr. H. Blochmann, Calcutta 1868; Aḥmad ʿAlī K͟hān Hās͟himī Sandīlawī, *Tad͟hkira-i mak͟hzan al-g͟harāʾib*, i, ed. Muḥammad Bāḳir, Lahore 1968.

2. Studies. S͟hams al-Dīn Sāmī, *Ḳāmus al-aʿlām*, v, Istanbul 1889; T.W. Beale, *An oriental biographical dictionary*, London 1894; *Indo-Iranica* (Calcutta), xii/1 (March 1959). (MUNIBUR RAHMAN)

ḲAṢR (A.), pl. *kuṣūr*, most probably from Grk. *kastron*, Latin *castrum*, has the general sense of "a fortified place", hence "residence of an *amīr* or ruler, palace, or any building on a larger scale than a mere house".

1. In the central and eastern Islamic lands. See for this, SARĀY, and note also that in the Persian lands, a synonym for this in early mediaeval usage (e.g. in Nars͟hak͟hī, Bayhaḳī, D͟jūzd͟jānī) is often *kūs͟hk* (MP *kōs͟hk*), yielding Eng. and Ger. *kiosk*, Fr. *kiosque*.

2. In the Mag͟hrib.

Here, from the vocalic changes frequent in Mag͟hribī dialects, we often find the pronunciation *ḳṣar*, pl. *ḳṣūr*. The term has here various semantic strata that have to be illuminated by close examination of the various texts available and by archaeological investigation, and in the light of the complex material factors concerning the Mag͟hribī habitat from mediaeval times until long afterwards. Hence it denotes here: (a) a palace, the place from which political authority is exercised, or an aristocratic residence; (b) a fortified place, a small fort or a full-scale fortress; (c) a fortified complex for community habitation; and (d) a collective granary or store house.

A. The evidence of mediaeval texts

The palace. The term is usually used in the texts to denote a palace, a place of residence for a person wielding authority, such as the *ḳaṣr al-ḳadīm* which the Ag͟hlabid *amīr* Ibrāhīm I had built in 184/800, on the site of the princely town of al-ʿAbbāsiyya, not far from al-Ḳayrawān [*q.v.*] (al-Balād͟hurī, *Futūḥ*, 328; al-Bakrī, *al-Masālik wa 'l-mamālik*, ed. and tr. de Slane, repr. Paris 1965, 28/64), or the palaces (*ḳuṣūr*) built in 263/876 by the *amīr* Ibrāhīm II in his new princely residence of Raḳḳāda [*q.v.*] (al-Bakrī, *op. cit.*, 27/62, 147/135; Ibn ʿId͟hārī, i, 299). Al-Mahdiyya [*q.v.*], the first royal residence founded by the Fāṭimids in Ifrīḳiya, additionally included the palaces of ʿUbayd Allāh and Abu 'l-Ḳāsim (Ibn Ḥawḳal, 71/67; al-Bakrī, *op. cit.*, 30/67-8). In the far Mag͟hrib, the fortress built by the Almoravids at the moment of the foundation of Marrākus͟h [*q.v.*] was called the Ḳaṣr al-Ḥad͟jar (Ibn ʿId͟hārī, iii, 20). The term served to designate at one and the same time palaces, including the governmental headquarters or princely residence, and also the residences (*ḳuṣūr*) of the Almohad leaders, each of which comprised houses (*diyār*), gardens (*basātīn*), a bathhouse (*ḥammām*) and stables (*iṣṭablāt*) (al-ʿUmarī, *Masālik al-abṣār fī mamālik al-amṣār*, B.N. Paris ms. No. 5868, fol. 67b, tr. M. Gaudefroy-Demombynes, Paris 1927, 179).

Fortresses, places for garrisons and the fortified community habitats. Although frequently used in texts from the mediaeval period, the term *ḳaṣr* has no homogenous geographical distribution. It is rare in the western regions, from Tilimsān/Tlemcen to the Atlantic, where toponyms like *ḥiṣn* and *ḳalʿa* are very clearly predominant, but places denominated as *ḳuṣūr* are numerous from Tripolitania to the region of Tāhart, passing through Ifrīḳiya, where they often correspond to fortresses whose construction goes back to Byzantine times (al-Bakrī, *Masālik*, 31/69, 50/108; al-Idrīsī, *Mag͟hrib*, 157/144-5). However, in their grouping, the fortified sites thus described as *ḳaṣr* or *ḳuṣūr* do not appear to be, above all, places for garrisons but rather centres for population, a role that certain fortresses dating from Byzantine times already played at the time of the Arab conquest (Ibn ʿAbd al-Ḥakam, *Futūḥ*, 224, 228, 239; al-Bakrī, *op. cit.*, 13/34). In Ifrīḳiya, as in the far Mag͟hrib, the term thus denotes a village or a fortified town (*ibid.*, 47/101, 153/292), or a fortified place where the surrounding people come to take refuge when necessary (al-Tid͟jānī, *Riḥla*, Tunis and Tripoli 1981, 56, 119). Corresponding to an agglomeration on a more important scale, the term finally denotes nuclei of people, and these may be of a pre-urban or an urban nature. Thus Tāhart was in origin made up of several *ḳuṣūr* (B. Zerouki, *L'imamat de Tahart, premier état musulman du Maghreb*, i, Paris 1987, 132-3); it was probably similarly the case at Sid͟jilmāsa (Ibn Ḥawḳal, 91/89).

B. The pre-modern *ḳṣūr* in the Mag͟hrib

The fortified villages of the Saharan wastes. In North African toponomy, Arabic *ḳṣar* frequently replaces its Berber equivalent *ig͟herm* (pl. *ig͟herman*) when applied to the fortified villages characteristic of a type of habitat peculiar to the ante-Saharan zones: in Morocco, in the valleys of the Zīz, Dadès and Draa, from the Sūs in the west to Tāfīlālt in the east, and from the Atlas from north of the Draa to the south; and in Algeria, the regions of Tuwāt [*q.v.*] and Gourara [*q.v.* in Suppl.] and that of Mzāb [*q.v.*]. In its "completed" form, i.e. pre-modern one, such as one still finds in Morocco, the *ḳṣar* appears as a fortified village with a rectangular plan, surrounded by a protective wall flanked with towers and with angled bastions; the space thus circumscribed, with a dense network of contiguous houses, is criss-crossed by several narrow streets whose pattern is based on more or less orthogonal axes. The regular form depends on the topographical conditions of the site; if the *ḳṣūr* of the plains of southern Morocco most often show a regular pattern, the mountain villages are made up of houses huddled together and presenting a continuous front view, whilst in the Algerian Sahara, the overwhelming majority of *ḳṣūr* simply consist of an agglomeration with a dense and complex pattern whose general contours attest an organic pattern of growth. As an economic centre and place of refuge, and as a nucleus for sedentarisation, the *ḳṣar* forms the basic political unit of these regions. In the southeast of Morocco, the management of the internal affairs of the *ḳṣar* is confided to two distinct political entities: the chief (*s͟hayk͟h* or *amg͟har*) elected once a year is seconded by the chiefs of the quarters or the great families (*mzarig* or *amur*) in order to avoid power being gathered up into the hands of a single kinship group. These balancing factors, which make up a small council (*d͟jamāʿa* [*q.v.*]), are guarantees of a social order that is expressed by means of prescribed forms and customary rules, often set down in writing.

The collective granary in the eastern Mag͟hrib. In southeastern Tunisia, the term *ḳṣar* further denotes a collective storehouse where the local people, living in the valleys near to cultivated fields, come to store their grain. The mountainous Tuniso-Libyan arc and its outliers, some 150 km/95 miles long, contains a hundred or so of these *ḳṣūr*, with similar ones in Algeria, in the region of Gourara. Built on a hilltop with escarpmented slopes, the *ḳṣar* here generally has a quadrangular plan, with its protective wall formed by the placing together of narrow rooms (*g͟hurfas*) with cradle vaulting, sometimes placed above each other on two or three levels, access to them being by an improvised outside ladder. Although nobody lives there, the *ḳṣar* is nonetheless a focus for the social life of peoples living a dispersed or troglodytic way of life. Sometimes it provides shelter for some artisanal activities, and it forms the point near to which an important market may on occasion be held. Likewise, one finds the mosque or *muṣallā* [*q.v.*], sometimes with a cemetery associated with it, at some distance away from the *ḳṣar* yet at the same time associated with it.

The overall view. It is extremely difficult, for reasons both historical and methodological, to trace the evolution of the habitat which finally contributed to the emergence of the "completed" form of the *ḳṣar*, the fortified village of the high plateaux of the Moroccan steppelands, more characteristic of certain regions which are in majority Berberophone than really "typical"—as has often been said—of a certain "Berber style of architecture". Various influences have been suggested in this regard: that of Africa, put forward at the time of the first exploratory travels, has speedily been forgotten, even if Terrasse perpetuated it in a certain manner by finding in the *ḳṣūr* an imprint of Pharaonic Egypt. The geometrical disposition of the Moroccan *ḳṣar*, above all the presence of a principal axis which serves the groups of dwelling places, has generated as many arguments in favour of the thesis of an influence from the Roman-Byzantine *castellum*, whilst the brick decoration which often ornaments the whole ensemble has raised the question of connections with the East and with Hispano-Moresque art. Suffice it to say that these suggestions still today do not go beyond simple formal or stylistic likenesses.

The problem of tracing the origin of the type is further exacerbated by the difficulty of dating these groupings, given the very fragmentary historical data and the absence of archaeological remains which can be firmly dated. Thus, although the Moroccan *ḳṣar* has for a long time been considered as an example of a "traditional" and "archaic" form of architecture, and therefore of an undateable nature, its existence is not attested by any sure material piece of evidence before at least the 17th and 18th centuries. The uncertainty over the dating—or at least, over the relative chronology—of these fortified villages has given rise to two postulates: (1) the prior dating of those with plans shows an organic growth compared with those having geometrical plans—*ḳṣūr* with regular plans are considered later than those which, in Tuwāt and elsewhere in the Sahara, show in their plans no concern for symmetry; and (2) *terre pisée* was substituted for stone—the *ḳṣūr* constructed of baked earth is seen as the end product of a process of change from the more ancient fortresses built in stone. These theories, even if they cannot be regarded as totally invalid, must, however, be approached with great prudence because of their neglect for the socio-economic and topographical considerations which brought about the conditions for the construction of these sites, and because of the *a priori* definition of a linear evolution of the construction techniques which they presuppose. Studies on the typologies involved, supported by the most rigorous possible surface explorations, are required to understand the phenomenon of the *ḳṣar* in all its breadth, geographical and chronological. J.-Cl. Echallier has accordingly made an exploration and inventory of over 300 *ḳṣūr* in the Gourara-Tuwāt region. Starting from formal criteria, he proposes classifying the ensemble of these sites into six main groups, ranging from storehouses used as refuges on rocky peaks (type I) to regular walled enclosures in unfired brick, displaying a sense of care in the organisation of the interior spaces (type VI). In southeastern Tunisia, some inscriptions on plasterwork placed on the arcading of the entrance vaulting, from which access leads into the *ḳṣar*, bear a date. A. Louis has studied and published the account of a granary which served as a place of refuge, the Ḳṣar Zanāta, which in this way dates to 475/1082-3, whilst at the Ḳṣar Djouama, an inscription dates either the building or the restoration of this part of the building to 1178/1764-5. The gap between these two dates indicates the degree of uncertainty which still reigns in the studies on the evolution of these forms of habitation in the Mag͟hrib.

Often placed in connection with the general phenomenon of a crisis which ruptured the complementary relationship between two types of economy, the nomadic and the sedentary, and which led to periods of conflict and change, it seems that the *ḳṣar* of southern Morocco and southern Algeria, like the communal storehouses of southeastern Tunisia, can be placed, in a more global and more nuanced way, in relationship to a situation of transition between nomadism and sedentarisation. This particular form of a place for keeping commodities and for refuge, or as a place for habitation, would thus form a nucleus for sedentarisation around which the territory of a given human group becomes organised. The *ḳṣar*, so characteristic of certain North African landscapes, is an architectural form on the verge of disappearing because of the major changes of recent decades in social relations and techniques. In these regions, it is now the village which has succeeded the *ḳṣar* as the basic element of social cohesion.

Bibliography: On the classical view of the Moroccan *ḳṣar*, see the basic works of E. Laoust, *L'habitation chez les transhumants du Maroc central (suite et fin)*, in *Hespéris*, xviii (1934), 109-96; H. Terrasse, *Kasbas berbères de l'Atlas et des Oasis*, Paris 1938; and BURD͟J. 4. On the storehouses of southeastern Tunisia, see A. Louis, *Tunisie du Sud. Ksars et villages de crêtes*, Paris 1975. For typology and corpus of monuments, see D. Jacques-Meunié, *Architectures et habitats du Dadès, Maroc présaharien*, Paris 1962; J.Cl. Echallier, *Villages désertés et structures agraires anciennes du Touat-Gourara (Sahara algérien)*, Paris 1972. For a new methodological approach, see W.J.R. Curtis, *Type and variation. Berber collective dwellings of the northwestern Sahara*, in *Muqarnas*, i (1983), 181-209; L. Mezzine, *Le Tafilalt, contribution à l'histoire du Maroc au XVIIe et XVIIIe siècles*, Rabat 1987 (fundamental work); P. Bonte, *L'habitat sédentaire "qsûrien" en Maurétanie saharienne*, in H.-P. Francfort (ed.), *Nomades et sédentaires en Asie centrale. Apports d'archéologie et de l'ethnologie*, Paris 1990, 57-67; P. Cressier, *La fortification islamique au Maroc. Éléments de bibliographie*, in *Archéologie islamique*, v (1995), 163-96, 203-4. (J.-P. VAN STAËVEL)

ḲAṢR ABĪ DĀNIS, a settlement of Islamic Portugal, revealed by archaeological excavations on the ancient site of Salacia, to the south of Lisbon, and on the site of the present convent of Aracoeli, the modern Alcácer do Sal.

It dates from the 3rd/9th century, when coastal defences were being erected against the Viking attacks which had begun in 230/844 [see AL-MAD͟JŪS]. The fortress occupied a major strategic site, up-river from the mouth of the Sado. According to Ibn Ḥazm and Ibn Ḥayyān, it was in the course of the *fitna* in this century, during the reign of the Umayyad *amīr* ʿAbd Allāh, that the Banū Dānis, Berbers driven from the region of Coimbra, besieged the place, which received their name. When ʿAbd al-Raḥmān III brought the region under his authority, he confirmed the Banū Dānis as chiefs in the town, which now became the capital of a *kūra* and grew into a prosperous centre. Ibn Abī ʿĀmir [see AL-MANṢŪR BI ʾLLĀH] made it into an important naval dockyard for attacking the shrine of St. James of Compostella in 387/997. As the main maritime outlet for the Afṭasids [*q.v.*] of Badajoz, Ḳaṣr Abī Dānis retained its role as a dockyard and arsenal and was also, according to al-Idrīsī, a prosperous commercial port. After the fall of Lisbon in 542/1147, the town was first taken by Afonso Henriques, but recovered by the Almohad caliph al-Manṣūr in 587/1191 before its definitive fall in 614/1217. Immediately after this, Muslim Alcácer declined in favour of Setúbal.

Bibliography: 1. Sources. Ibn Ḥayyān, *Muḳtabis*, reign of ʿAbd al-Raḥmān III, *Crónica del califa ʿAbd ar-Rahman III an-Nasir entre los años 912-942*, ed. Chalmeta, Corriente and Subh, Madrid 1979, tr. Viguera and Corriente, Saragossa 1981, 69, 167, 329; Ibn Ḥazm, *Djamharat ansāb al-ʿarab*, ed. Lévi-Provençal, Cairo 1948, 466; Ibn ʿIdhārī, *Bayān*, ed. Dozy, Leiden 1948-51, 238-9, tr. E. Fagnan, *Histoire de l'Afrique et de l'Espagne*, Algiers 1901-4, 394; Idrīsī, *Opus geographicum*, Naples-Rome 1975, 538, 544, tr. Dozy and De Goeje, ²Leiden 1968, 211, 219; Ḥimyarī, *Rawḍ*, ed. and tr. Lévi-Provençal, *La péninsule ibérique au Moyen-Age*, Leiden 1938, 193-4, tr. 161-2.

2. Studies. C. Tavarès da Silva *et alii*, *Escavações arqueológicas no Castelo de Alcácer do Sal (campanha de 1979)*, in *Setúbal arquelógica*, vi-vii (1980-1), 149-214; A.C. Paixão, J.C. Faria and A.R. Carvalho, *O castelo de Alcácer do Sal. Um projeto de arqueologia urbana*, in *IIIᵉ Encontro de arqueologia urbana, Braga 1994, Bracara Augusta*, xlv (1994), 97 (110); Ch. Picard, *L'océan Atlantique musulman de la conquête arabe à l'époque almohade*, Paris 1997; idem and I.C. Ferreira Fernandes, *La défense côtière à l'époque musulmane. L'exemple de la presqu'île de Setúbal*, in *Archéologie islamique*, viii (1999), 67-94. (CH. PICARD)

ḲAṢR AL-MUSHĀSH, an Umayyad period archaeological site in Jordan located 40 km/25 miles southeast of ʿAmmān. The core of the site consists of a *ḳaṣr*, a water reservoir and a bath, surveyed by King in 1980-1 and excavated by Bisheh in 1982-3. The *ḳaṣr* measures 26 m/85 feet square and consists of rooms around an open central courtyard, without any corner towers, and could accommodate up to 40 people. Re-used in one wall is a stone with a Kufic inscription asking for the forgiveness of the sins of an unknown Radjā b. Bashshār. Nearby is a plastered cistern 4.8 m/16 feet in diameter once roofed by stone slabs supported by arches, intended to supply the inhabitants of the *ḳaṣr* with drinking water. At 400 m/1,312 feet west of the *ḳaṣr* is a plastered water reservoir measuring 25 m/82 feet square. The excavated bath house was a simple structure with four rooms: an apodyterium, frigidarium, tepidarium and caldarium with a furnace. The bath has none of the lavish decorations characteristic of Ḳuṣayr ʿAmrā or Ḥammām al-Ṣarākh [*q.vv.*]. Other uninvestigated reservoirs, cisterns, walled enclosures and barrages dot the site. The pottery at the site is predominantly Umayyad. The function of the site, without a sizeable resident population, was to serve as a watering stop for caravans travelling between ʿAmmān and the northern Arabian Peninsula via the Wādī Sirḥān. Reduced traffic along that route after the ʿAbbāsid revolution soon led to the abandonment of the site.

Bibliography: G. King, C. Lenzen, and G. Rollefson, in *Annual of the Department of Antiquities of Jordan*, xxvii (1983), 386-91; G. Bisheh, *Qasr Mshash and Qasr ʿAyn al-Sil. Two Umayyad sites in Jordan*, in M.A. Bakhit and R. Schick (eds.), *Fourth International Conference on the History of Bilad al-Sham during the Umayyad period. English Section*, ii, ʿAmmān 1989, 81-104. (R. SCHICK)

ḲAṢR ṬŪBĀ, one of the so-called "desert castles" in Jordan, is located *ca.* 100 km/60 miles southeast of ʿAmmān. Since it is unfinished, information on the intended design of the elevations and the decorations are limited. The enclosure walls and the foundations were built of limestone, the remaining parts of brick. The building has a rectangular shape, measuring *ca.* 140 m (east-west) by *ca.* 70 m (north-south) and is flanked by five semicircular towers on the south side, two on the east and west sides. There was a round tower at each corner. In the north the arrangement is different (see below). The structure consists of two individual and identical halves, divided by a wall and connected with each other by a small passage. Each of the two buildings has a central courtyard of *ca.* 30 m by 30 m with rooms and/or smaller courtyards built around it. Entrance is given to each of the buildings by a gate flanked by square towers in the middle of northern façades. Between the two gates, a semicircular tower projects from the northern façade. Behind the gate, passages, *ca.* 6 m deep, lead into the courtyards. In each of the corners of the courtyards, traces of typical Umayyad *bayts*, i.e. two rooms flanking a central hall or courtyard on two sides, are to be found. This feature, in addition to the use of brick, the vaulting technique and the few decorations preserved, shows that the building must have been built in the late Umayyad period. Most authors consider al-Walīd II [*q.v.*] as the patron of this building.

Bibliography: A. Musil, *Ḳuṣejr ʿAmra*, Vienna 1907, 14-16; Jaussen-Sauvignac, *Mission archéologique en Arabie*, iii, Paris 1922, 29-50; G.L. Harding, *The antiquities of Jordan*, London 1967, 161-2; K.A.C. Creswell, *Early Muslim architecture*, i/2, Oxford 1969, 608-13. (H. GAUBE)

ḲASṬAL, one of the so-called Umayyad "desert castles", now in the Kingdom of Jordan. It lies *ca.* 15 km south of the centre of ʿAmmān. Its existence became known only at the beginning of the 20th century, following a publication by Brünnow and von Domaszewski (see *Bibl.*).

Until the 1970s, the period of its construction remained speculative, but since then there is little doubt that this desert castle was built in Umayyad times. The site consists of a palace and a mosque, the latter lying north of the palace. Changes in the construction as well as ceramic finds indicate that the place was used in the Ayyūbid-Mamlūk period as well as in later Ottoman times.

The palace is a square construction of *ca.* 59 × 59 m (without counting the towers), made of ashlars with cast work between the surfaces, with round corner towers and three semicircular intermediate towers on the northern, southern and western sides each, while the entrance was on the eastern side. The latter has four semicircular intermediate towers, two of which can be considered as part of the wings of the main entrance. Through a *ca.* 2 m-wide gate one enters into a space inside the tower, which is *ca.* 16 m deep and leads to an inner court of *ca.* 28 × 28 m. Around the inner court was a peristyle, behind which lay six groups of rooms, arranged *bayt*-wise (four on the eastern and western sides, with adjoining rooms in the corners, two on the northern and southern sides). Remains of an upper storey, which formerly surrounded the entire building, are only found in the neighbourhood of the tower room. The building thus resembles other Umayyad sites, the palace at Djabal Says [*q.v.* in Suppl.], Kharāna and Ḳaṣr al-Ḥayr al-Sharḳī [*q.vv.*] in particular.

A few metres off the western part of the northern palace wall lies a construction which originally was interpreted as a praetorium, but which is undoubtedly a mosque. Preserved are the remains of a rectangular surrounding wall of *ca.* 21 × 18 m, which encloses a courtyard and a prayer-house. Its north-western corner encloses a round tower with a diameter of *ca.* 6 m. From the southern side of the court a door leads to a rectangular prayer-room with a deeply vaulted *miḥrāb* [*q.v.*] in the middle of the southern wall. The mosque clearly shows three construction phases. The masonry of the earliest phase is the same as that of the inside constructions of the palace. It belongs to a mosque, which probably had a saddle roof. To this mosque also belonged the round tower, beyond all question one of the earliest minarets to survive. It proves that rectangular as well as round minarets were already erected in early Islamic times. In Ayyūbid-Mamlūk times the walls of the mosque were reinforced, and the original roof replaced by a barrel vault. In late Ottoman times, the mosque was further restored.

Bibliography: R.E. Brünnow and A. von Domaszewski, *Die Provincia Arabia*, Strasburg 1905, ii, 95-104, 676-85; H. Gaube, *ʿAmmān, Ḥarāna und Qaṣṭal*, in *ZDPV*, xciii (1977), 52-86; P. Carlier and F. Morin, *Recherches archéologiques au château de Qastal*, in *ADAJ*, xxviii (1984), 343-83. (H. Gaube)

KATHĪRĪ, a South Arabian tribal group and sultanate, the latter eventually becoming part of the Eastern Aden Protectorate prior to the departure of the British from South Arabia in 1967. Their origins were in the area of Ẓafār [*q.v.*] on the Indian Ocean, now within the Southern Region of the Sultanate of Oman [see ʿUMĀN], and they appear suddenly on the stage of history in the 9th/15th century. By the time the Eastern Aden Protectorate collapsed in 1967 after the departure of the British, the Kathīrī sultanate was made up of the centre and eastern end of the Wādī Ḥaḍramawt, tribal lands to the north of the Wādī towards the Empty Quarter [see AL-RUBʿ AL-KHĀLĪ] and to the south in the mountainous region towards the sea, although by this time they had no access to the sea. Their main towns were Sayʾūn [*q.v.*], the capital of the sultanate, Tarīm [*q.v.*], the intellectual centre, al-Ghuraf, Būr and al-Ghurfa, all within Wādī Ḥaḍramawt.

The Kathīrī tribe was of Ẓanna (sometimes written Ḍanna in the Arabic sources) and, according to al-Shāṭirī (*Adwār*, 234), Ḳaḥṭānīs of Sabaʾ, and not of Hamdān. Al-Shāṭirī adds (352) that Ẓanna are believed to have come from Muscat (Masḳaṭ) and Ẓafār.

The Kathīrīs first took Ẓafār in 807/1404 (al-ʿAlawī, *Taʾrīkh*, ii, 684). They took the important port of al-Shiḥr [*q.v.*] from the Ṭāhirids [*q.v.*] in 867/1462. The port, always vulnerable from the sea, was not only the emporium of Indian trade in the area but also handled the traffic of the pilgrims bound for Ḳabr Hūd in Wādī Ḥaḍramawt (Serjeant, *Portuguese*, 25 and see also his *Hūd*). Both trade and the pilgrimage traffic were huge sources of revenue. The exact situation is not clear, however, and it seems that the Kathīrīs on occasion held al-Shiḥr as governors of the Ṭāhirids.

The expansionist policies of the Kathīrīs are associated with the famous Badr Bū Ṭuwayriḳ (*r.* 922-77/1516-70). He fought the Mahra [*q.v.*] tribes to the east of al-Shiḥr, and endeavoured to keep the Portuguese and the Turks at bay as far as he could, playing them off against each other. He was able to pursue campaigns into Ḥaḍramawt, using Turkish-Portuguese rivalry to his own advantage. Badr even made use of the Turks and the Portuguese: with the aid of the former in 926/1520 he took Shibām, and with Portuguese musketeers he made gains in Wādī Ḥaḍramawt in 945/1539 (al-Kindī, *Taʾrīkh*, i, 164; Serjeant, *Portuguese*, 28). His successes in Ḥaḍramawt may well have been because of his access to firearms introduced by the Turks in the expedition against Shibām. He had no strong religious sentiment against the Portuguese, but this earned him the resentment of many Ḥaḍramīs who urged holy war against him (Serjeant, *Portuguese*, 27-30, 57).

Al-Kindī in his *Taʾrīkh* provides a whole catalogue of Kathīrī activities in mediaeval times in Ḥaḍramawt and on the coast. In 926/1520, for example, Badr went on to take both Tarīm and al-Ghurfa. In 934/1527, he struck coins in al-Shiḥr. Under the year 942/1535, the killing of a number of Portuguese is reported, others being shackled and plundered. The Kathīrīs were also in touch with the Turks and the Egyptians. In 943/1536, Badr began the building of the fortress of Ghayl Bā Wazīr in the coastal area. The year 944/1537 marked the arrival in al-Shiḥr of a Turkish galley to assist Badr against the Portuguese. It was announced that the *khuṭba* was to be pronounced in the name of the Ottoman sultan, Sulaymān Bā Yazīd (i.e. Süleymān the Magnificent). After Badr's death in 977/1569, there was less stability in the Kathīrī house. Reports for the following years reflect internecine squabbles (al-Kindī, *Taʾrīkh*, i, 164, 165, 180, 182, 185, 215, 216 and *passim*).

The struggle in 1064/1653 between the two Badrs of the Kathīrī family, Badr b. ʿUmar and Badr b. ʿAbd Allāh, brought the Zaydīs [see ZAYDIYYA] of the Yemen into the affairs of Ḥaḍramawt (al-Wazīr, *Ṭabaḳ al-ḥalwā*, 135 ff.). Badr b. ʿUmar al-Kathīrī, lord of Ḥaḍramawt, al-Shiḥr and Ẓafār, having already embraced the Zaydī rite, had the *khuṭba* pronounced in the name of the Zaydī Imām al-Mutawakkil (*r.* 1054-87/1644-76 [*q.v.*]). His nephew, Badr b. ʿAbd Allāh al-Kathīrī, had Badr b. ʿUmar arrested and imprisoned near Sayʾūn (Serjeant, *Omani naval activities*, 78). Al-Mutawakkil reacted swiftly to Badr b. ʿAbd Allāh's action against his uncle. Much correspondence passed between him and the Kathīrī, and the latter finally submitted, though Badr b. ʿAbd Allāh was resentful of the Imām's intervention and his submission was clearly a sham. Badr b. ʿUmar was obliged to flee Ẓafār, where the Imām had secured his governorship as part of his agreement with Badr b. ʿAbd Allāh, and finally arrived at the Imām's court in Ṣanʿāʾ [*q.v.*] in 1069/1659. This state of affairs now brought about a full-scale Zaydī military expedition into Ḥaḍramawt under the command of Ṣafī ʾl-Islām Aḥmad b. Ḥasan and accompanied by Badr b. ʿUmar. Ṣafī ʾl-Islām was able to subdue Ḥaḍramawt itself, but then experienced difficulties in supplying his large Zaydī army. He was thus unable to deal with the problem of Ẓafār, by this time under an ʿUmānī *amīr*. He returned from Sayʾūn to Ṣanʿāʾ (Serjeant, *Omani naval activities*, 79-80). By about 1080/1670, Zaydī influence in Ḥaḍramawt had declined and the Kathīrī sultans were in independent control there (*ibid.*, 84). Once again, sources provide a rather confused and lengthy catalogue of Kathīrī activities: military movements, battles, tribal problems and agreements, these involving also the Yāfiʿīs [see YĀFIʿ], who had entered the area, on occasion the Zaydīs, and from the mid-19th century onwards the Ḳuʿayṭīs.

The Government of Bombay's *Account of the Arab tribes*, compiled at the beginning of the 20th century, indicates (123) that Kat̲h̲īrī territory had originally been carved out of ʿAwlaḳī lands in the west and Mahra in the east, and included al-Mukallā on the coast, until 1881 when it passed to the Ḳuʿayṭī, and al-S̲h̲iḥr. The Kat̲h̲īrī sultanate lost much ground to the Yāfiʿīs and Ḳuʿayṭīs in the latter half of the 19th century. The *Account*, reporting on the Kat̲h̲īrī, also reports a total of 7,000 fighting males. Many Kat̲h̲īrī subjects were scattered over parts of India, Java, Singapore and East Africa, engaged in trade.

In 1883, Sultan ʿAbd Allāh b. Ṣāliḥ al-Kat̲h̲īrī visited the British Resident in Aden to assess the attitude of the British to his seizing al-Mukallā and al-S̲h̲iḥr from the Ḳuʿayṭī. The British answer was firm and to the point: if the Kat̲h̲īrī attacked the ports, the British would come to the aid of the Ḳuʿayṭī with a gunboat. The Kat̲h̲īrīs continued to smart at their loss of access to the sea (*Account*, 123).

It is interesting to note that in 1895, the Kat̲h̲īrīs still at this time had designs on their native region and they took Ẓafār, although they were unable to hang on to it for longer than two years. The *Account* also reports (124) that there was little contact between the Kathīrī and the Aden Residency in the 1860s and '70s and that there was none at all in the '80s and '90s. Unlike most of the other Aden Protectorate states, the Kat̲h̲īrī signed no 19th-century formal treaty of protection with Britain (*Account*, 130). They are, however, listed (154-5) among those states "having relations with Aden Residency". Their annual revenue is quoted as 24,000 rupees, although there was no stipend from the Residency. The sultan in 1906 when the *Account* was published was Manṣūr b. G̲h̲ālib.

It was only during the 1930s that relations between the Kat̲h̲īrī and the British became closer, the rapprochement occurring in the wake of the famous "Ingrams Peace", when the first British political officer in Ḥaḍramawt, Harold Ingrams, brought about a general peace between the years 1937-40 in the tribal lands of both Ḳuʿayṭī and Kat̲h̲īrī (Ingrams, *Arabia*, 10-19). This resulted in the political, social, agricultural, educational and medical development of both sultanates, including the completion of a road from Tarīm in Wādī Ḥaḍramawt to al-S̲h̲iḥr on the coast, and the increased British involvement in their affairs, culminating in the separate British administration of the Kat̲h̲īrī, Ḳuʿayṭī, Mahra and Wāḥidī [*q.v.*] sultanates as the Eastern Aden Protectorate. In March 1939, a treaty between the Kat̲h̲īrī and the British was finally signed (Smith, *"Ingrams Peace", Ḥaḍramawt, 1937-40*, see *Bibl.*; for the texts of the treaty, see *Records of Aden*, 239-40).

The sultanates of the Eastern Aden Protectorate never entered the Federation which was formed and fostered by the British in the Western Aden Protectorate. At the time of the withdrawal of the British in 1967, the Kat̲h̲īrī sultanate became a part of the People's Democratic Republic of Yemen. In 1990, with the unity of north and south Yemen, the whole of what had been the Eastern Aden Protectorate became a part of the Yemen Republic [see AL-YAMAN. 3(b)] with its capital at Ṣanʿāʾ.

Bibliography: Government of Bombay, *An account of the Arab tribes in the vicinity of Aden*, Bombay 1909; Muḥammad b. Hās̲h̲im, *Ḥaḍramawt. Taʾrīk̲h̲ al-dawla al-kat̲h̲īriyya*, Cairo 1948 (occasionally useful, but must be used with extreme care; there are clear errors); R.B. Serjeant, *Hūd and other pre-Islamic prophets of Ḥaḍramawt*, in *Le Muséon*, lxvii (1954), 121-79; idem, *The Portuguese off the Southern Arabian coast*, Oxford 1963; H. Ingrams, *Arabia and the Isles*, ³London 1966; Ṣāliḥ b. Ḥāmid al-ʿAlawī, *Taʾrīk̲h̲ Ḥaḍramawt*, 2 vols., Jeddah 1968; Serjeant, *Omani naval activities off the Southern Arabian coast in the late 11th/17th century from Yemeni chronicles*, in *Jnal. of Oman Studies*, vi (1983), 77-89; Muḥammad b. Aḥmad al-S̲h̲āṭirī, *Adwār al-taʾrīk̲h̲ al-ḥaḍramī*, Jeddah 1983; ʿAbd Allāh b. ʿAlī al-Wazīr, *Taʾrīk̲h̲ al-Yaman al-musammā Taʾrīk̲h̲ Ṭabaḳ al-ḥalwā wa-ṣiḥāf al-mann wa ʾl-salwā*, ed. Muḥammad ʿAbd al-Raḥīm D̲j̲āzim, Ṣanʿāʾ 1985; Sālim b. Muḥammad al-Kindī, *Taʾrīk̲h̲ Ḥaḍramawt al-musammā bi ʾl-ʿUdda al-mufīda al-d̲j̲āmiʿa li-tawārīk̲h̲ ḳadīma wa-ḥadīt̲h̲a*, ed. ʿAbd Allāh al-Ḥabs̲h̲ī, 2 vols., Ṣanʿāʾ 1991; Doreen and Leila Ingrams (eds.), *Records of Yemen 1798-1960*, 16 vols., [London] 1993; G.R. Smith, *"Ingrams Peace", Ḥaḍramawt, 1937-40. Some contemporary documents*, in *JRAS*, xii (2002), 1-30. (G.R. Smith)

AL-ḲAṬĪFĪ, Ibrāhīm b. Sulaymān, Imāmī S̲h̲īʿī jurist of the 9th-10th/15th-16th centuries.

He is most famous for his acrimonious dispute with his supposed classmate (or teacher), the influential ʿAlī b. ʿAbd al-ʿĀlī al-Karakī (d. 940/1534 [*q.v.*]). Al-Ḳaṭīfī moved from his birthplace Baḥrayn to ʿIrāḳ to study (some date this move to 913/1507). Apart from a pilgrimage to Mas̲h̲had, supposedly with al-Karakī, at some unknown date, he appears to have spent the rest of his academic life in southern ʿIrāḳ (Nad̲j̲af and later Ḥilla), teaching and writing. His academic output is mostly inspired by his personal and religious animosity towards al-Karakī. Al-Karakī had gained the favour of the Ṣafawid S̲h̲āh Ṭahmāsp I [*q.v.*], and al-Ḳaṭīfī accused him of egotism and legal chicanery aimed at personal enrichment. Such accusations can be found throughout al-Ḳaṭīfī's most famous work *al-Sirād̲j̲ al-wahhād̲j̲*, a detailed refutation of al-Karakī's *Ḳāṭiʿat al-lad̲j̲ād̲j̲*. The debate here concerned the legitimacy of land-tax (*k̲h̲arād̲j̲*) payable to the ruler. Whilst al-Karakī, benefiting personally from *k̲h̲arād̲j̲* revenue, argued that it was a permitted tax during the occultation (*g̲h̲ayba* [*q.v.*]) of the Imām, al-Ḳaṭīfī maintained that Ṣafawid rule was (legally speaking) illegitimate; no Ṣafawid tax could be legitimate and no gifts bestowed by the S̲h̲āh could be accepted. In one incident in Karbalāʾ, al-Ḳaṭīfī publicly refused to accept a gift brought by al-Karakī from S̲h̲āh Ṭahmāsp.

Most of al-Ḳaṭīfī's works remain in manuscript, and nearly all appear to be refutations of al-Karakī's views on subjects such as the *d̲j̲umʿa* prayer, fosterage and fasting. Some have linked al-Ḳaṭīfī to the emerging Ak̲h̲bārī school [see AKHBĀRIYYA, in Suppl.], but his juristic reasoning, though conservative, appears within the mainstream of S̲h̲īʿī jurisprudence. His date of death is unknown, but he is reported to have been alive as late as 951/1544.

Bibliography: 1. Texts. Ibrāhīm b. Sulaymān al-Ḳaṭīfī, *al-Sirād̲j̲ al-wahhād̲j̲ li-dafʿ ʿad̲j̲ād̲j̲ Ḳāṭiʿat al-lad̲j̲ād̲j̲* and *al-Risāla fi ʾl-riḍāʿ*, in *al-Riḍāʿiyyāt wa ʾl-k̲h̲arād̲j̲iyyāt*, Tehran 1313/1895; Yūsuf al-Baḥrānī, *Luʾluʾat al-baḥrayn*, Beirut 1406/1986, 159-66; Muḥammad Bāḳir al-K̲h̲ʷānsārī, *Rawḍāt al-d̲j̲annāt*, Beirut 1411/1991, i, 35-9; ʿAbd Allāh Afandī al-Iṣbahānī, *Riyāḍ al-ʿulamāʾ*, Ḳum 1403/1982, i, 15-19.

2. Studies. W. Madelung, *Shiʾite discussions on the legality of kharaj*, in *Proceedings of the Ninth Congress of the Union Européenne des Arabisants et Islamisants*, Leiden 1981; H.M. Tabataba'i, *Kharāj in Islamic law*, London 1983; A. Newman, *The development and political significance of the rationalist and traditionalist schools*

in Imāmī Shīʿī history, Ph.D. thesis, UCLA 1986, unpubl. (R. Gleave)

ḲAWĀʿID FIḲHIYYA (A.), legal principles, legal maxims, general legal rules (sing. *ḳāʿida fiḳhiyya*). These are *madhhab*-internal legal guidelines that are applicable to a number of particular cases in various fields of the law, whereby the legal determinations (*aḥkām*) of these cases can be derived from these principles. They reflect the logic of a school's legal reasoning and thus impart a "scaffolding" to the "case-law" (*furūʿ*).

Historically, general rules can be found already strewn throughout early *furūʿ* works. They were first collected by Ḥanafīs like Abu 'l-Ḥasan al-Karkhī (d. 340/952), but under the title of *uṣūl* rather than *ḳawāʿid*. (As a result, the term *aṣl* acquires, minimally, a fourfold meaning: (1) an act that has already been legally determined and now serves as a "model" for similar cases; (2) a scriptural pronouncement (Ḳurʾān or Ḥadīth) that is considered decisive for the legal determination of a given act; (3) a legal principle, under which several individual cases are subsumed; (4) a source of the law, such as the Ḳurʾān.) But this early start hardly bore fruit, and it is only around the 7th/13th century that all the legal schools began to produce books on *ḳawāʿid* (predominantly with this term in the title of their books), except (!) the Ḥanafīs. This strange gap in the latter's record is probably not to be attributed to a loss of their works, because the Ḥanafī scholar, Ibn Nudjaym (d. 970/1563 [*q.v.*]), complains about the fact that his school has nothing to compete with against the Shāfiʿīs in this respect (*Ashbāh*, 15)—a situation that he tries to redress by writing a *ḳawāʿid* book on the model of the Shāfiʿī Tādj al-Dīn al-Subkī's (d. 771/1370 [*q.v.*]) work. Some of the most influential *ḳawāʿid* works of the later period bear the title *al-Ashbāh wa 'l-naẓāʾir*, such as those of the Shāfiʿīs Ibn al-Wakīl (d. 716/1317), Tādj al-Dīn al-Subkī, and al-Suyūṭī (d. 911/1505), as well as that of the Ḥanafī Ibn Nudjaym. According to the co-editor of Ibn al-Wakīl's book, Aḥmad b. Muḥammad al-ʿAnḳarī, *ashbāh* refers to cases that are alike in appearance (*ẓāhir*) and legal status, while *naẓāʾir* denotes cases that are alike in appearance, but differ in legal status. Whether this is generally true remains to be seen. Look-alike cases of the latter type are dealt with in the *furūḳ* literature, the *farḳ* being the decisive difference that brings about a different legal determination (*ḥukm*). Since sections on *furūḳ* do occur in *ashbāh wa-naẓāʾir* works, one may consider such works an umbrella genre that comprises both the *ḳawāʿid* deduced from truly similar cases and the *furūḳ* indicating the differences between outwardly similar cases. Logically, and probably also historically, the establishment of similitudes among cases precedes the formulation of legal rules/maxims based on them as well as the recognition of *furūḳ* as obstacles to the subsumption of cases under a single rule.

However, with regard to the *ḳawāʿid*, this picture is too simple. Although generally valid rules (*al-ḳawāʿid al-kulliyya al-fiḳhiyya*) do exist, they are outnumbered by rules that are only "preponderant" (*al-ḳawāʿid al-aghlabiyya/al-aktharīyya*). In the *Īḍāḥ al-masālik ilā ḳawāʿid al-imām Mālik* of al-Wansharīsī (d. 914/1508 [*q.v.*]) the relationship of the two types is 17 to 101, and a number of legal scholars assert that legal rules, as opposed to other rules, are always preponderantly valid. The generally valid rules are couched in maxims, the preponderantly valid ones in double questions, thus e.g. *darʾ^u 'l-mafāsid^i muḳaddam^un ʿalā djalb^i 'l-maṣāliḥ* "warding off corruptions has the priority over bringing about benefits" is a *ḳāʿida kulliyya*, whereas *al-ẓann^u hal yunḳaḍ^u bi-'l-ẓann^i am lā* "can a presumption be canceled by [another] presumption or not?" is a *ḳāʿida aghlabiyya*. The term *aghlabī* refers to the fact that the non-subsumable cases are *istithnāʾāt* "exceptions" to the rule, rather than constituting a competing *ḳāʿida*.

The unmistakable blossoming of *ḳawāʿid* literature from the 7th/13th century onward expresses several tendencies:

(1) The focus of the *fuḳahāʾ* is *madhhab*-internal, not independent, *idjtihād* (*i. muṭlaḳ*). A good command of the *ḳawāʿid* will qualify the jurisprudent as a *mudjtahid al-fatwā*, someone who can issue a legal opinion on the basis of the *ḳawāʿid* of his school.

(2) The school-specific *ḳawāʿid* were collected from the *furūʿ* works or, where the imāms and other earlier authorities had not been explicit about their principles, were arrived at by induction from their *furūʿ* decisions (*ḳawāʿid istiḳrāʾiyya*). Ibn al-Wakīl (d. 716/1317) and Abū ʿAbd Allāh al-Maḳḳarī (d. 758/1357) are said to have done their own *istiḳrāʾ* of the major Shāfiʿī and Mālikī sources respectively (see al-Bāḥusayn, *Ḳawāʿid*, 324 and 328).

(3) There is a certain competitiveness among the schools to reduce the *ḳawāʿid* to the lowest possible number. The most extreme of these attempts is what Tādj al-Dīn al-Subkī imputes to ʿIzz al-Dīn Ibn ʿAbd al-Salām (d. 660/1262 [see AL-SULAMĪ]), that he reduced the whole of the Law to one principle, to wit *djalb al-maṣāliḥ wa-darʾ al-mafāsid* "bringing about benefits and warding off corruptions" (see al-Subkī, *al-Ashbāh*, i, 12, referring to Ibn ʿAbd al-Salām, *Ḳawāʿid al-aḥkām*, i, 6 and 11). These attempts at keeping the number small do not have any practical importance for the lawyer. They are an outcome of the desire to structure the law with the greatest economy.

Although the *ḳawāʿid* are mostly school-specific, some were generally accepted by all schools. Particularly famous are the so-called *al-ḳawāʿid al-khams* "Five Principles". Attested since the 8th/14th century, they are the following (there are variations in wording and sequence):

(1) *al-umūr^u bi-maḳāṣidihā* "Things [acts] are what they are through the intentions that bring them about";

(2) *al-ḍarar^u yuzāl* "Harm shall be removed";

(3) *al-ʿādat^u muḥakkama* "Custom is made the arbiter";

(4) *al-mashaḳḳat^u tadjlub^u 'l-taysīr* "Hardship brings about facilitation";

(5) *al-yaḳīn^u lā yazūl^u bi 'l-shakk* "Certainty is not erased (superseded) by doubt/uncertainty".

Restricting these principles, also called *al-ḳawāʿid al-kubrā*, the "Major Principles", to the number five may result from a desire for balance; an attendant saying goes: *buniya 'l-Islām^u ʿalā khams wa 'l-fiḳh^u ʿalā khams* "Islam has been built on five [sc. the *arkān*] and so has jurisprudence".

As for the position of the *ḳawāʿid* literature within legal studies, one may quote the Mālikī Shihāb al-Dīn al-Ḳarāfī (d. 684/1285), who says at the beginning of his *furūḳ* work that there are two kinds of *uṣūl*: *uṣūl al-fiḳh* and *al-ḳawāʿid al-fiḳhiyya al-kulliyya* (*al-Furūḳ*, i, 2), and the Ḥanafī Ibn Nudjaym who made the shocking statement that the *ḳawāʿid* are the real *uṣūl al-fiḳh* (*al-Ashbāh*, 15). While the latter statement seems exaggerated, it is clear that the *ḳawāʿid* were considered an important third "player" alongside the *uṣūl* and the *furūʿ*.

It should be mentioned that the *uṣūlīs* formulated hermeneutical principles that were called *ḳawāʿid uṣūliyya*; these are at times not carefully separated from the *ḳawāʿid fiḳhiyya*.

Bibliography: 1. Important *ḳawāʿid* texts. (a) Mālikīs. Abū ʿAbd Allāh al-Maḳḳarī (d. 758/1357), *al-Ḳawāʿid*, ed. Aḥmad b. ʿAbd Allāh b. Ḥumayd, Mecca n.d.; Wans̲h̲arīsī (d. 914/1508), *Īḍāḥ al-masālik ilā ḳawāʿid al-imām Mālik*, ed. Aḥmad Bū Ṭāhir al-K̲h̲aṭṭābī, Rabat 1400 A.H.; ed. al-Ṣādiḳ b. ʿAbd al-Raḥmān al-G̲h̲iryānī [?], Tripoli (Libya) 1401/1991. (b) Ḥanafīs. Abu ʾl-Ḥasan al-Kark̲h̲ī (d. 340/952), *al-Uṣūl* (plus Dabūsī, *Taʾsīs al-naẓar*), Cairo n.d.; Ibn Nud̲j̲aym (d. 970/1563), *al-As̲h̲bāh wa ʾl-naẓāʾir*, ed. ʿAbd al-ʿAzīz Muḥammad al-Wakīl, Cairo 1387/1968. (c) S̲h̲āfiʿīs. Ibn al-Wakīl, *al-Ashbāh wa ʾl-naẓāʾir*, i, ed. Aḥmad b. Muḥammad al-ʿAnḳarī, ii, ed. ʿĀdil b. ʿAbd Allāh al-S̲h̲uwayyik̲h̲, Riyāḍ 1413/1993; Ṣalāḥ al-Dīn al-ʿAlāʾī (d. 761/1317), *al-Mad̲j̲mūʿ al-mud̲h̲hab fī ḳawaʿid al-mad̲h̲hab*, ed. Muḥammad b. ʿAbd al-G̲h̲affār al-S̲h̲arīf, Kuwait 1414/1994; Tād̲j̲ al-Dīn al-Subkī, *al-As̲h̲bāh wa ʾl-naẓāʾir*, ed. ʿĀdil Aḥmad ʿAbd al-Mawd̲j̲ūd and ʿAlī Muḥammad ʿIwaḍ, 2 vols. Beirut 1411/1991; Badr al-Dīn al-Zarkas̲h̲ī (d. 794/1392), *al-Mant̲h̲ūr fī tartīb al-ḳawāʿid al-fiḳhiyya*, ed. Taysīr Fāʾiḳ Aḥmad Maḥmūd, 3 parts, Kuwait n.d. [1402/1982]; Suyūṭī, *al-As̲h̲bāh wa ʾl-naẓāʾir fī ḳawāʿid wa-furūʿ fiḳh al-S̲h̲āfiʿiyya*, ed. Muḥammad al-Muʿtaṣim bi ʾllāh al-Bag̲h̲dādī, Beirut 1407/1987. (d) Ḥanbalī. Ibn Rad̲j̲ab (d. 795/1393), *Taḳrīr al-ḳawāʿid wa-taḥrīr al-fawāʾid*, ed. Abū ʿUbayda Mas̲h̲hūr b. Ḥasan Āl Salmān. 4 vols. K̲h̲ubar 1419/1998. (e) Imāmī. al-S̲h̲ahīd al-Awwal (d. 782/1389), *al-Ḳawāʿid wa ʾl-fawāʾid*, ed. al-Sayyid ʿAbd al-Hādī al-Ḥakīm, 2 vols. Nad̲j̲af 1980.

2. Contemporary *ḳawāʿid* literature in Arabic. Yaʿḳūb b. ʿAbd al-Wahhāb al-Bāḥusayn, *al-Ḳawāʿid al-fiḳhiyya. al-Mabādiʾ – al-muḳawwimāt – al-maṣādir – al-dalīliyya – al-taṭawwur. Dirāsa naẓariyya taḥlīliyya taʾṣīliyya taʾrīk̲h̲iyya*, Riyāḍ 1418/1998; Muḥammad Ṣidḳī al-Būrnū, *al-Wad̲j̲īz fī īḍāḥ ḳawāʿid al-fiḳh al-kulliyya*, Beirut 1404/1983, and Riyaḍ 1410/1990; ʿAlī Aḥmad al-Nadwī, *al-Ḳawāʿid al-fiḳhiyya, mafhūmuhā, nas̲h̲ʾatuhā, taṭawwuruhā, dirāsat muʾallafātihā, adillatuhā, muhimmatuhā, taṭbīḳātuhā*, ⁴Damascus 1418/1998; idem, *al-Ḳawāʿid wa ʾl-ḍawābiṭ al-mustak̲h̲laṣa min al-Taḥrīr li ʾl-imām D̲j̲amāl al-Dīn al-Ḥaṣīrī (546-636 h), s̲h̲arḥ al-D̲j̲āmiʿ al-kabīr li ʾl-imām Muḥammad b. al-Ḥasan al-S̲h̲aybānī*, Cairo 1411/1991; Muḥammad al-Rūkī, *Naẓariyyat al-taḳʿīd al-fiḳhī wa-at̲h̲aruhā fī ʾk̲h̲tilāf al-fuḳahāʾ*, Riyāḍ 1414/1994; Ṣāliḥ b. Ghānim al-Sadlān, *al-Ḳawāʿid al-fiḳhiyya al-kubrā wa-mā tafarraʿa ʿanhā*, Riyāḍ A.H. 1417; Aḥmad Muḥammad al-Zarḳāʾ, *S̲h̲arḥ al-ḳawāʿid al-fiḳhiyya*, ed. ʿAbd al-Sattār Abū G̲h̲udda, Beirut 1403/1983; Muṣṭafā Aḥmad al-Zarḳāʾ, *al-Madk̲h̲al al-fiḳhī al-ʿāmm – Ik̲h̲rād̲j̲ d̲j̲adīd*, 2 vols. Damascus 1418/1998 [the third part is devoted to *al-ḳawāʿid al-kulliyya*, vol. ii, 965-1091]. Collections of *ḳawāʿid*. Muḥammad Ṣidḳī al-Būrnū, *Mawsūʿat al-ḳawāʿid al-fiḳhiyya*, 7 vols. Beirut 1416/1995 ff.; Bud̲j̲nūrdī, *al-Ḳawāʿid al-fiḳhiyya*, 6 vols. Nad̲j̲af n.d.

3. Studies. W. Heinrichs, *Structuring the law. Remarks on the Furūq literature*, in I.R. Netton (ed.), *Studies in honour of Clifford Edmund Bosworth*, i, *Hunter of the East. Arabic and Semitic studies*, Leiden 2000, 332-44; idem, Qawāʿid *as a genre of legal literature*, in B.G. Weiss (ed.), *Studies in Islamic legal theory*, Leiden 2002, 365-84 (with further bibl.).

(W.P. Heinrichs)

KAWĪR, DAS̲H̲T-I [see iran. i. 3].

KAYSŪM (modern Tkish. Keysun; Grk. Kaison; Arm. Kesun; Frankish Cressum and variants), a place situated to the south of Besni [*q.v.*], in eastern modern Turkey on the Keysun-çay, an affluent of the Sürfaz-çay, in the upper valley of the Euphrates. Considered in the 9th century A.D. as one of the marches of the Byzantine frontier, it commanded a col on the Besni road. Its fortress served as a base for the revolt of Naṣr b. S̲h̲abat̲h̲ [*q.v.*] but was dismantled after Naṣr's submission to al-Maʾmūn in 209/824-5.

Kaysūm was re-occupied by the Byzantines *ca.* 958, and at the end of the 11th century became the capital of the Armenian lord Gogh Vasil (d. 1112). The Franks annexed it in 1116 and it became part of the lands of the lord of Marʿas̲h̲. Baldwin of Marʿas̲h̲ (d. 1146) rebuilt the fortress in stone, but this has now disappeared. During this Frankish occupation, Kaysūm was the seat of a Latin bishopric. An Armenian bishopric is mentioned up to 1177 and a Jacobite one till 1174. It was even the place of residence of the Jacobite patriarch for a few years. All this indicates that there was living there an important Christian population.

Between 545/1150 and 568/1173 the Sald̲j̲ūḳs of Rūm and Nūr al-Dīn b. Zangī occupied it alternately. During Ayyūbid times it came within the territory of Aleppo, but its strategic role declined, and after the passage through it of the Mongols in 1260 it is mentioned only as a village under Armenian domination.

Bibliography: Yāḳūt, *Buldān*, ed. Beirut, iv, 497; Ibn S̲h̲addād, *Aʿlāḳ*, ed. and tr. A.-M. Eddé, in *BEO*, xxxii-xxxiii (1980-1), and see eadem, *Description de la Syrie du Nord*, Damascus 1984, index; Ibn al-ʿAdīm, *Bug̲h̲ya*, ed. S. Zakkār, Damascus 1988, i, 265; Michael the Syrian, *Chronicle*, tr. J.-B. Chabot, Paris 1899-1914, iii, 27, 55, 187, 269, 476; Matthew of Edessa, *Chronicle*, tr. A.E. Dostorian, London 1993, index; Cl. Cahen, *La Syrie du Nord*, Paris 1940, index; M. Canard, *H'amdanides*, Algiers 1951, 269; H. Hellenkemper, *Burgen der Kreuzritterzeit in der Grafschaft Edessa und im Königreich Kleinarmenien*, Bonn 1976, 67-71.

(Anne-Marie Eddé)

ḲAZAḲSTĀN, conventionally **KAZAKHSTAN**, a region of Inner Asia lying essentially to the south of Siberia and north of the older Islamic Transoxania [see mā warāʾ al-nahr]; the southern part of what is now the Ḳazaḳstān Republic includes what was in mediaeval Islamic times rather vaguely known as Mog̲h̲olistān [*q.v.*]. The modern Ḳazaḳstān Republic (formally, Ḳazaḳstān Respublikasï) is the largest state of Central Asia; it borders on its north and west with the Russian Federation of States, on the east with China and on the south with Ḳirgïzstān [*q.v.* in Suppl.], Uzbekistān [*q.v.*] and the northwestern tip of Turkmenistān [*q.v.*]. The capital since 1997 has been Astana (formerly Aḳmola), although the former capital Almatï (older Russian name, Alma Ata [*q.v.*]) remains the largest city.

1. Topography and climate.

Ḳazaḳstān covers an area of 2,724,900 km^2 and stretches from almost the lower Volga and the Caspian Sea in the west to the Altai and Tien Shan Mountains in the east. Deserts occupy the central and western parts of the country, while the northern part is largely covered by steppes. The highest point is K̲h̲antäṅgirï peak (6,995 m/22,944 feet) in the southeast. Main rivers are the Sïr Daryā [*q.v.*] which flows into the Aral Sea, the Ertïs (Irtïs̲h̲ [*q.v.* in Suppl.]) and Esïm (Is̲h̲im) which join the Obʾ river, the Ïle (Ili [*q.v.*]) which empties into Lake Balḳas̲h̲ (Balk̲h̲as̲h̲ [*q.v.*]), and the Oral (Ural [see yayïḳ]) river which drains into the Caspian Sea.

The average January temperature rises from -17° C

in the north to 0° C in the south, and the average July temperature increases from 19° C in the north to 28° C in the south. Annual precipitation levels are generally low, ranging from about 100 mm in the deserts to between 250 and 400 mm on the steppes, but higher levels of precipitation are observed in the foothills and mountains: e.g. in Almatï at the foot of the Alatau Mountains, it is 640 mm.

2. Demography and ethnography.

According to the results of the census in 1999, Ḳazaḳstān has a population of 14,953,100, giving it an average population density of 5.5 persons per km^2. The proportion of the urban population is the highest among the Central Asian states (56%).

The ethnic composition of the population underwent significant changes during the 20th century. In 1897, roughly 81% of the population of the present-day Ḳazaḳstān territory were Ḳazaḳs, and 11% were Russians. But due to continuous large influxes of Russians and other Europeans, as well as mass starvation of Ḳazaḳs during collectivisation and forcible sedentarisation in the late 1920s-1930s, the proportion of Ḳazaḳs decreased to 30% in 1959, while Russians then occupied 42.7%. Deportation by the Soviet authorities of Čečens, Germans, Koreans and others to Ḳazaḳstān on the eve of and during World War II also made the ethnic composition of the country diverse. In the 1970s, however, reverse migration of Russians to Russia started, and the proportion of Ḳazaḳs began increasing. In 1999, Ḳazaḳs formed 53.4% of the population; Russians, 30.0%; Germans, 2.4%; Ukrainians, 3.7%; and Uzbeks, 2.5%. The outflow of Russians, Germans and Ukrainians is so intense that the total population of Ḳazaḳstān has been decreasing since 1993.

Most Ḳazaḳs were nomadic people until they were forced to settle in the 1930s. They raised sheep, horses, goats and camels, and lived in felt-covered tents (*kiïz üy* in Ḳazaḳ, *yurta* in Russian) [see KHAYMA. iv]. Nomadism was the best form of adaptation to an arid environment before modern agricultural technology developed. Today, more than one-third of the Ḳazaḳs live in cities, whereas rural Ḳazaḳs engage in both farming and livestock breeding with limited seasonal migrations. In some areas during summer, Ḳazaḳs still live in felt-covered tents, which are also widely used as rest houses during festivals, even in cities.

Ḳazaḳs, except for the nobility and slaves, were traditionally divided into three large tribal confederations called Djuz (Ḳazaḳ form, Zhūz; the etymology of the term is unclear, though one thinks of Ar. *djuzʾ* "part, section"): Senior (Ulï Djuz, Middle (Orta) Djuz, and Junior (Kïshï) Djuz. The seniority among the Djuz was only nominal. The Senior Djuz occupied the southeastern part of Ḳazaḳstān, while the Middle Djuz occupied the eastern, northern and central parts, and the Junior Djuz occupied the western part. Each Djuz was divided into numerous tribes and clans. Although these tribal divisions were based on the nomadic way of life in the past, many Ḳazaḳs are still conscious of belonging to a Djuz and to tribes.

Ḳazaḳs also live in Sinkiang in western China (1,257,000 in 1996), Uzbekistān, Russia and other former Soviet countries, Mongolia, Afghānistān and Turkey.

3. Languages.

The Ḳazaḳ language belongs to the Ḳïpčaḳ group of the Turkic languages, together with Ḳaraḳalpaḳ, Noghay, Tatar, etc. Dialectal differences are not great. The written language of premodern times was a Ḳazaḳ version of Čaghatay Turkic, though its use was limited. The Ḳazaḳ literary language began to develop in the second half of the 19th century. In the early 20th century, Akhmet Baytūrsïnov and other intellectuals established the study of Ḳazaḳ linguistics and reformed the Arabic alphabet so that it would fit the phonetic characteristics of Ḳazaḳ. In 1928 the Latin alphabet was adopted, to be replaced in 1940 by the Cyrillic one [see further, TURKS. II. Languages, iv, v].

Ḳazaḳ became the state language in 1989, but most non-Ḳazaḳ citizens and some Ḳazaḳs do not understand it, while almost all citizens understand Russian. Russian was called "a language for inter-ethnic communication" by the language law in 1989, and the constitution in 1995 stipulated that Russian is to be used officially on equal terms with Ḳazaḳ.

4. Religion.

The Ḳazaḳs are Sunnī Muslims of the Ḥanafī *madhhab*. Islam was probably first introduced to a part of the sedentary population in southern Ḳazaḳstān by the incoming Arabs from the 8th century onwards, but nomadic people continued to worship Tañrï (the sky [*q.v.*]), fire and other natural beings and spirits. There were Nestorian Christians also. Because of the affinity between Ṣūfism and local traditional beliefs, Ṣūfīs, including Aḥmad Yasawī (1093?-1166 [*q.v.*]), who lived in Yasi (present-day "Türkïstan" or Turkistān in southern Ḳazaḳstān), greatly contributed to the propagation of Islam among both the sedentary and the nomadic populations. After the Mongol invasions, *khān*s of the Djočid *ulus* and the Čaghatayid *ulus* gradually came to support Islam. Ḳazaḳ *khān*s also maintained close relations with the *ʿulamāʾ* and Ṣūfīs of Transoxania.

Nevertheless, animistic beliefs and shamanistic customs were strongly maintained by Ḳazaḳs. Social and political affairs were usually regulated by customary law, *ʿādat*, not by the *Sharīʿa*. Although Tatar *mullā*s strengthened Islamic norms among the Ḳazaḳs, Ḳazaḳ intellectuals in the 19th and the early 20th centuries were more oriented towards European culture than towards Islam. Soviet anti-religious policies further weakened the influence of Islam on Ḳazaḳs.

From 1943, the Spiritual Directorate of Muslims of Central Asia and Ḳazaḳstān (known as SADUM), which collaborated with the Soviet government, controlled mosques in Ḳazaḳstān. In 1990, the Spiritual Directorate of Muslims of Ḳazaḳstān was separated from SADUM. At the same time, a certain degree of Islamic revival began both within and outside the framework of the Spiritual Directorate.

5. History.

From ancient times, present-day Ḳazaḳstān was the territory of various nomadic tribes and states: the Sakae, the Usun, the Kʿang-yüeh, the West Turkic Kaganate, the Türgesh, Ḳarluḳ and Oghuz Kaganates, the Ḳarakhānids, the Ḳarākhitāys, the Kimäks, the Ḳïpčaḳs, etc. Based on the Soviet theory which stresses the "autochthonness" of ethnogenetic processes, most Ḳazaḳ historians think that all these tribes are the Ḳazaḳs' direct ancestors; but most Western scholars are sceptical about it.

After the Mongol invasions, the Djočid *ulus* and the Čaghatayid *ulus* were established there. In the mid-15th century, most of present-day Ḳazaḳstān (the eastern Dasht-i Ḳïpčaḳ) was inhabited by the nomadic Özbeks, whose ruler was Abu 'l-Khayr, a descendant of Shïbān, Djočï's fifth son. In *ca.* 1460, descendants of another son of Djoči (the first son, Orda, or the thirteenth son, Toḳa Temür), Djānibek and Girey, split from Abu 'l-Khayr and moved to Mogholistān [*q.v.*] (southeastern Ķazaķstān). After they increased their power, they returned to the Dasht-i Ķipčaķ and replaced the Özbeks, who moved to the south of the Sīr Daryā. Their dynasty is known as the Ķazaķ Khānate, but its government structure and territory were unstable, and there is a dispute among Ķazaķstānī scholars on whether the khānate can be called a "state" or not. In any case, there is scant evidence of the ethnic consciousness of its inhabitants, and it is not clear whether the word "Ķazaķ", which originally means a "independent man" or a "wanderer", meant at this time a distinctive ethnic group.

In the late 17th and the early 18th centuries, fierce battles occurred between the Ķazaķs and the Oyirads or Oinats (Ķalmaķs [see KALMUK]) of the so-called Djungar Khānate (western Mongolia). This confrontation, on the one hand, consolidated the Ķazaķs' ethnic identity, and on the other hand, induced some Ķazaķ *khāns* to swear loyalty to the Russian Empress Anna Ivanovna, though in practice they remained independent. In the 1820s, Russia abolished the *khān*'s power in the Middle and the Junior Djuz, and started to rule directly most parts of Ķazaķstān. The territory of the Senior Djuz, which was under the rule of the Khoķand [*q.v.*] Khānate, was incorporated into Russia by the 1860s.

During the 1917 October Revolution and the ensuing civil warfare in Russia, Ķazaķ intellectuals established the Alash-Orda autonomous government. After it collapsed, the Autonomous Ķazaķ (mistakenly called "Kirgiz" in Russian usage until 1925) Socialist Soviet Republic was formed inside Soviet Russia. After receiving and abandoning some territories in 1925, it was in 1936 upgraded to the Ķazaķ SSR, one of the fifteen constituent republics of the USSR.

The 1920s and 1930s were especially hard times for Ķazaķstān: purges, mass collectivisation and forcible sedentarisation killed a large number of politicians, intellectuals, nomads and peasants. But at the same time, the Soviet government started the industrialisation of Ķazaķstān, which was accelerated during World War II, when factories were evacuated from Central Russia. The ethnic Ķazaķ cadre grew, especially since the 1960s under Dīnmŭkhamed Ķonaev, who served as first secretary of the Communist Party of Ķazaķstān for 25 years. When he resigned under pressure from Moscow in December 1986, Ķazaķ youths in Almatī and other cities held demonstrations, which were suppressed violently.

6. Post-Soviet Ķazaķstān.

Although the leadership of Ķazaķstān actively advocated maintaining and renovating the USSR, it declared independence in December 1991 when the USSR collapsed. Nŭrsŭltan Nazarbaev, who became first secretary of the Communist Party in 1989 and president in 1990, was known as a pragmatic and semi-democratic reformist. But in 1995 he took drastic measures to concentrate power in his own hands; the parliament was suddenly dissolved, the constitution of 1993 was abolished, and the new constitution increased the power of the president and restricted the functions of the parliament. The opposition's sphere of activity is very limited, though it has not been physically liquidated as in Uzbekistān and Turkmenistān.

Although the country is undergoing economic hardship, Ķazaķstān is rich in natural resources (especially oil and metals), which have not yet been fully exploited. Ķazaķstān's resources, as well as geopolitical importance, have drawn the attention of many foreign countries, and it maintains basically good relations with all neighbouring countries including Russia and China, as well as with the United States, Japan and European countries.

Bibliography: G.M. Wheeler, *The modern history of Soviet Central Asia*, London 1964; *Kazak Sov'et Éntsiklopediyasi*, 12 vols., Almatī 1972-8; A. Bennigsen and S.E. Wimbush, *Muslims of the Soviet empire. A guide*, London 1985, 63-73; E. Allworth (ed.), *Central Asia, 130 years of Russian dominance. A historical overview*, ³Durham N.C. and London 1993; *Kazakhi. Istoriko-etnografičeskoe issledovanie*, Almatī 1995; M.B. Olcott, *The Kazakhs*, ²Stanford, Calif. 1995; *Istoriya Kazakhstana s drevneishikh vremen do nashikh dnei*, Almatī 1996- (to be publ. in 4 vols.). (TOMOHIKO UYAMA)

KELANTAN, a state of northeastern Malaysia.

Lying on the coast adjoining the Malay areas of southern Thailand, Kelantan has long been a centre of devout Islamic scholarship and education, of Malay cultural creativity, and assertive forms of Malay-Islamic politics. Kelantan's traditional religious boarding school academies (*pondok* [see PESANTREN]) and their more illustrious teachers were well known throughout the Malay world; together with Malays from neighbouring Patani [*q.v.*] (Pattani) in southern Thailand, the Kelantanese constituted a sizeable component of the so-called *Djāwa* or Southeast Asian Malay community in 19th century Mecca. By the early 20th century, Kelantan was an important centre of publication of religious and Malay vernacular works and the site of important innovations in the collection and management of religious taxation (*zakat* and *fitra*) through its state religious council (*Majlis Ugama Islam*).

With its people intensely committed to their own local variants of the Malay language and culture, Kelantan has over time elaborated a powerful sense of its own distinctiveness within the wider Malay-Islamic world. It resisted Thai domination in the 19th century, succumbed to British rule in the first half of the 20th, and achieved independence in 1957 as part of the Federation of Malaya, later Malaysia. Since 1959 it has been the stronghold of PAS (*Parti Islam Se-Malaysia* [*q.v.*]), an avowedly Islamist party which, while playing a leading opposition role in national politics, has held power at the state level in Kelantan for much of the post-independence period (1959-78, and 1990 to present).

Since the 1980s, and especially since its return to power in Kelantan in 1990, PAS has promoted a strongly "*Sharīʿa*-minded" neo-traditionalistic Islamism. Since 1993, Kelantan has mounted a powerful challenge to the ascendancy of Malaysia's ruling multi-ethnic coalition by questioning the national government's Islamic credentials, most notably through its efforts to secure constitutionally-required federal assent to implement the *Sharīʿa* law, including the *ḥudūd* punishments, in Kelantan state.

Bibliography: W.A. Graham, *Kelantan, a state of the Malay Peninsula. A handbook of information*, Glasgow 1908; C. Snouck Hurgronje, *Mekka in the latter part of the 19th century*, Leiden 1931 (= Eng. tr. of orig. Dutch edition, 1888); W.R. Roff (ed.), *Kelantan. Religion, society and politics in a Malay state*, Kuala Lumpur 1974 (esp. ch. by Roff, *The origins and early years of the* Majlis Ugama, 101-52); C.S. Kessler, *Islam and politics in a Malay state. Kelantan 1838-1969*, Ithaca 1978; Shahril Talib, *History of Kelantan 1890-1940*, Kuala Lumpur 1995; Abdullah Alwi Haji Hassan, *Administration of Islamic law in Kelantan*, Kuala Lumpur 1996. (C.S. KESSLER)

KH^W^ĀDJAGĀN, a Ṣūfī brotherhood of Central Asia.

The movement of the Khʷādjagān belongs to the proto-history of the Naḳshbandiyya [*q.v.*] order, which often combines the two groups as the Khʷādjagān-Naḳshbandiyya. This movement, whose first figure is Abū Yaʿḳūb Yūsuf Hamadānī (d. 535/1140), took over a Ṣūfī tradition going back to the Prophet through Bāyazīd Bisṭāmī, Salmān al-Fārisī and the caliph Abū Bakr. This Ṣūfī tradition was at first known as the *Ṭarīḳat-i bakriyya* ("Abū Bakr's way") or *Ṭarīḳat-i Ṣiddīḳiyya*, and then at the time of Bisṭāmī, as the *Ṭayfūriyya* (from another name of Bisṭāmī). The main representatives of the Ṭayfūriyya were Abu 'l-Ḥasan Kharaḳānī, Abu 'l-Ḳāsim Gurgānī and Abū ʿAlī Fārmadī. It is only with Hamadānī, a pupil of the last-named, that the Ṭayfūriyya assumed the designation of *Ṭarīḳa-yi Khʷādjagān* ("way of the masters").

Yūsuf Hamadānī, having studied *fiḳh* at Baghdād and being connected with the Ḥanafī law school, spent his time between the cities of Marw and Harāt in Khurāsān. He was initiated into Ṣūfism by Abū ʿAlī Farmādī and founded a *khānaḳāh* [*q.v.*] at Marw, which became famous as "the Kaʿba of Khurāsān". Also, Hamadānī politely refused the support of the temporal power, in his time represented by the powerful Saldjūḳ sultan Sandjar [*q.v.*]. Conflicts over the manner of performing *dhikr*—whether out loud, *djahrī*, or inwardly and silently, *khafī*—caused divisions in Khʷādjagān circles and set these against the Yasawī Ṣūfīs [see YASAWIYYA], just as this later permitted the Naḳshbandīs to distinguish themselves from all other Ṣūfī brotherhoods. This conflict did not, however, exist in the time of Hamadānī, who practised *dhikr* of heart (*dhikr-i dil*) in preference to a public one (*dhikr-i ʿalāniyya*) but without rejecting this last; the *dhikr-i dil* was accompanied by the prolonged holding of the breath which made the Ṣūfī break out in violent sweats. In a short treatise, the *Rutbat al-ḥayāt*, attributed to Yūsuf Hamadānī, it is stated that "*dhikr* of the body", *dhikr-i tan*, which uses the tongue, *zabān*, is inferior to the *dhikr* of the heart. Moreover, it is averred, if *dhikr-i dil* is practised for forty days, lights will be manifested and will fill the heart.

Following the model of the Prophet and his preceptor Fārmadī, Hamadānī named four of his disciples as his successors. The first was ʿAbd Allāh Baraḳī, originally from Khʷārazm, who died and left his position to the second person, Ḥasan Andaḳī, from Bukhārā, who was in turn succeeded by the third, Aḥmad [*q.v.*] Yasawī (d. 562/1166-7), eponymous founder of the Yasawiyya and a native of Yasi (the present-day Turkistān [*q.v.*] in Kazakhstān). The hagiographies that later developed in Khʷādjagān and Naḳshbandī circles played down the role of Aḥmad Yasawī, and relate that Aḥmad, who had the reputation of a great spiritual master amongst the nomads, retired after having led the Khʷādjagān group for some time and installed the fourth of Hamadānī's disciples, ʿAbd al-Khāliḳ Ghudjduwānī (d. 617/1220 [*q.v.*]), who had not, however, apparently known Hamadānī himself. It is from this period that there dates the opposition between the groups claiming to stem from Aḥmad Yasawī, affirming that Yūsuf Hamadānī favoured *dhikr-i djahrī*, and the Khʷādjagān, who attribute to him *dhikr-i khafī*. According to the *Maḳāmāt-i Yūsuf Hamadānī*, attributed to Ghudjduwānī, *dhikr-i dil* was transmitted from Abū Bakr to Hamadānī's master Fārmadī, with an uninterrupted chain, and Hamadānī is reported on his death bed to have adjured his four disciples called to succeed him to only practise *dhikr-i dil* and avoid *dhikr-i djahrī*.

ʿAbd al-Khāliḳ Ghudjduwānī is the main figure in the Khʷādjagān movement, called "the first in the chain of the masters", *sar-daftar-i ṭabaḳa-yi khʷādjagān, sar-silsila-yi īn ʿazīzān*, although this title goes back to Yūsuf Hamadānī. Above all, he set forth and codified the main elements of Khʷādjagān doctrine, which were taken up by certain disciples of his, above all, by Bahāʾ al-Dīn Naḳshband (d. 791/1389 [*q.v.*]), eponymous master of the Naḳshbandiyya. Originally from a family of eastern Anatolia, ʿAbd al-Khāliḳ was born at Ghudjduwān in the Bukhārā oasis, and studied in Bukhārā. He soon evinced an interest in silent *dhikr*, to which he was initiated in a dream by the prophet Khiḍr. The hagiographical traditions recount that he then met Hamadānī in Bukhārā, becoming the latter's disciple, and Hamadānī authorised him to continue in the way of silent *dhikr*. The great merit of Ghudjduwānī was to have stated succinctly and codified, in the form of the eight adages or rules called "Holy Sayings", *kalimāt-i ḳudsiyya*, the essentials of Khʷādjagān doctrine and thought. Bahāʾ al-Dīn Naḳshband enriched these eight rules with three new ones, the whole making up his famous "Eleven Rules" of the Naḳshbandiyya, adopted and made the subject of lengthy commentaries by adepts of the order right up to the present day.

At the time of ʿAbd al-Khāliḳ, the "Holy Sayings" had the form of eight rules which, if followed, enabled the Ṣūfī to concentrate his attention and to organise for himself the contemplative life. ʿAbd al-Khāliḳ seems to have given preference to four of the rules, and these were the subject of a special commentary by such a Naḳshbandī author as Aḥmad Khʷadjagī Kāsānī (d. 949/1542; see his *Risāla-yi čahār kalima*, ms. 501/XVI, Bīrūnī Institute of Oriental Studies, Tashkent). The four rules were: (1) "assuming awareness in breathing", *hūsh dar dam*; (2) "observation of one's steps", *naẓar dar ḳadam*; (3) "journeying in the homeland", *safar dar waṭan*; and (4) "taking up a position of retreat within society", *khalwat dar andjuman*. The remaining four rules were: (5) "retaining in memory", *yād kard*; (6) "return [to God]", *bāz gasht*; (7) "maintaining awareness", *nigāh dāsht*; and (8) "keeping in mind", *yād dasht*.

Nevertheless, the Khʷādjagān movement had no doctrinal unity or agreement regarding the mystical exercises, and far from remaining united, Ghudjduwānī's disciples split into several rival groups after his death. One of these groups became known as the ʿAbd al-Khāliḳiyān, "the founder's partisans". The main Khʷādjagān who figure in the Naḳshbandī order's *silsila* after Ghudjduwānī are: ʿĀrif Rīwgarī (d. 649/1251); Maḥmūd Andjīr Faghnawī (d. 710/1310); ʿAlī ʿAzīzān-i Ramītanī (d. 716/1316 or 721/1321); Muḥammad Bābā-yi Sammāsī (d. 755/1354); and Sayyid Amīr Kulāl (d. 771/1370). Despite the importance laid on it by Ghudjduwānī, to be likewise stressed by Bahāʾ al-Dīn Naḳshband, silent *dhikr* was not followed by all Khʷādjagān circles. These circles developed a strong criticism of Ṣūfī movements contemporary with themselves and which they used to describe as corrupt. Above all, the Khʷādjagān held fast to a strict regard for the traditions of Islam, as reported in the *Rashaḥāt ʿayn al-ḥayāt*, where it is stated that Ghurdjduwānī encouraged his disciples to study Islamic law and the *Ḥadīth*, to avoid ignorant Ṣūfīs (*ṣūfiyān-i djāhil*), always to observe the Muslim worship, not to create any new *khānaḳāh* or to reside in such an institution, and not to be present at sessions of *samāʿ*.

There are two precious manuscripts, only brought to light and exploited in recent years, sc. the *Maslak al-ʿārifīn* of Muḥammad b. Asʿad al-Bukhārī (mid-8th/

14th century) and the *Manāḳib* of Khwādja ʿAlī ʿAzīzān-i Ramītanī (cf. D. DeWeese and J. Paul, below, in *Bibl.*), which are, at the present time, the two main sources on the practices and doctrines of the Khwādjagān before Bahāʾ al-Dīn Naḳshband. The Khwādjagān were mainly divided by the questions of *dhikr* and pious retreat (*khalwa*). In Bukhārā, the group headed by ʿĀrif Rīwgarī had good relations with that headed by Awliyā-i Kabī, but these deteriorated after the death of the former because his successor, Maḥmūd Andjīr Faghnawī, made the group adopt the open, vocal *dhikr*. The sources also tell us that Bahāʾ al-Dīn Naḳshband, who had been initiated into *dhikr khafī* by ʿAbd al-Khāliḳ Ghudjduwānī in a dream, came into conflict with his own master, Sayyid Kulāl, who was personally a proponent of *dhikr djahrī*. Ghudjduwānī's followers practised *dhikr* during which they held their breath, whilst concentrating on their *shaykh*'s heart, keeping their eyes closed, lips pressed together and tongue up against the palate. Amongst certain of the Khwādjagān, music and dancing were not formally proscribed. Likewise, *khalwa*, rejected by ʿAbd al-Khāliḳ as also rejected, later, by Bahāʾ al-Dīn Naḳshband, was nevertheless adopted by some members of the order; it was done in a darkened cell, where the adept had to struggle with his self by means of *dhikr*. A famous expression attributed to ʿAbd al-Khāliḳ, "close your door to *khalwa*, but open it to spiritual companionship (*ṣuḥba*)", shows the position of the early Khwādjagān on this subject and further reveals that ʿAbd al-Khāliḳ attributed a major importance to *ṣuḥba*, mystical discourse with the spiritual master, which was to become an essential feature for the Naḳshbandiyya. Like ʿAlī ʿAzīzān-i Ramītanī, ʿAbd al-Khāliḳ was opposed to the institution of Ṣūfī communal life *par excellence*, the *khānaḳāh*, but it is known that there existed amongst Sayyid Amīr Kulāl's disciples a form of association, whose precise nature is not clear, called a *djamāʿat-khāna* "house for social gatherings".

The Khwādjagān nevertheless remained essentially united in face of the other Ṣūfī currents in Central Asia, against the Ḳalandars [*q.v.*] and, in particular, against the Yasawī groups, whom they castigated for their lack of respect for the precepts of Islam. In sum, everything which symbolised Ṣūfism in general was rejected, from the *khānaḳāh* to the dervish cloak (*khirḳa*). The Khwādjagān were little attracted by asceticism, even if some of them preached abandonment of the secular world, *tark-i dunyā*, and encouraged *khalwa*, and Ramītanī went so far as to recommend that the Ṣūfī should have a trade (*ḥirfa*), a feature later found amongst the Naḳshbandiyya. In fact, a famous formula popularly attributed to Bahāʾ al-Dīn Naḳshband, "the heart should be with God and the hand with some piece of work", *dil bā-yār u dast ba-kār*, seems to have been inherited from a very similar maxim which one group of Khwādjagān held as a "Fifth Holy Saying" added to the four first ones: "the heart should be with God and the body in the market", *dil ba-yār wa tan ba-bāzār*. Another criticism of the Ṣūfīs on which they were united was rejection of the hereditary succession of *shaykh*s. This explains why, after the deaths of ʿAbd al-Khāliḳ and Bahāʾ al-Dīn Naḳshband, their communities of disciples split into several groups. In the 8th/14th century, Bahāʾ al-Dīn was unable to unite the various Khwādjagān groups and was only the master of one group out of many. Even if he did succeed in giving a more homogenous form to the doctrines and practices taught by ʿAbd al-Khāliḳ, and in retaining as vital principles for his own community, the one which was to become the Naḳshbandiyya, the obligation of a single, silent *dhikr*, the idea of *ṣuḥba*, adoption of the eight Holy Sayings and rejection of the practice of *khalwa* or retreat, it was only in the second half of the 9th/15th century, at Samarḳand, with Khwādja ʿUbayd Allāh Aḥrār [*q.v.* in Suppl.], that the Khwādjagān-Naḳshbandiyya were to take the form of a powerful, centralised Ṣūfī brotherhood.

Bibliography: 1. Sources. ʿAbd al-Khāliḳ Ghudjduwānī, *Risāla-yi ṣāḥibiyya*, in *Farhang-i Īrān-zamīn*, i/1 (1953); idem, *Maḳāmāt-i ʿAbd al-Khāliḳ Ghudjduwānī wa ʿĀrif-i Rīwgarī*, in *ibid.*, ii (1954); idem, *Maḳāmāt-i Yūsuf Hamadānī*, in Ḥarīrī-zāde Kemāl ul-Dīn Efendi, *Tibyān wasāʾil al-ḥaḳāʾiḳ*, Süleymaniye Ktph., Ibrahim Ef. collection, ms. 430, fols. 379a-389b, ed. N. Tosun, *Hayat nedir*, Istanbul 1998; Yūsuf Hamadānī, *Rutbat al-ḥayāt*, ed. Muḥ. Amīn Riyāḥī, Tehran 1983, Tkish tr. in Tosun, *op. cit.*, with information on Hamadānī's writings and Tkish tr. of two other texts by this author; Fakhr al-Dīn ʿAlī Kāshifī, *Rashaḥāt ʿayn al-ḥayāt*, Tehran 1978.

2. Studies. Khwādja Muḥammad, Pārsā, *Ḳudsiyya*, Tehran 1975; W. Madelung, *Yūsuf al-Hamadānī and Naqšbandiyya*, in *Quaderni di studi arabi*, v-vi (1987-8); H. Algar, *A brief history of the Naqshbandī order*, in M. Gaborieau, A. Popovic and Th. Zarcone (eds.), *Naqshbandis. Cheminement et situation actuelle d'un ordre mystique musulman*, Istanbul-Paris 1990; Algar, *Political aspects of Naqshbandī history*, in *ibid.*; D. DeWeese, *The Mashāʾikh-i Turk and the Khojagān. Rethinking the links between the Yasavī and Naqshbandī Sufi traditions*, in *JIS*, vii (1996); J. Paul, *Doctrine and organization. The Khwajagan Naqshbandiyya in the first generation after Baha'uddin*, Halle-Berlin 1998; F. Schwarz, *Bruderschaften, Gesellschaft, Staat im islamischen Mittelasien (Transoxanien) im 16. Jahrhundert*, Ph.d. diss., Univ. of Tübingen 1998; DeWeese, *Khojagani origins and the critique of Sufism. The rhetoric of communal uniqueness in the Manaqib of Khoja ʿAli ʿAzizan Ramitani*, in F. de Jong and B. Radtke (eds.), *Islamic mysticism contested. Thirteen centuries of controversies and polemics*, Leiden 1999; I. Togan, *The Khafi-Jahri controversy in Central Asia revisited*, in E. Özdalga (ed.), *Naqshbandis in Western and Central Asia: change and continuity*, Istanbul 1999; Zarcone, *Le "Voyage dans la patrie"* (safar dar waṭan) *chez les soufis de l'ordre naqshbandi*, in M.A. Amir-Moezzi (ed.), *Le voyage initiatique en terre d'Islam. Ascensions célestes et itinéraires spirituels*, Louvain-Paris 1999. (Th. Zarcone)

KHWĀDJAS, Khodjas, the designation of two lineages of spiritual and political leaders in Eastern Turkestan, the later Sinkiang [*q.v.*], and, more specifically, in the Altishahr ("six towns"), now in the western and southwestern parts of Sinkiang, where they played a decisive role from the late 10th/16th century to the last quarter of the 19th century. The lineages are distinguished as the White Mountain (Āfāḳiyya) line and the Black Mountain (Isḥāḳiyya) line (*aḳtaghlïk* vs. *ḳarataghlïk*, names possibly derived from the Tien Shan and Pamir [*q.v.*] mountain ranges, respectively).

Both lines were descended from the Khwādjagān-Naḳshbandī *shaykh* Aḥmad Khwādjagī-yi Kāsānī, known as Makhdūm-i Aʿẓam (d. 949/1542) (Bakhtiyar Babadžanov, *Političeskaya deyatel'nost' shaikhov Nakshbandiya v Maverannakhre (I polovina XVI v.)*. unpubl. diss., Tashkent 1996), who wielded considerable influence in the Shībānid [*q.v.*] internal struggles. One of his sons (the fourth or the seventh), Isḥāḳ, had to leave

Transoxania and came to Altî͟s͟hahr at an unspecified moment (between 990/1582 and 999/1591) where he stayed for some years; he died in Samarḳand in 1007/1599. He left behind an already powerful organisation that was to become the Black Mountain faction. Very much like their counterparts in Transoxania, the representatives of K͟hʷād͟ja Isḥāḳ acted as intermediaries between the Čag͟hatayid rulers and between the rulers, the begs and their subjects. They acquired considerable wealth (pious foundations, *waḳf*, and donations, *niyāzmandī*) on which their influence rested as well as on the communal affiliations of settled and nomadic communities. Almost from the start, they were active promoters of Islam among the still shamanistic Ḳîrg͟hîz [*q.v.*] and Ḳazak͟hs [see ḲAZAḲ] (J. Fletcher, *Confrontations between Muslim missionaries and nomad unbelievers in the late sixteenth century: notes on four passages from the 'Ḍiyāʾ al-qulūb'*, in *Tractata Altaica*, ed. W. Heissig, Wiesbaden 1976, 167-74). These endeavours must have gone on throughout. Later on, the White Mountain faction was instrumental in spreading Islam to China proper, beginning in the middle of the 17th century. (Fletcher, *The Naqshbandiyya in northwest China*, in his *Studies on Chinese and Islamic Inner Asia*, ed. B. Manz, Variorum, Aldershot 1995, no. XI, 1-46; this book also contains reprints of other relevant published texts by Fletcher).

It was unusual that a ruler came to occupy an elevated position in the spiritual hierarchy. This was, however, the case with Muḥammad K͟hān (*r.* 999-1018/1591-1609), who is even said to have been the Axis (*ḳuṭb*) (S͟hāh Maḥmūd Čurās, *Tārīk͟h (K͟hronika)*, ed. O.A. Akimus͟hkin, Moscow 1976 [Pamyatniki pis'mennosti vostoka, 45]). But apart from this, leadership in the Black as well as White Mountain group seems to have been hereditary, this principle extending even to the *k͟halīfa*s and sometimes to affiliations as well. The spiritual organisation adapted itself to the strongly localised political system of Altî͟s͟hahr: a city oasis governed by members of the ruling family or leading men of certain clans, with sometimes only nominal overlordship of the paramount k͟hān. The cities all had their *k͟halīfa*s. Whereas the centre of the Black Mountain faction was at Yārkand [*q.v.*], where the k͟hān also had his capital, the White Mountain faction centred on Kā͟s͟hg͟har [*q.v.*].

The Isḥāḳiyya K͟hʷād͟jas did not achieve a monopoly of spiritual guidance, however; at least in the north and northeast of Altî͟s͟hahr and beyond in the area where the Čag͟hatayid rulers held sway, other (sometimes local) groups were also active (in Ḳuld͟ja: see Masami Hamada, *De l'autorité religieuse au pouvoir politique: la révolte de Kūčā et Khwāja Rāshidīn*, in M. Gaborieau, G. Veinstein and Th. Zarcone (eds.), *Naqshbandis. Cheminements et situation actuelle d'un ordre mystique musulman*, Paris-Istanbul 1990, 455-89; in Turfan, the local shrine of Alpātā/Alfātā: see Akimus͟hkin, *op. cit.*, 165). To what extent other brotherhoods were active in the region remains open to question.

The Isḥāḳiyya supremacy did not last long. Sometime before the middle of the 17th century, another descendant of Mak͟hdūm-i Aʿẓam made his appearance in Altî͟s͟hahr in the person of Muḥammad Yūsuf (d. 1063/1653), son of Muḥammad Amīn, the eldest son of the Mak͟hdūm. He was able to gain a foothold in Kā͟s͟hg͟har and soon became influential with the Čag͟hatayid k͟hān. As a result of the rivalries that surrounded and followed his death, his son Hidāyat Allāh, better known as K͟hʷād͟ja Āfāḳ ("Master of the Horizons", whence the name by which the White Mountain faction was also known, sc. Āfāḳiyya) was compelled to take flight. The influence he had gained may be seen from the fact that he was given a Mog͟hul (although not Čingisid) princess in marriage. Āfāḳ then succeeded in persuading Galdan, the Zunghar k͟hān, to mount a campaign against Altî͟s͟hahr (1090/1679, when Galdan was only beginning his career as a conqueror). The report of Muḥammad Ṣādiḳ that this was achieved due to a letter from the Dalai Lama (the Zunghars had by then become Lamaist Buddhists) should perhaps also be seen as indicative of the view that spiritual leadership should prevail over military (Muḥammad Ṣādiḳ, *Tad͟hkira-yi k͟hʷād͟jagān*, epitome by R. Shaw, *A history of the Khojas of Eastern Turkistan*, in *JASB* [1897], extra number, pp. i-vi and 1-67, at 36-7; German version by M. Hartmann, *Ein Heiligenstaat im Islam. Das Ende der Caghataiden und die Herrschaft der Choğas in Kašgarien*, in *Der islamische Orient. Berichte und Forschungen*, vi-ix, Berlin 1905, 195-374, at 210-2). The Zunghars conquered Altî͟s͟hahr and reinstated K͟hʷād͟ja Āfāḳ as their vicegerent (*r.* 1090-1105/1679-94). The White Mountain faction now ruled with a degree of independence, but acknowledged Zunghar overlordship, paying them tribute (a comparatively heavy one, according to Fletcher's figures, unpubl. ms., ch. 3, 149-51) and accepting that members of their family be held as hostages. The area under this kind of K͟hʷād͟ja authority cannot have extended much over the four cities of K͟hotan, Yārkand, Kā͟s͟hg͟har and Aḳsu, the Oirot Zunghars having established their rule over the northeastern regions already in 1659. Nor had Čag͟hatayid rule come to an end; and even if the newly appointed k͟hān ʿAbd al-Ras͟hīd (who married his daughter to Āfāḳ, who thus became tied to the Čingisid house) was a puppet of the Zunghars, he was influential enough to build a faction together with the ousted Black Mountain followers; his attempt at a Mog͟hul-Black Mountain revival was, however, worsted in 1093-4/1682-3, and he was replaced by his brother. The White Mountain faction then set out to destroy their Black Mountain opponents, and after the Čag͟hatayid figurehead had died in 1103/1692, they tried to make do without a Mog͟hul k͟hān. In the ensuing strife, the deciding force in the southwestern part of Altî͟s͟hahr came to be the Ḳîrg͟hîz, but it was still a Mog͟hul who called back K͟hʷād͟ja Dāniyāl of the Black Mountain faction. Dāniyāl established himself with Ḳîrg͟hîz help, and until 1125/1713, when the Zunghars re-established their rule under Tsewang Rabtan, the oasis cities were under different nomad-K͟hʷād͟ja coalitions. After Dāniyāl had died *ca.* 1142/1730, the cities of Yārkand, K͟hotan, Kā͟s͟hg͟har and Aḳsu were divided up between his sons, thus furthering localisation. The next turn was induced by an attempt of the Black Mountain faction to break loose of the Zunghars, countered by their appeal to the White Mountain group (1166/1753); fights ensued between the two K͟hʷād͟ja factions, some Ḳîrg͟hîz begs, urban local begs, the nominal Zunghar ruler and his opponent Amursana, who was backed by the Chinese. As a result, the Zunghar empire was taken over by the Manchu Emperors, who consequently also came to be overlords of the Tarim [*q.v.*] basin as well.

The K͟hʷād͟jas failed because they were unable to build up a unified leadership, but more important still was their failure to gain a military basis of their own, not easily achieved under the circumstances. The resources available in the sedentary oasis economy could hardly support a state apparatus for revenue raising, and revenue was inadequate for building enough military strength to keep the nomads out.

Therefore, throughout this period, military power rested not with the urban-based Khwādjas, but essentially with their mainly nomadic Zunghar overlords and, as far as the region itself is concerned, with various Ḳirghiz groups.

It might appear that after the Chinese conquest of Altishahr, the fate of the Khwādjas was sealed, but this was not the case. After the first attempts at restoring White Mountain power had been crushed by the Manchus and their representatives in Altishahr (Amīn Khwādja of Turfan [*q.v.*], whose spiritual affiliation is not altogether clear), a period of relative stability ensued, which came to an end in 1820. By this period, the Khoḳand [*q.v.*] khānate had consolidated itself in the Farghāna basin, serving as a platform for repeated Khwādja incursions, the last of which occurred as late as the 1860s when Buzurg Khān, together with Yaʿḳūb Beg [*q.v.*], invaded Kāshgharia. It was only after the short-lived state of Yaʿḳūb Beg had been crushed in 1878 that the region was incorporated into the Chinese empire under the name of Sinkiang (1884) ("New dominion" [*q.v.*]), and this seems to have been the end of open Khwādja activity.

Bibliography: Partly given in the article. Islamic sources include hagiographic texts for both lineages as well as chronicles, many of them still remaining in manuscript; they are best discussed by Akimushkin and Fletcher. Chinese sources take prime importance only after the middle of the 18th century. *Tārīkh-i Kāshghar, faksimile rukopisi; izdanie teksta, vvedenie i ukazateli O.F. Akimushkina*, St. Petersburg 2001 (Pamyatniki kulʾturī vostoka, no. 8); Laura J. Newby, *The begs of Xinjiang; between two worlds*, in *BSOAS*, lxix (1998), 278-97; Isenbike Togan, *Islam in a changing society. The Khojas of Eastern Turkistan*, in Jo-Ann Gross (ed.), *Muslims in Central Asia. Expressions of identity and change*. Durham, N.C. and London 1992, 134-48; H. Schwarz, *The Khwājas of Eastern Turkestan*, in *CAJ*, xx (1976), 266-96 (to be used with caution); J. Fletcher, *China and Central Asia, 1368-1884*, in J.K. Fairbank (ed.), *The Chinese world order*, Cambridge, Mass. 1968, 106-224, 337-68; Fletcher, *Altishahr under the Khwajas*, unpubl. ms., Harvard University (chs. 2-4, "The Khojas of Eastern Turkestan", "The coming of the infidels" and "The triumph of the oasis nobility").

(J. Paul)

KHĀʾIR BEG (Khāyir or Khayr Bey), the last Mamlūk governor of Aleppo, subsequently first Ottoman viceroy of Egypt.

He was the son of Malbāy b. ʿAbd Allāh al-Djarkasī (*sic*), a Muslim Abaza trader in Circassian *mamlūks*. He was born at Samsun (on the Black Sea coast within the Ottoman Empire), and his father presented him, although not a slave, with his four brothers to the Mamlūk Sultan al-Ashraf Ḳāʾit Bāy [*q.v.*]. He was enrolled in the Royal Mamlūks, and was formally "emancipated" by the grant of a steed and uniform. He became an *amīr* of Ten in 901/1495-6, and subsequently an *amīr ṭablkhāna*, making his first contact with the Ottoman court as an envoy in 903/1498 to announce the accession of al-Nāṣir Muḥammad b. Ḳāʾit Bāy to Bāyezīd II. He was promoted *amīr* of a Hundred by al-Ashraf Djānbulāṭ (905-6/1500-1). Under al-Ashraf Ḳānṣawh al-Ghawrī, he held the important post of great chamberlain (*ḥādjib al-ḥudjdjāb*) until in 910/1504-5 he was appointed governor of Aleppo, where he was regarded as a severe but capable administrator. He was very wealthy, and maintained a large *mamlūk* household as his power-base, significantly including a company of arquebusiers "as in the Ottoman armies" (*kamā fī ʿasākir al-mamlaka al-rūmiyya: Durr*, i/2, 607). To Ḳānṣawh he must have seemed an overmighty subject, and the sultan unsuccessfully attempted to poison him.

His governorship of Aleppo ended with Selīm I's conquest of Syria, in which he colluded by going over to the Ottomans at the decisive battle of Mardj Dābiḳ [*q.v.*] (25 Radjab 922/24 August 1516). This act of treachery won him his final and supreme promotion, when Selīm, before leaving Cairo on 13 Shaʿbān 923/24 August 1517, appointed him viceroy of Egypt. He held this position until his death on 14 Dhu 'l-Ḳaʿda 928/5 October 1522, and although he kept up something of the state and usages of the defunct Mamlūk sultans, he remained ostentatiously loyal to his Ottoman suzerain. His viceroyalty began with the capture and execution of Ḳāsim Bey [see ḳāsim. 4], a grandson of Bāyezīd II, to whom Ḳānṣawh al-Ghawrī had given asylum. When Süleymān became sultan in 926/1520, and Djānbirdī al-Ghazālī [*q.v.*], the governor of Damascus and his former accomplice at Mardj Dābiḳ, rose in revolt, Khāʾir Beg studiously kept aloof, and prevented disaffected Mamlūks from joining him. Within Egypt, Khāʾir Beg's viceroyalty witnessed the restoration of stability. The terrorisation of the defeated Mamlūk soldiery ceased; they emerged from hiding, and resumed their traditional dress. Relations with the Ottoman troops, who envied their better pay and rations, were naturally uneasy. Although the former hierarchy of rank and office had fallen with the Mamlūk sultanate, the old administrative system largely survived, to be codified and perpetuated in the *ḳānūn-nāme* of Egypt, three years after Khāʾir Beg's death. Presiding over a crisis of transition in Egypt, Khāʾir Beg was thus one of the most successful survivors of the old régime.

Bibliography: For Khāʾir Beg's early history, see Ibn Iyās, *Badāʾiʿ al-zuhūr*, ed. Mohamed Mostafa, v, 253-4 n. 22, tr. G. Wiet, *Journal d'un bourgeois du Caire*, ii, 193-4; for his governorship of Aleppo, Ibn al-Ḥanbalī, *Durr al-ḥabab fī taʾrīkh aʿyān Ḥalab*, i/2, 603-9; for his vice-royalty of Egypt, Ibn Iyās, *Badāʾiʿ*, v, 203-486; Wiet, *Journal*, ii, 193-467; other references in respective indexes. Ibn Zunbul, *Taʾrīkh ghazwat al-Sulṭān Salīm Khān maʿa al-Sulṭān al-Ghawrī*, although apparently detailed, is essentially a prose saga forming a threnody on the passing of the Mamlūk sultanate.

(P.M. Holt)

KHALʿ (a.), the verbal noun from the verb *khalaʿa* "to take off (a garment), to remove, to discharge from an office, to depose" (sc. *ʿan ʿamalihī*, Lane, i, 2, 790a), "to dethrone (e.g. a ruler)", is the technical term for deposition. The modern Arabic term is *khalaʿa min al-ʿarsh* or *rafaʿa min al-manṣab*.

(i) *Historical development*. There are many cases of deposition or forced abdication throughout the course of Islamic history, e.g. in the Umayyad period (cf. Muʿāwiya II, 64/684 and Ibrāhīm, 126/744) and especially in ʿAbbāsid times. During this period, about a quarter of the rulers were deposed or forced to abdicate, pressured by the *de facto* ruling military leaders, after years of military disaster and misrule through favourites had amply demonstrated the incompetence of the caliphs. The unstable caliphs, many of whom had something of a genius for making bad situations worse, inevitably stimulated the claims of usurpers. After the war between the brothers al-Amīn and al-Maʾmūn, who each declared the other deposed [see khalīfa, at Vol. IV, 940a], the situation culminated in the anarchic period of Sāmarrāʾ and continued under Būyid rule (320-447/932-1055) and that of their successors, the Saldjūḳ sultans of ʿIrāḳ and western Persia (447-590/1055-1194), in whose hands the caliph was but a mere tool. The majority of the ʿAbbāsid caliphs were forced to abdicate, e.g. al-Mustaʿīn in 252/866 and his two successors, al-Muʿtazz in 255/869, and al-Muhtadī the following year. One ruler, al-Muḳtadir, had even to abdicate twice, in 296/908 and 317/929, and three caliphs, al-Ḳāhir in 322/934, al-Muttaḳī in 333/944 and al-Mustakfī in 334/946, were blinded, so that they were legally incapacitated from ever regaining power. Often the military leaders forced them, sometimes brutally, to abdicate, issuing an elaborate, sometimes falsified, document of the deposition, accusing them of treason, oath-breaking, etc., and insisting on a formal, written document of abdication. This act, considered as an essential part of the deposition process and registered officially by the judges, aimed at the nullification of the oath of allegiance. The forced abdication was accompanied by symbolic acts such as the taking off of clothes or shoes (cf. in the Old Testament, Ruth, iv. 7; see Goldziher, *Abhandlungen* i, 47-8), or turbans, or rings, and the yielding up of the insignia. Thus deprived of the sovereign dignity, the deposed caliph had to pay homage to his tractable successor, who was speedily installed. Often kept prisoner thereafter, many rulers were murdered, usually by rivals and relatives, or soon died. A striking example of a real deposition is the dethronement *in absentia* of al-Rās̲h̲id bi'llāh by al-Masʿūd b. Muḥammad in 530/1135. The practice of deposing rulers remained widespread throughout the Islamic world, particularly in the period of the Mamlūks and in Ottoman times. Often accused of alleged debility, a dozen Ottoman sultans were deposed, sc. Muṣṭafā I (1027/1618 and 1032/1623), ʿOt̲h̲mān II (1032/1622), Ibrāhīm (1058/1648), Meḥemmed IV (1099/1687), Muṣṭafā II (1115/1703), Aḥmed III (1143/1730), Selīm III (1222/1807), Muṣṭafā IV (1223/1808), ʿAbd al-ʿAzīz I (1293/1876), Murād V (1293/1876), ʿAbd al-Ḥamīd II (1327/1909) and Meḥemmed VI (1341/1922). Then, on 3 March 1924, the Grand National Assembly in Ankara definitively abolished the Ottoman caliphate, resulting in the creation of a secular Turkish state under Muṣṭafā Kemāl Atatürk [*q.v.*].

(ii) *Legal aspects.* The various instances of deposition became the starting point for subsequent discussions by Muslim writers. The question of the legitimacy of deposing a ruler was answered in different ways, but in general, Muslim writers denied to mere mortals the right of deposing rulers. The utterance *sulṭān ʿādil k̲h̲ayr min sulṭān ẓalūm wa-sulṭān ẓalūm g̲h̲as̲h̲ūm k̲h̲ayr min fitna tadūm* may demonstrate the attitude towards tyranny and the duty to obey even an unjust ruler (see details in U. Haarmann, *"Lieber hundert Jahre Zwangsherrschaft als ein Tag Leiden im Bürgerkrieg", ein gemeinsamer Topos in islamischen und frühneuzeitlichen europäischen Staatsdenken*, in U. Tworuschka (ed.), *Gottes ist der Orient, Gottes ist der Okzident. Festschrift für A. Falaturi*, Cologne-Vienna 1991, 262-9). The learned *ḳāḍī* al-Māwardī (d. 450/1058) defined in his *al-Aḥkām al-sulṭāniyya* (ed. M. Enger, Bonn 1853, 5, 23, 25-6, tr. E. Fagnan, Algiers 1915, 7-8, 30-1, 33) the office of the ruler and his duties. He laid down in his first chapter that any corrupt ruler who failed to meet the standards for the just, legitimate caliph might expect legitimate opposition and deposition, though he greatly feared misuse here. His exposition of the criteria for legitimate rulership played an important role in later times, and was cited again and again, for instance by Ibn D̲j̲amāʿa (d. 733/1333 [*q.v.*]) (see his *Taḥrīr al-aḥkām fī tadbīr ahl al-islām*, ed. H. Kofler, in *Islamica*, vi [1934], 349-414, vii [1935], 1-64, and [1938], 18-129, see ch. 1, § 3, and ch. 2, § 7). Other than a single passage in al-Fārābī's work on the perfect state (*Mabādiʾ ārāʾ ahl al-madīna al-fāḍila*, ed. F. Dieterici, Leiden 1895, repr. 1964, ch. 29, 63, tr. F. Dieterici, Leiden 1900, 100, ed. R. Walzer, Oxford 1985, 258, tr. R.P. Jaussen *et alii*, Cairo 1949, ch. 29, 87), the sources of political theory contain no distinction in the two bodies of the ruler, the visible individual and the objective institution, as in mediaeval European theories; see the exhaustive study of E. Kantorowicz, *Die zwei Körper des Königs. Eine Studie zur politischen Theologie des Mittelalters*, ²Munich 1994, esp. 385.

Bibliography: Besides the Arabic sources and the relevant historical studies, materials concerning Būyid times can be found in H. Busse, *Chalif und Grosskönig, die Buyiden im Iraq (945-1055)*, Beirut 1969, 28, 157-9, 500; see also C.E. Bosworth, *Notes on the lives of some ʿAbbāsid princes and descendants*, in *The Maghreb Review*, xix, 3-4 (1994), 277-84, esp. 278-9; for a single alleged case, that of al-Nāṣir li-Dīn Allāh, see A. Hartmann, *Wollte der Kalif sufi werden? Amtstheorie und Abdankungspläne des Kalifen an-Nāṣir li-Dīn Allāh (reg. 1180-1225)*, in *Egypt and Syria in the Fatimid, Ayyubid and Mamluk Eras*, Procs. of the 1st, 2nd, and 3rd International Colloquium, the Katholieke Universiteit, Leuven, in May 1992, 1993 and 1994, ed. U. Vermeulen and D. de Smet, Leuven 1995, 175-205; for the Mamlūks, see recently M. Espéronnier, *La mort violente à l'époque mamlouke. Le crime et le châtiment*, in *Isl.*, lxxi (1997), 137-55; for the Ottoman sultans, J. Matuz, *Das Osmanische Reich. Grundlinien seiner Geschichte*, Darmstadt 1985, index; and C. Kleinert, *Die Revision der Historiographie des Osmanischen Reiches am Beispiel von Abdülhamid II. Das späte Osmanische Reich im Urteil türkischer Autoren der Gegenwart (1930-1990)*, Berlin 1995, 130-41, 249-50; concerning juristic matters, see also the details in A.K.S. Lambton, *Theory and practice in medieval Persian government*, Variorum, London 1980, nos. II, III, V; further F.-C. Muth, *"Entsetzte" Kalifen. Depositionsverfahren im mittelalterlichen Islam*, in *Isl.*, lxxv (1998), 104-23. (F.-C. MUTH)

KHĀN, ʿABD AL-GHAFFĀR (1890-1988), Pathan leader and politician.

He was born at ʿUt̲h̲mānzay in the Peshawar district of the North West Frontier region of British India, his father Bahrām K̲h̲ān of the Muḥammadzay clan being a wealthy landowner and the chief k̲h̲ān of his village Hashtanagar. Educated first at a Ḳurʾān and then at a mission school, ʿAbd al-G̲h̲affār's early career was similar to those of many of the Muslim activists of his generation. From 1910 he began founding schools to stimulate social reform amongst the Pathans. At the same time, he was in close contact with the *ʿulamāʾ* of Deoband, in particular ʿUbayd Allāh Sindhi, and was strongly influenced by the pan-Islamic journalism of *al-Hilāl* and *Zamīndār*. After World War I he threw himself into the K̲h̲ilāfat movement [*q.v.*], and took part in the *Hid̲j̲rat* movement [see KHILĀFA, K̲H̲ILĀFAT MOVEMENT] to Afg̲h̲ānistān.

In the late 1920s, after performing the *Ḥad̲j̲d̲j̲*, the two guiding principles of ʿAbd al-G̲h̲affār's life became clear. The first was his concern to further the social and political advancement of the Pathans, or Pak̲h̲tūns as he called them. British rule had greatly enhanced Pathan identity by carving a Pathan province, the North West Frontier Province, out of the Punjab in 1901 to strengthen border security. The problem was that the British, given the province's strategic role and the relative backwardness of its people, were unwilling to give it the political advancement which had been given to the rest of India. To remedy this situation, ʿAbd al-Ghaffār founded in 1928 the *Pakhtun*, the first political journal in Pakhtu/Pashto, and in 1929, the *Khudāy Khidmatgār* or "Servants of God" organisation. *Khudāy Khidmatgārs*, who wore the uniform of a red shirt, did both social service and political tasks. ʿAbd al-Ghaffār's second guiding principle was non-violence. His *Khudāy Khidmatgārs*, though drilled in a military fashion, bore no arms and vowed to be non-violent, while he cooperated closely with India's leading apostle of non-violence, Mahatma Gandhi; in 1940, for instance, he resigned from the Working Committee of the Indian National Congress when it rejected a pacifist stance in World War II. Not once throughout a long life of protest did ʿAbd al-Ghaffār betray this principle, a remarkable fact given the warlike and vengeful traditions of his people.

From the early 1930s onwards, ʿAbd al-Ghaffār was the most influential figure amongst the Pathans, and between 1931 and 1947 he led large numbers of them in support of the Indian National Congress. From 1931, his Frontier Afghān Djirga [*q.v.* in Suppl.] became the Frontier Congress, and the *Khudāy Khidmatgārs*, the Congress Volunteers and their activities were largely responsible for bringing Congress ministries to power in the Province between 1937 and 1947. But why did these Pathans, staunch Muslims to a man, support the Congress which revealed, on occasion, strong elements of Hindu revivalism? The great personal influence of ʿAbd al-Ghaffār and his close relations with Gandhi and Nehru played some part. The power of the Congress in India played the major part, however: it offered the best chance of promoting Pathan interests—of winning provincial autonomy, of destroying British rule and of resisting inclusion within a Panjabi-dominated Pakistan. Only in this last and most vital matter was there ultimately disappointment; in 1947 the Congress abandoned ʿAbd al-Ghaffār and his Pathan Congressmen to their fate.

Within Pakistan, ʿAbd al-Ghaffār fought for the establishment of a Pathan state, Pakhtūnistān, although the area which it should include, and the degree of autonomy which it should have, remained ill-defined. He was not able to publish the *Pakhtūn*, the *Khudāy Khidmatgār* organisation was banned, and he spent most of his remaining days either in prison or in exile. In January 1988 he died at Peshawar but was buried in Afghānistān at Djalālābād, which he considered the original homeland of the Pakhtūns.

Bibliography: Sir William Barton, *India's North-West frontier*, London 1939; Sir Olaf Caroe, *The Pathans 550 B.C.-A.D. 1957*, London 1958; D.C. Tendulkar, *ʿAbdul Ghaffar Khan*, Bombay 1967; Bādshāh Khān (ʿAbd al-Ghaffār Khān), *My life and struggle*, Delhi 1969; M.S. Korejo, *The Frontier Gandhi: his place in history*, Karachi 1993.

(F.C.R. Robinson)

AL-**KHAṢṢĀF**, Abū Bakr Aḥmad b. ʿAmr (ʿUmar) b. Muhayr (Mahīr? also Mihrān and Mihrawān) al-Shaybānī al-Khaṣṣāf (d. 261/874), famous Ḥanafī jurist in the practical fields of *wakf*, *ḥiyal* [*q.vv.*], or legal stratagems and devices, and *adab al-ḳāḍī*, or laws of procedure and evidence. The sources speak of him as an expert also in the law of inheritance. He transmitted the doctrines of the Ḥanafī school from his father, who had transmitted them from Ḥasan b. Ziyād (d. 204/819-20) and Abū Yūsuf [*q.v.*], the students of Abū Ḥanīfa. He was also known as a student and transmitter of *ḥadīth* from no less than twenty scholars.

His family background, as well as the names of his father and grandfather, cannot be definitively determined, although the possible names of his grandfather suggest a Persian ancestry, as a client of the Arab tribe of Shaybān [*q.v.*]. In early life he must have worked as a cobbler (*khaṣṣāf*), since most sources say he lived off this calling. His scholarly endeavours nevertheless attracted the attention of the ʿAbbāsid court, then in Sāmarrāʾ. He was nominated by the former tutor of the caliph al-Muʿtazz [*q.v.*], with eight other scholars, for judgeships. But they were accused by palace personnel of being members of secessionist groups, so the caliph ordered their expulsion to Baghdād, and al-Khaṣṣāf was attacked by a mob (al-Ṭabarī, iii, 1683). Following the deposition of al-Muʿtazz in 255/869, and the start of the brief rule of al-Muhtadī (255-6/869-70 [*q.v.*]), al-Khaṣṣāf was brought back to the caliphal court as the court lawyer. It was during this period that he wrote a book about *kharādj* [*q.v.*], which unfortunately has been lost. Other books were also lost when his possessions were plundered following the murder of his patron, al-Muhtadī.

Ibn al-Nadīm, tr. Dodge, i, 509, says that al-Khaṣṣāf advocated the doctrines of the Djahmiyya [*q.v.*]. Since it is known that some Ḥanafīs advocated these doctrines, it is not unreasonable that al-Khaṣṣāf was one of them.

In the descending order of seven ranks of Ḥanafī jurists in the practice of *idjtihād* [*q.v.*], al-Khaṣṣāf has been placed in the third, following the first rank of Abū Ḥanīfa and the second rank of Abū Yūsuf and Muḥammad b. al-Ḥasan al-Shaybānī [*q.v.*]. Jurists of the third rank elucidated problems (*masāʾil*) not previously covered by jurists of higher rank (see Ṭashköprüzāde, *Ṭabaḳāt al-fuḳahāʾ*, Mawṣil 1954, 8-10).

His books, according to Ibn al-Nadīm, included the following: (1) *K. al-Kharādj*, which has been lost. (2) *K. al-Ḥiyal wa ʾl-makhāridj*. This book, which deals with legal devices and stratagems, was edited by Schacht, Hanover 1923, but Schacht thought that the book was written in the 4th/10th century and retrospectively attributed to al-Khaṣṣāf. An earlier printing appeared in Cairo in 1314/1896. (3) *K. Aḥkām al-awkāf*, Cairo 1322/1904, an early and authoritative treatise on *wakf*. (4) *K. al-Nafaḳāt*, ed. Abu ʾl-Wafāʾ al-Afghānī, Ḥaydarābād 1349/1930 and Beirut 1404/1984. (5) *K. Adab al-ḳāḍī*, which has been the subject of no less than ten commentaries (Ḥādjdjī Khalīfa, i, 72-3) including the commentary by Aḥmad b. ʿAlī al-Djaṣṣāṣ, ed. Farhat J. Ziadeh, Cairo 1978, and that by ʿUmar b. ʿAbd al-ʿAzīz b. Māza, ed. Muḥyī Hilāl al-Sirḥān, Baghdād 1397/1977. Other works mentioned by Ibn al-Nadīm, and not yet discovered/edited, may be looked up in Ibn al-Nadīm, tr. Dodge, i, 509-10.

Bibliography: In addition to the references given in the text, see ʿAbd al-Ḳādir b. Muḥammad al-Ḳurashī, *al-Djawāhir al-muḍiyya fī ṭabaḳāt al-Ḥanafiyya*, ed. ʿAbd al-Fattāḥ al-Ḥulū, Cairo 1398/1978, 230-2; ʿAbd al-Ḥayy al-Lakhnawī, *al-Fawāʾid al-bahiyya fī tarādjim al-Ḥanafiyya*, Banāras 1967, 23-4; Ḳāsim b. Ḳuṭlūbughā, *Tādj al-tarādjim fī ṭabaḳāt al-Ḥanafiyya*, Baghdād 1962, 12.

(F.J. Ziadeh)

KHATMIYYA [see mīrghaniyya].

KHAṬṬ.

vi. In Chinese Islam.

The evolution of the calligraphic art over almost a millennium amongst Chinese adherents of Islam (those now called the Hui) reflects the history of the implantation of Islam in China and its Sinicisation. During the first centuries of its presence in China,

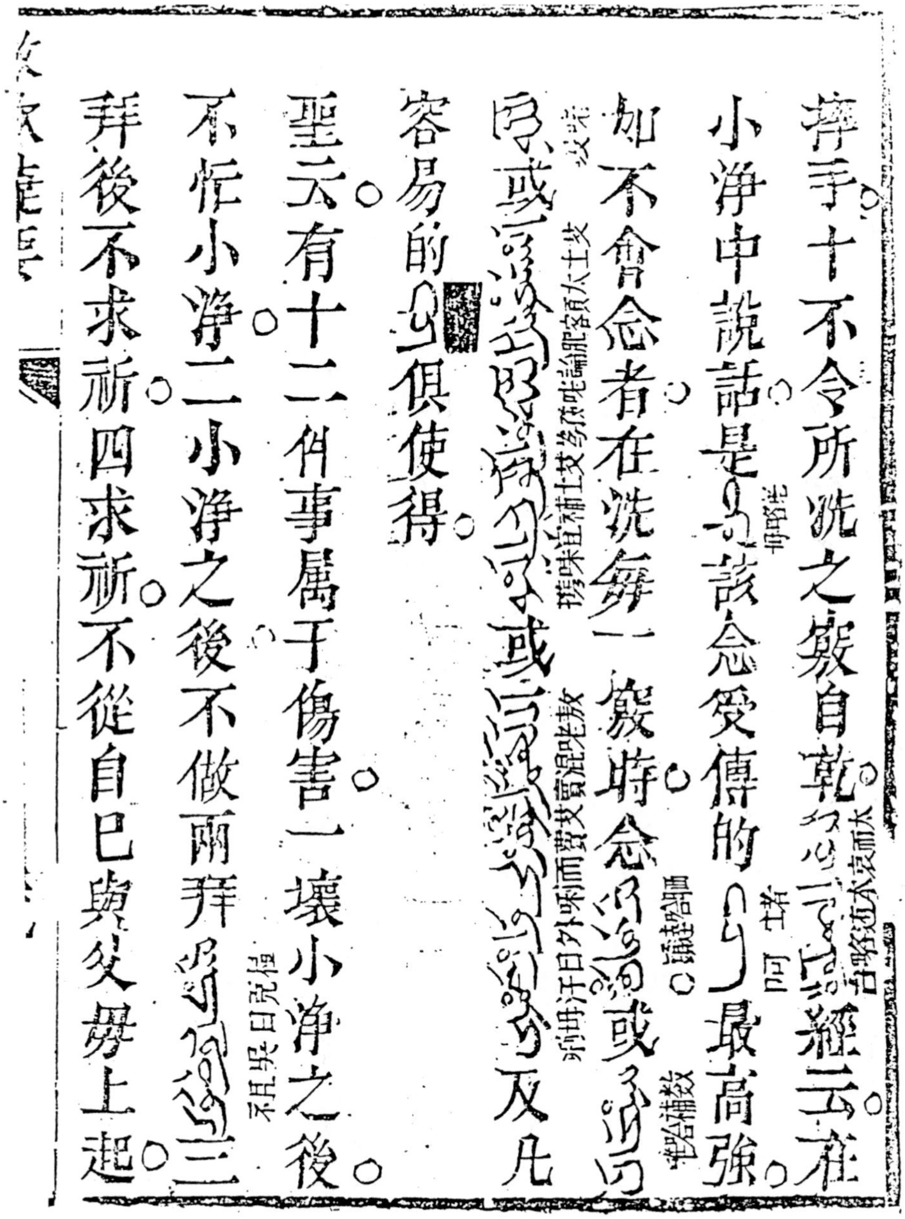
擦手十不令所洗之處自乾〇經云〇在
小淨中說話是該念受傳的最高強〇
如不會念者在洗每一般時念或
或或及凡
容易的俱使得〇
聖云〇有十二件事屬于傷害〇壞小淨之後〇
不作小淨〇一小淨之後不做兩拜三
拜後不求祈〇四求祈〇不從自已與父母上起〇

A cheap production, from Shantung/Shandong in 1874, in which the Arabic gloss (comprehensible by turning the book through 90°) has a supergloss of a transcription of the Arabic with the help of Chinese characters the *Chiao-k'uan chiai-yao/Jiaokuan jieyao* ("Quick résumé of the articles of the Faith") by Ma Po-liang/Ma Boliang, 1678.

A small Ḳurʾānic manual from 1912, in which the Chinese script tries to resemble Arabic writing.

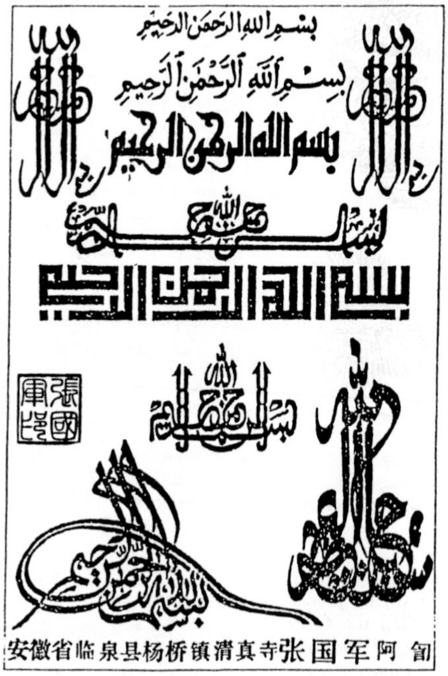

Examples of different types of artistic calligraphy made, as is stated in the lower part of the illustration, by the *imām* (*ahong*) Chang Kuo-chün/Zhang Guojun, of the mosque of Yang-chi'ao-chen/Yangqiaozhen ("town of the Yang bridge"), in the sub-prefecture (*hsien/xian*) of Chien-ch'üan/Jianquan in Anhui/Anhui province. In the centre, on the left-hand side, the Chinese seal of Chang Kuo-chün stands instead of a signature, according to Chinese custom (illustration taken from the journal of the Islamic Association of the PRC, the *Chung-kuo Mu-ssu-lin/Zhongguo Musilin* (1995), no. 6, at p. 45.

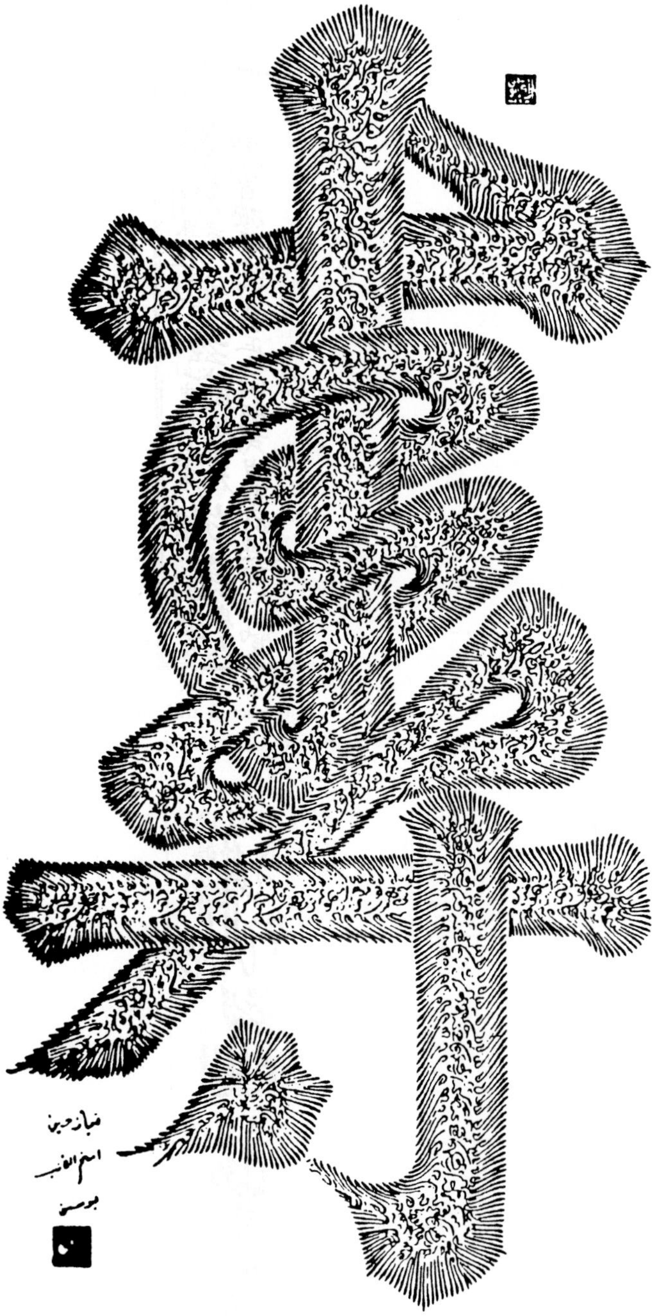

Written by a celebrated calligrapher of the present time, an *imām* (in Chinese, *ahong*) of Tientsin/Tianjin, Liu Ch'ang-ming/Liu Changming (b. 1927), the Chinese character, above all auspicious, *shou/shou*, is formed by the upright shafts of the Arabic letters. The artist's signature is given in Arabic below, and above, with a Chinese seal (work dating from 1985).

when this new faith was the achievement of merchants and of emigrants, temporary or permanent, coming from the Near East, Central Asia, Persia and India and mainly settled on the southern coastlands of China, the texts written in Arabic or Persian are to be found on tombstones and funerary stelae. Some date from the 12th century, but most are from the 13th and 14th centuries, the period when the Mongol rulers of China recruited foreigners for governing their Chinese subjects. They are first of all in an ornamental Kufic and then, later, in rounded characters—specimens of what one might call *muḥaḳḳaḳ*, or *riḳaʿ*, or *rīḥān* (see the corpus of some 200 examples existing in southeastern China made by a Chinese Islamic scholar, Chen Dasheng, and by an Arabic epigrapher, French by adoption, Ludvik Kalus, *Corpus d'inscriptions arabes et persanes en Chine. I. Province de Fujian*, Paris 1991). But from the 15th century onwards, funerary inscriptions are in Chinese, bearing witness to the integration of foreigners within the enveloping Chinese environment.

However, it was inevitable that, in a land where, in association with poetry, calligraphy was par excellence the art of cultivated persons, the Muslims should develop a personal calligraphic art once they were in possession of their own literature. They themselves characterise their calligraphic hands (see [in Chinese] Ch'en Chin-hui/Chen Jinhui, *Shih-lun a-la-po shu-fa tsai Chung-kuo Mu-ssu-lin chung-te ch'uan-po yü fa-chan/Shilun alabo shufa zai Zhongguo Musilin zhongde chuanbo yu fazhan* ["On the dissemination and development of Arabic calligraphy among Chinese Muslims"], in *Shih-chieh tsung-chiao yen-chiu/Shijie zongjiao yanjiu*, 1994, no. 2, 96-9) in terms of the actual instrument used for writing, whether a kind of bamboo reed or, more often, a brush made from the hairs of various animals, or in terms of a style inspired by Kufic, *naskh*, *thulth* or "Persian" (i.e. probably *nastaʿlīḳ*). But these styles are, in fact, all so strongly marked by Chinese influence that they speak of a "Chinese style" of their Arabo-Persian calligraphy, whence a cursive script which imitates the Chinese writing "of grass" (*ts'ao-tzu/caozi*), one almost unreadable for the uninitiated.

Another, more realistic, classification, operates substantially in terms of support for the writing and, consequently, of its destination. Books entirely in Arabic or Persian are extremely rare, Islamic literature being generally written in pure Chinese. Nevertheless, the Mission d'Ollone, which explored Western China during 1906-9, reported from the strongly Islamised region of Kansu [*q.v.*]/Gansu the existence of some ten manuscripts in Persian, locally written and in a good *naskhī* hand of the 18th or 19th century, and two in *nastaʿlīḳ* (see Mission d'Ollone, *Recherches sur les musulmans chinois*, Paris 1911, 284-93, or in *RMM*, viii-ix [1909]). Of a wider distribution, there are, from the 19th century, cheap, bilingual publications, in which the Arabic words, glossing the Chinese words and themselves accompanied by an approximate phonetic "transcription" in Chinese characters, are in a clumsy script (arising from the difficulty that Chinese engravers find in preparing plates for impression in the Arabic alphabet and, probably also, because of an imperfect education in local Ḳurʾān schools). Books where the Chinese characters are in a deformed state in imitation of Arabic characters are especially curious.

The type of calligraphy of which the Chinese Muslims are excessively fond, in the 1990s more often than not, is a stylised, decorative calligraphy in which "calligraphy and design make up a single whole (*shu-hua he-i/shuhua heyi*)" and which plays a role at the same time both propitiatory and displaying identity. These may be on paper, at the head of certain publications; or, above all, in the form of the so-called "designs of Ḳurʾānic letters" (*ching-tzu-hua/jingzihua*), with a composite Sino-Arabic technique and model, often found in vertical decoration (causing an extreme distortion of the Arabic script) or in a band in the centre of the prayer room, either in two parallel bands here and there in the mosque's *miḥrāb* [*q.v.*] or the prayer corner in a private house, or else in four bands put together on screens. In passing judgement on a piece of decorative calligraphy in Arabic characters, the believers are unconcerned about the form of the letters or the deformations necessary to fit them within a geometrical figure or to form the silhouette of an auspicious Chinese character; they make, rather, a general judgement using the same ideas with which they would judge a piece of Chinese calligraphy. Hence they recognise the use of the "northern style" for what is vigorous, and the more supple "southern style", that of the northwest being the most distinguished. In China, calligraphy, however Arabic it may be, forms an undeniable role in making up the Chinese culture of believers.

Bibliography: Given in the article, but see also Françoise Aubin, *L'art de l'écriture chez les musulmans de Chine*, in *Horizons maghrébiens*, xxxv-xxxvi/*Cahiers d'études maghrébines*, xi (1998), 29-43.

(FRANÇOISE AUBIN)

KHAWLA BT. **ḤAKĪM** b. Umayya b. Ḥāritha al-Sulamiyya, an early supporter of Muḥammad's cause at Mecca and an associate of his.

She was the daughter of a man of Sulaym [*q.v.*] who had come to Mecca and had become a confederate there of ʿAbd Manāf, and of a woman of ʿAbd Shams b. ʿAbd Manāf; hence Khawla was related maternally to the Prophet himself. She was an early convert to the new teaching, in company with her husband, the ascetic ʿUthmān b. Maẓʿūn [*q.v.*]. When he died in 3/624-5, Khawla is said to have "offered herself" (*wahabat nafsahā*) to Muḥammad, but the latter "put her off" (*ardjaʾahā*). She plays a role in Muḥammad's lifestory as the person who looked after him when Khadīdja [*q.v.*] died and who counselled him to marry the child virgin ʿĀʾisha and the widow Sawda b. Zamʿa [*q.vv.*].

Bibliography: Ibn Saʿd, viii, 113; Ibn Ḥanbal, *Musnad*, vi, 210-11, 409; Muḥammad b. Ḥabīb, *Muḥabbar*, 407; Ṭabarī, i, 1768-9; Ibn Ḥadjar, *Iṣāba*, iv, 691-2; Nabia Abbot, *Aishah, the beloved of Mohammed*, Chicago 1942, 2-4; W.M. Watt, *Muhammad at Medina*, Oxford 1956, 309.

(C.E. BOSWORTH)

KHAYRKH^WĀH-I HARĀTĪ, MUḤAMMAD RIḌĀ B. SULṬĀN ḤUSAYN, Nizārī Ismāʿīlī *dāʿī* and author. Born into a leading Nizārī Ismāʿīlī family in Ghūriyān near Harāt, in present-day Afghānistān, towards the end of the 9th/15th century, Muḥammad Riḍā b. Kh^wādja Sulṭān Ḥusayn Ghūriyānī, better known as Khayrkh^wāh-i Harātī, died not long after 960/1553, the latest date mentioned in his writings. Thus Khayrkh^wāh flourished in the early Andjudān period in post-Alamūt Nizārī history, when the Nizārī *daʿwa* and literary activities had begun to revive under the direct leadership of the Nizārī *imām*s themselves. In fact, Khayrkh^wāh represents the second most important literary figure, after Abū Isḥāḳ-i Ḳuhistānī (d. after 904/1498-9), in the contemporary Persian Nizārī Ismāʿīlī community; and his works are invaluable for understanding the Andjudān revival in Nizārī Ismāʿīlism and the Nizārī doctrine of the time.

In the autobiographical section of his *Risāla*, Khayrkhʷāh relates how his father, a *dāʿī* in the Harāt region, was murdered by brigands whilst on a journey to see the *imām* in Andjudān near Maḥallāt. Subsequently, the Nizārī *imām*, probably Mustanṣir bi ʾllāh III (d. 904/1498), better known as Shāh Gharīb, appointed Khayrkhʷāh, then only nineteen years of age, to the position of the chief *dāʿī* or *ḥudjdja*, then more commonly designated as *pīr* of Khurāsān and Badakhshān. Khayrkhʷāh also visited the Nizārī *imām* of the time at Andjudān and has preserved unique details in his *Risāla* on how the *imām* managed the affairs of the Nizārī *daʿwa* from his headquarters in Persia.

Khayrkhʷāh-i Harātī was a prolific writer and his works, all written in Persian, have been mainly preserved by the Nizārī Ismāʿīlī communities of Badakhshān (now divided between Afghānistān and Tādjikistān), Hunza and other northern areas of Pakistan. Khayrkhʷāh also composed poetry under the pen-name (*takhalluṣ*) of Gharībī, based on the name of his contemporary Nizārī *imām*. His writings include *Faṣl dar bayān-i shinākht-i imām* (ed. and tr. W. Ivanow in his *Ismailitica*, in *Memoirs of the Asiatic Society of Bengal*, viii [1922], 1-49; later editions and translations of this work by Ivanow were published in 1947, 1949 and 1960 in the series of publications of the Ismaili Society of Bombay), and the *Risāla-yi Khayrkhʷāh-i Harātī* (originally partially ed. and lithographed by Sayyid Munīr Badakhshānī in Bombay in 1333/1915), critically edited together with his *Ḳiṭaʿāt* and selections of his poetry (*ashʿār*) by Ivanow and published in a collection entitled *Taṣnīfāt* in Ismaili Society series A, no. 13, Bombay 1961. As Ivanow showed, Khayrkhʷāh also produced a plagiarised version of Abū Isḥāḳ-i Ḳuhistānī's *Haft bāb* (ed. Ivanow, Ismaili Society series A, no. 10, Bombay 1959, 3-8) under the title of *Kalām-i pīr* (ed. Ivanow, Islamic Research Association series, no. 4, Bombay 1935, introd.), attributing it to Nāṣir-i Khusraw in order to enhance its popularity among the Nizārī communities of Persia and Central Asia.

Bibliography (in addition to the works cited in the article): W. Ivanow, *Ismaili literature. A bibliographical survey*, Tehran 1963, 142-4; A. Berthels and M. Baqoev, *Alphabetic catalogue of manuscripts found by 1959-1963 expedition in Gorno-Badakhshan Autonomous Region*, Moscow 1967, 73, 104; I.K. Poonawala, *Biobibliography of Ismāʿīlī literature*, Malibu, Calif. 1977, 270, 275-7; F. Daftary, *The Ismāʿīlīs, their history and doctrines*, Cambridge 1990, 439, 469-71, 476-7, 481, 535.

(F. DAFTARY)

KHIFĀḌ [see KHAFḌ].

KHŌDJĀ-ZĀDE, Muṣliḥ al-Dīn Muṣṭafā b. Yūsuf, born into a well-to-do family in Bursa, was one of the leading Ottoman scholars of the 9th/15th century. Among others he studied with Khiḍr Beg [*q.v.*], and began his career as *ḳāḍī* in Ḳasṭal under Murād II [*q.v.*]. After 857/1453 he was appointed a private teacher of Meḥemmed II and held high positions in the law administration (*ḳāḍī ʿaskar* [*q.v.*], *ḳāḍī* in Edirne and Istanbul) and in the educational system of the empire (professor at the Sulṭāniyya in Bursa and in Istanbul). After 1470, following intrigues at the court, he was removed to Iznīk. Under Bāyezīd II [*q.v.*] he was rehabilitated and reappointed as professor and *muftī* [*q.v.*] in Bursa, where he died in 893/1488.

Most of his works have been lost, but those which have survived show the high level of his knowledge as well as of the educational system at the Ottoman universities in the 9th/15th century. Among the works that have survived are publications on the following subjects: (a) *Grammar*: a commentary on al-Zandjānī's *al-ʿIzzī fi ʾl-taṣrīf* (evidently composed as a textbook for Meḥemmed II); (b) *Fiḳh*: 1. Glosses to al-Taftāzānī's commentary on Maḥbūbī's *Tanḍīḥ*. 2. Glosses on al-Djurdjānī's glosses on al-Īdjī's commentary on Ibn al-Ḥādjib's *Mukhtaṣar Muntahā al-suʾāl*; (c) *Kalām*: 1. Commentary on al-Bayḍāwī's *Ṭawāliʿ al-anwār*. 2. Glosses on al-Khayālī's glosses on al-Taftāzānī's commentary on al-Nasafī's *ʿAḳāʾid*. 3. Glosses on al-Djurdjānī's commentary on al-Īdjī's *Mawāḳif* (this last work of Khodja-zāde, apparently unfinished, is critical of al-Djurdjānī); (d) *Philosophy*: 1. Glosses on Mawlānā-zāde's commentary on al-Abharī's *Hidāyat al-ḥikma*. 2. Commentary on al-Urmawī's *Maṭāliʿ al-anwār*.

Khodja-zāde's fame here is above all based on a work called *Tahāfut al-falāsifa* (printed in Cairo in 1321/1903-4, together with the *Tahāfut* of al-Ghazālī and the *Tahāfut al-tahāfut* of Ibn Rushd). The work was written at the instigation of Meḥemmed II, who organised a competition between Khodja-zāde and ʿAlāʾ al-Dīn Ṭūsī to answer the question who had been right in the dispute between al-Ghazālī and Ibn Rushd. Khodja-zāde gave a politic answer. Basically he sided with al-Ghazālī but corrected the latter's views on several points. At the same time, he emphasised that only the less important philosophers had made mistakes, while Ibn Rushd had a thorough command of his subject. This compromising attitude apparently carried approbation, for Khōdja-zāde was not only proclaimed winner by Meḥemmed II, but his *Tahāfut al-falāsifa* was still much read in the 10th/16th century and commented upon by several authors, among whom Kemāl-Pasha-zāde [*q.v.*].

Bibliography: Tāshköprüzāde, *Miftāḥ al-saʿāda*, Beirut n.d., ii, 161 ff.; idem, *al-Shaḳāʾiḳ al-nuʿmāniyya*, tr. O. Rescher, repr. Osnabrück 1978, 76-88; Muḥammad al-Shawkānī, *al-Badr al-ṭāliʿ*, Cairo 1348/1929-30, i, 306-8; Mübahat Türker, *Üç tahafut bakımından felsefe ve din münasebetleri*, Ankara 1956; Hassen Jarraï, *Tahāfut al-falāsifa par Khwādja Zāde*, diss., Paris 1972, unpubl.; Mustafa S. Yazıcıoğlu, *Le kalām et son rôle dans la société turco-ottomane aux XVe et XVIe siècles*, Ankara 1990, esp. 101 ff.

(U. RUDOLPH)

KHŌDJAS [see KHʷĀDJAS, in Suppl.].

AL-**KHULAFĀʾ** AL-**RĀSHIDŪN** (A.), literally, "the Rightly-Guided Caliphs", the four heads of the nascent Islamic community who succeeded each other in the thirty years or so after the death of the Prophet Muḥammad in Rabīʿ I 11/June 632. The qualifying term in the phrase has often been rendered as "Orthodox" (an anachronism, since there was no generally accepted corpus of Islamic belief and practice at this early time from which deviation could occur) or "Patriarchal", reflecting a view of this period as a heroic age for Islam.

The four caliphs in question comprised:

11-13/632-4	Abū Bakr b. Abī Ḳuḥāfa, called *al-Ṣiddīḳ*
13-23/634-44	ʿUmar (I) b. al-Khaṭṭāb, called *al-Fārūḳ*
23-35/644-56	ʿUthmān b. ʿAffān
35-40/656-61	ʿAlī b. Abī Ṭālib

All four were from the Prophet's own Meccan tribe of Ḳuraysh [*q.v.*], and all were already related to Muḥammad himself by marriage, whilst ʿAlī, as a first cousin on the father's side, was also a close blood relation. A strong feeling was thereby created that the caliph, as both military and religious head of the community, responsible for protecting the Muslim *umma* [*q.v.*] and its faith and for upholding the Prophetic heritage, should come from Ḳuraysh̲, a feeling later crystallised in a *ḥadīt̲h̲* attributed to the Prophet, "authority shall not depart from this tribe of Ḳuraysh̲."

It was Abū Bakr who first adopted the title of *k̲h̲alīfat Rasūl Allāh* "successor of the Messenger of God", with the implication of a necessity for the caliph to uphold and to further the Prophet's heritage; for the genesis of the title and its early development, see K̲H̲ALĪFA (I).

The three decades of the Rightly-Guided Caliphs saw the extraordinary expansion of the small Arab Muslim community based on Medina as the *mukātila* or warriors overran the outlying parts of the Arabian peninsula, Sāsānid ʿIrāḳ and Persia, and Byzantine Palestine, Syria and Egypt. By the time of ʿAlī's death, the Arabs were already raiding across the Oxus and into southern Afg̲h̲ānistān in the east, into Armenia and the Caucasus region in the north, and beyond Barḳa [*q.v.*] towards Tripoli and Fezzān in the west. The administrative and fiscal bases of the later caliphate also being laid down at this time, with ʿUmar's institution of the *dīwān* in which the pay allotments of the Arab warriors were registered, this military role became the requisite for full membership of the new community, creating the entitlement to share in its privileges [see ʿAṬĀʾ; DĪWĀN. I.]. The longer-term financial stability of the new state was ensured by the ruling authority's utilisation of a considerable proportion of the booty captured from the conquered lands for state and community purposes rather than it being shared out among the warriors and thereby dissipated [see BAYT AL-MĀL; FAYʾ; G̲H̲ANĪMA]. Hence by the end of the period of the Rightly-Guided Caliphs, the Islamic community was no longer a purely Arabian affair but was well established outside the peninsula. Although the Muslims were for long a minority in the conquered lands, the bases were being laid for the slow transformation of the societies of the conquered lands and their religious complexions. A pointer to this new orientation of the Muslim state was ʿAlī's move of the capital from Medina to the new military encampment of Kūfa in ʿIrāḳ; it was never to return to Arabia which, whilst remaining the locational focus for the Muslim cult, became from the political point of view, increasingly peripheral.

The end of ʿUt̲h̲mān's reign and the whole of that of ʿAlī's were marked by religio-political dissension. ʿUt̲h̲mān's murder accordingly inaugurated for the community a period of *fitna* [*q.v.*] or internecine strife, out of which eventually emerged such groups as the K̲h̲āridjites and the S̲h̲īʿa [*q.vv.*]. Hence the preceding part of the age of the Rightly-Guided Caliphs came in later times to be regarded through a nostalgic haze as a Golden Age of early Islam, when the community was undivided. The period was invested with the pristine virtues of piety, simplicity, justice, equality of all (male, free) Muslim believers, all the more so as later pietistic, traditionalist circles contrasted it with what they regarded as the worldly-oriented *mulk* or kingship of the Rightly-Guided Caliphs' immediate successors, the Umayyads [*q.v.*]; G.E. von Grunebaum coined the term "Rāshidūn classicism" for this backwards-looking feeling, discernible still in some contemporary fundamentalist currents of Islam.

Bibliography: See, in the first place, the separate articles on the four caliphs and the *Bibls.* there. There are relevant sections on the caliphs and their times in the general histories of Islam and its expansion, including Sir William Muir, *The Caliphate, its rise, decline, and fall*, revised ed. T.H. Weir, Edinburgh 1915; C. Brockelmann, *Geschichte der islamischen Völker und Staaten*, ²Munich 1943, Eng. tr., *History of the Islamic peoples*, London 1949; J.J. Saunders, *A history of mediaeval Islam*, London 1965; R. Mantran (ed.), *L'expansion musulmane (VIIᵉ-XIᵉ siècles)*, Paris 1969, ⁴1991; G.E. von Grunebaum, *Classical Islam, a history 600-1258*, London 1970; L. Veccia Vaglieri, *The Patriarchal and Umayyad caliphates*, in P.M. Holt *et alii* (eds.), *Camb. hist. of Islam*, i, Cambridge 1970; M.G.S. Hodgson, *The venture of Islam*, i, *The classical age of Islam*, Chicago 1974; H. Kennedy, *The Prophet and the age of the caliphs*, London 1986; A. Noth, *Früher Islam*, in U. Haarmann (ed.), *Geschichte der arabischen Welt*, Munich 1987. Specifically on the conquests of this period, see A.J. Butler, *The Arab conquest of Egypt*, 2nd ed. P.M. Fraser, Oxford 1978; F. McG. Donner, *The early Islamic conquests*, Princeton 1981; W.E. Kaegi, *Byzantium and the early Islamic conquests*, Cambridge 1992. On the internal evolution of the Islamic community and its stresses during this period, see Hichem Djaït, *La grande discorde. Religion et politique dans l'Islam des origines*, Paris 1989; W.F. Madelung, *The succession to Muhammad. A study of the early caliphate*, Cambridge 1997. For chronology, see C.E. Bosworth, *The New Islamic dynasties*, Edinburgh 1996, 1-2 no. 1. (C.E. BOSWORTH)

AL-**K̲H̲ULD**, ḲAṢR, the name of a palace of the early ʿAbbāsids in Bag̲h̲dād, so-called because of its being compared in splendour with the *djannat al-k̲h̲uld* "garden of eternity", i.e. Paradise.

It was built by the founder of the new capital Bag̲h̲dād, al-Manṣūr [*q.v.*], in 158/775 on the west bank of the Tigris outside the walled Round City, possibly on the site of a former Christian monastery (al-Ṭabarī, iii, 273; Yāḳūt, *Buldān*, ed. Beirut, ii, 382). It was strategically placed between the two great military areas of the Ḥarbiyya and al-Ruṣāfa on the eastern side [see AL-RUṢĀFA. 2.] and adjacent to the Upper or Main bridge across the river. The early ʿAbbāsid caliphs, and especially Hārūn al-Ras̲h̲īd and al-Amīn, resided in the K̲h̲uld palace, and the latter tried to escape by water from its riverside quay when Ṭāhir [*q.v.*] b. al-Ḥusayn's attackers were about to break into the city in 198/813 (al-Ṭabarī, iii, 917 ff.). It suffered badly from Ṭāhir's bombardment, and al-Maʾmūn stayed elsewhere on his first visit to Bag̲h̲dād from the East in 204/819. The seat of the caliphate was moved to Sāmarrāʾ some fifteen years later, and the K̲h̲uld palace must thenceforth have become completely ruinous; when, at the end of the century, al-Muʿtaḍid moved back to Bag̲h̲dād he occupied palaces on the eastern side. The site was only re-used when in 368/979 the Būyid ʿAḍud al-Dawla built there his Bīmāristān or hospital.

Bibliography: G. Le Strange, *Baghdad under the Abbasid caliphate*, Oxford 1900, 101-3; J. Lassner, *The topography of Baghdad in the early Middle Ages*, Detroit 1970, 55, 60, 105, 149, 154, 231, 243, 280. (C.E. BOSWORTH)

K̲H̲UMAYN, a small town in the province of Ḳum in modern Iran (lat. 33° 38' N., long. 50° 03' E.) some 70 km/42 miles to the south-south-east of Arāk/Sulṭānābād [*q.v.*]. It is unmentioned in the mediaeval Islamic geographers, but now has fame as the birthplace of the Āyatallāh Rūḥ Allāh K̲h̲umaynī (1902-89 [*q.v.* in Suppl.]). It is at present administratively in the *s̲h̲ahrastān* of Maḥallāt. In *ca.* 1950 it had a population of 7,038, which in 2003 had risen to 59,300.

Bibliography: Razmārā (ed.), *Farhang-i dju̲gh̲rāfiyā-yi Īrānzamīn*, i, 81-2. (Ed.)

KH̲UMAYNĪ, Sayyid Rūḥ Allāh Mūsawī (1902-89), Āyatullāh [*q.v.* in Suppl.] and prominent Iranian religious leader of the later 20th century.

He was born into a clerical family in the small town of K̲h̲umayn [*q.v.* in Suppl.] in central Iran, a few years before the Constitutional Revolution of 1906-11 [see dustūr. iv] opened the era of modern politics in Iran. Sayyid Rūḥ Allāh's father was murdered before he was a year old, and his mother died when he was in his teens. The reign of Riḍā S̲h̲āh (1925-41 [*q.v.*]), whose secularisation policies and dispossession of clerics he never forgot nor forgave, encompassed his formative years in Ḳum, where as an atypical seminarian he quietly studied mystical philosophy alongside jurisprudence, and began his teaching career. The popularity of his lectures on ethics in the latter part of the 1930s apparently caused the local police some apprehension. K̲h̲umaynī's entry into the public sphere began during World War II with the anonymous publication of *Kashf al-asrār*, a book written in defence of the S̲h̲īʿī hierarchy against a modernist anti-clerical pamphleteer. In it, he maintained that the *mud̲j̲tahids* had the authority to supervise parliamentary legislation and the deeds of the monarch. K̲h̲umaynī took a radically novel position in a tract on *id̲j̲tihād*, which was apparently written in the early 1950s but published in A.H. 1384/1964-5, in which he took the term *ḥākim* not only in the Arabic, technical, but also in the Persian everyday sense, to extend the judiciary authority of the *mud̲j̲tahid* to the political sphere as the right to rule (*Kungirih-i imām K̲h̲umaynī*, ix, 15-17).

K̲h̲umaynī first appeared on the national political scene in A.S.H. 1342/1963 as an outspoken critic of the S̲h̲āh and his reform program. The S̲h̲āh characterised his movement as "black reaction", and took repressive measures against it. K̲h̲umaynī was imprisoned in June 1963, and demonstrations by his supporters were violently suppressed. He was exiled to Turkey in November 1964, and moved on to the S̲h̲īʿī holy cities in ʿIrāḳ. In January 1965 a group of his followers assassinated the Prime Minister, Ḥasan-ʿAlī Manṣūr, with a plan for setting up a "unified Islamic government". While in exile in Nad̲j̲af, K̲h̲umaynī developed his theory of *wilāyat al-faḳīh* as the mandate of the jurist to rule, both in a series of lectures in Persian, which were published in Beirut in 1970 under the title of *Wilāyat-i faḳīh*, and in a work of jurisprudence on transactions, published in the second volume of *Kitāb al-Bayʿ* in A.H. 1391/1971. He argued that the right to rule devolves from the Imāms to the *mud̲j̲tahids* during the Occultation of the Twelfth Imām, and, further, that if one of them were able to exercise that right by establishing a government, it would be incumbent upon other *mud̲j̲tahids* to obey him. With this theory made public in clerical circles, K̲h̲umaynī began to prepare a beleaguered S̲h̲īʿī hierarchy for the takeover of a hostile, secularising state. His former students played the leading role in his movement and mobilised many younger clerics from humble rural and small town backgrounds in opposition to the monarchy and to Western cultural domination. As the leader of the Islamic revolutionary movement, K̲h̲umaynī assumed the title of *imām*, a title reserved for the twelve holy S̲h̲īʿī Imāms and not used by anyone else in Persian for over a thousand years.

On the victory of the Islamic revolution, Imām K̲h̲umaynī exercised his prerogatives according to the theory of *wilāyat al-faḳīh*, in ordering the confiscation of the property of the Pahlawī family and other industrialists of the old régime as war booty, and in appointing Mahdī Bāzargān, who represented the liberal and nationalist elements in the revolutionary coalition, as provisional prime minister. However, he was careful not to alienate the followers of the lay Muslim intellectuals and ideologues, such as D̲j̲alāl Āl-i Aḥmad and ʿAlī S̲h̲arīʿatī, and did not proclaim a theocratic government at once. The *wilāyat al-faḳīh* entered public debate only when a clerically-dominated Assembly of Experts was elected, in place of a constituent assembly, and bypassed the draft constitution prepared by the provisional government to institute theocratic government according to K̲h̲umaynī's theory. Some of the features of the original draft were retained, however, notably the elected president and parliament (*Mad̲j̲lis*), and a Council of Guardians (*s̲h̲ūrā-yi nigahbān*) which was modified to increase the number and power of its clerical jurists by giving them the exclusive right to veto any *Mad̲j̲lis* enactment they found in violation of Islamic standards. The new Constitution was approved by a referendum in December 1979, shortly after the occupation of the American embassy and the taking of its staff as hostages and the resignation of Bāzargān.

In the course of the ensuing power struggle of the early 1980s among the partners in the revolutionary coalition, K̲h̲umaynī sanctioned the violent suppression of the leftist and secular elements. Despite his apparent initial disinclination, the Iranian state and the revolutionary structures were brought under direct clerical control. Once the revolutionary power struggle ended with the complete victory of his supporters, K̲h̲umaynī sought to maintain unity between the conservative and the radical clerics and their respective allies, and intervened a number of times to prevent the tilting of the balance of power in favour of the former. Meanwhile, he oversaw the constitutional development of the Islamic theocratic republic he had founded. The failure of a variety of principles drawn from S̲h̲īʿī jurisprudence, including the distinctions between primary and secondary commandments (*aḥkām*) of the *S̲h̲arīʿa* and the introduction of a new category of "governmental (*ḥukūmatī*) commandments", to solve the impasse between the *Mad̲j̲lis* and the Council of Guardians had become evident by January 1988, when K̲h̲umaynī proclaimed a new idea of the "absolute (*muṭlaḳa*) mandate of the jurist". This gave priority to what has increasingly been called the "governmental commandments" of the *walī-yi faḳīh* over those of the *S̲h̲arīʿa*, including prayer and fasting. In the following month, overcoming the traditional reservations of the S̲h̲īʿī jurists regarding the principle of *maṣlaḥa* (public interest), he appointed a clerically-dominated Council for the Determination of the Interest of the Islamic Régime (*mad̲j̲maʿ-i tas̲h̲k̲h̲īṣ-i maṣlaḥat-i niẓām-i islāmī*) as the final arbiter of cases of disagreement between the *Mad̲j̲lis* and the Council of Guardians. In April 1989, he ordered the revision of the Constitution, and the amended Constitution of 1989, which was completed and ratified after his death, awkwardly incorporated the phrase "absolute mandate to rule" (*wilāyat-i muṭlaḳ-i amr*) into its Article 57, augmented the already considerable powers of the ruling jurist and gave the Council for the Determination of Interest the new function of setting the general policies of the state.

K̲h̲umaynī remained ruthlessly firm and resolute to his last days. He opposed the ending of the increasingly unpopular war with ʿIrāḳ (1980-8) until he finally decided to drink "the cup of poison", and accepted a ceasefire with ʿIrāḳ on 18 July 1988. Two days later, the ʿIrāḳ-based forces of the Islamic radical group, the *mudjāhidīn-i khalḳ*, attacked western Iran and were wiped out. In the following weeks, despite the vehement protest of his successor-designate, Āyatullāh Muntaẓirī (Muntaẓirī, chs. 9-10), he ordered the execution of about 3,000 Islamic radicals who had already served or were serving sentences given them by revolutionary courts. The incipient collapse of communism in the last year of his life renewed Khumaynī's optimism, and in January 1989, he told the Soviet leader Mikhail Gorbachev that he should learn about Islam as communism now belonged to the museum of history. Finally, Khumaynī caused another international crisis by issuing an injunction (*fatwā*) that sanctioned the death of Salman Rushdie, a non-Iranian writer who lived in England.

Khumaynī died on 14 Khurdād 1368/3 June 1989. He was a charismatic leader of immense popularity. Millions of Iranians massed to welcome him when he returned as the Imām from exile in 1979, and a million or more joined his funeral procession after he died ten years later.

Bibliography: Khumaynī, *Kashf al-asrār*, Tehran n.d. [1942 or 1943]; idem, *Wilāyat-i faḳīh*, Beirut 1970; idem, *K. al-Bayʿ*, ii, Nadjaf AH 1391/1971; Ḥ. Rūḥānī, *Barrasī wa taḥlīlī az nahḍat-i Imām Khumaynī*, 2 vols. Tehran ASH 1360-4/1981-5; S.A. Arjomand, *The turban for the crown. The Islamic Revolution in Iran*, New York 1988; Khumaynī, *Ṣaḥīfa-i nūr*, revised and expanded ed. 11 vols. Tehran ASH 1376/1997 (collected speeches, interviews and proclamations); B. Moin, *Khomeini. Life of the Ayatollah*, London 1999; *Kungirih-i Imām Khumaynī wa andishih-i ḥukūmat-i islāmī*, 22 vols. Tehran 1378/1999-2000 (centennial collection; vol. ix contains a serviceable bibliography, and vols. iv-viii occasional essays of interest); Arjomand, *Authority in Shīʿism and constitutional developments in the Islamic Republic of Iran*, in W. Ende and R. Brunner (eds.), *The Twelver Shia in modern times. Religious, cultural and political history*, Leiden 2000, 301-32; Ḥ.-ʿAlī Muntaẓirī, *Khāṭirāt* (Memoirs), www.montazeri.com.

(S.A. Arjomand)

KHUMS (A.), a one-fifth share of the spoils of war and, according to the majority of Muslim jurists, of other specified forms of income, set aside for variously designated beneficiaries.

1. In Sunnism.

For the Sunnīs, like the Shīʿīs, the starting point for the discussion of *khums* is Ḳurʾān, VIII, 41 (*āyat al-khums, āyat al-ghanīma*). The Sunnī exegetes take this verse to address the spoils of war specifically, but beyond that there is widespread disagreement about the circumstances of its revelation, its interpretation and the extent of its applicability after the death of the Prophet (Ibn al-ʿArabī, *K. al-Ḳabas*, ed. Walad Karīm, Beirut 1992, ii, 600). Although the institution of the *khums* is often regarded as replacing the pre-Islamic right of the commander to one-fourth (*mirbāʿ*) of the booty (al-Wāḳidī, *K. al-Maghāzī*, ed. J.M.B. Jones, Oxford 1966, i, 17; Muḥammad Rashīd Riḍā, *Tafsīr al-manār*, Beirut 1420/1999, x, 13; Lane, *Lexicon*, iii, 1015; Juynboll, *Handbuch*, 341), the acquisition of property, including the *khums*, through combat is regarded as unique to Islam among the revealed religions (Ibn al-Mulaḳḳin, *Ghāyat al-sūl fī khaṣāʾiṣ al-rasūl*, ed. ʿAbd Allāh, Beirut 1414/1993, 260-1; al-ʿAynī, *ʿUmdat al-ḳārī*, ed. Cairo, xv, 41-4).

It is generally held that Ḳurʾān, VIII, 41, abrogates Ḳurʾān, VIII, 1 (*āyat al-anfāl*), which put the spoils gained at Badr (2/624) entirely at the disposal of the Prophet to distribute as he saw fit (al-Ḳurṭubī, *al-Djāmiʿ li-aḥkām al-Ḳurʾān*, Cairo 1387/1967, viii, 2; al-Māwardī, *al-Aḥkām al-sulṭāniyya*, Cairo 1386/1966, 138-9). Ḳurʾān, VIII, 41 would thus have been revealed some time after Badr, and the rule of the *khums* was first implemented, according to some, in connection with the booty gained in the victory over the Jewish tribe of Banū Ḳaynuḳāʿ (2/624 [*q.v.*]). According to another account, ʿAbd Allāh b. Djaḥsh, shortly before the battle of Badr, on his own initiative set aside for the Prophet one-fifth of the spoils taken from Ḳuraysh at Nakhla, the first spoils gained under Islam, and this rule was later affirmed by the Ḳurʾān (Ibn Hishām, *al-Sīra al-nabawiyya*, ed. al-Saḳḳāʾ *et al.*, Cairo 1375/1955, i, 603-05, tr. Guillaume, Oxford 1955, 286-8). Some sources, however, place the introduction of the *khums* at other times: at Badr itself, at the victory over Banu ʾl-Naḍīr (4/625) or over Banū Ḳurayẓa (5/627), at the conquest of Khaybar (7/628) or as late as the battle of Ḥunayn (8/630) [*q.vv.*] (al-Ḳayrawānī, *al-Nawādir wa ʾl-ziyādāt*, ed. Ḥadjdjī, Beirut 1999, iii, 221; Ibn Ḳayyim al-Djawziyya, *Zād al-maʿād*, ed. al-Arnaʾūṭ, Beirut 1419/1998, v, 63).

Payment of the *khums* was taught by the Prophet as a cardinal religious obligation (*ʿUmdat al-ḳārī*, i, 302-11, *bāb adāʾ al-khums min al-īmān*, xv, 26-7; Ibn Baṭṭāl, *Sharḥ ṣaḥīḥ al-Bukhārī*, ed. Ibrāhīm, Riyāḍ 1420/2000, v, 257) and appears among the undertakings required of certain Bedouin tribes (Ibn Saʿd, i/2, 25, 30; Caetani, *Annali*, i, 682, ii/1, 303-04; W.M. Watt, *Muhammad at Medina*, Oxford 1955, 255-6). Two collectors of the *khums* who served the Prophet are named: Maḥmiya b. Djazʾ and ʿAbd Allāh b. Kaʿb al-Anṣārī (al-Khuzāʿī, *Takhrīdj al-dalālāt al-samʿiyya*, ed. ʿAbbās, Beirut 1405/1985, 509-10). ʿAlī b. Abī Ṭālib was charged by the Prophet with distributing the portion of the *khums* that went to the Prophet's next-of-kin, a position he continued to hold into the caliphate of ʿUmar (Abū Yūsuf, *K. al-Kharādj*, Cairo 1352, 20).

The common opinion is that, during the lifetime of the Prophet, the *khums* was divided into five shares, with that of God and the Prophet constituting a single share (*khums al-khums*), which the Prophet used for his own upkeep and that of his family, with any excess being spent on the needs of the community. A small minority, including the Baṣran Ḳurʾān scholar Abu ʾl-ʿĀliya Rufayʿ b. Mihrān al-Riyāḥī (d. 90/708 or 96/714 [*q.v.*]), and it is sometimes reported, his mentor Ibn ʿAbbās (d. 68/687-8 [*q.v.*]), were of the opinion that there was a distinct sixth portion for God. This portion, which was as much as the Prophet could grasp from the booty, was used for upkeep of the Kaʿba. According to Muḳātil b. Sulaymān (d. 150/767 [*q.v.*]), the *khums* was to be divided into four parts, with one part representing the shares of God, the Prophet, and the Prophet's next-of-kin (*K. Tafsīr al-khams miʾa āya*, ed. Goldfeld, Shfaram 1980, 271), a mode of division followed by the Ibāḍīs (Ibn Ḳays, *Mukhtaṣar al-khiṣāl*, ʿUmān 1403/1983, 192; al-Kindī, *Bayān al-sharʿ*, ʿUmān 1414/1993, lxx, 374).

The Shāfiʿīs and Ḥanbalīs continue to recognise five shares after the death of the Prophet: (1) the Prophet's share, now used to meet the needs of the community of Muslims (*sahm al-maṣāliḥ*), (2) the share of the Prophet's next-of-kin (*dhu ʾl-ḳurba*), which goes to the Hāshimīs and Muṭṭalibīs without regard to need, with males getting double the share of females, (3) the orphans (*yatāmā*) [see yatīm], defined as needy minors who have no father, (4) the indigent (*masākīn*), who correspond to the "poor and indigent" of Ḳurʾān, IX, 60 [see ZAKĀT. 5. xi], and (5) the traveller, defined as for *zakāt* (cf. al-Bādjūrī, *Ḥāshiya ʿalā Ibn Ḳāsim al-Ghazzī*, ed. Cairo, ii, 274). After the Prophet's death, his share and that of his family lapsed according to the Ḥanafīs, who appeal to the practice of the first four caliphs as evidence for this view (*K. al-Kharādj*, 19). The Ḥanafīs do, however, give preference to indigent members of the Prophet's family under the remaining three classes, in recognition of their ineligibility to receive *zakāt* [see ZAKĀT. 5. xi]. The Mālikīs regard the classes named in Ḳurʾān, VIII, 41, as illustrative (Ibn Rushd, *al-Muḳaddimāt*, ed. Ḥadjdjī, Beirut 1408/1988, i, 357) and treat the entire *khums* as *fayʾ* [*q.v.*] to be expended upon the needs of the Muslims as the ruler sees fit (Saḥnūn, *al-Mudawwana*, ed. Muḥammad, Beirut 1419/1999, ii, 604), a view also adopted by Ibn Taymiyya (d. 652/1254 [*q.v.*]). They do, however, recommend that distribution of the *khums* begin with grants to the Hāshimīs (*al-Khirshī ʿalā mukhtaṣar Khalīl*, ed. Beirut, iii, 129).

The obligation of paying the *khums* is incumbent on Muslims (cf. al-Dardīr, *al-Sharḥ al-ṣaghīr*, ed. Waṣfī, Cairo 1972, ii, 301, on Muslim slaves). Although it is sometimes stated that only Muslims are eligible to receive the *khums* (al-Shīrāzī, *al-Muhadhdhab*, ed. Cairo, ii, 247; Ibn Ḳudāma, *al-Kāfī*, ed. al-Shāfiʿī, Beirut 1421/2001, iv, 183), this restriction has been said not to apply to the expenditure of the share for the needs of the community (al-Ramlī, *Ghāyat al-bayān*, ed. Cairo, 345).

The rules for the *khums* apply specifically to *ghanīma* [*q.v.*], the spoils of war taken by armed force, except according to the Shāfiʿīs (al-Shāfiʿī, *K. al-Umm*, ed. Cairo, iv, 64; al-Māwardī, *al-Ḥāwī al-kabīr*, ed. Maṭradjī, Beirut 1414/1994, x, 429-30) and some Ḥanbalīs, notably al-Khiraḳī (d. 334/945) (Ibn Ḳudāma, *al-Mughnī*, ed. al-Turkī and al-Ḥulw, Cairo 1409/1989, ix, 284, 286), who fully extend the application of the *khums* to property taken from the enemy without such display of force, i.e. *fayʾ*, and the Mālikīs, who recognise an intermediate category, *al-mukhtaṣṣ*, between *ghanīma* and *fayʾ*, that includes property taken out of enemy territory by stealth, the *khums* of which must be privately distributed by its taker (al-Raṣṣāʿ, *Sharḥ ḥudūd Ibn ʿArafa*, ed. al-Adjfān and al-Maʿmūrī, Beirut 1993, i, 229-30). The extent to which *khums* is due on property seized by small groups of raiders acting on their own initiative is disputed (al-Ṭabarī, *Das konstantinopler Fragment des Kitāb Ikhtilāf al-Fuḳahāʾ*, ed. Schacht, Leiden 1933, 78-80; Schacht, *The origins of Muhammadan jurisprudence*, Oxford 1950, 286).

The booty subject to division does not include food consumed by the combatants or their animals (*al-Mudawwana*, ii, 612-14; al-Kāsānī, *Badāʾiʿ al-ṣanāʾiʿ*, ed. Muʾawwaḍ and ʿAbd al-Mawdjūd, Beirut 1418/1997, ix, 494-6) nor, during the Prophet's lifetime, such booty as he selected as a personal prize (*ṣafī*) (*K. al-Kharādj*, 22-3). The *khums* is calculated on the total booty net such expenses as those incurred for its transport and safekeeping, and, according to the Shāfiʿīs and Ḥanbalīs, after subtraction of the clothing, weapons, mounts, and other personal effects (*salab*) of enemy soldiers earned by the individual Muslim combatants who have killed or disabled them (cf. Schacht, *Origins*, 70-1). The Ḥanafīs and Mālikīs treat such claims to personal effects as rewards (*nafal*), for which they require an express grant by the ruler, preferably, according to the Mālikīs, after the battle has ended so as not to compromise the purity of motive of the combatants. The Mālikīs in all cases satisfy rewards from the *khums*; the Ḥanafīs from the *khums* if the grant has been made after the booty has been secured in Islamic territory (*iḥrāz*), otherwise from the four-fifths; the Ḥanbalīs from the four-fifths. The Shāfiʿīs pay rewards from the twenty-fifth share devoted to the needs of the community. Special allocations (*radkh*) of the booty granted to slaves, women, and children who participate in the battle but do not otherwise qualify as combatants, are distributed from the total booty according to the Ḥanafīs, from the four-fifths according to the Shāfiʿīs and Ḥanbalīs, and from the *khums* according to the Mālikīs, who in principle disapprove of such special allocations.

The rules for the *khums* apply in the first instance to moveable property, which includes the captured slaves of the non-Muslim enemy. In the case of combatants taken prisoner and captive women and children, the rule of the *khums* is applied most straightforwardly when these are enslaved and form part of the booty to be divided (cf. al-Dasūḳī, *al-Ḥāshiya ʿalā al-sharḥ al-kabīr*, ed. Cairo, ii, 184). There is disagreement as to real property: the Shāfiʿīs divide such property among the combatants and subject it to the *khums*; the Mālikīs do not, while the Ḥanafīs and Ḥanbalīs leave the matter of division to the discretion of the ruler. Where the division is of the booty itself, rather than of its sale price, the determination of what constitutes the *khums* is made by lot, with a special designation for the *khums* (*li ʾllāh, li ʾl-maṣāliḥ, li-rasūl Allāh*) (al-Wāḳidī, ii, 523-4; Ibn Abī Shayba, *al-Kitāb al-muṣannaf*, ed. al-Nadwī, Bombay 1402/1982, xii, 429-30; al-Ramlī, *Nihāyat al-muḥtādj*, Cairo 1386/1967, vi, 146; al-Ḥaṭṭāb, *Mawāhib al-djalīl*, ed. ʿUmayrāt, Beirut 1416/1995, iv, 584).

There is disagreement as to what extent the ruler can avoid the application of the general rules for the division of booty, including that of the *khums*, by declaring that what each combatant takes is his as a reward (*al-Nawādir wa ʾl-ziyādāt*, iii, 252; Ibn ʿAbd al-Barr, *al-Istidhkār*, ed. Ḳalʿadjī, Cairo 1414/1993, xiv, 102-3; Ibn al-Naḥḥās, *Mashāriʿ al-ashwāḳ*, ed. ʿAlī and Isṭanbūlī, Beirut 1410/1990, ii, 1035-6). According to many Ḥanafīs, the booty taken pursuant to such a general offer of reward (*tanfīl ʿāmm*), in the case of a detachment (*sariyya*), but not the entire army, dispatched from within enemy territory, is not subject to the *khums* (al-Djaṣṣāṣ, *Aḥkām al-Ḳurʾān*, ed. Istanbul, iii, 55; Ibn ʿĀbidīn, *Radd al-muḥtār*, Cairo 1386/1966, iv, 155-7; cf. Ibn Nudjaym, *al-Baḥr al-rāʾiḳ*, ed. Cairo, v, 92; C. Imber, *Ebu ʾs-Suʿud: the Islamic legal tradition*, Stanford 1997, 87 [with reference to a declaration of this sort on the part of the Ottoman sultan in 948/1541-2]).

The institution of the *khums* appears to have fallen into neglect from an early date. The students of Mālik (d. 179/796 [*q.v.*]) already addressed questions concerning the purchase of slave girls from sellers suspected of not having paid the *khums* (*al-Nawādir wa ʾl-ziyādāt*, iii, 215-6; *Mawāhib al-djalīl*, iv, 568-70) as well as the status of privately owned Andalusī estates on which *khums* was not known to have been paid at the time of their conquest and, according to the Mālikīs, irregular distribution to individuals (*al-Nawādir wa ʾl-ziyādāt*, iii, 364-65). Even revivalist movements such as that of the Almoravids and Almohads found it difficult to ensure consistent implementation of the law of the *khums* (J.F.P. Hopkins, *Medieval Muslim government in Barbary until the sixth century of the hijra*, London 1958, 28-9; al-Tadjkānī, *al-Iḥsān al-ilzāmī fi ʾl-islām wa-taṭbīḳātuhu fi ʾl-Maghrib*, al-Muḥammadiyya 1410/

1990, 592). The Ottoman *muftī* Abū Suʿūd (d. 982/ 1547) took it for granted that the spoils of war were not being divided in accordance with the law and put the burden of paying *khums* on the purchasers of slave girls (Imber, 87; al-Ḥaṣkafī, *al-Durr al-muntakā*, on the margin of Shaykhzāda, *Madjmaʿ al-anhur*, ed. Istanbul, i, 651; cf. *Radd al-muḥtār*, iv, 157-8).

Commonly treated by the jurists in connection with *zakāt* (cf. al-Zurḳānī, *al-Sharḥ ʿalā muwaṭṭaʾ al-imām Mālik*, ed. ʿAwaḍ, Cairo 1381/1961, ii, 321) but regarded by the Ḥanafīs, Mālikīs and Ḥanbalīs as analogous to the one-fifth payable from booty, is the one-fifth due upon the discovery under certain circumstances unrelated to combat of pre-Islamic treasure, as enjoined by the *ḥadīth* (*fī ʾl-rikāz al-khums*) (Mālik, *al-Muwaṭṭaʾ*, ed. ʿAbd al-Bāḳī, ed. Cairo, 170). The Shāfiʿīs limit this obligation to gold and silver, to which they apply the same minimum amount (*niṣāb*) as that for *zakāt* on gold and silver. While the Ḥanafīs distribute this one-fifth as they do the *khums* of booty (*Radd al-muḥtār*, iv, 139), the Mālikīs and Ḥanbalīs class it as *fayʾ* to be expended on the needs of the community, and the Shāfiʿīs treat it as *zakāt* (*ʿUmdat al-ḳārī*, ix, 104) [see ZAKĀT. 5. iv]. The Ḥanafīs, and to a limited extent the Mālikīs, extend the rule of one-fifth on treasure to the products of mining (*maʿdin*): malleable metals, according to the Ḥanafīs (al-Samarḳandī, *Tuḥfat al-fuḳahāʾ*, ed. ʿAbd al-Barr, Damascus 1377/1958, i, 505-09), pure or virtually pure pieces of gold and silver (*nadra*), according to the Mālikīs (al-Dardīr, *al-Sharḥ al-ṣaghīr*, i, 653). The opinions of certain early scholars that one-fifth was due on pearls, ambergris and other products of the sea, even fish, were not widely followed (Abū ʿUbayd al-Ḳāsim b. Sallām, *K. al-Amwāl*, ed. Fiḳī, ed. Cairo, 345-8; cf. *K. al-Kharādj*, 70).

The label *khums* is also found in other senses. Loosely related to the *khums* on booty is the early use of the term *takhmīs* in N. Africa for the taking of Berber captives for the service of the state, such slaves being termed *akhmās* (Hopkins, *Medieval Muslim government in Barbary*, 27-8; Dozy, *Suppl.*, i, 404). In Egypt the term *khums* was applied to a tax of variable percentage, apparently of Fāṭimid origin, that was imposed on the sale by foreign merchants of imported merchandise (H. Rabie, *The financial system of Egypt*, London 1972, 90-3).

Bibliography: In addition to references in the text, see Muḥammad al-Fātiḥ, *Aḥkām wa-āthār al-khums fī ʾl-iḳtiṣād al-islāmī*, *dirāsa muḳārana*, Cairo 1988; Najib Abdul Wahhab al-Fili, *A critical edition of Kitāb al-Amwāl by Abū Jaʿfar b. Naṣr al-Dāwūdī (d. 401/H)*, Ph.D. diss., Exeter University, 1989, unpubl., Arab. 3-24, English 78-94; Ibn al-ʿArabī, *Aḥkām al-Ḳurʾān*, ed. al-Bidjāwī, Cairo 1387/1967, ii, 823-8, 843-54; ʿUthmān Ibn Fūdī, *Bayān wudjūb al-hidjra ʿalā ʾl-ʿibād*, ed. El Masri, Khartoum 1978, 90-2, tr. 112-14; Ibn Ḥazm, *al-Muḥallā*, ed. al-Bindārī, Beirut n.d., v, 385ff.; Ibn Rushd, *Bidāyat al-mudjtahid*, ed. Cairo, i, 332-3, tr. I.A.K. Nyazee, *The distinguished jurist's primer*, London 1994, i, 466-8; Faradj b. Ḥasan al-ʿImrān al-Ḳaṭīfī, *al-Khums ʿalā ʾl-madhāhib al-khamsa*, Nadjaf 1961 (elementary); *al-Mawsūʿa al-fiḳhiyya*, Kuwayt 1400-/1980-, xi, 59-62 (*takhmīs*), xx, 10-21 (*khums*), xxiii, 98-108 (*rikāz*); Taḥāwī, *Sharḥ maʿānī al-āthār*, ed. al-Nadjdjār and Djād al-Ḥaḳḳ, Beirut 1414/1994, iii, 293-6 (epistle of ʿUmar b. ʿAbd al-ʿAzīz on *fayʾ* and booty, also in al-Mallāʾ, *al-Kitāb al-djāmiʿ li-sīrat ʿUmar b. ʿAbd al-ʿAzīz*, ed. al-Burnū, Beirut 1416/1996, i, 300-05; cf. Ibn ʿAbd al-Ḥakam, *Sīrat ʿUmar b. ʿAbd al-*

ʿAzīz, ed. ʿUbayd, Damascus 1385/1966, 96); N.P. Aghnides, *Mohammedan theories of finance*, New York 1916, 409-21; M. Ḥamīdullāh, *Muslim conduct of state*, Lahore 1945, 237-42; W.F. Madelung, *The Hāshimiyyāt of al-Kumayt and Hāshimī Shīʿism*, in *Stud. Isl.*, lxx (1989), 5-26; M.A.S. Siddiqi, *Early development of zakat law and ijtihad*, Karachi 1403/1983 (index); J.B. Simonsen, *Studies in the genesis and early development of the caliphal taxation system*, Copenhagen 1988, 63-7. (A. Zysow)

2. In Shīʿism.

Imāmī and Zaydī Shīʿī jurisprudence concerning *khums* differ in significant ways from those outlined in Sunnī *fiḳh*. The wealth liable for *khums*, the means of its collection and distribution and the constitution of the recipient categories (*aṣnāf*) form the major topics of debate within both juristic traditions. The main Ḳurʾānic reference is VIII, 41 ("Know that what you acquire, a fifth is for God, his Prophet, the near relatives, orphans, the needy and the wayfarer"). Whilst Sunnī exegetes consider this verse to relate to war booty (*ghanīma* [*q.v.*]), Imāmī and Zaydī writers associate the phrase *annamā ghanimtum* ("what you acquire") to refer to wealth more generally.

In the Imāmī tradition, there are reports to support such a definition. "Everything from which the people gain benefit is *ghanīma*," the Imām al-Riḍā (d. 203/818) is reported as saying. A number of *akhbār* refer to the Imām's original ownership of the world and its produce (e.g. "all the earth is ours, and what God brings forth from it is also ours," al-Kulaynī [d. 328/939], *Kāfī*, i, 408). The *khums*, therefore, was analogous to a tenant's payment of a fixed percentage of the harvest to the landowner.

Since the Ḳurʾānic verse appears in the midst of a discussion of war, some exegetical effort was required to reinforce this interpretation. This normally began with a grammatical analysis of the term *ghanīma* and the verb *ghanima* (see al-Ṭūsī [d. 460/1067], *Mabsūṭ*, ii, 64, where the verb means "acquiring something with the purpose of turning it to profitable use"). This was supported by other *akhbār* (e.g. "a fifth of the earth is ours, and a fifth of all things is ours," al-Ṭūsī, *Tahdhīb*, iv, 123).

The items liable for *khums* were defined in both collections of *akhbār* and works of *fiḳh*. In the earliest works of *fiḳh*, the discussions formed part of the *kitāb al-zakāt* or occasionally *kitāb al-fayʾ wa ʾl-ghanīma*; a separate *kitāb al-khums* (located after the *kitāb al-zakāt*) later became the norm (see e.g. Muḥammad b. Makkī, al-Shahīd al-Awwal (d. 786/1384), *al-Lumʿa al-dimashḳiyya*, 45-6). The earliest categorisation of taxable wealth comprised booty, produce of the sea, buried treasure, minerals and *malāḥa*. The last term, obscure in reference, was interpreted through juristic reasoning and the citation of other *akhbār* to refer to profit (from trade, agriculture and craft), *dhimmī* land bought by a Muslim and "*ḥalāl* goods mixed with *ḥarām* ones". This made seven categories in all (see such a categorisation in al-Muḥaḳḳiḳ [d. 676/1277], *Sharāʾiʿ*, i, 179-81). These categories, once established, remained remarkably stable in the subsequent tradition.

When present, the Imām receives and distributes the *khums* (though he may, it seems, appoint a representative). The *khums*, following Ḳurʾān, VIII, 41, is distributed amongst the six categories mentioned (God, the Prophet, the near relatives, the orphans, the needy and the wayfarers). A minority of jurists argued that the shares of God and the Prophet were actually one (hence there are five not six recipients, see Zayn al-Dīn ʿAlī al-Shahīd al-Thānī [d. 966/1588], *Masālik*, ii, 470), but this opinion was not popular. The juristic reasoning (authoritatively summed up in the later tradition by al-Nadjafī's [d. 1266/1850] commentary on al-Muḥaḳḳiḳ's *Sharāʾiʿ*: al-Nadjafī, *Djawāhir*, iv, 1-102) proceeded as follows: God's share was clearly owned by the Prophet, and he could dispose of it as he saw fit. After the Prophet's death, the two shares (of God and the Prophet) were, through inheritance, due to the Imām. The share of the "near relatives" was also due to the Imām, since they were the heads of the *ahl al-bayt* after the Prophet's death. The Imām, when present, was, then, due half the *khums*. The remaining shares were distributed by the Imām. The verse might indicate that the orphans, needy and wayfarers were from the population generally (as argued by Ibn Ḥamza [living in 566/1170] in his *al-Wasīla*, 718), though most jurists argued that these three categories applied to the family of the Prophet (the Banū Hāshim). A minority also argued that descendants of Hāshim's brother (Muṭṭalib) were also included (analogous to the *sayyid* status of descendants of both al-Ḥasan and al-Ḥusayn: see Zayn al-Dīn ʿAlī al-Shahīd al-Thānī, *Sharh al-lumʿa al-dimashkiyya*, 57-8), but this did not become the influential position.

The absence of the Imām through occultation provided the jurists with an opportunity to link the discussion with the vexed issue of community leadership during the *ghayba* [*q.v.*]. Was *khums* during the *ghayba* lapsed (*sāḳiṭ*) because the Imām could not collect it in person (a view attributed to Salār al-Daylamī [d. 463/1071])? This position was rejected quite early on in the tradition. Other solutions were proposed, such as burying one's *khums* in anticipation of the Imam's return (attributed to Ibn Barrādj [d. 481/1099]) or placing the *khums* in a perpetual will, until the Imam's return. Some jurists (Ibn Idrīs [d. 598/1202], *Sarāʾir*, i, 502-4) maintained that the option of a will applied only to the Imām's share (i.e. one half). The remaining three shares are distributed to the recipients (perhaps by the individual himself). Ibn Idrīs's assertion that the Imām's share must be preserved, pending his return, was not developed further. For al-Muḥaḳḳiḳ, the Imām had given the Shīʿa permission (*idhn*) to use his property generally, and his *khums* specifically, during his absence. This did not constitute using a person's property without permission. The *khums*, according to al-Muḥaḳḳiḳ, was distributed by "the one who possesses authority through delegation (*niyāba*)" (*Sharāʾiʿ*, i, 184). Al-ʿAllāma al-Ḥillī (d. 726/1325) identified the person as *al-ḥākim* (a reference to *al-ḥākim al-sharʿī*, sc. a member of the *fuḳahāʾ*). These terminological shifts became more nuanced until the time of the Ṣafawid jurist, al-Sabzawārī (d. 1090/1679), who wrote that the *khums* should be given to "the worthy recipients through the auspices of the just *faḳīh* who is qualified to give *fatwā*s" (*Kifāya*, 45); that is, the *mudjtahid*s should receive and distribute the *khums*. This continues to be the position up to the present day. Naturally, those *ʿulamāʾ* who were also *sayyid*s benefited financially, but, more importantly, the authority of the *fuḳahāʾ* (as in other areas of *furūʿ*) was enhanced. The contributions obviously aided the independence of the *ʿulamāʾ* from the Ḳādjār state, and may have provided part of the financial base for the *ʿulamāʾ* opposition movement in 20th-century Iran.

Zaydī discussions of *khums* bear some similarities to both Imāmī and Sunnī views. The important work, *al-Azhār*, of the Zaydī Aḥmad b. Yaḥyā al-Murtaḍā (d. 836/1432), provides a useful summary of three categories of produce liable for *khums*: the produce of the "land and sea" (*al-barr wa 'l-baḥr*), war booty and the ongoing revenue after a campaign. This represents an expansion of the Sunnī system of categorisation. In the subsequent commentaries on *al-Azhār*, Zaydī jurists (e.g. Ibn Miftāḥ [d. 877/1472] and al-Shawkānī [d. 1250/1834]) elaborated on this brief explanation. The produce of the land and sea included the produce gained from fishing and farming (with some restrictions) as well as precious stones and metals obtained through mining. Also included was treasure (*kunūz*) found by the Muslim but buried during the *djāhilī* period. War booty encompassed the booty from wars with both non-Muslims (*ahl al-ḥarb*) and non-Zaydī Muslims (*ahl al-baghy*). The ongoing revenue after a campaign included produce from land seized from the enemy, the *kharādj* (land-tax) and the *djizya* (the tax on non-Muslim communities living under Muslim control). It might be argued that Zaydī jurists envisaged an even larger amount of revenue as liable to *khums* than their Imāmī counterparts.

In Zaydī *fiḳh*, the *khums* is to be transferred to the Imām when he demands it. When there is no legitimate Imām in power, the *Azhār* records that the (Zaydī) Muslims must collect and distribute it themselves. The governance of an Imām does not affect the duty to give and distribute *khums*. The continued existence of a Zaydī Imām (though with limited suzerainty and disputed identity) did not encourage the discussion of delegation (*niyāba*) characteristic of the Imāmī tradition.

The distribution of *khums*, according to the Zaydīs, should be according to the established six categories of recipients. For al-Hārūnī (d. 424/1032), God's share is to be spent by the Imām on general benefits, such as mosques and roads (*maṣāliḥ*). The Prophet's share goes to the Imām who can spend it on his family, home and servants. The near-relatives' share is distributed, without regard for age, wealth or sex, to the descendants of the Prophets (with a broad definition of which lines of descent are to be included). The only restriction is that the descendants must recognise the Zaydī Imām (*mutamassik*^an^ *bi 'l-ḥaḳḳ li-imām al-muslimīn*). The three portions for the orphans, needy and wayfarers of the Prophet's descendants can be diverted if there are no such persons within the Prophet's descedants. First, the portions are available for the descendants of the Prophet. If unexhausted, the portions are distributed amongst the *muhādjirūn*; if not, then amongst the *anṣār*, and if not these last, then amongst the orphans, needy and wayfarers of the rest of the Muslim community (al-Hārūnī, *Taḥrīr*, i, 166). Though Zaydī thought on *khums* bears some resemblance to Imāmī *fiḳh* (e.g. the expansion of the definition of goods liable for *khums*), it avoids the contentious issues of *ʿulamāʾ* authority present in the Imāmī tradition.

The Ismāʿīlī Shīʿī tradition produced very little in terms of juristic literature, but one can conclude that, in terms of *khums*, it was much closer to the Sunnīs than either Zaydī or Imāmī *fiḳh*. In al-Ḳāḍī al-Nuʿmān's (d. 363/974 [*q.v.*]) *Daʿāʾim al-islām*, *khums* is discussed in the context of the *kitāb al-djihād*, mainly through citations of reports from Imām ʿAlī. The implication is that *khums* is only due on war booty. The resultant jurisprudence could fit well within the Sunnī *ikhtilāf* [*q.v.*] on the issue.

Bibliography: A. For Twelver Shīʿism. 1. *Texts*. Muḥammad b. Yaʿḳūb al-Kulaynī, *al-Kāfī fī ʿilm al-dīn*, Tehran 1388/1968; Ibn Ḥamza, *al-Wasīla*, in *al-Djawāmiʿ al-fiḳhiyya*, Ḳum 1279/1859; Muḥammad b. al-Ḥasan al-Ṭūsī, *al-Mabsūṭ*, Tehran

1378/1958; idem, *Tahdhīb al-aḥkām*, Nadjaf 1959; Muḥammad Ibn Idrīs, *Sarāʾir al-Islām*, Ḳum n.d.; al-Muḥaḳḳiḳ al-Ḥillī, *Sharāʾiʿ al-Islām*, Ḳum 1374/1954; Muḥammad b. Makkī al-Shahīd al-Awwal, *al-Lumʿa al-dimashkiyya*, Ḳum 1415/1994; Zayn al-Dīn b. ʿAlī al-Shahīd al-Thānī, *Masālik al-ifhām*, Beirut 1414/1993; idem, *Sharḥ al-lumʿa al-dimashkiyya*, Ḳum 1413/1992; Muḥammad Bāḳir al-Sabzawārī, *Kifāyat al-aḥkām*, Ḳum n.d.; Muḥammad Ḥasan al-Nadjafī, *Djawāhir al-kalām*, Beirut 1312/1992.

2. *Studies.* A. Sachedina, *Al-Khums: the fifth in the Imāmī Shīʿī legal system*, in *JNES*, xxxix (1980), 275-89; N. Calder, *Khums in Imāmī Shīʿī jurisprudence from the tenth to the sixteenth century AD*, in *BSOAS*, xlv (1982), 39-47; Sachedina, *The just ruler in Shīʾite Islam*, Oxford 1988, 237-45.

B. For Zaydī and Ismāʿīlī Shīʿism. 1. *Texts.* al-Ḳāḍī al-Nuʿmān, *Daʿāʾim al-Islām*, Cairo 1370/1951; Yaḥyā al-Hārūnī, *Kitāb al-Taḥrīr*, Ṣanʿāʾ 1418/1997; Aḥmad b. al-Murtaḍā and Ibn Miftāḥ, *Sharḥ al-Azhār*, Cairo 1357; Muḥammad b. ʿAlī al-Shawkānī, *al-Sayl al-djarrār*, Cairo 1390; Aḥmad b. Ḳāsim al-Yamānī, *al-Tādj al-mudhahhab, sharḥ matn al-Azhār*, Cairo 1380/1960. (R. GLEAVE)

KHURĀFA [see ḤIKĀYA. I].

KHUWWA (colloquial A., said to be of Nadjdī origin, Barthélemy, 224), also *khāwa*, both from the root ʾ-*kh-w* (Landberg, 71-2): terms used in the Syrian desert, its borderlands, and northern Arabia to refer to certain payments levied by the Bedouin (references in Henninger, 34-36). In these highly Bedouinised areas even tribute paid by one sedentary group to another was sometimes called *khāwa* (Musil, *Ar. Petr.*, iii, 67, 69; *Mid. Euphr.*, 72); in Syria the term *khuwwa* might also refer to a relationship of mutual assistance between an urban notable and a Bedouin *shaykh* (details in Oppenheim, ii, 65).

Wallin (122, 129) reported that *khāwa* was levied by almost all "genuine Bedouin tribes". Like Zakariyyā he distinguishes three groups who paid it: villagers, weak nomadic tribes (especially those not considered to be true Bedouin, for instance the *shāwiya* [*q.v.*]), and people crossing the desert (merchants, carriers, travellers). The Bedouin look on the regions where they live as being divided into tribal territories, and Wallin suggested that the payments to a tribe were made in exchange for the right to be in the territory of that tribe and to enjoy its protection. The degree of protection offered varied greatly: a village might receive no more from its "protectors" than the temporary cessation of their depredations, while a client tribe or a caravan might receive not merely protection against robbery and other offences (when committed by members of the protecting tribe, and sometimes at least also in other cases), but even indemnification. *Khuwwa* was paid (in cash or kind) to the *shaykh* or leading men of the Bedouin tribe. Some tributaries paid a fixed amount collected annually in an orderly fashion, but villagers often had nomadic "brothers" whose brutal *khuwwa*-collecting visits were scarcely distinguishable from raids (Schumacher, 144, offers an eye-witness account). For certain tribes—or for certain tribesmen—tribute must have been an important source of income (see Musil, *Ar. Petr.*, iii, 52-3 for an example); and at least in some instances, the right to *khuwwa* from a particular source was assignable (Lancaster, 122).

As governments became stronger during the 19th and 20th centuries, they were able to suppress exactions of this kind; and though *khuwwa* was still being paid in a remote corner of Lebanon as late as the 1960s (al-Rāʿī, 46), it may now be assumed to be a thing of the past.

It seems that *khuwwa* and words from the same root are, when used to refer to payments of some kind, confined to the Mashriḳ (though such terms are alleged to have been used in North Africa to refer to something related to tribute, see Abu-Lughod, 82, and Dunn, 76); but the practice of paying tribute to powerful nomadic tribes was once well-nigh universal in the Arab world [see ḤIMĀYA, ii (I) (3) (b)]. The terms most widely used in the Maghrib appear to be *khafāra* [*q.v.*] or *ghafāra* and other words from the same roots (Pröbster, 395); words from these roots in the same and related senses are also common in the Mashriḳ (Combe; Dozy, *Suppl.*, i, 386, ii, 217-18). Other terms are also attested in North Africa. Thus in the Western Desert of Egypt and in Cyrenaica, the Saʿādī tribes, who claimed that the land was theirs, used to receive a payment called *ṣadaḳa* from the subordinate Bedouin known as the *mrābṭīn al-ṣudḳān* (Djawharī, 172; Peters, 41), while in the Western Sahara the tribute paid by inferior to superior tribes went by the names of *ḥurma* and *gharāma* (and also *ghafar*), to say nothing of other words that referred to payments exacted from sedentary populations (Caro Baroja, 34-42; Stewart, 56-8).

Khuwwa is not sanctioned by Islamic law, and the tribute paid by settlements and nomadic tribes to pious rulers such as those of the Ibn Rashīd dynasty of Ḥāʾil was not called *khuwwa* (*pace* Al Rasheed, 113-15), but rather *zakāt* [*q.v.*] (Euting, ii, index s.v. *zékâ*; Musil, *N. Neğd*, 4; Zaʿārīr, 99-100).

Bibliography: G.A. Wallin, *Narrative of a journey*, in *JRGS*, xxiv (1854), 115-207, repr. in his *Travels in Arabia*, London 1979; C. Doughty, *Travels in Arabia Deserta*, Cambridge 1888, i, 35, 39, 123, 136, 152, 200, 287 *et passim*; E. Sachau, *Reise in Syrien und Mesopotamien*, Leipzig 1889, 311; J. Euting, *Tagbuch einer Reise in Inner-Arabien*, Leiden 1896-1914; M. von Oppenheim, *Vom Mittelmeer zum Persischen Golf*, Berlin 1899-1900; A. Musil, *Arabia Petraea*, iii, Vienna 1908; idem, *The Middle Euphrates*, New York 1927; idem, *Northern Neğd*, New York 1928; A. Jaussen and J. Savignac, *Mission archéologique en Arabie*, Paris 1909-22, i, 472-4; G. Schumacher, *Unsere Arbeiten im Ostjordanlande. VIII*, in *ZDPV*, xl (1917), 143-70; C. de Landberg, *Glossaire datînois*, Leiden 1920-42; E. Pröbster, *Privateigentum und Kollektivismus im muhammedanischen Liegenschaftrecht insbesondere des Maghrib*, in *Islamica*, iv (1931), 343-511; A. Barthélemy, *Dictionnaire arabe-français*, Paris 1935-69; E. Combe, *A note: qafar-khafara*, in *BSOAS*, x (1940-2), 790; J. Caro Baroja, *Estudios saharianos*, Madrid 1955; J. Henninger, *Das Eigentumsrecht bei den heutigen Beduinen Arabiens*, in *Zeitschr. für vergleichende Rechtswissenschaft*, lxi (1959), 6-56, repr. with additions in his *Arabica varia*, Freiburg 1989; Rifʿat al-Djawharī, *Sharīʿat al-ṣaḥrāʾ*, Cairo 1961; C.C. Stewart, *Islam and social order in Mauritania*, Oxford 1973; R.E. Dunn, *Resistance in the desert*, London 1977; W. Lancaster, *The Rwala Bedouin today*, Cambridge 1981, index s.v. *khuwa*; Aḥmad Waṣfī Zakariyyā, *ʿAshāʾir al-Shām*, Damascus 1983, 293-95 (copied in part from ʿAwda al-Ḳusūs, *al-Ḳaḍāʾ al-badawī*, ʿAmmān 1972, 104); Aḥmad ʿUwaydī al-ʿAbbādī, *Muḳaddima li-dirāsat al-ʿashāʾir al-urdunniyya*, ʿAmmān 1985, 243-7; I. Abu-Lughod, *Veiled sentiments*, Berkeley 1986; Lūrīs al-Rāʿī, *al-Taghayyur al-idjtimāʿī al-iḳtiṣādī fī mudjtamaʿ badawī*, Tripoli (Lebanon) 1987; E.L. Peters, *The Bedouin of Cyrenaica*, Cambridge 1990; Madawi Al Rasheed, *Politics in an Arabian oasis*, London 1991; Muḥammad ʿAbd Allāh al-Zaʿārīr,

Imārat Āl Rashīd fī Ḥā'il, ʿAmmān 1997; A. Shryock, *Nationalism and genealogical imagination*, Berkeley 1997, index s.v. *khawa*. (F.H. Stewart)

ḲIRGİZSTĀN, KIRGIZSTAN (official designations, Kyrgyzstan, Kyrgyz Respublikasy), the smallest of the five Central Asian republics emerging from the collapse of the Soviet Union, with an area of 198,500 km^2 (77,415 sq. miles), and with boundaries adjoining China 858 km, Ḳazaḳstān 1051 km, Tādjīkistān 870 km and Uzbekistān 1099 km. Kyrgyzstan is landlocked, like most of its neighbours. In 1999 it had a population of 4,823 million, its ethnic composition at various points in the 20th century being shown in Table 1 as percentages of the whole population.

Russians are concentrated in the capital and in the north, Uzbeks in the south (Ōsh and Djalālābād provinces). Changes in the ethnic composition of the Kyrgyzstani population are explained by much lower fertility among the Russians and other Europeans and massive outmigration of the "European" groups since the late 1980s. In the earlier Soviet period, the drop in the Kyrgyz population was linked to the crisis following collectivisation.

Kyrgyz, the official language, belongs to the northwestern group of Turkic languages [see TURKS. II (v), and for Kyrgyz literature, III. 6 (e)]. Russian was declared an official language in territories and work places where Russian dominates in March 1996, and is now termed the "language of inter-ethnic communication". Uzbek is granted no official status. The capital has been called Bishkek since 1993 (750,000 inhabitants in 1999), Frunze in Soviet times since 1926, and Pishpek [*q.v.*] before then. Other towns include Talas [see ṬARĀZ] in the northwest and Ōsh and Özkend [*q.v.*] in the Farghāna valley. Regarding natural resources, Kyrgyzstan, as a mountainous country, is rich in water and has a high potential in hydroelectric power (Toktogul dam on the Naryn river, built 1962-75). Coal was mined for Central Asian consumption. After independence, gold has been deemed to be worthwhile exploiting (the Komtur gold field).

The country is divided into two main geographic zones by the Tien Shan mountains, with their highest peaks in the far eastern corner (Pik Pobedy, Žengish Čokusu, 7,439 m), and the Pamir Alai range. To the north, the hills slope down to the great steppe zone of Semirečye [see YETI SU], to the south, they border on the Farghāna valley [see FARGHĀNA]. Most of Kyrgyzstan is thus mountainous (40% of it over 3,200 m/10,000 feet). Arable land makes up a mere 7% of the area, whereas pastures account for more than 40%.

1. *Pre-colonial history*.

The area where the Kyrgyz Republic is situated was never defined as a political unit before Soviet times. It was, however, at the centre of the Ḳarakhānid khānate [see ILEK-KHĀNS] from the 4th/10th to the 7th/13th centuries, and the khāns had one of their capitals at Bālāsāghūn [*q.v.*] with an appanage centre at Özkend, both situated within the boundaries of present-day Kyrgyzstan. A first wave of Islamisation occurred during this period; before, Buddhism, Nestorian Christianity and local cults prevailed. After the Mongol invasions, the area was part of the Čaghatay *ulus* [see MOGHOLISTĀN], and Islam receded as a consequence, primarily in the northern part of the country, remaining strong, however, in the Farghāna valley. It is not altogether clear when ethnic Kyrgyz came to the region; this point depends on whether the different groups thus called can be seen as ethnically and linguistically continuous [see ḲIRGHĪZ]. At any rate, many of the former Moghol/Čaghatayid subjects now became known as Kyrgyz. The second wave of Islamisation among these people began in the late 16th century, but Islamisation was apparently still going on under the influence of Kokand [see KHOḲAND] in the 19th century.

2. *The Russian colonial period*.

The Russian advance into what is now Kyrgyzstan was aided by a number of Kyrgyz delegations to St. Petersburg and to the Russian authorities in Siberia asking for help against the Khoḳand khānate, which, by 1830 had gained at least formal authority over the Kyrgyz tribes. In 1862, Kyrgyz contingents fought alongside Russian soldiers to take the fort of Pishpek, and when Russia liquidated the Khoḳand khānate in 1876, all of the Kyrgyz tribes had formally submitted to Russian rule (V.M. Ploskikh, *Kirgizî i kokandskoe khanstvo*, Frunze 1977). The area they inhabited fell into the Governorates of the Steppes and of Turkistan, and there was continuous reshuffling of the administrative organisation. Russian rule at first did not deeply affect local affairs, but this changed soon with the influx of settlers into the Semirečye region (northern Kyrgyzstan); migration reached its highest levels in the years immediately preceding World War I. In the Semirečye, between 1903 and 1913 about 4.5 million ha were allotted to settlers, thus provoking a drop of about one quarter in livestock. Land issues, as well as ethnic conflicts and accelerated social differentiation among the Kyrgyz, are seen behind the great steppe uprising in 1916, which was triggered by a decree to recruit local people as labourers in support of Russia's war effort. The rebellion was crushed, leaving an unknown number of Kyrgyz dead; about a third of the Kyrgyz population is said to have fled to China, partly returning after the Revolution in 1917. Again, the Kyrgyz herds decreased by about 60% (D. Brower, *Kyrgyz nomads and Russian pioneers. Colonization and ethnic conflict in the Turkestan revolt of 1916*, in *Jahrbücher für Geschichte Osteuropas*, N.F., xliv [1996], 41-53).

3. *Soviet times*.

The Russian Revolution provoked the creation of new Kyrgyz and Kyrgyz/Kazak organisations; at first, locals were reluctant to participate in the institutions created by Russians. Local ("Muslim") organisations included the Alash Orda [see ḲAZĀḲSTĀN, in Suppl.], *Shūrā-yi islāmiyya* (founded in Khoḳand in April 1917) and *Bukarā* (from Ar. *fuḳarā'* "paupers"). National demands came to the fore, and federal structures were demanded in a number of meetings (e.g. the First All-Russian Muslim Conference held at Moscow in May 1917). All of them were intent on preserving local interests, above all regarding the land question, against Russian encroachments.

During the civil war, Kyrgyzstan changed masters several times. The "Turkistan Autonomy" (November 1917-February 1918) was a short-lived attempt at creating a state structure in the Farghāna valley and one of the origins of the Basmači guerilla movement, which became strong enough to pose a threat to Ōsh, Djalālābād and Naryn in late 1919. In the north, Alash Orda struggled between Whites and Reds to conserve a measure of regional autonomy. But in the end, Mikhail Frunze led the Red Army to success.

In April 1918 the territory of the Kyrgyz was included into the Turkestan Autonomous Soviet Socialist Republic. Only in 1922 was the question of a separate representation of the Kyrgyz raised; until then, the ethnonym "Kyrgyz" had denoted those peo-

Table 1

Year	*Kyrgyz*	*Russian*	*Uzbek*	*Other groups*	*Others*
1924	63.5	16.8	15.4	Kazak 1.3	3.5
1970	45	30	11.3	Ukrainians 4 Germans 3 Tatars 2.3	4.5
1989	52.4	21.5	12.9	Ukrainians 2.5 Germans 2.4 Tatars 1.6	7.7
1999	64.9	12.5	13.8	Ukrainians 1.0 Germans 0.4 Tatars 0.9	6.5

ple whom we presently know as Ḳazaḳ, whereas the "real" Kyrgyz were called either Karakyrgyz "Black Kyrgyz" or otherwise, but in any case, were linked to the Ḳazaḳs. First, some former Alas͟h members (now within the Bolshevik party) worked for the creation of a "Kara-Kyrgyz Autonomous Mountain District", arguing that the splitting of the Kyrgyz over several administrative units was detrimental to their development as a nation. The district was to include the northern foothills as well. This move was at first viewed positively by party and state organs, but quashed later in 1922. Thus, the "Kara Kyrgyz" had to wait until the national demarcation (*razmeževanie*) in the second half of 1924 (the date retained was the decision taken by the Central Executive Committee of the USSR—TsIK SSSR—on 27 October 1924); this process provided them, for the first time in their recorded history, with a state-like structure in the form of an "autonomous district" (*avtonomnaya oblast'*) within the Russian Federation (not the Kazak ASSR). Soon afterwards, the structure was promoted into an Autonomous Soviet Socialist Republic (ASSR), still within the Russian Federation (1 February 1926). Status as a full member of the Soviet Union was achieved when the new Soviet Constitution was proclaimed on 5 December 1936, which counted eleven republics, among them the Kirgiz Soviet Socialist Republic.

Until then, the country had undergone significant change in line with the general evolution (for better or worse) within the Soviet Union. For the nomadic Kyrgyz the collectivisation of agricultural land (for which a ruthless campaign was launched in 1929) meant that they were forced to settle (R. Eisener, *"Konterrevolution auf dem Lande". Zur inneren Sicherheitslage in Mittelasien 1929/30 aus der Sicht der OGPU*, Berlin 1999 [ANOR, no. 6]). This again meant a sharp drop in livestock (from 3.8 million to 2.3 million in 1931-2; sheep and goats dropped from 3.1 million in 1924 to just under 1 million in 1932; livestock reached the levels of the late 1920s again only by the 1950s or later) and widespread famine; though the Ḳazaḳ steppe regions were hardest hit, Kyrgyzstan also was a disaster area. Repression was rampant; in 1932 during tax collection, more than 100 persons were shot (*U istokov kirgizskoy nats̲ional'noy gosudarstvennosti*, Bishkek 1996, 121). No reliable figures are available for human losses in this period, but they must have been massive. Hence by 1940, almost all Kyrgyz farmers worked on collective or state farms.

In 1938, as in other parts of the Soviet Union, the local intelligentsia was physically destroyed together with the "old guard" of revolutionaries. This included some of the former Alas͟h members who were involved in the affairs surrounding the "Social Turan Party".

Industrialisation was one of the main targets of Soviet development policies, and during the first Five-Year Plans, coal mining was developed, but also metal working and industries related to the agricultural production of the country (textiles, foodstuffs, meat). Nevertheless, Kyrgyzstan has remained a largely agricultural country.

In the post-Stalin period (beginning with the XXth Congress of the CPSU in 1956), developments in Kyrgyzstan closely followed the general Soviet pattern. This meant that a precarious balance was established by the Republic's leadership between utter devotion to the centre and the slow but irresistable localisation of decision making, using patron-client-relationships to a very large extent (O. Roy, *The new Central Asia. The creation of nations*, London 2000). These networks tend to have a regional basis; in Kyrgyzstan, this means the south-north divide. Whereas the last Soviet leaders were southerners, the new leadership is northern. During Turdakun Usunbaev's term as the party's first secretary (1961-85, when he was removed by the new leadership under Gorbachev), Kyrgyzstan was increasingly unable to attract new capital investment, and the republic was the second poorest part of the Soviet Union (after Tād͟jīkistān).

4. *Independence and after.*

In the case of Kyrgyzstan, national independence was spurred by an outburst of communal violence in Ōs͟h between Kyrgyz and Uzbeks in the summer of 1990, with land shortages and poor representation of Uzbeks as background. This led to the election of an outsider as chairman to the Supreme Soviet (28 October 1990), Askar Akaev, who came to be the only president in the new Central Asian republics not to have held high party office before. Akaev was re-elected president on 24 December 1995 (75% of expressed votes) and again on 29 October 2000 (74.5% of expressed votes, but major competitors were prevented from running).

Kyrgyzstan won its independence on 31 August 1991. The country has made rapid moves towards democracy and a market-oriented economy, earning the label of "Central Asia's island of democracy"; this characterisation has been questioned since more autocratic features have appeared. Economically, crisis has bordered on collapse during the first years of independence, the GDP plummeting by around 45% in 1992-5, industrial production by nearly two-thirds and agriculture by around one-third. Again, as in other crises all through the 20th century, reduction in livestock numbers is a good indicator: sheep and goats fell from 8,741,000 heads in 1993 to a mere 3,716,000 in 1997. Inflation has also been a major problem since the creation of a national currency, the *som*, in 1993; soaring up to more than 1000% in 1992-3, it has been down to 18% in 1998, rising again to 36% in 1999 in the aftermath of the financial crisis in Russia. In spite of this, the GDP was up by 3.6% in 1999, mainly due to over-average agricultural production. But economic prospects do not seem as bright now (2000-1) as in the latter 1990s.

Kyrgyzstan faces serious security problems, mainly in the Farg͟hāna region. In 1999 and 2000, Islamists from northern Tād͟jīkistān have made incursions into Kyrgyzstani territory. Previously, security had not been a priority issue for the Kyrgyzstani government, but in 2001, military expenditure was increased by 250%. Linked to this is the drug traffic (cannabis, but mostly opiates from Afg͟hānistān and Tād͟jīkistān), making Ōs͟h one of its major hubs in Central Asia. Other transnational problems include an increasing water problem (downstream Uzbekistān and Ḳazaḳstān depend on water supplies from Kyrgyzstani sources; water demand has increased by over 25% during the last decade).

The nation-building process involves a re-interpretation of the past, focussing on attempts at statehood in the more distant past and a re-evaluation of the early Kyrgyz nationalists, including those who fell victim to the Stalinist purges.

Bibliography (in addition to references given in the article): F. Willfort, *Turkestanisches Tagebuch*, Vienna 1930 (eye-witness of 1916 uprising and of events in 1917); G.K. Krongardt, *Naselenie Kirgizstana vo vtoroi polovine XIX-načale XX v.*, Bishkek 1997; *Istoriya Kirgizstana: XX vek*, Pod obs͟hčey redakts͟iey U. Ts͟otonova, Bishkek 1998; J. Anderson, *Kyrgyzstan. Central Asia's island of democracy?*, Amsterdam 1999; *Osnovnïe itogi pervoy nats͟ional'noy perepisi nasleniya Kirgizskoy Respubliki 1999 goda*, Bishkek 2000.

(J. Paul)

KIRMĀNĪ, ḤĀD͟JD͟J MUḤAMMAD KARĪM K͟HĀN [see S͟HAYK͟HIYYA. 2].

KISAKÜREK, Necip Fazil (1905-83), Turkish poet who wrote metaphysical poems of anxiety, darkness, loneliness and death, and whose tone became progressively mystical and, at the end, dogmatically religious. Already a bohemian as a student of philosophy in Istanbul, he continued a life of gambling, drinking and womanising as he worked first as a bank inspector and then as a teacher at various post-secondary schools in Ankara. Meeting the Naḳs͟hbandī *s͟heyk͟h* Abdülhakim Arvasi in 1934 became a turning point in his life by providing an answer in religion for his spiritual and intellectual crises. He quit his job in 1942 in order to devote all his time to writing and publishing. He published two journals: *Ağaç* ("Tree", 1936), and *Büyük doğu* ("The Great East", 1943-78). He was politically active in religious causes, and used especially *Büyük doğu* as an ideological platform.

Although he also wrote short stories, novels, monographs on as diverse topics as Imām ʿAlī, ʿAbd ül-Ḥamīd II and Nāmiḳ Kemāl, and plays of which the most noteworthy is *Bir adam yaratmak* ("To create a man", 1938), Kısakürek is first and foremost admired as a poet. With his first three books of poetry, he was hailed as a new voice in Turkish poetry. The tone of feverish nightmare in his early poems is created by striking, sometimes erotically charged images, by paradoxical metaphors of being and nothingness which dissolve into each other, and by experiments with the lengths of syllables that play with the traditional syllabic measure of Turkish folk poetry. After his conversion, he publicly disowned all but a few of his previous poems. His lifelong goal was to create one definitive book which would include all of his poems. He achieved this with *Çile* ("Suffering", 1974), which has 385 poems. In his later poems, the tone is of impatient waiting for death because he believed that the terror of death and loneliness ended in dying and uniting with God. He defines a poem as a thought stated in emotional terms, and argues that the structure of a poem should be completely absorbed by the theme. Details of his life can be found in his two books of memoirs: *O ve ben* ("He and I", 1974) and *Babıali* (1975).

Bibliography: 1. English translations of some of his poems appear in Talat Sait Halman, (ed.), *Contemporary Turkish literature*, New Jersey, London and Toronto 1982, 353-4; Feyyaz Kayacan Fergar (ed.), *Modern Turkish poetry*, Herts. 1992, 62-3; Kemal Silay (ed.), *An anthology of Turkish literature*, Indiana 1996, 394-6.

2. Studies. Hasan Çebi, *Bütün yönleriyle Necip Fazıl Kısakürek'in şiiri*, Ankara 1987; Ahmet Oktay, *Cumhuriyet dönemi edebiyatı* 1923-50, Ankara 1994, 989-1015; *Bütün yönleriyle Necip Fazıl*, Ankara 1994; M. Orhan Okay, *Necip Fazıl Kısakürek*, Istanbul 1998.

(Sibel Erol)

ḲIṬʿA (A.), pl. *ḳiṭaʿ*, or *muḳaṭṭaʿa*, pl. *muḳaṭṭaʿāt*, literally "piece, part cut off from the whole, segment". As a literary concept *ḳiṭʿa* denotes a form of poetry.

1. In Arabic poetry

A *ḳiṭʿa* or *muḳaṭṭaʿa* is a short monothematic poem or fragment of a poem, in contrast to the long (often polythematic) poem, the *ḳaṣīda* [*q.v.*]. The term *ḳiṭʿa* can actually denote a piece or part of a longer poem (e.g. poetic quotes in anthologies) [see MUK͟HTĀRĀT]. However, it is, in particular, independent short poems that are named thus (in rare cases, they are also termed *ḳiṣār al-ḳaṣāʾid*; see al-D͟jāḥiẓ, *K. al-Ḥayawān*, iii, 98). Western scholars usually equate *ḳaṣīda* and *ḳiṭʿa* with polythematic and monothematic poems respectively, while indigenous Arab critics in general consider only the length of a poem as a criterion for distinguishing between the two forms (cf. van Gelder, *Brevity*, 79 f.). They could, however, never agree on the number of verses that determines the borderline between the two forms. Ibn Ras͟hīḳ names seven or ten verses (*ʿUmda*, i, 188-9) as the lower limit for a *ḳaṣīda*; other numbers are mentioned as well, however (cf. van Gelder, 79-80). According to the Arab, and in contradistinction to the Persian, critics, the non-existence, of an opening verse (*maṭlaʿ*) with internal rhyming (*taṣrīʿ*) does not count as a criterion for the *ḳiṭʿa*. As a matter of fact, there are more than enough *ḳiṭʿa*s containing such opening verses even in the earliest times. Thoughts as to the purpose for which the ancient Arabs preferred short poems have already been formulated within the context of pre-systematic criticism. Abū ʿAmr b. al-ʿAlāʾ and al-K͟halīl b. Aḥmad [*q.vv.*] are said to have remarked on this: they were used whenever a poem had to be memorised. Others think that the *ḳiṭʿa* is especially useful for expressing disputes, proverbs and jests (cf. Ibn Ras͟hīḳ, i, 186).

*Ḳiṭʿa*s can be found in almost every *dīwān* of poetry and in numerous other works dealing with poetry and other topics (*inter alia* in the *ayyām al-ʿArab*, and also in many historical works, such as Ibn His͟hām's *Sīra*, al-Ṭabarī's *Taʾrīk͟h*, and al-Balād͟hurī's *Ansāb al-as͟hrāf*). The *ḳiṭʿa* is not subject to any thematic limitations. A classification and characterisation of the contents of the *ḳiṭʿa* among the ancient Arabs has been offered by Alfred Bloch. His principle of classification is the degree of the poem's "distance from life or from specific situations in life". As a result, the different categories are: (1) work-songs or songs that accompany a certain action (no or little "distance from life"; poetry of the moment); (2) poems containing a proclamation or message (medium distance from life; poetry of the occasion); (3) poems expressing a sentiment of life and poems of remembrance (timeless artistic poetry). (A group of verses of categories nos. 2 and 3 may form the final part of category no. 4, the *ḳaṣīda*.)

Category no. 1 is an impromptu poem of the moment, very often composed in the easiest metre, *radjaz*. Mainly war cries belong to this category, in addition to songs for round dances to which mothers let their children dance, and work-songs in the narrower sense that accompany real activities (rarely ever transmitted) (cf. Ullmann, *Untersuchungen*, 18 ff.). The contents of the war poems is mostly self-praise: "I am Ibn Wars, horseman without pusillanimity, who through his courage inspires admiration, who advances boldly when the weakling retreats, and on the day of horror with the sword I strike the towering (adversarial) hero until he falls" (al-Balādhurī, *Ansāb*, v, 268, 6).

Category no. 2 is most abundantly represented in ancient Arabic poetry and is, according to Bloch, its most characteristic genre. In proclamation poems the poet expresses his opinion on a certain event; they are occasional poems born out of daily life, "pamphlet verses", the contents of which are valid for a considerable amount of time. Since they are mostly disputes with distant opponents, many of them are composed as messages: *(a-lā) abligh banī fulān*[in] "send word to the Banū X that . . .", or *(a-lā) man mubligh*[un] *ʿannī fulān*[an] "who will send word from me to X that . . ."; numerous others present themselves as reactions to messages that have arrived: *nubbiʾtu anna* "it has been brought to my knowledge that . . .". As to content, these are poems of warning, blame (especially for poor hospitality), triumph, justification, challenge to blood revenge, etc. "To the Banū Dhuhl bring now . . . the message, that, as an atonement for your slaying of al-Muḳannā, we have slain ʿUbayda and Abu 'l-Djulāḥ. If you consider the matter settled now, then so will we; if not, the points of our lances [will await you]—[they are] pointed—and sharp swords, shining bright, cutting off heads and fingers" (*Sharḥ Dīwān al-Ḥamāsa*, recension of al-Marzūḳī, ii, 772, no. 259).

All poems in which the poet does not express his opinion on a certain event are subsumed by Bloch under category no. 3: the poems in which he puts in words, let us say, his view of life or remembers bygone pleasures and deeds of youth, or puts forward aphorisms about the transitoriness of life and all sorts of other practical wisdom (sententious poetry), or praises himself or his tribe without referring to a specific deed, etc. According to Bloch, most of the (monothematic) self-praise and praise poems are to be put into this category, because, in general, they have not been brought about by a specific event.

While this categorisation may still be sufficient for pre-Islamic and early Islamic poetry—it has, however, been criticised in that the dirge (*marthiya*) has not found its appropriate place therein (Wagner, *Grundzüge*, i, 68-9; Borg, *Mit Poesie*, 222-3)—it no longer covers the genres that came into being at the time of the Umayyads (and partly earlier) and unfolded their full potential at the time of the ʿAbbāsids. This new system is composed of genres that have, with good reason, been classified and named by the indigenous critics and, subsequently, by Western scholars primarily according to their topics (*ghazal* = love poetry; *khamriyya* = wine poetry, etc.). However, the topic often has additional characteristics of a genre-differentiating nature (e.g. the metre *radjaz* in hunting poems). According to their purely formal definition, poems belonging to the new genres are divided by the indigenous critics and editors of *dīwān*s into *ḳaṣīda*s and *ḳiṭʿa*s, depending on their length. This procedure shows up most prominently in Ḥamza al-Iṣfahānī's chapter headings of his recension of Abū Nuwās's *dīwān* (e.g. *al-bāb al-sābiʿ fi 'l-zuhdiyyāt wa-fīhi 20 ḳaṣīdat*[an] *wa-muḳaṭṭaʿat*[an]*; al-bāb al-tāsiʿ fi 'l-khamriyyāt . . . yashtamilu ʿalā 323 ḳaṣīdat*[an] *wa-muḳaṭṭaʿat*[an], etc.). The poems of the new genres are often short; there are, however, also very long poems, sometimes even containing several parts, which can especially be found among the *khamriyyāt*. These poems may also be seen as approaching the praise *ḳaṣīda* in their structure (they have—albeit seldom—a *nasīb*, or—very often—a parody of a *nasīb* as a prologue; the *raḥīl* can also be found). Among the so-called neo-classical poets (Abū Tammām, al-Buḥturī and al-Mutanabbī) the short poems, although abundant, stand entirely in the shadow of their *ḳaṣīda* poetry. However, there are cases like Abū Tammām's *ghazaliyyāt*, whose importance should not be underestimated (see Bauer, *Abū Tammām's Contribution*, 13 ff.). Most of them are short and it is noteworthy that pieces consisting of four verses are particularly numerous (cf. *ibid.*, 18-19; Seidensticker, *Die Herkunft*, 920). In al-Mutanabbī's *dīwān* one can find numerous short poems addressing more than one theme; al-Wāḥidī, in his commentary, criticises two *ḳiṭʿa*s that contain sundry descriptions—a genre not mastered by al-Mutanabbī, according to him (*Dīwān*, ed. Dieterici, 774). The themes of *ḳiṭʿa*s from the 3rd/9th to the 5th/11th century are extremely varied. Next to the short poems of the now established new genres one can find pieces that in their themes are close to the epigrams of late antiquity: descriptions (Ar. *awṣāf*, sing *waṣf* [*q.v.*], Greek *ekphrasis*) of a large variety of objects (especially in Ibn al-Rūmī, Kushādjim, al-Sarī al-Raffāʾ and al-Maʾmūnī), descriptions of flowers and gardens (*zahriyyāt* [*q.v.*] (in Ibn al-Rūmī, Ibn al-Muʿtazz and al-Ṣanawbarī; especially in the latter, one can also find long garden poems), reflective poetry (especially in Ibn al-Rūmī), jesting, riddles, requests for gifts, mockery, blame, excuses, thank-you notes, requests, invitations, etc. In Ibn al-Muʿtazz's praise poetry one can find a remarkably large amount of short pieces; al-Maʿarri, finally, in his philosophical poems (*luzūmiyyāt*) chooses the short form of the *ḳiṭʿa* as often as its long form.

2. In Persian literature

The Persian critics define the *ḳiṭʿa* or *muḳaṭṭaʿa* as a poem that has the same metre and rhyme throughout, and the opening verse (*maṭlaʿ*) of which does not contain internal rhyming (*taṣrīʿ*). Most often, two verses are named as the minimum amount whereas there is no upper limit as to the number of verses (Dihkhudā, s.v. *ḳiṭʿa*; Rückert-Pertsch, 64). This means that the length of a poem, which for the Arabs is its decisive feature, has been completely abandoned as a criterion. As with the Arabic *ḳiṭʿa* the choice of topic is arbitrary.

As can be expected, *ḳiṭʿa*s are found already among the poems of the oldest Neo-Persian poets (from Muḥammad b. Waṣīf via Rūdakī up to Manūčihrī). A sizeable number of the short poems of these old poets, however, begin with a *maṭlaʿ* that contains a *taṣrīʿ*, hence cannot be counted as *ḳiṭʿas*. Such is the case with the whole of Manūčihrī's wine and love poems (ed. de Biberstein Kazimirski, nos. 3, 4, 34, 69-75, 77-83, 85, 90, 92). Terminological *ḳiṭʿas* occur much more rarely in Manūčihrī. In the *dīwāns* of poets beginning in the 5th/11th century the *ḳiṭʿas* often occupy their own more or less voluminous chapter. Famous for their *ḳiṭʿas* are Anwarī (d. 587/1191 at the latest [*q.v.*]) and especially Ibn-i Yamīn (d. 769/1368 [*q.v.*]). Anwarī's *dīwān* contains a very large chapter comprising them. These are of extraordinary variety in their topics: in addition to praise, blame, mockery, threat, request (especially frequent is the request for wine), thanks, mourning, congratulation, complaint, description of personal circumstances (*ḥasb-i ḥāl*), one finds advice, admonishment, maxims, and reflective poems (occurring very frequently), jesting, epistles, riddles, chronograms, *munāẓaras*, and many others, among them very unusual topics, for instance, a poem about toothache, in which the word "tooth" occurs in every verse. Descriptions are remarkably rare; there are, however, a few descriptions of banquets and palaces. Poems containing 20 and even 30 verses do occur. As for the *ḳiṭʿas* of Ibn-i Yamīn who, all in all, is considered the most important Persian *ḳiṭʿa* poet, see the article on this poet. The *dīwān* of Ḥāfiẓ [*q.v.*] also contains a small section of *ḳiṭʿas*; in addition to the usual themes (praise, mourning, longing, wine, chronograms, maxims, congratulations, request for a reward, etc.), there are also some more remarkable poems like the one in which Ḥāfiẓ describes in many verses the loss of his poetic powers, which can only be restored by the ruler's grace. Kamāl Khudjandī's and Djāmī's [*q.vv.*] *ḳiṭʿas* are predominantly short. Most of them consist of only two verses, a peculiarity that is not found in the *ḳiṭʿas* of Kamāl's contemporary Ḥāfiẓ. Djāmī's three *dīwāns* contain altogether only 128 *ḳiṭʿas*; thematically, these do not offer anything out of the ordinary. It has been remarked, however, that Djāmī's "advice and admonishments" (*pand u mawʿiẓa*) are mostly of a sarcastic and pessimistic character, since, in any case, the *ḳiṭʿas* of this epoch are critical of society and complain about the upheavals of the day (H. Riḍā, in his introduction to the *Dīwān-i kāmil-i Djāmī*, Tehran 1341/1962, 84).

Bibliography: A. Bloch, *Qaṣīda*, in *Asiatische Studien*, iii-iv (1948), 106-32; M. Ullmann, *Untersuchungen zur Rağazpoesie*, Wiesbaden 1966; G.J. van Gelder, *Brevity: the long and the short of it in classical Arabic literary theory*, in *Proceedings of the Ninth Congress of the UEAI*, ed. R. Peters, Leiden 1981, 78-88; E. Wagner, *Grundzüge der klassischen arabischen Dichtung*, i, *Die altarabische Dichtung*, ii, *Die arabische Dichtung in islamischer Zeit*, Darmstadt 1987-8; Th. Bauer, *Abū Tammām's contribution to ʿAbbāsid* ghazal *poetry*, in *JAL* xxvii (1996), 13-21; G. Borg, *Mit Poesie vertreibe ich den Kummer meines Herzens. Eine Studie zur altarabischen Trauerklage der Frau*, Istanbul 1997; T. Seidensticker, *Die Herkunft des Rubāʿī*, in *Asiatische Studien*, liii (1999), 905-36; G. Schoeler, *Alfred Blochs Studie über die Gattungen der altarabischen Dichtung*, in *Asiatische Studien*, lvi (2002), 737-68. (G. Schoeler)

KITĀBA [see INSHĀʾ; KĀTIB; KHAṬṬ].

ḲOČO (Khocho, Chotscho, Kōśō) (Uyghur; in Chinese Kao-Ch'ang), also known as Idiḳut-shahri, and locally as "Asus (Ephesus), the town of Daḳyānūs", i.e. the Roman emperor Decius (*regn.* 249-51) [see AṢḤĀB AL-KAHF] (cf. A. Von Le Coq, *Auf Hellas' Spuren*, 41), the name of an Uyghur state (850-1250) and of an ancient, walled city, now in ruins, adjoining Ḳarakhodja in the desert to the east of Turfān [*q.v.*] in Eastern Sinkiang Uyghur Autonomous Region, China.

According to Von Gabain, the name is neither Turkish nor Chinese, but an ancient, indigenous one, meaning "highly brilliant". In the 7th century A.D. the Ḳočo state reached as far east as Tunhuang in Kansu [*q.v.*], famous for its "Cave of the Thousand Buddhas", and its "Jade Gate" (Chin. Yü-mön-kuan), where all the traffic between China and the West had to pass. In the north this state included the so-called "Four Garrisons", i.e. Bi̊shbali̊ḳ [*q.v.*], Kuča, Ḳarashahr and Ḳočo town itself, all on the northern branch of the Silk Route and described by the 7th-century Chinese traveller and monk Hsüan-tsang. In 791 the Tibetans, in alliance with the Ḳarluḳ [*q.v.*] and the Sha-t'o ("the People of the Sandy Desert"; see Chavannes, *Documents*, 96-9), defeated the Chinese and the Uyghur, and occupied the Tarim Basin [*q.v.*]. In 840 the Ḳi̊rgi̊z [*q.v.*] put an end to Uyghur power in Mongolia. Uyghur groups fled southward and settled in the Turfan region, where they established a state, with Ḳočo as its capital, which was recognised by the Chinese in 856. The earliest record of a Muslim presence in the oases along the northern branch of the Silk Route so far known seems to be the travel account which Sallām al-Tardjumān [*q.v.* in Suppl.] dictated to Ibn Khurradādhbih (Ar. text 164, Fr. tr. 126) of his journey from Sāmarrāʾ to Sinkiang in 230-2/842-4. Before reaching Ha-mi [see ḲOMUL, in Suppl.], he met followers of the Prophet who apparently had settled there more or less permanently since they had mosques and *madrasas*.

In 848 Chang I-ch'ao, the Chinese regent of Sha-chou, "the town of the sands" as Tun-hang had been renamed under the T'ang dynasty (618-907), began to oust the Tibetans from northwestern Kansu, and in 855 the Ḳočo Uyghur followed his example. In the 10th century they entertained good relations with the Tibetans, as they did with the Kitai (Liao) [see ḲARĀ KHIṬĀY], who in 924 toppled the Ḳi̊rgi̊z state of which Ḳočo had become a vassal. In 1001 the *khaḳan* of Ḳočo requested the emperor of China to wage war against the Tangut or Hsi Hsia, a people of Tibetan origin who lived in the great loop of the Yellow River [see ḤAMĀSA. iv; KANSU]. He boasted to the emperor about the large extension of his state. At that time the Ḳočo Uyghurs had moved their residence further westward to Kuča. In 1125 the Liao were overcome by the Jüchen, who until 1234 ruled over Manchuria, much of Central Asia and all of North China. With these new overlords, too, the Ḳočo Uyghurs had friendly relations. In 1209 King Barčuḳ of Ḳočo surrendered peacefully to Čingiz Khān in order to rid himself of pressure from the Naiman of Western Mongolia. He was adopted as "the fifth son". After the Mongolian conquest, Ḳočo was added to the Čaghatay khānate [*q.v.*]. The Mongols were instructed in Buddhism by the Ḳočo Uyghurs, Buddhism being strongly established in the region. But the famous Turfan finds also include fragments of Syrian manuscripts, most of them with texts from the Peshiṭta, while von Le Coq also found in Ḳočo a wall painting of Mani, the founder of Manicheism, dated to the 9th century A.D. The towns along the Silk Route thus had a rather mixed population of merchants who professed various religions. Over the centuries, Ḳočo seems to have adapted itself to its respective overlords in order to continue its lucrative trade.

Bibliography: E. Chavannes, *Documents sur les Tou-kine (Turcs) occidentaux*, St. Petersburg 1903;

A. von Le Coq, *Chotscho. Kõnigliche Preussische Turfan Expedition*, Berlin 1913; idem, *Buried treasures of Chinese Turkestan*, Berlin 1928; idem, *Auf Hellas' Spuren. Berichte und Abenteuer der II. und III. Deutschen Turfan Expedition*, Graz 1974; Sir Aurel Stein, *On ancient Central Asian tracks*, London 1933, repr. New York 1971; A. von Gabain, *Einführung in die Zentralasienkunde*, Darmstadt 1979; eadem, *Das Leben im uigurischen Königreich von Qočo (850-1250)*, Veröffentl. d. Societas Uralo-altaica, vi, Wiesbaden 1973; P. Zieme, *Religion und Gesellschaft im Uigurischen Königreich von Qočo*, Opladen 1992.

(E. van Donzel)

ḲOMUL (Uyg͟hur; Chin. Ha-mi), a town and oasis in Eastern Sinkiang Uyg͟hur Autonomous Region, China (42° 47' N., 93° 32' E.). The Chinese name Ha-mi is derived from K͟hamil, the Mongolian rendering of Uyg͟hur Ḳomul.

This important stage on the northern branch of the Silk Route was occupied by the Chinese under the Han dynasty (206 B.C.-A.D. 220) in A.D. 73 and again in 86. In the 5th century the Tarim Basin [*q.v.*], probably including Ḳomul, was dominated by the White Huns or Hephthalites [see hayāṭila]. During the so-called "forward policy" towards the west under the Chinese T'ang dynasty (618-907), Ḳomul, and subsequently Turfan [*q.v.*], were wrested from Turkish supremacy, though the Turkish nomads kept looking for grazing grounds, thus causing disturbances. Ḳomul became the seat of a regular prefecture under the name I-chou. In the 7th century the famous Buddhist monk and traveller Hsüan-tsang was hospitably received by the Uyg͟hur or Tog͟huzg͟huz [*q.v.*] ruler of Ḳomul, then a principality subordinate to the kingdom of Ḳočo [*q.v.* in Suppl.]. In 763 the town was taken by the Tibetans and in 840 it came under Uyg͟hur rule. In 231/843 Ḳomul was visited by the Arab traveller Sallām al-Tard͟jumān [*q.v.* in Suppl.] who calls it Īkku (إيكّة) (Ibn K͟hurradād͟hbih, Ar. text 164, Fr. tr. 126; cf. Beckwith, *The Tibetan empire*, 149) after the Chinese name I-chou. Sallām describes it as having a circumference of ten parasangs, with iron gates which were closed by letting them down; inside the enclosure were fields and mills. This description seems to correspond with a Chinese *kuan*, i.e. a large, walled-in fortification with barracks, arms depots, fields, and two gates (see Luo Zhewen, *The Great Wall*, 39-41). According to Sallām, the distance between this town and D͟hu 'l-Ḳarnayn's barrier (Ar. *sadd*), perhaps the famous "Jade Gate" in the western extension of the Great Wall of China (see Sir Aurel Stein, *On ancient Central Asian tracks*, 189), is three stages. The real distance is 350 km (Von Le Coq, *Buried treasures*). Sallām adds that D͟hu 'l-Ḳarnayn camped in Īkku, but this remark is probably part of what he thought he should report to the caliph al-Wāt͟hiḳ [*q.v.*], who had sent him on his mission. During his journey to Īkku/Ḳomul along the northern branch of the Silk Route, Sallām, before reaching Īkku/Ḳomul, met a community of Muslims who spoke Arabic and Persian and had mosques and *madrasas*. He was astonished that they did not know who the caliph was.

In the 13th century, Ḳomul was Čingiz K͟hān's temporary capital. After the Mongol domination, it became one of the small Uyg͟hur states in the region. At the end of the 13th century it was visited by Marco Polo, who describes it as a place known for its hospitality and where it is good to live. In 1473 Ḳomul was annexed by the sultanate of Turfan. In the late 16th century, Ḳomul town and region came under the control of the Dzungars, a western Mongolian people who conquered Central Asia and gave their name to Dzungaria and the Dzungarian Gate, at present the northern part of the Singkiang Uyg͟hur Autonomous Region. In 1696 the Chinese Ch'ing emperor defeated the Dzungar chief Dga'-Idan. After the death of the latter's grandson Dga'-Idan Cereng in 1745, internal Dzungarian strife led to their complete destruction in the war against China (1755-8), during which the Chinese used Ḳomul as a base. After the fall of the Dzungars, the Muslims of the Tarim Basin staged an independence movement, but by 1760 this was suppressed by the Ch'ing, who established control over the Basin by granting official status to the former rulers of its oasis states. In the 18th century, China's boundaries reached as far as Lake Balk͟has͟h [*q.v.*] and parts of the Kazak͟h steppe. During the great Muslim rebellion of 1862-78 under Ma Hua-lung [*q.v.*], Ḳomul was badly damaged. It was visited by Col. Mark Bell in 1886, by A.H. von Le Coq in 1904 and by Cable and French in 1940. Von Le Coq describes the riches of the palace of the Muslim *k͟hān* of Ḳomul: Chinese and Buk͟hārā carpets, porcelain, K͟hotan [*q.v.*] jade-carvings, silk embroideries, a cuckoo-clock and even French champagnes and Russian liqueurs. In 1932, after an abortive uprising, the town suffered terribly at the hands of the Chinese. Its population in 2003 is estimated at *ca.* 118,000.

Bibliography: Luo Zhewen and Zhao Luo, *The Great Wall of China in history and legend*, Beijing 1986; M.J. de Goeje, *De muur van Gog en Magog*, in *Verslagen en mededelingen Akademie van Wetenschappen Amsterdam*, 3e serie, vol. v (1888), 87 ff.; Yule-Cordier, *The book of Ser Marco Polo*, 3rd ed. London 1903; Sir Aurel Stein, *On ancient Central Asian tracks*, London 1933, repr. New York 1971; C.I. Beckwith, *The Tibetan empire in Central Asia*, Princeton 1987; Col. Mark Bell, V.C., *The great Central Asian trade route from Peking to Kashgaria*, in *Procs. Royal Geographical Society*, xii (1890); A.H. von Le Coq, *Buried treasures of Chinese Turkestan*, 1928; M. Cable and F. French, *The Gobi desert*, London 1942; P. Hopkirk, *Foreign devils on the Silk Road*, Oxford 1980. (E. van Donzel)

KONKAN, the coastal region of the western Deccan or Peninsular India lying roughly between Thālnēr and Bombay in the north and Goa in the south, i.e. between latitudes 19° 30' and 15° 30' N., and extending for some 560 km/350 miles. It has been known under this name in both mediaeval Islamic and modern times. Within British India, it was formerly in the Bombay Presidency, later Province, and is now in Maharashtra State of the Indian Union. It comprises a highly-forested, low-lying plain between the Arabian Sea and the inland mountain barrier of the Western Ghats.

In medieval Islamic times, the Tug͟hluḳids in the 14th century and then the Bahmanids [*q.v.*] in the course of the 15th century, endeavoured without much success to extend their authority from the Deccan plateau down to the ocean, until in 876/1472 the general Maḥmūd Gāwān [*q.v.*] finally established Bahmanid control over the Konkan strip. Konkan was subsequently divided between the Niẓām S͟hāhīs of Aḥmadnagar [*q.vv.*] (the northern part) and the ʿĀdil S͟hāhīs of Bīd͟japur [*q.vv.*] (the more southern part) in the 16th and early 17th centuries, then divided between the Mug͟hals and the ʿĀdil S͟hāhī sultans before the latter succumbed to the advance of the Mug͟hal Awrangzīb [*q.v.*] in 1097/1686. By the 18th century, Konkan was in the hands of the Śīvad͟ji and the Marāṭhās [*q.v.*], but after the peace settlements of

1816-17 with Britain at the end of the Marāthā Wars, the region was in 1818 incorporated into the Bombay Presidency. The local language, Konkani, is a dialect of Marāthī containing Dravidian elements probably borrowed from Kanarese.

Bibliography: *Gazetteers of the Bombay Presidency. Konkan*, i/2, *History*, Bombay 1896; *Imperial gazetteer of India*[2], xv, 394-5; G.M. Tibbetts, *Arab seafaring in the Indian Ocean before the coming of the Portuguese*, London 1971, index; H.K. Sherwani and P.M. Joshi (eds.), *History of medieval Deccan (1294-1724)*, Ḥaydarābād 1973, i, 17-22 and index; and see the map in HIND at Vol. III, 428. (C.E. BOSWORTH)

KÖSZEG, German Güns, a small Hungarian town near the Austrian border with a mediaeval castle which was sieged and symbolically taken by the Ottomans in 1532.

In the first decades of his reign, mainly under the influence of the Grand Vizier Ibrāhīm Pas̲h̲a, Süleymān the Magnificent cherished world-conquering ambitions. To achieve this goal, he intended, among other things, to defeat the Austrian Habsburgs by occupying their capital. After the unsuccessful 1529 campaign, he undertook another military operation in 1532 with the aim of marching against Vienna.

The Ottoman army proceeded slowly, holding sophisticated parades to imitate Charles V's shows of power and wealth. This time they followed a lesser known route, along which the castle of Köszeg was situated that did not seem to constitute a major obstacle. However, the garrison of approximately 1,000, mostly local peasants inexperienced in warfare, commanded by Miklós Jurisics (Nikola Jurišić), a Croatian landlord and the envoy of the Emperor Ferdinand I to Istanbul in 1529 and 1530, withstood the battle between 10 and 30 August. After long negotiations, the defenders surrendered, stipulating that, though Ottoman standards would be hoisted on the walls, none of their contingents would be stationed within the fort. One reason for procrastination was that the Ottomans wanted to avoid a pitched battle with the main forces of the Empire; similarly, the Habsburg side was reluctant to force a decisive clash.

For his valour, Jurisics was nominated royal councillor and received Köszeg as his hereditary property.

Bibliography: *Kőszeg ostromának emlékezete* ("The remembrance of the siege of Köszeg") ed. I. Bariska, Budapest 1982; P. Fodor, *Ottoman policy towards Hungary, 1520-1541*, in *Acta Orientalia Hungarica*, xlv (1991), 271-345; G. Necipoğlu, *Süleymân the Magnificent and the representation of power in the context of Ottoman-Habsburg-Papal rivalry*, in H. Inalcık and C. Kafadar (eds.), *Süleymân the Second and his time*, Istanbul 1993, 163-94. (G. DÁVID)

ĶUʿAYṬĪ, a South Arabian tribal group and sultanate, the latter eventually becoming part of the Eastern Aden Protectorate prior to the departure of the British from South Arabia in 1967. The full area of the sultanate was the whole of the coastal plain between the Wāḥidī [*q.v.*] in the west and Mahra in the east, the mountainous region north up to Wādī Ḥaḍramawt [see ḤAḌRAMAWT], the western end of the Wādī and some tribal lands north of the Wādī. One should add the area of the Wādīs Dawʿan (sometime spelt Dawʿān in the Arabic sources) and ʿAmd. The major towns of the sultanate were: al-Mukallā, the capital, and al-S̲h̲iḥr [*q.vv.*] (both ports on the Indian Ocean), G̲h̲ayl Bā Wazīr on the southern coastal plain, and S̲h̲ibām [*q.v.*] and al-Ḳaṭn in the Wādī itself (Government of Bombay, *Account*, 119).

It was the Kat̲h̲īrī [*q.v.*] Badr b. ʿAbd Allāh b. ʿUmar Ibn Abī Ṭuwayriḳ about the year 1270/1853 who began to bring in tribal mercenaries of Yāfiʿ [*q.v.*] from their lands in the west, as he strove to expand his territories in Ḥaḍramawt. Thereafter, there was a constant flow of Yāfiʿ immigration into the area (al-S̲h̲āṭirī, *Adwār*, ii, 401). The Ḳuʿayṭī were a tribal group (*baṭn*) of Yāfiʿ and they first settled in Wādī ʿAmd where ʿUmar b. ʿAwaḍ al-Ḳuʿayṭī, the founder of the dynasty, was born. In about 1246/1830, he went for the first time to Ḥaydarābād in South India where the *Nizām* employed Ḥaḍramīs and South Arabians as mercenary soldiers. ʿUmar did return to Ḥaḍramawt, but he died in India in 1282/1865 and was succeeded by his son, ʿAwaḍ b. ʿUmar, as *d̲j̲amaʿdār* (*jemadar* in the British sources). ʿUmar's three sons, Ṣalāḥ (called Barak Jung in India), ʿAwaḍ and ʿAbd Allāh, in particular, built fortunes in India and Arabia and had much influence on the later development of the dynasty.

During the 1280s/1860s and 1290s/1870s, full-scale wars were fought for control of Ḥaḍramawt between the Kat̲h̲īrī and the Ḳuʿayṭī (Government of Bombay, *Account*, 125; al-S̲h̲āṭirī, *Adwār*, ii, 405; Gavin, *Aden*, 160-62; Burrowes, *Dictionary*, 290-1; Dresch, *Yemen*, 21). In 1283/1866, the ports of al-Mukallā and al-S̲h̲iḥr were both controlled by Yāfiʿ, and when the latter called for help, Ṣalāḥ and ʿAbd Allāh sent funds from India and both Yāfiʿ and Indian troops were despatched to the area. In the following year, both ports were taken by the Ḳuʿayṭī, and the British became involved directly in the inter-dynasty struggles. The British, also fearing Turkish encroachment in the area, became apprehensive. In the confused situation, British policy was to cut off supplies and monies from India (Gavin, *Aden*, 162-8). In 1298/1881, they sanctioned Ḳuʿayṭī control of the southern coast and in 1299/1882 a treaty was drawn up between the two, the latter agreeing to accept British advice in exchange for an annual sum of 360 Maria Theresa dollars (Gavin, *Aden*, 171-2; for the text of the treaty, Government of Bombay, *Account*, 169-70).

In 1307/1888 a full protectorate treaty was signed between the Ḳuʿayṭī and the British, one of a number of such treaties. The British government agreed "to extend to Mokalla and Shehr and their dependencies which are under their authority and jurisdiction the gracious favour and protection of Her Majesty the Queen-Empress". In return, the Ḳuʿayṭī agreed "to refrain from entering into any correspondence, agreement or treaty with any foreign nation or power except with the knowledge and sanction of the British Government..." (Government of Bombay, *Account*, 186-7 for the full text). The Ḳuʿayṭī were in control of S̲h̲ibām and the western end of Wādī Ḥaḍramawt, as well as the coastal region in the south, and were able to deny the ports to the Kat̲h̲īrī. A generally cordial relationship developed between the British and the Ḳuʿayṭī (*ibid.*, 145; Gavin, *Aden*, 172-3; Ingrams, *Arabia*, 10).

In 1320/1902 the title of *jemadar* was finally abolished and ʿAwaḍ b. ʿUmar became Ḳuʿayṭī *sulṭān*. He died in India about 1325-7/1907-9 and was succeeded by his son G̲h̲ālib who himself died in 1340/1921. G̲h̲ālib was followed as *sulṭān* by his brother ʿUmar, who died in 1354/1935. Ṣāliḥ b. G̲h̲ālib became *sulṭān* in 1354/1935 and died in 1375/1955. ʿAwaḍ b. Ṣāliḥ reigned from that date until his death in 1386/1966 and ʿAwaḍ's son, G̲h̲ālib, was the last Ḳuʿayṭī *sulṭān* until the withdrawal of the British from the area about a year later (al-S̲h̲āṭirī, *Adwār*, ii, 407-8).

The year 1933 and the visit to Ḥaḍramawt of the

Political Resident in Aden, Sir Bernard Reilly, marks the beginning of the widespread development of the two sultanates, the Ḳuʿayṭī and the Kat̲h̲īrī, the peace which was negotiated among the tribes and the much closer involvement in their affairs by the British government, manifest in the establishment of an Eastern Aden Protectorate (EAP), quite separate from the Western Aden Protectorate (WAP). The peace, widely known as "Ingrams Peace" after its architect, Harold Ingrams, was finally brought about in 1355/1937 and was to last for three years. In 1937 also, an advisory treaty was signed between the Ḳuʿayṭī and the British in which an adviser was to be appointed, Ingrams himself (Smith, *"Ingrams Peace"*, 6-7, 21; for the text of the advisory treaty, see Ingrams, *Records*, ix, 236-7).

The Ḳuʿayṭī, along with the Kat̲h̲īrī, never entered the Federation which was formed and fostered by the British in the WAP. At the time of the withdrawal of the British in 1967, the Ḳuʿayṭī sultanate became a part of the People's Democratic Republic of Yemen. In 1990, with the unity of north and south Yemen, the whole of what had been the EAP became a part of the Yemen Republic [see AL-YAMAN. 3 (b)] with its capital at Ṣanʿāʾ.

Bibliography: Government of Bombay, *An account of the Arab tribes in the vicinity of Aden*, Bombay 1909; H. Ingrams, *Arabia and the Isles*, London 1966; R.J. Gavin, *Aden under British rule 1839-1967*, London 1975; Muḥammad b. Aḥmad al-S̲h̲āṭirī, *Adwār al-taʾrīk̲h̲ al-ḥaḍramī*, Jeddah 1983; Sālim b. Muḥammad al-Kindī, *Taʾrīk̲h̲ Ḥaḍramawt al-musammā bi 'l-ʿUdda al-mufīda al-d̲j̲āmiʿa li-tawārīk̲h̲ ḳadīma wa-ḥadīt̲h̲a*, ed. ʿAbd Allāh al-Ḥabs̲h̲ī, 2 vols., Ṣanʿāʾ 1991; Doreen and Leila Ingrams (eds.), *Records of Yemen 1798-1960*, 16 vols, [London] 1993; R.D. Burrowes, *Historical dictionary of Yemen*, Asian Historical Dictionaries no. 17, Lanham and London 1995; P. Dresch, *A history of modern Yemen*, Cambridge 2000; G.R. Smith, *"Ingrams Peace", Ḥaḍramawt, 1937-40. Some contemporary documents*, in *JRAS*, xii (2002), 1-30.

(G.R. SMITH)

KÜČÜK ʿALĪ OG̲H̲ULLARÎ, a line of Turkmen *derebey*s [*q.v.*] or local lords who controlled the region round Payās [*q.v.*], which was strategically situated near the head of the Gulf of Alexandretta (and now in the modern Turkish *il* or province of Hatay), and, for a while, Adana in Cilicia [*q.vv.*] for almost a century.

The founder, K̲h̲alīl Bey Küčük ʿAlī Og̲h̲lu, appears *ca.* 1770 as a bandit chief based on Payās, preying on shipping (including the ships of European powers) in the Gulf and on the land traffic which had to pass through the narrow gap between the Gâvur Daği mountains and the sea, levying dues on the Pilgrimage caravans from Anatolia to Syria and the Ḥid̲j̲āz, and even in 1801 capturing and imprisoning for ransom the Dutch consul-general in Aleppo. The efforts of the Porte in Istanbul at humbling him all failed, and it was obliged to come to an accommodation with him and accord to him the dignity of a *pas̲h̲a* of three *tug̲h̲*s.

When Küčük ʿAlī died in 1807, his equally rapacious son Dede Bey succeeded him, continuing to make a living by preying on shipping in the Gulf. An expedition sent against him under a rival *derebey*, Čapan Og̲h̲lu Amīn Pas̲h̲a of Yozgat, failed to dislodge him, but in 1818 the governor of Adana managed to capture him, and he was sent to Istanbul and executed.

His young son Mustuk (apparently a hypocoristic from Muṣṭafā; to be written as Muṣṭuḳ?) took refuge in Marʿas̲h̲ for nine years, out of the reach of the governors of Adana, but returned to Payās in 1827. During the 1830s he supported the Ottomans' enemy, Ibrāhīm Pas̲h̲a, son of Muḥammad ʿAlī [*q.vv.*], but rallied to the Sultans after the withdrawal of the Egyptian forces in 1840. William Burckhardt Barker, son of a British consul in the Levant, praises Mustuk for his polished manners and generous nature, a sharp contrast to his forebears, and Mustuk did try to discourage brigandage in his region. But the long-term policy of the Sultans at this time was the reduction and ending of the power of all *derebey*s. Mustuk fought off an attack by the governor of Adana in 1844, and it was not until 1863 that the then governor in Adana secured his capture. He was exiled, but the Payās region continued to be disturbed for another two years through the activity of two of his sons.

Bibliography: Barker's account of the family is the main Western source; see his *Lares and penates: or, Cilicia and its governors*, ed. W.F. Ainsworth, London 1853, 73 ff. Of modern studies, see A.G. Gould, *Lords or bandits? The derebeys of Cilicia*, in *IJMES*, vii (1976), 487-90; C.E. Bosworth, *William Burckhardt Baker's picture of Cilicia in the early 19th century*, forthcoming in *Graeco-Arabica*, ix (2003), with further references; and the *Bibl.* to DEREBEY.

(C.E. BOSWORTH)

KUFR [see KĀFIR].

AL-**KŪHĪ** or AL-ḲŪHĪ, ABŪ SAHL WAYD̲J̲ĀN b. Rustam, mathematician and astronomer who was originally from Ṭabaristān.

He worked in the second half of the 4th/10th century under the Būyid *amīr*s ʿAḍud al-Dawla and S̲h̲araf al-Dawla [*q.vv.*] and collaborated with the chief scholars of the time, notably Abu 'l-Wafāʾ al-Būzad̲j̲ānī, al-Sid̲j̲zī, al-Ṣag̲h̲ānī and ʿAbd al-Raḥmān al-Ṣūfī. Under the latter's direction, al-Kūhī took part in observation of the winter and summer solstices at S̲h̲īrāz (15 December 969 and 16 June 970), by means of a meridian circle 1.4 m in diameter having gradations of 5 in 5'. Subsequently, he built at Bag̲h̲dād an observatory equipped with instruments made after his own devising (a spherical segment with a diameter of *ca.* 13.5 m) and made observations of the entry of the Sun into the signs of Cancer and Libra on 16 June and 18 September 988. A certain Abu 'l-Ḥasan al-Mag̲h̲ribī (sc. ʿAlī b. Abi 'l-Rid̲j̲āl; cf. H. Suter, *Mathematiker*, no. 219) took part in these latter observations. At this time, urged on by his patron S̲h̲araf al-Dawla, who wished to emulate the achievements of the caliph al-Maʾmūn, he seems to have devoted himself enthusiastically to astronomy.

However, the greater—and best—part of his work was in the domain of mathematics and especially geometry. The number of his works here has increased over the years to the figure of 28 (Sezgin). One may mention his *Risāla fi 'l-birkār al-tāmm* (cf. Fr. Woepke, *Trois traités arabes sur le compas parfait*, in *NEMBN*, xxii/1 [1874], 1-21, 68-111, 145-75) and treatises on the construction of the heptagon (see Y. Dold-Samplonius, *Die Konstruktion des regelmässigen Siebenecks*, in *Janus*, 1/4 [1963], 227-49) and of the pentagon. He also wrote on the trisection of the angle (see A. Sayılı, *Al-Kūhī's trisection of the angle*, in *Actes du Xᵉ Congrès internat. d'Histoire des sciences*, i, Ithaca 1962, 545-6) and on the measurement of paraboloids (ed. Ḥaydarābād 1947, Ger. tr. Suter, *Die Abhandlungen Thābit b. Ḳurras und Abū Sahl al-Kūhīs über die Ausmessung der Paraboloide*, in *SBPMS Erl.*, xlviii-xlix [1916-17], 182-227). Others of al-Kūhī's works have titles analogous to those of certain treatises of Archimedes—of whom he was a good continuator—considered as apocryphal (e.g. *Marākiz al-dawā'ir al-mutamāssa; al-Masā'il al-handasiyya; K. al-Ma'khūdhāt*), or else are commentaries on Euclid or determinations of the value of π. The treatises on astronomical topics are much less numerous: on the construction of the astrolabe and of verticals (*dawā'ir al-sumūt*) on the tympanum of this last, preserved by Abū Naṣr Manṣūr b. ʿIrāķ, al-Bīrūnī's master (cf. J. Samsó, *Estudios sobre Abū Naṣr*..., Barcelona 1969, 63-4); on the determination of the *ķibla* [*q.v.*]; on the position of the Earth and the planets; etc. He was also the author of a *risāla* on kinetics (Eng. tr. Sayılı, *A short article... on the possibility of infinite motion in finite time*, in *Actes du VIIIe Congrès internat. d'Histoire des sciences*, Florence 1956, 248-9).

Bibliography: Ibn al-Nadīm, *Fihrist*, 283-4; Ķifṭī, 351-4; Suter, 75-6; C. Schoy, *Graeco-arabische Studien*, in *Isis*, viii (1926), 21-40; Sarton, *Introduction*, i, 665; G. Vajda, *Quelques notes sur le fonds de manuscrits arabes de la B.N. de Paris*, in *RSO*, xxv (1950), 1-10; Dold-Samplonius, in *Dict. sc. biogr.*, xi, New York 1975, 239; E.S. Kennedy, *A commentary upon Bīrūnī's Kitāb Taḥdīd al-amākin*, Beirut 1973; A.P. Youschkevitch, *Les mathématiques arabes (VIIIe-XVe siècles)*, tr. M. Cazenave and K. Jaouiche, Paris 1976, index; Brockelmann, I², 254, S I, 399; Sezgin, *GAS*, v, 314-21, vi, 218-19. (J. VERNET)

ĶULUZ, the Ottoman Turkish name for the Greek town of Vólos, a port on the northern shore of the Pagasetic Gulf or Gulf of Vólos in east-central Thessaly [see TESALYA] (lat. 39° 22' N., long. 22° 57' E.). The name probably stems from Slavonic *golosh* "seat of administration" and may be associated with the Slav presence in the area during middle Byzantine times.

Situated on the site of ancient Iolcos, the area received in *ca.* 1277 refugees from the Byzantine capital Constantinople who opposed the emperor Michael VIII Palaeologus's attempts at church union with the West, and in the late Byzantine period Vólos was known as a relatively new settlement. Together with neighbouring Demetrias (2 km to the south-west of modern Vólos), which had remained in Catalan hands until *ca.* 1381, Vólos experienced two Ottoman conquests, firstly between 1393 and 1397/796-800 and then *ca.* 805/1403, and passed definitively into Turkish hands *ca.* 826/1423. The conquerors strengthened the fortifications of the castle there in order to fend off an impending Venetian attack, and an Ottoman governor and garrison were installed, together with fresh Muslim settlers from Anatolia, whilst the local Christians moved to the slopes of Mt. Pélion to the north (refs. in A. Savvides, in *Thessalikó Hemerológio*, xxviii [1995], 51-2, 59-60).

In the early Ottoman period, the region of the Vólos fortress (but not Demetrias) is mentioned in the surviving testaments of the Turkish governors of Thessaly Turakhān Bey [*q.v.*] (850/1446), ʿÖmer Bey (889/1484) and Ḥasan Bey (937/1531), whilst it was also described in Pīrī Re'īs's [*q.v.*] *Kitāb-i Baḥriyye*. The first settlements outside the fortress grew up in the late 16th-early 17th centuries, a growth which stimulated local commerce and the transit trade. This was helped by a famed local fair held twice a week and the first works along the shore at the fortress beach, later to become Vólos's commodious port. In 1665 the fortress was attacked by Francesco Morosini and a Venetian force (P. Coronelli, *Memorie storio-geografiche*..., Venice 1692, 229), but soon recaptured and refortified by the Ottomans.

During the Greek Revolt of the early 19th century, the rebel Greeks of Pélion failed in May 1821 to capture the strongly-held fortress, although on 8 April 1827 the British naval commander and Philhellene Frank Abney Hastings seized five Turkish vessels in Vólos harbour and forced the Ottoman garrison temporarily to evacuate the fortress (see Tsopotós, *History*, 202 ff.). However, the region remained under Turkish rule till 1881 when, following the Berlin Conference, it passed between 2 and 22 November to the Kingdom of Greece and Turkish forces left the town (the citadel was unfortunately demolished a few years later). It was in this last phase of Ottoman rule that the initial settlements of the modern town of Vólos were established (1833-50), with consulates and commercial installations set up by Greeks, Austrians, British, French and Italians between 1838 and 1870 (see *ibid.*, 240 ff., 250 ff.).

Modern Vólos is now a major commercial and industrial centre (population in 1981: 70,000; in 2003: 83,600) and is the chef-lieu of the prefecture of Magnesia.

Bibliography: See also D. Tsopotós, *The Pagasetic Gulf and Vólos*... [in Greek], Athens 1930; idem, *Hist. of Vólos* [in Greek], Vólos 1991, with detailed bibl. at 326-33, 344-50; N. Papachatzés, *Historical and archaeological viewpoint of the Vólos area* [in Greek], Vólos 1946; J. Kordátos, *Hist. of the Vólos and Aghiá province* [in Greek], Athens 1960; A. Papathanassiou, *The Melisseni of Demetrias* [in Greek], Athens 1989; C. Liápes, *The fortress of Vólos through the ages* [in Greek], Vólos 1991; Papathanassiou, *Byzantine Demetrias* [in Greek], Vólos 1995, 150, 179, 251.

(A. SAVVIDES)

AL-**ĶUMMĪ**, ḤASAN B. MUḤAMMAD b. Ḥasan, the author of a local history of the town of Ķum [*q.v.*] in northern Persia, *fl.* in the 4th/10th century. He is said to have compiled his history originally in Arabic at the instigation of his brother, Abu 'l-Ķāsim ʿAlī, governor of Ķum for the Būyids, aiming to gather together and record all the traditions about the arrival of the Arabs in Ķum and the town's subsequent history. He dedicated the book to the famous vizier, the Ṣāḥib Ibn ʿAbbād [see IBN ʿABBĀD]. The Arabic original has not survived, but a Persian translation was made by one Ḥasan [b. ʿAlī] b. Ḥasan b. ʿAbd al-Malik Ķummī in 806/1403-4, though this seems to contain much less material than the original Arabic text did (ed. Djalāl al-Dīn Tihrānī, Tehran 1313/1934).

Bibliography: Storey, i, 348-9; Storey-Bregel, ii, 1008-9; A.K.S. Lambton, *An account of the Tārīkhi Qumm*, in *BSOAS*, xii (1947-8), 586-96. (ED.)

ĶŪRUS (present-day Shaykh Khuruz), the Classical Cyrrhus, capital of the Cyrrhestica, a stronghold in the north of modern Syria on the Sabun-suyu, a right-bank affluent of the Nahr ʿAfrīn.

As a Seleucid colony, it took the name of a place in Macedonia and remained a stronghold under the Romans. Three ancient bridges, still visible, allowed crossing of the Sabun-suyu and the ʿAfrīn. Archaeological researches have revealed several monuments, including an amphitheatre. In the necropolis to the southeast of the town is an ancient tomb which mediaeval Islamic tradition attributed to Uriah the Hittite and which includes a cenotaph of Mamlūk times.

Ķūrus enjoyed a fresh lease of life under the emperor Justinian I, who rebuilt its fortifications. The Muslims took it in 16/637, and later considered it as one of the marches of the empire, guarding the Antioch and Aleppo roads. Its military role thereafter declined. At the end of the 11th century it came under the domination of the Armenian Bagrat (Pakrad), brother of Gogh Vasil, before being taken by the Franks *ca.* 1114-15, who included it within the County of Edessa. It became the seat of a Latin bishopric, and had also a Jacobite one till at least 1042.

It was taken and destroyed by Nūr al-Dīn b. Zangī in 1150, but *ca.* 1165-6 ceded to the Armenian prince Mleh. In the 7th/13th century, Ḳūrus, coming within the territories of Aleppo, was ruinous but still gave its name to a district whose agricultural revenues formed an *iḳṭāʿ* [*q.v.*] supporting 40 cavalrymen.

Bibliography: Ibn Shaddād, *Aʿlāḳ*, ed. and tr. A.-M. Eddé, in *BEO*, xxxii-xxxiii (1980-1), and eadem, *Description de la Syrie du Nord*, Damascus 1984, index; Ibn al-ʿAdīm, *Bughya*, ed. S. Zakkār, Damascus 1988, i, 263; G. Le Strange, *Palestine under the Moslems*, London 1890, 489; *PW*, art. Kurros (E. Honigmann); Cl. Cahen, *La Syrie du Nord*, Paris 1940, index; Canard, *H'amdanides*, Algiers 1951, 231; J. Sourdel-Thomine, *Notes sur la cénotaphe de Qūrus (Cyrrhus)*, in *AAS*, ii (1952), 134-6; E. Frézouls, *Recherches sur la ville de Cyrrhus*, in *ibid.*, iv-v (1954-5); N. Elisséeff, *Nūr al-Dīn*, Damascus 1967, i, 184-5; Th. Bianquis, *Damas et Syrie sous la domination fāṭimide*, Damascus 1989, ii, 474; Eddé, *La principauté ayyoubide d'Alep*, Stuttgart 1999, index.

(Anne-Marie Eddé)

ḲUWAYḲ, Nahr, the name given by the Arabs to the ancient Chalos river in northern Syria. This stream, whose valley makes a shallow notch in the plateau of the Aleppo region, rises at the foot of the last outliers of the Taurus, to the east of al-Rāwandān [*q.v.*] in present-day Turkey. Fed by various springs, notably in the ʿAzāz region, it skirts Aleppo to the west, and to the south of this city receives the waters of the Blessed Spring (al-ʿAyn al-Mubāraka). After a course of some 110 km/70 miles, it peters out in the vicinity of Ḳinnasrīn [*q.v.*] in a swampy depression called al-Matkh.

This river, with an average flow of waters which is very feeble, enabled several mills up stream and below stream of Aleppo to turn, and it irrigated gardens to the north and west of the capital. Occasionally there were significant floodings from melting snows or violent rains, but it dried up in summer through absence of rainfall and because the villagers upstream used the little water which it carried for irrigating their fields.

In the mid-4th/10th century, the Ḥamdānid Sayf al-Dawla [*q.v.*] diverted the river so that it might flow through the palace he had had built in one of the western suburbs of Aleppo. At the beginning of the 8th/14th century, a canal was dug to carry part of the waters of the Sādjūr into the Ḳuwayḳ and thereby increase the latter's flow, but these works were destroyed by an earthquake in 1544, restored in 1644, but definitively abandoned in 1723.

Bibliography: Yāḳūt, *Buldān*, ed. Beirut, iv, 417; Ibn al-ʿAdīm, *Bughya*, ed. S. Zakkār, Damascus 1988, i, 347-56; Ibn Shaddād, *Aʿlāḳ*, ed. D. Sourdel, Damascus 1953, 138-43; Sibṭ Ibn al-ʿAdjamī, tr. J. Sauvaget, *Les trésors d'or*, Beirut 1950, 175-7; G. Le Strange, *Palestine under the Moslems*, London 1890, 61; S. Mazloum, *L'ancienne canalisation d'eau d'Alep*, Damascus 1936, 8-9; Sauvaget, *Alep*, Paris 1951, index; N. Elisséeff, *Nūr al-Dīn*, Damascus 1967, i, 178-82; H. Gaube and E. Wirth, *Aleppo*, Wiesbaden 1984, index.

(Anne-Marie Eddé)

ḲUZMĀN, Banū, a family of literary men of al-Andalus and connected with the city of Cordova. The name Ḳuzmān (Span. *Guzmán*, a personal name of Germanic origin) suggests an Iberian or Romance origin. As well as the most famous member of the family, the author of *zadjals* Ibn Ḳuzmān [*q.v.*], there are four other interesting members.

1. Abu 'l-Aṣbagh ʿĪsā b. ʿAbd al-Malik, poet and littérateur (4th/10th century), appointed by al-Manṣūr Ibn Abī ʿĀmir [*q.v.*] tutor of the young Hishām II al-Muʾayyad [*q.v.*] proclaimed caliph in Cordova in 366/976.

2. Abū Bakr Muḥammad b. ʿAbd al-Malik b. ʿUbayd Allāh (d. 508/1114), called al-Akbar "the eldest" in order to distinguish him from his nephew Ibn Ḳuzmān al-Aṣghar "the youngest" [*q.v.*], a famous poet, and secretary to the vizier of the Afṭasid prince Abū Ḥafṣ ʿUmar al-Mutawakkil [*q.v.*] of Badajoz, a colleague of Ibn ʿAbdūn [*q.v.*] and of Abū Bakr Ibn al-Ḳabṭūrnuh [see ḳabṭūrnuh, banu 'l-, in Suppl.]. After the advent of the Almoravids, nothing more is known of him.

3. Abū Marwān ʿAbd al-Raḥmān (479-593/1086 or 1087-1169), son of 2., a famous *faḳīh* and jurist, and one of the last traditionists of al-Andalus. He functioned as a *ḳāḍī*.

4. Abu 'l-Ḥusayn ʿUbayd Allāh (*ca.* 518-93/*ca.* 1124 to 1196-7), son of 3., poet, jurist and *ḳāḍī* in various districts of the province of Cordova.

Other possible members of the family are mentioned in Lévi-Provençal's article, see *Bibl.*

Bibliography: A genealogical tree in Ibn al-Abbār, no. 1517; Ḍabbī, *Bughyat al-multamis*, Cairo and Beirut 1989, nos. 992, 1151; Ibn Saʿīd, *Mughrib*, i, 99, 210; Ibn Bassām, *Dhakhīra*, ed. Iḥsān ʿAbbās, 8 vols. Beirut 1989, i/2, 774-86; Ibn Bashkuwāl, *Ṣila*, Cairo 1966, nos. 757, 1255; Ibn Khāḳān, *Ḳalāʾid*, ed. M.Ṭ. Ibn ʿĀshūr, Tunis 1990, 451-2; E. Lévi-Provençal, *Du nouveau sur Ibn Ḳuzmān*, in *And.*, ix (1944), 347-69; E. Garcia Gómez, *Todo Ben Quzmán*, Madrid 1972, ii, 889-99.

(I. Ferrando)

L

LAFẒ (a.), lit: "to spit out" (see *WbKAS*, letter L, ii/2, 989).

1. In grammar.

Here it denotes primarily the actual expression of a sound or series of sounds, hence "articulation" and, more broadly, the resulting "linguistic form". It has always been distinct from *ṣawt* "[individual] sound" (cf. Troupeau, *ṣ-w-t*, and see Bakalla, 39 ff. and 49 ff., for its use in Ibn Djinnī (d. 392/1002 [*q.v.*]), which provides the base for the modern Arabic terms for phonetics, *ʿilm al-aṣwāt*, and phonology, *ʿilm waẓāʾif al-aṣwāt* (and note also the neologism *ṣawtiyya* [*q.v.*] for the collective description of Arabic sounds). *Lafẓ* occurs mostly in morphological and syntactic contexts, but always indicates an actual acoustic event or a real utterance, usually at the word or sentence level, and thus often contrasts with implicit or semantic features of speech.

Definitions of speech using the term *lafẓ* may specify that it excludes elements which are not in the Arabic phoneme inventory [cf. ḤURŪF AL-HIDJĀʾ], as well as non-linguistic modes of communication such as gestures and context of situation and even writing, *khaṭṭ* [*q.v.*], when necessary; cf. Bakalla, 69. It was also established very early (Sībawayhi, *Kitāb*, ch. 4) that the lexical relationship between form (*lafẓ*) and meaning (*maʿnā* [*q.v.*]) was of three kinds, viz. (1) identity of form with difference of meaning (homonymy), e.g. *wadjada* "to find" and "to feel passion", (2) difference of form with identity of meaning (synonymy), e.g. *dhahaba* and *inṭalaḳa* "to go away", and (3) difference of both form and meaning, e.g. *dhahaba* "to go away" and *djalasa* "to sit".

In morphological contexts, *lafẓ* will typically contrast with *maʿnā*, i.e. opposing the phonological to the semantic properties of an element. For example, a distinction is made between absolute objects (*mafʿūl muṭlaḳ*) which are composed of the same radicals as their operating verb and are thus termed *lafẓī* "formal" (e.g. *djalastu djulūs^an^* "I sat right down") and those which are derived from a synonym of their operating verb and are thus termed *maʿnawī* "semantic" (e.g. *djalastu ḳuʿūd^an^* "I sat down with a squatting action").

At the syntactical level, the opposition is usually between the formal realisation (*lafẓī*) versus the implied, *muḳaddar* [see TAḲDĪR, where *lafẓī* is translated "literal")], i.e. the surface realisation is contrasted with some equivalent word or words assumed to underlie the forms actually expressed. This is not to be confused with modern notions of deep and surface structure, since the underlying forms are invariably stated as verbal paraphrases of the surface realisations and the question of transformation therefore does not arise. In this connection, it is worth mentioning that there are other, similar oppositions recognised by the grammarians, notably the explicit (*ẓāhir*) versus the suppressed (*muḍmar*), for the contrast between overt and implicit elements generally, and the visible (*bāriz*) versus the concealed (*mustatir*), for the pronouns in particular, to which must be added elision (*ḥadhf*) and the restoration of elided elements in the shape of "additions", *ziyādāt*, all of which point to a complex understanding of the relationship between the outward verbal features of speech and its inner contents. Understandably, the scrutiny of what was sometimes called the *kalām lafẓī* "the formal utterance" in the light of its internal implications, the *kalām nafsī* "mental or spiritual utterance", became a dominant preoccupation of the sciences of rhetoric, exegesis, law and theology.

Bibliography: Sībawayhi, *Le livre de Sībawaihi*, ed. H. Derenbourg, Paris 1881-9 (repr. Hildesheim 1970), *Kitāb Sībawayhi*, ed. Būlāḳ 1898-1900 (repr.) (the first seven, and also the last seven chapters of the *Kitāb*, which deal with phonological issues, are published in a hypertext version at <www.hf.uio.no/east/sibawayhi/HomePage>, general eds. M.G. Carter, A. Matveev and L. Edzard; G. Troupeau, *Lexique-index du Kitāb de Sībawayhi*, Paris 1976; M.G. Carter, *Arab linguistics, an introductory classical text with translation and notes*, Amsterdam, Philadelphia and New York 1981; M.H. Bakalla, *Ibn Jinni, an early Arab Muslim phonetician. An interpretative study of his life and contribution to linguistics*, London and Taipei 1982/1402; G. Bohas, J.-P. Guillaume and D.E. Kouloughli, *The Arabic linguistic tradition*, London and New York 1990, index s.v. *lafẓ*; K. Versteegh, *Landmarks in linguistic thought. III. The Arabic linguistic tradition*, London and New York 1997, index s.v. *lafẓ* and *maʿnā*.

(M.G. CARTER)

2. In theology.

Here it refers to the pronunciation of the Ḳurʾān. The term was introduced by Ḥusayn b. ʿAlī al-Karābīsī (d. 245/859 or 248/862 [*q.v.*]), a disciple of al-Shāfiʿī who, in theology, shared the position of Ibn Kullāb [*q.v.* in Suppl.]. Reacting against the Muʿtazilī doctrine of *khalḳ al-Ḳurʾān*, the latter had distinguished between *kalām Allāh*, God's speech which is eternal, and *ḳirāʾa*, the recitation of the Ḳurʾān which occurs in time. Al-Karābīsī replaced *ḳirāʾa* by *lafẓ* (or *nuṭḳ*) which was broader and meant any quoting of the Ḳurʾān, including beyond formal recitation. During the later phase of the *miḥna* [*q.v.*], his doctrine spread widely, to the Djazīra (Mawṣil, Niṣībīn and Ṭarsūs) and possibly even to Damascus, through Hishām b. ʿAmmār al-Sulamī (d. 245/859), who served as *khaṭīb* at the Umayyad Mosque. In Baghdād, however, al-Karābīsī encountered heavy opposition from Ibn Ḥanbal and his adherents, who denounced his approach as Djahmism, i.e. they equated it with the belief in the createdness of the Word of God, or at least banished any mention of it. In Persia, the situation was quite different. Ḥanbalī radicalism came under attack by al-Bukhārī (in his *K. Khalḳ al-afʿāl*) and Ibn Ḳutayba (in his *Ikhtilāf fi 'l-lafẓ*) who both virtually shared al-Karābīsī's opinion without explicitly referring to him. The so-called *Fiḳh akbar II* names the createdness of *lafẓ* as part of the creed. Theologians like Makḥūl al-Nasafī and al-Ghazālī adhered to it, as did even Ḥanbalīs like Ibn ʿAḳīl or Abū Yaʿlā Ibn al-Farrāʾ. This broad acceptation of the general idea was counterbalanced by an avoidance of the term *lafẓ* as such; al-Karābīsī's authorship was forgotten.

Bibliography: Ashʿarī, *Maḳālāt al-Islāmiyyīn*, 602 ll. 7-8; Wensinck, *The Muslim creed*, 189 §3; Makḥūl al-Nasafī, *Radd ʿalā 'l-bidaʿ*, ed. M. Bernand, in *Ann. Isl.*, xvi (1980), 113 ll. 7 ff.; H. Bauer, *Die Dogmatik al-Ghazālī's*, Halle 1912, 58-9; D. Gimaret, *La doctrine d'al Ashʿarī*, Paris 1990, 317-18; J. van Ess, *Theologie und Gesellschaft im 2. und 3. Jahrhundert Hidschra*, iv, Berlin 1997, 210-18.

(J. VAN ESS)

LAḤN (A.). In music. This is one of the basic terms of secular music in Islamic times, used in Arabic and Persian [see MŪSĪḲĪ]. In its early terminological sense, *laḥn* (pl. *luḥūn*, rarely *alḥān*) denoted a musical mode, comparable to the later terms *naghma* (pl. *anghām*) and *maḳām* [*q.v.*]. It was a loan from the Byzantine Greek concept of *ēchos*, adopted probably in Umayyad Syria. A *Kitāb al-Luḥūn al-thamāniya* ("Book on the modal system called *oktōēchos*"), wrongly attributed to Ptolemy, was known to Ibn al-Kalbī [*q.v.*], according to a quotation in Ibn ʿAbd Rabbih's *al-ʿIḳd al-farīd*, Cairo 1949, vi, 27. Al-Kindī [*q.v.*] equated *laḥn* with *ṭanīn* (= Greek *tónos*) in the same sense of musical mode. In its more general and more common meaning *laḥn* (pl. *alḥān, luḥūn*) stands for melody. Here it corresponds to the Greek term *mélos*. The notion of music (*mūsīḳī*) was therefore defined either as the "science of the modes" (*ʿilm al-luḥūn*) or as "composition of melodies" (*taʾlīf al-alḥān*). In the latter sense, the term was used and defined by many writers on music theory from al-Kindī to al-Lādhiḳī (see titles below). Al-Fārābī devoted several chapters of his *Kitāb al-Mūsīḳī al-kabīr* to an exhaustive treatment of melodics. "Reciting the Ḳur'ān with secular melodies" (*ḳirā'a* [*q.v.*] *bi 'l-alḥān*) was one of the crucial points in the discussion on decent music in Islamic society. The notion of *laḥn* (melody) has survived the centuries, as have its derivatives *laḥḥana* ("to chant; to set to music"), *talḥīn* ("chanting; composition"), *mulaḥḥin* ("composer") and *mulaḥḥan* ("set to music").

Bibliography: 1. Sources. Z. Yūsuf (ed.), *Mu'allafāt al-Kindī al-mūsīḳiyya*, Baghdād 1962, 54-7 (*laḥn* = mode), 60-5, 83-4, 114 (*laḥn* = melody); Fārābī, *K. al-Mūsīḳī al-kabīr*, Cairo [1967], 47-74, 107-13, 879-1189; Khʷārazmī, *Mafātīḥ al-ʿulūm*, Leiden 1895, 236; *Rasā'il Ikhwān al-Ṣafā'*, Beirut 1957, i, 188; Ibn Sīnā, *al-Shifā'*. *al-Riyāḍiyyāt*. 3. *Djawāmiʿ ʿilm al-mūsīḳī*, Cairo 1956, 9, 139-42; Ibn Zayla, *al-Kāfī fi 'l-mūsīḳī*, Cairo 1964, 17, 63-70; al-Ḥasan b. Aḥmad b. ʿAlī al-Kātib, *Kamāl adab al-ghinā'*, tr. A. Shiloah, *La perfection des connaissances musicales*, Paris 1972, index s.v. *laḥn*; Ibn al-Ṭaḥḥān, *Ḥāwī al-funūn wa-salwat al-maḥzūn*, Frankfurt 1990, 16-21, 31-3, 213-15; Ṣafī al-Dīn al-Urmawī, *al-Risāla al-Sharafiyya*, Baghdād 1982, 44; ʿAbd al-Ḳādir b. Ghaybī al-Marāghī, *Maḳāṣid al-alḥān*, Tehran 1965, 8-9; idem, *Djāmiʿ al-alḥān*, Tehran 1987, 7-8; idem, *Sharḥ-i Adwār*, Tehran 1991, 79-80; Muḥammad b. ʿAbd al-Ḥamīd al-Lādhiḳī, *al-Risāla al-Fatḥiyya*, Kuwait 1986, 37-8.

2. Studies. M. Ullmann, *Wa-ḫairu l-ḥadīṯi mā kāna laḥnan*, Munich 1979, 15; idem, *WKAS*, ii/1, Wiesbaden 1983, 376-89 (extensive references); M. Sitāyishgar, *Wāzhanāma-yi mūsīḳī-yi Īrānzamīn*, Tehran 1995-7, ii, 344-6; I. El-Mallah, *Arab music and musical notation*, Tutzing 1997, index 404, 406 (*laḥn* and *mulaḥḥin* today); E. Neubauer, *Zur Bedeutung der Begriffe Komponist und Komposition in der Musikgeschichte der islamischen Welt*, in *ZGAIW*, xi (1997), 307-63, esp. 310, 313, 319-20, 328, 356, 357, 360; idem, *Arabische Musiktheorie von den Anfängen bis zum 6./12. Jahrhundert*, Frankfurt 1998, index 379-80.

(E. Neubauer)

LĀLĀ, Lala (p.), a term found amongst the Turkmen dynasties of Persia and, especially, amongst the Ṣafawids, with the meaning of tutor, specifically, tutor of royal princes, passing also to the Ottoman Turks.

Under the Aḳ Ḳoyunlu [*q.v.*], both *atabeg* [see atabak] and *lālā* are found, but after the advent of the Ṣafawids (sc. after 907/1501), the latter term becomes more common, with the Arabic term *muʿallim* "instructor" also found. Such persons were already exalted figures in the state. The *lālā* of Shāh Ismāʿīl I's second son Sām Mīrzā was the *īshīk-āḳāsī* [*q.v.*] or Grand Marshal of the great *dīwān*, Durmish Khān Shāmlū, whilst the *muʿallim* of the first son, and succeeding ruler, Ṭahmāsp (I) Mīrzā, was a member of the religious classes, Mawlānā Niẓām al-Dīn Aḥmad Ṭabasī (R.M. Savory, *The principal offices of the Safawid state during the reign of Ismāʿīl I (907-30/1501-24)*, in *BSOAS*, xxiii [1960], 98; idem, *The principal offices of the Safawid state during the reign of Ṭahmāsp I (930-84/1524-76)*, in *ibid.*, xxiv [1961], 125). In the later Ṣafawid period, we hear also of *lalas* for the young eunuch pages of the royal court, the *ghulāmān-i khāṣṣa*, such as the (non-eunuch) Muḥibb ʿAlī Khān, whose importance was such that he was in 1029/1620 commissioned by Shāh ʿAbbās I to examine the possibility of diverting the headwaters of the Kārūn river [*q.v.*] in the Zagros mountains into the Zāyanda-rūd and the Iṣfahān plain. The tutor of Ṭahmāsp Mīrzā (the future Ṭahmāsp II, 1135-45/1722-32) when he was made *walī ʿahd* or heir to the throne, Muḥammad Āḳā, head of the royal *ghulāms*, was, on the other hand, obviously a eunuch himself (*Tadhkirat al-mulūk, a manual of Ṣafavid administration* (circa *1137/1725*), tr. V. Minorsky, London 1943, 56 n. 3, 57).

The title *lālā* passed, through Persian cultural influence, to the Ottoman Turks, amongst whom it was used for tutors attached to young princes, both at court and when, usually at the age of fourteen or fifteen, they were assigned provincial government (see İ.H. Uzunçarşılı, *Osmanlı devleti teşkilâtına medhal*, Istanbul 1941, 291-2; idem, *Osmanlı devletinin saray teşkilâtı*, Ankara 1945, 124-5; Pakalın, ii, 354; A.D. Alderson, *The structure of the Ottoman dynasty*, Oxford 1956, 18, 117). Again as in Persia, such tutors were prestigious figures, and could become senior *wezīrs* or leading commanders like Lala Muṣṭafā Pasha (d. 988/1580), tutor to the future Selīm II [see muṣṭafā pasha, lala].

It also made its way to the Muslim India of the Mughals, and in British Indian times, acquired a wider meaning of "child's tutor" in general and also, in northern India, became the title of a clerk or secretary in the local, vernacular languages (see Yule and Burnell, *Hobson-Jobson, a glossary of Anglo-Indian words and phrases* ²London 1903, 501-2).

Bibliography: Given in the article.

(C.E. Bosworth)

LĀSHĪN, Maḥmūd Ṭāhir (1894-1954), Egyptian writer of novels and short stories.

While neither the most famous nor the most productive of a group of Egyptian writers that came to prominence during the 1920s as the *Djamāʿat al-madrasa al-ḥadītha* ("The new school group"), Lāshīn was undoubtedly one of the first to display genuine mastery of the short story genre. Born into a family of Turko-Circassian origins, he studied engineering and then served in the Department of Public Works. While other colleagues in the group, such as Maḥmūd Taymūr (1894-1973) and Yaḥyā Ḥaḳḳī (1905-93), went on to illustrious careers in Egyptian literary life, Lāshīn appears to have become disillusioned with the reception of his work and published little after 1940. As critics have begun to appreciate the importance of his place in the development of modern Egyptian fiction, his relative obscurity among members of succeeding generations is being replaced by a deeper understanding of the extent of his achievement.

Lāshīn's family background allowed him to serve as a host for the early gatherings of the *Djamāʿat al-madrasa al-ḥadītha*. Already fascinated by the potential of the short story genre, the group soon became deeply influenced by the Russian school of writers, including Gogol, Turgenev, Chekov, and Dostoevsky. Lāshīn was writing stories as early as 1921, but it was the foundation in 1925 of the literary weekly *al-Fadjr* that afforded an outlet for his creativity. His first published collection, *Sukhriyyat al-nāy*, appeared in 1926, and he followed it with a second one, *Yuḥkā anna*, in 1929; a third, *al-Niḳāb al-ṭā'ir*, was published in 1940.

Like the short stories of his contemporaries. Lāshīn's examples focus on the environment with which he was most familiar, that of the urban middle class. Eschewing the more idealised and homiletic tone of his predecessors, he manages to create a convincing social reality through his gloomy portraits of the lives and struggles of various professional types—lawyers, merchants, and civil servants—utilising the short story genre to provide glimpses into both their public careers and family tensions. By contrast, *Ḥadīth al-ḳarya*

("Tale of the village") is set in the countryside; in an accomplished manner it explores the tension between rural and urban values that is such a frequent theme of modern Arabic fiction.

Lā<u>sh</u>īn's novel, *Ḥawwāʾ bi-lā Ādam* ("Eve without Adam", 1934), is also a major contribution to the development of that genre in the Egyptian context. While its date of publication places it within a decade during which most of Egypt's prominent littérateurs made initial attempts at penning novels (among them Tawfīḳ al-Ḥakīm, Ibrāhīm ʿAbd al-Ḳādir al-Māzinī, ʿAbbās Maḥmūd al-ʿAḳḳād and Maḥmūd Taymūr), Lā<u>sh</u>īn's work stands out both for the characteristically subtle way in which he portrays the tensions involved when a female tutor falls in love with her much younger charge and for the fact that the very fictionality of his narrative stands in marked contrast to the apparently autobiographical contexts of most of the efforts of his contemporaries. Like its author, however, *Ḥawwāʾ bi-lā Ādam* has, at least until recently, resided in an unmerited obscurity.

Bibliography: 1. Translations. *Eve without Adam*, tr. Saad El-Gabalawy, Fredericton, New Brunswick 1986; *Village small talk*, tr. Sabry Hafez, London 1993, in *The genesis of Arabic narrative discourse* (see 2. below).

2. Studies. Yaḥyā Ḥaḳḳī, *Fad<u>j</u>r al-ḳiṣṣa al-miṣriyya*, Cairo 1960; Ṣabrī Ḥāfiẓ, *Maḥmūd Ṭāhir Lā<u>sh</u>īn wa-mīlād al-uḳṣūṣa al-miṣriyya*, in *al-Ma<u>d</u>jalla*, Cairo (Feb.-March 1968); Hilary Kilpatrick, *Ḥawwāʾ bilā Ādam. An Egyptian novel of the 1930's*, in *JAL*, iv (1973), 48-56; Aḥmad Ibrāhīm al-Hawārī, *Maṣādir naḳd al-riwāya fi 'l-adab al-ʿArabī al-ḥadī<u>th</u> fī Miṣr*, Cairo 1979; Jad Ali, *Form and technique in the Egyptian novel, 1912-1971*, London 1983; Sabry Hafez, *The genesis of Arabic narrative discourse*, London 1993.

(R.M.A. Allen)

LEWNĪ, Ottoman miniature painter, born *ca.* 1680, died 1145/1732. Lewnī, meaning "colourful", and "varied", was the pseudonym used by the artist, whose real name was ʿAbd ül-<u>D</u>jelīl Čelebi. He was the most influential figure of early 18th-century Ottoman miniature painting, active during the reigns of Muṣṭafā II and Aḥmed III [*q.vv.*]. He came to Istanbul from Edirne after 1707. Since his name does not appear in the records of court artists, the *ehl-i ḥiref*, of this period it is thought that he either held a higher position at the imperial court or worked freelance. Lewnī was not only a painter but also a folk poet whose compositions have a close affinity to *dīwān* literature [see ʿothmānlı̊. III. Literature]. His poetry treated the themes of love, heroism and war, and his admonitory epic poem consisting of proverbs inspired other folk poets.

The unsigned engravings portraying Ottoman sultans that illustrate Demetrius Kantemir's [see ḳantimir, demetrius, in Suppl.] *Ottoman history* are thought to be based on early works by Lewnī. His series of Ottoman sultan portraits (Topkapı Palace Museum A 3109) display an innovative style characterised by an informal approach to his models, natural facial expression, and the use of colour shading and chiaroscuro to lend volume to the figures. Lewnī may have trained under the celebrated late 17th-century portraitist Muṣawwir Hüseyin.

Another of Lewnī's major works is the series of miniatures illustrating the *Surnāme-i Wehbī*, an account of the festivities for the circumcision of the sons of Aḥmed III in 1720 (Topkapı Palace Museum A 3593). These miniatures depict trade guild parades and public entertainments in a consistent narrative style, and the figures are portrayed with a vigorous sense of movement and suggestion of depth. An album containing forty-two full-length portraits signed by Lewnī magnificently reflects the atmosphere of the time (Topkapı Palace Museum H 2164). These portraits of men and women largely symbolise aspects of life during the so-called Tulip Era [see lāle devri] and were probably intended to illustrate the protagonists in contemporary stories.

At a time when Western influence was beginning to make itself felt, Lewnī masterfully rejuvenated Ottoman pictorial art without any loss of its essential character, and his work is regarded as a turning point in both style and approach.

Bibliography: Demetrius Cantemir, *The history of the growth and decay of the Ottoman Empire*, London 1734; Ḥāfiẓ Hüseyin Aywānsarāyī, *Me<u>d</u>jmūʿa-e tewārī<u>kh</u>* (1766), ed. F.Ç. Derin and V. Çubuk, Istanbul 1985, 175; M. Fuad Köprülü, *Türk sazşairleri*, Istanbul 1940, 330-61; Süheyl Ünver, *Ressam Lewnī, hayatı ve eserleri*, Istanbul 1949; idem, *Lewnī*, Istanbul 1967; I. Stchoukine, *La peinture turque d'après les manuscrits illustrés*, Paris 1971, ii, 74-84; Nurhan Atasoy-Filiz Çağman, *Turkish miniature painting*, Istanbul 1974; Esin Atil, *Lewnī and the Surname*, Istanbul 1999; A. Gül İrepoğlu, *Lewnī, painting – poetry – colour*, Istanbul 1999; eadem, *"From book to Canvas." The Sultan's portrait-picturing the House of Osman*, Istanbul 2000, 378-437.

(A. Gül İrepoğlu)

M

MĀʾ. 10. Irrigation in Transoxania.

The rivers of Inner Asia, extending from <u>Kh</u>ʷārazm in the west through Transoxania to eastern Turkistān (the later Sinkiang) and northwards to the Semirečye, have all been extensively used for irrigation purposes in the lands along those rivers and in oasis centres, providing a possibility for agriculture in favoured spots which were not too open to attack from the steppe nomads or more northerly forest peoples. Hence, as elsewhere in the Old World, the maintenance of irrigation works, surface canals and *kārīz*s or subterranean channels (these last to be found as far east as the Tarim basin and the fringes of China proper; see ḳanāt) depended on injections of capital from strong local rulers, on the mass mobilisation of labour for construction and maintenance work, and on vigorous defence policies to protect the settled lands. Such river systems as those of the Oxus, Zaraf<u>sh</u>ān and Syr Darya to the west of the Tien Shan mountains, and those of the Tarim river and its tributaries coming down from the Kun-Lun mountains, to the east of the Tien Shan, must have had irrigation works long antedating the coming of Islam, even where specific information is lacking and their existence can only be inferred from the sparse archaeological investigations in such regions.

Thus ground surveys and the results of aerial photography have enabled scholars like the late S.P. Tolstov to show how irrigation in K͟hʷārazm depended on a complex system of canals and channels from the lower Syr Darya and extending westwards towards the Caspian (these last, along the old channel of the Uzboi [see ĀMŪ DARYĀ], were investigated in an expedition of 1947; see Tolstov, *Auf den Spuren der altchoresmischen Kultur*, East Berlin 1953, 318 ff.).

The irrigation systems of what was the pre-Islamic Iranian region of Sogdia [see AL-ṢUG͟HD] are especially well known from the mediaeval Arabic and Persian geographers and local historians and were the subject of a special monograph by W. Barthold (*K istori oros͟heniya Turkestana*, St. Petersburg 1914, repr. in his *Sočineniya*, iii, Moscow 1965, 99-233). The river which flowed through the heart of Sogdia, the Nahr al-Ṣug͟hd or Zarafs͟hān [*q.v.*], watered an extensive agricultural region in which were located the great cities of Buk͟hārā and Samarḳand [*q.vv.*] and many significant smaller urban centres; under Islam, the zenith of their prosperity was reached under the local dynasty of the Sāmānids [*q.v.*] (3rd-4th/9th-10th centuries). The left bank tributaries of the Zarafs͟hān coming down from the Buttamān mountains (in what is now northern Tajikistan and the eastern part of the Kas͟hkadar'inskaya *oblast* of Uzbekistan) were fed by large quantities of melted snow in spring and early summer. There were along them diversionary dams which divided up the river flows and led them into irrigation channels, called from later mediaeval Islamic times onwards by the term used in Turkish *ariḳ*/*arig͟h* (but probably of non-Turkish origin, G. Doerfer, *Türkische und mongolische Elemente im Neupersischen*, Wiesbaden 1965-83, ii, 52-3 no. 469; Sir Gerard Clauson, *An etymological dictionary of pre-thirteenth century Turkish*, Oxford 1972, 214). A dam constructed four *farsak͟hs* from Samarḳand gave its name to the locality Warag͟hsar, lit. "head of the dam". The irrigation waters from there were regulated by an official resident in Samarḳand who had a staff of subordinates responsible for the upkeep of the banks of the channels, etc., whilst the inhabitants of Warag͟hsar itself were exempt from paying *k͟harād͟j* in return for maintenance work on the dam (Ibn Ḥawḳal, ed. Kramers, ii, 496-7, tr. Kramers and Wiet, ii, 475-6; Le Strange, *The lands of the Eastern Caliphate*, 465-6). The largest channels in the region were navigable, but probably for rafts rather than for boats, and timber was floated down along them to Samarḳand. Within the city itself, water was brought into the *s͟hahristān* or inner city along a channel which crossed the defensive ditch formed by excavating material for the walls, hence the channel was carried on an aqueduct into the *s͟hahristān* at the *ra᾿s al-ṭāḳ* "head of the arch". Alongside the channel, the properties were constituted as *awḳāf* for its upkeep, and the local community of Zoroastrians were free of the *d͟jizya* or poll-tax in return for maintaining the channel in good repair (Ibn Ḥawḳal, ii, 492-3, tr. ii, 473).

Such constructions and arrangements in Sogdia were undoubtedly of pre-Islamic origin. An early Arab governor of K͟hurāsān, His͟hām's nominee Asad b. ʿAbd Allāh al-Ḳasrī, in 117/735 tried to deprive the inhabitants of Samarḳand of water by blocking the channel at Warag͟hsar and diverting it from the city, at a time when Sogdia had thrown off short-lived Arab control and temporarily recovered its independence under the local king G͟hūrak, and had now to be reconquered by the Arabs (al-Ṭabarī, ii, 1586; H.A.R. Gibb, *The Arab conquests in Central Asia*, London 1923, 78-80). The dam at Warag͟hsar was obviously an ancient work. Further information on the irrigation system of Samarḳand, this time in the Ḳarak͟hānid period, is given by the local historian Abū Ḥafṣ ʿUmar al-Nasafī (early 6th/12th century) in his *Kitāb al-Ḳand fī ta᾿rīk͟h Samarḳand*; he enumerates the various *ariḳs* and gives the total area of irrigated land (Barthold, *Turkestan down to the Mongol invasion*, 3London 1968, 89, and on the irrigation system at Samarḳand in general, *ibid.*, 82-92).

The Arab geographers likewise give detailed information on the situation at Buk͟hārā, at the western end of the Zarafs͟hān basin, and this can be supplemented by items from the local historian Nars͟hak͟hī [*q.v.*]. According to the latter, the main irrigation channel through the city was known as the *rūd-i zar* "golden, or gold-bearing river" (*Tārīk͟h-i Buk͟hārā*, tr. R.N. Frye, *The history of Bukhara*, Cambridge, Mass. 1954, 31-2). Al-Muḳaddasī, 331-2, and Ibn Ḥawḳal, ii, 484-7, tr. ii, 465-7, describe how locks and sluices along the *ariḳs* through the city controlled the water flow at times of the river's spate and inundation; see also Barthold, *op. cit.*, 103-6.

There was a continuously-cultivated strip of agricultural land along the left bank of the Oxus from Āmul [*q.v.*] to K͟hʷārazm, with *ariḳs* led off the main channel of the river, some big enough for boats to sail on, until the extensive network of canals in K͟hʷārazm itself was reached (see above). Irrigation canals in the Syr Darya basin began in the Farg͟hāna [*q.v.*] valley, into which the river's most voluminous source, the Nahr D͟jidg͟hil (probably the modern Naryn), began; then as now, the Farg͟hāna valley was a land of intense cultivation, and the towns there, such as Ak͟hsikat͟h and K͟hud͟jand [*q.vv.*], derived their water supplies from conduits leading off the irrigation canals (see Le Strange, *op. cit.*, 477 ff.). Further down the Syr Darya basin, irrigation channels were a feature of such provinces as S͟hās͟h [see TAS͟HKENT], Īlāḳ and Isfīd͟jāb [*q.vv.* in Suppl.] until Sawrān and the frontier with the Og͟huz steppes were reached.

The Murg͟hāb river in northern K͟hurāsān (now mainly in Turkmenistan) had numerous canals and dams along its course, controlling the waters which came down from melted snows in the Paropamisus mountains of northern Afg͟hānistān. The situation there has been mentioned in section 6. above, at Vol. V, 868b, but one should add here that we possess especially valuable information for the very complex irrigation system in the Marw oasis from some of the Arab geographers and from the section on the terminology of the *dīwān al-mā᾿* in al-K͟hʷārazmī's concise encyclopaedia of the technical terms of the various sciences, the *Mafātīḥ al-ʿulūm*, composed in the later Sāmānid period by an author closely connected with the Sāmānid bureaucracy in Buk͟hārā; part of this last author's information on irrigation terminology deals specifically with conditions at Marw (see C.E. Bosworth, *Abū ʿAbdallāh al-Khwārazmī on the technical terms of the secretary's art*, in *JESHO*, xii [1969], 151-8). Ibn Ḥawḳal, ii, 436, tr. ii, 421-2, characterises the *mutawallī or muḳassim al-mā᾿* at Marw as a high-ranking *amīr* who had under him over 10,000 men, each with a specific task to perform, for keeping the irrigation system in repair. Al-Muḳaddasī, 330-1, mentions that the *amīr*'s staff included guards (*ḥurrās*) to keep watch over the canal banks and 4,000 divers (*ghawwāṣūn*) who watched the channels night and day and had to be ready to turn out for running repairs in all weather conditions; the allocation of water to its various users was determined by a special measure or gauge (*miḳyās*).

For all these hydraulic systems, the devastations of the Mongols must have had an adverse effect, although agriculture gradually revived and the systems were brought back into repair and use. Tīmūr took steps at restoration of the Sogdian irrigation system, especially when he made Samarḳand his capital. Under the succeeding lines of Özbeg Turkish khāns in Transoxania and Khʷārazm, internal prosperity continued to rest substantially on an agriculture supported by centrally-organised irrigation systems. Hence every canal and rural community dependent on it had its *mīrāb*, the official in charge of the construction and upkeep of the dams and channels. Some of these were comparatively humble local functionaries, but the vital importance of the irrigation systems for maintaining the economic health of Khʷārazm, in later times the khānate of Khīwa [*q.v.*] was ruled by the ʿArabshāhid ruler Abu ʾl-Ghāzī Bahādur Khān (*r.* 1054-74/1644-63 [*q.v.*]), who introduced various administrative reforms, including the appointment of four *mīrāb*s as members of his central council of ministers or *ʿamaldār*s. The historian of the dynasty, Shīr Muḥammad Muʾnis (1192-1244/1778-1829 [*q.v.*]), held the hereditary post of *mīrāb*, in succession to his deceased elder brother, until his death, and his *History* shows that he was indeed personally concerned with the practical affairs involved; his nephew and continuator Muḥammad Riḍā Āgāhī [*q.v.* in Suppl.], likewise functioned as a *mīrāb* (Yu. Bregel [tr.], *Firdaws al-iqbāl. History of Khorezm*, Leiden 1999, pp. xviii-xix, xxi). Some of the highest personages in the state gave personal attention to these matters. Muʾnis describes how the *amīr* ʿAwaḍ Biy Ināḳ in 1216/1802 supervised the dredging of the Khīwanik canal (the term for such operations being *ḳāzū*, apparently from *ḳazmaḳ* "to dig") the actual work being done by corvée labour (*hashar*, *bīgār*); and the Khān himself, Muḥammad Raḥīm, came personally in 1225/1810 for the re-opening of the head of this canal (Bregel, *op. cit.*, 162-3, 299).

Bibliography: Given in the article, but see also A. Mez, *Die Renaissance des Islâms*, Heidelberg 1923, Eng. tr. 449-50; D.R. Hill, in *The UNESCO history of the civilizations of Central Asia*, iv/2, Paris 2000, 265 ff.

(C.E. Bosworth)

MĀʾ AL-WARD, rose water (sometimes also found in the single word form *al-māward*, which suggests that among doctors and apothecaries, this commodity was perceived as something very specific), an essential preparation in Arab pharmacology.

Use of rose water is to be seen in the context of the knowledge professed by the Arabs of the medicinal and cosmetic properties of the rose and, clearly, their mastery of the technique of distillation. While the treatises evoke numerous varieties of rose, the generic term for which is *ward* (a word originally denoting, in classical Arabic, any flower of shrub or of tree) or indeed the Persian *gul*, they are not immune from ambiguity. Thus the red rose is sometimes called *ward aḥmar*, sometimes *ḥawdjam*, a term reserved by some for the damask rose. The varieties most frequently attested are three in number, if the wild rose is excluded (*nasrīn: Rosa canina*); white rose (*Rosa alba: ward abyaḍ, wathīr*); five-leaf rose (*Rosa centifolia: ḥawdjam*); damask rose (*Rosa damascena: ward djūrī, ward gūrī, ward baladī, ward shāmī*). Rose water was extracted from the petals of the last-named, pale red in colour and flowering from the spring to the end of summer. It may be noted that the rose was among the ingredients of various other concoctions such as rose honey (*djulandjubīn*) or julep (*djulāb*).

Rose water was thus obtained by the distillation of the damask rose (*ward djūrī*, the *nisba* referring to the town of Djūr in the south-west of Persia [see FĪRŪZĀBĀD], a technique described in detail by al-Nuwayrī (*Nihāyat*, xii, 123, 126-8), with reference to several recipes, on the basis of his usual source, namely the *Kitāb al-ʿArūs* of al-Tamīmī. But, contrary to what might be supposed, the majority of recipes for rose water blended this flower with other medicinal herbs such as aloes, saffron, musk, camphor or even cloves. This essence could be obtained from the petals (*waraḳ*) of the fresh flower (*ward ṭarī*) or of the dried flower (*ward yābis*), when they had been ground and set to macerate in the cucurbit (*ḳarʿa*, i.e. lower part of the alembic; then, by means of the alembic (*al-anbīḳ* [*q.v.*], here the coil) and its heating, the rose water was collected by distillation (*taḳṭīr*). The procedure of sublimation (rudimentary distillation, *taṣʿīd*) was also in use, according to al-Nuwayrī.

As regards the medicinal properties, the sources attest that distilled rose water was used, internally or externally, in the treatment of migraine, nausea and anxiety, but, especially, in eye-washes, to combat ophthalmia (Maimonides, *Sharḥ*, 59; Ibn Sīnā, *Ḳānūn*, i, 299-300). Mediaeval treatises on pharmacology and of ophthalmic medicine lay particular stress on the salutary properties of rose water as a wash for the treatment of numerous conditions of the eye, as well as for their prevention (*yamnaʿ ḳurūḥ al-ʿayn*, writes Dāwūd al-Antākī, *Tadhkira*, i, 339). The emollient and stabilising properties of rose water, often combined, in this case, with egg white, were appreciated after operations for cataract (Ibn Ḳassum al-Ghāfiḳī, *Kitāb al-Murshid*, 154; Ḥunayn b. Isḥāḳ, *K. al-ʿAshr maḳālāt fi ʾl-ʿayn*, 158, 160). Use of this essence as an eye-wash is still common today and traditionally-inclined doctors readily prescribe it (H. Ducros, *Droguier*, 66-7; G. Honda, *Herb drugs*, 19, 90; J. Bellakhdar, *Médecine traditionelle*, 302). Besides the purely medical use of this commodity, a number of texts refer to its benefits in the sphere of cosmetics and aesthetics, especially as a deodorant and as a cooling agent.

Bibliography: 1. Sources. Dāwūd al-Anṭākī, *Tadhkirat ulī al-albāb*, Cairo 1864, repr. Beirut n.d., 339; Ibn Sīnā, *al-Ḳānūn fi ʾl-ṭibb*, Cairo 1877, i, 299-300; M. Meyerhof (ed. and tr.), *The Book of the ten treatises on the eye ascribed to Hunain ibn Ishaq*, Cairo 1928; Nuwayrī, *Nihāyat al-arab fi funūn al-adab*, Cairo 1937, xii, 126-8; Meyerhof (ed. and tr.), *Kitāb al-Murshid fi ʾl-kuḥl ou Guide d'oculistique d'Ibn Qassum ibn Aslam al-Ghāfiqī*, Barcelona 1938; Maimonides, *Sharḥ asmāʾ al-ʿuḳḳār (L'explication des noms de drogues). Un glossaire de matière médicale*, ed. and tr. Meyerhof, Cairo 1939, 59; Ibn al-Bayṭār, *Traité des simples*, ed. and tr. L. Leclerc, Paris n.d., 284.

2. Studies. M.A.H. Ducros, *Essai sur le droguier populaire de l'inspectorat des pharmacies du Caire*, Mémoires de l'Institut d'Egypte, Cairo 1930; A. Issa Bey, *Dictionnaire des noms des plantes*, Cairo 1930, 157; E. Ghaleb, *al-Mawsūʿa fi ʿulūm al-ṭabīʿa*, Beirut 1965, ii, 634-5; J. Bellakhdar, *Médecine traditionelle et toxicologie ouest-sahariennes*, Rabat 1978; G. Honda, W. Miki and M. Saito, *Herb drugs and herbalists in Syria and North Yemen*, Tokyo 1990; E. Garcia-Sanchez, *Les techniques de distillation de l'eau de rose à al-Andalus*, in R. Gyselen (ed.), *Parfums d'Orient*, Res Orientales, xi, Paris 1999, 125-40.

(F. Sanagustin)

MADHHAB (A., pl. *madhāhib*), inf. n. of *dh-h-b*, meaning "a way, course, mode, or manner, of acting or conduct or the like" (Lane, i, 983b); as a term of religion, philosophy, law, etc. "a doctrine, a tenet, an opinion with regard to a particular case"; and in law specifically, a technical term often translated as "school of law", in particular one of the four legal systems recognised as orthodox by Sunnī Muslims, viz. the Ḥanafiyya, Mālikiyya, Shāfiʿiyya and Ḥanbaliyya [*q.vv.*], and the Shīʿī Djaʿfarī and Zaydiyya legal schools [see ITHNĀ ʿASHARIYYA; ZAYDIYYA].

For an exposé of *madhhab* development, see the second section of FIḲH, at Vol. II, 887b ff.; for recent writings questioning the Schachtian explanation of the "ancient schools of law" and for further bibliography on this, see N. Hurwitz, *Schools of law and historical context: Re-examining the formation of the Ḥanbalī madhhab*, in *ILS*, vii (2000), 37-64 and W.B. Hallaq, *From regional to personal schools of law? A reevaluation*, in *ILS*, viii (2001), 1-26. For new secondary studies on the *madhhab* since the *Bibl.* given in FIḲH, see the important publication of *Islamic Law and Society* (*ILS*), i (1994)-; N. Calder, *Studies in early Muslim jurisprudence*, Oxford 1993; C. Melchert, *The formation of the Sunni schools of law, 9th-10th centuries C.E.*, Leiden 1997; Nurit Tsafrir, *The beginnings of the Ḥanafī school in Isfahān*, in *ILS*, v (1998), 1-21; eadem, *The history of an Islamic school of law. The early spread of Hanafism*, Cambridge, Mass., in press [2004]; C. Adang, *From Mālikism to Shāfiʿism to Ẓāhirism: the 'conversions' of Ibn Ḥazm*, in Mercedes García-Arenal (ed.), *Conversions islamiques. Identités religieuses en Islam méditerranéen*, Paris 2001, 73-87; Hallaq, *Authority, continuity and change in Islamic law*, Cambridge 2001; Eyyup S. Kaya, *Mezheblerin teşekkulunden sonra fikhi istidlal* ("Legal reasoning after the formation of madhhabs"), unpubl. Ph.D. diss., Marmara University, Istanbul 2001; the forthcoming [2004] volume *The Islamic school of law. Evolution, devolution, and progress*, eds. P. Bearman, R. Peters and F.E. Vogel (Cambridge, Mass.) and the extensive bibliography there. See also G. Makdisi, *The rise of colleges. Institutions of learning in Islam and the West*, Edinburgh 1981; idem, *The rise of humanism in classical Islam and the Christian West*, Edinburgh 1990; É. Chaumont, *En quoi le maḏhab šāfiʿite est-il šāfiʿite selon le Muġiṯ al-ḫalq de Ǧuwaynī?*, in *AI*, xxxv (2001), 17-26; and Maribel Fierro, *Repertorio bibliográfico de derecho islámico*, Murcia 1999, s.v. "escuela". For the Shīʿī *madhhab* in particular, see Hossein Modarressi Tabātabāʾī, *An introduction to Shīʿī law: a bibliographical study*, London 1984, 23-58; D. Bredi, *I sistemi giuridici non sunniti: l'islamizzazione del diritto e l'alternativa jaʿfarita in Pakistan*, in *Annali di Ca'Foscari* (Rome), xxxv (1996), 313-34. For a list of *EI* articles on the schools and their jurists, see the entry LAW in the Encyclopaedia's *Index of Subjects* (Leiden [5]2002), and the sub-entries there. (ED.)

MADĪNA (A.), urbanism, the structure and planning of the Arab town and city.

This can be reconstructed as an historical reality from a vast body of literature, including chronicles and archival documents. It embodies enlightened ideas which seem to be commented on, as it were, by the remains of all the great Arab cities that can still be seen. The concept of a Muslim "city" was formulated chiefly by French orientalists (on this subject see R.S. Humphreys, *Islamic history: a framework for inquiry*, Princeton 1991, 228) between 1920 and 1950; in particular see G. and W. Marçais, J. Sauvaget and J. Weulersse. However, the most accomplished expression of this concept can be attributed to G. von Grunebaum in *The structure of the Muslim town*, in *The American Anthropologist*, lvii [1955].

It would be unnecessarily tedious to trace in detail the causes and conditions underlying the development of this concept (see J. Abu-Lughod, *The Islamic city*, in *IJMES*, xix [1987]; A. Raymond, *Islamic city, Arab city: orientalist myths and recent views*, in *BJMES*, xxi/1 [1994]). The importance accorded to it derived almost exclusively from religious factors, for Islam was assumed to underlie any form appearing in the Muslim domain.

The conception of a Muslim town *ne varietur*, scarcely affected by vicissitudes in the long history of Islam, was broadly extrapolated from Maghribī and Syrian examples. Furthermore it was supposed to be independent of the extremely diverse geographical conditions evident in the immense expanse of Muslim territory. It is altogether a very negative conception. The Muslim town, a structure devoid of any logical order, is said to have replaced the ancient organisation and model of regularity: it was irregular; its streets were winding cul-de-sacs; it was a maze, a labyrinth (R. Le Tourneau, *Les villes musulmanes de l'Afrique du Nord*, Algiers 1957); it was a dilapidated version of the ancient town; it had neither its own institutions nor administration (different, of course, not only from the cities of the ancient world but also from western mediaeval cities, which were endowed with communal institutions); and it had no legal existence. Thus Aleppo was like "a negation of urban order", a place where the influence of Islam had been "essentially negative"; the town had become "an inconsistent and inorganic collection of districts" (for these remarks see Sauvaget, *Alep*, 247-8). Weulersse describes such an internal dislocation in Antioch: the city is an amalgam of religious and national communities, a foreign body and a parasite in a country that it was exploiting (Weulersse, *Paysans de Syrie*, Paris 1946).

In the absence of any real precise information on Muslim town planning in any of the basic texts (the Ḳurʾān, *sunna* or *fikh* [*q.vv.*]), it is not surprising that the positive characteristics retained by such a "non-city" were reckoned to be few in number and, moreover, barely significant. It was inhabited by Muslims; as the seat of Muslim institutions (*ḳāḍī* [*q.v.*], *muḥtasib* [see ḤISBA]), it comprised a Friday mosque, normally located at its centre; it had a market (*sūḳ* [*q.v.*]), which was situated near the mosque and organised according to a strict professional specialisation; it was provided with public baths; and it was generally surrounded by ramparts. It is interesting to note that Arab researchers who are interested in the problem have generally adopted such a negative vision.

No further time will be wasted on the conditions under which a revision of this concept took place (the end of the colonial era, a more reasonable appreciation of the Arab cultural context and the "Turkish" period, and the discovery of Ottoman sources). A certain number of orientalists' pre-suppositions have been submitted to an excruciating revision, and a better acquaintance with later ancient cities has tempered any illusion about their supposed perfection (H. Kennedy, *From Polis to Madina*, in *Past and Present* [1985]). It was recognised that the variety of historical conditions should be taken into account (J.-Cl. Garcin, *Habitat médiéval et histoire urbaine*, in *Palais et maisons du Caire*, i, Paris 1982), as also the diversity of geographical and cultural conditions prevailing in the Muslim world (O. Grabar, *Reflections on the study of Islamic art*, in *Muqarnas*, i [1983]). Attention was drawn to the fact that the absence of administration in the Muslim town was not as absolute as had been suggested (see, for example, the role played by communities, *ṭawāʾif*, in the conduct of urban affairs). It was suggested that Muslim law and its interpreters were not silent on the subject of the town (see the early remarks of R. Brunschvig, in *Urbanisme médiéval et droit musulman*, in *REI*, xv [1947], which find an echo in the works of B. Johansen, *The claims of men and the claims of God*, in *Pluriformiteit en verdeling van de macht in het midden-oosten*, MOI publ. 4, Nijmegen 1980). It was admitted that the religious egalitarianism that characterised the *umma* did not preclude strong differentiation on socio-economic grounds, and traces of this could be found in urban organisation.

By concentrating on the modern, historically coherent period and by staying within the limits of the Arabo-Mediterranean region, which is both homogenous and clearly identifiable within the Ottoman domain, it is possible to define the major principles of the structure of traditional Arab towns at the beginning of the 19th century, just at the time when modernisation was beginning to alter their characteristics irretrievably (see Raymond, *La structure spatiale de la ville*, in M. Naciri and Raymond (eds.), *Sciences sociales et phénomènes urbains dans le monde arabe*, Casablanca 1997).

Through a study of the structure of the "traditional" Arab town we are able to demonstrate the existence of a coherent urban system. The fundamental characteristic of this system was a marked separation between the central "public" zone, where the principal economic, religious and cultural activities were developed, and the "private" zone, which was chiefly devoted to residence. This separation becomes apparent when a study is made of the localisation of urban functions. It is equally visible on street plans, where the relatively broad and regular road network of the centre is contrasted with the maze of narrow, irregular streets which had been seen to be a general feature of these towns; about 50% of the total length of the streets is represented by cul-de-sacs. This distinction has been recognised at length by jurists of the Ḥanafī school (B. Johansen).

The central region encloses the great markets (*sūḳs*), which are generally very specialised and assigned particular locations, and also the caravanserais, *funduḳs*, *khāns* and *wakālas*, according to the region and the period. It is here that big international business and wholesale trade took place and the centre of it was often the *ḳaysāriyya/bedestān*, devoted to the luxury trade (as in Fez or Cairo). This zone is assembled around the great university mosques (such as the Ḳarawiyyīn, the Zaytūna, al-Azhar and the Umayyad mosque), which are the centres of religious and cultural activities.

The surface area of this zone varies according to the importance of the towns and the extent of their commercial activity; it is about six hectares in Tunis, twelve in Aleppo and sixty in Cairo. The characteristics of the zone are so strongly marked that it sometimes has a particular name, such as "Mdineh" in Aleppo. Normally one or more main streets cross it, depending on the scale of traffic, which at that period consisted exclusively of transport on the backs of animals. At the beginning of the 19th century, 6 m represented an optimal breadth, according to the opinion of the Egyptian *ʿulamāʾ*. Some of these streets date back to ancient times, such as the "Street called Straight" in Damascus and the main street in Aleppo; others have been traced back to the Arab foundation (such as the Ḳaṣaba in Cairo). This zone is generally very stable, probably because it has a very strong structure and because it is closely linked with the principal mosque. In modern times there is only one case of a change of location known, at Mawṣil (D. Khouri, *Mosul, 1540-1834*, Cambridge 1997).

The areas spreading outside and around this central zone are chiefly devoted to housing, and from Morocco to Afghānistān these are organised into a system of neighbourhoods; in the Maghrib they are called *ḥawma*, in Egypt *ḥāra* and in the Near and Middle East *maḥalla*. They have a very consistent structure: there is one entrance point, which can be shut by a gate, and if necessary guarded; one main street, on to which alleys and cul-de-sacs are grafted. There are no specialised markets in these districts, only the *suwayḳas*, which have been analysed by Sauvaget and where the many activities necessary to daily existence take place. The life of the district is that of a community that is quite closed in upon itself; it is open only toward the centre, where the local inhabitants undertake their activities and towards which the network of roads leads in a hierarchically organised scheme (N. Messiri, *The concept of the Hara*, in *AI*, xv [1979]): this consideration, as well as the concern for security, justifies the statistical importance of the cul-de-sacs in this area. There does not seem to be any rule about homogeneity according to the origin or activity of the inhabitants, except in those cases where a district was inhabited by a community of a distinct religious or ethnic minority.

These general characteristics lead to a structure which may be described as doubly concentric, an arrangement such as is well known in the field of economic activities. Big international businesses and the main activities of craftsmen are located in the central regions, in the area near to the large mosque; nearby can be found in particular the markets for precious metals (*ṣāgha*) and the money changers (as noted by L. Massignon, *Enquête sur les corporations d'artisans*, in *RMM*, lviii [1924]). In Cairo the 62 caravanserais where the coffee trade took place were located in the area near the Ḳaṣaba. In Tunis, Damascus and Aleppo, the *sūḳs* for cloth and spices occupy a prominent place in the area immediately surrounding the mosque. From the centre outwards, activities spread over an increasingly great distance as their order of importance diminished, and also according to the growing inconvenience of particular trades. There could be found on the periphery of the town those domestic activities that needed space (such as the straw workers); those linked to the countryside (grain markets in the large squares, *raḥba*, *ʿarṣa* and livestock markets); those that were embarrassing and polluting (ovens of all sorts, abattoirs, tanneries). The moving of such trades to a more remote location could, moreover, be an indication of urban development, as was the case for the transfer of the tanneries in Aleppo (1570), Cairo (1600) and Tunis (1770) (see Raymond, *Le déplacement des tanneries*, in *REMMM*, lv-lvi [1990]).

By contrast, the orientalist vision of a fundamentally egalitarian, Muslim society was a factor in imposing a scheme according to which the rich and poor lived together in the same urban space, using a unique type of habitat qualified as "Muslim", although the house with a central patio may be found in Classical Antiquity, also, an idea strongly expressed by A. Abdel Nour, *Introduction à l'histoire urbaine de la Syrie ottomane*, Beirut 1982. Reality is quite different and corresponds logically to a strongly unequal socio-economic structure. Studies on this subject carried out in Cairo (Raymond, *Artisans et commerçants*, Damascus 1974),

Damascus (C. Establet and J.-P. Pascual, *Familles et fortunes à Damas*, Damascus 1994) and Algiers (T. Shuval, *La ville d'Alger*, Paris 1998) have shown a remarkable inequality in the range of wealth, insofar this can be measured through the successions registered in the courts: fortunes are in a proportion of 1 : 10,000 in Cairo and 1 : 3,000 in Damascus around 1700 (Establet, Pascual and Raymond, *La mesure de l'inégalité sociale dans la société ottomane*, in *JESHO*, xxxvii [1994]). It is therefore not surprising in these conditions that in the large Arab towns the population would be distributed according to a rather rigorous "classification": the comfortable residences occupied the zone near the centre (where the *ʿulamāʾ* preferably lived near to the mosque and traders near the *sūḳ*s); then there were the middle-class areas with increasingly poor living conditions, until one reached the often wretched housing for the common people on the periphery and in the suburbs. This roughly concentric arrangement can be clearly deduced from studies on Tunis (J. Revault, *Palais et demeures à Tunis*, Paris 1967-78), Cairo (N. Hanna, *Habiter au Caire*, Cairo 1991) and Aleppo (J.-Cl. David, *Alep, dégradation et tentatives actuelles de réadaptation*, in *BEO*, xxviii [1975]).

However, the central patio house only appears to be "unitary", and great differences evidently exist with regard to dimensions, whether there are one or more storeys, interior amenities and decoration between houses with courtyards of the rich, middle-class and poor (for Tunis, see G. Cladel and P. Revault, *Medina, approche typologique*, Tunis 1970). Moreover, examples of "atypical" houses are plentiful. There is the collective accommodation of the caravanserai type, the collective accommodation of the *rabʿ* type found in Cairo, vertical accommodation (Rosetta, Yemen), middle-class accommodation without a patio, poor community accommodation of the *ḥaws̲h̲* type, and cellular accommodation; mediaeval examples of this have been studied by Scanlon and Kubiak in their excavations of Fusṭāṭ.

Naturally, no existing town corresponds to this model of a round town, arranged in concentric rings around the centre, with its economic and residential activities classified according to a decreasing order of importance. There are a number of factors (natural, historical, economic and social) that explain the irregularities that are noted. The decentring of al-Ḳāhira, in the northeast quarter of ancient Cairo, is justified by natural considerations such as the presence of the Muḳaṭṭam Hills, which prohibited expansion towards the east; also by historical reasons, such as the construction of the citadel by Ṣalāḥ al-Dīn [*q.v.*], which favoured expansion towards the south, and the custom of dumping the rubbish from Cairo into the region today called "The Tells", which has restricted any expansion towards the northeast.

A similar analysis could be applied to Tunis, where the geography of the site dictates that expansion should develop only towards the north and the south, since expansion to the east and west is prevented by the two lagoons (*sabk̲h̲a*). It could be applied also to Aleppo, where for a long time the presence of the river Ḳuwayḳ has hindered any development of the city towards the west and the existence of cemeteries prevented expansion to the north and south. Mawṣil had the appearance of a round town until economic reasons, like the special attraction of the markets because of the commercial potential of the river Tigris, and probably also political reasons (the research into the proximity of the citadel) brought about the displacement of the centre towards the river, far from the great mosque. On the other hand, the locations of the districts for the minorities and for the élite followed a particular logic, which often led to their remoteness from the centre.

There is indeed good reason for emphasising the importance of the segregative factors in the way the "traditional" town is organised. The inegalitarian nature of Muslim society explains this discrimination by the standard of wealth and the difference in living conditions between the centre and the periphery. In Cairo, however, collective rented accommodation, the *rabʿ* [*q.v.*], allowed the middle classes to reside near the centre (Raymond, *Le* rabʿ, *un habitat collectif au Caire*, in *MUSJ*, 1 [1948]). Districts for the élite were often located on the periphery, where the powerful could find the space they needed for their houses and a certain isolation from the rest of the population. The vigour with which the "national" and/or religious Muslim minority communities regrouped depended on the degree of their differences with regard to the rest of the population: in Cairo, the Mag̲h̲ribīs and the Syrians regrouped less than the Turks; a Kurdish district had been in existence for a very long time in Damascus; while in Antioch, the Alawites were at one and the same time very much regrouped and pushed far from the centre. The non-Muslim minority communities (the People of the Book subject to the status of *d̲h̲immī*, "protected") were generally subjected from the point of view of space to strict segregation, expressing in terms of spatial location the discriminations and disabilities imposed upon them, despite the remarkable tolerance which these communities enjoyed under the Ottomans.

There were in all of the large towns Christian and Jewish districts, the location of which varied according to local conditions. The Jews of Tunis lived in a district (*al-ḥāra*) situated out of the way; those in Cairo were very close to the centre. The relative dispersion of the Copts in Cairo bore witness to the tolerance from which they benefited, but their districts were in the main situated to the west of K̲h̲alīd̲j̲, in a region that was occupied by Muslims only at a fairly late date. The evolution of the Christian district of Aleppo is significant from this point of view. There, from the end of the 16th century, the community experienced a remarkable development, and this expansion was marked by an eastwards advance of the Christians in the northern suburb of the town which was progressively occupied by them. The gradual retreat of the Muslims towards the east, a community that was none the less dominant, certainly tends to confirm that the religious groups preferred, for reasons of convenience, a segregated, collective life rather than a confessional mix, even though such a mix could exist in limited zones (Raymond, *Une communauté en expansion. Les chrétiens d'Alep*, in *La ville arabe, Alep*, Damascus 1998).

The traditional Arab cities were therefore strongly structured, an observation that seems self-evident, for one can hardly imagine how an anarchical town without an administration would have been able to continue in existence and even experience a strong expansion in modern times. Investigation into the constitutive elements of this specific urban system, the identification of the para-administrative structures which allowed the conduct of urban affairs, and the recognition of the major role played by the *waḳf*s [*q.v.*] in urban organisation and development (R. Deguilhem [ed.], *Le* waqf *dans l'espace islamique*, Damascus 1995) all lead to more positive conclusions than a discreditable comparison with other urban systems which were judged to have been more perfected.

However, an investigation such as this can be complete only when more can be learned about the origins of this urban system. Research on pre-Islamic towns in the Yemen (J.-F. Breton, *Le site et la ville de Shabwa*, in *Syria*, lxviii [1991]) and in Arabia (A.T. al-Anṣārī, *Qaryat al-Fāw*, London 1981) have brought important insights in this field. There is also a need for better information on the time of transition between the ancient period and the beginnings of the Muslim era (see the traces of Umayyad town planning discovered in the ancient sites of Palmyra and Beit Shean) and on the period of the foundation (for Fusṭāṭ, see R.P. Gayraud, *Iṣṭabl ʿAntar*, in *AI*, xxv [1991]).

The other crucial question is that of knowing to what extent the data on urban structure suggested by the study of the sources and the examinations of the remnants of ancient towns are equally valid for the "classical" Arab town, which we know from texts but which has to be the subject of reconstruction on the ground, since the urban tissue which subsists in the "madinas" of Arab towns dates only from the modern Ottoman period.

Bibliography (in addition to references in the article): On the city in general, see W. Marçais, *L'islamisme et la vie urbaine*, 1928, repr. in *Articles et conférences*, Paris 1961; G. Marçais, *L'urbanisme musulman*, 1939, repr. in *Mélanges*, Algiers 1957; I. Lapidus (ed.), *Middle Eastern cities*, Berkeley and Los Angeles 1969; A. Hourani and S.M. Stern (eds.), *The Islamic city*, Oxford 1970; L.C. Brown (ed.), *From Madina to metropolis*, Princeton 1973; L. Torrès Balbas, *Ciudades hispano-musulmanas*, 2 vols. Madrid 1972; E. Wirth, *Zum Problem des Bazars*, in *Isl.*, li (1974) and lii (1975); idem, *Die orientalische Stadt*, in *Saeculum*, xxvi (1975); D. Chevallier (ed.), *L'espace social de la ville arabe*, Paris 1979; A. Raymond, *La conquête ottomane*, in *ROMM*, xxvii (1979); N. Todorov, *La ville balkanique aux XVe-XIXe siècles*, Bucharest 1980; R. Serjeant (ed.), *The Islamic city*, Paris 1980; T. Khalidi, *Some classical Islamic views of the city*, in Wadad al-Qadi (ed.), *Studia arabica et islamica. Festschrift for Iḥsān ʿAbbās*, Beirut 1981; A. Bouhdiba and Chevallier (eds.), *La ville arabe dans l'Islam*, Tunis 1982; I. Serageldin and S. El-Sadek (eds.), *The Arab city*, n.p. 1982; Raymond, *The great Arab cities, an introduction*, New York 1984; idem, *Grandes villes arabes à l'époque ottomane*, Paris 1985; J.-Cl. Garcin, *Espaces, pouvoirs et idéologies de l'Égypte médiévale*, Variorum, London 1987; idem (ed.), *L'habitat traditionnel dans les pays musulmans autour de la Méditerranée*, GREPO, 3 vols. Cairo 1988-91; G. Veinstein, *La ville ottomane. Les facteurs d'unité*, in *La ciudad islamica*, Saragossa 1991; D. Panzac (ed.), *Les villes dans l'empire ottoman*, 2 vols. Paris 1991-4; M. Bonine *et alii* (eds.), *The Middle Eastern city and Islamic urbanism*, Bonn 1994; S. al-Hathlūl, *al-Madīna al-ʿarabiyya al-islāmiyya*, Riyāḍ 1414/1994; M. Naciri and Raymond (eds.), *Sciences sociales et phénomènes urbains dans le monde arabe*, Casablanca 1997; Raymond, *La ville arabe Alep à l'époque ottomane*, Damascus 1998; several articles by various specialists on the mediaeval and modern Arab town in Cl. Nicolle (ed.), *Mégapoles méditerranéennes, géographie urbaine retrospective*, Rome 2000; Garcin (ed.), *Grandes villes méditerranéennes*, Rome 2000; Wirth, *Die orientalische Stadt*, 2 vols. Mainz 2000; Raymond, *Arab cities in the Ottoman period*, Variorum, Aldershot 2002.

Amongst studies on specific towns and cities, see M. Clergé, *Le Caire*, 2 vols. Cairo 1934; J. Weulersse, *Antioche, essai de géographie urbaine*, in *BEO*, iv (1934); J. Sauvaget, *Alep*, Paris 1941; J. Caillé, *La ville de Rabat*, 3 vols. Paris 1949; R. Le Tourneau, *Fès avant le Protectorat*, Paris 1949; R. Mantran, *Istanbul dans la seconde moitié du XVIIème siècle*, Paris 1962; G. Deverdun, *Marrakech*, 2 vols. Rabat 1966; J. Revault, *Palais et demeures de Tunis*, 4 vols. Paris 1967-78; R. Serjeant and R. Lewcock (eds.), *Ṣanʿāʾ, an Arabian Islamic city*, London 1983; B. Maury, A. Raymond, Revault and M. Zakariya, *Palais et maisons du Caire. II. Époque ottomane*, Paris 1983; J.-P. Pascual, *Damas à la fin du XVIème siècle*, Damascus 1983; H. Gaube and E. Wirth, *Aleppo*, Wiesbaden 1984; Revault, L. Golvin and A. Amahan, *Palais et demeures de Fès*, 3 vols. Paris 1985-92; A. Marcus, *Aleppo in the eighteenth century*, New York 1989; J. Abdelkafi, *La medina de Tunis*, Paris 1989; A. Escher and Wirth, *Die Medina von Fes*, Erlangen 1992; Raymond, *Le Caire*, Paris 1993; P. Sebag, *Tunis, histoire d'un ville*, Paris 1998; Raymond *et alii*, *Le Caire*, Paris 2000; S. Auld and R. Hillenbrand, *Ottoman Jerusalem, the living city 1517-1917*, London 2000.

(A. Raymond)

MADĪNAT AL-NUḤĀS, "The city of brass," a story within the *Thousand and one nights* [see ALF LAYLA WA-LAYLA].

This story, that found its way, somewhat variably, into the 19th-century editions of the *Nights* (on the 18th-century manuscripts in which it appears, see the excellent discussion by D. Pinault, *Story-telling techniques in the Arabian Nights*, Leiden 1992, 150-80), is the most elaborate narrative about a city of copper, brass or bronze (on the proper meanings of *nuḥās* and *ṣufr*, and their indiscriminate use in non-scientific discourse, see M. Aga-Oglu, *A brief note on Islamic terminology for bronze and brass*, in *JAOS*, lxiv [1944], 218-23). Fabulous reports about such a place, set in remote reaches of the Maghrib or al-Andalus, appear already in the 3rd/9th century. In Ibn Ḥabīb's (d. 238/853 [*q.v.*]) *Kitāb al-Taʾrīkh* (ed. J. Aguadé, Madrid 1991, 144-5; authentic in the editor's view), Mūsā b. Nuṣayr's [*q.v.*] adventures include finding jars in which Solomon imprisoned rebellious demons, and a copper fortress (*madīna ʿalayhā ḥisn min nuḥās*) inhabited by *djinn*, which renders those who enter it unaware of their condition. Al-Masʿūdī tells us (*Murūdj*, i, 369 = ed. Pellat, i, 195-6, § 409) that beyond al-Sūs al-aḳṣā (southern Morocco) one comes to the River of Sand, then to the Black Castle, and at length to the sandy desert in which the City of Brass (*nuḥās*) and Domes of Lead are found. He also refers to a book in wide circulation dealing with the wondrous things that Mūsā b. Nuṣayr saw there. In another place (iv, 95 = § 1423) he refers to the same city (here as *madīnat al-ṣufr wa-ḳubbat al-raṣāṣ*), and says that those who flung themselves from the walls tasted (so they report) the pleasures of this world and the next. The *Mukhtaṣar* of Ibn al-Faḳīh's [*q.v.*] *Kitāb al-Buldān* is in several respects close to the *Nights* story, although the city is called al-Baht and no mention of metallic walls is made. After travelling through the "deserts of al-Andalus" Mūsā finds a city without an entrance, grim with brilliant battlements. Those who scale the walls laugh uncontrollably, and hurl themselves to their deaths below. (Mad laughter leading to death is the effect of the *baht* stone, cf. al-Bīrūnī, *K. al-Djamāhir fī maʿrifat al-djawāhir*, Ḥaydarābād 1355, 101.) A memento mori inscription (of which there are many in the *Nights* tale) refers to the mortality of Solomon, mightiest of kings. Mūsā renounces entering the City and moves on to "the lake". This lake is visited by al-Khaḍir [*q.v.*] once a year. Mūsā's divers recover a bronze (*ṣufr*) jar, from which, when opened, a brazen man escapes with the cry "O Prophet, I will not relapse!" Later it is explained that such bottles hold the rebellious *djinn* imprisoned by Solomon. The *Nights* story adds further Solomonic motifs to the journey and the City itself (cf. A. Hamori, *The art of medieval Arabic literature*, Princeton 1974, 149-53), as well as some other new details. The essential innovation is that in the *Nights*, Mūsā ultimately enters the City, to find it full of dead people who look deceptively alive. One of the leaders of the expedition, Ṭālib b. Sahl, is killed by robots when he tries to despoil the dead queen of her jewels.

The motifs in these narratives have their now inextricably tangled roots in Islamic (and Jewish) legends about Solomon, the Alexander Romance, Iranian legend, and, of course, in marvelling at ancient structures laid in massive desolation. Indeed, the sources show disagreement as to whether the builder of the City was Alexander or Solomon. Brazen or iron walls and palaces are a feature of many texts from Antiquity, and often occur in Iranian legend and poetry (cf. M. Barry, *Le Pavillon des sept princesses*, Paris 2000, 680-4, on Niẓāmī's *Tale of the red pavilion*). The principal source of the malefic City of Brass may well be the Iranian legend of the Brazen Hold, a subterranean (but brilliant) place of evil in the Avesta (cf. J. Darmesteter, *Le Zend-Avesta*, repr. Paris 1960, i, 111), which surfaces as the evil Ardjāsp's redoubt in the *Shāh-nāma* (ed. Mohl, iv, 493 and index). The Solomonic motifs became easily associated because of the Ḳur'ānic reference (XXXIV, 12-13) to the *ʿayn al-ḳiṭr*, mostly understood as a fountain of copper or brass, that God made to flow for Solomon, and to the *djinn* that built him palaces and statues. The journey to the ends of the world, cautionary inscriptions, automata and the overall memento mori mood are characteristic of all recensions of the Alexander Romance. In addition, as Ch. Genequand has pointed out (*Autour de la ville de bronze: d'Alexandre à Salomon*, in *Arabica*, xxxix [1992], 328-30), in his section on the Maghrib Ibn al-Faḳīh relates, before describing the City of Baht, versions of such details of the Alexander Romance as the River of Sand (which appears in some recensions) and Alexander's conversation with the gymnosophists (who are here an *umma* of the Banū Isrā'īl). Genequand suggests that Ibn al-Faḳīh's mysterious lake (in the *Nights*, the sea of Karkar) associated with al-Khaḍir derives directly from the Water of Life episode in the Alexander Romance via the traditional association of al-Khaḍir with Ḳur'ān, XVIII, 61-5 (cf. also Pinault, 180-6); and that the City of Brass itself derives from an episode in a late Byzantine recension (dated by its editor to the early 8th century A.D.) in which the gymnosophists' women live on an island surrounded by a brilliant brazen wall which no man can penetrate and live. The Water of Life episode is, indeed, likely to have been a major contributor to the shaping of the story. Whether the same is true of the women's island is harder to say, since this episode is itself an adaptation of the Amazons' self-segregation in the older recensions, and may have been elaborated under oriental influence.

Some commentators have considered the *Nights* story a clumsy grab-bag of motifs. At a minimum, one must agree with those who see in it a *zuhdī* homily (e.g. Pinault, 231-39). It has been suggested (Barry, 167-8, and Hamori, *loc. cit.*) that, in view of the mystical symbolism often attributed to various episodes in the Solomon legend, to dead bodies only seemingly alive, to spiritual famine, to al-Khaḍir, etc., an interpretation of the *Nights* story that assumes such symbolism to have been intended makes sense of some otherwise unmotivated details and offers the most coherent reading. It may be more prudent to say that, whatever the various narrators had in mind, in ages of deep popular Ṣūfism, such symbolic understanding would have been part of the reception of the story.

Bibliography (in addition to references given in the article): For the fullest discussion of classical Arabic references to the *Madīnat al-nuḥās* (or *ṣufr*), see M. Gaudefroy-Demombynes, *Les Cent et une nuits*, repr. Paris 1982, 261-70. The *Nights* story and its sources are also dealt with at length in M. Gerhardt, *The art of story-telling*, Leiden 1963, 195-235, and Julia Hernández Juberías, *La Península imaginaria*, Madrid 1996, 25-67. Literary criticism. A. Kilito, *L'Oeil et l'aiguille*, Paris 1992, 86-103; Pinault, *op. cit.*, 186-239. (A. Hamori)

AL-**MADJĀDHĪB**, a leading "holy family" among the Sudanese Djaʿaliyyūn [*q.v.*]. Their ancestors emerged in the 16th century as a family of religious specialists (*fugara*, sg. *fakī*) in the area of al-Dāmar. In 1117/1705-6, Muḥammad al-Madjdhūb ("the Enraptured"), the first of the family to bear this epithet, may have participated in the first revolt of the northern Sudanese provinces against their Fundj [*q.v.*] overlords. Under his son, *Fakī* Ḥamad wad al-Madjdhūb (1105-90/1694-1776), the family strengthened its position by accumulating private land titles and engaging in long-distance trade. Well trained in Mālikī law, Ḥamad adopted the Shādhiliyya *ṭarīḳa*. He and his sons—known since *ca.* 1800 as *awlād wad al-Madjdhūb* or *al-Madjādhīb*—taught Ḳur'ān and *fiḳh*, provided medical services, and mediated between peasants and nomads. Both their fame as scholars and their political importance grew rapidly. They maintained contact with al-Azhar, and their schools were of regional significance. The Turco-Egyptian conquest (1821-3) and economic hardship during the 19th century dispersed the Madjādhīb. Some returned to al-Dāmar; others remained in the Ethiopian borderlands or founded settlements in al-Ḳaḍārif, the Djazīra and the western Sudan.

Most important religiously was Ḥamad's grandson, Muḥammad Madjdhūb (b. 1210/1795-6, d. 1247/1831). After spending eight years in the Ḥidjāz where he was influenced by Aḥmad b. Idrīs [*q.v.*], he moved to Sawākin in 1829 to propagate his *ṭarīḳa*. A prolific writer, Madjdhūb did much to spread Islamic knowledge beyond the confines of the urban scholar-jurists. His nephew and *khalīfa* al-Ṭāhir Madjdhūb (1248-1307/1832-90) gained many followers in the eastern Sudan. In 1883 he joined the Mahdī [see AL-MAHDIYYA], and his influence among the eastern tribes was an important factor in their rallying behind the Mahdist cause. Al-Ṭāhir's son "al-Shaykh" b. al-Ṭāhir Madjdhūb (*ca.* 1860-1930) served as commander in the Mahdist army and was later venerated for his piety, poetry and learning. His successors moved the centre of the eastern Madjādhīb to Erkowit.

In 20th-century al-Dāmar, the heritage of *Shaykh* Muḥammad Madjdhūb was promoted by Madjdhūb Djalāl al-Dīn (1305-96/1888-96). Although efforts to create a centralised *Ṭarīḳa Madjdhūbiyya* failed, the *Shaykh* gradually displaced the clan ancestor, *Fakī* Ḥamad, as focal point of communal identification. A domed tomb was erected over his grave in 1996.

Bibliography: Muḥammad al-Ṭāhir Madjdhūb, *al-Wasīla ilā al-maṭlūb fī baʿd mā ishtahara min manāḳib wa-karāmāt walī Allāh al-Shaykh al-Madjdhūb*, Cairo 1914; *Madjmūʿat al-Madjdhūb*, Cairo 1941; A. Hofheinz, *Internalising Islam. Shaykh Muḥammad Madjdhūb, scrip-*

tural Islam and local context in the early nineteenth-century Sudan, dr. philos. thesis, Univ. of Bergen 1996, unpubl., and the sources given there.

(A. Hofheinz)

AL-**MADJDHŪBIYYA** [see AL-MADJĀDHĪB].

MADURA, MADURA'Ī, in mediaeval Islamic times a town, now the city of Madurai, in South India. It lies on the Vaidai river in lat. 9° 55' N., long. 78° 07' E. in the region known to the mediaeval Muslims as Maʿbar and to later European traders as Coromandel. For the historical geography and Islamic history of this coastal province, roughly extending from Cape Comorin northwards to Madras, see MAʿBAR.

In 734/1334 Sharīf Djalāl al-Dīn Aḥsan [*q.v.*], governor for the Dihlī Sultan Muḥammad b. Tughluḳ [*q.v.*], renounced his allegiance, and he and some seven of his successors ruled over a short-lived Muslim sultanate before it was overwhelmed in *ca.* 779/1377 by the rising Hindu power of Vidjayanagara [*q.v.*], (see on the Madura sultanate, H.K. Sherwani and P.M. Joshi (eds.), *History of medieval Deccan (1295-1724)*, Ḥaydarābād 1973, i, 57-75; C.E. Bosworth, *The New Islamic dynasties*, Edinburgh 1996, 318 no. 166; and for numismatics, E. Hultzsch, *The coinage of the Sultans of Madura*, in *JRAS* [1909], 667-83). Thereafter, Madura remained under Hindu control till the early 18th century, when the Nawwābs of Arcot [*q.v.*] or Ārkāt extended their power over it, provoking Marāthā [*q.v.*] intervention and then that of the British in favour of the Nawwābs. In 1801 the administration of the Madura region passed to the British East India Company as part of a treaty with the Nawwāb of Arcot, and then in 1855, to complete British control.

The modern city of Madurai, a municipality since 1866, is the chef-lieu of a District of the same name in the Indian Union State of Tamil Nadu; in 1971 it had a population of 548,000, and in 2003 its population totalled 959,200.

Bibliography (in addition to references given in the article): *Imperial gazetteer of India*², xvi, 386-407.

(C.E. Bosworth)

MAFRAḲ, lit. "place of separation, junction", a settlement, now a town, in the northeastern part of the Hashemite Kingdom of Jordan [see URDUNN]. It lies in lat. 32° 20' N., long. 36° 12' E. at an elevation of 600 m/1,960 feet in an arid area whose average rainfall is 150 mm per annum. The region lacks running water, hence local people have always depended on pools and reservoirs for water, and the settlement grew up near the "white pool" (*al-ghadīr al-abyaḍ*).

Archaeological investigations nevertheless show that the area was once well populated, and a large number of what were Greek Orthodox churches and their mosaics have been found; the Roman emperor Trajan in A.D. 108 had built a road passing south of the site of Mafraḳ. In Umayyad times, there may have been a *bādiya* [*q.v.* in Suppl.] there. The place had a certain importance in Islamic times from its position on the caravan and Pilgrimage route from Damascus to the Ḥidjāz, and the sources explain its name by saying some pilgrims used to separate there from the main road and go their own way, or that friends from Damascus used to accompany pilgrims southwards but return home from Mafraḳ. But the place only assumed real importance when the Ḥidjāz railway [*q.v.*] was built and a station opened there. After the Italian occupation of Libya, Libyan refugees, described as Maghāriba, settled there, and the city still has a quarter bearing their name. After 1918, it became an Arab Legion base. Economically, the place received an impetus in 1931 when the Iraq Petroleum Company established itself there, built an aircraft landing-ground and brought in labourers to construct a road to Baghdād and pipe lines and generators. A pipe line brought crude oil from Iraq via Mafraḳ to Haifa and the Mediterranean coast. The population further expanded with the settlement of Bedouin tribesmen, and the discovery of underground water supplies made a growth of industry as well as of population possible. In 1985 the region was promoted administratively from being a *mutaṣarrifiyya* to being a *muḥāfaẓa* or province. In 1994 the Āl al-Bayt University was established in the town's suburbs, bringing further expansion and development, and in 2003 the town had an estimated population of 67,400.

Bibliography: Naval Intelligence Division, Admiralty Handbooks, *Palestine and Transjordan*, London 1943, 510 and index; Abū Shāʿir Hind, *Irbid wa-djiwāruhā*, ʿAmmān 1995; ʿAbd al-Ḳādir al-Ḥiṣān, *Muḥāfaẓat al-Mafraḳ wa 'l-muḥīṭa*, ʿAmmān 1999.

(M.A. Bakhit)

MAḤAMMAD B. **AḤMAD** b. ʿAbd Allāh AL-**HUḌĪGĪ** al-Sūsī al-Djazūlī (1118-89/1706-75), Moroccan scholar and ascetic.

After a classic-type education in his native region of the Sūs, he left on the Pilgrimage in 1152/1739, en route following the courses of famous teachers, notably at Cairo; he gives details of these stays in his unpublished *Riḥla ḥidjāziyya*. On his return to Morocco, he spent the remainder of his life in his *zāwiya* [*q.v.*] of Wādī Īsī in the Sūs.

His main work, the *Manāḳib* or *Ṭabaḳāt al-Huḍīgī* (2 vols. Casablanca 1936-9) groups together alphabetically the names of personalities who lived essentially in the 11th-12th/17th-18th centuries. These comprise above all the scholars and mystics of the Sūs, but also persons from the rest of Morocco, though only rarely from neighbouring lands. The work contains important notices on persons otherwise unknown, increasing its value for the historian. Al-Huḍīgī also compiled several commentaries on manuals of *ḥadīth* and *fiḳh*, on poetry and on grammar; an important number of responsa; and a larger-scale *madjmūʿa* in which he mentions his masters, in the Maghrib and the Mashriḳ, the licenses to teach which he himself received and which he issued to others, and a few other sparse personal details. Apart from the *Manāḳib* mentioned above, the ensemble of his works, comprising some 20 titles, remains still unpublished. Al-Huḍīgī's intellectual progeny were numerous in the Sūs, but his fame as a Ṣūfī was equally great amongst his compatriots, with his asceticism and scrupulous orthodoxy impressing his contemporaries; numerous miracles and acts of intercession were attributed to him.

Bibliography: Ziriklī, *Aʿlām*³, vi, 15; Muḥammad Mukhtār al-Sūsī, *al-Maʿsūl*, Casablanca 1960, xi, 302-25; idem, *Sūs al-ʿālima*, Casablanca n.d., 193 (lists his works). For references to the mss. of his works, see M. Manūnī, *al-Maṣādir al-ʿarabiyya li 'l-taʾrīkh al-Maghrib*, Rabat 1404/1983, i, 222-3, 229-30.

(P. Lory and M. Zekri)

AL-**MAHDĪ LI-DĪN ALLĀH**, AL-**ḤUSAYN**, Yamanī Zaydī Imām.

He was born in 378/988-9 as one of the younger sons of Imām al-Manṣūr bi'llāh [*q.v.*] al-Ḳāsim b. ʿAlī al-ʿIyānī. In Ṣafar 401/September-October 1010 he proclaimed his imāmate at Ḳāʿa in al-Bawn and gained the support of tribes of Ḥimyar, Hamdān and the Magẖārib region. He faced the opposition of the Ḥusaynī ʿAlid Muḥammad b. al-Ḳāsim al-Zaydī, based in Dẖamār, and of the descendants of Yaḥyā al-Hādī, the founder of the Zaydī imamate in Yaman, whose stronghold was in Ṣaʿda. In 402/1011-12 he gained control of Ṣanʿāʾ from Muḥammad al-Zaydī and installed his elder brother Djaʿfar as governor there. In the following year, al-Zaydī re-entered Ṣanʿāʾ and destroyed the houses of some of al-Mahdī's partisans. Al-Mahdī defeated and killed him in al-Ḥaḳl. He also thwarted the efforts of Muḥammad al-Zaydī's son Zayd, who received financial backing from the Ziyādid ruler of Zabīd, to avenge his father's death. Next, al-Mahdī seized Ṣaʿda, where Yūsuf b. Yaḥyā b. Aḥmad al-Nāṣir, the claimant to the imāmate there, had died, and destroyed some houses of his opponents. Because of his severity in punishing dissent, however, he soon lost most of his tribal support. He suffered a serious defeat by the Hamdānī chief Aḥmad b. Ḳays b. al-Ḍaḥḥāk near Dẖībīn and was forced to seek refuge in the Djawf. When he returned with some hundred horsemen to recover al-Bawn, he was killed fighting fiercely by the Hamdān at Dẖū ʿArār near Rayda on 4 Ṣafar 404/15 August 1013.

Al-Mahdī's death was at first denied by his brother Djaʿfar, who thus became the founder of the Ḥusayniyya sect which expected his return as the Mahdī. The activity of the sect reached its peak during the successful resistance of Djaʿfar's sons al-Sẖarīf al-Fāḍil al-Ḳāsim (d. 468/1075) and Dẖu 'l-Sẖarafayn Muḥammad (d. 478/1085) in Sẖahāra against the Ṣulayḥid rule. It survived until the 9th/15th century.

Al-Mahdī had himself claimed to be the Mahdī whose advent was predicted by the Prophet. In the quarrels with his opponents, who impugned his scholarship, he is said to have made extravagant claims of being more learned than all former Imāms and more excellent even than Muḥammad. He denounced his critics with coarse abuse and curses. After repudiating one of his wives, he prevented a suitor from marrying her, relying on the Ḳurʾānic prohibition (xxxiii, 53) for anyone to marry a wife of the Prophet after him. Because of such conduct, his imāmate was widely denied by Zaydīs, apart from the Ḥusayniyya, during the two centuries following his death, and aspersions were cast on his sanity. Later, he was, however, generally recognised as an Imām on a par with others, and the accusations made against him by his opponents were considered as unfounded polemics. The Sayyid Ḥumaydān b. al-Ḳāsim (7th/13th century) composed a treatise defending his record.

Al-Mahdī is said to have left as many as 73 works, including a Ḳurʾān commentary. Only a few succinct treatises and pamphlets are extant, and it has been suggested that his writings may have been purged by his supporters. In religious law and theology he explicitly backed the authority of the Imāms al-Ḳāsim b. Ibrāhīm and Yaḥyā al-Hādī. He did not recognise the Caspian Zaydī Imāms and ignored their teaching.

Bibliography: Nasẖwān al-Ḥimyarī, *al-Ḥūr al-ʿīn*, Cairo 1367/1948, 157; Muḥallī, *al-Ḥadāʾiḳ al-wardiyya*, ii; Yaḥyā b. al-Ḥusayn b. al-Muʾayyad, *Gẖāyat al-amānī*, ed. Saʿīd ʿAbd al-Fattāḥ ʿĀsẖūr, Cairo 1388/1968, 235-8; W. Madelung, *Der Imam al-Qāsim ibn Ibrāhīm*, Berlin 1965, 198-201; Mufarriḥ b. Aḥmad al-Rabaʿī, *Sīrat al-amīrayn al-djalīlayn al-sẖarīfayn al-fāḍilayn*, ed. Riḍwān al-Sayyid and ʿAbd al-Gẖanī Maḥmūd ʿAbd al-ʿĀṭī, Beirut 1413/1993, esp. 36-46, 345-65; Ḥabsẖī, *Muʾallafāt ḥukkām al-Yaman*, ed. E. Niewöhner-Eberhard, Wiesbaden 1979, 23-27. (W. Madelung)

MĀHIR, ʿALĪ, Egyptian jurist and politician. Born on 9 November 1881 in Cairo, the son of Muḥammad Māhir Pasẖa, he was educated at the Khedivial Secondary School and the School of Law. ʿAlī Māhir held several posts in the Egyptian court system in the years before and during World War I, and briefly served as Dean of the School of Law (1923-4).

He began his active political career during the Revolution of 1919 as one of the organisers of civil servant petitions and protest. Made a member of the Wafd [q.v.] in November 1919, Māhir broke with the movement in March 1922, gravitating thereafter into the orbit of the Egyptian Palace. In 1922-3 he served on the commission which drafted the Egyptian Constitution of 1923. He sat briefly in the Chamber of Deputies (1925-6) and was a member of the Senate from 1930 to 1952. He held several ministerial posts in non-Wafdist governments in the 1920s and early 1930s.

Māhir's influence in Egyptian politics was greatest in the later 1930s, when as Royal Chamberlain he helped articulate the strategy of consolidating royal autocracy around the person of the young King Fārūḳ [q.v. in Suppl.]. Māhir twice served as Prime Minister at the close of the interwar era (January-May 1936 and August 1939-June 1940). He was forced out of office by the British in June 1940 because of presumed pro-Axis sentiments and was under house arrest from April 1942 until October 1944. He again headed a pro-Palace government in January-March 1952, after the king's dismissal of a Wafdist ministry. Partially because of his non-party status, Māhir was selected to serve as Prime Minister immediately after the military coup of July 1952. He was dismissed in September 1952 because of his opposition to agrarian reform, and died in Geneva on 24 August 1960.

Bibliography: A brief political biography is that of Rasẖwān Maḥmūd Djād Allāh, *ʿAlī Māhir*, Cairo 1987. His political approach is discussed in C. Tripp, *Ali Mahir and the politics of the Egyptian army, 1936-1942*, in idem (ed.), *Contemporary Egypt: through Egyptian eyes*, London 1993, 45-71. For his 1952 ministry, see J. Gordon, *Nasser's blessed movement. Egypt's Free Officers and the July Revolution*, New York 1992. (J. Jankowski)

MAḤKAMA.
4. xi. Algeria

When the French began their occupation of Algeria in 1830 there existed multiple legal traditions. The predominant Islamic tradition was the Mālikī one which had taken root in North Africa a thousand years earlier.

In the 10th/16th century, Algeria's Ottoman rulers had introduced the Ḥanafī tradition, which prevailed in the heartland of the empire. The Turkish military élite, and their offspring from marriages with local women, the *Ḳulugẖlīs* [see ḲUL-OGẖLU], tended to follow the Ḥanafī tradition. Appeals, and particularly difficult cases, might be referred to a *madjlis* or council of legal scholars.

In areas beyond firm Ottoman control, local traditions persisted. In the Mzāb [q.v.] oasis, some 500 km/250 miles south of Algiers, the Ibāḍī legal tradition [see IBĀḌIYYA] was applied. Immigrant Mzābī merchants in cities along the coast applied this tradition in their own internal matters. In the densely populated, Tamazigẖt-speaking Kabylia mountains, just to the south-east of Algiers, local customary law was applied.

Under French colonial rule, the mix of different

legal traditions was maintained, but Islamic and customary jurisdictions were gradually subordinated to the French courts. Areas of critical concern to the French, penal and commercial law, were annexed outright to the jurisdiction of French courts. Starting in the 1850s, the French sought to introduce their own principles of uniformity and hierarchy to the Muslim court system. In 1854, they instituted a standard, four-member *ma<u>dj</u>lis* as the court of appeal for all Islamic legal matters. The measure aroused opposition from settlers, and in some regions ran counter to traditions of negotiation over the size and composition of the *ma<u>dj</u>lis*. The *ma<u>dj</u>lis* was dismantled temporarily in 1859, revived in 1866, and permanently abolished in 1873, leaving French courts as the sole appeal jurisdiction.

In the 1850s and 1860s, the French promoted the reform of Islamic law by establishing a council of Muslim jurists to support change in areas of family law that either ran against humanitarian standards (the marriage of girls before they were capable of bearing children), or that seemed to run counter to scientific reason (the "sleeping baby" doctrine which held that a woman, abandoned for up to five years by her husband, might still produce his legitimate offspring). But as an autonomous institution at the national level, the council aroused the ire of French jurists and settlers and was soon dismantled. The French introduced an examination system for the selection of judicial personnel, and eventually required that all those entering the judiciary be graduates of one of three government-run provincial *madrasas*.

The most prominent urban Muslim spokesmen of this period were associated with the judicial system. These include al-Makkī Ibn Bādīs, long-time *ḳāḍī* of Constantine, and a forceful defender of the autonomy of the Muslim courts in the 1860s, and ʿAbd al-Ḳādir al-Ma<u>djdj</u>āwī, who made his career as a teacher in the law schools of Constantine and Algiers. Al-Ma<u>djdj</u>āwī was one of the first exponents of Islamic modernism in Algeria.

Though penal matters were early on entrusted to the French courts, colonial authorities concluded that they were not adequate to the task of maintaining order and that a more expeditious and severe form of justice was required. Thus was born in the 1870s the Code de l'Indigénat, a penal code administered by local French authorities. It focused on punishing the least hint of rebellious attitude on the part of Algerian Muslim subjects and on suppressing any action that might be construed as a threat to French economic interests. It was this aspect of French judicial policy, not only oppressive but also humiliating, that drew the most fire from the emerging nationalist movement starting in the 1920s.

In the early 20th century, Algeria-based French jurists with knowledge of Islamic law sought to produce a code of Islamic family law, known after its principal author as the Code Morand. Though the proposed code was published, it was never given official status. This was the result of opposition from powerful rural Muslim leaders, on whom the French leaned more and more for political support in the 1920s.

While the Muslim courts and law schools produced some outstanding figures in the period from the 1850s to 1914, they fell into eclipse after that time. With their jurisdiction restricted, the Muslim courts offered little prospect of reward for ambitious young men. Thus Malek Bennabi entered the court system in the mid-1920s but soon became disaffected. By 1930 he was studying at a technical school in Paris, launching what would be a career as one of Algeria's most original and prolific Islamic thinkers.

The turmoil of war in 1940-43 weakened French domination of Algeria. Two courses of action were possible for the French. One was to address Muslim grievances, including eliminating the Code de l'Indigénat. The other was severe repression, including the use of arbitrary detention, torture and execution. The period from 1943 to 1954 was one of competition between these tendencies. After the outbreak of revolution in November 1954, the repressive impulse quickly got the upper hand. It was this flouting of civilised legal standards, dramatically revealed by such incidents as the 1961 trial of Djamila Boupacha, that decisively eroded the French public's will to hold onto Algeria. But this severe repression also contributed to the development of a culture of extra-legal violence in Algeria that would dramatically resurface in the 1990s.

With independence in 1962, the new Algerian government's immediate concern was to restructure the court system so that it reflected the values of national unity and socialism. Toward this end, all Islamic and customary jurisdictions were absorbed into a unified national court system easily accessible to all citizens.

The next task was codification of law, beginning with the Penal Code, issued in 1966. An Economic Offences Ordinance, eventually incorporated into the code, upheld the socialist ideal of workers' participation and provided severe penalties to managers of state-run enterprises who let their own interests come before selfless dedication to the state. It also provided for the monopoly of the state in control of foreign trade and arranging contracts for the services of foreign enterprises. The notion that private individuals might serve as intermediaries was anathema in the socialist doctrines that guided these policies.

Even in areas where Islamic law might have appeared to have a clear-cut application, it was subordinated to the practical economic interests of the state, especially when they coincided with popular habit. Thus gambling on the state-run football pool was declared legal, while betting privately on horse races in France was not. Algerians were allowed to consume beer and wine produced by state-run enterprises. By the mid-1970s, the sale of alcohol was restricted by local authorities in those areas where there was strong public opposition.

Algeria had been independent for nearly a decade when the government finally began to deal with legal issues that were mainly cultural in character. As part of a larger campaign of Arabisation [see TAʿRĪB] launched by the Boumédienne régime in 1971, it was declared that court proceedings should be conducted in Arabic which, in practice, meant Algerian colloquial Arabic. By this time, the first law students whose training had been in Arabic graduated from the law school in Algiers. But as in many areas of the Algerian system, those with fluency in French, who tended to come from more affluent urban families, continued to have better opportunities. The question of opportunities in the court system for those proficient only in Arabic remained a smouldering issue that erupted in protests on Algerian campuses in 1976 in Constantine, and in 1980 in Algiers. The latter protests helped to launch an organised Islamist movement in Algeria, and resulted in President Chadeli's seeking to accommodate Arabic student grievances by intensifying the Arabisation of the judicial system.

This point also marks a change in orientation toward the task of codifying family law. Throughout the mid-1970s, the ideology of Algeria had been one of Islamic socialism, in which the interests of the state were paramount. Islam was given a place of honour, but this was still one subordinate to the state. This ideology was embedded in the National Charter, endorsed in a referendum in 1976. On family matters and the rights of women, the Charter pointed in a progressive direction, endorsing the principle of gender equality.

By the time intensive discussions of a family law code got under way in the early 1980s, the socialist emphasis of the charter was under attack from the emerging Islamist movement. But the debates were also shaped by economic questions, such as the acute shortage of urban housing—which made it costly to ensure the rights of a divorced wife—and the rapid growth in population. The Family Law Code finally passed in 1984 was a mix of conservative interpretations of Islamic law and the priorities of an embattled bureaucratic state facing the challenge of rapid population growth and high unemployment. Women were not protected against being married without their own freely-given consent, nor against being left economically helpless following divorce, nor against their husband deciding unilaterally to bring another wife into the household. Yet at the same time, in an effort to stem rapid population growth, the Code raised the minimum age of marriage to eighteen for women and twenty-one for men.

The late 1980s, rather like the 1940s, saw a relaxation of controls on political expression and the media. An important development in the legal realm was the founding of the Ligue Algérienne des Droits de l'Homme, founded in 1985 and given legal recognition in 1987. With the suppression of the Islamist opposition starting in 1992, many controls were restored and there was a resurgence of extra-legal violence on the part of both Islamic rebels and government forces. In dealing with the challenge of establishing clearly who was responsible for given violent incidents, the courts have often proved ineffective. Yet the glimmer of hope that they may occasionally rise to this challenge has sustained a small, dedicated group of Algerian human rights lawyers.

Bibliography: Simone de Beauvoir and Gisèle Halimi, *Djamila Boupacha*, Paris 1962; J.P. Charnay, *La vie musulmane en Algérie d'après la justice de la première moitié du vingtième siècle*, Paris 1965; A. Christelow, *Muslim law courts and the French colonial state in Algeria*, Princeton 1985; Hélène Vandevelde, *Le Code algérien de la famille*, in *Maghreb-Machrek*, cvii (janvier-mars 1985), 52-64; J. Entelis, *Algeria: the revolution institutionalized*, Boulder, Colo. 1986; Abu 'l-Ḳāsim Saʿd Allāh, *Taʾrīkh al-Djazāʾir al-thaḳāfī*, 8 vols., Beirut 1998; I. Taha, *L'indifference du droit algérien aux massacres*, in *An inquiry into the Algerian massacres*, Youcef Bedjaoui, Abbas Aroua and Meziane Aït-Larbi (eds.), Geneva 1999.

(A. Christelow)

4. xii. Tunisia

In the mid-19th century, Tunisia had a pluralist legal system. Although the respective spheres of competence and the various interrelations of the system's components were far from being clearly and strictly defined, the broad lines of its structures can be delineated as follows. There was a religious legal sphere covering matters of personal status and, in most cases, civil law, sc. a *sharʿī* jurisdiction for the Muslims (that of *ḳāḍīs*, Mālikī or Ḥanafī according to the defendant's rite, sitting as sole judges, plus *madjālis*, plural jurisdictions made up of *ḳāḍīs* and *muftīs*) and a rabbinical jurisdiction for the Jews. Alongside these was a jurisdiction of the central administration and its local agents, the *ḳāʾid*s [*q.v.*], who heard matters involving penal law and, in part, civil law. At the head of this structure was the Bey, the supreme authority according to the double principle of a delegated justice and one held in reserve. Disputes involving the representatives and subjects of foreign powers were the province of the consular courts [see imtiyāzāt].

In 1857 the Fundamental Pact (*ʿahd al-amān*), which proclaimed the equality of all subjects before the law, began a slow process of legal reform. Hence in 1861 there were promulgated at the same time a Constitution and a code of criminal and customary law (*ḳānūn al-djināyāt wa 'l-aḥkām al-ʿurfiyya*). The Constitution set up a hierarchic schema of new tribunals which were to be created within the entirety of the Regency. A tribunal for commercial cases organised under a code of commercial law had to be set up. However, although this last was actually promulgated on 1 April 1864, it could not be put into effect because of the outbreak of the rebellion in that year, which brought in its train the abrogation of the Constitution and the code of criminal and customary law. The idea of legal reform and codification was taken up again in the 1870s under the reformist Prime Minister Khayr al-Dīn (1822-90 [*q.v.*]), but without his efforts being fully accomplished.

In short, the modifications in the legal system attempted before the installation of the Protectorate were either of short duration or only touching upon the formal aspects of the existing legal jurisdictions. There was on one hand a reorganisation of the *sharʿī* jurisdiction at Tunis in 1856 and then in the interior of the Regency in 1876. Also, there were measures undertaken, notably between 1870 and 1873, to define more clearly the jurisdictions reserved to the central administration and its local representatives.

The installation of the French Protectorate in 1881 was to bring profound changes in the Tunisian legal system. By the Convention of La Marsa (1883), the Tunisian state undertook to "proceed to administrative, judicial and financial reforms as judged useful by the French government". In practice, French control over the beylical state was to be assured by the bias of the Resident-General as well as by the presence of French officials at all levels of the administration.

In the first place, following the doctrine of "double sovereignty", the protecting power undertook to install for its own nationals a French legal structure (law of 18 April 1883), comprising justices of the peace and courts of first instance; not till 1941 was an appeal court created. Furthermore, the French legal system thus installed was to replace, until 1884, the various consular jurisdictions of the European Powers. With the land law of 1885 there was set up a mixed court for land questions, an original jurisdiction (inspired by the Australian model) aimed at promoting the registration of land and buildings. This court, made up of a French president, with one-half French judges and the other half Tunisian judges, was at the same time to reduce the sphere of the *sharʿī* courts to embrace merely cases involving non-registered landed property.

Regarding the reform of justice dependent on the authority of the Tunisian state, apart from the regulation of the jurisdiction dependent on the central administration (the so-called *Ouzara* = *Wuzarāʾ*), whose competence was extended beyond the criminal law to all civil and commercial cases between Tunisians (except for personal status and matters connected with it), this was not really tackled till 1896, when an office for judicial affairs (*idārat al-umūr al-ʿadliyya*) was set up. At the same time regional courts of common law were created with an organisation modelled on that of the French courts of first instance. If the magistrates were Tunisians, they had nevertheless to be "assisted" from 1906 by "government commissioners" (French officials knowing Arabic). In 1921 a Commission of Pleas playing the role of an appeal court, as well as a Supreme Appeal Court and a criminal division with jurisdiction over the whole land, were installed at the side of the court of *Ouzara* in Tunis. Also in 1921 a real Ministry of Justice was created and the principle of delegated justice came formally to replace that of justice held by the Bey. Only the right of pardon was henceforth reserved to him. The year 1938 was marked by the multiplying of courts in the various counties of the land, with a wide sphere of competence largely replacing that of the *ḳāʾids*. From 1896, a commission was set up to prepare codifications based at one and the same time on French and on Muslim law and which were intended to become the laws applicable by the courts of common law. Codes of obligations and contracts (1906), of civil procedure (1910), of criminal law (1913), as well as for criminal procedure (1921) were successively promulgated. In certain spheres of economic life, French laws became directly applicable.

It was only much later that the *sharʿī* courts were remodelled. However, because of the reforms already in operation, their spheres of competence became reduced to cases of personal status and inheritance and also to those concerning family or private habous or *ḥubus* [see WAḲF. II. 3] and landed property which had not been registered. It was not till 1948 that a code of "procédure charaïque" governing the organisation and exact competence of these courts was set up. They then consisted of two *ḳāḍīs* and of two courts (*madjālis*) (for each of the two law schools, Ḥanafī and Mālikī) sitting in Tunis, with similar jurisdictions (with one or more judges) in the interior of the country where, however, the Ḥanafī law school was not represented. The demands by certain reformist circles seeking a more radical reform of the *maḥākim sharʿiyya*, as well as of the education system of the Zaytūna [*q.v.*], which trained future personnel for the legal system, were hardly taken into account by the Protectorate authorities.

A few months after the proclamation of independence in March 1956, the new Tunisian state issued a series of decrees aimed at reorganising and unifying the legal system. The jurisdiction of the *sharʿī* courts was transferred to the courts of common law and their members integrated within the framework of the state magistrature. In May 1956, the French commissioners attached to the Tunisian courts were relieved of their functions, and in March 1957 the Franco-Tunisian Legal Convention ended the French courts. In September 1957 it was the turn of the Rabbinical court to be suppressed.

After the installation of the republican régime in July 1957, Tunisia in 1959 acquired a Constitution which, in section IV devoted to legal powers, proclaimed notably the independence of judges and laid down that they should be appointed by presidential decree on the proposal of the Higher Council for Judges. The formal functioning of this unified and centralised legal system was embodied in Law no. 67-29 of 14 July 1967 concerning judicial organisation, the Higher Council for Judges and the position of the judiciary. This law fixed the Tunisian judicial hierarchy as follows: county courts, courts of first instance, a court for land questions, appeal courts and a supreme appeal court based at Tunis. Furthermore, alongside a High Court for cases of high treason, the 1959 Constitution equally made provision for an administrative court; this was effectively set up in 1974 and considerably reorganised in 1996.

In regard to the law applied by its courts, the Tunisian state undertook, from the time of independence onwards, to set up a new structure of national codifications. From among the legal texts dating from the colonial period, only the codes for obligations and contracts and the criminal code remained essentially in force. It is appropriate to mention that although the first article of the 1959 Tunisian Constitution made Islam the state religion, Islamic law does not appear amongst the formal sources of Tunisian law. Regarding the code of personal status, largely drawn from Islamic law, the legislating power showed a remarkable will for innovation, notably in abolishing polygamy, introducing judicial divorce and authorising adoption. However, an analysis of judicial practice in Tunisia has been able to show that there is a tendency amongst judges to refer, in certain cases, to non-codified Islamic law.

Bibliography: M. Bompard, *Législation de la Tunisie. Recueil des lois, décrets et règlements en vigeur dans la Régence de Tunis au 1er janvier 1888*, Paris 1888; A. Girault, *Principes de colonisation et la législation coloniale* (*V, L'Afrique du Nord: La Tunisie et le Maroc*), 5Paris 1928; L. Bercher, *L'organisation de la justice*, in *Initiation à la Tunisie*, Paris 1950, 270-80; J. Magnin, *Réformes juridiques en Tunisie*, in *IBLA*, xxi (1958), 77-92; R. Brunschvig, *Justice religieuse et justice laïque dans la Tunisie des Deys et des Beys jusqu'au milieu du XIXe siècle*, in 57, xxiii (1965), 27-70; G.S. van Krieken, *Khayr al-Din et la Tunisie (1850-1881)*, Leiden 1976; *Recueil des textes relatifs à l'organisation de la justice en Tunisie*, Tunis 1991; Muḥammad al-ʿAzīz Ibn ʿĀshūr, *Djāmiʿ al-Zaytūna, al-maʿlam wa-ridjāluhu*, Tunis 1991; Y. Ben Achour, *Politique, religion et droit dans le monde arabe*, Tunis 1992; M. Charfi, *Introduction à l'étude du droit*, 3Tunis 1997; E. Hélin, *La magistrature, de la marginalisation à la restructuration*, in *Monde arabe/Maghreb-Machrek*, clvii (1997), 40-6; S. Ben Nefissa, *Droit musulman, jurisprudence tunisienne et droit positif*, in *L'astrolabe*, ii (2000), 115-28.

(BETTINA DENNERLEIN and L. ROGLER)

5. The Indo-Pakistan subcontinent

After a century and a half of trade, the last few decades of which were characterised by increasing involvement in political intrigue and military adventurism—inspired initially by rivalry with European competitors (most particularly the French, with whom England was twice at war in the mid-18th century)—the East India Company emerged as a major political and military power in the subcontinent in the context of the disintegration of the Mughal empire into a collection of feuding regional powers. After the battle of Buxar (1764), which pitted the Company troops against the remnants of the Mughal army, the Company was in a position to conclude a treaty (*farmān* [*q.v.*]) with the titular head of the Mughal empire, Shāh ʿĀlam II [*q.v.*], who in 1765 ceded to the Company in perpetuity the *dīwānī* (civil and revenue administration) of three eastern provinces—Bengal, Bihar and Orissa—in exchange for an annual tribute of £260,000 (payment of which only continued until 1773). The Company thus became ruler of lands and peoples, ostensibly in the name of the emperor.

The modern period of judicial administration in South Asia commenced with the establishment by

Warren Hastings (Governor of Bengal, 1772-3; Governor-General of India, 1773-85) of courts serving the indigenous population of these three provinces; and the virtually simultaneous establishment by the Crown of a Supreme Court in Calcutta. Hastings' courts in the *mofussil* (the territory outside the seat of the Presidency, Ar. *mufaṣṣal* [*q.v.* in Suppl.] "separated") were creations of the East India Company. Hastings' plan—frequently revised during his own term, further modified by Lord Cornwallis (Governor-General, 1786-93), and cast by the latter in the Code of 1793—set the pattern for judicial administration in the territories subsequently acquired. Hastings proceeded to establish a *Dīwānī ʿAdālat* (civil court) and a *Fawdjdārī ʿAdālat* (criminal court) in each revenue district or Collectorship (the number of these courts was subsequently increased and their geographical jurisdiction decreased; courts subordinate to the *Dīwānī ʿAdālat* were also subsequently established). The Collector himself initially presided over the civil court; later judges were appointed from among the Company's covenanted civil servants. Indian Law Officers (Hindu *pundit*s and Muslim *mawlwī*s) were appointed to each *Dīwānī ʿAdālat* to expound the Hindu or Muslim law applicable to the case. The District Ḳāḍī and *Muftī* presided over the *Fawdjdārī ʿAdālat*, in which Muslim criminal law continued to be administered. Appeals from the *Dīwānī ʿAdālat*s lay to the *Ṣadr Dīwānī ʿAdālat* (chief civil court, initially comprised of the Governor-General and members of his Council), and, after 1781, to the King in Council. Appeals from the *Fauwdjdārī ʿAdālat* lay to the *Ṣadr Niẓāmat ʿAdālat*, initially headed by an appointee of the Niẓām.

The early bifurcation between civil and criminal jurisdiction derived from the terms of the 1765 grant, under which criminal jurisdiction remained with the representative of the Mug͟hal emperor. In 1790 criminal justice was (unilaterally) brought under the direct control of the Company; the *Fawdjdārī ʿAdālat*s were abolished and replaced by criminal courts, headed by covenanted servants of the Company, assisted by *ḳāḍī*s and *muftī*s. Although some of the rules of Muslim criminal law and evidence were gradually modified by government regulations, it was not until the Penal Code of 1860, the Code of Criminal Procedure, 1861, and the Evidence Act, 1872, that Muslim law in these respects was completely superseded. After 1790 the *Ṣadr Niẓāmat ʿAdālat* was comprised of the Governor-General and members of his Council, assisted by the Chief *Ḳāḍī* and two *muftī*s. In 1801 the Governor-General and his Council members were relieved of judicial responsibilities in both *Ṣadr ʿAdālat*s: the two appellate courts were united in a single *Ṣadr ʿAdālat* with civil and criminal sides, presided over by judges appointed from the ranks of the Company's covenanted servants.

In the Company settlements themselves, there had been courts established by royal charter since the Mayors' Courts of 1727. (Prior to this, what justice there was in the Company towns and factories was a very rough and ready, and often brutal, affair.) The Mayor's Court was a civil court of record, with compulsory jurisdiction only over Europeans to whom they applied English law; final appeal lay to the King in Council. (Although not compulsorily subject to the court, indigenous inhabitants might agree to such disposal of the dispute, in which case it would be adjudicated according to English law.) The Mayor's Court in Calcutta (the English town that had grown up around the Company's factory) was replaced by a Supreme Court, established by Royal Charter (1774) and Act of Parliament (1773, as amended in 1781 and 1784). The Supreme Court (after its jurisdiction had been more carefully defined by the latter acts) possessed civil jurisdiction over all British-born subjects and their descendants resident in the Bengal Presidency, and all persons residing in Calcutta, including its Indian inhabitants.

In Madras and Bombay, the Mayors' Courts were superseded in 1798 by Recorders' Courts, which possessed powers similar to those of the Supreme Court in Calcutta (and were subject to similar restrictions). The Recorder's Courts were upgraded to Supreme Courts in 1802 (Madras) and 1824 (Bombay). As these two Presidencies acquired *mofussil* territories—Bombay following the third Marāṭhā War (1818) [see MARĀṬHĀS]; Madras with the annexation of approximately half of Mysore after the defeat of Tīpū Sulṭān [*q.v.*] in 1799, followed by the annexation of the Carnatic—the establishment of *mofussil* courts in these territories followed the pattern of Hastings' plan as refined and codified by Cornwallis in 1793.

Bombay was in many ways unique. The island was ceded to the Crown by the Portuguese in 1661 and leased to the Company in 1668 on payment of £10 a year; the rights of the Company over Bombay thus derived from the British Crown, not from the Mug͟hal sovereign, or regional potentate, or military conquest. Further, the island of Bombay had, previous to being handed over to the English, been under Portuguese rule for over a century, and the territory conquered in 1818, was taken over not from Muslim but from Hindu rule; consequently, Muslim law did not enjoy in Bombay the pre-eminence that it did in Bengal and Madras. The Bombay *ʿAdālat* system underwent several changes and refinements until 1827, when all previous Regulations were repealed and replaced with a series of Regulations which came to be termed the Elphinstone Code. One of the interesting things contained in Elphinstone's Regulations was a Criminal Code for the Presidency, which was only superseded by the Indian Penal Code of 1860.

The dual system of courts—Royal Courts, whose judges were appointed by the Crown, in the Presidency headquarters (Calcutta, Bombay and Madras); and Company Courts, created by the East India Company and staffed by its officers, in the *mofussil*—persisted until, in the aftermath of the 1857-8 uprising, the Crown assumed all rights that the East India Company had acquired and exercised on Indian soil. One consequence was the integration of the Company and Crown courts and rationalisation of the judicial structure. In each presidency, the *Ṣadr* (appellate) Company Court was amalgamated with the Supreme Court to constitute a High Court.

Significantly, under the British—Company and Crown—there were not in South Asia separate religious courts for the religiously-derived personal laws; personal law of both Muslims and Hindus was administered as an integral part of their civil jurisdiction by both the *mofussil* civil courts and the Supreme Courts and, subsequently, the High Courts. Whether the litigation came before the Supreme Courts or the Company *mofussil* courts, the indigenous peoples of South Asia were guaranteed the application of their own system of personal law in a wide variety of civil matters. The phraseology of Hastings' formulation of 1772 and the Regulation of 1780 preserved to Muslims in the *mofussil* "the laws of the Koran" when the litigation concerned "inheritance, marriage, caste, and other religious usages and institutions". (The wording used in the Act defining the jurisdiction of the

Supreme Court was different but of similar import.) A Regulation of 1781 added "succession" to the topics concerning which the *mofussil* courts were to apply the personal law. The Regulation further provided that in the absence of statutory law, and in situations not covered by the earlier Regulation, the *mofussil* courts were to have recourse to "justice, equity and good conscience", with the result that the personal (Hindu or Muslim) law was often applied in matters other than those specifically enumerated. In essence, "justice, equity and good conscience" was used in numerous situations to render applicable the relevant personal law as the "proper law" of the contract or transaction; reference was to the law which the parties could be presumed to have expected would apply to the transaction. On the other hand, statutes took precedence over, and could and did oust, Muslim law. By the end of the 19th century, applicability of Muslim law was confined essentially to family law, inheritance and certain transfers of property. Even in these areas, the secular law made inroads; e.g. a Muslim father could be compelled by the magistrate to maintain his illegitimate child (a provision repealed in Pakistan in 1981); the apostate from Islam [see MURTADD] was not deprived of his share as an heir intestate (a provision repealed in West Pakistan in 1963).

Because the company officials appointed to judicial duties in the *mofussil* courts (and the barrister-judges of the Supreme Court) were not, at least initially, knowledgeable in the indigenous legal lore, Muslim Law Officers (*mawlwīs*) and Hindu Law Officers (*pundits*) were appointed to every civil court, original and appellate. These officers functioned, not as judges, but as resource personnel, to whom specific questions of law might be referred by the judge during the course of the proceedings before him. In order to displace the monopoly of specialised knowledge possessed by the Law Officers, work was undertaken to make authoritative source material directly available to lawyers and judges in English. The first Muslim text thus treated was the *Hidāya*, a 12th-century text by Burhān al-Dīn al-Marghīnānī [*q.v.*], translated by Charles Hamilton in 1791. This was followed in 1792 by William Jones' translation of the *Sirādjiyya*, together with an abstract of the *Sharīfiyya*; and by Neil Baillie's volumes on *Moohummadan law of inheritance* (1832) and *Moohummadan law of sale* (1850), the former an abridgement of the *Sirādjiyya* and *Sharīfiyya*, and the latter based on relevant chapters of the *Fatāwā-i-ʿĀlamgīrī* [see AL-FATĀWĀ AL-ʿĀLAMGĪRIYYA]. In 1865 appeared Neil Baillie's translation and abridgement of those portions of the *Fatāwā-i-ʿĀlamgīrī* likely to be relevant to litigation in India. This was followed in 1874 by Baillie's translation of the major Ithnā Ashʿarī Shīʿī text, the *Sharāʾiʿ al-Islām*. A collection of the questions submitted to Muslim Law Officers by judges of the Company Courts, together with their responses, was published by William Macnaghten in 1825 as the second part of his *Principles and precedents of Moohummudan law*. And toward the end of the century, Mahomed Yusoof, in his Tagore Law Lectures, 1891-2, translated the portions of the *Fatāwā-i-Ḳāḍī Khān* [see ḲĀḌĪ KHĀN] dealing with marriage and divorce. It was not until 1914 that E.C. Howard's English translation of the Shāfiʿī text *Minhaj et-talibin*, prepared for administrators and judges in Southeast Asia, became available. Textbooks and compilations by Indian scholars and scholars of Indian law also appeared. Ameer Ali's two volume work was first published in 1880 and 1884; Roland Knyvet Wilson's *Introduction* and *Digest* in 1894 and 1895, respectively. The first edition of Dinshah Fardunji Mulla's *Principles of Muhammadan law* was dated 1906; the first edition of Tyabji's learned tome, 1913. Meanwhile, systematic reporting of legal decisions of the High Courts, Judicial Commissioners' Courts and Chief Courts began in 1876 (under a statute of the previous year). The availability of published decisions enhanced the role of judicial precedent: a decision on a point of law by the Privy Council was binding on all British Indian Courts; and a decision of the High Court was binding on the subordinate Presidency Courts.

As part of the judicial reorganisation in the 1860s, the posts of Hindu and Muslim Law Officers were abolished; judges themselves, assisted by the lawyers appearing before them, were deemed capable of dealing with questions of Muslim and Hindu law, which continued to be dealt with as integral components of the civil jurisdiction. By the turn of the 20th century, virtually every superior provincial court of a province with a significant Muslim population had a Muslim among its sitting judges; the first two such High Court appointments were those of Justice Mahmood (son of Sir Syed Ahmed Khan [see AḤMAD KHAN]) to the Allahabad High Court in 1887, and Ameer Ali [see AMĪR ʿALĪ], appointed to the Calcutta High Court in 1890. From 1909 a series of distinguished Indian jurists sat on the Judicial Committee of the Privy Council (the ultimate court of appeal prior to independence and the establishment of national Supreme Courts); Ameer Ali, the first (and the only Muslim) Indian Privy Councillor, served from 1909 until his death in 1928.

Extremely significant is the fact that to this date Muslim law remains virtually entirely uncodified; this contrasts not only with the massive codification of Hindu law undertaken by India in the first decade of Independence, but also with the general trend in the Muslim world. (Major exceptions are the Dissolution of Muslim Marriages Act, 1939; the Pakistan Muslim Family Laws Ordinance, 1961; and the Indian Muslim Women [Protection of Rights on Divorce] Act, 1986.) Being uncodified, Muslim law is amenable to interpretation and/or reinterpretation by the court. This occurred during the British period, as in decisions holding that the post-pubescent Shāfiʿī girl could not be contracted in marriage without her permission; and that the pre-pubescent Ḥanafī girl contracted in marriage as a minor by a guardian other than father or paternal grandfather could extra-judicially renounce the marriage on attainment of puberty. (Incidentally, it was Ameer Ali who had proposed, in his *Mahomedan law*, the interpretation of Shāfiʿī and Mālikī law that was adopted by the courts in the former instance; and it was the same individual, in his capacity of judge of the Calcutta High Court, who delivered the decision establishing the point in the latter instance.) In the first decades of Independence, the new State of Pakistan appeared committed to a policy of *idjtihād*, as exemplified by the dramatic decisions, endorsed by the Supreme Court of Pakistan, holding that, within the Ḥanafī *madhhab*, wives are legally entitled to recover arrears of maintenance (1972); and that a Muslim woman is entitled to a judicial dissolution of her marriage (in spite of her husband's objection) merely on the ground that she finds the situation intolerable, provided that she is willing to return or forego her *mahr* [*q.v.*] and other "benefits" she may have received from her husband (1967).

Although the documents of the late 18th century reflect an assumption that "the laws of the Koran" constitute a single entity to which all Muslims owe allegiance, Muslim law is not a unified entity even at the textual level. The overwhelming proportion of South Asian Muslims are Ḥanafī Sunnīs, but on the southwestern coast of the subcontinent another Sunnī school, the Shāfiʿī, is locally significant. More important in British India was Shīʿism (brought to the subcontinent by the Persians), which had a considerable following, particularly in Oudh (annexed by the British in 1856 [see AWADH]). In spite of fact that since the mid-18th century the Nawāb Wazīr of Oudh had been a Shīʿī, Sunnī law, as the law of the Mughal empire, applied in the territory until 1847, when (three decades after the Oudh dynasty had assumed the title of "King," and nine years prior to the annexation of Oudh by the British) a Shīʿī *muftī* was appointed, and (Ithnā ʿAsharī) Shīʿī law began to be applied to Shīʿīs within the kingdom. Ironically, Shīʿī law was recognised by the Privy Council as the law applicable to Shīʿīs in British India six years before it was recognised by the indigenous government of the Oudh Kingdom; and by the Bengal *Ṣadr ʿAdālat* more than three decades before the matter reached the Privy Council. However, given the numerical prominence of the Ḥanafīs, the assumption of the South Asian courts is that a person, if a Muslim, is a Ḥanafī Sunnī; consequently, the term "Muslim law" or "Islamic law" as used in judicial decisions is usually synonymous with "Ḥanafī Sunnī law". The burden is on the person claiming to be a follower of a another Muslim school or sect to plead and establish this fact. Similarly, once it is established that a party is a Shīʿī, the assumption is that he is a member of the major sect, Ithnā ʿAsharī. Information on the law of the minority Shīʿī sect, the Ismāʿīlīs, is much less readily available, although a significant difference that was of some importance during the British period (and overlooked by the Privy Council in an 1890 case) is that the Ismāʿīlīs do not discriminate against the childless widow in matters of inheritance in the same way that Ithnā ʿAsharīs do. It was not until 1969 that Professor A.A.A. Fyzee published his *Compendium of Fatimid law*. The terms "Shīʿī" and "Shīʿī law" as used in South Asian judicial decisions are synonymous with "Ithnā ʿAsharī" and "Ithnā ʿAsharī law".

Textual Muslim law, of course, does not recognise customs in derogation of the law; but rural agrarian communities, particularly in North India, did. Customary law, applicable to Muslim (and Hindu) agrarian families in vast regions of the north-west (particularly the Punjab, the heartland of customary law and a province which was under Sikh, not Muslim, rule before conquered by the British in 1849) was essentially a retention and continuation of their pre-existing practices in "secular" matters, particularly succession and dealings with property, by converts to Islam (and their descendants); even those Muslim tribes—e.g. Pathans—who claimed to be descended from Muslim invaders had long ago fallen into line with the local practices. At the same time, these local practices were not consistent with Hindu law (and may well have predated the formal statement of Mitakshara Hindu law). Most of these people never had observed or been subject to Muslim law (or orthodox Hindu law), knew little if anything about it, were quite happy with the way things had always been managed in regard to succession and property and saw no reason to change—at least until well into the 20th century, when religious revivalists and political leaders trying to define a Muslim constituency and organise a Muslim political movement attempted to convince them to change, and eventually legislation in the new Muslim state forced them to submit to a new legal order.

Also problematic were communities whose ancestors had converted from Hinduism to Islam but retained many of their Hindu practices. Both Hinduism and Islam purport to govern more than an individual's religious devotion; both lay down rules concerning marriage, divorce, and other domestic concerns, as well as more "secular" matters, most importantly dealings with property and inter-generational transmission of property. Individuals and communities who converted to the faith of Islam from Hinduism not infrequently continued Hindu patterns of property holding and transmission: matters which may have struck them as having little to do with religious profession, and matters which the ancient practice managed entirely to their satisfaction. Such a course was undoubtedly facilitated by the fact that Ṣūfīs, who were responsible for much conversion to Islam in South Asia, were not particularly concerned with mundane things like worldly property and its inter-generational transmission. Prominent examples of groups which adopted Islam as a religion but continued their former Hindu practices were two commercial groups from western India, the Khōdjas and the Menons; both were judicially held amenable to Hindu law in regard to matters of inheritance in the mid-19th century. Further, an individual family (perhaps connected with or seeking favour from the Mughal court) might convert for political reasons, while at the same time continuing their previous practices concerning property dealing and succession. Other individuals or groups, most prominently exemplified by the Hindustani Kayasthas, who performed important roles in the Mughal administration, adopted many outward Muslim observances and customs (e.g. of dress, language, literature, and even burial) without converting; they remained Hindus by religion and followed Hindu law (although depreciated by their co-religionists as "half-Mussalmans").

Distinct both from those subject to agrarian custom in North India and from groups or families who converted from Hinduism without changing their practices (particularly concerning inheritance and property dealings) to conform to Muslim law were those aristocratic Muslim landowning families who, although unambiguously subject to Muslim law, observed "family customs" designed to keep the landed estate intact and/or control its devolution (e.g. primogeniture, exclusion of female heirs, appointment of an heir).

As the importance of "custom"—or behaviour and practices inconsistent with the religious affiliation of the parties—become more apparent, it was explicitly recognised in statutes governing the subsequently established courts, and in practice by all the courts. The burden of proving a custom in derogation of the (otherwise applicable) personal law was on the person pleading custom. To be accepted as a rule of law, a custom had to be ancient, certain, reasonable, and neither repugnant to morality or public policy nor contrary to any statutory law. It was usually sufficient to establish that the custom had been regularly and consistently observed in the family, tribe or locality for at least fifty years. Once judicially recognised, custom could not be altered by anything short of legislation.

One of the indirect (and doubtless unintended) effects of British policy in India was that anomalous communities and families became more aware of and conscious of their status and often moved to identify more closely with one or other orthodox tradition. The pressure to identify with one of the two great communities became more intense with the advent of rudimentary democratic institutions and the prospect of eventual self-government in which numbers would count. Both sides launched missionary activities; in addition to seeking fresh converts, the Muslim *tablīgh* movement [see TABLĪG͟HĪ DJAMĀʿAT] attempted to complete the conversion process in the case of anomalous communities and to induce groups following practices and customs inconsistent with the true faith to renounce such customs; the Hindu *shuddi* movement (launched by the reformist Arya Samaj) sought to "reclaim" descendants of former converts to Islam to the true faith of their more ancient ancestors.

In 1937, Muslim political leaders managed to secure enactment of the Muslim Personal Law (Shariat) Application Act, which substituted Muslim law as the rule of decision in preference to custom previously applicable, either by virtue of regulations specifically recognising custom and usage as the governing rule, or by virtue of the "justice, equity, and good conscience" clause. At the same time, the terms of this very statute demonstrate the importance of custom to a particular class of Muslims: the Muslim families of northern India holding large estates and frequently claiming aristocratic descent, whose support was essential to the Muslim League, insisted on being able to retain the control of the inter-generation transmission of family property—a right which "family custom" often guaranteed and Muslim law largely negated. It was at the insistence of this particular class that the Shariat Application Act, 1937, did not compulsorily cover either adoption (i.e. appointment of an heir) or testamentary disposition of property. By a fortuitous circumstance, however, the rural landlords were totally exempt from the terms of the Act as far as their agricultural land was concerned. The Government of India Act, 1935, had come into effect before the Bill which became the Act of 1937 was actually passed. Under the scheme of the Government of India Act, succession to agricultural land was a topic exclusively within the legislative competence of the provinces and the Central Legislature could not deal with it. (The 1937 statute did, of course, cover non-agriculture property and e.g. brought the urban property of the K͟hōdjas and Menons under the rule of Muslim law, as far as intestate succession was concerned.)

(West) Pakistan acted shortly after independence totally to negate custom as a rule of law applicable to Muslims, affirming in its stead Muslim law (of the appropriate sect). Several Indian states have passed supplementary legislation amending the 1937 Act to cover succession to agricultural land. The scope for the application of rules of custom to Muslims has considerably decreased in South Asia and has been totally ousted in Pakistan.

The new States of the subcontinent inherited, and very largely retained, the judicial structure as developed during the British period (with obvious exceptions; e.g. the ultimate court of appeal is no longer the Privy Council and High Court judges are not appointed by London), as well as procedural law and the major statutes enacted during the previous era. In every province a High Court sits at the apex of a hierarchy of subordinate civil and criminal courts, with ultimate appeal to the national Supreme Court. The most important post-Independence administrative development in regard to disputes to which Muslim law is applicable has been the introduction in each of the three countries of South Asia of special Family Courts with exclusive jurisdiction in regard to certain areas of matrimonial and family litigation. Pakistan took the lead with the (West Pakistan) Family Courts Act, 1964; India followed two decades later, 1984; and Bangladesh in 1985. Simplified and less formal procedures, designed to expedite the litigation, govern proceedings in the Family Courts, particularly in Pakistan and Bangladesh; and the rigorous requirements of the Evidence Act, 1908, have been mitigated in family litigation in India and Bangladesh. Although the Bangladesh statute itself declared all Munṣif's Courts (civil courts subordinate to the District Court) to be Family Courts and all Munṣifs to be Family Court Judges, and Pakistan had within two years appointed judges to function as Family Courts throughout the country, the Indian legislation only mandated Family Courts for urban areas of population one million or more, and implementation has proceeded slowly.

In Pakistan, General Zia-ul-Haq [see ZIYĀʾ AL-ḤAḲḲ], having seized power in July 1977 with the promise of elections within 90 days, justified holding power for eleven years (until his mysterious death in 1988) in the name of "Islamisation". His patronage of the Islamists—to whom he increasingly looked as providing some sort of "constituency" and creating the appearance of at least some popular support for his government, and whom he brought into a political prominence they had not previously enjoyed—received a tremendous international boast with the Soviet invasion of Afghanistan (1979) and United States' support of the "*mujahideen*" opposition. Money and arms poured into the region; thousands of *madrasas*, many of them training schools for Islamic warriors, sprang up in Pakistan. The Russians withdrew a decade later; the U.S. lost interest; and Afghanistan descended into civil war, which Pakistan thought it could control to its advantage.

The Zia era left his successors with a heady legacy, including the continuing fall-out of involvement in Afghanistan in the form of weapons, drugs, refugees and Islamic militants. Institutionally, the Zia legacy is represented by the Shariat Courts, created in 1978. These special courts possess jurisdiction to examine the Islamic vires of "any law", and if such law is found contrary to the "Injunctions of Islam, as laid down in the Holy Quran and the Sunnah of the Holy Prophet," to strike it from the statute book. Most recently this jurisdiction has been exercised (23 December 1999) to order that interest in all forms be abolished in Pakistan by June 2001; and (5 January 2000) to strike down many of the reforms achieved four decades previously by the Muslim Family Laws Ordinance 1961. (The Shariat Bench of the Supreme Court, affirming the 1991 decision of the Federal Shariat Court on *ribā*, set 30 June 2001 as the deadline for the conversion to a *ribā*-free system. On 15 June 2001, the same court extended the deadline by twelve months. The decision of the Federal Shariat Court on the various provisions of the Muslim Family Laws Ordinance has been stayed pending an appeal to the Shariat Bench of the Supreme Court, which may not be heard for some time, and which will probably not fully endorse the position of the Federal Shariat Court. For a concise introduction to and assessment of the *ribā* decision, see the booklet *Moving toward an Islamic financial regime in Pakistan* by P. Hassan and A. Azfar, available at www.law.harvard.edu/programs/ilsp/publications.html.). In terms of substantive law, Zia's program of "Islamisation" resulted in the promulgation in 1979 of the four *ḥudūd* ordinances (including the draconian *Zinā* Ordinance), introducing into Pakistan law the criminal offences (illicit intercourse, false imputation of unchastity, theft and consumption of alcohol), together with their respective punishments, defined in the *sharīʿa*; imposition (1980) of *zakāt* and *ʿushr* levies; promulgation (1982) of a blasphemy ordinance (defining an offence which carries a mandatory death sentence); repeal (1981) of the provision of the Criminal Procedure Code granting the illegitimate child a right to maintenance from his/her putative father; and the provisions in Pakistan's new Evidence Order (1984) which reintroduced the two-year period of gestation recognised by classical Ḥanafī jurists and devalued the evidence of women.

Other dimensions of the Zia legacy are the enhanced politicisation of Islam and a dramatic increase in sectarian violence, between one sect or community of Islam and another, as well as between Islamists and non-Muslims (including Aḥmadīs, who were constitutionally defined as non-Muslims by Zulfikar Ali Bhutto's government in 1974). Religion is opportunistically invoked by each of the major parties; implementation of the *Sharīʿa* is held forth as a panacea for the serious problems facing the country, and not merely by the Islamic parties on the fringe of electoral politics. The 15th Constitutional Amendment Bill, as projected by Nawaz Sharif during his second (and abruptly terminated) tenure as Prime Minister (1997-9), would have somehow ushered in an era of communal peace and social justice; ended corruption, maladministration, police excesses, judicial delays and economic problems, and would have created an "Islamic welfare state". Significantly watered down before being passed by the National Assembly (in which the Prime Minister had a comfortable and tame majority), the Bill declared the "Holy Quran and Sunnah of the Holy Prophet" to be the supreme law of Pakistan, above the Constitution itself and beyond the reach of judicial decrees, and it obliged the federal government "to take steps to enforce the Shariah, to establish *salat*, to administer *zakat*, to promote *amr bil maroof* and *nahi anil munkar* (to prescribe what is right and to forbid what is wrong), to eradicate corruption at all levels and to provide substantial socio-economic justice in accordance with the principles of Islam, as laid down in the Holy Quran and Sunnah." An unambiguous commitment to theocracy—but with all the relevant terms left undefined. The urban industrialist, the Prime Minister elected with a "heavy mandate" (because of low voter turnout as disillusioned Pakistan Peoples' Party cadres stayed at home) appropriated a page out of Zia's handbook in an attempt to consolidate power absolutely in his hands, without comprehending that it was a Pandora's box which he proposed to open. The Bill was pending before the Senate (where the Prime Minister had not yet mustered the requisite votes) at the time of the military take-over.

On 12 October 1999—after an eleven-year post-Zia interregnum, which had seen four civilian governments elected, and three of them prematurely (and constitutionally) removed—General Pervez Musharraf removed the fourth in a bloodless coup. The General appears to be following the same path as his predecessor, General Zia-ul-Haq. Banning political activities has created a vacuum which the Islamists (who have consistently failed dismally in electoral contests) are anxious to fill. At the same time, many of the announced intentions of General Musharraf (who initially expressed his admiration for Kemal Ataturk)—de-weaponising society, modernising the curriculum in *madrasas*, amending the blasphemy law, restoring the joint electorate and improving the human rights record—have floundered in the face of opposition from Islamists, and sectarian violence continues unabated.

In India, although the first decade of Independence saw the massive reform and codification of Hindu family law, nothing at all has been done in terms of reforming Muslim law and improving the position of Indian Muslim women. Pakistan's Ordinance of 1961—which, *inter alia*, requires that prior permission should be obtained for a polygamous marriage; renders all *ṭalāḳ* pronouncements (even the triple pronouncement) revocable; and denies legal effectiveness to any *ṭalāḳ* until a period of three months had passed following notification of the *ṭalāḳ* to a local official, who is to use the intervening time to attempt reconciliation—had no echoes in the neighbour to the south. The Congress party, which ruled India without interruption for its first thirty years (including seventeen years under Jawaharlal Nehru and eleven years under his daughter Indira Gandhi), was committed to secularism and democracy but was also pleased to have the Muslim "vote bank" securely on its side. When Mrs. Gandhi was assassinated in 1984, the Congress mantle passed to her son Rajiv Gandhi. It was on his watch (1986) that the (misnamed) Muslim Women (Protection of Rights on Divorce) Act was rushed through Parliament, over objections of his own Congress parliamentarians and by virtue of a three-line whip. The Act of 1986 reversed the (1985) *Shah Bano* judgment and deprived destitute divorced Muslim women (simply on the basis of their religious identity) of the minimal succour that section 125 of the (secular) Criminal Procedure Code, 1974, afforded to all such women. A harsh blow was struck against secularism (and against women). The dynastic link was broken with Rajiv's assassination in 1991 and—rudderless, faction-ridden, and tainted with scandal—the Congress party lost much of its appeal. The gathering clouds of Hindu activism, demanding an end to a policy of appeasement of minorities and emphatic affirmation of the Hindu-ness of India, broke over the North India city of Ayodhya when in 1992 the 16th-century Babri mosque was destroyed by a mob of Hindu militants, setting off a wave of Hindu-Muslim violence across the country. The Bhartiya Janata Party (BJP), with its "Hinduvta" (Hindu-ness) philosophy and agenda, rose to prominence on the rubble of the Babri mosque and emerged as the largest parliamentary party in the national elections of 1996, 1998, and again in 1999. A centre-left coalition (the United Front) managed to bring down the BJP government after only thirteen days in office in 1996, but itself fell seventeen months later. The BJP is the dominant member of the coalition (National Democratic Alliance) which has governed India since 1998. Although the exigencies of coalition require some dilution of the Hinduvta program, India under the BJP (1998 to the present) has seen a disconcerting amount of rhetoric and violence directed against religious minorities, Muslim and Christian.

In both countries, pseudo-revisionist historiography has subjected the discipline of scholarship to the service of cultural myth-making and political indoctrination.

Bibliography: 1. Works that are essentially translations of texts and of importance to the South Asian courts as repositories of the classical law. *The Hedaya*, tr. C. Hamilton, London 1791, 4 vols.; N.B.E. Baillie, *Moohummadan law of inheritance according to Aboo Huneefa and his followers* (abridgement of the *Siradjiyya* and *Sharifiyya*), 1832; idem, *Moohummadan law of sale*, (tr. of relevant chapters of the *Fatāwā-i-Ālamgīrī*), 1850; idem, *A digest of Moohummadan law. Part first: The doctrines of the Hanefea code of jurisprudence* (tr. and abridgement of those portions of the *Fatāwā-i ʿĀlamgīrī* likely to be relevant to litigation in India), 1865, [2]London 1875 (Reprints of the 2nd ed. are available, but must be used with caution. E.g., when the Premier Book House (Lahore) reprinted Baillie's Part I (the Ḥanafī *Fatāwā-i-ʿĀlamgīrī* and Part II (the Ithnā ʿAsharī *Sharāʾiʿ al-Islām*), pages from one were intermixed with the other, see e.g. pp. 73-80 of the 1974 reprint of Baillie I; these pages are from the Baillie II and represent Ithnā ʿAsharī, not Ḥanafī, law); A. Rumsey, *Al-Sirajiyyah on the Mahommedan law of inheritance* (repr. of Sir William Jones' 1792 translation of the *Sirādjiyya* and *Sharīfiyya*, with notes), Calcutta 1869, [2]1890; *The Hedaya*, tr. Charles Hamilton; ed. Standish Grady, 1870. (More convenient than the 1791 edition because comprising only one volume; reduction largely achieved by tighter, smaller print and the elimination of wide page margins, etc.; however, a few discussions have been omitted, including slavery (irrelevant in British India after slavery had been abolished in 1843) and much criminal law (irrelevant in British India after the Penal Code of 1860), but also including apostasy.) Reprints of this edition are readily available but must be used with caution; typographical errors in these reprints include not only numerous (and usually obvious) misspellings of individual words but also the occasional (and not always obvious) omission of a few lines, giving those lines remaining a totally different (and erroneous) meaning. Curiously, the same errors appear in the various reprints, regardless of date and publisher.; N.B.E. Baillie, *A digest of Moohummadan law. Part second: The doctrines of the Imameea Code of jurisprudence* (tr. essentially of major Ithnā ʿAsharī text, the *Sharāʾiʿ al-Islām*), 1874, [2]London 1887 (Reprints available, but see the entry under "Baillie 1865" for a word of caution.); Mahomed Yusoof Khan Bahadur, *Fatawa-i-Kazee Khan* (tr. of portions dealing with marriage and divorce), 1891-2, 3 vols. (Reprint, in which the first two volumes appear as volume I and volume 3 appears as volume 2, available.); E.C. Howard, *Minhaj et talibin. A manual of Muhammadan law according to the school of Shafii*, tr. into English from the French ed. by L.W.C. Van den Berg, London 1914; A.A.A. Fyzee, *Compendium of Fatimid law*, Simla 1969. (This text, edited by Fyzee in 2 vols., was published in Arabic in Cairo in 1951 and 1961.)

2. Works on Muslim law and its administration in South Asia. W.H. Macnaghten, *Principles and precedents of Moohummudan law*, 1825, [2]1870; W.H. Morley, *The administration of justice in British India*, London 1858; W.H. Rattigan, *A digest of civil law for the Punjab, chiefly based on the customary law as at present judicially ascertained*, Allahabad 1880 [6]1901; Ameer Ali, *Personal law of the Mahomedans* (later *Mahomedan Law*, vol. ii), London 1880; *Mahomedan Law*, vol. i, 1884. (Subsequent editions are available; fortunately, those appearing after 1928 have disturbed the author's text minimally.); R.K. Wilson, *An introduction to the study of Anglo-Muhammadan law*, London 1894; idem, *A digest of Anglo-Muhammadan law*, London 1895; Faiz Badruddin Tyabji, *Muslim law*, Bombay 1913, [4]1964; Mahabir Prasad Jain, *Outlines of Indian legal history*, New Delhi 1952, [5]1990; J.N. Hollister, *The Shia of India*, London 1953, repr. Delhi 1979; Tahir Mahood, *Muslim personal law. The role of the state in the Indian subcontinent*, New Delhi 1977, [2]1983; Lucy Caroll, *Muslim family law in South Asia. The right to avoid an arranged marriage contracted during minority*, in *Jnal. of the Indian Law Institute*, xxiii (1981), 149-80; eadem, *Nizam-i Islam. Processes and conflicts in Pakistan's programme of Islamisation, with special reference to the position of women*, in *Jnal. of Commonwealth and Comparative Politics*, xx (1982), 57-95; eadem, *The Muslim Women (Protection of Rights on Divorce) Act, 1986: a retrogressive precedent of dubious constitutionality*, in *Jnal. of the Indian Law Institute*, xxviii (1986), 364-76; eadem, *Marriage-guardiandship and minor's marriage in Islamic law*, in *Islamic and Comparative Law Quarterly*, vii (1987), 279-99; eadem, *Application of the Islamic law of succession: was the propositus a Sunni or a Shia?*, in *ILS*, ii (1995), 24-42; eadem, Qur'an 2:229: *"A charter granted to the wife"? Judicial khulʿ in Pakistan*, in *ibid.*, iii (1996), 91-126. (Lucy Carroll)

7. Singapore, Malaysia and Brunei

These three states share a common history of British colonial control. Colonial legal policy was founded on the principle that English law was the law of general application to all subjects. However, where the "religions, manners and customs" of the subject populations were concerned, an exception might be made consonant with (English notions of) "equity, justice and good conscience". This principle was established in 1781 in India and carried through into the Malayan possessions. The results for Islam was the development of a hybrid "Anglo-Muhammadan" law which had and still has family law and trusts as its area of jurisdiction. It was not until after the Second World War, and approaching independence, that any real effort was made to establish a separate Islamic court system. Prior to this time, the *syariah* (*sharīʿa* [*q.v.*]) or the English law version of *syariah* was a matter for the general courts. The colonial policy legacy remains important both for substantive law and for the structure of the contemporary *maḥkama* in each of the three states.

i. Singapore

The first religious court (Syariah Court) was formally established in 1957 under the Muslims Ordinance of that year. At this time, Singapore was still a Crown Colony and the main motive for the court's foundation was to attempt control over the very high divorce rates among Singaporean Muslims. For this reason, its jurisdiction was restricted to marriage, divorce, nullity of marriage, judicial separation, division of property on divorce, and maintenance. While the basic causes of action in these matters remain as in the *syariah*, the particular form in which they are put in the statute is derived from English law. The *syariah* has been reformulated. Further provisions in the statute reinforce this position. The language of the court could be English, professional advocates might appear, the laws on evidence were English, powers to compel attendance were the same as those applicable in the secular Magistrates Court, precedent was wholly English and the qualifications and appointment of judges was established by the Governor. Appeals lay to an Appeals Board over which the Governor exercised a general power of revision. Most important, the Ordinance did not exclude the overriding jurisdiction of the secular High Court. In a series of cases from the late 1950s, the High Court did not hesitate to overturn or amend Syariah Court decisions. There were severe criticisms of Syariah

Court procedure, lack of record keeping and misunderstanding of the rules of evidence. While justified, such criticisms could also be seen as somewhat unfair given that the *ḳāḍīs* were not formally trained in English law.

The Ordinance was replaced in 1966 by the Administration of Muslim Law Act which repeats and elaborates the 1957 Ordinance. The same subjects on family law are included and the 1966 Act, with later amendments, remains the law for Muslims in Singapore today. However, Singapore also has the "Women's Charter" of 1961. This is an Act intended to set out the law for marriage, divorce, guardianship and maintenance. It is essentially a copy of English matrimonial laws of the late 1950s, and thus does not sit all that well with the version of *syariah* which the Syariah Court in Singapore is supposed to administer. By copying an English statute, the government of Singapore had also imported all other English legislation on family laws, for example, the laws on maintenance, guardianship, matrimonial property and so on. The Syariah Court has been placed in an impossible position. On the one hand, it is constrained by statute, and on the other it is obliged to apply "Islamic" law. It is the definition of "Islamic" law which is the difficulty. It now means four things. (a) The Anglo-Muhammadan laws derived from British Indian precedent and elaborated in the colonial period. Textbooks of these laws remain authorities for the secular courts. (b) The classical textbooks of the Shāfiʿī school which are the primary reference for the Singaporean *ḳāḍī*. (c) The regulations made under the 1966 Act which are binding on the *ḳāḍī*. (d) The decisions of the *ḳāḍī* reported and followed by later *ḳāḍīs*—that is, a precedent. It is this last (d) which is likely to determine the future of the Syariah Court. While the *ḳāḍīs* derive their decisions from the classical texts (see (a) above), they also follow the earlier *ḳāḍīs* in an organised way through law reporting and analysis of the earlier judgements. In short, there is now a Muslim internal reformulation of *syariah* within the Syariah Court. While the substance of a rule may be *fiḳh*, the legal reasoning as to what it means and its application is English. This should occasion little surprise. Most if not all members of the Appeal Board have an English or English-derived legal education. For them, recourse to a precedent is perfectly normal. The fact that the structure and precedent of the court is English-derived merely reinforces this position. In extreme cases, the *syariah* presence is confined to quotations from the Ḳurʾān, not infrequently irrelevant. The result is an eclecticism of source of law in both the court and at the Appeal Board level. For example, a survey of recent Appeal Board decisions (1988-95) has shown recourse to (i) English principles of statutory interpretation, (ii) Anglo-Muhammadan rules from British India, (iii) citation from the Ḳurʾān, (iv) administrative rules on registration of marriage and divorce, and (v) earlier Syariah Court precedent. There is nothing from *fiḳh* as such; the whole complex is English. Even the *sūras* cited are not decisive but seem to be put in so as to provide "Islamic" colouring to a method of reasoning which is wholly outside the canons of Muslim jurisprudence. This is not to say that *fiḳh* does not play a part, at least at the lower level. It does, but increasingly now in a secularised form. At the Appeal Board level, however, the secularised form is dominant.

This state of affairs should come as no surprise. The intention of the Singaporean legislation was and is to control the family law of Muslims. This means that it has to approximate the secular family laws as closely as possible, consonant with the religion of Islam. The colonial legislation showed how this could be done. The Syariah Court, therefore, is limited in its function and jurisdiction and is ultimately answerable to the Supreme Court of Singapore which will apply an Anglo-Syariah law.

ii. Malaysia

This state [see MALAYSIA] is a Federation and under the Constitution (1957 and amendments), Islam is a state matter, not a federal matter. The result is that each of the states in the Federation has its own "Islamic" (or "Muslim") law legislation. However, the Malaysian Constitution also says (Art. 3) that "Islam is the religion of the Federation". Unlike Singapore, therefore, Islam has a constitutional presence at both the federal and state level in Malaysia and this has important implications for both the structure and jurisdiction of the Syariah Courts.

(a) A note of caution is necessary about structure. While all the states of the Federation have a Syariah Court with the same general structure, this does not mean that the courts have precisely the same jurisdiction. Details vary from state to state. To be fully informed, one must therefore reach each state enactment. The following description is taken from the Federal Territory Administration of Islamic Law Act, 1993, something of an exemplar Act for Malaysian Islam. Part IV (§§ 40-57) establishes a three-tier system, consisting of Syariah Subordinate Court, High Court and Appeal Court. The Appeal Court is headed by the Chief Syariah Judge who must be a citizen and who has had ten years Syariah Court experience, or "is a person learned in Islamic law". This last qualification is undefined. A quorum for the court is the Chief Judge plus two judges drawn from a panel of seven judges. Decision is by a majority and the Appeal Court is the final court in matters of family law, *wakf* [*q.v.*], offences against religion, inheritance and *bayt al-māl*. The Syariah Subordinate Court has a limited jurisdiction in the same matters. Appeals go to the Syariah High Court and, finally, to the Appeal Court, which also exercises a general supervisory jurisdiction over the lower courts. The Act also provides for the appointment of *syariah* prosecutors. Persons in proceedings in the Syariah courts may be represented by a *Perguam Syarie*, an advocate who has a sufficient degree of Islamic knowledge and who is admitted to practice in the Syariah courts. The procedure in all the courts is based on the secular model. It is government policy to standardise the Syariah court system nationwide on the Federal Territory model, but there is still some way to go at the moment.

(b) Islamic jurisdiction. The jurisdiction of the state Syariah Courts is as set out in their respective enactments. From the 1950s it has become increasingly elaborated to the extent that there is now a comprehensive jurisdiction which coexists with the secular court system (High Courts and Court of Appeal [formerly Federal Court]). Concurrent jurisdictions always raise the issue of which is superior, or more exactly, which forum decides the issue. The question only really arose in the 1950s and was not definitively decided in Malaysia until 1988. Before that date, it was the secular courts which had overriding jurisdiction because these courts derived from the Federal Constitution and not, as did the Syariah courts, from state legislation. This was always a matter of resentment in Syariah court circles, and in 1988 a new article, 121 (1A), was introduced into the Federal Constitution; which reads: "The courts referred to [the secular courts] shall have no jurisdiction in respect of any matters within the jurisdiction of the Syariah courts."

However, this does not really solve the issue; it merely puts it back one stage. It is still the secular courts, here the Court of Appeal of Malaysia, which actually decides whether a course of action is "within the jurisdiction of the Syariah Courts". There are a number of reported cases (1990s; see *Bibl.*) which demonstrate this; the Syariah courts have an inferior jurisdiction and have no power to determine the limits of that jurisdiction. It is the secular courts that interpret the Constitution just as they are the heirs to Anglo-Muhammadan jurisprudence.

Given the structure of the Syariah courts and the issue of jurisdiction, it is not surprising that the judgements in the courts show an increasing degree of secularisation of *fiḳh*. This has taken place in the area of family law, and the decisions are a case study of the fate of the *syariah* in the contemporary nation state. Fundamental to this is the fate of the classical text books themselves and here one can discern a consistent pattern from the late 1980s. Passages are cited as *hukum syariah* and then interpreted with reference to Malaysian legislation and, in some cases, Malay custom (*adat*) as to land. The Arabic texts (standard books and *ḥadīth* collections) get quite new meanings which derive from *adat*, from legislation, and from earlier Syariah court precedents. These new meanings are now what *fikh* means; thus the Arabic sources are beginning to be interpreted and distinguished on the basis of English-derived principles.

A second feature of the contemporary Syariah courts is the recourse to "modernist" legal reasoning with occasional but important recourse to Middle East authorities. Thus, from the late 1970s we find references to Syed Sabiq (his *Fiḳh al-Sunna*) and Ibn Ḳudāma (the latter's discussion of Abū Dāwūd).

These two trends seem now to be almost irreversible. The only surprising feature is the depth of penetration of secular (English) legal reasoning into the substantive *fiḳh* rules. There seem to be three reasons for this.

First, while it is true that the *syariah* in its "pure" form (*fiḳh* and *ḥadīth*) is now commonly cited, it is also true that the form of judicial records is in judicial precedent. Given that this is the form of the law, it is inevitable that the technical rules of English law will apply, and the result will be an Anglo-Syariah. Such has, of course, occurred before in British India and pre-independence British Malaya. The only difference in the present case is the greater quality of *fiḳh* in the *ḳāḍīs* jurisdiction. Even here, however, a lot of repetition appears. In short, the precedent law is decisive.

Second, the members of the Appeal Board are, almost without exception, trained in English and English-Malay universities and practice at the secular Bar or the judiciary. This, apart from being Muslim, is their primary qualification. When this is combined with the precedent form, it is not surprising that an increasingly secular form of judicial reasoning is apparent. This is not to say that judgements are "un-Islamic". Such would not be true in the substance (result) of a decision. It is certainly arguable, however, in terms of legal reasoning.

Third, the prevailing political climate for Islam in Malaysia is dictated by the Federal Government. It is one which encourages progress, "modernisation", "development" and the like. Whatever the rhetoric, Islam is controlled in all its aspects so far as possible. The religion must accommodate itself to the state and not the other way around. The same principle applies to *ḳāḍī* jurisdiction, and an increasing secularisation of Islam through administration and through the Syariah courts now seems inevitable.

iii. Brunei

The state of Brunei [*q.v.* in Suppl.] (independent in 1984) describes itself as a "Malay-Islamic-Sultanate" (*Melayu-Islam-Beraja*). The Sultan is Head of State and Head of Government; he is also the Head of the Religion of Islam which is thus entrenched in the Constitution. Prior to 1955, the laws as to Syariah courts were minimal, though a basic Kadi Court did exist. In 1955 Brunei adopted the Religious Council and Kadis Court Act which was based on the then Kelantan (Malaysia) Enactment. The Brunei Act has been amended and the current version is now cap. 77 of the Revised Laws (1984) with some later amendments.

The Act establishes a Court of Chief Kadi in the capital and subordinate Kadi Courts in outlying districts. The extent of jurisdiction is determined by the Sultan but is in fact specified in detail in the Act. These include family law, *wakf* and, in criminal matters, offences against religion. The latter include gambling, consumption of alcohol, sex outside marriage, preaching Islam without permission and the unlawful construction of mosques. Appeals are dealt with in the Chief Kadi's Court and above that by the Judicial Committee, which consists of the State Mufti and two other members appointed by the Sultan. This Committee also has authority to write an opinion on any question of Muslim law for a non-Islamic court if requested. Ultimate authority, however, still lies with the Sultan who, as Head of the Religious Council (one of the Councils of State), makes the final decision.

The language of the Courts is Malay and records are kept in Malay. Advocates may not appear if an appearance is "contrary to the provisions of Muslim law" but may be permitted at the discretion of the Court. Procedure is based on secular court procedure. So far as evidence is concerned, Muslim law is followed only with respect to witnesses. All other matters of evidence are governed by English law as adopted in Brunei. The Courts may summon non-Muslims to give evidence. Matters of arrest and search in relation to criminal activity, especially breach of the peace, are governed by the secular criminal proceedings in the Kadis Court. The execution of judgements is likewise governed by the Subordinate Courts Act. Generally, in civil matters the practice and procedure of the Magistrates Courts is followed in the Kadis Courts.

In essence, the Brunei Act repeats the Malaysian and Singaporean provisions. This is true for judicial process. However, it is important to realise that the constitutional position of Islam in Brunei and the position of the Sultan provides a unique context for the operation of the Kadi Courts. Unfortunately data on their actual working are not as yet available.

Bibliography: 1. Basic sources. These are the respective editions of the laws of each state. For Malaysia, there are variations from state to state. A useful overview, which notes the variations, is D. Horowitz, *The Quran and the Common Law*, in *American Journal of Comparative Law*, xlii (1994), 233-93. The other basic sources for Singapore and Malaysia are the *Malayan Law Journal* and *Current Law Journal*, both in English with Malay summaries and the *Jernal Hukum* in Malay. There are no reports for Brunei.

2. General accounts. M.B. Hooker, *Islamic law in South-East Asia*, Singapore 1974, chs. 2 and 4; idem, *Qadi jurisdiction in contemporary Malaysia and Singapore*, in M.A. Wu (ed.), *Public law in contemporary Malaysia*, Kuala Lumpur 1999, 57-75. The doyen of Islamic Studies in Malaysia was the late Professor Ahmad Ibrahim. His *Islamic law in Malaya*, Kuala Lumpur 1965, though now out of date, was an important work. In the 1970-1990s, he published important papers in *Journal of Malaysian Comparative Law* and in the *Annual Survey of Malaysian Law*.

(M.B. Hooker)

MAI, the official title of the Sayfuwa rulers of Kanem [*q.v.*], later Bornū [*q.v.*], an African kingdom situated in the area of Lake Chad. Arab geographers (al-Yaʿḳūbī, al-Muhallabī) depicted the ruler of pre-Islamic Kanem as a divine king. Although the rise to power of an Islamic line of rulers in the second half of the 11th century resulted in a number of radical changes in the political structure, some basic elements of divine kingship continued to shape the royal institution during the period of the Sayfuwa. Among the features of divine kingship which resisted the secularising tendencies of Islam were the seclusion of the king, shown by his concealment in a pavilion behind a silk curtain; the prevailing influence of women of the royal family in court life (queen-mother, principal queen and princesses); and the notion of a legendary protectress of the king during his youth (Aïsa Kili Ngirmaramma). Traditions associate the latter with the upbringing of the greatest rulers of Kanem-Bornū: Dūnama Dibalemī (1203-48), ʿAlī Gad͟jī (1455-87) and Idrīs Amsāmi (1564-96). The court ceremonies and institutions derived from divine kingship were abolished by *s͟hayk͟h* al-Amīn al-Kānimī, who founded a new dynasty in Bornū in the first half of the 19th century. By adopting the Arabo-Islamic *s͟hayk͟h* as a royal title instead of the earlier *mai*, he gave expression to his more strictly Islamic preferences.

Bibliography: D. Lange, *Le dīwān des sultans du [Kānem-] Bornū*, Wiesbaden 1977; idem, *Das Amt der Königinmutter im Tschadseegebiet*, in *Paideuma*, xxxvi (1990), 139-56.

(D. Lange)

MAI TATSINE (d. 1980), a nickname given to Muhammadu Marwa, a *mallam*, or Muslim religious leader in Kano, Nigeria, whose followers were involved in violent clashes from 18 to 28 December 1980. Over 4,000 people died in these disturbances.

He came from the region of Marwa in northern Cameroon, from a group classified as Kirdi. These are hill dwellers and followers of traditional religions, while the Muslim Fulani dominate the plains. Famine drove the young Mai Tatsine out of the hills, along with many fellow Kirdi, in the 1930s. In the city of Marwa he took up Islam.

He came to Kano in 1945 and began a career as a *mallam*. His teaching was evidently inflammatory for in 1962 he was jailed by Kano's chief Muslim judge for the offence of *shatima*, or verbal abuse. Following his sentence, Emir Sanusi deported him to Cameroon.

Such traditional forms of control were weakened following the abolition of the emirs' judicial authority in 1966. Mai Tatsine was able to return to Kano and establish a popular following by the late 1970s. The disturbances began when the police were overwhelmed by sect members in a confrontation near the emir's palace on December 18. Fighting continued for ten days until the Nigerian army finally dislodged the 'Yan Tatsine from their stronghold in a neighbourhood just outside the old walled city. Mai Tatsine was killed at this time. The sect survived and was involved in clashes in Maiduguri and Kaduna in following years.

The sect bears some resemblance to the Ḥamālliyya [*q.v.*], an offshoot of the Tid͟jāniyya [*q.v.*] that began in Mauritania in the 1920s. Both movements emphasised living as a separate community which regarded other Muslims as impure. Many of its followers were recent immigrants to Kano, drawn by the city's oil boom driven expansion, but it also had followers in rural areas.

Bibliography: J. Boutrais, *La colonisation des plaines par les montagnards au nord du Cameroun*, Paris 1973; A. Christelow, *The 'Yan Tatsine disturbances in Kano. A search for perspective*, in *MW*, lxxv (1985), 69-84; P. Lubeck, *Islam and urban labour in Northern Nigeria. The making of a Muslim working class*, Cambridge 1987.

(A. Christelow)

MAḲĀṢID AL-SHARĪʿA (A.), literally, "the aims or purposes of the law".

The term is used in works of legal theory (*uṣūl al-fiḳh* [*q.v.*]) and refers to the idea that God's law, the *S͟harīʿa* [*q.v.*], is a system which encompasses aims or purposes. If the system is correctly implemented, these aims will be achieved. From such a perspective, the *S͟harīʿa* is not merely a collection of inscrutable rulings. One who claims that the *S͟harīʿa* has *maḳāṣid* is, therefore, making a statement concerning the rational nature of the *S͟harīʿa*: that God intends to bring about a certain state of affairs by instituting particular laws. Most Sunnī legal theorists subscribe to the view that the *S͟harīʿa* has aims, and principal amongst these is the promotion of the "benefit for the believers" (*maṣāliḥ al-ʿibād*). As al-S͟hāṭibī (d. 790/1388), probably the most sophisticated of the classical exponents of the doctrine of *maḳāṣid al-s͟harīʿa*, states, "the laws were instituted only for the benefit of the believers in this world and the next" (*Muwāfaḳāt*, ii, 2). The laws themselves are only the means of achieving God's aims and intentions. They hold no intrinsic value, and if, on occasions, the strict application of the law compromises the aims of the *S͟harīʿa*, then for some supporters of the doctrine of *maḳāṣid*, the law can be set aside or modified so that God's intentions might be fulfilled. This possibility has made an appeal to *maḳāṣid al-s͟harīʿa* particularly popular amongst modern legal reformers in the Muslim word, as it enables them to alter some long-held elements of the law which they consider to be impracticable in a contemporary setting.

The doctrine of *maḳāṣid al-s͟harīʿa* has its roots in early Muslim attempts to rationalise both theology and law. In terms of theology, the ideas of the Muʿtazila [*q.v.*] undoubtedly influenced the emergence of the *maḳāṣid* doctrine. The Muʿtazilī doctrine that God's decrees are subject to, rather than the origin of, the ideas of good and evil (*al-taḥsīn wa 'l-taḳbīḥ* [*q.v.*]) ultimately resulted in an assertion that God is compelled to act in the interests (perhaps the best interests) of humankind. His law must be of benefit to his creation, for if it was not, his qualities of justice and goodness would be compromised.

In legal works, a bundle of related doctrines can be seen as precursors to al-S͟hāṭibī's elaboration. The development of *ḳiyās* [*q.v.*] as a legal tool provided the impetus for the doctrine of *maḳāṣid al-s͟harīʿa*; for, if rulings known to be true in one situation can be transferred to novel situations, then the law must, in some sense, be coherent. If it is coherent, then it must express the will of the Lawgiver. It is this underlying assumption (that the intentions of the Lawgiver could be known) that was so vehemently rejected by the Ẓāhirī Ibn Ḥazm (d. 456/1064 [*q.v.*]).

The Shāfiʿī jurist Abū Ḥamīd al-Ghazālī (d. 505/1111 [*q.v.*]), on the other hand, asserted that one way in which the *ratio* (*ʿilla* [*q.v.*]) of a ruling might be known is by comparing the candidate for the role of *ʿilla* with the general aim (*maḳṣūd*) of the law to "promote benefit and reduce harm". This means of identifying or verifying the *ʿilla* (known as *munāsaba*) rested upon the idea that the aims of the law were discernible (through reason or revelation).

The Ḥanbalī Nadjm al-Dīn al-Ṭūfī (716/1316 [*q.v.*]) went further than this, arguing that all rules derived from analogy (bar those not open to rational scrutiny such as the ritual *ʿibādāt*) are susceptible to change and development if the aims of the Lawgiver are not fulfilled. Discussion over the legitimacy of *istiḥsān* and *istiṣlāḥ* amongst Ḥanafīs and Mālikīs also rested on an acceptance that there were overall "aims" in the *Sharīʿa*. *Istiḥsān* [*q.v.*], originally used as an accusation of arbitrary preference, was rationalised by Ḥanafīs such as al-Sarakhsī (d. 483/1090 [*q.v.*]) to refer to the rejection of the strict application of *ḳiyās* in favour of a ruling which better promotes the benefits of the believers (*maṣāliḥ al-ʿibād*).

Istiṣlāḥ [*q.v.*] was discussed extensively by Mālikīs, in part because Mālik himself is reported to have advocated it; it refers to a jurist's ruling which has no precedent in the revelatory texts, and is based on the calculation of some benefit (*maṣlaḥa mursala*) [see MAṢLAḤA] to the individual or communities concerned. Mālikīs, such as al-Ḳarāfī (d. 684/1285 [see SHIHĀB AL-DĪN AL-ḲARĀFĪ]), recognised the theologically problematic nature of basing a ruling not on textual support but on a benefit perceived by a jurist. It is perhaps unsurprising then, given the Mālikī history of discussions of *istiṣlāḥ*, that the greatest exponent of *maḳāṣid al-sharīʿa* should come from the Mālikī school, sc. Abū Isḥāḳ al-Shāṭibī [*q.v.*], the 8th/14th-century Granadan jurist. Al-Shāṭibī, in his *Muwāfaḳāt*, takes the analysis of "benefits" accruing from the institution of the *Sharīʿa* used by previous jurists in relation to *ḳiyās*, *istiḥsān* and *istiṣlāḥ*, and declares, uncompromisingly, that the whole *Sharīʿa* exists to promote the welfare of the believers. The benefits which are promoted and preserved when the *Sharīʿa* is instituted are of three basic types. There are those elements which are necessary (*ḍarūra* [*q.v.*]) for human existence to prosper (there are, al-Shāṭibī argues, five of these: the preservation of life, property, progeny, mind and religion); there are those which are needed (*ḥādja*) in order to make obedience to the *Sharīʿa* less demanding; and there are those which, whilst not necessary or needed, improve (*taḥsīniyya*) the benefits already enjoyed by the believers. Each ruling in the *Sharīʿa* can be said to benefit the believers in one of these three areas. For example, it is necessary (*ḍarūra*) to human existence to preserve life, and God has instituted (in the *Sharīʿa*) rules concerning punishment and compensation for murder. In order to make the *Sharīʿa* easier to follow (*ḥādja*), the law permits sick people to miss prayer. Finally, the benefits to the believers are improved (*taḥsīniyya*) by supererogatory manumission, though community welfare would be maintained if this act was not performed.

Al-Shāṭibī's schema, which was innovative within the deeply conservative tradition of Sunnī *uṣūl al-fiḳh*, undoubtedly influenced subsequent writings, but it is in the modern period that these ideas have been developed and enhanced, and a genre of *maḳāṣid* writing can be said to have emerged. In particular, North African (Mālikī) jurists, such as Muḥammad Ṭāhir b. ʿĀshūr (d. 1973) and ʿAllāl al-Fāsī (d. 1973), composed works devoted to *maḳāṣid al-sharīʿa* which draw heavily on al-Ṭūfī and al-Shāṭibī. Ibn ʿAshūr, for example, adds equality and freedom to al-Shāṭibī's list of the five elements necessary for human existence to prosper. The modern emergence of a theology reminiscent of Muʿtazilī doctrine has enabled jurists to consider the *Sharīʿa* as more adaptable to change and distinguish between the unchanging aims of the law and mutable particular regulations.

Bibliography: 1. Sources. Ibn Ḥazm, *al-Iḥkām fī uṣūl al-aḥkām*, Cairo 1978; Sarakhsī, *al-Uṣūl*, Cairo 1973; Ghazālī, *al-Mustaṣfā min ʿilm al-uṣūl*, Beirut 1996; Ṭūfī, *ʿAlam al-djadhal fī ʿilm al-djadal*, Wiesbaden 1987; Ḳarāfī, *Sharḥ al-tanḳīḥ al-fuṣūl fī ikhtiṣār al-maḥṣūl fī 'l-uṣūl*, Cairo 1973; Shāṭibī, *al-Muwāfaḳāt fī uṣūl al-sharīʿa*, Cairo 1969-70.

2. Studies. ʿAllāl al-Fāsī, *Maḳāṣid al-sharīʿa al-islāmiyya wa-makārimuhā*, Casablanca 1963; A.-M. Turki, *Polémiques entre Ibn Ḥazm et Bāǧī sur les principes de la loi musulmane*, Algiers 1973; Muḥammad Ṭāhir Ibn ʿĀshūr, *Maḳāṣid al-sharīʿa al-islāmiyya*, Tunis 1978; K. Masood, *Islamic legal philosophy. A study of Abū Isḥāq al-Shāṭibī's life and thought*, Islamabad 1977; A. Zysow, *The economy of certainty. An introduction to the typology of Islamic legal theory*, Harvard Univ. Ph.D. thesis 1984, unpubl.; B. Weiss, *The search for God's law. Islamic jurisprudence in the writings of Sayf al-Dīn al-Āmidī*, Salt Lake City 1992; W. Hallaq, *A history of Islamic legal theories. An introduction to Sunni uṣūl al-fiqh*, Cambridge 1997. (R.M. Gleave)

MAḲBARA. 4. In Iran.

Islamic cemeteries in Iran, Transoxania and Afghanistan were generally located, in accordance with the practices of Zoroastrian, Christian or Jewish communities, *extra muros* of existing settlements and along main roads exiting from the city gates (al-Muḳaddasī, 438; al-Iṣfahānī, *Aghānī*[3], xix, 114 (for Iṣfahān, see Ibn al-Athīr, ed. Beirut, xi, 28; Harāt: T. Allen, *A catalogue of the toponyms and monuments of Timurid Herat*, Cambridge 1981, 165; Rayy: Ḥ. Karīmān, *Rayy-i bāstān*, Tehran 1345 A.S.H., i, 366-479; C. Adle, *Constructions funéraires à Rey circa Xᵉ-XIIᵉ siècle*, in *Akten des 8. Internationalen Kongresses für iranische Kunst und Archäologie*, Berlin 1979, 511-12; Samarḳand: N.B. Nemceva, *Etappen der Herausbildung der Ensembles Schah-i Sinda in Samarkand*, in *ZA*, N.S. xii [1978], 51-68). Al-Muḳaddasī, however, remarks on the noteworthy exception of Tustar where the cemetery was established on higher ground within the city because of frequent river floods (*ibid.*, 409). For a mediaeval visitor, the sight of cemeteries evoked feelings of sadness and a sense of disorientation (Abū Shāma, *Tarādjim ridjāl al-ḳarn al-sādis wa 'l-sābiʿ*, ed. M.Z. al-Kawtharī, Beirut 1974, 16). Nevertheless, tombs were often located as close as possible to the roads in the hope that compassionate passers-by would stop to offer prayers (Sibṭ Ibn al-Djawzī, *Mirʾat al-zamān*, Ḥaydarābād 1951, viii, 442). Not wanting to be constantly reminded of the inevitability of death, the Būyid ʿAḍud al-Dawla issued orders to enclose cemeteries with high walls (Djūzdjānī, *Ṭabaḳāt-i Nāṣirī*, ed. ʿAbd al-Ḥayy Ḥabībī, Kābul 1342/1963, 223). Visits to grave sites in Hamadhān or Shirāz included not only recitations of the Ḳurʾān but also offerings of food and drink (*zalla wa nawāla*) for the dead (Rāwandī, *Rāḥat al-ṣudūr*, ed. M. Iqbāl, London 1921, 300; Ibn Baṭṭūṭa, *Riḥla*, Beirut 1968, 209-10).

When Muslims lived with the indigenous population of Iran immediately after the conquest, they used existing pre-Islamic cemeteries and seem soon to have adopted local funerary customs. Muslim burials on

Tepe no. 2 at Bayram ʿAlī near Marw make use of earlier structures, so-called *nawāwīs* (M.E. Masson, *Materialī po arkheologii Merva*, in *Trudī YuTAKE*, xiv [1969], 7-12; O.V. Obel'čenko, *Nekropol' drevnego Merva*, in *ibid.*, 95-9). Burials in ossuaries and jars are mixed with regular Muslim graves in a 7th-10th century cemetery outside Tarāz near Dzhambul (Ḳazakhstān) (L.I. Rempel', *Nekropol' drevnego Taraza*, in *Kratkie Soobshčeniya Instituta Material'noy Kul'turī*, lxix [1957], 102). The best-known site for these hybrid practices, however, is the "Monumental Cemetery" (Site O) in Sīrāf [*q.v.*], situated on a spur of land overlooking the city's west end, that also had its own funerary mosque (D. Whitehouse, *Excavations in Siraf*, in *Iran*, xii [1974], 23-30). Dating back to the pre-Islamic period, the 100 × 150 m cemetery was dominated by a group of about forty monumental tombs (5 × 5 m to 9.5 × 10 m), built between the 9th and the 10th centuries, with graves grouped around them. Most appear to have been used for the collective disposal of the dead, who were buried inside without coffins and without separating the corpses according to gender. Most bodies were aligned in an orthodox manner north-south, with their heads turned towards the west, i.e. Mecca. The deceased, who appear to have been members of the wealthier society of Sīrāf, were buried with rings, beads, bracelets and ceramic jugs (*ibid.*, 25). Similar cemeteries are known from literary sources to have existed in Paykand, modern Karakul in Turkmenistān (anon., *Ḥudūd al-ʿālam*, tr. Minorsky², 113) and Yazd (Djaʿfarī, *Taʾrīkh-i Yazd*, ed. I. Afshār, Tehran 1337 A.S.H./1958, 130).

Cemeteries *intra muros* were often established in ruins or in buildings that were partially torn down for that purpose (Whitehouse, *ibid.*, 9; A. McNicoll, *Site G. Islamic Cemetery*, in McNicoll and W. Ball (eds.), *Excavations at Kandahar 1974 and 1975*, Oxford 1996, 214, 234-6), while growing settlements were laid out around pre-existing cemeteries, respecting and carefully enclosing the tombs (Whitehouse, *ibid.*, 12).

Local pre-Islamic cemeteries continued in use, but cemeteries also opened up in greater Iran around tombs ascribed to legendary *shuhadāʾ* of the Muslim conquest of Iran (Yāḳūt, iv, 418; E. Cohn-Wiener, *A Turanic monument of the twelfth century A.D.*, in *Ars Islamica*, vi [1939], 88-91); to saints (A.S. Melikian-Chirvani, *Remarques préliminaires sur une mausolée ghaznévide*, in *Arts Asiatiques*, xvii, 59-60) or to former rulers (Cohn-Wiener, *Die Ruinen der Seldschukenstadt von Merw und das Mausoleum Sultan Sandschars*, in *Festschrift F. Sarre*, Leipzig 1925, 116).

Only scarce documentation exists on remnants of some nomadic cemeteries in the Atrek valley in north-eastern Iran and in southwestern Iran dating from the 17th to the 19th centuries. The Turcoman Göklen tribe possessed a common burial ground 60 km/40 miles north of Djurdjān, scattered over hills, slopes, and plateaux of the Gökcheh mountain, to which the deceased were brought often from far away, after a preliminary burial for some time in the area around seasonal camps (D. Stronach, *Standing stones in the Atrek region. The Ḥālat Nabī cemetery*, in *Iran*, xix [1981], 147-51). In contrast to this, cemeteries of the Lur nomads in Luristān were established along the annual tribal migratory routes and may coincide with old camp sites. Tombs in these cemeteries were marked by pictorial stelae with gender-specific images and inscriptions (I.D. Mortensen, *Women after death. Aspects of a study on Iranian nomadic cemeteries*, in B. Utas [ed.], *Women in Islamic societies*, London 1983, 26-47; idem, *Nomadic cemeteries and tombstones from Luristan, Iran*, in J.-L. Bacqué-Grammont and A. Tibet [eds.], *Cimetières et traditions funéraires dans le monde islamique*, Ankara 1996, ii, 175-83).

In contemporary Iran, modern and efficiently-administered cemeteries have been established, often at some distance from major cities and pilgrimage centres, as more orderly alternatives to older, more scattered burial places. Between the 1970s and late 1980s, the city of Mashhad inaugurated the cemeteries of Bihisht-i Riḍā and Djawād-i Aʾimma 20 miles southwest of the city in the vicinity of an old cemetery named after the tomb of the 9th century Imāmzāda Khʷādja Abu 'l-Salṭ. Simultaneously, modern extensions to the Tīmūrid shrine of Imām ʿAlī al-Riḍā now include underground burial vaults, named al-Ḳuds and Mashhad-i Djumhūrī, for civilians and soldiers killed during the Revolution and the Iran-ʿIrāḳ War.

Used as a burial ground since the 1950s and opened officially in 1970, the sprawling Bihisht-i Zahrāʾ cemetery (Paradise of [Fāṭima] the Radiant) south of Tehran along the highway to Ḳum is today the city's main cemetery. During the late 1970s and early 1980s, Bihisht-i Zahrāʾ gained the reputation as a national symbol of the Revolution, as many of those killed during demonstrations against the Shāh or in post-Revolutionary factional fighting were buried there as martyrs. During the eight years of war with ʿIrāḳ, a vast, separate section was added for soldiers killed in action, whose tombs are typically surmounted by cases that exhibit a portrait photo of the deceased and Islamic and Revolutionary paraphernalia. The impressive visual expression of Bihisht-i Zahrāʾ as a cemetery dedicated to the commemoration of martyrs, a fountain that spouts red water, has been copied throughout Iran (Hamid Algar, art. *Behešt-e Zahrāʾ*, in *EIr*, iv, 108-9; D. Hiro, *Iran under the Ayatollas*, London 1985, 77).

Bibliography: Given in the article, but on the graveyards where British travellers, traders, missionaries, etc., were buried, see Sir Denis Wright, *Burials and memorials of the British in Persia*, in *Iran*, xxxvi (1998), 165-73, and *further notes and photographs*, in *ibid.*, xxx (1999), 173-4, xxxix (2001), 293-8. See also, on cemeteries in Persian folklore, *EIr* art. *Cemeteries* (Mahmoud Omidsalar). (T. Leisten)

MAKTŪBĀT (a.), literally "letters", a term used especially in Muslim India for the epistles of Ṣūfī leaders.

Apart from epistolary collections of political and literary significance (like *Iʿdjāz-i Khusrawī*, *Mukātabāt-i Rashīdī*, *Riyāḍ al-Inshāʾ*, *Inshāʾ-i Abu 'l-Faḍl*), there are collections of letters written by mystic teachers to their disciples. This epistolary literature, which throws valuable light on the mystic ideology and institutions of the period, may broadly be classified under four categories: (i) sundry correspondence limited mostly to one or two letters dealing with some religious problem, e.g. letters attributed to Shaykh ʿAbd al-Ḳādir Gīlānī, Khʷādja Ḳuṭb al-Dīn Bakhtiyār Kākī, Shaykh Farīd Gandj-i Shakar, Shaykh Niẓām al-Dīn Awliyāʾ and others; (ii) collections of letters in the nature of mystic lucubrations without any indication of the addressees, e.g. letters of ʿAyn al-Ḳuḍāt Hamadānī, Ḳāḍī Ḥamīd al-Dīn Nāgawrī and Sayyid ʿAlī Hamadānī; (iii) collections of letters bearing on mystical or religious themes addressed to disciples to resolve their difficulties, e.g. the letters of the Imām al-Ghazālī, Sanāʾī, Rifāʿī, Yaḥyā Manērī, Bū ʿAlī Ḳalandar, Ashraf Djahāngīr Simnānī, Gīsū Darāz, Nūr Ḳuṭb-i ʿĀlam, Djaʿfar Makkī, Shaykh ʿAbd al-Ḳuddūs, Shaykh ʿAbd al-Ḥaḳḳ Muḥaddith, Shāh Muḥibb Allāh of Allāhābād and others; and (iv) collections of letters having the consistent exposition of a specific ideological position and controlling the organisational direction and ideological drift of the disciples. The Naḳshbandī saints, particularly from the time of Shaykh Aḥmad Sirhindī, used letters as a regular channel for the communication of their trends of thought. His successors, Kh^wādja Muḥammad Maʿṣūm, Muḥammad Naḳshband-i Thānī, Kh^wādja Sayf al-Dīn, Mīrzā Maẓhar Djān-i Djānān, Shaykh Muḥammad Saʿīd, Shāh Ghulām ʿAlī, Shāh Aḥmad Saʿīd, ʿAbd al-Raʾūf and others, wrote large number of letters which are a veritable source for the study of Naḳshbandī thought and its reaction to different socio-religious situations. The thought of the silsila was so consolidated on their basis that, during the last three hundred years, the Naḳshbandīs have drawn spiritual guidance from these letters.

Taken as a whole, the Suhrawardī, the Ḳādirī and the Shaṭṭārī saints do not seem to have adopted correspondence as a regular means of communicating their ideology. Except for the Maktūbāt-i Ḳāḍī Shaṭṭar (ms. in Manēr Khānakāh) no saint of these orders seems to have left any significant collection of letters. The Naḳshbandīs, the Firdawsīs and the Čishtīs made use of this medium effectively. In Naḳshbandī discipline, the maktūbāt of Shaykh Aḥmad Sirhindī [q.v.] and his descendants assumed the same significance which malfūẓāt [q.v. in Suppl.] like Fawāʾid al-fuʾād and Khayr al-madjālis assumed in the Čishtī silsila. Shaykh Niẓām al-Dīn Awliyāʾ used to write letters on a large scale (Shaykh Mubārak Gopamawī had collected his hundred letters—Siyar al-awliyāʾ, Dihlī 1302, 310—and Amīr Khusraw also received a large number of letters which he had buried with him [ibid., 302-3], but these were of personal nature and were not collected in any compendium. Among the Čishtī saints, the most effective collections of maktūbāt are those of Nūr Ḳuṭb-i ʿĀlam, ʿAbd al-Ḳuddūs Gangōhī and Shāh Kalīm Allāh of Dihlī. The last-mentioned saint controlled and guided the Čishtī organisation in the Deccan through correspondence, at a time when Awrangzīb [q.v.] was showing his definite preference for the Naḳshbandī order. Perhaps Shāh Kalīm Allāh was influenced by the practice of his contemporary Naḳshbandī saints in giving importance to correspondence in organising the affairs of the silsila and in controlling its ideological slant.

Among the Firdawsīs, the letters of Shaykh Sharaf al-Dīn Yaḥyā succeeded in boosting the mystics' morale after their setback at the hands of Muḥammad b. Tughluḳ [q.v.].

The available maktūb literature throws light on the thought and activities, as also the problems and preferences, of the saints of different periods and different orders. Though some of the letters of the Imām al-Ghazālī are addressed to wazīrs and government officials, they help us in assessing the position of religion in the administration of those days. His communications to the ḳāḍīs, the jurists and theologians throw light on the nature of the religious problems and tensions of the period and have a sermonising tone. The letters of Sanāʾī, only seventeen in number, help us in understanding the mental climate of the late Ghaznawid period as much as his mystical poetry. The letters of Nūr Ḳuṭb-i ʿĀlam throw light on the socio-political crisis in Bengal in the 8th/14th century. The letters of Shaykh Sharaf al-Dīn Yaḥyā reveal the anxiety of the Firdawsī saint to salvage mystic institutions from ruin. The Maktūbāt of Shaykh ʿAbd al-Ḳuddūs of Gangōh [see GANGŌHĪ, in Suppl.] bring into focus the atmosphere immediately preceding the

rise of the Bhakti movement. The letters of Shaykh Aḥmad Sirhindī provide material for the study of reactions against Akbar's religious experiments. So also the letters of ʿAbd al-Ḥaḳḳ Muḥaddith reveal the anxiety of Muslim minds at the anarchy prevailing in Muslim religious life. The letters of Shāh Muḥibb Allāh, particularly those addressed to Dārā Shukōh [q.v.], show his anxiety to retrieve pantheistic thought from condemnation and conflict. When read with the letters of Kh^wādja Maʿṣūm and other Naḳshbandī saints, they reveal the nature of conflict in mystical thought at this time. Kh^wādja Maʿṣūm's letters highlight the atmosphere of religious revival that took place during the time of Awrangzīb. The letters of Shāh Walī Allāh [q.v.] illuminate his efforts to bridge the gulf between the devotees of waḥdat al-wudjūd and its critics on one side and his political activities, involving correspondence with Aḥmad Shāh Abdālī, Muḥammad Shāh and Nadjīb al-Dawla [q.vv.], on the other. The letters of Mīrzā Maẓhar show significant religious trends of the period which led to his declaration of Vedas as a revealed book and his according the status of Ahl-i Kitāb to the Hindus.

For a study of the actual application of mystic ideology to concrete socio-religious situations, the importance of Maktūbāt literature cannot be over-emphasised.

Bibliography: ʿAyn al-Ḳuḍāt, Maktūbāt, ms. B.L. Add 16,823; Ghazālī, Faḍāʾil al-Imām min rasāʾil ḥudjdjat al-Islām, ed. Sir Syed Ahmad, Akbarābād 1310/1892-3; Sanāʾī, Makātīb-i Sanāʾī, ed. Nāẓir Aḥmad, Kābul 1977; Rifāʿī, Maktūbāt, ms. Ḥabībgandj, ʿAlīgaŕh 21/139. Čishtīs. Kh^wādja Muʿīn al-Dīn, Maktūb, addressed to Kh^wādja Bakhtiyār Kākī, ms. Sherani Collection, Catalogue, ii, Lahore 255; Kh^wādja Ḳuṭb al-Dīn Bakhtiyār, Maktūbāt, ms. Sir Shah Sulayman Collection, ʿAlīgaŕh; Shaykh Niẓām al-Dīn Awliyāʾ, Maktūb, addressed to Ḥusām al-Dīn, ms. ʿAlīgaŕh, Farsiyya Madhhab 129; Shaykh Naṣīr al-Dīn Čirāgh, Ṣaḥāʾif al-sulūk, lith. Djadjjar n.d.; Djaʿfar Makkī, Baḥr al-maʿānī, Murādabād 1885; Gīsū Darāz, Maktūbāt, ed. ʿAṭā Ḥusayn, Ḥaydarābād 1326/1908-9; Nūr Ḳuṭb-i ʿĀlam, Maktūbāt, ms. personal collection; ʿAbd al-Ḳuddūs Gangōhī, Maktūbāt-i Ḳuddūsiyya, Dihlī n.d.; Shāh Muḥibb Allāh Allāhābādī, Maktūbāt, ms. ʿAlīgaŕh, Subḥan Allāh Collection 13/297; Sayyid Ashraf Djahāngīr, Maktūbāt-i Ashrafī, ms. B.L. 267; Shāh Kalīm Allāh, Maktūbāt-i Kalīmī, Dihlī 1315/1897-8. Firdawsīs. Sharaf al-Dīn Yaḥyā Manērī, Maktūbāt-i Ṣadī, Arrah 1870; idem, Maktūbāt-i bist wa hasht, Lucknow 1287. Naḳshbandīs. Kh^wādja Bāḳī Billāh, Maktūbāt-i Sharīfa, Urdu tr. Lahore n.d.; Shaykh Aḥmad Sirhindī, Maktūbāt-i Imām Rabbānī, ed. Nūr Aḥmad Amritsar 1336, Arabic tr. Murād Manzalwī, Beirut n.d., Turkish tr. Ḥusayn Ḥilmī, Istanbul 1972, Urdu tr. Ḳāḍī ʿAlam al-Dīn, Lahore 1913; Muḥammad Maʿṣūm, Maktūbāt, Kānpūr 1302/1884-5; idem, Wasīlat al-saʿādat, Lūdhīāna 1906; Muḥammad Naḳshband-i Thānī, al-Ḳubūl ilā Allāh wa ʾl-Rasūl, ed. Ghulām Muṣṭafā, Ḥaydarābād-Sind 1963; Sayf al-Dīn, Maktūbāt sharīfa, Ḥaydarābād-Sind 1331/1413; Shāh Walī Allāh, Kalimāt-i ṭayyibāt, Murādabād 1303/1885-6; idem, Shāh Walī Allāh kay siyāsī Maktūbāt, ed. K.A. Nizami, ²Dihlī 1969; Mīrzā Maẓhar Djān-i Djānān, Kalimāt-i ṭayyibāt, Murādabād 1303/1885-6; idem, Maktūbāt, ed. ʿAbd al-Razzāḳ Ḳurashī, Bombay 1966; Shaykh Muḥammad Saʿīd, Maktūbāt-i Saʿīdiyya, ed. ʿAbd al-Madjīd, Lahore 1385/1965-6; Shāh Ghulām ʿAlī, Makātib-i sharīfa, Istanbul 1396/1976; Shāh Aḥmad Saʿīd, Tuḥfat-i zawwāriyya

ADDENDA AND CORRIGENDA

VOLUME XI

P. 169[b], **WĀSIṬ**, *add after l. 37*, During the struggle for ʿIrāḳ under al-Maʾmūn, there were, however, small issues of silver from Wāsiṭ in the years 200 and 203, and occasional issues in copper in 147, 167, 177 and 187 or 9.

P. 174[a], **WASM**, *add to Bibl.*: A second general study is E. Littmann, *Zur Entzifferung der thamudenischen Inschriften*, Berlin 1904, 78-104, which argues that most of the brands originate from the South Semitic alphabet in its North Arabian form.

P. 292[a], **YARMŪK**, *add to Bibl.*: W.E. Kaegi, *Heraclius, Emperor of Byzantium*, Cambridge 2003, 237-44.

P. 364[a], **ẒĀʾ**, ll. 23-25, *read* a voiceless /ṯ̣/ for /ḏ̣/ is attested in some Northern Yemeni dialects . . ., and a voiceless /ṯ/ for /ḏ̣/ occurs in North African sedentary dialects
l. 42, *read* Uzbekistan-Arabic) with /ḏ̣/ > /y̧/,

SUPPLEMENT

P. 566[b], **MAḤKAMA**, *add to Bibl.*: See the writings by D. Pearl, in particular *Interpersonal conflict of laws in India, Pakistan, and Bangladesh*, London-Bombay 1981; idem and W. Menski, *Muslim family law*, London 1998 (rev. ed. of D. Pearl, *A textbook on Muslim personal law*, London [2]1987).

ISBN 90 04 12855 7

PRINTED IN THE NETHERLANDS

dar anfās-i Saʿīdiyya, Karachi 1955. Ḳādirīs. *Maktūbāt Shaykh Muḥiyy al-Dīn ʿAbd al-Ḳādir Gīlānī*, ms. Sherani Collection, *Catalogue*, Lahore 1969, ii, 257; Shaykh ʿAbd al-Ḥaḳḳ Muḥaddith, *Kitāb al-Makātīb wa ʾl-rasāʾil*, Dihlī 1297/1880. Miscellaneous. *Maktūb-i Shāh Madār*, addressed to Shihāb al-Dīn Dawlatābādī, ms. ʿAlīgaṙh, ʿAbd al-Salām collection 10/915; *Maktūbāt Bū ʿAlī Ḳalandar*, ms. Sherani collection, *Catalogue*, ii, 256; *Maktūbāt-i Aḥmad Kashmīrī*, ms. National Museum of Pakistan, *Catalogue*, ed. ʿĀrif Nawshabī, Lahore 1983, 222; *Tafsīr al-marām*, letters of Shukr Allāh, ms. B.L. Add. 18,883.

(K.A. Nizami)

MALAʾ (a.), lit. a "group (of people)", or a "host", or a "crowd", like *djamāʿa, ḳawm* [*q.vv.*], *nafar, raht*, and more generally, "the public", and hence, *fī malaʾ*, *fī ʾl-malaʾ* "publicly" (e.g. al-Bukhārī, *Ṣaḥīḥ*, 9 vols., Cairo 1958, ix, 148 = *kitāb* 97, *bāb* 15). The word also denotes decisions taken as a result of collective consultation, as in the phrase *ʿan [ghayri] malaʾin minnā* "[not] as a result of our consultation" (Aḥmad b. Ḥanbal, *Musnad*, 6 vols., Cairo 1313/1895, repr. Beirut n.d., i, 463). Since collective decisions are usually taken by the leaders of the group, *al-malaʾ* very often denotes the notables and leaders of the community (*wudjūh, ashrāf, ruʾasāʾ*) (e.g. Ibn Hishām, *al-Sīra al-nabawiyya*, ed. Muṣṭafā al-Saḳḳā *et alii*, 4 vols., repr. Beirut 1971, ii, 297-8; Lane, s.v.).

1. In the Ḳurʾān.

In II, 246 the *malaʾ* of the Children of Israel demands that a king be raised up for them by their prophet. The word is explained here in the sense of *al-ḳawm* "the people" (e.g. Ibn al-Djawzī, *Zād al-masīr fī ʿilm al-tafsīr*, 9 vols., Beirut 1984, i, 291-2 [from al-Farrāʾ]); al-Ḳurṭubī, *al-Djāmiʿ li-aḥkām al-Ḳurʾān*, 20 vols., Cairo 1967, iii, 243), although others perceived it in the sense of "the notables" (e.g. al-Zadjdjādj, *Maʿānī ʾl-Ḳurʾān wa-iʿrābuhu*, ed. ʿAbd al-Djalīl Shalabī, 5 vols., Beirut 1988, i, 325).

In most of its Ḳurʾānic occurrences the word *malaʾ* stands indeed for the notables of a given group, and they often represent the royal council, like that of the Queen of Sheba (XXVII, 29, 32), and of King Solomon (XXVII, 38). The *malaʾ* in the Ḳurʾān is often involved in the persecution of the messengers of God, as with the royal *malaʾ* of the Pharaoh. It denounces Moses as a sorcerer (VII, 109; XXVI, 34), incites the Pharaoh against him (VII, 127), and plots to kill him (XXVIII, 20). Other prophets who were persecuted by the *malaʾ* of their own peoples were Noah (VII, 60; XI, 27, 38; XXIII, 24), Hūd (VII, 66; XXIII, 33) Ṣāliḥ (VII, 75), and Shuʿayb (VII, 88, 90). In one instance, the contemporary *malaʾ* of Muḥammad's own people is mentioned as leading the opposition against him (XXXVIII, 6).

In two places the Ḳurʾān mentions the "upper" *malaʾ* (*al-malaʾ al-aʿlā*). In XXXVII, 8, it is stated that the rebellious devils may not listen to the upper *malaʾ*, and in XXXVIII, 69, the Prophet declares that he has no knowledge of what the members of the upper *malaʾ* are disputing about. In Ḳurʾānic exegesis, it is held that the upper *malaʾ* are the angels who have thus been named because they dwell in heaven, which differentiates them from the earthly *malaʾ*, i.e. the human beings (e.g. al-Ḳurṭubī, *Aḥkām al-Ḳurʾān*, xv, 65). According to this perception, *al-malaʾ al-aʿlā* denotes "the heavenly host" [see malāʾika]. On the other hand, *al-malaʾ al-aʿlā* of Ḳurʾān XXXVIII, 69, was also explained as though standing for the Ḳuraysh (al-Ḳurṭubī, *op. cit.*, xv, 226-7), which sets the term in an earthly context, meaning "the supreme council" (see below).

As a heavenly group consisting of angels, *al-malaʾ al-aʿlā* is considered superior to the earthly one which consists of the sons of Adam (*ibid.*, i, 289). This is indicated in a tradition of the Prophet stating that whenever a believer mentions God's name in public (*fī malaʾin*), God mentions his name in a better public (e.g. Aḥmad b. Ḥanbal, *Musnad*, ii, 251). A *malaʾ* of angels met the Prophet on his nocturnal journey to heaven (*ibid.*, i, 354), and in fact every human soul is about to pass by a *malaʾ* of angels at the time of death (*ibid.*, iv, 287).

Closely associated with *al-malaʾ al-aʿlā* in its heavenly significance is the expression *al-rafīḳ al-aʿlā* (the "upper company", cf. Ḳurʾān IV, 69). It appears in a widely current tradition in which the Prophet, on his deathbed, asks God to place him with *al-rafīḳ al-aʿlā*, and these constitute his last words (e.g. al-Bukhārī, *Ṣaḥīḥ*, vi, 18-19 = *kitāb* 64, *bāb* 84). According to one of the interpretations, this expression stands for angels belonging to *al-malaʾ al-aʿlā* (al-Ḳasṭallānī, *Irshād al-sārī li-sharḥ Ṣaḥīḥ al-Bukhārī*, 10 vols., Cairo 1305/1887, viii, 358).

2. In early Tradition.

In accounts containing episodes from Muḥammad's life, the *malaʾ* of Ḳuraysh [*q.v.*] is often mentioned, and the context indicates that it consists of Meccan notables. In most cases, this *malaʾ* is involved in acts of persecution perpetrated against Muḥammad. In a typical episode, it is related that the *malaʾ* of Ḳuraysh once told Muḥammad that they were ready to embrace Islam provided he turned away believers of the lower classes (Aḥmad b. Ḥanbal, *Musnad*, i, 420). The episode is usually recorded in the commentaries on Ḳurʾān VI, 52, in which the Prophet is instructed not to reject those who call upon their Lord in the morning and in the evening. Occasionally, the *malaʾ* of the Meccans is said to have convened in the Ḥidjr (a sacred enclosure and a meeting place near the Kaʿba [*q.v.*]) to discuss how to treat Muḥammad (*ibid.*, i, 303), and they are also said to have interrogated Muḥammad, offering him medical treatment to cure his supposed madness (al-Ḳurṭubī, *Aḥkām al-Ḳurʾān*, xv, 338). In another instance, specific names of the hostile *malaʾ* of Ḳuraysh are enumerated, in a tradition in which Muḥammad prays to God to punish them for having thrown a camel's placenta on him when he was prostrating during prayer. This was done to invalidate his prayer by causing him physical impurity (al-Bukhārī, *Ṣaḥīḥ*, iv, 127 = *kitāb* 58, *bāb* 21, v, 57 = *kitāb* 63, *bāb* 29).

According to modern scholars, the word *malaʾ* became a fixed term denoting the elected "senate" of the tribe of Ḳuraysh in pre-Islamic Mecca (e.g. W. Montgomery Watt, *Muhammad at Mecca*, Oxford 1953, 8. See also makka. 1). It was described as "a kind of urban equivalent of the tribal *majlis* [see madjlis. 1], consisting of notables and family chiefs elected by assent to their wealth and standing" (B. Lewis, *The Arabs in history*, repr. London 1985, 31). However, there is no evidence that a process of election to the *malaʾ* ever took place in pre-Islamic Mecca. That *malaʾ* essentially denoted no more than an occasional group of notables is evident from the fact that it is also used with reference to a group of Ḳuraysh acting in Medina after the Hidjra (e.g. al-Bukhārī, *Ṣaḥīḥ*, ii, 133 = *kitāb* 24, *bāb* 4; Aḥmad b. Ḥanbal, *Musnad*, v, 160).

The *malaʾ*, i.e. the notables, of the Arab tribes of Medina (of the Banu ʾl-Nadjdjār), are also mentioned in the sources, and they are described as being in contact with Muḥammad upon his arrival in Medina (al-Bukhārī, *Ṣaḥīḥ*, v, 86 = *kitāb* 63, *bāb* 46). A more typical form of a consultative body in Islamic times was, perhaps, the *shūrā* [*q.v.*].

Bibliography: Given in the article.

(U. Rubin)

MALAWI, Muslims in.

Historical background.

Islam is not a recent phenomenon in the interior East African state of Malawi (the former British protectorate of Nyasaland), since traders from Arabia, the Persian Gulf, India and Indonesia had dealings with the East African Coast since time immemorial and Islam was carried into the interior by such traders. The name Malawi was first used by the Portuguese to denote a variety of distinct ethnic groups. Amongst these, the Marawi established a hegemony over a considerable area, including the Makua on the coast around Mozambique [*q.v.*]. The penetration of Islam took place from two directions, i.e. along the Rovuma after the Portuguese occupation of Kilwa [*q.v.*] in 1505, and from Angoche, which, although it declined after 1530, remained an important centre for the spread of Muslim-Swahili influence into the interior.

The political turbulence on the northern parts of the East African coast during the 16th century did not affect the coastal region of the Mozambique channel. This comparatively peaceful area became conducive to new economic developments, particularly that of ship building at Mozambique and the local production of textiles which had implications for the influence of Islam in Malawi, the one enabling the building of boats to ply on Lake Nyasa, the other as gifts to or for the purchase of slaves, ivory and other goods from the local rulers. In the wake of ever-widening commercial enterprises between the coast and the interior from the end of the 16th century onwards, the Makua and Yao [*q.v.*] were the main traders, although agents from the coast had already settled in the interior at this time.

During the early part of the 18th century, the struggle between the Portuguese and the ʿUmānīs on the one hand, and the ʿUmānīs and the local population on the other, undermined the place of Islam along the coast and along the trade routes. Mozambique displaced Kilwa as the main centre of relations with Malawi. During the early 1750s, the Portuguese were making common cause with the *shuyūkh* of Sanculo and Quitangonha against the Makua, penetrating deep into Makua country. At around this time also, Indian trading interests on the coast, centred on Mozambique, began to penetrate inland; thus in 1727 the Viceroy granted a special license to a number of wealthy Indian Muslims that allowed them to trade with the Makua.

The next development of Islam in Malawi is connected with Sayyid Saʿīd of the Bū Saʿīd [*q.v.*] dynasty of ʿUmān (1806-56), who established himself as ruler of the coast in the early part of the 19th century and encouraged trade with the interior by establishing "forts" on the Kilwa-Lake Nyasa route. By 1861 Muslims had settled at the southern end of Lake Malawi and were operating west of the lake in 1863. In the 1870s Islamic influence could be seen in that petty chiefs were being addressed as *hakimu*. The first Yao chief to adopt Islam around 1870 was one Makanjila II Banali, who employed a Ḳurʾān teacher, and children were taught to read the Ḳurʾān and to write Swahili in Arabic script. Chief Mataka I Nyambi of Mwembe dressed like an Arab and built his houses in rectangular form representing a clear coastal influence.

The caravans from the coast usually had with them what has been termed "Muslim teachers", who taught the Ḳurʾān, instructing people in Islamic beliefs and practices and encouraging literacy in Arabic and Swahili in Arabic script. They are said to have disseminated commentaries and other literature dealing with the observance of customs connected with marriage, eating and drinking, the mode of killing animals, the efficacy of charms and the making of medicines, and encouraged the building of mosques. They also became involved in the training of young men, particularly the sons and nephews of the chiefs, as *walimu* on religious scholars. Some of them were sent to the coast for further training. Through such teachers, Swahili became the language predominantly spoken by Muslims in Malawi. Another spin-off of this work has been the number of Malawi Muslims acting as *imāms* and muezzins in South African mosques.

The anti-slavery campaign from 1873 onwards led to a revival of Islam, since Muslim slave traders who were suffering an economic recession, were as a consequence determined to extend their moral and religious influence. There was a growing self-consciousness and reaction to the colonial and mission presence.

When the British protectorate was established in 1889, the Muslim presence in Malawi can be said to have been represented by such chiefs as Mlozi, a half-caste Arab at the north end of the lake; by Salīm b. ʿAbd Allāh in the central region, where Nkota Kota had become an important centre; by Makanjila, who was established on the east side of the lake, where in 1891 an Arab said to have come from Aden originally owned a house at Saidi Mwazungu's town in the southern part of Makanjila's country; and by Mponda at the south end of the lake, where there were twelve *madāris* each with its own *mwalimu*.

The Islamic renaissance in Malawi in the early part of the 20th century was linked to the Maji-Maji disturbances in German East Africa in 1905-6. The so-called "Meccan Letter" purportedly sent by the head of the Uwaysiyya [*q.v.*] *ṭarīḳa* in Mecca giving instructions to the faithful to prepare for the final apocalyptic battle, played its part in the unrest in Muslim circles in Malawi in 1908. Rumours among the Yao were claiming that the Arabs would come and kill Europeans and Africans alike who refused to accept the Muslim faith. In Malawi, this was intensified by the appearance over Mua of Halley's Comet in 1910. The hostilities in East Africa connected with the First World War also played their part in deepening the commitment to Islam in Malawi. Letters from the German officer Count Falkenstein to Mwalimu Issa Chikoka at Losewa indicated to him that the Ottoman caliph, Sultan Meḥemmed V (1909-18), was the enemy of the British, and called on Mwalimu Issa to lead a *d̲j̲ihād* against the British during Ramaḍān. The growth of Islam was also encouraged by the recruitment of Muslims for the Nyasaland Police and the King's African Rifles. The general impact of these trends can partly be seen in the establishment of a Muslim boarding school for boys at Malindi and the proliferation of mosques from 1911 onwards.

During the early years of the Protectorate, Ḳurʾān schools offered the only education acceptable to Muslims. In 1918, the Governor recommended the establishment of Muslim schools in parallel to those run by various Christian mission societies. This development was encouraged by the Phelps-Stokes Commission and Ormsby-Gore reports of 1925 and led to the opening of a Muslim school in Liwonde in 1930. From 1946 Muslims were able to establish their own schools. Independence in 1964 brought major changes in the educational system. Islamic literature in English, particularly from South Africa, became more readily available. This and closer links with Muslims and Muslim institutions in East Africa and the wider Muslim world brought about a deeper awareness of the requirements of the faith. By the late 1950s, some Malawi Muslims were able to attend the teachers' college in Zanzibar.

The nature of Islam.

The Muslim community in Malawi is not homogeneous. The differences are not only ethnic but also due to membership of various *ṭuruḳ*. Nearly all people in the Kawinga, Liwonde, Jalasi and Nyambi chiefdoms are Muslims, and a group in the Jalasi chieftainship has been known as *twaliki* (Ar. *ṭarīḳa*). They represent the Ḳādiriyya order. The *twaliki* believe that their devotions should be accompanied by loud singing and chanting of Arabic texts and by vigorous dancing. Another group, the *sukutis*, centred around the Kawinga and Liwonde chieftainships, advocate a more orthodox type of Muslim devotion in which a quiet and restrained manner is emphasised (Ar. *sukūt* "quietness, silence"). The *sukutis* represent the stricter orthodoxy of the S͟hād͟hiliyya order. They are also known as *ahl al-sunna*. These differences undoubtedly reflect the variations in Muslim mystical practice involving both *d͟hikr d̲j̲alī*, audible remembrance of God, and *d͟hikr k͟hafī*, silent remembrance. Beside these differences regarding audible and silent *d͟hikr*, the *sukutis* also differ from other groups in their funeral practices, such as eating food before a funeral, singing and dancing and carrying flags on such occasions, as well as the propriety of dancing at the annual visits (*ziyala*, Ar. *ziyāra* [*q.v.*]) to the graves. They also differ regarding the legality of eating hippopotamus meat, the building of new mosques where there already are other mosques, and special prayers. The *ziyala* are also connected with the commemoration of the Prophet's birthday (Swa. *maulidi*) on 12 Rabīʿ I, which takes the form of feasting, *sikiri* (Ar. *d͟hikr*) and exhortations. The term *ziyala* is also used for the celebration of the anniversary of the founder of the *ṭarīḳa*. The Ḳādiriyya order, which was predominant until the 1930s, celebrates the birthday of the Prophet, the two main festivals and some other occasions, with sumptuous feasting and night-long *sikiri*, sometimes referred to as *zikara* and *bayan* (*ahd*), sc. an oath of loyalty to the *s͟hayk͟h*.

Muslims of Indian origin fall into various categories. The Sunnīs among them follow the Ḥanafī *mad͟hhab*, whereas the African Sunnī Muslims follow the S͟hāfiʿī school. Among the Indian Muslims, there are also a number of S͟hīʿa belonging to the Twelve, and the K͟hod̲j̲a Ismaʿīlī and Bohorā traditions. The majority of these arrived as traders from 1928 onwards, and some of them set up large commercial establishments.

The only ordinance in Malawi that directly concerns Muslim marriage (*nikāḥ* [*q.v.*]) is the Asiatics (Marriage, Divorce and Succession) Ordinance of 1929. Its wording allows for the application of the different systems of law followed by the various sects (*firaḳ*) and law schools (*mad͟hāhib*). It also includes any local variants that may become customary. Another particularity regarding marriage appears in the Marriage Ordinance of 1903 which, contrary to the *S͟harīʿa*, allows a Christian man to marry a Muslim girl. When it comes to a Muslim wife's rights in a marriage, particularly in relation to divorce, she has almost identical rights to those of her husband.

The month of fasting, has been observed for many years in Malawi. In 1889-90 Mponda II insisted on a proper observation of Ramaḍān, although it seems that the appropriate *tarāwīḥ* prayers were not observed. Muslims speak of *kumanga namasani* "binding on Ramaḍān", and though proud to observe the restrictions, many seem to *kumasula namasani* "to loosen the bonds of Ramaḍān" before the end of the month of fasting. The fast reaches its climax in the *ʿĪd al-Fiṭr* (*Bayram*) referred to as *Idi Balak* (Ar. *baraka*). The *ʿĪd al-Aḍḥā* (*Ḳurbān*), the feast of sacrifice, is known as *Idi Bakali*, a name adopted from the Indian sub-continent, where it is known as *Baḳara ʿĪd* (Ar. *baḳara* "cow", hence "the cow festival") an indication of an early Indian influence on Islam in Malawi, but also a local emphasis and appreciation of the significance of the festival. *Zakāt* is acknowledged, but is not strictly observed except in connection with the *ʿĪd al-Fiṭr*.

Noon prayers on Fridays, known locally as *juma* prayers are held at a central place, originally at the village of the main chief. Women join in the *juma* prayer, usually in a separate section of the mosque. Muslim headmen wear scarlet headbands around their white skullcaps known as *mzuli*. This may reflect the practice among Muslim scholars, who wear different colours to signify their status or the religious order to which they belong.

A number of traditional ceremonies have survived and have been given orthodox Islamic names. Thus the term *sadaka* in Malawi has nothing to do with alms but refers to a funeral feast. It is associated with a special dance, known among the Yao as *cindimba* and is connected with the brewing of a special beer. It has been partially Islamised through the *sikiri* (*d͟hikr*), which is now perceived purely as a dance. The *akika* (Ar. *ʿaḳīḳa*) ceremony is observed in some areas.

When a Muslim dies, the *s͟hayk͟h* is invited to bless the body and delivers an oration. The body is prepared for burial by having a hole cut in the neck and the intestines squeezed empty. It is then wrapped in long lengths of white cloth and taken to the graveyard on a stretcher, usually the bed on which the person died turned up-side down. The prayers and oblations (*ukana wacisoka*) offered to ancestral spirits at the root (*lipaka*) of a shrine tree has also taken on an Islamic air. It is explained by the more zealous Muslims as the gift of food to passers-by in order that God may forgive and bless the spirit of one's ancestors. Magical charms and talismans proliferated in the pre-Independence years. One of these was the *kirisi* (amulet; Swa. *hirizi* < Ar. *ḥirz*). Another is the charm called *alibadiri* consisting of Ḳurʾānic verses wrapped in leather.

Muslim organisations.

Formal organisations are a fairly recent phenomenon in Malawi, although the Muslim Association of Malawi (MAM) was founded in the 1940s by Asian Muslims. There have been associations concerned with the provision of *madrasa* education. The *walimu* as well as the heads of the *ṭuruḳ* owing allegiance to their *s͟hayk͟h*, *murs͟hid* or *pīr* also have their "informal" organisations, some of which co-operate over *ʿīd* celebrations. Some organisations, however, are supra-national, such as the *Tablīg͟hī D̲j̲amāʿat* [*q.v.*]. Muslims of Asian origin group together according to their particular trading or geographical background such as the Sunnī Memon, Punjabi, Surti and Khatri groups and the various S͟hīʿa communities. They make substantial contributions to the building of local mosques and Ḳurʾān schools. Mosques and *madāris* are often named after the person who organised and contributed to their construction. There are no *awḳāf* [see WAḲF] but trusts for mosques are registered under the Trustee Incorporation Act, and properties vested in Trustees and Office Bearers of the Associations. The socio-economic conditions of Muslims in Malawi have on the whole not enabled them to undertake the obligation of the Pilgrimage, and there has been no organisation looking after the welfare and travel arrangements for the pilgrims until recently. In 1981, 22 Malawians performed the Pilgrimage, and since then the number has grown.

Muslims expressed an interest in better educational facilities within the context of the Protectorate as early as 1916. A Department of Education was set up in 1926, but not until 1928 were three government schools established to cater primarily for Muslim children; these had to be closed after a few years due to lack of children and parental support. The following year an education ordinance was passed opening the schools to all regardless of religious affiliation. By 1962 there were, however, 29 schools under Muslim administration and owned by the Muslim community, seven of these grant aided. Today, all schools in the country are under government control through the Ministry of Education, both with respect to policy and standards. Muslim teachers instruct Muslim pupils in the basics of Islam at the times set aside in the timetable for Religious Education. The government has also encouraged schooling in predominantly Muslim areas through support for the building of classrooms and teacher accommodation. Contemporary-style education is pursued in the mornings in schools managed by Muslims. In the afternoon they become *madāris*, where Ḳur'ān, *ḥadīth*, *fiḳh* and *lugha* are taught; but Arabic is not taught. The Yao use their own language, including a fair amount of Swahili expressions; the reformists use Chewa or English, the two official languages of Malawi, employing some Arabic greetings and formulae. The Muslim Students' Association founded in 1982, which represents the reform movement and opposes the *ṭuruḳ*, and is supported by donations from Saudi Arabia and Kuwait, produced a syllabus in Islamic education for Muslims in primary and secondary schools in 1987. In 1988 Muslims were able to establish the first Islamic institute of higher learning, the Islamic Centre. Some young people have had the opportunity to study at Arabic institutions abroad. Contacts with the Muslim Youth Movement in South Africa from 1977 onwards led to the holding of the Southern Africa Islamic Youth Conference in Blantyre in 1981, and this met again in Malawi in 1987 when the Islamic Medical Assembly, a branch of the Muslim Association of Malawi, was formed. The Muslim Association of Malawi with its headquarters in Blantyre evolved out of a central Board for Muslim Education which was set up in the 1950s to co-ordinate the work and represent the interests of the Muslim community as a whole. The Association has received financial help from Kuwait in the form of a financial director as well as teachers from various parts of the Muslim world. Through its representations, time has been allocated on Radio Malawi for programmes on Islam in Chichewa. The organisation has also enabled women to hold regular conferences since 1982.

Local publications are limited. Some Muslims read the *Muslim digest* and *al-Ḳalam* published in South Africa. A pamphlet entitled *Tartibu 'l-salat* in Chichewa has been widely distributed. Publications by the International Islamic Federation of Student Organisations with its headquarters in Kuwait, and the writings of Abū 'l-Aʿlā Mawdūdī of Pakistan are also to be found.

The only outside links Muslims in Malawi had for long were with Muslims and Islamic institutions on the East African coast. Particularly important were the contacts with the late Shaykh Abdullah Saleh al-Farsy (d. 1982), Chief Ḳāḍī of Zanzibar and later of Kenya. Through the migrant labour force, contacts were also established with various organisations in South Africa that more recently have sought to help Muslims face the growing challenge presented by the socio-economic situation in Malawi. Contacts with the wider Muslim world began with a visit from representatives of the *Dār al-Iftā'* from Saudi Arabia in 1965. The African Muslims Committee, a charitable organisation based in Kuwait, has made considerable contributions to the Blantyre Islamic Mission which was founded in 1982 and has organised youth camps. The election and re-election of Bakili Mulunzi as president of Malawi in 1994 and 1999, reflects the degree Muslims have come to play in the country, and will strengthen and enhance the community's position.

Bibliography: Y.B. Abdallah, *The Yaos*, Zomba 1919; S.S. Murray, *Handbook of Nyasaland*, Zomba 1922; M. Sanderson, *Ceremonial purification among the Wayao, Nyasaland*, in *Man*, xxii, no. 55 (June 1922); J.C. Mitchell, *The Yao village*, Manchester 1956; F.J. Simoons, *The use and rejection of hippopotamus flesh as food in Africa*, in *Tanganyika Notes and Records*, no. 51 (December 1958), 195-7; *Documents on the Portuguese in Mozambique and Central Africa 1497-1840*, Lisbon 1962; W.H.J. Rangeley, *The Ayao*, in *Nyasaland Journal*, xvi/1 (1963), 7-27; J. McCracken, *The nineteenth century in Malawi*, in T.O. Ranger (ed.), *Aspects of Central African history*, London 1968; F. and L.O. Dotson, *The Indian minority of Zambia, Rhodesia and Malawi*, New Haven 1968; E. Alpers, *Towards a history of expansion of Islam in East Africa*, in Ranger and I. Kimabo (eds.), *The historical study of African religion*, London 1972, 172-201; P. Pachai, *Malawi. The history of a nation*, London 1973; Alpers, *Ivory and slaves in East Central Africa*, London 1975; idem, *The Mutapa and Malawi political systems*, in Ranger (ed.), *Aspects of Central African history*, London 1975; Macdonald (ed.), *From Nyasaland to Malawi*, Nairobi 1975; R.C. Greenstein, *The Nyasaland Government's policy towards African Muslims, 1900-1925*, in Macdonald (ed.), *From Nyasaland to Malawi*, Nairobi 1975, 144-68; idem, *Shaykhs and Tariqas. Early Muslim ʿUlama and Tariqa development in Malawi, c. 1895-1949*, Historical Research Seminar Papers 1976/77, Chancellor College, University of Malawi; J.N.D. Anderson, *Nyasaland Protectorate*, in *Islamic Law in Africa*, London 1978, 162-70; M. Newitt, *The Southern Swahili coast in the first century of European expansion*, in *Azania*, xiii (1978), 111-26; I.A.G. Panjwani, *Muslims in Malawi*, in *JIMMA*, i/2, ii/1 (1979-80), 158-68; G. Shepperson, *The Jume of Kota Kota and some aspects of the history of Islam in Malawi*, in I.M. Lewis (ed.), *Islam in Tropical Africa*, ^{2}London 1980, 253-65; G. Shepherd, *The making of the Swahili: a view from the southern end of the East African Coast*, in *Paideuma*, xxviii (1982), 129-48; D.S. Bone, *Islam in Malawi*, in *Jnal. of Religion in Africa*, xiii/2 (1982), 126-38; R. Ammah, *New light on Muslim statistics for Africa*, in *BICMURA*, ii/1 (January 1984); Bone, *The Muslim minority in Malawi and western education*, *JIMMA*, vi/2 (1985), 412-19; N.R. Bennett, *Arab versus European. Diplomacy and war in nineteenth-century East Central Africa*, New York 1986; A.P.H. Thorold, *Yao conversion to Islam*, in *Cambridge Anthropology*, xii/2 (1987), 18-28; A.J. Matiki, *Problems of Islamic educa-*

tion in Malawi, in *JIMMA*, xii/1 (1991), 127-34; Thorold, *Metamorphoses of the Yao Muslims*, in L. Brenner (ed.), *Muslim identity and social change in sub-Saharan Africa*, London 1993, 79-90; idem, *The Muslim population in Malawi*, in *Al-ʿIlm*, xiii (1993), 71-6; idem, *The politics of mysticism. Sufism and Yao identity in Southern Malawi*, in *Jnal. of Contemporary African Studies*, xv (1997), 107-17.

(S. von Sicard)

MALFŪẒĀT (a.), literally "utterances", in Ṣūfī parlance denotes the conversations of a mystic teacher.

Though some compilations of Ṣūfī utterances were made earlier in other lands, e.g. the *Ḥālāt wa-sukhanān-i Shaykh Abū Saʿīd* (Rieu, i, 342b ii) and *Asrār al-tawḥīd* (ed. Aḥmad Bahmanyār, Tehran 1934) [see abū saʿīd b. abi 'l-khayr], it was Ḥasan Sidjzī of Dilhī who gave it a definite literary form. In 707/1307 he decided to write a summary of what he heard from his spiritual mentor, Shaykh Niẓām al-Dīn Awliyā' [*q.v.*], and completed it under the rubric, *Fawā'id al-fu'ād* (Lucknow 1302). It marked the beginning of a new type of mystical literature, known as *malfūẓāt* (sing. *malfūẓ*). A few years later, in 711/1312, Sulṭān Bahā' al-Dīn Walad [*q.v.*], son of the famous Mawlānā Djalāl al-Dīn Rūmī [*q.v.*], completed a record of his father's utterances under the title *Fihi-ma-fihi* (ed. ʿAbd al-Mādjid, Aʿẓamgaṙh 1928). But Bahā' al-Dīn prepared this record on the basis of memory, some 39 years after the death of his father, without reference to dates on which specific discussions took place. Ḥasan Sidjzī gave dates of every discourse and referred to the queries and quests of the audience. Bahā' al-Dīn perhaps aimed at providing a philosophic basis for the *mathnawī*; Ḥasan presented through the conversations of his *Shaykh* the accumulated wisdom of the mystical creed with reference to specific problems of the people. Ḥasan's example inspired saints of different mystical orders, and a considerable *malfūẓ* literature appeared in India from Uččh to Manēr and from Dihlī to Deogīr.

The new genre of mystical literature developed mainly in India, but some collections of Ṣūfī utterances were prepared elsewhere also, e.g. the *Nūr al-ʿulūm*, utterances of Shaykh Abu 'l Ḥasan Khirkānī (ed. E. Berthels, Leningrad 1929), *Malfuẓāt-i Nadjm al-Dīn Kubrā* (ms. As. Soc. of Bengal 1250-3), *Mastūrāt* (discourses of Sayyid ʿAlī Hamadānī, ms. I.O. 1850) and *Anīs al-ṭālibīn* (conversations of Khwādjā Bahā' al-Dīn Nakshband, Lahore 1323).

Several disciples of Shaykh Niẓām al-Dīn Awliyā' emulated Ḥasan in compiling conversations of the Shaykh, e.g. *Anwār al-madjālis, Tuḥfat al-abrār wa-karāmāt al-akhyār, Ḥasrat-nāma* and *Durar-i niẓāmī*. Except the last one (ms. Buhar 183 and Salārdjang Museum, Ḥaydarābād) all are no longer extant. Conversations of Shaykh Burhān al-Dīn Gharīb, a *khalīfa* of Shaykh Niẓām al-Dīn Awliyā', were compiled in the Deccan under the titles *Aḥsan al-akwāl* (ms. ʿUthmāniyya, Ḥaydarābād 478 and 1479), *Nafā'is al-anfās* (ms. Nadwat al-ʿUlamā', Lucknow), *Shamā'il al-atkiyā* (lith. Ḥaydarābād 1347), etc. In Dihlī, Ḥamīd Ḳalandar compiled his *Khayr al-madjālis* (ed. K.A. Nizami, ʿAlīgaṙh 1959), which contains conversations of Shaykh Naṣīr al-Dīn Čirāgh, chief *khalīfa* of Shaykh Niẓām al-Dīn Awliyā'. In Nāgawr [*q.v.*] the conversations of Shaykh Ḥamīd al-Dīn Ṣūfī Nāgawrī were compiled in *Surūr al-ṣudūr* (ms. Ḥabīb Gandj, ʿAlīgaṙh). The Firdawsī saints produced *Maʿdin al-maʿānī* (2 vols. lith. Bihār 1301-3/1884-6). *Mukhkh al-maʿānī* (lith. Agra 1321/1903-4), *Rāḥat al-ḳulūb* (lith. Agra) and a few other works containing the conversations of Shaykh Sharaf al-Dīn Yaḥyā Manērī. Several saints of the Suhrawardī *silsila* produced conversations of their spiritual teachers. The conversations of Sayyid Djalāl al-Dīn Bukhārī were compiled under the titles *Sirādj al-hidāya* (ed. Ḳāḍī Sadjdjād Ḥusayn, Dihlī 1983), *Djāmiʿ al-ʿulūm* (ed. Ḳāḍī Sadjdjād Ḥusayn, Dihlī 1982), etc. Even the utterances of a *madjdhūb* of ʿAlā' al-Dīn Khaldjī's period, Khwādja Karak of Kara, were collected in *Asrār al-makhdūmīn* (lith. Fatḥpur-Haswa 1893).

The production of *malfūẓ* literature in India during the 8th/14th century synchronised with Shaykh Niẓām al-Dīn Awliyā''s decision to convert the mystical movement—hitherto confined to individual spiritual salvation—into a movement for mass spiritual culture (*Siyar al-awliyā'*, Dihlī, 346-7). This led to proliferation of *khānḳāh*s [*q.v.*] in South Asia and the adoption of local dialects for the communication of ideas (see ʿAbd al-Ḥaḳḳ, *The Sufis' work in the early development of Urdu language*, Awrangābād 1933). The *malfūẓ* literature differed from literature produced earlier in the form of mystical treatises which dealt with mystical thought or mystical litanies and lucubrations. The *malfūẓ* literature was intelligible to people at all levels and had a space-time context. Since the discussions contained in *malfūẓāt* took place before people belonging to different sections of society and referred to specific problems (see *Khayr al-madjālis*, 83, 185, 240, etc.; *Maʿdin al-maʿānī*, 3), this literature has assumed great historiographical significance. It acts as a corrective to the impressions created by the court chroniclers who, nurtured as they were in Persian traditions, restricted the conspectus of history to courts and camps. This literature views the historical landscape from a different angle and fills a gap in historical knowledge by providing a glimpse into the life of the common man, his problems, his hopes and fears. For example, the economic worries of the masses during the time of Fīrūz Shāh Tughluḳ, and the efforts of the Ṣūfīs to reorient mystical thought to meet the situation created by the ideology of Ibn Taymiyya [*q.v.*], can be read in the *Khayr al-madjālis*.

Malfūẓ literature continued to be produced in India all through the centuries. The conversations of Shaykh Aḥmad Maghribī of Khattū (*Tuḥfat al-madjālis*, I.O. Persian Collection DP 979) give an insight into the economic and cultural efforts that preceded the foundation of the city of Aḥmadābād. The utterances of Gīsū Darāz [*q.v.*], *Djawāmiʿ al-kalim* (ed. Ḥāmid Ṣiddīḳī, Kānpūr 1356/1937-8), give a lively picture of mystical activity in the South.

Widespread interest in *malfūẓ* literature encouraged the production of some apocryphal collections, e.g. *Anīs al-arwāḥ* (lith. Dihlī 1312), *Dalīl al-ʿārifīn* (lith. Lucknow 1311/1893-4), *Fawā'id al-sālikīn* (lith. Lucknow 1311/1893-4), *Asrār al-awliyā'* (lith. Kānpūr 1890), *Rāḥat al-ḳulūb* (lith. Lucknow 1311/1893-4), *Rāḥat al-muḥibbīn* (ms. personal collection), *Afḍal al-fawā'id* (lith. Dihlī 1304/1886-7), *Miftāḥ al-ʿāshiḳīn* (lith. Dihlī 1309/1891-2), etc. Critical scholarship has rejected this literature as spurious. The use of the term *malfūẓāt* for the apocryphal memoirs of Tīmūr is the solitary example of the application of the term to politcal literature.

The *malfūẓ* literature produced during the 9th/15th and 10th/16th centuries contains valuable information about the social, religious and literary activities of the people in the period preceding and following the foundation of the Mughal Empire. Particular reference may be made to the *Anwār al-ʿuyūn*, conversations of Shaykh Aḥmad ʿAbd al-Ḥaḳḳ (lith. ʿAlīgaṙh 1905), *Laṭā'if-i Ḳuddūsī*, conversations of Shaykh ʿAbd al-Ḳuddūs Gangohī [*q.v.* in Suppl.] (lith. Dihlī 1311/1893-4), *Kalimāt-i ṭayyibāt*, conversations of K͟hʷād͟ja Bāḳī billāh (lith. Dihlī 1332/1914) and *Malfūẓāt-i S͟hāh Mīnā* (Hardoi n.d.).

In the subsequent centuries appeared the conversations of S͟hayk͟h Muḥammad Čis͟htī (*Mad͟jālis al-ḥasaniyya*, ms. ʿAlīgaṙh), S͟hāh Kalīm Allāh S͟hāhd͟jahānābādī (*Mad͟jālis-i kalīmī*, lith. Ḥaydarābād 1328/1910), S͟hāh ʿAbd al-Razzāḳ (*Malfūẓāt*, lith. Fīrūzpur 1303/1885-6), S͟hayk͟h Burhān S͟haṭṭārī (*T͟hamarāt al-ḥayāt*, ms. As. Soc. of Bengal 448), S͟hayk͟h ʿĪsā of Burhānpūr (*Malfūẓāt*, ms. As. Soc. of Bengal 462), ʿAbd al-Raḥmān of Lucknow (*Anwār al-Raḥmān*, lith. Lucknow 1287/1870-1), and S͟hāh ʿAbd al-ʿAzīz of Dihlī (*Malfūẓāt-i ʿAzīzī*, lith. Meerut 1314/1896-7). This literature supplies background information about the intellectual and social crisis in a period of transition. For example, the *Anwār al-Raḥmān* throws invaluable light on the decadent culture of Awadh [*q.v.*], and the utterances of S͟hāh ʿAbd al-ʿAzīz reveal reaction and response to Western culture. In *Nāfiʿ al-sālikīn* (conversations of S͟hāh Sulaymān of Taunsa, Lahore 1285) the socio-religious scenario of the Pand͟jāb before 1857 is seen in all its details.

In the early decades of the 20th century, Mawlānā As͟hraf ʿAlī of Thana Bhaẁan made effective use of the *malfūẓ* medium in propagating his teachings, but his orations are more in the nature of *mawāʿiẓ* (sermons) than *malfūẓ* (table talk). In short, no study of Ṣūfism as a popular movement in India is possible without an intensive and critical use of the *malfūẓ* literature.

Bibliography: Important *malfūẓāt* collections are cited above. For assessment, see K.A. Nizami, *On history and historians of medieval India*, Dihlī 1988, ch. "Historical significance of the Malfuz literature", 163-97; idem, *The Ahsan al-Aqwal—a fourteenth-century Malfuz*, in *Jnal. Pak. Hist. Soc.* (Jan. 1955), 40-4; idem, *The Saroor-us-Sudur—a 14th century malfuz*, in *Procs. Indian Hist. Congr.*, Nagpur 1950, 167-9; idem, *The life and times of Shaikh Farid Ganj-i Shakar*, ʿAlīgaṙh 1955, 118-20; idem, *Malfūẓāt ki tārīk͟hī ahammiyyat*, in *Arshi presentation volume*, Dihlī 1966; M. Habib, *Chishti mystic records of the Sultanate period*, in *Medieval India Quarterly*, i/2, 15-42; Riaz ul-Islam, *Collections of the Malfuzat of Makhdum-i Jahaniyan*, in *Procs. Pak. Hist. Conf.*, Karachi 1951, 211-16.

(K.A. Nizami)

MALḲOČ-OGHULLARÎ, a line of Ottoman raiders from Bosnia who were active from the late 14th to the 17th centuries.

The origin of the name Malḳoč is unclear. The suggestions that it derived from the Greek Markos or Serbian Marković are not satisfactory. The Malḳoč-og͟hullarî were probably Christian converts to Islam. A Malḳoč is apparently first mentioned in the *Short chronicle of Ioannina* (*ca.* 1400) in connection with a war between two Epirot lords, perhaps in 1388-9. Murād I supposedly sent Malḳoč from Thessaloniki/Selānīk [*q.v.*] to help one of them, in the event, successfully. The first Ottoman chronicler to mention the name, Nes͟hrī (d. before 1520), seemingly refers to the same person as commander of 1,000 archers on the right wing of the Ottoman army at the Battle of Kosovo [see ḳoṣowa] (June 1389). He may also have participated in the Battle of Nicopolis (1395). Later, Malḳoč appears as the commander (*beg*) of Sīwās. He was captured by Tīmūr in 1402 but was subsequently sent as a messenger to Bāyezīd I.

The family held lands in northern Bosnia at the time of Meḥemmed II (second reign, 1451-81). They were given land there as march *beg*s. The most renowned member of the line was Bālī Beg Malḳoč-og͟hlu, who in 1444 fought the Hungarians under John Hunyádi outside Varna but fled the field. In 1462, he commanded the right wing of the army of Meḥemmed II against Vlad Tepesh in Wallachia, and during the next decade was the provincial military chief (*sand͟jaḳ beg*) of Smederovo in Serbia, burning the Croatian city of Varaždin in 1474. In 1475-6, he was the *sand͟jaḳ beg* of Bosnia, and in 1478, he led 3,000 raiders (*akînd͟jî* [*q.v.*]) before Scutari/Is͟hḳodra [*q.v.*, in Suppl.] in Albania. The following year he led another large force of raiders into Hungary and Transylvania. He became the governor of Silistria in the 1490s, raiding Aḳ Ḳirmān in 1496 and in 1498 twice raiding Poland and threatening Krakow. He had three sons, two of whom were killed at Čāldîrān [*q.v.*] in 1514, whilst the third became *sand͟jaḳ beg* of Kilia near the mouth of the Danube.

Subsequently, in the early 16th century, we hear of Ḳara ʿOt͟hmān Beg Malḳoč-oghlu as a leading landholder in Bosnia. The last known member of the dynasty was Yawuz ʿĀlī Pas͟ha, governor of Egypt, who became Grand Vizier in 1603 and died the following year at Belgrade. After this, the family seems to have lost its power and influence.

Bibliography: The basic study is F. Babinger, *Beiträge zur Geschichte des Geschlechtes der Malqoč-Oghlu's*, in *AISO Napoli*, N.S., i (1940), 117-35, repr. in idem, *Aufsätze und Abhandlungen zur Geschichte Südosteuropas und der Levante*, Munich 1962, i, 355-69; Branislav Đurđev *et al.*, *Historija naroda Jugoslavije*, Zagreb 1959, ii, 117; Dimitri Bogdanovich *et al.*, *Historija Srbska naroda*, Belgrade 1982, ii, 518; K. Setton, *The papacy and the Levant, 1204-1571*, Philadelphia 1984, iv, 694-5; C.H. Imber, *The Ottoman Empire 1300-1481*, Istanbul 1990, 48, 134, 228, 244-5; *Türk Ansikopedisi* and *Yeni Türk Ansiklopedisi*, arts. *Malkoçoğulları*.

(G. Leiser)

MAMLŪKS.

(iii) Art and Architecture

(a) *Architecture*

Within the history of Islamic art, the architecture of the Mamlūk period (648-922/1250-1517) occupies an intermediary position between what might be termed the early period predating the Mongol invasion and the later imperial arts of the Tīmūrids, Ṣafawids, Ottomans and Mug͟hals. Unlike its Tīmūrid counterpart, with which it is partly contemporary, Mamlūk architecture did not substantially impact on the later history of Islamic art once Egypt and Syria had become provinces of the Ottoman Empire. It lingered on in a reduced scale in Ottoman Egypt, until it was revived in modern times as a manifestation of a national style of mosque architecture.

Apart from the prestige accruing from their victories over the Mongols and the Crusaders, the Mamlūks were celebrated as guardians and patrons of orthodox Islam, an image they fostered by sponsoring religious foundations and creating centres of scholarship and Ṣūfī activities and other philanthropic institutions. The sheer number of mosques, *madrasa*s and *k͟hānḳāh*s which they established in Cairo proved without parallel in the Muslim world at the time, and is even believed to have exceeded the genuine requirements of the population. All the while remaining careful to cultivate the exclusive character of their ruling aristocracy, one based on their military slave origins, the Mamlūks directed their patronage at the man in the street. Instead of promoting an inward-looking court life, their chief concern was to obtain the enduring support of the religious establishment. The Mamlūk sultans ruled their capital in a very direct manner, involving themselves closely in the minutiae of religious and social policy. Sultans and *amīr*s themselves inspected monuments during the construction phase and, as supreme overseers of the *awḳāf*, ensured the maintenance of the buildings of their predecessors.

Mamlūk patronage was essentially religious, and one of its most significant aspects lay in the architecture and in the decorative arts which it helped to foster. Moreover, urban development was a major concern of the Mamlūks and the motivation behind the intensive building activity for which they became responsible in Cairo. Since sultans and *amīr*s incorporated their own lavish mausoleums within religious foundations, thereby setting up memorials for themselves in their capital, Cairo as a whole soon became an vast arena for Mamlūk art patronage. Most of the Mamlūk architectural legacy in Cairo was created by such sultans and *amīr*s, and only to a lesser extent by local dignitaries.

Although the Mamluks ruled over a territory including Egypt, Greater Syria and the Ḥidjāz, Mamlūk architectural identity is mainly discernible in Cairo. Even more decidedly than under other Islamic régimes, the metropolitan style of religious architecture rarely re-occurs outside the capital. The rulers' direct involvement in the building activity of the province of Egypt was confined to infrastructures, fortifications and commercial buildings, leaving the foundation of mosques and colleges to the governors and the local notables. The scarcity of significant royal mosques in the provinces accounts for a discrepancy in religious architectural style between the capital and the outlying regions. Religious architecture in Syria and the Ḥidjāz kept faith on the whole with the predominant regional building tradition, as was the case of the Egyptian province itself, where the cities of Ḳūṣ and Alexandria, in spite of their economic importance, retained a provincial type of architecture. Occasional mutual influences between Cairo and Syria were confined to decoration or individual elements that did not involve the architecture generally. The builders who erected the imperial mosques in Cairo were rarely employed beyond the confines of the capital. The exception confirming this rule is that of a late-9th/15th century initiative by Sultan Ḳāyitbāy, who is reported by chroniclers to have sent entire teams of craftsmen from Cairo to Jerusalem, Mecca and Medina. These reports themselves attest the singularity of this initiative. Indeed, *wakf* descriptions of his *madrasa*s in Jerusalem and Medina, as well as the remnants of his *madrasa* in Jerusalem, confirm that such patronage remained exceptional.

Moreover, the enormous quantitative discrepancy between Mamlūk architecture in Cairo and in Syrian cities, as well as the supremacy of the metropolitan religious foundations which functioned as the intellectual centres of the Mamlūk state, contributed to the stylistic singularity of Cairene Mamlūk architecture. With a few exceptions, such as the buildings of Tankiz al-Nāṣirī in Jerusalem (Burgoyne 1987, 223-48), urban schemes do not seem to have been a major concern of Mamlūk patrons in Syrian cities.

The evolution of Mamlūk architecture in Cairo shows an increasing tendency to adapt and adjust the layout of the buildings to the urban environment rather than to impose a large-scale or symmetrical architecture on the city. The portal, minaret and mausoleum dome were assigned a location that best responded to the specific aesthetic needs of the site rather than being forced to conform to a preconceived canon. A major factor in the architectural design was the founder's mausoleum dome, which was assured maximum visibility both through its position in the building and an increasingly lofty exterior transitional zone between the drum and dome (Kessler 1972; L. Ali Ibrahim 1975; and see ḳubba). This increased visibility required the builder to adjust both layout and architecture to the site. The patrons' challenge was to balance the status-enhancing placement of the mausoleum to the street with a juxtaposition with the mosque sanctuary. If the latter requirement could not be ensured because of the location, the preference was to place the mausoleum on the street side. In the city centre, royal foundations built round a courtyard were preferably located to the west side of the street so that the south-east, Mecca-oriented sanctuary could be on the street side. This allowed the mausoleum to lie adjacent to the sanctuary and overlook the street at the same time. Like their mosques, Mamlūk *madrasa*s and *khānḳāh*s were built along the axis of the orientation towards Mecca, as were the mausoleums which, with rare exceptions, included a *miḥrāb* (Kessler 1984). Owing to the aforementioned constraints, it often transpired that the orientation of the mosque's *miḥrāb* diverged from that of the mausoleum. Unlike in Syria, the minaret in Cairo was to be found not only in Friday mosques but in *madrasas*, *khānḳāhs* and minor oratories as well.

This interaction with the urban fabric, together with the pre-eminence of the metropolitan religious institutions housing Mamlūk mausoleums, created an architecture exclusively suited to Cairo. Furthermore, the overriding focus of Mamlūk monumental patronage in Cairo was in fact a response to the historical situation. It should be remembered that the history of Mamlūk Cairo begins at the same time as the fall of Baghdād from where Baybars transferred the ʿAbbāsid caliphate to his own capital [see mamlūks. i. History], a symbolic gesture that designated Cairo as Baghdād's successor. Already the possessor of a long undisturbed metropolitan tradition, unrivalled at that time by any other city in Egypt or in Syria, the Egyptian capital was the natural candidate to perpetuate Baghdād's glorious history.

Like any other architecture, that of the Mamlūks was based on that of its predecessors; and as such it inherited architectural devices and decorative techniques from the Fāṭimid and Ayyūbid periods. Far more monuments were erected than during the Ayyūbid era, however, and over a much longer period of time. Already al-Ẓāhir Baybars waived the Shāfiʿī rule applied by his predecessors which allowed only one Friday mosque to each agglomeration. Moreover, the inclusion of Syria and territories as far north as Cilicia, the migration of craftsmen escaping the Mongol invasions and others who came from al-Andalus, as well as the contacts with the Il-Khānids and with Christian kingdoms, introduced international features into the arts of the 7th-8th/13th-14th centuries.

A. Religious architecture in Cairo

(i) *The Baḥrī period*

From Shadjar al-Durr to al-Ẓāhir Baybars. The first building that can be securely attributed to the Mamlūk era is the funerary *madrasa* of Shadjar al-Durr [*q.v.*], the widow of the last Ayyūbid sultan al-Ṣāliḥ Nadjm al-Dīn Ayyūb, of which only the mausoleum is today extant. It was built in 648/1250 in the cemetery of Sayyida Nafīsa north of Fusṭāṭ [*q.v.*] as part of a complex that included a palace, a *ḥammām* and gardens.

In the same year, the short-lived sultana also added a mausoleum to her husband's *madrasa* in the heart of the Fāṭimid al-Ḳāhira, thus bringing to the city a tradition of princely funerary architecture which subsequently became a significant feature of Mamlūk Cairo (Creswell 1959, ii, 135f.-6; Behrens-Abouseif 1983). The profile of the mausoleum dome and its stucco decoration remain faithful to the tradition of the Ayyūbid period.

The *madrasa* of al-Muʿizz Aybak, Sha̲d̲jar al-Durr's second husband and her successor on the Mamlūk throne, was built in 654/1256-7 in the commercial centre of Fusṭāṭ (al-Maḳrīzī, *Sulūk*, iv, 302); it seems to have been part of an urban project which integrated pre-existing commercial structures. As it is not included in al-Maḳrīzī's *K̲h̲iṭaṭ*, it must have disappeared with the decline of Fusṭāṭ as al-Ḳāhira took over as Egypt's definitive capital during the 8th/14th century. It was the first and, indeed, only royal Mamlūk foundation within the city of Fusṭāṭ.

Sultan al-Ẓāhir Baybars I's [*q.v.*] first religious foundation—a *madrasa* next to that of his master al-Ṣāliḥ Nad̲j̲m al-Dīn—was built in al-Ḳāhira in 660-2/1262-3. The building itself, which was demolished in the last century, is reported to have consisted of four *īwān*s built around a courtyard to accommodate the four *mad̲h̲hab*s of Islamic law. It possessed no mausoleum. Nineteenth-century drawings and paintings convey some idea of the former exterior. The portal formed the shape of a semi-dome on *muḳarnas*, a pattern already applied in Ayyūbid Syrian architecture but the earliest of its kind to be documented in Cairo, a distinction that applies equally to the four-*īwān* plan. (Creswell 1959, ii, 142ff.)

When al-Ẓāhir Baybars built his monumental mosque on the site of his polo-ground in the northern outskirts of Ḥusayniyya (665-7/1266-9), it was the first Friday mosque to be founded in the Egyptian capital for some 150 years. The mosque, with its pointed arches and monumental entryways, contains references to the Fāṭimid mosque of al-Ḥākim. The major innovation and the most spectacular feature of the building was the size of the wooden dome over the *miḥrāb*, which covers the *maḳṣūra* of nine bays and is borne by piers. The space between the courtyard and the domed zone is furthermore emphasised by a transept running perpendicular to the arcades of the sanctuary. Creswell maintains that the dome was influenced by the Artuḳid mosque of Mayyāfāriḳīn [*q.v.*] built in the 6th/12th century. The building materials for Baybars' mosque had been seized as spolia from Crusader monuments during Baybars' triumphal campaign in Yaffa. The mosque was already falling into ruin during the mediaeval period (Creswell, 1950, ii, 155ff.; Bloom 1982). Baybars also founded in 671/1273 another monumental Friday mosque at Mans̲h̲ā' at al-Maharānī, between al-Ḳāhira and Fusṭāṭ, of which no trace exists today (Ibn Duḳmāḳ, iv, 119.). Baybars' reign produced a significant number of other secular and religious buildings in Egypt and Syria (Meinecke, ii, 6-51).

From al-Manṣūr Ḳalāwūn to al-As̲h̲raf K̲h̲alīl. The buildings of al-Manṣūr Ḳalāwūn [*q.v.*], his wife Fāṭima K̲h̲ātūn and his son al-As̲h̲raf K̲h̲alīl [*q.v.*], cannot be connected directly to those of their predecessors, neither do they seem to have had a marked impact on their successors'. Ḳalāwūn was the first Mamlūk sultan to build a religious complex with his own mausoleum in the city centre. The complex (683-4/1284-5) which included a *madrasa*, a mausoleum and a great hospital, displays many unprecedented features: the verticality of the façade and its decoration, the plan of the mausoleum centred on an octagonal domed baldachin, the basilical plan of the prayer *īwān*. Most remarkable is the treatment of the façade with pointed-arch recessed panels which include the windows, the upper ones forming a triple composition consisting of a pair of arched openings surmounted by a bull's eye. This treatment recalls the architecture of Norman Sicily, the façade of the Ḳalāwūn complex in fact exhibiting a striking resemblance to the original frontage of the Cathedral of Palermo. The marble mosaics decorating the opulent interior are once again closely related to those of Norman Sicily and southern Italy (Creswell 1959, ii, 190ff.; Meinecke 1971; Behrens-Abouseif 1995, *Sicily*). The adjustment of the Ḳalāwūn complex façade to the alignment of the streets—so deviating from the Mecca-oriented axis within—is a device of urban aesthetics created in the Fāṭimid period and faithfully maintained under the Mamlūks. The complex was erected on the street side to the west, with a passage between the mausoleum and the *madrasa* leading to the hospital. The massive masonry minaret stands at the northern edge of the complex, juxtaposing harmoniously with the mausoleum dome. The *madrasa* is built around a courtyard with two unequal axial *īwān*s and two lateral recesses between which the multi-storied dwelling units were located.

The mausoleum is one of the most lavishly decorated monuments of mediaeval Cairo, displaying the entire repertoire of techniques of that time: carved and painted wood, stucco, inlaid and carved marble as well as, in the *miḥrāb*, conch-glass mosaic. The hospital, no longer extant, was not visible from the street; it is described in its *waḳf* deed as a lavish construction built in two perpendicular axes around a courtyard (see Herz's plan, in Creswell 1959, ii, 207). The plan of the mausoleum and the massive shape of the minaret of Ḳalāwūn remained unique in Cairene architecture.

In the cemetery of Sayyida Nafīsa are the remains of a funerary *madrasa* attributed to Fāṭima K̲h̲ātūn (682-3/1283-4), a wife of Ḳalāwūn. Today only the funerary chamber with the gateway and the first storey of the rectangular minaret are extant. A photograph published by E. Diez (*Kunst der islamischen Völker*, Munich 1915) shows that this *madrasa* had arched recesses with the same triple-window composition that occurs on Ḳalāwūn's façade. Next to it, Ḳalāwūn's son, al-As̲h̲raf K̲h̲alīl, a ruler who left no architectural work in the city centre, built his own funerary *madrasa* of which only the mausoleum is extant (687/1288). The three domes of Ḳalāwūn, his wife and his son K̲h̲alīl, have in common a high octagonal drum with windows set in recessed arches, and an oval profile, whereas the interior treatment of the transitional zones is different in each case (Creswell 1959, ii, 180-1, 214-15); Meinecke 1992, i, 42ff.).

Al-Nāṣir Muḥammad and his immediate successors. Al-Nāṣir Muḥammad b. Ḳalāwūn [*q.v.*] was the greatest builder of the Baḥrī Mamlūk sultans. His long reign (693-741/1293-1341), interrupted by two interim periods (694-8/1294-99 and 708/1309) coincided with a period of relative peace and prosperity which was also the most fruitful for architectural achievement. Al-Nāṣir encouraged his *amīr*s to build mosques and palaces not only in the city itself but also in the outskirts on new land added to Cairo by the receding of the course of the Nile. Al-Nāṣir's second reign was already displaying the versatility characteristic of the architecture of the 8th/14th century (Meinecke-Berg 1977; J.A. Williams 1984; al-Harithy 2000).

The mosque (1262-3) of al-Ẓāhir Baybars

The mosque (1335) of al-Nāṣir Muḥammad at the Citadel with the eastern minaret and the dome over the *miḥrāb* (the dome is a modern reconstruction)

The funerary complex (1284-5) of Sultan Ḳalāwūn, with the funerary complex (1384-6) of Sultan Barḳūḳ in the back (B. O'Kane)

Interior view of the mausoleum of Sultan Ḳalāwūn (B. O'Kane)

The double mausoleum (1303-4) at the *kh̲ānḳāh/madrasa* of the *amīrs* Salār and Sanḏj̲ar

The funerary *kh̲ānḳāh* (1306-10) of Baybars al-Ḏj̲asẖankīr (Dept. of Egyptian Antiquities)

The double mausoleum known as Sulṭāniyya (1450s-60s) with the minaret of Ḳawṣūn to the left

The funerary *madrasa/djāmiʿ* (1356-62) of Sultan Ḥasan

The funerary *madrasa* (1356) of the *amīr* Ṣarg͟hitmis͟h (Dept. of Egyptian Antiquities)

The funerary mosque (1472-4) of Sultan Ḳāyitbāy

The *miḥrāb* of the mosque of Sultan Ḥasan

The minarets (1415-20) of Sultan al-Mu'ayyad on the Fāṭimid gate, the Bāb Zuwayla

The mausoleum dome of Sultan Ḳāyitbāy (B. O'Kane)

The interior of the mosque of Sultan Ḳāyitbāy

In 703/1304, al-Nāṣir Muḥammad completed the *madrasa* next to his father's during the first interval of his reign by Sultan Lādjīn [*q.v.*]. The construction possesses a narrow façade whose total width in the upper reaches was occupied by the minaret and the mausoleum dome. The dome, which like the top part of the minaret is no longer extant, has an octagonal drum similar to that of the previous Ḳalāwūnids. The *madrasa* is built with four axial *īwān*s with multi-storied living quarters between them. The Gothic portal is a spoil from a church in Palestine (Creswell 1959, ii, 234ff.; Meinecke 1992, i, 49).

Once the mausoleum dome became an integral part of the façade design, the evolution of urban religious and/or funerary architecture during the 8th/14th century stimulated the builders to display their versatility in the individual treatment of the minarets and the mausoleum domes, and most of all to create a consistently harmonious composition incorporating these two elements. At the funerary foundations of Salār and Sandjar (703/1303-4), which could have been a *madrasa* or a *khānḳāh*, the minaret is juxtaposed with a pair of unequal-sized mausoleum domes that formed a singular silhouette when viewed from the street. Here the mausoleums are Mecca-oriented, but, exceptionally, not the *madrasa*/*khānḳāh*.

At the *khānḳāh* of Baybars II al-Djashankīr (706-9/1306-10), too, the funerary dome adjoins the minaret harmoniously, leaving the prayer hall on the other side of the courtyard because of the placement of the four-*īwān khānḳāh* on the eastern side of the street. The mausoleum chamber, richly decorated in marble mosaic, contrasts with the rather plain interior of the Ṣūfī institution. In addition to the living units overlooking the courtyard, there was a separate dwelling compound (Fernandes 1983).

The funerary *madrasa* of Sunḳur al-Saʿdī (715-21/1315-21), of which only the façade with the mausoleum and the minaret remain extant, presents further variation on the shape of minaret and dome. The rectangular brick shaft is particularly slender and has lavish *muḳarnas*, while the dome, whose drum is decorated with stucco bands around the windows, stands on an elliptic base (Creswell 1959, ii, 267f.-8; M. ʿAbd al-Raḥmān Fahmī 1970). The small funerary mosque of Aydumur al-Bahlawān (747/1346), with one of the earliest masonry domes, is of the same composition.

Neither of the two major monuments of al-Nāṣir Muḥammad survives, sc. a great *khānḳāh* planned with his mausoleum at Siryāḳūs (a village to the north of Cairo) and his great mosque in the southern outskirts of al-Ḳāhira to the north of Fusṭāṭ (J.A. Williams 1984). However, his mosque at the Citadel completed in 735/1335 attests to artistic achievement under his patronage. The dome of its *maḳṣūra*, which is similar to but of lesser proportions than that of Baybars, was revetted in green tiles. Similarly, two unusual masonry minarets, one flanking the main entrance and another at the south-eastern corner, have a ceramic tilework mosaic in the Il-Khānid style decorating their upper part, which must have been the work of the Tabrīzī craftsmen reported to have come to Cairo at that time and to have been involved in the decoration of the no longer-extant mosque of Ḳawṣūn. Except for the use of ceramic on the dome and the minarets, the exterior is plain, in marked contrast to contemporary urban mosques.

Subsequent examples demonstrate that, due to urban constraints, the hypostyle courtyard mosque could no longer be accommodated within the city without sacrificing its symmetry. The Friday mosque of the *amīr* Almās al-Nāṣirī (729/1328-9), which also included the founder's mausoleum, has an irregular configuration (Karim 2000). The Friday mosque of Altinbughā al-Māridānī (739-40/1339-40), which in principle follows the plan of al-Nāṣir's mosque in the Citadel with three axial entrances and a large dome above the *miḥrāb*, has a corner of its sanctuary cut off to follow a bend of the street. At the mosque of Āḳsunḳur (747-8/1346-7), the façade is not parallel to the *ḳibla* wall but instead projects with the minaret out into the street. The minaret, originally with four instead of the usual three stories, could thus announce the mosque from an even greater distance (Behrens-Abouseif 1985, *Minarets*, 92-3). The heavily damaged interior of the mosque is characterised by cross-vaulted bays carried by piers, indicating Syrian influence (Meinecke 1973).

The funerary mosque (750/1349) of the *amīr* Shaykhū is also laid out according to an irregular plan. Together with Shaykhū's great *khānḳāh* built six years later across the street (757/1355), it forms an urban composition embracing the Ṣalība street with two symmetrical minarets and two similar portals. The *khānḳāh* has only the sanctuary with the *riwāḳ* or hypostyle plan, with living units on the three other sides of the courtyard. The enormous dwelling compound behind the prayer hall is the only one of its kind extant in Cairo. The use of the hypostyle sanctuary of traditional mosques in a *khānḳāh* had occurred already at the foundation of the *amīr* Ḳawṣūn (736/1335), built in the cemetery to the southeast of the Citadel. Today, only a stone minaret and a mausoleum dome stand. A reconstruction, however, shows that it had a double mausoleum on each side of the hypostyle sanctuary with the dwelling units most likely occupying the other sides of the court (Ali Ibrahim 1974).

The idea of building a religious complex on both sides of a street had been applied previously by the Amir Bashtāk (736/1336) with a *khānḳāh* connected to a mosque with a bridge; only a monumental minaret is extant.

The late Ḳalāwūnid period. Despite the political decline under the sons of al-Nāṣir Muḥammad and the devastation brought about by the Black Death (749/1348), the second half of the 8th/14th century was very productive and creative in terms of an architecture that continued to integrate exotic foreign patterns.

The *madrasa* of Ṣarghitmish (757/1356) displays the unusual combination of a four-*īwān* plan with a dome over the main *īwān*. The mausoleum dome projects boldly onto the street across the courtyard. The two domes are unexpected on the Cairene skyline; bulbous and with a high drum, their profile recalls Tīmūrid architecture, which, however, they pre-date. The mausoleum dome has a double shell, while that of the prayer hall was rebuilt with only one. Similarly recalling Tīmūrid dome profiles are the two ribbed onion-shaped masonry domes of the anonymous mausoleum known as Sulṭāniyya, which also have a double shell. The building has been assigned to the 750-60s/1350-60s. Despite the similarities, a direct influence from Samarḳand can be excluded on chronological grounds, but a common Iranian prototype from Western Persia or ʿIrāḳ must surely have influenced the Samarḳand and the Cairo domes (Meinecke 1976).

It is paradoxical that the mosque of Sultan Ḥasan, the most monumental of Mamlūk mosques and even of all mediaeval mosques at that time, was founded in the decade following the depredations of the Black Death. Although it took from 757/1356 to 764/1362 to build, its decoration was never completed. The funerary complex which includes a *madrasa* for the four *madhhabs* is the first Mamlūk teaching institution to be at the same time a Friday mosque, a combination that was subsequently adopted in all princely foundations. The complex stands beneath the Citadel, where it dominated an open square with the hippodrome, plainly visible from the palaces of the sultans at the Citadel. It is the only Mamlūk mosque to present a mausoleum behind the prayer hall that occupies the same width. The original dome, which collapsed in the 18th century, was described by an eyewitness as bulbous; it might have been similar to the wooden dome of the ablution fountain in the courtyard that has a rounded profile and no drum, or to the domes of Ṣarghitmish and the Sulṭāniyya mausoleum that possess a high drum, the latter with a pointed profile. Only one original minaret is extant, that flanking the mausoleum at the eastern corner. At *ca.* 80 m it was the tallest of its time, though the other one was replaced by a smaller structure in the Ottoman period. The placement of a dome between two minarets created a new perspective on the Cairo skyline (Kessler 2000). Two more minarets were planned at the entrance, according to al-Maḳrīzī, and as the buttresses themselves show; one was built and collapsed shortly afterwards so that the ambitious project of four minarets had to be abandoned. Like the design of the portal itself, the pair of minarets betray an Anatolian Saldjūḳ influence, albeit more than a century after the end of the Rūm Saldjūḳ period (Rogers 1972). The vestibule is roofed by a masonry dome flanked by three half-domes suggesting Byzantine inspiration, while remnants of glazed tile decoration in the lunettes of the mausoleum windows show the continuity of the Tabrīzī workshop. All the three-storey living units are arranged so as to overlook the street on the northern and southern façades of the complex. The interior has four gigantic vaulted *īwāns* around the courtyard, the sanctuary being the largest vault in the mediaeval Muslim world. The four sections of the *madrasa*, which are accessible from the corners of the courtyard have an analogous layout, with their cells overlooking the street on two sides. Although craftsmen from different parts of the Muslim world are reported to have worked at this monument, it is in essence and spirit a Mamlūk building.

The architecture of the Baḥri Mamlūks maintained an experimental and innovative character till the end of this period. Dome profiles, minarets and portals were not fully standardised; instead a variety of forms coexisted. The classical hypostyle courtyard mosque or *riwāḳ* mosque was gradually replaced by the more flexible *īwān* plan. This type of plan, whose exterior was not reflected in its interior of four unequal *īwāns* built around a courtyard, could better accommodate irregularities in the plot. Since Sultan Ḥasan the *madrasas* and *khānḳāhs* of the subsequent sultans and *amīrs* functioned as Friday mosques as well. Beside the rectangular-octagonal-cylindrical minaret (Salār and Sandjar, Baybars al-Djashankīr, Sunḳur al-Saʿdī, Ḳawṣūn) built in brick or masonry or in both materials with a ribbed domed pavilion (a disposition the Mamlūks inherited from their predecessors), the Baḥrī period created a new, more slender type with a stone shaft, either octagonal (Māridānī) or cylindrical (Āḳsunḳur, al-Nāṣir Muḥammad at the Citadel), and surmounted by an eight-sided pavilion crowned with a bulb on *muḳarnas*. Before masonry domes made an appearance in the mid-8th/14th century, Mamlūk domes were built either of brick or plastered wood. Two types of profiles were used for the domes, one that curves from the base (Baybars al-Djashankīr, Sunḳur al-Saʿdī) with a plain surface, and another that starts straight and curves at about one-third up the elevation. The second shape was used for ribbed and for carved masonry domes and is the characteristic form of later funerary architecture. During the Baḥrī period, initial experiments with masonry domes were undertaken. At first ribbed like their brick predecessors, they later appeared in other varieties. With the dome of Tankizbughā (769/1359), its surface carved with alternating concave-convex ribs, and that of Ildjāy al-Yūsufī (774/1373), carved with twisted ribs, Mamlūk dome builders opened up a new era in the design of masonry domes (Kessler 1976). For the transitional zones of brick or wooden domes, squinches and pendentives were used. The squinches were structured into niches with several tiers resembling a large *muḳarnas*. The pendentives of the domes of al-Nāṣir's mosque at the Citadel and of Sultan Ḥasan are made of wood. Stone domes were built mostly with angular pendentives carved with *muḳarnas*. Baḥrī Mamlūk decorators used largely stucco decoration on minarets and dome exteriors and in interiors, along with polychrome marble.

(ii) *The Circassian period*

Early Circassian (*784/1382 to the mid-9th/15th century*).

Notwithstanding economic decline and monetary instability, the sultans and *amīrs* of this period continued to build religious foundations on a large scale. The Circassian period sets out with the reign of Sultan Barḳūḳ (784-91/1382-89 [*q.v.*]), whose funerary religious complex in the heart of the city does not make use of any novelties. Its sanctuary, however, has a tripartite basilical composition with a wooden flat ceiling. The funerary *khānḳāh* of his son Faradj (801-15/1399-1412 [*q.v.*]) is the first to be built by a sultan in the northern cemetery and its layout takes full advantage of the available space, deploying perfect symmetry with a double mausoleum and a double minaret. Its zigzag carved stone domes are the largest built by the Mamlūks, with a diameter of over 14 m. It is built on the hypostyle courtyard plan with piers supporting domical bays. Living units occupying two storeys were placed along the lateral arcades of the courtyard (Lamei Mostafa 1968).

Sultan al-Muʾayyad Shaykh's [*q.v.*] monumental, multifunctional complex of *madrasa-khānḳāh*-mosque (821/1418) possesses a similar layout to that of Faradj. This mosque became a Cairo landmark because of its twin minarets erected on top of the Fāṭimid towers of the Bāb Zuwayla, which bear the only builder's signature to be found in Mamlūk architecture. The mosque also had a third minaret at the northeastern entrance.

The reign of Barsbāy (825-41/1422-38 [*q.v.*]) introduced masonry domes with carved star patterns. His funerary *khānḳāh* (835/1432) in the northern cemetery includes three star-carved mausoleum domes which exemplify the progress made in dealing with the difficult task of adapting a geometrical symmetrical design to a domical surface (Kessler 1976). The unique architecture of this *khānḳāh* demonstrates that the cemetery at that time had become an urban environment necessitating other than purely symmetrical layouts. Instead of being built around an inner courtyard, the elements of the complex are juxtaposed along the road. The mosque has a lateral format with the mausoleum chamber juxtaposed to it, occupying the same width and similarly overlooking the road. Further south is the *khānḳāh* proper with the living quarters. Other structures were built on the opposite side of the road, including a one-dome *zāwiya*.

Late Circassian (mid-9th/15th century to 923/1517).

Although the hypostyle courtyard mosque never totally disappeared, in the 9th/15th century, Friday mosques were increasingly built without an open courtyard (e.g. those of Īnāl, Ḳāyitbāy and Ḳānṣawh al-Ghawrī), adopting instead the plan of the *ḳāʿa* or reception hall current in Cairene residential architecture since pre-Mamlūk times. Already, the 8th/14th century had produced small covered mosques with an irregular plan which included *īwāns* around a covered courtyard, the adoption of the *ḳāʿa*, however, allowed the building of small covered mosques of a standard configuration. A major factor in the disappearance of the courtyard is the fusion of the functions of the *khānḳāh* with the *madrasa* and the Friday mosque; at the same time the abandonment of the original residential function of the *madrasa* and the *khānḳāh* rendered the cells around the courtyard superfluous (Behrens-Abouseif 1985).

The funerary mosque of Ḳidjmas al-Isḥāḳī (885-6/1480-1) is a genuine jewel of late Mamlūk architecture. It is remarkable not only for the refinement of its interior and innovative exterior decoration, but most of all for its almost triangular plan inserted between three streets, displaying an ingenious adaptation to the urban setting.

The reign of Ḳāyitbāy (827-901/1468-96 [see ḲĀʾIT BĀY] stimulated and refined architectural decoration, ushering in novel designs and techniques in both carving and marble inlay. The façade of his free-standing *sabīl-maktab* (879/1474) on Ṣalība Street and that of the mosque of Ḳidjmas al-Isḥāḳī present polychrome marble inlay of unprecedented intricacy.

During the 9th/15th century, domed *zāwiyas* and mosques were built. The earliest known belong to Barsbāy's funerary complex, two others were founded by Yashbak min Mahdī, the Great *Dawādār*, in the northern outskirts; the larger one, known as *Ḳubbat al-Fadāwiyya* (884-6/1479-81) was lavishly decorated with stucco, an unexpected choice at this period. Their architecture differs from that of funerary domes, built in brick and on squinches, the exterior being plain and lacking the conventional transitional zone (Behrens-Abouseif 1981, 1982, 1983).

The reign of Sultan Ḳānṣawh al-Ghawrī [*q.v.*] heralded a new era in the concept of architecture, with an emphasis on monumentality rather than minute decoration, at the same time bringing a new taste for ceramic revetment. At the Sultan's funerary complex (915/1501), the dome and the upper storey of the minaret were once entirely covered with lapis-blue tiles. This period also brought about an important change in the shape of minarets; the double bulb at the top was a new device and was used twice in combination with an entirely rectangular shaft at the two mosques of Ḳānibāy (908/1503, 911/1506), and once in combination with a facetted shaft at al-Ghawrī's tall minaret at the Azhar mosque. Al-Ghawrī's rectangular minaret at his own funerary mosque had four bulbs at the top. Ḳānibāy's funerary mosque (903/1503) beneath the Citadel unfolds a façade with an unusual broad format, inspired by its location overlooking the *maydān* from an elevated ground.

Ḳānṣawh al-Ghawrī managed to acquire a plot in the very centre of the city which allowed him to construct his foundation on both sides of the street, an unprecedented layout which may be considered as the peak of the urbanistic approach of Mamlūk religious architecture. The mosque and the minaret on the west side of the street face a monumental mausoleum, as deep as the *ḳibla īwān*, situated on the other side of the street and attached to a *khānḳāh* without dwellings and a *sabīl-maktab* projecting with three façades on to the street. A wooden roof covered the street, which widened to the north into a small piazza with booths and shops (Behrens-Abouseif 2002).

Although its layout is comparable to that of Ḳāyitbāy, the large funerary *khānḳāh* of the *amīr* Ḳurḳumās in the northern cemetery (911-13/1506-7) differs by its substantial proportions that make it one of the most monumental constructions in all Mamlūk architecture.

In the Circassian period, the harmonious juxtaposition of minaret and mausoleum dome continues to characterise the silhouette of funerary foundations. The increasing number of foundations of sultans and *amīrs* in the northern cemetery led to the urbanisation of its architecture that adopted the same street-oriented aesthetic criteria as in the city centre. This period maintained the tradition established in the late 8th/14th century of attaching to the religious foundation a *sabīl-maktab*, a structure consisting in a combination of fountain house with a primary school; the double structure was placed at a corner with the *sabīl* at ground level surmounted by the *maktab*. During the reign of Ḳāyitbāy, free-standing *sabīl-maktabs* were built, a tradition which was taken over in the Ottoman period. The reign of Ḳāyitbāy produced the domed *sabīl* recalling funerary architecture, such as the *sabīl* of Yaʿḳūb Shāh al-Mihmandār (901/1495-6) in Cairo and that of Ḳāyitbāy in the *ḥaram* of Jerusalem.

In the late Mamlūk period, the forms of portals, minarets, and domes were standardised, displaying a variety in their carved decoration, however, and reaching the peak of refinement at Sultan Ḳāyitbāy's mausoleum (877-9/1472-4).

Stucco decoration disappears from late Mamlūk architecture except for a short-lived revival in the reign of Ḳāyitbāy, namely at the Dome of Yashbak, albeit in a very different style. Stone-carving is more extensively used than in the past, and now adorns also *miḥrāb* conchs. Groin vaults become fashionable in the late 9th/15th and early 10th/16th century, also characterising portal vaults.

B. Residential and domestic architecture in Cairo

Mamlūk residential architecture [see ḲĀʿA; RABʿ] is less well preserved than religious (see Gracin *et al.* 1982). Half-a-dozen *ḳāʿas* and the vestiges of four monumental palaces, those of Ālīn Āḳ, Ḳawṣūn, Bashtāk and Ṭāz, date from the Baḥrī period. These great princely residences were continuously restored and remodelled, making it difficult to assess their original form. Our knowledge of the different types of residential architecture has to rely on the enormous resources of *waḳf* documents.

The courtyard of Cairene residences, to which the main entrance leads, is generally surrounded by stables and service rooms. Cairene residential architecture was not "inward-facing" in the sense that it overlooked the courtyard and remained blind to the street. The courtyard was not the centre of the house, as in Syrian or North African constructions, but simply a semi-private space. There was a general preference for giving the main rooms a view over the street or the available scenery, depending on the site. There could be more than one courtyard according to the size of the *dār*, and in large mansions a courtyard could fulfil the function of a garden.

The main reception hall or *ḳāʿa* lay on the first floor, occupying the height of several storeys where the smaller units or apartments (*riwāḳ* [*q.v.*]) were located. In the 9th/15th century, the *maḳʿad* becomes a salient feature of residential architecture. It is a loggia facing north and overlooking the courtyard on the first storey. Its origin seems to be associated with the architecture of 8th/14th century princely stables. The 9th/15th century presents another category of residences of less monumental, middle-size type of dwellings, such as the house of Zaynab K͟hātūn.

The palaces of the Citadel, which had undergone continuous restoration and refurbishment work by all Mamlūk sultans, are no longer extant. The most remarkable were the *īwān kabīr* and the *ḳaṣr* built by al-Nāṣir Muḥammad and maintained by all subsequent sultans (see Garcin *et alii* 1982, 41ff.; Behrens-Abouseif 1985; Rabbat 1995). The first was a basilical construction of gigantic dimensions employing Pharaonic columns. It had a ceramic green dome, as did the Sultan's mosque nearby.

As is to be expected, the decorative repertoire of residential architecture did not differ particularly from that of religious monuments. The royal palaces of the early Baḥrī period, however, did make use of murals depicting figures.

C. Religious architecture in Syria

As mentioned above, Mamlūk architecture of Greater Syria, including Palestine, followed regional schools autonomous from the capital, hence need to be dealt with separately. (The following brief summary is based on Meinecke for Aleppo and Damascus and Burgoyne for Jerusalem.) Whereas Cairene builders emphasised the verticality of their monuments with recessed panels around the windows, their Damascene colleagues stressed the horizontal configuration of their buildings with striped (*ablaḳ*) masonry as the essential exterior ornamental device. The use of recesses remained exceptional. In Damascus, the *madrasa* with the mausoleum of al-Ẓāhir Baybars built by his son Baraka K͟hān (676-8/1277-9) continues Ayyūbid traditions, with its four unequal-sized halls overlooking a courtyard; the prayer hall is connected to the domed funerary chamber. It is entirely decorated in glass mosaic, emulating the mosaics of the Great Mosque of Damascus (Meinecke 1992, i, 37-8). More characteristic, however, was a type of funerary foundations without a courtyard featuring two equal domes placed symmetrically on either side of the entrance, one of them with a *miḥrāb* to be used as a gathering and prayer hall, the other for funerary purposes. The *madrasa* of Fāridūn al-ʿAd͟jamī (744/1343-4), that recalls Cairene architecture with its four *īwāns* around a courtyard, was a special case. In the 9th/15th century, *madrasas* with two axial *īwāns* across a courtyard were constructed; plain Syrian *madrasas*, unlike the Cairene, were mostly built without a minaret, and Syrian minarets themselves were essentially rectangular with a sole balcony. Whereas octagonal shafts were also built throughout the Mamlūk period in Aleppo, in Damascus they appear only in the 9th/15th century. The Syrian dome profile remained close to the pattern established under the Ayyūbids, being rounded and occasionally ribbed.

In Aleppo, the plan of the hypostyle *riwāḳ* mosque built on piers supporting cross-vaulted bays, with or without courtyard, prevailed. The *madrasas*, built around a courtyard, have a lateral sanctuary roofed by a series of domes; cells and rooms of various sizes occupy the three other sides.

The holy city of Jerusalem enjoyed the most intensive Mamlūk patronage in Syria. Although no new Friday mosque was founded in this period, beside the one already existing at the Citadel, Mamlūk *amīrs* surrounded the Ḥaram on three sides with *madrasas*, *k͟hānḳāhs* or *ribāṭs*, or multifunctional institutions, most of them with mausoleums, usually domed, attached to them (Burgoyne 1987). The mausoleums attached to buildings around the *ḥaram* were always placed on the *ḥaram* side. There was no standard plan, most religious foundations possessing a covered courtyard surrounded by a varying number of *īwāns* and rooms. The complex of the mighty governor of Syria Tankiz (729/1328-9) had a four-*īwān madrasa* with a vaulted courtyard. It is the most important Mamlūk foundation in Jerusalem, since it served urban needs with two *ḥammāms*, a dwelling complex and a covered market called *sūḳ al-ḳaṭṭānīn*. The only *madrasa* built by a Mamlūk sultan is the As͟hrafiyya started by Sultan K͟hus͟hḳadam [*q.v.*] and rebuilt under the auspices of Ḳāyitbāy by Cairene craftsmen, hence its metropolitan style (Walls 1990).

In Jerusalem, unlike in other Syrian cities, minarets were attached to *madrasas* and *k͟hānḳāhs*; six extant ones are attributed to the Mamlūk period.

The city of Tripoli has a number of well preserved handsome Mamlūk monuments founded after Sultan Ḳalāwūn liberated it from the Crusaders in 688/1289. Throughout the following century, the city witnessed an intense building activity (Salam-Liebig 1983). Al-As͟hraf K͟halīl, the son of Ḳalāwūn, founded the Great Mosque which was completed by his successor al-Nāṣir Muḥammad in 714/1314-15. The architecture of the city is characterised by its masonry domes and vaulted spaces. In mosques and *madrasas* the larger dome is often not the one over the *miḥrāb*, but the central dome that covers the courtyard space (D͟jāmiʿ of Ṭaynāl, 1336; *Madrasa* of al-Burṭāsī, 1320s). The portals display half-domes on elaborate *muḳarnas* combined with carvings and *ablaḳ* masonry. Syrian *madrasas*, unlike those in Cairo, often lack living units.

An interesting feature of Mamlūk religious architecture in Syria is the carving of foundation deeds (*waḳfiyya*) on the external wall of the monument.

Bibliography: 1. Source material. For the study of Mamlūk architecture, beside the monuments themselves and their epigraphy (see van Berchem), an important number of *waḳf* documents are of prime importance to the study of the buildings in their original form and function as well as their urban context. The significance of al-Maḳrīzī's *K͟hiṭaṭ* does not need to be emphasised, as well as Ibn Duḳmāḳ's *K. al-Intiṣār li-wāsiṭat ʿiḳd al-amṣār*, Būlāḳ 1314/1896-7; see S. Denoix, *Décrire le Caire. Fusṭāṭ-Miṣr d'après Ibn Duqmāq et Maqrīzī*, Cairo 1992. Moreover, al-Maḳrīzī's *Sulūk* and all other Mamlūk chronicles and biographical encyclopaedias include valuable if scattered information on Mamlūk building activities. Ewliyā Čelebi's *Siyāhatnāmesi*, x, Istanbul 1938, which gives a description of Cairo and its monuments in the 11th/17th century in the tradition of al-Maḳrīzī's *K͟hiṭaṭ*, includes a valuable account. The *K͟hiṭaṭ al-tawfīḳiyya* of ʿAlī Mubārak (1888) continues, in the tradition of al-Maḳrīzī, the enumeration and description of Cairo's monuments down to his own time, often including information from *waḳf* documents.

A comprehensive collection of plans of Mamlūk monuments in Egypt and Syria is to be found in the first volume of Meinecke's *Mamlukische Architektur* (1992); the second volume lists all monuments known from the sources or from physical evidence to have been constructed in the Mamlūk period.

2. Studies. (a) General. M. Van Berchem, *Matériaux pour un Corpus Inscriptionum Arabicarum*, Mémoires publiés par les Membres de la Mission Archéologique Française au Caire, xix/1-4, Cairo 1894-1903; K.A.C. Creswell, *A brief chronology of the Muhammadan monuments of Egypt to A.D. 1517*, Cairo 1919; E. Pauty, *Les hammams du Caire*, Cairo 1933; L.A. Mayer, *Saracenic heraldry, a survey*, Oxford 1933; Ḥasan ʿAbd al-Wahhāb, *Taʾrīkh al-masādjid al-athariyya*, Cairo 1946; Farid Shafiʿi, *West Islamic influences on architecture in Egypt*, in *Bull. of the Fac. of Arts, Cairo University*, xvi/2 (December 1954), 1ff.; K.A.C. Creswell, *The Muslim architecture of Egypt*, 2 vols., Oxford 1952-9 repr. New York 1978; J.M. Rogers, *Seljuk influences on the monuments of Cairo*, in *Kunst des Orients* [= *KO*], vii/1 (1972), 40-68; M. Meinecke, *Zur mamlukischen Heraldik*, in *Mitteilungen des Deutschen Archäologischen Instituts, Abteilung Kairo* [= *MDAIK*], xxviii/2 (1972), 213-87; Ch. Kessler, *Funerary architecture within the City*, in *Colloque International sur l'Histoire du Caire (1969)*, Cairo 1972, 257-67; S. Humphreys, *The expressive intent of the Mamluk architecture of Cairo: a preliminary essay*, in *Stud. Isl.*, xxxv (1972), 69-119; Hayat Salam-Liebich, *The architecture of the Mamluk city of Tripoli*, Cambridge, Mass. 1975; Layla Ali Ibrahim, *The transitional zones of domes in Cairene architecture*, in *KO*, x/1-2 (1975), 5-23; Kessler, *The carved masonry domes of mediaeval Cairo*, Cairo and London 1976; Meinecke, *Die mamlukische Fayencemosaikdekorationen. Eine Werkstätte aus Tabriz in Kairo*, in *KO*, xi (1976-7), 85-144; V. Meinecke-Berg, *Quellen zur Topographie und Baugeschichte in Kairo unter Sultan an-Nāṣir Muḥammad b. Qalāʾūn*, in *ZDMG, Supplement ii* (1977), 539-50; D. Behrens-Abouseif, *The Qubba, an aristocratic type of* zāwiya, in *AI*, xix (1983), 1-7; J.A. Williams, *Urbanization and monument construction in Mamluk Cairo*, in *Muqarnas*, ii (1984), 33-45; Kessler, *Mecca-oriented urban architecture in Mamluk Cairo. The madrasa-mausoleum of Sultan Shaʿban II*, in A.H. Green (ed.), *In quest of an Islamic humanism. Arabic and Islamic studies in memory of Mohamed al-Nowaihi*, Cairo 1984, 97ff.; Meinecke, *Mamluk architecture. Regional architectural traditions. Evolution and interrelations*, in *Damaszener Mitteilungen*, ii (1985), 163-75; Behrens-Abouseif, *The minarets of Cairo*, Cairo 1985, repr. 1987; eadem, *Change in function and form of Mamluk religious institutions*, in *AI*, xxi (1985), 73-93; M.H. Burgoyne, *Mamluk Jerusalem*, London 1987; Behrens-Abouseif, *Islamic architecture in Cairo: an introduction*, Leiden, New York and Cairo 1989, repr. 1992; Mohamed-Moain Sadek, *Die mamlukische Architektur der Stadt Gaza*, Berlin 1990; Saleh Lamei Mostafa, *The Cairene sabil: form and meaning*, in *Muqarnas*, vi (1990), 33-42; Meinecke, *Mamlukische Architektur in Ägypten und Syrien*, 2 vols., Mainz 1993; Behrens-Abouseif, *Sicily, the missing link in the evolution of Cairene architecture*, in U. Vermeulen and D. De Smet (eds.), *Egypt and Syria in the Fatimid, Ayyubid and Mamluk eras*, Leuven 1995, 275-301; eadem, Muhandis, Shādd, Muʿallim. *Note on the building craft in the Mamluk period*, in *Isl.*, lxxii/2 (1995), 293-309; Kessler, *The "imperial reasons" that flawed the minaret-flanked setting of Sulṭān Ḥasan's mausoleum in Cairo*, in *Damaszener Mitteilungen*, xi (1999), 307-17; B. O'Kane, *Domestic and religious architecture in Cairo. Mutual influences*, in Behrens-Abouseif (ed.), *The Cairo heritage. Papers in honor of Layla Ali Ibrahim*, Cairo 2000, 149-83; Howyda al-Harithy, *The patronage of al-Nāṣir Muḥammad ibn Qalāwūn*, in *Mamluk Studies Review*, iv (2000), 219-44.

(b) Individual monuments. M. Herz, *La mosquée du Sultan Hassan au Caire*, Cairo 1899; idem, *La mosquée d'Ezbek al-Youssoufi*, in *Revue Egyptienne*, i (1899), 16ff.; idem, *Die Baugruppe des Sultans Qalawun*, Hamburg 1910; C. Prost, *Les revêtements céramiques dans les monuments musulmans de l'Egypte*, Cairo 1916; L.A. Mayer, *The buildings of Qaytbay as described in his endowment deeds*, London 1938; G. Wiet, *La Mosquée de Kāfūr au Caire*, in *Studies in Islamic art and architecture in honour of Professor K.A.C. Creswell*, Cairo 1965, 260-9; Saleh Lamei Mostafa, *Kloster und Mausoleum des Farağ ibn Barqūq in Kairo*, Abhandlungen des Deutschen Archäologischen Instituts, Abteilung Kairo [= ADAIK] Islamische Reihe ii, Glückstadt 1968; Layla Ali Ibrahim, *Four Cairene miḥrābs and their dating*, in *KO*, vii/1 (1970-1); ʿAbd al-Raḥmān Fahmī Muḥammad, *Bayna adab al-maḳāma wa-fann al-ʿimāra fi ʾl-madrasa al-saʿdiyya (ḳubba Ḥasan Ṣadaḳa)*, in *BIE*, lii (1970-71) 59-83, Arabic text section; M. Meinecke, *Das Mausoleum des Qalāʾūn in Kairo. Untersuchungen zur Genese der mamlukischen Architekturdekoration*, in *MDAIK*, xxvii/1 (1971), 47-80; Mostafa, *Moschee des Farağ ibn Barqūq in Kairo*, ADAIK, Islamische Reihe iii, Glückstadt 1972; Meinecke, *Die Moschee des Aqsunqur an-Nasiri in Kairo*, in *MDAIK*, xxxiv xxix/1 (1973), 9-48; Ibrahim, *The great Ḫānqāh of the Emir Qawsūn in Cairo*, in *ibid.*, xxx/1 (1974), 37-57; eadem, *The zāwiya of Shaikh Zain al-Dīn Yūsuf in Cairo*, in ibid., xxxiv (1978), 79-110; A Misiorowskij, *Mausoleum of Qurqumas in Cairo. An example of the architecture and building art of the Mamlouk period*, Warsaw 1979; Meinecke, *Die Restaurierung der Madrasa des Amirs Sābiq ad-Dīn Miṯqāl al-Ānukī und die Sanierung des Darb Qirmiz in Kairo*, Mainz 1980; D. Behrens-Abouseif, *Four domes of the late Mamluk period*, in *AI*, xvii (1981), 191-2; Mostafa, *Madrasa, Ḫānqāh und Mausoleum des Barqūq in Kairo (mit einem Beitrag von Felicitas Jaritz)*, ADAIK, Islamische Reihe iv, Glückstadt 1982; J. Bloom, *The mosque of Baybars al-Bunduqdārī*, in *AI*, *xviii* (1982), 45-78; Behrens-Abouseif, *An unlisted monument of the fifteenth century. The dome of* Zāwiyat al-Damirdāš, in *AI*, xviii (1982), 105-21; eadem, *The lost minaret of Shajarat ad-Durr at her complex in the cemetery of Sayyida Nafīsa*, in *MDAIK*, xxxix (1983), 1-16; J.A. Williams, *The Khanqah of Siryaqus: a Mamluk royal religious foundation*, in *In quest of an Islamic humanism. Arabic and Islamic studies in memory of Mohamed al-Nowaihi*, 109-19; L. Fernandes, *The foundation of Baybars al-Jashankīr. Its waqf, history and architecture*, in *Muqarnas*, iv (1987), 21-42; Chahinda Karim, *The mosque of Aṣlam al-Bahāʾī al-Silāḥdār (746/1345)*, in *AI*, xxiv (1988), 233-53; Behrens-Abouseif, *The Citadel of Cairo: stage for Mamluk ceremonial*, in *AI*, xxiv (1988), 25-79; Ibrahim and B. O'Kane, *The madrasa of Badr al-Dīn al-ʿAynī and its tiled miḥrāb*, in *AI*, xxiv (1988), 253-68; A.G. Walls, *Geometry and architecture in Islamic Jerusalem. A study of the Ashrafiyya*, London 1990; C. Williams, *The mosque of Sitt Hadaq*, in *Muqarnas*, xi (1944) 55-64; Howyda al-Harithy, *The complex of Sultan Ḥasan in Cairo. Reading between the lines*, in *Muqarnas*, xiii (1996), 68-79; Nasser Rabbat, *The citadel of Cairo*, Leiden and New York 1996; Behrens-Abouseif, *Sultan Qāytbāy's foundation in Medina: the* madrasah, *the* ribāṭ *and the* dashīshah, in *Mamluk Studies Review*, ii (1998), 61-71; eadem, *Qāytbāy's madrasahs in the Holy Cities and the evolution of Ḥaram architecture*, in *Mamluk Studies Review*, iii (1999), 129-49; Ch. Kessler, *The "imperial reasons" that flawed the minaret-flanked setting of Sulṭān Ḥasan's mausoleum in Cairo*, in *Damaszener Mitteilungen*, xi (1999), 307-17; al-Harithy, *Turbat al-Sitt. An identification*, in Behrens-Abouseif (ed.) *The Cairo heritage. Papers in honor of Layla Ali Ibrahim*. 103-22;

Chahinda Karim, *The mosque of Ulmas al-Ḥadjib*, in *ibid.*, 123-48; Behrens-Abouseif, *Sultan al-Ghawrī and the Arts*, in *Mamluk Studies Review*, vi (2002), 1-16.

(c) Domestic architecture. A. Lézine, *Les salles nobles des palais mameloukes*, in *AI*, x (1971), idem, *Persistance des traditions pré-islamiques dans l'architecture domestique du Caire*, in *AI*, xi (1972), 1-22; idem, *Trois palais d'époque ottomane*, Cairo 1972; Layla Ali Ibrahim, *Middle-class living units in Mamluk Cairo*, in *AARP*, xiv (1978), 24-30; J.C. Garcin, B. Maury *et al.*, *Palais et maisons du Caire*, i, *Époque mamelouke* Paris 1982; D. Behrens-Abouseif, *Quelques traits de l'habitation traditionnelle dans la ville du Caire*, in A. Bouhdiba and D. Chevalier (eds.), *La ville arabe dans l'Islam, histoire et mutations*, Tunis and Paris 1982, 447-59; Mona Zakarya, *Deux palais du Caire médiéval. Waqfs et architecture*, Paris 1983; Ibrahim, *Residential architecture in Mamluk Cairo*, in *Muqarnas*, ii (1984), 47-60.

(b) *The decorative arts*

Mamlūk art was less centralised than the other late imperial arts of the Muslim world as far as the decorative arts were concerned, a phenomenon due mainly to the absence of an equivalent of the Tīmūrid *kitābkhāna* or the Ottoman *naḳḳāshkhāna*. These royal workshops were in the first place set up to serve the arts of the book and thereby to fulfil the requirements of dynastic bibliophile patrons. While creating a repertory of designs for the illustration and illumination of books, they were involved in, and inspired, other media as well, the result being an interdisciplinary princely style. The Mamlūk rulers were not renowned as great book-lovers; the libraries which they sponsored were primarily part and parcel of their religious foundations in the city. However, in the Baḥrī period some crafts such as metalwork, glass and sgraffito ware advertised the aesthetic of titular epigraphy as the major decorative motif in art objects. Once the preponderance of titular epigraphy was no longer a characteristic feature of Mamlūk objects, i.e. by the end of the Baḥrī period, the decorative arts began to show different approaches to decoration across crafts as well as within the same craft.

A. Metalwork

The first period of Mamlūk metalwork continues the tradition established under the Ayyūbids. Zodiac and courtly themes (hunting and musicians) combined with animal friezes, along with epigraphic, geometric and floral designs, to decorate vessels in the second half of the 7th/13th century. At the same time, one final flowering of figural compositions rendered in an unprecedented monumental style and with great individuality occur shortly before figural themes were to disappear altogether from metalwork at the beginning of the 8th/14th century. This is apparent on the two vessels signed by Ibn al-Zayn, the so-called Baptistère de St Louis and the Vasselot bowl, both in the Louvre.

Mamlūk metalware is also strongly indebted to the Mawṣil tradition of silver inlay, as indicated by the large number of craftsmen signatures with the *nisba* of *al-mawṣilī* inscribed on objects until the mid-8th/14th century. Craftsmen from Mawṣil are believed to have migrated to the Mamlūk lands in order to escape the Mongol invasion. The continuity of *mawṣilī* signatures over a century after the end of the tradition in Mawṣil itself is a remarkable feature. During the first three quarters of the 8th/14th century, corresponding to the reign of al-Nāṣir Muḥammad and his sons, the Mamlūks produced a large number of exquisite brass objects with silver inlay decoration (and sometimes also with gold) with monumental epigraphic bands in *thuluth* script as main theme, delineating royal or princely titles combined with blazons. During this period chinoiserie floral patterns were integrated into the Mamlūk floral repertoire, along with the occasional Chinese dragon or bird motif. Among the objects produced were candlesticks, incense-burners, Ḳur'ān boxes with Ḳur'ānic inscriptions, trays and tray bases, pen-boxes, ewers, bowls and basins. The shapes tended to vary little; Islamic metalworkers in general were more interested in surfaces than in creating new forms.

The Mamlūks also produced various types of suspensed lighting implements unparalleled in the Muslim world, most of which are in the Islamic Museum in Cairo. There is a group of large open-work polycandelons (*tannūrs*) in cast bronze. Among them those bearing names of Amīr Ḳawṣūn, Sultan Ḥasan and Sultan Ḳānṣawh al-Ghawrī are remarkable. There are also polycandelons of pierced sheet-brass from the 9th/15th century. Composite lamps made of sheet-brass consisted of a tray, into which the glass lamps were inserted, surmounted by a spherical shade. The shade is densely pierced so as to form a translucent background against which inscriptions naming a sultan or an *amīr* stand out. Another group of lamps made of pierced sheet-brass was made in the shape of a truncated hexagonal pyramid, the base being the tray; it was produced throughout the entire Mamlūk period. Some metal lamps are signed but none has the Ḳur'ānic Verse of the Light which is so current on glass mosque lamps.

Very few metal art objects are known to have been produced between the last quarter of the 8th/14th century and the late 860-early 870s/1460s. With the revival of the production of metalware, a variety of new and disparate styles appear, without the monumental titular inscriptions characteristic of their Baḥrī predecessors. One group consists of dishes, bowls, basins, and lunch boxes made of tinned copper, and engraved with a series of interlocking bands forming cartouches and medallions filled with alternating inscriptions, knotted motifs and tight scrolls; the inscriptions are mostly benedictory verses, though princely names occasionally occur. This group, which lacks the calligraphic aesthetics of the earlier period, is indebted to Western Persian metalwork.

Another group consists of bowls with a rounded profile; their surface is plain except for a triple engraved band near the rim with inscriptions of a somewhat vernacular style with poetry and homilies. This group, too, harks back to some very similar Persian prototypes from 8th/14th century Shīrāz.

A group of spherical hand-warmers, lidded bowls and ewers with predominantly knotted and braided motives are attributed to late Mamlūk Syria. Some of the vessels combine a Mamlūk decoration with a European vessel, which indicate that objects were sent from Europe, mainly Italy, so as to be decorated in Egypt or Syria.

The group formerly known as Veneto-Saracenic and wrongly attributed to a Muslim workshop in Venice, has been now convincingly attributed to a late Mamlūk production (J. Allan 1986). The group differs strongly from mainstream Mamlūk metalware; their decoration is minutely engraved with unmatched refinement, recalling some Tīmūrid jugs, with new forms of scrolls and floral patterns against which silver-inlaid curved lines interlock to form neo-arabesques or lobed cartouches. The most famous of these vessels, many of which seem to possess European bodies, are signed by Mu'allim Maḥmūd al-Kurdī, one of about half-a-dozen identified craftsmen.

Fourteenth-century Mamlūk lamp in the Davis Collection, Copenhagen

Late Mamlūk tinned copper bowl in the Nasser D. Khalili Collection

Mamlūk scraffito ceramic bowl (14th century) in the Nasser D. Khalili Collection

Mamlūk underglaze-painted jar (14th century) in the Nasser D. Khalili Collection

Fourteenth-century Mamlūk enamelled glass bottle the Nasser D. Khalili Collection

Late Mamlūk lidded bowl, so-called "Veneto-Saracenic", in the Nasser D. Khalili Collection

There is also a group of high-quality, luxurious basins with shallow facetted forms mentioning the name of Sultan Ḳāyitbāy. The facets and the relief patterns also point to Persian influence. A magnificent piece in Istanbul is inlaid with silver and gold.

Bibliography: G. Wiet, *Catalogue général du musée arabe du Caire. Objets en cuivre*, Cairo 1932, repr. 1984; P. Ruthven, *Two metal works of the Mamluk period*, in *Ars Islamica* (1934), 230-4; D.S. Rice, *Two unusual Mamluk metal works*, in *BSOAS*, xxiii/2 (1950), 487-500; idem, *The blazons of the baptistère de St Louis*, in *ibid.*, xxiii/2 (1950), 367-80; idem, *Studies in Islamic metalwork*. I, in *ibid.*, xiv/3 (1952), 569-78; idem, *Studies in Islamic metalwork*. IV, in *ibid.*, xv/3 (1953), 489-503; idem, *The baptistère de St Louis*, Paris 1953; idem, *Studies in Islamic metalwork*. V. in *ibid.*, xvii/2 (1955), 207-31; idem, *Inlaid brasses from the workshop of Aḥmad al-Dhakī al-Mawṣilī*, in *Ars Orientalis*, ii (1957), 283-326; L.A. Mayer, *Islamic metalworkers and their work*, Geneva 1959; E. Baer, *Fish-pond ornaments on Persian and Mamluk metal vessels*, in *BSOAS*, xxxi (1968), 14-27; A.S. Melikian-Chirvani, *Cuivres inédits de l'époque de Qā'itbāy*, in *KO*, vi/2 (1969), 99-133; J.W. Allan, *Later Mamluk metalwork. A series of dishes*, in Oriental Art, xv/1 (1969), 38-43; idem, *Later Mamluk metalwork. II. A series of lunch-boxes*, in *Oriental Art*, xvii/2 (1971), 156-64; J.M. Rogers, *Evidence for Mamluk-Mongol relations*, in *Colloque International sur l'histoire du Caire (1969)*, Cairo 1972, 385-403; Melikian-Chirvani, *Venise, entre l'Orient et l'Occident*, in *BÉt.Or*, xxvii (1974), 1-18; E. Atıl, *Renaissance of Islam. The arts of the Mamluks*, Washington DC 1981; Allan, *Islamic metalwork. The Nuhad Es-Said Collection*, London 1982; idem, *Shaʿbān, Barqūq and the decline of the Mamluk metalworking industry*, in *Muqarnas*, ii (1984), 85-94; idem, *Venetian-Saracenic metalwork. The problem of provenance*, in *Venezia e l'Oriente Vicino Atti del Primo Simposio Internazionale sull' Arte Veneziana e l'Arte Islamica*, Venice 1986; idem, *Metalwork in the Islamic world. The Aaron Collection*, London 1986; J. Bloom, *A Mamluk basin in the L.A. Mayer Memorial Institute*, in *Islamic Art*, ii (1987), 15-26; D. Behrens-Abouseif, *The baptistère de St Louis. A reinterpretation*, in *Islamic Art* iii (1988-9), 3-13; S. Carboni, *Il periodo mamelucco Baḥrī (1250- 1390)*, in *Eredità dell'Islam. Arte Islamica in Italia*, Venice 1993, 278-89; Behrens-Abouseif, *Mamluk and post-Mamluk metal lamps*, Cairo 1995; eadem, *A late Mamluk [?] basin with Zodiac imagery*, in *AI*, xxix (1995), 1-21; R. Ward, *The "baptistere de St Louis", a Mamluk basin made for export to Europe*, in Ch. Burnett and A. Contadini (eds.), *Islam and the Italian Renaissance*, London 1999, 112-23.

B. Ceramics

Mamlūk pottery can be divided into seven decorative and technical categories: sgraffito, slip-painted, underglaze-painted, overglaze-painted lustre, celadon imitations, unglazed moulded and unglazed painted ware.

The Mamlūks both imported and also imitated China celadon ware, and it is this imitation product, comprising a buff body with copper or red glaze in Chinese-inspired forms, that forms the largest group of wares unearthed at Fusṭāṭ. Sgraffito forms the most characteristic group of Mamlūk pottery. It is made of a coarse red clay, the design being scratched through the slip to reveal red lines from underneath a brownish or green glaze. The forms are related to those of metalwork, as is the decoration, which consists essentially of titular epigraphy with benedictions and blazons, which date them to the first half of the 8th/14th century. Some of these objects were made for the kitchen, as is attested by an inscription on a bowl in the al-Ṣabāḥ Collection in Kuwait. Another type of coarse red bodied vessels show a white slip painted in brown, green or yellow.

Underglaze-painted ware constitutes a very different case. Produced in Egypt and Syria in large quantities, this group is rarely inscribed. Syrian ware is supposed to possess a firmer and finer body with a sharper executed design, and some pieces are made of red earthenware. The vessels (jars, albarelli, bowls, dishes, and goblets) have a porous greyish white frit body covered with a white slip painted in blue, black, green and turquoise under a transparent glaze. Their designs are mostly geometric, dishes and bowls displaying an interior radiating motif centred at the bottom of the vessel. The geometric design is filled in with floral motifs and sometimes adorned with calligraphic decoration. They can easily be, and are sometimes, confused with Persian Sulṭānābād ware. They also include representations of animals (birds, rabbits, fish and horses), and fragments with figural representations were also found. As mentioned above, craftsmen from Tabrīz worked in 8th/14th century Cairo in the production of ceramic for architectural decoration.

In the 9th/15th century, a new style of underglaze-painted ceramic was developed, imitating the Chinese Ming blue-and-white wares imported in large quantities to the Mamlūk lands. The vessels of this period very often bear craftsmen's signatures, which show that the same workshop could turn out a variety of styles. Some *nisbas* of craftsmen (*al-hurmuzī*, *al-tawrīzī*) point to a Persian connection. In the early 9th/15th century, ceramic revetment was used in Syria and in Egypt in the form of underglaze-painted tiles decorated similarly to contemporary vessels. The Mosque of Ghars al-Dīn al-Tawrīzī in Damascus (826/1424) contains a tile-clad *miḥrāb* signed by Ghaybī al-Tawrīzī, who also produced vessels and tiles in Cairo. Epigraphic blazons of supreme workmanship, inscribed with the name of Sultan Ḳāyitbāy set in a tympanum with blue-and-white floral decoration patterns, used to decorate a building of this sultan. The drum of al-Ghawrī's mausoleum dome, itself once covered with blue tiles, also presents a blue-black and white underglaze-painted inscription along its drum (Prost 1916, 11ff.). The mausoleum of the *amīr* Sulayman dated 951/1544 is adorned with a similar inscription on its drum; the tympanums of its exterior door and windows include ceramic tiles with underglaze painted epigraphic and floral patterns.

Although lustre-painted ware is generally attributed to Syria, wasters found at Fusṭāṭ confirm the existence of Egyptian production (A. Yusuf 2000). Mamlūk lustre-painted ware which was exported to Europe is characterised by its beautiful golden lustre in blue, turquoise and brownish red.

Bibliography: Aly Bahgat and F. Massoul, *La céramique musulmane de l'Egypte*, Cairo 1930; A. Abel, *Gaibi et les grands faïenciers égyptiens d'époque mamlouke*, Cairo 1930; M.A. Marzouk, *Three signed specimens of Mamluk pottery from Alexandria*, in *Ars Orientalis* ii (1957), 497-501; idem, *Egyptian sgraffiatio ware excavated at Kom ed-Dikka in Alexandria*, in *Bull. of the Fac. of Arts, Alexandria University*, xiii (1959), 3-23; Ahmad ʿAbd al-Raziq, *Documents sur la poterie d'époque mamlouke Sharaf al-Abwānī*, in *AI*, vii (1967), 21-32; J. Carswell, *Archaeology and the study of later Islamic pottery*, in D.S. Richards (ed.), *Islam and the Trade of Asia. A colloquium*, Oxford 1970, 63-5; idem, *Some fifteenth-century hexagonal tiles from the Near East*, in

Victoria and Albert Museum Yearbook, iii (1972), 59-75; idem, *Six Tiles*, in R. Ettinghausen (ed.), *Islamic art in the Metropolitan Museum of Art*, New York 1972, 99-109; K. Toueir, *Céramiques mameloukes à Damas*, in *BÉtO*, xxvi (1973), 209-17. Carswell, *Syrian Tiles from Sinai and Damascus*, in *Archaeology in the Levant. Essays for Kathleen Kenyon*, Warminster 1978, 269-92; idem, *Sin in Syria*, in *Iran* xvii (1979), 15-24; G. T. Scanlon, *Some Mamluk ceramic shapes from Fustat: 'Sgraff and 'Slip'*, in *Islamic Archaeological Studies*, ii (1980) 58-145; B. Petersen, *Blue and white imitation pottery from the Ghaibi and related workshops in medieval Cairo*, in *Bull. of the Museums of Far Eastern Antiquities*, lii (1980), 65-88; Scanlon, *Mamluk pottery. More evidence from Fustat*, in *Muqarnas*, ii (1984), 115-26; M. Jenkins, *Mamluk underglaze-painted pottery. Foundations for future study*, in *Muqarnas*, ii (1984), 95-114; M. Meinecke, *Syrian blue-and-white tiles of the 9th/15th century*, in *Damaszener Mitteilungen*, iii (1988), 203-14; Ahmad 'Abd al-Raziq, *Le sgraffiato de l'Egypte Mamluke dans la collection d'al-Ṣabāḥ* in *AI*, xxiv (1988), 1-23; C. Tonghini and E. Grube, *Towards a history of Syrian Islamic pottery before 1500*, in *Islamic Art*, iii (1988-9), 59-93; R. Ward, *Incense and incense burners in Mamluk Egypt and Syria*, in *Transactions of the Oriental Ceramics Society*, lx (1990-1), 68-82; eadem, *Tradition and innovation. Candlesticks made in Mamluk Cairo*, in J.W. Allan (ed.), *Islamic art in the Ashmolean Museum, Oxford Studies in Islamic Art*, x/2 (1995), 147-57; U. Staacke, *I metalli mamelucchi del periodo baḥrī*, Palermo 1997; E. Gibbs, *Mamluk ceramics (648-923H/A.D. 1250-1517)*, in *Transactions of the Oriental Ceramic Society*, lxiii (1998-99), 19-44; G. Fehérvári, *Ceramics of the Islamic world in the Tareq Rajab Museum*, London 2000; Abd al-Ra'uf Ali Yusuf, *Egyptian luster-painted pottery from the Ayyubid and Mamluk periods*, in. D. Behrens-Abouseif (ed.), *The Cairo heritage. Papers in honor of Layla Ali Ibrahim*, Cairo 2000, 263-75.

C. Glass

Like metalwork, Mamlūk enamelled and gilded glass continued the tradition of the Ayyūbids, using the same techniques and forms. After the craft reached its apogee, the production eventually came abruptly to an end in the late 8th/14th century. Although scholars have assigned the production of enamelled and gilded glass to Syria, where the technique was born, more recent research attributes a more preponderant role in this craft to Egypt, in light of the fact that the bulk of the consumption was there and that most of the objects concerned have been found in that region (Scanlon 1998). Tīmūr's sack of Damascus in 803/1401 is usually considered the reason for the abrupt end of this craft in Syria. However, Alexandria could have been another centre of production; a *waḳf* document of Sultan al-Nāṣir Muḥammad (published by Muḥammad Amīn in his edition of Ibn Ḥabīb's *Tadhkirat al-nabīh*, ii, Cairo 1982, 432) refers to a glass factory in Alexandria belonging to the Sultan's *waḳf* for his religious complex at Siryāḳūs. Unfortunately, it does not specify what kind of glass was produced there. The sack of Alexandria by Pierre de Lusignan of Cyprus in 1365 had a catastrophic effect on its economy. It may have had repercussions on its glass production and explain the fact that the few objects known to have been produced in the 770s/1370s show a marked decline in the quality and extent of enamelled decoration. Certain objects, such as beakers made for export, are not documented after the 770s/1370s. A short revival took place under Sultan Barḳūḳ, to whom about forty enamelled and gilded lamps are attributed. One should not exclude the presence of more than one centre of production. An enamelled lamp mentioning the name of Sultan Ḳāyitbāy (Wiet 1937), entirely different in style and techniques, testifies to endeavours during the artistic revival that took place under the auspices of this sultan.

Mamlūk glassmakers used a variety of shapes, sometimes in highly unusual large sizes, such as mosque lamps, goblets, bowls, flasks, bottles and vases, some of which are reminiscent of metalware. The glass was white or tinted, and never of perfect clarity. An outstanding group of enamelled and gilded vessels was those made of deep-blue glass, such as the famous Cavour vase (Newby 1998). The colours of the enamel—blue, red, yellow, green, brown, white and black—were applied as a vitreous paste, along with the gold, which fused with the surface upon firing.

As in metalwork, figural representations on secular objects were used until the 8th/14th century when they were replaced by epigraphy and blazons. The patterns, drawn with hair-thin lines, are extremely intricate. The mosque lamps made for Cairene religious buildings are among the most spectacular specimens of Mamluk glass; they bear a verse from the Sūra of Light (xxiv, 35) around the neck; whenever a patron's name is inscribed, it appears on the belly.

The Mamlūks also produced marvered and colourless vessels, as well as other types, moulded and/or with applied threads. Mamlūk glass was widely exported to all of Europe and to China.

Bibliography: G. Schmoranz, *Old oriental gilt and enamelled glass vessels*, Vienna-London 1899; C.J. Lamm, *Mittelalterliche Gläser und Steinschnitzarbeiten aus dem Nahen Osten*, 2 vols. Berlin 1929-30; G. Wiet, *Catalogue général du Musée Arabe du Caire. Lampes et bouteilles en verre émaillé*, Cairo 1929, repr. 1982; P. Ravaisse, *Une lampe sépulcurale en verre émaillé au nom d'Arghun en Nasiri*, Paris 1931; Wiet, *Les Lampes d'Arghun*, in *Syria*, xiv (1933), 203-6; L.A. Mayer, *Islamic glass makers and their works*, in *Israel Exploration Journal*, iv (1954), 262-5; R. Ward (ed.), *Gilded and enamelled glass from the Middle East*, London 1998, and especially the following articles there: G.T. Scanlon, *Lamm's classification and archaeology*, 27-9; R. Ward, *Glass and brass. Parallels and puzzles*, 30-5; M.S. Newby, *The Cavour vase and gilt and enamelled Mamluk coloured glass*, 35-9; H. Tait, *The Palmer Cup and related glasses exported to Europe in the Middle Ages*, 50-5; J.M. Rogers, *European inventories as a source for the distribution of Mamluk enamelled glass*, 69-74; V. Porter, *Enamelled glass made for the Rasulid Sultans of the Yemen*, 91-6; P. Hardie, *Mamluk glass from China?*, 85-91; and A. Contadini, *Poetry on enamelled glass. The Palmer cup in the British Museum*. See also M. Ribeiro, *Mamluk glass in the Calouste Gulbenkian Museum*, Lisbon 1999; J.M. Rogers, *Further thoughts on Mamluk enameled glass*, in D. Behrens-Abouseif (ed.), *The Cairo Heritage. Papers in Honor of Layla Ali Ibrahim*, Cairo 2000, 275–90; S. Carboni, *Glass of the Sultans*, New York 2001.

(Doris Behrens-Abouseif)

D. Arts of the book

Although little remains from the previous Fāṭimid and Ayyūbid periods, for the Mamlūks we have a wealth of material, both religious and secular, indicative of extensive book production and patronage. In fact, Mamlūk book production is comparable in volume and quality with that of major contemporary centres such as Il-Khānid Tabrīz and Tīmūrid Harāt. Many illustrated and illuminated examples survive, and we also have several original bindings.

(i) *Ḳurʾāns*

Despite the evident connections between Ḳurʾāns and secular books in terms of illumination and binding, for the sake of clarity they are best approached separately. As James (1992, 150) has pointed out, the particularly fine and grand Ḳurʾāns that survive, the best dating from the 14th century and the first decade of the 15th, were made under the patronage of a sultan who then endowed them as *wakf* to a particular religious foundation or mosque, where they were generally reserved for ceremonial use. They are mostly in single volume form; few multi-volume Ḳurʾāns withstood the intensive everyday use to which they were generally exposed.

One of the earliest outstanding Mamlūk Ḳurʾāns that we possess is, however, in seven volumes (London, B.L., Add. 22,406-22,413). It dates from 705/1305-6 (Lings and Safadi 1976, nos. 66-9, James 1988, no. 1) and was copied for Sultan Baybars by Ibn al-Wāḥid, an outstanding calligrapher of the early 8th/14th century (al-Ṣafadī, *Wāfī*, no. 1104, and Ibn Ḥajar al-ʿAsḳalānī, *al-Durar al-Kāmina*, Ḥaydarābād 1348-50/1929-32, no. 3740). The illumination was the work of three artists, Muḥammad b. Mubādir; the famous Muḥammad b. Abī Bakr, known as Ṣandal, who lived in Cairo at the beginning of the 8th/14th century; and his pupil Aydughdī b. ʿAbd Allāh al-Badrī, through whom Ṣandal's style maintained its influence until the 1330s. (see James 1988, ch. 3 for other works by these illuminators and for a discussion of the question of Il-Khānid influence; for Ṣandal, see Ṣafadī, no. 4843). Although there are evident differences between their individual styles, the general consistency of design indicates that one artist, almost certainly Ṣandal, had overall control. As is general in Mamlūk Ḳurʾāns, the illumination is concentrated in the frontispieces, opening pages of text and the final colophon page. Marginal ornaments in the main body of the text consist of the words *khamsa* and *ʿashara* in gold Kufic over a piece of arabesque scroll. But one may also argue that illumination is projected onto the text itself, for in contrast to the normal use of *naskh* in this period, its large *thuluth* unusually written in gold letters outlined in black, makes it visually special and rich.

Another Ḳurʾān signed by Ṣandal as the illuminator (Dublin, Chester Beatty Library, Is 1479; see Arberry 1967, no. 59; James 1980, no. 25; James 1988, no. 3), and datable to between 704-10/1305-10, has a similar type of illumination, but with the striking addition of the use of relief. On the two carpet-like opening pages, the geometric figures of the decoration are given an impression of three-dimensionality by the fact that alternating pentagons are in relief. The equally innovatory carpet-like design consists of a central block with a geometrical formation interrupted by borders surrounded on three sides by a thick band, from which protrude thin spikes almost like the fringes of a carpet.

It also occurs in combination with relief in other examples such as that dated 735/1334 and copied in Cairo by Aḥmad al-Mutaṭabbib (Cairo, Dār al-Kutub, Ḳurʾān ms. 81; see Atil 1981, no. 3, also James 1988, nos. 15-18). Both scribe and illuminator, he was responsible for a new type of Ḳurʾān, introduced by *ca.* 720/1320, which is characterised by a larger format with illumination of high quality, and in which the preferred script is *muḥaḳḳaḳ*.

From the 1330s to the 1360s, Damascus, too, was an important centre of manuscript production (for a discussion of illustrated secular manuscripts from Damascus, see below). It seems, moreover, to have been stylistically innovative, and a distinctive feature in Ḳurʾāns of this period that may have originated there (James 1992, 172-5) is the star polygon style, where the page is dominated by a large central starburst made up of symmetrically enmeshed small polygons. One such Ḳurʾān (London, Khalili Collection, Qur807; see James 1992, no. 43), datable to *ca.* 730-40/1330-40, has a colophon (fol. 296b) stating that the scribe worked on it in the Umayyad Mosque, and there is a stylistically related Arabic translation of the Four Gospels, copied in 741/1340 for a Damascene cleric (Cairo, Coptic Museum, Ms. 90; see Simaika Pasha 1939, pls. XVIII-XX). Like several other Christian manuscripts of the period, it was illuminated in the manner of contemporary Islamic manuscripts, so that it also has other features in common with the Khalili Ḳurʾān, and there are another two such manuscripts with similar illumination that are also known to have been produced in Damascus, one, a Gospel in Arabic, now in Istanbul (Topkapı Sarayı Library, Ahmet III, 3519; see Leroy 1967), the other, the Epistles and Acts of the Apostles in Arabic, in St. Petersburg (Academy of Sciences, D-228; see Khalidov, in Petrosyan (ed.) 1994, no. 23). The latter was commissioned by a certain "Jakomo", thought to have been an Italian Consul to Syria, and was copied by the monk Thomas (*Tūmā al-mutarahhib*), known as Ibn al-Ṣafī, in 742/1341 (for a list of eight manuscripts with some evidence of provenance from Damascus, see Contadini 1995, n. 8). To be noted also, from the 8th/14th century, is the diffusion of Mamlūk styles of illumination and binding from Damascus to Anatolia (see Tanındı 1991 and 2000).

There are also some superbly illuminated later Ḳurʾāns in the star polygon style from Cairo, datable to the reign of Sultan Shaʿbān II (*r.* 764-78/1363-76). During the latter part of his reign, however, between 770/1369 and 778/1376, an entirely new style of painting was introduced in Cairo by Ibrāhīm al-Āmidī. Its most important departure was the abandonment of the preceding norm of infinite recursivity in geometric patterning, so that there could now be large blocks incorporating irregular figures. But he was also innovative with regard both to his subtle use of colour reversal and to the wider range of his palette, which was much more like that of ʿIrāḳ and Persia in the first half of the 8th/14th century (Cairo, Dār al-Kutub, Ḳurʾān mss. 9, 10 and 15; see James 1988, nos. 31, 32, 34 and 35). This style was to be followed until the early 9th/15th century.

(ii) *Secular manuscripts*

Abundant evidence for the arts of the book is also provided by the numerous illustrated and/or illuminated secular manuscripts that survive. They represent various literary genres, some continuing earlier traditions, as, for example, scientific manuscripts and the great literary cycles of the *Maḳāmāt* and *Kalīla wa-Dimna*, others reflecting the particular interests of certain strata of Mamlūk society, as witnessed, for example, by the revival of the Furūsiyya [*q.v.*] genre.

The illustrated manuscripts show a variety of pictorial sources. Several contain what may be termed "classical" elements that link them to 7th/13th century styles as exhibited, for example, in the Syro-ʿIrāḳī al-Ḥarīrī *Maḳāmāt* in the Bibliothèque Nationale (Arabe 6094) dated 619/1222, and thus ultimately to Byzantine models of portraying the human figure and dress. Although incomplete, the al-Ḥarīrī *Maḳāmāt* in the British Library (Add. 7293), dated Rabīʿ II 723/April 1323 allows us to see the prolongation of this style into the Mamlūk period. (For both manuscripts see Grabar 1984, no. 2, pp. 8-9 and no. 9, pp. 14-15 respectively.)

Equally noteworthy is their frequent combination with elements of Saldjūḳ origin which provide links with North Djazīran 7th/13th-century manuscripts. They affect especially the human face, which is typically round, with narrow eyes, small mouth, straight, small nose and long hair, often with a curl in front of the ear (for lists of manuscripts with "classical" and Saldjūḳ influences, see Contadini 1988-9, nn. 29, 40). An early Mamlūk example showing strong Saldjūḳ influence is the Ibn Buṭlān *Risālat Daʿwat al-aṭibbāʾ* in the Ambrosiana Library in Milan (Ms. A. 125 Inf.) dated Djumādā I 672/December 1273 (see Miḥriz 1961; also Löfgren and Traini 1975, vol. i, no. LXX, col. pls. I-VI).

The pictorial repertoire also includes features of Il-Khānid origin as, for example, in a particularly striking early 8th/14th-century al-Ḳazwīnī *ʿAdjāʾib al-makhlūḳāt*, where they are combined in a masterly fashion with "classical" elements (see Carboni and Contadini 1990; for Mamlūk/Il-Khānid relationships, see Rogers 1972). But it is essentially the integration of "classical" and Saldjūḳ features that characterises Mamlūk style, whereas the Il-Khānid element, consisting of landscape features such as large lotus flowers, recessed planes to provide depth, and the use of free brush strokes (e.g. for leaves), normally affected specific features without resulting in a similar stylistic fusion.

There were doubtless several centres of production of illustrated manuscripts, but very few colophons identify a place. However, we can at least be certain about Damascus and Cairo. Damascus again comes to the fore at the beginning of the 8th/14th century, as demonstrated by a *Maḳāmāt* in the British Library (Or. 9718), which contains the name of the scribe and illuminator (fol. 53a), Ghāzī b. ʿAbd al-Raḥmān al-Dimashḳī, who lived and worked there and died in 709/1310 (see Mayer 1942; Grabar 1984, no. 7, p. 13. For al-Dimashḳī, see Ibn Ḥadjar al-ʿAsḳalānī 1929-32, vol. ii, p. 134).

A provenance from Damascus can also be argued for a further four illustrated manuscripts dated between 734/1334 and 755/1354 on the basis of stylistic affinity, allied to documentary evidence concerning the compiler of one of them, the Ibn Bakhtīshūʿ *Kitāb Manāfiʿ al-ḥayawān* in San Lorenzo del Escorial dated 755/1354 (Ar. 898; see Contadini 1988-9, with bibl.). Their illustrations have very similar characteristics, not all, however, shared by other Mamlūk manuscripts, such as the solid gold background of their miniatures and the frame consisting of one or more blue lines with decorative additions. At the same time, they conform to Mamlūk norms by containing pronounced Saldjūḳ features and, if in differing degrees, Il-Khānid ones. Further, the illumination in all four is very similar, when not identical, to that of the Khalili Ḳurʾān and the two Christian manuscripts mentioned above which also come from Damascus. This style of illumination will survive in Damascus until well into the 9th/15th century, as demonstrated by a copy of *Fākihat al-khulafāʾ wa-mufākahat al-ẓurafāʾ* (St. Petersburg, Academy of Sciences, C-651; see Khalidov, in Petrosyan (ed.) 1994, no. 32) by the Damascene Abu 'l-ʿAbbās Aḥmad b. Muḥammad b. ʿArabshāh, copied by Ismāʿīl b. ʿAbd al-Raḥmān al-Iṣfahānī in Rabīʿ I 852/June 1448 under the author's supervision.

For Cairo, on the other hand, we lack direct evidence for production, although it is generally thought that those manuscripts that have a more "classical", conservative style might have been produced there rather than in the more innovative Damascus.

The little that survives of late Mamlūk painting exhibits a rather striking stylistic blend which also absorbs Djalayirid, Turkmen and Ottoman influences, especially with regard to the depiction of landscape and costume. Representative examples are the late 8th/14th-century *Kashf al-asrār* by Ibn Ghānim al-Maḳdisī (Istanbul, Süleymaniye Library, Kara Ismail 565; see Ettinghausen 1962, pp. 158-9), the mid-9th/15th-century *Kitāb al-Ẓardaḳa* (Istanbul, University Library, inv. no. 4689; see Bittar 1996, 158), the *Iskandar-nāma* of Aḥmadī datable to 872/1467-8 (Istanbul, Univ. Library, T6044; see Atıl 1984) and the early 10th/16th-century *Shāh-nāma* (Istanbul, Topkapı Sarayı Library, Hazine 1519; see Zajączkowski 1965 and Atasoy 1966-8) made for Sultan Ḳānsawḥ al-Ghawrī (*r.* 906-22/1501-16).

(iii) *Bindings*

Numerous Mamlūk bindings have survived, consisting predominantly of leather with blind tooling, although often features are highlighted in gold.

There are resemblances between Mamlūk and Ottoman bindings of the 8th/14th and early 9th/15th centuries (Raby and Tanındı 1993, 7-11 and ch. 1), while at the same time 8th/14th-century examples may resemble contemporary Persian bindings, as is shown by two Ḳurʾāns in the Chester Beatty Library in Dublin, one (of *ca.* 746/1345, Is 1465, see James 1980, no. 33) made in Cairo, the other (dated 738/1338, Is 1470, see James 1980, no. 49) in Marāgha. Both have bindings in light brown leather with a pointed star in the centre of an empty field with a scalloped decoration at its outer border, the whole decorated with blind tooling. In other examples, the central ornament is an oval medallion, and in either case related designs appear in the four corners of the field.

This type of composition was to remain important, but more examples survive of a second type in which the whole field is covered. There are examples with arabesque or floral designs, but more frequently we find strapwork forming polygonal compartments which often contained tooled knotwork motifs, with the strapwork sometimes radiating out from a central star which echoes the star polygon style of illumination.

Bindings were sometimes lined with silk, but more often the doublures were decorated with block-pressed leather. During the period of Sultan Ḳāyitbāy (*r.* 872-901/1468-96), we witness an age of experimentation which includes the use of filigree for both inner and, especially, outer covers. This seems to reflect influence from Persia, where, in the 9th/15th century, filigree was already the norm. The use of filigree, together with other Mamlūk features of layout of design, were in turn to influence Italian bookbinders of the late 15th century (Hobson 1989, ch. 3).

Bibliography: K. Holter, *Die Galen-Handschrift und die Makamen des Hariri der Wiener Nationalbibliothek*, in *Jahrbuch der Kunsthistorischen Sammlung in Wien*, N.F., xi (1937), 1-48; L. Mayer, *A hitherto unknown Damascene artist*, in *Art Islamica*, ix (1942), 168; R. Ettinghausen, *Near Eastern book covers and their influence on European binding*, in *Ars Orientalis*, iii (1959), 113-31; S. Walzer, *The Mamluk illuminated manuscripts of Kalila wa Dimna*, in R. Ettinghausen (ed.), *Aus der Welt der islamischen Kunst. Festschrift für Ernst Kühnel*, Berlin 1959, 195-206; Dj. Miḥriz, *Min al-taṣwīr al-mamlūkī*, in *Revue des manuscrits arabes*, vii (1961), 75-80; Ettinghausen, *Arab painting*, Geneva 1962 (for general surveys on Mamlūk painting, see 143-60); M. Weisweiler, *Der*

Islamische Bucheinband des Mittelalters, Wiesbaden 1962 (for Mamlūk bindings, primarily from the Köprülü Library); A. Zajączkowski, *Turecka wersja Šāh-Nāme z Egiptu mameluckiego*, in *Zakładorientalistyki Polskiejakademii Nauk*, xv (1965); N. Atasoy, *1510 tarihli Memluk Şehnamesinin minyatürleri*, in *Sanat Tarihi Yıllığı* (1966-8), 49-69 (for the Mamlūk Shāh-nāma for Ḳānsawh al-Ghawrī); J. Leroy, *Un evangeliaire arabe de la Bibliothèque de Topqapi Sarayi à décor byzantin et islamique*, in *Syria*, xliv (1967), 119-30; M. Mostafa, *An illustrated manuscript on chivalry from the late Circassian Mamluk period*, in *Bulletin de l'Institut d'Egypte*, li (1969-70), 1-13 (for the Furūsiyya manuscript in the Keir Collection); J.M. Rogers, *Evidence for Mamluk and Mongol relations, 1260-1360*, in *Colloque Internationale sur l'Histoire du Caire, 1969*, Cairo 1972, 385-403; D. James, *Mamluk painting at the time of the Lusignan Crusade 1365-70*, in *Humaniora Islamica*, ii (1974), 73-87 (for the Furūsiyya manuscript in the Chester Beatty Library); O. Löfgren and R. Traini, *Catalogue of the Arabic manuscripts in the Biblioteca Ambrosiana*, 2 vols., Vicenza 1975-81 (for Ibn Buṭlān and al-Djāḥiẓ); E.J. Grube, *Pre-Mongol and Mamluk painting*, in B.W. Robinson (ed.), *The Keir Collection. Islamic painting and the arts of the book*, London 1976, 69-81; M. Lings and Y.H. Safadi, *The Qur'an. An exhibition at the British Library*, London 1976; D. Haldane, *Mamluk painting*, Warminster 1978; G.R. Smith, *Medieval Muslim horsemanship. A fourteenth-century Arabic cavalry manual*, London 1979; James, *Qur'ans and bindings from the Chester Beatty Library*, London 1980; C. Ruiz Bravo Villasante, *El libro de las utilidades de los animales de Ibn al-Durayhim al-Mawsili*, Madrid 1981 (facs. of Escorial Library, Ar. 898); E. Atıl, *Renaissance of Islam. Art of the Mamluks*, Washington D.C. 1981; eadem, *Kalīla wa Dimna. Fables from a fourteenth-century Arabic manuscript*, Washington D.C. 1981 (for Oxford, Bodleian Library, Pococke 400); G. Bosch, J. Carswell, and G. Petherbridge, *Islamic bindings and bookmaking*, Chicago 1981; H.C.G. von Bothmer, *Kalila wa Dimna. Ibn al-Muqaffa's Fabelbuch in einer mittelalterlichen Bildenschrift, Cod. Arab. 616 der Bayerischen Staatsbibliothek München*, Wiesbaden 1981; Haldane, *Islamic bookbindings in the Victoria and Albert Museum*, London 1983; Atıl, *Mamluk painting in the late fifteenth century*, in *Muqarnas*, ii (1984), 159-71; O. Grabar, *The illustrations of the Maqamat*, Chicago 1984; B. Gray, *The monumental Qur'ans of the Ilkhanid and Mamluk ateliers of the 1st quarter of the 14th century*, in *RSO*, lix (1985), 135-46 (for relationships between Mamlūk and Il-Khānid Ḳur'āns and bindings); A.S. Melikian-Chirvani, *Sulwān al-muṭā' fī 'udwān al-atbā'. A rediscovered masterpiece of Arab literature and painting*, 3 vols., Kuwait 1985; James, *Qur'ans of the Mamluks*, London 1988; A. Contadini, *The* Kitāb Manāfi' al-Ḥayawān *in the Escorial Library*, in *Islamic Art*, iii (1988-9), 33-57 (also for related manuscripts); A. Hobson, *Humanists and bookbinders*, Cambridge 1989; S. Carboni and Contadini, *An illustrated copy of al-Qazwīnī's The Wonders of Creation*, in *Sotheby's Art at auction*, London 1990, 228-33 (for the manuscript now in the Shaykh Sa'ūd collection); Grube, *Prolegomena for a corpus publication of illustrated Kalilah wa Dimnah manuscripts*, in *Islamic Art*, iv (1990-1), 301-481; idem, (ed.), *A Mirror for Princes from India*, Bombay 1991 (for articles on illustrated *Kalīla wa-Dimna*, also of the Mamlūk period); Tanındı, *Konya Mevlana Muzesi'nde 677 ve 665 yıllık kur'anılar. Karamanlı beyliği'nde kitap sanatı*, in *Kültür ve Sanat*, xii (1991), 42-4; James, *The master scribes. Qur'ans of the 11th to 14th centuries* (The Khalili Collection of Islamic Art, vol. ii), Oxford 1992; J. Raby and Z. Tanındı, *Turkish bookbinding in the 15th century. The foundation of an Ottoman court style*, London 1993; Y.A. Petrosyan (ed.), *De Bagdad à Ispahan. Manuscrits islamiques de la Filiale de Saint-Pétersbourg de l'Institut d'Études orientales, Académie des Sciences de Russie*, Lugano, Paris and Milan 1994; Contadini, *Islamic manuscripts and the ARCH Foundation*, in *Apollo* (February 1995), 29-30; eadem, *The horse in two manuscripts of Ibn Bakhtīshū''s Kitāb Manāfi' al-Ḥayawān*, in Alexander (ed.), *Furūsiyya. The horse in the art of the Near East*, i, 142-7; T. Bittar, *A manuscript of the Kitāb al-Bayṭara in the Bibliothèque Nationale, Paris*, in D. Alexander (ed.), *op. cit.*, 158-61; S. al-Sarraf, *Furusiyya literature of the Mamluk period*, in Alexander (ed.), *op. cit.*, 118-35; R. Pinder-Wilson, *Stone press-moulds and leatherworking in Khurasan*, in E. Savage Smith, *Science, tools and magic* (The Khalili Collection of Islamic Art, vol. xii), ii, London 1997, 338-55; Tanındı, *Seçkin bir mevlevi'nin tezhipli kitapları*, in I.C. Schick (ed.), *M. Uğur Derman 65 yaş armağanı*, Istanbul 2000, 513-36. (Anna Contadini)

(iv) Numismatics

While the coinage of the Mamlūks was manufactured from the usual metals: gold, silver and copper, with the traditional Islamic denominational names: dīnār, dirham and *fals* [*q.vv.*], it belonged to a distinctive currency family of its own which underwent a process of evolution unlike that of any other coinage series. Its 267-year history can be divided into three distinct periods that overlap one another to a greater or lesser extent.

The first period was little more than a continuation of the late Ayyūbid style of gold dīnārs and silver dirhams as struck by al-Ṣāliḥ Ayyūb. The field legends on the dīnārs were in circular fields with a single prominent marginal inscription, while those on the dirhams were in a square field with the remaining texts in the four marginal segments. This "pseudo-Ayyūbid" coinage was issued between 648 and 658/1250-60, from the accession of Shadjar al-Durr until that of al-Ẓāhir Baybars. While the weights of the dīnār and the dirham were not consistent enough for payments to be made by tail, individual pieces roughly approximated the weight of the coinage dīnār/*mithḳāl*, 4.25 gr, and the canonical dirham, 2.97 gr.

The second coinage type was initiated by al-Ẓāhir Baybars, the real founder of the Baḥrī Mamlūk state. While the legends on his dīnārs continued to be placed in a circle within a surrounding marginal legend, their calligraphy was carried out in a thinner and more refined *naskhī* script than that previously used. At the same time that the dies became wider in diameter, the flans upon which there were struck became thinner and more irregular in shape, so that large portions of the marginal legends are usually missing from the struck coins. Because these legends carried the mint and date formula, it is often difficult to place and date early Baḥrī Mamlūk dīnārs. With the passage of time, marginal legends became smaller and less legible until they shrank away altogether and their inscriptions were incorporated into the field legends. The Baḥrī Mamlūk dirham lost its original square in circle design and became a simple field legend inscribed in a circle with the mint and date around the edge in discontinuous words.

The Baḥrī Mamlūk-style dīnār was struck from 658/1260 until 830/1427 and the dirham from 658 until the early 800s/1400s. Both coins were beset by highly irregular weights and careless manufacture. The gold is usually regarded as no more than stamped ingots of totally random weights. The purity of the metal, however, was guaranteed by the sultan's stamp which ensured the high standard of its fineness as a trade commodity. The dirham, while less irregular in weight, was a shabby simulacrum of the attractive coinages of the preceding centuries. It was manufactured from silver approximately two-thirds fine then often struck cold on irregular flans. The variety usually regarded as a full dirham weighed around three grams, but there was a second type, regarded as a fractional dirham, whose flans were cut from bars with a chisel and then stamped with dies twice or more the size of the flans so that only one or two words of the legends were visible on their surface. Another method of manufacturing flans for fractional dirhams was to pour the molten metal over a cone of charcoal immersed in a bowl of water. The spattered droplets of base silver would then be stamped and placed in circulation.

Since Mamlūk gold had virtually ceased to be used in regular trade and silver was too rare to be a reliable standard of exchange, the Baḥrī Mamlūk state was forced to rely on the copper *fals* as its principal coinage metal. Copper was struck from the reign of Baybars onwards, initially with random weights and designs, but later, during the second reign of al-Nāṣir Ḥasan in 759/1358, the *fals* took on the status of an official coinage metal as the copper or trade dirham, probably due to the economic hardship caused by the Black Death in Egypt in the previous decade. As a result, enormous quantities were put into circulation, a perfect illustration of Gresham's Law, because silver became virtually unobtainable. Although these *fulūs* "dirhams" were theoretically struck at the familiar weight of one *mith̲ḳāl* apiece, their metallic value was purely nominal. The mints were therefore under no compulsion to maintain their theoretical weight or to put any concerted effort into maintaining the quality of their manufacuture. Thus it was that by the turn of the 8th/14th century the commercial classes of Egypt and Syria had lost all trust in their native currency and had turned, for lack of better, to the use of foreign coins.

In the second half of the 7th/13th century, the trading states of Italy were able to introduce and maintain stable gold coinages which became the standard commercial currencies of the Mediterranean and beyond. The first of these were the Florentine and Genoese florins which appeared in 1252 (A.H. 650), followed by the Venetian ducat in 1284 (A.H. 683). All three weighed slightly over 3.50 gr, with roughly the same diameter, and were thus easily exchanged against one another. The plentiful supply of these coins and their dependable value, much like the use of the U.S. dollar in financially-troubled countries today, made them the currency of choice in Levantine trade.

The pressure for currency reform grew to the point where the Burd̲j̲ī Mamlūk ruler Farad̲j̲ ordered his *ustād̲h̲ār*, Sayf al-Dīn Ilbug̲h̲ā b. ʿAbd Allāh al-Sālimī al-Ẓāhirī, to strike new dīnārs to the traditional monetary *mith̲ḳāl* standard alongside the stamped ingot gold. According to al-Maḳrīzī, this reform was initiated in A.H. 803, but the Sālimī dīnārs are known only from 804 and a few from 805. While the principal coin weighed the usual 4.25 gr, multiples of two and three dīnārs and fractions of half and quarters are known. This misdirected reform attempt failed utterly and left only a small handful of pieces to testify to its existence.

Farad̲j̲ made a second attempt at reform in 810, although al-Maḳrīzī records 811, introducing the new sequin, ducat or florin-style Nāṣirī dīnār. These coins, weighing 3.50 gr, were the Islamic equivalent of the Venetian ducat and were intended to supplant it in local trade. They, too, were issued concurrently with the ingot-style dīnārs between 810 and 815 in the name of al-Naṣr Farad̲j̲, the ephemeral ruler, the caliph al-Mustaʿīn in 815 and al-Muʾayyad S̲h̲ayk̲h̲ in 815 and 816.

The rulers and the mints were clearly in a quandary over how they could keep the Mamlūk gold coinage both Islamic in character and competitive in value with the ducat and could restore the silver dirham in its weight and alloy to become a reliable coinage for daily purposes. The silver reform began in 815/1412 and continued for at least the next seven years. The new coinage was struck on the dirham standard weighing 2.70 gr, with a half of 1.35 gr and a quarter of 0.67 gr. It imitated a well-known Ayyūbid design used on the Damascus coinage of al-ʿĀdil Abū Bakr I, a by-word for excellence from the distant past. Then, in about 820, al-Muʾayyad S̲h̲ayk̲h̲ followed up his reform silver with another attempt at a *mith̲ḳāl*-weight gold coinage. Two dīnārs are known dated 821 and 823 and a single half-dīnār from 823. This attempt at reform apparently went unnoticed by contemporary historians. Al-Muʾayyad S̲h̲ayk̲h̲ was succeeded after his death in 824/1421 by three ephemeral rulers until al-As̲h̲raf Barsbāy came to the throne in 825/1422. No gold of his is published dated between 825 and 829. The last ingot-style dīnārs to be recorded are rare issues of his dated 829 and 830. The former year, however, witnessed the re-introduction of the 3.50 gr ducat-style coinage, a reform which brought the Mamlūk lands into what became in effect an eastern Mediterranean monetary union. The new Mamlūk dīnār, as struck by al-As̲h̲raf Barsbāy, was known colloquially as the *as̲h̲rafī*, a name which followed it wherever the denomination went, to the Aḳ Ḳoyunlū, ʿOt̲h̲mānlīs and Ṣafawids in the East and to the Mag̲h̲rībī states in North Africa.

Because the new coin was of reasonably standard weight and alloy, prices could be established by numbers of actual coins rather than by weight of metal. In this connection, it is interesting to note that many Umayyad and ʿAbbāsid dīnārs originally struck on the monetary *mith̲ḳāl* standard have been found clipped down to the weight of the *as̲h̲rafī* in order to enable them to pass current in trade. This convenience was also available to those who paid in silver, the most popular coin being the half-dirham or *muʾayyidī*, later known as the medin, a denomination which, like the *as̲h̲rafī*, remained in use in ʿOt̲h̲mānlī lands until the early decades of the 12th/19th century.

The legends on the Mamlūk coinage are divided into the religious and the secular. The religious are drawn from the Holy Ḳurʾān, the principal text being the declaration of faith, or *kalima*: "There is no god but God" followed by the Divine Commission "Muḥammad is the Messenger of God", sūra XLVIII, 29, and then the words of prophetic witness in whole or in part: "He sent him with the guidance and [the] faith of the truth, so that he may proclaim it above every faith even if the polytheists dislike (it)", IX, 33 or LXI, 9. This text is frequently supplemented by a phrase from III, 122, which, because of its regular use, could be characterised as the Mamlūk "symbol" or motto: "For victory comes but from God". Occasionally another phrase from XI, 88, was used: "And my success [in my task] can only come from

God". While the *kalima* is only found on the obverse, the supplementary phrases appear above either the obverse or reverse fields, or on both.

The reverses on the gold and silver coinage carry the royal protocol. In the first Baḥrī Mamlūk period, the ruler was simply entitled *Malik*, or in the exceptional case of Shadjar al-Durr, *Malikat al-Muslimīn*. This was usually followed by a *laḳab*, e.g. Nūr al-Dīn, the ruler's name and that of his father, if of royal parentage. Rulers also placed the name of their spiritual overlord, the ʿAbbāsid caliph al-Mustaʿṣim bi'llāh, on the obverse field, but after his overthrow in 656/1258 his name was removed from the legends.

The establishment of the ʿAbbāsid caliphate in Cairo by al-Ẓahir Baybārs in 659/1261 reinforced the legitimacy of the Mamlūk state by relocating and naturalising the font of honour in the Islamic world and making the caliph an officer in the Mamlūk court. The first caliph, al-Mustanṣir, repaid the offer of refuge by granting Baybārs the double title of *al-Sulṭān al-Malik* and the honorific *Ḳāsim Amīr al-Muʾminīn* "Partner of the Prince of the Believers". After al-Mustanṣir's early death, Baybārs briefly recognised his successor al-Ḥakīm on the Syrian coinage, but thereafter the caliph's name was omitted. The title *Ḳāsim Amīr al-Muʾminīn* was also included in the royal protocols of Ḳalāwūn, Kitbughā, Baybārs II and the early coinage of Muḥammad I after which it, too, ceased to be used.

The early Baḥrī rulers of non-regal parentage proclaimed themselves as former royal Mamlūks, Baybārs and Ḳalāwūn used the *nisba* of *al-Ṣāliḥī* (after al-Ṣāliḥ Ayyūb) on their coins, while Kitbughā, Lādjīn and Baybārs II placed *al-Manṣūrī* (after al-Manṣūr Ḳalāwūn) on theirs. The use of the *nisba* was discontinued on the accession of al-Nāṣir Muḥammad I b. Ḳalāwūn because all subsequent Baḥrī rulers were either his sons, grandsons or great-grandsons. Thus the protocol of the penultimate Baḥrī ruler reads: *al-Sulṭān al-Malik al-Manṣūr ʿAlāʾ al-Dunyā wa 'l-Dīn ʿAlī b. al-Malik al-Ashraf Shaʿbān b. Ḥusayn b. Muḥammad ʿazza naṣruhu*. The succeeding Burdjī Mamlūk rulers included their royal paternity wherever possible, but as the great majority succeeded through the consensus of the *amīrs* or by *coup d'état*, the inclusion of a *kunya* in the royal protocol was used as a substitute for royal paternity. Thus: *al-Sulṭān al-Malik al-Ashraf Abu 'l-Naṣr Barsbāy ʿazza naṣruhu* or *al-Sulṭān al-Malik Abū Saʿīd Khushḳadam ʿazza naṣruhu*. Note that the protocol is followed by the pious invocation *ʿazza naṣruhu* "may his victory be glorious" or, occasionally, *khallada Allāh mulkahu*—"may God perpetuate his kingly rule". Many other Islamic dynasties made free use of these invocations to honour their rulers.

The Mamlūks operated mints in both their Egyptian and Syrian possessions. Cairo, *al-Ḳāhira*, struck coin for all rulers except for a few rebels or usurpers whose power base lay in Syria. Its principal responsibility was to coin gold and silver, while copper production only became important during the silver shortage from 759 to the end of Barḳūḳ's first reign in 791. The second Egyptian mint was Alexandria, *al-Iskandariyya*, which mainly struck gold between 650 and 693 and then again from 752 until 824. During the latter period it also participated in the ruinous production of copper dirhams.

The main Syrian mint (the second in the state) was located in Damascus, *Dimashk*. As might be expected, its silver and copper is very well known because silver was the more popular coinage metal in Syria, although gold is frequently found. The next in importance is Aleppo, *Ḥalab*, well known for its silver and copper, with occasional gold issues. The other Syrian mints are Ḥamā, *Ḥamāt*, Tripoli, *Ṭarābulus*, and the recently identified Latakia, *al-Lādhiḳiyya*. The first two produced sporadic issues of silver, but more often copper, while the third is known from only two silver pieces struck in the name of Muḥammad I.

All mints were occasionally given the epithet *al-maḥrūsa* "the guarded", while *thaghr* "frontier port" is sometimes found on gold from Alexandria. Aleppo is also known as *Madīnat Ḥalab* on some of its ingot-sized gold. Because of defects in the manufacturing process: off-centre striking, weak strikes, dies too large for the flans, plus the inevitable wear and tear of heavy circulation, a very large proportion of Mamlūk coins are difficult to attribute precisely and often many specimens are needed from various sources to make out the details of an individual issue.

While many of the Mamlūk sultans were no more than ephemeral rulers whose presence made little or no impact on the state other than having their names recited in the *khuṭba* and inscribed on their *sikka*, certain powerful rulers were acknowledged as overlords on the coinage of neighbouring states. Steven Album has recorded these issues as follows: Baḥrī Mamlūks, al-Nāṣir Muḥammad I: Beys of Ḥāmid, Antalya; local beys, ʿAlāʾiyya (Alanya), Silifke and Bazardjik; Eretnid, Ḳayṣariyya and other very rare Anatolian types; al-Nāṣir Ḥasan: Artuḳid, Āmid (Diyārbakr); al-Ashraf Shaʿbān II: Ḳaramānid, Ḳonya and Burdjī Mamlūks: al-Ẓāhir Barḳūḳ: Artuḳid, Āmid, Mārdīn; al-Ashraf Barsbāy, Ḳaramānid, al-ʿAlāʾī, Ḳonya, Lāranda, Beys of Alanya, ʿAlāʾiyya and other rare Anatolian types, al-Ashraf Aynāl, Malkish Kurds, Čemishkezek and al-Ẓahīr Khushḳadam, Aḳ Ḳoyunlu, Arzindjān and Āmīd. These issues should be regarded as evidence of political submission for local use rather than as tribute payments to be sent to Cairo. One well-known flow of tribute, however, is recorded from the reign of al-Nāṣir Muḥammad I. In 722-3/1322-3 the Mamlūks captured Sīs [*q.v.*], the capital of Cilician Armenia, seized its treasury and then imposed an annual tribute of 1,200,000 trams which was collected for many years thereafter. Balog observes that this treasure served to succour the chronically deficient Mamlūk silver currency. Part was probably melted down and restruck, part put into circulation directly (made possible because the Mamlūk dirham had no fixed weight standard itself) and part overstruck by dies bearing al-Nāṣir Muḥammad's name. Examples of these overstruck trams of Oshin (1308-20) and Levon IV (1320-42) are regularly found in silver hoards of the period.

The calligraphy and ornamentation seen on Mamlūk coins vary in quality from the superb dīnārs of al-Ashraf Khalīl to the crude late Baḥrī dīnārs of al-Ḳāhira and al-Iskandariyya. The die-sinkers generally employed various styles of *naskhī* script ranging from the well executed and highly legible to the hastily inscribed, virtually scribbled. For the later Baḥrī period it is easy to distinguish at a glance which coins came from Egyptian mints and which from Syria. The latter show the die-sinkers to be genuinely artistic craftsmen, while those of Egypt had only mediocre abilities. This disparity in calligraphic standards tended to disappear during the Burdjī period so that it is often difficult to tell the difference between Egyptian and Syrian issues. It is interesting to note that on the half-dirhams issued by the later Burdjī rulers from the mint of Ḥalab the *kalima* is inscribed in Turkoman Kufic. Turkish influence is also evident in the style of the many small knots of felicity, scrolls and flowerets that ornament the dies alongside seemingly random diacritical points and monumental *shaddas* over the word Allāh.

Much has been made by numismatists of the "heraldry" [see RANK] found on Mamlūk coins. However, heraldry in the European sense is totally foreign to Arab Islamic culture, although Turkish tribal *tamghas*, part of the folk culture of Central Asia, made their artistic influence and utility felt at a time when most people were illiterate. Traditionally, representations of animate objects on Islamic coins had been banned from the gold and silver coinage and restricted to the copper *fals*. The first major exception to this was when Ghiyāth al-Dīn Kayskhusraw II, the Saldjūḳ Sultan of Rūm, placed the lion and sun, depicting the "sun in Leo", on the silver dirhams he had struck in Ḳonya and Sīwās between 638 and 641/1240-4. While this depiction of royal power was hastily removed after his defeat by the Mongols, it may have been the precedent seized upon by al-Ẓāhir Baybārs when he placed his badge of a prowling lion or leopard on his gold, silver and copper coinage. His son al-Saʿīd Baraka Khān continued to use it during his brief reign, 676-8/1277-9, but after that the placing of all such devices on the gold and silver coinage was discontinued. Moreover, none was used on the long series of copper "dirhams" struck in Egypt in the second half of the 8th/14th century. A rich variety of animate and inanimate designs, the choice of which was probably left to the local die-sinker, were placed on the copper *fulūs* struck for local use to make it impossible for silver-washed copper to pass as silver dirhams. This anti-counterfeiting measure was also used by many other dynasties, including that of the ʿOthmānlis. While many designs may be associated with an individual Mamlūk ruler, and may also have been employed on metalwork made for his use, the *fulūs* were generally too insignificant for any consistency to be applied to their designs.

In conclusion, the evidence furnished by the Mamlūk coinage may be said to provide an accurate reflection of the political and economic challenges faced by late mediaeval Egypt and Syria during the time of the Black Death, uncertain political leadership and the growing European economic influence in the eastern Mediterranean world.

Bibliography: Mamlūk numismatics has been well served by the masterly study by P. Balog, *The coinage of the Mamlūk Sultans of Egypt and Syria*, ANS Numismatic Studies no. 12, New York 1964, with exhaustive source notes and supplemented by many additional articles by him and others since then. For a valuable modern summary, see the section *Mamlūk* in S. Album's *Checklist of Islamic coins*, [2]Santa Rosa, Calif. 1998, 51-5. (R. DARLEY-DORAN)

MANSHŪRĀT (A.), the term for the letters, *responsa* and edicts of Muḥammad (Aḥmad) b. ʿAbd Allāh (d. 1885), the Sudanese Mahdī [see AL-MAHDIYYA]. These individual documents were transcribed by his followers in numerous manuscript collections, three of which are described in P.M. Holt, *Three Mahdist letter-books*, in *BSOAS*, xviii [1956], 227-38. An authorised text was lithographed in Omdurman (Umm Durmān) during the Mahdiyya in four volumes: the first consists of general and doctrinal pieces, including Muḥammad Aḥmad's justification of his claim to be the Mahdī; the second (*al-indhārāt*) contains his letters and proclamations summoning various individuals and groups to join the Mahdiyya (cf. Holt, *The Sudanese Mahdia and the outside world*, in *BSOAS*, xxi [1958], 276-90); the third (*al-aḥkām*) gives his rulings on matters of law and custom; the fourth (*al-khuṭab*) comprises his sermons. Photographic reproductions of these volumes were published in Khartoum in 1963 under the auspices of the Sudanese Ministry of the Interior. The editor (not there named) was Dr. Muḥammad Ibrāhīm Abū Salīm, who has also produced an invaluable guide to the documents and their sources as *al-Murshid ilā wathāʾiḳ al-Mahdī*, Khartoum 1969, and a selection of these and later Mahdist documents in *Manshūrāt al-Mahdiyya*, n.p. [Beirut] 1969. He has now published a complete edition of the Mahdī's writings, *al-Āthār al-kāmila li 'l-Imām al-Mahdī*, 7 vols. Khartoum 1990-4.

Bibliography: Given in the article. (P.M. HOLT)

AL-MAR'A.

6. In Southeast Asia.

The Muslim peoples of Southeast Asia are found in the modern nation-states of Indonesia, Malaysia (and in these two states they comprise the majority), Thailand (in the five southern provinces, culturally very close to the neighbouring region of the northern Malay Peninsula) and in the Philippines (Mindanao). Islamisation of these populations has been ongoing since the 15th century and continues in the 21st century (total population conservatively estimated at 220 million). Travellers to the region from the earliest times have remarked on the prominence of women in commerce, agriculture and spiritual life. Bilateral kinship systems are still the norm for most societies in the region, with some notable exceptions such as the matrilineal Minangkabau of West Sumatra, also found throughout Indonesia and in Negeri Sembilan on the Malay Peninsula. Although Islam assumes a patrilineal descent system, the traditionally high status of women in Southeast Asian societies means that women continue to play a public role in many areas of social and, especially, economic life, which contrasts with the situation in many other Muslim cultures. In some cases, this has also led to local and particular interpretations and applications of the *Sharīʿa*, especially in matters of inheritance.

Before the 20th century, the traditional power structure of the region was based on small fiefdoms led by charismatic rulers and local chiefs. The fiefdoms in turn were oriented towards centres of influence (e.g. Sriwijaya, Melaka, Mahapahit, Aceh and Ayuthia), which shaped the cultural and religious forms of their satellites. The élites followed the prevailing aesthetic and religious fashions while the populace maintained older traditions. Thus, when Islam was accepted by the leaders of centres of power such as Melaka and Aceh, it was added to a spiritual armoury already consisting of a broad mix of animist and ancestor cults, and also of Hindu and Buddhist beliefs, in all of which women played important roles. There was an eclectic expression of Islam with a special appreciation of Ṣūfism and less concern with scriptural prescription. In this context, the traditional role of women as important figures in spiritual matters continued. This came under threat, however, in the early and mid-19th century when Southeast Asian pilgrims were influenced by Wahhābī concerns and attempted to institute "reforms" in their local areas (see b, below).

(a) *Status of women before the 19th century*

The status of women was such that at the courts of the Muslim kingdoms of Aceh (northern Sumatra) and Patani (now in southern Thailand), four queens ruled for extended periods during the 17th century. Female rule in Aceh ended late in the 17th century when court *ʿulamāʾ* obtained a *fatwā* from Mecca stating that women could not be rulers. It has been usual to regard the period of female rule as indicating a weakened monarchy vis-à-vis male chiefs. However, because it seems that the queens served as mediators and successfully intervened in disputes between chiefs, there are also grounds for arguing that the style of female rule provided an alternative model of kingship in which leadership was less important than the ability to maintain harmony. In both Aceh and Patani, the period of female rule was characterised by commercial prosperity and an increase in revenues from foreign trade; this has been attributed to the cooperation rather than rivalry between the queen and local merchants. This alternative model of female rule did not develop, and in the latter part of the 17th century the queens were followed by males. It was not until recent times that the issue of a woman as head of state again became a possibility with the success of Megawati Sukarnoputri as a political leader (see d, below).

In Java there are no records of female rulers, but several Sultans maintained large corps of women trained to bear arms and serve as palace bodyguards and sentries. More important was the contribution of women intellectuals in advice to rulers (as in India). For example, in the early 18th century, the grandmother of a teenage ruler of the Central Javanese kingdom of Mataram prepared three impressive texts for the guidance of the young sultan. Known as Ratu Pakubuwana (died 1732), she is celebrated for her Muslim piety and knowledge of Ṣūfism. Her manuscripts retell stories of the great Muslim warriors and heroes to emphasise the benefits of becoming a pious and ascetic Ṣūfī ruler. In the mid-18th century, there are references to other aristocratic Javanese women composing manuscripts also inspired by Islamic literature. Women of the court, in both Java and the Malay areas of the archipelago, were actively engaged in writing and collecting manuscripts from at least this period until the demise of the courts in the early 20th century.

Records from this period indicate that non-élite women (rather than men) organised domestic commercial activity, such as the buying and selling of local produce in the markets, with men dominating transactions with foreigners. However, it is clear that some élite women used their own wealth to provide the capital for overseas trade conducted on their behalf by men.

(b) *Status of women in the 19th century*

As with the earlier period, the historical record is incomplete and focussed on élite rather than non-élite women. However, it is possible to gain an impression of their status from descriptions of several notable women. In the early 19th century, for example, in the Malay-Bugis kingdom of Lingga-Riau (which encompassed Johor, Pahang and Singapore), one of the Sultan's wives was given an island, its appanages and revenues to remain in her family in perpetuity. In the mid-1820s, this woman was able to supply the capital for her brother to undertake a trading voyage to raise money for the *Ḥadjdj*. It was not apparently the custom at this time for women to cover their heads in public but, by the 1850s, the male rulers of this kingdom, influenced by their visits to Mecca, encouraged women to wear a veil when in public. This concern that women cover their heads was accompanied by similar requirements for men to dress modestly, and was a trend apparent also in other areas of Muslim Southeast Asia where returning pilgrims spread Wahhābī teachings.

If the élite women of this Riau-Lingga kingdom are in any way representative of the position of women in other Malay courts (and there is no reason not to extrapolate from their experience), then it is clear that they had the opportunity to learn to read and write and that they maintained their own collections of manuscripts and, later, of lithographed and printed works. One member of a leading Bugis-Malay family, Raja Aisyiyah Sulaiman (*ca.* 1870-1925), for example, began writing verse and prose in her teenage years and continued after marriage. She was one of at least six other women writers from the Lingga-Riau region who were composing a variety of works in the last quarter of the 19th century. Their writings indicate that they were well versed in the basic tenets of Islam and that they were concerned to apply Muslim teachings in their daily lives and to influence others to do the same, especially when raising children. Of particular interest is a compendium of charms beneficial for marital relations composed in 1908, just five years before the Dutch abolished the Riau-Lingga kingdom. Its author was a commoner, known as Khadijah Terong (1885-1955), who incorporated Ḳur'ānic verses into the charms in a manner which indicates her familiarity with and knowledge of more than just the basic tenets of Islam (see Mukherjee, in *Empowered women*, 1997). Khadijah's charms are designed to provide satisfaction and pleasure for both husband and wife, so ensuring that each is content in the marriage. The didactic writings of the women of Riau-Lingga may be described as forerunners of the "Guides for women" (*Panduan wanita*) which became popular in the 1980s and are still being produced and are selling well in Muslim bookshops in Indonesia and Malaysia.

Élite women were tutored in their own residences and were almost self-sufficient within their domains, although if they chose to travel (usually by sea) they were free to do so if accompanied by appropriate attendants or their husband. Non-élite women did not have the same degree of leisure nor the means to travel. Their access to intensive education, under the guidance of expert teachers, was also restricted, but the large number of local Ḳur'ān schools in southern Thailand, the northern Malay Peninsula and Java and Madura (late 19th century Dutch figures estimated there were 15,000 of these schools with about 230,000 pupils) suggest that girls as well as boys attended for basic religious instruction.

(c) *Status of women in the 20th century*

At the turn of the century, resistance to direct colonial rule was prolonged and violent in some areas. In this context, there are several notable examples of women joining or leading men in holy wars. In the late 19th century resistance to the Dutch control of Aceh (northern Sumatra), an area renowned for its devotion to Islam, a widow, Cut Nyak Dien, took over the leadership of a band of guerrilla fighters after her husband was killed by the Dutch in 1899. She continued to resist until captured in 1905. She died in exile in 1906 and is now an Indonesian national hero, whose struggle for Islam and her homeland has been celebrated in a very popular 1980s Indonesian film.

The adoption of new technologies such as printing, and improved communications, enabled greater contact between the heartlands of Islam and Southeast Asia. Of particular significance to women was the spread of modernist teachings, especially those of Muḥammad 'Abduh [*q.v.*], which were disseminated in a weekly publication, *al-Imām* (published in Singapore, 1906-8), which was clearly inspired by

Cairo's *al-Manār*. Widely read all over the Indonesian archipelago and through the Malay Peninsula, *al-Imām*'s articles urged Muslims in the region to improve their knowledge of Islam and to pay greater attention to education. To this end, *al-Imām* encouraged the establishment of new schools (*madrasah*) based on Egyptian models where Islamic doctrine, Arabic, English, and secular subjects such as mathematics and geography, were taught to both girls and boys. It was considered especially important that young women receive a "modern" education (including secular knowledge as well as religion), because as future mothers they bore the prime responsibility for the "correct" upbringing of the next generation.

In 1913 a number of co-educational schools offering both religious and secular subjects were established in Java by the *Jamʿiyyat al-Islah wa 'l-Irshad*, an organisation led by the reformist Sudanese teacher, Shaykh Aḥmad Surkati, while in 1915 the progressive co-educational Diniyah Schools were opened in the Minangkabau region of West Sumatra. By 1922 there were 15 Diniyah schools in West Sumatra which attracted young women from as far afield as the Malay Peninsula and Java. Graduates spread the message of responsible but active engagement in social life through their work as teachers and journalists and as modern-minded mothers. Further impetus for the education of women came from the writings of Sayyid Shaykh b. Aḥmad al-Hādī (1867-1934), a *Sharīʿa* lawyer, religious teacher, author and successful publisher who settled finally in Penang. He was an enthusiastic supporter of the ideas of Muḥammad ʿAbduh and Rashīd Riḍā [*q.v.*] and translated many of their writings into Malay for publication in *al-Imām*. He went on to use fiction to promote progressive interpretations of Islam, and in 1925 and 1926 published the two-volume best-seller *Faridah Hanom*. The eponymous heroine is an aristocratic Muslim woman living in Cairo, educated in both Islam and western teachings, and an admirer of ʿAbduh, who is written into the text. The popularity of the books, which were reprinted innumerable times up to the 1970s, ensured that the heroine's message of applying God's gift of intelligence to the understanding of Islamic teachings, linked with a dedication to improving contemporary social conditions, had wide exposure. The story of Faridah Hanom ends with a description of how the heroine uses her wealth to found schools for young women, and notes that from these schools came women who went on to lead the struggle for women's emancipation, citing real women such as Hudā Shaʿrāwī [*q.v.* in Suppl.], who founded *L'Union Féministe Égyptienne*. Sayyid Shaykh al-Hādī invested the profits from the success of this book in his printing business, and from it funded the publication of works of non-fiction. One of these, *Kitab Alam Perempuan* ("The world of women"), 1930, continued the themes of *Faridah Hanom* and argued forcefully that the most pressing matter for Muslims was the education of women so that the whole community would benefit.

In peninsula Malaya, Hajjah Zainon Suleiman (1903-1989) responded to Sayyid Shaykh's calls and worked actively for the education of Malay women. She was supervisor of one of the leading girls' schools for nearly 20 years and in 1930 founded the first Malay women's association, the Johor Women Teacher's Union, and a magazine for its members. The magazine, *Bulan Melayu*, became an influential publication for women and provided a forum for women writers to express their views on contemporary issues. Ibu Zain (as she was known) was an important advocate for the rights of Malay women within Islam in terms reminiscent of the heroine of *Faridah Hanom*. She was an influential figure in Malaya, and in the early 1950s led the women's wing of the UMNO (United Malays National Organisation).

The main Islamic women's organisations in Malaysia have been established since Independence in 1957, and almost all are subsections of a parent body which is male-dominated. The women's wing of PAS (*Partai Islam Se Malaysia* [*q.v*]) for example, was founded in 1958, and although extremely active in educating women, its members cannot be elected to the central board of PAS. There are at least four other Muslim women's organisations in Malaysia, each of which is engaged in welfare work among Muslim women, including marriage counselling, assistance for domestic violence victims and fund raising for charities. The most recently formed group, *Puteri Islam* (Sisters in Islam), was officially established in 1991 by a small group of professional women (lawyers and academics) to re-examine the sources of Islam for a better understanding of women's status in Islam. Through high-profile activities in the press and media and through seminars and workshops, members of Sisters in Islam have had considerable impact on the public perception of women's status in Malaysia. Their interpretations of the Ḳur'ān and Ḥadīth have aroused critical reactions from conservative religious scholars, and the resulting public debates have highlighted issues such as the role of Islamic law in a modern nation state.

In Indonesia (then the Netherlands East Indies) one of the earliest Islamic women's organisations, *Aisyiyah*, was established in 1917 by members of *Muhammadiyah*, a reformist movement which began in Java in 1912 and spread quite rapidly through the Indies. By 1938, *Aisyiyah* had set up over 1,700 schools (from primary to secondary levels) as well as teacher training colleges, health centres and orphanages. Members were encouraged to guide other women in their Islamic duties and to spread knowledge of Islam to diverse classes of women so as to increase their awareness of religious duties, rights and responsibilities.

The *Muslimat Nahdatul Ulama*, the women's branch of *Nahdatul Ulama*, the second Islamic mass movement in Indonesia (with a current following of over 30 million), was established in 1946. Like *Aisyiyah*, its members have been working to improve education and health care for women and they helped establish the "Advisory Council for Marriage and Divorce" (*Badan Penasehat Perkawinan dan Penyelesaian Perceraian*) which assists women who have to take marital disputes to court. Although the *Nahdatul Ulama* movement has been characterised as less progressive than *Muhammadiyyah*, during the 1980s, under the leadership of Abdurrahman Wahid, greater attention was given to social issues, including the status of women. One illustration is the work of the Association for Social and Pesantren Development (*Perhimpunan Pengembangan Pesantren dan Masyarakat*) whose work includes a successful education program for traditional religious teachers (both men and women) about women's reproductive rights.

In Indonesia, Malaysia, Singapore, the Philippines and Thailand, the post-colonial state has accommodated the *Sharīʿa* but restricted its formal application to matters of personal law [see SHARĪʿA. In South-East Asia]. The issue of polygamy has highlighted the differences between modernising and conservative elements in Southeast Asian Muslim communities, and has focussed on the absolute difference between revealed and secular authority. One example is the 1974 Indonesian Marriage Law, which was introduced in response to continued pressure from women's organisations and was to provide some security for women, particularly regarding divorce and polygamy. It was perceived by some Muslims as a strategy for secular (state) authority to displace Islamic jurisdiction and was fiercely opposed. The state was forced to enact an amended statute permitting polygamous marriages and unilateral divorce, with Sharīʿa courts retaining authority to make judgements in these areas (see Butt 1999). However, the jurisdiction of Sharīʿa courts has been steadily eroded by the Indonesian government, so that although polygamy has not officially been forbidden, it is extremely difficult to practise.

In Malaysia, the Federal Government introduced the Islamic Family Law Act in 1984 and set minimum ages for marriage and restrictions on polygamy and divorce. Although similar laws were enacted in each of the constituent states of Malaysia by 1991, Islamic authorities at the local levels have tried to undermine some of its provisions, particularly those concerning polygamy. When this occurs, and aggrieved women bring it to the attention of national activist groups (such as Sisters in Islam), there is widespread public debate and increasing pressure on traditional religious teachers to adapt to contemporary conditions.

In matters of inheritance, Muslims theoretically follow the Sharīʿa but detailed interviews with women in Indonesia and Malaysia indicate that many parents circumvent the provision of greater portions for male heirs by distributing some property to female heirs before death. This has been seen as maintaining the parity of sons and daughters as expressed in traditional (pre-Islamic) kinship systems.

(d) *Status of women in the 21st century*

The rise of the middle classes in the Muslim populations of Southeast Asia, with an increase in higher education and greater participation in the global cash economy, has caused some women in this group to seek to reaffirm their identity as Muslims. Participating fully in the public life of their nations, many of these women wish to understand Islam better and follow programmes to achieve this. It has also been noted that women as well as men are joining the new Ṣūfī groups which are being established in big cities to cater for those who seek to deepen their personal experience of Islam. Others are founding or playing leading roles in Muslim non-governmental organisations devoted to the needs of women, which have grown in numbers since the economic crisis affected Southeast Asia in the late 1990s.

The most visible statement about identity is obviously that of style of dress. A growing number of women in the region choose to fully cover their hair and to wear distinctively Muslim fashions, which has led to a new fashion industry. Only a small minority in the region choose to adopt a full body covering (including face) of black, and those who do are often subjected to critical comment and accused of being overly influenced by foreign Muslim (Middle-Eastern) traditions. The majority who adopt non-western dress do so to emphasise that they wish to identify themselves as followers of Islam. This is not necessarily linked with a desire to return to conservative religious practices. Many of the tertiary-educated women in Indonesia and Malaysia who fully cover their hair do so to show they are part of an international sisterhood of modern-minded (rather than tradition-bound) women. In nations where Muslims are in a minority, such as the Philippines and southern Thailand, many young Muslim women have adopted Islamic dress to indicate their resistance to the prevailing national political culture.

The improved economic conditions in both Indonesia and Malaysia since the 1970s have given large numbers of women access to tertiary education and the qualifications to enter public life. While Muslim women were represented in all areas of business, govenment administration and society in Indonesia and Malaysia, they were not elected as leaders of major political movements. This changed in the 1990s when Megawati Sukarnoputri headed a populist mass movement in Indonesia and in 1998, after her husband's arrest, Dr Wan Azizah Wan Ismail led the National Justice Party in Malaysia. The Indonesian general elections of 1999 delivered a huge vote to Megawati's party but in the political bargaining which followed she was defeated for the presidency by Abdul Rahman Wahid and had to accept the post of Vice-President. The possibility that Megawati might become President of Indonesia aroused heated debate in Indonesia with ordinary Muslim men and women unable to follow the complex legal reasoning based on the classical texts of Islam which some Indonesian scholars put forward. In 2001, Abdul Rahman Wahid lost the confidence of the Indonesian parliament and Megawati replaced him becoming the fifth president of the Republic of Indonesia. Political expediency overwhelmed the objections of a minority of *ʿulamāʾ*.

The debate over female leadership, however, is a useful point on which to conclude this survey of Muslim women in Southeast Asia because it exemplifies some of the features of Islam which are characteristic of the region. First, that it is not unusual for women to play prominent roles in public life; second, that women's leadership is seen as being distinctively different in style from that of males; third, that the religious arguments concerning the permissibility of a female head of state have revealed the division between traditional (conservative) approaches to Islamic law and more modern (liberal) interpretations; and finally, that specialist knowledge of Islam throughout Southeast Asia is still dominated by men.

Bibliography: 1. General. G.W. Jones, *Marriage and divorce in Islamic Southeast Asia*, Kuala Lumpur 1994; Anthony Reid, *Southeast Asia in the age of commerce, 1450-1680*, 2 vols., New Haven 1988, 1993; *Empowered women*, ed. Wendy Mukherjee, in *Review of Indonesian and Malaysian Affairs*, xxxi/2 (1997).

2. Indonesia. M.C. Ricklefs, *The seen and unseen worlds in Java 1726-1749*, Sydney 1998; Suzanne A. Brenner, *Reconstructing self and society. Javanese Muslim women and "the veil"*, in *American Ethnologist*, xxiii (1996); Andree Feillard, *Indonesia's emerging Muslim feminism. Women leaders on equality, inheritance and other gender issues*, in *Studia Islamika*, iv/1 (1997); S. Butt, *Polygamy and mixed marriage in Indonesia. The application of the marriage law in the courts*, in T. Lindsey (ed.), *Indonesia law and society*, Sydney 1999; Kathryn Robinson, *Women: difference versus diversity*, in D.K. Emmerson (ed.), *Indonesia beyond Suharto. Polity, economy, society, transition*, New York-London 1999; Robinson and Sharon Bessell (eds.), *Women in Indonesia. Gender, equity and development*, Singapore 2001.

3. Malaysia. Aihwa Ong, *State versus Islam. Malay families, women's bodies and the body politic*, in *Bewitching women, pious men. Gender and body politics in Southeast Asia*, ed. Aihwa Ong and M.G. Peletz, Berkeley 1995; Sharifah Zaleha Syed Hassan and S. Cederoth, *Managing marital disputes in Malaysia. Islamic mediators and conflict resolution in the Syariah courts*, Surrey 1997; Maila Stivens, *Becoming modern*

in Malaysia. Women at the end of the twentieth century, in *Women in Asia. Tradition, modernity and globalisation*, ed. Louise Edwards and Mina Roces, Sydney 2000; Maznah Mohamad, *At the centre and the periphery. The contribution of women's movements to democracy*, in F. Loh Kok Wah and Khoo Boo Teik (eds.), *Democracy in Malaysia. Discourses and practices*, Richmond, Surrey 2002; Maila Stivens, *(Re)Framing women's rights claims in Malaysia*, in V. Hooker and Norani Othman (eds.), *Malaysia: Islam, society and politics. Essays in honour of Clive S. Kessler*, Singapore 2003.

4. Philippines and Thailand. C. Prachuabmoh, *The role of women in maintaining ethnic identity and boundaries. A case of Thai Muslims in South Thailand*, in *South East Asian Review*, xiv/1-2 (1989); Jacqueline Siapno, *Gender relations and Islamic resurgence in Mindanao, southern Philippines*, in *Muslim women's choices. Religious belief and social reality*, ed. Camillia Fawzi El-Solh and Judy Mabro, Oxford-Providence 1994. (VIRGINIA MATHESON HOOKER)

MĀRID (A.), rebel or revolutionary, someone practising *murūd* or *tamarrud*, resistance to the established order, from the root *m-r-d* "to be refractory or rebellious".

The word *mārid* is strongly polysemantic; it includes both the idea of audacity and revolt, and also extreme pride and insolence (*al-ʿātī al-shadīd*, according to *LA*). Also present in the root is the idea of youth, with *amrad* meaning "young, beardless youth" (see Ibn al-ʿAdīm, *Zubda*, ed. S. Dahhān, Damascus 1951, i, 260, concerning beardless *ghilmān*), concomitant with the idea of a leafless tree (*shadjara mardāʾ*), and sometimes with that of a young slave boy, the equivalent of *ghulām* [*q.v.*], with, additionally, the connotations of violence, insolence, rebelliousness and, equally, of pederasty and homosexuality, as frequently found amongst young soldiers.

It should be noted that the central meaning of man's revolt is semantically associated with that of the rebellion of djinn and demons (*shayāṭīn*), as *LA* directly indicates. It follows that, in classical Arabic, the term *mārid* has negative connotations and that, in the unconscious collective mind, it goes back to the revolt of Iblīs against God and refers likewise to that of a member of the community against the ruling power, considered as a fatal source of trouble and instability. In Modern Standard Arabic it retains these two concepts, since it means, first, rebel, insurgent, refractory person, and second, demon or evil-working spirit. Other roots are more frequently used by mediaeval Arab historians to describe rebellion. Thus *shaghaba* "to wander away from the road, excite people against each other, kick up a row", and *ʿaṣā* "to rebel (to be connected with *ʿaṣā* "to strike with a stick"), go against other people", whence *al-ʿĀṣī* "the rebel", the name given to the Orontes river which flows from south to north, contrary to the rest of the rivers of western Asia (see al-Muḳaddasī, 32 l. 12, *aʿṣā* and *ashghab*). Likewise, *thāra* "to raise dust by galloping through the sands like a bull, to assault", whence *thāʾir* "rebel" and *thawra* [*q.v.*] "revolution"; and *ḳalaba* "to overturn, be reversed", whence *inḳilāb*, used in the 20th century for a *coup d'état* fomented by a small number of individuals, often military men. Only the verb *fatana* "to prove, test, trouble" refers to an activity more intellectual than physical, sc. *fitna* [*q.v.*], in origin a division voluntarily brought about within a homogenous group, which could be paralleled semantically with the Greek origin of the word for "devil", *diabolos*, "the divider", whence *fātin* (pl. *futtān*), intensive form *fattān*, meaning as much "seducer" as "agitator". The decision to go out from (*kharadja*) the ranks of ʿAlī's army, taken at Ṣiffīn [*q.v.*] by his most fervent followers when he agreed to the arbitration, has given rise to the epithet *khāridjī*, denoting a member of the sectarian group arising on this occasion [see KHĀRIDJITES] but, equally, a rebel in general, without any religious connotation (see Ibn al-Ḳalānisī, *Dhayl Taʾrīkh Dimashḳ*, ed. H. Amedroz, Beirut 1908, 87 l. 16).

Every aggressive action (*thawra, fitna, inḳilāb, tamarrud*) against the established social and institutional order involves both a political and religious aspect. The rebel is thus a doubly emblematic figure, condemned for breaking the consensual conformism of society and sometimes for a dangerous attachment to the purity of practice of the Islamic law and cult, but also admired for his devotion to the cause which he defends and for his physical courage, notable at the time of his public punishment after being defeated—this being generally the case—and condemned by the ruling power.

The Sunnīs, from the time of the establishment of the ʿAbbāsids to the 1970s (the execution in jail of Sayyid Ḳuṭb [*q.v.*] by ʿAbd al-Nāṣir [*q.v.* in Suppl.] was to give rise to the first, Sunnī Islamic doctrine justifying the use of violence and killing, not only against a power which was self-styled Muslim and Sunnī but not respecting the Islamic law, but also against every individual, Sunnī Muslim or of any belief or absence of belief, of either sex, child and adult, not joining in the revolt), were considering that challenging the ruling sovereign Muslim power, whether just or unjust, legitimate or having seized power for itself, was risking committing an offence against Islam and that a vacuum of power was worse than a corrupt ruling power [see AL-MĀWARDĪ; IBN TAYMIYYA].

In practice the *hidjra* of A.D. 622 enabled the Prophet Muḥammad to institutionalise Islam by creating at Yathrib/Medina the *umma* [*q.v.*], a society which involved personal commitment to the revealed Law, a concept opposed to those of *nasab* and *nisba* [*q.vv.*] acquired at birth by the newly-born, and by founding the tribal confederation at Mecca. At Medina, the individual was integrated of his own free will into the community of believers, in which was built up around the collective faith in the Ḳurʾānic revelation a solidarity between each believer, male or female, slave or free, Arab or black, or convert from other faiths. The survival of Islam required the strengthening of this bond which a common religion established between each believer. Ḳurʾān, III, 98/103, expresses this command: "Hold fast to the rope (or bond) of God and do not become divided into various groups; remember God's goodness to you when you were enemies; He established concord in your hearts" (see also IV, 63-4/60-1).

The fragility of the *umma* at the outset led to condemnation of any rebel who put in jeopardy the unity of Islam by disobedience, provocation or revolt. In appealing to ancient family, tribal, ethnic or territorial solidarities, the rebel thereby pushed the community back to the chaotic time of the *Djāhiliyya* [*q.v.*]. This is why, when Muḥammad died and the tribes thought themselves freed from this voluntary solidarity which they had entered with the person of the Prophet, Abū Bakr suppressed the *ridda* [*q.v.* in Suppl.]; from this time onwards, the Medinan concept of voluntary adhesion to Islam only functioned in that unique instance. The new convert, like all Muslims, including the child born of a Muslim father, saw himself constrained—before his birth, as at Mecca—and until his death, by his *nasab* of "Muslim" to profess Islam as long as he lived.

The traditional history of the first century of Islam is marked by a series of violent episodes, extending from the *ridda* in Abū Bakr's time to the murder of ʿU̲th̲mān, then the *fitna* in which ʿAlī and Muʿāwiya were opposed to each other and, finally, the intertribal conflicts under the Umayyads. For a symbolic interpretation of these stories at a later period, see J.-Cl. Garcin, *États, sociétés et cultures du Monde musulman médiéval*, i-ii, Paris 2000, index.

A typology of revolts in Sunnī Islam has so far not been attempted, according to our knowledge. Leaving aside purely S̲h̲īʿī and K̲h̲āridjite movements, one may put forward a very general classification of revolts within the Sunnī milieu.

In the first Islamic century, apart from revolts regarding the legitimacy of the caliph, there is a recurrent motif of disorder, the relative opportunities offered to the Ḳuras̲h̲īs or to Arabs from other tribal groupings, Ḳaysī or Yamanī, or even to the *mawālī*, to take over the functions of state. Certain groups wished to speed up the integration of the converts whilst others, on the contrary, wished to reserve the prestigious and financially rewarding posts for the Meccan aristocracy or the Arabs.

The revolts on the part of non-Muslims, Berbers, Copts, Christians of Lebanon or Armenians rarely marked a refusal to accept the installation of a Muslim state. A close examination shows that the motive here was, rather, revulsion against an oppressive tax system than against the political pre-eminence of Islam.

Over the succeeding centuries, revolts display most often a S̲h̲īʿī or K̲h̲āridjite motivation and in fact gather up violent recrudescences of pre-Islamic identities of ethnically homogenous groups in isolated regions, away from the prosperity of the great cities and the main commercial routes. It may then happen that other ethnic groups of the neighbourhood, without specific connections with the originally rebellious group but equally oppressed and adversely affected by the exercise of an arbitrary and corrupt power, join in the revolt. In any case, revolts against excessive tax burdens continue to break out regularly up to the Mamlūk period and beyond (see Tsugitaka Sato, *State and rural society in medieval Islam*, Leiden 1997, 162-7) in all the agricultural regions of the East. These rebellious groups were subject to exactions of the central exchequer, of urban landowners and, later on, of the owners of *iḳṭāʿ*s, at levels leaving no possibility of profit for the peasants or money for investment in increased productivity and therefore a rise in social status. The revolt of the Zand̲j̲ [*q.v.*] or Zunūd̲j̲ in lower ʿIrāḳ is another example of rural protest, that of agricultural labourers, in this case, black and impoverished, against the avidity of the city dwellers.

Amongst other causes of outbreaks, one should mention the grave disorders, in particular during the 2nd-4th/8th-10th centuries, amongst the Arab tribes (Ibn ʿAsākir, *Taʾrīk̲h̲ madīnat Dimas̲h̲ḳ* [ʿĀṣim-ʿĀyid̲h̲], Damascus 1977, Abu ʾl-Hayd̲h̲am al-Murrī, 393-418), and then those, more serious still, launched by the Bedouin tribes against the towns of lower ʿIrāḳ. In these they were protesting against the marginalisation which they considered was the policy of the town dwellers towards them. Whence the success among them of Ḳarmaṭī [*q.v.*] propaganda, which thus caught up for Ismāʿīlism the social and economic protest of peasants against the dues and taxes levied on them from the cities and that of Bedouin in revulsion against the spectacle of luxurious *ḥad̲j̲d̲j̲* caravans whilst they themselves were suffering from thirst and starvation. In the 5th/11th century, the nomads ceased for a while their intertribal fighting and came together—Arab Bedouin, Kurdish and Berber nomads—to attack the sedentary lands, from the D̲j̲azīra in northeastern Syria to Ifrīḳiya (see Th. Bianquis, *Damas et Syrie sous la domination fāṭimide*, Damascus 1989, ii, 415-65).

In the 5th-6th/10th-11th centuries, there were uprisings in the Mag̲h̲rib and al-Andalus, those of the Almoravids [see AL-MURĀBIṬŪN] and Almohads [see AL-MUWAḤḤIDŪN], launched from the austere and ascetic south against a corrupt and luxurious north and aiming at bringing régimes considered as lax back to the strict way of the Islamic law.

For the urban revolts, which have been well studied, see AḤDĀT̲H̲; ʿAYYĀR; SAFFĀRIDS; ZUʿʿĀR; etc.

Bibliography: See, in addition to the articles cited above, various contributions in M.A. al-Bakhit and R. Schick (eds.), *Bilād al-Shām during the Abbasid period. Procs. of the Fifth International Conference on the History of Bilād al-Shām, 1410/1990*, ʿAmmān 1991. M. Chokr, *Zandaqa et zindīqs in Islam, au second siècle de l'hégire*, Damascus 1993, has clearly shown how the ʿAbbāsid ruling power marshalled moral, political and sexual arguments in order to condemn every attempt at rebellion against the dynasty's official moral basis. See also the good bibl. in M. Bonner, *Aristocratic violence and holy war*, New Haven 1996. (TH. BIANQUIS)

MARḲIYŪNIYYA, the Arabic name for the Marcionites, an important non-monotheistic tendency in early Christianity. Marcion (Μαρκιων; Ar. Marḳiyūn) was a native of Sinope [see SĪNŪB] on the Black Sea who arrived in Rome in A.D. 138 (or somewhat later) and taught among the Christian community in the imperial capital. Marcion's doctrine was that the god described in the Old Testament (the creator, or just god) is different from the god described in the New Testament (the stranger, or good god), the father of Christ, and that men's souls, like their bodies, were made by and belonged to the creator, but that the stranger purchased these souls from their maker by sacrificing his own son to the other god. The later Marcionites elaborated this into various theological systems. One school taught four primal principles (the good god, the just god, matter, evil), another taught three principles (identifying evil with matter), but the "Neo-Marcionite" school (described most clearly in the second book of the *Dialogue of Adamantius* falsely attributed to Origen) equated the creator with the principle of evil and also maintained (against Marcion, but in broad agreement with the Manichaeans and Gnostics) that the good god sent his pneuma into the world already at the moment of creation and that it remained entrapped in the material world until it was set free by Christ.

The evidence for the survival of Marcionite communities in the mediaeval Near East is meagre, but not entirely negligible. The Christian writer Thomas of Margā (*Book of governors*, Syriac text, ed. Budge, London 1893, 261) reports that in the last decade of the 8th century A.D. the metropolitan of Gēlān and Daylam, S̲h̲uwḥālīs̲h̲ōʿ, travelled into the remote parts of his see, preaching "among the pagans, Marcionites and Manichaeans". Also, the Muslim bibliographer Ibn al-Nadīm, writing towards the end of the 4th/10th century, even claims that Marcionites are "numerous in K̲h̲urāsān" and that there "they practice openly, like the Manichaeans" (*Fihrist*, ed. Tad̲j̲addud, 402; for the Manichaeans in K̲h̲urāsān, see ZINDĪḲ). Elsewhere,

Ibn al-Nadīm quotes a reliable informant (*thiḳa*) who had seen Marcionite books and who reported that their script resembled that of the Manichaeans (*ibid.*, 19). These "numerous" Marcionites in Khurāsān do not seem to be mentioned in any other source.

Muslim writers on alien religions offer some data about the beliefs of the Marcionites. Some of this is manifestly taken from the standard Christian sources, e.g. when al-Masʿūdī (*Tanbīh*, 127) states, accurately enough, that the Marcionites taught "two principles, good and evil, and justice (read *al-ʿadl* with Ms. L) is a third (principle) between the two"; these three are clearly the good god, evil matter, and the just god. Ibn al-Malāḥimī (*al-Muʿtamad*, 586-9) has two conflicting accounts of the doctrines of the Marcionites. The second of these is credited explicitly to Abū ʿĪsā al-Warrāḳ, whose version was evidently used (directly or indirectly) by most of the other Muslim theologians who mention Marcionites (see Vajda's article, in *Bibl.*). This version claims that Marcion taught two polar principles, "light and darkness", plus a "third essence" who "mixed the light and darkness and mingled them by way of creating a balance between them". But this is pure fantasy, extrapolated from some vague notion that Marcionism is like Manichaeism, but with three rather than two principles.

The first account cited by Ibn al-Malāḥimī (possibly also from al-Warrāḳ, though this is not indicated unambiguously in the text) is totally different. This version is cited, much more briefly, also by ʿAbd al-Djabbār (*al-Mughnī*, v, 17-18; however, the translation in Vajda, *op. cit.*, 123-4, is incorrect) and by al-Shahrastānī (*al-Milal wa 'l-niḥal*, ed. Badrān, 643-5), who combines it, in a confused fashion, with the above-mentioned spurious account by al-Warrāḳ. What we have here is an essentially accurate account of the "Neo-Marcionite" doctrine: the primal beings here are God, the Devil (i.e. the demonised creator in Neo-Marcionism) and an "intermediate being" (evidently the divine pneuma). The Devil attacks and oppresses the intermediate, mixes himself with it and builds this world from that mixture. The stars and planets are the Devil's spirits, with which he rules the world. Animals and plants are likewise the creation of the Devil, and it is he who sends the false prophets and antagonistic religions. But the "highest one" (i.e. the good god) takes pity on the intermediate and sends his son Jesus into the world to liberate him from bondage. Ibn al-Malāḥimī says further that the Marcionites do not kill any being, are celibate, avoid "fatty meats" (*al-zuhūmāt*, presumably meaning that they did eat fish) and alcoholic drinks, and pray and fast all the time. The text contains also a very interesting Marcionite polemic against the adherents of the doctrine of the eternity of the world (*ahl al-dahr*), the monists (*muwaḥḥidūn*) and the dualists (*aṣḥāb al-ithnayn*, evidently Manichaeans). The passage contains much plausible information that is not found in other ancient or mediaeval accounts of Marcionism. It is therefore possible that it refers to the actual beliefs of a Neo-Marcionite community in the Islamic world, presumably in Khurāsān.

Bibliography: The basic work on Marcionism is still A. von Harnack, *Marcion: das Evangelium vom fremden Gott*, Leipzig 1921. For a different perspective, see F. de Blois, *Dualism in Iranian and Christian traditions*, in *JRAS* (2000), 1-19 (esp. 7-14). Most of the Arabic testimonia are collected and translated in G. Vajda, *Le témoignage d'al-Māturidī sur la doctrine des Manichéens, des Dayṣānites et des Marcionites*, in *Arabica*, xiii (1966), 1-38, with the "Note annexe", 113-28, repr. in his *Études de théologie et de philosophie arabo-islamiques à l'époque classique*, London 1986. Add to these Ibn al-Malāḥimī, *al-Muʿtamad fī uṣūl al-dīn*, ed. M. McDermott and W. Madelung, London 1991, 586-9; the relevant section is partially tr. in W. Madelung, *Abū ʿĪsā al-Warrāq über die Bardesaniten, Marcioniten und Kantäer*, in *Studien zur Geschichte und Kultur des vorderen Orients* (Festschrift B. Spuler), Leiden 1981, 210-24. For the Syriac sources, see J.-M. Fiey, *Les Marcionites dans les textes historiques de l'église de Perse*, in *Le Muséon*, lxxxiii (1970), 183-8. (F.C. de Blois)

MARTABA (a., pl. *marātib*), a term with a variety of meanings: class, rank, degree assigned by etiquette, rank, hierarchy, arrangement of places in an audience, a sofa, an upholstered piece of furniture.

The term presents an intriguing question in the domain of manners and etiquette. In pre-Islamic Arabic and the language of the very early Muslim generations, there was no well-developed conceptual vocabulary of ranks and categories, especially those perceived by the ruling class; there was a lack of terms dealing with the "distance" between the sovereign and his entourage, as well as among the different classes of courtiers. Therefore the writer and translator Ibn al-Muḳaffaʿ (d. *ca.* 139/756 [*q.v.*]) invented terms, adopted Persian images and improved existing vocables, such as *rutba* and *manzila* and others, for the purpose of indicating social standing and rank, both in his translations from Pahlavi Persian and in his original works, in which one can discern a measure of continuity with certain Sāsānid values which pre-date the Islamic period. One should remember, as background, that the Sāsānid sovereigns divided their population into a number of categories (A. Christensen, *L'empire des Sassanides*, 19ff., 93ff.; idem, *L'Iran sous les Sassanides*, 97ff., relying on Ps.-Djāḥiẓ, al-Masʿūdī, al-Thaʿālibī and other sources); neither the subjects of despised trades belonging to the lower ones, nor their descendants, would ever be permitted to serve at the royal court (Ps.-Djāḥiẓ, *K. al-Tādj*, [1914], 23-27; concerning the authorship and date of the latter source, see G. Schoeler, in *ZDMG*, cxxx [1980], 217-25, and *VOHD*, B/2, Wiesbaden 1990, 156-9; R. Brunschvig, in *Stud. Isl.* xvi [1962], 49 n. 1, hesitated to accept some details in this information reported by later Muslim historiographers). Thus the Shuʿūbiyya [*q.v.*], a cultural movement that stressed the contribution of the non-Arabic heritage (and often minimised the importance of certain Arab traditions that can be traced back to the culture of the desert), took great pride in the fact that the Persian kings (I. Goldziher, *Muslim Studies*, Eng. tr. i, 156-9 and n. 2 of 158, relying on al-Djāḥiẓ and al-Masʿūdī; namely, the "previous kings" as quoted from al-Masʿūdī) encouraged *al-ʿilm bi 'l-marātib*, as opposed to the pre-Islamic Arab tribal life, described by this movement in its own biassed judgment. The purpose of such boasting about this Persian distinction between social classes was to emphasise the fact that the early Arabs lived a life of uncontrolledness and of apparent anarchy, and that therefore it was the Persians to whom one had to turn in order to learn the concepts of government and etiquette (Sadan, *An admirable and ridiculous hero. Some notes on the Bedouin*, in *Poetics Today*, x [1989], 474, 487ff., with references to Goldziher, Gibb, al-Dūrī, al-Laythī, Monroe, Ṭalfāḥ and others). In Muslim society, in particular that of the ʿAbbāsid empire, the term *marātib* was used mainly in connection with court etiquette. Hārūn al-Rashīd (d. 193/809 [*q.v.*]) even divided his court singers into three *marātib*; in this case, the categories reflect not only the quality of the singing but also friendship, sympathy and taste for various singing abilities (al-Raḳīḳ al-Ḳayrawānī, *Ḳuṭb al-surūr*, B.N. Paris ms. 3302, fol. 162b; not identical to the part edited by al-Djundī; see also al-Shayzarī, *al-Manhadj al-maslūk*, Zarḳāʾ, Jordan 1987, 464-6, 578-9.

When approaching the ruler, one was expected to stop at a distance determined by one's *martaba*, and there await for a sign (the verb is *awmaʾa, ashāra*, to notify by a gesture) from the sovereign, permitting him to sit down. The participants at the ruler's audience were expected not to behave in a manner unfitting to their rank. The boon-companion, *nadīm* [*q.v.*], had the most difficult task of deciding when an audience with the ruler was public or official and when it was a private party (which included drinking as well) in which the rules of etiquette (*ādāb*) were not to be strictly applied, although even then one was supposed to try not to exceed one's *manzila* or *martaba* (*ibid.* and al-Ghuzūlī, *Maṭāliʿ al-budūr*, Cairo 2000, 165) and the minimal rules implied by it. The *ḥādjib*, who was the palace chamberlain and responsible for the system of granting and refusing entrance to the palace, also had the job of ascertaining that everyone sat according to the *marātib* (al-Djāḥiẓ, *al-Ḥidjāb*, in *Rasāʾil*, Cairo 1964-5, ii, 39).

Exceptionally, some people may in fact have wished to sit with those of a lower rank, since the people attending the audience with the sovereign sat in a circle (*madjlis, ḥalḳa*), and those who were near him were higher in rank but could not always see him, while those who were farther away could see him well and might in fact have been sitting just opposite him. We rarely find a courtier or a guest who would prefer to sit opposite, out of modesty, or in order to see more clearly his host (al-Rāghib al-Iṣbahānī, *Muḥāḍarāt al-udabāʾ*, ii, 706, describes the exception; al-Maḳrīzī, *Khiṭaṭ*, e.g. i, 386-7, 389, whereas i, 390, mentions the term *martaba*, describes the rule: no courtier would yield his place to an inferior person; i, 443, presents, however, the irregular behaviour of a courtier who "used to take a seat at the edge of the circle of guests [during the royal meal], in order to see the caliph better and not according to the rank this courtier deserved"). It is in fact well known that the Fāṭimids were particularly insistent on maintaining the appropriate distance between the ruler and the other ranks: at festivals only representatives of the four Islamic schools of law were permitted to come into the presence of the caliph and greet him. In fact, they only came up to the threshold of the hall or pavilion in which the caliph was at the time, and usually it was only the caliph's secretary who responded by uttering a greeting formula in the ruler's name, and not the caliph in person. However, it must be emphasised that M. Canard's comparison (see *Bibl.*) of the etiquette of the Fāṭimid and Byzantine courts was written at a time when important sources for the ceremonial customs of the ʿAbbāsid court had not yet been published (especially al-Ṣābī's *Rusūm dār al-khilāfa*, see D. Sourdel, in *Bibl.*). To the Fāṭimid court, it was obviously more important to vie with the ʿAbbāsid than with the Byzantine court, but the cross-cultural study which Canard undertook is still of value. It thus turns out that various courts, and some later sultans, would occasionally increase or decrease the distance between the ruler and his courtiers, for reasons of religious simplicity.

At times, the differences have a geographical character. In the northeastern parts of the Muslim empire, one can find, here and there, that facet of the Persian heritage that elevated the king almost beyond the human pale, much more so than at the centre of the empire, at the ʿAbbāsid court. Thus, for example, in Khwārazm (Sadan, *Ādāb, règles de conduite* [see *Bibl.*], 293-5), a certain person would not dare put a spoon (made of precious metal) in a dish into which the sovereign had also put his spoon, because of the reverence in which the latter was held. But in Baghdād, the ʿAbbāsid caliphs knew that it was unseemly for the ruler to wash his hands before the meal in the company of his friends and courtiers; rather, this should be done in a separate room only in the company of someone of the same rank, such as a brother or parent. It is, however, well known that this was not always adhered to; even from the way this rule is formulated by the author (Ps.-Djāḥiẓ, *K. al-Tādj*, 17) who commends this behaviour, it is clear that while this was proper for sovereigns, based probably on the code of behaviour at the court of the Sāsānids and the division of their society into classes, sadly it was not fully respected, as it should have been, in his days. Perhaps this indicates that the ʿAbbāsids did not blindly imitate the Sāsānid manners but only followed them up to a certain point.

Since the concept of rank also determined the seating order, it should come as no surprise that the word *martaba* ended up designating a cushion, a kind of low and soft seat. The reason for this is that cushions were the normal seats used at meetings (only the ruler himself would occasionally sit on a genuine throne, and the vizier would at times sit on a simpler chair, *kursī*). One finds this kind of *martaba* cushion in texts closer to the spoken language, such as stories of the *Arabian nights* variety and, even more so, in documents from the Cairo Geniza (in the dowry lists of young brides, see Sadan, *Martaba*, in *Bibl.*). It would appear that these mattress-seats were arranged by day for sitting (on the arrangement of cushions in book shops and reading rooms, see also idem, *Mobilier*, in *Bibl.*; idem, *Nouveaux matériaux*, in *REI*, xlv [1977], 51ff.) and by night for sleeping, a quite economical and efficient system for the common people.

Bibliography (in addition to references given in the article): F. Gabrieli, *Etichetta*, in *RSO*, xi (1928), 292-305; M. Canard, *Le cérémonial fatimite et le cérémonial byzantin*, in *Byzantion*, xxi (1951), 355-420; Ch. Pellat (tr.), *Le Livre de la couronne attribué à Ǧāḥiẓ*, Paris 1954; D. Sourdel, *Questions de cérémonial ʿabbāside*, in *REI*, xxviii (1960), 121-48; see especially Sadan, *A propos de martaba*, in *REI*, xli (1973), 51-69; idem, *Le mobilier au Proche orient médiéval*, Leiden 1976, 15, 16, 52-56, 99, 117, 118; idem, *Ādāb, règles de conduite*, in *REI*, lxv (1986), 283-300.

(J. Sadan)

al-**MAʿRŪF** wa ʾl-**MUNKAR** [see al-nahy ʿan al-munkar, in Suppl.].

MAʿRŪF BALKHĪ, Abū ʿAbd Allāh Muḥammad b. Ḥasan, early poet in New Persian, of whom almost nothing is known but who must have flourished in the middle decades of the 4th/10th century, since odd verses of his survive that were allegedly dedicated to the Sāmānid Amir ʿAbd al-Malik (I) b. Nūḥ (I) (343-50/954-61), and he may have been at the court of the Ṣaffārid ruler of Sīstān, Khalaf b. Aḥmad (352-93/963-1003). Fragments amounting to some 45 verses, mainly love poetry and satires, have been collected by G. Lazard, *Les premiers poètes persans (IXe-Xe siècles)*, Tehran-Paris 1964, i, 31, tr. 129-33, Persian text ii, 132-8.

Bibliography: See also Browne, *LHP*, i, 463; Dhabīḥ Allāh Ṣafā, *Tārīkh-i adabiyyāt dar Īrān*, ²Tehran 1335/1956, i, 422-3; F. de Blois, *Persian literature, a bio-bibliographical survey*, v, London 1997, 191. (C.E. Bosworth)

MĀRŪNIYYA, Mawārina (Syriac *Mārūnāyē*, presumed derivative from the personal name *Mārūn*, diminutive of *mār* "lord"), the Arabic name of the Syrian Christian sect of the Maronites, which first entered into union with the Roman Catholic Church in *ca.* A.D. 1180.

According to al-Masʿūdī (d. 345/956), the sect first emerged into existence as a Monothelite Christian communion during the reign of the Roman emperor Maurice (582-602), its Monothelite origin (contested by Maronite historians since the late 15th century) being also affirmed by al-Ḳāḍī ʿAbd al-Djabbār (d. 415/1024) and the Crusader historian William of Tyre (d. 1185). The first known base of the community was the monastic establishment of Dayr Mārūn (or Dār Mārūn), on the Orontes river, east of the town of Ḥamā, which had already fallen to ruins by al-Masʿūdī's time. This establishment allegedly carried the name of the Syrian hermit Mārō (Arabic Mārūn) of Cyrrus (d. 433), who is claimed by the Maronite church as its patron, although he is also revered by the Syrian Melchite (Chalcedonian Orthodox) church as a saint.

While the Maronites have traditionally used Syriac for their liturgy, they appear to have been Arab rather than Aramaeo-Arab in ethnic origin; their ecclesiastical and secular literature, as known directly or from reference from as early as the 10th century A.D., is entirely in Arabic. Their ethnic difference from other Syrian Christians, who were mainly Aramaean or Aramaeo-Arab, might explain in part why they came to be organised as a separate church. The claim of the community to be descended from the Mardaites [see djarādjima], first advanced by the Patriarch Isṭifān al-Duwayhī (1668-1704 [*q.v.*]), is historically incredible.

The Maronites signalled their break from the Syrian Melchite see of Antioch when they began electing patriarchs of their own in *ca.* 685. In that same year, the conclusion of a peace accord between the Byzantine emperor Justinian II and the Umayad caliph ʿAbd al-Malik b. Marwān seems to have enabled the Byzantines to regain control over the affairs of the Antiochene see. The Monothelite doctrine having been condemned by the Sixth Ecumenical Council (680) as a pernicious heresy, Justinian II, it appears, was bent on eradicating what remained of it in Syria.

According to Maronite tradition, the first Maronite Patriarch, Yuḥannā Mārūn, had barely assumed office when Byzantine persecution forced him to flee the Orontes valley and seek refuge in the rugged reaches of the northern Lebanon, where the Maronite patriarchate has remained ever since. When the Byzantines reoccupied Antioch and the adjacent parts of northern Syria, starting from 969, the Christian population of the Orontes valley was still largely, if not entirely, Maronite. This Byzantine reoccupation, however, was to last until *ca.* 1070, by which time the Maronites of the Orontes valley had been mostly, if not entirely, replaced by Melchites, presumably as a result of Byzantine persecution; the only notable Maronite community outside Mount Lebanon survived in the city of Aleppo, which the Byzantines had failed to occupy.

When the Crusader forces, having seized Antioch (1098), proceeded to advance southwards to Jerusalem in 1099, Maronite warriors met them outside Tripoli to offer their service as guides and auxiliaries. The first contacts between the Maronite patriarchate and the Roman Catholic Church followed, ending more than four centuries of Maronite ecclesiastical isolation. It was not before *ca.* 1180, however, that a body of leading Maronite clerics, meeting with the Latin Patriarch of Antioch, formally agreed to unite with the Roman Catholic Church and abandon the Monothelite doctrine in favour of Roman orthodoxy. To cement this union, Pope Innocent III (1198-1216), invited the Maronite Patriarch Jeremiah of ʿAmshīt (Irmiyā al-ʿAmshītī) to Rome in 1215, ostensibly to participate in the Lateran Council of that year.

Meanwhile, a split had occured in the Maronite church, in the course of which the party opposed to the union waged armed attacks against those in its favour. This split reached its climax in 1282-3, when, for a brief while, each side had its own Patriarch. Shortly after, however, the Mamlūks of Egypt, who were already in occupation of the Syrian interior, put an end to the Crusader County of Tripoli (1289); then Acre was conquered (1291) and the last Crusaders expelled from Syria (1291). Finding itself once more in isolation, the Maronite church was able to regain its unity under Patriarchs favouring the union with Rome. However, Maronite relations with the Papacy remained casual, because of the difficulty of maintaining regular contact between the two sides once the Crusaders had gone.

The Maronites suffered sporadic persecution under the rule of the Baḥrī Mamlūks (1291-1382), at which time some Maronites emigrated from Mount Lebanon to live under Crusader protection in Cyprus, where a few thousand Maronites remain to this day. With the replacement of the Baḥrī by the Burdjī Mamlūk régime, the fortunes of the community took a turn for the better. Starting from the reign of Barḳūḳ (1382-9, 1390-9 [*q.v.*]), the first of the Burdjī sultans, special favours were accorded to the Maronite *muḳaddamūn* (sing. *muḳaddam* "chief") of the district of Djubbat Bsharrī (the mountain hinterland of Tripoli), enabling them to manage the affairs of their district much as they pleased. Subsequently, in 1444, the seat of the Maronite patriarchate, which had never been fixed before, was established in the monastery of Ḳannūbīn, in Djubbat Bsharrī, where it remained until the 19th century.

The interest of the Roman Papacy in the Maronite Church had meanwhile been heightened following the failure of the Council of Florence (1439-44) to end the schism between the Roman Catholic and Byzantine Orthodox communions. Unable to attend this council in person, the Maronite Patriarch John of Jaj (Yuḥannā al-Djādjī) had sent a Franciscan missionary to represent him there, with a message indicating his fervent commitment to Roman Catholicism and requesting papal confirmation of his patriarchal title. (Since then, all Maronite Patriarchs, though elected by bishops of their own church, have been confirmed in office by the Popes; by implication, they came to derive their Apostolic authority from the Roman See.) Subsequently, the Franciscan mission in the Holy Land (Terra Sancta), which had an important base in Beirut, was entrusted with the maintenance of Maronite relations with Rome; and, starting from 1456, the Popes began to address the heads of the Maronite Church as Patriarchs of Antioch (a title which they might have traditionally claimed). Following the Catholic Counter-Reformation, the Capuchin and Jesuit fathers were charged by the Roman see to replace the Franciscans as religious mentors to the Maronites.

In 1585, Pope Gregory XIII (1572-85) established the Maronite College (*Collegium Maronitarum*) in Rome to train aspirants to Maronite church office in Roman Catholic orthodoxy and church discipline; and starting from 1608, graduates of this institution began to occupy the Maronite patriarchal see. By then, the first major reform of the Maronite Church had been undertaken, under Jesuit sponsorship, by the Synod of Ḳannūbīn (1596). Maronite church practice was brought closer to the Roman Catholic norm by the Synod of Luwayza (1736) (the trend has been continuing ever since). Meanwhile, the first Maronite monastic order following the Roman Catholic model had been chartered by Isṭifān al-Duwayḥī. Since the Second Vatican Council (1962), the Maronite liturgy has been largely Arabicised.

Starting from the early 17th century, the Maronites of the northern Lebanon entered into close political association with their Druze neighbours in the southern parts. A large-scale migration of Maronites to the Druze country followed, continuing through the 18th century to the early 19th, whereby the Maronites, in time, came to form the majority of the population of the Druze districts. Having the advantage over the Druze in numbers, and backed by the Roman Catholic European powers, especially by France, the Maronites began to entertain ambitions of dominating the whole of Mount Lebanon, thereby challenging Druze leaderships in their own home districts. Intermittent clashes between the two sides, starting from 1840, culminated in a massacre of Maronites and other Christians of the Druze regions in 1860, in which an estimated 15,000 were killed or died of destitution, and about 100,000 were left homeless. Intervention by the European powers, spearheaded by France, restored peace to the mountains, and in 1861, the Ottoman government was prevailed upon to grant Mount Lebanon the privileged status of a *mutaṣarrifiyya* administered by an Ottoman Catholic Christian *mutaṣarrif* or governor, who was appointed directly by the central government in Istanbul and assisted by a locally-elected administrative council. The decades that followed witnessed an Arabic literary revival in Beirut and Mount Lebanon, in which Maronite participation was particularly prominent.

Following the First World War, France, in 1920, was accorded the mandate over the territory of present-day Syria and Lebanon. The French thereupon expanded the territory of the Lebanese *mutaṣarrifiyya*, largely in response to Maronite ambitions, to form the State of Greater Lebanon, which became the Lebanese Republic in 1926, with the Maronites politically at the helm. In Lebanon, the Presidency of the Republic, the Army Command and a number of other key positions continue to be the preserve of the Maronites.

Since the 1880s, increasing numbers of Maronites have emigrated from Lebanon to North and South America, Australia, and other parts of the world. The community in Lebanon is estimated today at one million out of a total Lebanese population of about five million, the estimate of the Maronite population outside Lebanon being at least double that number.

Bibliography: Masʿūdī, *Tanbīh*; ʿAbd al-Djabbār, *al-Mughnī fī abwāb al-tawḥīd wa 'l-ʿadl*, v; William of Tyre, *Gesta rerum in patribus transmarinis gestarum*; Isṭifān al-Duwayḥī, *T. al-Azmina*, and *T. al-Ṭāʾifa al-Mārūniyya*; Pierre Dib, art. *Maronites*, in *Dictionnaire de Théologie catholique*, 1928; Matti Moosa, *The Maronites in history*, Beirut 1986; Kamal Salibi, *Maronite historians of mediaeval Lebanon*, Beirut 1959; idem, *The modern history of Lebanon*, London 1959; idem, *A house of many mansions. The history of Lebanon reconsidered*, Beirut 1988. (Kamal Salibi)

MASHHAD.

2. History and development since 1914.

In the course of the 20th century, Mashhad has become a regional metropolis (2,155,700 inhabitants in 2004), the capital of the vast province of Khurāsān, and well integrated into the economic and public life of Iran. At the same time, it has kept its character as a goal of pilgrimage, dominated by the strength of the economic and political authority of the Āstāna-yi ḳuds-i riḍawī, the administration of the Shrine *wakf*, probably the most important in the Muslim world.

In 1914, despite its religious importance, Mashhad was a marginal town in regard to the rest of the country. The population of some 70,000 was ethnically very diverse, with Azeris, Hazāras, Bukhārīs, Marwīs, Berberīs, Afghāns, and several thousand Jews who had been forcibly converted to Islam, called Djadīd al-Islām (Patai). About a hundred Europeans, mostly Russians, and as many again Indian subjects of the British crown, lived near their respective consulates. Trade with Russia was twice as important as that with Tehran, since the only modern road was that connecting Mashhad with ʿAshḳābād, opened in 1892 (Bharier, 14). Like most of the towns of Iran, it kept its traditional character for the first decades of the 20th century. The only modern street, lit by electricity since 1902, was the Bālā khiyābān leading from the entrance of the town on the western side to the Shrine and to the modest pilgrims' bazaar, since Mashhad never had a proper bazaar and the shops, just as the 37 caravanserais housing pilgrims, were dispersed throughout the town.

Riḍā Shāh [*q.v.*] and the Pahlavī dynasty showed a great interest in Mashhad and the Shrine of the Imām Riḍā. The ruler personally assumed the office of *mutawallī* of the Āstāna-yi ḳuds, and members of the royal family regularly made the pilgrimage to the town, where a palace was built at Bāk-i Malikābād; trusted servants were appointed as governors of Khurāsān and executive directors of the Shrine. A new town was laid out, with rectilinear streets, houses in the Russian style with two storeys and large windows; and businesses and offices were developed to the west of the holy city, which kept its houses of sun-dried brick, its alleys and the *musāfir-khānas* or hostels and the caravanserais for pilgrims. In 1935 Mashhad was linked with Tehran by a modern road, an aerial connection in 1928 (regular service in 1946), an oil pipeline in 1955 and a railway in 1957 (Bharier). At the end of the 1960s, there was a fresh wave of expansion. The Firdawsī University was opened in 1966, modern hospitals, amongst the best in Iran, were built, food and textile (carpets) industries were developed, whilst sources of natural gas at Sarakhs enabled the burgeoning city to be supplied with gas. An urban plan was successfully put into operation, since over half of the built-up area and 80% of the land available for building belonged to the Shrine. A French study centre, the SCET Iran, was given the task of making an inventory of the Shrine's possessions and of modernising its administration in order to increase its revenues (Hakami, Hourcade). To the west, at Abkūh, vast hotels for students, troops and officials of the Shrine were constructed. To the east, urbanisation swallowed up the small towns of Gulshahr, Sakhtimān and Ṭuruḳ, but was limited by the extensive agricultural holdings of the Shrine and by military lands.

After the oil boom of 1974, Muḥammad Riḍā

S̲h̲āh [*q.v.*] decided to make Mas̲h̲had the most important and most modern pilgrimage centre of the Muslim world. Under the direction of the governor, M. Waliyān, the reconstruction of the old town began in 1973 with the destruction of the bazaar, caravanserais, and traditional-type hotels near the Shrine and the avenue (*falaka*) which surrounded it. The only part left standing was a section of the carpet bazaar. The Bāzār-i Riḍā, a simple, modern gallery meant for the pilgrims' purchases, was opened in 1977 near the Ḥaram, whilst workshops and other commercial activities were dispersed to the town's periphery. From now on isolated in a vast open space, the Shrine was renovated and developed on a grandiose scale, making the Imām Riḍā's tomb the greatest religious architectural complex in the world, still in the course of construction in 2002 (library extension, schools, a new cemetery in the underground vaults, new courts and spaces for welcoming pilgrims). This policy of increased prestige was actively followed by the Islamic Republic, under the direction of the *āyatullāh* Wāʿiẓī Ṭabasī, the new *mutawallī* of the Shrine and no longer governor of the province. The city continued to expand towards the southwest along the Wakīlābād Avenue (new university campus, high-class residences) and, above all, to the northwest (agricultural lands towards the Kūčān road, where mass housing and industrial zones reach as far as the ancient Ṭūs, where Firdawsī's tomb is to be found).

From 1956 to 1996, Mas̲h̲had has had the greatest population growth (5.3% per annum) of the great cities of Iran, after Tehran itself. This development became very rapid after 1979 because of the influx of Afg̲h̲ān refugees in a new quarter to the northeast of the city. This new Afg̲h̲ān quarter evokes the traditional relations of Mas̲h̲had with the Harāt region and Central Asia, reinforced by the re-opening of the frontier with Turkmenistan in 1991 at Bad̲j̲girān and, above all, after the opening on 15 May 1996 of the new railway linking Mas̲h̲had, via Sarak̲h̲s, with the rail network of the former USSR. This opening towards the east of a town and a region long isolated from Tehran takes place, however, hand-in-hand with the strengthening of political, administrative and economic relations with the capital. The revolt of 1921 by Col. Muḥammad Taḳī K̲h̲ān Pisyān was one of the last manifestations of former isolation. Consequently, the population of Mas̲h̲had has participated actively in the crises and the political and social debates in Iran: the riots of 1963 against the White Revolution, and active participation in the Islamic Revolution (the thinker ʿAlī S̲h̲ariʿatī was a professor at the University of Mas̲h̲had, and Sayyid ʿAlī K̲h̲aminaʾī, who in 1989 became the Spiritual Guide of the Islamic Republic, was one of the most active of the local religious leaders).

As the second city of Iran in terms of population since 1975, Mas̲h̲had, now a modern city, remains the regional capital of eastern Iran, even though the province of K̲h̲urāsān, of which it is the capital, has been since 2002 divided into three different provinces. The passage through it of over ten million pilgrims each year accentuates more than ever before the religious identity and the economic activity of this regional metropolis, which now has the second-most important airport in Iran and the most important hotel complex (more than 25,000 beds in hotels and, above all, *musāfir-k̲h̲ānas*), well ahead of Iṣfahān.

Bibliography: G. Stratil-Sauer, *Meschhed. Eine Stadtbau am Vaterland Iran*, Leipzig 1935; K. Scharlau, *Moderne Umgestaltungen im Grundreiss iranischer Städte*, in *Erdkunde* (1961), 180-91; M.P. Pagnini Alberti, *Structure commerciali di una citta di pellegrinaggio: Mashad, Iran Nord-Orientale*, Udine Del Bianco 1971; SCET-Iran Ingenieurs-Conseils, Astaneh Ghods Razavi, *Les biens fonciers urbains de l'Astaneh Ghods, ville de Mashhad*, iii, *Rapport*, Tehran 1974; Pagnini Alberti, *Le commerce de détail dans les villes islamiques: une méthode d'analyse*, in *L'Espace géographique*, iv/3 (1975), 219-24; Planning Organisation and Budget and SCET-IRAN, *Aménagement du territoire. Développement urbain*, xi, *Mašhad*, Tehran 1977; E. Ehlers, *Iran. Grundzüge einer geographischen Landeskunde*, Darmstadt 1980, 365-7 and *passim*; Nasrine Hakami, *Pélérinage de l'Emâm Rezâ, étude socio-économique*, Institute for the Study of Languages and Cultures of Asia and Africa, Tokyo 1989; B. Hourcade, *Vaqf et modernité en Iran. Les agro-business de l'Astân-e qods de Mashad*, in Y. Richard (ed.), *Entre l'Iran et l'Occident. Adaptation et assimilation des idées et techniques occidentales en Iran*, Paris 1989, 116-41; E. Mafī, *Barrasī-yi kutāhī bar iktiṣād-i bak̲h̲s̲h̲-i k̲h̲ayr-i rasmī dar s̲h̲ahr-i Mas̲h̲had*, in *Faṣlnāma Taḥḳīḳāt-i D̲j̲ug̲h̲rāfiyā*, viii/1 (1372/1993), 37-51; R. Patai, *Jadid al-Islam. The Jewish "New Muslims" of Meshhed*, Detroit 1997; Stephanie Cronin, *An experiment in revolutionary nationalism. The rebellion of Colonel Muhammad Taqi Khan Pasyan in Mashhad, April-October 1921*, in *MES*, xxxiii/4 (1997), 693-750.

(B. Hourcade)

3. The Shrine, and Mas̲h̲had as a centre of S̲h̲īʿī learning and piety.

The location in Mas̲h̲had of the Shrine of the eighth Imām ʿAlī al-Riḍā [*q.v.*] has made Mas̲h̲had into the leading place of pilgrimage within Persia, the process whereby its veneration developed being accentuated by the fact that, for some four centuries, with one break of a few decades, the S̲h̲īʿī shrines of ʿIrāḳ were in the hands of the Sunnī Ottoman Turks, the powerful enemies and rivals of the Ṣafawids and their successors [see further, ʿatabāt, in Suppl.]. S̲h̲īʿī *ʿulamāʾ* place Mas̲h̲had as the seventh of the great sanctuaries of the Muslim world, after Mecca, Medina, and the four specifically S̲h̲īʿī *ʿatabāt* in ʿIrāḳ, al-Nad̲j̲af, Karbalāʾ, Samarrāʾ and Kāẓimayn [*q.vv.*] (see P.M. Sykes, *The glory of the Shia world*, London 1910, p. xiii), but some S̲h̲īʿī *ʿulamāʾ* would rank it next after Karbalāʾ (see G.N. Curzon, *Persia and the Persian question*, London 1892, i, 150 n. 2).

The Ḥaram containing the Shrine seems to be essentially the creation of the last six or seven centuries, its development receiving a powerful impetus when the Ṣafawids turned Persia into a S̲h̲īʿī state in the 10th/16th century. Previously, it had been easier for non-Muslims to visit the Shrine, since the Spanish ambassador Clavijo, en route for Tīmūr's court at Samarḳand, was able in 1404 to visit it. Thereafter, it was not till the first half of the 19th century that the British traveller J.B. Fraser was able, by dint of a feigned conversion to Islam, to enter the Shrine in 1822 long enough to make a drawing of the courtyard there (see Fatema Soudavar Farmanfarmaian, *James Baillie Fraser in Mashhad, or, the Pilgrimage of a nineteenth century Scotsman to the Shrine of the Imām Riḍā*, in *Iran, JBIPS*, xxxiv [1996], 101-15). Various other European travellers followed in the later 19th century (details in Curzon, *op. cit.*, i, 148 n. 1).

But the rise of the Mas̲h̲had shrine began well before the advent of the Ṣafawids, and especially after the sack of nearby Ṭūs by the Tīmūrid prince Mīran S̲h̲āh b. Tīmūr in 791/1389 dealt Ṭūs a death-blow and brought the Sanābad shrine into prominence as the nucleus of the later Mas̲h̲had [see ṭūs]. Already,

Ibn Baṭṭūṭa had gone on from Ṭūs to "the town of Mas̲h̲had al-Riḍā", which he describes as large and flourishing (*Riḥla*, iii, 77-8, Eng. tr. Gibb, iii, 582), and Tīmūrid rulers such as S̲h̲āh Ruk̲h̲ and his wife D̲j̲awhar-S̲h̲ad̲h̲ were great benefactors in the first half of the 9th/15th century; but members of the new dynasty of the Ṣafawids vied with each other in enriching and enlarging the Shrine. S̲h̲āh Ṭahmāsp I erected a minaret covered with gold in the northern part of the *Ṣaḥn-i kuhna* which, with the *Ṣaḥn-i naw*, bounds the Shrine on its northern and eastern sides, and he adorned the dome of the tomb with sheets of gold and put a golden pillar on top of it (this was to be carried off by the S̲h̲ībānids when in 997/1589 they invaded K̲h̲urāsān and sacked Mas̲h̲had). 'Abbās I laid out the main thoroughfare of the city, the *K̲h̲iyābān*, running from northwest to southeast and dividing the city into two roughly equal halves; the Shrine area divided this street into an upper (*bālā*) and a lower (*pā'īn*) part. 'Abbās II devoted his attention mainly to the decoration of the *Ṣaḥn-i kuhna*. Ṣafī II, the later Sulaymān I, restored the dome of the Imām's tomb. But there were benefactions during these times from outside potentates also, not only from the South Indian S̲h̲ī'ī Ḳuṭb-S̲h̲āhī ruler Sulṭān-Ḳulī Ḳuṭb al-Mulk in 918/1512 but also by the Sunnī Mug̲h̲al emperor Akbar, who made a pilgrimage to Mas̲h̲had in 1003/1595. Although likewise a Sunnī, Nādir S̲h̲āh Afs̲h̲ar was the greatest benefactor of the city and the Shrine in the 12th/18th century, devoting a great part of the plunder brought back from India to their embellishment. Before his accession to the throne, he had in 1142/1730 built a minaret covered with gold in the upper part of the *Ṣaḥn-i kuhna* as a counterpart to that of Ṭahmāsp I on on the north side of this. He now thoroughly restored the southern half of the *Ṣaḥn*, and decorated the southern gateway richly and covered it with sheets of gold, so that it acquired the historic name of "Nādir's Golden Gate"; in the centre of this court he placed his famous octagonal marble "water house", the *saḳḳā-k̲h̲āna-yi nādirī*. The Ḳād̲j̲ār S̲h̲āhs, from Fatḥ 'Alī to Nāṣir al-Dīn, likewise cherished the Shrine, despite the frequency with which the city of Mas̲h̲had was involved in rebellions against the central government at various points in the 19th century.

The Shrine area forms the so-called *Bast*, thus designated from the rights of asylum and sanctuary traditionally operating there for e.g. debtors, and, for a limited period, criminals (see Curzon, *op. cit.*, i, 155, and BAST). Nādir's Golden Gateway leads southwards to the area of the Imām's shrine itself and its ancillary buildings, what is strictly speaking the *Ḥaram-i muḳaddas*. The almost square shrine has the actual tomb in its northeastern corner. S̲h̲āh 'Abbās I provided the tomb with a gold covering, and he also covered the dome, 20 m/65 feet high, with gilded copper sheets. Notable also here is the *Dār al-siyāda* hall built by D̲j̲awhar S̲h̲ād̲h̲, a *Dār al-ḥuffāẓ*, and the fine mosque bearing D̲j̲awhar S̲h̲ād̲h̲'s name, regarded by many authorities as the most attractive building in the sacred area (see illustr. in Sykes, *op. cit.*, at 263). There are also teeming bazaars, caravanserais, baths, etc. in the Ḥaram, the property of the Shrine, but the Shrine also in pre-modern times held *awḳāf* [see WAḲF] all over Persia, and especially, in other parts of K̲h̲urāsān, contributing to the income of the Shrine and its upkeep. This last varied according to economic prosperity and peaceful or otherwise conditions in the land; information given to Curzon at the end of the 19th century put the Shrine revenues at 60,000 *tūmāns*, equivalent at that time to £17,000 sterling per annum (*op. cit.*, i, 162-3).

The Shrine was administered by a lay *Mutawallī-bāshī*, from the later 19th century onwards until Pahlavī times as an office held by the governor-general of K̲h̲urāsān, previous times having been often characterised by disputes between the Shrine administrator and the representatives of the central government; at the time of Curzon's visit, the *Mutawallī-bas̲h̲ī* was Nāṣir al-Dīn S̲h̲āh's brother Muḥammad Taḳī Mīrzā, Rukn al-Dawla (replaced in 1891 by a former governor of Fārs). The office was a lucrative one, since the administrator normally drew 10% of the Shrine's revenues. Beneath him was a large staff of lower *mutawallīs*, *mud̲j̲tahids* [*q.v.*] and *mullās*, some enjoying hereditary appointments.

Pilgrimage to the shrine of the Imām began at an early date. European travellers and visitors in the 19th century endeavoured to estimate their annual numbers: Ferrier (1845) gave 50,000; Khanikoff (1858) and Eastwick (1862), over 50,000; C.E. Yate (in the 1890s), 30,000. These numbers tended to rise at the times of special festivals such at the anniversary of 'Alī al-Riḍā's death and during Muḥarram. The rites of pilgrimage involved a triple circumambulation or *ṭawāf* and the three-fold cursing of the Imām's enemies, and especially of the caliphs Hārūn al-Ras̲h̲īd and al-Ma'mūn. The pilgrims enjoyed a support system of food kitchens and accommodation for three nights, and a pilgrim who had performed all the rites in the prescribed fashion was entitled to call himself a *Mas̲h̲hadī*.

As with the lands adjacent to al-Nad̲j̲af and Karbalā', the holiness of the Shrine and its environs made it very attractive for burials, and several large cemeteries lay round it, such as the *Maḳbara-yi ḳatl-gāh* ("killing ground cemetery") to its north. Since there was so much demand for places—not merely from Persians but also from S̲h̲ī'īs from the Indian subcontinent, Afg̲h̲ānistān and Central Asia—the same ground had to be used over and over again for burials. The fees for such burials—graves with proximity to the Shrine itself being the most expensive—brought in a not inconsiderable revenue to the Shrine. See also MAḲBARA. 4, in Suppl.

As well as a centre for piety and pilgrimage, Mas̲h̲had was an educational centre, with a considerable number of *madrasas*, whose number in the first decade or so of the 20th century approached twenty, the oldest still standing being the *Dūdār* one, founded by S̲h̲āh Ruk̲h̲ in 823/1420, the majority of them, however, dating from the later Ṣafawid period. From an architectural and artistic point of view, the Madrasa of Mīr D̲j̲a'far, built and endowed by the founder in 1059/1650, is regarded as especially fine. These colleges attracted students from Persia itself and also from the S̲h̲ī'ī communities of India; Sykes in 1910 put the number of students at that time at 1,200 (*The glory of the Shia world*, 267-8), many of whom at this time went on subsequently for further study at al-Nad̲j̲af.

For the Shrine, its administration and development in the 20th century, see 2. above.

Bibliography: Given in the article, and see that in the *EI*[1] art. *Mes̲h̲hed*. (M. STRECK*)

MASHSHĀ'IYYA (*mas̲h̲s̲h̲ā'ūn*, *mas̲h̲s̲h̲ā'iyyūn*, *mus̲h̲āt*), the Peripatetic or Aristotelian school of Greek philosophy and its Arabic-Islamic followers.

The Arabic term is a translation of the Greek *peripatētikoi*, the school of Aristotle, who is reported to have taught whilst "perambulating" (Greek, *peripatein*) with his students. While in the Greek sources the designation is restricted to Aristotle's personal disciples, the Arabic equivalent is used for the Hellenistic tradition of his philosophy in general. As a term of doxography, it occurs in the *Fihrist* of Ibn al-Nadīm (247, 16), and in the 5th/11th century *Ṣiwān al-ḥikma* (from the school of Abū Sulaymān al-Sidjistānī), where the term is explained historically. According to this, following the precept of Plato to train both body and soul, "Aristotle and Xenocrates used to teach philosophy to their pupils while walking to and fro", and so they were called the Peripatetics of the Academy (*al-mushāt al-akādhīmiyyūn*, 41, § 709); similarly al-Ḳifṭī, *Ta'rīkh al-ḥukamā'*, 26, in a classification of the various ways to designate schools of philosophy where both Platonists and Aristotelians are subsumed under this name; and likewise in al-Shahrastānī (*Milal*, 253, 296).

In the introduction to his work on the philosophy of the "Easterners" (*al-mashrikiyyūn*), Ibn Sīnā, while acknowledging the merit of Aristotle, blames those who "are infatuated with the Peripatetics (*al-Mashshā'ūn*) and who think that no one else was ever guided by God" (see Gutas, *Avicenna*, 45), announcing the evolution of his philosophy beyond the basis laid by Aristotle, who was henceforth called the First Teacher (*al-mu'allim al-awwal*; see e.g. Ibn Sīnā, *al-Shifā', al-Ilāhiyyāt*, ed. Anawati *et al.*, 392). The term "Peripatetics" is now used in explicit delimitation or criticism of Aristotle and his commentators (such as Alexander of Aphrodisias) against Ibn Sīnā's own doctrine (see Naṣīr al-Dīn al-Ṭūsī, *Sharḥ al-Ishārāt wa 'l-tanbīhāt*, Tehran 1959, ²1982, ii, 416, l. 10; iii, 174, l. 5, etc.) or other schools of thought.

In the subsequent development, however, it was the philosophy of Ibn Sīnā and his extensive following which, again from another standpoint, was designated as *mashshā'iyya*. It was not his principal critic al-Ghazālī, but Ibn Rushd [*q.vv.*] in his *Tahāfut al-Tahāfut* (ed. Bouyges, 178, l. 6), who pointed out *mā i'taraḍa bihi Abū Ḥāmid 'alā 'l-mashshā'īn*—using "Peripatetics" synonymously with *al-falāsifa* (*ibid.*, l. 8; and see ed. Bouyges, index, 605, § 139). Shihāb al-Dīn Yaḥyā al-Suhrawardī, in his turn, designates Avicennan concepts and doctrines as those of the *mashshā'īn* (*Opera*, ii, 13 and *passim*) in contrast to his own mystical philosophy. It is this general use of the term which appears in later doxography, blurring the difference between the Aristotelian and Platonic schools of Greek philosophy vis-à-vis the following of *ishrāḳī* mysticism [see ISHRĀḲ; ISHRĀḲIYYŪN]. In this sense, the 10th/16th century Iranian philosopher Ṣadr al-Dīn al-Shīrāzī [*q.v.*] is praised by his biographer for uniting *al-mashshā'iyya, al-ishrākiyya* and Islam (Muḥsin al-Amīn, *A'yān al-Shī'a*, Damascus and Beirut 1953-63, ix, 325).

Bibliography: Shihāb al-Dīn Yaḥyā al-Suhrawardī, *Opera metaphysica et mystica*, i-iii, ed. H. Corbin and S.H. Nasr, Istanbul 1945 and Tehran 1952-70, *index verborum*; D.M. Dunlop (ed.), *The Muntakhab Ṣiwān al-Ḥikma of Abū Sulaimān al-Sijistānī*, The Hague 1979; Shahrastānī, *Livre des religions et des sectes*, tr. J. Jolivet and G. Monnot, Louvain 1986-93, ii, 178, 246; D. Gutas, *Avicenna and the Aristotelian tradition*, Leiden 1988.

(G. ENDRESS)

MAṬAR, ILYĀS DĪB (1857-1910), Syro-Lebanese historian, medical doctor, pharmacist, lawyer and teacher. He was born into an Arab Orthodox middle-class family in the town of Ḥāṣbayyā, in present-day south Lebanon. The Druze-Maronite civil war, which erupted in 1860 and spread from Mount Lebanon to other parts of Syria, forced his family to move to the safety of the city of Beirut. His father, who was a prosperous merchant and a local notable of his community, managed to escape what became known as "The massacre of Ḥāṣbayyā" under the protection of the prominent Druze leader, Sa'īd Djunbulāṭ.

Ilyās Maṭar received his primary education at his confession's school, Les Trois Docteurs. He then entered the Catholic Patriarchal School, where he learned Arabic, French, Greek and other subjects. His studies widened in scope when he enrolled at the newly-established Syrian Protestant College (SPC), later renamed the American University in Beirut. There he studied chemistry, botany and pharmacy. During those formative years he was taught by a number of competent teachers, whose names were to become associated with the emergence of "the modern Arab renaissance" [see NAHDA] in the 19th century. These included Salīm Taḳlā (1849-92), founder of the celebrated Egyptian newspaper *al-Ahrām*; Nāṣīf al-Yāzidjī (1800-71), the accomplished Arabic scholar; and his fellow-townsman Fāris Nimr (1856-1952 [*q.v.*]) who taught Maṭar chemistry.

It seems that it was upon Nimr's suggestion that Maṭar decided to write a general history of his country, Syria. This was published in 1874 under the title, *al-'Uḳūd al-durriyya fī ta'rīkh al-mamlaka al-sūriyya*. It constituted the first historical work written on Syria as a well-defined entity by a native Arab historian. Its importance lies in the manner it deals with Maṭar's country as one single cultural and territorial unit. Thus Syria ceases to be a collection of Ottoman administrative units, and becomes a fatherland (*waṭan*) extending from the Taurus mountains in the north and the Sinai Peninsula in the south, and from the Euphrates in the east and the Mediterranean in the west. This fatherland is then shown to be endowed with an Arab national identity and an inherent capacity to acquire the new achievements of European civilisation. However, Syrian patriotism figures in this respect as an integral part of the wider movement of Ottomanism.

Maṭar's book is dedicated to the well-known Ottoman historian Aḥmed Djewdet Pasha (1822-95 [*q.v.*]), whom he met during his visit to Istanbul in 1874. This visit was undertaken in order to obtain his degree in pharmacy and secure the authorisation of the Ottoman Ministry of Education to publish his history. After this date, Maṭar became Djewdet's protégé, acting as his son's tutor, assistant and adviser. It was also upon Djewdet's encouragement that Maṭar qualified as a medical doctor and became a practising lawyer. He taught both medicine and law in Istanbul, while co-editing at the same time a legal journal, *al-Ḥuḳūḳ*.

Maṭar is credited with the authorship of over thirty books, both in Arabic and Ottoman Turkish. Apart from his pioneering historical text, his output includes works on a wide variety of subjects, such as jurisprudence, public health and education.

Owing to his affliction with a fatal disease, he returned to Beirut in 1909. He died the following year (March 1910) and was buried in his family's cemetery.

Bibliography: Ph. de Ṭarāzī, *Ta'rīkh al-ṣaḥāfa al-'arabiyya*, ii, Beirut 1913-33, 227-9; Yūsuf As'ad Dāghir, *Maṣādir al-dirāsa al-adabiyya*, iii/2, Beirut 1972, 1222-3; Y.M. Choueiri, *Arab history and the nation-state: a study in modern Arab historiography 1820-1980*, London-New York 1989, 34-9.

(YOUSSEF M. CHOUEIRI)

MATARAM, the name of an area in central Java where two kingdoms have developed.

1. The first kingdom bearing this name was founded by Sanjaya, who is recorded to have erected a *linga* in "Kunjarakunya". The inscription commemorating this event, written in Sanskrit in A.D. 732, was found in a Shaivite sanctuary at Changgal. Some time later, the Mahayana-Buddhist Shailendra appear as dominating dynasty of Mataram, and Sanjaya's successors submitted to them. The Shailendras probably came to central Java after the fall of the empire of Funan, centred in the south of present-day Kampuchea, after A.D. 627, continuing their royal titulature as "rulers of the mountains". They became famous for erecting the most outstanding Buddhist monuments such as the Borobudur, Mendut, Pawon, and others. After 832, however, their power declined, and thus the Shaivite dynastic line which had withdrawn to east Java returned to the centre. Obviously, both dynastic lines were linked together by intermarriage, and this paved the way for Mataram to reach the peak of its power, including the incorporation of most of central and east Java and parts of Bali into its territory. King Balitung (898-910) was the first king to use the name of "Mataram" in his inscriptions, and his successor Daksa (910-19?) is credited with the erection of the monumental Lara Djonggrang complex near Prambanan, consisting of 190 temples, the main one being dedicated to Shiva. King Sindok (929-47), however, moved the capital to the upper valley of the Brantas river in east Java, thus founding a new dynasty and ending the history of this first kingdom of Mataram.

2. The Islamic kingdom of Mataram was founded by the Panembahan Senopati Ingalaga (d. 1601). His father, Kyai Gedhe Pamanahan, is famed for his killing Arya Penangsang of Jipang, the powerful and frightening enemy of Adivijaya (Jaka Tingkir), ruler of the second Islamic (Shīʿī) kingdom of Java, Pajang (*r.* 1549-87). As a reward, he was given the central area of the ancient kingdom of Mataram where he founded the Kota Gedhe, later under his son to become the capital. After his death in 1584, his son was awarded the title of Senopati ("general") by the king, but Senopati soon fought against Demak and other principalities and eventually even attacked the king's troops. After the king's death, he rejected Pajang's supremacy, and he added to his magic powers through meditation and asceticism and a visit to the divine Queen of the Southern Sea, Nyai Lara Kidul, thus underlining the central cosmic position of his capital—and himself as ruler—between the volcano Mount Merapi to the north and the Sea in the south. With the support of two from among the "nine holy men" (*wali songo*) who are said to have brought Islam to the interior of Java, Sunan Giri and Sunan Kali Jaga, he made Islam the religion of his kingdom, which by now included most of the interior of central and east Java, but not the important sea ports on the north coast, from Surabaya in the east to Cirebon (Cheribon) and Banten in the west. Senopati's grandson Agung (*r.* 1613-46), the greatest ruler and warrior king of the dynasty, which now, according to the panegyric chronicle of Mataram *Babad Tanah Jawi*, claimed dynastic decent from the ruling family of Majapahit, the last Hindu kingdom in Java (until 1527), took the title of *susuhunan* in 1624, and in 1641 the title of *sulṭān* was added, legitimised by a special delegation from Mecca. He succeeded in subduing the northern seaports; even Surabaya surrendered in 1626, while its dependency Sukadana in southwestern Kalimantan had already been captured earlier. Even Palembang [*q.v.*] was captured after 1636. Thus Mataram developed as a maritime power as well. An attack on Batavia, then the stronghold of the Dutch *Vereenigde Oostindische Compagnie* (VOC) ended with a defeat. On his death, within the island of Java only Batavia and the sultanate of Banten, to the west of Batavia, refused to acknowledge Mataram's suzerainty. His wars had entailed an enormous loss of human lives and destruction of agriculture. Court literature, however, developed and presented a combination of Ṣūfī tradition and traditional Javanese cosmological mythology. His successor, his son Susuhunan Amengku Rat I (*r.* 1646-77) turned away from professing Islam, starting his increasingly tyrannical reign of continuous warfare and killing with the murder of about 6,000 Islamic teachers together with their families. Rebellions flared up, the biggest one led by Raden Trunajaya (1649-80) from Madura, who was also supported by many religious (Islamic) teachers who encouraged him to fight against the cruel king and his ally, the "Christian" VOC. The popular hope for the imminent arrival of a Messianic *ratu adil* ("just king") spread widely. The *susuhunan*'s son Amengku Rat II (*r.* 1677-1703) defeated his father's enemies and personally stabbed Trunajaya to death, but his throne, in the meantime, was occupied by his brother Pangeran Puger. Therefore the king established a new court in Kartasura, to the east of Kota Gedhe (Yogyakarta).

Madura and east Java remained, however, centres of rebellion. Under Amengku Rat III (*r.* 1703-8, d. in exile in Colombo in 1734), the son of his predecessor, the disintegration of Mataram took on a serious form, partly because of the insurgence of Surapati (d. 1706), a former Balinese slave and military trainee of the VOC who had established himself in Pasuruan and extended his territory to Madiun, partly because of the First Javanese War of Succession (1704-8) which broke out when the VOC recognised Pangeran Puger as Susuhunan Pakubuwana I (*r.* 1704-19). When he died and his son followed him as Amengku Rat IV (*r.* 1719-26), the Second Javanese War of Succession began (1719-23), involving the VOC even more in Javanese dynastic affairs. His death by poison brought his son Pakubuwana II (*r.* 1726-49) to the throne. Changing alliances, among others with the Chinese who had fled the massacre in Batavia in 1740, against the Dutch who, on their part, were allied for some time with Pangeran Cakraningrat IV of western Madura, or with the Dutch against other enemies, and continuous court intrigues weakened the position of the *susuhunan* continuously. The court, which in 1746 had been moved to the new capital Surakarta [*q.v.*], rose again in rebellion when the *susuhunan* agreed in a unilateral decision to the demand of the VOC to cede the ports on the north coast to Dutch administration. Thus began the Third Javanese War of Succession (1746-57), led by the rebellious brother of Pakubuwana II, Pangeran Mangkubumi, who, in his headquarters in Yogya, was declared Susuhunan Pakubuwana in 1749 (*r.* 1749-92); in 1755 he adopted the title Sultan—for the first time after Sultan Agung—Hamengkubuwana (I) which has been maintained until the present Sultan Hamengkubuwana X (since 1986), and made Yogyakarta [*q.v.* in Suppl.] his capital. Before his death, Pakubuwana II, however, had transferred sovereignty over his kingdom to the VOC, who agreed that the crown prince should become Pakubuwana III (*r.* 1749-88). This initiated the partition of Mataram into two major principalities, Surakarta and Yogyakarta.

The last major rebel in the court of Surakarta,

Pakubuwana III's cousin Mas Said, surrendered in 1757, and henceforth ruled, as Pangeran Adipati Mangkunegara I (*r.* 1757-95), over an area taken from Surakarta and inhabited by 4,000 households. During the temporary British occupation of the Dutch possessions (1811-16), the brother of Hamengkubuwana III (*r.* 1810-11; 1812-14), Natakusuma, was rewarded by the British with an appanage of 4,000 households and the title Pangeran Pakualam I (*r.* 1813-29), playing now a similar role in Yogyakarta territory as the Mangkunegara in Surakarta territory.

Ever-increasing colonial exploitation caused a general social and economic decline, and general unrest was growing. Hamengkubuwana's eldest son, Pangeran Dipanegara (1785-1855), avoiding the court and studying Islamic textbooks and Javanese wisdom with Islamic teachers, associated himself more and more with popular discontent, until finally the last great war in colonial times in Java, the Java War (1825-30), broke out. At its end, half of the population of Yogyakarta had died, and Dipanegara was exiled, first to Menado and then to Makassar.

From the two major and two minor principalities in the territory of Mataram, only the sultanate of Yogyakarta in the heartland of Mataram could maintain some limited degree of self-government, due to the merits of the late Sultan Hamengkubuwana IX (*r.* 1939-86) during the early years of independent Indonesia and his co-operation with the Pakualam VIII in modernising the administration of his territory, which is acknowledged in the Republic as the Daerah Istimewa Yogyakarta ("special district of Yogyakarta"), Sultan Hamengkubuwana X (1986-) being again its governor (since 1999).

Bibliography: *Babad Tanah Djawi*, ed. J.J. Meinsma, tr. W.L. Olthof, 2 vols. ²Dordrecht-Providence, R.I. 1987; G.W.J. Drewes, *The struggle between Javanism and Islam as illustrated in the Serat Dermagandul*, in *BKI*, cxxii (1966), 309-65; H.J. de Graaf, *De regering van Panembahan Sénopati Ingalaga*, in *VKI*, xiii (1954); idem, *De regering van Sultan Agung, vorst van Mataram 1613-1645, en die van zijn voorganger Panembahan Séda-ing-Krapyak 1601-1613*, in *VKI*, xxiii (1958); idem, *De regering van Sunan Mangku-Rat I 'Tegal Wangi', vorst van Mataram 1646-1677*, 2 vols., in *VKI*, xxxiii, xxxix (1961, 1962); idem, and Th.G.Th. Pigeaud, *De eerste Moslimse vorstendommen op Java*, in *VKI*, lxix (1974); D.G.E. Hall, *A history of South-East Asia*, London 1954, rev. ed. London 1964; Soemarsaid Moertono, *State and state-craft in old Java. A study of the later Mataram period, 16th to 19th century*, Ithaca 1968, rev. ed. 1981; Sir Thomas Stamford Raffles, *The history of Java*, London 1817; M.C. Ricklefs, *A history of modern Indonesia*, London and Basingstoke 1981 (S.E. Asian repr. 1982); idem, *Jogjakarta under Sultan Mangkubumi, 1749-1792. A history of the division of Java*, London 1974; M.R. Woodward, *Islam in Java. Normative piety and mysticism in the Sultanate of Yogyakarta*, Tucson 1989.

(O. Schumann)

MAṬBAʿA.

6. Early Arabic Presses in The Netherlands and England

The principal centre of Arabic printing in Protestant Europe was originally Leiden, where the scholar-printer Franciscus Raphelengius cut an Arabic fount and printed specimens in his *Specimen characterum Arabicorum officinae Plantinianae Raphelengii* (1595). The characters were modelled on the Medicean fount but were of inferior elegance. After being used for the posthumous printing of his Arabic-Latin lexicon (1613) and other works, the Raphelengian equipment was bought by the pioneer English Arabist William Bedwell (1563-1632), who left it to the University of Cambridge, intending that it should be used to print his own Arabic-Latin lexicon. His wishes remained unfulfilled, and no use seems to have been made of the fount since the earliest extant Arabic printing at Cambridge (1688) differs from the Raphelengian type. In the meantime, the great Arabist Thomas van Erpe (Erpenius), Professor of Arabic at Leiden (1612-24), had established his own press there, from which he published his own works. The Medicean Press again provided the model for the typeface. About this time oriental (and specifically Arabic) studies were encouraged at Oxford by Archbishop William Laud as chancellor of the university (1630-41). Laud established the chair of Arabic for Edward Pococke in 1636, and in the following year his agent bought printing equipment for Arabic and other oriental types from stock in Leiden. This provided the fount for *inter alia* Pococke's *Specimen historiae Arabum* (1648, 1650), and it continued to be used into the eighteenth century. A third Arabic fount was that used in London for the printing of the Polyglot Bible of 1653-57 and its great supplementary work, the *Lexicon Heptaglotton* of Edmund Castell, Professor of Arabic at Cambridge. Unlike the Raphelengian and Oxford founts, this was modelled on the characters of the Savarian Press, which had been set up by Savary de Brèves, the French ambassador at Rome (1608-14), when the Medicean Press there went out of production. Savary brought the press back to France, where it was acquired by the Imprimerie Royale and used in the production of the Parisian Polyglot (1645).

Bibliography: J. Fück, *Die arabischen Studien in Europa bis in den Anfang des 20. Jahrhunderts*, Leipzig 1955; J. Brugman and F. Schröder, *Arabic studies in the Netherlands*, Leiden 1979; J. Balagna, *L'imprimérie arabe en occident: XVIe, XVIIe et XVIIIe siècles*, Paris 1984; A. Hamilton, *William Bedwell the Arabist 1563-1632*, Leiden 1985; G. Roper, *Arabic printing and publishing in England before 1820*, in *BRISMES Bulletin*, xii/1 (1985), 12-32.

(P.M. Holt)

MAṬBAKH

3. In Persia.

The Persian word for kitchen, *ās̲h̲pazk̲h̲āna*, was not in general used before the 19th century, though the terms *ās̲h̲* "soup" and *ās̲h̲paz* "cook" do occur in earlier texts. Before the Ḳād̲j̲ār period, the Arabic *maṭbak̲h̲* was the common term for kitchen (Elahi, 790-91, with description of Persian kitchen).

A tradition with a long history, Persian cuisine ranks, with that of the French and the Chinese, as one of the great cuisines of the world. Its origins and influences are to be sought in the East, and more specifically in Transoxania. The traditional use of wheat as a staple and the basis of vegetable soups (*ās̲h̲*), the mixing of meat and fruit in dishes, the use of various types of yoghurt (*mast* and *kas̲h̲k*) and other dairy products, and ways of preparing meat, all point to Central Asian origins. Conversely, olives and olive oil, so abundant in the Mediterranean and Ottoman Turkish cuisine, are virtually absent in Persian cooking (except in the Caspian provinces); Persians traditionally cooked with animal fat (except for Jews, who used sesame oil). The important place of rice in Persian cooking similarly suggests Asian origins, in this case Southeast Asia and India (Bazin and Bromberger, 148; Fragner 1994a, 54-5).

Legend ascribes the art of cooking to Ahriman (the Zoroastrian spirit of evil) who is said to have taught a mythical King Zahāk to prepare the flesh of animals (Firdawsī, *Shāh-nāma*, 1988, i, 48-51, cited in Ghanoonparvar, 191). It is mainly Greek texts that offer some information on royal banquets, but otherwise we know little about food and ways of preparing it during the Achaemenid period, though borrowings from Lydia and Assyria seem plausible (Schmitt; Gunter, 13-21). The situation for the Sāsānid period is a little better, with information and recipes being available on the high cuisine of the court, including ingredients such as various types of hot and cold meat, stuffed vine leaves and sweet date purée (Amuzgar; Gunter, 44). The first five centuries of Islamic rule are again rather poorly documented. The available information, mostly from Muslim travellers and the occasional literary source, points to a heavy reliance on bread and cereals, an important role for (roasted) meat, including game, especially for nomads and soldiers, and the use of condiments such as pickled vegetables (*turshī*), sour grapes (*ghūra*), dried lemons and walnuts, which would remain essential to Persian cooking (Kasā'ī). It is only in the Mongol period that the current Persian cuisine became heavily influenced by Eastern traditions and took its current shape. Rashīd al-Dīn, who first entered Mongol employ as a head cook in the household of the khān and who later employed a Chinese cook in his own household, may have been instrumental in the transmission of Chinese cuisine to Iran (Allsen, 73-4).

The first period for which we have abundant information on eating and cooking practices is that of the Ṣafawids. European observers were struck at the frugality of eating habits. Chardin, iv, 28-9, 47, was among those who noted how Persians skipped breakfast except for a cup of coffee and only ate two proper meals a day. Food was cooked in earthenware or copper pots coated with tin (Olearius, 595). In areas where wood was scarce, such as the central plateau, cooked food was eaten at most only once a day, in the late afternoon, and instead of cooking, people in urban areas would get their pilaw and the ingredients for their soups from the ubiquitous cookshops. During other meals, bread and cheese were the main ingredients (Chardin, iv, 57; Tavernier, i, 545, 712). Meat included mutton and goat. Chicken and pigeon were also part of the menu of those who could afford it. Beef was rarely eaten. Chardin's observation, iv, 48-9, that beef, tough and dry, was only eaten by the poor in winter is echoed for the 19th century by Polak, i, 112, and Wills, 299. Even today, Persians do not favour beef, except those living in the Caspian provinces (Bromberger 1994, 191). Nor did game enjoy much popular appeal in Ṣafawid times, despite the enthusiasm for hunting on the part of the élite, in part because of the difficulty of abiding by ritual slaughter, in part because of its taste (Otter, i, 207). Game was often given as a present to Christians, who loved it as well as dark meat and fish. Turkey flesh seems to have caught on very slowly after its introduction from the New World via Europe (Tavernier, i, 712). Olearius, 596, claimed in the 1630s that turkey was not among the birds eaten, though under Shāh ʿAbbās I a Venetian merchant had once brought a few to Iṣfahān. A generation later, Tavernier wrote that the Armenians had brought turkeys and ways of raising them to Persia, adding that the meat was only for the court (i, 712). Some sources claim that horseflesh was the most esteemed type of meat (*Chronicle*, i, 155). The predilection for horseflesh at the court of Tīmūr (Clavijo, 106, 224) and the fact that the *Mihmān-nāma-i Bukhārā*, 318, calls it the most delicious meat, point to a Central Asian origin of the taste. Polak, i, 115, suggested regional variation by saying that Persians did not eat horseflesh with the exception of the people from Shīrwān and the Özbegs, who considered it a delicacy. Fish, not an ingredient of the nomadic diet, was naturally mostly confined to the Caspian coast and the Persian Gulf littoral, though trout from the Caspian region was also served at royal banquets (Tavernier, i, 545).

The information that has come to us from Ṣafawid times mostly concerns the food of the rich and eating practices at the royal court, as described by Western visitors who enjoyed the hospitality of the shāh and administrative officials. They offer information on the royal kitchen as well as on the types of food consumed at the court.

The royal kitchen prepared food only once a day for the royal household but twice a day for the shāh himself and his direct entourage. The daily food outlay for the shāh amounted to two sheep, four lambs, and thirty chickens for his midday meal and half as much for his supper, not counting small poultry, game and fish (Chardin, v, 350-1).

The royal kitchen was supervised by the *tūshmāl-bāshī*, an official who was subordinate to the *nāẓir al-buyūtāt*, the steward of the royal household. The *tūshmāl-bāshī* was responsible for the quantity and quality of the meat served at the court, preceded the procession of the meat dishes all the way from the kitchen to the royal quarters, and also acted as the royal taster (the *mihtar* "chamberlain" would taste all royal food a second time) (Minorsky, 137; Olearius, 672; Richard, ii, 15, 274; Chardin, v, 349-50, 378; Kaempfer, 279-80). Another important official was the *sufrači-bāshī*, who was in charge of arranging the floor cloth (*sufra*) on which food was consumed (Olearius, 672; Richard, ii, 15, 274; Chardin, v, 351). Other officials working in the royal food and drink department were the *ḳaṣṣābči-bāshī or sallākhči-bāshī* "the butcher", the *ḥawīdjār-bāshī*, who supervised the poultry yard and the scullery, the *sabziči-bāshī*, who was responsible for green salads, the *turshīči-bāshī*, who supervised the preparation of pickled vegetables, the *ḥalwači-bāshī*, or confectioner, the *sharbatči-bāshī*, or supervisor of the sherbets and syrups, the *ābdār-bāshī*, who was in charge of drinks, and the *ḳahwači-bāshī*, who headed the department of coffee making (Afshar, 1991, 409-11; Minorsky, 67, 94, 97, 98; Chardin, v, 352-53).

Meat was often eaten in the form of kababs, which Fryer, iii, 146, described as "rostmeat on skewers, cut in little round pieces no bigger than a sixpence, and ginger and garlic put between each". The same author, i, 147, notes that it was most often made into a pilaw, "their standing dish".

Rice had become an important ingredient in élite cookery after the Mongol domination of the country, gradually edging out pasta and groats (*bulghur*) (Fragner 1987, 789). Though it is not clear whether rice was grown in Persia before the advent of Islam, it has been part of the Persian diet since Sāsānid times (Balland and Bromberger, 148; Bazargan, 161). At least since early Ṣafawid times, Persians have eaten rice in various ways, either as chilaw or as pilaw. Unlike the situation in parts of China and India, where rice is a staple and a basic nutrient, in Persia rice has always been a prestige food and a luxury item not eaten by the poor on a regular basis. Its preparation has always been accordingly complex and time-consuming. Cooking is the same, involving a laborious process of soaking and steaming, resulting in rice that does not stick together, but the main difference is that chilaw consists of rice and clarified butter and sumac, which, served with kabab, a raw onion or herbs, has become in modern times a favourite restaurant meal. Pilaw, on the other hand, is rice mixed with a variety of ingredients (for cooking and types of pilaws, see Balland and Bromberger, 154; and Bazargan, 161). Fryer, iii, 147, describes the making of pilaw as follows: "To make pullow, the meat is first boiled to rags, and the broth or liquor being strained, it is left to drain, while they boil the rice in the same; which being tender, and the aqueous parts evaporating, the juice and gravy incorporates with the rice, which is boiled almost dry; then they put the meat again with spice, and at last as much butter as is necessary, so that it becomes not too greasy or offensive, either to the sight or taste; and it is then boiled enough when it is fir to be made into gobbets, not slabby, but each corn of rice is swelled and filled, not burst into pulp." Rice with lamb was the most common form of pilaw, but it was also prepared in numerous other ways, with spinach or cabbage, with roasted or boiled meat, with almonds and raisins, with onion and garlic, and it was served in various colours, depending on the condiment, which could be currant, pomegranate or saffron (Olearius, 595-6; Kaempfer, 278). Chardin, iii, 185-6, noted five or six different pilaws during a meal served by S̲h̲āh Sulaymān for a Russian envoy, with garlic crust, lamb, chicken, eggs stuffed with meat, and with fish. He also gave more than twenty as the total number of pilaw varieties (iv, 54). Twenty-five kinds of pilaw are mentioned in a Persian source from the Ṣafawid period (T̲h̲ābitiyān, 371; see Afs̲h̲ār 1378, 98).

Then as now, meals were consumed synchronically; unlike French cuisine, there was no time sequence to the order of eating the food and courses are not divided (Spooner, 253; Chehabi, 47). Kaempfer, 278, describing a royal banquet, noted, however, that confection and sweetmeats tended to precede the main course (see also *Lettres édifiantes et curieuses*, 115). All Europeans commented on the silence observed during meals, their short duration, and the fact that nothing was drunk until afterwards. They also noted that no silverware was used, except for a large wooden spoon that was used for eating soup and drinking the various juices that were served as part of the meal (Della Valle, i, 641; Olearius, 596; Kaempfer, 281; *Lettres édifiantes et curieuses*, 119). While ordinary Persians ate from porcelain or earthenware, at the court gold dishes were abundantly used as well (Herbert, 262; Kaempfer, 262; Kroell, 30). Kaempfer, 153, estimated the total value of the royal dishware at 10 million gold ducats. *Ād̲j̲ār* and *turs̲h̲ī* (pickled vegetables) served as condiments (Kaempfer, 278). Kaempfer, 262, describes the desserts served on the occasion of an audience: candied fruit, fresh fruit, various kinds of cake and sweetmeats. Jam, *murabbaʿ*, was very popular and came in many varieties (Afs̲h̲ār 1991, 417). Sugar was used in great quantities in the ubiquitous confectionery. According to De Bruyn, the Dutch East India Company annually brought 12,000 packs at 150 pounds each to Iṣfahān (De Bruyn, 178).

Common people ordinarily consumed bread, vegetables and fruit. Bread has always been the staple for the overwhelming majority of the population, and its central role in the diet is reflected in popular expressions and folklore (Kasāʾī, 112). The Caspian region, where bread has been spurned as unhealthy until modern times, is an exception (Orsolle, 171). Types of bread used in Ṣafawid times were remarkably similar to the ones eaten today; such as *lawas̲h̲*, thin unleavened bread that doubled as a spoon and a napkin, and *sangak*, long bread baked on pebbles (Chardin, iv, 50; Olearius, 596). Herbert noted how dates preserved in syrup mixed with buttermilk was seen as a precious food. He called the cheese dry, blue and hard, as being worst on the Gulf coast and best in Māzandarān (Herbert, 260, 262). Butter came from the tails of sheep. Nothing like restaurants existed. However, given the prohibitive cost of burning wood, many people ate at the ubiquitous public food stalls, *dukkān-i ṭabbāk̲h̲ī*, where simple hot rice dishes were prepared (Iskandar Beg Muns̲h̲ī, 188; Chardin, iv, 57).

Persia had since early mediaeval times been a crossroads for vegetables and fruits, serving as a source of diffusion or an east-west conduit for such plants and crops as sugar cane, lemons and sour oranges, spinach and eggplant (Watson, 26, 44-5, 62, 71). In the Ṣafawid period, the movement was generally in the opposite direction. Europeans introduced parsley, asparagus, artichokes and cauliflower into Persia, and these were cultivated in the vegetable gardens of S̲h̲īrāz and Iṣfahān (Ange de St. Joseph, 102-3; Tavernier, i, 422).

The first cookbooks—as opposed to texts in which food is described for its medicinal use—also date back to the Ṣafawid period (see Afs̲h̲ār 1360). Of the two that have come down to us, one, called *Kārnāma dar bāb-i ṭabbāk̲h̲ī wa ṣanʿat-i ān*, dates from the time of S̲h̲āh Ismāʿīl I (early 16th century) and was written as a gift to a nobleman. The second, *Maddat al-ḥayāt. Risāla dar ʿilm-i ṭabbāk̲h̲ī*, was probably written for S̲h̲āh ʿAbbās by his chief cook, Nūr Allāh, who may have been a descendant of Muḥammad ʿAlī Bāwarčī, and was perhaps even commissioned by the ruler. It is likely that both were composed for colleagues in the profession rather than as collections of recipes to serve as guidelines for the cooking of common people (Fragner 1984, 329; German tr. of the pilaw dishes in Nūr Allāh's *Maddat al-ḥayāt*, in *ibid.*, 343-60). For the Ḳād̲j̲ār period, we have the informative *Sufra-i aṭʿima*, a compendim of cooking and eating practices written for Nāṣir al-Dīn S̲h̲āh's personal physician, the Frenchman Tholozan, by the royal cook.

The menu in Ḳād̲j̲ār times does not seem to have differed greatly from that in the Ṣafawid period. Persian sources as well as foreign observers still note the bread and the cheese, the chilaw and pilaw, the *ās̲h̲* and the *āb-i gus̲h̲t*, the various legumes, such as beans, cucumbers, aubergines (egg plant), in addition to carrots, turnips, radishes and cabbages, as well as condiments in the form of *turs̲h̲ī*, and the prodigious quantities of fruit (Wills, 170-1; Nādir Mīrzā, 307-10, and see the references to food in Baṣīr al-Mulk, *Rūznāma*, introd. by Afs̲h̲ār, pp. XL-LII). Confectionery, too, continued to be an indispensable part of the Persian diet (Wilson, 249-50). A new feature was that food items originating in the New World, such as tomatoes and potatoes, began to make modest inroads into the country's kitchens. Potatoes, which were apparently introduced into Persia in the 18th century, were long called *ālū-yi Malkum* "plums of Malcolm", after the British envoy Sir John Malcolm, who is commonly but probably erroneously throught to have brought potatoes to Persia (Pūr-i Dāwūd, *Hurmazd-nāma*, 176; Binning, ii, 87-8). Though potatoes were cultivated in Persia, Muslim Persians in the early 19th century did not particularly care for them, and they mostly served the Armenian population and European residents

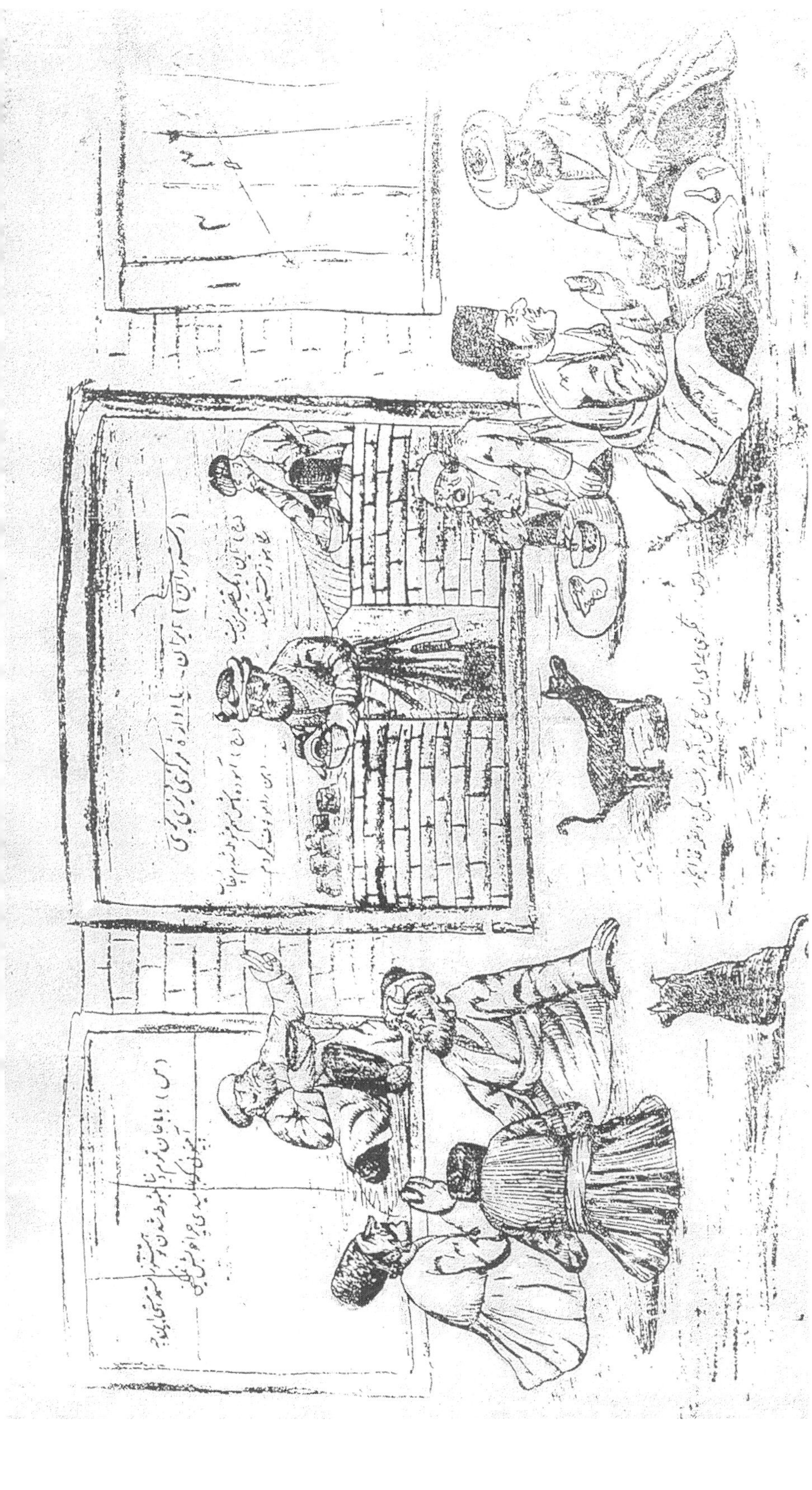

A cookshop at the turn of the 20th century. Source: Kashkūl (Tehran), 1st year, no. 31, p. 2, Saturday, 13 Dhu 'l-Ḥidjdja 1325/18 January 1908

(Binning, *loc. cit.*; Polak, *Persien*, 132; Wills, 170). This changed during the famine of 1861-2, when potatoes suddenly became popular as a substitute for scarce cereals (de Gobineau, 170). Strawberries, too, were gradually coming into cultivation in the late 19th century (Wills, 170, 300). Turkey at that point had become slightly more common, as had small game such as quail, partridge and pheasant, though these still only appeared on the tables of the rich (Polak, i, 113-21; Lycklama a Nijeholt, ii, 242; Bleibtreu, 70). The Caspian provinces continued to stand out for their different diet, including rice and the consumption of garlic, which was thought to neutralise the humid air (Fraser 1826, 16). Public cookshops, known from the Ṣafawid period, continued to exist all over Ḳād̲j̲ār Persia (Binning, ii, 62), yet the first places resembling real restaurants only opened their doors at the turn of the 20th century. Mostly patterned after Russian and Caucasian examples, with terraces and gardens, they first appeared in Tehran (Iʿtimād al-Salṭana, *Čihil sāl*, 153; Fragner 1987, 790).

Rich and poor naturally continued to eat differently both with regard to table manners as to ingredients. Beginning with the court, members of the élite began to adopt western cutlery in the late Ḳād̲j̲ār period, and the habit of sitting around a table on chairs was introduced in the early 20th century as well (Chehabi, 55-6). The rich used imported sugar while the poor made do with syrup and honey (Polak, ii, 154). The rich consumed different kinds of pilaw and *k̲h̲ūris̲h̲*, stews, with lamb meat, fowl or fish. The middling classes did not ordinarily eat pilaw and *k̲h̲ūris̲h̲* more than once or twice a week, but mostly had to satisfy themselves with *āb-i gus̲h̲t* (a stew on the basis of mutton stock, which seems to have become the staple of the poor in the course of the 19th century; see *EIr* art. *Ab-gūšt*). The poor ate mostly bread (and in times of scarcity, even acorn bread; A. Wilson, 63), cheese and fruit, could afford *āb-i gūs̲h̲t* only occasionally, and in the winter months rarely were in a position to eat any meat. They served pilaw and *k̲h̲ūris̲h̲* only during holidays and festivals. All ate large quantities of fruit, which was cheap (Dārābī, 247-8; Polak, i, 121; Ḳučānī, 18; Mustawfī, i, 284). Fish was a staple in the Caspian provinces, and dried and salted fish was also consumed inland. Fresh-water fish was little esteemed. On the Persian Gulf coast, prawn, *mīgū*, was eaten fresh, as it still is today; it was transported inland in dried form (Wills, 298).

Even today, chicken and turkey connote the food of the rich, while bread and cheese stand for the fare of simple folk. Bread continues to be the staple of the peasants and the urban poor in the arid and semi-arid interior, while rice is consumed by everyone in areas where it is cultivated, especially along the Caspian Sea. Elsewhere, rice is often still a luxury food, eaten on special occasions and offered to guests (Bazin, 245; Bazin and Bromberger, 154). With rising living standards, rice has become more common. Meat, formerly a food reserved for special occasion, has become much more standard as well, and traditionally vegetarian dishes such as *k̲h̲ūris̲h̲* are now often served with meat (Khosrowkhavar, 149). Beef has made inroads, necessitating its importation in large quantities and at great cost (Brun and Dumont, 14). The inhabitants of the Caspian provinces, and especially Gīlān, still enjoy a different diet. They eat rice, mostly in the form of *katih*, quickly prepared rice with clarified butter, with every meal, and as recently as the 1970s rice constituted from 45% to 65% of the daily diet of males in central Gīlān. They also like beef, and bread used to be unknown or at least spurned by them until quite recently (Bromberger 1994, 187, 189, 191).

The growing Western influence in the second half of the 20th century has led to the introduction of a number of new foods, most of them pale renderings of originally Western food. Often consumed as tokens of modernity, these include sausages, *kalbas*—until the Islamic Revolution prepared with pork—hamburgers and pizzas. During the reign of Muḥammad Riḍā S̲h̲āh Pahlavī, Iranians also took to eating frozen meat imported from Australia and New Zealand, and processed "Danish" cheese. The American-style "fast-food" restaurant, serving sandwiches, pizzas, hamburgers, and fried chicken, made its appearance in the late 1960s, followed by a variety of ethnic restaurants in the next decade. Soft drinks began to replace traditional juice beverages in the same period. The period following the Islamic Revolution did not fundamentally change this process. Hamburgers, pizza and hot dogs are now consumed by people from all classes in restaurants and pizzerias that imitate Western models. A new development is the appearance of self-styled "traditional" (*sunnātī*) restaurants and coffee-houses where waiters in "authentically Iranian" dress serve the customers (Chehabi, 59-60).

Other changes have occurred as well. Many traditional dishes, time-consuming to make, are no longer prepared on a regular basis (Khosrowkhavar, 149-52), and traditional cookbooks, a few of which are known from the Ḳād̲j̲ār period, were replaced in the 20th century by modern ones, the use of which remains unclear in a country where most women still learn the art of cooking from their mothers and grandmothers (Fragner 1984, 333; a list of modern cookbooks appears in *ibid.*, 332).

Bibliography: 1. Primary sources. I. Afs̲h̲ār (ed.), *ʿĀlam-ārā-yi S̲h̲āh Ṭahmāsb. Zindigī-dāstānī-yi duvvumīn pādshāh-i dawra-i Ṣafawī*, Tehran 1370/1991; idem (ed.), *Ās̲h̲pāzi-yi dawra-i Ṣafawī*, Tehran 1360/1981; Ange de St. Joseph, *Souvenirs de la Perse safavide et autres lieux de l'Orient (1664-1678)*, ed. and tr. M. Bastiaensen, Brussels 1985; Mīrzā ʿAlī Akbar K̲h̲ān Ās̲h̲pāzbās̲h̲ī, *Sufra-i aṭʿima*, Tehran 1353/1974; Baṣīr al-Mulk, *Rūznāma-i Baṣīr al-Mulk S̲h̲aybānī 1301-1306 ḳamarī*, ed. I. Afs̲h̲ār, Tehran 1374/1995; R.B.M. Binning, *A journal of two years' travel in Persia, Ceylon, etc.*, 2 vols. London 1857; J. Bleibtreu, *Persien. Das land der Sonne und des Löwen*, Freiburg 1894; C.A. de Bode, *Notes on a Journey in January and February 1841, from Behbehan to Shuster*, in *JRGeog. S.*, xiii (1843), 86-107; C. de Bruyn, *Reizen over Moskovie door Persie en Indie*, Amsterdam 1714; J. Chardin, *Voyages du chevalier Chardin en Perse, et autres lieux de l'Orient*, 10 vols. and atlas, Paris, 1810-11; *A chronicle of the Carmelites in Persia and the papal mission of the XVIIth and XVIIIth centuries*, ed. Chick, 2 vols. London 1939; R.G. de Clavijo, *Embassy to Tamerlane 1403-1406*, ed. G. Le Strange, London and New York 1928; J.B. Fraser, *Travels and adventures in the Persian provinces on the southern banks of the Caspian Sea*, London 1826; idem, *A winter's journey from Constantinople to Tehran*, 2 vols. London 1838; J. Fryer, *A new account of East India and Persia being nine years' travels, 1672-1681*, ed. W. Crooke, 3 vols., London 1909; A. de Gobineau, *Les dépêches diplomatiques du Comte de Gobineau en Perse*, ed. A.D. Hytier, Paris 1959; T. Herbert, *Travels in Persia 1627-1629*, London 1929; E. Kaempfer, *Am Hofe des persischen Grosskönigs 1684-1685*, ed. W. Hinz, Tübingen 1977; A. Kroell (ed.), *Nouvelles d'Ispahan 1665-1695*, Paris 1979; Iskandar Beg Muns̲h̲ī,

Tārīkh-i ʿālam-ārā-yi ʿAbbāsī, ed. Afshār, 2 vols., [2]Tehran 1350/1971; Iʿtimād al-Salṭana, *Čihil sāl-i tārīkh-i Īrān (Maʾāthir wa ʾl-āthār)*, ed. Afshār, Tehran 1363/1984; *Lettres édifiantes et curieuses*, 8 vols., new ed. Toulouse 1810; T.M. Lycklama a Nijeholt, *Voyage en Russie, au Caucase et en Perse*, 4 vols. Paris-Amsterdam 1873; ʿAbd Allāh Mustawfī, *Sharḥ-i zindigānī-yi man yā tārīkh-i idjtimāʿiyya idārī-yi dawra-i Ḳādjāriyya*, 3 vols. [3]Tehran 1371/1992; Nādir Mīrzā, *Tārīkh wa djughrāfiya-yi Dār al-Salṭana Tabrīz*, ed. G. Ṭabāṭabāʾī Madjd, Tabrīz 1373/1994; E. Orsolle, *Le Caucase et la Perse*, Paris 1885; J. Otter, *Voyage en Turquie et en Perse*, 2 vols., Paris 1748; J.E. Polak, *Persien, das Land und seine Bewohner. Ethnographische Schilderungen*, 2 vols., Leipzig 1865, repr. New York 1976; Āḳā Nadjafī Ḳūčānī, *Siyāḥat-i shark yā zindigīnāma-i Āḳā Nadjafī Ḳūčānī*, Tehran 1362/1983; F. Richard, *Raphaël du Mans, missionnaire en Perse au XVIIe s.*, 2 vols. Paris 1995, Dh. Thābitiyān, *Asnād wa namā-hā-yi tārīkhī wa idjtimāʿī-yi dawra-i Ṣafawiyya*, Tehran 1343/1964; P. della Valle, *Viaggi di Pietro della Valle il pellegrino*, 2 vols. Brighton 1843; C.J. Wills, *The land of the Lion and the Sun (modern Persia)*, London 1891; Sir Arnold Wilson, *Southwest Persia. A Political Officer's diary*, London 1941; S.G. Wilson, *Persian life and customs*, New York 1900.

2. Modern studies. Afshār, *Tāzahā va pāra-yi īrānshināsī*, in *Bukhārā*, 7 vii (1378/1999), 98; T. Allsen, *Two cultural brokers of medieval Eurasia: Bolad Aqa and Marco Polo*, in M. Gervers and Wayne Schlepp (eds.), *Nomadic diplomacy, destruction and religion from the Pacific to the Adriatic*, Toronto 1994, 63-78; Z. Amuzegar, art. *Cooking in Pahlavi literature*, in *EIr*, vi, 1991, 249-50; D. Balland and C. Bromberger, art. *Berenj (rice) in Iran*, in *EIr*, iv, 1990, 147-55; S. Bazargan, art. *Berenj (rice) in cooking*, in *ibid.*, 161-3; M. Bazin, *Quelques données sur l'alimentation dans la region de Qom*, in *St. Ir.*, ii (1973), 243-53; Bromberger, *Identité alimentaire et altérité culturelle dans le nord de l'Iran; le froid, le chaud, le sexe et le reste*, in P. Centlivres (ed.), *Identité alimentaire et altérité culturelle*, Neuchâtel 1985, 2-34, Eng. tr. as *Eating habits and cultural boundaries in northern Iran*, in S. Zubaida and R. Tapper (eds.), *Culinary cultures of the Middle East*, London 1994, 185-204; T. Brunn and R. Dumont, *Iran: des prétensions impériales à la dépendance alimentaire*, in *Peuples méditerranéens*, ii (1978), 3-24; H.E. Chehabi, *The westernization of Iranian culinary culture*, in *Iranian Studies*, xxxvi (2003), 43-62; ʿAbd al-Raḥīm Kālantar Dārābī (Suhayl Kāshānī), *Tārīkh-i Kāshān*, Tehran 1335/1956, repr. 1341/1962; E. Elahi, art. *Āš in modern Iran*, in *EIr*, ii, 1987, 692-3; idem, *Āšpāzkāna*, in *ibid.*, 790-91; B. Fragner, art. *Āšpāzī*, in *ibid.*, 788-90; idem, *From the Caucasus to the Roof of the World. A culinary adventure*, in Zubaida and Tapper (eds.), *op. cit.*, 49-62; idem, *Social realities and culinary fiction. The perspective of cookbooks from Iran and Central Asia*, in *ibid.*, 63-72; idem, *Zur Erforschung der kulinarischen Kultur Irans*, in *WI*, N.S. xxiii-xxiv (1984), 320-59; M.R. Ghanoonparvar, *Culinary arts in the Safavid period*, in K. Eslami (ed.), *Iran and Iranian studies. Essays in honour of Iraj Afshar*, Princeton 1998, 191-7; idem, art. *Principles and ingredients of modern Persian cooking*, in *EIr* vi, 1993, 250-1. A.C. Gunter, *The art of eating and drinking in ancient Iran*, in *Asian Art*, i/2 (1988), 7-54; N. Kasāʾī, *Khūrak va pūshak dar Āsyā-yi markazī, sada-i hidjrī ḳamarī 8-16 mīlādī*, in *Faṣlnāma-i Farhang*, ix/3 (1375/1996), 103-43; F. Khosrowkhavar, *La pratique alimentaire*, in Y. Richard (ed.), *Entre l'Iran et l'Occident*, Paris 1989, 143-9; I. Pūr-i Dāvūd, *Hurmazd-nāma*, Tehran 1331/1952; N. Ramazani and eds., art. *Ābgūsht*, in *EIr*, i, 1985, 47-8; M. Rāwandī, *Tārīkh-i idjtimāʿī-yi Īrān*, ix, Tehran 1371/1992; R. Schmitt, art. *Cooking in ancient Iran*, in *EIr*, vi, 1993, 246-8; B. Spooner, *Fesenjan and kashk. Culture and metaculture*, in *Folia Orientalia*, xxii (1981-4), 245-58; A. Watson, *Agricultural innovation in the early Islamic world. The diffusion of crops and farming techniques, 700-1100*, Cambridge 1983.

3. Modern cookbooks. N. Batmanglij, *New food of life. Ancient Persian and modern Iranian cooking and ceremonies*, Washington D.C. 1992; idem, *Persian cooking for a healthy kitchen*, Washington D.C. 1994; idem, *A taste of Persia. An introduction to Persian cooking*, London and New York 1999; N. Ramazani, *Persian cooking. A table of exotic delights*, New York 1974, repr. Bethesda 1997; M. Shaida, *The legendary cuisine of Persia*, London 1992/New York 2002.

(R. Matthee)

MAWĀKIB.

6. In the Mamlūk Sultanate

In the early Mamlūk sultanate, *mawkib* designates specifically the royal ride which formed an item in the sultan's installation ceremonies. The term is explicitly used by Ibn Taghrībirdī (*Nudjūm*, vii, 41) on the accession of al-Manṣūr ʿAlī b. Aybak: "He rode on Thursday, 2 Rabīʿ II [655/19 April 1257] with the insignia of the sultanate from the Citadel to Ḳubbat al-Naṣr in an awe-inspiring procession (*mawkib hāʾil*). Then he returned and entered Cairo by Bāb al-Naṣr. The *amīrs* dismounted and marched before him. . . . Then al-Manṣūr went up to the Citadel and took his seat in the palace of the sultanate." On the insignia of the sultanate (*shiʿār al-salṭana*), see al-Ḳalḳashandī, *Ṣubḥ*, iv, 6-9. Similar accounts in more or less detail, and not always using the term *mawkib*, are given in connection with the accession of several sultans down to al-Nāṣir Muḥammad b. Ḳalāwūn in 693/1294 (cf. *Nudjūm*, viii, 47). Ibn ʿAbd al-Ẓāhir gives an interesting account of the royal ride of al-Saʿīd Baraka Khān, when appointed joint sultan with his father, al-Ẓāhir Baybars, on 13 Shawwāl 662/8 August 1264: "He [Baybars] caused his son, al-Malik al-Saʿīd, to ride with the insignia of the sultanate. He himself went forth in the procession (*rikāb*), and going on foot carried the *ghāshiya* [*q.v.*; cf. P.M. Holt, *The position and power of the Mamlūk sultan*, in *BSOAS*, xxxviii (1975), 242-3] before him. The *amīrs* took it, . . . and the sultan returned to his royal residence, while the kings, the *amīrs* and everybody continued in attendance on him (sc. Baraka Khān) up to Bāb al-Naṣr. They entered Cairo, which had been magnificently decorated, on foot bearing the *ghāshiya*. The *amīrs* busied themselves with the raising of the [royal] parasols (?). He passed through the city with his *atābak*, the *Amīr* ʿIzz al-Dīn al-Ḥillī, riding at his side. Robes of satin, watered silk and so forth were spread before him until he returned to his Citadel" (*al-Rawḍ al-ẓāhir*, ed. Khuwayṭir, 204). After the time of al-Nāṣir Muḥammad, the procession through Cairo seems to have been discontinued, its place being taken by a short ride within the precincts of the Citadel to the throne-room, as described by al-Maḳrīzī (*Khiṭaṭ*, ii, 209): "It was also customary when one of the descendants of al-Malik al-Nāṣir Muḥammad b. Ḳalāwūn succeeded to the kingdom, that on his accession the *amīrs* would attend at his residence in the Citadel. He would be invested with the caliphal robe with a green robe (*faradjiyya*) beneath it and a round black turban, girt with the golden Arab sword, and mounted on the royal steed (*faras al-nawba*). He would proceed with the *amīr*s in front and the *ghāshiya* before him, while the *djāwīshiyya* chanted and the royal flutes played, surrounded by the halberdiers, until he had crossed from Bāb al-Nuḥās to the entrance of the great hall. Then he would dismount from the steed, go up to the throne and take his seat upon it." In this period, *mawkib* acquired the secondary meaning of "a session of the royal court", e.g. Ibn Taghrībirdī, *Nudjūm*, x, 61, of al-Nāṣir Aḥmad b. al-Nāṣir Muḥammad in 742/1342: "The sultan held another court (*mawkib ākhar*), and bestowed robes on all the *amīrs*, . . . and he went down in a great procession (*mawkib ʿaẓīm*) with those *amīr*s who were in his company."

The term *mawkib* was also used for other state appearances of the sultan in which there was a processional element, such as his attendance at congregational prayer on Fridays and the two Feasts, at polo in al-Maydān al-Akbar, at the cutting of the dam, and on royal progresses. Al-Ḳalḳashandī (*Ṣubḥ*, iv, 46-9) does not use the term consistently on each of these occasions, but it appears to apply to all of them. Uniquely Egyptian were the proceedings at the cutting of the dam at the height of the Nile-flood in Cairo. The sultan, when notified by the master of the Nilometer [see MIḲYĀS] that the flood was at its height, rode at once in modest state (without full insignia and with a reduced escort) to the Nilometer, where he held a banquet for the *amīr*s and Mamlūks. A vessel of saffron was given to the master of the Nilometer, who swam across the well and perfumed the column and then the sides of the well. The sultan's barge was brought alongside, and the sultan swam in the river, surrounded by the barges of the *amīr*s. Followed by the boats of spectators, the *amīrs*' barges and the sultan's great barge entered the mouth of the canal of Cairo, with the craft manoeuvring and cannons firing. The sultan sailed in his small barge to the dam, which was cut in his presence, and he then rode back to the Citadel.

Bibliography: Given in the article.

(P.M. HOLT)

MAWḲIF (A.), a term of Ṣūfī mysticism, referring to the intermediate moment between two "spiritual stations" (*maḳām*), represented as a halting (*wakfa*) and described as a state of stupor and of the loss of reference points acquired since the preceding stage. The *mawḳif* is a dynamic psychological state, in which the connection between the mystic and God becomes overturned, and sometimes suspended (annihilation in God, the so-called *fanāʾ* [see BAḲĀʾ WA-FANĀʾ]). The best example of the course of such an experience is given in the work of al-Niffarī (d. *ca.* 366/976-7 [*q.v.*]), his *K. al-Mawāḳif wa 'l-mukhāṭabāt*, ed. and Eng. tr. A.J. Arberry, London 1935, Fr. tr. M. Kâbbal, *Le Livre des stations*, Paris 1989; see also P. Nwyia, *Textes inédits de Niffarî*, in *Trois oeuvres inédites de mystiques musulmans*, Beirut 1973; idem, *Exégèse coranique et langage mystique*, Beirut 1970, 348-407. The term continued to be employed in classical Ṣūfism (e.g. by Ibn al-ʿArabī, *Futūḥāt*, Cairo 1329/1911, 392-3, who refers explicitly to al-Niffarī).

Bibliography: Given in the article.

(P. LORY)

MAWLID.

3. In the Maghrib.

Unlike the use of the term *mawlid* in other regions, e.g. in Egypt and the Sudan, where it also includes the celebration of the birthdays of various saints (see 1., in Vol. VI, 895), in the Maghrib the term *mawlid* is restricted to the birthday of the Prophet Muḥammad. In this part of the world, alongside the *ʿīd al-fiṭr* and the *ʿīd al-aḍḥāʾ* [*q.vv.*], the *mawlid* is among the most important festivals of the year.

The oldest known *mawlid* celebrations in the Maghrib were held in Sabta [*q.v.*]. This festival was introduced into this city by an *ʿālim* named Abu 'l-ʿAbbās al-ʿAzafī (d. 633/1236 [*q.v.*]) in order to call a halt to the participation of the people in Christian festivals and to strengthen the Muslim identity of Sabta in a period of Christian successes during the Reconquista, both at land and at sea.

After his son Abu 'l-Ḳāsim al-ʿAzafī had seized power in Sabta in 647/1250, he officially introduced the *mawlid* and propagated the festival throughout the rest of the Maghrib. Through this celebration of the *mawlid*, Abu 'l-Ḳāsim al-ʿAzafī was able to display his religious enthusiasm, and as the result of his largesse during the festivities he increased his popularity with the people. Moreover, during the *mawlid* celebration the hierarchical relationships among the various groups within the realm were confirmed and the loyalty to the ruler expressed in specially-composed poems.

Since then, in a similar way the celebration of the *mawlid* has always played a role at an official level in legitimising the power of various dynasties which have ruled over parts of the Maghrib: the Ḥafṣids (Eastern Maghrib); the ʿAbd al-Wādids (Central Maghrib); and the Marīnids, the Waṭṭāsids, the Saʿdids and the ʿAlawīs (Morocco) [*q.vv.*]. Today, the celebration of the *mawlid* plays a role in the consolidation of the power of the ʿAlawid king of Morocco, who traces his descent, together with the concomitant prestige, to the Prophet Muḥammad himself.

In addition to the state-sponsored celebrations at the courts and elsewhere, the *mawlid* always has been and still is immensely popular among the people, not only among the Arabicised sections of the population but also among the Berbers. The way in which the popular *mawlid* is celebrated displays an enormous variety, both in duration and in ritual, changing from one place to the other. Common elements in all celebrations are the taking of a holiday, the cheerful atmosphere, illuminated parades on the eve of the *mawlid*, festive meals, sweets, special dress, the exchange of gifts, music, dance and, under the influence of Ṣūfī brotherhoods, visits to shrines of saints and singing of mystical chants.

At times, these popular celebrations have given, and still give, rise to protests by the *ʿulamāʾ*, who do not consider these permissible from the point of view of the religious law because of the nature of the activities which take place during the celebrations, many of which are regarded as unlawful. The oldest discussions about this originate from the time of Abu 'l-ʿAbbās al-ʿAzafī, but the debate reappears with regular intervals. In the first decades of the 20th century, under the influence of Salafī ideas from Egypt [see SALAF. 1], there were various attempts to exclude certain practices from the *mawlid* celebration. In very recent times, inspired by Wahhābī ideas, the *mawlid* has again come under severe criticism. Despite these protests against the celebration of the festival, as a major manifestation of popular religion, the *mawlid* is as vital as ever.

Bibliography: P. Shinar, *Traditional and reformist mawlid celebrations in the Maghrib*, in Myriam Rosen-Ayalon (ed.), *Studies in memory of Gaston Wiet*, Jerusalem 1977, 371-413; Aḥmad al-Kharīṣī, *al-Mutaṣawwifa wa-bidʿat al-iḥtifāl bi-mawlid al-nabī*, al-Dār al-Bayḍāʾ 1403/1983; N.J.G. Kaptein, *Muḥammad's Birthday Festival. Early history in the Central*

Muslim lands and development in the Muslim West until the 10th/16th century, Leiden 1993; N. van den Boogert and H. Stroomer, *A Sous Berber poem on the merits of celebrating the Mawlid*, in *Études et Documents Berbères*, x (1993), 47-82; Y. Frenkel, Mawlid al-Nabī *at the court of Sulṭān Aḥmad al-Manṣūr al-Saʿdī*, in *JSAI*, xix (1995), 157-72.

(N.J.G. Kaptein)

MAWSŪʿA.

3. In Turkish.

The fascination which the Ottomans entertained for compendia of facts and the ordering of knowledge can be traced to their origins outside Anatolia. Although not strictly speaking an encyclopaedic work, the *Dīwān lughāt al-turk* written by Maḥmūd al-Kāshgharī in the second half of the 5th/11th century and providing a dictionary in Arabic or early Turkish, partakes also of the nature of a thesaurus, with information on the early Turks, including their onomastic, their folklore, proverbs, poetry, etc. [see al-kāshgharī].

As one would expect, the earliest examples of encyclopaedias in the Ottoman world were written in Arabic. It is clear that these types of encyclopaedic reference works were very closely modelled on existing Arabic language reference works on specialised subjects, biography and bibliography. The first phase in the emergence of the Ottoman encyclopaedia is represented by the work of translating encyclopaedic works from Arabic into Turkish, this being an important step in the development of reference tools for the use of Ottoman scholars.

As early as the reign of Meḥemmed I (816-24/1413-21), the first translations of encyclopaedic works appeared. In this period, Rukn al-Dīn Aḥmed made a translation of al-Ḳazwīnī's *ʿAdjāʾib al-makhlūḳāt* from Arabic into Turkish and presented it to the Sultan. It is most likely that the concept of the earth as an orb was introduced into Turkish scientific literature by this work. Meḥmed b. Süleymān made a Turkish translation of al-Damīrī's zoological encyclopaedia, the *Ḥayāt al-ḥayawān*, which listed the names of existing and, in some cases, fictitious animals, and subjects related to them. Aḥmad al-Miṣrī's *al-Ḳānūn fi 'l-dunyā* was translated into Turkish by Ḳāḍīʿ Abd al-Raḥmān in 983/1575. This work dealt with a variety of topics such as geography, astronomy, medicine, history, anecdotes, and signs and symbols.

The first original encyclopaedic works in the Ottoman empire can be dated to the 9th/15th century. These examples are mainly divided into two categories: general and specialised ones. The *Enmūzedj al-ʿulūm* was prepared by Mollā Fenārī [see fenārī-zade]. He classified subjects under one hundred headings which were termed "the sciences" (*ʿulūm*). He mainly used Fakhr al-Dīn al-Rāzī's *Ḥadāʾiḳ al-anwār*, adding forty more subject headings to it. It has been alleged that that the author of this work was not Molla Fenārī but his son, Meḥmed Shāh Čelebi. This claim, advanced most prominently by Adnan Adıvar in his *Osmanlı Türklerinde ilim*, is not however, supported with evidence.

A distinguished and gifted scholar in the 10th/16th century was Aḥmed ʿIṣām al-Dīn (901-68/1495-1561), who came from the scholarly family of the Ṭashköprüzādes [*q.v.*]. Ṭāshköprüzāde's work, the *Miftāḥ al-saʿāda wa-miṣbāḥ al-siyāda*, mainly discusses the virtues of teaching and learning. The first introduction explains the virtue of science while the second and the third discuss the obligations of students and teachers, respectively. After these introductory chapters, he classifies the sciences (*ʿulūm*) ontologically. The author not only gave the definitions of the sciences but also noted the names of the scholars who had worked on these subjects and their books, making his work an inventory of scholarly life and books taught in Istanbul in the 10th/16th century. Because of the popularity of this work his son, Ṭāshköprüzāde Kemāl al-Dīn Meḥmed, made a Turkish translation of it which is known as the *Mewḍūʿat al-ʿulūm*. Another important work by Ṭāshköprüzāde is a biographic account of the Ottoman empire, a typical example of the Turkish *tedhkire* tradition [see tadhkira. 3]. His *al-Shaḳaʾiḳ al-nuʿmāniyya* contains biographical information on the *ʿulemā* and *ṣuleḥāʾ* of the Ottoman empire, and it was arranged according to the reigns of the Sultans, comprising in total the biographies of 150 *sheykhs* and 371 scholars. Several translations of this work were also made into Turkish in the same century. There are also compilations of this work prepared in the same format. Another distinguished example of the bibliographic compendium is Ḥādjdjī Khalīfa's (Kātib Čelebi) *Kashf al-ẓunūn*. He started compiling it in 1042/1633 and took about twenty years to complete it. It contains bibliographic information on *ca.* 14,500 books and biographical information on *ca.* 10,000 authors.

Erzurūmī Ibrāhīm Ḥaḳḳī's *Maʿrifet-nāme* is the last example of the classical encyclopaedic works, reflecting the author's interest in Islamic mysticism. The work consists of selected topics chosen from arithmetic, geometry, astronomy, mineralogy, botany, zoology, anatomy, geography and physics.

After promising beginnings in compiling compendia of knowledge, the movement seems to have petered out, perhaps a victim of its own success; it was perhaps felt that there was no need to be filled by expanding or adding to these compendia. It is thus not surprising that the next stage of Ottoman compilation of encyclopaedias should be the introduction of European-styled encyclopaedias which surveyed European science. The first of these were introduced during the *Tanẓīmāt* [*q.v.*] period in the mid-19th century. Titles of these works reflect the lexicographic approach and understanding of their compilers, so that the word (*ḳāmūs*) "dictionary" was generally used in their titles. The first examples, are unfortunately incomplete. The first encyclopaedic work was planned by ʿAlī Ṣuʿāwī [*q.v.*] who escaped to France in 1867 because of his opposition to the ruling régime in the Ottoman empire. He attempted to publish this first encyclopaedic work as an appendix to his newspaper *ʿUlūm* in 1870. Entitled *Ḳāmūs al-ʿulūm we 'l-meʿārif*, it was published in fascicles and only five of these appeared, since it fell victim to the siege of Paris by the Prussian Army. In this encyclopaedia subjects were arranged in alphabetical order, contained illustrations, and each fascicle comprised sixteen pages. Other major, equally incomplete, attempts are, in chronological order: *Ḳaṭre* by Aḥmed Nāẓīm and Meḥmed Rüshdī, both of them officers in the Ottoman Army, in 1888, of which only one sample fascicle appeared; *Makhzen al-ʿulūm*, another general subject encyclopaedia, by Meḥmed Ṭāhir and Serkis Orpilyan, of which only one volume appeared in 1890; and a specialised subject encyclopaedia on mathematics and astronomy, the *Ḳāmūs-i riyāḍiyyāt*, prepared by Ṣāliḥ Dhekī (Zekī), a mathematician, in 1897, of which again only one volume appeared.

The *Muḥīṭ al-maʿārif* was prepared by Emr Allāh Efendī, who was the first philosophy lecturer at the Dār al-Fünūn in Istanbul, in 1900. Only one volume appeared, but it had importance as the first comprehensive general encyclopaedic work in Turkish, and its title was subsequently adopted as the Ottoman term for a general encyclopaedia. After Emr Allāh Efendī's appointment as the Minister of Education, a commission was set up under his chairmanship and consisting of 132 specialists. The aim was the preparation of his encyclopaedic work for the second time in 1910. The title of this new encyclopaedia accordingly became *Yeñi muhīṭ al-maʿārif*, but this attempt was also short-lived, and only one volume appeared.

The first complete work in the genre was, in fact, the *Lughat-i tārīkhiyye we djoghrāfiyye* "Historical and geographical dictionary", prepared by Yaghlîkdjîzāde Aḥmed Rifʿat in seven volumes in 1882-3. Although its title suggests that it was limited to historical and geographical matters, it in reality covered subjects such as new inventions, machinery, as well as the natural sciences physics, chemistry and botany.

The *Ḳāmūs al-ʿalām* of the linguist Shems el-Dīn Sāmī [*q.v.*] was compiled between 1888-98 as a historical and geographical encyclopaedic dictionary in six volumes. Sāmī relied on oriental and western sources for his work, and it remains a valuable reference source for historical research today, since the work contains not only historical and geographical terms and words used in the Ottoman language but also biographies of historical personalities and their works as well as the names, histories, and ethnic complexion of locations within the empire. It was issued fortnightly in fascicles, and its publication was completed in eleven years.

A similar work, the *Memālik-i ʿothmāniyyeʾniñ tārīkh we djoghrāfyā lughatî* "Dictionary of the history and geography of the Ottoman Empire", was prepared by ʿAlī Djewād, and published in 1893-9 in four volumes. It comprised two sections, the first, in three volumes, was devoted to the natural, historical, and economic aspects of the Ottoman provinces and their localities, while the second section, the fourth volume, contained biographical information on Ottoman statesmen and poets.

All these efforts were personal and self-motivated, and no financial or academic support was provided from any public or private institution. Within the same period, another initiative directed by a commission was launched in 1913 under ʿAli Reshād, ʿAlī Ṣeydī, Meḥmed ʿIzzet and L. Feuillet, the *Muṣawwer dāʾiret al-maʿārif* "Illustrated circle of knowledge", but only two volumes were issued 1913-17. The harsh social, economic and political conditions of the last decades of the Ottoman empire were certainly a contributing factor to the lack of success in completing these potentially promising works in the 19th and early 20th centuries.

Two notable biographical works appeared, however, towards the end of the 19th and the beginning of the 20th centuries. A national biography, the *Sidjill-i ʿOthmanī* "Ottoman register", was prepared by Meḥmed Thüreyyā [*q.v.*] in four volumes and published in 1890-4; it contained approximately 20,000 biographies of civil servants and statesmen. A bio-bibliographical compendium of Ottoman writers began to appear in 1914, *ʿOthmānlî müʾellifleri* "Ottoman authors", compiled by Bursalî Meḥmed Ṭāhir; it listed 1,600 books and gave the biographies of their authors. Its aim was to record the scientific and literary taste of the Ottomans for the new generation, and its subsequent was that it became one of the main sources for encyclopaedias published later.

After the establishment of the Republic in 1923, the government encouraged the publication of new books, especially for children, to alleviate the problem of illiteracy. The French word for encyclopaedia was used for the first time in Turkish as *ansiḳlopedi* with the publication of the *Čodjuk ansiklopedisi* "Children's encyclopaedia" in 1927. Four volumes appeared up to 1928, and after the change of alphabet in November 1928 the publication of this work was suspended until 1937. This encyclopaedia has a significance in Turkish encyclopaedic publication, being the last work begun in Arabic script before the change of alphabet, the first encyclopaedic work completely in the Latin script being that prepared on the initiative of a daily newspaper, *Cumhuriyet*, and published between 1932-6 in ten volumes. This publication was based on *Compton's pictured encyclopaedia* and *American educator*, and additional entries related to Turkey were written by specialists.

Several special-subject encyclopaedias have appeared in the Republican period. One of the most important of these is Reşad Ekrem Kocu's *İstanbul Ansiklopedisi*, which began in 1946 and ceased publication in 1975 on the death of the author. The significance of this incomplete work in eleven volumes is that the historian Kocu prepared it single-handed as a work limited to the city of Istanbul. Given the supreme importance of Constantinople/Istanbul in the history of the eastern Mediterranean world, further encyclopaedic works were prepared upon the death of Kocu. The *İstanbul kültür ve sanat ansiklopedisi* "Encylopaedia of the culture and art of Istanbul" was prepared by specialists and published by a daily newspaper, *Tercüman*, in 1982; unfortunately, it was never completed. The other encyclopaedia, *Dünden bugüne İstanbul ansiklopedisi* "Encyclopaedia of Istanbul from yesterday till today", was published by the Ministry of Culture and the Historical Foundation in eight volumes in 1993-4; although not as detailed as Kocu's work, it gives general information on almost every subject in 10,000 articles.

From the 1940s onward, the Ministry of National Education (*Maarif Vekaleti*) decided to initiate the publication of encyclopaedic works as well as its publications and translations of classical works. The first was the *İslam Ansiklopedisi* begun in 1940. A committee was set up, and the encyclopaedia was based on the original *Encyclopaedia of Islam* published in Leiden in 1913-36 [see MAWSŪʿA. 4]. However, amendments were carried out and in some cases, expansions were made in articles which were only briefly covered in the Leiden edition. The work was completed in 1988 in thirteen volumes, of which two volumes have two parts.

Meanwhile, a decision was made by the same Ministry to prepare a general, national encyclopaedia in 1943. The first four volumes were issued under the title of *İnönü ansiklopedisi*, the name of the President of Turkey at the time [see ISMET İNÖNÜ, in Suppl.], altered to *Türk ansiklopedisi* in 1951. The encyclopaedia consists of thirty-three volumes, and publication was completed in 1986. This work has a significant place in the history of official publications in the Turkish Republic. Since it was published over a span of forty-three years, it reflects the political approaches and the use of Turkish language by the various governments in power through the period, and it further illustrates how the publications of government agencies can be affected by the political ideology of these governments. The Ministry of National Education also commissioned Celal Esat Arseven and Mehmed Zeki Pakalın in 1943 and in 1946, respectively, to publish the *Sanat ansiklopedisi* "Encyclopaedia of the Arts" in five volumes and *Osmanlı tarih deyimleri ve terimleri sözlüğü* "Dictionary of Historical Phrases and Terms" in three volumes.

From that period until the 1960s, no new projects for a general encyclopaedia were initiated with the exception of the *Hayat ansiklopedisi* "Encyclopedia of life," begun by a private publisher in 1961 and by 1963 completed in six volumes. In a very short period, 100,000 copies were sold, indicating the need for a general encyclopaedia by an increasingly literate society.

The *Meydan Larousse büyük lugat ve ansiklopedi* is the largest Turkish encyclopaedic work initiated by a private publisher, with publication beginning in 1969. It is an encyclopaedia as well as a dictionary, being a translation of the *Grand Larousse encyclopédique* published in 1960-4 in ten volumes. Some subjects and entries related solely to French language and culture were omitted, and subjects related to Turkish and Islamic culture inserted. The encyclopaedia was issued in fascicles and was completed in 1973 in twelve volumes, with two supplementary volumes issued in 1974 and 1985, respectively. The publication of *Meydan Larousse* was a turning-point in the history of commercial publication of encyclopaedias in Turkey, and a result of the enthusiasm with which the *Meydan Larousse* was greeted by the public, other publishers have seen the commercial opportunities offered by publishing encyclopaedias.

Hence during these years, a handful of publishers began to specialise in such reference works. The major publishers today are Anadolu Yayıncılık, Gelişim, Görsel and İletişim, who publish not only general encyclopaedic works but also encyclopaedias on specialised subjects, such as *Yurt ansiklopedisi* "Encyclopedia of the Homeland", which gives information on the history, economic and social conditions of the cities of Turkey in alphabetical order; *Türk ve dünya ünlüleri ansiklopedisi*, a biographical reference source; *Gelişim genel kültür ansiklopedisi*, a general encyclopaedia; *Anadolu uygarlıkları ansiklopedisi*, an encyclopaedic publication on Anatolian civilisations; and *Cumhuriyet dönemi Türkiye ansiklopedisi*, which covers the development of various fields in the Republican period such as the constitution, archaeology, the press, energy, mining, librarianship, etc. *Ana Britannica ansiklopedisi* is a translation and adaptation of the *Encyclopaedia Britannica*, published in 1988 by Anadolu Yayıncılık. The publisher has also published yearbooks in order to update the necessary information. The second Turkish edition was initiated in 2000 and it is still in progress. Finally, *Türkiye diyanet vakfı islam ansiklopedisi*, an *Encyclopedia of Islam*, is being prepared and financially supported by the Turkish Religious Foundation. The publication started in 1988 and twenty-two volumes, covering the letters A-İ, have already appeared. The encyclopaedia contains not only subjects related to Islam but also wider aspects relating to the Islamic community throughout the world. Most of the Islamic subjects are very detailed, and the articles have comprehensive bibliographies.

Bibliography: A. Adnan Adıvar, *Osmanlı türklerinde ilim*, Istanbul 1943; Agah Sırrı Levend, *Türk edebiyatı tarihi*, Ankara 1973; *Türkiye'de dergiler ansiklopediler (1849-1984)*, Istanbul 1984; Ayhan Aykut, art. *Ansiklopedi*, in *TDV İslam ansiklopedisi*, iii, Istanbul 1991.

(A.O. Icimsoy)

5. In Urdu.

Here there does not seem to be any significant tradition of any antiquity, leaving aside modern Urdu translations of such reference works as *Chamber's Encyclopaedia*, the *Encyclopaedia Britannica* and, of course, the Urdu *Encyclopaedia of Islam*, which draws on material from the Western *Encyclopaedia of Islam*, published in Leiden.

MEḤMED ṬĀHIR, BURSALİ (1861-1925), Ottoman biographer and bibliographer.

Meḥmed Ṭāhir was born in Bursa in northwestern Turkey on 22 November 1861, the son of Rifʿat Bey, clerk to the city council, and grandson of Üsküdarlī Seyyid Meḥmed Ṭāhir Pas̲h̲a, formerly a commander in sultan ʿAbd ül-Med̲j̲īd's imperial guard. He studied at the Bursa military academy from 1875 and at the élite Ḥarbiyye (War) academy in Istanbul from 1880. Graduating in 1883 he spent the next twenty years teaching geography, history and rhetoric at military schools in Manāstir (and one year in Üsküb) in Macedonia, as part of the Ottoman Third Army. In 1904 he became director of the military high school in Selānik (Salonica). Whilst at the Ḥarbiyye academy he had become a member of the Melāmī order of dervishes, by whom he was profoundly influenced in his teaching, publications and political outlook. In Manāstir he first conceived the notion of collecting bio-bibliographical data on poets and learned men, and in 1897 published his first work *Türkler'in ʿulūm we funūna k̲h̲idmetleri* "The Turkish contribution to arts and sciences" (Istanbul 1314). In 1316/1899 he also published a full-length biographical study of the Arab mystic Ibn al-ʿArabī.

Meḥmed Ṭāhir was dismissed from his teaching post in December 1906 for his Ṣūfī involvement and his membership of the Ottoman Freedom Society (*ʿOt̲h̲mānlī ḥürriyyet d̲j̲emʿiyyeti*). From 1908 to 1911 he served as deputy for Bursa in the first representative assembly of the Second Constitutional period, and subsequently served in the Ministry of Charitable Endowments (*Ewḳāf nezāreti*) on a committee to inspect the holdings of institutional libraries. In 1915 he became director of the Ṭopkapi Sarāyī library. The date of Meḥmed Ṭāhir's death is uncertain, but was probably 1925. He was buried in Istanbul.

Meḥmed Ṭāhir's principal work is *ʿOt̲h̲mānlī mü'ellifleri*, a three-volume bio-bibliographical compendium published between 1915 and 1924, listing 1691 Ottoman authors and their works. Despite many lacunae and acknowledged errors, *ʿOt̲h̲mānlī mü'ellifleri* was unique in its comprehensive scope and immediately became a standard reference work. Aside from the works already mentioned, Meḥmed Ṭāhir also compiled over twenty lesser biographical works, either of particular individuals (e.g. Kātib Čelebi) or of groups of Ottoman *s̲h̲eyk̲h̲*s and *ʿulemā'*.

Bibliography: For a full bibliography, see the detailed article by Ömer Faruk Akün, in *Türkiye Diyanet Vakfı İslam Ansiklopedisi*, vi (1992), 452-61, on which the above is based.

(Christine Woodhead)

MEZISTRE, Mizistre, the Turkish name for Greek Mystras, Latin Mistra, a famous Byzantine necropolis on a hill slope west of modern Sparta in Laconia in the Peloponnese [see mora], which was a major centre of late mediaeval Greek civilisation and capital of the "Despotate of the Morea" till the Ottoman conquest. It has numerous Byzantine and Frankish monuments from the 13th-15th centuries, and was immortalised, albeit anachronistically, in Goethe's *Faust*. The name has been connected with the shape of the cone-shaped hill on which it stands.

The Frankish castle of 1249 was built by William II de Villehardouin of the Achaia Principality, but passed to the Byzantines in 1262. The ravages of Franks and Turkmens from Western Anatolia (see details in A. Savvides, *The origins and rôle of the Turkophone mercenaries in the Morea in the course of the Byzantine-Frankish war of 1263-4* [in Greek], in *Acts of the 4th Intern. Congr. of Peloponnesian Studies*, i, Athens 1992, 165-88) later compelled the local people to seek refuge in the citadel so that it developed into a fortified town. The 14th and early 15th centuries were, culturally, a Golden Age for Mistra, and notable for the humanist Plethon (d. 1452), whose connections with Islam are noteworthy; he was influenced, whilst in Edirne, by a Jewish scholar, Elissaeus, who initiated him into Zoroastrianism, Averroean Aristotelianism and Jewish mysticism of the Kabbalistic tradition. Plethon had connections with such more enlightened Muslim elements as the Akhīs [*q.v.*] and followers of the religio-social leader Badr al-Dīn Ḳāḍī Samawna [*q.v.*] (see F. Taeschner, *Plethon, ein Vermittler zwischen Morgenland und Abendland in Beginn der Renaissance*, in *Byz.-Neugrieschische Jb.*, viii [1930], 100ff.).

The earliest recorded battle of the Despot of Mistra against the Turks, sc. Turkmen arriving across the Aegean with a fleet, is variously placed in 1357-64. Subsequent Ottoman incursions were led by Ewrenos Beg [*q.v.*] in the late 1380s and 1390s, and by Turakhan [*q.v.*] in 1423, who reached the outskirts of Mistra (witnessed personally by Plethon). By 1446 the Despot Constantine Palaeologus had to acknowledge Ottoman suzerainty, and in spring 1460 Meḥemmed II decided to annex the Despotate, and Demetrios surrendered to him. An Albanian convert, Ḥamza Zenevisi, was made the first governor of Ottoman Mezistre (see von Hammer, *GOR*, ii, 379, iii, 9ff., 54ff.; F. Babinger, *Mahomet le Conquérant et son temps*, Paris 1954, 102ff., 210ff.; Savvides, *Notes on the Turkish raids in the Mystras area from c. 1360 to the Ottoman conquest of 1460*, in *Epeteris Etaireias Byzantinon Spoudon*, xlviii [1990-1], 45-51).

Under the first *Tourkokratia*, Mezistre was the favoured residence of the *sandjak bey* of Morea till the conquest of Nauplion (Anabolu) in 1540. It enjoyed relative tranquillity, with its architecture and urban topography largely unchanged except for the addition of a few mosques. The commerce of its bazaars and its local Jewish community were important, and Western travellers, from Coronelli (1681) onwards, describe the August "market fairs" (*emporopanegyreis*). The population *ca.* 1583-5 appears to have been, from the evidence of the Ottoman registers, 1,000 Christian families and 199 Jewish ones (see M.T. Gökbilgin, *Kanunî sultan Süleyman devri başlarında Rumeli eyaleti livaları*, in *Belleten*, xx [1956], 281), whilst Kātib Čelebi lists for the late 17th century *ca.* 15,000 inhabitants (von Hammer, *Rumeli und Bosna. Geogr. Beschreibung von . . . Hadschi Chalfa*, Vienna 1812, 117-18).

The Venetian Francesco Morosini captured Mezistre in August 1687, and the Venetians then made it the capital of their *territorium* of *Braccio di Maina*, second only in importance to the province of Laconia's capital of Monemvasia [see MENEKSHE]; yet their rule was rigorous and accordingly unpopular with the Greek inhabitants. Now, in the Venetian and second Turkish periods, the population of the town rose considerably and seems, from the travellers' accounts, to have reached 40-45,000. The Venetians abandoned Mistra in 1715 in face of a powerful approaching Turkish army, and Ottoman rule was re-established. But in the course of the Russo-Turkish war of 1768-74 and the Greek revolt of 1770 [see MORA. 2.], the Greeks, aided by the Russian fleet of the Orloffs, took the fortress of Mezistre and started a merciless slaughter of the small Turco-Albanian garrison, which was only saved through the intercession of the local metropolitan. But in autumn 1770 a Turco-Albanian force returned and sacked and burnt much of the town, not sparing even the metropolitan who had intervened to save their compatriots. From now onwards there began a gradual deserting of the fortress towards the lower slopes, which would eventually lead to the foundation of modern Mystras. With the outbreak of the Greek Revolt (1821), Mezistre surrendered to the powerful local Mainote clans of Mavromichales and Giatrakos and the Turkish garrison was allowed to flee to Tripolitza, but it was once again plundered and burned by Ibrāhīm Pasha's army in 1825, as vividly described by C. Swan in his *Voyages in the Eastern Mediterranean*, London 1826. These ravages signalled the town's abandonment, since—except for a few families—the exasperated inhabitants descended to the settlement of Neo-Mystras and thence to modern Sparta, inaugurated in 1834 by a decree of King Otto I and built by 1837-8.

Bibliography: For detailed references, see the *Bibls.* to MORA and NAVARINO; all relevant titles until 1989 in A. Savvides, *Medieval Peloponnesian bibliography for the period 396-1460*, Eng. ed. Athens 1990; additional refs. in T. Gritsopoulos, *Mystras* [in Greek], 1966, and M. Chatzidakes, *Mystras, medieval city and castle* [in Greek], 1987. Specialised monographs: I. Medvedev, *Mistra. Očerki istorii i kulturi pozdnevizantiiskogo goroda*, Leningrad 1973 (to the 15th century, rich refs., esp. on art and culture in chs. VI-VII); S. Runciman, *Mistra, Byzantine capital of the Peloponnese*, London 1980 (lucid popularised account to 1834). See also *Acts of Congress "Mystras' illustrious heritage in the Tourkokratia"* [in Greek], 1990 (esp. contributions by N. Drandakes, T. Gritsopoulos, H. Mpelia, C. Kotsones, K. Mamone and D. Vagiakakos). On the Frankish and Byzantine periods, see details in Miller-Lampros, i-ii; Miller, *Essays*; Zakythenos, *Despotat*, i-ii, 1975[2]; D. Sigalos, *Sparta and Lakedaimon*, ii, *The Mystras Despotate* [in Greek], Athens 1962; Bon, *Morée franque*, 1969; D. Nicol, *Last centuries of Byzantium 1261-1453*, [3]Cambridge 1993; Setton, *Papacy and Levant*, i-ii, 1976-8; still useful are A. Momferratos, *The Palaiologoi in Peloponnesos 1383-1458* [in Greek], Athens 1913, and R.-J. Loenertz, *Pour l'histoire de Péloponnèse 1382-1404*, in *Rev. ét. byz.*, i (1942), esp. on Turkish raids; cf. C. Amantos, *Relations between Greeks and Turks*, i [in Greek], Athens 1955, 83-4, 89, 139-40; P. Schreiner, *Byzant. Kleinchroniken*, i-ii, 1975-7 and A. Savvides, *Morea and Islam, 8th-15th centuries*, in *JOAS*, ii (1990), 55ff., 58ff. Finally, on the pre-1460 period, see surveys by J. Longnon and P. Topping, in K. Setton (ed.), *Hist. Crusades*, ii (1962[2]), 235ff., iii (1975), 104ff., 141ff.; G. Ostrogorsky and Setton, in *Camb. Med. Hist.*, iv/1 (1966[2]), 378ff., 401ff.; C. Maltezou, in *Istoria ellenikou ethnous*, ix (1979), 282ff. On the 1460 Ottoman annexation and the Turkish, Venetian and brief Greek periods (1821-5) until Ibrāhīm's withdrawal from the Morea, see İ.H. Uzunçarşılı, *Osmanlı tarihi*, ii-iv, 1949-59; Runciman, *Mistra*, chs. XI-XII and [in Greek]: C. Sathas, *Turkish-dominated Greece*, repr. Athens 1990; M. Sakellariou, *Peloponnesos during the 2nd Turkish domination*, repr. Athens 1978; on 17th-19th century travellers' accounts, see K. Simopoulos, *Foreign travellers*, ii, 1988[5], iii/1-2, 1989-90[3]; *How foreigners viewed Greece*, v, 1984, 424ff., and on contemporary figures, cf. B. Panagiotopoulos, *Population and settlements of Peloponnesos 13th-18th centuries*, Athens 1985.

(A. SAVVIDES)

MIHMĀN (p.), literally "guest", the equivalent of Ar. *ḍayf* [*q.v.* for this sense]. The Persian word occurs in various compounds, such as *mihmāndār* and *mihmān-khāna*. In Ṣafawid Persia, the *mihmāndārs* were officials appointed to receive and to provide hospitality for guests, including foreign ambassadors and envoys, with a court head official, the *mihmāndār-bāshī*, superintending these lesser persons. In Ḳādjār times, the *mihmāndārs* seem to have been appointed *ad hoc*. See the references to the accounts of European travellers in Ṣafawid Persia (Chardin, Kaempfer, Sanson) in the anonymous *Tadhkirat al-mulūk*, ed. and tr. V. Minorsky, London 1943, comm. 110 n. 2.

The institution of the *mihmān-khāna* in its more modern form goes back to Nāṣir al-Dīn Shāh Ḳādjār after his first visit to Europe in 1873 (cf. Sir Denis Wright, *The Persians amongst the English*, London 1985, 135). He had the laudable intention of providing rest houses along the routes to the capital Tehran, from such entry points to his kingdom as Enzeli on the Caspian coast, which would provide travellers with something better than the traditional caravanserais or *khāns* [*q.v.*] and the *čapar-khānas* (see a description of these last in Khurāsān given by the Hon. G.N. Curzon, *Persia and the Persian question*, London 1892, i, 249 ff., and cf. the remarks on the *čapar* system in general in *Murray's handbook for travellers in Asia Minor, Transcaucasia, Persia, etc.*, London 1895, 285-6) and which would possess in some degree the amenities of a western-type hotel. Western travellers in Persia during the later 19th century found the concept good, but its execution left much to be desired. E.G. Browne commented that the *mihmān-khāna* "has all the worse defects of a European hotel without its luxury"; he contrasted the insolence and rapacity of the servants there with the hospitality he had received in humble peasant homes, and the "new-fangled and extortionate" nature of the new buildings with the "venerable and commodious caravansaray" (*A year amongst the Persians*, London 1893, 85-8, 177-8). It was not until after the First World War that European-type hotels began to spread from the capital Tehran into the provinces.

Bibliography: Given in the article. See also MANZIL. 2. (C.E. Bosworth)

MILIANA [see MILYĀNA].

MĪR TAḲĪ MĪR [see MĪR MUḤAMMAD TAḲĪ].

MIʿRĀDJ.

6. In Persian literature.

The ascension of the Prophet of Islam is, for Persian literature, an account, *ḳiṣṣa-i miʿrādj*, one drawn from a long tradition, *ḥadīth-i miʿrādj* and an account that takes an autonomous form, *miʿrādj-nāma*. This account thus has a history. The progressive organisation of the narrative elements constituting the whole is derived from the world to which the text belongs. The world of Persian literature cannot be detached from its Muslim context (Ḳurʾān, tradition and exegesis) nor from its original milieu (Iranian and, furthermore, millennial).

The celestial journey was a familiar theme throughout the Near Eastern world. Having exclusive regard to the Iranian cultural domain, Zarathustra, according to the *Avesta*, had asked for immortality and this was granted: he did not die but departed, alive and intact, into the beyond through "assumption" (*ashi*-; Kellens 1999). From this point onward, according to another source, he spent ten years "in the best existence", guided by Vohū Manō "while maintaining contact with Ahura Mazda". Then, strengthened, he descended again to join his kinsmen (Molé 1967). As for the soul of the virtuous deceased, the *Avesta* describes the four stages through which it passes, guided by the same benevolent genie, before reaching the throne of Ahura Mazda (Duchesne-Guillemin 1962). The tale in Middle Persian of the magian Ardā Vīrāz, who used methods of a shamanic nature to make a journey to Heaven, was well known in its time. The magian visited Heaven and Hell, bringing back valuable advice for his community in the practice of the cult (Gignoux 1984). Also celebrated was the visit of the angel which began the prophetic vocation of the founder of Manicheism (Ibn al-Nadīm, *al-Fihrist*, tr. B. Dodge, ii, 774-5). As regards the Iranian calendar from the start of the Islamic era, al-Bīrūnī (*al-Āthār*, 216) relates that on Nawrūz [*q.v.*], the festival of the first day of the year, the ascension to Heaven of the great king of ancient times, Djamshīd, was celebrated. On his throne and in a kind of apotheosis, he went there to defeat death and the demons.

When Persian prose emerged, in the 4th/10th century, Ḳurʾānic exegesis had already travelled a considerable distance in constructing the account of the ascension of the Prophet. It was also at this time that the commemoration of this ascension began, in Jerusalem [see AL-ḲUDS, at Vol. V, 323]. The original translation into Persian of the commentary on the Ḳurʾān (*al-Tafsīr*) by al-Ṭabarī, on the initiative of the Sāmānid Manṣūr b. Nūḥ (d. 365/975 [*q.v.*]), is one of the greatest monuments of this early prose. Gathered here is the best of what exegesis had hitherto elaborated, on the basis of *ḥadīths* which focused the reading of notable passages of the Ḳurʾān on the "night journey" (*isrāʾ*) (Ḳurʾān, XVII, 1) and on the two visions of the Prophet (Ḳurʾān, LIII, 1-18 and LXXXI, 19-25). It may be noted that the *miʿrādj* is involved here three times. The account is first developed broadly at the end of the commentary on Sūra II (Persian *Tafsīr*, i, 182-98), while with Sūra XVII, that of the "night journey", the commentary offers at the end of the sūra only a summary (Persian *Tafsīr*, iv, 909-18). Through this style of repetition it can be understood what at that time constituted the nucleus of the story of the ascension. On arriving in the Seventh Heaven, Gabriel invites the Prophet to speak before God. The dialogue is contained in the verses 285-6 which conclude Sūra II. Then, for greater precision, Gabriel will say, in the account which follows Sūra XVII, that the object of the journey is "that you address your prayers to God" (Persian *Tqfsīr*, iv, 910). Thus at its birth, Persian prose was located at the end of a process of exegesis which had made from Ḳurʾānic verses which did not require it, an account of the ascent to Heaven, of dialogue with God and of re-descent, which had long been part of the religious and cultural ambience of the Near East.

But for a third time, at the end of the translation of Sūra LIII (Persian *Tafsīr*, vii, 1766-8) there is a further instance of *miʿrādj*. At Medina, the text relates, Arabs were competing at archery. The Prophet was then transported to Heaven, after which God told him that he had been closer to Him "than the distance of two bow-shots". This was the interpretation of the two well-known Ḳurʾānic verses LIII, 8-9. Secondly, where the Ḳurʾān says, "And he revealed to his servant what he revealed. His heart has not belied what he saw" (Persian *Tafsīr*, Sūra LIII, 10-11), the commentator has written: "The heart of the Prophet saw God more clearly than we see with the eyes in our heads, and it was not a deceitful vision" (vii, 1769). These few phrases were to be decisive in the development of Persian *miʿrādj*, focusing the interest of the story on the great proximity between the

Prophet and God, and on the vision of the heart. Bringing these elements together was all that remained to be accomplished.

The 5th/11th century saw a capital development in the story of the *miʿrādj* narrative in Persian. Attributed to Ibn Sīnā (370-427/980-1037 [*q.v.*]) is a "Book of the Ladder" (*miʿrādj-nāma*), consisting of a brief but substantial account of an ascension, drawn from tradition and accompanied by a long commentary. The account is composed of forty short pieces, a sort of *vade-mecum*, a *čihil sukhan* offered for meditation. Each piece receives a commentary in the typical style of Ibn Sīnā, with his angelology and his descriptive cosmology. The totality is known through several manuscripts, from the 6th/12th to the 8th/14th centuries. Nadjīb Māyil-i Hirawī was the discoverer of the manuscript which enabled him to prepare a critical edition (*Miʿrādj-nāma*, 1365/1986). The author of the text has reduced the narration to the essentials, copious as it is with the authors of the *Tafsīr*. His commentary interprets the ascension as a journey of the soul of the Prophet towards Primary Intelligence. Henry Corbin (1954, 1999) has rightly added his interpretation of the text to that of the three visionary accounts of Ibn Sīnā.

Ibn Sīnā's illustrious contemporary, al-Ḳushayrī (376-465/986-1072 [*q.v.*]), likewise a Khurāsānian, was of a totally different background: Ashʿarī, Shāfiʿī and a master of *ḥadīth* and of Ṣūfism. Shocked by those sceptical of the physical reality of the *miʿradj*, he undertook to establish, point by point, proof of the veracity of the events of the ascension of the Prophet. From a meticulous examination of all the *ḥadīth*s worthy of belief, he drew up a work in Arabic that concluded specifically that the Prophet "rose to Heaven with his body" (*K. al-Miʿrādj*, 65). Thus, two lines were drawn, between which numerous options were available: that of Ibn Sīnā, proponent of a journey of the spirit, and that of al-Ḳushayrī, an authority on Sunnism (Fouchécour 1996).

The 5th/11th and 6th/12th centuries constitute a decisive period of evolution of the *miʿrādj* story in Persian literature. In prose, the account of the ascension was developed within commentaries on the Ḳurʾān. Alongside them and in the Ḥallādjian tradition, works of spirituality dealt with the ascension of the Prophet as a prototype of the journey of the purified soul. Finally, poetry was directed towards an account of celebration of the event, which the *miʿrādj* was for the believer, and quickly blended, in its lyrical mode, with the spiritual mainstream.

The first commentary on the Ḳurʾān that went beyond the sole concern of translation into Persian was that of Shāhfūr-i Isfarāʾinī, the *Tādj al-tarādjim fī tafsīr al-Ḳurʾān li ʾl-aʿādjim*, composed between 430/1038 and 460/1067. This jurist, expert in *ḥadīth* and a committed Ashʿarī, used a style decidedly representative of Khurāsānian prose, close to the spoken language, pleasant and persuasive. His account of the *miʿrādj* (*Tādj al-tarādjim*, iii, 1229-51) is distinguished from that of al-Ṭabarī in several ways. It is not written in the same cosmic perspective, with the scholar making use of contemporary knowledge regarding the skies, the stars and planets. It is intentionally reduced to that which gives guidance in faith and which changes the proportions given to the sections of the account. The march from Mecca to Jerusalem has the nature of an important initiatory test; the approach to the Throne of God takes on the grandeur of court ceremonial. But the basis of the dialogue between God and the Prophet remains that which is said in Ḳurʾān, II, 285-6. Several of its original elements are not retained, but the account of Shāhfūr has left its mark on the story of the *miʿrādj*.

Another Khurāsānian, Abū Bakr ʿAtīḳ b. Muḥammad al-Harawī al-Sūrābādī, dedicated his *Tafsīr* to the Saldjūḳ Alp Arslan [*q.v.*], who reigned from 455/1063 to 465/1072. He composed his account of the *miʿrādj* in the same spirit as Shāhfūr, in a limpid Persian prose. His version was powerfully coherent and appropriate for various audiences, especially no doubt the community of preachers. In particular, they could find there two major affirmations: the importance of the Prophet's function as a mediator on behalf of his community, and the essential role of Gabriel as a guide on the celestial journey. On the other hand, the account is so well proportioned in its sections that it seems suitable for public reading, with the audience reciting the numerous Ḳurʾānic verses inserted in the text.

A little younger than al-Sūrābādī, an important translator of the Ḳurʾān from Transoxiana deserves mention. This is Abū Ḥafṣ Nadjm al-Dīn ʿUmar b. Muḥammad al-Nasafī (462-538/1069-1143 [see AL-NASAFĪ. III]). He used rhymed prose in his translation and showed himself an expert in the Persian literature of his time. His translation of Ḳurʾān, XVII, 1, for example, is already a form of commentary; he interprets Ḳurʾān, LIII, 8-9, as denoting the proximity of Gabriel with the Prophet. A brief account of the *miʿrādj* follows Ḳurʾān, LIII, 8-11 (*Tafsīr*, ii, 998-9), a short and powerful text which lends itself to serious consideration.

In the first half of the following century, Rashīd al-Dīn Abu ʾl-Faḍl Aḥmad al-Maybudī was the author of a large commentary on the Ḳurʾān, begun in 520/1126, He was not a Khurāsānian, but he revived a composition of al-Anṣārī (the eminent Ṣūfī master of Harāt, d. 481/1089 [see AL-ANṢĀRĪ AL-HARAWĪ]) which he called *pīr-i ṭarīḳat*. His account of the *miʿrādj* was, understandably, inspired by Ṣūfism, which was a novelty. He developed this story in its place, at the beginning of Sūra XVII (*Tafsīr*, 478-500). It is not certain that he knew al-Sūrābādī's account; he places objections to the miracle of ascension and the responses at the start of the text, or changes the dispositions of the inhabitants of the Heavens. His true originality is his way of addressing "the station of proximity" (*maḳām-i ḳurba*), describing in technical terms known in Ṣūfism the ecstasy of the Prophet before God.

Henceforward, no reader of the Ḳurʾān could miss the account of the *miʿrādj* nor ignore its implications regarding the personality of the Prophet and Islam, the ultimate destiny of men and their spiritual path. In his turn, a Shīʿī of Rayy, Abu ʾl-Futūḥ al-Rāzī, preacher and jurist, composed a major commentary on the Ḳurʾān, completed shortly before his death (552/1157). He took such care in the writing of his account of the Prophet's ascension to the point of turning it into a major classic, with the quality of his Persian and the organisation of the story (*Rawḍ al-djinān*, vi, 254-73), establishing the essentials for future generations.

But before him, Sanāʾī [*q.v.*] had for the first time introduced the theme of the *miʿrādj* into Persian poetry. He gave to the beautiful *mathnawī* which he composed at 33 years of age in 506/1112 (if he was born in 473/1080) the title of "Journey of the devotees towards the Place of Return" (*sayr al-ʿibād ilā ʾl-maʿād*), intentionally combining in this title two words taken from Ḳurʾān, XVII, 1, and from Ḳurʾān, XXVIII, 85, thus indicating that this journey is a *miʿrādj* (de Bruijn

1997), conceived in effect, in his description, as an ascension of the Ṣūfī. In his major work the *Ḥadīḳat al-ḥaḳīḳat*, incomplete at the time of his death (525/1131), he inaugurated the practice of eulogising the Prophet of Islam, giving special prominence to his night journey. The account is brief (*Ḥadīḳat*, 195-6), but it suffices to show how the Prophet has transcended everything which was traditionally related of this journey. The direct influence of the *Sawāniḥ* of Aḥmad al-Ghazālī (d. 520/1126) on Sanāʾī is very probable (Pūrdjawādī 1378/1999). A source for these two mystics was, it may be recalled, ch. ii of the *Tawāsīn* of al-Ḥallādj (Massignon, *Passion*, iii, 311-15). But Hudjwīrī (d. *ca.* 465/1072 [*q.v.*]), after his masters, was also an inspiration due to the magisterial fashion in which he addressed *miʿrādj* in general (*Kashf al-mahdjūb*, 306-7) and the Prophet's *miʿrādj* in particular (*op. cit.*, 364, 389).

Thus, in the space of a century, the story of the *miʿrādj* of the Prophet was to be imposed on several essential registers of Persian literature. In poetry especially, the two major authors who drew inspiration from Sanāʾī, sc. ʿAṭṭār and Niẓāmī [*q.vv.*], were intent on glorifying this ascent at the outset of their works. An example that can be given is the splendid text of the *Ilāhī-nāma* "The divine book" (*bayt*s 256-413, pp. 11-17; tr. J.A. Boyle, 12-19) composed before 586/1190. It takes considerable liberties in relation to the prose texts. The Prophet decides to ascend to the Heavens, and the reader witnesses a lengthy homage paid to him by all the previous prophets; the reader subsequently witnesses the meeting of the stars with him, and then the mystical transformation of the Chosen One is described at length, summarised at the end in the image of the arrow which struck the letter *m* from the name of Aḥmad, to give Aḥad, the image of unification. Niẓāmī, in his turn, composed five accounts of ascension as introductions to his five *mathnawī*s. The most successful was the one that he wrote, some years after ʿAṭṭār, for the *Haft paykar* "The seven princesses" (ed. Tharwatiyān 1998, 64-8), which shows excellent knowledge of the traditional tale and an incomparable spiritual and poetic sense (Fouchécour 1989).

The many Persian poets who were inspired, over the course of several centuries, by the *Pandj gandj*, the "Five treasures" of Niẓāmī, composed accounts of the *miʿrādj* in their turn. But with the 6th/12th century, the genre had matured and was growing stale. On the other hand, the perception of the *miʿrādj* of the Prophet "as a prototype of the experience of the mystic rising from Heaven to Heaven in his lifetime" (Corbin, *En Islam iranien*, iii, 1972, 346) formed the basis of numerous treatises on the fringes of literature and the science of religions. On these fringes, there remains a vast area of study which has been little explored, concerning the themes essential to the *miʿrādj*, such as the Opening of the Chest, the Celestial Mount, the Night of the Rescript (*shab-i barāt*), the Angel–Holy Spirit, the Tree of the Frontier, the Sails of Light, the shape of the Stars, the dwellings of Paradise, etc. And if "the nocturnal ascension is the nucleus of the religious vocation of Muḥammad" (Massignon), the account of it cannot be irrelevant to the essentials of Islam.

Bibliography: 1. Sources. Ph. Gignoux (ed. and tr.), *Le Livre d'Ardâ Vîrâz*, Paris 1984; Abū ʿAlī Ibn Sīnā, *Miʿrādj-nāma*, ed. Sh.I. Abarḳūhī, introd., ed. and notes N. Māyil Harawī, Mashhad 1365/1986; Ḳushayrī, *K. al-Miʿrādj*, ed. ʿA.H. ʿAbd al-Ḳādir, Cairo 1384/1964; Maybudī, *Kashf al-asrār wa-ʿuddat al-abrār*, ed. introd. and notes ʿA.A. Ḥikmat, 10 vols. Tehran 1331-8/1952-9; Nasafī, *Tafsīr*, i-ii, Tehran 1376/1997; Rāzī, *Rawḍ al-djinān wa-rūḥ al-djanān = Tafsīr*, ed. M.I. Kumshiʾī, 7 vols. Tehran 1325/1946; A.M. Piemontese, *Una versione persiana della storia del "miʿrāg"*, in *OM*, lx (1980), 225-43; Shāfūr-i Isfarāyinī, *Tādj al-tarādjim fī tafsīr al-Ḳurʾān li 'l-aʿādjim*, ed. M. Harawī and A.I. Khurāsānī, 3 vols. Tehran 1375-6/1995-7; Abū Bakr Sūrābādī, *Tafsīr*, in *Ḳiṣaṣ-i Ḳurʾān-i madjīd*, Tehran 1347/1968, 192-203; Ṭabarī, *Tardjuma-i Tafsīr-i Ṭabarī*, ed. Ḥabīb Yaghmāʾī, 7 vols. Tehran 1339/1960.

2. Studies. H. Corbin, *Avicenne et le récit visionnaire*, Paris 1954, repr. 1999, 206-22; J. Duchesne-Guillemin, *La religion de l'Iran ancien*, Paris 1962, 335; M. Molé, *La légende de Zoroastre*, Paris 1967; P. Nwyia, *Exégèse coranique et langage mystique*, Beirut 1970, 90-1, 98-9, 184-8; Ch.-H. de Fouchécour, *Les récits d'ascension (meʿrâj) dans l'oeuvre en persan du poète Nézâmi (XIIe siècle)*, in *Études irano-aryennes offertes à Gilbert Lazard*, Paris 1989, 99-108; J. van Ess, *Le* miʿrādj *et la vision de Dieu dans les premières spéculations théologiques en Islam*, in M.A. Amir Moezzi (ed.), *Le voyage initiatique en terre de l'Islam. Ascensions célestes et itinéraires spirituels*, Louvain-Paris 1996, 27-56; de Fouchécour, *Avicenne, al-Qosheyri et le récit de l'Échelle de Mahomet*, in *ibid.*, 173-98; H. Landolt, *La «double échelle» d'Ibn ʿArabî chez Simnânî*, in *ibid.*, 251-64; P. Ballanfat, *L'échelle des mots dans les ascensions de Rûzbihân Baqlî Shîrâzî*, in *ibid.*, 265-303; J.T.P de Bruijn, *Persian Sufi poetry*, London 1997, 88-92; N. Māyel-i Harawī, *Kitābshināsī-yi du risāla: miʿrādjiyya-i Bū ʿAlī wa tabṣira-i Ḳūnawī*, in *Sāyi ba sāyi*, Tehran 1378/1999, 363-71; J. Kellems, *Asi-, ou le Grand Depart*, in *JA*, cclxxxvii/2 (1999), 457-64; N. Pūrdjawardī, *Parwāna wa ātash*, in *Nashr-i Dānishī*, xvi/1 (1378/1999), 3-15.

(Ch.H. de Fouchécour)

MĪRZĀ SHAFĪʿ MĀZANDARĀNĪ (1159-1234/1744-1819) or Mīrzā Muḥammad Shafīʿ Bandpiʾī Māzandarānī, prime minister during the rule of Fatḥ ʿAlī Shāh Ḳādjār [*q.v.*].

He began his career as a statesman at the court of Āghā Muḥammad Khān [*q.v.*], the founder of the Ḳādjār [*q.v.*] dynasty, who promoted Mīrzā Shafīʿ to the rank of minister. After the murder of Āghā Muḥammad Khān in 1797, Mīrzā Shafīʿ continued in office at the court of the successor, Fatḥ ʿAlī Shāh, by whom in 1801 he was appointed prime minister. Mīrzā Shafīʿ's term of office coincided with Persia's being drawn into the strands of European diplomacy. In 1804, in an effort to reassert its former authority in Georgia and consequently to impede further Russian advances southwards, Persia entered into a war with Russia, which was finally concluded with the signing of the peace treaty of Gulistān [*q.v.*] in 1813. During the war, Mīrzā Shafīʿ attempted to make an alliance with France. He persuaded Fatḥ ʿAlī Shāh to despatch an envoy to the court of Napoleon Bonaparte in order to negotiate this. Accordingly, the Franco-Persian Treaty of Finkenstein was signed in 1807. However, the French soon ignored the treaty by reaching an agreement with the Russians at Tilsit in the same year, leaving Mīrzā Shafīʿ politically disillusioned. Much of his period of office was spent in military engagements and diplomatic negotiations. He died at Ḳazwīn in 1234/1819 and was survived by one daughter.

Bibliography: ʿAbd al-Razzāḳ b. Nadjaf-ḳulī, *Maʾāthir-i sulṭāniyya*, Tabriz 1826; Sir Harford Jones Brydges, *An account of the transaction of His Majesty's mission to the court of Persia in the years 1807-11*, London 1834; ʿAlī-ḳulī Mīrzā Iʿtimād al-Salṭana, *Iksīr al-tawārīkh*, repr. Tehran 1991; Lisān al-Mulk Sipihr, *Nāsikh al-tawārīkh*, Tabriz 1901; Maḥmūd Maḥmūd, *Tārīkh-i rawābiṭ-i Īrān wa Ingilīs*, Tehran 1949; Saʿīd Nafīsī, *Tārīkh-i idjtimāʿī wa siyāsī-i Īrān*, Tehran 1956; Mahdī Bāmdād, *Tārīkh-i ridjāl-i Īrān*, Tehran 1968; Ḥasan Fasāʾī, *Fārsnāma-yi Nāṣirī*, tr. H. Busse, *History of Persia under Qājār rule*, New York 1972; Iradj Amini, *Napoleon and Persia. Franco-Persian relations under the first Empire*, Richmond 1999.

(T. Atabaki)

MĪRZĀ SHAFĪʿ WĀḌIḤ TABRĪZĪ (b. 1794 Gandja, d. 1852 Tbilisi). Azerbaijani poet.

Born into a family from Tabrīz, at ten years old he lost his father, who was a stonemason, but with the assistance of his relatives he attended a traditional school where he learned literary Persian as well as Arabic. His knowledge of Persian literature introduced him to the works of renowned Persian poets such as Ḥāfiẓ and Niẓāmī. Because of his anti-clerical views, he was expelled from school and began to earn his living both as an accountant and a teacher in calligraphy. His position as accountant brought him the title of Mīrzā. As a teacher of calligraphy, he taught the young Mīrzā Fatḥ ʿAlī Ākhūndzāda [*q.v.*] and persuaded him to end his religious studies. In 1840, the persecutions that he endured from local clerics compelled him to leave Gandja and settle in Tbilisi. There, Ākhūndzāda assisted him in securing a teaching position in Persian and Azeri Turkish languages. In Tbilisi he published the first Azeri Turkish language guidebook, *Kitāb-i turkī*, and formed a cultural society known as *Dīwān-i ḥikmat*, where learned figures of the city occasionally gathered to debate literary, philosophical and social themes. Amongst those who attended these conventions was Friedrich Bodenstedt (1819-92), a German traveller who was interested in oriental studies. While following Mīrzā Shafīʿ's courses on Persian and Azeri Turkish, Bodenstedt collected the original manuscripts of Mīrzā Shafīʿ's poems, both in Persian and in Azeri Turkish. Returning to Germany in 1846, Bodenstedt translated these verses into German and published them in Berlin. The eventual translation of this book into almost all European languages soon made Mīrzā Shafīʿ a renowned Azerbaijani poet outside the Caucasus. In 1846 Mīrzā Shafīʿ left Tbilisi for Gandja and continued his teaching career. But *ca.* 1850 he returned to Tbilisi and taught in a local *Gymnasium* until his death.

Little remains of Mīrzā Shafīʿ's works, and it was not until the Soviet period that four of his *ghazals* and a few lines of his poems in Persian and Azeri Turkish were found and published. The German translation of his poetry has been surrounded by some controversy. While some scholars recognise Mīrzā Shafīʿ as a lyricist with an inclination towards oriental mysticism, others claim that Mīrzā Shafīʿ's understanding of poetry did not go beyond the common knowledge of the learned in the East. Bodenstedt himself was not consistent in his appreciation of Mīrzā Shafīʿ's literary status. While in his earlier writings he had acknowledged Mīrzā Shafīʿ as the original poet of the German translations, he later decreased Mīrzā Shafīʿ's role to being merely that of a source of inspiration for his own poetry.

Bibliography: F. Bodenstedt, *Tausend und Ein Tag im Orient*, Berlin 1850; idem, *Die Lieder des Mirza-Schaffy*, Berlin 1851; idem, *Gedichte*, Bremen 1853; idem, *Aus dem Nachlaß Mirza-Schaffys. Neues Liederbuch mit Prolog und erläuterndem Nachtrag*, Berlin 1874; art. s.v., in *Brockhaus*, 14th ed., Leipzig 1892; *Mīrzā Shafīʿ Wāḍiḥ*, Baku 1926; K. Sundermeyer, *Friedrich Bodenstedt und die "Lieder des Mirza-Schaffy"*, Kiel 1930; M. Rafili, *Mirze Feteli Akhundov, žizn' i tvorčestvo*, Moscow 1956; A. Ismailov (ed.), *Āzerbeydjān edebiyyātī*, ii, Baku 1960; Mīrzā Fatḥ ʿAlī Ākhūndov, *Alifbā-yi djadīd wa maktūbāt*, ed. Ḥāmīd Muḥammadzāda and Ḥamīd Ārāslī, Baku 1963; M. Ibrahimov (ed.), *Azerbaijanian poetry: classic, modern, traditional*, Moscow 1969; Farīdūn Ādamiyyat, *Andīshahā-yi Mīrzā Fatḥ ʿAlī Ākhūndzāda*, Tehran 1970.

(T. Atabaki)

MIṢR.

C. 2. vi. The city from 1798 till the present day.

The history of Cairo over the 19th and 20th centuries is primarily one of status: from being the important capital of an Ottoman province, it became the capital of independent Egypt. During the two centuries under consideration, the city experienced first of all a long period of stagnation; then, from the early 1870s, a strong political will brought an unprecedented development which pointed the way to the modern city. Some years later, the financial situation of Egypt put a brake on urban growth, which then entered upon a period of slow consolidation until the end of the First World War. The years 1920-50 are marked by a new departure, whose determinants are not so much political as migratory. After independence, and up to the end of the 1970s, Cairo became the city of superlatives, with municipal services expanding in all spheres. Then, the slowing down of the migratory movement, whose effects were felt from the beginning of the 1980s, allowed the municipal authorities to resume their policies. Hence the last two decades of the 20th century were devoted to replacing equipment and public services. At the end of the century, Cairo stretched out at the same time into the desert zones and also into the agricultural lands along the outskirts as far as some 30 km/18 miles from its historic core. The city's history during these two centuries is also one of the progressive slipping away of its centre. At the present time, the places making up the centre are spread out around several focuses without nevertheless the older centres, the ancient city as much as the quarters developed at the end of the 19th century, being abandoned.

A difficult start, 1800-68. In 1798 General Bonaparte established his headquarters at Cairo, at a time when the city had 263,000 inhabitants. The French plans for the improvement of the road system were ambitious, but the results were scanty. The re-establishment of Ottoman authority a few years later was unfavourable for the city, whose population declined. However, Cairo experienced some changes which were to be determining factors for later works. At the outset, the governor of Egypt Muḥammad ʿAlī Pasha [*q.v.*]. embarked upon the first act of the discontinuous development of the urban agglomeration: the building of a palace some 12 km/7 miles north of the city. Nearer to the centre, the strengthening of the embankments for containing the floodwaters of the Nile allowed the laying out of vast gardens and the construction of palaces between the fringes of the old structure of the city and the river banks. In regard to urban administration, Muḥammad ʿAlī took up again the structures of power from the previous century but put in place a new dividing out of the administrative which served as the base for the geographical extension of local public services. Heavy industry, whose development the Pasha embarked upon vigorously, was concentrated above all on Būlāḳ [*q.v.*], where several factories for metalworking, printing and spinning were set up at this time.

In the mid-19th century, ʿAbbās Pas͟ha, governor of Egypt 1848-54, developed—around important barracks, a palace and a school—a new quarter to the north of the city, sc. ʿAbbāsiyya. The first constructions for piping water began during this period but it was long before results were seen. Finally, in the framework of an agreement with the British, a railway was built between Alexandria and Suez via Cairo, with the Cairo railway station opening in 1856. At this time, the city's population was almost the same as it was a half-century previously.

A fillip to urbanisation, 1868-75. The succession of Ismāʿīl Pas͟ha [*q.v.*] at the beginning of the 1860s formed a turning-point. Taking as a pretext the need to receive fittingly European dignitaries for the opening of the Suez Canal at the end of 1869, he developed an immense project of extending the city westwards. Paris was the model, but Ismāʿīl retained only the general picture of the French model rather than the exact procedure; nevertheless, the permanent markets and properties strongly resisted the project. In order to promote the new quarters, the Khedive had several public buildings erected there and enormous buildings to be let out in flats, and he gave other stretches of land gratis to those who contracted to build there quickly. After several checks, the beginning of the 1870s was marked by a resumption of works. At that time, Ismāʿīl opened up for urban development the zones farthest away from the centre as far as the left bank of the Nile, and he founded the spa town of Ḥulwān [*q.v.*] some 30 km/18 miles to the south. More than 200 ha (the equivalent of one-fifth of the urbanised zone by *ca.* 1865) were offered to the land market over a few years. This development was interrupted as rapidly as it had been started up; in the mid-1870s, Egypt's bankruptcy dealt a brutal blow to the works. During this time, Cairo became the place of privileged exile for Syro-Lebanese intellectuals who formed the nucleus of the *Nahḍa* [*q.v.*] or Arab cultural awakening and who contributed considerably to the development of cultural life and the formation of the first press devoted to conveying opinion. It was also a high-point of the national movement whose activities were to lead to the British occupation of the country at the end of 1882.

Slowing down and consolidation, 1875-1918. This period was first of all one devoted to the servicing of the public debt. The greater part of resources was pledged to developing agricultural production for export. Cairo was in practice left to its own devices by the administration. After fifteen years of consolidating the quarters founded by Ismāʿīl, new works were begun. But the municipal services were now deprived of all means of state intervention; urban development was left to the initiative of private companies, utilising capital which for the most part emanated from outside the country. It was above all in the sphere of transport that these companies provided for the city's future. The first suburban railway dates from 1888, whilst the tramway system dates from a decade later. At this time, Cairo comprised 570,000 persons on the right bank of the Nile. In the wake of this process and the intense speculation which followed, numerous quarters were founded. In 1906, a Belgian tramway company obtained an authorisation to create a new city, in the desert a few kilometres to the northeast; Heliopolis (ʿAyn S͟hams [*q.v.*]) was thus born. But not all private capital was invested in land speculation. Industrial production also enjoyed a substantial development; this brought about the impoverishment of an important part of the population which was regrouped in a very dense and crowded precarious habitat, in quarters sometimes established in insalubrious areas. Two worlds and two cities were now established cheek-by-jowl, often in close proximity.

The period of growth, 1918-50. After the First World War, the slowing down of agricultural development and improvements in public health brought about an excess of population in the countryside, causing an acceleration of migration to the great cities. Cairo now became a great safety-valve for this rural population growth, with its population jumping from 791,000 in 1917 to 2,320,00 in 1947. During these thirty years, the city went through numerous changes. The construction sector, private as well as public, was very dynamic. The campus of the University at D̲j̲īza (Gizeh), the building for the Mixed Courts, the Parliament building, etc., all date from this period. Intervention by the public authorities in matters of urban development is less conclusive. Despite the first general development plan dating from the later 1920s, the works undertaken were largely those done from necessity. They affected mainly the structure of the old city, and if the public road system was improved, this was more a response to traffic problems than a project looking to the future. At the end of the 1940s, the first social housing appeared in Cairo. The period was also marked by a strong patriotic feeling expressed, in particular, in an abundant artistic and cultural production. Its exportation to the lands of both the Mag͟hrib and the Mas͟hriḳ made Cairo the cultural capital of the Arab world.

The period of bursting activity, 1950-80. After the Free Officers' *coup d'état* of July 1952, the rulers of Egypt adopted new approaches for the development of Cairo. Great projects multiplied, including expressways along the banks of the Nile, additional bridges, etc. The first master plan for the Cairo agglomeration, prepared in 1956, was soon out of date: the population predicted for the year 2000—5.5 millions—was reached before the end of the 1960s. However, on the basis of this plan, the state built large quantities of low-cost housing. But the problem of the living environment was not thereby solved, and it led to an intolerable increased density of the old quarters, whose service infrastructure was now revealed as inadequate. From 1950 onwards, the city spread out in all directions, but above all on the left bank, which now saw an unprecedented development. It became covered with new, planned quarters, with a fairly low density, of thousands of villas and small dwellings. The city also developed in favour of the dividing-out of agricultural lands on the outskirts near to the developing urban area, pushing into zones not prepared for building by the city authorities. In order to frustrate these further extensions, in the mid-1970s there were plans for creating several new towns in the desert regions. But the actual start on this work was long delayed, and the sector not subject to planning continued to swallow up the greater part of the urban expansion.

The period of overflowing development, 1980-2000. At the beginning of the 1980s, demographers predicted the worst possible catastrophes for Cairo. The publication of the 1986 census put a stop to these suggestions; it showed that the population growth was less and less the result of migration. This change gave rise to a lowering of the density of the ancient urban structure which, as a counterpart, became increasingly occupied by the sector of semi-artisanal production.

It also provided an adequate respite for the public services, allowing the preparation of a new master plan at the beginning of the 1980s and the inauguration of several great projects of re-developing public services; the city became an immense construction site. Between Cairo and Alexandria, the first new town, Madīnat al-Sādāt, saw the light. These constructions, large enough to accommodate three government ministries, were never to be occupied.

Despite the state's almost total withdrawal from the sphere of housing, the construction sector remains dynamic. Although the critical situation is obvious, with half the population of the agglomeration living in poverty in 1986, there has been a massive surge of house building for the middle classes. Areas of empty housing units, the result of pure speculation activities, reached several hundred thousands of units by the mid-1990s.

At the turn of the millennium, the urban agglomeration held *ca.* 12 million persons. The plan for establishing new towns has been scaled down, the results of these being much inferior to what was envisaged. The idea of balancing living units and industrial or artisanal units in these places is one check to their growth; they function at the price of the daily movement across the city of thousands of employees. If, with regard to population, Cairo is far behind the greatest cities of the world (fifteenth in 1990), it is one of the most dense, with *ca.* 250 persons per hectare. As a reaction to the inconveniences brought into being by this situation, a new form of development in the desert zone—houses or small properties grouped in an enclosure—appeared towards the end of the 1990s. It has caused a very rapid growth in the surface area of the agglomeration. In favour of these extensions, the groups of population become more homogeneous, but the distances between those living in security and the rest continue to deepen.

Bibliography: M. Clerget, *Le Caire, étude de géographie urbaine et d'histoire économique*, Cairo 1932-4; J. Abu-Lughod, *Cairo. 1001 Years of the city victorious*, Princeton 1971; *Colloque international sur l'histoire du Caire*, DDR 1972; J. Berque and M. Al-Chakka, *La Gamaliyya depuis un siècle: essai d'histoire sociale d'un quartier du Caire*, in *REI*, xlii/1 (1974), 45-99; R. Ilbert, *Héliopolis, Le Caire 1905-1922, genèse d'une ville*, Paris 1981; *Lettres d'information de l'Observatoire urbain du Caire contemporain*, nos. 1-49, Cairo 1985-2001; D. Stewart, *Cities in the desert: the Egyptian new town program*, in *Annals of the Association of American Geographers*, lxxxvi (1986), 459-80; J.-C. Depaule *et alii*, *Actualité de l'habitat ancien au Caire, le Rabʿ Qizlar*, Cairo 1985; *Les villes nouvelles en Égypte*, Cairo 1987; G. El Kadi, *L'urbanisation spontanée au Caire*, Tours 1987; G. Meyer, *Kairo. Entwicklungsprobleme einer Metropole der dritten Welt*, Cologne 1989; E.R. Toledano, *State and society in mid-nineteenth-century Egypt*, Cambridge 1990; A. Raymond, *Le Caire*, Paris 1993, 287-368; J. Gertel (gen. ed.), *The metropolitan food system of Cairo*, Fribourg 1995; D. Singerman, *Avenues of participation: family, politics, and networks in urban quarters of Cairo*, Princeton 1995; J.-L. Arnaud, *Le Caire, mise en place d'une ville moderne 1867-1907*, Arles 1998; E. Denis, *Croissance urbaine et dynamique socio-spatiale: Le Caire de 1950 à 1990*, in *L'espace géographique*, ii (1998), 129-42; Raymond *et alii*, *Le Caire*, Paris 2000, 361-464, with map and numerous illustrations. (J.-L. Arnaud)

D. 8. The British occupation and the Egyptian parliamentary monarchy, 1882-1952.

Great Britain's post-1882 occupation of Egypt was a classic case of indirect colonial domination. Formally, Egypt remained a province of the Ottoman Empire ruled by a Khedive [see khidīw] selected from the family of Muḥammad ʿAlī (Muḥammad Tawfīḳ 1882-92; his son ʿAbbās Ḥilmī II [*q.v.*] 1892-1914). A bureaucratic apparatus staffed overwhelmingly by Egyptians and members of the polyglot élite that had emerged over the course of the 19th century administered the day-to-day affairs of the country. They did so, however, under British supervision and in accord with British directives. A British military garrison was the ultimate guarantor of British control. The key British official in Egypt was its Consul-General. British policy and the course of Egyptian development were shaped particularly by the first Consul-General Sir Evelyn Baring, later Lord Cromer (1883-1907); Cromer's successors Sir Eldon Gorst (1907-11) and Sir Herbert Kitchener (1911-14) had shorter tenures and less impact. At lower levels, British advisers were gradually appointed to different Egyptian ministries and British nationals employed in the Khedivial bureaucracy.

Under this "veiled protectorate" from 1882 to 1914, Egypt experienced considerable economic growth but little structural change. Financial stabilisation, agricultural expansion and the maintenance of security were the main concerns of Egypt's British overlords. Egypt's financial situation was stabilised through the reduction of government expenditures and a new international agreement for debt repayment; the construction of new irrigation works contributed to a doubling of the total value of Egypt's agricultural output between 1886-7 and 1912-13; and the rough edges of Khedivial administration were smoothed under British supervision (e.g. the abolition of compulsory peasant labour on public works projects). On the other hand, little was done to encourage the development of an industrial base under the British. Egypt's social structure changed little between 1882 and 1914. The landed élite which had emerged earlier in the century consolidated its position and expanded its holdings after 1882, and the European/Levantine population which had become prominent in trade and banking under Muḥammad ʿAlī's successors continued to dominate the commercial and financial sectors of the economy.

Under the compliant Khedive Muḥammad Tawfīḳ, there was little overt opposition to British domination. ʿAbbās Ḥilmī II was more assertive, providing financial support for opposition newspapers and encouraging the formation of nationalist secret societies among Egyptian youth. Nationalist sentiment and activism became more pronounced in the decade prior to World War I. The catalyst was the Dinsh̲āway incident of 1906, when an altercation between a hunting party of British soldiers and Egyptian peasants near the Delta village of Dinsh̲āway resulted in one soldier dying and led to the arrest, trial by military tribunal, and subsequent execution, imprisonment, and public whipping of the peasants involved. Dinsh̲āway is credited with galvanising Egyptian opposition to the British occupation. Several political parties were formed in 1907, the most important being the firmly anti-occupation *al-Ḥizb al-waṭanī* led by the lawyer Muṣṭafā Kāmil [*q.v.*] and the more gradualist *Ḥizb al-umma*, whose chief spokesman was the journalist Aḥmad Luṭfī al-Sayyid [see luṭfī al-sayyid]. Despite a higher level of Egyptian opposition to occupation thereafter, Great Britain's position in Egypt was not significantly eroded before 1914.

Major change occurred during and after World War I. The entry of the Ottoman Empire into the war in late 1914 had immediate repercussions for Egypt. In December 1914 Great Britain severed the Ottoman connection by declaring a British Protectorate over Egypt. Simultaneously, it deposed the pro-Ottoman Khedive ʿAbbās Ḥilmī II, appointing his uncle Ḥusayn Kāmil [*q.v.*] as titular ruler with the new title of Sultan. The latter was succeeded by his brother Aḥmad Fuʾād [see FUʾĀD AL-AWWAL] in 1917.

The war itself generated massive pressures as well as new expectations within Egypt. Forced sales of grain and animals to British forces operating in the area; the use of Egyptian labourers to construct military facilities; wartime inflation; the behaviour of British and Imperial troops temporarily garrisoned in the country; not least Allied rhetoric pledging self-determination for subjugated peoples after the war: all these contributed to Egyptian discontent with the new Protectorate. On 13 November 1918 a delegation of Egyptian notables led by the lawyer-judge Saʿd Zag̲h̲lūl [*q.v.*] visited the High Commissioner, Sir Reginald Wingate, to request Egyptian representation at the Paris Peace Conference. Over the winter of 1918-19 Zag̲h̲lūl and associates organised a broadly-based nationalist front, the Wafd [*q.v.*] or "delegation", committed to working for Egyptian independence. When in March 1919 the British arrested Zag̲h̲lūl and two of his colleagues, Egypt exploded in protest. Daily demonstrations and work stoppages brought normal life to a standstill in Egyptian cities; the countryside witnessed attacks on British personnel and communications facilities.

The Revolution of 1919 set in motion a process of political change which eventually brought Egypt formal independence. The turbulence of 1919 inaugurated three years of negotiations between the British government and different Egyptian notables (sometimes the Wafd, sometimes ministers supported by the Sultan, Fuʾād) aimed at defining a new Anglo-Egyptian relationship. After three years of futile discussions, in February 1922 the British issued a unilateral declaration of Egyptian independence. It was ringed with qualifiers, however, the British reserving the four areas, those of Imperial communications, the defence of Egypt, the status of foreign minorities and the Sudan, as matters of British concern. But at last Egypt had independence—of a sort.

From 1922 to 1952, Egypt was a technically independent parliamentary monarchy. Sultan Fuʾād became King Fuʾād in 1922 and reigned until his death in 1936; he was succeeded by his son Fārūḳ [*q.v.* in Suppl.] from 1936 to 1952. A constitution establishing a parliamentary system of government, but reserving significant powers for the monarch, was drafted in 1923. An electoral law of the same year provided for a Chamber of Deputies elected by male sufferage and a partially-elected, partially-appointed Chamber of Notables. Egypt's first parliamentary elections in December 1923-January 1924 saw the Wafd emerge triumphant.

The dynamics of the parliamentary monarchy have often been described as a triangular struggle among the King, the British and the Wafd. The Wafd, the nation's premier popular movement at least through the interwar period, won every relatively free parliamentary election yet held ministerial office for only somewhat over eight of the 28-plus years from 1924 to 1952. Egypt was more often governed by "minority" parties of non-Wafdists or Wafdist dissidents ruling with the covert or overt backing of the King. British influence rested primarily on the continued presence of British troops in Egypt, and was exercised through the British High Commissioner (from 1936, the British Ambassador) meeting regularly with Egyptian Prime Ministers and rendering advice which the latter disregarded at the risk of incurring British opposition to their continued tenure in office. From its inception, the Egyptian parliamentary order was a flawed system characterised by the domination of politics by an élite, electoral corruption and frequent turnover in office, and—at least until after World War II—by a neglect of socio-economic adjustment or reform on the part of the country's politically dominant upper class. On the other hand, the period of the parliamentary monarchy was also one of political pluralism, of considerable freedom of expression, and of cultural efflorescence, as a galaxy of prominent intellectuals engaged in spirited debate on the relative merits of Egypt's inherited Arabo-Islamic culture versus patterns of social and political life modelled on those of the West.

The shortcomings of the parliamentary monarchy became more pronounced over time. The 1920s were years of economic prosperity and relative political optimism. The 1930s were a darker era marked by economic depression and extended periods of more overt royal autocracy. A Wafdist interlude in office in 1936-7 witnessed the main political development of the decade, the conclusion of the Anglo-Egyptian Treaty of Alliance in 1936 which regularised but did not totally eliminate the British military presence in Egypt. The years of the Second World War from 1939 to 1945 saw more overt British interference in the country's political life. Of particular importance was the "incident" of 4 February 1942, when British tanks surrounded the Egyptian Palace and threatened King Fārūḳ with forced abdication unless he complied with a British ultimatum to install the by-then more pro-British Wafd in office. The incident served to discredit both the Wafd, now seen as willing to accept British support in its quest for public office, and the King who had bowed to British power. The postwar years were ones of great political turmoil. Labour troubles and peasant unrest perturbed urban and rural Egypt respectively; anti-British demonstrations and agitation over the Arab-Jewish clash in neighbouring Palestine added to the turbulence of the later 1940s; deep-seated animosity between the supporters of rival political tendencies produced a wave of political violence, including the assassination of two prime ministers and of the charismatic leader of the anti-parliamentary Muslim Brotherhood (*al-Ik̲h̲wān al-Muslimūn* [*q.v.*]), Ḥasan al-Bannāʾ [*q.v.*], between 1945 and 1949; and in late 1951 to early 1952, the Wafd, once again in office, terminated the Anglo-Egyptian Treaty of Alliance and mounted a guerrilla campaign to pressure the British out of their remaining military base in the Suez Canal zone. The culmination of postwar unrest came on "Black Saturday", 26 January 1952, when huge crowds, angered by a British massacre of Egyptian police in the city of Ismāʿīliyya on the previous day, surged through Cairo, and organised bands of incendiaries undertook the systematic torching of commercial, primarily Western-owned, establishments in the city. The conventional narrative of 20th-century Egyptian history portrays the parliamentary monarchy as politically discredited and morally exhausted by 1952.

Bibliography: General works in Western languages which cover all or most of the 1882-1952 period include J. Berque, *Egypt, imperialism and revolution*, London 1972; M.W. Daly (ed.), *The Cambridge history of Egypt. II. Modern Egypt from 1517* to the end of the twentieth century, Cambridge 1998; P.J. Vatikiotis, *The modern history of Egypt*, London and New York 1969. The classic nationalist account of the politics of the era is in the works of ʿAbd al-Raḥmān al-Rāfiʿī, *al-Thawra al-ʿurābiyya wa ʾl-iḥtilāl al-indjilīzī*, Cairo 1937; *Muṣṭafā Kāmil*, Cairo 1950; *Muḥammad Farīd*, Cairo 1948; *Thawrat sanat 1919*, 2 vols. Cairo 1946; *Fī aʿḳāb al-thawra al-miṣriyya*, 3 vols. Cairo 1947-51; and *Muḳaddimat thawrat 23 Yulyū 1952*, Cairo 1957. For the period from 1882 to 1914, see esp. Lord Cromer, *Modern Egypt*, 2 vols. London 1908; P. Mansfield, *The British in Egypt*, London and New York 1971; Yūnān Labīb Rizḳ, *al-Ḥayāt al-ḥizbiyya fī Miṣr fī ʿahd al-iḥtilāl al-bīrīṭānī, 1882-1914*, Cairo 1970; Afaf Lutfi al-Sayyid, *Egypt and Cromer. A study in Anglo-Egyptian relations*, New York 1969; R.L. Tignor, *Modernization and British colonial rule in Egypt, 1882-1914*, Princeton 1966. For Egyptian political life under the parliamentary monarchy, see Ṭāriḳ al-Bishrī, *al-Ḥaraka al-siyāsiyya fī Miṣr 1945-1952*, Cairo 1972; Selma Botman, *Egypt from independence to revolution, 1919-1952*, Syracuse 1991; M. Colombe, *L'évolution de l'Égypte*, Paris 1951; Marius Deeb, *Party politics in Egypt. The Wafd and its rivals, 1919-1939*, London 1979; ʿĀṣim al-Dasūḳī, *Kibār mullāk al-arāḍī al-zirāʿiyya wa-dawruhūm fī ʾl-mudjtamʿa al-miṣriyya, 1914-1952*, Cairo 1975; Afaf Lutfi al-Sayyid Marsot, *Egypt's liberal experiment, 1922-1936*, Berkeley, etc. 1977; ʿAbd al-ʿAẓīm Muḥammad Ramaḍān, *Taṭawwur al-ḥaraka al-waṭaniyya fī Miṣr min sanat 1918 ilā sanat 1936*, Cairo 1968; idem, *Taṭawwur al-ḥaraka al-waṭaniyya fī Miṣr min sanat 1937 ilā sanat 1948*, 2 vols. Cairo 1973; Janice Terry, *Cornerstone of Egyptian political power. The Wafd, 1919-1952*, London 1982.

More specific studies include J. Beinin and Z. Lockman, *Workers on the Nile. Nationalism, communism, Islam, and the Egyptian working class*, Princeton 1987; E. Davis, *Challenging colonialism. Bank Misr and Egyptian industrialization, 1920-1941*, Princeton 1983; I. Gershoni and J. Jankowski, *Egypt, Islam, and the Arabs. The search for Egyptian nationhood, 1900-1930*, New York 1986; eidem, *Redefining the Egyptian nation, 1930-1945*, Cambridge 1995; Muḥammad Shafīḳ Ghurbāl, *Taʾrīkh al-mufāwaḍāt al-miṣriyya al-bīrīṭāniyya, 1882-1936*, Cairo 1952; E. Goldberg, *Tinker, tailor, and textile worker. Class and politics in Egypt, 1930-1954*, Berkeley 1986; J.P. Jankowski, *Egypt's young rebels. Young Egypt, 1933-1952*, Stanford 1975; Gudrun Kramer, *The Jews in modern Egypt, 1914-1952*, Seattle 1989; R.P. Mitchell, *The Society of the Muslim Brothers*, London 1969; R.L. Tignor, *State, private enterprise, and economic change in Egypt, 1918-1952*, Princeton 1984. See also ḤIZB. i. (J. JANKOWSKI)

D. 9. Republican Egypt 1952 to the present.

On 22-3 July 1952, a military coup effectively brought the era of the parliamentary monarchy to an end. The seizure of power was carried out by a clandestine movement within the army, the "Free Officers" (*al-ḍubbāṭ al-aḥrār*); the key figure in the movement was Colonel Djamāl ʿAbd al-Nāṣir [*q.v.* in Suppl.]. From July 1952 onwards, executive decisions were made by a committee of leading Free Officers, the Revolutionary Command Council (RCC).

A new political order emerged only gradually. On 26 July 1952 the sybaritic King Fārūḳ [*q.v.* in Suppl.] was hustled into exile. At first a civilian ministry held formal power. By September, General Muḥammad Nadjīb [*q.v.*], an associate but not a core member of the Free Officers, was appointed Prime Minister.

Existing political parties were banned in January 1953. On 18 June 1953 the monarchy was formally abolished and Egypt declared a Republic; Muḥammad Nadjīb became its first president. The crucial phase in the consolidation of the military régime came in early 1954, when President Nadjīb, supported by remnants of the old political order, mounted a challenge to continued RCC rule. In a month-long crisis marked by street clashes between partisans of the two camps, ʿAbd al-Nāṣir and the RCC outmanoeuvred Nadjīb and his supporters. By the end of 1954, after an abortive assassination attempt on ʿAbd al-Nāṣir by members of the Muslim Brotherhood (*al-Ikhwān al-Muslimūn* [*q.v.*]) provided the occasion for a crackdown on the Brotherhood, the military group reigned supreme in Egypt. A new constitution promulgated in January 1956 established a presidential form of government for Egypt. The constitution was ratified by popular referendum in June 1956; at the same time, Djamāl ʿAbd al-Nāṣir's nomination as President was also overwhelmingly approved.

There was occasional formal but little substantive change in Egypt's political structure from 1956 to 1970. ʿAbd al-Nāṣir remained President until his death in September 1970. The unexpected union of Egypt and Syria in the United Arab Republic (UAR) in early 1958 necessitated a new provisional constitution and the expansion of the National Assembly to include Syrian representatives; but real authority remained in the hands of ʿAbd al-Nāṣir. Syria's secession from the UAR in September 1961 prompted further adjustments. A Charter of National Action of 1962 now specified a socialist agenda for the United Arab Republic, as Egypt continued to be known until 1971. Another provisional constitution was promulgated in 1964, to remain in effect until 1971.

The years from 1952 to 1970 witnessed major changes in Egypt's economic policy, social structure, and international orientation. A policy of agrarian reform was inaugurated in 1952 and extended thereafter. By 1970, something over 800,000 *faddān*s of agricultural land, roughly one-eighth of the cultivated area, had been taken from large landlords and redistributed to some 340,000 peasant families. The foreign interests which had controlled much of the commercial sector of the economy were abruptly dispossessed as a consequence of the international crises of the later 1950s, their holdings now coming under state ownership. The heights of the domestically-owned urban economy also came under state control in the early 1960s, when Arab Socialism became the slogan of the UAR and the government nationalised much domestically-owned business and industry. The resulting economic structure was one of a privately-owned but state-directed agricultural sector and a huge state-owned public sector controlling most large-scale enterprises in the commercial and industrial sectors of the urban economy.

The social policies of the ʿAbd al-Nāṣir years were distinctly populist. The new revolutionary régime made major efforts to bring the benefits of modernity to the mass of Egyptians. Educational facilities were rapidly expanded; health care was extended to the countryside through a network of rural health clinics; new laws relating to hours of work, minimum pay, and social security entitlements attempted to improve the standard of living of Egypt's labouring population.

Externally, the ʿAbd al-Nāṣir years witnessed dramatic shifts. A negotiated Anglo-Egyptian agreement of 1954 arranged for the withdrawal of the last British troops from Egyptian soil in 1956. The mid-1950s witnessed major transformations in Egypt's international position. Egypt broke with the Western powers and turned to the Soviet bloc for military and economic assistance; simultaneously, it assumed a leadership role in both the Arab nationalist movement and the Afro-Asian bloc of non-aligned nations. Successful resistance to armed attack by Israel, Great Britain, and France in the Suez Crisis of late 1956 consolidated D̲j̲amāl ʿAbd al-Nāṣir's position as a major figure in world affairs. Thereafter he was unquestionably the leading personality in inter-Arab politics (leading to Syria's request for unity with Egypt in the UAR in 1958), as well as one of the most influential spokesmen in African and non-aligned politics. ʿAbd al-Nāṣir's regional dominance and international prominence eroded over the course of the 1960s. Syria's secession from the UAR in 1961 was a huge setback; inconclusive involvement in a prolonged civil war in Yemen from 1962 onwards drained the resources and prestige of the UAR; military defeat by Israel and the loss of the Sinai Peninsula in June 1967 irreparably damaged ʿAbd al-Nāṣir's aura as an Arab champion. Suffering from an unresolved military confrontation with Israel and a stagnant economy, the later 1960s were difficult years for Egypt/the UAR. The massive outpouring of Egyptian grief upon his death in September 1970 notwithstanding, D̲j̲amāl ʿAbd al-Nāṣir left a difficult legacy for his successor.

The Vice-President Anwar al-Sādāt [*q.v.*] assumed the presidency of the UAR upon ʿAbd al-Nāṣir's death. A popular referendum in October 1970 ratified Sādāt's accession. A veteran member of the Free Officers movement, at first Sādāt governed under ʿAbd al-Nāṣir's shadow. Rivalry with other members of ʿAbd al-Nāṣir's entourage and public discontent with the ongoing situation of no war–no peace with Israel marked the early 1970s. Sādāt consolidated his personal position only in October 1973, when a combined Egyptian-Syrian attack upon Israeli positions in the territories Israel had occupied in June 1967 created a new strategic situation in the region. From late 1973 onwards Sādāt was his own man, free to move Egypt in new directions.

He did so with a vengeance. Change was most pronounced in international relations. Sādāt signalled part of his orientation in 1971, when a new constitution changed the country's name from the United Arab Republic to the Arab Republic of Egypt. Over the course of the 1970s Egypt exchanged its reliance on the Soviet Union for material assistance and diplomatic support from the United States; abandoned the Nāṣirist commitment to Arab nationalism; and by 1979 made formal peace with Israel, in the process obtaining the return of the Sinai Peninsula to Egyptian control.

Shifts from the prevailing domestic patterns of the ʿAbd al-Nāṣir years were less sweeping but nonetheless appreciable. In the mid-1970s Sādāt presided over a limited liberalisation of Egypt's political system, dismantling part of the Nāṣirist security apparatus and allowing a degree of political pluralism including a greater measure of press freedom and the formation of opposition political parties. The scope for political expression became constricted again in the later 1970s, when growing criticism of his policies led to less tolerance by the regime of opposition voices and groups.

This political liberalisation was part of a more general "Opening" (*al-infitāḥ*) of Egypt under Sādāt; an opening to Western investment and expertise, to oil country investment, and to the previously-marginalised private sector of the economy. In the mid-1970s, the formally socialist orientation of the 1960s was jettisoned as new legislation gave incentives to foreign investors and to greater scope to private capital. Socially, the era of the Opening was one of an accentuation of class cleavages between Egypt's more affluent upper and middle classes, who were the main beneficiaries of the country's more open economic system, and the mass of Egyptians suffering from accelerating inflation and a decline in social benefits. This deepening social schism forms part of the context for the growth of Islamist activism and militancy in Egypt over the 1970s, a phenomenon which eventually cost Sādāt his life.

On 6 October 1981 Anwar al-Sādāt was assassinated by a group of Islamist militants. The Vice-President Ḥusnī Mubārak ascended to the presidency. A referendum in October 1981 ratified his accession; subsequent referenda in 1987, 1993, and 1999 extended Mubārak's term in office.

By and large, the hallmark of the Mubārak presidency has been continuity. Under Mubārak, Egypt has maintained its generally pro-Western stance, its strategic alliance with and material reliance upon the United States, and its peace with Israel. Sādāt's economic approach has also been echoed by Mubārak. The main features of the Opening remained in effect through the 1980s and accelerated in the 1990s as Egypt, under pressure from its international supporters and the IMF, moved more decisively towards a free-market economy. The early 1990s witnessed further measures of economic liberalisation in the line with IMF strictures (e.g. the elimination of many currency controls; accelerated deregulation; and a reduction in state subsidies), whilst the later 1990s saw a concerted effort to privatise public sector enterprises. The results have been mixed. Egypt's macro-economic performance over the 1990s was a robust one. The country's debt burden was reduced to managable levels; inflation was largely tamed; the rate of economic growth improved over that of the 1980s. The micro performance was more troubling. The rate of unemployment remained high; wages formed a decreasing share of GDP; and the reduction of state subsidies effected particularly the standard of living of poorer Egyptians.

A more relaxed political atmosphere prevailed in Mubārak's early years in power. The scope for political expression decreased thereafter. Greater political protest and violence in the later 1980s in turn led to more governmental repression of opposition voices and groups. Faced with a low-level Islamist insurgency in Egypt's sprawling shanty-towns and in the economically depressed countryside of Upper Egypt in the early and mid-1990s, the government asserted greater and greater control over political opinion and activism. Emergency laws first enacted in 1981 were renewed through the decade; Islamist violence was met with massive state repression and the brutalisation of families and communities suspected of harbouring militants; non-violent critics of the régime have been subjected to government harassment and muzzling; and the parliamentary elections of 1990 were boycotted by opposition groups in protest against electoral restrictions, and those of 1995 were marked by the systematic repression of the opposition as well as by unprecedented electoral violence and blatant fraud. Egypt at the close of the 1990s may have turned an economic corner, at least in terms of national economic indicators if not of popular well-being; its political situation, on the other hand, appeared to be one of increasing governmental authoritarianism and the progressive alienation of its leadership from the bulk of the population.

Bibliography: General studies surveying much or all of the post-1952 period include M.W. Daly (ed.), *The Cambridge history of Egypt. II. Modern Egypt from 1517 to the end of the twentieth century*, Cambridge 1998; D. Hopwood, *Egypt. Politics and society, 1945-1990*, ³London 1991; P.J. Vatikiotis, *The modern history of Egypt*, ⁴London and Baltimore, 1991.

The fullest Western-language biographies of ʿAbd al-Nāṣir are those of J. Lacouture, *Nasser*, Paris 1971, A. Nutting, *Nasser*, London and New York 1972 and R. Stephens, *Nasser. A political biography*, London and New York 1971; for a recent and more incisive portrait, see P. Woodward, *Nasser*, London 1992. For political developments between 1952 and 1970, see Anouar Abdel-Malek, *Égypte, société militaire*, Paris 1962; Nazih Ayubi, *Bureaucracy and politics in contemporary Egypt*, London 1980; K.J. Beattie, *Egypt during the Nasser years*, Boulder 1994; L. Binder, *In a moment of enthusiasm. Political power and the second stratum in Egypt*, Chicago 1978; R. Hrair Dekmejian, *Egypt under Nasser*, Albany 1971; J. Gordon, *Nasser's blessed movement: Egypt's Free Officers and the July Revolution*, New York 1992; Aḥmad Ḥamrūsh, *Ḳiṣṣat thawrat 23 Yulyū*, 5 vols. Cairo 1983-4; P.J. Vatikiotis, *The Egyptian army in politics*, Bloomington 1961; idem, *Nasser and his generation*, New York 1978; J. Waterbury, *The Egypt of Nasser and Sadat. The political economy of two regimes*, Princeton 1983.

Accounts of Egypt's international relations under ʿAbd al-Nāṣir include Muhammad Abd el-Wahab Sayed-Ahmed, *Nasser and American foreign policy, 1952-1956*, Cairo 1991; Fawzi Gerges, *The superpowers and the Middle East, 1955-1967*, Boulder 1994; Muḥammad Ḥasanayn Haykal, *al-Infidjār: 1967*, Cairo 1990; idem, *Sanawat al-ghulyān*, Cairo 1988; idem, *Milaffat al-Suwīs*, Cairo 1986; Mohamed Hassanein Heikal, *The Cairo documents*, New York 1973; M. Kerr, *The Arab Cold War. Gamal ʿAbd al-Nasir and his rivals, 1958-1970*, ³London 1971. Egypt's economic and social evolution under ʿAbd al-Nāṣir are the focus of Mahmoud Abdel-Fadil, *The political economy of Nasserism*, London 1980; Hamied Ansari, *Egypt. The stalled society*, Albany 1986; R. Baker, *Egypt's uncertain revolution under Nasser and Sadat*, Cambridge, Mass. 1978; C. Issawi, *Egypt in revolution*, London 1963; and R. Mabro, *The Egyptian economy, 1952-1972*, Oxford 1974.

Sādāt and the Opening are discussed in R. Baker, *Sadat and after*, Cambridge, Mass. 1990; Mohamed Hassanein Heikal, *Autumn of fury. The assassination of Sadat*, New York 1983; R. Hinnebusch, *Egyptian politics under Sadat*, Cambridge 1985; D. Hirst and Irene Beeson, *Sadat*, London 1981; G. Kepel, *Muslim extremism in Egypt. The Prophet and Pharaoh*, Berkeley, etc. 1986; Yoram Meital, *Egypt's struggle for peace. Continuity and change, 1967-1977*, Gainesville 1998; Anwar El Sadat, *In search of identity*, New York 1977; J. Waterbury, *The Egypt of Nasser and Sadat. The political economy of two regimes*, Princeton 1983.

Useful works on the Mubārak presidency include Sana Abed-Kotob and D. Sullivan, *Islam in contemporary Egypt. Civil society versus the state*, Boulder 1999; Nazih Ayubi, *The state and public policies in Egypt since Sadat*, Reading 1991; Diane Singerman, *Avenues of participation. Family, politics, and networks in urban quarters of Cairo*, Princeton 1995; and R. Springborg, *Mubarak's Egypt. Fragmentation of the political order*, Boulder 1989.

Economic studies relevant for the post-1970 period are Galal Amin, *Egypt's economic predicament, 1960-1990*, Leiden 1995; B. Hansen, *Egypt and Turkey. The political economy of poverty, equity, and growth*, Oxford 1991; Iliya Harik, *Economic policy reform in Egypt*, Gainesville 1997; Marcia Pripstein Posusney, *Labor and the state in Egypt, 1952-1994*, New York 1997.

(J. Jankowski)

MIZĀDJ (A., pl. *amzidja*), lit. "mixture", a basic term of mediaeval Islamic medicine, to be translated as "temperament, balance of elements within the body".

One has to go back to the fundamental features of human physiology as conceived by the Arabic physicians, although one cannot speak of a unified body of knowledge here, since the concepts can vary perceptibly from one medical expert to another. The great sources of Islamic medicine systematically devote a chapter to the *mizādj*, e.g. ʿAlī b. al-ʿAbbās [*q.v.*] al-Madjūsī's *K. al-Malakī*, Abū Sahl al-Masīḥī's [*q.v.*] *K. al-Miʾa fi 'l-ṭibb* and Ibn Sīnā's [*q.v.*] *al-Ḳānūn fi 'l-ṭibb*. As well as being part of physiology, the *mizādj* is directly involved in certain processes of morbidity. The physicians, like the philosophers, thought that the human body (like every other body in the world) was composed of four simple, homogeneous elements (*arkān, ustuḳuṣṣāt*): earth, water, air and fire. This doctrine is already central for ʿAlī b. Rabban al-Ṭabarī [*q.v.*], author in the 3rd/9th century of the *Firdaws al-ḥikma*.

With these elements were associated specific qualities: cold, dryness, humidity and heat. Thus these four primordial elements go to make up all living beings according to proportions which vary from one being to another. Their interaction, their connections in more or less equal measure, the effects of their interpenetration on the economy of the human body and the individual's general state are consequently called *mizādj*, a term corresponding to the *krasis* of the Ancient Greek physicians. A man's *mizādj* will depend on the balance between the different elements and their qualities. Hence he will be balanced (*muʿtadil*) when those are present in the organism in proportions corresponding to the norm, and from this, they are guarantors of an individual's health. He will be considered in a state of disequilibrium (*khāridj ʿan al-iʿtidāl*, Grk. *dyskrasis*) and, as a result, liable to some pathological occurrence, when a certain quality (cold, heat, etc.) or a certain element (watery, fiery, etc.) is in excess of or is below the norm.

Hence the great physicians pay great attention to the necessity of keeping the *mizādj* of their patients in equilibrium, since all "disequilibrium" was, in their eyes, the source of illness. Thus they recommend moderation in all things (food, drink, sleeping, sexual relations, etc.) in order to avoid *dyskrasis*. One says that a certain patient's temperament is hot if the fiery element predominates in him. Amongst certain physicians, such as Ibn Sīnā, this theory of temperament reached a high degree of elaboration, since, as well as taking into account internal aspects like the balance proper to each man (a kind of ideal balance) and to each vital organ (the heart, necessarily hot since it is the seat of vital heat, the brain, the liver, etc.), this physician-philosopher brought in external factors such as climate, the people to whom the individual belongs, age and sex (thus man is hotter and drier than woman). Thus, concerning the proper temperament for each age of one's life (*mizādj al-asnān*), the physicians considered that the "capital" of inner heat (*ḥarāra gharīziyya*) which a man has at birth, goes on decreasing when that person reaches the end of his life. They considered as proof of this the cold that old persons feel and that the physician can observe at the time of palpation, not to mention the coldness of a corpse after death. The corollary of the *mizādj* is the theory of humours, which the Greek and then the Arabic physicians developed. Even today, such ideas remain strongly connected in the popular imagination, since we speak of a person having a sanguine, a hot, a phlegmatic or a choleric temperament.

Bibliography: 1. Sources. ʿAlī Rabban al-Ṭabarī, *Firdaws al-ḥikma*, ed. M.Z. Siddiqi, Berlin 1928; Abū Sahl al-Masīḥī, *K. al-Miʾa fi 'l-ṭibb*, ed. F. Sanagustin, 2 vols. Damascus 2000; Ibn Sīnā, *Ḳānūn*, 3 vols. Cairo 1877.

2. Studies. M. Meyerhof, *An Arabic compendium of medico-philosophical definitions*, in *Isis*, x (1928), 340-9; idem, *ʿAlī at-Ṭabarī's Paradise of Wisdom, one of the oldest compendiums of medicine*, in *ibid.*, xvi (1931), 6-54; M. Ullmann, *Islamic medicine*, Edinburgh 1978, 56-60; G. Anawati, *Ishām Ibn Sīnā fi taḳaddum al-ʿulūm*, in *Ibn Sīnā bi-munāsabat al-dhikrā al-alfiyya li-mawtihi*, Damascus 1980, 72-3; S. Hussain, *Body fluids according to Avicenna*, in *Bull. Indian Inst. for the Hist. of Medicine*, xiii (1983), 52-8.

(F. Sanagustin)

MOGADOR [see al-suwayra].

MOZAMBIQUE, Islam in.

(a) The early period. For this, see mozambique, in Vol. VII.

(b) The 19th and earlier 20th centuries. The 19th century was for Islam a period of revival and *djihād* aided by the opening up of shipping across the Indian Ocean and the trade routes into Central Africa. Already at the beginning of the 19th century it was estimated that there were 15,000 Muslims in the Cape Delgado region and some 20,000 in the coastal hinterland of Mozambique Island. According to oral tradition, one Musa Momadi from Angoche, as a young man accompanied a relative who was a *sharīf* and a *ḥādjdjī* on an extended *daʿwa* expedition into the interior. His relative was concerned with converting the people he came across, including the Yao [*q.v.*] who by this time had migrated as far as the Shire valley. In light of this sort of occurence, it is not surprising to find the governor of Mozambique commenting on the extraordinary advance and infiltration of Islam in the interior in 1852. On Musa's return in the mid-1850s the records indicate that he led the defence of Angoche. By 1877 he controlled an area which covered most of the coast from Mozambique Island to Licungo River and stretching 100 miles inland. His successors repulsed Portuguese attacks until 1910. As in other parts of the coast, the diffusion was primarily undertaken by people of mixed Arab and African blood. It was Portuguese policy to supply *mestizos* and *wajoge* with goods so as to procure slaves. This came to an end with the anti-slavery proclamation of 26 May 1877. The successful penetration is indicated by the fact that by the 1870s, women in their mid-twenties are recorded as having Muslim names. In addition to the Makua, the Yao and the Machemba had accepted Islam. In the interior beyond Mogabo, the Mualia chief and elders observed the Islamic practices, as did Mtarika, Cuirassio and minor chiefs like Cattur in the Luambala valley. To the north of them, Mataka represented an important centre of Islam. The Arab chief of Matibane was licensed to deal in slaves by the ex-governor Vasco Guedes de Carvalho e Menezes. Tavares, writing to the Overseas Ministry in Lisbon on 8 November 1862, mentions that the slave trade is in the hands of Arabs whose religion permits them to buy slaves. Likewise, Andrade Corvo writing to the Duke of Saldanha, the Portuguese Minister in London, on 11 March 1876 comments that, "It is easy for the Muslims to make religious proselytes among the finest and most energetic of the aboriginal races and in this way they get active and not very scrupulous agents to provide them with slaves." Chief Matapwiri living near Kalanji was reported as selling slaves in 1886. Indian Muslims played their part, particularly in Angoche, where a Swahili dynasty was in power well into the 20th century. The slavers in this region were primarily from Surat in western India, supplying the Persian and Arab markets. At this stage, Islamic doctrine was not observed in a pure form but was mixed with local traditions. It would seem that by the 1880s most major Yao chiefs had embraced Islam. Their settlements were centres for the spreading of Islam through Ḳurʾān schools. Coutinho records meeting Yao caravan leaders at Quelimane who claimed to be Muslims and who carried the Ḳurʾān carefully wrapped in a fold of their clothes. Coastal Muslims, however, ridiculed the Yaos who claimed to be Muslims, saying that they were *mushrikūn*. The growing Muslim presence is documented in a report from 1893 which shows that Muslims were active along the Licungo River and Maganja de Costa north of Quelimane. The reasons for the growing Islamisation were varied and complex, but had to do with closer associations with Muslim trading partners on the coast, and the increased prestige of Islam through the influence of the Bū Saʿīd [*q.v.*] dynasty and its representatives along the coast. The South African influence on the development during the latter part of the 19th century can be seen in the establishment of a *madrasa* in Lourenço Marques by Abū Bakr Effendi (d. 1880), a Kurdish scholar sent to the Cape in 1862.

At the beginning of the 20th century there were 15 mosques and 10 Ḳurʾān schools in the Angoche region. All the *monhes* were said to be able to write their own language in Arabic script. The Portuguese, in seeking to subdue the north, considered that Muslims and local Africans were making common cause and sacked Angoche in 1903. In spite of Portuguese efforts, Muslim communities with a Ḳurʾān school were a growing force in the hinterland in 1905. Islam was spread by Muslim traders, as well as *walimu*, *shurafāʾ* with their religio-magical knowledge and *mafundi* (artisans) using a hut, a veranda or the shade of a tree to teach the children.

The *ṭuruḳ* [see ṭarīḳa] in any organised form did not appear in Mozambique until the end of the 19th century. By that time both the Ḳādiriyya and the Shādhiliyya [*q.vv.*] were established on Mozambique Island. The latter was established by students who went to a school in Kilwa founded by Ḥusayn b. Maḥmūd, himself a *khalīfa* of a Ḥaḍramī *sharīf*. In 1896 a member of the Yashrutiyya [*q.v.*] settled in Mozambique. The Ḳādiriyya seems to have been established by ʿAlī Msemakweli, a Yao who was a *khalīfa* of Ḥusayn b. ʿAbd Allāh al-Muʿīn. He spread the order to northern Mozambique from Kilwa [*q.v.*]. The Ḳādiriyya Sadate, a branch of the Uwaysiyya [*q.v.*], was established in Mozambique in 1904 by ʿĪsā b. Aḥmad from Zanzibar. When ʿĪsā b. Aḥmad returned to Zanzibar in 1925 he handed over the leadership to a local Muslim by the name of Momade Arune (Muḥammad Hārūn). A sub-branch of the *ṭarīḳa* was founded in Angoche at this time. After Momade

Arune's death in 1929 the *ṭarīḳa* was split by leadership rivalries leading in 1934 to the formation of the Ḳādiriyya Ba<u>gh</u>dādī branch, and further splits followed over the next decades. Developments which facilitated the growth of Islam during the second decade of the 20th century included the construction of the railroad from Lumbo, on the mainland opposite Mozambique Island, which began in 1913; the advance of Indian Muslim merchants beyond the coast; and towards the end of World War I, the presence of a considerable number of Muslims in the British forces engaged in the war in German East Africa with Von Lettow-Vorbeck's forces. As a result, the *ṭuruḳ* established branches in the principal settlements such as Nampula and Cabo Delgado. Mosques were constructed for the men and *zawāyā* (enclosed spaces) for women. As in the rest of the East African coast, Muslims from different parts of the Muslim world arrived bringing a variety of cultural and sectarian backgrounds. This has had its repercussions into the present, so that Muslims in different parts of Mozambique have tended to be and are isolated from one another.

Indian Muslims had their own mosques which were well built and ornate. They had cemeteries for their own exclusive use and brought and supported their own *imāms* from India. They observed the ordinances of the Ḳur'ān and the *<u>Sh</u>arī'a* strictly. They avoided what was *ḥarām*, fulfilled the requirements of ablutions and frequented the mosque assiduously. The African and *mestizo* Muslims had their own mosques which were like thatched huts, hence indistinguishable from other huts. Their observance of Islam was less rigorous. Their attendances at mosques were less frequent and their prayers and recitations less perfect because of their ignorance of Arabic and the absence of any of the required texts. All male Muslims, whether Indian or African, practiced circumcision. They wore the *malaia*, also referred to as *cabaia*, and the *cofio* or a turban.

The statistics available indicate that there were around 66,000 Muslims in Mozambique in the mid-1950s. By then it was estimated that there were 1,956 Orientals and 15,188 Indians. At the end of the 20th century, estimates of Muslims in Mozambique vary between 10 and 16% in a population of 19 millions. Muslims in Mozambique consist of *monhes*, those from the Indian sub-continent, as well as *moors* who have an Arab or Turkish origin, and the Swahili. They looked to Zanzibar as the centre of Sunnī Islam and source of Islamic publications; they viewed the Bū Sa'īdī Sultan as their protector, remembering his name during Friday *<u>kh</u>uṭba*, even though he was theologically an Ibāḍī. The leader of the Ḳādiriyya Sadate between 1929 and 1963 referred to himself as the Sultan's representative to Mozambique.

Historically, Islamic revivalist movements have opposed colonial rule in northern Mozambique. In the 1920s, some Muslim leaders protested against the abuses of forced labour, low wages and land appropriation in the Quelimane area. From the 1930s onwards, Muslim Africans and various Indians organised themselves into interest groups which carried out political action under the cover of social, mutual aid, cultural and athletic activities. The situation became even more acute from 1942, when Mozambique became *Portugal Ultramar*. Forced labour, arbitrary taxation, the obligation to plant cash crops and the lack of social improvement, produced a serious discontent among the Africans which led to the awakening of a national consciousness.

By the 1960s, the isolation of Muslims in Mozambique was breaking down. Muslims were seeking education in Tanzania and Arabia. Islamic publications from Cairo and Mumbai were available and Muslims were keen to acquire literacy in Arabic. People were listening to Cairo radio and were becoming aware of their religious roots. Arab and Islamic records and tapes from Egypt were circulating. African nationalism, linked to Arab anti-Portuguese propaganda, was gaining ground among the Muslims. It seems possible that clandestine Islamic associations were being established as early as the 1950s.

Given the total absence of liberty to form political organisations under the Portuguese, African Mozambicans living abroad in Tanzania, Zimbabwe and Malawi came together in a common front and formed the Frente de Libertação de Moçambique (FRELIMO) in 1962. An armed struggle began in 1964, but not until after the 1974 coup d'état in Portugal did Mozambique gain its independence (1975). During this period, a colonial policy was designed to win the support of the Muslim community against the forces of FRELIMO, which the colonial authorities thought had alienated the Muslims because of its Marxist tendencies. The policy was to work through the Muslim religious leadership, i.e. the *ṭuruḳ*, which they considered a conservative, local force against more radical, internationally organised expressions of Islam bent on political subversion. The Portuguese authorities, capitalising on the new situation that arose after the abolition of the Sultanate of Zanzibar in 1963, utilised the new links between the Muslim leadership in Northern Mozambique with the Comoros and invited the Mufti there to settle disputes between the *ṭuruḳ*. They also embarked on publishing an official, Portuguese-language version of abstracts of al-Bu<u>kh</u>ārī's *Ṣaḥīḥ*. In view of the fact that the liberation struggle was predominantly centred on the north, it is not surprising that the Muslims of Indian origin who lived in the southern part of the colony and adhered to the Ḥanafī legal tradition, with their orientation to Durban and Karachi, did not play an important role.

Nevertheless, the Muslim presence and growing Islamic influence can be seen by the fact that FRELIMO's representative in Cairo was a Muslim by the name of Shaffrudin Muhammad Khan, and an office was also opened in Algiers. Islam's influence received a boost when various Arab countries offered to train the "freedom fighters", and some 130 of them were sent to Algeria. FRELIMO established international relations with the Arab League and the Organisation of the Islamic Conference. There is no mention in FRELIMO's educational programme of Ḳur'ān schools, but traditional institutions like the *poro/sande* institutions were acknowledged, and it is possible that, to some extent, Muslim influence may have been spread through these. The Indian Muslim communities which represent non-Sunnī groups such as the Ith<u>n</u>ā' A<u>sh</u>arī, Ismā'īlī <u>Kh</u>o<u>dj</u>as and Bohorās ran small-scale commercial ventures, bush trading centres and small shops in towns. As closed communities, they had hardly any contact with Africans, Europeans or other Indian groups. Some Asian students attended universities or professional courses at technical schools in Portugal.

(c) Independence and after.

After independence in 1975, the Muslim leadership which had co-operated with the colonial authorities was discredited. Some Muslim associations were banned in 1976, while those which had had restrictions imposed on them during the colonial period gained some freedom; but the civil war which erupted soon after independence and lasted until 1992 between FRELIMO as a Marxist-Leninist party and the Resistência National Moçambicana (RENAMO), which sought to bring democracy to Mozambique, did not serve the Muslims well. By 1980 Mozambican Muslim students in exile in Dar es Salaam denounced the repression of Islam by the new government. Until 1982 the régime showed hostility to organised religion in general. There was considerable harassment of Muslims, including throwing pigs into mosques. Virtually all religious communities lost property through nationalisation. Religious associations were forbidden and attempts made to prevent religious activities anywhere but in mosques. Attitudes began to change after the establishment of RENAMO. FRELIMO found that its treatment of Muslims provided reasons for both Saudi Arabi and ʿUmān to send supplies to RENAMO. South Africa and the Comoro Islands also served as conduits for supplying RENAMO in 1983-9. That situation made any allies, including the religious communities, acceptable. Thus in 1983 FRELIMO officially recognised the new national Council of Muslims Mozambique (CISLAMO). There seems to have been an enthusiastic attitude to religion in RENAMO circles. Their bases exhibited this in the form of mosques and churches. With the accession of Chissano in 1987, FRELIMO began a gradual restoration of social legitimacy to religious bodies of all kinds. In that year, Mozambique hosted the fifth Southern Africa Islamic Youth Conference. By mid-1988, confiscated properties were being returned. The situation improved further when article 19 of the 1975 constitution was changed in 1990 to state that "The state shall respect the activities of religious denominations in order to promote a climate of social understanding and tolerance and to strengthen national unity."

The elections of 1994 returned FRELIMO to power. In further attempts to gain the support of Muslims, FRELIMO recognised the Islamic holy days of *ʿĪd al-Aḍḥā* and *ʿĪd al-Fiṭr* as national holidays in 1996. But in the 1999 elections it is revealing that, out of FRELIMO's 133 deputies, only one seems to be a Muslim, whereas out of RENAMO's 117, 12 were Muslims.

By the end of the 1990s, Mozambique had become a member of the Organisation of the Islamic Conference (OIC), thus securing economic benefits. Tensions between the Ṣūfī leaders of the majority of Muslims in the north and the more radical reformers based in the south have led the former to split off from CISLAMO to form the Congres Islâmico.

Bibliography: J. de A. da Cunha, *Estudo acerca dos usos e costumes dos Banianes, Bethias, Parses, Mouro e Indigenes*, Lisbon 1885; E.J. de Vilhena, *A influencia islamica na costa oriental d'Africa*, in *Boletin da Sociedade de Geografia de Lisbon* (1906), 133-46, 166-80, 197-218; E. do C. Lupi, *Angoche. Breve memoria sobre uma das capitanias mores*, Lisbon 1907; E. Axelson, *South East Africa 1488-1530*, London 1940; A.A. de Andrade, *Relações de Moçambique Setecentista*, Lisbon 1955; F. Balsan, *À la recherche des Arabes sur les côtes du Nord Mozambique*, in *Monumenta II*, 57-62; D.J.S. Rebelo, *Short notes on an east Indian group in Mozambique: the Ismailian Moslem community*, in *South African Journal of Science*, lviii (2 Feb. 1962), 41-4; J.J. Goncalves, *Influência ârabo-islâmica em Moçambique*, in *O Mundo Arabo-Islamico eo Ultramar Portugues*, Lisbon 1962, 247-87; F.J. Peirone, *A tribu Ajaua do alto Niassa (Moçambique) e alguns aspectos do sua problematica neo-islamica*, Lisbon 1967; E. Mondlane, *The struggle for Mozambique*, Harmondsworth 1969; A. and B. Isaacman, *Mozambique. From colonialism to revolution 1900-1982. Islam in Mozambique (East Africa)*, in *Islamic Literature*, xv, no. 9 (1969), 547-55; E.A. Alpers, *Ivory and slaves in East Central Africa. Changing patterns of international trade to the late nineteenth century*, London 1975; R.W. Beachey, *The Slave trade of Eastern Africa. A collection of documents*, London 1976; A. and B. Isaacman, *The tradition of resistance in Mozambique*. Berkeley 1976; *Islamic Council of Mozambique*, in *Arabia*, xxii (1983); F. Constantin, *Mozambique. Du colonialisme catholique à l'état marxiste. Les communautés musulmans d'Afrique orientale*, Pau 1983, 84-93; I. Asaria, *Back seat for Muslims in Mozambique*, in K. Siddiqui (ed.), *Issues in the Islamic movement 1981-82 (1401-1402)*, London 1983, 297-301; A.P. de Carvalho, *Notas para a história das confrarias islâmicas na Ilha de Moçambique*, in *Arquivo* (Maputo), iv, Outubro 1988, 59-66; F.N. Monteiro, *As communidades islamicas em Mocambique e mecanismos de communicacao*, in *Africana*, iv (March 1989), 65-89; B. Brito Joao, *Abdul Kamal-Megama (1892-1966). Pouvoir et religion dans un district du Nord-Mozambique*, in *Islam et sociétés au Sud du Sahara*, iv (Paris 1990), 137-41; R.T. Duarte, *Northern Mozambique in the Swahili world: an archaeological approach (Studies in African Archeology 4*, Stockholm/Maputo), Uppsala 1993; Duarte, *Sobre a actuacao corrente "Wahhabita" no Islao Mocambicano: algumas notas relativas ao periodo 1666-77*, in *Africana*, xii (March 1993), 85-111; idem, *I Islao, o poder e a guerra: Mozambique 1964-1974*, Oporto 1993; J.M. Penvenne, *Joao dos Santos Albasini (1876-1922). The contradictions of politics and identity in colonial Mozambique*, in *Jnal. of African History*, xxxvii (1996), 419-64; E. Medeiros, *Irmandades muculmanos do Norte de Mocambique*, in *Savana* (5 April 1996), 16-17; idem, *Abdul Kemal Megama*, in *Savana* (March 1996), Maputo; Alpers, *Islam in the service of colonialism? Portuguese strategy during the armed liberation struggle in Mozambique*, in *Lusotopie. Enjeux contemporains dans les espaces lusophones*, Paris 1999; Alpers, ch. *East Central Africa*, in *The history of Islam in Africa*, ed. N. Letzion and R.L. Pouwels, Athens, Ohio 2000, 303-25.

(S. VON SICARD)

MUʿĀHID (A.), literally, "one who enters into a covenant or agreement (*ʿahd*) with someone", applied in mediaeval Islamic times to those "People of the Book" who submitted to the Arab conquerors of the Middle East on condition of an *ʿahd* or of *d̲h̲imma* [*q.v.*] "protection". See for these *muʿāhidūn*, AHL AL-KITĀB, AMĀN, and in the context of al-Andalus, MOZARABS.

MUD̲J̲ĪR AL-DĪN BAYLAḲĀNĪ, a Persian poet of the second half of the 6th/12th century. He was, as his *nisba* indicates, a native of Baylaḳān [*q.v.*], in Transcaucasia, a compatriot and contemporary of the celebrated K̲h̲āḳānī [*q.v.*]. Mud̲j̲īr's *dīwān* contains a few poems to the S̲h̲arwān-s̲h̲āh Manūčihr II (d. not long after 555/1160-1), which must belong to the earliest part of his career, but the majority of his odes are addressed to the Atabegs Nuṣrat al-Dīn D̲j̲ahān-pahlawān b. Īldügüz (571-82/1175-86) and his successor Ḳïzïl Arslan (d. 587/1191) and to the Sald̲j̲ūḳid Arslan b. Toghrïl (556-71/1161-76), nominally the master, but in fact the puppet of D̲j̲ahān-pahlawān. Taḳī Kās̲h̲ī [see TAḲĪ AL-DĪN] puts his death in the year 594/1197-8, which (for once) must be roughly correct.

In his famous ode in praise of the town of Iṣfahān, K̲h̲āḳānī speaks of how an "accursed demon" (*dēw-i radjīm*) had mocked that city and how the Iṣfahānīs had in some way held Khāḳānī responsible for the attack, an accusation which he rejects energetically. The commentators identified this "demon" with Khāḳānī's supposed pupil Mudjīr (*radjīm* being an anagram for the latter's name) and there is in fact a *rubāʿī* in Mudjīr's *dīwān* poking fun at the people of Iṣfahān. Abu 'l-Radjā Ḳummī (*Taʾrīkh al-Wuzarāʾ*, ed. M.T. Dānish-pazhūh, Tehran 1985, 200-1), a nearly contemporary source, cites one verse from this quatrain and then a verse with which the "people of Iṣfahan" replied to Mudjīr's attack (and which in later sources is ascribed to Sharaf al-Dīn Shufurwa, see SHUFURWA). The story is expanded by later authors, some of whom claim that Mudjīr composed the quatrain when the Atabeg sent him to that town as a tax-collector and that he was subsequently murdered in a bath-house by the local mob. But this is perhaps merely a fanciful elaboration.

Mudjīr's *dīwān* contains several highly artificial poems (e.g. one in which he uses only the letters that do not take diacritical points) and a fair number in Arabic or with alternating Arabic and Persian verses. A critical edition was prepared by M. Ābādī, Tehran 1358 *sh*./1979.

Bibliography: de Blois, *Persian literature*, v, 425-8 (with further references); A.L.F.A. Beelaert, *La qaṣide en honneur d'Ispahan de Xâqânî*, in *Pand-o sokhan. Mélanges offerts à Charles-Henri de Fouchécour*, Tehran 1995, 53-63. (F.C. DE BLOIS)

AL-**MUFAḌḌAL** B. **SALAMA** B. ʿĀṢIM (with the erroneous *nisba* "al-Ḍabbī" since Ibn Khallikān [*q.v.*]) al-Kūfī, Abū Ṭālib (d. after 290/903), transmitter of historical materials (*akhbārī*) with wide interests and a philological-lexicographical background.

With this approach (Yāḳūt, *Udabāʾ*, vii, 170), he differed (a) from his father Salama (d. after 270/883; Ibn al-Djazarī, i, 311), a disciple and copyist (*warrāḳ*) of al-Farrāʾ [*q.v.*], the great authority of the Kūfan school of philologists, and (b) from his son Abu 'l-Ṭayyib Muḥammad al-Baghdādī (d. 308/920; Kaḥḥāla, xii, 43-4), a strict jurisprudent of the Shāfiʿī school in Baghdād (Ibn Khallikān, tr. de Slane, ii, 610-11). The three represent one of the early scholarly dynasties in ʿIrāḳ [see AL-YAZĪDĪ]. Apart from his father, the following philologists are mentioned among his teachers: Ibn al-Aʿrābī, Ibn al-Sikkīt, Thaʿlab, and—last but not least—the *adīb* ʿUmar b. Shabba [*q.vv.*]; among his students al-Ṣūlī [*q.v.*] is the best known. Al-Mufaḍḍal was also highly regarded as a calligrapher by the bibliophile and sponsor of poets and literati, al-Fatḥ b. Khāḳān [*q.v.*], and after the latter's murder (247/861) together with the caliph al-Mutawakkil, no less so by the vizier Ismāʿīl b. Bulbul [*q.v.*]. Neither of these two men was an Arab by descent. In the multicultural society of their time, they were probably receptive, besides the Arabic-Islamic tradition, not only to pre-Islamic Arabic transmissions (the "War of Dāḥis and al-Ghabrāʾ"; *Fākhir*, no. 442/360), but also to Christian, Jewish, Persian (see below) and Central Asian reports [see AFSHĪN].

Of al-Mufaḍḍal's œuvre, listed by the bio-bibliographers, little has been preserved or become known through quotations in the works of others. For an overview, see Sezgin, viii, 139-41, vii, 350, ix, 139-40. His best-known work is his much-used, unsystematic collection of proverbs (*amthāl*) and set turns of speech (*muḥāwarāt*, see MATHAL.1.i), containing 521 items:

(1) *al-Fākhir* (for partial prints and the two editions, see MATHAL.1.iii.4). The peculiarity of *al-Fākhir* is the fact that, in addition to 200 proverbs, all of which can be found in the better-known, extensive collection of al-Maydānī [see MATHAL.1.iii.12], it contains 321 turns of phrases (*muḥāwarāt*), such as greeting formulas, benedictions, curses, animal calls (no. 441) and similar things, not a few of them connected with the *awāʾil* [*q.v.*] angle. The same phrases can be found in Abū Bakr Ibn al-Anbārī's (d. 328/940) *al-Ẓāhir fī kalimāt al-nās*, also in Abū Hilāl al-ʿAskarī's (d. after 395/1005) *Djamharat al-amthāl* and in the large dictionaries, e.g. in the *Lisān al-ʿArab* of Ibn Manẓūr (d. 711/1311). The transmission of *al-Fākhir* can in part be traced back to Ibn al-Anbārī as well; he seems to have recognised that al-Mufaḍḍal had entered new "lexical" territory, which was then the motive for his composing the more comprehensive *al-Ẓāhir* [see MATHAL.1.iii.5]. Al-Mufaḍḍal was less of a philologist than a collector and an entertainer at court and in the city of Baghdād. Pointers towards this include his critique (cf. *Fihrist*, 43, 62, 63, 74, 82) of the *Kitāb al-ʿAyn* of the great al-Khalīl b. Aḥmad, bearing the title: *al-Radd* (var. *al-Istidrāk*) *ʿala 'l-Khalīl... fī K. al-ʿAyn wa-iṣlāḥ mā fīhi min al-ghalaṭ wa 'l-taṣḥīf*, which evidently did not convince the philologists and lexicologists, who felt called upon to contradict him, even in later centuries (for relevant passages, see Sezgin, viii, 140). Al-Mufaḍḍal had a preference in his work for what was novel, strange and contemporary. This can be seen in his renditions of the aetiological stories that go with the *amthāl/muḥāwarāt*: the clever Jew (no. 223), the loyal Jew (no. 482), the Seven Sleepers (no. 239), the Christian martyr (no. 517), and others, see MATHAL.1.ii.7, and W. Ebermann, *Bericht über arabische Studien in Russland während der Jahre 1914-1920*, in *Islamica*, iii [1927], 229-64 (see secs. V. "Christlich-arabisches", 248-51, and VI. "Jüdisch-arabische Literatur", 251-4). On the whole complex, see R. Sellheim, *Die klassisch-arabischen Sprichwörtersammlungen, insbesondere die des Abū ʿUbaid*, The Hague 1954, 114-21; Ar. tr. rev. and enlarged, *al-Amthāl al-ʿarabiyya al-ḳadīma*, tr. R. ʿAbd al-Tawwāb, Beirut 1391/1971, repr. [4]1408/1987, 167-75; *Oriens*, xxxii [1990], 472-5.

(2) *al-Malāhī* [*q.v.*], on musical instruments, a treatise on the justification for playing music, which al-Mufaḍḍal was the first (?) to compose; ed. J. Robson, *Ancient Arabic musical instruments in the handwriting of Yāḳūt al-Mustaʿṣimī, A.D. 1298*, text in facs. and tr. with notes, including notes on instruments by H.G. Farmer, Glasgow 1938 (Collection of Oriental Writers on Music, iv), repr. in ʿAbbās al-ʿAzzāwī, *al-Mūsīḳī al-ʿirāḳiyya*, Baghdād 1370/1951, 74-89; Farmer, *Islam*, Leipzig [1966], 8, 24, 26 (*Musikgeschichte in Bildern*, ed. H. Besseler and M. Schneider, Band 3, Lieferung 2), cf. E. Neubauer in *Oriens*, xxi-xxii [1968-9 (1971)], 418-31; A. Shiloah, *The theory of music in Arabic writings (c. 900-1900). Descriptive catalogue of manuscripts in libraries of Europe and the U.S.A.*, Munich 1979, 282-3 (Répertoire international des sources musicales = RISM B, x), cf. E. Neubauer in *ZGAIW*, i [1984], 290-6.

(3) *Mukhtaṣar al-Mudhakkar wa 'l-muʾannath*; no such grammatical opuscule on the masculine and the feminine is mentioned in the list of works drawn up by the bio-bibliographers. It is inspired by the work of the same name by al-Farrāʾ. As the technical term *mukhtaṣar* "abridgement", indicates, it might possibly be lecture notes [see MATHAL.1.iii]. Whether they should be traced back to al-Mufaḍḍal or whether a later anonymus is behind it will probably never be known. R. ʿAbd al-Tawwāb edited it in *RIMA*, xvii [1971], 277-346, with an introduction on the life and works of al-Mufaḍḍal.

(4) *Djalāʾ al-shabah fi ʾl-radd ʿala ʾl-Mushabbiha*, an extant treatise against the anthropomorphisation of God, by means of Ḳurʾānic verses and terms, see Sezgin, viii, 141, and R. Şeşen, *Nawādir al-makhṭūṭāt al-ʿarabiyya fi maktabāt Turkiyā*, Beirut 1400/1980, ii, 434.

Bibliography: In addition to the studies mentioned in the text, see G. Flügel, *Die grammatischen Schulen der Araber*, Leipzig 1862 (repr. Nendeln 1966), 162-4; Brockelmann, I², 121, S I, 181, 943 (!), S III, 1195 (!), O. Rescher, *Abriss der arabischen Litteraturgeschichte*, Stuttgart 1933, ii, 182-3 (repr. with addenda, Osnabrück 1983); Blachère, *HLA*, i, 137; Sarkīs, 1770; Ziriklī, *al-Aʿlām*, ⁴Beirut 1979, vii, 279; Kaḥḥāla, *Muʿdjam al-muʾallifīn*, Damascus 1380/1960, xii, 314; idem, *al-Mustadrak ʿalā Muʿdjam al-muʾallifīn*, Beirut 1406/1985, 797.

Further sources. Abu ʾl-Ṭayyib al-Lughawī, *Marātib al-naḥwiyyīn*, Cairo 1955, 97, ²Cairo 1974, 154; Marzubānī, *al-Muḳtabas*, Beirut-Wiesbaden 1964 (repr. Baghdād 1968; Tehran 1968), 339; *Fihrist*, 73-4, tr. Dodge, 161-2, and index, 1047; al-Khaṭīb, *Taʾrīkh Baghdād*, xiii, 124-5; Ibn al-Anbārī, *Nuzhat al-alibbāʾ*, Cairo 1967, 202; Ḳifṭī, *Inbāh al-ruwāt ʿalā anbāh al-nuḥāt*, Cairo 1374/1955, iii, 305-11 (Ḍabbī); Dhahabī, *Siyar aʿlām al-nubalāʾ*, Beirut 1403/1983, xiv, 362; Suyūṭī, *Bughya*, 396 (Cairo 1384/1964, ii, 396-7); idem, *Muzhir*, Cairo 1378/1958, 413, and index s.v.; Dāwūdī, *Ṭabaḳāt al-mufassirīn*, Cairo 1392/1972, ii, 328-9; Ismāʿīl Pasha, *Hadiyyat al-ʿārifīn*, Istanbul 1955, ii, 468. (R. SELLHEIM)

MUFAṢṢAL (A., lit. "separated", "hived off"), in Indo-Muslim pronunciation *mufaṣṣil*, whence the British Indian conventional form *Mofussil*, an informal term of British Indian administrative usage, attested in British usage from the later 18th century but probably going back to Mughal official usage. It denoted the provinces, the rural districts and stations, as opposed to the administrative headquarters of a Presidency, District or region, the *ṣadr* (in the Anglo-Indian usage of the Bengal Presidency, the *Sudder*); hence going into the *Mofussil* could mean something like going into the field, or into the bush or backwoods.

Bibliography: Yule and Burnell, *Hobson-Jobson, a glossary of Anglo-Indian words and phrases*, ²London 1903, 570, 862. (ED.)

MÜFETTISH (T.), the Ottoman Turkish form of Ar. *mufattish*, lit. "one who searches out, enquires into something". In the Ottoman legal system of the 12th/18th century, below the Great Mollās [see MOLLĀ] there was a layer of five judges called *müfettish*, whose duties were to oversee and enquire into the conducting of the Imperial *ewḳāf* or pious foundations [see WAḲF], three of them being resident in Istanbul and one each in Edirne and Bursa (see Gibb and Bowen, ii, 92). In the 19th century, and with the coming of the *Tanẓīmāt* [*q.v.*] reforms, *müfettish* was the designation for the overseers and inspectors of various new administrative mechanisms now set in motion within the empire. In modern Turkish, *müfettiş* remains a standard word for "inspector".

Bibliography: Given in the article. (ED.)

MUGHALMĀRĪ [see TUKARŌʾĪ].

MUḤALLIL (A.), literally, "someone who makes a thing legal, legaliser, legitimator", the figure who, in classical Islamic law acts as something like a dummy or a "man of straw", in order to authenticate or make permissible some legal process otherwise of doubtful legality or in fact prohibited. It thus forms part of the mechanisms and procedures subsumed under *ḥiyal*, legal devices, often used for evading the spirit of the law whilst technically satisfying its letter [see ḤĪLA].

Thus the *muḥallil* is found in gambling, racing for stakes, e.g. with horses or pigeons, and archery contests being a participant who does not contribute to the stakes; see F. Rosenthal, *Gambling in Islam*, Leiden 1975, 53, 98-106, and ḲIMĀR, at Vol. V, 109a. But *muḥallil* is also found in marriage and divorce law, as the person instructed, usually for payment, to marry a woman who has been three times divorced and cannot therefore remarry her original husband until a fourth, dummy marriage has been gone through and duly consummated. After this *taḥlīl* she can legally remarry her old husband. Such an intervention was generally allowed by the Ḥanafīs but disputed by the Mālikīs and Shāfiʿīs, whilst the Ḥanbalī Ibn Taymiyya denounced it as illegal in a treatise of his on divorce (cf. Brockelmann, II², 127, S II, 124) [see ṬALĀḲ. I. 7.].

The person acting as a *muḥallil* in marriage and divorce is not surprisingly a figure of contempt and obloquy in Islamic literature.

Bibliography: See also Ibn Ḳudāma, *Mughnī*, Beirut 1984, v, 459-553, vii, 397-400, viii, 476-8; Lane, *Lexicon*, 622c; Wahbī al-Zuḥaylī, *al-Fiḳh al-islāmī wa-adillatuhu*, Damascus 1985, v, 789, vii, 120-1; ʿAbd al-Raḥmān al-Djazāʾirī, *K. al-Fiḳh ʿalā ʾl-madhāhib al-arbaʿa*, Beirut 1986, iv, 437-9. (C.E. BOSWORTH)

MUḤAMMAD III B. ḤASAN, ʿALĀʾ AL-DĪN, Nizārī Ismāʿīlī *imām* and the penultimate lord of Alamūt, who was made famous in mediaeval Europe by Marco Polo as the "old man" Aloadin. The only son of Djalāl al-Dīn Ḥasan (r. 607-18/1210-21), he succeeded his father, at the age of nine, in Ramaḍān 618/November 1221. The vizier previously appointed by Djalāl al-Dīn Ḥasan acted for some time as the effective ruler of the Nizārī state, also generally retaining the then ongoing Nizārī policies of rapprochement with the ʿAbbāsids and Sunnī Islam. However, the observance of the Sunnī *sharīʿa*, imposed earlier, was gradually relaxed in the Nizārī communities of Persia and Syria.

Politically, Muḥammad III's long reign was a very turbulent period for the Persian world, which now experienced a forestate of the Mongol menace. However, the Nizārī leadership initially seems to have reached an understanding with the Mongols, who did not attack the Nizārī towns and fortresses of Persia for some time. Djūzdjānī, the Ghūrid historian and official who visited Ḳuhistān on diplomatic missions on several occasions during 621-3/1224-6, relates how the *muḥtashams* or the Nizārī chiefs in Ḳuhistān shared the stability and prosperity of their community with an increasing number of refugees, including many Sunnī scholars of Khurāsān, who fled before the invading Mongols and found asylum among the Nizārīs. Meanwhile, the Nizārīs extended their territories in Persia in the early years of Muḥammad III's reign. They seized Dāmghān and acquired or recaptured fortresses in Ḳūmis, Ṭārum and elsewhere, also extending their influence to Sīstān. In the wake of the Mongol invasions, relations between Alamūt and the Khʷārazmians, who had replaced the Saldjūḳs as the Nizārīs' foremost enemy, were characterised by warfare and diplomacy until Djalāl al-Dīn Mangubirtī, the last Khʷārazm-Shāh, was defeated by the Mongols in 628/1231. The shifting Nizārī-Khʷārazmian relations have been vividly recorded by al-Nasawī, Sultan Djalāl al-Dīn's secretary and chronicler, who was on one occasion dispatched as an ambassador to Alamūt where he conducted diplomatic negotiations with Muḥammad III on behalf of the Kh^w^ārazm-Shāh. In Muḥammad III's time, relations between Alamūt and the neighbouring Caspian provinces deteriorated. On the other hand, peace was finally established between the Nizārīs and their perennial enemy, the people of Ḳazwīn. Muḥammad III had personally developed a close association with a Ṣūfī *shaykh* of Ḳazwīn, Djamāl al-Dīn Gīlī (d. 651/1253), and regularly sent him an annual grant of 500 dīnārs. It seems that it was also in Muḥammad III's time that the Nizārī Ismāʿīlī *daʿwa* was introduced to the Indian subcontinent by *dāʿī*s dispatched originally to Sind.

Nizārī fortunes in Persia were rapidly reversed after the collapse of the Kh^w^ārazmian empire. The Nizārīs now directly confronted their most dangerous enemy, the Mongols, who were then making new efforts to conquer all of Persia. Following his abortive effort, in collaboration with the ʿAbbāsids, in 635/1238 to forge an alliance with the kings of France and England against the Mongols, Muḥammad III made one last peace overture to the new Great Khān Güyük in 644/1246. However, the Nizārī emissaries to Mongolia were dismissed with contempt by Güyük. Henceforth, Mongol-Nizārī relations deteriorated beyond repair. By 651/1253, under Güyük's successor Möngke [*q.v.*], the Mongols had destroyed numerous Nizārī towns and strongholds in Ḳuhistān and Ḳūmis. As the Mongols were incessantly conducting military campaigns against the Nizārī territories in Persia, ʿAlāʾ al-Dīn Muḥammad III was found murdered in Shīrkūh, near Alamūt, under obscure circumstances, on 29 Shawwāl 653/1 December 1255. He was succeeded by his eldest son Rukn al-Dīn Khurshāh [*q.v.*], who would rule for exactly one year as the last lord of Alamūt.

Muḥammad III's reign was also a period of intense intellectual activity in the Nizārī Ismāʿīlī community. In particular, Nizārī leadership at this time made a sustained effort to explain the various religious policies of the lords of Alamūt, since Ḥasan-i Ṣabbāḥ's time, within a coherent theological framework. The intellectual life of the Nizārī community was now particularly invigorated by the influx of outside scholars, non-Ismāʿīlī Muslims, who availed themselves of the Nizārī libraries and patronage of learning. Foremost among such outside scholars was Naṣīr al-Dīn al-Ṭūsī [*q.v.*], who spent some three decades in the Nizārī fortresses of Ḳuhistān, and later at Alamūt where he enjoyed the patronage of Muḥammad III and his successor until the collapse of the Nizārī state in 654/1256. Al-Ṭūsī made important contributions to the Nizārī thought of his time, and it is primarily through his Ismāʿīlī works, including especially his *Rawḍat al-taslīm* (ed. and tr. W. Ivanow, Leiden 1950), that modern scholars have come to possess an understanding of the Nizārī Ismāʿīlī teachings during the final decades of the Alamūt period.

Bibliography: Djuwaynī, iii, 249-59; Djuwaynī-Boyle, ii, 703-12; Rashīd al-Dīn Faḍl Allāh, *Djāmiʿ al-tawārīkh, ḳismat-i Ismāʿīliyān*, ed. M.T. Dānishpazhūh and M. Mudarrisī Zandjānī, Tehran 1338 *sh*./1959, 178-84; idem, *Djāmiʿ al-tawārīkh*, iii, ed. A.A. Alizade, Baku 1957, 20-1; Abu 'l-Ḳāsim ʿAbd Allāh b. ʿAlī Kāshānī, *Zubdat al-tawārīkh, bakhsh-i Fāṭimiyān wa Nizāriyān*, ed. Dānishpazhūh, ²Tehran 1366 *sh*./1987, 218-24; Nasawī, *Histoire du Djelal ed-Din Mankobirti*, ed. and tr. O. Houdas, Paris 1891-5, Ar. text, 129-30, 132-4, 143-6, 196, 212-5, Fr. tr., 215-16, 219-23, 237-42, 327, 353-60, anon. Persian tr. *Sīrat-i Djalāl al-Dīn Mīnkūbirnī*, ed. M. Mīnuwī, Tehran 1344 *sh*./1965, 161-6, 175-7, 229-33; Djūzdjānī, *Ṭabaḳāt-i Nāṣirī*, ed. ʿA. Ḥabībī, ²Kabul 1342-3 *sh*./1963-4, ii, 180-8, Eng. tr. H.G. Raverty, London 1881-99, ii, 1187-1214; M.G.S. Hodgson, *The order of Assassins*, The Hague 1955, 225 ff., 244-6, 250-62; B. Lewis, *The Assassins*, London 1967, 83-91, Fr. tr. A. Pélissier, *Les Assassins*, Paris 1982, 122-31; F. Daftary, *The Ismāʿīlīs. Their history and doctrines*, Cambridge 1990, 407-18, 421-2, 693-5 (with further bibl. refs.); idem, *The Assassin legends. Myths of the Ismaʿilis*, London 1994, 43, 59-60, 109-14, 166. (F. Daftary)

MUḤAMMAD b. ʿAbd Allāh, called **IBN SHABĪB**, Abū Bakr, Baṣran theologian who lived in the first half of the 3rd/9th century. He is possibly identical with Shabīb al-Baṣrī, "one of the best-known ascetics of his community and among the leading sages of his period" whom the Jewish *mutakallim* Dāwūd b. Marwān al-Muḳammiṣ reports defeating in a debate in Damascus. He was influenced by the Murdjiʾī Abū Shamir al-Ḥanafī and his school, but he studied with al-Naẓẓām [*q.v.*] and is therefore frequently called a Muʿtazilī. Al-Māturīdī extensively quotes a book of his, apparently the *K. al-Tawḥīd*, in which Ibn Shabīb described and refuted the doctrines of dualists, Christians and Ṣābians, of Aristotle and others who believed in the eternity of the world, of Indian sensualists (Sumaniyya [*q.v.*]) and the sceptics (Sūfisṭāʾiyya). In these polemics, especially those against the dualists, he followed al-Naẓẓām but frequently refined the arguments. The *ḳāḍī* ʿAbd al-Djabbār still found his book "excellent". Ibn Shabīb's Murdjiʾī leanings are apparent in a treatise on *irdjāʾ* which was refuted by Djaʿfar b. Mubashshir [*q.v.*], and another on the *waʿīd* (i.e. threat of eternal damnation), for which he was attacked by the Muʿtazilī Abū Djaʿfar al-Iskāfī [*q.v.*]. He did not accept the *manzila bayn al-manzilatayn* [*q.v.*] although he used the term *fāsiḳ*, for he believed that the mortal sinner remained a believer. In his definition of belief he omitted works, something which a Muʿtazilī would have never done, and based his definition on the intellect and will. In his view, Muslims could hope not to be punished eternally. The passages of the Ḳurʾān that speak of God's threat (*waʿīd*) in this respect are, he said, not clear enough. With this, he took up an old hermeneutical argument which the Murdjiʾa had carried into *uṣūl al-fiḳh*; it had been developed by Muways b. ʿImrān [*q.v.*] and discussed by Abu 'l-Hudhayl and al-Naẓẓām.

Bibliography: Djāḥiẓ, *al-Bayān wa 'l-tabyīn*, i, 15 ll. 15-16 and 36 ll. 12ff.; Ḳāḍī ʿAbd al-Djabbār, *Faḍl al-iʿtizāl*, 279 ll. 11ff.; idem, *Mughnī*, xvii, 35 ll. 12ff.; Ashʿarī, *Maḳālāt al-Islāmiyyīn*, index s.n.; Dāwūd al-Muḳammiṣ, *ʿIshrūn maḳāla*, ed. S. Stroumsa, Leiden 1989, 249 ll. 4ff. (tr. G. Vajda, in *Oriens*, xv, 1962, 68-71); Abū Ḥayyān al-Tawḥīdī, *al-Baṣāʾir wa 'l-dhakhāʾir*, ed. Wadād al-Ḳāḍī, Beirut 1408/1988, iv, 216 n. 784; Shahrastānī, *Livre des religions et des sectes*, tr. D. Gimaret, index s.n.; I.J.M. Pessagno, *The reconstruction of the thought of Muḥammad ibn Shabīb*, in *JAOS*, civ (1984), 445-53, including translations of many fragments; J. van Ess, *Theologie und Gesellschaft im 2. und 3. Jh. Hidschra*, Berlin 1991ff., iv, 124-31 and vi, 338-57; U. Rudolph, *Al-Māturīdī und die sunnitische Theologie in Samarkand*, Leiden 1997, 178-9 and index s.v.

(J. van Ess)

MUḤAMMAD b. ʿ**ABD** al-**KARĪM** al-Khaṭṭābī (*ca.* 1880-1963), Moroccan activist and leader in the Rīf War.

Ibn ʿAbd al-Karīm was born in the 1880s into the large Berber tribe (*ḳabīla*) Banū Waryāg͟hal in the Moroccan Rīf [*q.v.*], son of a *ḳāḍī* who had close relations with the Spanish in Melilla [*q.v.*] and Alhucemas Island. He studied at the Ḳarawiyyīn in Fās [*q.vv.*], and was influenced by the Salafiyya [*q.v.*] movement. From 1907 he worked in Melilla as a teacher, military interpreter, journalist and *ḳāḍī*. After the Moroccan Protectorate was established in 1912, he opposed French colonialism and during the First World War was briefly arrested by the Spanish for supposed German sympathies. In 1919, an inchoate movement emerged among the Banū Waryāg͟hal to resist the Spanish occupation, and Ibn ʿAbd al-Karīm returned to reorganise it on a more stable basis by imposing the *S͟harīʿa* and establishing a European-style military force.

After a rising against the Spanish in July 1921, he founded a government based on principles of modernisation and Salafī reform. In February 1923 various Rīfī tribes gave him *bayʿa*s as *imām*; he sometimes called himself *amīr al-muʾminīn* [*q.v.*], more to signify the religious nature of his movement than to claim universal leadership. His forces defeated the Spanish in 1924 and invaded the French Zone in 1925. After a joint invasion of the Rīf in the autumn of 1925, Spanish and French armies crushed his state in May 1926.

Ibn ʿAbd al-Karīm was exiled to Réunion until, in 1947, he escaped in Egypt on his way to France. He became the titular leader of the umbrella Committee for the Liberation of North Africa. After Moroccan independence (1956) he refused to return, saying that the American bases prevented Morocco from being truly independent. He died in Cairo in 1963.

Bibliography: D.M. Hart, *The Aith Waryaghar of the Moroccan Rif, an ethnography and history*, Tucson, Ariz. 1976 (useful on social background); G. Ayache, *Les origines de la guerre du Rif*, Paris and Rabat 1981; C.R. Pennell, *A country with a government and a flag. The Rif War in Morocco, 1921-1926*, Wisbech 1986; H. Munson, Jr., *Religion and power in Morocco*, New Haven 1993 (on ideological aspects); Ayache, *La guerre du Rif*, Paris 1996. (C.R. Pennell)

MUḤAMMAD b. ʿARAFA (d. 1976), ephemeral Sultan of Morocco 1953-5.

Muḥammad b. ʿArafa was the product of the Franco-Moroccan crisis of the early 1950s when sultan Muḥammad b. Yūsuf (after 1956, Muḥammad V) (d. 1961) defied the Protectorate authorities and openly supported the nationalists' demand for independence. In March 1952 the sultan addressed a letter to the President of the French Republic demanding the abrogation of the protectorate treaty of 1912. The French not only rejected the sultan's demand but started contemplating plans for his removal. A scheme for a dynastic change by which the Idrīsid ʿAbd al-Ḥayy al-Kattānī would be made sultan was quickly abandoned in favour of a more realistic alternative, that of finding a candidate for the throne from within the ʿAlawid house.

The idea of a new ʿAlawid sultan who would be more co-operative, if not in effect a French puppet, was judged to be more acceptable in view of the wide popularity that had built up round the ʿAlawid dynasty since the early 1930s. Upon the instructions of Augustin Guillaume, the French Resident General, Thāmī al-Glāwī, pasha of Marrakesh, and ʿAbd al-Ḥayy al-Kattānī toured the country to gather signatures for a petition demanding the removal of the sultan Muḥammad V. The new candidate for the throne was found in the person of Muḥammad b. ʿArafa, a retiring person from the ʿAlawid family. On 20 August 1953 the legal sultan was deposed and sent into exile in the French colony of Madagascar.

The enthronement of the new sultan was immediately met by a sweeping wave of opposition to the French policy. Ibn ʿArafa was dismissed by the overwhelming majority of the Moroccan people as "the sultan of the French" and they therefore refused to give him allegiance. Mosque *imām*s abstained from mentioning his name in the Friday sermon, and when they did this under French pressure, people simply deserted the mosques. His proclamation had for its immediate consequences the radicalisation of the nationalist movement and the outbreak of armed resistance to the French in many parts of the country. After two attempts on the sultan's life and the deterioration of security throughout the country, the French realised the seriousness of the situation. Internationally, the French action had been widely condemned, particularly by Spain which, as a co-partner in the protectorate system, felt deeply offended by the French unatilateral move. The Spanish authorities maintained allegiance to Muḥammad V, and at the United Nations the French government had also to face wide hostility to its Moroccan policy from the Arab and the Afro-Asian bloc.

For the Moroccan nationalist movement led by the Istiḳlāl party [see ḥizb. i, at Vol. III, 525], the return of the deposed sultan and the removal of Ibn ʿArafa became the most pressing demands and a rallying cry for all political tendencies. When the French finally decided to allow Ibn Yūsuf to return from exile, they had, in fact, accepted the principle of Morocco's independence. Ibn ʿArafa announced his abdication on 1 October 1955, and on 2 March 1956 the protectorate régime formally came to an end. Muḥammad b. ʿArafa went into exile in France and died at Nice on 18 July 1976.

Bibliography: S. Bernard, *Le conflit franco-marocain, 1943-1956*, 3 vols. Brussels 1963; Jamil M. Abun-Nasr, *A history of the Maghrib in the Islamic period*, Cambridge 1971; Ch. A. Julien, *Le Maroc face aux impérialismes, 1415-1956*, Paris 1978. (Mohamed El Mansour)

MUḤAMMAD b. ISMĀʿĪL al-MAYMŪN, the seventh *imām* of the Ismāʿīliyya [*q.v.*].

The eldest son of Ismāʿīl b. D͟jaʿfar al-Ṣādiḳ, Muḥammad was born around 120/738; and on the death of his grandfather, the *imām* D͟jaʿfar al-Ṣādiḳ, in 148/765 he was recognised as *imām* by a faction of the Imāmī S͟hīʿīs, who were later designated as the Mubārakiyya. These S͟hīʿīs, comprising one of the earliest Ismāʿīlī groups, affirmed the death of Muḥammad's father Ismāʿīl in the lifetime of the *imām* al-Ṣādiḳ. They further held that al-Ṣādiḳ had personally designated his grandson Muḥammad on Ismāʿīl's death. Muḥammad b. Ismāʿīl carried the epithet of al-Maymūn, the "fortunate one", and his followers were also originally referred to as the Maymūniyya, another designation of the nascent Ismāʿīliyya. Soon after 149/766, Muḥammad b. Ismāʿīl permanently left Medina, the residence of the ʿAlids, for the east and went into hiding; hence his additional epithet of al-Maktūm, the "hidden one". Subsequently, he maintained his contacts with the Mubārakiyya (Maymūniyya), centred in Kūfa. Muḥammad b. Ismāʿīl evidently spent his final years in K͟hūzistān, where he had some following, and died not long after 179/795-6 in the reign of the caliph Hārūn al-Ras͟hīd.

Until the schism of 286/899 in the early Ismāʿīlī

movement, the bulk of the Ismāʿīliyya acknowledged Muḥammad b. Ismāʿīl as their seventh and final *imām*; and as such, they denied his death and awaited his imminent return as the Mahdī or Ḳāʾim. In accordance with their cyclical view of the religious history of mankind, the early Ismāʿīlīs also believed that Muḥammad b. Ismāʿīl was the seventh and final speaker (*nāṭiḳ*); on his reappearance, he would initiate the final era or *dawr* [*q.v.*], fully revealing to all mankind the hitherto hidden esoteric truths (*ḥaḳāʾiḳ*) of all the preceding revelations. Muḥammad b. Ismāʿīl would rule the world in justice during that eschatological age of pure spiritual knowledge before the physical world ended; he was thus considered as the *Ḳāʾim al-ḳiyāma*. These beliefs were retained by the Ḳarmaṭīs [*q.v.*] who, in 286/899, split away from those Ismāʿīlīs who acknowledged continuity in the Ismāʿīlī imāmate and allowed for more than one heptad of *imāms* in the era of Islam. The latter, the Fāṭimid Ismāʿīlīs, denied the Mahdīship of Muḥammad b. Ismāʿīl; for them, the final age was gradually postponed indefinitely into the future and Muḥammad b. Ismāʿīl himself was no longer expected to return as the Mahdī.

Bibliography: Nawbakhtī, *Firaḳ al-Shīʿa*, ed. H. Ritter, Istanbul 1931, 58-64, 90; Saʿd b. ʿAbd Allāh al-Ḳummī, *al-Maḳālāt wa ʾl-firaḳ*, ed. M.J. Mashkūr, Tehran 1963, 80-86, 103; Kulaynī, *al-Uṣūl min al-kāfī*, ed. ʿAlī A. al-Ghaffārī, Tehran 1388/1968, i, 485-6; Abū Ḥātim al-Rāzī, *K. al-Zīna*, iii, ed. ʿA.S. al-Sāmarrāʾī in his *al-Ghuluw wa ʾl-firaḳ al-ghāliya*, Baghdād 1392/1972, 287-89; Djaʿfar b. Manṣūr al-Yaman, *K. al-Kashf*, ed. R. Strothmann, London, etc., 1952, 103-4, 109-10, 113-14, 132-3, 138, 143, 150, 169-70; idem, *Sarāʾir wa-asrār al-nuṭaḳāʾ*, ed. M. Ghālib, Beirut 1984, 21, 39, 109, 112, 259; al-Ḳāḍī al-Nuʿmān, *Sharḥ al-akhbār*, ed. S.M. al-Ḥusaynī al-Djalālī, Ḳumm 1409-12/1988-92, iii, 309-10; Idrīs ʿImād al-Dīn b. al-Ḥasan, *ʿUyūn al-akhbār*, iv, ed. Ghālib, Beirut 1973, 351-6; idem, *Zahr al-maʿānī*, ed. Ghālib, Beirut 1991, 204-8; Ashʿarī, *Maḳālāt al-islāmiyyīn*, ed. H. Ritter, Istanbul 1929-30, 26-7; Shahrastānī, 16, 127-8, 145-7, Fr. tr. D. Gimaret and G. Monnot, *Livre des religions et des sectes*, Louvain and Paris 1986, 138, 491-2, 551-3, Eng. tr. A.K. Kazi and J.G. Flynn, *Muslim sects and divisions*, London 1984, 23, 144, 163-5; Ibn ʿInaba, *ʿUmdat al-ṭālib*, ed. M.Ḥ. Āl al-Ṭāliḳānī, Nadjaf 1961, 233, 234ff.; Ḥ.F. al-Hamdānī, *On the genealogy of Fatimid caliphs*, Cairo 1958; W. Madelung, *Das Imamat in der frühen ismailitischen Lehre*, in *Isl.*, xxxvii (1961), 43-86; H. Halm, *Kosmologie und Heilslehre der frühen Ismāʿīlīya*, Wiesbaden 1978, 18-37; idem, *The empire of the Mahdi*, tr. M. Bonner, Leiden 1996, index; F. Daftary, *The Ismāʿīlīs, their history and doctrines*, Cambridge 1990, index; idem, *A major schism in the early Ismāʿīlī movement*, in *Stud. Isl.*, lxxvii (1993), 123-39; and idem, *A short history of the Ismailis*, Edinburgh 1998, index.

(F. Daftary)

MUḤAMMAD B. SAYF AL-DĪN, IBN AYDAMIR, compiler of a large anthology of Arabic poetry, d. 710/1310.

Born in Baghdād in 639/1240, he served the last ʿAbbāsid caliph as a youth. Trained both in the chivalrous and humanist disciplines, he was appointed to various civil offices by the Mongol Hülegü and his successors. Biographers mention that he wrote some good poetry and epistles. Ibn Aydamir (which is how he writes his own name, not Ibn Aydamur) died in Radjab 710/November-December 1310, some five years after completing his great anthology *al-Durr al-farīd*, of which an almost complete, beautifully written, autograph has been preserved and published in a facsimile edition. After an extensive introduction on stylistics and literary criticism, the main part of the work lists single lines of poetry, mostly of the gnomic and quotable kind. They are arranged strictly alphabetically, not according to rhyme-word, but, unusually and usefully, by their beginnings. The core of the book contains some 18,000 lines, a very large number, which is, however, easily outnumbered by the lines provided by the compiler in the margin, often giving the context or parallels of quoted lines. Biographical notes and philological commentary are also included. The poets date from all periods, many of them well known but also including lesser-known or obscure poets.

Bibliography: Muḥammad Ibn Sayf al-Dīn Aydamur, *al-Durr al-farīd wa-bayt al-qaṣīd/The priceless pearl a poetic verse* [sic], ed. [in facsimile] F. Sezgin, in collab. with M. Amawi, A. Jokhosha and E. Neubauer, 5 vols. (viii + 332, 384, 377, 377, 534 pp.), Frankfurt am Main 1988-9 (*Publications of the Institute for the History of Arabic-Islamic Science*, C, 45); G.J. van Gelder, *Arabic poetics and stylistics according to the introduction of* al-Durr al-farīd *by Muḥammad Ibn Aydamir (d. 710/1310)*, in *ZDMG*, cxlvi (1996), 381-414; R. Weipert, *Der* Durr al-farīd *des Muḥammad b. Aidamur. Ein Thesaurus gnomischer Poesie aus dem 7./13. Jahrhundert*, in W. Heinrichs and G. Schoeler (eds.), *Festschrift Ewald Wagner zum 65. Geburtstag. Band 2. Studien zur arabischen Dichtung*, Beirut-Wiesbaden 1994, 447-61. (G.J.H. van Gelder)

MUḤAMMAD B. SHIHĀB [see AL-ZUHRĪ].

MUḤAMMAD ʿABD ALLĀH, Shaykh (d. 1965), pioneer in the education of Muslim women in the Indian subcontinent.

He was born on 21 June 1874, in a Kashmīrī Sāsan (Hindu) Brahman family in the village of Bhān Tani (district of Punch in Kashmīr valley). Being a Hindu at birth, he was named Thākur Dās. His father, Mehta Gormukh Singh, was a local landlord. According to the traditions of his Kashmīrī Brahman family, his basic education in Persian was initiated under the tutorship of Ḳāḍī Ḳuṭb al-Dīn Kashmīrī. Later, he was admitted to the *maktab* of Miyān Niẓām al-Dīn Wazīr; there he was taught the *Shāh-nāma, Sikandar-nāma*, and *Yūsuf u Zulaykha*, among other Persian books. Here also he began learning Sanskrit. While still in his early teens, he studied *ṭibb-i yūnānī* (the Greek medical system) under the guidance of Mawlawī Nūr al-Dīn. Having been encouraged by both these scholars, he was sent to Djammū to continue his studies in the English system. In Djammū he remained under the guardianship of Mawlawī Nūr al-Dīn. In 1890, at the age of 16, he attended, in his company, the annual session of the Muhammadan Educational Conference at Lahore, where he enthusiastically listened to the speeches of Sir Sayyid Aḥmad Khān [*q.v.*] and other functionaries, being so inspired by these speeches that during the session he embraced Islam.

In 1891 he traveled to ʿAlīgaṙh with an introduction from Mawlawī Nūr al-Dīn addressed to Sir Sayyid, seeking admission to the Anglo-Muhammadan Oriental College (which later became Aligarh Muslim University). While filling in his admission form he, for the first time, wrote his Muslim name, Muḥammad ʿAbd Allāh, by which he was to be known all his remaining life. (It is not known when and how he acquired the title *Shaykh*.) While still an undergraduate student, he was privileged to have close acquaintance with Sir

Sayyid, under whose personal attention ʿAbd Allāh learnt writing for newspapers on various educational and social themes. It was, he stated, Sir Sayyid's guidance which inspired him actively to participate in the community's welfare work.

After graduation with a law degree and at the expressed desire of Sir Sayyid, ʿAbd Allāh settled down in ʿAlīgaŕh and began his career as a lawyer. In 1902 he was married to Waḥīd D̲j̲ahān Begam (from an established Muslim family of Dihlī), with whom he had four daughters and a son.

A few of his childhood experiences of witnessing cruelty and injustice to women left deep impressions on him which were to lead him later in life to a whole-hearted involvement in social welfare work for women, especially in education. He intensely believed that, with education, women's lot could alone be improved. With the then existing atmosphere in ʿAlīgaŕh, he became more and more concerned with the education of Muslim women.

During the 1896 session of the Muhammad Educational Conference, a section was established for women's education; but because of Sir Sayyid's involvement in other tasks, no practical steps were taken to attain any specific objectives toward education of Muslim women. In the 1902 session of the Conference, held at Dihlī, S̲h̲ayk̲h̲ Muḥammad ʿAbd Allāh, together with several of his friends, proposed to revive the section on women's education, which was enthusiastically approved: thereafter year after year he kept on propagating the necessity of providing adequate education to Muslim women in India. For this purpose he began publishing a monthly periodical *K̲h̲ātūn*, the first issue of which came out in 1904 and continued to be published for the next ten years. Also in the year 1904 he was permitted by the Conference session at Lucknow to open a normal (up to eighth grade) school for Muslim girls at ʿAlīgaŕh. After three years of hard work he succeeded in establishing the proposed normal school. The modest beginning of this school in 1907 in ʿAlīgaŕh attracted the attention of the government of the United Provinces (now known as Uttar Pradesh), which granted a sufficient sum for the purpose of buying land and constructing building for the school in 1908. The school at that initial stage had no boarding facilities for girls from outside the town. The increasing popularity of this pioneer institution for Muslim girls' education throughout the subcontinent meant that there was a need of residential facilities for girls from other nearby areas who wanted to join. In 1911 help came again from the U.P. government; Lady Porter, wife of the Lieutenant-Governor of the United Provinces, laid the foundation stone of the hostel adjacent to the school building. The school which had a modest beginning in 1907 had grown by 1936 into a renowned degree college leading up to B.A. classes. In that year it was affiliated to the Aligarh Muslim University.

Until 1947, education in all classes of the college and its affiliated primary and secondary schools was conducted under the strict rules of Islamic seclusion. The hostel followed also tradition both in observing *parda* and in religious obligations. In 1947, however, after the independence of the country and promulgation of a secular constitution, the basic structure of Islamic-oriented Western education remained untouched in all the affiliated insitutions of the Muslim University (Muslim Girls' College included), but seclusion of women students and obligatory religious observances were eliminated.

The attachment of S̲h̲ayk̲h̲ Muḥammad ʿAbd Allāh to the Muslim Girls' College was so deep that he built his spacious residential house close to the buildings of the College, and from the 1940s onwards, donated a large part of this house as the hostel for postgraduate girl students. His strong attachment to the girls' education and welfare was reciprocated by the affectionate title of "Pāpā Miyān" with which he came to be known in ʿAlīgaŕh.

In recognition of his pioneer work for Muslim women's education the British Government awarded him the title of "K̲h̲ān Bahādur", and Aligarh Muslim University honoured him with the award of honorary degree of Doctor of Laws. Towards the end of his life, in 1964 the post-Independence national government of India expressed its appreciation for his services by awarding him the title "Padam Bhūs̲h̲an". He died on 9 April 1965 at the age of 91, and was buried in the garden of his residential house, adjacent to the buildings of the Muslim Girls' College.

Bibliography: S̲h̲. ʿAbd Allāh, *Mus̲h̲āhidāt wa-taʾt̲h̲īrāt* [Urdu], 1969; idem, *Sawāniḥ ʿumrī ʿAbd Allāh Begam* [Urdu] Delhi ^{2}1954; *K̲h̲ātūn*, Urdu monthly journal, ʿAlīgaŕh, ed., S̲h̲. Muḥammad ʿAbd Allāh, 1904-10; T̲h̲urayyā Ḥusayn, *Bānī-e-Darsgāh: Doktor S̲h̲ayk̲h̲ Muḥammad ʿAbd Allāh, ḥayāt wa s̲h̲ak̲h̲ṣiyyat*, in *Women's College, Muslim University Aligarh Magazine* (1975). (Ghaus Ansari)

MUḤAMMAD ʿĀKIF PAS̲H̲A [see mehmed ʿākif pas̲h̲a].

MUḤAMMAD al-D̲J̲AWĀD [see muḥammad b. ʿalī al-riḍā].

MUḤAMMAD ḤĀKIM MĪRZĀ, Mug̲h̲al prince and half-brother of the emperor Akbar [*q.v.*], b. 960/1553, d. 993/1585.

In 973/1566 he was governor of Kābul and eastern Afg̲h̲ānistān for Akbar, but when temporarily forced out of his capital by the Tīmūrids of Badak̲h̲s̲h̲ān, he retreated towards India, where a group of dissident Özbeg nobles proclaimed him emperor at D̲j̲awpūr and incited him to invade India. He beseiged Lahore with his forces, but had to retreat to Kābul. For over a decade, he posed a threat on Akbar's northwestern frontier, offering a legitimate alternative to Akbar's rule. A fresh revolt of Mug̲h̲al and Afg̲h̲ān nobles broke out in 987-8/1579-80, in the wake of Akbar's *maḥḍar* or decree proclaiming himself supreme arbiter of religious affairs and claiming authority as caliph, and Muḥammad Ḥākim was again proclaimed counter-emperor. Akbar sent his chief minister Ṫōḋar Mal [*q.v.*] to supress the rebels in Bihār, and himself marched against Kābul, entering the town in Rad̲j̲ab 989/December 1581. He pardoned Muḥammad Ḥākim and reinstated him, but it was not until Muḥammad Ḥākim's death in S̲h̲aʿbān 993/August 1585 that all threats from Kābul were ended and the region brought under direct imperial rule.

Bibliography: See that for akbar, and add R.J. Majumdar (general ed.), *The history and culture of the Indian people*, vi, *The Mughul empire*, Bombay 1974, 141-5, and J.F. Richards, *The Mughal empire*, Cambridge 1993, 18-19. (Ç.E. Bosworth)

MUḤAMMAD ṢĀLIḤ KANBŌ LĀHAWRĪ, Indo-Muslim historian and stylist whose exact dates of both birth and death are unknown but who flourished in the 11th/17th century under the Mug̲h̲al emperors S̲h̲āh D̲j̲ahān and Awrangzīb [*q.vv.*]. He may have been the younger brother of the historian and littérateur ʿInāyat Allāh Kanbō (d. 1082/1671 [*q.v.*]), if Muḥammad Ṣāliḥ's reference to this last person, his master and patron, as *birādar-i kalān* "elder brother" is to be taken literally.

Virtually nothing is known of his life, but he was

a government official in Lahore, where his tomb still exists and where in 1079/1668-9 he had built a small mosque. He is famed for his detailed history of Shāh Djahān and his reign, the *ʿAmal-i Ṣāliḥ*, completed in 1070/1659-60, but with later additions (many mss.; ed. Ghulām Yazdānī, Bibl. Indica, 3 vols. Calcutta 1912-39), and also an *inshāʾ* collection, the *Bahār-i sukhan*, still in manuscript.

Bibliography: Storey, i, 579-81, 1317.

(C.E. Bosworth)

MUḤAMMAD-SHĀHĪ NIZĀRIYYA [see ismāʿīliyya].

MUḤAMMAD TAPAR [see muḥammad b. malik-shāh].

MUḤAMMAD ʿUTHMĀN DJALĀL (1829-16 January 1909, thus in Brockelmann, S II, 725), Egyptian translator and adapter of European drama into Arabic.

He played a crucial role in the transfer of the cultural milieu of European dramatic forms into an indigenous Egyptian language and format. After a traditional secondary education, he was sent to Rifāʿa al-Ṭahṭāwī's [see rifāʿa bey al-ṭahṭāwī] famous translation school, the *Madrasat al-alsun*, and became thereafter one of the foremost of its graduate translators from French to Arabic (both literary and colloquial). Alongside his achievements as a translator he also had a civil service career, firstly in the Khedive's office, then as a judge in the Mixed Courts, and later as a government minister. Various dates are given for his death, ranging from 1894 to 1909 (cf. Brockelmann, II[2], 627-8, S II, 725).

Moving from the practicalities of administrative manuals to the more complex stylistic issues of literary genres, Djalāl began his literary translation career with the *Fables* of La Fontaine, which he rendered into Arabic verse and published in 1858 (*al-ʿUyūn al-yawāḳiẓ fi 'l-amthāl wa 'l-mawāʿiẓ*). In 1872 he issued his famous translation of Bernardin de St. Pierre's *Paul et Virginie* (as *al-Amānī wa 'l-minna fī ḥadīth Ḳabūl wa-Ward Djanna*), using the lofty style of *sadjʿ* (rhyming prose) and "arabising" and "islamicising" many of the discourse elements of the original French text. He thereafter turned his attention to the dramatic genre, translating four comedies of Molière into colloquial Arabic poetry (using the form of *radjaz*) and once again cleverly transferring the cultural context from a European to an Egyptian milieu. The four plays in question (published as a group in 1889) were: *Tartuffe (al-Shaykh Matlūf), Les femmes savantes (al-Nisāʾ al-ʿālimāt), L'école des maris (Madrasat al-azwādj)*, and *L'école des femmes (Madrasat al-zawdjāt)*.

From comedy, he moved on to the French tragedians, translating (once more into colloquial Cairene dialect) a set of plays by Racine and Corneille: *Esthèr, Iphigénie*, and *Alexandre le Grand* by the former (as *al-Riwāyāt al-mufīda fī ʿilm al-tarādjīda*), and *El Cid* by the latter. His one excursion into dramatic writing on his own part, *al-Khaddāmīn wa 'l-mukhaddimīn* ("Servants and agents", 1904), was, like his translated plays, composed in colloquial verse.

In the lengthy and complex process of indigenising imported literary genres during the 19th century, Djalāl's role as a translator was a central one. That the translated versions of European works that he produced were successfully assimilated into Egyptian society can be convincingly demonstrated by the fact that *al-Shaykh Matlūf*, his Egyptianised *Tartuffe* and most masterful adaptation, has been revived on the Cairo stage in recent times (e.g. 1963, 1971) to tremendous popular acclaim.

Bibliography: M.M. Badawi, *Early Arabic drama*, Cambridge 1988; idem (ed.), *Modern Arabic literature* (*Cambridge History of Arabic Literature*), Cambridge 1992; P.C. Sadgrove, *The Egyptian theatre in the nineteenth century 1799-1882*, Reading 1996; Fāṭima Mūsā-Maḥmūd (ed.), *Ḳāmūs al-masraḥ*, Cairo 1996, ii, 493-4; Carol Bardenstein, *Matters of non-equivalence. Egyptianizing French literature*, in Lenore A. Grenoble and J.M. Kopper (eds.), *Essays in the art and theory of translation*, Lewiston 1997, 97-120; Shimon Ballas, *The translations of Muḥammad ʿUthmān Jalāl: between innovation and conservation*, in *Studies in canonical and popular arabic literature*, ed. S. Ballas and R. Snir, Toronto 1998, 47-53. For older literature, and biographical sources (including ʿAlī Pasha Mubārak, *al-Khiṭaṭ al-tawfīḳiyya al-djadīda*, xvii, 62ff.), see Brockelmann, *loc. cit.*

(R.M.A. Allen)

MUḤAMMAD ZAMĀN MĪRZĀ, perennially rebellious Mughal prince and brother-in-law of the emperor Humāyūn [*q.v.*].

On Humāyūn's accession in 937/1530, he allied with Bahādur Shāh of Gudjarāt, provoking an invasion by Humāyūn of Gudjarāt via Mālwā. Muḥammad Zamān was pardoned, but in 941/1534 rebelled again, this time in Bihār, but had to escape to Gudjarāt once more. This provoked a full-scale invasion and occupation of Gudjarāt by the Mughal emperor (941-2/1535-6). Muḥammad Zamān escaped; he tried to claim the throne of Gudjarāt for himself on Bahādur Shāh's death in 943/1537 but failed in the attempt, submitting at last to Humāyūn.

Bibliography: See that to humāyūn, and add R.J. Majumdar (general ed.), *The history and culture of the Indian people*, vi, *The Mughul empire*, Bombay 1974, 45-51, 395, 398.

(C.E. Bosworth)

MUḤDATHŪN (a.), "the Moderns", i.e., in classical Arabic literary history, those poets that came after the ancient poets (called *ḳudamāʾ*, *mutaḳaddimūn* or *awāʾil*) of the pre-Islamic and early Islamic periods. The term is first applied to some poets "of the two dynasties" (*mukhaḍramū 'l-dawlatayn*), who flourished in the middle and second half of the 2nd/8th century [see mukhaḍram]. No formal end of the period of the *Muḥdathūn* movement is recognised, but mostly the term applies to poets of the first few centuries of the ʿAbbāsid period. For poets from later times, one finds occasionally the term still used, or, more commonly, expressions such as *ahl al-ʿaṣr* and *muʿāṣirūn* "contemporary [poets]".

Critics were aware of the differences between the poetry of the pre-Islamic (*djāhilī*) poets and that of their successors, the *mukhaḍramūn* (straddling the *Djāhiliyya* and Islam), the *Islāmiyyūn* and the Umayyad poets. However, the changes in style, themes and motifs that arose from the mid-2nd/8th century—in the wake of the fundamental social and intellectual changes that took place in that period (such as the role of the *mawālī* [see mawlā] and the impact of Greek and Persian civilisation)—were considered so fundamental that the dichotomy between "old" (*ḳadīm*) and "modern" is dominant in traditional literary criticism. The distinction is important, too, in Arabic linguistics, since there was a general consensus among the grammarians and lexicographers that only early (pre-*muḥdath*) poetry could serve as attestation for the codification of the "pure" (*fuṣḥā*) language; as Ibn Djinnī, quoted by Ibn Rashīḳ (*ʿUmda*, Cairo 1953, ii, 236), put it: "Modern poets [he uses the term *muwalladūn*, on which see below] may be cited as authorities (*yustashhadu bihim*) on motifs (*maʿānī*), just as ancient poets may be cited as authorities on words (or expressions, alfāẓ)". Even though many grammarians appreciated the poetry of the *Muḥdathūn* for its literary qualities, it is likely that the term originally had pejorative connotations, just as a bad sword could be described as "modern, not cutting" (*muḥdath ghayr ṣārim*, Djarīr, in *Naḳā'iḍ*, ed. A.A. Bevan, Leiden 1905-12, 413). Well before the period of the *Muḥdathūn*, the poet Umayya b. Abī ʿĀ'idh (*fl.* 80/700) praises his own verse as "unlike the patchwork of the *muḥdathūn*" (*Aghānī*², xxiv, 6).

Resistance to the poetry of "moderns" had various grounds: its language, diction, style, contents, or even (though rarely) the fact that some prominent poets were not only non-nomads but also non-Arabs, witness the telling anecdote about Bashshār b. Burd [*q.v.*], often called "the father of the moderns", related in *Aghānī*², iii, 166. It took some time for the *Muḥdathūn* to be recognised by critics and anthologists. The *Ṭabaḳāt fuḥūl al-shuʿarā'* ("*The classes of the master poets*") by Ibn Sallām al-Djumaḥī (d. 231/845 [*q.v.*]) ignores them, as does, for instance, Ḳudāma b. Djaʿfar's [*q.v.*] *Naḳd al-shiʿr*. Abū Tammām (d. 231/846 [*q.v.*]), himself one of the greatest and most controversial of the "moderns", included only a few fragments that could be called *muḥdath* poetry in his influential anthology *al-Ḥamāsa* (his less famous anthology *al-Waḥshiyyāt*, on the other hand, has poems by Bashshār, Abū Nuwās, Abu 'l-ʿAtāhiya, Muṭīʿ b. Iyās, Muslim b. al-Walīd, Diʿbil [*q.vv.*] and other *Muḥdathūn*).

The recognition and esteem that many *Muḥdathūn* received in their lifetimes from patrons and other admirers is reflected in numerous reports and not long after in anthological and critical works, too. A contemporary of Abū Tammām, the poet Diʿbil (d. 246/860), compiled a (partly preserved) book on poets in which the *Muḥdathūn* are included; some later anthologies, such as Ibn al-Muʿtazz's [*q.v.*] *Ṭabaḳāt al-shuʿarā'*, are wholly devoted to the *Muḥdathūn*. This work opens with Ibn Harma (d. *ca.* 170/786 [*q.v.*]), who is more often considered "the last of the ancients" (al-Aṣmaʿī, quoted at 20, and cf. *Aghānī*², iv, 373) or "in the rearguard of poets" (*min sāḳat al-shuʿarā'*, Ibn Ḳutayba, *Shiʿr*, 473). Still quoted by linguists, but already indulging in very "modern" techniques such as writing a long poem without diacritical dots (*Aghānī*², iv, 378-9), Ibn Harma is a borderline case, like e.g. Ibn Mayyāda and Marwān b. Abī Ḥafṣa [*q.vv.*]. Even Bashshār, "father of the Moderns", is sometimes called "the last (*khātimat*) of the (ancient) poets" (*Aghānī*², iii, 143, 148, 150). It is rather surprising that Bashshār's coeval, the caliph al-Walīd b. Yazīd (d. 126/744 [*q.v.*]), in spite of his innovative poetry, is never counted among the *Muḥdathūn*, presumably because he did not live to reach the ʿAbbāsid period.

As Ibn Ḳutayba said, "God did not restrict knowledge, poetry and eloquence to one period . . .; Djarīr, al-Farazdaḳ, al-Akhṭal and other [pre-*muḥdath* poets] were once regarded as 'moderns'" (*Shiʿr*, 5). Of course, the distinction between *ḳadīm* and *muḥdath* is not merely a matter of chronology. The former is associated, or even equated, with the poetry of the *ʿArab*, the nomadic or semi-nomadic Bedouin, and the latter with the poetry of sedentary poets who were often non-Arab, like Bashshār, or of mixed descent (*muwallad*). Indeed, the term *muwalladūn* is sometimes used as a synonym of *muḥdathūn*, at other times for those poets who follow that school [see MUWALLAD. 2. In Arabic language and literature]. Al-Djāḥiẓ wrote (*Ḥayawān*, iv, 130), "The ʿArab and Aʿrāb, both the nomadic and sedentary Arabs (*al-badw wa 'l-ḥaḍar min sā'ir al-ʿarab*), are generally better poets than those poets who live in towns and villages and are not of pure Arab stock among the new generation (*min al-muwallada wa 'l-nābita*)." Confusingly, the term *muwallad* has occasionally been used for poets of pure Arab descent, even from the Umayyad period, such as "Umar b. Abī Rabīʿa, al-Kumayt b. Zayd and al-Ṭirimmāḥ [*q.vv.*] (al-Sidjistānī-al-Aṣmaʿī, *Fuḥūlat al-shuʿarā'*, Cairo 1991, 124, 132, and cf. Ibn Rashīḳ, *ʿUmda*, i, 90), presumably because they were not true nomads, some of them, such as al-Kumayt, having learned and taught grammar (al-Marzubānī, *al-Muwashshaḥ*, Cairo 1965, 302, 326-7).

It is a commonplace of traditional criticism to contrast the "purity" and solidity of the old style with the refinement and rhetoricisation of the new. The old poet built a house, the modern poet embellished and decorated it (e.g. *ʿUmda*, i, 92); the former is like a singer singing fine melodies with a coarse voice, the latter sings inferior melodies with a sweet voice (Ibn Wakīʿ, quoted in *ʿUmda*, i, 92). Modern verse is like a fragrant herb that smells deliciously but briefly, early poetry is like musk or ambergris, increasing in fragrance the more one rubs it (Ibn al-Aʿrābī, quoted in al-Marzubānī, *al-Muwashshaḥ*, 384). The *Muḥdathūn* are credited with introducing *badīʿ* [*q.v.*] consciously, a term referring to various rhetorical and poetic artifices and embellishments. "Muslim b. al-Walīd was the first to use *badīʿ* on a large scale, after Bashshār had first used it . . .; then came Abū Tammām, who used it excessively and immoderately" (quoted by Ibn al-Muʿtazz, *Ṭabaḳāt*, 235). Obviously, the contrast between old and new has been exaggerated and simplified: by no means all early poetry is stylistically rough and unadorned, some of it, notably Umayyad *radjaz* [*q.v.*], is highly rhetoricised. Conversely, much of "modern" poetry is unadorned and highly accessible, and its image is to some extent distorted because in literary criticism and theory it was mainly the rhetorical and embellished style that received attention. However, on the whole it is true that the most characteristic innovation of the *Muḥdathūn* lies precisely in the development of refined rhetorical techniques, a novel use of metaphor (cf. the distinction between the "old" and the "new" metaphor as pointed out by W. Heinrichs, *The hand of the Northwind*, Wiesbaden 1977), and of increasingly complex imagery and "conceits", on which see e.g. B. Reinert, *Der Concetto-Stil in den islamischen Literaturen*, in Heinrichs (ed.), *Neues Handbuch der Literaturwissenschaft. V. Orientalisches Mittelalter*, Wiesbaden 1990, 366-408.

It is difficult to generalise about "modern poetry", extremely varied as it is. Much of the ancient, Bedouin vocabulary and diction is abandoned, yet the so-called neo-classicist style of Abū Tammām and others indulges, at least in their formal *ḳaṣīda*s and other set-pieces, in archaic words and expressions. There were some prosodical innovations: a few new metres were created and truncated forms of existing metres became popular, yet all the old metres survived. Many oddities of grammar and prosody that were condoned in old and Bedouin poetry as poetic licences (*ḍarūrāt*) were deemed faults in new or urban poetry (e.g. Ibn Rashīḳ, *ʿUmda*, ii, 269; Ibn Djinnī, *Khaṣā'iṣ*, Cairo 1952, i, 323ff.).

The ʿAbbāsid critics themselves were aware that the originality and novelty of "modern" poetry were not as great as was sometimes claimed. Ibn al-Muʿtazz [*q.v.*] wrote his seminal treatise on rhetorical figures and tropes, *K. al-Badīʿ*, in order to demonstrate that these figures and tropes can be found already in early poetry and prose (Ḳur'ān and *Ḥadīth*); thus he provided a legitimisation of *badīʿ* while at the same time condemning some of its excesses, notably Abū Tammām's idiosyncratic techniques of metaphor, antithesis and paronomasia. The two brothers called al-Khālidiyyān [*q.v.*], in their *K. al-Ashbāh wa 'l-naẓā'ir*, traced many motifs and themes occurring in modern poetry to their early predecessors, in order to prove the superiority of the latter; it was written in response to those who preferred the moderns.

The poetry of the *Muḥdathūn* certainly was not, and could not have been, a wholly new start. The early poets were canonised by consensus and could not be ignored by the later ones. Modern poets had to choose between slavishly imitating them, which became increasingly archaic and inappropriate for urban poets, or reacting against them (e.g. by means of parody and in the "anti-*nasīb*" theme, common in Abū Nuwās [see NASĪB. d. ʿAbbāsid period]), or by transforming the early themes and motifs, by blending or subtly changing them, while transforming diction and style by means of rhetorical refinement. An important characteristic of modern poetry is the pervading presence of shorter and monothematic poems, with themes that in early poetry usually formed part of the polythematic ode or *ḳaṣīda* [*q.v.*]: the *khamriyya* [*q.v.*] or bacchic poem, the *ṭardiyya* [*q.v.*] or hunting poem, the *zuhdiyya* [*q.v.*] or ascetic, anti-worldly poem, the "floral" poem (called *nawriyya* [*q.v.*], *zahriyya*, *rawḍiyya* or *rabīʿiyya*), the epideictic epigram (*waṣf*), the gnomic epigram (*ḥikma*), the obscene or scatological poem (*mudjūn* [*q.v.*]) and several others. Here, too, there are precedents in early poetry, although it is not always possible to determine whether an early short poem was conceived as an independent epigram or is a fragment of an incompletely transmitted poem.

In any case, the *ḳaṣīda* retained its position as the most prestigious form. As before, one was not considered a great poet unless one could boast of the production of a substantial number of odes. It has been argued (M.M. Badawi, *From primary to secondary Qaṣīdas*, in *JAL*, xi [1980], 1-31 and see his chapter *ʿAbbasid poetry and its antecedents*, in J. Ashtiany *et al.* (eds.), *CHAL, ʿAbbasid belles-lettres*, Cambridge 1990, 146-66) that the coming of Islam brought about a more radical change in poetry than the *muḥdath* "revolution", a change seen in the shift from the tribal and ritualistic *ḳaṣīda* to the mostly panegyric ode modelled on the old type but being more strictly literary, and in the shift from oral to literate transmission. Important developments, too, took place in love-poetry in pre-*muḥdath* times (see GHAZAL. i. In Arabic poetry, and several more recent articles by Renate Jacobi and others). It is true that most of the changes of the period of the first *Muḥdathūn* were prepared by the early Islamic and Umayyad poets, yet on the whole the traditional distinction between them and the newer school is justified and the original contributions of such innovators as Bashshār, Abū Nuwās, Abu 'l-ʿAtāhiya, Abū Tammām and Ibn al-Rūmī cannot be denied. The new sensibility has been linked with the "discovery" of the individual, as a result of social and political changes, such as the dwindling of the old aristocracy, the individualistic egalitarianism espoused by Islam, and high social mobility (see Th. Bauer, *Liebe und Liebesdichtung in der arabischen Welt des 9. und 10. Jahrhunderts*, Wiesbaden 1998).

Among the characteristics of the *ḳaṣīda* among the *Muḥdathūn* is a greater concern for coherence and unity, or at least an avoidance of abrupt transitions. Even though such thematic jumps, such as from *nasīb* to the panegyric section, are still found, most poets devoted care to some kind of connecting motif (*takhalluṣ* [*q.v.*]). And whereas many early poems seem to end more or less fortuitously, often in mid-air as it were, the *Muḥdathūn* often conclude with a proper peroration, ending with topics appropriate to an envoi, such as a dedicatory passage or a blessing.

After the first few generations of *Muḥdathūn* poetry had become so artful, its techniques had developed to such an extent that it seemed to the following generations that it was difficult to come up with novel things: the poet and critic Ibn Ṭabāṭabā (d. 322/934), in his *ʿIyār al-shiʿr* (Riyāḍ 1985, 13) speaks of the "trial" (*miḥna*) of the poets in his days who try to please exacting patrons by means of their rhetorical subtleties and witticisms, while abandoning the truthfulness allegedly found in early poetry.

If there ever was a true *querelle des ancients et modernes* in Arabic literary history, it was mostly fought in moderate terms, the majority of critics professing their respect for the ancients, even though many pointed out the superior techniques of the moderns. Thus al-Ḥātimī (d. 388/998) notes that the latter excelled in *takhalluṣ* "because of the bright minds and subtle thoughts", surpassing the primitive methods of pre-Islamic and early Islamic poets (*Ḥilyat al-muḥāḍara*, Baghdād 1979, 215-16). Ḍiyā' al-Dīn Ibn al-Athīr (d. 637/1239 [*q.v.*]) calls Abū Tammām, al-Buḥturī and al-Mutanabbī "the al-Lāt, al-ʿUzzā and Manāt [*q.vv.*] of poetry" (*al-Mathal al-sā'ir*, Cairo 1962, iii, 226) and pronounces them superior to all others, ancient and modern (iii, 274). The Andalusian anthologist Ibn Bassām (d. 543/1147 [*q.v.*]), explaining why he only includes recent poets, speaks scathingly of ancient poetry (*al-Dhakhīra*, Beirut 1978-9, i/1, 13-14): "Everything that is recited over and over again is boring; the ear rejects 'O abode of Mayya . . .' "; he goes on to quote irreverently the opening words of several of the *Muʿallaḳāt* [*q.v.*], perhaps the most "canonical" of all Arabic poems. At the other extreme stands e.g. Ibn Khaldūn [*q.v.*], arch-conservative for once, who quotes with apparent approval the opinion that the rhymes of al-Mutanabbī and al-Maʿarrī [*q.v.*] cannot be considered true poetry, because they did not follow (ancient) Arab poetical methods (*al-Muḳaddima*, Cairo 1962, 1296, tr. F. Rosenthal, Princeton 1967, iii, 382). However, in the controversies such as arose on account of the style and motifs of Abū Tammām or al-Mutanabbī, it is usually not a matter of old vs. new.

Bibliography (in addition to references given in the article): I. Goldziher, *Alte und neue Poesie im Urtheile der arabische Kritiker*, in his *Abhandlungen zur arabischer Philologie*, i, Leiden 1896, 122-76; Ṭāhā Ḥusayn, *Ḥadīth al-arbiʿā'*, ii, Cairo 1968 (first publ. 1922-4); S.A. Bonebakker, *Poets and critics in the third century AH*, in G.E. von Grunebaum (ed.), *Logic in classical Islamic culture*, Wiesbaden 1970, 85-111; J.E. Bencheikh, *Poétique arabe*, Paris 1975; W. Heinrichs, *Paired metaphors in muḥdath poetry*, in *Occasional Papers of the School of Abbasid Studies*, i (1986), 1-22; Renate Jacobi, *Abbasidische Dichtung (8.-13. Jhdt.)*, in H. Gätje (ed.), *Grundriss der Arabischen Philologie. II. Literaturwissenschaft*, Wiesbaden 1987, 41-57; E. Wagner, *Grundzüge der klassischen arabischen Dichtung*, ii, Darmstadt 1988, 89-158; A. Arazi, *EI*² art. *Shiʿr*. 1. In Arabic. Relevant, too, are studies on *badīʿ*, such as Suzanne P. Stetkevych, *Abū Tammām and the poetics of the ʿAbbasid age*, Leiden 1991; Heinrichs, *Muslim b. al-Walīd und* badīʿ, in *Festschrift Ewald Wagner*, Beirut 1994, ii, 211-45; and P. Cachia, *The Arch rhetorician*, Wiesbaden 1998 (a summary of a late handbook of *badīʿ*). For a useful survey of mediaeval critical opinions, see Ibn Ras̲h̲īḳ, *ʿUmda*, i, 90-3 (*fi 'l-ḳudamāʾ wa 'l-muḥdat̲h̲īn*), 100-1 (section on famous poets), ii, 263-45 (section on "modern motifs", *al-maʿānī al-muḥdat̲h̲a*).

(G.J.H. van Gelder)

MUḤIBB al-DĪN al-K̲H̲AṬĪB, Sunnī Arab journalist, publisher and editor, an influential figure of the *Salafiyya* [*q.v.*] as well as of Arab nationalism [see ḳawmiyya. 1] in the 20th century (1886-1969). He was born in July 1886 in Damascus. Already in his youth his worldview was influenced by a number of Salafī thinkers such as Ṭāhir al-D̲j̲azāʾirī (d. 1920), and also by the writings of various Arab proto-nationalists, including al-Kawākibī [*q.v.*]. The gist of his views, which he advocated until the end of his life, can be described as a peculiar blend of Salafī and Arab nationalist positions (see Hurvitz, in *Bibl.*).

As a student of law in Istanbul (1905-7), and until the end of World War I, he was involved in the activities of a number of Arab secret societies such as *al-Nahḍa al-ʿArabiyya* and *al-ʿArabiyya al-Fatāt* (for details, see his own account in *al-K̲h̲aṭīb, ḥayātuhu bi-ḳalamihi*; also Burd̲j̲, *Muḥibb al-Dīn al-K̲h̲aṭīb*; Tauber, *The emergence*; idem, *The Arab movements*, in *Bibl.*).

From 1916 onwards, he served the "Arab Revolt", first as a member of the editorial staff of *al-Ḳibla* in Mecca, and later (summer 1919 to summer 1920) as chief editor of the Hās̲h̲imite official newspaper in Damascus, *al-ʿĀṣima*. However, a few days after the battle of Maysalūn (24 July 1920 [*q.v.*]) and the subsequent French occupation of Damascus, he left Syria for Egypt.

Having finally settled in Cairo, Muḥibb al-Dīn al-K̲h̲aṭīb in the following years rose to some prominence, in Egypt and far beyond, as owner of a printing press, a bookshop and a publishing house serving the causes of *ʿurūba* [*q.v.*] and Sunnī Islam, called *al-Maṭbaʿa al-Salafiyya wa-Maktabatuhā*. Further more, he gained recognition as founder and main author of two important journals, *al-Zahrāʾ* (1924-9) and *al-Fatḥ* (1926-48), and also as editor of mediaeval as well as modern Arabic texts.

Even before the fall of the Hās̲h̲imite rule in the Ḥid̲j̲āz (1925), he had declared his support for Ibn Suʿūd [see ʿabd al-ʿazīz, in Suppl.] and subsequently became an eloquent defender of Saudi-Wahhābī politics and religious practice [see wahhābiyya. 2]. In this connection, he came forward as one of the most influential Sunnī polemicists in modern times against the S̲h̲īʿa in general and their role in Islamic history in particular. As a result, he opposed all attempts at an ecumenical rapprochement between the two sides [see taḳrīb]. Even as chief editor of *Mad̲j̲allat al-Azhar* (1952-9) he maintained this view (see Brunner, esp. 193-208). He is also remembered as one of the modern authors who tried to restore the image of the Umayyads in the mind of the Sunnī Arab public (Ende, 91-110). He died in Cairo on 30 December 1969.

Bibliography: 1. Arabic works. Ḳuṣayy Muḥibb al-Dīn al-K̲h̲aṭīb, *Fihrist al-Maktaba al-Salafiyya*, Cairo 1399/1978-9 (on p. 4, a list of his most important publications, including editions, translations, etc., but without bibliographical details); *Muḥibb al-Dīn al-K̲h̲aṭīb, al-Ḥasanī al-Dimas̲h̲ḳī, ḥayātuhu bi-ḳalamihi*, ed. D̲j̲amʿiyyat al-Tamaddun al-Islāmī, Damascus 1399/1979; Anwar al-D̲j̲undī, *Taʾrīk̲h̲ al-ṣiḥāfa al-islāmiyya, ii, al-Fatḥ*, Cairo n.d. [1986]; Muḥammad ʿAbd al-Raḥmān Burd̲j̲, *Muḥibb al-Dīn al-K̲h̲aṭīb wa-dawruhu fi 'l-ḥaraka al-ʿarabiyya, 1906-1920*, Cairo 1990; Muḥammad Rad̲j̲ab al-Bayyūmī, *al-Nahḍa al-islāmiyya fī siyar aʿlāmihā 'l-muʿāṣirīn*, ii, Damascus and Beirut 1995, 311-28.

2. Western studies. W. Ende, *Arabische Nation und islamische Geschichte*, Beirut 1977; E. Tauber, *The emergence of the Arab movements*, London 1993; idem, *The Arab movements in World War I*, London 1993; N. Hurvitz, *Muhibb al-Din al-Khatib's Semitic wave theory and Pan-Arabism*, in *MES*, xxix (1993), 118-34; R. Brunner, *Annäherung und Distanz*, Berlin 1996; C. Mayeur-Jaouen, *Les débuts d'une revue néo-salafiste: Muḥibb al-Dīn al-K̲h̲aṭīb et* Al-Fatḥ *de 1926 à 1928*, in *RMMM*, nos. 95-8 (= Débats intellectuelles au Moyen-Orient dans l'entre-deux-guerres) (Aix-en-Provence 2002), 227-55.

(W. Ende)

MUʿĪNSIZ (a., t.), from Ar. *muʿīn* "supporter, helper" and Tkish. *siz* "without", a term connected with the introduction of the conscription system into the Ottoman Empire in the 19th century to indicate someone who has nobody to look after his family and other dependants if he is drafted, i.e. is a breadwinner. The decision as to who was regarded as sole breadwinner in a family depended on the age, sex and physical and mental condition of those left behind and on their degree of kinship to the potential *muʿīnsiz*. *Muʿīnsiz* were exempted from regular military service, but served as reservists: as *redīf* and *mustaḥfiẓ* [see radīf]. Once one was registered as a regular soldier, becoming a *muʿīnsiz* was rarely possible, even if personal circumstances had changed.

Although *muʿīnsiz*, as reservists, had only limited military obligations in times of peace, during times of mobilisation and war they were called up to the colours. In such cases, their families were left without breadwinners. To prevent these soldiers from worrying about their families and to obviate subsequent problems with morale and even desertion, the Ottoman state provided a separation allowance, the *Muʿīnsiz ʿĀʾile Maʿās̲h̲ī*. First applied during the Crimean War, the allowance and the terms under which it was assigned remained rather vague until the second decade of the 20th century. The First World War forced the Ottoman authorities to become more specific. Articles 49-55 of the *Mükellefiyyet-i ʿAskeriyye Ḳānūn-u Müwaḳḳatī* of May 1914 and its revised version of July-August 1915 dealt with the separation allowance. A bill for a separate, thirty-one article law on the allowance was discussed in the *S̲h̲ūrā-yi Dewlet* [see ʿabd al-ʿazīz; dustūr. ii. turkey] in October 1915, but did not reach the *Med̲j̲lis-i Wükelā* (Council of Ministers) and the Parliament until the end of 1918.

Bibliography: Pakalın, ii, 573; Nicole A.N.M. van Os, *Taking care of soldiers' families. The Ottoman state and the Muinsiz Aile Maaşı*, in E.J. Zürcher (ed.), *Arming the state. Military conscription in the Middle East and Central Asia, 1775-1925*, London and New York 1999, 95-110; Zürcher, *The Ottoman conscription system in theory and practice*, in *ibid.*, 79-94.

(Nicole A.N.M. van Os)

MUḲAWWIYĀT (a.), a medical term, originally denoting stimulants but gradually taking on the meaning of aphrodisiacs—probably as a form of euphemism—a meaning which it has retained into the present day. It will be noted, however, that in the *Ḳānūn fi 'l-ṭibb* of Ibn Sīnā [*q.v.*] the term *muḳawwī* is already in recurrent use in the section devoted to impotence (ii, 539-41). This is explained by the fact that aphrodisiacs were intended to restore to the deficient man all his vigour and all his strength and to excite his sexual desire (or that of the woman, evoked in some texts, although it is the male to whom most attention is given), whence this blurring of meanings. Mediaeval Arabic medical texts used, for these preparations, numerous words and expressions: *munʿiẓ, muhayyidj li 'l-shahwa, muhayyidj li 'l-bāh, ashyāʾ tuḳawwī ʿalā 'l-djimāʿ* and *al-mufradāt al-bāhiyya.* All these names refer to the notion of stimulating erection, exciting carnal desire and facilitating the sexual act.

In a society where virility remained a major factor, where guaranteeing the succession was an imperative for princes and where the presence of numerous concubines was still an element of social prestige in *khāṣṣa* circles—not to mention Ḳurʾānic verses calling for the "ploughing" of wives—it was to be expected that physicians should take an interest in aphrodisiacs and that texts of erotology as a literary genre should proliferate. Thus it is worth noting the significant fact that the last recipe given in the famous formulary of al-Kōhēn al-ʿAṭṭār is that of an aphrodisiac (*maʿdjūn al-saḳanḳūr,* in *Minhādj,* 169). This medical literature should be considered in association with the related tradition of works of erotology (*kutub al-bāh*), the existence of which is noted, from the 4th/10th century onward, by Ibn al-Nadīm in a section of his *Fihrist* entitled *Asmāʾ al-kutub al-muʾallafa fi 'l-bāh al-fārisī wa 'l-hindī wa 'l-rūmī wa 'l-ʿarabī* (436). He clearly points out the suggestive function of these works (*ʿalā ṭarīḳ al-ḥadīth al-mushabbiḳ*), most of which are undoubtedly of Indian origin. Consequently, there existed a science associated with sexuality, linking empirical observations, theoretical material inspired by the predominant medical doctrines, and psychological considerations. It is thus that the Shaykh al-Nafzāwī refers to six causes of sexual desire: intensity of desire, abundance of sperm, encounter with desirable individuals, physical beauty [of the object of desire], fortifying nourishment and petting. He supplements this list with reference to eight factors predisposing the male to coitus (*tuḳawwī ʿalā 'l-djimāʿ*): good health, absence of anxieties, happiness, relaxation, good diet, material well-being, variation of position and changing of partners (*al-Rawḍ al-ʿāṭir,* 143). Sexual problems described by doctors therefore included, besides physical malfunctions, inhibitions and psychological neuroses. Obviously, the form of treatment depended on the precise definitions of these psychosomatic disorders. Medical treatises also describe impotence (*ʿadjz, nuḳsān al-bāh*) and functional problems related to erection (*intishār, inʿāẓ*), generally known by the term *istirkhāʾ al-kadīb,* paralysis, slackening of the penis—but also female frigidity and anorgasm, which seem to be indicated by the expressions *bard al-raḥim* or *ṣalābat al-raḥim,* respectively: drying up of the uterus, sclerosis of its tissues (*Ḳānūn,* ii, 536-9).

The therapies applied in the treatment of these disorders thus rely on a wide variety of remedies ranging from potions to massages, ointments to auto-suggestion. Medications may be either simple or compound. Looking first at what could accurately be called auto-suggestion: for the physician, this consists, in recommending that his patient read pornographic works on the multiple positions and forms of intercourse (*al-kutub al-muṣannafa fi aḥwāl al-djimāʿ wa-ashkālihi*) or even listen to erotic anecdotes (*akhbār al-mudjāmiʿīn*). As regards aphrodisiac products as such, these are for the most part warming and stimulating items such as ginger, cinnamon, sandalwood, musk, camphor and asafoetida, combined with honey which remains a sovereign remedy. Types of compound aphrodisiacs are confections (*maʿdjūn*) and electuaries (*djawārshin*) which the invalid takes daily; oils (*duhn*) and pomades (*marham*), prescribed for external use and applied to the vagina, the penis, the pelvic region and the loins; and douches for female use (*ḥuḳna tuḳawwī 'l-marʾa li 'l-djimāʿ, Akrabādhīn al-Ḳalānisī,* 144).

One of the ingredients most often cited is the Egyptian skink (*saḳanḳūr, Scincus officinarum*), a variety of lizard which when dried and salted was credited—and is credited still in the traditional pharmacopoeia—with remarkable aphrodisiac qualities (*Minhādj,* 169), to such an extent that Dāwūd al-Anṭākī warns that this remedy can lead to death from excess of erection (*Tadhkira,* 194). The success of this animal seems to be explained by its phallic appearance, just as today, for the same reasons, the horn of the rhinoceros is credited, in Chinese medicine, with highly aphrodisiac qualities. This form of mind projection featured, in one manner or another, in the choice of certain other components utilised in the preparation of aphrodisiacs: bull's penis, "fox's testicles" (*khuṣā al-thaʿlab,* Satyrion, *Orchis hircina* L.) and testicles of the cock or the ram. It should be noted that, in traditional Arab medicine, use is still made, according to the theory of affinities, of the pulverised testicles of calf or bull, as well as the officinal skink (Bellakhdar, 98). In conclusion, account should be taken of the extent to which, in the mediaeval Arab medical tradition, coitus is seen as an activity particularly beneficial to man on the psychological and physiological level, and the degree of importance attached by physicians to the physiological aspect.

Bibliography: Dāwūd al-Anṭākī, *Tadhkira ulī 'l-albāb,* Beirut n.d.; Kōhēn al-ʿAṭṭār, *Minhādj al-dukkān wa-dustūr al-aʿyān,* Cairo 1870; Ibn Sīnā, *al-Ḳānūn fi 'l-ṭibb,* 3 vols. Cairo 1877, repr. Beirut n.d.; G.H. Bousquet, *L'éthique sexuelle de l'Islam,* Paris 1966; J. Bellakhdar, *Médecine traditionelle et toxicologie ouest-saharienne. Contribution à l'étude de la pharmacopée marocaine,* Rabat 1978; Ibn al-Nadīm, *Fihrist,* Beirut 1978; Badr al-Dīn al-Ḳalānisī, *Aḳrabādhīn,* ed. Z. al-Bābā, Aleppo 1983; B. Musallam, *Sex and society in Islam,* London 1983; F. Sanagustin, *Note sur un recueil ancien de recettes médicinales,* in *BEO,* xxxvi (1984), 163-200; A. Bouhdiba, *La sexualité en Islam,* Paris 1986; Shihāb al-Dīn al-Tifāshī, *Nuzhat al-albāb fīmā lā yūdjad fi kitāb,* London 1992; al-Shaykh al-Nafzāwī, *al-Rawḍ al-ʿāṭir fi nuzhat al-khāṭir,* London 1993. It should furthermore be noted that there is an abundant literature dealing with magical procedures for curing impotence (magical formulas, amulets and clay tablets), or guiding the choice of seasons and festive days for the sexual act (astronomical and agro-meteorological calendars).

(F. SANAGUSTIN)

MŪSĀ AL-ṢADR, SAYYID, Imāmī Shīʿī cleric and political leader in Lebanon (1928-78?). Born in Ḳum [*q.v.*] into a family of religious scholars with roots in southern Lebanon and ʿIrāḳ, he studied in the *madāris* of his home town and at the University of Tehran where he read (secular) law.

From 1954 to 1959, he pursued his studies in Nadjaf [*q.v.*], his principal teachers being Sayyid Muḥsin al-Ḥakīm (d. 1970) and Sayyid Abu 'l-Ḳāsim al-Khūʾī (d. 1992). From Nadjaf he began establishing personal contacts with the Lebanese branch of his family, and in particular with his uncle, the influential scholar Sayyid ʿAbd al-Ḥusayn Sharaf al-Dīn [*q.v.*]. Before the latter's death on 30 December 1957, he had apparently expressed the wish that Mūsā al-Ṣadr should succeed him as leader of the Imāmī Shīʿī community of Tyre [see ṢŪR].

In late 1959, Sayyid Mūsā al-Ṣadr took up residence

in Tyre. In the following years he gained influence both locally and further afield as teacher and preacher and also as a spokesman (called Imām) for the Shīʿīs of Lebanon [see also MUTAWĀLĪ], who felt socially and politically neglected by the government in Beirut. In the face of considerable resistance on the part of the old feudal leadership as well as from certain members of the Shīʿī clergy, he finally succeeded in setting up a Higher Shiʿite Council (*al-Madjlis al-Islāmī al-Shīʿī al-Aʿlā*) by resolution of the National Assembly in December 1967. In May 1969 Mūsā al-Ṣadr was elected president of this council, the first body to represent the Shīʿa of Lebanon.

In March 1974 he launched a mass movement called *Ḥarakat al-maḥrūmīn*, which was soon known to have formed a military wing called *Afwādj al-muḳāwama al-lubnāniyya* (AMAL). In late August 1978, more than three years after the outbreak of the civil war in Lebanon, Mūsā al-Ṣadr suddenly disappeared while on a visit to Libya. The circumstances of this affair remain mysterious, but after a few years he was presumed dead even by the majority of his followers. Both AMAL and its rival, *Ḥizb Allāh*, claim to be the heirs to his spiritual and political legacy.

Bibliography: 1. Arabic works. Markaz al-tawthīḳ fī Dār al-Khulūd (ed.), *Al-Ṣadr!?* [sic], Beirut 1979; ʿĀdil Riḍā, *Maʿ al-iʿtidhār . . . li 'l-imām al-Ṣadr*, Cairo 1981 (includes press reports etc. concerning his disappearance); Dār al-Ḥawrāʾ (ed.), *Minbar wa-miḥrāb. Al-Imām Mūsā al-Ṣadr 1960-1969 bi 'l-kalima wa 'l-ṣūra*, ²Beirut 1987 (speeches, articles, interviews); ʿAbd al-Ḥusayn Sharaf al-Dīn, *Bughyat al-rāghibīn*, ii, Beirut 1991, 619-35; *al-Imām Mūsā al-Ṣadr, al-radjul, al-mawkif, al-ḳadiyya*, Beirut 1993 (speeches, articles); ʿAdnān Faḥṣ, *al-Imām al-Ṣadr, al-sīra wa 'l-fikr 1969-1975*, Beirut 1996; Ḥusayn Sharaf al-Dīn, *al-Imām al-Sayyid Mūsā al-Ṣadr. Maḥaṭṭāt taʾrīkhiyya*, Tyre 1996; idem (ed.), *Abdjadiyyat al-ḥiwār. Muḥāḍarāt wa-abḥāth li 'l-Imām Mūsā al-Ṣadr*, Tyre 1997; Aḥmad Ḳaṣīr, *al-Imām Mūsā al-Ṣadr*, Beirut 1998; Hādī Faḍl Allāh, *Fikr al-Imām Mūsā al-Ṣadr al-siyāsī wa 'l-iṣlāḥī*, Beirut 1999; Ibrāhīm Khāzim al-ʿĀmilī, *Gharīb al-ʿaṣr āyatallāh al-mughayyab al-Ṣayyid Mūsā al-Ṣadr*, n.p. [Beirut?] 1421/2000-01; *Masīrat al-imām al-Sayyid Mūsā al-Ṣadr*, ed. Yaʿḳūb Ḍāhir, 12 vols., Beirut 2000.

2. In western languages. F. Ajami, *The vanished Imam*, London 1986; A.R. Norton, *Amal and the Shia*, Austin, Texas 1987; A. Rieck, *Die Schiiten und der Kampf um den Libanon*, Hamburg 1989; M. Halawi, *A Lebanon defied. Musa al-Sadr and the Shiʿa community*, Boulder, Col. 1992; A.W. Samii, *The Shah's Lebanon policy. The role of SAVAK*, in *MES*, xxxiii (1997), 66-91. (W. ENDE)

MUSĀBAḲA (A., pl. *musābaḳāt*) "race, competition, contest"; *musābaḳa tilāwat al-Ḳurʾān* is thus a "contest in the recitation of the Ḳurʾān". Such contests are held in many contemporary Muslim countries and contexts, such as Saudi Arabia, Egypt, Indonesia and North America. International competitions are held periodically in Mecca and in Kuala Lumpur, Malaysia.

There is a national level recitation competition held every two years in Indonesia. It is popularly known as "MTQ" (for *musābaḳah tilāwatil ḳurʾān*). Local, regional and provincial eliminations determine the selection of the final contestants, who represent all of Indonesia's provinces in a colourful and festive complex of events lasting about ten days. The Indonesian approach to the Ḳurʾān recitation *musābaḳa* conceives it to be a "national discipline" that affords Indonesia's Muslims a chance to strengthen their religious life while enhancing their pride as citizens of the Republic. Although recitation is at the core of the event, there are also Ḳurʾānic quiz shows for youth, who appear on provincial teams; an elaborate *daʿwa* (Islamic "missions") exhibit with displays of publications and programmes; a parade through the streets of the host city; colourful opening and closing ceremonies with processionals, special music, dance and recitation; and Islamic fashion shows. There is considerable national media coverage, as the MTQ is attended by the president, government ministers, the diplomatic corps, and distinguished Muslim leaders from Indonesia and abroad. Each MTQ is held in a different city, thus producing something like a royal progress about the country over the years.

Although recitation is governed by long-established *ādāb*, as far as the conduct of particular *musābaḳāt* is concerned, one needs to refer to specific cases. For example, the state television service in Surabaya, East Java, has sponsored a provincial *musābaḳa* that features groups of timed recitation selections (a standard procedure) interspersed with popular musical interludes performed by Muslim "seminarians" on guitars and other instruments (cf. Roman Catholic "rock" masses). In the Indonesian national-level tournament, the reciters are divided into categories of boys, girls, women, men and handicapped (usually blind). There are separate categories for those who read the Ḳurʾānic passages from a *muṣḥaf* and those who recite from memory. Judges evaluate the performances according to established criteria in *ādāb* (deportment, etiquette), *tadjwīd* (technical rules and procedures of recitation), and *naghamāt* (musical modes and melodies). Prizes and trophies are awarded to winning individuals and provincial teams, whose return home is marked by special festivities.

Bibliography: There is not much scholarly literature on Ḳurʾānic recitation competitions, although specific events are covered in the popular media. For Indonesia, see Khadijatus Shalihah, *Perkembangan seni baca al-Qurʾan dan Qiraat Tujuh di Indonesia* ("Developments in the art of reading the Ḳurʾān and the Seven Readings in Indonesia"), Jakarta 1983, 84-97; a more popular descriptive article is F.M. Denny, *The Great Indonesian Qurʾan-chanting tournament*, in *The World and I* (June 1986), 216-23, based on field work. The *musābaḳa* idea is motivated largely by a concern for maintaining and strengthening Ḳurʾānic literacy, especially in non-Arabic speaking countries. For ways in which Indonesians approach this, see Denny, *Qurʾān recitation training in Indonesia: a survey of contexts and handbooks*, in A. Rippin (ed.), *Approaches to the history of the interpretation of the Qurʾān*, Oxford 1988, 288-306. (F.M. DENNY)

MUSĀFIR (A.), literally, "traveller". For the genre of travel account literature, see RIḤLA. For the rest houses and caravanserais set up for travellers, see KHĀN, MANZIL, and MIHMĀN, in Suppl. For the commercial caravans of which travellers also usually formed part, see KĀRWĀN. For the Pilgrimage caravans, see ḤADJDJ. iii and AMĪR AL-ḤADJDJ. For the highways along which travellers passed, see SHĀRIʿ.

N

NADIRA.

2. In Swahili literature.

The word *nādira* is not well known in Swahili except in scholarly circles. The Swahili word *ngano* (common also in other Bantu languages) is in use for all invented tales including fables, as opposed to *hadithi*, which originally referred to Islamic legends about the Prophet Muḥammad and the characters he used to discuss with the *Ṣaḥāba*, while seated in the mosque at Medina after prayers. Today, such *hadithi* contain some of the most fantastic adventure tales, including the exploits of ʿAlī against the *d̲j̲inn* and *s̲h̲ayāṭīn*. Next to Arabian tales, such as Mad̲j̲nūn and Laylā, there are tales of Persian origin circulating on the Swahili coast, such as those of Sendibada (= Sindbād) or Farhād and S̲h̲īrīn. India is richly represented as a supplier of motifs for the Swahili storytellers. Fables from the *Pančatantra*, such as that of the monkey and the crocodile (who has become a shark in the Swahili version) are well known in Swahili, although they may have come via the Persian version of this work, the *Anwār-i Suhaylī*. Curiously, the Arabian version, *Kalīla wa-Dimna* [*q.v.*], is not known in Swahili. Some tales even go back to Sanskrit literature, such as the Tale of the Three Magic Objects from the *Vetālapancavimśatikā*, or the Tale of Moses (i.e. the Prophet Mūsā) and the two Angels, ultimately based on the Sanskrit *Kathāsaritsāgara*.

Swahili scholars are very well read in Arabic traditional literature, especially the *Ḳiṣaṣ al-anbiyāʾ* [*q.v.*], Creation and cosmology (*ibdāʿ wa-ʿilm al-samawāt*), the *Sīra, Mawlid, Miʿrād̲j̲*, and the fabulous tales of al-Iskandar and Nabī Sulaymān.

Finally, there is the vast African heritage of narration, which includes fables for children including the Aesop-type tales, as well as bloodcurdling stories about ghosts and monsters of every description; purely African, fresh original, well-structured tales of wonders.

Bibliography: E. Steere, *Swahili tales*, London 1869; C.B. Büttner, *Lieder und Geschichten der Suaheli*, Berlin 1894; C. Velten, *Märchen und Erzählungen der Suaheli*, Berlin 1898; L. Reinisch, *Die Somali Sprache. I. Texte*, Vienna 1900; Velten, *Prosa und Poesie der Suaheli*, Berlin 1907; C. Meinhof, *Afrikanische Märchen*, Jena 1917; E. Cerulli, *The folk literature of the Galla of Southern Abyssinia* (Harvard African Studies, III) Cambridge 1922; Alice Werner, *Myths and legends of the Bantu*, London 1933; M.M. Moreno, *Favole e rime galla*, Rome 1935; E. Damman, *Dichtungen in der Lamu Mundart des Suaheli*, Hamburg 1940; idem, *Die Quellen der Suahelidichtung*, in *Isl.*, xxvi (1942), 250-68; J.W.T. Allen, *Tendi*, London 1971; H.T. Norris, *Saharan myth and saga*, Oxford 1972; J. Knappert, *The epic in Africa*, in *Jnal. of the Folklore Inst.*, iv/2-3 (Bloomington 1967), 171ff.; idem, *The Qisaṣu ʾl-Anbiyāʾi as moralistic stories*, in *Procs. of the Seminar for Arabian Studies*, vi (London 1976), 103-16; idem, *Epic poetry in Swahili and other African languages*, Leiden 1983; idem, *Islamic legends*, Leiden 1985; idem, *Kings, gods and spirits from African mythology*, London 1986; idem, *Myths and legends of the Swahili*, Nairobi 1986.

(J. Knappert)

al-**NAD̲J̲ĀS̲H̲Ī**, Ḳays b. ʿAmr al-Ḥārit̲h̲ī, Arab poet of the 1st/7th century, probably called by this epithet because of his dark skin inherited from his Ethiopian mother, d. 49/669.

Born in Nad̲j̲rān, he and his clan became converts to Islam at Medina in 10/632. His bellicose nature led him to compose virulent satires against ʿAbd al-Raḥmān b. Ḥassān b. T̲h̲ābit, who replied with the aid of his father. On the advice of al-Ḥuṭayʾa and Ḥassān [*q.vv.*], the caliph ʿUmar had al-Nad̲j̲ās̲h̲ī imprisoned for his invectives against the B. ʿAd̲j̲lān and their poet Ibn Muḳbil [*q.v.*]. At the battle of Ṣiffīn, he joined ʿAlī and exchanged verses of a politico-religious nature with Muʿāwiya's poets, notably Kaʿb b. D̲j̲uʿayl. However, he left ʿAlī's side after the latter had him flogged for drinking wine during Ramaḍān, and he went over to Muʿāwiya's army, eventually dying at Laḥd̲j̲ in Yemen.

Al-Nad̲j̲ās̲h̲ī's poetic œuvre does not seem to have been gathered together in a *dīwān* by the early philologists, although Ibn al-Nadīm, *Fihrist*, ed. Cairo, 157, mentions a *kitāb al-Nad̲j̲ās̲h̲ī* attributed to al-Madāʾinī. Modern authors, such as Schultess, Cheikho and al-Nuʿaymī have endeavoured to piece together his surviving verses, and Ṭ. al-ʿAs̲h̲s̲h̲ās̲h̲, S. G̲h̲urāb and S. Bakkārī have tried to reconstitute the *dīwān*, based on some 50 sources, in *Annales de l'Université de Tunis*, xxi (1982), 105-201, comprising 333 verses in 64 pieces of unequal length from one to 43 verses. His themes are the usual main poetric ones: satire, praise, *fak̲h̲r*, elegy and erotic poetry, with his poetry reflecting the main phases of his life and times. Following al-ʿĀmilī, *Aʿyān al-S̲h̲īʿa*, xliii, 368-9, he may be considered as one of the main pro-ʿAlid poets of the period before 50/670, with his eulogies of ʿAlī and his supporters and insults against Muʿāwiya and his partisans at the time of Ṣiffīn forming over half of his surviving verses.

Bibliography: See, in addition to the works mentioned above, Brockelmann, S I, 73; Ziriklī, *Aʿlām*², vi, 58; Blachère, *HLA*, ii, 320; Sezgin, *GAS*, ii, 307-8; and El Achèche, doctorat d'état thesis, *La poésie shīʿite jusqu'au IIIe siècle de l'Hégire*, Paris 1988, unpubl., and corpus of S̲h̲īʿī poetry to the 3rd century A.H., *As̲h̲ʿār al-tas̲h̲ayyuʿ*, Beirut 1997.

(Taïeb El Achèche)

NAD̲J̲ĪB K̲H̲ĀN (see nad̲j̲īb al-dawla).

NAFAḲA (a.), in Islamic law, maintenance, i.e. of the necessities of life, consisting of food, clothing and shelter. The obligation to provide for a person's maintenance arises from kinship, ownership and marriage.

Kinship

Fathers are obliged to provide for their children, unless the latter have sufficient property to support themselves. The obligation lasts with regard to boys until puberty, and regarding girls, until they marry and their marriage is consummated. After puberty, boys are entitled to maintenance from their fathers if they are physically or mentally unfit to support themselves and their fathers have sufficient means. According to all schools of jurisprudence, children with sufficient means must support their parents if they are indigent. The S̲h̲āfiʿīs and Imāmī S̲h̲īʿīs hold that this obligation exists with regard to all ascendants. The Ḥanafīs extend it to all blood relatives within the forbidden degrees (*d̲h̲awū raḥim maḥram*).

Ownership

The owner of a slave has the duty to maintain him or her. If he fails to do so, the judge may sell the slave without the master's consent.

Marriage

The husband's duty to maintain his wife is regarded as a consideration for her being under her husband's control (*maḥbūsa*). As a consequence, her right to maintenance arises only after the consummation of her marriage, when cohabitation begins, and does not depend on her indigence. According to most schools, the level of maintenance depends on the status of both spouses. A wife is always entitled to be housed alone, preferably at some distance from her co-wives, and not to be forced to share her accommodation with her husband's relatives. If it is in accordance with the status of both spouses, the wife must be provided with a domestic servant.

The wife's right to maintenance ends with the termination of the marriage by her husband's decease or by repudiation. Since marriage persists after a revocable repudiation (*ṭalāḳ* [*q.v.*] *rad̲j̲ʿī*) until the expiry of the waiting period (*ʿidda* [*q.v.*]), the wife is entitled to maintenance during this period. Although after an irrevocable (*bāʾin*) repudiation the marriage comes immediately to an end, the husband must provide for his former wife during the ensuing waiting period if she is pregnant. If she is not, opinions vary.

The husband's obligation is suspended if his wife is disobedient (*nās̲h̲iza*). This is the case if she refuses to move to the marital home or leaves it without her husband's consent or a lawful reason. Her right to maintenance, however, is not affected if her behaviour is justified, e.g. if the home provided by her husband does not meet the legal requirements (*maskan s̲h̲arʿī*) or if he has exceeded the bounds of proper marital chastisement. All schools but the Ḥanafīs (who argue that such circumstances are practically impossible to prove) regard the wife's refusal to have sexual intercourse with her husband as disobedience entailing the suspension of maintenance.

Whereas most schools regard maintenance as an ordinary debt whose arrears are due and payable, the Ḥanafī view is different: if the husband for whatever reason does not provide maintenance, his obligation expires after one month, unless the amount of maintenance has been specified by agreement between the spouses or by judicial decree. All schools except the Ḥanafīs and the S̲h̲īʿīs regard the husband's failure to provide maintenance as a ground for divorce for the wife. Since the Ḥanafī doctrine on these two issues was prejudicial to women, the views of the other schools have now been introduced by legislation in many Ḥanafī countries.

For *nafaḳa* in the sense of expenditure, see RIZḲ. 3.

Bibliography: Muḥammad Abū Zahra, *al-Aḥwāl al-s̲h̲akh̲ṣiyya*, Cairo n.d., 243-73; Yūsuf al-Faḳīh, *al-Aḥwāl al-s̲h̲akh̲ṣiyya fī fiḳh Ahl al-Bayt*, Beirut 1989, 292-6; ʿAbd al-Raḥmān al-D̲j̲azīrī, *Kitāb al-fiḳh ʿalā ʾl-mad̲h̲āhib al-arbaʿa*, iv, *Ḳism al-aḥwāl al-s̲h̲akh̲ṣiyya*, 5th impr. Cairo n.d., 553-94; Y. Linant de Bellefonds, *Traité de droit musulman comparé*, Paris etc. 1965, ii, 256-86; D. Santillana, *Istituzioni di diritto musulmano malechita con riguardo anche al sistema sciafiita*, Rome 1938, i, 231-4, 243-7; Y. Meron, *L'obligation alimentaire entre époux en droit musulman hanéfite*, Paris 1971. (R. PETERS)

AL-NAHY ʿAN AL-MUNKAR (A.), "forbidding wrong", in full *al-amr bi ʾl-maʿrūf wa ʾl-nahy ʿan al-munkar*, "commanding right and forbidding wrong". The term is used to refer to the exercise of legitimate authority, either by holders of public office or by individual Muslims who are legally competent (*mukallaf*), with the purpose of encouraging or enforcing adherence to the requirements of the *S̲h̲arīʿa*. This article deals mainly with the duty of individual Muslims in this regard; technically, this is usually considered to be a collective obligation (*farḍ kifāya*) [see FARḌ].

1. Terminology.

The term is taken from the Ḳurʾān, where forbidding wrong is generally held to be imposed as a duty in III, 104: "Let there be one community of you, calling to good, and commanding right and forbidding wrong; those are the prosperers." Other verses making clear reference to forbidding wrong are III, 110, 114; VII, 157; IX, 71, 112; XXII, 41; XXXI, 17. However, there is little indication in the Ḳurʾān of the concrete character of the duty.

The most-cited Sunnī tradition uses a somewhat different wording. In the frame-story, a man reproves the Umayyad governor of Medina (the future caliph Marwān I [*q.v.*]) for infringing the *sunna* in the course of leading a ritual prayer. The Companion Abū Saʿīd al-K̲h̲udrī (d. 74/693) approves the man's action, and quotes the Prophet as saying: "Whoever of you sees a wrong (*munkar*), let him put it right (*fa-l-yug̲h̲ayyir-hu*) with his hand; if he cannot, then with his tongue; if he cannot, then with [or in] his heart" (Muslim, *Ṣaḥīḥ*, ed. M.F. ʿAbd al-Bāḳī, Cairo 1955-6, 69, no. 49). From this tradition is derived the term *tag̲h̲yīr al-munkar* "righting wrong", while a variant text supports the term *inkār al-munkar* "(manifesting) disapproval of wrong".

The Muslim scholars take it for granted that *al-nahy ʿan al-munkar, tag̲h̲yīr al-munkar* and *inkār al-munkar* all refer to the same duty. They occasionally make distinctions between *al-amr bi ʾl-maʿrūf* and *al-nahy ʿan al-munkar*, but normally assume that a single duty is involved. Al-G̲h̲azālī (d. 505/1111 [*q.v.*]), devised a new terminology for the duty of individuals based on the root *ḥ-s-b*; thus the duty itself is *ḥisba*, one who performs it is *muḥtasib*, etc. (*Iḥyāʾ ʿulūm al-dīn*, Cairo 1967-8, ii, 398). Hereafter the duty is referred to in this article as "forbidding wrong".

2. Forbidding wrong by holders of public office.

The sources speak of the exercise of authority by the legitimate ruler of the community as forbidding wrong. This usage is especially common in Imāmī, Zaydī and Ibāḍī texts, where forbidding wrong is closely linked to the imāmate (e.g. ʿAlī b. Ibrāhīm al-Ḳummī, *Tafsīr*, ed. Ṭ.M. al-D̲j̲azāʾirī, Nad̲j̲af 1386-7/1966-8, i, 306; ʿAlī b. Muḥammad al-ʿAlawī, *Sīrat al-Hādī ilā ʾl-Ḥaḳḳ Yaḥyā ibn al-Ḥusayn*, ed. S. Zakkār, Beirut 1972, 29; al-Bisyawī, *D̲j̲āmiʿ*, Ruwī 1984, iv, 192). But such language is also found in Sunnī sources (e.g. al-Masʿūdī, *Murūd̲j̲*, §3,111, on the caliph al-Muhtadī [*q.v.*]). Holders of subordinate offices may also be described as forbidding wrong, especially the officially-appointed *muḥtasib* (e.g. al-Māwardī, *al-Aḥkām al-sulṭāniyya*, ed. A.M. al-Bag̲h̲dādī, Kuwait 1989, 315) [see ḤISBA]. Despite the fact that such diction is widespread, it is not usually an object of scholastic reflection. Where scholars writing on the role of the *muḥtasib* pause to analyse the duty of forbidding wrong, they tend to borrow what they say from discussions of the duty of the individual (as in the chapter on the *muḥtasib* in K̲h̲und̲j̲ī, *Sulūk al-mulūk*, ed. M.ʿA. Muwaḥḥid, Tehran 1362 *s̲h̲amsī*/1983, 175-99, which includes much material going back to al-G̲h̲azālī). Opinion is divided on the question whether the state should have a monopoly of the use of violence in forbidding wrong.

3. Forbidding wrong by individuals in principle.

There is an extensive scholastic literature on this subject. Much material may be found in sources of the following types: Ḳurʾān commentaries under the relevant Ḳurʾānic verses; commentaries on Prophetic traditions under the relevant traditions; the handbooks of doctrine (*uṣūl al-dīn*) of some but not all theological schools; works on substantive law among the Imāmīs, Zaydīs and Ibāḍīs (but not the Sunnīs); and occasional monographs devoted to forbidding wrong. In terms of wealth of concrete detail, the richest body of material on the duty is a collection of responsa of Aḥmad b. Ḥanbal (d. 241/855 [*q.v.*]) (Abū Bakr al-K̲h̲allāl, *al-Amr bi ʾl-maʿrūf wa ʾl-nahy ʿan al-munkar*, ed. ʿA.A. ʿAṭā, Cairo 1975). In conceptual terms, the most sophisticated discussions stem from the Muʿtazila [*q.v.*] and their Zaydī and Imāmī heirs; by contrast, the As̲h̲ʿariyya and Māturīdiyya [*q.vv.*] have less to say. By far the most influential account of the duty is the substantial and very clear analysis that al-G̲h̲azālī included in his *Iḥyāʾ* (ii, 391-455, forming the ninth book of the second quarter, *rubʿ*, of the work). The influence of this treatment extended to all Sunnī schools, and also to the Imāmīs, Zaydīs and Ibāḍīs.

The central theme in formal discussions of the duty is often the set of conditions under which someone is obligated to confront a wrong. In the account of the Zaydī Muʿtazilī Mānkdīm (d. 425/1034), a pupil of the S̲h̲āfiʿī Muʿtazilī ʿAbd al-D̲j̲abbār b. Aḥmad al-Hamad̲h̲ānī (d. 415/1025 [*q.v.*]), these conditions are in outline as follows: (1) knowledge of law: the prospective performer of the duty must know that what he forbids is indeed wrong; (2) knowledge of fact: he must know, or have good reason to believe, that the wrong in question is in the making (*ḥāḍir*); (3) absence of worse side-effects: he must know that his action will not lead to a greater evil; (4) efficacy: he must know, or have good reason to believe, that his speaking out will be efficacious; (5) absence of danger: he must know, or have good reason to believe, that his action will not lead to harm to his person or property (Mānkdīm, *Taʿlīḳ S̲h̲arḥ al-Uṣūl al-k̲h̲amsa*, edited by ʿA. ʿUt̲h̲mān as the *S̲h̲arḥ al-Uṣūl al-k̲h̲amsa* of ʿAbd al-D̲j̲abbār b. Aḥmad, Cairo 1965, 142-3). Other scholars are likely to discuss these issues in somewhat different ways, and to disagree on details. Occasionally a scholar will reject a condition outright, but this is rare; a case in point is the S̲h̲āfiʿī al-Nawawī (d. 676/1277), who holds the uncommon view that one should proceed irrespective of the prospects of success, thus rejecting the fourth condition (cf. *S̲h̲arḥ Ṣaḥīḥ Muslim*, Beirut 1987, i, 382); he is followed in this by a good number of later S̲h̲āfiʿīs and some non-S̲h̲āfiʿīs.

The means by which the duty is to be performed are generally presented in an escalatory sequence (e.g. Mānkdīm, *Taʿlīḳ*, 144, 744-5; al-G̲h̲azālī, *Iḥyāʾ*, ii, 420-5; contrast the wording of the Prophetic tradition cited above). Thus one should speak politely to the offender before rebuking him harshly, and only proceed to physical action if words are of no avail. The major disagreement concerns the use of violence in forbidding wrong: can it be used by individuals, and if so, can it reach the point of recourse to arms? The use of arms finds favour among the Muʿtazilīs, Zaydīs and Ibāḍīs, and is sanctioned by some Sunnīs; but many Sunnīs reject it, as do the Imāmīs.

This is not the only issue on which tension arises between more activist and more quietist approaches to forbidding wrong. Thus there is a major disagreement in connection with the fifth condition. While it is generally accepted that danger voids the obligation (at least if the degree of prospective harm is significant), it is disputed whether, or in what circumstances, it may still be virtuous to proceed. Thus according to Mānkdīm, such action would be virtuous only if it secured the greater glory of the faith (*iʿzāz al-dīn*, see *Taʿlīḳ*, 143), whereas the Ḥanafī Muʿtazilī Abu ʾl-Ḥusayn al-Baṣrī (d. 436/1044 [*q.v.* in Suppl.]), likewise a pupil of ʿAbd al-D̲j̲abbār, held that no such distinction could be made, the greater glory of the faith being at issue in all such cases (cf. al-Ḥimmaṣī, *al-Munḳid̲h̲ min al-taḳlīd*, Ḳumm 1412-14/1991-4, ii, 219). By contrast, Imāmī authorities condemn such action (e.g. Murtaḍā, *D̲h̲ak̲h̲īra*, ed. A. al-Ḥusaynī, Ḳumm 1411/1990-1, 557-8).

A closely related question is whether it is virtuous to rebuke rulers harshly for their misdeeds. Al-G̲h̲azālī, representing a widespread view, was strongly in favour of this, and included in his discussion of the duty a substantial number of relevant anecdotes (*Iḥyāʾ*, ii, 437-55). Ibn Ḥanbal, by contrast, discouraged such activity (Ibn Abī Yaʿlā, *Ṭabaḳāt al-Ḥanābila*, ed. M.Ḥ. al-Fiḳī, Cairo 1952, i, 47), and the Ḥanbalī Ibn al-D̲j̲awzī (d. 597/1201) followed suit in his recension of al-G̲h̲azālī's *Iḥyāʾ* (see Aḥmad b. Ḳudāma al-Maḳdisī, *Muk̲h̲taṣar Minhād̲j̲ al-ḳāṣidīn*, Damascus 1389, 130). Likewise Muḥsin al-Fayḍ (d. 1091/1680), in his Imāmī recension of the *Iḥyāʾ*, disallows rudeness to rulers, and impugns the motives of the heroes of al-G̲h̲azālī's anecdotes (*al-Mahad̲j̲d̲j̲a al-bayḍāʾ fī tahd̲h̲īb al-Iḥyāʾ*, ed. ʿA.A. al-G̲h̲affārī, Tehran 1339-42 *s̲h̲amsī*/1960-3, iv, 112-13).

A final question of this kind, for those who accept recourse to arms, is whether forbidding wrong can take the form of rebellion against unjust rule. Such rebellion is usually condemned among the Sunnīs, although Ibn Ḥazm (d. 456/1064) is a striking exception (*Fiṣal*, Cairo 1317-21, iv, 175-6). Thus Abū Ḥanīfa (d. 150/767-8) is quoted as rejecting rebellion on the ground that its costs would exceed its benefits (Abū Ḥanīfa, *al-Fiḳh al-absaṭ*, ed. M.Z. al-Kawt̲h̲arī, Cairo 1368, 44). But rebellion under the aegis of forbidding wrong finds approval among, for example, the Ibāḍīs (cf. P. Crone and F. Zimmermann, *The epistle of Sālim ibn Dhakwān*, Oxford 2001, 140, §127 of the Arabic text), here continuing a K̲h̲ārid̲j̲ite tradition, and the Zaydīs (e.g. Muḥammad b. Sulaymān al-Kūfī, *Muntak̲h̲ab*, Ṣanʿāʾ 1993, 14).

One major concern (on which the systematic discussions in Muʿtazilī and related sources are surprisingly silent) is privacy: how far do its requirements override the duty of forbidding wrong? The basic idea is that for forbidding wrong to be in place, the wrong must in some way be public knowledge; a hidden sin, according to a Prophetic tradition, harms only the sinner (Ibn Abi ʾl-Dunyā, *ʿUḳūbāt*, ed. M.K.R. Yūsuf, Beirut 1996, 43, no. 40). Moreover, steps that would make hidden wrongs manifest are strongly discouraged. The Ḳurʾānic prohibition of spying (XLIX, 12) is widely quoted (e.g. Abū Yaʿlā Ibn al-Farrāʾ, *al-Muʿtamad fī uṣūl al-dīn*, ed. W.Z. Haddad, Beirut 1974, §355), as are versions of a Prophetic tradition that makes it a duty not to disclose shameful aspects of the lives of outwardly respectable Muslims (also quoted by Abū Yaʿlā; cf. Muslim, *Ṣaḥīḥ*, 1996, no. 2,580). The problematic cases arise in the grey area between public and private. Thus if one passes someone in the street who has a suspicious bulge under his cloak—suggesting that he is carrying a bottle of alcoholic liquor or a musical instrument—should one confront him (cf. Abū Yaʿlā Ibn al-Farrāʾ, *al-Aḥkām al-sulṭāniyya*, ed. M.Ḥ. al-Fiḳī, Cairo 1966, 296-7)?

4. Forbidding wrong by individuals in practice.

Some of the more concrete prescriptive literature also sheds light on the practice of the duty. Thus the responsa of Ibn Ḥanbal illustrate the kinds of wrong regularly confronted by individual Muslims in 3rd/9th century Bag͟hdād. The most frequent are making music and drinking alcoholic liquor, followed by sexual misconduct (cf. al-K͟hallāl, *al-Amr bi ʾl-maʿrūf*, no. 57); a variety of other wrongs appear from time to time, such as faulty prayer, chess-playing and the display of images. The mix seems to have been much the same at other times and places.

Biographical and historical sources preserve a considerable amount of scattered anecdotal material regarding the actual performance of the duty. On the whole, this material is richer for the earlier centuries of Islam than for later periods.

One respect in which the anecdotal material differs significantly from the prescriptive material is that it is much less ambivalent about confrontations involving danger. Thus many approving stories are told of pious Muslims who rebuked unjust rulers without regard for the consequences. An example is the reproof administered by S͟huʿayb b. Ḥarb (d. 196/811-12) to the caliph Hārūn al-Ras͟hīd [*q.v.*] on the road to Mecca, in which he addressed the caliph by name; he was released when he pointed out that he did the same to God (al-K͟haṭīb al-Bag͟hdādī, *Taʾrīk͟h Bag͟hdād*, Cairo 1931, ix, 239-40). At the same time, historical sources provide numerous examples of rebels who invoked forbidding wrong (see e.g. Ibn Ḥayyān, *Muḳtabis*, ed. M.M. Antuña, Paris 1937, 133, on the Andalusī rebel Ibn al-Ḳiṭṭ [*q.v.*] in 288/901).

While the anecdotal material normally takes the side of those who perform the duty, it also brings out the fact that they were often regarded by others as pious busybodies; thus when Abu ʾl-Ḥusayn al-Nūrī (d. 295/907-8) [see AL-NŪRĪ] concerns himself with a cargo of wine belonging to the caliph, the boatman calls him a "meddlesome Ṣūfī" (*ṣūfī kat͟hīr al-fuḍūl*) (al-D͟hahabī, *Siyar aʿlām al-nubalāʾ*, ed. S. al-Arnaʾūṭ *et al.*, Beirut 1981-8, xiv, 76).

5. Modern developments.

Discussion of forbidding wrong has played a significant part in the modern history of Islamic thought and practice, with Imāmī scholars tending to be more innovative than Sunnī ones.

One question that has naturally received increased attention is the role of women in forbidding wrong. In pre-modern times, a few authorities explicitly excluded women from performing the duty, a few (notably al-G͟hazālī and some Ibāḍīs) explicitly included them, but most said nothing either way (for al-G͟hazālī's view, see *Iḥyāʾ*, ii, 398). Modern authors, by contrast, often include women, even if they limit their role (e.g. K͟hālid b. ʿUt͟hmān al-Sabt, *al-Amr bi ʾl-maʿrūf wa ʾl-nahy ʿan al-munkar*, London 1995, 171-2, a conservative Sunnī view; Aḥmad Ṭayyibī S͟habistarī, *Taḳiyya; amr bah maʿrūf wa nahy az munkar*, Tehran 1350 *s͟hamsī*/1971, 208, a radical Imāmī view).

There has been a widespread trend towards greater political activism, most consistently among the Imāmīs.

Thus the view that it is wrong to proceed in the face of danger was qualified or rejected not just by K͟humaynī (d. 1409/1989 [*q.v.* in Suppl.]) (*Taḥrīr al-wasīla*, Beirut 1981, i, 472-6), but by numerous scholars of his and later generations. On the Sunnī side, one example among many of a strongly activist figure is the Algerian ʿAlī b. Ḥād̲j̲d̲j̲; thus in a talk distributed on cassettes, he quotes with enthusiasm a passage in which al-G͟hazālī sanctioned the recruitment of armed bands in the cause of forbidding wrong (*Iḥyāʾ*, ii, 425). But more quietist trends are also at work. Thus in Egypt, Ḥasan al-Bannā (d. 1368/1949) [see AL-BANNĀʾ] was against forbidding wrong "with the band" (ʿAbd al-K͟habīr al-K͟hūlī, *Ḳāʾid al-daʿwa al-Islāmiyya Ḥasan al-Bannā*, Cairo 1952, 73), and Sayyid Ḳuṭb (d. 1386/1966 [*q.v.*]) considered the duty to be in abeyance in the absence of an Islamic state (*Fī ẓilāl al-Ḳurʾān*, Beirut 1973-4, 949). K͟hālid al-Sabt, a mainstream Suʿūdī scholar, does not share such views, but bypasses the more subversive statements of al-Ghazālī (*al-Amr bi ʾl-maʿrūf*, 316ff.).

There has also been an unprecedented emphasis on the desirability of achieving greater organisation for the purpose of forbidding wrong (see e.g. Muḥammad Aḥmad al-Ras͟hid, *al-Munṭalaḳ*, Beirut 1976, 146-54, for a Sunnī view, and Ḥusayn al-Nūrī al-Hamadānī, *al-Amr bi ʾl-maʿrūf wa ʾl-nahy ʿan al-munkar*, Tehran 1990, 65, for an Imāmī view). In some Islamic countries, this has led to the creation of new organs of the state entrusted with the performance of the duty (but not to the revival of the traditional office of the official *muḥtasib*). Thus in Suʿūdī Arabia, a system of "committees (*hayʾāt*) for commanding right and forbidding wrong" emerged in the aftermath of the Suʿūdī conquest of the Ḥid̲j̲āz in 1343-4/1924-5, initially as a device to contain the zeal of the Wahhābī Ik͟hwān [*q.v.*] against the misdeeds of the Ḥid̲j̲āzīs and pilgrims (cf. Ḥāfiẓ Wahba, *D̲j̲azīrat al-ʿArab fi ʾl-ḳarn al-ʿis͟hrīn*, Cairo 1961, 309-12). In Iran, following the Islamic Revolution of 1399/1979, a plurality of organs of the state acquired responsibility for forbidding wrong; and in Afg͟hānistān, a single organisation was established to discharge the duty after the Ṭālibān conquered Kābul in 1417/1996.

Bibliography: See also *EIr*, art. "Amr be maʿrūf" (W. Madelung); M. Cook, *Commanding right and forbidding wrong in Islamic thought*, Cambridge 2000 (with extensive bibl.). Many of the works cited in the article contain substantial treatments of forbidding wrong, notably those of al-K͟hallāl, Mānkdīm and al-G͟hazālī. (M. COOK)

NAḲD (A.), "[literary] criticism", in modern Arabic, *al-naḳd al-adabī*, in mediaeval times most commonly used in the construct *naḳd al-s͟hiʿr* "criticism of poetry". The critic is *nāḳid* (pl. *nuḳḳād* or *naḳada*) or, more rarely, *naḳḳād*; the form VIII verbal noun *intiḳād* is a synonym of *naḳd*. The term originated in the figurative use (*mad̲j̲āz*) of *naḳd* in the sense of "assaying (coins) and separating the good from the bad" (for the *mad̲j̲āz* character, see al-Zamak͟hs͟harī. *Asās al-balāg͟ha*, Beirut n.d., col. 469c, and for an extended analogy between assayer and critic, see al-Tawḥīdī, *al-Muḳābasāt*, Cairo 1347/1929, 170). Outside the field of literary criticism the term is also used in *ḥadīt͟h* criticism (al-Tahānawī, *Kas͟hs͟hāf*, ed. A. Sprenger, Calcutta 1862, 1381, s.v. *intiḳād*); here, too, the analogy of the assayer is invoked (see Ibn Abī Ḥātim al-Rāzī, *ʿIlal al-ḥadīt͟h*, Cairo 1343/1924-5, i, 9).

Naḳd al-s͟hiʿr became the designation of a systematic discipline probably through the book of this title written by Ḳudāma b. Dja'far (d. *ca.* 337/948 [*q.v.*], and see below) in the first half of the 4th/10th century. The title should probably still be understood in the original metaphorical sense, "The Assaying of Poetry". Since Ḳudāma is very much aware of his innovative approach, the era preceding him may be called the pre-systematic period. This does not imply that all works after him were systematic, only that a standard had been set.

Pre-systematic literary criticism

Most of the material for this period is found in books on poets, such as Ibn Sallām al-Djumaḥī (d. 231-2/845-6 [*q.v.*]), *Ṭabaḳāt fuḥūl al-shuʿarā'*; Ibn Ḳutayba (d. 276/889 [*q.v.*]), *K. al-Shiʿr wa 'l-shuʿarā'*; and above all Abu 'l-Faradj al-Iṣbahānī (d. 356/967 [*q.v.*]), *K. al-Aghānī*, but also in *adab* encyclopaedias, such as Ibn Ḳutayba, *ʿUyūn al-akhbār*, and Ibn ʿAbd Rabbih (d. 328/940 [*q.v.*]), *al-ʿIḳd al-farīd*. In addition, there are works of a directly pertinent nature, namely al-Djāḥiẓ (d. 255/868-9 [*q.v.*]), *K. al-Bayān wa 'l-tabyīn*; and al-Marzubānī (d. 384/994 [*q.v.*]), *K. al-Muwashshaḥ fī ma'ākhidh al-ʿulamā' ʿalā 'l-shuʿarā'*. Information about the earliest phase of this period, up to the times of the great transmitters (*ruwāt*, sing. *rāwiya*) like Ḥammād al-Rāwiya (d. 155-6/772-3 [*q.v.*]) and Khalaf al-Aḥmar (d. *ca.* 180/796 [*q.v.*]) is anecdotal and mostly legendary. However, given the high degree of sophistication of even the earliest poetry, it is highly likely that there existed some implied rules of critical appreciation and at least a rudimentary technical vocabulary for discussions among the experts, i.e. poets and transmitters. There is some likelihood that the terms for rhyme mistakes (*ʿuyūb al-ḳāfiya*, or simply *ʿuyūb al-shiʿr*) go back to pre-Islamic times. Al-Akhfash al-Awsaṭ (d. 215/830 or 221/836 [*q.v.*]) points out that the *ʿarab* defined these terms only very loosely (*Ḳawāfī*, 43, 55, 67, 68), and early literary theorists such as Thaʿlab (d. 291/904 [*q.v.*]) (*Ḳawāʿid*, 67-70) and Ḳudāma (*Naḳd*, 108-11) include these mistakes in their works, although they normally abstain from all prosodical technicalities. Both facts suggest that this terminology was not of recent vintage. It is also quite likely that some of the terms that, later on, make up the varied taxonomy of plagiarism go back to the early days of Arabic poetry. This would in particular refer to *ighāra* (lit. "raiding"), the rather archaic procedure of a famous poet forcing a less famous one to give up a flawless line, because the more famous poet has a greater right to it. Finally, there are also a few glimpses of critical vocabulary in the poetry itself. The Umayyad poet ʿAdī b. al-Riḳāʿ (d. *ca.* 100/720), e.g., mentions that in careful revision of his poem at night he "straightens out" what is "crooked" in his poems (see *Dīwān shiʿr ʿA. b. al-R. ʿan . . . Thaʿlab*, ed. Nūrī Ḥammūdī al-Ḳaysī and Ḥātim Ṣāliḥ al-Ḍāmin, Baghdād 1407/1987, 88-90, and cf. M. Gaudefroy-Demombynes, *Ibn Qotaiba—Introduction*, 16-17, and notes 61-2, and al-Āmidī, *Muwāzana*, iii, 702-4, also for other early poets commenting on their poetry). As for rules of critical appreciation, the anecdotal material offers evaluative pronouncements on poets and their poems that may sometimes allow us to extract such rules. These aesthetic judgements may be classified as follows:

(a) Opinions expressed by means of an elative, either in general terms (*man ashʿaru 'l-nāsi* [or: *al-ʿarabi*]? *fulānun ḥīna yaḳūlu* . . . "Who is the best poet of all [or: of the Arabs]? So-and-so, where he says . . . [followed by a line]") or with reference to a specific theme or motif (*amdaḥu/ahdjā/ansabu/afkharu baytin ḳālat-hu 'l-ʿarabu* . . . "The best panegyrical/satyrical/amorous/self-glorifying line the Arabs have spoken is . . ." [followed by a line]). A characteristic feature of this type of criticism is that even in the former case the decision is based on a single, allegedly incomparable line. A similar mode of presentation is used by the early philologist Abū ʿAmr b. al-ʿAlā' (d. 144/771 or 147/774 [*q.v.*]) to express his high opinion of the poet Djarīr (d. 111/729 [*q.v.*]) by dividing poetry into four themes (*iftikhār, madīḥ, hidjā', nasīb*) and quoting one line in each category to prove that Djarīr is the best poet (ʿAbd al-Karīm al-Nahshalī, *Mumtiʿ*, 475-6). This one-line approach remains popular in later times.

(b) Opinions on the œuvre of certain poets expressed in similes and metaphors. Thus Ḥammād al-Rāwiya on the poetry of ʿUmar b. Abī Rabīʿa (d. 93/712 or 103/721): "That's shelled pistachios!" or Djarīr on a poem by the same poet: "That is poetry of the Tihāma (i.e. the hot coastal strip where ʿUmar's hometown Mecca is situated), which feels the cold, when it comes into the Nadjd (i.e. the central highlands)" (*Aghānī*[3], i, 75 and 81).

(c) The "psycho-literary" approach, i.e. the correlation of emotions and genres of poetry. E.g. Arṭāt b. Suhayya, asked by caliph ʿAbd al-Malik whether he could compose and recite some poetry on the spot, answered: "I am not drinking wine (*lā ashrabu*), I am not in an excited mood (*lā aṭrabu*), and I am not angry (*lā aghḍabu*); poetry happens only due to one of these three" (see Gaudefroy-Demombynes, *op. cit.*, 18).

(d) Sayings that define basic terms of the literary art, such as *balāgha, faṣāḥa*, and *bayān*. These belong in the present context only inasmuch as they are normative, as they often are. They are often attributed to "a Bedouin" but also to a "Greek", "Indian", or "Persian" (see a collection, including later definitions, in al-Ḥuṣrī, *Zahr al-ādāb*, 116-18). Combinations of these types also occur; e.g. (a) and (d) put together result in sayings like "the best verse is one whose beginning makes one anticipate its end."

Most of the critical terms and ideas mentioned so far refer to the homogeneous "timeless" body of ancient Arabic poetry, which means that the notion of literary history is absent from them. When this body was not allowed to fade into oblivion, as had been the fate of Arabic poetry in the centuries before our earliest specimens, but was collected into a corpus of "classical" models, a historical dimension was introduced and things gradually began to change also for criticism. The Umayyad poet al-Farazdaḳ (d. *ca.* 112/730 [*q.v.*]) devotes one of his poems to an enumeration of his literary forebears, twenty in all. To characterise his relationship to them, he uses the expressions *wahaba 'l-ḳaṣā'ida lī . . . idh maḍaw* "[they] gave the poems to me, when they passed away" and *warithtu* "I inherited" (three times). He even mentions a book that he has of the poetry of the pre-Islamic poet Bishr b. Abī Khāzim [*q.v.*] (cf. *Dīwān al-Farazdaḳ*, ed. ʿAlī Kharīs, Beirut 1416/1996, 435-6 [rhyme *-alu*]). Obviously, we are watching here the beginning of a conscious literary history, and this in more than one respect. Literary criticism would now have to take into account questions like imitation, plagiarism and deviation from the norm as embodied in the corpus.

Naḳd *as critical assessment of the genuineness of ancient poetry*

The situation became even more complex in early ʿAbbāsid times, when, on the one hand, the philologists began the codification of early literature and, on the other, a new "school" of poetry started to gain popularity, that of the "Moderns" [see MUḤDATHŪN, in Suppl.]. The most serious problem confronting the philologists, given the fluid state of transmission of the ancient texts, was the question "genuine (*ṣaḥīḥ*) or spurious?" If they assumed the latter, the spuriousness was due either to false attribution of an existing piece of poetry (*manḥūl*) or to outright forgery (*maṣnūʿ, mawḍūʿ, muftaʿal*). That this distinction was not lost on them is shown by the strange title of the second part of Abu 'l-Ḥasan al-Ṭūsī's redaction of the *Dīwān* of Imru' al-Ḳays: *al-ṣaḥīḥ al-ḳadīm al-manḥūl*, literally "the falsely attributed old genuine (part)", i.e. that part of the collection that is not included in the transmission of al-Ṭūsī's main authority, al-Mufaḍḍal al-Ḍabbī (d. after 163/780 [*q.v.*]), but which other transmitters attribute to Imru' al-Ḳays. Ibn Sallām al-Djumaḥī, who discusses these matters at the beginning of his book on the classes of poets, accuses the great transmitter Ḥammād al-Rāwiya of habitually and intentionally misattributing poetry (*wa-kāna yanḥalu shiʿra 'l-radjuli ghayrahū wa-yanḥaluhū ghayra shiʿrih* [*Ṭabaḳāt*, 48]). What is worse, he also accuses him of adding to the poems he transmits (*wa-yazīdu fi 'l-ashʿār* [*ibid.*]). But, as he states in another place (*Ṭabaḳāt*, 46-7), it is not only transmitters who are guilty of forgeries but also those tribes who in early Islamic times found themselves without an impressive poetic heritage and wanted to amend the situation. Ibn Sallām's passage is of sufficient interest to warrant translation in full: "When the Arabs [after the conquests] returned to the transmission of poetry and the narration of their battles and glorious deeds, some tribes found the poetry of their poets and the current narration of their battles to be scant. And there were people whose battles and poems were [in fact] few. So they wanted to catch up with those who did have battles and poems and [to do so] they composed poems attributing them to their poets (*ḳālū ʿalā alsinati shuʿarāʾihim*). Afterwards there came the transmitters and added to the poems that had been composed. To the experts (*ahl al-ʿilm*) the additions of the transmitters and what they have forged (i.e. separately, without adding it to an existing poem?) pose no problem, nor does what the *muwallads* [*q.v.*] have forged. However, [the experts] have been confounded, if a man from among the desert dwellers and belonging to the progeny of poets, or even a man who does not belong to their progeny, composes [spurious] poems. That can be somewhat difficult." This is followed by a story relating how a grandson of the poet Mutammim b. Nuwayra extended the latter's *dīwān* imitating his style (*yaḥtadhī ʿalā kalāmih*). The kind of critique that is necessary to recognise spurious poetry cannot, in Ibn Sallām's opinion, clearly be expressed in words (*Ṭabaḳāt*, 5-7, with parallels from other crafts and arts); it is a matter of intuition comparable to the art of physiognomy, and the famous transmitter Khalaf al-Aḥmar is called "the best physiognomist of all, when it comes to a line of poetry" (*kāna afrasa 'l-nāsi bi-bayti shiʿr* [*Ṭabaḳāt*, 23]). There is a famous anecdote, probably first attested by Ibn Sallām (*Ṭabaḳāt*, 7), which compares this ability with that of the money-changer who recognises a bad coin: "Someone said to Khalaf: 'If I hear a poem that I deem good, I do not care what you and your ilk say about it.' He replied: 'If you accept a dirham and consider it good and the money-changer tells you it is bad, does your good opinion of it help you at all?'" It seems evident, from this and the other references mentioned above, that the metaphorical application to poetry of the term *naḳd* originated in the context of distinguishing genuine from spurious, rather than good from bad poetry, although the dividing line between the two pairs can be rather fuzzy. (It should be mentioned *en passant* that, along with misattribution, scholarly forgery and tribal forgery, Ibn Sallām recognises also a fourth category of spurious poetry [*Ṭabaḳāt*, 7-8]: poems that are invented and attributed to legendary figures of the past; Ibn Sallām takes Ibn Isḥāḳ [*q.v.*] severely to task for including such material in his *Sīra* and refuses to call it *shiʿr*, since it is only "words put together and held together by rhymes" [*kalām^un muʾallaf^un maʿḳūd^un bi-ḳawāf^in*].)

Criticism of poetry among the philologists

At the same time, *naḳd* in the sense of literary criticism is represented by various approaches. The philologists who felt responsible for the integrity of ancient poetry also paid some attention to the question of its aesthetic quality. The evidence for this is partly implicit in the selections they made to produce the famous anthologies such as the *Muʿallaḳāt*, the *Mufaḍḍaliyyāt* [*q.vv.*] and the *Aṣmaʿiyyāt* [see AL-AṢMAʿĪ]. Most of the explicit evidence is anecdotal and in the form described above, but gradually certain critical yardsticks start being developed. Most of the early works on poetry and poets (*al-shiʿr wa 'l-shuʿarāʾ* and similar titles, mainly known from Ibn al-Nadīm's *Fihrist*) are unfortunately lost. The first extant *kitāb al-shiʿr wa 'l-shuʿarāʾ*, that of Ibn Ḳutayba, contains a remarkable introduction that delineates a number of basic critical ideas: (1) Poetry consist of wording (*lafẓ*) and meaning (*maʿnā*), both or either of which may be good or bad. (2) Poets are either "natural" (*maṭbūʿ* "poète de génie") or "painstaking" (*mutakallif* "poète d'étude"), (for the French renditions, see M. Gaudefroy-Demombynes, *op. cit.*, 15); the latter spend much time polishing their poems, a fact that shows in the final outcome. (3) In a passage much quoted in Western studies, he describes—and prescribes—the "movements" of the ancient ode (having in mind, however, the tripartite structure characteristic of the Umayyad rather than the pre-Islamic *ḳaṣīda* and describing it as a quadripartite sequence of themes: 1. sorrow at the vestiges of the encampment; 2. memory of the former beloved; 3. camel ride through the desert; and 4. praise of the addressee); he also disallows replacing the desert ambience by a sedentary one (no ruined buildings instead of the remnants of the encampment, no roses and myrtles for the thorny shrubs of the desert). On the other hand, he includes poets up to the early decades of the 8th century in his book and emphasises that the birthdate of a poet should not be held against him, as some of the philologists who considered only ancient poetry to be true poetry were inclined to do. Since Ibn Ḳutayba is not explicit about any awareness of the "Moderns" and their *badīʿ*, he may have considered the existing poetry as one homogeneous corpus, in which case every poet would be competing with all poets present and past. However, he may also have considered only the "official" *ḳaṣīda* immutable and sacrosanct, while the new genres were outside the realm of true *shiʿr*.

The philological approach to poetics has produced at least two books that are first attempts at systematisation, one before and one after Ibn Ḳutayba. The former is the *Fuḥūlat al-shuʿarāʾ* of al-Aṣmaʿī (d. 213/828, other dates are also given [*q.v.*]), or rather of his student, Abū Ḥātim al-Sidjistānī (d. 255/869 [*q.v.*]), who recorded al-Aṣmaʿī's utterances, often in answer to his questions. This is a critical attempt to evaluate the production of the ancient poets in order to see who would deserve the predicate *faḥl*, lit. "stallion". The exact semantic range of this term does not clearly emerge from al-Aṣmaʿī's pronouncements. But the profile of the *faḥl* contains certain traits that are not in doubt: he must have a prolific output and cannot be a *muḳill*; he may not compose only short poems; his descriptions (*naʿt*) must stand out; he must be free of plagiarisms (*sariḳāt*); he must not be a "righteous" man (*ṣāliḥ*), which *ipso facto* means that he must be pre-Islamic or, at least, have a *d̲j̲āhilī* bent (for a full list and discussion thereof, see Wen-Chin Ouyang, *Literary criticism*, 180-1). Due to the fact that al-Aṣmaʿī had, above all, pre-Islamic poetry in mind, his approach was not very influential (except on his student Ibn Sallām al-D̲j̲umaḥī, see above); the importance of *Fuḥūlat al-s̲h̲uʿarāʾ* resides in its being the first attempt on the part of a philologist to go beyond his usual concerns of a grammatical and lexical nature and enter the realm of criticism.

The other work of the philologist as critic is T̲h̲aʿlab's *Ḳawāʿid al-s̲h̲iʿr*. The attribution of this work to T̲h̲aʿlab is not entirely certain, but there is no proof that it is not by him. The focus of this little book is radically different from al-Aṣmaʿī's. It deals mostly with single lines of poetry, categorising them according to types of utterances, thematic content, embellishments (but T̲h̲aʿlab has no term for figures of speech) and, finally, structure (the best line being one in which the two hemistichs are meaningful on their own). This "atomistic" approach proved to be preponderant throughout the history of *naḳd al-s̲h̲iʿr*.

The real founders of naḳd: *the secretaries*

In an often quoted passage, al-D̲j̲āḥiẓ describes his search for true experts on poetry: "I searched for expertise in poetry (*ʿilm al-s̲h̲iʿr*) in al-Aṣmaʿī, but I found him only good at the rare words in it. Then I betook myself to al-Ak̲h̲fas̲h̲, but I found him expert only in its grammar. Then I turned to Abū ʿUbayda, but I found that he transmitted only [poetry] connected with historical reports or tied in with the battle-days [of the tribes] and genealogies. I did not gain what I wanted except from the men of letters among the secretaries (*udabāʾ al-kuttāb*), such as al-Ḥasan b. Wahb and ʿAbd al-Malik al-Zayyāt."

This statement in a way delineates the future of *naḳd al-s̲h̲iʿr*, in the further development of which the state secretaries clearly had the lion's share. This is easy to understand: The secretaries, especially those charged with writing official epistles, had a pressing professional need to refine and ornament their language and to develop critical acumen in this respect. They were in constant contact with poetry and poets, as the latter flocked to the seats of power to find sympathetic sponsors (caliphs, viziers, governors, etc.) who would enable them to live as professional poets. At some point there existed at the caliphal court an "Office of Poetry" (*Dīwān al-S̲h̲iʿr*), in which the incoming praise poetry was screened by *kuttāb* to see if it was worthy of the recipient. This distribution of power between poets and secretaries is a far cry from the ancient situation, where the poet had greater prestige than the producer of ornate prose, the tribal orator (*k̲h̲aṭīb*), and where, according to al-D̲j̲āḥiẓ (*Bayān*, i, 45-52), the talent for each art was clearly assigned: poetry and oratory were rarely combined in one person. In ʿAbbāsid society a radical change can be discerned. The secretaries not infrequently also composed poetry, though mainly in the private and intimate genres of love and wine poetry and the like, and not in the public and official genres of the professional poets, such as praise, congratulation, and condolence. When their official epistles began being collected, roughly from the 4th/10th century onward, it was not uncommon that a secretary's production was represented by two *dīwāns*, one dedicated to epistles and the other to poems. In this context the procedure of *ḥall al-manẓūm*, "dissolving the versified" (i.e. turning poetry into prose), became rather popular, especially with the secretaries who used it to add elegant conceits and allusions to their ornate epistles (on the theory and techniques of *ḥall*, see A. Sanni in *Bibl.*).

The close symbiosis between secretaries and poets was fertile ground for the development of literary criticism. We have a fair number of reports about gatherings in which questions of poetry and poetics were discussed, and we have some of the literature that sprang from these discussions. As already indicated, the book that made the term *naḳd al-s̲h̲iʿr* current was written by Ḳudāma b. D̲j̲aʿfar. He was a middle-level administrator in the caliphal chanceries, originally Christian and with a known interest in Greek philosophy, especially logic. This clearly had its effect on the very systematic presentation in his book: a definition of poetry ("metred rhymed speech referring to a meaning" [*Naḳd*, 2]) yields the four elements "metre rhyme, wording, meaning," which are then evaluated in isolation and in combination with each other (he finds that only the combinations wording/meaning, wording/metre, meaning/metre and meaning/rhyme are meaningful subjects for evaluation [*Naḳd*, 9]). In accordance with this, the book falls into two major parts, one on *nuʿūt* "good qualities", the other on *ʿuyūb* "bad qualities". It is worth noting that the vast majority of Ḳudāma's examples are from early poetry, although there is a sprinkling of "modern" poets as well, up to Abū Tammām (d. *ca.* 232/845 [*q.v.*]). The difference between "Ancients" and "Moderns" is, of course, known to him (*Naḳd*, 17, l. 7), but it does not inform the structure of his book.

His contemporary Ibn Ṭabāṭabā (d. 322/934) produced an entirely different book in his *ʿIyār al-s̲h̲iʿr*. "The criterion of poetry". Unfortunately, the little we know about his life does not tell us if he was a secretary in his hometown of Iṣfahān, but he certainly was a respectable poet. His book does not show a systematic arrangement; it is more like a collection of loosely connected but highly perceptive essays. He is almost painfully aware of the burden of tradition that the "Moderns" feel *vis-à-vis* the "Ancients". All the good things have already been said. However, there is an additional consideration, which makes the situation bearable: The Ancients aimed at the truth in their poems (except for approved hyperbole), while the Moderns (he says: "the poets of our time") meet approval only when they have to offer something subtle, novel, eloquent, witty, or elegant, without paying attention to the realities/truths (*ḥaḳāʾiḳ*) that might correspond to their words. As a result the latter's productions were "artificial" (*mutakallaf*), not springing from sound talent (*g̲h̲ayr ṣādir ʿan ṭabʿ ṣaḥīḥ*) (*ʿIyār*, 13). This is an admirable diagnosis of literary mannerism, in that (a) the poetic language moves away from reality, turning to inbreeding and the construction of ever more intricate conceits, (b) the craving of the public for innovation puts pressure on the poet to oblige and, consequently, (c) the poetry becomes ever more "artificial". Though this can only be considered a strong tendency, not a necessity, it is noteworthy that, in the section on poems that are without "artificiality" and prose-like in their easy flow, Ibn Ṭabāṭabā quotes twenty-four examples, twenty-two of which are "ancient". Of the remaining two, one is by ʿAbd al-Malik al-Ḥārit̲h̲ī, who is said by Ibn al-Muʿtazz (d. 296/908 [*q.v.*]) to be a poet in the Bedouin vein, while the other is the well-known *muḥdat̲h̲* Marwān b.

Abī Ḥafṣa (d. *ca.* 182/797 [*q.v.*]), who was rather conservative in his poetic ways (*Ṭabaḳāt*, 276-80). In another passage he indicates the way out for "modern" poets: he should take (*a<u>kh</u>d<u>h</u>, istiʿāra*) a poetic idea from a predecessor and improve on it (interestingly, he does not use the term *sariḳa*, as others often do) (*ʿIyār*, 123, 126).

However different Ḳudāma and Ibn Ṭabāṭabā may be in their presentations, they resemble each other in their basic goal: to identify the good and the bad in poetry, whether it reside in wording, meaning, rhyme or metre. Both have a preference for longish quotations to make their point (Ibn Ṭabāṭabā more so than Ḳudāma), an unusual phenomenon in the literature of *naḳd al-<u>sh</u>iʿr*. This is tied in with the question: do both works belong to the same "genre" of meta-discourse, i.e. do they give rules on how to compose poetry (a "poetics" in the strict sense) or on how to evaluate it (a theory of criticism)? Ibn Ṭabāṭabā uses language that tells the would-be poet what to do, while Ḳudāma does not.

Ibn Ṭabāṭabā is said to have greatly admired the poetry of Ibn al-Muʿtazz, an admiration that was reciprocated (Yāḳūt, *Ir<u>sh</u>ād*, ed. Rifāʿī, xvii, 144-5), although Ibn Ṭabāṭabā is not included in the latter's *Ṭabaḳāt al-<u>sh</u>uʿarāʾ al-muḥda<u>th</u>īn*. Ibn al-Muʿtazz was indeed a poet of the first magnitude but, as a member of the caliphal house, he was also in constant contact with high-level secretaries and was himself an accomplished prose stylist (see e.g. his *Fuṣūl al-tamā<u>th</u>īl fī tabā<u>sh</u>īr al-surūr*, ed. <u>Dj</u>ūr<u>dj</u> Ḳanāziʿ and Fahd Abū <u>Kh</u>aḍra, Damascus 1410/1989, and his *Kitāb al-Ādāb*, ed. Ṣabīḥ Radīf, Ba<u>gh</u>dād 1392/1972). He wrote the third important early work in the area of *naḳd al-<u>sh</u>iʿr*, the *Kitāb al-Badīʿ*, "The Book of the Novelty". The term *badīʿ* "novel, original" was already current at the time as a somewhat fuzzy technical term denoting the distinguishing trait of "modern" poetising. The transmitters of ancient poetry allegedly did not know this term (and, presumably, what it stood for); only the "modern" poets and critics did. Since some of the transmitters were also "modern" poets, this can only be a rule of thumb. Definitions are not offered in the literature preceding Ibn al-Muʿtazz. But wherever the term is applied to a line of poetry that is actually quoted, it invariably refers to what might be called the "loan metaphor", i.e. the type of metaphor, for which the term *istiʿāra* "borrowing" was originally coined (example: "claws of death", where the "claws" are taken from a "predator" and given "on loan" to "death") (cf. W. Heinrichs, Istiʿārah *and* Badīʿ *and their terminological relationship in early Arabic literary criticism*, in *ZGAIW*, i [1984], 180-211). While the ancient poets generated these metaphors on the basis of an analogy, comparing e.g. the inevitability of death with the relentlessness of the predator's attack, the "modern" poets often used a different generating mechanism: They started from an existing metaphor and, on the level of the analogue, moved to an adjacent element, which then became a "claws"-type metaphor. E.g. from the verb metaphor "drink" in "to make s.o. drink blame" (i.e. "make him swallow it") the adjacent element "water" is extracted, which forms the new genitive metaphor "the water of blame". The critics, though not aware of any differences in the generating mechanisms between "Ancients" and "Moderns", realised that many of the loan metaphors of the "Moderns" were surprising, farfetched, and at times outright abstruse, and they labelled them *badīʿ*, the "novelty". Since *badīʿ* is derived from the same root as *bidʿa* "religious innovation", it has a possible negative odour and was indeed abhorred by some more conservative critics. This is where Ibn al-Muʿtazz entered the picture. Being himself a "modern" poet and faced with *badīʿ* rejectionists, he declared the main objective of his book to be the proof that *badīʿ* was not "novel" at all, but occurred in all ancient text genres: Ḳurʾān, Ḥadī<u>th</u>, gnomic sayings and poetry. He thus attempted to legitimise the "novelty" by pointing to respectable precedents. The only "novelty" in "modern" poetry (and other genres), as he remarks, is the unbridled proliferation of this phenomenon, especially in the poetry of Abū Tammām, who was the focal point of much critical attention, pro and con. One has to be aware, though, that in Ibn al-Muʿtazz the term *badīʿ* has a more comprehensive meaning: according to the author it comprises the following five figures of speech: (1) loan metaphor (*istiʿāra*); (2) paronomasia (*ta<u>dj</u>nīs*); (3) antithesis (*muṭābaḳa*); (4) echoing the rhyme at the beginning of the line (*radd aʿ<u>dj</u>āz al-kalām ʿalā mā taḳaddamahā*); and (5) theologism (*ma<u>dh</u>hab kalāmī*, referring to imitations of the convoluted thinking and style of the dialectic theologians). He admits, however, his uncertainty as to whether all of these five subcategories really should be subsumed under *badīʿ* or whether additional figures of speech should be included, and he leaves that decision to the reader. In order not to be accused of being ignorant of other ornaments of speech, he later added an appendix of twelve figures which he called *maḥāsin* "beauties". The vagueness of his *badīʿ* concept makes it difficult to identify the criterion that separates the *badīʿ* figures from the *maḥāsin*. However, the loan metaphor is clearly of central importance in the book: (1) When *badīʿ* is exemplified at the beginning of the work, it is loan metaphors that are used as examples, without any warning that *badīʿ* might be something quite different. (2) The loan metaphor takes first place. (3) Most intriguingly, the other *badīʿ* figures, which are all characterised by repetition, are not seldom combined with a loan metaphor, the latter forming one of the terms of the repetition. This may lead one to believe that the other figures were first drawn into the *badīʿ* orbit due to cases that contained loan metaphors; subsequently, the term was extended also to non-metaphoric examples. Ibn al-Muʿtazz's uncertainty may reflect the vagaries of this intermediary stage.

The *Kitāb al-Badīʿ*, originally composed as a legitimation of the "novel" features of "modern" poetry, effectively launched the term *badīʿ* as a collective noun referring to "rhetorical figures", which found its scholastic culmination in the discipline called *ʿilm al-badīʿ*, as finally established as part of the "science of eloquence" (*ʿilm al-balā<u>gh</u>a*) by al-<u>Kh</u>aṭīb al-Ḳazwīnī (d. 739/1338 [*q.v.*]). The distinction between *badīʿ* and *maḥāsin* was not continued after Ibn al-Muʿtazz.

The controversy around Abū Tammām

One of the triggers for the composition of the *Kitāb al-Badīʿ* had been the controversy around the poet Abū Tammām, who was considered an addict of *badīʿ* and the prototype of the *ṣanʿa* poet (*maṣnūʿ*), who uses rhetorical figures to add a new point or even a new level to a line of poetry. Ibn al-Muʿtazz himself wrote a short treatise on the merits and defects of Abū Tammām's poetry (*Risāla fī maḥāsin <u>sh</u>iʿr Abī Tammām wa-masāwīhi*, preserved by al-Marzubānī, *al-Muwa<u>shsh</u>aḥ*, 277ff.), in which he mostly critiques single lines and mentions several times that he is not the first to voice that particular criticism. But the first large-scale critical appraisal is that of al-Ḥasan b. Bi<u>sh</u>r al-Āmidī (d. 371/981), which contrasts the "artful" (*maṣnūʿ*) Abū

Tammām with his counterpart (and disciple!), the "natural" (*maṭbūʿ*) poet al-Buḥturī (d. 284/897 [*q.v.*]); the fitting title of the book is "The weighing of the poetry of Abū Tammām and al-Buḥturī" (*al-Muwāzana bayn s̲h̲iʿr Abī Tammām wa 'l-Buḥturī*, see *Bibl.*). Al-Āmidī was a secretary, both in Baṣra and Bag̲h̲dād, and he was also an accomplished poet and a trained grammarian (Yāḳūt, *Irs̲h̲ād*, ed. Rifāʿī, viii, 75-93). This was clearly a good basis for his main claim to fame, his works on literary criticism. One might say that he established the field as a field, because he subjected a number of the existing *naḳd* works to a critical review. Unfortunately, we have only the titles of these works: "Mistakes to be found in the 'Criterion of Poetry' by Ibn Ṭabāṭabā" (*K. Mā fī ʿIyār al-s̲h̲iʿr li-(I)bn Ṭabāṭabā min al-k̲h̲aṭaʾ*), "Disclosure of the error of Ḳudāma b. D̲j̲aʿfar in his 'Assaying of Poetry'," (*K. Tabyīn g̲h̲alaṭ Ḳudāma. b. D̲j̲aʿfar fī Kitāb Naḳd al-s̲h̲iʿr*), and "Refutation of Ibn ʿAmmār in his faulting of Abū Tammām" (*K. al-Radd ʿalā Ibn ʿAmmār fīmā k̲h̲aṭṭaʾa fīhi Abā Tammām*) (for the last mentioned, Abu 'l-ʿAbbās Aḥmad b. ʿUbayd Allāh Ibn ʿAmmār al-T̲h̲aḳafī [d. *ca.* 314/926], see Yāḳūt, *Irs̲h̲ād*, ed. Rifāʿī, iii, 232-42).

In addition, he wrote the following works in the critical genre, of which again we have only the evocative titles (omitting the ubiquitous *Kitāb*):

"Unstringing the strung" (*Nat̲h̲r al-manẓūm*), i.e. turning poetry into prose, see above;

"That the ideas of two poets do not agree by chance" (*Fī anna 'l-s̲h̲āʿirayn lā yattafiḳu k̲h̲awāṭiruhumā*); the phenomenon negated here by al-Āmidī is also known as *tawārud al-k̲h̲āṭirayn* and is one of the ways to explain identical or similar lines, short of plagiarism;

"The difference between the individual and the shared with regard to the motifs of poetry" (*Farḳ mā bayn al-k̲h̲āṣṣ wa 'l-mus̲h̲tarak min maʿānī al-s̲h̲iʿr*), the distinction between attributable motifs and those in the public domain, an important issue in the discussion of plagiarism [see SARIḲA, in Suppl.];

"Preference of the poetry of Imruʾ al-Ḳays over [that of the other] pre-Islamic poets" (*Tafḍīl s̲h̲iʿr Imriʾ al-Ḳays ʿalā 'l-D̲j̲āhiliyyīn*); and "The motifs in the poetry of al-Buḥturī" (*Maʿānī s̲h̲iʿr al-Buḥturī*).

His main preserved work, the "Weighing", is the first serious attempt at applied criticism. Before entering into the actual comparison between the two poets, al-Āmidī collects and discusses what the adherents of either poet have already amassed in the way of critical opinions. But he first takes the opportunity to characterise the two poets as the two opposites on the *maṣnūʿ–maṭbūʿ* scale: al-Buḥturī is Bedouinic in his poetry, natural, in accordance with the "ancients"; he does not leave the well-known "mainstay of poetry" (*ʿamūd al-s̲h̲iʿr*); he shuns knotted syntax and forced expressions and uncouth words. Abū Tammām, on the other hand, is strenuously affectatious, a master of conceits who forces words and meanings, and his poetry does not resemble the poems of the "Ancients". Interestingly, he also describes the typical adherents of the two poets. In al-Buḥturī's case they are: the secretaries, the Bedouins, the "natural" poets, and the people of eloquence, while Abū Tammām has attracted the "people who are after conceits" (*ahl al-maʿānī*), the mannerist poets (*al-s̲h̲uʿarāʾ aṣḥāb al-ṣanʿa*), and those who incline to sophistication and speech philosophical (*al-tadḳīḳ wa-falsafī al-kalām*) (*Muwāzana*, i, 6). Al-Āmidī also remarks that the admirers of Abū Tammām allege that he invented a new style of poetising, but the followers of al-Buḥturī deny this saying that he followed the model of Muslim b. al-Walīd and pushed it to an extreme, and that even Muslim did not invent this style but found the *badīʿ* phenomena scattered in the old poetry and sought them out consciously in his own poetry (on Muslim's role in this respect, see W. Heinrichs, *Muslim b. al-Walīd und* Badīʿ, in Heinrichs and G. Schoeler (eds.), *Festschrift Ewald Wagner zum 65. Geburtstag*, Band 2: *Studien zur arabischen Dichtung*, Beirut and Stuttgart 1994, 211-45). In this context, he makes use of Ibn al-Muʿtazz's permission to redistrict the *badīʿ* phenomena by limiting them to three: loan-metaphor, antithesis and paronomasia (*istiʿāra, ṭibāḳ, tad̲j̲nīs* [*q.vv.*]) (*Muwāzana*, i, 14). This testifies to his experience as a poet and critic, as these three figures of speech are clearly the most pervasive and popular in *muḥdat̲h̲* poetry.

The overall structure of al-Āmidī's work is as follows. First, a literary debate between the follower (*ṣāḥib*) of Abū Tammām and that of al-Buḥturī, both anonymous (*Muwāzana*, i, 8-53); second, a collection of defects of either poet, including plagiarisms, defects in meaning, ugly loan metaphors, paronomasias and antitheses (only with Abū Tammām!), and metrical irregularities (*Muwāzana*, i, 54-388); third, the actual weighing of verses of the two poets against each other, arranged according to the themes and motifs that are usually taken up in the "official" long poem, the *ḳaṣīda* [*q.v.*]. Al-Āmidī promises, and tries hard, to be objective in his evaluation, but cannot really hide his preference for the "natural" style of al-Buḥturī.

The controversy around al-Mutanabbī

The next great literary controversy was sparked by the poetic œuvre of al-Mutanabbī (d. 354/955 [*q.v.*]). Unlike the literary fights about Abū Tammām that were fought posthumously, much of the new debate happened already during al-Mutanabbī's lifetime. Since he was on all accounts a difficult person, he made enemies easily, and the writings attacking him seem to be full of personal animus, which tends to cloud any valid points they might try to make. Al-Ṣāḥib Ibn ʿAbbād (d. 385/995 [*q.v.*]), vizier to two Buyid princes, poet and man of letters, sponsor of scholars and poets, had early on invited al-Mutanabbī to join him, but had not even received a reply (al-T̲h̲aʿālibī, *Yatīma*, ed. ʿAbd al-Ḥamīd, i, 138). His "Treatise on revealing the blemishes and defects of the poetry of al-Mutanabbī" (*Risāla fī 'l-Kas̲h̲f ʿan masāwī s̲h̲iʿr al-Mutanabbī wa-ʿuyūbih*) was, consequently, "written in a bitter spirit" and raised some eyebrows (Ouyang, *Literary criticism*, 150). It was clearly vengeful nitpicking, considering the fact that Ibn ʿAbbād later wrote a little collection with the title "Current proverb[ial line]s from the poetry of al-Mutanabbī" (*al-Amt̲h̲āl al-sāʾira min s̲h̲iʿr al-Mutanabbī*, ed. Muḥammad Ḥasan Āl Yāsīn, *Nafāʾis al-mak̲h̲ṭūṭāt*, iv, Bag̲h̲dād 1385/1965, 21-78) and used "prosified" versions (*ḥall*) of al-Mutanabbī's poetic lines in his ornate epistles (al-T̲h̲aʿālibī, *Yatīma*, ed. ʿAbd al-Ḥamīd, i, 139-42). He was thus fully aware of the qualities of al-Mutanabbī's poetry. Similarly, when al-Mutanabbī came to Bag̲h̲dād, he snubbed the Būyid vizier al-Muhallabī [*q.v.*] by failing to address a praise poem to him (alleging that he praised only kings), whereupon al-Muhallabī urged the literary critic al-Ḥātimī (d. 388/998 [*q.v.* in Suppl.]) to engage al-Mutanabbī in a polemical debate concerning the latter's poetry. Al-Ḥātimī subsequently wrote this up under the title "The scalp-cleaving treatise concerning the plagiarisms of Abu 'l-Ṭayyib al-Mutanabbī and his corrupt poetry" (*al-Risāla al-mūḍiḥa fī d̲h̲ikr sariḳāt Abi 'l-Ṭayyib al-Mutanabbī wa-sāḳiṭ s̲h̲iʿrih*). Although the bias is tangible and al-Mutanabbī appears obtuse and apologetic, the treatise does contain a number of interesting discussions of critical topics on the part of al-Ḥātimī. He was after all the author of a general book on poetics, the "Ornament of apt quotation, on the craft of poetry" (*Ḥilyat al-muḥāḍara fī ṣināʿat al-s̲h̲iʿr*). This work is mainly compilatory but brings a number of different angles to bear on literary criticism: figures of speech, best verses on specific themes and topics, a large section on plagiarism and related topics, and—for the first time in *naḳd*—a treatment of *mad̲j̲āz* in poetry; the latter is, however, not very successful, as al-Ḥatimī uses the term in its wide application as we know it from Ibn Ḳutayba, and not in the later sense of "figurative speech", which ʿAbd al-Ḳāhir al-D̲j̲urd̲j̲ānī (see below) introduced into the literary field (cf. Heinrichs, *Contacts between scriptural hermeneutics and literary theory in Islam. The case of* Majāz, in *ZGAIW*, vii [1991-2], 253-84). Another attack on al-Mutanabbī was launched by the Egyptian poet Ibn Wakīʿ al-Tinnīsī (d. 393/1003) in his "Dealing fairly with the lifter and the lifted, regarding the divulgation of the plagiarisms of Abu 'l-Ṭayyib al-Mutanabbī" (*al-Munṣif li 'l-sāriḳ wa 'l-masrūḳ fī iẓhār sariḳāt Abi 'l-Ṭayyib al-Mutannabī*). In an introductory section he discusses the figures of speech, basing himself on Ibn al-Muʿtazz, Ḳudāma, and (without naming him) al-Ḥātimī.

The author who tried to right the wrongs committed against al-Mutanabbī was al-Ḳāḍī al-D̲j̲urd̲j̲ānī (d. 392/1002) in his "Mediation between al-Mutanabbī and his adversaries" (*al-Wasāṭa bayn al-Mutanabbī wa-k̲h̲uṣūmih*). The author belonged to the entourage of Ibn ʿAbbād for a while and was later appointed chief *Ḳāḍī* of al-Rayy; he was also a recognised poet. His book is the apex of applied literary criticism: fair to the poet, cognisant of the existing critical literature and interested in the general problems of literary evaluation (as witnessed by a fifty-page introduction, before the *Wasāṭa* actually begins).

Alongside the books and treatises written about, and often against, al-Mutanabbī, there are also the commentaries on his *Dīwān* to consider, as they do at times go beyond the mere explanation of a line and offer evaluative comments. Moreover there is some disagreement among the commentators, which also may have critical implications. The earliest commentaries, the two written by al-Mutanabbī's friend, the grammarian Ibn D̲j̲innī (d. 392/1002 [*q.v.*]), contain a number of interpretations and justifications that were considered incorrect by other critics, such as al-Waḥīd (Abū Ṭālib Saʿd b. Muḥammad al-Azdī al-Bag̲h̲dādī, d. 385/995), Abu 'l-Faḍl al-ʿArūḍī (d. 416/1025) and Ibn Fūrrad̲j̲a (Muḥammad b. Aḥmad, d. after 437/1045) (on critics of Ibn D̲j̲innī, and especially al-Waḥīd, see I. ʿAbbās, *Taʾrīk̲h̲*, 279-85; for examples see also Heinrichs, *Obscurity in Classical Arabic poetry*, in *Mediaevalia*, xix [1996, for 1993], 239-59). They sometimes attacked Ibn D̲j̲innī rather violently, and often not without reason: he was after all, in spite of his enthusiasm for al-Mutanabbī, a grammarian and expert on ancient poetry. One of Ibn Fūrrad̲j̲a's "counter-commentaries" has been published (see *Bibl.*). He is also quoted about one hundred times in the commentary of al-Wāḥidī (d. 468/1075), often together with al-ʿArūḍī and here and there with other scholars, offering fascinating insights into their interpretive and critical activities.

The debate about al-Mutanabbī did not entirely cease after this first flurry of activity in the 4th/10th and 5th/11th centuries. Even much later, books were still composed about him, but they tend to be derivative, such as Yūsuf al-Badīʿī (d. 1073/1662), *al-Ṣubḥ al-munabbī ʿan ḥayt̲h̲iyyat al-Mutanabbī*, ed. Muṣṭafā al-Saḳḳā *et alii*, Cairo 1963. A notable exception is the critical comparison between al-Mutanabbī and Abū Tammām by the Andalusian author Ibn Labbāl (Abu 'l-Ḥasan ʿAlī b. Aḥmad al-S̲h̲arīs̲h̲ī, d. 582/1186), *Rawḍat al-adīb fī 'l-tafḍīl bayna 'l-Mutanabbī wa-Ḥabīb*, ed. M. Ibn S̲h̲arīfa in idem, *Abū Tammām wa-Abu 'l-Ṭayyib fī adab al-Mag̲h̲āriba*, Beirut 1986, 197-222.

Further systematical research: al-K̲h̲afād̲j̲ī and ʿAbd al-Ḳāhir al-D̲j̲urd̲j̲ānī

Later poets do not appear to have become the focus of critical attention on such a grand scale. But one unique work should at least be mentioned here: a rather original literary-critical treatment of the poetry of Imruʾ al-Ḳays by Nad̲j̲m al-Dīn al-Ṭūfī (d. 716/1316 [*q.v.*]) with the title "Tables laden with date-curd, on the finer points of Imruʾ al-Ḳays" (*Mawāʾid al-ḥays fī fawāʾid Imriʾ al-Ḳays*, ed. Muṣṭafā ʿUlayyān, ʿAmmān 1414/1994). However, in general, the *naḳd* literature returned to general treatments of the whole field. A transitional figure in this respect is the famous poet and sceptic, Abu 'l-ʿAlāʾ al-Maʿarrī (d. 449/1058 [*q.v.*]), who was also an expert philologist and an ardent admirer of al-Mutanabbī. He composed two commentaries on the latter's *Dīwān* (see *Bibl.* for *Muʿd̲j̲iz Aḥmad; al-Lāmiʿ al-ʿAzīzī* is in ms. Istanbul, Süleymaniye, Hamidiye 1148, for the Arabic text and translation of its introduction, see P. Smoor, *Kings and Bedouins in the palace of Aleppo as reflected in Maʿarrī's works*, Manchester 1985, 223-4). His other works are strewn with a number of critical ideas (see ʿAbbās, *Taʾrīk̲h̲*, 379-91), but he apparently did not treat this topic systematically in a separate book. However, his student Ibn Sinān al-K̲h̲afād̲j̲ī (d. 466/1074) did so in his *Sirr al-faṣāḥa* (see *Bibl.*), in which Abu 'l-ʿAlāʾ is quoted quite frequently. Ibn Sinān wrote poetry, but he was probably first and foremost a statesman (not a successful one, since as governor of the fort of ʿAzāz he paid with his life for his temerity in seceding from his Mirdāsid overlord in Aleppo). He says quite clearly that the discourse of the scribe is much more important than that of the poet (*Sirr*, 280): Poetry is a superfluity that can be dispensed with" (*al-s̲h̲iʿru faḍlᵘⁿ yustag̲h̲nā ʿanhu*). His book is thus more generally *naḳd al-kalām*. His approach is very systematic, starting with sounds and letters—unlike others he is aware of the difference between the two—and going on to words (*alfāẓ*) in isolation and in combination, this being the domain of *faṣāḥa*, and finally discussing meanings (*maʿānī*) as expressed in those words, in isolation and in combination; this is the domain of *balāg̲h̲a*. A certain similarity to Ḳudāma is unmistakable; he also explicitly quotes him. Among later critics, it is characteristically the scribe Ḍiyāʾ al-Dīn Ibn al-At̲h̲īr (d. 637/1239 [see IBN AL-AT̲H̲ĪR]), who has a predilection for him. Ibn Sinān's *kātib* attitude also emerges from his anti-mannerist insistence on clarity and avoidance of forced style (*Sirr*, 282, final advice at the end of the book).

The same attitude can also be found already earlier in al-Marzūḳī's (d. 421/1030 [*q.v.*]) important introduction to his commentary on the *Ḥamāsa* of Abū Tammām. One of the topics discussed there is the notion of *ʿamūd al-s̲h̲iʿr* "the mainstay of poetry". Taking this term from al-Āmidī and al-Ḳāḍī al-D̲j̲urd̲j̲ānī, who used to characterise the ancient poets and the "natural" ones among the "modern" poets as following the *ʿamūd al-s̲h̲iʿr*, al-Marzūḳī draws up a list of qualities that defines the notion, seven in all, namely, elevated appropriate meaning, firm wording, accurate description, apposite simile, coherence and choice of pleasant metre, affinity between donor and receptor of a metaphor, and close fit between wording and meaning. This is a veritable manifesto of anti-mannerist poetising; it clearly tries to curb the more outrageous innovations of the "Moderns".

A contemporary of al-Khafādjī in the Eastern Islamic world was the greatest genius of Arabic literary theory, ʿAbd al-Ḳāhir al-Djurdjānī (d. 471/1078 or 474/1081 [*q.v.* in Suppl.]). He was a grammarian and minor poet, but not a scribe. He never travelled *fī ṭalab al-ʿilm* and had few teachers of whom we know; al-Ḳāḍī al-Djurdjānī (see above) was apparently one of them. His two critical works, *Asrār al-balāgha* "The mysteries of eloquence", and *Dalāʾil al-iʿdjāz* "The signs of the [Ḳurʾān's] inimitability", do overlap to some extent, but the former deals with poetic discourse while the latter focuses on Ḳurʾānic discourse. Both are highly original and proved to be historically most important. The *Asrār* concentrate on imagery, i.e. the essence and the function of simile, simile-based metaphor, analogy and analogy-based metaphor. Al-Djurdjānī was the first, and in a way maybe the last, to identify a major constituent of *muḥdathūn* poetic language, the *takhyīl* [*q.v.*], "phantastic re-interpretation of facts", in the guise of mock aetiologies, mock analogies and a number of other techniques, often based on metaphors taken literally. This allowed him to distinguish between "rational" (*ʿaḳlī*) and "phantasmagorical" (*takhyīlī*) motifs and to sing the praises of the latter as nothing less than verbal alchemy; he still supports, nonetheless, the greater "ethical" value of the "rational" motifs, since *takhyīl* entails a poetic lie (and thus does not occur in the Ḳurʾān). While this work should thus clearly be reckoned a part of the *naḳd al-shiʿr* enterprise (this judgement is corroborated by the many perceptive interpretations of poetic prooftexts included in it), his book on the inimitability of the Ḳurʾān, though replete with valuable observations on poetry, focuses on *naẓm* [*q.v.*, section 2, in Suppl.], "syntactic ordering to achieve a certain meaning." *Naẓm* is the only criterion by which the *iʿdjāz* can be proven, since it applies to every text, and thus to every *āya*, while other textual phenomena that might be evaluated, as e.g. metaphors, occur only sporadically. Even metaphor itself is constituted by *naẓm*, i.e. the context determines the metaphoricalness of the expression at hand.

The influence of the Ḳurʾānic discourse

Despite the overlap between the two books of al-Djurdjānī, the *Dalāʾil* belongs to a different strand of tradition. The Ḳurʾānic discourse of the *Dalāʾil* had, of course, its forerunners, which need not detain us here, except inasmuch as they may have had an influence on *naḳd al-shiʿr*. There are, actually, at least two Ḳurʾānic discourses that have some bearing on *naḳd al-shiʿr*. One appears as part of the works on legal theory; it often forms a section called *bayān* ("clarity") and deals with linguistic questions of hermeneutics, such as literal (*ḥaḳīḳa*) vs. figurative language (*madjāz*). There is, however, comparatively little overlap between the *bayān* of the legal scholars and the *bayān* [*q.v.*] of the rhetoricians. More important is the other Ḳurʾānic discourse, that of the *iʿdjāz* [*q.v.*]. And here it is, in particular, one strand in the discussion of the inimitability of the Ḳurʾān, namely, the proof of the stylistic unsurpassedness of the revealed text, where contacts with *naḳd* arose. The central term, with many of the authors in this field, is *naẓm*, the "ordering" of meanings and words into larger units. However, this had little impact on *naḳd*. Strangely, the scholar who did not make use of the *naẓm* notion had the most influence on the field of *naḳd*: al-Rummānī (d. 384/994 [*q.v.*]). His little treatise, "Notes on the inimitability of the Ḳurʾān" (*al-Nukat fī iʿdjāz al-Ḳurʾān*), based on the central notion of *balāgha*, "eloquence", divides this notion into ten parts, a number of which are very pertinent also for evaluations of poetry: brevity (*īdjāz*), simile (*tashbīh*), substitution metaphor (*istiʿāra*) and emphasis (*mubālagha*). Al-Rummānī was used extensively, but without acknowledgment, by Abū Hilāl al-ʿAskarī (d. after 400/1010 [*q.v.*]) in his *K. al-Ṣināʿatayn*. This book might be called the first encyclopaedia of literary theory, as it is a compilation, though not devoid of original ideas, from most of the earlier literature on rhetoric (*khaṭāba*), *naḳd al-shiʿr* and *iʿdjāz*. Since these different strands of literary theory at times used the same term in different meanings (e.g. *istiʿāra* as "loan metaphor" in *naḳd*, "substitution metaphor" or even "figurative speech in general" in Ḳurʾānic discourse), certain contradictions in the materials collected by Abū Hilāl remain. This lack of homogeneity also besets other authors, such as Ibn Rashīḳ (d. 456/1063 or 463/1071 [*q.v.*]), who quote al-Rummānī. It was ʿAbd al-Ḳāhir al-Djurdjānī who in his two books (see above) cleaned up the terminological mess resulting from the confluence of the poetic and the Ḳurʾānic discourses. But before him there was one more interesting interface between the discourses, in al-Bāḳillānī's (d. 403/1013 [*q.v.*]) *Iʿdjāz al-Ḳurʾān*. Three parts of this book are especially pertinent here (these parts were translated by G.E. von Grunebaum, *Tenth-century document*): (a) an extensive section on *badīʿ* "rhetorical figures", which, however, according to him are not relevant for proving the *iʿdjāz*, since they are attainable by man through training and experience; (b) a critique of the *Muʿallaḳa* of Imruʾ al-Ḳays [*q.v.*]; and (c) a critique of a famous *lāmiyya* by al-Buḥturī (*Ahl^an bi-dhālikumu ʾl-khayāli ʾl-muḳbili*, see al-Buḥturī, *Dīwān*, ed. al-Ṣayrafī, 1741-52). Al-Bāḳillānī is fairly well read in the relevant literature, quoting Ḳudāma, Abū Hilāl al-ʿAskarī and al-Rummānī (the last one anonymously). His analyses of the two poems are, of course, intended to show their deficiency against the background of the inimitable divine style. Subsequent literary criticism was not influenced by them.

The Muslim West

At about the same time, there was a flourishing of poetry and literary criticism in Zīrid Ḳayrawān, which may also be considered the beginning of serious critical activities in the Muslim West. Much Eastern material was made accessible by the excellent anthologies of al-Ḥuṣrī (d. 413/1022 [*q.v.*]), in particular his "Flowers of maxims and fruits of keen minds" (*Zahr al-ādāb wa-thamar al-albāb*, ed. ʿAlī Muḥammad al-Bidjāwī, Cairo 1372/1953) and "Collection of jewels among jocosities and rarities" (*Djamʿ al-djawāhir fī ʾl-mulaḥ wa ʾl-nawādir*, ed. al-Bidjāwī, Cairo 1372/1953). Both of them contain many passages in which the author either reports or presents critical viewpoints. Al-Ḥuṣrī was the mentor of Ibn Rashīḳ (d. 456/1064 or 463/1071 [*q.v.*]) and Ibn Sharaf al-Ḳayrawānī (d. 460/1067 [*q.v.*]), both eminent poets and critics, and fierce competitors for most of their lives. Ibn Rashīḳ's main work, "The pillar, on the beauties, etiquette, and critique of poetry" (*al-ʿUmda fī maḥāsin al-shiʿr wa-ādābih wa-naḳdih*) is a comprehensive handbook on poetry that includes discussions of the major critical issues, such as wording and meaning (*lafẓ wa-maʿnā*), natural and "artificial" poetry (*maṭbūʿ wa-maṣnūʿ*) and plagiarism (*sariḳa, akhdh*). His slim volume "Gold filings, on the criticism of the poems of the Arabs" (*Ḳurāḍat al-dhahab fī naḳd ashʿār al-ʿarab*) gives the impression of a collection of notes on various topics of literary criticism, including very subtle instances of intertextuality (see especially the chapter on *talfīḳ, Ḳurāḍa*, 95-106, "piecing together" a line of poetry from two or more existing lines, a method skilfully used by Abu 'l-ʿAlāʾ al-Maʿarrī). Ibn Rashīḳ's rival, Ibn Sharaf, is less well known, due to the loss of most of his writings; his evaluation of earlier poets is preserved in a short work, probably fragmentary, with the title "Questions of [literary] criticism" (*Masāʾil al-intiḳād*, or more fully, as in the colophon, *al-maḳāma al-maʿrūfa bi-Masāʾil al-intiḳād*). The rather aphoristic critique of a large number of poets is followed by a second part in which general guidelines for the critic are developed, in part on the basis of a critical, and moralistic, reading of verses from the *Muʿallaḳa* and other poems by Imruʾ al-Ḳays [*q.v.*]. Particularly noteworthy is the literary genre of the *maḳāma* [*q.v.*] that Ibn Sharaf has chosen for his presentation: he attributes the critical opinions in his work to one Abu 'l-Rayyān and he says unmistakably in his introduction that he "invented" (*ikhtalaḳtu*) the narratives included in his work.

At about the same time, al-Andalus also entered the scene with important contributions (disregarding here the works that introduced Eastern transmissions and ideas into al-Andalus, like the *adab* encyclopaedia "The unique necklace", *al-ʿIḳd al-farīd* of Ibn ʿAbd Rabbih [d. 328/940 (*q.v.*)] and the "Dictations", *al-Amālī*, of al-Ḳālī [d. 356/967 (*q.v.*)]). The eminent poet Ibn Shuhayd (d. 426/1035 [*q.v.*]), needled by adverse criticism of his poetry, wrote an imaginative and imaginary report, full of wit and haughtiness, about his visit to the country of the jinn and his discussions with the familiar spirits of famous poets and prose writers, with literary critics among the jinn, and, finally, with two animals, a mule and a goose, who turn out to be the familiar spirits of two contemporaries. Much of the story revolves around the question of talent and training as prerequisites for successful poetic activity; the translator, James Monroe (see *Bibl.*), discovered a Neo-Platonic blueprint underlying the author's theory of "creativity".

Ibn Shuhayd's friend, Ibn Ḥazm (d. 456/1064 [*q.v.*]), should briefly be mentioned here, because his logical work "Bringing close to the definition of logic" (*al-Taḳrīb ilā ḥadd al-manṭiḳ*) leads over to the philosophical poetics in the next paragraph, although it is still very much "Arabic" in its contents. Two ideas stand out in his presentation. One is the notion that the essence of poetry is that it consists of false statements. This is not a new statement, being both part of the Greek tradition known to the Arab world (see below on Ibn al-Bannāʾ) as well as the indigenous one, where the adage *aḥsanu* (var. *khayru*) *'l-shiʿri akdhabuh* "the best poetry is the most untruthful one" is often quoted. However, the exclusivist view maintained by Ibn Ḥazm is rare (on the various non-formal definitions of prose and poetry, see Heinrichs, *Dichterische Rede*). The other unusual notion is his tripartite typology of poets: to the usual types characterised by *ṭabʿ* "natural talent" or *ṣināʿa* "artfulness" he adds a third one, distinguished by *barāʿa* "virtuosity". From his description this type appears like a synthesis of *ṭabʿ* and *ṣināʿa*; *barāʿa* is the ability to make intricate conceits appear natural (on this and related topics, see G. Schoeler, *Einige Grundprobleme der autochthonen und der aristotelischen arabischen Literaturtheorie* [*AKM*, Band xli, 4], Wiesbaden 1975, 33-56, and his additions in *ZDMG*, cxxvi [1976], *79*).

Philosophical poetics and the Maghribī "school"

A short aside on philosophical, or logical, poetics

is appropriate here. Aristotle's *Rhetoric* and *Poetics* were translated from Syriac into Arabic. The former exists in a *naḳl ḳadīm*, an "old" pre-Ḥunayn translation, the latter in the translation of Abū Bishr Mattā (d. 328/940 [see MATTĀ B. YŪNUS]) and, in the commentaries, also in a revision by Abū Bishr's disciple Yaḥyā b. ʿAdī (d. 363/974 [*q.v.*]). These translations remained for a very long time the domain of the logicians, because since the days of the Neo-Platonic Alexandrian commentators the *Rhetoric* and the *Poetics* had become part of the *Organon*, the logical writings of Aristotle. We have summaries and commentaries on these two books by a number of important philosophers, al-Fārābī, Ibn Sīnā and Ibn Rushd [*q.vv.*] among them, and many short characterisations of them in general exposés of logic. The basic notions of Arabic logical poetics are *takhyīl* "image-creation in the listener's mind" and *muḥākāt* "image-creation from reality", the latter going back to the Aristotelian *mimesis* but here reinterpreted as "imagery" (for further details, see TAKHYĪL). Probably due to the compartmentalisation of knowledge into Arabic and Ancient disciplines, the indigenous theorists of poetry did not show any interest in the logical approach, except in the Muslim West. While in the East Ḍiyāʾ al-Dīn Ibn al-Athīr, in a well-known passage of his *al-Mathal al-sāʾir* (ed. al-Ḥūfī and Ṭabāna, Cairo 379-81/1959-62, ii, 5-6), is the only indigenous theorist to take notice of the philosophers, by rejecting and scorning Ibn Sīnā's "Greek" poetics, in the Maghrib there are several authors who, in one way or another, make use of the basic terms and ideas of this unusual branch of logic. The first among these seems to have been Ibn ʿAmīra (d. 656/1258 or 658/1260 [*q.v.*]), who wrote his *al-Tanbīhāt ʿalā mā fī 'l-Tibyān min al-tamwīhāt* as a critique of a work by Ibn al-Zamlakānī (d. 651/1253) (see *al-Tibyān* in *Bibl.*). The polemical format of this work precludes a systematic introduction of technical terms; but the central terms of philosophical poetics, *takhyīl, muḥākāt* and *aḳyisa shiʿriyya*, are employed (see *Tanbīhāt*, 125, 134 and 135, respectively), and *muḥākāt* is used in the sense of "imaging" by means of similes or metaphors.

The most important among "philosophising" critics is Ḥāzim al-Ḳarṭādjannī (d. 684/1285 [*q.v.*]), who used the two basic notions of the logical approach, *takhyīl* and *muḥākāt* (the latter further reinterpreted as "image-creation by both descriptive and figurative processes"), in order to give a foundation to the hitherto more analytical and taxonomic indigenous approaches in the theory of poetry (for the details of his theory, see *Minhādj*, 62-129, translated in W. Heinrichs, *Arabische Dichtung und griechische Poetik*, 173-262).

His younger contemporary al-Sidjilmāsī (d. after 704/1304 [*q.v.*]), in his "Novel method in classifying the modes of figures of speech" (*al-Manzaʿ al-badīʿ fī tadjnīs asālīb al-badīʿ*), like Ḥāzim quotes al-Fārābī and Ibn Sīnā verbatim but understands *takhyīl* in the narrower sense of "imagery", including *tashbīh* "simile", *istiʿāra* "loan metaphor", *mumāthala* "analogy" and *madjāz* (see *Manzaʿ*, 218-61, 406-7; note that *takhyīl* here is used as a synonym of *muḥākāt*, due to a *pars pro toto* application of either term for the entire activity of the poet of shaping images from reality and creating corresponding images in the minds of the listeners). It is noteworthy that *madjāz* in al-Sidjilmāsī equals the Djurdjānian *takhyīl* (see above) (on this strange use of the term, see Suʿād al-Māniʿ, *Mafhūm muṣṭalaḥ "al-madjāz" ʿinda 'l-Sidjilmāsī fī ʿalāḳatihi bi-muṣṭalaḥ "al-takhyīl"*, in *Abḥāth al-Yarmūk*, xvii [1420/1999], 89-137).

The last of the "philosophising" Maghribī critics, who is known to us through his own work, is Ibn al-Bannā' (d. 721/1321 [*q.v.*]); there are a few others, about whose views we know little (see M. Ibn Sharīfa, *Muḳaddima* to Ibn ʿAmīra, *Tanbīhāt*, 32). Ibn al-Bannā' gives a short overview on the various truth values of the logical disciplines (*burhān, djadal, khaṭāba, shiʿr, mughālaṭa*) and defines poetry as "address by means of false, image-evoking (*mukhayyila*) statements based on image-making (*muḥākāt*), which result in the excitement (*istifzāz*) [of the listener] by those fancies (*tawahhumāt*)" (see *Rawḍ*, 81, and cf. 103). By stressing the falseness of the poetic statements he diverges from Ḥāzim and al-Sidjilmāsī, who declare "true" and "false" as immaterial in poetry; Ibn al-Bannā' resumes another tradition, which also has Greek roots and later Arab adherents (see above).

Much of the literature devoted to the criticism of poetry ultimately feeds into scholastic rhetoric (*ʿilm al-balāgha*), on which see BALĀGHA, BAYĀN, AL-MAʿĀNĪ WA-'L-BAYĀN, AL-SAKKĀKĪ and AL-KHAṬĪB AL-ḲAZWĪNĪ. But the main goal of rhetoric is as a tool to understand the *iʿdjāz al-Ḳurʾān* [*q.v.*]. The whole literature based on the third chapter of al-Sakkākī's *Miftāḥ al-ʿulūm* will thus not be treated here. The same is also true for most of the later works outside the al-Sakkākī tradition.

The main topics of naḳd

The historical outline presented so far should be complemented by a short topical outline of the basic themes of *naḳd al-shiʿr*. (1) *Poetry vs. prose.* The most popular definition of poetry is the formal one proposed by Ḳudāma, *Naḳd*, 2: *ḳawl^un mawzūn^un muḳaffā^n yadullu ʿalā maʿnā^n* "metrical rhymed utterance indicating a meaning". This would include didactic versification [see NAẒM] and thus cannot be considered satisfactory. Some authors have, therefore, tried to establish an essential difference between poetry and prose (cf. Heinrichs, *Dichterische Rede*). Three approaches can be distinguished:

(a) The first is based on the idea that reality can be expressed in different ways. Al-Zandjānī (d. 650/1262 [*q.v.* in Suppl.]) in his "Yardstick for students of the disciplines concerning poems" (*Miʿyār al-nuẓẓār fī ʿulūm al-ashʿār*) uses the threefold system of denotation (*dalāla*), i.e. *muṭābaḳa* ("congruence", "house" denotes a house), *taḍammun* ("implication", "house" denotes a ceiling) and *iltizām* ("concomitance", "ceiling" denotes a wall) and says that *muṭābaḳa* is the "original denotation" (*dalāla waḍʿiyya*) and is used in the rational sciences (*ʿulūm ʿaḳliyya*), while *taḍammun* and *iltizām* are "rational denotations" (*dalālatān^i ʿaḳliyyatān^i*, i.e. one has to think about their meaning) (*Miʿyār*, ed. al-Ashkar, 5-7). Of these, *iltizām* is the kind of denotation that matters in "eloquence" (*balāgha*), because the "concomitants" (*lawāzim*) are numerous and there are many ways, good and bad, in which a certain idea can be conveyed. Two points need emphasis here. (i) Although his book is devoted to poetry, in this passage he speaks about "eloquence", which, of course, extends to ornate prose as well; and (ii) the opposite of eloquent speech is scientific texts. Al-Zandjānī's approach may thus be somewhat askew when it comes to defining poetry. (As an aside, one might mention that al-Sakkākī uses the same theory of denotation but applies it only to imagery, *bayān*, see *Miftāḥ al-ʿulūm*, ed. Naʿīm Zarzūr, Beirut 1403/1983, 329-30.) There is a certain similarity between al-Zandjānī and Ḥāzim al-Ḳarṭādjannī in this respect. The latter defines poetry, with the help of terms from the Aristotelian-Fārābian tradition, as a speech that "imitates" (*muḥākāt*) the object by describing its accidents and then "generates representational images" (*takhyīl*) of the object in the mind of the listener/reader. Scientific propositions, on the other hand, consist in naming the essence of things and creating understanding (*ifhām*) (*Minhādj*, 98-9, 118-20). Again we have a dichotomy of poetic and scientific speech.

(b) The second attempt at defining poetry is based on the idea of "untruth" (*kadhib*). The adage *aḥsanu 'l-shiʿri akdhabuh* "the best poetry is the most untruthful one", sometimes said to be of Greek origin, has been interpreted as referring to (overblown) hyperbole (*ghulūw*) (Ḳudāma, *Naḳd*, 24-7) and to al-Djurdjānī's "phantastic re-interpretation" (*takhyīl*, see above), thus to "distortions" of reality (or of the mirror quality of language) in the course of increasing mannerism. Most critics did not conclude that all poetry was untrue, but at least two explicitly did so: the philologist Ibn Fāris (d. 395/1004 [*q.v.*]) in *al-Ṣāḥibī fī fiḳh al-lugha* (ed. al-Sayyid Aḥmad Ṣaḳr, Cairo 1977, 466) and Ibn Ḥazm (see above).

(c) The third approach contrasts the "obscurity" (*ghumūḍ*) of poetry with the "clarity" (*wuḍūḥ*) of literary prose. This was done by the *kātib* Ibrāhīm b. Hilāl al-Ṣābī (d. 384/994) in an epistle, in which he says that, due to the shortness and rigidity of the verse and the constraints of rhyme and metre, poems could not avoid being "obscure" (A. Arazi, *Une épître d'Ibrāhīm b. Hilāl al-Ṣābī sur les genres littéraires*, in M. Sharon (ed.), *Studies in Islamic history and civilization in honour of Professor David Ayalon*, Jerusalem and Leiden 1986). Later critics have usually not agreed, saying that the *balāgha* of both poetry and ornate prose required clarity (cf., e.g., Cantarino, *Poetics*, 195).

Since the middle ʿAbbāsid period, when the idea had taken hold that the *ḳaṣīda* and the *risāla* were identical but for formal differences, the terminology of the poetry-critics was to a large extent applied to ornate prose as well. But there are also some relatively early sets of terms that were developed by the state scribes for the description of the epistolary style. Ḳudāma b. Djaʿfar, in the introduction to his work on synonymous words and phrases, "Gems of words" (*Djawāhir al-alfāẓ*, 3-8), lists and exemplifies fourteen features that make for the highest degree of eloquence (*balāgha*) in ornate prose. His fellow-*kātib* al-Khʷārazmī (2nd half of 4th/10th cent. [*q.v.*]), in his "Keys of the sciences" (*Mafātīḥ al-ʿulūm*), has a chapter on "the conventions of the epistolographers" (*muwāḍaʿāt kuttāb al-rasāʾil*), which clearly harks back to Ḳudāma's list but also goes beyond it by adding a paragraph on defects (*Mafātīḥ*, 72-8). Al-Khʷārazmī is particularly instructive, because his encyclopaedia also contains a chapter on *naḳd al-shiʿr* (*Mafātīḥ*, 94-7); a comparison of the two lists shows surprisingly little overlap in terminology and only slightly more when the figures themselves are considered. A third list was compiled later by al-Yazdādī (dates unknown) in the introduction to his "Perfection of eloquence" (*Kamāl al-balāgha*, 19-32), a selection of epistles by Ḳābūs b. Wushmgīr (d. 403/1012 [*q.v.*]). The author says that he isolated, from the epistles themselves, such figures as Ḳudāma had not yet identified (*Kamāl*, 19); it is likely but not certain that he is referring to *Djawāhir al-alfāẓ* rather than to *Naḳd al-shiʿr*. All of this shows that, before the final confluence of terminologies, we have to assume separate traditions of poetic, rhetorical (epistolary) and Ḳurʾānic (see above) technical vocabulary.

For a critique of a piece of eloquent prose—not a very common event—one may point to al-Ḳāḍī ʿIyāḍ's (d. 544/1150 [see ʿIYĀḌ]) exhaustive interpretation of the *ḥadīth Umm Zarʿ* (on this text, see F. Rosenthal, *Muslim social values and literary criticism—reflections on the Ḥadīth of Umm Zarʿ*, in *Oriens*, xxxiv [1994], 31-56). This includes a chapter on *bayān* that deals with the literary aspects of the *ḥadīth* (*Bughyat al-rāʾid li-mā taḍammanahū ḥadīth Umm Zarʿ min al-fawāʾid*, ed. Ṣalāḥ al-Dīn b. Aḥmad al-Idlibī *et alii*, al-Muḥammadiyya 1395/1975, 186-214).

(2) *Truth vs. falsehood.* Ibn Rashīḳ states that most of poetry is *waṣf* "description" (*ʿUmda*, ii, 294), thus true. As mentioned, some critics have maintained the opposite (Ibn Ḥazm, Ibn Fāris, see above); this has to be seen against the background of the mannerist trends in "modern" poetry—with their irreal hyperboles (*ghulūw*), substratum-less metaphors (*istiʿāra [takhyīliyya]*), and phantastic re-interpretations (*takhyīl* of al-Djurdjānī). Critics often became a little nervous when confronted with "falsehoods" (*kadhib*) of this type, but the poets were not deterred. The idea of poetry being *per se* "untrue" is also highlighted by Abu 'l-ʿAlāʾ al-Maʿarrī's assertion that the sceptical poetry in his *Luzūmiyyāt* is *not* poetry, because it is true (ed., ʿA. Zand, Cairo 1891, 9, 42).

Explicit fiction is not of common occurrence in Arabic literature, and certainly not in poetry. There are, it is true, cases like the versification, in couplets, of *Kalīla wa-Dimna* and similar fictional works by Abān al-Lāḥiḳī (d. *ca.* 200/815 [*q.v.*]); but these would presumably be regarded as *naẓm* rather than poetry. However, the often stereotypical adventures that a poet, or his persona, would describe were, of course, known not to be the historical truth, but this kind of non-explicit fiction, because it could not be recognised from the poem itself, elicited little interest on the part of the critics. It is only Ḥāzim al-Ḳarṭādjannī who paid some attention to the notion of "fiction" (*ikhtilāḳ*, as he calls it) and who distinguished the type of fiction just mentioned from the one that is plainly fictional on the surface (e.g. the talking animals in *Kalīla wa-Dimna*) by calling the former "possibility-fiction" (*ikhtilāḳ imkānī*) and the latter "impossibility-fiction" (*ikhtilāḳ imtināʿī*) (*Minhādj*, 76-9).

(3) *The unit within the poem.* A large amount of poetic criticism is directed to the single line. This "molecular" approach is driven to the extreme by Thaʿlab, who considers lines with semantically independent hemistichs the best of all. Several critics do quote larger passages (e.g. Ibn Ṭabāṭabā), but they do not normally discuss the structure of larger entities. An exception is the analysis of transitions from one theme to the next in the polythematic *ḳaṣīda* (*takhalluṣ*). Al-Ḥātimī uses the image of the human body in order to stress the overall "organic" unity of the poem (see in general G.J.H. van Gelder, *Beyond the line. Classical Arabic literary critics on the coherence and unity of the poem*, Leiden 1982; the passage in question is translated and discussed at 82-3). But for a thorough discussion of "passages" (*fuṣūl*, sing. *faṣl*) as building-blocks within a poem, one has again to turn to Ḥāzim al-Ḳarṭādjannī (see van Gelder, 171-90).

(4) *Wording* (lafẓ) *vs. meaning* (maʿnā). This dichotomy is basic to all disciplines dealing with language. It was, e.g., used by the logicians in their dispute with the grammarians in the 4th/10th century, when they alleged that their domain was the *maʿānī*, while the grammarians dealt with the *alfāẓ*. This oversimplification did not go down well with the grammarians, who rightly claimed that they dealt with semantic matters as well. Among the earlier critics, the most commonly encountered attitude is that the *lafẓ* is the object of the poet's artistic endeavour, the "form" that he tries to achieve, while the *maʿnā* is the material that he works on. Poetry is thus a *ṣināʿa*, a "craft" like that of the carpenter, weaver or goldsmith, and indeed the poet's craft is often compared to these professions and many of the terms denoting figures of speech are taken in the way of metaphors from these other crafts. However, wording and meaning cannot easily be separated: if one wants to talk about the wording without any reference to the meaning, the topic becomes restricted to euphony, stylistic acceptability of words (cf. WAḤSHĪ), and grammatical features (everything covered by the term *faṣāḥa* [*q.v.*]). In most discussions of the critics *lafẓ* is used in the sense of a "particular expression" of a general idea (*maʿnā*); it thus clearly partakes in the *maʿnā* side of language. The term *maʿnā* itself acquires several meanings:

(a) the meaning of a specific verse (especially when it is difficult to gauge)—this is dealt with in early philological *maʿānī* works, such as al-Ushnāndānī (d. 256/870), *Maʿānī al-shiʿr* (ed. ʿIzz al-Dīn al-Tanūkhī, Damascus 1969);

(b) the motif expressed in a line, i.e. a popular poetic commonplace; these were collected, together with their most famous realisations, in motif catalogues, such as Ibn Ḳutayba, *K. al-Maʿānī al-kabīr* (Ḥaydarābād, Deccan 1949), Abū Hilāl al-ʿAskarī, *Dīwān al-maʿānī* (Cairo 1352 [1933-34]), al-Rāghib al-Iṣfahānī (d. 502/1108 [*q.v.*]), *Madjmaʿ al-balāgha* (ed. ʿUmar ʿAbd al-Raḥmān al-Sarīsī, 2 vols., ʿAmmān 1406/1986) and the anonymous *Madjmūʿat al-maʿānī* (ed. ʿAbd al-Salām Hārūn, Beirut 1992), as well as in catalogues of similes, such as Ibn Abī ʿAwn, *K. al-Tashbīhāt* (ed. ʿAbdul Muʿīd Khān, London 1950) and Ibn al-Kattānī, *K. al-Tashbīhāt min ashʿār ahl al-Andalus* (ed. Iḥsān ʿAbbās, Beirut 1967); and

(c) the specific meaning, which results from the application of rhetoric and imagery to a known motif, thereby refashioning it as a conceit (*concetto*)—these are the *maʿānī* that the admirers of Abū Tammām, al-Āmidī's *ahl al-maʿānī* (see above), cherish and which Ibn Rashīḳ calls the *maʿānī al-ṣanʿa* (*ʿUmda*, i, 133). An example would be Abū Tammām's notorious line: *lā tasḳinī māʾa 'l-malāmi fa-innanī/ṣabbun ḳad-i 'staʿdhabtu māʾa bukāʾī* "Do not pour for me the water of blame, for I am a man in love, I have come to find the water of my weeping sweet" (*Dīwān*, ed. Muḥammad ʿAbduh ʿAzzām, 4 vols. Cairo 1964-5, i, 22). Here the simple idea "Do not blame me, for I am in love and like weeping" has been transformed into a conceit, by "applying" to it (i) a loan metaphor ("the *water* of blame") and (ii) a *muḳābala* (the contrast of the two waters). It is clear from these literarily ever more meaningful uses of the term *maʿnā* that *maʿnā* and *lafẓ* become inextricably bound together; this *maʿnā-lafẓ* conglomerate came especially to the fore in discussions of the historical development of motifs, i.e. discussions of borrowings, imitations, and plagiarisms. ʿAbd al-Ḳāhir al-Djurdjānī realised the inefficiency of the rigid dichotomy "wording/meaning" and introduced the term *ṣūra* "form, structure" which he puts in the middle between the *lafẓ* as "linguistic material" (*adjrās al-ḥurūf* "the sounds of the letters") and the *maʿnā* as "thematic material" (*gharaḍ* "intention"); one could say that the *ṣūra* forms both the linguistic and the thematic material and thus creates a structured *lafẓ* and a structured *maʿnā* that are completely congruent.

(5) *Originality vs. plagiarism.* On the whole gamut of possibilities between *ikhtirāʿ* "original invention" and *sariḳa* crude "plagiarism", see SARIḲA, in Suppl.

Influence on other literatures

Arabic literary criticism and poetics have had an

influence on two linguistic-cultural domains outside of it. One is Persian literary theory. The first work in this field was Rādūyānī's [*q.v.*] "Interpreter of eloquence" (*Tardjumān al-balāgha*, ed. Ahmed Ateş, Istanbul 1949), written between 482/1089 and 507/1114 (see also Ateş, *Tarcumān al-Balāġa, das früheste neupersische Werk über rhetorische Figuren*, in *Oriens*, i [1948], 45-62). This work is based on an Arabic precursor, namely al-Marghīnānī's (middle of the 5th/11th century) "Beauties in poetry and prose" (*al-Maḥāsin fi 'l-naẓm wa 'l-nathr*, ed. van Gelder, *Two Arabic treatises on stylistics*, Istanbul 1987, 66-110).

The other cultural domain open to Arabic influence was the Jewish community, primarily in al-Andalus but also elsewhere, who had adopted Arabic prosody, or an adaptation thereof, for the composition of Hebrew poetry. This drew their attention also to the critical literature of the Arabs; this in turn confronted them with the notion of *iʿdjāz al-Ḳurʾān* and motivated them to discover rhetorical and figurative use of language in their own Scripture. The most important author here is Moshe b. ʿEzra (d. after 529/1135), who wrote two relevant works in Judaeo-Arabic: the *K. al-Muḥāḍara wa 'l-mudhākara* (ed. [in Hebrew script] and tr. into Hebrew by A.S. Halkin, Jerusalem 1975, ed. [in Arabic script] and tr. into Spanish by Montserrat Abumalhan Mas, 2 vols. Madrid 1985-6), dealing mainly with poetry, and the *Maḳālat al-Ḥadīḳa fi maʿnā 'l-madjāz wa 'l-ḥaḳīḳa*, ed. and tr. (into Hebrew) by P. Fenton (Jerusalem, forthcoming), see also Fenton, *Philosophie et exégèse dans le Jardin de la métaphore de Moïse Ibn ʿEzra* (Leiden 1997), with the main focus on scriptural issues. Recently, extant fragments of another Judaeo-Arabic work on poetics (including prosody), this time by a man from the East, have been published: J. Yahalom (ed. and tr. into Hebrew), *Perāḳīm be-tōrat ha-shīr le-Elʿāzār ben Yaʿaḳōv ha-Bavlī, Judaeo-Arabic poetics. Fragments of a lost treatise by Elazar ben Jacob of Baghdad* (Jerusalem 2001). Some early copies of this work and of Moshe b. ʿEzra's *K. al-Muḥāḍara* seem to have been written in Arabic script, as can be seen from mistakes attributable to misreadings of Arabic letters. This may point to some amount of give-and-take between Muslim and Jewish critics.

On the poetics of mediaeval dialect poetry, see ZADJAL (toward the end).

Bibliography: 1. General overviews. The most satisfactory is Iḥsān ʿAbbās, *Taʾrīkh al-naḳd al-adabī ʿinda 'l-ʿArab. Naḳd al-shiʿr min al-ḳarn al-thānī ḥattā 'l-ḳarn al-thāmin al-hidjrī*, 2nd enlarged and corrected ed. ʿAmmān 1993 ([1]Beirut 1971). An earlier attempt, still useful in parts but dealing only with the early period is Amjad Trabulsi, *La critique poétique des Arabes jusqu'au Ve siècle de l'Hégire (XIe siècle de J.C.)*, Damascus 1956. A combination of primary poetics, abstracted from the poetry itself, and *naḳd al-shiʿr*, is Jamel Eddine Bencheikh, *Poétique arabe*, Paris 1989 ([1]1975). The professionalisation of *naḳd* is described in Wen-Chin Ouyang, *Literary criticism in medieval Arabic-Islamic culture. The making of a tradition*, Edinburgh 1997. Specifically for Muslim Spain, see Muḥammad Riḍwān al-Dāya, *Taʾrīkh al-naḳd al-adabī fi 'l-Andalus*, Beirut 1388/1968. For an anthology of translated texts plus substantial introductions, see V. Cantarino, *Arabic poetics in the Golden Age*, Leiden 1975. Short presentations: W. Heinrichs, *Poetik, Rhetorik, Literaturkritik, Metrik und Reimlehre*, in *GaP*, ii, 177-207; K. Abu Deeb, *Literary criticism*, in *CHALABL*, 339-87.

2. Studies dealing with more than one author. S.A. Bonebakker, *Aspects of the history of literary rhetoric and poetics in Arabic literature*, in *Viator*, i (1970), 75-95; W. Heinrichs, *Literary theory: the problem of its efficiency*, in G.E. von Grunebaum (ed.), *Arabic poetry: theory and development, Third Levi Della Vida Biennial Conference*, Wiesbaden 1973, 19-69; idem, *The Hand of the Northwind. Opinions on metaphor and the early meaning of Istiʿāra in Arabic poetics*, Wiesbaden 1977 (AKM, Bd. XLIV, 2); idem, *Klassisch-arabische Theorien dichterischer Rede*, in H. Preissler and Heidi Stein (eds.), *Annäherungen an das Fremde. XXVI. Deutscher Orientalistentag vom 25. bis 29.9.1995 in Leipzig* (*ZDMG*, Supplement 11, Stuttgart 1998), 199-208; G.J. van Gelder, *Beyond the line. Classical Arabic literary critics on the coherence and unity of the poem*, Leiden 1982; Mansour Ajami, *The Alchemy of glory. The dialectic of truthfulness and untruthfulness in medieval Arabic literary criticism*, Washington, DC 1988; Djābir ʿUṣfūr, *Mafhūm al-shiʿr, dirāsa fi 'l-turāth al-naḳdī*, [4]Nicosia 1990 (on Ibn Ṭabāṭabā, Ḳudāma and Ḥāzim al-Ḳarṭādjannī); Sasson Somekh (ed.), *Studies in medieval Arabic and Hebrew poetics*, in *IOS*, xi (1991); Amidu Sanni, *The Arabic theory of prosification and versification: on ḥall and naẓm in Arabic theoretical discourse*, Beirut and Stuttgart 1998.

3. Editions and studies on individual authors. (The list contains a few additional authors not mentioned in the text.) Mediaeval lists of relevant literature are given by Ibn Abi 'l-Iṣbaʿ, *Taḥrīr al-taḥbīr fi ṣanʿat al-shiʿr wa-nathr wa-bayān iʿdjāz al-Ḳurʾān*, ed. Hifnī Muḥammad Sharaf, Cairo 1963 [in the introduction], and by Ṣafī al-Dīn al-Ḥillī, *al-Natāʾidj al-ilāhiyya fi sharḥ al-Kāfiya al-badīʿiyya*, ed. Nasīb Nashāwī, Damascus 1402/1982 [in the appendix]. A veritable encyclopaedia-cum-anthology of poetic figures is: Ibn Maʿṣūm [d. 1117/1705], *Anwār al-rabīʿ fi anwāʿ al-badīʿ*, 7 vols., ed. Shākir Hādī Shukr, Nadjaf 1968.) al-Akhfash al-Awsaṭ, Saʿīd b. Masʿada, *K. al-Ḳawāfī*, ed. ʿIzzat Ḥasan, Damascus 1390/1970; Aṣmaʿī and Abū Ḥātim al-Sidjistānī, *Suʾālāt Abī Ḥātim al-Sidjistānī li 'l-Aṣmaʿī wa-radduhū ʿalayhi—Fuḥūlat al-shuʿarāʾ*, ed. Muḥammad ʿAwda Salāma Abū Djarī, Cairo 1414/1994; Ibn Ḳutayba, *K. al-Shiʿr wa 'l-shuʿarāʾ*, *Muḳaddima*, ed. Gaudefroy-Demombynes, as *Ibn Qotaïba, Introduction au Livre de la poésie et des poètes*, Paris 1947; Thaʿlab, *Ḳawāʿid al-shiʿr*, ed. Ramaḍān ʿAbd al-Tawwāb, Cairo 1966; Ibn al-Muʿtazz, *K. al-Badīʿ*, ed. I. Kratchkovsky, London 1935; M. Canard, *Deux chapitres inédits de l'œuvre de Kratchkovsky sur Ibn al-Muʿtazz*, in *AIEO*, xx (1962), 21-111; S.A. Bonebakker, *Ibn al-Muʿtazz and* Kitāb al-Badīʿ, in *CHALABL*, 388-411; Ibn Ṭabāṭabā, *K. ʿIyār al-shiʿr*, ed. ʿAbd al-ʿAzīz b. Nāṣir al-Māniʿ, Riyāḍ 1405/1985; Ḳudāma b. Djaʿfar, *K. Naḳd al-shiʿr*, ed. S.A. Bonebakker, Leiden 1956; idem, *Djawāhir al-alfāẓ*, ed. Muḥammad Muḥyī 'l-Dīn ʿAbd al-Ḥamīd, Cairo 1932, repr. Beirut 1399/1979; Marzubānī, *al-Muwashshaḥ fi maʾākhidh al-ʿulamāʾ ʿalā 'l-shuʿarāʾ*, ed. Muḥibb al-Dīn al-Khaṭīb, [2]Cairo 1385; Isḥāḳ b. Ibrāhīm Ibn Wahb al-Kātib, *al-Burhān fi wudjūh al-bayān*, ed. Aḥmad Maṭlūb and Khadīdja al-Ḥadīthī, Baghdād 1387/1967; Khwārazmī, Abū ʿAbdallāh Muḥammad b. Aḥmad, *Mafātīḥ al-ʿulūm*, ed. G. van Vloten, Leiden 1895, repr. Leiden 1968; Āmidī, *al-Muwāzana bayn shiʿr Abī Tammām wa 'l-Buḥturī*, vols. i-ii, ed. al-Sayyid Aḥmad Ṣaḳr, Cairo 1380-4/1961-5, vol. iii, ed. ʿAbd Allāh Ḥamd Muḥārib, Cairo 1410/1990; Rummānī, *al-Nukat fi iʿdjāz al-Ḳurʾān*, ed. Muḥammad Khalaf Allāh and Muḥammad Zaghlūl Salām, in *Thalāth rasāʾil fi iʿdjāz al-Ḳurʾān*, Cairo

n.d.; Ḥātimī, *al-Risāla al-mūḍiḥa fī dhikr sariḳāt Abi 'l-Ṭayyib al-Mutanabbī wa-sāḳiṭ shiʿrih*, ed. Muḥammad Yūsuf Nadjm, Beirut 1385/1965 (cf. Bonebakker, *Ḥātimī and his encounter with Mutanabbī: a biographical sketch*, Amsterdam, etc. 1984, for the various extant versions of the *Risāla*); idem, *Ḥilyat al-muḥāḍara fī ṣināʿat al-shiʿr*, ed. Djaʿfar al-Kattānī, 2 vols. Baghdād 1979, ed. Hilāl Nādjī, Beirut 1978 (incomplete); Bonebakker, *Materials for the history of Arabic rhetoric: from the* Ḥilyat al-Muḥāḍara *of Ḥātimī (Mss 2934 and 590 of the Qarawiyyīn Mosque in Fez)*, Naples 1975; al-Ḳāḍī al-Djurdjānī, *al-Wasāṭa bayn al-Mutanabbī wa-khuṣūmih*, ed. Muḥammad Abu 'l-Faḍl Ibrāhīm and ʿAlī Muḥammad al-Bidjāwī, [3]Cairo n.d.; Ibn Wakīʿ, *K. al-Munṣif li 'l-sāriḳ wa 'l-masrūḳ minhu fī iẓhār sariḳāt Abi 'l-Ṭayyib al-Mutanabbī*, ed. Nadjm, pt. 1, Kuwait 1404/1984, also ed. as *al-Munṣif fī naḳd al-shiʿr wa-bayān sariḳāt al-Mutanabbī wa-mushkil shiʿrih*, by Muḥammad Riḍwān al-Dāya, Damascus 1402/1982; Muḥsin Ghayyāḍ ʿUdjayl (ed.), *Shurūḥ shiʿr al-Mutanabbī*, Baghdād 2000 [contains Abu 'l-Faḍl al-ʿArūḍī, *al-Mustadrak ʿalā Ibn Djinnī fīmā sharaḥahu min shiʿr al-Mutanabbī* (collection of fragments); Ibn Fūrradja, *al-Tadjannī ʿalā Ibn Djinnī* (collection of fragments); Ibn al-Ḳaṭṭāʿ al-Ṣiḳillī, *Sharḥ al-mushkil min shiʿr al-Mutanabbī* (edition)], Abū Hilāl al-ʿAskarī, *K. al-Ṣināʿatayn al-kitāba wa 'l-shiʿr*, ed. al-Bidjāwī and Ibrāhīm, [2]Cairo n.d. [1971]; G.J. Kanazi, *Studies in the Kitāb aṣ-Ṣināʿatayn of Abū Hilāl al-ʿAskarī*, Leiden, etc. 1989; Bāḳillānī, *Iʿdjāz al-Ḳurʾān*, ed. al-Sayyid Aḥmad Ṣaḳr, Cairo 1963; von Grunebaum, *A tenth-century document of Arabic literary theory and criticism: the section on poetry of al-Bâqillânî's Iʿjâz al-Qurʾân*, Chicago 1950, repr. 1974; Marghīnānī, *al-Maḥāsin fi 'l-naẓm wa 'l-nathr*, ed. van Gelder, in *Two Arabic treatises on stylistics*, Istanbul 1987; ʿAbd al-Karīm al-Nahshalī, *al-Mumtiʿ fī ʿilm al-shiʿr wa-ʿamalih*, ed. Mundjī al-Kaʿbī, Tunis 1398/1978; Ibn Rashīḳ, *al-ʿUmda fī maḥāsin al-shiʿr wa-ādābih wa-naḳdih*, ed. ʿAbd al-Ḥamīd, 2 vols. [3]Cairo 1383/1963-4, ed. ʿAbd al-Ḥamīd al-Hindāwī, Beirut 2001, ed. Muḥ. ʿAbd al-Ḳādir Aḥmad ʿAṭā, Beirut 2001, ed. al-Nabawī ʿAbd al-Wāḥid Shaʿlān, Beirut 1999, ed. Ṣalāḥ al-Dīn al-Hawwārī and Hudā ʿAwda, Beirut 1996; idem, *Ḳurāḍat al-dhahab fī naḳd ashʿār al-ʿarab*, ed. al-Shādhilī Bū Yaḥyā, Tunis 1972, ed. Munīf Mūsā, Beirut 1991; Ibn Sharaf al-Ḳayrawānī, *Masāʾil al-intiḳād*, ed. and tr. Ch. Pellat, as *Questions de critique littéraire*, Algiers 1953; idem, *Rasāʾil* [sic] *al-intiḳād*, ed. Ḥasan Ḥusnī ʿAbd al-Wahhāb, Beirut 1404/1983 ([1]1911); Rachel Arié, *Notes sur la critique littéraire dans l'Occident musulman au XIe siècle*, in eadem, *L'Occident musulman au bas moyen age*, Paris 1992, 1-21 (mainly on Ibn Rashīḳ and Ibn Sharaf); Abū ʿĀmir Ibn Shuhayd, *Risālat al-Tawābiʿ wa 'l-zawābiʿ*, ed. Buṭrus al-Bustānī, Beirut [2]1967, [Eng. tr.] *The treatise of familiar spirits and demons by Abū ʿĀmir ibn Shuhaid al-Ashjaʿī, al-Andalusī*, intro., tr. and notes by J.T. Monroe, Berkeley 1971; Ibn Bassām, *al-Dhakhīra fī maḥāsin ahl al-Djazīra*, 4 vols., ed. Iḥsān ʿAbbās, Lībiyā-Tūnis 1399/1979; Ibn Sinān al-Khafādjī, *Sirr al-faṣāḥa*, ed. ʿAbd al-Mutaʿāl al-Ṣaʿīdī, Cairo 1389/1969; ʿAbd al-Ḳāhir al-Djurdjānī, *K. Asrār al-balāgha*, ed. H. Ritter, Istanbul 1954; idem, *Dalāʾil al-iʿdjāz*, ed. Maḥmūd Muḥammad Shākir, Cairo 1404/1984; Kamal Abu Deeb, *Al-Jurjānī's theory of poetic imagery*, Warminster 1979; Abū Ṭāhir al-Baghdādī (d. 517/1123), *Ḳānūn al-balāgha*, ed. Muḥammad Kurd ʿAlī, in *Rasāʾil al-bulaghāʾ*, [4]Cairo 1374/1954, and ed. Muḥsin Ghayyāḍ ʿUdjayl, Beirut 1401/1981; Ibn Aflaḥ, *al-Muḳaddima*, ed. van Gelder, in *Two Arabic treatises on stylistics*; Abu 'l-Barakāt Ibn al-Anbārī (d. 577/1181), *K. al-Lumʿa fī ṣināʿat al-shiʿr*, in *RAAD*, xxx (1955), 590-607; Usāma b. Munḳidh (d. 584/1188), *al-Badīʿ fī naḳd al-shiʿr*, ed. Aḥmad Aḥmad Badawī and Ḥāmid ʿAbd al-Madjīd, Cairo 1960; Ḍiyāʾ al-Dīn Ibn al-Athīr, *al-Djāmiʿ al-kabīr fī ṣināʿat al-manẓūm min al-kalām wa 'l-manthūr*, ed. Muṣṭafā Djawād and Djamīl Saʿīd, Baghdād 1375/1956; idem, *al-Mathal al-sāʾir fī adab al-kātib wa 'l-shāʿir*, ed. Aḥmad al-Ḥūfī and Badawī Ṭabāna, 3 vols. [2]Riyāḍ 1403-4/1983-4; Ibn Abi 'l-Ḥadīd (d. 655-6/1257-8), *al-Falak al-dāʾir ʿalā 'l-Mathal al-sāʾir*, ed. al-Ḥūfī and Ṭabāna, [2]Riyāḍ 1984; al-Ṣafadī (d. 764/1353), *Nuṣrat al-thāʾir ʿalā 'l-Mathal al-sāʾir*, ed. Muḥammad ʿAlī Sulṭānī, Damascus n.d. [*ca.* 1391/1971]; Ibn al-Zamlakānī, *al-Tibyān fī ʿilm al-bayān al-muṭliʿ ʿalā iʿdjāz al-Ḳurʾān*, ed. Aḥmad Maṭlūb and Khadīdja al-Ḥadīthī, Baghdād 1383/1964; Ibn Abi 'l-Iṣbaʿ, *Taḥrīr al-taḥbīr fī ṣināʿat al-shiʿr wa 'l-nathr wa-bayān iʿdjāz al-Ḳurʾān*, ed. Ḥifnī Muḥammad Sharaf, Cairo 1963; al-Muẓaffar b. al-Faḍl al-ʿAlawī al-Ḥusaynī (d. 656/1258), *Naḍrat al-ighrīḍ fī nuṣrat al-ḳarīḍ*, ed. Nuhā ʿĀrif al-Ḥasan, Damascus 1396/1976; Zandjānī, *K. Miʿyār al-nuẓẓār fī ʿulūm al-ashʿār*, ed. Muḥammad ʿAlī Rizḳ al-Khafādjī, Cairo 1991; only pt. 3 on *ʿilm al-badīʿ*, ed. ʿAbd al-Munʿim Sayyid ʿAbd al-Salām al-Ashḳar, Cairo 1416/1995; and Ibn ʿAmīra, *al-Tanbīhāt ʿalā mā fi 'l-Tibyān min al-tamwīhāt*, ed. Muḥammad Ibn Sharīfa, Casablanca 1991; Ḥāzim al-Ḳarṭādjannī, *Minhādj al-bulaghāʾ wa-sirādj al-udabāʾ*, ed. Muḥammad al-Ḥabīb Ibn al-Khūdja (Belkhodja), Tunis 1966; W. Heinrichs, *Arabische Dichtung und griechische Poetik: Ḥāzim al-Qarṭāǧannīs Grundlegung der Poetik mit Hilfe aristotelischer Begriffe*, Beirut and Wiesbaden 1969; van Gelder, *Critic and craftsman: al-Qarṭājannī and the structure of the poem*, in *JAL*, x (1979), 26-48; Sidjilmāsī, *al-Manzaʿ al-badīʿ fī tadjnīs asālīb al-badīʿ*, ed. ʿAllāl al-Ghāzī, Rabat 1401/1980; Ibn al-Bannāʾ al-ʿAdadī, *al-Rawḍ al-marīʿ fī ṣināʿat al-badīʿ*, ed. Riḍwān Binshaḳrūn, Casablanca 1985; Yaḥyā b. Ḥamza al-ʿAlawī (d. 749/1348), *al-Ṭirāz al-mutaḍammin li-asrār al-balāgha wa-ʿulūm ḥaḳāʾiḳ al-iʿdjāz*, ed. Sayyid b. ʿAlī al-Marṣafī, 3 vols. Cairo 1914; ʿAbd al-Raḥmān b. ʿAlī al-Yazdādī, *Kamāl al-balāgha*, Cairo 1341.

(W.P. Heinrichs)

NAḲL.

1. In the central Islamic lands and North Africa. Add to the articles mentioned there the following article.

In the caliphal lands.

The emergence of Islam is known to have coincided with the disappearance of wheeled carts or wagons [see *ʿadjala*] in many parts of the Middle East, although the extinction of such transport cannot be conclusively proved. In fact, wheeled vehicles were in existence in the Middle East for many centuries after the rise of Islam, although they were rarely used.

The wheel was replaced by the camel in the Middle East during the era of the caliphates. Camels [see ibil] were a means of everyday transport which was eminently suitable for long-distance overland journey across deserts and valleys in Arabia, Syria, Egypt or North Africa, or Anatolia or in Central Asia along the Silk Road, being used for transport of goods or passengers or pilgrims in large caravans. Caravan trade and caravan cities existed in the Middle East since the pre-Islamic period, when the Arabs of Mecca used to go on seasonal caravan journeys for commerce to Yemen in the winter and to Syria in the summer (cf.

Kur'ān, CVI, 1-2). The nomadic peoples of Arabia, Syria and Persia were the camel-breeders who appreciated the value of their animals as the "ships of the land" (*al-sufun al-barriyya*); they knew that the skins of their animals provided them with water-bags (*kirab*) and that the animals' meat was a source of protein, and they could sell them in exchange for gold (cf. al-Thaʿālibī, *Thimār al-kulūb*, 284). At the beginning of Islam in the 7th century A.D. many individuals owned camels which they could use as a means of transport or as a source of milk or as a commodity for trade, but by the 8th century A.D., cameleers or professional camel-drivers emerged as a group of transport workers who used to hire out the camel(s) to travellers or traders (al-Wohaibi, *The northern Hijaz*, 393). The cameleers (see DJAMMĀL, in Suppl.) contributed much to the transport of pilgrims from all parts of the Middle East to Mecca and Medina. The Egyptian and North African pilgrims as well as traders started their caravan journey from Fusṭāṭ (Old Cairo) through Kulzum to Āʾila (ʿAkaba) and Yanbuʿ, thence to Mecca or Medina. The Anatolian and Syrian pilgrims assembled at Damascus and travelled through ʿAmmān and Tabūk to Medina and Mecca. Similarly, the pilgrims from Persia, Central Asia and ʿIrāk started their journey from Baghdād and travelled through Kūfa and the Arabian desert to Mecca or Medina, or they took the alternative route from Baghdād to Wāsiṭ, Baṣra, the Arabian desert and Mecca. Arab settlements grew up along the pilgrim routes and there were brisk seasonal trade during the pilgrimage season. Caravanserais were built throughout the Middle East to cater for travellers and traders and their mounts. Camels and horses were also used to transport arms and warriors to the battle front during the early Islamic conquests and the Umayyad period.

Among other means of transport, donkeys were the most popular among the tribesmen and the peasantry. Mules (Ar. *baghl* [*q.v.*], pl. *bighāl*) were also used as a means of transport especially in the hilly or mountainous terrains of Syria, Anatolia and Persia. Muleteers (Ar. *mukārī* [*q.v.*], *baghghāl*, or *ḥammāra*) emerged as a distinct group of transport workers during the ʿAbbāsid period (A.D. 750-1258). They could transport merchants or ordinary travellers from Baghdād along the Khurāsān trunk road to Nishāpūr or beyond (cf. al-Kazwīnī, *Āthār al-bilād*, 224-5) or transport pilgrims in a caravan of 50 donkeys from Kūfa to Mecca (al-Djāḥiẓ, *K. al-Bukhalāʾ*, 18). Mules were not popular animals in mediaeval Arab society, and al-Djāḥiẓ wrote a treatise on mules entitled *Kitāb al-Bighāl.* He voiced the public opinion of his time when he recorded the popular argument against the mules by saying that the Prophets rode on camels and donkeys but never on mules (cf. *Rasāʾil al-Djāḥiẓ*, ii, 326), but he refuted the popular prejudice against them by citing the evidence that the Prophet Muḥammad rode on a mule, as did the early caliphs like ʿUthmān and ʿAlī and the Umayyad caliph Hishām b. ʿAbd al-Malik. Moreover, al-Djāḥiẓ cited the fact that pilgrims from Syria went from Damascus to Mecca in a caravan of sixty mules during the reign of caliph ʿAbd al-Malik (cf. *Kitāb al-Bighāl*, 231).

The horse was a means of speedy transport which was owned mainly by the wealthy, for the price of an Arabian horse with a pedigree was very high. This last was also introduced into eastern Turkey and Persia as a means of transport. Horses were used for postal service by the Umayyad and ʿAbbāsid caliphs for the dispatch of royal mail and military intelligence from various provinces to the capital city [see BARĪD]. The ʿAbbāsid and Fāṭimid caliphs had stables full of horses ready as mounts kept near the royal palaces for riding by the caliphs and their family members, as well as by top officials both civilian and military (cf. Hilāl al-Ṣābiʾ, *Rusūm dār al-khilāfa*, 22-3).

The price of owning a pack and riding animal during the era of the ʿAbbāsīd caliphs was not, however, totally beyond the means of the common folk, but the maintenance of an animal involved extra expense. The income of a muleteer or a donkey-driver was meagre, but a cameleer (*djammāl*) or a boatman (*mallāḥ*) had an adequate income by hiring out camels or boats for transporting goods or passengers. A camel was sold for 2 or 3 dīnārs in Baṣra during the 4th/10th century (al-Tanūkhī, *Nishwār*, i, 89). The price of a donkey in Khurāsān was usually 5 dirhams, but it could go up to 50 dirhams or more in a year of scarcity during the ʿAbbāsid period (Yāķūt, *Muʿdjam*, iii, 412). The price of a horse in Khwārazm was an extraordinarily low cost of 4 dīnārs during the 14th century (Ibn Baṭṭūṭa, *Travels*, tr. Gibb, 167).

Inland transport in the Middle East also made use of boats and small ships in the navigable rivers like the Tigris, the Euphrates and the Orontes, part of the Kārūn river in Persia and the Nile in Egypt. The city of Baghdād was founded by the ʿAbbāsid caliph al-Manṣūr in 145/762 on the banks of the Tigris river *inter alia* to facilitate inland transport from Baghdād upstream to Mawṣil, Diyār Rabīʿa, etc., and downstream to the cities of Wāsiṭ, Baṣra and onwards to the Persian Gulf waters. There were many boats [see SAFĪNA] in the Baṭāʾiḥ [*q.v.*] (swamps) of the lower ʿIrāk. A port was built at Sāmarrāʾ on the Tigris by al-Wāthiķ. The Shaṭṭ al-ʿArab [*q.v.*] was very suitable for navigation by ships. The Euphrates river and the Shaṭṭ al-Gharrāf were also navigable, and goods could be transported from Diyār Muḍar and al-Rakka to Baghdād through the Nahr al-Malik canal (cf. Yaʿkūbī, *Buldān*, 234). There were thirty thousand river craft plying in the waters of the Tigris river to transport passengers or cargo during the 3rd/9th century (Ibn al-Djawzī, *Manākib*, 24; Shābushtī, *Diyārāt*, 158). The *muḥtasib* [see ḤISBA] supervised the transportation work by the boatmen so that the boats or ships were not overloaded, endangering the lives of the passengers by drowning or loss of cargo in mid-river. Similarly, the Nile was a busy highway of boat traffic for the people of Fusṭāṭ on the bank of the river.

The 5th/11th century Persian traveller Nāṣir-i Khusraw, travelled across the mediaeval Middle East by means of all available transport, including camels, horses, donkeys, boats and ships. While visiting the cities of Fusṭāṭ and Cairo (ca. 439/1047), he observed that traders rode on saddled donkeys. Everyday 50,000 beasts of burden were ready for hire. He saw that soldiers and militiamen rode on horses, while peasants, merchants and craftsmen were transported by donkeys (*Safar-nāma*, tr. 55).

On the whole, riding and pack animals such as donkeys, mules, camels and horses were the primary means of transport in the pre-industrial society of the Middle East during the Umayyad, ʿAbbāsid and Mamlūk periods, while horse- or camel-drawn wagons were hardly seen in the streets prior to the 13th-14th century A.D. Boats and coracles, and a kind of catamaran (Ar. *zaww/zawdj*), played a limited role in the inland transport network in the countries of the Middle East during the periods of the caliphates. The absence of wheeled vehicles on the streets had an impact on town planning in the Middle East, whose towns had consequently narrow streets and cul-de-sacs.

Bibliography: Ibn al-Aṯẖīr, *Usd*, Cairo 1970, ii, 527, iii, 528, iv, 280, 447, etc; Yaʿḳūbī, *Buldān*, 234; Tanūḵẖī, *Nisẖwār*, i, London 1921, 89; Ḳazwīnī, *Āṯẖār al-bilād*, Göttingen 1848, 224-5; Yāḳūt, *Muʿḏjam*, iii, Cairo 1906, 412; Ḏjāḥiẓ, *Buḵẖalāʾ*, Cairo 1958, 18, 54-5; Ḏjāḥiẓ, *Rasāʾil*, ed. Hārūn, Cairo 1965, ii (including *Kitāb al-Bigẖāl*), 220-223; 351-53; Thaʿālibī, *Ṯẖimār al-ḳulūb*, Cairo 1908, 284; Ibn al-Ḏjawzī, *Manāḳib Bagẖdād*, Baghdad 1923-24, 24; Sẖābusẖtī, *K. al-Diyārāt*, ed. G. ʿAwwād, Baghdad 1966, 158; Hilāl al-Ṣābiʾ, *Rusūm dār al-ḵẖilāfa*, Baghdad 1964, 22-3; Ibn Bāssām al-Muḥtasib, *Nihāyat al-rutba fī ṭalab al-ḥisba*, Baghdad 1968, 157; 165; Arculf, *The travels of Bishop Arculf in the Holy Land towards A.D. 700*, in *Early travels in Palestine*, ed. Thomas Wright, New York 1848; Nāṣir-i Ḵẖusraw, *Safar-nāma*, Eng. tr. W.M. Thackston, New York 1986, 55-6; Ibn Ḏjubayr, *The travels of Ibn Jubayr*, tr. R.J.C. Broadhurst, London 1952; Ibn Baṭṭūṭa, *Travels in Asia and Africa*, tr. H.A.R. Gibb, Cambridge and London 1958-2000; Le Strange, *Lands*; Abdulla al-Wohaibi, *The northern Ḥiḏjaz in the writings of the Arab geographers*, Beirut 1973, 393; R.W. Bulliet, *The camel and the wheel*, Cambridge, Mass. 1975; Per Sörbom (ed.), *Transport, technology and social change*, Stockholm 1980; M. Rostovtzeff, *Caravan cities*, tr. D. and T. Rice, Oxford 1932; Lane, *Lexicon*, 1145; G. Wiet, *Cairo—city of art and commerce*, Norman, Oklahoma 1964, 71-92; D.R. Hill, *The role of the camel and the horse in the early Arab conquests*, in *War, technology and society in the Middle East*, ed. V.J. Parry and M.E. Yapp, London 1975, 32-43; M.A.J. Beg, *A contribution to the economic history of the Caliphate*, in *IQ*, xvi (1972), 154; 158-59; idem, *The Mukārī: a group of transport workers in ʿAbbāsid Middle East*, in *J. Pak. H.S.*, xxiii/3 (1977), 143-51.   (M.A.J. BEG)

AL-NAʿL AL-**SHARĪF**, NAʿL RASŪL ALLĀH (A.), the sandal of the Prophet Muḥammad.

Sandals belong to the pre-Islamic Arabian clothing (see LIBĀS. 1), and are considered one of the features distinguishing Arabs from non-Arabs (ʿaḏjam). The scholar Mālik b. Anas (d. 180/796 [*q.v.*]) reportedly declared that only Arabs used to wear turbans and sandals (Ibn Abī Zayd, *al-Ḏjāmiʿ fī ʾl-sunan wa ʾl-ādāb wa ʾl-magẖāzī wa ʾl-taʾrīḵẖ*, Tunis 1982, 228). The Prophet himself reportedly advised the believers to wear sandals as well as boots to distinguish themselves from the People of the Book who only wore boots (Aḥmad b. Ḥanbal, *Musnad*, 6 vols., Cairo 1313/1895, repr. Beirut n.d., v, 264). Muslim tradition turned the sandals into a component of the legacy of Abraham and Ishmael, the prototypes of Arabian monotheism. In a letter of the caliph ʿUmar b. al-Ḵẖaṭṭāb [*q.v.*], the believers are requested to adhere to the clothes of their father Ismāʿīl and to wear sandals instead of boots (Ibn Ḥibbān, *al-Iḥsān fī taḳrīb Ṣaḥīḥ Ibn Ḥibbān*, *tartīb ʿAlāʾ al-Dīn al-Fārisī*, ed. Sẖuʿayb al-Arnāʾūṭ, 16 vols., Beirut 1988, xii, no. 5454). Abraham, says a Sẖīʿī tradition, was the first to wear sandals (al-Kulīnī, *al-Uṣūl wa ʾl-furūʿ min al-Kāfī*, ed. ʿAlī Akbar al-Gẖifārī, 8 vols., Beirut 1980, vi, 462). Wearing sandals is especially recommended during the pilgrimage to Mecca, which is the main centre of Abrahamic rites [see IḤRĀM].

The Prophet Muḥammad is regarded as the ultimate model of Arab piety, and sandals feature as an essential element in his descriptions as a messenger of God. Already Jesus is said to have announced the emergence of the Arabian prophet, whom he described as wearing sandals among other things (al-Bayḥaḳī,

Dalāʾil al-nubuwwa, ed. ʿAbd al-Muʿṭī Ḳalʿaḏjī, 7 vols., Beirut 1988, i, 378). Muḥammad himself is said to have stated that God instructed him to wear sandals and a seal (al-Ṭabarānī, *al-Muʿḏjam al-ṣagẖīr*, ed. ʿAbd al-Raḥmān Muḥammad ʿUthmān, 2 vols., Cairo 1981-3, i, 166).

Islamic tradition provides detailed descriptions of the Prophet's sandals. According to most of the earliest traditions, each sandal had two leather thongs (ḳibāl, zimām, sẖisʿ), which passed between the toes and were attached to the sole. The other end of the pair of thongs passed through two loops ("ears") to which were also attached the two arms of the sẖirāk, i.e. the folded strap that passed behind the wearer's ankle. In some versions, the sandal is said to have had a "heel" in the Yemeni style, i.e. a wide strap that embraced the wearer's heel. At the forepart of each sandal there was an extension shaped like a tongue (mulassan), and the middle part of the sole was narrow, with hollows (ḵẖaṣrānʿ) cut on each side. The sole consisted of two layers sewed or patched together (makẖṣūfa). It was made of tanned hide of oxen (Ibn Saʿd, *Ṭabaḳāt*, 8 vols., Beirut 1960, i, 478-82; Abu ʾl-Sẖayḵẖ, *Aḵẖlāḳ al-nabī*, ed. ʿIṣām al-Dīn Sayyid ʿAbd al-Nabī, Cairo 1993, 142-7; al-Zurḳānī, *Sẖarḥ al-mawāhib al-laduniyya li ʾl-Ḳasṭallānī*, Cairo 1911, repr. Beirut 1973, v, 44-52; al-Sẖāmī, *Subul al-hudā wa ʾl-rasẖād fī sīrat ḵẖayr al-ʿibād*, ed. Muṣṭafā ʿAbd al-Wāḥid, 11 vols., Cairo 1990, vii, 499-507). The colour of Muḥammad's sandal, according to the usual reports, was yellow (al-Zurḳānī, *op. cit.*, v, 46; al-Maḳḳarī, *Waṣf niʿāl al-nabī (ṣ) al-musammā bi-fatḥ al-mutaʿāl fī madḥ al-niʿāl*, ed. ʿAlī ʿAbd al-Wahhāb and ʿAbd al-Munʿim Faraḏj Darwīsẖ, Cairo 1997, 141-3).

A two-thong sandal remained a common fashion among pious believers, although it was sometimes regarded as extravagant (Ibn Ḥadjar al-ʿAsḳalānī, *al-Maṭālib al-ʿāliya bi-zawāʾid al-masānīd al-thamāniya*, ed. Ḥabīb al-Raḥmān al-Aʿẓamī, 4 vols., Beirut 1987, ii, no. 2231). Such sandals were said to have been worn by the Righteous Caliphs Abū Bakr and ʿUmar [*q.vv.*]. Only the third caliph, ʿUthmān b. ʿAffān [*q.v.*], reportedly began to wear sandals in which the two thongs were tied together and attached to a single strap passing between the toes (al-Tirmidẖī, *al-Sẖamāʾil al-muhammadiyya* (with commentary of Ibrāhīm al-Bādjūrī), Cairo 1925, 70; al-Ṭabarānī, *op. cit.*, i, 92; al-Zurḳānī, *op. cit.*, v, 45).

Sometimes the sole of Muḥammad's sandal was said to have consisted of only one layer, not two, and this was said to have been the style that the Arabs considered superior to the style of kings (al-Maḳḳarī, 89).

The fashion of cutting hollows on both sides of the middle part of the sole was preserved mainly among Sẖīʿīs, to whom soles without hollows represented a deplorable deviation from the Prophetic model (al-Kulīnī, vi, 463). Moreover, sandals without such hollows were considered Jewish by style (al-Ṭabrisī, *Makārim al-aḵẖlāḳ*, ed. Muḥammad al-Ḥusayn al-Aʿlamī, Beirut 1972, p. 123; al-Kulīnī, vi, 463-4). The habit of tying the sẖirāk of the sandal (and not simply folding it through the loop, as was reported concerning Muḥammad's sandal) was considered among Sẖīʿīs as a fashion set by Satan (al-Ṭabrisī, 123).

The supposedly original sandal or sandals of the Prophet were preserved by believers of later generations. Beginning with the generation of the Companions, the most prevalent is the tradition about the Baṣran Anas b. Mālik [*q.v.*], who is said to have exhibited to the believers the sandal with its two thongs (e.g. Ibn Saʿd, i, 478; Abu ʾl-Sẖayḵẖ, *Aḵẖlāḳ al-nabī*, no. 390).

He was reportedly the official keeper of Muḥammad's sandals (Ibn Saʿd, i, 482), but according to other traditions, the Kūfan Companion ʿAbd Allāh b. Masʿūd [see IBN MASʿUD, ʿABD ALLĀH] was in charge of them (e.g. al-Bukhārī, *Ṣaḥīḥ*, 9 vols., Cairo 1958, v, 31, 35 [*kitāb* 62, *bāb* 20, 27]).

ʿAlī's son, Muḥammad b. al-Ḥanafiyya [*q.v.*] was also able to show the relic (Ibn Saʿd, i, 478). The Meccan Hishām b. ʿUrwa (d. 146/763) claimed that he had seen the sandal and gave its description (Ibn Saʿd, i, 478).

As for the later history of the sandals, some reports relate that the descendants of the Syrian Companion Shaddād b. Aws (d. 46/683), who lived in Jerusalem, preserved them. He reportedly left them to his son Muḥammad, but the latter's sister got hold of one of them. This was passed on to her children. When the ʿAbbāsid caliph al-Mahdī visited Jerusalem, the sandal held by the sister's descendants was presented to him for a handsome reward. He summoned her brother Muḥammad b. Shaddād, by then a sick old man, and requested the other sandal, but Muḥammad refused to part with it and the caliph consented (Ibn Manẓūr, *Mukhtaṣar Taʾrīkh Dimashḳ li-Ibn ʿAsākir*, 29 vols., Damascus 1984–8, x, 278-9). A sandal of the Prophet was also claimed to have been in the possession of Ismāʿīl b. Ibrāhīm al-Makhzūmī who obtained it from his grandmother Umm Kulthūm, the daughter of Abū Bakr. She had received it from her sister ʿĀʾisha (al-Maḳḳarī, 175-6).

The last station of the "original" sandal seems to have been the Ashrafī *madrasa* at Damascus. It was placed there by the Ayyūbid of Egypt al-Malik al-Ashraf b. al-ʿĀdil, who had confiscated it in 625/1228 from the last descendant of the Companion Sulaymān Abu 'l-Ḥadīd, whose descendants claimed to have held it for centuries. Another sandal of the Prophet was kept elsewhere in Damascus, and during Tīmūr Lang's take-over of Damascus in 803/1400, both relics disappeared (Ibn Ḥadjar al-ʿAsḳalānī, *al-Iṣāba*, ed. ʿAlī Muḥammad al-Bidjāwī, 8 vols., Cairo 1970, iii, 173; Sibṭ Ibn al-ʿAdjamī, *Nūr al-nibrās ʿalā sīrat Ibn Sayyid al-Nās*, ms. B.L. Or. 8276, fol. 316b; al-Maḳḳarī, 513-24; Goldziher, *Muhammedanische Studien*, ii, 363-4).

The Prophet's sandals served as a model according to which shoemakers designed sandals for pious believers. A sandal of the Prophet, as seen at the house of Fāṭima, daughter of ʿUbayd Allāh b. ʿAbbās, was copied by a shoemaker who applied its two-thong style to sandals ordered by the eminent Baṣran scholar ʿAbd Allāh b. ʿAwn (d. 150/767). However, when the latter came to collect them, he found that Ibn Sīrīn (d. 110/728 [*q.v.*]) had already bought the sandals for himself (Ibn Ḥadjar, *Maṭālib*, ii, no. 2232; cf. Ibn Saʿd, i, 479).

Drawings (*mithāl, timthāl*) representing the supposedly original sandal were in circulation among scholars, especially in the Maghrib, where access to the sandal itself was more difficult than in the Mashriḳ (al-Maḳḳarī, 167-8). Such representations were also used by shoemakers for sandals ordered by pious believers (al-Ṭabrisī, 122; al-Maḳḳarī, 175-6). The representations became an object of veneration in their own right and were believed to provide one with safety in journeys, victory in battles, etc. Therapeutic powers were attributed to them and they were often hung up in houses for protection against the evil eye (al-Zurḳānī, v, 48; al-Maḳḳarī, 469-70; Goldziher, *op. cit.*, ii, 363). Some samples of them can be seen in al-Maḳḳarī's *Fatḥ al-mutaʿāl fī madḥ al-niʿāl*, where numerous *ḳaṣīdas* in praise of them are also recorded.

Closely associated with the veneration of the Prophet's sandals is that of his footprints [see ḲADAM SHARĪF].

Bibliography: Given in the article.

(U. RUBIN)

AL-**NAMIR** B. **ḲĀSIṬ**, BANŪ, a tribe of the Rabīʿa b. Nizār group [see RABĪʿA AND MUḌAR; NIZĀR B. MAʿADD]. It must be noted that not every Namarī mentioned in the sources belonged to the Namir b. Ḳāsiṭ, since tribal groups called al-Namir were also found among the Azd, the Ḳuḍāʿa and the Iyād. The fortunes of the Namir were closely linked to those of their relatives, the Taghlib [*q.v.*]. When the Taghlib migrated to the eastern part of the Djazīra [*q.v.*] or the Diyār Rabīʿa [*q.v.*] in the second half of the 6th century A.D., they were joined by part of the Namir. However, there were still Namarīs in Arabia after that time, more specifically in Yamāma and Baḥrayn. Some tribe members settled in al-Andalus. Most Namarīs remained Christian for at least two centuries after the advent of Islam.

The semi-legendary leader of the Namir, ʿĀmir al-Ḍaḥyān, would sit in judgement in the early part of the forenoon, hence his nickname al-Ḍaḥyān, or "the one exposing himself to the sun". Ibn al-Kalbī reported that the leadership of the Rabīʿa shifted among the Rabīʿa tribes. Leadership meant command in the battlefield, arbitration, the right to appoint the banner-carrier and entitlement to one-fourth of the spoils. When the leadership of the Rabīʿa reached the Namir, it was held by ʿĀmir al-Ḍaḥyān. After a long term in this role he was killed by a man of the ʿAbd al-Ḳays [*q.v.*]. Having received half the ransom for him, the Namir murdered the ʿAbd al-Ḳays hostages whom they held as a guarantee for the delivery of the other half. In the internecine war that followed, the Namir joined forces with the rest of the Rabīʿa against the ʿAbd al-Ḳays. Ibn al-Kalbī's account is quoted in a small genealogical treatise, *al-Inbāh ʿalā ḳabāʾil al-ruwāt*, by Ibn ʿAbd al-Barr [*q.v.*], himself a Namarī. Namarī partisanship on Ibn ʿAbd al-Barr's part is evident with regard to the origin of the Prophet's Companion Ṣuhayb b. Sinān, the most important individual in the genealogy of the Namir. Ṣuhayb's affiliation to the Namir, disputed by some, was for Ibn ʿAbd al-Barr beyond doubt, and in his Companion dictionary he emphasised that there was no dispute over it. But the claim that Ṣuhayb was of Arab stock stands in sharp contrast to a famous saying attributed to Muḥammad, namely, that he himself was the first Arab to enter Paradise, while Ṣuhayb was the first Byzantine, Salmān al-Fārisī the first Persian and Bilāl b. Rabāḥ the first Ethiopian.

While Ṣuhayb is invariably mentioned in the genealogies of the Namir, Ḥumrān b. Abān, a prominent figure in early Islamic history, is only mentioned in some. Ḥumrān, who was captured during the conquests in ʿAyn al-Tamr [*q.v.*], is supposed to have been Ṣuhayb's relative. But it is doubtful that Ḥumrān, said to have been of Jewish origin, was an Arab, since the claim of Arab descent originated with his offspring (*wa 'ddaʿā wulduhu fī 'l-Namir b. Ḳāsiṭ*). Family sources were likewise behind the claim that Ṣuhayb was an Arab.

The Namir boasted of a pre-Islamic link with the Ḳuraysh: the mother of the Prophet's uncle, al-ʿAbbās b. ʿAbd al-Muṭṭalib [*q.v.*], was one of them. She is supposed to have been the first Arab woman to provide a covering for the Kaʿba, following a vow she made when little al-ʿAbbās went lost.

Before Islam the Namir (like the Taghlib) were

within the sphere of influence of the Sāsānids and the Lakhmids [*q.vv.*] of al-Ḥīra. Mā᾿ al-Samā᾿, the mother of the Lakhmid king al-Mundhir III (*ca.* 505-54), who was of the Namir, was taken captive in a raid carried out by al-Mundhir's father; the fact that al-Mundhir had a half-brother among the Namir did not go unmentioned by the genealogists. One of the Arab units that fought on the Sāsānid side in the battle of Dhū Ḳār (*ca.* 605) included warriors from the Taghlib and the Namir. In the *ridda* [*q.v.*], there were Namarīs among the troops who came from the Djazīra with Sadjāḥ [*q.v.*], the false prophetess of the Tamīm [*q.v.*]. A whole subdivision of the Namir, the Aws Manāt b. al-Namir b. Ḳāsiṭ, was wiped out (*ubīrū*) during the *ridda* by Khalid b. al-Walīd. In ʿAyn al-Tamr during the conquests a Namarī led a large force made of Christians from the Namir, the Taghlib, the Iyād and others, which was defeated by Khālid. Later during the conquests Christians of the Namir fought alongside al-Muthannā b. Ḥāritha against the Sāsānids in the battle of al-Buwayb (near al-Ḥīra).

Some Namarīs who converted to Islam during the conquests settled in Kūfa together with members of the Taghlib and the Iyād. Members of these very tribes who fought as Sāsānid auxiliaries at Takrīt are said to have handed the town over to the Muslim besiegers. In the battle of Ṣiffīn [*q.v.*], there were Namarīs on both sides, probably because the Djazīra which was their homeland was divided at that time between ʿAlī and Muʿāwiya. The old association between the Taghlib and the Namir was still in place during the rebellion of ʿAbd Allāh b. al-Zubayr, when both tribes fought several battles in the Djazīra against the Ḳays ʿAylān [*q.v.*]

Bibliography: Caskel, *Ǧamharat an-nasab*, ii, 444; Ibn al-Kalbī, *Djamharat al-nasab*, ed. N. Ḥasan, Beirut 1407/1986, 576-81; idem, *Nasab Maʿadd wa ᾿l-Yaman al-kabīr*, ed. Ḥasan, Beirut 1408/1988, i, 96-100; Ibn Ḥazm al-Andalusī, *Djamharat ansāb al-ʿarab*, ed. Hārūn, Cairo 1382/1962, 300-2; Ibn ʿAbd al-Barr, *al-Inbāh ʿalā ḳabā᾿il al-ruwāt*, Cairo 1350/1931 (bound with *al-Ḳaṣd wa ᾿l-amam* by the same author), 97-100; Ṭabarī, index; F.M. Donner, *The early Islamic conquests*, Princeton 1981, index; M.G. Morony, *Iraq after the Muslim conquest*, Princeton 1984, index.

On the capture of Mā᾿ al-Samā᾿ by the king of al-Ḥīra, see al-Wazīr al-Maghribī, *Adab al-khawāṣṣ*, ed. Ḥ. al-Djāsir, Riyāḍ 1400/1980, 151. On the poet Manṣūr al-Namarī [*q.v.*], see also Sezgin, *GAS*, ii, 541-2. On Christianity among the Namir, see J.S. Trimingham, *Christianity among the Arabs in pre-Islamic times*, London and Beirut 1979, 176-7, and also NAṢĀRĀ. On the tribal groups of the Namir, particularly those living in the vicinity of Aleppo, see Ibn al-ʿAdīm, *Bughyat al-ṭalab*, ed. S. Zakkār, Damascus 1408/1988, i, 555-6. (M. LECKER)

NANDANA, the name of a hilly tract and a fortress of mediaeval India and Indo-Muslim times. It lies in a fold of the Salt Range, to the north of the Jhelum river in northern Pandjāb, and the place is still marked by ruins of a fortress and a Hindu temple near the modern Čao Saydān Shāh (lat. 32° 43' N., long. 73° 17' E.), in the Jhelum District of the Pandjāb province of Pakistan.

The place is mentioned in early mediaeval Indo-Muslim history. In 404-5/1013-14 Maḥmūd of Ghazna [*q.v.*] attacked the Hindūshāhīs [*q.v.*] of northwestern India and marched against the Rādjā Triločanapāla's son Bhīmapāla, besieging him in the fortress of Nandana and capturing an immense booty there (al-ʿUtbī, *al-Ta᾿rīkh al-Yamīnī*, with comm. of al-Manīnī, ii, 146-53 (calling the place Nardīn); Gardīzī, *Zayn al-akhbār*, ed. Nāẓim, 72; M. Nāẓim, *The life and times of Sulṭān Maḥmūd of Ghazna*, Cambridge 93, 91-3). Thereafter, the Ghaznawids tried to retain control of Nandana as a *thaghr* or entry point into the plains of northwestern India, as Abu ᾿l-Faḍl Bayhaḳī, *Tārīkh-i Masʿūdī*, ed. Ghanī and Fayyāḍ, 149, describes it.

In the early 7th/13th century, the fortress of Nandana, in what was then in Islamic sources called the Djūd hills, was held by a former commander of the Ghūrids, Ḳamar al-Dīn Karmānī (in the surmise of Boyle, to be equated with Nāṣir al-Dīn Ḳubāča, the ruler in Multān and Sind). Čingiz Khān, in his pursuit of the Khwārazm Shāh Djalāl al-Dīn Mingburnu, sent an army under Törbey Toḳshin which sacked Nandana in 618/1221, and then went on to attack Multān (Djūzdjānī, *Ṭabaḳāt-i Nāṣirī*, tr. Raverty, i, 534-5; Djuwaynī-Boyle, i, 141-2). Nandana was later temporarily captured by the Dihlī Sultan Iltutmish [*q.v.*], whose son and eventual successor Maḥmūd Shāh in 644-5/1247 ravaged the region in revenge for the local Rāna having guided a Mongol raid (Djūzdjānī, i, 677-9). It does not, however, seem thereafter to have played a significant role in history.

Bibliography: See also Djūzdjānī, i, 536-9 n.; *Punjab District gazetteers*, xxvii, Lahore 1904, 46-7; *Imperial gazetteer of India*[2], xviii, 349.

(C.E. BOSWORTH)

NATHR (A.), prose. The word is a noun denoting activity, derived from a verb meaning "to disperse, disseminate"; its opposite is *naẓm*, from a verb meaning "to join, set out in order", which is used to designate poetry. For Arab theorists, prose can be distinguished from poetry as the genre of literature which is not subjected to the order and constraints imposed by rhyme and metre. Such a formal definition is due to the fact that the prose they made the object of their attention was either the artistic prose of chancery documents, *rasā᾿il* (pl. of *risāla* [*q.v.*]), or the prose of the addresses or sermons, *khuṭab* (pl. of *khuṭba* [*q.v.*]). Whatever level of literary elaboration or rhetorical device required, they are all the same for the genres of prose and poetry, and are collectively referred to under the general term *balāgha* [*q.v.*]).

In a striking manner, this fact is shown, *inter alia*, by the procedures known as *ḥall al-manẓūm* and *naẓm al-manthūr*, setting a passage of prose into verse or verse into prose, in which the *maʿnā* [*q.v.*], the image of an idea expressed in the smallest unit of discourse, whether verse or colon, is launched in poetry or prose respectively. This procedure has been discussed since the 4th/10th century and was presented as a subtle form of plagiarism by theorists like Abū Hilāl al-ʿAskarī (d. 395/1005) in his *K. al-Ṣinaʿtayn*, ed. ʿA.M. Bidjāwī and A. Ibrāhīm, Cairo 1957, 198. The author al-Thaʿālibi (d. 429/1037), one of whose works was *Nathr al-naẓm wa-ḥall al-ʿaḳd*, and later on Ḍiyā᾿ al-Dīn Ibn al-Athīr (d. 637/1239) in his *al-Mathal al-sā᾿ir*, ed. A. al-Ḥūfī and B. Ṭabāna, 4 vols., Cairo 1959, i, 126-7, considered that rendering a verse into prose in a *risāla* was a way of achieving a higher level of literary expression. However, the formal point of view, which presumes a substantial literary equivalence between poetry and prose, did not exhaust the attention of the theorists to this problem. For example, they would raise the question of the superiority of one of the genres over the other, often basing their judgement more on sociological than on literary considerations; such considerations were the function of the chancery clerk or secretary (*kātib* [*q.v.*], *mutarassil*) and the poet, or the importance of the subjects they were dealing with, or the attitude adopted by the two genres towards religion and morals. Some authors (e.g. Ibn Khaldūn, *Muḳaddima, faṣl* 46), moreover, note that the essence of poetry does not reside in prosodic form but in the images that are expressed by this form.

The thinking of the Arab theorists developed from the 3rd/9th century onwards and was stimulated first of all by poetry. There is a detailed stylistic study of these ideas and of the scholars involved in Z. al-R. az-Zuʿbī, *Das Verhältnis von Poesie und Prosa in der arabischen Literaturtheorie des Mittelalters*, Berlin 1987, and the bibliography cited there; to this should be added A. Arazi, *Une épître d'Ibrāhīm b. Hilāl al-Ṣābī sur les genres littéraires*, in *Studies in Islamic history and civilization in honour of Professor David Ayalon*, ed. M. Sharon, Jerusalem-Leiden 1986, 473-505; also in M. Darabseh, *Die Kritik der Prosa bei den Arabern*, Berlin 1990, which is less careful and less original than the first work; see also Z. al-Zuʿbi, *Ibrāhīm b. Hīlāl al Ṣābī*, Risāla fi 'l-farḳ bayn al-mutarassil wa 'l-shāʿir, in *Abḥāth Yarmuk*, xi (1993), 129-65; A. Sanni, *The Arabic theory of prosification and versification*, Beirut 1998; see also SHIʿR.

The origins of prose

We can find examples of prose dating from the pre-Islamic period, such as proverbs (*mathal* [*q.v.*]), the prophesies of soothsayers (*sadjʿ* [*q.v.*] *al-kuhhān*) and sermons. Many formal characteristics of these documents, of which the authenticity in the literal meaning of that word can, of course, be debated, are the same as those of poetry: conciseness, allusive language and independent, paratactic clauses. These oral examples of prose can be connected with the remnants of prose of the same genre from the time of the Prophet and the very beginning of Islam. It was the arrival of Islam that saw one of the ancient literary genres, the *khuṭba*, the address or sermon, acquire new traits and gradually gain great popularity; for the importance of the orator in the pre-Islamic period see further KHAṬĪB.

While from the point of view of style these documents maintain the solidity and simplicity of pre-Islamic prose, far removed from the embellishments which these genres would later present, one is no longer faced with detached aphorisms (as in the case of the famous sermons of Ḳuss b. Sāʿida [*q.v.*] of the Iyād, al-Djāḥiẓ, *Bayān*, i, 308-9), but with contents that need to be communicated and thus articulated in a logical manner, the contents being of a religious nature as well as pertinent to the organisation of the new community. The new conditions were not without consequences on the level to which the prose could be elaborated. Similarly, the collections of *ḥadīth* [*q.v.*] take the form of short disjointed statements, often in the form of direct speech, and only a small number of fragments composed in literary prose remain from this period (cf. W. Fischer. *Ein Stück vorklassischer, arabischer Kunstprosa in der Umm Maʿbad Legende*, in *Festschrift W. Eilers*, Wiesbaden 1967, 318-27; he points out the similarities in this text with poetry).

Among the examples of prose from this period, the letters as well as other documents emanating from the Prophet and the first caliphs should be included. These documents from older sources have been collected by M. Hamidullah in *Documents sur la diplomatie musulmane à l'époque du Prophète et des Khalifes Orthodoxes*, Paris 1935; also an Arabic edition, *Madjmūʿat al-wathāʾiḳ al-siyāsiyya fi 'l-ʿahd al-nabawī wa 'l-khilāfa al-rāshida*, Cairo 1941.

The problem of their authenticity has been, of course, raised and the criterion most often used is that of linguistic usage (*op. cit.*, 4-5, in the French edition; B. Reichel-Baumgartner, *Parameter des Idiolekts des Propheten Muḥammad auf Grundlage des Ṣaḥīḥ von al-Buḫārī*, in *WZKM*, lxxviii [1988], 121-59). Problems of authenticity as well as of the transmission of ancient texts are examined by G.H.A. Juynboll, *On the origin of Arabic prose: reflections on authenticity*, in *Studies on the first century of Islamic society*, Carbondale, Ill. 1982; and R.B. Serjeant, *The Caliph ʿUmar's letters to Abū Mūsā al-Ashʿarī and Muʿāwiya*, in *JSS*, xxix [1984], 65-79.

The influence of the Ḳurʾān on the evolution of prose

Without any doubt, the Ḳurʾān is the primary example of a complex text in Arab literature that has not been composed in verse. The language that is used is one elaborated as a poetic koinè, the only one capable of communicating such a message. In form, especially in the more ancient sūras, it is close to poetic style. In the Muslim tradition, however, Scripture is distinguished from poetry as it is from prose, for literary as well as religious reasons; the deliberations of Muslim scholars about the form of the sacred text have taken on the form of the dogma of *iʿdjāz* [*q.v.*], the "stylistic uniqueness" of the Ḳurʾān.

Classical texts on poetry use the same criteria for analysis in order to show that the divide between the Ḳurʾān and literary discourse was uncrossable (see e.g. *Iʿdjāz al-Ḳurʾān* of al-Bāḳillānī, d. 403/1013 [*q.v.*]; G.E. von Grunebaum, *A tenth-century document of Arabic literary theory and criticism*, Chicago 1950). On the other hand there are some treatises drawn up to show that the decorative style of poetry could be found also in the Ḳurʾān (Ibn Abi 'l-Iṣbaʿ, d. 654/1256, *Badīʿ al-Ḳurʾān*, ed. Ḥ. Sharaf, Cairo 1957). In short, the Ḳurʾān plays an integral part in Arabic literary discourse, but it reaches a certain level of style which removes it far away from any other type of this discourse. In modern times, one typical example of this attitude is that of Ṭāhā Ḥusayn, who does not look at the Ḳurʾān when dealing with poetry and prose, for "it is neither poetry nor prose" (*Min ḥadīth al-shiʿr wa 'l-nathr*, Cairo 1936, 25).

It can therefore be concluded that, although the influence of the Ḳurʾān on the evolution of Arabic prose is immense from the point of view of religious content, the political and cultural effect its message has brought with it, and the status that has been imparted to the language in which it was transmitted, its influence on style is much more subtle to define. Treatises such as *Ḥusn al-tawassul ilā ṣināʿat al-tarassul* of Shihāb al-Dīn al-Ḥalabī (d. 725/1325), ed. A. Yūsuf, Baghdād 1980, insist that the strongest way for an argument to be confirmed is that citations from the Ḳurʾān must be inserted into a letter or into an official document, on condition that neither form nor basis is modified (72-3). Perhaps the earliest evidence for this exhortation to the *kātib*, secretary, to get to know and use quotations from the Ḳurʾān as part of his professional training dates from the *Risālat al-ʿAdhrāʾ* of Ibrāhīm al-Shaybānī (d. 298/910, ed. Z. Mubārak, Cairo 1931, under the name of Ibn al-Mudabbirī, 7; see Sanni, *op. cit.*, 6).

There is a more liberal attitude towards the text of the Ḳurʾān when it is approached from the viewpoint of *muʿāraḍa* [*q.v.*], "the fact of wishing to equal it". From the point of view of literary sentiment, and disregarding religious aspects, one could say that *muʿāraḍa* is to the Ḳurʾān what *sariḳa* is to poetry: there exists a threshold of literary propriety beyond which one should not tread without incurring blame, to be respected even more in the case of the Ḳurʾān. As stated by W. Marçais, "from very early on it appeared futile and even sacrilegious to want to imitate it" (see *Les origines de la prose littéraire arabe*, in *Rev. Afr.*, lxviii [1927], 15-28).

But at the outset, literary prose shows evidence of a different attitude. Systematic studies conducted by W. al-Ḳāḍī show that two prose writers adopted a more liberal attitude to the sacred text (*Bis̲h̲r b. Abī Kubār al-Balawī, namūd̲h̲adj̲ al-nat̲h̲r al-fannī al-mubakkir fi 'l-Yaman*, Beirut 1985 [a *kātib* from Yemen who was alive up to the end of the 2nd/8th century, and whom the author considered an intermediary between ʿAbd al-Ḥamīd and al-Dj̲āḥiẓ in the history of Arabic prose]; eadem, *The impact of the Qurʾān on the epistolography of ʿAbd al-Ḥamīd*, in G.R. Hawting and A.A. Shareef [eds.], *Approaches to the Qurʾan*, London and New York 1993, 285-313). Passages from the Ḳurʾān could be paraphrased to adapt them to the new syntax, and paraphrases and citations could even be combined; a quotation could be extended with phrases composed in the same rhythm.

On the other hand theorists recommended to the prose writers the *iḳtibās* of the Ḳurʾān, inserting a passage which is not an explicit quotation (for this see for example the presentation of Ibn al-At̲h̲īr, *al-Mat̲h̲al al-sāʾir*, i, 44). It is widely used as a literary device by *kuttāb* and orators; al-T̲h̲aʿālibī devotes a work to this, *al-Iḳtibās min al-Ḳurʾān al-karīm*, ed. I.M. al-Ṣaffār, Bag̲h̲dād 1975, see Sanni, *op. cit.*, 5-7; the work has recently been described by Cl. Gilliot in *Arabica*, xlvii (2000), 488-500. Of course, in contrast to poetry, the insertion of a fragment from the Ḳurʾān could be identified immediately (*Ḥusn al-tawassul*, 323) and within these limits did not appear to be taken as a tentative *muʿāraḍa*. Other studies, such as those undertaken by W. al-Ḳāḍī, are very much a desideratum; cf. recently K. Zakharia, *Les références coraniques dans les* Maqāmāt *d'al-Ḥarīrī*, in *Arabica*, xxxiv [1987], 275-86; U. Marzolph, *The Qoran and jocular literature*, in *Arabica*, xlvii [2000], 478-87.

Classical prose

The turbulent times of the Umayyad period found expression in the art of oratory. As it developed in this period, it represents the transition from oral to written Arabic prose. Al-Dj̲āḥiẓ (*K. al-Bayān wa 'l-tabyīn*) classified *k̲h̲uṭba* alongside poetry and noted the use of *sadj̲ʿ* as characteristic. A recent study has investigated the harangues that are to be found in this work and has uncovered a technique not only in the especially careful structure but also in the presence of recurring phraseology which the author is able to assemble at will; see M.-H. Avril, *Rhétorique et* ḫuṭba *dans le* Kitāb al-bayān wa-l-tabyīn *de Ǧāḥiẓ*, thesis, Université de Lumière-Lyon II 1994, 369; also I. Ḥāwī, *Fann al-k̲h̲iṭāba wa-taṭawwuruh ʿind al-ʿarab*, Beirut n.d.

However, Arabic prose of the classical period acquires its character from the written genre of the *risāla* as found in the Umayyad *kātib* ʿAbd al-Ḥamīd (d. 123/750 [*q.v.*]) and his contemporary Ibn al-Muḳaffaʿ (d. 139/756 [*q.v.*]) (see J.D. Latham, *Ibn al-Muqaffaʿ and early ʿAbbasid prose*, in *Camb. hist. of Ar. lit., ʿAbbasid belles-lettres*, Cambridge 1990, 48-77); it is versatile with an ease of expression, rich in rhythmic balance in the phrases used and in the parallelism. The latter characteristic in particular was not typical of ancient Arabic prose; instead it preferred a more concise style, like poetry (M. Kurd ʿAlī, *Umarāʾ al-bayān*, Cairo 1937, 18-19, 21; A. al-Maḳdisī, *Taṭawwur al-asālīb al-nat̲h̲riyya fi 'l-adab al-ʿarabī*, Beirut 1960, 151; I. ʿAbbās, *ʿAbd al-Ḥamīd b. Yaḥyā al-kātib wa-mā tabaḳḳā min rasāʾilih wa-rasāʾil Sālim Abi 'l-ʿAlāʾ*, ʿAmmān 1988, 145, who quotes the opinions of ancient writers on the style of ʿAbd al-Ḥamīd).

There is some discussion about whether these characteristics came into Arabic prose under the influence of Persian or Greek, because the master of ʿAbd al-Ḥamīd, Sālim Abu 'l-ʿAlāʾ, *kātib* of the Umayyad caliph His̲h̲ām, composed his epistles, probably intended for the same caliph, from a Greek original (Latham, *The beginnings of Arabic prose literature*, in *CHAL. Arabic literature to the end of the Umayyad period*, Cambridge 1983, 154-64; ʿAbbās, *op. cit.*, 141).

What one can say is that this prose was born in the atmosphere and under the influence of the chanceries, which were permeated with a Sāsānid ambience, particularly from the ʿAbbāsid period onwards. As they combined together, the influence of the intellectual customs of these environments and the activity of philologists concerned with the Arabic language produced this marvellous tool. Without contravening the rules or the spirit of the the Arabic language, it was used to express ethical thoughts, dialectic procedures, and philosophical and scientific ideas, none of which had been familiar in the circumstances in which this language first appeared. There are two particular areas in which the influence of non-Arab but Islamicised intellectual circles can be traced in particular: the dialectic and rhetorical procedures of the Muʿtazila [*q.v.*], and the moral and intellectual values upheld by the secretarial class. Ibn Ḳutayba (d. 276/889 [*q.v.*]) deplored the fact that the *kuttāb* of his time allowed themselves to be dazzled by a pompous-looking empty science, which took them away from the solid items of knowledge they required in their position and from the knowledge of the traditional sciences: "Right there we have the whole history of *kalām* and Muʿtazilism" (G. Lecomte, *L'introduction du* Kitāb adab al-kātib *d'Ibn Qutayba*, in *Mélanges L. Massignon*, Damascus 1956-7, iii, 55).

It was in this period and in this atmosphere that such major questions stopped being treated in verse (H.A.R. Gibb, *The social significance of the shuʿūbīya*, in *Studia orientalia Ioanni Pedersen, dicata*, Copenhagen 1953, 105-14). It was because of the role played by the *kuttāb*, the literary training demanded by their function and the intellectual climate created under their influence, that works appeared which claimed a position of superiority for prose above that of poetry, as we have seen earlier (e.g. Z. al-Zuʿbī; Ibrāhīm b. Hilāl al-Ṣābī, *Risāla fi 'l-Farḳ bayn al-mutarassil wa 'l-s̲h̲āʿir*, 143-4; or the introduction to the work already mentioned of al-T̲h̲aʿālibī, *Nat̲h̲r al-naẓm*).

At the beginning of the ʿAbbāsid period, a high peak in style was reached here by al-Dj̲āḥiẓ [*q.v.*], who had an inestimable influence on later Arabic prose and who contributed to the enunciation of a technical terminology for the *balāg̲h̲a*. Al-Dj̲āḥiẓ was a Muʿtazilī, and his belief can be seen in the dialectical skill of which he seeks to give proof in a number of his treatises, where he expounds arguments to praise and to condemn the same thing or the same idea (I. Geries, *Un genre littéraire arabe: al-Maḥāsin wa-l-Masāwī*, Paris 1977). But Al-Dj̲āḥiẓ was not the first, for there is preserved a fragment from Sahl b. Hārūn (d. 215/830 [*q.v.*]) in which he argues for glass to be given pre-eminence over gold (Ibn Nubāta, *Sarḥ al-ʿuyun, s̲h̲arḥ risālat Ibn Zaydūn*, Cairo 1957, 139).

Besides this, ʿAbd al-Ḥamīd, in his epistle addressed to the *kuttāb*, lists among the qualities necessary for the accomplishment of their duties a knowledge of ancient poetry, including its vocabulary and its themes; he himself proved his ability in a *risāla* describing a hunting expedition which has echoes of pre-Islamic verse on the same theme; more details on ʿAbd al-

Ḥamīd are to be found in e.g. H. Schönig, *Das Sendschreiben des ʿAbdalḥamīd b. Yaḥyā (gest. 132/750) an den Kronprinzen ʿAbdallah b. Marwān II*, Stuttgart 1985; and al-Ḳāḍī, *Early Islamic state letters: the question of authenticity*, in A. Cameron and L.I. Conrad (eds.), *The Byzantine and early Islamic Near East*, i, Princeton 1992, 215-75, which examines the transmission of these epistles.

The later development of prose

The way style evolved is the most obvious feature in the history of this prose, especially from the formal point of view in the use of richer and more laboured ornamentation (*badīʿ* [*q.v.*]) and *sadj*ʿ. Such a style figures primarily but not exclusively in documents emanating from the *kuttāb*, and it has been studied because, as has been seen, what interested the theorists was the *kitāba* (the prose of the literary secretaries [*q.v.*]). The fragments we have of Sahl b. Hārūn already display a style involving rhythmic scansion in short phrases; here the thought is developed in two or more colons, which has the double effect of the extension of the main idea and the musical quality of the form.

At the end of the 2nd/8th century, the chancery documents coming from the Barmakids [see AL-BARĀMIKA] are composed as *sadj*ʿ (*Bayān*, 3,215). The same is true for ʿAmr b. Masʿada, in the period of al-Maʾmūn, who belonged to an originally Turkish family known by the eponym Ṣūl; another member of this family was Ibrahim b. al-ʿAbbās al-Ṣūlī, the *kātib* of al-Mutawakkil (see AL-ṢŪLĪ, ABŪ BAKR; Sh. Ḍayf, *al-Fann wa-madhahibuh fi ʾl-nathr al-ʿarabī*, Cairo 1960, 197-9; M. Kurd ʿAlī, *Umarāʾ*, 191-217).

After the time of al-Muḳtadir (d. 320/932) there was a general use of *sadj*ʿ, as can be seen from the documents from this period transmitted by Hilāl b. al-Muḥassin al-Ṣābī (d. 448/1055), *Tuḥfat al-umarāʾ fī taʾrīkh al-wuzarāʾ*, Cairo 1958. There is a balance of rhythmic phrases and rhymes which is developed by accumulation and synonyms; it is permeated with stylistic figures (in particular, paranomasia and antithesis) which contribute to the overall sonority of the phrases. This rich and subtle use of words, polishing every detail before they become complicated and turgid, was much appreciated, not only because they were a proof of the dexterity and hence the value of the *kātib*, but also because they reduced once again the distance between poetry and prose. The *rasāʾil* of the three famous *kuttāb* of the Būyids, Ibn al-ʿAmīd (d. 360/970 [*q.v.*], al-Ṣāḥib Ibn ʿAbbād (d. 385/995 [*q.v.*]) and Abū Isḥāḳ al-Ṣābī (d. 384/994 [see ṢĀBIʾ] all share this style, in which a rhythmic symmetry of phraseology is accompanied by figurative language, which is compared to embroidery and drawing by Ḍayf (*op. cit.*, 209-10); he defines it as poetry in the form of prose (216) with the same qualities of lightness and elegance.

Incidentally, part of the *ikhwāniyya* letters exchanged between Abū Isḥāḳ al-Ṣābī and al-Sharīf al-Raḍī (ed. M.Y. Nadjm, Kuwait 1961) was composed in verse. But al-Tawḥīdī (*al-Imtāʿ wa ʾl-muʾānasa*, i, 64) considered the prose of Ibn ʿAbbād somewhat stiff in his choice of words (perhaps because of his preference for words with velar consonants) and complicated by the inclusion of numerous parenthetical phrases, attentive to form even to the detriment of the meaning. There is another bitter critique from a literary point of view of the *kuttāb* which is found in the work of an unknown author from the 4th/10th century (see J. Sadan, *La littérature vue par un administrateur frustré*, in *SI*, lxxi [1990], 29-36).

The principal sources for literary prose up to this period are: al-Djāḥiẓ, *al-Bayān wa ʾl-tabyīn*; al-Thaʿālibī, *Yatīmat al-dahr*; Yāḳūt, *Muʿdjam al-udabāʾ*; the collections of the epistles and of the other works of al-Ṣāḥib Ibn ʿAbbād and of Abū Isḥāḳ al-Ṣābī have been published; apparently for those of Ibn al-ʿAmīd, despite his fame, all we have is what has been mentioned in works cited here and in other encyclopaedias of *adab*. More modern collections include A.Z. Ṣafwat, *Djamharat khuṭab al-ʿarab fī ʿuṣūr al-ʿarabiyya al-ṭāhira*, i-iii, Cairo 1933, and *Djamharat rasāʾil al-ʿarab*, i-iv, Cairo 1937; Kurd ʿAlī, *Rasāʾil al-bulaghāʾ*, Cairo 1946. A state-of-the-art report on the general themes and the principal authors can be found in the recently-published *CHAL. ʿAbbasid belles-lettres*.

Literary prose from a non-scribal environment has retained something of this style: a diffuse tendency towards parallelism, the construction of a phrase through which variations of the same idea are expressed by using a structure of parallel segments; these can repeat the idea by using synonyms or by expressing its antithesis or by making it more complete and more precise (A.F.L. Beeston, *The role of parallelism in Arabic prose*, in *CHAL. Literature to the end of the Umayyad period*, 180-5).

In each segment the syntactic structure is the same, as also to a certain degree is the morphological structure, by the selection of the patterns of nouns and verbs. This confers on the phrase its typical rhythm, without any insistence on assonance or rhyme. Beeston (*op. cit.*, 185) underlines the difference between this elaborated style and the simplicity of the primitive *sadj*ʿ. Al-Djāḥiẓ makes very moderate use of the style; his arguments are developed in a full and diffuse manner; sometimes he uses the same syntactic device but without seeking any symmetry. In those parts of his work which are not a collection of *akhbār*, Ibn Ḳutayba likes to make use of the style here described, in the well-constructed introduction to *Adab al-kātib*, for example; some elegant examples of this style are to be found in Abū Ḥayyān al-Tawḥīdī (d. 414/1023 [*q.v.*]), or Ibn Ḥazm (d. 456/1064 [*q.v.*]) from al-Andalus.

Frequently, different registers of style can be found in the same author; e.g. Ibn al-Muḳaffaʿ uses a simple and uncontrived style in *Kalīla wa-Dimna* [*q.v.*], in contradistinction to the laboured style which he adopts for his original work and which was to influence later prose. Miskawayh (d. 421/1030 [*q.v.*]) has a sober, concise style of prose in his *Tadjārib al-umam*, but more expansive in *al-Hawamil wa ʾl-shawāmil*.

Prose which does not keep to the rules of *sadj*ʿ is called *al-nathr al-mursal*, and it is in this style that the majority of works in classical prose have been written; in them the use of *sadj*ʿ and the other stylistic conventions, if they exist at all, is often restricted to the author's opening prologue. Such is the case in e.g. Abu ʾl-Faradj al-Iṣfahānī (d. 363/972-3 [*q.v.*]), *Kitāb al-Aghānī*, where the introduction explains the purpose of the book without any literary embellishment; or Abū Djaʿfar al-Ṭabarī (d. 310/923 [*q.v.*], *Taʾrīkh al-Rusul wa ʾl-mulūk*, who commences his book with a praise to God in *sadj*ʿ.

Prose that relates a series of events, which is strictly concerned with facts, whether they be historical or scientific, and that uses in general short, juxtaposed phrases must be distinguished from prose whose purpose is argument or exhortation. This latter type of prose, whether or not it uses parallelism, displays a syntax consisting of complex phrases and a number of parentheses. A remarkable example of such prose is the style of the famous writer of verse ʿAbd al-Ḳāhir al-Djurdjānī (d. 471/1078 [*q.v.* in Suppl.]).

Evidently there was a technical vocabulary for each science (see e.g. L. Massignon, *Essai sur l'origine du lexique technique de la mystique musulmane*, Paris 1959; C.E. Bosworth, *Abū ʿAbdallāh al-Khwārazmī on the technical terms of the secretary's art*, in *JESHO*, xiii [1969], 113-64; A.M. Goichon, *Lexique de la langue philosophique d'Ibn Sînâ*, Paris 1938). There also existed stylistic conventions of form, like the fictitious dialogue, through which argument in theological texts was conducted; the earliest examples of this technique seem to date from the a period before the Muʿtazila, and have been investigated by J. van Ess, *Disputationspraxis in der islamischen Theologie*, in *REI*, xlv [1977]; idem, *Early development of kalām*, in *Studies on the first century*, 109-23; idem, *The logical structure of Islamic theology*, in von Grunebaum (ed.), *Logic in classical Islamic culture*, Wiesbaden 1970, 21-50. In this last study, the author makes a close investigation of the method and the terminology in the theological argumentation based on Aristotelian logic, and he shows how al-Ghazālī, once he had adopted this method as the only one capable of demonstrating religious truth, in order to get it accepted preserved the terminology of *uṣūl al-fiḳh* [*q.v.*]. This manner of argumentation goes beyond the field of theology and was followed, for example, in the grammar of ʿAlī b. ʿĪsā al-Rummānī (d. 384/994 [*q.v.*]) in his commentary on the *Kitāb* of Sībawayh (M. al-Mubārak, *al-Rummānī al-naḥwī fī ḍawʾ sharḥih li-Kitāb Sībawayh*, Damascus 1963). For the characteristics of the prose of the Ṣūfī, which often appears in the form of exhortation and advice addressed to a disciple, see the remarks of al-Ḳāḍī in her introduction to *al-Ishārāt al-ilāhiyya* of al-Tawḥīdī, Beirut 1973.

There is a classification of *Schrifttum* in Arabic to be found in M. Shakʿa, *Manāhidj al-taʾlīf ʿind al-ʿulamāʾ al-ʿarab*, Beirut 1973; see also now the organisation in *CHAL. Religion, learning and science in the ʿAbbasid period*, Cambridge 1990.

The development of decorative style

This technical refinement of style which was shown by the *kuttāb* of the 4th/10th century evolved during the course of the following century into a quest for effects, turning it into more and more complicated prose. Not only could the rhyme of the *sadjʿ* comprise two or more consonants, but the style decorates itself with archaic lexemes from ancient poetry, with historical allusions, with word-plays based on double meanings of technical grammatical, metrical and philosophical terms. This style goes beyond the administrative sphere and extends its influence also to literary works, such as first of all the *maḳāma* [*q.v.*] or the *Risāla Hazliyya* of Ibn Zaydūn (d. 463/1070 [*q.v.*]); also to historical works, such as ʿAbd al Djabbār al-ʿUtbī (d. *ca.* 427/1036 [*q.v.*]), *al-Kitāb al-Yamīnī*, see C.E. Bosworth, *Early sources for the history of the first four Ghaznavid sultans (977-1041)*, in *IQ*, vii [1963], 3-22, or ʿImād al-Dīn al-Iṣfahānī (d. 597/1201), *kātib* of Ṣalāḥ al-Dīn (for the differences in style of these historians see F. Gabrieli, *Storici arabi delle crociate*, Turin 1969; D.S. Margoliouth, *Lectures on Arabic historians*, Calcutta 1930). By contrast, al-Bīrūnī (d. 440/1048 [*q.v.*]) used *sadjʿ* when he wrote the introduction to his *al-Āthār al-bāḳiya*, ed. C. Sachau, Leipzig 1878, dedicated to Ḳābūs b. Wushmagīr (d. 403/1013 [*q.v.*]), the *amīr* of the Ziyārid dynasty, famous for his immoderate use of stylistic techniques. His *rasāʾil* have been collected by ʿA. al-Yazdādī, *Kamāl al-balāgha*, Cairo 1341/1922-3 (see Ḍayf, *op. cit.*, 255-9), but al-Bīrūnī's style is sober and tight in the introduction to the book *Fī taḥḳīḳ mā li 'l-Hind min maḳūla*, ed. Sachau, London 1887, and elegant in the description of the customs of the Indians.

The most remarkable representative of this ornate style is Abu 'l-ʿAlāʾ al-Maʿarrī (d. 443/1058 [*q.v.*]), whose prose was made deliberately obscure by the use of words that are not only rare but even obsolete, and by a profusion of erudite allusions to the world of ancient Arabia, including proverbs and the names of stars, wells and idols. Al-Maʿarrī has even provided a commentary to accompany his prose; ʿA. ʿAbd al-Raḥmān (Bint al-Shāṭiʾ), *al-Ghufrān li-Abi 'l-ʿAlāʾ al-Maʿarrī*, Cairo 1962, picks out examples of divergence from normal syntax into which the complications of his *sadjʿ* have led al-Maʿarrī; she lists those ancient critics who recognised a heaviness in that style, despite the prestige it enjoyed, and she analyses the use of different registers in the work.

For the history of prose works after the 6th/12th century, see *CHAL. ʿAbbasid belles-lettres*, in which the prose from the different areas (Yemen, Egypt) is discussed; see also *ibid.*, *Religion, learning and science*; and see further INSHĀʾ; MADRASA; NAHḌA; TAʾRĪKH; ʿULAMĀʾ.

Prose genres

As well as the *risāla*, there were other literary genres recognised by the ancient theorists, especially the *maḳāma*, the *khuṭba*, the *ḥikāya* [*q.v.*] and the *ḳiṣṣa* [*q.v.*]. In addition there were also "genres" that were less well recognised by those theorists but that form a part of *adab* and to which modern research devotes particular attention. They are designated by names such as *nawādir*, *mulaḥ*, *akhbār*, and *ḥikam* (see Sadan, *Death of a princess: episodes of the Barmakid legend in its late evolution*, in S. Leder (ed.), *Story-telling in the framework of non-fictional Arabic literature*, Wiesbaden 1998, 131, and ḤIKĀYA).

The *khabar* in particular, whether it derives from a work of history or of *adab*, presents itself as the report, seen from the outside, of a real event. A very valuable set of studies being undertaken now has produced an analysis of these stories from the standpoint of narrative structure. The results that have so far appeared tend on the one hand to bridge the gap between the "lack of fiction", which one can see in classical Arabic literature, and modern literary fiction, and on the other hand to examine the forms of awareness that the "reporter" of a *khabar* could have in composing in reality a work of literature. Further studies include those to be found in Leder, *op. cit.*; see Sh. Ayyād, *Fann al-khabar fī turāthinā al-ḳiṣaṣī*, in *Fuṣūl*, ii (1982), 11-18; Leder, *Features of the novel in early historiography*, in *Oriens*, xxxii (1990), 72-96; idem, *The literary use of the* Khabar: *a basic form of historical writing*, in Cameron and Conrad (eds.), *op. cit.*, 277-315; H. Kilpatrick, *Context and the enhancement of the meaning of* aḫbār *in the* Kitāb al-aġānī, in *Arabica*, xxxviii (1991), 351-68; eadem, Aḫbār manẓūma. *The romance of Qays and Lubnā in the* Aġānī, in *Festschrift E. Wagner*, 2 vols. Beirut 1994, 350-61.

Studies on the evolution of prose from the point of view of language are rare, but one may refer to some studies about an author's use of langauge, such as Schönig, *op. cit.*; or F. al-Djāmiʿī al-Ḥabbābī, *Lughat Abi 'l-ʿAlāʾ al-Maʿarrī fī Risālat al-ghufrān*, Cairo n.d.; or the works on syntax based on texts, such as Y. Peled, *Conditional structures in Classical Arabic*, Wiesbaden 1992; also the contributions in the *Beiträge zur Lexicographie des klassischen Arabisch*, in *Bayerische Akademie der Wissenschaften, phil. hist. Klasse* (1979-).

Bibliography: In addition to the references cited in the body of this article, see Z. Mubarak, *La prose arabe au IVᵉ siècle de Hégire*, Paris 1931;

ʿA. Balbaʿ, *al-Nat̲h̲r al-fannī wa-at̲h̲ar al-D̲j̲āḥiẓ fīh*, Cairo 1954; Ch. Pellat, *La prose arabe à Bag̲h̲dād*, in *Arabica*, ix (1962), 407-18; M. Cook, *Early Muslim dogma: a source-critical study*, Cambridge 1981, who presents and examines texts relative to the doctrinal controversies at the end of the 1st century; H. Kilpatrick, *Selection and presentation as distinctive characteristics of medieval Arabic courtly prose literature*, in K. Busby and E. Kooper (eds.), *Courtly literature, culture and context*, Amsterdam and Philadelphia 1990; A. Gully, *Epistles for grammarians: illustration from the* inshāʾ *literature*, in *BRISMES*, xxiii (1996), 147-66; R. Allen, *The Arabic literary heritage: the development of its genres and criticism*, Cambridge 1998; S. Leder, art. *Prose, non-fiction, medieval*, in *Encyclopedia of Arabic literature*, London and New York 1998, ii, 615-18; Leder and Kilpatrick, *Classical Arabic prose literature: a researcher's sketch map*, in *JAL*, xxiii (1999), 2-26; A. Ben Abdesselem, *La vie littéraire dans l'Espagne musulmane sous les* Mulūk al-ṭawāʾif *(V^e/XIe siècle)*, Damascus 2001.

(Lidia Bettini)

NĀY (P., in Tkish., *ney*), a rim-blown flute made of reed (*arundo donax* L.). The name, meaning basically "reed", is known from Pahlavi, in which it was a loanword from Aramaic *qnʾ* (cf. Assyrian *qanū, qanuʾu*, Hebr. *qnh*). However in early Arabic sources, such as the *Kitāb al-Ag̲h̲ānī*, the term *nāy* most probably denoted not a flute but a double-reed woodwind instrument of the *mizmār* [*q.v.*] family. The *mizmār*, because of its colour, was also called *nāy siyāh* "black *nāy*" in contrast to the *nāy safīd* "white *nāy*", i.e. the flute.

The rim-blown flute has been known since the 3rd millennium B.C. in Ancient Egypt as well as in Mesopotamia. For Ancient Egypt, written and iconographic testimonies of flute players are frequent. While the Sumerian flutes found at Ur are metal fragments, the Egyptian ones are of reed. The ancient Egyptian flutes that are preserved in the Egyptian Museum of Cairo were played and recorded by Maḥmūd ʿIffat in 1991. Some of them produced a pentatonic scale, others a heptatonic one.

After its peak in Antiquity, the rim-blown flute survived as a folk instrument until Ṣūfī movements in Islam gave it a new and prominent place in religious music (see below). The folk flutes do not conform to the norms of the classical instrument. They may be made of wood, reed or metal and have many local names, as e.g. the Palestinian and Syrian *s̲h̲abbāba*, the ʿIrāḳī *blūr*, the Turkish *kaval*, the Egyptian *kawala* and *salāmiyya*, the Algerian *gaṣba* or the Ethiopian *was̲h̲int*.

The *nāy/ney* is cut out of one naturally grown piece of reed of 15 to 25 mm diameter. Each end lies between two nodes; the whole instrument has 8 nodes and 9 internodes (persian *nāy*: 6 nodes/7 internodes). The *nāy* is held obliquely. It is blown upon the rim, which is the edge of the uppermost internode (*k̲h̲azna*). Persian players place the rim between their teeth ("Iṣfahān technique"); the rim of Persian instruments is often set in a metal ring. The Turkish *ney*, from Ottoman times onwards, has a mouthpiece (*baṣpare*) made of wood, ivory, gold or—in modern times—synthetic materials. The *nāy/ney* has 6 (Persian *nāy*: 5) fingerholes and one thumbhole.

The *nāy/ney* fits particularly well with oriental modes (*maḳāmāt* [see maḳām]), because its basic fingering includes the typical three-quartertone intervals. A set (*taḳm*) of 7 to 12 instruments of different length allows to transpose the *maḳāmāt* to nearly every note. Arabic *nāys* are named after their fundamental note, given by opening the last hole. A standard Arabic (Egyptian)

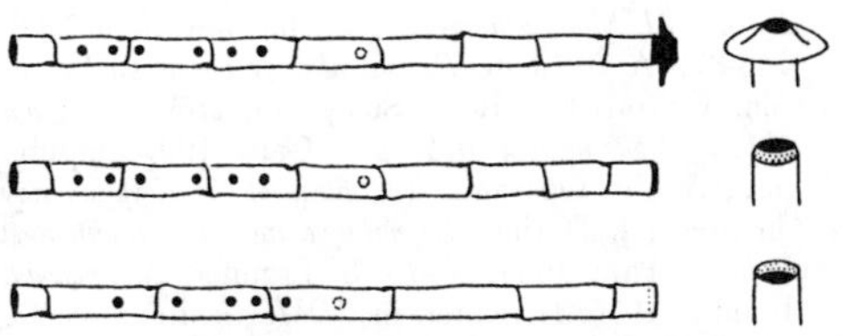

Turkish *ney*, Arabic and Persian *nāy* (from above)

taḳm consists of: *nāy Rāst* (C, length approximately 680 mm; the exact length depends on the width of the reed), *nāy Dūkāh* (D, 600 mm), *nāy Būsalīk* (E, 540 mm), *nāy Čehārkāh* (F, 510 mm), *nāy Nawā* (G, 445 mm), *nāy Ḥusaynī* (A, 405 mm) and *nāy ʿAd̲j̲am* (B^b, 375 mm). Higher, lower or "half-tone" *nāys* as e.g. *Dūkāh nisf* (D^b, 665 mm), are seldom in use. Turkish *neys* are longer and lower; the third step gives a higher *sīkāh* (three-quarter-tone) than the Arabic *nāy*. The Turkish set (*takım*) consists of: *Bolahenk ney* (length approximately 1040 mm); *Davud ney* (910 mm); *Şah ney* (858 mm); *Mansur ney* (806 mm), *Kız ney* (702 mm), *Müstahzen* (598 mm) and *Süpürde* (572 mm). For high levels, there are "half" (*nısfiye*) instruments, e.g. *Kız nisfiye* (350 mm). The Persian *nāys* vary from 400 to 800 mm in length.

Impressed by the modern European flute, several attempts have been made to technically improve and modernise the *nāy*. Until now, none of these attempts has been widely accepted. The simplicity of its construction and the naturalness of its sound are still essential for the instrument, which demands high skill of its players and plays an important role even in modern music.

The *nāy* has been the favoured wind instrument of art and court music from around the 8th/14th century onwards. As a court music instrument, the *nāy* is frequently represented in Persian miniature paintings. It is played solo or in mixed ensembles, but normally not with other *nāys*. Turkish ensembles, however, sometimes have many *neys* playing together. The dances of the Mevlevi dervishes, for example, are accompanied by drums and *neys* only. When playing with a singer, the *nāy* is especially used for short melodic formulas (*lāzima*, pl. *lawāzim*) and improvisations (*taḳsīm*, pl. *taḳāsīm*).

The sound of the *nāy* is regarded as particularly similar to the human voice. According to a legend in the *Mazhar al-ʿad̲j̲āʾib*, ascribed to Farīd al-Dīn ʿAṭṭār (*ca.* 513-618/1119-1221 [*q.v.*]), the *nāy* voices the Prophet's secret revelations which no other human being has ever heard. Before this, ʿAlī had told the secrets to a well at the edge of which reeds grew.

In Ṣūfī music, the *nāy* is the most prominent melodic instrument of all. The Ṣūfīs hear the sound of the *nāy* as the crying of the reed after it is cut. It is like the crying of the soul because of its separation from God. The famous *Mat̲h̲nawī* of D̲j̲alāl al-Dīn Rūmī (604-72/1207-73 [*q.v.*]) opens with a dramatic articulation of this symbolic meaning of the *nāy*.

Bibliography: H.G. Farmer, *EI*² art. *Mizmār*; S.Q. Hassan and J. During, in *The New Grove dictionary of musical instruments*, London 1984, art. *Nāy*; M. ʿIffat *et alii*, *Taḳrīr ʿan al-dirāsa allatī ḳāma bihā farīḳ mas̲h̲rūʿ dirāsat ālāt al-nāy al-firʿawniyya bi ʾl-matḥaf al-miṣrī li ʾl-taʿarruf ʿalā ʾl-sullam al-mūsīḳī ʾl-firʿawnī*, Cairo (unpub. ms. July 1991); D. Franke and E. Neubauer, *Museum des Institutes für Geschichte der Arabisch-Islamischen Wissenschaften: Beschreibung der*

Exponate. I. Musikinstrumente, Frankfurt am Main 2000, 166-87; ʿA. Mas͟hʿal, *Dirāsat al-nāy/The method of El Nay*, Cairo 1967; R.ʿA. Sulaymān, *al-Nāy al-ʿarabī al-ḥadīt͟h/The modern Arabic flute*, Cairo 1997 (unpubl. ms.); A. van Oostrum, *The music of the Egyptian nāy* (in press); J. During, *La musique iranienne: tradition et évolution*, Paris 1984, 67-73; S. Erguner, *Ney metodu*, Istanbul 1986; H. Ritter, in *ZDMG*, xcii (1938), 37.

(Claudia Ott)

NAẒM.

1. In metrical speech. Literally meaning "stringing (pearls, beads, etc.)", in early ʿAbbāsid times *naẓm* acquired the meaning of "versifying", "versification", and became almost synonymous with "poetry", *s͟hiʿr* [*q.v.*], especially when contrasted with prose, *nat͟hr*, literally "scattering". The comparison of a poem to a necklace, or verses to pearls, is apt in view of the relative independence of the individual verses, held together on the string of the uniform metre and rhyme. The image has pre-ʿAbbāsid origins, and although the noun *naẓm* was not used in the sense of "verse" until later (and Ḳudāma b. D̲jaʿfar [*q.v.*] still does not do so in his poetics), at least the related verb had already been used, when the 1st/7th century poet al-Nad̲jās͟hī said *Sa-anẓimu min ḥurri ʾl-kalāmi ḳaṣīdatan* "I shall string/compose an ode of noble speech" (al-Ḥātimī, *Ḥilyat al-muḥāḍara*, Bag͟hdād 1979, i, 426). Yet Abū Nuwās [*q.v.*] could still speak, in an ode addressed to al-Amīn, of "my scattering (*nat͟hrī*) pearls on you" (*Dīwān*, ed. Wagner, i, 241). The many discussions on the relative merits of prose and poetry regularly employ the terms *naẓm* and *nat͟hr* (on this debate, see e.g. Ziyad al-Zuʿbī, *Das Verhältnis von Poesie und Prosa in der arabischen Literatur-theorie des Mittelalters*, Berlin 1987). Not rarely, however, a distinction is made between *s͟hiʿr* as "true" poetry and *naẓm* as merely versifying, i.e. either prosodically correct but unintentionally bad poetry, or didactive verse (see e.g. Isḥāḳ b. Ibrāhīm b. Wahb, *al-Burhān*, Cairo 1969, 130; Ibn K͟haldūn, *The Muqaddimah*, tr. F. Rosenthal, Princeton 1967, iii, 381-2).

(G.J.H. van Gelder)

2. In Ḳurʾānic studies. Here, the "arrangement of pearls on a string" is used metaphorically to indicate "ordering of words-*cum*-meanings", i.e. "composition" (note that *taʾlīf* is sometimes used synonymously with *naẓm*), or, more freely, the "style" of the Ḳurʾān. In this sense it is closely connected with the discussions of the dogma of *iʿd̲jāz al-Ḳurʾān* [*q.v.*]; more particularly, it is evidently the backbone of the conception of *iʿd̲jāz* as "stylistic inimitability" of the Ḳurʾān.

The first known work devoted to this notion is the *K. fī ʾl-iḥtid̲jād̲j li-naẓm al-Ḳurʾān wa-salāmatihī min al-ziyāda wa ʾl-nuḳṣān* of al-D̲jāḥiẓ (d. 255/868-9 [*q.v.*]), which is unfortunately lost (Ch. Pellat's reference in *Nouvel essai d'inventaire de l'œuvre Ğāḥiẓienne*, in *Arabica*, xxxi [1984], 117ff., no. 191, to a ms. copy of this work preserved in the Escorial library is erroneous, see J. van Ess, *Theologie*, vi, 314). The work is usually cited with the brief title *Naẓm al-Ḳurʾān*. Al-K͟hayyāṭ describes it as follows: "No book is known concerning the argument for the well-orderedness (*naẓm*) and the wondrous composition of the Ḳurʾān, and that it is proof for the prophethood of Muḥammad—God bless him—, except the book of al-D̲jāḥiẓ" (*al-Intiṣār*, ed. A.N. Nader [Beirut 1957], 111). This description contains all the elements of the *iʿd̲jāz* concept, as generally adopted later. Al-D̲jāḥiẓ radically breaks with the *ṣarfa* notion of his teacher al-Naẓẓām [*q.v.*], who did not believe that the composition of the Ḳurʾān was stylistically unattainable and who thought that Muḥammad's pagan contemporaries, challenged to produce something like a sūra, were "turned away" by God from carrying out this task.

Claude Audebert has compiled a list of works on *naẓm* up to the time of al-K͟haṭṭābī, eight in all (*al-Ḫaṭṭābī*, 58-61). The most explicit title—and mostly we have but titles—is the one given to the Muʿtazilī al-Wāsiṭī's (d. 306/918 or 307/919) book: *K. Iʿd̲jāz al-Ḳurʾān fī naẓmihī wa-taʾlīfih* (*ibid.*, 59). It states the connection between *iʿd̲jāz* and *naẓm* and the near-synonymity of *naẓm* and *taʾlīf*. It is remarkable that the authors of these works are partly *mutakallimūn* and partly traditionists.

Al-K͟haṭṭābī (d. 386/996 or 388/998 [*q.v.*]), in his treatise *Bayān iʿd̲jāz al-Ḳurʾān*, postulates a triad of elements that make up "speech" (*kalām*), namely, *lafẓun ḥāmilun wa-maʿnan bihī ḳāʾimun wa-ribāṭun lahumā nāẓim* "words as carriers, meaning subsisting in them, and a connection that orders both of them" (ed. M. K͟halaf Allāh and M.Z. Salām, 24 l. 11; tr. Audebert, *al-Ḫaṭṭābī*, 120, cf. also 87). The third element is usually called *naẓm*; al-K͟haṭṭābī not infrequently also uses the plural *nuẓūm* to refer to the syntactic-stylistic "structures" or "molds" (this plural is not in the dictionaries). In all three elements the Ḳurʾān is the superior text, as the continuation of the quoted passage says. The workings of *naẓm* are several times metaphorically characterised (the various "types of ordering" [*rusūm al-naẓm*] are a "bridle on the words and a rein on the meanings" [*lid̲jām al-alfāẓ wa-zimām al-maʿānī*]; cf. ed., 33; tr. 128), but not defined and explicitly discussed. A large part of al-K͟haṭṭābī's *Bayān* is devoted to linguistic-stylistic criticisms (i.e. criticisms of the *naẓm*) of Ḳurʾānic passages by others, followed by the author's refutation (*al-Ḫaṭṭābī*, 97-102).

Al-Bāḳillānī (d. 403/1013 [*q.v.*]), in his *Iʿd̲jāz al-Ḳurʾān*, lists the excellent *naẓm* of the Ḳurʾān as the third reason for its inimitability (after [1] prophesysing passages, and [2] the illiteracy of the Prophet, which proves Divine instruction about creation, etc.). He enumerates ten aspects of this *naẓm*: (1) The Ḳurʾān is *sui generis* as a literary genre (35). (2) The Arabs had not produced any eloquent text of such enormous length (36). (3) The Ḳurʾān is homogeneously eloquent in all its subgenres (*wujūh*), such as narratives, admonitions, argumentations, etc., whereas a poet may excel in panegyrics but not in invective, or vice versa (36-8). (4) The smooth transition from one topic to the next in the Ḳurʾān is unrivalled (38). (5) Not only man is unable to produce anything similar to it, but so are the jinn (38-41). (6) All stylistic and rhetorical possibilities occur in the Ḳurʾān (42). (7) Expressing new ideas, rather than well-worn ones, with beautiful words is the highest level of language mastership (*barāʿa*); this the Ḳurʾān does when it speaks about legal and religious matters (42). (8) When a Ḳurʾānic phrase is quoted, it stands out in its new textual surrounding through its beauty (42-4). (9) The "mysterious letters" at the beginning of twenty-eight sūras show an amazingly regular selection of phonemes, when measured against the various groups of phonemes that the grammarians have established (44-6). (10) The style of the Ḳurʾān is easy though impossible to imitate (*ḳarīban ilā ʾl-afhāmi yubādiru maʿnāhu ʾl-lafẓa ilā ʾl-ḳalb . . . wa-huwa maʿa d͟hālika mumtaniʿu ʾl-maṭlab*); it is equally distant from lexical uncouthness (*waḥs͟hī*) and unusualness (*g͟harīb*) [*q.vv.*], on the one hand, and from affected artfulness (*al-ṣanʿa al-mutakkallafa*), on the other (46).

The list clearly shows that al-Bāḳillānī is not interested in the micro-analysis of what constitutes *naẓm*, nor does he establish, as al-Khaṭṭābī does, the strict correlation between *naẓm* and the two other elements of speech, "words" and "meaning". He focuses more on the overall linguistic-literary quality of the Ḳurʾānic text.

ʿAbd al-Ḳāhir al-Djurdjānī (d. 471/1078 or 474/1081 [*q.v.* in Suppl.]), in his *Dalāʾil al-iʿdjāz* ("Proofs for the Inimitability"), comes again closer to al-Khaṭṭābī, who may be called his precursor in matters of *naẓm*. But al-Djurdjānī surpasses him by far. Over hundreds of pages he subjects Ḳurʾānic phrases, or syntactic phenomena in general, to the most painstaking semantic analysis and thus manages to fill the notion of *naẓm* with real content. He defines it as *tawakhkhī maʿānī ʾl-naḥw* ("minding the meanings of syntactic relations"). The syntactic-semantic phenomena discussed include *inter alia*: word order (*taḳdīm wa-taʾkhīr*), ellipsis (*ḥadhf*), syndetic and asyndetic co-ordination (*waṣl wa-faṣl*), and the various functions of the sentence-initial particle *inna* (see also Weisweiler, in *Bibl.*)

The "ordering" (*naẓm*) creates a specific shape/form (*ṣūra*) for a general *gharaḍ* ("intention") in the mind and, parallel to it, in the language; the meaning (*maʿnā*) and the expression/wording (*lafẓ*) of a proposition (*kalām*) thus become mirror images. The inherited but, according to al-Djurdjānī, misunderstood dichotomy *lafẓ-maʿnā* is thus reinterpreted: the wording (*lafẓ*) is no longer a "garment" for a "naked" *maʿnā*. The two are inseparable, no "meaning" can be expressed by two "wordings" equally well; the two "wordings" would express two different "meanings".

K. Abu Deeb (*Poetic imagery*, 24-64) and, more recently, N. Kermani (*Gott ist schön*, 253-84, esp. 264, and n. 144) have argued that, with many of his deep-cutting analyses, al-Djurdjānī is a precursor of modern semanticists or even on a par with them. As a whole, his book is indeed highly original but not very well arranged. Fakhr al-Dīn al-Rāzī (d. 606/1209 [*q.v.*]) and al-Sakkākī (d. 626/1229 [*q.v.*]) later turned his ideas into a textbook format, thus creating the discipline called *ʿilm al-maʿānī* (i.e. *maʿānī ʾl-naḥw*) [see MAʿĀNĪ WA-BAYĀN].

All authors so far discussed restrict the notion of *naẓm* to single Ḳurʾānic or poetic phrases (lines, verses). Ibn Rashīḳ (d. 456/1063 or 463/1071 [*q.v.*]), in his handbook on poetry, includes a chapter on *naẓm*, in which this notion has at times a wider compass, referring as it does to the cohesion of consecutive lines (*ʿUmda*, i, 258-63). A similar approach to structures within a sūra can sometimes be found in books on the Ḳurʾān. Al-Khaṭīb al-Iskāfī (d. 421/1030), in his exegetical work *Durrat al-tanzīl wa-ghurrat al-taʾwīl fī bayān al-āyāt al-mutashābihāt fī Kitāb Allāh al-ʿazīz* (Beirut 1995), several times tries to do just that: a "knitting of part to part", as Hamori calls it (*Iskāfī*, 40-2). Some scholars seem to have gone even further and asked about the meaning of the place, within the Ḳurʾān, of individual sūras. Al-Zarkashī (d. 794/1392 [*q.v.*]) mentions one Abū Bakr al-Nīsābūrī, who "whenever the Koran was read to him, used to ask: Why is this verse put next to that one? For what reason does this *sūra* stand next to that one?" (G.J. van Gelder, *Beyond the line*, Leiden 1982, 100; the author suggests that we are possibly dealing here with Abu ʾl-Ḳāsim [!] al-Ḥasan b. Muḥammad al-Nisābūrī, who wrote a *Kitāb al-Tanzīl wa-tartībih*, see n. 214). However, al-Zarkashī also mentions that this subject did not attract much attention (*al-Burhān fī ʿulūm al-Ḳurʾān*, ed. M.A. Ibrāhīm, Cairo 1972, i, 36).

In the modern period this has changed. In the Indian subcontinent we find Ḥamīd al-Dīn ʿAbd al-Ḥamīd Farāhī (d. 1349/1930) and his disciple Amīn Aḥsan Iṣlāḥī (d. 1997) upholding the idea of the coherence (*naẓm*) of the Ḳurʾān on all levels (see M. Mir, *Coherence*, in *Bibl.*). The main motivation behind this seems to be traditional Orientalist criticism of the Ḳurʾān that stressed its structural incoherence on all levels. It should be noted that in more modern Western literary approaches the perceived "incoherence" is considered to be rather one of the strengths of the Holy Book (see Kermani, *Gott ist schön*, 281).

Bibliography: 1. Texts. Khaṭṭābī, *Bayān iʿdjāz al-Ḳurʾān*, ed. Muḥammad Khalaf Allāh and Muḥammad Zaghlūl Salām, in *Thalāth rasāʾil fī iʿdjāz al-Ḳurʾān*, Cairo n.d., 19-65, tr. C.F. Audebert, *al-Ḫaṭṭābī et l'inimitabilité du Coran: traduction et introduction au* Bayān iʿǧāz al-Ḳurʾān, Damascus 1982; Bāḳillānī, *Kitāb Iʿdjāz al-Ḳurʾān*, ed. al-Sayyid Aḥmad Ṣaḳr, Cairo 1963, 35-48; ʿAbd al-Ḳāhir al-Djurdjānī, *Dalāʾil al-iʿdjāz*, ed. Maḥmūd Muḥammad Shākir, Cairo 1404/1984; Ibn Rashīḳ, *al-ʿUmda fī maḥāsin al-shiʿr wa-ādābih*, ed. M.ʿA.A. ʿAṭā, 2 pts., Beirut 1422/2001.

2. Studies. J. van Ess, *Theologie und Gesellschaft im 2. und 3. Jahrhundert Hidschra. Eine Geschichte des religiösen Denkens im frühen Islam*, 6 vols., Berlin-New York 1991-7; Kamal Abu Deeb, *Al-Jurjānī's theory of poetic imagery*, Warminster, Wilts. 1979; Navid Kermani, *Gott ist schön. Das ästhetische Erleben des Koran*, Munich 1999; Aḥmad Abū Zayd, *Muqaddima fī ʾl-uṣūl al-fikriyya li ʾl-balāgha wa-iʿdjāz al-Ḳurʾān*, Rabat 1409/1989, 51-122; Andras Hamori, *Did medieval readers make sense of form? Notes on a passage of al-Iskāfī*, in A.H. Green (ed.), *In quest of an Islamic humanism. Arabic and Islamic studies in memory of Mohamed al-Nowaihi*, Cairo 1985, 39-47; Mustansir Mir, *Coherence in the Qurʾān. A study of Iṣlāḥī's concept of* naẓm *in* Tadabbur-i Qurʾān, Indianapolis 1986.

(W.P. Heinrichs)

NISSĪM b. YAʿḲŪB, IBN SHĀHĪN, outstanding leader and rabbi of North Africa and, Judaeo-Arabic author.

He was born *ca.* 300/990, and studied under his father and R. Ḥushiel, who emigrated from Italy and settled in al-Ḳayrawān [*q.v.*]. Like his father, Nissīm was head of the Academy there and the representative of the Academies of Sura and Pumbedita near Baghdād. He was famous as a scholar and enjoyed much glory, but the last period of his life was a sad time for him. His son died at an early age and his daughter was unhappily married to a son of Samuel ha-Nagid of the Banu ʾl-Naghralla, who served the Zīrids [*q.v.*] of Gharnāṭa. Nissim visited Granada and taught there. Of importance during his time was the disturbed political situation in North Africa, since the local Zīrid dynasty there was in conflict with the Fāṭimids, and when the Bedouin of the Banū Hilāl [*q.v.*] and the Sulaym attacked Ifrīḳiya, and the Zīrid ruler had to leave al-Ḳayrawān in 449/1057 and take refuge in al-Mahdiyya, Rabbi Nissīm fled to Sūsa [*q.v.*], where he died in 454/1062 after a serious illness.

The language of his important Judaeo-Arabic literary work, the *Kitāb al-Faradj baʿd al-shidda* ("Relief after hardship"), is one of the best examples of a Middle Arabic text that at times follows the rules of Classical Arabic, but at other times is influenced by the practice of Arabic dialects, with many hypercorrections. The contents of the text, which was more widely known in its early Hebrew translation called *Ḥibbur yafeh me-ha-yeshuʿah* ("A beautiful collection about relief", printed at Ferrara 1557), go back to the same genre as practiced by al-Madāʾinī (d. 225/840), Ibn Abi ʾl-Dunyā (d. 281/894) and al-Muḥassin al-Tanūkhī (d. 384/994), and have a religious, perhaps Jewish, origin. Nissīm Ibn Shāhīn's stories do not have a secular character like most of al-Tanūkhī's stories, but are embedded in a religious context. Some stories such as "The perfidious wife" and "The story of Kidor" found their way into other mediaeval bellestristic collections.

Bibliography: Shraga Abramson, *R. Nissim Gaon libelli quinque*, Jerusalem 1965; W. Brinner, *An elegant composition concerning relief after adversity*, New Haven and London 1977; G.D. Cohen, *The Book of Tradition (Sefer ha-Qabbalah) by Abraham ibn Daud*, London 1967, *index*, s.v. Ibn Shahin; J. Obermann (ed.), *The Arabic original of Ibn Shāhīn's Book of Comfort*, New Haven 1933; Rabbenu Nissim Bar Yaʿaqov, ed. H.Z. Hirshfeld, *Ḥibbur yafeh me-ha-yeshuʿah*, Jerusalem 1954 (new Hebrew translation).

(A. Schippers)

NIẒĀM ʿASKARĪ (a.), military organisation, the system of military rule in modern Islamic lands (for a consideration of military organisation before *ca.* 1900, see DJAYSH; ḤARB; ISTIʿRĀḌ).

1. In the modern Arab world
2. In modern Iran
3. In the late Ottoman Empire and the Turkish Republic
4. In Pakistan

1. In the modern Arab world.

The frequent appearance of military régimes in the Arab sector of the Muslim world during the second part of the 20th century owes less to a tradition of interaction between military conquest and the diffusion of Islam than to the heritage of the style of power exercised by the Ottoman Sultans [see ʿOTHMĀNLÎ. I.]. It is explained both by the game of the European imperialisms and the influence of the Kemālist model in the region since 1921. Colonial domination depended on the separation between an allogenic military organisation and local society. It took the form of political régimes (mandates, protectorates or direct colonisation) in which the military played a dominant role through the actual or potential use of brute force (D.A. Rustow, to S.N. Fischer 1963, 3). While the officer corps of the colonial army was European, there was a preference for recruiting the troops from among the ethnic and religious communities. Senior officers often exercised civil functions, such as that of the High Commissioner of the French Mandate in Syria and in Lebanon (1920-43), the British High Commissioner in Palestine (1920-46) or in ʿIrāḳ (1920-32) [see MANDATES]. Furthermore, the period of colonial domination was marked by the two World Wars which justified exceptional forms of government. It came to an end after sometimes prolonged and violent confrontation: in particular, the conflict in Palestine from 1936 onwards, the Algerian war (1954-62), and numerous suppressions of uprisings, as in Egypt by Great Britain in 1919 and 1924, in Syria by France in 1919, 1924-6 and 1945; and in ʿIrāḳ by Great Britain, in 1921 and 1941.

After independence, the incidence of military régimes in the Arab region can be correlated to the frequency and the intensity of inter-state conflicts, through the implementation of preparations for war by senior officers with the object of imposing constitutional forms, social control and economic priorities, which justified and prolonged their domination: Israeli-Arab wars (1948-9, 1956, 1967, 1973, 1982), the Yemeni conflict from 1960-7, the Algerian-Moroccan war in the Sahara in 1963, then the war of the eastern Sahara from 1975 onwards, the Iran-ʿIrāḳ war from 1980 to 1988, and the Gulf War of 1990-1. The regional and ethnic tensions within young states with fragile national identities also favoured the seizure of power by the military, as in ʿIrāḳ at the time of the 1958 revolution or in Sūdān from 1958 onwards. The principal motivating force was dissatisfaction with the poor economic performance of the civilian régimes.

After the Arab countries had gained their independence, the army became in the space of one or two decades the primary institution in terms of numbers—up to 30% of the workforce of certain countries—and of its budget, which often exceeded that of education, but also through the central place that it occupied in executive power. It permeated all the fields of political activity including the parties, exercised a tight control over the population using the force authorised by emergency laws and with recourse to the *mukhābarāt*, the intelligence and police services. Arab republics and monarchies were thus transformed into "military societies" (Abdelmalek 1962).

The analysis of Arab military régimes has given rise to three distinct interpretations of their nature and their effect on the state and the society of the countries concerned. The first credited the dominant participation of officers in the government with the qualities of order, efficiency and honesty as well as technical and organisational capacities. The army was seen as the best agency for the purpose of ensuring the development of the country, educating society and being the bearer of modern values and practices, since the generation of officers trained since independence belonged to a "new middle class" with modernising tendencies (Halpern 1962, 278); their nationalist sensibility, whether Arab (*ḳawmī*) or patriotic (*waṭanī*), manifested through various anti-colonial and revolutionary ideologies, gave them the legitimacy to impose on society a modernisation "from above" (industrialisation, agrarian reform) inspired by the Kemālist model (Allush 1968).

After the Arab defeat of 1967 and in view of the poor economic performance of Egypt and of Syria under military rule, then that of Algeria in the 1980s, a second analysis has prevailed. It described *niẓām ʿaskarī* as "praetorian", and considered the army an agency for the maintenance of order in the service of an authoritarian and barely representative political power, pursuing its corporatist interests rather than a social project (Perlmutter 1974).

Until the turn of the 1990s, oil revenues and the priority given to the war effort assured the perpetuation of the *niẓām ʿaskarī*. Subsequently, Arab armies had a tendency to return to their military function while a number of officers became economic entrepreneurs benefiting from the *infitāḥ*. The *niẓām ʿaskarī* progressively gave way to civilian governments, still under military control. A third analysis then placed the accent on the simultaneously policing and predatory nature of these regimes (R. Owen, *State, power and politics in the making of the modern Middle East*, London 1992).

(a) *Egypt*

Although it was not historically the first, the prototype of *niẓām ʿaskarī* in the Arab regions of the Muslim world in the 20th century is that of the *ḍubbāṭ al-aḥrār*, the Free Officers who on 23 July 1952 overthrew the Egyptian dynasty which had itself been founded by an officer of the Ottoman army, Muḥammad ʿAlī [*q.v.*]. This group of some three hundred officers (T. Aclimandos, *Les militaires égyptiens. Esprit de corps et révolution*, in *Peuples méditerranéens/ Mediterranean Peoples*, xli-xlii [1988], 87-104), graduates of the Military Academy after 1936 (the date of its opening to indigenous Egyptians), had particularly resented the indifference of the monarchical régime during the Palestine war of 1948-9. Their nine leaders, constituted into a *Madj̲lis ḳiyādat al-t̲h̲awra* (Revolutionary Command Council), installed military personnel in the higher ranks of the executive on a permanent basis. Originally, the RCC united personalities of diverse tendencies, Miṣr al-Fatāt, al-Ik̲h̲wān al-Muslimūn [*q.v.*] and Communists, who held in common the nationalist and socialist objectives summarised in the *Falsafat al-t̲h̲awra* of Dj̲amāl ʿAbd al-Nāṣir [*q.v.* in Suppl.]. In the competition for power, the leftists of the RCC led by Yūsuf al-Ṣiddīḳ, and the liberals led by K̲h̲ālid Muḥyī ʾl-Dīn, were ousted in March 1953 and March 1954 respectively. The rupture with the Muslim Brotherhood took place on 12 January 1954. Whether socialistic pan-Arabist as in the 1960s, or patriotic liberal as in the 1980s, Egyptian power henceforward depended on the alliance between the military institution and the bureaucracy of state.

The executive was the prerogative of generals: presidency of the Republic was taken by Muḥammad Nadj̲īb, on 18 June 1952, and after his ousting on 14 November 1954, by Nāṣir until his death on 28 September 1970, by Anwar al-Sādāt (assassinated 5 October 1981) and by Ḥusnī Mubārak, who began his fourth presidential period of power on 26 September 1999. In the government, one-fifth of the ministerial posts (in particular Defence, Military Production and the Interior) were occupied by senior officers under Nāṣir, and 7.5% under Sādāt (M. Cooper, *The demilitarization of the Egyptian cabinet*, in *IJMES*, xiv [1982], 209). More than 80% of the posts of provincial governors belonged to them. Of the five categories "allied to the régime"—workers, peasants, intellectuals, nationalist capitalists and army—only the latter was authorised to organise itself, whereas the political parties were abolished on 16 January 1953 and replaced by a single party. After the defeat of 1967 and until the expulsion of the Soviet advisers in July 1972, a policy of raising the standard of recruitment and of strategic co-operation with the USSR made the institution the best endowed financially and the most advanced in technological terms in the country (with the acquisition of the Mig-27), barely troubled by internal conspiracies in October 1972, April 1974 (attempted uprising at the Military Academy by the radical Islamist movement *al-Takfīr wa ʾl-Hidj̲ra* [*q.v.*] and October 1981 (assassination of Sādāt during a military parade).

According to the National Charter (*al-Mīt̲h̲āḳ al-waṭanī*) of 1962, the Egyptian military régime presented itself initially as revolutionary. It initiated economic and social reforms—the first agrarian reforms in September 1952 limiting property to 300 acres per family, Egyptianisation of British and French assets (nationalisation of the Suez Canal, 26 July 1956), nationalisation of heavy industry and textiles—and launched major works of infrastructure such as the Aswan Dam. However, the failures of economic policies combined with demographic growth of more than 3.5% per annum, and costly military defeats in Yemen and in the war of June 1967, impelled military leaders, in the second half of the decade of the 1970s, towards a liberalisation that opened the way for substantial investment by the military institution and by senior officers individually in the private sector. While the army was less visible on the political plane, its armaments enterprises such as the Arab Organisation for Industrialisation (*al-Hayʾa al-ʿArabiyya li ʾl-Taṣnīʿ*), founded in 1975 as a joint venture with Saudi Arabia, Qatar and the United Arab Emirates, and becoming exclusively Egyptian after the Camp David Accords with Israel (1978), exported more than a billion dollars worth of arms per year in the 1980s. Under the cover of ensuring security of food supplies (*al-amn al-g̲h̲idh̲āʾī*), the army also penetrated the civilian production sector, where it benefited from exemptions and privileges (Sadowski 1993).

The perpetuation of *niẓām ʿaskarī* went in tandem with a progressive sidelining of members of the Revolutionary Command Council by Nāṣir, who cultivated the image of a populist leader with no time for intermediary institutions and procedures. It was accentuated by Sādāt to the benefit of the Arab Socialist Union (*al-Ittiḥād al-ʿarabī al-is̲h̲tirākī*), the single party from 1961 to 1977, to which military personnel were not permitted to belong (J. Waterbury, *The Egypt of Nasser and Sadat: the political economy of two regimes*, Princeton 1983). It was accelerated following the adoption of the Constitution of 11 September 1971 authorising multi-partyism, while, in the context of the peace process with Israel, from October 1975 to March 1979 (the Washington Treaty), the army benefited by military assistance from the United States worth 1.3 billion dollars per year. In principle, the army did not control the political parties, legalised from June 1977 onwards. In practice, it drew inspiration from the Turkish model, constituting itself as informal guardian of the state and master of society, leading police operations at the time of the hunger riots in January 1977, and the uprising of the Interior Security Forces in 1986. From the 1990s onward, the Egyptian *niẓām ʿaskarī* became a security régime whose principal enemy was the Islamist movement and its extremist groups, both of these violently repressed.

(b) *Syria*

The developments of political life in the part of the Ottoman Bilād al-S̲h̲ām, which became Syria under French Mandate on 28 April 1920, hardly predisposed this country to a military régime. The civil, economic and religious élites were firmly based there and were dynamic, whilst the army numbered fewer than 5,000 men at Independence, recruited among the ethnic and religious minorities, and staffed by French officers (N. Bou-Nacklie, *The Special Troops: religious and ethnic recruitment, 1916-1946*, in *IJMES*, xxv [1993], 649-60). However, thirteen coups d'état followed the independence of the country and, after the seizure of power by Colonel Ḥusnī al-Zaʿīm [*q.v.*] on 30 March 1949, the army remained a dominant political actor, except during the period of the United Arab Republic (1 February 1958-28 September 1961).

The first three military régimes in Syria were the result of an *inḳilāb*, an uprising of officers discontented with the political direction of the country, in particular the treatment reserved for the armed forces and the circumstances of the defeat in Palestine. The Colonels Ḥusnī al-Zaʿīm, Sāmī al-Hinnāwī (14 August-19 December 1949) and Adīb al-S̲h̲īs̲h̲aklī (exiled 25 February 1954) were motivated more by personal ambition than by a political project. Like Zaʿīm, S̲h̲īs̲h̲aklī launched important constitutional reforms (5 September 1950 and 10 July 1953), including the reform of penal, civil and commercial codes as well as a first agrarian reform (30 July 1952). He granted the right to vote to literate women, and abolished the special treatment of Bedouin and the system of *awḳāf* [see WAKF]. The accession of Zaʿīm to the presidency of the Republic on 25 June 1949, and that of Shīshaklī on 10 July 1953, marked the apogee of authoritarian régimes characterised by the banning of political parties (replaced by Shīshaklī with the *ḍarakat al-taḥrīr al-ʿarabī* on 25 August 1952), censorship of the press and tight control of public life by an oppressive police force. The *niẓām ʿaskarī* was characterised also by a Syrian patriotism bordering on chauvinism in reaction to the "struggle for Syria"—real or imagined threats posed to the independence of the country by neighbouring states.

Returning to the shadows, the Syrian army nevertheless did not cease from intervention in the political arena during the parliamentary period of 1954-8. Fourteen senior officers made their way to Cairo on 12 January 1958 to demand from Marshal ʿAmr and from Nāṣir the creation of the United Arab Republic. The army subsequently gave its support to the parliamentary restoration of September 1961, implemented under the leadership of Colonel ʿAbd al-Karīm Naṣlawī, who intervened again to "rectify" the policy directions of the government in March 1962 (M. Colombe, *La République arabe syrienne à la lumière du coup d'état du 28 mars 1962*, in *Orient*, 1st trim. [1962]).

The type of *niẓām ʿaskarī* which came into effect following the coup of Colonel Ziyād Ḥararī on 8 March 1963 was simultaneously both specific to Syria and also evolutionary. Between 1963 and 1970 it was possible to speak of an army-party symbiosis (I. Rabinovich, *Syria under the Baʿth 1963-66: the army-party symbiosis*, Jerusalem 1972). It was not only a military Committee of between four and fourteen members set up in Cairo *ca.* 1959 (*al-ladjna al-ʿaskariyya*; see M. al-Razzāz, *al-Tadjriba al-murra*, Beirut 1967, 88) which played a clandestine role throughout this period, but in the Regional Command (*al-ḳiyāda al-ḳuṭriyya*), senior officers constituted 34.5% of members from September 1963 to February 1966, then 25% until November 1970 (H. Batatu, *Syria's peasantry, the descendants of its lesser rural notables, and their politics*, Princeton 1999, 165, 167). In this group, with its majority consisting of natives of the peripheral regions of the country, the revolutionary tendency and the representation of minority communities gradually gained the upper hand, ending with the installation of a clandestine dictatorship under Colonel Ṣalāḥ Djadīd, assistant general secretary of the Baʿth Party from the time of the disbandment of the civil wing of the Party on 23 February 1966. Nationalisations in industry and commerce (1965), international isolation and provocations on the Israeli front, favouring popular war, characterised revolutionary Syria under this régime weakened by the disaster of the war of June 1967.

Excluding his rivals by a display of force within the Regional Command of the Baʿth Party on 13 November 1970, General Ḥāfiẓ al-Asad turned the Syrian military régime in the direction of a more liberal economy through two *infitāḥs*, in 1971-4 and then from 1986 onwards. The legislative elections of 1990, and Law 10 of 1991 on investments, marked the entry of a new entrepreneurial bourgeoisie into the coalition of power and the increased participation of senior officers in the world of business. But this economic liberalisation was not accompanied by political liberation, despite the creation of a Progressive National Front of six parties, including the Communist Party and the Arab Socialist Union around the Baʿth (7 March 1972). The Constitution of 12 March 1973 installed a presidential régime. The state of emergency declared in 1963 remained in force. The army has maintained tight control of local life and internal security through its networks of *mukhābarāt*, and in 1978-81 there was a massive crackdown on Islamists (H.G. Lobmeyer, *Opposition und Widerstand in Syrien*, Hamburg 1995, 204-336). Finally, to succeed his father as Head of State on 17 July 2000, Bashshār al-Asad was obliged to re-invent himself in some haste as a military figure.

(c) *ʿIrāḳ*

The modern ʿIrāḳī state, where the élites surrounding King Fayṣal (Djaʿfar al-ʿAskarī, Yāsīn al-Hāshimī, Djamīl al-Midfaʿī and Nūrī al-Saʿīd) were in the main former officers of the Ottoman army, was born in the violent suppression of the anti-British uprising in November 1920 (P.-J. Luizard, *La formation d'Irak contemporain*, Paris 1991). Even though ʿIrāḳ [*q.v.*] has not lived continuously under *niẓām ʿaskarī*, the army has remained the primary political force in the country, appointing and deposing governments, and controlling ethnic and social groups through violence (H. Batatu, *The old social classes and the revolutionary movements of Iraq*, Princeton 1978, 319-61). The suppression of the Assyrian revolt in June 1933, then that of the tribal uprisings in 1935-6 under the command of General Bakr Ṣidḳī gave the latter the incentive to launch the first coup d'état inspired by Kemālism of the modern Arab world on 29 October 1936. His assassination on 11 August 1937 at the instigation of four nationalist officers ("the Gold Square"), led by Ṣalāḥ al-Dīn Ṣabbāgh, was the prelude to the seizure of power by them and the inauguration of a régime independent of the British, of which the public figurehead was Rashīd ʿAlī al-Ghaylānī (5 April-9 October 1941). From the creation of the state until the fall of the monarchy on 14 July 1958, the dominant personality of authority remained that of General Nūrī al-Saʿīd who had been prime minister for a total of 11 years and 9 months. While the monarchy neglected the institutionalisation of the state and the development of the country, governments supported by the army maintained order through repression.

After the revolution of July 1958 and the fall of the monarchy, General ʿAbd al-Karīm Ḳāsim [*q.v.*] quickly ousted the nine members of the Commanding Council of Free Officers, in particular Colonel ʿAbd al-Salām ʿĀrif, to impose himself as single leader (*al-zaʿīm* [*q.v.*] *al-awḥad*). His first government (27 July 1958) comprised five military figures out of sixteen members (Batatu 1978, 812) and the second (10 February 1959), six out of fourteen (Batatu 1978, 843). He authorised political parties, promulgated agrarian reforms (30 September 1958), inaugurated a state planification scheme (1959), partially nationalised the Iraq Petroleum Company (1961) and adopted measures to assist the disadvantaged urban classes. The régime of Ḳāsim was destabilised and its military character reinforced by confrontations between Communist and Nationalist Arabs in Mawṣil and Kirkūk (March-July 1959) and by the revival of the Kurdish revolt (September 1961). The military coup of 8 February 1963 perpetrated by Nāṣirist and Baʿthist officers led to a repetition of the same scenario: ʿAbd al-Salām ʿĀrif ousted the National Council of the Revolution and dismantled the Baʿthist National Guard to take for himself presidency of the Republic and supreme command of the armed forces (18 November 1963). He imposed the Arab Socialist Union as the sole party on 14 July 1964. Under the régime of his brother, Colonel ʿAbd al-Raḥmān ʿĀrif (13 April 1966-17 July 1968) a series of military governments ensued, their domination dependent on the use of force and the maintenance of martial law, while nationalised institutions were placed under the supervision of retired officers (M. Khadduri, *Republican Iraq: a study in Iraqi politics since the revolution of 1958*, London 1969, 280-9).

After the two coups which ensured the accession of the Baʿth Party to power (17 and 30 July 1968), the Revolutionary Command Council (R.C.C.), composed of five officers and led by General Ḥasan al-Bakr, carried out purges in the army to turn it into a *djaysh al-ʿaḳāʾidī*, an instrument of the Party alongside the militia, *djaysh al-shaʿb*, under the direction of the Military Bureau. The admission of ten civilians to the R.C.C. in November 1969 did nothing to alleviate the security-orientated character of the régime, which became a dictatorship after the accession of the (self-proclaimed) "General" Ṣaddām Ḥusayn, to the presidency of the R.C.C. and supreme authority over the state and the armed forces in July 1979. The state of civil war against the Kurds and the Shīʿīs, and external war against Iran (1980-88) and then against Ḳuwayt and the international coalition (1990-1), favoured a privatisation of public wealth which worked in particular to the benefit of military cadres (Isam al-Khafaji, *War as a vehicle for the rise and demise of a state-controlled society. The case of Baʿthist Iraq*, in Heydemann 2000, 272-5).

(d) *Sudan*

The "Free Officers" of Sudan [*q.v.*] who organised the overthrow of civil power two years after the independence of the country (1958) were strongly influenced by their Egyptian alter ego. The junta led by General Ibrāhīm ʿAbbūd until 1964 included radical officers close to the Sudanese Communist Party; in 1964 the rift between ʿAbbūd and this powerful ally brought to an end the first Sudanese *niẓām ʿaskarī*. After half a decade of civilian government, General Djaʿfār al-Numayrī in his turn imposed fifteen years of military dictatorship after a brief attempt at co-operating with civilians in the context of the Commanding Council of the Revolution, dissolved in October 1971. The Communist opposition was firmly suppressed on 22 July 1971 and the Arab Socialist Union became the sole authorised party, while the ministries of Defense, the Interior, Foreign Affairs, Information and Culture (*al-Irshād al-waṭanī*) remained in the hands of the military. Numayrī's régime formally recognised the right of the southern provinces to autonomy on 9 June 1969 and imposed radical nationalisation measures (Sequestration Act, May 1970). The second Sudanese civil war, provoked by the Islamising decrees of September 1983, accelerated the downfall of Numayrī in 1985, introducing a brief period of pluralism. The coalition between military figures and Islamists which characterised military régimes in Sudan returned to power following the coup d'état of General ʿUmar al-Bashīr on 30 June 1989. The National Salvation Revolutionary Command Council was based on a single party, the National Congress of Ḥasan al-Turābī. He imposed strict application of the *Sharīʿa*, banned parties and independent syndicates, organised popular local Islamist committees, and the Popular Defense Forces, an Islamist militia waging war against civilians in the south. Under pressure from humanitarian organisations and oil companies whose revenues were financing the war in the south, military leaders distanced themselves from the Islamists from 1997 onward. Bashīr re-established the state of emergency in 1998 to implement the institutional changes demanded for the survival of the régime and, on 12 December 1999, he suspended the parliament which was dominated by the Islamists of Turābī, arrested in February 2001.

(e) *Yemen*

The influence of the Egyptian Free Officers was felt as far away as Yemen [see AL-YAMAN] where a group of Nāṣirist officers led by Colonel ʿAbd Allāh Sallāl proclaimed the United Arab Republic on 26 September 1962 and received reinforcements of 26,000 Egyptian soldiers commanded by Marshal ʿAbd al-Ḥakīm ʿAmr—a contingent doubled over the next four years for the purpose of fighting a destructive Saudi-Egyptian war which lasted until the decision to withdraw, taken by Nāṣir at the Kharṭūm Summit in November 1967. Significant efforts in the fields of education and health were made by the new régime, which was characterised by the imposition of a heavy bureaucracy before its demise on 14 June 1970.

Military leaders, populists and developmentalists returned to the forefront of the stage with Colonel Ibrāhīm al-Ṣamadī (June 1974), and Colonel Aḥmad al-Ghāshimī (11 October 1977), both of them assassinated, then Colonel ʿAlī ʿAbd Allāh Khalīl, on 24 June 1978. The latter gradually handed over government to civilians (adoption of a constitution in October 1980, first legislative elections in July 1985) and guided the process of reunification with the Democratic and Popular Republic of Yemen: a constitutional reform in September 1994 legalising political pluralism, exclusion of armed forces from membership of parties (F. Djallūl, *Al-Yaman: al-thawratān al-djumhūriyatān, al-waḥda, 1962-94*, Beirut 1999, 272-97). As Marshal and President of the Republic of Yemen since 24 May 1990, Khalīl continues to control the state, supported by the Supreme Council of National Defense and by members of his entourage, occupying key posts in the security and armed forces.

Bibliography: A. Abdel Malek, *Egypte, société militaire*, Paris 1962; M. Halpern, *Middle Eastern armies and the new middle class*, Princeton 1962; G. Haddad, *Revolutions and military rule in the Middle East*, New York 1965; B. Vernier, *Armée et politique au Moyen-Orient*, Paris 1966; J.P. Vatikiotis, *Politics and the military in Jordan*, London 1967; E. Beeri, *Army officers in Arab politics and society*, New York 1970; A. Perlmutter, *Egypt: the praetorian state*, Brunswick 1974; M. Tarbush, *The role of the military in politics: a case study of Iraq to 1941*, London and Boston 1982; J.C. Hurewitz, *Middle East politics: the military dimension*, Boulder 1982; Kh.A. Ibrāhīm, *al-Djaysh wa 'l-mudjtamaʿ: dirāsāt fī ʿilm al-idjtimāʿ al-ʿaskarī*, Cairo 1985; J. Stork, *Arms industries in the Middle East*, in *MERIP Report*, cxliv (1987); Z. Ramzī (ed.), *al-Siyāsāt al-tashīḥiyya wa 'l-tanmiya fī 'l-waṭan al-ʿarabī: buḥūth wa-munāḳashāt nadwa ʿuḳidat bi 'l-Ḳuwayt fī 'l-fatra 20-22 fabrāʾīr 1988*, Beirut 1989; E. Picard, *Arab military in politics: from revolutionary plot to authoritarian state*, in G. Luciani, *The Arab state*, London 1990; A. Huwaydī, *al-ʿAskara wa 'l-amn fī 'l-sharḳ al-awsaṭ: taʾthīruhumā ʿalā 'l-tanmiya wa 'l-dīmūḳrāṭiya*, Cairo 1991; M. Barnett, *Confronting the costs of war, military power, state, and society in Egypt and Israel*, Princeton 1992; Y. Ṣāyigh, *Arab military industry: capability, performance and impact*, London and Washington 1992; Y.M. Sadowski, *Scuds or butter? The political economy of arms control in the Middle East*, Washington 1993; B. Korany, P. Noble and R. Brynen (eds.), *The many faces of national security in the Arab world*, London 1993; N. Van Dam, *The struggle for power in Syria: politics and society under Asad and the Baʿth party*, London 1996; R. Brooks, *Political-military relations and the stability of Arab regimes*, London 1998; S. Heydemann (ed.), *War, institutions, and social change in the Middle East*, Berkeley 2000. (ELIZABETH PICARD)

2. In modern Iran.

The period of military rule in Iran may be said to have been inaugurated by the coup d'état of 21 February 1921, and to have endured until the overthrow of Pahlavi rule in 1979. However, although the régime that resulted from the coup of 1921, and the Pahlavi state itself, was based on the army, there was no direct military rule, nor was there a military dictatorship in the straightforward sense.

The Pahlavi régime was one that owed its existence to military coups, in 1921 and in 1953, both Riḍā S̲h̲āh and his son, Muḥammad Riḍā S̲h̲āh [*q.vv.*], having been brought to power by the army. The army played a key role in the construction of the Pahlavi state, dominating both urban and rural opposition, and till 1979 remained, together with the various security forces, the main institution sustaining the régime internally.

Although the military occupied a pivotal position in Pahlavi Iran, it remained subordinate to the rule of the shahs. Both Riḍā S̲h̲āh and Muḥammad Riḍā S̲h̲āh were successful in dominating the military and in developing a monarchical system of government quite different from that found in conventional military régimes. Riḍā S̲h̲āh originally rose to power as an army officer, but in transforming his personal ascendancy into the form of a monarchy he distanced himself from other senior commanders and made a challenge from any one of them more difficult. Riḍā S̲h̲āh having established the dynasty, his son succeeded him and increased further the distance between the military and the throne, making it difficult for any army officer to challenge his authority without undermining the very structure of the régime (F. Halliday, *Iran, dictatorship and development*, London 1979, 51-2). Yet although both Pahlavi rulers secured and maintained their theoretical and actual control of the army, each also essentially relied on it to guarantee their régime.

In 1921 Riḍā S̲h̲āh arrived at the centre of political power using as an instrument a small Cossack force. He immediately embarked on the task of constructing a strong, modern, national army, organised and equipped on European lines, and based his rise to supremacy on the support of this army (Bāḳir Aḳalli, *Riḍā S̲h̲āh wa Ḳūs̲h̲ūn-i muttaḥid-i S̲h̲akl, 1300-1320*, Tehran 1377). He reorganised the system of military education inside Iran and began sending officers to France for training. He began a massive programme of arms purchases in Europe, including large numbers of tanks and aircraft. In 1925 he forced a conscription bill through the Mad̲j̲lis and the army mushroomed, rising from 42,000 men in 1930 to 127,000 men in 1941, with a total mobilisable force of 400,000. In the early 1920s, the army already accounted for approximately 40% of budget expenditure; between 1930 and 1941 spending on the army nearly quadrupled, and massive sums from oil revenues were allocated directly for weapons purchases.

Riḍā S̲h̲āh used this army to form a centralised state in Iran for the first time in the modern period. However, in the years 1921-5, although the army became dominant, it co-existed with a number of other political players and institutions. The cabinet was largely civilian in character, the constitution, although increasingly disregarded in practice, was not suspended, political parties functioned, elections were held, the Mad̲j̲lis passed legislation, and the Ḳād̲j̲ār shah remained nominally commander-in-chief of the army.

Although the military did not rule directly in the early Pahlavi period, Riḍā S̲h̲āh used the army both to intervene directly in the political process and also to manipulate, in a more subtle way, the political life of the country. His direct intervention began, of course, with the coup d'état itself, and continued with episodes such as the repeated cowing of the Mad̲j̲lis by the threat of armed force, in 1922 and, more seriously, after the failure of the republican movement in 1924. As well as openly intimidating the Mad̲j̲lis at certain key moments, the military, with its increasing control over elections, had by 1926 fatally compromised the independence of that body. The army also sponsored and orchestrated political movements and prepared the ground for constitutional change. Furthermore, Riḍā S̲h̲āh, having come to dominate the cabinet, reducing it largely to an appendage to his own position, systematically promoted the military at the expense of the civil authorities throughout the country. In fact, the army came to dominate the civil authorities throughout Iran, sometimes via the establishment of formal military government, sometimes through informal and unregulated mechanisms of pressure and control. Each military conquest of a recalcitrant area or population was invariably accompanied by the establishment of military government and there was considerable pressure from within the army to ensure that control, once established, remained in its own hands. Military government was especially important as a tool of tribal subjugation and control, army officers regularly replacing deposed tribal chiefs. Even when a provincial civil régime was officially in existence, the local military authorities encroached upon its sphere, appropriating its authority and many of its functions. The declaration of martial law and the establishment of military government was a frequent occurrence in both the capital and the provinces and gave the military authorities an opportunity to tighten their control over all aspects of civilian life, especially political dissent. The two periods of martial law in the capital, 1921-2 and 1924-6, were crucial to Riḍā S̲h̲āh's rise to supreme power. The role of the army was also positively enhanced by its transformation into a focus of nationalism and a pioneer of social progress, military personnel leading the way in clothing reform, the abolition of titles, rudimentary town planning, linguistic reform, etc. (Stephanie Cronin, *The army and the creation of the Pahlavi state in Iran, 1910-1926*, London and New York 1997, 182-221).

In the early Pahlavi period, the new Iranian army, although of questionable conventional military capability, was extremely successful in advancing the political ambitions of its chief and in safeguarding and extending his power. By far the most important function of the new army was to ensure the survival of the régime or, more narrowly interpreted, of Riḍā S̲h̲āh's personal position. This involved, first, the army's establishment of internal security throughout the country, and, second, the military authorities' enforcement of the subordination of all civilian political elements to their own dominance.

In making himself monarch, Riḍā S̲h̲āh profoundly altered the balance between the military and the centre of power. However, by 1926 the relationship between state and society in Iran had already been radically transformed, with the new, centralised army playing a crucial role. Furthermore the weight of the army vis-à-vis civil state institutions, the government, the Mad̲j̲lis, provincial civil governors, etc. had increased in a dramatic and wholly novel way. Although in becoming S̲h̲āh, Riḍā K̲h̲ān transformed what had been an incipient military dictatorship into a dynastic despotism, nonetheless the régime over which he presided was firmly marked by its military origins and continued to exhibit many features typical of military rule. Although institutions such as the Madjlis and a civilian government would continue to exist, their role was, after 1926, purely decorative and ornamental. Independent political activity would not resume until after the abdication of the Shāh in 1941.

Riḍā Shāh had risen to power as a career officer and he remained, even after ascending the throne, deeply involved in the day-to-day running of the army. His son, however, although he had attended Tehran military academy and frequently appeared on official occasions in military uniform, in reality lacked the connection with the army and with the upper echelons of the officer corps that his father had possessed.

In the 1940s the new Shāh, checked by a variety of social and political forces, was not able to utilise the army as his father had done. Between 1941 and 1953 the army receded into the background, reemerging only after the coup which overthrew Muṣaddiḳ [*q.v.*]. Immediately after the coup, the Shāh placed its leaders in key positions, General Faḍl Allāh Zāhidī became prime minister, General Taymūr Bakhtiyār military governor of Tehran and General ʿAbd Allāh Hidāyat chief of the general staff. But, most importantly, the Shāh also began to work towards restoring monarchical control of the army, and in 1955 dismissed Zāhidī, who left the country. The Shāh then began the serious rebuilding of the army while, at the same time, with the reorganisation and reinforcement of the gendarmerie and the police, the army's overt role in maintaining public order was reduced (M.J. Sheikh-ol-Islami, in *EIr*, art. *Army*. V. *Pahlavi period*, at ii, 510). From 1963 to 1978, the army remained garrisoned near towns and was sent into tribal areas on a number of small-scale campaigns. But the régime only resorted once to military force to crush urban civil unrest, sc. in June 1963 in Tehran and a number of other towns.

Although its public order duties were reduced, during the 1960s and 1970s the army became increasingly prominent in national life through its involvement in projects initiated under the White Revolution. Many high school and college conscripts served in the Literacy Corps, the Health Corps, and the Construction and Agricultural Development Corps, with such duties as building roads, schools, improving preventive medicine and teaching rudimentary reading and writing. In addition to these activities, which were largely carried out in rural areas, the military performed a host of other functions. In the administration of justice, the military courts had authority over a wide range of offences, including treason, armed robbery, hoarding, profiteering and trafficking in narcotics. The judgements were swift and the penalties harsh (Sheikh-ol-Islami, *loc. cit.*). The army gathered political intelligence and cooperated with SAVAK, the state security agency. Indeed, many of the SAVAK senior personnel came from the army. Many army officers also served in the Imperial Inspectorate, investigating inefficiency and corruption in the civil bureaucracy.

Although Riḍā Shāh had always used the army as a bulwark of his régime, he had been equally careful to prevent either military factions, or individual senior officers, from engaging in independent political activity or developing political ambitions of their own. During the 1930s, he had harboured a particular fear or assassination, believing that, were he to die while the Crown Prince was still young, the new dynasty would be threatened either from an overt challenge from the army or covertly, through the establishment of a regency exercised by one or more of the most powerful generals (Cronin, *The politics of radicalism within the Iranian army: the Jahansuz group of 1939*, in *Iranian Studies*, xxxii/1 [1999], 5-25). Muḥammad Riḍā Shāh, like his father, also feared the consequences of the military's involvement in politics. During the 1940s, while the new shah remained weak, the army became deeply politicised, visible political factions emerged, and certain generals began to establish their own followings (Halliday, *op. cit.*, 67). After 1953, however, and particularly after 1955, the Shāh worked consistently to depoliticise the army and to isolate the most powerful senior officers.

Muḥammad Riḍā Shāh employed various mechanisms to control his officer corps. The armed forces were highly compartmentalised. The chief of staff had little authority over the other chiefs, who all reported to the Shāh directly (W. Sullivan, *Mission to Iran*, New York 1981, 74-5). Each branch was literally headed by the Shāh and without the Shāh, the armed forces as a whole were structurally immobilised. The three services were not in fact allowed to communicate except via the Shāh's own staff. No general could visit Tehran or meet with another general without the Shāh's specific permission. The Shāh was reported to check all promotions above the rank of major, and personally vetted all entrants in the air force training school. He frequently moved senior commanders to ensure that they did not form power bases and used a personal secret police, the Imperial Organisation, as well as conventional military intelligence, to carry out surveillance of the officer corps. Occasionally, he purged officers suspected of disloyalty under the guise of waging anti-corruption campaigns (Halliday, *op. cit.*, 68-9).

As the political crisis of 1978 unfolded, the Shāh again fell back on the army, employing martial law and military government in the capital and a number of provincial cities. By the autumn, a number of generals were advocating direct military intervention. However, the army did not act, the Shāh's system of personal control still paralysing the high command, and the Shāh himself apparently feared that a military coup might prove to be simply another way of terminating his reign (Sepehr Zabih, *The Iranian military in revolution and war*, London and New York 1988, 13). By early 1979, after the Shāh's departure, the army was palpably disintegrating. Ten days after Āyatallāh Khumaynī's return, the Supreme Council of the Armed Forces issued the Declaration of Neutrality of the Armed Forces concerning the conflict between Khumaynī and Dr Shāhpūr Bakhtiyār's government (Zabih, 78).

Bibliography: In addition to references given in the article, see R.E. Huyser, *Mission to Tehran*, London 1986; ʿAbbās Ḳarābāghī, *Ḥaḳāyiḳ dar bāra-i buhrān-i Īrān*, Paris n.d. (Stephanie Cronin)

3. In the late Ottoman Empire and the Turkish Republic.

Although the ruling élite in the pre-*Tanẓīmāt* Ottoman Empire was referred to as military (*ʿaskerī*), it was in fact composed of both civilian and military elements. In the classical Ottoman Empire, this élite had three major branches: the *seyfiyye* (men of the sword), the *ʿilmiyye* [*q.v.*] (i.e. the *ʿulamāʾ*) and the *ḳalemiyye*, later referred to as *mülkiyye* (men of the pen, bureaucrats). In their explanations based on the idea of "circle of justice", the political thinkers of the classical Ottoman state likewise underscored the importance of statesmen and men of the sword, attributing the utmost importance to these two categories for the survival of the state (ʿAlī Ḳinalīzāde, *Akhlāḳ-i ʿAlāʾī*, iii, Būlāḳ 1833, 49; Naʿīmā, *Tārīkh*, Istanbul 1281/1866 i, 40). Despite the existence of these distinct categories within the ruling élite, and the various special rights of the military class (e.g. the *Yeñičeri Aghasi* and the Grand Admiral could judge certain cases between Janissaries or members of the Arsenal and could pronounce verdicts, see *Tewḳīʿī ʿAbd ul-Raḥmān Pasha ḳānūnnāmesi*, in *ʿOthmānlī ḳānūnnāmeleri*, in *Millī Tetebbuʿlar Medjmūʿasi*, i/3 [1915], 524-5, 536-7), the boundaries between these two branches were somewhat fluid, more than so in a modern state.

For example, many Grand Admirals later became Grand Viziers (in 1037/1628 the *Yeñičeri Aghasi* Khosrew Pasha became Grand Vizier); local governors enjoyed decision-making authority on military matters in their domains; and duties such as law enforcement and fire fighting were generally viewed as the military's responsibility (in Istanbul, Janissaries carried out these duties). Since the military played the most important role in succession and dethronement, it is difficult to speak of a civilian administration free of military intervention in the pre-reform Ottoman Empire. Nevertheless, while the power of the military fluctuated over this long period, it was always at the centre of policy and decision-making.

Late 18th and early 19th century Ottoman attempts at modernisation and Westernisation [see NIẒĀM-Ï DJEDĪD] had two important effects on the role of the military. First, since the reforms aimed at imitating superior Western military organisation and techniques, the Ottoman military was the first institution to be thus affected, and the process confirmed its clear superiority in relation to the other branches of the ruling class. Second, the eventual reorganisation of the entire state bureaucracy transformed the three branches of the old administration into more distinct entities. The destruction of the Janissaries in 1826 and their replacement with *Niẓāmiyye* troops resulted in the establishment of the *Bāb-i Serʿaskerī* (Office of the Commander of the Land Forces). The *Serʿasker* became the commander of all Ottoman land troops, and the old Ottoman practice of despatching the Grand Vizier to campaign with the title *Serdār-i Ekrem* was abandoned. In 1836 a *Dār-i Shūrā-yi ʿAskerī* (Military Council), similar to the *Dār-i Shūrā-yi Bāb-i ʿĀlī*, was charged with oversight of the military affairs of the empire. Other than a *muftī* and a representative of the *mülkiyye*, all members of this body were officers. Although the new military establishment initially inherited the Janissaries' duty of law enforcement in the capital, this was transferred to the *Ḍabṭiyye Neẓāreti* (Police Ministry) when it was established in 1845. In the state bureaucracy the title *Serʿasker* became the highest military rank, being on the same level as the Grand Vizier and the *Sheykh ül-Islām*. In 1843 the army was reorganised on the model of the French and Prussian armies. Commanders of the armies were now appointed by the *Serʿasker* and responsible to him. With the increasing distinction between the various branches of the Ottoman administration, the division of power between the military and civilian elements came to be formally regulated. The most important document showing the clear separation of military establishment from other branches of the state was the *Idāre-i ʿÖrfiyye Ḳarārnāmesi* (Martial Law Regulations) enacted by imperial decree on 24 September 1877 (*Düstūr*, 1st Series, iv, Istanbul 1295/1878, 71-2).

The third article of these regulations clearly distinguishes between the civilian and military administrations. Even after these formal arrangements, however, the military continued to enjoy a substantial role in the civil administration by the standards of a modern state. For instance, until the end of the empire, the Minister of War and the Minister of the Navy, who were both officers, and until 1908 the *Ṭopkhāne Müshīri* (Marshal of the Imperial Arsenal of Ordinance), served as members of the *Heyʾet-i Wükelāʾ* (Council of Ministers), and participated directly in decision-making on non-military matters. Although there were exceptions, it remained a common practice until the end of the empire to appoint a military commander to a remote province or sub-province, such as ʿAsīr or North African Tripoli, in the dual role of governor and commander. As in earlier times, during this late period many military figures, such as Aḥmed Djawād Pasha, Maḥmūd Shewkat Pasha Ghāzī Aḥmed Mukhtār Pasha and Aḥmed ʿIzzet Pasha [*q.vv.*], served as Grand Vizier.

During the pre-*Tanẓīmāt* era, the military element also played the leading role in major political events, often leading to drastic changes in the political shape of the empire. Thus the military element played a very important role in the deposition of ʿAbd ül-ʿAzīz in 1876. The 1908 revolution was initiated by a para-military committee, the Committee of Union and Progress [see ITTIḤĀD WE TERAḲḲĪ DJEMʿIYYETI] and various army units in Macedonia. The 1909 counter-revolution [see ITTIḤĀD-I MUḤAMMEDĪ DJEMʿIYYETI] was carried out by troops led by *alaylï*s (officers who had not attended military colleges); the military rebellion led by the Khalāṣkārān Ḍābiṭān ("Saviour Officers") in Macedonia and Albania in 1912 paved the way for the forming of the first government opposing the Committee of Union and Progress Committee since 1908. Finally, the Committee regained power in January 1913 through the Sublime Porte Raid led by Enwer Bey (Pasha) and other military leaders who were members of it.

Although ʿAbd ül-Ḥamīd II had kept the military establishment under strict control until the Young Turk Revolution of 1908, from this date onwards the military gained ground in the administration of the empire, though most of its power did not stem from legal adjustments but rather from the fact that many important figures within the Committee were officers. With the establishment of the authoritarian rule of the Committee in June 1913, the military share in the administration of the empire increased further, despite a temporary law of 11 October 1912 barring officers from participating in any political activity (*Düstūr*, 2nd Series, iv, 650-1). (Another temporary law, issued on the same day, disqualified military personnel from voting (*ibid.*, 651-2); because of this, Ottoman and, later, Turkish officers did not vote in elections until 1961.) A para-military intelligence service called the Special Organisation acted under the command of Enwer Pasha, reporting directly to him and working almost independently of the civilian administration. Yet despite the growing military grip on the administration, and despite the fact that martial law was in effect in the Ottoman capital during most of the decade from 1908 to 1918, no fully military régime was ever established in the Ottoman Empire.

The Ottoman military establishment led the Turkish resistance against the peace terms imposed upon the Ottoman government, and organised the armed struggle against the invasion of the Turkish heartland. Many leaders of the *Anadolu we Rūmeli Müdāfaʿa-i Ḥuḳūḳ Djemʿiyyeti*, and later of the Ankara government, were military figures including Muṣṭafā Kemāl (Atatürk [*q.v.*]). The latter led the armies and the Turkish (Grand) National Assembly while he was the speaker of this assembly, controlling all three branches of power. Despite this fact, the movement never turned into a fully military one.

Following the success of the Turkish War of Independence in 1922 and the establishment of the Turkish Republic in 1923, Muṣṭafā Kemāl instituted one of the most important principles of the new régime, according to which the army should play no part in politics. A law of 29 December 1923 required all army officers to resign from active duty if they wished to run for parliament. A law of 3 March 1924, abolished the Ministry of War and established the Office of the Commander-in-Chief, attached to the Ministry of Defence. Under the command of Marshal Fewzī Čaḳmaḳ [see ÇAKMAK, MUSTAFA FEVZI], who held the position from 1921 to 1944, the Turkish army remained loyal to the new republican régime, many founders of which were former military leaders, and to its principles. Even after Çakmak's retirement, the military did not show any interest in politics until the end of the single-party system in 1946. The first free elections in 1950 and the victory of the opposition caused many military leaders to rethink their role in Turkish politics and to reassess the loyalty of the political leaders to the tenets of the republican régime. Increasing political tension, clashes between law enforcement personnel and college students, and the Democrat Party government's strong measures against the opposition prompted a group of officers to form a revolutionary organisation and initiate a coup on 27 May 1960. This coup was not staged within the chain of command. In fact, the Commander-in-Chief and many high-ranking officers who had remained loyal to the Democrat Party government were arrested and expelled from the army. In a similar fashion, the Chamber of Deputies was dissolved, and the president, prime minister, cabinet members and leading figures of the Democrat Party were arrested and later tried by a special court. The leaders of the coup based their action on the 34th article of the Armed Forces Regulations, which charges the military with "defending and protecting the Turkish Republic and Turkish homeland". A special committee of law professors issued a document the day after the coup legitimising the revolutionary officers' action. Under the direction of General Cemal Gürsel, the Commander of the Land Forces and the highest-ranking officer to join the revolutionaries, an executive committee of thirty-six officers of various ranks, named the National Union Committee, was formed and assumed the power of issuing laws on 12 June 1960. Despite the formation of a government composed of civil and military leaders under Gürsel, the National Union Committee remained the most powerful institution in the country. On 13 November, a schism within the National Union Committee resulted in the elimination of fourteen of its members who had been promoting the idea of a prolonged military régime and more active participation in government. On 13 December, the committee issued a law for the establishment of a constitutional assembly; this would be composed of the members of the National Union Committee and of an Assembly of Representatives, members of which would be elected by various institutions, such as political parties, provincial administrations, the legal bars, and press and guild organisations. The new assembly was convened on 6 January 1961 and worked until 4 September. In the meantime, a new constitution was ratified by a referendum of 9 July. This constitution broadened individual liberties, and at the same time limited the power of the government. This was done by establishing new legal and bureaucratic bodies such as the Constitutional Court and the National Security Council, and by granting autonomy to various institutions such as the universities and the Turkish Radio administration. New elections for the Chamber of Deputies and the newly-established Senate were held on 15 October 1961, and the members of the National Union Committee became "natural" members of the Senate for life. As one of its last decisive actions, the National Union Committee discussed the death sentences pronounced by the special court against the leaders of the Democrat Party on 15 September 1961. By a vote of 13 to 9, the committee approved four death sentences out of sixteen, and three former ministers were hanged on 16 September 1961. The next day, Adnan Menderes [*q.v.*], former prime minister, was executed.

Despite the new elections and the formation of a new civilian government, the military continued to make its power felt in political life for two more years. New revolutionary organisations within the army attempted to dissolve the parliament even before its opening. Despite the agreement of right-wing parties on Ali Fuad Başgil as the next president, under heavy military pressure the deputies and senators elected the leader of the coup, Gürsel, to this post, and the military played a significant role in the formation of a new government under İsmet İnönü [*q.v.* in Suppl.]. On two occasions, 22 February 1962, and 21 May 1963, a group of officers led by Colonel Talât Aydemir attempted to stage a coup to establish a military régime. Both attempts were foiled by Prime Minister İnönü with the support of loyal forces. Following the first attempt, the leaders of the venture were only forced to retire; their second attempt led to the trial and hanging of Col. Talât Aydemir and Lt.-Col. Fethi Gürcan.

Military intervention in politics gradually receded after the second coup attempt in 1963, and normal political activity resumed. But in 1971, the military was prompted to intervene by increasing left-wing activity, and tension between the right-wing Justice Party government and civil-military bureaucratic institutions. There had been various military groups promoting the idea of the establishment of a military régime. One of these groups was also supported by renowned left-wing intellectuals, and promoted the idea of a régime of the Arab Baʿth type; it attempted a stillborn coup on 9 March 1971. Three days later, on 12 March, the military establishment presented an ultimatum to the President and the Speakers of the Chamber of Deputies and the Senate, accusing the Parliament and the government of not adhering to the Kemālist reforms, causing social and economic disorder and inviting anarchy. The military commanders threatened the Parliament and the government that they would take power unless a new Kemālist government was immediately established. Süleyman Demirel, the prime minister, tendered his resignation, and a new non-party government was established with the approval of the military. Up to the elections held on 14 October 1973, civilian governments under military control administered Turkey and made radical changes in the constitution, limiting many of the liberties granted in 1961. During this period, the major socialist party in Turkey, the Turkish Labour Party, was dissolved, along with the National

Order Party, the major Islamist one; new state courts with extraordinary powers were established, and many left-wing and Islamist politicians and activists were tried.

Following the 1973 elections, the army returned to its barracks and normal political activity resumed until 12 September 1980. However, increasing clashes between left-wing and right-wing groups, which resulted in the killing of approximately 5,000 people between 1977 and 1980, once again prompted the military to intervene. This time, a régime under a National Security Council composed of General Kenan Evren, Commander-in-Chief; three generals in command of the Land, Air and Gendarmerie forces; and the Admiral in charge of the Navy, ruled the country with the help of a government under former Admiral Bülend Ulusu, and a "House of Representatives" virtually hand-picked by the National Security Council; this continued until elections were held on 6 November 1983. In the meantime, thousands of left-wing and right-wing activists were arrested and tried, and all political parties were dissolved, their leaders being arrested or sent to military bases. A provisional article (no. 4) of the new constitution banned leaders of what had been the governing party and the major opposition party in the legislature at the time of the coup from any political activity for ten years, and deputies and senators belonging to these parties were excluded for five years. The 1982 constitution, which created a hybrid system of government involving the president and parliament and which pruned the liberties granted by the former constitution, was put into effect through a referendum. In accordance with a provisional article of the constitution, its ratification also conferred the presidency on the leader of the coup. General Kenan Evren, and made the other members of the National Security Council members of the Presidential Council for seven years. This constitution also remodelled the National Security Council by giving a 5 to 4 majority for the military members of this ten-person body under an impartial president (Article 118).

The importance of the National Security Council function in policy-making after 1983, and especially after 1996, and its role in imposing terms on a government led by the Islamist Prime Minister Necmettin Erbakan on 28 February 1997, have generally been interpreted as to mark a new period of military dominance in Turkish politics.

Bibliography: Given in the article.

(M. Şükrü Hanioğlu)

4. In Pakistan.

The pre-eminence of the Pakistani military within the country's political set-up, either through direct coups or by simply controlling the economic and external policies, has led to a growing academic debate on several inter-related issues. On the one hand, one notices an unbroken continuity of the British imperial tradition, as is evident through the recruitment, training and other organisational matters, while, simultaneously, the armed forces have taken upon themselves an extra-professional role justified in the name of national interests and ideology. Within the armed forces, it is the army, and not the navy or air force, which has frequently assumed such a flagship role. To its admirers, the army is the only stable institution that can keep the pluralistic country together, whereas to its detractors, the army is in league with secret agencies and a *de facto* state within a state. Certainly, the army is the steel frame of the country's administration, and its leadership reflects a nationwide representation whereas the lower echelons—*jawans*—are mainly recruited from the Northwestern Punjab and eastern districts of the Frontier Province (NWFP).

The Pakistani armed forces have retained the regimental character, with the gradual addition of newer and diverse corps and training facilities. The introduction of aircraft, gunships, tanks, mountain regiments, missiles and nuclear capabilities has collectively turned the Pakistani armed forces into a complex and quite a significant establishment. For decades, Pakistan's top military leadership has maintained close professional contacts with its U.S. and British counterparts, and while benefitting from huge budgetary allocations, they have established themselves as the most important politico-economic pressure group. Pakistan has been spending most of its revenues and foreign loans on the upkeep of a half-million strong military establishment, several cantonments and bases, besides a huge recurring expense on pensions, semi-private foundations and infrastructures to look after the welfare of the serving or retired officials.

Due to Pakistan's strategic and equally difficult location with a hostile neighbour separating the erstwhile two wings, and because of disputes such as that over Kashmir, her security perceptions have always centred around a "credible level and proportion of deterrence" to an Indian threat. In the 1950s and during the 1980s, the alliances with the United States led to a major inflow of military aid, which further strengthened the defence establishment. Growing intolerant of the political processes and, especially, of the criticism from the eastern wing, the generals decided to take over the country's leadership in 1958. Earlier on, their influence on national policies had been indirect; now they directly controlled the domestic and foreign policies. The first martial law led by General Ayub Khan was initially well received, but subsequently led to greater socio-ideological cleavages. A mass movement to dislodge General Khan led to the imposition of another martial law under General Yahya Khan, who promised unfettered elections in the country. However, following the split vote between East and West Pakistan in 1970, the junta refused to transfer power to the elected majority party—the Awami League of Shaikh Mujibur Rahman—and, instead unleashed a massive military operation in East Pakistan. The local insurgency, aided by India, resulted in the surrender of Pakistani troops at Dhaka in December 1971, and Bangladesh became an independent state. In the 1970s, Zulfikar Ali Bhutto, the elected Prime Minister, tried to reinvigorate the Pakistani military establishment, in addition to sponsoring Pakistan's nuclear programme. Despite his deep desire to rein in the generals, he was finally overthrown by General Zia-ul-Haq [see ziyāʾ al-ḥaḳḳ] in July 1977, who then ruled the country for the next eleven years. His death in an air crash led to the re-emergence of party-based politics, but the vital decisions were still being made by the Chief of Army Staff. The elected politicians Benazir Bhutto and Nawaz Sharif, in their own ways, tried to minimise the armed forces' interventionism, but to no avail. On 12 October 1999, Sharif was overthrown in another military coup, which brought in General Pervez Musharraf as the new Chief Executive. The new military rule stopped short of calling itself martial law, though Musharraf elevated himself to the presidency in July 2001. The relationship with India has remained very tense, and the Western countries also initially shunned the new military régime until the United States acquired vital Pakistani support and bases against Osama bin Laden and his Al-Qaeda organisation in Afghanistan.

Pakistan's army has not only ruled the country for almost three decades but it has also decided on vital policy matters. The development of the nuclear programme, support for specific groups in Afghanistan, the nature and extent of relationship with India, and active assistance for Kashmiris in their war against India, have all figured quite significantly in the recent past. The army has been engaged in the formulation and suspension of Pakistani constitutions, and has occasionally engaged itself in the formation and dissolution of numerous political alliances. Its various professional, political and other civilian roles make it the most crucial actor in the running of the country, whilst the security agencies such as the Military Intelligence (MI) and the Inter-Services Intelligence (ISI) implement such policies. The senior officials make up an élite class in which ethnic loyalties are considered unimportant. General Musharraf would like to revert to the old modernist postulation of the Ayub Khan-Yahya Khan era, i.e. away from Zia's Islamisation, but, given the conservative nature of khaki bureaucracy, the army may never undertake such radical steps. The relationship with India; the fragile nature of the country's economy, with defence accounting for a huge expenditure; the role in creating or denting political processes; and the extra-professionalism required, especially since the fall of Dhaka, are some of the main areas of debate and contestation amongst the supporters and the critics of the military élite. The army, through its information efforts, has been able to convince many Pakistanis in the upper Indus region of its own invincibility and its professional credentials, whereas lower Pakistan remains highly critical of the military's dictatorial role.

Bibliography: P.I. Cheema, *Pakistan's defence policy, 1947-58*, London 1958; H. Gardezi and J. Rashid (eds.), *Pakistan: the roots of dictatorship*, London 1983; M. Asghar Khan (ed.), *Islam, politics and the state: The Pakistan experience*, London 1983; C. Clapham and G. Philip (eds.), *The political dilemmas of the military regimes*, London 1985; Emma Duncan, *Breaking the curfew. A political journey through Pakistan*, London 1989; Ayesha Jalal, *The state of martial rule in Pakistan. The origins of Pakistan's political economy of defence*, Cambridge 1990; R. Sisson and L.E. Rose, *War and secession. Pakistan, India, and the creation of Bangladesh*, Berkeley and Los Angeles 1990; Altaf Gauhar, *Ayub Khan: Pakistan's first military ruler*, Lahore 1993; S. Cohen, *The Pakistan army*, Karachi 1994; Hasan-Askari Rizvi, *The military and politics in Pakistan*, Lahore 1995; I.H. Malik, *State and civil society in Pakistan. Politics of authority, ideology and ethnicity*, Oxford 1997; B. Cloughley, *A history of the Pakistani army: wars and insurrections*, Karachi 1999.

(Iftikhar H. Malik)

al-NUBĀHĪ (or, more probably, **al-BUNNĀHĪ**, see M. Bencherifa, *al-Bunnāhī lā al-Nubāhī*, in *Académia. Revue de l'Académie du Royaume du Maroc*, xiii [1998], 71-89), Abu 'l-Ḥasan ʿAlī b. ʿAbd Allāh al-Dju̲dh̲amī, equally known as Ibn al-Ḥasan, Andalusī jurist, *adīb* and historian of the period of the Naṣrids [*q.v.*], born at Malaga in 713/1313 and died, probably at Granada, after 798/1389-90.

He was *ḳāḍī al-d̲jamāʿa* [*q.v.*] during almost the whole reign of the Naṣrid sultan Muḥammad V. His name often appears linked with that of Lisān al-Dīn Ibn al-K̲h̲aṭīb [*q.v.*], with whom he had a relationship that passed from friendship and collaboration to emnity. This is why Ibn al-K̲h̲aṭīb presents an image of al-Bunnāhī in his later works (*Aʿmāl al-aʿlām*, ed. Lévi-Provençal, Beirut 1956, 78-80; *al-Katība al-kāmina*, ed. Iḥsān ʿAbbās, 146) completely opposite to what he had given in the biography consecrated to him in *Iḥāṭa*, iv, 88-100. Ibn al-K̲h̲aṭīb wrote, moreover, two opuscula bringing together anecdotes in which the personality of the *ḳāḍī* Ibn al-Ḥasan is presented as one of ridicule, the *Tanbīh al-sāhī ʿalā ṭuraf al-Bunnāhī* and *K̲h̲alʿ al-rasan fī 'l-taʿrīf bi-aḥwāl Ibn al-Ḥasan*.

As well as being a composer of epistles, poetry and other texts which the sources have preserved on account of their quality, he also wrote: 1. *al-Marḳaba* (var. *al-mirḳāt*) *al-ʿulyā fī man yastaḥikk* (var. *fī masāʾil*) *al-ḳaḍāʾ wa 'l-futyā*, ed. Lévi-Provençal, *Histoire des juges d'Andalousie*, Cairo 1948 (an edition which attracted important critical observations, e.g. by Ḥ. Zayyāt, in *al-Mashriq*, xlii [1948], 461-74, and was revised by A. Cuellas in his 1983 Univ. of Granada diss., unpubl.), 2. *Nuzhat al-baṣāʾir wa 'l-abṣār* (mss. Escorial 1653 and Bibl. Générale de Rabat 198 Ḳāf), commentary on a *maḳāma* by the same author *al-Iklīl fī tafḍīl al-nak̲h̲īl*, also called *al-maḳāma al-nak̲h̲liyya*. Some extracts from it were published by Müller in his *Beiträge*, i, 101-60, and 3. *D̲h̲ayl* (var. *tad̲h̲yīl*) *Taʾrīk̲h̲ Mālaḳa*, now lost, probably a continuation of Ibn ʿAskar's history [see mālaḳa].

Bibliography (in addition to references given in the article): R. Arié, *Notes sur la maqāma andalouse*, in *Hespéris-Tamuda*, ix/2 (1968), 212-13; J. Lalinde, *Una historia de los jueces en la España musulmana*, in *Anuario de historia del derecho español*, Madrid 1977, 683-740; M.I. Calero, *Los Banū l-Ḥasan al-Bunnāhī. Una familia de juristas malagueños (ss X-XV)*, in *Estudios árabes dedicados a D. Luis Seco de Lucena*, Granada 1999, 53-76.

(A. Carmona)

O

OIRATS, OYRAT [see kalmuk; wāfidiyya].

ÖREN ḲALʿE, in Russian Orenkale, a site in the southern part of the modern Azerbaijan Republic, in the mediaeval Islamic province of Arrān [*q.v.*]. It lies in lat. 39° 50' N., long. 47° 30' E. above the confluence of the Kur and Araxes rivers, close to an ancient canal, the Gyaur Ark̲h̲ [see mūḳān, at Vol. VII, 498b]. The site marks the mediaeval Islamic town of Baylaḳān [*q.v.*] conclusively established by the discovery of wasters of spheroconic vessels, stamped with the inscription *ʿamal Faḍlūn bi 'l-Baylaḳān*, in the course of excavations which began there in 1953 as part of a planned archaeological survey of the region above the confluence of the two rivers mentioned above. This last was, however, abandoned in 1959, and after the death of the director, A.A. Yessen, in

1963, the Ören Ḳal‘e excavations were abandoned also. Vol. II of the report (see *Bibl.*) is mostly devoted to sites in the surrounding area; a projected Vol. III on work at Ören Ḳal‘e in 1956-8 evidently never appeared. The excavation material is now in the reserves of the State Historical Museum at Bākū.

More contentious is the site's identification with the Late Antique fortress of P‘aytakaran, for the earliest remains at Ören Ḳal‘e, as attested by a copper coin of the Byzantine Emperor Anastasius (A.D. 491-518), are 6th century. But the only possible site for P‘aytakaran lies close to the modern village of Tazakend some 8 km/5 miles to the south-east, where Late Antique stone column bases for a palace or temple, together with a small hoard of denarii of Augustus, but no mediaeval glazed pottery, were brought to light. Ören Ḳal‘e was therefore a new foundation, connected with the Sāsānid Emperor Kawād͟h I (A.D. 488-531) and his fortifying of the Kur-Araxes steppes, though P‘aytakaran continues to figure in the Armenian historians' accounts of Heraclius's campaign in Atropatene.

Under the Umayyads, Baylaḳān was an important city of the province of Armīniya [*q.v.*] and was a notorious centre of K͟hārid͟jism, which persisted there until the mid-9th century. The local S͟haddādid rulers passed under the control of the Great Sald͟jūḳs *ca.* 1050 and, subsequently, of the Sald͟jūḳs of ‘Irāḳ, under the immediate administration of the Ildegizid Atabegs of Ād͟harbāyd͟jān [see ILDEÑIZIDS]. Though sacked by the Mongols late in 1221, it had recovered sufficiently for D͟jalāl al-Dīn K͟hwārazms͟hāh to install his harem and his treasury there in 1230. Under the Īl-K͟hānids it slowly declined, but was then rebuilt by Tīmūr in 1403, evidently to serve as his base in Transcaucasia. This long and varied history notwithstanding, the coin-finds were predominantly Ildegizid, especially of the last atabeg, Muẓaffar al-Dīn Özbeg.

The town at Ören Ḳal‘e was a square walled enceinte, with round towers at the corners and semi-circular towers between and a main gate on the south-west. The original walls, probably originally 6th-7th century, were of mud brick with a mud cladding. Later repairs were of mud brick with a fired brick revetment, but by the 12th century they had been abandoned. In the eastern corner was a smaller enceinte, 1,525 m^2, also walled: its dimensions are extraordinarily close to those given by S͟haraf al-Dīn ‘Alī Yazdī in his account of Tīmūr's restoration of the town. Excavations here brought to light a large bath, probably early 12th century in date, built on several levels, with walls of decoratively coursed fired brick, an entrance with terra cotta revetment plaques and a stalactite canopy, and one section with remains of wall-painting and carved or moulded plaster. Following its ruin, perhaps in an earthquake, it was intensively colonised, yielding abundant remains of both glazed and unglazed pottery.

Ören Ḳal‘e was one of a group of Transcaucasian potteries active in the pre-Mongol period—Gand͟ja, Ḳabāla, Bākū, Dwīn and especially Mingečawr, though none of the material from this last has been published. As at these sites, the 12th-13th century material from Ören Ḳa‘le, both in quantity and quality, is much more impressive than that from earlier periods. A trial excavation in the potters' quarter outside the walls to the south-west of the town brought four kilns to light, one of them containing spheroconic vessels. Unglazed 12th-13th century pottery included cooking pots, some decorated with spots of turquoise glaze; lavishly decorated storage jars, with barbotine stamped or incised ornament, sometimes with craftsmen's signatures; jugs and bowls, often with moulded decoration; and spheroconic vessels, with a characteristically yellowish-grey body and engraved, stamped or applied decoration. Of particular importance was a group of red-bodied storage vessels, perhaps wine jars with archaising friezes of horned animals, birds and fishes, and even crosses, recalling the impressions of cylinder-seals and, like these, applied with a cylinder. Such wares, with local peculiarities, are also known from Ānī, Gand͟ja, Dwīn, Garnī and Mingečawr.

The earlier locally manufactured glazed wares were mostly varieties of polychrome-stained splash- and drip-wares, characteristic of ‘Abbāsid Mesopotamia and Persia, though one fragment with a mounted huntsman was an imitation of opaque-glazed figural wares with polychrome decoration characteristic of the production of 10th-century Nīs͟hāpūr. In the 12th-13th centuries the pottery seems to show a change also in orientation, to the Caucasus, Anatolia and northern Syria, with many versions of polychrome-stained sgraffiato and champlevé wares. Particularly noteworthy are champlevé wares, one signed *‘amal K͟haṭṭāb*, with bold strapwork and panels of delicate scrolling arabesque, deriving from fine engraved K͟hurāsānī metalwork of *ca.* 1200; and a group of figural sgraffiato with animals clambering in foliage, so-called "Ag͟hkand" wares, which are, however, known from many sites, including Dmanisi and Urbnisi in Georgia. As at Gand͟ja, these may have been imports.

One important group of glazed wares, virtually exclusive to Baylaḳān, is red-bodied and underglaze-decorated, heavily potted but with exceptionally fine decoration scratched in a black manganese slip. They may be local versions of silicon-enriched 12th-century Kās͟hān "frit" wares painted in black slip under a colourless or a turquoise glaze, but here their repertoire makes use of Persian verse inscriptions, comparable in choice and execution to those on pre-Mongol Kās͟hān lustre wares, and elaborate knot patterns on grounds of fine scrolls. Several pieces were also signed *‘amal K͟haṭṭāb*. Among signatures on other pottery types from Ören Ḳa‘le, the most interesting is from an unglazed storage jar, with a distich incised in a fair hand and a signature, *‘amal Ibn ‘Alī b. ‘Azīzī al-fak͟hk͟hār* ("the potter"). Its phraseology is clear, if difficult to parallel, but errors in the transcription of the distich suggest that the signature, too, may contain mistakes.

Kiln furniture was abundant, including cockspurs, though most of the pottery recorded was fired without them. Most of the later glazed wares bore stamped designs on their bases, though, oddly, these were absent from the more highly decorated pieces and practically none of them are inscriptions. Similar stamps on wares of different groups show that the potters, like the decorator K͟haṭṭāb, did not specialise; they could have been bank marks, to identify the work of a craftsmen in a large workshop who was paid by the piece.

Imported wares included silicon-enriched lustre pottery (but not tiles) of most of the documented late 12th- to early 13th-century Kās͟hān types. Some of them, however, are characteristic of the 1260s-1270s, suggesting that the site may have continued to flourish under the Īl-K͟hānids and that the types of pottery discussed above may therefore have later termini than the Mongol invasion of 1221. Other Kās͟hān products, notably *mīnā'ī* and underglaze wares, do not seem to have been recorded.

Bibliography: For mediaeval Baylaḳān, see Le Strange, *The lands of the Eastern Caliphate*, 178; Schwarz, *Iran im Mittelalter*, 1144, 1296-8; *EIr* art. *Baylaqān* (C.E. Bosworth). For the Ören Ḳal'e excavations, see A.A. Yessen, *Trudî Azerbaydžanskoi (Orenkaliinskoi) ekspeditsii I. 1953-1955 gg.* (Materialî i issledovaniya po arkheologii, SSSR, 67), Moscow-Leningrad 1959; N. Nadžafova, *Khudžestvennaya keramika Azerbaydžana*, Baku 1964; Yessen and K.Kh. Kushnarëva, *Trudî ... II. 1956-1960 gg.* (Materialî ..., 125), Moscow-Leningrad 1965; Yessen, *Srednevekoviye pamyatniki Azerbaydžana* (Materialî ..., 133), Moscow 1965. (J.M. Rogers)

ÖZAL, Turgut, modern Turkish statesman (1927-93). He was born in 1927 in the province of Malatya in south-eastern Turkey. After graduating as an electrical engineer in 1950, he served in a number of important technical and economic posts between 1967 and 1980, initiating a programme of liberalising economic reforms in January 1980. Following the coup d'état led by General Kenan Evren on 12 September of that year, Özal continued these policies as Deputy Prime Minister, but he was forced to resign in July 1982 after a banking scandal. During the transition back to civilian rule in 1983, Özal established the Motherland Party, which won a comfortable majority in the general elections of November 1983. He thus became Prime Minister in the following month, increasing his party's majority in the next elections, held in November 1987. As premier, his main achievement was to free the economy from government constraints, producing high economic growth and an impressive increase in foreign trade; his main failures were the continuation of high inflation, and increasing allegations of corruption and disunity in his government during the late 1980s. When General Evren retired from the presidency in October 1989, Özal was elected to succeed him; however, his party lost its parliamentary majority in the general elections of October 1991, thus reducing his real political power. As President, Özal played a major role in foreign policy determination, controversially directing Turkey's support for the coalition powers in the Gulf crisis of 1990-1. His sudden death from a heart attack in April 1993 removed a towering figure in Turkish politics, distinguished by his attachment to economic and political liberalism, as well as the integration of moderate Islam into the country's political life.

Bibliography: Hasan Cemal, *Özal hikayesi*, Istanbul 1989; Üstün Ergüder, *The Motherland Party*, in Metin Heper and J.M. Landau (eds.), *Political parties and democracy in Turkey*, London 1991, 152-69; Nicole and H. Pope, *Turkey unveiled: Atatürk and after*, London 1997, chs. 11-15. (W. Hale)

P

PASHTO [see afghān. ii].

PĪRPANTHĪ (from Pers. *pīr* + *panth* "way of the spiritual master"), the name given in what is now Western India and in Pakistan to Hindus who follow Muslim *pīrs*, whether living or dead, these being generally Ṣūfīs or Ismāʿīlīs. To be precise, the term Pīrpanth is applied more strictly to two specific groups: (1) the disciples of Imām Shāh [*q.v.*], a dissident Ismāʿīlī who was one of the sons of the Ismāʿīlī *pīr* Ḥasan Kabīr al-Dīn, whose tomb is situated near Aḥmadābād [*q.v.*] in Gudjarāt; and (2) more rarely, to the Hindu disciples of Ṣūfī masters, Muslims or occasionally Hindus, originating from Sindh, Pandjāb or Rādjāsthān, such as Rāmdēv Pīr (or Rāmā Pīr), Pithoro Pīr, Paṭho Pīr, etc., with whom we are not concerned here.

The existence of the Pīrpanthīs attests the importance of interpenetration of Islam and Hinduism in this part of the subcontinent. Rather than speaking of syncretism, it would be more sensible to speak of a charismatic consensus at which these sects arrived. Sprung from the Mathīa Kanbī caste of agricultural labourers, the Pīrpanthīs were also known by the name of Momnahs (or Mōmnas). Established within Gudjarāt [*q.v.*] proper, but spilling out into Khāndesh and Kaččh [*q.vv.*], they are divided into several subsects according to whether they venerate Imām Shāh himself or one of his descendants or representatives. In the period from the late 19th century onwards, when confessional allegiances crystallised, fundamentalist Hindu organisations like the Āryā Samādj convinced a great number of them to revert to "orthodox" Hinduism. They generally assumed the name of Paṭel, and continued to venerate Imām Shāh, whom they considered as the *guru* who spoke in the name of the tenth *avatār* of Vishnu, Niklankī.

Bibliography: In addition to the *Bibls.* given for imām shāh and sathpanthīs, see J.M. Campbell (ed.), *Gazetteer of the Bombay Presidency*, ix/2, *Gujarat population: Musalmans and Parsis*, Bombay 1899; W. Ivanow, *The sect of Imam Shah in Gujerat*, in *Jnal. Bombay Branch of the RAS*, N.S. xii (1936), 19-70; Farhad Daftary, *The Ismāʿīlīs, their history and doctrines*, Cambridge 1990, 442-3, 480ff.; Dominique-Sila Khan, *Conversions and shifting identities. Ramdev Pir and the Ismailis in Rajasthan*, Dihlī 1997; M. Boivin, *Les Ismaéliens. Des communautés d'Asie du sud entre islamisation et indianisation*, Turnhout 1998; Dominique-Sila Khan and Zawahir Moir, *Coexistence and communalism in the shrine of Pirana in Gujarat*, in *South Asia*, xxii, Special issue (1999), 133-54. (M. Boivin)

PRESTER JOHN, the name of a mysterious potentate, said to be a Nestorian Christian and inimical to Islam, whom the Christians of medieval Europe placed beyond the Islamic lands in Inner or Far Asia.

The name Presbyter Johannes first occurs in the chronicle, called *Historia de duabus civitatibus*, of the German prelate Otto, Bishop of Freising, in which he describes, on the authority of a meeting in 1145 with the Latin Bishop Hugh of Djabala (= ancient Byblos, in Lebanon), how Prester John was a monarch, of the lineage of the Magi of the Gospels, living in the Far East (*in extremo oriente*) beyond Persia and Armenia. He had attacked the *Samiardi* brothers, kings of the Persians and Medes, had defeated them and had advanced to the Tigris in the hope of aiding the Church in Jerusalem, but had then been forced to turn back. The passage seems almost certainly to contain an allusion to the defeat of the Saldjūḳ sultan Sandjar [q.v.] (= the kings *Samiardos/Saniardos*, here made plural) and his Ḳaraḵẖānid allies by the Western Liao, known to the Muslims as the Ḳara Ḵẖiṭay [q.v.] at the battle of the Ḳaṭwān Steppe in Transoxania in 536/1141 (the remainder of Otto's story about Prester John's advance across Persia into Mesopotamia being unhistorical).

However, this does not necessarily mean that the later, elaborate stories of Prester John, which contained connections with the Indian Ocean coastlands and, above all, with Ethiopia, all had their origins in this battle. It is not impossible that stories of Prester John were known before the news of Sandjar's defeat percolated through to the Crusader principalities in the Levant, providing a convenient peg on which to hang the stories. In the opinion of the late Prof. C.F. Beckingham, such stories were probably connected with the legend of the shrine of St. Thomas in South India (modern Kerala) and the existence of an ancient Christian community there; but the intricacies of the later history of Prester John do not concern us here. It should be noted, however, that the assertion of B. Spuler in his article GÜRKHĀN at Vol. II, 1143b, that *Johannes* stems from the title *Gürḵẖān* (itself almost certainly Turkish in origin, according to G. Doerfer, *Türkische und mongolische Elemente im Neupersischen*, iii, Wiesbaden 1967, no. 1672) seems most unlikely.

Bibliography: The bibl. on this enigmatic figure is large, ranging from the pioneer work of F. Zarncke, *Der Priester Johannes*, in *Abh. Königl. Sächsischen Gesell. der Wiss.*, phil.-hist. Cl., vii-viii (1879-83), to C.F. Beckingham's *Prester John, the Mongols and the Ten Lost Tribes*, London 1995. A succinct and stimulating study is this same author's *The achievements of Prester John*, Inaugural Lecture, SOAS, London 1966. Most recently, see E. Ciurtin, *La mythologie asiatique et la légende africaine du Prêtre Jean*, in *Archaeus. Études d'Histoire des Religions*, v/3-4 (Bucarest 2001), 5-21.   (C.E. BOSWORTH)

PUASA, the Indonesian term for the month of fasting, Ramaḍān [q.v.].

During Ramaḍān in Indonesia all levels of local, indigenous and normative interpretations of Islam congregate. On the national level, the country converts into a large Ḳur'ān school with religious programmes dominating the news media, mobile Ḳur'ān schools, Ḳur'ān clinics and Ḳur'ān reciting marathons. In the month prior to Ramaḍān, many areas will hold "praise rallies" in order to prepare spiritually for Ramaḍān. These are nightly events of Ṣūfī-type *dhikr* that rotate from house to house.

Simultaneously, reaching back to the pre-Islamic, Hindu-Buddhist elements of Javanese culture, there is great stress on rituals surrounding the graves of ancestors. These take place in the weekend prior to the beginning of the fast and at the end. In certain areas, e.g. in Java, the so-called "Kraton culture" of the sultan's palace performs rituals that are entirely non-Islamic. For instance, after the 'Īd prayers a grand parade called *Gerebeg* is held in front of the Kraton with as its centre piece a magical "mount of blessing" that conveys some of the sultan's mystical power.

Attitudes toward the practice of fasting are influenced by Javanese ascetic practices that are followed for a variety of reasons year round. As a result of this, children as young as four years old start to practice abstinence for Ramaḍān. In general, the fast is broken in restrained manner with many Muslims limiting their first meal to a small snack and a glass of sweet juice.

Although Ramaḍān is a time of promoting unity among Muslims, differences between Reformist and Traditionalist Muslims are played out with fervour. This starts with the issue of identifying when the fast begins and ends, and is visible during Ramaḍān in different practices concerning the *tarāwīḥ* prayers and the 'Īd al-Fiṭr gatherings.

Celebrations for the 'Īd last up to one month, and serve to renew harmony and unity. People travel all over the country (*mudik*) in order to visit relatives and to ask forgiveness for wrongs committed during the past year. Neighbourhoods, businesses and schools organise special *halal bi 'l-halal* parties.

Bibliography: There are innumerable numbers of books about *puasa* in the Indonesian language. Many leading preachers and scholars of Islam have published their Ramaḍān sermons and reflections, such as Hamka, *Puasa 'tarawih dan Iedul Fitri*, Jakarta 1995; M. Ouraish Shihab, *Sahur bersama*, Bandung 1997.   (NELLY VAN DOORN-HARDER)

R

RADJA' B. ḤAYWA b. Ḵẖanzal al-Kindī, Abu 'l-Miḳdām or Abū Naṣr (full *nasab* in Gottschalk, 331, from Ibn 'Asākir), a rather mysterious *mawlā* or client who seems to have been influential as a religious and political adviser at the courts of the early Marwānid caliphs, from 'Abd al-Malik to 'Umar b. 'Abd al-'Azīz. His birth date is unknown, but he died in 112/730, probably around the age of seventy.

According to one account, Radjā''s family stemmed from Maysān in Lower 'Irāḳ, hence from the local Nabaṭ or Aramaeans, where the bond of *walā'* with the Arab tribe of Kinda [q.v.] must have been made, the Kinda being especially strong in Kūfa. The family moved westwards to the Palestine-Transjordan area, where again there were many Kindīs in such districts as the Balḳā' [q.v.], providing strong military support for the Umayyads. It is likely that Radjā' himself was from that area, from Baysān in the Jordan valley, as the *nisba*s sometimes applied to him, "al-Filasṭīnī" and "al-Urdunnī", would imply. He appears, together with Yāzid b. Sallām, a *mawlā* of the caliph 'Abd al-Malik and a native of Jerusalem, as being involved in the construction of the Dome of the Rock [see KUBBAT AL-ṢAKHRA], probably as financial controller (Mudjīr al-Dīn al-'Ulaymī, *al-Uns al-djalīl*, Cairo 1283/1866-7, i, 241-2 = 'Ammān 1973, i, 272-4), and he was also employed by al-Ḥadjdjādj b. Yūsuf [q.v.] on a diplomatic mission to conciliate the Ḳaysī Arab tribes of northern Syria under their leader Zufar b. al-Ḥāriṯẖ al-Kilābī.

Radjā' was further famed for his piety and knowledge of the religious sciences, and was high in the counsels of ʿAbd al-Malik and his son al-Walīd (I), accompanying the latter on his Pilgrimage of 90/709 or 91/710, when he first came into contact with the caliph's cousin ʿUmar b. ʿAbd al-ʿAzīz, governor of Medina, a relationship to be of significance later. During the short caliphate of Sulaymān b. ʿAbd al-Malik (96-9/715-17 [*q.v.*]), Radjā' appears as both an executive official and a spiritual adviser to the ruler and then to his successor ʿUmar (II) b. ʿAbd al-ʿAzīz; some sources make him head of Sulaymān's *dīwān al-khātam* or chancery. He clearly lent his religious backing to the caliphs, and his role thus marks a stage in the acceptance of *mawālī* in the sphere of legal and religious authority hitherto jealously guarded by the Arabs (cf. the role, parallel in many ways, of al-Ḥasan al-Baṣrī [*q.v.*]); one may also view it as an aspect of the increasing concern of the Umayyads with the religious and spiritual aspects of their authority.

The historical sources make Radjā''s great moment the events at Sulaymān's death in Ṣafar 99/September 717. It had been ʿAbd al-Malik's intention that his sons by free wives should succeed him, and there were still four of these eligible at Sulaymān's death. Yet a temporary re-routing of the succession was now achieved, to the collateral branch of ʿAbd al-Malik's brother ʿAbd al-ʿAzīz (in fact, it had been the wish of the founder of the Marwānid line, Marwān (I) b. al-Ḥakam [*q.v.*], that ʿAbd al-ʿAzīz should follow ʿAbd al-Malik in the caliphate).

What happened when Sulaymān was on his deathbed at Dābiḳ [*q.v.*], north of Aleppo, is related in detail by al-Wāḳidī, preserved by Ibn Saʿd, *Ṭabaḳāt*, v, 246-9, and al-Ṭabarī, ii, 1341-5, tr. in Bosworth, 52-9, and D.S. Powers (tr.), *The History of al-Tabarī*, xxiv, *The empire in transition*, Albany 1989 (with an *isnād* going back to Radjā'), with a few additional details in al-Dhahabī. According to these accounts, Radjā' was able to persuade Sulaymān to set aside his own children and half-brothers in favour of ʿUmar b. ʿAbd al-ʿAzīz, and secured adhesion to this arrangement by the device of requiring allegiance to the person named in a sealed *ʿahd* of Sulaymān. However, since much of the information on this episode goes back, directly or indirectly, to *riwāyas* stemming from Radjā' himself, it has been suggested that he may have exaggerated his personal share in events (see Eisener, *Zwischen Faktum und Fiktion*, 222ff., and idem, art. SULAYMĀN B. ʿABD AL-MALIK, at Vol. IX, 822a).

During ʿUmar's brief ensuing period of power (to Radjab 101/February 720), Radjā' may have been an adviser of the caliph, but specific detail is lacking; one would like to know whether, for instance, he had any part in ʿUmar's administrative and financial measures, including his famous "rescript". He apparently spent the last decade of his life in retirement, and died, in unknown circumstances, in 112/730, according to Ibn al-Athīr, ed. Beirut, v, 172, at Ḳussīn near Kūfa.

Bibliography: 1. Sources. There are brief entries on Radjā' in e.g. Ibn Saʿd, vii/2, 161-2; Khalīfa b. Khayyāṭ, *Ṭabaḳāt*, ed. Zakkār, Damascus 1966, ii, 773 no. 2924; Ibn Ḳutayba, *Maʿārif*, ed. ʿUkkāsha, 472-3; and a slightly longer one in Ibn Khallikān, ed. ʿAbbās, ii, 301-3, tr. de Slane, i, 526-7. For a full list of the sources mentioning him, see Gottschalk, 329-31. According to Eisener, 222 n. 290, the information in Ibn ʿAsākir on Radjā' stems from Ibn Saʿd.

2. Studies. Wellhausen, *Das arabische Reich*, 165-6, Eng. tr. *The Arab kingdom and its fall*, 261-2; H. Gottschalk, *Raǧā' ibn Ḥaiwa und der theologische Einfluss am Hofe der Marwaniden von Damaskus*, in *Festschrift für Wilhelm Eilers*, Wiesbaden 1967, 328-40; C.E. Bosworth, *Rajā' ibn Ḥaywa al-Kindī and the Umayyad caliphs*, in *IQ*, xvi (1972), 36-80, repr. in *Medieval Arabic culture and administration*, London 1982, no. III; R. Eisener, *Zwischen Faktum und Fiktion. Eine Studie zum Umayyadenkalifen Sulaimān b. ʿAbdalmalik und seinem Bild in den Quellen*, Wiesbaden 1987, 213ff. See also ʿUMAR II B. ʿABD AL-ʿAZĪZ.

(C.E. BOSWORTH)

RĀDJASTHĀN, a historic region of the western part of the Indian subcontinent, and now the name of a province in the Indian Union. It is bounded by the Pakistan provinces of Sind and Pandjāb on the west and northwest, and by the Indian states of Pandjāb, Haryana and Uttar Pradesh on the northeast, Madhya Pradesh on the east, southeast and south, and Gudjarāt on the south. With an area of 342,267 km^2/132,149 sq. miles, it is the second largest state in the Indian Union (after Madhya Pradesh), but because of its climate and habitat, has a less dense population than any other state. The population (1986 estimate) was 37,000,000. The state capital is at Jaipur, formerly the centre of a princely state [see DJAYPUR], and the state is divided into 26 Districts.

1. Geography and habitat.

The topography of Rādjasthān is dominated by the range of Aravalli Hills, which run in a transverse fashion across the state from northeast to southwest, culminating in Mount Abu (1,722 m/5,650 feet) at the southwestern end and ending just over the border of Gudjarāt State. The three-fifths of the state lying to the northwest are largely sandy, with the Great Indian or Thar Desert in the far west but with more fertile and habitable lands as one goes eastwards. The two-fifths lying to the southeast of the Aravalli Hills are diversified in character and more fertile, with the Districts of Kota and Bundi forming a tableland. In the south is the hilly tract of Mēwāṙ [*q.v.*], centred on Udaipur [see UDAYPŪR]. On the state's northeastern edge, the plains around Bharatpur form part of the Jumna/Yamunā basin. The only large perennial river is the Chambal, which flows northeastwards into the Jumna.

Rādjasthān is predominantly an agricultural and pastoralist state. Despite a low and erratic rainfall, with a subsequent need for irrigation, nearly all types of crops are grown, including various cereals, rice and vegetables. Despite the arid or semi-arid nature of more than half the state's area, there is a large livestock population in comparison with the rest of India, including camels and draught animals, and Rādjasthān is the largest produce of wool in the Union.

2. Ethnology.

There are aboriginal tribes in various parts of the state, especially to the east and south of the Aravalli Hills, including Bhīls, and various tribes of Rādjpūt stock, such as the Mēʾōs [*q.v.*], a part of whom was nominally converted to Islam in the 8th/14th century. Rādjpūts form the most significant element in Rādjasthān and have dominated its political and cultural history, even though, at present, Radjpūts form only a small proportion of the total population, with many more Rādjpūts outside the state in the Pandjāb, Uttar Pradesh, Bihar, Madhya Pradesh, etc. The princely states of Rādjasthān were almost all ruled by Hindu Rādjpūt princes, with the exceptions of Muslim Tonk [*q.v.*] in the east of the state whose founder was a Paṫhān chief, and the Djāṫ [*q.v.*] states of Dholpur and Bharatpūr in the northeast. The Rādjpūts claim to be the descendants of the Kshatriyas of Vedic times, and take great pride in their ancestry and their warlike traditions (Skr. *rādjaputra* "king's son"). But such claims are based on fictitious genealogies, and the Rādjpūts must be of very diverse ethnic origins, with some remains of the old Kshatriyas but with many later admixtures of invading peoples who became Hinduised, with new families recognised as Rādjpūt. The term Rādjpūt is, accordingly, not of racial significance but denotes a tribe, clan or warlike class whose members claimed aristocratic rank. At present, some 10% of the population of Rādjasthān State is Muslim.

Bibliography: *Imperial gazetter of India*[2], xxi, 82-93, 104-42; Government of India, District gazetteers, *Rajputana*, Calcutta 1908; H.A. Rose, *A glossary of the tribes and castes of the Punjab and North-West Frontier Province*, Lahore 1919, iii, s.v. *Rajputs*; O.K.H. Spate and A.T.A. Learmonth, *India and Pakistan, a general and regional geography*, [3]London 1967, 611-21; *Gazetteer of India, Provincial series, Rajasthan*, Delhi 1968; V.C. Misra, *The geography of Rajasthan*, New Delhi 1968; *EI*[1] art. *Rādjpūts*. (C.E. Bosworth)

3. Languages and literature.

The dialects of Rādjasthān belong to the Western Hindī group of New Indo-Aryan, with the Aravalli Hills marking the main internal divide between the north-western and the south-eastern dialects. Predictably closer in many respects to Brajbhāśā (and to standard Hindī), the main south-eastern dialects are Djaypūrī (Ḋhūnḋhāṙī) and its southern neighbours Mēwāṙī and Hāṙawṫī, in turn flanked to the east by Mēwāṫī and to the south by Mālwī. Possibly also reflected in the Romani of the European gypsies, earlier migrations from this region are certainly responsible for the close resemblances between south-eastern Rādjasthānī and the speech of several nomadic groups, including Lamānī in central India and the Godjrī (Gudjarī) spoken by the Muslim Gudjar herdsmen of Kashmīr and the adjacent areas of northern Pākistān. The Mārwāṙī dialects spoken in the desert areas of north-western Rādjasthān are collectively distinguished by such features as the distinction of implosives from explosives in the voiced series *g ḋ d b* or the retention of an organic passive in *-īdj-*, both with close parallels in Sindhī [*q.v.*] and Sirāikī [see LAHNDĀ], as well as individual shibboleths like the possessive marker *rō*.

Following a period of several centuries during which Old Gudjarātī (confusingly termed "Old Western Rādjasthānī" by Tessitori) was the common literary language of both Gudjarāt and Rādjasthān, Old Mārwāṙī emerged as an independent literary language around the middle of the 15th century, when it is attested in the semi-popular poetic treatments of romantic themes found in the *Vīsaḷadevarāsa* and the *Ḋholā-Mārū rā dūhā*. In the hands of the Chāraṅs, the hereditary bards of the ruling Rādjpūts [*q.v.*], Old Mārwāṙī was developed as a specialised literary medium for heroic poetry with the incorporation of numerous Sanskritisms and special poetic forms. This bardic language is known as Ḋingal, as opposed to "Pingal", the literary Brajbhāśā cultivated for other types of poetry in the period down until the later 19th century when both were replaced as literary standards by modern Hindī.

In its celebration of the chivalric ideals of the Rādjpūts and of their resistance to the Muslims, the heroic literature of Rādjasthān is of very great cultural importance. It finds its first classic statement in the Old Gudjarātī *Kānhaḋadē-prabandha* (1456) by Padmanābh, which celebrates the victories achieved over the Dihlī Sultan ʿAlāʾ al-Dīn Khaldjī [*q.v.*] and his generals by Kānhaḋadēv, the Rādjpūt ruler of Djalōr, until his final defeat (dated *ca.* 1312) is followed by his queens performing collective ritual self-immolation (*djawhar*). In addition to panegyrics and elegies (*marsiyā*), Ḋingal literature includes many similar treatments of such historical episodes, beginning with the mixed prose-verse *Achal Khīchī rī vachānikā* based on the resistance mounted by its eponymous Rādjpūt hero to the invasion in 1423 of Sultan Hūshang Ghūrī of Māndū [*q.v.*]. For stylistic as well as linguistic reasons, however, Ḋingal literature has attracted less interest from modern scholars than the more approachable prose chronicles of the Rādjpūt states dating from the early 17th century which were written in Middle Mārwāṙī, and whose most celebrated exemplar is the *Khyāt* by Nayṅasī, minister to Djaswant Singh of Mārwāṙ (d. 1670).

Bibliography: 1. Language. G.A. Grierson (ed.), *Linguistic survey of India*, ix/2, Calcutta 1908, 1-321; L.P. Tessitori, *A scheme for the bardic and historical survey of Rajputana*, in *JASB*, x, 10 (1914), 373-410; idem, *Notes on the grammar of the Old Western Rajasthani*, in *Indian Antiquary*, xliii-xlv (1914-16); R.L. Turner, *The position of Romani in Indo-Aryan*, in *Journal of the Gypsy Lore Society*, v (1926), 145-89; W.S. Allen, *Some phonological characteristics of Rājasthānī*, in *BSOAS*, xx (1957), 5-11; idem, *Notes on Rājasthānī verbs*, in *Indian Linguistics*, xxi (1960), 4-13; R.L. Trail, *A grammar of Lamani*, Norman, Okla., 1970; J.D. Smith, *An introduction to the language of the historical documents from Rājasthān*, in *Modern Asian Studies*, ix (1975), 433-64; idem (ed.), *The Vīsaḷadevarāsa*, Cambridge 1976; C.R. Rensch *et al.* (eds.), *Hindko and Gujari*, Islamabad 1992, 92-305.

2. Literature. L.P. Tessitori (ed.), *Bardic and historical survey of Rajputana*, Calcutta 1917-20; C. Vaudeville (*ed.*), *Les duhā de Ḍholā-Mārū*, Pondichery 1962; M. Prabhakar, *A critical study of Rajasthani literature*, Jaipur 1976; N.P. Ziegler, *Marvari historical chronicles*, in *Indian Economic and Social History Review*, xiii (1976), 219-50; H. Maheshwari, *History of Rajasthani literature*, New Delhi 1980; I.M.P. Raeside, *A Gujarati bardic poem: the Kānhaḍade-prabandha*, in C. Shackle and R. Snell (eds.), *The Indian narrative: perspectives and patterns*, Wiesbaden 1992, 137-53. (C. Shackle)

4. History.

Archaeological researches in western Rādjasthān show that people were living there in the 3rd and 2nd millennia B.C. who were close to the Harappan and post-Harappan cultures of the Indus valley. Late rulers of the whole or parts of the state included the Bactrian Greeks, Sakas, Guptas, and White Huns, until from the 7th century A.D. onwards, various Rādjpūt dynasties arose, including the Gurdjara-Pratīhāras, who fended off the Arab colonists in Sind; but for the most part, these Rādjpūt princely lines were involved in internecine warfare, which was to facilitate Muslim probes into the region. The last of the Čāhamāna or Čawhān line, Pṙithvīrādja III, was defeated and killed by the Ghūrid sultan Muʿizz al-Dīn Muḥammad b. Sām [*q.v.*] in the second battle of Taraʾin in 588/1192. The capital Adjmēr [*q.v.*] was briefly restored by the Ghūrid to Pṙithvīrādja's young son after the latter had accepted the Sultan's suzerainty over his lands. Only the strategic fortress of Ranthambhor in eastern Rādjasthān was occupied permanently, with a garrison under Kiwām al-Mulk

Rukn al-Dīn Ḥamza. In 591/1195 the Rādjpūts rebelled against Muslim control under the leadership of the chiefs Harirādjā and Djatrā'ī who occupied Adjmer [*q.v.*], threatened Ranthambhōr and fomented dissension in the region towards Dihlī, where Ḳuṭb al-Dīn Aybak [*q.v.*] resided as Muʿizz al-Dīn's viceroy. Aybak restored the situation and regained Adjmēr. Nāgawr [*q.v.*] in the region of Djōdhpūr [*q.v.*] seems to have been occupied at this time. Thangar, capital of the territory of Bayānā in this eastern part, was besieged and captured by Muʿizz al-Dīn in 592/1196 and then entrusted to Malik Bahā' al-Dīn Ṭoghril, who later transferred his capital to a newly-founded town, Sulṭānkōṭ, that later became known, from the name of the province, as Bayānā. Thus with the exception of the chief of Djālor in western Rādjasthān, most of the region had been nominally at least subdued. In the last years of the 6th/12th century, Khʷādja Muʿīn al-Dīn Ḥasan Sidjzī (d. 633/1236 [see ČISHTĪ]), founder of what was to become one of the most influential Ṣūfī orders in India, the Čishtiyya [*q.v.*], came to reside at the Čāhamāna capital Adjmēr, and his shrine there later became one of the most celebrated shrines, for both Muslims and Hindus, in the subcontinent. His disciple Shaykh Ḥamīd al-Dīn Suwalī Nāgawrī (d. 673/1274) was sent by Muʿīn al-Dīn to Nāgawr, which likewise became an important Čishtī shrine.

The relaxation of power in the Dihlī Sultanate [*q.v.*] on the death in 633/1236 of Iltutmish [*q.v.*] gave an opportunity for the Rādjpūt princes to reassert their power. A revolt in eastern Rādjasthān forced his daughter Sultan Raḍiyya [*q.v.*] to withdraw the Muslim garrison from Ranthambhōr, and except for the districts around Adjmēr and Nāgawr, the whole region reverted to Rādjpūt rule, allowing powerful lines like those of Ranthambhōr and Čitōr to come into existence; for the rest of the century no Muslim ruler was able to contemplate a reconquest. This only came in the reign of ʿAlā' al-Dīn Muḥammad Khaldjī (695-715/1296-1316), who aimed to secure at least eastern Rādjasthān in order to open a line of communication towards Mālwa and Gudjarāt, which he coveted. An army was sent in 700/1301 to besiege the powerful and prestigious ruler of Ranthambhōr, Rā'ī Hammīr Dēva, a descendant of Pṛithvīrādja III. This attempt failed ignominiously, and only after the Sultan had to come from Dihlī in person with reinforcements did Ranthambhōr fall after a year's struggle. It was then placed under the general Ulugh Khān, and in 701/1302 the Sultan invested the fortress of Čitōr, then ruled by another noted prince, Ratnasimha of the Guhila clan of Mēwāṛ and the grandson of Djatrā'ī, and captured it in the next year, annexing the territory of Čitōr to the Dihlī Sultanate and placing it under the governorship of the crown prince, Khiḍr Khān. Thereafter, the chiefs of smaller principalities either submitted or were overthrown by military force. Thus in 711/1311 the commander Malik Kamāl al-Dīn Gurg defeated Rā'ī Karan Dēva and seized his principality of Djālor, and after this, lesser chiefs in Djaysalmer, etc. likewise submitted and acknowledged Khaldjī suzerainty.

Thus throughout the 8th/14th century, Rādjasthān was controlled by the Dihlī Sultans and their governors from such centres as Adjmēr, Ranthambhōr, Nāgawr and Djālor. However, the invasion of northern India and sack of Dihlī by Tīmūr [*q.v.*] in 801/1398 eventually led to the end of the Tughluḳ Sultans and heralded a period of weakness for the Sultanate, with various Muslim powers arising in the provinces. It was also the opportunity for a re-assertion of power by the Rādjpūt chiefs, with the Rānā of Čitōr organising a confederacy of chiefs and with the Rādjpūts of Mēwāṛ driving the Muslims from Adjmēr, held by them till 859/1455 when the Sultan of Mālwa recaptured, with the rulers of Mālwa now holding it for almost eighty years. It was also an opportunity for Sultan Muẓaffar Shāh (I) of Gudjarāt [*q.v.*], now independent of Dihlī, to send his younger brother Shams al-Dīn Khān Dandānī against Nāgawr, at which his descendants established a local dynasty that endured till Dawlat Khān Nāgawrī was killed *ca.* 932/1525-6 by Rā'ī Māldēva of Djōdhpūr. Djalōr was ruled by a Nuhanī Afghan chief and his descendants until it was conquered by Māldēva after 932/1526, but the latter's power was then overthrown by the Dihlī Sultan Shīr Shāh Sūr (*r.* 947-52/1540-5 [*q.v.*]), who also attacked the Rādjā of Djōdhpūr in his principality of Mārwāṛ in 949/1542-3. Previous to this, Mēwāṛ had been built up into one of the most powerful principalities of northern India under its energetic ruler Rānā Sangrām Singh or Sāngā (*r.* 1509-28), who led successful campaigns against the Sultans of Mālwa and Gudjarāt. He went on to acquire imperial ambitions, defeating the Dihlī Sultan Ibrāhīm Lōdi [see LŌDĪS] in 929/1523 and made overtures to the Mughal adventurer Bābur [*q.v.*] for a concerted attack on the Lōdīs. He soon realised, however, that Bābur would be a powerful rival for power and turned against him; but in 933/1527 Bābur secured a decisive victory over Sāngā at Khānu'ā. This was a turning point in the history of northern India, for after this the Rādjpūt princes remained essentially on the defensive in their territories against the rising power of the Sūrs and then the Mughals.

Shīr Shāh Sūr's biographer ʿAbbās Sarwānī mentions the territories acquired by him in Rādjasthān as the *mulk-i Nāgawr u Adjmēr u Djōdhpūr*, and he also speaks of the desert regions of the west as the *zamīn-i rīgistān*. Shīr Shāh now divided up the whole region into extensive *sarkārs* [*q.v.* in Suppl.], each under a *fawdjdār* with his commander Khawāṣṣ Khān as *amīn* or overall governor. The emperor Akbar's policy in Rādjasthān was based on conquest and conciliation. The captures of Čitōr and Ranthambhōr made him master of the greater part of the region, with the exception of Mēwāṛ, not completely subdued until Djahāngīr's reign, when Rānā Amar Singh submitted at Udaypūr in 1023/1614. The emperor took Rādjpūt wives, and both his son Djahāngīr and the latter's son Shāh Djahān were born of Rādjpūt mothers. Rādjpūt troops, typically dismounting from their small horses to fight, formed contingents in the Mughal army under Akbar. Rādjasthān was organised into the *ṣūba* [*q.v.*] of Adjmēr under a *ṣūbadār* [*q.v.*], with seven component *sarkārs*: Adjmēr, Čitōr, Ranthambhōr, Sirohi, Nāgawr, Djōdhpūr and Bikāner. The districts of Alwār and Bharatpūr, which are now within modern Rādjasthān State, were included in the *ṣūba* of Āgra.

The reversing of Akbar's conciliatory policies under Awrangzīb [*q.v.*] left the emperor faced with such powerful enemies as the Rādjpūts in northern India and the Marāṭhās [*q.v.*] in the northwestern Deccan. The new policy of militant Muslim orthodoxy affected the emperor's relationship with the Rādjpūt nobility, who formed a highly influential element in the Mughal state apparatus; the highest-ranked noble in the empire was Mīrzā Radjā Djay Singh Kačhwaha of Djaypūr, and in 1090/1679 all Rādjpūts in the state service were excused the newly-imposed *djizya*, though the mass of Rādjpūt subjects were not. Nevertheless, the role of the Rādjpūt nobles now began to be curtailed by what seems to have been a deliberate policy on Awrangzīb's part. His attempt to interfere in the succession to the throne in Mārwāṙ and to impose a Rādjpūt candidate of his choice there led to a major Rādjpūt revolt in 1089-90/1679-80 at Mārwāṙ and then Mēwāṙ. Since the Rādjpūts had no field artillery, the Mughal army suppressed this, and occupied Udaypūr, but guerilla warfare against the Mughals continued for a generation in the hills.

Bharatpūr was taken over by a Djāt chief on Awrangzīb's death and the Rādjpūts were able to retake Adjmēr in 1133/1721; but internal dissensions prevented the Rādjpūts from making headway against the Marāthās, within whose confederation they now came. Adjmēr was captured in 1169/1756; the power of the Rādjpūt chiefs reduced to a low ebb, and the land suffered from Pindarī and Paṭhān plundering and oppressive levies. It may be noted that it is in the 18th century that the term Rādjpūtāna is found, so that a historian like Khāfī Khān uses the expressions *mulk-i Rādjpūtān* and also *Rādjpūtiyya*; it was essentially under British paramountcy in the 19th century that the designation Rādjpūtāna became usual.

With the defeat of the Marāthās by British forces in 1817-18, before the end of 1818, the group of principalities and chiefdoms which came to comprise the British Indian province of Rādjpūtāna had been taken under British protection. Their borders were now precisely delimited, with the whole of the province comprising these native states (totalling eighteen princely states and two chiefdoms) except for the small enclave of Adjmēr-Mērwāṙa which was a directly-ruled British Indian province. The chief commissioner of this last was also the political officer there, styled agent to the governor-general, for the Government of India, and there with various residents and political agents accredited to the native states. The outbreak of the Sepoy Mutiny in 1857 found Rādjpūtāna devoid of British troops; there were local disturbances, but the native princes, whose positions were often threatened, managed to restore order. The administrative system outlined above lasted until Partition and Indian independence in 1947; during the previous century or so, the province had, from its particular political constitution, remained largely outside the nationalist and westernising currents that affected other parts of the subcontinent. During the civil strife that raged around Partition, many Muslims were driven out of the Hindu princely states of Alwār and Bharatpūr. When the Indian Union was established, the central government in 1956 set up a Boundary Commission for the reorganisation of states on a linguistic basis. A recommendation, implemented in 1958, was that Alwār and Bharatpūr should be included in the new state of Rādjasthān, though linguistically they do not form part of it.

Bibliography: 1. Sources. Ḥasan Niẓāmī, *Tādj al-ma'āthir*, ms. Library of the Dept. of History, Aligarh Univ., ff. 121a, 123a-b; Djūzdjānī, *Ṭabaḳāt-i Nāṣirī*, ed. ʿAbd al-Ḥayy Ḥabībī, Kabul 1342-3/1963-4, i, 400-1, Eng. tr. H.G. Raverty, London 1881-99, i, 464-70; ʿIṣāmī, *Futūḥ al-salāṭīn*, ed. M. Usha, Madras 1948, 273-6, 279-80; Shaykh Rizḳ Allāh Mushtāḳī, *Wāḳiʿāt-i Mushtāḳī*, Eng. tr. Iqtidar Husain Siddiqi, New Delhi 1993; ʿAbbās Khān Sarwānī, *Tuḥfa-i Akbar-Shāhī* or *T.-i Shīr-Shāhī*, ed. S.M. Imām al-Dīn, Dacca 1964, 196-9; Abu 'l-Faḍl ʿAllāmi, *Āʾīn-i Akbarī*, ed. H. Blochmann, Calcutta 1867-77, repr. Lahore 1975, 386, 453, 508, 511-12; Muḥammad Khāfī Khān, *Muntakhab al-lubāb*, vol. ii., ed. Maulaví Kabír al-Dín Aḥmed and Ghulám Ḳádir, Calcutta 1860-74, 605, 737; Ghulām-Ḥusayn Ṭabāṭabāʾī, *Siyar al-mutaʾakhkhirīn*, Lucknow 1282-3/1866, ii, 45, 434, 452.

2. Studies. Col. J. Tod, *The annals and antiquities of Rajasthan*, 3 vols., London 1829-32; *Imperial gazetteer of India*², xxi, 93-104; Iqtidar Husain Siddiqui, *The evolution of the Vilayet, the Shiqq and the* Sarkar *during the Delhi Sultanate period*, in *Medieval India, a Quarterly*, v (Aligarh 1963), 10-32; R.C. Majumdar (ed.), *The history and culture of the Indian people. V. The struggle for empire*, ²Bombay 1966, 72-92, *VI. The Delhi Sultanate*, Bombay 1960, 326-61; V.S. Bhargava, *Marwar and the Mughal emperors*, Delhi 1966; R.C. Hallisey, *The Rajput rebellion against Aurangzeb*, Columbia, S.C. 1977; R. Jeffrey (ed.), *People, princes, and paramount power. Society and politics in the Indian princely states*, Delhi 1978; Siddiqui, *The early Chishti Dargahs in India*, in C.W. Troll (ed.), *Muslim shrines in India*, Delhi 1989; J.F. Richards, *The New Cambridge history of India*, 1.5, *The Mughal empire*, Cambridge 1993, 179-84 and bibl. on the Rādjpūts at 308-9; Shail Mayaram, *Resisting regimes. Myth, memory and the shaping of Muslim identity*, Delhi 1997 (on the fate of Mēʾō Muslims in Alwār and Bharatpūr at the time of Partition); S.C. Bhatt (ed.), *The encyclopedic district gazetteer of India*, New Delhi 1998; *EI*¹ art. *Rādjpūts*. See also the *Bibls.* to DJŌDH-PŪR; MĒWĀṘ.

(IQTIDAR H. SIDDIQUI)

RĀFIʿ AL-**DARADJĀT** b. Rāfiʿ al-Sha'n b. Shāh ʿĀlam I, Shams al-Dīn, great-grandson of the great Mughal emperor Awrangzīb [*q.v.*] and one of the ephemeral emperors in the last decades of independent Mughal rule, reigning for some four months in the spring of 1131/1719.

After Awrangzīb's death in 1118/1707, the main power in the empire was that of the Bārha Sayyids [*q.v.* in Suppl.], who in 1124/1712 raised to the throne Farrukh-siyar b. ʿAẓīm al-Sha'n Muḥammad ʿAẓīm [*q.v.*] but deposed him in Rabīʿ II 1131/February 1719 and substituted for him Rāfiʿ al-Daradjāt; but in June, the latter died of tuberculosis, to be succeeded by yet another puppet of the Bārha Sayyids, Shāh Djahān II b. Rāfiʿ al-Sha'n.

Bibliography: See that to FARRUKH-SIYAR, and add J.F. Richards, *The Mughal empire*, Cambridge 1993, 272. For chronology, see C.E. Bosworth, *The New Islamic dynasties*, Edinburgh 1996, 331 no. 175.

(C.E. BOSWORTH)

AL-**RAMLĪ**, MUḤAMMAD B. AḤMAD ABŪ BAKR **IBN** AL-**NĀBULUSĪ**, a traditionist originally from Nābulus [*q.v.*] who was the *raʾīs* of Ramla and who used often to make retreat with his disciples in the Akuwākh Bāniyās ("the huts of Bāniyās") at the foot of Mt. Hermon in the Syrian Djawlān.

He publicly opposed the Fāṭimid occupation of Syria. Taken from Damascus and sent in a cage to Egypt, on the orders of the caliph al-Muʿizz [*q.v.*] he was flayed alive in 363/973 at the Manẓar, the belvedere on the road connecting Fusṭāṭ with Cairo (the relevant Arabic texts and details of his biography and of the numerous famous *muḥaddiths* and historians whom he taught or frequented are to be found in Th. Bianquis, *Ibn al-Nābulusī, un martyr sunnite au IVᵉ s. de l'hégire*, in *AI*, xii [1974], 45-66; idem, *ʿAbd al-Ghanī b. Saʿīd, un savant sunnite au service des Fāṭimides*, in *Actes du XXIᵉ Congrès international des orientalistes*, Paris 1975, i, 39-47).

He exercised a more important influence on the historians of Damascus and Baghdād who tended towards the *ahl al-ḥadīth* than on those of Ashʿarī tendencies, so that Ibn al-ʿAsākir does not seem to hold many of his disciples in very high regard. One should mention in regard to him a curious *ḥadīth* which he transmitted and which after his death extended the mission of guiding the consciences of the Sunnī community entrusted collectively to the *ʿulamāʾ*. His Sunnī disciples, gathered together at the Akuwākh Bāniyās, lived a life close to nature which is described by al-Muḳaddasī (160, 188, tr. Miquel, 176, 238); these persons were mainly refugees from Tarsūs expelled by the Byzantines. The *nisba* of *al-Ballūṭī* borne by their head Abū Isḥāḳ seems to go back, not to their eating acorns but to a distant remembrance of Andalusī origins. After the Revolt of the Suburb at Cordova, these forebears had reached Alexandria, then Crete, then Ṭarsūs, and finally had sought refuge in Syria.

What made Ibn al-Nābulusī famous was the *fatwā* which he gave in reply to a question whether priority be given to the war against the Byzantines, who were regularly ravaging northern Syria, or to resistance against the Fāṭimid army which, it was true, could protect the province against Byzantine raids. He said, "If I had ten arrows, I would loose nine of them against the descendants of ʿUbayd Allāh (sc. the Fāṭimids) and one against the Byzantines." He justified his attitude thus: "In fact, the Byzantines are People of the Book, whereas the former are impious associators of others with God . . . enemies of all the prophets and all the scriptures that God has sent" (Ḳāḍī ʿAbd al-Djabbār, *Tathbīt*, ed. ʿA. al-K. ʿUthmān, Beirut 1970, ii, 608). According to Ibn al-Djawzī (*Muntaẓam*, Haydarābād 1375, vii, 82), he is even reported to have altered his reply when interrogated in Egypt, asserting that not merely nine arrows but also the tenth arrow should be launched against the Fāṭimids because they had improperly claimed for themselves the divine light. The later sources expatiate on his sufferings, which lasted for three days. The expressions attributed to the sufferer, about to be flayed alive, by a pitying Jew stem from the Ṣūfī vocabulary. Al-Dhahabī mentions that there was, at this same time as Ibn al-Nābulusī, another Sunnī who offered resistance, Abu 'l-Faradj al-Ṭarsūsī, who was subjected to humiliations in the Aḳṣā Mosque by the Fāṭimids' Maghribī soldiery, and he records for the year 364/974 the punishment, likewise at Jerusalem, of Abu 'l-Ḳāsim al-Wāsiṭī, who had his tongue cut out. Having been miraculously restored by the Prophet Muḥammad, al-Wāsiṭī climbed the minaret in order publicly to proclaim his Sunnī faith, and was then crucified, remaining on the cross for three days. His "corpse" was thrown down in a street, where some pious persons took it in order to wash it, but then discovered that he was still alive. Abū Bakr gave back to him his tongue, which had been cut out a second time and he climbed up to proclaim his faith from the top of a minaret. Tired of all this, the governor contented himself with expelling him from the city. References to Christ's life and crucifixion are frequent in the Ḥanbalī milieux of Palestine; accordingly, one finds an ascetic walking on the Lake of Tiberias. Ibn ʿAsākir does not hide his ironic scepticism when he mentions such occurences among the literalists, whom he despised and cordially hated, considering them to be liars who exploited the populace's credulity. It is furthermore known that militant Ḥanbalī Sunnism remained alive in Palestine up to the time of the Crusades (see H. Laoust, *Le précis de droit d'Ibn Qudāma*, Beirut 1950, introd.).

Bibliography: Given in the article.

(TH. BIANQUIS)

RAMY AL-DJIMĀR (A.), literally, "the throwing of pebbles", a practice which probably goes back to early Arabia and whose most celebrated survival is in the ritual throwing of stones in the valley of Minā by the pilgrims returning from ʿArafāt in the course of the Meccan Pilgrimage [see AL-DJAMRA; ḤADJDJ. iii. c]. In Fahd's view, the rite does not seem to have had any divinatory significance, but among suggestions regarding its origins is the one that it could have been a gesture of solidarity with a dead person, on whose tomb stones are placed. See the discussion in T. Fahd, *La divination arabe*, Leiden 1966, 188ff.

Bibliography: Given in the article. (ED.)

RA'Y (A.), a verbal noun of *raʾā*, the common Arabic verb for seeing with the eye, has among its various closely related meanings that of opinion (i.e. a seeing of the heart) on questions of Islamic law not within the literal scope of the revealed texts (*naṣṣ*) of the Ḳurʾān or *ḥadīth*. Although sometimes used for an opinion on a specific question of law (for which *ḳawl* is most common), *raʾy* is more often used for the body of such opinions held by a particular jurist (i.e. the *raʾy* of Abū Ḥanīfa) and for the reasoning used to derive such opinions. It is also found in the sense of the intellectual faculties that underlie such legal reasoning. Discrimination among these and other possible meanings of the term is not always easy (cf. Ch. Pellat, *Ibn al-Muqaffaʿ (mort vers 140/757), "conseilleur" du calife*, Paris 1976, 82) and *raʾy* never achieved the status of a fully technical legal term. Although the legal usage of *raʾy* is the most important historically, *raʾy* was also used for adherence to a body of theological doctrine (i.e. *raʾy al-Djahmiyya*), and its narrowest recorded sense appears to be that of adherence to the doctrine of the Khāridjīs (on the use of *raʾy* for the holding of specific theological dogmas, such as freewill, see al-Sharīf al-Murtaḍā, *al-Dharīʿa ilā uṣūl al-sharīʿa, ed.* Abu 'l-Ḳāsim Gurdjī, Tehran 1376/1956, ii, 673, where, however, the examples are all of the verb *raʾā* and the context is polemical). In all of the above senses, the singular *raʾy* is far more common than the plural *ārāʾ*.

As a process of deriving law *raʾy* does not constitute any single method of reasoning but can be used of such methods as *ḳiyās, istiḥsān*, and *istiṣlāḥ* [*q.vv.*], severally or together, although its use specifically in relation to *ḳiyās* is the most frequent (e.g. *yaḳīsūna bi-raʾyihim*). Consequently, identifying the precise forms of reasoning labelled as *raʾy* by one or another early jurist or school of jurists requires specific examination of their legal arguments (J. Schacht, *The origins of Muhammadan jurisprudence*, Oxford 1950, 98-132, 269-328, still of fundamental importance). Insofar as *raʾy* does not include the process of authenticating *ḥadīth* or interpreting texts, it constitutes only part of the scope of *idjtihād* [*q.v.*] as generally understood, although the expression *idjtihād al-raʾy* (the exercise of *raʾy*) figures prominently in the *ḥadīth* (e.g. the *ḥadīth* of Muʿādh b. Djabal, on which see al-Mubārakfūrī, *Tuḥfat al-aḥwadhī*, Beirut 1422/2001, iv, 637-9) and in the polemics concerning *raʾy*.

There is general agreement among both Sunnī and Shīʿī writers that there was some recourse to *raʾy* on the part of certain Companions (*ṣaḥāba* [*q.v.*]) of the Prophet, including such leading figures as Abū Bakr and ʿUmar, and then on the part of their Successors (*tābiʿūn*) (Ibn ʿAbd al-Barr, *Djāmiʿ bayān al-ʿilm wa-faḍlihi*, ed. al-Zuhayrī, al-Dammām 1414/1994, ii, 858-9). This early *raʾy* was accorded some measure of authority, at least by the mainstream of Muslims, and was transmitted by scholars together with Prophetic *ḥadīth*. This early *ra'y* is preserved in such collections as *al-Muṣannaf* of ʿAbd al-Razzāḳ al-Ṣanʿānī (d. 211/826) and *al-Muṣannaf* of Ibn Abī Shayba (d. 235/849) [*q.vv.*].

A critical development in the history of Islamic law occurred during the late Umayyad and early ʿAbbāsid periods with a dramatic growth in the scope and intensity of *ra'y* (cf. Ibn Taymiyya, *Madjmūʿat al-fatāwā*, ed. al-Djazzār and al-Bāz, al-Riyāḍ 1419/1998, xx, 175 which names Rabīʿa wa-Ibn Hurmuz (so read) [in Medina], ʿUthmān al-Battī (so read) in Baṣra, and Abū Ḥanīfa as the leading figures at the beginning of the ʿAbbāsid dynasty, cf. I. Goldziher, *Muslim studies*, tr. C.R. Barber and S.M. Stern, London 1971, 78-85 [on foreign influence], 201-2). The proponents of this new version of *ra'y* became known as the *ahl* or *aṣḥāb al-ra'y* [*q.v.*]. The *ahl al-ra'y* were met with opposition from a number of quarters: the scholars of tradition (the *ahl* or *aṣḥāb al-ḥadīth*) (Ibn Ḳutayba, *K. Mukhtalif al-ḥadīth*, Cairo 1326, 62-71; Shāh Walī Allāh al-Dihlawī, *Ḥudjdjat Allāh al-bāligha*, ed. Ḍamīriyya, al-Riyāḍ 1420/1999, i, 455-62 [explaining the dispute]), certain Muʿtazilī theologians, and large segments of the Shīʿī community. Although opposition to *ra'y* in these various groups was in its origin based on different considerations, anti-*ra'y* arguments developed by one group could come to be adopted by the others (Ibn Maʿṣūm, *al-Daradjāt al-rafīʿa*, Nadjaf 1382/1962, 26). The Muʿtazilī opponents of *ra'y* were particularly influential in propagating a epistemologically sophisticated anti-*ra'y* position that came to influence the opposition among the traditionists and Shīʿīs.

The opposition to *ra'y* from among the traditionists is extensively preserved in *ḥadīth* collections, above all that of al-Dārimī (d. 255/868), the writings of Ibn Ḥazm (d. 456/1064), Ibn ʿAbd al-Barr (d. 463/1070), and Ibn Ḳayyim al-Djawziyya (d. 751/1350) [*q.vv.*], and traditionist biographical works such as that of al-Fasawī, *K. al-Maʿrifa wa 'l-ta'rīkh*, (ed. Akram Ḍiyā' al-ʿUmarī, Baghdad 1394/1973). This material provides far richer historical resources for tracing the details of the development of the new *ra'y* movement than do the more dogmatic Muʿtazilī and Shīʿī anti-*ra'y* sources. The *ahl al-ra'y* were regarded by their traditionist opponents as undermining the authority of the *sunna* that the traditionists had dedicated their lives to preserving. Familiarity with the *sunna* (which included knowledge of the *ra'y* of the first generations) was sometimes labelled real knowledge (*ʿilm*) in contrast to subjective legal opinion (*ra'y, ẓann*). The *ahl al-ra'y* were set on a course of expanding Islamic law far beyond the resources of the traditionists and to this extent were inevitably led to expose the contradictions and limitations of the traditionist approach.

Although the traditionist anti-*ra'y* sources do point to the subjectivity and instability of the results of the new *ra'y* and to the many instances where the *ra'y* of the jurists was in contradiction to well-established *sunna*, their most frequent complaint concerns the relentless questioning on the most abstruse possible legal cases that was characteristic of the new *ra'y*. The anti-*ra'y* sources condemn the difficult questions (*muʿḍilāt, ughlūṭāt*) of the *ahl al-ra'y*, the relentlessness with which they were pursued (*tashdīd*), and the unwarranted speculative character of the answers these questions evoked (*takalluf, tanaṭṭuʿ*). Numerous anti-*ra'y* statements single out for criticism the annoying and virtually inescapable formula of eliciting a legal opinion (*ara'ayta*) (on the form and syntax of this expression, found in the Ḳur'ān and *ḥadīth*, see H.L. Fleischer, *Kleinere Schriften*, Leipzig 1885-8, i, 481-7; G. Bergsträsser, *Verneinungs- und Fragepartikeln*, Leipzig 1914, 93). The *ahl al-ra'y* are the *aṣḥāb ara'ayta* (al-Dārimī, *al-Sunan*, ed. Dahmān, Beirut n.d., i, 66). The expression is characteristic of certain genres of early legal literature from *ra'y* circles and sometimes appears in these works with unremitting frequency (e.g. al-Shaybānī, *K. al-Makhāridj fī 'l-ḥiyal*, ed. J. Schacht, Leipzig 1930). It was also employed to introduce an objection in debate (cf. Schacht, *Origins*, 120). The importance of this veritable flood of questions to the development of the Islamic law cannot be overstated. It was the questions that generated the growing scope of legal discussion (*ta'līd al-su'āl*, in Ibn Abī Zayd al-Ḳayrawānī, *al-Nawādir wa 'l-ziyādāt*, ed. ʿAbd al-Fattāḥ Ḥulw, Beirut 1999, i, 9) and led directly to the production of the large legal treatises that remain standard to this day (cf. the account of the Mālikī classic *al-Mudawwana* in Ibn Khaldūn, *al-Muḳaddima*, ed. al-Saʿīd al-Mandūh, Beirut 1414/1993, ii, 133; Ibn Taymiyya, *Madjmūʿat al-fatāwā*, xx, 180).

At the forefront of this new style of legal learning founded in posing questions were the ʿIrāḳī jurists headed by Abū Ḥanīfa. The questions posed by these jurists were often unabashedly hypothetical and among the jibes directed at Abū Ḥanīfa was that he was among the most knowledgeable about what has not occurred but among the most ignorant about what has occurred. The posing of such hypothetical questions enabled the jurists to gauge the extent to which they could found the law on general principles, and in fact the efforts of the *ahl al-ra'y* to render the law systematic are noted, sometimes critically (Ibn Abī Ḥātim, *Ādāb al-Shāfiʿī wa-manāḳibuhu*, ed. ʿAbd al-Khāliḳ, Cairo 1372/1952, 171).

The *ahl al-ra'y* were able to gain substantial successes in their competition with the *ahl al-ḥadīth* and to attract talented students of *ḥadīth* to their camp (Ibn Saʿd, vi, 270: Zufar b. al-Hudhayl). In such cases the sources speak of *ra'y* gaining mastery of the individual, and his eventual identification with *ra'y*. The most obvious examples of such an identification are the Medinan Rabīʿa Ibn Farrūkh (d. 136/753), known as Rabīʿat al-Ra'y and the Baṣran Ḥanafī Hilāl b. Yaḥyā (d. 245/859), known as Hilāl al-Ra'y. Often, however, *ra'y* was adopted but not in its most aggressive form, and the line dividing the *ahl al-ra'y* and *ahl al-ḥadīth* could not always be clearly drawn. Many writers, for example, include Mālik with the *ahl al-ḥadīth*, others with the *ahl al-ra'y* (Ibn Ḳutayba, *al-Maʿārif*, ed. ʿUkāsha, Cairo n.d., 498). Moderate forms of *ra'y* balanced by traditions were able to make some inroads among the *ahl al-ḥadīth*.

There is universal agreement on applying the label *ahl al-ra'y* to Abū Ḥanīfa and his followers in ʿIrāḳ, and Abū Ḥanīfa was the favoured target of the barbs of the traditionists, who sometimes portrayed him in satanic terms (there is an extensive collection of such denigrating remarks in al-Khaṭīb al-Baghdādī, *Ta'rīkh Madīnat al-Salām*, ed. Bashshār ʿAwwād Maʿrūf, Beirut 1422/2001, xv, 543-86). The many instances in which Abū Ḥanīfa was regarded as having contracted the *sunna* were collected (see Ibn Abī Shayba, *al-Kitāb al-muṣannaf*, Bombay 1403/1983, xiv, 148-282). Even Abū Ḥanīfa, however, did not lack entirely for admirers among the *ahl al-ḥadīth*, and one of these, ʿAbd Allāh Ibn al-Mubārak (d. 181/797 [*q.v.*]), approved of *ra'y* for the purpose of interpreting *ḥadīth*.

Al-Shāfiʿī was regarded by some leading representatives of the *ahl al-ḥadīth* as having supported their cause with arguments that the *ahl al-ra'y* could not dismiss, and Aḥmad b. Ḥanbal not only encouraged traditionists to study al-Shāfiʿī's *al-Risāla* (Ibn Abī Ḥātim, 61-3) but himself made a careful study of al-Shāfiʿī's legal works and was thus exposed to a moderate version of *ra'y*. The very development of the discipline of legal theory (*uṣūl al-fiḳh* [*q.v.*]) ushered in by al-Shāfiʿī's *al-Risāla* led to increased scrutiny of the epistemological foundations of the various methods of legal reasoning falling within *ra'y* and to a revaluation of *ra'y* in all its forms. The question was now raised, for example, of whether the Prophet himself had ever had recourse to *ra'y*, albeit infallibly, as suggested in the *ḥadīth* (Abū Dāwūd, *al-Sunan*, ed. al-Khālidī, Beirut 1416/1996, ii, 509; cf. Ḳur'ān, IV, 105: *bi-mā arāka Allāh*, a question to which al-Shāfiʿī was unable to give a definitive answer, cf. al-Bayhaḳī, *Maʿrifat al-sunan wa 'l-āthār*, ed. Aḥmad Ṣaḳr, Cairo n.d., i, 7-8).

Al-Shāfiʿī himself favoured the limitation of *ra'y* to *ḳiyās* to the exclusion of *istiḥsān* (Schacht, *Origins*, 120-8), and others in his wake reconciled the traditions for and against *ra'y* by identifying the *ra'y* that was acceptable with *ra'y* that was grounded in the revealed texts, that is, *ḳiyās*. Nonetheless the Ḥanafīs and Mālikīs continued to support a broader notion of *ra'y* and interpret the condemnation of *ra'y* in the *ḥadīth* to refer to *ra'y* in the sense of theological heresy (Ibn ʿAbd al-Barr, *Djāmiʿ bayān*, ii, 1052-4) or to offer accounts of *istiḥsān*, for example, that brought it within the scope of *ḳiyās*.

More radical forms of legal theory emerged, however, which imposed a standard of certainty for Islamic law in all its elements. Among the proponents of this elevated standard was the Baṣran Muʿtazilī al-Naẓẓām (d. between 220/835 and 230/845 [*q.v.*]) whose attack on probable reasoning in all forms including *ḳiyās* did not spare the Companions who resorted to *ra'y* (van Ess, *Das Kitāb an-Nakt des Naẓẓām und seine Rezeption im Kitāb al-Futyā des Ǧāḥiẓ*, Göttingen 1972). Among the Baghdādī Muʿtazilīs who took a similar position was Djaʿfar b. al-Mubashshir (d. 234/848-9), who unlike al-Naẓẓām sought to justify recourse to *ra'y* on the part of the Companions by way of compromise of a dispute or theoretical inquiry without practical consequences (ʿAbd al-Djabbār al-Hamadhānī, *al-Mughnī*, ed. Amīn al-Khūlī, Cairo 1962, xvii, 298).

The Ẓāhirī school of law, inaugurated by Dāwūd b. ʿAlī al-Iṣfahānī (d. 270/834 [see DĀWŪD B. KHALAF]) came from the ranks of the *ahl al-ḥadīth*, and Dāwūd, like Aḥmad b. Ḥanbal, was a fervent admirer of al-Shāfiʿī (I. Goldziher, *The Ẓāhirīs*, tr. W. Behn, Leiden 1971). Dāwūd's son Muḥammad (d. 297/910) impelled the Ẓāhirīs in a more independent direction and was unsparing in his critique of al-Shāfiʿī (D. Stewart, *Muḥammad b. Dā'ūd al-Ẓāhirī's manual of jurisprudence*: al-Wuṣūl ilā maʿrifat al-uṣūl, in B.G. Weiss, *Studies in Islamic legal theory*, Leiden 2002, 129-30). Each in somewhat different fashion propounded a version of Islamic law that excluded all forms of probable reasoning and both were in a position to draw upon their Muʿtazilī contemporaries (cf. al-Sarakhsī, *Uṣūl al-fiḳh*, ed. Abu 'l-Wafā' al-Afghānī, Cairo 1372, ii, 119). In the apparent absence of surviving writings by these early Ẓāhirīs, it is the extensive works of the Andalusī Ẓāhirī Ibn Ḥazm [*q.v.*] that shed light on the Ẓāhirī contribution to the anti-*ra'y* movement and exhibit the lingering influence of the Muʿtazilī theorists. According to Ibn Ḥazm, *ra'y* was already a feature of the period of the Companions before the appearance of analogy in the following generation (*Mulakhkhaṣ ibṭāl al-ḳiyās wa 'l-ra'y wa 'l-istiḥsān wa 'l-taḳlīd wa 'l-taʿlīl*, ed. Saʿīd al-Afghānī, Beirut 1379/1969, 4-5). He understands *ra'y* to involve the enunciation of legal opinion on the basis of sheer expediency and he regards the process as equivalent to *istiḥsān*, and *istinbāṭ* (derivation) (*al-Iḥkām fī uṣūl al-aḥkām*, ed. Aḥmad Muḥammad Shākir, Cairo 1347, vi, 16). He vigorously rejects the effort on the part of the jurists of his day to identify *ḳiyās* as a form of *ra'y*, in fact as identical to acceptable *ra'y*. There is no acceptable form of *ra'y*. The Companions' recourse to *ra'y* was misconceived, but in their case never amounted to an endorsement of *ra'y* as a method of deriving law because they did not, as did the later proponents of *ra'y*, regard their *ra'y* as God's law (*ḥukm*). They saw it rather as providing a rule they individually might follow out of pious precaution, or they offered their *ra'y* by way of compromise to settle a dispute. Insofar as any sound Prophetic traditions mandate recourse to *idjtihād al-ra'y*, what must be meant is exhaustive seeking for the applicable revealed texts.

Opposition to the movement of *ahl al-ra'y* was also found among the Twelver and Ismāʿīlī Shīʿīs, and resort to *ra'y* (also *irtiyā'*), *ḳiyās*, and *idjtihād* is condemned in numerous Shīʿī *ḥadīth*, sometimes in terms familiar from the Sunnī *ḥadīth*. Prominent in this connection are the *ḥadīth* going back to the Imām Djaʿfar al-Ṣādiḳ, who is portrayed as meeting with Abū Ḥanīfa, whose pretensions to legal understanding he quickly shows to be groundless (i.e. al-Madjlisī, *Biḥār al-anwār*, Tehran n.d., ii, 291-6, cf. Ḳāḍī al-Nuʿmān, *Daʿā'im al-Islām*, ed. Fayḍī, Cairo 1379/1960, ii, 266). Of particular interest is a purported letter from Djaʿfar to the proponents of *ra'y* and *ḳiyās* in which the Imām argues that if resort to *ra'y* were permitted, there would have been no point in God's sending of the prophets. He could have left humans to direct their own affairs (al-Barḳī, *al-Maḥāsin*, ed. Mahdī al-Radjā'ī, Ḳum 1413, i, 331-2). The same Imām is also found warning his followers against turning to *ra'y* when they are unable to find answers to their questions in the revealed texts, an injunction that is not always followed (Hossein Modarressi Ṭabāṭabā'ī, *An introduction to Shīʿī law*, London 1984, 30-1).

The anti-*ra'y* position was defended in the dogmatic writings of the Ismāʿīlī Ḳāḍī al-Nuʿmān [*q.v.*] b. Muḥammad (d. 363/974), whose polemics against *ra'y* were bolstered by arguments from Muḥammad b. Dāwūd al-Ẓāhirī (*K. Ikhtilāf uṣūl al-madhāhib*, ed. S.T. Lokhandwalla, Simla 1972, 202). A line of Twelver Shīʿī scholars, al-Shaykh al-Mufīd (d. 413/1002) and his students al-Sharīf al-Murtaḍā (d. 436/1044) and Muḥammad b. al-Ḥasan al-Ṭūsī (d. 460/1067) [*q.vv.*], writing under Muʿtazilī influence, maintained their community's rejection of *ra'y*. Even after the 7th/13th century when Twelver Shīʿī jurists came to recognise the validity of *idjtihād*, they continued to exclude *ra'y* and *ḳiyās* from their sources of law.

The competition between the proponents of *ra'y* and their various opponents ended in a clear victory for the *ahl al-ra'y*. Islamic law as it can be found in the enormous literature of the Sunnī schools is largely the product of *ra'y*; the books of *fiḳh* are the books of *ra'y*. It was this version of Sunnī law that formed a model for the elaboration of law in other circles, even those opposed to *ra'y*. In this sense al-Shāfiʿī was fully justified when he stated that "all are dependent on the ʿIrāḳīs in *fiḳh*" (Ibn Abī Ḥātim, 210, var. "in *ra'y*"). At another level, however, the deep division within Sunnism between *ahl al-ra'y* and *ahl al-ḥadīth* was never entirely bridged but continued to manifest itself to one degree or another within the

Sunnī schools of law (al-Khaṭṭābī, *Maʿālim al-sunan*, ed. Muḥammad Rāghib al-Ṭabbākh, Aleppo 1351/1932, i, 2-8 [on reconciling *ahl al-ḥadīth* and *ahl al-ra'y*]). Not only an Ibn Taymiyya (d. 728/1327 [*q.v.*]) (*Madjmūʿat al-fatāwā*, xix, 151) could take offence at the statement of the Shāfiʿī Ashʿarī al-Djuwaynī (d. 478/1085) that nine-tenths of the law depended on pure *ra'y* (*ra'y maḥḍ*) (*al-Burhān*, ed. ʿAbd al-ʿAẓīm al-Dīb, Cairo 1400, ii, 768). *Ra'y* was never entirely reputable as a source of law, and many centuries after the Central Asian Ḥanafī Abu 'l-Yusr al-Bazdawī (d. 493/1100) claimed that far from *aṣḥāb al-ra'y* being a label of opprobrium (reading *subba*) for the Ḥanafīs as some thought—it was in fact "one of the most beautiful names as indicating their special connection with knowledge of the heart" (*Kitāb fīhi maʿrifat al-ḥudjadj al-sharʿiyya*, ed. M. Bernand and E. Chaumont, Cairo 2003, 4)—Ḥanafīs and their allies felt called upon to address the label (Murtaḍā al-Zabīdī [d. 1205/1790], *K. ʿUḳūd al-djawāhir al-munīfa*, ed. al-Albānī, Beirut 1406/1985, i, 25; Ibn Hadjar al-Haytamī, *al-Khayrāt al-ḥisān*, ed. al-Barnī, Beirut n.d., 62-3).

A small but significant remnant of the *ahl al-ḥadīth* movement continued to take its inspiration from the anti-*ra'y* polemics of the early *ahl al-ḥadīth*, which remained accessible to them primarily through the writings of Ibn ʿAbd al-Barr and Ibn Ḳayyim al-Djawziyya. The latter in his *Iʿlām al-muwaḳḳiʿīn ʿan rabb al-ʿālamīn* (ed. Muḥammad Muḥyī al-Dīn ʿAbd al-Ḥamīd, Cairo 1374/1955, i, 67-85) had, in addition to citing a wealth of material on the *ra'y* debate, established an elaborate categorisation of *ra'y* under three headings: valid (*ṣaḥīḥ, maḥmūd*), invalid (*bāṭil, madhmūm*), and dubious (*mawḍiʿ, ishtibāh*). Ibn al-Ḳayyim is true to the early *ahl al-ḥadīth* in recognising the authority of the *ra'y* of the Companions but also admits the validity of *ḳiyās* in the absence of other sources. His dubious *ra'y* is *ra'y* employed under exigent circumstances when all else fails. It is not meant to establish a generally binding norm from which further rules can be derived, although in fact later jurists have developed this form of *ra'y* at the expense of the revealed texts and statements of early authorities (*al-nuṣūṣ wa 'l-āthār*). Those inspired by the writings of Ibn al-Ḳayyim shared his sense that much of the law of the schools was pure *ra'y* with very little in the way of textual support of any kind and thus of no authority. In their opposition to *taḳlīd* [*q.v.*] of such mere fallible opinions, they looked to the abolition of the existing schools. Among such jurists are Ṣāliḥ al-Fullānī (d. 1218/1803), Muḥammad b. ʿAlī al-Shawkānī (d. 1250/1834 [*q.v.*]) and Aḥmad b. Idrīs (d. 1253/1837 [*q.v.*]) (B. Radtke *et al.*, *The exoteric Aḥmad b. Idrīs*, Leiden 2000, including an edition and translation of his *Risālat al-radd ʿalā ahl al-ra'y*).

The arguments of these and other anti-*ra'y* writers were promoted during the twentieth-century reform movement inaugurated by Muḥammad ʿAbduh (d. 1905 [*q.v.*]) and continued by his disciple Muḥammad Rashīd Riḍā (d. 1935 [*q.v.*]). This movement has been quite successful in its intended goal of divesting the law of the schools of its aura of sanctity and revealing it as the body of *ra'y* that it is. It has, however, not put in its place a law that would have pleased the *ahl al-ḥadīth* but has inclined rather toward an eclecticism open to a wider body of *ra'y* than ever before (see the instructive preface of Riḍā to Ibn Ḳudāmā, *al-Mughnī*, Medina n.d., i, 21-8).

To a certain extent related to the great debate over *ra'y* in law is the prohibition reported in the *ḥadīth* of interpreting the Ḳur'ān according to *ra'y* (*al-tafsīr bi 'l-ra'y*) (Ibn Taymiyya, *Muḳaddima fī uṣūl al-tafsīr*, ed. Zarzūr, Kuwayt 1392/1972, 105-13; I. Goldziher, *Die Richtungen der islamischen Koranauslegung*, Leiden 1920, 61-2, 84), a prohibition frequently cited in the anti-*ra'y* material discussed above. Although the vast literature of Ḳur'anic commentary does contain works in which the interpretations given are entirely or largely in the form of transmitted explanations from the Prophet and his early followers, the prohibition did not prevent the rapid growth of exegetical works along more independent lines. In some cases this was justified by distinguishing between *tafsīr*, which depends on eyewitness knowledge of the circumstances surrounding the Ḳur'ānic revelations and was thus limited to the Companions, and *ta'wīl*, which, disclaiming knowledge of the real meaning of the Ḳur'ān, simply explores possible meanings of the Ḳur'ānic wording. This was the solution of the theologian al-Māturīdī (d. 333/944 [*q.v.*]) (*K. Ta'wīlāt ahl al-sunna*, ed. Muḥammad Mustafīḍ al-Raḥmān, Baghdād 1404/1987, i, 5-6). More commonly, the *ra'y* in the prohibition was understood to refer to theological heresy or subjective inclination, and interpretations not offered in defence of heretical doctrines or prompted by unlearned instinct without a basis in language or logic were deemed not to violate the prohibition (Ibn al-ʿArabī, *Ḳānūn al-ta'wīl*, ed. Muḥammad al-Sulaymānī, Beirut 1990, 366-8; Ibn Aṭiyya, *al-Muḥarrar al-wadjīz*, Beirut 1423/2003, 27; Muḥammad ʿAbd al-ʿAẓīm al-Zurḳānī, *Manāhil al-ʿirfān fī ʿulūm al-Ḳur'ān*, Cairo n.d., ii, 49-69 [defending *tafsīr bi 'l-ra'y*]; Muḥammad Ḥamad Zaghlūl, *al-Tafsīr bi 'l-ra'y ḳawāʿiduhu wa-ḍawābiṭuhu wa-aʿlāmuhu*, Damascus 1420/1999).

Bibliography: In addition to references in the text, see Muḥammad Mukhtār al-Ḳāḍī, *al-Ra'y fi 'l-fiḳh al-islāmī*, Cairo 1368/1949; Ahmad Hasan, *Early modes of ijtihad: ra'y, qiyas and istihsan*, in *Islamic Studies*, vi (1967), 47-79; Hossein Modarressi, *Rationalism and traditionalism in Shīʿī jurisprudence: a preliminary survey*, in *SI*, lix (1984), 141-58; M.I. Fierro Bello, *La pólemique à propos de* rafʿ al-yadayn fī l-ṣalāt *dans al-Andalus*, in *SI*, lxv (1987), 69-90 (conflict of *ra'y* and *ḥadīth*); eadem, *The introduction of ḥadīth in al-Andalus (2nd/8th-3rd/9th centuries)*, in *Isl.*, lxvi (1989), 68-93; M.H. Kamali, *The approved and disapproved varieties of ra'y (personal opinion) in Islam*, in *American Journal of Islamic Social Sciences*, vii (1990), 39-63; idem, *Freedom of expression in Islam*, Cambridge 1997; J. van Ess, *Theologie und Gesellschaft im 2. und 3. Jahrhundert Hidschra*, Berlin 1991-7, iv (index); Abdel-Majid Turki, *Le* Muwaṭṭa' *de Mâlik, ouvrage de* fiqh, *entre le* ḥadîth *et le* ra'y, *ou comment aborder l'étude du mâlikisme kairounais au IV/Xe siècle*, in *SI*, lxxxvi (1997), 5-35; Khalīfa Bā Bakr al-Ḥasan, *al-Idjtihād bi 'l-ra'y fī madrasat al-ḥidjāz al-fiḳhiyya*, Cairo 1418/1997; S. Stroumsa, *Freethinkers of medieval Islam: Ibn al-Rāwandī, Abū Bakr al-Rāzī and their impact on Islamic thought*, Leiden 1999 (*ra'y* in theology); B. Krawietz, *Hierarchie der Rechtsquellen im tradierten sunnitischen Islam*, Berlin 2002 (index, modern discussions).

(Jeanette Wakin and A. Zysow)

RIBĀ.

B. In modern commercial usage.

In the modern period, debates on *ribā* among Muslims followed the pre-modern conceptions and arguments developed in *fiḳh*. With the introduction of interest-based banks into Muslim lands, debate on the permissibility or otherwise of interest began, which intensified from the 1940s in the context of the emergence of the global Islamic neo-revivalist movements.

These movements such as the Muslim Brotherhood [see AL-IKHWĀN AL-MUSLIMŪN] of Egypt and Djamā'at Islāmī of Pakistan and those influenced by their ideological frameworks called for the transformation of the existing political, legal, social and economic institutions of Muslim societies to ones more in line with "Islamic" norms and principles. One such institution that was targeted for transformation was what they considered to be *ribā* (that is, interest)-based banking and finance in Muslim societies.

Ribā in its *fiḳhī* sense is associated with a range of contracts, from loans (*ḳarḍ*) to debts (*dayn*) to sales (*bay'*). However, in the mid-to late-20th century, in the Islamic finance literature, *ribā* came to be discussed mainly in the context of interest in financial transactions, and interpreted as interest. This close association between *ribā* and interest is generally accepted today among many Muslims. In his discussion on *ribā*, Khurshid Ahmad, a prominent advocate of Islamic finance in Pakistan, emphasised how *ribā* is to be understood today, and argued that Islam forbids "any premium or excess, small, moderate or large, contractually agreed upon at the time of lending money or loanable funds". (Ahmad, *Elimination of Riba*, 42). However, for some Muslims, *ribā* should not be interpreted simply as interest. For them, only some forms of interest may be *ribā*, and not others.

Muḥammad 'Abduh (d. 1905) and Rashīd Riḍā (d. 1935) [*q.vv.*] were among the first to address the question of interest on deposits. While uncomfortable with the idea, they were prepared to concede it if a *muḍāraba* (commenda [*q.v.*]) scheme could be devised to legitimise the interest (Mallat, *The debate on Riba*, 74). The Egyptian authority on Islamic law, 'Abd al-Razzāḳ Sanhūrī (d. 1971), saw compound interest as the main intent of the Ḳur'ān's prohibition of *ribā*. Interest on capital, in his view, could be justified on the basis of "need" (*ḥādja*), but to prevent misuse and exploitation the state should limit interest rates and control methods of payment (*Maṣādir al-ḥaḳḳ*, iii, 241-4). The contemporary Syrian thinker Doualibi argued that the Ḳur'ān prohibited interest on "consumption loans" specifically, presumably because of its concern for people who may have borrowed just to meet their basic needs. Following this line of thinking, some have argued that there is no *ribā* in interest paid or received by corporate bodies such as companies and governments, and others that Islam prohibits "usury" not "interest". There is also the idea that *ribā* should be equated with real interest, not nominal interest. Several scholars of the mid- to late-20th century also interpreted *ribā* from a "moral" perspective, away from the literalism that dominates much of the thinking on *ribā*. Muḥammad Asad (d. 1992), a modernist commentator on the Ḳur'ān, maintained that *ribā* involved "an exploitation of the economically weak by the strong and resourceful" (*The message*, 633). Fazlur Rahman (d. 1988), the Pakistani-American academic, argued that the *raison d'être* of the prohibition of *ribā* was injustice (*ẓulm*), as was stated in the Ḳur'ān (II, 279), and that "well-meaning Muslims with very virtuous consciences sincerely believe that the Ḳur'ān has banned all bank interest for all times in woeful disregard of what *ribā* was historically, why the Ḳur'ān denounced it as a gross and cruel form of exploitation and banned it" (*Islam: challenges*, 326).

Despite the appeal of these views, the neo-revivalists and their followers and sympathisers, who increasingly represent mainstream Muslim opinion today, have continued to reject any reinterpretation of *ribā* to accommodate bank interest. Mawdūdī (d. 1979), the founder of Djamā'at Islāmī of Pakistan, for example, asserted that there was no question that *ribā* was interest. The Council of Islamic Ideology of Pakistan (*Consolidated recommendations*, 7), which in the 1980s developed a blueprint for the transformation of the Pakistani financial system into an Islamic one, claimed that there was "complete unanimity among all schools of thought in Islam that the term *ribā* stands for interest in all its types and forms".

In the 1970s, the oil-producing Gulf states found themselves with massive cash surpluses to invest, which shifted the debate on *ribā* from the theoretical to the practical. One of the strategies adopted by these states was to develop financial institutions on an interest-free (that is, *ribā*-free, or Islamic) basis. Examples include the Islamic Development Bank based in Saudi Arabia, the Faisal Islamic Banks based in the Middle East, Kuwait Finance House and the Dubai Islamic Bank. *Sharī'a* advisers guided the design of contracts and products and the drawing up of principles for productive ventures, in which capital could be combined with the skill of entrepreneurs to lead to socially beneficial incremental returns. The system created is understood in Islamic finance today as Profit and Loss Sharing (PLS), in which both provider and user of the funds share in the outcome of the venture, be it positive or negative, and no interest is paid or received (Saeed, *Islamic banking*, 51-75). Contracts developed cover *muḍāraba* (commenda), *mushāraka* (partnership), *idjāra* (leasing), *istiṣnā'* (manufacturing or "made-to-order") and *murābaḥa* (mark-up finance based on sale of goods). Driven by these new strategies, Islamic banking and finance grew strongly in the 1980s and 1990s.

With the 21st century, the role of Islamic (that is, *ribā*-free) financial institutions in Muslim communities has become even more significant, with institutions ranging from village banks to major international development banks, to insurance (*takāful*) companies, to investment funds—all in competition with conventional interest-based institutions but often in co-operation with them as well. Several Muslim majority states such as Malaysia, Kuwait and Egypt, for instance, have dual banking and finance systems (one based on interest, the other based on Islamic principles). Even interest-based banks (including major international banks) now offer Islamic products or Islamic windows to their Muslim clientèle, and to interested non-Muslims.

The drive to develop modern, *ribā*-free banking, finance and insurance was accompanied by some serious difficulties and also pragmatic shifts in the understanding of *ribā*. Because of competition, Islamic financial institutions felt they had to provide their Muslim clients with "competitive" products, which at times meant interest-based products under different contractual arrangements and labels. These pragmatic adjustments tended to make the Islamic finance, at times, less distinguishable from interest-based finance in the eyes of their critics. What follows are some examples where critics argue that there are pragmatic shifts in the understanding of *ribā* by the proponents of Islamic finance.

First, Islamic bankers and their *Sharī'a* advisers came to see *ribā*, interpreted as interest, as a *legal* rather than an *economic* concept. For them, *ribā* occurred mainly in the context of contractual obligations on borrowers to pay an *increase* in a loan transaction (Nienhaus, *Islamic economics*, 44). Islamic law prohibited any positive return to the provider of capital in a purely financial transaction, such as where an entrepreneur received funds from a bank for utilisation at the entrepreneur's discretion. This was governed by the requirements of the contract of loan (*kard*). If the contract changed, e.g. from loan to sale (*bayʿ*), a return, even if in reality it might appear little different from fixed interest, was permissible. An example of this is the mark-up in *murābaḥa*, which from a *legal* point of view is not a purely financial transaction and therefore a positive return (= mark-up) is considered permissible.

Second, practical realities also meant that Islamic banks needed to compensate themselves if customers defaulted on contractual obligations, for example by failing to pay a debt on time. Thus, in such cases, a "fine" (compensation equivalent to the "opportunity cost" of the capital) became the practice, not without criticism, however. On the other hand, there are depositors who do not want to put their funds at risk in a PLS account but prefer to keep them in a non-PLS account to avoid any risk, primarily for safe-keeping purposes. While such depositors are not entitled to any profits, in practice in order to retain these deposits, Islamic banks have begun to offer "rewards" to such depositors saying that as long as no contractual obligations were involved, they had the discretion to offer incentives (Saeed, *Islamic banking*, 112).

Third, a question currently being debated is whether "profit" can be pre-determined in PLS contracts. In Islamic law, as well as in the literature on Islamic finance, the concept of legitimate profit is closely associated with the uncertainty of a positive return in a PLS venture or a sale transaction. One view, albeit a minority one, is that there is nothing wrong in determining profit in advance as long as this is done by the two parties by choice and consent. While this position is not accepted in the mainstream Islamic finance, it is possible that this position may become more acceptable at least in practice as more emphasis is put on developing investment products with less risk and more predictable returns.

Fourth, a further question is whether it is permissible to invest in a business which engages in an activity prohibited by Islamic law, for instance, in interest-based dealings. Since most publicly-listed companies in developed countries rely heavily on interest-based finance, paying and receiving of interest is normal. This is problematic from an Islamic finance perspective even if the businesses produce *ḥalāl* (permissible) goods or services. The debate has produced two camps, one declaring that investment in such companies is unambiguously prohibited and unlawful for Muslims according to *fiḳh*. In the other camp, the proponents of permissibility, relying on concepts such as "necessity", "public interest", "general need", and analogy (*ḳiyās*), have attempted to find a legal justification, a pragmatic position that recognises that such investment is a modern global phenomenon and difficult for Muslims to avoid. The pragmatists have accepted permissibility of investment in such companies with certain conditions and introduced concepts such as "cleansing" of investment profit from prohibited elements, i.e. the estimated interest component of the company.

Many Muslims who are interested in genuine *ribā*-free finance argue that these pragmatic adjustments have largely rendered Islamic banking and finance over to an interest-based system except in name. The trend to develop more and more products that are similar to those offered by the interest-based system would only blur any distinction that may exist between the Islamic and interest-based systems. Despite these reservations, "Islamic" banking and finance appear to be becoming increasingly acceptable among Muslims and their use consistently increasing, however pragmatic it may be.

Bibliography: Fazlur Rahman, *Riba and interest*, in *Islamic Studies* (March 1964); ʿAbd al-Razzāḳ Sanhūrī, *Maṣādir al-ḥaḳḳ fi 'l-fiḳh al-Islāmī*, Beirut 1967; Mohammed Uzair, *Interest-free banking*, Karachi 1978; Rahman, *Islam: challenges and opportunities*, in *Islam. Past influence and present challenge*, ed. A.T. Welch and P. Cachia, Edinburgh 1979; Council of Islamic Ideology, *Consolidated recommendations on the Islamic economic system*, Islamabad 1983; Muhammad Nejatullah Siddiqi, *Banking without interest*, Leicester 1983; idem, *Issues in Islamic banking. Selected papers*, Leicester 1983; Muhammad Asad, *The message of the Qurʾan*, Gibraltar 1984; Jordan Islamic Bank (JIB), *al-Fatāwā al-sharʿiyya*, ʿAmmān 1984; Uzair, *Impact of interest free banking*, in *Journal of Islamic Banking and Finance* (Autumn 1984); M. Umer Chapra, *Towards a just monetary system*, Leicester 1985; Nabil Saleh, *Unlawful gain and legitimate profit in Islamic law*, Cambridge 1986; Chibli Mallat, *The debate on Riba and interest in twentieth century jurisprudence*, in idem (ed.), *Islamic law and finance*, London 1988; Abu 'l-Aʿlā Mawdūdī, *Towards understanding the Qurʾan*, tr. Zafar Ishaq Ansari, Leicester 1988; Khurshid Ahmad, *Elimination of Riba: concept and problems*, in Institute of Policy Studies (ed.), *Elimination of Riba from the economy*, Islamabad 1994; F.E. Vogel and S.L. Hayes III, *Islamic law and finance: religion, risk, and return*, The Hague 1998; Abdullah Saeed, *Islamic banking and interest*, ²Leiden 1999. (Abdullah Saeed)

al-**RIDDA** (a.), lit: "apostasy", the name given in Islamic historiography to the series of battles against tribes, both nomadic and sedentary, which began shortly before the death of the Prophet Muḥammad and continued throughout Abū Bakr's [*q.v.*] caliphate.

In many cases the term *ridda* is, however, a misnomer since numerous tribes and communities had had no contact whatsoever with the Muslim state or had no formal agreements with it. Several tribes were led by chieftains who posed as prophets. These were ʿAbhala al-ʿAnsī, pejoratively nicknamed al-Aswad [*q.v.*] or the black one (also Dhu 'l-Khimār or the veiled one) in the Yemen, Maslama or Musaylima [*q.v.*] (the small or wretched Maslama) of the Ḥanīfa b. Ludjaym [*q.v.*] in Yamāma, Ṭalḥa or Ṭulayḥa [*q.v.*] (the small Ṭalḥa) of the Asad [*q.v.*] and Sadjāḥ [*q.v.*] of the Tamīm [*q.v.*]—both of them in Nadjd—and Dhu 'l-Tādj Laḳīṭ b. Mālik of the Azd [*q.v.*] in ʿUmān. Most of the tribes which prior to the *ridda* had been under Medinan domination merely refused to go on paying taxes, while stating their readiness to continue practicing Islam. Had it not been for Muḥammad's premature death, Islam would have gained a better foothold in tribal Arabia through his effective tactics. He would give a tribal representative—sometimes it was a tribesman who came on his own initiative—authority over both the Muslims and pagans in his tribe and instruct him to "fight against those who turn away with those who come forward". Consequently, in many tribes the Muslims and pagans neutralised each other. Among the Madhḥidj [*q.v.*], for example, Farwa b. Musayk, the Prophet's representative to the Murād [*q.v.*], the Zubayd and the rest of Madhḥidj, was confronted by a frustrated rival, ʿAmr b. Maʿdīkarib [*q.v.*] al-Zubaydī. When Muḥammad died, the latter rebelled. There were Muslim enclaves in many tribes, and consequently the Prophet and Abū Bakr could confront the rebels "by means of messengers and letters". Many Muslims were killed by the rebels and the Muslim representatives were driven out.

The reconstruction of the course of events beyond the general outline is complicated by the many contradictory accounts which are often of apologetic or polemical nature. Obviously, this problematic chapter of tribal history was of acute importance for the tribal informants who preserved the accounts for posterity, often improving the place in history of a tribal leader, rehabilitating an individual or a tribal group and vilifying an opponent.

When Abū Bakr ascended the throne, he defied threats from several nomadic tribes to attack Medina by dispatching to Syria an expedition force under Usāma b. Zayd. Some must have considered this move reckless, hence the claim that it was in fulfillment of a wish made by the dying Prophet. Yet the threat posed by the nomads must not be exaggerated. First, a nomadic takeover of a settlement was most unusual, although the risk of a raid for plunder was no doubt real. Second, the tribes living in the immediate vicinity of Medina remained unwavering. They included, among others, the Ashdjaʿ or part of them, the Aslam, the Dhuhayna [see ḲUḌĀʿA] and the Muzayna [*q.v.*]. These tribes were not major players in Arabian politics, but their combined military weight should not be underestimated. They provided Medina with an inner circle of defence, continuing their pre-Islamic links with its tribes. Indeed, Abū Bakr managed to organise the Muslim army in Dhu 'l-Ḳaṣṣa and send Khālid b. al-Walīd [*q.v.*] of the Ḳurashī clan of Makhzūm [*q.v.*] to Nadjd even before Usāma b. Zayd's return.

Yet on the whole the situation looked bleak. The sedentary false prophet Musaylima and the nomadic one Ṭulayḥa were amassing power. The latter was also followed by the Ṭayyiʾ [*q.v.*]. Most of the Ghaṭafān [*q.v.*] apostatised, as did parts of the Sulaym [*q.v.*], while the Hawāzin remained undecided with the exception of the Thaḳīf who remained steadfast. Also, the *ʿAdjuz/Aʿdjāz Hawāzin* "the rear part of the Hawāzin", that is, the Naṣr b. Muʿāwiya, Djusham b. Muʿāwiya and Saʿd b. Bakr, did not rebel, and the same is true of Djadīlat Ḳays, that is, the Fahm and ʿAdwān tribes.

The only battle which preceded the return of Usāma's force took place east of Medina against tribes of the Ghaṭafān group, namely, the ʿAbs and Dhubyān (more precisely, the former and the Murra subdivision of the latter). Following their defeat, the ʿAbs and Dhubyān killed the Muslims living in their midst, and their example was followed by other tribes. Ṭulayḥa al-Asadī lost the battle of Buzākha [*q.v.*], having been deserted by his non-Asadī allies. First the Ṭayyiʾ left unimpeded, having created the impression that their own tribe was threatened by the Muslims (whom they subsequently joined). Then the Ghaṭafān under ʿUyayna b. Ḥiṣn [*q.v.*] of the Fazāra [*q.v.*] defected.

The most important events of the *ridda* involved the Tamīm, the largest nomadic tribe in Arabia, and the sedentary Ḥanīfa who lived in Yamāma. Many of the Tamīm (perhaps even most of them) yielded to Muslim control during Muḥammad's lifetime. For example, the Saʿd b. Zayd Manāt, the most numerous subdivision of the Tamīm, had two tax-collectors appointed by Muḥammad: al-Zibriḳān b. Badr [*q.v.*] and Ḳays b. ʿĀṣim [*q.v.*]. Typically, the latter was waiting to see what the former would do with the camels which he had collected for Medina, in order to do the opposite. Indeed, Tamīm's subdivisions, not to mention the Tamīm as a whole, did not form a unified group and the same could be said of every single tribe, be it nomadic or sedentary. Two events dominate the accounts on the *ridda* of the Tamīm. First, the affair of the false prophetess Sadjāḥ, above all her infamous encounter with Musaylima. Now Musaylima required of his men strict asceticism, and the obscene descriptions of his meeting with Sadjāḥ were probably meant to call his ascetic image into question. Second, the killing of Mālik b. Nuwayra [*q.v.*] and the ensuing criticism concerning Khālid b. al-Walīd's conduct.

The sedentary Ḥanīfa who were unified (with the exception of the Suḥaym subdivision) under Musaylima were Medina's staunchest enemies. After an initial defeat, the Muslims pushed the Ḥanafīs to "the orchard of death" (*ḥadīḳat al-mawt*) in ʿAḳrabāʾ [*q.v.*], not far from Musaylima's home town al-Haddār (modern al-Hudaydīr). The historical traditions of the Ḳuraysh and the Anṣār preserved lists of the members of these groups who were killed in the battlefield, but one looks in vain for the names of the many nomads who died there. The fortresses of the Ḥanīfa remained intact and the Ḥanafī Mudjdjāʿa b. Murāra who had been taken captive at an earlier stage in the fighting and negotiated with Khālid on behalf of the Ḥanīfa tricked the latter by disguising the children, women and old people who remained in the fortresses as men, thus improving the terms of his tribe's capitulation. But the ruse may have been invented in order to protect Khālid's policy because the negotiated treaty—fortified by his marriage to Mudjdjāʿa's daughter—caused the Muslims great losses.

The story of al-Aswad in the Yemen which is full of intrigue involves a struggle between the Persian Abnāʾ [see AL-ABNĀʾ (II)] and several Arab tribes for the control of Ṣanʿāʾ and the rest of the Yemen. During this power struggle Medina remained in the background; when the Abnāʾ managed to regain control of Ṣanʿāʾ, Abū Bakr recognised them, precisely as the Prophet had done in his time. The Abnāʾ were then challenged by Ḳays b. al-Makshūḥ al-Murādī who took Ṣanʿāʾ, but they managed to drive him out shortly afterwards.

The road to the Yemen was secured by a Muslim expedition force which brought the rebellious ʿAmr b. Maʿdīkarib and Ḳays b. al-Makshūḥ back to the Muslim camp, and the Yemen as a whole could now be pacified. Then the Muslims turned to deal with the rebellion in Ḥaḍramawt. Here the dominant tribe Kinda [*q.v.*] yielded to superior forces, one under al-Muhādjir b. Abī Umayya (of the Makhzūm) arriving from the Yemen, and another under ʿIkrima b. Abī Djahl (also of the Makhzūm) arriving from the land of Mahra [*q.v.*]. The kingly family from the prestigious subdivision of Kinda, ʿAmr b. Muʿāwiya, was destroyed in a surprise night attack. Members from this subdivision and from the Ḥārith b. Muʿāwiya subdivision later surrendered in al-Nudjayr [*q.v.*]. Following the war against the Kinda, al-Ashʿath [*q.v.*] b. Ḳays of the Ḥārith subdivision rose to prominence. This shift in the leadership was atypical, since tribal leaderships usually survived the *ridda*. For example, ʿUyayna b. Ḥiṣn is said to have been the only Arab who received one *mirbāʿ* or a quarter of the captured booty in the Djāhiliyya and one *khums* or a fifth of the booty in Islam.

The war in Ḥaḍramawt was preceded by fighting in the southeastern corner of Arabia where Dhu 'l-Tādj Laḳīṭ b. Mālik al-Azdī pushed the sons of the Djulandā [*q.v.*, and see AZD and ṢUḤĀR] who were Abū Bakr's allies to the mountains and to the seaside of Ṣuḥār. Tribal forces sent by Medina to aid its allies besieged Laḳīṭ in Dabā and were joined by other tribal forces under ʿIkrima b. Abī Djahl. The Muslims were also supported by troops from the Nādjiya [cf. AL-KHIRRĪT] and the ʿAbd al-Ḳays [*q.v.*]. ʿIkrima continued his march to the land of Mahra with his tribal units (a subdivision of the Azd called Rāsib and the Saʿd b. Zayd Manāt of Tamīm are specifically mentioned). Among the Mahra there was internal strife, and the weaker party allied itself with the Muslims (in other words, it converted to Islam). After the stronger party was subdued, the leader of the weaker one brought to Medina one fifth of the spoils. When ʿIkrima continued his march to Ḥaḍramawt, his army also included warriors from the Mahra.

Shortly after the Prophet's demise, his governor in Baḥrayn, al-Mundhir b. Sāwā [*q.v.*] of the Tamīm, also died. The Ḳays b. Thaʿlaba of the Bakr b. Wāʾil [*q.v.*] "and the whole of the Rabīʿa" rebelled under al-Ḥuṭam, who was one of the Ḳays, while al-Djārūd of the ʿAbd al-Ḳays, among others, was steadfastly loyal to Islam. A client of the Ḳuraysh, al-ʿAlāʾ b. al-Ḥaḍramī, who had replaced al-Mundhir as governor of Baḥrayn fought against the rebels with the Arabs and Persians who joined him. Among others he was supported by a large force of the Tamīm. Al-Ḥuṭam controlled al-Ḳaṭīf [*q.v.*], Hadjar [see AL-ḤASĀ], Dārīn (modern Tārūt) and al-Khaṭṭ [*q.v.*], while the Muslims had been besieged in their stronghold, Djuwāthā, until they were rescued by al-ʿAlāʾ. The rebels were defeated on the mainland and fled to the island of Dārīn which the Muslims took after having miraculously crossed the sea.

The *ridda* can be seen as a prelude to the wider conquests. The Ḳurashī generals gained precious experience in mobilising large multi-tribal armies over long distances. They benefited from the close acquaintance of the Ḳuraysh with tribal politics throughout Arabia.

A crucial role was played by Khālid b. al-Walīd whose mother was a nomad. Indeed, the Bedouin way of life was not alien to him: he is said to have consumed a lizard, while Muḥammad who was watching loathed it. Already in the conquest of Mecca (8/630), Khālid was leading a troop of nomads (referred to as *muhādjirat al-ʿarab*), and in the battle of Ḥunayn [*q.v.*] shortly afterwards he led the nomadic Sulaym at the vanguard of the Muslim army.

The *ridda* changed for ever the relationship between the central government and the strong tribes of Arabia. The latter were trying to abolish whatever ascendancy the Muslim state had achieved during the lifetime of Muḥammad, but were overpowered by large expedition forces mobilised by able Muslim generals. The battlefield successes of the Muslims secured for them the cooperation of tribes living between Medina and the territories of the rebellious tribes. Medina re-established its prestige and dealt the severest forms of punishment to those who had killed Muslims earlier in the fighting.

New realities were created on the ground. Khālid's treaty with the Ḥanīfa prescribed that he receive one orchard and one field of his choice in every village included in the treaty. The villages in the Yamāma area which were not included in the treaty bore the full consequences of the defeat. The inhabitants of the Marʾāt village were enslaved and a tribal group of the Tamīm, the Imruʾ ʾl-Ḳays b. Zayd Manāt b. Tamīm, settled there. Musaylima's home town of al-Haddār was not part of the treaty. Khālid enslaved its people and settled there the Banu ʾl-Aʿradj, i.e., the Banu ʾl-Ḥārith b. Kaʿb b. Saʿd b. Zayd Manāt b. Tamīn. These changes demonstrate how local groups of the Tamīm benefited from their co-operation with Khālid in Yamāma. Other villages not included in the treaty were al-Suyūḥ, al-Ḍayḳ, al-ʿArika, al-Ghabrāʾ, Fayshān, al-Ḳurayya (one of the central villages of Yamāma), al-Ḳaṣabāt, al-Ḳaltayni, al-Kirs, Makhrafa and al-Maṣāniʿ. In addition, the al-Madjāza village was inhabited by the Hizzān of the ʿAnaza [*q.v.*] and by people of mixed descent (*akhlāṭ min al-nās*), including *mawālī* of the Ḳuraysh and others who settled there after the *ridda*, since it had not been included in Khālid's treaty.

The new balance of power between the central government and the tribes is reflected in the takeover by the state of tribal protected grazing grounds [see ḤIMĀ]. The thousands of camels and other beasts taken as booty in the last years of Muḥammad's life, in addition to those collected from the nomads in taxes, needed large grazing grounds. In addition, several influential Ḳurashīs, such as the future caliph ʿUthmān b. ʿAffān and also al-Zubayr b. al-ʿAwwām and ʿAbd al-Raḥmān b. ʿAwf, were competing with the state because they were themselves owners of large herds. ʿAbd al-Raḥmān left to his inheritors 1,000 camels, in addition to 3,000 ewes and 100 horses. The ewes and the horses were grazing in al-Naḳīʿ [see AL-ʿAḲĪḲ] (often written erroneously al-Baḳīʿ). It was Muḥammad who declared the Naḳīʿ, some 120 km/75 miles south of Medina a state *ḥimā* "for the horses of the Muslims", probably at the expense of the Sulaym, and put in charge of it a member of the Muzayna. Moreover, Muḥammad reportedly abolished the tribal grazing grounds by declaring that the only legitimate *ḥimā* belonged to God and His messenger, in other words to the state. Previously, the tribes feared the takeover of their land and water resources by other tribes, but now the powerful state and certain individuals coveted the same resources. The size of the state *ḥimās* grew constantly under the caliphs. A telling example of this is linked to the above-mentioned battle against the ʿAbs and Dhubyān which took place in al-Abraḳ in the area of al-Rabadha [*q.v.*] some 200 km/125 miles east of Medina. Abū Bakr actually conquered Dhubyan's territory (*ghalaba banī Dhubyān ʿalā ʾl-bilād*) and expelled (*adjlā*) its owners. He made al-Abraḳ a *ḥimā* for the horses of the Muslims (in other words, he made it state property) and permitted everybody to graze in the rest of al-Rabadha at the expense of the Thaʿlaba b. Saʿd b. Dhubyān. Later he declared the whole of al-Rabadha *ḥimā* for the camels collected as taxes (*ṣadaḳāt al-muslimīn*). One report attributes the expulsion of the Thaʿlaba from al-Rabadha to ʿUmar b. al-Khaṭṭāb, while another has it that the state *ḥimā* in al-Rabadha was created by Muḥammad, in which case Abū Bakr was merely reestablishing state authority there.

Bibliography: 1. Sources. Ṭabarī, i, 1795-8, tr. I.K. Poonawala, *The History of al-Ṭabarī*, ix, 164ff; Ṭabarī, i, 1851-2015, tr. F.M. Donner, *The History of al-Ṭabarī*, x, 18ff; Balādhurī, *Futūḥ*, passim; Sh. al-Faḥḥām, *Ḳitʿa fī akhbār al-ridda li-muʾallif madjhul*, in *Festschrift Nāṣir al-Dīn al-Asad* (*Fuṣūl adabiyya wa-taʾrīkhiyya* . . .), ed. Ḥ. ʿAṭwān, Beirut 1414/1993, 149-225; the relevant entries in Yāḳūt, *Muʿdjam al-buldān*.

2. Studies. E.S. Shoufani, *Al-Riddah and the Muslim conquest of Arabia*, Toronto and Beirut 1972; F.M. Donner, *The early Islamic conquests*, Princeton 1981, 82–90; M.J. Kister, ". . . illā bi-ḥaqqihi . . ." *A study of an early* ḥadīth, in *JSAI*, v (1984), 33-52; E. Landau-Tasseron, *Aspects of the ridda wars*, unpubl. Ph.D. thesis, Jerusalem 1981 (Hebrew with an

English summary; it deals with Ṭayyiʾ, Asad, Ghaṭafān, Sulaym and Tamīm); eadem, *The participation of Ṭayyiʾ in the* ridda, in *JSAI*, v (1984), 53-71; eadem, *Asad from Jāhiliyya to Islam*, in *JSAI*, vi (1985), 1-28, at 20-5; on the *ridda* of the Sulaym, see M. Lecker, *The Banū Sulaym*, Jerusalem 1989, index; on their *ḥimās*, see *ibid.*, 229-38; on the *ridda* of the Kinda, see idem, *Kinda on the eve of Islam and during the* ridda, in *JRAS*, 3rd ser., iv (1994), 333-56; also idem, *Judaism among Kinda and the* ridda *of Kinda*, in *JAOS*, cxv (1995), 635-50; J. Wellhausen, *Prolegomena zur ältesten Geschichte des Islams*, in *Skizzen und Vorarbeiten*, vi, Berlin 1899, 7-37.

(M. Lecker)

RIMĀYA [see ḳaws].

ROHTAK, the name of a region and a town of northwestern India, now in the Hariyana State of the Indian Union.

The region is not mentioned in the earliest Indo-Muslim sources, but from the Sultanate period onwards, its history was often linked with that of nearby Dihlī, to its southeast. In the 18th century, it was fought over by commanders of the moribund Mughals and the militant Sikhs [*q.v.*]; for its history in general, see hariyānā. In early British Indian times, till 1832, it was administered by a Political Agent under the Resident in Dihlī. During the Sepoy Mutiny of 1857-8, the whole of the Rohtak region fell into rebel hands. In contemporary Hariyana State, as in post-Mutiny British India, Rohtak forms an administrative District.

The town of Rohtak (lat. 28° 54' N., long. 76° 35' E.) lies 72 km/44 miles to the northwest of Dihlī; in British Indian times, Hindus and Muslims were fairly evenly balanced within its population, with a small preponderance of Hindus, a situation altered by the bloody aftermath of Partition in 1947.

Bibliography: *Imperial gazetteer of India*², xxi, 310-22. (C.E. Bosworth)

al-RUʿAYNĪ, Abū Djaʿfar Aḥmad al-Gharnāṭī (or al-Ilbīrī) al-Mālikī, d. 779/1377, Andalusī scholar, author of *al-Ḥulla al-siyarāʾ*, a voluminous commentary on the *Badīʿiyya* (a poem praising the Prophet Muḥammad while illustrating the *badīʿ* [*q.v.*]) of his companion, Ibn Djābir (d. 780/1378-9). The *Badīʿiyya* itself and important grammatical and lexicographical sections of the book have been published by ʿAlī Abū Zayd, Beirut 1405/1985, but numerous historical and geographical data, poetry, as well as a wealth of information in the domain of *adab* [*q.v.*] in the widest sense of the term remain unpublished, even though quotations from al-Ruʿaynī's book appear in acknowledged and unacknowledged borrowings, e.g. by al-Tanasī. Al-Ruʿaynī also wrote a commentary on a similar poem by Ibn Djābir consisting of *tawriyya*s [*q.v.*] on the sūras of the Ḳurʾān.

Both scholars began their careers in Spain and both were pupils of ʿAlī b. ʿUmar al-Ḳidjāṭī (d. 730/1329), a scholar of *fiḳh*, Ḳurʾān, grammar and philology, who lived in Granada. They left Spain together in 738/1337 on a pilgrimage having become, in the words of Lisān al-Dīn Ibn al-Khaṭīb, "like two souls in one body" and, Ibn Djābir being blind, they were also known as "the blind and the seeing". They lived in Egypt (where they attended the lectures of Abū Ḥayyān al-Gharnāṭī), Damascus, where they arrived in 741/1340-1, and Aleppo in 743/1342-3, before settling finally in al-Bīra.

Ibn Ḥadjar, *Durar*, iii, 300, claims that Ibn Djābir in composing his *Badīʿiyya* was inspired by a similar work by Ṣafī al-Dīn al-Ḥillī (d. 749, 750, or 752). Ibn Maʿṣūm in his *Anwār al-rabīʿ* (ed. Sh.H. Shukr, Nadjaf 1388/1968, i, 31-2) holds that the first *Badīʿiyya* was composed by one [Abu 'l-Ḥasan] ʿAlī b. ʿUthmān al-Irbilī al-Ṣūfī. The classical division between *maʿānī*, *bayān* and *badīʿ* [*q.vv.*] by Djalāl al-Dīn al-Ḳazwīnī (d. 739/1338) and Badr al-Dīn Ibn Mālik (d. 686/1287) in relation to the *Ṭirāz* as analysed by Soudan, 93-7, and Bonebakker cannot be discussed here. To illustrate the individual chapters of his friend's *Badīʿiyya*, al-Ruʿaynī uses examples in prose and poetry that are not limited to the Muslim West. Of special interest are the examples composed by Ibn Djābir and al-Ruʿaynī themselves. Though in some moving verses they express nostalgia, there is, so far, no indication that the two authors after settling in al-Bīra ever returned temporarily to Spain (which would explain the *nisba* al-Ilbīrī used by al-Ṣafadī, d. 764/1363). According to a report by Sibṭ Ibn al-ʿAdjamī quoted in Ibn Ḥadjar's *Durar*, their friendship ended when Ibn Djābir married, though Ibn Djābir composed a *marthiya* on al-Ruʿaynī when he died.

Bibliography: Brockelmann, G II², 136, S II, 138; N. Soudan, *Westarabische Tropik. Naẓm IV des Tanasī*, Wiesbaden 1980, 93-7; cf. 86-7; S.A. Bonebakker, *Ruʿaynī's commentary on the Badīʿiyya of Ibn Jābir*, in *Studi in onore di Francesco Gabrieli ... a cura di R. Traini*, Rome 1984, i, 73-83. The text of B.L. or 60, BS 6/7313, in particular the poetic quotations, can often be corrected with the help of Tanasī's *Naẓm*, Maḳḳarī, *Nafḥ al-ṭīb*, ed. I. ʿAbbās, Beirut 1388/1968, ii, vii, and Ibn Maʿṣūm, *Anwār al-rabīʿ fī anwāʿ al-badīʿ*, ed. Sh.H. Shukr, Karbalāʾ 1388-9/1968-9. See also Ibn Ḥidjdja al-Ḥamawī, *Khizānat al-adab*, Cairo 1304, *passim*; and for the terms used in individual chapters of the *Badīʿiyya*, A. Maṭlūb, *Muʿdjam al-muṣṭalaḥāt al-badīʿiyya*, Beirut (?) 1401/1981. (S.A. Bonebakker)

RŪḤ ALLĀH [see nafs. I. B.].

RUKHĀM (a.), in modern Arabic usage, the usual word for marble in general, whereas *marmar*, which clearly derives from the Greek *marmor*, usually refers to white marble or alabaster. Historically, however, *rukhām* and *marmar* were often used interchangeably to refer to a wide variety of hard stones, including marble, granite and diorite. Where the two terms were distinguished, it usually had to do with colour: *marmar* was white, whereas *rukhām* could assume various shades and hues.

Geographically, the use of marble in the Islamic world was largely restricted to those regions whose predominant building material was stone rather than brick or adobe. Generally speaking, places to the west and northwest of the Euphrates river—including Anatolia, Greater Syria, and Egypt, in addition to the Iberian peninsula and the Indian subcontinent—used stone and marble in their architectural monuments. Elsewhere, brick with a stucco or tile revetment predominated.

Marble in the Islamic world was obtained from two main sources: ancient buildings and quarries. Interestingly, the use of salvaged marble far outweighed that of freshly-quarried marble, which was only quarried by the later Islamic dynasties, especially the Ottomans and the Mughals. Exceptions did exist, such as the robust marble capitals in Madīnat al-Zahrāʾ in 4th/10th century al-Andalus and the exquisite columns and capitals in the Alhambra Palace in the 8th/14th one. But on the whole, marble in early and mediaeval Islamic monuments was taken from ancient, Christian, or even earlier Islamic buildings.

Historically, the use of marble in Islamic architecture may be divided into three characteristic phases: Late Antique and early Islamic (7th-10th centuries A.D.), mediaeval (11th-15th centuries) and pre-modern (10th-18th centuries). In the first period, which is dominated by Umayyad architecture, the use of marble shows direct continuities with Late Antique practice. Thus multi-coloured marble and granite columns and heavy marble architraves and arches are used in the Dome of the Rock in Jerusalem and the Great Mosque of Damascus. Perhaps more interesting is the continued use in both of these structures of split or quartered marble, whereby the distinctive pattern in a sheet of marble is displayed in mirror image along one or two axes. Equally impressive is openwork marble, which is used in the Great Mosque of Damascus as a series of window grilles, which most likely also existed at the Dome of the Rock (K.A.C. Creswell, *A short account of early Muslim architecture*, revised and supplemented by J.W. Allan, Cairo 1989).

With the exception of an outstanding series of Ghaznawid marble dadoes and cenotaphs dating to the 5th-6th/11th-12th centuries, the architectural use of marble goes into an extended decline after the Umayyads. But marble ornament and stone architecture undergo an important revival in the 6th/12th century, a revival centred in Aleppo during the time of the Ayyūbids. Polychrome marble ornament in the form of large interlaces around *miḥrābs*, *īwāns* and portals, and geometric patterns in pavements, soften and enliven an otherwise austere architectural style (Yasser Tabbaa, *Constructions of power and piety in medieval Aleppo*, Pittsburgh 1997).

These ornamental forms are transmitted in the 7th-8th/13th-14th centuries to the rest of Syria, as well as to Palestine, Egypt and Anatolia. Until the end of the 7th/13th century, marble revetments maintain their formal and stylistic affinities with Aleppo, as exemplified by the robust designs at the mausoleum of al-Ẓāhir Baybars al-Bunduḳdārī (constructed 675-80/1277-81) in Damascus and the portal to the complex of Ḳalāwūn in Cairo (684/1285). But an increasingly intricate ornamental style develops in the next century, lasting with few changes till the end of the Mamlūk period and beyond. Applied internally to *miḥrābs* and fountains, and externally to portals and window frames, this miniature style of polychrome marble inlay becomes a hallmark feature of Mamlūk architecture [see MAMLŪKS. 2. Art and Architecture, in Suppl.].

Although this Mamlūk ornamental style continued in Egypt and Syria under the Ottomans, it was largely shunned by classical Ottoman architecture, whose monuments demonstrated a marked preference for large stretches of lightly ornamented marble revetment. This return to an earlier style of marble decoration may have been motivated by the greater availability of marble, or perhaps by the emulation of nearby Byzantine structures.

In India, marble was rather sparingly used in Dihlī Sultanate architecture, often as a highlight to the predominant red sandstone. This attractive juxtaposition continues in early Mughal mosques and mausoleums, reaching an apogee in the tomb of Humāyūn at Dihlī. At first, white marble was reserved for saints' tombs, such as the spectacular tomb in Fatḥpūr Sikrī [*q.v.*] of Shaykh Salīm Čishtī (1573-7), which also boasts some of the earliest and finest openwork marble screens, commonly known as *Jali*. But by the 11th/17th century, various monuments were being sheathed in white marble inlaid with polychrome stones, including the Mosque of Iʿtimād al-Dawla (1031-6/1622-7), and the Tādj Maḥall (1041-53/1632-43 [*q.v.*]), both at Āgra [*q.v.*] (Ebba Koch, *Mughal architecture*, Munich 1991).

Bibliography (in addition to references given in the article): R. Lewcock, *Materials and techniques*, in G. Michell (ed.), *Architecture of the Islamic world, its history and social meaning*, New York 1978, 119-43; Luciana and T. Mannoni, *Marble, the history of a culture*, New York 1985. (YASSER TABBAA)

RŪSHANĪ, DEDE ʿUMAR, Turkish adherent of the Ṣūfī order of the Khalwatiyya [*q.v.*] and poet in both Persian and Turkish. He was born at an unspecified date at Güzel Ḥiṣār in Aydi̊n, western Anatolia, being connected maternally with the ruling family of the Aydi̊n Oghullari̊ [see AYDI̊N-OGHLU], and died at Tabrīz in Ādharbāydjān in 892/1487.

Dede ʿUmar was the *khalīfa* of Sayyid Yaḥyā Shīrwānī, the *pīr-i thānī* or second founder of the Khalwatī order, and as head of the Rūshanī branch of the order engaged in missionary work in northern Ādharbāydjān. He came to enjoy the patronage of the Aḳ Ḳoyunlu ruler Uzun Ḥasan [*q.v.*], whose wife built a *zāwiya* for him in the capital Tabrīz, and he lived there up to his death, being buried in the *zāwiya*. His *murīds* included the Turkish mystical poet from Diyārbakr, Ibrāhīm Gulshanī (d. 940/1533-4 [*q.v.*]), who founded his own order of the Gulshaniyya, and the Azeri Turk Muḥammad Demirdāsh Muḥammadī (d. 929/1524), founder of the Cairo order of the Demirdashiyya [*q.v.* in Suppl.]. Dede ʿUmar's *dīwān* included three Persian *mathnawīs*, in one of which, the *Nāynāma*, the influence of Djalāl al-Dīn Rūmī [*q.v.*] is especially clear, and poems in Turkish; one volume of the *dīwān* has been published as *Āthār-i ʿishḳ* (Istanbul 1315/1897-8).

Bibliography: Tāshköprüzāde, *al-Shaḳāʾiḳ al-nuʿmāniyya*, ed. A.S. Firay, Istanbul 1985, 264, Tkish. tr. M.M. Efendi, *Hadaik üş-şakayik*, Istanbul 1989, 281-2; Burṣali̊ Meḥmed Ṭāhir, *ʿOthmānli̊ müʾellifleri*, i, 69; M.ʿA. Tarbiyat, *Dānishmandān-i Ādharbaydjān*, Tehran ASH 1314/1935, 319-20. For further bibl., see *EIr*, vii, 202, art. *Dede ʿOmar Rūšanī* (Tahsin Yazıcı), on which the present article is based.

(C.E. BOSWORTH)

S

ṢABYĀ (Sabaya on Philby's map), a town in the Tihāmat ʿAsīr [see TIHĀMA; ʿASĪR and map] in south-western Saudi Arabia, at about 30 km/21 miles inland north-east of the port of Djayzān [*q.v.*]. In 1339/1920 Sayyid Muḥammad al-Idrīsī (see below) concluded a treaty with Ibn Suʿūd [see ʿABD AL-ʿAZĪZ

Al suʿūd, in Suppl.], but after his death in 1340/1922-3 internal dissensions among the Idrīsiyya led to a Suʿūdī protectorate. The Imām of Yemen maintained a claim to the Idrīsid territories, but the Treaty of al-Ṭāʾif (1353/1934) determined that they belong to Saudi Arabia, including Ṣabyā [see ʿasīr]. The town lies in what is called the central part of al-Mikhlāf al-Yamanī, a district which includes all the Tihāmat from al-Shuḳayḳ in the north to Wādī ʿAyn in the south. The central part extends from Umm al-Khashab to just south of Abū ʿArīsh [*q.v.*]. Being traversed by the wādīs Baysh, Ṣabyā, Damad and Djayzān, the region is among the most densely populated of the Tihāmat ʿAsīr. At the beginning of the 20th century, the largest part of the population was of Sudanese origin. They were partly unemancipated slaves but chiefly freedmen, the other inhabitants being *mutawallids* or Sudanese with an Arab strain, Arabs of pure blood, *sayyids* and *sharīfs* [*q.vv.*] (Cornwallis, 39-40).

In the 4th/10th century Ṣabyā, and a number of other places and wādīs, was ruled by the *Ḥakamiyyūn*, i.e. the Banū Ḥakam b. Saʿd al-ʿAshīra of the Ḳaḥtān [*q.v.*], with the Banū ʿAbd al-Djadd as the ruling family (al-Hamdānī, 120.5). In the 7th/13th century, Ṣabyā was one of the urban settlements (*ḳurā*) of ʿUshar, which was part of Yemen (Yāḳūt, iii, 367, 979, v, 23). The town does not seem to have played any role in early and mediaeval Islam. As in Ḳunfudha, Abhā and Bīsha [*q.vv.*], neighbouring tribes used to collect in Ṣabyā for a four-months' truce during the date season. In the 10th/16th century, it was one of the seats of the Sulaymānīs [*q.v.*], who are still to be found in the frontier districts between Saudi Arabia and Yemen [see khamīs mushayt; makramids].

In 1215/1800 Ṣabyā was drawn into Arabian politics when an inhabitant brought the Wahhābīs [*q.v.*] into the Tihāma (Serjeant and Lewcock, 87a), and even more so when Aḥmad b. Idrīs (d. 1253/1837 [*q.v.*]), the Moroccan *sharīf* and Ṣūfī who had preached in a school in Mecca, sought refuge in Ṣabyā in 1243/1827-8 from persecution for heresy by the Meccan *ʿulamāʾ*. In the Holy City he had admitted into the circle of his disciples the Algerian Ṣūfī Muḥammad b. ʿAlī al-Sanūsī, the founder of the Sanūsiyya [*q.vv.*]. Around 1250/1834-5 Ṣabyā became the centre of the Sanūsiyya and the capital of an Idrīsī semi-religious, semi-military state centred in al-Mikhlāf al-Yamanī with Djayzān and Midi (lat. 16° 18' N.) as its main ports. The ancestor of the Idrīsīs in ʿAsīr (see the family tree in Philby, 473) is Idrīs b. ʿAbd Allāh b. al-Ḥasan b. al-Ḥasan b. ʿAlī [see idrīs i] who, after the battle of Fakhkh [*q.v.*] in 169/786, fled via Egypt to the Maghrib where he founded the dynasty of the Idrīsids [*q.v.*]. Aḥmad's great-grandson Sayyid Muḥammad b. ʿAlī b. Muḥammad b. Aḥmad, born in Ṣabyā in 1293/1876, by 1328/1910 had reduced Turkish power in ʿAsīr with the support of the Italians, but had failed to hold Abhā against the *sharīf* of Mecca. Sayyid Muḥammad died in 1341/1922 and was buried in the cemetery that lies in the northern outskirts of Ṣabyā on the main road to Mecca. In 1344/1925-6 his son ʿAlī signed a treaty with the British resident in Aden against the Turks. He was supported by Ibn Suʿūd, but fiercely opposed by the Imām of Yemen. The Imām had at first concluded with ʿAlī a defensive alliance against the Turks, but in the end he sided with his former enemy. In 1345/1926-7 ʿAlī was forced to submit to Saudi Arabia [see aḥmad b. idrīs; ṭarīḳa. 3]. As followers of the Sanūsiyya, the tribes around Ṣabyā are Shāfiʿī, with no sympathy lost for the Zaydiyya [*q.v.*]. The Idrīsīs used to levy taxes on grain and animals, collected primarily by the *shaykhs* of the tribes, except the pro-Turkish ones, but also through travelling inspectors. The proceeds were sent to Ṣabyā. Some tribes refused to be regarded as taxpayers, but sent the Idrīsī rulers presents and helped them in war. Philby mentions the presses for the extraction of oil from sesame [see simsim] and remarks that the town spread over a considerable area, including Ṣabyā al-Baliyya and Bayt al-Sayyid, the original palace from which Ṣabyā al-Djadīda grew up. In Philby's days the population of the Ṣabyā area was estimated locally at some 25,000 souls.

Bibliography: Sir Kinahan Cornwallis, *Asir before World War I, a handbook*, London 1916, repr. 1976; Muḥammad ʿĪsā al-ʿUkaylī, *Min taʾrīkh al-Mikhlāf al-Sulaymānī*, al-Riyāḍ 1378, i, 83-93; Admiralty, Naval Intelligence Division, *A handbook of Arabia*, London 1916-7, i, 143; idem, *Western Arabia*, London 1946; H.St.J.B. Philby, *Arabian Highlands*, Ithaca, New York 1952; R.B. Serjeant and Ronald Lewcock, *Ṣanʿāʾ, an Arabian Islamic city*, London 1983.

(E. van Donzel)

SAʿD, Atabeg of Fārs [see salghurids].

SAʿD al-DĪN [see khodja efendi].

SADŌZAYS [see afghānistān. v. 3. a].

[al-]**SAHLA**, literally, "level, smooth place". There must have been several places in the Arabic lands named after this obvious topographical feature. Yāḳūt, *Buldān*, ed. Beirut, iii, 290-1, mentions a village in Baḥrayn and a *masdjid* of that name in Kūfa (perhaps the mosque also known as the Ẓāfir one or that of ʿAbd al-Ḳays, cf. Hichem Djaït, *Al-Kūfa, naissance de la ville islamique*, Paris 1986, 298).

Bibliography: Given in the article. (Ed.)

SAʿĪD b. **DJUBAYR** b. Hishām, an early Kūfan scholar of renown in the fields of Ḳurʾān recitation and exegesis, jurisprudence and *ḥadīth*. He was a *mawlā* of the Banū Wāliba b. al-Ḥārith, a branch of the Banū Asad b. Khuzayma. If the biographical traditions which say that he studied with Ibn ʿAbbās and Ibn ʿUmar are reliable, then he brought early Meccan and Medinan scholarship to Kūfa. There he had a circle of students but also held government positions. He functioned as secretary for two of the *ḳāḍīs* of Kūfa. When al-Ḥadjdjādj, the Umayyad governor of ʿIrāḳ, sent ʿAbd al-Raḥmān b. al-Ashʿath with an army to Sīstān, he put Saʿīd in charge of the troops' stipends. During the revolt of Ibn al-Ashʿath against al-Ḥadjdjādj (81-2/700-1), in which Saʿīd b. Djubayr participated, he was for a time in charge of levying the *zakāt* and the *ʿushr* [*q.vv.*] in Kūfa. In this revolt he was one of the active leaders of the *ḳurrāʾ*, the group of religious scholars and their followers, who joined the revolt of ʿIrāḳ's *ashrāf* against the Umayyads [see al-ḳurrāʾ and, more recent, R. Sayed, *Die Revolte des Ibn al-Ašʿaṯ und die Koranleser*, Freiburg i.Br. 1977]. After the revolt had failed, Saʿīd fled first to Iṣfahān and later to Mecca where he taught for some years. In 94 or 95 (711 or 712), more than a decade after the revolt, he was arrested by Khālid b. ʿAbd Allāh al-Ḳasrī [*q.v.*], then governor of Mecca, and sent to al-Ḥadjdjādj at Wāsiṭ, who had him beheaded. Saʿīd was then 49 or 57 years old. Some legends became woven around his capture, his examination by al-Ḥadjdjādj and his execution. They underline Saʿīd's piety and condemn al-Ḥadjdjādj's death sentence. Whether Saʿīd belonged to the Kūfan Murdjiʾa [*q.v.*] or not is a controversial issue. A few traditions say that he had good relations with and sympathy for members of the ʿAlid family.

Saʿīd's teachings in the fields of *fiḳh* and *tafsīr* were much sought after during the 2nd/8th century and played an important role in the development of *fiḳh* before the advent of the classical schools. Many traditions on his teachings have been collected in the two *Muṣannafs* of ʿAbd al-Razzāḳ and of Ibn Abī Shayba, as well as in ʿAbd al-Razzāḳ's and al-Ṭabarī's *Tafsīrs*. Ibn al-Nadīm mentions the existence of a *Kitāb Tafsīr Saʿīd b. Djubayr* (*Fihrist*, 34), but it is not clear whether this had been compiled by Saʿīd himself or a later scholar. An investigation of the traditions going back to Saʿīd b. Djubayr in ʿAbd al-Razzāḳ's *Muṣannaf* and *Tafsīr* shows that they were collected already during the first half of the 2nd century by scholars such as Sufyān al-Thawrī (d. 161/778), Maʿmar b. Rāshid (d. 153/770) and Ibn Djuraydj (d. 150/767). The legal traditions that they transmit from him via their informants reflect in most cases (*ca.* 75%) Saʿīd's own opinions (*raʾy*), more rarely traditions going back to Companions (*ca.* 17%) or to the Prophet (8%). Most of his Companion traditions give the legal opinion of Ibn ʿAbbās (70%) and Ibn ʿUmar (20%), and most of his traditions from the Prophet (70%) lack any *isnād*, i.e. they are *mursal*. These peculiarities of Saʿīd's scholarship correspond to what is known from his Meccan contemporary ʿAṭāʾ b. Abī Rabāḥ (d. 115/733), who was a pupil of Ibn ʿAbbās as well (see H. Motzki, *The origins of Islamic jurisprudence*, Leiden 2001, ch. III.B). In the exegetical traditions transmitted from Saʿīd by the early collectors mentioned above, and compiled in ʿAbd al-Razzāḳ's *Tafsīr*, the peculiarities are similar. Ibn ʿAbbās's opinion, however, is somewhat more strongly represented (*ca.* 40%) in comparison to Saʿīd's own exegesis (56%).

In ʿAbd al-Razzāḳ's *Muṣannaf* and *Tafsīr*, most of the material transmitted from Saʿīd by the three early collectors seems really to go back to him. However, some traditions of Saʿīd b. Djubayr transmitted by other informants of ʿAbd al-Razzāḳ and going back exclusively to Ibn ʿAbbās may be suspected of being falsely ascribed to Saʿīd. More Ibn ʿAbbās exegetical traditions allegedly going back to Saʿīd may be found in al-Ṭabarī's *Tafsīr* (see H. Berg, *The development of exegesis in early Islam*, Richmond, Surrey 2000, ch. 5).

Bibliography: Information on Saʿīd b. Djubayr can be found in many biographical compilations. In the following only the sources with the most detailed information are given. Ibn Saʿd, vi, 178-87 (Beirut vi, 256-67); Ṭabarī, ii, 1076, 1087, 1261-5; Abu 'l-ʿArab Muḥammad b. Aḥmad al-Tamīmī, *Kitāb al-Miḥan*, Beirut 1408/1988, 216-31; Mizzī, *Tahdhīb al-kamāl*, iii, 1418/1998, 141-45; Ibn Ḥadjar, *Tahdhīb al-tahdhīb*, iv, Ḥaydarābād 1325-7/1907-9, 11-14; Dhahabī, *Siyar aʿlām al-nubalāʾ*, Beirut 1413/1993, iv, 321-43 (with additional sources given by the editor, 321-2); ʿAbd al-Razzāḳ, *Muṣannaf*, i-xi, ²Beirut 1403/1983; idem, *Tafsīr*, al-Riyāḍ 1410/1989, i-iv; Ibn Abī Shayba, *Muṣannaf*, Bombay 1399-1403/1979-83, i-xv; A.J. Wensinck, *Concordance*, viii (for a listing of traditions in the "six books" and some earlier collections in which Saʿīd is mentioned as transmitter); Khaṭīb ʿAlī b. al-Ḥusayn al-Hāshimī, *Saʿīd b. Djubayr*, Baghdād 1380/1960 (not seen); W. Madelung, *Der Imam al-Qāsim ibn Ibrāhīm und die Glaubenslehre der Zaiditen*, Berlin 1965, 231-3, 237; F. Sezgin, *GAS*, i, Leiden 1967, 28-9; Salām Muḥammad ʿAlī, *Saʿīd b. Djubayr*, Nadjaf 1396/1976; R. Sayed, *Die Revolte*, quoted above, 352-3; J. van Ess, *Theologie und Gesellschaft im 2. und 3. Jahrhundert Hidschra*, i, Berlin-New York 1991, 151-61.

(H. Motzki)

SĀḲIYA [see MĀʾ. 3].

AL-**SĀḲIYA** AL-**ḤAMRAʾ**, conventionally Seguiat el Hamra, a region of the Western Sahara, situated in southwestern Morocco in lat. 27° N.

It is made up of low plateaux, dominated by rocky hamadas, sprinkled with numerous surface dayas and incised with the hydrographical network system of the Wādī al-Sāḳiya al-Ḥamrāʾ ("the red watercourse"), which runs westwards and includes long alluvial ribbons. At the Atlantic littoral, the end of its course is marked by vertical, abrupt cliffs, worn down by the general presence of the cold current of the Canaries, causing a misty haze almost permanently over the desert. But the aridness is attenuated by hardly visible forms of precipitation: condensation at night on the soil and the vegetation allows a well-spread carpet of vegetation (argan trees, euphorbias and groundsel), a carpet which becomes more narrowed towards the interior, with streaks of greenery and acacias, etc. along the wadis.

These austere conditions, together with the complete absence of any non-saline surface water, explain the almost total absence of oases. These lands have been used over the ages as pasture lands for herds of dromedaries and goats owned by the Reguibat and Tekna nomads. The bottoms of the wadis allow the occasional cultivation there of cereals.

Al-Sāḳiya al-Ḥamrāʾ has for long been a corridor of passage, in the context of trans-Saharan trade, between the southern Moroccan fringes and the trading posts of the Sahel. In the 15th and 16th centuries, it was a hive of maraboutic activity, a seed-bed of local saints, who would often depart along the roads leading eastwards to Mecca and establish themselves in some place along one of these axes (the Algerian countryside or the villages of Fezzan). The influence of these pious figures was such that, in this region, even today whole tribes consider themselves as their descendents.

It is partly within this context that one should mention the role of an exceptional figure of the 19th century, a religious reformer and political leader who took over control of the destiny of al-Sāḳiya al-Ḥamrāʾ, sc. Shaykh Māʾ al-ʿAynayn [*q.v.*]. Born in 1839, he studied in Tindūf and Chinguetti/Shinḳīt [*q.v.*], created his own dervish order, the ʿAyniyya, wrote several books, established links with the sultans of Morocco, fought against the French activities to the north and the south, and in 1898 founded the town of Ṣmāra, on the edge of the Wādī al-Sāḳiya al-Ḥamrāʾ, with its *ḳaṣaba*, mosque, *zāwiya* and a library of 500 manuscripts.

But the feeble state of the sultanate of Morocco brought with it an end to the Shaykh's dreams. In 1913, a corps of French troops bombarded the town of Ṣmāra. Established on the coast, the Spanish gradually penetrated into the interior, and in 1930 founded Laayoune. From that time onwards, al-Sāḳiya al-Ḥamrāʾ became the official name of one of the two colonies comprising the Spanish Sahara, the other being Rio de Oro (Wādī al-Dhahab).

In 1975, after the episode of the "Green March", reaching as far as Tarfaya, Spain evacuated the territories, and the Moroccan army and administration henceforth controlled their destinies. But they became the region for a political and military contest between Morocco and the Polisarios, a contest which the United Nations is still trying to resolve.

In the last 25 years, the Moroccan state has created a network of paved roads, built various installations and has begun exploiting the great deposits of phos-

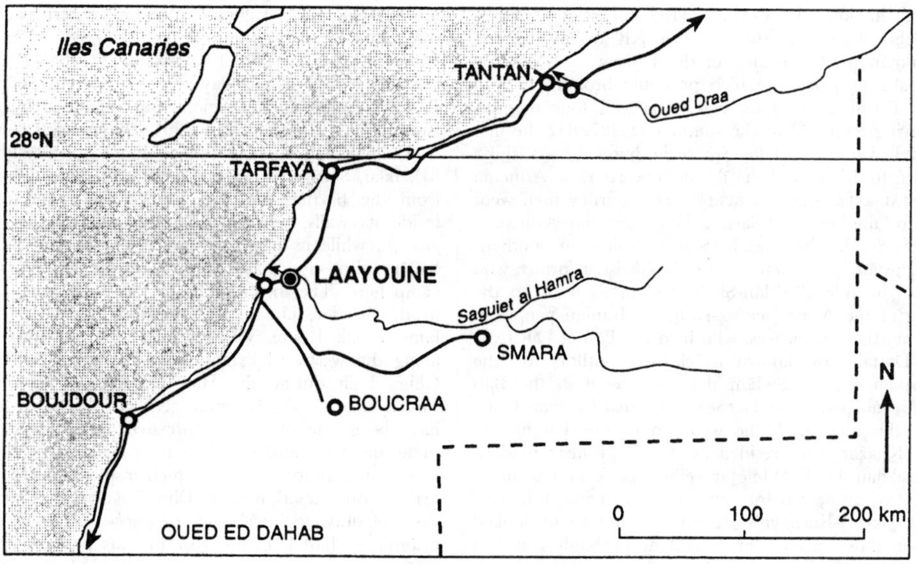

phates at Boucraa. Since the coast is full of fish, thanks to the Canaries current, fishing has become extensive and is an important activity through the creation of the ports of Tarfaya, Port Laayoune and Boudjour. The capital of al-Sāḳiya al-Ḥamrāʾ and the whole of the Western Sahara, Laayoune, has today 150,000 inhabitants, with another 35,000 at Ṣmāra.

Bibliography: F. Joly, *L'homme et le Sud au Maghreb Atlantique*, in *Mediterranée* (1979), 27-37; M. Vieuxchange, *Smara, carnets de route*, Paris 1993; M. Boughdadi, *Le passé et le présent marocains du Sahara (avec textes, documents et citations à l'appui)*, Maroc Soir, Rabat 1998. (M. CÔTE)

ṢAKK (A.), pl. *ṣikāk*, a technical term of early Islamic financial, commercial and legal usage, appearing in Persian, through a standard sound change, as *čak*, meaning "document, contract of sale, etc.", which has been suggested—for want of any other etymology—as the origin of Eng. "cheque", Fr. "chèque," Ger. "Scheck," see E. Littmann, *Morgenländische Wörter im Deutschen*, [2]Tübingen 1924.

The term's range of applications is wide, see Lane, *Lexicon*, 1709. In legal contexts, it has a similar meaning to *sidjill* [see SIDJILL. 1.], sc. a signed and sealed record of a judge's decision. In financial contexts, it often means "a written order for payment of a salary, allowance, pension, etc.", "a financial draft or assignment". Thus in Ḳudāma b. Djaʿfar's [*q.v.*] section on the ʿAbbāsid *dīwān* of military affairs contained in his *Kitāb al-Kharādj* (early 4th/10th century), a soldier displays at the pay session a certificate of assignment of pay (*ṣakk*) from the *dīwān* (W. Hoenerbach, *Zur Heeresverwaltung der ʿAbbāsiden. Studie über Abulfarağ Qudāma*: Dīwān al-ǧaiš, in *Isl.*, xxix [1950], 281). See for further references on the term's usage in mediaeval Islam, C.E. Bosworth, *Abū ʿAbdallāh al-Khwārazmī on the technical terms of the secretary's art. A contribution to the administrative history of mediaeval Islam*, in *JESHO*, xii (1969), 125-6.

Bibliography: Given in the article. (C.E. BOSWORTH)

ṢALĀT-I MAʿKŪSA (A., P.), literally, "the act of Muslim worship performed upside-down", one of the extreme ascetic practices found among extravagant members of the dervish orders, such as in mediaeval Muslim India among the Čishtiyya [*q.v.*], where it formed part of the forty days' retreat or seclusion (*khalwa, arbaʿīniyya, cilla*) undertaken to heighten spiritual awareness [see KHALWA]. This practice was one of those done in tortured or difficult circumstances, in this case hanging on the end of a rope over the mouth of a well; see ČISHTIYYA, at Vol. II, 55b, and HIND. v. Islam, at Vol. III, 432b. (ED.)

SALLĀM AL-TARDJUMĀN, early traveller in Central Asia, who has left an account of his alleged journey to the barrier of Yādjūdj wa-Mādjūdj [*q.v.*].

In 227/842 the caliph al-Wāthiḳ (*r.* 227-32/842-7 [*q.v.*]) reportedly saw in a dream that Dhu 'l-Ḳarnayn's barrier had been breached. Sallām al-Tardjumān ("the interpreter"), "who spoke thirty languages" and who, according to Ibn Rusta, 149, used to translate Turkish documents for the caliph, received the order to make inquiries about the barrier and to report about it. The account of his journey is given by Ibn Khurradādhbih (d. between 272/885 and 300/912 [*q.v.*], Ar. text in *BGA*, vi, 162-70; Eng. tr. Wilson, *The Wall*, 582-7; Fr. tr. Barbier de Meynard, *Le livre des routes*, 124-31 and Miquel, *Géographie*, ii, 498-507; Dutch tr. De Goeje, *De muur*, 104-9). He writes that Sallām told him the story of his journey and afterwards dictated to him the account he had drawn up for the caliph.

The dream is perhaps to be explained in relation to unrest caused by the Turks in Central Asia, e.g. by the movements of the Ḳirghiz [*q.v.*] around Lake Baykal in 226-7/841. Another reason for the mission may have been al-Wāthiḳ's wish to put an end to what Barbier de Meynard (*op. cit.*, 23) calls "ridiculous interpretations" current about "the people of the Cave" (Ḳurʾān, XVIII, 9-26; see AṢḤĀB AL-KAHF) and about Yādjūdj and Mādjūdj with whom the Turks were identified. Ibn Khurradādhbih, 106-7, relates that al-Wāthiḳ already had sent the famous mathematician and astronomer Abū Djaʿfar Muḥammad b. Mūsā al-Khwārazmī (d. 232/847 [*q.v.*]) to the land of Rūm in order to investigate the story of the men of *raḳīm* [see AṢḤĀB AL-KAHF]. As Sallām would do later, al-Khwārazmī informed Ibn Khurradādhbih personally about his journey. Al-Muḳaddasī, 362, relates that al-Wāt̲h̲iḳ had sent the same al-K̲h̲ʷārazmī to the Ṭark̲h̲ān [*q.v.*], the king of the K̲h̲azar.

Sallām's journey, which probably brought him to the Tarim Basin, took two years and four months. Leaving Sāmarrāʾ in the summer of 227/842, he first travelled north to Tiflis, where he handed al-Wāt̲h̲iḳ's letter to Isḥāḳ b. Ismāʿīl, the governor of Armenia [see AL-ḲABḲ; ḲARṢ; AL-ḲURDJ]. The journey then went on to "the lord of al-Sarīr", the present-day Avaristān, a district in the middle Köy-su valley in southern Dāg̲h̲istān [*q.v.*], then ruled by a Christian prince who bore the title of Fīlān-S̲h̲āh. Sallām went on to the king of the Alans [see AL-LĀN], an Iranian people in the northern Caucasus, who held the Bāb al-Lān [*q.v.*] or Darial Pass, known to classical authors as "the Caspian Gates". Sallām does not mention the Bāb al-Abwāb [*q.v.*] near Derbend, the real Caspian Gate. Via the Fīlān-S̲h̲āh, he went on to the Ṭark̲h̲ān of the K̲h̲azar, who resided at Atil [*q.v.*] near modern Astrakhan [*q.v.*]. While travelling back and forth in the Caucasus, Sallām must have convinced himself that D̲h̲u 'l-Ḳarnayn's barrier was not to be looked for in those regions. From Atil he probably travelled in an easterly direction to *Īkku*, which is identical with modern Ha-mi in Sinkiang (lat. 42° 47' N., long. 93° 32' E.). With Tiflis, this is the only town mentioned in Ibn K̲h̲urradād̲h̲bih's text. De Goeje (164 n. *g*; cf. 126 n. 4 and *De muur*, 109) remarks that the vocalisation of *Īkku* is a conjecture, but his identifying this town with *Igu* seems quite plausible. During the T'ang dynasty (618-907), and thus at the time of Sallām's arrival, Ha-mi was known as *I-chou*, which then was under the rule of the Uyg̲h̲urs (cf. *Encyclopaedia Britannica*, s.v. *Ha-mi*; see also ḲUMUL, in Suppl.). If Sallām indeed came to this town (see below), he may have travelled north of the Aral Sea. Al-Idrīsī, who used the now lost work of al-Djayhānī [*q.v.* in Suppl.], adds (*Opus geographicum*, 935) that Sallām travelled for twenty-seven days along the borders of the land of the Bas̲h̲d̲j̲irt (Bas̲h̲kurt) [*q.v.*], a Turkish people living in the southern Ural. He may have crossed the Dzungharian Basin and passed the Gate of that name in the northern spur of the T'ien Shan mountain system, on the border of modern Kazak̲h̲stān and China. But "the black, stinking land" (*arḍ sawdāʾ muntinat al-rāʾiḥa*) which he mentions (Ibn K̲h̲urradād̲h̲bih, 163) may also point to the neighbourhood of Lake Balk̲h̲as̲h̲ [*q.v.*], the evil smell being perhaps caused by asafoetida (De Goeje, *De muur*, 110). Sallām may then have followed the Ili river [*q.v.*] upstream. The "ruined towns" (*mudun k̲h̲arāb*) which he then reached are perhaps the ruins of Pei-ting (or Chin-man), the site of the ancient capital of the region. He may then have passed modern Urumchi, Guchen and Barkul (see map). If he took the southern route via Turfan, he may have seen the ruins of Yar-khoto, the capital of the Turfan region in Han times (206 B.C.-A.D. 220) (see Stein, *On ancient tracks*, 270; von Le Coq, *Auf Hellas' Spuren*, 41, 69ff.). The inhabitants told him that their towns had been destroyed by Yād̲j̲ūd̲j̲ and Mād̲j̲ūd̲j̲, perhaps a reference to the Ḳirg̲h̲iz invasions of 841, which had put an end to Uyg̲h̲ur rule north of the Great Wall of China. Sallām then came to "fortifications" (*ḥuṣūn*) in the neighbourhood of the barrier, where he met Muslims who spoke Arabic and Persian, who read the Ḳurʾān, and had Ḳurʾān schools and mosques, but did not know what the term *amīr al-muʾminīn* meant. These Muslims were probably merchants who had settled in an outpost far outside the world of Islam. The religion of the Prophet came to the Farg̲h̲ana [*q.v.*] valley, and to the western part of the Tarim Basin [*q.v.*] only around 225/840 under the Sāmānid governor Nūḥ b. Asad (d. 227/841-2) [see SĀMĀNIDS]. In Sallām's days the eastern part of the Basin, i.e. the Turfan region, was inhabited by the Ad̲h̲kas̲h̲ Turks (see al-Kās̲h̲g̲h̲arī, *Dīwān lug̲h̲āt al-turk*, tr. Dankoff and Kelly, i, 89; cf. Ibn K̲h̲urradād̲h̲bih, 31). Īkku, Sallām relates, lay at a three days' distance from the barrier and had farmed fields and mills inside its walls, which had a circumference of ten *farsak̲h̲s*, while its iron gates were let down at night. Sallām also says that D̲h̲u 'l-Ḳarnayn had pitched camp here. The fortifications on the road from Īkku to the barrier, i.e. on the northern branch of the famous Silk Route, were perhaps the watch-towers along the westward extension of the Great Wall of China built during the Han period (see Stein, *On ancient tracks*, ch. X; Hermann, *Atlas*, map 24). It may have been one of these impressive towers, fully 4.5 m at the base and standing to a height of over 9 metres (illustration no. 73), which inspired Sallām for his fantastic description of D̲h̲u 'l-Ḳarnayn's barrier (see the drawing in Miquel, *Géographie*, ii, 505). This inspiration, based on the Ḳurʾān, was perhaps influenced by the descriptions of Alexander's Gate, found e.g. in the Syriac Alexander Song of Jacob of Sarūd̲j̲ (see Reinink, *Das Syrische Alexanderlied*, 19) and the early Islamic poets.

According to Sallām, the barrier was a double-winged iron gate, 27 m high, over which was an iron lintel, *ca.* 64 m long and 3 m wide, on top of which was a wall of bricks, made of iron and brass. The barrier filled the gap between "the two mountains" (cf. Ḳurʾān, XVIII, 93, 96). Nearby, Sallām found two enormous fortresses, in one of which were the iron cauldrons and ladles used to form the bricks. Relics of them were stuck together with rust. The governor of the fortresses rode out every Monday and Thursday (according to al-Idrīsī, every Friday). One of his men knocked on the lock of the barrier and heard a noise as from a wasps' nest. He was then assured that Yād̲j̲ūd̲j̲ and Mād̲j̲ūd̲j̲ had done no harm to the barrier, since they realised that it was under constant guard. The governor assured Sallām that the only damage the barrier had suffered was a crack as thin as a thread. Sallām scraped half a dirham of iron dust from the crack to show to al-Wāt̲h̲iḳ. The people of the fortresses told him that they once had seen some individuals of Yād̲j̲ūd̲j̲ and Mād̲j̲ūd̲j̲ on the top of the mountain, their size being one span and a half. A "dark wind" had blown them back. On top of the right wing was an inscription in iron letters "in the primordial language" (*al-lisān al-awwal*), namely, Ḳurʾān, XVIII, 98: "But when the promise of my Lord shall come to pass, He will flatten it; and the promise of my Lord is true."

On his return journey, Sallām may have travelled to Lop Nor, from where he went to Nīs̲h̲āpūr via Ṭarāz, Isfīd̲j̲āb and Balk̲h̲ [*q.vv.*], having lost 36 men and 177 mules. Via al-Rayy he returned to Sāmarrāʾ, where he was well received by the caliph, to whom he showed the iron dust taken from D̲h̲u 'l-Ḳarnayn's barrier.

Ibn K̲h̲urradād̲h̲bih's text of Sallām's report was taken up over the next four or so centuries by Ibn al-Faḳīh, Ibn Faḍlān, Ibn Rusta, al-Muḳaddasī, al-Bīrūnī, al-Idrīsī, Ibn al-Djawzī and al-Nuwayrī [*q.vv.*]. Numerous other authors dealt with Yād̲j̲ūd̲j̲ and Mād̲j̲ūd̲j̲ but did not mention Sallām's journey. Ibn Rusta, 149, Sallām's and Ibn K̲h̲urradād̲h̲bih's contemporary, gives Sallām's report only to show how

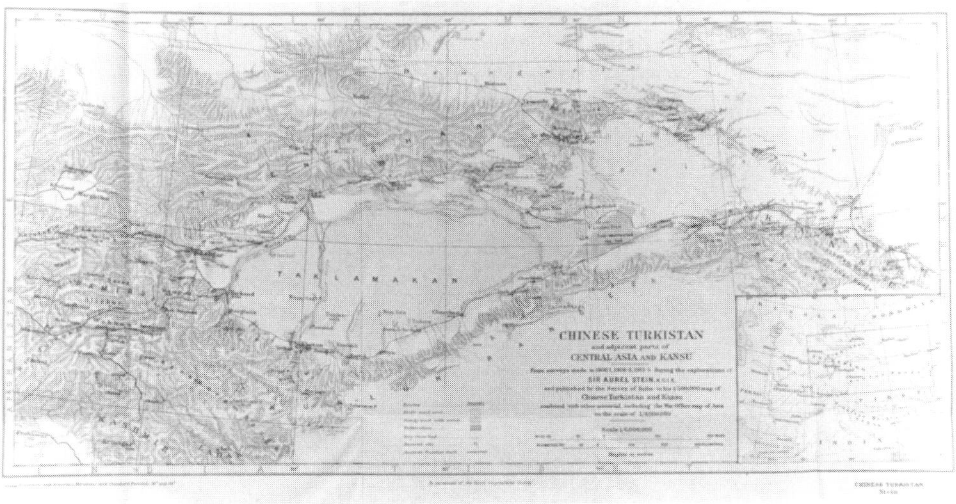

Chinese Turkestan and adjacent parts of Central Asia and Kansu. Source: Sir Aurel Stein, *On ancient Central Asian tracks. Brief narrative of three expeditions in innermost Asia and northwestern China*, London 1933, repr. New York 1971, p. 342.

Ruin of ancient Chinese fort marking the position of the "Jade Gate", seen from the northeast. Source: Sir Aurel Stein, *On ancient Central Asian tracks. Brief narrative of three expeditions in innermost Asia and northwestern China*, London 1933, repr. New York 1971, p. 180.

confused (*takhlīt*) and exaggerated (*tazayyud*) it is. Al-Bīrūnī (*al-Āthār*, 41) doubts Sallām's credibility because he cannot believe that there were Muslims who spoke Arabic and Persian but did not know about the caliph. Neither is there unanimity among the Western scholars who have dealt with Sallām's report. For Barbier de Meynard (*op. cit.*, 23), Sallām's journey at least had "a beginning", and he states that he does not see in it, as Sprenger did, an "impudent mystification". De Goeje does not leave any doubt about his view: "We have found the origin of the legend about the wall of Gog and Magog, as it appears in Pseudo-Callisthenes and the Ḳur'ān, in the Great Chinese Wall with the Jade Gate [*Yü-mönn*], and we have restored Sallām's travel account as the report of a real journey" (*De muur*, 116). Anderson (*Alexander's gate*, 95) argues that Sallām certainly did not go to the Chinese Wall. For Wilson (*The Wall*, 611), Sallām's story is nothing but a legend, while Miller (*Mappae arabicae*, iv, 93-5) holds that the place described by Sallām is the breach in the Altai mountains made by the river Irtish [*q.v.* in Suppl.]. Miquel finds in the account a "côtoiement d'un certain vraisemblable avec un légendaire certain" and adds "on mesure, à cet exemple, la place du merveilleux (*ʿaǧīb*) dans le goût du temps: il va jusqu'à se superposer chez un calife, aux nécessités de l'information objective" (*Géographie*, ii, 503).

Yet, there is some reason to support the view that Sallām did travel as far as Ha-mi. The data he gives about the Caucasus can be checked successfully in the sources available. Those for the journey from there to Īkku/Ha-mi are vague, it is true, the identification of landscapes, ruined towns and fortified places being speculative yet not absurd. Sallām did reach Ha-mi, since his *Īkku* is identical with this Chinese town [see ḲUMUL, in Suppl.]. It is thus quite likely that he saw the Jade Gate and the western extension of the Great Wall. His description of the town seems to be confirmed by Chinese publications (e.g. Luo Zhewen, *The Great Wall*, 7, 41), and his remark that the function of governor was hereditary agrees with later information by Abu 'l-Ghāzī [*q.v.*], according to whom some Turkish families had been charged by the Kitai [see ḲARA-KHIṬĀY] to guard, in return for payment, certain sections of the Great Wall. These Turks were called Öngüt ("wall") and their function was hereditary (cf. *Histoire des Mongols*, tr. Desmaisons, 47; Grousset, *L'Empire*, 287). The reports of Sven Hedin, Sir Aurel Stein, Albert von Le Coq *et alii* (see Hopkirk, *Foreign devils*, 243-5) seem to justify the view that Sallām did indeed travel to the eastern part of the Tarim Basin and saw part of the—by then already ruined—western extension of the Great Wall of China and at least one of its gates.

Bibliography: 1. Primary sources. Abu 'l-Ghāzī, *Histoire des Mongols*, tr. Desmaisons, Paris 1871-4; Bīrūnī, *al-Āthār al-bāḳiya ʿan al-ḳurūn al-khāliya*, ed. E. Sachau, Leipzig 1878, tr. idem, *The chronology of ancient nations*, London 1879; *Ḥudūd al-ʿālam*, tr. Minorsky, London 1937; Ibn Khurradādhbih, index; Ibn Rusta; Idrīsī, *Opus geographicum sive "Liber ad eorum delectationem qui terras peragrare studeant"*, Naples-Rome 1970-84; Idrīsī, tr. Jaubert; Iṣṭakhrī; Kāshgharī, *Dīwān lughāt al-turk*, tr. R. Dankoff and J. Kelly, *Compendium of the Turkish dialects*, Cambridge, Mass. 1982-4; Muḳaddasī, 362-5.

2. Secondary sources. A.R. Anderson, *Alexander's gate, Gog and Magog and the enclosed nations*, Cambridge, Mass. 1932; D.S. Attema, *De Mohammedaansche opvattingen omtrent tijdstip van den jongsten dag en zijn voorteekenen*, Amsterdam 1942; C. Barbier de Meynard, *Le livre des routes et des provinces par Ibn Khordadbeh*, in *JA*, v (1865); M.J. de Goeje, *De muur van Gog en Magog*, in *Mededel. Kon. Akad. van Wetenschappen*, Amsterdam, 3e Serie, v, 87-124; R. Grousset, *L'Empire des steppes*, [4]Paris 1960, Eng. tr. *The empire of the steppes. A history of Central Asia*, New Brunswick, N.J. 1970; A. Herrmann, *An historical atlas of China*, Edinburgh 1966; P. Hopkirk, *Foreign devils on the Silk Road. The search for the lost treasures of Central Asia*, Oxford 1980; A. von Le Coq, *Auf Hellas' Spuren. Berichte und Abenteuer der II. und III. Deutschen Turfan-Expedition*, Graz 1974; Luo Zhewen and Zhoa Luo, *The Great Wall of China in history and legend*, Beijing 1986; K. Miller, *Mappae arabicae. Arabische Welt- und Länderkarten des 9.-13. Jahrhunderts*, Stuttgart 1926-31; A. Miquel, *La géographie humaine du monde musulman jusqu'au milieu du 11e siècle*, ii, Paris-The Hague 1975, 497-511; Sir Aurel Stein, *On ancient Central Asian tracks. Brief narrative of three expeditions in innermost Asia and northwestern China*, London 1933, repr. New York 1971; C.E. Wilson, *The Wall of Alexander the Great against Gog and Magog and the expedition sent out to find it by the Khalif Wāthiq in 842 A.D.*, in *[Friedrich] Hirth anniversary volume* (*Asia Major*, 1) London 1922, 575-612.

(E. VAN DONZEL)

SALMĀN AL-FĀRISĪ or SALMĀN PĀK, a semi-legendary figure of early Islam, Companion of the Prophet and the person regarded in later tradition as the proto-convert to Islam from the Persian nation.

According to one tradition, the most complete version of which goes back to Muḥammad b. Isḥāḳ, he was the son of a *dihḳān* of the Persian village of Djayy (or Djayyān; cf. Yāḳūt, ii, 170) near Iṣfahān. According to other stories, he belonged to the vicinity of Rām-hurmuz and his Persian name was Māhbēh (Māyēh) or Rūzbēh (cf. Justi, *Iran. Namenbuch*, 217, 277). Attracted by Christianity while still a boy, he left his father's house to follow a Christian monk and, having changed his teachers several times, arrived in Syria; from there he went right down to the Wādi 'l-Ḳurā in western Arabia seeking the Prophet who was to restore the religion of Ibrāhīm, the imminence of whose coming had been predicted to him by his last teacher on his deathbed. Betrayed by Kalbī Bedouin, who were acting as his guides through the desert, and sold as a slave to a Jew, he had occasion to go to Yathrib where, soon after his arrival, the *hidjra* of Muḥammad took place. Recognising in the latter the marks of the prophet which the monk had described to him, Salmān became a Muslim and purchased his liberty from his Jewish master, after being miraculously aided by Muḥammad himself to raise the sum necessary to pay his ransom.

The name of Salmān is associated with the siege of Medina by the Meccans, for it was he who on this occasion advised the digging of the ditch (*khandak*) by means of which the Muslims defended themselves from the enemy. But, as Horovitz (see *Bibl.*) has shown, the earliest accounts of the *yawm al-khandaḳ* make no mention of Salmān's intervention, the story of which was probably invented in order to attribute to a Persian the introduction of a system of defence the name of which is of Persian origin. The other references to the career of Salmān (his part in the conquest of ʿIrāḳ and of Fārs, his governorship of al-Madā'in, etc.) are equally devoid of authority and almost all date from the historian Sayf b. ʿUmar, the bias of whose work is well known. Indeed, the fame of Salmān is almost entirely due to his Persian nationality: he is the prototype of the converted Persians, who played such a part in the development of Islam; as such, he has become the national hero of Muslim Persia and one of the favourite personages of the Shuʿūbiyya [*q.v.*] (see Goldziher, *Muh. Studien*, i, 117, 136, 153, 212). What explains the majority of the traditions relative to Salmān is the fact that the Prophet foretells to him that the Persians will form the better part of the Muslim community; he declares him a member of his own family (*ahl al-bayt*), etc. In reality, the historical personality of Salmān is of the vaguest, and it is with difficulty that one can even admit that his legend is based on the actual fact of the conversion of a Medinan slave of Persian origin.

The figure of Salmān has had an extraordinary development. Not only does he appear as one of the founders of Ṣūfism along with the *Aṣḥāb al-Ṣuffa* (*K. al-Lumaʿ*, ed. Nicholson, 134-5) but the alleged site of his tomb very early became a centre of worship (at latest in 4th/10th century) (cf. al-Yaʿḳūbī, *Buldān*, 321); it is still pointed out in the vicinity of the ancient al-Madā'in, at the place called after him Salmān Pāk ("Salmān the Pure") near the former Asbāndur suburb. His sepulchral mosque, which was seen in its older form by Pietro della Valle in 1617, was renovated by Sultan Murād IV [*q.v.*] and further restored in 1322/1904-5 (Herzfeld-Sarre, *Archäol. Reise im Euphrates- und Tigrisgebiet*, ii, 262, n. 1). It is the object of numerous pilgrimages, especially on the part of Shīʿīs, who do not fail to visit it when returning from Karbalā'. Other traditions locate the tomb of Salmān in the vicinity of Iṣfahān, where there is evidence of his cult in the 7th/13th century (Yāḳūt, ii, 170), and elsewhere, e.g. Lydda.

Salmān plays a remarkable part in the development of the *futuwwa* [*q.v.*] and the workmen's corporations. He is venerated as a patron of barbers, whence comes the tradition, unknown in ancient collections of traditions, which makes him the Prophet's barber. He is also one of the principal links in the mystic chain (*silsila*) in various dervish orders.

Among the extremist Shīʿī sects, he is placed immediately after ʿAlī in the series of divine emanations. The Nuṣayriyya [*q.v.*] make him the third member of the trinity formed by the three mystic letters ʿAyn (ʿAlī), M (Muḥammad) and S (Salmān), of which he forms the gate (*bāb*) (cf. R. Dussaud, *Histoire et religion des Nosaïris*, Paris 1900, 62).

The death of Salmān is placed in 35/655-6 or 36/656-7, a statement which has no value except to indicate that the historical tradition had no note of his activity after the accession of ʿAlī (end of 35/656). Like many other individuals, said to have embraced Islam after long experiences of other religions, he is credited with an extraordinary longevity: 200, 300, 350 and even 553 years (Goldziher, *Abhandl. zur arab. Philologie*, ii, p. LXVI).

Bibliography: Ibn Hishām, 136-42, Eng. tr. Guillaume, 95-8; Ibn Ḥanbal, *Musnad*, v, 441-4; Muṭahhar al-Maḳdisī, *K. al-Badʾ wa 'l-taʾrīkh*, 110-13, 345, 673, 677; Ibn Saʿd, iv/1, 53-67; Ṭabarī, i, 1465, 1467-9, tr. M. Fishbein, *The History of al-Ṭabarī*, viii, *The victory of Islam*, Albany 1997, 6, 10-12; Ibn al-Athīr, *Usd*, ii, 328-32; Cl. Huart, *Selmân du Fârs*, in *Mélanges H. Derenbourg*, Paris 1909, 297-310; idem, *Nouvelles recherches sur la légende de Selmân du Fârs*, in *Annuaire de l'École pratique des Hautes Études*, Section des sciences religieuses, Paris 1913; J. Horovitz, *Salmān al-Fārisī*, in *Isl.*, xii (1922), 178-83; L. Massignon, *Salmān Pāk et les prémices spirituelles de l'Islam iranien*, Publications de la Soc. des Études iraniennes no. 7, Paris 1934, repr. in *Opera minora*, Damascus 1957, i, 443-83.

(G. LEVI DELLA VIDA*)

SAMAW'AL B. YAḤYĀ AL-MAGHRIBĪ, ABŪ NAṢR (?520-70/?1126-75), prominent physician and mathematician who lived and practiced among the notables of Syria, ʿIrāḳ, Kurdistān and Ādharbāydjān. Born and raised as a Jew, he gives an account of his conversion to Islam, including a brief autobiography, in an appendix attached to the second edition of his anti-Jewish polemic, *Ifḥām al-yahūd* ("Silencing the Jews"). His father, Yehūdah Ibn Abūn, was a rabbi and poet from Fās whose family came from al-Andalus. Also known as Abu 'l-Baḳā' Yaḥyā b. ʿAbbās al-Maghribī, the father moved to Baghdād and married a literate and educated woman of a noble Jewish family named Ḥannah bt. Isḥāḳ b. Ibrāhīm al-Baṣrī al-Lawī (the Levite).

According to Samaw'al's autobiographical chapter, he began his studies like other Jewish boys with Hebrew writing, and the study of Torah and its commentaries. By the age of thirteen, however, the age marking adult maturity and ritual responsibility in Jewish law, his father moved him out of the traditional religious curriculum because of his perspicacity and introduced him to the study of mathematics and medicine. He excelled in these fields and wrote a number of works, most of which no longer survive. His only extant medical work, the *Nuzhat al-aṣḥāb*, centres around diseases and syndromes associated with sexual dysfunction, and it includes a collection of erotic stories and descriptions of being in love without recognising it. His most important scientific work is his book on algebra, *al-Bāhir*, written when he was nineteen. He set out to provide the same kind of systematisation for algebra that al-Karadjī did for geometry in his work, *al-Badīʿ*. He is the first Arab algebraist to undertake the study of relative numbers.

His early studies were taken under Abu 'l-Barakāt Hibat Allāh b. ʿAlī, another Jew who is said to have become Muslim, though late in life. Samaw'al is associated with yet another learned Jewish convert to Islam, Isaac the son of the famous biblical exegete, grammarian and philosopher, Abraham ben Ezra.

In al-Samaw'al's time, the science of medicine was closely associated with rationalistic philosophy. It has been suggested recently that the aforementioned conversions may have been "provisional". For example, Samaw'al's polemic against Judaism expresses a philosophical relativism that may have been influenced by or associated with the Nizārī Ismaʿīlī *ḳiyāma* (resurrection/resurgence) centred around Alamūt, a contemporary movement that transcended the normative boundaries of religion and law in the lands of Syria and Persia (S. Wasserstrom, following S. Stroumsa, J. Kraemer and H. Lazarus-Yafeh). If so, then Samaw'al's anti-Jewish *Ifḥām* may have been a safe way of criticising doctrinal thinking in general.

It has also been suggested that Samaw'al's conversion was a result of exactly the process about which Moses Maimonides later cautioned in his *Commentary on the Mishna*, that Jews should avoid the study of history because in the Islamic world such study was overwhelmingly anchored in Islamic perspectives and world views and would therefore encourage apostasy from Judaism. Samaw'al's conversion may have been a response to the difficult Jewish problem of accepting the negation of exile while accepting the need for infinite patience for a vague messianic redemption. Such a delicate balance of thought was difficult to sustain when confronted by the this-worldly reality of contemporary Muslim history, which fulfilled the Jewish longing for a polity, or *dawla*, a central concept in Samaw'al's polemical attack against Judaism (Husain).

Unlike his father, whose *kunya* Abu 'l-Baḳā' suggests longevity, Samaw'al died in 570/1175 at a relatively young age (Ibn Abī Uṣaybiʿa, *ʿUyūn al-anbāʾ*).

Bibliography: 1. Sources. Samaw'al al-Maghribī, *Ifḥām al-yahūd*, ed. and tr. M. Perlmann, in *Procs. American Academy for Jewish Research*, xxxii (1964); idem, *al-Bāhir fi 'l-djabr*, ed. Ṣalāḥ Aḥmad and Rushdī Rāshid, Damascus 1972; Ibn Abī Uṣaybiʿa, *ʿUyūn al-anbāʾ fī ṭabaḳāt al-aṭibbāʾ*, ed. A. Müller, Cairo-Königsberg 1882-4, Beirut 1955-6.

2. Studies. Suter, 124-5; M. Steinschneider, *Die Mathematiker bei den Juden*, Frankfurt 1901; Brockelmann, S I, 493-4; F. Rosenthal, *Al-Asturlābī and as-Samaw'al*, in *Osiris*, ix (1950), 560-4; A. Husain, *Conversion to history: negating exile and messianism in al-Samaw'al al-Maghribī's polemic against Judaism*, in *Medieval Encounters*, viii/1 (2002), 3-34; S. Wasserstrom, *False Messiahs and false conversion. Samaw'al al-Maghribi in the context of twelfth-century interconfessionalism*, in *Procs. XXVIII. Deutscher Orientalistentag, Bamberg 26-30 March 2001*, forthcoming.

(R. FIRESTONE)

SANAD (A.), pl. *asnād*, lit. "support, stay, rest", but in Islamic administrative usage coming to mean an administrative, financial or legal document on which reliance can formally be placed (*masnūd*), hence an authenticated document. From the same root *s-n-d* is derived the technical term of Islamic tradition, *isnād* [*q.v.* and ḤADĪTH], literally "the act of making something rest upon something else".

The Turkish form of *sanad*, i.e. *sened*, was used in Ottoman practice for a document with e.g. a seal attached, thereby authenticating it and supporting it with official proof; see Pakalın, iii, 173-4. In Indo-Muslim usage, *sanad* was used for government and similar decrees, hence the definition in J.T. Platts, *A dictionary of Urdū, Classical Hindī, and English*, [4]London 1911, 682: "ordinance, mandate, decree, grant, certificate, etc."

Bibliography: Given in the article.

(C.E. BOSWORTH)

ṢARF (A.), the Islamic legal term for exchanges of gold for gold, silver for silver, and gold and silver for each other. Although *ṣarf* in this sense appears in the *ḥadīth*, it is generally regarded as a term of art without prescriptive significance (Ibn al-ʿArabī, *Kitāb al-Ḳabas*, ed. Walad Karīm, Beirut 1992, ii, 822-3; al-Subkī, *Takmilat al-madjmūʿ*, Cairo n.d., x, 99; but see Ibn al-Murtaḍā, *al-Baḥr al-zakhkhār*, Beirut 1409/1988, iii, 386). According to another well-established usage (al-Baʿlī, *al-Muṭliʿ*, Beirut 1401/1981, 239; al-ʿAynī, *ʿUmdat al-ḳārī*, Beirut n.d., x, 293), followed by Mālikī jurists, *ṣarf* applies to exchanges of gold and silver, while exchanges (by weight) of gold for gold or silver for silver are termed *murāṭala*. Further variations in usage can be found (*Sharḥ al-Khirshī ʿalā mukhtaṣar Sīdī Khalīl*, Beirut n.d., v, 36 [including *fulūs*]; al-Subkī, x, 149 [*ṣarf* vs. *muṣārafa*]). In addition, *ṣarf* is commonly used in the sense of the rate of exchange of gold for silver, and is sometimes used for the money-changer's commission (S.D. Goitein, *A Mediterranean society*, Berkeley etc. 1967, i, 239-40) as well as for money in general (Dozy, *Supplément*, i, 829). It has been suggested that the sense of money-changing for the Arabic word *ṣarf* developed under Aramaic influence (S. Fraenkel, *Die aramäischen Fremdwörter im Arabischen*, Leiden 1886, 182-6). For a fanciful etymology from the clink (*ṣarīf*) of the metals as they are being weighed, see e.g. al-Bahūtī, *Kashshāf al-ḳināʿ*, ed. Hilāl, al-Riyāḍ n.d.

Ṣarf transactions are subject to particular stringencies. The parties, having entered into the contract, are required to take delivery before they separate. In addition, where the exchange is of gold for gold or silver for silver, the quantities on each side must be equivalent in weight. The rate of exchange of gold for silver, on the other hand, may be determined by the parties as they see fit, and even unascertained quantities (*djuzāf*) of these metals may be exchanged (cf. Mālik, *al-Muwaṭṭaʾ*, ed. ʿAbd al-Bāḳī, Cairo n.d., 393 [except coins]; al-Bādjī, *al-Muntaḳā*, Cairo 1332/1914 iv, 277-8, cf. al-Shaybānī, *K. al-Ḥudjdja*, ed. al-Kīlānī, Ḥaydarābād 1387/1968, ii, 571-2). The regulation of exchanges of gold and silver was introduced in the year 7/628 in the course of the division of the spoils of the conquest of Khaybar [*q.v.*] (Caetani, *Annali*, ii/1, 38-9). The legal rules governing these exchanges derive from the prohibition of *ribā* [*q.v.*] as expounded in the *ḥadīth*, general principles of contract law, and certain monetary conceptions.

The validity of *ṣarf* contracts requires that performance on both sides be due at once (*munādjaza, ḥulūl*); neither party may be granted a term in which to make delivery, which would constitute *ribā al-nasāʾ*. In fact, virtually all jurists require that delivery on both sides (*taḳābuḍ*) take place during the contractual session (*madjlis*) (but see al-Suyūrī, *al-Tanḳīḥ al-rāʾiʿ*, ed. al-Kūhkamarī, Ḳumm 1404/1985, ii, 97; al-Ṣadr, *al-Bank al-lā-ribawī fī 'l-Islām*, al-Kuwayt n.d., 147-8), which may, however, be protracted. To the extent otherwise available, the parties have the benefit of the right to rescind the executory contract while in their session (*khiyār al-madjlis*). The Mālikīs are stricter in this regard, insisting on prompt, if not immediate, mutual delivery, even a short delay making the exchange reprehensible (*makrūh*) (al-Ḥaṭṭāb, *Mawāhib al-djalīl*, Ṭarābulus, Libya n.d., iii, 302-3, cf. Ibn Ḥazm, *al-Muḥallā*, ed. Shākir, Beirut n.d., viii, 493). Thus while others prohibit the parties from reserving to themselves a right of rescission (*khiyār al-sharṭ*), Mālikī jurists go further and exclude delivery by assignment (*ḥawāla*) and the giving of either personal or real security for delivery, all of which are deemed repugnant to the required promptness of performance (Ibn Djuzayy, *Ḳawānīn al-aḥkām al-sharʿiyya*, Cairo 1975, 262-3; Ibn Djallāb, *al-Tafrīʿ*, ed. al-Dahmānī, Beirut 1408/1987, ii, 154, cf. the Ḥanafī al-Anḳirāwī, *Fatāwā*, Būlāḳ 1281/1864-5, i, 303). For the same reason, according to the Mālikīs, the *ṣarf* transaction is invalid if both parties borrow the gold or silver in order to make delivery (*al-ṣarf ʿalā al-dhimma*) (Saḥnūn, *al-Mudawwana*, Cairo 1323/1905, repr. Beirut n.d., iii, 396; al-Dardīr, *al-Sharḥ al-ṣaghīr*, ed. Waṣfī, Cairo 1972, iii, 50 gloss).

There is disagreement as to whether the requirement of mutual delivery is satisfied by a set-off of debts (*taṭāruḥ al-daynayn*). The Mālikīs regard the set-off as a valid *ṣarf* if both debts are presently due, the Ḥanafīs and Zaydīs as being valid whether or not due. The Shāfiʿīs and Ḥanbalīs, on the other hand, do not consider such a transaction a valid *ṣarf* (Ibn Rushd, *Bidāyat al-mudjtahid*, Cairo n.d., ii, 174; Ibn Ḳudāma, *al-Mughnī*, ed. al-Turkī and al-Ḥulw, Cairo 1408/1989, vi, 106; al-Subkī, x, 101; Ibn al-Murtaḍā, iii, 389).

Where there has been only part performance of the contract the Mālikīs treat the entire contract as void (*al-Mudawwana*, iii, 392; Ibn ʿAbd al-Barr, *al-Kāfī*, ed. al-Mūrītānī, al-Riyāḍ 1400/1980-1, ii, 634, cf. *al-Muntaḳā*, iv, 264). The other schools, following the principle of the severability of contracts (*tafrīḳ al-ṣafḳa*), uphold the *ṣarf* to the extent it has been executed (al-Nawawī, *al-Madjmūʿ*, Cairo n.d., ix, 461, cf. al-Shāfiʿī, *al-Umm*, Cairo n.d., iii, 26; al-Mardāwī, *al-Inṣāf*, ed. al-Fiḳī, Beirut n.d., v, 45; al-Suyūrī, ii, 98; Ibn al-Murtaḍā, iii, 387-8). Some jurists hold the view that the parties' failure to take delivery under the *ṣarf* contract not only voids the contract but amounts to a sin, unless they take the trouble to repudiate the contract before separating (*al-Madjmūʿ*, ix, 460-1, cf. al-Baḥrānī, *al-Ḥadāʾiḳ al-nāḍira*, ed. al-Īrawānī, Beirut 1405/1985, xix, 277).

The requirement that mutual delivery take place upon contracting makes it possible for either party to prevent the enforcement of an executory *ṣarf* contract by terminating the contractual session without taking delivery (*al-Muntaḳā*, iv, 264, cf. al-Shaybānī, *al-Amālī*, Ḥaydarābād 1360, 15-16). Furthermore, given the widespread circulation of different mintages and sub-standard coins in the mediaeval period, the jurists had to determine how far subsequent adjustments in the interest of a dissatisfied party were consistent with the rule of mutual delivery (e.g. *Mawāhib al-djalīl*, iv, 322-6; al-Mardāwī, v, 45-9).

The prohibition of *ribā* requires that exchanges of gold for gold or silver for silver involve equal quantities of the metals, any inequality constituting *ribā al-faḍl*, although some early authorities, most notably Ibn ʿAbbās (d. 68/687), are reported to have rejected the doctrine of *ribā al-faḍl*, at least for a time (e.g. al-Ṭaḥāwī, *Sharḥ maʿānī al-āthār*, ed. al-Nadjdjār, Cairo n.d., iv, 63-71, al-Subkī, x, 23-5), and thus to have permitted the exchange of unequal quantities of gold for gold and silver for silver—such unequal exchanges being termed *ṣarf* in the *ḥadīth* (al-Nasafī, *Ṭalibat al-ṭalaba*, Beirut n.d., 114; al-Nawawī, *Sharḥ ṣaḥīḥ Muslim*, Cairo n.d., xi, 23-4), a sense familiar to early lexicography, see Ibn Sīda, *al-Mukhaṣṣaṣ*, Beirut n.d., xii, 30 (quoting al-Khalīl b. Aḥmad [*q.v.*]). The requirement of strict equality (*tasāwī*) applies to all such exchanges, whatever the form of the metals, whether raw ore (*tibr*), ingots (*nuḳra, sabīka*), coins (*maḍrūb*) or manufactured articles (*maṣūgh, maṣnūʿ, ḥaly*), with the equality to be measured by weight (*wazn*), as in the time of the Prophet, without regard to the market value (*ḳīma*) of the objects (e.g. al-Bahūtī, iii, 262-3). The reasonableness and hence the validity of an exchange of exactly similar coins have been questioned (Ibn Nudjaym, *al-Baḥr al-rāʾiḳ*, ed. Cairo, vi, 193, cf. N.J. Coulson, *A history of Islamic law*, Edinburgh 1964, 42).

While campaigning in Syria, Muʿāwiya (d. 60/680) reportedly exchanged manufactured articles taken as booty for their value in the same metal, for which he was rebuked by other Companions, including the Caliph ʿUmar (al-Zurḳānī, *Sharḥ al-Muwaṭṭaʾ*, Beirut n.d., iii, 278-9; *al-Muntaḳā*, iv, 261-2), and this practice is said to have continued in Syria until ʿUmar b. ʿAbd al-ʿAzīz (d. 101/720) put an end to it (al-Subkī, x, 79). Nonetheless, the opinion that the value added by labour should be reflected in the rate of exchange continued to find support. This teaching is attributed to Dāwūd al-Ẓāhirī (d. 270/884) (al-Shaṭṭī, *Risāla fī masāʾil al-imām Dāwūd al-Ẓāhirī*, Damascus 1330, 21, cf. *al-Muḥallā*, viii, 493), and it is reported of both al-Shāfiʿī (Ibn al-Murtaḍā, iii, 387, cf. al-Shayzarī, *Nihāyat al-rutba fī ṭalab al-ḥisba*, ed. al-ʿArīnī, Beirut 1969, 75) and Aḥmad b. Ḥanbal (Ibn Ḳudāma, vi, 60) that they prohibited equal exchanges by weight of whole for broken coins because of the discrepancy in value. The most prominent later proponent of this doctrine was the Ḥanbalī Ibn Taymiyya (d. 728/1328), according to whom manufactured articles of gold or silver are outside the scope of the law of *ṣarf*, which is intended to promote monetary stability (al-Baʿlī, *al-Ikhtiyārāt al-fiḳhiyya*, ed. al-Fiḳī, Cairo n.d., 127; Ibn Ḳayyim al-Djawziyya, *Iʿlām al-muwaḳḳiʿīn*, ed. Saʿd, Cairo 1388/1968, ii, 154-63; al-Ḥaymī, *al-Rawḍ al-naḍīr*, Beirut n.d., iii, 229-31; Ibn al-Ālūsī, *Djalāʾ al-ʿaynayn*, Cairo 1400/1980, 628-44).

The attribution to Mālik of the view that coinage might be exchanged for its value in the same metal was vigorously denied by his followers (Ibn Ḳudāma, vi, 60; al-Subkī, x, 79-83, cf. J. Schacht, *The origins of Muhammadan jurisprudence*, Oxford 1950, 67). Many Mālikīs did, however, support the opinion expressed by Mālik that a traveller in dire need of coins might pay for them with the same metal in such a quantity as to cover the cost of minting (*al-Ḳabas*, ii, 822, cf. al-Khirshī, v, 43 [no longer applicable according to Ashhab, d. 204/819]; *al-Muntaḳā*, iv, 259; al-Mawwāḳ, *al-Tādj wa 'l-iklīl*, on the margin of *Mawāhib al-djalīl*, iv, 318 [only if life is in jeopardy]). Furthermore, the Mālikīs permit the exchange of up to six pieces of gold or silver currency passing by tale for an equal number of pieces made of the same metal even when the latter are up to one-sixth greater in weight. Such an exchange, termed *mubādala*, must be in the nature of an accommodation (*maʿrūf*) to the party with the underweight (*nāḳiṣ*) coins, and, according to some, must be expressly characterised by the parties as a *mubādala*, not a sale (*al-Muntaḳā*, iv, 259-60; al-Tasūlī, *al-Bahdja sharḥ al-tuḥfa*, Cairo, 1370/1951, ii, 27-9).

A further set of problems is posed when one or more objects, termed *ḍamīma* by Twelver Shīʿīs (al-Shahīd al-Awwal, *al-Lumʿa al-dimashḳiyya*, ed. Kalāntar, Ḳumm 1396/1976, iii, 441) and *djarīra* by Zaydīs (al-Ṣanʿānī, *Minḥat al-ghaffār*, Ṣanʿāʾ 1405/1985, iii, 1388), including objects subject to the laws of *ribā*, are introduced into the exchange of the same metals, for example one dirham and a measure of dates as consideration for two dirhams (*masʾalat mudd ʿadjwa*) (al-Muzanī, *al-Mukhtaṣar*, on the margin of *al-Umm*, ii, 145; Ibn Ḳudāma, vi, 92-4; Ibn Radjab, *al-Ḳawāʿid*, ed. Saʿd, Cairo 1392/1972, 267-70; *al-Muḥallā*, viii, 494-6). The Ḥanafīs, Twelver Shīʿīs and Zaydīs recognise the validity of such a transaction, by analysing it as a *ṣarf* of one dirham for another and a sale of the dates for the other dirham. The *ṣarf* contract meets the test for equality. Such transactions are valid when the gold or silver on the one side exceeds that on the other, so that the excess can be referred to the added object (*ṭarīḳ al-iʿtibār*) (Ibn al-Murtaḍā, iii, 338-40). The Mālikīs, Shāfiʿīs and Ḥanbalīs, on the other hand, regard this transaction as invalid, seeing in it the sale of a combination of things, with unascertained value, for two dirhams (cf. *Kitāb al-Ḥudjdja*, ii, 574-5; al-Ṭaḥāwī, iv, 72-3 [critical]). More pertinently perhaps, such a sale can be used to circumvent the prohibition of *ribā al-faḍl*, since an object of merely nominal value can be introduced to validate what is essentially an unequal *ṣarf* contract, and so should be prohibited as a preventive measure (*sadd al-dharāʾiʿ*) (cf. *al-Muwaṭṭaʾ*, 395; *al-Muntaḳā*, iv, 277). To obviate this result, some jurists, including the Zaydī Imām al-Hādī (d. 298/911) (*Kitāb al-Aḥkām*, Ṣanʿāʾ 1410/1990, ii, 73; al-Ḳāsim b. Muḥammad, *al-Iʿtiṣām bi-ḥabl Allāh al-matīn*, ed. al-Faḍīl, Ṣanʿāʾ 1404/1984, iv, 109) and, reportedly, Sufyān al-Thawrī (d. 161/778) (al-Mawwāḳ, iv, 301), insisted that the object introduced should correspond in value to the excess (*faḍl*) on the other side, and the Ḥanafī al-Shaybānī is supposed to have regarded an unequal exchange of this sort as valid but reprehensible (*makrūh*) (Ibn al-Humām, *Fatḥ al-ḳadīr*, repr. Kuwait n.d., vi, 271-2, cf. al-Nāṣir al-Uṭrūsh [d. 304/917], in R.B. Serjeant [ed.], *A Zaidī manual of Ḥisbah of the 3rd century (H)*, in *RSO*, xxviii [1957], 24 [better to exchange for the other metal]).

On the ground of hardship (*ḍarūra*), however, the Mālikīs permit the giving of up to one-half of a dirham as change in a sale with a purchase price of no more than a dirham, the exchange of currency being deemed ancillary to the sale (*al-radd ʿalā* or *fi 'l-dirham*) (al-Mawwāḳ, iv, 301; *Mawāhib al-djalīl*, iv, 318-21), whereas the Ḥanbalīs validate similar transactions by analysing them as made up of two distinct contracts, *ṣarf* and sale (al-Bahūtī, iii, 260-1).

The exchange of a dirham and a dīnār for a dirham and a dīnār (al-Khirshī, v, 36-7 gloss) is also invalid according to the Mālikīs, Shāfiʿīs and Ḥanbalīs, not to speak of the exchange of two dirhams and a dīnār for one dirham and two dīnārs. The Ḥanafīs, Twelver Shīʿīs and Zaydīs uphold the validity of these transactions, in the latter case by referring the silver coins on each side to the gold on the other, so that there is no requirement of equality (on the use of this principle as an evasive device, cf. al-Ābī, *Kashf al-rumūz*, Ḳumm 1408/1989, i, 500-1).

The Mālikīs' aversion to mixed transactions goes beyond that of the Shāfiʿīs and Ḥanbalīs, for they prohibit an exchange in which, for example, gold and another object is traded for silver, this constituting a combination of *ṣarf*, in the Mālikī sense, and an ordinary sale (*al-ṣarf wa 'l-bayʿ*) (*al-Mudawwana*, iii, 410), the incidents of which are deemed incompatible (al-Khirshī, v, 40-1, cf. Ibn Rushd, *Fatāwā*, ed. al-Talīlī, Beirut 1407/1987, i, 210; *Bidāyat al-mudjtahid*, ii, 175 [approving Ashhab's rejection of this doctrine]; al-Baghawī, *Sharḥ al-sunna*, ed. al-Arnāʾūṭ, Beirut 1403/1983, viii, 67 [no basis for it]). Here, too, however, the Mālikīs recognise exceptions on the ground of hardship for transactions with a purchase price of no more than one dīnār and transactions, however large, in which the *ṣarf* component involves the exchange of less than one dīnār for dirhams. In either of these cases, where no more than two dirhams are due as change for a payment in dīnārs, the *ṣarf* is treated as ancillary to the sale, and delivery of the coins need not take place at the time of the contract (*Hāshiyat al-Dasūḳī ʿalā al-sharḥ al-kabīr*, Cairo n.d., iii, 32-3).

The problems posed by the sale of objects with gold or silver ornamentation and by debased gold and silver coins are dealt with according to the rules for mixed transactions (but see Ibn Rushd, *Fatāwā*, i, 572; idem, *al-Bayān wa 'l-taḥṣīl*, ed. Aʿrāb, Beirut 1404/1984, vii, 30 [coins]). Where, however, the gold or silver ornamentation is in the form of a thin veneer that cannot be salvaged as saleable metal, the rules of *ṣarf* are deemed inapplicable (Ibn Ḳudāma, vi, 96; al-Dardīr, iii, 61-2; so also for coins, al-Kāsānī, *Badāʾiʿ al-ṣanāʾiʿ*, Cairo n.d., vii, 3137; al-ʿAbbādī, *al-Djawhara al-nayyira*, Istanbul n.d., i, 272; Ibn al-Ṣalāḥ, *Fatāwā wa-masāʾil*, ed. al-Ḳalʿadjī, Beirut 1406/1985, ii, 578; Ibn al-Ukhuwwa, *Kitāb Maʿālim al-ḳurba*, ed. Shaʿbān and Muṭīʿī, Cairo 1976, 124-5), so that, for example, a house with a gilded roof can be sold for gold although the gold in the roof exceeds the purchase price (*al-Fatāwā al-hindiyya*, Beirut n.d., iii, 224). Where, on the other hand, the gold or silver in the article or coin can be detached or melted down, the Mālikīs, Shāfiʿīs and Ḥanbalīs, following their rules for mixed transactions and the precedent found in the *ḥadīth* (*Sharḥ Ṣaḥīḥ Muslim*, xi, 17-19; al-Ṭaḥāwī, iv, 71-5, cf. al-Tilimsānī, *Miftāḥ al-wuṣūl*, ed. Ḳummī, Cairo n.d., 62-3), do not permit a sale for the same precious metal as in the ornament or coin. The metal must be detached and sold separately according to the rules of *ṣarf*. These stringencies, except according to the Mālikīs, do not apply when an article with gold ornamentation or a debased gold coin is sold for silver or *vice versa*; the Mālikīs do, however, make an exception when the ornamentation does not exceed one-third of the value (or weight, according to others) of the object (al-*Muwaṭṭaʾ*, 394; al-Dasūḳī, iii, 40, cf. Ibn Rushd, *al-Bayān wa 'l-taḥṣīl*, ed. Ḥabābī, Beirut 1404/1984, vi, 439-40 [gold and silver combined]). Furthermore, when the gold or silver is so affixed as to be detachable only with loss of value, the Mālikīs apply the one-third rule to exchanges for the same metal, and there is no restriction on exchanges for the other metal (Ibn Djuzayy, 264-5).

The Ḥanafīs, Twelver Shīʿīs and Zaydīs permit exchanges of objects with gold or silver ornamentation or debased coins for a greater quantity of the same precious metal, although for the Ḥanafīs, coins which are predominantly gold or silver are deemed equivalent to coins of pure metal. Where such objects or coins are exchanged for each other, the jurists of these schools cross-reference the precious metal on each side to the other component (cf. *al-Muḥallā*, viii, 498-501). For the purpose of upholding its validity, the transaction is analysed as consisting of two ordinary sales. The *ṣarf* requirement of mutual delivery, however, continues to apply (*Fatḥ al-ḳadīr*, vi, 275). This analysis would permit the unequal exchange of debased coins for each other, a consequence that the Central Asian Ḥanafīs, from fear that it would open the door to *ribā*, are reported to have refused to draw with respect to the greatly debased silver coins that served as their primary currency (*Fatḥ al-ḳadīr*, vi, 275, cf. Ḳāḍīkhān, *Fatāwā*, on the margin of *al-Fatāwā al-hindiyya*, ii, 252; Dāwūd b. Yūsuf al-Khaṭīb, *al-Fatāwā al-ghiyāthiyya*, Būlāḳ 1323, 141-2; on *ghiṭrīfī* dirhams, see al-Kirmilī, *al-Nuḳūd al-ʿarabiyya*, Beirut n.d., 150-1).

The extension of the law of *ṣarf* to copper coins functioning as currency (*al-fulūs al-rāʾidja* or *al-nāfiḳa*) is most strongly represented among the Mālikīs (*Mudawwana*, viii, 395-6), although there is also some support for this view in the Ḥanbalī (al-Mardāwī, v, 15), Shāfiʿī (al-Zabīdī, *Itḥāf al-sāda al-muttaḳīn*, Beirut n.d., v, 447), Ḥanafī (al-Shaybānī, cf. A.L. Udovitch, *Partnership and profit in medieval Islam*, Princeton, 1970, 52-5) and Zaydī (Ibn al-Murtaḍā; iii, 391) schools. There is disagreement among modern writers as to the applicability of the rules of *ṣarf* to transactions in paper currency (al-Rūḥānī, *al-Masāʾil al-mustaḥdatha*, Ḳumm 1385/1965, 33 [no]; al-Ṣadr, *al-Bank al-lā-ribawī fi 'l-Islām*, 149-52 [depends on the nature of the currency]; al-ʿUthmānī, *Takmilat fatḥ al-mulhim*, Karachi 1407/1988, i, 589-90 [yes]; *Ḳarārāt wa-tawṣiyāt Madjmaʿ al-Fiḳh al-Islāmī al-munbathiḳ min Munaẓẓamat al-Muʾtamar al-Islāmī*, Damascus 1418/1998, 40 [yes]; see also *Madjallat Madjmaʿ al-Fiḳh al-Islāmī*, iii [1408/1987], 1721-1965 cf. *ibid.*, v/3 [1409/1988], 1609-2261; and Bu 'l-Shinḳītī, *al-Ḳawl al-musaddad fī ḥukm zakāt al-awrāḳ*, n.p. [Beirut] 1420/1999).

The restrictiveness of the laws of *ṣarf* engendered evasive devices, *ḥiyal* [*q.v.*], sometimes included as part of the exposition of the subject, even when labelled reprehensible (e.g. al-Nawawī, *Rawḍat al-ṭālibīn*, ed.

ʿAbd al-Mawdjūd and Muʿawwaḍ, Beirut 1412/1992, iii, 44-5). Additional pressure for such devices came from the practice of some Muslim governments of minting debased silver coins and then imposing an exchange rate that inevitably involved a violation of the law of *ṣarf.* One expedient was to construe these exchanges as transactions by mutual delivery (*muʿāṭāt*), not *ṣarf* contracts, and thus not subject to the *ṣarf* restrictions (*al-Iʿtiṣām*, iv, 108-9; al-ʿĀmilī, *Kitāb al-Matādjir min miftāḥ al-karāma*, Cairo n.d., 7, 159, cf. *al-Baḥr al-rāʾiḳ*, vi, 192). Shāfiʿīs are reported to have upheld unequal exchanges as reciprocal gifts (al-Dardīr, iii, 57 gloss, cf. *Rawḍat al-ṭālibīn*, iii, 45), while Mālikīs validated small-scale unequal exchanges by appealing to the notion of hardship (al-Dasūḳī, iii, 35). Others insisted that the parties employ the device suggested in the *ḥadīth* of an intervening sale of one of the currencies for goods followed by a resale of the goods for the other currency (al-Shawkānī, quoted in Ṣiddīḳ Ḥasan Khān, *al-Rawḍa al-nadiyya*, Cairo n.d., ii, 116-18), although regular resort to this device was controversial (al-Subkī, x, 136, cf. *al-Muḥallā*, viii, 512-13). Against the inconvenience of this cumbersome practice, the Yemenī al-Maḳbalī (d. 1108/1696) argued for an analysis according to which the parties were granting each other a license (*ibāḥa*) in the exchanged coins, thus effectively freeing all except professional money-changers from the restrictions of the law of *ṣarf* (*al-Abḥāth al-musaddada*, ed. al-Iryānī, Ṣanʿāʾ 1403/1982, 286-7, 390-1, and *Minḥat al-ghaffār*, iii, 1389).

The complexity of the law of *ṣarf* made it difficult for those engaged in frequent exchanges to avoid violating the prohibition of *ribā*, which put the profession of money-changing (*ṣarrāf, sayraf, ṣayrafī, muṣarrif*) in a bad light (*al-Bayān wa 'l-taḥṣīl*, vi, 448 [better to exchange with merchants], cf. al-Dasūḳī, iii, 43 gloss), but this did not mean that its exercise by non-Muslims was encouraged (*al-Mudawwana*, viii, 403; Ibn ʿAbd al-Raʾūf, in N. Ziadeh, *al-Ḥisba wa 'l-muḥtasib fi 'l-Islām*, Beirut 1963, 141, cf. Goitein, i, 229-30). The condemnation of money-changers is particularly connected with the name of al-Ḥasan al-Baṣrī (d. 110/728 [*q.v.*]) (Ibn Rushd, *al-Muḳaddamāt al-mumahhadāt*, ed. Aʿrāb, Beirut 1408/1988, ii, 14), whose disapproval, according to a Shīʿī tradition, was countered by the Imām Djaʿfar al-Ṣādiḳ (d. 148/765 [*q.v.*]), when he noted that the *Aṣḥāb al-Kahf* [*q.v.*] of Ḳurān, XVIII, were money-changers (al-Ṭūsī, *al-Tahdhīb*, ed. al-Kharsān, Tehran 1390/1970, vi, 363; cf. al-Ṭurayḥī, *Madjmaʿ al-baḥrayn*, Beirut 1985, v, 79-80), but this did not prevent Twelver Shīʿī jurists from including money-changing among the reprehensible professions (*al-Lumʿa al-dimashḳiyya*, iii, 218). Instructing money-changers in the rules of *ṣarf* and supervision of their transactions were among the duties of the *muḥtasib* [see ḤISBA] (*Maʿālim al-ḳurba*, 227; al-Shayzarī, 74). For more information on the money-changer, see ṢARRĀF, in Suppl.

With the rise of Islamic banking in recent decades, there has been renewed interest in such old questions related to *ṣarf* such as the permissibility of non-binding agreements for future exchanges of currency at fixed rates (al-Bāz, *Aḥkām ṣarf al-nuḳūd wa 'l-ʿumulāt fi 'l-fiḳh al-islāmī*, ʿAmmān 1419/1999, 109-31). New questions have also arisen, such as the possibility of satisfying the requirement of delivery of the currency during the contractual session by issuance of a cheque, a practice recognised as valid by the Islamic Law Academy (Madjmaʿ al-Fiḳh al-Islāmī) of the Muslim World League (Rābiṭat al-ʿĀlam al-Islāmī) in 1409/1989, at the same time that it approved of delivery by entry of a record in the books of the bank (ʿA.A. al-Sālūs, *Mawsūʿat al-ḳaḍāyā al-fiḳhiyya al-muʿāṣira wa 'l-iḳtiṣād al-islāmī*, Bilbīsr [Egypt] 1423/2003, 630-1), and the same position was adopted by the Islamic Law Academy of the Organisation of the Islamic Conference (Munaẓẓamat al-Muʾtamar al-Islāmī) in 1410/1990 (*Ḳarārāt wa-tawṣiyāt Madjmaʿ al-Fiḳh al-Islāmī*, 113-4; also in *Madjallat Madjmaʿ al-Fiḳh al-Islāmī*, vi/1, [1410/1990], 771-2). To the extent that delivery of currencies is accomplished in accord with contemporary international banking usages, mutual delivery satisfying the law of *ṣarf* may extend over several days (Yūsuf al-Ḳaraḍāwī, *Fatāwā muʿāṣira*, Beirut 1421/2000, ii, 462-4).

Bibliography: In addition to the references in the text, see Santillana, *Istituzioni*, ii, 64-5, 185-92 (Mālikī); Ḳāsim b. Ibrāhīm *et al.*, *K. Taysīr al-marām fi masāʾil al-aḥkām*, Beirut 1407/1986, 79-81 (Zaydī); al-Ḳārī, *K. Madjallat al-aḥkām al-sharʿiyya*, Djidda 1401/1981, 191-3 (Ḥanbalī); R. Brunschvig, *Conceptions monétaires chez les juristes musulmans (viii-xiii siècles)*, in *Arabica*, xiv/2 (1967), 113-43, xv/3 (1968), 316; Goitein, *A Mediterranean society*, i, 234-40 (the profession of moneychanging); N.A. Saleh, *Unlawful gain and legitimate profit in Islamic law*, ²London 1992, 24-34 (*ribā al-faḍl*); ʿA.A. al-Sālūs, *al-Nuḳūd wa-istibdāl al-ʿumulāt*, Kuwayt and Cairo 1987; Wizārat al-Awḳāf wa 'l-Shuʾūn al-Islāmiyya, *al-Mawsūʿa al-fiḳhiyya*, Kuwayt 1412/1992, xxvi, 348-74; F.E. Vogel and S.L. Hayes, III, *Islamic law and finance*, The Hague 1998; ʿAlāʾ al-Dīn Djankū, *al-Taḳābuḍ fi 'l-fiḳh al-islāmī*, ʿAmmān 1423/2004, 111-8, 284-92.

(A. Zysow)

SARÏḲ, the name of a Türkmen [*q.v.*] tribe in Central Asia. Ethnonyms derived from colour-names are frequent in Turkic languages. Čaghatay and Uzbek have *sarik, sarïḳ* "yellow, yellowish, pale, blonde" where other historical and modern Turkic languages have *sarïγ or sarï* (Laude-Cirtautas, 64-8). The genealogy of the Sarïḳ is connected to the Salur [*q.v.*] tribal group, including the Salur proper, the Ersari, Teke and Yomut. In his work on the historical legends of the Türkmen, the *Shadjara-yi Tarākima*, Abu 'l-Ghāzī Bahādur Khān of Khīwa [*q.v.*] links the descent of the Sarïḳ and the Teke to Ṭoy Tutmaz of the Salur (ed. Kargı Ölmez, fol. 102a, ll. 4-5). The Salur are linked to Oghurdjïḳ Alp, a descendant of the eponymous progenitor of the Türkmen, Oghuz Khān. Drawing on Sarïḳ historical legends, Dshikijew connects the Sarïḳ to various groups of Tatars and other peoples of Central Asia, but his arguments lack convincing support. No historical details about the habitat and history of the Sarïḳ before the 16th century are available, except that since the Mongol period, they must have lived—along with other Türkmen tribes—between the Mangïshlaḳ [*q.v.*] peninsula and the Balkhān [*q.v.*] mountains. According to Abu 'l-Ghāzī Bahādur Khān (references in Bregel 1981), in the 16th century, the Teke, Yomut and Sarïḳ together paid a tax of 8,000 sheep to their Uzbek overlord, about half of what larger tribes like the Čowdur or Ersari paid at the time, or one-quarter of the tax of the Salur tribe proper. In the first Soviet census (1926), the Sarïḳ numbered 34,000 or 4% of the whole number of Türkmen (Bregel 1981, 13ff.). Sarïḳ were also to be found in Tadjïkistān, Afghānistān and Iran, but at the end of the 20th century, reliable figures are not available.

In the 17th century, the Salur confederation broke up and the Salur and Ersari left western Turkmenistan. Their place was taken by three junior tribes, the Teke, Yomut and Sarïḳ (Bregel 1981, 18). In the 18th century, the Sarïḳ nomadised between Khwārazm and the Marw oasis. Around 1800, they gradually became the dominant Türkmen tribal grouping among the population in and around the oasis, engaging in agriculture as well as in nomadic pastoralism (Wood 1998, 6-7, 70-5). Wood (1998) investigated the history of the Sarïḳ of Marw (a large part of the Sarïḳ tribal group) drawing on Western—including Russian—travel and political literature as well as on Persian, Bukhāran and, in particular, Khīwan sources such as the chronicles of the court historian Āgahī. By 1822, Khīwa succeeded in supplanting Bukhāran rule in the Marw area, keeping it until 1842 as an outpost in its frequent campaigns against Persia. At that time, the Sarïḳ began a prolonged struggle for independence from Khīwa which ended in 1855, both sides exhausted from the annual campaigns. The period of relative stability had proved profitable for the agriculture and caravan trade of the Sarïḳs, while the Khīwan khān had been able to draw revenues from them and use them as auxiliaries and border patrols. From 1857, under Persian pressure, the numerically superior Teke of Sarakhs moved into the Marw oasis and forced out the Sarïḳs who, replacing the Salur of Yolotan and Pandjdih [*q.v.*] on the middle course of the Murghāb river, remained there into the 20th century.

Bibliography: This article owes much to W.A. Wood, *The Sariq Turkmens of Merv and the khanate of Khiva in the early nineteenth century*, unpubl. diss., Bloomington, Ind. 1998 (with extensive bibl.); Ebulgazi Bahadır Han, *Şecere-i Terākime* (*Türkmenlerin soykütüğü*), ed., tr. and notes Z. Kargı Ölmez, Ankara 1996. The chronicle of Mu'nis and Āgahī, *Firdaws al-iḳbāl*, ed. and tr. Y. Bregel, Leiden 1988, [2]1998, regularly mentions the Sarïḳs; for excerpts from Āgahī's further chronicles, see A.K. Borovkov, A.A. Romaskevič and P.P. Ivanov, *Materialï po istorii turkmen i turkmenii, ii, XVI-XIX vv. Iranskie, bukharskie i khivinskie istočniki*, Moscow and Leningrad 1938. See further Bregel, *Nomadic and sedentary elements among the Turkmens*, in *CAJ*, xxv (1981), 3-37; A. Dshikijew, *Das turkmenische Volk im Mittelalter*, Berlin 1994, 252-62; I. Laude-Cirtautas, *Der Gebrauch der Farbbezeichnungen in den Türkdialekten*, Wiesbaden 1961.

(Barbara Kellner-Heinkele)

SARIḲA.

In literary criticism, "plagiarism".

Although the term *sariḳa* is used, no "theft" in the legal sense of the word is implied, as Islamic law does not recognise intellectual property. A modern booklet on intellectual theft stresses the moral turpitude involved, but does not invoke any *Sharīʿa* norms or punishments (ʿAbd al-Mannān, *al-Sariḳāt al-ʿilmiyya*). The victim of plagiarism could only have recourse to public opinion or approach a man of power (*istiʿdā'*) to redress the situation.

Literary theft occurred and was discussed predominantly, though not exclusively, in the field of poetry.

The term *sariḳa* does cover "plagiarism" in the strict sense of the word, i.e. appropriation of someone else's line or poem. But of greater importance and interest is its wider application, where it indicates any kind of "borrowing" and "developing" of an existing motif. As such it should be treated in the larger context of intertextuality, alongside other phenomena such as quotation (*taḍmīn*) and allusion (*talmīḥ*). Since the term came to cover both acceptable and unacceptable borrowings, qualifications like *sariḳa ḥasana* "good theft" and *sariḳa maḥmūda* "laudable theft" were introduced to characterise cases considered successful by the critics. Or else the inappropriate paradoxical term was avoided altogether and substituted by a neutral one, *akhdh* "taking".

True plagiarism

Already pre-Islamic poets mention literary theft as a known phenomenon by stressing that they do not have to rely on it. This is, of course, meaningful only on the background of a literary culture, in which poems are attributable to individual poets and the latter take pride in their craft. Alongside the general notion of "theft", the term *intiḥāl* "ascribing (verses) to oneself" is specifically used here. As later handbooks make clear, this means claiming other poets' verses as one's own without further ado (the obvious danger of anachronism involved in relying on these handbooks cannot be addressed here). It is difficult to judge the truth in the cases adduced by the later critics; one would need to ascertain if (a) they may not constitute quotations or formulae (see Bauer, in *Bibl.*) or (b) the victim of the plagiarism might not be an invention produced by intertribal hostilities.

While the idea of intellectual property seems to have been well developed, there is one strange phenomenon that in a way runs counter to this notion, to wit, the behaviour of some famous poets called *ighāra*, lit. "raiding". This occurs only between contemporaries and describes a situation in which a minor poet composes an outstanding line and is then forced by a major poet to relinquish it to him, on the pretext that he, the major poet, should have composed it. The victim, under threat of a stinging invective, would more often than not comply. Most notorious in this respect was the Umayyad poet al-Farazdaḳ [*q.v.*].

In the literate society of ʿAbbāsid times and later, outright plagiarism took the form of inserting extraneous material, often whole poems, into one's own *dīwān*. The term often used for this is *muṣālata* (see e.g. al-Thaʿālibī, *Yatīma*, ii, 119, 5), a post-classical word possibly derived from *ṣilt*, a variant—by metathesis—of *liṣt* "robber" (see Lane, *ṣ-l-t*). For an interesting plagiarism feud, see al-Sarī al-Raffā'. Even contemporary authorities admitted that it was very difficult to establish the truth in the case of poems recurring in various *dīwāns*. Al-Thaʿālibī, quoting two poems that he found both in a collection of al-Sarī al-Raffā''s poetry in the latter's own handwriting as well as in the *dīwān* of the Khālidī brothers in the hand of Abū ʿUthmān al-Khālidī, admits: "I do not know if I should attribute this situation to a confluence of minds (*tawārud [al-khāṭirayn]*) or to plagiary (*muṣālata*) (*Yatīma*, ii, 110, 5). The first possibility flows from the Muslim virtue of *ḥusn al-ẓann* which enjoins people always to think best about others. But with poems consisting of five lines each, the idea of *tawārud* strains credulity (while, with one or two lines, it would not be impossible in an environment of mannerist poetising). Another way of explaining duplication of poems is, of course, uncertainty of attribution on the part of redactors.

Borrowing

While crude plagiary may have exercised the literary public, a situation of truly literary interest arose only with the introduction of skilful changes into the borrowed verse. Critical literature developed along two lines: (1) general classifications and taxonomies of *sariḳa*, and (2) the collection and—to a lesser extent—critical evaluation of the *sariḳāt* of individual poets.

(1) *Classifications*

The *sariḳa* classifications are contained in a number of books on literary theory, sometimes also in the introductions to *sariḳa* collections of individual poets. They tend to be highly inhomogeneous in the early literature. The earliest example is al-Ḥātimī (d. 388/998 [*q.v.*]) in his *Ḥilyat al-muḥāḍara fī ṣināʿat al-shiʿr* (see *Bibl.*). His terminology seems to be tentative, partly based on earlier traditions that he quotes with their chains of authorities, but without establishing a clear system. As a consequence, there is much overlap between the terms and a certain opacity prevails (see S.A. Bonebakker's painstaking articles on al-Ḥātimī in the *Bibl.*). Ibn Rashīḳ (d. 456/1063 or later [*q.v.*]) is aware of this inadequacy of al-Ḥātimī's taxonomy, but he quotes him extensively all the same, with certain alterations and re-interpretations (see von Grunebaum, *Concept*, 238-40; note that the author did not yet have the text of al-Ḥātimī's *Ḥilya*).

Ibn Wakīʿ al-Tinnīsī (d. 393/1003) and Abū Hilāl al-ʿAskarī (d. 395/1005 [*q.v.*]) introduced the idea that one had to distinguish between good and bad "plagiary". The former did so in the introduction to his attack on al-Mutanabbī (*Munṣif*, 9-21, 22-39), the latter in the first encyclopaedic work on literary theory, the "Book of the Two Arts" (*Ṣināʿatayn*, 196-237, cf. Kanazi, *Studies*, 112-22). This approach takes into account the fact that mannerist poetry is in constant intertextual dialogue with past poetry (on the term "mannerism" in this context, see S. Sperl, *Mannerism in Arabic poetry*, Cambridge 1989); as a result, borrowing motifs and developing and improving them becomes a way of life.

Ibn Abī Ṭāhir Ṭayfūr (d. 280/893 [*q.v.*]) expressed this idea as follows: "The discourse of the Arabs hangs together, the later instances taking from the former. The original and newly invented of it (*al-mubtadaʿ minhu wa 'l-mukhtaraʿ*) is rare, if you go through it and check it. Even the cautious and watchful man, who is gifted in eloquence and poetry, whether ancient or modern, will not be safe that his discourse take [something] from the discourse of someone else, even if he does his utmost in being cautious. . . . How much more so with the affected constructer of conceits (*al-mutakallif al-mutaṣanniʿ*) who is intentionally seeking for them" (*apud* al-Ḥātimī, *Ḥilya*, ii, 28). The last sentence is the description of the mannerist poet, who cannot but have recourse to the existing poetry.

After a number of further attempts to instil some order into the traditionally transmitted terms, the taxonomy of plagiarism became homogenised and solidified in the scholastic *ʿilm al-balāgha* "science of eloquence" [see BALĀGHA], starting with al-Khaṭīb al-Ḳazwīnī (d. 739/1338 [*q.v.*]), in his *Talkhīṣ al-Miftāḥ*.

From the various endeavours of the theorists, some common notions emerge:

(a) The focus of the discussion is overwhelmingly the single line, which is, of course, the most common approach in literary criticism and theory.

(b) There is discussion about what is, and what is not, subject to a verdict of plagiary. Universally-known or well-worn motifs are in the public domain. Newly-invented motifs that are attributable to individual poets form the other extreme. These are rare and, according to Ḥāzim al-Ḳarṭādjannī, "infertile", because later poets would hardly dare to take them up again (*al-maʿānī 'l-ʿukm*, see *Minhādj*, 194, 14). Of greatest interest is the group of motifs in between the two extremes, those that have been treated, developed and improved upon (or, possibly, ruined) by a series of poets. Here a charge of plagiarism can only be avoided if the later poet introduces changes that confer a certain novelty on the borrowed motif. There are various ways of doing this: (1) by changing the context, by (a) inserting the motif into a different genre (e.g. from praise into love poetry), or (b) combining it with another motif of the same kind (see below); or (2) by changing the wording. If, by doing the latter, he improves on the rendition of the motif or adds a rhetorical twist to it, he can lay greater claim to it than the original poet. According to Ḥāzim, there are four relationships between a poet and his motif: "invention" (*ikhtirāʿ*), "greater claim" (*istiḥḳāḳ*), "partnership" (*sharika*, which is either "equal participation" [*ishtirāk*], when there is no quality difference between the earlier and later poet, or "falling short" [*inḥiṭāṭ*], if the later poet is not up to par), and finally "plagiarism" (*sariḳa*) (*Minhādj*, 192-4).

(c) Part of the taxonomy of plagiarism is based on the *lafẓ-maʿnā* dichotomy: does the alleged plagiariser take only the motif or also its wording? Taking both with only minimal changes of the wording is the worst kind of *sariḳa*.

(d) Plagiarism can only take place if the later poet consciously borrows from the earlier. Otherwise, identical or similar lines of poetry are due to a "confluence of two minds" (*tawārud al-khāṭirayn*): the two poets found the line independently of each other (see above).

(e) An identical line could also be explained as a quotation (*taḍmīn*, lit. "incorporation"). If it is not a very well-known line, the poet has to mark it as a quotation in order that it not be taken as a plagiarism.

(2) *Critical assessment of individual poets*

The other branch of literature devoted to *sariḳa* consists of collections of plagiarisms of individual poets, either in separate works or forming part of critical studies dealing with one or more poets. The most famous "modern" poets have all been made targets of such critiques: Abū Nuwās, Abū Tammām and especially al-Mutanabbī (at least six separate books have come down to us). There is usually very little in the way of naming and discussing their cases; the critics rather confine themselves instead to adducing the original (mostly by a "modern" poet) and the alleged plagiarism. They usually have a lenient approach, including many "laudable plagiarisms". They often manage to find several originals, either because the "plagiariser" has effected a combination of two "stolen" motifs or because there is some doubt as to the correct pedigree (the "originals" are sometimes not quite relevant, belonging, as it were, to a larger halo of motifs circling the motif in question). One is thus at times presented with little family trees of a motif (probably never more than four or five stages). This makes these works valuable for historical, systematic and critical research into the imbrication of motifs—molecular investigations, as it were, into the overlap of consecutive versions of the motif—, which in turn would lead, more importantly, to insights into the general tendencies governing such developments within a mannerist tradition of poetry.

The most sophisticated cases are those in which the "plagiariser" welds two different motifs together. An example would be the following (from al-ʿAmīdī, *Ibāna*, 31-2; the author starts with the pedigree verses and ends with the "plagiarising" verses by al-Mutanabbī):

al-Buḥturī:	*Malaʾta aḥshāʾa 'l-ʿadūwi balābilan* *fa-'rtadda yaḥsudu fīka man lam yaḥsudi*
al-ʿAbartāʾī:	*Ḳaṭṭaʿa aḥshāʾa ḥāsidīhi wa-lam* *yathub* [s.l.] *ghalīlu 'l-ḥashā mina 'l-ḥasadi*
al-Mutanabbī:	*Ḳaṭṭaʿtahum ḥasadan arāhum mā bihim* *fa-taḳaṭṭaʿū ḥasadan li-man lā yaḥsudu*

Here we have two motifs and their confluence in al-Mutanabbī: Motif no. 1: People envy [in you] someone who does not have envy [because you are the best anyway, or because envy is an evil character trait that you do not have]; motif no. 2: The praised one tears the entrails of the enviers to shreds.

(a) al-Buḥturī: The first motif is there in the second hemistich without further ado. The second motif is lacking, but note that the entrails appear as a seat of emotion in the first hemistich.

(b) al-ʿAbartāʾī: The second motif appears in the first hemistich without further ado. The second hemistich is an elaboration on it (again with *ḥashā*).

(c) al-Mutanabbī: The entrails are gone, but the tearing apart is still there. Motif no. 2 is in the first hemistich (with an addition, namely, that this envy shows the enviers what [evil] is in them). Motif no. 2 recurs in the second hemistich, inextricably bound together with motif no. 1.

Al-Mutanabbī achieves a logical confluence of the two motifs, and in addition a pleasant balance between the two hemistichs: root *q-ṭ-ʿ* followed by *ḥasadan*, followed by a contrast between "them" and "him".

This technique of knitting together two independent motifs seems to be subsumed under the term *talfīḳ*. Ibn Ras̲h̲īḳ deals with it in one chapter of his *Ḳurāḍat al-d̲h̲ahab* (ed. Mūsā, 95-106). He says that al-Mutanabbī and Abu 'l-ʿAlāʾ al-Maʿarrī are the outstanding masters of this procedure. (Note that al-T̲h̲aʿālibī's use of *talfīḳ* in his *K. al-Tawfīḳ li 'l-talfīḳ*, ed. Hilāl Nād̲j̲ī and Zuhayr Zāhid, Beirut 1417/1996, seems to differ from Ibn Ras̲h̲īḳ's, coming closer to *murāʿāt al-naẓīr* "harmony of images".)

Bibliography: 1. Important texts. (a) Taxonomies: Ḥātimī, *Ḥilyat al-muḥāḍara fī ṣināʿat al-s̲h̲iʿr*, ed. D̲j̲aʿfar al-Kattānī [on title-page: "al-Kitānī"], 2 vols. Bag̲h̲dād 1979, ii, 28-98 (unreliable edition); selection by Maẓhar Ras̲h̲īd al-Ḥid̲j̲d̲j̲ī [?], *Min Ḥilyat al-muḥāḍara*, 2 pts. Damascus 2000, 323-81 (attempts to correct the edition, but is not itself a critical ed.); substantial quotations also in Muḥammad Ibn Sayf al-Dīn Aydamir (d. 710/1310), *al-Durr al-farīd wa-bayt al-qaṣīd. The priceless pearl, a poetic verse*, facs. ed. F. Sezgin, in collaboration with M. Amawi, A. Jokhosha and E. Neubauer, 5 vols., Frankfurt am Main 1988-9, i, 116-55 (see also G.J. van Gelder, *Arabic poetics and stylistics according to the introduction of* al-Durr al-Farīd *by Muḥammad Ibn Aydamir (d. 710/1310)*, in *ZDMG*, cxlvi (1996), 381-414, a short section on the plagiary chapter, 409-12); Abū Hilāl al-ʿAskarī, *Kitāb al-Ṣināʿatayn al-kitāba wa 'l-s̲h̲iʿr*, ed. ʿA.M. al-Bid̲j̲āwī and M.A.F. Ibrāhīm, 2nd ed. Cairo n.d. [1971], 200-37; Ibn Ras̲h̲īḳ, *al-ʿUmda fī maḥāsin al-s̲h̲iʿr wa-ādābih*, ed. M.ʿA.A. ʿAṭā, 2 vols., Beirut 1422/2001, ii, 216-30; idem, *Ḳurāḍat al-d̲h̲ahab fī naḳd as̲h̲ʿār al-ʿArab*, ed. M. Mūsā, Beirut 1991 (other ed. Chedli Benyahya [al-Shād̲h̲ilī Bū Yaḥyā], Tunis 1972); ʿAbd al-Ḳāhir al-D̲j̲urd̲j̲ānī, *K. Asrār al-balāg̲h̲a*, ed. H. Ritter, Istanbul 1954, paragr. 20, Ger. tr. idem, *Geheimnisse der Wortkunst*, Wiesbaden 1969, paragr. 20; al-Muẓaffar al-Ḥusaynī (d. 656/1258), *Naḍrat al-ig̲h̲rīḍ fī nuṣrat al-ḳarīḍ*, ed. Nuhā ʿĀrif al-Ḥasan, Damascus 1396/1976, 203-26; Ḥāzim al-Ḳarṭād̲j̲annī, *Minhād̲j̲ al-bulag̲h̲āʾ wa-sirād̲j̲ al-udabāʾ*, ed. Muḥammad al-Ḥabīb Ibn al-K̲h̲ūd̲j̲a [Belkhodja], Tunis 1966, 192-6. (b) Studies of individual poets: Muhalhil b. Yamūt b. al-Muzarraʿ (d. after 334/946), *Sariḳāt Abī Nuwās*, ed. M.M. Haddāra, Cairo 1958; Āmidī (d. 371/981), *al-Muwāzana bayn s̲h̲iʿr Abī Tammām wa 'l-Buḥturī*, ed. al-Sayyid Aḥmad Ṣaḳr, 2 vols. Cairo 1380-[4]/1961-5 (*sariḳāt Abī Tammām*, i, 55-129; *sariḳāt al-Buḥturī*, i, 292-350); al-Ṣāḥib Ibn ʿAbbād (d. 385/995), *al-Risāla fī 'l-kas̲h̲f ʿan masāwiʾ al-Mutanabbī*, in ʿAmīdī, *Ibāna*, 219-50; Ḥātimī, *al-Risāla al-mūḍiḥa fī d̲h̲ikr sariḳāt Abi 'l-Ṭayyib al-Mutanabbī wa-sāḳiṭ s̲h̲iʿrih*, ed. M.Y. Najm, Beirut 1965 (cf. also S.A. Bonebakker, *Ḥātimī and his encounter with Mutanabbī: a biographical sketch*, Amsterdam etc. 1984 [Verhandlingen der Koninklijke Nederlandse Akademie van Wetenschappen, Afd. Letterkunde, nieuwe reeks, cxxii]); al-Ḳāḍī al-D̲j̲urd̲j̲ānī (d. 392/1001), *al-Wasāṭa bayn al-Mutanabbī wa-k̲h̲uṣūmih*, ed. M.A.-F. Ibrāhīm and ʿA.M. al-Bid̲j̲āwī, 3rd ed., Cairo n.d., 183-411; Ibn Wakīʿ al-Tinnīsī, *Kitāb al-Munṣif li 'l-sāriḳ wa 'l-masrūḳ minhu*, ed. ʿU.K̲h̲. ibn Idrīs, Bing̲h̲āzī 1994 (other eds.: *al-Munṣif fī 'l-dalālāt ʿalā sariḳāt al-Mutanabbī*, ed. Ḥ. Zayn al-Dīn ʿAbd al-Mas̲h̲hadānī, Beirut 1414/1993; *al-Munṣif fī naḳd al-s̲h̲iʿr wa-bayān sariḳāt al-Mutanabbī wa-mus̲h̲kil s̲h̲iʿrih*, ed. Riḍwān al-Dāya, i, Damascus n.d. [preface dated 1401/1981]; *K. al-Munṣif li 'l-sāriḳ wa 'l-masrūḳ minhu fī iẓhār sariḳāt Abi 'l-Ṭayyib al-Mutanabbī*, ed. Muḥ. Yūsuf Nad̲j̲m, 2 vols. Beirut 1412/1992 [[1]Kuwait 1404/1984] [the theoretical part is on pp. 9-38]); Thaʿālibī (d. 429/1038), *Yatīmat al-dahr fī maḥāsin ahl al-ʿaṣr*, ed. M. Muḥyī 'l-Dīn ʿAbd al-Ḥamīd, 4 vols., 2nd ed. Cairo n.d. (finished 1377/1958) (contains substantial sections on *sariḳāt* of the various poets treated in this anthology); al-ʿAmīdī (d. 433/1041), *al-Ibāna ʿan sariḳāt al-Mutanabbī*, ed. I. al-Dasūḳī al-Bisāṭī, Cairo 1961; Ibn Bassām al-S̲h̲antarīnī (d. 543/1147), *Sariḳāt al-Mutanabbī wa-mus̲h̲kil maʿānīh*, ed. M. al-Ṭāhir ibn ʿĀs̲h̲ūr, [Tūnis] 1970 (the material in the section *Sariḳāt uk̲h̲rā nusibat ilā 'l-Mutanabbī*, ed. I. al-Dasūḳī, in al-ʿAmīdī, *Ibāna*, 199-217, seems to be mostly taken from Ibn Bassām, though not in the same sequence); on the later scholastic system see A.F.M. von Mehren, *Die Rhetorik der Araber*, Copenhagen and Vienna 1853, repr. Hildesheim and New York 1970, 147-54 (also containing the Ar. text of al-K̲h̲aṭīb al-Ḳazwīnī, *Talk̲h̲īṣ al-Miftāḥ*, Ar. pag. 94-104, and of al-Suyūṭī's versification *ʿUḳūd al-d̲j̲umān*, 133-8).

2. Studies. G.E. von Grunebaum, *The concept of plagiarism in Arabic theory*, in *JNES*, iii (1944), 234-53, rev. Ger. version *Der Begriff des Plagiats in der arabischen Kritik*, in idem, *Kritik und Dichtkunst*, Wiesbaden 1955, 101-29; ʿAlī ʿAbd al-Razzāḳ al-Sāmarrāʾī, *al-Sariḳāt al-adabiyya fī s̲h̲iʿr al-Mutanabbī*, Bag̲h̲dād n.d. [1969]; Muḥammad Muṣṭafā Haddāra, *Mus̲h̲kilat al-sariḳāt fī 'l-naḳd al-ʿarabī*, [2]Beirut 1395/1975; Badawī Ṭabāna, *al-Sariḳāt al-adabiyya, dirāsa fī ibtikār al-aʿmāl al-adabiyya wa-taḳlīdihā*, [3]Beirut 1394/1974; W.P. Heinrichs, *Literary theory: the problem of its efficiency*, in von Grunebaum (ed.), *Arabic poetry: theory and development*, Wiesbaden 1973 (the fourth part deals with "plagiarism" cases from al-ʿAmīdī, *Ibāna*), idem, *An evaluation of sariqa*, in *QSA*, v-vi (1987-8), 357-68; S.A. Bonebakker, *Sariqa and formula: three chapters from Ḥātimī's* Ḥilyat al-Muḥāḍara, in *AIUON*, xlvi (1986), 367-89; idem, *Ancient Arabic poetry and plagiarism: a terminological labyrinth*, in *QSA*, xv (1997), 65-92; idem, *The root* n-ḥ-l *in Arabic* sariqa *terminology*, in *Dutch Studies of the Near Eastern Languages and Literatures Foundation*, i-ii (1997), 133-61; G.J. Kanazi, *Studies in the Kitāb aṣ-Ṣināʿatayn of Abū Hilāl al-ʿAskarī*, Leiden 1989, 112-22; M. Peled, *On the concept of literary influence in classical Arabic criticism*, in *IOS*, xi (1991), 37-46; Th. Bauer, *Formel und Zitat: Zwei Spielarten von Intertextualität in der alt-arabischen Dichtung*, in *JAL*, xxiv (1993), 117-38; ʿAbd al-Laṭīf Muḥammad al-Sayyid al-Ḥadīdī, *al-Sariḳāt*

al-sh̲i̲ʿriyya bayn al-Āmidī wa 'l-Ḏj̲urdj̲ānī fī ḍawʾ al-naḳd al-adabī al-ḳadīm wa 'l-ḥadīt̲h̲, al-Manṣūra 1415/1995; Ḥassān ʿAbd al-Mannān, al-Sariḳāt al-ʿilmiyya, ʿAmmān and Beirut 1416/1996.

(W.P. Heinrichs)

SARKĀR (p.), lit. "head [of] affairs", a term used in Mug̲h̲al Indian administration and also in the succeeding British Indian domination of the subcontinent.

1. In the structure of Mug̲h̲al provincial government, as elaborated under the Emperor Akbar [q.v.] in 989/1580, there was a hierarchy of the ṣūba [q.v.] or province, under the ṣūbadār [q.v.] (also called sipāhsālār, nāẓim and ṣāḥib-i ṣūba); the sarkār, or district, under the fawd̲j̲dār [q.v.], who combined both administrative and military functions, corresponding to the two separate officials of British India, the District Magistrate and the Superintendent of Police; and the pargana [q.v.] or maḥall, i.e. subdistrict, headed by various officials with specific functions, such as the ḳāḍī for the administration of justice and the ḳānūngo and čawd̲h̲arī concerned with revenue collection. Thus in Akbar's time, Abu 'l-Faḍl ʿAllāmī enumerated with in the province of Awadh [q.v.] (Oudh) 5 sarkārs and 38 parganas [see PARGANA and MUG̲H̲ALS. 3].

2. As a term in the historical geography of more recent India, sarkār appears Anglicised as "the [Northern] Circars", specifically for the coastal territory north of Madras and the Coromandel Coast in peninsular South India, in part to the south of the delta of the Godāvarī river but mostly to its north (hence now in the northeasternmost tip of Andhra Pradesh State in the Indian Union). This territory was ceded to the British East Indian Company in 1765 by the Mug̲h̲al ruler in Dihlī, S̲h̲āh ʿĀlam II, but claimed by the Niẓām of Ḥaydarābād, leading to a treaty of 1766 whereby the Niẓām gave up his claim in return for the provision of a force of British troops to be at his disposal [see further, ḤAYDARĀBĀD, at Vol. III, 320b-322a].

3. In informal Anglo-Indian usage, the Sarkār (local pronunciation, Sirkār, often written "Sircar") meant the state or the government, and this continued to be the usage all through British Indian times. It may be noted that the term now popularly and almost ubiquitously used to denote the British domination in India, its government and administration, sc. "the Raj" (in Hindi and the modern Indo-Aryan languages, rād̲j̲ is a regular derivative of rād̲j̲ya "kingship, rule", cognate with rād̲j̲a "ruler"), is a neologism of the post-1947 period, probably from the later 1950s, when what had been "the Raj" had in fact for several years ceased to be.

Bibliography: See the *Bibls.* to the various administrative terms of Mug̲h̲al provincial administration cited above, and also Yule and Burnell, *Hobson-Jobson, a glossary of Anglo-Indian colloquial words and phrases*, [2]London 1903, 222, 754, 840-1; P. Saran, *The provincial government of the Mughals*, Allahabad 1941; S.R. Sharma, *Mughal government and administration*, Bombay 1951; information from Prof. Christopher Shackle.　　　(C.E. Bosworth)

ṢARRĀF (A.), lit. "money-changer", such persons often functioning as bankers in pre-modern Islam.

In fiḳh [q.v.], ṣarf is a contract of sale (bayʿ [q.v.]). It applies to currency exchange, originally of gold (dīnārs) to silver (dirhams) and vice-versa. The Ḥadīt̲h̲ provides basic rules for currency exchange, such as that the transaction should be on the spot (yadⁿ bi-yad) [see RIBĀ]. Among the famous ḥadīt̲h̲s relating to

ṣarf is "Gold for silver is ribā except hand-to-hand" (Mālik, Muwaṭṭaʾ, ṣarf).

Money-changing was an activity apparently engaged in by the earliest Muslims. This was related to their involvement in trade, including by the Prophet himself [see TĀD̲JIR; TID̲JĀRA]. However, several ḥadīt̲h̲s warn of the dangers of ribā in currency exchange if parties do not follow the rules of ṣarf. Thus money-changing as a profession was not held in high esteem by the fuḳahāʾ. The popular view was that non-Muslims (particularly Jews and Christians) were better suited to it than Muslims, who were constrained by the prohibition on ribā (for money-changing and banking in the mediaeval Arab world, see D̲JAHBAD̲H̲, and ṢARF, in Suppl.).

In the Ottoman Empire, ṣarrāfs were more than money-changers; they were also moneylenders and brokers, and pawnbrokers. In time, many ṣarrāfs became large financiers with well-recognised international connections, and played a significant role in the economy and politics of the empire. They were based mainly in the capital, Istanbul, but also operated in provincial capitals. Greeks, Jews, Armenians and Muslims were involved in the profession.

With the Ottoman conquest of Constantinople in 857/1453, the Italian predominance in finance in that city ended, to be replaced by that of Ottoman non-Muslim subjects, particularly Greeks. Meḥemmed II (r. 848-50/1444-6 and 855-86/1451-81) favoured Greeks who played an active role in Ottoman finance, taxation through tax-farming (e.g. administration of customs zones and mines) and politics during his reign. From the mid-10th/16th century, Jewish bankers (ṣarrāfs) and tax-farmers challenged Greek dominance in both finance and long-distance trade. Because of the activities of the Inquisition in Catholic countries in that century, under the protection of the Ottoman Sultans, several wealthy Marrano Jewish families came to settle in Istanbul. Many were to be involved in large-scale banking operations, international trade, and investment in tax farms. Financial expertise and close links to the Sultan and ruling élite gave them considerable power. Well-known Jewish names of this period include Dona Gracia Mendes, Don Joseph Nasi and Alvaro Mendes. Later, the role of the Jews declined, and Armenians became prominent as ṣarrāfs, with some of their members rising to prominence; for example, Muṣṭafā III (1171-87/1757-74) appointed a member of the Armenian Duzuoglu family as manager of the imperial mint. The ability of the Duzuoglu family to mobilise credit for the state, domestically and abroad, enabled them to retain control of the day-to-day activities of the mint until the 1820s (Pamuk, *Monetary history*, 202).

Until the 10th/16th century especially, the ṣarrāfs functioned in a context of expanding trade both within and without the empire. Facilitated by networks, their business was enhanced by increased credit or bartering as a result of the limited supply of gold and silver coins. They used several financial instruments, e.g. the ḥavale (Ar. ḥawāla [q.v.]) was "an assignation of a fund from a distant source of revenue by a written order. It was used in both state and private finances to avoid the dangers and delays inherent in the transport of cash" (Inalcik and Quataert, *An economic and social history*, 208). Letters of credit were also widely used, particularly from the mid-11th/17th century, by merchants and for government payment. The increase in trade also meant more opportunities for currency exchange, which was abetted by the problem of a universally acceptable currency, the fluctuations in the purity of the coinage and currency values.

From the 11th/17th to the 19th centuries, the state continued to need and encourage the activities of the *ṣarrāfs*, tax-farming being one. Until the late 10th/16th century, the empire's financial situation had been strong, with the major part of taxation being collected locally and mostly in kind by the *sipahīs* under the *tīmār* system. These funds were used locally. The *tīmār* system then began to be abandoned in favour of tax-farming [see MÜLTEZIM], and tax units (*muḳāṭaʿs*) began to be auctioned off at Istanbul. *Ṣarrāfs* based on Istanbul were thus able to purchase tax-farming privileges or to lend money to purchasers. *Ṣarrāfs* also became direct lenders to the treasury and were considered the most dependable source of liquid funds. As the empire sank further into fiscal decline after the 1760s, it relied on the *ṣarrāfs* to use their connections with European organisations to arrange short-term direct loans to the state. The *ṣarrāfs* also became personal financiers to the sultans and many leading Ottoman bureaucrats. It is estimated that, e.g. in 1860, the short-term debts of various government offices to private banking firms (*ṣarrāfs*) alone amounted to 250 million francs (Kasaba, *The Ottoman empire*, 80). By the mid-19th century, the power of *ṣarrāfs* as well as of tax-farmers and merchants equalled and perhaps surpassed the power of the bureaucratic élite.

Not all *ṣarrāfs* prospered. Of the hundreds, especially in the capital, who combined petty exchange with other small-scale money lending, relatively few became extremely rich, particularly through their dealings with the central or provincial authorities. Towards the end of the 11th/17th century, the *ṣarrāfs* of Istanbul organised around a guild and began to move their business to the Istanbul suburb of Galata [see GHALAṬA, in Suppl.], later to be known as "Galata bankers". Consolidation was also taking place. For instance, in the early 1840s, eighty members of the guild of *ṣarrāfs* were accredited by the government; by the mid-1850s, the number was down to 18. The *ṣarrāf* families included the Baltazzis, the Rallis, Zarafis, the Rodoconachis and Duzuoglus. These families played prominent roles in most of the major private and public banks that were established in the second half of the 19th century, starting with the Istanbul Bankasî (Bank of Istanbul) in 1845 (Kasaba, *The Ottoman empire*, 76).

The stereotypical view of *ṣarrāfs* is that they were on the whole non-Muslims. However, Muslims appear to have been involved in all aspects of *ṣarrāf* business, including tax-farming, currency exchange, money lending and international trade. A sample of 534 tax farms in the 10th/16th and 11th/17th centuries shows that around 60% of tax farmers were Muslims (Cizakca, *Comparative evolution*, 154-7). Research into the 10th/16th and 11th/17th century court records of specific regions (primarily Anatolia) of the Ottoman Empire also challenges the view that Muslims were not involved in money-lending or in the traditionally problematic area of interest. While there is debate among historians as to any marked difference between the Arab and "Turkish" parts of the Empire in regard to the acceptability of lending at interest, there is evidence that such transactions were carried out by Muslims in Anatolia on a relatively large scale, and that the practice was supported by the highest religious authorities of the time and approved by the *ḳāḍīs* (judges) who were responsible for implementing the *Sharīʿa* and *ḳānūn*. The best-known example was the cash *wakf* controversy and the associated charging of lending. Many of the *fatwās* of the time, even by the *Sheykh al-Islām* and other religious authorities, declared the permissibility not only of the cash *wakf* but also of interest charged on loans advanced therefrom (see Mandaville, *Usurious piety*). However, towards the end of the 19th century, the Muslim role in *ṣarrāf* business was radically curtailed by the increasing importance of non-Muslim *ṣarrāf* families and the emergence of banks, established largely by Europeans and by Armenian and Greek *ṣarrāfs*.

Bibliography: R.C. Jennings, *Loans and credit in early 17th century Ottoman judicial records*, in *JESHO*, xvi/2-3 (1973), 168-216; J.E. Mandaville, *Usurious piety: the cash waqf controversy in the Ottoman empire*, in *IJMES*, x (1979), 289-308; N.A. Saleh, *Unlawful gain and legitimate profit in Islamic law*, Cambridge 1986; Halil Inalcik and D. Quataert, *An economic and social history of the Ottoman empire 1300-1914*, Cambridge 1994; Reşat Kasaba, *The Ottoman empire and the world economy: the nineteenth century*, New York [1988]; M. Cizakca, *A comparative evolution of business partnerships, the Islamic world and Europe with specific reference to the Ottoman archives*, Leiden 1996; Şevket Pamuk, *A monetary history of the Ottoman empire*, Cambridge 2000.

(ABDULLAH SAEED)

SĀṬIʿ AL-ḤUṢRĪ, Ottoman official, educator, Arab Minister and theorist of Arab nationalism, d. 1968.

He was born in Ṣanʿāʾ, Yemen in 1880 to an Arab family of Aleppo. Both his father and mother were of prominent Aleppine mercantile families. His father, Muḥammad Hilāl al-Ḥuṣrī (b. 1840), served as an Ottoman judge after his graduation from al-Azhar University, becoming at the time of his son's birth Director of the Court of Criminal Appeals in the Yemeni capital. Owing to the pattern of his father's shifting appointments in accordance with Ottoman practice, Sāṭiʿ accompanied his family to a number of countries. Receiving his early education at home, Sāṭiʿ learnt Ottoman Turkish, Arabic and French. At the age of thirteen, he began his formal education at the College of Mülkiyye Mektebi in Istanbul, studying mathematics, history, botany, French and chemistry. Graduating with distinction in 1900, he chose to serve as a natural science teacher in a secondary school in the Balkans. During this period, he began to develop a lifelong interest in the question of nationalism and the rights of national communities. Shortly before the eruption of the Young Turk revolution in 1908, he came into contact with members of the Committee of Union and Progress [see ITTIḤĀD WE TERAḲḲĪ DJEMʿIYETI]. He also assumed in the same period the post of district governor in Kosovo and Florina.

After the revolution, al-Ḥuṣrī returned to Istanbul with the determination to propagate and implement his belief in a modern education system, coupled with his desire to articulate a secular notion of Ottomanism. This he did by founding new journals, publishing new school textbooks on various scientific subjects and taking part in public debates relating to contemporary issues. Furthermore, between 1909 and 1912 he assumed the directorship of the Teachers' Training College in Istanbul, restructuring and modernising in the process its entire curricula and management. He also visited a number of European countries to acquaint himself with the latest methods of pedagogy. By the end of his directorship, al-Ḥuṣrī had become one of the most influential educators throughout the Ottoman Empire.

His most distinctive intellectual contribution in the Ottoman period of his life was five lectures he delivered in Istanbul in 1913 on the significance of patriotism. In those lectures, entitled *Vatan için*, he called for building a new Ottoman community based on the idea of the fatherland as an object of love. Moreover, these lectures were to form the basis of his Arab nationalist theory in the wake of his decision to leave the Ottoman capital in 1918 and join the newly formed government of Amīr Fayṣal in Damascus.

In his Arab phase, al-Ḥuṣrī resumed his interrupted career by acting as Director General of Education, and then Minister of Education in the Syrian government until its liquidation by the French in 1920. After a short sojourn in Italy and Egypt, he once again joined Fayṣal, the new king of British-mandated ʿIrāḳ, and became Director General of Education from 1923 to 1927. He used this opportunity to create a new system of instruction geared towards the inculcation of Arab nationalism, coupled with his insistence on high standards and rigorous methods of promotions. Meeting resistance or obstruction in the course of his duties, he resigned his post and devoted himself to lecturing at the Teachers' College and publishing a new journal on education. In 1935 he assumed the deanship of the Law College and was appointed Director of Antiquities between 1936 and 1941. Following the second British occupation of ʿIrāḳ in 1941, al-Ḥuṣrī was, along with other non-ʿIrāḳī Arab nationalists, deported to Syria and stripped of his ʿIrāḳī citizenship. In 1944 he was invited by the Syrian government to modernise and overhaul its system of education. The foundation of the Arab League in 1945 afforded al-Ḥuṣrī the opportunity to develop its cultural and educational policies. After acting as a cultural adviser, he was appointed the first director of its Institute of Higher Arab Studies in 1953. After his retirement in 1957, al-Ḥuṣrī wrote and published a number of studies on pan-Arabist subjects, including his memoirs, which dealt with his ʿIrāḳī period. He died in 1968.

Bibliography: L.M. Kenny, *Satiʿ al-Husri's views on Arab nationalism*, in *MEJ*, xvii (1963), 231-56; W.L. Cleveland, *The making of an Arab nationalist. Ottomanism and Arabism in the life and thought of Sāṭiʿ al-Ḥuṣrī*, Princeton 1971; Aḥmad Yūsuf Aḥmad *et al.*, *Sāṭiʿ al-Ḥuṣrī, thalāthūn ʿāman ʿalā al-raḥīl*, Beirut 1999; Youssef Choueiri, *Arab nationalism, a history*, Oxford 2000, ch. 4. (Youssef M. Choueiri)

SATR (A.), "concealment", a term used in a variety of senses particularly by the Ismāʿīliyya [*q.v.*] The Ismāʿīlīs originally used it in reference to a period in their early history, called *dawr al-satr*, stretching from soon after the death of *imām* Djaʿfar al-Ṣādiḳ in 148/765 to the establishment of the Fāṭimid state in 297/909. The Ismāʿīlī *imām*, recognised as the *ḳāʾim* or *mahdī* by the majority of the early Ismāʿīlīs, was hidden (*mastūr*) during this period of concealment; in his absence, he was represented by *ḥudjdjas* (see Djaʿfar b. Manṣūr al-Yaman, *Kitāb al-Kashf*, ed. R. Strothmann, London 1952, 98-9; al-Shahrastānī, 146). Later, the Ismāʿīlīs of the Fāṭimid period, who allowed for continuity in their imāmate, recognised a series of three such "hidden *imāms*" (*al-aʾimma al-mastūrūn*) between Muḥammad b. Ismāʿīl b. Djaʿfar, their seventh *imām*, and ʿAbd Allāh al-Mahdī, founder of the Fāṭimid dynasty (see H.F. al-Hamdani, *On the genealogy of Fatimid caliphs*, Cairo 1958, text 11-14).

In the aftermath of the Nizārī-Mustaʿlī schism of 487/1094 in Ismāʿīlism, the early Nizārī Ismāʿīlīs experienced another period of *satr*, when their *imāms*, descendants of Nizār b. al-Mustanṣir (d. 488/1095 [*q.v.*]), remained hidden for several decades. The inaccessible Nizārī *imāms* were now once again represented by *ḥudjdjas*, starting with Ḥasan-i Ṣabbāḥ [*q.v.*], who also ruled over the Nizārī state from Alamūt [*q.v.*]. The period of *satr* in early Nizārī history ended with the declaration of the *ḳiyāma* at Alamūt in 559/1164 and the resulting open emergence of the Nizārī imāmate. Subsequently, the term *satr* acquired a new meaning for the Nizārīs. As explained by Naṣīr al-Dīn al-Ṭūsī, the Nizārīs had by the late Alamūt period formulated what may be called a new doctrine of *satr*. In this context, *satr* no longer referred to the physical concealment of the *imāms*; instead, it referred to a time when spiritual reality or religious truths (*ḥaḳāʾiḳ*) were hidden in the *bāṭin* of religion, requiring the observance of *taḳiyya* in any necessary form, including the adoption of the Sunnī *Sharīʿa* as demanded earlier by the sixth lord of Alamūt, Djalāl al-Dīn Ḥasan (607-18/1210-21).

The Mustaʿlī Ismāʿīlīs, who survived only in the Ṭayyibī form after the downfall of the Fāṭimid dynasty, have experienced a period of *satr*, in the original Ismāʿīlī sense of the term, since their twentieth *imām*, al-Āmir bi-Aḥkām Allāh [*q.v.*], was murdered in 524/1130. It is the belief of the Ṭayyibī Ismāʿīlīs that all their *imāms*, starting with al-Āmir's son al-Ṭayyib who disappeared in infancy, have remained hidden to the present day. In their absence, *dāʿī muṭlaks*, or supreme *dāʿīs*, have led the affairs of the Ṭayyibiyya (*q.v.*).

Satr found expression also in the Ismāʿīlīs' cyclical conception of religious history of humankind. The Ismāʿīlīs believed from early on that this hierohistory was comprised of seven eras or *dawrs*, all except the last one being eras of *satr*, because the inner, immutable truths of religions or the *ḥaḳāʾiḳ* remained undisclosed. In this scheme, only in the seventh and final eschatological era initiated by the *ḳāʾim* before the end of the physical world, would the *ḥaḳāʾiḳ* be fully revealed to humankind. This final age, designated as the *dawr al-kashf* or the era of manifestation, would be an age of pure spiritual knowledge when there would no longer be any distinction between the *ẓāhir* and *bāṭin* dimensions of religion, and between religious laws and their inner meanings. On the basis of astronomical calculations, the Ṭayyibīs of Yaman introduced further innovations into this cyclical scheme. They conceived of a grand aeon (*kawr al-aʿẓam*) composed of countless cycles, each one divided into seven eras. This grand aeon would progress through successive cycles of concealment (*satr*) and manifestation (*kashf*), and it would be finally concluded by the Great Resurrection (*ḳiyāmat al-ḳiyāmāt*) proclaimed by the final *ḳāʾim*.

Bibliography (in addition to the works cited in the article): 1. Sources. Ibrāhīm b. al-Ḥusayn al-Ḥāmidī, *K. Kanz al-walad*, ed. M. Ghālib, Wiesbaden 1971, 149ff., 205-7, 232ff., 258-72; Naṣīr al-Dīn Muḥammad al-Ṭūsī, *Rawḍat al-taslīm*, ed. and tr. W. Ivanow, Leiden 1950, text 61, 62-3, 83-4, 101-2, 110, 117-19, 128-49; al-Ḥusayn b. ʿAlī al-Walīd, *Risālat al-Mabdaʾ wa ʾl-maʿād*, ed. and Fr. tr. H. Corbin, in his *Trilogie ismaélienne*, Paris and Tehran 1961, text 100ff., 121-8.

2. Studies. M.G.S. Hodgson, *The Order of Assassins*, The Hague 1955, 225-38; W. Madelung, *Das Imamat in der frühen ismailitischen Lehre*, in *Isl.*, xxxvii (1961), 48ff., 61ff., 101-14; Corbin, *Histoire de la philosophie islamique*, i, Paris 1964, 127-32; idem, *Cyclical time and Ismaili gnosis*, London 1983, 37-58, 78-84, 117ff.; H. Halm, *Kosmologie und Heilslehre der*

frühen Ismāʿīlīya, Wiesbaden 1978, 18-37, 99-100; F. Daftary, *The Ismāʿīlīs. Their history and doctrines*, Cambridge 1990, 102-5, 126-8, 136-40, 177-8, 257, 294-5, 404ff., 408, 409-11 (containing further bibliographical references).

(F. Daftary)

ṢAWLADJĀN (a.), said to be an Arabised form of Pers. *čawgān* "polo stick" [see čawgān]. The intrusive *l* makes this difficult, but D.N. MacKenzie, *A concise dictionary of Pahlavi*, London 1971, 22, has **caw(l)agān* ("of doubtful transcription"). At all events, the curve of a polo stick makes it a suitable figurative expression, either as a simile [see tashbīh] or as a metaphor [see istiʿāra], in classical Arabic, Persian and Turkish literatures, for the curving eyebrows and locks or tresses of hair of a beautiful girl; see Annemarie Schimmel, *The two-colored brocade. The imagery of Persian poetry*, Chapel Hill N.C. and London 1992, 284-5.

(C.E. Bosworth)

SEGBĀN (t., from Pers. *sagbān* "servant in charge of dogs, or keeper of the sultan's hounds". In Ottoman Turkish, it was often spelled *sekbān*, and also written as *segmen* or *seymen*, following popular pronunciation), a term of Ottoman palace and military organisation.

In the Ottoman Empire, the term had three general uses which evolved over time: first used for the guardians of the sultan's hunting dogs, it was then applied to members of various salaried infantry units within the Janissaries, surviving until the corps itself was abolished in 1826, and finally, as the name of groups of infantry auxiliaries or militias. Officially prohibited as a military term in the latter use at the beginning of the 18th century, it was briefly revived again in the 19th. In present-day provincial Turkish, *seğmen* refers to an armed ceremonial escort in national dress.

The first use of the term *segbān* occurs in a *waḳf* deed of the late 8th/14th century. Hunting and dogs were an integral part of the early Ottoman court, especially that of Bāyezīd I [*q.v.*], who is credited with greatly expanding the number of *segbān*s. Servants for the hunting parties were probably recruited from war captives or as part of the military levy (*devs̲h̲irme* [*q.v.*]). Early records indicate that villagers sought protection from recruitment, or from other obligations to *segbān*s, indicating the burden which hunting could impose on the populace. Murād I [*q.v.*] explicitly recognised the service of his *segbān*s and falconers in his will, emancipating them at his death. *Segbān*s figure prominently in Ottoman miniature painting. Süleymān I [*q.v.*] himself was portrayed as a great hunter, and surrounded by dogs and their keepers (see ʿot̲h̲mānlî. viii. Painting, Pl. X, for an example).

In the 9th/15th century, the evolution of courtly retinue to fighting units became more marked, and it is at this point that *segbān*s became part of the Janissaries. In 855/1451, Meḥemmed II added 7,000 *segbān*s to the Janissaries, with a separate commander, the *segbān bas̲h̲î*, who joined the ranks of the high officials of the empire (Chalcondyles, ed. Bonn 1848, bk. vii, 377). Other officers of the *segbān*s included a *ketk̲h̲üdā* and a *kātib*. After the middle of the 10th/16th century, the *segbān bas̲h̲î* was subordinated to second-in-command after the *ag̲h̲a*, and generally remained in Istanbul when the *ag̲h̲a* left on campaign. The *segbān*s formed the 65th *orta* of the Janissaries, and were divided into two sections: a small cavalry *orta* of 40-70 men, most of whom were sons of Janissary officers, and 34 *bölük*s (companies of infantry), known as the *segbān bölükleri*. Hunting traditions survived in the 33rd *bölük*, called the *awd̲j̲î* (hunter) *bölük*, which accompanied the sultan on hunting parties but not on campaign; sons of Janissaries and statesmen alike made up its rolls.

A second general use of the term was for provincial auxiliary mercenary or militia troops, like the *lewend* [*q.v.*], who served the official appointees to the provinces, the *pas̲h̲as*, *mīr-i mirān*s, *beglerbegi* or *sand̲j̲aḳ begleri* [*q.vv.*]. Initially the entourage of the governor (*pas̲h̲a*), his private retinue and army (*ḳapî ḥalḳî*), *segbān* also came to be applied to troops called to campaign, and paid out of the central treasury (*mīrī segbān*s, *mīrī lewend*). Provincial officials were the recruiters of the *segbān-lewend* style of troops, and by the end of the 18th century, they were each required to mobilise 1,000-2,000 cavalry or infantry for campaigns. The essential characteristic of such auxiliaries was that they carried firearms, were recruited for short periods, and were drawn from the countryside, often from among the landless and lawless [see bārūd. iv]. Their first significant appearance in that military capacity was during the Ottoman-Habsburg War of 1593-1606, when a few hundred were noted among the troops in Hungary. They were organised as other Ottoman troops, into companies or standards (*bayraḳ*), the latter generally numbering 50 or 100 men. Their use was increased in the latter 11th/17th century, as both Janissary and *sipāhī*s [*q.v.*] proved inadequate for facing the better-armed Habsburgs.

The demobilisation of such troops led to countryside unrest, as they often stayed together as armed bands, and participated in uprisings such as the D̲j̲elālī rebellions [see d̲j̲alālī, in Suppl.] or revolts of their provincial masters. The central government endeavoured unsuccessfully to eliminate the designation *segbān* around 1700, but military necessity dictated its continuance, although the term *mīrī lewend* was the preferred usage for such troops by the mid-18th century.

Such mercenary or militia troops could be found in all the territories of the empire, as armies of provincial officials, as the fighting units described above, or as guards of towns, where they were often in conflict with local Janissaries. They included Christian recruits, Serbians and Croatians, especially in the Principalities, where they were called *seymen*, and could be found in the fighting forces of Moldavia and Wallachia well into the 18th century. In general, however, Muslims were the primary recruits, and Albanians and Bosnians the most prized for their military prowess.

The term *segbān* was revived in military usage in 1808, when Muṣṭafā Pas̲h̲a Bayrakdār [*q.v.*] tried to continue the reforms of Selīm III [*q.v.*] by renaming the detested *niẓām-î d̲j̲edīd* [*q.v.*] troops *segbān-î d̲j̲edīd*, and incorporating them as the eighth *od̲j̲aḳ* of the Janissaries. The new troops allied with the Janissaries, however, and were instrumental in Muṣṭafā's own downfall that same year. The term *segbān* disappeared when Maḥmūd II [*q.v.*] eliminated the corps in 1826.

Bibliography: See gönüllü for further discussion; *IA*, art. *Sekbân* (M.T. Gökbilgin); Pakalın, iii, 145-9; Hammer-Purgstall, *Staatsverfassung*, i, 56, 48, ii, 37, 191, 203, 207-09; Uzunçarşılı, *Osmanlı devleti teşkilâtından kapıkulu ocakları*, i, Ankara 1943, 162-6 and *passim*; Halil İnalcık, *Fatih devri üzerinde tetkikler ve vesikalar I*, Ankara 1954, repr. 1987, 207, for Murād I's will; M. Cezar, *Osmanlı tarihinde levendler*, Istanbul 1965; İnalcık, *Military and fiscal transformation in the Ottoman Empire, 1600-1700*, in *Archivum ottomanicum*, vi (1980), 283-337; H.G. Majer, *Albaner und Bosnier in der osmanisichen Armee. Ein Faktor in der Reichsintegration im 18. und 19. Jahrhundert*, in K.-D. Grothusen (ed.), *Jugoslawien. Interpretationsprobleme in Geschichte und Gegenwart*, Göttingen 1984, 105-17; Esin Atil, *Süleymanname. The illustrated history of Süleyman the Magnificent*, New York 1986, pls. 10-11, for illustrations of hunting parties; Karen Barkey, *Bandits and bureaucrats. The Ottoman route to state centralization*, Ithaca 1994; V. Aksan, *Whatever happened to the Janissaries? Mobilization for the 1768-1774 Russo-Ottoman War*, in *War in History*, v (1998), 23-36.

(Virginia H. Aksan)

SEMENDIRE, the Ottoman Turkish form of the Serbian town of Smederovo, older form Semendria. Lying on the Danube downstream from Belgrade [*q.v.*] (lat. 44° 40' N., long. 20° 56' E.), it was in pre-modern times a fortified town and, under the Ottomans, the chef-lieu of a *sandjaḳ* of the same name. Since the break-up of Yugoslavia, it has come within the Serbian Republic.

A first conquest under Murād II (842/1438) did not lead to permanent incorporation into the Ottoman Empire, since due to the crisis of 847-8/1444 the sultan thought it necessary to preserve the Serbian despotate as a buffer state between his own lands and those of the king of Hungary (Halil İnalcık and Mevlut Oğuz (eds.), *Gazavât-i Sultân Murâd b. Mehemmed Hân, İzladi ve Varna savaşları (1443-1444) üzerinde anonim Gazavâtnâme*, Ankara 1978, 31-5, 102-3). According to Theodore Spandunes, it was George Kantakuzenos, surnamed Sachatai, a brother of the Byzantine princess Irene, consort of the Despot of Serbia George Branković, who came from the Morea to Serbia and built the fortified town of Smederovo. In 858/1454, this was one of the major centres of the Serbian despotate, with fortifications solid enough to withstand an Ottoman attack. In 860-1/1456 a Hungarian attempt to take the town was also beaten back by the same George Kantakuzenos (Th. Spandunes, *On the origin of the Ottoman Emperors*, tr. and ed. D. Nicol, Cambridge 1997, 29, 35; *Memoiren eines Janitscharen oder Türkische Chronik*, tr. Renate Lachmann, with comm. by eadem, C.-P. Haase and G. Prinzing, Graz 1975, 117, 210, this being the text supposedly written by Constantine of Ostrovica, an ex-Janissary or Janissary auxiliary; Th. Stavridis, *The Sultan of Vezirs: the life and times of the Ottoman Grand Vezir Mahmud Pasha Angelović (1453-1474)*, Leiden 2001, 82-95).

After the death of George Branković and that of his son Lazar two years later, Smederovo was inherited by the latter's son-in-law, the Bosnian king Stepan Tomasević, who in 863-4/1459 surrendered the city to Maḥmūd Pas̲h̲a, then *beylerbeyi* of Rumeli. Born a member of the Byzantino-Serbian aristocratic family of the Angelović, Maḥmūd Pas̲h̲a had been commissioned to take over the region in the name of Sultan Meḥemmed II. Pope Pius II viewed the Ottoman conquest of the Serbian despotate and the concomitant acquisition of Smederovo as a calamity all but equivalent to the end of the Byzantine Empire. Most possessions of the Serbian despotate within the kingdom of Hungary were confiscated by the local ruler as a measure of retaliation for the surrender of Smederovo (F. Babinger, *Mehmed der Eroberer und seine Zeit. Weltenstürmer einer Zeitenwende*, Munich 1953, 174-5).

These events had been preceded, in 862/early 1458, by an attempt on the part of Michael Angelović, Maḥmūd Pas̲h̲a's (probably elder) brother, a member of the regency council that took over after the death of Lazar, to make himself despot with the backing of the Ottoman sultan and take power in Smederovo. He had gained the support of Serbian nobles who were worried about a possible subjection to the Pope, in case the Hungarian party should gain the upper hand. However, the takeover failed, and Michael Angelović was arrested by members of the pro-Hungarian party in the regency council and sent to Dubrovnik, where—probably at Hungarian behest—he was held captive by a local patrician (C. Jireček, *Geschichte der Serben*, Gotha 1918, ii, 207-15). If this version of events is the true one, Michael Angelović thus cannot have negotiated the surrender of Smederovo to his brother on the Ottoman side (Stavridis, *op. cit.*, 102; most Ottoman chronicles, however, take the agreement between brothers for granted; see for example *ʿĀs̲h̲ïkpas̲h̲azāda tārīk̲h̲ï*, ed. ʿAlī Bey, Istanbul 1332/1914, 152. On a divergent version of these campaigns, compare *The History of Mehmed the Conqueror by Tursun Beg*, comments and tr. by Halil Inalcik and R. Murphey, Minneapolis and Chicago 1978, 40-5; Ṭursun Beg claims that the outer fortress of Smederovo was conquered by force of arms, and only the inner citadel ultimately surrendered). Subsequently, King Matthias Corvinus of Hungary made various projects for a conquest of the fortress, now known in Ottoman as Semendire, but none of these led to any concrete results (Babinger, *op. cit.*, 385).

Within the Ottoman realm, the Semendire area became a *sandjaḳ* and was divided up into *tīmār*s and *ziʿāmet*s [*q.vv.*], itself forming part of the *beylerbeylik* of Rumeli; in the early 10th/16th century, Belgrade was part of this *sandjaḳ*, albeit producing far less revenue than the Semendire area (M. Tayyib Gökbilgin, *Kanuni Sultan Süleyman devri başlarında Rumeli eyaleti, livaları, şehir ve kasabaları*, in *Belleten*, xx [1956], 252-7). After the conquest of Hungary, Semendire was transferred to the newly formed *vilāyet* of Buda. In addition to the cavalry supplied by *tīmār*s and *ziʿāmet*s, the local Eflāḳ (Vlach) were accorded tax remissions in return for military services (N. Beldiceanu and Irène Beldiceanu-Steinherr, *Quatre actes de Meḥmed II concernant les Valaques des Balkans slaves*, in Beldiceanu, *Le monde ottoman des Balkans (1420-1566): institutions, société, économie*, London 1976, no. III; on Vlach-related issues in the reign of Bāyezīd II, see *Osmanlılarda divân-bürokrasi-aklam, II. Bâyezid dönemine ait 906/1501 tarihli ahkâm defteri*, ed. by İlhan Şahin and Feridun Emecen, Istanbul 1994, nos. 208, 209).

Entries in the 10th/16th-century *Mühimme defterleri* reflected the position of Semendire as a military base during the wars of Süleymān the Magnificent against the Habsburgs: its governor was called upon to purchase timber for bridge-building, see to the construction of boats to be used on the Danube and organise supplies of flour and barley for the needs of the army. The town also possessed a cannon-foundry (*ṭopk̲h̲āne*). A text from 951-2/1544-6 refers to the fact that much of the town had been destroyed by fire, and enjoined the *ḳāḍī* to make sure that the new houses were not built so close to the walls as to endanger their military function (Hacı Osman Yıldırım *et alii* [eds.], *7. numaralı mühimme defteri 975-976/1567-69*, 5 vols. Ankara 1997, i, 273. For one of the oldest extant *Mühimme* registers, see Halil Sahillioğlu [ed.], *Topkapı Sarayı arşivi H. 951-952 tarihli ve E-12321 numaralı mühimme defteri*, Istanbul 2002, 24-5, 192-3, 219, 306; for a selection of relevant texts from this register in French tr., see Mihnea Berindei and G. Veinstein, *L'Empire ottoman et les pays roumains 1544-1545*, Paris and Cambridge, Mass. 1987, 8-9, 14-15, 18-19, 29, 40-3, 46, 65-6, 69-70).

Economic life was based on agriculture, stock-raising and fishing; Semendire functioned as a small-scale market for rural produce, while crafts seem to have been of limited importance and many townsmen cultivated fields and gardens (B. McGowan, *Food supply and taxation on the Middle Danube (1568-79)*, in *Archivum Ottomanicum*, i [1969], 139-96; Mihnea Berindei, Annie Berthier, Marielle Martin and G. Veinstein, *Code de lois de Murâd III concernant la province de Smederovo*, in *Südost Forschungen*, xxxi [1972], 140-63). Timber was brought in from the surrounding forests, while imports from further afield included metals, Asian spices and also slaves; the Danube seems to have functioned as a barrier at which internal customs could be conveniently collected.

After the peace of Zsitvatorok (1015/1606 [*q.v.*]) had ended the Long War between Habsburgs and Ottomans, the embassy of Adam Freiherr von Herberstein was, on its return from Istanbul (1016-18/1608-9), permitted to view the fortifications of Semendire (M. Brandstetter, *Itinerarium oder Raisbeschreibung*, in K. Nehring, *Adam Freiherr zu Herbersteins Gesandtschaftsreise nach Konstantinopel: ein Beitrag zum Frieden von Zsitvatorok (1606)*, Munich 1983, 174-5). This permission may have been granted because Ottoman military men regarded the fortifications as obsolescent: Brandstetter described a once powerful stronghold that he did not, however, consider very suitable for contemporary warfare. Roofs and floors had been neglected, while heavy artillery could only be placed in the towers and on the bare ground; but the fortress did suffice to control traffic on the Danube. Brandstetter also noted the existence of an inner citadel protected by its own water-filled ditch and five towers, as well as the presence of a garrison commander, but he made no reference to a civilian population.

An 11th/17th-century description from an Ottoman perspective is owed to Ewliyā Čelebi, who visited Semendire as a participant in several Balkan campaigns (*Evliya Çelebi Seyahatnâmesi. Topkapı Sarayı Bagdat 307 yazmasının transkripsyonu–dizini*, v, ed. Yücel Dağlı, Seyit Ali Kahraman and İbrahim Sezgin, Istanbul 2001, 316-17). Ewliyā relates a set of partly counterfactual traditions concerning the Ottoman acquisition of the town, seventeen years before Constantinople, possibly an allusion to the ephemeral conquest under Murād II. These stories are, however, important because they possibly circulated among the local military men and show the "ideological" importance of Semendire even at this date. Other conquest traditions involve a marital union between Sultan Bāyezīd I Yïldïrïm and a daughter of the Serbian despot which resulted in the conclusion of peace between the two states—this was possibly a reminiscence of the marriage of the Serbian princess Mara to Murād II. These stories also include an account of military conquest on the part of Meḥemmed II and a subsequent return of the town to the unbelievers in exchange for the liberation of the commander Bali̇ Bey, who had been taken prisoner in battle. After his return, Bali̇ Bey supposedly attacked and took Semendire, so that he was regarded as its second conqueror, his memory perpetuated by a *zāwiye* slightly to the west of the town. This latter story probably refers to one of the first *sandjak beyis* of the province, Bali̇ Bey Malkoč-oghlu, who became famous for his two campaigns against Poland and other feats of derring-do (Babinger, *Beiträge zur Geschichte des Geschlechtes der Malqoč-Oghlus*, repr. in *Aufsätze und Abhandlungen zur Geschichte Südosteuropas und der Levante*, i, Munich 1962, 355-70; and see MALKOČ-OGHULLARÏ, in Suppl.).

As in the late 10th/16th century, Semendire in Ewliyā's time was a centre of the homonymous *sandjak*, famous on account of the numerous soldiers domiciled in this place ('Ayn-i̇ 'Alī Efendi, *Kawānīn-i āl-i 'Othmān der khülāṣa-i meḍāmīn-i defter-i dīwān*, preface by Gökbilgin, Istanbul 1979, 17; compare also the description by Kātib Čelebi, *Rumeli und Bosna*, tr. J. von Hammer, Vienna 1812). The fortress supposedly consisted of an inner and an outer section, with a circumference of 4,000 paces and four gates, protected by the Danube on three sides and in addition by 36 towers. Apart from the garrison officers, the urban élite consisted of the *kāḍī*, the *shehir ketkhudāsi̇* and the teachers in two local *medreses*, while four Friday mosques, one of them bearing the name of Meḥemmed the Conqueror, were available for worship. There was a settlement outside of the walls (*warosh*) that supposedly contained 3,000 houses and 300 shops, accessible by wooden bridges crossing the river or else the water-filled ditch that made the fortress into a virtual island. Due to the marshy ground, few buildings were of stone, roofs were often covered in wooden shingles and even the streets were paved with boards. Although Ewliyā claims that an abundance of goods was available in the two local *khāns* and elsewhere, the lack of a covered market probably indicates that this was not a town noted for its commerce (on the limited economic activity of the entire area, see McGowan, *The Middle Danube cul de sac*, in Huri İslamoğlu-İnan (ed.), *The Ottoman Empire and the world-economy*, Paris and Cambridge 1987, 170-7).

In the Ottoman-Habsburg war of 1094-1111/1683-99, Semendire shared the fate of nearby Belgrade: it was first taken by the Habsburgs and then re-conquered by the Ottomans. The Orthodox bishop moved to Belgrade in 1140-1/1728; this was probably a sign of the town's declining relative importance (Adolph Kunike [ed.], *Zwey hundert vier und sechzig Donau-Ansichten nach dem Laufe des Donaustromes*, comments by Georg C.B. Rumy, Vienna 1826, repr. Munich n.d.; non-paginated brochure appended to the lithographs). Nevertheless, in the early 13th/19th century, Semendire formed one of the centres of a Serbian movement for autonomy; in 1219-20/1805 local troops in rebellion against the Ottoman central government took the town, before moving on to Belgrade (J. Stoye, *Marsigli's Europe, 1680-1730: the life and times of Luigi Ferdinando Marsigli, soldier and virtuoso*, New Haven 1994, 57, 74-5, 78, 95, 109; Barbara Jelavich, *History of the Balkans*, i, *Eighteenth and nineteenth centuries*, Cambridge 1983, 91, 198).

Documenting the physical shape of the town at the beginning of that century, there survive two remarkable lithographs published in 1241-2/1826 (Kunike *op. cit.*, nos. 180, 181). These show that the town preserved quite a few of the characteristics described one and a half centuries earlier by Ewliyā Čelebi. While according to Rumy's comments, the fortress lay partially in ruins, this is not apparent from the images, which show a wall surmounted by towers of different shapes and sizes and protected by a palisade. The town proper was located not on the peninsula/island but on the river banks, and there was a Muslim section surmounted by many minarets, more than the four existing in Ewliyā's time. Semendire possessed a sizeable Christian quarter as well, for there was also a church with a high steeple, rather Central European in character. Roofs and walls made for shingles still formed a notable feature of the local architecture, and the Austrian commentator remarked that the town had "a handsome appearance".

Bibliography: Given in the article. See also Olga Zirojević, *The Constantinople road from Beograd to Sofija (1459-1683)* (Zbornik istorijskog muzeja Srbije, 7), Belgrade 1970; and the *Bibls.* to SIRB.

(SURAIYA FAROQHI)

SHĀH DAGH, a peak of the southeasternmost tip of the Caucasus range (4,253 m/13,951 feet high), the mountainous region which in mediaeval Islamic times separated the districts of Ḳubba from Shamākha [see ḲUBBA]. It now lies in the northeasternmost part of the Azerbaijan Republic.

SHĀHBANDAR (P.), lit. "harbourmaster", an official of the ports in Ṣafawid Persia and one also known on other shores of the Indian Ocean.

A lack of information from before the advent of the European maritime companies notwithstanding, it is likely the office of *shāhbandar* first appeared in Persia, and from there spread throughout the Indian Ocean basin. The precise status of the *shāhbandar* remains unclear for the early period. Moreland concluded that, while elsewhere around the Indian Ocean the term had a wide range of meaning in the 10th/16th century, in Hurmuz [*q.v.*] it clearly referred to the harbourmaster. He documents a *shāhbandar* in that port for 1521, and for 1584 the Portuguese sources identify a person with the title of *goarda mor da praya*, chief warden of the beach and customs house. The Portuguese sources also mention an official called *juiz da alfandega*, judge of the tollhouse. Already at that time the function had a political dimension as well, for at some point in the early 10th/16th century, the vizier of Hurmuz combined his position as governor of the port with that of head of customs.

Most of the subsequent information on the *shāhbandar* concerns the position in Bandar ʿAbbās [*q.v.*] after the arrival in the Persian Gulf of the English and Dutch East India Companies in the early 17th century, and is a function of the documents generated by their agents. In the Persian sources the *shāhbandar* appears as the *ḍābiṭ-i wudjūh wa khurūdj*, commander of imports and exports, but he is rarely mentioned, reflecting the fact that, although the Persian Gulf trade was important to the state and the official served the central administration, the region itself was not at the centre of official attention.

The *shāhbandar* wielded considerable power in the port. He administered the payment of tolls on incoming and outgoing goods, which generally amounted to 10% *ad valorem* for both. In order to secure smooth relations, merchants were forced periodically to hand him gifts, which was really a form of taxation. Thus the Dutch and the English typically paid the *shāhbandar* of Bandar ʿAbbās 50 *tūmāns* annually, but in 1654 we hear of local merchants being forced to pay a sum of 1,000 *tūmāns*, and in 1661 the resident Indian merchant community was made to pay a similar amount. *Shāhbandars* were also wont to make private deals with brokers, who bribed them to let goods pass. *Shāhbandars* had their own agents in other Persian Gulf ports and India and elsewhere in Persia who tried to entice merchants to patronise Bandar ʿAbbās. There are also reports of the *shāhbandar* of Bandar ʿAbbās terrorising the local merchants and interfering with their trade, demanding the choicest wares available at below market prices and refusing to give a transport license when they demurred.

While sharing many of his responsibilities and traits with *shāhbandars* in other parts of Asia, the *shāhbandar* in Persia resembles the ones in India and South East India more than his colleagues in the Ottoman Empire. Whereas in a place like Aleppo the *shāhbandar* was chosen from among the wealthy local merchants, and was sometimes a Jew or an Armenian, in 11th/17th-century Persia he was invariably a political official with a fixed salary, who was sent down by the central government with the task of collecting customs revenue for the shāh. At the end of his term in office he had to account for his dealings and submit his financial report to the crown's financial council. The fact that in the late 1620s Mulāyim Beg was simultaneously the shāh's commercial factor and *shāhbandar* of Bandar ʿAbbās suggests this strong nexus between politics and commerce. The reports of the maritime companies also make clear that the *shāhbandar* was a shadowing official, sent down to supervise and report on the *khān* of the town. As this surveillance was mutual, it often led to rivalry and even violent confrontations between the retinue of both officials. As was the case for most positions in Ṣafawid Persia, the post of *shāhbandar* tended to be hereditary, yet no single family managed to establish a hold over it for any length of time. For most of the 1650s, Muḥammad Beg, who later became Grand Vizier, and his family furnished a series of *shāhbandars*, beginning with Muḥammad Beg himself. Of Armenian descent, he was a *ghulām* [*q.v.*], one of the many originally Christian slaves from the Caucasus region who attained high political positions in Ṣafawid Persia. Georgian *ghulāms*, who by the 11th/17th century had taken over most of the administration in the country, infiltrated the position as well. In 1669 it was reported that the new *shāhbandar* was a Georgian *ghulām*.

Several changes occurred in this same period. Until 1656 the port of Kung fell under the jurisdiction of Lār [see LĀR, LĀRISTĀN]. When ʿAvaḍ Beg left his post as *khān* of Lār, a separate governor-cum-*shāhbandar* was appointed for Kung, apparently in order to improve the central government's control over its revenues. A similar motivation underlay the changes effected in the smaller ports of the Persian Gulf, which until the second half of the 11th/17th century did not have a customs house and therefore no *shāhbandar*. As this prompted those merchants keen to evade tolls and harassment in Bandar ʿAbbās to turn to those ports, the Ṣafawid government in the mid-1660s conducted an investigation and decided to establish a customs house in Bandar Rīg. Būshihr [*q.v.*], which was of minor importance, had a *shāhbandar*, too, at this point. Smaller ports must have remained under the jurisdiction of local *shaykhs*.

In a more structural change, the position of *shāhbandar* of Bandar ʿAbbās began to be farmed out in this period. Until the reign of Shāh Sulaymān (1077-1105/1666-94), each individual port had its own customs official and the office of *shāhbandar* had rotated on an annual basis. Mismanagement, corruption and the attendant dwindling income from customs in the early 1670s prompted the Ṣafawid government to consolidate the customs administration by bringing it under the control of one official, who now farmed the post for six to eight years at a fixed salary and a stipulated revenue of 24,000 *tūmāns*. (Chardin claims that the change came in 1674, but it is more likely that it was part of a series of reforms effected by the Grand Vizier Shaykh ʿAlī Khān in 1671-2.) The term of a given official might be prolonged after expiration. Thus in 1684, Mīrzā Murtaḍā, having served one term, received the post for seven more years. He was also reinstated as *shāhbandar* of Kung. Various other sources report that, ten years later, the *shāhbandar* of Kung acted both as customs official and as *dārūgha* [*q.v.*], or mayor of the town, and that he farmed the customs of Kung, Bandar ʿAbbās and Bandar Rīg, for an annual sum of 20,000 *tūmāns*.

Būs͟hihr in the mid-12th/18th century offers an example of an Armenian *s͟hāhbandar*—as opposed to a *g͟hulām* who had been made to convert to Islam. This person, named K͟hʷad͟ja Mellelsk, was a subordinate of the *s͟hāhbandar* of Bandar ʿAbbās. In 1748 the town's governor, S͟hayk͟h Nāṣir, usurped the position. This may have set a precedent, for in the 19th century the head of customs in Būs͟hihr appears to have been the port's *k͟hān* or *kalantar* [*q.v.*] or mayor, rather than a *s͟hāhbandar.* Beginning in *ca.* 1850, when the port's trade began to flourish, customs were collected by a private functionary called the *ḥammālbās͟hī*. In Bandar ʿAbbās the term *s͟hāhbandar* long remained in use, but here, too, it was the *ḥammālbās͟hī* who in the 19th century collected customs fees. In the smaller ports, tribal chiefs or government officials called *ḍābiṭs* were usually the ones to manage the port's customs. Having become obsolete for the port towns of Persia, the term *s͟hāhbandar* was now used for the official who represented the interests of the Turkish merchants operating within Persia.

Bibliography: 1. Sources. (a) Archives. *Algemeen Rijksarchief*, The Hague (ARA), *Verenigde Oost Indische Compagnie; India Office Records* (IOR). (b) Printed. H. Dunlop (ed.), *Bronnen tot de geschiedenis der Oostindische Compagnie in Perzië, 1630-38*, The Hague 1930; E. Kaempfer, *Am Hofe des persischen Grosskönigs, 1684-1685*, tr. W. Hinz, Tübingen 1977, 121; J. de Thévenot, *Relation d'un voyage fait au Levant*, iii, *Livre troisième du suite du voyage de Mr. De Thévenot au Levant*, Paris 1689, 609; J. Chardin, *Voyages du chevalier Chardin en Perse et en autres lieux de l'Orient*, ed. C. Langlès, 10 vols. and atlas, Paris 1810-11, v, 402-03; J. Aubin (ed.), *L'ambassade de Gregório Pereira Fidalgo à la cour de Châh Soltân Hosseyn 1696-1697*, Lisbon 1971, 33; G.F.G. Careri, *Giro del mondo*, 6 vols., Naples 1699, ii, 282; C. de Bruyn, *Reyse over Moskovië door Perzië en Indië*, Amsterdam 1711; Abbé Carré, *The travels of the Abbé Carré in India and the Near East*, tr. Lady Fawcett, 3 vols., London 1848, iii, 834-5; Muḥammad Mahdī b. Muḥammad Hādī S͟hīrāzī, *Tārīk͟h-i ṭahmāspiyya*, Staatsbibliothek Berlin, ms. Or. Sprenger 204, fol. 129a; C. Niebuhr, *Reisebeschreibungen nach Arabien und andren umliegenden Ländern*, 2 vols., Copenhagen 1774-8, ii, 92; E.S. Waring, *A tour to Sheeraz*, London 1807, 73, 148; W.A. Shepherd, *From Bombay to Bushire and Bussora*, London 1857; O. Blau, *Commercielle Zustände Persiens*, Berlin 1858; J.G. Lorimer (ed.), *Gazetteer of the Persian Gulf, 'Oman and Central Arabia*, i, *Historical*, Calcutta 1915; D͟j. Ḳā'im-maḳāmī (ed.), *Yak ṣad wa pand͟ja sanad-i tārīk͟hī az D͟jalā'iriyān tā Pahlawī*, Tehran 1348/1969, 49-50; Muḥammad ʿAlī Sadīd al-Salṭana, *Bandar ʿAbbās wa k͟halīd͟j-i Fars*, ed. ʿAlī Sitāyis͟h, Tehran 1363/1984.

2. Studies. J. Aubin, *Le royaume d'Ormuz au début du XVIe siècle*, in *Mare Luso-Indicum*, ii (1972), 148; W. Floor, *The customs in Qājār Iran*, in *ZDMG*, cxxvi (1976), 281-311; S.R. Grummon, *The rise and fall of the Arab Shaykhdom of Būshire 1750-1850*, Ph.D. diss., Johns Hopkins University 1985; B. Masters, *The origins of Western European dominance in the Middle East. Mercantilism and the Islamic economy in Aleppo, 1600-1750*, New York 1988, 57-8; R. Matthee, *Politics and trade in late Safavid Iran. Commercial crisis and government reaction under Shah Solayman (1666-1694)*, Ph.D. diss., University of California, Los Angeles 1991, 329-83; R. Klein, *Trade in the Safavid port city of Bandar Abbas and the Persian Gulf area (ca. 1600-1680). A study of selected aspects*, Ph.D. diss., University of London 1993-4, 82-8; Floor, *A fiscal history of Iran in the Safavid and Qajar periods 1500-1925*, New York 1998, 163-6; Masters, *Aleppo, the Ottoman Empire's caravan city*, in E. Eldem, D. Goffman and Masters (eds.), *The Ottoman city between east and west: Aleppo, Izmir, and Istanbul*, Cambridge 1999, 39; Matthee, *The politics of trade in Safavid Iran. Silk for silver, 1600-1730*, Cambridge 1999, 164.

(R. Matthee)

SHĀʿIR.

1. B. From the ʿAbbāsid period to the *Nahḍa*.

Poetic communication is part of a larger system of social communication governed by a particular set of rules and carried out by participants who are more or less aware of the value and meaning of these rules. The role of the poet is only one of several roles which are mutually co-formative. Any discussion of one of these social roles must perforce take into account the other roles. S.J. Schmidt (1992) described four action roles which are used below to inform the discussion of *s͟hāʿir*.

(a) *Production*. In the period between 750 and 1850, poetry was composed by a very different range of people from all walks of society in the Arab speaking world. Among the producers of poetry we find caliphs and craftsmen, secretaries and slaves, religious scholars and rogues, members of noble Arab tribes or people of non-Arab descent, rich and poor, famous and infamous. Of the three main panegyrists of the 3rd/9th century, Abū Tammām (d. *ca.* 231/845 [*q.v.*]) was of Christian descent (and embarrassed by this fact), and had to earn his living as a weaver's assistant and a water carrier in his early years; Ibn al-Rūmī (d. 283/896 [*q.v.*]) was of Christian (Byzantine) descent as well (and proud of it), whereas al-Buḥturī (d. 284/897 [*q.v.*]) was of pure Arab stock and grew up in a tribal milieu.

There was no uniform group of poets, nor was being a poet considered a specific profession with an established and definitive course of study or a canon of specific knowledge to be learned. Instead, everybody who had learned to compose poetry that met with common approval was called *s͟hāʿir.* Professional poets during the ʿAbbāsid period were primarily court poets who were financially dependent on the favour of a patron. In later periods, poets most typically came from the ranks of the *ʿulamā*ʾ. During the whole of the period in question, however, it was taken for granted that every educated person had the ability to take part in poetic communication, at least in the role of a receptive listener/reader. Therefore, poetry composed by professional poets forms only one segment of the poetry composed, esteemed and transmitted. Even those poets who can be considered professional poets often played more than the role of producer of poetry and engaged in processing literature as anthologists, critics, or philologists. Given this multi-layered situation, the role of poets and poetry in Arabic-Islamic society can be appreciated properly only if the whole of the system of poetic communication is taken into account. This is even more important given that poetic communication played an incomparably much higher role in pre-modern Arabic societies than in modern societies.

(b) *Mediation*. The oral recitation of a poem by its producer has always been considered the basic means by which poetry was made accessible to others. Professional singers were not only important but often even famous transmitters of poetry from the latter

Umayyad period onwards, not only in courtly arenas but also in other well-to-do households. Written transmission in the form of letters or books also played an increasingly important role. The output of individual poets was often collected in the form of a *dīwān*, frequently by those other than the original poets themselves. For example, it was Abū Bakr al-Ṣūlī (d. *ca.* 335/947 [*q.v.*]) who collected the *dīwān*s of Abū Nuwās, Abū Tammām, Ibn al-Rūmī and others. Of enormous importance for the transmission of poetry were anthologies [see MUKHTĀRĀT] and other works of *adab*. Both linguistic and historiographical works as well as collections of biographies contain a great deal of poetry. Religious texts of an edifying nature and Ṣūfī works are hardly to be found without poetry. After the rise of the *madrasa* [*q.v.*], the formal parameters of poetry (metre, rhyme) and peculiarities of literary language [see AL-MAʿĀNĪ WA 'L-BAYĀN] would become part of the propaedeutic discipline of *adab* (in this case meaning the whole of linguistic disciplines). Poetry itself, however, was not a regular subject in the curriculum. Only the most famous works, such as the *Dīwān* of al-Mutanabbī and the *Maḳāmāt* of al-Ḥarīrī, were taught within an academic framework. Story-tellers and preachers [see ḲĀṢṢ] included poems in their speeches and thus contributed to their own popularity among the masses. As a whole, the process by which poetry was imparted has not yet been studied adequately.

(c) *Reception.* Poetry was an everyday commodity. A poet could "réciter une *qaṣīda* à son entourage, à ses amis, à des confères. Qu'il aille dans les souks de la ville, parcourt ses rues, fréquente les cabarets de ses faubourgs et leurs jardins, descende son fleuve, ses canaux ou se poste sur l'un des ponts . . . ou sous les arcades de mosquées, dans le demeure d'un bourgeois ou d'un prince, partout . . . il peut déclamer sans étonner, parler d'amour sans surprendre, pleurer de douleur sans choquer" (Bencheikh, 38). Poetry was an effective system of communication in which a substantial part of the population took part and by which the emotional and affective requirements of the people were met. People listened to poetry for its social, emotional, and intellectual effect [see ṬARAB; TAʿADJDJUB], and it was considered the poet's task to convey information and to stir emotions, curiosity and interest rather than to express his own feelings. Modern modes of reception, influenced by the cult of the poet as a genius who is expected to be more in touch with deeper feelings and thoughts than other people, and the individualistic notion of poetry as a means to express one's very own and specific emotions, have often lead to misconceptions about pre-modern Arabic poetry. Whereas modern and individualistic conceptions of poetry have fostered an acceleration of literary change, they have also led to an increasing social marginalisation of poetic communication. By contrast, although the pre-modern understanding of poetry as a social activity resulted in a greater stability of literary forms and content, it nonetheless allowed poetry to remain effective and meaningful for a wide range of people over the whole period considered here and thus allowed a greater sector of the population to participate in elaborate artistic activities.

(d) *Processing.* The Arabic pre-Islamic literary and cultural heritage forms, next to Islam itself, one of the two foundations of Arabic-Islamic culture. The collection of and commentary on pre- and early Islamic poetry therefore was one of the primary activities in the first centuries of Islamic scholarship. The disciplines of grammar and lexicography owed their development more to the need to comment upon ancient Arabic poetry than upon the normative texts of Islam. This creation of a consciousness of poetry was one of the prerequisites for the rise of the scientific study of contemporary poetry and of literary criticism by the 3rd/9th century. These disciplines cannot be dealt with here (see the overview by Ouyang), but it should be remarked that, during the ʿAbbāsid period, literary history and criticism was a discourse clearly separated from the production of poetry itself, notwithstanding the exertion of mutual influence. Among the major poets, only Ibn al-Muʿtazz and Ibn Rashīḳ were famed theorists as well. The Mamlūk period, in which the merger of a secular and religious discourse had already been perfected, witnessed the complete synthesis of poetic production, on the one hand, and literary theory and rhetorics on the other in the form of the *badīʿiyya* commentaries by Ṣafī al-Dīn al-Ḥillī (d. probably 749/1348 [*q.v.*]) and Ibn Ḥidjdja al-Ḥamawī (d. 837/1434 [*q.v.*]), among others.

Other important forms by which literature was processed are various forms of intertextuality such as the *muʿāraḍa* or the *takhmīs* [*q.vv.*], in which a poet transforms a given poem into a new work of literature following special rules. These techniques should be understood within the framework of similar forms of appropriation-cum-transformation of the scholarly, cultural and literary heritage of Islamic culture, such as the commentary (*sharḥ* [*q.v.*]) or the abbreviation (*mukhtaṣar* [*q.v.*]).

Four important social environments provided a framework for educated poetic communication between the Umayyad and the modern period.

i. *The Court*

Throughout the entirety of the ʿAbbāsid period, the courts of the caliph(s), provincial rulers, governors and the court-like households of viziers, generals, and other high officials served as centres of literary activity of preeminent importance. Two kinds of literary activities should be distinguished here: first, the recitation of panegyric poems as part of the official representation of the ruler; and second, poetry as part of court entertainment.

Panegyric poems [see MADĪḤ] formed the most important political discourse throughout a great deal of Islamic history. In panegyric poems, the subject personage was described as an embodiment of royal virtue, above all in terms of military prowess and generosity. The recollection of these virtues simultaneously confirmed and reinforced them, for society as well as for the ruler himself, and by confirming the ruler's ideal fulfillment of these normative values, the poems contributed to his legitimisation. Further, they served to spread the news of important events (such as battles won), and helped to memorialise them and to locate them and their protagonists within a broader historical context.

To understand the mechanism of the panegyric poem, it is important to bear in mind that the patron, to whom the poem is addressed (the *mamdūḥ*), is not identical with the intended public of the poem. Of course, panegyric poems could fulfil their political and social role only if a general interest in them was granted. Therefore, the dichotomy of the poet and the *mamdūḥ*, which appears in the texts themselves, should be expanded to a triangle with the "public" as third participant. Each of the three participants in this form of communication acted in a mutually informative give and take. This triadic interplay can be generally schematized as follows:

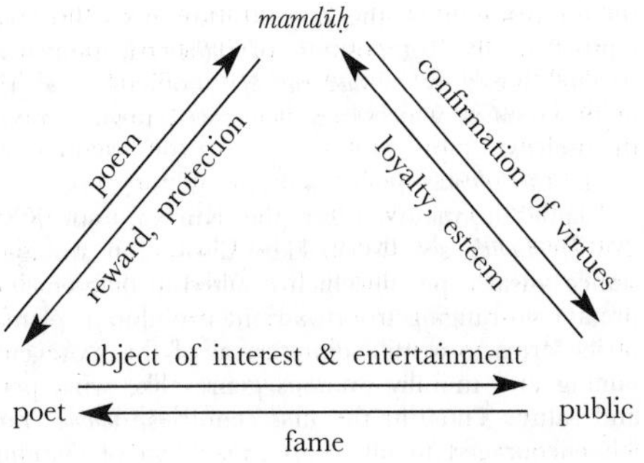

Given the first-rank importance of the panegyric-political discourse as a means of representation and legitimisation, even rulers who had no feeling for poetry could hardly afford not to patronise poets. On the other hand, many rulers and princes pursued an intense interest in poetry, had expert knowledge at their disposal, and often composed poetry themselves. Just to mention a few, the caliph Hārūn al-Rashīd (d. 193/809; his sister the princess ʿUlayya bt. al-Mahdī (d. 210/825); the prince Ibn al-Muʿtazz (d. 296/908), one of the greatest men of letters of the ʿAbbāsid period; the caliph al-Rāḍī bi ʾllāh (d. 392/940); the Ḥamdānid Sayf al-Dawla (d. 356/967); and the Ayyūbid Abu ʾl-Fidāʾ (d. 732/1331) [*q.vv.*] and other members of this dynasty. In such cases, where the *mamdūḥ* assumed both the role of the patron as well as the role of the public, poets had to accommodate their poems not only to general panegyric standards but also to the personal taste of the patron. To mention two examples: al-Buḥturī replaced the traditional *nasīb* [*q.v.*] with all its intertextual strands with the more modern genre of *ghazal* [*q.v.*] in order to meet the taste of al-Mutawakkil, who had less literary training than his predecessors. Ibn Nubāta al-Miṣrī (d. 750/1349 [*q.v.*]) faced the opposite problem after the death of Abu ʾl-Fidāʾ and tried to win the favour of his pious and ascetic successor by replacing the *nasīb* of his panegyric odes with ascetic poetry.

Panegyric poets hoped for an immediate reward for any given poem, which often reached rather exorbitant sums of money. Considering the fact that generosity was one of the main virtues praised in the panegyric odes and that the poet offered himself as a first object for the demonstration of this generosity, the exchange of poem for reward assumed the character of a ritual exchange. If successful, poets could even hope for a permanent patronage of the ruler, thus being spared having to wander from patron to patron. Al-Mutanabbī, the pre-eminent panegyric poet of the times, spent several years in search of a permanent patron, eulogising Bedouin chiefs and second-rank provincial dignitaries until he found the favour of Sayf al-Dawla, at whose court he spent nine untroubled years, only to start the search anew after an intrigue by his fellow-poets forced him to flee Sayf al-Dawla's court. In addition to material gains, success at a court could also provide for a broader fame of a poet due to the public nature of his task as a panegyrist. In any case, gaining the favour of patrons through panegyric poetry was nearly the only way to make a living as a professional poet during the ʿAbbāsid period. Poets who did not have an administrative or scholarly position as a starting-point therefore had to earn their living as a copyist or craftsman, or with similar jobs until they gained enough fame to be able to live as a full-time poet. Competition for a position as court poet must have been rather rigorous. Therefore, it is small wonder that the relations between the poets enjoying the favour of a certain patron is often characterised by envy, polemics and intrigues. The relations between al-Mutanabbī, Abū Firās and the Khālidī brothers offer a good example. Dependent as poets were on the favour of their patron, they were not completely powerless in turn. If they felt that they were treated unjustly, they had the possibility of taking revenge by composing satires (*hidjāʾ* [*q.v.*]), and the satires of a famous poet could prove to be a sharp weapon indeed. Again, al-Mutanabbī—an extraordinary self-confident poet—provides us with examples in his invectives against the Ikhshīd ruler Kāfūr [*q.v.*]. Many poets, however, experienced feelings of humilation when forced to "beg" for monetary reward for their poems, as is repeatedly told in their biographies.

The circumstances under which courtly panegyric poetry was performed have been only little studied so far. Obviously, panegyric poems were often performed as part of public ceremonies, during a *madjlis* or a banquet. The poems that were recited may have been pre-selected by court officials (al-Ḳifṭī, *Inbāh*, iv, 149). How these poems became known by a broader public has not yet been explored in detail. The poets themselves, philologists, compilers of anthologies and literary critics may have participated as mediators in this process. In the end, however, this process must have been rather effective, since in most books on literary criticism, panegyric poetry is given privileged interest, and anthologies and chronicles overflow with quotations of eulogies. Since without the participation of the recipients, the process of panegyric communication must have been ineffective as a whole, the study of this part must be considered a major desideratum.

In addition to the ritual and public performance of panegyric poetry, courtly life offered a great many other opportunities for poetry making. Hunting excursions provided an opportunity for the recitation of hunting poetry (*tardiyya* [*q.v.*]); banquets and musical gatherings gave rise to the presentation of wine poetry [see KHAMRIYYA], love poetry and other genres. On these occasions, the ruler was accompanied by his *nudamāʾ* "boon-companions" (sing. *nadīm* [*q.v.*]), a group of talented people from various fields. Even the office of the *nadīm* was institutionalised at the ʿAbbāsid court. Poetry played a prominent role in the gatherings of the ruler and his *nudamāʾ*, and was practiced not only by professional poets but also by *nudamāʾ* with other professions. And poetry itself, both ancient and contemporary, was often the subject of conversation in the *madjlis*. It must be stressed that the kind of poetry recited and sung in these courtly environments was not fundamentally different from that practised outside the court in urban milieux. Therefore, a common term like "courtly love" characterising the relations between lover and beloved in a current type of love poetry (*ghazal*, *nasīb*) is misleading, since love poetry sung at caliphal banquets in no way differed from the poetry that was popular in other social environments. Instead, it was rather the ideals, ethical models, and literary tastes of the *udabāʾ* and *kuttāb* which dominated at the courts [see ẒARF]. *Nudamāʾ* circles also existed in the households of viziers and high-ranking *kuttāb*, and the same people practised their poetic skill in circles of philologists and *udabāʾ* as well as in their role as *nadīm* at the court.

In the period after the fall of the ʿAbbāsids and

Ayyūbids, the importance of the court for Arab literary culture decreased considerably. Though panegyric poems in the Arabic language were still composed about Mamlūk and Ottoman sultans (and poets duly rewarded for them), the Mamlūk and Ottoman courts no longer offered the resources for a vivid literary culture in Arabic language. One of the main reasons for this development is, of course, the fact that rulers of these dynasties often had only limited (if any) command of the Arabic language. But it should also be borne in mind that, whereas in the ʿAbbāsid period political authorities were part of the culture of the civilian non-religious élite of the *kuttāb* and were eager to see their legitimisation expressed in the medium of poetry common to both, the post-ʿAbbāsid period witnessed the merger of a religious and non-religious élite, which now formed a counterpart to the military élite which no longer shared this culture. Rather than poetry, Mamlūks instead patronised architecture to an hitherto unprecedented extent.

ii. *The kuttāb*

At least in the 3rd and 4th/9th and 10th centuries, the class of the secretaries (*kuttāb*, sing. *kātib* [*q.v.*]), which formed a rather homogenous group with a distinct group consciousness, had no lesser influence on the shaping of Islamic culture than the group of religious scholars. This is especially true in the field of literature. The *kuttāb* were the bearers and main exponents of the culture of *adab* [*q.v.*], which meant not only producing a certain type of literature but also adhering to an ideal of education, knowledge, manners and conduct, which became manifest in the literature called *adab*. Of course, not every *adīb* was a *kātib*, but the *kuttāb* serve as its most typical embodiment.

For the *kuttāb*, poetry had a multitude of functions. Some of them, to mention a few, are as following:

(a) Perfection in artistic prose and poetry was a prerequisite for other responsibilities. These included drafting and writing official letters and administrative correspondence in which they showed their mastery of linguistic correctness and stylistic sophistication.

(b) *Kuttāb* were expected to be able to compose poetry. In this context, it seems plausible that the first dictionary that was arranged according to rhyme consonants and rhyme schemes, the *Kitāb al-Taḳfiya* by al-Bandanīdjī (d. 284/897; Sezgin, *GAS*, viii, 170-1) was in all probability addressed to the *kuttāb* who needed to find rhyme words for their poetic compositions.

(c) Poetry formed part of the encyclopaedic knowledge *kuttāb* were supposed to have.

(d) Genres like love and wine poetry, besides being entertaining and emotionally affective at an individual level, were especially suitable for not only expressing the refined *Weltanschauung* of this group [see ẒARĪF] but also for displaying their literary taste.

(e) Literature of the *adab* type in prose and poetry was part of the *kuttāb*'s life-style and its practice served to strengthen their group identity.

Some of the *kātib* poets typical of the 3rd/9th and 4th/10th centuries were: al-ʿUtbī (d. 228/852-3), Ibn al-Zayyāt (d. 233/847), the *ghazal* poet Khālid b. Yazīd al-Kātib (d. *ca.* 262/876), al-Nāshiʾ al-Akbar (d. 293/906), Ibn Bassām (d. 303-4/914-15), Abū Isḥāq al-Ṣābiʾ (d. 384/994), Ibn ʿAbbād (d. 385/995) [*q.vv.*], and Ibrāhīm al-Ṣūlī (d. 243/857). The influence of the *kuttāb*, however, went far beyond their activity as poets: more importantly, they shaped the culture of *adab*, which proved equally dominant in courtly milieux as well as in the urban middle class in general. A sharp distinction between the court and the *kuttāb* cannot be drawn in any event, since *kuttāb* were themselves part of the courts. Many of them participated in the composition of panegyric poetry and fulfilled the duty of *nadīm*. Many officials had risen to positions in which they acted as patrons for poets themselves.

iii. *The ʿulamāʾ*

Islamic normative texts (the Ḳurʾān, esp. XXVI, 224-7; *Ḥadīth*, see Bonebakker) display an ambiguous stance towards poetry which resulted in different interpretations, ranging from outright prohibition of many of its forms to a mild disapproval of the more entertaining and morally dubious genres like wine poetry and satire. Thus, in the first centuries, *ʿulamāʾ* rarely felt encouraged to take part in a form of communication that was dominated by the secular élite. Yet religious scholars required knowledge of pre- and early Islamic poetry in order to be able to comment upon Ḳurʾān and *Ḥadīth*, and some of them composed at least poetry of the *zuhdiyya* [*q.v.*] genre, as the collection of poetry ascribed to al-Shāfiʿī (d. 204/820 [*q.v.*]) demonstrates. Due to its emotional effectiveness, poetry of the *zuhdiyya* genre, as well as love poetry was used in sermons. However, scholars were rarely proficient poets, and in his collection of the biographies of linguistic scholars, al-Ḳifṭī repeatedly speaks with derision of grammarians and other scholars who "composed verses of the kind of the poetry of grammarians (*nuḥāt*)/scholars (*ʿulamāʾ*)" (al-Ḳifṭī, *Inbāh*, iii, 219, 263, 267, 288, 343, iv, 165). Nevertheless, from the latter ʿAbbāsid period onwards, there is an increase in the number of *ʿulamāʾ* who were composing poetry in different genres. A few *ḳāḍīs* and *muḥaddithūn* are already mentioned in al-Thaʿālibī's [*q.v.*] anthology titled *Yatīmat al-dahr*, which contains poetry from the second half of the 4th/10th century. By the time of ʿImād al-Dīn al-Iṣfahānī's [*q.v.*] anthology, the *Kharīdat al-ḳaṣr*, which covers poets from the 6th/12th century, the number of *ʿulamāʾ* composing poetry and the quality of their poems had obviously increased considerably. Here, in this period of transition, we can witness the gradual merger between the *adab*-oriented culture of the *kuttāb* and the *sunna*-oriented culture of the *ʿulamāʾ* (Bauer, *Raffinement*; Homerin, *Preaching poetry*). From the Saldjūḳ period onwards, the *kuttāb* gradually ceased to be a distinct social group with their own cultural values. Instead, the duties of the *kātib* came to be fulfilled by people who had received the training of a religious scholar. The result, as it becomes very obvious during the Mamlūk period, was a rather homogeneous group of *ʿulamāʾ* who had become the bearers of Islamic religious as well as secular culture. Remarkably, this development did not prove detrimental to literary culture. Instead, the process of "'*ulamāʾ*isation of *adab*" was counterbalanced by a process of "*adab*isation of the *ʿulamāʾ*", who in the meantime had made the *adab* discourse of the *kuttāb* their own. Though the political relevance of poetry decreased, its relevance for the civil élite increased, so that one can speak of a process of privatisation of poetry. Poetry became a pre-eminent medium of communication between *ʿulamāʾ*, and this medium included panegyric poetry, which now became addressed from one *ʿālim* to the other rather than to rulers and military leaders. For the *ʿulamāʾ*, it would become more and more important to be able to take part in this form of poetic communication. Consequently, the poetry of the Mamlūk period grew more personal and more interested in private matters. The merger of the secular and religious élite into a new group which shared to a considerable extent the values and ideas of the old religious élite, but which also had appropriated the literary culture of the old secular élite, led to an unprecedented rise of religious poetry. Since also the boundaries between high and popular culture became blurred, the percentage of the population taking part in a rather homogeneous literary culture became larger than ever. The Mamlūk period, therefore, may have been the period which displayed the broadest literary culture in Arab history.

The Ottoman period has not been studied well enough to allow a more detailed assessment. At least, it is beyond doubt that the *ʿulamāʾ* still played the most important role in poetry. Arabic poetry at this time may have witnessed a decrease in its local importance, but at the same time could expand its geographical range due to the increasingly global and cosmopolitan character of the *ʿulamāʾ*. Texts displaying a very similar literary taste were composed in Sub-Saharan Africa as well as in the Indian subcontinent. Locally, Ṣūfī circles seem to have developed into one of the main centres of the production of poetry.

iv. *Urban milieux*

A study of the involvement of different social environments of the urban middle classes in the poetic discourse has not yet been carried out. However, it is clear from countless hints in the sources that poetry in the standard language and the established genres was esteemed and even produced among craftsmen, merchants, and in similar milieux. The site of Abū Nuwās's (d. *ca.* 196/813 [*q.v.*]) wine poems is not only the courtly banquet but also the tavern. Another and rather different urban milieu was that of the *ẓurafāʾ*, in which the poems of al-ʿAbbās b. al-Aḥnaf [*q.v.*] are set. Several little-known poets mentioned in Ibn al-Muʿtazz's *Ṭabaḳāt al-shuʿarāʾ* bear names pointing to crafts, and even professional poets like Abū Tammām had to earn their living by manual work before they were famous enough to live from their poetry. In any case, social boundaries were not as strict as in Europe, and people of low descent and non-privileged social positions were not in principle excluded from taking part in high culture.

In the 4th/10th century we find a baker (al-Khabbāz al-Baladī, see Sezgin, *GAS*, ii, 625-6), a fruit-seller (al-Waʾwāʾ [*q.v.*]), and a darner (al-Sarī al-Raffāʾ [*q.v.*]) among the well-known poets of the age. Another poet, al-Khubzaʾaruzzī [*q.v.*], was a baker of rice bread in Baṣra and became famous as a *ghazal* poet. Young men from all over the town used to visit his shop in the hope of becoming the object of one of his love poems. By quoting poems by al-Aḥnaf al-ʿUkbarī, al-Thaʿālibī (*Yatīma*, ii, 122-4) allows a glimpse of the poetry of the vagabonds [see SĀSĀN, BANŪ]. These poets owe their lasting fame to the fact that representatives of high culture took an interest in their productions, but they may also be taken as evidence of the kind of interest in poetry that cut across different levels of society.

Sources are much more copious for the Mamlūk period, during which a convergence between high and popular culture is attested. The most representative figures of popular poetry (in standard Arabic, as well as in dialect), appealing to *ʿulamāʾ* and people of the street alike, were Ibrāhīm al-Miʿmār for the 7th/13th and Ibn Sūdūn for the 8th/14th century. These and quite a few of other similar, often illiterate figures represent a "missing link" between modern forms of popular literature and time-honoured forms, themes, and motives, and thus point to the fact that Arabic literary culture was not the exclusive prerequisite of a small élitarian group, but was, at least in its fundamental parameters, ideas and way of achieving emotional effects, shared by a broad sector of the population.

During the Mamlūk and Ottoman periods, religious poetry was extremely popular in all urban environments. Ṣūfī poetry, prayers [see WIRD] and poems in praise of the prophet [see MAWLIDIYYA] were composed and recited among adherents of the Ṣūfī orders [see ṬARĪḲA and TAṢAWWUF], which were deeply rooted in the middle classes.

During all periods, different forms of folk poetry co-existed alongside poetry which was eventually written down. In many environments, both written and oral forms of poetry influenced each other, and sometimes it is not easy to draw a clear boundary between them. Other forms of poetry transmitted only orally existed without being noticed by the educated. So, for example, Bedouin poets continued to compose poetry in a style reminiscent of pre-Islamic poetry throughout the centuries. This can be deduced by the existence of the so-called *nabaṭī* poetry [*q.v.*] which has been recorded from the 19th century onwards and is still practised in the Arabian peninsula even today. For further information about the complex of folk poetry, see SHĀʿIR. 1. E. The folk poet in Arab society, at Vol. IX, 233b.

Bibliography: Only a small selection of relevant sources and studies can be noted here. In principle, all *dīwāns*, anthologies, and biographical dictionaries are fruitful sources of relevant information. See also the *Bibl.* of the article SHIʿR. 1(a), and Abu 'l-Faradj al-Iṣbahānī, *Aghānī*[3]; Ibn al-Muʿtazz, *Ṭabaḳāt al-shuʿarāʾ al-muḥdathīn*, Cairo 1956; al-ʿImād al-Iṣfahānī, *Kharīdat al-ḳaṣr* (different eds.); (Ibn) al-Ḳifṭī, *Inbāh al-ruwāt*, 4 vols., Cairo 1955-73; Abū Bakr al-Ṣūlī, *Akhbār Abi 'l-Tammām*, Cairo 1937; idem, *Akhbār al-Buḥturī*, Damascus 1948; idem, *Akhbār al-Rāḍī wa 'l-Muttaḳī*, ed. J.H. Dunne, Cairo 1935; Ṣafadī, *al-Wāfī*; Thaʿālibī, *Yatīma*, Cairo 1375-7/1956-8; A. Arazi, *Amour divin et amour profane dans l'Islam médiéval. A travers le Dīwān de Khālid al-Kātib*, Paris 1990; T. Bauer, *Raffinement und Frömmigkeit. Säkulare Poesie islamischer Religionsgelehrter der späten Abbasidenzeit*, in *Asiatische Studien*, v (1996), 275-95; idem, *Liebe und Liebesdichtung in der arabischen Welt des 9. und 10. Jahrhunderts*, Wiesbaden 1998; idem, *Ibrāhīm al-Miʿmār. Ein dichtender Handwerker aus Ägyptens Mamlukenzeit*, in *ZDMG*, clii (2002), 63-93; J. Bencheikh, *Poetique arabe: essai sur les voies d'une création*, Paris 1975; idem, *Les secrétaires poètes et animateurs de cénacles aux IIe et IIIe siècles de l'hégire*, in *JA*, clxiii (1975), 265-315; idem, *Le cénacle poétique du calife al-Mutawakkil*, in *BEO*, xxix (1977), 33-52; S.A. Bonebakker, *Religious prejudice against poetry in early Islam*, in *Medievalia et humanistica*, n.s. vii (1976), 77-99; G.J. van Gelder, *The bad and the ugly. Attitudes towards invective poetry (Hijāʾ) in Classical Arabic literature*, Leiden 1988; B. Gruendler, *Ibn al-Rūmī's ethics of patronage*, in *Harvard Middle Eastern and Islamic Review*, iii (1996), 104-60; G.E. von Grunebaum, *Aspects of Arabic urban literature mostly in ninth and tenth centuries*, in *Islamic Studies (Islamabad)*, viii (1969), 281-300; A. Hamori, *On the art of medieval Arabic literature*, New York 1974; Th.E. Homerin, *Preaching poetry*, in *Arabica*, xxxviii (1991), 87-101; ʿAbd al-Ḥasanayn al-Khiḍr, *al-Shuʿarāʾ al-Ayyūbiyyūn*, 2 vols., Damascus 1993-6; H. Kilpatrick, *Making the great Book of Songs*, London 2003; E. Neubauer, *Musiker am Hof der frühen ʿAbbasiden*, Frankfurt 1965; W. Ouyang, *Literary criticism in medieval Arabic-Islamic culture. The making of a tradition*, Edinburgh 1997; E.K. Rowson and

S.A. Bonebakker, *A computerized listing of biographical data from the Yatīmat al-Dahr by al-Thaʿālibī*, Malibu 1980; S.J. Schmidt, *Conventions and literary systems*, in M. Hjort (ed.), *Rules and conventions*, Baltimore 1992, 215-49; A. Vrolijk, *Bringing a laugh to a scowling face*, Leiden 1998; E. Wagner, *Abū Nuwās*, Wiesbaden 1965. (T. Bauer)

SHAKHAB, (Battle of) [see mardj al-ṣuffar].

SHĀLĪSH, also written Djālīsh, a term referring to either the vanguard of an army or a flag raised to signal the announcement of a campaign. The word is of Turkish origin, derived from *Čalïsh*, meaning "battle" or "conflict" (see G. Doerfer, *Türkische und mongolische Elemente in Neupersischen*, Wiesbaden 1963-75, iii, 32). It appears in Persian during the late Saldjūḳ era (Rāwandī, *Rāḥat al-ṣudūr*, ed. M. Iqbál, GMS, NS, 2, London 1921, 347), with the meaning of "battle"; in Arabic, it is found in works of the Ayyūbid and Mamlūk times (see below). It is unclear whether it entered Arabic via the Persian or was adopted in the former language directly from Turkish military men.

1. In the sense of advance troops of a rather general nature, the term is found in the description of the battle of Ḥiṭṭīn [*q.v.*] in 584/1187, where we find *djālīshiyya* (Bahā' al-Dīn Ibn Shaddād, *Nawādir al-sulṭāniyya*, Cairo n.d., 61 = tr. D.S. Richards, *The rare and excellent history of Saladin*, Aldershot 2001, 73; Ibn al-Athīr, *Kāmil*, Beirut 1987, xi, 146). In the early Mamlūk period, it is used on the one hand as a synonym for *ṭalīʿa*, advanced scouts or vanguard, as at the battle of ʿAyn Djālūt [*q.v.*] in 658/1260 (cf. Ibn al-Dawādarī, *Kanz al-durar*, viii, ed U. Haarmann, Freiburg-Cairo 1971, 49, with al-Maḳrīzī, *Sulūk*, Cairo 1934-73, i, 430). On the other hand, in the battle of Ḥimṣ [*q.v.*] in 680/1281, *djālīsh* is used in the sense of *muḳaddama*, i.e. the large forward division of the Mamlūk army (Baybars al-Manṣūrī, *Zubda*, ed. Richards, Beirut 1998, 197). The term was not only applied to the Mamlūk army; in 699/1299, the *djālīsh* of the Il-Khān Ghāzān [*q.v.*] passed by Ḥalab on the way south (al-Maḳrīzī, *Sulūk*, i, 885); the exact intention, i.e. whether it was a small reconnaissance unit or a large advance division, is unclear from the context.

2. In the sense of a flag raised above the *ṭablkhāna* [*q.v.*], see D. Ayalon, art. ḥarb. iii, above, Vol. III, at 184. Ibn Khaldūn (*Muḳaddama*, ed. Muṣṭafā Muḥammad, Cairo n.d. = tr. Rosenthal, ii, 52), writes that in the Mamlūk state (*dawlat al-turk*), a large flag (*rāya*) surmounted by a big tuft of hair (probably of a horse) was called a *shalīsh*, and that it was a sign of the sultan. It would seem that the use of the word for the flag used to declare preparations for a campaign was secondary to the meaning given above, sc. the advance force or vanguard. The sense of flag was derived perhaps from the advance force which may have carried it.

Bibliography: Besides the sources and studies given above, see E. Quatremère, *Histoire des sultans mamlouks de l'Égypte*, Paris 1837-45, i/1, 225-7 (with numerous examples from the Ayyūbid and Mamlūk sources giving both contemporary meanings); Dozy, *Supplément*, i, 168. (R. Amitai)

SHAMIR (also al-Shamir, commonly Shimr) b. **DHI 'l-DJAWSHAN** Abu 'l-Sābigha, often portrayed as one of the killers of al-Ḥusayn b. ʿAlī [*q.v.*]. Shamir's father, Shuraḥbīl (or Aws) b. Ḳurṭ (various forms of the name are given), was a Companion of the Prophet who settled in al-Kūfa.

Shamir fought at Ṣiffīn [*q.v.*] on ʿAlī's side, receiving a sword wound to his face (al-Minḳarī, *Waḳʿat Ṣiffīn*, ed. ʿA. Hārūn, Cairo 1401/1981, 268; al-Ṭabarī, i, 3305). Subsequently he changed sides and became a supporter of the Umayyads. In 51/671 he testified against Ḥudjr b. ʿAdī [*q.v.*] (*ibid.*, ii, 133); nine years later, ʿUbayd Allāh b. Ziyād [*q.v.*] recruited him and other tribal notables to quell the revolt of Muslim b. ʿAḳīl [*q.v.*]. When al-Ḥusayn was intercepted at Karbalā', he appealed in vain to Shamir and others to let him go to the caliph Yazīd (*ibid.*, ii, 285). Shamir prevailed upon Ibn Ziyād to adopt an uncompromising attitude towards al-Ḥusayn; Ibn Ziyād thereupon gave him a letter ordering ʿUmar b. Saʿd to kill al-Ḥusayn should he refuse to submit to Ibn Ziyād's authority, and warning ʿUmar that if he failed to obey this order he would be replaced as commander by Shamir (*ibid.*, ii, 315-6). ʿUmar reluctantly obeyed and put Shamir in charge of the foot-soldiers (al-Balādhurī, iii, 391; al-Ṭabarī, ii, 317). On 9 Muḥarram 61/9 October 680, as ʿUmar was making final preparations to do battle with al-Ḥusayn, Shamir offered a safe-conduct to three (or four) sons of ʿAlī by Umm al-Banīn bt. Ḥizām, who belonged to Shamir's tribe, the Banū Kilāb; the sons rejected the offer, insisting that al-Ḥusayn, too, should be granted safe-conduct (al-Balādhurī, iii, 391; Ibn Aʿtham, iii, 105; cf. al-Ṭabarī, ii, 316-7).

The next morning—the Day of ʿĀshūrā'—ʿUmar put Shamir in command of the army's left wing (*ibid.*, ii, 326). Shamir intended to burn down al-Ḥusayn's tent with the women and children inside, but was shamed into withdrawing (*ibid.*, ii, 346-7) and acceded to al-Ḥusayn's request to spare them (al-Balādhurī, iii, 407; al-Ṭabarī, ii, 362). Shamir's role in the death of al-Ḥusayn is disputed in the sources. While some accounts merely refer to his participation in the battle (e.g. Ibn ʿAsākir, xxiii, 186), he is more usually said to have instigated the final assault, while yet other reports explicitly mention him as having killed al-Ḥusayn (al-Wāḳidī, in al-Balādhurī, iii, 418; al-Iṣfahānī, 119; Ibn Ḥazm, *Djamharat ansāb al-ʿarab*, ed. ʿA. Hārūn, Cairo 1382/1962, 287), as having decapitated his corpse (al-Ṣafadī, xii, 425, xvi, 180), or both (al-Madjlisī, xlv, 56; cf. al-Ṭabrisī, 250). This conflicts with reports that it was Sinān b. Anas al-Nakhaʿī who killed al-Ḥusayn and decapitated his body (Abū Mikhnaf, in al-Ṭabarī, ii, 366), or that Sinān killed him and Khawalī b. Yazīd al-Aṣbaḥī cut off his head (al-Balādhurī, iii, 418; cf. Ibn ʿAbd al-Barr, i, 393). In the *taʿziya* [*q.v.*] passion plays, Shamir is habitually presented as al-Ḥusayn's killer (Chelkowski, 15, 106, 110, 146-7, 159, 165; Ayoub, 127) and as more evil even than Sinān (Virolleaud, 94-5; Chelkowski, 160).

After the battle, Shamir was about to kill al-Ḥusayn's son ʿAlī [see zayn al-ʿābidīn], but was prevented from doing so (Ibn Saʿd, i, 480). Shamir led the Hawāzin, who formed one of the contingents that brought the heads of the fallen warriors to Ibn Ziyād (al-Ṭabarī, ii, 386; Ibn Ṭāwūs, 85); later he accompanied the survivors to Damascus (al-Ṭabarī, ii, 375). An address is preserved in which he recounts to Yazīd the events of Karbalā' (al-Dīnawarī, 260-1, cited in D.M. Donaldson, *The Shiʿite religion*, London 1933, 102-3; this same address, however, is also ascribed to Zaḥr b. Ḳays al-Djuʿfī: see al-Ṭabarī, ii, 374-5). Back in al-Kūfa, Shamir is said to have repented of his actions, explaining that he had been duty-bound to obey Ibn Ziyād (al-Dhahabī, *Mīzān al-iʿtidāl*, ed. ʿA. Muʿawwaḍ and ʿA. ʿAbd al-Mawdjūd, Beirut 1416/1995, iii, 385; cf. Ibn Saʿd, i, 499; Ibn ʿAsākir, xxiii, 189).

In 66/686 Shamir was among the Kūfan *ashrāf* who rose against al-Mukhtār [*q.v.*]. After they had been defeated at Djabbānat al-Sabīʿ (in al-Kūfa), al-Mukhtār sent his slave Zirbī in pursuit of Shamir, but Shamir attacked and killed him (al-Balādhurī, vi, 407; al-Ṭabarī, ii, 661). Unlike many of the defeated leaders, Shamir did not flee to al-Baṣra, but went to Sādamā/Sātīdamā (apparently between al-Kūfa and al-Baṣra) (al-Dīnawarī, 302; al-Ṭabarī, ii, 662) and then encamped by the village of al-Kaltāniyya (or al-Kalbāniyya) (*ibid.*, ii, 662; Ibn ʿAsākir, xxiii, 191). From there he sent a letter to Muṣʿab b. al-Zubayr [*q.v.*] in al-Baṣra. The letter was intercepted by one of Abū ʿAmra's men [see KAYSĀN], and its carrier revealed Shamir's hiding-place, to which cavalrymen were dispatched. Shamir, realising that he was surrounded, tried to fight his way out but was killed by one of the attackers (al-Balādhurī, vi, 407; al-Ṭabarī, ii, 663). According to one report, Abū ʿAmra sent the badly wounded Shamir to al-Mukhtār, who killed him (al-Madjlisī, xlv, 338). Elsewhere Shamir is said to have been killed at al-Madhār (on the Tigris) and his head brought to al-Mukhtār, who sent it on to Muḥammad Ibn al-Ḥanafiyya [*q.v.*] in Medina (al-Dīnawarī, 305).

Shamir's grandson al-Ṣumayl b. Ḥātim [*q.v.*] played a prominent role in al-Andalus before the establishment there of the Umayyad dynasty.

Bibliography (in addition to references given in the article): 1. Sources. Ibn al-Kalbī-Caskel, *Ǧamharat an-nasab*, Leiden 1966, i, table 98; Ibn Saʿd, *al-Ṭabaḳāt al-kubrā: al-ṭabaḳa al-khāmisa min al-ṣaḥāba*, ed. M. al-Sulamī, al-Ṭāʾif 1414/1993, i, 465-6, 469, 473, 499-500; Khalīfa b. Khayyāṭ, *Taʾrīkh*, ed. A. al-ʿUmarī, Nadjaf 1386/1987, i, 225; Ibn Ḳutayba, *al-Maʿārif*, ed. Th. ʿUkāsha, Cairo 1981, 481, 582; Balādhurī, *Ansāb*, ed. S. Zakkār and R. Ziriklī, Beirut 1417/1996, iii, 383, 390, 395-7, 399, 401, 402, 407-9, 412, 416, 418-19, 423, 425, v, 263, vi, 389, 398, 399; Dīnawarī, *al-Akhbār al-ṭiwāl*, ed. ʿA. ʿĀmir and Dj. al-Shayyāl, Cairo 1960, index; Ṭabarī, index; Ibn Aʿtham, *al-Futūḥ*, Beirut 1406/1986, iii, 99, 103-5, 110-11, 134-6, 138; Abu 'l-Faradj al-Iṣfahānī, *Maḳātil al-ṭālibiyyīn*, ed. A. Ṣaḳr, Beirut n.d., 114, 116, 118; Ibn Bābawayh, *Amālī*, Nadjaf 1389/1970, 137, 144; al-Shaykh al-Mufīd, *al-Irshād*, Beirut 1399/1979, 229-30, 233-4, 237-8, 240-3, 245; Ibn ʿAbd al-Barr, *al-Istīʿāb fī maʿrifat al-aṣḥāb*, Cairo 1380/1960, i, 393-5, 467-8; Ṭabrisī, *Iʿlām al-warā*, Nadjaf 1390/1970, 236, 240, 245, 248-51, 253; Ibn ʿAsākir, *Taʾrīkh madīnat Dimashḳ*, ed. al-ʿAmrawī, Beirut 1415/1995 ff., xxiii, 186-92; Ibn Shahrāshūb, *Manāḳib āl Abī Ṭālib*, Beirut 1405/1985, iv, 77, 97-8, 106, 111, 112; Ibn al-Athīr, *al-Lubāb fī tahdhīb al-ansāb*, Beirut n.d., ii, 258-9; Ibn Ṭāwūs, *al-Luhūf fī ḳatlā 'l-Ṭufūf*, Beirut 1414/1993, 54, 71, 84, 101-2; Irbilī, *Kashf al-ghumma*, Beirut 1405/1985, ii, 258, 262, 265, 268, 276; Ibn Ḥadjar al-ʿAsḳalānī, *Lisān al-mīzān*, Beirut 1407-8/1987-8, iii, 185; Madjlisī, *Biḥār al-anwār*, Tehran 1376-94/1956-74, xliv, 198, 322, 349, 386, 390-1, xlv, 4-7, 20-1, 27, 31, 51, 54-7, 60-2, 107, 127, 130, 246, 264, 273, 283, 289, 312, 337, 342, 372, 373-4.

2. Studies. Ch. Virolleaud, *Le théâtre persan ou Le drame de Kerbéla*, Paris 1950, 44-9, 58-9. 94-8, 102; M. Ayoub, *Redemptive suffering in Islām*, The Hague 1978, index; S.H.M. Jafri, *The origins and early development of Shīʿa Islam*, London 1979, 187, 189-192; P.J. Chelkowski (ed.), *Taʿziyeh. Ritual and drama in Iran*, New York 1979, index.

(E. KOHLBERG)

AL-**SHARAF**, more exactly Sharaf Ḥadjūr or Sharaf Ḥadjdja, the mediaeval name of a mountainous region of northern Yemen, some 100-120 km/62-75 miles northwest of Ṣanʿāʾ, today called al-Sharafān/al-Sharafayn. The extended forms of the name are to distinguish it from several homonymous al-Sharafs, Ḥadjūr being a tribal name and Ḥadjdja a nearby town. The form al-Sharaf survives today only in the toponym Kuḥlān al-Sharaf, a local town (lat. 16° 02' N. and long. 43° 28' E.) and its district. The dual form appears already in Ayyūbid times, when al-Sharaf al-Asfal and al-Sharaf al-Aʿlā are distinguished (see e.g. G.R. Smith, *The Ayyūbids and early Rasūlids in the Yemen*, London 1974-8).

The chain of the Djibāl al-Sharafayn reaches an altitude of 2,180 m/7,150 feet, forming an arc overlooking the coastal Tihāma. The massif gives its name to a *ḳaḍāʾ*, with the chef-lieu of al-Maḥābisha in the province (*muḥāfaẓa*) of Ḥadjdja. In the early 1980s, the population of the region was *ca.* 220,000, these being Zaydīs, with the Banu 'l-Sharafī, ʿAlid descendants of the founder of the Zaydī dynasty of Yemen, being the most important lineage there.

Al-Sharaf al-Aʿlā denotes the northern part of al-Sharafān, whereas al-Sharaf al-Asfal denotes the slightly lower, more southern region, although it seems that in the time of al-Hamdānī (4th/10th century), the former denoted another region, that of Sharaf Akyān or Shibām Akyān (modern Shibām Kawkabān), to the southeast (ed. Müller, 107 ll. 17-18, 135 l. 8). The name of al-Sharafān appears very often in the Yemeni chronicles.

In fact, there are numerous al-Sharafs in Yemen, reflecting the term's basic meaning of "eminence, height", hence it is not surprising that Yāḳūt had difficulty distinguishing various homonyms (see Ismāʿīl al-Akwaʿ, *al-Buldān al-yamāniyya ʿind Yāḳūt al-Ḥamawī*, Kuwait 1405/1985, 155).

Al-Sharaf does not appear in pre-Islamic inscriptions, but Ḥadjūr is attested once as *Hgr Lmd* (Ja 616/25) for a small tribe belonging to the Dawʾat federation confronting the Sabaean king Nashaʾkarib Yuhaʾmin Yuharḥib *ca.* A.D. 260-270 (A. Jamme, *Sabaean inscriptions from Mahram Bilqîs (Mârib)*, Baltimore 1962, 113-17).

Bibliography: Given in the article. See also R.T.O. Wilson, *Gazetteer of historical North-West Yemen in the Islamic period to 1650*, Hildesheim, etc. 1989.

(CH. ROBIN and AHMAD AL-GHUMARI)

AL-**SHARAF**, the modern Aljarafe, an *iḳlīm* or county situated within the *kūra* or province of Ishbīliyya/Seville in the Gharb of mediaeval al-Andalus. The extent of this *iḳlīm* varies: in al-Rāzī, 7,000 km² and in al-Idrīsī, 1,650 km². Beginning from the neighbourhood of Seville, it stretched to the limit of the *kūra* of Labla in the Guadiamar or Tinto river valleys.

The Arabic sources describe the richness of its olive trees and the quality of their oil. The Sevillans sold this, after keeping it for two years, not only within the Iberian peninsula but also as far as the Far Maghrib, Egypt and the Atlantic regions of Christian Europe; this was an exceptional case of a specialised culture oriented towards distant markets. The most important writers of agronomy in al-Andalus practiced their skills in al-Sharaf, including Ibn Ḥadjdjādj (5th/11th century), Abu 'l-Khayr (5th-6th/11th-12th centuries) and Ibn al-ʿAwwām (6th-7th/12th-13th centuries).

Within the *kūra* of Ishbīliyya, the link between political authority and the great landowners is clear. The Banu 'l-Ḥadjdjādj and the Banū Khaldūn owned the greater part of the land—according to the Arabic sources, as the result of a marriage between an Arab chief of the conquest period and Sara the Visigoth—and these two families long governed Seville.

The enemies of the Sevillans on various occasions launched raids which ravaged the *iḳlīm* of al-Sharaf, e.g. the Berbers, during the early part of the *fitna*, Alfonso VI during the reign of al-Muʿtamid Ibn ʿAbbād [*q.v.*] and the Portuguese during the Almohad period.

The *iḳlīm* was very densely populated in Hispano-Roman and Islamic times, with al-Idrīsī mentioning a figure of over 800 *kuwar* or villages. In regard to demography, two periods should be distinguished. During the pre-Almohad period (i.e. from the Arab conquest to the second half of the 6th/12th century), al-Sharaf formed, as from Hispano-Roman times onwards, a very populous region with many small villages spread along the watercourses which crossed the region (the Majalberraque and the Repudio). The two *ḥiṣns* at that time were Ḳawra (Coria del Rio) and Ḥiṣn al-Ḳaṣr (Aznalcazar). The function of both was to guard lines of communication, that of the Guadalquivir in the first case, and the Guadiamar in the second, as well as the east-west land routes.

In Almohad times (second half of the 6th/12th century to the mid-7th/13th one), there was a change. The Almohads built two new fortified points, Shalūḳa (Sanlucar la Mayor) after 1189 to defend this region against Portuguese attacks; and Ḥiṣn al-Faradj (San Juan de Aznalfarache) in 1195 as a garrison for the troops of the ruler Abū Yūsuf Yaʿḳūb and to control access to Seville across the Guadalquivir, becoming a royal residence during that caliph's time. The population of the region continued to be densely spread. The territorial limits of the *ḥuṣūn* can be reconstructed thanks to Christian documentation from the post-conquest period. Thus in regard to Ḥiṣn al-Faradj, its territory covered 227.6 km^2 and included 69 *ḳarya*s, whose acreage for olive and fig cultivation is equally known. Cuatrovitas (Bollulos de la Mitacíon) is a remarkable instance; a minaret and many surface archaeological traces, from the Almohad period, can be found.

Of the Andalusī fortifications of al-Sharaf, there are important remains at Sanlucar la Mayor and San Juan de Aznalfarache. Coria has disappeared, and one can only see the *tell* on which the fortress was situated, and at Aznalcázar there are just some traces of the walls and of the town gate.

Bibliography: M. El Faiz, *L'Aljarafe de Seville. Un jardin d'essai pour les agronomes de l'Espagne musulmane*, in *Hésperis-Tamuda*, xxix (1992); M. Valor *et alii*, *Espacio rural y territorio en el-Aljarafe de Sevilla*, in *Asentiamentos rurales y territorio en el mundo mediterráneo, Berja, Almeria, 2-4 November 2000*, Granada 2001.

(M. VALOR and J. RAMÍREZ)

SHAʿRĀNIYYA, a mystical brotherhood (*ṭarīḳa* [*q.v.*]) whose eponymous master was the Ṣūfī ʿAbd al-Wahhāb b. Aḥmad al-Shaʿrānī (d. 973/1565 [*q.v.*]).

The Shaʿrāniyya cannot be defined as the branch of an older, original *ṭarīḳa*, since al-Shaʿrānī had several masters, notably those stemming from the Suhrawardiyya [*q.v.*] and Aḥmadiyya; he was, moreover, himself affiliated to twenty-six orders in order to pile up *baraka* [*q.v.*]. Although he was considerably influenced by the Shādhiliyya [*q.v.*] and although his successors retained clear links with the later manifestation of that order, nothing authorises us to class the Shaʿrāniyya amongst the Egyptian Shadhilī groups (see J.S. Trimingham, *The Sufi orders in Islam*, Oxford 1971, 279).

Starting from the *zāwiya* that had been built for al-Shaʿrānī at the Bāb Shaʿriyya in Cairo, the order was handed down from father to son. Hereditary transmission of the function of *shaykh* was in fact dominant during the Ottoman period. None of the master's successors possessed his spiritual charisma; they were content to manage the order amongst rich notables and to keep up good relations with the ruling classes. Through the prestige of their ancestor, they nevertheless retained an initiatory role until the opening of the 19th century. The historian al-Djabartī [*q.v.*] mentions several *shaykhs* of the order, his own contemporaries, at the end of the 18th century (*ʿAdjāʾib al-āthār fī tarādjim wa 'l-akhbār*, Cairo 1870, i, 364, ii, 213), and Lane makes a brief mention of them (*The manners and customs of the modern Egyptians*, ch. X "Superstitions").

The Shaʿrāniyya seem to have lost their identity during the course of the 19th century, since ʿAlī Bāshā Mubārak, our main source for Egyptian Ṣūfism in the later 19th century, does not cite any Ṣūfī order bearing that name in his *al-Khiṭaṭ al-tawfīḳiyya al-djadīda li-Miṣr al-Ḳāhira*, Cairo 1887-9). Another indication of its disappearance at this time is that the Shādhilī *shaykh* and author Muḥammad b. Khalīl al-Ḳāwuḳdjī (d. 1305/1888) was the disciple of an ʿAbd al-Wahhāb al-Shaʿrānī, who initiated him into the path of his illustrious and hononymous ancestor, but this ʿAbd al-Wahhāb seems to have grown up amongst the Shādhiliyya rather than the Shaʿrāniyya (M. Winter, *Society and religion in early Ottoman Egypt. Studies in the writings of ʿAbd al-Wahhāb al-Shaʿrānī*, New Brunswick, N.J. 1982, 70). However, the anniversary of al-Shaʿrānī's birth (*mawlid*) continued into the 20th century (*ibid.*, 85 n. 111).

Bibliography: Given in the article.

(E. GEOFFROY)

AL-**SHARTŪNĪ**, SAʿĪD b. ʿABD ALLĀH b. MĪKHAʾĪL b. ILYĀS b. YŪSUF AL-KHŪRĪ (1849-1912), linguist and literary figure of the Arab literary Renaissance (*nahḍa* [*q.v.*]) in the 19th and early 20th centuries, and a good example of the prominent group of vocational intellectuals of this period. Born in Shartūn in Lebanon, he studied under American missionaries before devoting himself to a lifetime of scholarly activities. He taught in Damascus and in the Jesuit schools of Beirut and Cairo, and also worked for many years as a proof reader of Jesuit publications whilst carrying out his intellectual pursuits. Like a number of his contemporaries, he worked for many years as a newspaper editor and contributed articles to respected journals, mainly on linguistic issues. His eclectic interests are reflected further in his involvement in the publication of a number of works on Maronite history. Although most sources concur on the years of his birth and death, variant dates given for the former include 1848 or even 1847, and for the latter as early as 1907.

His principal scholarly interests lay in the fields of *inshāʾ* [*q.v.*] "[the art of] composition, style" through which he is generally held to have been a major influence on a new generation of "stylists"; grammar; and lexicography. Some sources maintain that his most enduring contribution to the Arabic linguistic heritage is his dictionary entitled *Aḳrab al-mawārid fī fuṣaḥ al-ʿarabiyya wa 'l-shawārid* (Beirut 1992, 2 vols., based on ed. Beirut 1889-91, 2 vols., with a supplement in 1893). In this work he sets out to demonstrate the original purity of the Arabic language which, he argues, was being eroded, particularly as a result of the growing influence of foreign languages on Arabic. This was a common, if ultimately unachievable, goal of some scholars of the language at that time who worked assiduously to prevent it from further degeneration, thus underlining the status of the Arabic language as a form of nationalistic expression. In his dictionary, al-Shartūnī scrutinised closely the content of previous lexicographical works based on the classical sources, claiming that the editors had made errors in their transmission of material from the original manuscripts. In both these regards his scholastic approach to scholarship was no different from the techniques of many of his contemporaries and pre-modern scholars. This work was heavily influenced by the famous dictionary *Muḥīṭ al-muḥīṭ* compiled by his friend Buṭrus al-Bustānī [*q.v.*]; e.g. in the simplified presentation of the root entries and the attempts to extract the increasing number of colloquialisms infiltrating the written language. The close friendship between al-Bustānī and al-Shartūnī also manifested itself in the various scholarly and personal disputes that arose between the so-called conservative group of scholars which included al-Shartūnī, al-Bustānī and al-Yāzidjī [*q.v.*], and the reformists such as al-Shidyāḳ [*q.v.*]. Al-Shartūnī also produced an edition of a pre-modern lexicographical work by Saʿīd b. Aws Abū Zayd al-Anṣārī (d. 3rd/9th century), *al-Nawādir fi 'l-lugha* (Beirut 1967, repr. with indexes of Beirut 1894 ed.) and a dictionary arranged according to semantic categories entitled *Nadjdat al-yarāʿ fi 'l-lugha* (Beirut 1905, vol. i only). His legacy of stylistic works is contained in three principal publications, two on *inshāʾ* and one on oratory. The pedagogical intent of these works is unequivocal. His *K. al-Muʿīn fī ṣināʿat al-inshāʾ* (Beirut 1899) is a practical manual for school pupils in which he addresses various aspects of style and composition through a series of chapters in which pupils are required to identify superfluous sentences in a passage or explain underlined words or phrases, for instance. He also gives the outline of a number of scenarios of a practical or moral nature about which the student must write a piece of composition or construct a letter. His other major work on *inshāʾ*, *al-Shihāb al-thāḳib fī ṣināʿat al-kātib* (Beirut 1884), is an extensive collection of model letters on informal and formal subjects in a very similar style to that of many of the works from the pre-modern epistolary genre. His manual on oratory style entitled *al-Ghuṣn al-raṭīb fī fann al-khaṭīb* (Beirut 1908) prescribes the rhetorical, stylistic and structural components of an oration based mainly on the principles of those of the pre-modern period. An interesting feature is the description of metalinguistic elements such as the recommended tone of voice, body language and standing position of the orator. He wrote a more general work on eloquence and style entitled *Maṭāliʿ al-aḍwāʾ fī manāhidj al-kuttāb wa 'l-shuʿarāʾ* (Beirut 1908), using the question-and-answer technique throughout the book. In the introduction, he states that he wrote it mainly as a reaction to the growing negative influence of foreign languages on Arabic, and out of a desire to clarify and simplify the fundamentals of eloquence and good style. His main work on poetry and prose entitled *Ḥadāʾiḳ al-manthūr wa 'l-manẓūm* was published in Beirut in 1902. On grammar he also wrote works of a practical nature, such as his unpublished eight-volume work for teachers and students on morphology and syntax, and a gloss on Germānūs Farḥāt's [*q.v.*] *Baḥth al-maṭālib*. But his best known published grammatical tract is his *al-Sahm al-ṣāʾib fī takhṭiʾat ghunyat al-ṭālib* (Beirut 1874). This work is a strident refutation of much of al-Shidyāḳ's *Ghunyat al-ṭālib* in which al-Shartūnī employs the polemical technique of some of the grammarians from the pre-modern period.

Bibliography: Kaḥḥāla, *Muʿdjam al-muʾallifīn*, Damascus 1961, iv, 226; Y.A. Dāghir, *Maṣādir al-dirāsāt al-adabiyya: al-fikr al-ʿarabī al-ḥadīth fī siyar aʿlāmihi*, Beirut 1955, ii, 482-4; A. Gully, *Arabic linguistic issues and controversies of the late nineteenth and early twentieth centuries*, in *JSS*, xlii (1997), 113-15; P.D. Ṭarrāzī, *Taʾrīkh al-ṣiḥāfa al-ʿarabiyya*, ii, Beirut 1913, 154-5; Y.I. Sarkīs, *Muʿdjam al-maṭbūʿāt al-ʿarabiyya wa 'l-muʿarraba*, i, Baghdād 1965, repr. of 1928 Cairo ed., 1112-13; Ziriklī, *al-Aʿlām*, Beirut 1969, iii, 151; R. Ḳāsim, *Ittidjāhāt al-baḥth al-lughawī al-ḥadīth fi 'l-ʿālam al-ʿarabī*, Beirut 1982, i, 327-8, ii, 217-20; L. Shaykhū, *Taʾrīkh al-ādāb al-ʿarabiyya fi 'l-rubʿ al-awwal min al-ḳarn al-ʿishrīn*, Beirut 1926, 67; R. ʿAṭiyya, *Saʿīd al-Shartūnī*, in *al-Muqtaṭaf*, xli (Nov. 1912), 425-30; Brockelmann, S II, 769.

(A.J. Gully)

SHATM (A.), an act of insult, vilification, defamation, abuse, or revilement. Other words derived from the Arabic root *sh-t-m* denote mutual vilification (*mushātama*, *tashātum*), a person who vilifies (*shātim*, *shattāma*) or who is vilified (*mashtūm*, *shatīm*) and are often treated as synonymous with corresponding forms of the root *s-b-b* (Lane, iv, 1503).

Shatm and *sabb* as phenomena of ordinary interpersonal relations are described in works of different literary genres. When directed against God, the prophet Muḥammad, other Ḳurʾānic prophets, Muḥammad's Companions, historical personalities or objects venerated by the Muslim community or by different groups within this community, *shatm* is considered as an act of blasphemy and unbelief (*kufr*) which may entail legal prosecution. Other terms that are used less frequently in order to describe particular acts of blasphemy and that can be treated as synonymous with *shatm* in a broader sense are *laʿn* (cursing, malediction), *ṭaʿn* (accusing, attacking), *īdhāʾ* (harming, hurting), or the verb *nāla* with the preposition *min* (to do harm to somebody, to defame).

As a punishable act, religiously motivated insult is a subject of Islamic legal literature. However, there is no occurrence of the term *shatm* or other words that are derived from the root *sh-t-m* in the primary material source of Islamic jurisprudence (*fiḳh*), i.e. the Ḳurʾān. The act of insult is described in the Holy Book by a word derived from the root *s-b-b* in one verse, namely, sūra VI, 108: *wa-lā tasubbū al-ladhīna yadʿūna min dūni Allāhi fa-yasubbū Allāha ʿadwᵃⁿ bi-ghayri ʿilmⁱⁿ* "abuse not those to whom they pray, apart from God, or they will abuse God in revenge without knowledge". Here, the Muslims are told not to abuse the idols that are venerated by the polytheists. Further, it is implied that those who insult God in this manner are acting out of ignorance. In IX, 12, the verb *ṭaʿana* describes revilement of the Muslim faith as an act of the polytheists, and the Muslims are urged to fight their, i.e. the polytheists', leaders. The six canonical *ḥadīth* collections refer to offences of insult and blasphemy described as *shatm* or *sabb* on several occasions. An episode contained in a *ḥadīth* collection that does not belong to the canonical books but is regarded as the literary foundation of one of the Sunnī *madhhabs* sc. Ibn Ḥanbal's (d. 241/855) *Musnad* (Cairo 1913, ii, 436), reports a case in which Abū Bakr, the first caliph and one of Muḥammad's close Companions (*ṣaḥāba*), is insulted by an unidentified person in the presence of the Prophet. Abū Bakr is surprised by the Prophet's behaviour, since Muḥammad fails to defend him against the stranger's abuse and, at one point, appears to be amazed and smiles without any discernible reason. When Abū Bakr begins to return the abuse, Muḥammad becomes angry and, eventually, springs to his feet. After the dispute has finished, Abū Bakr asks Muḥammad why he did not support him, but instead became angry when he, Abū Bakr, attempted to defend himself. Muḥammad replies that an angel had been with Abū Bakr replying in the latter's place. But when Abū Bakr returned some of the abominable words to his adversary the devil entered the scene and he, Muḥammad, was unable to remain in a place where the devil is present. This episode from Ibn Ḥanbal's *Musnad*, like other similar passages in the canonical *ḥadīth* collections, suggests that the vilification of the Prophet or his Companions was considered intolerable and therefore forbidden by some of the religious scholars at the time when the respective *ḥadīth* books were compiled. This impression is corroborated by a report describing possible legal consequences of insulting the Prophet Muḥammad (*sabb al-rasūl*) in the 2nd/8th century. According to this report, a certain Muḥammad b. Saʿīd b. Ḥassān al-Urdunnī was executed in 153/770, in all probability because he had supplemented the *ḥadīth* "I am the seal of the prophets; there will not be any Prophet after me" with the phrase "if God does not intend otherwise"—an addition that, apparently, was considered blasphemous by the scholarly and political authorities at that time (J. van Ess, *Theologie und Gesellschaft im 2. und 3. Jahrhundert Hidschra*, Berlin 1991, i, 136-7). However, the extent to which these *ḥadīth*s reflect theological disputes about the role of the Prophet and his Companions in the first two centuries of Islam still remains to be analysed in depth.

In any case, early legal literature confirms the assumption that blasphemy against the Prophet Muḥammad was regarded an intolerable act in the 2nd/8th century. The chapter on *al-muḥāraba* of ʿAbd Allāh b. Wahb's (d. 197/812) *Muwaṭṭaʾ* contains a paragraph on the blasphemer in which the one who insults (*sabb*) the Prophet Muḥammad is threatened with the death penalty. Ibn Wahb states that Mālik b. Anas (d. 179/795) held the opinion that a blasphemer against Muḥammad, be he Christian or Muslim, must not be granted repentance. In the same passage, the caliph ʿUmar b. ʿAbd al-ʿAzīz (*r.* 101-4/717-20) is reported as having stated that the vilification of Muḥammad, but not of any other person, is to be punished (M. Muranyi, *ʿAbd Allāh b. Wahb (125/743-197/812). Leben und Werk. Al-Muwaṭṭaʾ. Kitāb al-muḥāraba*, Wiesbaden 1992, 287-8). However, a 3rd/9th-century legal manual, the *ʿUtbiyya* by the Mālikī *faḳīh* Muḥammad al-ʿUtbī (d. 255/869 [*q.v.*]), mentions blasphemy against Muḥammad's Companions as a punishable act (*al-ʿUtbiyya*, printed with Ibn Rushd, *al-Bayān wa 'l-taḥṣīl*, Beirut 1986, xvi, 420). Also, an opinion ascribed to the Ḥanafī legist al-Ṭaḥāwī (d. 321/933 [*q.v.*]) suggests that hatred of the Companions (*bughḍ al-ṣaḥāba*) indicates unbelief (al-Subkī, *al-Fatāwā*, Beirut n.d., ii, 590).

It has been observed that blasphemy against God, the Prophet Muḥammad, and his Companions, when committed by a Muslim, was discussed by the legal scholars in the context of apostasy (*ridda*) and unbelief (*kufr*), that is, of two matters that were regarded to warrant capital punishment under certain circumstances. However, in the relevant chapters of the formative texts of the *madhhab*s, insulting the Prophet or the *ṣaḥāba* is not mentioned among the punishable acts that constitute *ridda* or *kufr*. Neither in Mālik's *Muwaṭṭaʾ*, nor in Saḥnūn's (d. 240/854) *Mudawwana*, nor in al-Shāfiʿī's (d. 204/820) *al-Umm*, nor in al-Shaybānī's (189/805) *Kitāb al-Aṣl*, is *sabb al-rasūl* or *sabb al-ṣaḥāba* listed as an offence tantamount to *ridda*. However, from information on legal practice in the 3rd/9th century it may be inferred that the opinion that *sabb al-ṣaḥāba* must entail certain legal consequences was held by particular functionaries. A biographical note on al-Ḥārith b. Miskīn, a Mālikī jurist who took over the judgeship of Egypt in 237/854, informs us that during his tenure capital punishment (*ḥadd*) was enforced against a person who had insulted Muḥammad's wife ʿĀʾisha (al-Kindī, *The governors and judges of Egypt or Kitāb el ʿUmarāʾ (el Wulāh wa Kitāb el Quḍāh of el Kindī)*, ed. R. Guest, Leiden 1912, 469-70). The awareness of insulting the Prophet or his Companions as an offence for which a penalty must be established by the law appears to have become stronger about the end of the 3rd/9th and the beginning of the 4th/10th centuries. While al-Muzanī (d. 264/878), like his master al-Shāfiʿī, does not mention the blasphemer against God, His Prophet, or the Prophet's Companions among those who apostatise from Islam (*murtadd*), his fellow Shāfiʿī, Ibn al-Mundhir (d. 318/930) briefly discusses insult against the Prophet Muḥammad in the chapter on the apostate in his book on consensus, *idjmāʿ*. The Muslim scholars, Ibn al-Mundhir states, are in agreement that the one who insults the Prophet should be put to death (*al-Idjmāʿ*, ed. Fuʾād ʿAbd al-Muʾmin Aḥmad, Ḳaṭar 1402/1982, 122). A later work of the Shāfiʿī *madhhab*, al-Nawawī's (d. 676/1276) *Minhādj al-ṭālibīn*, counts the blasphemer against any Prophet (not only Muḥammad) among the apostates (ed. L.W.C. van den Berg, Batavia 1889-91, iii, 205). Yet al-Nawawī, like some of his later commentators, does not discuss insulting Muḥammad's Companions in the chapter on *ridda*. However, the 11th/17th-century *faḳīh* Shihāb al-Dīn al-Ḳalyūbī (d. 1069/1658) again explicitly includes insulting the Prophet's Companions in the chapter on *ridda*. Shams al-Dīn al-Ramlī (d. 1004/1596) underscores the fact that a person who claims that there are prophets after Muḥammad is classified as *kāfir* (*Nihāyat al-muḥtādj ilā maʿrifat al-Minhādj*, Cairo 1938, vii, 395). But whereas the Shāfiʿī *faḳīh* al-Shirbīnī (977/1570) counts those who brand the *ṣaḥāba* as infidels among the unbelievers (*Mughnī al-muḥtādj*, Cairo 1933, ii, 125), al-Ramlī does not mention blasphemy against the *ṣaḥāba* among acts that constitute *kufr*. Again, al-Ramlī's 11th/17th-century commentator, Nūr al-Dīn al-Shabrāmallisī (d. 1096/1685), treats blasphemy against the Companions as an act of *kufr*.

Altogether it may be said that, at the latest since the 7th/13th century, insult against the Prophet(s) is often mentioned among the acts that constitute *kufr* in the chapters on apostasy (*ridda*) of the Shāfiʿī manuals of positive law (*furūʿ*). Insult against the *ṣaḥāba*, however, is mentioned only occasionally and apparently only in manuals written from the 11th/17th century onwards in the chapters on *ridda*. However, the veneration of the *ṣaḥāba* and the inadmissibility of insulting them had become a salient point of *idjmāʿ* among Sunnī jurists by the 8th/14th century. As the majority of the legal manuals quoted above contain a paragraph that declares that the one who violates the consensus of the Muslim community (*idjmāʿ al-umma*) is a *kāfir*, the charge of unbelief can be extended to include those who insult the Prophet's Companions. A reading of historiographical works suggests that this conclusion had an impact also on the relation between Sunnī and Shīʿī Muslims. For example, Ibn Kathīr (d. 774/1373) reports in his *al-Bidāya wa 'l-nihāya* (Beirut 1977, xiv, 250) the case of a Shīʿī Muslim from the town of Ḥilla, who in Damascus in 755/1354 insulted some of the Prophet's closest companions like Abū Bakr, ʿUmar b. al-Khaṭṭāb, and ʿUthmān b. ʿAffān as violators of the rights of the Prophet's descendants. When he refused to revoke his blasphemous attacks against these *ṣaḥāba*, his case was presented to the chief judges of the four Sunnī *madhhabs* in the *Dār al-saʿāda*. As a result of this session, the blasphemer was sentenced to death by the Mālikī deputy chief judge (*al-nāʾib al-mālikī*) and executed immediately after judgement had been issued. His body was burnt by the plebs of Damascus who later walked through the city showing his head and exclaiming that this would be the punishment of the one who abuses the Companions of the Prophet. A closer look at the religio-political situation of 8th/14th-century Egypt and Syria suggests that insult against the Prophet's Companions or even against the Prophet Muḥammad himself, on the part of some Shīʿīs, or accusations brought forward by the Sunnīs against alleged Shīʿī blasphemers, are an expression of the strong Shīʿī-Sunnī hostilities at that time.

The offence of insult against the Prophet and his Companions continues to be an issue of legal debate and political discourse in Islamic societies until the present time. The controversy on Salman Rushdie's novel *The Satanic verses* has been the most prominent among a number of cases in which Islamic communities and their leaders have reacted to acts that were conceived of as an insult against Muḥammad and other venerated personalities. As has been shown, the legal foundations for this reaction date back to the 2nd/8th century.

Bibliography (in addition to the references in the text): Ibn Taymiyya, *al-Ṣārim al-maslūl ʿalā shātim al-rasūl*, Ḥaydarābād 1322/1905; Abu 'l-Faḍl b. Mūsā b. ʿIyād, *Kitāb al-Shifā bi-taʿrīf ḥuḳūḳ al-Muṣṭafā*, Istanbul 1312/1894; T. Andrae, *Die Person Muḥammads in Lehre und Glauben seiner Gemeinde*, Stockholm 1917, 263-9; L. Bercher, *L'apostasie, le blasphème et la rebellion en droit musulman malekite*, in *RT* (1923), 115-30; Maria I. Fierro, *Andalusian "Fatāwā" on Blasphemy*, in *AI*, xxv (1990), 103-17; L. Wiederhold, *Blasphemy against the prophet Muḥammad and his companions* (sabb al-rasūl, sabb al-ṣaḥābah): *The introduction of the topic into Shāfiʿī legal literature and its relevance for legal practice under Mamluk rule*, in *JSS*, xlii (1997), 39-70; Victoria LaPorte, *An attempt to understand the Muslim reaction to the Satanic verses*, Lewiston 1999; D.S. Powers, *From Almohadism to Malikism. The Case of al-Haskurī, the mocking jurist*, in idem (ed.), *Law, society and culture in the Maghrib, 1300-1500*, Cambridge 2002; Wiederhold, *Some remarks on Mālikī judges in Mamluk Egypt and Syria*, in S. Conermann and Anja Pistor-Hatam (eds.), *Die Mamluken. Studien zu ihrer Geschichte und Kultur. Zum Gedenken an Ulrich Haarmann (1943-1999)*, Schenefeld 2003, 403-13.

(L. Wiederhold)

SHAYKHZĀDE II [see sheykh-zāde. 3].

SHIʿR.

5. In Malay and in Indonesian.

In line with their strong preference for theology and Ṣūfī mysticism over literature and philology, the interest of the Muslims of the Malay-Indonesian world in Arabo-Persian *shiʿr* has been predominantly drawn by religious poetry as found in the Arabic *ḳaṣīda* and its derivative verse forms. It was initially mainly in the north Sumatran kingdom of Aceh [see atjeh]—in the early 17th century the dominant power in the region around the Straits of Malacca and an important centre of Islamic learning—that this religious poetry was closely studied (Braginsky 1996, 372-3) and it was there that most local forms of Islamic poetry were developed under its influence, subsequently to spread among the Muslim communities of the Archipelago.

A case in point is the genre of Malay poetry, called *nazam* (from the Arabic synonym for *shiʿr, naẓm*). It consists of a long sequence of couplets (*bayt* [*q.v.*]) comprising two hemistiches, each usually numbering from nine or ten up to twelve syllables, that rhyme with each other on one of the following patterns: (a) *aa, bb, cc*...; (b), *aa, aa, aa*...; (c) *aa, ba, ca*... Couplets rhyming *ab, ab* are rare. The oldest specimens of *nazam*, teaching good rulership, are found in the Mirror for Princes, *Tādj al-salāṭīn* (1012/1603-4) by the Acehnese *ʿālim* Bukhārī al-Djawharī (Braginsky 2000, 183-209). Some of these (pattern [a]) are modelled on the Persian *mathnawī* [*q.v.*], while others (pattern [b]) resemble the poetry of Arabic versified treatises of scholarly or religious content (*urdjūza* [see radjaz]), whereas still others (pattern[c]) imitate the Arabic *ḳaṣīda* or *ghazal* [*q.vv.*] with its monorhyme (Braginsky 1996, 377-80).

Malay *nazam*, containing religious teachings, praise of the Prophet and suchlike, have subsequently continued to be written. In Malaysia and Indonesia they are sung (*nashīd* [*q.v.*]) as a monotone or with varied melodies on a variety of occasions, alongside *ḳaṣīdas* in Arabic: in religious schools as a means of memorising the basic tenets of Islam; at weddings; after the completion of studies of the Ḳurʾān [see mawlid]; at Mawlūd celebrations, etc. Arabo-Malay or purely Malay *nazam* are also sung at *berdikir* gatherings (Malay, from Arabic *dhikr* [*q.v.*]) to various melodies and rhythms, accompanied by instrumental music and bodily movements (Harun Mat Piah 1989, 282-309).

In 18th and 19th century Aceh, a genre of Acehnese literature called *nalam* was practised, which, like the Malay *nazam*, was probably also created using partly Arabic *urdjūza*, partly *ḳaṣīda* as a model. Although the *nalam*'s verse line seems to be patterned on the Arabic *radjaz* and *ṭawīl* [*q.vv.*] metres, it has remained closely tied to indigenous conventions. According to the demands of its metre (*sanja*, from Arabic *sadjʿ* [*q.v.*]), it usually comprises two hemistiches and numbers sixteen metric units of one to three syllables each, the latter being arranged to form eight feet of a sort. The fourth foot, that is, the last foot of the first hemistich, is connected by a compulsory internal rhyme to the sixth foot, that is, the second foot of the second hemistich, while all lines have an external monorhyme represented by words ending with the vowel *a*. Thus the *rajat* (from the Arabic *radjaz*) metre of the *nalam* is an eight-foot modification of the *sanja* metre and its *tawi* (from the Arabic *ṭawīl*) metre, one with nine feet (Snouck Hurgronje, ii, 1906, 73-8; Djajadiningrat, ii, 1934, 279, 462, 664, 988).

The most important new genre of poetry to emerge in the early 17th century Malay literature is the *syair* (in the Malay version of the Arabic script, Jawi, this word is usually written *sh-y-ʿ-r* but sometimes *sh-ʿ-r*). The *syair* consists of a chain of quatrains, each of them with monorhyme of the type *aaaa, bbbb, cccc*... The metre of its lines, which tend to comprise four full words of a length of two to three syllables including their bound morphemes, is based on a relative tendency towards isosyllabism. Each line may contain between nine to twelve syllables, a ten-syllable line being the dominant tendency, and is divided by a caesura into two roughly equal hemistiches that tend to form complete syntactic units (Braginsky 1998, 225-6). The following sample is from the poetry of the

Acehnese Ṣūfī mystic Ḥamza Fanṣūrī [*q.v.*] (active *ca.* 1600), who is now generally accepted to have created the genre: "Baḥr al-Ḥaḳḳ terlalu *dalam* / ombaknya menjadi *ʿālam* / aṣalnya tiada bersiang *malam* / di laut itu ʿālam nin *karam* // Dengarkan hai anak *dagang* / lautnya tiada bersurut *pasang* / muaranya tiada bersawang-*sawang* / banyaklah orang sana ter*karang*" (Drewes and Brakel 1986, 134) ("The Sea of the Truth is immensely deep, / The world has sprung from Its waves, / Its beginning is foreign to day and to night, / And the world will sink again in that Sea. / /Hear ye, oh wanderer, / There is neither ebb nor flow in that Sea, / You won't see the sky in the mouth of Its rivers, / There many sailors have been stranded on the reefs.")

There are different opinions on the origin of the *syair* (Teeuw 1966; Al-Attas 1968; Sweeney 1971). According to the argument of Braginsky (1996, 383-7), if it is correct to read a corrupt passage describing the *syair* in Ḥamza Fanṣūrī's treatise *Asrār al-ʿārifīn* ("Secret of the Gnostics") (Doorenbos 1933, 120-1) as saying that in each of its *bayt*s four *sadj̲ʿ* are used, this indicates that Ḥamza may well in part have modelled it on a variety of *ḳaṣīda* or *g̲h̲azal*, widespread in Persian, Ottoman and Urdu Ṣūfī poetry, which is called *musammaṭ* [*q.v.*] or *s̲h̲iʿr-i musadjdjaʿ* in Persian poetics (Tabrīzī 1959, 128). Because in the classical *musammaṭ*, as written, for instance, by ʿIrāḳī and D̲jāmī [*q.vv.*], a *bayt* is divided into four lines with *sadj̲ʿ* placed at the end of the first three lines and a monorhyme (*ḳāfiya* [*q.v.*]) in the fourth, Ḥamza here probably meant to say that, differing from the classical *musammaṭ*, he had made use of one and the same *sadj̲ʿ* in all four lines, doing away with the final monorhyme, a feature that was hard to assimilate in Malay literature. A poem of this type was written by the 11th century Persian poet Manūčihrī [*q.v.*] (Browne, *LHP*, ii, 42). Perhaps because the four-line *musammaṭ* was known as *murabbaʿ* ("four-fold"), Ḥamza's followers called his poems *rubāʿ* (with the same meaning). Consisting of a chain of between thirteen to twenty stanzas and ending with mentioning his name, Ḥamza's *syair*s resemble the *g̲h̲azal* "with *sadj̲ʿ*", with its chain of between four and fifteen stanzas, which since the time of ʿAṭṭār (d. *ca* 627/1230 [*q.v.*]) ends with the writer's *tak̲h̲alluṣ* [*q.v.*] or pen-name.

Ḥamza's *syair*s lack any traces of Arabo-Persian metrics (*ʿarūḍ* [*q.v.*]). They manifest their relation to indigenous Malay poetry, *inter alia* in the use of a specific "interrupted" or "assonanced" rhyme (see the italicised rhyme words in the sample above) and the similarity to the "tirade poem", a verse form widely used in popular poetry of the Archipelago. Like in Old French and Turkic epic "tirades" or in the *sadj̲ʿ* of the Ḳurʾān, the individual verse lines in Malay-Indonesian "tirade poems" are united, by continuous rhyme or assonances, into groups of varying lengths. Therefore Ḥamza's *syair bayt*s may be viewed as a regularisation of the loosely structured "tirade poems" into a chain of quatrains, each having its own continuous rhyme, through adopting features of *g̲h̲azal* with the non-classical *s̲h̲iʿr-i musadjdjaʿ* (Braginsky 1998, 229-31).

After Ḥamza Fanṣūrī and his followers, such as Ḥasan Fanṣūrī and ʿAbd al-D̲jamāl, had in the 17th century popularised the *syair* as an instrument for Ṣūfī homiletics and allegory, it spread rapidly through the Archipelago wherever Malay literature was produced. Developing into a poem that could attain a length of thousands of quatrains, by the late 18th and the early 19th centuries it had become a verse form covering a wide range of topics, as can be gleaned from the catalogues of the collections of Malay manuscripts (Chambert-Loir and Oman Fathurahman 1999). It could now teach Islamic dogma, instruct the reader about how to perform his prayers or admonish him of the terrors that could await him in the grave. It could tell of the lives of Muslim prophets, of historical events such as wars with the Dutch, of fictional loves between princes and princesses in the days of yore or, in parodied romance, between animals or flowers, and it could aim the barb of satire at historical or political events in allegorical animal fables (Braginsky, 1998, 236; Harun Mat Piah 1989, 243-66; Koster 1997).

In the transition of Malay literature to modernity that began to manifest itself in the major colonial cities of the Archipelago beween 1850 and 1870, concomitant with the rise of the printing press and the newspaper, the *syair* was enthusiastically taken up by non-Muslim writers as well (ethnic Chinese and Eurasians) and was published in profuse numbers, in lithographs, printed booklets and newspapers. At the same time, it underwent yet another widening of its thematic scope, treating, for instance, sensational events, as it adapted itself to its urban milieu and usage (Harun Mat Piah 1989, 262-4; Lombard-Salmon 1977, *passim*; Salmon 1981, 25-6 and *passim*; Proudfoot 1993).

In the love stories in the early novels of Modern Indonesian and Malay literature written around 1920, *syair*s were inserted at moments of climax, and both literatures used them for lyric (sometimes nationalistic) poetry, in Indonesia until about 1930 and in Malaya until about 1950 (Harun Mat Piah 1989, 260-1; Johan Jaafar *et al.* 1992, i, 67-83, ii, 58-60; Teeuw 1967, 49-51). In the modern poetry of the Malay-Indonesian world, except that of the Sultanate of Brunei (Harun Mat Piah 1989, 258), there is now no longer any place for the *syair*, but its place as an Islamic genre of poetry is still acknowledged; among the Malays, *syair*s continue to be performed at important religious feasts and events in the Islamic lifecycle alongside *ḳaṣīda*s in Arabic and *nazam* (Harun Mat Piah 1989, 266-82).

On Java's northern coast and in east Java, in particular in Ponorogo which is well known for its religious schools, a form of Islamic poetry is found called *singir* or *geguritan*, treating themes similar to those of religious *syair*s. To what extent this genre can be related to Arabo-Persian *s̲h̲iʿr* is still an open question. Like the *syair*, it consists of verse lines of between eight to ten syllables in length. These may be grouped into rhyming couplets or, as in the *syair*, into quatrains, but may also be arranged into groups of variable lengths as in "tirade poems". The *singir* is performed by singers to the accompaniment of musical instruments (*angklung, terbang*) (Darnawi 1964, 53-4; Pigeaud 1938, 304, 321).

Bibliography: P.P. Roorda van Eysinga, *Tadj oes-Salatin. De kroon aller koningen* ("Tadj oes-Salatin. The crown of all kings"), Batavia 1827; Browne, *LHP*, ii, London 1906; C. Snouck Hurgronje, *The Achehnese*, ii, Leiden 1906; J. Doorenbos, *De geschriften van Hamzah Pansoeri*, Leiden 1933; H. Djajadiningrat, *Atjehsch-Nederlandsch woordenboek*, ii, Batavia 1934; Th.G.Th. Pigeaud, *Javaansche volksvertoningen*, Batavia 1938; Waḥīd Tabrīzī, *Jām-i Muk̲h̲tasar, Traktat o poetike* ("A treatise on poetics"), ed., tr. and notes A. Y̲e̲. Berthels, Moscow 1959; S. Darnawi, *Pengantar puisi Djawa* ("Introduction to Javanese poetry") Djakarta 1964; A. Teeuw, *The Malay shaʿir. Problems of origin and tradition*, in *Bijdragen tot de Taal-, Land-*

en Volkenkunde, cxxii (1966), 429-46; idem, *Modern Indonesian literature*, i, The Hague 1967; S.M.N. Al-Attas, *The origin of the Malay shaʿir*, Kuala Lumpur 1968; A. Sweeney, *Some observations on the Malay shaʿir*, in *Jnal. Malaysian Branch of the RAS*, xliv/1 (1971), 52-90; C. Lombard-Salmon, *La littérature en Malais romanisé des Chinois de Malaisie. Première enquête*, in *Archipel*, xiv (1977), 79-109; C. Salmon, *Literature in Malay by the Chinese of Indonesia. A provisional annotated bibliography*, Paris 1981; G.W.J. Drewes and L.F. Brakel, *The poems of Hamzah Fansuri*, Dordrecht-Cinnaminson 1986; Harun Mat Piah, *Puisi Melayu tradisional. Satu pembicaraan genre dan fungsi* ("Traditional Malay poetry. A discussion of its genres and their function"), Kuala Lumpur 1989; Johan Jaafar, Mohd. Thani Ahmad and Safian Hussain (eds.), *History of modern Malay literature*, i-ii, Kuala Lumpur 1992; I. Proudfoot, *Early Malay printed books*, Kuala Lumpur 1993; V.I. Braginsky, *On the Qasida and cognate poetic forms in the Malay-Indonesian world*, in S. Sperl and C. Shackle (eds), *Qasida poetry in Islamic Asia and Africa*, i, Leiden 1996, 370-88; G.L. Koster, *Roaming through seductive gardens. Readings in Malay narrative*, Leiden 1997; Braginsky, *Yang indah, berfaedah dan kamal. Sejarah sastra Melayu dalam abad 7-19* ("The beautiful, the profitable and the perfect. A history of Malay literature from the 7th to the 19th Centuries"), Jakarta 1998; Braginsky, *Tajus Salatin ("The crown of sultans") of Bukhari al-Jauhari*, in D. Smyth (ed.), *The canon in Southeast Asian literatures*, London 2000.

(V.I. Braginsky and G.L. Koster)

SHŪRĀ-yi DEWLET [see madjlis al-shūrā].

SĪBA, Bilād al-, a term borrowed from local speech by the French colonial authorities to designate the absence of control by the Sultan of Morocco over a considerable part of his territory at the end of the 19th century. It presupposes a congenital disorder threatening the existence of the "auspicious empire". The origins of the term go back to explorers like Charles de Foucauld, academic professors like Alfred Le Chatelier and Augustin Bernard, and military men like Lyautey, eager to conquer Morocco from the contiguous French territory of Algeria. It forms the concept behind the Comité du Maroc, a lobby operating at a level below the decision makers in Paris with the idea of extending French power over the land, given shape in the Protectorate of 30 March 1912. These experts put together an imagery based on a dichotomy between the Bilād al-sība and the Bilād al-makhzan [see makhzan]. The former was a land outside the authority of the Sultan, hence free from taxes and conscription, whose people lived in an insolent, free fashion impervious to all outside influences. The latter was the land over which government authority levied taxes in an iniquitous fashion and recruited tribal militias, driving rural society into a state of non-submission, *sība*.

Colonial terminology equated the antagonistic dichotomy of the two terms with a semi-racial cleavage, setting the autochthnous Berbers against the Arab invaders, who imposed themselves on a refractory indigenous element. The Berbers lived under customary law, *ʿurf*, whilst the Arabs were subject to the *Sharīʿa*, an expression of Muslim theocracy and a pliant system under the Sultans' despotism which the Berbers continuously rejected. It was postulated that the Berbers were spirits basically inspired by laicity under their Islamic coating and that they had attained a form of republican local democracy in their strongholds of mountain towns and regions. This vision of Morocco gave further life to the Kabyle myth so active in the constituting of French Algeria and converged on a policy of separating the Berbers, the "good savages", in their mountain retreats, from the Arabic-speaking peoples of the plains and the great Muslim cities, as illustrated in the famous Berber *dahir* of 1930 [see ẓahīr], which did much do crystallise national sentiment in Morocco.

The Bilād al-sība rightly appeared to post-colonial Moroccan historians as a fantastic intellectual construction meant exclusively to bolster the Berber policy of the French Protectorate. However, the term appears, if only rarely, in the correspondence of the Makhzan in the 19th century, for stigmatising local tribal groups hostile to all the local authorities (*ḳāʾid, muḳaddim, zāwiya* and *kabīr* over tribal sections) who tended to interpose themselves between the Makhzan and the segmentary base of society. In fact, the term Bilād al-sība is an ancient one going back to early times, and its usage, current in al-Andalus from the 11th century onwards, became generalised in the vocabulary of Maghribī *ʿulamāʾ* from the 15th century onwards for condemning the backward rural areas living in a state close to *djāhiliyya* since they ignored injunctions of the *Sharīʿa* and transgressed the prescriptions of *fikh*.

These Maghribī scholars were correctly following the original sense of the term *sāʾiba*, one which denoted, within a semantic and spatial complex, successively: a beast brought out of the herd for offering to the gods of ancient Arabia; a freed slave, but one foot-loose and without a patron in early Islam; by extension, a woman left to herself, a rebel or a prostitute; the breaking of allegiance to a sovereign and, from that time onwards, the territory where this dissidence was rife, when the term passed from the East to the West via al-Andalus. *Bilād sāʾiba* appears, probably for the first time, in a commentary of Mālikī law on Saḥnūn's *Mudawwana* by Abū ʿImrān al-Fāsī (d. 430/1039), a scholar of Moroccan origin settled in Ḳayrawān.

The Term Bilād al-sība was never, however, used by those Maghribīs to whom it applied. Most of these were vacillating and uncontrolled subjects. They were vacillating because they oscillated between rallying to the sovereign and rejecting the central power's local agents, between being dogs and wolves, when they could not be sheepdogs, to use Ernest Gellner's metaphor. They were uncontrolled, as the maxim in the Tunisian Djerīd says, *lā bayy, lā rayy*. They feared subjection to the central power which would entail their being shorn like sheep by its local agents. This is why, except for some islands in the mountains and along the Sub-Saharan fringes, the Bilād al-sība never corresponded to a fixed territorial entity which could raise up a lasting counter-force able to divide up the area over which three powers claimed control since the 16th century. In a certain way, the Bilād al-sība was everywhere, as appeared from the difficulty of travelling without a safe-conduct negotiated with the tribal peoples. It insinuated itself over almost all the territory through the institution of the *maḥalla* [*q.v.*], a splendour which inspired local riches but also redistributed them, in such a way that all the prince's subjects were in a relationship, more or less asymmetrical according to place and time, with the sovereign and his local representatives. In practice, when it became a concrete entity, the Bilād al-sība was sought after for bringing to heel the Bilād al-makhzan. Some rebellious tribes acted as guard dogs over the tribes which had submitted, showing how far they were integrated in a unified system personified by a Bey in the Ottoman Maghrib, and by the Sultan, the Commander of the Faithful, in Morocco.

Bibliography: Ch. de Foucauld, *Reconnaissance du Maroc, 1883-1884*, Paris 1888; R. Montagne, *Les Berbères et le Makhzen dans le sud du Maroc. Essai sur la vie politique des Berbères sédentaires (groupe chleuh)*, Paris 1930; E. Gellner, *The saints of the Atlas*, London 1969; Abdallah Laroui, *Les origines sociales et culturelles du nationalisme marocain (1830-1912)*, Paris 1977; J. Berque, *L'intérieur du Maghreb, XVe-XIXe siècles*, Paris 1978; Abderrahaman El Moudden, *État et société rurale à travers la harka au Maroc du XIXème siècle*, in *The Maghreb Review*, viii/5-6 (1983), 141-5; Mohamed Ennaji and Paul Pascon, *Le makhzen et le sous al-aqsa, la correspondance politique de la maison d'Illigh (1821-1894)*, Paris and Casablanca 1988; Jocelyne Dakhlia, *L'oubli de la cité. La mémoire collective à l'épreuve du lignage dans le jérid tunisien*, Paris 1990; Houari Touati, *Le prince et la bête. Enquête sur une métaphore pastorale*, in *Stud. Isl.*, lxxxiii (1996), 101-20. (D. Rivet)

ṢIḤĀFA.

4. Persia.

During the century and a half of its existence, the Iranian press has experienced several periods of expansion and contraction. From 1851 to 1880 the press had only a limited audience, as it was meant only for civil servants. In all, some seven newspapers (*rūznāma-hā*) were published. From 1880 to 1906, the press began publishing for all Persians, although few could afford a newspaper. By the end of the century almost forty newspapers and journals had been published. From 1906 to 1925 the number of newspapers grew enormously and editors were able to influence the course of events in the country. During the period 1925-41, the press was reduced to an instrument in the hands of a strong authoritarian state. The period 1941-53 marked the country's return to a free and expanding press. From 1953 to 1977 the press was basically muzzled; after 1965 it became a cheerleader for the régime. From 1978 to the present the press experienced, first, four years of freedom, followed by the severest censorship it had ever known. Since 1998, however, the press has become more expansive and is trying to become a free agent of change.

The first Persian newspaper, *A<u>kh</u>bār-i Waḳāyiʿ*, was published in Muḥarram 1253/April-May 1837 in Tehran (*JRAS*, v [1839], 355-71), but it lasted less than two years. It was only in February 1851 that a new government weekly newspaper, *Waḳāyiʿ-i Ittifāḳiyya*, was published. The stated purpose of the newspaper was to explain government activities. By royal order, all leading government bureaucrats had to subscribe to the newspapers. From 1871, the press was under the control of the newly-created Ministry of the Press with its censorship office. The rationale for censorship was published in issue 522 (22 December 1863) of the government newspaper *Dawlat-i ʿĀliya-yi Īrān*, sc. to bar publications harmful to infants and contrary to religion. The text was addressed not to readers but to listeners, which confirms what Eichwald noted in 1826, sc. that literature or news was read out loudly for the entire community (E. Eichwald, *Reise auf dem Caspischen Meere und in den Caucasus unternommen in den Jahren 1825-1826*, 2 vols., Stuttgart und Tübingen 1834, i, 384). Given the very low level of literacy (about 5%), this is understandable, and confirms that the actual readership of the newspapers was much larger than the number of subscribers. The "journalists" were civil servants reporting on non-controversial and approved events (government, religion, foreign, literature, science). After 1880, political reformists started to publish newspapers but to avoid the censors they printed their papers outside Iran. Once published, they smuggled them into Iran. These newspapers published abroad had an enormous influence inside Iran and on the reformist movement.

After 1896 censorship was reduced, although the restrictive press rules (to inhibit things harmful to morality and the state) were repeated in 1901, when the government at the same time banned the importation of all Persian newspapers published abroad. With the establishment of the constitutional government in 1906 [see dustūr. iv. Iran] the press was basically free (art. 20 of the 1906 Constitution). In 1907, there were some 84 newspapers, whereas only 40 in all had been published prior to that date. During this period of intermittent press freedom in Iran (1896-1925), political activity merged with journalistic vocation. The various interest groups, which soon developed into parties, defined a number of emerging social themes and political ideas, which they explained and propagated in the editorials of various journals. Thus the often fiery editorial page of most journals became the main battleground for the opposing schools of thought. With the suppression of parliament in 1908, Muḥammad ʿAlī <u>Sh</u>āh [*q.v.*] also suppressed the press, and its leading members were imprisoned and some executed. After the overthrow of the <u>Sh</u>āh in 1909, the press started a new life. This period was the coming of age of the press, and representatives from left and right of the spectrum were to be found. Until the First World War, a total of 371 newspapers and journals were published. During the First World War the Allies often suppressed the press, because of its wide use of slander and invective. After 1918, the press resurged, but in the early 1920s, government pressure on the media intensified. Riḍā <u>Kh</u>ān, the Minister of War, had a journalist flogged, while the outspoken poet-journalist ʿI<u>sh</u>ḳī [*q.v.* in Suppl.] was killed in 1924, allegedly by the authorities. One year later, the Pahlavī régime was established, which did not allow any discussion of political subjects, and certainly not criticism of government. The number of newspapers dropped from 150 to 50 between 1925 and 1941. They served to propagate the government's programmes and were censored by the Department of Press and Propaganda prior to publication.

After the fall of Riḍā <u>Sh</u>āh [*q.v.*] (1941), the press was controlled by the Allies (1941-6) and by martial law (1941-8), although there was considerable freedom of expression. The Allies, as well as national interest groups, wanted certain positions taken, and thus editorials were again mostly marked by their extremely partisan tones and aggressive styles. Most newspapers were small, limited in circulation, and short-lived. The journalist (*rūznāma-niwīs, rūznāma-nigār*) was usually both editor and publisher. The topics were mainly analysis and criticism of personalities in public life, and discussion of contemporary social-economic-political problems. Although nobody wanted censorship or banning of newspapers, both methods were used, for the new 1941 Press Law could not rein in excessive vituperation in the press. However, suppressed papers would often immediately reappear under the name of a legally-licensed other periodical. Attempts to bring about a more responsible press failed, because often financing of papers was provided to attack certain political issues (blackmail of politicians; subsidies from foreign powers). The strongest group was the pro-Soviet Tudeh (*Tūda*) press that formed the Freedom

Front in 1943. There also was a pro-British, nationalist coalition of papers, and some independents. The suppression of separatist movements in Ādharbāydjān and Kurdistān in 1946 led to a clamp-down on the local language press. This had a negative impact on the journalistic role of Tabrīz that had been in the forefront from the beginning.

In the first few years after the fall of Muṣaddiḳ's [*q.v.*] government (1953), which had widespread press support, press restrictions were mainly imposed through the application of martial law. Later, the responsibility for enforcing censorship was divided between the Ministry of Information and the Ministry of Culture, together with the newly-founded security agency, SAVAK. The usual grounds for suspension were: slander of the monarchy, or of relations of Iran with friendly countries, and inflammatory articles against the government or religion. These were incorporated into the 1955 Press Law. In this period of extended press censorship and government control, the tone and style of editorial writing underwent considerable change towards blandness and conformity to what was tolerated, and often government-designed norms of political, cultural and social expression. In March 1963, the Press Law was amended. It formulated the criteria for persons who could obtain a license to publish and it limited the number of periodicals; the grounds for suppressing newspapers remained the same.

Most papers had serious financial difficulties due to low circulation, except for a few large ones. In 1963, *Kayhān* and *Iṭṭilāʿāt* accounted for 65% of newspaper circulation. Five magazines accounted for more than 50% of total magazine circulation. Because of financial pressure (rising cost, falling revenues, competition from radio and TV), newspapers accepted government-written articles. Consequently, the quality of the newspapers was bad, in part because there was a shortage of staff, which was lowly paid. Papers used "scissor editors" to cut articles from other newspapers. Also, they used translators to translate foreign articles, so that there was often more news on foreign countries than on Iran. Specialised publications, such as literary and humorous ones, also depended much on donations and government articles to survive. Hence papers improved their appearance rather than their substance. This in turn led to loss of readership, due to mistrust of government propaganda, irrelevance of foreign news, and the ignoring of what most concerned people's daily lives. The two major dailies, along with some quality periodicals, created and supported a class of professional journalists who challenged the government by focusing on failures and shortcomings in regard to what government had promised to deliver. In response to criticism from the government to encourage better reporting and tell the "truth", the papers reacted by telling the government, as the major newsmakers, to provide more, better, and timely information, to allow better and freer contacts with government agencies, and to respect the letter and spirit of the Press Law.

After the fall of the Pahlavī régime in 1979, more than two hundred periodicals were published whose variety and number were unprecedented in the modern history of Iran. Press freedom was, however, short-lived. Soon the country's ruling clergy ordered the closure of more than twenty publications, and more followed later, despite the 1985 Press Law that banned censorship. Art. 4 defined the press limits, including, slander of the Leader and *ʿulamāʾ*, inflammatory articles against the government or religion, and reporting on classified information on the military and parliament. Only two unions are officially recognised, the Islamic Society of Journalists and the Professional Society of Journalists, belonging to hardliners and the Islamic reformist factions respectively. The Iranian press under President Khātamī (since 1997) is freer than it has been in many years and political journalism is flourishing. The struggle between the conservatives and those who favour greater press freedom has become a major issue in Iran, resulting in banning of newspapers and jailing of journalists. Following the 1999 student uprising, parliament passed new laws banning any publication other than those specifically sanctioned, holding the licensee, editors, writers and even typists directly responsible for any unauthorised article or publication.

From 1956, a School of Journalism offered a four-year B.A. course. In 1960, an advanced course was added. There were 137 graduates in 1969, when Tehran University announced that it would close the school. The two major dailies also offered courses on journalism in the 1960s. The major papers also started to hire more qualified, academically trained staff. Although the Universities again offer Journalism as a subject for study, its effect is minimal. Since 1966, about 900 people have graduated from journalism courses in Iranian universities, of whom 93% are not working for the press. Although 68% of current journalists have a university education, only 4.6% have received academic education in communications.

Bibliography: Iʿtimād al-Salṭana, *K. al-Āthār wa ʾl-maʾāthir*, Tehran 1306/1889, 117; L.P. Elwell-Sutton, *The press in Iran today*, in *JRCAS*, xxxv (1948), 209-19; Iṭṭilāʿāt, *Iṭṭilāʿāt dar yak rubʿ ḳarn*, Tehran 1329/1950; Mehrangiz Doulatschahi Ansari, *Die religions-politische Entwicklung der Publizistik in Iran und die Entstehung der freien Press infolge der Revolution von 1906*, diss. Heidelberg 1953; *Iran Almanac*, issues 1963-76; Masʿūd Barzīn, *Sayri dar maṭbūʿāt-i Īrān*, Tehran 1344/1965; Elwell-Sutton, *The Iranian press 1941-47*, in *Iran JBIPS*, vi (1968), 65-104; Barzīn, *Maṭbūʿāt-i Īrān 1343-1353*, Tehran 1354/1975; Yaḥyā Aryānapūr, *Az sabā tā nīmā*, 2 vols. Tehran 1354/1975; Kūʾīl Kūhan, *Tārīkh-i-sansūr dar maṭbūʿāt-i Īrān*, 2 vols. Tehran 1360/1981; W.H. Behn and W.M. Floor, *Twenty years of Iranian power struggle*, Berlin 1982; Muḥīṭ Ṭabāṭabāʾī, *Tārīkh-i taḥlīlī-yi maṭbūʿāt-i Īrān*, Tehran 1366/1987; Mushaffaḳ Hamadānī, *Khāṭirāt-i nīm ḳarn-i rūznāma-nigārī*, Los Angeles 1370/1991; P. Avery, *Printing, the press and literature in modern Iran*, in *Camb. hist. Iran*, vi, Cambridge 1991, 815-61; Mehdi Mohsenian-Rad and Ali Entezari, *Problems of journalism education in Iran*, in *Rasaneh. A Research Quarterly of Mass Media Studies*, v/2 (1994), 75; *Īrān-nāma*, xvi/1-2 (1998), special issue on journalism; Cyrus Masroori, art. *History of censorship in Iran up to 1941*, in D. Jones (ed.), *Censorship. An international encyclopedia*, 2001.

(W. FLOOR)

5. Turkey.

(a) Up to *ca.* 1960 [see DJARĪDA. iii].

(b) Since the 1960s.

The 1960s

The military take-over of 27 May 1960 put an end to the period when freedom of the press had been seriously threatened in Turkey due to the increasingly repressive policy of the *Demokrat Parti* [*q.v.*] (DP). For the most part the Turkish press welcomed the *coup* and the resultant "Government of National Unity" (*Millî Birlik Hükûmeti*). The Constitution of 1961 (articles 22-7) guaranteed freedom of the press, and laws restricting it were abolished. A new press law assured the rights of journalists in their working place, much to the chagrin of certain newspaper barons. The restrictive Penal Code remained in force. The "Press Advertising Organisation" (*Basın İlân Kurumu*) was established in 1961 for the purpose of an impartial distribution of advertisements from public institutions and organisations. The Turkish press decided to institute a system of self-control: a code of press ethics (*Basın ahlâk yasası*) was signed by all major newspapers.

The principal successor to the DP, the "Justice Party" (*Adalet Partisi*: AP), which won the general elections of 1965 and remained in power until the *muhtıra* of 1971 (see below), remained tolerant towards the press. The leftist press, often supporting the newly-founded "Labour Party of Turkey" (*Türkiye İşçi Partisi*; TİP), flourished during the 1960s in a hitherto unknown way: the weekly *Yön* (1961-7) founded by Doğan Avcıoğlu (1926-83), was one of the most discussed periodicals in Turkey for a while. It was followed by *Ant* (1967-71), and *Devrim* (1969-71) (see on these J.M. Landau, *Radical politics in modern Turkey*, Leiden 1974, 49-87). Among the newly-founded papers of the 1960s, the *Yeni Gazete* (1964-71) was the first daily paper printed in the offset technique. Another new type of paper for Turkey was the tabloid (*bulvar gazetesi*) *Günaydın*, founded in November 1968 by Haldun Simavi. Among its editorialists (*köşe yazarları*) was Aziz Nesin (1916-95) who also edited its weekly humoristic supplement *Ustura*. The rise of the conservative-nationalist paper *Tercüman* (founded in 1955) also began after 1961. *Hürriyet* [see ḎJARĪDA. iii] was the first newspaper whose circulation exceeded one million in the middle of the 1960s (Gevgilili, *Türkiye basını*, 225). Television was introduced in Turkey in 1968, but there was only one black-and-white channel until the mid-1980s.

The 1970s

Increasing violence in the country brought about a second military intervention, through the memorandum (*muhtıra*) issued by the armed forces on 12 March 1971. Martial law was proclaimed in eleven provinces. This intervention did not abolish the parliament, but governments of that period exerted pressure, especially on the leftist press. Journalists were arrested, papers banned and publications forbidden. The 1973 elections paved the way for a return to parliamentary democracy. The work of journalists was then, however, seriously disturbed by something like a civil war which ravaged the country. Numerous journalists, both rightists and leftists, became victims of attempts on their lives. A climax was reached with the assassination of Abdi İpekçi (1929-79), editor of *Milliyet* [see ḎJARĪDA. iii] by Mehmed Ali Ağca (who later attempted to kill Pope John Paul).

Social and political polarisation was also reflected in the media. Apart from the conservative papers *Tercüman, Son Havadis, Hakikat* (founded in 1970, it changed its name to *Türkiye* in 1971), and *Güneş* (founded in 1975), there were left-wing periodicals like the dailies *Yeni Ortam* (1972-6; close to the *Devrimci İşçiler Sendikaları Konfederasyonu* [DİSK]) and *Politika* (1975-7), whose director Ali İhsan Özgür was assassinated in 1978. A paper close to the AP was *Yeni Asya* (founded in 1970). The Islamist *Millî Selâmet Partisi* (MSP) had the support of the *Millî Gazete* (founded in 1973). The ideas of the neo-fascist *Millî Hareket Partisi* (MHP) were voiced by *Hergün, Millet* (1975-86) and *Ortadoğu* (1972), whose director İhsan Darendelioğlu was assassinated in 1979. Several old-established newspapers ceased publication in the 1970s: the mouthpiece of the CHP, *Ulus* (1934; founded in 1920 in Ankara as *Hākimiyyet-i milliyye*), ended its existence in July 1971, *Vatan* (1923 [see ḎJARĪDA. iii]), whose orientation had changed several times since 1950, in 1978. Important news magazines of the 1970s were *Yankı* (founded 1971 by the correspondent of *Time*, Mehmet Ali Kışlalı), *7 Gün* and *Toplum*. *Gırgır*, founded in 1972, was to become, after *Krokodil* and *Mad*, the third largest satirical paper in the world.

The 1980s

After the third intervention of the military on 12 September 1980 (12 Eylül), all political parties were banned. Printing houses of newspapers were closed down, and four papers (the leftist papers *Demokrat, Politika, Aydınlık* and *Hergün*, the organ of the MHP) were banned immediately after the *coup*. Between 12 September 1980 and 12 March 1984 publication of eight national papers was suspended seventeen times, for 195 days. In total, 181 journalists and writers were arrested and 82 of them sentenced during the same period (details in *Basın '80-84*, 197-230).

The influence of the military decreased after the general elections of 1983 were won by Turgut Özal's "Motherland Party" (*Anavatan Partisi*; ANAP) with a clear majority. This victory inaugurated a new period of economic liberalisation. The Turkish press had a share in the relatively rapid re-democratisation of the régime and became a significant factor in politics. Most papers were eventually fiercely opposed to the ANAP governments. In the late 1980s, Prime Minister Özal used the control of paper supplies against the hostile press. The freedom of the press continued to be restricted on the basis of the restrictive Constitution passed in 1982 (esp. articles 22, 24-30), the Press Law, the "Law on Harmful Publications", and the Penal Code (esp. articles 312 and 158). A series of government regulations in the spring of 1990 and later the "Law on Terrorism" also brought censorship to the press. In 1984, the "Kurdistan Workers' Party" (PKK), founded in 1978, had started its first action.

A number of papers was founded in the 1980s among which *Dünya* (1981), *Sabah* (1985), *Zaman* (1986; see below) are still published today (2003). The circulation of *Sabah*, founded by the dynamic Dinç Bilgin (b. 1940), publisher of the İzmir-based *Yeni Asır*, exceeded that of *Hürriyet* in 1987. *Akşam*, by then the oldest newspaper of Turkey (founded in 1918 [see ḎJARĪDA. iii]), ceased publication in 1982, *Yeni İstanbul* (founded 1949) in 1986, and *Son Havadis* in 1988. In the second half of the 1980s most papers adopted the editorial system (computer system, first used by *Yeni Asır*). The tabloid *Güneş* (1982-91) gave new impetus to give-away and lottery campaigns in the Turkish press which only *Cumhuriyet* refused to join. There was an explosion of weekly and monthly magazines in the 1980s, including cultural reviews of superior quality. *2000'e Doğru* (1986) was one of the best-known news magazines. A Turkish version of *Playboy* came on the market in 1985. The world of the press was shaken by the Asil Nadir affair in 1989. This Cypriot businessman had acquired, thanks to his contacts with government circles, the tabloids *Günaydın* and *Tan*, as well as several magazines, including the news magazine *Nokta* (founded in 1983 with the French *Le Point* as a model).

Most papers had left at that period the Avenue of the Sublime Porte (*Bâbıâli Caddesi*) in Istanbul, the Turkish Fleet Street. In 1988 a Press Museum (*Basın Müzesi*) was opened in the same area thanks to the Newspapermen's Association (*Gazeteciler Cemiyeti*).

The 1990s and beyond

The downfall of the ANAP government in 1991

has been in part attributed to the mobilisation of public opinion by the press. Tansu Çiller became the first female prime minister in 1993. The end of Kemalism seemed to have arrived with the general elections of December 1995 when Necmettin Erbakan's Islamist "Welfare Party" (*Refah Partisi*; RP) obtained 21% of the votes. A coalition government, the first Islamist-led government in Republican Turkey, was formed in July 1996. But once more, the military started to play a more active role. An ultimatum issued by the generals in February 1997 to restrict the influence of Islamists compelled the prime minister Erbakan to resign. His downfall was speeded by a sustained campaign in some sections of the press. Subsequently, the country was governed by various coalition governments formed by Kemalist and nationalist leaders. The PKK-led Kurdish insurgency came to an end after the capture of Abdullah Öcalan in Kenya in 1999. The country was shaken by a severe economic crisis in 2001. In November 2002, Recep Tayyip Erdoğan won the general election with his moderate Islamist "Justice and Development Party" (*Adalet ve Kalkınma Partisi*; AKP).

These developments were also reflected in the Turkish press at the turn of the 21st century with the rise of a "Kurdish" press and a growing importance of Islamic and Islamist papers (see below). Violence against journalists continued in the 1990s. *Cumhuriyet* lost seven of its writers through attacks, the most prominent victim being Uğur Mumcu (1942-93), known for his investigative journalism, who was killed by a car bomb in 1993.

Concentration and monopolisation (*tekelleşme*) became one of the major problems faced by the Turkish press. There was also serious concern about the media moguls', journalists' and columnists' increasingly close relations with the political establishment. Most national newspapers belonged (in 2003) to three important press groups which also controlled the country's largest private TV channels. Traditional ownership had almost disappeared from the media market. *Cumhuriyet* remained the only independent paper. Twelve papers, including the mass circulation papers *Hürriyet, Milliyet* and *Radikal* (founded in 1996 and considered by some as the most "Western" paper), and the sports paper *Fanatik*, belong to Aydın Doğan's *Doğan Media Group*. It is said to control nearly 40% of the country's advertising revenues and 80% of distribution (2003). The *Sabah* group plunged into crisis when its head Dinç Bilgin was jailed in 2001. Thanks to its promotional activities, the paper *Sabah* had reached a circulation of 1.5 million in October 1992. A law (*promosyon yasası*) eventually prohibited in 1997 *promosyons* except those of cultural value. *Tercüman* ceased publication in 1994, but two papers bearing the same name re-emerged after 2000. The leading news magazines in the 1990s were *Aktüel* (circulation: 40,000), *Tempo* (28,000), *Aksiyon* (18,000) and *Nokta* (3,000).

The "Kurdish" press

The 1990s also saw the emergence of a new type of papers focussing on Kurdish issues which appeared in Istanbul and Ankara, usually in Turkish. All of them were accused of being close to the PKK. The first of them, *Özgür Gündem*, founded in 1992 and banned by the Ankara State Security Court (DGM) in 1994, lost seven of its writers and correspondents and thirteen vendors to killings. It was followed by *Özgür Ülke* (1994-5), whose premises in Istanbul were the target of a devastating bomb attack in December 1994. *Yeni Politika* (13 April-16 August 1995) was one of the most often censored papers in Turkey. Its successors (*Demokrasi, Ülkede Gündem, Özgür Bakış, 2000'de Yeni Gündem*) had a similar fate, and functioned usually in a most precarious situation. *Yeniden Özgür Gündem* (founded in September 2002) had a circulation of *ca.* 10,000 in November 2003. In the 1990s, many Kurdish weekly or monthly magazines also began to appear, including local papers. The Kurdish language paper *Rojname* was soon banned after its first publication in December 1991. In the same year, the prohibition of Kurdish publications had been removed. There is now (2003) a Kurdish-language literary magazine, *Azadiya Welat*, published in Istanbul. However, most papers destined for Kurds from Turkey are published in Western countries known for their large Kurdish immigrant population (e.g. Sweden, etc.). The paper *Özgür Politika* is published in Europe. Kurdish satellite TV and numerous internet sites have created what has been called a "virtual Kurdistan".

Islamic and Islamist press

The spectacular rise of the Islamic and Islamist press dates from the 1980s. Prior to 1980, its percentage in terms of newspapers and periodicals was 7%, in 1993 it had reached 47% (G. Seufert, *Politischer Islam in der Türkei*, Istanbul 1997, 392n.). Many periodicals (including newspapers like *Yeni Asya, Türkiye, Millî Gazete*) have been associated with religious orders and groups in the Muslim world, the Naḳshbandī dervish order and its branches [see NAḲSHBANDIYYA] being particularly influential. *Yeni Şafak* (founded in 1995) was financed by a pious industrialist. The paper *Zaman* (see above), organ of the group around Fethullah Gülen of the *Nurcus* [see NURCULUK], is now (2003) among the top five national daily newspapers in Turkey, with an average circulation of 300,000. It boasts of having been the first Turkish daily newspaper to appear on-line (since 1995). It has bureaus and correspondents in many countries all over the world. It has special international editions for twelve foreign countries, those for the new Turkish Caucasian and Central Asian republics being printed in their own alphabets and languages. *Zaman* also owns the weekly news magazine *Aksiyon*, a children's monthly, a news agency, and the private TV channel *Samanyolu*.

Islamist reviews and magazines include weeklies, numerous monthly magazines (*Sızıntı*, Izmir, published by the *Türkiye Öğretmenler Vakfı*, founded in 1978), and publications for women: *Kadın ve Aile* (founded 1985) was the largest Muslim women's magazine, reputed to have sold 60,000. It was closely associated with that branch of the Naḳshbandī order whose major mouthpiece is the magazine *İslâm* (circulation 100,000). *Bizim Aile* (published since 1988) is a spin-off of the magazine *Köprü*, published since 1977 and representing the views of a section of the Nurcu order.

Local newspapers

National newspapers based in Istanbul account for about 90% of total circulation. But there have been registered up to 745 local newspapers published in Turkey, almost half of them being dailies. The circulation figures vary according to the economic development of the region. *Yeni Asır*, published in Izmir (founded in 1924; its predecessor, *ʿAṣîr*, was founded in Ottoman Salonika in 1895), remains the biggest newspaper with a regional character (circulation 43,000 in November 2003). The local press has been trying to renew itself technologically in recent years and many papers are produced by printing houses with offset printing facilities.

Turkish papers published in Europe

The first Turkish papers printed in Europe were *Akşam* and *Hürriyet* (Munich 1969). They were followed by *Tercüman* (1970), *Milliyet* (1972) and the *Millî Gazete* (1973). In the 1980s appeared *Türkiye* (1987), in the 1990s *Zaman* (1990), the weeklies *Cumhuriyet-Hafta* (1993) and *Dünya-Hafta* (1995), *Özgür Politika* (1995), *Sabah* (1996), *Emek* (leftist; 1996), and *Ortadoğu* (1996). *Hürriyet, Milliyet, Fanatik* and *Hafta Sonu*, all belonging to the Doğan Group, had a circulation of 189,000 (of which *Hürriyet* alone comprised 84,000), i.e. 80% of the Turkish newspapers sold in Europe.

The minority press

The decline of the Greek community in Istanbul from the 1960s onwards was also reflected in the Greek minority papers. *Elevtherê Phônê* and *Empros*, which figure among the signatories of the *Basın ahlâk yasası*, disappeared in 1965. Two Greek dailies still appear in Istanbul for a community of 2,000-3,000 souls: *Απογευματινή/Apoyevmatini* (founded in 1925), which until the death of its founder, Gr. Yaverides, in the 1970s, used to employ some ten journalists; and *Ηχώ/Iho* (1977), initially a weekly, which became a daily in 1979 (circulation: about 800 copies).

The Armenian press (for a population estimated at 60,000) counted some ten titles in 2001, including the bulletin of the Saint Saviour (*Surp Pırgiç* [Սուրբ Փրկիչ]) Hospital (a monthly founded in 1949), *Kulis* (a literary and artistic bi-monthly founded in 1946 by Agop Ayvaz) ceased publication in 1996. There are two daily papers: *Jamanak* [*Ժամանակ*] (founded in 1908, the oldest daily published in Turkey). Its circulation has decreased during the last years, from 15,000 to 1,500. Another daily, *Marmara* (Մարմարա ; founded in 1940) has been directed by Robert Haddeler, a writer and critic. It is also published in Armenian but since 2001 it has contained a Turkish supplement. The weekly *Agos* [*Ակօս*] was founded in 1996; it is published mainly in Turkish (circulation some 5,000). Two journalists of this paper were tried in 1999 because of an article on the *Varlık Vergisi* of 1942.

The once flourishing Jewish press in Judaeo-Spanish and French is now limited to the weekly *Şalom* (founded in 1947). It is, however, published in Turkish, with a few articles written in Judaeo-Spanish. The last Jewish French language daily, the *Journal d'Orient* (founded in 1917 by Albert Carasso), disappeared in 1971.

Whereas attempts to revive the French language press proved little successful, there is one English-language daily paper, *Turkish Daily News* (founded in 1961) published in Ankara. *Dünya* has an English-language daily news page; *Zaman* also has an English on-line edition.

Conclusion

The Turkish printed press has made considerable progress during the last two decades of the 20th century which have witnessed the industrialisation of the media. The number of newspapers with an average daily circulation over 10,000 was 11 in 1983, 14 in 1990 and 32 in 1997. According to August 2003 figures, the average total daily sales of 35 major daily papers was about 4 million. Some 25 of them had their own website in 2004, including several regional papers. The number of magazines has increased with extraordinary speed. Its total number, which was 20 in 1990, reached 110 in 1999 (total circulation around 2,300,000). They include magazines with foreign brand names like *Marie Claire, Cosmopolitan, Harper's Bazaar, Esquire, Votre Beauté*, or *National Geographic*. As far as printing techniques are concerned, the Turkish press has attained in most domains European standards.

But some basic issues remain: press readership is still far from assuming European proportions. According to official sources (*Facts about Turkey*, 412), the average number of newspapers sold to 1,000 persons is 58 (cf. Germany: 314). The habit of reading newspapers regularly has remained the privilege of a relatively small group, around 15% of the population (estimated at 67 million in 2000). The visual media have emerged as the most influential institution shaping public opinion. The number of private TV channels has exceeded twenty within a few years.

In spite of numerous amendments to the restrictive Constitution (the last ones in February 2003), press freedom in Turkey remains limited by various laws and a frequently restrictive interpretation of press freedom and freedom of expression by the judiciary. There is no functioning journalist's trade union. Journalists continue to be arrested and sentenced to prison terms. Leftist, Islamist and pro-Kurdish media are the primary targets. For many modern Turkish writers and intellectuals, criminal prosecution has been an indispensable part of their *curriculum vitae*. But even members of the mainstream media occasionally face legal action, although these papers usually practice a sort of self-censorship and avoid sensitive issues such as criticising the military and high-level corruption.

Bibliography: F.S. Oral, *Türk basın tarihi*, 2 vols., Ankara 1969; E.B. Şapolyo, *Türk gazetecilik tarihi ve her yönüyle basın*, Ankara 1969; H.R. Ertuğ, *Basın ve yayın hareketleri tarihi I*, Istanbul 1970; *Türkiye basın-yayın tarihi kaynakçası*, Ankara 1981; *Türkiye basın-yayın tarihi kaynakçası (Ek-1)*, 1982; A. Gevgilili, art. *Türkiye basını*, in *Cumhuriyet Dönemi Türkiye Ansiklopedisi*, i, Istanbul 1983, 202-28; G. Groc and İ. Çağlar, *La presse française de Turquie de 1795 à nos jours. Histoire et catalogue*, Istanbul 1985 (Varia turcica II); O. Koloğlu, *La presse turque: évolution et orientations depuis 1945*, in A. Gokalp (ed.), *La Turquie en transition*, Paris 1986, 177-98; N. Benbanaste, *Örneklerle türk musevi basının tarihçesi*, Istanbul 1988; H. Topuz *et al.*, *Basında tekelleşmeler*, Istanbul 1989; N. Clayer *et al.* (eds.), *Presse turque et presse de Turquie*, Istanbul 1992 (Varia turcica XXIII); M. Nuri Inuğur, *Türk basın tarihi*, Istanbul 1992; O. Koloğlu, *Türk basını—Kuvayi Milliye'den günümüze*, Istanbul 1993; M. Orhan Bayrak, *Türkiye'de gazeteler ve dergiler sözlüğü (1831-1993)*, Istanbul 1994; M. Bülent Varlık, *Türkiye basın-yayın tarihi bibliyografyası (Ek-2)*, Ankara 1995; Yusuf Tavus, *Basın rehberi*, [4]1995 ([1]1996); H. Topuz, *100 soruda türk basın tarihi*, Istanbul 1996 ([1]1973); Turkish News Agency for the Directorate General of Press and Information of the Prime Ministry, *Facts about Turkey*, Ankara 1998; Ç. Akkaya *et al.*, *Länderbericht Türkei*, Darmstadt 1998; M. Heper and T. Demirel, *The press and the consolidation of democracy*, in S. Kedourie (ed.), *Turkey. Identity, democracy, politics*, [2]London 1998, 109-23; A. Kabacalı, *Cumhuriyet öncesi ve sonrası matbaa ve basın sanayii*, Istanbul 1998. (J. Strauss)

SILĀḤ (A.), masc. and fem. noun according to the lexicographers, standard pl. *asliḥa*, with *sulūḥ, sulḥān* and *silāḥāt* also found in the lexica, the general term in Arabic for both offensive weapons and protective armour and equipment. This collective sense of the word is also often included in the general term *ʿudda*, literally "equipment, gear, tackle". The sense of "weapon" has clearly no connection with that of the common Arabic verb *salaḥa* "to defecate". Attestations of any parallel form of *silāḥ* are weak in Old South Arabian. One can only cite Biblical Hebrew *šelaḥ*, of obscure meaning in general but with the meaning of "javelin" or "some sort of weapon that can be carried and thrown" in such contexts as

II Chron. xxiii. 10, Joel ii. 8, etc., and as a possible parallel, despite the phonetic problems, Akk. *šêlu* "to sharpen weapons", *šēlūtu* "dagger blade" (*CAD, Letter Š*, ii, 275).

1. The pre-Islamic period.

The weapons of the pre-Islamic Arabs were essentially the bow, the sword and the spear or lance. Our knowledge of these weapons of theirs is almost entirely a bookish one, and it was from the evidence of pre-Islamic poetry that F.W. Schwarzlose compiled his *Die Waffen der alten Araber aus ihren Dichtern dargestellt* (Leipzig 1886, repr. Hildesheim 1982), a work concerned primarily with the nomenclature of weapons and their component parts.

Fighting was a prominent aspect of desert life, in which tribes often competed over pasture grounds, sought to drive off opponents' herds or were involved in protracted vendettas entailed by the unwritten laws of revenge, retaliation and the exacting of compensation for losses to the tribe's fighting strength [see DIYA; ḲIṢĀṢ; THA'R]. Hence a rich vocabulary evolved for weapons and armour, often descriptive, by metonymy, of some special characteristic ("shining", "incisive") or of some origin, real or supposed ("Indian", "Yemeni", "Khaṭṭī"). This vocabulary naturally attracted the philologists of Islamic times, concerned to elucidate the names of weapons, armour and their synonyms in early poetry. Whence the composition of works with titles like *Kitāb al-Silāḥ*, such titles being attributed to the Baṣran scholar al-Naḍr b. Shumayl (d. 204/820), al-Aṣmaʿī, Ibn Durayd [*q.vv.*] and Shamir b. Ḥamdawayh (d. 255/869) (see Schwarzlose, 11 n. 1). Few of these works have survived (Sezgin, *GAS*, viii, 257, lists a fragmentarily surviving *K. al-Silāḥ* by a disciple of al-Aṣmaʿī's), but lexicographical and philological studies like al-Thaʿālibī's *Fiḳh al-lugha* and Ibn Sīduh's *Mukhaṣṣaṣ* are rich sources of information on the nomenclature of weapons and their component parts. It is highly improbable that any of these works gave any actual descriptions of weapons or their use—the authors were literary men, who probably never wielded a weapon in anger in their lives, and not practical warriors—and on these points we have virtually no information. It is not till later mediaeval times that practical treatises on the art of war and the use of weapons are known (see below, 2.; FURŪSIYYA; ḤARB. 1.). The only direct, contemporary source which might conceivably give us some idea of pre-Islamic weapons lies in possible representations in petroglyphs and similar drawings. There are quite a lot of depictions of warriors wielding lances and bows, and possibly swords, on horseback and on foot, in the Thamudic and Safaitic materials, cf. also the frontispiece photograph of a rock graffito showing an archer, and the drawing of a South Arabian spear, of uncertain age, at p. 65 of R.B. Serjeant, *South Arabian hunt*, London 1976.

The weapon most frequently mentioned in the ancient literary sources is the sword (*sayf*), for which special works by the philologists are recorded, e.g. Abū ʿUbayda's *Kitāb al-Sayf* and a work by Abū Ḥātim al-Sidjistānī, a *Kitāb al-Suyūf wa 'l-rimāḥ* (Schwarzlose, 124 n. 1). These must have been stabbing swords for close, hand-to-hand fighting rather than cavalry swords. There emerges that swords of Indian steel (*hindī, muhannad*) were particularly prized; whether the Hind envisaged here relates to the Indian subcontinent or to lands beyond in Southeast Asia, such as Malaya or Sumatra, is unclear, but any such weapons were presumably imported via the Persian Gulf ports. Nearer home, the ancient Arabs prized blades forged by the smiths of Syria, e.g. of Boṣrā [*q.v.*] (see below), a land which had access to supplies of iron ore and to wooded terrains for the production of charcoal. On the other hand, it is unlikely that "Yemeni" swords were actually made in Yemen; more probably, blades or complete swords were imported from lands further east to the ports of Hadramawt and Yemen, thus acquiring this territorial name. See in general on swords of this period, Schwarzlose, 124-209.

The spear or lance (*rumḥ, ʿanaza, ḳanāt*, the latter term, originally "bamboo, reed shaft" being used by synecdoche for the whole weapon) was, it seems, included in the work by Abū Ḥātim al-Sidjistānī on swords and spears mentioned above (see also Schwarzlose, 210 n. 1). It was used as a thrusting weapon in close fighting, but spears which could be thrown at the enemy like javelins (*nayzak* < Pers. *nīza, miṭrad, ḥarba*) are also mentioned, and the designation *miṭrad* indicates that such throwing weapons could be used for hunting as well as war. Spears with a bamboo or strong reed shaft (*ḳanāt*) are often described as *khaṭṭī*, from al-Khaṭṭ [*q.v.*] in Baḥrayn or Hadjar, where a certain Samhar is said to have been an expert fashioner of spears, whence *samharī* ones. Whether these shafts were made from the stems of the vegetation growing along the Gulf shores, or were imported from further east, as the term *ḳanāt al-Hind* implies, is unclear. Various trees are also mentioned as providing wood for spear shafts, such as the *washīdj* or ash (?). Spears had a head (*sinān*) and a tapered iron butt at their lower end which could be stuck into the ground when the weapon was not being carried (*zudjdj*). See, in general, Schwarzlose, 210-45.

The bow and arrow were used by the ancient Arabs, and the sources distinguish "Arab" from "Persian" bows. See further ḲAWS, and Schwarzlose, 246-319.

As well as all these offensive weapons, there are frequent mentions of protective body armour in the shape of coats of mail (*dirʿ* or *sard, zarad, muzarrad* < Pers. *zard*, traceable back, according to Fraenkel, *Die aramäischen Fremdwörter im arabischen*, 241-2, to a Persian form preceding MP *zrēh* with a final *d*, Avestan *zrādhā; sard* appears in Ḳurʾān, XXXIV, 10/11, in a passage concerning King David's skill as a maker of closely-woven mail, cf. Jeffery, *The foreign vocabulary of the Qurʾān*, Baroda 1938, 169). The manufacture of chain armoured coats must have been basically in the settled fringes around the Arabian peninsula, as the Persian origin of some of its nomenclature shows. Also, Boṣrā in the Ḥawrān region of southern Syria was in Byzantine times a noted centre for the forging of weapons and the making of armour, and the Byzantine authorities tried on occasion to stop the export of these to the nomads. In *awāʾil* [*q.v.*] lore, the original making of mailed coats is attributed to King David (or, as some Arab commentators on ancient poetry averred, to a celebrated Jewish (?) smith called Dāwūd or to his son, but the identification of the inventor of mailed coats with the Biblical David was already made in pre-Islamic times [see DĀWŪD]). This skill was also attributed to the Tubbaʿ kings of Yemen. See, in general, Schwarzlose, 322-49. Mailed coats were accounted valuable in desert fighting, and it was weapons and coats of mail which the poet and prince of Kinda, Imruʾ al-Ḳays, allegedly entrusted to the Jewish Arab poet and lord of Taymāʾ al-Samawʾal b. ʿĀdiyāʾ [*q.v.*] and which the latter refused to give up to the Ghassānid king al-Ḥārith b. Djabala.

Iron helmets were termed *bayḍa*, from their resemblance in shape to an ostrich egg, see Schwarzlose, 349-51, and also *khūdha* < Pers. *khūd*. Although not mentioned extensively in poetry, which prefers to extol fearless warriors who scorned to protect themselves in battle behind shields, the pre-Islamic Arabs do seem to have employed shields on such occasions (*turs, dj̲unna, midj̲ann, daraḳa*). Such shields were probably made of hide (as is specifically said of the *daraḳa*) stretched over a wooden frame, enough to deflect the indifferent weapons of the nomads. See Schwarzlose, 351-6.

Bibliography: Given in the article.

(C.E. Bosworth)

2. The Islamic period.

The military technologies of Arabia at the time of the Prophet Muḥammad remain little known, but they were still clearly under strong influence from neighbouring technologically advanced neighbours such as the Byzantine Empire, Sāsānid Persia and India via maritime trade contacts. Not surprisingly, early Byzantine styles dominated in the north and west, Persian in the east and, to a less certain extent, Indian in southern Arabia. Swords and spears remained the favoured weapons, while archery played a minor role and only amongst foot soldiers. Most armour was of mail although leather defences were also widespread, much of this latter probably being manufactured in Yemen (see 1. above). Similarly, the people of prosperous but strife-torn trading regions such as the Ḥidj̲āz appear to have been relatively rich in weaponry.

With the rapid Muslim Arab conquest of vast regions from Central Asia and India to Spain and the Atlantic Ocean, other military techniques began to appear in the arms and armour of Muslim armies during the 8th and 9th centuries. After the establishment of an Islamic "empire", such armies became largely territorial which further encouraged the development of regional styles. Thus Central Asian Turkish military techniques had their first impact in 8th to 9th-century Transoxania and what is now eastern Persia, while Sāsānid Persian military styles remained dominant in western Persia and eastern parts of the Arab world until the 9th-10th centuries. Early Byzantine military styles survived in areas like eastern Anatolia well into the 10th century, and in Syria and Egypt well into the 12th century. Yet the situation was less clear in North Africa and the Iberian peninsula. Here pre-Islamic military techniques had generally been more primitive than those of the conquering Muslim Arabs, despite a residual early Byzantine military heritage.

This is not to say that the Muslim Arabs merely adopted the military styles of those whom they conquered. Nevertheless, the Muslim Arabs' contribution to the development of a specifically Islamic military tradition, and to the history of military technology as a whole, was primarily to open up a vast area to differing military influences. Thus Persian influence was eventually felt in North Africa, Byzantine technology reached Iberia and, above all, the Turkish Central Asian military tradition spread throughout the Middle East. Such Turkish influence also served as a channel whereby Chinese military techniques spread westward and may even have reached the Iberian peninsula, though in a very diluted form.

A truly Islamic tradition of arms, armour and their associated tactics developed rapidly, yet this was neither uniform nor monolithic. Large variations could always be seen between different regions resulting both from local traditions or conditions, and from the recruitment of troops from specific geographical zones which had their own distinctive styles.

In general, however, it could be said that Persian and Turkish influences were the most powerful, whereas those of the Byzantine or Mediterranean countries were of secondary importance, at least after the first century of Islamic history. Such a pattern persisted until early modern times as peoples and dynasties of essentially Turkish origin rose to political dominance in most of the militarily significant Islamic countries. Only in the late 18th and 19th centuries, with the rise of European military power and its accompanying colonialism, did indigenous or Turkish military practice rapidly give way to a widespread adoption of European weaponry and of the tactics associated with such modern technologies.

Weapons

For Islamic bows and archery, see ḲAWS; for firearms, see BĀRŪD; for siege weaponry, see ḤIṢĀR; and see also DJAYS̲H̲.

Since ancient and pre-Islamic times the long bamboo-hafted spear or *rumḥ* had been regarded as a typically Arab weapon. It was used on foot, on horseback and when riding camels. In the early Islamic centuries the Arabs were also renowned for their use of a relatively short sword (*sayf*). This was probably a broad-bladed weapon reflecting Roman and Byzantine infantry traditions rather than the cavalry traditions of Persia, where long-bladed slashing swords had been widespread for some centuries. Whereas the typical Arab *rumḥ* spear remained in use until modern times, the Arabs' short *sayf* was soon replaced by longer-bladed weapons suitable for mounted combat, though these were still largely known as *suyūf*. Only in southern and eastern Arabia (Yemen, Ḥaḍramawt and ʿUmān), and in a few other isolated parts of the Arabian peninsula, did short swords persist along with a tradition of infantry-dominated warfare.

Long, single-edged cavalry swords were already characteristic of Turco-Mongol Central Asia and had appeared in Persia and the Byzantine Empire shortly before the Islamic conquests of the 7th and 8th centuries. Thereafter, they become increasingly popular throughout most of the Islamic world, becoming the dominant cavalry sword by the 15th century although the single-edged sword or sabre never entirely replaced the double-edged weapon. The curved or true sabre spread from Turkish Central Asia into Islamic Persia by the 11th century, or perhaps slightly earlier. Thereafter, in a great variety of forms, it spread throughout most of the Islamic world reaching Granada, the last bastion of Andalusian Islam, by the 15th century. Heavier straight and double-edged weapons were, nevertheless, still used in many parts of the Islamic world in the 19th century, particularly in Islamic sub-Saharan Africa.

Smaller weapons, including those which fell between the categories of sword and dagger, were similarly used in most areas at most times. Here there may have been a greater degree of similarity across the Islamic world, perhaps because a particular type or shape of personal weapon was often worn as a mark of religious or cultural identity. The most obvious example was a heavy dagger or short stabbing sword widely known as a *k̲h̲andj̲ar* (for variations on this and other weapons terminology, see the *Glossary* below). Although the development of the *k̲h̲andj̲ar* drew on many regional traditions and evolved into various shapes of dagger in different parts of the Islamic world, the basic weapon again appears to have been of eastern Iranian or Turkish origin. Other sometimes highly distinctive styles of dagger were limited to smaller areas, generally on the fringes of the Islamic world such as Morocco, the Caucasus and the East Indies. In the latter region, the double-edged *kēris* dagger or short sword was retained from pre-Islamic times and continued to have an almost magical and pagan significance amongst a population sometimes only superficially converted to Islam.

Other weapons where a distinctly Islamic style developed were war-axes and maces. The latter were occasionally described as a "friendly" weapons, suitable for use during conflicts with fellow-Muslims as a lighter mace, when skilfully used, could incapacitate without killing a foe. Both also involved a large and complex terminology which distinguished between sometimes minor varieties of weapon but which nevertheless remains in part obscure. This terminology, along with surviving weapons and abundant pictorial representations, show that axes ranged from those with large "half-moon" to narrow spiked blades, while maces varied considerably in weight, shape of head, length of haft or handle and in the material from which they were made.

The javelin was widely used during the early period (7th-13th centuries), particularly by Arab and Persian troops, and remained in use by cavalry in most Islamic countries at least until the 15th century, certainly long after the javelin had been abandoned in western Europe. This probably reflected the more mobile and more disciplined character of Islamic armies during the mediaeval period, at least when compared to their European rivals, as well as the lighter styles of armour associated with Islamic tactics. The fact that such an apparently simple weapon as a javelin came in a large variety of sizes, weights and types of blade, along with an equally complex terminology, further illustrates the importance of the javelin in the hands of both foot soldiers and horsemen. It is also worth noting that cavalry training exercises or "games" involving the javelin were not only developed within the Islamic world but were copied by neighbours ranging from Spaniards and Ethiopians to Armenians [see DJERĪD and FURŪSIYYA].

Armour

Islamic armies have been widely regarded as lightly armoured when compared to their Western European rivals, but this is a misleading over-simplification. The amount of armour available to early mediaeval European forces such as those of the Crusaders has been exaggerated, while that available to Islamic armies from the time of the first conquests onwards has generally been underestimated. Nevertheless, there were wide variations between regions resulting from the differing availability of iron and of wealth to pay for the manufacture or importation of expensive military equipment.

Four types of body armour dominated throughout Islamic military history. These were mail (inter-linked metal rings, usually of iron); lamellar (small scales of iron, bronze, hardened leather or other rigid materials laced to each other but not to a flexible fabric or leather backing); so-called soft-armour of felt, quilted material or flexible buff leather; and a distinctive later form known as mail-and-plate armour. A fifth system of construction has only recently been recognised on the basis of archaeological finds rather than obscure textual references and barely decipherable artistic representations. This is a form of flexible protection consisting of partial hoops of hardened or apparently reconstituted leather which may have been of Central Asian or even Chinese derivation. Hardened and apparently reconstituted leather was also used in the construction of helmets, as shown in written sources such as Marḍī or Murḍā b. ʿAlī al-Ṭarsūsī [see AL-ṬARSŪSĪ] (*Tabṣirat arbāb al-lubāb*, ed. and tr. Cl. Cahen, *Un traité d'armurerie composé pour Saladin*, in *BEO*, xii [1948], 103-63), and confirmed by recent though as yet unpublished archaeological finds in Syria. Carbon dating tests on wood and sinew amongst these finds have produced an optimum date at the end of the 12th century, while tests on the leather have produced an optimum date of A.D. 1220. It is however, worth noting that a leather helmet or reinforced hat amongst these Syrian finds incorporates small piece of wood; supposedly "wooden" helmets have been mentioned in previously inexplicable texts.

Full plate armour consisting of large shaped pieces of iron buckled or rivetted together, of the type known in western Europe from the 14th century to early modern times, remained rare though not entirely unknown in the Islamic world. Where they seem to have been occasionally used, as in al-Andalus, southern India and the Philippines, they almost invariably reflected direct Western European military influence.

The body-covering mail hauberk (coat or tunic-like protective garment) generally known as the *dirʿ*, and the coif (hood) known as the *mighfar*, were by far the most common form of metallic protection throughout the Mediterranean lands, the Middle East and Persia at the time of the Prophet Muḥammad. It subsequently evolved into a greater variety of forms than was seen elsewhere, ranging from ordinary hauberks, given names describing their overall size or shape, to the *kazāghand* which had its own integral padded lining and a decorative outer layer of cloth.

Only in eastern Persia, Afghanistan and Transoxania was lamellar armour common, although it was used in the late Roman Middle East and Sāsānid Persia during earlier centuries and remained known if only occasionally worn. The period from the 8th to 14th centuries saw such lamellar armour spread westwards in the Islamic world along with other essentially Turkish Central Asian military styles. As a result, the lamellar *djawshan* became widespread throughout most Islamic countries (with the possible exception of North Africa and the Iberian peninsula) by the 12th century, and even in the Islamic West, lamellar was known if not popular. Nor was mail armour abandoned in favour of such lamellar protections. Instead, the two were often worn together, usually with the lamellar *djawshan* on top, until the development of mail-and-plate protections combining the advantages of both forms made it unnecessary to wear two armours at once.

Such mail-and-plate armour appeared in a variety of forms and used varied terminology, some of it stemming from earlier and different usage. In the Ottoman Empire, however, such the new style of body protection was often called a *ḳorazin*, from the common European term cuirass and its various Balkan dialect forms. In this mail-and-plate armour, pieces of iron plate of varied shapes and sizes designed to protect different parts of the body were linked by pieces of mail of varying widths depending on the degree of flexibility required. It was an essentially Islamic technological development, perhaps first appearing in ʿIrāḳ or western Persia in the 14th century, from where it spread to become the most typical 15th to 18th-century form of Islamic armour for both men and horses. As such it was characteristic of the late Mamlūk, Ottoman, later Persian and Indo-Muslim states.

So-called soft armours were widespread in early Islamic centuries and seem to have remained popular until the early 14th century, thereafter largely being relegated to the hottest regions such as India and Sudan. These should not, however, be seen only as a cheap alternative to metallic armour. Rather, they were a light, effective and easily-made protection suitable for the highly mobile cavalry-dominated warfare which characterised Islamic military history. Soft armour could also be combined with other forms of protection. In particular, it was worn beneath or combined with mail protections. Soft armours were also suitable in the hot climates characteristic of some Islamic countries and survived throughout the 19th century in the sub-Saharan Sudan.

The history of Islamic helmets differed from that of Europe, generally reflecting a preference for good visibility and mobility at the cost of less protection. Little is yet known about helmets in the early Islamic period (7th to 9th centuries), but in general they seem to have continued previous Romano-Byzantine and Persian shapes and forms of construction, most of which were based on two pieces joined along a central comb. Unfortunately, the terminology, though varied, cannot usually be identified with one specific form of helmet. In fact, it seems that the naming of helmets, though not entirely interchangeable, was generally unspecific (see the *Glossary* below).

Central Asian types of pointed and segmented helmet were already spreading into the Middle East and eastern Europe before the coming of Islam. Thereafter, such helmets, in which iron segments were rivetted either to each other or to an iron frame, spread throughout the Islamic countries. Meanwhile, advances in metallurgy within Islam during the 8th to 11th centuries, and perhaps even earlier, led to the production of one-piece iron helmets in relatively large numbers long before such defences appeared in Europe or even the Byzantine Empire. By and large, this one-piece form was known as the *bayḍa*. Helmets were an obvious and popular object on which wealth or prestige could be demonstrated, as a result of which most of the techniques of inlay and surface decoration found in other forms of Islamic metalwork also came to be seen on helmets. Meanwhile, lighter helmets made of leather and, apparently, a form of reconstituted hardened leather were also used in most regions.

Facial and neck protection was provided by mail coifs (hoods) and mail or lamellar aventails (veil-like skirts hanging from the rim of a helmet). Only rarely were rigid metallic face-guards or hinged visors seen on Islamic helmets. Nevertheless, they did appear in Central Asia and Persia during the 12th to 14th centuries and, in a very different form, in the Iberian peninsula around the same period. These exceptions probably reflected special military circumstances, such as an enhanced threat from horse-archery composite bows in the east and from a greater use of handheld crossbows in Iberia. Elsewhere, flexible mail or lamellar head and neck protections, often pulled across the face to leave only small apertures for the eyes, were considered an adequate defence.

Shields of wood, hardened leather, wickerwork and, in later centuries, of iron were all used by Muslim warriors. Most were round and relatively small, being suitable for light cavalry warfare. Yet there were plenty of other variations. Tall, kite-shaped shields for infantry use were used in the Middle East during the 11th to 13th centuries. These included the flat-based *djanūwiyya* whose name might indicate that it was initially imported from Genoa, since identical flat-based infantry shields or mantlets were also characteristic of Italy though not of other parts of western Europe at this time. Large shields which were apparently mantlets (shields that could be rested on the ground), made of woven reeds, were probably widespread in Arabia at the time of the Prophet and appear to have continued in use, at least in ʿIrāḳ, until at least the 9th century.

Large and flexible shields made from various animal hides were used in the Sahara, North Africa, Egypt and the Iberian peninsula during the mediaeval period and subsequently developed into the smaller but characteristic kidney-shaped "Moorish" *adarga* of 14th to 17th-century Spain and Portugal (this name stemming from the Ar. *daraḳa* meaning a small shield, usually of leather). Shields of purely European form were also used by Muslim Andalusian soldiers during periods when western European military fashions dominated, most obviously in the 13th century.

Meanwhile, the typical Turkish *ḳalḳan* shield was constructed from a spiral of cane bound together with cotton or silk thread. This formed an exceptionally light and effective cavalry shield in which the threads gave almost unlimited scope for colour and decoration. Iron shields were known by the 12th century, the earliest known example being of segmented construction, but they only became more widespread and of one-piece construction in the 16th and 17th centuries. These later metal shields had developed in response to guns, as they had in Europe, and were as rapidly abandoned when advances in firearms rendered them redundant.

Armour of a rigid or semi-rigid type for the limbs was used in several Islamic countries long before it became more than a localised novelty in mediaeval Europe. This almost certainly resulted from the importance of close-combat cavalry warfare with swords. Nevertheless, Islamic warriors never took limb defences to the extremes seen in later mediaeval and early modern Europe. Early Islamic arm protections such as the *bāzūband, kaff* and *sāʿid* (7th to 14th centuries), though never very widespread, followed in the Byzantine and Turco-Persian traditions. The latter consisted of segmented vambraces for the lower arms, probably of iron or bronze but perhaps also of hardened leather, while the upper arms were protected by the sleeves of a mail hauberk or by flaps of lamellar armour attached to the body of a lamellar cuirass. A style of long-hemmed, half-sleeved lamellar cuirass became more widespread after the Mongol invasions of the 13th century but was rarely seen west of Persia. A rigid tube-like iron vambrace for the lower arms, known in Turkish as the *ḳolčaḳ* or *ḳulluḳ*, appeared in the second half of the 13th or early 14th century and was almost certainly of Sino-Mongol origin. Thereafter it remained popular in Central Asia, Persia, Turkey and Mamlūk Egypt.

Leg protections of similar construction to arm defences were known in pre-Islamic Transoxania but seem to have declined in popularity after the coming of Islam. Mail leg protections appeared in Islamic and Byzantine sources in the 11th century, slightly before they did so in western Europe. These and other forms, included those of mail-and-plate construction, reappeared in later years being known as *budluḳ, dizček, kalsāt zarad, rānāt ḥadīd* and *sāḳ al-mūza*. Nevertheless, such items of armour were generally reserved for a small élite of heavily-armoured cavalry.

Horse-armour

It has often been assumed that horse-armour was rare or even unknown in the early Islamic period because it is virtually unknown in art before the 14th century. Documentary sources, however, make it clear that various forms of horse-armour were widespread. The most popular type appears to have been of quilted or padded construction; this being reflected in the most common Arabic term for horse-armour, *tidjfāf*. Before the late 13th century, references to horse-armours of scale, lamellar or mail are rare, though they can be found.

In most parts of the world, and during most periods, horse-armour was primarily a defence against arrows or other such missiles. Even in these circumstances it was more effective against long-range harassment than close-range shooting. This was clearly true in the Islamic world where, even in the later period (15th to 17th centuries) light horse-armours of quilted, leather, lamellar, mail or mail-and-plate construction were relatively widespread, whereas plated iron horse-armour was virtually unknown. Generally speaking, the construction of horse-armour reflected that used for the rider's own armour, though there tended to be a certain time lag between the introduction of new styles for the rider and for his horse. Thus a rider might wear a mail-and-plate cuirass while riding a horse still protected by hardened leather lamellae.

The chamfron or armour for the animal's head was also used, being known as a *burḳuʿ*, *kashka*, *sarī* and probably *tishtaniyya*; the variety of terms indicates that this form of protection was more widespread than is sometimes thought. This was probably of hardened leather until plated metal forms, along with fully lamellar horse-armours, became common in the 14th century. Nevertheless, there is some evidence that rigid metal chamfons were known in Egypt and neighbouring Islamic territories some centuries earlier and that these were almost certainly descended from Roman forms of horse-armour.

A few surviving head protections for camels date from the Ottoman period but these are likely to have been for parade rather than war use. Much elephant-armour was, however, used in war. Naturally, it was most highly developed in Islamic India although war-elephants continued to be used elsewhere in the eastern parts of the Muslim world, as they had been in the pre-Islamic period [see FĪL. 2. As beasts of war]. Little is known about such early Islamic elephant-armour, although enormous circular shields to protect the animal's vulnerable ears do appear in art sources from the 12th or 13th centuries.

Terminology

The terminology of Islamic arms and armour is huge and embraces several languages with the same terms, or minor variations on such terms, being used within several languages. Many other terms are merely descriptive or poetic. The following list includes only the most important.

GLOSSARY

ʿabbāsī: curved sword, Mughal India
absad: cheek-piece of helmet, Mughal India
abṣar: leather shield (Ar. and Pers.)
adaga: small shield or parrying device, Mughal India (from Ar. *daraḳa*; Indo-Pers.)
ʿadī: helmet, probably of riveted plates (Ar.)
afaru: sabre (Berber)
afru: knife, Algeria (Berber)
afru ghanim: lit. "rose petal"; dagger, Morocco (Berber)
aghash: baton or staff, equivalent of Ar. *ʿaṣā* (Ḳîpčaḳ Tk.)
ʿāʾid: central part or grip of spear-shaft (Ar.)
ʿalāḳa: connections of a *djawshan* cuirass (Ar.)
alla: long spear or javelin with a large blade (Ar.)
ʿamūd: heavy form of mace, probably with flanged head (Ar.)
anābīb: spaces between knots of a bamboo spear-shaft (Ar.)
ʿanaza: short spear or staff weapon with a large elongated blade (Ar.)
ʿanāza: short infantry spear, Mughal India (Indo-Pers.)
anf: nasal of helmet (Ar.)
ʿarāḍ: blade of large-bladed spear (Ar.)
ʿarḍ: flat surface of sword-blade (Ar.)
artak-i kājim: horse-armour, Mughal India (Indo-Pers.)
ʿaṣā: club, cudgel, iron staff or light form of mace (Ar.)
asbād: possibly the cheek-pieces of a helmet (Ar.)
ashîk: helmet, equivalent of Ar. *khūda* (Ḳîpčaḳ Tk.)
aṣl: shaft of spear (Ar.)
aṣm: staff weapon in which the blade is longer than the haft (Ar.)
ʿayna: individual lamellae or pieces of a lamellar cuirass (Ar.)
ʿayr: central ridge of a spear-blade (Ar.)
badan: short hauberk or shirt of mail, sometimes sleeveless (Ar.)
baghlṭāḳ: horse-armour, usually quilted (Pers.)
bakhta-kalaghī, *bagta-kalagi*: feathered helmet crest or plume, Mughal India
bakhtar-zillu: scale or scale-lined armour of Mongol origin, Mughal India
ballam: broad-bladed short spear, Mughal India
balṭa: war-axe (Ḳîpčaḳ Tk. and Ar.)
baltū: war-axe, Mughal India
band-mawdj: "watering" pattern on sword-blade (Indo-Pers.)
bank: dagger with extravagantly curved blade (Hindi)
baračhā: spear all of metal, Mughal India
barāsim: horse-armour or caparison (Ar.)
bardhanb: crupper, piece of horse-armour covering the rump or tail (see also *pār dum*) (Ar.-Pers.)
bargustuwān, *barkustuwān*: horse-armour, also elephant armour (Pers.)
bayḍ: type of sword-blade (Ar.)
bayḍa: helmet, probably of one-piece construction (Ar.)
bāzūband: vambrace, lower arm protection (Pers.)
bekter: cuirass, usually lamellar (Mongol)
bhala, *bhallā*: spear or cavalry javelin (Indo-Pers.)
bhandju, *bhandjī*: armour with throat-guard, Mughal India
bhudj: combined axe and dagger, Mughal India
bîchak: knife (Ḳîpčaḳ Tk.)
bichāḳ: single-edged dagger, Mughal India
birmāhan, *birmān*: Indian sword-blade (Pers.)
bitčhawa: dagger with looped guard on the grip, southern India
bozdaghan: type of mace, lit. "grey falcon" (Tk.)
budluḳ: thigh defences (Tk.)
bughlutāḳ: quilted soft armour (Pers.)
bukhtar: body armour of Mongol origin, Mughal India
burḳuʿ, pl. *barāḳiʿ*: chamfron (lit. "veil"; Ar.)
čahār āʾīna, *chār āʾīna*: lit. "four mirrors"; body armour basically consisting of four linked plates (Pers.)
čakar: throwing disc (Indo-Pers.)
čakh: sheath or scabbard (Pers.)
čakhī: infantry mantlet (Indo-Pers.)
čamchāḳ: cavalry axe, Mughal India
čaray: single-edge sword or large dagger with a reinforced back, known in Europe as a "Khyber knife", Mughal India (see also *salawar* and *čhura*)
čashmak: face-covering aventail of helmet (Pers.)
čhura: single-edge sword or large dagger with a reinforced back, known in Europe as a "Khyber knife", Mughal India (see also *salawar* and *čaray*)
čičak: helmet with a neck-guard, pendant ear-pieces and a sliding nasal (Tk.)
čilamum: dagger, Mughal India
čirwā: small shield, Mughal India

čūb: staff or club, or shaft of spear or mace (Pers.)
čūbhā-i āhan: probably long form of infantry mace (Pers.)
čuḳal: mail hauberk (Tk.)
čuḳmar, shuḳmar: mace (Ḳîpčaḳ Tk.)
čumuḳ, shumuḳ: mace (Ḳîpčaḳ Tk.)
dabbūs, dabbūṣ: general term for mace (Ar.)
dabīra: rear part of a helmet, neck-guard or aventail (Ar.)
dahra: curved dagger (Pers.)
daraḳa: small shield, usually of leather but sometimes of other materials (Ar.)
dās: agricultural implement sometimes used as a weapon (Pers.)
dashna, dashan: large dagger (Pers.)
dast: edge of sword-blade (Pers.)
dastānā: vambrace, Mughal India
ḍawārī: javelin with a long socket to the blade, like Roman *pilum* or Frankish *angon* (Ar.)
deste-chūb: mace (Tk. from Pers.)
dhāl: shield, Mughal India
dhāl-baftā: shield of folded silk, Mughal India
dhu'āba: decorative tassels on spear or sword, also wrist-strap of sword (Ar.)
dhubba: point or top part of sword (Ar.)
dhūp: straight sword with enclosed basket-hilt, Mughal India
dir': mail hauberk (Ar.)
dizček: thigh and knee defences (Ott. Tk.)
djaba: fabric-covered mail hauberk; also quilted soft-armour or incorporating such a soft-armour (see also *djubba*; Tk.)
djafn: scabbard (Ar.)
djaghnul: axe with narrow blade shaped like a bird's beak, Mughal India
djah: throwing disc (Indo-Pers.)
djāk: form of mace (Pers.)
djamadhar: broad thrusting dagger with a horizontal grip, Mughal India
djanūwiyya: kite-shaped infantry shield with flattened base (perhaps originally "from Genoa"; Ar.)
djarīd: light cavalry javelin (Ar. "palm branch stripped of its leaves")
djawb: shield or mantlet of wood and leather, or perhaps of leather-bound cane (Ar.)
djawshan: lamellar or laminated cuirass (Ar. and Pers.)
djibā: quilted soft armour, Mughal India (see also *djubba*)
djināwī: style of dagger, Algeria, lit. "Genoese" (Ar.)
djirāb: cover for scabbard and perhaps also sword (Ar.)
djirī: Indian dagger (Ar.)
djīwarak: unclear form of Indian armour (Pers.)
djubba: large form of quilted soft armour, sometimes incorporating a layer of mail (Ar. and Pers.)
djunna: shield, normally wood (Ar.)
dodhārā: double-edged short-sword or dagger, Mughal India
du-sanga: spear or pike with two-pronged blade (Indo-Pers.)
dubulghā: domed helmet without ear-pieces, Mughal India
dumchī: crupper, armour for rump of horse, Mughal India
dūrbāsh: infantry spear with a doubled-point, later perhaps an infantry axe with half-moon blade (Pers.)
dushnī: small dagger (see *dashna*; Ar.)
falākhan: sling (Pers.)
faṭīr: rivets of mail links (Ar.)
firind: "watering" pattern on damascene sword-blade (Ar.)
fuḳra: groove down sword-blade (Ar.)
furandjiyya, furaydjiyya: infantry spear or staff weapon, possibly with European-style flanges or "wings" below the blade (Ar.)
gandja: quillons of Malayan *kēris* dagger (Malay)
gara: knot or lacing or armour (Pers.)
gardanī: gauntlet, Mughal India
gārwa, gāruwa: quilted leather soft-armour, or a form of quilted shield or mantlet (Pers.)
ghilāf: scabbard, sheath or container for armour (Ar.)
ghilāla: rivets in construction or armour or weapons (Ar.)
ghimd: scabbard (Ar.)
ghirār: edges of sword-blade (Ar.)
ghughwāh: mail hauberk with integral coif, Mughal India
girah kusha: hooked spear (Indo-Pers.)
girībān: aventail, gorget or tippet (Pers.)
gudhār: infantry javelin or staff-weapon (Pers.)
gundar: javelin (Tk.)
gūpāl: form of mace (Pers.)
guptī kard: small thrusting knife with integral gauntlet, Mughal India
gurz: mace, probably asymetrical, animal-headed form (Pers.)
gustuwān: horse-armour (see *bargustuwān*; Pers.)
ḥabīka: coif or more likely aventail (Ar.)
ḥadd: point or perhaps edge of sword-blade (Ar.)
ḥadjaf: shield, usually leather, of Africa and Andalus (Ar.)
ḥadjārat al-yad: hand-thrown stone (Ar.)
ḥalḳa: ring, either as part of a mail hauberk or for other purposes (Ar.)
ḥamīla, ḥimāla: baldric, or attachment points on scabbard for a baldric or sword-belt (Ar.)
ḥandjer: dagger (see *khandjar*; Ott. Turk.)
ḥarba: large-bladed infantry spear or staff-weapon (Ar.)
ḥarf: edge of sword-blade (Ar.)
harrī: Indian dagger (Ar.)
ḥashw: padded garment or soft armour (Ar.)
ḥilya: decorative elements on scabbard and sword (Ar.)
hirāwa: thick haft of a staff weapon or spear (Ar.)
ḥusām: edges of sword-blade (Andalusian Ar.)
kabastin: ball and chain (Urdu)
ḳabḍa: grip or hilt of sword (Pers.)
ḳabīʿa: pommel of sword-hilt (Ar.)
kabūra: heavy form of cuirass (Ar. prob. from Pers.)
ḳadd: sword-blade (Ar.)
ḳaddara: straight two-edged sword (Pers.)
kādjam, kadjīm, kadjīn: horse armour of mail (Pers.)
kaff: gauntlet or extension to a vambrace; also perhaps an upper arm defence attached to body armour (Ar.)
kāfir-kūbat: form of mace (Ar.)
ḳahzana: thick haft of spear or staff weapon (Ar.)
ḳā'im: hilt of sword (Ar.)
ḳalaʿ: form of straight broad sword-blade (Ar.)
ḳalāchūr, ḳalādjūrī, ḳaldjūrī: curved sword or early form of sabre (poss. from Turk. *ḳilič*; Pers. and Ar.)
kalaghī: helmet-crest, Mughal India
kalb: ring on scabbard to attached baldric or straps to belt (Ar.)
ḳalb: centre of shield, over the grip (Ar.)
ḳalḳan: spiral cane shield bound with silk or cotton (Turk.)
kalsāt zarad: mail chausses (Ar.)
kamand: lasso (Pers.)
kamarband: waist and abdomen protecting armour or the central part of a *djawshan* cuirass (Pers.)
ḳanāt: long spear (Ar.)
kanbūsh: caparison or horse-cloth (Ar.)
kantha-shubha: gorget for neck and throat, Mughal India

kantup: one-piece helmet, Mug̲h̲al India
ḳarāčul: sword associated with Central Asian Turks, probably a corruption of *ḳalāčūr* (Indo-Pers.)
kārd: knife or small dagger (Pers.)
ḳarḳal: quilted soft armour or arming coat, later incorporating iron scales or plates (Ar.)
ḳarṭal: Indian curved sword or dagger (Ar.)
karud: straight-bladed narrow-bladed dagger, Mug̲h̲al India
kārwa: leather mantlet padded with cotton (see also *gārwa*; Indo-Pers.)
kas̲h̲ka, ḳas̲h̲ḳā: chamfrom or the front part of horse-armour, Mug̲h̲al India
kaskara: Sudanese straight double-edged sword
katāra: Indian sword or large dagger (Pers.)
ḳatīr: rivet-heads of a mail hauberk (Ar.)
ḳawnas: point or decorated summit of helmet (Ar.)
kazāg̲h̲and, kaz̲h̲āgand, kaz̲h̲āgan, kāzig̲h̲and: fabric-covered mail hauberk with integral padded lining (Ar. and Pers.)
ḳazāḳand: fabric-covered, mail-lined and padded armour (see also *kazāg̲h̲and*; Pers.)
ḳazākanda: (Tk. from Pers.; see *ḳazāḳand*)
kēris, kris: Malay & Indonesian dagger of varied form, usually with its blade expanding towards the grip and with a slightly angled grip (Malay)
kēris suluk: large form of *kēris* for cutting rather than thrusting (Malay)
k̲h̲aftān: padded soft armour in the same shape as the similarly named garment (Pers.)
k̲h̲alal: lining of fur or skin inside scabbard (Ar.)
k̲h̲ančar: large dagger (see *k̲h̲anjar*, Tk.)
k̲h̲āndā, k̲h̲anda: broad straight-bladed sword (Indo-Pers.)
k̲h̲and̲j̲ar: large dagger (Pers. and Ar.)
k̲h̲apwā: double-curved dagger, Mug̲h̲al India
k̲h̲arātagīn: unclear form of infantry armour also protecting the legs (Pers.)
k̲h̲atangku dehel: padded or felt soft armour, later also lined with scales or plates (Mongol)
k̲h̲aṭil: longest form of Arab spear (Ar.)
k̲h̲aydaʿa: heavy form of helmet, possibly local form of the European Great Helm (Andalusian Ar.)
k̲h̲end̲j̲er: large dagger (from Ar. *k̲h̲and̲j̲ar*, Berber)
k̲h̲irā: small round shield, Mug̲h̲al India
k̲h̲irṣ: short infantry spear (Andalusian Ar.)
k̲h̲is̲h̲t: javelin (Ar. and Pers.)
k̲h̲ud, k̲h̲ūd, k̲h̲ūd̲h̲, k̲h̲ūd̲h̲a: helmet, usually of segmented construction; can also be made of hardened leather segments (Pers. and Ar.)
k̲h̲ūdās̲h̲īkan: mace, lit. "helmet breaker" (Pers.)
k̲h̲umm g̲h̲is̲h̲ān: false sleeve protecting the upper arm (Ar.)
k̲h̲urz: mace (see *gurz*; Ar.)
k̲h̲uyag̲h̲: lamellar cuirass (Mongol)
ḳilič: sword, usually a curved sabre (Tk.)
ḳin: scabbard (Tk.)
ḳind̲j̲al: broad double-edged dagger, originally from Caucasus
ḳirāb: sheath of dagger (Ar.)
ḳolčaḳ: vambrace (Ott. Turk.)
konpal: mace with flower-shaped head, India
ḳorazin: cuirass or mail-and-plate construction, Ottoman (Turk. from Latin)
kris: (see *kēris*)
ḳubaʿ: lining or skull-cap of a helmet, or an arming cap (Ar.)
kūbad̲j̲: shield-boss (Ar.)
kulāh: helmet (Pers.)
kulah-zirih: mail coif or helmet of mail-and-plate (Pers.)
ḳulluḳ: arm protection (Tk.)
kummiya: sabre or curved dagger (Berber)
ḳunṭāriyya: relatively short cavalry spear for thrusting only (from Greek *Kontarion*; Ar.)
kūpal: mace (see *gūpāl*; Pers.)
ḳurūn: edges of spear-blade (Ar.)
kurz: mace (see *gurz*; Pers.)
ḳus̲h̲a: belt for sword and archery equipment (Tk.)
lak̲h̲h̲ī: form of mace (see *latt*; Pers.)
lamṭ: Berber and Saharan large leather shield (Ar.)
latt: mace with elongated head (Ar.)
lit̲h̲ām: aventail also covering the throat, lit. "veil" (Ar.)
lkummiyt: sabre or curved dagger (Berber)
maʿālīḳ: tassels on sword (Ar.)
mābiḍ: grip of sword-hilt, probably corruption of *miḳbaḍ* (Ar.)
madas: Berber javelin (Andalusian Ar.)
māḍī, māḍiya: swords (Ar.)
mad̲j̲inn, mid̲j̲ann: shield (see *d̲j̲unna*; Ar.)
madya: knife or dagger used by Europeans (Ar.)
maḥwar: nail fixing blade to haft of spear (Ar.)
mak̲h̲mūs: short cavalry spear (Ar.)
makk: short infantry spear or javelin (Pers.)
mamarr al-watar: horizontal lacing of a lamellar cuirass (Ar.)
manābid̲h̲: individual links of a mail hauberk (Ar.)
manāṭiḳ: sword-belt (Ar.)
marbūʿa: short spear (poss. from Greek *riptaria*; Ar.)
mard gīr: spear with a hook beneath the blade (Indo-Pers.)
mas̲h̲rafī: early Arabian sword, largely in poetic usage (Ar.)
masrūda, misrūda: possibly the scales of a coat-of-plates (Ar.)
mig̲h̲far: hood or coif, usually of mail, to protect the head; later sometimes referring to the mail aventail attached to a helmet (Ar.)
mig̲h̲fer: helmet (Ott. Tk. from Ar.)
miḳbaḍ: hilt or grip of sword (Ar.)
miḳḍab: curved or single-edged sword (Ar.)
miḳlāʿ: sling (Ar.)
miḳraʿa: club or cudgel (Ar.)
mirkiz: foot or shoe of spear-shaft (Ar.)
mirzaba: foot or shoe of spear-shaft (Ar.)
mismār: nail or rivet attaching hilt to tang of sword (Ar.)
missyurka: form of helmet largely consisting of mail with a small skull-top, mostly used in the Caucasus (from Tk.)
miṭrad, miṭrād: short hunting spear, javelin or staff weapon, later used as a standard (Ar.)
miyān: sheath or strap to hold mace (Pers.)
mizrāḳ: javelin with armour piercing blade (Ar.)
mudāk̲h̲ala: possibly a scale armour (Ar.)
mud̲j̲allida: protective leather costume worn by fire-troops (Ar.)
muḥaddab: curved or single-edged sword (Ar.)
murhafa: slender sword-blade (Andalusian Ar.)
murrāna: infantry spear with flexible wooden haft (Ar.)
mustawfiya: long hafted mace, probably ceremonial (Ar.)
muza-i āhanī: iron leg armour, Mug̲h̲al India (Pers.)
nāčak̲h̲: war-axe, perhaps with half-moon blade and often with a hammer at the back (Pers.)
nad̲j̲ag̲h̲: war-axe (see *nāčak̲h̲*; Tk.)
nād̲j̲ik̲h̲: war-axe (see *nāčak̲h̲*; Ar.)
nahd: shield-boss or nails to hold grip, North Africa (Ar.)
naʿl, naʿla: chape of scabbard (Ar.)
naṣl: blade of Indian or Yemeni sword (Ar.)
nawk: point of spear-blade (Pers.)
nayzak: short spear with a pointed foot (Ar.)
naz̲h̲aḳ: war-axe, equivalent of Arabic *ṭabar* (Ḳîpčaḳ Tk.)
nid̲j̲ād: scabbard-mounts for rings to baldric or sword-belt (Ar.)

niḳāb: moveable nasal or visor of helmet (Tk. from Ar.)
nīm nīza: short infantry spear, lit. "half spear" (Pers.)
nimdjā: short sword or large dagger (from Persian *nīmča*; Ar.)
nimsha: Moroccan short sabre (from Persian *nīmča*; Ar.)
niṣāb: grip of a dagger-hilt (Ar.)
niyām: scabbard (Pers.)
nīza: spear (Pers.)
nīzayi mard-gīr: spear with a curved blade or incorporating a hook, of Mongol-Chinese origin (Pers.)
pahrī: shield of cane or bamboo, Mughal India (see also *phari*)
pāk'har, pākhar: elephant armour, Mughal India
palārak: sabre or large dagger of damascene steel (Pers.)
pār dum: crupper, piece of horse-armour covering the rump or tail (Pers.)
parālak: sword of damascene steel (from Pers. *palārak*; Tk.)
parand: glittering sword-blade (Pers.)
pari magas: sword, largely poetic (Pers.)
paywand: fastenings of a *kamarband* cuirass or armoured girdle (Pers.)
pēdang: early form of Malay sword (Malay)
peshkabz: slender dagger, Mughal India
phari: Indian version of the Turkish *kalḳan* spiral cane shield bound with silk or cotton
piazi: ball attached to shaft by leather strap (Urdu)
pīl kash, bīl kash: short infantry spear or staff weapon, apparently for use against elephants (Indo-Pers.)
purda: aventail, Mughal India
rabā'ith: Bedouin Arab light javelins (prob. from Greek *riptaria* via Syriac; Ar.)
rabiʿa: local form of helmet (Andalusian Ar.)
rāg, rāk: leg armour of mail-and-plate, Mughal India
rānāt ḥadīd: cuisses, probably of mail (Ar.)
raṣā'iʿ: ends of baldric, perhaps in form of knots to attach to scabbard (Ar.)
ri'ās: entire sword-hilt (Ar.)
rumḥ: spear or lance (Ar.)
ṣabarbara: long hafted infantry staff weapon or heavy javelin (Ar.)
sābigh, sābigha: long-hemmed, long-sleeved form of mail hauberk, also lower part or hem of a coif (Ar.)
sābiriyya: long style of mail hauberk (Ar.)
ṣaffa: sword-blade from India (Ar.)
ṣafḥa, ṣafīḥa: broad sword-blade (Ar.)
ṣafīḥa: individual lamellae of a lamellar cuirass (Ar.)
sāʿid: vambrace, lower arm protection (Ar.)
sāḳ, sāḳ al-mūza: leg protections (Ar.)
saḳī: "watering" pattern on damascene sword-blade (Ar.)
salawar: single-edge sword or large dagger with a reinforced back, known in Europe as a "Khyber knife", Mughal India (see also *čaray* and *čhura*)
sallārī: quilted soft armour with short sleeves (Ar.)
ṣamṣām: broad sword-blade with fuller groove or grooves (Ar.)
sanbuk: edge of sword-blade (Andalusian Ar.)
sang: short cavalry spear (Indo-Pers.)
sanglakh: knobbed mace, India
sannāha: body armour, Mughal India
sar: collar of an armour or military garment, also part of sword blade beneath quillons, or point or summit of helmet (Pers.)
sār, sārī: mace or club (Pers.)
sard: individual ring of an armour of mail construction (Ar.)
sarī: form of chamfron (Ar.)
sayāl: part of sword-hilt enclosing the tang (Ar.)
sayf: sword (Ar.)
saynthī: javelin or short spear (Indo-Pers.)
sbula: slender dagger (Berber)
shabh: iron foot of spear (Ar.)
shafra: edge of sword-blade (Ar.)
shahadast: early Yemeni sword, perhaps single-edged (Ar.)
shaʿīra: peg or rivet fastening sword-hilt to tang of blade (Ar.)
shalīl: arming coat or soft armour worn beneath a mail hauberk (Ar.)
shamshīr: sword (Pers.)
shārbān: quillons (Ar.)
shārib: locket around open end of scabbard (Ar.)
shashbur, shishpar: flanged made (Indo-Pers.)
shasḳa: Caucasian sabre without quillons
shathab: fuller groove down sword-blade (Ar.)
shīl: barbed light javelin (Indo-Pers.)
shirāstrāṇa: helmet, Mughal India
shūshak: large lute-shaped shield used in sieges (Pers.)
sīkh: dagger (Ar.)
sikkīn, sikkīna: knife or small dagger (Ar.)
sīlān: tang of sword (Ar.)
sinān: spear blade or point (Ar.)
sinkh: tang of sword (Ar.)
sipar: shield (Pers.)
sipar-i farākh: infantry shield or mantlet (Pers.)
sirash: aventail (Pers.)
sirbāl: large form of cloth-covered or lined mail hauberk with a raised collar (Ar.)
siyābiḥa: form of cavalry war-axe made by the Armenian people of Siyāwurdiya or Sevordikʿ (Ar.)
sosum patta: form of sword (Indo-Pers.)
sunbula: form of sword (Andalusian Ar.)
sundang: large sword (Malay)
süngi, süngü: spear (Ḳipčaḳ Tk.)
sunu: spear (Tk.)
sutūn: iron staff (Pers.)
taʿālīḳ: suspension straps from belt to scabbard, or perhaps tassets of a cuirass (Ar.)
tabar zaghnol: double-headed axe or with a pointed blade on the back, India
ṭabar: war-axe (Pers. and Ar.)
ṭabarzīn: cavalry axe; lit. "saddle-axe" (Pers. and Ar.)
tafrat mekkurn: small sabre or cutlass (Berber)
tafrut, tafrat: general term for bladed weapon, Morocco, or working knife, Algeria (Berber)
ṭāḳ: ring at end of baldric to attach scabbard (Ar.)
taḳallada: style of carrying sword from baldric (Ar.)
takouba: straight sword of Saharan Tuareg (Berber)
tāla: shield of wood or leather, Mughal India
ṭalā: clothing covered, lined or impregnated with fire-resistant chemicals, worn by fire-troops (Ar.)
tālamūla: wooden shield, Mughal India
taʿlib: part of spear-shaft entering socket of blade (Ar.)
talwar: form of sword (Indo-Pers.)
tämür kömläk: mail armour, lit. "iron clothes" (Ḳipčaḳ Tk.)
tannūr, tanūrigh: early form of large cuirass, possibly of scales and associated with the Sāsānid period (Pers.)
tanutrāṇa, tanutra: body armour, Mughal India
ṭaraf: point of spear (Ar.)
tarā'ik: segments of a segmented helmet (Ar.)
tarangala: axe with a spike on top and a hammer at the back, India
tarangar: multi-pronged infantry spear (Indo-Pers.)
targ (see *tark*; Pers.)
tarīk, tarīka: rounded helmet, possibly fluted (Ar.)
ṭārika: tall or kite-shaped shield with pointed base (Ar.)
tark: helmet (Pers.)
tasbult: dagger (Berber)
teber: war-axe (Ott. Tk., see *tabar*)

teneke: individual lamellae of a lamellar cuirass (Tk.)
thafrut: sabre, Morocco (Berber)
thaḳad: soft armour quilted with camel hair (Ar.)
thaʿlab: part of spear-shaft entering socket of blade (see *taʿlib*; Ar.)
tidjfāf: horse-armour of quilted material or felt (Ar.)
tifratin: knife or small-sword (Berber)
tīgh: sword-blade (Pers.)
tilwā: cavalry shield, Mughal India
tīr-i andāzān: light infantry javelins (Pers.)
ṭirfil: sheath or holder for mace (Tk.)
tīsha: long-hafted battle axe or halberd (Pers. and Ar.)
tishtaniyya: probably chamfron, armour for horse's head (Ar. from Latin)
tūra: wooden mantlet, Mughal India
turs: shield (Ar.)
ukkāz: Berber infantry mace (Ar.)
ʿurā, pl. of *ʿurwa*: loops or holes in the rim of a helmet by which it is attached to an arming cap or an aventail (Ar.)
valahkānta: bamboo or leather shield, Mughal India
varman: mail hauberk or body armour, Mughal India
waḍaf: Berber sling (Ar.)
wahaḳ: lasso (Ar.)
yāfūrt, yāfrūt: slender thrusting dagger, Berber (prob. from Berber *tāfrūt*; Ar.)
yakbandī: sword-belt, Mughal India
yataghān, yataghan: reverse-curved short sword (Ott. Tk.)
yazanī: early Southern Arabian spear or javelin (Ar.)
zaghnol: axe with a pointed rather than curved blade, India
zāhiḳa: local form of helmet (Andalusian Ar.)
zarad: mail armour in general (Ar.)
zaradiyya: mail coif or helmet largely of mail construction (Pers.; see also *zardiyya*)
zarāfayn: rings to attach scabbard to baldric (Ar.)
zardiyya: mail hauberk or layer of mail forming part of an armour (Ar.)
zāriḳ: javelin (see *mizrāḳ*; Ar.)
zırh gömlek: mail-and-plate cuirass (Ott. Tk.)
zirih: mail hauberk or mail armour in general (Pers.)
zuba: edge of sword-blade (Ar.)
zūbīn, zūpīn, zhūpīn: heavy javelin with a pointed foot or second blade (Pers.)
zudjdj: iron foot of spear (Ar.)

Bibliography: 1. Specialised works on Islamic arms and armour. J. Hammer-Purgstall, *Sur les lames des Orientaux*, in *JA*, 5th ser., iii (1854), 66-80; F. Fernández y González, *Espadas hispano-árabes, espadas de Abindarraez y de Aliatar, espada de hoja tunecina atribuida vulgarmente a Muhammad Boabdeli (Boabdil)*, in *Bol. Museo Español de Atigüedades*, i (1872), 573-90, and v (1875), 389-400; E. Rehatsek, *Notes on some old arms and instruments of war, chiefly among the Arabs*, in *Jnal. Bombay Branch RAS*, xiv (1880), 219-63; F.W. Schwarzlose, *Die Waffen der alten Araber*, Leipzig 1886; Y. Artin Pasha, *Un sabre de l'Eybek*, in *Bull. de l'Institut d'Egypte*, ix (1899), 219-59; idem, *Les armes de l'Egypte aux XVe et XVIe siècle*, in *Bull. de l'Institut d'Egypte*, iv (1906-7), 87-90; M. Herz, *Armes et armures arabes*, in *BIFAO*, vii (1910), 1-14; C. List, *Die Waffen*, in F. Sarre, *Die Ausstellung von Meistermerken muhammadanischer Kunst in München*, Munich 1910; Capt. Belhomme, *Les armes dans le Sous Occidental*, in *Archives Berberes*, ii (1917); idem, *Les poignards du Sous*, Rabat 1917; C.P. Davis, *Persian arms and armor*, in *Bull. City Art Museum of St. Louis*, vii (1922); P. de Vigy, *Les sabres marocains*, in *Hespéris*, iv (1924), 117-31; H. Stocklein, *Ein türkische Helm*, in *Jahrbuch für Asiatische Kunst*, ii (1925), 163-9; E.A. Gessler, *Der Kalotten-Helm von Chamoson*, in *Zeitschr. für Historische Waffen- und Kostümkunde*, iii (1930), 121-7; M. du Buisson, *Tête de lance arabe*, in *Bull. de la Société Nationale des Antiquaires de France* (1931); W.W. Arendt, *Sigeron-Kubetschi*, in *Zeitschr. für Historishe Waffen- und Kostümkunde*, iv (1932-4); idem, *Türkische Säbel aus den VII-IX Jahrhundert*, in *Archaeologia Hungarica*, xvi (1934); H. Stocklein, *Die Waffenschätze im Topkapu Sarayi Müzesi*, in *Ars Islamica*, i (1934), 200-18; S. Grancsay, *The George C. Stone Bequest. Indian and Persian arms and armour*, in *Bull. Metropolitan Museum of Art*, xxxii (1937); idem, *The George C. Stone Bequest. Turkish, Balkan, Caucasian and North African arms and armour*, in *ibid.*, xxxii (1937); H. Stocklein, *Arms and armour*, in A.U. Pope, *Survey of Persian art*, 2555-85; Hamete Ben Cobexi, *Espadas hispano-arabes*, in *Mauretania*, xv (1942), 135-7; J. Ferrandis Torres, *Espadas granadinas dela Jineta*, in *Archivo Español de Arte*, xvi (1943), 142-66; L.A. Mayer, *Saracenic arms and armour*, in *Ars Islamica*, x (1943), 2-; H. Goetz, *The Kris of the first Muslim Sultan of Malacca in the colletion of H.H. the Maharaja Gaekwad of Baroda*, in *Jnal. of the Greater India Society*, xii (1945), 49-52; R. Bullock, *Oriental arms and armour*, in *Bull. Metropolitan Museum of Art*, n.s., v (1947); G.C. Wooley, *The Malay Keris: its origins and development*, in *Jnal. Malay Branch RAS*, xx (1947), 60-103; Cl. Cahen, *Un traité d'armurerie composé pour Saladin*, in *BEO*, xii (1947-8), 103-63; B.W. Robinson, *The sword of Islam*, in *Apollo Annual* (London 1949); A.B. De Hoffmeyer, *Middelalderens islamiske svaerd*, in *Vaabenhistoriske Aalboger*, viii (1956); F. Buttin, *Les Adargues de Fès*, in *Hespéris-Tamuda*, i (1960), 409-55; A.R. Zaki, *Centres of Islamic sword-making in the Middle Ages*, in *Bull. de l'Institut d'Egypte*, xxxviii (1960); D. Jacques-Meunié, *Le nom berbère d'un poignard maghrébin au XIe siècle d'après un texte arabe de l'Egypte*, in *JA*, ccl (1962), 613-8; Mayer, *Islamic armourers and their works*, Geneva 1962; M.R. Bajraktarović, *Epée et yatagan de Petrovo Selo*, in *Vesnik Vojnog* (Belgrade), viii-ix (1963), 301; A.D. Bivar, *Nigerian panoply: arms and armour of the Northern Regions*, Lagos 1964; S.Q. Fatimi, *Malaysian weapons in Arabic literature: a glimpse of early trade in the Indian Ocean*, in *Islamic Studies*, i (1964), 199-217; A.R. Zaki, *On Islamic swords*, in *Studies in Islamic art and architecture in honour of Prof. K.A.C. Creswell*, Cairo 1965; idem, *Important swords in the Museum of Islamic Art in Cairo*, in *Vaabenhistoriske Aaboger*, xiii (1966), 143-57; H. Siruni, *Armes turques du XVIe XIXe siècles au Musée Militaire Centrale de Bucharest*, in *Studia et Acta Orientalia*, vii (1968), 277-93; J.M. García Fuentes, *Las armas hispano-musulmanas al final de la Reconquista*, in *Crónica Nova*, iii (1969), 38-55; R. Djanpoladian and A. Kirpicnikov, *Mittelalterlicher Säbel mit einer Armenischen Inschrift, gefunden im subpolaren Ural*, in *Gladius*, x (1972), 15-23; H. Nickel, *A Mamluk axe*, in R. Ettinghausen (ed.), *Islamic art in the Metropolitan Museum of Art*, New York 1972, 213-25; L. Kalus, *Boucliers circulaires de l'Orient musulman*, in *Gladius*, xii (1974), 59-133; idem, *Un bouclier mamelouke dans les collections du Musée de l'Homme à Paris*, in *Armi Antiche* (1975), 23-8; A. Bahnassi, *Fabrication des épées de Damas*, in *Syria*, liii (1976), 281-94; G. Fehérvári, *Islamic metalwork of the eighth to the fifteenth century in the Keir collection*, London 1976; D.C. Nicolle, *Early medieval Islamic arms and armour*, Madrid 1976; A. North, *Islamic arms and armour*, in *The Connoisseur* (London 1976); H.T. Norris, *The Hauberk, the Kazāghand and the ʿAntar Romance*, in *Jnal. of the Arms and Armour Society*, ix (1978), 93-101; M.R. Zamir-Dahncke, *Ein persischer Rundschild mit Jagdmotiven*, in *Archäologische Mitteilungen aus Iran*, xi (1978), 205-9; R. Elgood (ed.) *Islamic arms and armour*, London 1979; M.V. Gorelick, *Oriental armour of the Near and Middle East from the eighth to the fifteenth centuries as shown in works of art*, in Elgood (ed.), *op. cit.*, 30-63; Nicolle, *an introduction to arms and warfare in Classical Islam*, in Elgood (ed.), *op. cit.*, 162-86; F.K. Wiest, *The sword of Islam: edged weapons of Mohammedan Asia*, in *Arts of Asia*, ix (1979), 73-82; Nicolle, *Arms and armour in the album paintings*, in *Islamic Art*, i (volume dedicated to the Fatih Albums in the Topkapı Library), New York 1981, 145-9; idem, *Islamische Waffen*, Graz 1981; Davids-Samling, *Islamiske vaben i dansk privateje/Islamic arms and armour from private Danish collections*, Copenhagen 1982; H. Ricketts, *Some early collectors and scholars of oriental arms and armour*, in Davids-Samling, *op. cit.*; A.S. Melikian-Chirvani, *The westward journey of the Kazhagand*, in *Jnal. of the Arms and Armour Society*, xi (1983), 8-35; Nicolle, *Arms production and the arms trade in South-Eastern Arabia in the early Muslim period*, in *Jnal. of Oman Studies*, v (1984), 231-8; D.G. Alexander and Ricketts, *Armes et armures*, in S.C. Welch (ed.), *Trésors de l'Islam (collection Rifaat Shaikh al Ard)*, Geneva 1985, 296-8; North, *Islamic arms*, London 1985; J.K. Schwarzer and E.C. Deal, *A sword-hilt from the Serçe Liman shipwreck*, in *MASCA Jnal.*, iv (1986), 50-9; Melikian-Chirvani, *On Indian saddle-axes*, in *Apollo*, cxxvii (1988), 117-20; North, *Swords and hilted weapons*, London 1989; S.Z. Haidar, *Islamic arms and armour of Muslim India*, Lahore 1991; Nicolle, *Armi bianche; Islam*, in *Enciclopedia dell'Arte Medievale*, ii, Rome 1991, 498-500; Schwarzer, *Arms from an eleventh century shipwreck*, in *Graeco-Arabica*, iv (1991), 327-50; Alexander, *The arts of war, arms and armour of the 7th to 19th centuries*, in *The Nasser D. Khalili collection of Islamic Art, vol. XXI*, Oxford 1992; Nicolle, *Byzantine and Islamic arms and armour; evidence for mutual influence*, in *Graeco-Arabica*, v (1992), 299-325; A. Collet, *Dans la salle orientale du Musée de l'Armée: les casques turcs (XVe-XVIe siècle)*, in *Revue de la Société des Amis du Musée de l'Armée*, cvi (1993), 25-31; A.N. Kirpichnokov, *Medieval sabres with brands from the collections of the National Museum of Finland*, in P. Purhonen (ed.), *Fenno-Ugri et Slavi 1992. Prehistoric economy and means of livelihood*, Helsinki 1994, 26-33; Nicolle, *Saljûq arms and armour in art and literature*, in R. Hillenbrand (ed.), *The arts of the Saljûqs in Iran and Anatolia*, Costa Mesa 1994, 247-56; idem, *The reality of Mamluk warfare: weapons, armour and tactics*, (= tr. of Ch. Two, Lesson Seven of the *Nihāyat al-su'l*), in *Al-Masāq*, v (1994), 77-111; A.R. Williams, *Ottoman military technology: the metallurgy of Turkish armour*, in Y. Lev (ed.), *War and society in the Eastern Mediterranean, 7th-15th centuries*, Leiden 1996, 363-97; Nicolle, *Arms of the Umayyad era: military technology in a time of change*, in *ibid.*, 9-100.

2. General works including Islamic arms and armour. W. Egerton (Lord Egerton of Tatton), *A description of Indian and Oriental armour*, London 1896, repr. London 1968; A. Robert, *Les cottes de mailles de la Mosquée du Sid el Djoudi*, in *Recueil des notices et mémoires de la Societé Archéologique de Constantine*, xl (1906), 105-9; B. Dean, *Handbook of arms and armor, European and Oriental, including the William H. Riggs Collection*, New York 1915; N. Fries, *Das Heereswesen der Araber zur Zeit der Omaijaden nach Ṭabarî*, Tübingen 1921; Ibn Hudhayl al-Andalusī, tr. L. Mercier, *La parure des cavaliers et l'insigne des preux*, Paris 1922, tr. idem, *L'ornament des armes*, Paris 1939, tr. M.J. Viguera, *Gala de caballeros, blason de paladines*, Madrid 1977; J.G. Mann, *Notes on the armour worn in Spain from the tenth to the fifteenth century*, in *Archaeologia*, lxxiii (1933), 285-305; F. Wolff, *Glossar zu Firdosis Schahname*, Berlin 1935, repr. Hildesheim 1965; R. Zeller and E.F. Rohrer, *Orientalische Sammlung Henri Moser, Charlottenfels*, Bern 1955; A. Mazahéri, *Le sabre contre l'épée*, in *Annales, ESC*, xiii (1958), 670-86; G.C. Stone, *A glossary of the construction, decoration and use of arms and armour in all countries and in all times*, New York 1961; B. Thomas, *Aus der Waffensammlung in der Neuen Burg zu Wien: Orientalische Kostbarkeiten*, in *Bustan* (1963-4); G.F. Laking, *The Wallace Collection. Catalogue of Oriental arms and armour*, repr. London 1964; J.J. Rodriguez Lorente, *The XVth century ear dagger. Its Hispano-Moresque origins*, in *Gladius*, iii (1964); G. Pant, *A study of Indian swords*, in *Itihāsa-Chayanikā, Jnal. of the Panjab University Historical Society*, xi-xiii (1965), 75-86; G. Vianello, *Armi e armature orientali*, Milan 1966; E. García Gómez, *Armas, banderas, tiendas de campaña, monturas y correos en los "Anales de al Ḥakam II" por ʿĪsā Rāzī*, in *And.*, xxxii (1967), 163-79; H.R. Robinson, *Oriental armour*, London 1967; P.S. Rawson, *The Indian sword*, London 1968; O. Kurz, *A gold helmet made in Venice for the Ottoman Sultan Sulayman the Magnificent, 1532*, in *Gazette des Beaux Arts*, iii (1969), 249-58; Pant, *Studies in Indian weapons and warfare*, New Delhi 1970; Y. Zoka, *The Tofang and its antecedents in Iran*, in *Historical Studies in Iran*, i (1971), 53-9; A.B. De Hoffmeyer, *Arms and armour in Spain, a short survey*, i, Madrid 1972, ii, Madrid 1982; Z. Zygulski, *Turkish trophies in Poland in the Imperial Ottoman style*, in *Armi Antiche* (1972); Jarnuszkiewicz, *The oriental sabre: a comprehensive study of the oriental sabre and its origins*, London 1973; E. Esin, *L'arme zoomorph du guerrier turc (étude iconographique)*, in G. Hazai and P. Zieme (eds.), *Sprache, Geschichte und Kultur der altaischen Völker*, Berlin 1974, 193-217; Robinson, *Il Museo Stibbert, vol. i (Oriental armour)*, Florence 1974; K.U. Uray-Köhalmi, *La périodisation l'histoire des armaments des nomades des steppes*, in *Études Mongoles*, v (1974); J. Schöbel, *Princely arms and armour*, London 1975; M.A. Hindi, *Bibliography of Arabic mss. on Islamic military arts, arms and armour*, in *International Symposium for the History of Arabic Science (Aleppo, April 1977)*, Aleppo 1978; J.W. Allan, *Persian metal technology, 700-1300 AD*, Oxford 1979; E. Atil, *Art of the Mamluks*, Washington 1981; Melikian-Chirvani, *Notes sur le terminologie de la metallurgie et des armes dans l'Iran Musulman*, in *JESHO*, xxiv (1981), 310-16; Pant, *Medieval arms and armour*, in *Salar Jang Museum Bi-Annual Research Jnal.*, xv-xvi (1981-2), 51-82; Allan, *Nishapur metalwork of the early Islamic period*, New York 1982; L. Tarassuk and C. Blair (eds.), *The complete encyclopedia of arms and weapons*, London 1982; Pant, *The Indian shield*, New Delhi 1983; O.D. Sherby and J. Wadsworth, *Damascus steels*, in *Scientific American* (Feb. 1985), 112-20; A.Y. al-Hasan and D.R. Hill, *Islamic technology, an illustrated history*, Cambridge 1986; A. Soler del Campo, *El armamento medieval hispano*, in *Cuadernos de Investigacion Medieval*, iii (1986), 1-51; F. Bodur, *Türk maden sanatı/Turkish metalwork*, Istanbul 1987; Nicolle, *The arms and armour of the Crusading era 1050-1350*, New York 1988; Ricketts and P. Missillier, *Splendeur des armes orientales*, Paris 1988; Pant, *Mughul weapons in the Bābur-Nāmā*, Delhi 1989; Zygulski, *Sztuka islamu w zbiorach polskic*, Warsaw 1989; J.D. Verhoeven and A.H. Pendray, *Studies of Damascus steel blades*, in *Materials Characterisation* (1992, 1993); Pant, *Horse and elephant armour*, New Delhi 1993; Soler del Campo, *La evolucion del armamento medieval en el reino castellano-léones y al-Andalus (siglos XII-XIV)*, Madrid 1993; M. Sachse, *Damascus steel: myth, history, technology, applications*, 1994; D.G. Alex-

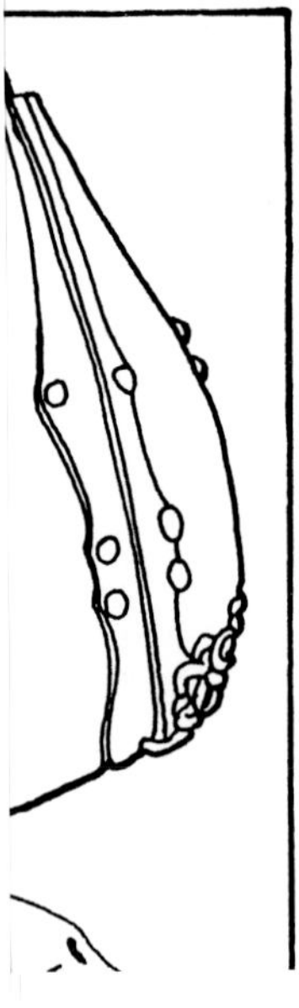

ander (ed.), *Furusiyya*, i. *The horse in the art of the Near East*, ii. *Catalogue*, Riyāḍ 1997; C. Beaufort-Spontin, *The Schwendi booty of Archduke Ferdinand of Tyrol*, in Alexander (ed.), *Furusiyya*, i, 184-9; Nicolle, *The origins and development of cavalry warfare in the early Muslim Middle East*, in *ibid.*, 92-103.

Captions

1. A hardened crocodile-skin helmet with an iron lamellar neck-guard and one remaining crocodile-skin cheek-piece; said to be from Wadī Garāra east of Kalabsha in Nubia. Although this helmet is sometimes considered to be from the "Roman" era, the presence of a neck-guard made of iron lamellae over camel skin could indicate a later origin, perhaps from the 5th to 8th centuries. Until the helmet is carbon-dated, the question remains unresolved; meanwhile, the helmet itself is an interesting example of non-metallic Middle Eastern military technology. (Staatliche Museen zu Berlin, Preussischer Kulturbesitz, Antikensammlung, inv. nr. 30882, Germany)

2. A very corroded iron helmet made of two pieces joined beneath a flat comb, from Ḥadītha on the eastern shore of the Dead Sea, Jordan. This typical late Roman helmet is generally considered to date from the 4th or 5th centuries, though the history of Ḥadītha as a Romano-Byzantine military outpost could make a late 6th to mid-7th century date more likely. This helmet was also found in conjunction with a dagger or short-sword identical to one found in Pella [see FAḤL] and undoubtedly dating from the mid-8th century. Comparable helmets continued in use elsewhere in the Byzantine Empire and parts of Western Europe at least until the 8th century, and are likely to have similarly continued in use in the early Islamic Middle East. (Castle Museum, Karak, Jordan)

3. An iron and bronze helmet excavated at Nineveh in northern ʿIrāḳ. It is a late and undecorated version of the so-called Parthian Cap style characteristic of Sāsānid troops. The style and context suggest that this helmet dated from the very end of the Sāsānid Empire in the early 7th century, though some pictorial evidence from the first century of Islamic civilisation indicates that comparable helmets continued in use for a century after the coming of Islam. (British Museum, inv. 22497, London, England)

4. A second iron helmet found at Nineveh is in a completely different *Spangenhelm* style stemming from Central Asian military techniques. It also retains a fragment of its mail aventail. This helmet represents a major technological shift which would also be seen in much of Europe. It is again assumed to date from the very end of the Sāsānid period, but is just as likely to have been made during the first century of Islamic rule. (British Museum, inv. 22495, London, England)

5. A well-preserved iron helmet in a version of the *Spangenhelm* form of construction in which the "frame-plates" are actually broader than the "infill-plates". It probably dates from the 8th or 9th centuries and was found at Stary Oskol, near Voronezh in Russia. Yet it was probably imported from Islamic Persia or Transoxania, where identical helmets are shown on fragmentary wall-paintings dating from the 8th to 10th centuries. (State Hermitage Museum, St. Petersburg, Russia)

6. The earliest known helmet forged from a single piece of iron is this low-domed protection with a row of iron rings. These were probably the attachment for a lamellar or mail aventail rather than being the uppermost row of mail links. It was found in the early 8th century stratum in a ruined temple at Waraghsar near Samarḳand in Uzbekistan. Whether such advanced metallurgy originated in Transoxania, the Islamic Middle East or reflected Chinese influence remains unknown, but it is interesting to note that one contemporary Arabic chronicler differentiated between enemies "wearing round helmets" and those "wearing pointed helmets" on the north-eastern frontier of the Islamic world. (From a drawing by the archaeologist, Masud Samibayev; present whereabouts unknown)

7. A much better-known one-piece iron helmet came from Chamosen in Switzerland and dates from the 9th or 10th century. It is believed to be of Arab-Islamic origin and, beneath its purely decorative "frame-straps" and more functional brow-band, this helmet has essentially the same narrowing around its rim seen on the earlier one-piece helmet from Waraghsar. (Schweizerisches Landesmuseum, Zürich, Switzerland)

8. A third one-piece iron helmet was found in Tunisia. Though provisionally dated to the Ḥafṣid period (13th to 16th centuries), it has a virtually identical outline to the helmet from Chamosen. As such, it might have been made as early as the 10th century. (Museum of Islamic Studies, Raḳḳāda, Tunisia)

9. Another very distinctive form of iron helmet, of which this appears to be the only surviving example, appears in Christian Iberian art from the 12th to early 14th centuries. It is generally worn by "evil" figures which might indicate that it was originally associated with Muslim troops from al-Andalus. This style of helmet may, indeed, have originated in the Islamic south of the Iberian peninsula. (W. Scollard private coll., Los Angeles, USA)

10. This apparently unique helmet is so unusual that it might initially be dismissed as a fake, except that a very similar form of helmet is illustrated in a Moroccan manuscript dating from 621/1224. If it is genuine, then it could be a very late development of the Roman two-piece helmet seen in figure 2. (From a drawing by Dr. Michael Brett, made in the local archaeological museum at Ḳayrawān in the 1970s; present whereabouts unknown)

11. One of two very similar late 13th or early 14th century Turkish helmets, still with their long neck and shoulder covering mail aventails. This one has a bowl either strengthened by widely spaced "ribs" or made from plates joined by "rolled joints". The other has a one-piece bowl, though both are characterised by exceptionally deep brow-bands and decorative eyebrows. (Askeri Müzesi store, Istanbul, Turkey)

12. A simple *Spangenhelm* helmet from southern Persia. It was found with the remains of a lamellar cuirass and perhaps a lamellar aventail to be fastened to the rim of this helmet. The ring on the finial suggests that it dates from after the Mongol conquest, as this was a feature of perhaps Chinese origin which was introduced to many areas by the Mongols. The helmet probably dates from the later 13th or early 14th centuries. (After a drawing by V.V. Ovsyannikov; present whereabouts unknown)

13. A damaged but still recognisable lacquered leather or rawhide helmet, lined with small blocks of wood judging by a second fragmentary example, which came from the Euphrates region of northeastern Syria. It was decorated with black and red lacquer (shown here in black) which included a heraldic lion on one side. This heraldic cartouche, plus inscriptions on other pieces of equipment from the same location, indicates that they were of Mamlūk origin, the optimum

radiocarbon dating being A.D. 1285. (Private collection, London, England)

14. One-piece helmet with an inscription dedicated to the second Ottoman ruler Or<u>kh</u>an <u>Gh</u>āzī; mid-14th century. It is the earliest known example of the so-called "turban helmet" style which probably originated in Anatolia or western Persia and would become particularly associated with Ottoman armies of the 15th century. (Askeri Müzesi, Istanbul, Turkey)

15. A magnificent though extremely practical late 13th or early 14th century iron helmet with an original mail aventail to protect the wearer's neck and shoulders. By this period, armourers in the central Islamic lands, including Persia and the expanding Ottoman Empire, had reached their metallurgical and stylistic pinnacle. Their products were also very different to those made by European armourers to the west and Chinese armourers to the east. (State Hermitage Museum, St. Petersburg, Russia)

16. At the end of the mediaeval period, a very distinctive style of helmet appeared in the Islamic Middle East, thereafter being almost universal in Persian speaking regions, Islamic India and parts of the eastern Arab world. The example shown here may be one of the earliest surviving examples since the dedicatory inscription (X) names the early 8th/14th-century Mamlūk ruler Nāṣir al-Dīn Muḥammad b. Ḳalāwūn. It is, however, possible that this dedication was a later anachronism. (Musée de la Porte de Hal, Brussels)

17. As Islam spread across the Eurasian steppes, a number of very distinctive forms of helmet appeared, particularly in the western steppes where Turkish, Mongol, Persian and perhaps also Byzantine influences combined. One result was a form of tall one-piece iron helmet based upon the segmented *Spangenhelms* of earlier years, but incorporating an anthropomorphic visor which seemed to reflect European artistic values. These helmets are generally thought to date from the immediate pre-Mongol period but are more likely to stem from the late 13th-early 14th centuries A.D. This was a period of cultural transition when the western Mongol <u>Kh</u>ānate was evolving into the Islamic Golden Horde. (State Hermitage Museum, St. Petersburg, Russia)

18. This late 7th/13th or early 8th/14th-century helmet, probably from Mamlūk Egypt or Syria, has some features in common with the visored helmet from the Golden Horde while remaining very different in other respects. It is forged from one piece of iron, then richly decorated with arabesques and Arabic dedicatory inscriptions. (After a drawing by H. Russell Robinson; present whereabouts unknown)

19. Though now lacking its characteristic mail aventail and sliding nasal bar, this 8th/14th-century Persian helmet is a fine example of a form that would be used throughout most of the eastern Islamic world from the late 14th to 19th centuries. (Wawel Collection, Cracow, Poland)

20. During the 15th and 16th centuries an apparently new form of cavalry helmet came into use in Mamlūk and Ottoman armies. It proved so successful that it was adopted throughout most of Europe, spreading as far as England where it became known as the "Cromwellian pot helmet". In reality, it was of neither European nor Islamic origin but seems to have been developed by the Mongols or their successor <u>kh</u>ānates from a Chinese original. Thereafter, it was copied and developed by Mamlūk and Ottoman armourers. The crudely-constructed example shown here is one of the earliest. It was found in a Turco-Mongol grave near Plysky in the Ukraine, from the superficially Islamised Golden Horde and dating from between 1290 and 1313. (After a drawing by M. Gorelik; present whereabouts unknown)

(D. NICOLLE)

AL-ṢĪN.

5. Chinese Islamic literature.

Muslims settled in Kuang-chou (Canton, <u>Kh</u>ānfū [*q.v.*]) and possibly in Ch'ang-an (Hsi-an) and Ch'üan-chou (Zaytūn) as early as the T'ang dynasty, 2nd/8th century, thereafter also in Hang-chou (<u>Kh</u>ansā [*q.v.*]) and Pei-ching (<u>Kh</u>ānbaliḳ [*q.v.*]), and throughout China [see also MĪNĀ']. Extant tombstone and other inscriptions in Arabic and Chinese, however, date only from the 7th/13th and 8th/14th centuries (Ch'en Ta-sheng; Leslie, *Guide*, 28-31; *Beijing National Library list of rubbings of inscriptions*).

The most significant are three stelae in Chinese, from 749/1348 in Ting-chou, 751/1350 in Ch'üan-chou, and 751/1350 in Kuang-chou. The first two describe the supposed visit to China of Waḳḳāṣ (the Companion Sa'd b. Abī Waḳḳāṣ [*q.v.*], a maternal cousin of the Prophet, and a famous general) in the 1st/7th century, sent, it is suggested, as an envoy of the Prophet himself (Yang and Yü, 91-106; Devéria; Tasaka, *Wakkas*). One should also mention an inscription dated 770/1368, set up in Nan-ching and copied in Wu-ch'ang, supposedly written by the first Ming Emperor T'ai-tsu, the *Hung-wu* Emperor (Low). Most intriguing is an undated inscription in Ch'ang-an, claiming a permit to build a mosque as early as 86/705 (Pickens).

These Chinese-style inscriptions served four main purposes: to record the history of the community; to explain Islamic ideas to the Muslims themselves and to non-Muslim Chinese; to demonstrate Confucian attitudes; and to protect the community. They are invaluable for the history of Islam in China, but of less value for the religious beliefs and practices of Chinese Muslims.

Islamic astronomy and medicine were influential in China in the Yuan and Ming dynasties. Four volumes (out of 36) of the large medical translation *Hui-hui yao-fang* are extant, preserved in the *Yung-lo ta-tien*, 811/1408.

One should note, too, the Sayyid A<u>dj</u>all, Muslim official of the Mongols in China, about whom much has been written [see AL-ṢĪN, at Vol. IX].

Three books written about the voyages between 808/1405 and 837/1433 to Africa and Arabia of Cheng Ho, the famous Muslim admiral of the Ming, include the *Ying-yai sheng-lan*, written by a Muslim who accompanied him, Ma Huan [*q.v.*], in 837/1433 (Mills).

It is only with the Ming dynasty (1389-1644), that Islamic literature in Chinese as such developed. The earliest extant full-length Islamic book written in Chinese is the *Cheng-chiao chen-ch'üan* by Wang Tai-yü, in 1052/1642. This gives a full account of the Islamic religion, with some criticism of Chu Hsi, the Sung dynasty Aquinas of Confucianism. The main aim was probably to educate Muslims living in China, who by now could be called Chinese Muslims. A large stream of Islamic books, some in Arabic, some in Arabic and Chinese, and several only in Chinese, were written soon after this, some translations, some original. Most significant are: Ma Chu, *Ch'ing-chen chih-nan* ("The compass of Islam"), in 8 volumes, 1095/1683 (Hartmann); and *Hui-hui yüan-lai* ("The origin of Islam in China"), possibly 1135/1722 (Devéria).

The peak of Islamic literature in Chinese was reached around 1704 to 1724, when Liu Chih [*q.v.*] (Liu Chieh-lien, Liu I-chai) wrote his three main works:

T'ien-fang hsing-li about Islamic philosophy; *T'ien-fang tien-li* about Islamic laws and rites (this book was reviewed by the prestigious *Ssu-k'u ch'üan-shu tsung-mu t'i-yao*); and *T'ien-fang chih-sheng shih-lu*, a biography of the Prophet, probably based on the *Tard͟juma-yi Mawlid i-Muṣṭafā*, a Persian translation from the Arabic work by Saʿīd (al-Dīn Muḥammad) b. Masʿūd b. Muḥammad al-Kāzarūnī, d. 758/1357 (a partial translation is given by Mason). Two other works by Liu are *Wu-kung shih-i* and *Chen-kung fa-wei* (Palladius).

The first two works include lists of sources with titles in transliterated Chinese, Chinese paraphrases of the title, and Arabic originals, many of which can be identified with the help of Brockelmann, Storey, etc. (Leslie and Wassel; and see also Leslie, Yang and Youssef, *Qianlong*, for other lists of Arabic and Persian Islamic works available in China). Liu was clearly influenced by the Ḥanafī school of law of the Sunnīs and by Ṣūfism, in particular, by the Kubrawiyya order [see KUBRĀ], and the Persian Nak͟shbandī Ṣūfī poet D͟jāmī [*q.v.*].

Liu's main sources were:

1. *Tafsīr (Chen-ching chu)* (one or more);
2. *Lawāʾiḥ (Chen-ching chao-wei)*, by D͟jāmī, d. 898/1492;
3. *As͟hiʿʿat al-lamaʿāt (Fei-yin ching* or *E-shen-erh-ting)* by D͟jāmī;
4. *Mirṣād al-ʿibād (Kuei-chen yao-tao* or *T'ui-yüan cheng-tao)*, by the Kubrawī Nad͟jm al-Dīn Rāzī Dāya [*q.v.*], Abū Bakr Asadī, d. *ca.* 654/1256;
5. *Maḳṣad-i aḳṣā (Yen-chen-ching* or *Kuei-chen pi-yao)* probably by the Kubrawī writer ʿAzīz al-Nasafī, d. 661/1263 [see KUBRĀ, at Vol. V, 301a];
6. *Mawāḳif (Ko-chih ch'üan-ching)*.

Nos. 2-5 of these had already been translated into Chinese. Other translations included *Munabbihāt; Irs͟hād; Tanbīh; ʿAḳāʾid* (by Abū Ḥafṣ al-Nasafī, d. 537/1142 [*q.v.*]; *Wiḳāya* (a commentary by Maḥmūd Burhān al-S͟harīʿa, 7th/13th century, to the *Hidāya* by al-Marg͟hīnānī, d. 593/1197 [*q.v.*]); and the Persian *Gulistān* by Saʿdī d. 691/1292 [*q.v.*].

Liu's biography of the Prophet has an introduction with the main Manchu edicts concerning Islam (see also Ma Sai-pei), and two large appendices, vol. XIX being a description of Arab and other countries overseas, and vol. XX being absolutely invaluable as a source book for the history of Islam in China, with inscriptions. Liu's works clearly show an attempt to accommodate Confucianism. The writings of Confucius and Mencius are referenced, as are Confucian and Taoist terms. At this time, several Muslims were succeeding in the Confucian literati examinations and becoming scholars and officials.

The works of Wang Tai-yü and Liu Chih were original creations. In addition, over the centuries a large number of translations, some from Persian, some from Arabic, have been made, so that there is a rich variety of Islamic works available in Chinese. In the 19th century, Ma Fu-ch'u (Ma Te-hsin) and Ma An-li continued to write significant Islamic literature in Chinese.

Other influential works are: *T'ien-fang cheng-hsüeh*, by Lan Tzu-hsi (1861), which includes a large number of fanciful biographies of Biblical and Muslim personalities; *Ch'ing-chen hsien-cheng yen-hsing lüeh*, by Li Huan-i (1875), which gives short biographies of 90 Chinese Muslims; *Ch'ing-chen shih-i pu-chi*, by T'ang Ch'uan-yu (1880), a valuable source book for Islam in China; and *T'ien-fang ta-hua li-shih*, by Li T'ing-hsiang (1919), a translation of the *Badāʾiʿ al-zuhūr (umūr) fī waḳāʾiʿ al-duhūr* (sic. This is according to the Chinese postscript. However, the contents of the Chinese work seem to be from a different, less well-known work by the same author, sc. the *Mard͟j al-zuhūr fī waḳāʾiʿ al-duhūr*), by Abu 'l-Barakāt Muḥammad b. Aḥmad b. Iyās (or Ayās) Zayn (S͟hihāb) al-Dīn al-Nāṣirī al-D͟jarkasī al-Ḥanafī, d. 930/1524 [see IBN IYĀS].

The main works have been republished, edited by Chang Hsiu-feng and Ma Sai-pei, in 55 volumes (1987). These works are to be found also in various libraries in China, Japan, Europe and America. Key collections outside China are those of Palladius (St. Petersburg); d'Ollone (Musée Guimet, Paris); Vissière (École des Langues Orientales Vivantes, Paris); Mason (N.Y. Public Library); Toyo Bunko, Tokyo; and Tenri University, Tenri (Leslie, *Islamic literature*; idem, *Guide*, 21-5; Panskaya).

One should note also a number of extant *Chia-p'u* (family records), notably those found by Nakada Yoshinobu in the Diet Library in Tokyo for the Mi and Sha families; and also some for the P'u family, possibly tracing descent from P'u Shou-Keng of the Yuan (Mongol) period.

A renaissance of Islamic literature occurred in the 1920s, with original works and translations by Wang Ching-chai, Yang Ching-hsiu and others. From this time a series of translations of the Ḳurʾān was made, including some into classical Chinese, others into modern *Kuo-yü* (Yü and Yang, 1-32), and these were used, together with Arabic and Persian works, by Islamic schools in various cities. Chinese Muslim bookshops of this time had catalogues of books in Chinese and in Arabic and Persian, most notably the Niu-chieh (Ox Street) mosque catalogue of the 1920s (extant in Tenri University Library), and dozens of Muslim journals in Chinese flourished at this time (Loewenthal).

A second renaissance occurred in the 1980s and thereafter, with hundreds of books about Chinese communities all over China and about the history of Islam in China and also many about the history and duties of the religion (Yü and Yang). Several large encyclopaedias have been written (e.g. by Ch'iu Shu-sen, 1992; Yang Hui-yün, 1993; the *Chinese Encyclopedia of Islam*, 1994), and for the first time, histories of Islam in China in Chinese (by Ch'iu Shu-sen, 1996, and by Li Hsing-hua *et al.*, 1998) to rival Tasaka Kōdō's masterly 1964 history in Japanese. There are also invaluable bibliographical and biographical reference works by Pai Shou-i (1948 [mostly reprinted in 1982-3], and 1985, 1988, 1992, 1997); Ma En-hui (1983); Yü Chen-kuei and Yang Huai-chung (1993); Li Hsing-hua and Feng Chin-yüan, (1985); Chin I-chiu (1997); and by Leslie, Yang and Youssef (to be published by Monumenta Serica).

There are also several works written analysing the voyages of the Muslim admiral Cheng Ho to Africa and Arabia.

Bibliography: Palladius (P.I. Kafarov), *Kitaiskaya literatura magometan*, in *Trudî imperatorskago Russkago ark͟heologičeskago obs͟hčestva*, xviii (1887), ed. Nikolai (Adoratskii), repr. St. Petersburg 1909, 163-494; G. Devéria, *Origine de l'Islamisme en Chine*, in *Centenaire de l'École des Langues Orientales Vivantes*, Paris 1895, 305-55; H.M.G. d'Ollone, *Mission d'Ollone 1906-1909. Recherches sur les mussulmans chinois*, Paris 1911, see section XVIII (by A. Vissière); Vissière, *Ouvrages chinois mahométans*, in *RMM*, xiii (Jan. 1911), 30-63; M. Hartmann, *Vom chinesischen Islam*, in *WI* (1913), 178-210; I. Mason, *The Arabian Prophet (a life of Mohammed from Chinese and Arabic sources) (a Chinese-Moslem work by Liu Chai-lien)*, Shanghai 1921; idem,

Notes on Chinese Mohammedan literature, in *Jnal. of the North China Branch of the Royal Asiatic Society*, lvi (1925), 172-215; C.L. Pickens, *The Great West Mosque of Ch'ang An (Sian)*, in *Friends of Moslems*, ix/3 (July 1935), 44-5; P.C. Low, *100-character Psalm on Islam by the first Ming Emperor*, in *Friends of Moslems*, xi/2 (April 1937), 39; R. Loewenthal, *The Mohammedan press in China. Digest of the Synodal Commission*, 1940; Tasaka (Tazaka) Kōdō, *Chūgoku Kaikyō shijō ni okeru Wakkas denkyō no densetsu ni tsuite*, 391-406, in *Wada Festschrift*, Tokyo 1951; idem, *Chūgoku ni okeru kaikyō no denrai to sono gutsū, Tokyo* 1964; J.V.G. Mills, *Ma Huan, Ying-yai sheng-lan, "The overall survey of the ocean's shores" (1433)*, Cambridge 1970; D.D. Leslie, *Islam in China to 1800, a bibliographical guide*, in *Abr Nahrain*, xvi (1976), 16-48; Ludmilla Panskaya (with Leslie), *Introduction to Palladii's Chinese literature of the Muslims*, Canberra 1977; Leslie, *Islamic literature in Chinese, Late Ming and Early Ch'ing: books authors and associates*, Canberra College of Advanced Education, Canberra 1981, Chinese tr. by Yang Daye 1994; Leslie and M. Wassel, *Arabic and Persian sources used by Liu Chih*, in *CAJ*, xxvi (1982), 78-104; Ch'en Ta-sheng (Chen Dasheng), *Ch'üan-chou l-ssu-lan-chiao shih-k'e*, Fu-chou 1984; Chang Hsiu-feng (Zhang Xiufeng) and Ma Sai-pei (Ma Saibei), *Hui-tsu ho Chung-kuo l-ssu-lan-chiao ku-chi tzu-liao hui-pien*, Tienjing 1987; Ma Sai-pei (Ma Saibei), *Ch'ing shih-lu Mu-ssu-lin tzu-liao chi-lu*, Yin-ch'üan 1988; *Pei-ching t'u-shu-kuan tsang Chung-kuo li-tai shih-k'o t'uo-pen hui-pien* ("Beijing National Library list of rubbings of stone inscriptions"), ed. Hsü Tzu-ch'iang (Xu Ziqiang), Pei-ching 1989-91; Yü Chen-kuei (Yu Zhengui) and Yang Huai-chung (Yang Huaizhong), *Chung-kuo l-ssu-lan wen-hsien chu-i t'i-yao*, Yin-ch'üan 1993; Yang Huai-chung and Yü Chen-kuei, *l-ssu-lan yü Chung-kuo wen-hua*, Yin-ch'üan 1995; Leslie, Yang Daye, and Ahmed Youssef, *Arabic works shown to the Qianlong Emperor in 1782*, in *CAJ*, xlv (2001), 7-27; eidem, *Islam in traditional China, a bibliographical guide* (to be publ. by Monumenta Serica). (D.D. LESLIE)

SINDHĪ [see SIND. 3.].

SINDHU, the Sanskrit name for the Indus river. See for this MIHRĀN, and for the lands along its course, SIND, MULTĀN, PANDJĀB and KASHMĪR.

AL-**SINDĪ**, ABŪ ʿALĪ, mystic of the 3rd/9th century.

He is said to have imparted to the famous Abū Yazīd al-Bisṭāmī (al-Basṭāmī) (d. 261/874 [*q.v.*]) the doctrine of "annihilation in God" (*fanāʾ*; see BAḲĀʾ WA-FANĀʾ). Moreover, because of his *nisba* al-Sindī, he was thought to be of Indian origin, and therefore it was assumed that his views could be traced back to Indian, i.e. Hindu or Buddhist, influences. However, the basis for such an assumption as provided by the sources is very weak. In fact, hardly anything is known about Abū ʿAlī al-Sindī. The *nisba* may also refer to a place in Khurāsān (Yāḳūt, *Buldān*, s.v. *Sind*). The only reference in early literature to Abū ʿAlī's influence on al-Bisṭāmī is found in a saying of the latter, mentioned in Abū Naṣr al-Sarrādj (d. 378/988 [*q.v.*]), *al-Lumaʿ* (275/70.3): "I was a companion of Abū ʿAlī al-Sindī. I used to give him instructions that enabled him to fulfil his religious duty. In turn, he enlightened me on the doctrine of God's uniqueness (*tawḥīd* [*q.v.*]) and on the mystical realities in a pure form (*ḥaḳāʾiḳ ṣirfa*)." It is only in a later variant of this saying that the term *fanāʾ* is used, see Rūzbihān b. Abī Naṣr al-Baḳlī al-Shīrāzī (d. 606/1209 [*q.v.*]), *Sharḥ-i shaṭhiyyāt* (ed. H. Corbin, 35 ll. 12-13). Moreover, Ṣūfī currents have tended to consider not Abū Yazīd as the founder of the doctrine of *fanāʾ* but rather his contemporary Abū Saʿīd al-Kharrāz al-Baghdādī (d. 277/890-1 [*q.v.*]).

Bibliography: Sources and bibl. in R. Gramlich, *Die schiitischen Derwischorden Persiens*, Wiesbaden 1970, ii, 317 n. 1965. (B. RADTKE)

ṢIRB.

1. The Ottoman period to 1800.

A. SERBIA BEFORE THE OTTOMANS

(a) *The origins of the Serbian kingdom.* The arrival of Slavic peoples in the Balkan peninsula took place in the second half of the 6th century and the beginning of the 7th one. These peoples, later to be called "South Slavs", were grouped round three main tribes: those of the Serbs, the Croats and the Slovenes, who had occupied Pannonia towards the end of the 6th century and who had moved from there towards the Adriatic coast, slowly assimilating the various Romanised peoples of Illyria. The most numerous of these "South Slavs", the Serbs, became implanted, towards the end of the 8th century, in a territory defined by the rivers Ibar (in the east), Neretva (in the southwest), Bosna (in the west) and Sava (in the north). At that time they were organised into petty principalities, governed by *joupans*, and when one of them secured an ascendancy over the rest, he would assume the tide of great *joupan*. Under the political tutelage of Byzantium, the Serbs became Christian in *ca.* 874. Serbia became independent towards the mid-9th century, thanks to the first princes of Raška (Rascie), i.e. the "Old Serbia", whose capital was at that time in the town of Ras (on the Ibar, to the northeast of Skadar/Scutari/Shkodër [see YEÑI BĀZĀR]. Under pressure from its enemies, notably the Byzantine emperors and the Bulgarian kings, the Serbian state's centre of gravity then moved towards the Zeta (the modern Montenegro and the extreme northwest of modern Albania) and then, at the time of Stevan/Stephen Nemanja (*r. ca.* 1166-96) and his successors (sc. the dynasty of the Nemanjići or Nemanids, *ca.* 1166-1371) towards the valley of the river Morava, towards Kosovo [see ḲOṢOWA and PRISHTINA] and towards Macedonia [see ÜSKÜB]. In 1219, one of the sons of Stevan Nemanja, Rastko (the future great saint of the Serbian Church, under the name of St. Sava), obtained from the Patriarch at Nicea archiepiscopal consecration and the autocephalous status of the Serbian Church, an action which was going to play an important role in preserving Serbian identity during the five centuries of Ottoman domination. The mediaeval Serbian state's apogee was in 1346, under Stephen IX Uroš IV Dušan (*r.* 1331-55), who had himself crowned "Emperor (*tsar*) of the Serbs and Greeks" and had the *Sabor* or Assembly at Skoplje set out the *Dušanov Zakonik* "Code of Dusan" (1349). The anarchy which followed his premature death at the age of 47 favoured the beginnings of Ottoman expansion in the Balkans during the next decades. (On the Nemanid tradition and the introduction of "sacral kingship" in Serbia and in general, see B.I. Bojović, *L'hagiographie dynastique et l'idéologie de l'État serbe au Moyen-Âge (XIII*ᵉ*-XV*ᵉ *siècles)*, in *Cyrillomethodianum*, xvii-xviii [Thessalonica 1993-4], 73-92.)

(b) *The first contacts with the Ottomans.* It was in the time of Tsar Dušan that Turkish units (at that time still only mercenaries or allies of the Byzantines) inflicted their first defeats on Serbian forces: first before Stephaniana in 1344 and then near Dimetoḳa [*q.v.*] in 1352. But the real Ottoman conquest of Rumelia (this time, undertaken on their own account) began in 1354 by the seizure of the fortress of Gallipoli on the Dardanelles [see GELIBOLU], or, to pinpoint the moment when the Serbian state felt the Ottomans pressingly, seventeen years later, in 1371, at the battle of the Maritsa [see MERIČ], in the course of which the Serbian king Vukašin Mrnjavčević (who ruled western Macedonia) and three of his sons, plus his own brother Uglješa, Despot of Serres [see SIROZ], were killed. However, this was only felt within the Serbs' collective memory as a baneful prelude to the disaster suffered by the troops of Prince Lazar (the "Tsar Lazar" in popular memory) on 15 June 1389 at the "Field of Blackbirds", the battle better known as that of Kosovo [see ḲOṢOWA, KOSOVO]. On the one hand, this event gave rise to the "myth of Kosovo" and, on the other hand, to a famous cycle of Serbian popular epic poetry (gathered together by Vuk Karadžić at Vienna from 1814 onwards, which was to attract very close interest from European intellectuals of the time; see, most recently, *Kosovo, six siècles de mémoires croisées*, in *Les annales de l'autre Islam*, no. 7, INALCO [Paris 2001], with further references).

B. SERBIA UNDER OTTOMAN DOMINATION (TO 1804)

The first four centuries of this history can be divided into three phases: (a) from the battle of Kosovo to 1552, the date when all the Serbian territories came under Ottoman control; (b) from 1552 to 1699, the date of the Treaty of Carlowitz, which marked the beginning of the Ottoman retreat in Danubian Europe after their maximal expansion in those lands; and (c) the slow but irreversible decline of Ottoman power in the Balkans up to 1804, the date of the first Serbian revolt.

(a) *The period 1389-1552*. The result of Kosovo was that Serbia became a vassal state of the Ottomans, forced to pay tribute and to furnish troops. With that said, the Serbian state did not disappear from existence after that date, but its centre of gravity moved much further north, where Serbian principalities were to subsist, for good or ill, for some 60 years. In the first place, there was that of the prince of Northern Serbia (the son of the Tsar Lazar, put to death by the Ottomans after the battle of Kosovo), the despot Stevan/Stephen Lazarević (*r*. 1389-1427), succeeded by his nephew George Branković (*r*. 1427-56), who in 1439 fixed his capital at Smederovo (at that time, on the Danube) [see SEMENDIRE, in Suppl.] and became involved in a double vassal status with the Ottomans and the kings of Hungary. Profiting from the Ottomans' difficulties in Anatolia (sc. the defeat at Ankara in 1402 at the hands of Tīmūr Lang [*q.v.*], the episode of Muṣṭafā Čelebi, Düzme [*q.v.*], the revolt of Sheykh Bedr al-Dīn [see BADR AL-DĪN B. ḲĀḌĪ SAMĀWNĀ], etc., the Serbian despots formed close and enduring alliances with the kings of Hungary in the hope, always to be disappointed, of "driving the Turks back to Asia". Thus in 1412, e.g., the king of Hungary Sigismund offered to cede to Stevan Lazarević the town of Belgrade as a fief, so that this last became, for the first time in its history, the capital of a Serbian prince.

But contrary to these hopes, the events of the period 1389-1552 were finally settled by the very strong and lasting implantation of Ottoman power in the Balkan peninsula (and beyond its frontiers). The main dates are: 1439, occupation of a great part of Serbia by Sultan Murād II [*q.v.*]; 1443, victories by Serbian and Hungarian troops; 1444, signature of the peace treaty of Edirne; 1453, fall of Constantinople; 1455, fresh Ottoman conquests in Serbia; 1458, fall of the Serbian despotate; 1459, surrender of the fortress of Smederovo; 1520, beginning of the reign, with its conquests, of Süleymān [*q.v.*] the Magnificent; 1526, defeat of the Hungarians at Mohácz [*q.v.*]: 1529, fall of Šabac and the first campaign against Vienna; 1541, fall of Buda; and 1552, fresh capture of Belgrade, which now made, from this date onwards, all Serbian territories subject to the Ottomans.

Two other topics important for this period must be touched upon here, if only briefly: the survival of the Serbian Orthodox Church (the only remaining "Serbian" institution during the centuries to come) and the situation of the Serbian people at this period.

Regarding the position of the Serbian Church, it should be noted that, in the course of raids by *aḳindjis* [*q.v.*] and in the course of the more regular military campaigns, neither monasteries nor churches were spared. Without the Church being singled out as such, its treasures were plundered, its buildings were burnt down and a certain number of priests and monks massacred or made prisoners-of-war. But this very dark picture needs also to be nuanced. The Serbian principalities lived for several decades as Ottoman vassals, guarding their internal organisation, including the Church, more or less intact. In some cases at least, one can even speak of a certain cultural florescence of the Serbian Orthodox Church, especially in the remoter regions, e.g. in Pomoravlje (sc. in the basin of the Morava river and its affluents), through the arrival of Bulgarian, Macedonian, Serbian and other monks and craftsmen fleeing from the lands invaded by the Turks. Then, little by little, once the disasters brought by the battles and the Ottoman campaigns were over, certain monasteries acquired official charters from the new authorities guaranteeing them a certain status within the Ottoman state, or at least, certain privileges. Unfortunately, we know little about the Church during this first period. But we do know that many monasteries were devastated, such as e.g. that of Visoki Dečani, that the greater part of their immense estates were confiscated and that, in the towns, certain churches (usually the finest) were transformed into mosques. Other churches suffered destruction later in order to provide materials for building various structures such as mosques, caravanserais, etc. Nevertheless, the Church did not lose all its lands, and not all monasteries—far from it—were devastated and left abandoned. Thus e.g. the monastery of Ravanica secured certain privileges from the time of the first Ottoman period onwards (that of 1439-44), and during this time, sultan Murād II awarded privileges to certain other Serbian monasteries. Some of these last were even excused payment of taxes, or else they were given the status of small *tīmār*s [*q.v.*] with the obligation to furnish one or two *djebelis* at the times of military campaigns (i.e. auxiliary troops, supplied and equipped by the beneficiaries of sources of revenue given by the state). But those mostly involved here were the monasteries in the frontier zones, or along the axes for provisioning the Ottoman army at times of campaigns (see A. Popovic, *Les rapports entre l'Islam et l'orthodoxie en Yougoslavie*, in *Aspects de l'orthodoxie. Structures et spiritualité, Colloque de Strasbourg, septembre 1978*, Paris 1981, 169-89).

As for the Serbian people, with the Ottoman conquest a more or less irreversible phenomenon is observable the definitive division of Serbian society into three groups. First, the group that, for various reasons, became converts to Islam and thus became separated (relatively quickly, and, even, very quickly) from the "common trunk", espousing not only a new belief and ideology but also cutting themselves off, in the long term, from anything in common with their past. Then there was the group of those who fled the lands occupied by the Ottomans (for Hungary in the first place, then for Austria, and then, much later, for Russia), certain of whose descendants were to play a great role in Serbian political and cultural life when the state was rebuilt in the 19th century. And finally, by far the most numerous, there were those who stayed behind, where they were forced to live under the new status of *dh̲immīs* [see DH̲IMMA and RAʿIYYA], a way of life punctuated by long periods of submission and daily collaboration with the Ottoman authorities but also by insurrections against these authorities, providing backing for Hungarian and Austrian armies in turn, according to the different phases of the international situation, risings which were regularly bloodily suppressed. This schema repeated itself regularly throughout the four centuries of history dealt with in this article, a history that should nevertheless be considered not only by events and by political and diplomatic processes, but also by a very close examination of the extremely complex processes going on within the central Ottoman empire and within its society in general.

(b) *The period 1552-1699.* The period that followed was to be marked, for the Serbian population, by a certain number of new occurences. The advance of Ottoman troops towards European Danubia, and the conquest of new territories, ended up by moving the "frontiers" of Serbia, as noted above, further northwards and northwestwards in relation to its original territory, that of Nemanid times. Henceforth, Serbia was to find itself, on the one hand, part of the "central provinces" of Ottoman Rumelia [see RŪMELI], and on the other, directly on the routes leading to the future theatre of military operations, viz. those leading to Vienna. Hence in 1557 (probably as part of the long-term plans of the Grand Vizier of Serbian origin, Meḥmed Pas̲h̲a Soḳollu [see SOḲOLLU]), the Porte decided to re-establish the Patriarchate of Peć. This was apparently a political act which was aimed mainly at securing peace within the central provinces of the Balkans, whilst at the same time keeping an eye on the highest levels of the revived Serbian Church, but, as G. Veinstein has noted [see SOḲOLLU, at Vol. IX, 708b], "one may also see an additional factor at work here, a wider policy of conciliating the Serbs to make them a support of Ottoman policy in the Balkans." This restored Patriarchate of Peć covered an enormous territory (part of Macedonia and Bulgaria, Serbia, Montenegro, the Voivodina and Bosnia, plus certain parts of Croatia, Dalmatia and Hungary). But, contrary to what was envisaged, this period of collaboration between the Serbian Orthodox Church and the Ottoman power was merely a flash in the pan.

The reasons for this deterioration in relations between the Serbian Church and the Porte probably resided from the start in the ambiguity of Serbian Orthodoxy's attitude *vis-à-vis* the authorities, but the reasons must above all be found in the transformation of Ottoman society itself. The first task of the renewed Serbian Church was obviously to rally the Serbian people. It thus became not only a religious organisation but also a truly political one, becoming the focus for the feelings and aspirations of the people. The basis of such an ideology could only be a glorification of the work of St. Sava, an action that was logically based on the Nemanid tradition and, in particular, on the myth of Kosovo, and because of this, Serbian Orthodoxy was compelled sooner or later to emerge from this contradiction and to break with the Ottomans and proclaim war against them. It was to be hastened very rapidly along this road by the great crisis of Ottoman society at the end of the 16th century, when non-Muslims were deprived of the possibility of becoming *tīmār*-holders, *ipso facto* throwing such persons back into the category of *reʿāyā* and thereby uniting all classes of the Orthodox population against the Ottomans.

Revolts soon broke out. One of the first occurred in the Banat in 1594, when the insurgents had, it seems, banners bearing the picture of St. Sava. It was bloodily suppressed and then, on the orders of the Grand Vizier Sinān Pas̲h̲a [*q.v.*], St. Sava's relics were brought from the monastery of Mileševo to Belgrade and publicly burnt on the Vračar hill there. The break was thus definitively made, above all in people's minds. Despite all tentative attempts and political moves to improve relations and to soothe the situation (e.g. under the Patriarch Pajsije Janjevac, between 1614 and 1647), both sides knew perfectly well what the future situation was going to be like. The deterioration rapidly accelerated. The crisis in Ottoman society led the state and its ruling classes to press down on the non-Muslim population and the Serbian Orthodox Church with increasingly heavier taxes and by all sorts of illegal abuses and practices. The churches and monasteries that were unable to satisfy these demands were sold up, bought at low prices by Muslim dignitaries and then transformed into mosques or public buildings, or even demolished for their materials to be re-used in new building works. Yet here, too, everything cannot be viewed as black and white. Thus we have cases where monasteries, under attack from Orthodox peasants coveting their lands, appealed to the Ottoman authorities. But in general, there was definitely a feeling of a certain unity between the Orthodox population and its Church and clergy, who existed within the same conditions and in an implicit connecting bond, one that was reinforced by the actions of certain Patriarchs and their being put to death by the Ottoman authorities.

The process of pressure–revolt–suppression was soon to compel the Church to seek external support: in Austria, in Italy, from the Pope, and finally, from Russia. But such support was only symbolic until the Austrian counter-offensive after the Turks' failure before Vienna in 1683. This offensive led the Christian powers far into the interior of the Ottoman lands (even the patriarchal seat, Peć, would be taken) and was to be marked by an active participation of the more energetic parts of the Serbian people, with the Patriarch Arsenije III Crnojević at their head. The Austrian troops' withdrawal had grave consequences, not only for the subsequent history of the Orthodox Church but also for the Serbian people themselves. Too compromised by these events to await the return of the Ottomans, the Patriarch in 1690 decided to lead a grand emigration of the Serbian people and their church from Kosovo to the north, beyond the Sava and Danube. The arrival of Ottoman troops brought acts of reprisal of a savagery easy to imagine, and the region of Kosovo-Metohija, the ancient centre of the Serbian state, left partly empty by its people, was gradually filled by Muslim Albanians (since a large part of the Catholic Albanians was to become rapidly Islamised), whose colonisation there was strongly supported, and extensively assisted, by the Porte.

The key dates during this century and a half are: 1557, reestablishment of the Patriarchate at Peć; 1593, Ottoman defeat before Sisak [see SISḲA]; 1593-1606, the "Long War" between Austria and Turkey; 1594, Serbian revolts (in the Banat and elsewhere); 1595, the public destruction of the relics of St. Sava at Belgrade; 1606, the peace treaty of Zsitvatorok [*q.v.*]; 1614, the Patriarch Pajsije renews the policy of compromise with the Ottoman authorities; 1683, the Ottoman check at Vienna; 1686, definitive loss of Buda; 1687, the Holy League against the Ottomans; 1688, Serbian rising and conquest of Belgrade; 1689, Austrian troops reach as far as "Old Serbia"; 1690, great Serbian emigration from Kosovo and return of the Ottomans; and 1699, the peace treaty of Carlowitz (Sremski Karlovci) [see ḲARLOVČA].

(c) *The period 1699-1804.* As during the preceding two periods, the 18th century was to bring the non-Muslim Serbian people a fresh lot of "vain hopes" and "bitter disillusionments". All this had its basis in the slow decline of the Ottoman empire, which did not, however, lead to its disintegration, supported as it was at that time by France, Britain and the Netherlands, who looked with a jaundiced eye on the subsequent successes of the Austrian Hapsburgs and the Russian Tsars (thus confirming the foresights of Montesquieu). On quite a different plane, the social and religious divisions between the Muslim and non-Muslim populations of Rumelia were to crystallise, impelling the non-Muslim Serbians to participate actively in fighting against the "Turks" in the course of each new war launched by Austria into their territory. But the ephemeral victories and the long-lasting defeats of the 18th century (notably from that time when the Serbian population had to suffer a long occupation by the Austrians, in 1718-39, one whose methods were no different from those of the Ottomans) made the Serbian people conscious of the political implications of their fight.

Here follows a chronology of events: the renewed Austro-Turkish war (of 1716-18) ended in practice with the greatest success the Hapsburgs had ever enjoyed since these last took possession, under the Treaty of Passarowitz/Požarevac [see PASAROFČA], of the eastern part of Sirmia (Srem); the Banat (with Temesvar), Lesser Wallachia, all the northeastern part of Serbia, including Belgrade; and the northern zone of Bosnia (along the Sava), territories they retained for some 20 years. (On the desert aspect of Serbia in 1717, with the encroachment of virgin forests with strips of cultivation abandoned for many years, with miserable, scattered village populations, see Lady Mary Stuart Wortley Montague, *Turkish letters*, London 1763, with many later editions.) The measure of disenchantment of the non-Muslim population during these years (faced with the Austrians' attitudes, their arbitrary taxes and the missionary activities of the Roman Catholic Church) can be simply measured by the numerous cases of flight by the Serbian Orthodox people back to Ottoman territory.

Then, twenty years later, a fresh Austro-Turkish war broke out (1737-9) which, after great initial successes by the Austrians and the insurgent Serbs (conquest of southwestern Serbia, with Alleksinac, Kruševac, Novi Pazar, Pri<u>sh</u>tina and Ni<u>sh</u>), ended in a terrible defeat before Grocka (not far from Belgrade), and by the Treaty of Belgrade (1739) the Hapsburgs lost all the territories captured twenty years before. Naturally, there were more waves of emigration by Serbs into southern Hungary, one of which, under the Patriarch Arsenije IV Jovanović Šakabenta, became known as "the second Serbian migration from Kosovo".

The years that followed, generally called "the thirty years of peace", were marked by the suppression in 1766 of the Patriarchate of Peć (whose increasingly frequent flirtations with the Russian Orthodox Church ended by seriously worrying the Porte, but which had already, for a fair amount of time, been in a lamentable state (see O. Zirojević, 152-5), and by attempts by Russia (from 1751-2 onwards) to attract Serbian emigrants from Hungary to settle in the Ukraine. (These events are described in a magistral fashion by M. Crnjanski [1893-1977] in his novel *Seobe* ["Migrations"], Belgrade 1929, ^{2}1962, etc., Fr. tr. Paris 1986.)

Then a third Austro-Turkish war broke out in 1788 (as a prolongation of the Russo-Turkish war that had begun the previous year), in which a large part of the Serbian population took part, notably in the famous volunteer bands of *Frajkori* (< Ger. *Freikorps*), led by their own offices. These troops, led by the famous Koča Andjelković (hence the name "Kočina Krajina"), succeeded in conquering western and northern Serbia (sc. Šumadija and the Požarevac region) and in 1789 (in collaboration with the Austrians), the city of Belgrade itself. However, two years later, in 1791, the peace treaty of Svištov [see ZI<u>SH</u>TOWA] deprived the insurgents of their conquests and authorised the return of the Ottomans. Finally, at the end of the 18th century, the reforms undertaken by Selīm III [*q.v.*] provoked plots and risings of the Janissaries in various parts of Rumelia. Amongst these, more specifically, was the rising in Serbia of 1804, provoked by the excesses and violence of the Janissaries; this was genuinely a rising with a national character, affecting the greater part of the Serbian people and conducted by one of their chiefs, George Petrović, called Kara ("black") George (see R. Mantran, in idem [ed.], *Histoire de l'Empire ottomane*, 430-1). It was in these conditions that there broke out in 1804 the "First Serbian Revolt", which allowed, by successive stages and three decades later, the definitive freeing of Serbia from the Ottoman empire and the beginnings of its independence.

The key dates, which spanned a century (1699-1804), are the following: 1716, a new Austro-Turkish war; 1717, the conquest of Belgrade by Prince Eugène of Savoy's army; 1718, the peace treaty of Požarevac, with Belgrade becoming the capital of Northern Serbia under Austrian occupation; 1737-9, a new Austro-Turkish war; 1739, the peace treaty of Belgrade, by which the Ottomans re-occupied their former Serbian territories; 1739-74, the so-called "thirty years of peace"; 1766, suppression of the Patriarchate of Peć; 1768-74, Russo-Turkish war; 1774, the peace treaty of Küčük Ḳaynar<u>dj</u>a [*q.v.*]; 1788, fresh Austro-Turkish war; 1789, conquest of Belgrade by Austrian troops and Serbian insurgents; 1791, peace treaty of Svištov stipulating the return of the Ottomans in Serbia; 1792, revolt of the Janissaries of Serbia against the Porte and Selīm III's reforms: 1794-7, conquest of the *pa<u>sh</u>alïḳ* of Belgrade by the rebel *pa<u>sh</u>a* of Vidin [see WIDIN], Paswan-o<u>gh</u>lu [*q.v.*]; 1801-3, reign of terror by the four rebel Janissary chiefs, installed in Belgrade; 1804, the First Serbian Revolt led by Kara George.

In the course of this rapid survey, several important questions have remained unexplored: economic topics (agriculture, stockrearing, exploitation of mines, large-scale colonisation by the Ottoman authorities through the intermediacy of installing pastoralist nomads and "Wallachs/Vlachs"—whose name, however, poses certain problems—etc.); the formation and growth of the towns, and the town-and-country relationships (taking into account the minimal representation of Serbs in the towns and of "Turks" in the villages); the Serbian patriarchal society and the system of *zadruga* (extended families living under the same roof); the very numerous migrations and emigrations (notably towards southern Hungary, south-western Bosnia, Southern Russia and the Croatian "Krajina"); the demographic evolution of the Serbian population; brigandage, and the question of guerilla bands against the Ottoman authorities (the *hajduks* and *uskoks*); the results of the wars and the continual devastations (shrinking of the economy from primitive agricultural methods and exhaustion of the soil); famines and epidemics (cholera and plague); the increasing authority of the Serbian Church and the crystallisation of Serbian national feeling; and cultural topics and the rule played here by Jovan Rajić (1726-1801), Zaharije Orfelin (1726-85), Dositej Obradović (1739-1811) and Vuk Stefanović Karadžić (1787-1864). These subjects can be explored through titles listed below in the *Bibl.*

Bibliography (in addition to references given in the article): I.I. Tkalac, *Das serbische Volk in seiner Bedeutung für die orientalische Frage und für die europäische Zivilisation*, Leipzig 1853; B. Kallay, *Geschichte der Serben (1780-1815)*, Budapest-Vienna-Leipzig 1878, [2]1910; S. Novaković, *Srbi i Turci XIV i XV veka*, Belgrade 1893, [2]1933, [3]1960; J. Radonić, *Zapadna Evropa i balkanski narodi prema Turcima u prvoj polovini 15 veka*, Novi Sad 1905; Novaković, *Tursko carstvo pred srpski ustanak 1780-1804*, Belgrade 1906; S. Stanojević, *Istorija srpskog naroda*, Belgrade 1908, [3]1926; C. Jireček, *Geschichte der Serben*, 2 vols., Gotha 1911-18; A. Ivić, *Istorija Srba u Ugarskoj. Od pada Smedereva do seobe pod Čarnojevićima (1459-1690)*, Zagreb 1914; G. Gravier, *Les frontières historiques de la Serbie*, Paris 1919; Ivić, *Migracije Srba u Slavoniji tokom 16., 17. i 18. stoljéća*, Belgrade 1923; J. Ancel, *Peuples et nations des Balkans*, Paris 1926, [2]1992; D. Pantelić, *Beogradski pašaluk posle Svištovskog mira, 1791-1794*, Belgrade 1927; V. Popović, *Istočno pitanje*, Belgrade 1928, [2]Sarajevo 1965, [3]Belgrade 1996; É. Haumant, *La formation de la Yougoslavie (XVe-XXe s.)*, Paris 1930; D. Pantelić, *Kočina Krajina*, Belgrade 1930; D. Popović, *O hajducima*, 2 vols., Belgrade 1930-1; A. Hajek, art. *Serbia*, in *EI*[1] Suppl.; Ivić, *Istorija Srba u Vojvodini*, Novi Sad 1939; L. Hadrovics, *Le peuple serbe et son Église sous la domination turque*, Paris 1947; Pantelić, *Beogradski pašaluk pred Prvi srpski ustanak (1794-1804)*, Belgrade 1949; idem, *Srbi u Sremu*, Belgrade 1950; B. Djurdjev, *Uticaj turske vladavine na razvitak naših naroda*, in *Godišnjak ist. dr. BiH*, ii (Sarajevo 1950), 19-82; idem, *Osnovni problemi srpske istorije u periodu turske vlasti nad našim narodima*, in *Istoriski Glasnik*, iii-iv (Belgrade 1950), 107-18; idem, *Uloga srpske crkve u borbi protiv osmanske vlasti*, dans *Pregled*, i (Sarajevo 1953), 35-42; *Istorija naroda Jugoslavije*, 2 vols., Belgrade-Zagreb-Ljubljana 1953-60; D. Popović, *Velika seoba Srba*, Belgrade 1954; Pantelić, *Srbi u Banatu do kraja osamnaestog veka*, Belgrade 1955; idem, *Srbi u Vojvodini*, 3 vols., Novi Sad 1957-63; R. Veselinović, *Vojvodina, Srbija i Makedonija pod turskom vlašću u drugoj polovini XVII veka*, Novi Sad 1960; Dj. Slijepčević, *Istorija srpske pravoslavne crkve*, 2 vols., Munich 1962-6; M. Mirković, *Pravni položaj i karakter srpske crkve pod turskom vlašću (1459-1766)*, Belgrade 1965; G. Stanojević, *Srbija u vreme Bečkog rata*, Belgrade 1976; *Istorija srpskog naroda*, 10 vols., Belgrade 1981-93; D.Lj. Kašić, *Pogled u prošlost srpske crkve*, Belgrade 1984; R. Mantran (ed.), *Histoire de l'Empire ottoman*, Paris 1989; O. Zirojević, *Srbija pod turskom vlašću (1459-1804)*, Novi Pazar 1995; and, for the ensemble of publications which have appeared in Yogoslavia 1945-75, J. Tadić (ed.), *Dix années d'historiographie yougoslave 1945-1955*, Belgrade 1955; idem (ed.), *Historiographie yougoslave 1955-1965*, Belgrade 1965; D. Janković (ed.), *The historiography of Yugoslavia 1965-1975*, Belgrade 1975. (A. Popovic)

SIRR (a.), lit. "secret", denotes in Islamic spirituality two notions, at first sight distinct but which certain adepts did not hesitate to combine (al-Djurdjānī, 218; al-Tahānawī, i, 653; on the combination of the two senses, see e.g. al-Sulamī, 1953, 213, 216, 282).

1. The first notion is that of secret, mystery, arcana, in the sense of a teaching, a reality or even a doctrinal point, hidden by nature or which is kept hidden from persons considered unworthy of knowing it. If there is a secret, says al-Sarrādj al-Ṭūsī (d. 378/998), probably taking up the Shīʿī concept of two levels of reality (Amir-Moezzi, 1997), it is because the object of knowledge sought by the individual has an obvious, exoteric (*ẓāhir*) aspect and a hidden, esoteric (*bāṭin*) one. The Ḳurʾān, the Ḥadīth, knowledge, Islam, etc., all have these two distinct, complementary levels. In order to attain the esoteric level, a person must so dispose his body (lit. "his members", *djawāriḥ*), since this level can only be reached by the "esoteric organ", sc. the heart (*ḳalb*). The *bāṭin* of objects of knowledge as well as the interior realities of a man are secrets that only the initiates can discover and which they must protect (al-Sarrādj, 43-4). The mass of people, prisoners of their own ignorance and blindly attached to the letter only of religion, can only become violent if the secret is revealed to them, even if only partially (Lāhidjī, 100, 498; al-Ḳaysarī, 41; Ḳāḍī ʿAbd al-Nabī, ii, 167). Even the Ḳurʾān, in two places, authorises the faithful to dissimulate their beliefs in cases of danger (III, 28; XL, 28), whence the adage, untiringly repeated in the mystical works, "the breasts of free men are repositories (lit. 'tombs') of secrets" (*ṣudūr al-aḥrār ḳubūr al-asrār*, see e.g. al-Tahānawī, 92).

According to the Shīʿa (for whom "everything has a secret; the secret of Islam is Shīʿism," al-Kulaynī, ii, 14), this—i.e. essentially the Imāms' teachings, which has several esoteric levels, *bāṭin* and *bāṭin al-bāṭin*—contains secrets that must be protected at all costs (al-Ṣaffār, 28-9). The duty of keeping such secrets (*taḳiyya, kitmān, khabʾ*) is thus a canonical obligation for them (Kohlberg, 1975, 1995; Amir-Moezzi, 1992, index, s.v. *taqiyya*).

For the Ṣūfīs likewise, such notions as "protection of the secret" (*ḥifẓ al-sirr*, around which expression, above all, certain mystics combine the two senses of *sirr*), "concealing, changing the guise of something to make it appear other than it is" (*talbīs*), or further, "hiding the real nature of the particular interior state" (*ikhfāʾ al-ḥāl*), make up practices and disciplines which are particularly important (al-Suhrawardī 1983, 72; Hudjwīrī, 500-1; ʿAfīfī, 89, 117; al-Shaybī, 20ff.). In the literature of mysticism, constant reference is made to the trial of al-Ḥallādj [*q.v.*], who was executed in 309/922 for having divulged the Secret *par excellence*, by putting forward the famous *shaṭḥ* "I am the Real" (*anā 'l-ḥaḳḳ*), *ḥaḳḳ* being a Name of God. The greatest Persian mystical poets, such as ʿAṭṭār, ʿIrāḳī and Ḥāfiẓ, very often allude to the "crucified one of Baghdād" (sc. al-Ḥallādj) and call the real spiritual masters "the people of the Secret" (Khurramshāhī, s.v. *ahl-i rāz*). This is why mystical authors, from their oldest writings onwards, devised an "allusive language" (*ishāra*), a coded form of discourse which was later to assume very numerous forms (technical vocabularies, symbolic lexica, fables, poetic images, etc.), reflecting esoteric realities and distinguishing themselves from "literal language" (*ʿibāra*) which is unsuitable for exoteric topics (al-Sarrad̲j̲, 414, concerning *ramz*; al-Kalābād̲h̲ī, ch. iii, 30ff.; Hud̲j̲wīrī, 480ff.; and see Amir-Moezzi 2002b).

2. The second notion is that of a "subtle organ", one of the layers of the "heart", making up the human spiritual anatomy, which may be translated by "secret, inner consciousness". It seems that, for the K̲h̲urāsān school of mystics, the Malāmatiyya [*q.v.*] comprise the progression of levels of consciousness, "organs" of invocation (*d̲h̲ikr*) and vision (*mus̲h̲āhada*), going through the soul (*nafs*) to the spirit (*rūḥ*), passing by the heart (*ḳalb*) and the inner consciousness (al-Tustarī, 16, 19, 34, 45, 78; al-Sulamī 1991, 16). It should be noted that al-Ḥakīm al-Tirmid̲h̲ī (d. *ca.* 318/936 [*q.v.*]), one of the oldest of the K̲h̲urāsānian theoreticians of the elements making up the "heart", seems to be the only one of them not counting the *sirr* amongst these last (*Bayān*, *passim* and esp. 427; Gobillot 1996, 197-8). Al-Ḳus̲h̲ayrī (d. 465/1072 [*q.v.*]), conveying the system of the ʿIrāḳī Ṣūfīs, sets forth another progression which omits the soul, the seat of the ego, and the *sirr* is said to be the seat of vision, whilst the spirit is the seat of love (*maḥabba*) and the heart that of knowledge (*maʿārif*). Here, the inner consciousness is considered as amongst the most subtle and the noblest parts of man, as the innermost secret between the created man and God, the most interiorised part of a man's being (al-Ḳus̲h̲ayrī, 45; Gobillot and Ballanfat, 175-6); it is in this context that one should probably understand the formula pronounced over a dead person: *ḳaddasa Allāh sirrahu al-ʿazīz* "may God sanctify his noble inner consciousness". Such great mystics as ʿAmr b. ʿUt̲h̲mān al-Makkī (d. 291/903-4) or al-Ḥallād̲j̲ seem close to this system (Massignon, i, 113, ii, 411ff.), whilst others, like al-K̲h̲arrāz (d. 286/899 [*q.v.*]) for example, develop a much more complex spiritual anatomy, comprising instinct (*ṭabʿ*), soul, heart, will (*irāda*), spirit, inner consciousness and spiritual aspiration (*himma*) (Nwyia, 243-5, 272, 301).

After the attempt at a synthesis of the different systems by ʿUmar al-Suhrawardī (d. 632/1235 [*q.v.*]) (1983, 454ff., 1986, 181, 203), one often finds amongst the later mystics a sevenfold division, admittedly with other nomenclatures, to which they add new touches derived from mystical theories and practices like *d̲h̲ikr* formulae corresponding to each level, interior prophetology or coloured lights accompanying each layer of the "heart". We have here the theory of "subtle organs" (*laṭīfa*, pl. *laṭāʾif*, or also *ṭūr*, pl. *aṭwār*) especially developing from the time of Nad̲j̲m al-Dīn Kubrā (d. 617/1220-1 [*q.v.*]) and the mystics of his school (Corbin 1971; al-Isfarāyinī, 1986, introd., 60-2; Landolt, 287-8; Kubrā 2001, index s.v. *organe subtil*), from Ibn al-ʿArabī's followers such as Muʾayyid al-Dīn D̲j̲andī or Dāwūd al-Ḳaysarī (Gobillot and Ballanfat, 189-90), up to the modern and even contemporary Ṣūfīs Muḥammad b. ʿAlī al-Sanūsī of Algeria (d. 1276/1879 [*q.v.*]) (105ff.) and the Kurd Muḥammad Amīn al-Naḳs̲h̲bandī (d. 1324/1914-15) (548-58). In the different progressions of the "subtle organs", *sirr* is almost always present, most often associated with the colour white. The *d̲h̲ikr* corresponding to it varies greatly according to authors or mystical orders. The most often-found is: *ṭabʿ*, *nafs*, *ḳalb*, *rūḥ*, *sirr*, *k̲h̲afī* ("what is hidden") and *ak̲h̲fā* ("what is most hidden") (Kās̲h̲ānī, 82ff., 101 and the editor's notes).

In S̲h̲īʿī mysticism, allusions of varying precision to the subtle "layers" of the "heart" and vision by means of the heart, are found from the time of the oldest compilations of *ḥadīt̲h̲* onwards (Amir-Moezzi 1992, 112ff.). However, the S̲h̲īʿī Ṣūfīs (Niʿmatullāhiyya, D̲h̲ahabiyya and K̲h̲āksar), organised in brotherhoods from the 16th-17th centuries onwards, went on to adopt one or another of the systems used by Sunnī orders like the Ḳādiriyya, Kubrawiyya or Naḳs̲h̲bandiyya (Gramlich, ii, 207 n. 1073, 247-50; Amir-Moezzi 1992, 129ff.; idem 2002, *passim*).

Bibliography: 1. Sources. Hud̲j̲wīrī, ed. V.A. Z̲h̲ukovski, repr. Tehran 1979; Isfarāyinī, *Kās̲h̲if al-asrār*, Fr. tr. H. Landolt, *Le révélateur des mystères*, Paris and Lagrasse 1986; D̲j̲urd̲j̲ānī, *K. al-Taʿrīfāt*, Fr. tr. M. Gloton, Tehran 1994 (based on four printed texts, beginning with that of Flügel, Leipzig 1845); Kalābād̲h̲ī, *K. al-Taʿarruf*, ed. ʿA.M.ʿA. Surūr, Beirut 1400/1980; Kās̲h̲ānī, *Miṣbāḥ al-hidāya*, ed. D̲j̲. Humāʾī, Tehran 1323/1945; Nad̲j̲m al-Dīn Kubrā, *Fawātiḥ al-d̲j̲amāl*, Fr. tr. P. Ballanfat, Nîmes 2001; Kulaynī, *al-Rawḍa min al-Kāfī*, ed. R. Maḥallātī, Tehran 1389/1969; Lāhid̲j̲ī, *Mafātīḥ al-iʿd̲j̲āz fī s̲h̲arḥ Guls̲h̲an-i rāz*, ed. K̲h̲āliḳī-Karbāsī, Tehran 1992; Naḳs̲h̲bandī, *Tanwīr al-ḳulūb*, [6]Cairo 1348/1929; Ḳāḍī ʿAbd al-Nabī Aḥmadnagarī, *Dustūr al-ʿulamāʾ*, Ḥaydarābād 1331/1912; Ḳaysarī, *S̲h̲arḥ Fuṣūṣ al-ḥikam*, Tehran 1299/1881; Ḳus̲h̲ayrī, *al-Risāla al-ḳus̲h̲ayriyya*, Beirut n.d.; al-Ṣaffār al-Kummī, *Baṣāʾir al-darad̲j̲āt*, ed. M. Kūčibāg̲h̲ī, Tehran *ca.* 1960; Sanūsī, *K. al-Masāʾil al-ʿas̲h̲ar* (incl. also *al-Salsabīl al-maʿīn*), Cairo 1353/1932; al-Sarrād̲j̲ al-Ṭūsī, *K. al-Lumaʿ*, ed. Surūr, Cairo and Bag̲h̲dād 1380/1960; Suhrawardī, *ʿAwārif al-maʿārif*, Beirut 1983; idem, *Ras̲h̲f al-naṣāʾiḥ al-īmāniyya*, ed. Māyil Harawī, Tehran 1365/1986; Sulamī, *Ṭabaḳāt al-ṣūfiyya*, ed. N. S̲h̲urayba, Cairo 1953; idem, *al-Risāla al-malāmatiyya*, ed. A.ʿA. al-ʿAfīfī, Cairo 1364/1945, Fr. tr. R. Deladrière, *La lucidité implacable, épître des hommes du blâme*, Paris 1991; Tahānawī, *Kas̲h̲s̲h̲āf iṣṭilāḥāt al-funūn*, Calcutta 1862; Tirmid̲h̲ī, *Bayān al-farḳ bayn al-ṣadr wa ʾl-ḳalb wa ʾl-fuʾād wa ʾl-lubb*, ed. M. Heer, Cairo 1958; Tustarī, *Tafsīr al-Ḳurʾān al-ʿaẓīm*, Cairo n.d.

2. Studies. A.ʿA. al-ʿAfīfī, *al-Malāmatiyya wa ʾl-taṣawwuf wa-ahl al-futuwwa*, Cairo 1945; K.M. al-S̲h̲aybī, *al-Taḳiyya, uṣūluhā wa-taṭawwuruhā*, in *Revue de la Fac. des Lettres de l'Univ. d'Alexandrie*, xvi (1962-3), 14-40; P. Nwyia, *Exégèse coranique et langage mystique*, Beirut 1970; H. Corbin, *L'Homme de Lumière dans le soufisme iranien*, [2]Paris 1971; L. Massignon, *La passion d'Hallâj*, 4 vols. repr. Paris 1975; E. Kohlberg, *Some Imāmī-Shīʿī views on taqiyya*, in *JAOS*, xcv (1975), 395-402; R. Gramlich, *Die schiitischen Derwischorden Persiens*, 3 vols. Wiesbaden 1976-81; H. Landolt, *Deux opuscules de Semnânî sur le moi théophanique*, in S.H. Nasr (ed.), *Mélanges offerts à Henry Corbin*, Tehran 1977, 279-319; B. K̲h̲urrams̲h̲āhī, *Ḥāfiẓ-nāma*, Tehran 1366/1987; M.A. Amir-Moezzi, *Le Guide divin dans le shīʿisme originel*, Paris and Lagrasse 1992; Kohlberg, *Taqiyya in Shīʿī theology and religion*, in H.G. Kippenberg and G. Stroumsa (eds.), *Secrecy and concealment. Studies in the history of Mediterranean and Near Eastern religions*, Leiden 1995, 345-80; Amir-Moezzi, *Du droit à la théologie. Les niveaux de réalité dans le shiʿisme duodécimain*, in *L'Esprit et la nature: Colloque tenu à Paris les 11 et 12 mai 1996*, Milan 1997, 37-63; G. Gobillot, *Le livre de la profondeur des choses (Ghawr al-umūr d'al-Ḥakīm al-Tirmidhī)*, Paris 1996; eadem and P. Ballanfat, *Le coeur et la vie spirituelle chez les mystiques musulmans*, in *Connaisance des Religions*, no. 57-9 (1999), 170-204; Amir-Moezzi, *Visions d'Imam en mystique imamite moderne et contemporaine*

(Aspects de l'imamologie duodécimaine VIII), in *Autour du regard. Mélanges offerts à Daniel Gimaret*, Louvain 2002; idem, art. *Dissimulation*, in *Encycl. of the Qur'ān*, i, Leiden 2002, 540-2.

(Mohammad Ali Amir-Moezzi)

SOLTANGALIEV [see sulṭān ʿalī ūghlī].

SOUTH AFRICA, Islam in.

2. Afrikaans in Arabic script.

Arabic-Afrikaans denotes the script whereby Muslims in 19th-century South Africa rendered a creolised dialect of the Afrikaans language. A phonetically adapted Arabic script was used to write Muslim religious literature of this spoken dialect. Afrikaans itself owes its origins to these creolised varieties of the colonial dialect of Netherlandic (Cape Dutch) that was spoken among the Khoisan and slave community of the Cape. Arabic-Afrikaans is the patrimony of this distinct Cape Muslim community, whose major ancestral ties can be traced to the Malay-speaking world, from where many of them arrived after 1652.

Cape Muslims, possibly as far back as the late 18th and early 19th centuries, spoke a more distinct creole variety of Cape Dutch that was heavily affected by word borrowings from Malayu but also contained some Bughanese and Arabic words. The grammatical structure of Arabic-Afrikaans writings shows unmistakable resemblances to the grammar of what later develops into the Afrikaans language. The written script of this Cape Muslim creole Afrikaans is derived from the Djāwī [*q.v.*] script that modifies the Arabic alphabet, in order to create specific phonetic renderings unavailable in Arabic.

As a written script, Arabic-Afrikaans served as a vehicle for the transmission of a knowledge of religion in the course of educating mostly slaves and free blacks among the Muslims of the Cape *ca.* 1810 or thereafter. Members of this community were literate but not in the Roman script; they could read languages based on Arabic orthography and could read the Ḳur'ān for liturgical purposes.

One of the earliest Arabic-Afrikaans manuscripts can be dated back to 1840, according to Achmat Davids (d. 1998), whose seminal writings pioneered this field of study (Davids 1991, 56). Texts in circulation that were written in Arabic-Afrikaans covered subjects such as the elementary rules of Islamic law (*fiḳh*), catechism and theology (*tawḥīd* and *ʿilm al-kalām*) for the instruction of adults and children. Handwritten and later printed editions known as *koples boeke*, mnemonic texts written for the purpose of memorising religious teachings, circulated widely at the Cape and its hinterland for much of the 19th century and were still in use during the early part of the 20th century.

However, with the gradual growth of literacy in English and Afrikaans among Cape Muslims, many *ʿulamā'* switched to the Roman script, while continuing to write in the distinct Cape Muslim idiom of Afrikaans that is different from standard Afrikaans. Apart from literacy in the Roman script, easy access to mechanised printing facilities was the main reason for the change, since Arabic-Afrikaans texts had to be published outside South Africa.

Accredited as the first and best-known of Arabic-Afrikaans texts is the *Bayān al-dīn* "The exposition of religion" of Abu Bakr Effendi (d. 1880), a Kurdish religious scholar who was sent to the Cape by the Ottomans. His book was completed in 1869, but only published at Istanbul in 1877. In the mid-20th century Mia Brandel-Syrier translated it into English. Hans Kähler believed that the *Tuḥfat al-ikhwān*, "Gifts to friends", a manuscript written by Imām ʿAbd al-Ḳahhār b. ʿAbd al-Malik *ca.* 1856 could have been the earliest text, but this document, now in Germany, has not been properly verified. The Dutch orientalist Adrianus van Selms (d. 1984) believed that the earliest attempt to print Arabic-Afrikaans at the Cape could have taken place as early as 1856. Since no copy of this work remains extant, Davids doubted this claim.

Three other figures deserve mention for their prolific contribution to the genre of Arabic-Afrikaans writing. One was Shaykh ʿAbd al-Raḥīm b. Muḥammad al-ʿIrāḳī (d. 1942), a native of Baṣrā who settled in the Cape around the 1880s. He quickly mastered the local patois and began writing in Arabic-Afrikaans, producing smaller tracts directed at an adult audience. Texts were also produced for the local *madrasa* education system that students attended in the afternoon after their schooling in the secular educational system. The second person was Imām ʿAbd al-Raḥmān Ḳāsim Gamieldien (d. 1921), his creolised family name being possibly a corruption of Djamīl al-Dīn or Ḥāmil al-Dīn (Davids 1991, 147), who wrote several texts for the *madrasa* curriculum. The third person was the son of Abū Bakr Effendi, sc. Hishām Niʿmat Allāh Effendi (d. *ca.* 1945), who published several Arabic-Afrikaans books in his desire to advance education among the local Muslims.

According to an inventory made by Davids, some 74 Arabic-Afrikaans publications have been identified, with the possibility of more being discovered in private collections and libraries. Further investigation of these texts should shed light on how knowledge from the metropolises of the Islamic world was transferred to marginal and smaller communities, thereby increasing local knowledge and introducing new practices.

Bibliography: A. van Selms, *Die oudste boek in Afrikaans: Isjmoeni se betroubare woord*, in *Hertzog Annale* (Nov. 1953); Abu Bakr Effendi, *The religious duties of Islam as taught and explained by Abu Bakr Effendi*, tr. Mia Brandel-Syrier, Leiden 1960; H. Kähler, *Studien über die Kultur, die Sprache und die arabisch-afrikaansche Literatur der Kap Malaien*, Berlin 1971; Achmat Davids, *Words the Cape slaves made. A socio-historical linguistic study*, in *South African Jnal. of Linguistics*, viii/1 (1990); idem, *The Afrikaans of the Cape Muslims from 1815 to 1915. A socio-linguistic study*, M.A. diss., Faculty of Humanities, Dept. of Afrikaans and Nederlands, Univ. of Natal (Durban) 1991, unpubl.

(Ebrahim Moosa)

al-**SUFYĀNĪ**, a descendant of the Umayyad Abū Sufyān [*q.v.*] figuring in apocalyptic prophecies as the rival and opponent of the Mahdī [*q.v.*] and ultimately overcome by him.

The bulk of these prophecies dates from the 2nd/8th century. The largest collection of them was assembled by the Sunnī traditionist Nuʿaym b. Ḥammād (d. 227/842) in his *Kitāb al-Fitan*. Different views have been expressed about the origins of this figure. The Zubayrid Muṣʿab b. ʿAbd Allāh (d. 236/851) claimed that Khālid, son of the caliph Yazīd I [see khālid b. yazīd b. muʿāwiya], had invented it out of resentment of the usurpation of his title to the caliphate by the caliph Marwān I. Khālid thus wanted to arouse popular hopes for a restorer of the Sufyānid branch of the house of Umayya. This view that the figure at first represented Sufyānid interests against the Marwānid caliphate was in modern times endorsed by Th. Nöldeke and Ch. Snouck Hurgronje, who held that it was later transformed by orthodox religious tradition into an Umayyad Antichrist. Following suggestions by J. Wellhausen, H. Lammens questioned this view and connected the figure with the abortive anti-ʿAbbāsid rising of Abū Muḥammad al-Sufyānī in Syria in 133/751. The Syrians denied his death and believed that he was hiding in the mountains of al-Ṭāʾif from where he would return in triumph. S͟hīʿī and pro-ʿAbbāsid traditionists then turned this "Syrian national hero" into a figure resembling the Dad͟jd͟jāl [*q.v.*]. Combining the two views, R. Hartmann argued that the Sufyānī was at first an anti-Marwānid messianic figure which, after the overthrow of the Umayyad dynasty, was turned by Syrian advocates of an Umayyad restoration into an anti-ʿAbbāsid messiah. The Syrians, Hartmann suggested, may at that time have longed for a return of the caliph Yazīd I. Only thereafter was the figure taken over by the ʿAbbāsids and their S͟hīʿī backers and transformed into an opponent of the Mahdī.

The image of the opposition between the Mahdī and the Sufyānī goes back to a *ḥadīt͟h* (fully quoted in the art. AL-MAHDĪ at Vol. V, 1232a), which predicted the rise to power of a political refugee from Medina in Mecca and the subsequent rise in Syria of "a man whose maternal uncles are of Kalb", who would send an army of Kalb against the rebel in Mecca. This army, however, would be utterly defeated, and the rebel caliph in Mecca would justly rule Islam for seven or nine years. The first part of this *ḥadīt͟h* reflected, as pointed out by D.S. Attema, the career of ʿAbd Allāh b. al-Zubayr, and the prediction dates from shortly after the death of the caliph Yazīd (64/683). In the later Umayyad age, this prediction was widely spread as a prophetic *ḥadīt͟h* by the highly regarded Baṣran traditionist Ḳatāda b. Diʿāma (d. 117/735). As its contents were now projected into the apocalyptic future, the rebel caliph in Mecca came to be identified with the Mahdī and his rival, whose maternal uncles were of Kalb, with a Sufyānī opponent.

As the Mahdī in the later Umayyad age was more and more identified with a descendant of Muḥammad, the figure of his Sufyānī opponent was commonly appropriated from the originally pro-Zubayrid Ḳatāda *ḥadīt͟h* and developed by S͟hīʿī and pro-ʿAlid Kūfan circles. The appearance of the Sufyānī was thus closely connected with the advent of the Mahdī. A Kūfan prophecy foretold that the Sufyānī and the Mahdī would come forth like two racehorses. Each one would subdue the region next to him. The S͟hīʿī *imām* Muḥammad al-Bāḳir was quoted as predicting that the Sufyānī would reign for the time of the pregnancy of a woman (*ḥaml marʾa*). The prediction of a "swallowing up (*k͟hasf*)" of a Syrian army by the desert between Mecca and Medina, which according to the Ḳatāda *ḥadīt͟h* was to occur under the predecessor of the Sufyānī (historically the caliph Yazīd), was now integrated into the career of the Sufyānī. S͟hīʿīs referred to the Sufyānī also as the Son of the Liver-eating Woman (*ibn ākilat al-akbād*) after Abū Sufyān's wife Hind bt. ʿUtba [*q.v.*], who was said to have bitten the liver of Muḥammad's uncle Ḥamza after he was killed in the battle of Uḥud. The Sufyānī, it was predicted, would first come forth in the Wādī al-Yābis near Damascus. In the later Imāmī S͟hīʿī standard doctrine, the appearance of the Sufyānī in the Wādī al-Yābis in the month of Ramaḍān and the *k͟hasf* of an army sent by him in the desert are counted among the indispensable signs for the advent of the Mahdī or Ḳāʾim [see ḲĀʾIM ĀL MUḤAMMAD].

There is no sound evidence for an early anti-Marwānid expectation of a restorer of Sufyānid rule. The apocalyptic Sufyānī figure came to Syria and Egypt together with that of the Fāṭimid Mahdī and represented a minority view there in the late Umayyad age. The great Berber rebellion in the Mag͟hrib in 123/740-1 aroused fears of an invasion of Egypt and Syria, the *fitna* of the Mag͟hrib inaugurating the end of time, and there were predictions of the appearance of the Sufyānī connected with it. In post-Umayyad Sufyānī prophecies, the coming of a rebel Berber army, often described as carrying yellow flags, became a standard element.

After the overthrow of the Umayyad caliphate by the ʿAbbāsids, the apocalyptic Sufyānī was in Syria given the role of a successful challenger of the eastern conquerors. Already during the anti-ʿAbbāsid revolt of Abū Muḥammad al-Sufyānī in 133/751, word was spread by his supporters that he was "the Sufyānī who had been mentioned". The Sufyānī was now associated with a prediction that the Syrians would march against an eastern caliph in Kūfa, which would be razed to the ground "like a leather skin (*tuʿraku ʿark al-adīm*)". Bag͟hdād was soon added as a town to be destroyed by the Sufyānī, who would send his armies to the east, the Mag͟hrib, Yemen and ʿIrāḳ. Such anti-ʿAbbāsid prophecies were first spread by pro-ʿAlid Syrian narrators, who invariably portrayed the Sufyānī as a ruthless forerunner of the just Fāṭimid Mahdī to whom he would ultimately lose out. In some prophecies, the Sufyānī was described as "handing over the caliphate to the Mahdī (*yadfaʿ al-k͟hilāfat^a^ li ʾl-Mahdī*)". The themes of these S͟hīʿī prophecies were taken over and further developed by Sunnī traditionists, especially in Ḥimṣ. The largest contribution was made by Arṭāt b. al-Mund͟hir (d. 162-3/779-80), an ascetic worshipper highly regarded as a transmitter who produced lengthy predictions, either attributing them to Kaʿb al-Aḥbār [*q.v.*] and his stepson Tubayʿ b. al-ʿĀmir al-Ḥimyarī or in his own name. Arṭāt's predictions turned the Sufyānī into a thoroughly repulsive and monstrous figure resembling the Dad͟jd͟jāl. Sometimes Arṭāt divided the Sufyānī into two figures. The first one, named ʿAbd Allāh b. Yazīd, would be al-Azhar or al-Zuhrī b. al-Kalbiyya, the deformed Sufyānī (*al-Sufyānī al-mus͟hawwah*). He would take the *d͟jizya* from the Muslims, enslave their children and split open the wombs of pregnant women. After he had died from a carbuncle, another Sufyānī would come forth in the Ḥid͟jāz. He, too, would be deformed, flat-headed, with scarred forearms and hollow eyes.

In Egypt, the apocalyptic Sufyānī figure was promoted and elaborated by ʿAbd Allāh b. Lahīʿa (d. 174/790 [*q.v.*]) in numerous traditions spuriously ascribed to early authorities including Companions and the Prophet. Although one-eyed (*aʿwar*) and the perpetrator of massacres of ʿAbbāsids and ʿAlids, Ibn Lahīʿa's Sufyānī could not compete with Arṭāt's in repulsive ugliness and bestiality nor be described as a forerunner of the Dad͟jd͟jāl.

The Umayyad rebel Abu ʾl-ʿAmayṭar, a grandson of K͟hālid b. Yazīd b. Muʿāwiya, who rose against the ʿAbbāsid caliphate in Damascus in 195/811, gained some support as the expected Sufyānī. Already before the eruption of the revolt, the Damascene traditionist al-Walīd b. Muslim spread the prediction that the Sufyānī would inevitably come forth even if only a single day remained of the year 195. Umayyad backers claimed that the signs for the Sufyānī mentioned in the prophecies were present in Abu ʾl-ʿAmayṭar and that Kalb would be his supporters. A prophecy describing the reign of Hārūn al-Ras͟hīd and the succession of his son al-Amīn foretold the appearance of the Sufyānī during the latter's reign and the collapse of the ʿAbbāsid caliphate. Abu 'l-ʿAmayṭar, however, rejected the Sufyānī title for himself, evidently because of the negative implications in the apocalyptic tradition.

Bibliography: Nuʿaym b. Ḥammād, *al-Fitan*, ed. S. Zakkār, Beirut 1993; Zubayrī, *Nasab*, 129; *Aghānī*, xvi, 88; Snouck Hurgronje, *Verspr. Geschr.*, i, 155-6; H. Lammens, *Le "Sofyani", héros national des Arabes syriens*, in *Études sur le siècle des Omayyades*, Beirut 1930; R. Hartmann, *Der Sufyānī*, in *Studia orientalia Ioanni Pedersen dicata*, Copenhagen 1953; T. Nagel, *Rechtleitung und Kalifat*, Bonn 1975, 253-7; W. Madelung, *The Sufyānī between tradition and history*, in *Religious and ethnic movements in medieval Islam*, Variorum, Aldershot 1992; idem, *Abu 'l-ʿAmayṭar the Sufyānī*, in *JSAI*, xxiv (2000), 327-42.

(W. Madelung)

al-SUHAYLĪ, ʿAbd al-Raḥmān b. ʿAbd Allāh, Abu 'l-Ḳāsim (508-81/1114-85), Andalusī scholar of the religious sciences.

He was born either in the village of Suhayl, modern Fuengirola, or in nearby Málaga, and studied Ḳur'ān, *ḥadīth* and philology there as well as in Cordova and Granada. His most famous teacher was Ibn al-ʿArabī [*q.v.*], under whom he studied for a while in Seville. Settled in Málaga, he led a quiet scholarly life. Since he had lost his sight at the age of seventeen, he relied for his reading and writing on, among others, Ibn Diḥya [*q.v.*], his best-known pupil. At the Almohad court in Marrākush, where he stayed for some time, he achieved fame and wealth; he died during a visit to Morocco in 581/1185.

His fame rests on his *Rawḍ al-unuf*, a commentary on Ibn Hishām's biography of the Prophet. This contains old material which has not been preserved elsewhere, sc. *sīra* texts by al-Zuhrī, Mūsā b. ʿUḳba [*q.vv.*], Yūnus b. Bukayr and others. It also provides evidence for fragments of Ibn Isḥāḳ in versions other than that of Ibn Hishām. The *Rawḍ* was commented upon and criticised by Mughulṭāy [*q.v.*].

Bibliography: 1. Texts by al-Suhaylī, in addition to editions mentioned in Brockelmann, I, 413, S I 206, 734; and Sezgin, *GAS*, ix, 91: (a) *al-Taʿrīf wa 'l-iʿlām, bi-mā ubhima fi 'l-Ḳur'ān min al asmā' wa 'l-aʿlām*, ed. Maḥmūd Rabīʿ, Cairo 1356/1938; (b) *al-Rawḍ al-unuf fī sharḥ al-sīra al-nabawiyya li-Ibn Hishām*, ed. ʿAbd al-Raḥmān al-Wakīl, Cairo 1387-90/1967-70; (c) *Adjwiba fī masā'il sa'alahu ʿanhu . . . Abū Ḳurḳūl*, ed. Muḥammad Ibrāhīm al-Bannā as *Amālī al-Suhaylī fi 'l-naḥw wa 'l-lugha wa 'l-ḥadīth wa 'l-fiḳh*, n.p. (Baghdād?) 1970; and by Ṭāhā Muḥsin in *Masā'il fi 'l-naḥw wa 'l-lugha wa 'l-ḥadīth wa 'l-fiḳh li-Abi 'l-Ḳāsim al-Suhaylī*, in *al-Mawrid* (Baghdād), xviii (1989), 84-109.

2. Modern studies. Maher Jarrar, *Die Prophetenbiographie im islamischen Spanien. Ein Beitrag zur Überlieferungs- und Redaktionsgeschichte*, Frankfurt, etc. 1989, 176-210; H.M.A. Shaʿbān, *al-Buḥūth al-lughawiyya fi 'l-Rawḍ al-unuf*, Cairo 1984.

(W. Raven)

SŪḲ.

5. In mediaeval ʿIrāḳ.

Before the Arab conquest of ʿIrāḳ there were markets frequented by Arabs in ancient cities, such as al-Ḥīra and al-Madā'in [*q.vv.*]. There was also a so-called "sūḳ Baghdād" on the west bank of the Tigris, where a monthly market was held during the Sāsānid period. The latter was raided by Arab troops as early as the caliphate of Abū Bakr (Le Strange, *Baghdad*, 12, 101). Following the Arab conquest of ʿIrāḳ, the founders of the garrison towns of Baṣra and Ḳūfa designated an open space close to the mosque for use as a market. In this they were emulating the Prophet Muḥammad who had designated an open space in Medina for a similar use. A distinctive method in the organisation of markets began to emerge in the new Islamic cities of Wāsiṭ, Baghdād and Sāmarrā' during the late Umayyad and early ʿAbbāsid periods. Evidence from the ʿAbbāsid period suggests that there were often a series of markets (*aswāḳ*) adjacent to each other and separated only by roads and streets. Outside the central market in Baghdād and Sāmarrā', other markets were created for local residents and there were also a number of smaller markets known by the diminutive *suwayḳa*.

Markets, according to al-Shayzarī (d. 589/1193), author of the earliest *ḥisba* manual, should be as spacious and wide as possible (like the Roman market), and every kind of craft or profession (*ṣanʿa*) represented in it should be allocated its own market (*sūḳ*). The reference to separate space for each product sold or manufactured probably implies a series of markets or a row of shops and workshops producing and selling similar goods. Thus al-Shayzarī recommends that a market should allocate space to a concentration of shops selling the same product. The shops were arranged in a linear fashion along roads, streets and lanes. The author further recommends that traders who used fire in the preparation of their products, such as bakers (*khabbāzūn*), cooks (*ṭabbākhūn*) and blacksmiths (*ḥaddādūn*) should for safety reasons have their shops at some distance from others, for instance, perfumers (*ʿaṭṭārūn*) and cloth merchants (*bazzāzūn*). A similar market layout was endorsed by Ibn Bassām al-Muḥtasib. Other principles applied to the organisation of shops in a market took into account non-topographical considerations. For instance, Ibn al-Djawzī (d. 597/1200), writing about the markets of Baghdād, noted that in the markets of al-Karkh the perfumers did not associate with traders selling noisome goods nor with sellers of fancy or of secondhand goods. People of refined culture lived in special residential areas. No working-class people lived in the Saffron Road (*darb al-zaʿfarān*) in Karkh; the only residents there were the cloth merchants and perfume traders (cf. *Manāḳib Baghdād*, 28). The segregation of the traders in products that smelled nice (perfumes, sweets, jewellery, silk cloth, etc.) from those dealing in smelly things, such as tanners, dyers, garbage collectors and bric-à-brac merchants, was a principle which seems to have been widely applied in laying out these markets. Such social custom, according to Massignon, was responsible for the practice of housing the markets of the jewellers (*sūḳ al-ṣāgha*) with those of the moneychangers (*sūḳ al-ṣayārif*) (*Khiṭaṭ Baghdād*, 84). Another reason for grouping the shops of jewellers and moneychangers together was probably the fact that these commercial enterprises were monopolised by Jews and Christians.

Al-Shayzarī's views on the topographical organisation of markets, in which shops and workshops were grouped together for manufacturing or selling similar goods, reflect the broadly-accepted principles followed by Arab town-planners in the early Islamic period. Our knowledge of the early ʿIrāḳī markets goes back to the 1st/7th century, when Baṣra and Kūfa were laid out using these principles, according to al-Ṭabarī.

Baṣra was founded in 16/637 on the site of the base camp established by ʿUtba b. Ghazwān, whose first action was to select the site of the mosque. At the same time, Bilāl b. Abī Burda marked out a makeshift market, which was gradually expanded, thus contributing to Baṣra's success as a trading centre.

It seems that a site for the town's market was not originally allocated. The governor ʿAbd Allāh b. ʿĀmir later chose a particular site, which came to be known as *sūḳ ʿAbd Allāh*. His successor Ziyād b. Abīhi encouraged the settlers to establish a permanent market. The *sūḳ ʿAbd Allāh*, which was located within the residential quarters, proved inadequate for a rising population (cf. Naji and Ali, 298-309), and the old market was transferred to the Bilāl canal (*nahr Bilāl*). Most of the early markets of Baṣra were on designated open space, and permanent shops (*ḥānūt*) were not built until the 3rd/9th century.

During the 1st-2nd/7th-8th centuries Baṣra's markets selling specialised wares were located in a single space or road; for instance, the leather market (*sūḳ al-dabbāg̲h̲īn* (lit. tanners' market), the camel market (*sūḳ al-ibl*), market of the straw sellers (*sūḳ al-tabbānīn*) and the locksmith's market (*sūḳ al-ḳaffālin*). The Mirbad [*q.v.*] market was situated at the caravan station on the edge of the desert, where town-dwellers and Bedouin gathered to sell camels and other animals and to listen to poets reciting poems and orators speaking on current affairs. By the 3rd-4th/9th-10th centuries, the great market (*sūḳ al-kabīr*) was located at the junction between the Maʿḳil Canal and the Ibn ʿUmar Canal, where a variety of products, including glassware, bottles, combs, textiles, cooked food, flour, fish, fruits and vegetables were sold. Carpenters and tailors also had their shops there. The shore market (*sūḳ al-kallā*) lay in the residential area along the Fayl canal. It also had a food market (*sūḳ al-ṭaʿām*), which sold flour, rice, dates, meat, vinegar and secondhand goods. In addition, there was a money-changers' market, a goldsmiths' market and a slave market (*sūḳ al-nak̲h̲k̲h̲āsīn*).

Baṣra's trade with foreign merchants was conducted through the ancient port of al-Ubulla [*q.v.*], which was linked to the garrison city through a canal dug by Ziyād b. Abīhi (Yāḳūt, *Buldān*, Cairo 1906, i, 89-90). One traveller noted in 443/1051 that al-Ubulla was located to the south-west of Baṣra, and the S̲h̲aṭṭ al-ʿArab [*q.v.*] lay to the east of this port, which had thriving markets, caravanserais, mosques and luxury villas. The Ubulla canal was busy with boats carrying merchandise to and from Baṣra. Nāṣir-i K̲h̲usraw visited the city in the mid-5th/11th century and found that Baṣra's markets opened for business at different times of the day. For instance, a morning market was held at *sūḳ al-K̲h̲uzāʿa*, a mid-day one at *sūḳ ʿUt̲h̲mān* and a late-afternoon one at *sūḳ al-kaddāḥin* (the flint-makers' market) (*Safar-nāma*, 91-5).

Kūfa, which was founded shortly after Baṣra, was a better planned town. However, al-Ṭabarī does not specify the sites of its markets. Ḳūfa began with an open-air market. ʿAlī b. Abī Ṭālib, who moved his capital from Medina to Ḳūfa, is reported to have said "For the Muslims, the market is similar to the place of worship: he who arrives first can hold his seat all day until he leaves it" (al-Balād̲h̲urī, *Futūḥ*, tr. Hitti, 463-4). The same theory that a seller had a right to a space in the market was upheld by the governors al-Mug̲h̲īra b. S̲h̲uʿba and Ziyād b. Abīhi, who held that a trader who sat in a specific space in a market place could claim the spot so long as he occupied it. This suggests that no permanent shops were built in the market of Kūfa during the early Umayyad period and that these were only erected during the caliphate of His̲h̲ām by K̲h̲ālid b. ʿAbd Allāh al-Ḳaṣrī. Endorsing al-Balād̲h̲urī's statement, al-Yaʿḳūbī affirms that K̲h̲ālid al-Ḳaṣrī built markets and constructed a room and an arch (*ṭāḳ*) for every trader (*K. al-Buldān*, 311). Yāḳūt, on the other hand, recorded that the Asad Market (*sūḳ Asad*) built at this time in Ḳūfa was the work of Asad b. ʿAbd Allāh al-Ḳaṣrī (*Buldān*, v, 175). Setting up a temporary stall/shop in a market incurred no tax during the 1st/7th century.

According to one account, artisans and craftsmen worked in an open space near the central mosque. Al-D̲j̲āḥiẓ recorded that much of Ḳūfa was in ruins in his time (*K. al-Buldān*, 500). Moreover, the cost of living was higher in Ḳūfa than in Baṣra. For instance, building a house in Ḳūfa or Bag̲h̲dād cost 100,000 dirhams, whereas a similar house in Baṣra cost half as much (*ibid.*, 503-4). According to Massignon, the market in Ḳūfa during the 3rd-4th/9th-10th centuries, included the following craftsmen: the book and paper-sellers were sited on the *ḳibla* side of the city's major mosque; other crafts nearby included date-sellers (*tammārūn*), the manufacturers and sellers of soap (*aṣḥāb al-ṣābūn*) and grocers (*baḳḳālūn*). There were also carpet-sellers (*aṣḥāb al-anmāṭ*) and cloth merchants; laundrymen (*kaṣṣārūn*) at Dār al-Walīd, butchers (*d̲j̲azzārūn*) and wheat merchants (*ḥannātūn*); sellers of roast meat (*sawwāḳūn*); other merchants who were neighbours of the tradesmen were money-changers (*ṣayārifa*) and goldsmiths (*ṣayyāg̲h̲ūn*) (*Explication du plan de Kūfa*, in *Opera minora*, iii, 50-1). The markets of Ḳūfa flourished throughout the ʿAbbāsid period, and after, according to Ibn D̲j̲ubayr and Ḥamd Allāh al-Mustawfī, but details of commercial activities are lacking in most of our sources. While visiting Ḳūfa, the Spanish traveller Benjamin of Tudela (*ca.* 1173) reported that the Jewish population of about 70,000 had an impressive synagogue (*The world of Benjamin of Tudela*, 228). These population figures were probably exaggerated; nevertheless, they remain significant. Jews in the mediaeval Middle East were well known for their commercial activities and their craftsmanship as jewellers, and were also famed as bankers and money-changers. Their presence in large numbers in the predominantly S̲h̲īʿī city of Ḳūfa (only 2,000 Jews lived in Sunnī-dominated Baṣra) would tend to suggest that the former was still an important commercial centre in the late ʿAbbāsid period. But when Ibn Baṭṭūṭa (*ca.* 1325-54) visited Ḳūfa, he found that it was merely a caravan station for pilgrims from Mawṣil and Bag̲h̲dād travelling to Mecca; the commercial city had fallen into ruins as a result of attacks by Bedouin. However, he found the neighbouring Nad̲j̲af a populous town with a thriving market, admiring the fine and clean *sūḳ* which he entered through the Bāb al-Ḥaḍra. He then offers details of the layout of the Nad̲j̲af *sūḳ*, beginning with the food and vegetable shops, markets of the greengrocers, cooks and butchers, the fruit market, the tailors' market, followed by the covered market (*ḳayṣariyya*) and the perfumers' bazaar, which was close to the alleged tomb of the Imām ʿAlī b Abī Ṭālib.

Al-Wāsiṭ [*q.v.*] was founded by al-Ḥad̲j̲d̲j̲ād̲j̲, and its markets, according to the local historian Bahs̲h̲al (d. 292/905), were well planned. The layout of the market allotted to every trade a separate plot of land and segregated each craft or trade. Each group of tradesmen was given its own money-changer (*Taʾrīk̲h̲ Wāsiṭ*, 44). Iyās b. Muʿāwiya was appointed inspector of the Wāsiṭ market. A kind of toll or rent was collected from the tradesmen. The *sūḳ* was divided into two broad sections. On the right side of the market the shops of the food-sellers, cloth merchants, money-changers and perfume traders were located; on the left side, the greengrocers, fruit vendors (*aṣḥāb al-fākiha*) and sellers of second-hand goods (*aṣḥāb al-suḳaṭ*) established their shops or stalls. Day labourers (*ruzdjāriyyūn*) and craftsmen (*ṣunnā*ʿ) waited for work on a space stretching from the sandal-makers' road (*darb al-kharrāzūn*) towards the Tigris river. The market was thus an elaborately laid-out affair. This main market was on the western side of the town.

In planning a circular-shaped double-walled citadel city at Baghdād, with four massive arcaded gates, the ʿAbbāsid caliph al-Manṣūr was also responsible for laying out the city's markets in the arcaded space of the four city gates, following the practice of ancient cities such as Jerusalem. However, after ten years or so, Abū Djaʿfar is said to have been advised by a visiting envoy, the Patricius, from Byzantium that siting markets near his palace posed danger to a ruler from foreign spies visiting the markets in the guise of traders. Shortly before the removal of the markets from the arcades (measuring 15 × 200 cubits) of the four gates, there was a riot incited by a certain Yaḥyā b. ʿAbd Allāh, whom Abū Djaʿfar had appointed the city's *muḥtasib*, for which Yaḥyā was executed. Nevertheless, the emergence of the *muḥtasib* in Baghdād heralded the rise of this urban institution which regulated the ethical behaviour of traders and craftsmen in the ʿAbbāsid markets [see HISBA].

Following the riots of 157/774, the city's markets were transferred to the district of al-Karkh [*q.v.*] where shops and workshops were laid out on the principle of selling homogenous products in adjacent shops/stalls systematically arranged in rows of roads (*darb*, pl. *durūb*) and streets (*sikka*, pl. *sikak*). The markets of the butchers, who carried sharp tools, were allotted a space at the far end of the market. Thus according to al-Khaṭīb al-Baghdādī, al-Manṣūr instructed his officers Ibrāhīm b. Ḥubaysh al-Kūfī and Khirāsh b. al-Musayyab al-Yamanī to develop the central business district at al-Karkh on the west bank of the Tigris. Al-Manṣūr's successor al-Mahdī was later responsible for laying out the markets at the Bāb al-Ṭāḳ and Bāb al-Shaʿīr on the east bank of the Tigris, around the palace of Khuld [*q.v.* in Suppl.], in the Ruṣāfa district, and also for establishing the west bank markets in the Ḥarbiyya quarter to the north of the Round City. This quarter was inhabited by Central Asians, who traded with Khʷārazm and Transoxania. Both Ibn al-Faḳīh and al-Yaʿḳūbī describe the markets of Baghdād in the later 3rd/9th century and early 4th/10th century.

The markets in east Baghdād included the *sūḳ Yaḥyā* (named after Yaḥyā al-Barmakī). The land on which this market stood war later awarded by al-Maʾmūn to Ṭāhir b. al-Ḥusayn at the end of the civil war between the sons of Hārūn al-Rashīd (Ibn al-Faḳīh, 55). During the 5th/11th century, when the Saldjūḳs were controlling Baghdād, there were many reports of arson in the city's markets. In 485/1092 fire raged in the markets of the goldsmiths' and of the money-changers (*sūḳ al-ṣāgha wa 'l-ṣayārif*) resulting in great loss of life; and in 512/1118 the *sūḳ al-rayāḥīn* (the spice market) and the market of ʿAbdūn caught fire, resulting in extensive damage to property in east Baghdād, including the money-changers' shops, millers' inn, the royal mint (*dār al-ḍarb*) and public baths, all of which were destroyed (*Khiṭaṭ Baghdād*, 56-7, 61). Ibn al-Djawzī describes the layout of east Baghdād's markets in the 6th/12th century, which contained high-rise buildings owned by rich merchants, such as the millers (*daḳḳāḳūn*), bakers and sellers of sweets (*ḥalwayiyyūn*). There was also a nearby shoe-makers' market (*sūḳ al-asākifa*), then a market selling all kinds of birds (*sūḳ al-ṭayr*), one for aromatic plants/spices, and in the vicinity of this lay the bankers' or money-changers' shops. Next came shops selling food (*sūḳ al-maʾkūl*), such as those of the bakers and butchers (*ḳaṣṣābūn*). Alongside them there was the goldsmiths' market housed in a most splendid building. Next to it, there was a big market of booksellers and copyists (*sūḳ al-warrāḳīn*) in which scholars and poets congregated (*Manāḳib Baghdād*, 26). All these markets of east Baghdad were located close to the market of al-Ruṣāfa and its congregational mosque.

There was an element of competition in the setting up of *sūḳ*s. For instance, the *sūḳ al-ʿaṭash* (Thirst Market) formerly known as *suwaykat al-Ḥarashī* was built by Saʿīd al-Ḥarashī for al-Mahdī as a means of transferring some of the business to the east bank at the expense of al-Karkh. Among the smaller markets of east Baghdād were the *suwayḳat Naṣr* (attributed to Naṣr b. Mālik), *suwayḳat Khālid* (referring to Khālid b. Barmak) at the Shammāsiyya Gate, and *suwayḳat al-Ḥadjdjādj* (related to al-Ḥadjdjādj b. Waṣīf, a client of al-Mahdī, and the *suwayḳat Aḥmad b. Abī Khālid*. Similarly, west Baghdād had, besides the great markets of al-Karkh and al-Ḥarbiyya, many other markets, including the *sūḳ al-Haytham* (referring to al-Haytham b. Muʿāwiya), the *sūḳ ʿAbd al-Wahhāb* and the fruit market of *dār al-baṭṭīkh* (Ibn al-Faḳīh, 45). At Ḳaṣr Waḍḍāḥ, named after the client of the caliph who was in charge of the arsenal (*ṣāḥib khizānat al-silāḥ*), there were markets selling all kinds of goods; these included over a hundred shops selling paper and books and the shops of copyists (al-Yaʿḳūbī, *Buldān*, 245). These bookshops spread from the Ṭāḳ al-Ḥarrānī to the new bridge on the Sarāt Canal, occupying both sides of the road and on the bridge itself.

Al-Yaʿḳūbī, 246, states that, in his time, the market of al-Karkh occupied an area two *farsakh*s in length from Ḳaṣr Waḍḍāh to the *sūḳ al-thulātha* (Tuesday Market) and one *farsakh* from the Ḳaṭīʿat al-Rabīʿ towards the Tigris. Each trade was located in a well-known street and the shops and workshops were arranged in rows of shops. Craftsmen of one kind did not mix with another kind and were segregated from those of other markets, each market constituting a separate unit. The Ḥarb b. ʿAbd Allāh Street was the largest street around which people from Balkh, Marw, Bukhārā, Khuttal, Kābul and Khʷārazm settled (248). In the same locality was located the *dār al-raḳīḳ*, where slaves were bought and sold under the supervision of al-Rabīʿ b. Yūnus. When the Andalusian traveller Ibn Djubayr visited Baghdād in the 6th/12th century, he found that the Ḥarbiyya markets and residential areas had declined. He also noted that the market of the hospital (*sūḳ al-māristān*) where physicians attended the sick every Monday and Thursday, was located at the old Baṣra Gate in west Baghdād. The shops and workshops of leather workers (*dabbāghūn*) were situated at the ʿĪsā Canal on the west bank of the Tigris away from the main market of al-Karkh, and not far from a rubbish dump (*kunāsa*) and an ancient graveyard (*Travels*, tr. Broadhurst, 234-5, 244). In 449/1057, a fire caused extensive damage to the food market (*sūḳ al-ṭaʿām*), the wood-sellers' market (*sūḳ al-khashshābīn*), the carpenters' market (*sūḳ al-nadjdjārīn*), the butchers' market (*sūḳ al-djazzārīn*), the dyers' market (*sūḳ al-ṣabbāghīn*) and the market of the perfumers and chemists (*sūḳ al-ʿaṭṭārīn*) which were sited in adjacent buildings (*Khiṭaṭ Baghdād*, 41-3).

On the east bank, construction for the palace of al-Khuld began in 143/760 for the prince al-Mahdī, and this had its own markets: the fief of Badr al-

Waṣīf housed the *sūḳ al-ʿaṭash*; among the five streets in east Baghdād, there was a *sūḳ Khuḍayr*, where Chinese wares were sold. Rents collected from the markets during the 3rd/9th century on both banks of Baghdād, including those from the Mills of the Patricius (*arḥāʾ al-Baṭrīk*), amounted to 12 million dirhams annually. The traders in the markets of Baghdād imported goods from Central Asia and from the Far East as far as China, and al-Djāḥiẓ in his *K. al-Tabaṣṣur bi 'l-tidjāra* gives a list of exotic products available in ʿIrāḳ's markets.

When al-Muʿtaṣim built the city of Sāmarrāʾ [*q.v.*], he followed the established pattern for earlier markets in Islamic cities such as Baghdād. After laying out the palace and public buildings, he marked out the site of the chief mosque and built the markets around it; the rows of shops and workshops were made spacious and every kind of product was sold in adjacent shops. In the north of Sāmarrāʾ some groups of Turkish soldiers were allotted land on which to build their houses, but the barracks of the Turks and the men of Farghāna were established far away from the markets so that these troops did not mix with local people and traders. Some folk were settled further north, in the area of al-Dūr, where small markets, some shops and butchers' stalls were built for the *muwalladūn*. The *ḳaṭīʿa* or fief of Ḥizām on which the slave market was situated, was near the guard headquarters and prison. Shops and rooms for housing slaves were located there, and on this main thoroughfare there were houses for the common people and markets where craft and product were sold separately. This was Sāmarrāʾ's second big market. Outside the old Sāmarrāʾ, al-Mutawakkil built a new satellite town, where all the traders of demeaning status, such as the sellers of barley beer, *harīsa* soup and wine (*aṣḥāb al-fuḳḳāʿ wa 'l-harāʾis wa 'l-sharāb*) were isolated from the rest of the market. Market taxes and rents (*ghalla wa-mustaghillāt*) collected in Sāmarrāʾ amounted to ten million dirhams a year.

Mawṣil also had its markets, and its Wednesday (*sūḳ al-arbaʿāʾ*) and Sunday Markets (*sūḳ al-aḥad*) were well known as early as the 2nd/8th century. The local historian al-Azdī mentions others markets, including the hay market (*sūḳ al-ḥashīsh*) and market of sellers of saddles stuffed with straw (*sūḳ al-ḳattābīn*) and food market (363). Al-Muḳaddasī noted that Mawṣil had fine markets, which extended to the tanners' road and gypsum sellers' road (*darb al-djaṣṣāṣīn*). In the city's square (*murabbaʿa*), near the inns, was the Wednesday Market, where farm labourers (*akara*) and harvesters (*ḥawāṣid*) came from the surrounding countryside to seek temporary or seasonal work in the city. From Mawṣil's covered markets, provisions for Baghdād were transported by boats and caravans. Among other towns, al-Muḳaddasī cites Ḳaṣr Ibn Hubayra, which had a large concentration of weavers and Jews in a thriving market economy. At the same time, Tikrīt was a sizeable town, where a monastery provided the focal point for local Christian pilgrimage and many woollen workers settled there in order to meet the demands of the pilgrims.

Bibliography: 1. Sources. Djāḥiẓ, *K. al-Tabaṣṣur bi 'l-tidjāra*, ed. Ḥ.Ḥ. ʿAbd al-Wahhāb, Beirut 1966, 1-48; idem, *K. al-Buldān*, ed. Ṣ.A. al-ʿAlī, Baghdād 1970, 462-506; Yaʿḳūbī, *Buldān*, 232-360; Ibn Rusta, 180-7; Ibn al-Faḳīh al-Hamadānī, *Baghdād, Madīnat al-Salām*, ed. al-ʿAlī, Baghdād and Paris 1977, 5, 117; Iṣṭakhrī[1], 78-88; Abū Ḥayyān al-Tawḥīdī, *al-Risāla al-baghdādiyya*, ed. Abbood Shalghy, Beirut 1980, 42-106; Muḳaddasī, 116-23, 138; al-Khaṭīb al-Baghdādī, i, 25-6, 69, 79-81; Aslam b. Sahl al-Wāsiṭī, called Bahshal, *T. Wāsiṭ*, ed. G. ʿAwwād, Baghdād 1967, 44, 92-3; Azdī, *T. Mawṣil*, ed. ʿAlī Ḥabība, Cairo 1967, 24, 83, 157, 229, 350; Ibn al-Djawzī, *Muntaẓam*, ed. Ḥaydarābād, x, 170; idem, *Manāḳib Baghdād*, ed. M. Bahdjat al-Atharī, Baghdād 1342/1923, 26; Samʿānī, *Ansāb*, ed. Ḥaydarābād, i, 378, x, 344-5; Ibn Djubayr, *Riḥla*, tr. R.J.C. Broadhurst, London 1952, 221-44; Shayzarī, *Nihāyat al-rutba fī ṭalab al-ḥisba*, ed. al-Arīnī, Cairo 1946, 11-12; Yāḳūt, *Buldān*, Cairo 1906, ii, 196-9, v, 175-7, viii, 382-31; Ibn Baṭṭūṭa, *Riḥla*, tr. Gibb, ii, 271-81.

2. Studies. Le Strange, *Baghdad during the Abbasid Caliphate*, 12, 92, 101, 356; idem, *Lands*, 24-85; Ch. Pellat, *Le milieu baṣrienne et la formation de Ğāḥiẓ*, Paris 1953, 2ff.; ʿAbbās ʿAzzāwī, *Taʾrīkh al-ḍarāʾib al-ʿirāḳiyya*, Baghdād 1958, 10-37; ʿAbd al-Ḳādir Bāshā Aʿyān al-ʿAbbāsī, *al-Baṣra fī adwārihā al-taʾrīkhiyya*, Baghdād 1961, 7-87, 7-87; L. Massignon, *Opera minora*, Beirut 1963, iii, 35-93; J. Lassner, *The topography of Baghdad in the early Middle Ages*, Detroit 1970, 602, 78-102, 172-88; A.A. Duri, ch. *Government institutions*, in R.B. Serjeant (ed.), *The Islamic city*, Paris 1980, 52-65; P. Chalmeta, ch. *Markets*, in *ibid.*, 104-13; A.J. Naji and Y.N. Ali, *The Sūqs of Basra. Commercial organisation and activity in an Islamic city*, in *JESHO*, xxiv (1981), 298-309; M.A.J. Beg, *The Islamic city from al-Madinah to Sāmarrāʾ*, in idem, *Historic cities of Asia*, Kuala Lumpur 1986, 245-6, 255; Hichem Djaït, *Al-Kūfa, naissance de la ville islamique*, Paris 1986, 274-7; Sandra Benjamin (ed.), *The world of Benjamin of Tudela, a medieval Mediterranean travelogue*, Madison 1995, 226-8. (M.A.J. Beg)

SUKARNO, Soekarno, the first President of the independent Republic of Indonesia [*q.v.*] from 1945 to 1967 (b. 6 June 1901, d. 21 June 1970).

His father, Raden Sukemi, came from lower Javanese nobility and worked as a teacher and civil servant, while his mother originated from a Balinese *brāhmaṇa* family but was excluded after her marriage to her Muslim husband. Sukarno's name in his childhood was Kusno. Later his father renamed him Sukarno, referring to the hero Adipati Karno in the Hindu epic *Mahābhārata*. Already as a small boy, while living with his grandfather in a village, he paid more attention to *wayang* (shadow play) performances, where the stories of the *Mahābhārata* are displayed, than to his homework for school, thus acquainting himself with the ethics of the *kśatriya*, namely, fighting without compromise against evil and injustice but open to mercy and compromise in one's own quarter, and firmly believing in the victory of the righteous ones. Much of his later political vocabulary was rooted in the symbols of *wayang*.

After having finished a European primary school in Mojokerto where he also had to learn Dutch, he moved, aged 15, to Surabaya for further studies. There he stayed in the "open house" of (Hajji) Omar Said (abbrev. HOS) Tjokroaminoto, the charismatic leader of the Sarekat Islam [*q.v.*] (since 1912), which was the first Indonesian nationalist organisation, founded in 1911. Tjokroaminoto's strong identification with those who suffered under the colonial administration made many people think he might be the *Ratu Adil*, a just ruler expected to arrive before the end of this aeon and end the sufferings of the suppressed people. This expectation had first appeared in Java in the 17th century. Tjokroaminoto himself, however, is said to have stressed that the movement for independence did not involve establishing the rule of a *Ratu Adil*, but of a *ratuning adil*, a realm of righteousness ruled by the people and their representatives.

During his five years in the Hogere Burger School (HBS) in Surabaya (1916-21) Sukarno became not only acquainted with the aims and targets of the Sarekat Islam (SI), but C. Hartogh, teacher of the German language at the HBS and co-founder of the "Indische Sociaal Democratische Vereeniging" in 1914, introduced Sukarno to socialism and Marxism, warning, however, against too radical action against Western capitalism and favouring an accelerated evolution of the indigenous society and its economy. Among the Indonesian leaders of that time, a controversy between more universal, international, socialist and radical options on the one hand and visions dealing more with the "national" problems in the Dutch colony and favouring stepped-up co-operation with the government for achieving freedom on the other, led finally to a split in the Sarekat Islam. In 1921 the Communist Party (PKI) was established and communists were expelled from the SI, albeit against the will of Tjokroaminoto, who feared a decay of the Nationalist Movement, but thus urged by Hajji Agus Salim, another SI leader. It is noteworthy that the communists in their statements frequently used Islamic or Hindu terminology, particularly that of the modernist movements in both communities, Atatürk and Gandhi being among their favourites. After 1921, the SI became more receptive to the Islamic international movement (so-called Pan-Islamism [*q.v.*]).

After his successful graduation from the HBS and his marriage with a daughter of Tjokroaminoto, Sukarno moved to Bandung in 1921 and there enrolled as a student in the newly-established Technical High School, where he graduated in 1926 as a civil engineer. In Bandung, Sukarno met with more radical nationalists like Douwes Dekker and Tjipto Mangunkusumo, both co-founders of the Nationaal Indische Partij (NIP) whose leaders resided in Bandung. Deeply disappointed with the reviving colonial attitudes and measures after World War I, they refused to co-operate with the government and its institutions, including the Volksraad (consulting body). Sukarno adopted their position and thus estranged himself from Tjokroaminoto and even from his wife, whom he divorced. Thus he became what he remained: a convinced and fervent nationalist advocating religious and ethnic tolerance and equal rights for all Indonesians as internal goals, and fighting capitalism and co-operation with the unjust government as external measures. In contrast to nationalist students who had spent some time in the Netherlands and experienced there a democratic society and a well-functioning administration of the law, Sukarno, lacking such experience, viewed everything Western with deep suspicion and antipathy.

After his graduation, Sukarno dedicated his time and energies to efforts towards uniting the different anti-colonial parties and groups, all of which were pursuing quite different options. Nationalism was endangered from two sides: internationalism and regionalism. Therefore he urged the three strongest groups, namely, the Nationalists (NIP), the Islamic Nationalists (SI), and the Marxists (PKI), to find one voice in fighting against the "Kaurawas", the representatives of colonialism. All nationalists should be united in one goal: achieving *Indonesia merdeka* (an independent Indonesia). On this point Sukarno was not only an analytical thinker, but also—based on the world view of the *wayang*—a bit of a mystic: the notion of nationalism, national unity, resembles a revelation (*wahy*) given by God, and to strive for it is like an act of liturgy or service (*bakti*), the work of a true *kśatriya*. The space of nationalism was as "wide as the air", a perception already present in the early Sarekat Islam, where Marxists, Christians and others were active together.

After both the failure of the new ruler in Arabia (since 1924), ʿAbd al-ʿAzīz of the Āl Suʿūd, to call a conference of the Islamic world, and the founding of the Nahdatul Ulama party in early 1926 in Java, with the aim of safeguarding traditionalist Islamic teaching in the Holy Places, the SI lost interest in pan-Islamic visions. Sukarno and Tjokroaminoto became reconciled, and Hajji Agus Salim encouraged Sukarno to proceed with his plan to establish a Federation of the biggest nationalist organisations, including his own, the "Nationalist Union of Indonesia" (Perhimpunan Nasional Indonesia: PNI) founded in July 1927. Because of communist riots, the PKI had been outlawed in 1927, leaving the struggle for independence to the nationalists and the national Islamists.

Sukarno's self-confidence grew apace. Those who did not agree with his radical attitude but favoured a more consultative way to deal with the Dutch, while firmly striving also for independence, like the socialists, were not included in his front of the "Pendawas". But the colonial government's actions seemed to justify his suspicion and adversary attitude: even people ready for compromise like Tjipto Mangunkusumo, were attacked by the Dutch with false accusations and exiled.

In 1930 the outbreak of a Pacific war was expected, one which, it was hoped, would bring colonial rule in Asia to its end. In Indonesia, old prophecies related to Jayabaya, a Javanese king of the 12th century, who is said to be the source of the *Ratu Adil* expectations as well, foretold the victory of a "yellow people"; Sukarno, and with him many other people from India to China, expected the Japanese to take the leading role in this forthcoming anti-colonial revolution, remembering their victory over Russia in 1905. Combining Jayabaya with Karl Marx's prediction of the final victory of the suppressed proletariat, Sukarno firmly believed in the imminent victory of the "brown" people, or Pendawas. Although imperialistic themselves, the Japanese would at least crush the power of the U.S. and England and other colonial powers from the West and thus pave the way for final liberation. But to prevent such expectations causing unrest, on 29 December 1929 the colonial government detained all leaders of Sukarno's PNI, including himself. Although it was impossible during the subsequent trials to prove that the PNI or Sukarno himself had any concrete plans for an insurrection, he was sentenced to four years imprisonment in December 1930, thereby becoming an innocent martyr for many Indonesians. After an act of clemency by the then departing Governor-General De Graef, Sukarno was released at the end of December 1931. But both organisations led by him, the PNI and the Federation, did not survive his detention and were dissolved by the remaining leaders. This was criticised by a leader of the Perhimpunan Indonesia (PI, "Indonesian Union") in the Netherlands, Moh. Hatta, who accused Sukarno of only provoking the government and not trying to educate the people at the same time.

For Sukarno and his supporters, these events only showed how important he himself was for the independence movement. Thus the nationalists split into two groups: one gathered into the PNI Baru ("New"

PNI) around the socialist Sutan Sjahrir who, like Moh. Hatta, originated from West Sumatra, preferring incisive analyses of the political and societal situation and the functional role of organisations, and the other gathered around Sukarno in the Partindo (Partai Indonesia), which emphasised more strongly a feeling of unity that took in specific dissent. Partindo now became the platform for Sukarno's new concept of "Marhaenism", which he also called "Socio-Nationalism"; Marhaen was a common name mainly among Sundanese farmers (cf. Dahm, 110). A feeling of social responsibility would unite all Indonesians—not only the proletariat—to establish social justice in the nation. No opposition or deviation would be tolerated. The leadership of a Marhaenist party would have the right to punish anyone who disturbed the consensus by exclusion. For this attitude, Sukarno was much criticised by Sutan Sjahrir and Moh. Hatta, who urged the acceptance of democratic rules. On 1 August 1933, Sukarno was again detained and consequently exiled to the island of Flores. He terminated his membership in Partindo, which later (1936) dissolved itself. His isolation in Flores encouraged him to revive old acquaintances in the SI, which meanwhile had become Partai Sarekat Islam Indonesia (PSII), trying to harmonise Islamic internationalism with Indonesian nationalism. Friendly contact with Catholic missionaries seems to have strengthened his religious awareness. In 1938 he was transferred to Bengkulu (Bencoolen), West-Sumatra, where he became a member of the reformist Muhammadiyah social organisation. There he joined those who pleaded for a radical new interpretation of Ḳurʾān and Sunna, one which was sometimes too rationalist for other members like Moh. Natsir, who urged obedience to tradition in matters of faith first and then revision of social rules. To justify his more radical position, Sukarno pointed to the progress Atatürk and the Kemalists had achieved in Turkey. He pleaded for a separation of state and religion, which led to another emotional controversy with Moh. Natsir in 1941.

When Japan started occupying Indonesia in 1941, Sukarno, who returned to Java in July 1942, was open for co-operation with the proviso that the Japanese should help the Indonesians to achieve their independence in accord with Jayabaya's prophecy. The foundation of the "putera" (Pusat Tenaga Rakyat, centre for people's work; *putera* means literally "son"), intended as a basis of the people's support for Japan, became Sukarno's basis of action.

The ambiguous policy of the Japanese—sometimes treating "the Southern Regions" as a colony, occasionally also promising self-government, and sometimes favouring the Islamist nationalists, while on other occasions preferring the religiously neutral nationalists—led to an estrangement between Sukarno and the Japanese government, which added to Sukarno's popularity. But after the announcement of Prime Minister Koiso on 7 September 1944 that all Indonesian peoples should be granted independence, and despite the people's continued distrust of and contempt for those who co-operated with the Japanese, Sukarno on the one hand urged support for the Japanese, who faced the advancing Allied forces, and on the other hand urged the Japanese to speed up their plans lest the Allies return to a still-occupied Indonesia and therefore re-establish colonial rule. His violent pro-Japanese agitation and loyalty to Japan, and his emotional anti-Western rhetoric, again earned him much criticism. But on 28 May 1945, the Investigating Board for Preparatory Work on Indonesian Independence (the BPUPKI), appointed by the Japanese, started its work. On 1 June, Sukarno presented his famous concept of the Pancasila (Pantjasila, "Five Principles"), meant to become the *weltanschauliche* basis of the Indonesian Constitution to which all Indonesians could consent (Eng. tr. in Mangullang, 198ff.): Nationalism (one nation, *kebangsaan*), Internationalism or Humanity (*perikemanusiaan*), People's Rule (*kerakyatan*, always striving for consent, *mufakat*, from Ar. *muwāfaḳa*), Social Justice (*keadilan sosial*, originally social welfare, *kesejahteraan social*) and Divine Oneness (*Ketuhanan yang Maha Esa*). These could also be reduced to three: socio-nationalism, socio-democracy and Divine Oneness, or to one: *gotong royong* (the Javanese principle of mutual co-operation), as Sukarno stated. Complaints from the side of the Islamists led to a compromise on 22 June, stating the *Ketuhanan* as first principle with the addition that all Muslims are obliged to follow the *Sharīʿa*; this compromise became known as the Jakarta Charter. Encouraged by the Japanese, who referred to "Asian traditions", and very much to the liking of Sukarno, it was also agreed that the independent state should resemble a presidential democracy with a parliament (Dewan Perwakilan Rakyat: DPR) only serving as a consultative body. A People's Consultative Assembly (Dewan Permusyawaratan Rakyat: MPR), consisting of the members of the DPR and other members nominated by the government or by people's organisations, meeting once every five years, was to elect the president and define the general political guidelines for the government. In the general anti-colonial mood, Sukarno and others favoured the inclusion into Indonesia Merdeka of peninsular Malay and territories on Borneo and Timor still claimed by the British and Portuguese. This proposal was rejected by the Japanese, who wanted Indonesia restricted to the former Dutch possessions. Under pressure from external and internal events, Sukarno, assisted by Moh. Hatta, declared the independence of Indonesia in the early morning of 17 August 1945.

During the following days the Preparatory Committee for Indonesian Independence, inaugurated by the Japanese on 7 August, met and passed the provisional constitution (Basic Law), with a modified Pancasila, included in the Preamble: as second principle there now stands Internationalism, with Nationalism becoming the third principle. The provision of the Jakarta Charter for the Muslims was omitted because it implied a special relation with the Muslims which would endanger the neutrality of the state in religious matters. Sukarno was elected president and Moh. Hatta his vice-president. A Central National Indonesian Committee (Komite Nasional Indonesia Pusat: KNIP) was to support the government until a parliament could be elected, and Sukarno favoured the formation of one political party only, a Partai Nasional Indonesia. In this, however, he was opposed by Sutan Sjahrir, Moh. Hatta and some of the Islamist nationalists. To avoid an open domestic crisis, Sukarno agreed to the formation of different parties and he accepted also that ministers should be accountable to the parliament or the KNIP. Thus Sukarno's short-lived presidential government came to its end, and on 14 November 1945, a parliamentary government was elected with Sutan Sjahrir as prime minister.

Sukarno's popularity increased again when he, Hatta, Sjahrir and other leaders of the young republic were detained by the Dutch, who wanted to re-establish their rule and punish at the same time those who had collaborated with the Japanese. After the end of the Dutch police actions and acknowledgement of Indonesia's independence in late 1949, Sukarno was accepted as president, an office still to his own dislike, however, as it was hampered by the liberal constitutions that were drafted in 1949 and 1950. He met other challenges from the militant Islamists, who staged insurrections in West Java and Sulawesi, and from regionalists, who opposed the strong political and economic centralisation in Java. His international reputation increased in 1955 when, inspired by the second principle of Pancasila, he succeeded in hosting in Bandung the first conference of independent "Third World" leaders (his opening speech is in Feith and Castles, 454 ff.). During the political campaigns preceding the 1955 elections to the first parliament, and, some months later, to a Constitutional Assembly (Konstituante) to design a final constitution, Sukarno made it clear that he wanted a presidential republic based on the Pancasila, against the option of an Islamic state, and also a unitary state, against demands for more autonomy in the areas outside of Java. In opposition to Sukarno's agitation, Moh. Hatta resigned as vice-president in 1956. Anticipating a great majority of votes in favour of liberal democracy, Sukarno issued a presidential decree on 5 July 1959 dissolving the Konstituante and declaring the Basic Law of 1945 as the final constitution. Guided Democracy (*demokrasi terpimpin*) was the name of the new system, himself being the Great Leader (of the Revolution), as he explained in his independence speech on 17 August 1959, which later became known as his "Political Manifesto" (Manipol), elaborated later by "USDEK": the Basic Law of 1945, Indonesian Socialism, Guided Democracy, Guided Economy and Indonesian Identity. In 1960, Sukarno also dissolved the parliament and later in the same year he banned the modernist Islamic party Masyumi, chaired by Moh. Natsir, and the socialist Party of Sutan Sjahrir, both of whose leaders and some followers were detained.

But opposition came now also from the anti-Communist armed forces under Gen. A.H. Nasution. Sukarno tried to balance the antagonising forces by showing favour to the traditionalist Islamic party Nahdatul Ulama (NU) and the Communist Party (PKI), both of which had strong roots in Java. Under the leadership of the PNI, the old triad from the 1920s reappeared, now styled as "Nasakom": Nasionalisme, Agama (religion, represented by NU), and socialist Communism. The ideological controversies and power play among military leaders inflamed the domestic situation, some of them profiting from the Irian crisis in 1961-2 and the "confrontation" with Malaysia [*q.v.*], the new independent federation (1963) supported by the British and condemned by Sukarno. The PKI, strengthening its ties with Maoist China, increasingly dominated the streets and therefore caused an estrangement with the other allied elements in Nasakom who, on their side, approached some of the military leaders critical of Sukarno, these being mainly in the army, while most of the air force was pro-Sukarno. Anti-American and anti-Soviet agitation prepared the withdrawal of Indonesia from the UNO in early 1965, thus strengthening its alliance with Beijing and other Communist states in South and East Asia. Corruption, mismanagement and nepotism in the bureaucracy and military brought the state close to collapse. In the evening of 30 September 1965, a *coup d'état* was launched, but to this date it is not clear who were the real initiators and what were their aims. Some leading generals of the army close to Sukarno were murdered, and the later official version under Suharto's rule laid responsibility with the Communists. Sukarno, contrary to his own perception, became a spectator to the events, and on 11 March 1966, he had to sign a letter transferring all executive power and the military command to General Suharto because of his alleged inability to maintain any longer the unity of Indonesia and its people. A few weeks later the PKI was banned, and its leaders and members and many other people killed, imprisoned or detained in camps. One year later, the new Provisional People's Consultative Assembly stripped Sukarno of the presidency and proclaimed Gen. Suharto acting president. Sukarno spent his last years virtually under house arrest in Bogor until his death. His grave in Blitar, East Java, has become a sacred shrine for many Javanese.

Bibliography: Notonagoro, *Pancasila dasar falsafah negara*, Jakarta 1951, [2]1974; G.McT.T. Kahin, *Nationalism and revolution in Indonesia*, Ithaca and New York 1952; H. Feith, *The decline of constitutional democracy in Indonesia*, Ithaca 1962; *Dibawah bendera revolusi*, Jakarta 1963; Sukarno, *Sukarno. An autobiography as told to Cindy Adams*, Hong Kong 1965; B. Dahm, *Sukarnos Kampf um Indonesiens Unabhängigkeit. Werdegang und Ideen eines asiatischen Nationalisten*, Frankfurt/Main and Berlin 1966; M.P.M. Muskens, *Indonesië. Een strijd om nationale identiteit*, Bussum 1969, [2]1970; Feith and L. Castles (eds.), *Indonesian political thinking 1945-1965*, Ithaca and London 1970; Dahm, *History of Indonesia in the 20th century*, London 1971; B.R.O'G. Anderson, *Java in a time of revolution: occupation and resistance, 1944-1946*, Ithaca and London 1972; J.D. Legge, *Sukarno. A political bibliography*, London 1972; A. Katoppo (ed.), *80 Tahun Bung Karno*, Jakarta 1980, [2]1990; M. Bonneff *et al.*, *Pantjasila. Trente années de débats politiques en Indonésie*, Paris 1980; Eka Darmaputera, *Pancasila and the search for identity and modernity in Indonesian society*, Leiden 1988; Achmad C. Manullang, *Die Staatssoziologie der Pancasila*. Würzburg 1988; Adnan Buyung Nasution, *The aspiration for constitutional government in Indonesia. A socio-legal study of the Indonesian Konstituante 1956-1959*, Jakarta 1992; Marsillam Simanjuntak, *Pandangan negara integralistik*, Jakarta 1994; Pamoe Rahardjo and Islah Gusmian (eds.), *Bung Karno dan pancasila. Menuju revolusi nasional*, Yogyakarta 2002.

(O. Schumann)

SULAYMĀN b. al-**ḤAKAM** b. Sulaymān al-**MUSTAʿĪN**, Umayyad caliph of al-Andalus, proclaimed at Cordova in 400/1009, died in 407/1016. The two phases of his reign are located in the period of the Andalusī *fitna* following the "Revolution of Cordova", at the time of the serious political crisis which was to lead to the demise of the Umayyad caliphate in 422/1031.

When the Cordovans put an end to the ʿĀmirid régime in Dj̲umādā II-Rad̲jab 399/February-March 1009, and replaced the incompetent caliph His̲h̲ām II with one of his cousins, Muḥammad al-Mahdī, the latter, on account of his political blunders, speedily aroused opposition, in particular that of the Mag̲h̲ribī Berber contingents of the Umayyad army, whose families had been the object of harassment on the part of the Cordovans. These soldiers, numbering several hundreds, rallied around Sulaymān b. al-Ḥakam, who was a great-grandson of the first caliph of Cordova, ʿAbd al-Raḥmān III, and whom they put forward as a claimant to the caliphate. With him, they made their way to the frontier zone of Medinaceli in search of support. Confronted by the former slave governor of this region, Wāḍiḥ, they obtained the aid of the Count of Castile, Sancho Garcia, in exchange for a promise to cede frontier fortresses to him. Having defeated the forces of Wāḍiḥ in Dhu 'l-Ḥidjdja 400/August 1010, they returned to Andalusia to march on Cordova, which they entered after overpowering the quite significant, but disparate and ineffective troops of al-Mahdī. The latter was forced to take refuge in the capital where Sulaymān was proclaimed caliph on 17 Rabīʿ I/9 November, with the *laḳab* of al-Mustaʿīn bi 'llāh.

Having placed himself under the protection of Wāḍiḥ, who henceforward became his "strong man", al-Mahdī rallied supporters in the north and, crucially, obtained the support of Count Raymond Borrell III of Barcelona and of his brother Armengol (Ermengaud) of Urgel, in order to march in his turn against Cordova with some 40,000 men, including 9,000 Franks. The defeat of El Vacar (*ʿaḳabat al-baḳar*, in Shawwāl 400/June 1010), 20 km/12 miles to the north of the capital, forced al-Mustaʿīn to flee and enabled al-Mahdī and Wāḍiḥ to enter Cordova and restore the caliphate of the former. But this success could not be consolidated, and on 6 Dhu 'l-Ḳaʿda 400/21 June 1010 Sulaymān's Berbers inflicted a heavy defeat near Ronda on the forces of al-Mahdī and their Frankish allies. Henceforth, it was Sulaymān al-Mustaʿīn and his Berbers who found themselves again in a position to lay siege to the capital, which resisted until its surrender on 26 Shawwāl 403/9 May 1013. The town was sacked by the Berbers and numerous Cordovans were killed, including probably the caliph al-Mahdī, although a rumour was later put about claiming that he had escaped.

Little is known about the second reign of the caliph al-Mustaʿīn, which lasted three years until the insurrection against him by the Maghribī chieftain of Idrīsid origin ʿAlī b. Ḥammūd, whom he had appointed governor of Ceuta. The latter took the capital, killed al-Mustaʿīn and obtained the *bayʿa* of the Cordovans, who recognised him under the name of al-Nāṣir li-dīn Allāh (22 Muḥarram 407/1 July 1016).

Sulaymān al-Mustaʿīn seems to have been endowed with more qualities than his rival al-Mahdī, reasonably cultivated but of irresolute character and very much dependent on the Berbers who had put him in power. A large portion of the territory of al-Andalus eluded his authority. He consolidated the local power of certain chieftains who were in process of becoming "party kings" [see MULŪK AL-ṬAWĀʾIF], such as the Tudjibid al-Mundhir b Yaḥyā, who had lent him his support at Saragossa. In particular, he appointed his Berber supporters to command regional "fiefs" which were in fact virtually amirates, the most important being that of the Ṣanhādjī Zīrids of Granada which was to last until the arrival of the Almoravids.

Bibliography: A. Prieto y Vives, *Los reyes de taifas. Estudio histórico-numismático de los musulmanes españoles en el siglo V de la hégira (XI de J.C.)*, Madrid 1926; Ibn ʿIdhārī, *Kitāb al-Bayān al-mughrib*, ed. E. Lévi-Provençal, Paris 1930; Lévi-Provençal, *Histoire de l'Espagne musulmane*, Paris-Leiden 1953, ii; J. Pellicer i Bru, *Suleiman Al-Mostaîn 400-1010/407-1014 (revisión de las acuñaciones de plata a su nombre)* in *Acta Numismática*, xiv (1984), 143-60; M.J. Viguera Molins, *Los reinos de taifas y las invasiones magrebies*, Madrid-Mapfre 1992; D.J. Wasserstein, *The Caliphate in the West. An Islamic political institution in the Iberian Peninsula*, Oxford 1993; P.C. Scales, *The fall of the Caliphate of Córdoba. Berbers and Andalusis in conflict*, Leiden 1994. (P. GUICHARD)

SULAYMĀN KHĒL, a Pashtūn tribe [see AFGHĀN. (i) The people].

Ghalzay [*q.v.*] Pashtūns were principal actors in 18th century political and military events in Afghānistān and Persia. By 1800 a political identity had congealed around the largest Ghalzay tribal confederation, the Sulaymān Khēl, whose landholdings increased throughout eastern Afghānistān, particularly in and south of the area roughly bounded by Ghazna, Djalālābād, and Kābul [*q.vv.*], during the 19th century. The largest Sulaymān Khēl tribe, the Aḥmadzay, remain prominent in this region. The Djabār Khēl are the *khān khēl* of the Sulaymān Khēl and all eastern Ghalzays.

The Sulaymān Khēl were strongly represented in the consistent Ghalzay political opposition and military resistance to Durrānī [*q.v.*] government initiatives from 1747 to 1978. However, from the late 1800s onwards a small but growing number of Sulaymān Khēl individuals and families became dependent upon state patronage. The ethnic composition of all central governments in the increasingly Kābul-centred Afghān political environment after 1978 reflects a growing presence of Ghalzays. Aḥmadzay Sulaymān Khēl visibility in post-monarchal Afghān state politics is illustrated by Dr. Nadjībullāh's tenure of office as President (1986-92).

Like all Ghalzay, the Sulaymān Khēl are notable for socio-cultural heterogeneity and vibrant commercial activity during annual nomadic migrations in and between Turkistān, Khurāsān and India.

Bibliography: Mountstuart Elphinstone, *An account of the Kingdom of Caubul*, London 1839, repr. Karachi 1992, i, 212-14, 237, ii, 137-41, 147-58, 329-31; H. Priestly, *Afghanistan and its inhabitants*, Lahore 1874 (= tr. of S.M. Hayat Khan, *Ḥayāt-i Afghānī*, 1865), 162-76; H.G. Raverty, *Notes on Afghanistan and parts of Baluchistan*, Calcutta 1878, repr., Quetta 1982, i, 57, 60, 85, ii, 413, 490-2, 669, 679; J.A. Robinson, *Notes on nomad tribes of eastern Afghanistan*, 1934, repr. Quetta 1980, 52-126; L. Adamec, *Historical and political gazetteer of Afghanistan*, vi, *Kabul*, Graz 1985, 20, 202-9, 270-3. (SHAH MAHMOUD HANIFI)

SÜLEYMĀN DHĀTĪ, Ottoman poet and Ṣūfī adherent of the Khalwatiyya order and *khalīfat* of Sheykh Ismāʿīl Ḥaḳḳī, b. in Gallipoli, d. 1151/1738-9 as *pūst-neshīn* of the Khalwatī *tekke* in Keshan. He left behind a *dīwān* of Ṣūfī-inspired verse and a verse treatise, *Sawāniḥ al-nawādir fī maʿrifat al-anāṣir* or *Madjmaʿ al-anāṣir* (printed together, Istanbul 1289/1872); *Sharḥ-i ḳaṣīda yi-Ḥaḍrat Ismāʿīl Ḥaḳḳī*, a commentary on a Ṣūfī poem; and *Miftāḥ al-masāʾil*, dealing with various theological questions, such as predestination, the nature of the afterlife, etc. (all these works preserved in Istanbul mss.).

Bibliography: Bursalî Meḥmed Ṭāhir, *ʿOthmānlî müʾellifleri*, i, 72-3; Meḥmed Thüreyyā, *Sidjill-i ʿothmānī*, ii, 342; Sheykh Sāmī, *Ḳāmūs al-aʿlām*, iii, 2224; *IA*, art. *Ẓātī, Süleyman* (M. Kanar).

(TH. MENZEL*)

SULṬĀN ʿALĪ ŪGHLĪ (SOLTANGALIEV), MĪR SAYYID (*ca.* 1885-28 January 1940), leader of the Muslim Communist movement in Russia.

Son of a *muʿallim* (teacher), in a village in the Urals, Karmaskaly (in the canton of Sterlitamak, currently the Republic of Bashkortostan), Mīr Sayyid studied in his father's *mäktäb*—a reformed school where, in addition to religion and *ädäb*, reading was taught according to the "new method" (*uṣūl-i djadīd*) based on phonetics introduced by the Tatar from the Crimea, Ismāʿīl Ghāṣpîralî (Gasprinskiy, 1851-1914 [see GASPRALI (GASPRINSKI) ISMĀʿĪL]) as well as some secular subjects such as arithmetic and the rudiments of geography and modern history. His knowledge of Russian, which he learned from his father, enabled him to study at the Tatar High School (*Tatarskaya učitel'skaya shkola*) of Ḳazan, the only state-sponsored secondary education facility available to the Muslims of the Empire. From the mid-1890s onwards, a group of pupils formed a secret revolutionary society there, led by the writer Muḥammad ʿAyyāḍ Isḥāḳī (1878-1954) and influenced by Russian populism; it was to make a profound and lasting impression on the young Soltangaliev. After 1905, as an employee of the Municipal Library of Ufa, he was to participate in the *Iṣlāḥī* movement of the young Tatar intelligentsia, of which ʿAyyāḍ Isḥāḳī was the most prominent figure. Soltangaliev contributed, under various pseudonyms, to the leading journals of the Urals, most notably *Ṭūrmush* ("Life"), a reformist Tatar review in which he published translations of the later works of Tolstoy. From 1911 onward he published stories and articles in the *Musul'manskaya gazeta* ("Muslim Journal") of Moscow, showing the influence of his Tatar and Russian literary models; his themes (reform of education, the status of women, the parasitism of the mullahs, the political vocation of students committed to the public good), borrowed from Russian populism, had been promulgated from Ḳazan since the beginning of the century by authors sympathetic to the *Iṣlāḥī* movement such as ʿAyyāḍ Isḥāḳī or the novelist and poet ʿAbd Allāh Ṭuḳāy (1886-1913). During the First World War, Soltangaliev took up a teaching appointment in Baku; from there he contributed to various Russian Muslim periodicals.

December 1917-March 1919. Revolution as an instrument of conquest of political autonomy.

In April 1917, Soltangaliev was summoned to Moscow to direct the executive committee of the "Muslim Congress", before making his way to Ḳazan where he joined the "Muslim Socialist Committee". Created the 7 [19] April on the basis of Muslim workers' committees, the MSC was led by Mullā Nūr Waḥīdov (Vahitov) (1885-1918) whose project was to unite the revolutionary forces of the Tatar lands into a militarised group. The political ideas of Waḥīdov—who was to be killed in the early stages of the Civil War—constituted the basis of what would later be called "Soltangalievism"; they centred on the struggle against traditionalism, the liberation of Muslims from Russian domination and the extension of Socialism to all of Islam. However the Bolshevik *coup d'état* of 26 October [8 November] 1917, imposed Russian power in the Volga-Ural region, since Russians dominated the urban and provincial soviets of Ḳazan. The party of Lenin was nevertheless seen as constituting a superb school of political theory; Muslim nationalist leaders like Waḥīdov understood that by imitating him they could, perhaps, neutralise him. After all, Lenin's "April Decrees" (1917) were perceived as allowing the minorities of the former Empire to hope for a right of secession.

The leadership of the MSC (Waḥīdov, and his lieutenant Soltangaliev) sought to exploit the anarchy into which Russia had been plunged to exact concessions from the Bolshevik leaders, who needed all the support they could get. At the end of 1917, Stalin, Commissar of the People for the Nationalities, called on Soltangaliev to direct the Muslim section of his ministry. On 19 January 1918, Stalin created the "Central Commissariat for Muslim Affairs of the Russian Interior and Siberia" (*Muskom*), headed by Waḥīdov; Soltangaliev was recruited in June to take charge of propaganda in Muslim circles. Until the offensive mounted by the White Armies on the Volga in July 1918, the regions populated by Muslims in European Russia were covered by a network of regional and local commissariats dominated by nationalist partisans, independent of the local soviets which were dominated by Russians. Controlled by the *Muskom*, these commissariats were to form the nucleus of the great "Tatar and Bashkir Republic" promised by Stalin to the Communist Muslim leaders. In a parallel development, Waḥīdov and Soltangaliev created in Moscow, on 8 March, the Muslim Socialist-Communist Party (replaced in June by the "Party of Communist (Bolshevik) Muslims of Russia").

Autonomous in its relations with the Russian CP, the new party severed links with the "bourgeois" Muslim organisations which were henceforward isolated (an example of this being the dismal episode of the short-lived "Republic of Transbulakia" in Ḳazan), but sought to gather Muslim revolutionaries into a united front. Waḥīdov and Soltangaliev concentrated their efforts on the training of political cadres (with the projected Muslim University of Ḳazan, a long-standing demand of the *Iṣlāḥī* movement), and on the mobilisation throughout the Volga-Ural region of the Muslim regiments of the Red Army. From August onward, however, these regiments were incorporated into Russian units, after the fall of Ḳazan into the hands of the Whites, who executed Waḥīdov. In November 1918, at the "First Congress of Communist Muslims", Soltangaliev and Ismāʿīl Firdäws (1888-1937) a Tatar from the Crimea, sought confirmation of the autonomy of the Muslim Communist Party. But Stalin, intent on retaining control of the "colonial revolution", rejected this demand; the crucial moment when the Tatars could argue with the Russians over the direction of the revolutionary movement seemed to have passed. In fact, from the spring of 1919 onward, the Civil War turned on the eastern front in favour of the Bolsheviks, and in the Muslim territories reconquered by the Red Army, the civil and military apparatus installed by Waḥīdov was dismantled.

March 1919-April 1923. Russian monolithism against Muslim polycentrism.

From March 1919, the 8th Congress of the Russian Communist Party (in Moscow, 18-23 March) proposed the suppression of all national communist organisations. The "Bureau of Muslim Organisations"—which had replaced the Muslim Communist Party—was replaced in its turn by a "Central Bureau of Communist Organisations of the Peoples of the Orient". It was the principle of the distinctness and unity of the Muslim world, dear to the former leaders of the *Iṣlāḥī* movement, which was thus negated. The "oriental" revolution was making rapid progress, in Persia especially, where the *Djangalī* movement [*q.v.*] was supported militarily by the Bolsheviks. But the policy of the Komintern in the Middle East was also to be marked by a fundamental divergence between Russians, supporters of monolithism, and Muslims, supporters of decentralisation. At the "Congress of Oriental Peoples" in Baku, September 1920, the ideas of Soltangaliev regarding the liberation of colonial peoples were in collision with those of the Komintern, which was only interested in the East as a source of temporary assistance to the western industrial proletariat, through the weakening of colonial powers. Soltangaliev sought to bypass the obstacle of the RCP by approaching the "Organisation of Communist Youth" (Komsonol); between 12 and 18 September

1920 he convened in Moscow the "First Pan-Russian Conference of Communist Organisations of the Lands of the Orient" where he evoked for the first time, it seems, the notion of a "colonial Communist International", independent of the Komintern. Cast in a minority, he succeeded nevertheless in transforming the komsonols of the Muslim republics of Russia into power-bases of his movement.

In the autumn of 1920, after the victories of the Red Army on all fronts, the civil war came to an end. As the Muslim communist party no longer existed and the dream of a great Tatar and Bas̲h̲kir Muslim State had been frustrated (Stalin had opted for the creation of two small and distinct republics, Tatar and Bas̲h̲kir), the Muslim nationalist communists turned their efforts towards the new national republics. At the same time, they promoted their ideas externally: Soltangaliev won over an international audience at the Communist University of Workers from the East, founded in Moscow in 1921. Refusing to reject outright the Tatar heritage and the religion of Islam, he also maintained contact with the principal reformist *ʿulamāʾ*, among whom ʿĀlimd̲j̲ān Bārūdī (*muftī* of Russia between 1917 and 1921) and Riḍā al-Dīn Fak̲h̲r al-Dīn (*muftī* from 1922 till his death in 1936), and sought to maintain their role as cultural intermediaries between the Soviet authorities and the Muslim, essentially rural, masses. Islam was presented as an oppressed religion, whose historical evolution, cherishing among its adherents a strong sense of solidarity, had to some extent resisted the anti-religious campaigns of the early Soviet period. Stalin was soon to see, in these efforts, an aspiration to found an "Islamic Communism" opposed to Marxism-Leninism.

April 1923-November 1928. East versus West?

In the spring of 1921, the 10th Congress of the Russian Communist Party pushed the nationalist Communist Muslims towards clandestine opposition, by denouncing "nationalist deviants". The notion of a non-Russian socialist party, mooted in the spring of 1919, was revived in November of the same year: a number of leaders, assembled in Moscow by Soltangaliev, decided to create an independent socialist Muslim party, which came into being the following year under the name of *Ittiḥād wa Taraḳḳī* ("Unity and Progress"). In parallel, from the start of the year 1921, the Tatar Republic underwent a period of intense nationalist agitation, which continued throughout the following two years. At a regional conference of the Russian CP in Ḳazan, March 1923, the Tatar majority went as far as to pass a motion demanding the expulsion of Russian colonists as well as a radical "nativisation" of the administrative apparatus of the republic; the Tatar communists refused, furthermore, to purge their organisation of its non-proletarian elements.

Shortly after this, in the wake of the 12th Congress of the CP, which witnessed, in April, the denunciation of "local nationalisms", Soltangaliev was arrested in Moscow on a personal order from Stalin, countersigned by the principal Bolshevik leaders. Excluded from the Russian CP, Soltangaliev, like many former *Iṣlāḥī* activists (such as Čulpān in Central Asia), seems to have been preoccupied by awareness of an insoluble conflict between East and West, and to have been convinced that the Bolshevik revolution was the most dangerous, because the most penetrating, attempt by the West to perpetuate its domination. Soltangaliev was soon at the heart of a secret organisation led by Communist Tatars and linked with various clandestine groups in European Russia, the Caucasus and Central Asia (*Ālās̲h̲ Orda* in Ḳazakstan, *Millī Firḳa* in the Crimea, the former *Hümmet* in Azerbaidjan and *Millī Ittiḥād* in Uzbekistan). The political thought of Soltangaliev, from 1923 onward, is known only from the criticisms voiced by his opponents, and the "confessions" extracted in the course of his successive trials. His political programme hinged on the creation of a great Turkish national state in Russia, the "Republic of Turan", governed by a single party, but based on state capitalism and with economic independence assured by orientation towards the lands of the Far and the Middle East.

An attack on the part of the commissars of the people of the Tatar Republic led to the second arrest of Soltangaliev in November 1928, the prelude to a series of large-scale and bloody purges which were to be inflicted periodically on all the republican communist parties until 1939, not sparing the national intelligentsias. Sentenced in 1929 to ten years of hard labour as an agent of imperialism, Soltangaliev was deported to the camp of the Solovki islands on the White Sea. He took advantage of early release in 1934, only to be arrested again in 1937 and tortured, then executed 28 January 1940. On the eve of the Second World War, Soltangalievism seems to have been eradicated in Russia. In Central Asia and in the Caucasus, as the Muslim nations had made good the lack of cultural development which in the early 20th century had separated them from the Tatars, the latter had lost their status as models to be copied. Born in a land of secular confrontation between Muslims and Christians, Tatar nationalism, initially supposed to be spread beyond the zone of the Middle Volga, was ultimately to withdraw, confined to its place of origin. Soltangaliev, mythologised outside the USSR as the father of non-European, even anti-European revolution, enjoyed in Russia itself only a belated rehabilitation—today virtually limited to the territory of Tatarstan, of which he was not a native. His memory has helped the Turkish-speaking peoples of the former USSR to consider themselves protagonists in their own modern history. But the rediscovery of this history tends to relativise the role played by communist nationalists, giving more credit to the great figures of Muslim reformism. The former and the latter shared, between 1920 and the Second World War, the same conviction of a cataclysmic confrontation between Tatars and Russians, Muslims and Christians, East and West, rural and industrial worlds—a parallelism given insufficient emphasis in studies of Soltangalievism, and in studies of the Muslim reformisms, of which the *Iṣlāḥī* movement was a component.

Bibliography: In the absence of complete works, the most important collection of texts of Soltangaliev is the very selective anthology published by I.G. Gizzatullin and D.R. S̲h̲arafutdinov: Mirsäet Soltangaliev, *Saylanma k̲h̲äzmätlär/Izbrannïe trudï* ("Selected works"), Ḳazan 1998; however, this volume ignores the manuscript writings and correspondence of Soltangaliev (a general trait of studies of the *Iṣlāḥī* movement and of national communism, which prefer normative and programmatic publications) as well as all texts later than 1923, other than numerous transcripts of Soltangaliev's successive interrogations. Among a sparse list of monographic studies, the irreplaceable reference source remains A. Bennigsen and Chantal Lemercier-Quelquejay, *Sultan Galiev. Le père de la révolution tiers-mondiste*, Paris 1986, with a very thorough critical bibl., a work which, in spite of its title, establishes the most subtle distinction that has yet been drawn between the personality of Soltangaliev and the various myths to which he gave rise; for an equally documented, but more global approach, see Azade-Ayşe Rohrlich, *The Volga Tatars. A profile in national resilience*, Stanford 1986, in particular 125-56. Also available for reference, although this is essentially a work based on second-hand sources, nourished by pan-Asiatic sympathies, is the recent synthesis by Masayuki Yamauchi, *Surutangariefu no yume to genjitsu. Shio* ("Dreams and Realities of Soltangaliev. Documents"), Tokyo 1998 (tr. into Turkish by Hironao Matsutani under the title *Sultan Galiev. Islam dünyası ve Rusya* ["Soltangaliev. The world of Islam and Russia"], Ankara 1998.

(S.A. Dudoignon)

ṢUMĀDIḤ, Banū, Arab dynasty of al-Andalus, ruling in Almeria from 420/1038 to 484/1091, in the epoch of the "party kings" [see MULŪK AL-ṬAWĀʾIF].

The Banū Ṣumādiḥ were a branch of the powerful Arab family of the Banū Tudjīb of the Upper March (region of Saragossa). At a time when the caliphate was in disarray, a certain Muḥammad b. Aḥmad b. Ṣumādiḥ was governing Huesca, but, before 414/1023, he was expelled from there by his distant cousins of Saragossa, and took refuge in Valencia as a guest of the local sovereign, the ʿĀmirid ʿAbd al-ʿAzīz al-Manṣūr, who gave two of his daughters in marriage to his two sons, Abu 'l-Aḥwas Maʿn and his brother Abū ʿUtba Ṣumādiḥ. This Muḥammad b. Aḥmad died soon afterwards at sea, having set out on the Pilgrimage. After the death in 429/1038 of the former slave and *amīr* of Almeria, Zuhayr [*q.v.*], the inhabitants of this town placed themselves under the authority of the prince of Valencia, who seems to have sent his son-in-law Maʿn b. Ṣumādiḥ to govern Almeria, with the title of *dhu 'l-wizāratayn*. In circumstances that are unclear, and apparently with the agreement of the populace, the latter declared himself independent, thus founding a new dynasty, but not adopting a *laḳab* and not striking his own coinage. Furthermore, for the years 430-5/1038-43 or 1044, there are examples extant of coins of al-Manṣūr of Valencia struck at Almeria, which tends to support one of the versions supplied by the sources, according to which this independence did not involve a rift with the prince of Valencia.

In 443/1052, Abū Yaḥyā Muḥammad b. Maʿn succeeded his father, initially under the tutelage of his uncle Abū ʿUtba on account of his youth. It was during his reign that the power of the Banū Ṣumādiḥ took on the "royal" forms current under the taifas: he replaced the "amiral" title of Muʿizz al-Dawla which he bore at the time of his accession to power, with the more "caliphal"-sounding one of al-Muʿtaṣim bi 'llāh and al-Wāthiḳ bi-faḍl Allāh. He did not differ in this respect from numerous other sovereigns of taifas in the second half of the 5th/11th century. Coins on which these *laḳabs* appeared were minted at Almeria. But it seems that under his reign and in his name, only dirhams of poor quality were minted at Almeria, and in limited quantities, judging by the standard and the rarity of the examples preserved in numismatic collections.

The contemporary geographer and historian al-ʿUdhrī, a native of the region of Almeria and probably a visitor to the court of the Banū Ṣumādiḥ, gives in his *Tarṣīʿ al-akhbār* a rapturous description of the splendid palace maintained by al-Muʿtaṣim in the *ḳaṣaba* which dominates the town of Almeria. Furthermore, it is known that there existed a substantial royal entertainment complex, situated *extra muros* at the edge of the town, known as the Ṣumādiḥiyya. Although apparently lacking serious politico-military ambitions, this prince was engaged in rivalry, sometimes armed, with his neighbours in Valencia and Granada; these limited conflicts had no effect on the apparent prosperity of a state of considerably reduced dimensions, effectively confined to the region surrounding the major port city of Almeria.

When the Almoravids disembarked in the peninsula in 479/1086, al-Muʿtaṣim sent troops commanded by his son Muʿizz al-Dawla and presents to the *amīr* Yūsuf b. Tāshufīn, excusing himself, on the grounds of age, from participating in the campaign which culminated in the victory of Zallāḳa/Sagrajas. The following year, he was present at the siege of Aledo with troops from Almeria, and even supplied a siege-engine constructed in the form of an elephant. He died in the summer of 484/1091, just as Almoravid troops, having taken possession of Granada, were moving agaist Almeria; his son resisted for only a few weeks in the *ḳaṣaba* before leaving the city by sea to spend the rest of his life in Bougie [see BIDJĀYA], then governed by the Ḥammādids. In Ramaḍān 484/October-November 1091, the Almoravids absorbed Almeria and the taifa into their empire.

Like other courts of the taifas, that of the Banū Ṣumādiḥ was a literary centre, which seems to have maintained a certain ideal of Arabism: it was in response to a poet at the court of al-Muʿtaṣim who had insisted on the Arab origins of the dynasty, that Ibn Garcia, secretary and court poet to Mudjāhid, prince of Denia, composed a *Risāla* known as the principal text of the *Shuʿūbiyya* movement in al-Andalus.

Bibliography: R. Dozy, *Essai sur l'histoire des Todjibides: les Beni Hachim de Saragosse et les Beni Çomadih d'Almerie*, in *Recherches sur l'histoire et la littérature de l'Espagne pendant le Moyen Age*, ³Leiden 1881; A. Prieto y Vives, *Los reyes de taifas. Estudio histórico-numismático de los musulmanes españoles en el siglo V de la hégira (XI de J.C.)*, Madrid 1926; H. Pérès, *La poésie andalouse en arabe classique au XIᵉ siècle*, Paris 1937; ʿUdhri, *Fragmentos geográfico-históricos de* al-Masālik ilā djamīʿ al-mamāliḳ, ed. ʿAbd al-ʿAzīz al-Ahwānī, Madrid 1965; M. Sánchez Martínez, *La cora de Ilbīra (Granada y Almeria) en los siglos X y XI, según Al-ʿUdhrī*, in *Cuadernos de Historia del Islam*, ii (1975-6); E. Molina López, *Los Banū Sumādiḥ de Almeria (siglo XI) en* el Bayan *de Ibn ʿIdhārī*, in *Andalucia islámica: textos y estudios*, i (1980), 123-40; M.J. Viguera Molins (ed.), *Los reinos de taifas. Al-Andalus en el siglo XI*, vol. viii of the *Historia de España Menéndez Pidal*, Madrid 1994; D. Wasserstein, *The rise and fall of the Party-Kings. Politics and society in Islamic Spain, 1002-1086*, Princeton 1985.

(P. Guichard)

AL-**SUNĀMĪ**, ʿUmar b. Muḥammad b. ʿIwaḍ, Ḥanafī scholar of mediaeval Muslim India whose importance comes from his work on *hisba* [*q.v.*], the *Niṣāb al-iḥtisāb*, which refers to the author's own role in this office. Judging by the number of surviving mss., some sixty, the work was highly popular in the eastern Islamic lands. Previous scholars have been uncertain about the author's origins and life (cf. e.g. Brockelmann, S II, 427). It now seems clear from internal evidence in his book that he stemmed from Sunām, a place that still exists in the modern Indian province of Panjab, to the south-west of Patiala; that he lived under the Dihlī Sultans [*q.v.*], in particular, in the time of Muḥammad b. Tughluḳ (*r.* 725-52/1325-51 [*q.v.*]); and that he died at the newly-founded

Deccan capital of the Tug̲h̲luḳids, Dawlatābād [*q.v.*], the ancient Dēōgīrī, around or after 743-4/1333-4.

The value of the *Niṣāb* lies in the fact that it is the first known Ḥanafī text on *ḥisba*, with its practical and theoretical approaches reflecting al-Sunāmī's dual functions as a lawyer and a *muḥtasib*. The author tackles the common problems facing the *muḥtasib* in accordance with the Ḥanafī *mad̲h̲hab*, and his insights show the importance of local Indian customs and the practices of daily life, often denounced by him as *bidaʿ*, within the formal framework of Islamic law.

Bibliography: M. Izzi Dien, *The theory and the practice of market law in medieval Islam. A study of Kitāb Niṣāb al-iḥtisāb of ʿUmar b. Muḥammad al-Sunāmī (fl. 7th-8th/13th-14th century)*, GMS, Cambridge 1997.

(MAWIL Y. IZZI DIEN)

SÜRGÜN (T., lit. "expulsion"), a term of Ottoman administrative and social policy.

It encompasses a wide range of practices employed by the Ottomans, not just to remove dissident elements from politically troubled provinces, but also more constructively to achieve vital state-defined economic and military objectives. The term is better translated as population transfer or strategic resettlement, and its purpose was fundamentally different from the purely punitive sentence of internal exile or banishment (*nefy*) temporarily imposed on individual members of the ruling élite who had incurred the sultan's disfavour. The use of *sürgün* forcibly to remove fractious elements such as uncooperative tribes or rebellious city populations from persistently troublesome areas is documented as part of the Ottomans' attempts to impose control over Anatolia, especially during the closing decades of the 8th/14th and the first part of the 9th/15th century. However, its use as a weapon for political suppression without concomitant social or economic benefits was frowned on in Muslim popular opinion (see Ibn Kēmal's remarks on the mass deportations from Lārende to Istanbul in 872/1467-8, as cited in *Bibl.*: . . . *etdi, Larendeye bir is̲h̲ etti ki üzerine düs̲h̲man-i bed-kīs̲h̲ dak̲h̲ī gelse, böyle etmezdi*). In principle, *sürgün* was designed not to punish the source area which contributed a part of its labour force as emigrants but to provide some advantage to the target area to which they were being dispatched as immigrants. It had the real potential for providing the double benefit of relieving population and land pressure in the source territory while at the same time acting as a stimulus to the growth and development of the target territory. It also facilitated the transfer of groups with essential skills to the areas where they were most needed. The underlying purpose, whether it was the repopulating of Istanbul after its capture in 856/1453 by the transfer of population groups with specific commercial and artisan skills from provincial cities in Anatolia and (after 880/1475) the Crimea, or the settling of rural populations as agriculturalists in newly-conquered territories in Rumelia, was essentially the same: the settlement and development (*iskān we iʿmār*) of key strategic areas identified as either economically fragile or militarily insecure. This logic applied with particular force to the period of Ottoman territorial expansion in the Balkans lasting until the end of the 10th/16th century, but strategic resettlement of tribes and displaced peasants also formed an important dimension of Ottoman rural development initiatives in subsequent periods of territorial contraction. The creation of new settlements on the Upper Euphrates in the 1100s/1690s using tribes transferred from contiguous regions of Anatolia is just one example of the continuing use of *sürgün* in later centuries (see the study by Orhonlu cited in *Bibl.*, and, for developments in the 19th century following territorial losses in the Balkans and Russian expansion in Crimea and the Caucasus, see MUHĀD̲J̲IR. 2.)

Bibliography: 1. Sources. Ö.L. Barkan (ed.), *Kanunlar*, Istanbul 1943, 272-7 (*Kanunname-i liva-i Silistre*, 274, §8, on the tax and residence obligations of *sürgün* populations from Anatolia); idem (ed.), text and analysis of the *sürgün hükmü* sent in 980/1572 to districts of southern Anatolia to promote population transfers to Cyprus after its conquest in the previous year, *İktisat Fakültesi Mecmuası*, xi (1952), 550-3 (text transcription), 562-4 (facs. of *mühimme* document); Ibn Kemāl, *Tevarih-i Al-i Osman. VII. defter*, facs. ed. S. Turan, Ankara 1954, see esp. 290 ll. 6-8.

2. Studies. Barkan, *Osmanlı imparatorluğunda bir iskan ve kolonizasyon metodu olarak sürgünler*, 3 parts, in *İktisat Fakültesi Mecmuası*, xi (1951), 624-69, xiii (1953), 56-78, xv (1955), 209-37; M.T. Gökbilgin, *Rumelide yürükler, tatarlar ve evlâd-i Fatihan*, Istanbul 1957; C. Orhonlu, *Osmanlı imparatorluğunda aşiretleri iskan teşebbüsü, 1691-1696*, Istanbul 1963; H. Inalcik, *The policy of Mehmed II towards the Greek population of Istanbul*, in *Dumbarton Oaks Papers*, xxiii-xxiv (1969-70), 231-49; Y. Halaçoğlu, *XVIII. yüzyılda osmanlı imparatorluğunun iskan siyaseti ve aşiretlerin yerleştirilmesi*, Ankara 1988; M.H. Şentürk, *Osmanlı devletinin kuruluş devrinde Rumelide uyguladığı iskan siyaseti ve neticeleri*, in *Belleten*, lvii, no. 218 (1993), 89-112.

(R. MURPHEY)

AL-**SUWAYNĪ**, SAʿD B. ʿĀLĪ BĀ MAD̲H̲ḤID̲J̲ (d. 857/1453), ʿAlawī *sayyid* of Ḥaḍramawt. He was the student of ʿAbd al-Raḥmān Bā ʿAlawī of Tarīm, from the Saḳḳāf branch of the *sayyids* [see BĀ ʿALAWĪ], and in turn the *s̲h̲ayk̲h̲* of Abū Bakr b. ʿAbd Allāh al-ʿAydarūs, the patron saint of Aden [see ʿADAN], d. 914/1508 [see ʿAYDARŪS]. It was this last who was to compose the *manāḳib* of al-Suwaynī.

Bibliography: See R.B. Serjeant, *The Saiyids of Hadramawt*, London 1957.

(ED.)

T

TAʿALLUḲ (A.), or more often **TAʿALLUḲA**, literally "dependence, being related to, dependent on", a revenue term of late Mug̲h̲al India, which meant a jurisdiction, a fiscal area from which a fixed amount of taxes was to be collected by a revenue official called *taʿalluḳdār* or *taʿalluḳadār*. The word *taʿalluḳ* with this meaning appeared in the second half of the 11th/17th century during the reign of Awrangzīb [*q.v.*], in the context of increasing tax farming [see ḌARĪBA. 6. c]; it was distinguished from the older

Indo-Persian term *zamīndārī*, which included also feudal rights for the *zamīndār* [*q.v.*] who was in charge of it, while the *taʿallukdār*, originally considered as a tax farmer, was only in charge of collecting the revenue of his *taʿalluk*, except for a small part of it on which he had *zamīndārī* rights. For this reason, *taʿallukdārs* ranked lower than *zamīndārs*.

From the 18th to the 20th centuries, under the late Mug͟hals, the successor states and colonial rule, the words *taʿalluk* and *taʿallukdār* came to mean different things according to place and time. In Northern India, the *taʿallukdārs* were men of substance who acquired hereditary and transferable rights on their *taʿalluk* and were barely distinguishable from the *zamīndārs*: in Bengal before the British conquest, working as the subordinates of powerful *zamīndārs*, they brought large tracts of land under cultivation; in Awadh [*q.v.*], they collected taxes over large estates and constituted a rich feudal class of landlords whose fortunes lasted up to the end of the British period. Elsewhere, the word *taʿalluk* meant only a fiscal jurisdiction of varying size, equivalent to a district in the state of Ḥaydarābād [*q.v.*] and only to a fraction of a village in Nepal; the office of *taʿallukdār* as that of tax collector died out during the British period, except in Nepal where it was still common in the 1960s.

Bibliography: H.H. Wilson, *A glossary of judicial and revenue terms . . .*, London 1855, repr. Delhi 1968, 497-8 under "taâlluk", "taâllukdâr"; H. Yule and A.C. Burnell, *Hobson-Jobson. A glossary of Anglo-Indian words and phrases . . .*, 2nd ed. W. Crooke, London 1903, repr. London 1969, Delhi 1969, 894, under "Talook", "Talookdar"; I. Habib, *The agrarian system of Mughal India*, 2nd rev. ed. Delhi 1999, 173, 183, 211-12, 554 ([1]Bombay 1963); N.A. Siddiqi, *Land revenue administration under the Mughals, 1700-1750*, Bombay 1970, 47; M. Gaborieau, *Le partage du pouvoir entre les lignages dans une localité du Népal central*, in *L'Homme*, xviii/1-2 (1978), 37-67; T.R. Metcalf, *Land, landlords, and the British Raj. Northern India in the nineteenth century*, Berkeley 1979, index s.v. "Taluqdar"; M. Alam, *The crisis of Empire in Mughal North India: Awadh and the Punjab, 1707-1748*, Delhi 1986, 217-18; R.M. Eaton, *The rise of Islam and the Bengal frontier, 1204-1760*, Berkeley 1993, 220-3.
(M. Gaborieau)

TABANNIN (a.), adoption. This term—*maṣdar* or verbal noun of the form V verb derived from the biliteral root *b n*, which is also the source of *ibn* ("son")—is used, just as in Western languages, in the literal sense (adoption of a child) and in the figurative sense (adoption of a doctrine, etc.). This article is concerned only with adoption in the literal sense.

Since the Ḳurʾān (XXXIII, 5, 37; two verses from the Medinan period) is clear on this point, there is no disagreement among Muslim jurists of the different schools regarding the strict prohibition of plenary adoption.

The occasion (*sabab*) of the revelation of these two verses that prohibit adoption—forbidding anyone to give his name to another who does not belong within his "natural" descendance, which amounts to banning all adoptive filiation—is provided by these verses themselves. The Prophet Muḥammad, perpetuating, according to Muslim sources, a practice of pre-Islamic Arabia, the *D̲j̲āhiliyya*, had adopted one of his slaves, Zayd b. Ḥārit̲h̲a [*q.v.*], offered by his wife K̲h̲adīd̲j̲a [*q.v.*]. He had emancipated Zayd (an important figure in the early years of Islam: one of the first converts to Islam, if not the first, according to al-Zuhrī, and the only person, besides the prophets, to be named in the Ḳurʾān), and he was henceforward known without any ambiguity as "Zayd, son of Muḥammad" (Zayd b. Muḥammad), even though his ancestry was known (his father tried to buy him back, but Zayd refused to leave Muḥammad, see al-D̲j̲aṣṣāṣ, *Aḥkām al-Ḳurʾān*, i-iii, n.p. [Beirut], n.d., iii, 361).

Adoption as practised before the revelation of Ḳurʾān, XXXIII, 5, 37, was plenary, entailing the same legal consequences as natural filiation (the right to inherit, etc.), and more significantly, the same prohibitions applied to marriage; the verses abrogate adoptive filiation and, explicitly, the prohibitions applying to marriage which would result from it. This is a good example, according to the Ḥanafī al-D̲j̲aṣṣāṣ, of abrogation of the *sunna* by the Ḳurʾān (a theoretical remark directed against al-S̲h̲āfiʿī [*q.v.*], who did not agree that the Ḳurʾān could abrogate the *sunna*). Muḥammad intended to marry Zaynab bt. D̲j̲aḥs̲h̲ [*q.v.*], the repudiated wife of Zayd b. Ḥārit̲h̲a, who, if plenary adoption had remained valid, would have been absolutely forbidden to him. The marriage of Muḥammad with Zaynab bt. D̲j̲aḥs̲h̲ would not have been legally permissible without the abrogation of plenary adoption (see al-Māwardī, *al-Nukat wa 'l-ʿuyūn. Tafsīr al-Māwardī*, 6 vols. Beirut 1412/1992, iv, 370ff. and 405ff.).

Numerous students of Islamic Studies have seen this episode from the marital life of Muḥammad as a sign of the moral weakness of the Prophet of Islam. It is true that certain *ʿulamāʾ* of the classical epoch had difficulty hiding their embarrassment, and it is certainly no accident that Fak̲h̲r al-Dīn al-Rāzī [*q.v.*] undertook to show that the marital life of the Prophet was in no way governed by his carnal appetites, with his commentary on Ḳurʾān, XXXIII, 37: "Here is evidence that the marital life of the Prophet (*al-tazwīd̲j̲ min al-nabī*) did not have the purpose of satisfying the carnal appetite of the Prophet (*ḳaḍāʾ s̲h̲ahwat al-nabī*), but on the contrary, its purpose was to render the Law explicit though his agency." In other words, there was nothing here other than one example among others of "clarification of the Law through the agency [of the Prophet]" (*bayān al-S̲h̲arīʿa bi-fiʿlihi*), see al-Rāzī, *al-Tafsīr al-kabīr aw mafātīḥ al-g̲h̲ayb*, 32 vols. and index, Beirut 1411/1990, xxv, 184).

The prohibition of adoption under the terms of the revealed Law (*S̲h̲arīʿa*) is no doubt more easily understood if it is remembered that Islam regards the "natural" nuclear family, rather than the tribe, as the basis of the community (*umma*). From this perspective, which is that of Abrahamic monotheism in general, adoption appears as a disruptive element, confusing "lineages" (*nasab*, pl. *ansāb*), or the lines of "natural" filiation which reflect the familial order as willed by the Divine Legislator (see Ps.-al-S̲h̲āfiʿī, *Aḥkām al-Ḳurʾān*, ed. Kawt̲h̲arī, 2 vols., Damascus n.d., ii, 164).

If reference is made to the "occasion" of the Ḳurʾānic prohibition of adoption—or the case of Zayd—it can well be understood why, in classical doctrines, a *de facto* distinction is imposed between, on the one hand, the child whose genealogy is known (*maʿrūf al-nasab*) and on the other, the child whose genealogy is unknown (*mad̲j̲hūl al-nasab*), the *laḳīṭ* [*q.v.*] ("foundling"), who is the object of a specific chapter in treatises of *fiḳh*. In the second case, a recognition of paternity, with transference of the *nasab* (*istilḥāḳ* or *iḳrār bi 'l-nasab*) by the finder of the child proves possible, under certain circumstances, and even facilitated, since Muslim jurists show themselves very flexible on this point, demanding only indications of "probability" in such recognitions and not formal proof (see M.S. Sujimon, *The treatment of the foundling according to the Ḥanafīs*, in *ILS*, ix/3 [2002], 358-85). As for the possibility of passing from one known genealogy to another, it is unequivocally barred *de jure* according to all legal schools. In the Muslim legal order, the creation of a genealogy *ex nihilo* thus proves easier than a change of *nasab*.

At the present time, only one Arab Muslim country, Tunisia, has had the audacity to contravene openly the Ḳurʾānic prohibition of plenary adoption. In 1958, the Tunisian legislature, more aware of new social realities than others, established adoptive filiation in the full sense. It seems nevertheless that in the tribunals interpretation of statutes of adoption is often restrictive and sometimes expressly infringes the terms of the legislation in force (see L. Pruvost, *Intégration familiale*..., in *Recueil d'articles offert à Maurice Borrmans par ses collègues et amis*, Rome 1996, 155-80).

Modern and contemporary ethnology has shown that despite its theoretical prohibition, adoption used to be practised in numerous Muslim societies. Adoption in Islam probably constitutes one of those instances where custom, in the event more favourable to this institution, has been only very superficially Islamised.

Bibliography: 1. Surveys of the classical doctrine. References given in the article; the corpus of commentaries on Ḳurʾān, XXXIII, 5, 37; and for an unusual point of view, cautiously favourable to adoption, Zamak̲h̲s̲h̲arī, *al-Kas̲h̲s̲h̲āf ʿan ḥaḳāʾiḳ al-Ḳurʾān*, Beirut n.d. [1947] on Ḳurʾān, XXXIII, 5. Treatises of *fiḳh* barely mention the question of the prohibition of adoption.

2. Studies. Few works have been devoted to adoption as such in Islam, but see nevertheless G.H. Bousquet and A. Demeerseman, *L'adoption dans la famille tunisienne*, in *R.Afr.*, ccclxxii-iii (1937), 127-59; A.R. Naqvi, *Adoption in Muslim law*, in *Islamic Studies*, xix (1980), 283-392; U. Vermeulen, *De gezagsvoorzieningen in de Islam: adoptie en hoederecht*, in *Recht van de Islam*, iv (1986), 4-17; K. Dilger, *Die Adoption im modernen Orient. Ein Beitrag zu den Hiyal im islamischen Recht*, in *Recht van de Islam*, vii (1988), 42-62; A. al-A. Sonbol, *Adoption in Islamic society, a historical survey*, in E. Warnock Fernea (ed.), *Children in the Muslim Middle East*, Cairo 1996, 45-67; O. Pesle, *L'adoption en Islam*, Algiers n.d.

(E. Chaumont)

ṬABĪʿIYYĀT (a.), an abstract noun formed from the adjective *ṭabīʿī* "natural" (antonym, *maṣnūʿ*), physics, or natural sciences.

Aristotle divided the theoretical sciences into mathematics, physics and metaphysics. Islamic philosophers, starting from al-Kindī [*q.v.*], were familiar with this division and it forms part of the various classifications of the sciences that were drawn up by Islamic scholars, such as in the *Iḥṣāʾ al-ʿulūm* by al-Fārābī [*q.v.*] and in many subsequent ones. In these classifications, physics was subdivided into parts that mostly corresponded to the Aristotelian works on natural science, including those that are now known to have originated in his school. Such a division was also maintained in the encyclopaedic works of Ibn Sīnā [*q.v.*] and his followers, such as Bahmanyār b. al-Marzubān, Abu 'l-Barakāt al-Bag̲h̲dādī, Fak̲h̲r al-Dīn al-Rāzī, al-Abharī and others.

For instance, the part of Ibn Sīnā's *Kitāb al-S̲h̲ifāʾ* that deals with *ṭabīʿiyyāt* constains the following eight sections: lectures on physics; the heaven and the world; generation and corruption; actions and passions; meteorological phenomena; the soul, plants; and the natures of animals. Except for the section entitled "Actions and passions", each of these sections corresponds to a work from the Aristotelian school; in fact, the section "Actions and passions" together with the next section "Meteorological phenomena" discusses the subjects from Aristotle's *Meteorology*.

Furthermore, Islamic philosophers such as Ibn Bād̲j̲d̲j̲a and Ibn Rus̲h̲d [*q.vv.*] wrote individual commentaries on several of Aristotle's physical works.

It should be mentioned that the Islamic theologians (*mutakallimūn*) also discussed subjects that fall under *ṭabīʿiyyāt*, such as the structure of matter and the nature of change.

The Islamic philosophers writing on subjects of natural science remained within the framework of Aristotelian natural philosophy: they used concepts such as potentiality/actuality, matter/form, natural place and natural motion *vs.* non-natural place and forced motion; they adopted Aristotle's definition of motion; and they denied the existence of the void and conceived matter as continuous, not atomistic. However, it appears that the work of Philoponos [see yaḥyā al-naḥwī], who opposed Aristotle in several respects, was also well studied, and that often Islamic philosophers took sides with him against Aristotle. Moreover, they often had a different way of discussing things and brought forward new arguments. A few examples follow.

In their discussion of infinity, Islamic philosophers adopted Aristotle's definition, but they used a way to prove that infinite quantities cannot actually exist, which was first propounded by Philoponos. His proof was based on the (mistaken) idea that a part of an infinite collection cannot be infinite, for if something is smaller than infinite, it must be finite. Al-Kindī and al-G̲h̲azālī [*q.vv.*] used this method also to prove, against Aristotle, that time cannot be infinite, but must have a beginning. Objections against this again were raised by Ibn Sīnā and Ibn Rus̲h̲d. It is worth mentioning that T̲h̲ābit b. Ḳurra [*q.v.*] recognised that infinite collections may have parts that are also infinite; this in fact invalidates the proofs of Philoponos and his Islamic followers.

In opposition to the Aristotelian explanation of motion, that "every body that moves is moved by another body", Islamic philosophers adopted the concept of impressed force such as conceived by Philoponos; this was further developed by Ibn Sīnā and his school, and became known as *mayl* ("inclination").

Aristotle's "law of motion", stating that the velocity of a body moving through a medium is inversely proportional to the density of that medium, was criticised by Philoponus and subsequently Ibn Bād̲j̲d̲j̲. Aristotle's law implies that motion through a void (if void existed) would occur with infinite velocity, that is, any distance would be covered in no time, and this absurd consequence was an argument for Aristotle to assert the impossibility of the void. However, Philoponus and Ibn Bād̲j̲d̲j̲ stated that covering a distance always needs a finite time, even in void, if it existed, and that the effect of the presence of a medium will be that more time is needed to cover that distance.

Atomism was discussed by Ibn Sīnā in a way not found in Greek philosophy, for he wrote in opposition to the atomism of the *mutakallimūn*, who defended atomism with their own arguments.

The discussions of meteorological phenomena [see al-āt̲h̲ār al-ʿulwiyya] are mostly based on Aristotle's assumption that they are caused by the two exhalations, the dry one from the earth and the moist one from the water. However, in their explanation of some phenomena, such as precipitation, wind, earthquakes, thunder, rainbow and the climates, al-Kindī and Ibn Sīnā do not always follow Aristotle. They show an independent way of thinking and criticise Aristotle on the basis of personal observation of these phenomena.

Much of the discussions of the above-mentioned subjects remained speculative or philosophical. The discipline that is nowadays called physics also had its scholars in the period of the flourishing of Islamic science. Statics was the subject of the *Kitāb al-Karasṭūn* by Thābit b. Ḳurra and *Kitāb Mīzān al-ḥikma* by al-Khāzinī [*q.v.*]. Hydrostatics and the determination of specific weights were discussed in the same book of al-Khāzinī and by al-Bīrūnī in his *Maḳāla fī nisab*. These scholars were able to execute very precise measurements of specific weights with their diverse instruments.

Although the work of Ibn al-Haytham [*q.v.*] on optics also contains much speculation, it stands out as one of the first examples of a systematic experimental investigation of the behaviour of light. This work was continued by Kamāl al-Dīn al-Fārisī [*q.v.*] who made a considerable contribution to the explanation of the rainbow by recognising that it is due to refraction of light in drops of water in a cloud [see MANĀẒIR].

Bibliography: J. van Ess, *Theologie und Gesellschaft im 2. und 3. Jahrhundert Hidschra*, i-iii, v-vi, Berlin, New York 1991-5; P. Lettinck, *Aristotle's* Physics *and its reception in the Arabic world: with an edition of the unedited parts of Ibn Bādjdja's* Commentary on the Physics, Leiden 1994; R. Rashid (ed.), *Encyclopedia of the history of Arabic science*, ii, London and New York 1996, 614-715; Lettinck, *Aristotle's* Meteorology *and its reception in the Arab world: with an edition and translation of Ibn Suwār's* Treatise on meteorological phenomena *and Ibn Bādjdja's* Commentary on the Meteorology, Leiden 1999; idem, *Ibn Sīnā on atomism. Translation of Ibn Sīnā's Kitāb al-Shifāʾ, al-Ṭabīʿiyyāt 1: al-Samāʿ al-Ṭabīʿī, Third treatise, chapters 3-5,* in *Al-Shajarah, Journal of the International Institute of Islamic Thought and Civilization (ISTAC)*, iv/1 (1999), 1-50.

(P. LETTINCK)

TAʿBĪR AL-RUʾYA (A.), "the interpretation of dreams".

As well as this expression, *tafsīr al-aḥlām* is employed, with *taʿbīr*, basically "the passage of one thing to another, one sense to another", hence "explanation" and *tafsīr*, lit. "commenting, explaining", from roots occurring in other Semitic languages and with the two Arabic verbal nouns found, once each, in the Ḳurʾān, at XII, 43, and XXV, 33, with *taʾwīl* [*q.v.*] also at XII, 44-5. In current usage, *taʿbīr* is confined to the sense of "interpretation of dreams", whilst *tafsīr* [*q.v.*] is used for commentaries on e.g. the Bible and the Ḳurʾān.

For the terminology of dreams and for the development of literature in Arabic on them, see RUʾYĀ. Here, their interpretation is considered, i.e. the skill of oneirocriticism.

In origin, oneiromancy was the province of the *kāhin* [*q.v.*] and custodians of inspired knowledge. It depended on divination, which was both intuitive and deductive: the first when in dreams, the divinity itself or its messenger appears to announce future happenings; the second, in regard to dreams of daily life, with their own obvious interpretation. In Islam, the two methods existed, the first in regard to the great Islamic dynasties (see Fahd, *Le rêve dans la société islamique du Moyen Age*) and in apparitions in dreams of the Prophet himself to privileged or pious persons and mystics. The second is seen in the immense oneirocritical literature in Islam (see idem, *La divination arabe*, 247-367). To these types of knowledge of the future a third may be added, incubation, in which a revealing angel is prompted to get in contact with the supernatural world and bring back knowledge of the future, a procedure already known from the Gilgamesh epic (J. Bottéro, *Les songes et leurs interpretations*, Paris 1959).

From oneiromancy, said by the Prophet to be one part of prophesy, following the Talmudic tradition (*Berakhot*, 57b, with comm. of Maimonides, *Le guide des égarés*, ii, 136), to oneirocriticism, the transition was made by two simultaneous impulses from the ancient Babylonian and Hellenistic traditions. In fact, by its symbolism and its formulation, the interpretation of dreams shows close links with the most ancient Semitic tradition, seen in Oppenheim's reconstitution of the Assyrian book of dreams and his exhaustive study of oneiromancy in the Near East. The transmission can, of course, only have been oral, as one would expect with a popular tradition.

After the 4th/10th century, under the impulsion of the Arabic translation of Artemidorus of Ephesus (2nd century A.D.), oneirocriticism borrowed from this last not only its plan and method of classification but also a considerable number of symbolic elements (see e.g. al-Dīnawarī's work). This injection of new blood led to the prodigious development of the Islamic genre of this literature (180 works listed in Fahd, *op. cit.*, 330 ff.), and the double heritage was developed and perfected through numerous generations.

The first codifier here was the Medinan Ibn al-Musayyab (*flor.* in the caliphate of the Umayyad ʿAbd al-Malik (later 1st/7th century A.D.). He left behind a list of thirteen dreams which his contemporaries had asked him to interpret, given by Ibn Saʿd, *Ṭabaḳāt*, v, 91-3, tr. in Fahd, *op. cit.*, 310-11). He was followed by Ibn Sīrīn [*q.v.*], whose fame here has come down to us and who figures amongst the forefathers of Arabic oneirocriticism.

At this stage, Arabic skill lacked a method of classifying dreams into precise categories illustrated by clear examples showing the constant symbolism. The translator of Artemidorus, Ḥunayn b. Isḥāḳ [*q.v.*], filled this gap, and it was exploited by Abū Saʿīd al-Dīnawarī in his work of 397/1006-7 dedicated to the ʿAbbāsid caliph al-Ḳādir (see *Bibl.*), of which over 25 mss. survive, the oldest work in the genre to have reached us integrally. This immense compilation not only contains materials on the interpretation of dreams but also on the range of man's activities, social and religious, and on his hopes and fears as experienced by a man of Baghdādī society in the 4th/10th century. This work also allows us to reconstitute, *grosso modo*, the six books of the work of Artemidorus, and its classification of themes became normative in later tradition, with only slight modifications appearing.

For the Muslim oneirocritics, the interpretation of dreams was the first of the sciences, practised from the start by the prophets and messengers of God so that the greater part of their pronouncements were made by means of dreams. For Ibn Khaldūn, it is a science whose light is a reflection of prophesy, with which it is closely connected. Both involve the permanent preoccupations of the Revelation (iii, 84, Eng. tr. iii, 103, Fr. tr. ii, 118). He details the skills required for interpretation of dreams, essentially those for religious piety, including discretion and the avoidance of careless talk and divulgence of confidences.

The oneirocritic should consider all aspects of the phenomenon and give a clear, measured response.

Note must be taken of the status, age, etc. of the person involved, the conditions in which the dream has been experienced, etc. Faced with a difficulty, the oneirocritic must go back to basic principles, but if after all that, he can find no answer, he must confess this, and no-one will reproach him, since this has happened to the prophets themselves. The dreams of all classes of men must be interpreted, after a rigorous enquiry into the status, etc. of the questioner. If no progress can, however, be made, recourse must be had to one's own personal opinion. Above all, discretion is vital (al-Dīnawarī, fols. 41-3).

All the authors stress the need to have a vast knowledge of all the sciences; all branches of knowledge are useful, including mathematics, law, etymology, onomastic, literature, proverbs, the practices of the Islamic cult, etc. Nothing has changed in the ancient principles of oneirocriticism; the only differences revealed in the course of time come from the conditions of men and their preoccupations, morals and whether they prefer immediate, present gains at the expense of the Afterlife, whereas previously, religious affairs formed the main activities of men. When the Prophet's Companions dreamed of dates, they saw there the sweetness of their religion; for them, honey signified the delights gained for them from reading the Ḳurʾān, knowledge and justice (Ibn Sīrīn, *Munta<u>kh</u>ab*, i, 21ff.).

One should say in conclusion that, despite the efforts of the oneirocritics to furnish their art with principles and techniques, they were forced to recognise that "the interpretation of dreams remains based on analogy, relationship, comparison and probability. One cannot base a course of action, nor refer to its findings, before their accomplishment in the waking state and even before proof for it is put forward" (*ibid.*, i, 4). In fact, wrote E. Doutté, *Magie et religion dans l'Afrique du Nord*, Algiers 1909, 407, "la pluralité des méthodes, l'arbitraire avec lequel on les emploie, l'abus de symbolisme font de l'oniromancie une pure fantaisie et il n'est pas un songe qui ne puisse, au gré du devin, être interprété d'une façon favorable ou défavorable aux intérêts de son client".

Nevertheless, the severe judgements of both ancients and moderns do not reduce the considerable value of oneirocritical literature for the light it throws on psychology, sociology and mysticism. Beneath dreams, simple or incoherent, there is a complex of passions, ambitions and dynastic rivalries. Whether spontaneous or fabricated, they are the vehicles for conceptions and ideas issuing from the popular milieu, one not widely revealed in other literary genres. Since the dream forms part of the life of rich and poor alike, it forms something like a screen between the dead past and the present, which can be used to reconstruct, with great precision and realism, the social life and aspirations of any given class at any fixed time.

Bibliography: 1. Sources. Artemidorus of Ephesus, *Book of dreams*, Ar. tr. from the Greek by Ḥunayn b. Isḥāḳ (d. 210/873), ed. T. Fahd, Damascus 1964; Abū Saʿīd Naṣr b. Yaʿḳūb al-Dīnawarī, *al-Ḳādirī fi 'l-taʿbīr*, ms. B.N. Paris, fonds ar. 2745; Ibn <u>Kh</u>aldūn, *Muḳaddima*, ed. Quatremère, Fr. tr. de Slane, Eng. tr. Rosenthal, ch. VI, § 17; Ps.-Ibn Sīrīn, *Munta<u>kh</u>ab al-kalām fī tafsīr al-aḥlām*, 3 vols. Būlāḳ 1294/1877.

2. Studies. A.L. Oppenheim, *The interpretation of dreams in the Ancient Near East*, in *Trans. Amer. Philosophical Soc.*, N.S. xliii/3, Philadelphia 1956, 179-373; T. Fahd, *Les songes et leurs interpretation en Islam*, Sources orientales 2, Paris 1959, repr. in *Études d'histoire et de civilisation islamiques*, Istanbul 1997, 37-60; idem, *Le rêve dans la société musulmane du Moyen Age*, in *Les rêves et les sociétés humaines. Colloque de Royaumont*, ed. G.E. von Grunebaum and R. Caillois, Paris 1967, 335-67, Span tr. Buenos Aires 1964, 193-230, Eng. tr. Berkeley and Los Angeles 1966, 351-79, repr. in Fahd, *Études*, 61-93; idem, *Le divination arabe*, Leiden 1965, repr. Paris 1987; idem, *L'oniromancie orientale et ses repercussions sur l'oniromancie de l'Occident médiéval*, in *Oriente e Occidente nel Medioeve. Filosofia e Scienze, 13° Convegno Internazionale della Fondazione Alessandro Volta, Rome-Florence 1969*, Rome 1971, 347-74, repr. in *Studies*, 95-119; idem, in *Dict. critique de l'esotérisme*, Paris 1998, arts. *Divination*, 412-21, *Rêve*, 107-9; Nadia al-Bagdadi, *The* Other-Eye. *Sight and insight in Arabic classical dream literature*, contrib. to colloquium on *Le regard dans la civilisation arabe classique*, Paris 2002, 22, with refs. to other recent works on the subject.

(T. FAHD)

TABRĪZĪ, <u>DJ</u>ALĀL AL-DĪN, Abu 'l-Ḳāsim, a saint of the Suhrawardiyya [*q.v.*] order (date of death perhaps 642/1244; <u>Gh</u>ulām Sarwar-i Lāhawrī, *<u>Kh</u>azīnat al-asfiyāʾ*).

Together with Bahāʾ al-Dīn Zakariyyā [*q.v.*], <u>Dj</u>alāl al-Dīn is to be counted as the founder of the order in India (Saiyid Athar Abbas Rizvi, *A history of Sufism in India*, New Delhi 1978, i, 190). After the death of his teacher Badr al-Dīn Abū Saʿīd Tabrīzī, <u>Dj</u>alāl al-Dīn went to Ba<u>gh</u>dād to join Abū Ḥafṣ ʿUmar al-Suhrawardī (d. 632/1234 [*q.v.*]), the eponym of the order, as a disciple, when al-Suhrawardī was already old. <u>Dj</u>alāl al-Dīn stayed with al-Suhrawardī for nearly a decade and he accompanied him on his annual pilgrimages to Mecca and Medina. In the company of Bahāʾ al-Dīn Zakariyyā who was to found a *<u>kh</u>ānaḳāh* in Multān, <u>Dj</u>alāl al-Dīn set out to travel to India (<u>Dj</u>āmī, *Nafaḥāt*, 504). However, they separated on the way, a fact explained by legend as follows: <u>Dj</u>alāl al-Dīn met the mystical poet ʿAṭṭār (d. 618/1221 [*q.v.*]) in Nī<u>sh</u>āpūr and was asked by him, who in Ba<u>gh</u>dād was to be included among the mystics. Impressed by the poet's spiritual presence <u>Dj</u>alāl al-Dīn is said not to have uttered the name of al-Suhrawardī (Či<u>sh</u>tī, *Mirʾāt al-asrār*, Staatsbibliothek zu Berlin SPK, Ms. orient. Quart. 1903, 284b). At the beginning of the 7th/13th century, during the reign of Iltutmi<u>sh</u> (607-33/1210-36 [*q.v.*]), <u>Dj</u>alāl al-Dīn arrived in India where he was warmly welcomed by the Sultan. The *<u>Sh</u>ay<u>kh</u> al-Islām* Na<u>dj</u>m al-Dīn, however, resented this and tried to influence the Sultan against the Ṣūfī (Či<u>sh</u>tī, *loc. cit.*). An accusation was concocted and in 1228 the Sultan organised an investigation, which was presided over by Bahāʾ al-Dīn Zakariyyā. Though the charge was soon found to be false, <u>Dj</u>alāl al-Dīn left Dihlī for Badāʾūn. There again <u>Dj</u>alāl al-Dīn became friendly with the ruling classes, viz. the local administrator Ḳāḍī Kamāl al-Dīn, who enrolled his son as <u>Dj</u>alāl al-Dīn's disciple.

Finally, <u>Dj</u>alāl al-Dīn reached Bengal where he settled down. In recruiting followers, <u>Dj</u>alāl al-Dīn converted many Hindus and Buddhists to Islam (Rizvi, ii, 398; Trimingham, 232). In accordance with the policy of the Suhrawardī order of supporting enforced conversion, <u>Dj</u>alāl al-Dīn demolished, at Devatalla in northern Bengal, a large temple that a *kāfir* (Hindu or Buddhist) had erected and constructed a monastery in its place. In the *Riḥla* of Ibn Baṭṭūṭā [*q.v.*], <u>Dj</u>alāl al-Dīn Tabrīzī is confused with <u>Sh</u>āh <u>Dj</u>alāl of Sylhet, one of the Bengali warrior saints (Rizvi, i, 314). In the Kāmrūp hills of Assam <u>Dj</u>alāl al-Dīn was said to have been met by the Moroccan traveller (*Riḥla*, iv,

216-22) who had reached India only in 734/1333. Djalāl al-Dīn's sanctuary in Sylhet is still visited by the devout to this very day (Lawrence, *Notes from a distant flute*, Tehran 1978, 63). Reliable information of his successors in Bengal is not available (Rizvi, i, 202).

Bibliography (in addition to references given in the article): Firis̲h̲ta, Muḥammad Ḳāsim Hindūs̲h̲āh, *Tārīk̲h̲-i Firis̲h̲ta*, Bombay 1831, ii, 760; Ḥāmid b. Faḍl Allāh Dihlawī "Djamālī", *Siyar al-ʿārifīn*, Dihlī 1311/1893; ʿAbd al-Ḥaḳḳ Muḥaddit̲h̲, *Ak̲h̲bār al-ak̲h̲yār*, Dihlī 1309, 44-6; Muḥammad ʿAlī Tarbiyat, *Dānis̲h̲mandān-i Ād̲h̲arbāyd̲j̲ān*, Tehran 1314/1935, 97; Storey, ii, 971 and n. 7.   (F. Sobieroj)

TABS̲H̲ĪR (A.), lit. "proclamation, spreading of the good news", a term used in modern works for Christian proselytism in various forms and the work of missionaries (*mubas̲h̲s̲h̲irūn*) within the Islamic world.

The use of the word, if not the activity which it denotes, does not seem to go back beyond the end of the 19th century, being at one and the same time contemporaneous with the Arab renaissance (*Nahḍa* [*q.v.*]), European colonialism and the development of Christian missions. It seems to be a term of Christian origin, corresponding to its usage in Arabic translations of the Bible for Grk. *evangelion* "announcement of good news", as evidenced in the Protestant (London-Beirut 1831) and the Roman Catholic (Beirut 1898) translations, where in Mark, xvi, 16, we have, however, *aʿlinū al-bis̲h̲āra* without, however, the form *tabs̲h̲īr*. *Tabs̲h̲īr* does not appear in such classical dictionaries as *LʿA* and *TA*, and *bis̲h̲āra* is found for the first time in Freytag's Arabic-Latin dictionary (Halle 1830-7, i, 124) in the sense of *evangelium*, uncapitalised and without any connotation of the Gospel itself. Lane, *Lexicon*, i, 208, simply has *mubas̲h̲s̲h̲ir* in the general sense of "one who announces good news". Buṭrus al-Bustānī in his *Muḥīṭ* (Beirut 1867, i, 95) is the first person to give a reasoned definition, citing the expression *bis̲h̲ārat al-ind̲j̲īl*, where the origin of this neologism is explained: *id̲āfa bayyina li-anna al-Ind̲j̲īl maʿnāhu al-bis̲h̲āra bi 'l-yūnāniyya*. Curiously, and in which he is followed by the author of the dictionary *Aḳrab al-mawārid* (1889), he mentions (96) that *al-bas̲h̲īr* means, in a general way, *al-mubas̲h̲s̲h̲ir wa 'l-d̲j̲amīl* and that it is the epithet given to St. Luke by the Christians, *laḳab Mār Lūḳā ʿind al-Naṣārā*. Words from this root *b-s̲h̲-r* occur several times in the Ḳurʾān (ʿAbd al-Bāḳī, *Muʿd̲j̲am al-mufahras*, Cairo 1378/[1945], 119-21), especially in the verbal forms *bas̲h̲s̲h̲ara* and *abs̲h̲ara*, whose ambivalent sense can announce some good news but also, in menacing tones, the coming of bad news; *mubas̲h̲s̲h̲ir* is attested in speaking, *inter alios*, of the Prophet, but not *tabs̲h̲īr* in regard to him.

It is impossible to discuss here the innumerable books and articles devoted directly or indirectly to *tabs̲h̲īr*; only a few representative ones, in Arabic, of the mediaeval period will be given. The enquiry ought, however, to be extended beyond the Arab to the wider Islamic world, notably to India and Indonesia.

Reading these works, one notes that, at different levels, the authors treat various aspects of the subject. Two forms of *tabs̲h̲īr* are distinguished. The direct one is an effort by churches and missionaries in the strict sense, *mubas̲h̲s̲h̲irūn*, to announce to Muslims the Christian "good news". It involves, then, an individual or collective enterprise of the Christians, openly proclaimed. Distinguished from it is a more radical notion, sometimes confused with the first, envisaging directly "conversion" or more precisely, Christianisation, *tanṣīr*, a *maṣdar* or verbal noun of Form II from the collec-

tive designation of Christians, *al-Naṣārā* [*q.v.*], traditional among the Muslims.

The *tabs̲h̲īr* in these works can denote proselytisation aimed directly at Muslims but equally, and frequently, aimed at whole populations, as in Black Africa or amongst certain ethnic minorities not connected with Judaism or Islam, as in the Sudan, in Chad or in other countries of Africa and elsewhere. These Christian missionary activities, openly declared, have for the most part their origins in Western, traditionally Christian—Catholic or Protestant—countries, but do not stem, above all in the Near East, from the churches or members of the Eastern Christian churches, present in that region for two millennia. However, according to authorities consulted, certain members of these local churches may have been involved in the missionary activities, *tabs̲h̲īriyya*, of missionaries of Western origin. Finally, the term "the West" embraces not only Europe, but also North America, especially the United States, even though colonisation activities in predominantly Muslim lands have never been directly launched, so these authors state, from the USA.

Alongside this direct, avowed missionary work, numerous authors devote—some more, perhaps, than others—an important place to the indirect form of *tabs̲h̲īr*, one that is "hidden" or "stealthy", which, with concealed motives, uses diversionary means (cultural, charitable and political) to achieve its aims indirectly. The authors who denounce this indirect missionary work connect it to two main trends, which, they allege, are its main inspirers, viz. colonisation (*istiʿmār*) and orientalism (*istis̲h̲rāḳ*).

The titles of certain works on this theme, placing *tabs̲h̲īr* in direct connection with colonisation, are revelatory enough of this fact. One may cite e.g. Muṣṭafā K̲h̲ālidī and ʿUmar Farrūk̲h̲, whose work is often cited as a reference work on the topic, *al-Tabs̲h̲īr wa 'l-istiʿmar fi 'l-bilād al-ʿarabiyya: ʿard li-d̲j̲uhūd al-mubas̲h̲s̲h̲irīn allatī tarmī ilā ik̲h̲bāʾ al-s̲h̲ark li 'l-istiʿmār al-g̲h̲arbī* (Beirut 1953) and, more recently, ʿAbd al-Fattāḥ Aḥmad Abū Zāyida, *al-Tabs̲h̲īr al-ṣalībī wa 'l-g̲h̲azw al-istiʿmārī* (Malta 1988) (see Ṭalāl ʿAtrīsī, *al-Baʿt̲h̲a al-yasūʿiyya: muhimmat īʿdād al-nak̲h̲ba al-siyāsiyya fī Lubnān*, 1987), which emphasise the school, University and charitable activities of certain religious orders, in general French- or English-speaking, practising this indirect form of *tabs̲h̲īr*. Limiting ourselves to the Near East, the main University institutions envisaged are the American University of Beirut (AUB), the Jesuit Université Saint-Joseph, also at Beirut, and the American University in Cairo (AUC), the first two of which have a religious orientation and were founded in the second half of the 19th century, that of the *Nahḍa* and of colonisation [see DJĀMIʿA].

On the same track, there is a great stress on the introduction of foreign languages, English and French, as hidden means of detaching student élites of the Near East from their own language, Arabic, and their original culture, that of the Ḳurʾān and Islam, and as a means of making favourable comparisons in favour of the West, especially in the domains of technical and industrial progress. Another of the means (*wasāʾil*) of this second form of *tabs̲h̲īr* is the encouragement by these educational establishments of developing, on the one hand, the use of the various Arabic dialects, *al-lahad̲j̲āt al-ʿāmmiyya*, and on the other, the use of non-Arabic local languages, Syriac, Kurdish, Berber, Armenian, etc., in order to perpetuate divisions between the peoples of the Near East, to "divide and rule", and thereby prevent the wider diffusion of Islam. This is an argument already used, in a slightly different context, by authors of the Salafiyya [*q.v.*] at the end of the 19th and beginning of the 20th centuries, admittedly without recourse to the term *tab<u>sh</u>īr*, e.g. in the commentary of the *Manār* [see AL-MANĀR] on sūra V, 82. Also attacked are the endeavours of these establishments to promote or to favour various forms of bilingualism or trilingualism to the detriment of the one language, Arabic.

Certain authors go even further and allege that these missionary enterprises find agents (*ʿumalāʾ*) to aid them within the heart of the Arabic and Islamic worlds themselves, and they cite in particular passages from the famous work of Ṭāhā Ḥusayn [*q.v.*], *Mustaḳbal al-<u>th</u>aḳāfa fī Miṣr*, or that of Ḳāsim Amīn [*q.v.*], *al-Marʾa al-<u>dj</u>adīda* (see ʿAbd al-ʿAẓīm al-Murtaḍā, *al-Tab<u>sh</u>īr al-ʿālamī ḍidd al-Islām, ahdāfuhu, wasāʾiluhu, ṭuruḳuhu, muwā<u>dj</u>ahātuhu*, Miṣr al-<u>Dj</u>adīda 1992, 37 ff.).

Orientalism, *isti<u>sh</u>rāḳ*, is often mentioned and denounced as one of the indirect means of *tab<u>sh</u>īr*. Without always avoiding a facile juxtaposition, but with some persons recognising the positive aspects of *isti<u>sh</u>rāḳ*, this link between the two notions brought together in this fashion often goes on to an analysis of the "religious and missionary impulse" of the orientalists' activities, *al-dāfiʿ al-dīnī al-tab<u>sh</u>īrī* (see Ṣulṭān ʿAbd al-Ḥamīd Ṣulṭān, *Min ṣuwar al-<u>gh</u>azwī al-fikrī li 'l-Islām: al-tab<u>sh</u>īr, al-isti<u>sh</u>rāḳ al-ʿilmāniyya*, Cairo 1990, 166). The idea that *tab<u>sh</u>īr* and *isti<u>sh</u>rāḳ* are linked derives its origin from the fact that a certain number of orientalists, above all those who lived or published works in the Arab-Muslim lands, were indeed members of religious orders or missionary societies. Hence in a general way, some of their more critical attitudes, if not the whole body of their works, are considered to be hidden methods of sapping the foundations of the doctrines of Islam, especially by dwelling on the controversial aspects of the Ḳurʾān and the life of Muḥammad, or, on another level, by an exclusive orientation towards certain aspects of Islamic mysticism, etc. On this negative role of the orientalists, allied hand-in-hand with *tab<u>sh</u>īr*, one may refer to the opinions of ʿAbd al-Laṭīf al-<u>Sh</u>uwayrif, *Ā<u>th</u>ār al-isti<u>sh</u>rāḳ wa-kayfa muwā<u>dj</u>ihatuhu*, in *<u>Dj</u>awhar al-Islām*, vi/1 (Tunis 1973).

One may conclude this summary sketch with some reflections. The first is that this idea of *tab<u>sh</u>īr* and the positions taken up by those involved with it, should be placed in a much wider and more ancient context, often far from eirenic, of Islamo-Christian relations in general, and, since the end of the 19th century, of relations between Islam and the West, regarded as an emanation of and as being representative of Christianity. On the more particular level of the basic choices of the two religions regarding *tab<u>sh</u>īr*, one may add that these two religions see themselves equally, although employing differing means, as faiths dealing with universal final ends, bearers of a message meant for men of all places and ages, a message which can bring into action an expansionist dynamism that explains, even if it does not justify, some of the methods used by the Islamic side regarding the idea of *tab<u>sh</u>īr* studied here. Finally, let it be said that the examples discussed above and their tentative analysis do not in any way represent the positions of the most authoritative and representative of the faithful of each of the two religions.

Bibliography: As indicated above, this cannot be exhaustive. In addition to references given in the article, see ʿAbd al-Wadūd <u>Sh</u>alabī, *Afīḳū ayyuhā al-muslimīn ḳabl an tadfaʾū al-<u>dj</u>izya*, Cairo 1997; Saʿd al-Dīn al-Sayyid Ṣāliḥ, *Iḥ<u>dh</u>arū al-asālīb al-ḥadī<u>th</u>a fī muwā<u>dj</u>ahāt al-islām*, Cairo 1998, esp. 25-109. For a global presentation of *tab<u>sh</u>īr* in the first half of the 20th century, which highlights its relative check in face of Islam, above all in Africa and Asia, see the art. *Tab<u>sh</u>īr*, in Muḥammad Farīd Wa<u>dj</u>dī, *Dāʾirat al-maʿārif al-ḳarn al-rābiʿ a<u>sh</u>ar/al-ʿi<u>sh</u>rīn*, 1937, i, 205-20, and see also Ḥasan Ḥanafī, *Mā<u>dh</u>ā yaʿnī ʿilm al-isti<u>gh</u>rāb*, Beirut 2000, Preface. On the links between orientalism and *tab<u>sh</u>īr*, E. Said, *Orientalism*, London 1978, Fr. tr. 1980, Ar. tr. 1981; *EI*², art. MUSTA<u>SH</u>RIḲŪN (J.J. Waardenburg), Vol. VII, 745ff.; *al-Fikr al-ʿarabī*, xxxi (Jan.-March 1983), xxxii (April-June 1983), on *isti<u>sh</u>rāḳ*; *Études arabes*, lxxxiii (1992/2), PISAI, Rome, dossier on *al-musta<u>sh</u>riḳūn*. For the views of an Arab academic on European orientalists, see ʿAbd al-Raḥmān Badawī, *Mawsūʿat al-musta<u>sh</u>riḳūn*, ³Beirut 1992. Also E. Rudolph, *Westlische Islamwissenschaft im Spiegel muslimischer Kritik*, Berlin 1991. On earlier relations of Islam and the West, see N. Daniel, *Islam and the West, the making of an image*, Edinburgh 1960, Fr. tr. *L'Islam et l'Occident*, Paris 1993; idem, *The Arabs and mediaeval Europe*, ²London and New York 1979; F. Cardini, *Europe e islam. Storia di un malinteso*, Rome-Bari 2000, Fr. tr. *Europe et Islam, histoire d'un malentendu*, Paris 2000.

(L. POUZET)

ṬĀHIR BEG, MEḤMED, late Ottoman journalist, publisher, and owner of journals, newspapers, and a printing-house in Istanbul (1864-1912). He was one of the journalists and publishers who were supported by ʿAbd al-Ḥamīd II, being awarded various medals and decorations by the Sultan.

Information about his family and education is limited. Re<u>dj</u>āʾī-zāde Ekrem [*q.v.*] reports that Ṭāhir Beg's mother looked after his older son. It is known that he was working as a reporter at *<u>Th</u>erwet*, the newspaper published in Turkish by Dimitraki Nikolaidi between 1307/1891 and 1324/1908. That he was a well-known figure in the press and publishing world can be deduced from the names of the staff of his journals and newspapers, from the variety of the authors of the books he published at his printing-house, from the fact that he introduced Aḥmed Rāsim [*q.v.*] into journalism, and from his getting articles from Re<u>dj</u>āʾī-zāde to publish in his journals and printing a book translated by Aḥmed Iḥsān Tokgöz [see AḤMAD IḤSĀN] at his printing-house, although he had many conflicts with both of these in later years. Thanks to his high connections, he was able to resume publishing his journal *Maʿlūmāt* very soon after it was suppressed or confiscated for various reasons.

He was notorious in the world of Turkish press and publication as the first person in the history of Turkish journalism to produce false news and then to take bribes for publishing denials of it, so that his *laḳab* (*Baba Ṭāhir*) is given as an example for such situations. First, abusing his proximity to the Ottoman Sultan, he supplied the latter with names to be given ranks, decorations and medals, these persons being close to him, and he published those names in his newspaper. Then he printed bogus certificates at his printing-house, employed an Italian engraver to produce spurious decorations and sold them, especially to foreigners. In addition, he printed publications opposing the Palace and then informed the Palace that the "Young Turks" were printing such journals in Egypt. In 1901, together with Dr. M. Pa<u>sh</u>a, he denounced the journal *<u>Th</u>erwet-i Fünūn* [*q.v.*] and caused it to be suppressed for 40 days and its owner and writers to be arraigned in court. He published Re<u>dj</u>āʾī-zāde Ekrem Beg's *<u>Sh</u>emsā* in his journal *Maʿlūmāt* without his permission.

When his offences were revealed, he was arrested, tried and in 1903 sentenced to 15 years' imprisonment. But, only after five years, benefiting from the amnesty declared after the *Meshrūṭiyyet* in 1908, he returned to Istanbul. He was then kept under surveillance by the police authorities and not permitted to publish his newspaper again. Having been involved in the incident of 31 March 1325/13 April 1909, he was exiled to Tripoli, but after a while escaped from there to Naples and then to Paris. In both places he established businesses, but these failed. From the fact that A.I. Tokgöz's article on his death is dated 16 February 1912, it appears that he died at the beginning of that month in Paris.

He published five journals and newspapers: *Bahār* (1299/1883, 19 issues, fortnightly), *Therwet* (1314-18/1898-1903, 2088 issues, daily), *Irtiḳā'* (1315-19/1899-1904, 251 issues, weekly), *Maʿlūmāt* (1311-18/1895-1903, journal-newspaper, 2443 issues, weekly-daily) and *Muṣawwer Fenn we Edeb* (1315-19/1899-1903, 222 issues, weekly). Initially 48 issues of the *Maʿlūmāt* were published by the Artin Asadoryan Press weekly (1309-11/1894-5). *Maʿlūmāt*, with its writers and contents, filled an important gap during the period when it was published. Since it attracted attention through photographs and illustrations having also French subtitles, it was also known as the *Muṣawwer Maʿlūmāt*. The journal was distributed throughout the Ottoman lands, Persia and Russia. It was also printed locally in Filibe [*q.v.*] under the title *Āfāḳ-ī Sharḳiyyeden Ṭulūʿ Eden Maʿlūmāt* (1314/1896). Readers' letters sent from places like Cyprus, the Mediterranean shores, the Aegean Islands, Algeria and Egypt, show the extent of the domain where it was being read. Some of its issues were in Arabic and Persian, and it had supplements on diverse themes (*Khanïmlara Maḥṣūṣ Maʿlūmāt, Ilāwe-i Maʿlūmāt*, etc.). The journals *Maʿlūmāt* and *Therwet-i Fünūn* were always in a state of rivalry, but while *Therwet-i Fünūn* was the journal supporting modern literature, *Maʿlūmāt* was the journal of supporters of a more moderate line (*mutawassiṭ*) in literature.

Apart from these, Ṭāhir Beg also published books at his printing-house. According to Seyfettin Özege's catalogue, 95 books were printed at the *Maṭbaʿa-i Ṭāhir Beg* between the years 1311-19/1895-1903. Among these were books printed in three languages: in Turkish-Arabic-French or in Persian-Turkish-French. Moreover, it is known that some French books were also printed by him. Some of the books have the name of the series *Maʿlūmāt Kütüphanesi* or *Ṭāhir Beg Kütüphanesi* and the publisher's name as *Maʿlūmāt ve Therwet gazeteleri ṣāḥib-i imtiyāzï es-Seyyid Meḥmed Ṭāhir*. In the books, the name of the printing-house is given as *Maṭbaʿa-i Ṭāhir Beg, Ṭāhir Beg Maṭbaʿasï, Ṭāhir Beg'in 40 numaralï Maṭbaʿasï* and *Maʿlūmāt Gazeteleri ve Ṭāhir Beg Maṭbaʿasï*. The relation with Ṭāhir Beg's printing-house of the 20 books that appeared in Seyfettin Özege's catalogue as having been printed at the *Maʿlūmāt Maṭbaʿasï* between 1311-17/1894-1901, is a matter which still needs to be examined. Ṭāhir Beg had received the privilege of printing official documents at his printing-house during the period when the *Maṭbaʿa-i ʿĀmire* was closed.

Bibliography: Maḥmūd, *Khafiyelerin listesi: ikindji djüzʿde 988 khafiyye var!*, djüzʿ 2, Istanbul 13[2]4/1909, 65-7; Aḥmed Iḥsān [Tokgöz], *ʿOthmānlï maṭbūʿātï. Maʿlūmātdjï Baba Ṭāhir*, in *Therwet*, no. 1080 (9 Shubāṭ 1327/4 Rebīʿ ül-ewwel 1327/20 February 1912), 337-40; Aḥmed Rāsim, *Maṭbūʿāt khāṭiralarïndan: muharrir, shaʿir, edīb*, Istanbul 1342/1924, 89-94; Münir Süleyman Çapanoğlu, *Basın tarihine dair bilgiler ve hatıralar*, Istanbul 1962, 8-11, 155; idem, *Basın tarihimizde parazitler*, Istanbul 1967, 11-4; Halid Ziya Uşaklıgil, *Kırk yıl*, Istanbul 1969, 423; Seyfettin Özege, *Eski harflerle basılmış Türkçe eserler kataloğu*, 5 vols. Istanbul 1971-82; Hasan Duman (ed.), *İstanbul kütüphaneleri Arap harfli süreli yayınlar kataloğu: 1828-1928*, Istanbul 1986, 5, 180-1, 229, 234-5, 354; Ahmed İhsan Tokgöz, *Matbuat hatıralarım*, ed. Alpay Kabacalı, Istanbul 1993, *passim*; art. *Malumat*, in *Türk Dili ve Edebiyat Ansiklopedisi*, vi, Istanbul 1996, 128-9; Bilge Ercilasun, *Ahmet Ihsan Tokgöz*, Ankara 1996, 23, 77-80.

(Hatice Aynur)

TAḲĀLĪD (a.), pl. of the *maṣdar* or verbal noun *taḳlīd*, the Form II verb *ḳallada* having the meaning, *inter alia*, "to mimic, imitate" (for *taḳlīd* in its legal and theological context, see the art. s.v.), is used in Arabic today for the ensemble of inherited folk traditions and practices, popular customs and manners, and folklore in general, although the loanword from English *fulklūr*, is often used, especially for the discipline and its study at large. In recent years also, the term *al-turāth al-shaʿbī* "folk inheritance" is being used to denote the common Arabic heritage of popular culture.

According to the common definition of the term "folklore", it denotes the cultural popular traditions which are passed on from generation to generation and their study. Folklore may be divided into five main categories: (1) Oral traditions: folktales, legends, myths, fables, riddles, jokes; popular poems, common expressions, expletives and oaths; (2) Written materials: proverbs, amulets and talismans; (3) Traditional practices: food and drinks, clothes, embroidery, cosmetics, jewellery, household tools and furniture; popular medicine, witchcraft; customs and manners; (4) Beliefs and superstitions; and (5) Popular art: popular theatre, songs, dances, musical instruments, paintings, drawings and sculpting.

1. In the Arab world.

Although descriptions of popular traditions and customs among Arabs, mainly the Bedouin, appear already in early Arab literature, and, in particular, within travel literature, serious discussion of Arab folklore only started in the 19th century with the appearance of works such as E.W. Lane's (1801-76) *An account of the manners and customs of the modern Egyptians* (1836). However, research of this field was not very common until the second half of the 20th century. This omission is clearly illustrated by Aḥmad Amīn (1878-1954) in the introduction to his *Ḳāmūs al-ʿādāt wa 'l-taḳālīd wa 'l-taʿābīr al-miṣriyya* (²Cairo 1953) in which he says: "I sincerely believe that historians have deliberately neglected popular aspects in their books of history, showing off their aristocracy, although popular literature, in many respects, is not of less importance than the literary Arabic language and literature. . . . It is quite possible that some aristocratic scholars will look askance and be bewildered as to how an academic professor degrades himself by recording manners and popular expressions which concern the populace" (pp. II-III).

This attitude among Arab scholars towards their popular heritage in the past resembles their attitude towards the study of Arabic dialects, which also won recognition as a discipline worth investigating only during the second half of the 20th century after the appearance of works by non-Arab scholars who valued both Arab heritage and Arabic dialects and consequently published extensively on both subjects.

Oral traditions have been known for generations and in particular the art of the story-telling of folktales (*ḳiṣaṣ sha'biyya*; in colloquial Arabic *ḥikāya* [*q.v.*] or *ḥaddūta* (from *uḥdūtha* "speech, tale"), which was usually carried out by an elder member of the family or by the local "professional" teller (*ḥakawātī*). The best example of such a genre is the famous *Thousand and One Nights* [see ALF LAYLA WA-LAYLA]. The genre of fables is represented by *Kalīla wa-Dimna* [*q.v.*] attributed to the Indian philosopher Bidpai (4th century B.C.) and rendered into Arabic by Ibn al-Muḳaffa' (721-57 [*q.v.*]). Another genre is that of amusing anecdotes (*nawādir, mulaḥ*), e.g. the funny stories of Djuḥā [*q.v.*] (Turkish: Nāṣir al-Dīn Khodja [*q.v.*]), about whose real existence or non-existence scholars are divided. It is mainly the Bedouin and the inhabitants of rural areas around the Middle East who still continue with the long tradition of story-telling which, together with riddles (*ḥazzūrāt* or *ḥazāzīr*), and jokes (*nukat*), are the most common and basic forms of entertainment. Several collections have been published and new editions continue to appear, sometimes offering the reader different versions of the same story or anecdote.

Another important genre which has been very popular from old times are poems composed by professional or amateur poets to commemorate a special occasion or event, such as parties in honour of a person, weddings, eulogies or obituary speeches. Although these poems usually take the form of the Arabic *ḳaṣīda* [*q.v.*], which is composed in literary Arabic, some are recited in colloquial or something resembling Middle Arabic, similar to common songs which are performed on such occasions.

So far as common expressions, expletives and oaths are concerned, they are usually associated with special situations and circumstances or etiquette, such as weddings, the birth of a child, bereavement, etc., which are often connected with local customs. These are usually recorded in the various dialect dictionaries. What most of them, however, have in common is the fact that many of them contain the word *Allāh*, including the commonest expression used for encouragement and urging: *yalla* (in the name of God), and the word *walla(hi)* (by God!), used customarily to express astonishment or as an oath. Other common words used as oaths are: *wi-ḥyāt rabbina* (by God), *wi 'l-nabi* (by the Prophet), *wa-ḥayātī/wa-ḥayātak* (by my/your life), *wa-ḥayāt rāsī/rāsak* (by my/your head), *wa-ḥayāt wlādī* (by my children), *wi-ḥyāt* or *bi-raḥmat ummī/abūy* (by the memory of my mother/father), *bi-sharafī* (by my honour) and *ḥalaft bi 'l-ṭalāḳ* (I swear I will divorce my wife). Common expressions often used are: e.g. when a person sneezes, people say to him *raḥimaka allāh* (may God have mercy upon you), or simply *te'īsh* (may you live long), and when a person leaves, others wish him *Allāh ma'ak* (may God be with you). The word *mabrūk* is the commonest wish to congratulate people on the occasion of an engagement, marriage, birth, new house, car, job, clothes, etc. Sometimes the dual, and the number one thousand are used in good or bad wishes for emphasis: *ṣaḥtēn* (bon appetit); *marḥabtēn* (hello); *'amayēn* ("double blindness", i.e. Hell!); *alf mabrūk* (lit. a thousand blessings, i.e. congratulations!); *alf dāhiya* ("thousand hells"). A reference to shoes, dogs and donkeys (and in some areas to a woman) is immediately followed by the speaker with the expressions *ba'īd 'annak* (lit. far from you) or *adjallak* (lit. you are more respected than the object mentioned).

Written materials include proverbs (*amthāl*) [see MATHAL], a genre well known in classical Arabic literature as one of the earliest and most common compositions in prose, even though some of them are based on Arabic poetry. The thousands of proverbs found in Arabic demonstrate the important role they play in writing and in daily discourse. Moreover, as many proverbs depict a situation or give advice or warning, it is customary among Arabic speakers or writers to use them in order to illustrate their speech/written work to draw conclusions of a comparable situation. Old collections of Arabic proverbs, such as that of al-Maydānī (d. 518/1124 [*q.v.*]), are constantly being reprinted while new collections of proverbs, arranged by countries, continue to appear.

Amulets and talismans (*tamā'im, ruḳayāt, ta'āwīdh, ṭalāsim, 'azā'im, ḥudjub*) are very popular, especially in rural areas [see RUḲYA; TAMĪMA]. Many of these are meant to protect the bearer against the evil eye [see 'AYN], bring blessing and prosperity, speed the recovery from an illness or bring good luck in general. The most popular amulet is the one in the shape of an open hand called *khamsa*, i.e. "five", referring to the five fingers of the hand, which are meant "to stop" bad luck or envy. The amulet may be a copy of the Ḳur'ān, a few verses from it or brief statements such as: *'eyn al-ḥasūd lā tasūd* (May the eye of the one who envies never prevail) or *'eyn al-ḥasūd fīhā 'ūd* (The eye of the one who envies will have a piece of wood in it), but may also be simple blue beads, a piece of blue cloth (since the eyes of the devil are believed to be blue), leaves or flowers of certain plants and even a pinch of salt. It is customary to give such amulets to children or hang them at home, in the car, at work and even on animals. There are also talismans which are written in a code or contain numerals and other symbols which are only known to the writer. Moreover, although the traditional rosary, commonly used by men (*misbaḥa*), is more associated with a ritual based on the custom of mentioning on every occasion God's Most Beautiful Names (*al-asmā' al-ḥusnā* [*q.v.*]), it may also be regarded as a kind of talisman.

Traditional practices vary from region to region and from one society to another. That is to say, daily practices of the urban society may differ from those of the rural one in the same way that they may be different between one Arab country and another and between sedentary and nomad society. Hence, what, for example, is generally known in the West as Oriental cuisine may have different recipes, names of ingredients and occasions for their consumption. Thus *harīsa* is the term for a dish of meat and bulgur, but in Egypt it refers to a sweet pastry made of flour, melted butter and sugar (see Wehr, under *harīsa*). Bread is called in Syro-Palestine *khubz*, whereas in Egypt it is called *'eysh* (which has the same meaning as "life"). Flesh of lamb (*kharūf*) is usually consumed in festivals such as Ramaḍān and the two 'Īds, as well as sweets (*ḥalwayyāt*) such as *kunāfa, baḳlawa, ghurayba* and *ma'mūl*. Sweets, mainly for children, such as *ghazl al-banāt* ("girls' spinning") are also popular on special occasions. Incidentally, the ingredients used for these dishes or the method of their preparation may differ from one region to another. Traditional food served in family celebrations such as weddings, birth of a child or bereavement may also vary in accordance with the local customs, except for bereavements when sweet dishes are normally avoided.

Coffee (*ḳahwa* [*q.v.*]) and tea (*shāy* [see ČAY]) are the most popular drinks all around the Middle East. Black coffee, usually with cardamon (*hēl*), may be served with sugar (*maḍbūṭ*) or without (*sāda*) in small cups, after being boiled a few times, first without sugar and then with. Tea is always strong and very sweet and is usually served with mint leaves (*naʿnaʿ*). The popularity of coffee has, over the years, given rise to a whole ethos: it is offered to guests, and in addition, to mark reaching an agreement concerning engagement, transactions or settlement of feud. It is also customary to offer bitter coffee in the house of a bereaved family to people who have come to express their condolences. Several customs are current in various areas which are associated with coffee drinking, such as, shaking the cup to indicate that no more coffee is wanted or using the word *dāyman* or *al-ḳahwe dāyme* ("always", i.e. may coffee always be in this house) to thank the host after finishing drinking, or the word *ʿāmir* (lit. fully inhabited, i.e. may this house never again suffer the loss of any of its members), when finishing drinking coffee in a house of a bereaved family. The third cup of coffee, when offered to a guest, may symbolise, in some areas, a start of enmity or it may politely hint that the meeting is over and that the guest is expected to leave. Telling the fate of the drinker by a "coffee reader", who scrutinises the dregs of the coffee in the bottom of his cup, is also a very popular custom around the Middle East. Finally, drinking coffee in cafés while smoking a hookah (*arḏjīla, narḏjīla* or *s̲h̲īs̲h̲a*), and reading or chatting with friends is another daily popular custom for one's leisure.

Traditional Arab clothes vary: upper and middle class urban citizens are increasingly wearing western clothes, while the lower class males among the fellahin and the Bedouin usually wear the *gallabiyya, ḏjilbāb, ḳufṭān, ḳumbāz* (or *ḳunbāz*), *ʿabāʾa* (or *ʿabāya*), *ḏjubba, dis̲h̲dās̲h̲a; sirwāl* (or *s̲h̲irwāl*) and cover their heads with the *kūfiyya* and *ʿaḳāl, ṭaḳiyya* (cap) or *laffe* (lap kerchief). Few men wear today the *ṭarbūs̲h̲* (or fez) or *ʿaraḳiyya*, while the European *burnēṭa* is hardly seen. Often a combination of the ordinary European *banṭalōn* (trousers), *ḳamīṣ* (shirt) and *ḏjakita* (jacket) are worn, while the head is covered with a *kūfiyya* and *ʿakāl*. Religious leaders, orthodox people or teachers at rural schools, however, still cover their heads with a *laffe* or *ʿimāma* (turban). Most women who belong to the upper and middle classes normally wear European dresses (*fustān*) or suits (*ṭaḳm*), while those who belong to the lower class usually wear the traditional *milāya* and cover their head with a *mindīl*. In strict Muslim society, only married women cover their faces with a veil (*burḳuʿ, lit̲h̲ām, ṭarḥa* or *yas̲h̲mak*). It is worth mentioning that both sexes of the upper and middle classes often wear traditional clothes at home and on special occasions. The traditional clothes, in general, are embroidered and often made in deep colours [see further, LIBĀS].

Traditional jewellery is still worn by women, and is mainly made of gold or silver. Diamonds may be worn by women of means, while the middle and lower classes wear various precious and cheap stones. It is often customary for a woman to wear several necklaces, bracelets, earrings and rings, and Bedouin women wear in addition noserings and anklets. Many of these are made of coloured beads or old coins that are no longer in circulation. The names of women's jewellery differ from area to area. Men adorn themselves mainly with rings, gold watches and ornamented daggers, whereas some women and men, especially Bedouin, have in addition various tattoos [see WAS̲H̲M]. The most popular make-up, which is also associated with good luck and used against the evil eye, is henna [see ḤINNĀʾ], used mainly by women though many men also use it. Henna constitutes part of the wedding ceremony preparations all around the Middle East.

Traditional household tools, furniture, fixtures and fittings are still in use especially in rural regions and by the lower class. They vary from one area to another and have different names. Thus one still may find in the kitchen the traditional *hāwin* or *ḏjurn* (mortar) used for grinding coffee and spices; *bakraḏj* or *dalla* (coffee pot), *finḏjān* (coffee cup) and many more articles. The same applies to traditional furniture which often has names of non-Arabic origin, e.g. *mūbīlya* (furniture), *dikka* (sofa-like bench), *ṭāwla* (table), *burdāi* (curtain), *lamba* (lamp).

Popular medicine is still practised in rural areas and by some Bedouin tribes, and even the urban and the higher classes often resort to traditional methods for curing less complicated illnesses. Various herbs, fruit, oil and special liquids may be used as medications. Thus onion drops are still used in Egypt against trachoma and watermelon seeds are prescribed for high blood pressure. Smallpox may be treated by burning dung near the sick child. Fig juice is used against corns or calluses, while burning or cauterising the skin against pain, fear and paralysis is believed to alleviate suffering.

Witchcraft and magic are used for three main purposes: to avert the evil eye, to cure illnesses and to regain the affections of the husband. The first involves various customs such as writing on a piece of a paper the name of the person who is believed to have put the evil eye on one, then setting it on fire while pouring salt on it and reciting some formulae that basically wish the person total destruction or blindness. The second witchcraft practice mainly involves the use of talismans or "blessed" objects or plants prepared usually by older people known for their piety [see TILSAM], and the third, which is called *s̲h̲abs̲h̲aba*, denotes a ritual mostly current in Egypt in which a woman casts a spell by beating her genitals with a slipper while pronouncing a magic formula to jinx an inattentive husband or a female rival. (See Hinds-Badawi, under *s̲h̲.b.s̲h̲.b.*)

Customs and manners. Since the Arabs themselves often describe their society as devout, emotional and fatalist, it is not surprising that scores of customs and manners are current within the Arab world, making the discussion of even a fraction of them an impossible task within the present article. Moreover, the diversity and heterogeneity of Arab society with its long history and contacts with other cultures (e.g. Persian and Turkish) prevent any attempt at formulating a monolithic ethos.

Among the characteristics typical of the Arabs are hospitality, generosity and strong commitment to the family and tribe. Hence most of the customs and manners current among Arab society revolve around those. Moreover, the general attitude towards life and death is of resignation to fate. Hence it is customary to accept happiness and tragedy with the same dictum, expressing praise to God (*ḥamdala*) and bearing in mind that, in the case of death, the deceased will eventually reach a better world.

Many customs are mentioned in the *Ḥadīt̲h̲* literature as practices attributed to the Prophet Muḥammad, hence are *sunan* which should obviously be adhered to by all Muslims. For example, customs concerning hygiene, such as bathing or the need to clean the teeth (*taswīk*) with a toothpick (*sawwāk* or *siwāk* [see MISWĀK]), or food. Eating "procedures" include washing the hands before and after the meal; saying the *basmala* before starting; encouraging the guest to eat more. Satiety is indicated by leaving some food on the plate (in some communities, satiety is indicated by burping), and wishing the host that his table will always be full (*al-sufra dāyma*), or wishing the lady of the house that her hands will be protected by God (*tislam/yislamū* or *yesallem idēkī*).

Many customs recorded by classical Arabic literature not only suggest that the Arabs paid considerable attention to good manners but that some of these older customs are still current in the society. For example, the custom of holding food with the right hand and with three fingers is mentioned by D̲j̲alāl al-Dīn al-Suyūṭī (d. 911/1505), who explains that using one finger in order to hold the food is abominated, two fingers show arrogance, while four fingers indicate gorging (*al-Kanz al-madfūn*, 182).

Other customs concerning etiquette are numerous. Most of them concern family life, e.g. a husband and wife may address each other in front of other people as *umm*... (the mother of...) or *abū*... (the father of...) followed by the name of the first-born, or as *ibn ʿammī* or *bint ʿammī* (my cousin). A non-member of the family must not show interest in any female. Hence, when wishing to ask about the health of any female, he should refer to *al-karīma* (the respected, for the daughter of the person he speaks to); *al-wālida* (the one who gave birth, i.e. the mother) and *al-ahl* (the home/family, i.e. the wife). The divorce procedure [see ṬALĀḲ] includes usually the statement *anti ṭāliḳ* (you are divorced) repeated by the husband three times in the presence of two adult witnesses. A request for a favour, within reason, must be fulfilled if the asking party grabs the hem of a person's cloak and states: *anā dak̲h̲īlak*, i.e. "I am under your protection".

Some tribal customs, such as circumcision of females [see K̲H̲AFḌ], blood revenge [see ḲIṢĀṢ], killing in order to protect family or tribal honour [see ʿIRḌ] or "marriage of pleasure" (*nikāḥ al-mutʿa* [see MUTʿA]) are still current in some places, though they are gradually declining.

Beliefs and superstitions and some customs associated with them are very common in Arab society. The most popular are a strong belief in the devil (*al-S̲h̲ayṭān* [see S̲H̲AYṬĀN]), who has several names and epithets in the Ḳurʾān and other Muslim literature, spirits (*arwāḥ* or *as̲h̲bāḥ*) and demons (*ʿifrīt*, *g̲h̲ūl* or *d̲j̲inn*) (hence an insane person is called *mad̲j̲nūn*, i.e. someone whose body has been possessed by a *d̲j̲inn*). Since the devil and demons are mentioned in the Ḳurʾān, no Muslim doubts their existence. The *d̲j̲inn* and the demons may harm but they may also protect. Thus one should please them by offering them bread when they come out at night, prowling for food (this custom is referred to in Ṭāhā Ḥusayn's *al-Ayyām*, i, 7-8). Appeasing of the *d̲j̲inn*s in ʿIrāḳ, such as *ṭanṭal*, *dew* and *siʿluwa* was carried out by pouring water mixed with sugar and salt. This "ceremony" was known as *dalḳ*. Another custom aiming at the protection of people from the harms of the *d̲j̲inn* involves the fastening of chicken legs and seven onions on a skewer and leaving them hung for forty days over the bed of a woman who has given birth.

The custom called *zār* [*q.v.*] (exorcism) is particularly popular in Egypt. It refers to a "ritual of sacrifices, incantations, drumming and dancing performed for the purpose of appeasing any one of a number of spirits by which a person may be believed to be possessed" (Hinds-Badawi, 363).

People, and in particular, children and the house should be protected against the evil eye. Hence after the visit of a stranger to the house it is customary to spread salt on the children. It is also customary to say after seeing a handsome child: *mā abs̲h̲aʿaka* (How ugly you are!) and even nickname a girl *ḳabīḥa* (ugly), in order to nullify the harm of evil eye. A guest is expected to say *mā s̲h̲āʾa Allāh* (God willing) or *smalla ʿalēh* (the name of Allah on him) when speaking of or looking at a child.

A strong belief in luck and fortune is also common. Hence the family who has suffered a disaster may resort to using amulets, pray and give money to charity and even go to live elsewhere. In some areas, the days of the week are either good or bad. Hence they may influence actions. Thus Monday, Wednesday, Thursday and Friday are regarded as "good" days while the other days are usually "bad". This division may differ from area to area. The eclipse of the sun and the moon [see KUSŪF] indicate bad luck. Hence it is customary that when an eclipse occurs, people pray to God to save the world. Some believe that in the case of the eclipse of the moon, it has in fact been swallowed up by a big whale or leviathan (*ḥūt*) and therefore people should pray to God calling on him to "let it go". Strong belief in the good luck brought by the first customer (*istiftāḥ*), makes a shopkeeper do anything to persuade the first customer to buy something, even at a loss. Moreover, it is customary for a shop-keeper to open his business in the morning, reciting a short dictum consisting of four of the Most Beautiful Names of God (see above): *yā fattāḥ yā ʿalīm yā razzāḳ yā karīm* in which he invokes God that the day will be profitable.

Many beliefs are well known from the time of the D̲j̲āhiliyya [*q.v.*], some of which are still current, e.g. the belief associated with the flight of birds, called *taʿayyuf* or *taṭayyur* (augury), and more specifically, the belief that certain birds may bring bad luck, such as the crow (whose sound indicates separation and enmity) and the owl (whose sound indicates desolation) [see FAʾL; ʿIYĀFA]. When describing al-Azhar, Aḥmad Amīn recalls the existence of a small box on the right side of the big *miḥrāb* [*q.v.*] which contained a talisman against birds (31). Similarly, fear of bad luck is associated with the hyena (*ḍabʿ*) which is still widespread in the region. It also appears in a number of folktales which aim at warning recalcitrant children.

Many other older beliefs are current in the area, though no one can trace back their origin. Examples include the belief that a creeping baby indicates the arrival of guests; and when someone sneezes while a name of a deceased person is mentioned, he/she will certainly come to harm unless the lobe of his/her ear is pulled, while the expression *falāt al-k̲h̲ēr* (favourable redemption) is normally cited.

The Arabs also believe in the magic power of dreams and have several classical works attempting to interpret them [see TAʿBĪR AL-RUʾYA, in Suppl.]. Examples are: dreaming of a snake symbolises a long life, probably because a snake is an old symbol for cure, and also the word "snake" (*ḥayya*) shares the same root as of that for "living, life" (*ḥayy*/*ḥayā*); dreaming of water or oil portends imminent disaster, whereas dreaming of a donkey bodes the receipt of a present.

Customs associated with the belief in saints (*awliyāʾ* [see WALĪ]) are also current in the Middle East. The *walī* is usually the patron of the area whose grave is visited mainly on special dates (*mawālid*) or in certain seasons. This usually involves rituals around the tomb in which people pray and place their requests, e.g. for a cure for an illness, for becoming pregnant, for finding a husband, etc. Among the famous saints are al-Sayyid al-Badawī and al-Sayyida Zaynab in Egypt and al-Nabī Shuʿayb in Israel. Many other tombs of famous pious personalities which are visited regularly (*ziyāra* [*q.v.*]) are the tomb of the Prophet Muḥammad in Medina, the tombs of the Patriarchs in Hebron and some of the prophets who are mentioned in the Ḳurʾān, as well as other local saints (some of whom were famous Ṣūfīs or *darwīshs*) [*q.v.*]).

Popular art which is based on old traditions and customs may be divided into two main branches: the "performed" art, which includes popular shows, singing and dancing, and the "produced" art, which includes artifacts, embroidery and weaving and drawing and sculpting. The popular show includes the puppet show (*ḳaragöz* [*q.v.*]) and performances by local artists, e.g. amateur comedians who entertain people at weddings. Acrobats (*bahlawān*), clowns (*muharridj*) and snake charmers (*ḥāwi*) are also popular, especially in North Africa. There are singers of different types of songs (e.g. the *mawwāl* [see MAWĀLIYA]), when the lyric is usually written in the local dialect. Some of the well-known singers in the last century were Umm Kulthūm [*q.v.*], Farīd al-Aṭrash and ʿAbd al-Wahhāb, whose fame and popularity around the Middle East continue long after their deaths. Various types of traditional popular dancing, usually performed by men or women separately (e.g. *dabka*), exist in the area. However, the famous oriental belly-dancing performed usually by one woman (called in the past *ghāziya*, but today usually called *raḳḳāṣa*) in nightclubs or at weddings is still very popular. Traditional musical instruments used in all these performances include string instruments such as the *rabāba* (one/two-string violin), *ʿūd* (lute), *ḳānūn* (psaltery) and *kamandja* (violin). Wind instruments include different kinds of flutes and pipes, such as the *mizmār, muzmār turkī, arghūl, nāy(e), shabāba* and *būḳ*. Percussion instruments include the *daff, ṭabl, durbakke, ṭanbūr* (kinds of drums) and *ṣandj* (cymbals).

The "produced" popular art includes household articles, furniture and clothes. Among these one may find e.g. the *miṣbāḥ* or *ḳandīl* (oil or kerosene lamp), *tisht* (basin), *ibrīḳ* (ewer), *sudjdjāda* (carpet), *ṣiniyyeh* (tray), [*n*]*ardjīla* or *shīsha* (hookah), and clothes, as described above. In modern Egypt, a very successful industry of papyri products and other artifacts associated mainly with ancient Egypt has been flourishing for several decades.

The interest in Arab folklore is certainly growing both inside and outside the Arab world. Scores of institutes, centres and museums have been opened, making it impossible to list them. In general, one may conclude that in every Arab state there can be found at least one centre or museum of ethnography or folklore, usually called *muʾassasat* or *maʿhad* or *matḥaf* or *markaz al-turāth al-shaʿbī* or *al-funūn al-shaʿbiyya*. Moreover, some countries, such as Egypt, Syria, ʿIrāḳ, Jordan and Palestine, are particularly known for their efforts to preserve the past by encouraging research on Arab folklore. Consequently, scores of publications appear and conferences are held annually in different parts of the Middle East and North Africa. Conservation work is in progress, to which one should add the growing amount of research, based on field-work, carried out by scholars and amateurs, who have originated from minority communities previously living in Arab countries, especially Jews from Yemen, ʿIrāḳ and North Africa and who now live in Israel.

Bibliography: 1. Studies. J.L. Burckhardt, *Notes on the Bedouins and Wahabys*, London 1831; E.W. Lane, *The manners and customs of the modern Egyptians*, London 1836 and many subsequent reprints; R.P.A. Dozy, *Dictionnaire détaillé des noms des vêtements chez les Arabes*, Amsterdam 1843; Anne Blunt, *Bedouin tribes of the Euphrates*, 2 vols., London 1879; eadem, *A pilgrimage to Nejd*, London 1881; E.W. Lane, *Arabian society in the Middle Ages*, London 1883; C. Doughty, *Travels in Arabia Deserta*, 2 vols., London 1885; I.G.N. Keith-Falconer, *Kalilah and Dimnah*, Cambridge 1885; F.E. Hulme, *Proverb lore*, London 1902; E.S. Stevens, *By Tigris and Euphrates*, London 1923; R. Basset, *Mille et un contes, récits et légendes arabes*, 3 vols., Paris 1924-6; W. Blackman, *The Fellahin of Upper Egypt*, London 1927; Tewfik Canaan, *Muhammadan saints and sanctuaries in Palestine*, London 1927; A. Musil, *Manners and customs of the Rwala Bedouin*, New York 1928; G. Dalman, *Arbeit und Silte in Palästina*, 7 vols., Gütersloh 1928-42; T.S. Knowlson, *The origins of popular superstitions and customs*, London 1930; E. Westermarck, *Wit and wisdom in Morocco*, London 1930; A. Wilson, *Folk-tales of Iraq*, Oxford 1931; Khalid Chatila, *Le mariage chez les musulmans en Syrie*, Paris 1934; J. Walker, *Folk medicine in modern Egypt*, London 1934; Yosef Meyuhas, *The Fellahin*, Jerusalem 1937; M. von Oppenheim, *Die Bedouinen*, 4 vols., Leipzig-Wiesbaden 1939-68; Ester Panetta, *Pratiche credence popolari Libiche*, Roma 1940; Ṭāhā Ḥusayn, *al-Ayyām*, Cairo 1942; Moshe Stavsky, *The Arab village*, Tel-Aviv 1946; Jacob Shimoni, *The Arabs in Palestine*, Tel-Aviv 1947; Josef Waschitz, *The Arabs in Palestine*, Palestine 1947; A.S. Tritton, *Folklore in Arabic literature*, in *Folklore*, lx (1949), 332-9; idem, *Folklore in Islam*, in *MW*, xl (1950), 167-75; Djaʿfar Khayyāṭ, *al-Ḳarya al-ʿirāḳiyya*, Beirut 1950; Aḥmad Amīn, *Ḳāmūs al-ʿādāt wa ʾl-taḳālīd wa ʾl-taʿābīr al-miṣriyya*, ²Cairo 1953; F. de Grand'combe, *La superstition*, Paris 1955; M.S. al-Ḥūt, *Fī ṭarīḳ al-mīthōlōdjiya ʿind al-ʿarab*, Beirut 1955; H. Ringgren, *Studies in Arabian fatalism*, Uppsala 1955; Saʿd al-Khādim, *Taʾrīkh al-azyāʾ al-shaʿbiyya fī Miṣr*, Cairo 1956; Touvia Ashkenazi, *The Bedouins: manners and customs*, Jerusalem 1957; J.M. Landau, *Studies in the Arab theater and cinema*, Philadelphia 1958; Dj.N. Al-Rayyis, *Fann al-ṭabkh*, Beirut 1958; G. Baer, *The Arabs of the Middle East, population and society*, Tel-Aviv 1960; M.J.L. Hardy, *Blood feuds and the payment of blood money in the Middle East*, Beirut 1963; Anīs Frayḥa, *al-Fuḳāhaʾ ʿind al-ʿarab*, Beirut 1962; ʿAbd al-Karīm al-ʿAllāf, *al-Mawwāl al-baghdādī*, Baghdād 1963; K.S. Goldstein, *A guide for field workers in folklore*, Pennsylvania 1964; *Larousse Encyclopaedia of mythology*, London 1964; A. Aarne and Stith Thompson, *The types of the folktale. A classification and bibliography*, Helsinki 1964; Hilma Granquist, *Muslim death and burial. Arab customs and traditions studied in a village in Jordan*, Helsinki 1965; Fawzī al-ʿAnṭīl, *al-Fulklūr mā huwa?*, Cairo 1965; ʿAbd al-Ḥamīd al-ʿAlūsī, *Min turāthinā al-shaʿbī*, Baghdād 1966; S.D. Goitein, *Studies in Islamic history and institutions*, Leiden 1966; Tawfiq Fahd, *La divination arabe, études religieuses sociologiques et folkloriques sur le milieu natif de l'Islam*, Leiden 1966; H.R.P. Dickson, *The Arab of the desert*, London 1967; E. Marx, *Bedouin of the Negev*, Manchester 1967; Muḥammad al-Marzūḳī, *al-Adab al-shaʿbī fī Tūnis*, Tunis 1967; ʿAbd al-Laṭīf al-Dulayshī, *al-Alʿāb al-shaʿbiyya fī Baṣra*, Baghdād 1968; ʿAbd al-Ḥamīd Yūnus, *al-Ḥikāya al-shaʿbiyya*, Cairo 1968; Y. al-Sh.I. al-Sāmarrāʾi, *al-ʿĀdāt wa ʾl-taḳālīd al-ʿāmmiyya*, Baghdād 1969; S. Jargy, *La poésie populaire traditionnelle chantée au proche-orient Arabe*, The Hague 1970; Aḥmad al-Khashshāb, *Dirāsāt anthrōpōlōdjiyya*, Cairo 1970; Aḥmad Mursī, *al-Ughniyya al-shaʿbiyya*, Cairo 1970; Abū ʿĀmir Ibn Shuhayd, *The treatise of familiar spirits and demons*, tr. and notes by J.T. Monroe,

Los Angeles 1971; A.R. Ṣāliḥ, *al-Adab al-sha'bī*, Cairo 1971; *Encyclopaedia judaica*, Jerusalem 1972; M. Gilsenan, *Saint and Sufi in modern Egypt*, London 1973; Ṣafwat Kamāl, *Madkhal li-dirāsat al-fulklūr al-kuwaytī*, Kuwait 1973; anon., *Dirāsa fi 'l-mudjtamaʿ wa 'l-turāth al-shaʿbī al-filasṭīnī*, Beirut 1973; A.B. Sāʿi, *al-Ḥikāyāt al-shaʿbiyya fi 'l-lādhikiyya*, Damascus 1974; M.A. Maḥdjūb, *Muḳaddima li-dirāsat al-mudjtamaʿāt al-badawiyya*, Kuwait 1974; Nabīla Ibrāhīm, *Ashkāl al-taʿbīr fi 'l-adab al-shaʿbī*, Cairo 1974; Fāṭima al-Maṣrī, *al-Zār*, Cairo 1975; ʿAli al-Zayn, *al-ʿĀdāt wa 'l-taḳālīd fi 'l-ʿuhūd al-iḳṭāʿiyya*, Beirut-Cairo 1977; Laḥd Khāṭir, *al-ʿĀdāt wa 'l-taḳālīd al-lubnāniyya*, 2 vols. Beirut 1977; Muḥammad al-Djawharī, *Dirāsat al-fulklūr al-ʿarabī*, Cairo 1978; Philippa Waring, *A dictionary of omens and superstitions*, London 1978; M. Zwettler, *The oral tradition of classical Arabic literature*, Ohio 1978; P. Underwood, *Dictionary of the occult and supernatural*, Bungay, Suffolk 1979; M.E. Meeker, *Literature and violence in North Arabia*, Cambridge 1979; Moshe Piamenta, *Islam in everyday Arabic speech*, Leiden 1979; F.E. Planer, *Superstition*, London 1980; H.M. el-Shamy, *Folktales of Egypt*, Chicago 1980; ʿUthmān al-Kaʿʿāk, *al-Taḳālīd wa 'l-ʿādāt al-tūnisiyya*, Tunis 1981; W. Lancaster, *The Rwala Bedouin today*, Cambridge 1981; F.A. Muṣṭafā, *al-Mawālid, dirāsa li 'l-ʿādāt wa 'l-taḳālīd al-shaʿbiyya fī Miṣr*, Alexandria 1981; Mādjida ʿAbd al-Munʿim, *Aṭbāḳ al-sharḳ*, Alexandria 1982; Shawḳī ʿAbd al-Ḥakīm, *Mawsūʿat al-fulklūr wa 'l-asāṭīr al-ʿarabiyya*, Beirut 1982; idem, *Madkhal li-dirāsat al-fulklūr wa 'l-asāṭīr al-ʿarabiyya*, Beirut 1983; Muḥammad al-Djawharī, *Maṣādir dirāsat al-fulklūr al-ʿarabī*, Cairo 1983 (particularly rich bibliography, containing 4175 entries); idem, *al-Dirāsa al-ʿilmiyya li 'l-muʿtaḳadāt al-shaʿbiyya*, 2 vols., Alexandria-Cairo, 1983-90; Yosef Saddan, *Humour in classical Arabic*, Tel-Aviv and Acre 1983; G.H. Miller, *The dictionary of dreams*, Devon 1983; Moshe Piamenta, *The Muslim conception of God and human welfare*, Leiden 1983; ʿAbd al-Ḥamīd Yūnus, *Muʿdjam al-fulklūr*, Beirut 1983; Y.F. Dūkhī, *al-Aghānī al-kuwaytiyya*, Kuwait 1984; M.T. al-Duwayk, *al-Ḳaṣaṣ al-shaʿbī fī Ḳaṭar*, 2 vols. Qatar 1984; H.R. al-Ḥārib, *Mawāwīl min al-khalīdj*, Qatar 1984; H.M. al-Amily, *The Arabian treasure*, n.p. 1985; L.S. Al-Bassam, *Traditional inheritance of women's clothing in Najd*, Qatar 1985; Nadjla al-Izzi, *Traditional costumes of the Gulf*, Qatar 1985; S. al-A. al-Suwayyān, *Djamʿ al-maʾthūrāt al-shafahiyya*, Qatar 1985; Ḥasan Budayr, *Āthār al-adab al-shaʿbī fi 'l-adab al-ḥadīth*, Cairo 1986; Bridget Connelly, *Arab folk epic and identity*, Berkeley 1986; F. Maʿtūḳ, *al-Taḳālīd wa 'l-ʿādāt al-shaʿbiyya al-lubnāniyya*, Tripoli 1986; Suyūṭī, *Laghṭ al-mirdjān fī aḥkām al-djānn*, ed. M.A. al-K. ʿAṭāʾ, Beirut 1986; Aḥmad Abū Saʿd, *Ḳāmūs al-muṣṭalaḥāt wa 'l-taʿābīr al-shaʿbiyya*, Beirut 1987; Sāmya ʿAṭallāh, *al-Amthāl al-shaʿbiyya al-miṣriyya*, Cairo 1987; Shabtai Levi (Shabo), *The Bedouins in Sinai Desert*, Tel-Aviv 1987; anon., *The complete book of fortune*, Exeter 1988; P. Cachia, *Popular narrative ballads of modern Egypt*, Oxford 1989; Heather Colyer Ross, *The art of Bedouin jewellery*, Montreux 1989; Iona Opie and Moira Tatem, *A dictionary of superstitions*, Oxford 1989; Abū Saʿd, *Muʿdjam faṣīḥ al-ʿāmma*, Beirut 1990; C. Bailey, *Bedouin poetry from Sinai and the Negev*, Oxford 1991; S. Moreh, *Live theatre and dramatic literature in the medieval Islamic world*, Edinburgh 1992; R. Strijp, *Cultural anthropology of the Middle East. A bibliography*, 2 vols., Leiden 1992-7; W.C. Hazlitt, *Dictionary of faiths and folklore*, London (1905) 1995; A.E. Waite, *Book of spells*, Ware, Herts. 1995; H.M. el-Shamy, *Folk traditions of the Arab world, a guide to motif classification*, 2 vols., Bloomington and Indianapolis 1995; A. Fodor and A. Shivtiel (eds.), *Proceedings of the colloquium on logos, ethos, mythos in the Middle East and North Africa*, Budapest Studies in Arabic 18, Budapest 1996; S. Moreh, *The tree and the branch*, Jerusalem 1997; G. Fehérvári, *The Tareq Rajab Museum*, Kuwait 1997; S. Leder (ed.), *Story-telling in the framework of non-fictional Arabic literature*, Wiesbaden 1998; J.S. Meisami and P. Starkey (eds.), *Encyclopedia of Arabic literature*, 2 vols., London and New York 1998, arts. *Folklore; Popular literature; Proverbs; Alf Layla wa-Layla*; ʿAfīf ʿAbd al-Raḥmān, *Ḳāmūs al-amthāl al-ʿarabiyya al-turāthiyya*, Beirut 1998; Eli Yassif, *The Hebrew folktale: history, genre, meaning*, Bloomington, Indiana 1999; Tamar Alexander, *The beloved friend-and-a-half: studies in Sepharadic folk-literature*, Jerusalem 1999; Yadida Stillman, *Arab dress: A short history, from the dawn of Islam to modern times*, Leiden 2000; A.M. al-ʿAkkād, *Djuḥa al-ḍāḥik al-mudḥik*, Cairo n.d.; Nabīla Ibrāhīm, *al-Dirāsāt al-shaʿbiyya bayn al-naẓariyya wa 'l-taṭbīḳ*, Cairo n.d.; Naṣr al-Dīn Djuḥa, *Nawādir Djuḥa al-kubrā*, Beirut n.d.; Fāṭima Naʿīm, *ʿĀlam al-naksh bi 'l-ḥinnāʾ*, Rabat n.d.

2. Periodicals. *al-Turāth al-shaʿbī*, quarterly, Baghdad, since 1964; *Dirāsāt*, University of Jordan, ʿAmmān, since 1974; *al-Funūn al-shaʿbiyya Folklore*, quarterly, Cairo, since 1982; *Arab food magazine*, monthly, London, since August 1985; *al-Maʾthūrāt al-shaʿbiyya*, Markaz al-turāth al-shaʿbī, quarterly, Al-Doha, Qatar, since January 1986.

(A. Shivtiel)

2. In Persia.

The term "folklore", which has been accepted in Persian as well as in a number of other Middle Eastern languages, was first proposed by William John Thoms (1803-85). In a letter to the *Athenaeum* 22 August 1846, Thoms, writing under the pseudonym Ambrose Merton, proposed that the term "folklore" be adopted in place of the more cumbersome "Popular Antiquities", or "Popular Literature", to describe "the Lore of the People, . . . their manners, customs, observances, superstitions, ballads, proverbs, etc. of the olden time" (Dorson, 1968, 1, 80-4). Thoms' suggestion gained acceptance within a year of its proposal. The term refers not only to rural but also to urban "lore" these days. However, the debate concerning the exact definition of the term "folklore" rages on. The general atmosphere of ambiguity that surrounds this word may be deduced from the decision of the editors of the standard *Dictionary of folklore, mythology, and legend* (1949) to include no less than twenty-one definitions of it (s.v. *Folklore*).

Driven by the kind of nationalist zeal that propels many Muslim scholars to coin and use native words in place of foreign vocabulary, indigenous Persian scholars have proposed a bewildering variety of terms to denote "folklore". Some of these are: *farhang-i mardum* literally "people's culture", *farhang-i ʿāmma, farhang-i tūda* "culture of the masses", *ʿaḳāyid, rusūm, bāwardāsht-hā-yi ʿāmma* (or *ʿawāmm* or *ʿawāmmāna* or *mardum* or *tūda*) "beliefs, customs, notions of the general public (or common folk, people, masses)". Whereas the words *ʿāmma* and *mardum* "folk", are clearly used in contradistinction to *khāṣṣa* "the élite", and are more innocuous, the form *tūda* "masses" (cf. *ḥizb-i tūda* "the Communist Party") has ideological associations of a leftist nature because many of the intellectuals who began the systematic study of Persian folklore were inspired by socialist or communist ideologies. Be that as it may, of these, the term *farhang-i mardum*, a literal

Persian translation of the English "folklore", is probably the most widely accepted. However, the loan word "folklore", spelled *fwlklwr* in Persian, continues to be used side-by-side with it and there may even be a movement toward its adoption in specialised publications. This is signalled not only by the early uses of it, its Persian plural *fwlklwr-hā* and its adjectival form *fwlklwrī* (Katīrāʾī 1357/1978, 93, 135, 138) but also by the fact that the word *fwlklwr* is used interchangeably with *farhang-i mardum* in the first two issues of the *Iranian Folklore Quarterly* in Spring 2002 (i, 7-8, 9-16; ii, 43, 132).

Scholarship on Persian folklore, which is concentrated chiefly on verbal lore, may be divided into two groups. That conducted by Iranians, and that which is undertaken by Westerners. Although the Persian study of folklore is typically traced to the Āḳā Dj̲amāl-i Kh̲ʷānsārī's (d. *ca.* 1121-5/1709-13) satirical treatise on superstitions of the Iṣfahānī women, which was entitled *Kulth̲ūm-nama* (for an edition see Katīrāʾī 1349/1970), this attribution appears unreasonable. Kh̲ʷānsārī intended to ridicule these women's beliefs as a way of combating superstition; he was neither trying to collect folklore nor present an accurate account of the female lore of his time. By the same token, attributing folklore collection activity to Persian novelists (e.g. Ṣādiḳ-i Čūbak, or even Dj̲amālzāda), who happen to use a significant number of "folksy" expressions in their writing as a matter of style, would be stretching the point.

Although brief collections of Persian folk expressions, beliefs and especially proverbs are scattered throughout Persian and Arabic literatures, none may be called systematic until the appearance of Dihkh̲uda's (1297-1375/1879-1955) four-volume *Amth̲āl wa ḥikam* ("Proverbs and dicta") in (1308-11/1929-32. Dihkh̲uda's collection is, however, no more than an alphabetical list of literary and folk proverbs, which rarely provides contextual information. The systematic collection of Persian folklore had to await the attentions of Ṣādiḳ Hidāyat (1281-1330 *sh̲*./1902-51), who, inspired by Arnold van Gennep's (1873-1957) classificatory system, published several tales, folk songs and collections of Persian folklore between the years 1310/1931 and 1324/1945 (e.g. Hidāyat 1312/1933 and 1344/1965, 447-83). Of these, the two volumes, *ūsāna* "fairytales", and *nīrangistān* (a title adopted from a Middle Persian treatise on counter-magical incantations), published respectively in 1310/1931 and 1312/1933, are the most extensive. Hidāyat later published two articles on folklore and the method of its collection, the methodological aspects of which were inspired by Pierre Saintyve's (1870-1935) *Manuel de folklore* (1936). These essays later inspired the work of the most important Persian collector of folklore, Abū 'l-Ḳāsim Indj̲awī (d. 1993), who in the spring of 1340/1961 began a radio programme that aimed to collect folklore data by direct appeal to its listeners, who were also provided with training as well as with supplies (e.g. paper, forms, pencils). Indj̲awī's appeals generated an enormous public response. Soon a flood of data from his listeners began to come in, and he was thus able to amass a vast archive of Persian folklore data, some of which he published in a series called *Gandj̲īna-yi farhang-i mardum* ("the treasury of folklore"; see Indj̲awī 1352 *sh̲*./1973, 1352-5 *sh.*/1973-7). This massive archive, that represented some two decades of systematic collection, contained some 120,000 folklore texts, hundreds of objects, 3,000 documents of cultural history, thousands of phonograph recordings, cassettes, films, videos and over 2000 photos (Dālwand, 1377/1998, 3-4). This material was preserved in the *Markaz-i farhang-i mardum* (Folklore Centre).

Since the 1970s, folklore had enjoyed significant backing from the royal family and other wealthy organisations. During this period, folklore research was promoted and even an international congress on folklore was held in Iṣfahān in the summer of 1977 (for an excellent summary, see Marzolph, art. *Folklore studies*, in *EIr*). Folklore studies fared poorly after the Islamic Revolution of 1978-9. Folklore was viewed as promoting superstitious and even pagan beliefs, and most funding for it came to a halt. In spite of this, the Folklore Centre continued an anaemic existence until the early 1980s when Indj̲awī's radio programme was discontinued. The discontinuation of the programme not only brought the process of collection to a virtual halt but also signalled the final fall of folklore from grace. Much of the holdings of the Persian folklore archives, especially its audio-visual collection, was unceremoniously dispersed among other centres or was sent to storage. Only some written documents, especially texts that were submitted by the public, were allowed to remain at the archives of the Folklore Centre. Moreover, the Centre was placed under the control of the Islamic Republic's broadcasting agency (*ṣadā u sīmā-yi dj̲umhūrī-yi islāmī*).

This unfortunate situation continued until 1374/1995, when following a speech by the leader of the Islamic Republic of Iran in which dangers of assimilation into Western culture were pointed out and Iranians were called back to their native cultural values, folklore studies were revived. This new interest in folklore has led to attempts that seek to impose some order on the chaotic mass of the existing folklore data in Iran. R.S. Boggs' art. "Types and classifications" in the *Dictionary of folklore, mythology and legend* has been used as a guide in an experimental effort to classify this material (Dālwand 1377/1998). Folklore publication and research continues, and a number of important Western studies on folklore have been translated (e.g. Propp 1368 *sh̲*./1989, 1371 *sh̲*./1992).

The earliest European interest in Persian folklore came about as a result of the British and Russian political interests in the Persian-speaking world. Alexander Chodzko (1804-91), Valentin Zh̲ukovski (1858-1918), D.C. Phillot (1860-1930), D.L.R. Lorimer (1876-1962), B. Nikitin (1885-1960), L.P. Elwell-Sutton (1912-84) and above all the Danish Iranist Arthur Christensen (1875-1945) and the French Persianist Henri Massé (1886-1969), made significant contributions to Persian folklore studies (see Chodzko 1842; Christensen 1918, 1958; Lorimer 1919; Massé 1938; Nikitin 1922; Pillot 1905-7; Zh̲ukovski 1902; cf. also Radhayrapetian 1990, and Marzolph, *art. cit.* Massé drew on the resources of his Iranian connections to collect and publish the most extensive body of Persian folklore of his time. He worried about the disappearance of the rural Iranian folklore as a result of rapid modernisation (Massé 1938, i, 13). Therefore, early in the 1920s, he embarked on a research trip to Persia in order to collect Persian rural folklore. Interestingly enough, his data came almost exclusively from city dwellers. Religious and ethnic minorities such as Zoroastrians, Armenians and Jews were intentionally excluded (i, 16). In spite of his concern for the endangered rural tradition he accordingly finished by gathering one of the best existing collections of the Persian urban folklore (i, 15). The classification and arrangement of Massé's data follows that of Van Gennep. The most important contemporary western scholar of Persian folklore is Ulrich Marzolph, who compiled the first tale-type index of Persian narratives (Marzolph 1984), and has contributed many important monographic studies and essays to Persian folklore; the best study in depth on the history of Persian folklore studies to date remains his discussion of the subject in *EIr.*

Bibliography: A.B. Chodzko, *Specimens of the popular poetry of Persia*, London 1842; V.A. Zhukovski, *Obrazt͟sī persidskogo narodogo tvorčestva*, St. Peterburg 1902; D.C. Phillott, *Some current Persian tales, collected in the south of Persia from professional story-tellers*, in *Memoirs Asiatic Soc. of Bengal*, i/18 (1905-7), 375-412; A. Christensen, *Contes persans en langue populaire*, Copenhagen 1918; D.L.R. and E.S. Lorimer, *Persian tales, written down for the first time in the original Kermani and Bakhtiari*, London 1919; B. Nikitin, *La vie domestique kurde*, in *Revue d'éthnographie et des traditions populaires*, iii (1922), 334-44; Ṣādiḳ Hidāyat, *Ūsāna*, Tehran 1310 *s͟h.*/1931; idem, *Nīrangistān*, Tehran 1312 *s͟h.*/1931; H. Massé, *Croyances et coutumes persans suivies de contes et chansons populaires*, Paris 1938; Bess Allen Donaldson, *The wild rue. A study of Muhammadan magic and folklore in Iran*, London 1938; M. Leach (ed.), *Dictionary of folklore, mythology and legend*, New York 1949; L.P. Elwell-Sutton, *The wonderful sea-horse and other Persian tales*, London 1950; idem, *Persian proverbs*, London 1954, and see several articles on folklore listed in the bibl. of this author's works in E. Bosworth and Carole Hillenbrand (eds.), *Qajar Iran. Political, social and cultural change 1800-1925*, Edinburgh 1983, nos. 29, 30, 49, 52, 56, 57, 62, 65, 89, 90, 122, 124; Christensen, *Persische Märchen*, Düsseldorf-Köln 1958; Hidāyat, *Fūlklūr yā farhang-i tūda* ("Folklore, or the culture of the masses"), in *Niwis͟hta-hā-yi parākanda* ("Collected papers"), ²Tehran 1344 *s͟h.*/1965, 447-83; R.M. Dorson, *The British folklorists, a history*, Chicago 1968; Mahmūd Katīrā'ī (ed.), *ʿAḳāyid al-nisāʾ wa mirʾāt al-bulahāʾ. Du risāla-yi intiḳādī dar farhang-i tūda* ("Women's beliefs and the mirror of the stupid ones. Two critical treatises on folklore"), Tehran 1349 *s͟h.*/1970; Abu 'l-Ḳāsim Indjawī, *Tamt͟hīl u mat͟hal*, i, Tehran 1352 *s͟h.*/1973; idem, *Ḳiṣṣa-hā-yi ʿāmmiyāna* ("Folktales"), 3 vols. Tehran 1352-5 *s͟h.*/1973-8; Katīrā'ī, *Zabān u farhang-i mardum* ("The people's language and culture"), Tehran 1357 *s͟h.*/1979; U. Marzolph, *Typologie des persischen Volksmärchens*, Beirut 1984; V. Propp, *Rīk͟ht-s͟hināsī-yi ḳiṣṣa-hā-yi pariyān* ("The morphology of the fairy-tale"), Pers. tr. F. Badrā'ī, Tehran 1368 *s͟h.*/1989; Juliet Radhayrapetian, *Iranian folk narrative. A survey of scholarship*, New York 1990; Propp, *Ris͟ha-hā-yi tārīk͟hī-yi ḳiṣṣa-hā-yi pariyān* ("Historical roots of fairy tales"). tr. Badrā'ī, Tehran 1371 *s͟h.*/1992; Marzolph, *Dāstān-hā-yi shīrīn. Fünfzig persische Volksbüchlein aus der zweite Hälfte des zwanzigsten Jahrhunderts*, Stuttgart 1994; idem, *EIr* art., *Folklore studies. i. Of Persia.*

(Mahmoud Omidsalar)

TAKLA MAKAN [see tarim].

TAḲRĪẒ (a.), lit. "the act of praising", a minor genre of mediaeval Arabic literature which consisted of statements praising the virtues of a particular work, some composed after the death of the author of the work in question but probably for the most part composed at the time of the work's appearance with the aim of giving it a puff and thus advertising it; such statements must have been solicited by the author from obliging friends and colleagues, the more eminent the better. F. Rosenthal (see below) has felicitously compared them to modern "blurbs" of publishers to advertise their books. Ahlwardt, in his Berlin catalogue, seems to have been the first Western scholar to isolate and identify the genre as *Lobschriften*. *Taḳrīẓ*s tended to be formulaic in form and style, invariably in rhymed prose (*sadj*ʿ [*q.v.*]) and with a stock of fairly trite images for praising the recipient. See Rosenthal, *Blurbs (Taqrîẓ) from fourteenth-century Egypt*, in *Oriens*, xxvii-xxviii (1981), 177-96, who here translates two *taḳrīẓ*s from the Yale and Berlin mss. of a collection dating from 795/1393, by Ibn K͟haldūn and Ibn Ḥadjar [*q.vv.*] respectively, these being aimed at puffing one Ibn al-Damāmīnī.

Bibliography: Given in the article. See also A. Gacek, *The Arabic manuscript tradition. A glossary of technical terms and bibliography*, HdO, Section 1, Vol. 58, Leiden 2001, 114-15.

(Ed.)

TAḲWĀ (a.), a term of Islamic religion denoting piety.

1. Etymology and range of meanings.

Taḳwā is a verbal noun from *taḳā* "to fear [God]", itself a secondary formation from form VIII of *w-ḳ-y*, *ittaḳā* "to fear [God]" (see on this phenomenon, Wright, *Arabic grammar*, I, § 148 Rem. *b*). From this same secondary formation is derived the adjective *taḳī*, pl. *atḳiyāʾ* "pious, God-fearing", in fact a synonym of the form VIII participle *muttaḳī*.

Depending on context, the denotations of the term in classical Islamic religious and mystical literature include "godliness", "devoutness", "piety", "God-fearing", "pious abstinence" and "uprightness". As a social ideal, *taḳwā* originally connoted "dutifulness", "faithful observance", a meaning which was discarded in most later Islamic ethical thought. In the poetry of Labīd (d. 40/660), for instance, the social connotation of *taḳwā* as "moral behaviour" or "reverential dutifulness" with respect to one's tribe or relatives appears to have fused with the Ḳurʾānic religious ideal of "fear of God", so that "concepts for a 'respectful relationship' between the members of a tribe and the 'reverential behavior' towards God seem even to be interchangeable and identical" (M.M. Bravmann, *The spiritual background of early Islam*, Leiden 1972, 117), but this combination of social and spiritual meanings of *taḳwā* is now obsolete.

The Persian dictionaries (cf. the references in Dihk͟hudā, *Lug͟hāt-nāma*, s.v. *taḳwā*) render the word as synonymous with the Persian *tarsīdan* "fear" and *parhīzgarī* "abstinence", precisely the same connotations of *taḳwā* found in early Muslim mystical theology. In English, various translations which approach the Islamic spirit of *taḳwā* are "pious God-fearing", "God-fearing piety", "devout uprightness" and "holy fear"; William Chittick has proposed the rendition "god-wariness", a neologism which, he claims, "makes *taqwā*'s orientation toward God explicit, brings out the implication of being aware and mindful, and avoids the negative and sentimental undertones of words such as 'piety', 'dutifulness', and 'righteousness' . . ." (*Faith and practice of Islam. Three thirteenth century Sufi texts*, Albany 1992, 12).

In fact, *taḳwā* in many respects equals a particularly Protestant kind of religious notion, the spiritual significance of which is exactly conveyed by the Anglican ascetic and mystic William Law (1686-1761) in his *A serious call to a devout and holy life*, ed. P. Stanwood, London 1978, where he evokes that "true devotion" which requires that we "live as pilgrims in spiritual watching, in holy fear, and heavenly aspiring after another life" in one passage (31); and in another passage (256), insists that we "do everything in His fear and abstain from everything that is not according to His will". As a religious concept in Islam, *taḳwā*, as will be seen below, has definite extra-Islamic resonances.

William Law's two principles of "fear of God" and "abstinence" from all ungodly affairs are found, in fact, in the earliest work in Persian on Ṣūfism: the *S̲h̲arḥ-i Taʿarruf* by Abū Ibrāhīm Mustamlī Buk̲h̲ārāʾī (d. 434/1042-3), where *taḳwā* is described as having "two principles: fear and abstinence. Thus the devotee's attitude of *taḳwā* towards God has two senses: either fear of chastisement (*ʿiḳāb*) or fear of separation (*firāḳ*)". The attitude of fear generates observance of the commandments of God, while "fear of separation" means that "the devotee is content with nothing less than God, and does not find ease in aught beside Him" (from the anonymous *K̲h̲ulāṣa-yi S̲h̲arḥ-i Taʿarruf*, ed. ʿA. Rad̲j̲āʾī, Tehran 1349 A.S.H./1970, 294, an 8th/14th-century summary of this work). In an almost identical definition by the great Kubrawī master Muḥammad Lāhīd̲j̲ī (d. 912/1507) in the *Mafātīḥ al-iʿd̲j̲āz fī s̲h̲arḥ-i Guls̲h̲an-i rāz*, ed. Muḥammad Riḍā Barzgar K̲h̲āliḳī and ʿIffat Karbāsī, Tehran 1371 A.S.H./1992, 250 *taḳwā* is described as the "fear of God regarding the final consequences of one's affairs, or else fear of one's own passional self (*nafs*) lest it play the brigand, casting one into the perdition of separation and being veiled from God". After over half a millennium of theosophical speculation—from Buk̲h̲ārāʾī to Lāhīd̲j̲ī—the two foundations of *taḳwā*: fear and abstinence, remain completely intact.

2. *Taḳwā in the Ḳurʾān and Ḥadīt̲h̲.*

In general Ḳurʾānic usage, the moral virtue of *taḳwā* denotes piety, abstinence and God-fearing obedience, suggesting the idea of a faith animated by works, and works quickened by a genuine experience of faith; in brief, such *taḳwā* is the substance of all godliness. *Taḳwā* is one of the most frequently mentioned religious concepts in the Ḳurʾān, having entered into the world of Islam upon the very first appearance of the angel Gabriel to the Prophet. "Have you seen him who tries to prevent a servant when he would pray? Have you considered if such a one has any divine guidance or enjoins [others] to piety (*taḳwā*)", Gabriel asks Muḥammad in the very early sūra, XCVI, 9-12, revealed in the cave on Mt. Ḥirā [*q.v.*] near Mecca. An allusion to *taḳwā* reappears in the second verse of the first sūra revealed in Medina (II), where the Ḳurʾān is described as "a guidance for all endowed with piety (*hud^an li 'l-muttaḳīn*)". In XLIX, 10, the believers are described as "naught but brothers" and, in a kind of communal participation in their "pious vigilant awareness of God" (*taḳwā Allāh*), are enjoined to establish fraternal peace amongst themselves. Another verse (IX, 123), devoted to the theme of being harsh on the enemies of Islam, assures believers that "God is with the godfearing pious devotees (*maʿa 'l-muttaḳīn*)". This latter verse may be compared with the *ḥadīt̲h̲* which situates *taḳwā* as the "aggregate of all good things" alongside *d̲j̲ihād* which is described as "the monasticism [of the Muslim]" (al-Ḳus̲h̲ayrī, *al-Risāla*, ed. Maʿrūf Ẓarīf and ʿAlī ʿAbd al-Ḥamīd Balṭand̲j̲ī, Beirut 1990, 105).

Ultimately, salvation in both this world and the next is attained through *taḳwā*; with it the saints gain "their deserts and are untouched by evil and they have no grief" (XXXIX, 61; an idea also repeated in X, 62-3); while those with *taḳwā* "are driven into Paradise" (XXXIX, 73). The true mosque must also be "built upon *taḳwā*" (IX, 108-9) if it is to be consecrated (an echo of Luke, vi. 47-9?). This connotation of *taḳwā* is echoed in an early Ḳurʾān commentary—by Muḳātil b. Sulaymān (d. 150/767 [*q.v.*])—where *taḳwā* is "considered as synonymous with *ik̲h̲lāṣ*, pure sincerity, [and] *ittaḳā* is translated as *taraka* in the sense of 'to abstain' from what is evil, such as disobedience (*maʿṣiya*) or associationism (*s̲h̲irk*)" (P. Nwyia, *Exégèse coranique et langage mystique*, Beirut 1970, 59).

While *taḳwā* is, in particular, the universal measurement and the final criterion of the sincere religious life of the faithful Muslim who is enjoined to "avoid suspicion" and instead to "fear God" (*taḳwā Allāh*, XLIX, 12; cf. II, 41), in a more general sense *taḳwā* appears as the common ecumenical characteristic of the universal man of faith, regardless of sectarian divisions and political differences based on nationality and ethnic origin in the verse: "We have created you male and female, and made you nations and tribes to know one another. Indeed, the noblest of you in the sight of God is the most God-fearing (*akramakum ʿind Allāh atḳākum*)" (XLIX, 13). In al-Sulamī's recension of the text of the Ḳurʾānic *Tafsīr* ascribed to D̲j̲aʿfar al-Ṣādiḳ (d. 148/765 [*q.v.*]) (ed. Nywia, in *MUSJ*, xliii/4 [1967], 181-230), the Imām explains the verse as follows (221): "the generous person (*al-karīm*) is one who is, in truth, piously God-fearing (*al-muttaḳī*), and one who is piously God-fearing is one who has severed all his ties to created things for God's sake".

The idea of *taḳwā* as specifically the *Islamic* species of piety appears in the Prophet's saying: "Faith is naked and *taḳwā* its dress" (*al-īmān ʿuryān wa-libāsuhu al-taḳwā*) (cited by ʿAyn al-Ḳuḍāt Hamadānī, *Tamhīdāt*, ed. ʿA. ʿUsayrān, Tehran 1962, 325). Another *ḥadīt̲h̲* recounts that someone asked the Prophet, "Who are the Family of Muḥammad?" He replied: "Every pious God-fearing person (*kull taḳī*)" (al-Ḳus̲h̲ayrī, *al-Risāla*, 105). From such traditions, it is evident that *taḳwā*, as a religious concept, was seen to represent the robes of the *Islamic faith*, as well as to personify the very garments which cloak the Sacred appearing within diverse cultures and religions.

3. *Taḳwā and īmān.*

Taḳwā was regarded as an essential element of the interior dimension of the act of faith, of *īmān ʿan ʿilm* "enlightened faith" (see L. Gardet, ĪMĀN, at Vol. III, 1173). "The Prophet said: 'Submission is public and faith is in the heart.' Then, he pointed to his breast three times, repeating: 'Fear of God (*taḳwā*) is here, fear of God is here'." (Ibn Ḥanbal, and Aḥmad b. Mād̲j̲a, cited by C. Ernst, *Words of ecstasy in Sufism*, Albany 1985, 56).

As an element of Faith, *taḳwā* thus embodies the purely internal and contemplative attitude of heart rather than merely external ritual practice; the same interiorisation of *īmān* which is, in fact, reflected in XXII, 37, which, regarding such purely physical practices as the sacrifice of animals to feed the poor, a ritual part of the ceremony of Muslim pilgrimage, affirms that "it is not their flesh nor their blood that reaches God: it is your piety (*taḳwā*) that reaches Him". Commenting on this verse in his *Iḥyāʾ*, al-G̲h̲azālī notes that "What is meant here by 'devotion' (*taqwā*) is a quality that gains control of the heart, disposing it to comply with the commands it is required to obey" (cited in *Al-Ghazālī. Inner dimensions of Islamic worship*, tr. Muhtar Holland, repr. London 1992, 35). Indeed, interpreting the Ḳurʾānic reference to "heart-piety" (*taḳwā al-ḳulūb*) in the same sūra (XXII, 32), Ibn al-ʿArabī (d. 638/1240) was to point out that just as the human heart is in constant fluctuation in every breath, so genuine *taḳwā* must by understood as a kind of "'pious-wariness-awareness' of God with every breath, which is the ultimate end of what God desires from man" (*al-Futūḥāt al-makkiyya,* Cairo 1911, repr. Beirut n.d., ii, 672, 29-37); cf. Chittick's definition and translation of *taḳwā*, cited above.

Taḳwā was sometimes considered the supreme proof of the certitude of faith (*yaḳīn*). Abū Bakr al-Warrāḳ, (d. 294/906-7), an early Khurāsānian mystic, observed that "certitude (*yaḳīn*) is a light by means of which the devotee's spiritual condition is illuminated. After he experiences such enlightenment, he is enabled to realise the rank of the pious (*muttaḳīn*)" (ʿAṭṭār, *Tadhkirat al-awliyāʾ*, ed. M. Istiʿlāmī, Tehran 1372 A.S.H./1993, 538). Underlining the esoteric nature of piety in the spiritual life, al-Kalābadhī's (d. 380/990) *K. al-Taʿarruf*, Cairo 1933, 69, cites the statement of Sahl al-Tustarī (d. 283/896), author of one of the earliest mystical Ḳurʾān commentaries, that "piety is to contemplate mystical states in the act of isolation [from aught but God]".

Such a radically interiorised outlook, which evokes *taḳwā* as the soul of *īmān*—piety as the inner life of faith—of course, was not always understood by exoteric members of the *ʿulamāʾ*. Ibn Taymiyya, an opponent of the Ṣūfism of Ibn al-ʿArabī and scholastic philosophy, for instance, in his *K. al-Īmān*, interprets piety in its most exoteric meaning, considering *īmān, birr* (righteousness) and *taḳwā* to be synonymous with each other when used in an "absolute" sense in the Ḳurʾān (as, for instance, II, 177, V, 2), holding that the believers (*muʾminūn*) are equivalent to the God-fearing (*muttaḳūn*), who, in turn, are identical to the upright (*abrār*) (T. Izutsu, *The concept of belief in Islamic theology*, repr. Salem, N.H. 1988, 72-4).

4. The mystical theology of *Taḳwā*.

(a) *Taḳwā*-as-abstinence

In Muslim mystical theology, the general notion of *taḳwā* is that of holy fearfulness, pious vigilance over and abstemious fear of following one's passions; in a word, the heart's awe of God who is ever-present in the contemplative life of the soul (cf. al-Sharīf al-Djurdjānī, *K. al-Taʿrīfāt*, ed. I. al-Abyārī, Beirut 1985, 90). Sahl al-Tustarī's maxim "There is no helper besides God; no guide besides the Prophet. There is no spiritual sustenance besides *taḳwā*, nor any other work than patience (*ṣabr*)" quoted by al-Ḳushayrī, *Risāla*, 105) declares *taḳwā* to be the mainstay, if not the very sustenance, of Ṣūfī spiritual practice. In its perfect form, *taḳwā* involves abstention from everything but God, for, as Ibn Khafīf (d. 371/981) states, "Piety is to distance yourself from everything which distances you from God" (ʿAṭṭār, *Tadhkirat*, 578). The connotation of "*taḳwā*-as-abstinence" is also captured in another al-Tustarī maxim: "Whoever wishes to perfect his piety, tell him to refrain from all sins" (ʿAṭṭār, *op. cit.*, 313).

(b) *Taḳwā*-as-heart-abstinence

The contemplative interiority of *taḳwā*, with the connotation of "*taḳwā*-as-the heart's-abstinence" from all but God, is summed up in one of the earliest definitions of the term given by Djaʿfar al-Ṣādiḳ that "for those who traverse the spiritual path (*ahl al-sulūk*), piety (*taḳwā*) is that you do not find within your heart anything but Him" (al-Tahānawī, *Kashshāf iṣṭilāḥāt al-funūn. A dictionary of the technical terms used in the sciences of the Musalmans*, Calcutta 1862, ii, 1527). Abū Saʿīd al-Kharrāz (d. 277/890 or 286/899), an important Ṣūfī of the school of Baghdād, in his *K. al-Ḥaḳāʾiḳ* devoted to the vocabulary of Ṣūfī mystical experience on the two-fold levels of rational expression (*ʿibāra*) and mystical allusion (*ishāra*), combined this interiorised vision of *taḳwā* with the more traditional Ḳurʾānic understanding of the term in his statement that *taḳwā* is "to have a heart vigilant not to let itself pursue passion, and a soul which guards itself against occasions of sin and error" (cited by Nywia, *Exégèse coranique et langage mystique*, 289). Another leading member of the Baghdād school of Ṣūfīs, Abu 'l-Ḥusayn al-Nūrī (d. 295/907), in the first chapter of his *Maḳāmāt al-ḳulūb* discovered and edited by Nywia, *Textes mystiques inédits*, in *MUSJ*, xliv/9 [1968], 132), in a section devoted to "the qualities of the house of the heart of the faithful believer", mentions *taḳwā* as the Light of Piety, the soul of Ṣūfī ethics, for the contemplative "Light of Piety" illuminates both faith and works.

This interiorised concept of *taḳwā* of the heart more or less disappeared but did not altogether die out from the vocabulary of Ṣūfism after the 5th/11th century. Thus Rūzbihān Baḳlī (d. 606/1209 [*q.v.*]) wrote in his *Mashrab al-arwāḥ* that "The root of God-fearing piety is detachment of one's inmost consciousness (*sirr*) from everything but God, whether from the material or spiritual realms, during contemplation of the proofs of the divine Attributes and flashes of the divine Essence. In this manner, one's inmost consciousness melts away before the onslaught of the majesty of the manifestation of the lights of Post-Eternity. That is the esoteric meaning of the Prophet's saying: Faith is naked and *taḳwā* its dress" (ed. N.M. Hoca, Istanbul 1973, 30).

5. *Taḳwā* in the spiritual stations of Ṣūfism.

From the late 3rd/9th to the 5th/11th centuries, *taḳwā* was regularly featured in classifications devoted to the spiritual transactions (*muʿāmalāt*) or moral virtues (*akhlāḳ*) of the Ṣūfīs' spiritual journey, being closely aligned to the analogous concepts of fear (*khawf*), asceticism (*zuhd*), and abstinence (*waraʿ*). Al-Ḥārith al-Muḥāsibī (d. 243/857) propounded in his *K. al-Riʿāya* that all piety stems from fear and dread of God Almighty. According to him, "Obedience [to God's commands and prohibitions] is the road to salvation, and knowledge is the guide to the road, and the foundation of obedience is abstinence (*waraʿ*), and the foundation of abstinence is godfearing piety (*taḳwā*), and the foundation of that is self-examination (*muḥāsaba*), and self-examination is based on fear (*khawf*) and hope (*radjāʾ*)" (Margaret Smith, *Al-Muhāsibī, an early mystic of Baghdad*, Cambridge 1935, 89, 112). If *taḳwā* appears in this description as an essential "foundation" of ascetic theology, the emphasis on piety is even more accentuated later on in the same book: "O brother, let godliness (*taḳwā*) be your chief concern, for it is your capital stock, and works of supererogation beyond that represent your profit" (*ibid.*, 129), cf. also Massignon, *Essai sur les origines du lexique technique de la mystique musulmane*, Paris 1928, 149.

Al-Muḥāsibī's emphasis on piety-as-godliness in early Islamic mysticism was formally integrated into the Ṣūfī methodological approach to the spiritual stations (*maḳāmāt*) in al-Ḳushayrī's *Risāla* (91-140), where *taḳwā* is placed fourth among the first ten spiritual stations, in the following sequence: [1] repentance (*tawba*) → spiritual struggle (*mudjāhida*) → spiritual retreat, withdrawal (*khalwa, ʿuzla*) → God-fearing piety (*taḳwā*) → abstinence (*waraʿ*) → asceticism (*zuhd*) → silence (*ṣamt*) → fear (*khawf*) → hope (*radjāʾ*) → [10] grief (*ḥuzn*). Despite al-Ḳushayrī's traditional classification of *taḳwā* among the rudimentary spiritual stations of the Path, the term often seemed to fall out of usage among some of the later classical authors who wrote on the *maḳāmāt*. Thus, there is no mention of *taḳwā* (whether as a station or a technical term) in Nicholson's index of technical terms to his critical edition of al-Sarrādj's (d. 378/988) *K. al-Lumaʿ*, nor in the *Ḳūt al-ḳulūb* by Abū Ṭālib al-Makkī (d. 386/996), nor in the *Ṭabaḳāt al-ṣūfiyya* of Abū ʿAbd al-Raḥmān al-Sulāmī (d. 412/1021), nor in ʿAbd Allāh Anṣārī of Harāt's (d. 481/1089) manual on the *Stages of the Ṣūfī wayfarers*, nor even in Abū Manṣūr Iṣfahānī's (d. 417/1026) *Nahdj al-khāṣṣ*, which had considerable influence on Anṣārī's theory of mystical stations.

The early notion of the fundamental place of *taḳwā* in the ascetic theology of Islam does sometimes resurface in later works, particularly those written in the Persian language. In his treatise *Ṣad maydān* ("The hundred fields", in *Manāzil al-sāʾirīn*, 299-300), which Anṣārī also devoted to the mystical stations, he set up *taḳwā* as the sixteenth station, subsequent to the field of abstinence (*waraʿ*), in the following order: [11] self-examination (*muḥāsaba*) → awakening (*yaḳẓa*) → asceticism (*zuhd*) → detachment (*tadjrīd*) → abstinence (*waraʿ*) → God-fearing piety (*taḳwā*) → spiritual transactions (*muʿāmalāt*) → mindfulness (*mubālāt*) → certitude (*yaḳīn*) → [20] insight (*baṣīra*). The field of *taḳwā* [16] is described as follows:

"Those who fear God with proper piety (*muttaḳiyān*) are three [kinds of] men: the lesser, intermediate, and the great.

"He who possesses the least degree [of *taḳwā*] does not corrupt his profession of divine Unity with associating others with God (*shirk*), or debase his sincerity (*ikhlāṣ*) with hypocrisy, or contaminate his worship with innovation (*bidʿa*).

"He who possesses the medial degree does not vitiate his service (*khidma*) with false shows (*riyāʾ*), or adulterate his sustenance with food of a doubtful nature, or let his mystical state (*ḥāl*) become perverted by heedlessness.

"He who possesses the greatest degree does not blemish his gratefulness with complaints; or dilute his sins by arguments [of his innocence], or ever cease to be beholden to God for His grace towards him."

As a key technical term or spiritual station, *taḳwā* is rarely present in any late classical Ṣūfī texts—among some of the more important of which may be mentioned Abu 'l-Nadjīb al-Suhrawardī's (d. 563/1168) *Ādāb al-murīdīn* (ed. N.M. Harawī, Arabic text with Pers. tr. Tehran 1363 A.S.H./1984), and ʿIzz al-Dīn Maḥmūd Kāshānī's (d. 735/1335) *Miṣbāḥ al-hidāya wa-miftāḥ al-kifāya* (ed. Djalāl al-Dīn Humāʾī, 2nd ed. Tehran 1325 A.S.H./1946); it is even absent from Shihāb al-Dīn Abū Ḥafṣ ʿUmar al-Suhrawardī's (d. 632/1234) *ʿAwārif al-maʿārif*, which formed the literary model for Kāshānī's book, and was later to become the foremost manual of Ṣūfism in the Indian subcontinent.

Wherever the term turns up in later works it is usually considered as a necessary corollary of *waraʿ* or *zuhd*. For instance, in Saʿīd al-Dīn al-Farghānī's (d. 699/1300) *Mashāriḳ al-darārī. Sharḥ-i Tāʾiyya Ibn Fāriḍ* (ed. Djalāl al-Dīn Āshtiyānī, Tehran 1979, 150-1), *taḳwā* is placed among the stations belonging to the first of three ascending degrees of "annihilation" (*fanāʾ*). The first degree of *fanāʾ* involves annihilation by means of "faring through and realisation of the spiritual stations, stages and mystical states such as repentance (*tawba*), self-examination (*muḥāsaba*), contemplative vigilance (*murāḳaba*), spiritual struggle (*mudjāhada*), sincerity (*ikhlāṣ*), God-fearing piety (*taḳwā*), abstinence (*waraʿ*), asceticism (*zuhd*) and similar related degrees. . . ." As in al-Ḳushayrī's schema, al-Farghānī's classification places God-fearing piety among those virtues which the mystic must struggle to realise by *his own* will; for aspirants still bound in the bonds of egocentric personality, *taḳwā* is a knife to cut through the cords of Selfhood. In the writings of the Persian mystics of the Kubrawī school, the virtue of *taḳwā* featured quite prominently. In his monumental conspectus of Ṣūfī doctrine, the *Mirṣād al-ʿibād* (ed. M.A. Riyāḥī, Tehran 1352 A.S.H./1973, 257-60), Nadjm al-Dīn Rāzī (d. 654/1256) cites some twenty qualities (*ṣifāt*) with which the disciple must be characterised in a chapter devoted to "the conditions, manners and qualities of a disciple", and here *taḳwā* is the fifth of his *sulūk*; and a similar conception of the place of *taḳwā* in Ṣūfī ethics appears in the third book of the *Kashf al-ḥaḳāʾiḳ* (ed. Aḥmad Dāmghānī, Tehran 1359/1980, 131-2)—"an exposition of the conditions for wayfaring (*sulūk*) the mystical path"—by Rāzī's fellow Kubrawī Shaykh ʿAzīz Nasafī (d. between 1281-1300).

As in the Rule of St. Benedict, for the Persian mystics of the Kubrawī order, God-fearing piety had come to be viewed as an essential virtue in the practical ethics of the master-disciple relationship, so that religious devotion is indistinguishable from unhesitating obedience to the order's superior.

6. *Taḳwā*'s apophasis in mediaeval Ṣūfism. In the mediaeval period, the master-disciple relationship and the role of the master in spiritual practice, and, in particular, the need for the novice to be guided by an enlightened master, came to the forefront of Ṣūfī theory and practice, replacing the previous emphasis on the ethics of *taḳwā* as the cornerstone of spirituality and devotional worship in Islam. Djalāl al-Dīn Rūmī stated that "The gnostic is the soul of the Law (*sharʿ*) and religious piety (*taḳwā*): gnosis is the fruit of past ascetic effort. . . . He [the gnostic] is both the command to righteousness and righteousness itself; he himself is both hierophant and mystery" (*Mathnawī*, ed. and tr. Nicholson, vi, vv. 2090, 2093). This redirection of Islamic piety towards cultivation of, and concentration on, the elect "Perfect Man" [see AL-INSĀN AL-KĀMIL] with the consequent devaluation of the devotee's own private ascetic vigilance, is visible in the thought of most Ṣūfī poets of the Mongol period. One such poet, Maḥmūd Shabistarī [*q.v.*], in his *Gulshan-i rāz* thus describes the Perfect Man as "endowed with praiseworthy qualities, celebrated for knowledge (*ʿilm*), asceticism (*zuhd*) and piety (*taḳwā*)" (*Madjmūʿa-yi āthār-i Shaykh Maḥmūd Shabistarī*, ed. Ṣamad Muwaḥḥid, Tehran 1365 A.S.H./1986, v. 351), relegating *taḳwā*, as did the classical masters of the School of Baghdād, to being a rudimentary but not insignificant principle of the Ṣūfī ethical system. However, a discernible difference in accentuation has occurred, so that the Perfect Man is the source of piety rather than piety being the animus of individual spirituality. Ultimately, the Perfect Man may decide to dispense with all pious fear as well, since he is "free of the ties of master and disciple, beyond all asceticism (*zuhd*) and all the fictions of piety (*taḳwā*)" (*ibid.*, v. 862).

In the works of Saʿdī and Ḥāfiẓ, the two greatest Persian Ṣūfī lyricists, another kind of de-accentuation on individual piety is evident, with *taḳwā* often denigrated as a kind of spiritual attitude characteristic of cold-hearted ascetics (*zāhid*) and formalist preachers. "Wherever the Sultan of Love appears, no power is left in the arm of *taḳwā*," asserts Saʿdī in the *Gulistān* (ed. Kh. Khaṭīb-Rahbar, Tehran 1348/1969, 337), and in his *ghazals* he cries out: "Stand on your feet, so we can cast aside this blue [Ṣūfī] cloak/Throw to the winds of antinominianism this idolatry which bears the name of piety (_shirk-i takwā-nām rā_)" (_Ghazalhā-yi Saʿdi_, ed. N. Īzadparast, Tehran 1362/1983, 23). Saʿdī probably knew of al-Ḳushayrī's notion that "the root of _takwā_ is fear of all idolatrous associationism (_al-shirk_)" (_Risāla_, 105), and in this verse no doubt merely wished to criticise the element of self-consciousness which _takwā_ often engendered in less sincere adepts, re-evoking the classical concept of _takwā_ which had recognised the need to develop an apophatic discourse capable of expressing the interior subtleties of its ideal (Abū Bakr al-Wāsiṭī, d. 320/931, a member of the Baghdād School, stated "piety is that you piously abstain from your own [self-indulgent] piety", cited in ʿAṭṭār, _Tadhkirat_, 745).

This paradoxical approach to the classical ideal of piety in Islam, expressed—in order to avoid meta-physical reification—in the wish to transcend the dichotomy of piety/impiety, godliness/ungodliness (understanding the affirmation of faith and piety as a subtle form of delimitation, an idolatry of a mundane doctrine instead of adoration of the Transcendent), is best expressed in the poetry of Ḥāfiẓ, as in the fol-lowing verse:

In the way of the Ṣūfī it's total infidelity
to put your trust in knowledge and piety;
Although a pilgrim boast a hundred arts
Just the same, he must have trust.
(_Dīwān_, ed. Khānlarī, 2nd ed. Tehran 1362 A.S.H./1983, 559).

Elsewhere he asks: "What relation does libertinism (_rindī_) have to purity and piety (_takwā_)?/How wide the gap between the priest's homily and the rebeck's refrain!" (_Dīwān_, 20). In another place, he boasts, "So many nights I've strayed from Piety's path (_rah-i takwā_) with harp and daff/but now they say, I'll set my foot on the strait and narrow path—indeed, a likely tale" (_ibid._, 324, no. 154 l. 2), scorning to sully the hon-our of his dervish cloak by following the pedestrian rites of canonical piety. Indeed, Ḥāfiẓ's libertinism seems a far cry from the religious sentiment of Abū 'l-Dardāʾ (d. 32/652-3 [_q.v._]), the celebrated Com-panion of the Prophet greatly venerated by early Ṣūfīs, who was reported to have preferred piety (_takwā_) above forty years of ritual worship and observances (_ʿibāda_) (Massignon, _Essai_, 158).

With Ḥāfiẓ and his followers, the austere ideals of early Islamic piety reached both a moral threshold and a metaphysical apex, as the journey from Ḳurʾānic religious concept to ascetic doctrinal ideal based on fear and abstinence, to the interiorised Ṣūfī notion of piety as the faith of the heart culminated in the irony of the paradox which dissolves the mystic's need for the _scala perfectionis_ of his own _via negativa_.

Bibliography (apart from the references already cited): Dj. Nūrbakhsh, _Maʿārif al-ṣūfiyya_, iv, London 1987, ch. 4 "Takwā", 71-80, Eng. tr. W.C. Chittick, _Sufism IV_, London 1988, ch. 4 "Wariness", 69-77); idem and S. Murata, _The vision of Islam_, New York 1994, 282-5.   (L. Lewisohn)

ṬĀLIB AL-ḤAḲḲ, "Seeker of the Truth", the title given to the Ibāḍī Khāridjite leader ʿABD ALLĀH b. YAḤYĀ, d. end of 130-beginning of 131/August-September 748.

According to the chronicler al-Shammākhī (d. 928/1522), the full name of this leader from the Banū Shayṭān of Kinda was Abū Yaḥyā ʿAbd Allāh b. Yaḥyā b. ʿUmar b. al-Aswad b. ʿAbd Allāh b. al-Ḥārith b. Muʿāwiya b. al-Ḥārith al-Kindī (_Siyar_, 98). He adopted the title of "Seeker of the Truth" at the beginning of the year 129/746 on receiving the oath of allegiance as _Imām_ of the Ibāḍī community of

Ḥaḍramawt and Yemen. The Arabic sources give scanty information on him. A biography written by an anonymous Ibāḍī author, the _Sīrat al-Imām ʿAbd Allāh b. Yaḥyā_, together with a collection of his poems, was still available in the 9th/15th century, but has not survived until now (A. de C. Motylinski, _Bibliographie du Mzab_, in _Bulletin de Correspondance Africaine_, iii [1885], 20, nos. 29-30).

ʿAbd Allāh b. Yaḥyā was _ḳāḍī_ to Ibrāhīm b. Djabala b. Makhrama al-Kindī, the Umayyad vice-governor of Ḥaḍramawt. He was a pious man and an ener-getic leader, and his inflexible attitude towards in-fringements of Ḳurʾānic precepts, which were still widespread, won over the hearts of those Yemenis who were dissatisfied with the Umayyad régime. He was in touch with the Ibāḍīs of Baṣra, who had spread their propaganda across the Arabian peninsula using the Meccan Pilgrimage to disseminate their principles. Abū ʿUbayda Muslim b. Abī Karīma, the leader of the Ibāḍīs of Baṣra, encouraged him to revolt against the Umayyad government and sent to him not only weapons and funds but also some prominent person-alities, amongst them Abū Ḥamza al-Mukhtār and Baldj b. ʿUḳba al-Azdī, who came to the Ḥaḍramawt with the aim of organising an imāmate. The revolt appears to have taken place towards the end of 127 or the beginning of 128/745-6. Having gained con-trol in Ḥaḍramawt, the rebels then in 129/747 crossed into Yemen and occupied the capital Ṣanʿāʾ. There ʿAbd Allāh b. Yaḥyā distributed the wealth of the Umayyad treasury to the poor and, as _Imām_, showed himself to be of a mild disposition. He organised a new system of administration but nevertheless kept the former officials in their old ranks. Many Khāridjites from other regions flocked to him, attracted by his honesty and rectitude. At the end of the year 129/747, at the time of pilgrimage, ʿAbd Allāh b. Yaḥyā decided to occupy the two Holy Cities, Mecca and Medina. The Ibāḍī army, only 900 or 1,000 strong, under the command of Abū Ḥamza al-Mukhtār, took Mecca with ease, and then went on to occupy Medina.

From Ḥidjāz, the Ibāḍīs now became an immedi-ate threat to the Umayyads in Syria, so that, despite his waning might, the caliph Marwān II assembled sufficient strength to overcome the rebels. Around the beginning of Djumādā I 130/January 748, a strong army composed of 4,000 Syrian soldiers, led by ʿAbd al-Mālik b. ʿAṭiyya, marched against Medina. Abū Ḥamza was defeated and killed. At the end of 130 A.H. the Syrian army marched against Yemen. On receiving news of this, ʿAbd Allāh b. Yaḥyā, at the head of an Ibāḍī force, left Ṣanʿāʾ to prevent the Syrians from penetrating the land. The encounter between the two armies took place not far from Djurash, where the Ibāḍī army suffered a serious defeat. Ṭālib al-Ḥaḳḳ was killed and his head sent to Marwān II, while the rest of the Ibāḍīs took cover in the fortified town of Shibām [_q.v._]. A long elegy on the fallen leaders is quoted in _Aghānī_, xxiii, 148 ff. While this serious Ibāḍī rising was quelled, it is nev-ertheless true that the anarchy that it provoked con-tributed to the final undoing of Umayyad power and enabled the ʿAbbāsid insurrection to penetrate more easily to the heart of the empire. Having defeated ʿAbd Allāh b. Yaḥyā, ʿAbd al-Mālik b. ʿAṭiyya took Ṣanʿāʾ and brought Ḥaḍramawt into submission, but afterwards received from the caliph Marwān b. Muḥammad an order to return to Mecca. He was thus forced to conclude a peace with the Ibāḍīs and to recognise their independence in Ḥaḍramawt. After the death of Ṭālib al-Ḥaḳḳ, ʿAbd Allāh b. Saʿīd al-Ḥaḍramī was recognised as his successor by the Ibāḍīs of both Ḥaḍramawt and Baṣra.

Bibliography: 1. Sources. *Ag̲h̲ānī*[3], xxiii, 111 ff.; Dard̲j̲īnī, *K. Ṭabaqāt al-mas̲h̲āyik̲h̲ bi 'l-Mag̲h̲rib*, ed. I. Ṭallāy, 2 vols. Constantine 1394/1974, ii, 258-61; Ibn Sallām al-Lawātī al-Ibāḍī, *Kitāb Ibn Sallām. Eine ibaditisch-magribinische Geschichte des Islams aus dem 3./9. Jahrhundert*, ed. W. Schwartz and Sālim b. Ya'ḳūb, Bibliotheca Islamica 33, Wiesbaden 1986, 112-13, 117; *Kas̲h̲f al-g̲h̲umma al-d̲j̲āmi' li-ak̲h̲bār al-umma li-muṣannif mad̲j̲hūl*, ed. 'Ubaydalī, Nicosia 1985, 162 ff.; Mas'ūdī, *Murūd̲j̲*, vi, 66-7; S̲h̲ammāk̲h̲ī, *K. al-Siyar*, lith. Cairo 1301/1883, 98-102; *[al-]Siyar wa 'l-d̲j̲awābāt li-'ulamā' wa-a'imma 'Umān*, ed. I. Kās̲h̲if, 2 vols. 'Umān 1410/1989, i, 133, 204-5; Ṭabarī, ii, 1981-3, 2006-14.

2. Studies. J. Wellhausen, *Die religiöspolitischen Oppositionsparteien im alten Islam*, Berlin 1901, 52 ff.; Ch. Pellat, Le *milieu baṣrien et la formation de Ǧāḥiz*, Paris 1952, 212-14; T. Lewicki, *Les Ibāḍites dans l'Arabie du Sud*, in *Folia Orientalia*, i (1959), 6-9; H. Laoust, *Les schismes dans l'Islam. Introduction à une étude de la religion musulmane*, Paris 1965, 43-4; A.M. Khleifat (K̲h̲ulayfāt), *Nas̲h̲'at al-ḥaraka al-ibāḍiyya*, 'Ammān 1978, 116-26; J. van Ess, *Theologie und Gesellschaft im 2. und 3. Jahrhundert der Hidschra*, 6 vols. Berlin-New York 1991-7, ii, 656-7.

(Ersilia Francesca)

ṬĀLIBĀN, Pers. plural of Arabic *ṭālib* "student", a term coming into use in the last years of the 20th century for a radical Islamist group in Afghānistān.

These "religious students" became the face of radical Islam during the late 1990s, when they controlled most of Afg̲h̲ānistān. They emerged in reaction to widespread lawlessness in south-western Afg̲h̲ānistān in the summer of 1994 and went on to become the dominant force in Afg̲h̲ānistān until their defeat by a US-led coalition of forces in the autumn of 2001. Core leaders of the Ṭālibān were trained in the *madrasas* or religious colleges of Pakistan's North-West Frontier Province (NWFP) and Balūchistān affiliated to or run by the conservative Islamist Pakistani political movement, the D̲j̲ami'at al-'Ulamā-i Islāmī/Jamiat-ul-Ulema-i-Islami (JUI) party, whose ideology blended Wahhābī influences from Arabia with the Dēobandi tradition of South Asia.

Led by a former *mud̲j̲āhid* in the Afghan-Soviet War of the 1980s, Mullā Muḥammad 'Umar, the early Ṭālibān were primarily young former *mud̲j̲āhidīn*, mostly southern Pus̲h̲tūns. There is debate about whether the Ṭālibān were essentially an indigenous movement that Pakistan supported to advance its own foreign policy goals, or whether the Ṭālibān were from the beginning a creation of Pakistan, which had seen its Afghan policy frustrated by the civil war between *mud̲j̲āhidīn* factions following the fall of the Communist government in April 1992 and was seeking an alternative faction to support, especially in the fractious Ḳandahār area. Regardless of the source of their genesis, the Ṭālibān gained prominence and power through deep, early, and multi-faceted support from Pakistan's Interior Ministry, Inter-Services Intelligence Directorate (ISI), army, and society and were Pakistan's proxy army in Afg̲h̲ānistān by 1995. From a strategic standpoint, the Ṭālibān provided Pakistan with a militia that could possibly settle the power struggle within Afg̲h̲ānistān, but at the minimum could control the southwest of the country and make possible a stable route for trade with Central Asia.

After their unexpected emergence near Ḳandahār in October 1994, the Ṭālibān steadily advanced to gain control of almost all of Afg̲h̲ānistān, despite some setbacks, such as the massacre of their forces at Mazār-i-S̲h̲arīf in May 1997 and Northern Alliance leader Aḥmad S̲h̲āh Mas'ūd's counter-attack north of Kābul in August 1999. Following their capture of Ḳandahār in November 1994, the Ṭālibān advanced through Pus̲h̲tūn tribal areas toward Kābul, ultimately forcing Gulbuddīn Ḥikmatyār's Ḥizb-i Islāmī to evacuate its positions south of the city. The then Defence Minister, Aḥmad S̲h̲āh Mas'ūd soundly defeated the Ṭālibān and drove them out of range of Kābul in the spring of 1995, so the Ṭālibān turned their attention to western Afg̲h̲ānistān, capturing Harāt in September 1995. In September 1996 the Ṭālibān flanked Kābul to the east and captured D̲j̲alālābād, then drove up the main road through steep gorges toward Kābul, which fell without a fight later that month. Having taken control of the capital and most of Afg̲h̲ānistān after only two years, in 1997 the Ṭālibān sought to conquer the north of Afg̲h̲ānistān and finish off the remnants of the Burhānuddīn Rabbānī government.

Divisions within the Northern Alliance made possible the temporary Ṭālibān capture of Mazār-i-S̲h̲arīf in May 1997, but after four days local militias rebelled and destroyed the Ṭālibān forces there, while a Ṭālibān force that had come up from Kābul through the Salang Pass was cut off and surrounded in Ḳunduz. In the summer of 1998 the Ṭālibān pushed resolutely into the north once again, this time capturing Mazār-i-S̲h̲arīf in August and Bāmiyān in September. Following the fall of both cities, the Ṭālibān killed or forcibly relocated thousands of the residents. After the campaigns of 1998, the Ṭālibān controlled all but 10-15% of the country, primarily the rugged north-eastern mountains where Aḥmad S̲h̲āh Mas'ūd's well-organised Tad̲j̲ik army held on. Combat ebbed and flowed in and out of this area over the next three years, with Mas'ūd having great success in August 1999, but his assassination on 9 September 2001 by al-Ḳā'ida (al-Qaeda) operatives coincided with the beginning of a final Ṭālibān push into his salient that might have been successful had the events of 11 September 2001 not brought the United States into Afg̲h̲ānistān with the goal of destroying the Ṭālibān.

Afg̲h̲ānistān's long war destroyed or discredited most of its traditional leadership and led to a deep Islamisation of its society, providing the milieu in which the Ṭālibān could arise. The Ṭālibān were the last and most vehement of Afg̲h̲ānistān's Islamist leaders, but they were simultaneously a Pus̲h̲tūn ethnic movement and a militia for Pakistan. Thus, their rise to power hardened ethnic divisions in Afg̲h̲ānistān and heightened the regional competition between Pakistan, Saudi Arabia, Iran and Russia for control within the country. The multiple sources of Ṭālibān identity gave the movement a plasticity that enhanced its resiliency over time. The Ṭālibān leadership was comprised of Ḳandahār-area Pus̲h̲tūns of different tribal and sub-tribal lineages, but most of the Inner S̲h̲ūrā (council) knew each other from shared combat experiences during the Afghan-Soviet War and/or shared time in Pakistani *madrasas*. As the movement expanded its territorial control, its ranks grew to include eastern and northern G̲h̲ilzai Pus̲h̲tūns, some ethnic minority militias, and former Afghan Communist soldiers from the K̲h̲alḳ/Khalq faction (introduced by the Pakistanis to provide the Ṭālibān with specialised military skills in which they were lacking; following the conquests of 1998 most of the ex-Communists were purged).

The Ṭālibān also were an international force, with

thousands of Pakistani "volunteers" (over 100,000 had served by the time of the Ṭālibān's defeat) and an "international brigade" of largely Arab fighters under the command of Usāma b. Lādin/Osama bin Laden. When the Ṭālibān captured Dj̲alalābād in 1996 they began a partnership with Osama bin Laden and his al-Ḳāʿida organisation that was based in that area. Over the next few years, the Ṭālibān-al-Ḳāʿida nexus became more puritanical and intolerant of Afg̲hānistān's northern minorities, and increasingly larger numbers of Pakistani "volunteers" joined the movement. Thus, what was initially seen in the southwest of Afg̲hānistān as a local Pus̲h̲tūn movement came to be seen by its northern opponents as a front for Pakistani aspirations in Afg̲hānistān.

As the Ṭālibān grew more numerous, tensions between the different factions within the movement occurred on several levels. The early core of Ṭālibān leaders kept most of the positions of authority, and many of them remained in Ḳandahār near to Mullā ʿUmar, who ruled from there rather than moving to Kābul when it fell in 1996. Over time, a moderate faction led by Premier Muḥammad Rabbānī and Foreign Minister Wakīl Aḥmad lost ground to the growing influence of a hard-line faction affiliated with Osama bin Laden. This cost the Ṭālibān international recognition (only Pakistan, Saudi Arabia, and the United Arab Emirates ever recognised the movement) and support. During the late 1990s, al-Ḳāʿida became increasingly aggressive, targeting the U.S. in several high-profile operations, which led to U.S. cruise missile attacks on Afg̲hānistān in August 1998, increased U.S. pressure on the Ṭālibān to give up Bin Laden, and sanctions by the U.S. and U.N. on the Ṭālibān régime starting in 1999. The struggle between moderates and hard-liners within the Ṭālibān shifted in favour of the latter group with the destruction of the cliff Buddhas of Bāmiyān in March 2001 and the death of Muḥammad Rabbānī in April 2001. Ultimately, the attacks by al-Ḳāʿida on the U.S. on 11 September 2001 brought about the destruction of the Ṭālibān and al-Ḳāʿida rule and the implementation of an interim government in December 2001 headed by Ḥamīd Kārzai, a Durrānī Pus̲h̲tūn tribal leader.

The Ṭālibān were a tribal militia, a Pakistani proxy army, and a movement for social change in Afg̲hānistān. Their early success on the battlefield was due to the shared ethnicity and war-weariness of the populations in the areas that they conquered during 1994-6. They also presented themselves as simple men motivated by piety and a desire to Islamise Afghan society, holding themselves in contrast to the formerly noble *mud̲j̲āhidīn* whose lust for power had caused them to stray from the straight path of Islamic governance. Ultimately, though, the Ṭālibān extended their control over almost all of Afg̲hānistān due to extensive Pakistani support, including money, weapons, training, military advisers, direct military involvement, logistical support, and recruits. The return of tens of thousands of these recruits to Pakistan exacerbated and deepened Islamist trends in that society, producing an effect referred to within that country as the "Talibanisation" of Pakistan.

Although they ruled most of Afghānistān for several years, Ṭālibān governance was mostly non-existent. Perhaps this was by design, and Afg̲hānistān's state failure under the Ṭālibān was a conscious effort to destroy a Western model of government there, but more likely it reflected Ṭālibān incompetence at government. Rule was by decree from Mullā ʿUmar, or from organisations such as the Ministry for the Promotion of Virtue and Prevention of Vice (*Amr bi 'l-Maʿrūf wa-Nahy ʿan al-Munkar*), a religious police modelled on the similar organisation that exists in Saudi Arabia. A 30 to 40-man S̲h̲ūrā advised Mullā ʿUmar. There were few funds for routine government, and most of the 27 ministries sat idle, as such funds as the Ṭālibān did have went into the war effort against the Northern Alliance. Traditional social welfare functions of government such as infrastructure re-building were carried out by international aid organisations in Afg̲hānistān, although the Ṭālibān frequently constrained their operations.

The centrepiece of Taliban Islamisation policy was the maltreatment of women and girls, denying them access to adequate health care, education, jobs and basic human rights. Women's status and position in Afghan society had come to be symbolic of all that the Ṭālibān opposed, and their mistreatment of females helped keep their young male fighters unified and supportive, since most of them had learned in the Pakistani *madrasas* that women were supposed to be constrained in the ways practiced by the Ṭālibān leadership. Other notable Ṭālibān social policies included applying *S̲h̲arīʿa* punishments (based on Ṭālibān interpretation of the *S̲h̲arīʿa*, which was influenced by Pus̲h̲tūnwālī, or code of the Pus̲h̲tūns), such as execution for adultery and amputation of hands for theft; forcing men to attend mosque services and grow beards as signs of piety; bans on all forms of secular entertainment, such as sports, music and television; and ultimately the destruction of images in Afg̲hānistān, including the world-famous Bāmiyān Buddhas.

The Ṭālibān were a by-product of Afg̲hānistān's long and highly destructive war and capped a decades-long movement to Islamise Afghan society, itself a reaction to an even longer attempt by Afghan urban élites to modernise the country. The collapse of the Afghan state, the Islamisation of the Afghan resistance movement and refugee population, and the regional geopolitical struggle following the Cold War combined to create the unique conditions that gave rise to the Ṭālibān. U.S.-led military operations beginning in late 2001 have now almost destroyed the Ṭālibān movement, but the underlying ideology of Islamising the state and society remains and continues to influence Afg̲hānistān.

Bibliography: R. Moshref, *The Taliban*, New York 1997; R.H. Magnus, *Afghanistan in 1996 – year of the Taliban*, in *Asian Survey*, xxxvii/2 (February 1997), 111-17; idem and E. Naby, *Afghanistan – mullah, Marx, and mujahid*, Boulder 1998; W. Maley (ed.), *Fundamentalism reborn? Afghanistan and the Taliban*, New York 1998 (excellent collection of articles); P. Marsden, *The Taliban: war, religion, and the new order in Afghanistan*, London 1998; Physicians for Human Rights, *The Taliban's war on women: a health and human rights crisis in Afghanistan*, Boston 1998; K. Matinuddin, *The Taliban phenomenon: Afghanistan 1994-1997*, Karachi 1999 (useful); B.R. Rubin, *Afghanistan under the Taliban*, in *Current History*, xcviii/625 (February 1999), 79-91; A. Rashid, *The Taliban: exporting extremism*, in *Foreign Affairs*, lxxviii/6 (November-December 1999), 22-35; idem, *Taliban: militant Islam, oil, and fundamentalism in Central Asia*, New Haven 2000 (fundamental); M. Griffin, *Reaping the whirlwind: the Taliban movement in Afghanistan*, London 2001; L.P. Goodson, *Afghanistan's endless war: state failure, regional politics, and the rise of the Taliban*, Seattle 2001 (fundamental); idem, *Perverting Islam: Taliban social policy toward women*, in *Central Asian Survey*, xx/4 (December 2001), 415-26.

(L.P. Goodson)

TARĀ'ŌRI, an alternative name for the place mentioned in Indo-Muslim history as Nārdīn or Nandana in the Jhelum District of the Western Pandjāb, now in Pakistan; see on it NANDANA, in Suppl.

TARDJAMA.

4. (b) The 20th century.

In the 20th century, translation into Arabic contributed noticeably to the shaping of modern Arabic literatures and cultures. It arose in historical circumstances which considerably differed from those of the Arabic translation movement (*ḥarakat al-tardjama*) in the previous century (see 4. (a) at Vol. X, 232b). The colonial experience, the rise of nationalist and anti-colonial movements, and the subsequent formation of independent Arab nation states exercised a strong ideological impact on Arab societies. The specific developments of translation as an integral part of Arabic national cultures embodied their changing interests and priorities.

In the early decades of the century, the proliferation of privately-owned periodicals and publishing houses in Egypt, Lebanon, Syria, Palestine and ʿIrāḳ made possible the broader transmission of texts into Arabic. New centres of translation emerged in the communities of Arab immigrants in Northern and Southern America [see MAHDJAR]. Journalists, writers and scholars participated, along with trained professionals, in thriving translation practices. As the number of translated works increased on an unprecedented scale, the sources, methods and forms of individual translations diversified.

For the first time in Arabic cultural history, the translation of literature took precedence over other forms of linguistic and cultural import. This new cultural phenomenon was related to a massive translation of Western fiction prompted by the growing demand of readers dissatisfied with traditional forms of literary discourse. Their manifest interest in translated narratives, especially short stories, met a strong response on the part of Arab authors searching for new ways of artistic expression. Transmission of Western literature became an integral part of their creative activity, along with composition of original works in the new fictional genres discovered through the experience of translation. Prominent early contributors to Arabic literary translation were the writers and poets Ḥāfiẓ Ibrāhīm, Muṣṭafā al-Manfalūṭī [*q.vv.*], the first school of modern Egyptian writing, *madrasat al-dīwān* (the Dīwān school); Nadjīb al-Ḥaddād, Salīm al-Naḳḳāsh and Niḳūlā Ḥaddād in Lebanon; Khalīl Baydās, Anṭūn Ballān, and Nadjātī Ṣidḳī in Palestine; Muḥammad Kurd ʿAlī and Tanyūs ʿAbduh in Syria; Salīm Baṭṭī and Maḥmūd Aḥmad al-Sayyid in ʿIrāḳ; and the leading figures of *madrasat al-mahdjar* (the literary school of Arab immigrants in the United States) Nasīb ʿArīḍa, ʿAbd al-Masīḥ Ḥaddād and Mīkhā'īl Nuʿayma [*q.v.*].

The involvement of writers and poets broadened the scale of literary translation. While the majority of translated texts represented short stories, novellas and novels, since the beginning of the century more attempts were made at translation of European drama and poetry. In addition to French classical plays by Corneille, Rostand and Molière, Shakespeare's works—especially *Romeo and Juliet*—inspired several early Arabic adaptations. Ṭāhā Ḥusayn [*q.v.*] translated and published an anthology of Greek dramatic poetry (1920), Racine's *Andromaque* (1935) and a selection of Western drama (1959). Poems by Victor Hugo, Lamartine and Shelley were amongst the first rendered into Arabic. Typically, Arab translators dealt with differences of prosody between the traditions of Western and classical Arabic poetry by rendering Western poetic forms into prose. Further generic changes as in al-Manfalūṭī's radical transformation of a rhymed play—Rostand's *Cyrano de Bergerac* (1921)—into a novel were uncommon. The modern Arabic poetic free-verse style developed since the 1950s offered translators of poetry a new tool.

French literature remained an essential source of translation in the first decades of the century: reportedly, by 1930 more than 150 French authors were represented in Arabic translations, and about 15 English ones. The contributions of *madrasat al-mahdjar* included the introduction of Arab readers to classical works of American and Russian literatures. In 1920, Aḥmad Ḥasan al-Zayyāt's eloquent Arabic rendition of Goethe's *Die Leiden des jungen Werthers* from the German original was still a rare occurrence. In the inter-war period, single works by Italian, Greek and Turkish authors attracted translators' attention as embodiments of national cultures to which they related by way of human and intellectual experience.

Not all Western source texts selected for translation, nor all of their Arabic versions, were of high literary and cultural value. A great deal of translators' production catered to the needs of a growing popular market for romantic stories, mysteries and adventures. Translation techniques involving rewritings (*tardjama mawḍūʿa*), adaptations (*tardjama bi 'l-taṣarruf*), additions (*iḍāfāt*), abridgements (*tardjama mulakhkhaṣa*), and various changes of the genre, set, plot and characters of the original, did not always yield good quality in the target language. Yet the substantial body of Arab fictional texts that those early translations built contributed, by its sheer mass, to familiarising Arabic readers with new genres of fiction. At their best, the pioneers of Arabic literary translation created works, which, like original writings, expressed and affirmed their own cultural identity and traditions through the forms of Western literature. The appreciation of their audiences accounts for the longevity of such creative translations. They continued to flourish well into the 1940s, long after the genres of Western fiction had been adopted in Arabic writing, replacing traditional forms of literary discourse.

A similar symbiosis between translation and creation of literature is observed in many national cultures at the formative stage, when writers commonly use translation as a creative device and for addressing what they perceive as the pressing issues and actual cultural needs of their societies and time. Since the 1920s, modern Arabic literary theory and criticism have contributed to the emergence of new perceptions of translation, which have determined its subsequent evolution as a creative activity with specific social and cultural functions.

Extensive transmission of Western scientific knowledge and intellectual thought continued. Translated contemporary works of history, philosophy and literary theory were an integral part of the critical debates of the day (e.g. the translation of Thomas Carlyle's *On heroes, hero-worship, and the heroic in history* (1911) by the Dīwān school). Translations of Herbert Spencer's *On education* (1908) and Lebon's work on pedagogy (by Ṭāhā Ḥusayn, 1921) reflected the edifying priorities of Arab intellectuals. Aḥmad Luṭfī al-Sayyid's [*q.v.*] renderings of Aristotle from the original (1924-35) introduced the classical tradition of Western intellectual thought. At that time, major influences on modern Arabic literary theory and criticism (Freud's psychoanalysis, the ideas of the Russian formalists, etc.) were also exercised through the intermediary of Western languages different from the original.

In the second half of the century, translation entered a new phase of development under the aegis of the independent Arab nation states. The cultural policy of *taʿrīb* [*q.v.*] (arabisation) adopted by Arab governments placed special emphasis on translation as a means of interaction with other cultures meant to serve what they deemed the interest of Arab societies and their comprehensive advancement.

Efforts have been made to support the study of translation and develop translators' professional skills. Translation is a commonly taught subject within foreign language acquisition programmes at the high school level. Arab translators receive modern professional training in independent academic institutions (e.g. al-Mustanṣiriyya School in ʿIrāḳ; King Fahd School for Translation in Morocco), or through academic programmes in translation offered in a number of universities (e.g. the King Suʿūd University in Saudi Arabia; Yarmūk University in Jordan; Alexandria University in Egypt, etc.). The academic institutions develop translation studies as well (e.g. the Translation Center at the King Suʿūd University worked in the last decade on a major project designed to catalogue 20th-century Arabic translations). Pan-Arab conferences provide forums for discussion of policies and issues of translation (e.g. al-Tunis, 1979, on developing common criteria for selecting texts for translation, reassessing the status and training of Arab translators, etc.; Jordan, 1992, on translation studies; Egypt, 1995, on scientific translation; etc.).

At the national level, the ministries of culture and education oversee translation activities. In many countries, translators are syndicated in professional organisations and unions, and some are individual members of the International Translators' Union (Geneva).

At the regional level, two organisations formulate pan-Arab strategies of translation. The objective of the Arabisation Coordination Bureau (1961, Rabat) is to create and update a unified system of modern Arabic terminology. The Arab Center for Arabisation, Translation, Authorship and Publication (1989, Damascus) supports translation into Arabic of materials for higher and university education in all areas of academic and technical specialisation, and of distinguished works in the fields of the sciences, literature and arts. Both organisations are affiliated with ALECSO. Recent contributions of Arab translators to ALECSO's cultural programmes include publications of *Basic Arabic dictionary* (1988) and *Trilingual thesaurus: Arabic, English, French* (1995); and the ongoing projects *Translations of distinguished books on science and technology*, and *Arabic unified dictionaries*. The Islamic Organisation for Culture and Science also retains translation programmes.

Over the last five decades, translation production has increased everywhere in the Arab world. Egypt and Syria hold leading positions, with more than 100 publishers of translations in each country (here and further below, statistics by UNESCO, *Index translationum*). Lately, Saudi Arabia and Kuwait have emerged as major translation centres.

French and English remain the important sources of Arabic translation, used also as intermediaries for transmission of texts written in other original languages. Since the 1930s, and especially with the influx of American culture in the post-World War II period, English became the main source language of translation into Arabic. In the course of the most recent decades, the source languages diversified, reflecting new cultural priorities on the part of Arab authors, audiences and institutions related to the acquisition of modern technologies and know-how; to the interest in literatures and cultures traditionally not represented, or under-represented by Arabic translation, etc. The pool of languages from which translations are currently undertaken includes Japanese, Chinese, and other less common foreign languages. The leading languages from which books were translated into Arabic in the last 20 years are: English (3188 translations), Russian (1388), French (929), German (263), Spanish (149), Persian (77), Italian (58) and Turkish (49).

The majority of texts translated in the second half of the century represent fiction of European origin: Shakespeare is the most translated foreign author, with a total of 49 Arabic translations, closely followed by Agatha Christie with 47. Emerging since the interwar period new concepts of the nature of translation and its cultural functions manifested themselves in a more attentive approach to the selection and transmission of original texts. Translators' creativity was employed to best express the ideas of the original using the tools of the modern Arabic language. The resulting more accurate renditions of classics by Balzac, Turgenev, Dickens, Baudelaire, Guy de Maupassant, Sartre, Gorky, Thomas Mann, Camus, James Joyce, T.S. Eliot, Virginia Woolf and Apollinaire exposed readers to a variety of writing styles, and encouraged since the 1950s new trends in Arabic prose (realism, modernism, stream-of-consciousness), and poetry (the free-verse movement). In drama, Chekhov, Henrik Ibsen and Harold Pinter elicited many translations (the latter's works compiled in a three-volume edition appeared in Cairo in 1987). Since 1983, Kuwait's Ministry of Information has published a series of modern translations from classical Greek of Euripides' tragedies.

Among the significant American writers translated in that period (e.g. Faulkner, Hemingway, Fitzgerald, Henry Miller), Edgar Allan Poe was better known for his mystery stories than as a poet, but Mark Twain remained most popular, his early Arabic renditions revisited by later translators. Lately, Arabic versions of Walt Disney's books head the growing production of children's literature in translation, including classic tales by Leo Tolstoy, Wilhelm and Jacob Grimm, Hans Christian Andersen, and modern Western authors.

In the 1960s to early 1980s, publishers in Moscow, Leipzig and other cultural centres of the then Communist countries produced a large number of Arabic translations introducing classics of their national literatures. The collaboration between Arab and European translators and publishing houses continues to broaden the perspective of Arab readers on European literary traditions (e.g. Arab and Swedish translators at present render from the original poems by Tomas Tranströmer, one of Sweden's most important contemporary poets, whose forthcoming Arabic anthology will be published by al-Muʾassasa al-ʿArabiyya li 'l-Dirāsāt wa 'l-Nashr in 2003).

Numerous translations of works by Milan Kundera (Czech Republic), Wole Soyinka (Nigeria), Gabriel Garcia Marquez (Colombia) and Aziz Nesin (Turkey) in the course of the last decade testify to lasting aspirations by leading Arab translators and publishers to bring the best of modern world literature to their audiences.

In literary translation, transmission through intermediary languages remains a problem (e.g. Kundera and Marquez were first translated from French; Italo

Calvino and Ibsen from English; etc.). Duplications (e.g. four recent renderings of George Orwell's *1984*) could be avoided through better professional communication (al-ʿAysawī, 11-12).

Translations of non-fictional literature range from the modern sciences, business, social theories, philosophy (e.g. Foucault), psychoanalysis (e.g. Freud, Pierre Daco), literary theory (e.g. Barthes), general history, history of religions and religious writings, psychology and social behaviour (e.g. Edward De Bono), to popular science adaptations, textbooks at all educational levels, etc. Randomly selected and outdated source texts are by no means an exception.

Works which represent Western points of view on the history and culture of the region, have always aroused interest among Arab translators and readers (e.g. the latest accomplishment of the Egyptian National Translation Project, the 2002 translation of Marilyn Booth's study on Bayram al-Tūnisī; the recent translations of studies on modern Palestinian and Egyptian history by the German scholar Alexander Schölch; on Libyan history by the Italian scholar Francesco Coro; etc.).

A growing transmission of modern scientific knowledge has emphasised the need for an even closer cooperation between professionals in specific fields and in translation in the search for Arabic equivalents of foreign terms and modes of scientific expression (al-ʿAysawī, 15).

During the entire modern period, translations have been made primarily in *al-fuṣḥā*. While the part of *al-ʿāmmiyya* increases in original fictional writings, and the performing arts of Arabic theatre and cinema, it remains limited in fictional translation. The colloquial versions of Arabic are entirely absent from non-fictional translation. As a target language, *al-fuṣḥā* has shown flexibility, adjusting its structures to fit new forms of discourse brought by translation. In the process of giving shape to new ideas and meanings, translation has constantly perfected its linguistic vehicle. By modernising the vocabulary, amplifying the semantics, and modifying and simplifying the sentence structure of the language, translation contributes to building a modern, informative and to-the-point style of expression in literary Arabic. Modern translation has enriched the cultures of Arab nations and shared their best achievements with the world: in the last two decades of the 20th century alone, 6881 books were translated into Arabic, and 6756 from Arabic into other languages.

Bibliography: M. Mahir and W. Ule, *Deutsche Autoren in arabischer Sprache, Arabische Autoren in deutscher Sprache*, Saur n.d.; H. Pérès, *Le roman, le conte et la nouvelle dans la littérature arabe moderne*, in *AIEO*, iii (1937), 266-337 (esp. list of trs. from the French, 289-311); Tawfīḳ al-Ḥakīm, *Ḳalbunā al-masraḥī*, Cairo 1967 (tr. of drama); Budayr Ḥilmī, *al-Muʾaththirāt al-adjnabiyya fī 'l-adab al-ʿarabiyy al-ḥadīth*, Cairo 1982; Aḥmad ʿIṣām al-Dīn, *Ḥarakat al-tardjama fī Miṣr fī 'l-ḳarn al-ʿishrīn*, Cairo 1986; Saʿīd ʿAllūsh, *Khiṭāb al-tardjama al-adabiyya: min al-izdiwādjiyya ilā 'l-muthāḳafa; al-Maghrib al-ḥadīth (1912-1956)*, Rabat 1990; Ḥussām Khāṭib, *Ḥarakat al-tardjama al-filasṭīniyya: min al-nahḍa ḥattā awākhir al-ḳarn al-ʿishrīn*, Beirut 1995; Bashīr al-ʿAysawī, *al-Tardjama ilā 'l-ʿarabiyya: ḳaḍāyā wa-ārāʾ*, Cairo 1996; Salīm ʿAys, *al-Tardjama fī khidmat al-thaḳāfa 'l-djamāhīriyya*, Damascus 1999; UNESCO, *Index Translationum Database*, Paris 2002.

Periodicals on translation. *al-Lisān al-ʿArabī*, ALECSO; *Arabic Journal of Arabisation*, ALECSO (lexicology; terminology); *Turdjumān*, The King Fahd School for Translation, Tangier; *Madjallat al-alsun li 'l-tardjama*, Cairo; *Tawāṣul*, Aden; *Madjallat al-adab wa 'l-tardjama*, Université Saint-Esprit, Kazlik, Lebanon. (Mirena Christoff)

TAʿRĪB.

2. Arabicisation as a weapon of modern political policy.

Given that the Arabic language is commonly identified as a vital, if not the most important, aspect of Arab nationalist ideologies—whether they are pan-Arab, regional, or state-specific—Arabicisation has played a significant role in modern Arab politics. In the early 19th century, before Arab nationalist discourse began to emerge, Muḥammad ʿAlī [*q.v.*] of Egypt laid the foundations for the use of Arabic as an instrument of state-building. As part of his efforts to modernise education in Egypt, particularly military, medical and scientific education, Muḥammad ʿAlī authorised the establishment of a School of Languages (*Madrasat al-Alsun*) in 1835. The school was closed in 1850 during the reign of ʿAbbās Ḥilmī I [*q.v.*] but reopened in 1863 on orders of Ismāʿīl. Under the leadership of Rifāʿa al-Ṭahṭāwī (1801-73 [*q.v.*]) during both of its phases, the school undertook an ambitious program of not only training translators, but also of translating and publishing European texts in Arabic. Thus, the School of Languages pioneered the ideology and the methodology of *taʿrīb*. The European works chosen for translation reflected the interests of the State as determined mainly by al-Ṭahṭāwī, who remained loyal to the house of Muḥammad ʿAlī throughout his life. These works included texts in geography, history, medicine, military sciences and politics. In translating modern European works into Arabic, the staff of the School of Languages devised not only the principles for rendering foreign languages into a clear, modern Arabic idiom, but also coined Arabic vocabulary to express novel technical terms. In many ways, therefore, the school provided the intellectual resources for the Arab nationalist movement that gained ground in the latter half of the 19th century and provided Arab nationalists with grounds for asserting the continuing vitality and centrality of Arabic in their nationalist programs.

The work of European and American missionaries, primarily in the Levant, provided a second catalyst for the revitalisation of Arabic during the 19th century. American and British Protestant missions, eager to distinguish themselves from the French Catholics, who insisted upon and actively promoted the use of French, encouraged the translation of the Bible and liturgical readings into Arabic. The schools established by Protestant missionaries also promoted the study of Arabic in their curricula. The political consequences of these policies were perhaps more significant and long-lasting than the religious: The missionaries helped to nurture a sense of Arab national identity among both Muslims and Christians that distinguished them linguistically from the other constituents of the Ottoman Empire.

Arabicisation in Arab nationalist discourse

The unifying factor of language in Arab nationalism is a theme developed at length by a number of intellectuals during the late 19th and early 20th centuries. ʿAbd al-Raḥmān al-Kawākibī (*ca.* 1849-1902 [*q.v.*]) viewed Arab political unity and cultural revival as a necessary precursor to pan-Islamic unity and revival. In *Umm al-ḳurā*, as part of his argument for Arab leadership of the Islamic world, he claims that the language of the Arabs is the language common to all Muslims. Yet he also prepares the foundation for later secular Arab nationalists by acknowledging that Arabic is the native language of both Muslims and non-Muslims. The Lebanese Maronite scholar Ibrāhīm al-Yāzid̲j̲ī (1847-1906 [see AL-YĀZID̲J̲Ī. 2.]) equated nationhood with language. The standard Arabic of the educated classes provides an integrative force that surpasses the disintegrative tendencies of religion and culture. For this reason, al-Yāzid̲j̲ī championed the revival and dissemination of the standard literary language (*al-lug̲h̲a al-fuṣḥā*), based on classical Ḳurʾānic Arabic, in opposition to various suggestions for replacing it with colloquial dialects (*al-lug̲h̲āt al-ʿāmma*). He participated in efforts to modernise and simplify Arabic pedagogy, arguing that the proper use and teaching of a language is necessary to political, economic and cultural modernisation efforts. The standard Arabic also demarcates, for al-Yāzid̲j̲ī, the boundaries between the Arab nation and other peoples. To maintain their cultural distinctiveness and by implication their eventual political autonomy, the Arabs had to preserve their language from foreign corruption, including the use of loan words and especially the adoption of the Latin script in place of the Arabic, as suggested by some reformers of the time. Instead, he proposed rules for Arabicisation of foreign words and names that would either assimilate them into Arabic phonology and morphology or distinguish them clearly as foreign proper nouns.

The most powerful stimulus for the rise of an Arab nationalist discourse came from the Turkification policy pursued by the Young Turks after they seized power in Istanbul in 1908. The Ottoman constitution of 1876 had established Turkish as the official language of the empire but had provided no details for the practical enforcement of this provision. The political program adopted by the Committee of Union and Progress [see ITTIḤĀD WE TERAḲḲĪ D̲J̲EMʿIYYETI] in 1908 not only reaffirmed that "the official language of the state will remain as Turkish" but it also stipulated provisions for enacting this policy (see Kayalı 1997, 90-4). All civil servants and government officials, including members of parliament, were instructed to conduct business in Turkish. The teaching of Turkish was made compulsory in elementary schools and Turkish was imposed as the medium of instruction in all secondary and higher education. As a result of this policy, Arabic was taught in the state secondary schools of the Arab provinces as a foreign language, with instruction in Arabic grammar provided in Turkish by Arab teachers who were often not conversant in Turkish or by Turkish teachers who were frequently not expert in the intricacies of Arabic grammar. Arab students caught speaking Arabic outside the classroom were subject to punishment. The imposition of Turkish was coupled with a campaign conducted through the Turkish newspapers to paint Arabic as a stagnant language and its speakers as an obstacle to the progressive reforms launched by the Young Turks.

Arab responses to the Turkification policy came from a number of political, literary and educational societies, some based in Arab cities, others in Europe. The Arab Congress of 1913, a gathering of Arab intellectuals and political activists in Paris, adopted a resolution demanding in part: "La langue arabe doit être reconnue au Parlement ottoman et considérée comme officielle dans les pays syriens et arabes" (Zeine 1966, 161). Another group, the Arab Revolutionary Society (*al-d̲j̲amʿiyya al-t̲h̲awriyya al-ʿarabiyya*), called in the same year for a more drastic measure: complete Arab independence from the Ottoman Empire. The society's "Proclamation (*balāg̲h̲*) to the Arabs, the Sons of Ḳaḥṭān" expounded the superiority of Arabic over Turkish and denounced Turkish attempts to substitute the "sacred" language of Islam with Turkish translations of such things as the call to prayer and the ritual prayer itself. The proclamation also appeals to Christians and Jews to recognise that their common language unites them with Muslims in a single Arab nation: "Let the Muslims, the Christians, and the Jews be as one in working for the interest of the nation (*umma*) and of the country (*bilād*). You all dwell in one land, you speak one language, so be also one nation and one hand." The fanaticism that divides the religious communities is deliberately cultivated by the Turkish authorities, the proclamation avers. Religious hostilities will subside when "our affairs, our learning, and the verdicts of our courts will be conducted in our own language" (*ibid.*, 174-7; Haim 1976, 83-8).

Opposition to the Turkification policy also figures prominently in the works of individual intellectuals. In his newspaper *al-Mufīd*, ʿAbd al-G̲h̲anī al-ʿUraysī (1891-1916) wrote incessantly on the need for Arabs to resist attempts to undermine their language. He demanded that Arabic be recognised in the Ottoman constitution as the primary official language in the Arab provinces of the empire, and that it be enforced as such in the schools and civil administration. He urged Arabs to insist that all foreign schools teach Arabic as the national language of the students they were educating, alongside Turkish, the official language of the empire, and a foreign language, such as English or French. Al-ʿUraysī also campaigned for the use of a simple, pure Arabic idiom in private communications, one that avoided flowery expressions that he blamed on Turkish influences or words and phrases borrowed from French, the language popular among many educated Arabs, especially his fellow Lebanese. Al-ʿUraysī's growing influence among Arab nationalists led to his execution by Turkish authorities in Beirut in 1916.

Arab nationalist writing in the period after World War I continued to emphasise the role of the Arabic language, but with the imposition of English and French mandates in much of the former Ottoman Arab provinces, the perceived threat to Arabic came from English and French, not Turkish. ʿAbd Allāh al-ʿAlāyilī's (b. 1914) *Dustūr al-ʿarab al-ḳawmī*, published in 1941, is a not so veiled attack on the dissemination of French in his native Lebanon: "The duty of nationalists who are imbued with a burning and true belief is to persuade society by all possible means to free itself from all languages except the one which it is desirable to impose, attachment to which must be fanatical. . . . In such a fanaticism we must mingle hate and contempt for anyone who does not speak that national language, which we hold sacred and venerate as a high ideal" (Haim 1976, 121-2). In his 1952 article *al-Islām wa 'l-ḳawmiyya al-ʿarabiyya* ʿAbd al-Raḥmān al-Bazzāz (1913-73) declared the Arabic language to be the "soul of our Arab nation and the primary aspect of its national life" (*ibid.*, 181). Zakī al-Arsūzī (1900-68) argued that the true Arab genius lies in the Arabic language, which had flowered well before the advent of Islam. Thus, for al-Arsūzī, the origins of the Arab nation lie in its pre-Islamic antiquity, and the Prophet Muḥammad becomes simply one among many who forged an Arab national consciousness. The challenge of all modern Arabs, Christians and Muslims, according to al-Arsūzī, is to reinvigorate this national identity by reviving the language, for which he suggested a number of radical reform measures (see Suleiman 2003, 146-57).

The period between the two World Wars saw increasing opposition to French rule in Algeria, Morocco and Tunisia as well. French colonialism in all three countries had meant the imposition of a policy of *francophonie* that made French the sole official language. The independence movements in the Maghrib would consequently stress Arabic along with Islam as the unifying and authentic markers of nationhood. In 1931, Shaykh ʿAbd al-Ḥamīd Ben Bādīs (1889-1940 [see IBN BĀDĪS]) and his colleagues in the Association of Algerian Muslim ʿUlamāʾ adopted the motto "Islam is our religion, Arabic is our language, Algeria is our country".

More than any other writer, it was Sāṭiʿ al-Ḥuṣrī (1880-1968 [*q.v.* in Suppl.]) who most firmly established the common Arabic language as the basis for Arab nationalism. Unlike other writers who included such factors as shared culture, customs, interests and physical environment in their definitions of Arab nationalism, al-Ḥuṣrī limited his idea to a shared language and a shared history. The priority he attaches to the two is clearly articulated in the following passage from *Muḥāḍarāt fī nushūʾ al-fikra al-ḳawmiyya*: "Language constitutes the life of a nation. History constitutes its feeling. A nation which forgets its history loses its feeling and consciousness. A nation which forgets its language loses its life and [very] being" (Suleiman 2003, 132).

Al-Ḥuṣrī was keenly aware, however, that linguistic unity was largely a fiction, that the common standard Arabic was shared by only a small fraction of Arabs, namely, the literate classes, whereas the vast majority of Arabic speakers were divided by widely divergent colloquial dialects. In order to realise his vision of a language-based Arab identity, al-Ḥuṣrī devoted much of his career to promoting the modernisation and simplification of classical Arabic grammar, with the intention of reconciling standard Arabic with the dialects, and then disseminating this modern standard Arabic in the new educational system of Arab countries. At the same time, he waged a fierce intellectual battle against advocates of regional vernaculars as the basis for an Egyptian, Syrian or ʿIrāḳī nationalism. Salāma Mūsā (1887-1958 [*q.v.*]), for example, campaigned for replacing standard Arabic, which he considered a dead language, with a refined Egyptian colloquial as the medium of writing, communication and education in his vision of Egyptian nationalism. Al-Ḥuṣrī bitterly denounced the suggestion that the teaching of standard Arabic was an anachronism akin to the teaching of Latin. The analogy between Latin and its Romance language successors is inapplicable to classical Arabic and its regional vernaculars because of the continuing use by modern Arabs of the *fuṣḥā*. Similarly, in response to Ṭāhā Ḥusayn's (1889-1973 [*q.v.*]) contention that Egypt should look to its pharaonic past as the basis for its modern national identity, al-Ḥuṣrī caustically asked whether a modern Egyptian would be able to speak with a revived Egyptian pharaoh or with Ibn Khaldūn.

Arabicisation in Arab politics

Arabicisation has been pursued to some degree by all post-colonial Arab states as an integral part of their state-building enterprise, and Arabicisation has generally meant the promotion of modern standard Arabic as the common language within individual Arab states as well as among them. The goal of Arabicisation programs has been to cultivate a national identity in opposition to the European imperialist legacy that left behind pockets of anglophone or francophone élites or in opposition to ethnic fragmentation caused by indigenous languages such as Berber, Kurdish or various Nilo-Saharan and other African languages spoken in southern Sudan. Promoting standard Arabic also targets the disintegrative tendencies of the spoken Arabic dialects and thus serves an important ideological function in pan-Arabist schemes and a very practical function in more specific national projects, where sometimes different regional vernaculars exist within a single state. Finally, Arabicisation has been bolstered by the rise of Islamist groups that accentuate the connection between Arabic and the Islamic identity of the vast majority of the populations of Arab states. Arabic is today designated as an official language in the constitutions of nearly all 22 members of the Arab League, and it is the sole official language in some 16 states.

Egypt was among the first Arab states to react to the dissemination of English and French as a deliberate policy of imperialism. In 1888, the British colonial administration in Egypt announced that the language of instruction in all Egyptian schools should be either English or French. This policy was coupled with the promotion of the Egyptian colloquial over the literary Arabic as the "authentic" language of Egypt. Various British officials, most famously William Wilcox in a speech in 1892, argued that Egypt's adherence to literary Arabic was a major reason for its backwardness and that the key to Egypt's progress lay in making the spoken language Egypt's written language as well. The British language policies were not met with immediate resistance, but to the contrary the policies found champions among many influential Egyptian reformers. Calls for a restoration of standard Arabic in the national life of Egypt became pronounced when the independence movement gained ground in the early 20th century. Saʿd Zaghlūl [*q.v.*], in his capacity of Minister of Education (1906-10), worked to replace English with Arabic in Egypt's schools. The Pedagogy Committee of the University of Cairo (est. 1908), headed by the then Prince Fuʾād, recommended that the official language of instruction at the university be Arabic, but, given the poverty of instructional material in that language, French and English would serve by necessity and temporarily as the medium of instruction in many faculties. Despite these early efforts, as late as the 1940s Arabic was rarely the medium of instruction in Egypt's educational system, except for the religious schools supervised by al-Azhar. The foreign-language schools, where most of Egypt's élite were educated, continued to exclude Arabic altogether, leading Ṭāhā Ḥusayn in *Mustaḳbal al-thaḳāfa fī Miṣr* (1938) to warn of the cultural and political consequences for the nation. Ṭāhā Ḥusayn's demand that Arabic be taught in all foreign schools (though the medium of instruction remained English or French) became government policy in the early 1940s.

Syria and then ʿIrāḳ launched Arabicisation policies under the direction of Sāṭiʿ al-Ḥuṣrī, who served as an advisor and education minister to Fayṣal b. Ḥusayn [see FAYṢAL I]. The short-lived Arab national government in Damascus (October 1918-July 1920) undertook several measures to build Arab national consciousness in the country, including the implementation of an Arabic curriculum at all grade levels, requiring the rapid translation into Arabic of textbooks and the training of qualified instructors. Al-Ḥuṣrī continued the aborted Arabicisation program in Syria when he relocated to ʿIrāḳ with Fayṣal. The teaching of foreign languages was eliminated in state primary schools, and the foreign-sponsored schools were forced to adopt much of the nationalist-oriented curriculum developed for the state schools.

The ascendancy of pan-Arab politics during the 1950s raised the language issue to new levels of political saliency. Both of the dominant ideologies of pan-Arabism, namely, Nasserism and Baʿthism, emphasised the alleged unity of language as a key constituent of the single Arab nation. The result was the further curtailment, if not outright elimination, of the influence of foreign languages in Egypt, Syria and ʿIrāḳ. In Egypt, standard Arabic was promoted as the language of instruction in all subjects, including technical and scientific subjects generally taught in universities in English. The debates on the place of colloquial Egyptian in Egyptian national life faded, but did not die entirely, as evinced by the controversy engendered by the publication of Luwīs ʿAwaḍ's (1915-90) *Muḳaddima fī fiḳh al-lugha al-ʿarabiyya* in 1980. This work, which attempts to sever the link between Arabic and Egyptian nationhood, was published, perhaps not by coincidence, following Egypt's expulsion from the Arab League because of its peace treaty with Israel.

Lebanon was the Arab state most torn by the advent of pan-Arab ideologies, and language figured prominently in its political disputes. In 1962, Père Selim Abou, a young Lebanese Jesuit teaching at the University of St. Joseph in Beirut, published *Bilinguisme arabe-français au Liban*, in which he argued that Lebanon's bilingual character is unique among Arab countries and not the result of foreign domination. Much of the Christian population and many of the Muslim élites as well used French well before the French Mandate, he pointed out. French has been voluntarily adopted, Père Abou suggests, by a segment of the Lebanese population, especially the Maronites, "to express their deepest spiritual needs" (Sayigh 1965, 121). Such views were strongly challenged by other Lebanese writers, including a number of prominent Maronites. Kamāl Yūsuf al-Ḥādjdj (1917-76), for example, argued that Lebanon's bilingualism was largely a myth, since only a small percentage of the élite classes in each confessional group commanded native mastery of both Arabic and French. French was the language of Lebanon's European coloniser, and its continued use instead of Arabic by the Lebanese marked their inferior status and dependence upon Europe.

Similar controversies involving the role of French have occurred in the countries of the Maghrib. Algeria, Morocco and Tunisia have all pursued efforts to promote standard Arabic as a marker of their national identities as well as their solidarity with the broader Arab world. But the three countries have exhibited varying degrees of official hostility to the use of French in national life. Algeria, which experienced the longest and most intensive process of Gallicisation, has pursued the most zealous Arabicisation agenda. During the 1960s, under President Houari Boumedienne, the government adopted the goal of total Arabicisation in government and education. Subsequently, laws were passed requiring fluency in standard Arabic as a qualification for a government job, and standard Arabic became the medium for broadcasting on state-controlled television and radio. In the private sector, however, businesses continued to give preference to those with command of French. The discrimination faced by young Arabic-speaking university graduates led to a series of student demonstrations and strikes in the mid-1980s during the presidency of Chadli Benjedid. In an effort to quell the unrest, the Benjedid government issued a directive to employers to end language-based preferences in hiring, but little changed in actual hiring practices. Continued student protests in 1990, coupled with the rise of the Islamic movement in Algerian politics, led to new legislation to limit the use of French in public spheres and to restrict the number of French-language newspapers and magazines imported into the country.

By contrast, Morocco and Tunisia have demonstrated much less hostility to the legacy of French. Moroccan governments have pursued deeply ambivalent policies. The first government initiated a full Arabicisation program for the country's schools and bureaucracy in 1956, only to reverse itself two years later. King Ḥassān II extolled the virtues of Arabicisation while doing little to implement it, particularly as he sought greater economic and political ties with France. In Tunisia, the government of Ḥabīb Bourguiba encouraged bilingualism in its efforts to maintain close ties with France and the rest of Europe, a policy that has been continued by Bourguiba's successor, Zayn al-ʿĀbidīn Ben ʿAlī. Islamic opposition groups in Tunisia, mainly the Islamic Nahḍa Party, include the government's lack of commitment to Arabicisation in their criticisms.

In addition to European languages and the colloquial Arabic dialects, the politics of Arabicisation has targeted indigenous regional languages. The status of Berber dialects has been especially problematic in Morocco and Algeria, the two countries with the largest Berber-speaking populations and the most organised Berber political movements. In response to Berber agitation in southern Morocco during 1994, Ḥassān II declared in a speech on August 20, 1994, that Berber dialects and Moroccan Arabic should be included in the national educational system, at least in primary schools. This statement signalled a greater visibility of Berber in the state media, but its critics charge that it has effectively undermined the recognition of Berber as a national language alongside Arabic. In Algeria, the political liberalisation from 1988 to 1991 led to a resurgence of Berber political activity. The Mouvement Culturel Berbère (MCB) organised large demonstrations and boycotts of schools and universities, demanding that the government officially recognise the Berber dialect of Tamazight [*q.v.*]. The government responded by creating the Haut Commissariat à la Amazighité in 1993 for the promotion of Tamazight in education and mass communication. In April 2004 Tamazight was recognised as a second national language in Algeria. The recognition fell short of Berber demands that it be acknowledged as an official language, which the government reaffirmed throughout the 1990s as being standard Arabic.

The Kurdish minorities in Syria and ʿIrāḳ have faced similar obstacles to gaining official status for their language. Kurdish-language publications were banned in Syria after independence. Its 1973 constitution declared Arabic alone to be the official language. ʿIrāḳ's 1925 constitution also established Arabic as the sole official language of the country, but the use of Kurdish in schools and other public spheres was always accepted by the government in the predominantly Kurdish regions of the north. The ʿIrāḳī law of administration for the transition period, promulgated in March 2004 following the American occupation of the country, recognises both Arabic and Kurdish as official languages.

The constitution of Sudan designates Arabic as the official language of the republic, but adds that "the state shall allow the development of other local and international languages". The reference to other local languages is presumably to the 100 or so African languages spoken in the southern, mainly non-Muslim part of the country. The British colonial administration cultivated these regional dialects along with English in an openly espoused policy of divide and rule. Post-independence Sudanese governments have pursued Arabicisation with the argument that a common language is the most effective means of maintaining the unity of the country. Yet Arabicisation has been strongly resisted in the south as merely one aspect of Khartoum's attempts to Arabise and, since the late 1980s, Islamise the Christian and animist regions of the country.

Organisations promoting Arabicisation

A number of organisations have been founded by Arab governments and by the Arab League to promote the policy of Arabicisation. The Arab Academy was created in 1919 in Damascus as part of the intensive Arabicisation program launched under Sāṭiʿ al-Ḥuṣrī. Its principal mission was to coin Arabic terms for scientific and technological applications. The Royal Academy of the Arabic Language (*al-Madjmaʿ al-malakī li 'l-lugha al-ʿarabiyya*) in Cairo was established in December 1932 by a royal decree of King Fuʾād. Its mandate was to explore all means by which the Arabic language could be revitalised. The King personally took an interest in orthographic reform, advocating the use of different characters to function as capital letters, dubbed the *ḥurūf al-tādj*. This experiment was ultimately abandoned, but the academy continued to debate various measures for orthographic and grammatical simplification for years to come. Under Nasser [see ʿABD AL-NĀṢIR, in Suppl.], the academy diverted its attention away from internal reform of the language to formulating new terminology for scientific and technical applications. This shift reflected the régime's argument that Arabicisation should proceed with minimal internal alterations to classical Arabic, the bearer of the common Arab heritage, and should focus instead on only those reforms necessary for economic and scientific progress. Other Arabic language academies have been established in Baghdād (1947) and ʿAmmān (1976).

The need to coordinate the work of the various national language academies was acknowledged in 1961 by the Arab League. The Bureau for the Coordination of Arabicisation in the Arab World was established the following year in Rabāṭ. The bureau has organised a number of international scholarly conferences on Arabic reform and pedagogy and publishes the journal *al-Lisān al-ʿArabī*. In 1989, the Arab Center for Arabization, Translation, Authorship and Publication (ACATAP) was established in Damascus by an agreement between the government of Syria and the Arab League Educational, Cultural and Scientific Organization (ALECSO). ACATAP's goals include translating foreign works into Arabic and translating key Arabic texts in science, art and literature into selected foreign languages. The centre also publishes a semi-annual journal titled *al-Taʿrīb*.

Bibliography: E. Shouby, *The influence of the Arabic language on the psychology of the Arabs*, in *MEJ*, v/3 (Summer 1951), 284-302; Rosemary Sayigh, *The bilingualism controversy in Lebanon*, in *The World Today*, xxi/3 (March 1965), 120-30; Z.N. Zeine, *The emergence of Arab nationalism, with a background study of Arab-Turkish relations in the Near East*, Beirut 1966; Sylvia G. Haim (ed.), *Arab nationalism: an anthology*, Berkeley and Los Angeles 1976; M. Sayadi (al-Ṣayyādī), *Le bureau de coordination de l'arabisation dans le monde arabe à Rabat (Maroc)*, Lille 1980; idem, *al-Taʿrīb wa-tansīḳuhu fī 'l-waṭan al-ʿarabī*, Beirut 1980; idem, *al-Taʿrīb wa-dawruhu fī tadʿīm al-wudjūd al-ʿarabī wa 'l-waḥda al-ʿarabiyya*, Beirut 1982; G. Grandguillaume, *Arabisation et politique linguistique au Maghreb* (Islam d'hier et d'aujourd'hui, no. 19), Paris 1983; S. Ḥammād *et al.*, *al-Lugha al-ʿarabiyya wa 'l-waʿy al-ḳawmī*, Beirut 1984; A. Ayalon, *Language and change in the Arab Middle East: the evolution of modern political discourse*, New York 1987; B. Lewis, *The political language of Islam*, Chicago 1988; Y. Suleiman (ed.), *Arabic sociolinguistics: issues and perspectives*, Richmond, Surrey 1994; idem (ed.), *Language and identity in the Middle East and North Africa*, Richmond, Surrey 1996; H. Kayalı, *Arabs and Young Turks: Ottomanism, Arabism, and Islamism in the Ottoman Empire, 1908-1918*, Berkeley 1997; J.M. Landau (ed.), *Language and politics: theory and cases*, in *International Journal of the Sociology of Language*, cxxxvii (1999); Suleiman (ed.), *Language and society in the Middle East and North Africa: studies in variation and identity*, Richmond, Surrey 1999; idem, *The Arabic language and national identity: a study in ideology*, Edinburgh 2003.

(SOHAIL H. HASHMI)

ṬARĪḲ (A., pls. *ṭuruḳ*, *ṭuruḳāt*, etc.), "road, route, way, path", apparently a native Arabic word, and with the idea of a way which has been prepared for traffic to some extent by levelling, by the spreading of stones, etc. (see C. de Landberg, *Glossaire datînois*, Leiden 1920-42, iii, 2204-5). The word shares a common field of geographical reference with similar terms like *ṣirāṭ* [*q.v.*], *darb* (see R. Hartmann, *EI*[1] art. s.v.), *maslaka* and *shāriʿ* [*q.v.*], though each is to be distinguished in its usage.

In the Ḳurʾān, Moses is bidden to strike a dry road or path (*ṭarīḳ*) through the sea in order to escape Pharaoh (XX, 79/77) and thus achieve physical salvation. However, the Ḳurʾān usually employs *al-ṣirāṭ [al-mustaḳīm]* for the spiritual highway to Paradise (I, 6; XLII, 52-3; XLIII, 42/43) and never *al-ṭarīḳ al-mustaḳīm*; clearly, *ṣirāṭ* has a more religious and spiritual connotation than *ṭarīḳ*. This last is more like the Latin *via* in terms of its topographical role, although the physical layout and mode of construction of the two might differ considerably. The Roman Empire had many famous roads like the Vias Appia, Flaminia and Valeria. Many of these were of antique, pre-Roman origin, and the same was true of Near Eastern trade routes which ran from Syria to the towns of the Ḥidjāz and South Arabia, linking the Byzantine empire with the Arabian peninsula and the lands across the Arabian Sea towards India. In ancient Rome, the *viae* played a vital role in buttressing Roman military power and in facilitating trade. In early Islamic times, the *ṭuruḳ* likewise performed these functions, and furthermore, conveyed pilgrims journeying on the Ḥadjdj [*q.v.*] to the Holy Places. Piety was accordingly an additional motive for rulers, governors and others who built and maintained roads, supplied waymarks (*ʿalam*) and constructed caravanserais [see KHĀN], and the Arab geographers record in detail the Pilgrimage routes which crossed the Islamic lands, such as the Darb Zubayda [*q.v.* in Suppl.] across Nadjd from ʿIrāḳ to Mecca, as do figures like Ibn Djubayr and Ibn Baṭṭūṭa [*q.vv.*] in their travel accounts; the Ḳurʾān itself (XXII, 28/27) implies a diversity of ways with the Kaʿba as their goal. *Maslaka* was in many ways a synonym of *ṭarīḳ*, but figures prominently in Arabic geographical literature in the name of what R. Blachère defined as an important sub-genre of this last, the "road books" or *al-masālik wa 'l-mamālik* [*q.v.*], an important element of which was also the fixing of the geographical co-ordinates of places (see Blachère, *Extraits des principaux géographes arabes du Moyen Âge*, Beirut-Algiers 1934, ²Paris 1957, 110-200; DJUGHRĀFIYĀ, at Vol. II, 575); at all events, Ibn Khurradādhbih [*q.v.*] may be accounted the father of this sub-genre.

Those *ṭuruḳ* which were major highways of the Islamic world for trade and communication naturally stimulated the growth of staging posts (*manāzil* [see MANZIL]) and important towns along them. Mecca may have been along one of these *ṭuruḳ*, the route from Syria down the Wādī 'l-Ḳurā [*q.v.*] (but cf. the thesis of Patricia Crone in her *Meccan trade and the rise of Islam*, Oxford 1987, that the importance of Mecca as a centre for pre-Islamic trade has been much exaggerated). Yet undoubtedly, Samarḳand [*q.v.*] lay at the intersection of trade routes coming from India and Afghānistān and from Khurāsān and western Persia and then leading northwards and eastwards along the "Silk Route" to eastern Turkistan and China—the "Golden Road to Samarqand" which forms the culmination and envoi of the James Elroy Flecker's (d. 1915) poetic drama *Hassan*. The famous Silk Route, or better, Silk Routes, ran westwards from Xi'an in China through Lanzhou to Dunhuang, where the ways split, proceeding either along the northern or southern rims of the Tarim basin [*q.v.*] to Tashkent, Samarḳand, Bukhārā, and thence to the caliphal lands of Persia and ʿIrāḳ, and through Anatolia or along the Black Sea coast to Byzantium (see M. Mollat du Jourdin, ch. "Des routes continentales à la voie maritime (fin du Moyen Âge)", in UNESCO, *Les routes de la soie. Patrimoine commun, identités plurielles*, Paris 1994, 1-19; K. Baipakov, ch. VIII/2 "The Silk Route across Central Asia", in C.E. Bosworth and Muhammad Asimov (eds.), *UNESCO History of the civilizations of Central Asia*, iv, *The age of achievement: A.D. 750 to the end of the fifteenth century*, pt. 2, Paris 2000, 221-6; Frances Wood, *The Silk Road*, London 2000, 13). At the other side of the Islamic world, caravan routes across the Sahara Desert brought the slaves and gold of ancient Mali and Ghana to the North African cities (see E.W. Bovill, *The golden trade of the Moors*, London 1958), whilst the Darb al-Arbaʿīn [*q.v.*] "Route which took forty days" linked Egypt and Nubia with the eastern lands of the Bilād al-Sūdān, bringing slaves, ivory, ostrich feathers, etc. [see SŪDĀN, BILĀD AL-].

It should be noted that *ṭarīḳ* should not be confused with the related term *ṭarīḳa*, pl. *ṭarāʾiḳ*, Ṣūfī "path" or order; for these, see ṬARĪḲA.

Bibliography (in addition to references given in the article): A. Mez, *Die Renaissance des Islams*, Heidelberg 1922, Eng. tr. Patna 1937, ch. XXVIII; A. Miquel, *La géographie humaine du monde musulman*, Paris 1967-88, i, ch. 8, iv, ch. 7; I.R. Netton (ed.), *Golden roads. Migration, pilgrimage and travel in mediaeval and modern Islam*, Richmond, Surrey 1993; S. Hornblower and A. Spafforth, *The Oxford classical dictionary*, ³Oxford 1999, arts. "Roads", "Via".

(I.R. NETTON)

TA'RĪKH.

II. 1. In the Arab world.

(c) The period 1500 to 1800.

i. *The Ottoman occupation of the central Arab lands*

The Ottoman Empire, in a few decisive battles, destroyed the Mamlūk Sultanate (1250-1517 [see MAMLŪKS]), which included Egypt, Syria and parts of Anatolia (with the Ḥidjāz within its sphere of influence). Egypt, the centre of empires for centuries, and also Syria became tax-paying Ottoman provinces for the next three, nominally four, centuries. Later in the 16th century, the Yemen, ʿIrāḳ and North Africa (with the exception of Morocco) were also incorporated into the Ottoman Empire with varying degrees of centralisation.

For Egypt in particular, the change of rule was traumatic. It is true that like the Mamlūks, the Ottomans were Turcophone Sunnīs and were ruled by a foreign-born military caste. Yet the language of administration under the Mamlūks had been Arabic; now, under the Ottomans, it was Turkish. Under the new régime, all governors, chief government officials, *ḳāḍīs* and soldiers came from the Turkish provinces and spoke Turkish. Thus the foreign presence in the Arab lands was much more massive than before. At the beginning, many of the natives of Syria, Egypt and other Arab lands regarded the Ottomans as bad Muslims, negligent of the religious ordinances and disrespectful of the *Sharīʿa*. This judgment entailed automatically a view of the rulers as unjust. Later this negative image of the Ottomans changed, however, as the Ottomans, starting with the long and stable reign of Sultan Süleymān Ḳānūnī (the Magnificent, 1520-66 [*q.v.*]), became themselves more devout. The dynasty emphasised its role as pious Muslim rulers and defenders of Islam against Christian infidels in the west and Shīʿī heretics in the east. Nevertheless, anti-Turkish sentiments persisted, beside a genuine loyalty toward the Ottoman dynasty itself and the distant sultan in Istanbul. Such seemingly contradictory sentiments could coexist in that pre-national age and are reflected in the writings of Arab historians.

The Mamlūk sultanate was extremely rich in historiography (see (b) at Vol. X, 276a-280a), more than any other period in pre-modern Islam. Yet research into the history of the Arab provinces of the Ottoman Empire has also been increasing recently, and there is a better appreciation of the wealth of Arabic historiography under Ottoman rule (see *Bibl.*).

EGYPT

The political, diplomatic and military events leading to the Mamlūk-Ottoman conflict and the occupation of Egypt (Muḥarram 923/January 1517), and then the first six years of Ottoman rule (until Dhu 'l-Ḥidjdja 928/November 1522) are superbly narrated by the Cairene chronicler Muḥammad b. Iyās [see IBN IYĀS]. The fifth volume of his *Badāʾiʿ al-zuhūr fī waḳāʾiʿ al-duhūr* (ed. Muḥammad Muṣṭafā, v, ²Cairo 1961) is a most valuable work that has few equivalents in describing day by day how a new régime steps into the shoes of the old one. Ibn Iyās not only reports the decisions and moves undertaken by the Ottomans in Egypt but his writing reflects the people's attitudes and feelings toward their new masters.

Ibn Iyās's hostility towards the Ottomans is obvious throughout his chronicle. He identified with the fallen Mamlūks, since he was one of *awlād al-nās* [*q.v.*] "the sons of the (important) men", namely, the Mamlūks. He judged all the Ottomans—Sultan Selīm, who defeated the Mamlūks, his soldiers, and his *ḳāḍīs*—as cruel and ignorant.

The problem with this chronicle is that it is almost isolated. Ibn Iyās was one of the best, but also the last, representatives of the great Egyptian Mamlūk historiographical tradition. This tradition stops abruptly after the Ottoman occupation. It cannot be determined whether that happened because Egypt was relegated from an empire to a province, or because the greater part of the 10th/16th century in Egypt passed peacefully and without major political upheavals. Some information about the history of Egypt in the 10th/16th century is provided by non-Egyptian Arabic sources, such as by the important histories of the Meccan historian Ḳuṭb al-Dīn al-Nahrawālī (d. 990/1582 [q.v.]), who wrote a detailed account of the exploits of the Ottomans in the Yemen. He was familiar with developments in Egypt, in the Ḥidjāz and, to a certain extent, in Istanbul as well, since he travelled to the Ottoman capital where he met some of the most influential men. Al-Nahrawālī wrote a lengthy history of the Ottoman Empire up to his time, which comprises a great part of his book about the history of Mecca (al-Barḳ al-yamānī fi 'l-fatḥ al-ʿuthmānī, ed. Ḥamad al-Djāsir, al-Riyāḍ 1967; K. al-Iʿlām bi-aʿlām bayt Allāh al-ḥarām, Beirut 1964). His attitude towards the Ottoman state is positive in the extreme, and his works influenced Egyptian historians for a long time.

Since contemporary chroniclers did not cover the greater part of the 16th century, the information about that period is cursory and episodic. The historiography of the period organises its coverage of events by what has been called by scholars the "sultan-pasha" type of chronicle. The pasha is the central figure in the narratives. The chroniclers characterise each viceroy by his personality and religious profile.

One of the two notable historians of this period is Muḥammad ʿAbd al-Muʿṭī al-Isḥāḳī (the chronicle ends in 1033/1623-4). In his Kitāb Akhbār al-uwal fī-mā taṣarrafa fī Miṣr min arbāb al-duwal he gives a most laudatory chronicle of the Ottoman dynasty and a history of Egypt up to his time. Of far greater importance are the numerous historical writings of Muḥammad b. Abi 'l-Surūr al-Bakrī al-Ṣiddīḳī (d. ca. 1071/1661 [see AL-BAKRĪ]), the leading historian of the 11th/17th century. He was a member of a famous aristocratic Ṣūfī family of Ashrāf, who also claimed descent from Abū Bakr, the first caliph [see BAKRIYYA]. The Bakrīs played a role in Egypt's religious and public life until the middle of the 20th century. Ibn Abi 'l-Surūr himself had close relations with the Ottoman authorities in Egypt, and his attitude toward the Ottomans is extremely laudatory, describing the sultans as impeccably orthodox. Almost all his chronicles are about Ottoman Egypt, but he also wrote a history of the Ottoman Empire, naturally with a strong emphasis on Egypt (al-Minaḥ al-raḥmāniyya fī 'l-dawla al-ʿuthmāniyya, ed. Laylā al-Ṣabbāgh, Damascus 1995).

It was only towards the end of the 11th/17th century and during the 12th/18th century that Arabic history writing in Egypt became really mature and rich. We have many chronicles, some of them very valuable, which fall into two main categories: (a) literary chronicles, written by educated ʿulamāʾ or scribes in standard literary Arabic, and (b) the popular chronicles or "soldiers' narratives". The "soldier" language is ungrammatical, and the narratives have the characteristics of stories told before an audience. The chronicles of this category were created in the milieu of the seven odjaḳs, or the regiments of the Ottoman garrison in Cairo, more specifically in the ʿAzab odjaḳ, the second largest regiment in Cairo (after the Janissaries). These five manuscripts are known as the Damurdāshī group, since their authors are related in one way or another to officers in the ʿAzab regiment called by this surname. The most important chronicler of this group is Aḥmad al-Damurdāshī Katkhudā ʿAzabān [see AL-DAMURDĀSHĪ] (meaning an officer below the rank of the regimental commander in the ʿAzab corps), whose chronicle ends in 1170/1756 (al-Durra al-muṣāna fī akhbār al-Kināna, ed. ʿA. ʿAbd al-Raḥīm, Cairo 1989, ed. and tr. D. Crecelius and

ʿAbd al-Wahhāb Bakr, Al-Damurdāshī's chronicle of Egypt, 1688-1755, Leiden 1991). His narrative is lively, detailed and trustworthy, and is full of information about military and political events, as well as anecdotes that throw light on various economic, religious and cultural aspects of Egyptian civilian society. It is important to note that Aḥmad al-Damurdāshī was aware of the de facto autonomy of Egypt within the Empire. He calls the régime in Egypt dawlat al-Mamālīk, namely, the Mamlūk government, as it appears in the book's sub-title Fī akhbār mā waḳaʿa bi-Miṣr fī dawlat al-Mamālīk "that which happened in Egypt under the Mamlūk government".

The historians of the period describe in detail the political struggles that they witnessed in Egypt, again, particularly in Cairo. After the pashas' authority declined from the latter part of the 10th/16th century, power passed in the next century to the military grandees, called amīrs, beys or sanādjik (the arabised plural of the Turkish sandjaḳ or sandjaḳ beyi). In the late 17th and early 18th centuries, power shifted to the odjaḳs, primarily to the Janissaries and the ʿAzab, in that order. For most of the 12th/18th century, the supremacy belonged to the constantly-feuding Mamlūk beys until 1798, when the French occupation put an end to the Mamlūk régime.

Aḥmad Shalabī (Čelebi) b. ʿAbd al-Ghanī's chronicle, Awḍaḥ al-ishārāt fī-man tawallā Miṣr al-Ḳāhira min al-wuzarāʾ wa 'l-bāshāt, ed. ʿA.R. ʿAbd al-Raḥīm (Cairo 1978), covers the period from the Ottoman occupation in 923/1517 to the year 1150/1737. He was an ʿālim, and like many ʿulamāʾ at the time, also had Ṣūfī connections. He is unusually revealing personally, often telling about himself, his impressions of the events and the personalities that he witnessed, together with his personal opinions and his sources of information. Like other contemporary historians, he notes the declining power of the central Ottoman government and its representatives in Egypt. Sometimes he expresses contempt towards an Ottoman pasha or a ḳāḍī, while fully acknowledging the role of the Sultan as the supreme ruler of Islam. In addition to political events, Aḥmad Shalabī, like other historians in Ottoman Egypt, writes about economic, social and cultural, mainly religious, subjects. For example, Aḥmad Shalabī and his near contemporary Yūsuf al-Mallawānī (also called Ibn al-Wakīl) write about the devaluation of the currency, droughts, plague, and the flooding of the Nile and its effect on food shortages and prices. Occasionally, information is provided concerning Arab tribes and their chiefs, since these were often involved in the power struggles in the capital, and more rarely about the common people, the city poor and the fellaheen. Events concerning the religious minorities, Christians and Jews are also mentioned.

We come now to the monumental work of ʿAbd al-Raḥmān b. Ḥasan al-Djabartī (1168-1241/1754 to 1825-6 [q.v.]), the last and the greatest of the historians of Ottoman Egypt. His importance as a chronicler has been long recognised. He became a historian under the influence of the French occupation of Egypt in 1798. This was a traumatic event, and the Egyptians' first taste of the overwhelming military supremacy of modern Europe. Al-Djabartī wrote a detailed description of the occupation and the people's reaction to the French. The Frenchmen's claims that they were Muslims, or at least friends of Islam, were met with ridicule; the ideas of the Revolution were totally and naturally misunderstood. For all his hatred of the occupiers, al-Djabartī was impressed by their love of learning and science and by their system of justice (see S. Moreh [ed. and tr.], *Al-Jabartī's chronicle of the first seven months of the French occupation of Egypt*, Leiden 1975). After the departure of the French army and the return of the Ottomans to Egypt, he wrote another account of the occupation that was much more hostile to the French and much more favourable to the Ottomans (*Maẓhar/Muẓhir al-taḳdīs bi-zawāl dawlat al-Faransīs*, Cairo 1958). Finally, he wrote his *magnum opus*, *ʿAdjāʾib al-āthār fī 'l-tarādjim wa 'l-akhbār* (4 vols., Būlāḳ 1297/1880). This work is a chronicle of Egypt from the end of the 12th *Hidjrī* century (1099/1688), setting the stage for the rivalry within the *amīrs*' ranks between the Faḳārī and the Ḳāsimī [see ḲĀSIMIYYA] factions. The chronicle ends in the year 1821 (end of A.H. 1236), under Muḥammad ʿAlī's [*q.v.*] rule. As the book's title indicates, it is a combination of narrative (*akhbār*), organised by the *Hidjrī* years followed by obituaries (*tarādjim*) of the notables who died during the previous year. Al-Djabartī's coverage of events, which took place since his maturity, starting around 1770, is a masterpiece of history writing. The detailed description and evaluation of the French occupation and, later, the early stages of Muḥammad ʿAlī's rule, are written with precision, honesty and insight. The historian's grasp of political events and of his society, with all its shades and nuances, is truly impressive. He presents to the reader a panoramic view of Egyptian, primarily Cairene, society, economy and culture, with several important glimpses of the Bedouin and the fellaheen as well. His obituaries of *amīrs*, Arab *shaykhs*, *ʿulamāʾ*, Ṣūfīs and other outstanding persons, and his chronicle, actually a diary, of the events that he witnessed and experienced, are among the best in Islamic historiography. Al-Djabartī was a man of strong religious faith, an ardent orthodox Muslim, who hated infidels and the vulgar sides of popular Islam. He admired the reformed orthodox Ṣūfī order of the Khalwatiyya [*q.v.*], to which even the chief *ʿulamāʾ* of al-Azhar (*shuyūkh al-Azhar*) belonged. On the other hand, he condemned and detested the excesses of the vulgar dervish orders. He often criticised the *ʿulamāʾ* for their selfishness and the Mamlūk *amīrs* for their behaviour, but he leaves no doubt that in his mind they were better Muslims than the Ottomans, the Turkish soldiers who massacred them at the order of Muḥammad ʿAlī. He hated the latter's tyranny, but acknowledged his talents. Al-Djabartī's education and approach were thoroughly traditional, but he was the first modern historian, and he experienced "the impact of the West".

SYRIA

Arabic historiography during the Ottoman period in *Bilād al-Shām*, Greater Syria, is at least as rich in quality and quantity as its Egyptian counterpart. A central and obvious reason was that Egypt had only one political and intellectual centre, Cairo, while Syria had at least three centres where historical works were written—Damascus, Lebanon and Ḥalab (Aleppo)—and, far behind, smaller towns such as Ḥims, Ḥamāt, Ṣafad and Jerusalem.

The majority of the Arabic historians in Syria were men of religion, *ʿulamāʾ*, members of families of religious scholars and functionaries, almost all of them with some Ṣūfī affiliations, in accord with the spirit of the times. Several of the leading Lebanese chroniclers were Christian clerics or bureaucrats in the service of powerful rulers. The topics covered by the chronicles were local politics, power struggles between men and factions, careers of *ʿulamāʾ*, Ṣūfī *shaykhs*, prominent *Ashrāf*, and other *aʿyān* (notables). Special attention was paid to religious matters, both among Muslims and Christians. Since Damascus was a major station on the Pilgrimage route, much information is provided about the Pilgrimage. The chronicles are good sources for social, economic and urban history, giving details about food prices, construction projects, and the like.

By far the most important and prolific historian of the late Mamlūk and the early Ottoman period is an *ʿālim*, a native of the al-Ṣāliḥiyya [*q.v.*] suburb of Damascus, called Muḥammad b. ʿAlī Shams al-Dīn b. Ṭūlūn al-Ṣāliḥī al-Dimashḳī al-Ḥanafī (880-953/1475-1546 [see IBN ṬŪLŪN]). Like Ibn Iyās, his Egyptian contemporary, Ibn Ṭūlūn witnessed the Ottoman occupation of his town, which he described in detail. He was a professional and devoted *ʿālim*, however, and his judgment of the Ottomans, from the Sultan downwards, was more balanced than that of Ibn Iyās. His Arabic style is literary, unlike that of Ibn Iyās, whose Arabic is lively but ungrammatical. Ibn Ṭūlūn wrote no less than 753 treatises, many about Islamic learning, but he owes his fame to his many historical writings. He also wrote an autobiography. His best and most detailed historical work is *Mufākahat al-khullān fī ḥawādith al-zamān*, a chronicle covering the last decades of Mamlūk Syria, Damascus in particular (from 884/1489), and the first years of Ottoman rule in Damascus until the year 926/1520 (ed. Muḥammad Muṣṭafā, 2 vols. Cairo 1381/1962; ed. Khalīl al-Manṣūr, Beirut 1418/1998). He reveals a humanistic sense of justice.

Ibn Ṭūlūn wrote also a book about al-Ṣāliḥiyya, his native suburb, which is an important source of lives of notables, primarily religious functionaries and *ʿulamāʾ*, and of information on religious institutions (*al-Ḳalāʾid al-djawhariyya fī taʾrīkh al-Ṣāliḥiyya*, ed. M.A. Dahmān, Damascus 1401/1980). He also wrote two important books about the personalities and careers of office-holders in Damascus, who served in that city under the Mamlūks and the Ottomans, one about governors of the Province of Damascus (*Iʿlām al-warā bi-man wulliya nāʾiban min al-Atrāk bi-Dimashḳ al-Shām al-Kubrā*, ed. Dahmān, Damascus 1984) and the second about the chief *ḳāḍīs* in that city (*Ḳuḍāt Dimashḳ al-Thaghr al-bassām fī dhikr man wulliya ḳaḍāʾ al-Shām*, ed. Ṣalāḥ al-Dīn al-Munadjdjid, Damascus 1376/1956).

Two biographical works on the governors of Damascus were written by Ibn Djumʿa al-Maḳarrī and Ibn al-Ḳārī. The former (d. after 1156/1743) was a Ḥanafī *ḳāḍī* and a Ḳādirī Ṣūfī. Sayyid Raslān Ibn al-Ḳārī wrote his book in the first half of the 19th century.

Another outstanding historian of the period, whom Ibn Ṭūlūn regarded as his teacher, was ʿAbd al-Ḳādir al-Nuʿaymī, the author of the important historical encyclopaedia of the schools and houses of worship of Damascus, entitled *al-Dāris fī taʾrīkh al-madāris* (several eds., inc. Djaʿfar al-Ḥasanī, Damascus 1988). Al-Nuʿaymī was an expert on *awḳāf* [see WAḲF]. The work is organised by *madhāhib* and types of institutions—Ḳurʾān schools, *madrasas*, *zāwiyas* (Ṣūfī centres) and the like, and includes biographies of teachers and also details about relevant *awḳāf*.

An important historical source for Syria in the 10th/16th century is Nadjm al-Dīn's al-Ghazzī's *al-Kawākib al-sāʾira fī aʿyān al-miʾa al-ʿāshira*, the first of the three centennial dictionaries of Ottoman Syria (3 vols. Beirut, Jounieh and Harissa 1945-59). Al-Ghazzī (977-1061/1570-1651) was a member of a family of *ʿulamāʾ* and an orthodox Ṣūfī of the Ḳādirī order, who lived in Damascus where he held several religious offices. The biographies in the *Kawākib* are arranged by generations (*ṭabaḳāt*) of 33 years each. The order is alphabetical. Among his biographies there are Ottoman officials, *ḳāḍīs*, and governors. He had to rely extensively on information he found in works of earlier historians.

Al-Ghazzī continued the *Kawākib* with a dictionary of lives of notables in the first *ṭabaḳa* of the 11th/17th century entitled *Luṭf al-samar wa-ḳaṭf al-thamar min tarādjim a'yān al-ṭabaḳa al-ūlā min al-ḳarn al-ḥādī 'ashar* (2 vols., ed. Muḥammad al-Shaykh, Damascus 1981). It has 254 biographies, including those of Ottoman judges, military personnel, poets, dervishes, physicians and guild chiefs. From approximately the same time we have the biographical dictionary of Ḥasan b. Muḥammad al-Būrīnī (d. 1024/1615), *Tarādjim al-a'yān min abnā' al-zamān* (ed. al-Munadjdjid, 2 vols. Damascus 1959-66).

A popular collection of biographies from early Islam to the year A.H. 1000, the *Shadharāt al-dhahab fī akhbār man dhahab* (8 vols., Cairo 1350/1931) was written by Ibn al-'Imād, another Ḥanbalī *'ālim* born in the al-Ṣāliḥiyya suburb of Damascus (d. 1089/1622).

This survey of the biographical dictionaries of the 10th/16th century should include the work of Ṭāshköprüzāde Aḥmad b. Muṣṭafā (d. 968/1560 [see ṬASHKÖPRÜZĀDE.2]), a Turkish historian whose *al-Shaḳā'iḳ al-nu'māniyya* is a collection in Arabic of lives of Ottoman *'ulamā'* and Ṣūfīs since the establishment of the Empire. The biographies are arranged by the sultans' reigns.

The centennial dictionary for 11th/17th-century Syria is the *Khulāṣat al-athar fī a'yān al-ḳarn al-ḥādī 'ashar* by Muḥammad al-Amīn al-Muḥibbī (d. 1111/1699 [*q.v.*]) (4 vols. Cairo 1284/1868 and subsequent prints). Al-Muḥibbī also was a member of a wealthy family of Damascene *'ulamā'*. The work consists of 1,289 biographies of distinguished persons. It provides important information about politics, religion and culture in the Ottoman Middle East and the Ḥidjāz. There are also biographies about personages from India and Kurdistan.

The history of Damascus in the 12th/18th century is recorded in a detailed and uninterrupted manner by several reliable contemporary chronicles. The earliest is Ibn Kannān's history covering the period between 1111/1699 and 1153/1740 (Muḥammad b. 'Īsā b. Kannān al-Ṣāliḥī, *Yawmiyyāt shāmiyya*, ed. A.H. al-'Ulābī, Damascus 1994).

The immediate continuer of Ibn Kannān's narrative was a chronicler who, unlike the great majority of the historians of Ottoman Syria, was not a scholar but a barber, called Aḥmad al-Budayrī al-Ḥallāḳ ("the Barber"). His work, *Ḥawādith Dimashḳ al-yawmiyya* (ed. Aḥmad 'Izzat 'Abd al-Karīm, Damascus 1959), covers the period between 1154/1740 or 1741 and 1176/1762; hence, with Ibn Kannān, we have a continuous chronological narrative of Damascus for 63 years. Al-Budayrī was a Ṣūfī, but his order was the Sa'diyya [*q.v.*], which was notoriously unorthodox.

Another Damascene chronicler, a Greek Orthodox priest of Damascus named Mīkhā'īl Breik, brings the historical coverage of the city to 1782 with his *Ta'rīkh al-Shām* (ed. Ḳusṭanṭīn al-Bāshā, Harissa 1930). He explains that he began his history at the year 1720 because this was the time when the rule of the governors (*wālīs*) of the 'Aẓm family started. He makes a point that they were the first native Arabs (*awlād 'Arab*, as distinct from the Turks) who rose to this office. Breik reports of conflicts in Damascus between Catholics and Greek Orthodox. He stands out among his contemporaries as the only historian who wrote also about events that were taking place outside the Ottoman Empire, mainly in Europe.

The last centennial dictionary for the period under survey is *Silk al-durar fī a'yān al-ḳarn al-thānī 'ashar* (4 vols. Beirut 1997) by the Damascene *'ālim* Muḥammad Khalīl al-Murādī (d. 1206/1791-2 at the age of 31 [*q.v.*]). He came from a family of Ḥanafī *'ulamā'* originating from Samarḳand. Like his father before him, he served as the Ḥanafī *muftī* of Damascus and the *naḳīb al-Ashrāf* there. The book, which comprises 1,000 biographies, is a most valuable source for the political, social and cultural history of Syria in the 12th/18th century. In addition to using contemporary chronicles, al-Murādī corresponded with other *'ulamā'* in Syria and Egypt, asking them to collect materials for his biographical dictionary.

LEBANON

Mount Lebanon was a separate political and administrative unit, and had its own history owing to its unique topography [see LUBNĀN]. It often enjoyed a degree of independence, and had a predominantly non-Muslim population of Christians and Druze. During the Ottoman period, Lebanon had many well-educated historians, several of whom were clergymen, others were bureaucrats. The former were preoccupied with the history of their communities, defending their creed and describing the quarrels among different Christian churches. The Lebanese historians wrote about the politics of the region (some recorded the history of other parts of Syria as well), struggles between factions, the great feudal families of the Mountain, and the leaders. They also wrote about the history of the two semi-autonomous dynasties that ruled Lebanon during the Ottoman period, the Ma'nids [see MA'N, BANŪ] and the Shihābs [see SHIHĀB, BANŪ].

The Patriarch Iṣṭifān al-Duwayhī (1630-1704 [*q.v.*]), the greatest of the Maronite church historians, was the author of the only history of Syria with an emphasis on Lebanon in the 16th and 17th centuries by a contemporary writer. He wrote about the Maronite community and church with the purpose of defending their Catholic orthodoxy and attacking other Christian churches, such as the Jacobites, whom he considered as hostile to his church as the Mamlūk sultans. His general history, *Ta'rīkh al-azmina* (ed. F. Taoutel (Tawtal), in *al-Mashriḳ*, xliv [Beirut 1950]; another ed. by P. Fahed, Jounieh 1976, covering the period from the rise of Islam until 1098/1686) is a chronicle of Syria from the Crusades until the end of the 17th century, but the fullest and the most informative account is about the two last centuries. Al-Duwayhī's emphasis is on northern Lebanon where the population was Maronite, and which was ruled by Druze *amīrs* or by Muslims, who were appointed by the Mamlūks, and later by the Ottomans.

Ḥananiyā al-Munayyir (d. 1823), a Greek monk of the Shuwayrite religious order, wrote a history of the Shūf region of Lebanon and the Shihābīs. He concentrated on his own religious order and on other Christian religious topics (*al-Durr al-marṣūf fī ta'rīkh al-Shūf*, ed. I. Sarkīs, in *al-Mashriḳ*, xlviii-li [1954-7]). The most important historian of that period is Aḥmad Ḥaydar al-Shihābī (1761-1835), a cousin of the Amīr Bashīr II. He had access to official documents, such as Bashīr's correspondence with Ottoman governors. He wrote a history of Lebanon from the rise of Islam until 1827, called *Ghurar al-ḥisān fī akhbār al-zamān*. Aḥmad Ḥaydar was a Maronite convert from Islam. In his history he expresses unmitigated support for the Shihābīs, in particular for Bashīr II, against their

Lebanese and Ottoman enemies (his books have been published in several editions, e.g. *Lubnān fī ʿahd al-umarāʾ al-Shihābiyyīn*, Beirut 1969, and *Taʾrīkh al-Amīr Ḥaydar Aḥmad al-Shihābī*, Beirut 2000).

ʿIRĀḲ

For the 10th/16th century, no historical parallel to Ibn Iyās or Ibn Ṭūlūn describing ʿIrāḳ's conditions under the Ottomans—who conquered the country in 941/1534—has come down to us, and the few works that were written are in Turkish. The historians tended to write about the main cities—Baghdād, Baṣra, Mawṣil—and several smaller towns. As expected, power struggles among the rulers are constant features in the chronicles. As for foreign affairs, wars between Persia and Ottoman ʿIrāḳ are the main theme. Baghdād itself was occupied by the Ṣafawids from 1622 until 1632. The attacks of the Persians under Nādir Shāh during the first half of the 12th/18th century (1733 until 1746, including sieges of Baghdād, Mawṣil and Kirkūk) were the most traumatic events in the political history of ʿIrāḳ, and are reported in detail by the chroniclers.

The first historian of Ottoman ʿIrāḳ worthy of the name was ʿAlī al-Ḥuwayzī (d. 1075/1664). He lived in the court of the *amīrs* of the Afrasiyāb house, founded at the end of the 10th/16th century by a local magnate who administered the Province of Baṣra as his private domain. Al-Ḥuwayzī's history of Baṣra in the first half of the century is entitled *al-Sīra al-murḍiyya fī sharḥ al-farḍiyya*.

Aḥmad b. ʿAbd Allāh al-Ghurābī from Baghdād (d. 1690/1102) wrote the first chronicle that is arranged by years. For his information, he relied on Turkish official documents and eyewitnesses' reports. His book, *ʿUyūn akhbār al-aʿyān mimmā maḍā min sālif al-ʿuṣūr wa ʾl-azmān*, is a chronicle of the political events in Baghdād in the 11th/17th century.

Similar to the situation in Syria, 12th/18th-century ʿIrāḳ saw the emergence of governors (*wālīs*) of local families. Maḥmūd al-Raḥabī, a *muftī*, wrote the biography of *pashas* who confronted the Persians in 1145/1736. ʿAbd al-Raḥmān al-Suwaydī (d. 1175/1761), an important chronicler, wrote the history of Baghdād in the first half of the century. His book, *Taʾrīkh Baghdād* or *Ḥadīḳat al-zawrāʾ fī sīrat al-wuzarāʾ* (Baghdād 1962), tells the history of the city through the biography of the governors Ḥasan Pasha and his son Aḥmad Pasha.

One may conclude by mentioning two brothers from Mawṣil who wrote about the history of ʿIrāḳ until their own time. Yāsīn b. Khayr Allāh al-Khaṭīb al-ʿUmarī (d. after 1816), the more important of the two, wrote a general historical work from the Hidjrā until 1811, with an emphasis on ʿIrāḳ, and also on Mawṣil and Baghdād (*Zubdat al-āthār al-djaliyya fī ʾl-ḥawādith al-arḍiyya*, ed. ʿAbd al-Salām Raʾūf, Nadjaf 1974; *Ghāyat al-marām fī taʾrīkh maḥāsin Baghdād dār al-salām*, Baghdād 1986; *Munyat al-udabāʾ fī taʾrīkh al-Mawṣil al-ḥadbāʾ*, Mawṣil 1955). Muḥammad Amīn al-ʿUmarī, Yāsīn's brother, wrote *Manhal al-awliyāʾ*, another book about Mawṣil.

ii. *Concluding remarks*

Despite the differences between the various Arab provinces of the Ottoman Empire, certain common features emerge in their historiography. With the notable exception of ʿIrāḳ, local chronicles reasonably cover the first decades or at least the first years after the Ottoman occupation in the early 10th/16th century. The rest of that century has much less historiographical coverage (it should be noted, however, that there was a rich historiography in Yemen for the 10th/16th and early 11th/17th centuries; see the book of Frédérique Soudan, below, in *Bibl.*, and AL-MAWZAʿĪ). The 11th/17th century witnessed more intensive historical writings in Arabic, which came to full maturity and richness in the 12th/18th century (this being true with regard to ʿIrāḳ as well).

The differences between the societies of the various Arab lands and cities notwithstanding, there are strong similarities owing to the common religion (at least for the Muslim majority) and the common language and culture. The roles and status of the *ʿulamāʾ*, *Ashrāf*, Ṣūfīs, guilds, leaders of city quarters and the like were as a general rule similar in Cairo, Aleppo, Baghdād and Jerusalem.

Latent or even explicit patriotism is discernible in the writings of the local historians. The writers (and no doubt their readers) accepted Ottoman rule and hegemony as legitimate and natural, despite occasional expressions of criticism of the régime or even antipathy toward the Turks. However, as Ottoman rule became more decentralised after the 10th/16th century, and as local forces, such as the Mamlūks in Egypt or the leaders of strong Arab families elsewhere, were entering the ruling élites in Egypt, Syria, Lebanon and ʿIrāḳ, the Sultan and the Ottoman capital seemed more distant and even irrelevant.

Bibliography (in addition to references given in the article): Only a few items of the extensive research literature on Arabic historiography during the Ottoman period can be mentioned here. On Egypt. D. Crecelius (ed.), *Eighteenth century Egypt: the Arabic manuscript sources*, Claremont, CA, 1990, which consists of several important essays and has a very rich and useful bibliography in the text and footnotes. Some of the papers also discuss the earlier centuries. References are made to earlier historiographical studies by D. Ayalon, P.M. Holt, Muḥammad Anīs, Laylā ʿAbd al-Laṭīf and others. On Syria. Ṣalāḥ al-Dīn al-Munadjdjid, *al-Muʾarrikhūn al-dimashkiyyūn fī ʾl-ʿahd al-ʿuthmānī wa-āthāruhum al-makhṭūṭa*, Damascus 1964; Abdul-Karim Rafeq, *The Province of Damascus, 1723-1783*, Beirut 1966, 320-33; Laylā al-Ṣabbāgh, *Min aʿlām al-fikr al-ʿArabī fī ʾl-ʿaṣr al-ʿuthmānī al-awwal: Muḥammad al-Amīn al-Muḥibbī wa-kitābuhu Khulāṣat al-athar fī aʿyān al-ḳarn al-ḥādī ʿashar 1061-1111/1651-1699*, Damascus 1406/1986. On Lebanon. A.H. Hourani, *Historians of Lebanon*, in B. Lewis and P.M. Holt (eds.), *Historians of the Middle East*, London 1962, 226-45. On ʿIrāḳ. ʿAbd al-Salām Raʾūf, *al-Taʾrīkh wa ʾl-muʾarrikhūn al-ʿIrāḳiyyūn fī ʾl-ʿaṣr al-ʿuthmānī*, Baghdād 1983. On Yemen. F. Soudan, *Le Yemen ottoman d'après la chronique d'al-Mawzaʿī*, Cairo 1999.

(M. WINTER)

(e) North Africa.

A. *The period up to 1450*

As far as written documentation goes, the historiography of the mediaeval Maghrib proceeds, *grosso modo*, out of the Arab-Islamic historical tradition of the East. As well as the implicit teleological element, it follows the divisions and techniques of elaboration of those of the East, but nevertheless develops quite early lines of demarcation, which will be examined below, together with points of divergence.

1. Emergence and starting-points.

The newly-emerging Maghribī historiography should be understood as both a result and a support of the mainstream tradition. A certain number of points need to be recognised:

(i) Because of the late character of the conquest of the Maghrib, and its being a peripheral sector of

Islam, an Arabic historiography was fairly late in emerging. Taking into account the loss of the account called *Futūḥ Ifrīḳiya* still attributed on weak grounds to Abu 'l-Muhādjir [*q.v.*], the effective appearance of this historiography seems to have been in the second half of the 3rd/9th century, at a moment when the historical tradition in ʿIrāḳ and Syria was firmly enough established to provide an accomplished model. The first text written by a Maghribī in Arabic language is generally considered to be the Ibāḍī work composed by Ibn Sallām *ca.* 273/876-7 on the self-Islamisation of the Maghrib along the Khāridjite route from Tāhart to Barḳa, which manuscript was discovered in 1964 (ed. W. Schwartz and Shaykh Sālim Ibn Yaʿḳūb, Wiesbaden 1986).

(ii) As with the above work, after the fashion of the Mashriḳ, the next works were also closely linked to politico-ideological questions. In this same Eastern tradition, they included, in addition to chronicles (*akhbār, ta'rīkh*), the various fields of biography (*tarādjim*), the classification of élite groups (*ṭabaḳāt*), stories of the conquests (*maghāzī*) and collective genealogies (*ansāb*).

(iii) As well as Maghribī writings, there was early on a contribution from outside authors; it was probably difficult to ignore Ifrīḳiya and the Far Maghrib (= Morocco) when dealing with Spain or Egypt. In this regard, towards the first half of the 3rd/9th century, the Egyptian Ibn ʿAbd al-Ḥakam [*q.v.*], in his *Futūḥ Miṣr*—dealing with the conquest of Egypt and the Maghrib—is a notable example. A similar instance, older but more debatable as to the early age of the whole text, would be that of al-Wāḳidī [*q.v.*] and his *Futūḥ Ifrīḳiya.* As for the overlapping of the two traditions of al-Andalus and the Maghrib, the first tentative steps are seen in the surviving extracts of the *K. al-Rāyāt* of the Persian Muḥammad al-Rāzī of Cordova (d. 273/886 or 277/890), which was still used in the Far Maghrib at the opening of the 8th/14th century (El-Mennouni, 17-18; Lévi-Provençal, *Hist. Esp. mus.*, iii, Paris 1953, 501-3).

(iv) Although uneven, this relative interest by non-Maghribī authors seems to have been motivated by the social and political repercussions of the conquest. As well as these texts by al-Wāḳidī and Ibn ʿAbd al-Ḥakam, the theme is tackled in the first corpora of *fiḳh* and *ḥadīth* in the course of the 4th/9th century, e.g. in the *Futūḥ* of al-Balādhurī, the *Ta'rīkh* of al-Ṭabarī and, later, in the *Kāmil* of Ibn al-Athīr. In connection with the latter two works, it should be noted that they not only convey the historical tradition of the conquests but at times depend also on what seems to have been oral tradition, cf. al-Ṭabarī, i, 2813-18, tr. R.S. Humphreys, *The History of al-Ṭabarī*, xv, *The crisis of the early caliphate*, Albany 1990, 18-24, year 27, and Ibn al-Athīr, ed. Beirut, iii, 92-3.

(v) This apart, it is notable that, once it developed, the Maghribī historiographical tradition tended in general to restrict itself within its own geographical sphere, apart from the association with the Iberian peninsula. Also, from the time of the first Muslim conquest, it always looks forwards, and almost never backwards; what is pre-Islamic is qualified as *azalī*, outside time, hence History for the Maghrib begins, it seems, with Islam.

2. The process of development, and its salient features.

At first sight, one notes that the relative stability of Ifrīḳiya permitted, in a first stage of development up to the end of the 5th/11th century, an activity in composing works which had only its equal in Muslim Spain. For the rest of the Maghribī region, such an activity seems to come only with the installation, during the second stage of development, of powerful, centralising dynasties, under which the same outburst of historiographical writing now appears in the Far Maghrib.

The disparate nature of the historical works and the primacy of Ifrīḳiya, mid-3rd/8th to late 5th/11th centuries

After a void following on from the conquests, from the mid-3rd/9th century, various initiatives appear, independently of each other, in Fās and Tāhart and, above all, in Ifrīḳiya. However, most of the works from this period have been lost. We possess Ibn Sallām's Ibāḍī text and the chronicle of Ibn al-Ṣaghīr [*q.v.*] on the Rustamid Imāms of Tāhart from the end of this same century (ed. and Fr. tr. C. de Motylinski, in *Actes du XIVe Congrès International des Orientalistes*, Paris 1908, 2-132, new ed. Tunis 1976), and the contemporary collection of biographies by Abu 'l-ʿArab [*q.v.*], the *Ṭabaḳāt ʿulamā' Ifrīḳiya* (ed. M. Ben Cheneb, Algiers 1915), but the first chronicles dealing with the Idrīsids of Fās, the Khāridjites of Sidjilmāsa, the Aghlabids and the Fāṭimids of Ifrīḳiya, and the works on the heretical Barghawāṭa and the Ghumāra [*q.vv.*] of the Atlantic seaboard, have not survived. There have likewise disappeared the only two contemporary or near-contemporary accounts of the Idrīsids, viz. a chronicle on the Imāms of Fās by Ibn al-Waddūn (4th/10th century), allegedly called the *T. al-Adārisa*, and one from the previous century, apparently better known since it was still cited by al-Bakrī [*q.v.*] in the mid-5th/11th century and by Ibn ʿIdhārī two centuries later, the *al-Madjmūʿ al-muftarik* of al-Nawfalī (El-Mennouni, 18, 27). Three works written under the Aghlabids, apparently detailed and of extended length, have also failed to survive: the *T. Bani 'l-Aghlab* by the prince Muḥammad b. Ziyādat Allāh (d. 283/896); a second chronicle with the same name; and an important *Ṭabaḳāt al-ʿulamā'* by Muḥammad b. Saḥnūn (d. 256/870), son of the famous Mālikī jurist of al-Ḳayrawān.

Apart from Fāṭimid Ifrīḳiya, our knowledge of the Maghrib during the 4th-5th/10th-11th centuries stems essentially from eastern sources or late Andalusī ones, and only after that from later Maghribī sources. Hence the immense *al-Muḳtabas* of the Cordovan Ibn Ḥayyān [*q.v.*], from the mid-5th/11th century, forms one of the basic chronicles for the Far Maghrib, at that time pulled between the two influences of the Umayyads and the Fāṭimids or Fāṭimids-Zīrids. In this context, the contemporary Ifrīḳiyan sources would have been a counterpoise to these, in particular the lost, slightly earlier chronicle of Ibn al-Raḳīḳ [*q.v.*] called *T. Ifrīḳiya wa 'l-Maghrib.* Of this most important source, a supposedly authentic fragment has been recovered and twice published (Tunis 1967, Beirut 1990). We also have, in its entirety, a text equally important for Ifrīḳiyan history but one which is not a chronicle and which only concerns in a subordinate way the rest of the Maghrib, sc. the *Riyāḍ al-nufūs* of al-Mālikī (d. 460/1068 [*q.v.*]), a work essentially concerned with the biographies of Mālikī scholars and ascetics in Ifrīḳiya up to the mid-4th/9th century.

For the rest, other contemporary Ifrīḳiyan texts are known only from paraphrases or from quotations by later authors. Here one would include the work called *Fī masālik Ifrīḳiya wa-mamālikihā*, plus a range of opuscula concerning strategically-placed towns such as Tāhart, Ténès, Oran, Sidjilmāsa, Nakkūr and al-Baṣra in the northwestern Far Maghrib. Gathered together for al-Ḥakam II [*q.v.*] of Cordova, these writings stem from Abū ʿAbd Allāh Muḥammad b. Yūsuf al-Warrāḳ (292-363/904-74 [*q.v.*]), of Ḳayrawānī birth and education, who was accordingly to be of great value for al-Bakrī, Ibn Ḥayyān and Ibn ʿIdhārī. To these works by al-Warrāḳ, one may add those of Ibn al-Djazzār [*q.v.*], whose oeuvre included also geography (the *ʿAdjāʾib al-buldān*) as well as history (*K. al-Taʿrīf bi-ṣaḥīḥ al-taʾrīkh*) as well as *maghāzī and ṭabaḳāt*, likewise utilised by al-Bakrī and Ibn Ḥayyān.

The losses of major sources are paralleled by similar losses of writings for tribal or family history and for the first attempts at Berber genealogy, the compilation of Ibn Shaddād [*q.v.*], a Zīrid prince exiled in Syria, as well as two continuations of Ibn al-Raḳīḳ's work, that of Ibn Sharaf (d. 460/1068 [*q.v.*]) and that of Abu 'l-Ṣalt (d. 529/1134 [*q.v.*]), who continued, according to Ibn ʿIdhārī, the previous work. Nevertheless, since it happens that a good number of these writings were sufficiently utilised up to the time of Ibn Khaldūn, their legacy remains, despite everything, appreciable.

Furthermore, there exist various sources, more or less contemporary and spread across time, which can be used to fill gaps. Thus, in connection with intellectual and religious life in the Maghrib up to the beginning of the 6th/12th century, the *Madārik* of al-Ḳāḍī ʿIyāḍ (d. 544/1149 [see ʿIYĀḌ B. MŪSĀ]) of Ceuta, provide information often of first-rate importance. As for court life under the first Fāṭimid Imāms in North Africa, we can comprehend the impact of the Fāṭimid system on wider society and the obvious dysfunctions of the system, from the contemporary documents used in the *Sīrat al-Ustādh Djawdhar* (Cairo 1954) of al-Manṣūr al-Djawdharī [*q.v.*] and thanks to the contemporary witness of the *ḳāḍī* al-Nuʿmān. As well as this witness displayed in his *K. al-Madjālis wa 'l-musāyarāt*, this *ḳāḍī* has in his *K. Iftitāḥ al-daʿwa* left us a precious account of the Fāṭimids' rise to power. One may deplore the obviously partisan tone of these texts, but this in fact may well have been one of the reasons for their survival. Certainly, for many mediaeval Ismāʿīlī authors, these last two works were, even in the Mashrīḳ, basic reference works.

On the margins of this local production tested over the centuries, there existed, too, other non-Maghribī sources. The most relevant relate to the geography of the region. Composed for the most part in ʿIrāḳ and for various motives, these works dealt with the lands of the Maghrib in detail, describing road networks, financial assessments, main economic activities, morals, customs and beliefs. For their works, geographers and literary men had recourse to direct observation or to information which had been transmitted and followed after careful examination. This last procedure may have been the main one, since neither al-Yaʿḳūbī nor Ibn Khurradādhbih nor even al-Bakrī, living as he did in nearby al-Andalus, knew the Maghrib first-hand (*bi 'l-ʿiyān*); only al-Muḳaddasī and Ibn Ḥawḳal were exceptions to this rule, and it is undoubtedly this first-hand knowledge that informs the great originality of these two eastern authors, especially of the latter.

Variations, and the Almoravid-Almohad domination (late 5th/11th to mid-7th/13th centuries)

With the installation of the Almoravids in the Far Maghrib and their annexation of the western part of the Central Maghrib and of al-Andalus of the *taifas*, there existed at the end of the 5th/11th century the Almoravid empire and the Zīrid-Ḥammādid grouping. Both belonged to the great Berber group of the Ṣanhādja [*q.v.*]. These two powers co-existed, through thick and thin, till the rise, at their expense, of the Almohads in the mid-6th/12th century.

Transposed to the level of history writing, this evolution was going to cause a draining away of effort towards the West. Hence till the mid-7th/13th century, the fundamental works were written either in al-Andalus or in Morocco, and consequently reflect the new environment dominated by the Almoravids and Almohads. Despite this trend, there were many irreparable losses of works, a need to rely on later compilations and even the intervention of eastern authors. Nevertheless, there appear fresh nuances when compared with the earlier period.

Almoravid historical writing

One of the characteristic traits of this is that it was reduced, over the centuries, to a summation of later, general accounts. Apart from the important information of al-Bakrī, one can hardly distinguish, right up to the mid-20th century, many witnesses who were near to the events described. The only contemporary narrative, that of Ibn al-Ṣayrafī (d. 557/1162 [*q.v.*]), *al-Anwār al-djaliyya fī akhbār al-dawla al-murābiṭiyya*, has not survived, although it is known that this chronicle, covering the Almoravid period up to 530/1135-6, was in current use right to the end of the mediaeval period. Authors distant in time and space, such as Ibn Khallikān (d. 681/1282), Ibn al-Abbār (d. 658/1260), Ibn Abī Zarʿ (d. between 710-20/1310-20) and Ibn al-Khaṭīb (d. 776/1375) [*q.vv.*] either drew material directly from it or refer to it. Moreover, the anonymous author of the chronicle *al-Ḥulal al-mawshiyya* (written 783/1381) probably drew upon it more than he explicitly reveals. Although poor in surviving chronicles, it is possible to construct a fairly precise chronology of Almoravid history. The publication of leaves discovered of the Almoravid *Bayān* (in *Hespéris-Tamuda*, ii [1961], 43-111) makes a large contribution to this process, as do a certain number of Almohad writings, especially for the transition phase between the two dynasties.

The canvas thus delineated can fairly often be enriched, at the level of content, by varied sources ranging from simple accounts to collections of *tarādjim*, travel accounts (*riḥla*), official correspondence, personal writings and juridical literature. This is how the chronicle of Abū Zakariyyā on the Ibāḍī state of Tāhart (partial Fr. tr. E. Masqueray, Paris-Algiers 1878), was put together at the turn of the 6th/12th century. Also from this period date the summa of the *Madārik* of al-Ḳāḍī ʿIyāḍ as well as the *Ghunya* which he wrote, setting out his own masters. In parallel to this, one should mention the *Dhakhīra* of Ibn Bassām (552/1147 [*q.v.*]), meant primarily for Andalusī scholars without, however, systematically excluding Maghribīs, whilst Ibn Khāḳān (d. 529/1134) included in his *Ḳalāʾid al-ʿiḳyān* distinguished poets, men of letters, government officials and men of state of both shores. Regarding such men, one should note the *Tibyān*, the memoirs of the Zīrid prince of Granada ʿAbd Allāh (d. 469/1077) (ed. Lévi-Provençal, Cairo 1955; Sp. tr. idem and E. García Gómez, Madrid 1980; Eng. tr. Amin Tibi, Leiden 1992; ed. A.T. Ṭībī, Rabat 1995), which give an excellent impression of the struggles of the *reyes de taifas* with Yūsuf b. Tāshufīn [*q.v.*]. Of the same type of narration, there is the account left by Abū Bakr Ibn al-ʿArabī (d. 543/1148 [*q.v.*]) concerning the official mission of his father, whom he accompanied to the East to seek the ʿAbbāsid caliph's investiture of the same Yūsuf b. Tāshufīn (see *Tres textos árabes sobre Berbéres*, ed. M. Yaʿlā, Madrid 1996, 275-315).

As well as this documentation concerned with the élites, Almoravid history writing also includes works depicting social-economic realities and governmental practices. The two treatises on *ḥisba* of al-Saḳaṭī [*q.v.*] of Malaga (ed. Lévi-Provençal, Paris 1931) and Ibn ʿAbdūn [*q.v.*] of Seville (ed. idem, Cairo 1954; Fr. tr. Paris 1947) are significant here. Although primarily concerned with the situation in al-Andalus, both of them, and especially the latter, have material relevant for the dominant power on both shores, the Almoravids. Their content is quite often confirmed by legal material contained in the collections of *nawāzil* of the *ḳāḍī* Ibn Rushd (d. 520/1126 [*q.v.*]), forebear of the philosopher, and later, in the *Miʿyār* of al-Wansharīsī (d. 914/1508-9 [*q.v.*]). Many of the problems raised in these *nawāzil* (e.g. the status of the Christians of al-Andalus, the behaviour of the Banū Hilāl in Ifrīḳiya, the appearance of Almohad rebels, etc.) are reflected in the *Nuzhat al-mushtāḳ*, the *riḥla* of al-Idrīsī [*q.v.*], completed in 548/1154, and also in the substantial body of official correspondence emanating from the Almoravid court (see *Revista de Estudios Islámicos en Madrid*, ii [1954], 55-84, vii-viii [1959-60], 109-98).

Almohad historical writing

Inasmuch as the Almohad system rested on the Imām's infallibility, all innovation, from any source outside himself, was in principle inadmissible. Whence the complete absence at the documentary level of all traces of *fatwās* [*q.v.*] and decisions on specific cases (*nāzila* [*q.v.*]). However, this same system witnessed the spread of a mystical movement more or less tolerated which produced its own literature at the popular level, using, amongst other things, the *manāḳib* [*q.v.*]. In effect, this genre, immortalising the lives and deeds of "men of God", can be placed with that of the *tarādjim*, with the formal qualification that al-Andalus was the favoured field for *tarādjim* whilst *manāḳib* literature was to flourish above all in North Africa.

Thus on one side there are the collections of *tarādjim* published since the end of the 19th century, such as the *Fahras* of the Sevillan Ibn Khayr (d. 575/1179 [*q.v.*]); the *K. al-Ṣila* of the Cordovan Ibn Bashkuwāl (d. 578/1182 [*q.v.*]); and the *K. al-Takmila*, a continuation of the preceding, by the Valencian Ibn al-Abbār. On the other side, there are the *Mustafād* (still in ms.) on the ascetics of Fās and its region by al-Tamīmī (d. 603/1206); the *Tashawwuf* on the lives of saints of southern Morocco by al-Tādilī (d. 628 or 629/1230-1 [see IBN AL-ZAYYĀT]) (ed. A. Toufiq, Rabat 1984; Fr. tr. M. de Fenoyl, Casablanca 1995); al-Bādisī's [*q.v.*] *Maḳṣad*, written *ca.* 711/1311-12, on the saints of the Rīf in the Almohad period; the *Diʿāmat al-yaḳīn* of al-ʿAzafī (d. 633/1236 [*q.v.* in Suppl.]) (ed. A. Toufiq, Rabat 1989); and, to a certain extent, *al-Dhurr al-munaẓẓam*, also by al-ʿAzafī, in which he invites people to the celebration, at that time (mid-7th/13th century) still a timid one, of the Prophet's birthday (ed. and Sp. tr. F. de la Granja, in *al-And.*, xxxiv [1969], 19-53).

Taking a wide conspectus of relevant literature, one should include the great Ibn al-ʿArabī of Murcia (d. 638/1240 [*q.v.*]), who left behind works on education in the mystical way such as *al-Futūḥ al-makkiyya* and the *Muḥāḍarāt al-akhyār* in which *karāmāt* [see KARĀMA] and *manāḳib* play a great part. Conversely, the Andalusī biographical dictionaries were to have a North African counterpart in such works as the anonymous *Siyar al-mashāyikh* and the *K. al-Siyar* of al-Wisyānī, both written in the second half of the 6th/12th century on notable figures amongst the Khāridjites of Tāhart and Ifrīḳiya, as also the *ʿUnwān al-dirāya* of al-Ghubrīnī of Bidjāya (d. 714/1314-15 [*q.v.*]) (Algiers 1910; new ed. Beirut 1969) and *al-Dhayl wa 'l-takmila* of Ibn ʿAbd al-Malik al-Marrākushī (d. 703/1303 [*q.v.*]), dealing, amongst other things, with well-known Maghribī figures unduly absorbed into the host society or simply ignored by Andalusī authors (Beirut n.d. and 1965; Rabat 1984). Furthermore, in his *Taʿrīf*, Muḥammad b. ʿIyāḍ included interesting information on his father, the famous judge, on his masters and on his fellow-disciples (ed. Ben Chrifa, Rabat n.d.).

The impact of theological dogma was to generate a genre of popularised doctrine. As well as an *ʿaḳīda* (creed) and a *murshida* (breviary) spread during his lifetime in the Berber language, Ibn Tūmart [*q.v.*] is said to have dictated to his disciple and successor ʿAbd al-Muʾmin educational texts and epistles which the latter collected into *al-Taʿālīḳ* ("The commentaries"), and made known as *Le livre d'Ibn Toumert* (ed. L. Luciani, Algiers 1903) or under the title *Aʿazz mā yuṭlab* (Marrākush 1997). Like the letters addressed to the Almoravid ruler ʿAlī b. Yūsuf (*Documents inédits d'histoire almohade*, ed. Lévi-Provençal, Paris 1927, 11-13, tr. 19-21), this collection is an attempt at spreading the Almohad doctrines whilst stigmatising the distortions of their religious opponents.

The preoccupation of the Almohad state with informing its followers probably explains the profusion of circulars and notes scattered throughout the sources or isolated as documents in archives or collections of official matter. One example of these collections would be the one collated by Ibn ʿAmīra [*q.v.*] towards the mid-7th/13th century. The diversity of the archive material can be appreciated through the *Trente-sept lettres officielles almohades* (ed. Lévi-Provençal, Rabat 1941, Fr. tr. in *Hespéris* [1941], 1-70) and *Nouvelles lettres almohades* (ed. A. Azzaoui, Casablanca 1995). The information in these texts is often first-hand, and they illuminate, in general, the underlying aspect of facts generally lacking in cohesion at the level of the narrative sources.

Regarding these latter sources it is, of course, true that they hardly ever deal with real situations, but there is nevertheless an exception in the work of al-Baydhaḳ [*q.v.*], in which he describes from memory, towards the middle of the 6th/12th century, the peregrinations and stages of ascension of Ibn Tūmart. From a greater distance and probably because of the distance, ʿAbd al-Wāḥid al-Marrākushī (d. 633/1235 [*q.v.*]) undertook, from Egypt, to give a lively account in his *al-Muʿdjib* of the contemporary Maghrib, using his own observations and the memories of an aged member of the Almohad court (Cairo 1949, Fr. tr. E. Fagnan, Algiers 1893). Another text now lost seems to have corresponded to the same schema, *al-Mughrib fī maḥāsin ahl al-Maghrib*, whose author, Ilyasaʿ b. ʿĪsā al-Ghāfiḳī (d. 575/1179) likewise chose to settle in Egypt where he wrote his work at the request of Ṣalāḥ al-Dīn. For the rest, the Almohad accounts, above all utilising this last chronicle, had recourse to compilation, gradually adopting the method of the classical annalists. Out of these accounts, one of the most notable is the *Naẓm al-djumān* written by Ibn al-Ḳaṭṭān [*q.v.*] for al-Murtaḍā, the penultimate Almohad ruler, in the mid-7th/13th century, and of which only the part describing the beginnings of Ibn Tūmart's movement has survived (ed. M.A. Makkī, Tetouan n.d.). It was much used by authors of the immediate succeeding period and later, and depends, in addition to al-Baydhaḳ's work, on *al-Mann bi 'l-imāma* of Ibn Ṣāḥib al-Ṣalāt (d. 594/1198) (ed. A. Tazi, Beirut 1979, new ed. 1987). The author dwells particularly on the events of the Almohad lands between 554-68/1159-73. From this same period stem Abū Marwān al-Warrāḳ's *al-Miḳbās fī akhbār al-Maghrib wa 'l-Andalus wa-Fās*, and Ibn Ḥamādu(h) of Ceuta's *al-Muktabis fī akhbār al-Maghrib wa-Fās wa 'l-Andalus*, both now lost but widely used up to Ibn Khaldūn's time. As for the so-called Almohad *Bayān* of Ibn ʿIdhārī, it is recognised as the chronicle par excellence for the whole period (ed. A. Huici Miranda, Tetuan 1960, new ed. Beirut-Casablanca 1985). Completed in 712/1312, it appears to reflect an undoubted serenity. Using rare or lost sources, the author obviously aimed at exhaustiveness and scholarly rigour. On the level of the finer points, he does not hesitate to sort out the information, when required, in order the better to achieve a synthesis or even to discern long-term effects.

It remains to mention geographical works. Outside the very unoriginal work of Ibn Saʿīd of Granada (d. 685/1286 [*q.v.*]), the *K. Basṭ al-arḍ fī 'l-ṭūl wa 'l-ʿarḍ* (Beirut 1970) and that, at second hand, of al-Zuhrī (d. after 546/1151-2), *al-Sufra* (ed. M. Hadj-Sadok, Paris 1968), one should emphasise the originality of Ibn Djubayr's (d. 614/1217 [*q.v.*]) *Riḥla* (Fr. tr. M. Gaudefroy-Demombynes, Paris 1949-65, Eng. tr. R.J.C. Broadhurst, London 1952) and also the anonymous *al-Istibṣār* (Alexandria 1958). Coming from the last quarter of the 6th/12th century, these two descriptions can be taken, it seems, as pure travel narratives, but with the difference that Ibn Djubayr starts from the Maghrib through the Mediterranean without omitting the Mashriḳ nor the opposite shores of the Sea, whilst the author of *al-Istibṣār* limits himself to describing from the interior the ensemble of the region, whilst highlighting the Far Maghrib. Also, the first author is interested in morals and the resulting abuses of government, whilst the second is, rather, although an acute observer, simply a writer with a thesis.

Post-Almohad developments

With the disintegration of the Almohad empire, there came a certain renewal of historiography dealing with the Maghrib, with biography and chronicles—with their nuances blurred—seeming to be under a similar impulsion, as also the *riḥla* and local genealogical works.

Regarding chronicles, this was to benefit from the rival inheritors of the Almohad empire, and these lent themselves to manipulation by the victors. This may explain the disappearance and eventual loss of certain texts. Also, there was a decline in the use of circulars and a complete uninterest, it seems, in preserving for posterity archival documents. However, some documents have survived by chance, such as the collection of al-ʿAzafī (Rabat 1979) and the later anthologies like al-Ḳalḳashandī's (d. 821/1418 [*q.v.*]) *Ṣubḥ al-aʿshā* (Cairo 1913-19) or al-Maḳḳarī's (d. 1041/1631 [*q.v.*]) *Azhār al-riyāḍ* (Rabat 1979-80), but above all, this has been thanks to the rich collections of Barcelona, Italy, Spain and Portugal.

Leaving aside archive material, we have the following:

Chronicles. Between the mid-7th/13th century and the end of the 9th/15th one, the chronicle in the Maghrib is above all the product of Ifrīḳiya and the Far Maghrib, reflecting the politico-military situation. Accordingly, apart from Abu 'l-ʿAbbās al-Dardjīnī's [*q.v.*] *K. Ṭabaḳāt al-mashāyikh*, dealing with the Ibāḍī community in the mid-7th/13th century (ed. I. Ṭallāy, 2 vols. Constantine 1974) and the late *K. al-Siyar* of al-Shammākhī (d. 928/1522 [*q.v.*]), dealing with personalities and events at Mzāb (Cairo 1301/1883-4), the Central Maghrib was to have no reference work except for the great historian Ibn Khaldūn's brother Yaḥyā's *Bughyat al-ruwwād* (ed. and Fr. tr. A. Bel, Algiers 1903-10, new ed. A. Hadjiat, Algiers 1980), whilst the land of the Ḥafṣids, in addition to the masterwork *K. al-ʿIbar*, pan-Islamic in its sweep, has left behind works of more limited range, such as Ibn Ḳunfudh's (d. 810/1407-8 [*q.v.*]) *al-Fārisiyya* (ed. M. Nifer and A. Turki, Tunis 1968), Ibn Shammāʿ's *al-Adilla al-bayyina*, written in 861/1457 (ed. Kaak, Tunis 1936), and the *T. al-Dawlatayn* attributed to al-Zarkashī (d. after 894/1489) (new ed. Tunis 1966, Fr. tr. Fagnan, Constantine 1895). From the Marīnid kingdom, we have the *radjaz* work of al-Malzūzī (d. 697/1297-8), *Naẓm al-sulūk*, in which he lauds his masters' rise to power (Rabat 1963). This same version of events was soon produced in prose and included in the anonymous *al-Dhakhīra al-saniyya* (Rabat 1972) before being included in the *Rawḍat al-ḳirṭās* (ed. C.J. Tornberg, Upsala 1843-6, Rabat 1936, 1972, Fr. tr. Beaumier, Paris 1860, Sp. tr. A. Huici Miranda, Valencia 1948). In this, the supposed author Ibn Abī Zarʿ [*q.v.*] seems to be an innovator in introducing the idea of historical continuity, leading, with Fās as the centre, from the "founding" state of the Idrīsids to the Marīnids, to stop in the year 726/1326 towards the end of Abū Saʿīd I's reign. In the next reign, there was a further innovation in al-Kafīf al-Zarhūnī's use of the Arabic colloquial of Morocco to describe, in an *urdjūza* called *Malʿaba* comprising 497 verses, Sultan Abu 'l-Ḥasan's [*q.v.*] campaign in Ifrīḳiya. Much later, and further from the lively eye-witness account of the Marīnids of Ibn Khaldūn, another *urdjūza* by al-Kurrāsī (d. 964/1556-7), his *ʿArūsat al-masāʾil* dedicated to the Waṭṭāsid dynasty, closes, in literary Arabic, the list of chronicles dealing with the region.

Of works written in the Mashriḳ and concerning the Maghrib at this time, were Abu 'l-Fidā's (d. 732/1331) *Taʾrīkh*, al-Dhahabī's (d. 748/1347) *K. al-ʿIbar* (Kuwait 1960-6), Ibn Kathīr's (d. 774/1373) *K. al-Bidāya wa 'l-nihāya* (Cairo 1351-8/1932-9), al-Sakhāwī's (d. 902/1497) *al-Ḍawʾ al-lāmiʿ* and al-Djannābī's (d. 999/1590) *al-Baḥr al-zakhkhār* (Fr. tr. Fagnan, Algiers 1924).

Biographical literature. In post-Almohad times, the focus seems to have been placed apart from on collections of usage, on the elaboration of *fihrist*s and *barnāmadj*s indicating particular themes.

The biographical collections all have different provenances. Ibn al-Zubayr (d. 708/1309 [*q.v.*]) tried to follow in the path of his Andalusī compatriots in composing his *Ṣilat al-ṣila* (ed. Lévi-Provençal, Rabat 1938), whilst Ibn Nādjī of al-Ḳayrawān (d. 837/1433-4 [*q.v.*]) followed the work of Ibn al-Dabbāgh (d. 696/1297) on the religious figures of his city, and completed his *Maʿālim al-īmān* (Tunis 1325/1907-9). Further to the west, Ibn Ḳunfudh in Constantine composed his *Wafayāt* (Rabat 1976), whilst throughout his *Nathīr al-djumān* (Beirut 1976), his contemporary Ismāʿīl Ibn al-Aḥmar (d. 808/1405) dealt with the poets of al-Andalus and Morocco. Outside the region, the jurist Ibn Farḥūn (d. 799/1397 [*q.v.*]), of Andalusī origins, wrote in his native town of Medina a dictionary of celebrated Mālikīs, the *Dībādj* (Cairo 1315/1897-8), including the Maghribī ones. The Sudanese Aḥmad Bābā (d. 1036/1627 [*q.v.*]) continued and completed the same work in his *Nayl al-ibtihādj* (Cairo 1315/1897-8); and the Egyptian Ibn Ḥadjar (d. 852/1449 [*q.v.*]) devoted considerable space in his *al-Durar al-kāmina*, to noted figures from the 8th/14th century Maghrib (Ḥaydarābād 1348-50/1929-32).

As well as these general works, there were others devoted to the itineraries of their authors, built round famous masters of the time, each itinerary being the object of a *Fihrist* or *Barnāmadj*. We have extant the *Barnāmadj* of al-Ishbīlī (d. 688/1289), that of al-Ḳāsim al-Tudjībī of Ceuta (d. 730/1329-30) (both publ., the latter in Tunis 1981); and the *Fihrists*, still in ms., of Ibn Rushayd of Ceuta (d. 721/1321 [*q.v.*]) and al-Sarradj of Fās (d. 805/1402), plus the encyclopaedic *Barnāmadj* of al-Mantūrī of Granada (d. 834/1431).

Also important are two biographical portraits, in part convergent: one drawn by Ibn Marzūḳ (d. 781/1379 [*q.v.*]) in his *Musnad* (ed. M.-J. Viguera, Algiers 1981, Sp. tr. Madrid 1977), devoted to the Marīnid Abu 'l-Ḥasan; and the other from the pen of Ibn Khaldūn, *al-Ta'rīf*, in which the life, education and career of the author are traced (ed. M.T. al-Ṭandjī, Cairo 1951, Fr. tr. A. Cheddadi, Paris 1980).

Genealogical works. Far from being an isolated phenomenon, these texts stem from the natural prolongation, it seems, of the old polemics between Maghribīs and Andalusīs, especially from Almoravid times onwards; these polemics became, after the downfall of the Almohads, a sub-genre everywhere cultivated. One can cite three texts as testimony here: the anonymous *Mafākhir al-barbar* [*q.v.*] (ed. Lévi-Provençal, Rabat 1941, new ed. M. Ya'lā, in *Tres textos árabes*, 123-272), which celebrates, at the opening of the 8th/14th century, the scholars, ascetics and heroes, legendary or historic, from the Berber past. The equally anonymous *Ṭurmat al-ẓarīf fī ahl al-Djazīra wa-Ṭarīf* (ed. Ben Chrifa, in *Madjallat Kulliyyat al-Ādāb*, Rabat, i [1977], 7-50) from a few decades earlier aimed at revealing the failings of the Andalusīs and, finally, the opposing situation in Ibn al-Khaṭīb's *Mushāhadāt* (Alexandria 1958, 55-66) between Malaga and Salé, in which, through the two opposing cities, the lively tension between the two cultures is delineated.

Whilst being set on the cultural plane, these writings seem to be the vehicles for consideration of the basic problem of origins, leading to the question of connections with the ruling power. Whilst Ibn Tūmart, in the *K. al-Ansāb* attributed to him (in *Documents inédits*, 18-49, Fr. tr. 25-74), could be given a Sharīfian genealogy, the legitimising process which speedily followed, as Ibn Khaldūn notes (*Muḳaddima*, Fr. tr. de Slane, Paris 1863, i, 53-6), was challenged at this same period precisely when there was a strong current displaying Berber origins, with an insistence on salient figures since the beginning of Islam. Another *K. al-Ansāb*, anonymous but written in 712/1312, was also composed to celebrate openly these origins (ed. Ya'lā, in *op. cit.*, 13-121).

There developed in parallel to this, under the impulsion of Marīnid power, the cult of Sharīfian lineage, linked with the city of Fās, it meant a predilection for the Idrīsid branch, whence numerous references to this fact in the works of Ibn al-Khaṭīb and Ibn Khaldūn as well as in late compilations like those of al-Maḳḳarī, the *Nafḥ al-ṭīb* (ed. I. 'Abbās, Beirut 1968) and the *Azhār al-riyāḍ*. Also connected with it were separate monographs like the anonymous collection on the *Buyūtāt Fās al-kubrā* (Rabat 1972) and the *Nusḥ mulūk al-islām* (lith. Fās n.d.) of Ibn al-Sakkāk (d. 818/1415), followed, especially from the 10th/16th century onwards, by a host of opuscula on the genealogies of each branch of the Sharīfs.

Socio-religious works. These include *manāḳib* texts, those meant for edification and concerned with *bid'as* [*q.v.*] and legal texts (*nawāzil*).

Regarding *manāḳib*, it would be tedious to rehearse here all the collections devoted to a particular saint or to a group of them. On the general level, for Ifrīḳiya there is the *Ma'ālim al-īmān* of Ibn al-Dabbāgh, and Ibn Ḳunfudh's *Uns al-faḳīr* (Rabat 1965), in which the author concentrates on the Far West of the Maghrib. For the Central Maghrib, there is the late-period *al-Bustān* of Ibn Maryam (d. 1014/1605 [*q.v.*]), devoted to the saints and scholars of Tlemcen, Oran and Nedroma (Algiers 1928). For the Far Maghrib, there are *al-Minhadj al-wāḍiḥ* of al-Mādjarī (d. at the opening of the 8th/14th century) (Cairo 1933), and the *Salsal al-'adhb* of al-Ḥaḍramī, a contemporary of the preceding author (ed. M. Fassi, in *RIMA*, x/1 [1964], 37-98), heralding the *Dawḥat al-nāshir* of Ibn 'Askar (d. 986/1578 [*q.v.*]) (ed. M. Hajji, Rabat 1976, Fr. tr. A. Graulle, Paris 1913). As for the edificatory works denouncing innovations (*bida'*), the most significant come from the mid-8th/14th century and from the end of the following century. As well as *al-Durr al-thāmin* of Ibn Hilāl (d. 903/1497), in which the author details the imprecations against Abu 'l-Ḥasan al-Ṣughayyir (d. 719/1319) (lith. Fās 1319/1901-2), there is *al-Madkhal* of Ibn al-Ḥādjdj al-'Abdarī al-Fāsī (d. 737/1336 [*q.v.*]), in which the author draws up a review of *bida'* current in the Far West of the Maghrib and in his natal city, Cairo. Two famous mystics contributed through their writings to the reformation of morals: Ibn 'Abbād (d. 792/1390 [*q.v.*]) in his *Rasā'il al-kubrā* (lith. Fās 1320/1902), his *Rasā'il al-ṣughrā* (ed. P. Nwiya, Beirut 1974) and his epistles, still in ms., addressed directly to governors; and Aḥmad Zarrūḳ (d. 899/1493-4), through numerous works, including the *'Uddat al-murīd al-ṣādiḳ* and the *I'ānat al-mutawadjdjih al-miskīn* (ed. A.F. Khashīm, Tunis-Libya 1979). Finally, the same situations giving rise to similar interventions are developed in a good number of *nawāzil* compiled in the *Djāmi' al-masā'il* of al-Burzulī (d. 841/1438), still in ms. although well established, and the *Mi'yār* of al-Wansharīsī (ed. M. Hajji, Beirut-Rabat 1981).

Descriptive works and travel accounts. This literature is witness to the strength of contacts, and is to be distinguished from the *Masālik* type of literature, although there are two exceptions: the *Masālik al-abṣār fī mamalīk al-amṣār* of the Syrian Ibn Faḍl Allāh al-'Umarī (d. 749/1348 [*q.v.*]) (section on the Muslim West, new ed. M. Aboudayf, Casablanca 1988, partial Fr. tr. de Gaudefroy-Demombynes, Paris 1927), and *al-Rawḍ al-mi'ṭār* of the Ifrīḳiyan al-Ḥimyarī (d. 726/1326), who often confines himself to reproducing the oldest texts (new ed. 'Abbās, Beirut 1975). Around these two extended works, it seems that there are only monographs on local topics or accounts emanating from various motivations.

The monographs relate almost exclusively to towns and cities. Ibn al-Khaṭīb drew up a comparative table in his *Mi'yār al-ikhtiyār* between two groups of localities in Spain and North Africa (ed. M. Abbadi, Alexandria 1958), but he also wrote his imposing *al-Iḥāṭa* on the city of Granada (ed. M. 'Inān, Cairo 1973-7; complement, A. Chakkour, Tetuan 1988). At the same period, al-Djaznā'ī (d. 766/1365) dedicated his precious *Djanā zahrat al-ās* to Fās (ed. and Fr. tr. A. Bel, Algiers 1920-2, new ed. Rabat 1967). Much later, in 825/1441, Muḥammad b. al-Ḳāsim al-Anṣārī bore witness to Muslim Ceuta, now become Portuguese, with a minute description in his *Ikhtiṣār al-akhbār* (new ed. Rabat 1969). Miknāsa/Meknès was the subject of a monograph known under the abridged title of *al-Rawḍ al-hatūn*, written by Ibn Ghāzī (d. 919/1513), a learned magistrate in Fās, for his natal town.

There remain the *riḥlas*, which comprehend spatial journeys and/or varied themes. Whilst the *riḥla* of al-Abdārī is a description of the intellectual centres and of the state of knowledge obtaining towards the end of the 7th/13th century, comprising the Maghrib and the lands stretching to the Ḥidjāz (Rabat 1968), that by al-Tidjānī at the turn of the 8th/14th century has a setting of military considerations and describes the position of the tribes along the eastern littoral of Ifrīḳiya, at the same time noting the socio-cultural peculiarities and traditions of the inhabitants there (new ed. H.H. Abdul-Wahab, Tunis 1958, Fr. tr. in *JA*, 4th series, xx, 57-208, 5th series, i, 101-68). The *riḥla* called *Malʾ al-ʿayba* of Ibn Rushayd (Tunis n.d.) and the *Mustafād* of al-Tudjībī of Ceuta (Tunis-Libya n.d.) bring out the impacts of cultural relations between the Maghrib and the Mashriḳ at their various periods. Further, the *Notes of the journey of an Andalusi in Morocco* of Ibn al-Ḥādjdj al-Numayrī (d. after 768/1367) (ed. and Fr. tr. A.L. de Prémare, Lyons 1981) are a sketch of the same relations between al-Andalus and the southern shores of the western Mediterranean in the mid-8th/14th century, whilst his *Fayḍ al-ʿubāb* is rather a field report tracing the situation in the Central Maghrib at the time of the Marīnid Sultan Abū ʿInān's [*q.v.*] expedition towards Ifrīḳiya 757-8/1356-7. Soon afterwards, a fairly different account was to be the subject of a holiday *riḥla* written up by Ibn al-Khaṭīb, the *Nufāḍat al-djirāb*, in which the society and countryside of the Moroccan southwest are described in a magistral fashion, in spite of artificialities (ed. M. Abbadi, Cairo n.d.; complement ed. F. Faghya, Rabat 1989). Somewhat later, in the second half of the next century, there are two accounts to note: one written in Latin by the Fleming Anselm Adornus on Ḥafṣid Ifrīḳiya in 1470, and the other in Arabic by the Egyptian ʿAbd al-Basīṭ b. Khalīl (d. 920/1515), illuminating, for the same period, the socio-political situation in Fās and Tlemcen (R. Brunschvig, *Deux récits de voyage inédits en Afrique du Nord au XVe siècle*, Paris 1936).

Finally, there are two essential pictures of the situation in North Africa of their time, though distant from each other, sc. the *riḥla*, called *Tuḥfat al-nuẓẓār*, of Ibn Baṭṭūṭa (d. after 770/1368 [*q.v.*]) and the *Description of Africa* by al-Ḥasan al-Wazzān, called Leo Africanus [*q.v.*], completed in Italy in the local language.

Bibliography (in addition to references in the text): R. Brunschvig, *La Berbérie orientale sous les Ḥafṣides des origines à la fin du XVe siècle*, i, Paris 1940, pp. xv-xii and *passim*; idem, *Ibn ʿAbd al-Ḥakam et la conquête de l'Afrique du Nord par les Arabes, étude critique*, in *AIEO* (1942), 108-55; idem, *Un aspect de la littérature historico-géographique de l'Islam*, in *Mélanges Gaudefroy-Demombynes*, Cairo 1935-45, 147-58; A. Huici Miranda, *Historia política del Imperio almohade*, 2. vols. Tetuan 1956-7; T. Lewicki, *Les historiens, biographes et traditionnistes ibāḍites-wahbites de l'Afrique du Nord du VIIIe au XVIe siècle*, in *Folia Orientalia*, iii (1961), 1-134; H.R. Idris, *La Berbérie orientale sous les Zīrides (X^e^-XIIe siècles)*, i, Paris 1962, pp. xiii-xxv; M. Talbi, *L'emirat aghlabide (184-296/800-909)*, Paris 1966, 9-15; Maya Shatzmiller, *L'historiographie mérinide*, Leiden 1982; Mohammed El-Mennouni, *al-Maṣādir al-ʿarabiyya li-taʾrīkh al-Maghrib*, i, Rabat 1983; W. Schwartz, *Die Anfänge der Ibāḍiten in Nordafrika*, Wiesbaden 1983; Cl. Cahen, *L'historiographie arabe, des origines au VIIIe s. H.*, in *Arabica*, xxxiii (1986), 133-98, esp. 166-71, 191-2; M. Kably, *Société, pouvoir et religion au Maroc à la fin du Moyen-Age (XIVe-XVe siècles)*, Paris 1986, pp. xxii-xxxi and *passim*; H.L. Beck, *L'image d'Idrīs II, ses descendants de Fès et la politique sharīfienne des sultans marīnides (656-869/1258-1465)*, Leiden 1989, ch. 1; V. Lagardère, *Les Almoravides*, Paris 1989, 9-16 and *passim*.

(M. Kably)

B. *The post-1450 period*

In Maghribī historiography, which to a great extent follows the patterns of mediaeval Arab historiography, *taʾrīkh* represents a wide range of knowledge; it thus has a broader semantic charge than its equivalents—e.g. history, histoire, historia—in European languages. It is a source of information for those in government, a gallery for the display of former political régimes, a repertory of significant religious events (e.g. the life of the Prophet), biographies of devout men who left to posterity commentaries and compilations of *ḥadīth*, etc. Considered from a simply formal point of view, *taʾrīkh* is the science of the narration of events, especially religious and political, and the art of arranging them logically or chronologically. In the introduction to his *Muḳaddima*, Ibn Khaldūn writes that "History (*taʾrīkh*) is a noble science . . . It conveys to us the biography of prophets, the chronicles of kings, their dynasties and their policies (*siyāsa*)" (Beirut 1967; Fr. tr. V. Monteil, i, 13, Eng. tr. F. Rosenthal, New York 1958, i, 15).

Maghribī historical science affirms its autonomy in relation to the historiography of the Muslim lands of the Orient, from the end of the Middle Ages onwards, as a function of the changes in political organisation, the object of its study, which unfolded in the lands of the Muslim West: the end of the Marīnid empire, and the beginning of a long period of instability affecting the lands of the western Mediterranean at the end of the 15th century and the beginning of the 16th. The territorial individualities which henceforward took the specific names of *al-Maghrib al-aḳṣā*, *al-Maghrib al-awsaṭ*, *Ifrīḳiya*, etc., gave the intellectuals of each country the idea of belonging to a particular nation, unique and different from all others. Religion was no longer the cement of cohesion. Also, the presence of Ottoman Turks on the coasts of the Maghrib, and that of Christians, Spanish and Portuguese in certain ports where concessions and consulates were established, constituted the driving force contributing to the emergence and affirmation of history specific to each state. Thus, as a result of politics, the idea of the nation was gradually crystallised in the lands of the Maghrib. And history, *taʾrīkh*, fixed these successive events in time and space and was to give rise to another, hitherto little-known phenomenon, sc. that of nationalism.

Akhbār "facts, information, news" (on this subject, see Cl. Cahen, *Introduction à l'histoire du monde musulman médiéval, VIIe-XVe siècle. Methodologie et éléments de bibliographie*, Paris 1982, 69-70) constitute the basis of all historical narration. They are the essential source of chronicles, the object of which is to narrate, from day to day, events concerning princes and dynasts, thus compiling royal annals (see below for examples relating to al-Maghrib al-Aḳṣā). The constitution of a corpus of *akhbār* might have as its object the description (not analysis nor explanation, since either of these may engender indifference towards the prince) of dynastic politics, or of a wide-ranging social change; compilations of *akhbār* may show features reminiscent of *ḥadīths*.

From the 15th century onwards, Maghribī historical science abandoned the style of the major epic to concentrate on the history of more circumscribed territories, focusing on towns and local politics, and on peoples whose ways and customs were known. Ibn Khaldūn remains the master in this field. In the first book of the *Muḳaddima*, the *Kitāb al-ʿIbar* ("book of examples") he set out his theory, indeed his philosophy, of history. He opened the way not only for historiographers of the Maghrib, but for those of other nations as well. But this science is not within the reach of the novice, according to him; it demands qualities and extensive knowledge. "He who practises this science (*taʾrīkh*) needs to know the rules of the political art, the nature of existing things and the difference between nations, regions and tribes in terms of way of life, qualities of character, customs, sects, schools of thought, etc. He must distinguish the similarities and the differences between the present and the past, and know the diverse origins of dynasties and of communities."

In the 16th century, the centres of study and diffusion of the culture of the Muslim West would henceforward be Fās, Marrakesh, Tlemcen, Tunis and Ḳayrawān. The authors whose historical works are known to us passed through at least one of these centres, articulating and formulating local themes. The best representative of this period is without doubt al-Ḥasan Muḥammad al-Wazzān al-Fāsī, better known by the name of Leo Africanus [*q.v.*]. His work, *Historical description of Africa*, 1556, translated from Italian, is made up of a series of monographs on cities, regions, populations and kingdoms (of Fās, Marrakesh, Tlemcen, Bougie, Tunis and Tripoli). This study reflects the brilliant personality of the author, as well as the ideas that were current at the time. It was to be imitated and plagiarised by numerous Arab and Christian writers, but it would never be equalled. As for Luis del Marmol y Carvajal, *Descripcion general de Africa* (Granada 1573-99, 3 vols.), his texts are sometimes overloaded with detail but are not lacking in interest. His debt is considerable, not only to Leo Africanus but also to other "Arab" authors—Maghribīs in this instance. The author lays emphasis on the natural riches of the Maghrib, and his work is extremely useful for the study of historical geography and the history of agricultural practices.

In the central Maghrib, where political unity had long been hindered by the absence of a central authority and the existence at certain times of numerous kingdoms, authors exercised their talents in the domain of urban monography, with such titles as *Constantine, and some Arab authors of Constantine* (see Ch. Saint-Calbre, in *RA*, vii [1913], 70-93). Each author evoked, in his own fashion, the history of his town and of the Maghribī town in general. Not all of these studies were published; most remained in manuscript state and were ignored even by a cultured public.

In the conceptions of history held by Maghribī scholars, there is a perennial need to return to the sources, to the origins of life and mankind as far back as Adam, Eve or Noah when they are dealing with anthropology; or to the Prophet Muḥammad when religious questions are being addressed. Genealogy, an area of knowledge dear to scholars, is considered a branch of history in its own right. A text belonging to this genre of writing can be the work of one or several persons, and may be the private chronicle of a family. The object of writers of this genre is to show their illustrious origins, either by associating themselves with the family of the Prophet or with some saintly person whose religious aura is recognised in the West as well as in the East; Berber dynasties, such as the Marīnids and Waṭṭāsids, had recourse to this stratagem to bolster their legitimacy. The *Kitāb al-Nasab*, by ʿAbd al-Salām b. Abī ʿAbd Allāh (who wrote at Fās in 1098/1687; see A. Giacobetti, in *RA*, xlvi-xlviii [1902-4]), is a good example of this. The first part of this work begins with the eulogy of the Prophet, followed by the biography of Sīdī ʿAbd al-Ḳādir al-Djīlānī. The second part (by ʿAbd al-Salām b. al-Ṭayyib, written 1089/1678), deals with the descendants of this saint, among whose number the authors of the work claim to be.

The Tunisian historian Ibn Abī Dīnār al-Ḳayrawānī [*q.v.*], considered a successor to Ibn Khaldūn although several centuries separate them, displays in his historical study of Ifrīḳiya a certain reserve, even scorn, towards those Arabs who settled in Tunisia in former times, following invasions and migrations. The period which he describes (the 17th century) is far removed, however, from the major invasions of the Arab tribes which left nothing but desolation in their wake. It is evident that these considerations move him closer to the author of *al-Muḳaddima*.

Al-Ḳayrawānī reclaimed the autonomy and the maturity of Tunisian scholarship. His writings may be used in the service of the history of political ideas or of Tunisian nationalism.

In Morocco, al-Maghrib al-Aḳṣā, historical research and historiography have been fertile in the modern period and even in the 19th century. The number of titles is impressive, but the quality sometimes mediocre. Even religious history, which once enjoyed particular esteem, remained largely incomprehensible. Its new style, sententious and emphatic, had the effect of erecting a barrier between the scholars and those whom they addressed. Although Ibn Khaldūn was known and even admired, no one took him for a model. His unequivocal statements of truth, his criticisms of governments as unscrupulous, indolent, violent, power-hungry, self-seeking, etc., as applied to Morocco, could have endangered those expressing such views. The majority of Moroccan scholars turned at that time towards chronology, literature (on condition that it was not subversive), biography, hagiography and geographical descriptions. The essentials, meaning general history and political history, were utterly neglected.

In sum, the majority of Moroccan historians of the modern and contemporary eras have been chroniclers: most if not all have been historiographers in the service of Saʿdian or ʿAlawī sultans. The following may be cited: Abū Fāris, known by the name of ʿAbd al-ʿAzīz al-Fishtālī and his history, *Manāhil al-ṣafā fī akhbār al-mulūk al-shurafāʾ*; al-Ifrānī [*q.v.*] and his *Nuzhat al-hādī bi-akhbār mulūk al-ḳarn al-hādī*; and Abu 'l-Ḳāsim al-Zayyānī, *al-Turdjumān al-mughrib* (for these works, see E. Lévi-Provençal, *Chorfas*).

In the 17th-18th centuries, Maghribī history was enriched by increasingly numerous European accounts, such as *Histoire des conquêtes de Moulay Archy et de Muley Ismaël* by Germain Mouette (1683) on the first ʿAlawī sultans of Morocco; the *Topografia e historia general de Argel* by D. Haedo (1612); and the *Mémoires* of the Chevalier d'Arvieux (1735), who was French consul in Algiers at the end of the 18th century.

In the 17th, 18th and 19th centuries, accounts of journeys proliferated—not least stories of Christian captives and of their ransoming by religious figures who travelled frequently to the Maghrib and to the Orient. Particular mention should be made of the work of Père Dan, *Histoire de la Barbarie et de ses corsaires* (Paris 1637, 1649), the Redemptorist priest who for almost half a century made it his business to ransom Christian captives and who supplied copious information on the three regions of North Africa.

Finally, since the middle of the 19th century, research in European archives (national archives, archives of foreign and marine affairs, chambers of commerce in France and in other maritime states in western Europe) has led to the study of a large number of documents relating to the three above-mentioned lands or to those further east, comprising various treaties, commercial accords, and official correspondence, and some of these have been published, e.g. *Documents inédits sur l'occupation espagnole en Afrique*, published in 1875-77 by de la Primaudaiae; the monumental collection of *Sources inédites de l'Histoire du Maroc*, undertaken in 1905 in Paris by Colonel H. de Castries, in which are published documents drawn from the archives of France, Spain, the Netherlands, Portugal and Britain, from the 16th century onwards; and the *Correspondence des deys d'Alger avec la Cour de France (1579-1833)*, Paris 1898, published by E. Plantet.

It is to be noted that the work of the chroniclers continued into the 19th century, exemplified in the very important book written by al-Nāṣir al-Salāwī [*q.v.*], *K. al-Istiḳṣā li-akhbār duwal al-maghrib* (Cairo 1844).

In the 1970s, Abdallah Laroui, in his *Histoire du Maghreb*, has become the reference source for the understanding, recording and analysing of the history of the Muslim West. His novel method of approaching documentation facilitates the comparison of texts of diverse origins, and the establishment of more pertinent syntheses.

Bibliography: Given in the article.

(Ahmed Farouk and Chantal de La Véronne)

(g) Christian Arabic historiography.

The information on the course of Muslim history, especially on the early conquests or the struggles and relations with foreign powers, as well as the sometimes one-sided perception of events found in Muslim historiographical sources, is usefully complemented by information provided by Christian historiographers, whose writings are partly based on sources in Syriac, Greek or Coptic—not accessible to Muslim authors—and which were written from a different perspective, that of the conquered peoples who were later to become the Christian minorities. It should be emphasised, however, that the perspective of these Christian writings, even when composed in Arabic, is often not determined by their general Christian background so much as by their more specific communitarian affiliation (Jacobites [see ya'ḳūbiyyūn], Nestorians [see nasṭūriyyūn], Melkites, Copts [see al-ḳibṭ] and Maronites [see marūniyya, in Suppl.]). Especially in the Universal Chronicles, Christian historiographers did not hesitate to use different genres of Muslim material, sometimes copying it in a most literal way, without comments or corrections on their side.

The aim of the present article is to give an overview of the historiographical material written by Christians till the end of the 'Abbāsid period and the first years of the Mamlūks in Egypt insofar as it deals with general history and is relevant for aspects of the relations between Muslims and Christians. Chronicles describing mainly the internal life of the Christian communities, such as the recently discovered East Syrian Ecclesiastical Chronicle *Mukhtaṣar al-akhbār al-bī'iyya* (ed. B. Ḥaddād, Baghdād 2000) are not taken into consideration. This article is, for this period somewhat artificially, limited to the production in Arabic. As a matter of fact, Christian historiography written in the Christian national languages, especially in Syriac, in many aspects shows the same characteristics as the works composed by Christians in Arabic.

Melkites

The first important historiographer is Euthychius, Patriarch of Alexandria from 323/935 till 328/940, known in Arabic as Sa'īd b. al Biṭrīḳ [*q.v.*]. He is the author of a universal history: *Kitāb al-Ta'rīkh al-madjmū' 'alā 'l-taḥḳīḳ wa 'l-taṣdīḳ*, also known as *Naẓm al-djawhar*. This work exists in two different recensions. The first, shorter recension (by the editor designated as "Alexandrian") is preserved only in ms. Sinaiticus Arab. 582 (10th century), possibly an autograph. Mutilated in the beginning and at the end, it gives the history from Moses till the Muslim conquest of Egypt and some subsequent events in Jerusalem (*Das Annalenwerk des Eutychios von Alexandrien. Ausgewählte Geschichten und Legenden kompiliert von Sa'īd ibn Baṭrīq um 935 A.D.*, ed. and tr. M. Breydy, CSCO 471-2, Leuven 1985). The longer recension ("Antiochian") enjoyed greater popularity, but contains an important number of later additions and interpolations (ed. L. Cheikho, *Eutychiii Patriarchae Alexandrini annales*, i, Beirut, 1905, ii, 1909, 1-88 (repr. in CSCO 50-1, Leuven 1954, tr. E. Pococke, *Contextio gemmarum seu Eutychiae patriarchae Alexandrini annales*, Oxford 1658, repr. in *PG*, cxi, cols. 889-1156, and B. Pirone, *Eutychi, Patriarca di Alessandria (877-940). Gli annali*, Cairo 1987). It covers the period from the creation of Adam till the year 326/938, two years before the death of the author. The work exploits several Muslim sources, among which is historical, juridical and traditionist material. The Alexandrian recension presents the conquest of Egypt according to a version by the local traditionist 'Uthmān b. Ṣāliḥ.

In the manuscripts containing the Antiochian recension, Eutychius's *Ta'rīkh* is continued by a chronicle composed by Yaḥyā b. Sa'īd al-Anṭākī [*q.v.*] covering the period between 326/937-8 to 425/1033-4 (best ed., *Histoire de Yaḥyā-Ibn-Sa'īd d'Antioche*, ed. and tr. I. Kratchkovsky and A. Vassiliev, in *PO*, xviii/5, xxiii/3, Paris 1924, 1932, crit. ed. I. Kratchkovsky, Fr. ann. F. Micheau and G. Troupeau, in *PO*, xlvii/4, Paris 1997, with extensive bibliography). The objective of this work is clearly indicated by the author in the introduction: to write the continuation (*dhayl*) of the work composed by Sa'īd b. al-Biṭrīḳ according to the method adopted by the latter. After the discovery of new sources, the author felt, however, obliged to rework the first recension, a first time in Egypt, a second time (in 405/1014-15) in Antioch. The *dhayl* is an important source for our knowledge of the history of Egypt and Syria, especially the regions of Antioch and Aleppo, and the Arab-Byzantine relations during this period. It is based on various Greek (unidentified) and Arabic sources, among which are on the Muslim side, Thābit b. Sinān, an anonymous 'Irāḳī source, Ibn Zulāḳ, 'Alī b. Muḥammad al-Shimshāṭī and al-Musabbiḥī. A Christian-Arabic source is the *vita* of the Melkite patriarch of Antioch Christopher (959-67) by Ibrāhīm b. Yūḥannā (J.A. Forsyth, *The Byzantine-Arab chronicle (938-1034) of Yaḥyā b. Sa'īd al-Anṭākī*, Ph.D. diss. Ann Arbor, University of Michigan 1977). The *dhayl* was known to later Muslim authors, such as Ibn al-'Adīm, who used it for the composition of his *Zubdat al-ḥalab fī ta'rīkh Ḥalab* (ed. S. Dahan, Damascus 1951).

Agapius (Maḥbūb Ḳusṭanṭīn), bishop of Manbidj (10th century) wrote a universal history, known as the *Kitāb al-'Unwān*, beginning with the Creation and continuing till the reign of the Byzantine Emperor Leo IV (775-80) and the Caliph al-Mahdī. Most information on the Muslim period was drawn from the so-called *Syriac common source*, a work well known to later Syriac historiographers, presumably composed by the Melkite Theophilus of Edessa, an astrologer in the service of al-Mahdī, who may also have used an unidentified Muslim chronology. Agapius's work was edited by L. Cheikho (*Agapius episcopus Mabbugensis. Historia universalis/Kitāb al-ʿUnwān*, CSCO 65, Paris 1912, and by A. Vassiliev, *Kitāb al-ʿUnvan, histoire universelle écrite par Agapius (Mahboub) de Menbidj*, *PO*, v/4, vii/4, viii/3. The *K. al-ʿUnwān*, together with the work by Saʿīd b. al-Biṭrīḳ, was much appreciated by al-Masʿūdī (*Tanbīh*, 154).

According to al-Nadīm's *Fihrist* (ed. Flügel, i, 1871, 295), Ḳusṭā b. Lūḳā (9th century [*q.v.*]) is said to be the author of a (lost) universal (?) chronicle, *al-Firdaws fi 'l-ta'rīkh*.

West Syrians

The most important historiographical work in Arabic composed by a Syrian Orthodox author is the *Mukhtaṣar ta'rīkh al-duwal* of Gregorius Barhebraeus (Syriac: Bar ʿEbrōyō) or Ibn al-ʿIbrī (1226-86 [*q.v.*]). According to information found in his *Ecclesiastical chronicle* (*EC*), he allegedly composed this chronicle at the request of some Muslim friends in Marāgha [*q.v.*], who apparently had heard about Barhebraeus's fame as a historiographer and as author of a voluminous universal history, written in Syriac. This *Chronography* was divided into two parts, an ecclesiastical chronicle and a so-called civil chronicle, which were sometimes considered as two separate works. The structure of the *Mukhtaṣar* (ed. A. Ṣālḥānī as *Ta'rīkh Mukhtaṣar al-duwal*, Beirut 1898, [2]1958, new ed. Kh. Manṣūr, Beirut 1997) is comparable to that of the *Civil chronicle* (*CC*), the *Mukhtaṣar* being divided into ten dynasties and its Syriac counterpart into eleven dynasties; but both works are universal histories covering the period from Adam till the time of the Mongols. The Arabic title suggests that the *Mukhtaṣar* is merely a summary of the *CC*. As a matter of fact, the *Mukhtaṣar* contains much information not found in the *CC*, e.g. many short biographical notices on Islamic scholars. Sometimes the information given in the *Mukhtaṣar* differs considerably from the *CC* or is written from a different perspective. A good example is the attitude towards Muḥammad, depicted positively in the *Mukhtaṣar* as an instrument in the hands of God, whereas the *CC* emphasises forced conversions and the spread of Islam "by the sword". A possible reason for these differences, as suggested by the *EC*, might be the public the author had in mind when he composed his chronicle. A study by L.I. Conrad, *On the Arabic Chronicle of Barhebraeus: his aims and audience*, in *Parole de l'Orient*, xix [1994], 319-78, shows that it is too simplistic to consider Muslims as the intended readership of the *Mukhtaṣar*, since a number of passages are of interest only to Christians. The best way to explain the differences between both works is to consider them as independent histories, which are to an important extent based on different sources (H. Teule, *The Crusaders in Barhebraeus' Syriac and Arabic secular chronicles*, in K. Ciggaar *et alii* (eds.), *East and West in the Crusader states*, Louvain 1996, 39-49). In the case of the *Mukhtaṣar*, the author used more Islamic historiographical material, such as the *Ta'rīkh al-Ḥukamā'* of al-Ḳifṭī or the *Ṭabaḳāt al-umam* by Ṣaʿīd al-Andalusī. Written at the end of his life, he did not bother to harmonise the sometimes divergent views expressed in the *Mukhtaṣar* and the *CC*.

East Syrians

Ḥunayn b. Isḥāḳ [*q.v.*], the most renowned ʿIrāḳī Christian in Muslim literature, is the author of a lost chronicle in Arabic describing the period from Creation till the time of al-Mutawakkil (cf. Ibn Abī Uṣaybiʿa, *ʿUyūn al-anbā'*, 273). Yaʿḳūb b. Zakariyyā al-Kashkarī composed a seemingly important chronicle, now lost, comparable to the work of Agapius and Eutychius. It was highly praised by al-Masʿūdī (*Tanbīh*, 155). Elias, bishop of Nisibis (975-after 1049) is the author of a bilingual (Syriac-Arabic) chronicle, divided into two parts, preserved in only one manuscript, documenting the period from Creation till 409/1018 (*Eliae Metropolitae Nisibenae opus chronologicum*, i, ed. and tr. E.W. Brooks, ii, ed. and tr. J.B. Chabot, CSCO 62-3, Rome, Paris and Leipzig 1910). The second part consists mainly of conversion tables and descriptions of the different Christian, Muslim and Jewish calendars. The Muslim sources quoted by name in the first part are: Muḥammad b. Mūsā al-Khʷārazmī, Abū Djaʿfar al-Ṭabarī, ʿUbayd Allāh b. Aḥmad, Abū Bakr Muḥammad b. Yaḥyā al-Ṣūlī and Thābit b. Sinān. This work was also highly praised by Ibn Abī Uṣaybiʿa (*op. cit.*, 72). The voluminous *K. al-Ta'rīkh* or *K. al-Tawārīkh* ("Book of Dates") composed by Yuḥannā al-Mawṣilī in 1332 is, in fact, more a theological encyclopaedia than a work of history. The historical section only deals with inner-Christian developments (cf. B. Landron, *Chrétiens et musulmans en Irak*, Paris 1994, 140).

Maronites

According to al-Masʿūdī (*Tanbīh*, 154), a certain Ḳays al-Mārūnī is said to have written a beautiful historical work beginning with Creation and ending with the caliphate of al-Muktafī. The language of this lost work was supposedly Arabic. Al-Masʿūdī states that generally speaking the Maronites, unlike the Melkites, the Jacobites and the Nestorians, were not active in the field of historiography.

Copts

Traditionally ascribed to Sawīrus b. al-Muḳaffaʿ (flor. 10th century [see IBN AL-MUḲAFFAʿ, Severus] the *History of the Patriarchs of Alexandria* (Ar. *Siyar al-Bīʿa al-muḳaddasa* "biographies" of the Holy Church) is a collective work, the main redaction of which was completed by Mawhūb b. Manṣūr b. Mufarridj al-Iskandarānī (*ca.* 1025-1100). Mawhūb, who frequently acted as an intermediary between the Fāṭimid authorities and the Coptic community, is himself the author of the lives of the Patriarchs Christodoulos and Cyril II. His work was continued till the early 13th century by three subsequent authors. Later lives do not belong to the original work. This history (ed. B. Evetts, *History of the Coptic Church of Alexandria*, *PO* 1.2, 1.4, 5.1, 10.5, Paris 1904-15, continued by Y. ʿAbd al-Masīḥ *et alii* as *History of the Patriarchs of the Egyptian Church*, Cairo 1943-74) describes the history of the Coptic Church, arranged according to the reigns of the Patriarchs. Many *siyar*, including those by Mawhūb, deal, however, not only with ecclesiastical life but also record events pertaining to the field of general political history. The work was known to Ibn Khaldūn and al-Maḳrīzī.

Nushū' Abū Shākir Ibn al-Sanā' al-Rāhib (13th century), or Ibn al-Rāhib [*q.v.* in Suppl.], is the author of a *K. al-Tawārīkh* consisting of three parts: a treatise on astronomy and chronology; an elaborate universal history, dealing with world events, Islamic history and ecclesiastical matters; and a short history of the Ecumenical Councils. The so-called *Chronicon orientale*, ascribed by the editor to Ibn al-Rāhib (ed. Cheikho, CSCO scriptor. ar. 1-2, Beirut, Paris and Leipzig 1903), is only a later abridgment of Ibn al-Rāhib's universal history composed by an anonymous author.

The 13th century al-Makīn b. al-ʿAmīd [*q.v.*] wrote a universal history, called *al-Madjmūʿ al-mubārak*, extending from Creation to the time of Sultan Baybars (658/1260). It exists of two parts, the second Islamic part being based on al-Ṭabarī or the *Ta'rīkh Ṣāliḥī* of Ibn Wāṣil or one of its sources. The section on the Ayyūbids (ed. Cl. Cahen, in *BÉO*, xv [1955], 109-84), describing contemporary events is, however, more original and based on personal observations.

Bibliography (in addition to references given in the article): L. Cheikho, *al-Tawārīkh al-naṣrāniyya fi 'l-ʿarabiyya*, in *al-Mashrik*, xii (1909), 481-506 (also surveys works no longer extant); G. Graf, *GCAL*, Rome 1944-53, 5 vols.; A. Sidarus, *Ibn al-Rāhibs Leben und Werk. Ein koptisch-arabischer Enzyklopädist des 7./13. Jahrhunderts*, Freiburg 1975; P. Kawerau, *Christlich-arabische Chrestomathie aus historischen Schriftstellern des Mittelalters, 1.1. Texte, 1.2. Glossar, 2. Übersetzung*, CSCO 370, 374, Louvain 1976, 385, Louvain 1977; Samir Khalil Samir, *Trois manuscrits de la chronique arabe de Barhebraeus à Istanbul*, in *Orientalia Christiana Periodica*, xlvi (1980), 142-4; M. Breydy, *Études sur Saʿīd ibn Baṭrīq et ses sources*, CSCO 450, subsidia 69, Leuven 1983; J.M. Fiey, *Importance et limites des écrivains "dimmī" pour l'histoire de l'Orient*, in *Dirāsāt*, xxiii (1988), 5-13; Y.M. Isḥāḳ, *Maṣādir Abi 'l-Faradj al-Malaṭī al-ta'rīkhiyya wa-atharuhā fī manāhidjihi*, in *Aram*, i (1989), 149-72; J. den Heijer, *Mawhūb ibn Manṣūr ibn Mufarriğ et l'historiographie copto-arabe. Étude sur la composition de l'Histoire des Patriarches d'Alexandrie*, CSCO 513, subsidia 83, Leuven 1989; Samir, *Christian Arabic literature in the ʿAbbasid period*, in M.J.L. Young *et alii* (eds.), *CHAL. Religion, learning and science in the ʿAbbasid period*, Cambridge 1990, 446-60 esp. 455-9; den Heijer, art. *History of the Patriarchs of Alexandria*, in *Coptic Encyclopaedia*, iv (1991), 1238-42; R. Hoyland, *Arabic, Syriac and Greek historiography in the first Abbasid century: an enquiry into intercultural traffic*, in *Aram*, iii (1991), 211-33; idem, *Seeing Islam as others saw it. A survey and evaluation of Christian, Jewish and Zoroastrian writings on early Islam*, Princeton 1997; J. Nasrallah, *Histoire du mouvement littéraire dans l'Église melchite du Vᵉ au XXᵉ siècle. Contribution à l'étude de la littérature arabe chrétienne*, II.2, III, Leuven-Paris 1990. (H.G.B. TEULE)

II. 8. In the Nilotic Sudan.

The extant Arabic historical writings of the Nilotic Sudan (including the outlying western provinces of Kordofān and Dār Fūr [*q.vv.*]) before 1899 are exhaustively listed in R.S. O'Fahey, *Arabic literature of Africa*, i, *The writings of eastern Sudanic Africa to c. 1900*, Leiden 1994. Most of these works are extant only in mss. Of the few published works, the most important are:

(1) "The Fundj Chronicle", the conventional name of a chronicle extant in several mss. and recensions. It covers the period from the emergence of the Fundj kingdom of Sinnār, traditionally in 910/1504-5, to (at latest) 1288/1871. The original author of the Chronicle was Aḥmad b. al-Ḥādjdj Abū [*sic*] ʿAlī, known as Kātib al-Shūna from his post in the government grain-store. He was born near al-Masallamiyya (Blue Nile) in 1199/1784-5, and died after Rabīʿ I 1254/May-June 1838, where his Chronicle ends. Beginning as a king-list with added blocks of information (some of anthropological interest), a continuous detailed narrative starts with the reign of Bādī IV, on whose overthrow in 1175/1762 power passed to a clan of regents, the Hamadj Shaykhs, ruling over an ever-dwindling region of the Blue Nile until the invasion of the Sudan by the forces of Muḥammad ʿAlī Pasha of Egypt [*q.v.*] in 1235/1820, and the establishment of the Turco-Egyptian régime (*al-Turkiyya*). The later editors and continuators were, like Kātib al-Shūna, formed by a traditional Sudanese Islamic education, and had appointments under the Turco-Egyptian administration. They were thus members of a group which had little to regret at the passing of the Fundj kingdom and the ending of the anarchic Hamadj regency. They show no hostility to the Turco-Egyptian régime as such, which brought greater security and the consolidation under the aegis of the Islamic Ottoman Empire, although they criticise individual officers and administrators. While the later part of the Chronicle is in no sense an official history, it was written by men who accommodated themselves reasonably comfortably to the régime of Muḥammad ʿAlī and his successors.

The Chronicle has been published twice: (a) its last recension by Makkī Shubayka, *Ta'rīkh mulūk al-Sūdān*, Khartoum 1947; (b) Kātib al-Shūna's text (some collation with other mss.) by al-Shāṭir Buṣaylī ʿAbd al-Djalīl, *Makhṭūṭat Kātib al-Shūna*, Cairo 1963. An annotated English summary translation of the final recension was published by H.A. MacMichael, *A history of the Arabs in the Sudan*, Cambridge 1922, ii, 354-430. A fuller translation from a collation of the principal mss. is provided by P.M. Holt, *The Sudan of the three Niles. The Funj Chronicle 910-1288/1504-1871*, Leiden 1999.

(2) *Kitāb al-Ṭabaḳāt fī khuṣūṣ al-awliyā' wa 'l-ṣāliḥīn wa 'l-ʿulamā' wa 'l-shuʿarā' fi 'l-Sūdān* (some minor variants of title in the published editions). As the title indicates, this is a biographical dictionary of the Muslim holy men of the Nilotic Sudan, perhaps the only representative of the genre from the region. It was written and compiled (since there is internal evidence of sources of various kinds) by Muḥammad al-Nūr b. Ḍayf Allāh, and hence is usually referred to as the *Ṭabaḳāt* of Wad (i.e. Walad) Ḍayf Allāh. From internal evidence it was compiled about 1219/1804-5. Wad Ḍayf Allāh resembled the authors of the Fundj Chronicle in being a member of the traditionally educated Muslim élite. He was born in 1139/1727 at Ḥalfāyat al-Mulūk, north of present-day Khartoum North. Like his father, he taught in the mosque, acted as a *muftī*, and became celebrated for his religious writings. He died before the Turco-Egyptian conquest in 1224/1809-10.

The *Ṭabaḳāt* was published twice in 1930 in Cairo, by Ibrāhīm Ṣadīḳ (? Ṣuddayḳ) and Sulaymān Dāwūd Mandīl, respectively. A critical edition, prepared by Yūsuf Faḍl Ḥasan, was published in Khartoum in 1971 (²1974). It contains 270 biographical notices, predominantly of Ṣūfī *shaykhs* (mainly from the Ḳādiriyya *ṭarīḳa*) and jurists, chiefly of the Mālikī *madhhab*. There are a few notices of persons holding formal appointments, and a small number of legendary saints are included. No full English translation has been made, but an annotated summary translation with excerpts from the Arabic text is given by MacMichael, *op. cit.*, ii, 217-323. The text and translation of three notices appear in S. Hillelson, *Sudan Arabic texts*, Cambridge 1935, 172-203. One family of holy men is studied in Holt, *The Sons of Jābir and their kin*, in *BSOAS*, xxx/1 (1967), 142-58.

The roles of charismatic holy man and Islamic reformer were momentously fused in Muḥammad (Aḥmad) b. ʿAbd Allāh, the Sudanese Mahdī [see AL-MAHDIYYA], a hagiography of whom was written by Ismāʿīl b. ʿAbd al-Ḳādir al-Kurdufānī (perhaps his court chronicler), and entitled *Kitāb Saʿādat al-mustahdī bi-sīrat al-Imām al-Mahdī*. The unique extant copy of this and its sequel, *al-Ṭirāz al-manḳūsh bi-bushrā ḳatl Yuḥannā malik al-Ḥubūsh*, describing the war between the Mahdists and the Ethiopians in 1889, is now in the

Sudan Archive (Box 99/6) of Durham University. The former was edited by Muḥammad Ibrāhīm Abū Salīm and published under its own title at Beirut in 1972; an English summary translation with a useful introduction was published by Haim Shaked, *The life of the Sudanese Mahdi*, New Brunswick, N.J. 1978. An edition of *al-Ṭirāz* was published by Abū Salīm and Muḥammad Saʿīd al-Ḳaddāl as *al-Ḥarb al-Ḥabashiyya al-Sūdāniyya 1885-1888* [*sic*], Khartoum 1972.

The establishment of the Anglo-Egyptian Condominium in 1899 was followed by the development of westernised education. This, continuing under independence, has produced a growing number of professional historians, among their pioneers the late Professor Makkī Shubayka (see above), and an increasing body of scholarly historical writing in Arabic and English. A link between the old and new types of historians was Muḥammad ʿAbd al-Raḥīm (b. 1878, d. after 1935), the self-styled *mu'arrikh al-Sūdān*, whose writings of historical, literary and political import, include *Nafathāt al-yarāʿ fi 'l-adab wa 'l-ta'rīkh wa 'l-idjtimāʿ*, Khartoum n.d.

Bibliography: Given in the article.

(P.M. Holt)

ṬAYYIBIYYA, a Ṣūfī brotherhood of the Maghrib (also Tuhāmiyya in western Morocco, or, further, Wazzāniyya [*q.v.*]). Add to the *Bibl.* of wazzāniyya, O. Depont and X. Coppolani, *Les confréries religieuses musulmanes*, Algiers 1897, 484-90, and P.J. André, *Contribution à l'étude des confréries musulmanes*, Algiers 1956, 241-5, for an evaluation of the numerical importance of the orders's adherents in the 19th and 20th centuries. See also Ḥamdūn al-Ṭāhirī, *Tuḥfat al-ikhwān bi-baʿḍ manāḳib shurafā' Wazzān*, Fās 1324/1906; Muhammad al-Miknāsī, *al-Kawkab al-asʿad fī manāḳib mawlānā sayyidinā ʿAlī b. Aḥmad*, lith. on the margins of the preceding work; ʿAbd al-Salām al-Ḳādirī, *al-Tuḥfa al-ḳādiriyya*, ms. Gen. Library of Rabat no. 2331, I and II (these three sources stem from affiliates of the order); Muḥammad b. al-Ṭayyib al-Ḳādirī, *Nashr al-mathānī li-ahl al-ḳarn al-ḥādī ʿashar wa 'l-thānī*, ed. M. Ḥādjdjī and A. Tawfīḳ, Rabat 1407/1986; and for a detailed bibl. of studies on the order, H. Elboudrari, *La maison du cautionnement. Les shorfa d'Ouezzane de la sainteté à la puissance*, diss., EHESS, Paris 1984.

(Ahmed Toufiq)

THAṬṬĀ.

2. Monuments.

Over the centuries Thaṭṭā has endured invasions, destruction as well as the fluctuations of the Indus river bed. This is reflected in the chequered history of its monuments. Two early mausoleums of saints remain in the most western part of the city by what was once an enlarged part of the river bed. Presumably after the sack of the town by the Portuguese in 1555, boats were built in that area under Akbar. Two *maḥallas* formed the western part of the town and in the northern part stood the *masdjid* Walī-i-Ni'mat, which appears to have been used as the *Djāmiʿ masdjid* before a new structure was ordered by Shāhdjahān. The Shāhī bazaar was the link to the later eastern half of the town. This is a slightly depressed area which could have been the site of a Mughal irrigation channel. In the north-eastern *maḥalla*, Dabgīrān, the wooden box makers' area, now outside the town, there remains part of the Dabgīr mosque ordered by Khusrau Khān Čarkas in 966/1588. Its measurements are about 25 m by 11 m and the brick building, similar to other important constructions, stands on a stone base. The prayer hall, akin to that of a Lōdī mosque, is still extant with the remains of an octagonal drum and squinches from the collapsed central dome. Two lower lateral domes cover the rest of the area. Panels of glazed square tiles with vegetal designs in blues, white and yellow still remain on some areas of the building. Part of the visible *ṣaḥn* is paved with flat stones.

The Khirzī mosque standing in the Shāhī bazaar dates from 1022/1613 and was built by ʿAbd al-Razzāḳ Muẓaffar Khān prior to his governorship of Thaṭṭā. A small domed entrance leads to the *ṣaḥn*; each side of the prayer chamber measures 16 m. Some of the tilework remains in place. The square Amīr Muḥammad Khān mosque (1039/1629) with slightly tapered walls, each side measuring 17 m, consists of an entrance portal, a dome on squinches and a square hall. The flower tile decoration on the dado is akin to Mughal flower designs. Other tiles follow Sindhi geometric patterns.

Persian inscriptions give several dates for the building and repairs of the *Djāmiʿ masdjid*: start 1053/1644, completion 1056/1648, stone paving 1068/1657, first repairs in 1104/1692. During the substantial restoration of the 1970s, the area around the mosque was cleared to make way for a *čahār-bāgh*. The mosque was ordered by Shāhdjahān, and is built along an east-west axis. It follows the Saldjūḳ four-*īwān* plan used in India since the 9th/15th century; cf. the Aṭalā mosque in Djawnpūr (810/1408). The overall size is 93 m by 52 m. The main dome rising from a drum of sixteen panels covers the square prayer hall. Two lesser domed chambers at the main entrance lead into the *ṣaḥn*, with smaller ones over each lateral entrance in the middle of the side *riwāḳs*, while its arcades are covered with a series of small domes. There is no minaret. Although the restored glazed tiles on an earthen body look rather crude, the general impact is still effective, with dense geometric patterns including stars and floral designs. The colours include light and dark blue, white and yellow. Here the continuation of the tradition tilework of Multān, Uččh and the tombs of the Maklī Hills, is beset with the same technical problems of loose glazing encountered in earlier times.

Bibliography: H. Cousens, *Sindh tiles*, 1906, repr. Karachi 1993; M.I. Siddiqi, *Thatta*, Karachi 1979; A.H. Dani, *Thatta. Islamic architecture*, Islamabad 1982.

(Yolande Crowe)

ṬIBBIYYE-I ʿADLIYYE-I SHĀHĀNE, the Ottoman Imperial Medical School of Maḥmūd II (*r.* 1223-55/1808-39 [*q.v.*]), opened in 1254/1838, in the renovated Ghalaṭa-Sarāyi [*q.v.*]. It was a reorganisation of the *Ṭibbkhāne-i ʿĀmire*, a medical school founded at Istanbul in 1827. The official opening day of the original *Ṭibbkhāne* was 14 March 1827, adopted by the medical community of the Turkish Republic as Medicine Day (Tıp Bayramı), to celebrate modern medicine. In the *Ṭibbiyye-i ʿAdliyye-i Shāhāne*—as in the original *Ṭibbkhāne-i ʿĀmire*—European and Ottoman doctors taught modern Western medicine, not the traditional Muslim medicine based still on the humouralistic system from Antiquity.

During the 19th century, medicine in the Middle East underwent profound changes. European medicine was introduced on a much larger scale, and many European texts were translated into Muslim languages. Translations by ʿAṭā' Allāh Muḥammad Shānīzāde (d. 1826 [*q.v.*]) were especially important in this regard. The aim of these reforms was to improve the health of the armed forces as the measures in the medical realm were part of military modernisation. Thus medical schools, shaped according to the Western model, and at which French, Italian,

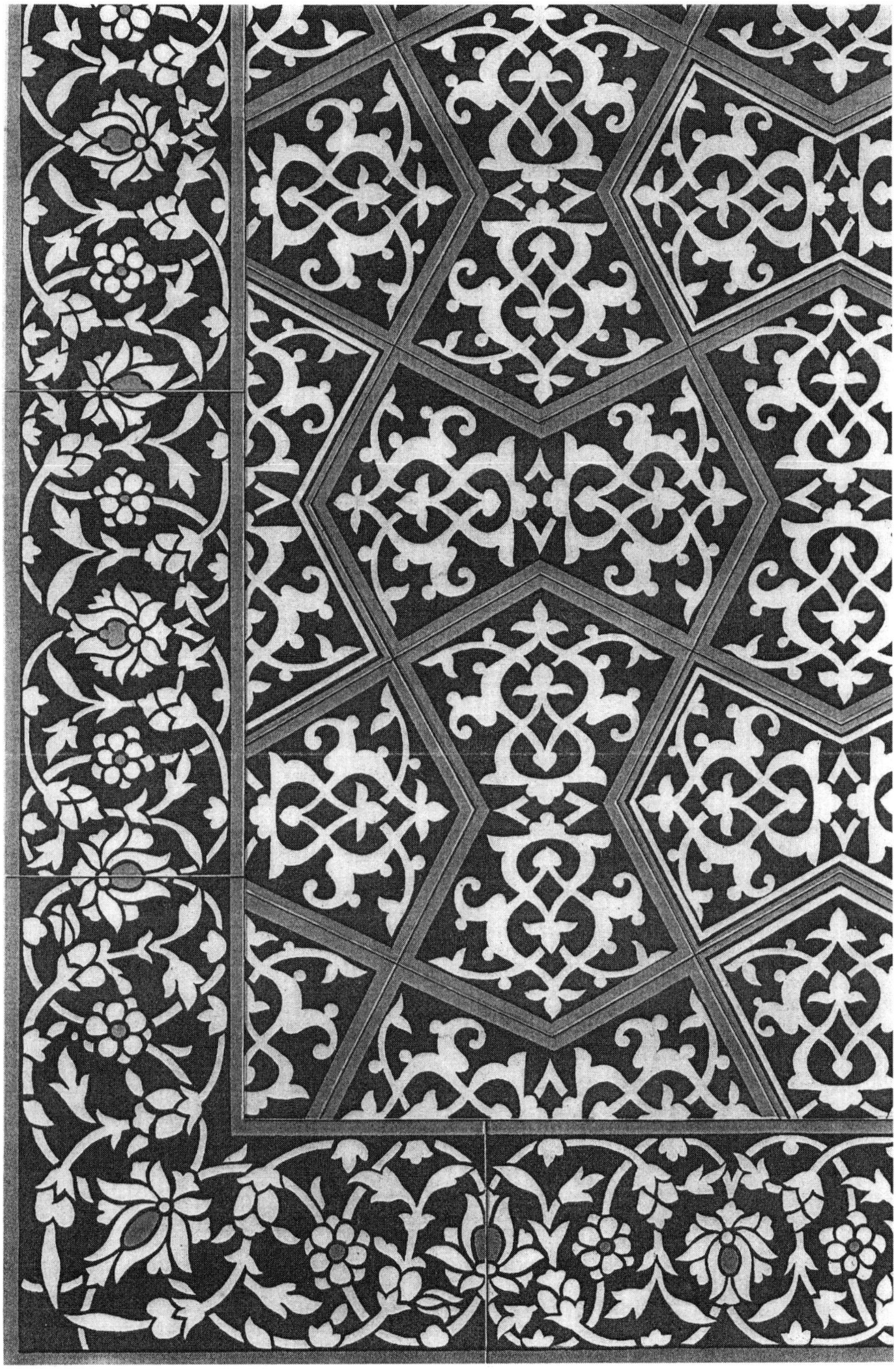

Fig. 2. *D̲j̲āmiʿ masd̲j̲id*, part of a tile panel, from Plate 2 in H. Cousens, *Sindh tiles*, 1906.

Austrian and German professors taught European medicine in French, were founded in all major capitals of the Middle East during the first half of the 19th century. Muḥammad ʿAlī Pās̲h̲ā [*q.v.*] established the first one in 1827 near Cairo, followed only a month later by Maḥmūd II's military medical school in Istanbul. The third, another military medical school, was included in the *Dār al-Funūn*, a polytechnic school founded in Tehran in 1850-1.

The changes in medicine in the Ottoman Empire during Maḥmūd II's reign were part of a wide range of reforming measures. Under his rule, government functions proliferated well beyond the traditional realms of administering justice, collecting taxes and maintaining the armed forces. Matters that had traditionally been left to private hands gradually came under government administration. The final aim was to create a new generation of able administrators. Two methods were employed to achieve this. First, Ottoman students were sent to universities in Europe to acquire a profession in selected valued fields; second, new schools were established and given precedence over the traditional Muslim *madrasas*. One of them was the *Ṭibbiyye-i ʿAdliyye-i S̲h̲āhāne*. The many documents and letters produced by the Ottoman bureaucracy dealing with salaries and hiring, teaching aids brought over from Europe, the school's physical setting, etc., reflect the close attention of the central government to this school. Even everyday matters and decisions were not left to the discretion of the school administration.

The curriculum at the *Ṭibbiyye-i ʿAdliyye-i S̲h̲āhāne*, where the language of instruction was French, was decidedly Western. Teaching aids pertaining to medical instruction were imported from Europe. In this it parted ways from the traditional medical schools in the Ottoman Empire. The few of these that existed, for example at the Süleymāniyye complex, reproduced Arab-Muslim medicine based still to a large extent on interpretations of, and additions to, mediaeval Muslim texts. In contrast, the four-year course at the *Ṭibbiyye-i ʿAdliyye-i S̲h̲āhāne* followed a syllabus combining general and medical subjects. The general syllabus included languages (Arabic and Turkish, but also French and Latin). French was mandatory in order to help the students communicate with the teachers, many of whom were Europeans. There was another reason for the French classes. As the sultan explained in his opening address, the first graduates of the medical school were to master French in order to be able to translate the much-needed European medical texts into Ottoman Turkish. Other non-medical subjects included arithmetic and geometry, drawing, geography, history and zoology. The general curriculum was taught by Ottoman Muslim teachers. Medical studies, taught mainly by non-Muslim and non-Ottoman teachers, comprised anatomy, dissection, pathology, chemistry, botany and pharmacology, diagnostics, ophthalmology and medical devices.

Despite the pronounced French influence, the school was the product of the close relationship at the time between the Ottoman and Habsburg empires. Dr. Karl Ambros Bernard, a medical doctor and surgeon and a graduate of the Vienna medical faculty, was brought in 1838 from the Austrian capital at the instigation of Abdülhaḳ Efendi, the *ḥekīmbas̲h̲ī* (Ottoman head physician [*q.v.*]), to found the school. Dr. Bernard served as its first manager till his death at the early age of 38 in 1844. His widow and family were granted a stipend by the empire as a sign of respect to the man and his services to Ottoman medical education. Dr. Bernard was not the only example. Other Austrians teaching at the school were Dr. Neuner and Dr. Riegler, and in the 1840s an Austrian midwife was given a contract to teach gynaecology and obstetrics at the school.

The student body comprised mainly Muslims but also included Christians. Their numbers fluctuated from around 200 at the beginning to over 400 by the end of the 1840s. Similarly, the teaching cadre rose from fewer than ten in the 1830s to several dozen a decade later. The *Ṭibbiyye-i ʿAdliyye-i S̲h̲āhāne* functioned in G̲h̲alaṭa for ten years; a fire in August 1848 then obliged the medical school to move to the Golden Horn.

Bibliography: Many archival documents can be found in the Başbakanlık Osmanlı Arşivi (The Archives of the Ottoman Prime Minister) in the İrade, Cevdet and Hatt-i Hümayun classifications. For publications that include primary sources, see Arslan Terzioğlu, *Türk Avustraya tıbbı ilişkerileri*, Istanbul 1987; idem, *Türk tıbbının batılılaşması*, Istanbul 1993; Ayten Altıntaş, *Karl Ambros Bernard'in Mekteb-i Tibbiye-Şahane'nin kurucusu olduğu meselesi ve görevi hakkında*, in *II. Türk Tip Tarihi Kongresi (20-21 Eylül 1990)*, Ankara 1999, 91-9; Rengin Dramur, *Mekteb-i Tibbiye-i Şahane'de öğretin üzerine bazı belgeler*, in *ibid.*, 137-47. (Miri Shefer)

TONGUÇ, Ismail Hakki (1893-1960), Turkish educator.

He was born, the son of a peasant family, in Tataratmaca village, Silistre. He attended Kastamonu Teachers' College and later the Istanbul Teachers' College, graduating in 1918. He continued his educational career at the Karlsruhe State Academy for the Graphic Arts and Ettlingen Teachers' College in Germany during 1918-19 and 1921-2. After returning to Turkey, Ismail Hakkı worked in several schools both in administrative posts and as a teacher of painting, handicrafts and physical education. In 1935, he was appointed Director General of Primary Education in the Ministry of Education where he had been working as the Director of School Museums since 1926. The fame of İsmail Hakkı rests basically on his views concerning the educational problems of village children in the early Republican period, which found concrete expression in the project of Village Institutes [see köy enstitüleri], his major achievement. Being the brain behind the Institute, he played a leading role during their establishment and development. Forced into resigning office in 1946, because of an extensive campaign attacking the Institutes, he was first appointed a member of the *Talim ve Terbiye Kurulu* (Instruction and Training Board) and later in 1949 a teacher at the Atatürk Lycée, where he worked until the Ministry's decision to remove him in 1950. İsmail Hakkı retired, following the annulment of the decision by the Council of State in 1954, and died in Ankara on 23 June 1960.

Throughout his career as an educator, İsmail Hakkı wrote several books and articles. In most of his works, he elaborated the educational problems from theoretical and practical perspectives and stressed the significance of vocational training in the developmental process.

Bibliography: 1. Selected works. *Elişleri rehberi*, Istanbul 1927; *İlk, orta ve muallim mekteplerinde resim-elişleri ve sanat terbiyesi*, Istanbul 1932; *İş ve meslek terbıyesi*, Ankara 1933; *Köyde eğitim*, Istanbul 1938; *Canlandırılacak köy*, Istanbul 1939; *İlköğretim kavramı*, Istanbul 1946; *Resim iş dersleri*, Istanbul 1951; *Öğretmen ansiklopedisi ve pedagoji sözlüğü*, Istanbul 1952; *Pestalozzi çocuklar köyü*, Ankara 1960; *Mektuplarla köy enstitüsü yılları*, Istanbul 1976.

2. Studies. M. Başaran, *Tonguç yolu*, Istanbul 1974; *Tonguç'a kitap*, Istanbul 1961; M. Cimi, *Tonguç baba. Ülkeyi kucaklayan adam*, Istanbul 1990; E. Tonguç, *Bir eğitim devrimcisi. Ismail Hakkı Tonguç* (*yaşamı, öğretisi, eylemi*), i, Ankara 1997; P. Türkoğlu, *Tonguç ve enstitüleri*, Istanbul 1997.

(Aylin Özman)

ṬUGHDJ b. Djuff b. Baltakīn (or Yaltakīn) (b. Furān) b. Fūrī b. Khaḳān, military commander of Farghānan origin, d. at Baghdād in 310/922-3. His father had left Farghāna to serve as an officer in the caliph al-Muʿtaṣim's army, also serving his successors al-Wāthiḳ and al-Mutawakkil. Djuff, said to have received *ḳaṭāʾiʿ* at Sāmarrā, died in 247/861 on the same night that al-Mutawakkil was assassinated.

Ṭughdj left ʿIrāḳ at the *ghulām* Luʾluʾ's invitation to enter the service of Aḥmad b. Ṭūlūn [*q.v.*], the governor of Fusṭāṭ-Miṣr, in 254/868. He is said to have acted as governor of Egypt, Diyār Miṣr, for the latter or, according to a variant reading, of Diyār Muḍar. According to Ibn Khallikān, he allegedly recognised the governor of the Djazīra, Isḥāḳ b. Kundādj, set there by al-Muwaffaḳ to uphold the ʿAbbāsid cause against Ibn Ṭūlūn, but Isḥāḳ later rallied to the latter. At all events, Ṭughdj, after placing himself at Ibn Ṭūlūn's service, must have returned once more to ʿIrāḳ since his son Muḥammad, the future Ikhshīd [see muḥammad b. ṭughdj] was born at Baghdād, in the Bāb Kūfa street, in mid-Radjab 268/January 882.

According to Ibn ʿAsākir, Abu 'l-Djaysh Khumārawayh [*q.v.*] nominated Ṭughdj governor of Damascus after the death of his father Ibn Ṭūlūn in 269/882, a post in which Khumārawayh's two sons and successors, Djaysh (d. 283/896) and then Hārūn (d. 292/904-5), confirmed him. He was apparently governor during the whole of al-Muʿtaḍid's caliphate (279-89/892-902) and at the beginning of the next reign, that of al-Muktafī. According to Ibn Saʿīd al-Andalusī, he was also governor of Tiberias, in which his son Muḥammad acted as deputy. An ʿAlid, one Abu 'l-Ṭayyib Laḥḥā Muḥammad b. Ḥamza, who enjoyed great authority in Tiberias, was executed on Hārūn b. Khumārawayh's orders for collusion with the Carmathians (see M. Gil, *A history of Palestine 634-1099*, Cambridge 1992, §§ 467, 473, 487). According to Ibn ʿAdīm, Ṭughdj had previously for long acted as governor of Aleppo for Khumārawayh.

In 279/892-3, state al-Ṭabarī and Ibn al-Athīr, Ṭughdj led at Aleppo, acting for Khumārawayh, an expedition involving ʿAbbāsid and Ṭūlūnid generals in the Djazīra and northern Syria, and in 281/894, a summer plunder raid deep into Byzantine Anatolia.

In 283/896, a group of Ṭūlūnid *ghulāms*, having failed in a revolt against the incompetent buffoon Djaysh b. Khumārawayh, sought *amān* in Baghdād. One of the fugitives was Badr b. Djuff, but his brother Ṭughdj remained in his post as governor of Damascus, nevertheless showing more and more autonomy from Fusṭāṭ-Miṣr. Certain sources allege that, at the beginning of Hārūn's reign, Badr b. ʿAbd Allāh al-Ḥammāmī was sent from Miṣr with an army and compelled Ṭughdj temporarily to evacuate Damascus. At all events, he was still governor in 289/902 when he had to face the Carmathian revolt in Syria; an army under Bashīr which he sent against Ibn Zakrawayh was wiped out and he himself besieged in Damascus, losing a large number of troops [see kalb b. wabara]. The Ṭūlūnids' incapacity, faced with the Carmathians, led to the ʿAbbāsids deciding to resume direct control in Syria and Egypt.

On the fall of the Ṭūlūnids in 292/905, Ṭughdj left Damascus, with other commanders, to submit to the new ʿAbbāsid authorities in Miṣr, who sent them back as a garrison in the *djund* of Ḳinnasrīn. He later returned to Baghdād where, according to Ibn Khallikān, he died in prison.

He left six sons, as well as Muḥammad, the future Ikhshīd, and at least one daughter who, in 326/938 married the son of the grand Amīr Ibn Rāʾiḳ [*q.v.*], at the same time as the vizier Abu 'l-Faḍl's [*q.v.*] son married Ibn Rāʾiḳ's daughter (al-Hamdānī, *Dhayl Taʾrīkh al-Ṭabarī*, ed. M. Abu 'l-Faḍl Ibrāhīm, Cairo 1977, 314).

Ṭughdj was known for his passion for perfumes; when travelling, he had in his train fifty camels loaded with perfumes [*sic*]. He is said to have built at Damascus a cupola with latticework, forming a giant censer, from which he had wafted the aroma of perfumes for all the population of the city. Even if these accounts are clearly exaggerated, they do show how the standard of living in the Syrian-Egyptian lands, at the end of the 3rd/9th and beginning of the 4th/10th centuries, had risen, allowing the élites to enjoy a significant amount of luxury goods (see also Ibn Saʿīd, *al-Mughrib*, 154-5).

Bibliography: Many sources have information on Ṭughdj, often contradictory. For the present article, the following only have been used: Ṭabarī, iii, index; Ibn ʿAsākir, *Tahdhīb*, vii, 57; ʿAẓīmī, *T. Ḥalab*, ed. Zaghrūr, 283; Ibn al-ʿAdīm, *Zubda*, ed. Dahhān, i, index; idem, *Bughya*, ed. Zakkār, ii, ix, index; Ibn Khallikān, ed. ʿAbbās, v, 56-7; Ibn al-Athīr, vii, index; R. Guest, *The governors and judges of Egypt*, Leiden 1912, index. The richest, but not always the most reliable, source is Ibn Saʿīd al-Andalusī, *al-Mughrib fī ḥulā al-Maghrib*, ed. Zakī Muḥammad Ḥasan *et alii*, Cairo 1954, index. See also J. Bacharach, *The career of Muhammad b. Tughj al-Ikhshīd*..., in *Speculum*, 1 (1975), 586-612.

(Th. Bianquis)

TURKS.

II. Languages.

(vi) Turkic languages in non-Arabic and non-Latin scripts.

During their history of over fifteen centuries Turkic peoples interacted with peoples and cultures of three continents. As a result of this process they became acquainted with many writing systems, used in various regions between Central Asia and Europe. The historical scene of the emergence of the first written and literary languages of Turkic peoples is Inner Asia, the territory of modern Mongolia, the Tarim Basin (in Sinkiang) and Kansu. The first epigraphic monuments written in a Turkic idiom belong to the Orkhon Turks (A.D. 552-744) and Uyghurs (744-840), who created empires in the steppe region. These monuments are written in the so-called runic or runiform script. After the collapse of their empire, the Uyghurs left the steppes and moved to the Tarim Basin and Kansu, founding the Kingdom of Kočo (866-1124) and Kan-tsu (880-1028), both becoming centres of the Uyghur culture and offering in abundance written documents mainly of religious (Manichaean, Buddhist and Nestorian) content. These monuments are written in Sogdian, Manichaean, Uyghur, and Nestorian scripts (all of Semitic origin), in Brāhmi script (of Indian origin) and in Tibetan script (in the case of the latter, also in its variant, the Phags-pa script).

1. *The Khazar and Karaim languages*

Judaism and Jewish culture played an important role in the Khazar empire [see khazars] in the region of the Black and Caspian Seas (7th-11th centuries).

Therefore it is very probable that the Hebrew script was in use by this Turkic people, although, unfortunately, no written documents have survived.

The Hebrew script was adopted later by the Karaim, of Jewish religion, living originally in the Crimea [see KARAITES]. A large part of this people migrated, probably before the 14th century, to the western Ukraine and Lithuania. They lived there until the end of the Second World War, when they moved to Poland. The rich written culture of the Karaim is represented by many manuscripts and printed works. Today, the Karaim language is an especially endangered language; some dialects of it can be considered as extinct.

The generally suggested, supposed historical continuity between the Khazars and the Karaim remains unproven.

2. *The Armenian-Ḳïpčaḳ language*

After the collapse of the Armenian Asa empire in the middle of the 11th century, Armenians moved to the Crimea, and later to the western Ukraine. As a result of intensive contact with the Ḳïpčaḳ Turks, they adopted their language for purposes of administration and religious practice, keeping their original Armenian language for secular life. These documents, which have come down to us from between the 16th and 17th centuries, are written in Armenian script.

3. *The Armenian-Ottoman language*

After the Turkicisation of Asia Minor, Armenians living in different provinces of Anatolia seem very soon to have become bilingual. Turcophone Armenians created their own Turkish literature in the so-called Armeno-Turkish language, written in Armenian script. As a result of this activity, a large body of literature (original works, translations, inscriptions, later also journals) was created. This written documentation, which is especially rich from the 17th century onwards, can be traced back until the 14th century.

4. *The Greek alphabet used in the Ottoman Empire for Turkish*

The Orthodox Christian Karamans (Turkish *Ḳarāmānlïlar*), living in northeastern Anatolia until the Greek-Turkish population exchanges of 1924, created a special literature, the products of which were written in Greek script. The history of this well-documented group of monuments can be traced back to the 16th century. It is obvious that these products (at the outset, works of a religious and historical content, later also journals and newspapers, etc.) written in the so-called Karaman (*Ḳarāmānlï*) language (in fact, in a special dialect of Ottoman Turkish), were also used by the bilingual Greeks living in other regions, especially in the Ottoman capital. Many written texts in the Turkish language but Greek alphabet have also come down to us from this large ethnic and religious group of the empire.

5. *Other alphabets used in the Ottoman Empire for Turkish*

The Syriac script was used for Turkish by a small Christian community. These texts, mainly preserved in the University Library of Bonn, were destroyed during the Second World War.

At the same time, the Hebrew alphabet was also used by the Jewish community for Turkish, the best-known surviving example being a copy of an Ottoman chronicle in this script.

The Institute of Manuscripts of the Georgian Academy of Sciences in Tbilisi has a large collection of Ottoman Turkish texts written in the Georgian alphabet. Unfortunately, we do not possess any survey of or study on this precious material, so that neither its quantity nor its character and chronology are so far known. Scholars agree, however, that a systematic analysis of these materials could throw interesting light on the history of the Ottoman Turkish language in this region of the empire.

The Cyrillic alphabet was used in the Balkans for Turkish by intellectuals interested in the official language of the empire. We possess a few manuscripts and printed books, mainly from the 19th century.

6. *Other Turkic languages written in Cyrillic script*

Turkic peoples living in Eastern Europe and Siberia (Chuvash, a part of the Volga Tatars, Yakuts, Turkic peoples in the Altai Region, etc.), due to the Russian colonial expansion from the 18th century onwards, experienced Russian missionary activities, and thereby an acquaintance with the Cyrillic alphabet. All other Turkic peoples living in the former Soviet Union adopted the Cyrillic script in the second phase of the Soviet writing reform (1939-40), after a very short period of using the Latin script, introduced to these peoples between 1922 and 1930 as a replacement for the Arabic alphabet.

The collapse of the Soviet Union in 1991 created a new situation for rethinking the language and script policies of the former imperial power. In the sometimes heated discussions, all possible solutions found their supporters (keeping the Cyrillic script; reintroduction of the Latin, or even of the Arabic alphabets). In the course of the 1990s, Azerbaijan, Turkmenistan and Uzbekistan have reintroduced the Latin alphabet with some special signs. In these countries, a transition period, in which both Latin and Cyrillic scripts may be used, has been allowed. Efforts to create a Latin alphabet on a common theoretical and practical basis for all Turkic peoples have until now had no results.

Bibliography: U. Marazzi, *Tevārīḫ-i āl-i ʿOs̱mān. Cronaca anonima ottomana in trascrizione ebraica (dal manoscritto Heb. E 63 della Bodleian Library)*, Naples 1980; A. Stepanjan, *Bibliografiya knig na turetskom yazïke, napisannikh armyanskimi bukvami (1727-1968)*, Erevan 1985; E. Balta, *Karamanlidika. Additions (1584-1900). Bibliographie analytique*, Athens 1987; idem, *Karamanlidika. XXᵉ siècle. Bibliographie analytique*, Athens 1987; A. Hetzer, *Dačkerēn. Texte. Eine Chrestomathie aus Armenier-drucken des 19. Jahrhunderts in türkischer Sprache. Unter dem Gesichtspunkt der fonktionalen Stile des Osmanischen ausgewählt und bearbeitet*, Wiesbaden 1987; G. Hazai (ed.), *Handbuch der türkischen Sprachwissenschaft. Teil I*, Budapest-Wiesbaden 1990; I. Baldauf, *Schriftreform und Schriftwechsel bei den muslimischen Russland- und Sowjet-Türken 1850-1937*, Budapest-Wiesbaden 1993; K.H. Menges, *The Turkic languages and peoples. An introduction to the history of Turkic peoples*, ²Wiesbaden 1995; W.E. Scharlipp, *Türkische Sprache, arabische Schrift. Ein Beispiel schrifthistorischer Akkulturation*, Budapest 1995; N. Ruji, *An introduction to Uighur scripts and documents*, Ürümqi 1997 [in Chinese]; T. Tekin, *Tarih boyunca türkçenin yazımı*, Ankara 1997; P.T. Daniels and W. Bright (eds.), *The world's writing systems*, Oxford 1996; Balta, *Karamanlidika. Nouvelles additions et compléments*, Athens 1997; L. Johanson and É.Á. Csató (eds.), *The Turkic languages*, London and New York 1998; V. Adam, J.P. Laut and A. Weiss, *Bibliographie alttürkischer Studien, nebst einem Anhang: Alphabetisches Siglen verzeichnis zu Klaus Röhrborn: Uigurisches Wörterbuch, Lieferung 1-6 (1977-1988)*, Wiesbaden 2000; H. Jensen, *Die Schrift. Die Schrift in Vergangenheit und Gegenwart*, ³Berlin 2000; *PTF*, ed. J. Deny *et alii*, i-ii, Wiesbaden 1959-64, iii, ed. H.R. Roemer, Berlin 2000; J.M. Landau and B. Kellner-Heinkele, *Politics of language in the ex-Soviet Muslim states. Azerbayjan, Uzbekistan, Kazakhstan, Kyrgyzstan, Turkmenistan and Tajikistan*, London 2001; D. Shapira, *Miscellanea judaeo-turkica. Four Judaeo-Turkic notes. IV*, in *JSAI*, xxvii (2002), 475-96.

(G. Hazai)

III. Literature.

6. (m) Turkish literature in Muslim India. The constant stream of Turkish migrants started pouring on to Indian soil from the 5th/11th century onwards, but hardly anything is known of the role Turkish language played in the Ghaznawid, Ghūrid and Sultanate periods. Turkish seems to have been used mainly as a medium of communication in the army, but also in court circles (see Amīr Khusraw Dihlawī, *Nuh sipihr*, ed. Muhammad Wahid Mirza, Oxford 1950, 173). The hitherto unearthed sole remnants of Turkish from this period are the Turkish words contained in a Persian dictionary, the *Farhang-i zufān-gūyā wa djahān pūyā* (see R. Dankoff, *The Turkish vocabulary of the Farhang-i zafān-gūyā*, Bloomington 1987).

The Tīmūrid conquest and then the establishment of the Mughal dynasty altogether changed this situation. The Tīmūrids and their Turkish military élite arrived in India with a cultural legacy that included support for and cultivation of a Turko-Persian literary tradition which was in a sense founded and elaborated by the activities of ʿAlī Shīr Nawāʾī [*q.v.*]. Tīmūrids in India remained true to their Central Asian Turkish legacy till the 19th century, and it was a custom for Mughal princes to be trained in Turkish as well as in the other great Islamic languages. The last member of the family whose skills in Turkish grammar, lexicography and poetry were well known in Hindūstān was Mīrzā ʿAlī-bakht Gurgānī "Aẓfarī" [*q.v.*].

Tīmūrid and thus also Mughal rulers and princes were not only passive patrons of culture but also played an active role in literary life (see Muḥammad Khālidī, *Gulistān-i Tīmūrī*, Lakhnaw 1973). Quite a few of them displayed outstanding literary skills but only some of them are known to have contributed to Turkish literary output in India. Except for the first generation of Indian Tīmūrids, the sources do not yield much information on possible Turkish works by members of the royal family. The Turkish oeuvre of Bābur [*q.v.*] is, of course, well known, and some Turkish lines by Humāyūn [*q.v.*] and a full *dīwān* by Kāmrān [*q.v.*] have been preserved. Due to the ruler's political aims and policies, Turkish seems to have been pushed into the background in court circles during the reign of Akbar [*q.v.*]. Nevertheless, later rulers seem to have been able at least to appreciate Turkish poetry, as was the case with Shāh ʿĀlam II (1760-88, 1788-1806; see Aẓfarī, *Wāḳiʿāt-i Aẓfarī*, ed. T. Chandrashekharan, Madras 1957, 17). Turkish manuscripts copied in India indicate that Nawāʾī was the most often read author, but contemporary sources remain silent on these rulers' literary activities in Turkish.

The benefits which the Mughal empire could offer in its heyday attracted many immigrants from the neighbouring lands. Soldiers, poets and scholars flocked to Hindūstān to try their luck by entering imperial service or by being employed at one of the numerous noble courts. Many of these came from regions inhabited by Turkish peoples. Though contemporary sources do not devote much space to achievements in Turkish, their references being random, it is still possible to draw a fairly detailed picture of those persons who cultivated Turkish.

The brother of the historian Bāyazīd Bayāt, Shāh-berdi, writing under the pseudonym Saḳḳā Čaghatay (d. *ca.* 1558) composed poetry in Turkish. Mīr Muḥammad, the brother-in-law of Akbar's wet-nurse, Djidji-anägä, was a renowned art lover who not only supported poets but also composed verses both in Persian and Turkish under the *takhalluṣ* "Ghaznawī". He is supposed to have written a great number of poems, but nothing has so far been found from his oeuvre. Well known is the poetic achievement of the Turkmen statesman Bayrām Khān [*q.v.*], whose Persian and Turkish *dīwān* has been published. His son, ʿAbd al-Raḥīm Khān, Khān-i Khānān [*q.v.*], following his father's footsteps, acted as both a generous patron of outstanding literary talents and a dedicated poet who was able to compose poetry in several languages including various dialects of Turkish. The *mushāʿiras* [*q.v.*], meetings of poets organised at his court, were attended by poets who excelled in Turkish poetry as well. Reference should be made here to Kalb-i ʿAlī, a Turkmen from the Bahārlū tribe, Siyānī Hamadānī, or the Aleppo-born Turkish poet Darwīsh Mithlī. Though their complete poetical works do not seem to have survived, a few of their couplets in Turkish are preserved in our sources.

One of the most honoured poets of the 17th century, Mīrzā Ṣāʾib Tabrīzī [*q.v.*] who received the title of *malik al-shuʿarāʾ* or laureate from Shāh ʿAbbās II, was also attracted to the Mughal court. He is famous for his Persian poetry that set a trend which was followed even in Ottoman Turkey, but one should not forget that he was an equally gifted poet in Turkish. This side of his poetic talent almost faded into oblivion because only a handful of the manuscripts of his Persian *dīwān* contain Turkish pieces. At some point during the reign of Awrangzīb, there migrated to Hindūstān Ḥusayn Farīdūn Iṣfahānī, whose Persian *dīwān* has preserved a couple of Turkish lines as well. Dīwālī Singh (d. 1896) a well-known poet and a great stylist in Persian, became famous under his *takhalluṣ* "Ḳatīl". Following the practice of members of the Mughal élite in the 17th-18th centuries, he also learnt Turkish and wrote two short stories in this tongue. His famous work on Persian style titled *Čār sharbat* contains a sketchy Turkish grammar explained in Persian.

In a multi-ethnic society like India, it is not considered an extraordinary feat if someone learns several languages, but even in such an environment the achievements of Inshā-allāh Khān "Inshā" [*q.v.*] earned him fame. Born to a family of Turkish immigrants from Nadjaf, he not only spoke Arabic, Persian, Urdu, Kashmīrī, Purbi, Pashto and Turkish but was also able to compose poetry in these tongues. His Turkish output consists of a couple of *ḳaṣīdas*, *mukhammas*, a few *bayts* in his *Shikār-nāma* and a prose diary entitled *Turkī rūznāmča*. One of his most intimate friends and fellow poet was Saʿādat-yār Khān "Rangīn" [*q.v.*], whose father Ṭahmāsp Beg Khān Iʿtiḳād-Djang arrived in India with the army of Nādir Shāh and later wrote his memoirs, the *Aḥmad-nāma*. Rangīn spent most of his life in Lucknow in the service of Mīrzā Sulaymān-Shukūh. His works in Turkish includes a Turkish-Urdu vocabulary titled *Niṣāb-i turkī* and a few Turkish lines in his *Madjmūʿa-yi Rangīn*.

It should be noted, however, that contemporary chronicles and *tadhkiras* are full of references to poets of Turkish origin whose literary achievements in their mother-tongue have not yet come to light. There is further the fact that libraries, mainly throughout the former British Indian Empire, preserve manuscripts written in or on Turkish whose authors are either not mentioned in historical sources or literary antholo-gies, or even when contemporary records provide some information on them, their knowledge of Turkish is not mentioned. One should mention here Ḳaplan Beg, Yolḳulï Beg "Anīsī" S̲h̲āmlū, Mullā S̲h̲aydā'ī Tekkelü, Ustād Mīrzā 'Alī Ḳipčāḳī and also Pīr Muḥammad "Ag̲h̲ar K̲h̲ān" an Uzbek from the Ag̲h̲ar tribe who distinguished himself in the wars of Awrangzīb's reign. He composed verses filling a full dīwān that is pre-served in an Indian institution, but contemporary sources remain silent on his contribution to Indo-Turkish literature.

Beside being a medium for artistic expression Turkish was also used for more mundane purposes in Mug̲h̲al India up to the 19th century, as a lan-guage quite common in court circles, in the army and in diplomatic correspondence, mainly with Russia and the Ottoman Empire.

Bibliography: H.K. Hofman, *Turkish literature. A bio-bibliographical survey*, Utrecht 1969; S.A. Garriev (ed.), *Türkmen édebiyatǐnǐng tarǐk̲h̲ǐ*, i, As̲h̲gabat 1975, 351-93; M. Fuat Köprülü, art. *Çağatay edebiyatı*, in *IA*, iii, 270-323; A. Schimmel, *Türkisches in Indien*, in *Scholia. Beiträge zur Turkologie und Zentralasienkunde. Annemarie von Gabain zum 80. Geburtstag am 4. Juli 1981 dargebracht von Kollegen, Freunden und Schülern*, Wiesbaden 1981, 156-62; A.F. Bilkan, *Hindistan kütüphanelerinde bulunan türkçe el yazmaları*, in *Türk Dili* (Nisan 1996), 1096-1105; B. Péri, *A török írás- és szóbeliség nyomai a mogul-kori Indiában: Mīrzā 'Alī-baxt Gurgānī Azfarī Mīzān at-turkī cǐmǘ grammatikai értekezése és ami körülötte van* ("Traces of Turkish language use in Mughal India. The Mīzān at-turkī by Mīrzā 'Alī-bak̲h̲t Gurgānī Azfarī and its background"), Ph.D. diss., Budapest 2000, unpubl. (B. Péri)

AL-ṬŪSĪ, 'ALĀ' AL-DĪN 'ALĪ b. Muḥammad, important religious scholar of the 9th/15th cen-tury. He grew up in Iran (in Samarḳand, according to al-Suyūṭī [q.v.]), where he also finished his studies. During the reign of the Ottoman Sultan Murād II [q.v.] (probably in the second phase of his rule, i.e. between 850/1446 and 855/1451), he came to Anatolia and was appointed as a teacher at the *madrasa al-sulṭāniyya* in Bursa [q.v.]. After the conquest of Constantinople in 1453, Meḥemmed II [q.v.] assigned him to a professorship, first in Istanbul, afterwards in Edirne [q.v.]. It was around this time that the con-test between al-Ṭūsī and K̲h̲odja-zāde [q.v.] took place. Both had been summoned by the sultan to compose a work of advice on the famous discussion between al-G̲h̲azālī [q.v.] and the philosophers. A jury classi-fied al-Ṭūsī's treatise as the one of lesser interest. As a consequence, he renounced his academic post in Edirne and returned, via Tabrīz [q.v.], to Samarḳand. He is said to have returned there to live as a Ṣūfī, allegedly under the guidance of 'Ubayd Allāh Aḥrār [see AḤRĀR, K̲H̲ᵂĀDJA 'UBAYD ALLĀH, in Suppl.]. He is reported to have died in Samarḳand in 877/1472 (according to al-Suyūṭī) or in 887/1482 (according to

Tās̲h̲köprüzāde and Ḥādjdjī K̲h̲alīfa [q.vv.]).

Notwithstanding the above-mentioned failure, re-corded in several sources, al-Ṭūsī was able to compose a considerable number of scientific works. As was the case with many scholars of the 9th/15th century, al-Ṭūsī's writings deal with the various disciplines that were taught at the *madrasa* [q.v.]. His works can be divided into the following categories:

Ḳur'ān exegesis: superglosses on the glosses of al-Djurdjānī [q.v.] on the *al-Kas̲h̲s̲h̲āf* of al-Zamak̲h̲s̲h̲arī [q.v.];

Fiḳh: glosses on the commentary of al-Taftāzānī [q.v.] on al-Maḥbūbī's *Tawḍīḥ*, and also glosses on the commentary of al-Īdjī [q.v.] on the *Muk̲h̲taṣar muntahā al-su'āl* of Ibn al-Ḥādjib [q.v.];

Kalām: glosses on al-Djurdjānī's commentary on al-Īdjī's *al-Mawāḳif* as well as on al-Djurdjānī's com-mentary on al-Īdjī's *al-Aḳā'id*;

Logic and philosophy: superglosses on al-Djurdjānī's glosses on Ḳuṭb al-Dīn al-Taḥtānī's commentary on Sirādj al-Dīn al-Urmawī's *Maṭāli' al-anwār fi 'l-manṭiḳ*, as well as the above-mentioned treatise on the dis-cussion between al-G̲h̲azālī and the philosophers, which has become known under the title *al-Dhak̲h̲īra* (*fi 'l-muḥākama bayna al-G̲h̲azālī wa 'l-ḥukamā'*).

Several of these texts have survived in manuscript (see Brockelmann, II², 261-2, S II 279, 292a). So far, however, only the *Dhak̲h̲īra* has appeared in print (Ḥaydarābād 1899; recently also under the title *Tahāfut al-falāsīfa*, ed. R. Sa'āda, Beirut 1990; cf. the Turkish translation by R. Duran, Ankara 1990). The work shows that al-Ṭūsī, following al-G̲h̲azālī, tried to com-bine classical doctrines of Sunnī theology with philo-sophical concepts. Among other things, he underlines that the rules of logic and the results of mathemat-ics and astronomy are incontestable; should the state-ments of revelation be in contradiction with them, they must be interpreted allegorically. In the doctrine on the soul, too, al-Ṭūsī is a representative of philo-sophical notions (the soul lives on after death; spiri-tual enjoyments have precedence over physical pleasures, in both this world and the hereafter). In the question of causality, on the contrary, he insists that the occasionalistic theory of the early As̲h̲'arī theo-logians is correct.

Bibliography: Laknawī, *al-Fawā'id al-bahiyya*, Cairo 1906, 145-6; Suyūṭī, *Naẓm al-'iḳān*, ed. P. Hitti, New York 1927, 132; Tās̲h̲köprüzāde, *al-S̲h̲aḳā'iḳ al-nu'māniyya*, Ger. tr. O. Rescher, Constantinople-Stuttgart 1927-34, repr. Osnabrück 1978, 58-60; Brockelmann, II², 261-2, S II, 279; Ḥādjdjī K̲h̲alīfa, *Kas̲h̲f al-ẓunūn*, ed. Ṣ. Yaltkaya and R. Bilge, Istanbul 1941-3, 497, 513, 825, 1144, 1479, 1856, 1892; Mübahat Türker, *Üç tahafut bakımından felsefe ve din münasebetleri*, Ankara 1956; Mustafa S. Yazıcıoğlu, *Le kalâm et son rôle dans la société turco-ottomane aux XVe et XVIe siècles*, Ankara 1990; T. Nagel, *Geschichte der islamischen Theologie*, Munich 1994, 203-4.

(U. Rudolph)

U

ʿUBAYD ALLĀH SULṬĀN KHĀN, ruler in Transoxania of the Uzbeks or Özbegs [*q.v.*] 940-6/1533-9.

He was the son of Maḥmūd Sulṭān, son of Shāh-Būdāgh, son of the founder of the Uzbek confederacy, Abu ʾl-Khayr Khān, a descendant of Čingiz Khān's grandson Shībān (hence the epithet "Shībānī," or "Shaybānī" [see SHĪBĀNIDS]). During his youth, ʿUbayd Allāh accompanied his uncle Muḥammad Shībānī Khān (*r.* 905-16/1500-10) on his sweeping victories over the Tīmūrids throughout Central Asia and Khurāsān in order to re-establish Čingizid rule in the area. On 7 Muḥarram 913/19 May 1507 the Uzbek forces under ʿUbayd Allāh and Temür Sulṭān defeated the Tīmūrids outside Harāt. As a victory prize, ʿUbayd Allāh was given in marriage Mihrangīz Begim, a daughter of Muẓaffar-Ḥusayn Mīrzā, who shared the throne of Harāt with his brother Badīʿ al-Zamān Mīrzā after the death of their father, Sulṭān-Ḥusayn Mīrzā, in 912/1506. With the consolidation of his rule over Khurāsān and Central Asia, Muḥammad Shībānī Khān appointed ʿUbayd Allāh as governor of Bukhārā.

In Radjab 917/October 1511, Bābur [*q.v.*] re-occupied Samarḳand, his ancestral capital, with the help of the Ṣafawid Shāh Ismāʿīl I [*q.v.*]. The Uzbeks were not slow to retaliate, and in Ṣafar 918/April 1512 Bābur launched an ill-prepared attack on the Uzbeks under ʿUbayd Allāh at Köl-i Malik near Bukhārā, and although Bābur had been winning, suddenly "through the machinations of heaven, the evil eye struck" and Bābur lost. After the battle he left Transoxania forever. On 3 Ramaḍān 918/12 November 1512, ʿUbayd Allāh defeated the Ṣafawid general Nadjm-i Thānī (Amīr Yār-Aḥmad Iṣfahānī) at the Battle of Gizhduvan (Ghudjduwān). The next winter, Shāh Ismāʿīl returned to western Persia to deal with incursions by the Ottoman Sultan Selīm I, and Ḳāsim Khān of the Ḳirghiz-Ḳazakhs returned to Siberia to tend to his realm, leaving the Uzbeks a free hand in Central Asia. That winter ʿUbayd Allāh took Hissar, to the north of the upper Oxus, from the Moghuls. In 920/1514 the Uzbeks headed for Andizhān, where the Moghul Sulṭān-Saʿīd Khān was. Since by then Bābur had withdrawn to Kābul, the khān went to Kāshghar, leaving Hissar to fall to the Uzbeks.

ʿUbayd Allāh became the khān of the Shībānids in 940/1533, although, as Mīrzā Ḥaydar reports, "from the year 911 [1505] until the end of the reign of the latter khāns, it was really he who had conducted the affairs of the Shībānids, and had he accepted to be khān, no-one would really have opposed him; nonetheless, he maintained the ancient custom and let the office of khān be given to whoever was the eldest—until after Abū Saʿīd Khān, when there was no one older than him" (*Tārīkh-i-Rashīdī*, 181-2). During his ascendancy, six advances were made against Khurāsān. In 930/1523 there was an abortive siege of Harāt. In 932/1525 Mashhad was taken, and ʿUbayd Allāh proceeded to Astarābād and drove the governor out. Astarābād was given to ʿUbayd Allāh's son ʿAbd al-ʿAzīz, but he could not hold out against Ṣafawid reinforcements and had finally to abandon the territory. When the Uzbeks advanced on Khurāsān the third time, they clashed with the Ṣafawid army at Saru Ḳamish near Djām on 10 Muḥarram 935/24 September 1528, and although the battle was going badly against the Ṣafawids, they managed to turn it into a resounding defeat of the Uzbeks. An eyewitness account of this battle is included in Bābur's memoirs (*Bābur-nāma*, fol. 354), where it is incorrectly recorded that ʿUbayd Allāh was killed. The fifth invasion of Khurāsān was launched in 937/1530-1, but the Uzbeks again pulled out when Shāh Ṭahmāsp I advanced on them and entered Harāt on 22 Djumādā II 939/19 January 1533. The sixth and last invasion was made in 942/1535, when the Uzbeks again took Mashhad. Harāt was evacuated by the Uzbeks in Shaʿbān 943/January 1537 and re-occupied by the Ṣafawids under the command of Khudābanda and Muḥammad Khān Sharaf al-Dīn-oghlu Täkälü.

In 945/1538-9, ʿUbayd Allāh's forces occupied Khʷārazm, but subsequently they were dealt a crushing defeat by Dīn-Muḥammad Khān, another Čingizid descendant with whom Shāh Ṭahmāsp had formed an alliance and to whom he had given the territory of Nasā and Abīward. Returning to Bukhārā in 946/153, "in answer to the cries of the oppressed, ʿUbayd Allāh took to his bed, overtaken by a severe illness, and while pining for Harāt and yearning to stroll along the banks of the Mālān Bridge, he hastened to the next world, and the residents of Khurāsān were released from the oppression and cruelty of that heathen butcher" (Iskandar Beg, *T.-i ʿĀlam-ārā*, 66). He left two sons, ʿAbd al-ʿAzīz and Muḥammad-Raḥīm Sulṭān, but the khānate went to ʿAbd Allāh Khān; the son of ʿUbayd Allāh's predecessor, Küčüm Khān, although ʿAbd al-ʿAzīz continued to rule autonomously in Bukhārā. A valuable eyewitness accounts of events in Bukhārā, Samarḳand and Tashkent during ʿUbayd Allāh's reign is Zayn al-Dīn Maḥmūd Wāṣifī's *Badāyiʿ al-waḳāyiʿ*.

Bibliography: Bābur, *Bābur-nāma*; Faḍl Allāh Rūzbihān Iṣfahānī, *Mihmān-nāma-yi Bukhārā*, Moscow 1976; Ḥasan Rūmlū, *Aḥsan al-tawārīkh*, Tehran 1357/1978; Mīrzā Ḥaydar Dughlāt, *Tārīkh-i-Rashīdī*, Eng. tr. W.M. Thackston, Cambridge, Mass. 1996; Iskandar Beg Türkmän, *Tārīkh-i ʿĀlam-ārā-yi ʿAbbāsī*, Tehran 1350/1971; Khʷāndamīr, *Ḥabīb al-siyar*, Tehran 1353/1974; Wāṣifī, *Badāyiʿ al-waḳāyiʿ*.

(W.M. Thackston)

ʿUḲALĀʾ AL-MADJĀNĪN (A.), "wise fools", a general denomination for individuals whose actions contradict social norms, while their utterances are regarded as wisdom. It is not altogether clear whether or not wise fools were particularly numerous in the early ʿAbbāsid period. At any rate, several authors of classical Arabic literature have treated the phenomenon in specific works that belong to the literary genre dealing with unusual classes of people, such as the blind or misers. While the first collection devoted specifically to wise fools was apparently a work written by al-Madāʾinī (d. 228/843 [*q.v.*]), the only surviving work is the *Kitāb ʿUḳalāʾ al-madjānīn* by Abu ʾl-Ḳāsim al-Ḥasan b. Muḥammad al-Naysābūrī (d. 406/1015 [*q.v.*]) (ed. ʿUmar al-Asʿad, Beirut 1407/1987).

Al-Naysābūrī, while drawing upon earlier authors such as al-Djāḥiẓ (d. 255/868 [*q.v.*]) or Ibn Abi ʾl-Dunyā (d. 281/894 [*q.v.*]), introduces his subject from a theological point of view. For him, God has created the world in splendour and incapacity at the same time: good is blended with evil, and health with illness. In this way, madness, even though apparently a contradiction to God's benevolence, is a perfectly normal constituent of the human condition. In the following, the author discusses the terms used to denote madness, besides classifying different connotations of madness, such as *aḥmaḳ, maʿtūh, mamsūs, mamrūr*, etc. The main part of his work is devoted to anecdotes about specific characters known as wise fools. He begins with Uways al-Ḳaranī [*q.v.*], Madjnūn [*q.v.*], Saʿdūn and Buhlūl [*q.v.*], all of whom share a relatively ascertained historical existence. After these, al-Naysābūrī lists a large number of tales about other, less popular wise fools, details about whose lives become progressively more limited. The names he mentions include ʿUlayyān, Abu ʾl-Dīk, ʿAbd al-Raḥmān b. al-Ashʿath, Abū Saʿīd al-Ḍabʿī, Djuʿayfirān and many others; the final chapters of his work deal with Bedouin (including Imruʾ al-Ḳays [*q.v.*] and Habannaḳa), women, and anonymous persons.

Though each of the characters known as wise fools behaved in an individual manner, several traits were germane to all or most of them (Dols 1992, 349-65): wise fools were indifferent to appearance, often walking around naked or half-clad; they were oblivious to social conventions such as greeting or paying respect; they were ascetics, living on charity and not caring for worldly possessions; they lived in the streets of the cities without any specific abode, while their favourite place of residence was the cemetery. Those of the wise fools whose actions were considered harmful to society were held in hospitals. Wise fools would constantly remind their fellow citizens, particularly the powerful, of their worldliness and vanity, quoting pious verses and admonishing them with stories or allegories alluding to the hereafter; some of them even acted as unofficial preachers. In particular, their quality as free-wheeling admonishers makes the Islamic wise fools appear as precursors of the mediaeval European phenomenon of the court fool (Mezger 1991). Hence it is not surprising to see Buhlūl, who in later tradition all over the Islamic word was to become the stereotypical figure for the character of the wise fool (Marzolph 1983), being listed in European literature as the court fool of Hārūn al-Rashīd (K.F. Flögel, *Geschichte der Hofnarren*, Leipzig 1789, 172 ff.).

Other works of Islamic literature, while more or less drawing upon the same data, interpreted the phenomenon in various directions. Ibn al-Djawzī (d. 597/1200 [*q.v.*]) in his *K. Ṣifat al-ṣafwa*, regards the wise fools as important figures in the early history of Ṣūfism (Dols 1992, 376), and Ibn al-ʿArabī (d. 638/1240 [*q.v.*]) in his *al-Futūḥāt al-makkiyya* elevates the holy fools to the position of spiritual leaders (*ibid.*, 408-9). In Persian literature, wise fools figure prominently in the mystical *mathnawī*s of Farīd al-Dīn ʿAṭṭār (d. 617/1220 [*q.v.*]), for whom the character is licensed to speak his mind in a way beyond that permissible to ordinary human beings (Ritter 1978, 159-80).

Bibliography: H. Ritter, *Das Meer der Seele*, ²Leiden 1978; U. Marzolph, *Der Weise Narr Buhlūl*, Wiesbaden 1983; W. Mezger, *Narrenidee und Fastnachtsbrauch*, Konstanz 1991; M. Dols, *Majnūn. The madman in medieval Islamic society*, Oxford 1992.

(U. MARZOLPH)

ʿUKBARĀ, a town of mediaeval ʿIrāḳ, lying, in the time of the classical Arabic geographers (3rd-4th/9th-10th centuries) on the left, i.e. eastern, bank of the Tigris, ten *farsakh*s to the north of Baghdād, roughly halfway between the capital and Sāmarrāʾ.

As Yāḳūt noted (*Buldān*, ed. Beirut, iv, 142), the name is orginally Aramaic (*sūriyānī*), sc. ʿOkbarā, and the history of the place can be traced back at least to early Sāsānid times. In the reign of the emperor Shāpūr I (mid-3rd century A.D.), Roman captives were settled there, and by the reign of Khusraw Anūsharwān (mid-6th century A.D.), it was the chef-lieu of the subdistrict (*ṭassūdj*) called Buzurdjsābūr in the *kūra* or province of Khusrāwma (see M.G. Morony, *Iraq after the Muslim conquest*, Princeton 1984, 138-9).

When the Arabs started raiding into Sāsānid ʿIrāḳ, Khālid b. al-Walīd in 12/633-4 sent the commander al-Nuṣayr b. Daysam al-ʿIdjlī to the region north of al-Madāʾin, and the people of ʿUkbarā and the nearby Baradān made agreements for *amān* or a peace settlement with the incomers. Therafter, the town flourished as part of the rich, irrigated agricultural region stretching along the Tigris banks; al-Muḳaddasī, 122, praises its fruits, and in particular its grapes, and Ibn Ḥawḳal, ed. Kramers, i, 219, tr. Kramers and Wiet, i, 213, mentions the watermills (*ʿurūb*) there, a feature characteristic of the whole river valley between al-Mawṣil and Baghdād (see A. Mez, *Die Renaissance des Islâms*, Heidelberg 1922, 438-9, Eng. tr. Patna 1937, 466-7). The town was large and populous in the 4th/10th century, and a Jewish community there is mentioned in the early 3rd/9th century. But from Saldjūḳ times onwards, mentions of it in the historical and geographical sources dwindle. It appears that the bed of the Tigris above Baghdād began to shift its course, for al-Masʿūdī, *Murūdj*, i, 223, ed. and tr. Pellat, §235, already mentions disputes and lawsuits (*muṭālabāt*) between proprietors along the eastern and western banks. Le Strange noted that the author of the *Marāṣid al-iṭṭilāʿ* (*ca.* A.D. 1300) clearly mentions ʿUkbarā as by that time standing a considerable distance to the west of the Tigris, the river's bed having shifted eastwards into the channel then known as al-Shuṭayṭa "the little *shaṭṭ* [*q.v.*]", and the ruins of ʿUkbarā lie at the present day on the left bank of the old channel of the Tigris (see G. Le Strange, *Description of Mesopotamia and Baghdad written about the year 900 A.D. by Ibn Serapion*, in *JRAS* [1895], 37-9; A. Musil, *The Middle Euphrates, a topographical itinerary*, New York 1927, 137-8).

Al-Samʿānī, *K. al-Ansāb*, ed. Ḥaydarābād, ix, 345-8, mentions a considerable number of scholars stemming from ʿUkbarā, and at a slightly later date, the parents of the Ḥanbalī *faḳīh* and philologist ʿAbd Allāh b. al-Ḥusayn al-ʿUkbarī [*q.v.*] came from the town.

Bibliography: Given in the article; see also Le Strange, *The lands of the Eastern Caliphate*, 50-1.

(C.E. BOSWORTH)

ʿUMĀN.

iii. Social structure.

ʿUmān is overwhelmingly an Arab, Muslim society, and tribal organisation remains an important element in national identity. The country's rapid development since 1970 has introduced a measure of physical and social mobility, as well as creating an influx of emigrants.

The migration of Arab tribes into ʿUmān predates Islam, with Ḳaḥṭānī or South Arabian tribes moving along the southern Arabian Peninsula from Yemen into ʿUmān around the 2nd century A.D. They were followed several centuries later by ʿAdnānī or North Arabian tribes who penetrated from the west along the Gulf coast. The Islamisation of ʿUmān resulted in the eviction of the Persianised ruling class stemming from Sāsānid influences and completed the organisation of the tribal framework that continues today.

On the local level, the competition for scarce resources in water and arable land created a mosaic of tribal settlement. Many settlements stretch alongside the courses of *wādī*s and attendant *faladj*s (water channels); frequently the *ʿalāya* or upper quarter is inhabited by a tribe in traditional rivalry with another tribe occupying the *sifāla* or lower quarter. Regionally, a rough balance was obtained through two competing alliances and this balance was replicated on the national level by association with either the Hināwiyya confederation or the opposing Ghāfiriyya confederation. Above these confederations stood the Ibāḍī imāmate [see IBĀḌIYYA] which served as a supertribal or quasi-national institution. Because the tribal confederations acted principally as balancers of power, membership in one or the other tended to be fluid over time. This has tended to blur earlier tendencies for al-Hināwiyya to consist of Ibāḍī and ʿAdnānī tribes and al-Ghāfiriyya to consist of Sunnī and Ḳaḥṭānī tribes.

The power of the Ibāḍī imāmate derived directly from the personal standing of the *imām*, who was both dependent on the support of the principal *shaykh*s of the major tribes of both confederations for his position and the mediating figure between them and between tribes on the regional and local levels. This system gave enormous power to the leading *shaykh*s who dominated the confederations, and especially powerful *shaykh*s were able to use their power to determine the election of *imām*s. During the second half of the 19th century, the powerful shaykhly family of the Hināwī al-Ḥirth tribe of al-Sharḳiyya region orchestrated a series of attempts to oust the Āl Bū Saʿīd [*q.v.*] rulers in Masḳaṭ in order to restore the imāmate. But by the early 20th century, the head of the Ghāfirī Banū Riyām had become the predominant political figure in the interior, and the imām elected in 1920 came from a Ghāfirī tribe.

The reassertion of sultanate control over interior ʿUmān in the mid-1950s, with the attendant demise of the imāmate, reduced the autonomy of the tribes and restricted the role of the *shaykh*s. For the first time, order and authority was maintained by a permanent army presence and, with a single exception, the *shaykh*s found their responsibilities restricted to leadership of their own tribes. When a new development-minded government appeared as a result of a palace *coup d'état* in 1970, the role of the *shaykh*s was further reduced. The government assumed responsibility for public works and welfare. Social service ministries carried out improvements throughout the country, and a new system of courts and national police usurped many of the traditional functions of the *shaykh*s.

But even though the political power of the tribes has waned considerably since 1970, their social functions remain undiminished. Marriages take place by and large within the tribe, if not within the extended family. The government issues identity cards classifying the holder by tribal membership. Tribesmen seek the assistance of fellow tribesmen in obtaining employment, business help, and resolving problems with the police.

The great majority of the ʿUmānī population is Arab and either Ibāḍī or Sunnī Muslim. The more prominent of these two divisions is the Ibāḍī sect, which, until the second half of the 20th century, provided the national leadership of ʿUmān through an elected *imām*. Perhaps slightly less than half of ʿUmān's total population is Ibāḍī, all in the northern half of the country. Sunnīs are thought to form slightly more than half of the ʿUmānī population. While the north contains both Ibāḍī and Sunnī tribes, the southern province Ẓafār [*q.v.*] (Dhofar) is entirely Sunnī. While Sunnī tribes in northern ʿUmān may be Shāfiʿī or Mālikī, Ẓafārīs are all Shāfiʿīs. Much of the Sunnī population of Ṣūr and its hinterland is Ḥanbalī.

There are also several small Shīʿī communities, mostly located in the capital area of Masḳaṭ, all of which are Djaʿfarī or Twelver. Al-Lawātiyya form the largest Shīʿī community, numbering perhaps 10,000 and traditionally residing in a closed quarter of Maṭraḥ, Masḳaṭ's sister settlement. The community seems to be Indian in origin, and at one time was in close connection with Agha Khānī Ismāʿīlīs, all of whom have since converted or left ʿUmān. The Lawātiyya have been settled in Maṭraḥ for at least three centuries. The Arab Shīʿī community of al-Baḥārina, formerly concentrated in Masḳaṭ itself, is considerably smaller in size and consists of a few families that immigrated to ʿUmān independently of each other. ʿAdjam, people of Persian origin whose arrival in ʿUmān may be supposed to have occurred gradually over the course of centuries, comprises the third Shīʿī group. Their numbers are similarly small and they appear to be assimilating into broader ʿUmānī society.

The largest non-Arab component of the ʿUmānī population is Balūč, mostly residing along al-Bāṭina coast of the Gulf of Oman and in the capital area. Often included with the Balūč, but nevertheless distinct, is a smaller group known as al-Zadjāl. Masḳaṭ is also home to a few Hindu families, some of whom can trace back their arrival in ʿUmān approximately a century and a half. Most of these families hold Indian citizenship and form marriages with relations in India.

Arabic is the predominant language of ʿUmān, but nearly a dozen languages are spoken by ʿUmānīs. Balūč undoubtedly produces the second-largest proportion of native speakers. The Zadjāl and Lawātiyya speak their own languages, both akin to Gujarātī. The long ʿUmānī association with East Africa has resulted in a significant number of ʿUmānīs either born in or formerly resident in Zanzibar and neighbouring African countries. Some of these speak Swahili as their primary language, with English second and Arabic third.

Ẓafār is distinct from ʿUmān in several respects. Separated by the north by extensive gravel-plain desert, the region traditionally was linked with the Mahra and Ḥaḍramawt regions of Yemen. The widespread Kathīr tribe is perhaps the most extensive group in the region, with subgroups including nomadic sections on the Nadjd (the stony inland plain) and three clans that traditionally have been prominent in Ṣalāla, Ẓafār's largest settlement and now a small city. Another transhumant section, the Bayt Kathīr, inhabits a narrow band of mountainous territory.

The other mountain tribes, commonly known as *djibbālī*s and traditionally transhumant as well, occupy similar strip territories, all running perpendicular to the coast and including parts of the coastal plain. These tribes speak a South Arabian language, Ḳarawī, apparently adopted from the indigenous inhabitants whom they conquered some six or more centuries ago. The latter, al-Shahra, maintain a separate but socially inferior identity.

Mahra tribes are also found in Ẓafār, mainly camel-herding nomads in either the northeastern Nadjd or along the Yemen border in the west. Some have established themselves recently on the mountains. In addition to al-Shahra, other *ḍaʿīf* or socially inferior peoples are also present in Ẓafār, amongst them al-Mashāyikh and al-Barāʿima. Ṣalāla and the smaller coastal towns are also inhabited by mixed-race *baḥḥār*s and descendants of African slaves. Several small groups speaking South Arabian languages have been pushed out into the deserts northwest of Ẓafār; among these are al-Baṭāhira, al-Ḥikmān, and the larger and more important al-Ḥarasīs.

Following the end of the civil war in Ẓafār in the late 1970s, the region has undergone rapid socio-economic development. Most *djibbālī*s have built permanent homes in the mountains, often clustered in new settlements, and some maintain second homes in Ṣalāla.

Traditionally, ʿUmān was a rural country, with most of its population scattered in small agricultural settlements or coastal fishing villages. The process of development since 1970, however, has produced considerable urbanisation. The capital region, consisting in 1970 of the twin towns of Masḳaṭ and Maṭraḥ with a combined population then of perhaps 25,000, grew to nearly half a million at the beginning of the 21st century. Ṣalāla's population grew over the same period to nearly 200,000 and Ṣuḥār (on the northwestern al-Bāṭina coast), Nizwā (in the interior), and Ṣūr (near the eastern coastal tip) have become relatively large regional centres.

ʿUmānī society is relatively free from social stratification, although members of the ruling Āl Bū Saʿīd family, tribal leaders, religious figures, and wealthy merchants occupy the upper rungs of society. A small middle class has emerged since 1970, but many ʿUmānīs in the Masḳaṭ region are employed as government employees, soldiers, drivers, and skilled and unskilled labour. The majority of the population outside the capital remains engaged in subsistence agriculture, fishing, or animal husbandry.

The government has used its modest oil revenues to extend roads, electricity, communications, schools, and health-care facilities throughout the country. The country remains dependent on oil income, however, and diversification into natural gas exports and tourism has had limited success. The first university opened in 1986.

Up to 25% of the total population is expatriate, with the greatest numbers coming from south and southeast Asia. While the heaviest concentration is in the capital area, expatriates are dispersed throughout the country and the government periodically has extended bans on expatriate labour to a growing number of occupations in an effort to "Omanise" the labour force and provide employment for a burgeoning indigenous population.

Bibliography: J.G. Lorimer, *Gazetteer of the Persian Gulf, 'Umān and Central Arabia*, 2 vols. Calcutta 1908-15; J.E. Peterson, *Oman in the twentieth century. Political foundations of an emerging state*, London and New York 1978; F. Barth, *Sohar. Culture and society in an Omani town*, Baltimore 1983; Christine Eickelman, *Women and community in Oman*, New York 1984; J. Janzen, *Nomads in the Sultanate of Oman. Tradition and development in Dhofar*, Boulder, Colo. 1986; J.C. Wilkinson, *The Imamate tradition of Oman*, Cambridge 1987; F. Scholz, *Muscat-Sultanat Oman. Geographische Skizze einer einmaligen arabischen Stadt*, Berlin 1990; Dawn Chatty, *Mobile pastoralists. Development planning and social change in Oman*, New York 1996.

(J.E. Peterson)

URA-TEPE (Ūrā-Tipa, Ūrā-Tīpa), Russian Ura-Tyube, a town and a district on the northern slope of the Turkestan chain, now the town and district of Ūroteppa in Tādjīkistān. The town is located in lat. 39° 55' N. and long. 69° 00' E. at 1040 m/3,425 feet above sea level. Lying in the foothills between the steppe plains and the mountains, and on a major route linking Samarḳand with Tashkent and the Farghāna valley, the historical Ura-Tepe both connected and separated adjacent ecological and political regions.

The place name, signifying a "high hill" (*örä tübe/töpä/tepä*) in Ḳïpčaḳ and Čaghatay vernaculars, emerges in the Tīmūrid period. It is first mentioned in the course of events in early Muḥarram 812/late May 1409 when the royal camp of Shāh Rukh [*q.v.*] was pitched in the "summer pasture (*yaylāḳ*) of Ūrā-Tipa" (ʿAbd al-Razzāḳ Samarḳandī, *Maṭlaʿ al-saʿādayn*, ed. M. Shafīʿ, Lahore 1941-9, ii, 141). Several 10th/16th century authorities confirm that the new toponym had come to gradually replace the earlier "Usrūshana" (Bābur, ed. Mano, 13), "Ūstrūshana" (Muḥammad Ḥaydar, *Tārīkh-i Rashīdī*, ed. W.M. Thackston, 91), or "Ustrūshana" (Ḥāfiẓ-i Tanish, *Sharaf-nāma-i shāhī*, ed. Salakhetdinova, i, facs. fol. 88b; and see USRŪSHANA).

At the turn of the 10th/16th century, the district's centre was a fortified town (*ḳūrghān*) surrounded by high walls and a moat, amidst cultivated lands and pastures for horses and sheep (Muḥammad Ṣāliḥ, *Shībānī-nāma*, ed. and tr. H. Vambéry, 174-9). In 908/1503 the former Tīmūrid stronghold fell to the Özbegs led by Muḥammad Shībānī Khān. During the Shībānid and early Ashtarkhānid periods, the Ura-Tepe district (*wilāyat, ḳalamraw*) at times was alloted as an individual appanage to ruling princes, and at times it was attached to larger entities, such as Tashkent or Samarḳand.

From the middle of the 11th/17th century, the Özbeg tribe of the Yūz, established in Ura-Tepe, as well as in Khodjand and Ḥiṣār (to the north and the south of Ura-Tepe, respectively), came to play an increasingly important political role, which was not strictly confined to the realm of Ura-Tepe.

One line of Yūz chiefs can be traced back to Bāḳī Biy Yūz, who around 1641-4 served as chief military and administrative adviser (*atālīḳ*) to an Ashtarkhānid prince (i.e. Bahrām Sulṭān b. Nadr Muḥammad Khān) ruling at Tashkent. Bāḳī Biy's grandson, Muḥammad Raḥīm Biy Yūz (b. Ghāzī Biy), who held Ura-Tepe in 1091/1680 and 1105/1693-4, proved to be loyal to the Bukhāran court, at a time when another leading figure of the Yūz joined a rebellion (Mukhtarov, *Materiali*, 24, 29). Subsequently, Muḥammad Raḥīm was named governor (*ḥākim*) of Samarḳand. In 1114/1702, when he was further raised to the rank of an *atālīḳ* and "Pillar of the Amirs" (*ʿumdat al-umarāʾ*), one of Muḥammad Raḥīm's major assets was said to be his prestige among the warlike tribes of "Andigān, Khodjand, Āḳ-Kūtal and Tāshkand, up to the regions of Sayrām, Turkistān and Ulugh-Tāgh", which enabled him to provide auxiliaries for the Bukhāran rulers (Muḥammad Amīn Bukhārī, *ʿUbayd Allāh-nāma*, ms. Tashkent, no. 1532, fols. 20b, 28b, tr. Semenov, 34-5, 43-4). While Muḥammad Raḥīm reached the zenith of his career, his son, Muḥammad Āḳbūta Biy, followed his father's footsteps in Ura-Tepe and Khodjand, where he ruled from 1113/1701 up to 1144/1731

(Mukhtarov, *op. cit.*, 33-9). Sometime between 1731 and 1734, he was killed by a Ming chief of the expanding Khoḳand state [*q.v.*].

A second line of Yūz chiefs emerges with Muḥammad Fāḍil Biy (b. Ṣādiḳ Biy). Fāḍil Beg Yūz was one of the commanders of the Bukhāran army that surrendered to Nādir Shāh in 1153/1740. Subsequently, he guided a Nādirid military campaign against "the rebellious Yūz and Ming tribes seated in the mountain and on the banks of the Sīr-Daryā" (Muḥammad Kāẓim, *ʿĀlam-ārā-yi nādirī*, ed. Riyāḥī, ii, 790, 802, 819). While ruling in Ura-Tepe, Fāḍil Biy supported the Khoḳand chief ʿAbd al-Karīm Biy against the Ḳalmāḳs (Muḥammad Ḥakīm Khān, *Muntakhab al-tawārīkh*, ii, 378), i.e. the Djunghars, who repeatedly invaded Khoḳand between 1153/1740 and 1158/1745 (Moiseev 1991, 162-3, 167, 173; Nabiev, 14). His own decrees, issued upon the order of an unnamed khān, confirm Fāḍil Biy's rule over Ura-Tepe in 1164/1750-1 and 1187/1774-5 (Mukhtarov, *op. cit.*, 40, 42). Under Fāḍil Biy, one of the most stubborn opponents of the rising Manghït dynasty of Bukhārā, Ura-Tepe turned into a strong and nearly independent statelet dominating neighbouring territories such as Khodjand, Djizzāḳ, and even Samarḳand. Around 1780, however, when the town with four gates was under Fāḍil Biy's son Muḥammad Khudāyār, the ruler's authority was confined to the environment of the town (Yefremov, 114). In 1800, Khudāyār's son Beg-Murād Biy, having ruled less than a year, was deposed by the ruler of Bukhārā Shāh Murād.

In the 19th century, Ura-Tepe lost its independence and became a disputed border area between Bukhārā and Khoḳand. From 1800 to 1866, the two rival states launched dozens of military campaigns into Ura-Tepe, where more than twenty governors succeeded each other. Both sides often chose Yūz representatives as local governors, such as Muḥammad Raḥīm Parwānačī b. Muḥammad Khudāyār, who ruled in 1234/1818 (Mukhtarov, *op. cit.*, 56).

When Filipp Nazarov visited Ura-Tepe in 1814, it had recently been taken by Khoḳand. He observed that the town "is very large and surrounded by two high walls, separated from each other by a deep moat; openings made in these walls allow the use of fire-arms, if need be. This town is densely populated, the streets are narrow, and the houses built of clay. There are manufactories producing goat wool shawls. The inhabitants trade with the Turcomans, the Persians and the Arab nomads who are subjects of Bukhārā" (Nazarov, 65-6).

On 2 October 1866, the Imperial Russian army conquered the town. Having been ceded by the Bukhāran *amīr* to Russia in 1868, Ura-Tepe became part of the Khodjand *uyezd*. The population of Ura-Tepe at that time was variously estimated to be between 10 and 15,000 people. There were 854 shops of artisans and traders in the town. When the Soviet Republic of Tādjīkistān was founded in 1929, Ura-Tepe was its second largest city after Khodjand. In the decade 1976-85 there were *ca.* 38,000 inhabitants in the town and 143,000 inhabitants in the district (*Entsiklopediyai sovetii todjik*, viii, Dushanbe 1988, 339). By a presidential decree of 10 November 2000, the town has been officially renamed Istravshan.

Bibliography: P. Nazarov, *Voyage à Khokand entrepris en 1813 et 1814*, in *Magasin Asiatique*, i (1825), 1-80; A. Mukhtarov, *Materialī po istorii Ura-Tyube. Sbornik aktov XVII-XIX*, Moscow 1963; idem, *Očerk istorii Ura-Tyubinskogo vladeniya v XIX v.*, Dushanbe 1964; R. Nabiev, *Iz istorii Kokandskogo khanstva*, Tashkent 1973; B.A. Akhmedov (ed.), *Materialī po istorii Srednei i Tsentralniy Azii X-XX vv.*, Tashkent 1988; V.A. Moiseev, *Džungarskoe khanstvo i kazakhi, XVII-XVIII vv.*, Alma-Ata 1991; A. Mukhtorov, *Istoriya Ura-Tyube*, Dushanbe 1999.

(W. Holzwarth)

W

WADD, a god of pre-Islamic Arabia, mentioned in the Ḳurʾān in a speech of Noah: "They have said: Forsake not your gods. Forsake not Wadd, nor Suwāʿ, nor Yaghūth, Yaʿūḳ and Nasr!" (LXXI, 22/23).

Traditionists and commentators have exercised their ingenuity in the pursuit of the identity of Wadd, but their quest has not been very productive. In his "Book of the Idols" (*Kitāb al-Aṣnām*, §§ 7c, 9d, 45e, 49c-51b), Ibn al-Kalbī (d. 204/819 or 206/821) considers that Wadd was a divinity of the tribe of Kalb at Dūmat al-Djandal, the great oasis of north-western Arabia (on the composition of *Kitāb al-Aṣnām*, see Hawting, *The idea of idolatry*, 88-9).

At first sight, the information supplied by Ibn al-Kalbī regarding this god is exceptionally precise. He invokes the direct testimony of Mālik b. Ḥāritha al-Adjdārī (collected apparently by his father Muḥammad al-Kalbī, d. 146/763: see § 51b), according to which the statue of the god represented a man of great height, dressed, armed with a sword, a bow and a lance. In his youth, Mālik is said to have been instructed by his father to offer milk to Wadd (§ 49f). The statue was allegedly destroyed by Khālid b. al-Walīd after the expedition of Tabūk (§§ 49f, 50a-d, 51a). The *nisba* al-Adjdārī associates Mālik with the Banu ʿĀmir al-Adjdar, one of the two clans (with the Banū ʿAbd Wadd) that opposed the destruction of the statue (§ 50b).

Ibn al-Kalbī also seeks to explain how it was that mankind, monotheistic at the time of creation, came to worship such a multiplicity of divinities. For his purposes, he supposes that originally Wadd was a devout man; after his death, he was commemorated by a statue, then promoted to the rank of intercessor in the presence of God. It was the Flood which would have brought his idol into Arabia, near Djudda; there it was said to have been found by ʿAmr b. Luḥayy who is supposed to have entrusted it to the tribe of Kalb (§§ 45e-47b).

Ancient Arabian nomenclature recognised two theophoric forms involving Wadd: ʿAbd Wadd (Caskel 1966, ii, 133, nine entries, divided between various tribes of South and North, including one for Kalb), and Wahab Wadd (Abdallah 1975, 76, one instance in the genealogies of Ḥimyar).

The data supplied by Tradition hardly accord with those of pre-Islamic inscriptions. According to the latter, Wadd (*Wd* or *Wd*^{m}), who is an important divinity in southern Arabia, is almost unknown in the rest of Arabia. It is in the kingdom of Maʿīn (capital Ḳarnaw, *Ḳrnw*, today Maʿīn, in the D̲j̲awf of the Yemen) that Wadd occupies the most eminent position: he is one of the divinities of the official pantheon, always included in invocations. He had a temple at Yat̲h̲ill (*Yt̲l*, today Barāḳis̲h̲) (*M* 244 = *RES* 3019/1) and another in the Minaean colony of Dedan (today al-ʿUlā) in the north of the Ḥidjāz (*M* 356 = *RES* 3695/2). A clan of Yat̲h̲ill (the Banū *Dmr*^{n}) considers itself the "clients of Wadd^{um} S̲h̲ahrān (*ʾdm Wd*^{m} *ᵒhr*^{n}) (*M 222* = *RES* 2999/2). Finally, the permanent river that irrigates the D̲j̲awf bears his name: (*Hr*^{n}) *ǧyl Wd* "(Hirrān), torrent of Wadd" (Maʿīn 1 = *M* 29 = *RES* 2774/6; Maʿīn 13 = *M* 43 = *RES* 2789/5; Shaqab 1/11).

The god Wadd was also venerated at Sabaʾ where, not far from Maʾrib, a small temple was dedicated to him, and in the Sabaean tribes of the environs of Ṣanʿāʾ (Schmidt 1982, 1987; Müller 1982, 1987). In the kingdom of Awsān, based around the Wādī Mark̲h̲a, one of the sovereigns, Yaṣduḳʾil Fariʾ^{um} S̲h̲araḥʿat, son of Maʿaddʾīl Salḥīn (*Yṣdḳʾl Frʿm ᵒrḥʿt bn Mʿdʾl Sʾlḥn*) alleged that the god Wadd was his father; he is the only South Arabian sovereign to have claimed such divine parentage; and the only one to be honoured by statues, like a god, in the Niʿmān (*Nʿm*^{n}) temple which was dedicated to Wadd. This sovereign probably dates from the 1st century A.D., judging by the foreign influences shown by his statue (preserved in the Museum of Aden) and by the script of his inscriptions (*CIAS* F58/s4/49.10 no. 3; 49.10/ol no. 2; Louvre 90).

To protect persons and property, the South Arabians made use of the formula "Wadd is father" (*Wdm ʾb*^{m}, with variants), which is found on amulets (Louvre 186) and on numerous buildings. It is an interesting fact that this apotropaic formula is more widely diffused than the cult of Wadd; it is found in all the regions of southern Arabia and on the Arabian shore of the Arabo-Persian Gulf (Robin 1994, 85).

South Arabian nomenclature includes a number of theophoric anthroponyms composed with Wadd: these are most notably *ʾgrwd, Bnwd, Hwfwd, Mrʾtwd, Nʿmwd, ᵒrḥwd, Whbwd, Wdʾb, Wdʾl* or *Ẓydwd*.

The god Wadd is not attested in Nabataean inscriptions, not even in nomenclature. In Safaitic, anthroponyms such as *Wdʾl* do not necessarily imply the existence of a god name Wadd, since the radical *wd* can have the sense of "love, affection". At Dedan, finally, the god Wadd seems to be known, according to JS lih. 49/1-9: "ʿAbdwadd priest of Wadd and his sons Salām and Zēdwadd have dedicated . . . to d̲h̲u-G̲h̲abāt . . ." (*ʿbdwd ʾfkl Wd w-bn-h Slm w-Ẓdwd hwdqw . . . l-d̲-Ġbt . . .*)—with two theophoric forms with Wadd and the title "priest of Wadd". It may be noted, however, that except for this text, Wadd is almost unknown (see the theophoric *bnwd* in AH 11 and possibly 1); one may therefore wonder if the author of JS 49 did not come from the Yemen.

Inscriptions do not confirm the opinion of His̲h̲ām Ibn al-Kalbī, who sites the cult of Wadd at Dūmat al-D̲j̲andal: mentioned there are *Lh, Dṯn, Rḍw, ʿtrsm* and *Nhy* [see THAMUDIC], but not this god. This is not enough to lead to the conclusion that Ibn al-Kalbī made a mistake, or relayed a tendentious tradition, but a degree of doubt is permissible. Furthermore it is not impossible that the idol of Dūmat al-D̲j̲andal may have borne a name resembling Wadd and that the traditionists were confused. Conversely, the god Wadd enjoyed great popularity in Yemen, a fact totally ignored by Tradition. This would seem to prove that Ibn al-Kalbī was ill-informed and that his principal source was indeed the Ḳurʾānic text.

Bibliography: 1. Texts and studies. Maria Hofner, *Die Stammesgruppen Nord- und Zentralarabiens im vorislamischer Zeit*, in H.W. Haussig (ed.), *Götter und Mythen im Vorderen Orient* (Wörterbuch der Mythologie, 1. Abt., *Die alten Kulturvölker*, Bd. 1), Stuttgart 1965, 407-81 ("Wadd", 476-7); W. Caskel, *Ǧamharat an-nasab. Das genealogische Werk des Hišām ibn Muḥammad al-Kalbī*, 2 vols., Leiden 1966; His̲h̲ām Ibn al-Kalbī, *Le Livre des idoles de Hicham ibn al-Kalbi*, text ed. and tr. Wahib Atallah, Paris 1969; Yusuf Abdallah, *Die Personennamen in al-Hamdānī's al-Iklīl und ihre Parallelen in den altsüdarabischen Inschriften. Ein Beitrag zur jemenitischen Namengebung*, diss. Tübingen 1975; W. Müller, *Die Inschriften vom Tempel des Waddum Dū-Masmaʿim*, in *Archäologische Berichte aus dem Yemen*, i (1982), 101-6 and pl. 37: J. Schmidt, *Der Tempel des Waddum Dū-Masmaʿim*, in *ibid.*, 91-9 and pls. 35-6; Müller, *Weiterer altsabaische Inschriften vom Tempel des Waddum Dū-Masmaʿim*, in *ibid.*, iv (1987), 185-9 and pls. 33-6; Schmidt, *Der Tempel des Waddum Dū-Masmaʿim*, in *ibid.*, 179-84 and pls. 33-5; C. Robin, *Documents de l'Arabie antique III*, in *Raydan*, vi (1994), 69-90 and pls. 35-46 (179-90); G.R. Hawting, *The idea of idolatry and the emergence of Islam. From polemic to history*, Cambridge 1999.

2. Sigla. RES: *Répertoire d'épigraphie sémitique*, published by the Commission of *Corpus Inscriptionum Semiticarum* (Académie des Inscriptions et Belles-Lettres), Paris 1900-67, i-viii; M: [G. Garbini], *Iscrizioni sudarabiche*, i. *Iscrizioni minee* (Ricerche, X), Naples 1974; CIAS: *Corpus des Inscriptions et des Antiquités Sud-arabes* (Académie des Inscriptions et Belles-Lettres), i, sections 1 and 2, Louvain 1977; ii, fasc. 1 and 2, Louvain 1986; Shaqab: see G. Gnoli, *Shaqab al-Manaṣṣa* (Inventaire des inscriptions sudarabiques, 2), Paris and Rome 1993; JS lih. 49: Jaussen and Savignac, *Mission archéologique en Arabie* (Publications of the Société française des fouilles archéologiques), Paris 1909-22, repr. Institut français d'Archéologie orientale, Cairo 1997, ii, 379-86; Louvre: see Y. Calvet and C. Robin, *Arabie heureuse, Arabie deserte. Les antiquités arabiques du Musée du Louvre* (Notes et documents des Musées de France, 31), Paris 1997; Maʿīn: see F. Bron, *MaʿSʾn* (Inventaire des inscriptions sudarabiques, 3), Paris and Rome 1998; AH 1 and 11: see A. Sima, *Die lihyanischen Inschriften von al-ʿUd̲ayb (Saudi Arabien)* (Epigraphische Forschungen auf der Arabischen Halbinsel, Band 1) Rahden/Westf. 1999, 35, 37.

(CH. ROBIN)

WĀDĪ LAKKU, a river of the Iberian peninsula, on the banks of which the decisive encounter took place between Ṭāriḳ b. Ziyād [*q.v.*], the first Muslim conqueror of the Iberian peninsula, and Roderic, the last Visigothic king, on 28 Ramaḍān 92/19 July 711.

Identification of the toponym is difficult on account of the lack of clarity of the Arabic language sources. On the one hand, all do not give the same variant of the name: Wādī Lakku, or perhaps Wādī Lagu (the hard *g* sound being conventionally represented in mediaeval script by a *kāf*, surmounted by a *s̲h̲adda*, which can be pronounced *kku* or *gu*), Wādī Lakka or Wādī Bakka—while on the other hand they sometimes give a different name to this battle: the battle of Faḥṣ Sharīsh ("plain of Jerez"), al-Sawāḳī ("the canals"), Karḍādjanna (Cartagena), Wādī Umm Ḥakīm, al-Buḥayra ("the lake": Laguna de la Janda?), Wādī 'l-Ṭīn, al-Djazīra, etc. (cf. J. Vallvé, *La Cora de Tudmir*, in *And.*, xxxvii [1972], 146 n. 3), although it is the form of Wādī Lakku, the phonetic origin of the Spanish Guadalete, which appears most often. In the Romance transcriptions of the Arabic name one also encounters Guadalac, Guadalec, Guadalet or Guadalete. The intermingling of geographical and historical sources does not permit precise localisation of the site of the encounter, on account of the lack of clarity and above all the numerous contradictions which characterise these texts.

For example, the geographer al-Zuhrī (6th/12th century) states that the Wādī Lakka is a river forty parasangs in length which descends from the mountains of Tākurūnna to discharge into the Atlantic Ocean (*Djaghrāfiya*, 167). Furthermore he asserts "on the basis of what is said by the Christians in their chronicles", that the inhabitants of Cadix drink the water of a great river called Wādī Lakka, spanned by a bridge of thirty arches (*ibid.*, 218). This river is said to have flowed into the ocean at a place known as Shant Bāṭaru. For al-Rāzī, quoted by al-Maḳḳarī, the battle allegedly took place on the banks of the Wādī Lakka, the river into which the last Visigothic king, Roderic, was supposedly thrown, in armour, to disappear there without trace (Maḳḳarī, *Analectes*, i, 162). Ibn ʿIdhārī also quotes al-Rāzī (*Bayān*, ii, 10). In the 6th/12th century, al-Idrīsī refers in his geography to the locality of Bakka, a possible variant of Lakka, in the district, or *iḳlīm*, of al-Buḥayra, a stretch of water identified by R. Dozy as being the Laguna de la Janda (al-Idrīsī, *Description*, 174, tr. 208). According to the notice which al-Ḥimyarī devotes to this locality, at the start of the 8th/14th century (*Rawḍ al-miʿṭar*, no. 159), Lakku, the ruins of which were said to have survived until his time, was an ancient city boasting "one of the best thermal springs in al-Andalus". It was on the banks of the river flowing through the city that the encounter took place between the Christians (*ʿadjam*) of Roderic and the Muslim contingents of Ṭāriḳ b. Ziyād. This locality of Lakku would correspond to Bolonia, the ancient Baelo, and the Wādī Lakku to Guadalete or to Rio Barbate. The author states (no. 186) that the encounter between Ṭāriḳ b. Ziyād, the freedman of Ibn Nuṣayr, with Roderic, sovereign of al-Andalus and last king of the Goths, allegedly took place on the Wādī Lakku, in the territory of Algeciras, on the southern coast of al-Andalus.

This is why the exact placing of the encounter between Ṭāriḳ and Roderic remains uncertain, and why historians, starting with Gayangos, Dozy, Lafuente Alcántara, Simoney and Saavedra in the 19th century, have discussed at length its precise location. For some, like Dozy and Lévi-Provençal, Wādī Lakku denoted the Laguna de la Janda, source of the Rio Barbate; for others, the place in question was the banks of the Guadalete, between Medina Sidonia, Arcos and Jerez de la Frontera, in the territory of Cadix. Others tend towards the Rio Salado, a small coastal river which has its estuary close to the village of Conil.

Whatever the precise location, the majority of mediaeval Muslim sources concur in situating this battle on the banks of a watercourse (*wādī, nahr*) of the *kūra* of Shadhūna (Medina Sidonia). In Radjab 92/May 711, on the orders of his master, the Umayyad governor of Ifrīḳiya, Mūsā b. Nuṣayr, Ṭāriḳ is said to have embarked with 7,000 Berbers (Matghāra, Madyūna, Miknāsa and Nawāra) and a few Arabs (ranging between a dozen and several hundreds, according to the sources). Arriving at the foot of Mount Calpe (the future Djabal Ṭāriḳ, Gibraltar), Ṭāriḳ repulsed Theodemir, the Visigothic governor of the region, who appealed to his king, Roderic (710-11), occupied in the north of the Iberian peninsula in suppressing an uprising. The latter made haste towards Cordova. Learning of the arrival of the Visigothic troops, Ṭāriḳ called for reinforcements from Mūsā, who sent him an extra 5,000 Berber soldiers. The total strength of his army thus rose to 12,000 fighters, most of them foot-soldiers, not counting certain partisans of Akhila, the dispossessed son of Witiza, the preceding Visigothic king (700-10). Ṭāriḳ decided to halt in the region of Algeciras and there to await the Visigothic army on the banks of the Rio Barbate, Guadalete, Salado or the Laguna de la Janda.

Although superior in numbers (the sources speak of between 40,000 and 100,000 Christians), Roderic's troops, confident of victory, were defeated. According to some authors, both wings of the Visigothic army were commanded by partisans, or actual brothers of Akhila, and at the start of the engagement, they changed sides. Roderic, in the centre, resisted, but was ultimately forced to retreat, and his troops were cut to pieces by the Muslims. According to al-Rāzī, quoted by Ibn ʿIdhārī (*Bayān*, ii, 10, tr. 13) and by al-Maḳḳarī (*Analectes*, i, 163) the battle lasted a whole week, from 28 Ramaḍān to 5 Shawwāl 92/19 to 26 July 711. Captives of all social conditions were taken: nobles, plebeians and slaves, recognisable respectively by their gold, silver and leather rings (al-Ḥimyarī, *Rawḍ al-miʿṭār*, 204). According to certain sources, Roderic lost his life in the battle and Ṭāriḳ sent his head to Mūsā b. Nuṣayr; according to others, he succeeded in escaping. The victory for Muslim arms opened the gates of the Iberian peninsula.

Bibliography: *Akhbār madjmūʿa*, ed. Lafuente y Alcántara, Madrid 1867, ²1984, 9-10 (*al-Buḥayra*); Elias Teres, *Materiales para el studio de la toponimia hispanoárabe. Nómina fluvial*, i, Madrid 1986, 346-59; Maḳḳārī, *Analectes*, i, 156ff., and *Nafḥ al-ṭīb*, ed. M.K. Ṭawīl and Y.ʿA. Ṭawīl, Beirut 1995, i, 219-23, 231, 239, 240-2, 257-9; *Fatḥ al-Andalus*, ed. J. de González, 6-7, tr. 7; Ibn al-Abbār, *Ḥullat al-siyarā'*, ii, 332-4 (*nahr Lakku*); Ibn al-Shabbāṭ, *Ta'rīkh al-Andalus*, 29, 48, 145; Ibn Ghālib, *Furḥat al-anfus*, 25; Ibn Hudhayl, *Tuḥfat al-anfus*, 81-2; Ibn al-Khaṭīb, *Iḥāṭa*, ed. ʿInān, i, 106; Ibn Khallikān, *Wafayāt*, v, 321-2. (P. Buresi)

WAHM.

2. In mysticism.

In the doctrinal texts of Muslim mysticism, the term *wahm* can appear with either the general sense of "illusory, uncertain personal conjecture" or the more precise sense of "estimative faculty" acquired through the intermediary of Hellenistic philosophy and medicine. However, in the context of the description of spiritual progress, it takes on specific connotations: it denotes a natural faculty of comprehension capable of giving sense only to sensible phenomena, inclined towards anthropomorphism (*tashbīh*) in religious matters and unsuited to the perception of the divine: "Imagination (*wahm*) is a cloud of dust between intelligence (*ʿaḳl*) and profound comprehension (*fahm*). It relates neither to intelligence, of which it is not an attribute, nor to comprehension, nothing in which corresponds to any of its attributes (. . .). It resembles the drowsiness between deep sleep and waking, which is being neither asleep nor awake. Waking, it is the transition between intelligence and comprehension, and comprehension and intelligence, without there being any fog of obscurity between the two" (Ibrāhīm al-Khawwāṣ, quoted by al-Sarrādj, *K. al-Lumaʿ*, ed. A.H. Maḥmūd and T.ʿA.B. Surūr, Cairo 1960, 298; and R. Gramlich, *Schlaglichter über das Sufitum*, Stuttgart 1990, 345). It is in this sense that al-Ḥallādj declares in a celebrated poem: "No estimation (*wahm*) could relate to the subject of You, in such a way that in imagination it could be decided where You are!" (*K. al-Tawāsīn*, ed. P. Nwyia, v, 11-12). And subsequently, evoking the spiritual *miʿrādj*, he writes: "Overturn your discourse, abandon conjectures (*al-awhām*), pick up your feet behind and before!" (*ibid.*, v, 21).

While imagination is a natural faculty, sometimes useful for meditation (see al-Muḥāsibī, *K. al-Tawahhum*), it needs to be mastered and left behind. More profoundly still, illusion, the fundamental *wahm*, consists from the Ṣūfī point of view in believing that existence and, *a fortiori*, human activities, exist independently of God, outside Him. Men assume an illusory existence (*wudjūd wahmī*), when this is entirely dependent on pure divine existence (*wudjūd ḥaḳīḳī*). Spiritual exercises, as well as the use of discursive reasoning, amount here to means of waking up and of being freed from this illusion. The most expansive treatment of the functions of imagination is to be found in the works of Ibn al-ʿArabī [*q.v.*]. Although he sometimes employs the terms *wahm* and *khayāl* as synonyms, he propounds a doctrine of precise human imagination where *wahm* regains the connotations mentioned above (for example, *al-Futūḥāt al-makkiyya*, Cairo 1911, iii, 364-5). Basically, he disassociates imagination deriving from simple individual mental representation from that which links the spirit of the person to the superior worlds. Only this second imaginative faculty constitutes a genuine way of knowledge and can become the setting for an authentic theophanic experience (see H. Corbin, *L'imagination créatrice dans le soufisme d'Ibn ʿArabī*, Paris 1958, Eng. tr. R. Mannheim, *Creative imagination in the Sufism of Ibn ʿArabī*, Princeton 1969; W.C. Chittick, *The Sufi path of knowledge: Ibn al-ʿArabi's metaphysics of imagination*, Albany 1989).

Bibliography: Given in the article.

(P. Lory)

WAḲF.

II. In the Arab Lands

2. In Syria.

A survey of the history of endowments in Syria, in the geographical sense of Bilād al-Shām [see al-shām], has to take into account a broad range of changing and often localised rules and practices. This article will focus primarily on Syria's main urban centres, Damascus [see dimashḳ], Jerusalem [see al-ḳuds] and Aleppo [see ḥalab], and occasionally refer to smaller cities.

In general, endowments in Syria have not solicited as much scholarly attention as those in Egypt, particularly before the Ottoman period. To a certain extent, this is due to the fact that access to sources and documentation is less centralised than in Cairo and not always facilitated by adequate research instruments. Large collections of *waḳf*-related documents are housed in the National Archives and other institutions in Syria, Lebanon, Jordan, Israel and the Palestinian territories. The putatively rich archives of the Waḳf Ministries are not easily accessible for researchers. Important holdings concerning Syrian endowments can be found in Istanbul, Ankara, Cairo and various archives, libraries and collections in Europe and the United States as well.

If archival holdings are particularly rich for the Ottoman period owing to series of local court registers [see sidjill.3 and 4], they tend to become comparatively thin for earlier periods. A notable exception are the documents from the Mamlūk period found in the Ḥaram of Jerusalem [see al-ḥaram al-sharīf] (D.P. Little, *A catalogue of the Islamic documents from al-Ḥaram al-Sharīf in Jerusalem*, Beirut 1984). Otherwise, researchers have to rely on legal literature (especially *waḳf* treatises and *fatāwā*), *ḥadīth* collections and the different genres of historical writing (chronicles, biographical dictionaries, travelogues, topographies, *faḍāʾil*). Much can be learned from archaeological findings, inscriptions in particular (*Matériaux pour un Corpus Inscriptionum Arabicarum [CIA]*, Cairo 1903-56; *RCEA*, ed. E. Combe, J. Sauvaget, G. Wiet, Cairo 1931-2; H. Gaube, *Arabische Inschriften aus Syrien*, Beirut 1978).

i. *Umayyads and ʿAbbāsids*

Only in the 3rd/9th century did various forms of charitable giving (*ṣadaḳa* [*q.v.*]) and of immobilisation of property (*ḥabs* in a strict sense) crystallise into the legal institution that is known thereafter, synonymously, as *waḳf* or *ḥabs* [see waḳf. I. In Classical Islamic Law, at Vol. XI, 59b]. It is often difficult to put the earliest traces of charitable practices under Islamic rule in their proper context. It is therefore impossible to determine the exact nature of the acts that are known as the earliest endowments in Syria. A freedman of the Prophet named Abū ʿAbd Allāh Thawbān b. Yuḥdad (d. 54/673-4) is said to have given away his house in Ḥims [*q.v.*] as *ṣadaḳa* (Ibn Ḳutayba, *K. al-Maʿārif*, 72; al-Ṭabarī, i, 1178; Gil, *Early endowments*, 129). An incomplete inscription found in the perimeter of the Dome of the Rock in Jerusalem, dated around 290/902-3, mentions a house inalienable for eternity designated for an unknown purpose (*al-dār . . . muḥabbasa abad^{an} ʿalā*) (*CIA Jérusalem. II*, no. 218). Two *waḳf* inscriptions from Ramla, dated around 300/912-13, however, show that by this time the legal terminology had been fully developed and that endowing followed established procedures, including the deposition of the *kitāb al-waḳf* in front of a *ḳāḍī* (Sharon). Yet even legendary early acts of piety could be transformed into real endowments that endured for centuries. A pertinent example is the endowment for Tamīm al-Dārī [*q.v.*] in Hebron [see *EI*[1], art. *al-Khalīl*] which allegedly had been given to him by the Prophet himself. Later, it was sanctioned several times by different authorities, among them the British mandatory administration of Palestine in the 1920s (Massignon).

Hebron was of special significance to early Muslims because of its close connection with the prophet Ibrāhīm [*q.v.*]. Palestine and the rest of Syria possessed a considerable number of such holy places which attracted pious and charitable donations from early on (see e.g. the *waḳf* inscription dated 400/1009-10 for the *mashhad* of the prophet Lūṭ in Banī Nāʿīm near Hebron, *Répertoire*, no. 2148). For Muslims, the most eminent of these places was Jerusalem, ceding in sanctity only to Mecca (Makka [*q.v.*]) and Medina [see al-madīna], but it was seen as a spiritual centre by other religious communities as well. In early Islamic legal thinking, the devotional practices of Christians and Jews were obviously points of discussion, but they were eventually declared permissible (al-Khaṣṣāf, *Aḥkām al-awḳāf*, Cairo 1904, 341), and donations reached Jerusalem even from Christian Europe (Gil, *Donations*).

Little is known about endowments in Syria of the Umayyad period. Some of the most prestigious religious buildings of early Islam were built there, financed by funds from the Muslim treasury [see BAYT AL-MĀL]. In Jerusalem, the Dome of the Rock was completed in 72/691-2 and the al-Aḳṣā Mosque in the reign of al-Walīd b. 'Abd al-Malik (86-96/705-15 [q.v.]) [see AL-ḲUDS. B. Monuments]. This caliph also ordered the construction of the Umayyad Mosque in Damascus in 86/705, approximately at the same time as the Great Mosque of Aleppo was built.

Founding a mosque (masdjid [q.v.]) was one of the few uncontested early forms of waḳf. Opening a building for the prayers of the Muslim community made it the property of God (al-Khaṣṣāf, op. cit., 113). Yet evidently not all mosques were endowed with assets that secured their upkeep and provided for the needs of the community, as this was carefully noted in the listings of mosques in early topographical writing (e.g. Ibn 'Asākir; Ibn Shaddād; Ibn al-Shihna; Mudjīr al-Dīn).

When the 'Abbāsids removed their capital to 'Irāḳ, the Syrian regions lost much of their importance. The following centuries were characterised by warfare, insecurity and changing ruling dynasties [see ṬŪLŪNIDS; IKHSHĪDIDS; ḤAMDĀNIDS; MARWĀNIDS; ARṬUKIDS]. The north was temporarily reoccupied by Byzantine troops, and Jerusalem and Damascus came under the domination of the Ismā'īlī Fāṭimids [q.v.] of Cairo. According to the legal treatises which have to be situated in the 'Irāḳī context, various types of waḳf must have existed in this period. And even though a special agency, the dīwān al-birr [see DĪWĀN], was established in Baghdād in the early 4th/10th century to supervise pious endowments and charity (wuḳūf and ṣadaḳāt) (Miskawayh, i, 151-2, 257), nothing is known about a similar institution in Syria.

ii. Fāṭimids and Saldjūḳids

Only in the first half of the 5th/11th century when, under a precarious balance of power between Fāṭimids [q.v.], Buwayhids [q.v.] and the Byzantine empire, commerce resumed, are there some examples of commercial gains being invested in endowments, not surprisingly destined for defence purposes: The historian al-Fāriḳī mentions the case of a cloth merchant in Mayyāfāriḳīn [q.v.], north of Aleppo, who bought a village and endowed it to secure the upkeep of three forts (Bianquis, 606).

Helping the war effort against enemies of Islam (fī sabīl Allāh) was by this time a time-honoured waḳf type. Such endowments belonged to the category designated for the Muslim community as a whole or groups of an undetermined number of people being in need of charity that are supposed to exist continually till the end of time (waḳf 'āmm). Thus the ultimate recipients of all charity are the poor and destitute (al-fuḳarā' wa 'l-masākīn) as prescribed in Ḳur'ān IX, 60 and LI, 19. The other category included endowments for descendants, other family members, clients, liberated slaves or other named persons, i.e. endowments for a limited number of people (waḳf khāṣṣ) who would eventually die out and thus allow the waḳf to reach its ultimate stage as everlasting charity (al-Khaṣṣāf, op. cit., 135-7; al-Māwardī, K. Aḥkām al-sulṭāniyya, Bonn 1853, 118, 139-40; al-Ṭarābulsī, K. al-Is'āf fī aḥkām al-awḳāf, Cairo 1902, 28-9). The second type—a sub-category of which was later known as the family waḳf (waḳf ahlī or dhurrī)—was rather popular if we count the cases discussed in the extant legal literature. One of the earliest documented examples in Syria belonged to a group of ashrāf [q.v.] in

Fāṭimid Damascus. In 435/1043 several descendants of the endower fought over their allotted shares, which resulted in a document that also presented a list of the waḳf's assets (Sourdel-Thomine and Sourdel) [see WAḴF. II. 3. ii, at Vol. XI, 70a, for a discussion of family endowments in North Africa]. Compared with al-Maḳrīzī's statement that in early Egyptian endowments urban properties prevailed over agricultural lands, it is of interest to note that in this case the assets consisted of six agricultural domains (ḍay'a). They were situated in the grain-growing regions around Damascus, the Ḥawrān [q.v.], in the plains at the foot of Hermon, and the Biḳā' [q.v.] valley near Ba'labakk [q.v.]. The distribution of assets within a rather limited geographical region proved rather typical for Syrian endowments in the centuries to come. There were, however, always notable exceptions to this rule: endowments spanning great distances between faraway regions, in particular for the benefit of the Ḥaramayn [q.v.] and in Mamlūk and Ottoman times.

The waḳf was not only a means to gain rewards in the afterlife for the sake of one's soul [thawāb] or to secure the material well-being of one's descendants. In the hands of various élite groups it became an eminent instrument for the propagation of status, wealth and power. Charitable giving, aiming at otherworldly rewards, was no longer done preferably in secret, but led to open displays of worldly riches and splendour (Korn). At the same time, new forms of burying and remembering the dead appeared. Funerary art and architecture [see ḲABR] became more elaborate, and saintly persons or the rich and powerful were frequently buried in mausolea [see ḲUBBA; TURBA] and other buildings of public character. We still do not fully comprehend these complex phenomena, but endowments clearly played a significant role in them, resulting in the "constructions of power and piety" (Tabbaa) that give Syrian cityscapes their distinct character till today.

Thus the building type of the mosque, which had been used simultaneously as place of worship, for learning and for sheltering the needy, was complemented by a number of new institutions with more specific purposes. The separation between places of prayer and places of learning had far-reaching implications not only for urban and architectural history. The new urban complexes which were generally financed by endowments had a profound impact on the social, economic, intellectual and educational life of the cities (Makdisi; Pouzet; Chamberlain). Waḳf stipulations now provided for the regular payment of fixed sums to a growing number of people who worked in and for the foundations. Salaried posts were established for professors and assistant professors, but also for the administration and the physical upkeep of the institutions. Endowments financed the professional reading of the Ḳur'ān which became more widespread and organised at this time (Pouzet, 169).

This feature decisively altered the notion of poverty that was at the core of the concept of waḳf (Sabra). The early legal texts had maintained that a recipient of waḳf income had preferably to be poor in a material sense, excluding groups like the blind or those who were in charge of calling for prayer (mu'adhdhin [see ADHĀN]) in a mosque as lawful beneficiaries, because they presumably included poor and rich people (al-Khaṣṣāf, op. cit., 276). Yet this criterion evidently no longer applied, and to receive such payments became a sign of group affiliation or social distinction. Thus the waḳf could be used as a prop for the formation and reproduction of social groups, as e.g.

the *as͟hrāf*, Ṣūfī brotherhoods [see ṬARĪḲA; ZĀWIYA], professional guilds [see ṢINF] or diaspora communities.

The first of the new institutions, the *k͟hānḳāh* [*q.v.*], was introduced from the Persian world to look after the needs of travelling Ṣūfīs. Some of the earliest examples in Syria were founded in Damascus. The best known goes back to the famous Ṣūfī, historian and astronomer, Abu 'l-Ḳāsim ʿAlī b. Muḥammad al-Sulamī al-Sumaysāṭī (d. 453/1061) (al-Nuʿaymī, ii, 118-26; Bianquis, 634; Elisséeff, *Nūr al-Dīn*, iii, 767). Passing through Damascus in 580/1184, Ibn D̲j̲ubayr [*q.v.*] saw the *k͟hānḳāh* still working as stipulated and remarked that it was a beautiful way to remember the departed and his good works (*Riḥla*, ed. M.J. de Goeje, Leiden 1907, 290).

During the second half of the 5th/11th century the advance of the Sald̲j̲ūḳids [*q.v.*] led to hostilities with the Fāṭimids. Contemporaries saw the *umma* [*q.v.*] even more threatened when, at the end of the century, the armies of the Crusaders [see CRUSADES] occupied considerable tracts of Syria, among them Jerusalem in 492/1099. In this period, the *madrasa* was introduced into the Syrian cities, an institution specialising in the teaching of Sunnī jurisprudence and law. Endowing a *madrasa* was often part of a larger building programme. The Sald̲j̲ūḳ ruler Duḳāḳ and his mother, for instance, founded after 491/1097-8 the first *bīmāristān* [*q.v.*] of Damascus, a *madrasa* for the Ḥanafiyya and a *k͟hanḳāh* which also became their own tomb. Women of the ruling dynasties start to figure prominently among the endowers in this period (Tabbaa, 46).

iii. *Zangids and Ayyūbids*

The political and spiritual significance of endowments becomes more pronounced when, after 541/1146, Nūr al-Dīn Maḥmūd b. Zankī [*q.v.*] came to control the parts of Syria that were not under the domination of the Crusaders. Particularly after 558/1162-3, the Zangid ruler adopted a public image of strict religiosity following the model of the Prophet. As part of this policy, he ordered religious and other buildings serving the Muslim community all over Syria to be restored, and he assured their functioning by supplementing their endowments. Among his most important new foundations are the famous *bīmāristān* in Damascus, as well as his tomb *madrasa* and the first *dār al-ḥadīt͟h* [*q.v.*] in Islamic history, and in Aleppo, another *bīmāristān* and several colleges of law (for a list, see Elisséeff, *op. cit.*, iii, 913-35).

Only for this period do the historical sources mention a state official in charge of the *wakf* system for Syria. The supervision of endowments (*naẓar al-awḳāf*) was among the functions attributed to the *ḳāḍī 'l-ḳuḍāt* [*q.v.*] of Damascus, the Ḥanafī Kamāl al-Dīn Abu 'l-Faḍl Muḥammad b. ʿAbd Allāh al-S͟hahrazūrī (d. 572/1176-7) (Pouzet, 29). The way in which he exercised his prerogatives was the reason for a legal debate which allows interesting insights into contemporary legal thinking on *wakf*. To finance defence measures, the *ḳāḍī* had been authorised to use the surplus income (*faḍl*) of endowments which occurred after the stipulated purposes had been paid for (Abū S͟hāma, i, 11). The debate is related by Abū S͟hāma [*q.v.*] as having taken place in the Citadel of Damascus in 554/1159: Nūr al-Dīn convened several experts of the S͟hāfiʿī, Ḥanbalī and Mālikī schools of law. He wanted to know which of the Umayyad mosque's assets were part of its *wakf* and which were merely additions (*muḍāf*) belonging to the treasury (*op. cit.*, i, 17). The distinction was significant, because it allowed the diversion of income of the mosque for other purposes. The second question aimed specifically at the surplus income of endowments. Asked whether it was permissible to spend such funds for the defence of the *umma*, the S͟hāfiʿī *ḳāḍī* Ibn Abī ʿAṣrūn forcefully denied it and maintained that the ruler should borrow the needed sums in the name of the treasury. *Wakf* income could only be spent for the designated beneficiaries (*op. cit.*, i, 18). It is, however, manifest in Abū S͟hāma's account that not all jurists held the same opinion, and later on even the S͟hāfiʿiyya adopted the opposite position. These discussions highlight the tensions resulting from the overlapping political and social fields of *wakf*, *bayt al-māl*, personal income of the ruler [see K͟HĀṢṢ], and claims in the name of the general good [see MAṢLAḤA].

The impact of the Crusades is even more apparent under the Ayyūbids [*q.v.*]. After the reconquest of Jerusalem, Ṣalāḥ al-Dīn pursued his policy of propagating a strict Sunnī Islam, already adopted in Fāṭimid Cairo, in order to turn it into a truly Muslim city. Endowing was an important part of this programme to repossess the properties of Frankish institutions. In 585/1189, Ṣalāḥ al-Dīn established in the former residence of the Latin patriarch a hospice for Ṣūfīs, which was named after him *al-Ṣalāḥiyya*. The deed of this foundation is the earliest extant example of a complete *wakfiyya* for Syria (ʿAsalī, i, 83-100). In the case of his *madrasa*, the foundation deed of 588/1192 explicitly stated that the sultan had officially purchased the properties which formerly had belonged to two Latin churches from the *bayt al-māl* (Frenkel, *Political and social aspects*; Pahlitzsch).

The return to Muslim rule affected also the status of agricultural land that had been occupied by non-Muslims. In analogy with early Islamic history, several and often contradicting solutions could be drawn from the explanations of the different schools of law. In practice, some of these lands were left with those in possession of them. Others were given out as grants [see IḲṬĀʿ] (Frenkel, *Impact*, 239-47). Many of these were later incorporated into a growing number of endowments founded by members of the ruling dynasty, its military and administrative functionaries and increasingly also by *ʿulamāʾ* (Humphreys; Tabbaa). A considerable portion of these foundations can be attributed to women. The proliferation of public buildings which resulted from these endowment activities can be traced into the smaller cities and settlements of the region.

iv. *Mamlūks*

Many features of these *wakf* policies continued under the Mamlūks [*q.v.*], who after their victory over the Mongols [*q.v.*] in ʿAyn D̲j̲ālūt [*q.v.*] in 658/1260 and numerous campaigns against the Franks, came to dominate the whole of Syria. The military triumph of the Muslim forces was followed by an extensive building programme which aimed at propagating the Islamic character of the new rulers. Hence special reverence was shown for the "Sanctuaries" [see AL-ḤARAMAYN AL-S͟HARĪFAYN], which was used to refer not only to Mecca and Medina but also to Jerusalem and Hebron. Sultan al-Ẓāhir Baybars I [*q.v.*] is attributed with a considerable number of endowments in these cities and other places of religious interest, and many of his successors followed his example (Meinecke).

The centre of Mamlūk endowment activities was undisputedly Cairo, but in the Syrian cities, mostly in ruins after the destructions caused by the Crusades and the Mongol invasion, building and restoring also resumed on a large scale. Tripoli [see ṬARĀBULUS AL-S͟HĀM] was rebuilt in a new location (Luz). Aleppo was slow in regaining its former glory, but new urban quarters developed in the north and north-east (Sauvaget; Gaube-Wirth). Damascus witnessed a period of considerable growth, illustrated by the endowment of several new Friday mosques outside the old city walls (Meinecke). These building activities came to an abrupt halt in 803/1400-1 when the army of Tīmūr Lang [q.v.] invaded Syria. For Damascus, the extent of the destruction can be gleaned from a document which enumerates the assets of the Umayyad Mosque and describes their actual state (to be published by S. Atāsī and B. ʿUlabī, IFPO, Damascus).

Although the written documentation becomes denser for this period, what we know about endowing is still very much an élite phenomenon. This is evident in the appearance of a novel waḳf type: At first sight it appears as a typical charitable endowment (waḳf khayrī), yet founders began to stipulate that any surplus (faḍl) from the waḳf's income was not to be reinvested, but was destined for themselves and their descendants (Amīn, Awḳāf, 73-8). It was still customary to endow new mosques and other institutions with rather small incomes (Mudjīr al-Dīn; al-Nuʿaymī; al-Ghazzī), but some foundations started to produce much higher revenues than warranted by their specified purposes. Such arrangements allowed founders and, after them, their descendants, as administrators and beneficiaries, to pursue their own interests, protected from interference and confiscation by the state by the sanctity of the waḳf (Petry).

Administrators of such endowments were often accused of embezzling funds belonging to all the Muslims. Such accusations were all the more difficult to refute, as endowments increasingly were made of land that previously had belonged to the treasury and had been given out as military or administrative grants [see IḲṬĀʿ]. This practice, known as irṣād or in Ottoman times as waḳf ghayr ṣaḥīḥ (see al-Ṭarābulsī, op. cit., 20; Cuno), was not acknowledged as a sound waḳf by the jurists. In legal theory, it was only allowed for the purposes specified for the bayt al-māl. Stipulations could be altered by later rulers.

The Mamlūk administration tried to control this complex waḳf system [see WAḲF. II. 1. In Egypt, at Vol. XI, 63b] by putting it under the supervision of local governmental agencies: In Damascus, the second capital of the realm, the naẓar al-awḳāf belonged within the duties of the Shāfiʿī ḳāḍī al-ḳuḍāt. This official was also charged with the supervision of the awḳāf of the Umayyad Mosque, whereas the al-Nūrī bīmāristān was put under the responsibility of the governor. Similar arrangements can be found in other Syrian towns (al-Ḳalḳashandī, Ṣubḥ, Cairo 1914-28, iv, 191-2, 220-1).

By the end of the Mamlūk period, the waḳf as an institution built on the initiative of individuals had taken over many functions that the treasury had fulfilled in earlier times. This is evident for instance in the dīwān al-asrā, responsible for the liberation of Muslim war prisoners: it was now financed by endowments, but stayed under the supervision of an appointed agent of the state (op. cit., iv, 191). Ibn Baṭṭūṭa who travelled from Cairo to Damascus in 726/1326, was struck by the "varieties of the endowments of Damascus and their expenditure . . ., so numerous are they. There are endowments in aid of persons who cannot undertake the Pilgrimage. . . . There are endowments for supplying wedding outfits to girls, to those namely whose families are unable to provide them. There are endowments for the freeing of prisoners, and endowments for travellers, out of which they are given food, clothing, and the

expenses of conveyance to their countries. There are endowments for the improvement and paving of the streets. . . . Besides these there are endowments for other charitable purposes." And he went on to relate a story how an endowment "for utensils" (ālāt) helped a slave to replace a broken porcelain dish (Ibn Baṭṭūṭa, tr. Gibb, i, 148-9).

v. *Ottomans*

The Ottoman conquest of Bilād al-Shām in 922/1516-17 did not radically change the waḳf regime [see WAḲF. IV. In the Ottoman Empire, at Vol. XI, 87b]. To establish a secure hold on the tax income of the new provinces which stemmed mainly from agricultural revenues, the Ottoman administration began early on to survey all rights concerning land or access to its produce. These tax registers (taḥrīr [q.v.], later called the daftar al-khāḳānī [q.v.] or al-sulṭānī) are a valuable source for Mamlūk and Ottoman waḳf history, because they allow insights into number, types, composition and lifespan of endowments.

According to the Ottoman provincial regulations (ḳānūn [q.v.]), waḳf properties were subject to an imposition, in many cases, one-tenth of their share (ʿushr māl al-waḳf) (Venzke). Only the waḳf al-Ḥaramayn al-sharīfayn, those for Jerusalem and Hebron, and the great imperial endowments, were tax-exempt. Studies of the tax régime tend to focus on the early period of Ottoman rule in Syria. Yet endowments continued as part of rural life and were involved in the conflicts over resources between the different social groups trying to control them. Many court cases and fatāwā refer to the necessity of defending the interests of endowments against iḳṭāʿ-holders and tax-farmers [see ILTIZĀM; MÜLTEZIM] (Johansen).

The importance of land is highlighted by the issue of the appropriation of state lands [see MĪRĪ]. Especially during the first century of Ottoman rule in Syria, highly-placed Ottoman officials included in their endowments large tracts of land, in different regions or even provinces (e.g. the endowments of Lālā Muṣṭafā Pasha and his wife Fāṭima Khātūn). In fact, most of these foundations are formally genuine awḳāf because a deed of possession (tamlīk) from the sultan authorised such transfers. Later on, endowing agricultural land became less frequent, with the exception of privately-owned gardens and orchards. Even in the case of prominent officials and notables, only the rights of cultivation (mashadd maska) and the plantations standing on the land were endowed. Agricultural revenues were appropriated by more indirect means like long-term rents and sublease contracts (Rāfiḳ).

Ottoman endowment practice is more visible in the urban context. Like other rulers before them, the Ottoman sultans showed a marked interest in the Ḥaramayn of Jerusalem and Hebron. At the same time, they and members of their households founded large urban complexes in other towns, which added a distinctly Ottoman element to their cityscapes. The most outstanding examples in Damascus are the endowment of sultan Selīm I [q.v.] around the tomb of Ibn al-ʿArabī [q.v.] in al-Ṣāliḥiyya [q.v.], or the takiyya [q.v.] of sultan Süleymān [q.v.]. In Jerusalem, it was the latter's wife, Khurrem Sulṭān [q.v.], who founded the famous Khāṣṣekī Sulṭān complex, including a soup-kitchen [see ʿIMĀRET] (Singer). Numerous foundations of Ottoman officials and local notables helped to develop urban quarters and contributed in some cases to the establishing of new city centres. Yet the waḳf was also used by a growing number of persons of rather modest means, among them a high proportion of women. The majority of these endowments are rather small, consisting of one house or even a part of a house.

It may be stating the obvious to stress that endowing as a social practice was influenced by gender, economic means, social distinction, ethnic and religious affiliations, membership of guilds or Ṣūfī groups, etc. Ongoing research, however, reveals how much there is still to be learned to come to a better understanding of such distinctions. The use of *wakf* by Christian and Jewish communities is an important field of research in this context (Oded). Other approaches stress the significance of localised practices. The cash *wakf*, for instance, was quite widespread in Jerusalem, but in the other parts of Syria its introduction was slow and confined to certain social groups from the administrative and military milieu (Arnāʾūṭ). Local practice also influenced notions of family and the modes by which property was transferred from one generation to the next, as shown in a comparative study of late Ottoman Nābulus [*q.v.*] and Tripoli (Doumani).

Decisive changes in the *wakf* régime of the Syrian provinces occurred under the *Tanẓīmāt* [*q.v.*] reforms. A Wakf Ministry had been gradually established in Istanbul between 1826 and 1838. Under the impact of the reforms, the state forcefully claimed to be the sole legitimate representative of public interests. In this context, the administration introduced new *wakf* classifications along the lines of private and public property. The single steps of the reforms are not altogether clear, but a state agency was introduced into the provincial administrations in the late 1830s which cut back the ancient prerogatives of the *kāḍī*. The new functionaries (*nāẓir [muʿadjdjalāt] al-awkāf* and *mudīr al-awkāf*) were directly paid from Istanbul to prevent the notorious embezzling of funds. Other laws concerning changes in *wakf* administration followed in 1863 and 1870 (Barnes, 103-54; Gerber, 178-98; Meier).

During the 19th century, the *wakf* institution as a whole came under severe criticism, being denounced as an obstacle on the way to progress and modernity. The family *wakf*, in particular, was accused of being a mere circumvention of the inheritance laws of the Kurʾān. These controversies ceased only in the middle of the 20th century, when many of the independent states decided on severe legal restrictions for family endowments or, in the case of Syria, even abolished them completely (see WAKF. II. 5, at Vol. XI, 78b).

Bibliography (in addition to references given in WAKF. IV): 1. Historical writing. Abū Shāma, *K. al-Rawḍatayn fī akhbār al-dawlatayn*, 2 vols., Cairo 1287-8/1870-2; Ibn al-Shihna, *al-Durr al-muntakhab li-taʾrīkh Ḥalab*, ed. Y. Sarkis, Beirut 1909 (tr. J. Sauvaget, *Les perles choisies*, Beirut 1933); Ghazzī, *Nahr al-dhahab fī taʾrīkh Ḥalab*, 3 vols., Aleppo 1922-6; Nuʿaymī, *K. al-Dāris fī taʾrīkh al-madāris*, ed. Djaʿfar al-Ḥasanī, 2 vols. Damascus 1948-51; J. Sourdel (ed.), *La description d'Alep d'Ibn Shaddād*, Damascus 1953; N. Elisséeff (ed.), *La description de Damas d'Ibn ʿAsākir*, Damascus 1959; Mudjīr al-Dīn al-ʿUlaymī, *al-Uns al-djalīl bi-taʾrīkh al-Kuds wa 'l-Khalīl*, Cairo 1866.

2. Publications of *wakf*-related documents (*wakfiyyāt*, etc.). *K. Wakf al-wazīr Lālā Muṣṭafā Pāshā wa-yalīhi K. Wakf Fāṭima Khātūn bt. Muḥammad Beyk b. al-Sulṭān al-Malik al-Ashraf Kānṣūh al-Ghawrī*, ed. Kh. Mardam Beyk, Damascus 1925; *K. Wakf al-kāḍī ʿUthmān b. Asʿad b. al-Munadjdjā*, ed. Ṣ. Munadjdjid, Damascus 1949; L. Massignon, *Documents sur certains waqfs de lieux saints de l'Islam*, in *REI*, xix (1951), 73-120; J. Sourdel-Thomine and D. Sourdel, *Biens fonciers constitués waqf en Syrie fatimide pour une famille de Sharīfs Damascains*, in *JESHO*, xv (1972), 269-96; A. ʿAlamī, *Wakfiyyāt al-maghāriba*, Jerusalem 1981; K.J. ʿAsalī, *Wathāʾik makdisiyya taʾrīkhiyya*, 3 vols. ʿAmmān 1983-9; M. Salati, *Un documento di epoca mameluca sul waqf di ʿIzz al-Dīn Abu 'l-Makārim Ḥamza b. Ẓuhra al-Ḥusaynī al-Isḥāqī al-Ḥalabī (ca. 707/1307)*, in *Annali di Ca'Foscari*, xxv (1994), 97-137; M. Sharon, *A waqf inscription from Ramla c. 300/912-13*, in *BSOAS*, lx (1997), 100-08; H.N. Ḥarithy (ed.), *The waqf document of Sultan al-Nāṣir Ḥasan b. Muḥammad b. Qalāwūn for his complex in al-Rumaila*, Beirut and Berlin 2001 (edited rather carelessly, but of interest because of many references to Syrian topography).

3. *Wakf* studies, urban and general history. J. Sauvaget, *Alep. Essai sur le développement d'une grande ville syrienne, des origines au milieu du XIXe siècle*, Paris 1941; N. Elisséeff, *Nūr al-Dīn. Un grand prince musulman de Syrie au temps des croisades (511-569 H./1118-1174)*, 3 vols. Damascus 1967; M.M. Amīn, *al-Awkāf wa 'l-ḥayāt al-idjtimāʿiyya fī Miṣr 648-923/1250-1517*, Cairo 1980; G. Makdisi, *The rise of colleges. Institutions of learning in Islam and the West*, Edinburgh 1981; M. Gil, *Dhimmī donations and foundations for Jerusalem (638-1099)*, in *JESHO*, xxvii/2 (1984), 156-74; H. Gaube and E. Wirth, *Aleppo. Historische und geographische Beiträge zur baulichen Gestaltung, zur sozialen Organisation und zur wirtschaftlichen Dynamik einer vorderasiatischen Fernhandelsmetropole*, Wiesbaden 1984; H. Gerber, *Ottoman rule in Jerusalem 1890-1914*, Berlin 1985 (ch. on *wakf* reform); J.R. Barnes, *An introduction to religious foundations in the Ottoman Empire*, Leiden 1986; M.L. Venzke, *Special use of the tithe as a revenue-raising measure in the 16th-century sanjaq of Aleppo*, in *JESHO*, xxix (1986), 239-334; T. Bianquis, *Damas et la Syrie sous la domination fatimide (359-468/968-1076). Essai d'interprétation de chroniques arabes médiévales*, 2 vols. Damas 1986-9; M.H. Burgoyne, *Mamluk Jerusalem. An architectural study*, Buckhurst Hill, Essex 1987 (with extensive bibl.); B. Johansen, *The Islamic law on land tax and rent. The peasants' loss of property rights as interpreted in the Hanafite legal literature of the Mamluk and Ottoman periods*, London 1988; R.S. Humphreys, *Politics and architectural patronage in Ayyubid Damascus*, in C.E. Bosworth *et al.* (eds.), *The Islamic world from classical to modern times. Essays in honor of Bernard Lewis*, Princeton 1989, 151-74; L. Pouzet, *Damas au VIIe/XIIIe siècle. Vie et structures religieuses d'une métropole islamique*, ²Beirut 1991; M. Meinecke, *Die mamlukische Architektur in Ägypten und Syrien*, 2 vols. Glückstadt 1992; M. Chamberlain, *Knowledge and social practice in medieval Damascus 1190-1350*, Cambridge 1994; Y. Tabbaa, *Constructions of power and piety in medieval Aleppo*, University Park 1997; ʿA. Rāfiḳ, *al-Arāḍī 'l-zirāʿiyya al-wakfiyya fī bilād al-Shām bayn al-fiʾāt al-idjtimāʿiyya wa 'l-madhāhib al-fikhiyya fī 'l-ʿahd al-ʿuthmānī*, in ʿA. Tamīmī (ed.), *Mélanges Halil Sahillioğlu*, Tunis 1997, i, 169-86; Y. Frenkel, *The impact of the Crusades on the rural society and religious endowments. The case of medieval Syria*, in Y. Lev (ed.), *War and society in the eastern Mediterranean, 7th-15th centuries*, Leiden 1997, 237-48; C.F. Petry, *Fractionalized estates in a centralized regime. The holdings of al-Ashraf Qāytbāy and Qansūh al-Ghawrī according to their waqf deeds*, in *JESHO*, xli/1 (1998), 96-117; B. Doumani, *Endowing family. Waqf, property devolution, and gender in Greater Syria*, in *Comparative Studies in Society and History*, xl/1 (1998), 3-41; K.M.

Cuno, *Ideology and juridical discourse in Ottoman Egypt. The uses of the concept of irṣād*, in *ILS*, vi/2 (1999), 136-63; Frenkel, *Political and social aspects of Islamic religious endowments* (awqāf). *Saladin in Cairo (1169-73) and Jerusalem (1187-93)*, in *BSOAS*, lxii (1999), 1-20; A. Sabra, *Poverty and charity in medieval Islam. Mamluk Egypt, 1250-1517*, Cambridge 2000; M. Arnā'ūṭ, *Studies in cash waqf*, Tunis 2001; L. Korn, *Ayyubidische Bautätigkeit aus der Sicht der Chronisten*, in U. Vermeulen and J. van Steenbergen (eds.), *Egypt and Syria in the Fatimid, Ayyubid and Mamluk eras*, iii, Leuven 2001, 123-39; P. Oded, *Christianity under Islam in Jerusalem. The question of the holy sites in early Ottoman times*, Leiden 2001; N. Luz, *Tripoli reinvented. A case of Mamluk urbanization*, in Y. Lev (ed.), *Towns and material culture in the medieval Middle East*, Leiden 2002, 53-71; A. Meier, *"Waqf only in name, not in essence". Early Tanẓīmāt waqf reforms in the province of Damascus*, in J. Hanssen, Th. Philipp and S. Weber (eds.), *The empire in the city. Arab provincial capitals in the late Ottoman empire*, Beirut 2002, 201-18; A. Singer, *Constructing Ottoman beneficence. An imperial soup kitchen in Jerusalem*, New York 2003; J. Pahlitzsch, *The transformation of Latin religious insititutions into Islamic endowments by Saladin in Jerusalem*, in L. Korn and J. Pahlitzsch (eds.), *Governing the Holy City. The interaction of social groups in medieval Jerusalem*, Wiesbaden, forthcoming. (ASTRID MEIER)

WARD.

In Arabic literature.

The rose is easily the most sung flower in Arabic poetry. Its natural place is in flower, garden and spring poetry (*zahriyyāt, rawḍiyyāt* and *rabīʿiyyāt*), but the rose also figures prominently in the setting of wine poetry (*khamriyyāt*), which is actually the place of origin for flower poems. Abū Nuwās (d. *ca.* 198/813 [*q.v.*]) still keeps the bacchic framework of his flower descriptions, and it may have been ʿAlī b. al-Djahm (d. 249/863 [*q.v.*]) who first wrote pure floral pieces, all of them devoted to the rose (see Schoeler 71-2, 128). Poetic descriptions of it may be individual or part of the description of a garden with a variety of flowers. The vast majority of rose poems deal with the red variety, but the white, yellow, black and blue varities (the last created artificially with the use of indigo) have also attracted some attention (see al-Nuwayrī, *Nihāya*, xi, 193-6).

Gem imagery

The description (*waṣf* [*q.v.*]) of the rose is rarely a simple recreation of the visual impression it presents. The first step to transcend the natural is the use of similes, which introduce a second layer of imagery; the next step is to omit the particle of comparison, thus creating a metaphorical identification. Two "genres" of the phantastic are the outcome of this procedure. One consists in turning the rose into an aggregate of precious materials, mainly gems. The first stage (similes) may be exemplified by the following example, by Muḥammad b. ʿAbd Allāh b. Ṭāhir (d. 237/851 [*q.v.*]):

"Don't you see the rose bushes presenting to us wonderments that have been mounted on branches,
"Their petals are red, their insides are yellow embers, and around them are green boughs.
"It is as if they were rubies framed with emeralds, in the midst of which are chippings of gold."
(al-Sarī al-Raffāʾ, *Muḥibb*, iii, 89 [no. 147]).

The analogues of the simile in the third line form a parallel to the topics in the second line, so this is a very cautious introduction of the precious materials as a new sphere of imagery.

The next step (metaphorical equation) may be seen in the following example (of multiple attribution):

"Don't you see the roses inviting [us] to go down to be 'watered' with aged wine whose color is amber.
"[They are] ointment pots made of rubies laid on top of emeralds, inside of which is gold. . . ."
(al-Nuwayrī, *Nihāya*, xi, 189).

The same kind of imagery is also used with other flowers. The unusual "freezing" into gems of the various parts of the blossom may historically be explained as a result of the emergence of flower poems from wine poetry: the latter, especially in Abū Nuwās, is rife with gem similes and metaphors to evoke the wine and the cup (cf. Schoeler, 72-5). Since the materials used as analogues are noble and incorruptible, an additional effect is that time itself freezes (cf. Hamori, 78-87). Finally, one should not forget that the recreation of natural objects, especially animals and plants, with the use of gems was not uncommon in courtly circles.

Personification

The other way of introducing a phantastic dimension is the personification of the rose, which in turn allows the poet to attribute a reason or motivation to its outward appearance or its "actions"—the phenomenon called *takhyīl* [*q.v.*] by ʿAbd al-Ḳāhir al-Djurdjānī (d. 471/1078 or later [*q.v.* in Suppl.]).

Al-Buḥturī (d. 284/897 [*q.v.*]) composed the following famous lines:

"Gay spring has come to you, strutting [and] laughing with beauty, almost talking even.
"In the darkness before daybreak, Nawrūz has awakened the first roses that yesterday had still been sleeping,
"the coolness of the dew slitting them open, and it was as if it [sc. spring or Nawrūz] were spreading news that yesterday had been concealed (*fa-ka'annahū yabuththu ḥadīth^an kāna amsi mukattamā*)."
(*Dīwān*, ed. al-Ṣayrafī, p. 2090; the "improved" version in al-Nuwayrī, *Nihāya*, xi, 189, has *fa-ka'annamā yabuththu ḥadīth^an baynahunna mukattamā* "and it was as if it were spreading news that had been concealed among them [sc. the roses]").

The idea that the opening of the buds is a broadcasting of something previously secret is cautiously formulated as an "as if". The second step (full personification) appears in the following line by ʿAlī b. al-Djahm:

"The roses started laughing only when the beauty of the flower beds and the sound of the chirping birds excited it.
"They appeared, and the world showed them its beauties, and, in the evening the wine came in its new clothes. . . ."
(al-Sarī al-Raffāʾ, *Muḥibb*, iii, 92, with slight divergences from the *Dīwān* version).

"Laughing" is "coming into bloom". The roses wait until the stage is set for them. The possibilities of *takhyīl*, the poetic re-interpretation of reality, are made use of in two specific contexts: the rose–cheek equation, and the rose vs. narcissus debate.

Rose = cheek

The term "rose" became part of the poetic jargon of the Moderns, where it simply meant "cheek"—alongside "narcissus" for "eye" and "chamomile (petals)" for "teeth", to name but these. Underlying this usage is, of course, the comparison of the red cheek with the red rose. But by reversing the comparison (*ḳalb*) the rose is often perceived as a cheek. Abū Hilāl al-ʿAskarī says (*Dīwān al-maʿānī*, ii, 23):

"Comparing it to the cheek is an appropriate simile (*tashbīh muṣīb*), but I refrained from indulging in it (*al-ikthār minhu*) because of its fame and frequency". Here are a few more sophisticated examples of the rose–cheek identification, showing in particular the phenomenon called "harmony of imagery" (*murāʿāt al-naẓīr*).

al-Walīd b. al-Djannān al-Shāṭibī:

"On the cheek of the rose are tears, dripping from the eyes of the clouds."

(al-Nawādjī, *Ḥalbat al-kumayt*, 239).

Abū Bakr al-Khālidī:

"They protected the roses of their cheeks, so that we could not pluck them due to the scorpions of their forelocks."

(al-Khālidiyyān: *Dīwān*, 70).

Ibn al-Rūmī:

"Those tears resemble drops of dew that fall from a narcissus (eye) onto a rose (cheek)."

(Ibn Abī ʿAwn, *Tashbīhāt*, 83, 7ff.; 89, 16).

One of the dandies (*aḥad al-ẓurafāʾ*):

"A fawn whose cheek and whose eyes are my rose and my narcissus."

(Ibn Abī ʿAwn: *Tashbīhāt*, 90, 2).

Kushādjim:

"If you like, it [the wine] is, from his hands, wine and, from his cheeks, roses."

(*Dīwān*, 140 [no. 129]).

Rose vs. narcissus

The debate about the precedence of the rose over the narcissus or vice versa was mostly decided in favour of the rose. The rose was considered the king of the flowers. The caliph al-Mutawakkil [*q.v.*] is supposed to have said: "I am the king of the rulers and the rose is the king of the fragrant plants, and each one of us is the most suitable for his counterpart" (al-Nawādjī, *Ḥalbat al-kumayt*, 235). Similarly, Abū Hilāl al-ʿAskarī says:

"The one who is sitting in an assembly is not like the one who is standing in it."

(Abū Hilāl al-ʿAskarī, *Dīwān al-maʿānī*, ii, 23, quoting himself; but it also occurs in Ibn al-Rūmī, *Dīwān*, 1242 [no. 1022], which, however, is strange in view of his well-known predilection for the narcissus).

I.e. the rose blossom is sitting on the bush like the ruler, while the narcissus is standing on its stem like his attendant.

It was Ibn al-Rūmī (d. 283/895 [*q.v.*]) who objected and declared his preference for the narcissus (*Dīwān*, 643-4 [often quoted], also 665 [no. 36], 1234 [a little prose text]; 1458 [no. 1112]). This he emphasised in a notorious invective against the rose, in which he compared it to a mule's anus with remnants of faeces in its midst (*Dīwān*, 1452 [no. 1107]). S. Boustany has offered a political-symbolic interpretation of Ibn al-Rūmī's favouring the narcissus (*Ibn ar-Rūmī. Sa vie et son œuvre. I. Ibn ar-Rūmī dans son milieu*, Beirut 1967, 339-40), but this has been effectively refuted by Schoeler (213-5). If it is not a simple personal predilection, it seems appropriate to consider Ibn al-Rūmī's position a somewhat sensationalist game in the tradition of *al-maḥāsin wa 'l-masāwī* [*q.v.*], especially if he did indeed on another occasion toot the usual horn (see above). His poem elicited a number of counterpoems, the best known being a six-liner by the famous garden poet al-Ṣanawbarī (*Dīwān*, 498 [no. 123]). On the "proofs" offered by Ibn al-Rūmī and al-Ṣanawbarī, most of them in the *takhyīl* category, see Heinrichs, *Rose versus narcissus*, 184-6. Notable is the fact that al-Ṣanawbarī offers a real *munāẓara*, i.e. the two flowers debate each other, if only in a rudimentary way, while Ibn al-Rūmī does use personification, but not in a sustained way and without letting the "protagonists" speak.

Some poets, such as Abū Bakr al-Khālidī, refrain from taking sides in the debate; he says:

"I disclosed to the narcissus of al-Raḳḳa my love, and I have no strength to avoid the roses.

"Both brothers are beloved, and I consider judging between them foolishness.

"In the army of flowers one is the vanguard that marches, the other the rear guard.

(al-Khālidiyyān, *Dīwān*, 143 [no. 125]).

The most interesting developments in the rose vs. narcissus debate are in prose (prosimetrum, to be exact). From 11th-century al-Andalus we have two *risālas*, one by Abu Ḥafṣ Aḥmad b. Burd al-Aṣghar (d. 1053-4), addressed to Abu 'l-Walīd b. Djahwar, ruler of Cordova (*r.* 1043-69), the other by Abu 'l-Walīd al-Ḥimyarī (d. *ca.* 440/1048) and addressed to Abu 'l-Ḳāsim Muḥammad b. Ismāʿīl b. ʿAbbād, ruler of Seville (*r.* 1023-42) (both in al-Ḥimyarī, *Badīʿ*, 53-8, 58-67). The first tells a story of certain leaders among the flowers agreeing on recognising the rose as their king and drawing up a contract (*a contrat social*) that would be binding also on those flowers as are spatially or temporally absent. After quoting the *risāla* of Aḥmad b. Burd, Abu 'l-Walīd al-Ḥimyarī responds to it by entering the fictional realm created by Ibn Burd and continuing the story by pointing out that the recognition of the rose as ruler was an error and that the narcissus should have been in that position (one of the arguments being that the "eye" [narcissus] is much nobler than the "cheek" [rose], which latter is not even a sense organ!).

A political interpretation of the two flower epistles imposes itself. After the recent breakdown of the Umayyad caliphate in al-Andalus, both addressees, Ibn Djahwar and Ibn ʿAbbād, ruled their respective city states, Cordova and Seville, with the consent of their people (people of substance, no doubt) and without any regnal title. This democratic, or aristocratic, model was unusual. Both Ibn Burd and al-Ḥimyarī were or had been high-ranking administrators; it is hardly strange that they attempted to make a constitutional statement in "flowery" language, most likely in the sense that they suggested to their addressees to adopt the caliphal title (for further details, see Heinrichs, *Rose versus narcissus*, 186-93).

In a purely literary vein, there are two more prose *munāẓaras* between rose and narcissus, one by Tādj al-Dīn Ibn ʿAbd al-Madjīd (d. 744/1343), with the title *Anwār al-saʿd wa-nuwwār al-madjd fi 'l-mufākhara bayn al-narjis wa 'l-ward* (in al-Nuwayrī, *Nihāya*, ii, 207-13), and one by Abu 'l-Ḥasan al-Māridīnī (2nd half of 15th century), entitled *al-Djawhar al-fard fī munāẓarat al-narjis wa 'l-ward* (in al-Shirwānī, *Nafḥat al-Yaman*, Hooghly 1841, 107-17). Of interest here is the way in which they establish the fictionality of their debates: Ibn ʿAbd al-Madjīd states that he wanted "to personify the two" (*ushakhkhiṣahumā*), while al-Māridīnī uses the phrase: "I represented them (*maththaltuhumā*) as two adversaries in a debate and I made the tongue of their state speak in the way of conversation (*wa 'stanṭaḳtu lisāna ḥālihimā ʿalā sabīli 'l-muḥādara*)" (for further details see Heinrichs, *op. cit.*, 193-8).

Rose as emblem

Given the general interest in the rose–narcissus debate, it is surprising that in two books, each of which contains a chapter on the rose, no such "enmity" is mentioned at all. Al-Washshāʾ (d. 325/937 [*q.v.*]) compiled a handbook of correct etiquette for the "refined" people (*ẓurafāʾ, ahl al-ẓarf*). The rose chapter contains mainly two ideas: (l) The rose represents everything beautiful and auspicious. (2) However, according to some, it is inauspicious, because it is shortlived. As such it is called *al-ghaddār*, the "traitor", as opposed to the myrtle that stays fresh for a long time (al-Washshā', *Muwashshā*, tr. D. Bellmann, ii, 92-6). The idea of the ephemeral and thus disloyal rose and its counterpart, the longlived loyal myrtle, finds expression in some poetry as well. Thus Abū Dulaf al-ʿIdjlī, writing to ʿAbd Allāh b. Ṭāhir, said:

"I see your love like the rose inconstant, there is nothing good in someone whose timespan does not last;

"And my love is like the myrtle in beauty and freshness, which has a white blossom that lasts, when the roses fade away."

The latter answered:

"You have compared my love with the rose, and it is similar to it: Is there any flower whose overlord is not the rose?!

"And your love is like the myrtle, bitter of taste; with regard to scent it has neither before nor after."

(al-Nuwayrī, *Nihāya*, xi, 192-3).

Finally, it needs to be said that in Arabic mystical literature the rose does not even come close to the symbolic value it has in Persian and Persianate literature, where it represents the divine Beloved. Ibn Ghānim al-Maḳdisī (d. 678/1279 [*q.v.*]), in his book on the symbolic or emblematic meaning of flowers and birds, devotes one chapter to the rose and another to the narcissus, but there is no cross-reference whatsoever (*Kashf al-asrār*, 12-13 and 16-17, tr. 10-12 and 13-14). The book resembles the *munāẓara*s in that the flowers speak in the first person. The self-characterisation of the rose revolves mainly around suffering, both from its own thorns that prick it and stain its petals with blood, and from the torment of destillation, when the rosewater is extracted from it.

Bibliography: 1. Texts. (a) Anthologies. Abū Hilāl al-ʿAskarī, *Dīwān al-maʿānī*, 2 parts, Cairo 1352h; al-Sarī al-Raffāʾ, *al-Muḥibb wa-maḥbūb wa 'l-mashmūm wa 'l-mashrūb*, 4 vols., ed. Miṣbāḥ Ghalāwundjī *et al.*, Damascus 1405/1986, iii, 89-95; Thaʿālibī, *Yatīmat al-dahr wa-maḥāsin ahl al-ʿaṣr*, ed. Muḥammad Muḥyī 'l-Dīn ʿAbd al-Ḥamīd, 4 vols., Cairo n.d. [*ca.* 1956]; Abu 'l-Walīd al-Ḥimyarī, *al-Badīʿ fī waṣf al-rabīʿ*, ed. H. Pérès, new ed. [Casablanca] 1410/1989, 94-100; Nawādjī, *K. Ḥalbat al-kumayt fi 'l-adab wa 'l-nawādir wa 'l-fukāhāt al-mutaʿallika bi 'l-khamriyyāt*, Cairo 1357/1938, 235-46; Nuwayrī, *Nihāyat al-arab*, xi, Cairo n.d., 184-213. (b) Books on similes. Ibn Abī ʿAwn, *Kitāb al-Tashbīhāt*, ed. M. ʿAbdul Muʿīd Khān, GMS, NS, xvii, London 1950 (see index of *prima comparationis* under *ward* [and under *khadd*]); Ibn al-Kattānī, *Kitāb al-Tashbīhāt min ashʿār ahl al-Andalus*, ed. Iḥsān ʿAbbās, Beirut n.d. [1966], 50-3; ed. ʿAbdel Sattār M.I. Ḥasanein, *Ibn al-Kattānī's "Dichterische Vergleiche der Andalus-Araber"*, Ph.D. Kiel 1969, 23-5, Ger. tr. W. Hoenerbach, *Dichterische Vergleiche der Andalus-Araber*, Bonn 1973, 52-4. (c) Dīwāns. Khālidiyyān (Abū Bakr Muḥammad and Abū ʿUthmān Saʿīd), *Dīwān*, ed. Sāmī al-Dahhān, Damascus 1388/1969; Kushādjim, *Dīwān*, ed. Khayriyya Muḥammad Maḥfūẓ, Baghdād 1390/1970; Ṣanawbarī, *Dīwān*, ed. Iḥsān ʿAbbās, Beirut 1970; al-Sarī al-Raffāʾ, *Dīwān*, ed. Ḥābīb Ḥusayn al-Ḥusaynī, 2 vols. [Baghdād] 1981 (with index of *mawṣūfāt*); Ibn al-Rūmī, *Dīwān*, ed. Ḥusayn Naṣṣār, Cairo 1973ff. (d) Other works. Washshā', *K. al-Muwashshā*, ed. R. Brünnow, Leiden 1886, 136-8, tr. D. Bellmann, *Das Buch des buntbestickten Kleides*, 3 pts. Bremen 1984, ii, 92-6; Ibn Ghānim al-Maḳdisī, *Kashf al-asrār ʿan ḥikam al-ṭuyūr wa 'l-azhār*, ed. Garcin de Tassy, Paris 1821, repr. London 1980 [with Eng. tr.] *Revelation of the secrets of the birds and flowers*, 12-13 (Ar.), 10-12 (Eng.).

2. Studies. A. Hamori, *On the art of medieval Arabic literature*. Princeton 1974; H. Pérès, *La poésie andalouse en arabe classique au XIe siècle*, ²Paris 1953; G. Schoeler, *Arabische Naturdichtung. Die Zahrīyāt, Rabīʿīyāt und Rauḍīyāt von ihren Anfängen bis aṣ-Ṣanawbarī. Eine gattungs-, motiv- und stilgeschichtliche Untersuchung*, Beirut 1974, 53-72, 83, 115, 128-31, 178, 204-17, 256-9, 286-9, 312-27; W.P. Heinrichs, *Rose versus narcissus. Observations on an Arabic literary debate*, in G.J. Reinink and H.L.J. Vanstiphout (eds.), *Dispute poems and dialogues in the ancient and medieval Near East. Forms and types of literary debates in Semitic and related literatures*, Louvain 1991, 179-98.

(W.P. Heinrichs)

AL-WASHM.

1. In older Arab society.

Tattooing was a custom among women in pre-Islamic times. The parts of the body mentioned as recipients are the hand ([*ẓāhir al-*]*yad*), the wrist (*miʿṣam*), the arm (*dhirāʿ*), the posterior (*ist*) and the gums (*litha*). The motifs used are not mentioned; going by modern-day tattooing in Islamic countries they were probably abstract designs. The tattoo was created by pricking (*gharaza*) the skin with a needle (*ibra, misalla*) or—more specifically—with a tattooing needle (*mīsham*, pl. *mawāshim*, see Lewin, *Vocabulary*, 471), so that a trace (*athar*) remained. This was then filled with soot (*naʾūr*, explained as *dukhān al-shaḥm* "smoke of grease"), antimony (*kuḥl*), or indigo (*nīl*). As a result the tattoo would become either darkish-green (*yakhḍarru*) or blue (*yazraḳḳu*). An existing tattoo could be touched up or retraced (*rudjdjiʿa*) when it had become weak (*mankūs*) (see *Mufaḍḍaliyyāt*, ed. Shākir and Hārūn, 105, 7 [no. 19, v. 2]).

In the *nasīb* section of the *ḳaṣīda*, the traces of former encampments (*aṭlāl*) are sometimes compared to a tattoo, or tattoos, in the same way that they are sometimes likened to foreign writing. The most famous example is the beginning of the *muʿallaḳa* of Ṭarafa, where the traces "appear like the remainder of a tattoo on the back of a hand" (see *Dīwān*, ed. M. Seligsohn, Paris 1901, 5). See also *Mufaḍḍaliyyāt*, ed. Shākir and Hārūn, 114, 3 (no. 21, v. 7) and 181, 2 (no. 38, v. 2).

In the *Ḥadīth* there are several traditions in which the Prophet is portrayed as cursing women who tattoo others (*wāshimāt*) as well as those who ask to be tattooed (*mustawshimāt*). The curse is often extended to other embellishing procedures that involve changing the body. The common denominator is that one should not alter God's creation (the women are called *al-mughayyirātu khalḳa 'llāh*) (see e.g. al-Bukhārī, *Ṣaḥīḥ*, part 7, Būlāḳ 1312h., 164, ult.–167, 7, and for further references see A.J. Wensinck, *A handbook of early Muhammadan tradition*, Leiden 1927, s.v. "tattooing"; and idem, *Concordance*, v, Leiden 1969, s.v. *washama*). It seems that there was some hesitation in the early community in this respect: After one of the Prophet's condemnations of *washm* whose chain goes back via Nāfiʿ to Ibn ʿUmar, Nāfiʿ remarks: *al-washmu fi 'l-litha* "tattooing of the gums [is intended]" (al-Bukhārī, *op. cit.*, 165, penult.). Ibn Manẓūr remarks with regard to this that "what is known nowadays is that tattooing is on the skin and the lips" (*LA*, xii, 639b, 10-11).

Bibliography: B. Lewin, *A vocabulary of the Hudailian poems*, Göteborg 1978; *Mufaḍḍaliyyāt*, ed. Aḥmad M. Shākir and ʿAbd al-Salām M. Hārūn, Cairo 1964; *LA*, xii, 638a-b. (W.P. Heinrichs)

WIṢĀL, Mīrzā Muḥammad Shafīʿ b. Muḥammad Ismāʿīl, Persian poet of the early Ḳādjār period, also known as Mīrzā Kūčik ("the little Mīrzā"). He was born in 1197/1782 at Shīrāz in a family of officials who had served the rulers of Persia since the time of the Ṣafawids. His studies not only included Arabic and the literary sciences, but also the arts. It is said that Wiṣāl was a graceful person with a beautiful voice and an excellent performer of *ghazals*. He also became a famous calligrapher, proficient in all the current styles of writing (see the autograph in Browne, *LHP*, iv, facing 300). In addition, he was educated as a mystic by Mīrzā Abu 'l-Ḳāsim Sukūt, a *shaykh* of the Dhahabiyya order. He died in 1262/1845 and was buried near the shrine of Shāh Čirāgh in Shīrāz.

As a poet, Wiṣāl was a typical representative of the neo-classicism that had set in with the Return Movement (*bāzgasht-i adabī*) of the mid-12th/18th centuries. He wrote panegyrics after the fashion of the mediaeval poets, in particular Manūčihrī, Anwarī and Khāḳānī [*q.vv.*], and *ghazals* in the style of Saʿdī [*q.v.*]. Among his patrons were, besides the governor and other notables of the province of Fārs, the Ḳādjār kings Fatḥ-ʿAlī Shāh and Muḥammad Shāh, as well as people residing in the Deccan, which made him also popular on the Subcontinent. His *mathnawīs* include *Bazm-i Wiṣāl*, a lyrical account of an excursion into the mountains of Fārs, and the continuation of *Farhād va Shīrīn*, more a treatise on love than a story, which had been left unfinished by Waḥshī [*q.v.*] and is usually printed together with the latter's text (see e.g. *Kulliyyāt-i dīwān-i Waḥshī-yi Bāfḳī*, ed. Bīdār, Tehran 1373 *sh.*/1994, 476-526). In prose, he wrote an imitation of Saʿdī's *Gulistān* and he translated *Aṭwāḳ al-dhahab*, an Arabic *adab* work by al-Zamakhsharī [*q.v.* in Suppl.]. Another aspect of his work are his religious poems, such as elegies (*marāthī*) mourning the martyrs of Karbalā.

Modern critics have pointed to the lack of originality in his poetry, the main merit of which is the perfect imitation of the old masters. Nevertheless, his reputation as a refined poet and artist lasted throughout the Ḳādjār period and his works were printed several times both in India and Persia. A substantial selection from his poetry is to be found in the anthologies of Riḍā Ḳulī Khān. The sons of Wiṣāl followed in the footsteps of their father. One of them is Dāwarī (d. 1283/1866-7), who acquired a reputation as a poet and a painter (see further, Browne, *LHP*, iv, 319-25).

Bibliography: Biographical data are to be found in ʿAlī-Akbar Bismil Shīrāzī, *Tadhkira-yi dilgushā* (cf. Storey, i/2, 888); Riḍā Ḳulī Khān, *Madjmaʿ al-fuṣaḥāʾ*, Tehran 1295/1878, ii, 528-47; idem, *Riyāḍ al-ʿārifīn*, Tehran 1305/1888, 337-50. See further: A. von Kegl, *Viṣāl und seine Söhne, eine Dichterfamilie des modernen Persiens*, in *WZKM*, xii (1898), 113-27; E.G. Browne, *LHP*, iv, 300-1, 316-25; idem, *A year amongst the Persians*, ²Cambridge 1926, 130, 292; Nūrānī Wiṣāl, *Gulshan-i Wiṣāl*, Tehran 1319 *sh.*/1940; Māhyār Nawābī, *Khāndān-i Wiṣāl-i Shīrāzī*, in *Nashriyya-yi Dānishkada-yi Adabiyyāt-i Tabrīz*, vii (1334 *sh.*/1955), 190-239, 288-356, 392-459; Dhabīḥ-Allāh Ṣafā, *Gandj-i sukhan*, ²Tehran 1340 *sh.*/1961, iii, 197-200; J. Rypka, *History of Iranian literature*, Dordrecht 1968, 331-2; Aḥmad Munzawī, *Fihrist-i nuskhahā-yi khaṭṭī-yi fārsī*, iii, Tehran 1350 *sh.*/1971, 2599-2600; Khānbābā Mushār, *Fihrist-i kitābhā-yi čāpī-yi fārsī*, Tehran 1352 *sh.*/1973, 389, 501, 1593, 1678, 2136, 2413; Yaḥyā Āryanpūr, *Az Ṣabā tā Nīmā*, Tehran 1976, ii, 40-4; Abu 'l-Ḳāsim Rādfar (ed.), *Čand marthiya az shāʿirān-i pārsigūy*, Tehran 1369 *sh.*/1990, 96-104; Dāwarī Shīrāzī, *Dīwān*, n.p. 1370 *sh.*/1991. (J.T.P. de Bruijn)

Y

YAGHŪTH, a god of pre-Islamic Arabia, mentioned in the Ḳurʾān in a speech of Noah: "They have said: Forsake not your gods. Forsake not Wadd, nor Suwāʿ, nor Yaghūth, Yaʿūḳ and Nasr (LXXI, 22-3).

Traditionists and commentators (see the references given by Hawting, *The idea of idolatry*, 113 and n. 6) have exercised their ingenuity in the search for the traces of Yaghūth in Arabia. Ibn al-Kalbī (d. 204/819 or 206/821) in his *Book of the Idols* (*Kitāb al-Asnām*, §§ 7c, 9d, 45e, 52a) relates in laconic style: "[the tribe of] Madhḥidj and the people of Djurash adopted Yaghūth . . .; it was located on a hill in the Yemen known as Madhḥidj; Madhḥidj and allied tribes worshipped it." Djurash is today an important archaeological site in the south-west of Saudi Arabia, at ʿAsīr, 42 km east-south-east of Abhā. The tribe of Madhḥidj [*q.v.*] is first attested (1st century A.D. or thereabouts) at Ḳaryat al-Fāw (280 km north-north-east of Nadjrān), then in the regions situated between Nadjrān and Maʾrib, and finally in the highlands of southern Yemen (10th century A.D.) where it is still found today. Shortly before the advent of Islam, the famous battle of al-Razm, which pitted Murād (a subsection of Madhḥidj) against Hamdān, is said to have been provoked by a quarrel over the stewardship of the idol (Fahd, *Le panthéon*, 193-4).

On the divinities of Madhḥidj and of Djurash, the ancient inscriptions of southern Arabia tell us nothing, either because they do not indicate the tribal affiliation of their authors (where they are numerous, as at Ḳaryat al-Fāw and at Nadjrān), or because they are quite rare (as in the region of Djurash). Direct verification of Ibn al-Kalbī's statements is thus impossible; however, the fact that the god Yaghūth is completely unknown in South Arabian epigraphy (including onomastics) inspires some doubt as to their reliability. The only epigraphic attestation of the word *Ygṯ* is to be found in a Sabaean inscription (RES 5002) as an attributive personal name.

Two Nabataean inscriptions from Petra and possibly a third from Sinai mention the anthroponym *ʾmrʾ-yʿwt* (Cantineau, *Le Nabatéen*, ii, 64, 104), composed of *ʾmrʾ* (Arabic *imruʾ*) and *Yʿwt* (Aramaean graphic of

Yag̲h̲ūt̲h̲, with notation of *g̲h̲ayn* by means of *ʿayn*). In these anthroponyms, the second element could be the name of a divinity or that of a particularly venerated individual. Safaitic epigraphy knows the anthroponym *Ygt̲* (see, for example, Winnett and Harding, *Inscriptions*, 625).

Finally, Arabic nomenclature attests the anthroponym ʿAbd Yag̲h̲ūt̲h̲ (Caskel, *Ǧamhara*, ii, 133-4, 42 entries). It is known that the element ʿAbd governs either the name of a divinity (see especially ʿAbd d̲h̲i ʾl-S̲h̲arā, ʿAbd Manāf, ʿAbd Manāt, ʿAbd Ruḍā, ʿAbd Suwāʿ, ʿAbd S̲h̲ams, ʿAbd al-S̲h̲āriḳ, ʿAbd al-ʿUzzā or ʿAbd Wadd) or the name of a person or a group (compare with ʿAbd ʿAdī, ʿAbd Ahlih, ʿAbd ʿĀmir, ʿAbd ʿAmr, ʿAbd ʿAwf, ʿAbd Bakr, ʿAbd Hind, ʿAbd al-Ḥārit̲h̲, ʿAbd Ḥārit̲h̲a, ʿAbd al-Mund̲h̲ir, ʿAbd al-Nuʿmān, etc.). The distribution of ʿAbd Yag̲h̲ūt̲h̲ in the genealogies does not make it possible to identify the tribes which particularly appreciated this name, with the exception of Mad̲h̲ḥid̲j̲ (18 entries out of 42). But regarding this tribe, there is no knowing whether it is the frequency of the name which has led traditionists to associate the god with it, or conversely whether it is the association with the god which has multiplied the instances of ʿAbd Yag̲h̲ūt̲h̲.

Ibn al-Kalbī also seeks to explain how it was that mankind, monotheistic at the time of creation, came to worship such a multiplicity of divinities. For his purposes, he supposes that, originally, Yag̲h̲ūt̲h̲ was a devout man; after his death, he was commemorated by a statue, then promoted to the rank of intercessor in the presence of God. It was the Flood which allegedly brought his idol into Arabia near D̲j̲udda; there it is said to have been found by ʿAmr b. Luḥayy who entrusted it to the tribe of Mad̲h̲ḥid̲j̲, more specifically to Anʿam b. ʿAmr al-Murādī (§§ 45e-52a; note that for the traditionists, Murād is attached to Mad̲h̲ḥid̲j̲).

The root *g̲h̲-w-t̲h̲* from which the name of Yag̲h̲ūt̲h̲ is derived (imperfect of *g̲h̲āt̲h̲a* "to help") is current in Arabic nomenclature; see Ar. G̲h̲awt̲h̲, al-G̲h̲awt̲h̲, G̲h̲iyāt̲h̲, G̲h̲uwayt̲h̲ or G̲h̲uwāt̲h̲a (Caskel, *Ǧamhara*, ii, 274-6). It is also attested in North Arabian epigraphy; in South Arabia, on the other hand, it is more rare and probably indicates a North Arabian influence.

Like other commentators, Yāḳūt was struck by the similarity of the names Yag̲h̲ūt̲h̲ and Yaʿūḳ, and by a possible opposition in the sense of the two words; he speculates that it may be necessary to recognise two aspects of one and the same divinity, who "sometimes sends the rain, sometimes prevents the rainfall" (Fahd, *Le panthéon*, 194). It is clear that all the developments of the tradition depend on the Ḳurʾānic text and are based on anthroponyms formed on the root *g̲h̲-w-t̲h̲*; as for the origin of the mention of Yag̲h̲ūt̲h̲ in the Ḳurʾān, it remains unexplained.

Bibliography: J. Cantineau, *Le Nabatéen*, 2 vols., Paris 1930-2; M. Hofner, *Die Stammesgruppen Nord- und Zentralarabiens im vorislamischer Zeit*, in H.W. Haussig (ed.), *Götter und Mythen im Vorderen Orient*, Stuttgart 1965, 407-81 ("Yaġūṯ, Yaġūt", 478); T. Fahd, *Le panthéon de l'Arabie centrale à la veille de l'hégire*, Paris 1968; His̲h̲ām Ibn al-Kalbī, *[Kitāb al-Aṣnām] Le Livre des idoles de Hicham ibn al-Kalbi*, text ed. and tr. Wahib Atallah, Paris 1969; F.V. Winnett and G.L. Harding, *Inscriptions from fifty Safaitic cairns*, Toronto 1978; G.R. Hawting, *The idea of idolatry and the emergence of Islam. From polemic to history*, Cambridge 1999.

(Ch. Robin)

YAḤYĀ, S̲h̲eyk̲h̲ al-Islām, Ottoman legal scholar and poet, d. 1053/1644.

The son of S̲h̲eyk̲h̲ al-Islām Bayrāmzāde Zekeriyyā Efendi, Yaḥyā was born in Istanbul in 969/1561 (some sources give the birth date 959). As the scion of an important *ʿulemāʾ* family, he underwent a rigorous private education under the tutelage of his father and several other noted scholars, including ʿAbd al-D̲j̲ebbārzāde Dervī̲s̲h̲ Meḥmed Efendi and Maʿlūlzāde Seyyid Meḥmed Efendi. In 988/1580, at 19 years of age, he was granted a *mulāzimet* and went on to teach in the most important *madrasas* of the day. In 1004/1595 Yaḥyā was appointed *ḳāḍī* of Aleppo and he subsequently served as *ḳāḍī* in various parts of the empire until 1013/1604, when he was elevated to the position of *ḳāḍī ʿasker* of Anatolia. After several dismissals and reappointments, he was appointed *S̲h̲eyk̲h̲ al-Islām* in Rad̲j̲ab 1031/May 1622. A brief but turbulent tenure, during which he presided over the funeral of Sultan ʿOt̲h̲mān II [*q.v.*], ended in D̲h̲u ʾl-Ḳaʿda 1032/September 1622 when a powerful vizier, angered by Yaḥyā's opposition to the practice of selling government positions, forced the young Murād IV [*q.v.*] to dismiss him. Between 1034/1625 and 1041/1632 he again served as *S̲h̲eyk̲h̲ al-Islām* and was re-appointed in 1043/1634 for a period that lasted until his death in 1053/1644.

Yaḥyā was noted as a legal scholar. Kātib Čelebi (*Fed̲h̲leke*) reports that, in delivering legal opinions, he embodied the perfection of Abu ʾl-Suʿūd [*q.v.*] and was its seal. He served in an important position during a period of great turmoil and was a powerful supporter of the reforms instituted by Murād IV. He was widely known as an honest and decent person in a time when few like him rose to power.

Nonetheless, Yaḥyā's most enduring fame has derived from his talent as a *g̲h̲azal* poet. He was said to possess a poet's inborn nature: witty of speech, a cheerful countenance, a pleasant conversationalist. His poetry, in the manner of Bāḳī [*q.v.*], consists primarily of five-couplet *g̲h̲azals*, most on the transitoriness of this world and life's bitter and sweet aspects. His style is simple and flowing, free from the excesses of rhetorical complexity that marked the poetry of many of his contemporaries.

His works include: a *dīwān*, the *S̲h̲arḥ D̲j̲āmiʿ al-dürer* (commentary on Muḥsin-i Ḳayserī's *Ferāʾiḍ*), *Nigāristān čevirisi* (a Turkish translation of Kemāl-Pās̲h̲āzāde's Persian parallel to Saʿdī's [*q.v.*] *Gulistān*) and *Fetāwā-yi Yaḥyā Efendi* (a collection of legal opinions).

Bibliography: Yaḥyā is mentioned in the *ted̲h̲kires* of Ḳafzāde Fāʾiḍī, Riḍā, Yümnī, ʿĀṣim, Ṣafāyī, Tewfīḳ, Kātib Čelebī's *Fed̲h̲leke* (Istanbul 1287), and in the addenda to the *S̲h̲aḳāʾiḳ al-Nuʿmāniyya* by ʿUs̲h̲s̲h̲āḳīzāde and S̲h̲eyk̲h̲ī Meḥmed. There are three editions of his *dīwān*: İbnülemīn M. Kemāl Ināl, *Dīwān-ı S̲h̲eyk̲h̲ülislām Yaḥyā*, Istanbul 1334/1915-16 (in Arabic script); Rekin Ertem, *Şeyhülislam Yahya divanı*, Ankara 1995; and Hasan Kavruk, *Şeyhülislam Yahya divanı*, Ankara 2001 (Latin script transcriptions). See also Lütfi Bayraktutan, *Şeyhülislam Yahya divanından seçmeler*, Istanbul 1990; Ismail Hakkı Uzunçarşılı, *Osmanlı tarihi*, III. cild, Ankara 1995; Gibb, *HOP*, iii, 273-84; von Hammer-Purgstall, *Gesch. d. Osm. Dichtkunst*, ii, 378-85; A. Bombaci, *Storia della letteratura turca*, Milan 1956, 371-2.

(W.G. Andrews and Mehmet Kalpakli)

YAS̲H̲, the Ottoman Turkish form of the name of the Romanian town of Iaşi, conventionally Jassy. It lies on the plain of northeastern Moldavia near the confluence of the Bahlui river with the Prut (lat. 47° 10′ N., long. 27° 35′ E.).

In Ottoman times, it was the capital of the principality of Boghdān [*q.v.*] or Moldavia. Dimitri Cantemir, from 1121-2/1710 to 1122-3/1711 resident in this town as prince of Moldavia, stated that the seat of government had been transferred to Yash by Stephen the Great (838 or 9-909 or 10/1435-1504; in reality this was done by Alexander Lapusneanu in 972-3/1565); as a reason for this, Cantemir maintained that, due to its geographical position, Yash was better suited to warfare with the Ottomans and Tatars than its predecessor, the more remote fortress town of Suceava (Demetrius Cantemir, *Beschreibung der Moldau*, facs. repr. Bucarest 1973, 52). Ewliyā Čelebi, who visited Yash around 1075/1665, called it Yashḳa Ruhbān, due to the importance of the local monasteries. In his account, Yash appears as a town of 20,000 thatched *ḳorta* (from Romanian *curte* "court"); he noted the absence of (private?) buildings covered with lead or roof-tiles, but commented on the existence of palaces and monasteries built of stone or brick (*Evliya Çelebi Seyahatnâmesi. Topkapı Sarayı Bagdat 307 yazmasının transkripsyonu–dizini*, v, ed. Yücel Dağlı, Seyit Ali Kahraman and İbrahim Sezgin, Istanbul 2001, 180-6).

Among ecclesiastical institutions, the Ottoman traveller refers to the Yashḳa Deyri, that Ewliyā believed had been a mosque in the reigns of sultans Bāyezīd and Süleymān, in addition to the Menokola, Galata and Lipul Beğ monasteries; the latter must be identical to that of the Trei Erachi/Trieh Svetiteilei, built by Vasile Lupu in 1049-50/1640—Ewliyā hoped to see it one day transformed into a mosque. As to the Menokola, it was probably identical to the St. Nicholas Church, where a newly-arrived prince was blessed by a church authority (Miron Costin, *Grausame Zeiten in der Moldau. Die Moldauische Chronik des Miron Costin 1593-1661*, tr. and comments by A. Armbruster, Graz, Vienna and Cologne 1980, 196, for a monastery called Galata, see *ibid.*, 207; on the affairs of local monasteries in general, see C. Zach, *Über Klosterleben und Klosterreformen in der Moldau und in der Walachei im 17. Jahrhundert*, in Kálmán Bénda *et alii* (eds.), *Forschungen über Siebenbürgen und seine Nachbarn. Festschrift für Atilla T. Szabó und Zsigmund Jakó*, Munich 1987, 111-22). Ewliyā also referred to the monastery supposedly founded by Duna Bānū, the wife of Prince Lipul Beğ/Vasile Lupu, which contained an "uncorrupted body" of a young woman that Ewliyā claimed was the daughter of the mythical architect Yanḳō b. Mādyān; this may well be the relic that Lupu had brought to his capital and that was believed to be the body of St. Paraschiva (Costin, *op. cit.*, 160-1).

To the south of Yash there was an artificial lake full of fish, that Ewliyā thought had been constructed by Prince Lipul Beğ/Vasile Lupu with the permission of Sultan Murād IV. The traveller also admired the princely palace with its grand reception room and numerous pavilions looking out upon the water (judging from a map of the early 20th century, the core of the palace was located at some distance from the one major lake in the town; however, the body of water seen by Ewliyā may have been drained later on; see *Meyers Reisebücher, Türkei, Rumänien, Serbien, Bulgarien*, Leipzig and Vienna, 1908, 93). Costin confirms that Vasile Lupu greatly augmented the palace, constructing gardens, stables and bath-houses; some of the buildings supposedly were covered in tiles of "Chinese porcelain" (Costin, *loc. cit.*). Ewliyā also claims that there were 2,060 shops covered with timber or reeds, six *khāns* used by merchants and a guest house that also accommodated visiting Ottoman and Tatar dignitaries.

Complementary to Ewliyā's account is that of a near-contemporary embassy chaplain (*Conrad Jacob Hiltebrandts Dreifache Schwedische Gesandtschaftsreise nach Siebenbürgen, der Ukraine und Constantinopel (1656-1658)*, ed. with comm. by F. Babinger, Leiden 1937, 82 ff.) Hiltebrandt served the Swedish embassy that was received at the court of Prince George Stephen, who after his deposition by Meḥemmed IV (1067-68/1657) emigrated to the Swedish kingdom. The author stressed the commercial activity of Yash, which was, however, unfortified; numerous Jewish traders were active here, in addition to both local and Greek merchants. At the court, where it was customary to accord a visiting Ottoman *čawush* absolute precedence, there was a guard of German-speaking soldiers, yet Ewliyā commented on the presence of Ottoman gunners. According to Hiltebrandt, the numerous churches of Yash rather resembled mosques without minarets; he also commented on the local folklore, including dances and fairground amusements specific to the Easter season.

Throughout the early modern period, the Polish-Lithuanian commonwealth attempted to influence the decision-making of the Moldavian princes, which meant that Polish-Tatar-Cossack rivalries also were fought out on Moldavian soil. In 918-19/1513 Yash was thus fired on by the Tatars, while Ottoman and Russian attacks in 944-5/1538 and 1097-8/1686 had similar consequences (art. "Jassy" in *Encyclopedia Britannica*, ed. 1963, xii, 972). Ewliyā Čelebi even claimed that the conditions of Moldavian subjection included the right of the Tatars to pillage the country once every ten years. In 1123/1711 Peter the Great briefly occupied the town, receiving the homage of the learned prince Dimitri Cantemir. On this occasion, numerous Ottoman merchants present in Yash were murdered and their goods pillaged (Akdes Nîmet Kurat, *Prut seferi ve barışı 1123 (1711)*, 2 vols., Ankara 1951-3, i, 234 and *passim*); similar atrocities were repeated in 1236-7/1821, when the Greek uprising began in both the Peloponnesus and the Principalities. Russian armies advanced as far as Yash once again in 1148-9/1736, but were not able to hold on to the town due to the defeats suffered at Ottoman hands by their Austrian ally (Barbara Jelavich, *History of the Balkans*, i, *Eighteenth and nineteenth centuries*, Cambridge 1983, 66-8, 105, 121; H. Uebersberger, *Russlands Orientpolitik in den letzten zwei Jahrhunderten*, i, *Bis zum Frieden von Jassy*, Stuttgart 1913, *passim*). On the level of international diplomacy, the Moldavian capital was known through the peace of Jassy concluded between the Ottoman and Russian empires (Djumādā II-Radjab 1206/January 1792); this agreement confirmed many of the stipulations of the earlier treaty of Küčük Ḳaynardja [*q.v.*], especially the loss of the Crimea. A coastal strip between Bug and Dniestr was also ceded to Russia, where the town of Odessa was founded the following year. From this time onwards, Russia maintained an influential position in Yash, which was to continue throughout the 13th/19th century.

In the late 12th/18th century, when Istanbul Greek families known as the *hospodars* represented Ottoman authority in Yash, the town possessed a small but active educated stratum that purchased books both religious and secular in Greek, Italian, Romanian and other languages, with an emphasis on the Greek authors of Antiquity, as well as grammars and dictionaries covering modern European languages. Such works were procured by merchants for whom dealing in books must have formed a sideline. These educated traders maintained links to the Athos but also to Leipzig and Vienna, in addition to stocking works printed in Moldavia itself (Mihail Carataşu, *La bibliothèque d'un grand négotiant du XVIII*^{e} *siècle: Grégoire Antoine Avramios*, in *Symposium l'époque phanariote, 21-25 octobre 1970, à la mémoire de Cléobule Tsourkas*, Salonica 1974, 135-43). A princely academy founded by Antioh Cantemir was attended not only by the sons of local noblemen but also by young people of more modest backgrounds; from 1173-4/1760 onwards, this school began to teach Enlightenment philosophy as well as the natural sciences (Ariadna Camariano-Cioran, *Écoles grecques dans les principautés danubiennes au temps des Phanariotes*, in *ibid.*, 49-56). However, given the frequency of warfare, the depressed condition of the peasantry and the relative weakness of urban life in Moldavia, the level of general education remained low even in the 13th/19th century (Jelavich, *op. cit.*, i, 270).

In the mid-19th century, Jassy came within the principality of Moldavia, now united with Wallachia to form the kingdom of Romania. Though Bucharest became the political capital of the new state, Jassy continued to be the most important cultural centre of the realm. The first book in Romanian had been printed there (1643), and it was the seat of an Orthodox archbishop. Now, in 1860, the University of Jassy was founded. The large Jewish population of the town, approximately one-half, perished in the course of World War II. After 1947, Jassy was within the People's Republic of Romania. In 1996 it was the third city of Romania, with a population of 346,613, whilst the county of the same name, with the town of Jassy as its chef-lieu, had 823,800 inhabitants.

Bibliography: Given in the article.

(Suraiya Faroqhi)

YAʿŪḲ, a god of pre-Islamic Arabia, mentioned in the Ḳurʾān in a speech of Noah: "They have said: Forsake not your gods. Forsake not Wadd, nor Suwāʿ, nor Yaghūth, Yaʿūḳ and Nasr!" (LXXI, 22-3).

Traditionists and commentators have exercised their ingenuity in the effort to track down the god Yaʿūḳ, with little success. In his "Book of the Idols" (*Kitab al-Aṣnām*, §§ 7d, 9d, 45e, and 52b), Ibn al-Kalbī (d. 204/819 or 206/821), relates that: "Khaywān adopted Yaʿūḳ; he was in one of their villages called Khaywān, in the region of Ṣanʿāʾ, two nights from Mecca." But he adds immediately: "I have heard neither Hamdān nor any other Arab [tribe] giving a name [composed] with it", explaining this silence by the Judaisation of Hamdān under the reign of Dhū Nuwās [*q.v.*, where his name needs to be corrected in the Sabaean form, which is Yūsuf Asʾar Yathʾar, *Ys^{3}f ʾs^{1}ʾr Yṯʾr*].

The information provided by Ibn al-Kalbī on the location and tribal associations of the township of Khaywān is precise. Khaywān is situated well to the north of Sanʿāʾ in the direction of Mecca, at a distance of 105 km, midway between Ṣanʿāʾ and Ṣaʿda. In the 4th/10th century, the township marked the boundary between Ḥāshid and Bakīl, the two tribal groups constituting the Hamdān confederation (al-Ḥasan al-Hamdānī, *Ṣifat Djazīrat al-ʿArab*, ed. Müller, 66); it is today the last outpost of Ḥāshid (the al-ʿUṣaymāt clan) before entering Sufyān. On the other hand, no divinity named Yaʿūḳ is attested in Hamdān. However, the pantheons of the tribes of this confederation, which give the highest rank to Taʾlab Riyām and Almaḳah, are quite well known through many inscriptions and the vestiges of a large number of temples. A god named Yaʿūḳ is not attested elsewhere in Yemen or in Arabia.

It is clear that Ibn al-Kalbī or his source felt the need to manipulate the available information to provide a basis for the Ḳurʾānic text. It was all the easier to locate Yaʿūḳ in Yemen, not only because it was a distant country, but also because polytheism had been officially banned there since the end of the 4th century A.D. and any indications to the contrary had been obliterated.

However, the epigraphy of Yemen is acquainted with the appellation of Yaʿūḳ. It is the name of a synagogue (*mkrb*) constructed in A.D. January 465 (*ḏ-dʾw*^{n} 574 of the Ḥimyarite era), at Ḍulaʿ apparently (some 12 km to the north-west of Ṣanʿāʾ), according to the inscription Ry 520/4 (*Yʿḳ*) and 9 (*Yʿwḳ*). In a relief inscription on the island of Suḳutra [*q.v.*], *Yʿḳ* is apparently an anthroponym (Robin and Gorea, *Les vestiges antiques*).

Among traditionists and Muslim scholars, the cult of Yaʿūḳ was the object of hypotheses other than that of Ibn al-Kalbī: they localise it in the tribes of Khawlān-Ḳuḍāʿa, Murād or Kināna (Fahd, *Le panthéon*, 195 n. 1) or at Balkhaʿ (a Sabaean town known only through traditions relating to idols: see Hawting, *The idea of idolatry*, 107 and n. 15) but without further evidence.

Ibn al-Kalbī also seeks to explain how it was that mankind, monotheistic at the time of creation, came to worship such a multiplicity of divinities. For his purposes, he assumes that originally, Yaʿūḳ was a devout man; after his death, he was commemorated by a statue, then promoted to the rank of intercessor in the presence of God. It was the Flood that would have brought his idol into Arabia near Djudda; there it is said to have been found by ʿAmr b. Luḥayy who entrusted it to the tribe of Hamdān (§§ 45e-52b).

Attestations and the senses of the root from which the name of Yaʿūḳ is derived offer nothing further by way of clarification. One may note only that Yāḳūt underlines the similarity between the names Yaghūth and Yaʿūḳ and wonders whether it is necessary to recognise two aspects of one and the same divinity, who "sometimes sends the rain, sometimes prevents the rainfall" (Fahd, *Le panthéon*, 194).

It is thus difficult to follow Toufic Fahd when he affirms that "The conclusion cannot be avoided that Yaʿūḳ and the other four divinities cited by Noah belong to the most primitive pantheon of central Arabia" (*op. cit.*, 196); to this day, nothing has been established with certitude as to the origin of the mention of Yaʿūḳ in the Ḳurʾān.

Bibliography: Hamdānī, [*Ṣifat Djazīrat al-ʿArab*], D.H. Müller, *al-Hamdânî's Geographie der arabischen Halbinsel*, 2 vols., Leiden 1884-91, repr. 1968; G. Ryckmans, *Inscriptions sud-arabes. Onzième série*, in *Le Muséon*, lxvii (1954), 99-105 and pl. 1; M. Höfner, *Die Stammesgruppen Nord- und Zentralarabiens im vorislamischer Zeit*, in H.W. Haussig (ed.), *Götter und Mythen im Vorderen Orient*, Stuttgart 1965, 407-81 ("Yaʿūq", 479); T. Fahd, *Le panthéon de l'Arabie centrale à la veille de l'hégire*, Paris 1968; Hishām Ibn al-Kalbī, [*Kitāb al-Aṣnām*] *Le Livre des idoles de Hicham ibn al-Kalbi*, text ed. and tr. Wahib Atallah, Paris 1969; G.R. Hawting, *The idea of idolatry and the emergence of Islam. From polemic to history*, Cambridge 1999; Ch. Robin and Maria Gorea, *Les vestiges antiques de la grotte de Ḥôq (Suquṭra, Yémen)*, in *Académie des Inscriptions et Belles-Lettres, Comptes rendus*, 2002, 409-45.

(Ch. Robin)

YAZÎDJÎ, Ṣāliḥ b. Süleymān, the early Ottoman author of the *Shemsiyye*, one of the earliest works on astrology known to be written in Anatolia. He was the father of Yāzīdjīoghlu Meḥmed and Aḥmed Bīdjān [*q.vv.*], two important religious figures and writers of the 9th/15th century.

The place and date of his birth are uncertain. However, due to the fact that he dedicated his work (the *Shemsiyye*) to Iskender b. Ḥādjī Pasha from the Dewlet Khān family living in Ankara, it is supposed that he was also from Ankara. On the other hand, in the introduction (*sebeb-i teʾlif*) of his *Shemsiyye*, he wrote that he was strongly attached to ʿAlī Beg, the son of Ḳaṣṣāb-oghlu Maḥmūd Pasha, who was the tutor (*lala*) of Sulṭān Meḥmed Fātiḥ and vizier to Murād II and Fātiḥ, and that he served him from the year 775/1373 for 36 years until ʿAlī Beg's death. Ḳaṣṣāb-oghlu Maḥmūd Pasha founded a *masdjid*, a *madrasa* and a hospital in Malḳara [*q.v.*] and appointed his son ʿAlī Beg to administer them, so Yazīdjī Ṣāliḥ also lived in Malḳara and in later years he settled in Gallipoli (Gelibolu) probably after ʿAlī Beg's death. The date of his death is unknown. The story that his grave is near the graves of his sons Meḥmed and Aḥmed Bīdjān (outside Gelibolu, on the road to Istanbul) is unauthenticated.

That his father's name was Süleymān, although Ewliyā Čelebi calls him Shüdjāʿ al-Dīn, is certain, because in the manuscript of the *Muḥammediyye*, by his son Yazīdjī-oghlu Meḥmed, and also in his other works, he speaks of himself as Meḥmed b. Ṣāliḥ b. Süleymān. As a consequence of writing in his work his name as Ṣalḥ al-Dīn, from the exigencies of the metre, in some sources his name has mistakenly appeared as Ṣalāh al-Dīn.

Although the available information about his education is uncertain, some facts, e.g. that he was a scribe, so that he was given the *laḳab* Yazīdjī, that he was a very knowledgeable person about astrology, and that he used Arabic and Persian quotations and titles in his *Shemsiyye*, imply a certain level of education.

The number of his works is unknown. His only extant work is the *Shemsiyye* on astrology. Although Ewliyā Čelebi mentions a *Sebʿ al-Methānī, a Taʿbīr-nāme* and works on medicine, no copy of them has so far been found. The work which has appeared in some sources as the *Melḥame* is part of the *Shemsiyye*. The question whether the *Shemsiyye* was a compilation or a translation was long discussed. However, considering the manner of book writing of the time and also the fact that Yazīdjī Ṣāliḥ mentions the works and people from whom he profited (like Ebu 'l-Faḍl Ḥubeysh b. Ibrāhīm b. Muḥammed al-Tiflisī), it is recognised as a compilation.

Yazīdjī Ṣāliḥ writes in the introduction of his work that he completed it in 811/1408-9, naming it the *Shemsiyye*, and submitted it to Iskender b. Ḥādjī Pasha. The *Shemsiyye* was written in the form of a *methnewī* and in the metre *fāʿilātün fāʿilātün fāʿilün*. Since no autograph ms. exists and no critical edition has been done, the number of original verses is unknown; they differ in each copy (e.g. in ms. Süleymaniye Kütüphanesi-Pertevniyal no. 776, 4724 verses). The fact that over 30 mss. of it survive shows that it was widely read. If not great literature, it is nevertheless important linguistically as a text of 15th-century Turkish. It is composed of three sections. In the first section there is the introduction (*tewḥīd, naʿt, mirʿādjiyye, sebeb-i teʾlif*), which is to be found in works written in the *methnewī* form; the second section is divided into twelve *bābs*, each referring to one of the months, and each divided again into 25 *faṣls*; and in the third section, three characteristics of the moon are narrated, with their subdivisions. It was rendered by his younger son Aḥmed Bīdjān into prose form, also including some verse sections, as the *Bostānü 'l-ḥaḳāyiḳ*. Apart from this, there is the *Rūz-nāme-i Melḥame*, which is composed of selections, summaries and explanations from the *Shemsiyye* (Topkapı Sarayı Müzesi Kütüphanesi-Hazine no. 1740, 129a-141b), printed as the *Melḥame* at Kazan in 1891.

Bibliography: ʿĀlī, *Künh al-akhbār*, Millet Kütüphanesi, Tarih no. 4225, 75b; Bursalī Meḥmed Ṭāhir, *Yazīdjī Ṣalāḥ al-Dīn*, in *Türk Yurdu*, v/6 (1329/1914), 1021-2; idem, *ʿOthmānlī müʾellifleri*, iii, 308-9; Halil İnalcık, *Fatih devri üzerinde tetkikler ve vesikalar*, i, ³Ankara 1995, 71 n. 8; Âmil Çelebioğlu, *Muhammediyye*, i, Istanbul 1996, 9-16; idem, *Yazıcı Salih ve Şemsiyye'si*, in *Eski türk edebiyatı araştırmaları*, Istanbul 1998, 55-91; Atilla Batur, *Yazıcı Salih ve Şemsiyye'si*, unpubl. M.A. thesis, Erciyes Üniversitesi, 1996; Evliya Çelebi b. Derviş Mehemmed Zıllî, *Evliya Çelebi seyahatnâmesi. Topkapı Sarayı Bağdat 307 yazmasının transkripsiyonu dizini*, vols. i, ii, v, Istanbul 1995-2001, i 139, ii, 228, v, 166.

(Hatice Aynur)

YEDI ADALAR, the Turkish name of the Greek Seven (Ionian) Islands (Gk. *Heptanesos/-a*), an insular group off the western coast of north-western Peloponnese (Morea) and mainland Greece, stretching northwards in the following order: Zakynthos, Kephallenia (Cephalonia), Ithake (Ithaca), Leukas, Paxoi (Antipaxos and Paxos) and Kerkyra (Corfu). Sometimes the island of Kythera or Cerigo [see čoka adasī], off the southeastern tip of the Morea, is also included, albeit erratically, in the Seven Islands group (mainly by scholars of the area's Latin domination period). The relevant Arabic names of the islands appear in al-Idrīsī [*q.v.*], while the Ottoman Turkish names of Zaklise [*q.v.*], Kifalonia, Siyaki (Ithake), Levkas/Levkada [*q.v.*] (only the island's main town and fortress was called Aya Mavra by the Ottomans), Bakshiler (Paxoi islands) and Körfüz/Körfüs [*q.v.*] (stemming, like Corfu, from the island's Byzantine appellation of *Koryphō*) appear in the early 16th-century *Kitāb-i Baḥriyye* by Pīrī Reʾīs [*q.v.*] (see detailed comm. in the recent Greek tr. by D. Loupes, Athens 1999, 312-16, 322-37), although Ottoman rule in the Ionian area, usually commencing from 1479 with the ousting of the Italian Tocco dynasty from Benevento, was never definitively established during the Ottoman domination period except for the case of Levkas, where it lasted for almost two centuries. The Toccos' last dukes had retreated to the islands in the 1460s from mainland Eriros in view of the Ottoman conquest there, completed between 1449 and 1479.

In the Byzantine period lasting to the early 13th century (from 1204 onwards the area gradually passed under Latin control), the Heptanese sustained severe attacks, mainly from Muslims and Normans. Of particular importance here are the two attacks, first on Kephallenia and Zakynthos between 878 and 881 by the North African Arabs [see ifrīḳiya], repulsed by the celebrated Byzantine admiral Ooryphas (see Elisabeth Malamut, *Les îles de l'Empire byzantin, VIIIe-XIIe s.*, Paris 1988, 77 n. 236 and table on p. 110; sources and refs. in A. Savvides, in *Mésogeios*, i [1998], 91-2), and secondly on Corfu in 1033 by Saracens from Sicily [see ṣiḳilliya], who burned the island's main town (refs. in A. Savvides, *The Byzantine Heptanese, 11th-early 13th century* [in Gk.], Athens 1986, 19). Other references to possible Muslim attacks in the area, mainly appearing in *Saints' lives*, cannot be corroborated by parallel sourcess. Also of importance is the information provided by al-Idrīsī, who *ca.* 1153 visited Byzantium and gave in his *Kitāb Rudjdjar, inter alios,* details on Tanu (Othonoi), Ḳurfus (Corfu), Lḳata (Leukas), Djefaluniya (Kephallenia), Faskyu (Ithake?) and Djandjnt or Gagni (Zakynthos) (French tr. Jaubert, ii, 121, 123; cf. Soustal-Koder, 168, 176, 179, 195, 278; Savvides, *Byz. Heptanese,* 46-8, and idem, in *Byzantinoslavica,* lx/2 [1999], 454). About 12 years later (1164-5) the Spanish Jew from Tudela, Benjamin, also visited Korypho (Corfu) and Lachta or Lekat (Leukas and not Arta in the Epitor mainland, as in the Eng. tr. by Adler, 10, and in Soustal-Koder, 57-8 n. 97, 113; on this see the recent Gk. tr. by Photeine Vlachopoulou, introd. and comm. by K. Megalommates and A. Savvides, Athens 1994, 34-5 n. 8, 62).

From the second half of the 14th century onwards, Latin control in the Ionian Islands was divided between the Toccos on the southern (until *ca.* 1479) and Venice on the northern group (until 1797). Since there is no fixed pattern for a unified and lasting Ottoman presence in the area, this article will discuss the islands separately, beginning with Leukas, which sustained the longest Ottoman occupation.

Leukas. In Leukas (Leucata or Santa Maura in western sources) the Ottoman occupation lasted from 1479 until the final Venetian capture of 1684, with an interval between 1502-3 when the Venetians succeeded in seizing it during the Second Venetian-Ottoman war of 1499-1502. By the 1503 treaty, it was returned to Sultan Bāyezīd II [*q.v.*], who in turn recognised the Venetian occupation of Kephallenia (1500-1). Leukas' conqueror in 1479, the *bey* of Avlonya (Valona) Aḥmad Pasha Gedik [*q.v.*], carried out Meḥemmed II's plans of repopulating Istanbul with deportations, among others, of a significant part of Leukas', Zakynthos' and Kephallenia's populations. In the 16th and 17th centuries, the island's town and fortress of Aya Mavra developed as the largest settlement of the *sandjaḳ* of Ḳarlî-Ili [*q.v.*] and as an important Ottoman naval base in the area, with interesting samples of Ottoman fortifications and building activity (refs. in LEVKAS). The Venetian capture of 1684 was ratified by the treaty of Carlowitz [see ḲARLOFČA] in 1699.

Zakynthos. A Tocco possession since 1357, Zakynthos (Zante in western sources) was briefly seized (with Kephallenia and Leukas) by the Ottomans (1479); the Toccos soon recovered it (1480), but they were driven out by the Venetians (1482-3), who in 1485 purchased it by special treaty with Bāyezīd II. The 1503 treaty secured Zakynthos and Kephallenia for the Republic of St. Mark in exchange for an annual tribute of 500 ducats, a situation maintained until the Carlowitz treaty (1699). In the 16th century, the island had suffered from raids conducted by Khayr al-Dīn Pasha Barbarossa, Torghud Re'īs and Ulūdj ʿAlī [*q.vv.*]; Zakynthians participated against the Ottomans at Lepanto [see AYNABAKHTÎ] (1571), the Russian-instigated Orloff insurrection of 1770 and—after the overthrow of Venetian rule (1797)—in the 1821 Greek War for Liberation (refs. in ZAKLISE, and in Savvides, in *Mésogeios,* v [1999], 81-2, 84-5 nn. 26-38).

Kephallenia. Also a Tocco possession since 1357, the island (mentioned as Zeffalonia by Westerners) was also seized by the Ottomans in 1479 and held until 1481, when the Toccos reclaimed it until 1482-3, at which time the Venetians took over; in 1485, however, Kephallenia was ceded, in a state of depopulation, to Bāyezīd II, who extended the second Ottoman rule until 1500-1, when Venice assumed definitive control there (as well as in Ithake), resettling the island with Zakynthians and Ithakiotes in the course of the Second Venetian-Ottoman war (see G. Moschopoulos, *History of Cephalonia* [in Gk.], i, Athens 1985, 67-83). From then onwards, the Venetian presence was uninterrupted until 1797, despite two destructive Ottoman raids in 1537-8 and 1570-1 (Moschopoulos, *op. cit.*, 83-6). Kephallenians, like other Heptanesians, participated on the side of Venice in the long siege of Crete (1645-69) (Moschopoulos, 86ff.), while Kephallenia and the other islands were to receive hosts of refugees from Crete [see IḲRĪTISH] following its fall to the Sultanate (see A. Vakalopoulos, *History of modern Hellenism* [in Gk.], iii, Thessalonica 1968, 532ff.).

Ithake. Known as Val de Compare to the Latins, Ithake, following a period of Frankish rule, was laid waste in 1430 and again in the period 1479-85 by Meḥemmed II's and Bāyezīd II's fleets, in the attempt of the Sultanate to consolidate its hold on the western Greek littoral. In 1500-1 it was captured (with Kephallenia) by the Venetians, who, on account of its depopulated state, resettled it in 1504 with Kephallonians and Zakynthians. The Venetian hold on the island ended in 1797.

Paxos. The island was sold by Venice to a wealthy Corfiote, whose oppressive government forced its inhabitants to flee to the Ottoman-dominated Epirote mainland. On 22 July 1537 an allied Western fleet under Andrea Doria defeated near Paxos the Ottoman vice-admiral ʿAlī Čelebi, seizing 12 Ottoman vessels, but in 1577 the Ottomans, recovering from their defeat at Lepanto (1571) and realising the island's vulnerability, attacked and plundered it before the Venetians took over again (until 1797).

Corfu. Although it never experienced a period of Ottoman domination, the island was severely threatened by three Ottoman attacks [see also KÖRFÜZ]. In 1386 it was ceded by the Navarrese Company to Venice, whose control there lasted until 1797, while after the fall of Constantinople in 1453, Corfu was to become a place of Byzantine refugees and exiles. In 1537-8, Khayr al-Dīn Pasha Barbarossa and the Grand Vizier Luṭfī Pasha [*q.vv.*] besieged the island but, failing to seize it, they plundered Kephallenia (see Vakalopoulos, *op. cit.*, iii, 143 ff.). Another threatening attack against Corfu took place in the reign of Sultan Aḥmed III, in 1716, in the course of the Seventh Venetian-Ottoman war of 1714-18; despite a stifling blockade by sea (by the *ḳapudan-pasha* Meḥmed) and land (by the *serʿasker* Ḳara Muṣṭafa Pasha), the Venetians and Corfiotes held out (see G. Athanasainas, *The assedio of Corfu, 1716* [Gk. adaptation], Athens 2001, and D. Chatzopoulos, *The last Venetian-Ottoman war of 1714-18* [in Gk.], Athens 2002, 235-97). Finally, following the end of Venetian rule in the Heptanese (1797) and in the reign of Sultan Selīm III, the French were besieged in Corfu (Nov. 1798-March 1799) by a united Russo-Ottoman fleet under Admiral Feodor Ushakov, who had also seized Zakynthos, Kephallonia, Ithake (Oct. 1798) and Leukas (Nov. 1798) and whose operations were supported also by the Orthodox ecumenical patriarch Gregory V (detailed description of the operations by the priest Petros-Polykarpos Voulgares, in a recent modern Gk. adaptation by S.-C. Voulgares, *Chronicle of a siege, 1798-9,* Athens 2001; cf. N. Moschonas, in *IEE*, xi, 389ff.). Russo-Ottoman control, in the course of which both the first independent small Greek "Ionian State" was created (1800-7) under the sovereignty of the Porte and treaties were signed with ʿAlī Pasha Tepedelenli [*q.v.*] of

Ioannina [see YANYA] (on these treaties, see E. Protopsaltes, in *Deltion historikes kai ethnologikes hetaireias hellados*, xi [1956], 59-77), lasted until 1807, when the French took over again until 1814, at which time the British prevailed in the area until its eventual cession to Greece (1864).

Bibliography: Given in the article; see also references in the articles KÖRFÜZ, LEVKAS, ZAKLISE; on the temporary Ottoman occupation of some of the Ionian islands, see D. Pitcher, *An historical geography of the Ottoman Empire*, Leiden 1972, 87ff., index and maps (esp. XV-XVI). Detailed references on the Arab and Ottoman raids in P. Soustal and J. Koder, *Nikopolis und Kephallenia (Tabula Imperii byzantini 3)*, Vienna 1981, and A. Savvides, *Notes on the Ionian Islands and Islam in the Byzantine and post-Byzantine periods (Arab and Ottoman raids)*, in *Journal of Oriental and African Studies*, xii (Athens 2003-4); cf. idem, *Notes on Edessa/Vodena/Wodina, Volos/Gološ/Wolos/Kuluz and Zakynthos/Zante/Zaklise in the Byzantine and Turkish domination periods*, in *Mésogeios*, v (1999). See also K. Setton, *The Papacy and the Levant, 1204-1571*, 4 vols. Philadelphia 1976-84, *passim*; Alexandra Krantonelle, *History of piracy*, 3 vols. (periods 1390-1538, 1538-1699, and 18th century until the Greek War for Liberation), Athens 1985, 1991, 1998 (in Gk.). Good bibliographies on the Byzantine and post-Byzantine (Latin) Heptanese in the collective *Historia tou hellenikou ethnous (IEE) (= History of the Hellenic nation)*, ix (1979), 463-5, x (1974), 465-6, and xi (1975), 496, and in the collection of studies by G. Leontsines, *Problems in Heptanesian social history* (in Gk.), Athens 1991, 615-99. (A. SAVVIDES)

YEMENLI ḤASAN PAS̲H̲A (d. 1016/1607), Ottoman Turkish governor in the Yemen.

In the absence of tribal consensus and an agreed successor to the Zaydī imāmate following the death of al-Muṭahhar [*q.v.*] in 980/1572, the Ottomans were offered an unprecedented opportunity to extend their zone of influence beyond the Tihāma [*q.v.*] into the Yemeni interior. Earlier Ottoman advances and the securing of Ṣanʿāʾ [*q.v.*] in 954/1547 had still left large areas of the north—including strongholds such as Kawkabān and T̲h̲ulā [*q.vv.*] situated perilously close to the governor's seat itself—incompletely pacified, and it was only during Ḥasan Pas̲h̲a's exceptionally long term of office as provincial governor between D̲j̲umādā I 988/June 1580 and Muḥarram 1013/June 1604 (Rās̲h̲id, i, 154, 186) that the Ottoman administration began to make serious inroads against local resistance forces. Throughout the period of Ḥasan Pas̲h̲a's governorship in the Yemen, the Ottomans were preoccupied by wars on both the eastern and northwestern frontiers of their empire (against the Ṣafawids 986-98/1578-90 and the Habsburgs 1001-15/1593-1606, so that Ḥasan was given a free hand to secure the consolidation of Ottoman rule within his jurisdiction by his own means. One method he employed to good effect in the early years of his governorship was deportation (*nafy*) of prominent members of the Zaydī leadership. In 994/1586 he sent five of al-Muṭahhar's sons and potential successors to Istanbul for incarceration at Yedi Kule (Rās̲h̲id, i, 161), where they remained until the end of his governorship (see *ibid.*, i, 185, noting the death in captivity of Luṭf Allāh b. al-Muṭahhar in 1010/1601-2).

To reinforce his authority locally, Ḥasan Pas̲h̲a made extensive use of an inner core of long-term associates of proven military ability and unswerving personal loyalty such as his deputy (*ketk̲h̲üdā*) Sinān Pas̲h̲a and another right-hand man called Amīr ʿAlī al-D̲j̲azāʾirī. In 997/1589 he appointed the latter with the rank of *pas̲h̲a* as lieutenant-governor in Ṣaʿda [*q.v.*] with key responsibilities for securing the northern districts. When at a later stage in his governorship Ḥasan Pas̲h̲a faced a resumption of the Zaydī challenge with al-Manṣūr al-Ḳāsimī's declaration of independence in 1006/1597 [see AL-MANṢŪR BI 'LLĀH], he turned for assistance to his former associate ʿAlī Pas̲h̲a who was called in from his then current post as governor of Eritrea (for ʿAlī Pas̲h̲a's term as *beylerbeyi* of the *eyālet-i Ḥabes̲h̲* between Rad̲j̲ab 1002/April 1594 and Ramaḍān 1010/March 1602, see C. Orhonlu, *Habeş eyaleti*, Istanbul 1974, 183) to lend his help in the crisis. Through a combination of swift communications, rapid reaction and effective teamwork, the Ottomans succeeded in capturing al-Manṣūr's base of operations at S̲h̲ahāra in 1011/1602 and in forcing his re-submission, albeit temporary, to Ottoman rule. In sum, although Ottoman control over the province remained precarious at the close of Ḥasan Pas̲h̲a's twenty-four year term as governor in 1013/1604, there is no question but that he had contributed significantly to Yemen's fuller incorporation into the Ottoman imperial system.

After Ḥasan Pas̲h̲a's recall at his own request to Istanbul, he served a brief term as governor of Egypt between the early part of 1014/summer 1605 and 3 D̲h̲u 'l-Ḥid̲j̲d̲j̲a 1015/2 March 1607 (*Tārīk̲h̲-i Naʿīmā*, i, 462). Shortly after his return to the capital, he died on 9 Rad̲j̲ab 1016/3 October 1607 (*ibid.*, ii, 23).

Bibliography (in addition to references in the article): 1. Sources. Burṣalî Meḥmed Ṭāhir, *Sid̲j̲ill-i ʿot̲h̲mānī*, ii, 128-9; Aḥmed Rās̲h̲id, *Tārīk̲h̲-i Yemen we Ṣanʿāʾ*, 2 vols. Istanbul 1294/1877 (Ḥasan Pas̲h̲a's governorship being covered in detail, i, 153-86).

2. Studies. Fuad I. Khuri, *Imams and Emirs. State, religion and sects in Islam*, London 1990, 118-23 and map on 61; C.G. Brouwer, *Al-Mukha. Profile of a Yemeni sea port as sketched by servants of the Dutch East India Company (VOC) 1614-1640*, Amsterdam 1997, 106-11. (R. MURPHEY)

YOGYAKARTA, the name of a city in central Java, Indonesia, capital of the former sultanate and present-day Special District of Yogyakarta. Inhabitants (in 2002): *ca.* 448,760 (city) or *ca.* 3,068,000 (whole district).

Together with the city and area of Surakarta [*q.v.*] it was formerly part of the kingdom of Mataram [*q.v.*] located in the southern parts of central Java. The first *kraton* (palace) of Mataram was built in 1582 in Kuṭa Gĕdé, a present suburb of Yogyakarta, by Kyai Gĕdé Pamanahan. After his death in 1584 his son took over the *kraton* and military installations and was recognised by Sultan Adivijaya of Pajang as Sénopati-ing-Alaga, a military leader ("general"). After the ruler's death in 1587 Sénopati established and enlarged his new kingdom. He died in 1601. The greatest ruler among his descendants was Sultan Agung (*r.* 1613-45), who conquered most of central and eastern Java including Surabaya, and even some regions on other islands. Besides his deep roots in Javanese monistic traditions as *susuhunan* (originally a spiritual title), he also supported the spread of Islam to the interior of the island and obtained the title of *sulṭān* by a special mission from Mecca in 1641. Under his successors, however, the Islamic elements were extensively eliminated once more.

After three wars of succession and the move of the capital city to Kartasura (1677) and Surakarta (Solo, 1745), the kingdom of Mataram was divided in 1755; the Pangĕran Mangkubumi III choose again

Yogyakarta as place for his *kraton*, thus reviving the traditions of Sénopati and Sultan Agung. As Sultan Hamengku Buwono I (d. 1792) he became the founder of the dynasty of Nga Yogyakarta Hadiningrat. The situation of his *kraton* was just beside a sacred line reaching from Mt. Merapi in the north to the mouths of the rivers Opek and Progo, the meeting place with the goddess of the South Sea Nyai Lara Kidul, thus underlining his central role in sacred geography, above all, in the cosmos. More than the *susuhunan* in Surakarta, the *sulṭān* of Yogyakarta gave dominance to Islamic symbols and precepts, combining them to the special brand of Javanese Islam: the normative expressions of Islam, in confession and *S̲h̲arīʿa*, as the vessel for mystical practice; divine decree (*taḳdīr, waḥy, wangsit, pulung*) combined with the magical power (*kesaktèn, sĕkti*, from Sanskr. *śakti*) of the ruler, and thus the subordination of the religious scholar to the king (Woodward, 152). The tradition of Yogyakarta relates these teachings to Sunan Kali Jaga, one of the nine revered teachers of Islam (*wali songo*) in Java who was a particular adviser to Sénopati.

The Java War (1825-30) broke out when Pangĕran Diponegoro (1785-1855), son of Sultan Hamengku Buwono III and a person well trained in mystical practices, was taken to fight against the alliance of the court and the Dutch because of new administrative regulations. He was supported by the people, by members of the nobility and the Islamic *ʿulamāʾ* led by Kiyai Maja. After being treacherously taken prisoner, he was exiled to Makassar [*q.v.*], while Kiyai Maja was exiled to Menado.

In 1912 Yogyakarta witnessed the founding of the *Muhammadiyah* by K.H. Ahmad Dahlan as a modernist social and educational organisation which is at present the second largest Islamic organisation in Indonesia. The great popularity of Sultan Hamengku Buwono IX (1912-88, *r.* since 1939), a modernising reform of the village administration in 1946 in his district, and his close co-operation with the republican leaders after 1945, particularly 1946-9 when Yogyakarta was the interim capital of Indonesia because of the Dutch occupation of Jakarta, saved the special status of the district. Its role as a centre of academic learning (1946: founding of Gajah Mada University; 1959: Institute for Higher Islamic Learning, *IAIN*; and others, including Protestant and Catholic seminaries) has been further developed by Sultan Hamengku Buwono X (b. 2 April 1946, succeeded his father in 1988).

Bibliography: *EI*[1], *s.v. D̲j̲okyâkartâ*; *Babad Tanah Djawi*, rev. repr. J.J. Ras, 2 vols. [2]Dordrecht and Providence, R.I. 1987; M.C. Ricklefs, *Jogjakarta under Sultan Mangkubumi 1749-1792. A history of the division of Java*, London 1974; M.R. Woodward, *Islam in Java. Normative piety and mysticism in the Sultanate of Yogyakarta*, Tucson 1989. (O. Schumann)

YOMUT, a Türkmen tribe, or rather a tribal confederacy, in Central Asia.

Today, most of them live in the Republic of Türkmenistan (1926: *ca.* 100,000; contemporary state policy takes no cognisance of individual tribes). About 130,000 (in the 1960s, cf. Irons 1974) inhabit Iran (east of the Caspian sea, from the Gurgān plain north to the border of Türkmenistan), and between 125,000 and 400,000 (Adamec) live in northwestern Afg̲h̲ānistān (north of the Paripamisus range). The etymology of the name is unclear. The Yomut do not appear among the pre-Mongol Türkmen tribes listed by al-Kās̲h̲g̲h̲arī in his *Dīwān lug̲h̲āt al-Turk* (tr. R. Dankoff and J. Kelly 1982-5), nor in Ras̲h̲īd al-Dīn's *D̲j̲āmiʿ al-tawārīk̲h̲* (*Die Geschichte der Oġuzen*, tr. Karl Jahn, 1969, 46-7). Abu 'l-G̲h̲āzī Bahādur K̲h̲ān [*q.v.*] mentions Yomut, a remote descendant of Salur, the son of the legendary Og̲h̲uz K̲h̲ān's son Ṭag̲h̲ K̲h̲ān (*S̲h̲ad̲j̲ara-yi Tarākima*, fol. 100b, ed. and Turkish tr. Z.K. Ölmez, 1996). Dshikijew (1994) collected among the Yomut in the Turkmen SSR some divergent genealogical tales all of which show that the Yomut believe that they have the same ancestor Salur (Ḳazan Alp), one of the most famous heroes of Türkmen lore [see dede ḳorḳut], as the Teke, Ersari, Sarïḳ and Salor tribes [*q.vv.*]. According to Bregel (1981), in the 16th century the Yomut, along with other tribal groups such as the Ersari, Salor, Sarïḳ and Teke, practised pastoral nomadism in the region between the Mangïs̲h̲laḳ peninsula and the Balk̲h̲ān mountains. Due to ecological factors and the pressure of the Ḳalmuḳs and Ḳazak̲h̲s from the north, probably in the second half of the 17th century, some Yomut moved to the Gurgān plain while others migrated towards the oases of K̲h̲ʷārazm in the first half of the 18th century. Eventually they received permission from the k̲h̲ān to remain on the northwestern periphery of the K̲h̲īwa oasis.

In the *Firdaws al-iḳbāl*, a 19th century chronicle of K̲h̲īwa, written by Mūnis and Āgahī [*q.vv.*], from the early 18th century onward the Yomut are frequently mentioned among the tribal enemies whom several k̲h̲āns had to subdue at regular intervals. The Yomut also played a certain role in K̲h̲īwan history since, as auxiliaries, they often joined the K̲h̲ān's army, mostly in his fights with the S̲h̲īʿī Persians in K̲h̲urāsān, but also in campaigns against Buk̲h̲ārā. They were also prone to ally themselves with a k̲h̲ān's rebellious relatives or governors. Between 1178/1764-5 and 1184/1770-1, the Yomut even succeeded in capturing twice the city of K̲h̲īwa and also most other strongholds of the k̲h̲ānate. After the Russians had reduced K̲h̲īwa to a protectorate (1873) and annexed the Türkmen territory from Mangïs̲h̲laḳ down to the Persian border (1881-4), the Yomut incursions continued across the Russian-Persian border but on a much reduced scale.

From the early 19th to the second half of the 20th century, all the Gurgān (Astarābād) Yomut tribes had either predominantly pastoral (*čarva*) or predominantly agricultural (*čomur*) members producing for monetary economy. Their most famous product were carpets. Up to the 1950s, they were also able to preserve slave and lifestock raiding as an additional source of income, since the Iranian government exerted firmer political and fiscal control only in the 1930s and, again, from the middle of the century onwards (Irons 1994).

Bibliography: Y. Bregel, *Nomadic and sedentary elements among the Turkmens*, in *CAJ*, xxv (1981), 5-37; Mūnis and Āgahī, *Firdaws al-iḳbāl*, ed. and tr. Bregel, *Firdaws al-iqbāl. History of Khorezm*, Leiden 1988-98 (with copious notes on the details of Yomut-K̲h̲īwan relations accompanying the tr.); L.W. Adamec, *Historical dictionary of Afghanistan*, Metuchen, N.J. and London 1991; B. Rosetti, *Die Turkmenen und ihre Teppiche*, Berlin 1992; A. Dshikijew, *Das turkmenische Volk im Mittelalter*, Berlin 1994; W. Irons, *Why are the Yomut not more stratified?*, in Claudia Chang and H.A. Koster (eds.), *Pastoralists at the periphery*, Tucson and London 1994, 175-96 (with refs. to earlier articles by Irons based on fieldwork in the 1960s and 1970s).

(Barbara Kellner-Heinkele)

YURTČÏ (t.) (from *yurt* "tribal territory, camp site, tent site", a general term in the Turkic languages, cf. Türkmen *yūrt* ~ *yuwïrt*, Ḳaraḳalpaḳ, Ḳazaḳ and Ḳïrghïz *žurt*; see KHAYMA. iv, to whose *Bibl.* should be added G. Doerfer, *Türkische und mongolische Elemente im Neupersischen*, Wiesbaden 1965-70, iv, 212-16 no. 1914), Pers. *yūrtdjī*, the salaried officer responsible for choosing camp sites for the army or court, organising them, and supervising their use.

Djuwaynī's use of *yūrt* for the appanages granted by Činggiz Ḳan to his brother, sons and grandsons demonstrates that *yurt* then included both summer and winter quarters, the whole territory of an *ulus* (i, 31). Rashīd al-Dīn uses it in the same way, saying, for example, that "the dwelling and territories, *maḳām wa yūrt-hā*" of Činggiz Ḳan were next to those of the Ong Ḳan (Berezin, *Činggiz*, text, i, 118). The *yurtčī*'s duties are set out by Nakhčiwānī [*q.v.*] in 1360, in two specimen charters (ii, 64-6): his appointment is to be recognised by all, from the viziers downwards through commanders of ten thousands and thousands to the tribes themselves. He alone is to designate camp sites, *yūrt-hā*, in a pleasant district, giving priority to the ruler, and then to his counsellors and lords wherever the camps, *urdū-hā*, are to be pitched in summer and winter quarters, *mawāḍiʿ-i yāylāḳ wa ḳīshlāḳī*. His choices in all districts are to take account of the local population's separate needs: they should be far from the arable land of village peasants, or troops of horse-herders, or those settled in *obas*, or nomads; the site should not be irksome, to the detriment of people's land, and for this reason nothing should be demanded of anyone. No-one should exceed the camp site which he had designated for them. It is emphasised that the *yurtčī* was selected on the basis of his long experience, and knowledge of where camp sites with plenty of water and grazing were to be found in all the districts for summer and winter quarters, and of all the communication routes used by the camp. In whatever direction a royal expedition was undertaken, he was to go in the vanguard and establish the site for royal use, and those for the principal members of the court, so that the troops on arrival at the stage [see MANZIL] should know exactly where to encamp. It is mentioned specifically that these must be far from the courses of rivers which might flood. The office was thus a highly responsible one, in which the experience and competence to be found in those living a largely nomadic life were integrated with a system of state finance and administration. Besides the *yurtčī*, three other officials were particularly responsible for the management of the camp: the *farrāsh*, or tent-pitcher, the *bularghučī* or keeper of lost property, and the *sārbān* or cameleer. The superintendent of the tent department, *mihtar-i farāsh-khāna*, was accountable for the supply and maintenance of the royal tents. Such camps had to operate under a wide variety of conditions, which must have strained the vigilance of these officials. Though at times the movement from recognised summer quarters to winter quarters was regular enough, the use of at least seven different summer sites by Ghāzān in the course of his nine-year reign shows the extent to which movement was possible in the north of Persia alone. Some sites were preferred for ceremonial purposes, most probably because of their proximity to Tabrīz: a grand assembly was held at Ḳārābāgh in 1295, and a great public festival of 1302 in the meadows at Ūdjān. Some of these sites at least were registered as royal domains, *indjü*: Lār, for example, belonged to Arghūn.

Bibliography: Muḥammad b. Hindūshāh Nakhčiwānī, *Dastūr al-kātib fī taʿyīn al-marātib*, text ed. A.A. Alizade, 2 vols. in 3, Moscow 1964, 1971, 1976 (Pamyatniki literaturui narodov vostoka. Tekstui bolshoya seriya, ix); Rashīd al-Dīn Faḍl Allāh, Ṭabīb, Hamadānī, *Djāmiʿ al-tawārīkh*, text ed. I.N. Berezin with tr. as *Sbornik letopisey, Istoriya Mongolov. Istoriya Čingiz-khana*, 2 vols. St Petersburg 1868, 1888 (Trudi vostočnago otdeleniya Imperatorskago Arkheologičeskago Obshčestva, xiii, xv); Doerfer, *op. cit.*, iv, 216-17 no. 1915.

(P.A. ANDREWS)

YŪSUF B. AL-ḤASAN (I), MAWLĀY, sultan of Morocco, *r.* 1330-46/1912-27.

He was born in 1298/1880-1 of a Circassian mother, Āmina. His early life in the royal palace remains obscure. He received education from private tutors in a traditional curriculum and did not emerge into public life until 1330-1/1912 when his brother, sultan ʿAbd al-Ḥāfiẓ (*r.* 1325-30/1908-12) appointed him as his *khalīfa* (viceroy) at Fez. Later that year, he was named sultan (19 Shaʿbān 1330/12 August 1912) after his brother was forced to abdicate by Marshal Lyautey, Resident-General and principal architect of the French Protectorate then being established in Morocco.

Dignified, pious, intelligent, affable, possessed of no political experience or ambitions, and apparently friendly toward France, Mawlāy Yūsuf seemed an ideal choice for an office meant by the French Protectorate authorities to serve as a legitimating symbol and façade for their governance in the country. Under Lyautey's tutalage (1912-25) he would serve this role well: lending his prestige as an ʿAlawī *sharīf* to French military campaigns against Moroccan resistance to the imposition of French and Spanish rule, and generally remaining publicly co-operative and uncritical of France and its Protectorate policies. He was routinely associated with the inauguration of a wide range of Protectorate initiatives in the areas of government, finance, administration, the judiciary, the education system, infrastructure and economic development.

At the same time, he gradually emerged as a more active and interested participant in the creation of a revitalised sultanate and government (*makhzan* [*q.v.*]) that linked traditional forms—embodied especially in the person and reign of his father Mawlāy al-Ḥasan (*r.* 1290-1311/1873-94)—and modern innovation represented and advocated by France. He took an active interest in the reform and encouragement of Islamic education, and gave generous royal patronage to the repair and construction of mosques, *madrasas* and other public buildings. He effectively opposed French efforts to reduce or replace *Sharīʿa* courts in the country's Berber-speaking areas, and was an increasingly vocal opponent of the Protectorate's ongoing expropriation of rural and urban property. Unknown and unpopular at first, his travels throughout the country, extensive publicity and increasing association with the development of a modern Morocco that respected and preserved religious and cultural traditions, gained for him broadening popular acceptance. Recent scholarship (e.g. Rivet) shows him and his relationship to the French Protectorate to be much more complex than earlier interpretations have allowed. Though never enjoying real power, the sultanate during Mawlāy Yūsuf's reign became more than a mere façade lending itself uncritically and unawares to the policies of the Protectorate authorities. Over the course of time, he took on substance sufficient to begin a transition from the status of a perplexed and diffident pupil to that of respected mentor, perhaps, in some ways, even partner, in the governance of the sultanate.

Yūsuf died on 22 Djumādā I 1346/17 November 1927 from the effects of uraemia. He was succeeded by his third son Muḥammad (V) [*q.v.*].

Bibliography: *Rapport général sur la situation du Protectorat du Maroc*, Rabat 1914; *RMM*, xxix (1914); *Renseignements Coloniaux*, vi (1916); Ibn Zaydān, *al-Yumn al-wāfir fī imtidāḥ al-djānab al-mawlāy al-yūsufī*, Fez 1923; A.G.P. Martin, *Quatre siècles d'histoire marocaine*, Paris 1923; *Bulletin du Comité de l'Afrique française* (Nov. 1927); Ibn Zaydān, *al-Durar al-fākhira*, Rabat 1937; ʿAllāl al-Fāsī, *al-Ḥarakāt al-istiḳlāliyya fī 'l-maghrib*, Cairo 1948, Eng. tr., repr. New York 1970; P. Lyautey, *Lyautey l'Africain*, 4 vols. Paris 1954; R. Bidwell, *Morocco under colonial rule*, London 1973; Ch.-A. Julien, *Le Maroc face aux imperialismes*, Paris 1978; D. Rivet, *Lyautey et l'institution du Protectorat francais au Maroc*, 3 vols. Paris 1988; W. Hoisington, *Lyautey and the French conquest of Morocco*, New York 1995. (W. ROLLMAN)

YÜZBASHİ (T.), lit. "head of a hundred [men]", a term used in later Ottoman and now modern Turkish armies for the rank of captain, and in the form *yūzbashī* in modern Arab armies for this same rank. It was further used in Muslim Indian minting practice for the engraver of coin dies; see DĀR AL-ḌARB, at Vol. II, 121a.

Z

AL-ZAMAKHSHARĪ, ABU 'L-ḲĀSIM MAḤMŪD B. ʿUMAR.

2. Contributions in the fields of theology, exegesis, *ḥadīth* and *adab*.

His father, as imām of the local mosque in Zamakhshar, taught him the Ḳur'ān, but since he lacked the means to support the further education of his son, he wanted him to become a tailor. Yielding to his son's wishes, however, he brought him to the capital of Khwārazm, Djurdjāniyya, which henceforth became his permanent home and where he first earned his sustenance by copying for a wealthy patron. His ambition was a high secretarial career in government. For his literary education, he studied first with Abū ʿAlī al-Ḥasan b. al-Muẓaffar al-Naysābūrī (the death date of 442/1050 commonly given for him is mistaken, since his son ʿUmar died only in 536/1142), the leading man of letters in Khwārazm at the time, and after the arrival there of Abū Muḍar Maḥmūd b. Djarīr al-Ḍabbī al-Iṣfahānī (d. 507/1114), with the latter, who became his most influential teacher and generous patron. Al-Zamakhsharī also visited Bukhārā to study and hear *ḥadīth*. On his way there he fell from his mount and broke a leg, which had to be amputated and replaced by a wooden substitute.

In his ambition for a high position in government, he first addressed panegyric poems to the famous Saldjūḳ vizier Niẓām al-Mulk (d. 485/1092 [*q.v.*]), referring to his teacher Abū Muḍar, but his hopes were disappointed. Later he travelled widely in Khurāsān and western Persia, pursuing his scholarly interests and addressing similar poems to Saldjūḳ dignitaries such as Mu'ayyid al-Mulk b. Niẓām al-Mulk (d. 495/1102) and Mudjīr al-Dīn Abu 'l-Fatḥ al-Ardastānī and even to the Sultans Muḥammad b. Malikshāh (d. 511/1118) and Sandjar. Although he received some monetary rewards for these eulogies, he failed to secure any position. This was largely due to his open espousal of Muʿtazilī doctrine, which in the Saldjūḳ period came increasingly to be viewed as heretical. When he fell seriously ill in 512/1118, he vowed never again to visit a court or praise a ruler, seeking thereby a position, and vowed to lead an ascetic life devoted to religion and teaching. After his recovery, he visited Baghdād where he engaged in studies and debates with scholars. He assembled with the Ḥanafī jurist Aḥmad b. ʿAlī al-Dāmghānī and the grammarian al-Sharīf Hibat Allāh b. al-Shadjarī. As he made the Pilgrimage in that year, he was welcomed by the *amīr* of Mecca, the Sharīf ʿAlī b. ʿĪsā b. Ḥamza b. Wahhās, a Muʿtazilī Zaydī man of letters and learning. A close friendship developed between the two, and al-Zamakhsharī stayed with the *amīr* for two years as a greatly honoured guest, during which he also visited parts of Arabia and Yemen. Then he returned to Djurdjāniyya, where he was honoured in this period by the Khwārazmshāhs Muḥammad b. Anūshtakīn (d. 521/1127) and his son Atsïz. A decade later, he again set out for Mecca and stayed for an extended time in Damascus, where he composed eulogies for the Būrid ruler Tādj al-Mulūk Ṭughtakīn (d. 526/1131) and his son Shams al-Mulk. He reached Mecca for the Pilgrimage in 526/1132 and stayed there for three years, again hospitably received by Ibn Wahhās, who encouraged him to assemble his *dīwān* of poetry and to compose his Ḳur'ān commentary *al-Kashshāf*. Al-Zamakhsharī completed the latter after two years in 528/1133. In 533/1138 he made a further trip to Mecca and passed through Baghdād, where he visited Abū Manṣūr Mawhūb b. al-Djawālīḳī [*q.v.*], a famous man of letters, and received his *idjāza*. He died in Djurdjāniyya on 9 Dhu 'l-Ḥidjdja 538/14 June 1144 and was buried near the town. On account of his prolonged stay in Mecca—he lived there for five years and performed the Pilgrimage seven times according to his own testimony—he claimed the title Djār Allāh, under which he remained widely known. In his home country he was commonly referred to as Fakhr Khwārazm "the Glory of Khwārazm".

Although of Persian origin, al-Zamakhsharī was most basically motivated in his scholarship to serve and promote the Arabic language. Arabic was in his view the most perfect language which God had preferrred to all languages as He preferred the Ḳur'ān and Islam over all scripture and religions (see 1., at Vol. XI, 432b-434a). In the work on which his fame primarily rests, the Ḳur'ān commentary *al-Kashshāf ʿan ḥaḳā'iḳ al-tanzīl*, his efforts in explaining the Holy Book's grammatical, lexicographical and rhetorical features, variant readings and the miraculous nature (*iʿdjāz* [*q.v.*]) of its beautiful language earned him universal admiration. He did so adducing quotations from a wide variety of early prose texts, including the *tafsīr* of the grammarian al-Zadjdjādj [*q.v.*] and poetry, rather than relying on traditional exegesis. His rationalist Muʿtazilī interpretations, however, provoked criticism among traditionalist Sunnīs. While some of these interpretations were adopted from earlier Muʿtazilī exegetes such as Abū Bakr al-Aṣamm and al-Rummānī, he also frequently presented views of his own. In concord with his Muʿtazilī outlook, he emphasised ethical and ascetic aspects and denounced Ṣūfī antinomian tendencies and belief in miracles of saints, Shuʿūbīs and the Umayyad caliphs. In legal questions, he occasionally backed al-Shāfiʿī and other positions against his own Ḥanafī school. The popularity of his work was in the eastern Muslim world not seriously impaired by the attempt of al-Bayḍāwī [*q.v.*] to furnish an orthodox counterpart to it in his *Anwār al-tanzīl*. Opposition to his Muʿtazilī tendency was stronger in the Muslim West, where the Mālikī Aḥmad b. Muḥammad b. al-Munayyir (d. 683/1284) wrote a refutation of his Muʿtazilī interpretations entitled *K. al-Inṣāf min al-Kashshāf*, which is sometimes printed on the margins of the *Kashshāf*.

In Muʿtazilī theology, al-Zamakhsharī was familiar with the school doctrine of Ḳāḍī ʿAbd al-Djabbār through the literary transmission of al-Ḥākim al-Djushamī [*q.v.*], which he received from his teacher Aḥmad b. Muḥammad b. Isḥāḳ al-Khwārazmī. In addition, he studied the school doctrine of Abu 'l-Ḥusayn al-Baṣrī [*q.v.*], which was first introduced into Khwārazm by his teacher Abū Muḍar al-Iṣfahānī, with his colleague Rukn al-Dīn Ibn al-Malāḥimī. In his Muʿtazilī creed *al-Minhādj fī uṣūl al-dīn* he appears partly influenced by the doctrine of Abu 'l-Ḥusayn al-Baṣrī but generally avoids taking side in the conflict between the two schools.

In the field of *ḥadīth*, he composed a large, alphabetically-arranged dictionary of unusual words, *al-Fāʾiḳ fī gharīb al-ḥadīth*. The relevant *ḥadīth*s are fully quoted and explained. In his *Mukhtaṣar al-Muwāfaḳa bayna ahl al-bayt wa 'l-ṣaḥāba* he abridged the work of the Muʿtazilī Zaydī traditionist Abū Saʿīd Ismāʿīl b. ʿAlī al-Sammān al-Rāzī (d. 443/1051), omitting the *isnād*s. The book was intended to demonstrate the concord between the family of Muḥammad and the major Companions (see Ḥādjdjī Khalīfa, ii, 1890). He assembled biographical data and reports about the virtues of the ten Companions whom the Prophet had promised paradise in his *Khaṣāʾiṣ al-ʿashara al-kirām al-barara*. His *al-Kashf fi 'l-ḳirāʾāt al-ʿashar* deals with the canonical variant readings of the Ḳurʾān.

In the field of *adab*, he collected an extensive dictionary of Arabic proverbs *al-Mustaḳṣā fī amthāl al-ʿArab* which rivalled the *Madjmaʿ al-amthāl* of his contemporary al-Maydānī. Completed in 499/1106, it contains 3,461 proverbs alphabetically arranged according to their beginnings with explanation of their origin and use. His voluminous *Rabīʿ al-abrār wa-nuṣūṣ al-akhbār* contains extracts from literary and historical works arranged according to 92 topics. It was meant to be a companion reader to his Ḳurʾān commentary. His *K. al-Amkina wa 'l-djibāl* is a small dictionary of Arabic geographical names.

In his own artistic prose works, his predilection was for ethical admonition and preaching. His *Maḳāmāt*, also entitled *al-Naṣāʾiḥ al-kibār*, contain fifty *maḳāmāt* [*q.v.*] in the older meaning of the term, moral exhortations which he addressed to himself. He composed them after his illness in 512/1118 and later added his own philological commentary. His *Aṭwāḳ al-dhahab* or *al-Naṣāʾiḥ al-ṣighār* consists of 100 pious maxims with allusions to the Ḳurʾān, Sunna and proverbial expressions. It was dedicated to Ibn Wahhās and the people of Mecca. His *Nawābigh al-kalim* or *al-Kilam al-nawābigh* is a small collection of apophthegms. A commentary on it, *al-Niʿam al-sawābigh*, was written by al-Taftāzānī [*q.v.*].

His poetry, collected into his *dīwān*, reflects his technical skill and understanding of the classical tradition of Arabic poetry more than an original poetical talent. An influence of the poetry of Djarīr and al-Mutanabbī is occasionally apparent. He wrote a substantial commentary on al-Shanfarā's *Lāmiyyat al-ʿArab*, the *K. Aʿdjab al-ʿadjab fī sharḥ Lāmiyyat al-ʿArab*. His *al-Ḳisṭās al-mustaḳīm fī ʿilm al-ʿarūḍ* is a treatise on prosody.

Bibliography: Samʿānī, *Ansāb*, ed. ʿAbd Allāh b. ʿUmar al-Bārūdī, Beirut 1988, iii, 163-4; Andarasbānī, *Muʿdjam al-siyar*, in ʿAbd al-Karīm al-Yāfī, *Fī sīrat al-Zamakhsharī*, in *RAAD*, lvii (1982), 365-82; Ibn al-Ḳifṭī, *Inbāh al-ruwāt*, ed. M. Abu 'l-Faḍl Ibrāhīm, Cairo 1986, iii, 265-72; Yāḳūt, *Udabāʾ*, vii, 147-51; Ibn Khallikān, ed. Iḥsān ʿAbbās, v, 168-74; Muṣṭafā al-Ṣāwī al-Djuwaynī, *Manhadj al-Zamakhsharī fī tafsīr al-Ḳurʾān*, Cairo 1959; A.M. al-Ḥūfī, *al-Zamakhsharī*, Cairo 1966; A. Yüksel, *Al-Zamakhshari's life and a critical edition of his Dīwān*, thesis Durham 1979; S. Schmidtke, *A Muʿtazilite creed of az-Zamaḫšarī*, Stuttgart 1997.

(W. MADELUNG)

ZANDAḲA [see ZINDĪḲ].

AL-**ZANDJĀNĪ**, ʿIZZ AL-DĪN ʿABD AL-WAHHĀB b. Ibrāhīm b. ʿAbd al-Wahhāb al-Kharadjī (often given as: al-Khazradjī) al-Shāfiʿī, Abu 'l-Maʿālī (*fl.* in the middle of the 7th/13th century), grammarian and *adīb*, who *ca.* 625/1228 wrote a celebrated treatise on morphology (*ṣarf* [*q.v.*]), *Mabādiʾ al-taṣrīf* or *(Kitāb) al-Taṣrīf al-ʿIzzī*, extant in numerous mss. and the subject of many commentaries, the most popular one being that of al-Taftāzānī (see *Bibl.*).

The *Kitāb al-Taṣrīf* was the third grammatical treatise (after Ibn al-Ḥādjib's *Kāfiya* and the *Ādjurrūmiyya*) to be made available in the West, in an edition and two Latin translations, one literal and one idiomatic, by the director of the Medici press, J.B. Raymundus (Giovanni Battista Raimondi), *Kitāb al-Taṣrīf taʾlīf al-Shaykh al-Imām, Liber Tasriphi compositio est Senis Alemami, traditur in ea compendiosa notitia conjugationum verbi Arabici*, Rome 1610 (see Chr.F. Schnurrer, *Bibliotheca arabica*, Halle 1811, 25-7, no. 47). The name of the author sometimes appears as al-ʿIzzī (see e.g. J. Fück, *Die arabischen Studien in Europa*, Leipzig 1955, 56); this seems to have arisen from a careless rendition of the title as *Taṣrīf al-ʿIzzī* rather than *al-Taṣrīf al-ʿIzzī* (the *nisba* refers to the author's *laḳab* ʿIzz al-Dīn). In addition to other works in the fields of, *inter alia*, grammar and lexicography, al-Zandjānī wrote works also in *adab*. One is an anthology of poetic snippets (not entire poems) with the title *al-Madnūn bihī ʿalā ghayr ahlih*. It deals with the following themes: books, praise, yearning, love, congratulations, dirges, complaints and invective. An extensive commentary on it was written by ʿUbayd Allāh b. ʿAbd al-Kāfī b. ʿAbd al-Madjīd al-ʿUbaydī, who finished it in 724/1324. The other book, with the title *K. Miʿyār al-nuzzār fī ʿulūm al-ashʿār*, deals with prosody and rhetoric. It is divided into three parts: metrics (*ʿilm al-ʿarūḍ*), rhyme taxonomy (*ʿilm al-ḳawāfī*), and rhetoric (*ʿilm al-badīʿ*). This arrangement of the poetic disciplines imitates al-Khaṭīb al-Tibrīzī's *al-Kāfī fi 'l-ʿarūḍ wa 'l-ḳawāfī*, which likewise contains an unexpected section on *al-badīʿ* (ed. al-Ḥassānī Ḥasan ʿAbd Allāh, Cairo n.d., 170-204). Interestingly, one of his sources is the *Ḥadāʾiḳ al-siḥr fī ḥaḳāʾiḳ al-shiʿr*, written in Persian by Rashīd al-Dīn Waṭwāṭ [*q.v.*]. Knowledge of Persian on the part of al-Zandjānī is also shown by a line of Persian poetry in *al-Madnūn* (ed. Yahuda, 25). The *Miʿyār* is often quoted in later rhetorical literature.

Bibliography (N.B. ʿAbd al-Wahhāb b. Ibrāhīm al-Zandjānī is not infrequently confused with his father Ibrāhīm b. ʿAbd al-Wahhāb [both having the *laḳab* ʿIzz al-Dīn!]): 1. Biographical and bibliographical. Ziriklī, *Aʿlām*, ²Damascus 1373-8/1954-9, iv, 330; Brockelmann, I², 336-7 (ʿAbd al-Wahhāb b. Ibrāhīm), S I, 497-8 (Ibrāhīm b. ʿAbd al-Wahhāb, referring to the same person!); Kaḥḥāla, i, 57 (Ibrāhīm, with the *al-Taṣrīf al-ʿIzzī* attributed to him); vi, 216-17 (ʿAbd al-Wahhāb, author of the remaining works mentioned above).

2. Works. Saʿd al-Dīn al-Taftāzānī, *Sharḥ Mukhtaṣar al-Taṣrīf al-ʿIzzī fī fann al-ṣarf*, ed. ʿAbd al-ʿĀl Sālim Makram, Kuwait 1983; ʿUbaydī, *Sharḥ al-Madnūn bihī ʿalā ghayr ahlih*, ed. I.B. Yahuda, Cairo 1913-15, repr. Beirut and Baghdād n.d. [1993 or before] (with a new title-page that omits the name of the editor and with omission of the two, Arabic and French, prefaces of the editor); ed. Faradj Allāh Dhakī al-Kurdī, Cairo 1342; *K. Miʿyār al-nuẓẓār fī ʿulūm al-ashʿār*, ed. Muḥammad ʿAlī Rizḳ al-Khafādjī, 2 vols, Cairo 1991; ed. of Pts. 1-2 by Maḥmūd Fadjdjāl (forthcoming [?], cf. al-Ashḳar, introd. to Pt. 3, 3, n. 1); ed. of Pt. 3 by ʿAbd al-Munʿim Sayyid ʿAbd al-Salām al-Ashḳar, Cairo 1416/1995 (with valuable introd., based in part on Maḥmūd Fadjdjāl's unpublished study and ed. of al-Zandjānī, *al-Kāfī fī sharḥ al-Hādī li-dhawī 'l-albāb fī ʿilm al-iʿrāb*, doctoral thesis, Kulliyyat al-Lugha al-ʿArabiyya, Djāmiʿat al-Azhar 1398/1978). (Eds.)

AL-**ZARKASHĪ**, Abū ʿAbd Allāh Badr al-Dīn Muḥammad b. ʿAbd Allāh b. Bahādur (or Muḥammad b. Bahādur b. ʿAbd Allāh, according to some), prolific writer who lived in Mamlūk Cairo at a time of flourishing intellectual activity.

Born in Cairo in 745/1344, he studied *ḥadīth* in Damascus with ʿImād al-Dīn Ibn Kathīr (d. 774/1373 [*q.v.*]), *fiḳh* and *uṣūl* in Aleppo with Shihāb al-Dīn al-Adhraʿī (d. 783/1381; see Brockelmann, S II, 108), and Ḳurʾān and *fiḳh* in Cairo with the head of the Shāfiʿī school in Cairo at the time, Djamāl al-Dīn al-Asnawī (d. 772/1370, see Gilliot, *Textes arabes anciens édités en Égypte au cours des années 1996 à 1999*, in *MIDEO*, xxiv [2000], 252, entry no. 135, item 4), as well as with Sirādj al-Dīn al-Bulḳīnī (d. 805/1403 [*q.v.*]) and ʿAlāʾ al-Dīn Mughulṭay (d. 762/1361 [*q.v.*]). He died in Cairo on 3 Radjab 794/27 May 1392 and was buried in the smaller al-Ḳarāfa cemetery in the area of the tomb of the Amīr Baktamur al-Sāḳī. He was called al-Zarkashī because he learned embroidery while he was young; he also became known as al-Minhādjī because he learned the text of Muḥyī al-Dīn al-Nawawī (d. 676/1277 [*q.v.*]), the *Minhādj al-ṭālibīn*, by heart. Al-Zarkashī is spoken of as naturally reserved, having spent most of his time in his house or in the bookstores where he would take copious notes in order to avoid spending money to buy books.

According to the study by Muḥammad Abu 'l-Faḍl Ibrāhīm, the modern editor of one of al-Zarkashī's more famous works, *al-Burhān fī ʿulūm al-Ḳurʾān* (Cairo 1957, ²1972; see i, 5-13, for the biography of al-Zarkashī), some 33 works are attributed to him, 23 of which are apparently still in existence. ʿAbd al-Ḳādir ʿAbd Allāh al-ʿĀnī, the editor of al-Zarkashī's *al-Baḥr al-muḥīṭ fī uṣūl al-fiḳh* (6 vols., Kuwait 1401/1989; see i, 7-19, for the biography of al-Zarkashī), manages to increase this total to 46 works, although many are attested only by single mentions in historical bibliographies. Brockelmann, II, 91-2, S II, 108, lists 22 works, all in existence.

About 14 of al-Zarkashī's works are available in published form today, displaying the broad spectrum of his interests. A jurist of the school of al-Shāfiʿī, al-Zarkashī's works cover the full range of traditional scholarship: *ḥadīth, tafsīr, fiḳh, adab* and *kalām*. In *fiḳh*, al-Zarkashī wrote his summary *al-Baḥr al-muḥīṭ fī uṣūl al-fiḳh* in 777/1376 when he was only 32. Among his many other legal works of note is a book on hashish, *Ẓahr al-ʿarīsh fī taḥrīm al-ḥashīsh*, which details the physical hazards of hashish consumption and the moral effects the substance has, which are deemed to be parallel to those associated with wine and intoxication. Al-Zarkashī did, however, admit to some of hashish's positive (and legal) anaesthetising abilities. It was the use of hashish for enjoyment and pleasure that raised the ire of al-Zarkashī, as it did for almost every Muslim jurist.

His achievements have only recently started to be properly recognised. He lived at a time of significant scholarly activity and his works certainly drew the attention of those in the immediate generations thereafter. His *al-Burhān fī ʿulūm al-Ḳurʾān*, for example, was the first all-encompassing work of its type, only to be eclipsed a century later by al-Suyūṭī's *al-Itḳān fī ʿulūm al-Ḳurʾān*, even though (or perhaps because) al-Suyūṭī benefited from al-Zarkashī's work in terms of providing the structuring and content of his own work. In a total of 47 chapters in *al-Burhān*, al-Zarkashī brings together every major topic related to understanding the Ḳurʾān, devoting what is essentially a monograph to each one; he mentions previous authors who have treated each subject and compares the opinions of the traditionists, the theologians, the exegetes and the grammarians on many of the topics. Al-Suyūṭī also created his own work *al-Durar al-muntathara fi 'l-aḥādīth al-mushtahara* (Beirut 1995) on the basis of al-Zarkashī's now lost treatise *al-Tadhkira fi 'l-aḥādīth al-mushtahira*.

Bibliography: 1. Biographical sources. Dāwudī, *Ṭabaḳāt al-mufassirīn*, Cairo 1392, ii, 157-8 (no. 504); Ibn Ḥadjar, *al-Durar al-kāmina fī aʿyān al-miʾa al-thāmina*, Ḥaydarābād 1348-50, iii, 397-8 (no. 1059); other sources cited in G.C. Anawati, *Textes arabes anciens édités en Égypte au cours de l'année 1957*, in *MIDEO*, iv (1957), 223-7, entry no. 18 (on the edition of *al-Burhān*) and Cl. Gilliot, *Textes arabes anciens édités en Égypte au cours des années 1996 à 1999*, in *MIDEO*, xxiv (2000), 247-49, entry no. 131.

2. Studies. K.E. Nolin, *The* Itqān *and its sources: a study of* al-Itqān fī ʿulūm al-Qurʾān *by Jalāl al-Dīn al-Suyūṭī with special reference to* Al-Burhān fī ʿulūm al-Qurʾān *by Badr al-Dīn al-Ẓarkashī*, Ph.D. thesis, Hartford Seminary Foundation 1968; F. Rosenthal, *The Herb. Hashish versus medieval Muslim society*, Leiden 1971 (includes a summary and ed. of Zarkashī's *Ẓahr al-ʿarīsh*); ʿAbd al-Ḥamīd Aḥmad Muḥammad ʿAlī, *Mabāḥith al-tashbīh ʿind al-imām Badr al-Dīn al-Ẓarkashī*, Cairo 1984; A. Rippin, *Al-Ẓarkashī and al-Suyūṭī on the "occasion of revelation" material*, in *IC*, lix (1985), 243-58, repr. in Rippin, *The Qurʾān and its interpretative tradition*, Aldershot 2001, ch. XVIII; Muḥammad Kamāl al-Dīn ʿIzz al-Dīn, *al-Badr* [sic] *al-Ẓarkashī muʾarrikh^an^*, Beirut 1989; I.L. Camara, *Tres tratados arabes siobre el* Cannabis Indica. *Textos para la historia del hachis en las socoedades islamicas S. XIII-XVI*, Madrid 1990, 45-146, with an ed. and tr. of al-Zarkashī's *Ẓahr al-ʿarīsh*. (A. Rippin)

ZAWDJ.

3. Usage in the dialects of the Muslim East.

The original meaning of *zawdj* in Classical Arabic was "one of a pair or couple" (see 1., at Vol. XI, 464b). Its dual in a phrase such as *zawdjān min al-ḥamām* meant "a pair of pigeons" (i.e. one male, one female). *Zawdj* also naturally came to mean "spouse, married person" of either gender. Later, a morphologically marked female form *zawdja* "wife" was coined, as a consequence of which *zawdj* came to designate specifically "husband". In Modern Standard Arabic, as well as the meaning "husband", *zawdj* retains the original Classical meaning "one of a pair", but is also now used to mean "pair", as in *zawdj min al-ḥidhāʾ* "a pair of shoes".

In the major (urban) Arabic dialects of the eastern Mediterranean (Cairo, Damascus, Jerusalem, Beirut), the first and third radicals of *zawdj* became metathesised (and modified phonetically in well-known ways), so that one typically hears *gōz* (Cairo), *žōz* (Jerusalem, Damascus, Beirut) for both the "pair" and "husband" meanings, but the non-metathesised forms for the feminine form, e.g. *zōga* (Cairo), *zawže* (Damascus) "wife". In rural areas, there is a considerable amount of variation between metathesised and non-metathesised forms, as there is in the phonetic realisation of the two consonants. Thus in parts of the Nile valley and Delta, *zawz, zōz, gōz* and even *gaz* "two, (the) pair, both" may be heard, as in *gōz saʿāt* "two hours", *gaz t-ushhur* "two months", *ig-gaz zayyi baʿḍ* "the pair/the two are alike", *hum iz-zawz* "both of them". The use of *gōz*, etc. for "two" is reminiscent of the general Maghribī form *žūž* "two" (see 2., at Vol. XI, 464b).

In ʿIrāḳ and Arabia, the non-metathesised forms *zōdj* "pair"; "husband" and *zōdja* "wife" are the normal realisations, though these are koinè terms when used to refer to marital partners (which in "pure" dialect are usually words whose basic meaning is "man" and "woman", e.g. Baḥrayn *radjdjāl/rayyāl* and *mara*). In some derivatives from this root, metathesised forms are also heard among less educated speakers, e.g. *djawāz* "marriage" (Gulf States), instead of *zawādj* and *djawwaz* "to marry" (Nadjd), instead of *zawwadj*.

It is interesting to speculate on the reasons for the metathesis so widely encountered in this root. One possible reason may be a meaning coalescence in the dialects, because of a similarity of sound, of the originally separate verbs *zawwadj* "marry, (legitimately) couple" (< *z-w-dj*) and *djawwaz* "to deem or make permissible" (< *dj-w-z*)—a process which has been referred to by Voigt as *Wurzelangleichung*. There is already a similarity in meaning between them, in that an imām who "marries" (*yizawwidj*) a man to a woman thereby makes her "permissible" (*yidjawwizhā*) to him. From this coalescence of sound and meaning may have arisen a secondary fusion of other words from the same root, such as we see in the vacillation between the modern dialectal variants *zawdj* and *djawz*, which were separate words in Classical Arabic.

Bibliography: C. Denizeau, *Dictionnaire des parlers arabes de Syrie, Liban et Palestine*, Paris 1960; M. Hinds and El-Said Badawi, *A dictionary of Egyptian Arabic*, Beirut 1986; R. Voigt, *Die infirmen Verbaltypen des Arabischen und das Biradikalismus-problem*, Stuttgart 1988; B. Ingham, *Najdi Arabic*, Amsterdam 1990; P. Behnstedt and M. Woidich, *Die ägyptische-arabischen Dialekte. Band 4. Glossar arabisch-deutsch*, Wiesbaden 1994; C. Holes, *Dialect, culture and society in Eastern Arabia. Volume I. Glossary*, Leiden 2001.

(C. Holes)

ZĪRĪ b. **ʿAṬIYYA** b. ʿAbd Allāh b. Khazar, Abū Yūsuf, Berber chief of the Maghrib whose fate was linked, at the end of the 4th/10th century and the beginning of the 5th/11th, on the one hand to that of the *ḥādjib* al-Manṣūr b. Abī ʿĀmir [*q.v.*] and on the other to that of the Maghrāwa [*q.v.*], who were caught between the forces of the caliphate of Cordova, to the north, and those of the Fāṭimid caliphate and the Zīrid principality of Ifrīḳiya, to the east. In fact, following the proclamation of the caliphate of Ḳayrawān, the Maghrāwa were compelled by circumstances to pay allegiance to one or other of the neighbouring powers.

Zīrī b. ʿAṭiyya belonged to an illustrious family, the Banū Khazar, whose ancestors were already guiding the Maghrāwī confederation at the time of the conquest of the Maghrib by the Muslims. In 351/962, on the death of his grandfather, Muḥammad b. al-Khayr b. Muḥammad b. Khazar became the leader of the Maghrāwa. Extending his territory at the expense of the Fāṭimid zone of influence established by Djawhar [*q.v.*], the new chieftain established a short-lived Maghrāwī state in the central Maghrib, within the orbit of the Umayyad caliphate of Cordova. But in 360/971, the Fāṭimid governor of Ifrīḳiya, Buluggīn b. Zīrī [*q.v.*] defeated, close to Tlemcen, the Maghrāwa and the Zanāta. From this date onwards, the history of these tribes, which had formerly established a confederation, is closely linked with the history of what is now Morocco, where the different princes of the family of the Banū Khazar created three states, around the cities of Fās, Sidjilmāsa and Aghmāt. Among these Maghrāwī *amīrs* who went in search of new territories in the far Maghrib were Zīrī b. ʿAṭiyya and his brother Muḳātil b. ʿAṭiyya. Theoretically dependent on the caliph of Cordova, the two brothers deferred sometimes to the authority of the Umayyad caliph in the region, and sometimes to that of his chamberlain, Ibn Abī ʿĀmir.

Towards 365/975-6, Muḥammad b. al-Khayr b. Muḥammad seems to have lost control of the northern group of Maghrāwī Moroccans. In fact, at this time Zīrī and Muḳātil b. ʿAṭiyya were in the entourage of the Umayyad governor of the Maghrib, the general Djaʿfar b. ʿAlī b. Ḥamdūn, appointed by the caliph al-Ḥakam II. The Maghrib served at this time as a source for the provision of fighters in the struggle against the Iberian Christians. The Maghrāwa, the leadership of whom had just been taken over by Zīrī and Muḳātil, and the Banū Īfran [*q.v.*], commanded by Yaddu b. Yaʿlā, supported this policy and supplied horsemen to al-Andalus.

The news of the death of the Umayyad caliph al-Ḥakam II arrived in North Africa just as negotiations were in progress between Djaʿfar b. Ḥamdūn, Yaddu b. Yaʿlā, Zīrī b. ʿAṭiyya and his brother Muḳātil. The minority of Hishām II, leading to the accession of the *ḥādjib* Ibn Abī ʿĀmir (366-71/976-81), perceptibly modified the traditional policies of Cordova in this region. In fact, al-Manṣūr played on the rivalries between the Zanāta chiefs; in 376/986, he sent a new governor-general to the Maghrib, Ḥasan b. Aḥmad b. ʿAbd al-Wadūd al-Sulamī, who moved his headquarters from Sabta to Fās. On the orders of al-Manṣūr, Ibn ʿAbd al-Wadūd overtly favoured the Maghrāwa to the detriment of the other Zanāta chiefs and especially the Īfranid Yaddu b. Yaʿlā, known for his rebellious tendencies. When Muḳātil died in 378/988, Zīrī took over the leadership of the Maghrāwa and became the sole interlocutor of the Cordovan power.

In 379/989, for example, al-Manṣūr invited Zīrī to pay an official visit to Cordova. The latter brought with him numerous recruits for al-Manṣūr's armies, who were incorporated into the regular army. He was received in princely style and was awarded on this occasion the title of vizier. On his return to the Maghrib, Zīrī seems to have demonstrated some independence towards the ʿĀmirid master of Cordova, founding in the north of Morocco a principality with Fās as its capital. Seeking the support of the Īfranid, al-Manṣūr made overtures of Yaddu b. Yaʿlā which the latter rejected, moving openly into dissidence. The reaction of al-Manṣūr was immediate: Ibn ʿAbd al-Wadūd received the order to call upon Zīrī b. ʿAṭiyya to subdue Yaddu. On 18 Muḥarram 381/6 April 991, on the banks of the Wadi Moulouya, an encounter took place in the course of which Yaddu b. Yaʿlā crushed the Cordovan army and the Maghrāwī reinforcements.

For Umayyad policy in the Maghrib, this constituted a serious reverse, temporarily alleviated by the unexpected support of a Ṣanhādjī prince of Ifrīḳiya. In fact, the paternal uncle of the Zīrid king al-Manṣūr b. Buluggīn, Abu 'l-Bahār b. Zīrī, rebelled against the Ḳayrawān government and declared himself for that of Cordova. According to certain authors, this allegiance was short-lived and Zīrī b. ʿAṭiyya attacked Abu 'l-Bahār who took refuge first at Ceuta, in Shawwāl 382/end of 992, and then, after being reconciled with his relatives, in Ifrīḳiya; Zīrī took over all his domains and announced his victory, in 381/391, to al-Manṣūr, who invited him to pay a second visit. Arriving at Cordova in 382/992, Zīrī brought numerous presents with him on this occasion, as recorded by the sources (although they are sometimes attributed to a diplomatic mission sent by Zīrī in 384/November 994): 200 racehorses, some 20 of them with a documented pedigree, camels, weapons and shields of antelope hide (*lamṭ*), a parrot, a gigantic panther and a giraffe, which died en route and was stuffed, all these last for the menagerie of the Caliph's palace. On his return to the Maghrib, Zīrī learned that the Īfranid Yaddu b. Yaʿlā had taken possession of Fās. After a bloody battle, Zīrī regained his throne and sent Yaddu's head to al-Manṣūr.

No doubt finding the location of Fās too remote in relation to the assemblage of regions which recognised his authority, in 383/994 Zīrī founded the town of Oujda (Wadjda [*q.v.*]), on the border between Morocco and what is now Algeria, with the aim of establishing his court and his household garrison there. Subsequently, relations with Cordova deteriorated. The precise reasons for the conflict between Zīrī and al-Manṣūr are not known, but it is possible that Zīrī had emerged as the champion of Hishām II in his claims against al-Manṣūr: in 388/998, his battle cry (*shiʿār*) was *yā Hishām yā Manṣūr*, while that of the ʿĀmirids was only *yā Manṣūr* (Lévi-Provençal, *Fragments*, 29). In 386/997, al-Manṣūr sent troops to the Maghrib to intimidate Zīrī, who affirmed his independence without going so far as to repudiate overtly his oath of fealty to Hishām II. In Shawwāl 387/October 997, al-Manṣūr deprived him of his title of vizier and sent against him one of his best generals, the former slave Wāḍiḥ, who commanded the middle march of al-Andalus (*al-thaghr al-awsaṭ*). In Tangier, the latter received the allegiance of numerous local chiefs who came to rally beneath his banner. Then he set out with all these forces to attack Zīrī, who had taken up positions in a mountainous region of northern Morocco, the Djabal Ḥabīb (Ibn Khaldūn, *Histoire des Berbères*, iii, 244).

As a first step, Wāḍiḥ took possession of Arcila on the Atlantic and of Nakūr on the Mediterranean. In Radjab 388/July 998, he succeeded in surprising the bulk of Zīrī's forces in a mountain pass and inflicted a severe defeat on the Maghrāwa. Some weeks later, wanting to reap the rewards of victory, al-Manṣūr sent his own son ʿAbd al-Malik with fresh reinforcements. ʿAbd al-Malik joined forces with Wāḍiḥ and then both of them marched against Zīrī. The second encounter, which took place on 19 Shawwāl 388/13 October 998, was at first indecisive. But Zīrī's army, on hearing that its leader had been severely wounded, disintegrated; forced into flight, Zīrī abandoned his camp and his wealth to the Cordovans.

Having tried in vain to take refuge in Fās, where his wives and children were, Zīrī took the Sahara road. In fact, the town refused to open its gates to him and it was occupied by ʿAbd al-Malik. Having barely recovered from his injuries, Zīrī refrained from attempting anything in the north of Morocco, which was strongly held by the Umayyad army. But taking advantage of the death of Zīrid king al-Manṣūr b. Buluggīn and the quarrels between the latter's son and successor, Badīs, and his great-uncles Maksan and Zawī, Zīrī b. ʿAṭiyya laid siege to Tāhart, which he took in 388/998. Then he successively conquered the Ṣanhādjī centres of Tlemcen, Chélif, Ténès and al-Masīla, where he had the prayer celebrated in the name of the Umayyad caliph Hishām II and his *ḥādjib* al-Manṣūr, whose pardon he sought, asking to have his former prerogatives reinstated. His appeal was accepted.

In 391/1001, Zīrī laid siege to Ashīr [*q.v.*], the capital of the Ṣanhādja, but his state of health obliged him to raise the siege after a month, and he died shortly afterwards. On the death of Zīrī, his son, al-Muʿizz, took his place at the head of the federation of Maghrāwa, and declared himself the loyal vassal of Cordova, continuing the struggle against the Ṣanhādja until the death of al-Manṣūr. A little later, al-Muʿizz asked the new *ḥādjib*, ʿAbd al-Malik, to award him an official investiture. A letter of ʿAbd al-Malik dated Dhu 'l-Kaʿda 396/August 1006, the text of which has been preserved (Ibn Khaldūn, *Berbères*, iii, 248-50, and al-Warrāḳ, *Fragments historiques sur les Berbères*, 40-1) is addressed to the inhabitants of Fās, inviting them to recognise al-Muʿizz b. ʿAṭiyya as governor of the whole Maghrib, with the exception of the territory of Sidjilmāsa, the personal fief of Wānūdīn b. Khazrūn b. Falfūl. The rest of the reign of al-Muʿizz was turbulent, but on his death in 417/1026, the general revolt of al-Andalus smashed once and for all the ties which for almost a century had linked the Zanāta North African bloc with the Umayyads of Cordova. The fortunes of the Zanāta [*q.v.*] declined in the Maghrib, before the increasing power of the Almoravids, who relied for support on the Ṣanhādja tribes.

Bibliography: 1. Sources. The principal source is Ibn Ḥayyān, reproduced in full by the author of the *Mafākhir al-Barbar, fragments historiques sur les Berbères du Maghreb*, ed. É. Lévi-Provençal, 15-36, and ed. Maḥmūd Yaʿlā, *Tres textos árabes sobre beréberes en el occidente islámico*, Madrid 1996, 143; 153-85; Ibn Abī Zarʿ, *Rawḍ al-ḳirṭās*, Rabat 1972, 92, 101-8, 116; ʿAbd al-Malik al-Warrāḳ, *Miḳbas*, 37-9; Ibn Khaldūn, *Histoire des Berbères*, iii, 217-21, 235-48.

2. Studies. H.R. Idris, *La Berbérie orientale sous les Zīrides, X^e^-XIIe s.*, 2 vols., Paris 1962, and bibl. in J.-Cl. Garcin (ed.), *États, sociétés et cultures du monde musulman médiéval, X^e^-XVe s.*, Paris 1995, i, p. xlix.

(P. Buresi)